From BEOWULF to MODERN BRITISH WRITERS

Edited by JOHN BALL

*Based on Robert Shafer's*

From BEOWULF to THOMAS HARDY

# From BEOWULF
# to MODERN
# BRITISH WRITERS

THE ODYSSEY PRESS · INC · New York

# PREFACE

*From Beowulf to Modern British Writers* is an inclusive single volume designed to provide a balanced set of resources for the study of English literature; it combines the features of a survey anthology, a series of texts of major works by major writers, a history of English literature, and a social, political, and cultural study of the backgrounds of English literature.

Its selections offer not a sampling but a substantial representation of the best work of the chief British writers; thus there is abundant material to permit different emphases in different courses. Where there is inadequate time to cover all, the course may concentrate on the two dozen major writers from the author of *Beowulf* to T. S. Eliot; alternatively, the course may include all the writers but move some of the longer works into supplementary or suggested reading assignments. Wherever possible the use of small excerpts from major works has been avoided.

The seven Historical and Critical Introductions form the equivalent of a separate work of 35,000 words, tracing the development of the English language, the English viewpoint, and the English achievement in the literary arts from the beginnings to the present time. Inevitably the Introductions have also something to say more generally, in relation to literature, toward the interpretation of man's motives and goals, and of his quest for answers to the basic questions *who* is man, *why* is man, and *what* is important; and toward the understanding of the relationship of man's life to his art, and of the conflicts and creative tensions between individualism and the expectations of others, between change and tradition.

Robert Shafer's *From Beowulf to Thomas Hardy* was among the first of the English literature anthologies, and it set a widely-imitated pattern and a high standard. Used by nearly every college and university in America, and by the United States Armed Forces Institute during and after World War II, it became the best-known of all the anthologies, and its title almost a generic term for the survey course. Because of the strength and range of its historical and critical introductions, and the quality and depth of its selections, it was not vulnerable to the criticism aimed at some survey texts—that they take the student on a hasty bus tour of literature without stopping long enough anywhere to find out anything.

Certainly the survey course can be superficial—as can any course in the college— but it need not be. A survey course based on a good text, well taught, can be one of the broadest and soundest of humanities courses. When the student has completed it he has entered the worlds of Chaucer, Spenser, Shakespeare, Milton, Swift, Wordsworth, Keats, Browning, Shaw, Forster, Eliot—and a score of other exceptionally perceptive observers of mankind he dare not miss. Not only has he been caught up in the developing stream of Western thought, in the Renaissance and in the Age of Reason, in the Romantic Movement and in the complex interactions of the Age of Anxiety; he has also gained insight into the nature of literature both as implicit in each work he has read, and as discussed explicitly, for example, by Sidney, Dryden, Johnson, Coleridge, and Matthew Arnold. His experience has, besides its value in and of itself, great worth in illuminating history and philosophy, economics and sociology, religion and art. It provides a firm basis for his advanced courses in the literature of England, or of America, or of any other country; a backlog of educated interest to stimulate further reading throughout his life; and if he keeps his textbook, a useful reference work of literary examples and of literary biography and history.

This new one-volume edition has retained a great deal and changed a great deal. The first six Historical and Critical Introductions, which carry English literature from the beginnings to about 1914, retain as much as possible of Dr. Shafer's language and style as well as of his approach to literature. The major changes in these six essays are made to effect a reduction in their length and to make more readily available to the under-graduate student concepts and critical commentary which in the earlier editions seemed at times to be aimed at the graduate level. A number of lesser writers and works have also been omitted to make this one-volume edition possible.

The chief additions include works by twenty-one authors not represented previously, five from the nineteenth century and sixteen from the twentieth, and an introduction to the literature of the present time. Elizabeth Barrett Browning, Meredith, Christina Rossetti, Henley, and Hopkins are now represented. The modern section is strong in drama, with the inclusion of Shaw's *Don Juan in Hell,* Synge's *In the Shadow of the Glen,* and Eliot's *Murder in the Cathedral.* Modern poetry is given a balanced showing, with poems by Yeats, Joyce, Lawrence, Eliot, Brooke, Owen, Auden, Spender, and Dylan Thomas. The inclusion of Herbert Read's "A World within a War" is worthy of special note. Modern criticism and essay are represented by Eliot and Virginia Woolf. The additions in fiction are by Joyce, Lawrence, Virginia Woolf, Katherine Mansfield, and Aldous Huxley, with E. M. Forster's *The Machine Stops* a particularly notable inclusion.

The practice of identifying omissions by asterisks (*), and at times by footnotes, has been carried over from the earlier editions. The Chronological Outline, a valuable aid for reference and review, has been brought up to date. A few dates and ascriptions of authorship about which there is some uncertainty have been included anyway on the basis of the best evidence available. The Glossary has been retained. Pictures have been omitted to provide more space for the literature itself.

The present editor's obligation and gratitude to the late Robert Shafer are far greater than can be recorded. Dr. Shafer was a devoted scholar and friend, whose breadth of view, wide range of knowledge, depth of learning, and great humility made a profound impression and remain as permanent standards. Without the encouragement and access to materials provided by Dr. Shafer's widow, Mrs. Giuditta G. Shafer, this edition would have appeared much later, if at all. The present volume owes a continuing debt to the colleagues of Dr. Shafer who aided him in the preparation of previous editions; also to Professor Lawrence J. Hynes of Miami University, who made valuable suggestions on Shaw and Joyce; to Anne Beard, who gave expert help with proof and indexing; to Jane Denham, who typed and prepared the manuscript with patience and care; and to the many students who have served both as experimental audience and as inspiration.

JOHN BALL

# CONTENTS

# III. The Renaissance and the Protestant Revolt, 1485-1660

# IV. The Restoration and the Eighteenth Century, 1660-1784

# V. The Romantic Reaction and Triumph, 1784-1837

# VI. The Victorian Era and After, 1837-1914

An Interlude 1100
Hertha 1101
To Walt Whitman in America 1103
The Oblation 1104
Ave atque Vale, in Memory of Charles
  Baudelaire 1105
A Ballad of François Villon, Prince of
  All Ballad-Makers 1108
First Footsteps 1108
The Roundel 1108

## Selected Victorian and Edwardian
Poetry 1109

Elizabeth Barrett Browning
*From* Sonnets from the Portuguese
  1, 3, 4, 6, 7, 14, 20, 22, 26, 35,
  43 1111
George Meredith
*From* Modern Love
  1, 16, 17, 43, 47, 50 1113
Christina Georgina Rossetti
Song (When I am dead, my dear-
  est) 1114
A Better Resurrection 1114
A Birthday 1114
Life and Death 1114
Sleeping at Last 1115
Thomas Hardy
Hap 1115
Nature's Questioning 1115
The Slow Nature 1115
God-Forgotten 1116
On a Fine Morning 1116
The Well-Beloved 1116
The Curate's Kindness 1117
The Dawn After the Dance 1118
Misconception 1118
The Homecoming 1118
To Sincerity 1119
George Meredith 1120
The Face at the Casement 1120
Lost Love 1120
Ah, Are You Digging on My Grave? 1121
The Sweet Hussy 1121
You Were the Sort That Men
  Forget 1121
To the Moon 1121
Life Laughs Onward 1122
Gerard Manley Hopkins
God's Grandeur 1122
The Windhover 1122
Pied Beauty 1122
Binsey Poplars 1123
Spring and Fall: To a Young Child 1123
As Kingfishers Catch Fire 1123
Inversnaid 1123

I Wake and Feel the Fell of Dark 1123
William Ernest Henley
*From* In Hospital
  1. Enter Patient 1124
  4. Before 1124
  28. Discharged 1124
Invictus 1124
I. M. Margaritae Sorori 1124
Space and Dread and the Dark 1125
Oscar Wilde
Helas! 1125
Symphony in Yellow 1125
The Ballad of Reading Gaol 1125
Francis Thompson
The Hound of Heaven 1132
Alfred Edward Housman
A Shropshire Lad
  II. (Loveliest of trees, the
    cherry now) 1134
  IV. Reveille 1134
  VIII. ("Farewell to barn and
    stack and tree") 1134
  XIX. To an Athlete Dying
    Young 1134
  XXVII. ("Is my team plow-
    ing?") 1135
  XXXIV. The New Mistress 1135
  XLVIII. (Be still, my soul, be
    still; the arms you
    bear are brittle) 1135
  LIV. (With rue my heart is
    laden) 1135
  LXII. ("Terence, this stupid
    stuff") 1136
Last Poems
  VII. (In valleys green and still) 1136
  IX. (The chestnut casts his
    flambeaux, and the flow-
    ers) 1136
  XI. (Yonder see the morning
    blink) 1137
Rudyard Kipling
Tomlinson 1137
Tommy 1139
"Fuzzy-Wuzzy" 1140
Gunga Din 1140
Mandalay 1141
Recessional 1142
When 'Omer Smote 'Is Bloomin'
  Lyre 1142
John Masefield
Cargoes 1142
Captain Stratton's Fancy 1143
The West Wind 1143
C. L. M. 1144
On Growing Old 1144

# VII. The Present Time: 1914-

From BEOWULF to MODERN BRITISH WRITERS

# I     EARLIEST TIMES: THE ANGLO-SAXONS, 449-1066

Britain first appears on the page of history with Julius Caesar's invasion of its southern coast in 55 B.C. Before that time there are no recorded accounts, but there is much that we can learn about it from inference. We know, for instance, that Britain was very rich in natural resources—that its forests were full of game, that its rivers were full of fish, that its fields were fertile and open, that its earth contained valuable deposits of tin and gold, and that its climate was even and favorable. And we know that this rich land was very attractive to residents of the Continent; traders from the more civilized countries of southern Europe brought goods to trade with the Britons, raiders from the northern coasts of Europe made quick forays to the island to steal what they wanted, and dissatisfied peoples from diverse parts of Europe sailed to England to live, confident that in this new land they would find abundance. One group of colonist-invaders followed another; and each new group pushed the others farther west. The people encountered by Caesar were Celts, who were closely related to the Gallic tribes then living in northern Europe.

The Roman conquerors made sweeping changes in Britain; they built substantial towns and solid straight roads, and they gave encouragement and improved methods to agriculture. But these effects of the Conquest were not lasting; when the Roman soldiers were withdrawn from Britain to fight on the Continent, the Celts relapsed into their old ways.

## THE COMING OF THE ANGLO-SAXONS

Before the Conquest the country had been divided up into small "kingdoms," the Celtic "kings" being really not much better than tribal chiefs whose principal occupation was warfare against their neighbors. Robber tribes from the German and Danish coasts were quick to see the island's defenseless condition, and during the fourth century A.D. they began raiding the British coast. Once the robbers had discovered how attractive the island was, they began to settle there; gradually they took from the Celts practically all of what is now England. Although the date of this new conquest is generally said to be A.D. 449, there was no sudden, complete victory; actually the conquest took more than a hundred and fifty years.

According to old tradition, the invaders belonged to three tribal groups—the Angles, the Saxons, and the Jutes. The Angles, or English, eventually gave their name to the greater part of the island, and to its inhabitants, and to the language which has spread over a large part of the modern world, wherever Englishmen have established themselves as settlers and rulers.

## THE LANGUAGE OF THE ANGLO-SAXONS

All of the invaders spoke a common language—a variety of what we now call Low German. Its appearance and its sound are very strange to us, as the late West-Saxon version of the first thirteen verses of the first chapter of the Gospel According to St. John will show:

On frymthe waes Word, and thaet Word waes mid Gode, and God waes thaet Word. Thaet waes on fruman mid Gode. Ealle thing waeron geworhte thurh hyne; and nan thing naes geworht butan him. Thaet waes lif the on him geworht waes; and thaet lif waes manna leoht. And thaet leoht lyht on thystrum; and thystro thaet ne genamon.

1

Mann waes fram Gode asend, thaes nama waes Johannes. Thes com to gewitnesse, thaet he gewitnesse cythde be tham leohte, thaet ealle menn thurh hyne gelyfdon. Naes he leoht, ac thaet he gewitnesse forth baere be tham leohte.

Soth leoht waes thaet onlyht aelcne cumendne man on thisne middaneard. He waes on middanearde, and middaneard waes geworht thurh hine, and middaneard hine ne underfengon. Sothlice swa hwylce swa hyne underfengon, he sealde him anweald thaet hi waeron Godes bearn, tham the gelyfath on his naman: tha ne synt acennede of blodum, ne of flaesces willan, ne of weres willan, ac hig synt of Gode acennede.

Here are the same verses as they appear in the Bible used today:

In the beginning was the Word, and the Word was with God, and the Word was God. The same was in the beginning with God. All things were made by Him; and without Him was not anything made that was made. In Him was life; and the life was the light of men. And the light shineth in darkness; and the darkness comprehended it not.

There was a man sent from God, whose name was John. The same came for a witness, to bear witness of the Light, that all men through him might believe. He was not that Light, but was sent to bear witness of that Light.

That was the true Light, which lighteth every man that cometh into the world. He was in the world, and the world was made by Him, and the world knew Him not. He came unto His own, and His own received Him not. But as many as received Him, to them gave He power to become the sons of God, even to them that believe on His name: which were born, not of blood, nor of the will of the flesh, nor of the will of man, but of God.

These versions are much more nearly alike than they appear to be at first sight. The Anglo-Saxon language is the foundation and framework upon which our own modern English has been built, and for this reason it is sometimes called Old English rather than Anglo-Saxon.

The term "Old English" has one advantage —it helps to emphasize the real continuity of English life and speech from the fifth century to the present. After the Anglo-Saxon conquest both the people and their language had a long rough road to travel before they could come to maturity and greatness; but the road *was continuous*, and if we are to understand English literature we must begin studying it with the earliest surviving writings of the Anglo-Saxons, even though these writings seem now to be in a foreign language.

## CONVERSION TO CHRISTIANITY

By the end of the sixth century the Anglo-Saxons had firmly established themselves throughout the eastern and southern parts of Britain. Nobody knows to what extent they absorbed the Celtic population, but it appears likely that most of the Celts were either killed where they were found or pushed back into Cornwall and Wales or up into Scotland. Many went across to Ireland, and others to the northwest corner of France (Brittany).

Roman Britain had become Christianized along with the rest of the Empire, and some of its clergy knew Latin and had some classical learning. In their retreat the Celts carried with them both their religion and their culture. Thus Christianity and Latin passed into Ireland, and for several centuries flourished there. Irish monasteries became centers of learning, and Irish missionaries went forth to the coast of Scotland and into England and Wales, and even to remote parts of the continent of Europe.

The Anglo-Saxons brought their own ancient religion with them, but it was weakened by passage across the sea. The practice of human sacrifice, for example, which had been a part of their religion, apparently was not carried over to Britain. Many of the Anglo-Saxon gods gave us names we still use: there was the god of war and warriors, Woden (Wednesday); the thunder-god, Thunor or Thor (Thursday); the Northern Venus, Frig (Friday); a minor war-god, Tiw (Tuesday); and a dawn-goddess, Eostra (Easter). Supreme above all gods and spirits was Wyrd (Fate), who for centuries remained a real force in the minds and imaginations of the English. Below these gods, and more real to the people than any of them except Wyrd, was a confused mass of elves, mysterious monsters, dragons, and spirits of the wheat field, of the sunlight, of the rain, and the like. Many sacrifices to these powers were believed to be necessary, and magical charms were used for many purposes, such as to ward off rheumatism, to help the field if crops were poor, or to bring back strayed cattle.

By the end of the sixth century the pagan belief of the Anglo-Saxons had declined, and the people were willing to change to the new faith that was offered them. In 597 Augustine and forty Benedictine monks landed on the southeastern coast of England to preach the gospel of Christ. They had been sent from Rome by Pope Gregory the Great. Gregory is said to have exclaimed years before, on seeing some fair-haired English boys in the slave-market at Rome, that they were "not Angles, but Angels," and to have decided on the spot to carry Christianity to the land from which the boys came. Gregory was never able to go himself, but he finally succeeded in sending Augustine and his band of monks. King Ethelbert of Kent—whose Christian wife from the Continent probably had a great deal to do with his attitude—received the monks courteously, gave them an old Roman Church in Canterbury, and promptly accepted baptism. His subjects soon followed their king's example, and within a year some 10,000 had been converted.

Probably the most important reason for the rapid conversion of the English was the failure of Germanic paganism to hold its own in its new environment. The ancient beliefs had become shadowy, had begun to seem childish, and offered little to an awakening reason. The Christian interpretation of life won its way with the English because it seemed better than any they had known—better in itself and better in its effects. Augustine and the other monks lived what they preached; they were men of evident holiness, strong character, and remarkable practical intelligence. And they brought not only a system of worship and a rule of life, but all that still survived within the Roman Church of classical civilization. Along with Christianity came some part of Greek and Roman philosophy, some classical literature, an elementary but firm educational discipline, and Roman standards of administration. The acceptance of Christianity, then, opened to the English the door to civilization. Roman churchmen introduced improvements in law and administration and promoted the ideal of unity among the English kingdoms. But above all they brought in education; and Latin, then necessary to education, became the language of the Church and of educated men.

The English grasped eagerly the opportunities thus placed before them, thereby showing from the very beginnings of their history a characteristic which through the centuries has been of primary importance in their development. The background of English intellectual, literary, and artistic history is a series of external or foreign influences, so that a student who does not go into the matter deeply may be tempted to wonder if English literature is not merely a series of borrowings and imitations. The truth is that the English have been receptive to foreign influences but have never been overpowered by them; rather, they have discovered themselves through them, have made the foreign things their own, and have built upon them, impressing them firmly with the unmistakable English character.

## THE VENERABLE BEDE

One of the earliest English writers, the Venerable Bede, insisted that the English lost nothing by their conversion except what was "trivial or vain." We can also see in him much that was gained by this conversion. Bede was born in Northumbria, the northeastern part of England, while the Christian influence was yet young. From the age of seven he spent his entire life in a monastery where there were competent teachers and a library. He learned Latin and Greek, and acquired, for his time, a considerable knowledge of the classics. He liked to study, to teach, and to write: he spent his life in these pursuits. We can see from his carefully-written *Ecclesiastical History of the English Nation* that Bede had a composed assurance and an inward strength, that he was capable and intelligent. If we could encounter him today we would find that he could meet us, across all the centuries, on equal terms. We could understand him, and he, with little effort, could understand us.

## CAEDMON

Since all of Bede's books were written in Latin they are often not considered a part of English literature. From Bede, however, we learn the name and the story of the earliest known English poet. This was Caedmon, a devout layman associated with a monastery, who made English verses about parts of the Bible which had been translated for him. He wrote most of his poetry between 660 and 670; none of it has survived except a few lines translated by Bede into Latin. Caedmon stands at the beginning of a short era, extending through the first third of the eighth century, in which the kingdom of Northumbria was the center of a "golden age" in Anglo-Saxon education, literature, and art.

## THE EARLIEST ENGLISH POETRY

A piece of literature is something written; and the Anglo-Saxons did not write until they were taught the use of the Roman alphabet. Before that they had used an alphabet adapted from Greek and Roman characters, not for writing, but chiefly for carving inscriptions in stone. Its letters were called runes, and certain of its characters or marks were believed to have a magic significance. Writing, however, did not develop as a native art from runes, but was introduced with Christianity and formal education.

Any general account of our earliest English literature must be based on information which is incomplete, because only fragments of the literature of that time have been preserved. Such Old English manuscripts as we now have are copies made much later in the south of England. And there is no means of knowing how much was not copied, or how many manuscripts moldered away or were otherwise lost through neglect.

This much, however, we know: the Angles and Saxons possessed a traditional poetry, remembered and handed down by word of mouth since before their settlement in England. It was probably of two kinds, aristocratic and popular. The aristocratic poetry consisted of short narratives about warriors and their exploits, and was chanted by minstrels. The popular kind consisted of charms for many occasions and of short narratives sung to simple tunes—poems similar to those of a much later time which we know as popular ballads.

We cannot be sure that any of this pre-literary, pre-Christian poetry has been preserved unaltered. All of the Old English poetry we possess was written in its present form by Christians; practically all of it is to some degree influenced by Christianity. This does not mean that the older poetry which had been transmitted by word of mouth has completely perished. For example, some of the ancient charms to cure rheumatism and the like were not suppressed but were simply altered to a Christian appearance. And even in the writing of sacred poetry the Angles remained true to themselves and their own past. *Genesis, Daniel,* and *Exodus,* which were probably composed about 700, are in part loose poetical translations of books of the Old Testament. Yet they are written in the verse-form which the English had inherited from their pagan past, and even the subject-matter is distorted to conform to Anglo-Saxon experience.

In *Exodus,* for instance, the poet has confined himself chiefly to the thirteenth, fourteenth, and fifteenth chapters. His imagination was aroused by the stir and movement of the flight of the Jews from Egypt and their pursuit by the Egyptians, and by the dramatic incident of the dry path miraculously made for the Jews through the Red Sea. To the poet's eye, Jews and Egyptians became armies of northern warriors, equipped like the fighting men he knew, with northern habits and outlook, and an eye on treasure to be won. Ravens wheeled over them and gray wolves circled nearby ready to devour the slain. Moses became a "lord of men" a "bold folk-captain"—like the leaders the poet knew—and he was surrounded by "earls." There was, to be sure, no battle, and this difficulty appears to have bewildered the poet, though he made the best of such bloody destruction as did occur. Even the deeply felt Christian purpose—to glorify God, the righteous King, who rewarded His faithful followers and destroyed those who strove against Him—reflects the old Anglo-Saxon ethical principle of loyalty to the king.

## BEOWULF

Even more striking proof of the fact that Christianity brought no sharp break with the past is given by *Beowulf,* which was probably written about 740 in the kingdom of Northumbria. The author of *Beowulf* was probably a churchman connected with a royal court. He had received a classical education, and appears in some parts of *Beowulf* to have been inspired by Virgil's *Aeneid.* He knew and was influenced by *Genesis, Exodus,* and *Daniel;* he loved the past reflected in the heroic lore of his people, with its aristocratic standards of conduct and bearing. *Beowulf* is an excellent example of foreign source material adapted by the English to their own use—not merely an imitation, but a distinctive new creation. Inspired by classical example to produce an epic, the author of *Beowulf* used traditional tales of heroism then current among the Northern peoples, faithfully representing the Germanic atmosphere, but giving his poem a pervasive Christian interpretation. The result was a thoroughly English poem. The material the author had to work with was not of the high quality of the Homeric epics, nor was it well unified. Nevertheless, he made from it a large poem in the heroic manner. His Christianity enabled him to see Beowulf's conflicts with monsters as symbols of the opposition in this world between good and evil; it is this interpretation of the pagan subject-matter which dignified alike the monsters and their opponent, and gives us the really heroic substance along with the heroic manner.

*Beowulf* possesses enduring human and literary interest. It is almost the only composition surviving from the Old English period—except two spirited short battle pieces, *Brunanburh* and *Maldon,* written in the tenth century—for which such interest can be claimed. It is also an unrivaled source of information about the early life and standards of the Germanic peoples.

The kind of life depicted in *Beowulf* is aristocratic; the common people do not appear. We are in the presence of royalty and of those who make up the royal court. These are first of all warriors, bound to loyal service; lasting disgrace is the lot of any man who betrays or deserts his leader, no matter how hopeless the cause. If the leader and his band are trapped, it is the warrior's duty to stand his ground and die, if need be, in defense of his lord. In return for this loyalty the king or leader is expected to support his warriors splendidly, to reward them generously, and to treat them with kindness. The great king is strong and brave, a terror to his foes, but to his followers the mildest of men. For entrance into this aristocratic society, birth and family connections are important, but not so important as personal bravery. Once a member of the fellowship, the warrior is above productive labor. When not fighting and gathering spoil, he is idle, eating and drinking to excess and listening to tales of brave adventure to keep his spirits up. He needs to keep his spirits up, because he leads an extremely dangerous life; even when he sits safely by the fire he has many things to fear, and is made more uneasy by the fact that he does not know what some of them are.

We know there were other heroic tales stored in the minds of the contemporaries of the poet who wrote *Beowulf*, but we cannot know whether or not any of them were fashioned into epics. The few fragments of other heroic poetry which survive are too incomplete to enable anyone to feel sure what they were originally. We do have, however, two short poems, *Widsith* and *Deor*, in which the professional minstrel speaks for himself. From them one can learn a little of the life lived by these singers, and something of the range of the tales they told. Both poems contain some reflective passages, and are thus allied with such reflective pieces as *The Wanderer* and *The Seafarer*. Most of the personal poetry of the time seems to be moody, gloomy, and fatalistic.

## CYNEWULF

Besides Caedmon we know the name of only one Old English poet. That one is Cynewulf, and of him, besides his name, we know only what his poems imply. We gather that he came of a noble family, that in his youth he was carefree, and that as a man he was converted to Christianity, devoted himself to religion, and probably entered a monastery. He wrote in the early years of the ninth century; he may have been either a Northumbrian or a Mercian. We happen to know his name, and to know at the same time that four poems were written by him, because into the text of each of these he worked runic characters which form his name, and so constitute a kind of signature. The poems so signed are *Juliana*, *Elene*, *Fates of the Apostles*, and that portion of *Christ* called *The Ascension*.

Anglo-Saxon Christian culture was beginning to decline in the early years of the ninth century when Cynewulf wrote, and neither his signed pieces nor any other surviving poems of this period possess much interest or importance except to the historian or the scholar. All of them are translations or paraphrases of Latin originals. *Andreas*, *Guthlac*, and Cynewulf's *Juliana* and *Elene* are saints' lives retold in verse. *Andreas* and *Elene* are the most readable of the four, the former being an exciting tale of marvelous adventure. Another poem which deserves mention is *The Dream of the Rood*, which has elements of real beauty. The "dream" is a vision of the True Cross (or Rood) which rises, adorned with gold and jewels and giving forth light, before the poet. As he watches it in awe its appearance changes and it is bathed in blood; then it speaks, telling its history, and how it is honored among men, and how those who hope to dwell with God must seek His Kingdom through it. It is interesting that this personification was presented through a dream; the dream was a favorite device of medieval literature, and we shall meet with other dream-poems before the close of the Middle Ages in England.

## LIMITATIONS OF OLD ENGLISH POETRY

Among the surviving examples of Old English poetry are a group of ninety-five short pieces, all of which are riddles. They are mentioned here because they can help us to understand the poetic taste of the Anglo-Saxons, and also to understand one reason why Old English poetry failed to develop beyond the point reached in *Beowulf*. The Anglo-Saxons were fond of riddles. Their enjoyment of hearing someone talk in a roundabout way, flinging out hints for them to puzzle over, is shown by all of their poetry. The riddle-like style which was evidently the most prominent characteristic of the traditional Germanic poetry unfortunately encouraged in the Old English poets the habit of talking all around what they intended to say. And no Old English poet appeared who had the originality to break away from poetic tradition.

Old English poetry as a whole looks, not forward, but—as we see the poet himself doing in *Beowulf*—backward to a dying past. In that fine and interesting poem Old English poetry came to an early climax, and then declined.

## VIKINGS

The creative energy generated in England by religion and learning was a small flame which burned bravely, but soon began to flicker amid wind and storms. And in the ninth century the flame was snuffed out in Northumbria by new invaders. Fortunately, sparks had been carried to Mercia, to be cherished there and passed on later to the south of England, so that the work which had begun so well in the north was never lost.

The new invaders were Vikings from the coast of Norway and from the Danish peninsula. Although they were closely related to the Angles and Saxons in language and race, they were still pagan barbarians. To the Britons they seemed to be monsters of cruelty and savagery, as the Angles and Saxons had themselves seemed to the Celts centuries before. In Britain the Viking migration followed a similar course to the Anglo-Saxon migration. The Vikings, however, in the north sailed as far as Iceland, Greenland, and America; and in the south they ravaged the coasts of France and Spain, and sailed the length of the Mediterranean. The Vikings made an extremely profitable business of piracy, and combined trade with massacre. They discovered that the British Isles and Europe, lacking seapower, were defenseless against them, and promptly made the most of this advantage. Just as the Angles and Saxons had begun coming to England for plunder, but had ended by settling there, the Vikings were soon settling thickly in Northumbria and the east Midlands, besides forming isolated smaller settlements on the west coast and in Ireland.

The Vikings, however, did not kill or drive out the English as the Anglo-Saxons had killed or driven out the Celts. The new invaders were gradually absorbed into the English population, altering it, but in time accepting its religion and language and becoming a part of it. But the Vikings were never able to overrun all England; for in Wessex, in the south, a great leader appeared who successfully opposed them, and at the same time reformed the government of his kingdom and revived there the cause of Christianity and education.

## ALFRED THE GREAT

This leader was Alfred, justly called Alfred the Great, who ruled Wessex from 871 until his death in 899. Early in life he developed a quality extraordinary in his time: a willingness to place the interests of his people and of his family first, and his own interests second. In addition, he had a keen sense of reality. He could see through appearances; he could size up men and situations; and his deepest concern was not just to save his land from the Vikings, but to civilize his people and to revive Christianity. We are chiefly concerned with this educational and religious side of Alfred's achievement, because out of it arose the earliest English prose literature. But we should remember that Alfred's real greatness lay in his many-sidedness. Besides being an educator and a religious reformer, he was a capable and successful warrior, he created the first English navy, he revised and simplified the law, he rebuilt and improved the structure of government, and he transformed the old Germanic social relationships into the beginnings of English feudalism. We know, too, that Alfred was a devoted sportsman, and that he loved to hear old English poems, such as *Beowulf*, recited by minstrels.

Alfred believed that wisdom could not fail, and that the chief trouble of the English was their ignorance. For this reason he surrounded himself with learned men—chiefly from abroad, since there were none at all in Wessex —and set up a school as a part of his household. His officials and their children were forced to learn all they could, and he himself struggled to learn Latin after he was forty years old. He realized, however, that it would take a long time for his officials and churchmen to learn enough Latin to benefit from the Latin works which at that time contained practically all organized knowledge; therefore he decided upon a plan which seems simple and obvious now, but which at the time was revolutionary. He decided to translate some of the most essential books into the language of the people, Anglo-Saxon.

Alfred's translations were co-operative works, though all were made under his direction.

Some he made himself; others he made in part; and still others were made entirely by associates such as Bishop Werferth. Translations were made of Gregory the Great's *Dialogues* and *Pastoral Care*, Bede's *Ecclesiastical History*, the *History of the World* by Orosius, *The Consolation of Philosophy* by Boethius, and the *Soliloquies* of St. Augustine of Hippo. In addition, it seems likely that the *Anglo-Saxon Chronicle* was written under Alfred's direction, so that with the *History* of Orosius and the *Chronicle* together the English might have a continuous view of history from the beginning to their own time. We also owe to Alfred such eighth-century and ninth-century poetry as we have, because it all survives only in West-Saxon versions made under his influence.

Several of the Alfredian translations were really free adaptations, with some passages omitted and others inserted; and these throw light on Alfred's widely ranging curiosity and on his thinking. We see, for instance, Alfred's special interest in his own part of the world when he puts into his version of Orosius descriptions of all the regions in which Germanic languages were spoken, and when he puts in also narratives given to him by two sailors of their voyages in the north. To take a quite different example, Alfred speaks to his readers from his inmost self in the passage from his version of St. Augustine's *Soliloquies:* "I would know whether after the parting of the body and the soul I shall ever know more than I now know of all that which I have long wished to know; for I cannot find anything better in man than that he know, and nothing worse than that he be ignorant."

Besides their personal interest these translations possess considerable interest because of their language and style. One finds upon looking into them that English speech in the ninth century was developing in the direction of our own speech of today. Many of Alfred's sentence-structures are almost exactly like our own, and his words, too, although their forms appear strange to us, are often our words. It can therefore be said with substantial truth that in Alfred's prose we have the beginnings

of English literature. Old English poetry looks back, but Old English prose looks forward.

In general Alfred's efforts did not quickly or strikingly bear fruit. Yet his successors in the tenth century did become kings of all England; and in spite of frequent wars, the struggle to keep learning alive was not abandoned. At least two churchmen appeared, Aelfric in the latter half of the tenth century and early part of the eleventh, and Wulfstan in the first quarter of the eleventh century, who in their homilies, or sermons, show that much progress had been made since Alfred's time in the writing of literary prose.

### THE LAST ANGLO-SAXON KING

But the times were still troubled and uncertain. Evidently there could be no secure or considerable advance towards civilization as long as violence and disorder continued. And disorder and violence were still normal in the tenth century and in the eleventh, with no leader appearing who was able to form a firm government. Danish raids were renewed towards the end of the tenth century, and were so successful that soon the southern part of England was paying heavy tribute to Sweyn Forkbeard, King of Denmark, to keep peace. Then in 1016 Sweyn's son, Canute, forcibly seized the English crown. He was a wise and good ruler; and as king also of Denmark, conqueror of Norway, and lord of the Hebrides, he held a North-Sea empire which, under capable successors, might have greatly altered European history. But with the death of the man who had erected it this empire fell apart, and Edward the Confessor, son of the last Saxon king before Canute, became king of England. Edward had been living in exile in Norway, and had been influenced by French piety and French feudal civilization, so that on his return he did what he could to sway England toward the Norman-French way of life. Thus he prepared the way for the last invasion of England, and for the momentous changes which followed and which brought England once and for all within the circle of Latin civilization.

# Beowulf [1]

There is only one extant manuscript of Beowulf. It is bound with some other Old English texts in a volume belonging to the collection of Sir Robert Cotton (1571–1631), which is now in the British Museum. This manuscript was written by two scribes about A.D. 1000. The poem was probably composed in the first half of the eighth century. Of its author nothing is directly known, though the internal evidence of the poem enables us to picture him to ourselves "as a man connected in some way with an Anglian court, a royal chaplain or abbot of noble birth or, it may be, a monk friend of his, who possessed an actual knowledge of court life and addressed himself to an aristocratic, in fact a royal audience. A man well versed in Germanic and Scandinavian heroic lore, familiar with secular Anglo-Saxon poems of the type exemplified by Widsith, Finnsburg, Deor, and Waldere, and a student of Biblical poems of the Caedmonian cycle, a man of notable taste and culture and informed with a spirit of broad-minded Christianity" (Fr. Klaeber, Beowulf, p. cxxii). The poem consists of two parts, joined to each other only by the person of the hero. The first part has three divisions: Beowulf's fight with Grendel, his fight with Grendel's mother, and his return to his own land. In the second part is narrated his struggle, after the passage of many years, with a dragon. The events of the poem take place entirely in Denmark and southern Sweden, and England is nowhere mentioned in it. It is considered practically certain that the stories of the conflict with the Grendel race and of the slaying of the dragon are of direct Scandinavian origin. The Anglian author, however, fuses with these many other elements from other sources—notably the pervasive Christian coloring, which deeply affects the character of the poem. But notwithstanding the latter, Beowulf gives us a faithful picture of many phases of ancient Germanic life, moral as well as material, and particularly of Germanic military ideals. Practically the only direct historical data of the poem are the several allusions to the raid of Hygelac which took place between A.D. 512 and 520. It has been conjectured that a person named Beowulf actually accompanied Hygelac on this raid and so distinguished himself by exceptional bravery that he gradually became a center of heroic legend. Whether this be so or not, the Beowulf of the poem is obviously an idealized, heroic figure, not an historical character.

The original poem, although it makes no use of rime, is written in a meter. Each verse contains four accented syllables together with a freely varying number of unaccented ones, and each verse contains a marked pause between the second and third accented syllables. The accented syllables are, with the exceptions presently to be noted, distinguished by alliteration—that is, they begin with the same sound. They occur at the beginning of a word, save that prefixes are disregarded. Like consonant sounds alliterate with each other, whether they are indicated by the same letter or not; thus card and kitchen alliterate with each other, as also noon and knight, and bedeck and indict. Any vowel sound alliterates with any other vowel sound. The fourth accented syllable never alliterates with the third in Old English verse of the best period; but the third always alliterates with the first or second, and in the majority of cases with both. Occasionally the fourth accented syllable alliterates with the second, and more rarely with the first, when either of these is not in alliteration with the third.

The first eleven lines of Beowulf are subjoined in their original form:

[1] From *Old English Poetry*, translated by J. Duncan Spaeth. Copyright 1922 by Princeton University Press. Used by permission.

Hwæt, we Gar-Dena     in geardagum,
Þeodcyninga     þrym gefrunon,
huþa æþelingas     ellen fremedon!

Oft Scyld Scefing        sceaþena þreatum,
monegum mægþum        meodo-setla ofteah,
egsode eorl[as],        syððan ærest wearð
feasceaft funden;        he þæs frofre gebad,
weox under wolcnum,        weorðmyndum þah,
oð þæt him æghwylc        þara ymbsittendra
ofer hron-rade        hyran scolde,
gomban gyldan;        þæt wæs god cyning!

*A good edition of the original text, together
with an excellent summary of the scholarship
which has grown up around the poem, is* Beowulf and the Fight at Finnsburg, *ed. Franz
Klaeber (Boston, 1922). The historical and
literary background is discussed more fully by
Raymond W. Chambers,* Beowulf; an Introduction to the Study of the Poem, with a Discussion of the Stories of Offa and Finn *(Cambridge, 1921), and by William W. Lawrence,*
Beowulf and Epic Tradition *(Cambridge,
U. S. A., 1928). For a standard work on the
whole period see Francis B. Gummere,* Germanic Origins: A Study in Primitive Culture
*(New York, 1892; reissued under new title,*
Founders of England, *1930).*

### The Myth of the Sheaf-Child [2]

List to an old-time lay of the Spear-Danes,
Full of the prowess of famous kings,
Deeds of renown that were done by the heroes;
Scyld the Sheaf-Child from scourging foemen,
From raiders a-many their mead-halls wrested.
He lived to be feared, though first as a waif, [6]
Puny and frail he was found on the shore.
He grew to be great, and was girt with power
Till the border-tribes all obeyed his rule,
And sea-folk hardy that sit by the whale-path [10]
Gave him tribute, a good king was he.
Many years after, an heir was born to him,
A goodly youth, whom God had sent
To stay and support his people in need.
(Long time leaderless living in woe, [15]
The sorrow they suffered He saw full well.)
The Lord of Glory did lend him honor,
Beowulf's [3] fame afar was borne,
Son of old Scyld in the Scandian lands.
A youthful heir must be open-handed, [20]
Furnish the friends of his father with plenty,
That thus in his age, in the hour of battle,
Willing comrades may crowd around him
Eager and true. In every tribe
Honorable deeds shall adorn an earl. [25]
The aged Scyld, when his hour had come,
Famous and praised, departed to God.
His faithful comrades carried him down
To the brink of the sea, as himself had bidden,
The Scyldings' friend, before he fell silent, [30]
Their lord beloved who long had ruled them.

[2] The Sheaf-Child, Scyld, is the mythical ancestor
of Hrothgar, King of the Spear-Danes.

[3] Not the Beowulf of this poem, but another of
the same name.

Out in the bay a boat was waiting
Coated with ice, 'twas the king's own barge.
They lifted aboard their bracelet-bestower,
And down on the deck their dear lord laid, [35]
Hard by the mast. Heaped-up treasure
Gathered from far they gave him along.
Never was ship more nobly laden
With wondrous weapons and warlike gear.
Swords and corslets covered his breast, [40]
Floating riches to ride afar with him
Out o'er the waves at the will of the sea.
No less they dowered their lord with treasure,
Things of price, than those who at first
Had launched him forth as a little child [45]
Alone on the deep to drift o'er the billows.
They gave him to boot a gilded banner,
High o'er his head they hung it aloft.
Then set him adrift, let the surges bear him.
Sad were their hearts, their spirits mournful; [50]
Man hath not heard, no mortal can say
Who found that barge's floating burden.

## I

### The Line of the Danish Kings and the Building of Heorot

Now Beowulf was king in the burgs of the
        Scyldings,
Famed among folk. (His father had left
The land of the living.) From his loins was
        sprung
Healfdene the royal, who ruled to old age,
Gray and battlegrim, the bold-hearted Scyld-
        ings. [5]
Children four to this chief of the people
Woke unto life, one after another;
Heorogar and Hrothgar, and Halga the brave,
And winsome Sigeneow, a Scylfing she wedded;
Saewela's queen they say she became. [10]
To Hrothgar was given such glory in battle,
Such fame he won, that his faithful band
Of youthful warriors waxed amain.
So great had grown his guard of kinsmen,
That it came in his mind to call on his people
To build a mead-hall, mightier far [16]
Than any e'er seen by the sons of men,
Wherein to bestow upon old and young,
Gifts and rewards, as God vouchsafed them,
Save folk-share lands and freemen's lives. [20]
Far and wide the work was published;
Many a tribe, the mid-earth round,
Helped to fashion the folk-stead fair.
With speed they built it, and soon 'twas fin-
        ished,
Greatest of halls. Heorot [4] he named it, [25]
Whose word was law o'er lands afar;
Nor failed in his promise, but freely dealt
Gifts at the feast. The fair hall towered
Wide-gabled and high, awaiting its doom,
The sweep of fire; not far was the time [30]
That ancient feuds should open afresh,
And sword-hate sunder sons from fathers.

[4] The word means hart.

In the darkness dwelt a demon-sprite,
Whose heart was filled with fury and hate,
When he heard each night the noise of
revel                                    35
Loud in the hall, laughter and song.
To the sound of the harp the singer chanted
Lays he had learned, of long ago;
How the Almighty had made the earth,
Wonder-bright lands, washed by the ocean; 40
How he set triumphant, sun and moon
To lighten all men that live on the earth.
He brightened the land with leaves and
branches;
Life he created for every being,
Each in its kind, that moves upon earth.   45
So, happy in hall, the heroes lived,
Wanting naught, till one began
To work them woe, a wicked fiend.
The demon grim was Grendel called,
March-stalker huge, the moors he roamed.   50
The joyless creature had kept long time
The lonely fen, the lairs of monsters,
Cast out from men, an exile accurst.
The killing of Abel, on offspring of Cain
Was justly avenged by the Judge Eternal.   55
Nought gained by the feud the faithless mur-
derer;
He was banished unblest from abode of men.
And hence arose the host of miscreants,
Monsters and elves and eldritch sprites,
Warlocks and giants, that warred against God;
Jotuns and goblins; He gave them their due. 61

## II

### *The Ravaging of Heorot Hall by the Monster Grendel*

When night had fallen, the fiend crept near
To the lofty hall, to learn how the Danes
In Heorot fared, when the feasting was done.
The aethelings all within he saw
Asleep after revel, not recking of danger,   5
And free from care. The fiend accurst,
Grim and greedy, his grip made ready;
Snatched in their sleep, with savage fury,
Thirty warriors; away he sprang
Proud of his prey, to repair to his home,   10
His blood-dripping booty to bring to his lair.
At early dawn, when day-break came,
The vengeance of Grendel was revealed to all,
Their wails after wassail were widely heard,
Their morning-woe. The mighty ruler,      15
The aetheling brave, sat bowed with grief.
The fate of his followers filled him with sorrow,
When they traced the tracks of the treacherous
foe,
Fiend accurst. Too fierce was that onset,
Too loathsome and long, nor left them respite.
The very next night, anew he began        21
To maim and to murder, nor was minded to
slacken
His fury of hate, too hardened in crime.

'Twas easy to find then earls who preferred
A room elsewhere, for rest at night,        25
A bed in the bowers, when they brought this
news
Of the hall-foe's hate; and henceforth all
Who escaped the demon, kept distance safe.

So Grendel wrongfully ruled the hall,
One against all till empty stood           30
That lordly mansion, and long remained so.
For the space of twelve winters the Scyldings'
Friend [5]
Bore in his breast the brunt of this sorrow,
Measureless woe. In mournful lays
The tale became known; 'twas told abroad    35
In gleemen's songs, how Grendel had warred
Long against Hrothgar, and wreaked his hate
With murderous fury through many a year,
Refusing to end the feud perpetual,
Or decently deal with the Danes in parley,   40
Take their tribute for treaty of peace;
Nor could their leaders look to receive
Pay from his hands for the harm that he
wrought.
The fell destroyer kept feeding his rage
On young and old. So all night long        45
He prowled o'er the fen and surprised his vic-
tims,
Death-shadow dark. (The dusky realms
Where the hell-runes haunt are hidden from
men.)
So the exiled roamer his raids continued;
Wrong upon wrong in his wrath he heaped.   50
In midnights dark he dwelt alone
'Mongst Heorot's trophies and treasures rich.
Great was the grief of the gold-friend of Scyld-
ings,
Vexed was his mood that he might not visit
His goodly throne, his gift-seat proud,    55
Deprived of joy by the judgment of God.
Many the wise men that met to discover
Ways of escape from the scourge of affliction.
Often they came for counsel together;
Often at heathen altars they made          60
Sacrifice-offerings, beseeching their idols
To send them deliverance from assault of the
foe.
Such was their practice, they prayed to the
Devil;
The hope of the heathen on hell was fixed,
The mood of their mind. Their Maker they
knew not,                                   65
The righteous Judge and Ruler on high.
The Wielder of Glory they worshipped not,
The Warden of Heaven. Woe be to him
Whose soul is doomed through spite and envy,
In utter despair and agony hopeless         70
Forever to burn. But blessed is he
Who, after this life, the Lord shall seek,
Eager for peace in the arms of the Father.

[5] Hrothgar.

## III

### The Voyage of Beowulf to the Hall of Hrothgar

Thus boiled with care the breast of Hrothgar;
Ceaselessly sorrowed the son of Healfdene,
None of his chieftains might change his lot.
Too fell was the foe that afflicted the people
With wrongs unnumbered, and nightly hor-
rors.                                               5
Then heard in his home king Hygelac's thane,[6]
The dauntless Jute,[7] of the doings of Grendel.
In strength he outstripped the strongest of men
That dwell in the earth in the days of this life.
Gallant and bold, he gave command         10
To get him a boat, a good wave-skimmer.
O'er the swan-road, he said, he would seek the
king
Noble and famous, who needed men.
Though dear to his kin, they discouraged him
not;
The prudent in counsel praised the adven-
ture,                                              15
Whetted his valor, awaiting good omens.

So Beowulf chose from the band of the Jutes
Heroes brave, the best he could find;
He with fourteen followers hardy,
Went to embark; he was wise in seamanship,
Showed them the landmarks, leading the
way.                                              21
Soon they descried their craft in the water,
At the foot of the cliff. Then climbed aboard
The chosen troop; the tide was churning
Sea against sand; they stowed away         25
In the hold of the ship their shining armor,
War-gear and weapons; the warriors launched
Their well-braced boat on her welcome voyage.

Swift o'er the waves with a wind that favored,
Foam on her breast, like a bird she flew.   30
A day and a night they drove to seaward,
Cut the waves with the curving prow,
Till the seamen that sailed her sighted the
land,
Shining cliffs and coast-wise hills,
Headlands bold. The harbor opened,         35
Their cruise was ended. Then quickly the
sailors,
The crew of Weder-folk clambered ashore,
Moored their craft with clank of chain-mail,
And goodly war-gear. God they thanked
That their way was smooth o'er the surging
waves.                                            40

High on the shore, the Scylding coast-guard
Saw from the cliff where he kept his watch,

[6] Beowulf.
[7] The people are called Geats in the original; the
translator assumes that they are Jutes from Jutland
on the Baltic.

Glittering shields o'er the gang-plank carried,
Polished weapons. It puzzled him sore,
He wondered in mind who the men might be.
Down to the strand on his steed came riding  46
Hrothgar's thane, with threatening arm
Shook his war-spear and shouted this challenge:
"Who are ye, men, all mailed and harnessed,
That brought yon ship o'er the broad sea-ways,
And hither have come across the water,      51
To land on our shores? Long have I stood
As coast-guard here, and kept my sea-watch,
Lest harrying foe with hostile fleet
Should dare to damage our Danish land.      55
Armed men never from overseas came
More openly hither. But how do ye know
That law of the land doth give ye leave
To come thus near. I never have seen
Statelier earl upon earth than him,—        60
Yon hero in harness. No house-carl he,
In lordly array, if looks speak true,
And noble bearing. But now I must learn
Your names and country, ere nearer ye come,
Underhand spies, for aught I know,          65
In Danish land. Now listen ye strangers,
In from the sea, to my open challenge:
Heed ye my words and haste me to know
What your errand and whence ye have come."

## IV

### Beowulf's Words with the Coast-Guard

Him the hero hailed with an answer,
The war-troop's leader, his word-hoard un-
locked:
"In truth we belong to the tribe of the Jutes;
We are Hygelac's own hearth-companions.
Far among folk my father was known,         5
A noble chieftain; his name was Ecgtheow.
Honored by all, he ended his days
Full of winters and famed in the land.
Wise men everywhere well remember him.
Hither we fare with friendly purpose        10
To seek thy lord, the son of Healfdene,
The land-protector. Instruct us kindly.
Bound on adventure we visit thy lord,
The prince of the Danes. Our purpose is open;
Nought keep we secret; thou surely wilt know
If the tale we were told is true or not:    16
That among the Scyldings a monster strange,
A nameless demon, when nights are dark,
With cruel cunning, for cause unknown,
Works havoc and slaughter. I have in mind 20
A way to help your wise king Hrothgar,
Your ruler to rid of the ravening foe,
If ever his tide of troubles shall turn,
The billows of care that boil in his breast
Shall cool and subside, and his sorrow be cured;
Else, failing my purpose, forever hereafter  26
He shall suffer distress, while stands on its hill,
Mounting on high, his matchless hall."
Straight answered the coast-guard, astride his
horse,

The warrior brave: "Twixt words and deeds 30
A keen-witted thane, if he thinks aright,
Must well distinguish and weigh the difference.
Your words I believe, that you wish no evil
To the Scylding lord. I will let you bring
Your shields ashore and show you the way. 35
My comrades here shall keep the watch,
From meddling foe defend your craft,
Your fresh-tarred boat, fast by the beach,
And faithfully guard her till again she bear
With curving bow, o'er the bounding main, 40
Her master well-loved to the Wedermark.
Fortune oft favors the fighter who yields not;
Hero unflinching comes unhurt from the fray."
Landward they hastened, leaving behind them
Fast at her moorings the full-bosomed boat, 45
The ship at anchor. Shone the boar-heads,
Gleaming with gold, o'er the guards of their
    helmets;
Bright and fire-forged the beast kept watch.
Forward they pressed, proud and adventurous,
Fit for the fight, till afar they descried      50
The high-peaked radiant roof of the hall.
Of houses far-praised 'neath heaven by the
    people
That inhabit the earth, this house was most
    famous,
The seat of King Hrothgar; its splendor
    gleamed bright
O'er many a land. Their leader well-armed 55
Showed them the shining shield-burg of
    heroes,
And set them right on the road to their goal.
Then, wheeling his steed, he wished them fare-
    well:

" 'Tis time that I leave you; the Lord of
    Heaven,
The Father Almighty in mercy keep you      60
Safe on your journey; seaward I turn,
Watch to keep and ward against foe."

## V

### Beowulf's Arrival at the Hall and the Manner of his Reception

The street was stone-paved; straight it led
To the goal of their journey. Glistened their
    byrnies
Stout and strong-linked; sang the rings
Of their iron mail as they marched along,
In armor and helmet right up to the hall.      5
Sea-voyage-sated, they set their shields,
Their linden-woods broad, along the wall.
As they bent to the bench, their byrnies clat-
    tered.
They stacked their spears that stood in a row,
Ashwood tipped with iron above;      10
Well-equipped was the warlike band.
A stately Dane the strangers addressed,
Asked who they were and whence they had
    come:
"Whence do ye bear your burnished shields,

Your visored helmets and harness gray      15
Your heap of spear-shafts? A servant of Hroth-
    gar's,
His herald, am I. Hardier strangers,
Nobler in mien, have I never seen.
'Tis clear you come to the court of Hrothgar,
Not outlaws and beggars, but bent on adven-
    ture."      20
To him gave answer the hero brave,
The lord of the Weders these words returned,
Bold 'neath his helmet: "We are Hygelac's
    men,
His board-companions. I am Beowulf called."
Ready am I the ruler to answer,      25
To say to thy lord, the son of Healfdene,
Why we have come his court to seek,
If he will graciously grant us a hearing."
Wulfgar replied (he was prince of the Wen-
    dles,
His noble renown was known to many,      30
His courage in war, and wisdom in counsel):
"I will carry thy quest to the king of the Danes,
And ask him whether he wishes to grant
The boon thou dost ask of the breaker-of-rings,
To speak to himself concerning thy journey; 35
And straight will I bring thee the answer he
    sends."
Swiftly he hied him where Hrothgar sat,
White-haired and old, his earls around him.
Stately he strode, till he stood in the presence
Of the king of the Danes,—in courtly ways 40
Was Wulfgar skilled; he spoke to his lord:
"Hither have fared from a far country,
A band of Jutes o'er the bounding sea.
Their leader and chief by his chosen comrades
Is Beowulf called; this boon they ask:      45
That they may find with thee, my lord,
Favor of speech; refuse them not,
But grant them, Hrothgar, gracious hearing.
In armor clad, they claim respect
Of choicest earls; but chiefly their lord      50
Who lately hither hath led his comrades."

## VI

### Hrothgar's Welcome to Beowulf

Hrothgar spoke, the Scyldings' protector:
"Beowulf I knew in his boyhood days;
His aged father was Ecgtheow named.
To him, to take home, did Hrethel give
His only daughter. Their dauntless son      5
Now comes to my court in quest of a friend.
My sea-faring men whom I sent afar
To the land of the Jutes, with generous gifts,
In token of friendship, have told me this,
That the power of his grip was so great it
    equalled      10
The strength of thirty stout-armed thanes.
Him bold in battle, the blessed God
Hath sent in his mercy, to save our people
—So I hope in my heart—from the horror of
    Grendel.
I shall offer him gold for his gallant spirit.      15

Go now in haste, and greet the strangers;
Bid to the hall the whole of the company;
Welcome with words the warrior band,
To the home of the Danes." To the hall door went
Wulfgar the courtly, and called them in:  20
"My master commands me this message to give you,
The lord of the Danes your lineage knows;
Bids me to welcome you, brave-hearted warriors,
Bound on adventure o'er the billowy main.
Ye may rise now and enter, arrayed in your armor,  25
Covered with helmets, the king to greet.
But leave your shields, and your shafts of slaughter,
Here by the wall to await the issue."
Then rose the leader, around him his comrades,
Sturdy war-band; some waited without,  30
Bid by the bold one their battle-gear to guard.
Together they hastened where the herald led them,
Under Heorot's roof. The hero went first,
Strode under helmet, till he stood by the hearth.
Beowulf spoke, his byrnie glistened,  35
His corslet chain-linked by cunning of smith-craft:
"Hail, king Hrothgar! Hygelac's thane
And kinsman am I. Known is the record
Of deeds of renown I have done in my youth.
Far in my home, I heard of this Grendel;  40
Sea-farers tell the tale of the hall:
How bare of warriors, this best of buildings
Deserted stands, when the sun goes down
And twilight deepens to dark in the sky.
By comrades encouraged, I come on this journey.  45
The best of them bade me, the bravest and wisest,
To go to thy succor, O good king Hrothgar;
For well they approved my prowess in battle,
They saw me themselves come safe from the conflict  49
When five of my foes I defeated and bound,
Beating in battle the brood of the monsters.
At night on the sea with nicors I wrestled,
Avenging the Weders, survived the sea-peril,
And crushed in my grip the grim sea-monsters
That harried my neighbors. Now I am come
To cope with Grendel in combat single,  56
And match my might against the monster, alone.
I pray thee therefore, prince of the Scyldings,
Not to refuse the favor I ask,
Having come so far, O friend of the Shield-Danes,  60
That I alone with my loyal comrades,
My hardy companions, may Heorot purge.
Moreover they say that the slaughterous fiend
In wanton mood all weapons despises.
Hence,—as I hope that Hygelac may,  65

My lord and king, be kind to me,—
Sword and buckler I scorn to bear,
Gold-adorned shield, as I go to the conflict.
With my grip will I grapple the gruesome fiend,
Foe against foe, to fight for our life.  70
And he that shall fall his faith must put
In the judgment of God. If Grendel wins
He is minded to make his meal in the hall
Untroubled by fear, on the folk of the Jutes,
As often before he fed on the Danes.  75
No need for thee then to think of my burial.
If I lose my life, the lonely prowler
My blood-stained body will bear to his den,
Swallow me greedily, and splash with my gore
His lair in the marsh; no longer wilt then  80
Have need to find me food and sustenance.
To Hygelac send, if I sink in the battle,
This best of corslets that covers my breast,
Heirloom of Hrethel, rarest of byrnies,
The work of Weland.[8] So Wyrd[9] will be done."  85

## VII

### *The Feasting in Heorot and the Customs of the Hall*

Hrothgar spoke, the Scyldings' defender:
"Thou hast come, dear Beowulf, to bring us help,
For the sake of friendship to fight our battles.

Fifteen lines are omitted, in which Hrothgar recounts the exploits of Beowulf's father.

Sad is my spirit and sore it grieves me
To tell to any the trouble and shame  5
That Grendel hath brought me with bitter hate,
The havoc he wrought in my ranks in the hall.
My war-band dwindles, driven by Wyrd
Into Grendel's grasp; but God may easily
End this monster's mad career.  10
Full often they boasted, my beer-bold warriors,
Brave o'er their ale-cups, the best of my fighters,
They'd meet in the mead-hall the mighty Grendel,
End his orgies with edge of the sword.
But always the mead-hall, the morning after,
The splendid building, was blood-bespattered;  16
Daylight dawned on the drippings of swords,
Soiled with slaughter were sills and benches.
My liegemen perished, and left me poor.  19
Sit down to the board; unbend thy thoughts;
Speak to my men as thy mood shall prompt."
For the band of the Jutes a bench was cleared;
Room in the mead-hall was made for them all.
Then strode to their seats the strong-hearted heroes.

---

[8] The smith of Norse legend.   [9] Fate.

The warriors' wants a waiting-thane served;
Held in his hand the highly-wrought ale-cup,
Poured sparkling mead, while the minstrel sang
Gaily in Heorot. There was gladness of heroes,
A joyous company of Jutes and of Danes.    25

## VIII

### *Unferth Taunts Beowulf*

Then up spoke Unferth, Ecglaf's son,
Who sat at the feet of the Scylding ruler;
He vented his jealousy. The journey of Beowulf,
His sea-adventure, sorely displeased him.
It filled him with envy that any other    5
Should win among men more war-like glory,
More fame under heaven than he himself:
"Art thou the Beowulf that battled with Brecca,
Far out at sea, when ye swam together,
What time you two made trial of the billows,
Risking your lives in reckless folly,    11
On the open sea? None might dissuade you,
Friend nor foe, from the fool-hardy venture,
When straight from the shore you struck for the open,
Breasted the waves and beat with your arms    15
The mounting billows, measured the sea-paths
With lusty strokes. Stirred was the ocean
By wintry storms. Seven days and nights
Your sea-strife lasted; at length he beat you,
His strength was the better; at break of day    20
He made the beach where the Battle-Reamas
Dwell by the shore; and straightway returned
To his people beloved in the land of the Brondings,
Where liegemen and towns and treasure were his.
In sooth I say, the son of Beanstan    25
His boast against thee made good to the full.
But now I ween a worse fate awaits thee
Though thy mettle be proved in many a battle
And grim encounter, if the coming of Grendel
Thou darest abide, in the dead of the night."
Beowulf spoke, the son of Ecgtheow:    31
"What a deal of stuff thou hast talked about Brecca,
Garrulous with drink, my good friend Unferth.
Thou hast lauded his deeds. Now listen to me!
More sea-strength had I, more ocean-endurance,    35
Than any man else, the wide earth round.
'Tis true we planned in the pride of our youth
This ocean-adventure, and vowed we would risk
Our lives in the deep, each daring the other.
We were both of us boys, but our boast we fulfilled.    40
Our naked swords as we swam from the land,
We held in our grasp, to guard against whales.
Not a stroke could he gain on me, strive as he would,

Make swifter speed through the swelling waves,
Nor could I in swimming o'ercome him at sea.    45
Side by side in the surge we labored
Five nights long. At last we were parted
By furious seas and a freezing gale.
Night fell black; the norther wild    49
Rushed on us ruthless and roughened the sea.
Now was aroused the wrath of the monsters,
But my war-proof ring-mail, woven and hand-locked,
Served me well 'gainst the sea-beasts' fury;
The close-linked battle-net covered my breast.
I was dragged to the bottom by a blood-thirsty monster,    55
Firm in his clutch the furious sea-beast
Helpless held me. But my hand came free,
And my foe I pierced with point of my sword.
With my battle-blade good 'twas given me to kill    59
The dragon of the deep, by dint of my blow."

## IX

### *Beowulf Completes the Story of his Swimming Adventure with Brecca. Hrothgar's Departure from the Hall*

"Thus sore beset me sea-beasts thronging,
Murderous man-eaters. I met their charges,
Gave them their due with my goodly blade.
They failed of their fill, the feast they expected
In circle sitting on the sea-floor together    5
With me for their meal. I marred their pleasure.
When morning came, they were cast ashore
By the wash of the waves; their wounds proved fatal;
Bloated and dead on the beach they lay.
No more would they cross the course of the ships,    10
In the chop of the channel charge the sailors.
Day broke in the east, bright beacon of God;
The sea fell smooth. I saw bold headlands,
Windy walls; for Wyrd oft saveth
A man not doomed, if he dauntless prove.    15
My luck did not fail me, my long sword finished
Nine of the nicors. Ne'er have I heard
Of fiercer battle fought in the night,
Of hero more harried by horrors at sea.
Yet I saved my life from the sea-beasts' clutch.
Worn with the struggle, I was washed ashore    21
In the realm of the Finns by the run of the tide,
The heave of the flood. I have failed to hear
Of like adventure laid to thee,
Battle so bitter. Brecca did never,—    25
Neither of you was known to achieve
Deed so valiant, adventure so daring,
Sword-play so nimble; not that I boast of it,
But mark me Unferth, you murdered your brothers,

Your closest of kin. The curse of hell 30
For this you will suffer, though sharp be your
 wit.
In sooth I say to you, son of Ecglaf,
Never had Grendel such grim deeds wrought,
Such havoc in Heorot, so harried your king
With bestial fury, if your boasted courage 35
In deeds as well as in words you had proved.
But now he has found he need not fear
Vengeance fierce from the Victory-Scyldings,
Ruthless attack in return for his raids.
He takes his toll of your tribe as he pleases,
Sparing none of your spearmen proud. 41
He ravens and rages and recks not the Dane
 folk,
Safe from their sword-play. But soon I will
 teach him
How the Jute-folk fight. Then freely may go
To the mead-hall who likes, when the light of
 morning, 45
The next day's dawn, the dark shall dispel,
And the heaven-bright sun from the south shall
 shine."

Glad in his heart was the giver of rings,
Hoped to have help, the hoar-headed king; 49
The Shield-Danes' shepherd was sure of relief,
When he found in Beowulf so firm a resolve.
There was laughter of heroes. Loud was their
 revelry,
Words were winsome as Wealhtheow rose,
Queen of Hrothgar, heedful of courtesy,
Gold-adorned greeted the guests in the hall.
First to her lord, the land-defender, 56
The high-born lady handed the cup;
Bade him be gleeful and gay at the board,
And good to his people. Gladly he took it,
Quaffed from the beaker, the battle-famed
 king. 60
Then leaving her lord, the lady of the Helm-
 ings
Passed among her people in each part of the
 hall,
Offered the ale-cup to old and young,
Till she came to the bench where Beowulf sat.
The jewel-laden queen in courteous manner
Beowulf greeted; to God gave thanks, 66
Wise in her words, that her wish was granted,
That at last in her trouble a trusted hero
Had come for comfort. The cup received 69
From Wealhtheow's hand the hardy warrior,
And made this reply, his mind on the battle;
Beowulf spoke, the son of Ecgtheow:
"I made up my mind when my mates and I
Embarked in our boat, outbound on the sea,
That fully I'd work the will of thy people, 75
Or fall in the fight, in the clutch of the fiend.
I surely shall do a deed of glory,
Worthy an earl, or end my days,
My morning of life, in the mead-hall here."
His words pleased well the wife of Hrothgar,
The Jutish lord's boast. The jewelled queen 81
Went to sit by the side of her lord.

Renewed was the sound of noisy revel,
Wassail of warriors. Brave words were spoken.
Mirth in the mead-hall mounted high, 85
Till Healfdene's son [10] the sign did give
That he wished to retire. Full well he knew
The fiend would find a fight awaiting him,
When the light of the sun had left the hall,
And creeping night should close upon them, 90
And shadowy shapes come striding on
Dim through the dark. The Danes arose.
Hrothgar again gave greeting to Beowulf,
Wished him farewell; the wine-hall lofty
He left in his charge. These last words spoke
 he: 95
"Never before have I fully entrusted
To mortal man this mighty hall,
Since arm and shield I was able to lift.
To thee alone I leave it now,
To have and to hold it. Thy hardihood prove!
Be mindful of glory; keep watch for the foe!
No reward shalt thou lack if thou live through
 this fight." 102

## X

### Beowulf's Watch in Heorot

Then Hrothgar went with his warrior-band,
The Arm-of-the-Scyldings, out of the hall,
Would the war-lord Wealhtheow seek,
The queen for his bed-mate. The best of kings
Had placed in the hall, so heroes report, 5
A watch against Grendel, to guard his house,
Deliverance bring to the land of the Danes.
But the lord of the Jutes joyfully trusted
In the might of his arm and the mercy of God.
Off he stripped his iron byrnie, 10
Helmet from head, and handed his sword,
Choicest of blades, to his body-thane,
And bade him keep the battle armor.
Then made his boast once more the warrior,
Beowulf the bold, ere his bed he sought, 15
Summoned his spirit; "Not second to Grendel
In combat I count me and courage of war.
But not with the sword will I slay this foeman,
Though light were the task to take his life.
Nothing at all does he know of such fighting,
Of hewing of shields, though shrewd be his
 malice 21
Ill deeds to contrive. We two in the night
Shall do without swords, if he dare to meet me
In hand to hand battle. May the holy Lord
To one or the other award the victory, 25
As it seems to Him right, Ruler all-wise."
Then he sought his bed. The bolster received
The head of the hero. In the hall about him,
Stretched in sleep, his sailormen lay.
Not one of them thought he would ever return
Home to his country, nor hoped to see 31
His people again, and the place of his birth.
They had heard of too many men of the Danes
O'ertaken suddenly, slain without warning,
In the royal hall. But the Ruler on High 35

[10] Hrothgar.

Through the woof of fate to the Wederfolk
    gave
Friendship and help, their foes to o'ercome,
By a single man's strength to slay the destroyer.
Thus all may learn that the Lord Almighty
Wields for aye the Wyrds of men. . . .    40

## XI

### Beowulf's Fight with Grendel

Now Grendel came, from his crags of mist
Across the moor; he was curst of God.
The murderous prowler meant to surprise
In the high-built hall his human prey.
He stalked 'neath the clouds, till steep before
    him    5
The house of revelry rose in his path,
The gold-hall of heroes, the gaily adorned.
Hrothgar's home he had hunted full often,
But never before had he found to receive him
So hardy a hero, such hall-guards there.    10
Close to the building crept the slayer,
Doomed to misery. The door gave way,
Though fastened with bolts, when his fist fell
    on it.
Maddened he broke through the breach he had
    made;
Swoln with anger and eager to slay,    15
The ravening fiend o'er the bright-paved floor
Furious ran, while flashed from his eyes
An ugly glare like embers aglow.
He saw in the hall, all huddled together,
The heroes asleep. Then laughed in his heart 20
The hideous fiend; he hoped ere dawn
To sunder body from soul of each;
He looked to appease his lust of blood,
Glut his maw with the men he would slay.
But Wyrd had otherwise willed his doom;    25
Never again should he get a victim
After that night. Narrowly watched
Hygelac's thane how the horrible slayer
Forward should charge in fierce attack.
Nor was the monster minded to wait:    30
Sudden he sprang on a sleeping thane,
Ere he could stir, he slit him open;
Bit through the bone-joints, gulped the blood,
Greedily bolted the body piecemeal.
Soon he had swallowed the slain man wholly,
Hands and feet. Then forward he hastened, 36
Sprang at the hero, and seized him at rest;
Fiercely clutched him with fiendish claw.
But quickly Beowulf caught his forearm,
And threw himself on it with all his weight. 40
Straight discovered that crafty plotter,
That never in all midearth had he met
In any man a mightier grip.
Gone was his courage, and craven fear
Sat in his heart, yet helped him no sooner.    45
Fain would he hide in his hole in the fenland,
His devil's den. A different welcome
From former days he found that night!
Now Hygelac's thane, the hardy, remembered
His evening's boast, and bounding up,    50

Grendel he clenched, and cracked his fingers;
The monster tried flight, but the man pursued;
The ravager hoped to wrench himself free,
And gain the fen, for he felt his fingers
Helpless and limp in the hold of his foe.    55
'Twas a sorry visit the man-devourer
Made to the Hall of the Hart that night.
Dread was the din, the Danes were frighted
By the uproar wild of the ale-spilling fray.
The hardiest blenched as the hall-foes wrestled
In terrible rage. The rafters groaned;    61
'Twas wonder great that the wine-hall stood,
Firm 'gainst the fighters' furious onslaught,
Nor fell to the ground, that glorious building.
With bands of iron 'twas braced and stiffened
Within and without. But off from the sill    66
Many a mead-bench mounted with gold
Was wrung where they wrestled in wrath
    together.
The Scylding nobles never imagined
That open attack, or treacherous cunning,    70
Could wreck or ruin their royal hall,
The lofty and antlered, unless the flames
Should some day swallow it up in smoke.
The din was renewed, the noise redoubled;
Each man of the Danes was mute with dread,
That heard from the wall the horrible wail, 76
The gruesome song of the godless foe,
His howl of defeat, as the fiend of hell
Bemoaned his hurt. The man held fast;
Greatest he was in grip of strength,    80
Of all that dwelt upon earth that day.

## XII

### The Defeat of Grendel

Loath in his heart was the hero-deliverer
To let escape his slaughterous guest.
Of little use that life he deemed
To human kind. The comrades of Beowulf
Unsheathed their weapons to ward their leader,
Eagerly brandished their ancient blades,    6
The life of their peerless lord to defend.
Little they deemed, those dauntless warriors,
As they leaped to the fray, those lusty fighters,
Laying on boldly to left and to right,    10
Eager to slay, that no sword upon earth,
No keenest weapon, could wound that mon-
    ster:
Point would not pierce, he was proof against
    iron;
'Gainst victory-blades the devourer was
    charmed.
But a woful end awaited the wretch,    15
That very day he was doomed to depart,
And fare afar to the fiends' domain.

Now Grendel found, who in former days
So many a warrior had wantonly slain,
In brutish lust, abandoned of God,    20
That the frame of his body was breaking at
    last.
Keen of courage, the kinsman of Hygelac

Held him grimly gripped in his hands.
Loath was each to the other alive.
The grisly monster got his death-wound:    25
A huge split opened under his shoulder;
Crunched the socket, cracked the sinews.
Glory great was given to Beowulf.
But Grendel escaped with his gaping wound,
O'er the dreary moor his dark den sought,    30
Crawled to his lair. 'Twas clear to him then,
The count of his hours to end had come,
Done were his days. The Danes were glad,
The hard fight was over, they had their desire.
Cleared was the hall, 'twas cleansed by the hero    35
With keen heart and courage, who came from afar.
The lord of the Jutes rejoiced in his work,
The deed of renown he had done that night.
His boast to the Danes he bravely fulfilled;
From lingering woe delivered them all;    40
From heavy sorrow they suffered in heart;
From dire distress they endured so long;
From toil and from trouble. This token they saw:
The hero had laid the hand of Grendel
Both arm and claws, the whole forequarter    45
With clutches huge, 'neath the high-peaked roof.

## XIII

### The Celebration of the Victory and the Song of the Gleeman

When morning arrived, so runs the report,
Around the gift-hall gathered the warriors;
The folk-leaders fared from far and near,
The wide ways o'er, the wonder to view,
The wild beast's foot-prints. Not one of them felt    5
Regret that the creature had come to grief,
When they traced his retreat by the tracks on the moor;
Marked where he wearily made his way,
Harried and beaten, to the haunt of the nicors,
Slunk to the water, to save his life.    10
There they beheld the heaving surges,
Billows abrim with bloody froth,
Dyed with gore, where the gruesome fiend,
Stricken and doomed, in the struggle of death
Gave up his ghost in the gloom of the mere,    15
His heathen soul for hell to receive it.
Then from the mere the thanes turned back,
Men and youths from the merry hunt,
Home they rode on their horses gray,
Proudly sitting their prancing steeds.    20
Beowulf's prowess was praised by all.
They all agreed that go where you will,
'Twixt sea and sea, at the south or the north,
None better than he, no braver hero,
None worthier honor could ever be found,    25
(They meant no slight to their master and lord
The good king Hrothgar, their ruler kind.)

Now and again the noble chiefs
Gave rein to their steeds, and spurred them to race,
Galloped their grays where the ground was smooth.    30
Now and again a gallant thane,
Whose mind was stored with many a lay,
With songs of battle and sagas old,
Bound new words in well-knit bars,
Told in verse the valor of Beowulf,    35
Matched his lines and moulded his lay.

Here is introduced an episode of the Nibelungen Legend. The gleeman tells how Sigmund the Volsung, with his son and nephew Fitela, ranged the forests and slew wild beasts. Later, when Fitela was no longer with him, Sigmund killed a dragon and won a great treasure. [44 lines are omitted.]

When the lay was ended they urged once more
Their racers fleet to fly o'er the plain.
As the morning sped, and the sun climbed higher,
Many went in, the marvellous sight    40
More closely to scan. The king himself
With a troop of trusty retainers about him
Strode from his bower; the bestower-of-rings
Came, and with him the queen, in state,
The meadow-path trod, by her maidens attended.    45

### XIV

### Hrothgar's Praise of Beowulf, and Beowulf's Reply

Hrothgar spoke when he reached the hall,
Stood on the step, and stared at the roof
Adorned with gold, and Grendel's hand:
"Prompt be my heart to praise the Almighty
For the sight I behold. Much harm have I suffered,    5
And grief from Grendel, but God still works
Wonder on wonder, the Warden of Glory.
But a little while since, I scarcely dared,
As long as I lived, to look for escape
From my burden of sorrow, when blood-stained stood    10
And dripping with slaughter, this stately hall.
Wide-spread woe my warriors scattered;
They never hoped this house to rid,
While life should last, this land-mark of people,
Of demons and devils. 'Tis done by the hero.
By the might of the Lord this man has finished    16
The feat that all of us failed to achieve
By wit or by war. And well may she say,
—Whoever she be,—that bore this son,
That the Ancient of Days dealt with her graciously,    20
And blest her in child-birth. Now Beowulf, hear!
I shall henceforth hold thee, hero beloved,

As child of my own, and cherish thee fondly
In kinship new. Thou shalt never lack
Meed of reward that is mine to give.     25
For deeds less mighty have I many times
     granted
Fullest reward to warriors feebler,
In battle less brave. Thy boldness and valor
Afar shall be known; thy fame shall live
To be great among men. Now God the Al-
     mighty     30
With honor reward thee, as ever he doth."

Beowulf spoke, the son of Ecgtheow:
"Gladly we fought this good fight through,
Fearlessly faced the foe inhuman,     34
Grappled him gruesome; it grieves me sore
That the man-beast himself you may not see,
Dead in the hall, fordone in the fray.
I meant to master the monster quickly,
To his death-bed pin him by power of my grip,
Hold him hard till my hand could strangle
     him,     40
Bringing him low, but he broke away.
In vain I tried to prevent his escape.
The Lord was unwilling; I lost my hold
On the man-destroyer; too strong was the
     monster,
Too swift on his feet. But to save his life     45
He left behind him the whole of his fore-paw,
Arm and shoulder. 'Twas a useless shift,
Profiting nothing. He ne'er will prolong
His life by the loss, the loathly slayer,
Sunk in sin; but sorrow holds him,     50
Caught in the grasp of its grip relentless,
In woful bonds to await in anguish,
Guilty wretch, the rest of his doom,
As the Lord Almighty shall mete it to him."

More silent seemed the son of Ecglaf,[11]     55
Less boastful in bragging of brave deeds done,
When all of them, looking aloft, beheld
The hand on high, where it hung 'neath the
     roof,
The claw of the fiend; each finger was armed
With a steel-like spur instead of a nail,     60
The heathen's handspikes, the horrible paw
Of the evil fiend. They all declared
No iron blade could e'er have bit
On the monstrous bulk of the man-beast's
     hide,
Or hewn away that woful talon.     65

## XV

### The Feasting and Giving of Treasure in the Hall

Now orders were given the guest-hall to
     cleanse,
And furnish it fresh. Forth went hurrying
Men and maids. To the mead-hall they went
And busily worked. Woven tapestries,
Glinting with gold, hung gay on the walls,     5

[11] Unferth.

Marvellous wonders for men to look upon.
Ruin and wreck had been wrought in the
     building,
Though braced within by iron bands,
The hinges were wrenched, the roof alone
     stood
Undamaged and sound, when the sin-spotted
     wretch,     10
The demon destroyer, in despair of his life,
Turned and made off,—not easy it is
To escape from death, essay it who will.
(So each of us all to his end must come,
Forced by fate to his final abode     15
Where his body, stretched on the bier of death,
Shall rest after revel.) Now right was the hour
For Healfdene's heir to enter the hall;
The king himself would come to the feast.
I never have heard of nobler bearing     20
'Mongst ranks of liegemen surrounding their
     lord
As they took their seats, the trusty comrades,
And fell to feasting. Freely quaffed
Many a mead-cup the mighty kinsmen,
Hrothgar and Hrothulf, the high hall within.
Heorot was filled with a friendly host.     26
(Far was the day when the Scylding host
Should treachery plot, betraying each other.)
Then Healfdene's son bestowed on Beowulf
A gold-adorned banner for battle-reward,     30
A rich-broidered standard, breast-plate and
     helmet.
The swordmen assembled saw the treasures
Borne before the hero. Beowulf drank
The health of Hrothgar, nor had reason to feel
Ashamed before shieldmen to show his reward.
Never were offered by earls that I heard of,     36
In token of friendship four such treasures,
Never was equalled such ale-bench bounty.
Round the ridge of the helmet a rim of iron,
Wound with wire, warded the head,     40
That the offspring of files, with fearful stroke,
The hard-tempered sword-blade, might harm
     it not,
When fierce in the battle the foemen should
     join.
At a sign from the king, eight stallions proud,
Bitted and bridled, were brought into hall.     45
On the back of one was a wondrous saddle,
Bravely wrought and bordered with jewels,
The battle-seat bold of the best of kings
When Hrothgar himself would ride to the
     sword-play.
(Nor flinched from the foe the famous war-
     rior     50
In the front of the fight where fell the slain.)
To the hero delivered the lord of the Scyldings,
The heir of Ing, both armor and horses,
Gave them to Beowulf, and bade him enjoy
     them.
Thus royally, the ruler famous,     55
The heroes' hoard-guard, heaped his bounty;
Repaid the struggle with steeds and trophies,
Praised by all singers who speak the truth.

## XVI

### The King's Gifts to Beowulf's Men, and the Gleeman's Lay of Finn

The Lord of the earls then added gifts,
At the mead-bench remembered the men, each one,
That Beowulf brought o'er the briny deep,
With ancient heirlooms and offered to pay
In gold for the man that Grendel had slain,    5
As more of them surely the monster had killed
Had not holy God and the hero's courage
Averted their doom. (So daily o'errules
The Father Almighty the fortunes of men.
Therefore is insight ever the best,    10
And prudence of mind; for much shall suffer
Of lief and of loath who long endures
The days of his life in labor and toil.)
Now music and song were mingled together,
In the presence of Hrothgar, ruler in war.    15
Harp was struck and hero-lays told.
Along the mead-bench the minstrel spread
Cheer in hall when he chanted the lay
Of the sudden assault on the sons of Finn.

The episode which follows alludes obscurely to details of a feud between Frisians and Danes. The Finnsburg fragment contains a portion of the same story; and one of the heroes, Hnaef, is also mentioned in Widsith. [91 lines are here omitted.]

## XVII

### The Lay of Finn Ended. The Speech of the Queen

The lay was ended,
The gleeman's song. Sound of revelry
Rose again. Gladness spread
Along bench and board. Beer-thanes poured
From flagons old the flowing wine.    5
Wealhtheow the queen walked in state,
Under her crown, where uncle and nephew
Together sat,—they still were friends.
There too sat Unferth, trusted counsellor,
At Hrothgar's feet; though faith he had broken
With his kinsmen in battle, his courage was proved.    11
Then the queen of the Scyldings spoke these words:
"Quaff of this cup my king and my lord,
Gold-friend of men. To thy guests be kind,
To the men of the Jutes be generous with gifts.
Far and near thou now hast peace.    16
I have heard thou dost wish the hero for son
To hold as thy own, now Heorot is cleansed,
The jewel-bright hall. Enjoy while thou mayest,
Allotment of wealth, and leave to thy heirs    20
Kingdom and rule when arrives the hour
That hence thou shalt pass to thy place appointed.
Well I know that my nephew Hrothulf
Will cherish in honor our children dear

If thou leavest before him this life upon earth;
He will surely requite the kindness we showed him,    26
Faithfully tend our two young sons,
When to mind he recalls our care and affection,
How we helped him and housed him when *he* was a child."
She turned to the bench where her two boys sat,    30
Hrethric and Hrothmund, and the rest of the youth,
A riotous band, and right in their midst,
Between the two brothers, Beowulf sat.

## XVIII

### The Queen's Gifts to Beowulf

With courteous bow the cup she offered,
Greeted him graciously and gave him to boot
Two armlets rare of twisted gold,
A robe and rings, and the rarest collar;
A better was never known among men,    5
Since Hama brought to his bright-built hall
The jewelled necklace, the gem of the Brisings.

The 15 lines omitted here interrupt the narrative to tell of the subsequent history of Wealhtheow's gift; how Beowulf gave it to Hygelac, who wore it on his famous raid against the Frisians, in which he was slain by the Franks.

Before the warriors Wealhtheow spoke:
"Accept, dear Beowulf, this bright-gemmed collar;
Make happy use of this heirloom jewelled,    10
This ring and robe and royal treasure;
Be brave and bold. My boys instruct
In gentle manners; mine be the praise.
Thou hast done such a deed that in days to come
Men will proclaim thy might and valor    15
To the ends of the earth, where the ocean-wave
Washes the windy walls of the land.
I wish thee joy of thy jewelled treasure,
Long be thy life; enlarge thy prosperity,
Show thee a friend to my sons in deed.    20
Here each earl to the other is faithful,
True to his liege-lord, loyal and kind.
My warriors obey me, willing and prompt.
The Danes carousing, do as I bid."
She went to her seat, the wine flowed free;    25
'Twas a glorious feast. The fate that impended,
None of them knew, though near to them all.

When darkness came, the king of the Danes
Went to his rest in the royal bower;
But a throng of his kinsmen kept the hall    30
As they used to do in the days of old.
They cleared the boards and covered the floor
With beds and bolsters. One beer-thane there
Lay down to sleep with his doom upon him.

They placed by their heads their polished
shields,                                    35
Their battle-boards bright, on the bench
nearby.
Above each earl, within easy reach,
Was his helmet high and his harness of mail
And the spear-shaft keen. 'Twas their custom
so,
That always at rest they were ready for war 40
At home or abroad, where'er they might be,
At what hour soever for aid might call
Their lord and king; they were comrades true.

### END OF THE FIRST ADVENTURE

## XIX

*The Coming of Grendel's Dam to Avenge her
Son*

Then sank they to sleep, but sorely paid
One poor wretch for his sleep that night.
The same thing fell, as in former days
When Grendel his raids on the gold-hall made,
Before the fiend had found his match,     5
Caught in his sins. 'Twas seen that night
An avenger survived the villainous fiend,
Although they had ceased from their sorrow
and care.
'Twas Grendel's mother, a monstrous hag.
She remembered her loss. She had lived in the
deep,                                       10
In a water-hell cold, since Cain had become
The evil slayer of his only brother,
His kin by blood; accursed he fled,
Marked by murder, from men's delights,
Haunted the wilds; from him there sprung  15
Ghastly demon-shapes, Grendel was one.

The 10 lines omitted here break the narrative to
turn back to the Grendel fight.

              Now grim and vengeful
His mother set out on her errand of woe,
Damage to wreak for the death of her son.
Arrived at Heorot, the Ring-Danes she found
Asleep in the hall. Soon was to come    21
Surprise to the earls when into the hall
Burst Grendel's dam. (Less grim was the
terror,
As terror of woman in war is less,
—The fury of maidens, than full-armed men's,
When the blood-stained war-blade with wire-
bound hilt,                               26
Hard and hammer-forged, hurtling through air,
Hews the boar from the helmet's crest.)
Many the swords that were suddenly drawn,
Blades from the benches; buckler and shield
Were tightly grasped; no time for the hel-
met,                                      31
For harness of mail, when the horror was on
them.
The monster was minded to make for the open;
Soon as discovered, she sought to escape.

Quickly she seized a sleeping warrior,     35
Fast in her clutch to the fens she dragged him.
He was to Hrothgar of heroes the dearest,
Most trusted of liegemen between the two seas,
Comrade the nearest, killed in his sleep,
The bravest in battle. Nor was Beowulf there,
They had elsewhere quartered the earl that
night,                                     41
After the giving of gifts in the hall.
There was shouting in Heorot; the hand she
seized,
The bloody talon, she took away.
Sorrow was renewed in the nearby dwellings,
Bad was the bargain that both had made    46
To pay for their friends with further lives lost.
With grief overcome was the gray-haired king,
When he learned that his thane was alive no
more,
His dearest comrade by death o'ertaken;    50
Quick from his bower was Beowulf fetched,
The hero brave. At break of dawn
He with his comrades came to the place
Where the king in sorrow was waiting to see
Whether God the Wielder of All would grant
him                                        55
A turn in his tide of trouble and woe.
Then entered the room the ready hero;
With his band of brave men the boards re-
sounded.
He eagerly greeted the aged ruler,
Delayed not to ask the lord of the Ingwines 60
If his night had passed in peace and quiet.

## XX

*Hrothgar Describes the Haunt of the Monster
and Asks Beowulf to Undertake
a Second Adventure*

Hrothgar spoke, the Scylding defender:
"Speak not of peace for pain is renewed
'Mongst all the Danes. Dead is Æschere,
Elder brother of Irmenlaf,
My comrade true and counsellor trusted,    5
My right-hand friend when in front of the
combat
We stood shoulder to shoulder, when shield-
burg broke,
And boar-crests crashed in battle together.
Earls should ever like Æschere be.
On Heorot's floor he was foully slain     10
By warlock wild. I wot not whither
The prey-proud fury hath fled to cover,
Glutted and gorged. With gruesome claws
And violence fierce she avenged thy deed,
The slaying of Grendel her son last night, 15
Because too long my loyal thanes
He had hunted and hurt. In the hall he fell,
His life was forfeit. To the fray returned
Another as cruel, her kin to avenge;
Faring from far, the feud re-opened.      20
Hence many a thane shall mourn and think
Of the giver of gifts with grief renewed
And heart-woe heavy. The hand lies low

That fain would have helped and defended
    you all.
I have heard my people, the peasant folk  25
Who house by the border and hold the fens,
Say they have seen two creatures strange,
Huge march-stalkers, haunting the moorland,
Wanderers outcast. One of the two
Seemed to their sight to resemble a woman; 30
The other manlike, a monster misshapen,
But huger in bulk than human kind,
Trod an exile's track of woe.
The folk of the fen in former days
Named him Grendel. Unknown his father,  35
Or what his descent from demons obscure.
Lonely and waste is the land they inhabit,
Wolf-cliffs wild and windy headlands,
Ledges of mist, where mountain torrents
Downward plunge to dark abysses,    40
And flow unseen. Not far from here
O'er the moorland in miles, a mere expands:
Spray-frosted trees o'erspread it, and hang
O'er the water with roots fast wedged in the
    rocks.
There nightly is seen, beneath the flood,  45
A marvellous light. There lives not the man
Has fathomed the depth of the dismal mere.
Though the heather-stepper, the strong-horned
    stag,
Seek this cover, forspent with the chase,
Tracked by the hounds, he will turn at bay, 50
To die on the brink ere he brave the plunge,
Hide his head in the haunted pool.
Wan from its depths the waves are dashed,
When wicked storms are stirred by the wind,
And from sullen skies descends the rain.   55
In thee is our hope of help once more.
Not yet thou hast learned where leads the way
To the lurking-hole of this hatcher of outrage.
Seek, if thou dare, the dreaded spot!
Richly I pay thee for risking this fight,    60
With heirlooms golden and ancient rings,
As I paid thee before, if thou come back alive."

## XXI

### The Arrival of Hrothgar and Beowulf at Grendel's Mere

Beowulf spoke, the son of Ecgtheow:
"Sorrow not, gray-beard, nor grieve o'er thy
    friend!
Vengeance is better than bootless mourning.
To each of us here the end must come
Of life upon earth: let him who may    5
Win glory ere death. I deem that best,
The lot of the brave, when life is over.
Rise, O realm-ward, ride we in haste,
To track the hag that whelped this Grendel.
I tell thee in truth, she may turn where she
    will,    10
No cave of ocean nor cover of wood,
No hole in the ground shall hide her from me.
But one day more thy woe endure,
And nurse thy hope as I know thou wilt."

Sprang to his feet the sage old king,  15
Gave praise to God for the promise spoken.
And now for Hrothgar a horse was bridled,
A curly-maned steed. The king rode on,
Bold on his charger. A band of shield-men
Followed on foot. Afar they saw    20
Footprints leading along the forest.
They followed the tracks, and found she had
    crossed
Over the dark moor, dragging the body
Of the goodliest thane that guarded with
    Hrothgar
Heorot Hall, and the home of the king.  25
The well-born hero held the trail;
Up rugged paths, o'er perilous ridges,
Through passes narrow, an unknown way,
By beetling crags, and caves of the nicors.
With a chosen few he forged ahead,  30
Warriors skilled, to scan the way.
Sudden they came on a cluster of trees
Overhanging a hoary rock,
A gloomy grove; and gurgling below,
A stir of waters all stained with blood.  35
Sick at heart were the Scylding chiefs,
Many a thane was thrilled with woe,
For there they beheld the head of Æschere
Far beneath at the foot of the cliff.
They leaned and watched the waters boil  40
With bloody froth. The band sat down,
While the war-horn sang its summons to
    battle.
They saw in the water sea-snakes a many,
Wave-monsters weird, that wallowed about.
At the base of the cliff lay basking the nicors,
Who oft at sunrise ply seaward their jour-
    ney,    46
To hunt on the ship-trails and scour the main,
Sea-beasts and serpents. Sudden they fled,
Wrathful and grim, aroused by the hail
Of the battle-horn shrill. The chief of the
    Jutes,    50
With a bolt from his bow a beast did sunder
From life and sea-frolic; sent the keen shaft
Straight to his vitals. Slow he floated,
Upturned and dead at the top of the waves.
Eager they boarded their ocean-quarry;  55
With barb-hooked boar-spears the beast they
    gaffed,
Savagely broached him and brought him to
    shore,
Wave-plunger weird. The warriors viewed
The grisly stranger. But straightway Beowulf 59
Donned his corslet nor cared for his life.

The 30 lines here omitted break the narrative with
a description of Beowulf's armor and the sword
Hrunting, lent him by Unferth.

## XXII

### Beowulf's Fight with Grendel's Dam

To Hrothgar spoke the son of Ecgtheow:
"Remember O honored heir of Healfdene,
Now that I go, thou noble king,

Warriors' gold-friend, what we agreed on,
If I my life should lose in thy cause,          5
That thou wouldst stand in stead of my father,
Fulfil his office when I was gone.
Be guardian, thou, to my thanes and kinsmen,
My faithful friends, if I fail to return.
To Hygelac send, Hrothgar beloved,          10
The goodly gifts thou gavest to me.
May the lord of the Jutes, when he looks on
       this treasure,
May Hrethel's son, when he sees these gifts,
Know that I found a noble giver,
And joyed, while I lived, in a generous lord.  15
This ancient heirloom to Unferth give,
To the far-famed warrior, my wondrous sword
Of matchless metal, I must with Hrunting
Glory gain, or go to my death.''

After these words the Weder-Jute lord          20
Sprang to his task, nor staid for an answer.
Swiftly he sank 'neath the swirling flood;
'Twas an hour's time ere he touched the bot-
       tom.
Soon the sea-hag, savage and wild,
Who had roamed through her watery realms
       at will,                                   25
For winters a hundred, was 'ware from below,
An earthling had entered her ocean domain.
Quickly she reached and caught the hero;
Grappled him grimly with gruesome claws.
Yet he got no scratch, his skin was whole;    30
His battle-sark shielded his body from harm.
In vain she tried, with her crooked fingers,
To tear the links of his close-locked mail.
Away to her den the wolf-slut dragged
Beowulf the bold, o'er the bottom ooze.       35
Though eager to smite her, his arm was help-
       less.
Swimming monsters swarmed about him,
Dented his mail with dreadful tusks.
Sudden the warrior was 'ware they had come
To a sea-hall strange and seeming hostile,    40
Where water was not nor waves oppressed,
For the caverned rock all round kept back
The swallowing sea.[12] He saw a light,
A flicker of flame that flashed and shone.
Now first he discerned the sea-hag monstrous, 45
The water-wife wolfish. His weapon he raised,
And struck with his sword a swinging blow.
Sang on her head the hard-forged blade
Its war-song wild. But the warrior found
That his battle-flasher refused to bite,       50
Or maim the foe. It failed its master
In the hour of need, though oft it had cloven
Helmets, and carved the casques of the doomed
In combats fierce. For the first time now
That treasure failed him, fallen from honor.   55
But Hygelac's earl took heart of courage;
In mood defiant he fronted his foe.
The angry hero hurled to the ground,
In high disdain, the hilt of the sword,

[12] Perhaps a cave behind a waterfall.

The gaudy and jewelled; rejoiced in the
       strength                                   60
Of his arm unaided. So all should do
Who glory would find and fame abiding,
In the crash of conflict, nor care for their lives.
The Lord of the Battle-Jutes braved the en-
       counter;
The murderous hag by the hair he caught;      65
Down he dragged the dam of Grendel
In his swelling rage, till she sprawled on the
       floor.
Quick to repay in kind what she got,
On her foe she fastened her fearful clutches;
Enfolded the warrior weary with fighting;      70
The sure-footed hero stumbled and fell.
As helpless he lay, she lept on him fiercely;
Unsheathed her hip-knife, shining and broad,
Her son to avenge, her offspring sole.
But the close-linked corslet covered his breast,
Foiled the stroke and saved his life.          76
All had been over with Ecgtheow's son,
Under the depths of the ocean vast,
Had not his harness availed to help him,
His battle-net stiff, and the strength of God. 80
The Ruler of battles aright decided it;
The Wielder all-wise awarded the victory:
Lightly the hero leaped to his feet.

## XXIII

### *Beowulf's Victory and Return to Heorot*

He spied 'mongst the arms a sword surpassing,
Huge and ancient, a hard-forged slayer,
Weapon matchless and warriors' delight,
Save that its weight was more than another
Might bear into battle or brandish in war;      5
Giants had forged that finest of blades.
Then seized its chain-hilt the chief of the
       Scyldings;
His wrath was aroused, reckless his mood,
As he brandished the sword for a savage blow.
Bit the blade in the back of her neck,         10
Cut the neck-bone, and cleft its way
Clean through her flesh; to the floor she sank;
The sword was gory; glad was the hero.
A light flashed out from the inmost den,
Like heaven's candle, when clear it shines      15
From cloudless skies. He scanned the cave,
Walked by the wall, his weapon upraised;
Grim in his hand the hilt he gripped.
Well that sword had served him in battle.
Steadily onward he strode through the cave,    21
Ready to wreak the wrongs untold,
That the man-beast had wrought in the realm
       of Danes.

[Here are omitted 6 lines.]

He gave him his due when Grendel he found
Stretched as in sleep, and spent with the battle.
But dead was the fiend, the fight at Heorot    25
Had laid him low. The lifeless body
Sprang from the blows of Beowulf's sword,
As fiercely he hacked the head from the carcass.

But the men who were watching the water with
Hrothgar
Suddenly saw a stir in the waves,    30
The chop of the sea all churned up with blood
And bubbling gore. The gray-haired chiefs
For Beowulf grieved, agreeing together
That hope there was none of his home-
returning,
With victory crowned, to revisit his lord.    35
Most of them feared he had fallen prey
To the mere-wolf dread in the depths of the sea.
When evening came, the Scyldings all
Forsook the headland, and Hrothgar himself
Turned homeward his steps. But sick at heart
The strangers sat and stared at the sea,    41
Hoped against hope to behold their comrade
And leader again.
                    Now that goodly sword
Began to melt with the gore of the monster;
In bloody drippings it dwindled away.    45
'Twas a marvellous sight: it melted like ice,
When fetters of frost the Father unlocks,
Unravels the ropes of the wrinkled ice,
Lord and Master of months and seasons.
Beheld in the hall the hero from Juteland    50
Treasures unnumbered, but naught he took,
Save Grendel's head, and the hilt of the sword,
Bright and jewelled,—the blade had melted,
Its metal had vanished, so venomous hot
Was the blood of the demon-brute dead in the
cave.    55

Soon was in the sea the slayer of monsters;
Upward he shot through the shimmer of waves;
Cleared was the ocean, cleansed were its waters,
The wolfish water-hag wallowed no more;
The mere-wife had yielded her miserable life.
Swift to the shore the sailors' deliverer    61
Came lustily swimming, with sea-spoil laden;
Rejoiced in the burden he bore to the land.
Ran to meet him his mailéd comrades,
With thanks to God who gave them their
leader    65
Safe again back and sound from the deep.
Quickly their hero's helmet they loosened,
Unbuckled his breastplate. The bloodstained
waves
Fell to a calm 'neath the quiet sky.
Back they returned o'er the tracks with the foot-
prints,    70
Merrily measured the miles o'er the fen,
Way they knew well, those warriors brave;
Brought from the holm-cliff the head of the
monster;
'Twas toil and labor to lift the burden,
Four of their stoutest scarce could carry it    75
Swung from a spear-pole, a staggering load.

[Here are omitted 3 lines.]

Thus the fourteen of them, thanes adventurous,
Marched o'er the moor to the mead-hall of
Hrothgar.
Tall in the midst of them towered the hero;

Strode among his comrades, till they came to
the hall.    80
In went Beowulf, the brave and victorious,
Battle-beast hardy, Hrothgar to greet.
Lifting by the hair the head of Grendel,
They laid it in the hall, where the heroes were
carousing,
Right before the king, and right before the
queen;    85
Gruesome was the sight that greeted the Danes.

## XXIV, XXV

### *Beowulf's Story of His Fight, and Hrothgar's Counsel*

Beowulf spoke, the son of Ecgtheow:
"Gladly we offer this ocean-booty,
That here thou lookest on, lord of the Scyld-
ings,
For sign of victory, son of Healfdene.
Hard was the fight I fought under water;    5
That combat nearly cost me my life.
Soon had been ended the ocean-encounter,
Had God in his mercy not given me aid.
No help I got from the good blade Hrunting;
The well-tried weapon worthless proved.    10
By the grace of God, who guided me friendless,
A splendid old sword I spied on the wall,
Hanging there, huge; by the hilt I grasped it,
And seeing my chance, I struck amain
At the sea-cave's wardens, when sudden the
blade    15
Melted and burned, as the blood gushed out,
The battle-gore hot. The hilt I saved
From the villainous fiends, and avenged their
crimes,
The murder of the Danes, as was meet and due.
I promise thee now, in peace thou shalt sleep
In Heorot hall, with the whole of thy band.    21
Thou and thy thanes may throng within
As ye used of yore, both young and old.
Thou need'st not fear renewal of strife,
Harm to thy folk at the hands of the fiends."
The golden hilt was given to the king;    26
The jewelled work of the giants of old
Came into hand of the hoary warrior.
On the death of the demons, the Danish lord
kept it,
Wondersmiths' work. When the world was rid
Of the evil fiend, the enemy of God,    31
Guilty of murder, and his mother too,
The trophy passed to the peerless lord,
The goodliest king, that gave out treasure
Between the two seas on Scandia's isle.    35
Hrothgar gazed on the golden hilt,
Relic of old, where was writ the tale
Of a far-off fight, when the flood o'erwhelmed,
The raging sea, the race of the giants
(They wantonly dared to war against God;    40
Then rose in his wrath the Ruler Eternal,
'Neath the heaving billows buried them all.)
On the polished gold of the guard of the hilt,
Runes were writ that rightly told,

To him that read them, for whom that weapon,
Finest of sword-blades, first was made,                46
The splendid hilt with serpents entwined.
All were silent, when the son of Healfdene,
The wise king spoke: "Well may he say,
The aged ruler, who aye upholds                        50
Truth and right, 'mid the ranks of his people,
Whose mind runs back to by-gone days,
This guest is born of a goodly breed.
Thy fame shall fly afar among men,
Beowulf my friend, firmly thou holdest                 55
Both wisdom and might. My word will I keep,
The love that I proffered. Thou shalt prove a
    deliverer
To thy folk and followers in far-off years,
A help to the heroes. Not Heremod thus,
Ecgwela's heir, did offer at need                      60
His strength to the Scyldings; instead, he
    brought
Slaughter and death on the sons of the Danes.
Swoln with wrath he slew his comrades,
His friends at the board and fled alone,
Ill-famed earl, an outcast from men.                   65
Though God endowed him with gifts of
    strength,
With boldness and might above all men,
And prospered him greatly, yet he grew to be
Blood-thirsty and cruel. No bracelets he gave
To the Danes as due, but dwelt in gloom,
Reaped the reward of the woful strife,                 71
And wearisome feud. Take warning from him."

Hrothgar now delivers a long sermon to Beowulf
on the dangers of pride, the fickleness of fortune, and
the brevity of life, and ends by asking him to sit
down to the feast, promising more gifts on the morrow. [43 lines are omitted.]

Beowulf hastened, happy in mood,
To seek his bench as bid by the king.
Once more, as of old, for the earls in hall,           75
The famous in battle, the board was set
For feasting anew. When night with its
    shadows
O'erwhelmed the world, the heroes arose.
The gray-haired ruler his rest would seek,
The Scylding his bed; and Beowulf too,                 80
The lusty warrior, longed for his sleep.
Soon an attendant showed the way
To the stranger from far, spent with his faring.
With courtly custom, he cared for his needs,
All that to warriors, overseas wandering,              85
Was due in those days, he did for the guest.
High-gabled and gold-decked, the gift-hall
    towered;
The stout-hearted hero slept soundly within,
Till the raven black, with blithe heart hailed
The bliss of heaven, and bright the sun                90
Came gliding o'er earth. Then, eager to start,
The warriors wakened; they wished to set out
On their homeward journey. The hero brave
Would board his ship, and back again sail.
The hardy one bade that Hrunting be
    brought                                             95

To the son of Ecglaf: [13] the sword he offered
    him;
Thanked him for lending the lovely weapon;
Called it a war-friend, keen in the battle;
Not a word in blame of the blade he uttered,
Great-hearted hero. Now hastened the guests,
Eager to part, and armed for their voyage.             101
Their dauntless leader, beloved of the Danes.
Came to the high-seat, and to Hrothgar the
    king
The bold-in-battle now bade farewell.

## XXVI
### Beowulf's Leave-Taking of Hrothgar

Beowulf spoke, the son of Ecgtheow:
"Now we sea-farers would make known our
    desire;
Far-travelled wanderers, we wish to return
To Hygelac now. A hearty welcome
We here have found, thou hast harbored us
    well.                                              5
If ever on earth I may anywise win,
Master of men, more of thy love
Than now I have won, for another adventure
Of arms and war I am eager and willing.
If ever I hear, o'er the ocean-ways                    10
That neighbor-tribes threaten annoyance or
    war,
As feud-seeking foemen aforetime assailed thee,
A thousand thanes to thee will I bring,
Heroes to help thee. For Hygelac, I know,
Though young in years will yield me aid;               15
The people's Shepherd will surely help me
By word and deed to do thee service,
And bring thee spear-shafts to speed thee in
    battle,
Thy might to strengthen when men thou need-
    est.
If ever Hrethric, heir of thy line,                    20
Should come to sojourn at the court of the
    Jutes,
A host of friends he will find awaiting him.
Who boasts himself brave, abroad should
    travel."
The aged Hrothgar answering spoke:
"To utter these words, the All-wise Lord              25
Hath prompted thy heart; more prudent coun-
    sel
From one in years so young as thou,
I never have heard. Thou art hardy in strength,
And sage in spirit, and speakest well.
If ever it happen that Hrethel's heir                  30
Be stricken by spear and slain in battle,
If sickness or sword assail thy lord,
And thou survive him, I think it likely
The Sea-Jutes in vain will seek for a better
As choice for their king, their chief to become
And rule o'er the thanes, if thou be willing          36
The lordship to hold. The longer I know thee
The better I like thee, Beowulf my friend.

[13] Unferth.

Thou hast brought it about that both our
  peoples,
Jutes and the Spear-Danes, shall be joined in
  peace.                                          40
They shall cease from war, the strife shall be
  ended,
The feuds of aforetime, so fiercely waged.
While I rule this realm, our riches we share;
Many shall travel with treasure laden,
Each other to greet, o'er the gannet's bath;  45
O'er the rolling waves the ringéd prow
Tokens of friendship shall freely bring
And bind our people in peace together,
Toward friend and foe, in faith as of old."

Still other treasures, twelve in all,           50
Healfdene's heir in the hall bestowed
On Beowulf brave, and bade him take them
And seek his people, and soon return.
Then kissed the king, of kin renowned,
The thane beloved. The lord of the Scyldings 55
Fell on his neck. Fast flowed the tears
Of the warrior gray; he weighed both chances,
But held to the hope, though hoary with years,
That each should see the other again,
And meet in the mead-hall. The man was so
  dear                                            60
That he could not restrain the storm in his
  breast.
Locked in his heart, a hidden longing
For the man he loved so, left him no peace,
And burnt in his blood. But Beowulf went;
The gold-decked hero the grass-way trod,      65
Proud of his booty. The boat awaited
Its owner and master, where at anchor it rode.
As they went on their way, the warriors praised
The bounty of Hrothgar, the blameless king.
None was his equal till age snatched away    70
The joy of his manhood,—no mortal it spares.

## XXVII

### Beowulf's Return Voyage to Hygelac

Then came to the coast the comrades brave,
The lusty warriors, wearing their ring-nets,
Their chain-linked corslets. The coast-guard
  saw them,
The same that at first had spied them coming;
This time he chose not to challenge them
  harshly,                                         5
But gave them his greeting, galloping toward
  them.
Said the Weder-folk would welcome the sight
  of them,
Boarding their ship in shining armor.
Then by the sands, the seaworthy craft,
The iron-ringed keel, with arms was laden,   10
With horses and treasure. On high the mast
Towered above the treasures of Hrothgar.
To the man who had waited as watchman
  aboard,
Beowulf gave a gold-bound sword.

(Oft on the mead-bench that heirloom pre-
  cious                                           15
Its owner would honor.) When all had em-
  barked,
They drove for the deep, from Daneland's
  shore.
Then soon did the mast its sea-suit wear,
A sail was unfurled, made fast with ropes,
The sea-wood sang as she sped o'er the ocean,
No baffling head-wind hindered her course;  21
The foamy-necked floater flew o'er the billows,
The sea-craft staunch o'er the salt-sea waves,
Till they came in sight of the cliffs of Jutland
The well known capes, and the wind-driven
  keel,                                           25
Grating the sand, stood still on the shore.
Soon was at hand the harbor-watch eager.
Long had he looked for his loved companions,
Scanning the sea for their safe return.
The broad-bosomed boat to the beach he
  moored                                          30
With anchor-ropes fast, lest the force of the
  waves
That comely craft should cast adrift.
Then Beowulf bade them bring ashore
His treasure-cargo of costly gold
And weapons fine; not far was the way       35
To Hygelac's hall, where at home he dwelt,
The king and his comrades, close by the sea.

## END OF THE SECOND ADVENTURE

After the death of Hygelac and his son, Beowulf
became king of the Jutes, and ruled over them fifty
years. In his old age his people were harried by a
fire-dragon, whom the hero went out to fight. It
seems that an outlaw, banished and flying for shelter,
had come upon a treasure hid in a deep cave or
barrow, guarded by a dragon. Long years before,
an earl, the last of his race, had buried the treasure.
After his death the dragon, sniffing about the stones,
had found it and guarded it three hundred years,
until the banished man discovered the place, and
carried off one of the golden goblets. In revenge
the dragon made nightly raids on Beowulf's realm,
flying through the air, spitting fire, burning houses
and villages, even Beowulf's hall, the "gift-stool"
of the Jutes. Beowulf had an iron shield made
against the dragon's fiery breath, and with eleven
companions, sought out the hill-vault near the sea.
These events are related in Sections XXVIII–XXXV
of the *Beowulf* MS.

## XXXV

### Beowulf's Fight with the Fire-Dragon

Before attacking the fire-dragon, Beowulf once
more, and for the last time, makes his "battle-boast"
in the presence of his followers.

Beowulf said to them, brave words spoke he:
"Brunt of battles I bore in my youth,
One fight more I make this day.
I mean to win fame defending my people,

If the grim destroyer will seek me out,          5
Come at my call from his cavern dark."
Then he greeted his thanes each one,
For the last time hailed his helmeted warriors,
His comrades dear. "I should carry no sword,
No weapon of war 'gainst the worm should
     bear,          10
If the foe I might slay by strength of my arm,
As Grendel I slew long since by my hand.
But I look to fight a fiery battle,
With scorching puffs of poisonous breath.
For this I bear both breastplate and shield;    15
No foot will I flinch from the foe of the bar-
     row.
Wyrd is over us, each shall meet
His doom ordained at the dragon-cliff!
Bold is my mood, but my boast I omit
'Gainst the battle-flier. Abide ye here,          20
Heroes in harness, hard by the barrow,
Cased in your armor the issue await:
Which of us two his wounds shall survive.
Not yours the attempt, the task is mine.
'Tis meant for no man but me alone          25
To measure his might 'gainst the monster fierce.
I get you the gold in glorious fight,
Or battle-death bitter shall bear off your lord."
Uprose with his shield the shining hero,
Bold 'neath his helmet. He bore his harness  30
In under the cliff; alone he went,
Himself he trusted; no task for faint-heart.
Then saw by the wall the warrior brave,
Hero of many a hard-fought battle,
Arches of stone that opened a way;          35
From the rocky gate there gushed a stream,
Bubbling and boiling with battle-fire.
So great the heat no hope was there
To come at the hoard in the cavern's depth,
Unscathed by the blast of the scorching dragon.
He let from his breast his battle-cry leap,      41
Swoln with rage was the royal Jute,
Stormed the stout-heart; strong and clear
Through the gloom of the cave his cry went
     ringing.
Hate was aroused, the hoard-ward knew      45
The leader's hail. Too late 'twas now
To parley for peace. The poisonous breath
Of the monster shot from the mouth of the
     cave,
Reeking hot. The hollow earth rumbled.
The man by the rock upraised his shield,      50
The lord of the Jutes, 'gainst the loathly dragon.
Now kindled for battle the curled-up beast;
The king undaunted with drawn sword stood,
'Twas an heirloom olden with edge of light-
     ning.
Each was so fierce he affrighted the other.    55
Towering tall 'neath tilted shield,
Waited the king as the worm coiled back,
Sudden to spring: so stood he and waited.
Blazing he came in coils of fire
Swift to his doom. The shield of iron          60
Sheltered the hero too short a while,—
Life and limb it less protected

Than he hoped it would, for the weapon he
     held
First time that day he tried in battle;
Wyrd had not willed he should win the fight.
But the lord of the Jutes uplifted his arm,    66
Smote the scaly worm, struck him so fierce
That his ancient bright-edged blade gave way,
Bent on the bone, and bit less sure
Than its owner had need in his hour of peril. 70
That sword-stroke roused the wrath of the cave-
     guard;
Fire and flame afar he spirted,
Blaze of battle; but Beowulf there
No victory boasted: his blade had failed him,
Naked in battle, as never it should have,      75
Well-tempered iron. Nor easy it was
For Ecgtheow's heir,[14] honored and famous,
This earth to forsake, forever to leave it;
Yet he must go, against his will
Elsewhere to dwell. So we all must leave      80
This fleeting life.—Erelong the foes,
Bursting with wrath, the battle renewed.
The hoard-ward took heart, and with heaving
     breast
Came charging amain. The champion brave,
Strength of his people, was sore oppressed,    85
Enfolded by flame. No faithful comrades
Crowded about him, his chosen band,
All aethlings' sons, to save their lives,
Fled to the wood. One of them only
Felt surging sorrow; for nought can stifle      90
Call of kin in a comrade true.

## XXXVI

### Wiglaf's Reproach to his Comrades. Beowulf Mortally Wounded.

The shield-thane beloved, lord of the Scylfings,
Wiglaf was called, 'twas Weohstan's son,
Ælfheré's kinsman. When his king he saw
Hard by the heat under helmet oppressed,
He remembered the gifts he had got of old,      5
Lands and wealth of the Waegmunding line,
The folk-rights all that his father's had been;
He could hold no longer, but hard he gripped
Linden shield yellow and ancient sword.

     The intervening lines tell the history of the sword
and the feuds in which it has participated. [14 lines
are omitted.]

For the first time there the faithful thane,    10
Youthful and stalwart, stood with his leader,
Shoulder to shoulder in shock of battle.
Nor melted his courage, nor cracked his blade,
His war-sword true, as the worm found out
When together they got in grim encounter.    15

Wiglaf in wrath upbraided his comrades,
Sore was his heart as he spake these words:
"Well I mind when our mead we drank
In the princely hall, how we promised our lord

[14] Beowulf.

Who gave us these rings and golden armlets, 20
That we would repay his war-gifts rich,
Helmets and armor, if haply should come
His hour of peril; us hath he made
Thanes of his choice for this adventure;
Spurred us to glory, and gave us these treasures
Because he deemed us doughty spearmen, 26
Helmeted warriors, hardy and brave.
Yet all the while, unhelped and alone,
He meant to finish this feat of strength,
Shepherd of men and mightiest lord     30
Of daring deeds. The day is come,—
Now is the hour he needs the aid
Of spearmen good. Let us go to him now,
Help our hero while hard bestead
By the nimble flames. God knows that I     35
Had rather the fire should ruthlessly fold
My body with his, than harbor me safe.
Shame it were surely our shields to carry
Home to our lands, unless we first
Slay this foe and save the life     40
Of the Weder-king. Full well I know
To leave him thus, alone to endure,
Bereft of aid, breaks ancient right.
My helmet and sword shall serve for us both,
Shield and armor we share to-day."     45

Waded the warrior through welter and reek;
Buckler and helmet he bore to his leader;
Heartened the hero with words of hope:
"Do thy best now, dearest Beowulf,
Years ago, in youth, thou vowedst     50
Living, ne'er to lose thine honor,
Shield thy life and show thy valor.
I stand by thee to the end!"
After these words the worm came on,
Snorting with rage, for a second charge;     55
All mottled with fire his foes he sought,
The warriors hated. But Wiglaf's shield
Was burnt to the boss by the billows of fire;
His harness helped not the hero young.
Shelter he found 'neath the shield of his kins-
     man,     60
When the crackling blaze had crumbled his
     own.
But mindful of glory, the mighty hero
Smote amain with his matchless sword.
Down it hurtled, driven by anger,
Till it stuck in the skull; then snapped the
     blade,     65
Broken was Nægling, Beowulf's sword,
Ancient and gray. 'Twas granted him never
To count on edge of iron in battle;
His hand was too heavy, too hard his strokes,
As I have heard tell, for every blade     70
He brandished in battle: the best gave way,
And left him helpless and hard bestead.
Now for a third time neared the destroyer;
The fire-drake fierce, old feuds remembering,
Charged the warrior who wavered an instant; 75
Blazing he came and closed his fangs
On Beowulf's throat; and throbbing spirts
Of life-blood dark o'erdrenched the hero.

## XXXVII

### The Slaying of the Dragon

Then in the hour of utmost peril,
The stripling proved what stock he came of;
Showed his endurance and dauntless courage.
Though burnt was his hand when he backed
     his kinsman,
With head unguarded the good thane charged,
Thrust from below at the loathly dragon,     6
Pierced with the point and plunged the blade
     in,
The gleaming-bright, till the glow abated
Waning low. Ere long the king
Came to himself, and swiftly drew     10
The war-knife that hung at his harness' side,
And cut in two the coiléd monster.
So felled they the foe and finished him bravely,
Together they killed him, the kinsmen two,
A noble pair. So needs must do     15
Comrades in peril. For the king it proved
His uttermost triumph, the end of his deeds
And work in the world. The wound began,
Where the cave-dragon savage had sunk his
     teeth,
To swell and fever, and soon he felt     20
The baleful poison pulse through his blood,
And burn in his breast. The brave old warrior
Sat by the wall and summoned his thoughts,
Gazed on the wondrous work of the giants:
Arches of stone, firm-set on their pillars,     25
Upheld that hill-vault hoar and ancient.

Now Beowulf's thane, the brave and faithful,
Dashed with water his darling lord,
His comrade and king, all covered with blood
And faint with the fight; unfastened his helmet.
Beowulf spoke despite his hurt,     31
His piteous wound; full well he knew
His years on earth were ended now,
His hours of glad life, gone for aye
His days allotted, and death was near:     35
"Now would I gladly give to a son
These weapons of war, had Wyrd but granted
That heir of my own should after me come,
Sprung from my loins. This land have I ruled
Fifty winters. No folk-king dared,     40
None of the chiefs of the neighboring tribes,
To touch me with sword or assail me with ter-
     ror
Of battle-threats. I bided at home,
Held my peace and my heritage kept,
Seeking no feuds nor swearing false oaths.     45
This gives me comfort, and gladdens me now,
Though wounded sore and sick unto death.
As I leave my life, the Lord may not charge me
With killing of kinsmen. Now quickly go,
Wiglaf beloved, to look at the hoard,     50
Where hidden it rests 'neath the hoary rock.
For the worm lies still, put asleep by his wound,
Robbed of his riches. Then rise and haste!
Give me to see that golden hoard,

Gaze on the store of glorious gems, 55
The easier then I may end my life,
Leave my lordship that long I held."

## XXXVIII

### The Rescue of the Hoard and the Death of Beowulf

Swiftly, 'tis said, the son of Weohstan
Obeyed the words of his bleeding lord,
Maimed in the battle. Through the mouth of
the cave
Boldly he bore his battle-net in.
Glad of the victory, he gazed about him; 5
Many a sun-bright jewel he saw,
Glittering gold, strewn on the ground,
Heaped in the den of the dragon hoary,
Old twilight-flier,—flagons once bright,
Wassail cups wondrous of warriors departed 10
Stript of their mountings, many a helmet
Ancient and rusted, armlets a many,
Curiously woven. (Wealth so hoarded,
Buried treasure, will taint with pride,
Him that hides it, whoever it be.) 15
Towering high o'er the hoard he saw
A gleaming banner with gold inwoven,
Of broidure rare, its radiance streamed
So bright, he could peer to the bounds of the
cave,
Survey its wonders; no worm was seen. 20
Edge of the sword had ended his life.
Then, as they say, that single adventurer
Plundered the hoard that was piled by the
giants;
Gathered together old goblets and platters,
Took what he liked; the towering banner, 25
Brightest of beacons, he brought likewise.
The blade of Beowulf, his brave old chief,
With edge of iron had ended the life
Of him that had guarded the golden hoard
For many a year, and at midnight hour 30
Had spread the terror of surging flames
In front of the den, till death o'ertook him.
So Wiglaf returned with treasure laden.
The high-souled hero hastened his steps,
Anxiously wondered if he should find 35
The lord of the Weders alive where he left him
Sapped of his strength and stretched on the
ground.
As he came from the hill he beheld his com-
rade,
His lord of bounty, bleeding and faint,
Near unto death. He dashed him once more 40
Bravely with water, till burden of speech
Broke from his breast, and Beowulf spoke,
Gazing sad at the gold before him:
"For the harvest of gold that here I look on,
To the God of Glory I give my thanks. 45
To the Ruler Eternal I render praise
That ere I must go, he granted me this,
To leave to my people this priceless hoard.
'Twas bought with my life; now look ye well
To my people's need when I have departed. 50

No more I may bide among ye here.
Bid the battle-famed build on the foreland
A far-seen barrow when flames have burnt me.
High o'er the headland of whales it shall tower,
A beacon and mark to remind my people. 55
And sailors shall call it in years to come
Beowulf's Barrow, as bound from afar
Their tall ships stem the storm-dark seas."

The great-hearted king unclasped from his
neck
A collar of gold and gave to his thane, 60
The brave young warrior, his bright-gilt helmet,
Breastplate and ring. So bade him farewell:
"Thou are the last to be left of our house.
Wyrd hath o'erwhelmed our Wægmunding
line,
Swept my kinsmen swift to their doom. 65
Earls in their prime. I must follow them."
These words were the last that the warrior gray
Found, ere the funeral-flames he chose.
Swift from his bosom his soul departed
To find the reward of the faithful and true. 70

In Section XXXIX of the MS. the narrative
doubles back upon itself to repeat the description
of Beowulf and the Dragon lying dead before the
cave, and to report Wiglaf's second reproach to the
deserters.

## XL

### Beowulf's Death Announced to the People. The Speech of the Herald.

Then Wiglaf bade the battle-work tell
To the sorrowful troop that had sat all day
At the sea-cliff's edge, their shields in hand,
In dread and in hope, yet doubtful of either:
Their dear lord's return, or his death in the
fight. 5
The herald that came to the headland riding,
Nought kept back of the news that befell,
But truthfully told them the tidings all:
"Now lies low the lord of the Weders;
The generous giver of gifts to the Jutes, 10
Sleeps his battle-sleep, slain by the worm.
At his side lies stretched his slaughterous foe,
Fordone by the dagger. The dragon fierce
Would take no wound from touch of sword;
Its blade would not bite. At Beowulf's side 15
Wiglaf sits, the son of Weohstan;
By the hero dead, the hero living
At his head keeps watch with woful heart
O'er friend and foe."

· · · · · · ·

The herald now warns of renewed attacks on the
Jutes by Franks and Frisians, and alludes to the
origin of the feud in the famous raid in which
Hygelac was slain. He further warns of renewed attacks by the Swedes, now that Beowulf is dead, and
refers to the origin of the wars between Swedes and
Jutes and to a famous battle at "Ravenswood." The
episodic digression over, the herald returns to present
events. [97 lines are omitted.]

## XLI

### *The Herald's Speech Concluded.*

" 'Tis time we hasten
To see where lies our lord and king,
Our giver of bounty, and bear him away
To the funeral pyre; of precious gems
Not a few shall melt in the fire with him.    5
The hoard he won, the wealth untold,
The priceless treasure he purchased so dear,
And bought with his life at the bitter end,
The flame shall enfold it, the fire consume.
No warrior one keepsake shall carry away,    10
No necklace be worn by winsome maid.
In sorrow rather, and reft of her gold,
Alone she shall tread the track of an exile,
Now our lord lies low, his laughter stilled,
His mirth and revel. Now many a spear    15
Shall morning-cold be clasped in the hand
And held on high. No harp shall sound
The warriors to wake, but the wan-hued raven
Shall croak o'er the carcass and call to the eagle,
To tell how he fared at the feast after battle    20
When he and the gray wolf gorged on the
    slain."
Thus ended his tale, his tidings of woe,
The faithful thane, nor falsely reported
Wyrd or word. The warriors rose;
To the Eagles' Cliff they came in sadness,    25
With welling tears, the wonder to see.
Lying helpless, their lord they found
Stretched on the ground, the giver of rings.
The end had come to him, open-handed
King of the Weders, warrior brave.    30
That day a fearful death he had found.
A stranger thing they saw near by:
The loathsome monster lying dead
On the field where they fought, the fiery
    dragon,
The gruesome beast was burnt and charred.    35
Fifty feet in full he measured
In length, as he lay, along the ground.
'Twas his wont at night to wing aloft
And dip to earth as his den he sought;
Now he lay dead, his night-revels over.    40
Scattered about were bowls and flagons,
Golden platters, and priceless swords,
With rust eaten through, as though they had
    lain
Winters a thousand in the womb of the earth.
O'er that heritage huge, the hoard of afore-
    time,    45
A spell had been woven to ward off despoilers,
And none might touch the treasure-vault hid-
    den;
Save that God alone, the Lord of victory,
The Guardian of men, might grant the power
To unlock the hoard, and lift the treasure,    50
To such a hero as to Him seemed meet.

[18 lines are here omitted.]

.    .    .    .    .    .    .    .    .

## XLII

### *Beowulf's Body Carried to the Funeral Pyre and the Dragon Cast into the Sea.*

Wiglaf spoke, the son of Weohstan:

[24 lines are here omitted.]

"Let us go once more to gaze at the marvels
Still left 'neath the rock; I will lead you in
Where your hands may touch great heaps of
    gold,
Bracelets and rings. Let the bier be ready    5
When out of the cave we come again,
To bear away the warrior brave,
Our lord beloved, where long he shall bide,
Kept in the sheltering care of God."
The son of Weohstan, warrior brave,    10
Called on the folk-men, far and wide,
From house and home to hasten and bring
Wood for the pyre of the peerless man,
His funeral pile. "Now fire shall consume,
The wan flame wax o'er the warrior strong,    15
Who oft stood firm in the iron shower,
When the storm of arrows, sent from the bow-
    string,
Flew o'er the shield-wall, and the fleet-winged
    shaft,
Feathered behind, pushed home the barb."
Now the wise young warrior, Weohstan's son,
Seven men called, of the king's own thanes,    21
The best of the band; the bravest he gathered;
Himself the eighth, they sought the den
Of the hateful beast; one bore in his hand
A lighted torch and led the way.    25
No lots were drawn for the dragon's hoard
When they saw it lying, loose in the cave,
Uncared for, unguarded, unclaimed by a soul;
There was none to hinder as they hurried away,
Laden with spoils and splendid heirlooms.    30
O'er the edge of the cliff they cast the dragon,
Into the sea, the scaly worm;
Let the waves engulf the gold-hoard's keeper.
On a wagon they loaded the wondrous treasure,
Gold past counting. The gray-haired king    35
They bore to the pyre, on the Point of Whales.

## XLIII

### *The Burning of Beowulf's Body*

Then built for Beowulf the band of the Jutes
A funeral pyre; 'twas firmly based.
They hung it with helmets as he had bidden,
With shining byrnies and battle-shields.
In the midst they laid, with loud lament,    5
Their lord beloved, their leader brave.
On the brow of the cliff they kindled the blaze,
Black o'er the flames the smoke shot up;
Cries of woe, in the windless air,
Rose and blent with the roar of the blast,    10
Till the frame of the body burst with the heat
Of the seething heart. In sorrowing mood
They mourned aloud their leader dead.

Joined in the wail a woman old,
With hair upbound for Beowulf grieved,    15
Chanted a dreary dirge of woe,
Dark forebodings of days to come,
Thick with slaughter and throes of battle,
Bondage and shame. The black smoke rose.
High on the headland they heaped a barrow,    20
Lofty and broad 'twas built by the Weders,
Far to be seen by sea-faring men.
Ten days long they toiled to raise it,
The battle-king's beacon. They built a wall
To fence the brands of the funeral burning,    25
The choicest and best their chiefs could devise.
In the barrow they buried the bracelets and
    rings,
All those pieces of precious treasure
That bold-hearted men had brought from the
    cave,
Returned to earth the heirloom of heroes,    30

The gold to the ground, again to become
As useless to men as of yore it had been.

Around the barrow the battle-brave rode,
Twelve in the troop, all true-born æthelings,
To make their lament and mourn for the king;
To chant a lay their lord to honor.    36
They praised his daring; his deeds of prowess
They mentioned in song. For meet it is
That men should publish their master's praise,
Honor their chieftain, and cherish him dearly
When he leaves this life, released from the
    body.    41

Thus joined the men of the Jutes in mourning
Their hero's end. His hearth-companions
Called him the best among kings of the earth,
Mildest of men, and most beloved,    45
Kindest to kinsmen, and keenest for fame.

# The Venerable Bede

## 672?-735

Bede, or Baeda, as his name is written in Latin, was born near Jarrow in Northumbria about A.D. 672. Two years later a monastery was founded at Wearmouth in the same neighborhood by a certain Benedict Biscop, a learned churchman; here Bede was placed by his family at the age of seven. Soon after 681 Benedict established another house, also under his guidance, at Jarrow; and to this the boy seems to have been immediately transferred. At Jarrow Bede passed the whole of his maturity, probably leaving the monastery for short periods only, and never, as far as it is known, departing from England. He must have given early evidence of his abilities, for he became a deacon at the age of nineteen although canon law forbade that any man should do so before he became twenty-five; Bede, however, was ordained a priest only after he had reached the canonical age of thirty. He was employed by the monastery, not as an administrator, but as a teacher and a scholar. Benedict had brought a fair number of manuscripts from the Continent, and books could be borrowed from other monastic libraries in England. With the materials available, scanty as they may seem today, Bede composed scientific treatises on orthography, metrics, and chronology; but the majority of his works deal with theological subjects. He wrote the lives of several Northumbrian abbots; a martyrology, or calendar of the martyrs; and, what he undoubtedly regarded as his chief title to fame, a commentary on several books of the Bible. But from the modern point of view his masterpiece is the Ecclesiastical History of the English Nation, which he completed in 731. He died four years later, on 25 May, 735, engaged even to his last moments, if we may believe a contemporary account, in scholarly writing. At the time of his death he was about sixty-three; he has been called "the Venerable," not because he attained a great age, but as a tribute to his sanctity.

The Ecclesiastical History is modeled to some extent on the work of Eusebius which bears the same title, and on the History of the Franks by Gregory of Tours. In his opening chapters Bede epitomizes the affairs of England from Caesar's first invasion to the mission of Augustine in 597; he devotes the body of his work to the conversion of the English and the vicissitudes of their church between 597 and 731. His account is on the whole well ordered and well informed; it reveals a scholarly grasp of his material and a regard for accuracy which are unique among the histories written in that period; but it likewise enjoys the advantage of Bede's pure and lucid style as well as of his narrative skill. The immediate popularity of the Ecclesiastical History is indicated in a curious way: after the disappearance of Roman authority from western Europe it was customary for each kingdom to number years from the beginning of the reign of each of its kings; where, as in England, several small kingdoms existed side by side, this expedient was complex and awkward; although the modern system of dating the years uniformly from the incarnation of Christ had been invented about two centuries before Bede's time, the Ecclesiastical History was the first important work to adopt the improvement; and as soon as the Ecclesiastical History had adopted it, the modern system of dating became common throughout western Europe.

The standard edition of the original Latin is the Venerabilis Baedae Historiam Ecclesiasticam Gentis Anglorum, ed. Charles Plummer (Oxford, 1896); the so-called "Alfredian" translation is printed as The Old English Version of Bede's Ecclesiastical History of the English People, ed. Thomas Miller for the Early English Text Society (London, 1890–1898). Bede, his Life, Times, and Writings, ed. A. Hamilton Thompson (Oxford, 1935), is a convenient summary, by several experts, of all that is known about Bede and his background. The history of the Old English period is presented, largely through translations of original sources, by Raymond W. Chambers, England before the Norman Conquest (*London, 1926*).

# The Ecclesiastical History of the English Nation [1]

### The Coming of Augustine

## BOOK I

### CHAPTER XXIII

*How Pope Gregory Sent Augustine, with Other Monks, to Preach to the English Nation, and Encouraged Them by a Letter of Exhortation Not to Cease from Their Labor.*

IN the year of our Lord 582, Mauritius, the fifty-fourth from Augustus, ascended the throne [2] and reigned twenty-one years. In the tenth year of his reign Gregory,[3] a man renowned for learning and behavior, was promoted to the apostolical see of Rome and presided over it thirteen years, six months, and ten days. He, being moved by divine inspiration, in the fourteenth year of the same emperor, and about the one hundred and fiftieth after the coming of the English into Britain, sent the servant of God, Augustine, and with him several other monks who feared the Lord, to preach the word of God to the English nation. They having, in obedience to the pope's commands, undertaken that work, were, on their journey, seized with a sluggish fear and began to think of returning home rather than proceed to a barbarous, fierce, and unbelieving nation, to whose very language they were strangers; and this they unanimously agreed was the safer course. In short, they sent back Augustine, who had been appointed to be consecrated bishop in case they were received by the English, that he might, by humble entreaty, obtain of the holy Gregory that they should not be compelled to undertake so dangerous, toilsome, and uncertain a journey. The pope, in reply, sent them a hortatory epistle, persuading them to proceed in the work of the divine word and rely on the assistance of the

Almighty. The purport of which letter was as follows:—

"*Gregory, the servant of the servants of God, to the servants of our Lord.* Forasmuch as it had been better not to begin a good work than to think of desisting from that which has been begun, it behooves you, my beloved sons, with the greatest zeal to fulfill the good work which, by the help of our Lord, you have undertaken. Let not, therefore, the toil of the journey, nor the tongues of evil-speaking men, deter you; but with all possible earnestness and zeal perform that which, by God's direction, you have undertaken; being assured that much labor is followed by the greater glory of an eternal reward. When Augustine, your chief, returns, whom we also constitute your abbot, humbly obey him in all things; knowing that whatsoever you shall do by his direction, will, in all respects, be available to your souls. Almighty God protect you with his grace and grant that I may, in the heavenly country, see the fruits of your labor; inasmuch as, though I cannot labor with you, I shall partake in the joy of the reward, because I am willing to labor. God keep you in safety, my most beloved sons. Dated the twenty-third of July in the fourteenth year of the reign of our pious and most august lord, Mauritius Tiberius, the thirteenth year after the consulship of our said lord, the fourteenth indiction." [4]

### CHAPTER XXV

*How Augustine, Coming into Britain, First Preached in the Isle of Thanet to King Ethelbert and, Having Obtained License, Entered the Kingdom of Kent in Order to Preach Therein.*

AUGUSTINE, thus strengthened by the confirmation of the blessed father, Gregory, returned to the work of the word of God with the servants of Christ, and arrived in Britain. The powerful Ethelbert was at that time king of Kent; he had extended his dominions as far as the great river Humber, by which the southern English are divided from the northern. On the east coast of Kent is the large Isle of Thanet containing, according to the English way of reckoning, six hundred families,[5] divided from the other land by the river Want-

---

[1] From the translation of John Stevens (1723), revised by John A. Giles (1840); the passages included here have again been revised after a comparison with the Latin text.

[2] As emperor of the Western Roman Empire.

[3] Gregory I (later called the Great), who actually became pope in 590.

[4] In 596, the fourteenth year of the fifteen-year cycle (indiction), which began with the year in which Mauritius came to the throne.

[5] Containing land enough to support six hundred families.

sum,[6] which is about three furlongs over and fordable only in two places, for both ends of it run into the sea. In this island landed the servant of our Lord, Augustine, and his companions, being, as is reported, nearly forty men. They had, by order of the blessed Pope Gregory, taken interpreters of the nation of the Franks and, sending to Ethelbert, signified that they were come from Rome and brought a joyful message, which most undoubtedly assured to all that took advantage of it everlasting joys in heaven and a kingdom that would never end, with the living and true God. The king, having heard this, ordered them to stay in that island where they had landed, and that they should be furnished with all necessaries, till he should consider what to do with them. For he had before heard of the Christian religion, having a Christian wife of the royal family of the Franks, called Bertha;[7] whom he had received from her parents upon condition that she should be permitted to practice her religion with the Bishop Luidhard, who was sent with her to preserve her faith. Some days after, the king came into the island and, sitting in the open air, ordered Augustine and his companions to be brought there into his presence. For he had taken precaution that they should not come to him in any house, lest, according to an ancient superstition, if they practiced any magical arts, they might by surprise impose upon him and so get the better of him. But they came furnished with divine, not with magic[8] virtue, bearing a silver cross for their banner, and the image of our Lord and Savior painted on a board; and singing the litanies, they offered up their prayers to the Lord for the eternal salvation both of themselves and of those to whom and for whose sake they were come. When they had sat down, pursuant to the king's commands, and preached to him and his attendants there present the word of life, the king answered thus:—"Your words and promises are very fair, but as they are new to us and of uncertain import, I cannot approve of them so far as to forsake those things which I have so long followed with the whole English nation. But because you are come from far into my kingdom and, as I conceive, are desirous to impart to us those things which you believe to be true and most beneficial, we will not molest you, but give you favorable entertainment and take care to supply you with your necessary suste-

nance; nor do we forbid you to preach and gain as many as you can to belief in your religion." Accordingly he permitted them to reside in the city of Canterbury, which was the metropolis of all his dominions, and, pursuant to his promise, besides allowing them sustenance, did not refuse them liberty to preach. It is reported that, as they drew near to the city after their manner, with the holy cross and the image of our sovereign Lord and King, Jesus Christ, they, in concert, sung this litany: "We beseech Thee, O Lord, in all Thy mercy, that Thy anger and wrath be turned away from this city and from Thy holy house, because we have sinned.[9] Hallelujah."

## CHAPTER XXVI

*How St. Augustine in Kent Followed the Doctrine and Manner of Living of the Primitive Church, and Settled His Episcopal See in the Royal City.*

As soon as they entered the dwelling-place assigned them, they began to imitate the course of life practiced in the primitive Church; applying themselves to frequent prayer, watching, and fasting; preaching the word of life to as many as they could; despising all worldly things as not belonging to them; receiving only their necessary food from those they taught; living themselves in all respects conformably to what they prescribed to others, and being always disposed to suffer any adversity and even to die for that truth which they preached. In short, several believed and were baptized, admiring the simplicity of their innocent life and the sweetness of their heavenly doctrine. There was on the east side of the city a church dedicated to the honor of St. Martin, built whilst the Romans were still in the island, wherein the queen, who, as has been said before, was a Christian, used to pray. In this they first began to meet, to sing, to pray, to say mass, to preach, and to baptize, until the king, being converted to the faith, allowed them greater freedom to preach and build or repair churches in all places.

When he among the rest, gladdened by the unspotted life of these holy men and their delightful promises, which, by many miracles, they proved to be most certain, believed and was baptized, greater numbers began daily to flock together to hear the word and, forsaking their heathen rites, to associate themselves, by believing, to the unity of the Church of Christ.

[6] Branch of the Stour.
[7] Daughter of Charibert, king of Paris.
[8] Diabolic.

[9] Daniel, 9:16.

Their faith and conversion the king so far encouraged as that he compelled none to embrace Christianity, but only showed closer affection to the believers, as to his fellow-citizens in the heavenly kingdom. For he had learned from the instructors and authors of his salvation that the service of Christ ought to be voluntary, not by compulsion. Nor was it long before he gave his teachers a residence suitable to their degree [10] in his metropolis of Canterbury, with such possessions of different kinds as were necessary for their subsistence.

### CHAPTER XXIX

*How the Same Pope Sent Augustine the Pall,[11] an Epistle, and more Ministers of the Word.*

MOREOVER, the same Pope Gregory, hearing from Bishop Augustine that he had a great harvest and but few laborers, sent to him, together with his aforesaid messengers,[12] more fellow laborers and ministers of the word, of whom the first and principal were Mellitus, Justus, Paulinus, and Rufinianus, and by them all things in general that were necessary for the worship and service of the church, *viz.*, sacred vessels and vestments for the altars, also ornaments for the churches and vestments for the priests and clerks, as likewise relics of the holy apostles and martyrs, besides many books. He also sent a letter wherein he signified that he had transmitted the pall to him, and at the same time directed how he should constitute bishops in Britain.

\*    \*    \*

### CHAPTER XXX

*A Copy of the Letter Which Pope Gregory Sent to the Abbot Mellitus, Then Going into Britain.*

THE aforesaid messengers [13] being departed, the holy father, Gregory, sent after them a letter worthy to be preserved in memory, wherein he plainly shows what care he took of the salvation of our nation. The letter was as follows:—

"To *his most beloved son, the Abbot Mel-*

---

[10] His own palace.
[11] Cloak, bestowed as mark of ecclesiastical honor.
[12] Lawrence and Peter, whom Augustine had sent to Rome with the report of his success (chapter xxvii).
[13] Lawrence, Peter, Mellitus, Justus, Paulinus, and Rufinianus.

*litus, Gregory, the servant of the servants of God.* We have been much concerned, since the departure of our congregation that is with you, because we have received no account of the success of your journey. When, therefore, Almighty God shall bring you to the most reverend Bishop Augustine, our brother, tell him what I have, upon mature deliberation on the affair of the English, determined upon, *viz.*, that the temples of the idols in that nation ought not to be destroyed; but let the idols that are in them be destroyed; let holy water be made and sprinkled in the said temples; let altars be erected and relics placed. For if those temples are well built, it is requisite that they be converted from the worship of devils to the service of the true God; that the nation, seeing that their said temples are not destroyed, may remove error from their hearts and, knowing and adoring the true God, may the more familiarly resort to the places to which they have been accustomed. And because they have been used to slaughter many oxen in the sacrifices to devils, some solemnity must be exchanged for them on this account, as that on the day of the dedication, or the nativities of the holy martyrs whose relics are there deposited, they may build themselves huts of the boughs of trees about those churches which have been turned to that use from temples, and celebrate the solemnity with religious feasting, and no more offer beasts to the Devil but kill cattle to the praise of God in their eating, and return thanks to the Giver of all things for their abundance; to the end that, whilst some gratifications are outwardly permitted them, they may the more easily consent to the inward consolations of the grace of God. For there is no doubt that it is impossible to efface everything at once from their obdurate minds; because he who endeavors to ascend to the highest place, rises by degrees or steps, and not by leaps. Thus the Lord made Himself known to the people of Israel in Egypt; and yet He allowed them the use of the sacrifices which they were wont to offer to the Devil, in His own worship; so as to command them in His sacrifice to kill beasts, to the end that, changing their hearts, they might lay aside one part of the sacrifice, whilst they retained another; that whilst they offered the same beasts which they were wont to offer, they should offer them to the true God and not to idols; and thus they would no longer be the same sacrifices. This it behooves your affection to communicate to our aforesaid brother, that he, being there present, may consider how he is to order all things. God preserve you in safety, most beloved son.

"Given the eighteenth of July, in the nineteenth year of the reign of our lord, the most pious emperor, Mauritius Tiberius, the eighteenth year after the consulship of our said lord, the fourth indiction."[14]

## BOOK II

### CHAPTER I

*On the Death of the Blessed Pope Gregory.*

At this time, that is, in the year of our Lord 605,[15] the blessed Pope Gregory, after having most gloriously governed the Roman apostolic see thirteen years, six months, and ten days, died and was translated to the eternal see of the heavenly kingdom. Of him, in regard that he by his zeal converted our nation, the English, from the power of Satan to the faith of Christ, it behooves us to discourse more at large in our Ecclesiastical History, for we may and ought rightly to call him our apostle; because, as soon as he bore the pontifical power over all the world and was placed over the churches already reduced to the faith of truth, he made our nation, till then given up to idols, the Church of Christ, so that we may be allowed thus to attribute to him the character of an apostle; for though he is not an apostle to others, yet he is so to us; for we are the seal of his apostleship in our Lord.

\* \* \*

To his works of piety and righteousness this also may be added, that he saved our nation, by the preachers he sent hither, from the teeth of the old enemy, and made it partaker of eternal liberty; in whose faith and salvation rejoicing and worthily commending the same, he in his exposition on holy Job says, "Behold, the tongue of Britain, which only knew a barbarous gnashing, has long since begun to resound the Hebrew Hallelujah! Behold, the once swelling ocean now serves prostrate at the feet of the saints; and its barbarous motions, which earthly princes could not subdue with the sword, are now, through the fear of God, bound by the mouths of priests with words only; and he that when an infidel stood not in awe of fighting troops, now a believer, fears the tongues of the humble! For by reason that the virtue of the divine knowledge is infused into it by precepts, heavenly words, and conspicuous miracles, it is curbed by the dread of the same divinity, so as to fear to act wickedly, and bends all its desires to arrive at eternal glory." In which words holy Gregory declares this also, that St. Augustine and his companions brought the English to the knowledge of truth, not only by the preaching of words, but also by showing of heavenly signs.

\* \* \*

Nor is the account of St. Gregory which has been handed down to us by the tradition of our ancestors to be passed by in silence in relation to his motives for taking such interest in the salvation of our nation. It is reported that some merchants, having just arrived at Rome on a certain day, exposed many things for sale in the market-place, and abundance of people resorted thither to buy: Gregory himself went with the rest, and, among other things, some boys were set to sale, their bodies white, their countenances beautiful, and their hair very fine. Having viewed them, he asked, as is said, from what country or nation they were brought? and was told, from the island of Britain, whose inhabitants were of such personal appearance. He again inquired whether those islanders were Christians or still involved in the errors of paganism? and was informed that they were pagans. Then fetching a deep sigh from the bottom of his heart, "Alas! what pity," said he, "that the author of darkness is possessed of men of such fair countenances; and that being remarkable for such graceful aspects, they should have minds void of inward grace." He therefore again asked what was the name of that nation? and was answered that they were called Angles. "Right," said he, "for they have an angelic face, and it becomes such to be co-heirs with the angels in heaven. What is the name," proceeded he, "of the province from which they are brought?" It was replied that the natives of that province were called Deiri.[16] "Truly are they *De ira*," said he, "withdrawn from wrath and called to the mercy of Christ. How is the king of that province called?" They told him his name was Aella; and he, alluding to the name, said, "Hallelujah, the praise of God, the Creator, must be sung in those parts."

Then repairing to the bishop of the Roman apostolical see [17] (for he was not himself then made pope), he entreated him to send some

---

[14] The fourth year in the second indiction of Mauritius.

[15] According to a corrected computation, 604.

[16] Inhabitants of Deifyr, the district south of the Tees or the Tyne.

[17] Pope Benedict I.

ministers of the word into Britain to the nation of the English, by whom it might be converted to Christ; declaring himself ready to undertake that work, by the assistance of God, if the apostolic pope should think fit to have it so done. Which not being then able to perform, because, though the pope was willing to grant his request, yet the citizens of Rome could not be brought to consent that he should depart so far from the city; as soon as he was himself made pope, he perfected the long-desired work, sending other preachers but himself by his prayers and exhortations assisting the preaching, that it might be successful. This account, as we have received it from the ancients, we have thought fit to insert in our Ecclesiastical History.

## *The Conversion of Edwin*

### BOOK II

#### CHAPTER IX

*Of the Reign of King Edwin, and How Paulinus, Coming to Preach the Gospel to Him, First Instructed His Daughter and Others in the Mysteries of the Christian Faith.*

At this time [1] the nation of the Northumbrians, that is, the nation of the English that live on the north side of the river Humber, with their king, Edwin, received the faith through the preaching of Paulinus, above mentioned.[2] This Edwin, as an omen of his receiving the faith and of his share in the heavenly kingdom, received an increase of that which he enjoyed on earth, for he reduced under his dominion all the borders of Britain that were provinces either of the aforesaid nation,[3] or of the Britons, a thing which none of the English had ever done before; and he in like manner subjected to the English the Mevanian Islands, as has been said above.[4] The first whereof, which is to the southward, is the largest in extent and most fruitful, containing nine hundred and sixty families according to the English computation; the other, above three hundred.

The occasion of this nation's embracing the faith was that their aforesaid king was allied to the kings of Kent, having taken to wife Ethelberga, otherwise called Tata, daughter to King Ethelbert. He, having by his wooers asked her in marriage of her brother Eadbald, who then reigned in Kent, was answered, "That it was not lawful to marry a Christian virgin to a pagan husband, lest the faith and the mysteries of the heavenly King should be profaned by her cohabiting with a king that was altogether a stranger to the worship of the true God." This answer being brought to Edwin by his messengers, he promised in no manner to act in opposition to the Christian faith which the virgin professed; but would give leave to her and all that went with her, men or women, priests or ministers, to follow their faith and worship after the custom of the Christians. Nor did he deny but that he would embrace the same religion, if, being examined by wise persons, it should be found more holy and more worthy of God.

Hereupon the virgin was promised and sent to Edwin, and pursuant to what had been agreed on, Paulinus, a man beloved of God, was ordained bishop, to go with her and by daily exhortations and celebrating the heavenly mysteries to confirm her and her company, lest they should be corrupted by the company of the pagans. Paulinus was ordained bishop by the Archbishop Justus on the twenty-first of July in the year of our Lord 625, and so he came to King Edwin with the aforesaid virgin as a companion of their union in the flesh. But his mind was wholly bent upon reducing the nation to which he was sent to the knowledge of truth; according to the words of the apostle, "To espouse her to one husband, that he might present her as a chaste virgin to Christ." [5] Being come into that province, he labored much, not only to retain those that went with him, by the help of God, that they should not revolt from the faith, but, if he could, to convert some of the pagans to a state of grace by his preaching. But, as the apostle says, though he labored long in the word, "The god of this world blinded the minds of them that believed not, lest the light of the glorious Gospel of Christ should shine unto them." [6]

The next year there came into the province a certain assassin, called Eumer, sent by the king of the West-Saxons, whose name was Cuichelm, in hope at once to deprive King Edwin of his kingdom and his life. He had a two-edged short sword, dipped in poison to the end that if the wound were not sufficient to kill the king, it might be aided by the venom.

---

[1] About 625.    [2] Cf. Book I, chapter xxix.
[3] The Angles.
[4] Book II, chapter v. The Mevanian Islands are Anglesey and Man.

[5] II Corinthians, 11:2.
[6] II Corinthians, 11:4.

He came to the king on the first day of Easter at the river Derwent, where then stood the regal city, and being admitted as if to deliver a message from his master, whilst he was in an artful manner delivering his pretended embassy, he started on a sudden and, drawing the sword from under his garment, assaulted the king; which Lilla, the king's beloved minister, observing, having no buckler at hand to secure the king from death, interposed his own body 10 to receive the stroke; but the wretch struck so home that he wounded the king through the slain knight's body. Being then attacked on all sides with swords, he in that confusion also slew another soldier, whose name was Forthhere, with the same unlucky weapon.

On that same holy night of Easter Sunday the queen had brought forth to the king a daughter, called Eanfled. The king, in the presence of Bishop Paulinus, gave thanks to 20 his gods for the birth of his daughter; and the bishop, on the other hand, returned thanks to Christ and endeavored to persuade the king that by his prayers to Him he had obtained that the queen should bring forth the child in safety and without much pain. The king, delighted with his words, promised that in case Christ would grant him life and victory over the king by whom the assassin who had wounded him had been sent, he would cast 30 off his idols and serve Him; and as a pledge that he would perform his promise, he delivered up that same daughter to Paulinus, to be consecrated to Christ. She was the first baptized of the nation of the Northumbrians, on Whitsunday, with eleven others of her family. At that time, the king, being recovered of the wound which he had received, marched with his army against the nation of the West-Saxons; and having begun the war, either 40 slew or subdued all those that he had been informed had conspired to murder him. Returning thus victorious unto his own country, he would not immediately and unadvisedly embrace the mysteries of the Christian faith, though he no longer worshiped idols ever since he made the promise that he would serve Christ; but thought fit first at leisure to be instructed by the venerable Paulinus in the knowledge of faith, and to confer with such as 50 he knew to be the wisest of his prime men, to advise what they thought was fittest to be done in that case. And being a man of extraordinary sagacity, he often sat alone by himself a long time, silent as to his tongue but deliberating much in his heart how he should proceed, and which religion he should adhere to.

## CHAPTER XII

*How King Edwin Was Persuaded to Believe by a Vision Which He Had Seen When He Was in Exile.*

BUT a heavenly vision, which the Divine Mercy was pleased once to reveal to this king when he was in banishment at the court of Redwald, king of the Angles, was of no little use in urging him to embrace and understand the doctrines of salvation. Paulinus, therefore, perceiving that it was a very difficult task to incline the king's lofty mind to the humility of the way of salvation and to embrace the mystery of the cross of life, and at the same time using both exhortation with men and prayer to God, for his and his subjects' salvation; at length, as we may suppose, it was shown him in spirit what and of what nature was the vision from heaven that had been formerly revealed to the king. Nor did he lose any time, but immediately admonished the king to perform the vow which he made when he received the oracle, promising to put the same in execution, if he were delivered from the trouble he was at that time under and should be advanced to the throne.

The vision was this. When Ethelfrid, his predecessor, was persecuting him, he for many years wandered in a private manner through several places and kingdoms, and at last came to Redwald, beseeching him to protect his life against the snares of his powerful persecutor. Redwald willingly admitted him and promised to perform what he requested. But when Ethelfrid understood that he had appeared in that province, and that he and his companions were hospitably entertained by Redwald, he sent messengers to offer that king a great sum of money to murder him, but without effect. He sent a second and a third time, bidding more and more money each time and threatening to make war on him if he refused. Redwald, either terrified by his threats or gained by his gifts, complied with his request and promised either to kill Edwin or to deliver him up to the ambassadors. This being observed by a trusty friend of his,[7] he went into his chamber where he [8] was going to bed, for it was the first hour of the night; and calling him out, discovered what the king had promised to do with him, adding, "If, therefore, you think fit, I will this very hour conduct you out of this province, and lead you to a place where neither

[7] Edwin's.     [8] Edwin.

Redwald nor Ethelfrid shall ever find you." He answered, "I thank you for your good will, yet I cannot do what you propose, or be guilty of breaking the compact I have made with so great a king, when he has done me no harm, nor offered me any injury; but, on the contrary, if I must die, let it rather be by his hand than by that of any meaner person. For whither shall I now fly, who have for so many years been a vagabond through all the provinces of Britain, to escape the hands of my enemies?" His friend being gone, Edwin remained alone without, and sitting with a heavy heart before the palace, began to be overwhelmed with many thoughts, not knowing what to do or which way to turn himself.

When he had remained a long time in silence, brooding over his misfortunes in silent anguish of mind and pent-up misery, he, on a sudden, in the dead of night, saw approaching a person whose face and habit were equally strange, at which unknown and unexpected sight he was not a little frightened. The stranger, coming close up, saluted him and asked him, "Why he sat there alone and melancholy on a stone, keeping watch at that time when all others were taking their rest and were fast asleep?" Edwin, in his turn, asked, "What it was to him, whether he spent the night within doors or abroad?" The stranger, in reply, said, "Do not think that I am ignorant of the cause of your grief, your watching, and sitting alone without. For I know who you are, and why you grieve, and the evils which you fear will fall upon you. But tell me what reward you will give the man, if such there be, that shall deliver you out of this anguish and persuade Redwald neither to do you any harm himself nor to deliver you up to be murdered by your enemies." Edwin replied, "That he would give that person all that he was able for so singular a favor." The other further added, "What if I also assure you that you shall overcome your enemies, and surpass in power, not only all your own progenitors, but even all that have reigned before you over the English nation?" Edwin, encouraged by these questions, did not hesitate to promise that he would make a suitable return to him who should so highly oblige him. Then spoke the other for the third time, "But if he who foretells so much good as is to befall you can also give you better and more profitable advice for your life and salvation than any of your progenitors or kindred ever heard of, do you consent to submit to him and to follow his wholesome counsel?" Edwin did not hesitate

to promise that he would in all things follow the directions of that man who should deliver him from so many and so great calamities and raise him to a throne.

Having received this answer, the person that talked to him laid his right hand on his head, saying, "When this sign shall be given you, remember this present discourse that has passed between us, and do not delay the performance of what you now promise." Having uttered these words, he is said to have immediately vanished, that the king might understand it was not a man, but a spirit, that had appeared to him.

Whilst the royal youth still sat there alone, glad of the comfort he had received, but preoccupied and seriously considering who he was, or whence he came, that had so talked to him, his above-mentioned friend came to him, and saluting him with a pleasant countenance, "Rise," said he, "go in and compose your mind and limbs to sleep without care or fear; for the king's resolution is altered, and he designs to do you no harm, but rather to perform the promise which he made you; for when he had privately acquainted the queen with his intention of doing what I told you before, she dissuaded him from it, declaring it was unworthy of so great a king to sell his good friend in such distress for gold and to sacrifice his honor, which is more valuable than all other ornaments, for the love of money." In short, the king did as he was advised and not only refused to deliver up the banished man to his enemy's messengers, but assisted him to recover his kingdom. For as soon as the ambassadors were returned home, he raised a mighty army to make war on Ethelfrid; who, meeting him with much inferior forces (for Redwald had not given him time to gather and unite all his power), was slain on the borders of the kingdom of Mercia,[9] on the east side of the river that is called Idle.[10] In this battle Redwald's son, called Regnhere, was killed; and thus Edwin, pursuant to the oracle he had received, not only escaped the danger from the king his enemy but, by his death, succeeded him in the throne.

King Edwin, therefore, delaying to receive the word of God at the preaching of Paulinus and using for some time, as has been said, to sit alone at suitable hours and seriously to ponder with himself what he was to do and what religion he was to follow, the man of

---

[9] The kingdom which embraced the central portion of what is now England.

[10] A tributary of the Trent.

God came to him, laid his right hand on his head, and asked, "Whether he knew that sign?" The king, in a trembling condition, was ready to fall down at his feet, but he raised him up and in a familiar manner said to him, "Behold, by the help of God you have escaped the hands of the enemies whom you feared. Behold, you have of his gift obtained the kingdom which you desired. Take heed not to delay the third part, that which you promised to perform; embrace the faith and keep the precepts of Him who, delivering you from temporal adversity, has raised you to the honor of a temporal kingdom; and if, from this time forward, you shall be obedient to His will, which through me He signifies to you, He will not only deliver you from the everlasting torments of the wicked, but also make you partaker with Him of His eternal kingdom in heaven."

## CHAPTER XIII

*What Counsel the Same Edwin Held with His Chief Men about Embracing the Faith of Christ, and How the High Priest Profaned His Own Altars.*

THE king, hearing these words, answered that he was both willing and bound to receive the faith which he taught; but that he would confer about it with his principal friends and counselors, to the end that if they also were of his opinion, they might all together be cleansed in Christ, the Fountain of Life. Paulinus consenting, the king did as he said; for, holding a council with the wise men, he asked of every one in particular what he thought of this hitherto unknown doctrine and the new divine worship that was preached? To which the chief of his own priests, Coifi, immediately answered, "O king, consider what this is which is now preached to us; for I verily declare to you that the religion which we have hitherto professed has, as far as I can certainly learn, no virtue nor advantage in it. For none of your people has applied himself more diligently to the worship of our gods than I; and yet there are many who received greater favors from you, and are more preferred than I, and are more prosperous in all they seek to do and to get. Now if the gods were good for anything, they would rather forward me, who have been more careful to serve them. It remains, therefore, that if upon examination you find those new doctrines which are now preached to us better and more efficacious, we immediately receive them without any delay."

Another of the king's chief men, approving of his prudent words and exhortations, presently added: "The present life of man on earth, O king, seems to me, in comparison of that time which is unknown to us, like to the swift flight of a sparrow through the room wherein you sit at supper in winter with your commanders and ministers, a good fire burning in the midst whilst the storms of rain and snow rage everywhere abroad; the sparrow, I say, flying in at one door and immediately out at another, whilst he is within is safe from the wintry storm; but after a short space of fair weather, lasting only a moment, he immediately vanishes out of your sight into the dark winter from which he had emerged. So this life of man appears for a short space, but of what went before or what is to follow we are utterly ignorant. If, therefore, this new doctrine contains something more certain, it seems justly to deserve to be followed." The other elders and king's counselors, by divine inspiration, spoke to the same effect.

But Coifi added that he wished more attentively to hear Paulinus discourse concerning the God whom he preached; which he having by the king's command performed, Coifi, hearing his words, cried out, "I have long since been sensible that there was nothing in that which we worshiped; because the more diligently I sought after truth in that worship, the less I found it. But now I freely confess that such truth evidently appears in this preaching as can confer on us the gifts of life, of salvation, and of eternal happiness. For which reason I advise, O King, that we instantly curse and set fire to those temples and altars which we have consecrated without reaping any benefit from them." In short, the king publicly gave his license to Paulinus to preach the Gospel and, renouncing idolatry, declared that he received the faith of Christ; and when he inquired of the aforesaid priest of his sacrifices who should first profane the altars and temples of their idols with the enclosures that were about them, he answered, "I; for who as an example to all others can now more properly than myself, through the wisdom which has been given me by the true God, destroy those things which I worshiped through my folly?" Then immediately, in contempt of his vain superstitions, he desired the king to furnish him with arms and a stallion, on which he might mount and set out to destroy the idols; for it was not lawful before for the high priest either to carry arms or to ride on any but a mare. Having, therefore, girt a sword about him, with a spear in his hand he mounted the king's stallion and proceeded to the idols. The multitude, beholding it, concluded he was distracted; but he lost no time, for as soon as he drew near the temple he profaned the same, casting into it the spear which he held; and rejoicing in the knowledge of the worship of the true God, he commanded his companions to destroy the temple, with all its enclosures, by fire. This place where the idols 10 once were is still shown not far from York, to the eastward beyond the river Derwent, and is now called Godmundingham, where the high priest, by the inspiration of the true God, profaned and destroyed the altars which he had himself consecrated.

### CHAPTER XIV

*How King Edwin and His Nation Became 20 Christians, and Where Paulinus Baptized Them.*

KING EDWIN, therefore, with all the nobility of his nation and a large number of the common sort, received the faith and the washing of regeneration, in the eleventh year of his reign, which is the year of the incarnation of our Lord 627, and about one hundred and eighty after the coming of the English 30 into Britain. He was baptized at York on the holy day of Easter, being the twelfth of April, in the church of St. Peter the Apostle which he himself had there hastily built of timber whilst he was catechizing and instructing in order to receive baptism. In that city also he appointed the see of the bishopric of his instructor and bishop, Paulinus. But as soon as he was baptized, he took care, by the direction of the same Paulinus, to build in the same place 40 a larger and nobler church of stone, in the midst whereof that same oratory which he had first erected should be enclosed. Having therefore laid the foundation, he began to build the church square, encompassing the former oratory. But before the wall was raised to the proper height, the wicked assassination of the king left that work to be finished by Oswald his successor. Paulinus for the space of six years from that time, that is, till the end of the 50 reign of that king, by his consent and favor, preached the word of God in that country, and all that were preordained to eternal life believed and were baptized; among whom were Osfrid and Eadfrid, King Edwin's sons, who were both born to him whilst he was in

banishment, of Quenberga, the daughter of Cearl, king of the Mercians.

\*        \*        \*

### *Caedmon*

### BOOK IV

### CHAPTER XXIV

*That There Was in the Same Monastery* [1] *a Brother on Whom the Gift of Writing Verses Was Bestowed by Heaven.*

THERE was in this abbess's monastery a certain brother particularly remarkable for the grace of God, who was wont to make pious and religious verses, so that whatever was interpreted to him out of Scripture, he soon after put the same into poetical expressions of much sweetness and humility, in English, which was his native language. By his verses the minds of many were often excited to despise the world and to desire the heavenly life. Others after him attempted, in the English nation, to compose religious poems, but none could ever compare with him, for he did not learn the art of poetry from men or through human help, but received it as a gift freely bestowed by God; for which reason he never could compose any trivial or vain poem, but only those which relate to religion suited his religious tongue; for having lived in a secular habit until he was well advanced in years, he had never learned anything of versifying; for which reason being sometimes at entertainments, when it was agreed for the sake of mirth that all present should sing in their turns, when he saw the harp come towards him, he rose up from the middle of the feast and returned home.

Having done so at a certain time and gone out of the house where the entertainment was, to the stable where he had to take care of the horses that night, he there composed himself to rest at the proper time; a person appeared to him in his sleep and, saluting him by his name, said, "Caedmon, sing some song to me." He answered, "I cannot sing; for that was the reason why I left the entertainment and retired to this place because I could not sing." The other who talked to

---

[1] The monastery of the Abbess Hilda at Whitby on the east coast of what is now Yorkshire; Bede, who supplies all that is known about Caedmon, apparently dates the discovery of the poet not long before the death of Hilda in 680.

him replied, "However, you have to sing to me."—"What should I sing?" rejoined he. "Sing the beginning of created beings," said the other. Hereupon he presently began to sing to the praise of God, the Creator, verses which he had never heard, the purport whereof was thus:—"We are now to praise the Maker of the heavenly kingdom, the power of the Creator and His counsel, the deeds of the Father of glory. How He, being the eternal God, became the Author of all miracles, who first, as almighty Preserver of the human race, created heaven for the sons of men as the roof of the house, and next the earth." This is the sense, but not the words in order as he sang them in his sleep; for verses, though never so well composed, cannot be literally translated word by word out of one language into another without losing much of their beauty and loftiness. Awaking from his sleep, he remembered all that he had sung in his dream, and to these words soon added many more, in the same measure and worthy of the Deity.

In the morning he came to the steward, his superior, and, having acquainted him with the gift he had received, was conducted to the abbess, by whom he was ordered, in the presence of many learned men, to tell his dream and repeat the verses, that they might all give their judgment what and whence was the thing which he reported. They all concluded that heavenly grace had been conferred on him by our Lord. They expounded to him a passage in Holy Writ, either historical or doctrinal, ordering him, if he could, to put the same into verse. Having undertaken it, he went away and, returning the next morning, gave it to them composed in most excellent verse; whereupon the abbess, embracing the grace of God in the man, instructed him to quit the secular habit and take upon him the monastic vow; which being accordingly done, she associated him to the rest of the brethren in her monastery and ordered that he should be taught the whole series of sacred history. Thus Caedmon, keeping in mind all he could hear and learn and, as it were chewing the cud, converted the same into most harmonious verse; and sweetly repeating the same, made his masters in their turn his hearers. He sang the creation of the world, the origin of man, and all the history of Genesis; the departure of the children of Israel out of Egypt and their entering into the land of promise, with many other histories from Holy Writ; the incarnation, passion, resurrection of our

Lord, and his ascension into heaven; the coming of the Holy Ghost and the preaching of the apostles. He also made many verses on the terror of future judgment, the horror of the pains of hell, and the delights of heaven, as well as many more about the divine benefits and judgments, by all of which he endeavored to turn away men from the love of vice and to excite in them the love of, and application to, good actions; for he was a very religious man, humbly submissive to regular discipline but full of zeal against those who behaved themselves otherwise; for which reason he ended his life happily.

For when the time of his departure drew near, he labored for the space of fourteen days under a bodily infirmity which seemed to prepare the way, yet so moderate that he could talk and walk the whole time. In his neighborhood was the house to which those that were sick and like shortly to die were wont to be carried. He desired the person that attended him, in the evening, as the night came on in which he was to depart this life, to make ready a place there for him to take his rest. This person, wondering why he should desire it, because there was as yet no sign of his dying soon, did what he had ordered. They accordingly went there; and, conversing pleasantly in a joyful manner with the rest that were in the house before, when it was past midnight, Caedmon asked them whether they had the Eucharist there? They answered, "What need of the Eucharist? for you are not likely to die, since you talk so merrily with us, as if you were in perfect health."—"However," said he again, "bring me the Eucharist." Having received the same into his hand, he asked whether they were all in charity with him and without any enmity or rancor? They answered that they were all in perfect charity and free from anger; and in their turn asked him whether he was in the same mind towards them? He immediately answered, "I am in charity, my children, with all the servants of God." Then strengthening himself with the heavenly viaticum,[2] he prepared for the entrance into another life and asked how near the time was when the brothers were to be awakened to sing the nocturnal praises of our Lord? They answered, "It is not far off." Then he said, "Well, let us wait that hour"; and signing himself with the sign of the cross, he laid his head on the pillow and,

[2] The Eucharist.

falling into a little slumber, ended his life so in silence.

Thus it came to pass that, as he had served God with a simple and pure mind and undisturbed devotion, so he now departed to His presence, leaving the world by a quiet death; and that tongue which had composed so

many salutary words in praise of the Creator uttered its last words in His praise whilst he was in the act of signing himself with the cross and recommending himself into His hands; and by what has been here said, he seems to have had foreknowledge of his death.

# Old English Poetry

## The Wanderer [1]

This poem is preserved in the Exeter Book, a manuscript volume left with other books to his church by Leofric (first bishop of Exeter, died A.D. 1071). The volume is still in the cathedral library at Exeter. The author of the poem is unknown, as well as the date of its composition, though it has been conjectured that this elegiac lyric was written probably in the first quarter of the eighth century. "Over the body of the poem lie the shadows of fatalism, and a profound sense of the instability of the earth and its joys" (J. Duncan Spaeth, Old English Poetry, p. 247). This theme is a characteristic one in Old English literature.

The text of the original may be found in An Anglo-Saxon Book of Verse and Prose, ed. W. J. Sedgefield (Manchester, 1928), pp. 28–31. For a discussion of this and related Old English poems see Bernhard Ten Brink, Early English Literature (to Wiclif), trans. Horace M. Kennedy (New York, 1883), pp. 59–67; and also Charles W. Kennedy, Old English Elegies (Princeton, 1936).

"Still the lone one and desolate waits for his
    Maker's ruth—
God's good mercy, albeit so long it tarry, in
    sooth.
Careworn and sad of heart, on the watery ways
    must he
Plow with the hand-grasped oar—how long?
    —the rime-cold sea,
Tread thy paths of exile, O Fate, who art
    cruelty."       5
    Thus did a wanderer speak, being heartfull
    of woe, and all
Thoughts of the cruel slayings, and pleasant
    comrades' fall:
"Morn by morn I, alone, am fain to utter my
    woe;
Now is there none of the living to whom I
    dare to show

Plainly the thought of my heart; in very sooth
    I know       10
Excellent is it in man that his breast he
    straightly bind,
Shut fast his thinkings in silence, whatever he
    have in his mind.
The man that is weary in heart, he never can
    fate withstand;
The man that grieves in his spirit, he finds not
    the helper's hand.
Therefore the glory-grasper full heavy of soul
    may be.       15
So, far from my fatherland, and mine own good
    kinsmen free,
I must bind my heart in fetters, for long, ah!
    long ago,
The earth's cold darkness covered my giver of
    gold brought low;
And I, sore stricken and humbled, and winter-
    saddened, went
Far over the frost-bound waves to seek for the
    dear content     20
Of the hall of the giver of rings; but far nor near
    could I find
Who felt the love of the mead-hall, or who with
    comforts kind
Would comfort me, the friendless. 'T is he
    alone will know,
Who knows, being desolate too, how evil a
    fere [2] is woe;
For him the path of the exile, and not the
    twisted gold;     25
For him the frost in his bosom, and not earth-
    riches old.
    "O, well he remembers the hall-men, the
    treasure bestowed in the hall;
The feast that his gold-giver made him, the joy
    at its height, at its fall;
He knows who must be forlorn for his dear
    lord's counsels gone,
Where sleep and sorrow together are binding
    the lonely one;     30
When himthinks he clasps and kisses his leader
    of men, and lays
His hands and head on his knee, as when, in
    the good yore-days,
He sat on the throne of his might, in the
    strength that wins and saves.

[1] The translation is by Emily H. Hickey. It is reprinted here with the permission of the editors and publishers from Select Translations from Old English Poetry, edited by A. S. Cook and C. B. Tinker, and published by Ginn and Company.

[2] Comrade.

But the friendless man awakes, and he sees the
yellow waves,
And the sea-birds dip to the sea, and broaden
their wings to the gale,                             35
And he sees the dreary rime, and the snow
commingled with hail.
O, then are the wounds of his heart the sorer
much for this,
The grief for the loved and lost made new by
the dream of old bliss.
His kinsmen's memory comes to him as he lies
asleep,
And he greets it with joy, with joy, and the
heart in his breast doth leap;                       40
But out of his ken the shapes of his warrior-
comrades swim
To the land whence seafarers bring no dear old
saws for him;
Then fresh grows sorrow and new to him whose
bitter part
Is to send o'er the frost-bound waves full often
his weary heart.
For this do I look around this world, and
cannot see                                           45
Wherefore or why my heart should not grow
dark in me.
When I think of the lives of the leaders, the
clansmen mighty in mood;
When I think how sudden and swift they
yielded the place where they stood.
So droops this mid-earth and falls, and never a
man is found
Wise ere a many winters have girt his life
around.                                              50
Full patient the sage must be, and he that
would counsel teach—
Not over-hot in his heart, nor over-swift in his
speech;
Nor faint of soul nor secure, nor fain for the
fight nor afraid;
Nor ready to boast before he know himself well
arrayed.
The proud-souled man must bide when he
utters his vaunt, until                               55
He know of the thoughts of the heart, and
whitherward turn they will.
The prudent must understand how terror and
awe shall be,
When the glory and weal of the world lie waste,
as now men see
On our mid-earth, many a where, the wind-
swept walls arise,
And the ruined dwellings and void, and the
rime that on them lies.                              60
The wine-halls crumble, bereft of joy the
warriors lie,
The flower of the doughty fallen, the proud
ones fair to the eye.
War took off some in death, and one did a
strong bird bear
Over the deep; and one—his bones did the gray
wolf share;
And one was hid in a cave by a comrade
sorrow-faced.                                        65

O, thus the Shaper of men hath laid the earth
all waste,
Till the works of the city-dwellers, the works
of the giants of earth,
Stood empty and lorn of the burst of the
mighty revelers' mirth.
"Who wisely hath mused on this wall-stead,[3]
and ponders this dark life well,
In his heart he hath often bethought him of
slayings many and fell,                              70
And these be the words he taketh, the thoughts
of his heart to tell:
'Where is the horse and the rider? Where is
the giver of gold?
Where be the seats at the banquet? Where be
the hall-joys of old?
Alas for the burnished cup, for the byrnied[4]
chief to-day!
Alas for the strength of the prince! for the time
hath passed away—                                    75
Is hid 'neath the shadow of night, as it never
had been at all.
Behind the dear and doughty there standeth
now a wall,
A wall that is wondrous high, and with wondrous snake-work wrought.
The strength of the spears hath fordone the
earls and hath made them naught,
The weapons greedy of slaughter, and she, the
mighty Wyrd;[5]                                       80
And the tempests beat on the rocks, and the
storm-wind that maketh afeard—
The terrible storm that fetters the earth, the
winter-bale,
When the shadow of night falls wan, and wild
is the rush of the hail,
The cruel rush from the north, which maketh
men to quail.
Hardship-full is the earth, o'erturned when the
stark Wyrds say:                                     85
Here is the passing of riches, here friends are
passing away;
And men and kinsfolk pass, and nothing and
none may stay;
And all this earth-stead here shall be empty and
void one day.' "

# The Seafarer [1]

*This poem is, like* The Wanderer, *preserved
in the Exeter Book. Its author and date of
composition are unknown, though it was written probably in the eighth century. The first
part has been thought by some scholars to be
a dialogue between an old mariner who knows
the sea from bitter experience and a young man
eager to become a sailor. This is only conjec-*

[3] Wall-place, earth.          [4] Mail-coated.
[5] Fate.
[1] The translation is by LaMotte Iddings. It is reprinted here with the permission of the editors and
publishers from *Select Translations from Old English Poetry,* edited by A. S. Cook and C. B. Tinker,
and published by Ginn and Company.

ture, though it is plain that two opposed moods are realized by the poet and expressed. It has also been supposed that the second part is by a different and later hand, but this too is only conjecture.

The text of the original may be found in An Anglo-Saxon Book of Verse and Prose, ed. W. J. Sedgefield (Manchester, 1928) pp. 32–4. In addition to the references cited for The Wanderer (p. 43), see Dorothy Whitelock, "The Interpretation of the Seafarer," in The Early Cultures of Northwest Europe, ed. C. Fox and B. Dickins (Cambridge, 1950).

## PART I

I can sing of myself a true song, of my voyages telling,
How oft through laborious days, through the wearisome hours
I have suffered; have borne tribulations; explored in my ship,
Mid the terrible rolling of waves, habitations of sorrow.
Benumbed by the cold, oft the comfortless night-watch hath held me   5
At the prow of my craft as it tossed about under the cliffs.
My feet were imprisoned with frost, were fettered with ice-chains,
Yet hotly were wailing the querulous sighs round my heart;
And hunger within me, sea-wearied, made havoc of courage.
This he, whose lot happily chances on land, doth not know;   10
Nor how I on the ice-cold sea passed the winter in exile,
In wretchedness, robbed of my kinsmen, with icicles hung.
The hail flew in showers about me; and there I heard only
The roar of the sea, ice-cold waves, and the song of the swan;
For pastime the gannets' cry served me; the kittiwakes' chatter   15
For laughter of men; and for mead-drink the call of the sea-mews.
When storms on the rocky cliffs beat, then the terns, icy-feathered,
Made answer; full oft the sea-eagle forebodingly screamed,
The eagle with pinions wave-wet. There none of my kinsmen
Might gladden my desolate soul; of this little he knows   20
Who possesses the pleasures of life, who has felt in the city
Some hardship, some trifling adversity, proud and wine-flushed.
How weary I oft had to tarry upon the seaway!
The shadows of night became darker, it snowed from the north;

The world was enchained by the frost; hail fell upon earth;   25
'Twas the coldest of grain. Yet the thoughts of my heart now are throbbing
To test the high streams, the salt waves in tumultuous play.
Desire in my heart ever urges my spirit to wander,
To seek out the home of the stranger in lands afar off.
There is no one that dwells upon earth, so exalted in mind,   30
So large in his bounty, nor yet of such vigorous youth,
Nor so daring in deeds, nor to whom his liege lord is so kind,
But that he has always a longing, a seafaring passion
For what the Lord God shall bestow, be it honor or death.
No heart for the harp has he, nor for acceptance of treasure,   35
No pleasure has he in a wife, no delight in the world,
Nor in aught save the roll of the billows; but always a longing,
A yearning uneasiness, hastens him on to the sea.
The woodlands are captured by blossoms, the hamlets grow fair,
Broad meadows are beautiful, earth again bursts into life,   40
And all stir the heart of the wanderer eager to journey,
So he meditates going afar on the pathway of tides.
The cuckoo, moreover, gives warning with sorrowful note,
Summer's harbinger sings, and forebodes to the heart bitter sorrow.
The nobleman comprehends not, the luxurious man,   45
What some must endure, who travel the farthest in exile.
Now my spirit uneasily turns in the heart's narrow chamber,
Now wanders forth over the tide, o'er the home of the whale,
To the ends of the earth—and comes back to me. Eager and greedy,
The lone wanderer screams, and resistlessly drives my soul onward,   50
Over the whale-path, over the tracts of the sea.

## PART II

The delights of the Lord are far dearer to me than this dead,
Fleeting life upon earth, for I cannot believe that earth's riches
For ever endure. Each one of three things, ere its time comes,
Is always uncertain: violence, age, and disease

Wrench the soul away, doomed to depart. This
  is praise from the living,                         5
From those who speak afterwards, this the best
  fame after death—
That ere he departed he labored, and wrought
  daring deeds
'Gainst the malice of fiends, and the devil; so
  men shall extol him,
His praise among angels shall live, ever, world
  without end,
His the blessing of life everlasting, and joy mid
  the hosts.                                         10
  The days have departed, all pomps of earth's
  kingdom have vanished;
There now are no kings, no emperors now, no
  gold-givers
As of yore, when they wrought in their midst
  the most glorious deeds,
And lived in the lordliest power. This glory has
  fallen,
Delights have all vanished away; the weak ones
  remain,                                            15
And these govern the world, obtaining their
  pleasure with effort.
Power has declined, earth's glory grows aged
  and sear,
Like every man now in the world; old age
  overtakes him,
His countenance loses its color, gray-haired he
  laments;
He has seen his old friends, sons of princes,
  consigned to the earth.                            20
  This garment of flesh has no power, when
  the spirit escapes,
To drink in the sweet nor to taste of the bitter;
  it then
Has no power to stretch forth the hands or to
  think with the mind.
Though the grave should be covered with gold
  by the nearest of kin,
Be buried along with the dead in masses of
  treasure,                                          25
Still that will not go with them. Gold can no
  substitute be
For the fear of the Lord, to the soul which is
  laden with sin,
Which aforetime, so long as it lived, kept that
  treasure concealed.
Great is the fear of the Lord; the earth
  trembles before it;
He established the unmovable earth, the world
  and the heavens.                                   30
Foolish is he who stands not in awe of the
  Lord—
Unexpectedly death comes upon him; but
  happy is he
Who lives humble in mind, to him cometh
  honor from heaven;
God doth establish the soul that believes in
  His might.
  One should check a strong will, and should
  govern it firmly,                                  35
Be true unto men, and be clean in his manner
  of life. . . .

Fate, God the Creator, is stronger than any
  man's will.
  Come, let us reflect where our home is,
  consider the way
By which we go thither; then let us each strive
  to press forward
To joy everlasting, where life has its source
  in God's love,                                     40
Where is heavenly hope. Then to Him who is
  holy be thanks,
Because He hath honored us; thanks to the
  Ruler of Heaven,
The Lord everlasting, throughout all the ages!
  Amen.

# The Battle of Brunanburh [1]

*This poem is preserved in four of the six
extant manuscripts of the Anglo-Saxon Chronicle—in the Parker MS. in the library of Corpus
Christi College, Cambridge, and in three Cotton MSS. in the British Museum. Its author is
unknown, but the date under which it is entered in the Chronicle is A.D. 937. The poem
describes an historical event. Tennyson, whose
translation is printed here, prefixed to it the following note: "Constantinus, King of the Scots,
after having sworn allegiance to Aethelstan,
allied himself with the Danes of Ireland under
Anlaf, and invading England, was defeated by
Aethelstan and his brother Edmund with great
slaughter at Brunanburh in the year 937."
Aethelstan reigned over the West Saxons and
Mercians from A.D. 925 to 940, and extended
his influence throughout England. The site of
Brunanburh is unknown. The most likely conjecture hitherto advanced is apparently that it
is Bramber, near Preston in Lancashire.*

  *The text of the original may be found in An
Anglo-Saxon Book of Verse and Prose, ed. W.
J. Sedgefield (Manchester, 1928), pp. 68–70.
For a discussion and a literal translation of the
poem see Bernhard Ten Brink, Early English
Literature (to Wiclif), trans. Horace M. Ken-
nedy (New York, 1883), pp. 90–92.*

### I

Athelstan King,
Lord among Earls,
Bracelet-bestower and
Baron of Barons,
He with his brother,                                 5
Edmund Atheling,
Gaining a lifelong
Glory in battle,
Slew with the sword-edge
There by Brunanburh,                                10
Brake the shield-wall,

[1] This translation is by Alfred Tennyson. Tennyson stated that he more or less availed himself of his
son's prose translation of the poem published in the
*Contemporary Review*, November, 1876.

Hewed the linden-wood,
Hacked the battle-shield,
Sons of Edward with hammered brands.

### II

Theirs was a greatness        15
Got from their grandsires—
Theirs that so often in
Strife with their enemies
Struck for their hoards and their hearths and
    their homes.

### III

Bowed the spoiler,        20
Bent the Scotsman,
Fell the ship-crews
Doomed to the death.
All the field with blood of the fighters
Flowed, from when first the great        25
Sun-star of morning-tide,
Lamp of the Lord God
Lord everlasting,
Glode over earth till the glorious creature
Sank to his setting.        30

### IV

There lay many a man
Marred by the javelin,
Men of the Northland
Shot over shield.
There was the Scotsman        35
Weary of war.

### V

We the West-Saxons,
Long as the daylight
Lasted, in companies
Troubled the track of the host that we hated; 40
Grimly with swords that were sharp from the
    grindstone,
Fiercely we hacked at the fliers before us.

### VI

Mighty the Mercian,
Hard was his hand-play,
Sparing not any of        45
Those that with Anlaf,
Warriors over the
Weltering waters
Borne in the bark's-bosom,
Drew to this island—        50
Doomed to the death.

### VII

Five young kings put asleep by the sword-
    stroke,
Seven strong Earls of the army of Anlaf
Fell on the war-field, numberless numbers,
Shipmen and Scotsmen.        55

### VIII

Then the Norse leader—
Dire was his need of it,
Few were his following—
Fled to his war-ship;
Fleeted his vessel to sea with the king in it,        60
Saving his life on the fallow flood.

### IX

Also the crafty one,
Constantinus,
Crept to his North again,
Hoar-headed hero!        65

### X

Slender warrant had
*He* to be proud of
The welcome of war-knives—
He that was reft of his
Folk and his friends that had        70
Fallen in conflict,
Leaving his son too
Lost in the carnage,
Mangled to morsels,
A youngster in war!        75

### XI

Slender reason had
*He* to be glad of
The clash of the war-glaive—
Traitor and trickster
And spurner of treaties—        80
He nor had Anlaf
With armies so broken
A reason for bragging
That they had the better
In perils of battle        85
On places of slaughter—
The struggle of standards,
The rush of the javelins,
The crash of the charges,
The wielding of weapons—        90
The play that they played with
The children of Edward.[2]

### XII

Then with their nailed prows
Parted the Norsemen, a
Blood-reddened relic of        95
Javelins over
The jarring breaker, the deep-sea billow,
Shaping their way toward Dyflen[3] again,
    Shamed in their souls.

[2] Athelstan and Edmund.        [3] Dublin.

### XIII

Also the brethren,                                    100
King and Atheling,
Each in his glory,
Went to his own in his own West-Saxonland,
Glad of the war.

### XIV

Many a carcase they left to be carrion,     105
Many a livid one, many a sallow-skin—
Left for the white-tailed eagle to tear it, and
Left for the horny-nibbed raven to rend it, and
Gave to the garbaging war-hawk to gorge it,
    and
That gray beast, the wolf of the weald.[4]   110

[4] Moorland.

### XV

Never had huger
Slaughter of heroes
Slain by the sword-edge—
Such as old writers
Have writ of in histories—                     115
Hapt in this isle, since
Up from the East hither
Saxon and Angle from
Over the broad billow
Broke into Britain with                            120
Haughty war-workers who
Harried the Welshman, when
Earls that were lured by the
Hunger of glory gat
Hold of the land.                                      125

# II  THE LATE MIDDLE AGES, 1066-1485

In 1066 Edward the Confessor died childless. Since his chief interest had been in religious matters, the actual government of his kingdom had been gradually taken over by a few powerful noblemen; Harold, Earl of Wessex, had become, in almost everything but name, the real ruler of England. On his deathbed Edward named Harold his successor, and the choice was afterwards confirmed by the king's council.

Across the Channel, however, William, Duke of Normandy, had been awaiting Edward's death. He now asserted his claim to England, gathered an army, secured the Pope's blessing upon the undertaking, and landed on the south coast of England late in September, 1066. William based his claim in part on his relationship, through his mother, to Edward, and in part to promises he said he had received from Edward and Harold.

Whether or not William had justice on his side, the expedition was successful. Harold's army was, fortunately for William, diverted by the King of Norway, who landed in the north of England. Harold defeated the Norse army near York, but then had to hasten immediately south to encounter William. And in the battle which followed, at Hastings, in October, Harold was killed and his army routed. William was soon accepted by the English, and he was crowned king in Westminster Abbey on Christmas. William had some rebellions to put down during the next few years, but he eventually made it clear that he had come to stay and that all England was to be firmly united under his rule.

## FEUDALISM

William was indeed an extraordinary man, and the measures he took to consolidate his position were ingenious and effective. His fellow adventurers expected rewards, and he of course needed their continued aid. Hence he gave them land which had been owned by the English who fought against him, but he so divided up the land that none of the new owners had a large amount in any one place. Thus when he gave his more important followers several small estates, or manors, in different parts of the country, instead of a large estate all in one place, he scattered their strength, and made it as important to them as it was to him that the country should have a strong central government, able everywhere to force obedience and orderly conduct. Moreover, he made no outright gifts, but rather grants of land to be held subject to conditions. In this he introduced the principles of feudalism as practiced on the continent.

Under feudalism a king was, in theory, the sole absolute owner of all his country's land. He merely granted the use of his land to his peers or noblemen, in return for their acknowledgment of loyalty and service due him. The service exacted was both military and administrative. The great noblemen held large estates, and administered them, in part, by dividing them into portions and granting the use of these portions to lesser men who swore loyalty and promised services. These in turn divided their estates and granted the use of small holdings, in return for loyalty and services, to still lesser men, until the end was reached with the peasants who actually tilled the soil.

Social organization under feudalism may be compared to a pyramid. The broad base was composed of peasants or serfs. Some of these were bound to the soil; they had some rights to balance their services and so were not slaves, but they could not leave the estates to which they were attached. In England they gradually won their freedom before the close of the Middle Ages. The next tier of the pyramid was composed of the smallest land-holders—and so it went up, with the king at the top. This was a graded order, with an assigned place and prescribed duties for every man; no one was independent, though everyone received a certain measure of security as compensation for what he gave up. This meant that the several ranks were bound together by ties of personal loyalty extending through the whole social structure, besides being bound by contracts which governed the use of land. It also meant that society was divided sharply into classes, and that every man's station in life was determined largely by the social rank and material circumstances of his parents.

### FEUDALISM AND THE CHURCH

The organization of the Catholic Church was similar in many ways to the feudal structure, with the important difference that position within the Church could not be passed on by inheritance. But the medieval Church was a vast world in itself, owing its power and its prosperity to its great accumulation of property. Theoretically Church and State were two separate worlds existing side by side; but practically each penetrated into the other, and actually they were often in conflict. Rulers of the State could not, or would not, allow the land acquired by the Church to pass completely beyond their control. Further, as bishops and abbots came to have great wealth and power, these positions were sought by ambitious men whose desire for luxury or for important political or social position was stronger than their interest in religion.

In general, in England, William and his successors managed to force abbots of monasteries and some bishops into the feudal structure; so that these lords of the Church became, in so far as their lands were concerned, subjects of the king, bound by oaths of loyalty and obligated to military service. The king, however, could not rest content with this; he

sought to control the appointment of abbots and bishops for his own purposes rather than for the purposes of religion. Sometimes he wished to reward a favorite or a follower for distinguished service; sometimes he wished to place an able man in a position of power in the State; always he wished to maintain or increase his own power. The clergy, on their side, could not ignore the State, because it was only at the expense of the State that they could maintain or increase the power of the Church.

Life in the Middle Ages can only be understood in terms of these two institutions, feudalism and the Roman Catholic Church: uneasy bedfellows, both born of the effort to achieve order and security in the period of social disorder which followed the breakup of the ancient Roman Empire and the resettlement of Europe by hordes of Germanic barbarians. This, of course is said of the Church considered only, for the moment, as a form of social organization.

### NORMAN CULTURE AND SHREWDNESS

William and his followers were themselves, by descent, Vikings. Their Danish ancestors had in the ninth century taken possession of that part of the north coast of France which was later called Normandy. They did not long retain their Viking culture, however; by 1066 they had become in effect Frenchmen—and this at a time when France was the center of the new social order and the new civilization which were now rapidly taking form after some centuries of chaos. They had become mixed, by intermarriage, with the Franks among whom they had settled, and had besides promptly accepted Christianity, the French language, and French usages and manners. Yet in becoming Frenchmen they had lost nothing of their native energy, shrewdness, and strength, and were still capable of acting unscrupulously when there was a purpose to be served by it.

William therefore brought to England not merely an army capable of holding his new kingdom by force, but also a rising civilization and culture, and well-trained educators and administrators for both Church and State, who were able rapidly to alter the social organization, the intellectual outlook, and the manners of the English. For the small group of Normans soon held throughout England all the positions of power and influence, and from these they dominated the life of the island. Their hold was secure because of William's shrewdness in profiting by what he had seen, in France, of the dangers of feudalism. The chief danger was that a nobleman might become powerful enough within his own estate to defy his king; it was William's greatest achievement that he succeeded in avoiding this danger. He managed to *use* feudalism in England, giving his foreign aristocracy power and responsibility, yet keeping his central government so strong that the unity of the realm was not seriously endangered for centuries.

## CONTINUITY OF ENGLISH CIVILIZATION

The success of the Norman Conquest was made easier by the fact that it did not really break the continuity of English civilization. The English were already Christian and Catholic; feudalism had been developing naturally for some time; and Norman-French influence had begun to be felt strongly under Edward the Confessor. These things we need to remember, because the changes which were brought about by the Norman invasion were so impressive that students have at times been wrongly led to think of this last foreign conquest of England as a sharp break and a new beginning.

For example, the English language seems, as we look back, almost to disappear in the years following the Conquest. Throughout the Middle Ages in Europe Latin was the universal language of the Church and of the learned. And the Normans brought in their own French for daily use, and imposed it upon the Englishmen who had to deal with them. The immediate result was that French became the language of all kinds of officials, of the law courts, even of the English stewards and other employees or servants of the Norman nobility. Moreover, England did not seem to be affected by an upswing in native literature in the eleventh century—an upswing which began in France, moved on to Germany and Italy, and led the way for the modern literature of England. It is obvious that the reason this new movement seemed for a while to have passed over England was that French was now the language in England of the aristocracy for whom the new literature was written. Indeed some of this new French native literature was written in England; and it appears altogether probable that any enlightened and observant Englishman a century after the Conquest must have thought that England's language and culture would be swallowed up by those of

France, and that England's political destiny was permanently linked with that of France. For almost three centuries France and England seemed destined to share a common future, though during all this time the English national consciousness was gradually awakening. It was not until the end of the Hundred Years' War, which began in 1338 and ended in 1453, that it became finally clear that England and France were to face each other across the Channel as independent countries, very different in temper, in political organization, and in language and literature.

The changes made in England during the Middle Ages were so great as to be almost revolutionary; yet they do not mark a break between Old and Modern English language or literature. The period is one of transition, but of transition through which threads of historical continuity firmly bind Old English to Modern. The term used to designate both the language and the literature of the period is Middle English, which properly emphasizes the fact of continuity persisting amidst great change.

## THE MIDDLE ENGLISH LANGUAGE

We must notice first what happened to the language. We have already seen how French became the official speech of England immediately after the Conquest. English, however, remained continuously the speech of the common people; and the Normans, though they held all the important positions in State and Church, remained so greatly in the minority that it was not long, as such things go, until they began to be absorbed into the English majority. This meant that in the end it was not the English, but the descendants of the Normans who had first to speak both languages and then gradually give up the use of their own. Barely three centuries after the Conquest, in 1362, Edward III opened Parliament by a speech in English; and in the same year he sought to stop the use of French in law courts. It was also about the middle of this century that English began to be taught in schools. In the contest of tongues English had decisively won.

English as it was spoken in 1362, however, was very different from English as it was spoken before the Conquest. During the three centuries between, two causes had been at work to produce change. One was the tendency to abandon inflectional endings; the other was the importation into English of a host of

French and Latin words. Several hundred Latin words had come into Old English in the last centuries before the Conquest, but these made only a slight addition to the resources of the language in comparison with the great number which were imported from both Latin and French in the years between 1100 and 1500. About thirty-four hundred words from French alone had entered Middle English before 1400. Very considerable changes in pronunciation were also taking place in these centuries; and in London and the surrounding country pronunciation was much closer to French than it is now.

Altogether it is not surprising that some students formerly thought of Middle English as practically a new language made up principally from French and Latin in the thirteenth and fourteenth centuries. But they judged hastily, and were wrong, as a single instance may show: in Chaucer's "Prologue" to his *Canterbury Tales* the French and Latin words number only thirteen per cent of the whole. In general it is true that the words in commonest use, in the fourteenth century and still today, have come down from Old English, and that the foreign words, then and since, have been drawn into the language and completely assimilated. In this the English ran true to form, showing a remarkable power to draw in the foreign thing and make it their own, until it no longer was foreign. Some notion of what happened can be gained from the example used by Sir Walter Scott in *Ivanhoe*, where the jester is made to remark that living animals, under the care of English serfs, kept their native names—"ox," "sheep," "calf," "swine," "deer"—while the flesh of those animals when used for food, eaten by Norman nobles, came to be called by French names—"beef," "mutton," "veal," "pork," "bacon," "venison." So also the words "master," "servant," "butler," "buttery," "bottle," "dinner," "supper," "banquet" are derived from the French. One could go on almost indefinitely giving familiar English words relating to law, government, property, trades, warfare, and the like, which had come in from French by the fourteenth century, but our conclusion would remain the same—that Middle English was English, and did take all these words into itself instead of being swallowed up by French and Latin.

Before leaving the subject of language, however, it should be said that the form of Middle English which was destined to survive and become the foundation of standard Modern English was the dialect spoken in and around London. This is the form of Middle English used by Chaucer, the greatest poet of the period and the most finished artist; it has survived as the foundation of Modern English, however, not because Chaucer used it, but because of the unique importance of London in the life and developing civilization of England.

## THE CONTINUITY OF ENGLISH LITERATURE: INFLUENCE OF THE CHURCH

When we turn from language to literature we again find a real continuity between the pre-Conquest time and the later Middle Ages. Though we do not know as much about the use of English during the first two hundred years after the Conquest as we should like to, we know that English throughout this period remained indispensable in at least one literary field, that of religious instruction.

There is much truth in the characterization of the Middle Ages as the ages of faith; serious churchmen of the time were filled with a remarkable religious zeal and an intense desire to spread the principles of Christianity. In order to do this they used every means which ingenuity could suggest to bring Christianity home to the mass of the people. And one vital means was instruction in English. Aelfric, who died about 1020, wrote a number of sermons, or homilies, in the simple, direct prose he had inherited from Alfred and his contemporaries. After the Conquest these sermons continued to be used, as was also the English translation of the first seven books of the Old Testament which Aelfric had supervised. After the Conquest, also, new discourses were composed in English upon the model furnished by Aelfric. This stream of good prose, confined by the Normans to the one service of popular religious instruction, was a slender trickle, which at the close of the twelfth century appeared to be dwindling away to nothing.

Yet just at the beginning of the thirteenth century a churchman wrote in English a set of directions for three young women who wished to lead a devout life in retirement and who had appealed to him for guidance. His book is called the *Ancren Riwle*, or *Rule of Anchoresses* (nuns), and it is one of the masterpieces of English medieval literature. And the *Ancren Riwle* is but one of half a dozen surviving prose pieces written about 1200 for the guidance of nuns. All are written with a competence and finish which would have been impossible had their authors not been in touch with a still-living tradition of good English prose; and they served to give this tradition a new lease on life. For the fine quality in the *Ancren Riwle* was immediately felt; the book became a classic, was rewritten for general use, and for three centuries was one of the most widely read books in England. Its long-continued popularity enabled it to become a principal means of giving the great English religious writers of the fourteenth century a living, developed, flexible medium to work in.

We do not know the names of some of these writers, but the most important of those whose names are known are Richard Rolle of Hampole, Walter Hilton, Juliana of Norwich, and Margery Kempe. They gave England in this period a great prose literature of Christian piety and mystical contemplation, and some used a style which, in spite of its strange spelling, is surprisingly close to modern English. Their writings have been neglected, however, by students of English literature, partly because of the greater interest today in John Wiclif, who wrote at about the same time. Wiclif's writings have more life in them because of their controversial nature: Wiclif was a herald of the Protestant Reformation, and, more than a century before Luther, he defied the papacy, attacked the worldliness and corruption—as well as some of the beliefs—of the Catholic Church, and encouraged all men to read the Bible and interpret it for themselves. To aid the English people in interpreting the Bible, Wiclif translated part of it into English and directed the translation of the rest. Although today Wiclif is so well thought of that he is sometimes called "the father of English prose," his prose is much inferior to and much less like Modern English than that of Rolle or that of Hilton; and, because of the religious attitude of the people of that time, Wiclif's writing was not nearly so popular as theirs, and therefore did not do nearly so much to maintain the continuity of English prose.

## THE FOURTEENTH CENTURY: MATURITY AND INDEPENDENCE

Discussion of Rolle and Hilton and Wiclif has brought us into the great century of medieval English literature. By the early years of the fourteenth century the education of medieval man in England was complete. As the century advanced it became unmistakably clear that English was to be at any rate the spoken and literary tongue of England, and that a great deal had been accomplished in the development of English style. Above all, men themselves had become mature. Oxford had become a center of higher learning before the end of the twelfth century and Cambridge early in the thirteenth, so that the English no longer were dependent on the continental universities for their scholarly education. Though it is not easy to say just how important medieval university training was in the development of literature, certainly by the fourteenth century Englishmen's wits were sharpened, and they were thoroughly at home in the fields of medieval learning and thought and story, could move about at their ease, and could handle traditional themes and forms with sure mastery—mastery and independence.

Often we associate independence with rebelliousness, because rebellion against the established order of things is an obvious sign of independence. In the fourteenth century the spirit of rebellion was active, as we have already seen in the case of Wiclif; and it was not confined to religion, but spread out into the whole field of social organization. The famous, though unsuccessful, Peasants' Rising of 1381 illustrated the flood of energy which burst loose and animated the English people in the fourteenth century. So many men died of the plague in 1348 and 1349 that a very serious labor shortage developed; wages rose, and serfs began loudly to demand their freedom. They were already winning freedom gradually, which in part explains the situation. But now suddenly they began to demand freedom as a right. This was something new, and in it we can catch our first glimpse of that sturdy self-respecting independence of spirit which in time came to be regarded as the peculiar characteristic of all Englishmen. This doctrine of "freedom as a right" was revolutionary, and needed respectable and powerful support; it was immediately discovered that this had all along been the teaching of Christianity, though a teaching which the Church had seriously neglected.

John Ball, a poor priest, was the chief leader of the Peasants' Rising. For some twenty years before 1381 he had been going about the countryside attacking both Church and State. This vivid account of his activities comes from the French historian Froissart:

Ball was accustomed every Sunday after Mass, as the people were coming out of the church, to preach to them in the market-place and assemble a crowd around him, to whom he would say, "My good friends, things cannot go well in England, nor ever will until everything shall be in common; when there shall be neither vassal nor lord and all distinctions leveled, when the lords shall be no more masters than ourselves. How ill have they used us? And for what reason do they thus hold us in bondage? Are we not all descended from the same parents, Adam and Eve? And what can they show or what reasons give, why they should be more masters than ourselves?—except perhaps in making us labor and work for them to spend. They are clothed in velvets and rich stuffs, ornamented with ermine and other furs, while we are forced to wear poor cloth. They have handsome seats and manors, when we must brave the wind and rain in our labors in the field; but it is from our labor they have wherewith to support their pomp. We are called slaves, and if we do not perform our services we are beaten."

And the noblemen, who based all their claims on birth and inheritance, not on their usefulness to society, were unable to answer him.

When we look at the fourteenth century as a whole, what we see is a quite general awakening of the critical or questioning spirit, just as much awake and active in the author of *Piers Plowman* and in Chaucer as in the rebels Wiclif and John Ball. Neither Langland nor Chaucer was a rebel, however; Langland was passionately indignant over the corruption and abuses which he saw around him—but he was equally indignant at those who were preaching communism as a quick and simple remedy. And Chaucer was not blind to any of the abuses and discontents of the time; his moral judgments are sound, even severe. Nevertheless, he was content to accept all he saw as part of a lively and varied picture which it would be no more sensible to attempt to change than it would be to wish for the moon —a picture which, too, was endlessly interesting and amusing just as it was.

### THE NEW VERSE

But when we turn from the prose literature we have been discussing to Chaucer's verse, we instantly see that a literary revolution has occurred. Chaucer writes verse in accordance with the principles which, in general, have governed English versification from his day to ours—and does it with a finished skill which has never been excelled. Chaucer uses rime, and his lines have a regular number of syllables with the accents evenly distributed. He also uses a number of forms of stanzas, one of which, rime royal, he introduced into English.

Now this marks a complete break with the Old English system of versification. But Chaucer did not invent it; he found it, and had the good sense to use it, and the talent to use it with perfect ease and sureness. The new versification came from France, but it had first appeared quite early in the Middle Ages when Catholic writers of hymns in Latin substituted it for the ancient classical forms. These Latin hymns, many of them strikingly beautiful, served as examples in the matter of form when poets in the south of France, towards the beginning of the twelfth century, began to write lyric poems in their own language. And this French poetry served in turn as example and inspiration for all Europe.

As early as the beginning of the thirteenth century some English writers were trying to imitate in their own language the form of the Latin hymns. And the reason was that they were translating the hymns into English, and wanted their English versions to fit the music. English poets liked the music of these Latin hymns, and soon began to compose original songs which could be sung to this music. Such a song is the "Cuckoo Song," one of the earliest Middle English lyrics to be written on a subject not religious:

> Sumer is icumen in,
> Lhude sing cuccu!
> Growth sed and bloweth med
> And springth the wude nu.
> Sing cuccu!
>
> Awe bleteth after lomb,
> Lhouth after calve cu,
> Bulluc sterteth, bucke verteth,
> Murie sing cuccu!
> Cuccu, cuccu,
> Wel singes thu cuccu,
> Ne swik thu naver nu!
>
> Sing cuccu nu, Sing cuccu!
> Sing cuccu, Sing cuccu nu!

However, though all of the surviving lyric poetry of the thirteenth and fourteenth centuries is in the new versification, by far the greater part of it is devotional or moral in content.

### THE OLD ALLITERATIVE VERSE

At the same time the Old English alliterative verse form was not forgotten. In the second half of the fourteenth century it was used by the author of *Piers Plowman*, and also by the poet from the northwestern part of England who wrote *Sir Gawain and the Green Knight*, and, probably, *The Pearl*, *Purity*, and *Patience*. It continued to be used occasionally even into the sixteenth century, but it was a dying form. *Piers Plowman* is the last poem of any importance in strict alliterative verse, and it in effect proves that the old form would no longer do. For one thing, the result is very different from that obtained in Old English by the same form. And here we see another influence which helped to establish the new versification: the changes in the language which have already been discussed made the language really a new kind of medium, with a new movement of its own, lighter and quicker than that of Old English. The rhythm of *Piers Plowman* is neither one thing nor the other; it seems merely awkward and slovenly. We continue to value *Piers Plowman*, not because its author was a great artist, but because he had deep feeling and keen insight and vivid imagination, and so contrived to give us a picture of his age which still lives and breathes—a picture, moreover, which is complementary to Chaucer's, so that anyone who hopes to understand the latter half of the fourteenth century must always study both writers.

In *Sir Gawain* and *The Pearl* and in other poetry of the fourteenth century we see more what we might expect—an attempt to combine the traditional alliteration with the new verse forms. In these poems, however, the actual effect was due mostly to what was new —new and French; for the French influence on both form and content had by then become unmistakable and strong. From this poetry to Chaucer is only a step or two; nevertheless, there was no gradual development from the old verse forms to the new. The two systems are genuinely different, and the attempts made in the fourteenth century to effect a compromise between them led to nothing.

## THE BALLADS

It is difficult to fit the popular poetry of the time into its proper place in the pattern of change. Since popular ballads existed first in the oral tradition, and were passed along only by word of mouth from the singer to his audience, there is no way to date their origin accurately. We know that the verse form of the thirteenth and fourteenth century ballads which have come down to us is the verse form of the Latin hymns, and of Chaucer. Whether European ballads had the verse form before the Latin hymns, or adapted the verse form from the Latin hymns or the French poems of the twelfth century, cannot be determined. Certainly the fact that the popular ballads used the same verse form as the poems produced by the literary artist contributed to the establishment of the form in literature.

The impact of the popular ballad is strikingly direct and intense even though we cannot hope ever to hear the ballad sung as it was sung originally. It must have been exciting to be a part of an audience of the time and to participate in the emotional experience of hearing "Edward" or "The Hunting of the Cheviot" sung and of joining in the chorus of "The Three Ravens" or "The Cruel Brother." In many of the ballads we find a perception of the tragic quality of life which is elsewhere lacking in medieval literature—a perception suggesting that the ballad authors were looking directly at realities of experience, undistracted by literary conventions.

## PROVENÇAL LOVE POETRY AND FRENCH ROMANCES

The new French poetry which transformed the literature not only of England, but of Europe, was novel and dazzling in content as well as in versification. The new poetry of the south of France (from the region known as Provence) was chiefly lyrical, and its theme was love—the love of man for woman. On the other hand, the new poetry of northern France was chiefly narrative, and its theme was adventure, expressed through a framework of history. The first thing to strike us is that both kinds of poetry were not religious but secular: men's active interests in their immediate affairs of this world had begun to develop at the expense of interest in a promised life beyond death. The change of outlook was slow, and certainly not always conscious or consistent; even today it is not completed, and there is no reason to suppose it will ever be. Yet it is clear that the French poetry of the twelfth and thirteenth centuries showed a tacit rebellion against the all-embracing claims of medieval Christianity.

The new narrative poems of adventure composed in northern France were called romances, simply because *romance* was the term used to denote the language in which these poems were written. The word was not long, however, in acquiring a new and distinct literary meaning, derived from the special character of the French narratives. They were, in the beginning, merely tales of remote and strange adventures. Remoteness was necessary because it helped belief; medieval people were sharp-witted, and could readily detect error in the fields where they had knowledge gained by experience or direct observation. The difference between them and ourselves is that their knowledge of the external world was very limited, and that they all had an overwhelming sense of inferiority to the great men of ancient times, so that they tended to accept without question whatever they found in old books. The world was large in those days, and might very well be full of wonders.

The French romances, then, were written for people who were not childishly credulous, but who nevertheless could believe very strange things on the authority of tradition. The material of these tales came from old books which were inaccurately considered to be histories, and the characters were historical figures out of the mighty past. Three spacious fields of history, or of presumed history, had the strongest appeal: stories were told of Charlemagne and his peers, of King Arthur of Britain and his Knights of the Round Table, and of "Rome the Great." This last field really included all of classical antiquity, and within it fell tales of Alexander the Great, of Thebes, and of Troy. The fact that these stories were supposed to have a basis in history gave them a considerable part of their value. Hence as the demand grew for more tales, writers did not go out into new fields, but multiplied incidents and characters related to what was already familiar. So cycles grew up and, particularly in the case of King Arthur, an immense body of legend accumulated which formed in a rough way a detailed account of Arthur's whole life and of the lives and adventures of all his knights. Thus the story of Sir Gawain, exquisitely retold in English by a northern poet late in the fourteenth century, is part of the Arthurian cycle because, though it is an episode complete in itself, it is told about one of Arthur's knights and has its beginning and its end at Arthur's court.

So far, these romances, though obviously not sacred in their theme and intent, may not appear to bear out the assertion that they represent a movement of rebellion against medieval Christianity. But though the characters and events of these tales were historical and remote, the dress, the manners, customs, social relationships, the whole atmosphere and life were contemporary. Although the poets pretended to be writing history they actually drew idealized pictures of the feudal society around them, and put into graphic form the code of conduct and the scale of values which governed that society. And that code of conduct and that scale of values were in a large part independent of Christianity, and frequently in opposition to the spirit and letter of Christian belief. In this scale of values birth and breeding were of more importance than religion or good works, and gallantry to women became as important as worship of God.

Indeed, as the most important achievement of the lyric poets of Provence in the twelfth century there was developed, in fundamental opposition to Christianity, what could only be called a rival religion. This was the worship of gentle-born women—"romantic love." Briefly, it demanded that a gentlewoman be regarded as the incarnation of a spirit as worthy of worship as the true God—there is no other way to express it—and that she receive abject and wholehearted devotion from her knightly lover. He was to submit himself humbly to her every wish; whatever he did, whatever warlike exploits he performed, whatever adventures he undertook—all were to be looked upon as services in honor of his lady. In sum, the knight owed his lady the kind of loyalty he owed his feudal lord. Normally the medieval knight devoted himself to another man's wife, as Launcelot devoted himself to Guinevere, the wife of King Arthur. Romantic love was opposed to Christianity because it was earthly love—such devotion paid to a creature as could properly be paid only to the Creator. However it began, it took fast hold upon medieval courtly society; and when priests condemned it, the poets retaliated by centering all knightly virtues more and more in love as a noble and ennobling passion which alone could kindle honor, courtesy, and true loyalty.

## ALLEGORY AND ROMANCE

The French romances which began as supposedly historical tales of knightly adventure were rapidly transformed by this new discovery of the Provençal poets into love stories. The persons in these tales had been at first only pegs on which to hang the action; characters began, however, with the growth of sentiment, to be individualized, and action tended to be subordinated to inward conflicts of feeling. In order to portray such conflicts the medieval poet inevitably turned to allegory. Allegory is simply the representation of something immaterial by a visible or picturable embodiment. The more appropriate the embodiment seems to be, the more effective the allegory; but, in general, allegory is simply an emblematic way of speaking. Although allegory was not invented in the Middle Ages, there is much reason for associating it with that period, because it was then important in all fields of thought and art. Christian preachers had interpreted everything in the Bible as possessing an emblematic significance lying behind its apparent meaning; and this habit had been extended to the whole visible world and the course of human history. Thus it was natural that when the medieval poet wished to represent something invisible he should personify it.

The classical example of this, and the source of much that followed it in English as well as French poetry, is *The Romance of the Rose*, written in the thirteenth century by Guillaume de Lorris and Jean de Meung. The narrator falls asleep and in his dream finds himself by a walled garden which Idleness invites him to enter. The garden represents the world of courtly society, and in it the poet finds a rose which represents a young girl. His efforts to win the rose are aided by persons representing Pity, Innocence, and Fair Welcome, and opposed by persons representing such abstractions as Danger and Shame. It seems hard to believe that through these means the poet was really engaged in representing the conflicts of feelings within the mind and heart of the young girl; but that is what he was doing, and doing with striking success.

## PROGRESS OF ROMANCE IN ENGLAND

All the stages in the development of romance can be illustrated by English poems of the late thirteenth and the fourteenth centuries. Thus *Guy of Warwick* and *Sir Bevis of Hampton* illustrate the first stage, in which interest was centered in battles and combat. A reader of *Sir Bevis* has calculated that this hero, aside from slaughter which he effected with others in set battles, killed more than six hundred and fifty human beings with his own hand before he settled down into tranquil domestic life.

From this beginning, which did not concern itself with knightly ideals or virtues, there gradually developed the romance in which the representation of knights and ladies as embodiments of the courtly ideals became a chief object. The fourteenth century *Sir Launfal* is an important step in this direction; in this tale politeness and good breeding are shown, but there is no regard for serious characterization. Not until we come to *Sir Gawain and the Green Knight* do we find that the interest in characterization has become strong, and the ability to satisfy it mature.

And then finally in *The Pearl* and in *Piers Plowman* and in Chaucer's *House of Fame* we have English examples of the dream which furnishes the setting for an allegory in which the poet emblematically sets forth his theme. In writing the greatest of English medieval love romances, *Troilus and Criseyde*, however, Chaucer cast aside the allegorical method, although he left the center of attention where the French allegorical romance had finally placed it—in characterization and in inward conflicts of feeling. In this poem, as in *The Canterbury Tales*, we see Chaucer stepping outside of the enchanted realm of romance, into the more familiar field of direct observation and realistic treatment. He saw the unreality of the high-flown heroes and ladies of romance; he parodied chivalrous adventure and courtly love in *Sir Thopas*, and frequently poked fun at them throughout *The Canterbury Tales*.

This kind of thing, we say, shows that Chaucer is "modern." But he was by no means alone in perceiving that the proper home of the heroes and ladies of chivalry was in fairyland. Many before him had revolted against the violation of common sense, or common observation, of which the writers of conventional romance were guilty. Characteristic of this anti-romantic revolt are the numerous beast stories, similar to Chaucer's own *Nuns' Priest's Tale*, which exhibit a humorous but determined worldly wisdom—shrewd, selfish, practical, close to reality as medieval people knew it in their own experience. Similar in effect were the comic and often coarse prose tales called *fabliaux*, a literary development to which modern prose fiction owes much.

## MIRACLE PLAYS

That in the fourteenth century the English were fond of broad realistic comedy is further proved by the miracle plays of that time. In the wreck of ancient civilization drama had disappeared from view more completely than other kinds of literature, and in the Middle Ages it had a new birth. This came as a direct result of the varied and determined efforts of religious teachers to impress the gospel story on those who could not read. There is a certain element of drama in the ceremonial of the mass itself; and in the ninth and tenth centuries the Divine Office for Easter, and then that for Christmas, began to be elaborated in order to make more vivid the sacred events which they commemorated. During the Divine Office at Easter there was a representation of the three Marys at the Sepulchre, and at Christmas a representation of the Shepherds seeking the Manger and also of the Magi kneeling before the infant Christ. All these representations were accompanied by brief dialogues sung, not spoken, in Latin. These new methods proved so popular that they were gradually expanded; and by the end of the twelfth century fairly well-developed dramatic scenes were being presented, with the dialogues no longer sung in Latin, but spoken in French.

As the thirteenth century opened, sacred dramatizations were outgrowing the churches. First they were banished to the church porch, and then in time they were banished wholly from the church grounds, while some of the clergy tried without success to abolish them altogether. The miracles, as they were now called, had become too popular—too popular in the sense that they were being enjoyed, not for the light they cast on sacred stories, but for their own dramatic qualities. They were becoming too popular, too, in another sense: they were being transformed into comic skits.

Although the miracle plays were banished from the churches, the people would not let them die. They were taken over by the guilds, or merchants' associations, which performed them each Corpus Christi day. During the fourteenth century the miracles began to be written and spoken in English, and by this time they had grown until they formed series, or cycles, of scenes representing in order the whole course of sacred history. These cycles were under the control of the towns where they were performed, and plays were assigned to different guilds. At the town of York, the Armorers, appropriately enough, had the responsibility of staging the Expulsion from Paradise; the Shipwrights, the Building of Noah's Ark; the Fishermen and Mariners, the Flood; the Bakers, the Last Supper; and so on. The York Cycle was made up of fifty-four scenes, of which forty-eight have come down to us.

Because Corpus Christi day was celebrated with processions in which the guilds marched with great banners, the cycles usually were played processionally. For each scene there was a raised platform on wheels, with space under the platform to which the actors retired in the intervals between their appearances and in which stage properties were kept. At various points along the streets were stations at which each movable stage stopped in turn, while the scene for which it was designed was enacted. As the cycles grew, more time was required for their presentation, and the annual performances could not be confined to Corpus Christi day. At the town of Chester three days were needed, during which the town was crowded, and there was a joyful holiday spirit much in evidence.

In general it cannot be said that the writers of the miracles advanced very far towards drama in the full sense, for they were for the most part restricted by their source, the Bible. They followed popular taste wherever possible, however, and the taste for dramatic representation which they had stimulated expanded in the fifteenth century into a demand for a less restricted drama in which there would be more scope for comedy. To satisfy this demand short plays called interludes, which had no connection with religion, and were enacted by strolling companies of professional players, were developed. They formed an essential connecting link between the miracle plays and the fully developed English drama of the late sixteenth century.

## MORALITY PLAYS

Another service performed by the writers of the miracles was the precedent they set for the mixture of the comic with the serious. And they did, in some of their scenes, make an advance towards the study and representation of individual character. But as the interest in character developed, the same thing happened that had happened in the case of the romances. At the end of the fourteenth century and in the fifteenth, dramatic writers turned to allegory, personifying all inward conflicts of feeling or motive. The subject most often treated in this fashion was the universal one—the conflict between the vices and the virtues for the soul of man. This is why these pieces are called morality plays. There are about thirty of them existing today, all dating from the fifteenth and early sixteenth centuries. By far the best is the famous play entitled *Everyman*. The moralities suffered from a number of limitations, but in the fifteenth century they marked an important advance toward fully developed drama. Drama is basically a situation—a conflict between two sides—and this was exactly what was achieved in the moralities.

## FIFTEENTH CENTURY DECADENCE

In the field of poetry the fifteenth century achieved nothing of great importance. The internal condition of England at the time was very unsettled. The medieval social organization was breaking up, and no one saw what was to come next, nor was there a strong central government able to preserve even the appearance of order. Political and social unrest certainly were not favorable to literature, but these factors alone cannot account for the stagnation into which England fell in the fifteenth century. Probably the best explanation is simply this: the framework of belief and aspiration which had sufficed for the Middle Ages had lost its compelling force under disillusioning experience, and nothing was yet in sight to take its place. In the absence of a living literature, English people of the fifteenth century who were not wholly absorbed with their own day-to-day practical affairs could only look back with longing to the good old days, or amuse themselves with accounts of the marvelous things to be observed in distant lands. For those who liked the good old days, a number of imitators of Chaucer wrote. Among those who wished to hear about the marvelous, such books as the English translation of the French *Voiage and Travaile of Sir John Maundeville* had a great vogue. "Maundeville" was supposed to have been a fourteenth century Englishman, but he was really an invented character who entertained his readers with many decidedly curious observations. He would not have believed these things himself, he says, had he not actually seen them. In Ethiopia, for example, he saw men with only a single foot who could travel extraordinarily fast by hopping, "and the foot is so large that it shades all the body from the sun when they lie down to rest." Elsewhere he saw dog-headed men, ant-hills of gold dust, and diamonds which were the size of hazelnuts and were alive and grew.

## SIR THOMAS MALORY

We look at such writing as that in *Maundeville* because it tells us something about the time in which it was written rather than because it has worth in itself; it obviously has not the stuff of greatness in it. But there was in this century one work which had great

value in its own right—a work which came out of longing for the grandeur of the departed age of chivalry. This is the *Morte d'Arthur*, written by Sir Thomas Malory, and printed by Caxton in 1485. Malory drew his material from a great many French romances, adapting and condensing them, and loosely binding them together. In effect he gives a view of Arthur's whole imagined career, interrupted by accounts of the adventures of the Knights of the Round Table—one of these being the long search for the Holy Grail. The *Morte d'Arthur* possesses unity of style and atmosphere, and both, one feels, are exactly right. The prose of Malory is almost childlike, the right kind for a fairy story; and the atmosphere is that of an enchanted world, so different from the real one that a reader is perplexed to find creatures of flesh and blood with very human passions moving about in it. All in all, Malory caught better than any other English writer the unreality, the noble and moving aspiration, the beauty, the brutality, the aristocratic courtliness, and the vague conventionalized scenery of medieval romance, and in so doing caught a great part of what is most distinctive in the Middle Ages and bequeathed it to following generations.

## CAXTON

It was said above that the *Morte d'Arthur* was printed by Caxton in 1485. William Caxton deserves a place in any account of English literature, because he introduced printing into England. He learned the art on the Continent, and then set up a press at Westminster in 1475. He was a translator and editor as well as a printer, however; he himself translated twenty of the more than seventy different books he printed. Caxton admired the clarity and ease of French prose and attained both qualities in some of his own writing, thus helping to develop English prose style. Although his printing press brings us to the threshold of the modern age, Caxton himself, like so many others of his own time, looked back toward the Middle Ages. The fact that Caxton printed so many medieval poems, chivalrous romances, moral allegories, and books of devotion was due to his anxiety to please the existing popular taste. The net result was that in England the modern age was ushered in by a flood of books recalling and in a sense renewing the atmosphere and spirit of medievalism.

# Sir Gawain and the Green Knight[1]

This poem is preserved in a manuscript of the Cotton collection in the British Museum. The manuscript dates from the end of the fourteenth century or early in the fifteenth, but Sir Gawain and the Green Knight was probably composed about 1370. Of the author nothing is known save what can be gathered from this work—or from this work and from The Pearl, Purity, and Patience (three other poems found in the same manuscript), if, as most scholars think on the basis of internal evidence, all four are by the same author. In either case we can say that he was probably a native of Lancashire, as he uses the West Midland dialect; he was also a highly educated and cultivated gentleman, familiar with the best society of his day. "He had a keen eye, a vivid imagination, and a love for external phenomena, that gave him a power for description unequaled in Middle English literature. He was a lover of details; but he handled the details with a constructive power and a picturesqueness that create vivid impressions or realistic scenes. His observation of dress, of color, of position, of relative location, of deportment, enabled him at the opening of the piece to make of a conventional situation an intense, rich, dramatic scene with a splendid background. . . . He caught, and makes us feel, the very spirit of nature in varied moods, spring, summer, autumn—but especially nature in her wilder aspects, the biting winter, the icy rain, the dreary forest, the rugged rocks, the snow-covered country, and the cold hills lost in mist" (J. E. Wells, Manual of the Writings in Middle English, pp. 56–57). It should be added that this author had, too, real feeling for the higher spirit of chivalry and an uncommon fineness of nature. It is believed that he drew the materials for his story from a Norman-French romance now lost—which, in turn, was based on Celtic legend—but that his delicate treatment of the materials is all his own. Sir Gawain and the Green Knight is by general consent the best of the English romances. It is also interesting for the picture it gives of the earlier Gawain; for in the beginning he was without peer for courage and courtesy among the Knights of the Round Table. It was only later that he came to be depreciated for the sake of others, and it is unfortunate that both Malory and Tennyson have contributed to make him best known as an "empty-headed, empty-hearted worldling."

For the Middle English text see Sir Gawain and the Green Knight, ed. with Introduction, full notes, and glossary by J. R. R. Tolkien and E. V. Gordon (Oxford, corrected edition 1930); and Sir Gawayne and the Grene Knight, ed. Sir Israel Gollancz, with introductory essays by Mabel Day and Mary S. Serjeantson, the Early English Text Society (Oxford, 1940). A new critical edition is being prepared by Henry L. Savage. The original manuscript has been reproduced in Pearl, Cleanness, Patience and Sir Gawain, ed. Sir Israel Gollancz, the Early English Text Society (Oxford, 1923). Commentary and background are supplied by Jessie L. Weston in The Legend of Sir Gawain; Studies upon its Original Scope and Significance (London, 1897), by G. L. Kittredge in A Study of Gawain and the Green Knight (Cambridge, U. S. A., 1916), and by Henry L. Savage in The Gawain-Poet: Studies in His Personality and Background, (Chapel Hill, 1956). Miss Weston has given complete translations, in the original meters, of Sir Gawain and the three other poems attributed to the same poet in a volume entitled Romance, Vision, and Satire (Boston, 1912).

## I

AFTER the siege and the assault of Troy, when that burg was destroyed and burnt to ashes, and the traitor tried for his treason, the noble

---

[1] This translation is by Miss Jessie L. Weston. It forms the first volume in the series of "Arthurian Romances unrepresented in Malory's Morte d'Arthur" published by David Nutt.

Aeneas and his kin sailed forth to become princes and patrons of well-nigh all the Western Isles. Thus Romulus built Rome (and gave to the city his own name, which it bears even to this day); and Ticius turned him to Tuscany; and Langobard raised him up dwellings in Lombardy; and Felix Brutus sailed far over the French flood, and founded the kingdom of Britain, wherein have been war and waste and wonder, and bliss and bale, ofttimes 10 since.

And in that kingdom of Britain have been wrought more gallant deeds than in any other; but of all British kings Arthur was the most valiant, as I have heard tell; therefore will I set forth a wondrous adventure that fell out in his time. And if ye will listen to me, but for a little while, I will tell it even as it stands in story stiff and strong, fixed in the letter, as it hath long been known in the land. 20

King Arthur lay at Camelot upon a Christmas-tide, with many a gallant lord and lovely lady, and all the noble brotherhood of the Round Table. There they held rich revels with gay talk and jest; one while they would ride forth to joust and tourney, and again back to the court to make carols;[2] for there was the feast holden fifteen days with all the mirth that men could devise, song and glee, glorious to hear, in the daytime, and dancing at night. 30 Halls and chambers were crowded with noble guests, the bravest of knights and the loveliest of ladies, and Arthur himself was the comeliest king that ever held a court. For all this fair folk were in their youth, the fairest and most fortunate under heaven, and the king himself of such fame that it were hard now to name so valiant a hero.

Now the New Year had but newly come in, and on that day a double portion was 40 served on the high table to all the noble guests, and thither came the king with all his knights, when the service in the chapel had been sung to an end. And they greeted each other for the New Year, and gave rich gifts, the one to the other (and they that received them were not wroth, that may ye well believe!), and the maidens laughed and made mirth till it was time to get them to meat. Then they washed and sat them down to the feasting in fitting 50 rank and order, and Guinevere the queen, gaily clad, sat on the high daïs. Silken was her seat, with a fair canopy over her head, of rich tapestries of Tars, embroidered, and studded with costly gems; fair she was to look upon, with her shining gray eyes, a fairer woman might no man boast himself of having seen.

But Arthur would not eat till all were served, so full of joy and gladness was he, even as a child; he liked not either to lie long, or to sit long at meat, so worked upon him his young blood and his wild brain. And another custom he had also, that came of his nobility, that he would never eat upon an high day till he had been advised of some knightly deed, or some strange and marvelous tale, of his ancestors, or of arms, or of other ventures. Or till some stranger knight should seek of him leave to joust with one of the Round Table, that they might set their lives in jeopardy, one against another, as fortune might favor them. Such was the king's custom when he sat in hall at each high feast with his noble knights; therefore on that New Year tide, he abode, fair of face, on the throne, and made much mirth withal.

Thus the king sat before the high tables, and spake of many things; and there good Sir Gawain was seated by Guinevere the queen, and on her other side sat Agravain, *à la dure main*;[3] both were the king's sister's sons and full gallant knights. And at the end of the table was Bishop Bawdewyn, and Ywain, King Urien's son, sat at the other side alone. These were worthily served on the daïs, and at the lower tables sat many valiant knights. Then they bare the first course with the blast of trumpets and waving of banners, with the sound of drums and pipes, of song and lute, that many a heart was uplifted at the melody. Many were the dainties, and rare the meats; so great was the plenty they might scarce find room on the board to set on the dishes. Each helped himself as he liked best, and to each two were twelve dishes, with great plenty of beer and wine.

Now I will say no more of the service, but that ye may know there was no lack, for there drew near a venture that the folk might well have left their labor to gaze upon. As the sound of the music ceased, and the first course had been fitly served, there came in at the hall door one terrible to behold, of stature greater than any on earth; from neck to loin so strong and thickly made, and with limbs so long and so great that he seemed even as a giant. And yet he was but a man, only the mightiest that might mount a steed; broad of chest and shoulders and slender of waist, and all his features of like fashion; but men marveled

---

[2] Dances accompanied by song.

[3] Of the hard hand.

much at his color, for he rode even as a knight, yet was green all over.

For he was clad all in green, with a straight coat, and a mantle above; all decked and lined with fur was the cloth and the hood that was thrown back from his locks and lay on his shoulders. Hose had he of the same green, and spurs of bright gold with silken fastenings richly worked; and all his vesture was verily green. Around his waist and his saddle were 10 bands with fair stones set upon silken work, 't were too long to tell of all the trifles that were embroidered thereon—birds and insects in gay gauds of green and gold. All the trappings of his steed were of metal of like enamel, even the stirrups that he stood in stained of the same, and stirrups and saddle-bow alike gleamed and shone with green stones. Even the steed on which he rode was of the same hue, a green horse, great and strong, and hard to 20 hold, with broidered bridle, meet for the rider.

The knight was thus gaily dressed in green, his hair falling around his shoulders; on his breast hung a beard, as thick and green as a bush, and the beard and the hair of his head were clipped all round above his elbows. The lower part of his sleeves was fastened with clasps in the same wise as a king's mantle. The horse's mane was crisp and plaited with many a knot folded in with gold 30 thread about the fair green, here a twist of the hair, here another of gold. The tail was twined in like manner, and both were bound about with a band of bright green set with many a precious stone; then they were tied aloft in a cunning knot, whereon rang many bells of burnished gold. Such a steed might no other ride, nor had such ever been looked upon in that hall ere that time; and all who saw that knight spake and said that a man 40 might scarce abide his stroke.

The knight bore no helm nor hauberk, neither gorget nor breast-plate, neither shaft nor buckler to smite nor to shield, but in one hand he had a holly-bough, that is greenest when the groves are bare, and in his other an ax, huge and uncomely, a cruel weapon in fashion, if one would picture it. The head was an ell-yard long, the metal all of green steel and gold, the blade burnished bright, 50 with a broad edge, as well shapen to shear as a sharp razor. The steel was set into a strong staff, all bound round with iron, even to the end, and engraved with green in cunning work. A lace was twined about it, that looped at the head, and all adown the handle it was clasped with tassels on buttons of bright green richly broidered.

The knight rideth through the entrance of the hall, driving straight to the high daïs, and greeted no man, but looked ever upwards; and the first words he spake were, "Where is the ruler of this folk? I would gladly look upon that hero, and have speech with him." He cast his eyes on the knights and mustered [4] them up and down, striving ever to see who of them was of most renown.

Then was there great gazing to behold that chief, for each man marveled what it might mean that a knight and his steed should have even such a hue as the green grass; and that seemed even greener than green enamel on bright gold. All looked on him as he stood, and drew near unto him, wondering greatly what he might be; for many marvels had 20 they seen, but none such as this, and phantasm and faërie did the folk deem it. Therefore were the gallant knights slow to answer, and gazed astounded, and sat stone still in a deep silence through that goodly hall, as if a slumber were fallen upon them. I deem it was not all for doubt, but some for courtesy that they might give ear unto his errand.

Then Arthur beheld this adventurer before his high daïs, and knightly he greeted him, for fearful was he never. "Sir," he said, "thou art welcome to this place—lord of this hall am I, and men call me Arthur. Light thee down, and tarry awhile, and what thy will is, that shall we learn after."

"Nay," quoth the stranger, "so help me He that sitteth on high, 't was not mine errand to tarry any while in this dwelling; but the praise of this thy folk and thy city is lifted up on high, and thy warriors are holden for 40 the best and most valiant of those who ride mail-clad to the fight. The wisest and the worthiest of this world are they, and well proven in all knightly sports. And here, as I have heard tell, is fairest courtesy; therefore have I come hither as at this time. Ye may be sure by the branch that I bear here that I come in peace, seeking no strife. For had I willed to journey in warlike guise I have at home both hauberk and helm, shield and 50 shining spear, and other weapons to mine hand, but since I seek no war, my raiment is that of peace. But if thou be as bold as all men tell, thou wilt freely grant me the boon I ask."

[4] Surveyed.

And Arthur answered, "Sir Knight, if thou cravest battle here thou shalt not fail for lack of a foe."

And the knight answered, "Nay, I ask no fight; in faith here on the benches are but beardless children; were I clad in armor on my steed there is no man here might match me. Therefore I ask in this court but a Christmas jest, for that it is Yule-tide and New Year, and there are here many fain for sport. If any one in this hall holds himself so hardy, so bold both of blood and brain, as to dare strike me one stroke for another, I will give him as a gift this ax, which is heavy enough, in sooth, to handle as he may list, and I will abide the first blow, unarmed as I sit. If any knight be so bold as to prove my words, let him come swiftly to me here, and take this weapon; I quit claim to it, he may keep it as his own, and I will abide his stroke, firm on the floor. Then shalt thou give me the right to deal him another, the respite of a year and a day shall he have. Now haste, and let see whether any here dare say aught."

Now if the knights had been astounded at the first, yet stiller were they all, high and low, when they had heard his words. The knight on his steed straightened himself in the saddle, and rolled his eyes fiercely round the hall; red they gleamed under his green and bushy brows. He frowned and twisted his beard, waiting to see who should rise, and when none answered he cried aloud in mockery, "What, is this Arthur's hall, and these the knights whose renown hath run through many realms? Where are now your pride and your conquests, your wrath, and anger, and mighty words? Now are the praise and the renown of the Round Table over-thrown by one man's speech, since all keep silence for dread ere ever they have seen a blow!"

With that he laughed so loudly that the blood rushed to the king's fair face for very shame; he waxed wroth, as did all his knights, and sprang to his feet, and drew near to the stranger and said, "Now by heaven, foolish is thy asking, and thy folly shall find its fitting answer. I know no man aghast at thy great words. Give me here thine ax and I shall grant thee the boon thou hast asked." Lightly he sprang to him and caught at his hand, and the knight, fierce of aspect, lighted down from his charger.

Then Arthur took the ax and gripped the haft, and swung it round, ready to strike.

And the knight stood before him, taller by the head than any in the hall; he stood, and stroked his beard, and drew down his coat, no more dismayed for the king's threats than if one had brought him a drink of wine.

Then Gawain, who sat by the queen, leaned forward to the king and spake, "I beseech ye, my lord, let this venture be mine. Would ye but bid me rise from this seat, and stand by your side, so that my liege lady thought it not ill, then would I come to your counsel before this goodly court. For I think it not seemly when such challenges be made in your hall that ye yourself should undertake it, while there are many bold knights who sit beside ye; none are there, methinks, of readier will under heaven, or more valiant in open field. I am the weakest, I wot, and the feeblest of wit, and it will be the less loss of my life if ye seek sooth. For save that ye are mine uncle, naught is there in me to praise, no virtue is there in my body save your blood, and since this challenge is such folly that it beseems ye not to take it, and I have asked it from ye first, let it fall to me, and if I bear myself ungallantly, then let all this court blame me."

Then they all spake with one voice that the king should leave this venture and grant it to Gawain.

Then Arthur commanded the knight to rise, and he rose up quickly and knelt down before the king, and caught hold of the weapon; and the king loosed his hold of it, and lifted up his hand, and gave him his blessing, and bade him be strong both of heart and hand. "Keep thee well, nephew," quoth Arthur, "that thou give him but the one blow, and if thou redest [5] him rightly I trow thou shalt well abide the stroke he may give thee after."

Gawain stepped to the stranger, ax in hand, and he, never fearing, awaited his coming. Then the Green Knight spake to Sir Gawain, "Make we our covenant ere we go further. First, I ask thee, knight, what is thy name? Tell me truly, that I may know thee."

"In faith," quoth the good knight, "Gawain am I, who give thee this buffet, let what may come of it; and at this time twelvemonth will I take another at thine hand with what-soever weapon thou wilt, and none other."

Then the other answered again, "Sir Gawain, so may I thrive as I am fain to take this buffet at thine hand," and he quoth

[5] Handlest.

further, "Sir Gawain, it liketh me well that I shall take at thy fist that which I have asked here, and thou hast readily and truly rehearsed all the covenant that I asked of the king, save that thou shalt swear me, by thy troth, to seek me thyself wherever thou hopest that I may be found, and win thee such reward as thou dealest me to-day, before this folk."

"Where shall I seek thee?" quoth Gawain. 10 "Where is thy place? By him that made me, I wot never where thou dwellest, nor know I thee, knight, thy court, nor thy name. But teach me truly all that pertaineth thereto, and tell me thy name, and I shall use all my wit to win my way thither, and that I swear thee for sooth, and by my sure troth."

"That is enough in the New Year, it needs no more," quoth the Green Knight to the gallant Gawain, "if I tell thee truly when I 20 have taken the blow, and thou hast smitten me; then will I teach thee of my house and home, and mine own name, then mayest thou ask thy road and keep covenant. And if I waste no words then farest thou the better, for thou canst dwell in thy land, and seek no further. But take now thy toll, and let see how thou strikest."

"Gladly will I," quoth Gawain, handling his ax. 30

Then the Green Knight swiftly made him ready; he bowed down his head, and laid his long locks on the crown that his bare neck might be seen. Gawain gripped his ax and raised it on high; the left foot he set forward on the floor, and let the blow fall lightly on the bare neck. The sharp edge of the blade sundered the bones, smote through the neck, and clave it in two, so that the edge of the steel bit on the ground, and the fair head fell 40 to the earth that many struck it with their feet as it rolled forth. The blood spurted forth, and glistened on the green raiment, but the knight neither faltered nor fell; he started forward with out-stretched hand, and caught the head, and lifted it up; then he turned to his steed, and took hold of the bridle, set his foot in the stirrup, and mounted. His head he held by the hair, in his hand. Then he seated himself in his 50 saddle as if naught ailed him, and he were not headless. He turned his steed about, the grim corpse bleeding freely the while, and they who looked upon him doubted them much for the covenant.

For he held up the head in his hand, and turned the face towards them that sat on the high daïs, and it lifted up the eyelids and looked upon them and spake as ye shall hear. "Look, Gawain, that thou art ready to go as thou hast promised, and seek loyally till thou find me, even as thou hast sworn in this hall in the hearing of these knights. Come thou, I charge thee, to the Green Chapel; such a stroke as thou hast dealt thou hast deserved, and it shall be promptly paid thee on New Year's morn. Many men know me as the Knight of the Green Chapel, and if thou askest, thou shalt not fail to find me. Therefore it behooves thee to come, or to yield thee as recreant."

With that he turned his bridle, and galloped out at the hall door, his head in his hands, so that the sparks flew from beneath his horse's hoofs. Whither he went none knew, no more than they wist whence he had come; and the king and Gawain they gazed and laughed, for in sooth this had proved a greater marvel than any they had known aforetime.

Though Arthur the king was astonished at his heart, yet he let no sign of it be seen, but spake in courteous wise to the fair queen: "Dear lady, be not dismayed, such craft is well suited to Christmas-tide when we seek jesting, laughter, and song, and fair carols of knights and ladies. But now I may well get me to meat, for I have seen a marvel I may not forget." Then he looked on Sir Gawain, and said gaily, "Now, fair nephew, hang up thine ax, since it has hewn enough," and they hung it on the dossal [6] above the daïs, where all men might look on it for a marvel, and by its true token tell of the wonder. Then the twain sat them down together, the king and the good knight, and men served them with a double portion, as was the share of the noblest, with all manner of meat and of minstrelsy. And they spent that day in gladness, but Sir Gawain must well bethink him of the heavy venture to which he had set his hand.

## II

This beginning of adventures had Arthur at the New Year; for he yearned to hear gallant tales, though his words were few when he sat at the feast. But now had they stern work on hand. Gawain was glad to begin the jest in the hall, but ye need have no marvel if the end be heavy. For though a man be merry in mind when he has well

[6] Tapestry.

drunk, yet a year runs full swiftly, and the beginning but rarely matches the end.

For Yule was now over-past, and the year after, each season in its turn following the other. For after Christmas comes crabbed Lent, that will have fish for flesh and simpler cheer. But then the weather of the world chides with winter; the cold withdraws itself, the clouds uplift, and the rain falls in warm showers on the fair plains. Then the flowers come forth, meadows and grove are clad in green, the birds make ready to build, and sing sweetly for solace of the soft summer that follows thereafter. The blossoms bud and blow in the hedgerows rich and rank, and noble notes enough are heard in the fair woods.

After the season of summer, with the soft winds, when zephyr breathes lightly on seeds and herbs, joyous indeed is the growth that waxes thereout when the dew drips from the leaves beneath the blissful glance of the bright sun. But then comes harvest and hardens the grain, warning it to wax ripe ere the winter. The drought drives the dust on high, flying over the face of the land; the angry wind of the welkin wrestles with the sun; the leaves fall from the trees and light upon the ground, and all brown are the groves that but now were green, and ripe is the fruit that once was flower. So the year passes into many yesterdays, and winter comes again, as it needs no sage to tell us.

When the Michaelmas moon was come in with warnings of winter, Sir Gawain bethought him full oft of his perilous journey. Yet till All Hallows Day he lingered with Arthur, and on that day they made a great feast for the hero's sake, with much revel and richness of the Round Table. Courteous knights and comely ladies, all were in sorrow for the love of that knight, and though they spake no word of it, many were joyless for his sake.

And after meat, sadly Sir Gawain turned to his uncle, and spake of his journey, and said, "Liege lord of my life, leave from you I crave. Ye know well how the matter stands without more words; to-morrow am I bound to set forth in search of the Green Knight." Then came together all the noblest knights, Ywain and Erec, and many another. Sir Dodinel le Sauvage, the Duke of Clarence, Launcelot and Lionel, and Lucan the Good, Sir Bors and Bedivere, valiant knights both, and many another hero, with Sir Mador de la Porte, and they all drew near, heavy at heart, to take counsel with Sir Gawain. Much

sorrow and weeping was there in the hall to think that so worthy a knight as Gawain should wend his way to seek a deadly blow, and should no more wield his sword in fight. But the knight made ever good cheer, and said, "Nay, wherefore should I shrink? What may a man do but prove his fate?"

He dwelt there all that day, and on the morn he arose and asked betimes for his armor; and they brought it unto him on this wise: first, a rich carpet was stretched on the floor (and brightly did the gold gear glitter upon it), then the knight stepped upon it, and handled the steel; clad he was in a doublet of silk, with a close hood, lined fairly throughout. Then they set the steel shoes upon his feet, and wrapped his legs with greaves, with polished knee-caps, fastened with knots of gold. Then they cased his thighs in cuisses closed with thongs, and brought him the byrnie [1] of bright steel rings sewn upon a fair stuff. Well burnished braces they set on each arm with good elbow-pieces, and gloves of mail, and all the goodly gear that should shield him in his need. And they cast over all a rich surcoat, and set the golden spurs on his heels, and girt him with a trusty sword fastened with a silken bawdrick. When he was thus clad his harness was costly, for the least loop or latchet gleamed with gold. So armed as he was he hearkened Mass and made his offering at the high altar. Then he came to the king, and the knights of his court, and courteously took leave of lords and ladies, and they kissed him, and commended him to Christ.

With that was Gringalet ready, girt with a saddle that gleamed gaily with many golden fringes, enriched and decked anew for the venture. The bridle was all barred about with bright gold buttons, and all the covertures and trappings of the steed, the crupper and the rich skirts, accorded with the saddle; spread fair with the rich red gold that glittered and gleamed in the rays of the sun.

Then the knight called for his helmet, which was well lined throughout, and set it high on his head, and hasped it behind. He wore a light kerchief over the ventail, that was broidered and studded with fair gems on a broad silken ribbon, with birds of gay color, and many a turtle [2] and true-lover's knot interlaced thickly, even as many a maiden had wrought diligently for seven winters long. But the circlet which crowned his helmet was yet more precious, being adorned with a device in diamonds. Then they brought him his shield, which was

---

[1] Coat of mail.   [2] Turtle-dove.

of bright red, with the pentangle painted thereon in gleaming gold. And why that noble prince bare the pentangle I am minded to tell you, though my tale tarry thereby. It is a sign that Solomon set ere-while, as betokening truth; for it is a figure with five points and each line overlaps the other, and nowhere hath it beginning or end, so that in English it is called "the endless knot." And therefore was it well suiting to this knight and to his 10 arms, since Gawain was faithful in five and five-fold, for pure was he as gold, void of all villainy and endowed with all virtues. Therefore he bare the pentangle on shield and surcoat as truest of heroes and gentlest of knights.

For first he was faultless in his five senses; and his five fingers never failed him; and all his trust upon earth was in the five wounds that Christ bare on the cross, as the Creed tells. And wherever this knight found him- 20 self in stress of battle he deemed well that he drew his strength from the five joys which the Queen of Heaven had of her Child. And for this cause did he bear an image of Our Lady on the one half of his shield, that whenever he looked upon it he might not lack for aid. And the fifth five that the hero used were frankness and fellowship above all, purity and courtesy that never failed him, and compassion that surpasses all; and in these five virtues was 30 that hero wrapped and clothed. And all these, fivefold, were linked one in the other, so that they had no end, and were fixed on five points that never failed, neither at any side were they joined or sundered, nor could ye find beginning or end. And therefore on his shield was the knot shapen, red-gold upon red, which is the pure pentangle. Now was Sir Gawain ready, and he took his lance in hand, and bade them all farewell, he deemed it had been for ever. 40

Then he smote the steed with his spurs, and sprang on his way, so that sparks flew from the stones after him. All that saw him were grieved at heart, and said one to the other, "By Christ, 't is great pity that one of such noble life should be lost! I' faith, 't were not easy to find his equal upon earth. The king had done better to have wrought more warily. Yonder knight should have been made a duke; a gallant leader of men is he, 50 and such a fate had beseemed him better than to be hewn in pieces at the will of an elfish man, for mere pride. Who ever knew a king to take such counsel as to risk his knights on a Christmas jest?" Many were the tears that flowed from their eyes when that goodly knight rode from the hall. He made no delaying, but

went his way swiftly, and rode many a wild road, as I heard say in the book.

So rode Sir Gawain through the realm of Logres,[3] on an errand that he held for no jest. Often he lay companionless at night, and must lack the fare that he liked. No comrade had he save his steed, and none save God with whom to take counsel. At length he drew nigh to North Wales, and left the isles of Anglesey on his left hand, crossing over the fords by the foreland over at Holyhead, till he came into the wilderness of Wirral,[4] where but few dwell who love God and man of true heart. And ever he asked, as he fared, of all whom he met, if they had heard any tidings of a Green Knight in the country thereabout, or of a Green Chapel? And all answered him, "Nay," never in their lives had they seen any man of such a hue. And the knight wended his way by many a strange road and many a rugged path, and the fashion of his countenance changed full often ere he saw the Green Chapel.

Many a cliff did he climb in that unknown land, where afar from his friends he rode as a stranger. Never did he come to a stream or a ford but he found a foe before him, and that one so marvelous, so foul and fell, that it behooved him to fight. So many wonders did that knight behold, that it were too long to tell the tenth part of them. Sometimes he fought with dragons and wolves; sometimes with wild men that dwelt in the rocks; another while with bulls, and bears, and wild boars, or with giants of the high moorland that drew near to him. Had he not been a doughty knight, enduring, and of well-proved valor, and a servant of God, doubtless he had been slain, for he was oft in danger of death. Yet he cared not so much for the strife; what he deemed worse was when the cold clear water was shed from the clouds, and froze ere it fell on the fallow ground. More nights than enough he slept in his harness on the bare rocks, near slain with the sleet, while the stream leapt bubbling from the crest of the hills, and hung in hard icicles over his head.

Thus in peril and pain, and many a hardship, the knight rode alone till Christmas Eve, and in that tide he made his prayer to the Blessed Virgin that she would guide his steps and lead him to some dwelling. On that morning he rode by a hill, and came into a thick forest, wild and drear; on each side were high hills, and thick woods below them of great

---

[3] England.        [4] In Cheshire.

hoar oaks, a hundred together, of hazel and hawthorn with their trailing boughs intertwined, and rough ragged moss spreading everywhere. On the bare twigs the birds chirped piteously, for pain of the cold. The knight upon Gringalet rode lonely beneath them, through marsh and mire, much troubled at heart lest he should fail to see the service of the Lord, who on that self-same night was born of a maiden for the cure of our grief; and there- 10 fore he said, sighing, "I beseech thee, Lord, and Mary thy gentle Mother, for some shelter where I may hear Mass, and thy matins at morn. This I ask meekly, and thereto I pray my Paternoster, Ave, and Credo." Thus he rode praying, and lamenting his misdeeds, and he crossed himself, and said, "May the Cross of Christ speed me."

Now that knight had crossed himself but thrice ere he was aware in the wood of a 20 dwelling within a moat, above a lawn, on a mound surrounded by many mighty trees that stood round the moat. 'T was the fairest castle that ever a knight owned; built in a meadow with a park all about it, and a spiked palisade, closely driven, that enclosed the trees for more than two miles. The knight was ware of the hold from the side, as it shone through the oaks. Then he lifted off his helmet, and thanked Christ and Saint Julian that they had 30 courteously granted his prayer, and hearkened to his cry. "Now," quoth the knight, "I beseech ye, grant me fair hostel." Then he pricked Gringalet with his golden spurs, and rode gaily towards the great gate, and came swiftly to the bridge end.

The bridge was drawn up and the gates close shut; the walls were strong and thick, so that they might fear no tempest. The knight on his charger abode on the bank of the deep 40 double ditch that surrounded the castle. The walls were set deep in the water, and rose aloft to a wondrous height; they were of hard hewn stone up to the corbels, which were adorned beneath the battlements with fair carvings, and turrets set in between with many a loophole; a better barbican Sir Gawain had never looked upon. And within he beheld the high hall, with its tower and many windows with carven cornices, and chalk-white chimneys on 50 the turreted roofs that shone fair in the sun. And everywhere, thickly scattered on the castle battlements, were pinnacles, so many that it seemed as if it were all wrought out of paper, so white was it. The knight on his steed deemed it fair enough, if he might come to be sheltered within it to lodge there while that the holyday lasted. He called aloud, and soon there came a porter of kindly countenance, who stood on the wall and greeted this knight and asked his errand.

"Good sir," quoth Gawain, "wilt thou go mine errand to the high lord of the castle, and crave for me lodging?"

"Yea, by Saint Peter," quoth the porter. "In sooth I trow that ye be welcome to dwell here so long as it may like ye."

Then he went, and came again swiftly, and many folk with him to receive the knight. They let down the great drawbridge, and came forth and knelt on their knees on the cold earth to give him worthy welcome. They held wide open the great gates, and courteously he bade them rise, and rode over the bridge. Then men came to him and held his stirrup while he dismounted, and took and stabled his steed. There came down knights and squires to bring the guest with joy to the hall. When he raised his helmet there were many to take it from his hand, fain to serve him, and they took from him sword and shield.

Sir Gawain gave good greeting to the noble and the mighty men who came to do him honor. Clad in his shining armor they led him to the hall, where a great fire burned brightly on the floor; and the lord of the household came forth from his chamber to meet the hero fitly. He spake to the knight, and said: "Ye are welcome to do here as it likes ye. All that is here is your own to have at your will and disposal."

"Gramercy!" quoth Gawain, "may Christ requite ye."

As friends that were fain each embraced the other; and Gawain looked on the knight who greeted him so kindly, and thought 't was a bold warrior that owned that burg.

Of mighty stature he was, and of high age; broad and flowing was his beard, and of a bright hue. He was stalwart of limb, and strong in his stride, his face fiery red, and his speech free: in sooth he seemed one well fitted to be a leader of valiant men.

Then the lord led Sir Gawain to a chamber, and commanded folk to wait upon him, and at his bidding there came men enough who brought the guest to a fair bower. The bedding was noble, with curtains of pure silk wrought with gold, and wondrous coverings of fair cloth all embroidered. The curtains ran on ropes with rings of red gold, and the walls were hung with carpets of Orient, and the same spread on the floor. There with mirthful speeches they took from the guest his byrnie and all his shining armor, and brought him rich robes of the choicest in its stead. They were long and flowing, and became him well, and when he was clad in them all who looked on the hero thought that surely God had never made a fairer knight: he seemed as if he might be a prince without peer in the field where men strive in battle.

Then before the hearth-place, whereon the fire burned, they made ready a chair for Gawain, hung about with cloth and fair cushions; and there they cast around him a mantle of brown samite, richly embroidered and furred within with costly skins of ermine, with a hood of the same, and he seated himself in that rich seat, and warmed himself at the fire, and was cheered at heart. And while he sat thus, the serving men set up a table on trestles, and covered it with a fair white cloth, and set thereon salt-cellar, and napkin, and silver spoons; and the knight washed at his will, and set him down to meat.

The folk served him courteously with many dishes seasoned of the best, a double portion. All kinds of fish were there, some baked in bread, some broiled on the embers, some sodden,[5] some stewed and savored with spices, with all sorts of cunning devices to his taste. And often he called it a feast, when they spake gaily to him all together, and said, "Now take ye this penance, and it shall be for your amendment." Much mirth thereof did Sir Gawain make.

Then they questioned that prince courteously of whence he came; and he told them that he was of the court of Arthur, who is the rich royal king of the Round Table, and that it was Gawain himself who was within their walls, and would keep Christmas with them, as the chance had fallen out. And when the lord of the castle heard those tidings he laughed aloud for gladness, and all men in that keep were joyful that they should be in the company of him to whom belonged all fame, and valor, and courtesy, and whose honor was praised above that of all men on earth. Each said softly to his fellow, "Now shall we see courteous bearing, and the manner of speech befitting courts. What charm lieth in gentle speech shall we learn without asking, since here we have welcomed the fine father of courtesy. God has surely shown us His grace since He sends us such a guest as Gawain! When men shall sit and sing, blithe for Christ's

birth, this knight shall bring us to the knowledge of fair manners, and it may be that hearing him we may learn the cunning speech of love."

By the time the knight had risen from dinner it was near nightfall. Then chaplains took their way to the chapel, and rang loudly, even as they should, for the solemn evensong of the high feast. Thither went the lord, and the lady also, and entered with her maidens into a comely closet, and thither also went Gawain. Then the lord took him by the sleeve and led him to a seat, and called him by his name, and told him he was of all men in the world the most welcome. And Sir Gawain thanked him truly, and each kissed the other, and they sat gravely together throughout the service.

Then was the lady fain to look upon that knight; and she came forth from her closet with many fair maidens. The fairest of ladies was she in face, and figure, and coloring, fairer even than Guinevere, so the knight thought. She came through the chancel to greet the hero; another lady held her by the left hand, older than she, and seemingly of high estate, with many nobles about her. But unlike to look upon were those ladies, for if the younger were fair, the elder was yellow. Rich red were the cheeks of the one, rough and wrinkled those of the other; the kerchiefs of the one were broidered with many glistening pearls, her throat and neck bare, and whiter than the snow that lies on the hills; the neck of the other was swathed in a gorget, with a white wimple over her black chin. Her forehead was wrapped in silk with many folds, worked with knots, so that naught of her was seen save her black brows, her eyes, her nose, and her lips, and those were bleared, and ill to look upon. A worshipful lady in sooth one might call her! In figure was she short and broad, and thickly made—far fairer to behold was she whom she led by the hand.

When Gawain beheld that fair lady, who looked at him graciously, with leave of the lord he went towards them, and, bowing low, he greeted the elder, but the younger and fairer he took lightly in his arms, and kissed her courteously, and greeted her in knightly wise. Then she hailed him as friend, and he quickly prayed to be counted as her servant, if she so willed. Then they took him between them, and talking, led him to the chamber, to the hearth, and bade them bring spices, and they brought them in plenty with the good wine that was wont to be drunk at such

---

[5] Boiled.

seasons. Then the lord sprang to his feet and bade them make merry, and took off his hood, and hung it on a spear, and bade him win the worship thereof who should make most mirth that Christmas-tide. "And I shall try, by my faith, to fool it with the best, by the help of my friends, ere I lose my raiment." Thus with gay words the lord made trial to gladden Gawain with jests that night, till it was time to bid them light the tapers, and Sir Gawain took leave of them and gat him to rest.

In the morn when all men call to mind how Christ our Lord was born on earth to die for us, there is joy, for his sake, in all dwellings of the world; and so was there here on that day. For high feast was held, with many dainties and cunningly cooked messes. On the daïs sat gallant men, clad in their best. The ancient dame sat on the high seat with the lord of the castle beside her. Gawain and the fair lady sat together, even in the midst of the board when the feast was served; and so throughout all the hall each sat in his degree, and was served in order. There was meat, there was mirth, there was much joy, so that to tell thereof would take me too long, though peradventure I might strive to declare it. But Gawain and that fair lady had much joy of each other's company through her sweet words and courteous converse. And there was music made before each prince, trumpets and drums, and merry pipings; each man hearkened his minstrel, and they too hearkened theirs.

So they held high feast that day and the next, and the third day thereafter, and the joy on Saint John's Day was fair to hearken, for 't was the last of the feast and the guests would depart in the gray of the morning. Therefore they awoke early, and drank wine, and danced fair carols, and at last, when it was late, each man took his leave to wend early on his way. Gawain would bid his host farewell, but the lord took him by the hand, and led him to his own chamber beside the hearth, and there he thanked him for the favor he had shown him in honoring his dwelling at that high season, and gladdening his castle with his fair countenance. "I wis, sir, that while I live I shall be held the worthier that Gawain has been my guest at God's own feast."

"Gramercy, sir," quoth Gawain, "in good faith, all the honor is yours, may the High King give it you, and I am but at your will to work your behest, inasmuch as I am beholden to you in great and small by rights."

Then the lord did his best to persuade the knight to tarry with him, but Gawain answered that he might in no wise do so. Then the host asked him courteously what stern behest had driven him at the holy season from the king's court, to fare all alone, ere yet the feast was ended?

"Forsooth," quoth the knight, "ye say but the truth: 't is a high quest and a pressing that hath brought me afield, for I am summoned myself to a certain place, and I know not whither in the world I may wend to find it; so help me Christ, I would give all the kingdom of Logres an I might find it by New Year's morn. Therefore, sir, I make request of you that ye tell me truly if ye ever heard word of the Green Chapel, where it may be found, and the Green Knight that keeps it. For I am pledged by solemn compact sworn between us to meet that knight at the New Year if so I were on life; and of that same New Year it wants but little—I' faith, I would look on that hero more joyfully than on any other fair sight! Therefore, by your will, it behooves me to leave you, for I have but barely three days, and I would as fain fall dead as fail of mine errand."

Then the lord quoth, laughing, "Now must ye needs stay, for I will show you your goal, the Green Chapel, ere your term be at an end, have ye no fear! But ye can take your ease, friend, in your bed, till the fourth day, and go forth on the first of the year and come to that place at mid-morn to do as ye will. Dwell here till New Year's Day, and then rise and set forth, and ye shall be set in the way; 't is not two miles hence."

Then was Gawain glad, and he laughed gaily. "Now I thank you for this above all else. Now my quest is achieved I will dwell here at your will, and otherwise do as ye shall ask."

Then the lord took him, and set him beside him, and bade the ladies be fetched for their greater pleasure, tho' between themselves they had solace. The lord, for gladness, made merry jest, even as one who wist not what to do for joy; and he cried aloud to the knight, "Ye have promised to do the thing I bid ye: will ye hold to this behest, here, at once?"

"Yea, forsooth," said that true knight, "while I abide in your burg I am bound by your behest."

"Ye have traveled from far," said the host, "and since then ye have waked with me, ye are not well refreshed by rest and sleep, as I know. Ye shall therefore abide in your chamber, and lie at your ease tomorrow at

Mass-tide, and go to meat when ye will with my wife, who shall sit with you, and comfort you with her company till I return; and I shall rise early and go forth to the chase." And Gawain agreed to all this courteously.

"Sir knight," quoth the host, "we will make a covenant. Whatsoever I win in the wood shall be yours, and whatever may fall to your share, that shall ye exchange for it. Let us swear, friend, to make this exchange, however our hap may be, for worse or for better."

"I grant ye your will," quoth Gawain the good; "if ye list so to do, it liketh me well."

"Bring hither the wine-cup, the bargain is made," so said the lord of that castle. They laughed each one, and drank of the wine, and made merry, these lords and ladies, as it pleased them. Then with gay talk and merry jest they rose, and stood, and spoke softly, and kissed courteously, and took leave of each other. With burning torches, and many a serving-man, was each led to his couch; yet ere they gat them to bed the old lord oft repeated their covenant, for he knew well how to make sport.

### III

Full early, ere daylight, the folk rose up; the guests who would depart called their grooms, and they made them ready, and saddled the steeds, tightened up the girths, and trussed up their mails.[1] The knights, all arrayed for riding, leapt up lightly, and took their bridles, and each rode his way as pleased him best.

The lord of the land was not the last. Ready for the chase, with many of his men, he ate a sop hastily when he had heard Mass, and then with blast of the bugle fared forth to the field. He and his nobles were to horse ere daylight glimmered upon the earth.

Then the huntsmen coupled their hounds, unclosed the kennel door, and called them out. They blew three blasts gaily on the bugles, the hounds bayed fiercely, and they that would go a-hunting checked and chastised them. A hundred hunters there were of the best, so I have heard tell. Then the trackers gat them to the trysting-place and uncoupled the hounds, and the forest rang again with their gay blasts.

At the first sound of the hunt the game quaked for fear, and fled, trembling, along the vale. They betook them to the heights, but the liers in wait turned them back with

loud cries; the harts they let pass them, and the stags with their spreading antlers, for the lord had forbidden that they should be slain, but the hinds and the does they turned back, and drave down into the valleys. Then might ye see much shooting of arrows. As the deer fled under the boughs a broad whistling shaft smote and wounded each sorely, so that, wounded and bleeding, they fell dying on the banks. The hounds followed swiftly on their tracks, and hunters, blowing the horn, sped after them with ringing shouts as if the cliffs burst asunder. What game escaped those that shot was run down at the outer ring. Thus were they driven on the hills, and harassed at the waters, so well did the men know their work, and the greyhounds were so great and swift that they ran them down as fast as the hunters could slay them. Thus the lord passed the day in mirth and joyfulness, even to nightfall.

So the lord roamed the woods, and Gawain, that good knight, lay ever a-bed, curtained about, under the costly coverlet, while the daylight gleamed on the walls. And as he lay half slumbering, he heard a little sound at the door, and he raised his head, and caught back a corner of the curtain, and waited to see what it might be. It was the lovely lady, the lord's wife; she shut the door softly behind her, and turned towards the bed; and Gawain was shamed, laid him down softly and made as if he slept. And she came lightly to the bedside, within the curtain, and sat herself down beside him, to wait till he wakened. The knight lay there awhile, and marveled within himself what her coming might betoken; and he said to himself, " 'T were more seemly if I asked her what hath brought her hither." Then he made feint to waken, and turned towards her, and opened his eyes as one astonished, and crossed himself; and she looked on him laughing, with her cheeks red and white, lovely to behold, and small smiling lips.

"Good morrow, Sir Gawain," said that fair lady; "ye are but a careless sleeper, since one can enter thus. Now are ye taken unawares, and lest ye escape me I shall bind you in your bed; of that be ye assured!" Laughing, she spake these words.

"Good morrow, fair lady," quoth Gawain blithely. "I will do your will, as it likes me well. For I yield me readily, and pray your grace, and that is best, by my faith, since I needs must do so." Thus he jested again, laughing. "But an ye would, fair lady, grant me this grace that ye pray your prisoner to rise. I

---

[1] Bags.

would get me from bed, and array me better, then could I talk with ye in more comfort."

"Nay, forsooth, fair sir," quoth the lady, "ye shall not rise, I will rede ² ye better. I shall keep ye here, since ye can do no other, and talk with my knight whom I have captured. For I know well that ye are Sir Gawain, whom all the world worships, wheresoever ye may ride. Your honor and your courtesy are praised by lords and ladies, by all who live. Now ye are here and we are alone, my lord and his men are afield; the serving men in their beds, and my maidens also, and the door shut upon us. And since in this hour I have him that all men love I shall use my time well with speech, while it lasts. Ye are welcome to my company, for it behooves me in sooth to be your servant."

"In good faith," quoth Gawain, "I think me that I am not him of whom ye speak, for unworthy am I of such service as ye here proffer. In sooth, I were glad if I might set myself by word or service to your pleasure; a pure joy would it be to me!"

"In good faith, Sir Gawain," quoth the gay lady, "the praise and the prowess that pleases all ladies I lack them not, nor hold them light; yet are there ladies enough who would liever now have the knight in their hold, as I have ye here, to dally with your courteous words, to bring them comfort and to ease their cares, than much of the treasure and the gold that are theirs. And now, through the grace of Him who upholds the heavens, I have wholly in my power that which they all desire!"

Thus the lady, fair to look upon, made him great cheer, and Sir Gawain, with modest words, answered her again: "Madam," he quoth, "may Mary requite ye, for in good faith I have found in ye a noble frankness. Much courtesy have other folk shown me, but the honor they have done me is naught to the worship of yourself, who knoweth but good."

"By Mary," quoth the lady, "I think otherwise; for were I worth all the women alive, and had I the wealth of the world in my hand, and might choose me a lord to my liking, then, for all that I have seen in ye, Sir Knight, of beauty and courtesy and blithe semblance, and for all that I have hearkened and hold for true, there should be no knight on earth to be chosen before ye."

"Well, I wot," quoth Sir Gawain, "that ye have chosen a better; but I am proud that ye should so prize me, and as your servant do I hold ye my sovereign, and your knight am I, and may Christ reward ye."

² Manage.

So they talked of many matters till midmorn was past, and ever the lady made as though she loved him, and the knight turned her speech aside. For though she were the brightest of maidens, yet had he forborne to show her love for the danger that awaited him, and the blow that must be given without delay.

Then the lady prayed her leave from him, and he granted it readily. And she gave him good-day, with laughing glance, but he must needs marvel at her words:

"Now He that speeds fair speech reward ye this disport; but that ye be Gawain my mind misdoubts me greatly."

"Wherefore?" quoth the knight quickly, fearing lest he had lacked in some courtesy.

And the lady spake: "So true a knight as Gawain is holden, and one so perfect in courtesy, would never have tarried so long with a lady but he would of his courtesy have craved a kiss at parting."

Then quoth Gawain, "I wot I will do even as it may please ye, and kiss at your commandment, as a true knight should who forbears to ask for fear of displeasure."

At that she came near and bent down and kissed the knight, and each commended the other to Christ, and she went forth from the chamber softly.

Then Sir Gawain rose and called his chamberlain and chose his garments, and when he was ready he gat him forth to Mass, and then went to meat, and made merry all day till the rising of the moon, and never had a knight fairer lodging than had he with those two noble ladies, the elder and the younger.

And ever the lord of the land chased the hinds through holt and heath till eventide, and then with much blowing of bugles and baying of hounds they bore the game homeward; and by the time daylight was done all the folk had returned to that fair castle. And when the lord and Sir Gawain met together, then were they both well pleased. The lord commanded them all to assemble in the great hall, and the ladies to descend with their maidens, and there, before them all, he bade the men fetch in the spoil of the day's hunting, and he called unto Gawain, and counted the tale of the beasts, and showed them unto him, and said, "What think ye of this game, Sir Knight? Have I deserved of ye thanks for my woodcraft?"

"Yea, I wis," quoth the other, "here is the fairest spoil I have seen this seven year in the winter season."

"And all this do I give ye, Gawain," quoth the host, "for by accord of covenant ye may claim it as your own."

"That in sooth," quoth the other, "I grant you that same; and I have fairly won this within walls, and with as good will do I yield it to you." With that he clasped his hands round the lord's neck and kissed him as courteously as he might. "Take ye here my spoils, no more have I won; ye should have it freely, 10 though it were greater than this."

"'T is good," said the host, "gramercy thereof. Yet were I fain to know where ye won this same favor, and if it were by your own wit?"

"Nay," answered Gawain, "that was not in the bond. Ask me no more: ye have taken what was yours by right, be content with that."

They laughed and jested together, and sat them down to supper, where they were served 20 with many dainties; and after supper they sat by the hearth, and wine was served out to them; and oft in their jesting they promised to observe on the morrow the same covenant that they had made before, and whatever chance might betide, to exchange their spoil, be it much or little, when they met at night. Thus they renewed their bargain before the whole court, and then the night-drink was served, and each courteously took leave of the other 30 and gat him to bed.

By the time the cock had crowed thrice the lord of the castle had left his bed; Mass was sung and meat fitly served. The folk were forth to the wood ere the day broke; with hound and horn they rode over the plain, and uncoupled their dogs among the thorns. Soon they struck on the scent, and the hunt cheered on the hounds who were first to seize it, urging them with shouts. The others hastened to 40 the cry, forty at once, and there rose such a clamor from the pack that the rocks rang again. The huntsmen spurred them on with shouting and blasts of the horn; and the hounds drew together to a thicket betwixt the water and a high crag in the cliff beneath the hillside. There where the rough rock fell ruggedly they, the huntsmen, fared to the finding, and cast about round the hill and the thicket behind them. The knights wist well what beast was 50 within, and would drive him forth with the bloodhounds. And as they beat the bushes, suddenly over the beaters there rushed forth a wondrous great and fierce boar; long since had he left the herd to roam by himself. Grunting, he cast many to the ground, and fled forth at his best speed, without more mischief. The

men hallooed loudly and cried, "Hay! Hay!" and blew the horns to urge on the hounds, and rode swiftly after the boar. Many a time did he turn to bay and tare the hounds, and they yelped, and howled shrilly. Then the men made ready their arrows and shot at him, but the points were turned on his thick hide, and the barbs would not bite upon him, for the shafts shivered in pieces, and the head but leapt again wherever it hit.

But when the boar felt the stroke of the arrows he waxed mad with rage, and turned on the hunters and tare many, so that, affrightened, they fled before him. But the lord on a swift steed pursued him, blowing his bugle; as a gallant knight he rode through the woodland, chasing the boar till the sun grew low.

So did the hunters this day, while Sir Gawain lay in his bed lapped in rich gear; and the lady forgat not to salute him, for early was she at his side, to cheer his mood.

She came to the bedside and looked on the knight, and Gawain gave her fit greeting, and she greeted him again with ready words, and sat her by his side and laughed, and with a sweet look she spoke to him:

"Sir, if ye be Gawain, I think it a wonder that ye be so stern and cold, and care not for the courtesies of friendship, but if one teach ye to know them ye cast the lesson out of your mind. Ye have soon forgotten what I taught ye yesterday, by all the truest tokens that I knew!"

"What is that?" quoth the knight. "I trow I know not. If it be sooth that ye say, then is the blame mine own."

"But I taught ye of kissing," quoth the fair lady. "Wherever a fair countenance is shown him, it behooves a courteous knight quickly to claim a kiss."

"Nay, my dear," said Sir Gawain, "cease that speech; that durst I not do lest I were denied, for if I were forbidden I wot I were wrong did I further entreat."

"I' faith," quoth the lady merrily, "ye may not be forbid, ye are strong enough to constrain by strength an ye will, were any so discourteous as to give ye denial."

"Yea, by heaven," said Gawain, "ye speak well; but threats profit little in the land where I dwell, and so with a gift that is given not of good will! I am at your commandment to kiss when ye like, to take or to leave as ye list."

Then the lady bent her down and kissed him courteously.

And as they spake together she said, "I would learn somewhat from ye, and ye would not be wroth, for young ye are and fair, and so courteous and knightly as ye are known to be, the head of all chivalry, and versed in all wisdom of love and war—'t is ever told of true knights how they adventured their lives for their true love, and endured hardships for her favors, and avenged her with valor, and eased her sorrows, and brought joy to her bower; and ye are the fairest knight of your time, and your fame and your honor are everywhere, yet I have sat by ye here twice, and never a word have I heard of love! Ye who are so courteous and skilled in such love ought surely to teach one so young and unskilled some little craft of true love! Why are ye so unlearned who art otherwise so famous? Or is it that ye deemed me unworthy to hearken to your teaching? For shame, Sir Knight! I come hither alone and sit at your side to learn of ye some skill; teach me of your wit, while my lord is from home."

"In good faith," quoth Gawain, "great is my joy and my profit that so fair a lady as ye are should deign to come hither, and trouble ye with so poor a man, and make sport with your knight with kindly countenance; it pleaseth me much. But that I, in my turn, should take it upon me to tell of love and such like matters to ye who know more by half, or a hundred fold, of such craft than I do, or ever shall in all my lifetime, by my troth 't were folly indeed! I will work your will to the best of my might as I am bounden, and evermore will I be your servant, so help me Christ!"

Then often with guile she questioned that knight that she might win him to woo her, but he defended himself so fairly that none might in any wise blame him, and naught but bliss and harmless jesting was there between them. They laughed and talked together till at last she kissed him, and craved her leave of him, and went her way.

Then the knight rose and went forth to Mass, and afterward dinner was served and he sat and spake with the ladies all day. But the lord of the castle rode ever over the land chasing the wild boar, that fled through the thickets, slaying the best of his hounds and breaking their backs in sunder; till at last he was so weary he might run no longer, but made for a hole in a mound by a rock. He got the mound at his back and faced the hounds, whetting his white tusks and foaming at the mouth. The huntsmen stood aloof, fearing to draw nigh him; so many of them had been already wounded that they were loath to be torn with his tusks, so fierce he was and mad with rage. At length the lord himself came up, and saw the beast at bay, and the men standing aloof. Then quickly he sprang to the ground and drew out a bright blade, and waded through the stream to the boar.

When the beast was aware of the knight with weapon in hand, he set up his bristles and snorted loudly, and many feared for their lord lest he should be slain. Then the boar leapt upon the knight so that beast and man were one atop of the other in the water; but the boar had the worst of it, for the man had marked, even as he sprang, and set the point of his brand to the beast's chest, and drove it up to the hilt, so that the heart was split in twain, and the boar fell snarling, and was swept down by the water to where a hundred hounds seized on him, and the men drew him to shore for the dogs to slay.

Then was there loud blowing of horns and baying of hounds; the huntsmen smote off the boar's head, and hung the carcass by the four feet to a stout pole, and so went on their way homewards. The head they bore before the lord himself, who had slain the beast at the ford by force of his strong hand.

It seemed him o'er long ere he saw Sir Gawain in the hall, and he called, and the guest came to take that which fell to his share. And when he saw Gawain the lord laughed aloud, and bade them call the ladies and the household together, and he showed them the game, and told them the tale, how they hunted the wild boar through the woods, and of his length and breadth and height; and Sir Gawain commended his deeds and praised him for his valor, well proven, for so mighty a beast had he never seen before.

Then they handled the huge head, and the lord said aloud, "Now, Gawain, this game is your own by sure covenant, as ye right well know."

"'T is sooth," quoth the knight, "and as truly will I give ye all I have gained." He took the host round the neck, and kissed him courteously twice. "Now are we quits," he said, "this eventide, of all the covenants that we made since I came hither."

And the lord answered, "By Saint Giles, ye are the best I know; ye will be rich in a short space if ye drive such bargains!"

Then they set up the tables on trestles, and covered them with fair cloths, and lit waxen tapers on the walls. The knights sat and were served in the hall, and much game and glee was there round the hearth, with many songs, both at supper and after; song of Christmas, and new carols, with all the mirth one may think of. And ever that lovely lady sat by the knight, and with still stolen looks made such feint of pleasing him, that Gawain marveled much, and was wroth with himself, but he could not for his courtesy return her fair glances, but dealt with her cunningly, however she might strive to wrest the thing.

When they had tarried in the hall so long as it seemed them good, they turned to the inner chamber and the wide hearth-place, and there they drank wine, and the host proffered to renew the covenant for New Year's Eve; but the knight craved leave to depart on the morrow, for it was nigh to the term when he must fulfill his pledge. But the lord would withhold him from so doing, and prayed him to tarry, and said:

"As I am a true knight I swear my troth that ye shall come to the Green Chapel to achieve your task on New Year's morn, long before prime.[3] Therefore abide ye in your bed, and I will hunt in this wood, and hold ye to the covenant to exchange with me against all the spoil I may bring hither. For twice have I tried ye, and found ye true, and the morrow shall be the third time and the best. Make we merry now while we may, and think on joy, for misfortune may take a man whensoever it wills."

Then Gawain granted his request, and they brought them drink, and they gat them with lights to bed.

Sir Gawain lay and slept softly, but the lord, who was keen on woodcraft, was afoot early. After Mass he and his men ate a morsel, and he asked for his steed; all the knights who should ride with him were already mounted before the hall gates.

'T was a fair frosty morning, for the sun rose red in ruddy vapor, and the welkin was clear of clouds. The hunters scattered them by a forest side, and the rocks rang again with the blast of their horns. Some came on the scent of a fox, and a hound gave tongue; the huntsmen shouted, and the pack followed in a crowd on the trail. The fox ran before them, and when they saw him they pursued him with noise and much shouting, and he wound and turned through many a thick grove, often cowering and hearkening in a hedge. At last by a little ditch he leapt out of a spinney, stole away slily by a copse path, and so out of the wood and away from the hounds. But he went, ere he wist, to a chosen tryst, and three started forth on him at once, so he must needs double back, and betake him to the wood again.

[3] Probably nine o'clock.

Then was it joyful to hearken to the hounds; when all the pack had met together and had sight of their game they made as loud a din as if all the lofty cliffs had fallen clattering together. The huntsmen shouted and threatened, and followed close upon him so that he might scarce escape, but Reynard was wily, and he turned and doubled upon them and led the lord and his men over the hills, now on the slopes, now in the vales, while the knight at home slept through the cold morning beneath his costly curtains.

But the fair lady of the castle rose betimes, and clad herself in a rich mantle that reached even to the ground, left her throat and her fair neck bare, and was bordered and lined with costly furs. On her head she wore no golden circlet, but a network of precious stones, that gleamed and shone through her tresses in clusters of twenty together. Thus she came into the chamber, closed the door after her, and set open a window, and called to him gaily, "Sir Knight, how may ye sleep? The morning is so fair."

Sir Gawain was deep in slumber, and in his dream he vexed him much for the destiny that should befall him on the morrow, when he should meet the knight of the Green Chapel, and abide his blow; but when the lady spake he heard her, and came to himself, and roused from his dream and answered swiftly. The lady came laughing, and kissed him courteously, and he welcomed her fittingly with a cheerful countenance. He saw her so glorious and gaily dressed, so faultless of features and complexion, that it warmed his heart to look upon her.

They spake to each other smiling, and all was bliss and good cheer between them. They exchanged fair words, and much happiness was therein, yet was there a gulf between them, and she might win no more of her knight, for that gallant prince watched well his words—he would neither take her love, nor frankly refuse it. He cared for his courtesy, lest he be deemed churlish, and yet more for his honor lest he be traitor to his host. "God forbid," quoth he to himself, "that it should so befall." Thus with courteous words did he set aside all the special speeches that came from her lips.

Then spake the lady to the knight, "Ye deserve blame if ye hold not that lady who sits beside ye above all else in the world, if ye have not already a love whom ye hold dearer, and like better, and have sworn such firm faith to that lady that ye care not to loose it—and that am I now fain to believe. And now I pray ye straitly that ye tell me that in truth, and hide it not."

And the knight answered, "By Saint John" (and he smiled as he spake) "no such love have I, nor do I think to have yet awhile."

"That is the worst word I may hear," quoth the lady, "but in sooth I have mine answer; kiss me now courteously, and I will go hence; I can but mourn as a maiden that loves much."

Sighing, she stooped down and kissed him, and then she rose up and spake as she stood, "Now, dear, at our parting do me this grace, give me some gift, if it were but thy glove, that I may bethink me of my knight, and lessen my mourning."

"Now, I wis," quoth the knight, "I would that I had here the most precious thing that I possess on earth that I might leave ye as love-token, great or small, for ye have deserved forsooth more reward than I might give ye. But it is not to your honor to have at this time a glove for reward as gift from Gawain, and I am here on a strange errand, and have no man with me, nor mails with goodly things—that mislikes me much, lady, at this time; but each man must fare as he is taken, if for sorrow and ill."

"Nay, knight highly honored," quoth that lovesome lady, "though I have naught of yours, yet shall ye have somewhat of mine." With that she reached him a ring of red gold with a sparkling stone therein, that shone even as the sun (wit ye well, it was worth many marks); but the knight refused it, and spake readily.

"I will take no gift, lady, at this time. I have none to give, and none will I take."

She prayed him to take it, but he refused her prayer, and sware in sooth that he would not have it.

The lady was sorely vexed, and said, "If ye refuse my ring as too costly, that ye will not be so highly beholden to me, I will give you my girdle as a lesser gift." With that she loosened a lace that was fastened at her side, knit upon her kirtle under her mantle. It was wrought of green silk, and gold, only braided by the fingers, and that she offered to the knight, and besought him though it were of little worth that he would take it, and he said nay, he would touch neither gold nor gear ere God give him grace to achieve the adventure for which he had come hither. "And therefore, I pray ye, displease ye not, and ask me no longer, for I may not grant it. I am dearly beholden to ye for the favor ye have shown me, and ever, in heat and cold, will I be your true servant."

"Now," said the lady, "ye refuse this silk, for it is simple in itself, and so it seems, indeed; lo, it is small to look upon and less in cost, but whoso knew the virtue that is knit therein he would, peradventure, value it more highly. For whatever knight is girded with this green lace, while he bears it knotted about him there is no man under heaven can overcome him, for he may not be slain for any magic on earth."

Then Gawain bethought him, and it came into his heart that this were a jewel for the jeopardy that awaited him when he came to the Green Chapel to seek the return blow—could he so order it that he should escape unslain, 't were a craft worth trying. Then he bare with her chiding, and let her say her say, and she pressed the girdle on him and prayed him to take it, and he granted her prayer, and she gave it him with good will, and besought him for her sake never to reveal it but to hide it loyally from her lord, and the knight agreed that never should any man know it, save they two alone. He thanked her often and heartily, and she kissed him for the third time.

Then she took her leave of him, and when she was gone Sir Gawain rose, and clad him in rich attire, and took the girdle, and knotted it round him, and hid it beneath his robes. Then he took his way to the chapel, and sought out a priest privily and prayed him to teach him better how his soul might be saved when he should go hence; and there he shrived him, and showed his misdeeds, both great and small, and besought mercy and craved absolution; and the priest assoiled [4] him, and set him as clean as if doomsday had been on the morrow. And afterwards Sir Gawain made him merry with the ladies, with carols, and all kinds of joy, as never he did but that one day, even to nightfall; and all the men marveled at him, and said that never since he came thither had he been so merry.

Meanwhile the lord of the castle was abroad chasing the fox; awhile he lost him, and as he rode through a spinney he heard the hounds near at hand, and Reynard came creeping through a thick grove, with all the pack at his heels. Then the lord drew out his shining brand, and cast it at the beast, and the fox swerved aside for the sharp edge, and would have doubled back, but a hound was on him ere he might turn, and right before the horse's feet they all fell on him, and worried him fiercely, snarling the while.

---

[4] Absolved.

Then the lord leapt from his saddle, and caught the fox from the jaws, and held it aloft over his head, and hallooed loudly, and many brave hounds bayed as they beheld it; and the hunters hied them thither, blowing their horns; all that bare bugles blew them at once, and all the others shouted. 'T was the merriest meeting that ever men heard, the clamor that was raised at the death of the fox. They re- 10 warded the hounds, stroking them and rubbing their heads, and took Reynard and stripped him of his coat; then blowing their horns, they turned them homewards, for it was nigh nightfall.

The lord was gladsome at his return, and found a bright fire on the hearth, and the knight beside it, the good Sir Gawain, who was in joyous mood for the pleasure he had had with the ladies. He wore a robe of blue, that reached even to the ground, and a surcoat 20 richly furred, that became him well. A hood like to the surcoat fell on his shoulders, and all alike were done about with fur. He met the host in the midst of the floor, and jesting, he greeted him, and said, "Now shall I be first to fulfill our covenant which we made together when there was no lack of wine." Then he embraced the knight, and kissed him thrice, as solemnly as he might.

"Of a sooth," quoth the other, "ye have 30 good luck in the matter of this covenant, if ye made a good exchange!"

"Yet, it matters naught of the exchange," quoth Gawain, "since what I owe is swiftly paid."

"Marry," said the other, "mine is behind, for I have hunted all this day, and naught have I got but this foul fox-skin, and that is but poor payment for three such kisses as ye have here given me." 40

"Enough," quoth Sir Gawain, "I thank ye, by the Rood."

Then the lord told them of his hunting, and how the fox had been slain.

With mirth and minstrelsy, and dainties at their will, they made them as merry as a folk well might till 't was time for them to sever, for at last they must needs betake them to their beds. Then the knight took his leave of the lord, and thanked him fairly. 50

"For the fair sojourn that I have had here at this high feast may the High King give ye honor. I give ye myself, as one of your servants, if ye so like; for I must needs, as you know, go hence with the morn, and ye will give me, as ye promised, a guide to show me the way to the Green Chapel, an God will suffer me on New Year's Day to deal the doom of my weird." [5]

"By my faith," quoth the host, "all that ever I promised, that shall I keep with good will." Then he gave him a servant to set him in the way, and lead him by the downs, that he should have no need to ford the stream, and should fare by the shortest road through the groves; and Gawain thanked the lord for the honor done him. Then he would take leave of the ladies, and courteously he kissed them, and spake, praying them to receive his thanks, and they made like reply; then with many sighs they commended him to Christ, and he departed courteously from that fold. Each man that he met he thanked him for his service and his solace, and the pains he had been at to do his will; and each found it as hard to part from the knight as if he had ever dwelt with him.

Then they led him with torches to his chamber, and brought him to his bed to rest. That he slept soundly I may not say, for the morrow gave him much to think on. Let him rest awhile, for he was near that which he sought, and if ye will but listen to me I will tell ye how it fared with him thereafter.

## IV

Now the New Year drew nigh, and the night passed, and the day chased the darkness, as is God's will; but wild weather waking therewith. The clouds cast the cold to the earth, with enough of the north to slay them that lacked clothing. The snow drave smartly, and the whistling wind blew from the heights, and made great drifts in the valleys. The knight, lying in his bed, listened, for though his eyes were shut, he might sleep but little, and hearkened every cock that crew.

He arose ere the day broke, by the light of a lamp that burned in his chamber, and called to his chamberlain, bidding him bring his armor and saddle his steed. The other gat him up, and fetched his garments, and robed Sir Gawain.

First he clad him in his clothes to keep off the cold, and then in his harness, which was well and fairly kept. Both hauberk and plates were well burnished, the rings of the rich byrnie freed from rust, and all as fresh as at first, so that the knight was fain to thank them. Then he did on each piece, and bade them bring his steed, while he put the fairest raiment on himself; his coat with its fair cognizance,

[5] To take the judgment of my fate.

adorned with precious stones upon velvet, with broidered seams, and all furred within with costly skins. And he left not the lace, the lady's gift, that Gawain forgot not, for his own good. When he had girded on his sword he wrapped the gift twice about him, swathed around his waist. The girdle of green silk set gaily and well upon the royal red cloth, rich to behold, but the knight ware it not for pride of the pendants, polished though they were with fair gold that gleamed brightly on the ends, but to save himself from sword and knife, when it behooved him to abide his hurt without question. With that the hero went forth, and thanked that kindly folk full often.

Then was Gringalet ready, that was great and strong, and had been well cared for and tended in every wise; in fair condition was that proud steed, and fit for a journey. Then Gawain went to him, and looked on his coat, and said by his sooth, "There is a folk in this place that thinketh on honor; much joy may they have, and the lord who maintains them, and may all good betide that lovely lady all her life long. Since they for charity cherish a guest, and hold honor in their hands, may He who holds the heaven on high requite them, and also ye all. And if I might live anywhile on earth, I would give ye full reward, readily, if so I might." Then he set foot in the stirrup and bestrode his steed, and his squire gave him his shield, which he laid on his shoulder. Then he smote Gringalet with his golden spurs, and the steed pranced on the stones and would stand no longer.

By that his man was mounted, who bare his spear and lance, and Gawain quoth, "I commend this castle to Christ, may He give it ever good fortune." Then the drawbridge was let down, and the broad gates unbarred and opened on both sides; the knight crossed himself, and passed through the gateway, and praised the porter, who knelt before the prince, and gave him good-day, and commended him to God. Thus the knight went on his way, with the one man who should guide him to that dread place where he should receive rueful payment.

The two went by hedges where the boughs were bare, and climbed the cliffs where the cold clings. Naught fell from the heavens, but 't was ill beneath them; mist brooded over the moor and hung on the mountains; each hill had a cap, a great cloak, of mist. The streams foamed and bubbled between their banks, dashing sparkling on the shores where they shelved downwards. Rugged and dangerous was the way through the woods, till it was time for the sun-rising. Then were they on a high hill; the snow lay white beside them, and the man who rode with Gawain drew rein by his master.

"Sir," he said, "I have brought ye hither, and now ye are not far from the place that ye have sought so specially. But I will tell ye for sooth, since I know ye well, and ye are such a knight as I well love, would ye follow my counsel ye would fare the better. The place whither ye go is accounted full perilous, for he who liveth in that waste is the worst on earth, for he is strong and fierce; and loveth to deal mighty blows; taller he is than any man on earth, and greater of frame than any four in Arthur's court, or in any other. And this is his custom at the Green Chapel; there may no man pass by that place, however proud his arms, but he does him to death by force of his hand, for he is a discourteous knight, and shows no mercy. Be he churl or chaplain who rides by that chapel, monk or mass-priest, or any man else, he thinks it as pleasant to slay them as to pass alive himself. Therefore, I tell ye, as sooth as ye sit in saddle, if ye come there, and that knight know it, ye shall be slain, though ye had twenty lives; trow me that truly! He has dwelt here full long and seen many a combat; ye may not defend ye against his blows. Therefore, good Sir Gawain, let the man be, and get ye away some other road; for God's sake seek ye another land, and there may Christ speed ye! And I will hie me home again, and I promise ye further that I will swear by God and the saints, or any other oath ye please, that I will keep counsel faithfully, and never let any wit the tale that ye fled for fear of any man."

"Gramercy," quoth Gawain, but ill-pleased. "Good fortune be his who wishes me good, and that thou wouldst keep faith with me I will believe; but didst thou keep it never so truly, an I passed here and fled for fear as thou sayest, then were I a coward knight, and might not be held guiltless. So I will to the chapel let chance what may, and talk with that man, even as I may list, whether for weal or for woe as fate may have it. Fierce though he may be in fight, yet God knoweth well how to save His servants."

"Well," quoth the other, "now that ye have said so much that ye will take your own harm on yourself, and ye be pleased to lose your life, I will neither let [1] nor keep ye. Have here your

---

[1] Hinder.

helm and the spear in your hand, and ride down this same road beside the rock till ye come to the bottom of the valley, and there look a little to the left hand, and ye shall see in that vale the chapel, and the grim man who keeps it. Now fare ye well, noble Gawain; for all the gold on earth I would not go with ye nor bear ye fellowship one step further." With that the man turned his bridle into the wood, smote the horse with his spurs as hard as he 10 could, and galloped off, leaving the knight alone.

Quoth Gawain, "I will neither greet [2] nor moan, but commend myself to God, and yield me to His will."

Then the knight spurred Gringalet, and rode adown the path close in by a bank beside a grove. So he rode through the rough thicket, right into the dale, and there he halted, for it seemed him wild enough. No sign of a 20 chapel could he see, but high and burnt banks on either side and rough rugged crags with great stones above. An ill-looking place he thought it.

Then he drew in his horse and looked round to seek the chapel, but he saw none and thought it strange. Then he saw as it were a mound on a level space of land by a bank beside the stream where it ran swiftly; the water bubbled within as if boiling. The knight 30 turned his steed to the mound, and lighted down and tied the rein to the branch of a linden; and he turned to the mound and walked around it, questioning with himself what it might be. It had a hole at the end and at either side, and was overgrown with clumps of grass, and it was hollow within as an old cave or the crevice of a crag; he knew not what it might be.

"Ah," quoth Gawain, "can this be the 40 Green Chapel? Here might the devil say his matins at midnight! Now I wis there is wizardry here. 'T is an ugly oratory, all overgrown with grass, and 't would well beseem that fellow in green to say his devotions in devil's wise. Now feel I in five wits, 't is the foul fiend himself who hath set me this tryst, to destroy me here! This is a chapel of mischance: ill-luck betide it, 't is the cursedest kirk that ever I came in!" 50

Helmet on head and lance in hand, he came up to the rough dwelling, when he heard over the high hill beyond the brook, as it were in a bank, a wondrous fierce noise, that rang in the cliff as if it would cleave asunder.

'T was as if one ground a scythe on a grindstone; it whirred and whetted like water on a mill-wheel and rushed and rang, terrible to hear.

"By God," quoth Gawain, "I trow that gear is preparing for the knight who will meet me here. Alas! naught may help me, yet should my life be forfeit, I fear not a jot!" With that he called aloud. "Who waiteth in this place to give me tryst? Now is Gawain come hither: if any man will aught of him let him hasten hither now or never."

"Stay," quoth one on the bank above his head, "and ye shall speedily have that which I promised ye." Yet for a while the noise of whetting went on ere he appeared, and then he came forth from a cave in the crag with a fell weapon, a Danish ax newly dight, wherewith to deal the blow. An evil head it had, four feet large, no less, sharply ground, and bound to the handle by the lace that gleamed brightly. And the knight himself was all green as before, face and foot, locks and beard, but now he was afoot. When he came to the water he would not wade it, but sprang over with the pole of his ax, and strode boldly over the bent [3] that was white with snow.

Sir Gawain went to meet him, but he made no low bow. The other said, "Now, fair sir, one may trust thee to keep tryst. Thou art welcome, Gawain, to my place. Thou hast timed thy coming as befits a true man. Thou knowest the covenant set between us: at this time twelve months agone thou didst take that which fell to thee, and I at this New Year will readily requite thee. We are in this valley, verily alone; here are no knights to sever us, do what we will. Have off thy helm from thine head, and have here thy pay; make me no more talking than I did then when thou didst strike off my head with one blow."

"Nay," quoth Gawain, "by God that gave me life, I shall make no moan whatever befall me, but make thou ready for the blow and I shall stand still and say never a word to thee, do as thou wilt."

With that he bent his head and showed his neck all bare, and made as if he had no fear, for he would not be thought a-dread.

Then the Green Knight made him ready and grasped his grim weapon to smite Gawain. With all his force he bore it aloft with a mighty feint of slaying him: had it fallen as straight as he aimed he who was ever doughty of deed had been slain by the blow. But Ga-

---

[2] Weep.　　　　　　　　　　　　　　　　　[3] Field.

wain swerved aside as the ax came gliding down to slay him as he stood, and shrank a little with the shoulders, for the sharp iron. The other heaved up the blade and rebuked the prince with many proud words:

"Thou art not Gawain," he said, "who is held so valiant, that never feared he man by hill or vale, but thou shrinkest for fear ere thou feelest hurt. Such cowardice did I never hear of Gawain! Neither did I flinch from thy blow, or make strife in King Arthur's hall. My head fell to my feet, and yet I fled not; but thou didst wax faint of heart ere any harm befell. Wherefore must I be deemed the braver knight."

Quoth Gawain, "I shrank once, but so will I no more; though an my head fall on the stones I cannot replace it. But haste, Sir Knight, by thy faith, and bring me to the point, deal me my destiny, and do it out of hand, for I will stand thee a stroke and move no more till thine ax have hit me—my troth on it."

"Have at thee, then," quoth the other, and heaved aloft the ax with fierce mien, as if he were mad. He struck at him fiercely but wounded him not, withholding his hand ere it might strike him.

Gawain abode the stroke, and flinched in no limb, but stood still as a stone or the stump of a tree that is fast rooted in the rocky ground with a hundred roots.

Then spake gaily the man in green, "So now thou hast thine heart whole it behooves me to smite. Hold aside thy hood that Arthur gave thee, and keep thy neck thus bent lest it cover it again."

Then Gawain said angrily, "Why talk on thus? Thou dost threaten too long. I hope thy heart misgives thee."

"For sooth," quoth the other, "so fiercely thou speakest I will no longer let thine errand wait its reward." Then he braced himself to strike, frowning with lips and brow, 't was no marvel that it pleased but ill him who hoped for no rescue. He lifted the ax lightly and let it fall with the edge of the blade on the bare neck. Though he struck swiftly, it hurt him no more than on the one side where it severed the skin. The sharp blade cut into the flesh so that the blood ran over his shoulder to the ground. And when the knight saw the blood staining the snow, he sprang forth, swift-foot, more than a spear's length, seized his helmet and set it on his head, cast his shield over his shoulder, drew out his bright sword, and spake boldly (never since he was born was he half so blithe), "Stop, Sir Knight, bid me no more blows; I have stood a stroke here without flinching, and if thou give me another, I shall requite thee, and give thee as good again. By the covenant made betwixt us in Arthur's hall but one blow falls to me here. Halt, therefore."

Then the Green Knight drew off from him and leaned on his ax, setting the shaft on the ground, and looked on Gawain as he stood all armed and faced him fearlessly—at heart it pleased him well. Then he spake merrily in a loud voice, and said to the knight, "Bold sir, be not so fierce; no man here hath done thee wrong, nor will do, save by covenant, as we made at Arthur's court. I promised thee a blow and thou hast it— hold thyself well paid! I release thee of all other claims. If I had been so minded I might perchance have given thee a rougher buffet. First I menaced thee with a feigned one, and hurt thee not for the covenant that we made in the first night, and which thou didst hold truly. All the gain didst thou give me as a true man should. The other feint I proffered thee for the morrow: my fair wife kissed thee, and thou didst give me her kisses—for both those days I gave thee two blows without scathe—true man, true return. But the third time thou didst fail, and therefore hadst thou that blow. For 't is my weed thou wearest, that same woven girdle, my own wife wrought it, that do I wot for sooth. Now know I well thy kisses, and thy conversation, and the wooing of my wife, for 't was mine own doing. I sent her to try thee, and in sooth I think thou art the most faultless knight that ever trod earth. As a pearl among white peas is of more worth than they, so is Gawain, i' faith, by other knights. But thou didst lack a little, Sir Knight, and wast wanting in loyalty, yet that was for no evil work, nor for wooing either, but because thou lovedst thy life—therefore I blame thee the less."

Then the other stood a great while, still sorely angered and vexed within himself; all the blood flew to his face, and he shrank for shame as the Green Knight spake; and the first words he said were, "Cursed be ye, cowardice and covetousness, for in ye is the destruction of virtue." Then he loosed the girdle, and gave it to the knight. "Lo, take there the falsity, may foul befall it! For fear of thy blow cowardice bade me make friends with covetousness and forsake the customs of largess and loyalty, which befit all knights.

Now am I faulty and false and have been afeared: from treachery and untruth come sorrow and care. I avow to thee, Sir Knight, that I have ill done; do then thy will. I shall be more wary hereafter."

Then the other laughed and said gaily, "I wot I am whole of the hurt I had, and thou hast made such free confession of thy misdeeds, and hast so borne the penance of mine ax edge, that I hold thee absolved from that sin, and purged as clean as if thou hadst never sinned since thou wast born. And this girdle that is wrought with gold and green, like my raiment, do I give thee, Sir Gawain, that thou mayest think upon this chance when thou goest forth among princes of renown, and keep this for a token of the adventure of the Green Chapel, as it chanced between chivalrous knights. And thou shalt come again with me to my dwelling and pass the rest of this feast in gladness." Then the lord laid hold of him, and said, "I wot we shall soon make peace with my wife, who was thy bitter enemy."

"Nay, forsooth," said Sir Gawain, and seized his helmet and took it off swiftly, and thanked the knight: "I have fared ill, may bliss betide thee, and may He who rules all things reward thee swiftly. Commend me to that courteous lady, thy fair wife, and to the other my honored ladies, who have beguiled their knight with skilful craft. But 't is no marvel if one be made a fool and brought to sorrow by women's wiles, for so was Adam beguiled by one, and Solomon by many, and Samson all too soon, for Delilah dealt him his doom; and David thereafter was wedded with Bathsheba, which brought him much sorrow—if one might love a woman and believe her not, 't were great gain! And since all they were beguiled by women, methinks 't is the less blame to me that I was misled! But as for thy girdle, that will I take with good will, not for gain of the gold, nor for samite, nor silk, nor the costly pendants, neither for weal nor for worship, but in sign of my frailty. I shall look upon it when I ride in renown and remind myself of the fault and faintness of the flesh; and so when pride uplifts me for prowess of arms, the sight of this lace shall humble my heart. But one thing would I pray, if it displease thee not: since thou art lord of yonder land wherein I have dwelt, tell me what thy rightful name may be, and I will ask no more."

"That will I truly," quoth the other. "Bercilak de Hautdesert am I called in this land. Morgain le Fay dwelleth in mine house, and through knowledge of clerkly craft hath she taken many. For long time was she the mistress of Merlin, who knew well all you knights of the court. Morgain the goddess is she called therefore, and there is none so haughty but she can bring him low. She sent me in this guise to yon fair hall to test the truth of the renown that is spread abroad of the valor of the Round Table. She taught me this marvel to betray your wits, to vex Guinevere and fright her to death by the man who spake with his head in his hand at the high table. That is she who is at home, that ancient lady; she is even thine aunt, Arthur's half-sister, the daughter of the Duchess of Tintagel, who afterward married King Uther. Therefore I bid thee, knight, come to thine aunt, and make merry in thine house; my folk love thee, and I wish thee as well as any man on earth, by my faith, for thy true dealing."

But Sir Gawain said nay, he would in no wise do so; so they embraced and kissed, and commended each other to the Prince of Paradise, and parted right there, on the cold ground. Gawain on his steed rode swiftly to the king's hall, and the Green Knight got him whithersoever he would.

Sir Gawain, who had thus won grace of his life, rode through wild ways on Gringalet; oft he lodged in a house, and oft without, and many adventures did he have and came off victor full often, as at this time I cannot relate in tale. The hurt that he had in his neck was healed, he bare the shining girdle as a baldric bound by his side, and made fast with a knot 'neath his left arm, in token that he was taken in a fault—and thus he came in safety again to the court.

Then joy awakened in that dwelling when the king knew that the good Sir Gawain was come, for he deemed it gain. King Arthur kissed the knight, and the queen also, and many valiant knights sought to embrace him. They asked him how he had fared, and he told them all that had chanced to him—the adventure of the chapel, the fashion of the knight, the love of the lady—at last of the lace. He showed them the wound in the neck which he won for his disloyalty at the hand of the knight; the blood flew to his face for shame as he told the tale.

"Lo, lady," he quoth, and handled the lace, "this is the bond of the blame that I bear in my neck, this is the harm and the loss I have suffered, the cowardice and covetousness in which I was caught, the token of my covenant in which I was taken. And I must needs wear it so long as I live, for none may hide his harm, but undone it may not be, for if it hath clung to thee once, it may never be severed."

Then the king comforted the knight, and the court laughed loudly at the tale, and all made accord that the lords and the ladies who belonged to the Round Table, each hero among them, should wear bound about him a baldric of bright green for the sake of Sir Gawain. And to this was agreed all the honor of the Round Table, and he who ware it was honored the more thereafter, as it is testified in the book of romance. That in Arthur's days this adventure befell, the book of Brutus bears witness. For since that bold knight came hither first, and the siege and the assault were ceased at Troy, I wis

> Many a venture herebefore
> Hath fallen such as this:
> May He that bare the crown of thorn
> Bring us unto His bliss.
> *Amen.*

# William Langland(?)

The Vision of William concerning Piers the Plowman *has been traditionally attributed to one William Langland, to whom Skeat assigned, for convenience' sake, the conjectural dates c. 1332–c. 1400. On the basis of the author's supposed references to himself within the poem a biography has also been made up. His name, however, has been disputed, and likewise the identification with him of the "Will" of the poem; as a matter of fact nothing is certainly known about the authorship of the work. Piers Plowman exists in three versions, known as the A-, B-, and C-texts. The A-text was written in* 1362 *or shortly thereafter. It is* 2567 *lines in length. The B-text was written probably in* 1376 *or* 1377; *for this the A-text was taken as a basis, was thoroughly made over, and was considerably enlarged, the number of lines in this text being* 7242. *The C-text was written probably some time between* 1393 *and* 1399; *it is a revision of the B-text with many comparatively small changes, and contains* 7357 *lines. Until a generation ago these versions were accepted as the work of one writer. In* 1906, *however, Professor J. M. Manly asserted that the A-text was the work of three writers, and that the B- and C-texts were by two different authors, each other than the writers of the A-text. Proof of these assertions has not yet appeared, and the published work of other scholars since* 1906 *has on the whole gone to show that their proof would be more difficult than may have been at first supposed. Consequently, although the question of single or multiple authorship remains an open one and can perhaps never be settled, it seems justifiable to retain, at least provisionally, the traditional name William Langland.*

Piers Plowman *was in its own age and in the fifteenth century one of the most popular and valued pieces of literature in the English language, as is evinced by the fact that no less than forty-seven manuscripts of it are still ex-* tant. This popularity was deserved. The poem is, after The Canterbury Tales of Chaucer, "the greatest piece of Middle English literature; it is one of the greatest of the medieval vision poems, and as a vision poem, in many respects second only to the Divine Comedy; it is one of the foremost of the writings in English in which allegory is used" (J. E. Wells, Manual of the Writings in Middle English, p. 264). Moreover, to any student of the fourteenth century the poem is a necessary complement to the work of Chaucer, picturing as it does the life of the lower classes, and reflecting as it does the convictions and aspirations of simple-hearted men of deep feeling. Piers Plowman *has little of conscious art, its language is rough and broken, and it is written in the old alliterative meter, but its author felt intensely, saw deeply, and dealt greatly with the great issues of life.*

*A good critical edition of the A-text has recently appeared: T. A. Knott and D. C. Fowler, eds.,* Piers the Plowman: a Critical Edition of the A-Version *(Baltimore,* 1952). *The A-, B-, and C-texts are reproduced in parallel columns in* The Vision of William concerning Piers the Plowman, *ed. Walter W. Skeat (Oxford,* 1954). *Greta Hort's* Piers Plowman and Contemporary Religious Thought *(London,* 1938) *is a valuable study of a side of the poem which is too often neglected at the present time. A number of other studies have recently appeared:* Piers Plowman, the C-Text and its Poet, *by E. T. Donaldson (New Haven,* 1949); Piers Plowman and the Pursuit of Poetry, *by A. H. Smith (London,* 1951); *and* Piers Plowman and Scriptural Tradition, *by D. W. Robertson and B. F. Huppé (Princeton,* 1951). *For the medieval background see also D. Chadwick,* Social Life in the Days of Piers Plowman *(Cambridge,* 1922), *and* Life in the Middle Ages, *ed. and trans. George G. Coulton (Cambridge,* 1928–1930). The Vision of Piers Plowman *is the title of a complete translation into modern English by Henry W. Wells, with Introduction by Nevill Coghill (London and New York, 1935); Visions from Piers Plowman Translated into Modern English Verse by Nevill Coghill (London, 1949) is an excellent selection.*

# The Vision of Piers the Plowman [1]

## PROLOGUE

### THE FIELD FULL OF FOLK

In a summer season, when soft was the sun,
I enshrouded me well in a shepherd's garb,
And robed as a hermit, unholy of works,
Went wide through the world, all wonders to hear.
And on a May morning, on Malvern Hills,[2] 5
Strange fancies befell me, and fairy-like dreams.
I was weary of wand'ring, and went to repose
On a broad green bank, by a burn-side;
As I lay there and leaned and looked on the waters, 9
I slumbered and slept, they sounded so merry.

Came moving before me a marvelous vision;
I was lost in a wild waste; but *where*, I discerned not.
I beheld in the east, on high, near the sun,
A tower on a hill-top, with turrets well wrought;
A deep dale beneath, and a dungeon therein, 15
With deep ditches and dark, and dreadful to see.
A fair field, full of folk, I found there between,[3]
Of all manner of men, the mean and the rich,
All working or wand'ring, as the world requires.

Some plowed with the plow; their play was but seldom; 20
Some sowing, some earning, with sweat of their brows,
The gain which the great ones in gluttony waste.

In pride of apparel some passed on their way,
And in costliest clothing were quaintly disguised.
In prayer and in penance some placed their delight, 25
And all for our Lord's love lived strictly and hard,
In hope to have after their heavenly meed;
These hermits and anchorites held to their cells,
Not caring to roam through the country around

For doles of sweet dainties, their flesh to delight. 30

Some chose to be chapmen, to chaffer for gain;
As it seems to our sight, such surely succeed.
And some, to make merry, as minstrels are wont,
Getting gold with their glee, yet guiltless, I trust.
As for jugglers and jesters, all Judas's children,
That feign silly fancies, appareled as fools, 36
Having wit, if they willed it, to work as they ought—
I pass o'er what Paul would have preached of these sinners; [4]
For the speaker of evil is Satan's own son.

Next beggars and beadsmen were bustling about, 40
Their bags and their bellies with bread were well crammed.
By falsehood they fed them, and fought o'er their ale,
As greedy as gluttons they go to their beds,
And rise up as ribalds, these robberlike knaves;
Sleep and vile sloth pursue them forever. 45

Next, pilgrims and palmers would plight them together
To seek out Saint James [5] and saints known in Rome;
They went on their way with many wise tales,
And had leave to tell lies all their lifetime after.
Some saw I that said they had sought out the saints; 50
In each tale that they told their tongue fashioned lies
Much sooner than sooth, as it seemed by their speech.

Of hermits a huge heap, with hooks to their staves,
To Walsingham [6] went; and their wenches went after;
Great lubbers and long, that to labor were loath; 55
They clothed them in cloaks, to be known from all others
And arrayed them as hermits, more ease to enjoy.

I found there some friars of all the four orders,[7]
Who preached to the people for personal profit;
As it seemed to them good, put a gloss on the gospel, 60

[1] From the translation of W. W. Skeat in "The Medieval Library."
[2] In Worcestershire.
[3] The world, midway between heaven and hell.
[4] "If any would not work, neither should he eat" (II Thessalonians, 3:10).
[5] The shrine of St. James at Compostella in Spain.
[6] The shrine of our Lady at Walsingham in Norfolk.
[7] Carmelites, Augustinians, Dominicans, and Minorites or Franciscans.

And explained it at pleasure; they coveted copes.

Many of these masters may wear what they will;

Their money and merchandise meet well together;

Since Charity was chapman, and chief to shrive lords,

What sights we have seen in a few short years!

Unless they and the Church keep closer together,                                                          66

The most mischief e'er made will be mounting up fast.

There preached, too, a pardoner, a priest, as he seemed,

Who brought forth a bull, with the bishop's seals,

And said he himself might absolve them all    70

Of falsehood in fasting, or vows they had broken.

The laymen believed him, and liked well his words,

Came up and came kneeling, to kiss the said bull;

He blessed them right bravely, and blinded their eyes,

And won with his roll both their rings and their brooches.                                                          75

Thus they give up their gold for such gluttons to spend,

And lose to loose livers their lawful gains.

If the bishop were wiser, or worth both his ears,

His seal ne'er were sent, to deceive so the people.

Small blame of the bishop such boys will express;                                                          80

For the parish-priest and pardoner part all the silver

That the poor of the parish would otherwise share.

The parsons and parish-priests complained to the bishop

That their parishes were poor since the pestilence-year,[8]

Asking license and leave in London to dwell,   85

To sing there for simony; for silver is sweet.

Bishops and bachelors, both masters and doctors,

Having cures [9] under Christ, and crowned with the tonsure

To show they should hear their parishoners' shrift,

Preaching and praying, and feeding the poor,  90

Are lodged now in London, in Lent-time and ever.

Some serve there the king, and count out his silver,

In chancery and exchequer make claims of his dues

From wards and from ward-motes,[10] his waifs and his strays.

And some serve as servants both ladies and lords,                                                          95

Are as stewards enstalled, or as judges take seat.

Their masses and matins and many of their prayers

Are done undevoutly. I dread, at the last,

Lest Christ, at the Judgment, will curse not a few.

I pondered on the power that Peter had to keep—                                                          100

"To bind and to unbind"—as the Book tells us.[11]

How he left it, with love, as our Lord him bade,

In trust of four virtues—the best of all virtues—

As "cardinal" known, or "the closing of gates,"

Where Christ's in His kingdom, to close and to shut,                                                          105

Or to open to good men the glory of heaven.[12]

But for cardinals at court, who have caught up the name,

And presume on their power a pope to appoint,

To have Peter's own power—impugn it I dare not;

To learning and love that election belongeth;                                                          110

I might, but I must not, say more of that court.

Then came there a king, with knights in a troop;

The might of the commons had made him to reign;

And then came Kind-Wit,[13] and clerks he appointed

To counsel the king, and the commons to save.

The king and his knights, and the clergy also 116

Decreed that the commons must toil for their bread.

The commons contrived for the craftsmen their trades,

And for profit o' the people set plowmen to work,

To till and to travail, as true life requires;   120

While the king and the commons, with Kind-Wit as third,

Made laws for protecting all loyal men's goods.

Then looked up a lunatic, a lean man withal,

Knelt down to the king, and full clerk-like spake:—

[8] Probably 1348–9, the year of the Great Pestilence.

[9] Spiritual duties.

[10] Ward-meetings.    [11] Matthew, 16:19.

[12] Prudence, Temperance, Fortitude, and Justice are called the four "cardinal," or all-important, virtues. The poet puns on the derivation of "cardinal" from *cardo*, the Latin word for a door-hinge, and connects this idea with that of St. Peter's keys.

[13] Common Sense; or perhaps the natural intelligence enlightened by revelation.

"Christ keep thee, sir king! and thy kingdom
    eke,    125
So to reign in thy land that thy lieges may love
    thee,
And thy righteous rule be rewarded in heaven!"

Then, high in the air, an angel from heaven
Spake loudly in Latin, that laymen might fail
To object or to judge, or justly to doubt,    130
But suffer and serve:—and thus said the
    angel—
"Know, prince, that thy power soon passes
    forever;
Thy kingdom is Christ's, and in keeping His
    laws
Thou 'rt just; but let justice be joined to dis-
    cretion!
Array naked justice in raiment of mercy;    135
Sow wisely such grain as thou gladly wouldst
    reap.
Who deals in bare justice, bare justice be
    dealt him;
To him who has mercy shall mercy be meted."

A riotous rich one, who rambled in talk,
To the angel on high made answer in anger:—
"Since *rex* is derived, sure, from *rego*, I rule,    141
Kings rule by the laws, or they rule but in
    name."

Then cried out the commons, exclaiming in
    Latin,
To the king and his knights (let him construe,
    who will)—
*Precepta regis sunt nobis vincula legis:*    145
"Commandments of kings are the canons of
    law."

Then forth ran a rout of great rats, all at
    once,
Where met them small mice, yea, more than a
    thousand;
All came to a council for their common profit.[14]
For a cat of the court would come, when he
    liked,    150
And chase them and clutch them, and catch
    them at will,
Play with them perilously, and push them
    about:—
"For dread of the danger, look round us we
    dare not;
If we grudge him his game, he will grieve us
    the more,
Tease us or toss us, or take in his claws,    155

[14] "This fable refers to events following the Good
Parliament (1376). The King, Edward III, is the
cat. The rats are certain nobles, desiring to depose
the king (to 'bell the cat'), but lacking the power
and courage to put their plan into effect. The poet
sympathizes with the desire of the nobles to bring
pressure on the rulers, but refuses to go so far as to
favor the deposition of the aged king and the establishment of a regency" (Henry W. Wells).

That we loathe our own lives, ere he lets us
    go free.
If by wit or by wile we his will might with-
    stand,
We might lord it aloft, and might live at our
    ease."

Then a rat of renown, very ready of tongue,
Said, for a sovereign help to themselves,    160
"Some cats have I seen, in the city of London,
Wear chains on their necks of the choicest gold,
Or collars of crafty work; uncoupled they go
Both in warren and waste, as their will inclines,
And elsewhere at odd times, as I hear tell.    165
If they bore each a bell, by its ringing, me
    thinketh,
One might wit where they were, and away
    soon run!
Right so," quoth the rat, "doth reason suggest
To buy a bell of brass or of bright silver,
To be bound on a collar, for our common
    profit,    170
On the cat's neck to hang; then each hearer
    can tell
If he rambles or rests him, or runs out to play!
When mild is his mood, we can move as we
    list
And appear in his presence, when playful and
    pleased,
Or, when angry, beware; and away will we
    run!"    175

All the rout of great rats to his reasons
    assented,
But when bought was the bell, and well bound
    on the collar,
Not a rat in the rout, for the realm of all
    France,
Durst bind the said bell about the cat's neck,
Nor hang it beside him, all England to win!    180
They owned they were cowards, and their
    counsel weak;
So their labor was lost, and all their long study.

Then a mouse of mind, who had merit, me-
    thought,
Strode forth sternly, and stood before them all,
And to the rout of rats rehearsèd these words:
"Though we killed the old cat, yet another
    would come    186
To catch all our kin, though we crept under
    benches.
I counsel the commons to let the cat be;
Be we never so bold as to show him the bell.
For I heard my sire say, some seven years since,
'Where the cat is a kitten, the court is a sad
    one';    191
So witnesseth Scripture, who willeth may read
    it,
*Woe to thee, land, when thy king is a child!* [15]
For no one could rest him, for rats in the night!

[15] Ecclesiastes, 10:16.

While the cat catches rabbits, he covets us less,
But is fed as with venison; defame we him
    never!    196
Better a little loss than a livelong sorrow,
By loss of a loathed one to live in disorder!
For many men's malt we mice would destroy,
And ye, rout of rats, would rend men's clothes,
If the cat of the court could not catch you at
    will!    201
Ye rats, if unruled, could not rule o'er your-
    selves.
I see," quoth the mouse, "such a mischief
    might follow,
Neither kitten nor cat, by my counsel, shall
    suffer;
Nor care I for collars that have cost me noth-
    ing;    205
Had they cost me a crown, I would keep it
    unknown,
And suffer our rulers to rove where they like,
Uncoupled, or coupled, to catch what they can.
I warn well each wise man to ward well his
    own."
What this vision may mean, ye men that are
    merry,    210
Discern ye! I dare not discern it myself!

I saw then a hundred, in hoods all of silk,
All serjeants, it seemed, that served at the bar,
Pleading their causes for pence or for pounds,
But for love of our Lord their lips moved
    never!    215
Sooner measure the mist upon Malvern Hills
Than see a mouth mumble ere money be
    shown!

Barons and burgesses, and bondmen also
I saw in this assembly, as soon ye shall hear;
Bakers and brewers, and butchers full many, 220
Websters of woollen, and weavers of linen,
Tailors and tinkers, and tollers [16] in markets,
Masons and miners, and many other crafts.
Of laborers of all kinds there leapt forth some,
Such as dikers and delvers; ill done was their
    work;    225
They drawled through the day, singing, *Dieu
vous save, dame Emme!* [17]

Cooks and kitchen-lads cried—"Hot pies,
    hot!"—
"Good geese and good bacon!"—"Good din-
    ners! come, dine!"
Taverners touted—"A taste here, for nothing!"
"White wine of Alsace!"—"Red Gascony
    wine!"
"Here's Rhine wine!" "Rochelle wine, your
    roast to digest!"    231
All this saw I sleeping, and seven times more.

[16] Takers of toll.
[17] God save you, Lady Emma! (Evidently the refrain of some popular song.)

## PASSUS V [1]

### THE SEVEN DEADLY SINS

The king and his knights to the kirk went
To hear matins of the day, and the mass after.
Then I waked from my sleep, and was woful
    withal
That I had not slept sounder, and seen much
    more.
Scarce fared I a furlong, ere faintness o'er-
    came me,    5
Nor further could foot it, for default of repose.
Sat I softly adown, and said my belief, [2]
And babbled o'er my beads; which brought me
    asleep.

Then saw I much more than I marked
    hitherto;
The field full of folk I saw, as before,    10
Where Reason was ready to preach to the
    realm;
With a cross, 'fore the king, he commenced
    his teaching.

He proved that the pestilences were purely
    for sin,
And the south-west wind, on Saturday at even, [3]
Was plainly for our pride, and for no point else.
Pear-trees and plum-trees were puffed to the
    earth    16
For example to sinners, to serve God better.
Beeches and broad oaks were blown to the
    ground,
Turning upward their tails, as a token of dread
That deadly sin, at Doomsday, would condemn
    us all.    20

I might, of this matter, be muttering long;
But I say what I saw—so God be my help!—
How plainly Sir Reason 'gan preach to the
    people.

He bade Waster to work at what he knew
    best,
To win what he wasted, with wise employ.    25
Maid Parnel he prayed fine apparel to leave,
And keep it in chests, as a chattel at need.

[1] Canto V. The sections which follow the Prologue describe a series of dreams which come to the
poet while he is resting on Malvern Hills: Holy
Church instructs him in Truth and Love, and warns
him against Falsehood and Flattery; he sees arrangements made for the marriage of Falsehood to
Lady Meed (Reward or Bribery); when the legality
of the union is called in question, Lady Meed is
brought before the king at Westminster; and in the
end her plea is overcome by the arguments of Reason. At the opening of Passus V the poet awakes
for a moment from his dream of the trial at Westminster.
[2] Creed.
[3] The violent tempest on Saturday, 15 January,
1362.

Tom Stow then he taught to take two staves,
And fight for his Phyllis, when ducked for a
    scold!

He warned also Wat that his wife was to
    blame, 30
For her head [4] cost a half-mark, his hood not
    a groat.
He bade also Bat cut a bough or e'en twain,
And beat Betty therewith, unless she would
    work.
He charged also chapmen to chasten their
    children,
Not spoil them, though wealthy, the while
    they were young, 35
Nor please them too fondly, in pestilence-time.
"My sire to me said once, and so did my dame,
'The liefer [5] the child, the more lore it be-
    hooveth';
And Solomon likewise, in Sapience, wrote,
*He that spareth his rod hateth his son.*[6] 40
The sense of this saying, if some one would
    know,
Is, 'who spareth the birch-sprig, his children
    he spoileth.'"

And next he prayed prelates and priests
    together,
"What ye preach to the people, first prove on
    yourselves,
And do so in deed; it will draw you to good; 45
If ye live by your lore, we believe you the
    better."

Religion he counseled his rule to observe,
"Lest the king and his council your commons [7]
    impair,
And be stewards of your steads, till ye're better
    established."

Then he counseled the king the commons to
    love, 50
"'Tis thy treasure 'gainst treason, an antidote
    true."

Then prayed he the pope to have pity on
    the Church;
Ere he granted a grace, first to govern himself.
"Ye that laws have to keep, first covet the
    truth
More than gold or great gifts, if God ye would
    please. 55
The traitor to truth has been told in the Gospel
That neither God knows him, nor saints in the
    skies:
*Verily I say unto you, I know you not.*[8]
Ye that seek [9] to Saint James, and the saints in
    Rome,
Seek rather Saint Truth, who can save you all; 60

Who with Father and Son: [10]—fair hap them
    befall
Who assent to my sermon!"—And thus said
    Sir Reason.

With that ran Repentance, rehearsing the
    text,
And making Will [11] weep many watery tears.

### The Confession of Pride

Maid Parnel Proud-heart fell prone on the
    earth, 65
Lying long ere she looked up, and "Lord,
    mercy!" cried.
She vowed then a vow to the Father in heaven,
Her smock to unsow, and a hair-shirt to wear,
To enfeeble her flesh, that so fierce was to
    sin:—
"Shall no high heart upheave me; I'll hold my-
    self low, 70
And suffer men slight me—and so did I never!
I pray for more meekness, and mercy beseech
For all I have hitherto hated in heart."

### The Confession of Lechery

Then said Lecher, "Alas!"—to our Lady he
    cried
To have mercy, for misdeeds, 'twixt God and
    his soul, 75
And said that on Saturdays, seven years after,
He would drink with the duck, and would dine
    only once!

### The Confession of Envy

Next Envy, with heavy heart, asked to have
    shrift;
As a sorrowful sinner his sins he confessed.
He was pale as a stone, in a palsy he seemed, 80
And clothed in a coarse suit I scarce can de-
    scribe,
In a short coat and kirtle,[12] a knife by his side.
Of a friar's frock were the two fore-sleeves;
Like a leek that has lain too long in the sun
He looked, with his lean cheeks, lowering on
    all. 85
With wrath swelled his body, he bit both his
    lips,
Fast clenching his fists; to avenge him he
    thought
With works or with words, still awaiting his
    time.
He uttered his tales with an adder's tongue;
Chiding and challenging chose he as food; 90
To backbite and blacken, and bear false witness
Was his care and his courtesy, whereso he came.

"I'd be shriven," quoth this shrew, "if for
    shame I might dare;

---

[4] Head-covering.      [5] Dearer.
[6] Proverbs, 13:24.      [7] Provisions.
[8] Matthew, 15:12.      [9] Resort.

[10] An abbreviated formula for ending sermons.
[11] Probably the poet himself and not a personification of the will.
[12] Under-jacket.

My gladness is greater, when Gib fares amiss,
Than in winning a wey [13] of your fine Essex
   cheese!
                              95

   "I've a neighbor full nigh, I annoy him full
     oft,
And belie him to lords, till he loses his pelf;
His friends are made foes through my false re-
   port;
His gains and his good luck oft grieve me full
   sore.
'Twixt household and household such hatred I
   raise                         100
That both lives and limbs have been lost by
   my means.
When I meet him at market whom most I de-
   test,
I heartily hail him in haste, as a friend;
He's more doughty than I, so I dare do naught
   else;
Had I mast'ry and might, God knows my de-
   sire!                       105

   "When I come to the kirk, and should kneel
     to the cross,
And pray for the people, as teacheth the priest,
For pilgrims and palmers, and people at large,
Then I cry on my knees, 'may Christ give him
   sorrow
Who bore off my bowl, or my broken plate!' 110
Away from the altar then turn I mine eyes,
And note how Elaine hath a new-made gown;
I wish it were mine, with the rest of the web.

   "I laugh when men lose, for that my heart
     liketh;
I weep when they win, and bewail the time; 115
I doom the ill-doer, myself doing worse;
With him that upbraids me I'm angry forever.
I would that each wight were my servant and
   slave;
Who hath what I have not, him hate I full sore.
Thus loveless I live, like a low-bred cur,   120
That my body nigh bursts for bitterest gall.

   "I oft cannot eat, as a man ought to do,
For envy and ill-will are hard to digest.
Can no sugar nor sweet thing assuage my
   swelling,
Nor medicinal drug drive it out of my heart,
Nor yet shrift nor shame, save my maw be
   scraped?"                  126

   "Yes; readily," said Repentance, "this rule is
     the best—
Sorrow for sins is salvation of souls."

   "I am sorry," quoth that sinner, "I am sel-
     dom aught else;
This makes me so meager—I miss my revenge!
I have been among burgesses, dwelling in Lon-
   don,                       131

[13] Weight of 336 pounds.

Getting brokers to backbite and blame men's
   ware.

   "If my neighbor could sell, while I sold not,
     right soon
Would I lower and lie, and lay on him blame.
I'll amend, if I may, by th' Almighty's
   help!"                      135

### The Confession of Wrath

Now Wrath awaketh, with two white eyes;
He sniveled with his nose, with a neck low
   bent.

   "I am Wrath," quoth he; "I once was a friar,
And the convent-gardener, to graft young
   shoots.
On limiters and lectors such lies I engrafted, [14]
They bore leaves of low-speech, great lords for
   to please,               141
And then blossomed abroad, to hear shrifts in
   bowers, [15]
Till there fell this fruit—that folk would far
   rather
Show shrifts unto them than be shriven by
   priests.

   "Now that priests have perceived how friars
     claim part,              145
These prebend'ries preach, and deprave the
   friars.
Then friars find fault, as the folk bear witness,
And preach to the people in places around;
I, Wrath, with them rove, and teach them to
   rail.
Thus clerks of the Church one another con-
   temn                   150
Till both are but beggars, and live by their beg-
   ging,
Or else all are rich, and go riding about.
I, Wrath, never rest, but rove evermore,
And follow these false ones; for such is my
   grace.

   "My aunt is a nun, and an abbess to boot; 155
She sooner would swoon than once suffer a
   pain.
I was cook in her kitchen, the convent I served
For many a month; and with monks have I
   stayed;
Made pottage for the prioress, and other poor
   dames.
Their broth was to backbite—'Dame Joan is a
   bastard'—              160
'Dame Clarice, a knight's girl, a cuckold's her
   sire'—
'Dame Parnel's a priest's wench, a prioress
   never;

[14] I taught such lies to those sent out by their convents to beg within certain limits, and to church-
readers.
[15] Ladies' chambers.

She childed in cherry-time, the chapter all
    know it.'

"Their worts [16] I commingled with wicked
    words,
Till 'liar!' and 'liar!' leapt forth from their
    lips,   165
And each hit the other just under the cheek;
They had dealt many deaths, had daggers been
    near!

"Saint Gregory, pope,[17] had a good fore-
    knowledge,
And granted no prioress power to shrive;
For surely, with women, no secret is safe!  170

"To remain among monks I mostly refuse;
Too keen are some brothers my counsels to spy,
Such as prior, sub-prior, and *pater* [18] the abbot.
If I tell any tales, they take me to task,
And make me fast Fridays on bread and on
    water.  175
I am chidden in chapter-house, like to a child,
And beaten on bare flesh, rebuked and abused.
With such men to linger small liking is mine;
Salt fish is their diet, and feeblest of ale.
If wine, once a while, in my way comes at
    eve,  180
I defame them, with foul mouth, some five days
    after.
All sins I had seen any brother consent to
I discussed in the cloister; the convent soon
    knew them."

"Repent," quoth Repentance; "rehearse
    nevermore
Such facts as thou findest by favor or right; [185]
Nor drink over deeply, nor delicate drafts,
Lest rashly thy will unto wrath should incline.
Be sober," he said; and absolved him thereafter,
Bade him weep with good will, and his wicked-
    ness mend.

### The Confession of Avarice

Next Coveting came; whom I scarce can
    describe;  190
So hungry and hollow Sir Harvey appeared.
He had beetling brows, coarse bulging lips,
And two bleary eyes, like a blind old hag;
Like a leathern purse were his loose-hung
    cheeks,
Lower than his chin low-drooping with age. [195]
His beard, like a boor's, was beslobbered with
    bacon;
A hood on his head, and a lousy old hat;
In a tawny tabard, some twelve years old,
All tattered and torn, with lice for its tenants;—
By nature a louse is a lively leaper,  200
Or it could not have crawled on that thread-
    bare cloth.

"I've been covetous," quoth that caitiff, "I
    confess it here;
For some time I served old Sim at-the-Stile,
And was plighted his 'prentice, his profit to
    serve.
First learnt I, in lying, a lesson or twain;  205
Wickedly to weigh was my first lesson;
To Weyhill [19] and Winchester I went to the
    fair
With all manner of wares, as my master bade;
If Guile had not given some grace to my ware,
It had still been unsold, were it seven years
    since!  210

"Then I drew me to drapers, my duties to
    learn,
To stretch out the stuff, till it looked the longer.
One lesson I learnt as to long striped cloths;
To pierce them with a needle, and piece them
    together,
Put them in a press, and press them thereunder
Till ten yards or twelve were turned to thir-
    teen!  216

"My wife was a weaver, and woollen cloth
    made;
She spoke to the spinners to spin it well out;
But the pound that she paid by surpassed by a
    quarter
The standard of weight that the steelyard [20]
    gave!  220
I barley-malt bought her, she brewed it to sell,
Thick ale and thin ale she thoroughly mingled
For laborers and low folk; this lay by itself.
The best ale in bower or bed-room we kept;
He that tasted thereof was contented to buy it,
A groat for a gallon; he gave never less;  226
Yet it came forth in cups; [21] such craft would
    she use.
Rose the Retailer she rightly was named;
The trade of a huckster is hers, as at first.
I swear now, so thrive I! that sin will I leave,
Nor chaffer so falsely, nor false measures use,
But wend unto Walsingham, and with me my
    wife,  232
And pray Bromholm-rood [22] to reprieve me
    from sin."

"Hast never repented, nor made restitution?"
"Yes; once was I housed with a host of chap-
    men;  235
I rose while they rested, and rifled their bags."

"That was no restitution, but a robber's deed;
For which thou more highly hast claim to be
    hanged
Than for all the misdeeds thou hast hitherto
    done."

[16] Vegetables.      [17] Gregory IX, d. 1241.
[18] Father.

[19] In Hampshire.      [20] Scales.
[21] To prevent accurate measurement.
[22] The Cross of Bromholm, in Norfolk.

"I thought theft restitution; for read could I
    never;    240
Such French as I know is of further Norfolk."

"Was usury ever a usage of thine?"
"Nay, soothly!" he answered, "except in my
    youth.
I learnt among Lombards and Jews this lesson,
To weigh the king's pence, and the heavy ones
    pare,    245
And lend them (to lose them) for love of the
    pledge;
So I worded the deed, if the day should be
    broken.
More manors are mine through arrears than
    mercy.

"I have lent things to lords, and to ladies
    also,
And then been their broker, and bought them
    myself.    250
Exchanges and loans are the chaffer I deal with.
When I lend, of each noble [23] a portion they
    lose;
And with letters of Lombards bear money to
    Rome,
Here take it by tally, there tell it as less."

"Hast lent aught to lords, for love of their
    aid?"    255
"I have lent oft to lords, that ne'er loved me
    thereafter,
And made of a knight both a mercer and
    draper [24]
Who paid, as apprentice, not one pair of
    gloves!"

"Hast thou pity on poor men, persuaded to
    borrow?"
"Such pity on poor men, as a pedlar on cats;
Could he catch them, he'd kill them; he cov-
    ets their skins."    261

"Dost deal out to neighbors thy drink and
    thy meat?"
"I'm as courteous," he cried, "as a cur in a
    kitchen;
Such a name, among neighbors, is noted as
    mine!"

"Now God never grant thee, unless thou
    repent,    265
His grace, on this ground, thy goods to bestow,
Nor thine heirs have, after thee, aught of thy
    gains,
Nor executors spend well the silver thou leavest!
What was wrongfully won will be wickedly
    spent.
Were I friar of a house, where faith is and
    love,    270

Thy coin should not clothe us, nor our kirk
    amend,
Nor a penny of thine should our pittance im-
    prove
For the best book we have, though bright gold
    were the leaves,
If I knew for a sooth thou wert such as thou
    sayest,
Or could witness, by watching, thy works and
    thy ways.    275
*Seek a man's feasts, and you serve him as slave;*
*Live on thy loaf, and thy life then is free!*
Thou'rt a creature unkind, whom I cannot
    assoil
Till thou make restitution, and reckon with all.
Till Reason enroll, i' th' register of heaven,    280
Thou hast made full amends, I may not ab-
    solve thee:—
*The sin is not remitted, till the stolen thing be*
    *restored.*
All that gain by thy goods, so God have my
    troth!
At the high day of doom, must help thee re-
    store.
Who sees not this sooth, let him seek in the
    Psalter,    285
In *Miserere-mei*,[25] that I mean the truth:—
*Behold, thou desirest truth in the inward*
    *parts.*[26]
No workman i' th' world shall thrive on thy
    winnings;
*Cum sancto eris sanctus*; expound that in Eng-
    lish:—
*With the holy thou shalt be holy.*" [27]    290

Then lost he all hope, and himself would
    have hanged,
Had not quickly Repentance the wretch reas-
    sured—
"Keep mercy in mind, and with mouth implore
    it;
God's mercy is more than His mightiest
    works:—
*His mercy is over all his works.*[28]    295
All the wickedness i' th' world that men work
    or devise
Is no more, to God's mercy, than sparks in the
    main:—
*All iniquity, compared with God's mercy, is as*
    *a spark in the midst of the sea.*
Keep mercy in mind, and thy merchandise
    leave;
Thou hast no better way to win thee a loaf    300
Than by aid of thy tongue or thy two good
    hands.
The gain thou hast gotten began with deceit,
And while buying therewith, thou wast bor-
    rowing ever!

"If thou wit not whereby or to whom to re-
    store,

---

[23] A gold coin.
[24] Since he had to take part of the loan in goods.

[25] Have mercy on me.    [26] Psalms, 51:6.
[27] Psalms, 18:25.    [28] Psalms, 145:9.

Bear it to the bishop; beseech him, of grace, [305]
To bestow it himself as is best for thy soul.
He shall answer for thee, at the awful doom,
For thee and for many that man shall ac-
count—
As his lore was in Lent (believe this is true)—
How the Lord's grace he lent you, to lead you
from sin." [310]

### The Confession of Gluttony

Now beginneth Sir Glutton to go to his
shrift;
His course is to kirkward, as culprit to pray.
But Betty the brewster just bade him "Good-
morrow,"
And asked him therewith as to whither he went.

"To holy church haste I, to hear me a
mass, [315]
And straight to be shriven, and sin nevermore."
"Good ale have I, gossip; Sir Glutton, assay it!"
"But hast thou hot spices at hand, in thy bag?"
"I have pepper and peony-seed, and a pound of
garlic,
And a farthingworth of fennel-seed, for fasting-
days." [320]

Then Glutton goes in, and with him great
oaths.
Cicely the shoe-seller sat on the bench,
The warrener [29] Wat, and his wife also,
Timothy the tinker, with two of his lads,
The hackney-man Hick, the needle-man Hugh,
Clarice of Cock-lane,[30] the clerk of the
church, [326]
Davy the ditcher, and a dozen others;
Sir Piers the priest, and Parnel of Flanders,
A fiddler, a ratcatcher, a Cheapside raker,[31]
A rider,[32] a rope-seller, dish-selling Rose, [330]
Godfrey of Garlickhithe, Griffin of Wales,
And a heap of upholsterers, early assembled,
Gave Glutton, with glad cheer, a treat of good
ale.

Then Clement, the cobbler, cast off his cloak,
Which he offered to any, by way of ex-
change; [335]
Hick the hackney-man hitched off his hood,
And bade Bat the butcher to be on his side.
Then chapmen were chosen the choice to ap-
praise;
He that hath but the hood shall have more for
amends.

Two rose up in haste, and reasoned to-
gether, [340]
Appraising these pen'orths apart by themselves.
They could not, in conscience, accord together

Till Robin the roper arose from his place,
And was ordered, as umpire, to end the dispute,
And tell the true value between them at
last. [345]

So Hickey the ostler laid hold of the cloak,
In covenant that Clement should fill up his
cup,
And have Hick's hood, the ostler's, and hold
him content;
Who soonest repented must after arise,
And grant to Sir Glutton a gallon of ale. [350]

There was laughing and lowering, and "let
go the cup!" [33]
They sat so till evensong, and sung now and
then,
Till Glutton had gulped down a gallon and a
gill.[34]

\* \* \*

He neither could step, nor without a staff
stand;
Then began he to go like a gleeman's dog,[35] [355]
Sometimes aside, and sometimes arear,
Like one that lays lines, young larks to en-
snare.

As he drew to the door, then dim grew his
eyes,
He was tripped by the threshold and thrown to
the earth.
Clement the cobbler him caught by the mid-
dle, [360]
To lift him aloft, and he laid on his knees;
But Glutton, that great churl, was grievous to
lift,
And coughed up a caudle in Clement's lap;
So hungry no hound is in Hertfordshire lane
As would lap up the leavings, unlovely of
scent. [365]

With all woe in the world his wife and his
wench
Bore him home to his bed, and brought him
therein,
And after this surfeit he slept, in his sloth,
All Saturday and Sunday, till sunset had come.
Then woke he in wonder, and wiped both his
eyes; [370]
The word he first uttered was—"Where is the
bowl?"
His wife sadly warned him, how wicked his
ways,
And Repentance full rightly rebuked him of
sin:—
"Both in words and in works thou hast wrought
much evil,

---

[29] Game-keeper.
[30] A section of London inhabited by women of ill
repute.
[31] Scavenger.    [32] Groom.

[33] Pass the cup round.
[34] Skeat here omits five lines in which some of the
first consequences of Glutton's drinking are graphi-
cally described.
[35] A dog who led a blind minstrel.

Now shrive thee with shame, and show me thy
   sins."             375

"I, Glutton," he granted, "am guilty indeed;
I have trespassed with tongue, I can tell not
   how oft,
Have sworn 'by God's soul,' and 'so help me
   the saints,'
Where never was need, nine hundred of times.
I'd a surfeit at supper, and sometimes at
   noon,             380
Till I, Glutton, it gulped up, ere gone was a
   mile,
And spilt what should spared be, and spent on
   the hungry.
Too delicately, on fast-days, I drank and ate
   both,
And sat sometimes so long that I slept while I
   ate.
To hear tales, in taverns, to drink more, I
   dined,           385
And feasted ere noon, when the fasting-days
   came."
"This showing of shrift shall be to thy merit."

   Then Glutton 'gan groan; great mourning he
   made
For the loathsome life he had lived such a
   while;
And vowed he would fast:—"For hunger or
   thirst           390
Shall no fish on the Friday be found in my maw
Till Abstinence, my aunt, hath accorded me
   leave;
And yet have I hitherto hated her ever!"

### The Confession of Sloth

   Then came Sloth all beslobbered, with two
   slimy eyes;
"I must sit," quoth this sinner, "or else shall I
   doze;           395
I stand not, nor stoop, nor kneel without stool.
Were I brought to my bed, save for bitterest
   need,
Should no ringing arouse me, ere ripe time for
   dinner."
*Benedictite* he began, and smote on his breast;
He grumbled, and stretched him, and grunted
   at last.           400

   "Awake!" quoth Repentance, "make ready
   for shrift."

"This day should I die, no duties for me!
*Paternoster* I know not, as priests intone it,
But rhymes of Robin Hood, or Randolph of
   Chester; [36]
Of our Lady or Lord, not the least ever made!
Forty vows have I made, and forgot them the
   morrow;         406

[36] Earl of Chester, 1181–1231 or 1232.

I performed never penance as the priest ap-
   pointed;
Right sorry for my sins as yet was I never.
If I bid any beads,[37] but it be in my wrath,
What I tell with my tongue is two miles from
   my heart.         410
Each day am I occupied, holidays and others,
With idle tales at ale-house, and sometimes in
   churches;
God's pain and His passion I ponder on seldom.

   "I visit no feeble men, or fettered men in
   jails;
I'd soon hear ribaldry, or summer-games [38] of
   cobblers,         415
Or lying tales to laugh at, and belie my neigh-
   bors,
Than all that e'er Mark wrote, John, Matthew,
   or Luke.
All vigils and fastdays I simply let slide,
And lie abed in Lent, in a lazy sleep,
Till past matins and mass; then I move to the
   friars;         420
To come to the mass-end, for me, is enough.
I seldom am shriven, save sickness impel me,
Not twice in two years; when I shrive me by
   guess!
I've been parson and priest past thirty long
   years,
Yet I sing not, nor *sol-fa*,[39] nor Saints' Lives
   read;         425
I can find in a field or a furlong [40] a hare
Better than in *beatus-vir* or in *beati-omnes*.[41]
Construe a clause, or full clearly expound it.
I can hold well lovedays,[42] or hear a reeve's
   reckoning,
But in canon-law and decretals can read not a
   line.         430

   "If I buy aught and pledge it—but it be on
   the tally—
I forget it right soon; and, when settlement's
   sought,
Six times or seven I forswear it with oaths;
Thus true men I trouble ten hundred of times.

   "My servingmen's salary is sometimes be-
   hind;         435
Rueful is the reckoning, to read the accounts;
With wrath and ill-will all my workmen I pay.

   "If a service is shown me, or succor at need,
I requite it unkindly; I cannot conceive it;
For I have, and have had, the ways of a
   hawk,         440
Being lured, not by love, but by meat in the
   hand.

   "The favors my fellows once fondly accorded,
I, Sloth, have forgotten them sixty times since;

[37] Say any prayers.      [38] Probably May games.
[39] Sing by notes.      [40] Furrow.
[41] In Psalms, 1 or 128.
[42] Days for the arbitration of disputes.

In speech, or in sparing speech, spoilt many
   times
Both flesh-meat and fishes, and many such
   victuals:       445
Both bread and eke ale, milk, butter, and
   cheese,
Would I waste in my service, till none would
   they serve.

"I ran wild in youth, still refusing to learn,
And since, for my sloth, as a beggar subsisted.
*How barren, alas! was the life of my youth!"* 450

"Dost repent?" quoth Repentance; and
   straightway he swooned;
V*igilate*, the watchful, drew water from his eyes
Which he flung in his face, and with firmness
   of speech
Said, "Beware of Despair, that will work thee
   but woe;
'I am sorry for my sins,' thus say to thyself, 455
And beat on thy breast, and beseech God's
   grace;
No guilt is so great but His goodness is more."

Then sat Sloth up, made the sign of the
   cross,
And vowed, before God, for his foul neglect:—
"Each Sunday, for seven years, except I am
   sick,    460
Will I draw me, ere day, to the dear-loved
   church,
To hear matins and mass, like a monk devout.
No ale after meat shall hold me thence
Till I've evensong heard; so help me the Rood!
Of wealth will I strip me, and strive to re-
   store    465
What I wickedly won by my cunning wits.
Though I lack good living, no labor I'll spare
Till each have his own, ere I hence depart;
And with help of the remnant, by the rood of
   Chester,
Will I seek Saint Truth, ere I see far Rome!"

Robert the robber was fain to restore;   471
But wealth had he none, wherefore sorely he
   wept.
The sorrowing sinner thus said to himself:—
"Christ, that on Calvary didst die on the cross,
When Dismas my brother besought Thee for
   grace,    475
And had mercy on the man who 'Remember
   me' said,[43]
Have ruth on the robber that naught can re-
   store,
Nor ween to win wealth with skill of my own.
Mitigation I pray for; Thy mercy is great,
Nor condemn me at Doomsday for deeds I did
   ill."    480

What befell of this felon I failed to discern;
With both his eyes water, I wot well, he wept,

[43] Luke, 23:42.

And acknowledged moreover his crimes unto
   Christ
Till Penitence, his pike-staff, was polished
   anew,
To leap with, o'er land, while his life should
   endure.[44]    485

\*    \*    \*

Then Repentance had ruth, and advised
   them to kneel:—
"For sinners I pray to our Savior for grace
To amend our misdeeds, and show mercy to all.
Now, God! that in goodness the great world
   didst make,
Of naught madest all, and man most like Thy-
   self,    490
And didst suffer him to sin, which was sickness
   to all,
Yet all for the best, as the book [45] hath ex-
   pressed:—
*Oh happy fault! Oh necessary sin of Adam!*
Thy Son, through that sin, was sent to this
   earth,
Made man of a maid, mankind for to save; 495
Like Thyself and Thy Son we sinners were
   made;
*Let us make man in our image, after our like-
ness.*[46]
*He that dwelleth in love, dwelleth in God, and
God in him.*[47]
And since, in Thy Son, in our suit didst die
On Good Friday, for man's sake, at full time
   of day;    500
Nor Thyself, nor Thy Son, didst feel sorrow
   in death,
In our suit [48] was the sorrow; Thy Son led it
   captive:—
*He led captivity captive.*[49]

"The sun then, for sorrow, lost sight for a
   time;
At midday, when's most light, the mealtime of
   saints,    505
Thou fed'st, with Thy fresh blood, our forefathers in darkness;—
*The people that walked in darkness have seen
a great light.*[50]
By the light that then leapt out was Lucifer
   blinded;
It blew all Thy blessèd to Paradise' bliss.

"The third day thereafter saw Thee in our
   suit;    510
Frail Mary beheld Thee ere Mary Thy mother;
To solace all sinners Thou sufferedst thus:—
*I am not come to call the righteous, but sin-
ners to repentance.*[51]

[44] Skeat here omits a line which may be translated:
"For he had lain with Latro (Robbery), Lucifer's
aunt."
[45] The Sarum Missal.    [46] Genesis, 1:26.
[47] I John, 4:16.    [48] Flesh.
[49] Psalms, 68:18.    [50] Isaiah, 9:2.
[51] Matthew, 9:13.

All that Mark ever made, John, Matthew, and
Luke—
Thy doughtiest deeds—were done in our ar-
mor:—                                            515
*The word was made flesh, and dwelt among
us.*[52]
By so much, me seemeth, more surely may we
Both pray and beseech, if it be Thy will,
Our Father and Brother, Thy mercy be shown
us;
Have ruth on these ribalds, repenting them
sorely                                            520
They wrought Thee to wrath, in word, thought,
or deed."

Then Hope seized a horn, *Thou-shalt-
quicken-us-again,*[53]
And blew it with *blessed-is-he-whose-sin-is-
forgiven,*[54]
Till saints high in heaven all sang in accord:—
*O Lord, Thou preservest man and beast; how
excellent is Thy loving-kindness.*[55]     525

A thousand of men then came thronging to-
gether,
Crying upward to Christ and His kindly mother
That grace might go with them, to seek Saint
Truth.

No wight was so wise that the way there he
knew;
They blundered, like beasts, over banks and
o'er hills,                                       530
A long while, till late, when a lithe one they
met,
Appareled as a pagan, in pilgrim's guise.
He bare him a staff, with a broad strip bound,
That round it was twined like a woodbine's
twist;
A bowl and a bag he bare by his side;        535
A hundred of vials[56] were set on his hat,
Signs from Sinai, Galician[57] shells;
With crosses on his cloak, and the keys of
Rome,
And the vernicle[58] before, for that men should
discern
And see by his signs what shrines he had
sought.                                          540

Then fain would this folk know from whence
he had come?
"From Sinai," he said, "and the Sepulcher
Holy,
Bethlehem and Babylon, I've been in them
both,

Armenia, Alexandria, and other like places.
Ye may see by the signs that here sit on my
hat                                              545
I have walkèd full widely, in wet and in dry,
And sought out good saints, for the health of
my soul."
"Know'st thou a saint men entitle Saint Truth?
Canst thou walk in the way now, to where He
resides?"

"Nay," said the good man, "so God be my
guide,                                           550
I saw never palmer with pikestaff or scrip
That asked for Him ever, ere now in this
place!"

"By Peter!" quoth a plowman,[59] and put
forth his head,
"I know him as closely as clerk doth his books!
Through Conscience and Kind-Wit I ken
where He dwelleth;                               555
They safely ensured me to serve Him forever,
Both to sow and to set, while my strength shall
endure.
I have faithfully followed Him fifty long years,
Both sown Him His seed, and His cattle pre-
served;
Within and without have I watched o'er His
profit.                                          560
I dike and I delve, and do that He biddeth;
Sometimes I sow, and sometimes I thrash;
I am tailor or tinker, as Truth doth appoint;
I weave or I wind, doing what so He biddeth.

"Though I say it myself, my service He
values;                                          565
I have meed in good measure, and sometimes
have more;
None prompter to pay can a poor man find,
He withholds none His hire; He hath it at
even.
He's lowly as a lamb, and loving in speech;
And would ye now wit well, where that He
dwelleth,                                        570
Full well can I wend on my way to His place."

"Yea, Piers!" quoth the pilgrims, and proffered him hire
To teach them the true way to Truth's own
abode.

"By my soul's health," quoth Piers, and was
fain for to swear,
"Not a farthing I finger, for Saint Thomas's
shrine!                                          575
Truth would love me the less for a long time
after.
But would ye now wend there, the way there
is this
That I set now before you; I say you the
sooth.—

---

[52] John 1:14.             [53] Psalms, 71:20.
[54] Psalms, 32:1.          [55] Psalms, 36:6.
[56] Signifying that he had visited the shrine of St.
Thomas at Canterbury.
[57] From the shrine of St. James at Compostella in
Galicia, Spain.
[58] Copy of St. Veronica's handkerchief, impressed
with the image of Christ. It signified that he had
made a pilgrimage to Rome.
[59] Piers the plowman. This is his first appearance
in the poem.

Commence it through Meekness, ye men and
    ye women,
Till ye come unto Conscience; let Christ know
    the truth         580
How ye love well our Lord as the liefest of
    things,
And your neighbor the next, and in no wise
    requite him
Otherwise than thou wouldst he should do to
    thyself.
Bend forth by a brook named Be-courtly-of-
    speech,
Till ye find there a ford, called Honor-your-
    fathers:—       585
*Honor thy father and thy mother:* [60]
Wade through that water, and wash you well
    there;
Ye shall leap then the lightlier, your lifetime
    after!
Then see shall ye Swear-not-except-ye-have-
    need-
And-name-not-in-vain-the-great-name-of-the-
    Lord.       590

    "Next come near a croft, but ne'er come
    ye therein;
That croft is called Covet-not-men's-cattle-or-
    wives-
And-none-of-their-servants-that-might-them-an-
    noy;
So break ye no boughs there, save boughs of
    your own.
Two stocks there are standing, but stay ye not
    there,       595
Named Steal-not and Slay-not, but slip by them
    both,
Leave them on the left hand, and look not upon
    them;
And Hold-well-thy-holiday-holy-till-even.
Next bend past a barrow, Bear-no-false-witness,
'Tis fenced in with florins and other like fees;
Then pluck thou no plant there, for peril of
    thy soul.       601
Then see shall ye Say-Sooth-as-sooth-is-indeed-
And-otherwise-never-at-no-one's-request.
Next come to a court, as clear as the sun,
Its moat is of Mercy, the manor around,     605
The walls are of Wit, to guard against Will,
Embattled with Christendom, Christians to
    save,
Buttressed with Believe-so-or-savéd-be-never.
The house is all covered, both chambers and
    halls,
Not with lead, but with Love, and Low-speech-
    of-brethren;       610
The bridge is of Pray-well-the-better-to-speed;
Each pillar, of Penance or Prayers-to-the-Saints,
And of Almsdeeds, the hooks whereon hung are
    the gates.

    "Grace is the gate-ward, a good man for-
    sooth;

[60] Exodus, 20:12.

His man is Amend-you, full many men know
    him.       615
Tell him this token, which Truth will approve,
'I performed all the penance the priest did en-
    join,
And am sorry for my sins, and so shall be ever
When thoughts of them throng me, yea,
    though I were pope!'
Pray Amend-you full meekly his Master to
    ask       620
To throw wide the wicket the woman once shut
When Adam and Eve ate their apples un-
    roasted:—
*Through Eve was it closed to all, and through*
    *the Virgin Mary was it opened again.*
For His is the key, though the king should
    slumber.
If Grace shall once grant thee to go through
    the gate,       625
Thou shalt see, in thyself, Truth sit in thine
    heart,
In a chain of Charity, a child as thou wert,
To suffer but say naught, gainst will of thy sire.
Beware then of Wrath-thee, most wicked of all,
He hath envy of Him that should sit in thine
    heart,       630
And putteth forth Pride and the Praise-of-
    thyself;
Thy boasting of benefits maketh thee blind,
Till out thou art driven, and the door shut fast,
And closed with a key, to keep thee outside
A hundred years, haply, ere ever thou en-
    ter.       635
Thus thou losest His love, by uplifting thy-
    self,
Ne'er, haply, to enter, save only by grace.

    "There are seven sweet sisters that serve
    Truth forever.
Porters of posterns assigned to that place.
Abstinence is one, and Humility next,     640
Charity and Chastity, chief of His maidens,
Patience and Peace, many people they help;
And Largesse, the lady that lets many in;
From the pinfold of hell she hath helped out
    a thousand.
He that kinship can claim with these sisters
    seven       645
Is wondrously welcome, and well is receivéd.
And except ye're akin to some one of the seven
'Tis full hard, by my head, for any of you all
To go through the gate there, save grace may
    be yours."

    "By Christ!" quoth a cutpurse, "no kin have
    I there!"       650
"Nor I," quoth an ape-ward, "for aught that I
    know."
"Wist I," quoth a wafer-man,[61] "such were the
    truth,
No further I'd foot it, by friars' advice!"

[61] Confectioner, whose occupation frequently allowed him to serve as a go-between.

"Yes!" quoth Piers Plowman (their profit he
  sought),
"Mercy's a maid there, hath might over all, 655
Akin to all sinners, as her Son is also;
By help of these two (there is hope in none
  other)
Grace shalt thou get there, by going betimes."

"By Saint Paul," quoth a pardoner, "perhaps
  I'm unknown there;
Where's my brief-box, my bull, and my bishop's
  letters?"                                   660

A common wench cried—"Thy companion
  I'll be,
And say I'm thy sister; but see! they are gone!"

# Geoffrey Chaucer

## c. 1340 - 1400

Chaucer was born in London, the son of a wine-merchant who was in some way connected with the court of Edward III. He is the earliest English writer about whose life and works we have reasonably full knowledge. Though our knowledge of his life is confined almost exclusively to its external course, still, what we do know is definite and dependable. The reason is that Chaucer from an early age was connected with the English court or government, so that the outlines of his public career can be traced from documentary evidence. We first hear of him as attached to the household of the wife of Prince Lionel, the third son of Edward III, in 1357. The only known evidence concerning the date of Chaucer's birth is contained in testimony he gave in a suit in 1386, when he stated that he was forty years or more of age and had borne arms for twenty-seven years. This statement agrees with the record of his service with the English army in France in 1359 (when he was taken prisoner by the French), and suggests 1340 as a probable date for his birth. In the absence of knowledge this generally accepted date is open to question, and an attempt has been made to show, from what has been learned of the ages at which youths took arms, that Chaucer may have been born as late as 1345. This seems improbable, though perhaps he was born in 1342 or 1343. He may have studied law at some time between 1360 and 1367; in the latter year he was granted a pension for his services as valet in the king's household. Probably about this time Chaucer married Philippa, a lady who is thought to have been a sister-in-law of John of Gaunt. In 1372–1373 he was sent on a diplomatic mission to Italy. In 1374 he was given a post in the customs. In 1377 he was in Flanders and France on diplomatic service, and in 1378 went again to Italy. In 1382 he was given an additional post in the customs and three years later was allowed to exercise his office through a deputy. In 1386 he sat as a member of Parliament for Kent; in the same year he was for some reason deprived of his offices in the customs. Later he again held public offices, being appointed clerk of the king's works at Westminster in 1389 and holding the same office at Windsor in 1390, while he received a pension which was increased in 1394 and again in 1399; but despite this help Chaucer seems to have been in some financial difficulty from the time of his reverses in 1386 until shortly before his death. He died in 1400 and was buried in Westminster Abbey.

Chaucer's literary career has been divided into three periods: the French and Latin period (to 1373), the Italian period (1373–1385), and the English period (1385–1400). This division is convenient and is roughly in accordance with the facts. It should be kept in mind, however, that it is only approximate and that the so-called periods are not mutually exclusive. As a young man Chaucer made himself familiar with what was closest to hand—the Latin literature that was known to everyone of any education, and French poetry of his own time or shortly before. His acquaintance with the work of Dante, Petrarch, and Boccaccio probably dates from his first Italian journey in 1373. All that he learned from these varied sources was of use to him throughout his life, and what is meant in terming his last fifteen years an "English" period is that his apprenticeship was definitely over, and that he then wrote with a free command of his material which enabled him, more clearly than before, to exhibit himself in his work. In his first period Chaucer translated at least parts of the French Romance of the Rose, an allegorical poem of the thirteenth century, and wrote the Book of the Duchess, which shows the influence of French allegorical love poetry. In his second period he began, but did not finish, The House of Fame, he wrote The Parliament of Fowls, he translated Boethius' Consolation of Philosophy, *and he wrote* Troilus and Criseyde, *a long and highly finished narrative poem based upon, and in part translated from, Boccaccio's Filostrato. In his third period he wrote* The Legend of Good Women *and* The Canterbury Tales, *leaving both unfinished.*

*Chaucer won for himself immediately a foremost place in literature, and his works exerted a dominating influence upon later poets in the fifteenth and sixteenth centuries. He was a supreme story-teller, and a keen observer of human nature; his tolerance and breadth of view have seldom been equalled among writers in any language. Chaucer loved life, and made the most of it; his good humor and spirit of affirmation are infectious.*

*The editions of Chaucer which are most useful to the scholar are* The Complete Works, *ed. Walter W. Skeat (Oxford, 1894–1897) and (of the tales alone)* The Text of the Tales, Studied on the Basis of All Known Manuscripts, *edited in 8 volumes by J. M. Manly and Edith Rickert (Chicago, 1940); a good compact edition is* The Complete Works of Geoffrey Chaucer, *ed. F. N. Robinson, the "Cambridge Poets" (Boston, 1957).*

*Information about the poet and his work is found in Robert D. French's* Chaucer Handbook *(New York, 1947). Interpretative and background studies include George L. Kittredge,* Chaucer and his Poetry *(Cambridge, U. S. A., 1915); John L. Lowes,* Geoffrey Chaucer and the Development of his Genius *(Boston, 1934); Robert K. Root,* The Poetry of Chaucer; a Guide to its Study and Appreciation, *revised edition (Boston, 1922); Muriel Bowden,* A Commentary on the General Prologue *(New York, 1948); Nevill Coghill,* The Poet Chaucer *(Oxford, 1949); J. S. P. Tatlock,* The Mind and Art of Chaucer *(Syracuse, 1950); John Speirs,* Chaucer The Maker *(London, 1951); and G. H. Gerould,* Chaucerian Essays *(Princeton, 1952). For the contemporary background see George G. Coulton,* Chaucer and his England *(London, 1908), and Jules J. Jusserand,* English Wayfaring Life in the Middle Ages, *trans. L. Toulmin Smith, revised edition (London, 1921).*

# The Canterbury Tales

## The Prologue [1]

Whan that Aprille with his shoures sote
The droghte of Marche hath perced to the rote,
And bathed every veyne in swich licour,

[1] The *Prologue*, besides describing the pilgrims, outlines Chaucer's general design. This calls for

Of which vertu engendred is the flour;
Whan Zephirus eek with his swete breeth    5
Inspired hath in every holt and heeth
The tendre croppes, and the yonge sonne
Hath in the Ram [2] his halfe cours y-ronne,
And smale fowles maken melodye,
That slepen al the night with open yë,    10
(So priketh hem nature in hir corages):
Than longen folk to goon on pilgrimages
(And palmers for to seken straunge strondes)
To ferne halwes, couthe in sondry londes;
And specially, from every shires ende    15
Of Engelond, to Caunterbury they wende,
The holy blisful martir [3] for to seke,
That hem hath holpen, whan that they were
    seke.
    Bifel that, in that seson on a day, [4]
In Southwerk at the Tabard as I lay    20
Redy to wenden on my pilgrimage
To Caunterbury with ful devout corage,
At night was come in-to that hostelrye
Wel nyne and twenty in a companye,
Of sondry folk, by aventure y-falle    25
In felawshipe, and pilgrims were they alle,
That toward Caunterbury wolden ryde;
The chambres and the stables weren wyde,
And wel we weren esed atte beste.
And shortly, whan the sonne was to reste,    30
So hadde I spoken with hem everichon,
That I was of hir felawshipe anon,
And made forward erly for to ryse,
To take our wey, ther as I yow devyse.
    But natheles, whyl I have tyme and space,    35
Er that I ferther in this tale pace,
Me thinketh it acordaunt to resoun,
To telle yow al the condicioun
Of ech of hem, so as it semed me,
And whiche they weren, and of what degree;    40
And eek in what array that they were inne:
And at a knight than wol I first biginne.
    A KNIGHT ther was, and that a worthy man,
That fro the tyme that he first bigan
To ryden out, he loved chivalrye,    45
Trouthe and honour, fredom and curteisye.
Ful worthy was he in his lordes werre,
And therto hadde he riden (no man ferre)
As wel in Cristendom as hethenesse,
And ever honoured for his worthinesse.    50
    At Alisaundre he was, whan it was wonne;
Ful ofte tyme he hadde the bord bigonne
Aboven alle naciouns in Pruce.
In Lettow hadde he reysed and in Ruce,
No Cristen man so ofte of his degree.    55

about 120 stories, two told by each pilgrim on the way to Canterbury, and two on the way back. Chaucer seems later to have modified this plan, reducing the number of tales by one-half. But even so he left the work far from completed. We have only 24 tales, several of them unfinished.

[2] Sign of the zodiac, Aries.

[3] Thomas à Becket.

[4] The day was 16 April, and the year may be supposed to be 1387 (Skeat).

In Gernade at the sege eek hadde he be
Of Algezir, and riden in Belmarye.
At Lyeys was he, and at Satalye,
Whan they were wonne; and in the Grete See
At many a noble aryve hadde he be.　　60
At mortal batailles hadde he been fiftene,
And foughten for our feith at Tramissene
In listes thryes, and ay slayn his fo.
This ilke worthy knight had been also
Somtyme with the lord of Palatye,　　65
Ageyn another hethen in Turkye:
And evermore he hadde a sovereyn prys.
And though that he were worthy, he was wys,
And of his port as meke as is a mayde.
He never yet no vileinye ne sayde　　70
In al his lyf, un-to no maner wight.
He was a verray parfit gentil knight.
But for to tellen yow of his array,
His hors were gode, but he was nat gay.
Of fustian he wered a gipoun　　75
Al bismotered with his habergeoun;
For he was late y-come from his viage,
And wente for to doon his pilgrimage.

　　With him ther was his sone, a yong SQUYER,
A lovyere, and a lusty bacheler,　　80
With lokkes crulle, as they were leyd in presse.
Of twenty yeer of age he was, I gesse.
Of his stature he was of evene lengthe,
And wonderly deliver, and greet of strengthe.
And he had been somtyme in chivachye,　　85
In Flaundres, in Artoys, and Picardye,
And born him wel, as of so litel space,
In hope to stonden in his lady grace.
Embrouded was he, as it were a mede
Al ful of fresshe floures, whyte and rede.　　90
Singinge he was, or floytinge, al the day;
He was as fresh as is the month of May.
Short was his goune, with sleves longe and
　　wyde.
Wel coude he sitte on hors, and faire ryde.
He coude songes make and wel endyte,　　95
Juste and eek daunce, and wel purtreye and
　　wryte.
So hote he lovede, that by nightertale
He sleep namore than dooth a nightingale.
Curteys he was, lowly, and servisable,
And carf biforn his fader at the table.　　100

　　A YEMAN hadde he, and servaunts namo
At that tyme, for him liste ryde so;
And he was clad in cote and hood of grene;
A sheef of pecok-arwes brighte and kene
Under his belt he bar ful thriftily;　　105
(Wel coude he dresse his takel yemanly:
His arwes drouped noght with fetheres lowe),
And in his hand he bar a mighty bowe.
A not-heed hadde he, with a broun visage.
Of wode-craft wel coude he al the usage.　　110
Upon his arm he bar a gay bracer,
And by his syde a swerd and a bokeler,
And on that other syde a gay daggere,
Harneised wel, and sharp as point of spere;
A Cristofre on his brest of silver shene.　　115
An horn he bar, the bawdrik was of grene;

A forster was he, soothly, as I gesse.
　　Ther was also a Nonne, a PRIORESSE,
That of hir smyling was ful simple and coy;
Hir grettest ooth was but by sëynt Loy;　　120
And she was cleped madame Eglentyne.
Ful wel she song the service divyne,
Entuned in hir nose ful semely;
And Frensh she spak ful faire and fetisly,
After the scole of Stratford atte Bowe,[5]　　125
For Frensh of Paris was to hir unknowe.
At mete wel y'taught was she with-alle;
She leet no morsel from hir lippes falle,
Ne wette hir fingres in hir sauce depe.
Wel coude she carie a morsel, and wel kepe,　　130
That no drope ne fille up-on hir brest.
In curteisye was set ful muche hir lest.
Hir over lippe wyped she so clene,
That in hir coppe was no ferthing sene
Of grece, whan she dronken hadde hir draughte.
Ful semely after hir mete she raughte,　　136
And sikerly she was of greet disport,
And ful plesaunt, and amiable of port,
And peyned hir to countrefete chere
Of court, and been estatlich of manere,　　140
And to ben holden digne of reverence.
But, for to speken of hir conscience,
She was so charitable and so pitous,
She wolde wepe, if that she sawe a mous
Caught in a trappe, if it were deed or bledde.
Of smale houndes had she, that she fedde　　146
With rosted flesh, or milk and wastel-breed.
But sore weep she if oon of hem were deed,
Or if men smoot it with a yerde smerte:
And al was conscience and tendre herte.　　150
Ful semely hir wimpel pinched was;
Hir nose tretys; hir eyen greye as glas;
Hir mouth ful smal, and there-to softe and reed;
But sikerly she hadde a fair forheed;
It was almost a spanne brood, I trowe;　　155
For, hardily, she was nat undergrowe.
Ful fetis was hir cloke, as I was war.
Of smal coral aboute hir arm she bar
A peire of bedes, gauded al with grene;　　159
And ther-on heng a broche of gold ful shene,
On which ther was first write a crowned A,
And after, *Amor vincit Omnia*.[6]

　　Another NONNE with hir hadde she,
That was hir chapeleyne, and PREESTES THREE.

　　A MONK ther was, a fair for the maistrye,　165
An out-rydere, that lovede venerye;
A manly man, to been an abbot able.
Ful many a deyntee hors hadde he in stable:
And, whan he rood, men mighte his brydel here
Ginglen in a whistling wind as clere,　　170
And eek as loude as dooth the chapel-belle
Ther as this lord was keper of the celle.
The reule of seint Maure or of seint Beneit,
By-cause that it was old and som-del streit,
This ilke monk leet olde thinges pace,　　175
And held after the newe world the space.

[5] A convent near London.

[6] Love conquers all things (Virgil, *Eclogues*, x, 69).

He yaf nat of that text a pulled hen,
That seith, that hunters been nat holy men;
Ne that a monk, whan he is cloisterlees,
Is lykned til a fish that is waterlees;          180
This is to seyn, a monk out of his cloistre.
But thilke text held he nat worth an oistre;
And I seyde, his opinioun was good.
What sholde he studie, and make him-selven
    wood,
Upon a book in cloistre alwey to poure,          185
Or swinken with his handes, and laboure,
As Austin bit? How shal the world be served?
Lat Austin have his swink to him reserved.
Therfore he was a pricasour aright;
Grehoundes he hadde, as swifte as fowel in
    flight;                                190
Of priking and of hunting for the hare
Was al his lust, for no cost wolde he spare.
I seigh his sleves purfiled at the hond
With grys, and that the fyneste of a lond;
And, for to festne his hood under his chin,      195
He hadde of gold y-wroght a curious pin:
A love-knotte in the gretter ende ther was.
His heed was balled, that shoon as any glas,
And eek his face, as he had been anoint.
He was a lord ful fat and in good point;          200
His eyen stepe, and rollinge in his heed,
That stemed as a forneys of a leed;
His botes souple, his hors in greet estat.
Now certeinly he was a fair prelat;
He was nat pale as a for-pyned goost.             205
A fat swan loved he best of any roost.
His palfrey was as broun as is a berye.

   A FRERE ther was, a wantown and a merye,
A limitour, a ful solempne man.
In alle the ordres foure [7] is noon that can     210
So muche of daliaunce and fair langage.
He hadde maad ful many a mariage
Of yonge wommen, at his owne cost.
Un-to his ordre he was a noble post.
Ful wel biloved and famulier was he               215
With frankeleyns over-al in his contree,
And eek with worthy wommen of the toun:
For he had power of confessioun,
As seyde him-self, more than a curat,
For of his ordre he was licentiat.                220
Ful swetely herde he confessioun,
And plesaunt was his absolucioun;
He was an esy man to yeve penaunce
Ther as he wiste to han a good pitaunce;
For unto a povre ordre for to yive                225
Is signe that a man is wel y-shrive.
For if he yaf, he dorste make avaunt,
He wiste that a man was repentaunt.
For many a man so hard is of his herte,           229
He may nat wepe al-thogh him sore smerte.
Therfore, in stede of weping and preyeres,
Men moot yeve silver to the povre freres.
His tipet was ay farsed ful of knyves
And pinnes, for to yeven faire wyves.
And certeinly he hadde a mery note;               235

   [7] Dominicans, Franciscans, Carmelites, and Augustinians.

Wel coude he singe and pleyen on a rote.
Of yeddinges he bar utterly the prys.
His nekke whyt was as the flour-de-lys;
Ther-to he strong was as a champioun.
He knew the tavernes wel in every toun,           240
And everich hostiler and tappestere
Bet than a lazar or a beggestere;
For un-to swich a worthy man as he
Acorded nat, as by his facultee,
To have with seke lazars aqueyntaunce.            245
It is nat honest, it may nat avaunce
For to delen with no swich poraille,
But al with riche and sellers of vitaille.
And over-al, ther as profit sholde aryse,
Curteys he was, and lowly of servyse.             250
Ther nas no man no-wher so vertuous.
He was the beste beggere in his hous;
And yaf a certeyn ferme for the graunt;
Noon of his bretheren cam ther in his haunt;
For thogh a widwe hadde noght a sho,              255
So plesaunt was his "*In principio*," [8]
Yet wolde he have a ferthing, er he wente.
His purchas was wel bettre than his rente.
And rage he coude, as it were right a whelpe.
In love-dayes ther coude he muchel helpe.         260
For there he was nat lyk a cloisterer,
With a thredbar cope, as is a povre scoler,
But he was lyk a maister or a pope.
Of double worsted was his semi-cope,
That rounded as a belle out of the presse.        265
Somwhat he lipsed, for his wantownesse,
To make his English swete up-on his tonge;
And in his harping, whan that he had songe,
His eyen twinkled in his heed aright,
As doon the sterres in the frosty night.          270
This worthy limitour was cleped Huberd.

   A MARCHANT was ther with a forked berd,
In mottelee, and hye on horse he sat,
Up-on his heed a Flaundrish bever hat;
His botes clasped faire and fetisly.              275
His resons he spak ful solempnely,
Souninge alway th'encrees of his winning.
He wolde the see were kept for any thing
Bitwixe Middelburgh and Orewelle. [9]
Wel coude he in eschaunge sheeldes selle.         280
This worthy man ful wel his wit bisette;
Ther wiste no wight that he was in dette,
So estatly was he of his governaunce,
With his bargaynes, and with his chevisaunce.
For sothe he was a worthy man with-alle,          285
But sooth to seyn, I noot how men him calle.

   A CLERK ther was of Oxenford also,
That un-to logik hadde longe y-go.
As lene was his hors as is a rake,
And he nas nat right fat, I undertake;            290
But loked holwe, and ther-to soberly.
Ful thredbar was his overest courtepy;

   [8] In the beginning (opening words of the Gospel of St. John, a text much quoted by the friars).
   [9] The former a port on an island off the coast of The Netherlands, the latter an English port at the mouth of the Orwell River. He wanted the sea-route between the two kept open at any expense.

For he had geten him yet no benefyce,
Ne was so worldly for to have offyce.
For him was lever have at his beddes heed ²⁹⁵
Twenty bokes, clad in blak or reed,
Of Aristotle and his philosophye,
Than robes riche, or fithele, or gay sautrye.
But al be that he was a philosophre,
Yet hadde he but litel gold in cofre; ¹⁰    ³⁰⁰
But al that he mighte of his freendes hente,
On bokes and on lerninge he it spente,
And bisily gan for the soules preye
Of hem that yaf him wher-with to scoleye.
Of studie took he most cure and most hede. ³⁰⁵
Noght o word spak he more than was nede,
And that was seyd in forme and reverence,
And short and quik, and ful of hy sentence.
Souninge in moral vertu was his speche,    ³⁰⁹
And gladly wolde he lerne, and gladly teche.

A SERGEANT OF THE LAWE, war and wys,
That often hadde been at the parvys,
Ther was also, ful riche of excellence.
Discreet he was, and of greet reverence:
He semed swich, his wordes weren so wyse. ³¹⁵
Justyce he was ful often in assyse,
By patente, and by pleyn commissioun;
For his science, and for his heigh renoun
Of fees and robes hadde he many oon.
So greet a purchasour was no-wher noon.    ³²⁰
Al was fee simple to him in effect,¹¹
His purchasing mighte nat been infect.
No-wher so bisy a man as he ther nas,
And yet he semed bisier than he was.
In termes hadde he caas and domes alle,    ³²⁵
That from the tyme of king William were falle.
Therto he coude endyte, and make a thing,
Ther coude no wight pinche at his wryting;
And every statut coude he pleyn by rote.
He rood but hoomly in a medlee cote    ³³⁰
Girt with a ceint of silk, with barres smale;
Of his array telle I no lenger tale.

A FRANKELEYN was in his companye;
Whyt was his berd, as is the dayesye.
Of his complexioun he was sangwyn.    ³³⁵
Wel loved he by the morwe a sop in wyn.
To liven in delyt was ever his wone,
For he was Epicurus owne sone,
That heeld opinioun, that pleyn delyt
Was verraily felicitee parfyt.    ³⁴⁰
An housholdere, and that a greet, was he;
Seint Julian ¹² he was in his contree.
His breed, his ale, was alwey after oon;
A bettre envyned man was no-wher noon.
With-oute bake mete was never his hous, ³⁴⁵
Of fish and flesh, and that so plentevous,
It snewed in his hous of mete and drinke,
Of alle deyntees that men coude thinke.
After the sondry sesons of the yeer,

So chaunged he his mete and his soper.    ³⁵⁰
Ful many a fat partrich hadde he in mewe,
And many a breem and many a luce in stewe.
Wo was his cook, but-if his sauce were
Poynaunt and sharp, and redy al his gere.
His table dormant in his halle alway    ³⁵⁵
Stood redy covered al the longe day.
At sessiouns ther was he lord and sire;
Ful ofte tyme he was knight of the shire.
An anlas and a gipser al of silk
Heng at his girdel, whyt as morne milk.    ³⁶⁰
A shirreve hadde he been, and a countour;
Was no-wher such a worthy vavasour.

An HABERDASSHER and a CARPENTER,
A WEBBE, a DYERE, and a TAPICER,
Were with us eek, clothed in o liveree,    ³⁶⁵
Of a solempne and greet fraternitee.
Ful fresh and newe hir gere apyked was;
Hir knyves were y-chaped noght with bras,
But al with silver, wroght ful clene and weel,
Hir girdles and hir pouches every-deel.    ³⁷⁰
Wel semed ech of hem a fair burgeys,
To sitten in a yeldhalle on a deys.
Everich, for the wisdom that he can,
Was shaply for to been an alderman.
For catel hadde they y-nogh and rente,    ³⁷⁵
And eek hir wyves wolde it wel assente;
And elles certein were they to blame.
It is ful fair to been y-clept "ma dame,"
And goon to vigilyës al bifore,
And have a mantel royalliche y-bore.    ³⁸⁰

A COOK they hadde with hem for the nones,
To boille the chiknes with the mary-bones,
And poudre-marchant tart, and galingale.
Wel coude he knowe a draughte of London ale.
He coude roste, and sethe, and broille, and frye,
Maken mortreux, and wel bake a pye.    ³⁸⁶
But greet harm was it, as it thoughte me,
That on his shine a mormal hadde he;
For blankmanger, that made he with the beste.

A SHIPMAN was ther, woning fer by weste;
For aught I woot, he was of Dertemouthe. ³⁹¹
He rood up-on a rouncy, as he couthe,
In a gowne of falding to the knee.
A daggere hanging on a laas hadde he
Aboute his nekke under his arm adoun.    ³⁹⁵
The hote somer had maad his hewe al broun;
And, certeinly, he was a good felawe.
Ful many a draughte of wyn had he y-drawe
From Burdeux-ward, whyl that the chapman
    sleep.¹³
Of nyce conscience took he no keep.    ⁴⁰⁰
If that he faught, and hadde the hyer hond,
By water he sente hem hoom to every lond.¹⁴
But of his craft to rekene wel his tydes,
His stremes and his daungers him bisydes,    ⁴⁰⁴
His herberwe and his mone, his lodemenage,
Ther nas noon swich from Hulle to Cartage.
Hardy he was, and wys to undertake;

---

¹⁰ The reference is to the alchemists, who were also termed philosophers. It was commonly believed that they could turn base metals into gold.
¹¹ The meaning is that he could untie any entail, or restriction on land.
¹² The patron saint of hospitality.

¹³ He had stolen wine from the casks he was carrying from Bordeaux.
¹⁴ Threw them overboard.

With many a tempest hadde his berd been
    shake.
He knew wel alle the havenes, as they were,
From Gootlond to the cape of Finistere,    410
And every cryke in Britayne and in Spayne;
His barge y-cleped was the Maudelayne.

    With us ther was a Doctour of Phisyk,
In al this world ne was ther noon him lyk
To speke of phisik and of surgerye;    415
For he was grounded in astronomye.[15]
He kepte his pacient a ful greet del
In houres, by his magik naturel.
Wel coude he fortunen the ascendent
Of his images for his pacient.    420
He knew the cause of everich maladye,
Were it of hoot or cold, or moiste, or drye,
And where engendred, and of what humour;
He was a verrey parfit practisour.
The cause y-knowe, and of his harm the rote,
Anon he yaf the seke man his bote.    426
Ful redy hadde he his apothecaries,
To sende him drogges and his letuaries,
For ech of hem made other for to winne;
Hir frendschipe nas nat newe to beginne.    430
Wel knew he th'olde Esculapius,
And Deiscorides, and eek Rufus,
Old Ypocras, Haly, and Galien;
Serapion, Razis, and Avicen;
Averrois, Damascien, and Constantyn;    435
Bernard, and Gatesden, and Gilbertyn.[16]
Of his diete mesurable was he,
For it was of no superfluitee,
But of greet norissing and digestible.
His studie was but litel on the bible.    440
In sangwin and in pers he clad was al,
Lyned with taffata and with sendal;
And yet he was but esy of dispence;
He kepte that he wan in pestilence.
For gold in phisik is a cordial,    445
Therfore he lovede gold in special.

    A good Wyf was ther of bisyde Bathe,
But she was som-del deef, and that was scathe.
Of clooth-making she hadde swiche an haunt,
She passed hem of Ypres and of Gaunt.    450
In al the parisshe wyf ne was ther noon
That to the offring bifore hir sholde goon;
And if ther dide, certeyn, so wrooth was she,
That she was out of alle charitee.
Hir coverchiefs ful fyne were of ground;    455
I dorste swere they weyeden ten pound
That on a Sonday were upon hir heed.
Hir hosen weren of fyn scarlet reed,
Ful streite y-teyd, and shoos ful moiste and
    newe.
Bold was hir face, and fair, and reed of hewe.
She was a worthy womman al hir lyve,    461
Housbondes at chirche-dore she hadde fyve,
Withouten other companye in youthe;

But therof nedeth nat to speke as nouthe.
And thryes hadde she been at Jerusalem;    465
She hadde passed many a straunge streem;
At Rome she hadde been, and at Boloigne,
In Galice at seint Jame,[17] and at Coloigne.
She coude muche of wandring by the weye:
Gat-tothed was she, soothly for to seye.    470
Up-on an amblere esily she sat,
Y-wimpled wel, and on hir heed an hat
As brood as is a bokeler or a targe;
A foot-mantel aboute hir hipes large,
And on hir feet a paire of spores sharpe.    475
In felawschip wel coude she laughe and carpe.
Of remedyes of love she knew per-chaunce,
For she coude of that art the olde daunce.

    A good man was ther of religioun,
And was a povre Persoun of a toun;    480
But riche he was of holy thoght and werk.
He was also a lerned man, a clerk,
That Cristes gospel trewely wolde preche;
His parisshens devoutly wolde he teche.
Benigne he was, and wonder diligent,    485
And in adversitee ful pacient;
And swich he was y-preved ofte sythes.
Ful looth were him to cursen for his tythes,
But rather wolde he yeven, out of doute,
Un-to his povre parisshens aboute    490
Of his offring, and eek of his substaunce.
He coude in litel thing han suffisaunce.
Wyd was his parisshe, and houses fer a-sonder,
But he ne lafte nat, for reyn ne thonder,
In siknes nor in meschief, to visyte    495
The ferreste in his parisshe, muche and lyte,
Up-on his feet, and in his hand a staf.
This noble ensample to his sheep he yaf,
That first he wroghte, and afterward he taughte;
Out of the gospel he tho wordes caughte;[18]  500
And this figure he added eek ther-to,
That if gold ruste, what shal iren do?
For if a preest be foul, on whom we truste,
No wonder is a lewed man to ruste;
And shame it is, if a preest take keep,    505
A shiten shepherde and a clene sheep.
Wel oghte a preest ensample for to yive,
By his clennesse, how that his sheep shold live.
He sette nat his benefice to hyre,
And leet his sheep encombred in the myre,  510
And ran to London, un-to sëynt Poules,
To seken him a chaunterie for soules,[19]
Or with a bretherhed to been withholde;[20]
But dwelte at hoom, and kepte wel his folde,
So that the wolf ne made it nat miscarie;   515
He was a shepherde and no mercenarie.
And though he holy were, and vertuous,
He was to sinful man nat despitous,
Ne of his speche daungerous ne digne,

[17] Compostella in Spain.
[18] St. Matthew, 5:19.
[19] There were thirty-five chantries at St. Paul's,
served by fifty-four priests who said masses for the
dead.
[20] "Or to remain in retirement with some fraternity."

[15] "Astronomye." This is really astrology. The
physician knew well how to watch for a favorable
astrological hour for the making of images to be
used as charms in the treatment of his patient.
[16] All great medical authorities.

But in his teching discreet and benigne. 520
To drawen folk to heven by fairnesse
By good ensample, was his bisinesse:
But it were any persone obstinat,
What-so he were, of heigh or lowe estat, 524
Him wolde he snibben sharply for the nones.
A bettre preest, I trowe that nowher noon is.
He wayted after no pompe and reverence,
Ne maked him a spyced conscience,
But Cristes lore, and his apostles twelve,
He taughte, and first he folwed it him-selve. 530

    With him ther was a PLOWMAN, was his brother,
That hadde y-lad of dong ful many a fother,
A trewe swinker and a good was he,
Livinge in pees and parfit charitee.
God loved he best with al his hole herte 535
At alle tymes, thogh him gamed or smerte,
And thanne his neighebour right as himselve.
He wolde thresshe, and ther-to dyke and delve,
For Cristes sake, for every povre wight,
Withouten hyre, if it lay in his might. 540
His tythes payed he ful faire and wel,
Bothe of his propre swink and his catel.
In a tabard he rood upon a mere.

    Ther was also a Reve and a Millere,
A Somnour and a Pardoner also, 545
A Maunciple, and my-self; ther were namo.

    The MILLER was a stout carl, for the nones,
Ful big he was of braun, and eek of bones;
That proved wel, for over-al ther he cam, 549
At wrastling he wolde have alwey the ram.[21]
He was short-sholdred, brood, a thikke knarre,
Ther nas no dore that he nolde heve of harre,
Or breke it, at a renning, with his heed.
His berd as any sowe or fox was reed,
And ther-to brood, as though it were a spade.
Up-on the cop right of his nose he hade 556
A werte, and ther-on stood a tuft of heres,
Reed as the bristles of a sowes eres;
His nose-thirles blake were and wyde.
A swerd and bokeler bar he by his syde; 560
His mouth as greet was as a greet forneys.
He was a janglere and a goliardeys,
And that was most of sinne and harlotryes.
Wel coude he stelen corn, and tollen thryes;
And yet he hadde a thombe of gold, pardee. 565
A whyt cote and a blew hood wered he.
A baggepype wel coude he blowe and sowne,
And ther-with-al he broghte us out of towne.

    A gentil MAUNCIPLE was ther of a temple,
Of which achatours mighte take exemple 570
For to be wyse in bying of vitaille.
For whether that he payde, or took by taille,
Algate he wayted so in his achat,
That he was ay biforn and in good stat.
Now is nat that of God a ful fair grace, 575
That swich a lewed mannes wit shal pace
The wisdom of an heep of lerned men?
Of maistres hadde he mo than thryes ten,
That were of lawe expert and curious;

Of which ther were a doseyn in that hous 580
Worthy to been stiwardes of rente and lond
Of any lord that is in Engelond,
To make him live by his propre good,
In honour dettelees, but he were wood,
Or live as scarsly as him list desire; 585
And able for to helpen al a shire
In any cas that mighte falle or happe;
And yit this maunciple sette hir aller cappe.

    The REVE was a sclendre colerik man,
His berd was shave as ny as ever he can. 590
His heer was by his eres round y-shorn.
His top was dokked lyk a preest biforn.
Ful longe were his legges, and ful lene,
Y-lyk a staf, ther was no calf y-sene.
Wel coude he kepe a gerner and a binne; 595
Ther was noon auditour coude on him winne.
Wel wiste he, by the droghte, and by the reyn,
The yelding of his seed, and of his greyn.
His lordes sheep, his neet, his dayerye,
His swyn, his hors, his stoor, and his pultrye,
Was hoolly in this reves governing, 601
And by his covenaunt yaf the rekening,
Sin that his lord was twenty yeer of age;
Ther coude no man bringe him in arrerage.[22]
Ther nas baillif, ne herde, ne other hyne, 605
That he ne knew his sleighte and his covyne;
They were adrad of him, as of the deeth.
His woning was ful fair up-on an heeth,
With grene treës shadwed was his place.
He coude bettre than his lord purchace. 610
Ful riche he was astored prively,
His lord wel coude he plesen subtilly,
To yeve and lene him of his owne good,
And have a thank, and yet a cote and hood.
In youthe he lerned hadde a good mister; 615
He was a wel good wrighte, a carpenter.
This reve sat up-on a ful good stot,
That was al pomely grey, and highte Scot.
A long surcote of pers up-on he hade,
And by his syde he bar a rusty blade, 620
Of Northfolk was this reve, of which I telle,
Bisyde a toun men clepen Baldeswelle.
Tukked he was, as is a frere, aboute,
And ever he rood the hindreste of our route.

    A SOMNOUR was ther with us in that place,
That hadde a fyr-reed cherubinnes face, 626
For sawcefleem he was, with eyen narwe.
As hoot he was, and lecherous, as a sparwe;
With scalled browes blake, and piled berd;
Of his visage children were aferd. 630
Ther nas quik-silver, litarge, ne brimstoon,
Boras, ceruce, ne oille of tartre noon,
Ne oynement that wolde clense and byte,
That him mighte helpen of his whelkes whyte,
Nor of the knobbes sittinge on his chekes. 635
Wel loved he garleek, oynons, and eek lekes,
And for to drinken strong wyn, reed as blood.
Than wolde he speke, and crye as he were wood.
And whan that he wel dronken hadde the wyn,

---

[21] The prize.

[22] Catch him in arrears.

Than wolde he speke no word but Latyn.    640
A fewe termes hadde he, two or three,
That he had lerned out of some decree;
No wonder is, he herde it al the day;
And eek ye knowen wel, how that a jay    644
Can clepen "Watte," as well as can the pope.
But who-so coude in other thing him grope,
Thanne hadde he spent al his philosophye;
Ay *"Questio quid iuris"* [23] wolde he crye.
He was a gentil harlot and a kinde;
A bettre felawe sholde men noght finde.    650
He wolde suffre, for a quart of wyn,
A good felawe to have his concubyn
A twelf-month, and excuse him atte fulle:
Full prively a finch eek coude he pulle.
And if he fond o-wher a good felawe,    655
He wolde techen him to have non awe,
In swich cas, of the erchedeknes curs,
But-if a mannes soule were in his purs;
For in his purs he sholde y-punisshed be.
"Purs is the erchedeknes helle," seyde he.    660
But wel I woot he lyed right in dede;
Of cursing oghte ech gilty man him drede—
For curs wol slee, right as assoilling saveth—
And also war him of a *significavit*.[24]
In daunger hadde he at his owne gyse    665
The yonge girles of the diocyse,
And knew hir counseil, and was al hir reed.
A gerland hadde he set up-on his heed,
As greet as it were for an ale-stake;
A bokeler hadde he maad him of a cake.    670
    With him ther rood a gentil PARDONER
Of Rouncival,[25] his freend and his compeer,
That streight was comen fro the court of Rome.
Ful loude he song, "Com hider, love, to me."
This somnour bar to him a stif burdoun,    675
Was never trompe of half so greet a soun.
This pardoner hadde heer as yelow as wex,
But smothe it heng, as dooth a strike of flex;
By ounces henge his lokkes that he hadde,
And ther-with he his shuldres overspradde;    680
But thinne it lay, by colpons oon and oon;
But hood, for jolitee, ne wered he noon,
For it was trussed up in his walet.
Him thoughte, he rood al of the newe jet;
Dischevele, save his cappe, he rood all bare.    685
Swiche glaringe eyen hadde he as an hare.
A vernicle hadde he sowed on his cappe.
His walet lay biforn him in his lappe,
Bret-ful of pardoun come from Rome al hoot.
A voys he hadde as smal as hath a goot.    690
No berd hadde he, ne never sholde have,
As smothe it was as it were late y-shave;
I trowe he were a gelding or a mare.
But of his craft, fro Berwik into Ware,
Ne was ther swich another pardoner.    695
For in his male he hadde a pilwe-beer,
Which that, he seyde, was our lady veyl:
He seyde, he hadde a gobet of the seyl

That sëynt Peter hadde, whan that he wente
Up-on the see, til Jesu Crist him hente.    700
He hadde a croys of latoun, ful of stones,
And in a glas he hadde pigges bones.
But with thise relikes, whan that he fond
A povre person dwelling up-on lond,
Up-on a day he gat him more moneye    705
Than that the person gat in monthes tweye.
And thus, with feyned flaterye and japes,
He made the person and the peple his apes.
But trewely to tellen, atte laste,
He was in chirche a noble ecclesiaste.    710
Wel coude he rede a lessoun or a storie,
But alderbest he song an offertorie;
For wel he wiste, whan that song was songe,
He moste preche, and wel affyle his tonge,
To winne silver, as he ful wel coude;    715
Therefore he song so meriely and loude.
    Now have I told you shortly, in a clause,
Th'estat, th'array, the nombre, and eek the
        cause
Why that assembled was this companye
In Southwerk, at this gentil hostelrye,    720
That highte the Tabard, faste by the Belle.
But now is tyme to yow for to telle
How that we baren us that ilke night,
Whan we were in that hostelrye alight.
And after wol I telle of our viage,    725
And al the remenaunt of our pilgrimage.
But first I pray yow, of your curteisye,
That ye n'arette it nat my vileinye,
Thogh that I pleynly speke in this matere,
To telle yow hir wordes and hir chere;    730
Ne thogh I speke hir wordes properly.
For this ye knowen al-so wel as I,
Who-so shal telle a tale after a man,
He moot reherce, as ny as ever he can,
Everich a word, if it be in his charge,    735
Al speke he never so rudeliche and large;
Or elles he moot telle his tale untrewe,
Or feyne thing, or finde wordes newe.
He may nat spare, al-thogh he were his brother;
He moot as wel seye o word as another.    740
Crist spak him-self ful brode in holy writ,
And wel ye woot, no vileinye is it.
Eek Plato seith, who-so that can him rede,
The wordes mote be cosin to the dede.[26]
Also I prey yow to foryeve it me,    745
Al have I nat set folk in hir degree
Here in this tale, as that they sholde stonde;
My wit is short, ye may wel understonde.
    Greet chere made our hoste us everichon,
And to the soper sette us anon;    750
And served us with vitaille at the beste.
Strong was the wyn, and wel to drinke us leste.
A semely man our hoste was with-alle
For to han been a marshal in an halle;
A large man he was with eyen stepe,    755
A fairer burgeys is ther noon in Chepe:[27]
Bold of his speche, and wys, and wel y-taught,

[23] What is the law on this point?
[24] A writ of excommunication, which usually began with this word.
[25] An hospital near Charing Cross, London.

[26] Chaucer took this from Boethius, *De Consola-
tione*, bk. III, pr. 12. Cf. Plato, *Timaeus*, 29B.
[27] Cheapside.

And of manhod him lakkede right naught.
Eek therto he was right a mery man,
And after soper pleyen he bigan,                 760
And spak of mirthe amonges othere thinges,
Whan that we hadde maad our rekeninges;
And seyde thus: "Now, lordinges, trewely,
Ye been to me right welcome hertely:
For by my trouthe, if that I shal nat lye,       765
I ne saugh this yeer so mery a companye
At ones in this herberwe as is now.
Fayn wolde I doon yow mirthe, wiste I how.
And of a mirthe I am right now bithoght,
To doon yow ese, and it shal coste noght.        770
    "Ye goon to Caunterbury; God yow spede,
The blisful martir quyte yow your mede.
And wel I woot, as ye goon by the weye,
Ye shapen yow to talen and to pleye;
For trewely, confort ne mirthe is noon           775
To ryde by the weye doumb as a stoon;
And therfore wol I maken yow disport,
As I seyde erst, and doon yow some confort.
And if yow lyketh alle, by oon assent,
Now for to stonden at my jugement,               780
And for to werken as I shal yow seye,
To-morwe, whan ye ryden by the weye,
Now, by my fader soule, that is deed,
But ye be merye, I wol yeve yow myn heed.
Hold up your hond, withouten more speche."
    Our counseil was nat longe for to seche;     786
Us thoughte it was noght worth to make it wys,
And graunted him withouten more avys,
And bad him seye his verdit, as him leste.
    "Lordinges," quod he, "now herkneth for the
        beste;                                   790
But take it not, I prey yow, in desdeyn;
This is the poynt, to speken short and pleyn,
That ech of yow, to shorte with your weye,
In this viage, shal telle tales tweye,
To Caunterbury-ward, I mene it so,               795
And hom-ward he shal tellen othere two,
Of aventures that whylom han bifalle,
And which of yow that bereth him best of alle,
That is to seyn, that telleth in this cas
Tales of best sentence and most solas,           800
Shal have a soper at our aller cost
Here in this place, sitting by this post,
Whan that we come agayn fro Caunterbury.
And for to make yow the more mery,
I wol my-selven gladly with yow ryde,            805
Right at myn owne cost, and be your gyde.
And who-so wol my jugement withseye
Shal paye al that we spenden by the weye.
And if ye vouche-sauf that it be so,
Tel me anon, with-outen wordes mo,               810
And I wol erly shape me therfore."
    This thing was graunted, and our othes swore
With ful glad herte, and preyden him also
That he wold vouche-sauf for to do so,
And that he wolde been our governour,            815
And of our tales juge and reportour,
And sette a soper at a certeyn prys;
And we wold reuled been at his devys,
In heigh and lowe; and thus, by oon assent,

We been acorded to his jugement.                 820
And ther-up-on the wyn was fet anon;
We dronken, and to reste wente echon,
With-outen any lenger taryinge.
    A-morwe, whan that day bigan to springe,
Up roos our host, and was our aller cok,         825
And gadrede us togidre, alle in a flok,
And forth we riden, a litel more than pas,
Un-to the watering of seint Thomas.[28]
And there our host bigan his hors areste,
And seyde, "Lordinges, herkneth, if yow leste.
Ye woot your forward, and I it yow recorde.      831
If even-song and morwe-song acorde,
Lat see now who shal telle the firste tale.
As ever mote I drinke wyn or ale,
Who-so be rebel to my jugement                   835
Shal paye for al that by the weye is spent.
Now draweth cut, er that we ferrer twinne;
He which that hath the shortest shal biginne.
Sire knight," quod he, "my maister and my
        lord,
Now draweth cut, for that is myn acord.          840
Cometh neer," quod he, "my lady prioresse;
And ye, sir clerk, lat be your shamfastnesse,
Ne studieth noght; ley hond to, every man."
    Anon to drawen every wight bigan,
And shortly for to tellen, as it was,            845
Were it by aventure, or sort, or cas,
The sothe is this, the cut fil to the knight,
Of which ful blythe and glad was every wight;
And telle he moste his tale, as was resoun,
By forward and by composicioun,                  850
As ye han herd; what nedeth wordes mo?
And whan this gode man saugh it was so,
As he that wys was and obedient
To kepe his forward by his free assent,
He seyde: "Sin I shal biginne the game,          855
What, welcome be the cut, a Goddes name!
Now lat us ryde, and herkneth what I seye."
    And with that word we riden forth our weye;
And he bigan with right a mery chere
His tale anon, and seyde in this manere.[29] 860

### The Prioresses Prologue

"Wel seyd, by *corpus dominus*," [1] quod our
        hoste,
"Now longe moot thou sayle by the coste,
Sir gentil maister, gentil marineer!
God yeve this monk a thousand last quad yeer!
A ha! felawes! beth ware of swiche a jape!    5
The monk putte in the mannes hood an ape,
And in his wyves eek, by seint Austin!
Draweth no monkes more un-to your in.
    "But now passe over, and lat us seke aboute,
Who shal now telle first, of al this route,    10
Another tale"; and with that word he sayde,

[28] Two miles from Southwark.
[29] Here follow the tales of the Knight, the Miller, the Reeve, and the Cook, the last unfinished. On the morning of the second day the Man of Law tells the first tale, then the Shipman tells one, and then the Host turns to the Prioress.
[1] By the body of our Lord.

As curteisly as it had been a mayde,
"My lady Prioresse, by your leve,
So that I wiste I sholde yow not greve,
I wolde demen that ye tellen sholde          15
A tale next, if so were that ye wolde.
Now wol ye vouche-sauf, my lady dere?"
    "Gladly," quod she, and seyde as ye shal here.

### The Prioresses Tale
#### Domine, dominus noster.[2]

O Lord our lord, thy name how merveillous
Is in this large worlde y-sprad—quod she:—
For noght only thy laude precious
Parfourned is by men of dignitee,
But by the mouth of children thy bountee      5
Parfourned is, for on the brest soukinge
Som tyme shewen they thyn heryinge.

Wherfor in laude, as I best can or may,
Of thee, and of the whyte lily flour
Which that thee bar, and is a mayde alway,     10
To telle a storie I wol do my labour;
Not that I may encresen hir honour;
For she hir-self is honour, and the rote
Of bountee, next hir sone, and soules bote.—

O modor mayde! o mayde moder free!           15
O bush unbrent, brenninge in Moyses sighte,
That ravisedest doun fro the deitee,
Thurgh thyn humblesse, the goost that in
        th'alighte,
Of whos vertu, whan he thyn herte lighte,
Conceived was the fadres sapience,             20
Help me to telle it in thy reverence!

Lady! thy bountee, thy magnificence,
Thy vertu, and thy grete humilitee,
Ther may no tonge expresse in no science;
For som-tyme, lady, er men praye to thee,       25
Thou goost biforn of thy benignitee,
And getest us the light, thurgh thy preyere,
To gyden us un-to thy sone so dere.

My conning is so wayk, o blisful quene,
For to declare thy greate worthinesse,          30
That I ne may the weighte nat sustene,
But as a child of twelf monthe old, or lesse,
That can unnethes any word expresse,
Right so fare I, and therfor I yow preye,
Gydeth my song that I shal of yow seye.         35

#### HERE BIGINNETH THE
#### PRIORESSES TALE[3]

Ther was in Asie, in a greet citee,
Amonges Cristen folk, a Jewerye,

[2] O Lord, our Lord.
[3] Chaucer probably based this tale on some Latin prose legend current in his day. The theme, the murder of a Christian child by Jews, was a popular one in the Middle Ages, and at least 29 versions of it are known.

Sustened by a lord of that contree
For foule usure and lucre of vilanye,
Hateful to Crist and to his companye;           40
And thurgh the strete men mighte ryde or
        wende,
For it was free, and open at either ende.

A litel scole of Cristen folk ther stood
Doun at the ferther ende, in which ther were
Children an heep, y-comen of Cristen blood,     45
That lerned in that scole yeer by yere
Swich maner doctrine as men used there,
This is to seyn, to singen and to rede,
As smale children doon in hir childhede.

Among thise children was a widwes sone,         50
A litel clergeon, seven yeer of age,
That day by day to scole was his wone,
And eek also, wher-as he saugh th'image
Of Cristes moder, hadde he in usage,
As him was taught, to knele adoun and seye      55
His *Ave Marie*,[4] as he goth by the weye.

Thus hath this widwe hir litel sone y-taught
Our blisful lady, Cristes moder dere,
To worshipe ay, and he forgat it naught,
For sely child wol alday sone lere;             60
But ay, whan I remembre on this matere,
Seint Nicholas stant ever in my presence,
For he so yong to Crist did reverence.

This litel child, his litel book lerninge,
As he sat in the scole at his prymer,           65
He *Alma redemptoris*[5] herde singe,
As children lerned hir antiphoner;
And, as he dorste, he drough him ner and ner,
And herkned ay the wordes and the note,
Til he the firste vers coude al by rote.        70

Noght wiste he what this Latin was to seye,
For he so yong and tendre was of age;
But on a day his felaw gan he preye
T'expounden him this song in his langage,
Or telle him why this song was in usage;        75
This preyde he him to construe and declare
Ful ofte tyme upon his knowes bare.

His felaw, which that elder was than he,
Answerde him thus: "this song, I have herd
        seye,
Was maked of our blisful lady free,             80
Hir to salue, and eek hir for to preye
To been our help and socour whan we deye.
I can no more expounde in this matere;
I lerne song, I can but smal grammere."

"And is this song maked in reverence            85
Of Cristes moder?" seyde this innocent;
"Now certes, I wol do my diligence

[4] Hail Mary (the first two words of a short prayer made up from St. Luke, 1:28 and 42).
[5] Gracious Mother of the Redeemer. There is more than one medieval hymn with this beginning.

To conne it all, er Cristemasse is went;
Though that I for my prymer shal be shent,
And shal be beten thryës in an houre,          90
I wol it conne, our lady for to honoure."

His felaw taughte him homward prively,
Fro day to day, til he coude it by rote,
And than he song it wel and boldely
Fro word to word, acording with the note;          95
Twyës a day it passed thurgh his throte,
To scoleward and homward whan he wente;
On Cristes moder set was his entente.

As I have seyd, thurgh-out the Jewerye
This litel child, as he cam to and fro,          100
Ful merily than wolde he singe, and crye
O *Alma redemptoris* ever-mo.
The swetnes hath his herte perced so
Of Cristes moder, that, to hir to preye,
He can nat stinte of singing by the weye.          105

Our firste fo, the serpent Sathanas,
That hath in Jewes herte his waspes nest,
Up swal, and seide, "O Hebraik peple, allas!
Is this to yow a thing that is honest,
That swich a boy shal walken as him lest          110
In your despyt, and singe of swich sentence,
Which is agayn your lawes reverence?"

Fro thennes forth the Jewes han conspyred
This innocent out of this world to chace;
An homicyde ther-to han they hyred,          115
That in an aley hadde a privee place;
And as the child gan for-by for to pace,
This cursed Jew him hente and heeld him faste,
And kitte his throte, and in a pit him caste.

I seye that in a wardrobe they him threwe          120
Wher-as these Jewes purgen hir entraille.
O cursed folk of Herodes al newe,
What may your yvel entente yow availle?
Mordre wol out, certein, it wol nat faille,          124
And namely ther th'onour of god shal sprede,
The blood out cryeth on your cursed dede.

"O martir, souded to virginitee,
Now maystou singen, folwing ever in oon
The whyte lamb celestial," quod she,
"Of which the grete evangelist, seint John,          130
In Pathmos wroot, which seith that they that
          goon
Biforn this lamb, and singe a song al newe,
That never, fleshly, wommen they ne knewe."

This povre widwe awaiteth al that night
After hir litel child, but he cam noght;          135
For which, as sone as it was dayes light,
With face pale of drede and bisy thoght,
She hath at scole and elles-where him soght,
Til finally she gan so fer espye
That he last seyn was in the Jewerye.          140

With modres pitee in hir brest enclosed,
She gooth, as she were half out of hir minde,

To every place wher she hath supposed
By lykihede hir litel child to finde;
And ever on Cristes moder meke and kinde          145
She cryde, and atte laste thus she wroghte,
Among the cursed Jewes she him soghte.

She frayneth and she preyeth pitously
To every Jew that dwelte in thilke place,
To telle hir, if hir child wente oght for-by.          150
They seyde, "nay"; but Jesu, of his grace,
Yaf in hir thought, inwith a litel space,
That in that place after hir sone she cryde,
Wher he was casten in a pit bisyde.

O grete god, that parfournest thy laude          155
By mouth of innocents, lo heer thy might!
This gemme of chastitee, this emeraude,
And eek of martirdom the ruby bright,
Ther he with throte y-corven lay upright,
He "*Alma redemptoris*" gan to singe          160
So loude, that al the place gan to ringe.

The Cristen folk, that thurgh the strete wente,
In coomen, for to wondre up-on this thing,
And hastily they for the provost sente;
He cam anon with-outen tarying,          165
And herieth Crist that is of heven king,
And eek his moder, honour of mankinde,
And after that, the Jewes leet he binde.

This child with pitous lamentacioun
Up-taken was, singing his song alway;          170
And with honour of greet processioun
They carien him un-to the nexte abbay.
His moder swowning by the bere lay;
Unnethe might the peple that was there
This newe Rachel bringe fro his bere.          175

With torment and with shamful deth echon
This provost dooth thise Jewes for to sterve
That of this mordre wiste, and that anon;
He nolde no swich cursednesse observe.
Yvel shal have, that yvel wol deserve.          180
Therfor with wilde hors he dide hem drawe,[6]
And after that he heng hem by the lawe.

Up-on his bere ay lyth this innocent
Biforn the chief auter, whyl masse laste,
And after that, the abbot with his covent          185
Han sped hem for to burien him ful faste;
And whan they holy water on him caste,
Yet spak this child, whan spreynd was holy
          water,
And song—"*O Alma redemptoris mater!*"

This abbot, which that was an holy man          190
As monkes been, or elles oghten be,
This yonge child to conjure he bigan,
And seyde, "o dere child, I halse thee,
In vertu of the holy Trinitee,
Tel me what is thy cause for to singe,          195
Sith that thy throte is cut, to my seminge?"

[6] *Sc.* to the gallows.

"My throte is cut un-to my nekke-boon,"
Seyde this child, "and, as by wey of kinde,
I sholde have deyed, ye, longe tyme agoon,
But Jesu Crist, as ye in bokes finde,          200
Wil that his glorie laste and be in minde;
And, for the worship of his moder dere,
Yet may I singe 'O *Alma*' loude and clere.

"This welle of mercy, Cristes moder swete
I lovede alwey, as after my conninge;          205
And whan that I my lyf sholde forlete,
To me she cam, and bad me for to singe
This antem verraily in my deyinge,
As ye han herd, and, whan that I had songe,
Me thoughte, she leyde a greyn up-on my
          tonge.          210

"Wherfor I singe, and singe I moot certeyn
In honour of that blisful mayden free,
Til fro my tonge of-taken is the greyn;
And afterward thus seyde she to me,
'My litel child, now wol I fecche thee          215
Whan that the greyn is fro thy tonge y-take;
Be nat agast, I wol thee nat forsake.'"

This holy monk, this abbot, him mene I,
His tonge out-caughte, and took a-wey the
          greyn,
And he yaf up the goost ful softely.          220
And whan this abbot had this wonder seyn,
His salte teres trikled doun as reyn,
And gruf he fil al plat up-on the grounde,
And stille he lay as he had been y-bounde.

The covent eek lay on the pavement          225
Weping, and herien Cristes moder dere,
And after that they ryse, and forth ben went,
And toke awey this martir fro his bere,
And in a tombe of marbul-stones clere
Enclosen they his litel body swete;          230
There he is now, god leve us for to mete.

O yonge Hugh of Lincoln, slayn also
With cursed Jewes, as it is notable,
For it nis but a litel whyle ago;
Preye eek for us, we sinful folk unstable,          235
That, of his mercy, god so merciable
On us his grete mercy multiplye,
For reverence of his moder Marye. Amen.

### The Prologue of the Nonne Preestes Tale [1]

"Ho!" quod the knight, "good sir, namore of
          this,
That ye han seyd is right y-nough, y-wis,
And mochel more; for litel hevinesse

[1] After the Prioress's tale the Host asks Chaucer for a story. He begins *Sir Thopas*, a burlesque of the popular romances of the day, but is soon interrupted by the Host, who is bored. Thereupon Chaucer begins anew, and tells the edifying prose *Tale of Melibeus*. The Monk's tale which follows consists of a series of "tragedies," or sad stories, illustrating the instability of human good fortune; these prove to be too much for the patience of the Knight.

Is right y-nough to mochel folk, I gesse.
I seye for me, it is a greet disese          5
Wher-as men han ben in greet welthe and ese,
To heren of hir sodeyn fal, allas!
And the contrarie is joie and greet solas,
As whan a man hath been in povre estaat,
And clymbeth up, and wexeth fortunat,          10
And ther abydeth in prosperitee,
Swich thing is gladsom, as it thinketh me,
And of swich thing were goodly for to telle."
"Ye," quod our hoste, "by seint Poules belle,
Ye seye right sooth; this monk, he clappeth
          loude,          15
He spak how 'fortune covered with a cloude'
I noot never what, and als of a 'Tragedie'
Right now ye herde, and parde! no remedie
It is for to biwaille, ne compleyne
That that is doon, and als it is a peyne,          20
As ye han seyd, to here of hevinesse.
Sir monk, na-more of this, so god yow blesse!
Your tale anoyeth al this companye;
Swich talking is nat worth a boterflye;
For ther-in is ther no desport ne game.          25
Wherfor, sir Monk, or dan Piers by your name,
I preye yow hertely, telle us somwhat elles,
For sikerly, nere clinking of your belles,
That on your brydel hange on every syde,
By heven king, that for us alle dyde,          30
I sholde er this han fallen doun for slepe,
Although the slough had never been so depe;
Than had your tale al be told in vayn.
For certeinly, as that thise clerkes seyn,
'Wher-as a man may have noon audience,          35
Noght helpeth it to tellen his sentence.'
And wel I woot the substance is in me,
If any thing shal wel reported be.
Sir, sey somwhat of hunting, I yow preye."
"Nay," quod this monk, "I have no lust to
          pleye;          40
Now let another telle, as I have told."
Than spak our host, with rude speche and bold,
And seyde un-to the Nonnes Preest anon,
"Com neer, thou preest, com hider, thou sir
          John,
Tel us swich thing as may our hertes glade,          45
Be blythe, though thou ryde up-on a jade.
What though thyn hors be bothe foule and
          lene,
If he wol serve thee, rekke nat a bene;
Look that thyn herte be mery evermo."
"Yis, sir," quod he, "yis, host, so mote I go,          50
But I be mery, y-wis, I wol be blamed."—
And right anon his tale he hath attamed,
And thus he seyde un-to us everichon,
This swete preest, this goodly man, sir John.

### The Nonne Preestes Tale [2]

A povre widwe, somdel stape in age,
Was whylom dwelling in a narwe cotage,

[2] The immediate source of this story is not known, but there were popular cycles dealing with Reynard the Fox.

Bisyde a grove, stonding in a dale.
This widwe, of which I telle yow my tale,
Sin thilke day that she was last a wyf,    5
In pacience ladde a ful simple lyf,
For litel was hir catel and hir rente;
By housbondrye, of such as God hir sente,
She fond hir-self, and eek hir doghtren two.
Three large sowes hadde she, and namo,    10
Three kyn, and eek a sheep that highte Malle.
Ful sooty was hir bour, and eek hir halle,
In which she eet ful many a sclendre meel.
Of poynaunt sauce hir neded never a deel.
No deyntee morsel passed thurgh hir throte;    15
Hir dyete was accordant to hir cote.
Repleccioun ne made hir never syk;
Attempree dyete was al hir phisyk,
And exercyse, and hertes suffisaunce.
The goute lette hir no-thing for to daunce,    20
N'apoplexye shente nat hir heed;
No wyn ne drank she, neither whyt ne reed;
Hir bord was served most with whyt and blak,
Milk and broun breed, in which she fond no lak,
Seynd bacoun, and somtyme an ey or tweye,    25
For she was as it were a maner deye.
A yerd she hadde, enclosed al aboute
With stikkes, and a drye dich with-oute,
In which she hadde a cok, hight Chauntecleer,
In al the land of crowing nas his peer.    30
His vois was merier than the mery orgon
On messe-dayes that in the chirche gon;
Wel sikerer was his crowing in his logge,
Than is a clokke, or an abbey orlogge.
By nature knew he ech ascencioun    35
Of equinoxial in thilke toun;
For whan degrees fiftene were ascended,[3]
Thanne crew he, that it mighte nat ben amended.
His comb was redder than the fyn coral,
And batailed, as it were a castel-wal.    40
His bile was blak, and as the jeet it shoon;
Lyk asur were his legges, and his toon;
His nayles whytter than the lilie flour,
And lyk the burned gold was his colour.
This gentil cok hadde in his governaunce    45
Sevene hennes, for to doon al his plesaunce,
Whiche were his sustres and his paramours,
And wonder lyk to him, as of colours.
Of whiche the faireste hewed on hir throte
Was cleped faire damoysele Pertelote.    50
Curteys she was, discreet, and debonaire,
And compaignable, and bar hir-self so faire,
Sin thilke day that she was seven night old,
That trewely she hath the herte in hold
Of Chauntecleer loken in every lith;    55
He loved hir so, that wel was him therwith.
But such a joye was it to here hem singe,
Whan that the brighte sonne gan to springe,
In swete accord, "my lief is faren in londe."
For thilke tyme, as I have understonde,    60
Bestes and briddes coude speke and singe.
  And so bifel, that in a daweninge,

[3] When an hour had passed.

As Chauntecleer among his wyves alle
Sat on his perche, that was in the halle,
And next him sat this faire Pertelote,    65
This Chauntecleer gan gronen in his throte,
As man that in his dreem is drecched sore.
And whan that Pertelote thus herde him rore,
She was agast, and seyde, "O herte dere,
What eyleth yow, to grone in this manere?    70
Ye been a verray sleper, fy for shame!"
And he answerde and seyde thus, "madame,
I pray yow, that ye take it nat a-grief:
By god, me mette I was in swich meschief
Right now, that yet myn herte is sore afright.
Now god," quod he, "my swevene recche aright,    76
And keep my body out of foul prisoun!
Me mette, how that I romed up and doun
Withinne our yerde, wher-as I saugh a beste,
Was lyk an hound, and wolde han maad areste    80
Upon my body, and wolde han had me deed.
His colour was bitwixe yelwe and reed;
And tipped was his tail, and bothe his eres,
With blak, unlyk the remenant of his heres;
His snowte smal, with glowinge eyen tweye.    85
Yet of his look for fere almost I deye;
This caused me my groning, doutelees."
  "Avoy!" quod she, "fy on yow, hertelees!
Allas!" quod she, "for, by that god above,
Now han ye lost myn herte and al my love;    90
I can nat love a coward, by my feith.
For certes, what so any womman seith,
We alle desyren, if it mighte be,
To han housbondes hardy, wyse, and free,
And secree, and no nigard, ne no fool,    95
Ne him that is agast of every tool,
Ne noon avauntour, by that god above!
How dorste ye seyn for shame unto your love,
That any thing mighte make yow aferd?
Have ye no mannes herte, and han a berd?    100
Allas! and conne ye been agast of swevenis?
No-thing, god wot, but vanitee, in sweven is.
Swevenes engendren of replecciouns,
And ofte of fume, and of complecciouns,
Whan humours been to habundant in a wight.    105
Certes this dreem, which ye han met to-night,
Cometh of the grete superfluitee
Of youre rede *colera*, pardee,
Which causeth folk to dreden in here dremes
Of arwes, and of fyr with rede lemes,    110
Of grete bestes, that they wol hem byte,
Of contek, and of whelpes grete and lyte;
Right as the humour of malencolye
Causeth ful many a man, in sleep, to crye,
For fere of blake beres, or boles blake,    115
Or elles, blake develes wole hem take.
Of othere humours coude I telle also,
That werken many a man in sleep ful wo;
But I wol passe as lightly as I can.    119
  "Lo Catoun,[4] which that was so wys a man,

[4] Dionysius Cato, a medieval writer.

Seyde he nat thus, ne do no fors of dremes?
Now, sire," quod she, "whan we flee fro the
    bemes,
For Goddes love, as tak som laxatyf;
Up peril of my soule, and of my lyf,
I counseille yow the beste, I wol nat lye,   125
That bothe of colere and of malencolye
Ye purge yow; and for ye shul nat tarie,
Though in this toun is noon apotecarie,
I shal my-self to herbes techen yow,
That shul ben for your hele, and for your
    prow;   130
And in our yerd tho herbes shal I finde,
The whiche han of hir propretee, by kinde,
To purgen yow binethe, and eek above.
Forget not this, for goddes owene love!
Ye been ful colerik of compleccioun.   135
Ware the sonne in his ascencioun
Ne fynde yow nat repleet of humours hote;
And if it do, I dar wel leye a grote,
That ye shul have a fevere terciane,
Or an agu, that may be youre bane.   140
A day or two ye shul have digestyves
Of wormes, er ye take your laxatyves,
Of lauriol, centaure, and fumetere,
Or elles of ellebor, that groweth there,
Of catapuce, or of gaytres beryis,   145
Of erbe yve, growing in our yerd, that mery is;
Pekke hem up right as they growe, and ete hem
    in.
Be mery, housbond, for your fader kin!
Dredeth no dreem; I can say yow namore."
   "Madame," quod he, "*graunt mercy* of [5]
    your lore.   150
But nathelees, as touching daun Catoun,
That hath of wisdom such a greet renoun,
Though that he bad no dremes for to drede,
By god, men may in olde bokes rede
Of many a man, more of auctoritee   155
Than ever Catoun was, so mote I thee,
That al the revers seyn of his sentence,
And han wel founden by experience,
That dremes ben significaciouns,
As wel of joye as tribulaciouns   160
That folk enduren in this lyf present.
Ther nedeth make of this noon argument;
The verray preve sheweth it in dede.
   "Oon of the gretteste auctours that men
    rede [6]
Seith, thus, that whylom two felawes wente
On pilgrimage, in a ful good entente;   166
And happed so, thay come into a toun,
Wher-as ther was swich congregacioun
Of peple, and eek so streit of herbergage,
That they ne founde as muche as o cotage   170
In which they bothe mighte y-logged be.
Wherfor thay mosten, of necessitee,
As for that night, departen compaignye;
And ech of hem goth to his hostelrye,
And took his logging as it wolde falle.   175

That oon of hem was logged in a stalle,
Fer in a yerd, with oxen of the plough;
That other man was logged wel y-nough,
As was his aventure, or his fortune,
That us governeth alle as in commune.   180
   "And so bifel, that, longe er it were day,
This man mette in his bed, ther-as he lay,
How that his felawe gan up-on him calle,
And seyde, 'allas! for in an oxes stalle
This night I shal be mordred ther I lye.   185
Now help me, dere brother, er I dye;
In alle haste com to me,' he sayde.
This man out of his sleep for fere abrayde;
But whan that he was wakned of his sleep,
He turned him, and took of this no keep;   190
Him thoughte his dreem nas but a vanitee.
Thus twyës in his sleping dremed he.
And atte thridde tyme yet his felawe
Cam, as him thoughte, and seide, 'I am now
    slawe;
Bihold my blody woundes, depe and wyde!   195
Arys up erly in the morwe-tyde,
And at the west gate of the toun,' quod he,
'A carte ful of dong ther shaltow see,
In which my body is hid ful prively;
Do thilke carte aresten boldely.   200
My gold caused my mordre, sooth to sayn';
And tolde him every poynt how he was slayn,
With a ful pitous face, pale of hewe.
And truste wel, his dreem he fond ful trewe;
For on the morwe, as sone as it was day,   205
To his felawes in he took the way;
And whan that he cam to this oxes stalle,
After his felawe he bigan to calle.
   "The hostiler answered him anon,
And seyde, 'sire, your felawe is agon,   210
As sone as day he wente out of the toun.'
This man gan fallen in suspecioun,
Remembring on his dreames that he mette,
And forth he goth, no lenger wolde he lette,
Unto the west gate of the toun, and fond   215
A dong-carte, as it were to donge lond,
That was arrayed in the same wyse
As ye han herd the dede man devyse;
And with an hardy herte he gan to crye
Vengeaunce and justice of this felonye:— 220
'My felawe mordred is this same night,
And in this carte he lyth gapinge upright.
I crye out on the ministres,' quod he,
'That sholden kepe and reulen this citee;
Harrow! allas! her lyth my felawe slayn!'   225
What sholde I more un-to this tale sayn?
The peple out-sterte, and caste the cart to
    grounde,
And in the middel of the dong they founde
The dede man, that mordred was al newe.
   "O blisful god, that art so just and trewe! 230
Lo, how that thou biwreyest mordre alway!
Mordre wol out, that see we day by day.
Mordre is so wlatsom and abhominable
To god, that is so just and resonable,
That he ne wol nat suffre it heled be;   235
Though it abyde a yeer, or two, or three,

---

[5] Many thanks for.
[6] Cicero in *De Divinatione.*

Mordre wol out, this my conclusioun.[7]
And right anoon, ministres of that toun
Han hent the carter, and so sore him pyned,
And eek the hostiler so sore engyned,     240
That they biknewe hir wikkednesse anoon,
And were an-hanged by the nekke-boon.

"Here may men seen that dremes been to
    drede,
And certes, in the same book I rede,
Right in the nexte chapitre after this     245
(I gabbe nat, so have I joye or blis),
Two men that wolde han passed over see,
For certeyn cause, in-to a fer contree,
If that the wind ne hadde been contrarie,
That made hem in a citee for to tarie,     250
That stood ful mery upon an haven-syde.
But on a day, agayn the even-tyde,
The wind gan chaunge, and blew right as hem
    leste.
Jolif and glad they wente un-to hir reste,
And casten hem ful erly for to saille;     255
But to that oo man fil a greet mervaille.
That oon of hem, in sleping as he lay,
Him mette a wonder dreem, agayn the day;
Him thoughte a man stood by his beddes syde,
And him comaunded, that he sholde abyde,     260
And seyde him thus, 'if thou to-morwe wende,
Thou shalt be dreynt; my tale is at an ende.'
He wook, and tolde his felawe what he mette,
And preyde him his viage for to lette;
As for that day, he preyde him to abyde.     265
His felawe, that lay by his beddes syde,
Gan for to laughe, and scorned him ful faste.
'No dreem,' quod he, 'may so myn herte agaste,
That I wol lette for to do my thinges.
I sette not a straw by thy dreminges,     270
For swevenes been but vanitees and japes.
Men dreme al-day of owles or of apes,
And eke of many a mase therwithal;
Men dreme of thing that never was ne shal.
But sith I see that thou wolt heer abyde,     275
And thus for-sleuthen wilfully thy tyde,
God wot it reweth me; and have good day.'
And thus he took his leve, and wente his way.
But er that he hadde halfe his cours y-seyled,
Noot I nat why, ne what mischaunce it eyled,
But casuelly the shippes botme rente,     281
And ship and man under the water wente
In sighte of othere shippes it byside,
That with hem seyled at the same tyde.
And therfor, faire Pertelote so dere,     285
By swiche ensamples olde maistow lere,
That no man sholde been to recchelees
Of dremes, for I sey thee, doutelees,
That many a dreem ful sore is for to drede.

"Lo, in the lyf of seint Kenelm, I rede,     290
That was Kenulphus sone, the noble king
Of Mercenrike, how Kenelm mette a thing;
A lyte er he was mordred, on a day,
His mordre in his avisioun he say.
His norice him expouned every del     295

His sweven, and bad him for to kepe him wel
For traisoun; but he nas but seven yeer old,
And therfore litel tale hath he told
Of any dreem, so holy was his herte.
By god, I hadde lever than my sherte     300
That ye had rad his legende, as have I.
Dame Pertelote, I sey yow trewely,
Macrobeus, that writ th'avisioun
In Affrike of the worthy Cipioun,
Affermeth dremes, and seith that they been     305
Warning of thinges that men after seen.

"And forther-more, I pray yow loketh wel
In th'olde testament, of Daniel,
If he held dremes any vanitee.
Reed eek of Joseph, and ther shul ye see     310
Wher dremes ben somtyme (I sey nat alle)
Warning of thinges that shul after falle.
Loke of Egipt the king, daun Pharao,
His bakere and his boteler also,
Wher they ne felte noon effect in dremes.     315
Who-so wol seken actes of sondry remes,
May rede of dremes many a wonder thing.

"Lo Cresus, which that was of Lyde king, [8]
Mette he nat that he sat upon a tree,
Which signified he sholde anhanged be?     320
Lo heer Andromacha, Ectores wyf,
That day that Ector sholde lese his lyf,
She dremed on the same night biforn,
How that the lyf of Ector sholde be lorn,
If thilke day he wente in-to bataille;     325
She warned him, but it mighte nat availle;
He wente for to fighte nathelees,
But he was slayn anoon of Achilles.
But thilke tale is al to long to telle,
And eek it is ny day, I may nat dwelle.     330
Shortly I seye, as for conclusioun,
That I shal han of this avisioun
Adversitee; and I seye forther-more,
That I ne telle of laxatyves no store,
For they ben venimous, I woot it wel;     335
I hem defye, I love hem never a del.

"Now let us speke of mirthe, and stinte al
    this;
Madame Pertelote, so have I blis,
Of o thing god hath sent me large grace;
For whan I see the beautee of your face,     340
Ye ben so scarlet-reed about your yën,
It maketh al my drede for to dyen;
For, also siker as *In principio*,
*Mulier est hominis confusio*; [9]
Madame, the sentence of this Latin is—     345
Womman is mannes joye and al his blis.
For whan I fele a-night your softe syde,
Al-be-it that I may nat on you ryde,
For that our perche is maad so narwe, alas!
I am so ful of joye and of solas     350
That I defye bothe sweven and dreem."
And with that word he fley doun fro the beem,
For it was day, and eek his hennes alle;

[7] Cf. the Prioress's tale, l. 124.

[8] The story of Croesus had been the last of the tragedies told by the Monk before the Knight interrupted him.

[9] In the beginning woman is man's undoing.

And with a chuk he gan hem for to calle,
For he had founde a corn, lay in the yerd.  355
Royal he was, he was namore aferd;
He fethered Pertelote twenty tyme,
And trad as ofte, er that it was pryme.
He loketh as it were a grim leoun;
And on his toos he rometh up and doun,  360
Him deyned not to sette his foot to grounde.
He chukketh, whan he hath a corn y-founde,
And to him rennen thanne his wyves alle.
Thus royal, as a prince is in his halle,
Leve I this Chauntecleer in his pasture;  365
And after wol I telle his aventure.

    Whan that the month in which the world
      bigan,
That highte March, whan god first maked man,
Was complet, and [y]-passed were also,
Sin March bigan, thritty dayes and two,  370
Bifel that Chauntecleer, in al his pryde,
His seven wyves walking by his syde,
Caste up his eyen the brighte sonne,
That in the signe of Taurus hadde y-ronne  374
Twenty degrees and oon, and somwhat more;
And knew by kynde, and by noon other lore,
That it was pryme, and crew with blisful
    stevene.
"The sonne," he sayde, "is clomben up on
    hevene
Fourty degrees and oon, and more, y-wis.
Madame Pertelote, my worldes blis,  380
Herkneth thise blisful briddes how they singe,
And see the fresshe floures how they springe;
Ful is myn herte of revel and solas."
But sodeinly him fil a sorweful cas;
For ever the latter ende of joye is wo.  385
God woot that worldly joye is sone ago;
And if a rethor coude faire endyte,
He in a cronique saufly mighte it wryte,
As for a sovereyn notabilitee.
Now every wys man, lat him herkne me;  390
This storie is al-so trewe, I undertake,
As is the book of Launcelot de Lake,[10]
That wommen holde in ful gret reverence.
Now wol I torne agayn to my sentence.

    A col-fox, ful of sly iniquitee,  395
That in the grove hadde woned yeres three,
By heigh imaginacioun forn-cast,
The same night thurgh-out the hegges brast
Into the yerd, ther Chauntecleer the faire
Was wont, and eek his wyves, to repaire;  400
And in a bed of wortes stille he lay,
Til it was passed undern of the day,
Wayting his tyme on Chauntecleer to falle,
As gladly doon thise homicydes alle,
That in awayt liggen to mordre men.  405
O false mordrer, lurking in thy den!
O newe Scariot, newe Genilon![11]
False dissimilour, O Greek Sinon,
That broghtest Troye al outrely to sorwe!
O Chauntecleer, acursed be that morwe,  410
That thou into that yerd floug fro the bemes!

[10] A prose romance.
[11] The betrayer of Roland.

Thou were ful wel y-warned by thy dremes,
That thilke day was perilous to thee.
But what that god forwoot mot nedes be,
After the opinioun of certeyn clerkis.  415
Witnesse on him, that any perfit clerk is,
That in scole is gret altercacioun
In this matere, and greet disputisoun,
And hath ben of an hundred thousand men.
But I ne can not bulte it to the bren,  420
As can the holy doctour Augustyn,
Or Boëce, or the bishop Bradwardyn,
Whether that goddes worthy forwiting
Streyneth me nedely for to doon a thing
(Nedely clepe I simple necessitee);  425
Or elles, if free choys be graunted me
To do that same thing, or do it noght,
Though god forwoot it, er that it was wroght;
Or if his witing streyneth nevere a del
But by necessitee condicionel.  430
I wol not han to do of swich matere;
My tale is of a cok, as ye may here,
That took his counseil of his wyf, with sorwe,
To walken in the yerd upon that morwe
That he had met the dreem, that I yow tolde.
Wommennes counseils been ful ofte colde;  436
Wommannes counseil broghte us first to wo,
And made Adam fro paradys to go,
Ther-as he was ful mery, and wel at ese.—
But for I noot, to whom it mighte displese,
If I counseil of wommen wolde blame,  441
Passe over, for I seyde it in my game.
Rede auctours, wher they trete of swich matere,
And what thay seyn of wommen ye may here.
Thise been the cokkes wordes, and nat myne;
I can noon harm of no womman divyne.—  446

    Faire in the sond, to bathe hir merily,
Lyth Pertelote, and alle hir sustres by,
Agayn the sonne; and Chauntecleer so free
Song merier than the mermayde in the see;  450
For Phisiologus [12] seith sikerly,
How that they singen wel and merily.
And so bifel that, as he caste his yë,
Among the wortes, on a boterflye,
He was war of this fox that lay ful lowe.  455
No-thing ne liste him thanne for to crowe,
But cryde anon, "cok, cok," and up he sterte,
As man that was affrayed in his herte.
For naturelly a beest desyreth flee
Fro his contrarie, if he may it see,  460
Though he never erst had seyn it with his yë.

    This Chauntecleer, whan he gan him espye,
He wolde han fled, but that the fox anon
Seyde, "Gentil sire, allas! wher wol ye gon?
Be ye affrayed of me that am your freend?  465
Now certes, I were worse than a feend,
If I to yow wolde harm or vileinye.
I am nat come your counseil for t'espye;
But trewely, the cause of my cominge
Was only for to herkne how that ye singe.  470
For trewely ye have as mery a stevene
As eny aungel hath, that is in hevene;

[12] The Bestiary, a popular collection containing moralized descriptions of animals.

Therwith ye han in musik more felinge
Than hadde Boëce, or any that can singe.
My lord your fader (god his soule blesse!) 475
And eek your moder, of hir gentilesse,
Han in myn hous y-been, to my gret ese;
And certes, sire, ful fayn wolde I yow plese.
But for men speke of singing, I wol saye,
So mote I brouke wel myn eyen tweye, 480
Save yow, I herde never man so singe,
As dide your fader in the morweninge;
Certes, it was of herte, al that he song.
And for to make his voys the more strong,
He wolde so peyne him, that with bothe his yën 485
He moste winke, so loude he wolde cryen,
And stonden on his tiptoon ther-with-al,
And strecche forth his nekke long and smal.
And eek he was of swich discrecioun,
That ther nas no man in no regioun 490
That him in song or wisdom mighte passe.
I have wel rad in daun Burnel the Asse,[13]
Among his vers, how that ther was a cok,
For that a preestes sone yaf him a knok
Upon his leg, whyl he was yong and nyce, 495
He made him for to lese his benefyce.
But certeyn, ther nis no comparisoun
Bitwix the wisdom and discrecioun
Of youre fader, and of his subtiltee.
Now singeth, sire, for seinte Charitee, 500
Let see, conne ye your fader countrefete?"
This Chauntecleer his winges gan to bete,
As man that coude his tresoun nat espye,
So was he ravisshed with his flaterye.

    Allas! ye lordes, many a fals flatour 505
Is in your courtes, and many a losengeour,
That plesen yow wel more, by my feith,
Than he that soothfastnesse unto yow seith.
Redeth Ecclesiaste of flaterye;[14]
Beth war, ye lordes, of hir trecherye. 510

    This Chauntecleer stood hye up-on his toos,
Strecching his nekke, and heeld his eyen cloos,
And gan to crowe loude for the nones;
And daun Russel the fox sterte up at ones,
And by the gargat hente Chauntecleer, 515
And on his bak toward the wode him beer,
For yet ne was ther no man that him sewed.
O destinee, that mayst nat been eschewed!
Allas, that Chauntecleer fleigh fro the bemes!
Allas, his wyf ne roghte nat of dremes! 520
And on a Friday fil al this meschaunce.
O Venus, that art goddesse of plesaunce,
Sin that thy servant was this Chauntecleer,
And in thy service dide al his poweer,
More for delyt, than world to multiplye, 525
Why woldestow suffre him on thy day to dye?
O Gaufred,[15] dere mayster soverayn,
That, whan thy worthy king Richard was slayn
With shot, compleynedest his deth so sore,

Why ne hadde I now thy sentence and thy lore, 530
The Friday for to chyde, as diden ye?
(For on a Friday soothly slayn was he.)
Than wolde I shewe yow how that I coude pleyne
For Chauntecleres drede, and for his peyne.
    Certes, swich cry ne lamentacioun 535
Was never of ladies maad, whan Illioun
Was wonne, and Pirrus with his streite swerd,
Whan he hadde hent king Priam by the berd,
And slayn him (as saith us *Eneydos*),[16]
As maden alle the hennes in the clos, 540
Whan they had seyn of Chauntecleer the sighte.
But sovereynly dame Pertelote shrighte,
Ful louder than dide Hasdrubales wyf,
Whan that hir housbond hadde lost his lyf,
And that the Romayns hadde brend Cartage;
She was so ful of torment and of rage, 546
That wilfully into the fyr she sterte,
And brende hir-selven with a stedfast herte.
O woful hennes, right so cryden ye,
As, whan that Nero brende the citee 550
Of Rome, cryden senatoures wyves,
For that hir housbondes losten alle hir lyves;
Withouten gilt this Nero hath hem slayn.
Now wol I torne to my tale agayn:—

    This sely widwe, and eek hir doghtres two,
Herden thise hennes crye and maken wo, 556
And out at dores sterten they anoon,
And syen the fox toward the grove goon,
And bar upon his bak the cok away;
And cryden, "Out! harrow! and weylaway! 560
Ha, ha, the fox!" and after him they ran,
And eek with staves many another man;
Ran Colle our dogge, and Talbot, and Gerland,
And Malkin, with a distaf in hir hand;
Ran cow and calf, and eek the verray hogges
So were they fered for berking of the dogges 566
And shouting of the men and wimmen eke,
They ronne so, hem thoughte hir herte breke.
They yelleden as feendes doon in helle;
The dokes cryden as men wolde hem quelle;
The gees for fere flowen over the trees; 571
Out of the hyve cam the swarm of bees;
So hidous was the noyse, a! *benedicite!*[17]
Certes, he Jakke Straw,[18] and his meynee,
Ne made never shoutes half so shrille, 575
Whan that they wolden any Fleming kille,
As thilke day was maad upon the fox.
Of bras thay broghten bemes, and of box,
Of horn, of boon, in whiche they blewe and pouped,
And therwithal thay shryked and they houped;
It semed as that heven sholde falle. 581
Now, gode men, I pray yow herkneth alle!
    Lo, how fortune turneth sodeinly

---

[13] A Latin poem by Nigellus Wireker entitled *Burnellus or the Mirror of Fools* (written towards the close of the twelfth century).

[14] Ecclesiasticus (in *Apocrypha*), 12:10, 11, 16.

[15] Geoffrey de Vinsauf, Anglo-Norman trouvère.

[16] *Aeneid*, II, 544.

[17] Literally, "Blessings on you."

[18] Leader of an insurrection in 1381. Thomas Walsingham states that when he and his men killed Flemings they raised a "most horrible clamor."

The hope and pryde eek of hir enemy!
This cok, that lay upon the foxes bak,     585
In al his drede, un-to the fox he spak,
And seyde, "sire, if that I were as ye,
Yet sholde I seyn (as wis god helpe me),
Turneth agayn, ye proude cherles alle!
A verray pestilence up-on yow falle!     590
Now am I come un-to this wodes syde,
Maugree your heed, the cok shal heer abyde;
I wol him ete in feith, and that anon."—
The fox answerde, "in feith, it shal be don,"—
And as he spak that word, al sodeinly     595
This cok brak from his mouth deliverly,
And heighe up-on a tree he fleigh anon.
And whan the fox saugh that he was y-gon,
"Allas!" quod he, "O Chauntecleer, allas!
I have to yow," quod he, "y-doon trespas,     600
In-as-muche as I maked yow aferd,
Whan I yow hente, and broghte out of the
          yerd;
But, sire, I dide it in no wikke entente;
Com doun, and I shal telle yow what I mente.
I shal seye sooth to yow, god help me so."     605
"Nay than," quod he, "I shrewe us bothe two,
And first I shrewe my-self, bothe blood and
          bones,
If thou bigyle me ofter than ones.
Thou shalt na-more, thurgh thy flaterye,
Do me to singe and winke with myn yë.     610
For he that winketh, whan he sholde see,
Al wilfully, god lat him never thee!"
"Nay," quod the fox, "but god yeve him
          meschaunce,
That is so undiscreet of governaunce,
That jangleth whan he sholde holde his pees."
Lo, swich it is for to be recchelees,     616
And necligent, and truste on flaterye.
But ye that holden this tale a folye,
As of a fox, or of a cok and hen,
Taketh the moralitee, good men.     620
For seint Paul seith, that al that writen is,
To our doctryne it is y-write, y-wis.[19]
Taketh the fruyt, and lat the chaf be stille.
Now, gode god, if that it be thy wille,
As seith my lord,[20] so make us alle good
          men;     625
And bringe us to his heighe blisse. Amen.

## Words of the Host [1]

Our Hoste gan to swere as he were wood,
"Harrow!" quod he, "by nayles and by blood!

[19] II Timothy, 3:16.

[20] A note in one of the manuscripts explains this as referring to the Archbishop of Canterbury.

[1] Following the Nun's Priest's Tale there is an evident break, after which, in the now accepted arrangement of the tales, come the Physician's Tale (immediately preceding the above "words of the Host") and the Pardoner's Tale. The Physician's Tale, to which the Host refers, was one of afflicted innocence, the story of Appius and Virginia, in which the latter's father slays her as the only means

This was a fals cherl and a fals justyse!
As shamful deeth as herte may devyse
Come to thise juges and hir advocats!     5
Algate this sely mayde is slayn, allas!
Allas! to dere boghte she beautee!
Wherfore I seye al day, as men may see,
That yiftes of fortune or of nature
Ben cause of deeth to many a creature.     10
Hir beautee was hir deeth, I dar wel sayn;
Allas! so pitously as she was slayn!
Of bothe yiftes that I speke of now
Men han ful ofte more harm than prow.
But trewely, myn owene mayster dere,     15
This is a pitous tale for to here.
But natheles, passe over, is no fors;
I prey to god, so save thy gentil cors,
And eek thyne urinals and thy jordanes,
Thyn Ypocras, and eek thy Galianes,     20
And every boist ful of thy letuarie;
God blesse hem, and our lady seinte Marie!
So mot I theen, thou art a propre man,
And lyk a prelat, by seint Ronyan! [2]
Seyde I nat wel? I can nat speke in terme;     25
But wel I woot, thou doost my herte to erme,
That I almost have caught a cardiacle.
By corpus bones! but I have triacle,
Or elles a draught of moyste and corny ale,
Or but I here anon a mery tale,     30
Myn herte is lost for pitee of this mayde.
Thou bel amy, thou Pardoner," he seyde,
"Tell us som mirthe or japes right anon."
"It shall be doon," quod he, "by seint Ronyon!
But first," quod he, "heer at this ale-stake     35
I wol both drinke, and eten of a cake."

But right anon thise gentils gonne to crye,
"Nay! lat him telle us of no ribaudye;
Tel us som moral thing, that we may lere
Som wit, and thanne wol we gladly here."     40
"I graunte, y-wis," quod he, "but I mot thinke
Up-on som honest thing, whyl that I drinke."

## The Prologue of the Pardoners Tale

*Radix malorum est Cupiditas: Ad Thimotheum, sexto.*[3]

"Lordings," quod he, "in chirches whan I
          preche,
I peyne me to han an hauteyn speche,
And ringe it out as round as gooth a belle,
For I can al by rote that I telle.
My theme is alwey oon, and ever was—     5
'Radix malorum est Cupiditas.'

"First I pronounce whennes that I come,
And than my bulles shewe I, alle and somme.
Our lige lordes seel on my patente,
That shewe I first, my body to warente,     10

of protecting her from shame at the hands of Appius.

[2] St. Ronan, whose name will be familiar to readers of Scott. Little besides his name is known of him.

[3] Greed is the root of all evil (I Timothy, 6:10).

That no man be so bold, ne preest ne clerk,
Me to destourbe of Cristes holy werk;
And after that than telle I forth my tales,
Bulles of popes and of cardinales,
Of patriarkes, and bishoppes I shewe;     15
And in Latyn I speke a wordes fewe,
To saffron with my predicacioun,
And for to stire men to devocioun.
Than shewe I forth my longe cristal stones,
Y-crammed ful of cloutes and of bones;     20
Reliks been they, as wenen they echoon.
Than have I in latoun a sholder-boon
Which that was of an holy Jewes shepe.
'Good men,' seye I, 'tak of my wordes kepe;
If that this boon he wasshe in any welle,     25
If cow, or calf, or sheep, or oxe swelle
That any worm hath ete, or worm y-stonge,
Tak water of that welle, and wash his tonge,
And it is hool anon; and forthermore,
Of pokkes and of scabbe, and every sore     30
Shal every sheep be hool, that of this welle
Drinketh a draughte; tak kepe eek what I
    telle.
If that the good-man, that the bestes oweth,
Wol every wike, er that the cok him croweth,
Fastinge, drinken of this welle a draughte,     35
As thilke holy Jewe our eldres taughte,
His bestes and his stoor shal multiplye.
And, sirs, also it heleth jalousye;
For, though a man be falle in jalous rage,
Let maken with this water his potage,     40
And never shal he more his wyf mistriste,
Though he the sooth of hir defaute wiste;
Al had she taken preestes two or three.
    "Heer is a miteyn eek, that ye may see.
He that his hond wol putte in this miteyn,     45
He shal have multiplying of his greyn,
Whan he hath sowen, be it whete or otes,
So that he offre pens, or elles grotes.
    " 'Good men and wommen, o thing warne I
    yow.
If any wight be in this chirche now,     50
That hath doon sinne horrible, that he
Dar nat, for shame, of it y-shriven be,
Or any womman, be she yong or old,
That hath y-maad hir housbond cokewold,
Swich folk shul have no power ne no grace     55
To offren to my reliks in this place.
And who-so findeth him out of swich blame,
He wol com up and offre in goddes name,
And I assoille him by the auctoritee
Which that by bulle y-graunted was to me.'     60
    "By this gaude have I wonne, yeer by yeer,
An hundred mark sith I was Pardoner.
I stonde lyk a clerk in my pulpet,
And whan the lewed peple is doun y-set,
I preche, so as ye han herd bifore,     65
And telle an hundred false japes more.
Than peyne I me to strecche forth the nekke,
And est and west upon the peple I bekke,
As doth a dowve sitting on a berne.
Myn hondes and my tonge goon so yerne,     70
That it is joye to see my bisinesse.

Of avaryce and of swich cursednesse
Is al my preching, for to make hem free
To yeve her pens, and namely un-to me.
For my entente is nat but for to winne,     75
And no-thing for correccioun of sinne.
I rekke never, whan that they ben beried,
Though that her soules goon a-blakeberied!
For certes, many a predicacioun
Comth ofte tyme of yvel entencioun;     80
Som for plesaunce of folk and flaterye,
To been avaunced by ipocrisye,
And som for veyne glorie, and som for hate.
For, whan I dar non other weyes debate,
Than wol I stinge him with my tonge smerte
In preching, so that he shal nat asterte     86
To been defamed falsly, if that he
Hath trespased to my brethren or to me.
For, though I telle noght his propre name,
Men shal wel knowe that it is the same     90
By signes and by othere circumstances.
Thus quyte I folk that doon us displesances;
Thus spitte I out my venim under hewe
Of holynesse, to seme holy and trewe.
    "But shortly myn entente I wol devyse;     95
I preche of no-thing but for coveityse.
Therfor my theme is yet, and ever was—
'Radix malorum est cupiditas.'
Thus can I preche agayn that same vyce
Which that I use, and that is avaryce.     100
But, though my-self be gilty in that sinne,
Yet can I maken other folk to twinne
From avaryce, and sore to repente.
But that is nat my principal entente.
I preche no-thing but for coveityse;     105
Of this matere it oughte y-nogh suffyse.
    "Than telle I hem ensamples many oon
Of olde stories, longe tyme agoon:
For lewed peple loven tales olde;
Swich thinges can they wel reporte and holde.
What? trowe ye, the whyles I may preche,     111
And winne gold and silver for I teche,
That I wol live in povert wilfully?
Nay, nay, I thoghte it never trewely!
For I wol preche and begge in sondry londes;
I wol not do no labour with myn hondes,     116
Ne make baskettes, and live therby,
Because I wol nat beggen ydelly.
I wol non of the apostles counterfete;
I wol have money, wolle, chese, and whete,     120
Al were it yeven of the povrest page,
Or of the povrest widwe in a village,
Al sholde hir children sterve for famyne.
Nay! I wol drinke licour of the vyne,
And have a joly wenche in every toun.     125
But herkneth, lordings, in conclusioun;
Your lyking is that I shal telle a tale.
Now, have I dronke a draughte of corny ale,
By god, I hope I shal yow telle a thing
That shal, by resoun, been at your lyking.     130
For, though myself be a ful vicious man,
A moral tale yet I yow telle can,
Which I am wont to preche, for to winne.
Now holde your pees, my tale I wol beginne."

## The Pardoners Tale [4]

In Flaundres whylom was a companye
Of yonge folk, that haunteden folye,
As ryot, hasard, stewes, and tavernes,
Wher-as, with harpes, lutes, and giternes,
They daunce and pleye at dees bothe day and
    night,    5
And ete also and drinken over hir might,
Thurgh which they doon the devel sacrifyse
With-in that develes temple, in cursed wyse,
By superfluitee abhominable;
Hir othes been so grete and so dampnable,  10
That it is grisly for to here hem swere;
Our blissed lordes body they to-tere;
Hem thoughte Jewes rente him noght y-nough;
And ech of hem at otheres sinne lough.
And right anon than comen tombesteres  15
Fetys and smale, and yonge fruytesteres,
Singers with harpes, baudes, wafereres,
Whiche been the verray develes officeres
To kindle and blowe the fyr of lecherye,
That is annexed un-to glotonye;  20
The holy writ tak I to my witnesse,
That luxurie is in wyn and dronkenesse.
   Lo, how that dronken Loth, unkindely,
Lay by his doghtres two, unwitingly;
So dronke he was, he niste what he wroghte.  25
   Herodes (who-so wel the stories soghte),
Whan he of wyn was replet at his feste,
Right at his owene table he yaf his heste
To sleen the Baptist John ful gilteless.
   Senek seith eek a good word doutelees;  30
He seith, he can no difference finde
Bitwix a man that is out of his minde
And a man which that is dronkelewe,
But that woodnesse, y-fallen in a shrewe,
Persevereth lenger than doth dronkenesse.  35
O glotonye, ful of cursednesse,
O cause first of our confusioun,
O original of our dampnacioun,
Til Crist had boght us with his blood agayn!
Lo, how dere, shortly for to sayn,  40
Aboght was thilke cursed vileinye;
Corrupt was al this world for glotonye!
   Adam our fader, and his wyf also,
Fro Paradys to labour and to wo
Were driven for that vyce, it is no drede;  45
For whyl that Adam fasted, as I rede,
He was in Paradys; and whan that he
Eet of the fruyt defended on the tree,
Anon he was out-cast to wo and peyne.
O glotonye, on thee wel oghte us pleyne!  50
O, wiste a man how many maladyes
Folwen of excesse and of glotonyes,

He wolde been the more mesurable
Of his diete, sittinge at his table.
Allas! the shorte throte, the tendre mouth,  55
Maketh that, Est and West, and North and
    South,
In erthe, in eir, in water men to-swinke
To gete a glotoun deyntee mete and drinke!
Of this matere, o Paul, wel canstow trete,
"Mete un-to wombe, and wombe eek un-to
    mete,  60
Shal god destroyen bothe," as Paulus seith.[5]
Allas! a foul thing is it, by my feith,
To seye this word, and fouler is the dede,
Whan man so drinketh of the whyte and rede,
That of his throte he maketh his privee,  65
Thurgh thilke cursed superfluitee.
   The apostel weping seith ful pitously,
"Ther walken many of whiche yow told have I,
I seye it now weping with pitous voys,
[That] they been enemys of Cristes croys,  70
Of whiche the ende is deeth, wombe is her
    god." [6]
O wombe! O bely! O stinking cod,
Fulfild of donge and of corrupcioun!
At either ende of thee foul is the soun.
How greet labour and cost is thee to finde!  75
Thise cokes, how they stampe, and streyne,
    and grinde,
And turnen substaunce in-to accident,[7]
To fulfille al thy likerous talent!
Out of the harde bones knokke they
The mary, for they caste noght a-wey  80
That may go thurgh the golet softe and swote;
Of spicerye, of leef, and bark, and rote
Shal been his sauce y-maked by delyt,
To make him yet a newer appetyt.
But certes, he that haunteth swich delyces  85
Is deed, whyl that he liveth in tho vyces.
   A lecherous thing is wyn, and dronkenesse
Is ful of stryving and of wrecchednesse.
O dronke man, disfigured is thy face,
Sour is thy breeth, foul artow to embrace,  90
And thurgh thy dronke nose semeth the soun
As though thou seydest ay, "Sampsoun, Samp-
    soun";
And yet, god wot, Sampsoun drank never no
    wyn.
Thou fallest, as it were a stiked swyn;
Thy tonge is lost, and al thyn honest cure;  95
For dronkenesse is verray sepulture
Of mannes wit and his discrecioun,
In whom that drinke hath dominacioun,
He can no conseil kepe, it is no drede.
Now kepe yow fro the whyte and fro the rede,
And namely fro the whyte wyn of Lepe,[8]  101
That is to selle in Fish-strete or in Chepe.[9]

---

[4] The story is of Eastern origin, and its theme
has been often used from early times to the present
day—for example by Boccaccio, *Decameron*, 6th
Day, 10th Tale (apparently not Chaucer's source,
which is unknown) and by Kipling, *The King's
Ankus*. The Pardoner's final comment makes the
tale a sort of sermon or *exemplum* of avarice.

[5] I Corinthians, 6:13.    [6] Philippians, 3:18–19.
[7] An allusion to disputes between the realists and
the nominalists among medieval philosophers. The
meaning is that cooks so changed the very nature
of the things they prepared that those who ate them
could not tell what they originally were.
[8] Near Cadiz.    [9] Cheapside, London.

This wyn of Spayne crepeth subtilly
In othere wynes, growing faste by,[10]
Of which ther ryseth swich fumositee,     105
That whan a man hath dronken draughtes
    three,
And weneth that he be at hoom in Chepe,
He is in Spayne, right at the toune of Lepe,
Nat at the Rochel, ne at Burdeux town;
And thanne wol he seye, "Sampsoun, Samp-
    soun."                                 110
But herkneth, lordings, o word, I yow preye,
That alle the sovereyn actes, dar I seye,
Of victories in th'olde testament,
Thurgh verray god, that is omnipotent,
Were doon in abstinence and in preyere;    115
Loketh the Bible, and ther ye may it lere.
    Loke, Attila, the grete conquerour,
Deyde in his sleep, with shame and dishonour,
Bledinge ay at his nose in dronkenesse;
A capitayn shoulde live in sobrenesse.     120
And over al this, avyseth yow right wel
What was comaunded un-to Lamuel—[11]
Nat Samuel, but Lamuel, seye I—
Redeth the Bible, and finde it expresly
Of wyn-yeving to hem that han justyse.     125
Na-more of this, for it may wel suffyse.
    And now that I have spoke of glotonye,
Now wol I yow defenden hasardrye.
Hasard is verray moder of lesinges,
And of deceite, and cursed forsweringes,   130
Blaspheme of Crist; manslaughtre, and wast
    also
Of catel and of tyme; and forthermo,
It is repreve and contrarie of honour
For to ben holde a commune hasardour.
And ever the hyër he is of estaat,         135
The more is he holden desolaat.
If that a prince useth hasardrye,
In alle governaunce and policye
He is, as by commune opinioun,
Y-holde the lasse in reputacioun.          140
    Stilbon,[12] that was a wys embassadour,
Was sent to Corinthe, in ful greet honour,
Fro Lacidomie, to make hir alliaunce.
And whan he cam, him happede, par chaunce,
That alle the grettest that were of that lond,
Pleyinge atte hasard he hem fond.          146
For which, as sone as it mighte be,
He stal him hoom agayn to his contree,
And seyde, "ther wol I nat lese my name;
N'I wol nat take on me so greet defame,    150
Yow for to allye un-to none hasardours.
Sendeth othere wyse embassadours;
For, by my trouthe, me were lever dye,

Than I yow sholde to hasardours allye.
For ye that been so glorious in honours    155
Shul nat allyen yow with hasardours
As by my wil, ne as by my tretee."
This wyse philosophre thus seyde he.
    Loke eek that, to the king Demetrius
The king of Parthes, as the book seith us,[13] 160
Sente him a paire of dees of gold in scorn,
For he hadde used hasard ther-biforn;
For which he heeld his glorie or his renoun
At no value or reputacioun.
Lordes may finden other maner pley         165
Honeste y-nough to dryve the day awey.
    Now wol I speke of othes false and grete
A word or two, as olde bokes trete.
Gret swering is a thing abhominable,
And false swering is yet more reprevable.  170
The heighe god forbad swering at al,
Witnesse on Mathew;[14] but in special
Of swering seith the holy Jeremye,[15]
"Thou shalt seye sooth thyn othes, and nat lye,
And swere in dome, and eek in rightwisnesse";
But ydel swering is a cursednesse.         176
Bihold and see, that in the firste table
Of heighe goddes hestes honourable,
How that the seconde heste of him is this—
"Tak nat my name in ydel or amis."[16]     180
Lo, rather[17] he forbedeth swich swering
Than homicyde or many a cursed thing;
I seye that, as by ordre, thus it stondeth;
This knowen, that his hestes understondeth,
How that the second heste of god is that.  185
And forther over, I wol thee telle al plat,
That vengeance shal nat parten from his hous,
That of his othes is to outrageous.
"By goddes precious herte, and by his nayles,
And by the blode of Crist, that it is in
    Hayles,[18]                           190
Seven is my chaunce, and thyn is cink and
    treye;
By goddes armes, if thou falsly pleye,
This dagger shal thurgh-out thyn herte go"—
This fruyt cometh of the bicched bones two,
Forswering, ire, falsnesse, homicyde.      195
Now, for the love of Crist that for us dyde,
Leveth your othes, bothe grete and smale;
But, sirs, now wol I telle forth my tale.

    Thise ryotoures three, of whiche I telle,
Longe erst er pryme rong of any belle,     200
Were set hem in a taverne for to drinke;

---

[10] The Pardoner says that the mixture must come from the closeness of the vineyards to each other, but means that it comes from the closeness of the casks in the vintners' cellars. The wines of La Rochelle and Bordeaux were milder than the Spanish wines.

[11] Lemuel. Proverbs, 31: 1, 4, 5.

[12] Should be Chilon. The story is in John of Salisbury's *Policraticus*, bk. I, ch. 5.

[13] *Policraticus*, bk. I, ch. 5.

[14] St. Matthew, 5:34.     [15] Jeremiah, 4:2.

[16] Formerly the first and second commandments were considered as one, the tenth being divided into two to make up the number; hence the Pardoner refers to the third commandment as the second. It is in the first table, i. e., the group teaching man's duty to God, those in the second table teaching his duty to his neighbor.

[17] Earlier in the list of commandments.

[18] The Abbey of Hailes, or Hales, in Gloucestershire.

And as they satte, they herde a belle clinke
Biforn a cors, was caried to his grave;
That oon of hem gan callen to his knave,
"Go bet," quod he, "and axe redily,          205
What cors is this that passeth heer forby;
And look that thou reporte his name wel."
"Sir," quod this boy, "it nedeth never-a-del.
It was me told, er ye can heer, two houres;
He was, pardee, an old felawe of youres;      210
And sodeynly he was y-slayn to-night,
For-dronke, as he sat on his bench upright;
Ther cam a privee theef, men clepeth Deeth,
That in this contree al the peple sleeth,       214
And with his spere he smoot his herte a-two,
And wente his wey with-outen wordes mo.
He hath a thousand slayn this pestilence:
And, maister, er ye come in his presence,
Me thinketh that it were necessarie
For to be war of swich an adversarie:          220
Beth redy for to mete him evermore.
Thus taughte me my dame, I sey na-more."
"By seinte Marie," seyde this taverner,
"The child seith sooth, for he hath slayn this
    yeer,
Henne over a myle, with-in a greet village,     225
Both man and womman, child and hyne, and
    page.
I trowe his habitacioun be there;
To been avysed greet wisdom it were,
Er that he dide a man a dishonour."
"Ye, goddes armes," quod this ryotour,          230
"Is it swich peril with him for to mete?
I shal him seke by wey and eek by strete,
I make avow to goddes digne bones!
Herkneth, felawes, we three been al ones;
Lat ech of us holde up his hond til other,       235
And ech of us bicomen otheres brother,
And we wol sleen this false traytour Deeth;
He shal be slayn, which that so many sleeth,
By goddes dignitee, er it be night."
    Togidres han thise three her trouthes plight,
To live and dyen ech of hem for other,           241
As though he were his owene y-boren brother.
And up they sterte al dronken, in this rage,
And forth they goon towardes that village,
Of which the taverner had spoke biforn,          245
And many a grisly ooth than han they sworn,
And Cristes blessed body they to-rente—
"Deeth shal be deed, if that they may him
    hente."
    Whan they han goon nat fully half a myle,
Right as they wolde han troden over a style,
An old man and a povre with hem mette.          251
This olde man ful mekely hem grette,
And seyde thus, "now, lordes, god yow see!"
    The proudest of thise ryotoures three
Answerede agayn, "what? carl, with sory grace,
Why artow al forwrapped save thy face?          256
Why livestow so longe in so greet age?"
    This olde man gan loke in his visage,
And seyde thus, "for I ne can nat finde
A man, though that I walked in-to Inde,          260
Neither in citee nor in no village,

That wolde chaunge his youthe for myn age;
And therfore moot I han myn age stille,
As longe time as it is goddes wille.
"Ne deeth, allas! ne wol nat han my lyf;        265
Thus walke I, lyk a resteless caityf,
And on the ground, which is my modres gate,
I knokke with my staf, bothe erly and late,
And seye, 'leve moder, leet me in!
Lo, how I vanish, flesh, and blood, and skin!   270
Allas! whan shul my bones been at reste?
Moder, with yow wolde I chaunge my cheste,
That in my chambre longe tyme hath be,
Ye! for an heyre clout to wrappe me!'
But yet to me she wol nat do that grace,        275
For which ful pale and welked is my face.
    "But, sirs, to yow it is no curteisye
To speken to an old man vileinye,
But he trespasse in worde, or elles in dede.
In holy writ ye may your-self wel rede,         280
'Agayns an old man, hoor upon his heed,
Ye sholde aryse'; [19] wherfor I yeve yow reed,
Ne dooth un-to an old man noon harm now,
Na-more than ye wolde men dide to yow
In age, if that ye so longe abyde;              285
And god be with yow, wher ye go or ryde.
I moot go thider as I have to go."
    "Nay, olde cherl, by god, thou shalt nat so,"
Seyde this other hasardour anon;               289
"Thou partest nat so lightly, by seint John!
Thou spak right now of thilke traitour Deeth,
That in this contree alle our frendes sleeth.
Have heer my trouthe, as thou art his aspye,
Tel wher he is, or thou shalt it abye,
By god, and by the holy sacrament!              295
For soothly thou art oon of his assent,
To sleen us yonge folk, thou false theef!"
    "Now, sirs," quod he, "if that yow be so leef
To finde Deeth, turne up this croked wey,
For in that grove I lafte him, by my fey,        300
Under a tree, and ther he wol abyde;
Nat for your boost he wol him no-thing hyde.
See ye that ook? right ther ye shul him finde.
God save yow, that boghte agayn mankinde,
And yow amende!"—thus seyde this olde man.
And everich of thise ryotoures ran,              306
Til he cam to that tree, and ther they found
Of florins fyne of golde y-coyned rounde
Wel ny an eighte busshels, as hem thoughte.
No lenger thanne after Deeth they soughte,
But ech of hem so glad was of that sighte,       311
For that the florins been so faire and brighte,
That doun they sette hem by this precious hord.
The worste of hem he spake the firste word.
    "Brethren," quod he, "tak kepe what I seye;
My wit is greet, though that I bourde and
    pleye.                                       316
This tresor hath fortune un-to us yiven,
In mirthe and jolitee our lyf to liven,
And lightly as it comth, so wol we spende.
Ey! goddes precious dignitee! who wende         320
To-day, that we sholde han so fair a grace?

[19] Leviticus, 19:32.

But mighte this gold be caried fro this place
Hoom to myn hous, or elles un-to youres—
For wel ye woot that al this gold is oures—
Than were we in heigh felicitee.      325
But trewely, by daye it may nat be;
Men wolde seyn that we were theves stronge,
And for our owene tresor doon us honge.
This tresor moste y-caried be by nighte
As wysly and as slyly as it mighte.      330
Wherfore I rede that cut among us alle
Be drawe, and lat see wher the cut wol falle;
And he that hath the cut with herte blythe
Shal renne to the toune, and that ful swythe,
And bringe us breed and wyn ful prively.      335
And two of us shul kepen subtilly
This tresor wel; and, if he wol nat tarie,
Whan it is night, we wol this tresor carie
By oon assent, wher-as us thinketh best."      339
That oon of hem the cut broughte in his fest.
And bad hem drawe, and loke wher it wol
      falle;
And it fil on the yongeste of hem alle;
And forth toward the toun he wente anon.
And al-so sone as that he was gon,
That oon of hem spak thus un-to that other,      345
"Thou knowest wel thou art my sworne
      brother,
Thy profit wol I telle thee anon.
Thou woost wel that our felawe is agon;
And heer is gold, and that ful greet plentee,
That shal departed been among us three.      350
But natheles, if I can shape it so
That it departed were among us two,
Hadde I nat doon a freendes torn to thee?"
      That other answerde, "I noot how that may
      be;      354
He woot how that the gold is with us tweye,
What shal we doon, what shal we to him
      seye?"
"Shal it be conseil?" seyde the firste shrewe,
"And I shal tellen thee, in wordes fewe,
What we shal doon, and bringe it wel aboute."
      "I graunte," quod that other, "out of
      doute,      360
That, by my trouthe, I wol thee nat biwreye."
      "Now," quod the firste, "thou woost wel we
      be tweye,
And two of us shul strenger be than oon.
Look whan that he is set, and right anoon
Arys, as though thou woldest with him pleye;
And I shal ryve him thurgh the sydes tweye      366
Whyl that thou strogelest with him as in game,
And with thy dagger look thou do the same;
And than shal al this gold departed be,
My dere freend, bitwixen me and thee;      370
Than may we bothe our lustes al fulfille,
And pleye at dees right at our owene wille."
And thus acorded been thise shrewes tweye
To sleen the thridde, as ye han herd me seye.
      This yongest, which that wente un-to the
      toun,      375
Ful ofte in herte he rolleth up and doun
The beautee of thise florins newe and brighte.

"O lord!" quod he, "if so were that I mighte
Have al this tresor to my-self allone,
Ther is no man that liveth under the trone      380
Of god, that sholde live so mery as I!"
And atte laste the feend, our enemy,
Putte in his thought that he shold poyson beye,
With which he mighte sleen his felawes tweye;
For-why the feend fond him in swich lyvinge,
That he had leve him to sorwe bringe,      386
For this was outrely his fulle entente
To sleen hem bothe, and never to repente.
And forth he gooth, no lenger wolde he tarie,
Into the toun, un-to a pothecarie,      390
And preyed him, that he him wolde selle
Som poyson, that he mighte his rattes quelle;
And eek ther was a polcat in his hawe,
That, as he seyde, his capouns hadde y-slawe,
And fayn he wolde wreke him, if he mighte,
On vermin, that destroyed him by nighte.      396
      The pothecarie answerde, "and thou shalt
      have
A thing that, al-so god my soule save,
In al this world ther nis no creature,
That ete or dronke hath of this confiture      400
Noght but the mountance of a corn of whete,
That he ne shal his lyf anon forlete;
Ye, sterve he shal, and that in lasse whyle
Than thou wolt goon a paas nat but a myle;
This poyson is so strong and violent."      405
      This cursed man hath in his hond y-hent
This poyson in a box, and sith he ran
In-to the nexte strete, un-to a man,
And borwed [of] him large botels three;
And in the two his poyson poured he;      410
The thridde he kepte clene for his drinke.
For al the night he shoop him for to swinke
In caryinge of the gold out of that place.
And whan this ryotour, with sory grace,
Had filled with wyn his grete botels three,      415
To his felawes agayn repaireth he.
      What nedeth it to sermone of it more?
For right as they had cast his deeth bifore,
Right so they han him slayn, and that anon.
And whan that this was doon, thus spak that
      oon,      420
"Now lat us sitte and drinke, and make us
      merie,
And afterward we wol his body berie."
And with that word it happed him, par cas,
To take the botel ther the poyson was,
And drank, and yaf his felawe drinke also,      425
For which anon they storven bothe two.
      But, certes, I suppose that Avicen [20]
Wroot never in no canon, ne in no fen,
Mo wonder signes of empoisoning
Than hadde thise wrecches two, er hir ending.
Thus ended been thise homicydes two,      431
And eek the false empoysoner also.

[20] Avicenna (A.D. 980–1037), celebrated Arabian
physician and philosopher. As Chaucer (or the
Pardoner) perhaps did not understand, "Canon" is
the general title of Avicenna's treatise on medicine.

O cursed sinne, ful of cursednesse!
O traytours homicyde, o wikkednesse!
O glotonye, luxurie, and hasardrye!    435
Thou blasphemour of Crist with vileinye
And othes grete, of usage and of pryde!
Allas! mankinde, how may it bityde,
That to thy creatour which that thee wroghte,
And with his precious herte-blood thee boghte,
Thou art so fals and so unkinde, allas!    441
    Now, goode men, god forgeve yow your
        trespas,
And ware yow fro the sinne of avaryce.
Myn holy pardoun may yow alle waryce,
So that ye offre nobles or sterlinges,    445
Or elles silver broches, spones, ringes.
Boweth your heed under this holy bulle!
Cometh up, ye wyves, offreth of your wolle!
Your name I entre heer in my rolle anon;
In-to the blisse of hevene shul ye gon;    450
I yow assoile, by myn heigh power,
Yow that wol offre, as clene and eek as cleer
As ye were born; and, lo, sirs, thus I preche.
And Jesu Crist, that is our soules leche,
So graunte yow his pardon to receyve;    455
For that is best; I wol yow nat deceyve.
    But sirs, o word forgat I in my tale,
I have relikes and pardon in my male,
As faire as any man in Engelond,
Whiche were me yeven by the popes hond.    460
If any of yow wol, of devocioun,
Offren, and han myn absolucion,
Cometh forth anon, and kneleth heer adoun,
And mekely receyveth my pardoun:
Or elles, taketh pardon as ye wende,    465
Al newe and fresh, at every tounes ende,
So that ye offren alwey newe and newe
Nobles and pens, which that be gode and trewe.
It is an honour to everich that is heer,
That ye mowe have a suffisant pardoneer    470
T'assoille yow, in contree as ye ryde,
For aventures which that may bityde.
Peraventure ther may falle oon or two
Doun of his hors, and breke his nekke atwo.
Look which a seuretee is it to yow alle    475
That I am in your felaweship y-falle,
That may assoille yow, bothe more and lasse,
Whan that the soule shal fro the body passe.
I rede that our hoste heer shal biginne,
For he is most envoluped in sinne.    480
Com forth, sir hoste, and offre first anon,
And thou shalt kisse the reliks everichon,
Ye, for a grote! unbokel anon thy purs.
    "Nay, nay," quod he, "than have I Cristes
        curs!    484
Lat be," quod he, "it shal nat be, so thee'ch!
Thou woldest make me kisse thyn old breech,
And swere it were a relik of a seint,
Thogh it were with thy fundement depeint!
But by the croys which that seint Eleyne fond,
I wolde I hadde thy coillons in myn hond    490
In stede of relikes or of seintuarie;
Lat cutte hem of, I wol thee helpe hem carie;

They shul be shryned in an hogges tord."
    This pardoner answerede nat a word;
So wrooth he was, no word ne wolde he seye.
    "Now," quod our host, "I wol no lenger
        pleye    496
With thee, ne with noon other angry man."
But right anon the worthy Knight bigan,
Whan that he saugh that al the peple lough,
"Na-more of this, for it is right y-nough;    500
Sir Pardoner, be glad and mery of chere;
And ye, sir host, that been to me so dere,
I prey yow that ye kisse the Pardoner.
And Pardoner, I prey thee, drawe thee neer,
And, as we diden, lat us laughe and pleye."    505
Anon they kiste, and riden forth hir weye.[21]

# Chaucers Wordes unto
# Adam, His Owne Scriveyn

Adam scriveyn, if ever it thee bifalle
Boece or Troilus to wryten newe,
Under thy lokkes thou most have the scalle,
But after my making thou wryte trewe.
So ofte a daye I mot thy werk renewe,    5
Hit to correcte and eek to rubbe and scrape;
And al is through thy negligence and rape.

# Truth

## Balade de Bon Conseyl

Flee fro the prees, and dwelle with soth-
        fastnesse,
Suffyce unto thy good, though hit be smal;
For hord hath hate, and climbing tikelnesse,
Prees hath envye, and wele blent overal;
Savour no more than thee bihove shal;    5
Werk wel thy-self, that other folk canst rede;
And trouthe shal delivere, hit is no drede.

Tempest thee noght al croked to redresse,
In trust of hir that turneth as a bal: [1]
Gret reste stant in litel besinesse;    10
And eek be war to sporne ageyn an al;
Stryve noght, as doth the crokke with the wal.
Daunte thy-self, that dauntest otheres dede;
And trouthe shal delivere, hit is no drede.

That thee is sent, receyve in buxumnesse,    15
The wrastling for this worlde axeth a fal.
Her nis non hoom, her nis but wildernesse:
Forth, pilgrim, forth! Forth, beste, out of thy
        stal!
Know thy contree, look up, thank God of al;
Holde the hye wey, and lat thy gost thee lede:
And trouble shal delivere, hit is no drede.    21

[21] The Pardoner's tale concludes what, in the present arrangement of The Canterbury Tales, is the
third group. There follow six more groups, in
which eleven stories are told.
[1] Fortune.

Therfore, thou vache,[2] leve thyn old wrecch-
 ednesse
Unto the worlde; leve now to be thral;
Crye him mercy, that of his hy goodnesse
Made thee of noght, and in especial            25
Draw unto him, and pray in general
For thee, and eek for other, hevenlich mede;
And trouthe shal delivere, hit is no drede.

## The Compleint of Chaucer to His Empty Purse [3]

To you, my purse, and to non other wight
Compleyne I, for ye be my lady dere!
I am so sory, now that ye be light;

[2] It is now known that this poem was addressed
to one of Chaucer's friends, Sir Philip la Vache;
"vache" (beast) is therefore used with double meaning.
[3] This is probably one of the last poems Chaucer
wrote, inasmuch as the envoy, at least, cannot have
been written before 30 September, 1399, when Parliament formally acknowledged Henry IV's right
to the English throne. Chaucer's appeal, it may be
added, was successful.

For certes, but ye make me hevy chere,
Me were as leef be leyd up-on my bere;         5
For whiche un-to your mercy thus I crye:
Beth hevy ageyn, or elles mot I dye!

Now voucheth sauf this day, or hit be night,
That I of you the blisful soun may here,
Or see your colour lyk the sonne bright,       10
That of yelownesse hadde never pere.
Ye be my lyf, ye be myn hertes stere,
Quene of comfort and of good companye:
Beth hevy ageyn, or elles mot I dye!

Now purs, that be to me my lyves light,        15
And saveour, as doun in this worlde here,
Out of this toune help me through your might,
Sin that ye wole nat been my tresorere;
For I am shave as nye as any frere.
But yit I pray un-to your curtesye:            20
Beth hevy ageyn, or elles mot I dye!

### LENVOY DE CHAUCER

O conquerour of Brutes Albioun!
Which that by lyne and free eleccioun
Ben verray king, this song to you I sende;
And ye, that mowen al our harm amende,         25
Have minde up-on my supplicacioun!

# Popular Ballads

A *popular ballad* is "a song that tells a story," and that has come out of the past through oral tradition: the word-of-mouth passage of the cultural inheritance of an unlettered people from generation to generation. The story is the thing in the ballad: generally it is a single, highly dramatic action, such as a battle or a murder. The ballad often concentrates its attention on the moment of climax, or on some intensely felt human situation following the climax of the action; a listener who is curious to know the details leading up to the action will generally find that curiosity unsatisfied by the ballad. As the ballad changes through the generations the universal qualities of the dramatic situation tend to remain, while non-essential detail is lost.

Perhaps the outstanding characteristic of the ballad is its impersonality, its apparent objectivity. The singer makes no comment, sheds no tears, seems outside the context of the situation entirely. He speaks as Edward's mother, and then as Edward; the dialogue between the two moves the plot rapidly to its bitter ending. Nowhere does the singer speak for himself, or for the social group that he represents. There is no place for sentimentality, no place for the intrusive self-awareness of the artist. It is as if the ballads exist apart from the artist.

There has been much speculation about the authorship of the ballads. It was thought by some nineteenth-century scholars that they were produced at a very early stage of culture by a kind of spontaneous creation of the "singing, dancing throng": that there was no single author but rather that the members of a whole community contributed lines more or less on the spur of the moment as the song was being sung. It is certainly true that the process of passing a song from generation to generation produces changes which make the ballad a product of the entire community in a very

real sense; it also seems certain that each ballad was originally the production of one singer. One of the chief arguments against the theory of communal origin is that the "very early stage of culture" assumed in the theory did not exist in Western Europe in the Middle Ages.

The ballads are not the crude product of a primitive people, but are rather the highest achievement of an accomplished and complex culture which expressed itself in an oral rather than in a written tradition.

More than three hundred ballads are extant. Of these only eleven come from manuscripts older than the seventeenth century, but the time when a ballad reached its final form through writing or printing is not significant of its real age. The oldest of the English and Scottish ballads may have had their origin in the thirteenth century or earlier, and others which are founded on historical events can be definitely assigned to the fourteenth and fifteenth centuries. In the eighteenth century Bishop Percy discovered a folio manuscript, written about 1650, which still remains the most important collection of ballads. He printed his famous Reliques of Ancient English Poetry in 1765. The book was at once a sign of growing interest in ballad-literature and a stimulant to further search for additional material. A little later Sir Walter Scott became a collector of ballads of the Scottish border.

The ballads give an appearance of simplicity, primarily because of the directness of their language and their avoidance of polysyllabic words. Conventional epithets and standing phrases abound. A dramatic framework is frequently assumed. Stanzas consist generally either of a couplet of verses of four lines riming a b c b, of which the first and third have four accents and the second and fourth three. The usual themes fall into a few broadly popular types—domestic tragedy, supernatural occurrences, the lives of outlaws, riddles, historical events, and humorous incidents.

The English and Scottish Popular Ballads, ed. Francis J. Child (Boston, 1882–1898), contains all save a few ballads, which have been discovered since; this collection has been published in an abridged form, under the same title, ed. Helen C. Sargent and George L. Kittredge (Boston, 1904). The Popular Ballad, by F. B. Gummere (Boston, 1907), has historical interest as a critical study. The theory that the ballads were of communal origin, which was accepted by Gummere, is notably attacked by Louise Pound in Poetic Origins and the Ballad (New York, 1921). For a more inclusive commentary see Gordon H. Gerould, The Ballad of Tradition (Oxford, 1932). A recent study by Evelyn K. Wells, The Ballad Tree (New York, 1950), analyzes the ballad subject-matter.

## Riddles Wisely Expounded

There was a lady of the North Country,
  Lay the bent to the bonny broom
And she had lovely daughters three.
  Fa la la la, fa la la la ra re.

There was a knight of noble worth     5
Which also livéd in the North.

The knight, of courage stout and brave,
A wife he did desire to have.

He knockéd at the ladie's gate
One evening when it was late.     10

The eldest sister let him in,
And pinned the door with a silver pin.

The second sister she made his bed,
And laid soft pillows under his head.

The youngest daughter that same night,     15
She went to bed to this young knight.

And in the morning, when it was day,
These words unto him she did say:

"Now you have had your will," quoth she,
"I pray, sir knight, will you marry me?"     20

The young brave knight to her replied,
"Thy suit, fair maid, shall not be denied.

"If thou canst answer me questions three,
This very day will I marry thee."

"Kind sir, in love, O then," quoth she,     25
"Tell me what your [three] questions be."

"O what is longer than the way,
Or what is deeper than the sea?

"Or what is louder than the horn,
Or what is sharper than a thorn?     30

"Or what is greener than the grass,
Or what is worse then a woman was?"

"O love is longer than the way,
And hell is deeper than the sea.

"And thunder is louder than the horn,     35
And hunger is sharper than a thorn.

"And poyson is greener than the grass,
And the Devil is worse than woman was."

When she these questions answered had,
The knight became exceeding glad.     40

And having [truly] tried her wit,
He much commended her for it.

And after, as it is verified,
He made of her his lovely bride.

So now, fair maidens all, adieu,     45
This song I dedicate to you.

I wish that you may constant prove
Unto the man that you do love.

## The Douglas Tragedy

"Rise up, rise up, now Lord Douglas," she says,
  "And put on your armour so bright;
Let it never be said that a daughter of thine
  Was married to a lord under night.

"Rise up, rise up, my seven bold sons,     5
  And put on your armour so bright,
And take better care of your youngest sister,
  For your eldest's awa the last night."

He's mounted her on a milk-white steed,
  And himself on a dapple grey,     10
With a bugelet horn hung down his side,
  And lightly they rode away.

Lord William lookit o'er his left shoulder,
  To see what he could see,
And there he spyed her seven brethren bold,     15
  Come riding over the lea.

"Light down, light down, Lady Margret,"
  he said,
  "And hold my steed in your hand,
Until that against your seven brethren bold,
  And your father, I mak' a stand."     20

She held his steed in her milk-white hand,
  And never shed one tear,

Until that she saw her seven brethren fa',
   And her father, who loved her so dear.   24

"O hold your hand, Lord William!" she said,
   "For your strokes they are wondrous sair;
True lovers I can get many a ane,
   But a father I can never get mair."

O she's ta'en out her handkerchief,
   It was o' the holland sae fine,   30
And aye she dighted her father's bloody
   wounds,
That were redder than the wine.

"O chuse, O chuse, Lady Margret," he said,
   "O whether will ye gang or bide?"
"I'll gang, I'll gang, Lord William," she said,
   "For ye have left me no other guide."   36

He's lifted her on a milk-white steed,
   And himself on a dapple grey,
With a bugelet horn hung down by his side;
   And slowly they baith rade away.   40

O they rade on, and on they rade,
   And a' by the light of the moon,
Until they came to yon wan water,
   And there they lighted down.

They lighted down to tak' a drink   45
   Of the spring that ran sae clear,
And down the stream ran his gude heart's
   blood,
And sair she gan to fear.

"Hold up, hold up, Lord William," she says,
   "For I fear that you are slain";   50
"'Tis naething but the shadow of my scarlet
   cloak,
That shines in the water sae plain."

O they rade on, and on they rade,
   And a' by the light of the moon,
Until they cam to his mother's ha' door,   55
   And there they lighted down.

"Get up, get up, lady mother," he says,
   "Get up, and let me in!
Get up, get up, lady mother," he says,
   "For this night my fair lady I've win.   60

"O mak my bed, lady mother," he says,
   "O mak it braid and deep,
And lay Lady Margret close at my back,
   And the sounder I will sleep."

Lord William was dead lang ere midnight,   65
   Lady Margret lang ere day,
And all true lovers that go thegither,
   May they have mair luck than they!

Lord William was buried in St. Mary's kirk,
   Lady Margret in Mary's quire;   70

Out o' the lady's grave grew a bonny red rose,
   And out o' the knight's a briar.

And they twa met, and they twa plat,
   And fain they wad be near;
And a' the warld might ken right weel   75
   They were twa lovers dear.

But bye and rade the Black Douglas,
   And wow but he was rough!
For he pulld up the bonny briar,
   And flang 't in St. Mary's Loch.   80

# Robin Hood and Guy of Gisborne [1]

When shawes beene sheene, and shradds full
   fayre,
   And leeves both large and longe,
Itt is merry, walking in the fayre fforrest,
   To heare the small birds songe.

The woodweele sang, and wold not cease,   5
   Amongst the leaves a lyne:
And it is by two wight yeomen,
   By deare God, that I meane.

.   .   .   .   .

"Me thought they did mee beate and binde,
   And tooke my bow mee froe;   10
If I bee Robin a-live in this lande,
   I 'le be wrocken on both them towe."

"Sweavens are swift, master," quoth John,
   "As the wind that blowes ore a hill;
Ffor if itt be never soe lowde this night,   15
   To-morrow it may be still."

"Buske yee, bowne yee, my merry men all,
   Ffor John shall goe with mee;
For I 'le goe seeke yond wight yeomen
   In greenwood where the bee."   20

They cast on their gowne of greene,
   A shooting gone are they,
Untill they came to the merry greenwood,
   Where they had gladdest bee;

[1] Tradition has it that Robin Hood was an historical character, an outlaw of the early fourteenth century. This is, to say the least, extremely improbable. As he is portrayed in the ballads, at any rate, he is a typical figure, an idealized outlaw, the champion of common folk against oppression. As such he was extremely popular, there being some 40 ballads about him. We know from a reference in the B-text of *Piers Plowman* that he was a familiar character at least as early as 1377.

A few verses are lost between stanzas 2 and 3, and the story itself has suffered some derangement. Robin dreams that two yeomen beat and bind him, and goes to seek them. One is Sir Guy, the other the sheriff of Nottingham; but we are not told how Robin knew that the sheriff was out against him, had attacked his camp, and had taken John prisoner.

There were the ware of [a] wight yeoman, 25
    His body leaned to a tree.

A sword and a dagger he wore by his side,
    Had beene many a mans bane,
And he was cladd in his capull-hyde,
    Topp, and tayle, and mayne. 30

"Stand you still, master," quoth Litle John,
    "Under this trusty tree,
And I will goe to yond wight yeoman,
    To know his meaning trulye."

"A, John, by me thou setts noe store, 35
    And that's a ffarley thinge;
How offt send I my men beffore,
    And tarry my-selfe behinde?

"It is noe cunning a knave to ken,
    And a man but heare him speake; 40
And itt were not for bursting of my bowe,
    John, I wold thy head breake."

But often words they breeden bale,
    That parted Robin and John;
John is gone to Barn[e]sdale, 45
    The gates he knowes eche one.

And when hee came to Barnesdale,
    Great heavinesse there hee hadd;
He ffound two of his fellowes
    Were slaine both in a slade, 50

And Scarlett a ffoote flyinge was,
    Over stockes and stone,
For the sheriffe with seven score men
    Fast after him is gone.

"Yett one shoote I 'le shoote," says Litle John,
    "With Crist his might and mayne; 56
I 'le make yond fellow that flyes soe fast
    To be both glad and ffaine."

John bent up a good veiwe bow,
    And ffetteled him to shoote; 60
The bow was made of a tender boughe,
    And fell downe to his foote.

"Woe worth thee, wicked wood," sayd Litle
    John,
    "That ere thou grew on a tree!
Ffor this day thou art my bale, 65
    My boote when thou shold bee!"

This shoote it was but looselye shott,
    The arrowe flew in vaine,
And it mett one of the sheriffes men;
    Good William a Trent was slaine. 70

It had beene better for William a Trent
    To hange upon a gallowe
Then for to lye in the greenwoode,
    There slaine with an arrowe.

And it is sayd, when men be mett, 75
    Six can doe more then three:
And they have tane Little John,
    And bound him ffast to a tree.

"Thou shalt be drawen by dale and downe,"
    quoth the sheriffe,
    "And hanged hye on a hill": 80
"But thou may ffayle," quoth Little John,
    "If itt be Christs owne will."

Let us leave talking of Litle John,
    For hee is bound fast to a tree,
And talke of Guy and Robin Hood, 85
    In the green woode where they bee.

How these two yeomen together they mett,
    Under the leaves of lyne,
To see what marchandise they made
    Even at that same time. 90

"Good morrow, good fellow," quoth Sir Guy;
    "Good morrow, good ffellow," quoth hee;
"Methinkes by this bow thou beares in thy
    hand,
A good archer thou seems to bee."

"I am wilfull of my way," quoth Sir Guye, 95
    "And of my morning tyde":
"I 'le lead thee through the wood," quoth
    Robin,
    "Good ffellow, I 'le be thy guide."

"I seeke an outlaw," quoth Sir Guye;
    "Men call him Robin Hood; 100
I had rather meet with him upon a day
    Then forty pound of golde."

"If you tow mett, itt wold be seene whether
    were better
Afore yee did part away;
Let us some other pastime find, 105
    Good ffellow, I thee pray.

"Let us some other masteryes make,
    And wee will walke in the woods even;
Wee may chance mee[t] with Robin Hoode
    Att some unsett steven." 110

They cutt them downe the summer shroggs
    Which grew both under a bryar,
And sett them three score rood in twinn,
    To shoote the prickes full neare.

"Leade on, good ffellow," sayd Sir Guye, 115
    "Lead on, I doe bidd thee":
"Nay, by my faith," quoth Robin Hood,
    "The leader thou shalt bee."

The first good shoot that Robin ledd
    Did not shoote an inch the pricke ffroe; 120
Guy was an archer good enoughe,
    But he cold neere shoote soe.

The second shoote Sir Guy shott,
　He shott within the garlande;
But Robin Hoode shott it better then hee, 125
　For he clove the good pricke-wande.

"Gods blessing on thy heart!" sayes Guye,
　"Goode ffellow, thy shooting is goode;
For an thy hart be as good as thy hands,
　Thou were better then Robin Hood. 130

"Tell me thy name, good ffellow," quoth Guy,
　"Under the leaves of lyne":
"Nay, by my faith," quoth good Robin,
　"Till thou have told me thine."

"I dwell by dale and downe," quoth Guye, 135
　"And I have done many a curst turne;
And he that calles me by my right name
　Calles me Guye of good Gysborne."

"My dwelling is in the wood," sayes Robin;
　"By thee I set right nought; 140
My name is Robin Hood of Barnesdale,
　A ffellow thou has long sought."

He that had neither beene a kithe nor kin
　Might have seene a full fayre sight,
To see how together these yeomen went, 145
　With blades both browne and bright.

To have seene how these yeomen together
　foug[ht],
　Two howers of a summers day;
Itt was neither Guy nor Robin Hood
　That ffettled them to flye away. 150

Robin was reacheles on a roote,
　And stumbled at that tyde,
And Guy was quicke and nimble withall,
　And hitt him ore the left side.

"Ah, deere Lady!" sayd Robin Hoode, 155
　"Thou art both mother and may!
I thinke it was never mans destinye
　To dye before his day."

Robin thought on Our Lady deere,
　And soone leapt up againe, 160
And thus he came with an awkwarde stroke;
　Good Sir Guy hee has slayne.

He tooke Sir Guys head by the hayre,
　And sticked itt on his bowes end:
"Thou hast beene traytor all thy liffe, 165
　Which thing must have an ende."

Robin pulled forth an Irish kniffe,
　And nicked Sir Guy in the fface,
That hee was never on a woman borne
　Cold tell who Sir Guye was. 170

Saies, Lye there, lye there, good Sir Guye,
　And with me be not wrothe;

If thou have had the worse stroakes at my hand,
　Thou shalt have the better cloathe.

Robin did off his gowne of greene, 175
　Sir Guye hee did it throwe;
And hee put on that capull-hyde,
　That cladd him topp to toe.

"The bowe, the arrowes, and litle horne,
　And with me now I 'le beare; 180
Ffor now I will goe to Barn[e]sdale,
　To see how my men doe ffare."

Robin sett Guyes horne to his mouth,
　A lowd blast in it he did blow;
That beheard the sheriffe of Nottingham, 185
　As he leaned under a lowe.

"Hearken! hearken!" sayd the sheriffe,
　"I heard noe tydings but good;
For yonder I heare Sir Guyes horne blowe,
　For he hath slaine Robin Hoode. 190

"For yonder I heare Sir Guyes horne blow,
　Itt blowes soe well in tyde,
For yonder comes that wighty yeoman,
　Cladd in his capull-hyde.

"Come hither, thou good Sir Guy, 195
　Aske of mee what thou wilt have":
"I 'le none of thy gold," sayes Robin Hood,
　"Nor I 'le none of itt have.

"But now I have slaine the master," he sayd,
　"Let me goe strike the knave; 200
This is all the reward I aske,
　Nor noe other will I have."

"Thou art a madman," said the shiriffe,
　"Thou sholdest have had a knights ffee;
Seeing thy asking [hath] beene soe badd, 205
　Well granted it shall be."

But Litle John heard his master speake,
　Well he knew that was his steven;
"Now shall I be loset," quoth Litle John,
　"With Christs might in heaven." 210

But Robin hee hyed him towards Litle John,
　Hee thought hee wold loose him belive;
The sheriffe and all his companye
　Fast after him did drive. 214

"Stand abacke! stand abacke!" sayd Robin;
　"Why draw you mee soe neere?
Itt was never the use in our countrye
　One's shrift another shold heere."

But Robin pulled forth an Irysh kniffe,
　And losed John hand and ffoote, 220
And gave him Sir Guyes bow in his hand,
　And bade it be his boote.

But John tooke Guyes bow in his hand—
　His arrowes were rawstye by the roote;
The sherriffe saw Litle John draw a bow　225
　And ffettle him to shoote.

Towards his house in Nottingam
　He ffled full fast away,
And soe did all his companye,
　Not one behind did stay.　230

But he cold neither soe fast goe,
　Nor away soe fast runn,
But Litle John, with an arrow broade,
　Did cleave his heart in twinn.

## Robin Hood and the Monk [1]

In somer, when the shawes be sheyne,
　And leves be large and long,
Hit is full mery in feyre foreste
　To here the foulys song:

To se the dere draw to the dale,　5
　And leve the hilles hee,
And shadow hem in the levës grene,
　Under the grene-wode tre.

Hit befel on Whitsontide,
　Erly in a May mornyng,　10
The son up feyre can shyne,
　And the briddis mery can syng.

"This is a mery mornyng," seid Litull John,
　"Be hym that dyed on tre;
A more mery man then I am one　15
　Lyves not in Cristiantë."

"Pluk up thi hert, my dere mayster,"
　Litull John can sey,
"And thynk hit is a full fayre tyme
　In a mornyng of May."　20

"Ye, on thyng greves me," seid Robyn,
　"And does my hert mych woo;
That I may not no solem day
　To mas nor matyns goo.

"Hit is a fourtnet and more," seid he,　25
　"Syn I my savyour see;
To day wil I to Notyngham," seid Robyn,
　"With the myght of mylde Marye."

Than spake Moche, the mylner sun,
　Ever more wel hym betyde!　30
"Take twelve of thi wyght yemen,
　Well weppynd, be thi side.
Such on wolde thi selfe slon,
　That twelve dar not abyde."

[1] This is the oldest of the extant Robin Hood ballads. It comes from a manuscript of about 1450 which is now in the Cambridge University Library.

"Of all my mery men," seid Robyn,　35
　"Be my feith I wil non have,
But Litull John shall beyre my bow,
　Til that me list to drawe."

"Thou shall beyre thin own," seid Litull Jon,
　"Maister, and I wyl beyre myne,　40
And we well shete a peny," seid Litull Jon,
　"Under the grene-wode lyne."

"I will not shete a peny," seyd Robyn Hode,
　"In feith, Litull John, with the,
But ever for on as thou shetis," seide Robyn,
　"In feith I holde the thre."　46

Thus shet thei forth, these yemen too,
　Bothe at buske and brome,
Til Litull John wan of his maister
　Five shillings to hose and shone.　50

A ferly strife fel them betwene,
　As they went bi the wey;
Litull John seid he had won five shillings,
　And Robyn Hode seid shortly nay.

With that Robyn Hode lyed Litul Jon,　55
　And smote hym with his hande;
Litul Jon waxed wroth therwith,
　And pulled out his bright bronde.

"Were thou not my maister," seid Litull John,
　"Thou shuldis by hit ful sore;　60
Get the a man wher thou w[ilt],
　For thou getis me no more."

Then Robyn goes to Notyngham,
　Hym selfe mornyng allone,
And Litull John to mery Scherwode,　65
　The pathes he knew ilkone.

Whan Robyn came to Notyngham,
　Sertenly withouten layn,
He prayed to God and myld Mary
　To bryng hym out save agayn.　70

He gos in to Seynt Mary chirch,
　And kneled down before the rode;
Alle that ever were the church within
　Beheld wel Robyn Hode.

Beside hym stod a gret-hedid munke,　75
　I pray to God woo he be!
Fful sone he knew gode Robyn,
　As sone as he hym se.

Out at the durre he ran,
　Fful sone and anon;　80
Alle the gatis of Notyngham
　He made to be sparred everychon.

"Rise up," he seid, "thou prowde schereff,
　Buske the and make the bowne;

I have spyed the kynggis felon, 85
    Ffor sothe he is in this town.

"I have spyed the false felon,
    As he stondis at his masse;
Hit is long of the," seide the munke,
    "And ever he fro us passe. 90

"This traytur name is Robyn Hode,
    Under the grene-wode lynde;
He robbyt me onys of a hundred pound,
    Hit shalle never out of my mynde."

Up then rose this prowde shereff, 95
    And radly made hym gare;
Many was the moder son
    To the kyrk with hym can fare.

In at the durres thei throly thrast,
    With staves full gode wone; 100
"Alas, alas!" seid Robyn Hode,
    Now mysse I Litull John."

But Robyn toke out a too-hond sworde,
    That hangit down be his kne;
Ther as the schereff and his men stode thyckust,
    The durwarde wolde he. 106

Thryes thorowout them he ran then,
    For sothe as I yow sey,
And woundyt mony a moder son,
    And twelve he slew that day. 110

His sworde upon the schireff hed
    Sertanly he brake in too;
"The smyth that the made," seid Robyn,
    "I pray to God wyrke hym woo!

"Ffor now am I weppynlesse," said Robyn, 115
    "Alasse! agayn my wylle;
But if I may fle these traytors fro,
    I wot thei wil me kyll."

Robyn in to the churchë ran,
    Throout hem everilkon, 120

.  .  .  .  .

Sum fel in swonyng as thei were dede,
    And lay stil as any stone;
Non of theym were in her mynde
    But only Litull Jon.

"Let be your rule," seid Litull Jon, 125
    "Ffor his luf that dyed on tre,
Ye that shulde be dugty men;
    Het is gret shame to se.

"Oure maister has been hard bystode
    And yet scapyd away; 130
Pluk up your hertis, and leve this mone,
    And harkyn what I shal say.

"He has servyd Oure Lady many a day,
    And yet wil, securly;

Therfor I trust in hir specialy 135
    No wyckud deth shal he dye.

"Therfor be glad," seid Litul John,
    "And let this mournyng be;
And I shal be the munkis gyde,
    With the myght of mylde Mary. 140

.  .  .  .  .

    "We will go but we too;
And I mete hym," seid Litul John,

"Loke that ye kepe wel owre tristil-tre,
    Under the levys smale,
And spare non of this venyson, 145
    That gose in thys vale."

Fforthe then went these yemen too,
    Litul John and Moche on fere,
And lokid on Moch emys hows,
    The hye way lay full nere. 150

Litul John stode at a wyndow in the mornyng,
    And lokid forth at a stage;
He was war wher the munke came ridyng,
    And with hym a litul page.

"Be my feith," seid Litul John to Moch, 155
    "I can the tel tithyngus gode;
I see wher the munke cumys rydyng,
    I know hym be his wyde hode."

They went in to the way, these yemen bothe,
    As curtes men and hende; 160
Thei spyrred tithyngus at the munke,
    As they hade bene his frende.

"Ffro whens come ye?" seid Litull Jon,
    "Tel us tithyngus, I yow pray,
Off a false owtlay, [callid Robyn Hode,] 165
    Was takyn yisterday.

"He robbyt me and my felowes bothe
    Of twenti marke in serten;
If that false owtlay be takyn,
    Ffor sothe we wolde be fayn." 170

"So did he me," seid the munke,
    "Of a hundred pound and more;
I layde furst hande hym apon,
    Ye may thonke me therfore."

"I pray God thanke you," seid Litull John, 175
    "And we will when we may;
We wil go with you, with your leve,
    And bryng yow on your way.

"Ffor Robyn Hode hase many a wilde felow,
    I tell you in certen; 180
If thei wist ye rode this way,
    In feith ye shulde be slayn."

As thei went talking be the way,
  The munke and Litull John,
John toke the munkis horse be the hede,   185
  Fful sone and anon.

Johne toke the munkis horse be the hed,
  Ffor sothe as I yow say;
So did Much the litull page,
  Ffor he shulde not scape away.   190

Be the golett of the hode
  John pulled the munke down;
John was nothyng of hym agast,
  He lete hym falle on his crown.

Litull John was so[re] agrevyd,   195
  And drew owt his swerde in hye;
This munke saw he shulde be ded,
  Lowd mercy can he crye.

"He was my maister," seid Litull John,
  "That thou hase browgt in bale;   200
Shalle thou never cum at our kyng,
  Ffor to telle hym tale."

John smote of the munkis hed,
  No longer wolde he dwell;
So did Moch the litull page,   205
  Ffor ferd lest he wolde tell.

Ther thei beryed hem bothe,
  In nouther mosse nor lyng,
And Litull John and Much infere
  Bare the letturs to oure kyng.   210

He knelid down upon his kne:
  "God yow save, my lege lorde,
  Ihesus yow save and se!

"God yow save, my lege kyng!"
  To speke John was full bolde;   215
He gaf hym the letturs in his hond,
  The king did hit unfold.

The kyng red the letturs anon,
  And seid, "So mot I the,
Ther was never yoman in mery Inglond   220
  I longut so sore to se.

"Wher is the munke that these shuld have
    brought?"
  Oure kyng can say:
"Be my trouth," seid Litull John,
  "He dyed after the way."   225

The kyng gaf Moch and Litul Jon
  Twenti pound in sertan,
And made theim yemen of the crown,
  And bade theim go agayn.

He gaf John the seel in hand,   230
  The sheref for to bere,

To bryng Robyn hym to,
  And no man do hym dere.

John toke his leve at oure kyng,
  The sothe as I yow say;   235
The next way to Notyngham
  To take, he gede the way.

Whan John came to Notyngham
  The gatis were sparred ychon;
John callid up the porter,   240
  He answerid sone anon.

"What is the cause," seid Litul Jon,
  "Thou sparris the gates so fast?"
"Because of Robyn Hode," seid [the] porter,
  "In depe prison is cast.   245

"John and Moch and Wyll Scathlok,
  Ffor sothe as I yow say,
Thei slew oure men upon our wallis,
  And sawten us every day."

Litull John spyrred after the schereff,   250
  And sone he hym fonde;
He oppyned the kyngus prive seell,
  And gaf hym in his honde.

Whan the scheref saw the kyngus seell,
  He did of his hode anon:   255
"Where is the munke that bare the letturs?"
  He seid to Litull John.

"He is so fayn of hym," seid Litul John,
  "Ffor sothe as I yow say,
He has made hym abot of Westmynster,   260
  A lorde of that abbay."

The scheref made John gode chere,
  And gaf hym wyne of the best;
At nygt thei went to her bedde,
  And every man to his rest.   265

When the scheref was on slepe,
  Dronken of wyne and ale,
Litul John and Moch for sothe
  Toke the way unto the jale.

Litul John callid up the jayler,   270
  And bade hym rise anon:
He seyd Robyn Hode had brokyn prison,
  And out of hit was gon.

The porter rose anon sertan,
  As sone as he herd John calle;   275
Litul John was redy with a swerd,
  And bare hym to the walle.

"Now wil I be porter," seid Litul John,
  "And take the keyes in honde":
He toke the way to Robyn Hode,   280
  And sone he hym unbonde.

He gaf hym a gode swerd in his hond,
  His hed [ther] with for to kepe,
And ther as the walle was lowyst
  Anon down can thei lepe.    285

Be that the cok began to crow,
  The day began to spryng;
The scheref fond the jaylier ded,
  The comyn bell made he ryng.

He made a crye thoroout al the tow[n],    290
  Wheder he be yoman or knave,
That cowthe bryng hym Robyn Hode,
  His warison he should have.

"Ffor I dar never," said the scheref,
  "Cum before oure kyng;    295
Ffor if I do, I wot serten
  Ffor sothe he wil me heng."

The scheref made to seke Notyngham,
  Bothe be strete and stye,
And Robyn was in mery Scherwode,    300
  As ligt as lef on lynde.

Then bespake gode Litull John,
  To Robyn Hode can he say,
I have done the a gode turne for an evyll,
  Quyte the whan thou may.    305

"I have done the a gode turne," seid Litull
  John,
"Ffor sothe as I yow say;
I have brougt the under grene-wode lyne;
  Ffare wel, and have gode day."

"Nay, be my trouth," seid Robyn Hode,    310
  "So shall hit never be;
I make the maister," seid Robyn Hode,
  "Off alle my men and me."

"Nay, be my trouth," seid Litull John,
  "So shalle hit never be;    315
But lat me be a felow," seid Litull John,
  "No noder kepe I be."

Thus John gate Robyn Hod out of prison,
  Sertan withoutyn layn;
Whan his men saw hym hol and sounde,    320
  Ffor sothe they were full fayne.

They filled in wyne, and made hem glad,
  Under the levys smale,
And gete pastes of venyson,
  That gode was with ale.    325

Than worde came to oure kyng
  How Robyn Hode was gon,
And how the scheref of Notyngham
  Durst never loke hym upon.

Then bespake oure cumly kyng,    330
  In an angur hye:

"Litull John hase begyled the schereff,
  In faith so hase he me.

"Litul John has begyled us bothe,
  And that full wel I se;    335
Or ellis the schereff of Notyngham
  Hye hongut shulde he be.

"I made hem yemen of the crowne,
  And gaf hem fee with my hond;
I gaf hem grith," seid oure kyng,    340
  "Thorowout all mery Inglond.

"I gaf theym grith," then seid oure kyng;
  "I say, so mot I the,
Ffor sothe soch a yeman as he is on
  In all Inglond ar not thre.    345

"He is trew to his maister," seid our kyng;
  "I sey, be swete Seynt John,
He lovys better Robyn Hode
  Then he dose us ychon.

"Robyn Hode is ever bond to hym,    350
  Bothe in strete and stalle;
Speke no more of this mater," seid oure kyng,
  "But John has begyled us alle."

Thus endys the talkyng of the munke
  And Robyn Hode i-wysse;    355
God, that is ever a crowned kyng,
  Bryng us all to his blisse!

## Robin Hood's Death

When Robin Hood and Little John,
  Down a down a down a down,
Went oer yon bank of broom,
  Said Robin Hood bold to Little John,
We have shot for many a pound.    5
  Hey, *etc.*

But I am not able to shoot one shot more,
  My broad arrows will not flee;
But I have a cousin lives down below,
  Please God, she will bleed me.    10

Now Robin he is to fair Kirkly gone,
  As fast as he can win;
But before he came there, as we do hear,
  He was taken very ill.

And when he came to fair Kirkly-hall,    15
  He knocked all at the ring,
But none was so ready as his cousin herself
  For to let bold Robin in.

"Will you please to sit down, cousin Robin,"
  she said,
  "And drink some beer with me?"    20
"No, I will neither eat nor drink,
  Till I am blooded by thee."

"Well, I have a room, cousin Robin," she said,
  "Which you did never see,
And if you please to walk therein,    25
  You blooded by me shall be."

She took him by the lily-white hand,
  And led him to a private room,
And there she blooded bold Robin Hood,
  While one drop of blood would run down. 30

She blooded him in a vein of the arm,
  And locked him up in the room;
Then did he bleed all the live-long day,
  Until the next day at noon.

He then bethought him of a casement there, 35
  Thinking for to get down;
But was so weak he could not leap,
  He could not get him down.

He then bethought him of his buglehorn.
  Which hung low down to his knee;    40
He set his horn unto his mouth,
  And blew out weak blasts three.

Then Little John, when hearing him,
  As he sat under a tree,
"I fear my master is now near dead,    45
  He blows so wearily."

Then Little John to fair Kirkly is gone,
  As fast as he can dree;
But when he came to Kirkly-hall,
  He broke locks two or three:    50

Until he came bold Robin to see,
  Then he fell on his knee;
"A boon, a boon," cries Little John,
  "Master, I beg of thee."

"What is that boon," said Robin Hood,    55
  "Little John, [thou] begs of me?"
"It is to burn fair Kirkly-hall,
  And all their nunnery."

"Now nay, now nay," quoth Robin Hood,
  "That boon I'll not grant thee;    60
I never hurt woman in all my life,
  Nor men in woman's company.

"I never hurt fair maid in all my time,
  Nor at mine end shall it be;
But give me my bent bow in my hand,    65
  And a broad arrow I'll let flee
And where this arrow is taken up,
  There shall my grave digged be.

"Lay me a green sod under my head,
  And another at my feet;    70
And lay my bent bow by my side,
  Which was my music sweet;
And make my grave of gravel and green,
  Which is most right and meet.

"Let me have length and breadth enough,    75
  With a green sod under my head;
That they may say, when I am dead,
  Here lies bold Robin Hood."

These words they readily granted him,
  Which did bold Robin please:    80
And there they buried bold Robin Hood,
  Within the fair Kirkleys.

## The Hunting of the Cheviot [1]

The Persë owt off Northombarlonde,
  and avowe to God mayd he
That he wold hunte in the mowntayns
  off Chyviat within days thre,
In the magger of doughtë Dogles,    5
  and all that ever with him be.

The fattiste hartes in all Cheviat
  he sayd he wold kyll, and cary them away;
"Be my feth," sayd the dougheti Doglas agayn,
  "I wyll let that hontyng yf that I may."    10

The[n] the Persë owt off Banborowe cam,
  with him a myghtee meany,
With fifteen hondrith archares bold off blood
  and bone;
  the wear chosen owt of shyars thre.

This begane on a Monday at morn,    15
  in Cheviat the hillys so he;
The chylde may rue that ys un-born,
  it wos the more pittë.

The dryvars thorowe the woodës went,
  for to reas the dear;    20
Bomen byckarte uppone the bent
  with ther browd aros cleare.

Then the wyld thorowe the woodës went,
  on every sydë shear;
Greahondes thorowe the grevis glent,    25
  for to kyll thear dear.

This begane in Chyviat the hyls abone,
  yerly on a Monnyn-day;
Be that it drewe to the oware off none,
  a hondrith fat hartës ded ther lay.    30

[1] This is probably a later and confused account
of the fight dealt with in the ballad called *The
Battle of Otterburn*. The battle took place in 1388.
Sir Philip Sidney's famous praise is generally referred to this ballad, though it would fit *Otterburn* almost as well: "Certainly I must confess my
own barbarousness. I never heard the old song of
Percy and Douglas that I found not my heart
moved more than with a trumpet," *etc.* (*Defense
of Poesie*). Addison criticized with high praise a
younger and more corrupted version (*Chevy Chase*)
of *The Hunting of the Cheviot*, in Nos. 70 and 74
of the *Spectator*.

The blewe a mort uppone the bent,
  the semblyde on sydis shear;
To the quyrry then the Persë went,
  to se the bryttlynge off the deare.

He sayd, "It was the Duglas promys    35
  this day to met me hear;
But I wyste he wolde faylle, verament";
  a great oth the Persë swear.

At the laste a squyar off Northomberlonde
  lokyde at his hand full ny;    40
He was war a the doughetie Doglas commynge,
  with him a myghttë meany.

Both with spear, bylle, and brande,
  yt was a myghtti sight to se;
Hardyar men, both off hart nor hande,    45
  wear not in Cristiantë.

The wear twenti hondrith spear-men good,
  withoute any feale;
The wear borne along be the watter a Twyde,
  yth bowndës of Tividale.    50

"Leave of the brytlyng of the dear," he sayd,
  "and to your boÿs lock ye tayk good hede;
For never sithe ye wear on your mothars borne
  had ye never so mickle nede."

The dougheti Dogglas on a stede,    55
  he rode alle his men beforne;
His armor glytteryde as dyd a glede;
  a boldar barne was never born.

"Tell me whos men ye are," he says,
  "Or whos men that ye be:    60
Who gave youe leave to hunte in this Chyviat
  chays,
  in the spyt of myn and of me."

The first mane that ever him an answear mayd,
  yt was the good lord Persë:
"We wyll not tell the whoys men we ar," he
  says,    65
  "nor whos men that we be;
But we wyll hounte hear in this chays,
  in the spyt of thyne and of the.

"The fattiste hartës in all Chyviat
  we have kyld, and cast to carry them away":
"Be my troth," sayd the doughetë Dogglas
  agay[n],    71
  "therfor the ton of us shall de this day."

Then sayd the doughtë Doglas
  unto the lord Persë:
"To kyll alle these giltles men,    75
  alas, it wear great pittë!

"But, Persë, thowe art a lord of lande,
  I am a yerle callyd within my contrë;

Let all our men uppone a parti stande,
  and do the battell off the and of me."    80

"Nowe Cristes cors on his crowne," sayd the
  lord Persë,
  "who-so-ever ther-to says nay!
Be my troth, doughttë Doglas," he says,
  "thou shalt never se that day.

"Nethar in Ynglonde, Skottlonde, nar France,
  nor for no man of a woman born,    86
But, and fortune be my chance,
  I dar met him, on man for on."

Then bespayke a squyar off Northombarlonde,
  Richard Wytharyngton was him nam;    90
"It shall never be told in Sothe-Ynglonde," he
  says,
  "To Kyng Herry the Fourth for sham.

"I wat youe byn great lordës twaw,
  I am a poor squyar of lande;
I wylle never se my captayne fyght on a fylde,
  and stande my selffe and loocke on,    96
But whylle I may my weppone welde,
  I wylle not [fayle] both hart and hande."

That day, that day, that dredfull day!
  The first fit here I fynde;    100
And youe wyll here any mor a the hountynge
  a the Chyviat,
  yet ys ther mor behynde.

The Yngglyshe men hade ther bowys yebent,
  ther hartes wer good yenoughe;
The first off arros that the shote off,    105
  seven skore spear-men the sloughe.

Yet byddys the yerle Doglas uppon the bent,
  a captayne good yenoughe,
And that was sene verament,
  for he wrought hom both woo and wouche.

The Dogglas partyd his ost in thre,    111
  lyk a cheffe cheften off pryde;
With suar spears off myghttë tre,
  the cum in on every syde;

Thrughe our Yngglyshe archery    115
  gave many a wounde fulle wyde;
Many a doughetë the garde to dy,
  which ganyde them no pryde.

The Ynglyshe men let ther boÿs be,
  and pulde owt brandes that were brighte;    120
It was a hevy syght to se
  bryght swordes on basnites lyght.

Thorowe ryche male and myneyeple,
  many sterne the strocke done streght;
Many a freyke that was fulle fre,    125
  ther undar foot dyd lyght.

At last the Duglas and the Persë met,
    lyk to captayns of myght and of mayne;
The swapte togethar tylle the both swat,
    with swordes that wear of fyn myllan.    130

Thes worthë freckys for to fyght,
    ther-to the wear fulle fayne,
Tylle the bloode owte off thear basnetes
    sprente,
    as ever dyd heal or ra[y]n.

"Yelde the, Persë," sayde the Doglas,    135
    "and i feth I shalle the brynge
Wher thowe shalte have a yerls wagis
    of Jamy our Skottish kynge.

"Thoue shalte have thy ransom fre,
    I hight the hear this thinge;    140
For the manfullyste man yet art thowe
    that ever I conqueryd in filde fighttynge."

"Nay," sayd the lord Persë,
    "I tolde it the beforne,
That I wolde never yeldyde be    145
    to no man of a woman born."

With that ther cam an arrowe hastely,
    forthe off a myghttë wane;
Hit hathe strekene the yerle Duglas
    in at the brest-bane.    150

Thorowe lyvar and longës bathe
    the sharpe arrowe ys gane,
That never after in all his lyffe-days
    he spayke mo wordës but ane:
That was, "Fyghte ye, my myrry men, whyllys
    ye may,    155
    for my lyff-days ben gan."

The Persë leanyde on his brande,
    and sawe the Duglas de;
He tooke the dede mane by the hande,
    and sayd, "Wo ys me for the!    160

"To have savyde thy lyffe, I wolde have partyde
    with
    my landes for years thre,
For a better man, of hart nare of hande,
    was nat in all the north contrë."

Off all that se a Skottishe knyght,    165
    was callyd Ser Hewe the Monggombyrry;
He sawe the Duglas to the deth was dyght,
    he spendyd a spear, a trusti tre.

He rod uppone a corsiare
    throughe a hondrith archery:    170
He never stynttyde, nar never blane,
    tylle he came to the good lord Persë.

He set uppone the lorde Persë
    a dynte that was full soare;

With a suar spear of a myghttë tre    175
    clean thorow the body he the Persë ber,

A the tothar syde that a man myght se
    a large cloth-yard and mare:
Towe bettar captayns wear nat in Cristiantë
    then that day slan wear ther.    180

An archar off Northomberlonde
    say slean was the lord Persë;
He bar a bende bowe in his hand,
    was made off trusti tre.

An arow that a cloth-yarde was lang    185
    to the harde stele halyde he;
A dynt that was both sad and soar
    he sat on Ser Hewe the Monggombyrry.

The dynt yt was both sad and sar
    that he of Monggomberry sete;    190
The swane-fethars that his arrowe bar
    with his hart-blood the wear wete.

Ther was never a freake wone foot wolde fle,
    but still in stour dyd stand,
Heawyng on yche othar, whylle the myghte dre,
    with many a balfull brande.    196

This battell begane in Chyviat
    an owar befor the none,
And when even-songe bell was rang,
    the battell was nat half done.    200

The tocke . . . on ethar hande [2]
    be the lyght off the mone;
Many hade no strength for to stande,
    in Chyviat the hillys abon.

Of fifteen hondrith archars of Ynglonde    205
    went away but seventi and thre;
Of twenti hondrith spear-men of Skotlonde,
    but even five and fifti.

But all wear slayne Cheviat within;
    the hade no streng[th]e to stand on hy;    210
The chylde may rue that ys unborne,
    it was the mor pittë.

Thear was slayne, withe the lord Persë,
    Ser Johan of Agerstone,
Ser Rogar, the hinde Hartly,    215
    Ser Wyllyam, the bolde Hearone.

Ser Jorg, the worthë Loumle,
    a knyghte of great renowen,
Ser Raff, the ryche Rugbe,
    with dyntes wear beaten dowene.    220

For Wetharryngton my harte was wo,
    that ever he slayne shulde be;

[2] Words are missing in the manuscript. "Rest" has been suggested to fill the gap; and also "them off"—i. e., "they took themselves off." "No respite" also seems possible.

For when both his leggis wear hewyne in to,
    yet he knyled and fought on hys kny.

Ther was slayne, with the dougheti Duglas, 225
    Ser Hewe the Monggombyrry,
Ser Davy Lwdale, that worthë was,
    his sistars son was he.

Ser Charls a Murrë in that place,
    that never a foot wolde fle;    230
Ser Hewe Maxwelle, a lorde he was,
    with the Doglas dyd he dey.

So on the morrowe the mayde them byears
    off birch and hasell so g[r]ay;
Many wedous, with wepyng tears,    235
    cam to fache ther makys away.

Tivydale may carpe off care,
    Northombarlond may mayk great mon,
For towe such captayns as slayne wear thear
    on the March-parti shall never be non.  240

Word ys commen to Eddenburrowe,
    to Jamy the Skottishe kynge,[3]
That dougheti Duglas, lyff-tenant of the
    Marches,
    he lay slean Chyviot within.

His handdës dyd he weal and wryng,  245
    he sayd, "Alas, and woe ys me!
Such an othar captayn Skotland within,"
    he sayd, "ye-feth shuld never be."

Worde ys commyn to lovly Londone,
    till the fourth Harry our kynge,  250
That lord Persë, leyff-tenante of the Marchis,
    he lay slayne Chyviat within.

"God have merci on his solle," sayde Kyng
    Harry,
    "good lord, yf thy will it be!
I have a hondrith captayns in Ynglonde," he
    sayd,    255
    "as good as ever was he:
But, Persë, and I brook my lyffe,
    thy deth well quyte shall be."

As our noble kynge mayd his avowe,
    lyke a noble prince of renowen,  260
For the deth of the lord Persë
    he dyde the battell of Hombyll-down;

Wher syx and thrittë Skottishe knyghtes
    on a day wear beaten down;
Glendale glytteryde on ther armor bryght,  265
    over castille, towar, and town.

This was the hontynge off the Cheviat,
    that tear begane this spurn;
Old men that knowen the grownde well
    yenoughe
    call it the battell of Otterburn.  270

    [3] James I of Scotland.

At Otterburn begane this spurne,
    uppone a Monnynday;
Ther was the doughtë Doglas slean,
    the Persë never went away.

Ther was never a tym on the Marche-partës 275
    sen the Doglas and the Persë met,
But yt ys mervele and the rede blude ronne
    not,
    as the reane doys in the stret.

Ihesue Crist our balys bete,
    and to the blys us brynge!  280
Thus was the hountynge of the Chivyat:
    God send us alle good endyng!

## Sir Patrick Spens

The king sits in Dunfermlin town,
    Sae merrily drinkin the wine:
"Whare will I get a mariner,
    Will sail this ship o mine?"

Then up bespak a bonny boy,  5
    Sat just at the king's knee:
"Sir Patrick Spence is the best seaman,
    That eer set foot on sea."

The king has written a braid letter,
    Seald it wi his ain hand;  10
He has sent word to Sir Patrick,
    To come at his command.

"O wha is this, or wha is that,
    Has tald the king o me?
For I was never a good seaman,  15
    Nor ever intend to be."

They mounted sail on Munenday morn,
    Wi a' the haste they may,
And they hae landed in Norraway,
    Upon the Wednesday.  20

They hadna been a month, a month
    In Norraway but three,
Till lads o Norraway began to say,
    "Ye spend a' our white monie.

"Ye spend a' our good kingis goud,  25
    But and our queenis fee":
"Ye lie, ye lie, ye liars loud,
    Sae weel's I hear you lie.

"For I brought as much white money
    as will gain my men and me;  30
I brought half a fou o good red goud
    Out oer the sea with me.

"Be 't wind or weet, be 't snaw or sleet,
    Our ships maun sail the morn:"
"O ever alack! my master dear,  35
    I fear a deadly storm.

"I saw the new moon late yestreen,
  Wi the auld moon in her arm;
And if we gang to sea, master,
  I fear we'll suffer harm."    40

They hadna sailed a league on sea,
  A league but barely ane,
Till anchors brak, and tap-masts lap;
  There came a deadly storm.

"Whare will I get a bonny boy    45
  Will tak thir sails in hand,
That will gang up to the tap-mast,
  See an he ken dry land?"

Laith, laith were our good Scots lords
  To weet their leathern shoon;    50
But or the morn at fair day-light,
  Their hats were wat aboon.

Mony was the feather bed,
  That flottered on the faem,
And mony was the good Scots lord    55
  Gaed awa that neer cam hame,
And mony was the fatherless bairn
  That lay at hame greetin.

It's forty miles to Aberdeen,
  And fifty fathoms deep;    60
And there lyes a' our good Scots lords,
  Wi Sir Patrick at their feet.

The ladies crackt their fingers white,
  The maidens tore their hair,
A' for the sake o their true loves,    65
  For them they neer saw mair.

Lang, lang may our ladies stand,
  Wi their fans in their hand,
Ere they see Sir Patrick and his men
  Come sailing to the land.    70

## The Three Ravens

There were three ravens sat on a tree,
  Downe a downe, hay down, hay downe,
There were three ravens sat on a tree,
  With a downe,
There were three ravens sat on a tree,    5
They were as blacke as they might be.
  With a downe, derrie, derrie, derrie, downe,
    downe.

The one of them said to his mate,
"Where shall we our breakefast take?"

"Downe in yonder greene field,    10
There lies a knight slain under his shield.

"His hounds they lie downe at his feete,
So well they can their master keepe.

"His haukes they flie so eagerly,
There's no fowle dare him come nie."    15

Downe there comes a fallow doe,
As great with yong as she might goe.

She lift up his bloudy hed,
And kist his wounds that were so red.

She got him up upon her backe,    20
And carried him to earthen lake.

She buried him before the prime,
She was dead herselfe ere even-song time.

God send every gentleman,
Such haukes, such hounds, and such a leman.    25

## Edward

"Why dois your brand sae drap wi bluid,
          Edward, Edward,
"Why dois your brand sae drap wi bluid,
  And why sae sad gang yee O?"
"O I hae killed my hauke sae guid,    5
          Mither, mither,
O I hae killed my hauke sae guid,
  And I had nae mair bot hee O."

"Your haukis bluid was nevir sae reid,
          Edward, Edward,    10
Your haukis bluid was nevir sae reid,
  My deir son I tell thee O."
"O I hae killed my reid-roan steid,
          Mither, mither,
O I hae killed my reid-roan steid,    15
  That erst was sae fair and frie O."

"Your steid was auld, and ye hae gat mair,
          Edward, Edward,
Your steid was auld, and ye hae gat mair,
  Sum other dule ye drie O."    20
"O I hae killed my fadir deir,
          Mither, mither,
O I hae killed my fadir deir,
  Alas, and wae is mee O!"

"And whatten penance wul ye drie, for that,    25
          Edward, Edward?
And whatten penance will ye drie for that?
  My deir son, now tell me O."
"Ile set my feit in yonder boat,
          Mither, mither,    30
Ile set my feit in yonder boat,
  And Ile fare ovir the sea O."

"And what wul ye doe wi your towirs and your
    ha,
          Edward, Edward?
And what wul ye doe wi your towirs and your
    ha,    35
  That were sae fair to see O?"

"Ile let thame stand tul they doun fa,
        Mither, mither,
Ile let thame stand tul they doun fa,
    For here nevir mair maun I bee O."    40

"And what wul ye leive to your bairns and your
    wife,
        Edward, Edward?
And what wul ye leive to your bairns and your
    wife,
    Whan ye gang over the sea O?"
"The warldis room, late them beg thrae life, 45
        Mither, mither,
The warldis room, late them beg thrae life,
    For thame nevir mair wul I see O."

"And what wul ye leive to your ain mither deir,
        Edward, Edward?  50
And what wul ye leive to your ain mither deir?
    My deir son, now tell me O."
"The curse of hell frae me sall ye beir,
        Mither, mither,
The curse of hell frae me sall ye beir,  55
    Sic counseils ye gave to me O."

# Babylon; or, The Bonnie
# Banks o Fordie

There were three ladies lived in a bower,
    Eh vow bonnie
And they went out to pull a flower.
    On the bonnie banks o Fordie.

They hadna pu'ed a flower but ane,  5
When up started to them a banisht man.

He's taen the first sister by her hand,
And he's turned her round and made her stand.

"It's whether will ye be a rank robber's wife,
Or will ye die by my wee pen-knife?"  10

"It's I'll not be a rank robber's wife,
But I'll rather die by your wee pen-knife."

He's killed this may, and he's laid her by,
For to bear the red rose company.

He's taken the second ane by the hand,  15
And he's turned her round and made her stand.

"It's whether will ye be a rank robber's wife,
Or will ye die by my wee pen-knife?"

"I'll not be a rank robber's wife,
But I'll rather die by your wee pen-knife."  20

He's killed this may, and he's laid her by,
For to bear the red rose company.

He's taken the youngest ane by the hand,
And he's turned her round and made her stand.

Says, "Will ye be a rank robber's wife,  25
Or will ye die by my wee pen-knife?"

"I'll not be a rank robber's wife,
Nor will I die by your wee pen-knife.

"For I hae a brother in this wood,
And gin ye kill me, it's he'll kill thee."  30

"What's thy brother's name? come tell to me."
"My brother's name is Baby Lon."

"O sister, sister, what have I done!
O have I done this ill to thee!

"O since I've done this evil deed,  35
Good sall never be seen o me."

He's taken out his wee pen-knife,
And he's twyned himsel o his ain sweet life.

# The Twa Sisters

There was twa sisters in a bowr,
    Edinburgh, Edinburgh
There was twa sisters in a bowr,
    Stirling for ay
There was twa sisters in a bowr,
There came a knight to be their wooer.
    Bonny Saint Johnston stands upon Tay

He courted the eldest wi glove an ring,
But he lovd the youngest above a' thing.

He courted the eldest wi brotch an knife,  10
But lovd the youngest as his life.

The eldest she was vexéd sair,
An much envi'd her sister fair.

Into her bowr she could not rest,
Wi grief an spite she almos brast.  15

Upon a morning fair an clear,
She cried upon her sister dear:

"O sister, come to yon sea stran,
And see our father's ships come to lan."

She's taen her by the milk-white han,  20
And led her down to yon sea stran.

The younges[t] stood upon a stane,
The eldest came an threw her in.

She tooke her by the middle sma,
An dashd her bonny back to the jaw.  25

"O sister, sister, tak my han,
An Ise mack you heir to a' my lan.

"O sister, sister, tak my middle,
An yes get my goud and my gouden girdle.

"O sister, sister, save my life,     30
An I swear Ise never be nae man's wife."

"Foul fa the han that I should tacke,
It twin'd me an my wardles make.

"Your cherry cheeks an yallow hair
Gars me gae maiden for evermair."     35

Sometimes she sank, an sometimes she swam,
Till she came down yon bonny mill-dam.

O out it came the miller's son,
An saw the fair maid swimmin in.

"O father, father, draw your dam,     40
Here's either a mermaid or a swan."

The miller quickly drew the dam,
An there he found a drownd woman.

You coudna see her yallow hair
For gold and pearle that were so rare.     45

You coudna see her middle sma
For gouden girdle that was sae braw.

You coudna see her fingers white,
For gouden rings that was sae gryte.

An by there came a harper fine,     50
That harpéd to the king at dine.

When he did look that lady upon,
He sighed and made a heavy moan.

He's taen three locks o her yallow hair,
An wi them strung his harp sae fair.     55

The first tune he did play and sing,
Was, "Farewell to my father the king."

The nextin tune that he playd syne,
Was, "Farewell to my mother the queen."

The lasten tune that he played then,     60
Was, "Wae to my sister, fair Ellen."

## The Twa Brothers

There were twa brethren in the north,
    They went to school thegithar;
The one unto the other said,
    Will you try a warsle afore?

They warsled up, they warsled down,     5
    Till Sir John fell to the ground,
And there was a knife in Sir Willie's pouch,
    Gied him a deadlie wound.

"Oh brither dear, take me on your back,
    Carry me to yon burn clear,     10

And wash the blood from off my wound,
    And it will bleed nae mair."

He took him up upon his back,
    Carried him to yon burn clear,
And washd the blood from off his wound,     15
    But aye it bled the mair.

"Oh brither dear, take me on your back,
    Carry me to yon kirk-yard,
And dig a grave baith wide and deep,
    And lay my body there."     20

He's taen him up upon his back,
    Carried him to yon kirk-yard,
And dug a grave baith deep and wide,
    And laid his body there.

"But what will I say to my father dear,     25
    Gin he chance to say, Willie, whar's John?"
"Oh say that he's to England gone,
    To buy him a cask of wine."

"And what shall I say to my mother dear,
    Gin she chance to say, Willie, whar's John?"
"Oh say that he's to England gone,
    To buy her a new silk gown."

"And what will I say to my sister dear,
    Gin she chance to say, Willie, whar's John?"
"Oh say that he's to England gone,     35
    To buy her a wedding ring."

"But what will I say to her you loe dear,
    Gin she cry, Why tarries my John?"
"Oh tell her I lie in Kirk-land fair,
    And home again will never come."     40

## The Cruel Brother

There was three ladies playd at the ba,
    With a hey ho and a lillie gay
There came a knight and played oer them a'.
    As the primrose spreads so sweetly

The eldest was baith tall and fair,     5
But the youngest was beyond compare.

The midmost had a graceful mien,
But the youngest lookd like beautie's queen.

The knight bowd low to a' the three,
But to the youngest he bent his knee.     10

The ladie turned her head aside,
The knight he woo'd her to be his bride.

The ladie blushd a rosy red,
And sayd, "Sir knight, I'm too young to wed."

"O ladie fair, give me your hand,     15
And I'll make you ladie of a' my land."

"Sir knight, ere ye my favor win,
You maun get consent frae a' my kin."

He's got consent frae her parents dear,
And likewise frae her sisters fair.    20

He's got consent frae her kin each one,
But forgot to spiek to her brother John.

Now, when the wedding day was come,
The knight would take his bonny bride home.

And many a lord and many a knight    25
Came to behold that ladie bright.

And there was nae man that did her see,
But wishd himself bridegroom to be.

Her father dear led her down the stair,
And her sisters twain they kissed her there. 30

Her mother dear led her thro the closs,
And her brother John set her on her horse.

She leand her oer the saddle-bow,
To give him a kiss ere she did go.

He has taen a knife, baith lang and sharp, 35
And stabbd that bonny bride to the heart.

She hadno ridden half thro the town,
Until her heart's blude staind her gown.

"Ride softly on," says the best young man,
"For I think our bonny bride looks pale and
    wan."    40

"O lead me gently up yon hill,
And I'll there sit down, and make my will."

"O what will you leave to your father dear?"
"The silver-shode steed that brought me here."

"What will you leave to your mother dear?"
"My velvet pall and my silken gear."    46

"What will you leave to your sister Anne?"
"My silken scarf and my gowden fan."

"What will you leave to your sister Grace?"
"My bloody cloaths to wash and dress."    50

"What will you leave to your brother John?"
"The gallows-tree to hang him on."

"What will you leave to your brother John's
    wife?"
"The wilderness to end her life."

This ladie fair in her grave was laid,    55
And many a mass was oer her said.

But it would have made your heart right sair,
To see the bridegroom rive his haire.

# The Wife of Usher's Well

There lived a wife at Usher's Well,
    And a wealthy wife was she;
She had three stout and stalwart sons,
    And sent them oer the sea.

They hadna been a week from her,    5
    A week but barely ane,
Whan word came to the carline wife
    That her three sons were gane.

They hadna been a week from her,
    A week but barely three,    10
Whan word came to the carlin wife
    That her sons she'd never see.

"I wish the wind may never cease,
    Nor fashes in the flood,
Till my three sons come hame to me,    15
    In earthly flesh and blood."

It fell about the Martinmass,
    When nights are lang and mirk,
The carlin wife's three sons came hame,
    And their hats were o the birk.    20

It neither grew in syke nor ditch,
    Nor yet in ony sheugh;
But at the gates o Paradise,
    That birk grew fair eneugh.

        .        .        .

"Blow up the fire, my maidens,    25
    Bring water from the well;
For a' my house shall feast this night,
    Since my three sons are well."

And she has made to them a bed,
    She's made it large and wide,    30
And she's taen her mantle her about,
    Sat down at the bed-side.

Up then crew the red, red cock,
    And up and crew the gray;
The eldest to the youngest said,    35
    " 'Tis time we were away."

The cock he hadna crawd but once,
    And clappd his wings at a',
When the youngest to the eldest said,
    "Brother, we must awa."    40

"The cock doth craw, the day doth daw,
    The channerin worm doth chide;
Gin we be mist out o our place,
    A sair pain we maun bide."

"Fare ye weel, my mother dear!    45
    Fareweel to barn and byre!
And fare ye weel, the bonny lass
    That kindles my mother's fire!"

## Kemp Owyne [1]

Her mother died when she was young,
    Which gave her cause to make great moan;
Her father married the warst woman
    That ever lived in Christendom.

She servéd her with foot and hand,         5
    In every thing that she could dee,
Till once in an unlucky time,
    She threw her in ower Craigy's sea.

Says, "Lie you there, dove Isabel,
    And all my sorrows lie with thee;        10
Till Kemp Owyne come ower the sea,
    And borrow you with kisses three,
Let all the warld do what they will,
    Oh borrowed shall you never be!"

Her breath grew strang, her hair grew lang,   15
    And twisted thrice about the tree,
And all the people, far and near,
    Thought that a savage beast was she.

These news did come to Kemp Owyne,
    Where he lived, far beyond the sea;      20
He hasted him to Craigy's sea,
    And on the savage beast lookd he.

Her breath was strang, her hair was lang,
    And twisted was about the tree,
And with a swing she came about:          25
    "Come to Craigy's sea, and kiss with me.

"Here is a royal belt," she cried,
    "That I have found in the green sea;
And while your body it is on,
    Drawn shall your blood never be;         30
But if you touch me, tail or fin,
    I vow my belt your death shall be."

He steppéd in, gave her a kiss,
    The royal belt he brought him wi;
Her breath was strang, her hair was lang,    35
    And twisted twice about the tree,
And with a swing she came about:
    "Come to Craigy's sea, and kiss with me.

"Here is a royal ring," she said,
    "That I have found in the green sea;     40
And while your finger it is on,
    Drawn shall your blood never be;
But if you touch me, tail or fin,
    I swear my ring your death shall be."

He steppéd in, gave her a kiss,            45
    The royal ring he brought him wi;
Her breath was strang, her hair was lang,

[1] Owyne is Owain or Ywain, one of King Arthur's
knights. Disenchantment by a kiss is common in
romance, but none is known in which Ywain has
this adventure.

And twisted ance about the tree,
And with a swing she came about:
    "Come to Craigy's sea, and kiss with me.   50

"Here is a royal brand," she said,
    "That I have found in the green sea;
And while your body it is on,
    Drawn shall your blood never be;
But if you touch me, tail or fin,          55
    I swear my brand your death shall be."

He steppéd in, gave her a kiss,
    The royal brand he brought him wi;
Her breath was sweet, her hair grew short,
    And twisted nane about the tree,         60
And smilingly she came about,
    As fair a woman as fair could be.

## Thomas Rymer [1]

True Thomas lay oer yond grassy bank,
    And he beheld a ladie gay,
A ladie that was brisk and bold,
    Come riding oer the fernie brae.

Her skirt was of the grass-green silk,      5
    Her mantel of the velvet fine,
At ilka tett of her horse's mane
    Hung fifty silver bells and nine.

True Thomas he took off his hat,
    And bowed him low down till his knee:    10
"All hail, thou mighty Queen of Heaven!
    For your peer on earth I never did see."

"O no, O no, True Thomas," she says,
    "That name does not belong to me;
I am but the queen of fair Elfland,         15
    And I'm come here for to visit thee.

"But ye maun go wi me now, Thomas,
    True Thomas, ye maun go wi me,
For ye maun serve me seven years,
    Thro weel or wae as may chance to be."   20

She turned about her milk-white steed,
    And took True Thomas up behind,
And aye wheneer her bridle rang,
    The steed flew swifter than the wind.

For forty days and forty nights             25
    He wade thro red blude to the knee,
And he saw neither sun nor moon,
    But heard the roaring of the sea.

[1] This story is told in fuller detail in the poem
called *Thomas of Erceldoune*, a fifteenth-century
romance and probably the source of the ballad.
Thomas of Erceldoune is an historical character;
he lived in southern Scotland in the thirteenth century.

O they rade on, and further on,
  Until they came to a garden green:   **30**
"Light down, light down, ye ladie free,
  Some of that fruit let me pull to thee."

"O no, O no, True Thomas," she says,
  "That fruit maun not be touched by thee,
For a' the plagues that are in hell   **35**
  Light on the fruit of this countrie.

"But I have a loaf here in my lap,
  Likewise a bottle of claret wine,
And now ere we go farther on,
  We'll rest a while, and ye may dine."   **40**

When he had eaten and drunk his fill,
  "Lay down your head upon my knee,"
The lady sayd, "ere we climb yon hill,
  And I will show you fairlies three.

"O see not ye yon narrow road,   **45**
  So thick beset wi thorns and briers?
That is the path of righteousness,
  Tho after it but few enquires.

"And see not ye that braid braid road,
  That lies across yon lillie leven?   **50**
That is the path of wickedness,
  Tho some call it the road to heaven.

"And see not ye that bonny road,
  Which winds about the fernie brae?
That is the road to fair Elfland,   **55**
  Whe[re] you and I this night maun gae.

"But Thomas, ye maun hold your tongue,
  Whatever you may hear or see,
For gin ae word you should chance to speak,
  You will neer get back to your ain countrie."

He has gotten a coat of the even cloth,   **61**
  And a pair of shoes of velvet green,
And till seven years were past and gone
  True Thomas on earth was never seen.

# Sir Hugh; or, The Jew's Daughter [1]

Four and twenty bonny boys
  Were playing at the ba,
And by it came him sweet Sir Hugh,
  And he playd oer them a'.

He kicked the ba with his right foot,   **5**
  And catchd it wi his knee,
And throuch-and-thro the Jew's window
  He gard the bonny ba flee.

[1] This is based on an alleged murder which took place in 1255. The popularity of such stories in the Middle Ages has been mentioned in the note to Chaucer's Prioress's tale, which has the same theme.

He's doen him to the Jew's castell,
  And walkd it round about;   **10**
And there he saw the Jew's daughter,
  At the window looking out.

"Throw down the ba, ye Jew's daughter,
  Throw down the ba to me!"
"Never a bit," says the Jew's daughter,   **15**
  "Till up to me come ye."

"How will I come up? How can I come up?
  How can I come to thee?
For as ye did to my auld father,
  The same ye'll do to me."   **20**

She's gane till her father's garden,
  And pu'd an apple red and green;
'T was a' to wyle him sweet Sir Hugh,
  And to entice him in.

She's led him in through ae dark door,   **25**
  And sae has she thro nine;
She's laid him on a dressing-table,
  And stickit him like a swine.

And first came out the thick, thick blood,
  And syne came out the thin,   **30**
And syne came out the bonny heart's blood;
  There was nae mair within.

She's rowd him in a cake o lead,
  Bade him lie still and sleep;
She's thrown him in Our Lady's draw-well,   **35**
  Was fifty fathom deep.

When bells were rung, and mass was sung,
  And a' the bairns came hame,
When every lady gat hame her son
  The Lady Maisry gat nane.   **40**

She's taen her mantle her about,
  Her coffer by the hand,
And she's gane out to seek her son,
  And wanderd oer the land.

She's doen her to the Jew's castell,   **45**
  Where a' were fast asleep:
"Gin ye be there, my sweet Sir Hugh,
  I pray you to me speak."

She's doen her to the Jew's garden,
  Thought he had been gathering fruit:   **50**
"Gin ye be there, my sweet Sir Hugh,
  I pray you to me speak."

She neard Our Lady's deep draw-well,
  Was fifty fathom deep:
"Whareer ye be, my sweet Sir Hugh,   **55**
  I pray you to me speak."

"Gae hame, gae hame, my mither dear,
  Prepare my winding sheet,
And at the back o merry Lincoln
  The morn I will you meet."   **60**

Now Lady Maisry is gane hame,
  Made him a winding sheet,
And at the back o merry Lincoln
  The dead corpse did her meet.

And a' the bells o merry Lincoln        65
  Without men's hands were rung,
And a' the books o merry Lincoln
  Were read without man's tongue,
And neer was such a burial
  Sin Adam's days begun.                70

## The Daemon Lover

"O where have you been, my long, long love,
  This long seven years and mair?"
"O I'm come to seek my former vows
  Ye granted me before."

"O hold your tongue of your former vows,    5
  For they will breed sad strife;
O hold your tongue of your former vows,
  For I am become a wife."

He turned him right and round about,
  And the tear blinded his ee:           10
"I wad never hae trodden on Irish ground,
  If it had not been for thee.

"I might hae had a king's daughter,
  Far, far beyond the sea;
I might have had a king's daughter,     15
  Had it not been for love o thee."

"If ye might have had a king's daughter,
  Yer sel ye had to blame;
Ye might have taken the king's daughter,
  For ye kend that I was nane.           20

"If I was to leave my husband dear,
  And my two babes also,
O what have you to take me to,
  If with you I should go?"

"I hae seven ships upon the sea—        25
  The eighth brought me to land—
With four-and-twenty bold mariners,
  And music on every hand."

She has taken up her two little babes,
  Kissd them baith cheek and chin:      30
"O fair ye weel, my ain two babes,
  For I'll never see you again."

She set her foot upon the ship,
  No mariners could she behold;
But the sails were o the taffetie,      35
  And the masts o the beaten gold.

She had not sailed a league, a league,
  A league but barely three,
When dismal grew his countenance,
  And drumlie grew his ee.              40

They had not saild a league, a league,
  A league but barely three,
Until she espied his cloven foot,
  And she wept right bitterlie.

"O hold your tongue of your weeping," says he,
  "Of your weeping now let me be;       46
I will shew you how the lilies grow
  On the banks of Italy."

"O what hills are yon, yon pleasant hills,
  That the sun shines sweetly on?"      50
"O yon are the hills of heaven," he said,
  "Where you will never win."

"O whaten a mountain is yon," she said,
  "All so dreary wi frost and snow?"
"O yon is the mountain of hell," he cried,  55
  "Where you and I will go."

He strack the tap-mast wi his hand,
  The fore-mast wi his knee,
And he brake that gallant ship in twain,
  And sank her in the sea.             60

## Get Up and Bar the Door

It fell about the Martinmas time,
  And a gay time it was then,
When our goodwife got puddings to make,
  And she's boild them in the pan.

The wind sae cauld blew south and north,    5
  And blew into the floor;
Quoth our goodman to our goodwife,
  "Gae out and bar the door."

"My hand is in my hussyfskap,
  Goodman, as ye may see;               10
An it should nae be barrd this hundred year,
  It's no be barrd for me."

They made a paction tween them twa,
  They made it firm and sure,
That the first word whaeer shoud speak,     15
  Shoud rise and bar the door.

Then by there came two gentlemen,
  At twelve o clock at night,
And they could neither see house nor hall,
  Nor coal nor candle-light.           20

"Now whether is this a rich man's house,
  Or whether is it a poor?"
But neer a word wad ane o them speak,
  For barring of the door.

And first they ate the white puddings,      25
  And then they ate the black;
Tho muckle thought the goodwife to hersel,
  Yet neer a word she spake.

Then said the one unto the other,
 "Here, man, tak ye my knife; 30
Do ye tak aff the auld man's beard,
 And I'll kiss the goodwife."

"But there's nae water in the house,
 And what shall we do than?"
"What ails ye at the pudding-broo, 35
 That boils into the pan?"

O up then started our goodman,
 An angry man was he:
"Will ye kiss my wife before my een,
 And scad me wi pudding-bree?" 40

Then up and started our goodwife,
 Gied three skips on the floor:
"Goodman, you've spoken the foremost word,
 Get up and bar the door."

# Everyman

The authorship of *Everyman* is not known. The play made its appearance some time during the fifteenth century. Its text is preserved in four early editions, none of which is dated, though all must have appeared between 1493 and 1537—dates which mark the limits of the period during which the two printers of the editions, Pynson and Skot, did their work. It is considered probable by some scholars that *Everyman* is a translation of a Dutch play, *Elckerlijk* (ascribed to Dorlandus), which was in print before the earliest edition of *Everyman*. This, however, is by no means certain, as *Everyman* may be really the earlier of the two, or both may go back to some common source now unknown. The importance of this unsettled question, moreover, may easily be exaggerated, inasmuch as *Everyman* as it now stands is a thoroughly English play, with none of the earmarks of a mere translation, and has its inherent right to the place it has won in English literature.

The English moralities, of which *Everyman* is an outstanding example, were in the beginning vehicles of religious and moral instruction; later the type was made the instrument of religious controversy and was also used in exhibiting the value of learning. The chief theme of the earlier moralities was the life of man conceived as a conflict between good and evil, a conflict which begins with birth and ends only with death. In its entirety this is a practically endless subject, and writers tended to narrow its scope, with a proportionate gain in simplicity of structure, in directness, and in power. Thus some moralities exhibit a crucial conflict between two groups, virtues and vices, for possession of the soul of man. Another plan was to picture the coming of death, and this is done in *Everyman*. The play shows the measure of dramatic quality and power which the morality was capable of attaining when it was at its best.

A good text of *Everyman* may be found in

Chief Pre-Shakespearean Dramas, *ed. Joseph Q. Adams (Boston, 1924), pp. 288–303. For a discussion of the morality play and its background see Hardin Craig*, English Religious Drama of the Middle Ages (Oxford, 1955).

## CHARACTERS

| | |
|---|---|
| EVERYMAN | STRENGTH |
| GOD: ADONAI | DISCRETION |
| DEATH | FIVE-WITS |
| MESSENGER | BEAUTY |
| FELLOWSHIP | KNOWLEDGE |
| COUSIN | CONFESSION |
| KINDRED | ANGEL |
| GOODS | DOCTOR |
| GOOD-DEEDS | |

Here beginneth a treatis how the High Father
   of Heaven sendeth death to summon every
   creature to come and give account of their
   lives in this world and is in manner of a
   moral play.

MESSENGER. I pray you all give your audience,
   And hear this matter with reverence,
   By figure a moral play—
   The *Summoning of Everyman* called it is,
   That of our lives and ending shows   5
   How transitory we be all day.
   This matter is wondrous precious,
   But the intent of it is more gracious,
   And sweet to bear away.
   The story saith,—Man, in the beginning, 10
   Look well, and take good heed to the ending,
   Be you never so gay!
   Ye think sin in the beginning full sweet,
   Which in the end causeth thy soul to weep,
   When the body lieth in clay.   15
   Here shall you see how *Fellowship* and
     *Jollity*,
   Both *Strength, Pleasure,* and *Beauty*,
   Will fade from thee as flower in May.
   For ye shall hear how our Heaven King
   Calleth *Everyman* to a general reckoning: 20
   Give audience, and hear what he doth say.

God. I perceive here in my majesty,
  How that all creatures be to me unkind,
  Living without dread in worldly prosperity:
  Of ghostly sight [1] the people be so blind, 25
  Drowned in sin, they know me not for their
    God;
  In worldly riches is all their mind,
  They fear not my rightwiseness, the sharp
    rod;
  My law that I showed, when I for them died,
  They forget clean, and shedding of my blood
    red;                                        30
  I hanged between two, it cannot be denied;
  To get them life I suffered to be dead;
  I healed their feet, with thorns hurt was my
    head:
  I could do no more than I did truly,
  And now I see the people do clean forsake
    me.                                         35
  They use the seven deadly sins damnable;
  As pride, covetise, wrath, and lechery,
  Now in the world be made commendable;
  And thus they leave of angels the heavenly
    company;                                    39
  Everyman liveth so after his own pleasure,
  And yet of their life they be nothing sure:
  I see the more that I them forbear
  The worse they be from year to year;
  All that liveth appaireth [2] fast,
  Therefore I will in all the haste            45
  Have a reckoning of Everyman's person;
  For and I leave the people thus alone
  In their life and wicked tempests,
  Verily they will become much worse than
    beasts;
  For now one would by envy another up eat;
  Charity they all do clean forget.            51
  I hoped well that Everyman
  In my glory should make his mansion,
  And thereto I had them all elect;
  But now I see, like traitors deject,         55
  They thank me not for the pleasure that I
    to them meant,
  Nor yet for their being that I them have
    lent;
  I proffered the people great multitude of
    mercy,
  And few there be that asketh it heartily;
  They be so cumbered with worldly riches, 60
  That needs on them I must do justice,
  On Everyman living without fear.
  Where art thou, *Death*, thou mighty mes-
    senger?
Death. Almighty God, I am here at your will,
  Your commandment to fulfil.                  65
God. Go thou to *Everyman*,
  And show him in my name
  A pilgrimage he must on him take,
  Which he in no wise may escape;
  And that he bring with him a sure reckoning
  Without delay or any tarrying.               71

Death. Lord, I will in the world go run over
    all,
  And cruelly outsearch both great and small;
  Every man will I beset that liveth beastly
  Out of God's laws, and dreadeth not folly:
  He that loveth riches I will strike with my
    dart,                                       76
  His sight to blind, and from heaven to
    depart,
  Except that alms be his good friend,
  In hell for to dwell, world without end.
  Lo, yonder I see *Everyman* walking;        80
  Full little he thinketh on my coming;
  His mind is on fleshly lusts and his treasure,
  And great pain it shall cause him to endure
  Before the Lord Heaven King.
  *Everyman*, stand still; whither art thou going
  Thus gaily? Hast thou thy Maker forget? 86
Everyman. Why askst thou?
  Wouldest thou wete? [3]
Death. Yea, sir, I will show you;
  In great haste I am sent to thee             90
  From God out of his majesty.
Everyman. What, sent to me?
Death. Yea, certainly.
  Though thou have forgot him here,
  He thinketh on thee in the heavenly sphere,
  As, or we depart, thou shalt know.          96
Everyman. What desireth God of me?
Death. That shall I show thee;
  A reckoning he will needs have
  Without any longer respite.                 100
Everyman. To give a reckoning longer leisure
    I crave;
  This blind matter troubleth my wit.
Death. On thee thou must take a long journey:
  Therefore thy book of count with thee thou
    bring;
  For turn again thou cannot by no way, 105
  And look thou be sure of thy reckoning:
  For before God thou shalt answer, and show
  Thy many bad deeds and good but a few;
  How thou hast spent thy life, and in what
    wise,
  Before the chief lord of paradise.          110
  Have ado that we were in that way,
  For, wete thou well, thou shalt make none
    attournay. [4]
Everyman. Full unready I am such reckoning
    to give.
  I know thee not: what messenger art thou?
Death. I am *Death*, that no man dreadeth. [5]
  For every man I rest [6] and no man spareth;
  For it is God's commandment               117
  That all to me should be obedient.
Everyman. O *Death*, thou comest when I had
    thee least in mind;
  In thy power it lieth me to save,          120
  Yet of my good will I give thee, if ye will be
    kind,

---

[1] Spiritual insight.    [2] Is impaired.

[3] Know.                         [4] Mediator.
[5] That respecteth no man.        [6] Arrest.

Yea, a thousand pound shalt thou have,
And defer this matter till another day.
DEATH. *Everyman*, it may not be by no way;
I set not by gold, silver, nor riches, 125
Nor by pope, emperor, king, duke, nor
princes.
For and I would receive gifts great,
All the world I might get;
But my custom is clean contrary.
I give thee no respite: come hence, and not
tarry. 130
EVERYMAN. Alas, shall I have no longer respite?
I may say *Death* giveth no warning:
To think on thee, it maketh my heart sick,
For all unready is my book of reckoning.
But twelve year and I might have abiding,
My counting book I would make so clear, 136
That my reckoning I should not need to
fear.
Wherefore, *Death*, I pray thee, for God's
mercy,
Spare me till I be provided of remedy.
DEATH. Thee availeth not to cry, weep, and
pray: 140
But haste thee lightly that you were gone the
journey,
And prove thy friends if thou can.
For, wete thou well, the tide abideth no
man,
And in the world each living creature
For *Adam's* sin must die of nature. 145
EVERYMAN. *Death*, if I should this pilgrimage
take,
And my reckoning surely make,
Show me, for saint *charity*,
Should I not come again shortly?
DEATH. No, *Everyman*; and thou be once there,
Thou mayst never more come here, 151
Trust me verily.
EVERYMAN. O gracious God, in the high seat
celestial,
Have mercy on me in this most need;
Shall I have no company from this vale
terrestrial 155
Of mine acquaintance that way me to lead?
DEATH. Yea, if any be so hardy,
That would go with thee and bear thee
company.
Hie thee that you were gone to God's mag-
nificence, 159
Thy reckoning to give before his presence.
What, weenest thou thy life is given thee,
And thy worldly goods also?
EVERYMAN. I had wend so, verily.
DEATH. Nay, nay; it was but lent thee;
For as soon as thou art go, 165
Another awhile shall have it, and then go
therefro
Even as thou hast done.
*Everyman*, thou art mad; thou hast thy wits
five,
And here on earth will not amend thy life,
For suddenly I do come. 170

EVERYMAN. O wretched caitiff, whither shall I
flee,
That I might scape this endless sorrow!
Now, gentle *Death*, spare me till tomorrow,
That I may amend me
With good advisement. 175
DEATH. Nay, thereto I will not consent,
Nor no man will I respite,
But to the heart suddenly I shall smite
Without any advisement.
And now out of thy sight I will me hie; 180
See thou make thee ready shortly,
For thou mayst say this is the day
That no man living may scape away.
EVERYMAN. Alas, I may well weep with sighs
deep;
Now have I no manner of company 185
To help me in my journey, and me to keep;
And also my writing is full unready.
How shall I do now for to excuse me?
I would to God I had never be gete! [7]
To my soul a full great profit it had be; 190
For now I fear pains huge and great.
The time passeth; Lord, help that all
wrought;
For though I mourn it availeth nought.
The day passeth, and is almost a-go;
I wot not well what for to do. 195
To whom were I best my complaint to make?
What, and I to *Fellowship* thereof spake,
And showed him of this sudden chance?
For in him is all mine affiance;
We have in the world so many a day 200
Be on good friends in sport and play.
I see him yonder, certainly;
I trust that he will bear me company;
Therefore to him will I speak to ease my
sorrow.
Well met, good *Fellowship*, and good mor-
row! 205
FELLOWSHIP *speaketh*. *Everyman*, good mor-
row by this day.
Sir, why lookest thou so piteously?
If any thing be amiss, I pray thee, me say,
That I may help to remedy.
EVERYMAN. Yea, good *Fellowship*, yea, 210
I am in great jeopardy.
FELLOWSHIP. My true friend, show to me your
mind;
I will not forsake thee, unto my life's end,
In the way of good company.
EVERYMAN. That was well spoken, and lov-
ingly. 215
FELLOWSHIP. Sir, I must needs know your
heaviness;
I have pity to see you in any distress;
If any have you wronged ye shall revenged
be,
Though I on the ground be slain for thee,—
Though that I know before that I should
die. 220

[7] Been born.

EVERYMAN. Verily, *Fellowship*, gramercy.
FELLOWSHIP. Tush! by thy thanks I set not a
    straw.
Show me your grief, and say no more.
EVERYMAN. If I my heart should to you break,
And then you to turn your mind from me,
    And would not me comfort, when you hear
      me speak,     226
Then should I ten times sorrier be.
FELLOWSHIP. Sir, I say as I will do in deed.
EVERYMAN. Then be you a good friend at need:
    I have found you true here before.   230
FELLOWSHIP. And so ye shall evermore;
    For, in faith, and thou go to Hell,
I will not forsake thee by the way!
EVERYMAN. Ye speak like a good friend; I
    believe you well;
I shall deserve it, and I may.   235
FELLOWSHIP. I speak of no deserving, by this
    day.
For he that will say and nothing do
Is not worthy with good company to go;
Therefore show me the grief of your mind,
As to your friend most loving and kind. 240
EVERYMAN. I shall show you how it is;
    Commanded I am to go a journey,
A long way, hard and dangerous,
And give a strait count without delay
Before the high judge Adonai.[8]   245
Wherefore I pray you, bear me company,
As ye have promised, in this journey.
FELLOWSHIP. That is matter indeed! Promise is
    duty,
But, and I should take such a voyage on me,
I know it well, it should be to my pain: 250
Also it make me afeard, certain.
But let us take counsel here as well as we
    can,
For your words would fear a strong man.
EVERYMAN. Why, ye said, If I had need,
Ye would me never forsake, quick nor dead,
Though it were to hell truly.   256
FELLOWSHIP. So I said, certainly,
But such pleasures be set aside, thee sooth
    to say:
And also, if we took such a journey,
When should we come again?   260
EVERYMAN. Nay, never again till the day of
    doom.
FELLOWSHIP. In faith, then will not I come
    there!
Who hath you these tidings brought?
EVERYMAN. Indeed, *Death* was with me here.
FELLOWSHIP. Now, by God that all hath
    bought,[9]   265
If *Death* were the messenger,
For no man that is living to-day
I will not go that loath journey—
Not for the father that begat me!
EVERYMAN. Ye promised other wise, pardie. 270
FELLOWSHIP. I wot well I say so truly;

And yet if thou wilt eat, and drink, and
    make good cheer,
Or haunt to women, the lusty company,
I would not forsake you, while the day is
    clear,
Trust me verily!   275
EVERYMAN. Yea, thereto ye would be ready;
To go to mirth, solace, and play,
Your mind will sooner apply
Than to bear me company in my long
    journey.
FELLOWSHIP. Now, in good faith, I will not
    that way.   280
But and thou wilt murder, or any man kill,
In that I will help thee with a good will!
EVERYMAN. O that is a simple advice indeed!
Gentle *fellow*, help me in my necessity;
We have loved long, and now I need, 285
And now, gentle *Fellowship*, remember me.
FELLOWSHIP. Whether ye have loved me or no,
By Saint John, I will not with thee go.
EVERYMAN. Yet I pray thee, take the labor, and
    do so much for me
To bring me forward, for saint charity, 290
And comfort me till I come without the
    town.
FELLOWSHIP. Nay, and thou would give me a
    new gown,
I will not a foot with thee go;
But and you had tarried I would not have
    left thee so.
And as now, God speed thee in thy journey,
For from thee I will depart as fast as I
    may.   296
EVERYMAN. Whither away, *Fellowship*? will
    you forsake me?
FELLOWSHIP. Yea, by my fay, to God I be-
    take[10] thee.
EVERYMAN. Farewell, good *Fellowship*; for this
    my heart is sore;
Adieu for ever, I shall see thee no more. 300
FELLOWSHIP. In faith, *Everyman*, farewell now
    at the end;
For you I will remember that parting is
    mourning.
EVERYMAN. Alack! shall we thus depart indeed?
Our Lady, help, without any more comfort,
Lo, *Fellowship* forsaketh me in my most
    need:   305
For help in this world whither shall I resort?
*Fellowship* herebefore with me would merry
    make;
And now little sorrow for me doth he take.
It is said, in prosperity men friends may find,
Which in adversity be full unkind. 310
Now whither for succor shall I flee,
Since that *Fellowship* hath forsaken me?
To my kinsmen I will truly,
Praying them to help me in my necessity;
I believe that they will do so,   315
For kind will creep where it may not go.

---

[8] God.      [9] Redeemed.      [10] Commit.

I will go say,[11] for yonder I see them go.
Where be ye now, my friends and kinsmen?
KINDRED. Here be we now at your command-
  ment.
  *Cousin*, I pray you show us your intent 320
In any wise, and not spare.
COUSIN. Yea, *Everyman*, and to us declare
  If ye be disposed to go any whither,
  For wete you well, we will live and die to-
  gether.
KINDRED. In wealth and woe we will with you
  hold,     325
  For over his kin a man may be bold.
EVERYMAN. Gramercy, my friends and kins-
  men kind.
  Now shall I show you the grief of my mind:
  I was commanded by a messenger,
  That is an high king's chief officer;   330
  He bade me go a pilgrimage to my pain,
  And I know well I shall never come again;
  Also I must give a reckoning straight,
  For I have a great enemy, that hath me in
  wait,
  Which intendeth me for to hinder.   335
KINDRED. What account is that which ye must
  render?
  That would I know.
EVERYMAN. Of all my works I must show
  How I have lived and my days spent;
  Also of ill deeds, that I have used   340
  In my time, since life was me lent;
  And of all virtues that I have refused.
  Therefore I pray you go thither with me,
  To help to make mine account, for saint
  *charity*.
COUSIN. What, to go thither? Is that the mat-
  ter?   345
  Nay, *Everyman*, I had liefer fast bread and
  water
  All this five year and more.
EVERYMAN. Alas, that ever I was bore! [12]
  For now shall I never be merry
  If that you forsake me.   350
KINDRED. Ah, sir; what, ye be a merry man!
  Take good heart to you, and make no moan.
  But one thing I warn you, by Saint Anne,
  As for me, ye shall go alone.
EVERYMAN. My *Cousin*, will you not with me
  go?   355
COUSIN. No, by Our Lady; I have the cramp
  in my toe.
  Trust not to me, for, so God me speed,
  I will deceive you in your most need.
KINDRED. It availeth not us to tice.
  Ye shall have my maid with all my heart; 360
  She loveth to go to feasts, there to be nice,
  And to dance, and abroad to start:
  I will give her leave to help you in that
  journey,
  If that you and she may agree.

EVERYMAN. Now show me the very effect of
  your mind.   365
  Will you go with me, or abide behind?
KINDRED. Abide behind? yea, that I will and I
  may!
  Therefore farewell until another day.
EVERYMAN. How should I be merry or glad?
  For fair promises to me make,   370
  But when I have most need, they me for-
  sake.
  I am deceived; that maketh me sad.
COUSIN. Cousin *Everyman*, farewell now,
  For verily I will not go with you;
  Also of mine own an unready reckoning 375
  I have to account; therefore I make tarrying.
  Now, God keep thee, for now I go.
EVERYMAN. Ah, *Jesus*, is all come hereto?
  Lo, fair words maketh fools feign;   379
  They promise and nothing will do certain.
  My kinsmen promised me faithfully
  For to abide with me steadfastly,
  And now fast away do they flee:
  Even so *Fellowship* promised me.
  What friend were best me of to provide? 385
  I lose my time here longer to abide.
  Yet in my mind a thing there is;—
  All my life I have loved riches;
  If that my good now help me might,
  He would make my heart full light.   390
  I will speak to him in this distress.—
  Where art thou, my *Goods* and riches?
GOODS. Who calleth me? *Everyman*? what
  haste thou hast!
  I lie here in corners, trussed and piled so
  high,
  And in chests I am locked so fast,   395
  Also sacked in bags, thou mayst see with
  thine eye,
  I cannot stir; in packs low I lie.
  What would ye have, lightly me say.
EVERYMAN. Come hither, *Good*, in all the
  haste thou may,
  For of counsel I must desire thee.   400
GOODS. Sir, and ye in the world have trouble
  or adversity,
  That can I help you to remedy shortly.
EVERYMAN. It is another disease [13] that grieveth
  me;
  In this world it is not, I tell thee so.
  I am sent for another way to go,   405
  To give a straight account general
  Before the highest *Jupiter* of all;
  And all my life I have had joy and pleasure
  in thee.
  Therefore I pray thee go with me,
  For, peradventure, thou mayst before God
  Almighty   410
  My reckoning help to clean and purify;
  For it is said ever among,
  That money maketh all right that is wrong.
GOODS. Nay, *Everyman*, I sing another song,

[11] Put it to the trial.
[12] Born.

[13] Trouble.

I follow no man in such voyages;      415
For and I went with thee
Thou shouldst fare much the worse for me;
For because on me thou did set thy mind,
Thy reckoning I have made blotted and
   blind,      419
That thine account thou cannot make truly;
And that hast thou for the love of me.
EVERYMAN. That would grieve me full sore,
When I should come to that fearful answer.
Up, let us go thither together.
GOODS. Nay, not so, I am too brittle, I may not
   endure;      425
I will follow no man one foot, be ye sure.
EVERYMAN. Alas, I have thee loved, and had
   great pleasure
All my life-days on good and treasure.
GOODS. That is to thy damnation without
   lesing,[14]
For my love is contrary to the love ever-
   lasting.      430
But if thou had me loved moderately during,
As, to the poor give part of me,
Then shouldst thou not in this dolor be,
Nor in this great sorrow and care.
EVERYMAN. Lo, now was I deceived or I was
   ware,      435
And all I may wyte[15] my spending of time.
GOODS. What, weenest thou that I am thine?
EVERYMAN. I had wend so.
GOODS. Nay, *Everyman*, I say no;
As for a while I was lent thee,      440
A season thou hast had me in prosperity;
My condition is man's soul to kill;
If I save one, a thousand I do spill;
Weenest thou that I will follow thee?
Nay, from this world, not verily.      445
EVERYMAN. I had wend otherwise.
GOODS. Therefore to thy soul *Good* is a thief;
For when thou art dead, this is my guise
Another to deceive in the same wise
As I have done thee, and all to his soul's
   reprief.      450
EVERYMAN. O false *Good*, cursed thou be!
Thou traitor to God, that hast deceived me,
And caught me in thy snare.
GOODS. Marry, thou brought thyself in care,
Whereof I am glad,      455
I must needs laugh, I cannot be sad.
EVERYMAN. Ah, *Good*, thou hast had long
   my hearty love;
I gave thee that which should be the Lord's
   above.
But wilt thou not go with me in deed?
I pray thee truth to say.      460
GOODS. No, so God me speed,
Therefore farewell, and have good day.
EVERYMAN. Oh, to whom shall I make my
   moan
For to go with me in that heavy journey?
First *Fellowship* said he would with me gone;

His words were very pleasant and gay,      466
But afterward he left me alone.
Then spake I to my kinsmen all in despair,
And also they gave me words fair;
They lacked no fair speaking;      470
But all forsake me in the ending.
Then went I to my *Goods* that I loved best,
In hope to have comfort, but there had I
   least!
For my *Goods* sharply did me tell
That he bringeth many into hell.      475
Then of myself I was ashamed,
And so I am worthy to be blamed;
Thus may I well myself hate.
Of whom shall I now counsel take?
I think that I shall never speed      480
Till that I go to my *Good-Deeds*.
But alas, she is so weak,
That she can neither go nor speak;
Yet will I venture on her now.—
My *Good-Deeds*, where be you?      485
GOOD-DEEDS. Here I lie cold in the ground;
Thy sins hath me sore bound,
That I cannot stir.
EVERYMAN. O, *Good-Deeds*, I stand in fear;
I must you pray of counsel,      490
For help now should come right well.
GOOD-DEEDS. *Everyman*, I have understanding
That ye be summoned account to make
Before *Messias*, of Jerusalem King;
And you do by me[16] that journey with you
   will I take.      495
EVERYMAN. Therefore I come to you, my moan
   to make;
I pray you, that ye will go with me.
GOOD-DEEDS. I would full fain, but I cannot
   stand verily.
EVERYMAN. Why, is there anything on you
   fall?
GOOD-DEEDS. Yea, sir, I may thank you of all;
If ye had perfectly cheered me,      501
Your book of account now full ready had be.
Look, the books of your works and deeds eke;
Oh, see how they lie under the feet,
To your soul's heaviness.      505
EVERYMAN. Our Lord *Jesus*, help me!
For one letter here I cannot see.
GOOD-DEEDS. There is a blind reckoning in
   time of distress!
EVERYMAN. *Good-Deeds*, I pray you, help me
   in this need,
Or else I am for ever damned indeed;      510
Therefore help me to make reckoning
Before the redeemer of all things,
That king is, and was, and ever shall.
GOOD-DEEDS. *Everyman*, I am sorry of your fall,
And fain would I help you, and I were able.
EVERYMAN. *Good-Deeds*, your counsel I pray
   you give me.      516
GOOD-DEEDS. That shall I do verily;
Though that on my feet I may not go.

---

[14] Lying.      [15] Blame.      [16] If you take my counsel.

I have a sister, that shall with you also,
Called *Knowledge*, which shall with you
    abide,    520
To help you to make that dreadful reckon-
    ing.
KNOWLEDGE. *Everyman*, I will go with thee,
    and be thy guide,
In thy most need to go by thy side.
EVERYMAN. In good condition I am now in
    every thing,
And am wholly content with this good thing;
Thanked be God my Creator.    526
GOOD-DEEDS. And when he hath brought thee
    there,
Where thou shalt heal thee of thy smart,
Then go you with your reckoning and your
    *Good-Deeds* together
For to make you joyful at heart    530
Before the blessed Trinity.
EVERYMAN. My *Good-Deeds*, gramercy;
I am well content, certainly,
With your words sweet.    534
KNOWLEDGE. Now go we together lovingly,
To *Confession*, that cleansing river.
EVERYMAN. For joy I weep; I would we were
    there;
But, I pray you, give me cognition
Where dwelleth that holy man, *Confession*.
KNOWLEDGE. In the house of salvation:    540
We shall find him in that place.
That shall us comfort by God's grace.
Lo, this is *Confession*; kneel down and ask
    mercy,
For he is in good conceit [17] with God Al-
    mighty.
EVERYMAN. O glorious fountain that all un-
    cleanness doth clarify,    545
Wash from me the spots of vices unclean,
That on me no sin may be seen;
I come with *Knowledge* for my redemption,
Repent with hearty and full contrition;    549
For I am commanded a pilgrimage to take,
And great accounts before God to make.
Now, I pray you, *Shrift*, mother of salvation,
Help my good deeds for my piteous exclama-
    tion.
CONFESSION. I know your sorrow well, *Every-
    man*;
Because with *Knowledge* ye come to me,    555
I will you comfort as well as I can,
And a precious jewel I will give thee,
Called penance, wise voider of adversity;
Therewith shall your body chastised be,
With abstinence and perseverance in God's
    service:    560
Here shall you receive that scourge of me
Which is penance strong, that ye must
    endure,
To remember thy Savior was scourged for
    thee
With sharp scourges, and suffered it pa-
    tiently;
[17] Esteem.

So must thou, or thou scape that painful
    pilgrimage;    565
*Knowledge*, keep him in this voyage,
And by that time *Good-Deeds* will be with
    thee.
But in any wise, be sure of mercy,
For your time draweth fast, and ye will saved
    be;
Ask God mercy, and He will grant truly.    570
When with the scourge of penance man doth
    him bind,
The oil of forgiveness then shall be find.
EVERYMAN. Thanked be God for his gracious
    work!
For now I will my penance begin;
This hath rejoiced and lighted my heart,    575
Though the knots be painful and hard with-
    in.
KNOWLEDGE. *Everyman*, look your penance
    that ye fulfil,
What pain that ever it to you be,
And *Knowledge* shall give you counsel at
    will,    579
How your accounts ye shall make clearly.
EVERYMAN. O eternal God, O heavenly figure,
O way of rightwiseness, O goodly vision,
Which descended down in a virgin pure
Because he would *Everyman* redeem,
Which *Adam* forfeited by his disobedi-
    ence;    585
O blessed Godhead, elect and high-divine,
Forgive my grievous offense;
Here I cry thee mercy in this presence.
O ghostly treasure, O ransomer and redeemer
Of all the world, hope and conductor,    590
Mirror of joy, and founder of mercy,
Which illumineth heaven and earth thereby,
Hear my clamorous complaint, though it late
    be;
Receive my prayers; unworthy in this heavy
    life
Though I be, a sinner most abominable,    595
Yet let my name be written in *Moses*' table;
O *Mary*, pray to the Maker of all thing,
Me for to help at my ending,
And save me from the power of my enemy,
For *Death* assaileth me strongly;    600
And, Lady, that I may by means of thy
    prayer
Of your Son's glory to be partaker,
By the means of his passion I it crave,
I beseech you, help my soul to save.—
*Knowledge*, give me the scourge of pen-
    ance;    605
My flesh therewith shall give a quittance:
I will now begin, if God give me grace.
KNOWLEDGE. *Everyman*, God give you time
    and space:
Thus I bequeath you in the hands of our
    Savior,    609
Thus may you make your reckoning sure.
EVERYMAN. In the name of the Holy Trinity,
My body sore punished shall be:

Take this body for the sin of the flesh;
Also thou delightest to go gay and fresh,
And in the way of damnation thou did me
    bring;            615
Therefore suffer now strokes and punishing.
Now of penance I will wade the water clear
To save me from purgatory, that sharp fire.
GOOD-DEEDS. I thank God, now I can walk
    and go;           619
And am delivered of my sickness and woe.
Therefore with *Everyman* I will go, and not
    spare;
His good works I will help him to declare.
KNOWLEDGE. Now, *Everyman*, be merry and
    glad;
Your *Good-Deeds* cometh now; ye may not
    be sad;
Now is your *Good-Deeds* whole and sound,
Going upright upon the ground.     626
EVERYMAN. My heart is light, and shall be ever-
    more;
Now will I smite faster than I did before.
GOOD-DEEDS. *Everyman*, pilgrim, my special
    friend,
Blessed be thou without end;       630
For thee is prepared the eternal glory.
Ye have me made whole and sound,
Therefore I will bide by thee in every
    stound.[18]
EVERYMAN. Welcome, my *Good-Deeds*; now I
    hear thy voice,
I weep for very sweetness of love.     635
KNOWLEDGE. Be no more sad, but ever rejoice;
God seeth thy living in his throne above;
Put on this garment to thy behove,
Which is wet with your tears,
Or else before God you may it miss,   640
When you to your journey's end come shall.
EVERYMAN. Gentle *Knowledge*, what do you it
    call?
KNOWLEDGE. It is a garment of sorrow:
From pain it will you borrow;
Contrition it is,            645
That getteth forgiveness;
It pleaseth God passing well.
GOOD-DEEDS. *Everyman*, will you wear it for
    your heal?
EVERYMAN. Now blessed be *Jesu, Mary's* Son!
For now have I on true contrition.    650
And let us go now without tarrying;
*Good-Deeds*, have we clear our reckoning?
GOOD-DEEDS. Yea, indeed I have it here.
EVERYMAN. Then I trust we need not fear;
Now, friends, let us not part in twain.   655
KNOWLEDGE. Nay, *Everyman*, that will we not,
    certain.
GOOD-DEEDS. Yet must thou lead with thee
Three persons of great might.
EVERYMAN. Who should they be?
GOOD-DEEDS. *Discretion* and *Strength* they
    hight,[19]              660

And thy *Beauty* may not abide behind.
KNOWLEDGE. Also ye must call to mind
Your *Five-Wits* as for your counselors.
GOOD-DEEDS. You must have them ready at all
    hours.
EVERYMAN. How shall I get them hither?   665
KNOWLEDGE. You must call them all together,
And they will hear you incontinent.
EVERYMAN. My friends, come hither and be
    present,
*Discretion, Strength*, my *Five-Wits*, and
    *Beauty*.
BEAUTY. Here at your will we be all ready.   670
What will ye that we should do?
GOOD-DEEDS. That ye would with *Everyman*
    go,
And help him in his pilgrimage,
Advise you, will ye with him or not in that
    voyage?
STRENGTH. We will bring him all thither,   675
To his help and comfort, ye may believe me.
DISCRETION. So will we go with him all to-
    gether.
EVERYMAN. Almighty God, loved thou be,
I give thee laud that I have hither brought
*Strength, Discretion, Beauty*, and *Five-Wits*;
    lack I nought;           680
And my *Good-Deeds*, with *Knowledge* clear,
All be in my company at my will here;
I desire no more to my business.
STRENGTH. And I, *Strength*, will by you stand
    in distress,
Though thou would in battle fight on the
    ground.                685
FIVE-WITS. And though it were through the
    world round,
We will not depart for sweet nor sour.
BEAUTY. No more will I unto death's hour,
Whatsoever thereof befall.
DISCRETION. *Everyman*, advise you first of all;
Go with a good advisement and delibera-
    tion;                 691
We all give you virtuous monition
That all shall be well.
EVERYMAN. My friends, hearken what I will
    tell:
I pray God reward you in his heavenly
    sphere.                695
Now hearken, all that be here,
For I will make my testament
Here before you all present.
In alms half my good I will give with my
    hands twain
In the way of charity, with good intent,   700
And the other half still shall remain
In quiet to be returned there it ought to be.
This I do in despite of the fiend of hell
To go quite out of his peril
Ever after and this day.         705
KNOWLEDGE. *Everyman*, hearken what I say;
Go to priesthood, I you advise,
And receive of him in any wise
The holy sacrament and ointment together;

[18] Season.     [19] Are called.

Then shortly see ye turn again hither; 710
We will all abide you here.
FIVE-WITS. Yea, *Everyman*, hie you that ye
ready were;
There is no emperor, king, duke, nor baron,
That of God hath commission, 714
As hath the least priest in the world being;
For of the blessed sacraments pure and
benign,
He beareth the keys and thereof hath the
cure
For man's redemption, it is ever sure;
Which God for our soul's medicine
Gave us out of his heart with great pine; 720
Here in this transitory life, for thee and me
The blessed sacraments seven there be,
Baptism, confirmation, with priesthood good,
And the sacrament of God's precious flesh
and blood,
Marriage, the holy extreme unction, and
penance; 725
These seven be good to have in remem-
brance,
Gracious sacraments of high divinity.
EVERYMAN. Fain would I receive that holy
body,
And meekly to my ghostly [20] father I will go.
FIVE-WITS. *Everyman*, that is the best that ye
can do: 730
God will you to salvation bring,
For priesthood exceedeth all other thing;
To us Holy Scripture they do teach,
And converteth man from sin heaven to
reach;
God hath to them more power given 735
Than to any angel that is in heaven;
With five words he may consecrate
God's body in flesh and blood to make,
And handleth his maker between his hands;
The priest bindeth and unbindeth all bands,
Both in earth and in heaven; 741
Thou ministers all the sacraments seven;
Though we kissed thy feet thou were worthy;
Thou art surgeon that cureth sin deadly:
No remedy we find under God 745
But all only priesthood.
*Everyman*, God gave priests that dignity,
And setteth them in his stead among us to
be;
Thus be they above angels in degree.
KNOWLEDGE. If priests be good it is so surely;
But when Jesus hanged on the cross with
great smart 751
There he gave, out of his blessed heart,
The same sacrament in great torment:
He sold them not to us, that Lord Omnipo-
tent.
Therefore Saint Peter the apostle doth say
That Jesu's curse hath all they 756
Which God their Savior do buy or sell,
Or they for any money do take or tell.

[20] Spiritual.

Sinful priests giveth the sinners example
bad;
Their children sitteth by other men's fires,
I have heard; 760
And some haunteth women's company,
With unclean life, as lusts of lechery:
These be with sin made blind.
FIVE-WITS. I trust to God no such may we
find;
Therefore let us priesthood honor, 765
And follow their doctrine for our souls' suc-
cor;
We be their sheep, and they shepherds be
By whom we all be kept in surety.
Peace, for yonder I see *Everyman* come,
Which hath made true satisfaction. 770
GOOD-DEEDS. Methinketh it is he indeed.
EVERYMAN. Now Jesu be our alder speed.[21]
I have received the sacrament for my re-
demption,
And then mine extreme unction:
Blessed be all they that counseled me to take
it! 775
And now, friends, let us go without longer
respite;
I thank God that ye have tarried so long.
Now set each of you on this rod your hand,
And shortly follow me:
I go before, there I would be; God be our
guide. 780
STRENGTH. *Everyman*, we will not from you go
Till ye have gone this voyage long.
DISCRETION. I, *Discretion*, will bide by you also.
KNOWLEDGE. And though this pilgrimage be
never so strong,
I will never part you fro: 785
*Everyman*, I will be as sure by thee
As ever I did by Judas Maccabee.
EVERYMAN. Alas, I am so faint I may not stand,
My limbs under me do fold;
Friends, let us not turn again to this land,
Not for all the world's gold. 791
For into this cave must I creep
And turn to the earth and there to sleep.
BEAUTY. What, into this grave? alas!
EVERYMAN. Yea, there shall you consume more
and less. 795
BEAUTY. And what, should I smother here?
EVERYMAN. Yea, by my faith, and never more
appear.
In this world live no more we shall,
But in heaven before the highest Lord of all.
BEAUTY. I cross out all this; adieu by Saint
John; 800
I take my tap in my lap and am gone.[22]
EVERYMAN. What, *Beauty*, whither will ye?

[21] Jesu help us all.
[22] A proverbial expression used to describe a hasty
departure. In the beginning it was used literally of
a woman taking her tap—a quantity of flax for
spinning—and distaff in her lap or apron, in going
to or from a friend's house.

BEAUTY. Peace, I am deaf; I look not behind
me,
Not and thou would give me all the gold in
thy chest.
EVERYMAN. Alas, whereto may I trust?     805
*Beauty* goeth fast away hie;
She promised with me to live and die.
STRENGTH. *Everyman*, I will thee also forsake
and deny;
Thy game liketh me not at all.
EVERYMAN. Why, then ye will forsake me all.
Sweet *Strength*, tarry a little space.     811
STRENGTH. Nay, sir, by the rood of grace
I will hie me from thee fast,
Though thou weep till thy heart brast.[23]
EVERYMAN. Ye would ever bide by me, ye
said.     815
STRENGTH. Yea, I have you far enough con-
veyed;
Ye be old enough, I understand,
Your pilgrimage to take on hand;
I repent me that I hither came.
EVERYMAN. *Strength*, you to displease I am to
blame;     820
Will you break promise that is debt?
STRENGTH. In faith, I care not;
Thou art but a fool to complain,
You spend your speech and waste your brain;
Go thrust thee into the ground.     825
EVERYMAN. I had wend surer I should you have
found.
He that trusteth in his *Strength*
She him deceiveth at the length.
Both *Strength* and *Beauty* forsaketh me,
Yet they promised me fair and lovingly.     830
DISCRETION. *Everyman*, I will after *Strength* be
gone,
As for me I will leave you alone.
EVERYMAN. Why, *Discretion*, will ye forsake
me?
DISCRETION. Yea, in faith, I will go from thee,
For when *Strength* goeth before     835
I follow after evermore.
EVERYMAN. Yet, I pray thee, for the love of the
Trinity,
Look in my grave once piteously.
DISCRETION. Nay, so nigh will I not come.
Farewell, every one!     840
EVERYMAN. O all thing faileth, save God alone;
*Beauty*, *Strength*, and *Discretion*;
For when *Death* bloweth his blast,
They all run from me full fast.
FIVE-WITS. *Everyman*, my leave now of thee
I take;     845
I will follow the other, for here I thee for-
sake.
EVERYMAN. Alas! then may I wail and weep,
For I took you for my best friend.
FIVE-WITS. I will no longer thee keep;
Now farewell, and there an end.     850
EVERYMAN. O Jesu, help, all hath forsaken me!

GOOD-DEEDS. Nay, *Everyman*, I will bide with
thee,
I will not forsake thee indeed;
Thou shalt find me a good friend at need.
EVERYMAN. Gramercy, *Good-Deeds*; now may
I true friends see;     855
They have forsaken me every one;
I loved them better than my *Good-Deeds*
alone.
*Knowledge*, will ye forsake me also?
KNOWLEDGE. Yea, *Everyman*, when ye to death
do go:
But not yet for no manner of danger.     860
EVERYMAN. Gramercy, *Knowledge*, with all my
heart.
KNOWLEDGE. Nay, yet I will not from hence
depart,
Till I see where ye shall be come.
EVERYMAN. Methinketh, alas, that I must be
gone,
To make my reckoning and my debts pay,
For I see my time is nigh spent away.     866
Take example, all ye that this do hear or see,
How they that I loved best do forsake me,
Except my *Good-Deeds* that bideth truly.
GOOD-DEEDS. All earthly things is but vanity:
*Beauty*, *Strength*, and *Discretion* do man
forsake,     871
Foolish friends and kinsmen, that fair spake,
All fleeth save *Good-Deeds*, and that am I.
EVERYMAN. Have mercy on me, God most
mighty;
And stand by me, thou Mother and Maid,
holy *Mary*.     875
GOOD-DEEDS. Fear not, I will speak for thee.
EVERYMAN. Here I cry God mercy.
GOOD-DEEDS. Short our end, and minish our
pain;
Let us go and never come again.
EVERYMAN. Into thy hands, Lord, my soul I
commend;     880
Receive it, Lord, that it be not lost;
As thou me boughtest, so me defend,
And save me from the fiend's boast,
That I may appear with that blessed host
That shall be saved at the day of doom.     885
*In manus tuas*—of might's most
For ever—*commendo spiritum meum*.[24]
KNOWLEDGE. Now hath he suffered that we all
shall endure;
The *Good-Deeds* shall make all sure.
Now hath he made ending;     890
Methinketh that I hear angels sing
And make great joy and melody,
Where *Everyman's* soul received shall be.
ANGEL. Come, excellent elect spouse to Jesu:
Hereabove thou shalt go     895
Because of thy singular virtue:
Now the soul is taken the body fro;
Thy reckoning is crystal-clear.
Now shalt thou into the heavenly sphere,

---

[23] Burst.

[24] To thy hands I commend my soul.

Unto the which all ye shall come    900
That liveth well before the day of doom.
DOCTOR. This moral men may have in mind;
Ye hearers, take it of worth, old and young,
And forsake pride, for he deceiveth you in
    the end,
And remember *Beauty*, *Five-Wits*, *Strength*,
    and *Discretion*,    905
They all at the last do *Everyman* forsake,
Save his *Good-Deeds*, there doth he take.
But beware, and they be small
Before God, he hath no help at all.
None excuse may be there for *Everyman*;
Alas, how shall he do then?    911

For after death amends may no man make,
For then mercy and pity do him forsake.
If his reckoning be not clear when he do
    come,
God will say—*ite, maledicti, in ignem aeter-*
    *num.*[25]    915
And he that hath his account whole and
    sound,
High in heaven he shall be crowned;
Unto which place God bring us all thither
That we may live body and soul together.
Thereto help the Trinity,    920
Amen, say ye, for saint *charity*.

[25] Hence, accursed one, into eternal fire.

Very little is known about the life of Malory. The year generally given as that of his birth is approximate only. He lived at Newbold Revell, in Warwickshire. He served in the French wars with Richard Beauchamp, Earl of Warwick, a renowned representative of the chivalric ideal. Malory was also conspicuous on the Lancastrian side in the Wars of the Roses, and for this reason he was imprisoned towards the close of his life. In 1445, he was a member of Parliament for Warwickshire. He was "a gentleman of an ancient house, and a soldier"—a man whose career, as far as we know anything about it, seems eminently appropriate to the compiler of the Morte d'Arthur. This book Malory finished in 1469 or 1470, and it was first printed in 1485, by William Caxton (c. 1421–1491), the earliest English printer.

Caxton tells us in the Preface printed below that Malory took the Morte d'Arthur "out of certain books of French, and reduced it into English." Malory, in fact, used some English material; but he translated the greater part of his work from a number of French romances, whose volume is said to be about ten times as great as that of the Morte d'Arthur itself. These romances told no connected story; on the contrary, they were frequently inconsistent with each other, and this, together with their number, probably accounts sufficiently for the incongruities in Malory's book. He seems to have chosen the stories that pleased him best, with the general design of giving an account of Arthur's life from birth to death. This is done only in the loosest fashion, but it is a mark of originality on Malory's part, inasmuch as Arthur is thus given an importance which he does not have in the old romances.

The Works of Sir Thomas Malory, ed. Eugène Vinaver (Oxford, 1947; text reprinted in one volume, Oxford, 1954), is based on a fifteenth-century manuscript. Vinaver has re-edited one of the works with corrections and additional notes: The Tale of the Death of King Arthur (Oxford, 1955). Le Morte Darthur, ed. H. Oskar Sommer (London, 1889–1891), is based on the text published by Caxton. A good interpretation is given in English Literature at the Close of the Middle Ages, by Sir Edmund K. Chambers (Oxford, 1945). For a full discussion of Malory's life and sources see Eugène Vinaver, Sir Thomas Malory (Oxford, 1929).

# Le Morte D'Arthur

## CAXTON'S PREFACE

AFTER that I had accomplished and finished divers histories, as well of contemplation as of other historical and worldly acts of great conquerors and princes, and also certain books of ensamples and doctrine, many noble and divers gentlemen of this realm of England came and demanded me, many and ofttimes, wherefore that I have not do made [1] and imprinted the noble history of the Sangreal, and of the most renowned Christian king, first and chief of the three best Christian and worthy, King Arthur, which ought most to be remembered among us English men tofore all other Christian kings. For it is notoriously known through the universal world that there be nine worthy and the best that ever were. That is, to wit, three paynims, three Jews, and three Christian men. As for the paynims they were tofore the Incarnation of Christ, which were named, the first Hector of Troy, of whom the history is come both in ballad and in prose; the second Alexander the Great; and the third Julius Caesar, Emperor of Rome, of whom the histories be well-known and had. And as for the three Jews which also were tofore the Incarnation of our Lord, of whom the first was Duke Joshua which brought the

[1] Had made.

154

children of Israel into the land of behest; the second David, King of Jerusalem; and the third Judas Maccabaeus: of these three the Bible rehearseth all their noble histories and acts. And sith the said Incarnation have been three noble Christian men stalled [2] and admitted through the universal world into the number of the nine best and worthy, of whom was first the noble Arthur, whose noble acts I purpose to write in this present book here following. The second was Charlemagne or Charles the Great, of whom the history is had in many places both in French and English; and the third and last was Godfrey of Bouillon, of whose acts and life I made a book unto the excellent prince and king of noble memory, King Edward the Fourth. The said noble gentlemen instantly required me to imprint the history of the said noble king and conqueror, King Arthur, and of his knights, with the history of the Sangreal, and of the death and ending of the said Arthur; affirming that I ought rather to imprint his acts and noble feats, than of Godfrey of Bouillon, or any of the other eight, considering that he was a man born within this realm, and king and emperor of the same; and that there be in French divers and many noble volumes of his acts, and also of his knights. To whom I answered, that divers men hold opinion that there was no such Arthur, and that all such books as be made of him be but feigned and fables, by cause that some chronicles make of him no mention nor remember him no thing, nor of his knights. Whereto they answered and one in special said, that in him that should say or think that there was never such a king called Arthur, might well be credited great folly and blindness; for he said that there were many evidences of the contrary: first ye may see his sepulture in the Monastery of Glastonbury. And also in Polichronicon,[3] in the fifth book the sixth chapter, and in the seventh book the twenty-third chapter, where his body was buried and after found and translated into the said monastery. Ye shall see also in the history of Bochas,[4] in his book *De Casu Principum*, part of his noble acts, and also of his fall. Also Galfridus [5] in

his British book recounteth his life; and in divers places of England many remembrances be yet of him and shall remain perpetually, and also of his knights. First in the Abbey of Westminster, at Saint Edward's shrine, remaineth the print of his seal in red wax closed in beryl, in which is written *Patricius Arthurus, Britannie, Gallie, Germanie, Dacie, Imperator*.[6] Item in the castle of Dover ye may see Gawaine's skull and Craddock's mantle: at Winchester the Round Table: at other places Launcelot's sword and many other things. Then, all these things considered, there can no man reasonably gainsay but there was a king of this land named Arthur. For in all places, Christian and heathen, he is reputed and taken for one of the nine worthy, and the first of the three Christian men. And also he is more spoken of beyond the sea, more books made of his noble acts than there be in England, as well in Dutch, Italian, Spanish, and Greek, as in French. And yet of record remain in witness of him in Wales, in the town of Camelot,[7] the great stones and marvelous works of iron, lying under the ground, and royal vaults, which divers now living hath seen. Wherefore it is a marvel why he is no more renowned in his own country, save only it accordeth to the Word of God, which saith that no man is accept for a prophet in his own country. Then, all these things foresaid alleged, I could not well deny but that there was such a noble king named Arthur, and reputed one of the nine worthy, and first and chief of the Christian men; and many noble volumes be made of him and of his noble knights in French, which I have seen and read beyond the sea, which be not had in our maternal tongue, but in Welsh be many and also in French, and some in English, but no where nigh all. Wherefore, such as have late been drawn out briefly into English I have after the simple conning that God hath sent to me, under the favor and correction of all noble lords and gentlemen, emprised [8] to imprint a book of the noble histories of the said King Arthur, and of certain of his knights, after a copy unto me delivered, which copy Sir Thomas Malory did take out of certain books of French, and reduced it into English. And I, according to my copy, have done set it in imprint, to the intent that noble men may see and learn the noble acts of chivalry, the gentle and virtuous deeds that some knights used in

[2] Installed.
[3] A history of the world, written in Latin by Ranulph Higden (died *c.* 1364).
[4] Boccaccio. The book (*On the Fall of Princes*) tells of the misfortunes of illustrious men.
[5] Geoffrey of Monmouth, whose *History of the Kings of Britain* (written in Latin, probably about 1140) contains much fabulous matter.

[6] Noble Arthur, Emperor of Britain, Gaul, Germany, and Dacia.
[7] A legendary town, where Arthur held his court.
[8] Undertaken.

those days, by which they came to honor; and how they that were vicious were punished and oft put to shame and rebuke; humbly beseeching all noble lords and ladies, with all other estates, of what estate or degree they be of, that shall see and read in this said book and work, that they take the good and honest acts in their remembrance, and to follow the same. Wherein they shall find many joyous and pleasant histories, and noble and renowned 10 acts of humanity, gentleness, and chivalries. For herein may be seen noble chivalry, courtesy, humanity, friendliness, hardiness, love, friendship, cowardice, murder, hate, virtue, and sin. Do after the good and leave the evil, and it shall bring you to good fame and renown. And for to pass the time this book shall be pleasant to read in; but for to give faith and believe that all is true that is contained herein, ye be at your liberty; but all is written for our 20 doctrine, and for to beware that we fall not to vice nor sin; but to exercise and follow virtue; by which we may come and attain to good fame and renown in this life, and after this short and transitory life, to come unto everlasting bliss in heaven, the which He grant us that reigneth in heaven, the blessed Trinity. Amen.

Then to proceed forth in this said book, which I direct unto all noble princes, lords 30 and ladies, gentlemen or gentlewomen, that desire to read or hear read of the noble and joyous history of the great conqueror and excellent king, King Arthur, sometime king of this noble realm, then called Britain. I, William Caxton, simple person, present this book following, which I have emprised to imprint; and treateth of the noble acts, feats of arms of chivalry, prowess, hardiness, humanity, love, courtesy and very gentleness, with many 40 wonderful histories and adventures. And for to understand briefly the content of this volume, I have divided it into twenty-one books, and every book chaptered as hereafter shall by God's grace follow. The first book shall treat how Uther Pendragon gat the noble conqueror King Arthur, and containeth twenty-eight chapters. The second book treateth of Balin the noble knight, and containeth nineteen chapters. The third book treateth of the mar- 50 riage of King Arthur to Queen Guenever, with other matters, and containeth fifteen chapters. The fourth book, how Merlin was assotted,[9] and of war made to King Arthur, and containeth twenty-nine chapters. The fifth book treateth of the conquest of Lucius the em-

peror, and containeth twelve chapters. The sixth book treateth of Sir Launcelot and Sir Lionel, and marvelous adventures, and containeth eighteen chapters. The seventh book treateth of a noble knight called Sir Gareth, and named by Sir Kay, Beaumains, and containeth thirty-six chapters. The eighth book treateth of the birth of Sir Tristram the noble knight, and of his acts, and containeth forty-one chapters. The ninth book treateth of a knight named by Sir Kay, La Cote Male Taile, and also of Sir Tristram, and containeth forty-four chapters. The tenth book treateth of Sir Tristram and other marvelous adventures, and containeth eighty-eight chapters. The eleventh book treateth of Sir Launcelot and Sir Galahad, and containeth fourteen chapters. The twelfth book treateth of Sir Launcelot and his madness, and containeth fourteen chapters. The thirteenth book treateth how Galahad came first to King Arthur's court, and the quest how the Sangreal was begun, and containeth twenty chapters. The fourteenth book treateth of the quest of the Sangreal, and containeth ten chapters. The fifteenth book treateth of Sir Launcelot, and containeth six chapters. The sixteenth book treateth of Sir Bors and Sir Lionel his brother, and containeth seventeen chapters. The seventeenth book treateth of the Sangreal, and containeth twenty-three chapters. The eighteenth book treateth of Sir Launcelot and the queen, and containeth twenty-five chapters. The nineteenth book treateth of Queen Guenever and Launcelot, and containeth thirteen chapters. The twentieth book treateth of the piteous death of Arthur, and containeth twenty-two chapters. The twenty-first book treateth of his last departing, and how Sir Launcelot came to revenge his death, and containeth thirteen chapters. The sum is twenty-one books, which contain the sum of five hundred and seven chapters, as more plainly shall follow hereafter.

## BOOK XXI

### CHAPTER I

*How Sir Mordred Presumed and Took on Him to Be King of England, and Would Have Married the Queen, His Uncle's Wife*

As Sir Mordred was ruler of all England, he did do make[1] letters as though that they came from beyond the sea, and the letters specified that King Arthur was slain in battle with Sir Launcelot. Wherefore Sir Mordred made a

---

[9] Besotted.

[1] Have made.

parliament, and called the lords together, and there he made them to choose him king; and so he was crowned at Canterbury, and held a feast there fifteen days; and afterward he drew him unto Winchester, and there he took the Queen Guenever, and said plainly that he would wed her which was his uncle's wife and his father's wife. And so he made ready for the feast, and a day prefixed that they should be wedded; wherefore Queen Guenever was passing heavy. But she durst not discover her heart, but spake fair, and agreed to Sir Mordred's will. Then she desired of Sir Mordred for to go to London, to buy all manner of things that longed unto the wedding. And by cause of her fair speech Sir Mordred trusted her well enough, and gave her leave to go. And so when she came to London she took the Tower of London, and suddenly in all haste possible she stuffed it with all manner of victual, and well garnished it with men, and so kept it. Then when Sir Mordred wist [2] and understood how he was beguiled, he was passing wroth out of measure. And a short tale for to make, he went and laid a mighty siege about the Tower of London, and made many great assaults thereat, and threw many great engines unto them, and shot great guns. But all might not prevail [3] Sir Mordred, for Queen Guenever would never for fair speech nor for foul, would never trust to come in his hands again. Then came the Bishop of Canterbury, the which was a noble clerk and an holy man, and thus he said to Sir Mordred: Sir, what will ye do? will ye first displease God and sithen [4] shame yourself and all knighthood? Is not King Arthur your uncle, no farther but your mother's brother, and on her himself King Arthur begat you upon his own sister, therefore how may you wed your father's wife? Sir, said the noble clerk, leave this opinion or I shall curse you with book and bell and candle. Do thou thy worst, said Sir Mordred, wit thou well I shall defy thee. Sir, said the Bishop, and wit you well I shall not fear me to do that me ought to do. Also where ye noise where my lord Arthur is slain, and that is not so, and therefore ye will make a foul work in this land. Peace, thou false priest, said Sir Mordred, for an thou chafe me any more I shall make strike off thy head. So the Bishop departed and did the cursing in the most orgulist [5] wise that might be done, and then Sir Mordred sought the Bishop of Canterbury, for to have slain him. Then the Bishop fled, and took part of

his goods with him, and went nigh unto Glastonbury; and there he was as priest hermit in a chapel, and lived in poverty and in holy prayers, for well he understood that mischievous war was at hand. Then Sir Mordred sought on Queen Guenever by letters and sondes, [6] and by fair means and foul means, for to have her to come out of the Tower of London; but all this availed not, for she answered him shortly, openly and privily, that she had lever slay herself than to be married with him. Then came word to Sir Mordred that King Arthur had araised the siege for Sir Launcelot, and he was coming homeward with a great host, to be avenged upon Sir Mordred; wherefore Sir Mordred made write [7] writs to all the barony of this land, and much people drew to him. For then was the common voice among them that with Arthur was none other life but war and strife, and with Sir Mordred was great joy and bliss. Thus was Sir Arthur depraved, [8] and evil said of. And many there were that King Arthur had made up of nought, and given them lands, might not then say him a good word. Lo ye, all Englishmen, see ye not what a mischief here was! for he that was the most king and knight of the world, and most loved the fellowship of noble knights, and by him they were all upholden, now might not these Englishmen hold them content with him. Lo thus was the old custom and usage of this land; and also men say that we of this land have not yet lost nor forgotten that custom and usage. Alas, this is a great default of us Englishmen, for there may no thing please us no term. And so fared the people at that time, they were better pleased with Sir Mordred than they were with King Arthur; and much people drew unto Sir Mordred, and said they would abide with him for better and for worse. And so Sir Mordred drew with a great host to Dover, for there he heard say that Sir Arthur would arrive, and so he thought to beat his own father from his lands; and the most part of all England held with Sir Mordred, the people were so newfangle. [9]

## CHAPTER II

*How after that King Arthur Had Tidings, He Returned and Came to Dover, where Sir Mordred Met Him to Let [10] His Landing; and of the Death of Sir Gawaine*

AND so as Sir Mordred was at Dover with his host, there came King Arthur with a great navy

---

[2] Heard.    [3] Avail.
[4] Afterwards.    [5] Insolent.

[6] Messages.    [7] Had written.    [8] Slandered.
[9] New-fashioned.    [10] Prevent.

of ships, and galleys, and carracks. And there was Sir Mordred ready awaiting upon his landing, to let his own father to land upon the land that he was king over. Then there was launching of great boats and small, and full of noble men of arms; and there was much slaughter of gentle knights, and many a full bold baron was laid full low, on both parties. But King Arthur was so courageous that there might no manner of knights let him to land, and his knights fiercely followed him; and so they landed maugre [11] Sir Mordred and all his power, and put Sir Mordred aback, that he fled and all his people. So when this battle was done, King Arthur let bury his people that were dead. And then was noble Sir Gawaine found in a great boat, lying more than half dead. When Sir Arthur wist that Sir Gawaine was laid so low, he went unto him; and there the king made sorrow out of measure, and took Sir Gawaine in his arms, and thrice he there swooned. And then when he awaked, he said: Alas, Sir Gawaine, my sister's son, here now thou liest, the man in the world that I loved most; and now is my joy gone, for now, my nephew, Sir Gawaine, I will discover me unto your person: in Sir Launcelot and you I most had my joy, and mine affiance,[12] and now have I lost my joy of you both; wherefore all mine earthly joy is gone from me. Mine uncle, King Arthur, said Sir Gawaine, wit you well my death day is come, and all is through mine own hastiness and willfulness; for I am smitten upon the old wound the which Sir Launcelot gave me, on the which I feel well I must die; and had Sir Launcelot been with you as he was, this unhappy war had never begun; and of all this am I causer, for Sir Launcelot and his blood, through their prowess, held all your cankered enemies in subjection and danger. And now, said Sir Gawaine, ye shall miss Sir Launcelot. But alas, I would not accord with him, and therefore, said Sir Gawaine, I pray you, fair uncle, that I may have paper, pen, and ink, that I may write to Sir Launcelot a cedle [13] with mine own hands. And then when paper and ink was brought, then Gawaine was set up weakly by King Arthur, for he was shriven a little tofore; and then he wrote thus, as the French book maketh mention: Unto Sir Launcelot, flower of all noble knights that ever I heard of or saw by my days, I, Sir Gawaine, King Lot's Son of Orkney, sister's son unto the noble King Arthur, send thee greeting, and let thee have knowledge that the tenth day of May I was smitten upon the old

wound that thou gavest me afore the city of Benwick,[14] and through the same wound that thou gavest me I am come to my death day. And I will that all the world wit, that I, Sir Gawaine, knight of the Table Round, sought my death, and not through thy deserving, but it was mine own seeking; wherefore I beseech thee, Sir Launcelot, to return again unto this realm, and see my tomb, and pray some prayer more or less for my soul. And this same day that I wrote this cedle, I was hurt to the death in the same wound, the which I had of thy hand, Sir Launcelot; for of a more nobler man might I not be slain. Also, Sir Launcelot, for all the love that ever was betwixt us, make no tarrying, but come over the sea in all haste, that thou mayst with thy noble knights rescue that noble king that made thee knight, that is my lord Arthur; for he is full straitly bestad [15] with a false traitor, that is my half-brother, Sir Mordred; and he hath let crown him king, and would have wedded my lady Queen Guenever, and so had he done had she not put herself in the Tower of London. And so the tenth day of May last past, my lord Arthur and we all landed upon them at Dover; and there we put that false traitor, Sir Mordred, to flight, and there it misfortuned me to be stricken upon thy stroke. And at the date of this letter was written, but two hours and a half afore my death, written with mine own hand, and so subscribed with part of my heart's blood. And I require thee, most famous knight of the world, that thou wilt see my tomb. And then Sir Gawaine wept, and King Arthur wept; and then they swooned both. And when they awaked both, the king made Sir Gawaine to receive his Savior. And then Sir Gawaine prayed the king for to send for Sir Launcelot, and to cherish him above all other knights. And so at the hour of noon Sir Gawaine yielded up the spirit; and then the king let inter him in a chapel within Dover Castle; and there yet all men may see the skull of him, and the same wound is seen that Sir Launcelot gave him in battle. Then was it told the king that Sir Mordred had pyghte a new field [16] upon Barham Down. And upon the morn the king rode thither to him, and there was a great battle betwixt them, and much people was slain on both parties; but at the last Sir Arthur's party stood best, and Sir Mordred and his party fled into Canterbury.

[11] Despite.    [12] Trust.    [13] Note.

[14] Launcelot had, in fact, wounded him twice on the head (Book XX, Chaps. xxi, xxii).

[15] Hard pressed.

[16] Taken up a new position.

## CHAPTER III

*How after, Sir Gawaine's Ghost Appeared to King Arthur, and Warned Him that He Should Not Fight That Day*

AND then the king let search all the towns for his knights that were slain, and interred them; and salved them with soft salves that so sore were wounded. Then much people drew unto King Arthur. And then they said that Sir Mordred warred upon King Arthur with wrong. And then King Arthur drew him with his host down by the seaside westward toward Salisbury; and there was a day assigned betwixt King Arthur and Sir Mordred, that they should meet upon a down beside Salisbury, and not far from the seaside; and this day was assigned on a Monday after Trinity Sunday, whereof King Arthur was passing glad, that he might be avenged upon Sir Mordred. Then Sir Mordred araised much people about London, for they of Kent, Southsex, and Surrey, Estsex, and of Southfolk, and of Northfolk, held the most part with Sir Mordred; and many a full noble knight drew unto Sir Mordred and to the king: but they that loved Sir Launcelot drew unto Sir Mordred. So upon Trinity Sunday at night, King Arthur dreamed a wonderful dream, and that was this: that him seemed he sat upon a chaflet [17] in a chair, and the chair was fast to a wheel, and thereupon sat King Arthur in the richest cloth of gold that might be made; and the king thought there was under him, far from him, an hideous deep black water, and therein were all manner of serpents, and worms, and wild beasts foul and horrible; and suddenly the king thought the wheel turned up so down, and he fell among the serpents, and every beast took him by a limb; and then the king cried as he lay in his bed and slept: Help. And then knights, squires, and yeomen awakened the king; and then he was so amazed that he wist not where he was; and then he fell on slumbering again, not sleeping nor thoroughly waking. So the king seemed verily that there came Sir Gawaine unto him with a number of fair ladies with him. And when King Arthur saw him, then he said: Welcome, my sister's son; I weened thou hadst been dead, and now I see thee on live, much am I beholding unto almighty Jesu. O fair nephew and my sister's son, what be these ladies that hither be come with you? Sir, said Sir Gawaine, all these be ladies for whom I have foughten when I was man living, and all these are those that I did

battle for in righteous quarrel; and God hath given them that grace at their great prayer, by cause I did battle for them, that they should bring me hither unto you: thus much hath God given me leave, for to warn you of your death; for an ye fight as tomorn with Sir Mordred, as ye both have assigned, doubt ye not ye must be slain, and the most part of your people on both parties. And for the great grace and goodness that almighty Jesu hath unto you, and for pity of you, and many more other good men there shall be slain, God hath sent me to you of His special grace, to give you warning that in no wise ye do battle as tomorn, but that ye take a treaty for a month day; and proffer you largely,[18] so as tomorn to be put in a delay. For within a month shall come Sir Launcelot with all his noble knights, and rescue you worshipfully, and slay Sir Mordred, and all that ever will hold with him. Then Sir Gawaine and all the ladies vanished. And anon the king called upon his knights, squires, and yeomen, and charged them wightly [19] to fetch his noble lords and wise bishops unto him. And when they were come, the king told them his avision, what Sir Gawaine had told him, and warned him that if he fought on the morn he should be slain. Then the king commanded Sir Lucan the Butler, and his brother, Sir Bedivere, with two bishops with them, and charged them in any wise, an they might, Take a treaty for a month day with Sir Mordred, and spare not, proffer him lands and goods as much as ye think best. So then they departed, and came to Sir Mordred, where he had a grim host of an hundred thousand men. And there they entreated Sir Mordred long time; and at the last Sir Mordred was agreed for to have Cornwall and Kent, by Arthur's days: after, all England, after the days of King Arthur.

## CHAPTER IV

*How by Misadventure of an Adder the Battle Began, where Mordred Was Slain, and Arthur Hurt to the Death*

THEN were they condescended that King Arthur and Sir Mordred should meet betwixt both their hosts, and every each of them should bring fourteen persons; and they came with this word unto Arthur. Then said he: I am glad that this is done: and so he went into the field. And when Arthur should depart, he warned all his host that an they see any sword drawn:

[17] Platform.          [18] Make generous proposals.          [19] Quickly.

Look ye come on fiercely, and slay that traitor, Sir Mordred, for I in no wise trust him. In likewise Sir Mordred warned his host that: An ye see any sword drawn, look that ye come on fiercely, and so slay all that ever before you standeth; for in no wise I will not trust for this treaty, for I know well my father will be avenged on me. And so they met as their appointment was, and so they were agreed and accorded thoroughly; and wine was fetched, 10 and they drank. Right soon came an adder out of a little heath bush, and it stung a knight on the foot. And when the knight felt him stung, he looked down and saw the adder, and then he drew his sword to slay the adder, and thought of none other harm. And when the host on both parties saw that sword drawn, then they blew beamous,[20] trumpets, and horns, and shouted grimly. And so both hosts dressed them together. And King Arthur took 20 his horse, and said: Alas, this unhappy day! and so rode to his party. And Sir Mordred in likewise. And never was there seen a more dolefuller battle in no Christian land; for there was but rushing and riding, foining[21] and striking, and many a grim word was there spoken either to other, and many a deadly stroke. But ever King Arthur rode throughout the battle of Sir Mordred many times, and did full nobly as a noble king should, and at all 30 times he fainted never; and Sir Mordred that day put him in devoir,[22] and in great peril. And thus they fought all the long day, and never stinted till the noble knights were laid to the cold earth; and ever they fought still till it was near night, and by that time was there an hundred thousand laid dead upon the down. Then was Arthur wood[23] wroth out of measure, when he saw his people so slain from him. Then the king looked about him, and then 40 was he ware, of all his host and of all his good knights, were left no more on live but two knights; that one was Sir Lucan the Butler, and his brother Sir Bedivere, and they were full sore wounded. Jesu mercy, said the king, where are all my noble knights become? Alas that ever I should see this doleful day, for now, said Arthur, I am come to mine end. But would to God that I wist where were that traitor Sir Mordred, that hath caused all this 50 mischief. Then was King Arthur ware where Sir Mordred leaned upon his sword among a great heap of dead men. Now give me my spear, said Arthur unto Sir Lucan, for yonder I have espied the traitor that all this woe hath

wrought. Sir, let him be, said Sir Lucan, for he is unhappy; and if ye pass this unhappy day ye shall be right well revenged upon him. Good lord, remember ye of your night's dream, and what the spirit of Sir Gawaine told you this night, yet God of his great goodness hath preserved you hitherto. Therefore for God's sake, my lord, leave off by this, for blessed be God ye have won the field, for here we be three on live, and with Sir Mordred is none on live; and if ye leave off now this wicked day of destiny is past. Tide me death, betide me life, saith the king, now I see him yonder alone he shall never escape mine hands, for at a better avail shall I never have him. God speed you well, said Sir Bedivere. Then the king gat his spear in both his hands, and ran toward Sir Mordred, crying: Traitor, now is thy death day come. And when Sir Mordred heard Sir Arthur, he ran until him with his sword drawn in his hand. And there King Arthur smote Sir Mordred under the shield, with a foin of his spear, throughout the body, more than a fathom. And when Sir Mordred felt that he had his death wound he thrust himself with the might that he had up to the bur[24] of King Arthur's spear. And right so he smote his father Arthur, with his sword holden in both his hands, on the side of the head, that the sword pierced the helmet and the brain pan, and therewithal Sir Mordred fell stark dead to the earth; and the noble Arthur fell in a swoon to the earth, and there he swooned ofttimes. And Sir Lucan the Butler and Sir Bedivere ofttimes heaved him up. And so weakly they led him betwixt them both, to a little chapel not far from the seaside. And when the king was there he thought him well eased. Then heard they people cry in the field. Now go thou, Sir Lucan, said the king, and do me to wit what betokens that noise in the field. So Sir Lucan departed, for he was grievously wounded in many places. And so as he yede,[25] he saw and hearkened by the moonlight, how that pillers[26] and robbers were come into the field, to pill and to rob many a full noble knight of brooches, and beads, of many a good ring, and of many a rich jewel; and who that were not dead all out, there they slew them for their harness and their riches. When Sir Lucan understood this work, he came to the king as soon as he might, and told him all what he had heard and seen. Therefore by my rede,[27] said Sir Lucan, it is best that we bring you to some town. I would it were so, said the king.

---

[20] Horns.     [21] Thrusting.     [22] Duty.
[23] Mad.

[24] Ring to prevent the hand from slipping.
[25] Went.     [26] Pillagers.     [27] Counsel.

## CHAPTER V

*How King Arthur Commanded to Cast His
Sword Excalibur into the Water, and How
He Was Delivered to Ladies in a Barge*

But I may not stand, mine head works so.
Ah Sir Launcelot, said King Arthur, this day
have I sore missed thee; alas, that ever I was
against thee, for now have I my death, whereof
Sir Gawaine me warned in my dream. Then
Sir Lucan took up the king the one part, and
Sir Bedivere the other part, and in the lifting
the king swooned; and Sir Lucan fell in a
swoon with the lift, that the part of his guts
fell out of his body, and therewith the noble
knight's heart brast.[28] And when the king
awoke, he beheld Sir Lucan, how he lay foaming at the mouth, and part of his guts lay
at his feet. Alas, said the king, this is to me a
full heavy sight, to see this noble duke so die
for my sake, for he would have holpen me, that
had more need of help than I. Alas, he would
not complain him, his heart was so set to help
me: now Jesu have mercy upon his soul! Then
Sir Bedivere wept for the death of his brother.
Leave this mourning and weeping, said the
king, for all this will not avail me, for wit
thou well an I might live myself, the death of
Sir Lucan would grieve me evermore; but my
time hieth fast, said the king. Therefore, said
Arthur unto Sir Bedivere, take thou Excalibur, my good sword, and go with it to yonder
water side, and when thou comest there I
charge thee throw my sword in that water, and
come again and tell me what thou there seest.
My lord, said Bedivere, your commandment
shall be done, and lightly [29] bring you word
again. So Sir Bedivere departed, and by the way
he beheld that noble sword, that the pommel
and the haft was all of precious stones; and
then he said to himself: If I throw this rich
sword in the water, thereof shall never come
good, but harm and loss. And then Sir Bedivere hid Excalibur under a tree. And so, as
soon as he might, he came again unto the king,
and said he had been at the water, and had
thrown the sword in the water. What saw thou
there? said the king. Sir, he said, I saw nothing
but waves and winds. That is untruly said of
thee, said the king, therefore go thou lightly
again, and do my commandment; as thou art
to me lief and dear, spare not, but throw it in.
Then Sir Bedivere returned again, and took
the sword in his hand; and then him thought
sin and shame to throw away that noble sword,

and so eft [30] he hid the sword, and returned
again, and told to the king that he had been at
the water, and done his commandment. What
saw thou there? said the king. Sir, he said, I
saw nothing but the waters wappe [31] and waves
wanne.[32] Ah, traitor untrue, said King Arthur,
now hast thou betrayed me twice. Who would
have weened that, thou that hast been to me so
lief and dear? and thou art named a noble
knight, and would betray me for the richness of
the sword. But now go again lightly, for thy
long tarrying putteth me in great jeopardy of
my life, for I have taken cold. And but if thou
do now as I bid thee, if ever I may see thee, I
shall slay thee with mine own hands; for thou
wouldst for my rich sword see me dead. Then
Sir Bedivere departed, and went to the sword,
and lightly took it up, and went to the water
side; and there he bound the girdle about the
hilts, and then he threw the sword as far into
the water as he might; and there came an arm
and an hand above the water and met it, and
caught it, and so shook it thrice and brandished, and then vanished away the hand with
the sword in the water. So Sir Bedivere came
again to the king, and told him what he saw.
Alas, said the king, help me hence, for I dread
me I have tarried over long. Then Sir Bedivere
took the king upon his back, and so went with
him to that water side. And when they were
at the water side, even fast by the bank hoved
a little barge with many fair ladies in it, and
among them all was a queen, and all they had
black hoods, and all they wept and shrieked
when they saw King Arthur. Now put me into
the barge, said the king. And so he did softly;
and there received him three queens with great
mourning; and so they set them down, and in
one of their laps King Arthur laid his head.
And then that queen said: Ah, dear brother,
why have ye tarried so long from me? alas, this
wound on your head hath caught over-much
cold. And so then they rowed from the land,
and Sir Bedivere beheld all those ladies go from
him. Then Sir Bedivere cried: Ah, my lord
Arthur, what shall become of me, now ye go
from me and leave me here alone among mine
enemies? Comfort thyself, said the king, and
do as well as thou mayest, for in me is no trust
for to trust in; for I will into the vale of Avil-
ion [33] to heal me of my grievous wound: and
if thou hear never more of me, pray for my
soul. But ever the queens and ladies wept and
shrieked, that it was pity to hear. And as soon
as Sir Bedivere had lost the sight of the barge,

[28] Burst.          [29] Swiftly.

[30] Again.          [31] Ripple.          [32] Grow dark.
[33] Avalon, home of spirits of the departed.

he wept and wailed, and so took the forest; and so he went all that night, and in the morning he was ware betwixt two holts [34] hoar, of a chapel and an hermitage.

## CHAPTER VI

*How Sir Bedivere Found Him on the Morrow Dead in an Hermitage, and How He Abode There with the Hermit*

Then was Sir Bedivere glad, and thither he went; and when he came into the chapel, he saw where lay an hermit groveling on all four, there fast by a tomb was new graven.[35] When the hermit saw Sir Bedivere he knew him well, for he was but little tofore Bishop of Canterbury, that Sir Mordred flemed.[36] Sir, said Bedivere, what man is there interred that ye pray so fast for? Fair son, said the hermit, I wot not verily, but by deeming. But this night, at mid- 20 night, here came a number of ladies, and brought hither a dead corpse, and prayed me to bury him; and here they offered an hundred tapers, and they gave me an hundred besants.[37] Alas, said Sir Bedivere, that was my lord King Arthur, that here lieth buried in this chapel. Then Sir Bedivere swooned; and when he awoke he prayed the hermit he might abide with him still there, to live with fasting and prayers. For from hence will I never go, said 30 Sir Bedivere, by my will, but all the days of my life here to pray for my lord Arthur. Ye are welcome to me, said the hermit, for I know ye better than ye ween that I do. Ye are the bold Bedivere, and the full noble duke, Sir Lucan the Butler, was your brother. Then Sir Bedivere told the hermit all as ye have heard tofore. So there bode Sir Bedivere with the hermit that was tofore Bishop of Canterbury, and there Sir Bedivere put upon him poor 40 clothes, and served the hermit full lowly in fasting and in prayers. Thus of Arthur I find never more written in books that be authorized nor more of the very certainty of his death heard I never read, but thus was he led away in a ship wherein were three queens; that one was King Arthur's sister, Queen Morgan le Fay; the other was the Queen of Northgalis; the third was the Queen of the Waste Lands. Also there was Nimue, the chief lady of the 50 lake, that had wedded Pelleas the good knight; and this lady had done much for King Arthur, for she would never suffer Sir Pelleas to be in

no place where he should be in danger of his life; and so he lived to the uttermost of his days with her in great rest. More of the death of King Arthur could I never find, but that ladies brought him to his burials; and such one was buried there, that the hermit bare witness that sometime was Bishop of Canterbury, but yet the hermit knew not in certain that he was verily the body of King Arthur: for this tale 10 Sir Bedivere, knight of the Table Round, made it to be written.

## CHAPTER VII

*Of the Opinion of Some Men of the Death of King Arthur; and How Queen Guenever Made Her a Nun in Almesbury*

YET some men say in many parts of England that King Arthur is not dead, but had 20 by the will of our Lord Jesu into another place; and men say that he shall come again, and he shall win the holy cross. I will not say it shall be so, but rather I will say, here in this world he changed his life. But many men say that there is written upon his tomb this verse: *Hic jacet Arthurus Rex, quondam Rexque futurus.*[38] Thus leave I here Sir Bedivere with the hermit, that dwelled that time in a chapel beside Glastonbury, and there was his her- 30 mitage. And so they lived in their prayers, and fastings, and great abstinence. And when Queen Guenever understood that King Arthur was slain, and all the noble knights, Sir Mordred and all the remnant, then the queen stole away, and five ladies with her, and so she went to Almesbury; and there she let make herself a nun, and ware white clothes and black, and great penance she took, as ever did sinful lady in this land, and never creature could make her 40 merry; but lived in fasting, prayers, and almsdeeds, that all manner of people marveled how virtuously she was changed. Now leave we Queen Guenever in Almesbury, a nun in white clothes and black, and there she was abbess and ruler as reason would; and turn we from her, and speak we of Sir Launcelot du Lake.

## CHAPTER VIII

*How when Sir Launcelot Heard of the Death* 50 *of King Arthur, and of Sir Gawaine, and Other Matters, He Came into England*

AND when he heard in his country that Sir Mordred was crowned king in England, and

---

[34] Wooded hills. Later (Chap. x) they are spoken of as cliffs.

[35] Dug.     [36] Put to flight.

[37] Coin first made at Byzantium (Constantinople).

[38] Here lies King Arthur, King formerly and so to be in the future.

made war against King Arthur, his own father, and would let him to land in his own land; also it was told Sir Launcelot how that Sir Mordred had laid siege about the Tower of London, by cause the queen would not wed him; then was Sir Launcelot wroth out of measure, and said to his kinsmen: Alas, that double traitor Sir Mordred, now me repenteth that ever he escaped my hands, for much shame hath he done unto my lord Arthur; for all I feel by the doleful letter that my lord Sir Gawaine sent me, on whose soul Jesu have mercy, that my lord Arthur is full hard bestad. Alas, said Sir Launcelot, that ever I should live to hear that most noble king that made me knight thus to be overset with his subject in his own realm. And this doleful letter that my lord, Sir Gawaine, hath sent me afore his death, praying me to see his tomb, wit you well his doleful words shall never go from mine heart, for he was a full noble knight as ever was born; and in an unhappy hour was I born that ever I should have that unhap to slay first Sir Gawaine, Sir Gaheris the good knight, and mine own friend Sir Gareth, that full noble knight. Alas, I may say I am unhappy, said Sir Launcelot, that ever I should do thus unhappily, and, alas, yet might I never have hap to slay that traitor, Sir Mordred. Leave your complaints, said Sir Bors, and first revenge you of the death of Sir Gawaine; and it will be well done that ye see Sir Gawaine's tomb, and secondly that ye revenge my lord Arthur, and my lady, Queen Guenever. I thank you, said Sir Launcelot, for ever ye will my worship. Then they made them ready in all the haste that might be, with ships and galleys, with Sir Launcelot and his host to pass into England. And so he passed over the sea till he came to Dover, and there he landed with seven kings, and the number was hideous to behold. Then Sir Launcelot spered [39] of men of Dover where was King Arthur become. Then the people told him how that he was slain, and Sir Mordred and an hundred thousand died on a day; and how Sir Mordred gave King Arthur there the first battle at his landing, and there was good Sir Gawaine slain; and on the morn Sir Mordred fought with the king upon Barham Down, and there the king put Sir Mordred to the worse. Alas, said Sir Launcelot, this is the heaviest tidings that ever came to me. Now, fair sirs, said Sir Launcelot, show me the tomb of Sir Gawaine. And then certain people of the town brought him into the Castle of Dover, and showed him the tomb.

Then Sir Launcelot kneeled down and wept, and prayed heartily for his soul. And that night he made a dole, and all they that would come had as much flesh, fish, wine and ale, and every man and woman had twelve pence, come who would. Thus with his own hand dealt he this money, in a mourning gown; and ever he wept, and prayed them to pray for the soul of Sir Gawaine. And on the morn all the priests and clerks that might be gotten in the country were there, and sang mass of *requiem*; [40] and there offered first Sir Launcelot, and he offered an hundred pound; and then the seven kings offered forty pound apiece; and also there was a thousand knights, and each of them offered a pound; and the offering dured from morn till night, and Sir Launcelot lay two nights on his tomb in prayers and weeping. Then on the third day Sir Launcelot called the kings, dukes, earls, barons, and knights, and said thus: My fair lords, I thank you all of your coming into this country with me, but we came too late, and that shall repent me while I live, but against death may no man rebel. But sithen [41] it is so, said Sir Launcelot, I will myself ride and seek my lady, Queen Guenever, for as I hear say she hath had great pain and much disease; and I heard say that she is fled into the west. Therefore ye all shall abide me here, and but if I come again within fifteen days, then take your ships and your fellowship, and depart into your country, for I will do as I say to you.

## CHAPTER IX

*How Sir Launcelot Departed to Seek the Queen Guenever, and How He Found Her at Almesbury*

THEN came Sir Bors de Ganis, and said: My lord Sir Launcelot, what think ye for to do, now to ride in this realm? wit ye well ye shall find few friends. Be as be may, said Sir Launcelot, keep you still here, for I will forth on my journey, and no man nor child shall go with me. So it was no boot to strive, but he departed and rode westerly, and there he sought a seven or eight days; and at the last he came to a nunnery, and then was Queen Guenever ware of Sir Launcelot as he walked in the cloister. And when she saw him there she swooned thrice, that all the ladies and gentlewomen had work enough to hold the queen up. So when she might

---

[39] Asked.

[40] Mass for the dead.   [41] Since.

speak, she called ladies and gentlewomen to her, and said: Ye marvel, fair ladies, why I make this fare. Truly, she said, it is for the sight of yonder knight that yonder standeth; wherefore I pray you all call him to me. When Sir Launcelot was brought to her, then she said to all the ladies: Through this man and me hath all this war been wrought, and the death of the most noblest knights of the world; for through our love that we have 10 loved together is my most noble lord slain. Therefore, Sir Launcelot, wit thou well I am set in such a plight to get my soul heal; and yet I trust through God's grace that after my death to have a sight of the blessed face of Christ, and at domesday to sit on His right side, for as sinful as ever I was are saints in heaven. Therefore, Sir Launcelot, I require thee and beseech thee heartily, for all the love that ever was betwixt us, that thou 20 never see me more in the visage; and I command thee, on God's behalf, that thou forsake my company, and to thy kingdom thou turn again, and keep well thy realm from war and wrake; [42] for as well as I have loved thee, mine heart will not serve me to see thee, for through thee and me is the flower of kings and knights destroyed; therefore, Sir Launcelot, go to thy realm, and there take thee a wife, and live with her with joy and bliss; and I pray thee 30 heartily, pray for me to our Lord that I may amend my misliving. Now, sweet madam, said Sir Launcelot, would ye that I should now return again unto my country, and there to wed a lady? Nay, madam, wit you well that shall I never do, for I shall never be so false to you of that I have promised; but the same destiny that ye have taken you to, I will take me unto, for to please Jesu, and ever for you I cast me specially to pray. If thou wilt 40 do so, said the queen, hold thy promise, but I may never believe but that thou wilt turn to the world again. Well, madam, said he, ye say as pleaseth you, yet wist you me never false of my promise, and God defend but I should forsake the world as ye have done. For in the quest of the Sangreal I had forsaken the vanities of the world, had not your love been. And if I had done so at that time, with my heart, will, and thought, I had passed 50 all the knights that were in the Sangreal except Sir Galahad, my son. And therefore, lady, sithen ye have taken you to perfection, I must needs take me to perfection, of right. For I take record of God, in you I have had mine

earthly joy; and if I had found you now so disposed, I had cast to have you into mine own realm.

## CHAPTER X

*How Sir Launcelot Came to the Hermitage Where the Archbishop of Canterbury Was, and How He Took the Habit on Him*

But sithen I find you thus disposed, I ensure you faithfully, I will ever take me to penance, and pray while my life lasteth, if I may find any hermit, either gray or white, that will receive me. Wherefore, madam, I pray you kiss me and never no more. Nay, said the queen, that shall I never do, but abstain you from such works: and they departed. But there was never so hard an hearted man but he would have wept to see the dolor that they made; for there was lamentation as they had been stung with spears; and many times they swooned, and the ladies bare the queen to her chamber. And Sir Launcelot awoke and went and took his horse, and rode all that day and all night in a forest, weeping. And at the last he was ware of an hermitage and a chapel stood betwixt two cliffs; and then he heard a little bell ring to mass, and thither he rode and alit, and tied his horse to the gate, and heard mass. And he that sang mass was the Bishop of Canterbury. Both the Bishop and Sir Bedivere knew Sir Launcelot, and they spake together after mass. But when Sir Bedivere had told his tale all whole, Sir Launcelot's heart almost brast for sorrow, and Sir Launcelot threw his arms abroad, and said: Alas, who may trust this world. And then he kneeled down on his knee, and prayed the Bishop to shrive him and assoil [43] him. And then he besought the Bishop that he might be his brother. Then the Bishop said: I will gladly; and there he put an habit upon Sir Launcelot, and there he served God day and night with prayers and fastings. Thus the great host abode at Dover. And then Sir Lionel took fifteen lords with him, and rode to London to seek Sir Launcelot; and there Sir Lionel was slain and many of his lords. Then Sir Bors de Ganis made the great host for to go home again; and Sir Bors, Sir Ector de Maris, Sir Blamore, Sir Bleoberis, with more other of Sir Launcelot's kin, took on them to ride all England overthwart [44] and endlong, to seek Sir Launcelot. So Sir Bors by fortune rode so long till he

---

[42] Ruin.     [43] Absolve.     [44] Across.

came to the same chapel where Sir Launcelot was; and so Sir Bors heard a little bell knell, that rang to mass; and there he alit and heard mass. And when mass was done, the Bishop, Sir Launcelot, and Sir Bedivere came to Sir Bors. And when Sir Bors saw Sir Launcelot in that manner clothing, then he prayed the Bishop that he might be in the same suit. And so there was an habit put upon him, and there he lived in prayers and fasting. And within half a year, there was come Sir Galihud, Sir Galihodin, Sir Blamore, Sir Bleoberis, Sir Villiars, Sir Clarras, and Sir Gahalantine. So all these seven noble knights there abode still. And when they saw Sir Launcelot had taken him to such perfection, they had no list to depart, but took such an habit as he had. Thus they endured in great penance six year; and then Sir Launcelot took the habit of priesthood of the Bishop, and a twelvemonth he sang mass. And there was none of these other knights but they read in books, and holp for to sing mass, and rang bells, and did bodily all manner of service. And so their horses went where they would, for they took no regard of no worldly riches. For when they saw Sir Launcelot endure such penance, in prayers and fastings, they took no force [45] what pain they endured, for to see the noblest knight of the world take such abstinence that he waxed full lean. And thus upon a night, there came a vision to Sir Launcelot, and charged him, in remission of his sins, to haste him unto Almesbury: And by then thou come there, thou shalt find Queen Guenever dead. And therefore take thy fellows with thee, and purvey them of an horse bier, and fetch thou the corpse of her, and bury her by her husband, the noble King Arthur. So this avision came to Sir Launcelot thrice in one night.

### CHAPTER XI

*How Sir Launcelot Went with His Seven Fellows to Almesbury, and Found There Queen Guenever Dead, Whom They Brought to Glastonbury*

THEN Sir Launcelot rose up or [46] day, and told the hermit. It were well done, said the hermit, that ye made you ready, and that you disobey not the avision. Then Sir Launcelot took his seven fellows with him, and on foot they yede [47] from Glastonbury to Almesbury, the which is little more than thirty mile. And thither they came within two days, for they were weak and feeble to go. And when Sir Launcelot was come to Almesbury within the nunnery, Queen Guenever died but half an hour afore. And the ladies told Sir Launcelot that Queen Guenever told them all or she passed, that Sir Launcelot had been priest near a twelve-month, And hither he cometh as fast as he may to fetch my corpse; and beside my lord, King Arthur, he shall bury me. Wherefore the queen said in hearing of them all: I beseech Almighty God that I may never have power to see Sir Launcelot with my worldly eyen; and thus, said all the ladies, was ever her prayer these two days, till she was dead. Then Sir Launcelot saw her visage, but he wept not greatly, but sighed. And so he did all the observance of the service himself, both the dirge at night, and on the morn he sang mass. And there was ordained an horse bier; and so with an hundred torches ever burning about the corpse of the queen, and ever Sir Launcelot with his seven fellows went about the horse bier, singing and reading many an holy orison, and frank-incense upon the corpse incensed. Thus Sir Launcelot and his seven fellows went on foot from Almesbury unto Glastonbury. And when they were come to the chapel and the hermitage, there she had a dirge, with great devotion. And on the morn the hermit that sometime was Bishop of Canterbury sang the mass of *requiem* with great devotion. And Sir Launcelot was the first that offered, and then also his seven fellows. And then she was wrapped in cered cloth of Raines,[48] from the top to the toe, in thirtyfold; and after she was put in a web [49] of lead, and then in a coffin of marble. And when she was put in the earth Sir Launcelot swooned, and lay long still, while the hermit came and awaked him, and said: Ye be to blame, for ye displease God with such manner of sorrow making. Truly, said Sir Launcelot, I trust I do not displease God, for He knoweth mine intent. For my sorrow was not, nor is not, for any rejoicing of sin, but my sorrow may never have end. For when I remember of her beauty, and of her noblesse that was both with her king and with her, so when I saw his corpse and her corpse so lie together, truly mine heart would not serve to sustain my careful [50] body. Also when I remember me how by my default, mine orgulity [51] and my pride, that they were both laid full low, that were peerless that ever was living of Christian people, wit you

[45] Account.    [46] Before.    [47] Went.
[48] Waxed cloth from Rennes, in Brittany.
[49] Thin sheet.    [50] Distressed.    [51] Arrogance.

well, said Sir Launcelot, this remembered, of their kindness and mine unkindness, sank so to mine heart, that I might not sustain myself. So the French book maketh mention.

*How Sir Launcelot Began to Sicken, and After Died, Whose Body Was Borne to Joyous Gard for to Be Buried*

THEN Sir Launcelot never after ate but little meat, ne drank, till he was dead. For then he sickened more and more, and dried, and dwined [52] away. For the Bishop nor none of his fellows might not make him to eat, and little he drank, that he was waxen by a cubit [53] shorter than he was, that the people could not know him. For evermore, day and night, he prayed, but sometime he slumbered a broken sleep; ever he was lying groveling on the tomb of King Arthur and Queen Guenever. And there was no comfort that the Bishop, nor Sir Bors, nor none of his fellows could make him, it availed not. So within six weeks after, Sir Launcelot fell sick, and lay in his bed; and then he sent for the Bishop that there was hermit, and all his true fellows. Then Sir Launcelot said with dreary steven: [54] Sir Bishop, I pray you give to me all my rites that longeth to a Christian man. It shall not need you, said the hermit and all his fellows, it is but heaviness of your blood, ye shall be well mended by the grace of God tomorn. My fair lords, said Sir Launcelot, wit you well my careful body will into the earth, I have warning more than now I will say; therefore give me my rites. So when he was houseled and enelid,[55] and had all that a Christian man ought to have, he prayed the Bishop that his fellows might bear his body to Joyous Gard. Some men say it was Alnwick, and some men say it was Bamborough. Howbeit, said Sir Launcelot, me repenteth sore, but I made mine avow sometime, that in Joyous Gard I would be buried. And by cause of breaking of mine avow, I pray you all, lead me thither. Then there was weeping and wringing of hands among his fellows. So at a season of the night they all went to their beds, for they all lay in one chamber. And so after midnight, against day, the Bishop that was hermit, as he lay in his bed asleep, he fell upon a great

laughter. And therewithal the fellowship awoke, and came to the Bishop, and asked him what he ailed. Ah Jesu mercy, said the Bishop, why did ye awake me? I was never in all my life so merry and so well at ease. Wherefore? said Sir Bors. Truly, said the Bishop, here was Sir Launcelot with me with more angels than ever I saw men in one day. And I saw the angels heave up Sir Launcelot unto heaven, and the gates of heaven opened against him. It is but dretching of swevens,[56] said Sir Bors, for I doubt not Sir Launcelot aileth nothing but good. It may well be, said the Bishop; go ye to his bed, and then shall ye prove the sooth. So when Sir Bors and his fellows came to his bed they found him stark dead, and he lay as he had smiled, and the sweetest savor about him that ever they felt. Then was there weeping and wringing of hands, and the greatest dole they made that ever made men. And on the morn the Bishop did his mass of *requiem;* and after, the Bishop and all the nine knights put Sir Launcelot in the same horse bier that Queen Guenever was laid in tofore that she was buried. And so the Bishop and they all together went with the body of Sir Launcelot daily, till they came to Joyous Gard; and ever they had an hundred torches burning about him. And so within fifteen days they came to Joyous Gard. And there they laid his corpse in the body of the quire, and sang and read many psalters and prayers over him and about him. And ever his visage was laid open and naked, that all folks might behold him. For such was the custom in those days, that all men of worship should so lie with open visage till that they were buried. And right thus as they were at their service, there came Sir Ector de Maris, that had seven years sought all England, Scotland, and Wales, seeking his brother, Sir Launcelot.

*How Sir Ector Found Sir Launcelot His Brother Dead, and How Constantine Reigned Next after Arthur; and of the End of This Book*

AND when Sir Ector heard such noise and light in the quire of Joyous Gard, he alit and put his horse from him, and came into the quire, and there he saw men sing and weep. And all they knew Sir Ector, but he knew

---

[52] Dwindled.    [53] About eighteen inches.
[54] Voice.
[55] Given the Holy Sacrament and anointed.

[56] The troubling of dreams.

not them. Then went Sir Bors unto Sir Ector, and told him how there lay his brother, Sir Launcelot, dead; and then Sir Ector threw his shield, sword, and helm from him. And when he beheld Sir Launcelot's visage, he fell down in a swoon. And when he waked it were hard any tongue to tell the doleful complaints that he made for his brother. Ah Launcelot, he said, thou were 10 head of all Christian knights, and now I dare say, said Sir Ector, thou Sir Launcelot, there thou liest, that thou were never matched of earthly knight's hand. And thou were the courteoust knight that ever bare shield. And thou were the truest friend to thy lover that ever bestrad horse. And thou were the truest lover of a sinful man that ever loved woman. And thou were the kindest man that ever struck with sword. And thou 20 were the goodliest person that ever came among press of knights. And thou were the meekest man and the gentlest that ever ate in hall among ladies. And thou were the sternest knight to thy mortal foe that ever put spear in the rest. Then there was weeping and dolor out of measure. Thus they kept Sir Launcelot's corpse on loft fifteen days, and then they buried it with great devotion. And then at leisure they went all 30 with the Bishop of Canterbury to his hermitage, and there they were together more than a month. Then Sir Constantine, that was Sir Cador's son of Cornwall, was chosen king of England. And he was a full noble knight, and worshipfully he ruled this realm. And then this King Constantine sent for the Bishop of Canterbury, for he heard say where he was. And so he was restored unto his Bishopric, and left that hermitage. And Sir 40 Bedivere was there ever still hermit to his life's end. Then Sir Bors de Ganis, Sir Ector de Maris, Sir Gahalantine, Sir Galihud, Sir Galihodin, Sir Blamore, Sir Bleoberis, Sir Villiars le Valiant, Sir Clarrus of Clermont, all these knights drew them to their countries. Howbeit King Constantine would have had them with him, but they would not abide in this realm. And there they all lived in their

countries as holy men. And some English books make mention that they went never out of England after the death of Sir Launcelot, but that was but favor of makers.[57] For the French book maketh mention, and is authorized, that Sir Bors, Sir Ector, Sir Blamore, and Sir Bleoberis went into the Holy Land thereas Jesu Christ was quick and dead, and anon as they had stablished their lands. For the book 10 saith, so Sir Launcelot commanded them for to do, or ever he passed out of this world. And these four knights did many battles upon the miscreants [58] or Turks. And there they died upon a Good Friday for God's sake.

*Here is the end of the book of King Arthur, and of his noble knights of the Round Table, that when they were whole together there was ever an hundred and forty. And here is the end* 20 *of the death of Arthur. I pray you all, gentlemen and gentlewomen that readeth this book of Arthur and his knights, from the beginning to the ending, pray for me while I am on live, that God send me good deliverance, and when I am dead, I pray you all pray for my soul. For this book was ended the ninth year of the reign of King Edward the Fourth, by Sir Thomas Maleore, knight, as Jesu help him for his great might, as he is the servant of Jesu* 30 *both day and night.*

*Thus endeth this noble and joyous book entitled Le Morte Darthur. Notwithstanding it treateth of the birth, life, and acts of the said King Arthur, of his noble knights of the Round Table, their marvelous enquests and adventures, the achieving of the Sangreal, and in the end the dolorous death and departing out of this world of them all. Which book was reduced into English by Sir Thomas Malory,* 40 *knight, as afore is said, and by me divided into twenty-one books, chaptered and imprinted, and finished in the abbey Westminster the last day of July the year of our Lord* MCCCCLXXXV.

*Caxton me fieri fecit.*[59]

---

[57] The fiction of poets.   [58] Misbelievers.
[59] Caxton caused me to be made.

# III
# THE RENAISSANCE AND THE PROTESTANT REVOLT, 1485-1660

*Renaissance* is a word of French origin which means literally "rebirth." It is used by all historians to denote the period following the Middle Ages—the period when the modern world took form. This was a period of extraordinary and far-reaching change. And the men of that time, participating in the movement, felt that what was taking place was a rebirth of civilization after a long night of barbarism. They knew all along that Europe had enjoyed a remarkable civilization before the coming of Christianity. They knew that early in the Christian era this civilization had been shattered, seemingly by the barbarian invasions. They now began to feel that through the intervening centuries until their own time men had been sunk in shameful ignorance, had remained blind to the good possibilities of earthly life and so had gradually declined into a state of corruption. At length, however, men's eyes were being opened; men were becoming conscious of what they had neglected and lost, were reaching out to recover it, and civilization was being reborn.

This conscious effort at recovery had its beginnings in Italy in the fourteenth century, and spread out from Italy over Europe. The Renaissance was a lengthy period of complex change, however, and it did not effectively touch England or English literature until the close of the fifteenth century. The effect of the Renaissance upon the English gives us yet another chance to observe their perhaps unique power to absorb foreign influences without being overmastered by them. Hence we should not be surprised to find that though the English Renaissance was part and parcel of a large movement, it was also markedly different from its continental sources in its character and results.

## THE AGE OF DISCOVERY AND INVENTION

If now we ask what were the great impersonal causes of change which were altering the medieval conditions of life and giving men a new outlook and new hopes, we find standing in front of all others three late medieval inventions: the mariner's compass, gunpowder, and the art of printing with movable type. Printing was the latest of these inventions, and can be said to come before the Renaissance only because that movement traveled somewhat slowly northward. Printing is generally supposed to have begun about 1440 in the German city of Mainz, and its invention is attributed to Johann Gutenberg. Gunpowder was apparently invented in the thirteenth century by an Englishman, Friar Roger Bacon. No one attempts to say who invented the mariner's compass; but the earliest known description of the instrument occurs in a manuscript written in 1269, and it had come into general use by the early part of the fifteenth century.

The social importance, or usefulness, of the feudal nobility of Europe tended to disappear as rapidly as it became apparent that a common man with a gun could defeat the best armed and mounted knight without one. The whole character of warfare suffered a revolution, and besides the social consequences within Europe, the possession of firearms gave European powers a military advantage which enabled them to dominate the rest of the world. At the same time, thanks to the mariner's compass, the rest of the world was being discovered and opened up for commerce and colonization. Commerce was the stimulus which brought the mariner's compass into use and sent a host of adventurous and bold explorers out on the sea. The Crusades had a lasting and important effect here in opening the eyes of Europeans to Oriental luxuries and thus creating a demand which resulted in permanent commercial relations between Europe and the East. The development of trade affected the basic economy of feudalism: the self-sufficient community, producing and consuming its own goods. This economy broke down everywhere as soon as opportunities for commerce among regions were seen. It is scarcely too much to say that the gradual collapse of the feudal social system in the face of growing commercial opportunity during the later Middle Ages was the one great underlying cause of the Renaissance.

Commerce between Europe and the East was carried on principally through Venice, and was so profitable that it aroused the envy of other states and caused them to try to open up a sea route to the Indies and China which could compete with the overland route controlled by the Venetians. The discovery of America by Christopher Columbus was only an unsuccessful episode in this long-continued effort to reach Asia by sea. Success was achieved five years later by the Portuguese when Vasco da Gama sailed around the Cape of Good Hope to India. In the same year England entered the race, sending John Cabot on a western voyage which finally took him to Newfoundland.

It did not take long for the Spaniards, for whom Columbus had made his voyages, to learn that though their explorer had not reached Asia, he had led them to a country rich in gold and silver, and of vast extent, whose very existence had not been suspected.

No words can be adequate to describe, no effort of the imagination can be sufficient to grasp, the full effect of these exploits upon the life of Europe. They forced a revolution in thought which was at once exhilarating and bewildering. The world was proved to be larger, more various, richer than had been dreamed; and human capacities were proved to be equal to the challenge. Life here and now was a better thing than Christian teachers had admitted—life was action, which could lead to earthly power and earthly happiness. There came, then, a definite enlargement of the sense

of personality; a conviction of the worth of present earthly life considered simply in and for itself, without necessary reference to a life of the soul after death; and a new self-confidence. This was a growth of individualism, and individualism was further promoted by the development of commerce which had stimulated exploration. Commerce gave scope for personal initiative, ambition, and even heroism; it was the open door out of the medieval world of inherited place in life; and the wealth which was its end, when achieved, gave further opportunity for the expression of individuality.

## REDISCOVERY OF THE ANCIENT WORLD

The economic development which awakened individualism, and the prosperity which enabled men to seek the refinements of life came earliest in Italy. And accordingly it was first in Italy that men began, more than a century before the spectacular successes of the explorers, to look back to classical civilization with a new sense of what had been lost throughout the Middle Ages. In the thousand years before the fourteenth century the barbarians who had overrun Europe had become humanized, had built up a distinctive culture of their own which had rather quickly reached its limits, and were now at length ready, and anxious, to learn more from antiquity.

## INFLUENCE OF PETRARCH

The great and justly celebrated pioneer in this attempt was Francis Petrarch, who was born near Florence in 1304 and died in 1374. Someone has called him the first man who felt contempt for the Middle Ages. Petrarch had a boundless and lifelong enthusiasm for classical culture, born of the conviction that the great writers of antiquity were more completely developed human beings, were wiser, and were far more accomplished artists than any the Middle Ages could show. He communicated this enthusiasm wherever he went; and his aim was not merely the study of classical literature, but study to the end that men might again become fully and maturely human, and might again write great poetry.

Petrarch remains endlessly interesting because of his own clear consciousness of the opposition between the Christian and the classical views of life. The classical view of life is a pagan one, and Petrarch wrestled unsuccessfully with the opposition between Christian and pagan through a great part of his life. Indeed, it is this inner contradiction, and the self-consciousness which issues from it, that earns for Petrarch the title of "the first modern man." He had to choose between two philosophies, that of the Greeks and Romans, where human life was significant and full of solid worth in and for itself, and that of the Christians, where human life was only a means to an end beyond itself. The Greeks and the Romans had studied to obtain the most from life; they had held determinedly to a belief in the dignity and greatness of human nature, and in the possibility of a sufficing happiness in this life, regardless of any life to come. The Christians, on the other hand, believed that the soul of man lived on eternally after death, in perfect happiness in Heaven or in complete torment in Hell, and that life on earth was just a way of determining which of the two it would be—no more.

Petrarch saw no way of reconciling these two views of life, yet he could not let go of either; consequently he remained a troubled and divided spirit, trying somehow to make the best of both worlds. In this divided allegiance—which forced Petrarch to keep trying to make independent judgments—we see not only the birth of individualism and of the modern critical intelligence, but also the beginning of a progressive movement away from the unity of thought and feeling achieved in Europe in the twelfth and thirteenth centuries.

## HUMANISM

Those who followed Petrarch as students of Greek and Latin were called humanists—that is, the exponents of *humanism*. The important thing to grasp is that the word "humanism" denotes not the study of Greek and Roman literature, but the object of this study. Petrarch and the scholars who succeeded him aimed to bring in and encourage the study of "humanity" as a subject no less worthy of attention than the "divinity" or study of religion which in the Middle Ages held the supreme place in the field of higher learning. They were all convinced that the best material for studying mature and cultivated humanity was to be found in Greek and Roman literature.

## HUMANISTIC EDUCATIONAL AND LITERARY STANDARDS

From the study of classical civilization came the humanistic ideal of life as an art. This ideal received unsurpassed expression in the famous book entitled *The Courtier* by Castiglione, as did the idea of education as a discipline calculated for the equal and harmonious development of all human abilities. Only the well-rounded man, whose training developed his body, emotions, and mind, who possessed varied accomplishments but was not too expert in any of them, could be called fully human.

In art and literature it seemed reasonable to ask for the same balance, symmetry, restraint, and smoothness that were required for acceptable practice of the art of living. Whatever was whimsical or merely fanciful, extreme, impulsive, disordered, or vague was therefore condemnable. It was confidently believed that the poet, no matter how great his genius, must be disciplined and formed, taught to avoid faults, to observe decorum, and to subdue native wildness to reason. "Decorum" here meant simply appropriateness in characterization: a prince must act and talk like a prince, a merchant like a merchant, and so on. Though merchants do not always act and talk like merchants in real life, it was felt that the poet should be concerned not with the exceptional, but with the typical human being. Poetry should not be the mirror of particular fact, but of generalized truth. It was held to be the office of the poet to represent life, not photographically as it is, but as it might be and should be. Thus the poet himself must be an informed and critical observer, capable in selection and rejection, with a view to making his picture more real than actual life, and more significant and impressive. Thus too the poet accepts a fearful responsibility, because he must see more clearly and deeply than ordinary men, and rise equal to the demands of his theme, and so become a leader and teacher of mankind.

## MEDIEVAL SURVIVALS IN THE RENAISSANCE

Today, when we look back on the Renaissance, we cannot see it as did those who took part in it. It often seemed to them that the Renaissance was a sharp break from the Middle Ages, a bold new thing. Practically everything which seemed to be the innovation of the Renaissance, however, was developing unmistakably in the later Middle Ages. Furthermore, both in literature and in thought much that is characteristically medieval persisted through the Renaissance. The truth is that even the greatest changes are slower and less complete than we like to imagine, and the generations of men are bound to one another by invisible ties not easily severed. In retrospect we can always see this; thus we see in Spenser, Marlowe, and Shakespeare not the sharp break their contemporaries saw, but continuity with the later Middle Ages. Spenser in writing his *Faerie Queene* consciously looked back to Chaucer, to the romances of chivalry, and to the moralities, and felt that there he was on firm ground. Marlowe's *Doctor Faustus* is in form really a morality play; and Shakespeare's plays have intimate bonds of connection with the whole native medieval conception of courtesy, the medieval discovery of romantic love, and medieval symbolism or allegory carried on into and through the Renaissance—until we may begin to doubt the very existence of the Renaissance.

## MINGLING OF OLD AND NEW: MARLOWE'S *Doctor Faustus*

To doubt the existence of the Renaissance, however, would be a grave mistake. For the evidence that along with the old there is also something in this literature which is distinctly new and transforming is spread everywhere, and cannot be escaped. When we first look at *Doctor Faustus* we see personified virtues and vices contesting for man's soul, with the hero reduced to a passive role. But soon we see that the old symbolical framework has been put to a new kind of use; despite his passive role, Faustus begins to have for us a personal interest. The colorless "Mankind" or "Everyman" of the old moralities has become an individual with positive qualities, with a boundless curiosity, a soaring desire for knowledge and power and full experience of life, and daring self-confidence. Faustus is still a type, but he is the typical new man of the Renaissance, determined to see and learn and experience all things for himself, at whatever cost.

In studying the English Renaissance, therefore, we must constantly remember that though the new literature of the sixteenth century had vital connections with the native medieval past, it was also really new—shot through with the Renaissance spirit of worldliness and also with influences from the Renaissance literature of Italy and from ancient classical literature. And whether or not they were right, we must remember that Englishmen of the later sixteenth century felt that they were living in a new world of thought and aspiration, felt a deep opposition between themselves and the Middle Ages, and felt that they were pioneers in literature and in life.

## FORCES OF CHANGE

One of the most important reasons that men in the sixteenth century felt that they were sharply separated from the Middle Ages was the constant change in the language. Before printing, Shakespeare, and the English Bible combined to standardize modern English, the language had changed so rapidly that less than a hundred years after Chaucer's death no one knew how his Middle English language had been pronounced. The principal change was the dropping of the final "e" so frequent in Chaucer, but there were other important changes as well. Men of the Renaissance were disgusted with this barbarous language, so subject to rapid and capricious change. They felt, therefore, that they were pioneers, confronted with the task of shaping and refining a rude tongue so that it might become a fit and sufficient medium for the literary use of cultivated people.

The other important reasons for the feeling of separation from the Middle Ages cannot be disentangled from one another for discussion. They can be summarized at the outset, however, as the accession of the new Tudor dynasty, the entrance of humanism into England, and the Protestant Reformation. To understand these changes we have to look at them in their interrelations; but we must remember as we proceed that we are trying to see why Englishmen in the sixteenth century began to feel that they were living in a new world.

## THE TUDORS

During the later Middle Ages England had had a number of relatively weak monarchs, and political uncertainty and dissension were the general rule. The country had become a battleground for hostile factions, and a reign of lawlessness had set in.

When Henry Tudor won the crown in 1485, then, another great break with the Middle Ages occurred. For Henry was steady, capable, and strong. He founded a new dynasty, and he gave the English people the new deal which they so desperately needed. He and his successors in the next century were practically absolute sovereigns, but they were gratefully supported by the people because they gave the people as a whole exactly what they desired. Under the Tudors England enjoyed peace, great and constantly increasing prosperity, and rising national prestige, which reached a magnificent climax in the defeat of the Spanish Armada in the latter half of the long reign of Elizabeth.

## THE ENTRANCE OF HUMANISM INTO ENGLAND

Although the spirit of the Renaissance was seen in England as early as Chaucer, Duke Humphrey of Gloucester appears to have been the first English scholar actively interested in Renaissance humanism. He studied classical Latin literature, learned to read the new Italian literature, and collected manuscripts. At his death in 1447 he was followed by some younger men who were eager not only to partake of the new classical learning but to implant it in England. The most notable of these were Thomas Linacre, William Grocyn, and John Colet. These men all learned Greek in Italy and returned to England to establish the classical curriculum in English schools and colleges.

Another important founder of humanism in England was the famous Dutch scholar Erasmus. He was influenced especially by Colet to become a serious student of Greek, and in the course of several long visits he made himself a co-founder of Greek learning in England. From 1511 to 1514 he taught Greek at Cambridge University. The closest and most congenial friend Erasmus made in England was St. Thomas More, who had learned some Greek and become thoroughly imbued with the humanistic spirit under Linacre and Grocyn at Oxford.

## RELIGIOUS REFORM

The effect everywhere of the new classical learning was to awaken the independent critical intelligence, and to give form and direction to the gradually strengthening revolt against medieval Catholicism.

The earliest English humanists were serious

men, to whom religion was the basis of the good life. This does not mean that they were narrow and sadly solemn. St. Thomas More had high spirits, wit, abundant geniality, and eager interest in all that the new classical learning could contribute to cultivated life. To all appearances he was an urbane man of the world—yet next to his skin he wore the hair shirt of the medieval penitent with no feeling of incongruity between his outward life and his religious faith. To men like St. Thomas More, therefore, it was natural that the critical frame of mind awakened by the new learning should suggest, not abandonment of Christianity for classical culture, but a reformation of the clergy and of Christian institutions. John Colet led the way in lectures he gave at Oxford on the epistles of St. Paul. Colet said that medieval interpreters of the Bible made it appear to say anything they wanted it to through their method of explaining "hidden" meanings. He said that only one meaning of St. Paul's epistles was important—their real or literal meaning. Colet's approach seems so sensible to us now that it is hard for us to realize how revolutionary it was at the time. Yet such treatment of any part of the Bible *was* revolutionary, and shows us clearly as anything we have discussed the really sharp line of division between the medieval spirit and the modern critical spirit.

## SOCIAL REFORM: MORE'S *Utopia*

More's contribution to the cause of enlightenment and reform was a small book written in Latin and entitled *Utopia*, which is Greek for "nowhere." This book is a picture, inspired by Plato's *Republic* and *Laws*, of an imaginary commonwealth, supposed to have been found by one of the adventurous mariners of the early sixteenth century in the New World beyond the Atlantic. More's humanistic training encouraged the free play of reason, and his aim was to describe the kind of commonwealth which could be imagined as issuing logically from the use of reason in conjunction with the human virtues—wisdom, fortitude, temperance, and justice. More's description of Utopia is preceded by a picture of the England and Europe of his time as he saw them, made poor by the expense of arms, distracted by constant warfare, governed by corrupt statesmen, while real social welfare and justice were neglected, and general unemployment was causing waves of crime. And More's object was simply to emphasize the shameful contrasts between his two pictures.

## HENRY VIII AND THE
## NEW COURTLY POETRY

In 1509 Henry VII died and Henry VIII ascended the throne. It has been said that St. Thomas More is one of the two most vivid and significant figures in the England of the early sixteenth century. Henry VIII is the other. His accession seemed unmistakably to mark a new and happy era. His subjects were filled with unbelievable enthusiasm for him, and looked forward to a golden age unmatched in history. Probably no one could have satisfied such anticipations; certainly Henry did not, yet to the end he commanded a more complete loyalty from the mass of his people than we today find it easy to understand. And for a while things went very well. Modern English poetry was born in Henry's court, and this alone is enough to prove that the court promptly became a center of Renaissance influences.

Poetry, which had been sinking steadily through the fifteenth century, continued in the early years of the sixteenth to be imitative, dull, lifeless, and metrically almost formless. But as Henry VIII entered manhood there was new life stirring in poetry; John Skelton, one of Henry's tutors, wrote rough but energetic verses which promised well for the future.

Though Henry did not reward the high hopes of English humanists, he did have some real interest in the new learning, and he was fond of music, which meant at this time chiefly song. He is said himself to have been a creditable composer, and he encouraged song writing at his court. The importance of this can hardly be exaggerated. Music had been popular in England through the later Middle Ages, and now again it was to exercise an influence for the good when the secret of writing smooth verse in English had to be rediscovered. Henry's encouragement made song writing fashionable, and led directly to the great age of English music in the reigns of Elizabeth and James. This is the great age also of English lyric poetry, when poets were writing directly for music, and were often skilled musicians themselves.

What we know of the new kinds of poems written in the first half of the sixteenth century we owe almost entirely to the enterprise of Richard Tottel, who in 1557, ten years after the death of Henry VIII, gathered together 271 poems and printed them under the title *Songs and Sonnets*.

## TWO COURTLY POETS:
## WYATT AND SURREY

*Tottel's Miscellany*, as it is generally called, stands at the threshold of the poetry of the English Renaissance, and owes its fame to this position. Its most notable poems are two groups which make up just over half of the pieces printed. One group contains ninety-six poems by Sir Thomas Wyatt, and the other, forty by Henry Howard, Earl of Surrey. Wyatt had been to Italy and had there encountered Petrarch's famous sonnets. He introduced into England the lyric of courtly love and the Petrarchian or Italian sonnet form, the most popular verse form of the Renaissance. Both Wyatt's sonnets and Surrey's are in many cases simply translations from Petrarch, though many are moving and beautiful English poems.

We see other important beginnings in *Tottel's Miscellany* which show that Renaissance impulses at this time were really striking home in England. There are odes, epigrams, satires, and reflective lyrics, all in the classical manner. We also owe to Surrey a translation of two books of Virgil's *Aeneid*, published by Tottel though not in the *Miscellany*, in which he used blank verse—iambic pentameter lines without rime. This was taken up and used by Thomas Sackville and Thomas Norton in *Gorboduc*, the earliest English classical tragedy, and so was passed on to Marlowe, who finally showed its possibilities and made it the verse of Elizabethan drama, above all of Shakespearean drama. Thence it passed to Milton to become the verse of *Paradise Lost*, and since then it has been the verse most commonly used in England for long poems.

When all is said, however, none of the verse written by Surrey or by other courtly poets of the first half of the sixteenth century has much value beyond its historical importance, with the exception of certain songs, chiefly by Wyatt. In the best of his songs Wyatt has a sure control over metrical form without sacrifice of spontaneity, and he raises poetry "in small parcels" to a position of dignity and strength which it has held to our own day. And though they do have dignity, there is nothing heavy or over-formal in these songs. On the contrary, they are simple, and full of a light grace which reminds us that Wyatt was an accomplished courtier.

## THE PROTESTANT REFORMATION

But behind the exquisite song, the gaiety and splendor of Henry's court, storms were brewing. They were to burst forth with violence in the 1530's and were to continue for many years, plaguing and dividing the English people, even to the point of civil war in the next century. The first open sign of division appeared in the German town of Wittenberg in 1517, when Martin Luther nailed the celebrated ninety-five theses to the door of the Schlosskirche. This proved to be the first decisive step leading to the Protestant Reformation. Luther's defiance of the Pope almost immediately found sympathizers in England.

A movement for reform of the Catholic Church had already sprung up among the earliest English humanists toward the end of the fifteenth century. It was born of the critical attitude awakened by the Renaissance learning; not only was it distinct from the earlier Lollard movement, but also it was much deeper than a mere outcry against the ignorance, self-seeking, and worldliness of the clergy. Thus a few young men, principally at Cambridge University, were already so deeply convinced of the necessity of radical reform that they promptly welcomed Luther's leadership. Among them was William Tyndale.

### TYNDALE AND THE ENGLISH BIBLE

Tyndale remains personally somewhat obscure, but there is no doubt that he was a man of genius and of heroic determination. He became convinced that it was an immediate necessity, for the revival of Christianity among his countrymen, to translate the Bible into English. After great difficulties he succeeded; the first printed New Testament in English was completed abroad in 1528, and immediately began to circulate in England.

Tyndale produced a version which is almost miraculously good. He had an extraordinary command of idiomatic English, and he aimed to convey the meaning of the Gospel in a form which the simplest reader might grasp. He had a spirit which responded nobly to the height and dignity of his text. He went on at once to learn Hebrew in order to translate the Old Testament directly from the language in which it had been written, and published his version of the first five books in 1530. He completed other books of the Old Testament, but was not allowed to finish his task. Branded as an arch heretic, he had to live in hiding. In the late spring of 1535 he was betrayed, condemned, tied to a stake, strangled, and his body burned.

### THE REFORMATION IN ENGLAND

Meanwhile in England Henry VIII had been having his own troubles, of a very different kind, with the Papacy. Henry desired a male heir, and he therefore wished to have his marriage with Catherine of Aragon annulled so that he could marry Anne Boleyn. Catherine was the aunt of the king of Spain, the most powerful ruler on the Continent, however, and the Pope did not dare to grant the annulment.

The consequence was the English Reformation. Henry in effect appealed to English national feeling against foreign dictatorship over internal affairs of the kingdom. He carried his subjects with him because there was acute dissatisfaction over the amount of property held by the Church and over the amount of money annually drawn out of England into the Papacy. He also carried many Englishmen with him who were convinced of the necessity of a religious reformation, and who were willing to seize any opportunity for a separation from Rome. In 1533 Thomas Cranmer, Archbishop of Canterbury, annulled Henry's marriage on the findings of an English court. Before this, Henry had forced the clergy to acknowledge him as the supreme head of the Church in England "as far as the law of Christ allows." The break with the Roman Catholic Church had been made.

Henry did not at any time desire the slightest change in Catholic doctrine, worship, or clerical organization. But he had spent his father's treasure and did need money. For this reason he proceeded to dissolve the English monasteries and to confiscate their vast estates. Also, after he had been excommunicated and "deposed" by the Pope, he was forced to make concessions to Protestant demands, the most important being his authorization in 1539 of the use of an English Bible in the churches. The Bible used was one which included as much of Tyndale's translation as he had been able to finish.

After Henry's death in 1547 English feeling tended to favor a position midway between Catholic claims and Protestant wishes. The reformers carried things too far in the Protestant direction during the brief reign of Edward VI, but the reversal to Catholicism under Mary also provoked strong opposition. When Elizabeth succeeded to the throne in 1558, then, there was general rejoicing. Elizabeth aimed to effect a characteristically English compromise, and during her long and brilliant reign she did succeed in holding an even course between extremists on both sides. The question at issue, however, was not one that could be settled so easily, and the great queen accomplished no more than a postponement of conflict.

## THE ELIZABETHAN VOYAGERS

Meanwhile, Elizabeth did give England nearly a half century of relative quiet and peace at just the time the opportunity could be used to the greatest advantage. In the first half of the sixteenth century England took practically no part in the work of exploration of the new world. It appeared that both the glory and the prizes were to go to Spain and Portugal. But in the second half of the century English sailors, with Elizabeth's encouragement, began to make up for lost time.

Of all these sailors the greatest was Sir Francis Drake. He personified the daring, expanding, conquering Elizabethan spirit in action as perfectly as Marlowe personified it in the world of imagination. And Drake did what all the explorers and sailors dreamed of doing, but what none of the others so wonderfully achieved. When he returned from his three years' voyage around the world in the *Golden Hind* he paid the shareholders in the venture a profit of 4700 per cent.

No one could have foreseen at the time that by the shift from the Mediterranean to the Atlantic as the all-important highway of trade, England was removed from the position of a remote border-state to the most advantageous place among nations for carrying on world commerce. No one could have foreseen that the Elizabethan voyagers were laying the foundations of a vast British Empire of the nineteenth century. Yet what contemporaries did see was enough to arouse their enthusiasm and wonder, to give them a sense of expanding opportunity for themselves, and to make them glow with exuberance and self-confidence. All that they felt received full confirmation when in the summer of 1588 the Spanish Armada of Philip II, which had been expected to destroy British sea power, was decisively defeated and nearly destroyed. English enthusiasm for voyages was reflected in *The Principal Navigations, Voyages, and Discoveries of the English Nation*, which appeared in 1589. This collec-

tion of heroic narratives, which has been called "the prose epic" of modern England, was the life work of Richard Hakluyt.

## THE ELIZABETHAN TRANSLATORS

Hakluyt's great collection gives the background of action against which Elizabethan life and letters took form. But the sea captains were not the only explorers who were at work. The task of opening up the riches of classical literature, and also of the newer literatures of Italy and France, had been carried on steadily in England throughout the sixteenth century but gained a new momentum in the reign of Elizabeth. The age is notable not least for its wealth of translations, which often were very unscholarly but were nearly always vivid and lively.

Sir Thomas North's translation of Plutarch's *Lives of the Noble Grecians and Romans* was published in 1579. It stands out above other translations both because of the use made of it by Shakespeare and because it has won an important place of its own in English literature. Outstanding also were George Chapman's translations of Homer. He completed the *Iliad* in 1611 and the *Odyssey* in 1616.

The age was not less interested in the Renaissance literature of Italy, France, and Spain than in ancient classical literature. We have already noticed this in speaking of the sonnet, and everywhere in Elizabethan verse scholars find evidence that the Continental Renaissance poets were being studied and used. But popular interest was most strongly attracted by the short stories in prose which had become fashionable in Italy during the Renaissance. Boccaccio's *Decameron*, written in the middle of the fourteenth century, set the fashion for such stories. The first English collection of such tales, translated from Italian and other languages, was compiled by William Painter, under the title *The Palace of Pleasure*. It was first published in 1566. In its final form, *The Palace of Pleasure* contains one hundred tales, including the story of Shakespeare's *Romeo and Juliet* and the source of his *All's Well that Ends Well*.

There is not space here to give a complete picture of the wealth of foreign literature made into English in the Tudor period. The most important translations can be discussed, however, and the most important of all is the Authorized, or King James, Version of the Bible which appeared in 1611. This was the culmination of nearly a century's work by various men, beginning with Tyndale's New Testament. It owes more to Tyndale than to anyone else, and we must therefore think of Tyndale as chiefly responsible for the most influential book in English that has ever been published from the beginning to the present.

## THE ELIZABETHAN CHRONICLERS

Our glance at the Elizabethan voyagers and the Elizabethan translators does not quite cover the work of exploration which was carried on in the latter half of the sixteenth century, and which formed the rich and varied background of Elizabethan literature. The pride of nationality had been growing in England, as we have noticed, in the later Middle Ages; it greatly increased in the sixteenth century, and especially in the reign of Elizabeth. It then showed itself in a heightened interest in English history and antiquity.

The greatest achievement in the realm of history in this period was the composite work known as *Holinshed's Chronicle*, which first appeared in 1578. It goes under Raphael Holinshed's name because he supervised the work of the other writers and himself wrote the most important part, the *History of England*. Holinshed freely used the work of previous chroniclers, and his compilation became a classic. It is the principal source not only for Shakespeare's historical plays, but for other Elizabethan plays dealing with England's past.

We can now see the first part of Elizabeth's reign for what it was: a time when the accustomed framework of life and thought and imagination, the medieval scheme of things, had fallen apart; and when men with youthful energy and confidence were busily exploring new worlds—a new physical world, the whole field, new to them, of classical literature and culture, the brave new field of continental literature inspired by the Italian Renaissance, and finally their own national history seen with new eyes and a growing pride.

## POETRY AND DRAMA

The student looking at literature alone does not find much to reward him in the first twenty years after Elizabeth became queen. The one really fine piece of verse these years have to show was composed about 1560. This is the *Induction*, or preface, written by Thomas Sackville for an enlarged edition of *The Mirror for Magistrates*. The *Mirror* is a series of narratives showing the way in which Fortune or Fate has brought great persons—most of them characters in English history—from high estate to low. It was exceedingly popular for half a century, though as poetry it is almost worthless except for Sackville's *Induction* in the second edition. The *Mirror* as a whole shows the persistence of the medieval spirit; Sackville's *Induction* shows the Renaissance spirit entering in. It is a thoroughly humanistic poem; but there is nothing to compare it with until we reach Spenser's *Faerie Queene*, which began to appear in 1590.

In the twenty years from 1560 to 1580 there was a certain amount of literary activity. Verse "in small parcels" continued to be written, and the popularity of *Tottel's Miscellany* suggested the publication of additional miscellanies. In the quite varied works of George Gascoigne one can see how the new influences from classical studies and from the Italian Renaissance were being assimilated. Gascoigne and his contemporaries, however, were only able to do what may be called apprentice work. Importance has been conferred upon it by the literature which followed.

This is true, on the whole, in the field of drama as well as in the field of non-dramatic poetry. There was throughout the sixteenth century a constantly increasing interest in dramatic performance, and many plays were written or revived to satisfy this interest. Most of those plays we study now not because of their worth in themselves, but because we can see in the changes occurring and in the different kinds of plays the development which brought the drama in England to the point where Shakespeare and his contemporaries took it up.

Drama, as the word has been understood from Shakespeare's time to the present, is the representation, through speech and act, by persons on a stage, of a conflict of some kind. As a play opens, we are confronted by a situation which has in it possibilities of trouble; and the situation more or less rapidly develops to the point of conflict—conflict between two persons, or two groups of persons, or conflict within one person. The point of actual conflict is the climax of the play, and this is followed by the outcome of the conflict, which ends the play. In accordance with the medieval use of the two words, a play in which the conflict was happily resolved was called a comedy, and a play in which the conflict came out unhappily was called a tragedy—the most effective tragic event being the death of the hero after he has gained our sympathies.

Hence a play in the full sense of the word must have a plot whose essential element is a conflict and its resolution. The early moralities met these requirements; they had, however, only one theme—the conflict between virtues and vices for the soul of man. At the beginning of the sixteenth century the method or framework of the morality was used for other themes: interests aroused by humanism were allegorically treated; later, towards the middle of the century, religious controversy. At the same time, writers of interludes were getting away from allegory and exploring the possibilities of realistic presentation of human characters, with comic scenes depending for their effect upon character rather than upon mere clowning. There was also during the sixteenth century an independent development of the dramatized presentation of heroic stories from history or legend, out of which grew the chronicle-plays.

### CLASSICAL DRAMA IN ENGLAND

The fatal trouble with the chronicle-plays was that they lacked plot. It is true also of all the native efforts that they were structurally very poor, and that they showed very little understanding of the relation between character and real dramatic conflict. In contrast, the new knowledge of classical literature included a strong emphasis on structure. Latin comedies and tragedies were not only being read; at schools and the universities they were being acted by the students, and new plays were being written in Latin modeled upon them. Presently the next step was taken, and plays modeled upon Latin tragedy and comedy were written in English for performance before learned audiences.

The London Inns of Court, the law schools of England, were at this time centers of humanistic learning and culture. Queen Elizabeth, moreover, had been taught the classics by Roger Ascham, and her court was the dominating center of culture in England. Hence learned audiences were to be found not only at the universities and at schools, but also at the court of Elizabeth and in the London law schools. The earliest English plays modeled on Latin comedy were *Gammer Gurton's Needle*, written by a Cambridge man; and *Ralph Roister Doister*, written by Nicholas Udall, who was Headmaster at Eton and later at Westminster. *Gorboduc*, by Sackville and

Norton, has already been mentioned as the earliest English classical tragedy.

These plays and other similar ones which followed them were enjoyed only by those who shared the new classical learning, and were not publicly performed for popular audiences. Public demand for dramatic spectacle was eager, but was being satisfied in the 1560's and 1570's by beggarly professional actors who wandered about performing chronicle-plays and interludes with a liberal addition of clowning and ribaldry. If a genuine English drama was to appear, somehow a union would have to be brought about between these two kinds.

### THE GREAT ELIZABETHAN WRITERS AND THE NEW LEARNING

We can now see the first twenty years of Elizabeth's reign as a period, in the field of literature, of continuing experiment with apparently small result. It was a time of exploration in many fields, all of which could contribute something to a new literature, if only the writers should appear who could take full advantage of the opportunity. And suddenly at the end of the 1570's and in the 1580's they did appear, not merely one or two, but a whole group. They felt keenly the bewildering variety of influences and changes we have been reviewing; they had confidence, energy, and genius; and they rapidly proceeded to make the end of the sixteenth century the great age of English literature. Almost without exception these new writers were university men. Sir Philip Sidney, Edmund Spenser, Sir Walter Ralegh, John Lyly, Christopher Marlowe, Robert Greene, George Peele, Thomas Lodge, Thomas Nashe, and Francis Bacon went to either Oxford or Cambridge; Thomas Kyd received a classical education at the Merchant Taylors' School in London.

The least learned of them all, as it happened, was Shakespeare, not only the greatest poet and dramatist of the age, but the greatest poet in the whole range of English and of modern European literature. Shakespeare's formal education was obtained at the grammar school in Stratford, where he was born, and it was early concluded. Traditionally he is said to have had "small Latin and less Greek." Somehow or other it is often implied that Shakespeare's slender education is a commentary on the usefulness of learning. It may therefore be well to say at once that his extraordinary ability by no means took the place of education, and that he had to pick up as best he could outside of school a great deal that he could have learned more readily with the help of teachers. No amount of inborn genius, not even Shakespeare's, can ever enable anyone to create a work of art without materials. The truth about Shakespeare consequently is, not that he rose to a supreme height of literary achievement without education, but that he was better able to educate himself than most men. Of equal importance is the fact that he came to London at just the time when enough had been done by others to enable him, with his keen eye and perceptive mind, to enter into a heritage which we may think was almost providentially prepared for him. This in fact is one of the secrets of his achievement—that he did not build from the ground up, but took what others had done and immeasurably improved it.

## SPENSER'S *Shepherd's Calendar*

Before anything more is said of Shakespeare's achievement we should glance at what was done in the first years of this great period. The publication of Edmund Spenser's *Shepherd's Calendar* in 1579 was the beginning. The book created a stir; it was recognized promptly as something new and promising, by a talented poet. Thus its historical importance is very great, but, except for a few passages, it is scarcely readable today. Nor is this surprising. The poems are too consciously and purely experimental. But to his contemporaries Spenser seemed a pioneer, and his Eclogues were rightly recognized as the herald of a new day, because of the attempt he made in them to join humanism and native tradition.

He was thoroughly indoctrinated with Renaissance humanism, and fired with the wish to create a new English poetry which might satisfy humanistic criteria. He would go back to the undefiled source of the English poetic tradition in Chaucer, and found his language and poetic style and verse, as far as he could, directly on Chaucer. He would also look to English scenery for his pastoral setting, and make his shepherds English in their customs and beliefs as well as in their names. Thus he would create a poetry truly English in substance and form, but filled with the spirit of classical pastoral, handled freely as Virgil himself had handled it.

This was the central aim, and it is worth pausing over because here we see Spenser engaged in the characteristic English task of assimilating a new foreign influence, and using

it, while maintaining a real continuity of native tradition. Spenser's practice in *The Shepherd's Calendar* was not so successful as his intention was sound. But his talent saved the enterprise from looking ridiculous, and he was encouraged, fortunately, to continue what he had begun. His work culminated in *The Faerie Queene*, which has placed him securely among the five or six greatest English poets.

## The Faerie Queene

Now *The Faerie Queene* should be considered first of all as a continuance of the kind of effort made in *The Shepherd's Calendar*. It is Spenser's English embodiment of the aims of Renaissance humanism. In it he meant to accomplish for England what it seemed to him Homer had done for Greece, and Virgil for Rome. He meant to write an heroic poem which should teach by example, not by rule, the art of living, with a due value set upon all the good and enjoyable possibilities of present life, and a due emphasis upon the life to come. His characters were to be, not men and women as they are, but living embodiments of ideal types or qualities—men and women as they ought to be, or as they ought not to be. Everything was to be harmonized with his central purpose; for instance, the landscapes of *The Faerie Queene* were to be not only subordinated to the action but as far removed from crude true-to-life landscapes as were the characters from crude true-to-life people. Further, the style was to be worthy of the height and seriousness of the theme. As it is fit that the crown of an emperor should be elaborately and curiously carved and encrusted with jewels, so the heroic poem should have a stately movement, a formal elaborated style, and magnitude.

All of this Spenser accomplishes, yet *The Faerie Queene* is strikingly different from the *Iliad* or the *Odyssey*. Spenser set out to write, not an *Iliad* or an *Aeneid* in English, but an English heroic poem—a poem rooted in the native English past, using everything medieval and familiar that could be used. In *The Shepherd's Calendar* Spenser went back to Chaucer; now he went back to Malory's *Morte d'Arthur*. Also, *The Faerie Queene* is a series of medieval allegories, and the allegory of the first book is identical with the theme of the earlier morality plays. Nevertheless, the poem is inconceivable except as the production of a writer of the Renaissance. And although Spenser's direct classical learning was meager, he was widely read in the French and Italian literature of the Renaissance. He was not a "classical" poet, but he was certainly and completely a Renaissance poet, carrying out the aims of Renaissance humanism.

One of the most significant things about *The Faerie Queene* is the way in which Spenser has sought to bring together in it the whole range of matter, thought, and feeling which the age presented to him. The poem is medieval, yet Protestant; Christian and pagan; ethical, yet sensuous in the extreme; idyllic, but also heroic. If proof were needed, this would be enough to prove how completely the poem is the product of Renaissance influence. Spenser was certainly no less aware than Petrarch had been of contradictions between things which still irresistibly appealed to him. Since they did irresistibly appeal, he somehow got everything into his poem; and while we read it we feel that all is subdued and harmonized to his slow and stately music, which is, after all, the best of Spenser. But when the spell of the music is broken, and we look for intellectual, or even emotional, harmony, we are disappointed. Spenser is "modern" as Petrarch is. Both are divided souls, unable to reconcile flesh and spirit, unable to cleave to either, and so trying to make the best of both worlds.

## SIR PHILIP SIDNEY

Spenser's *Shepherd's Calendar* had been dedicated to Sir Philip Sidney; and though Sidney wrote nothing which can place him beside the author of *The Faerie Queene*, anyone who would understand the English Renaissance must know Sidney as well as Spenser. There are interesting points of contact between the two. Sidney was the paragon of his age, the living embodiment of the hero as Spenser thought of that ideal type. He was a thorough aristocrat, early famous for his courtesy and taste, and the best example England could show of humanistic education and of the symmetrically developed man of many accomplishments. His *Defense of Poesy* is almost the earliest piece of formal literary criticism in the language and is an eloquent and distinguished presentation of Renaissance literary theory. Spenser agreed with practically all that Sidney says in the *Defense*. For Sidney, however, as an independent gentleman, the writing of poetry—indeed all writing—was only a kind of hobby. A gentleman should be able to write a copy of verses, on occasion, as he should be

able to play a musical instrument, or take his part in a song, or acquit himself well on the tennis court or in a fencing bout. And Sidney did write, but, because it was the gentlemanly thing, he published nothing. His writings found their way into print only after his early death. His series of sonnets, *Astrophel and Stella*, contains some of the best sonnets written in the Elizabethan period—better than any Spenser wrote, better than any except some of Shakespeare's. Sidney also wrote a very long prose romance, the *Arcadia*, which contains some charming lyrics, although it is almost as disconnected as Spenser's *Faerie Queene*. The interest of Sidney's romance, in fact, lies partly in the extent to which it is a prose counterpart of *The Faerie Queene*. The *Arcadia* is an heroic tale in a pastoral setting, whose characters are much occupied with love and with everything that can be said about love.

## THE THEMES OF ELIZABETHAN LITERATURE

Spenser and Sidney between them in all their writings supplement and bear out each other. From either we can learn the three chief subjects of English literature at the end of the sixteenth century: courtly love, heroism, and pastoralism. Heroism was a subject which the Renaissance owed directly to humanism—to the efforts of the humanists to give full credit to this earthly life. Courtly love was a pretense that the lover cared only for the spiritual, or divine, qualities of the beloved. Pastoral poetry was the expression of an enticing dream of simple kindly people leading an easy life, in company with their sheep, in unspoiled natural surroundings: a way of life idealized because of its remoteness from the uncertainty and complexity of court and city life.

## JOHN LYLY

Spenser and Sidney also illustrate, in different ways, the Elizabethan exuberance which led, with rapidly growing wealth, to such extravagances as the unrestrainedly and, to us today, unbelievably fancy costume of courtiers. In literature this exuberance led finally to the over-elaborate and too-decorative writing style known as "fine writing." Better than by Spenser or Sidney, however, or than by anyone else of the period, "fine writing" is illustrated by John Lyly. His *Euphues, the Anatomy of Wit*, which appeared in 1578, excited so much interest that Lyly wrote a sequel to it, and Lodge, Greene, and others wrote popular imitations.

Lyly's book is really a humanistic treatise on the art of living. The story is a framework for chapters on education, friendship, manners, morals, religion, and clothes, all intended for gentle folk. But it was the literary style, not the subject-matter, which at once attracted attention. No one had previously written English prose so formal, so highly elaborated, so rich in decorative qualities as Lyly's; and the effects he achieved were vastly admired by a generation in love with words and with all the wonderful things to be done with them. Euphuism was so obviously an extreme, however, that a reaction against it soon set in.

## THE FIRST THEATER

English love of clowning and buffoonery; Elizabethan love of gaudy display, elaborate pageantry, and high-flown language; spreading humanistic passion for the heroic and for earthly glory—all these interests came, as the reign of Elizabeth continued, to find their fullest satisfaction in the theater. We have noticed how widespread the love for dramatization steadily grew through the sixteenth century, and have seen the various steps towards drama, in the full sense of the word, which were being taken. Now we must see what these preparatory gropings led to.

In 1576 James Burbage, a carpenter who had turned professional actor, became convinced that it would be profitable to erect a building in London exclusively for dramatic performances. He was not permitted to do so within the City, but had to build his theater in the suburbs. Outside the City were already facilities for other popular amusements—pits for cock-fighting, butts for archery, playing fields for football, and rings for bull-baiting and bear-baiting. Burbage's notion of a theater came partly from a bear-baiting ring and partly from courtyards of inns, where traveling players had for some time been giving their performances. The building was circular, with tiers of galleries running towards the stage from either side of the entrance, and with the center open to the sky. The stage was a platform projecting into the unroofed center, so that the audience surrounded three sides of the stage. There was no front curtain. There was also no painted scenery, and not very much in the way of stage properties. But these deficiencies were made up for as fully as possible by expensive and gaudy costumes and much impressive display.

## THE NEW PLAYS OF THE 1580's

Burbage's instinct for business was excellent. His theater more than paid its way, and soon had rivals. And since these theaters could not continue to make money if they showed the same old plays night after night, there arose an active market for new plays. A talented man who was desperate for money could earn a living by writing—not much of a living, to be sure, but enough to attract certain very needy and dissolute young university men who could find nothing else to do for their bread and wine. These young men had learned a great deal from the Latin tragedies and comedies they had studied, and they had some Renaissance learning, besides talent and plenty of exuberance. They had to meet a commercial demand, and were restricted by it; but they succeeded in bringing about a fusion of classical structure and motifs with native liveliness and freedom which was something new and unique. Elizabethan drama could not have come into being without this fusion.

## WILLIAM SHAKESPEARE

When Shakespeare came to London, in the late 1580's, the groundwork had been completed. He found the theater a thriving business into which, somehow, he entered. By combining in his own career the offices of actor, playwright, manager, and theater owner he was able to make a good thing out of it, and toward the close of his life he was able to retire to Stratford as a gentleman and property-holder.

Shakespeare was not a pioneer or experimenter. The themes of almost all his plays are those which have been named as the themes of Elizabethan literature in general—courtly or romantic love, pastoralism, and the heroic character. In his early dramas he shows the same exuberance, and the same delight in rich effects and in play with words, that we have seen in other writers of the time. Shakespeare, then, accepted what he found, grew into it as any apprentice might unquestioningly learn a craft, and finally wrote plays with the mastery of supreme genius. This is the difference between Shakespeare and his fellow-dramatists; he did what they were doing, but did it better. We cannot say that Shakespeare is "better," however, without at least briefly suggesting what this means. Though he is often careless, even slovenly, sometimes bombastic, sometimes barbaric, he triumphs over all his faults in the matchless expressiveness of his poetry. He could be expressive of the whole range of human moods, the whole range of human character, the whole range of human perceptions. The English vocabulary had more than doubled itself during the sixteenth century, and Shakespeare had all of it under his command —the word and phrase so perfect for whatever he needed to say that we can only call it a kind of magic. By his wealth of imagery, so appropriate for his meaning and intention that his pictures have entered into the mind of the race, he seems not so much to *say* a thing as to express it directly after the fashion of the painter or the musician. And he was a subtle and effortless musician who with a touch of his bow could summon the one perfectly right tone for every utterance of every character.

Shakespeare, we know, wrote rapidly, sometimes too rapidly; but, in compensation, there is nothing labored, painfully forced out, in his plays. The man himself seems puzzling to many; he seems completely impersonal—an unexpressive mask looking down impartially on his multitude of extraordinarily varied characters. He became possessed by a plot, by a character, and was himself merely the recording instrument. This objectivity is another reason for his "betterness." He had the dramatic imagination in its greatest purity and intensity; he did not engage in self-expression, but in dramatic expression.

No one has ever equalled Shakespeare in this, and he was so perfectly equipped with wide sympathies, right feeling, and sound perception that he succeeded in making his characters life-like to the point of giving them a kind of existence outside of and beyond his plays. In this he had no notion of what was later to be called "realism." He was trying to create dramatic effectiveness, and to this purpose he did not hesitate to make his characters act at times in most improbable ways. But he succeeds better than any magician in creating his illusions because of the amount and kind of human truth which conceals the wires and pulleys by which his puppets are directed. The Elizabethan audience wanted to be thrilled, shocked, staggered by a tragic performance. Dramatists gave the audience what it wanted by boldly making their characters larger and livelier than people are in real life, and by using every device to make situations more clear-cut and striking than they are in real life.

The tragic writer wrestles with a problem— in Milton's famous words, he seeks to "justify the ways of God to men." Expressing this more generally, we may say that the tragic writer seeks to show that justice is not really violated, though it seems to be. What is Shakespeare's solution of this problem? Up to a point the answer is obvious: Shakespeare's heroes, for all their nobility or grandeur of nature, have fatal flaws of character, which explain and in a sense justify the calamities by which they are overwhelmed. But here we stop in perplexity— and perhaps one reason Shakespeare continues to hold his supreme place with us is that here too the modern world stops in perplexity. "What a piece of work is a man! how noble in reason! how infinite in faculty! in form and moving how express and admirable! in action how like an angel! in apprehension how like a god! the beauty of the world! the paragon of animals!" And yet man is born to suffer, born to encounter the one trial he is least able to face, born to calamity, born to die and, for all we know, to be swallowed up for ever by the earth. Why should it be so? Shakespeare does not know. Is there a law of justice by which all is swayed? or a covenant of grace? Shakespeare does not know. Quite possibly we are all mere creatures of illusion, as truly as the feigned characters of the stage:

Tomorrow, and tomorrow, and tomorrow,
Creeps in this petty pace from day to day
To the last syllable of recorded time,
And all our yesterdays have lighted fools
The way to dusty death. Out, out, brief candle!
Life's but a walking shadow, a poor player
That struts and frets his hour upon the stage
And then is heard no more: it is a tale
Told by an idiot, full of sound and fury
Signifying nothing.

Of Prospero in *The Tempest* an English critic has said that he "is the supreme manifestation in poetry of the full-grown wisdom of humanism"; yet Prospero has nothing different to say from Macbeth, except in the manner:

Our revels now are ended. These our actors,
As I foretold you, were all spirits, and
Are melted into air, into thin air:
And, like the baseless fabric of this vision
The cloud-capp'd towers, the gorgeous palaces,
The solemn temples, the great globe itself,
Yea, all which it inherit, shall dissolve
And like this insubstantial pageant faded
Leave not a wrack behind. We are such stuff
As dreams are made on, and our little life
Is rounded with a sleep.

## LATER PLAYS AND THE COMEDY OF MANNERS

Plays continued to be written in very large numbers from the time of Shakespeare's retirement until the London theaters were closed by the Puritans in 1642. In general the drama suffered a sharp decline into sensationalism; but one kind of play, which began to appear towards the end of the 1590's and which flourished especially in the early years of the seventeenth century, continued to be written later with no decline of power or zest. This, moreover, is the one type of Elizabethan play which has real and influential connections with later English drama of the Restoration and eighteenth century. It may be described as the comedy, often satirical, of London life and manners. Thomas Dekker's *Shoemakers' Holiday* is one of the earliest, pleasantest, and most successful of the comedies of this type.

## BEN JONSON

Another dramatist who wrote comedies with a London setting was Ben Jonson; but his comedies were satirical, and the satire was directed against follies not confined to any one time or place. In these plays, in other words, Jonson aimed directly at the criticism of life for "the correction of manners." From his study of classical literature he had derived his conception of comedy as something which could be "throughout pleasant and ridiculous" and yet should stick close to real life and serve a useful purpose.

Jonson had been apprenticed to his stepfather's trade of bricklaying, but had come under the influence of William Camden, antiquarian, classical scholar, and Headmaster of Westminster School. With Camden's help Jonson had acquired a wide and close knowledge of Greek and Latin literature, which enabled him to take a critical view of Elizabethan drama and poetry. He reacted strongly against Elizabethan exuberance, extravagance, facility, and fancifulness, and tried by his own example to show the way to a more controlled and mature literary art. His classical "missionary work" came at a fortunate time, for by 1600 Elizabethan high spirits were evidently beginning to fail. Moreover, though Jonson was arrogant and fierce, he had good sense and real talent. It was he who said that classical writers should be accepted as guides, not commanders; and he had no notion of leading to

an imitation classical literature, but aimed at something very different, assimilation of the foreign thing and growth through it.

Jonson wrote not only satirical comedies, but tragedies, and many poems after classical models. He was also the great master of that courtly and elaborate form of entertainment called the masque, in which spoken dialogue, song, and dancing were mingled. The masques were performed not only with expensive costumes, but with magnificent scenery and other stage devices, mostly designed by Inigo Jones, a great architect; and it is from these performances that the painted scenes of the modern stage are descended.

Ben Jonson was one of the earliest all-round professional men of letters in England. His whole life was centered in the cause of literature, and he gained among writers of his time a position of leadership comparable to that attained much later by Samuel Johnson. His influence among the lyric poets of the first half of the seventeenth century is shown by the fact that a definite school of followers learned his classical lessons and wrote the most finely controlled and exquisitely designed lyrics in the language. Among this "tribe of Ben" were Randolph, Carew, Lovelace, Suckling, Waller, and—the best of them—Robert Herrick.

## JOHN DONNE

Jonson was not the only one who reacted critically against Elizabethan literature at the end of the sixteenth century, or who attracted a following among later writers. The poetry of the first half of the seventeenth century can be roughly classified as of three kinds—a sign that culture as well as society was now fast losing its unity. First, there were a number of poetic followers of Spenser, including the brothers Giles and Phineas Fletcher, George Wither, and William Browne of Tavistock. The other two schools had far more vitality and are of much greater importance—the school of Jonson and the school of John Donne.

Donne reacted against the "sugared sweetness" of Elizabethan love poetry, against what had come to be the conventional praise of ladies as models of constancy, purity, and all other virtues, and as surpassingly beautiful. Like Jonson, he wanted to bring literature down to earth and reality, but his method was more simply and purely a *reaction* than was Jonson's. Since he found Elizabethan love-poems diffuse, obvious, cloyingly sweet, false in their "idealistic" pictures of womankind and in their pretense that love was purely spiritual, he would write poems about love in a completely opposite style. Hence his poems tend to be crabbed, compressed, hard to understand, sometimes bitter, sometimes cynical, realistic in the modern sense, and seemingly contradictory. Donne had in him as a young man a good deal of that impudent desire to shock conventional people which was to reappear in English literature in the 1890's. But he had also a kind of dark intensity of feeling, and a wretched sense that love was really at one and the same time both a devil and a saint; hence his poems express an inward struggle and a strange uneasiness. What particularly struck readers at the time, however, was Donne's new literary style, the most remarkable feature of which was the conceit. The word is the equivalent of the Italian *concetto*, and means an ingenious, unexpected comparison or turn of thought. *Unexpected* is the most important word in this definition, and the quality which readers found most striking.

When he was forty-three, Donne became a priest of the Anglican Church, and six years later was made Dean of St. Paul's Cathedral in London. He continued to write poetry, with not much change in style, but with an appropriate change in subject. This later verse is religious and devotional. And it was this that influenced George Herbert in the style of his devotional poetry. Herbert in turn exerted an influence on Henry Vaughan; and these three, together with the Roman Catholic poet Richard Crashaw, are the best of the school of Donne—or "metaphysical" poets, as they are called.

## FRANCIS BACON

We have noticed how the first fruits of humanism in England were a sharpening of the critical sense—the awakening of the spirit of independent, fresh inquiry, which turned men away from tradition and back to sources. This is the key to the age. The new impulse was slow and fitful in its development, but at the end of the sixteenth century it acquired a new force. It reappeared not only in poetry and drama, but in religion, and also extended itself to philosophy. There it found voice in Francis Bacon.

It is important to remember that Bacon was limited like others by the conditions of his age, and inspired also by the same impulse

that others felt. What is distinctive in him is that he came into the field of philosophic thought with the mind and something of the experience of the politician engaged in managing men for their own good. He was a searcher after truth, but he tended to value truth largely for its practical uses. Bacon's vision was the improvement of man's earthly estate through the increase of exact knowledge of the physical world.

The question was just how to go about this new search for real, as against merely pretended, knowledge. Bacon had a clear understanding of the distinction between the two, as well as of the aim just set forth; he also had a profound belief in the great importance both of that distinction and of that aim. He himself never worked out a useful scientific method; his works are a mass of fragments, of great beginnings left incomplete, and of notes. But he did succeed in expressing more eloquently and impressively than anyone else the inestimable value of scientific inquiry, in words which seem prophetic of the revolution in our ways of life and in our thinking which science has progressively brought about since the seventeenth century. And in so acting as the missionary of modern science he made a deeper impression on his own age than has always been realized. Sir Thomas Browne was a delightful follower of Bacon; and the founders and early members of the Royal Society were all influenced by Bacon. He did, in short, a very great deal to turn men's minds toward science and keep them working energetically and hopefully, until at the end of the seventeenth century the new kind of inquiry gained irresistible prestige and momentum from the discoveries of Sir Isaac Newton.

## PROSE OF THE FIRST HALF OF THE SEVENTEENTH CENTURY

In the seventeenth century we find very little imaginative work in prose; the *ends* writers set before themselves are not literary. Outside of Bacon, we have Robert Burton, whose extraordinary *Anatomy of Melancholy* is, in intention, a medical treatise; and Sir Thomas Browne, whose works are antiquarian, or speculative, or ethical; and Izaak Walton, who wrote biographical sketches of his friends or of men he admired, and a treatise on fishing. If we look beyond these we encounter the succession of divines of the Anglican Church, whose treatises and sermons during the first half of the century are indeed one of the glories of English literature too much neglected —but, still, they are writings composed to serve a cause not literary.

## RELIGIOUS WRITINGS AND CONTROVERSY

The works of the divines fall into two classes: they are either, like the eloquent sermons of Donne and of Lancelot Andrewes, primarily devotional; or they are treatises in defense of Anglican Protestantism, some directed against Rome, and some against Calvinists and other kinds of Protestants who felt that the Church of England was not sufficiently reformed to be genuinely Protestant. The significant feature of these treatises, from Richard Hooker's *Of Ecclesiastical Polity* to Jeremy Taylor's *Liberty of Prophesying*, is that their writers place their reliance on human reason as the final authority man can appeal to, even in questions of religion. The Roman Catholic Church, on the other hand, held the Roman Catholic Church itself to be the final authority, while the extreme reformers believed authority to come from private inspiration. This conflict in ideologies was an early manifestation of the more serious conflict which lay ahead.

The Reformation in England and the Renaissance were not two separate movements which happened to take place at the same time. The Reformation as a return to the sources of Christianity was a movement back to the early Christian writers and thus inevitably to a revival of the otherworldly attitude of historical Christianity. The Renaissance as a return to the sources of culture, as we have seen, was a movement back to classical pre-Christian civilization. In England the two were really united into one complex movement of change; and this for some years covered up their fundamental opposition, and helped to make possible the compromise which Elizabeth maintained, through a Church which claimed to be Catholic though reformed. The more extreme Protestants under Elizabeth, however, felt strongly that the English Church still savored in its ritual and organization of "popery," and wanted thoroughly to purify it of the taint. Hence arose the term "Puritanism," which happened to stick, so that we have it yet.

There were, then, at the close of Elizabeth's reign, three main divisions of religious loyalty. Least important were the Roman Catholics, who were to play but a small part in the conflict to come. At the other extreme were the Protestant reformers, the Calvinists and Puritans who were the vanguard of the Reformation, and who hated "popery" and any compromise with it. In the middle, product of the Renaissance, was the Church of England, the characteristically English compromise, trying desperately to maintain its dominant position but beset with attacks from both of the other divisions.

The attempt to justify separation from Rome and yet hold Englishmen together in one Christian Church founded on reason might have succeeded had it had a fair chance. But it did not. James Stuart, Elizabeth's successor, was a foolish king who held that he ruled by Divine Right, and who had none of Elizabeth's ability to see what Englishmen would willingly endure. Obstinate in asserting claims to absolute arbitrary power, he inevitably succeeded in alarming many of his subjects and so encouraged the spirit of rebellion against both Church and State. His son, Charles I, added fuel to flame, and did so especially by handing the administration of the Church to Archbishop Laud, who was suspected of wanting to lead the English Church back to Rome.

The consequence, during the years from 1603 to about 1640, was that the growth of fanatical Protestant beliefs among the extreme reformers was accelerated, that Puritan grievances became combined with political grievances, and that finally open rebellion against Church and State broke out, and civil war followed. The Puritans found an able military commander in Oliver Cromwell, and through his ability won the war. They then were guilty of the cardinal blunder of beheading Charles I, in 1649, and so of making a royal martyr of him. But this was only the beginning of their troubles. They had fought against despotism. Split into factions as they were, however, they found it necessary to establish a strong form of government to preserve their union. As a result, and against his own desire, Cromwell was forced to govern England by a military dictatorship. By the time he died, in 1658, it seemed evident to most Englishmen that they had merely jumped out of the frying pan into the fire.

## JOHN MILTON

The last representative of the English Renaissance was John Milton, who grew up amid the thickening clouds and the increasing discords that led to the Civil War. As a young man he seemed wholly unconscious of the actual state of the country. He *was* conscious of his own ability, and determined to prepare himself for the writing of an heroic poem—the great crowning literary achievement which was the dream and the ambition of poets wherever Renaissance humanism penetrated. When Civil War came, however, he had no hesitation in allying himself with the Puritan cause, put aside his poetical ambition, and spent some ten years as official propagandist and as a member of Cromwell's government. During all that time he nursed his early intention, and after his years of public service, when old and blind, returned to it, to write *Paradise Lost, Paradise Regained*, and *Samson Agonistes*.

Milton acknowledged Spenser as his master, and this should be remembered and pondered, because what strikes most readers is the

great difference between the two. Yet there is no doubt that Milton did feel himself to be really indebted to Spenser, and the fact may help us to place Milton justly. He is often regarded as a lonely figure, out of relation to the highway of literary development. He was, of course, monumentally self-dependent; but he only appears isolated in his final triumphant literary activity because by the middle of the century he was the last man still trying to unite in himself discordant elements which Spenser had not so much united as simply accepted. Milton, then, was the product of Renaissance culture, and of a wonderfully complete assimilation of classical art, and of Protestant individualism. For better, for worse, what he did represents what could be done with this combination, by a man possessed of genius and an iron determination proof against every difficulty.

# John Lyly

## 1554?-1606

Of Lyly's life not much is known. He was born in either 1553 or 1554. In the spring of 1569 he entered Magdalen College, Oxford, taking his bachelor's degree in 1573 and his master's degree in 1575. In the following year he was perhaps at Cambridge; he became a master of arts of that university in 1579. In 1578 he published the book for which he is still most widely known, Euphues, the Anatomy of Wit, the immediate success of which led to the publication of a second part, Euphues and his England, in 1580. Lyly's comedies, which he produced in the years that followed, are chiefly important for the part they played in helping to affect the transition from medieval to Elizabethan drama; the best known of them are Endimion, Sapho and Phao, Campaspe, and Gallathea. In 1588 Lyly obtained a minor post in the Revels Office which he held until 1604. He sat in Parliament four times between 1589 and 1601.

Euphues is a tale, and it has been called "the earliest English novel," but this unduly stretches the meaning of "novel," for the story is slight and of secondary importance, serving really as a framework to hold together a collection of letters and moral discussions. Moreover, the content of the book as a whole is primarily a means to an end. That is to say, it was meant as a vehicle for a certain kind of style, Euphuism, as it is called, which has three chief characteristics: (1) Balanced sentences are the rule, with frequent use of antithesis and alliteration. Euphues is described, for example, as having more wit than wealth, yet more wealth than wisdom. (2) Every fact is referred to some ancient authority, usually classical. (3) Besides the profusion of classical references, Lyly's pages are filled with allusions to natural history, mostly fabulous. Shakespeare's Falstaff knew that a lion will not harm a true prince; and Lyly gathered and used an extraordinary amount of this kind of lore. Lyly's prose, in short, is extremely mannered and arti-

ficial. But Lyly was a literary pioneer; we owe it to him probably more than to any other one man that prose came to be regarded equally with verse as an artistic medium. If his style now seems merely quaint and curious, it should be remembered that Lyly was one who showed the way, and that our better standards have been made possible by the fact that later writers were able to take advantage of his successes as well as of his failures.

The best edition of Euphues: The Anatomy of Wit; Euphues & his England is that edited by Morris W. Croll and Harry Clemons (New York, 1916). The Complete Works of John Lyly, ed. R. Warwick Bond (Oxford, 1902), supplies a voluminous scholarly apparatus. For a discussion of the whole development of which Euphues is a part see George P. Krapp, The Rise of English Literary Prose (New York, 1915).

# Euphues, the Anatomy of Wit

Very pleasant for all Gentlemen to read, and most necessary to remember: wherein are contained the delights that Wit followeth in his youth by the pleasantness of Love, and the happiness he reapeth in age by the perfectness of Wisdom.

## A COOLING CARD [1] FOR PHILAUTUS AND ALL FOND LOVERS [2]

MUSING with myself, being idle, how I might be well employed, friend Philautus, I could find nothing either more fit to continue our friendship, or of greater force to dissolve our folly, than to write a remedy for that

[1] Guide; sailor's compass.
[2] A "pamphlet" written by Euphues to "bridle the overlashing affections" of his friend Philautus, "yet generally to be applied to all lovers."

which many judge past cure; for love, Philautus, with the which I have been so tormented that I have lost my time, thou so troubled that thou hast forgot reason, both so mangled with repulse, inveigled by deceit, and almost murdered by disdain, that I can neither remember our miseries without grief, nor redress our mishaps without groans. How wantonly, yea, and how willingly have we abused our golden time and misspent our gotten treasure! How curious were we to please our lady, how careless to displease our Lord! How devout in serving our goddess, how desperate in forgetting our God! Ah, my Philautus, if the wasting of our money might not dehort us, yet the wounding of our minds should deter us; if reason might nothing persuade us to wisdom, yet shame should provoke us to wit. If Lucilla[3] read this trifle, she will straight proclaim Euphues for a traitor, and, seeing me turn my tippet,[4] will either shut me out for a wrangler, or cast me off for a wiredrawer;[5] either convince me of malice in bewraying their sleights, or condemn me of mischief in arming young men against fleeting minions. And what then? Though Curio be as hot as a toast, yet Euphues is as cold as a clock;[6] though he be a cock of the game, yet Euphues is content to be craven and cry creek;[7] though Curio be old huddle, and twang *"ipse, he,"*[8] yet Euphues had rather shrink in the wetting than waste in the wearing. I know Curio to be steel to the back, standard-bearer in Venus's camp, sworn to the crew, true to the crown, knight marshal to Cupid, and heir apparent to his kingdom. But by that time that he hath eaten but one bushel of salt with[9] Lucilla, he shall taste ten quarters[10] of sorrow in his love; then shall he find for every pint of honey a gallon of gall, for every dram of pleasure an ounce of pain, for every inch of mirth an ell of moan. And yet, Philautus, if there be any man in despair to obtain his purpose, or so obstinate in his

opinion that, having lost his freedom by folly, would also lose his life for love, let him repair hither, and he shall reap such profit as will either quench his flames or assuage his fury; either cause him to renounce his lady as most pernicious, or redeem his liberty as most precious. Come, therefore, to me, all ye lovers that have been deceived by fancy, the glass of pestilence, or deluded by women, the gate to perdition; be as earnest to seek a medicine as you were eager to run into a mischief; the earth bringeth forth as well endive to delight the people as hemlock to endanger the patient; as well the rose to distill as the nettle to sting; as well the bee to give honey as the spider to yield poison.

If my lewd life, gentlemen, have given you offense, let my good counsel make amends; if by my folly any be allured to lust, let them by my repentance be drawn to continency. Achilles's spear could as well heal as hurt; the Scorpion, though he sting, yet he stints the pain; though the herb Nerius poison the sheep, yet is it a remedy to man against poison; though I have infected some by example, yet I hope I shall comfort many by repentance. Whatsoever I speak to men, the same also I speak to women; I mean not to run with the hare and hold with the hound, to carry fire in the one hand and water in the other; neither to flatter men as altogether faultless, neither to fall out with women as altogether guilty; for, as I am not minded to pick a thank with the one, so am I not determined to pick a quarrel with the other; if women be not perverse, they shall reap profit by remedy of pleasure. If Phyllis were now to take counsel, she would not be so foolish to hang herself, neither Dido so fond to die for Aeneas, neither Pasiphaë so monstrous to love a bull, nor Phedra so unnatural to be enamored of her son.

This is, therefore, to admonish all young imps and novices in love not to blow the coals of fancy with desire, but to quench them with disdain. When love tickleth thee, decline it, lest it stifle thee; rather fast than surfeit; rather starve than strive to exceed. Though the beginning of love bring delight, the end bringeth destruction. For, as the first draught of wine doth comfort the stomach, the second inflame the liver, the third fume into the head, so the first sip of love is pleasant, the second perilous, the third pestilent. If thou perceive thyself to be enticed with their wanton glances or allured with their wicked guiles, either enchanted with

---

[3] Lucilla was betrothed to Philautus, but, when she saw Euphues, fell in love with him, he returning her love. This broke the friendship of Euphues and Philautus; but a little later Lucilla fell in love anew with one Curio and married him, whereupon Euphues and Philautus renewed their friendship.

[4] Proverbial expression meaning to change sides.

[5] An over-precise person.

[6] As free from passion as a machine.

[7] Confess himself beaten.

[8] Though Curio be embraced as her loved one and sing "I am the man."

[9] Seen a great deal of.

[10] There are eight bushels to the quarter.

their beauty or enamored with their bravery, enter with thyself into this meditation: What shall I gain if I obtain my purpose? nay, rather, what shall I lose in winning my pleasure? If my lady yield to be my lover, is it not likely she will be another's leman? and if she be a modest matron, my labor is lost. This, therefore, remaineth, that either I must pine in cares or perish with curses.

If she be chaste, then is she coy; if light, then is she impudent; if a grave matron, who can woo her? if a lewd minion, who would wed her? if one of the Vestal Virgins, they have vowed virginity; if one of Venus's court, they have vowed dishonesty. If I love one that is fair, it will kindle jealousy; if one that is foul, it will convert me into frenzy. If fertile to bear children, my care is increased; if barren, my curse is augmented; if honest, I shall fear her death; if immodest, I shall be weary of her life.

To what end, then, shall I live in love, seeing always it is life more to be feared than death? for all my time wasted in sighs and worn in sobs, for all my treasure spent on jewels and spilled in jollity, what recompense shall I reap besides repentance? What other reward shall I have than reproach? What other solace than endless shame? But haply thou wilt say, "If I refuse their courtesy I shall be accounted a mecock,[11] a milksop, taunted and retaunted with check and checkmate, flouted and reflouted with intolerable glee."

Alas, fond fool, art thou so pinned to their sleeves that thou regardest more their babble than thine own bliss, more their frumps than thine own welfare? Wilt thou resemble the kind spaniel,[12] which, the more he is beaten the fonder he is, or the foolish eyas,[13] which will never away? Dost thou not know that women deem none valiant unless he be too venturous?—that they account one a dastard if he be not desperate, a pinch-penny if he be not prodigal; if silent, a sot, if full of words, a fool? Perversely do they always think of their lovers and talk of them scornfully, judging all to be clowns[14] which be no courtiers, and all to be pinglers[15] that be not coursers.

Seeing therefore the very blossom of love is sour, the bud cannot be sweet. In time prevent danger, lest untimely thou run into a thousand perils. Search the wound while it is green; too late cometh the salve when the sore festereth, and the medicine bringeth double care when the malady is past cure.

Beware of delays. What less than the grain of mustard seed?—in time, almost what thing is greater than the stalk thereof? The slender twig groweth to a stately tree, and that which with the hand might easily have been pulled up will hardly with the ax be hewn down. The least spark, if it be not quenched, will burst into a flame; the least moth in time eateth the thickest cloth; and I have read that, in a short space, there was a town in Spain undermined with conies, in Thessaly with moles, with frogs in France, in Africa with flies. If these silly worms in tract of time overthrow so stately towns, how much more will love, which creepeth secretly into the mind (as the rust doth into the iron and is not perceived), consume the body, yea, and confound the soul. Defer not from hour to day, from day to month, from month to year, and always remain in misery.

He that to-day is not willing will tomorrow be more willful. But, alas, it is no less common than lamentable to behold the tottering estate of lovers, who think by delays to prevent dangers, with oil to quench fire, with smoke to clear the eyesight. They flatter themselves with a feinting farewell, deferring ever until to-morrow, when as their morrow doth always increase their sorrow. Let neither their amiable countenances, neither their painted protestations, neither their deceitful promises, allure thee to delays. Think this with thyself, that the sweet songs of Calypso were subtle snares to entice Ulysses; that the crab then catcheth the oyster when the sun shineth; that hyena, when she speaketh like a man, deviseth most mischief; that women when they be most pleasant pretend most treachery.

Follow Alexander, which, hearing the commendation and singular comeliness of the wife of Darius, so courageously withstood the assaults of fancy that he would not so much as take a view of her beauty. Imitate Cyrus, a king endued with such continency that he loathed to look on the heavenly hue of Panthea; and, when Araspus told him that she excelled all mortal wights in amiable show, "By so much the more," said Cyrus, "I ought to abstain from her sight; for if I follow thy counsel in going to her, it may be I shall desire to continue with her, and by my light affection neglect my serious affairs." Learn of Romulus to refrain from wine, be

---

[11] A tame-spirited man.    [12] True-bred spaniel.
[13] Nestling or unfledged bird.    [14] Peasants.
[15] Loiterers.

it never so delicate; of Agesilaus to despise costly apparel, be it never so curious; of Diogenes to detest women, be they never so comely. He that toucheth pitch shall be defiled; the sore eye infecteth the sound; the society with women breedeth security in the soul, and maketh all the senses senseless. Moreover, take this counsel as an article of thy creed, which I mean to follow as the chief argument of my faith, that idleness is 10 the only nurse and nourisher of sensual appetite, the sole maintenance of youthful affection, the first shaft that Cupid shooteth into the hot liver of a heedless lover. I would to God I were not able to find this for a truth by mine own trial, and I would the example of others' idleness had caused me rather to avoid that fault than experience of mine own folly. How dissolute have I been in striving against good counsel, how resolute in stand- 20 ing in mine own conceit, how forward to wickedness, how wanton with too much cockering,[16] how wayward in hearing correction! Neither was I much unlike these abbey lubbers in my life (though far unlike them in belief) which labored till they were cold, ate till they sweat, and lay in bed till their bones ached. Hereof cometh it, gentlemen, that love creepeth into the mind of privy craft, and keepeth this hold by main courage. 30

The man being idle, the mind is apt to all uncleanness; the mind being void of exercise, the man is void of honesty. Doth not the rust fret [17] the hardest iron if it be not used? Doth not the moth eat the finest garment if it be not worn? Doth not moss grow on the smoothest stone if it be not stirred? Doth not impiety infect the wisest if it be given to idleness? Is not the standing water sooner frozen than the running stream? Is 40 not he that sitteth more subject to sleep than he that walketh? Doth not common experience make this common unto us, that the fattest ground bringeth forth nothing but weeds if it be not well tilled, that the sharpest wit inclineth only to wickedness if it be not exercised? Is it not true which Seneca reporteth, that as too much bending breaketh the bow, so too much remission spoileth the mind? Besides this, immoderate sleep, im- 50 modest play, unsatiable swilling of wine doth so weaken the senses and bewitch the soul that, before we feel the motion of love, we are resolved into lust. Eschew idleness, my Philautus, so shalt thou easily unbend the

bow and quench the brands of Cupid. Love gives place to labor; labor, and thou shalt never love. Cupid is a crafty child, following those at an inch [18] that study pleasure, and flying those swiftly that take pains. Bend thy mind to the law, whereby thou mayest have understanding of old and ancient customs; defend thy clients; enrich thy coffers; and carry credit in thy country. If law seem loathsome unto thee, search the secrets of physic, whereby thou mayest know the hidden natures of herbs; whereby thou mayest gather profit to thy purse and pleasure to thy mind. What can be more exquisite in human affairs than for every fever, be it never so hot, for every palsy, be it never so cold, for every infection, be it never so strange, to give a remedy? The old verse standeth as yet in his old virtue: That Galen giveth goods, Justinian honors. If thou be so nice that thou canst no way brook the practice of physic, or so unwise that thou wilt not beat thy brains about the institutes of the law, confer all thy study, all thy time, all thy treasure to the attaining of the sacred and sincere knowledge of divinity; by this mayest thou bridle thine incontinency, rein thine affections, restrain thy lust. Here shalt thou behold, as it were in a glass, that all the glory of man is as the grass; that all things under heaven are but vain; that our life is but a shadow, a warfare, a pilgrimage, a vapor, a bubble, a blast; of such shortness that David saith it is but a span long; of such sharpness that Job noteth it replenished with all miseries; of such uncertainty that we are no sooner born but we are subject to death; the one foot no sooner on the ground but the other ready to slip into the grave. Here shalt thou find ease for thy burden of sin, comfort for the conscience pined with vanity, mercy for thine offenses by the martyrdom of thy sweet Savior. By this thou shalt be able to instruct those that be weak, to confute those that be obstinate, to confound those that be erroneous, to confirm the faithful, to comfort the desperate, to cut off the presumptuous, to save thine own soul by thy sure faith, and edify the hearts of many by thy sound doctrine. If this seem too strait a diet for thy straining disease,[19] or too holy a profession for so hollow a person, then employ thyself to martial feats, to jousts, to tourneys, yea, to all torments, rather than to loiter in love and spend thy life in the laps of ladies; what more monstrous can there be than

---

[16] Coddling.　　　　[17] Eat.　　　　[18] Close behind.　　　　[19] Craving for freedom.

to see a young man abuse those gifts to his own shame which God hath given him for his own preferment? What greater infamy than to confer the sharp wit to the making of lewd sonnets, to the idolatrous worshiping of their ladies, to the vain delights of fancy, to all kind of vice, as it were against kind and course of nature? Is it not folly to show wit to women, which are neither able nor willing to receive fruit thereof? Dost thou not know that the tree Silvacenda beareth no fruit in Pharos? [20] That the Persian trees in Rhodes do only wax green but never bring forth apple? [21]

That amomus and nardus will only grow in India, balsamum only in Syria; that in Rhodes no eagle will build her nest, no owl live in Crete, no wit spring in the will of women? Mortify, therefore, thy affections, and force not nature against nature to strive in vain. Go into the country, look to thy grounds, yoke thine oxen, follow thy plow, graft thy trees, behold thy cattle, and devise with thyself how the increase of them may increase thy profit. In autumn pull thine apples, in summer ply thy harvest, in the spring trim thy gardens, in the winter, thy woods, and thus, beginning to delight to be a good husband,[22] thou shalt begin to detest to be in love with an idle housewife; when profit shall begin to fill thy purse with gold, then pleasure shall have no force to defile thy mind with love. For honest recreation after thy toil, use hunting or hawking; either rouse the deer, or unperch the pheasant; so shalt thou root out the remembrance of thy former love, and repent thee of thy foolish lust. And, although thy sweetheart bind thee by oath always to hold a candle at her shrine, and to offer thy devotion to thine own destruction, yet go, run, fly into the country; neither water thou thy plants, in that thou departest from thy pigsny,[23] neither stand in a mammering [24] whether it be best to depart or not; but how much the more thou art unwilling to go, by so much the more hasten thy steps, neither feign for thyself any sleeveless excuse whereby thou mayest tarry. Neither let rain nor thunder, neither lightning nor tempest, stay thy journey; and reckon not with thyself how many miles thou hast gone

—that showeth weariness; but how many thou hast to go—that proveth manliness. But foolish and frantic lovers will deem my precepts hard, and esteem my persuasions haggard;[25] I must of force confess that it is a corrosive to the stomach of a lover, but a comfort to a godly liver to run through a thousand pikes [26] to escape ten thousand perils. Sour potions bring sound health; sharp purgations make short diseases; and the medicine, the more bitter it is, the more better it is in working. To heal the body we try physic, search cunning, prove sorcery, venture through fire and water, leaving nothing unsought that may be gotten for money, be it never so much or procured by any means, be they never so unlawful. How much more ought we to hazard all things for the safeguard of mind, and quiet of conscience! And, certes, easier will the remedy be when the reason is espied; do you not know the nature of women, which is grounded only upon extremities?

Do they think any man to delight in them unless he dote on them? Any to be zealous except they be jealous? Any to be fervent in case he be not furious? If he be cleanly, then term they him proud; if mean in apparel, a sloven; if tall, a longis; if short, a dwarf; if bold, blunt; if shamefaced, a coward; insomuch as they have neither mean in their frumps, nor measure in their folly. But at the first the ox wieldeth not the yoke, nor the colt the snaffle, nor the lover good counsel; yet time causeth the one to bend his neck, the other to open his mouth, and should enforce the third to yield his right to reason. Lay before thine eyes the slights and deceits of thy lady, her snatching in jest and keeping in earnest, her perjury, her impiety, the countenance she showeth to thee of course,[27] the love she beareth to others of zeal, her open malice, her dissembled mischief.

O, I would in repeating their vices thou couldst be as eloquent as in remembering them thou oughtst to be penitent! Be she never so comely, call her counterfeit; be she never so straight, think her crooked. And wrest all parts of her body to the worst, be she never so worthy. If she be well set, then call her a boss; if slender, a hazel twig; if nutbrown, as black as a coal; if well colored, a painted wall; if she be pleasant, then is she a wanton; if sullen, a clown; if honest, then is she coy; if impudent, a harlot.

Search every vein and sinew of their dispo-

---

[20] The island near Alexandria on which Ptolemy I built a lighthouse.

[21] Lyly has in mind Pliny's statement (*Natural History*, xvi, 58) that in general trees do not bear except where they are indigenous.

[22] Husbandman.    [23] Thy loved one.

[24] Hesitation.

[25] Wild? A haggard is a wild hawk.

[26] Rocks.    [27] Outwardly.

sition; if she have no sight in descant,[28] desire her to chant it; if no cunning to dance, request her to trip it; if no skill in music, proffer her the lute; if an ill gait, then walk with her; if rude in speech, talk with her; if she be jag-toothed, tell her some merry jest to make her laugh; if pink-eyed, some doleful history to cause her weep: in the one her grinning will show her deformed; in the other her whining, like a pig half roasted.

It is a world to see how commonly we are blinded with the collusions of women, and more enticed by their ornaments being artificial than their proportion being natural. I loathe almost to think on their ointments and apothecary drugs, the sleeking of their faces, and all their slibber [29] sauces which bring queasiness to the stomach and disquiet to the mind.

Take from them their periwigs, their paintings, their jewels, their rolls, their bolsterings, and thou shalt soon perceive that a woman is the least part of herself. When they be once robbed of their robes, then will they appear so odious, so ugly, so monstrous, that thou wilt rather think them serpents than saints; and so like hags that thou wilt fear rather to be enchanted than enamored. Look in their closets, and there shalt thou find an apothecary's shop of sweet confections, a surgeon's box of sundry salves, a pedlar's pack of new fangles. Besides all this, their shadows,[30] their spots,[31] their lawns, their lyfkies,[32] their ruffs, their rings, show them rather cardinals' courtesans than modest matrons, and more carnally affected than moved in conscience. If every one of these things severally be not of force to move thee, yet all of them jointly shall mortify thee.

Moreover, to make thee the more stronger to strive against these sirens, and more subtle to deceive these tame serpents, my counsel is that thou have more strings to thy bow than one; it is safe riding at two anchors; a fire divided in twain burneth slower; a fountain running into many rivers is of less force; the mind enamored on two women is less affected with desire and less infected with despair: one love expelleth another, and the remembrance of the latter quencheth the concupiscence of the first.

Yet, if thou be so weak, being bewitched with their wiles that thou hast neither will to eschew nor wit to avoid their company, if thou be either so wicked that thou wilt not, or so wedded that thou canst not abstain from their glances, yet at the least dissemble thy grief. If thou be as hot as the mount Etna, feign thyself as cold as the hill Caucasus; carry two faces in one hood; cover thy flaming fancy with feigned ashes; show thyself sound when thou art rotten; let thy hue be merry when thy heart is melancholy; bear a pleasant countenance with a pined [33] conscience, a painted sheath with a leaden dagger.[34] Thus, dissembling thy grief, thou mayest recure thy disease. Love creepeth in by stealth, and by stealth slideth away.

If she break promise with thee in the night, or absent herself in the day, seem thou careless, and then will she be careful; if thou languish, then will she be lavish of her honor, yea, and of the other strange beast, her honesty. Stand thou on thy pantofles,[35] and she will veil bonnet. Lie thou aloof, and she will seize on the lure; if thou pass by her door and be called back, either seem deaf and not to hear, or desperate, and not to care. Fly the places, the parlors, the portals wherein thou hast been conversant with thy lady; yea, Philautus, shun the street where Lucilla doth dwell, lest the sight of her window renew the sum of thy sorrow.

Yet, although I would have thee precise in keeping these precepts, yet would I have thee to avoid solitariness—that breeds melancholy; melancholy, madness; madness, mischief and utter desolation. Have ever some faithful fere [36] with whom thou mayest communicate thy counsels: some Pylades to encourage Orestes, some Damon to release Pythias, some Scipio to recure [37] Laelius. Phyllis in wandering the woods hanged herself; Asiarchus, forsaking company, spoiled himself with his own bodkin; [38] Biarus, a Roman, more wise than fortunate, being alone, destroyed himself with a potsherd. Beware solitariness. But, although I would have thee use company for thy recreation, yet would I have thee always to leave the company of those that accompany thy lady; yea, if she have any jewel of thine in her custody, rather lose it than go for it, lest in seeking to recover a trifle thou renew thine old trouble. Be not curious to curl thy hair, nor careful to be neat in thine apparel; be not prodigal of thy gold nor precise in thy going; be not like the Englishman, which preferreth every strange

---

[28] No knowledge of musical harmony.
[29] Dirty.
[30] Borders attached to bonnets to shield complexion.
[31] Patches.          [32] Bodices.

[33] Tortured.
[34] A proverbial expression for false appearances.
[35] A proverbial expression for pride.
[36] Comrade.      [37] Recover.      [38] Small dagger.

fashion before the use of his country; be thou dissolute,[39] lest thy lady think thee foolish in framing thyself to every fashion for her sake. Believe not their oaths and solemn protestations, their exorcisms and conjurations, their tears which they have at commandment, their alluring looks, their treading on the toe, their unsavory toys.

Let every one loathe his lady and be ashamed to be her servant. It is riches and ease that nourisheth affection; it is play, wine, and wantonness that feedeth a lover as fat as a fool; refrain from all such meats as shall provoke thine appetite to lust, and all such means as may allure thy mind to folly. Take clear water for strong wine, brown bread for fine manchet,[40] beef and brewis [41] for quails and partridge; for ease, labor; for pleasure, pain; for surfeiting, hunger; for sleep, watching; for the fellowship of ladies, the company of philosophers. If thou say to me, "Physician,

heal thyself," I answer that I am meetly well purged of that disease; and yet was I never more willing to cure myself than to comfort my friend. And, seeing the cause that made in me so cold a devotion should make in thee also as frozen a desire, I hope thou wilt be as ready to provide a salve as thou wast hasty in seeking a sore. And yet, Philautus, I would not that all women should take pepper in the nose,[42] in that I have disclosed the legerdemains of a few, for well I know none will wince unless she be galled, neither any be offended unless she be guilty. Therefore I earnestly desire thee that thou show this cooling card to none except thou show also this my defense to them all. For, although I weigh nothing the ill will of light housewives, yet would I be loath to lose the good will of honest matrons. Thus, being ready to go to Athens, and ready there to entertain thee whensoever thou shalt repair thither, I bid thee farewell, and fly women.

Thine ever,

Euphues.

---

[39] Disheveled.  
[40] The finest white bread.  
[41] Broth obtained from boiling salted beef.  
[42] Take offense.

# Christopher Marlowe

## 1564 - 1593

Marlowe was born at Canterbury in February, 1564. His father belonged to the shoemakers' and tanners' guild of the town. In 1579 the boy entered the King's School at Canterbury, and two years later passed thence to Corpus Christi College, Cambridge. He was graduated B. A. in 1584, M. A. in 1587. While at the King's School he had held a scholarship, and during his Cambridge years he held another—one created in 1575 by the will of Archbishop Matthew Parker. After 1584 his periods of residence at the University were much broken, and in the spring of 1587 his absence apparently gave opportunity for the spread of damaging rumors concerning him, which threatened to prevent his receiving his higher degree. He seems to have been in reality engaged in some secret governmental service on the Continent, and he obtained his degree as a consequence of the intervention of the Privy Council. His retention of his scholarship for six years implied the intention of taking orders in the Anglican Church; it has been inferred that his failure to do so was the result of "the growth of his speculative views" (F. S. Boas, Marlowe and his Circle). At all events, he went from Cambridge to London, and at once began writing for the theaters, chiefly for the Lord Admiral's Company. On 18 September, 1589, he engaged in a duel with a certain William Bradley, whom a friend of Marlowe's, joining the fight, proceeded to slay; Marlowe, after being imprisoned and then released on bond, was finally cleared of the charge of murder. Three years later, at the petition of two constables, he was bound over to keep the peace. In May, 1593, he was summoned before the Privy Council, but before the month was out he lay murdered in a Deptford tavern. He had gone thither on 30 May with three companions, Ingram Frizer, Nicholas Skeres, and Robert Poley. The four had spent most of the day in the tavern of Eleanor Bull, and in the evening Frizer and Marlowe had begun to quarrel over the payment of the reckoning. Marlowe, in sudden anger, had seized Frizer's dagger and inflicted two wounds on his head; whereupon the latter, struggling with Marlowe, had managed to get back his dagger and had given Marlowe a mortal wound over his right eye, causing instant death. This is the account returned by the coroner's jury of sixteen men, and there is no good reason to doubt its substantial accuracy. Frizer was soon pardoned on the ground that he had acted in self-defense, and he survived—a churchwarden during his last twenty-two years—until August, 1627.

Marlowe's Tamburlaine, Part I, was performed in 1587, Doctor Faustus at some time between 1588 and 1592, and The Jew of Malta in 1589. In these three plays and in Tamburlaine, Part II, and Edward II he wrote such poetry as England had not before known. To a lofty and intense imagination he united a command of language and a skill in versification which put him easily above the other dramatists who preceded Shakespeare. He wrote his plays in blank verse, and with such mastery that he established it as the verse of Elizabethan tragedy. And in the pictures he drew, in Tamburlaine of the craving for universal political power, in Doctor Faustus of the craving for unlimited power got through knowledge, and in The Jew of Malta of the craving for boundless wealth, he exhibited an important—if not indeed the central—aspect of the Renaissance, with its sudden accession of unbounded confidence in human capacity and its corresponding expansion of desires. In so doing he seems, it is true, to be curiously remote from the ways and life of his time—but this is a mere deceptive appearance. "The Elizabethan world is never photographed or portrayed in his works; but its ideas and aspirations find nowhere a truer revelation; none of his contemporaries reflect its spirit, its desires and efforts better than he. A simple instance of such transmutation comes to mind. To us, *looking back over 300 years, one of the most significant series of events in that age is the vast enterprise which inspired and organized the voyages of discovery. . . . The wonders and highly-colored fantasies reported by the voyagers appealed to the credulity of poets and public alike; Shakespeare clothes with concrete forms the marvels of the Bermudas. But if we turn back to the year 1593 when much of this was already current, Marlowe has little to tell us of the wonders and marvels, of dogheaded men and the sun coming up like thunder out of the far East. . . . Yet this is not the whole truth."* For *"deep in Marlowe's mind lay certain memories, the impressions left by those Westward voyages."* Witness the dying words of Mortimer in *Edward II*:

> Weep not for Mortimer
> That scorns the world, and as a traveler
> Goes to discover countries yet unknown.

*"The lives and deaths of the voyagers had made no emotional—far less any sentimental—appeal to him. But they had remained an image of eternal forth-faring."* And in fact *"Marlowe is, of all Elizabethans, the truest explorer. His career is a long voyage of discovery; his America is always just beyond the horizon. He endeavors, blindly and passionately at first, later with more sureness and clarity, to map new territory; new thought, and truths ascertained by thought; new dreams, visions and ecstasies created by the imagination"* (U. M. Ellis-Fermor, *Marlowe*).

The Works and Life of Christopher Marlowe, ed. R. H. Case (London, 1930–1933), is the best edition; it contains a concise life of Marlowe, by C. F. Tucker Brooke, in vol. I, and Faustus, ed. Frederick S. Boas, in vol. V. A revision of this edition is in progress; the first volume of the revision to appear was Edward II (1955). Dr. Faustus has been edited in parallel texts (1604 and 1616) by Sir W. W. Greg (Oxford, 1950); see also Tragical History of the Life and Death of Dr. Faustus: a Conjectural Reconstruction, by Sir W. W. Greg (Oxford, 1950). There have been many recent interpretative and biographical works, including Marlowe: A Biographical and Critical Study, by F. S. Boas (Oxford, 1953); The Tragical History of Marlowe, by John Bakeless (Cambridge, U. S. A., 1942); and The Overreacher: a Study of Marlowe, by Harry Levin (Cambridge, U. S. A., 1952). For the dramatic background see Edmund K. Chambers, The Elizabethan Stage (Oxford, 1923); for the intellectual background, Hardin Craig, The Enchanted Glass; the Elizabethan Mind in Literature (*New York*, 1936).

# The Tragical History of Doctor Faustus [1]

## DRAMATIS PERSONAE

| | |
|---|---|
| THE POPE. | SCHOLARS, FRIARS, |
| CARDINAL OF LOR- | and ATTENDANTS. |
| RAIN. | DUCHESS OF VAN- |
| THE EMPEROR OF | HOLT. |
| GERMANY. | LUCIFER. |
| DUKE OF VANHOLT. | BELZEBUB. |
| FAUSTUS. | MEPHISTOPHILIS. |
| VALDES and | GOOD ANGEL. |
| CORNELIUS, friends | EVIL ANGEL. |
| to Faustus. | THE SEVEN DEADLY |
| WAGNER, servant to | SINS. |
| Faustus. | DEVILS. |
| CLOWN. | SPIRITS in the shapes |
| ROBIN. | of Alexander the |
| RALPH. | Great, of his Par- |
| VINTNER. | amour, and of |
| HORSE-COURSER. | Helen. |
| A KNIGHT. | CHORUS. |
| AN OLD MAN. | |

*Enter* CHORUS.

CHORUS. Not marching now in fields of Thrasymene,
Where Mars did mate [2] the Carthaginians;
Nor sporting in the dalliance of love,
In courts of kings where state is overturned;
Nor in the pomp of proud audacious deeds, 5
Intends our Muse to vaunt her heavenly verse:
Only this, gentlemen,—we must perform
The form of Faustus' fortunes, good or bad:
To patient judgments we appeal our plaud,
And speak for Faustus in his infancy.    10
Now is he born, his parents base of stock,
In Germany, within a town called Rhodes: [3]
Of riper years, to Wertenberg he went,

---

[1] The earliest edition of *Doctor Faustus* extant is the quarto of 1604, on which the present reprint is based. In 1616 and in 1663 appeared versions which differ widely from the text of 1604, but the generally accepted opinion is that the earliest version of the play is the one nearest to what Marlowe wrote. The German *Faustbuch*, as it is usually called, in which the legend of Faustus first appeared in print, was published at Frankfurt in 1587. It instantly attained wide popularity, and from it Marlowe drew the material for his play. There is difficulty in the question whether he used the German book or had access to a manuscript translation (the English translation was apparently not printed before 1590 at the earliest); the latter supposition, however, is the more probable one.

[2] Pit himself against.

[3] Roda, not far from Jena.

Whereas his kinsmen chiefly brought him up.
So soon he profits in divinity,                    15
The fruitful plot of scholarism graced,[4]
That shortly he was graced [5] with doctor's
    name,
Excelling all whose sweet delight disputes
In heavenly matters of theology;
Till swol'n with cunning,[6] of a self-conceit,
His waxen wings did mount above his
    reach,                                          21
And, melting, heavens conspired his over-
    throw; [7]
For, falling to a devilish exercise,
And glutted now with learning's golden gifts,
He surfeits upon curséd necromancy;                25
Nothing so sweet as magic is to him,
Which he prefers before his chiefest bliss:
And this the man that in his study sits.
                                   [*Exit.*

FAUSTUS *discovered in his study.*

FAUST. Settle thy studies, Faustus, and begin
    To sound the depth of that thou wilt pro-
    fess: [8]                                       30
Having commenced, be a divine in show,
Yet level [9] at the end of every art,
And live and die in Aristotle's works.
Sweet Analytics,[10] 'tis thou hast ravished me!
*Bene disserere est finis logices.*[11]            35
Is to dispute well logic's chiefest end?
Affords this art no greater miracle?
Then read no more; thou hast attained the
    end:
A greater subject fitteth Faustus' wit:
Bid *ὸν καὶ μὴ ὄν* [12] farewell; Galen come,    40
Seeing, *Ubi desinit philosophus, ibi incipit
    medicus:* [13]
Be a physician, Faustus; heap up gold,
And be eternized for some wondrous cure:
*Summum bonum medicinae sanitas,*[14]
The end of physic is our body's health.            45
Why, Faustus, hast thou not attained that
    end?
Is not thy common talk sound aphorisms?
Are not thy bills [15] hung up as monuments,
Whereby whole cities have escaped the
    plague,
And thousand desperate maladies been
    eased?                                          50
Yet art thou still but Faustus, and a man.
Wouldst thou make men to live eternally,

Or, being dead, raise them to life again,
Then this profession were to be esteemed.
Physic, farewell! Where is Justinian?              55
                                  [*Reads.*
*Si una eademque res legatur duobus, alter
    rem, alter valorem rei, etc.*[16]
A pretty case of paltry legacies!      [*Reads.*
*Exhaereditare filium non potest pater, nisi,
    etc.*[17]
Such is the subject of the institute,
And universal body of the law:                     60
His [18] study fits a mercenary drudge,
Who aims at nothing but external trash;
Too servile and illiberal for me.
When all is done, divinity is best:
Jerome's Bible,[19] Faustus, view it well.         65
                                  [*Reads.*
*Stipendium peccati mors est.* Ha! *Stipen-
    dium, etc.*
The reward of sin is death: that's hard.
                                  [*Reads.*
*Si peccasse negamus, fallimur, et nulla est in
    nobis veritas;*
If we say that we have no sin, we deceive
    ourselves, and there's no truth in us. Why,
    then, belike we must sin, and so conse-
    quently die:                                    72
Ay, we must die an everlasting death.
What doctrine call you this, *Che sera, sera,*
What will be, shall be? Divinity, adieu!           75
These metaphysics of magicians,
And necromantic books are heavenly;
Lines, circles, scenes, letters, and characters;
Ay, these are those that Faustus most desires.
O, what a world of profit and delight,             80
Of power, of honor, of omnipotence,
Is promised to the studious artisan!
All things that move between the quiet poles
Shall be at my command: emperors and
    kings
Are but obeyed in their several provinces, 85
Nor can they raise the wind, or rend the
    clouds;
But his dominion that exceeds in this,
Stretcheth as far as doth the mind of man;
A sound magician is a mighty god:
Here, Faustus, try thy brains to gain a
    deity.                                          90

*Enter* WAGNER.

Wagner, commend me to my dearest friends,
The German Valdes and Cornelius;
Request them earnestly to visit me.
WAG. I will, sir.                       [*Exit.*
FAUST. Their conference will be a greater help
    to me                                           95
Than all my labors, plod I ne'er so fast.

---

[4] I. e., gracing.      [5] Took his degree.
[6] Knowledge.
[7] Like Icarus who flew too near the sun.
[8] Teach.      [9] Aim.      [10] Logic.
[11] To argue well is the end of logic.
[12] Being and not being (an Aristotelian phrase).
[13] Where the philosopher leaves off the physician
begins.
[14] Translated in the following line. Other passages in Latin translated in the text are left without note.
[15] Pronouncements.

[16] If one and the same thing is willed to two persons, one receives the thing, the other the value of
the thing, etc.
[17] A father cannot disinherit his son, unless, etc.
[18] Its.      [19] The Vulgate.

*Enter* GOOD ANGEL *and* EVIL ANGEL.

G. ANG. O Faustus, lay thy damnéd book aside,
And gaze not on it, lest it tempt thy soul,
And heap God's heavy wrath upon thy head!
Read, read the Scriptures:—that is blas-
    phemy.                                      100
E. ANG. Go forward, Faustus, in that famous
    art
Wherein all Nature's treas'ry is contained:
Be thou on earth as Jove is in the sky,
Lord and commander of these elements.
                              [*Exeunt* ANGELS.
FAUST. How am I glutted with conceit [20] of
    this!                                       105
Shall I make spirits fetch me what I please,
Resolve me of all ambiguities,
Perform what desperate enterprise I will?
I'll have them fly to India for gold,
Ransack the ocean for orient pearl,           110
And search all corners of the new-found
    world
For pleasant fruits and princely delicates;
I'll have them read me strange philosophy,
And tell the secrets of all foreign kings;
I'll have them wall all Germany with brass,
And make swift Rhine circle fair Werten-
    berg;                                       116
I'll have them fill the public schools with
    silk,
Wherewith the students shall be bravely
    clad;
I'll levy soldiers with the coin they bring.
And chase the Prince of Parma from our
    land,[21]                                   120
And reign sole king of all our provinces;
Yea, stranger engines for the brunt of war,
Than was the fiery keel at Antwerp's bridge,
I'll make my servile spirits to invent.

*Enter* VALDES *and* CORNELIUS.

Come, German Valdes and Cornelius,       125
And make me blest with your sage confer-
    ence.
Valdes, sweet Valdes, and Cornelius,
Know that your words have won me at the
    last
To practice magic and concealéd arts:
Yet not your words only, but mine own fan-
    tasy,                                       130
That will receive no object; for my head
But ruminates on necromantic skill.
Philosophy is odious and obscure;
Both law and physic are for petty wits;
Divinity is basest of the three,             135
Unpleasant, harsh, contemptible, and vile:
'Tis magic, magic, that hath ravished me.
Then, gentle friends, aid me in this attempt;
And I, that have with concise syllogisms
Graveled the pastors of the German Church,
And made the flowering pride of Werten-
    berg                                        141

[20] Thought.            [21] The Netherlands.

Swarm to my problems, as the infernal spirits
On sweet Musaeus when he came to hell,
Will be as cunning as Agrippa was,
Whose shadow made all Europe honor
    him.                                        145
VALD. Faustus, these books, thy wit, and our
    experience,
Shall make all nations to canonize us.
As Indian Moors [22] obey their Spanish lords,
So shall the subjects of every element
Be always serviceable to us three;           150
Like lions shall they guard us when we
    please;
Like Almain rutters [23] with their horsemen's
    staves.
Or Lapland giants, trotting by our sides;
Sometimes like women, or unwedded maids,
Shadowing more beauty in their airy brows
Than have the white breasts of the queen of
    love:                                       156
From Venice shall they drag huge argosies,
And from America the golden fleece
That yearly stuffs old Philip's treasury;
If learnéd Faustus will be resolute.          160
FAUST. Valdes, as resolute am I in this
As thou to live: therefore object it not.
CORN. The miracles that magic will perform
Will make thee vow to study nothing else.
He that is grounded in astrology,            165
Enriched with tongues, well seen [24] in min-
    erals,
Hath all the principles magic doth require:
Then doubt not, Faustus, but to be re-
    nowned,
And more frequented for this mystery
Than heretofore the Delphian oracle.       170
The spirits tell me they can dry the sea,
And fetch the treasure of all foreign wrecks,
Ay, all the wealth that our forefathers hid
Within the massy entrails of the earth:
Then tell me, Faustus, what shall we three
    want?                                       175
FAUST. Nothing, Cornelius. Oh, this cheers my
    soul!
Come, show me some demonstrations magi-
    cal,
That I may conjure in some lusty grove,
And have these joys in full possession.
VALD. Then haste thee to some solitary
    grove,                                       180
And bear wise Bacon's [25] and Albertus'
    works,
The Hebrew Psalter, and New Testament;
And whatsoever else is requisite
We will inform thee ere our conference
    cease.
CORN. Valdes, first let him know the words of
    art;                                        185
And then, all other ceremonies learned,
Faustus may try his cunning by himself.
VALD. First I'll instruct thee in the rudiments,

[22] American Indians.      [23] Troopers.
[24] Versed.                [25] Roger Bacon's.

And then wilt thou be perfecter than I.

FAUST. Then come and dine with me, and, after meat, 190

We'll canvass every quiddity [26] thereof;

For, ere I sleep, I'll try what I can do:

This night I'll conjure, though I die therefore. [*Exeunt.*

### *Enter two* SCHOLARS.

FIRST SCHOL. I wonder what's become of Faustus, that was wont to make our schools ring with *sic probo*.[27] 196

SEC. SCHOL. That shall we know, for see, here comes his boy.

### *Enter* WAGNER.

FIRST SCHOL. How now, sirrah! where's thy master? 200

WAG. God in heaven knows.

SEC. SCHOL. Why, dost not thou know?

WAG. Yes, I know; but that follows not.

FIRST SCHOL. Go to, sirrah! leave your jesting, and tell us where he is. 205

WAG. That follows not necessary by force of argument, that you, being licentiates, should stand upon; therefore acknowledge your error, and be attentive.

SEC. SCHOL. Why, didst thou not say thou knewest? 211

WAG. Have you any witness on't?

FIRST SCHOL. Yes, sirrah, I heard you.

WAG. Ask my fellow if I be a thief.

SEC. SCHOL. Well, you will not tell us? 215

WAG. Yes, sir, I will tell you; yet, if you were not dunces, you would never ask me such a question, for is not he *corpus naturale*?[28] and is not that *mobile*?[29] then wherefore should you ask me such a question? But that I am by nature phlegmatic, slow to wrath, and prone to lechery (to love, I would say), it were not for you to come within forty foot of the place of execution, although I do not doubt to see you both hanged the next sessions. Thus having triumphed over you, I will set my countenance like a precisian,[30] and begin to speak thus:—Truly, my dear brethren, my master is within at dinner, with Valdes and Cornelius, as this wine, if it could speak, it would inform your worships: and so, the Lord bless you, preserve you, and keep you, my dear brethren, my dear brethren! [*Exit.* 236

FIRST SCHOL. Nay, then, I fear he is fallen into that damned art for which they two are infamous through the world.

SEC. SCHOL. Were he a stranger, and not allied to me, yet should I grieve for him. But,

come, let us go and inform the Rector, and see if he by his grave counsel can reclaim him.

FIRST SCHOL. Oh, but I fear me nothing can reclaim him! 245

SEC. SCHOL. Yet let us try what we can do. [*Exeunt.*

### *Enter* FAUSTUS *to conjure.*

FAUST. Now that the gloomy shadow of the earth,

Longing to view Orion's drizzling look,

Leaps from th' antarctic world unto the sky,

And dims the welkin with her pitchy breath,

Faustus, begin thine incantations, 251

And try if devils will obey thy hest,

Seeing thou hast prayed and sacrificed to them.

Within this circle is Jehovah's name, 254

Forward and backward anagrammatized,

Th' abbreviated names of holy saints,

Figures of every adjunct to [31] the heavens,

And characters of signs and erring stars,[32]

By which the spirits are enforced to rise:

Then fear not, Faustus, but be resolute, 260

And try the uttermost magic can perform.—

*Sint mihi dei Acherontis propitii! Valeat numen triplex Jehovae! Ignei, aërii, aquatici spiritus, salvete! Orientis princeps Belzebub, inferni ardentis monarcha, et Demogorgon, propitiamus vos, ut appareat et surgat Mephistophilis; quid tu moraris? Per Jehovam, Gehennam, et consecratam aquam quam nuncspargo, signumque crucis quod nunc facio, et per vota nostra, ipse nunc surgat nobis dicatus Mephistophilis!* [33] 272

### *Enter* MEPHISTOPHILIS.

I charge thee to return, and change thy shape;

Thou art too ugly to attend on me:

Go, and return an old Franciscan friar; 275

That holy shape becomes a devil best.

[*Exit* MEPHISTOPHILIS.

I see there's virtue in my heavenly words:

Who would not be proficient in this art?

How pliant is this Mephistophilis,

Full of obedience and humility! 280

Such is the force of magic and my spells:

[26] Subtlety.     [27] Thus I demonstrate.

[28] Natural body.     [29] Movable.

[30] I. e., a puritan.

[31] Every star belonging to.

[32] Planets.

[33] Gods of Acheron, grant me your aid! The triple deity of Jehovah assist me! Spirits of fire, air, water, all hail! Belzebub, Prince of the East, ruler of the fiery realms, and Demogorgon, I supplicate you, that Mephistophilis may rise and appear; why do you delay? By Jehovah, Gehenna, and the holy water I now sprinkle, and the sign of the cross I now make, and by my prayer, may Mephistophilis now called by me arise!

Now, Faustus, thou art conjurer laureate,
That canst command great Mephistophilis:
*Quin regis Mephistophilis fratris imagine.*[34]

*Re-enter* MEPHISTOPHILIS *like a Franciscan friar.*

MEPH. Now, Faustus, what wouldst thou have
    me do?                                                285
FAUST. I charge thee wait upon me whilst I live,
    To do whatever Faustus shall command,
    Be it to make the moon drop from her
      sphere,
    Or the ocean to overwhelm the world.
MEPH. I am a servant to great Lucifer,          290
    And may not follow thee without his leave:
    No more than he commands must we per-
      form.
FAUST. Did not he charge thee to appear to me?
MEPH. No, I came now hither of mine own
    accord.
FAUST. Did not my conjuring speeches raise
    thee? speak.                                       295
MEPH. That was the cause, but yet *per ac-
    cidens*,[35]
    For, when we hear one rack the name of
      God,
    Abjure the Scriptures and his Saviour Christ,
    We fly, in hope to get his glorious soul;
    Nor will we come, unless he use such means,
    Whereby he is in danger to be damned.  301
    Therefore the shortest cut for conjuring
    Is stoutly to abjure the Trinity,
    And pray devoutly to the prince of hell.
FAUST. So Faustus hath                             305
    Already done; and holds this principle,
    There is no chief but only Belzebub;
    To whom Faustus doth dedicate himself.
    This word "damnation" terrifies not him,
    For he confounds hell in Elysium:       310
    His ghost be with the old philosophers!
    But, leaving these vain trifles of men's souls,
    Tell me what is that Lucifer, thy lord?
MEPH. Arch-regent and commander of all
    spirits.
FAUST. Was not that Lucifer an angel once?
MEPH. Yes, Faustus, and most dearly loved of
    God.                                                316
FAUST. How comes it, then, that he is prince
    of devils?
MEPH. Oh, by aspiring pride and insolence;
    For which God threw him from the face of
      heaven.
FAUST. And what are you that live with Lucifer?
MEPH. Unhappy spirits that fell with Luci-
    fer,                                                 321
    Conspired against our God with Lucifer,
    And are for ever damned with Lucifer.
FAUST. Where are you damned?

MEPH. In hell.                                          325
FAUST. How comes it, then, that thou are out
    of hell?
MEPH. Why, this is hell, nor am I out of it.
    Think'st thou that I, who saw the face of
      God,
    And tasted the eternal joys of heaven,
    Am not tormented with ten thousand hells,
    In being deprived of everlasting bliss?  331
    O, Faustus, leave these frivolous demands,
    Which strike a terror to my fainting soul!
FAUST. What, is great Mephistophilis so pas-
    sionate [36]
    For being deprivéd of the joys of heaven? 335
    Learn thou of Faustus manly fortitude,
    And scorn these joys thou never shalt possess.
    Go bear these tidings to great Lucifer:
    Seeing Faustus hath incurred eternal death
    By desperate thoughts against Jove's deity,
    Say, he surrenders up to him his soul,     341
    So he will spare him four-and-twenty years,
    Letting him live in all voluptuousness;
    Having thee ever to attend on me,
    To give me whatsoever I shall ask,         345
    To tell me whatsoever I demand,
    To slay mine enemies, and aid my friends,
    And always be obedient to my will.
    Go and return to mighty Lucifer,
    And meet me in my study at midnight, 350
    And then resolve me of thy master's mind.
MEPH. I will, Faustus.                          [*Exit.*
FAUST. Had I as many souls as there be stars,
    I'd give them all for Mephistophilis.
    By him I'll be great emperor of the world, 355
    And make a bridge through the moving air,
    To pass the ocean with a band of men;
    I'll join the hills that bind the Afric shore,
    And make that country continent to Spain,
    And both contributory to my crown:     360
    The Emperor shall not live but by my leave,
    Nor any potentate of Germany.
    Now that I have obtained what I desired,
    I'll live in speculation [37] of this art,
    Till Mephistophilis return again. [*Exit.* 365

*Enter* WAGNER *and* CLOWN.

WAG. Sirrah boy, come hither.
CLOWN. How, boy! swowns, boy! I hope you
    have seen many boys with such pick-
    adevaunts [38] as I have: boy, quotha!    369
WAG. Tell me, sirrah, hast thou any comings
    in?
CLOWN. Ay, and goings out too; you may see
    else.                                            373
WAG. Alas, poor slave! see how poverty jesteth
    in his nakedness! the villain is bare and
    out of service, and so hungry that I know
    he would give his soul to the devil for a

---

[34] Verily you have power in the image of your brother Mephistophilis.
[35] By accident.
[36] Saddened.          [37] Study.
[38] Beards trimmed to a sharp point.

shoulder of mutton, though it were blood-raw. 379

CLOWN. How! my soul to the devil for a shoulder of mutton, though 'twere blood-raw! not so, good friend: by'r lady, I had need have it well roasted, and good sauce to it, if I pay so dear. 384

WAG. Well, wilt thou serve me, and I'll make thee go like *Qui mihi discipulus?* 39

CLOWN. How, in verse? 387

WAG. No, sirrah; in beaten silk and staves-acre.40

CLOWN. How, how, knaves-acre! 41 ay, I thought that was all the land his father left him. Do you hear? I would be sorry to rob you of your living. 393

WAG. Sirrah, I say in staves-acre.

CLOWN. Oho, oho, staves-acre! why then, be-like, if I were your man I should be full of vermin. 397

WAG. So thou shalt, whether thou beest with me or no. But, sirrah, leave your jesting, and bind yourself presently unto me for seven years, or I'll turn all the lice about thee into familiars, and they shall tear thee in pieces. 403

CLOWN. Do you hear, sir? you may save that labor; they are too familiar with me already: swowns, they are as bold with my flesh as if they had paid for their meat and drink. 408

WAG. Well, do you hear, sirrah? hold, take these guilders. [*Gives money.*

CLOWN. Gridirons! what be they?

WAG. Why, French crowns. 412

CLOWN. Mass, but for the name of French crowns, a man were as good have as many English counters. And what should I do with these? 416

WAG. Why, now, sirrah, thou art at an hour's warning, whensoever and wheresoever the devil shall fetch thee.

CLOWN. No, no; here, take your gridirons again.

WAG. Truly, I'll none of them. 422

CLOWN. Truly, but you shall.

WAG. Bear witness I gave them him.

CLOWN. Bear witness I give them you again.

WAG. Well, I will cause two devils presently to fetch thee away—Baliol and Belcher!

CLOWN. Let your Baliol and your Belcher come here, and I'll knock them, they were never so knocked since they were devils: say I should kill one of them, what would folks say? "Do ye see yonder tall fellow in the round slop? 42 he has killed the devil." So I should be called Kill-devil all the parish over. 435

*Enter two* DEVILS; *and the* CLOWN *runs up and down crying.*

WAG. Baliol and Belcher,—spirits, away!
[*Exeunt* DEVILS.

CLOWN. What, are they gone? a vengeance on them! they have vile long nails. There was a he-devil and a she-devil: I'll tell you how you shall know them; all he-devils has horns, and all she-devils has clifts and cloven feet. 442

WAG. Well, sirrah, follow me.

CLOWN. But, do you hear? if I should serve you, would you teach me to raise up Banios and Belcheos?

WAG. I will teach thee to turn thyself to any-thing, to a dog, or a cat, or a mouse, or a rat, or anything. 449

CLOWN. How! a Christian fellow to a dog or a cat, a mouse or a rat! no, no, sir; if you turn me into anything, let it be in the likeness of a little pretty frisking flea, that I may be here and there and everywhere: Oh, I'll tickle the pretty wenches' plackets! I'll be amongst them, i'faith.

WAG. Well, sirrah, come. 457

CLOWN. But, do you hear, Wagner?

WAG. How!—Baliol and Belcher!

CLOWN. O Lord! I pray, sir, let Baliol and Belcher go sleep. 461

WAG. Villain, call me Master Wagner, and let thy left eye be diametarily 43 fixed upon my right heel, with *quasi vestigias nostras insistere.*44 [*Exit.*

CLOWN. God forgive me, he speaks Dutch fustian. Well, I'll follow him; I'll serve him, that's flat. [*Exit.* 468

*FAUSTUS discovered in his study.*

FAUST. Now, Faustus, must
Thou needs be damned, and canst thou not be saved:
What boots it, then, to think of God or heaven? 471
Away with such vain fancies, and despair;
Despair in God, and trust in Belzebub:
Now go not backward; no, Faustus, be resolute:
Why waver'st thou? Oh, something soundeth in mine ears, 475
"Abjure this magic, turn to God again!"
Ay, and Faustus will turn to God again.
To God? he loves thee not;
The god thou serv'st is thine own appetite,
Wherein is fixed the love of Belzebub: 480
To him I'll build an altar and a church,
And offer lukewarm blood of new-born babes.

39 Who will be my pupil?
40 Species of larkspur, used for destroying vermin.
41 Name given to Poultney Street, London.
42 Wide knickerbockers.
43 Diametrically.
44 As if to follow in my footsteps.

*Enter* Good Angel *and* Evil Angel.

G. Ang. Sweet Faustus, leave that execrable
art.

Faust. Contrition, prayer, repentance—what
of them?

G. Ang. Oh, they are means to bring thee
unto heaven!                                485

E. Ang. Rather illusions, fruits of lunacy,
That make men foolish that do trust them
most.

G. Ang. Sweet Faustus, think of heaven and
heavenly things.

E. Ang. No, Faustus; think of honor and of
wealth.                      [*Exeunt* Angels.
                                            490

Faust. Of wealth!
Why, the signiory of Emden shall be mine.
When Mephistophilis shall stand by me,
What god can hurt thee, Faustus? thou art
safe:
Cast no more doubts.—Come, Mephistoph-
ilis,
And bring glad tidings from great Lucifer;—
Is't not midnight?—come, Mephistophilis,
*Veni, veni, Mephistophile!* [45]

*Enter Mephistophilis.*

Now tell me what says Lucifer, thy lord?

Meph. That I shall wait on Faustus whilst he
lives,
So he will buy my service with his soul. 500

Faust. Already Faustus hath hazarded that
for thee.

Meph. But, Faustus, thou must bequeath it
solemnly,
And write a deed of gift with thine own
blood;
For that security craves great Lucifer.
If thou deny it, I will back to hell.       505

Faust. Stay, Mephistophilis, and tell me, what
good will my soul do thy lord?

Meph. Enlarge his kingdom.

Faust. Is that the reason why he tempts us
thus?

Meph. *Solamen miseris socios habuisse
doloris.* [46]                              510

Faust. Why, have you any pain that tortures
others?

Meph. As great as have the human souls of
men.
But, tell me, Faustus, shall I have thy soul?
And I will be thy slave, and wait on thee,
And give thee more than thou hast wit to
ask.                                        515

Faust. Ay, Mephistophilis, I give it thee.

Meph. Then, Faustus, stab thine arm coura-
geously,
And bind thy soul, that at some certain day
Great Lucifer may claim it as his own;
And then be thou as great as Lucifer.       520

[45] Come, come, Mephistophilis!
[46] Misery loves company.

Faust. [*Stabbing his arm*] Lo, Mephistophilis,
for love of thee,
I cut mine arm, and with my proper blood
Assure my soul to be great Lucifer's,
Chief lord and regent of perpetual night!
View here the blood that trickles from mine
arm,                                        525
And let it be propitious for my wish.

Meph. But, Faustus, thou must
Write it in manner of a deed of gift.

Faust. Ay, so I will [*Writes*]. But, Mephistophilis,
My blood congeals, and I can write no
more.                                       530

Meph. I'll fetch thee fire to dissolve it straight.
                                          [*Exit.*

Faust. What might the staying of my blood
portend?
Is it unwilling I should write this bill?
Why streams it not, that I may write afresh?
*Faustus gives to thee his soul:* ah, there it
stayed!                                     535
Why shouldst thou not? is not thy soul
thine own?
Then write again, *Faustus gives to thee his
soul.*

*Re-enter* Mephistophilis *with a chafer of
coals.*

Meph. Here's fire; come, Faustus, set it on.

Faust. So, now the blood begins to clear again;
Now will I make an end immediately.    540
                                          [*Writes.*

Meph. O, what will not I do t' obtain his
soul!                                   [*Aside.*

Faust. *Consummatum est;* [47] this bill is ended,
And Faustus hath bequeathed his soul to
Lucifer.
But what is this inscription on mine arm?
*Homo, fuge;* [48] whither should I fly?     545
If unto God, he'll throw me down to hell.
My senses are deceived; here's nothing
writ:—
I see it plain; here in this place is writ,
*Homo, fuge:* yet shall not Faustus fly.

Meph. I'll fetch him somewhat to delight his
mind.         [*Aside, and then exit.*  550

*Re-enter* Mephistophilis *with* Devils, *who
give crowns and rich apparel to* Faustus,
*dance, and then depart.*

Faust. Speak, Mephistophilis, what means this
show?

Meph. Nothing, Faustus, but to delight thy
mind withal,
And to show thee what magic can perform.

Faust. But may I raise up spirits when I
please?

[47] It is finished.         [48] O man, flee!

MEPH. Ay, Faustus, and do greater things than these. 555

FAUST. Then there's enough for a thousand souls.

Here, Mephistophilis, receive this scroll,
A deed of gift of body and of soul:
But yet conditionally that thou perform
All articles prescribed between us both. 560

MEPH. Faustus, I swear by hell and Lucifer
To effect all promises between us made!

FAUST. Then hear me read them. [*Reads.*]
*On these conditions following. First, that Faustus may be a spirit in form and substance. Secondly, that Mephistophilis shall be his servant, and at his command. Thirdly, that Mephistophilis shall do for him, and bring him whatsoever he desires. Fourthly, that he shall be in his chamber or house invisible. Lastly, that he shall appear to the said John Faustus, at all times, in what form or shape soever he please. I, John Faustus, of Wertenberg, Doctor, by these presents, do give both body and soul to Lucifer, prince of the East, and his minister Mephistophilis; and furthermore grant unto them that, twenty-four years being expired, the articles above-written inviolate, full power to fetch or carry the said John Faustus, body and soul, flesh, blood, or goods, into their habitation wheresoever. By me, John Faustus.* 583

MEPH. Speak, Faustus, do you deliver this as your deed?

FAUST. Ay, take it, and the devil give thee good on't!

MEPH. Now, Faustus, ask what thou wilt.

FAUST. First will I question with thee about hell.

Tell me, where is the place that men call hell?

MEPH. Under the heavens.

FAUST. Ay, but whereabout? 590

MEPH. Within the bowels of these elements,
Where we are tortured and remain for ever:
Hell hath no limits, nor is circumscribed
In one self place; for where we are is hell,
And where hell is, there must we ever be:
And, to conclude, when all the world dissolves, 596
And every creature shall be purified,
All places shall be hell that are not heaven.

FAUST. Come, I think hell's a fable.

MEPH. Ay, think so still, till experience change thy mind. 600

FAUST. Why, think'st thou, then, that Faustus shall be damned?

MEPH. Ay, of necessity, for here's the scroll
Wherein thou hast given thy soul to Lucifer.

FAUST. Ay, and body too: but what of that?
Think'st thou that Faustus is so fond [49] to imagine 605

[49] Foolish.

That, after this life, there is any pain?
Tush, these are trifles and mere old wives' tales.

MEPH. But, Faustus, I am an instance to prove the contrary,
For I am damnéd, and am now in hell.

FAUST. How! now in hell! 610
Nay, an this be hell, I'll willingly be damned here:
What! walking, disputing, etc.
But, leaving off this, let me have a wife,
The fairest maid in Germany;
For I am wanton and lascivious, 615
And cannot live without a wife.

MEPH. How! a wife!
I prithee, Faustus, talk not of a wife.

FAUST. Nay, sweet Mephistophilis, fetch me one, for I will have one. 620

MEPH. Well, thou wilt have one? Sit there till I come: I'll fetch thee a wife in the devil's name. [*Exit.*

*Re-enter* MEPHISTOPHILIS *with a* DEVIL *dressed like a woman, with fireworks.*

MEPH. Tell me, Faustus, how dost thou like thy wife?

FAUST. A plague on her for a hot whore! 625

MEPH. Tut, Faustus,
Marriage is but a ceremonial toy;
If thou lovest me, think no more of it.
I'll cull thee out the fairest courtesans, 629
And bring them every morning to thy bed:
She whom thine eye shall like, thy heart shall have,
Be she as chaste as was Penelope,
As wise as Saba,[50] or as beautiful
As was bright Lucifer before his fall. 634
Hold, take this book, peruse it thoroughly:
[*Gives book.*
The iterating of these lines brings gold;
The framing of this circle on the ground
Brings whirlwinds, tempests, thunder, and lightning;
Pronounce this thrice devoutly to thyself,
And men in armor shall appear to thee, 640
Ready to execute what thou desir'st.

FAUST. Thanks, Mephistophilis: yet fain would I have a book wherein I might behold all spells and incantations, that I might raise up spirits when I please.

MEPH. Here they are in this book. 646
[*Turns to them.*

FAUST. Now would I have a book where I might see all characters and planets of the heavens, that I might know their motions and dispositions. 650

MEPH. Here they are too. [*Turns to them.*

FAUST. Nay, let me have one book more,—and then I have done,—wherein I might see all plants, herbs, and trees that grow upon the earth. 655

[50] Queen of Sheba.

MEPH. Here they be.

FAUST. Oh, thou art deceived.

MEPH. Tut, I warrant thee.

[*Turns to them. Exeunt.*

*Enter* FAUSTUS *in his study, and* MEPHI-
STOPHILIS.

FAUST. When I behold the heavens, then I
repent,

And curse thee, wicked Mephistophilis, 660

Because thou hast deprived me of those joys.

MEPH. Why, Faustus,

Thinkest thou heaven is such a glorious
thing?

I tell thee, 'tis not half so fair as thou,

Or any man that breathes on earth.     665

FAUST. How prov'st thou that?

MEPH. 'Twas made for man, therefore is man
more excellent.

FAUST. If it were made for man, 'twas made
for me:

I will renounce this magic and repent.

*Enter* GOOD ANGEL *and* EVIL ANGEL.

G. ANG. Faustus, repent; yet God will pity
thee.                                          670

E. ANG. Thou art a spirit; God cannot pity
thee.

FAUST. Who buzzeth in mine ears I am a
spirit?

Be I a devil, yet God may pity me;

Ay, God will pity me, if I repent.     674

E. ANG. Ay, but Faustus never shall repent.

[*Exeunt* ANGELS.

FAUST. My heart's so hardened, I cannot
repent:

Scarce can I name salvation, faith, or heaven,

But fearful echoes thunder in mine ears,

"Faustus, thou art damned!" Then swords,
and knives,

Poison, guns, halters, and envenomed steel
Are laid before me to dispatch myself; 681

And long ere this I should have slain myself,

Had not sweet pleasure conquered deep
despair.

Have not I made blind Homer sing to me

Of Alexander's love and Oenon's death?

And hath not he that built the walls of
Thebes                                        686

With ravishing sound of his melodious harp,

Made music with my Mephistophilis?

Why should I die, then, or basely despair!

I am resolved; Faustus shall ne'er repent.—

Come, Mephistophilis, let us dispute again,

And argue of divine astrology.           692

Tell me, are there many heavens above the
moon?

Are all celestial bodies but one globe,

As is the substance of this centric earth? 695

MEPH. As are the elements, such are the
spheres,

Mutually folded in each other's orb,

And, Faustus,

All jointly move upon one axletree,

Whose terminus is termed the world's wide
pole;                                         700

Nor are the names of Saturn, Mars, or
Jupiter

Feigned, but are erring stars.

FAUST. But, tell me, have they all one motion,
both *situ et tempore?* [51]                704

MEPH. All jointly move from east to west in
twenty-four hours upon the poles of the
world; but differ in their motion upon
the poles of the zodiac.

FAUST. Tush,

These slender trifles Wagner can decide: 710

Hath Mephistophilis no greater skill?

Who knows not the double motion of the
planets?                                      713

The first is finished in a natural day;

The second thus; as Saturn in thirty years;

Jupiter in twelve; Mars in four; the Sun,
Venus, and Mercury in a year; the Moon
in twenty-eight days. Tush, these are
freshmen's suppositions. But, tell me, hath
every sphere a dominion or *intelligentia?*

MEPH. Ay.                                     721

FAUST. How many heavens or spheres are
there?

MEPH. Nine; the seven planets, the firmament,
and the empyreal heaven.               725

FAUST. Well, resolve me in this question: why
have we not conjunctions, oppositions,
aspects, eclipses, all at one time, but in
some years we have more, in some less?

MEPH. *Per inaequalem motum respectu
totius.* [52]

FAUST. Well, I am answered. Tell me, who
made the world?                          732

MEPH. I will not.

FAUST. Sweet Mephistophilis, tell me.

MEPH. Move me not, for I will not tell thee.

FAUST. Villain, have I not bound thee to tell
me anything?                             737

MEPH. Ay, that is not against our kingdom;
but this is.

Think thou on hell, Faustus, for thou art
damned.

FAUST. Think, Faustus, upon God that made
the world.                               740

MEPH. Remember this.              [*Exit.*

FAUST. Ay, go, accursèd spirit, to ugly hell!

'Tis thou hast damned distressèd Faustus'
soul.

Is't not too late?

*Re-enter* GOOD ANGEL *and* EVIL ANGEL.

E. ANG. Too late.                         745

G. ANG. Never too late, if Faustus can repent.

E. ANG. If thou repent, devils shall tear thee
in pieces.

[51] In direction and time.

[52] On account of their unequal motion in relation
to the whole.

G. Ang. Repent, and they shall never raze thy
  skin.            [*Exeunt* Angels.
Faust. Ah, Christ, my Savior,
  Seek to save distresséd Faustus' soul! 750

*Enter* Lucifer, Belzebub, *and* Mephi-
STOPHILIS.

Luc. Christ cannot save thy soul, for he is
  just:
  There's none but I have interest in the same.
Faust. Oh, who art thou that look'st so ter-
  rible?
Luc. I am Lucifer,
  And this is my companion-prince in hell. 755
Faust. O Faustus, they are come to fetch
  away thy soul!
Luc. We come to tell thee thou dost injure
  us;
  Thou talk'st of Christ, contrary to thy
  promise:
  Thou shouldst not think of God: think of
  the devil,
  And of his dam too.          760
Faust. Nor will I henceforth: pardon me in
  this,
  And Faustus vows never to look to heaven,
  Never to name God, or to pray to him,
  To burn his Scriptures, slay his ministers,
  And make my spirits pull his churches
  down.         765
Luc. Do so, and we will highly gratify thee.
  Faustus, we are come from hell to show
  thee some pastime: sit down, and thou
  shalt see all the Seven Deadly Sins ap-
  pear in their proper shapes.    770
Faust. That sight will be as pleasing unto me
  As Paradise was to Adam the first day
  Of his creation.
Luc. Talk not of Paradise nor creation; but
  mark this show: talk of the devil, and
  nothing else.—Come away!    776

*Enter the* Seven Deadly Sins.

Now, Faustus, examine them of their several
  names and dispositions.
Faust. What art thou, the first?    779
Pride. I am Pride. I disdain to have any
  parents. I am like to Ovid's flea; I can
  creep into every corner of a wench; sometimes, like a periwig, I sit upon her brow;
  or, like a fan of feathers, I kiss her lips;
  indeed, I do—what do I not? But, fie,
  what a scent is here! I'll not speak another
  word, except the ground were perfumed,
  and covered with cloth of arras.
Faust. What art thou, the second?    790
Covet. I am Covetousness, begotten of an old
  churl, in an old leathern bag: and, might
  I have my wish, I would desire that this
  house and all the people in it were turned
  to gold, that I might lock you up in my
  good chest: O my sweet gold!

Faust. What art thou, the third?    798
Wrath. I am Wrath. I had neither father
  nor mother: I leaped out of a lion's
  mouth when I was scarce half an hour
  old; and ever since I have run up and
  down the world with this case [53] of
  rapiers, wounding myself when I had
  nobody to fight withal. I was born in hell;
  and look to it, for some of you shall be my
  father.[54]
Faust. What art thou, the fourth?    808
Envy. I am Envy, begotten of a chimney-
  sweeper and an oyster-wife. I cannot read,
  and therefore wish all books were burned.
  I am lean with seeing others eat. O that
  there would come a famine through all the
  world, that all might die, and I live alone!
  then thou shouldst see how fat I would
  be. But must thou sit, and I stand? come
  down, with a vengeance!
Faust. Away, envious rascal!—What art thou,
  the fifth?    820
Glut. Who I, sir? I am Gluttony. My parents
  are all dead, and the devil a penny they
  have left me, but a bare pension, and that
  is thirty meals a day, and ten bevers,[55]
  —a small trifle to suffice nature. Oh, I
  come of a royal parentage! my grandfather
  was a Gammon of Bacon, my grandmother
  a Hogshead of Claret-wine; my godfathers
  were these, Peter Pickle-herring and Martin Martlemas-beef; O but my godmother,
  she was a jolly gentlewoman, and well-
  beloved in every good town and city; her
  name was Mistress Margery March-beer.
  Now, Faustus, thou hast heard all my
  progeny; [56] wilt thou bid me to supper?
Faust. No, I'll see thee hanged: thou wilt eat
  up all my victuals.    838
Glut. Then the devil choke thee!
Faust. Choke thyself, glutton!—What art
  thou, the sixth?    841
Sloth. I am Sloth. I was begotten on a sunny
  bank, where I have lain ever since; and
  you have done me great injury to bring
  me from thence: let me be carried thither
  again by Gluttony and Lechery. I'll not
  speak another word for a king's ransom.
Faust. What are you, Mistress Minx, the seventh and last?    850
Lechery. Who I, sir? I am one that loves
  an inch of raw mutton better than an ell
  of fried stock-fish; and the first letter of
  my name begins with L.
Luc. Away, to hell, to hell!    855
                [*Exeunt the* Sins.
Now, Faustus, how dost thou like this?
Faust. Oh, this feeds my soul!

[53] Pair.
[54] I. e., one of the devils must be my father.
[55] Refreshments between breakfast and dinner.
[56] Lineage.

Luc. Tut, Faustus, in hell is all manner of delight.

Faust. O might I see hell, and return again,
How happy were I then! 861

Luc. Thou shalt; I will send for thee at midnight.

In meantime take this book; peruse it thoroughly,

And thou shalt turn thyself into what shape thou wilt.

Faust. Great thanks, mighty Lucifer! 865
This will I keep as chary as my life.

Luc. Farewell, Faustus, and think on the devil.

Faust. Farewell, great Lucifer.
[*Exeunt* Lucifer *and* Belzebub.
Come, Mephistophilis. [*Exeunt.* 870

*Enter* Chorus.

Chor. Learnéd Faustus,
To know the secrets of astronomy
Graven in the book of Jove's high firmament,
Did mount himself to scale Olympus' top,
Being seated in a chariot burning bright, 875
Drawn by the strength of yoky dragons' necks.
He now is gone to prove cosmography,
And, as I guess, will first arrive in Rome,
To see the Pope and manner of his court,
And take some part of holy Peter's feast,
That to this day is highly solemnized. 881
[*Exit.*

*Enter* Faustus *and* Mephistophilis.

Faust. Having now, my good Mephistophilis,
Passed with delight the stately town of Trier,[57]
Environed round with airy mountain-tops,
With walls of flint, and deep-entrenchéd lakes, 885
Not to be won by any conquering prince;
From Paris next, coasting the realm of France,
We saw the river Maine fall into Rhine,
Whose banks are set with groves of fruitful vines;
Then up to Naples, rich Campania, 890
Whose buildings fair and gorgeous to the eye,
The streets straight forth, and paved with finest brick,
Quarter the town in four equivalents:
There saw we learnéd Maro's[58] golden tomb,
The way he cut, an English mile in length,
Thorough a rock of stone, in one night's space; 896
From thence to Venice, Padua, and the rest,
In one of which a sumptuous temple stands,
That threats the stars with her aspiring top.

[57] Trèves.
[58] Virgil's, who in the Middle Ages was thought to have been a magician.

Thus hitherto hath Faustus spent his time:
But tell me now what resting-place is this?
Hast thou, as erst I did command, 902
Conducted me within the walls of Rome?

Meph. Faustus, I have; and, because we will not be unprovided, I have taken up[59] his Holiness' privy-chamber for our use. 906

Faust. I hope his Holiness will bid us welcome.

Meph. Tut, 'tis no matter, man; we'll be bold with his good cheer.
And now, my Faustus, that thou mayst perceive 910
What Rome containeth to delight thee with,
Know that this city stands upon seven hills
That underprop the groundwork of the same:
Just through the midst runs flowing Tiber's stream
With winding banks that cut it in two parts; 915
Over the which four stately bridges lean,
That make safe passage to each part of Rome:
Upon the bridge called Ponte Angelo
Erected is a castle passing strong,
Within whose walls such store of ordnance are, 920
And double cannons framed of carvéd brass,
As match the days within one complete year;
Besides the gates, and high pyramidés,[60]
Which Julius Caesar brought from Africa.

Faust. Now, by the kingdoms of infernal rule, 925
Of Styx, of Acheron, and the fiery lake
Of ever-burning Phlegethon, I swear
That I do long to see the monuments
And situation of bright-splendent Rome:
Come, therefore, let's away. 930

Meph. Nay, Faustus, stay: I know you'd fain see the Pope
And take some part of holy Peter's feast,
Where thou shalt see a troop of bald-pate friars,
Whose *summum bonum*[61] is in belly-cheer.

Faust. Well, I'm content to compass then some sport, 935
And by their folly make us merriment.
Then charm me, that I
May be invisible, to do what I please,
Unseen of any whilst I stay in Rome.
[Mephistophilis *charms him.*

Meph. So, Faustus; now 940
Do what thou wilt, thou shalt not be discerned.

*Sound a Sennet.*[62] *Enter the* Pope *and the* Cardinal of Lorrain *to the banquet, with* Friars *attending.*

Pope. My lord of Lorrain, will't please you draw near?

[59] Engaged.    [60] Obelisks.    [61] Highest good.
[62] Set of notes on trumpet or cornet.

FAUST. Fall to, and the devil choke you, an you spare!    945

POPE. How now! who's that which spake?—Friars, look about.

FIRST FRIAR. Here's nobody, if it like your Holiness.

POPE. My lord, here is a dainty dish was sent me from the Bishop of Milan.    951

FAUST. I thank you, sir.    [*Snatches the dish.*

POPE. How now! who's that which snatched the meat from me? will no man look?—My lord, this dish was sent me from the Cardinal of Florence.    956

FAUST. You say true; I'll ha't.
    [*Snatches the dish.*

POPE. What, again!—My lord, I'll drink to your grace.

FAUST. I'll pledge your grace.    960
    [*Snatches the cup.*

C. OF LOR. My lord, it may be some ghost newly crept out of purgatory, come to beg a pardon of your Holiness.

POPE. It may be so.—Friars, prepare a dirge to lay the fury of this ghost.—Once again, my lord, fall to.    966
    [*The* POPE *crosses himself.*

FAUST. What, are you crossing of yourself?
    Well, use that trick no more, I would advise you.
    [*The* POPE *crosses himself again.*
    Well, there's the second time. Aware [63] the third;
    I give you fair warning.    970
    [*The* POPE *crosses himself again, and* FAUSTUS *hits him a box on the ear; and they all run away.*
    Come on, Mephistophilis; what shall we do?

MEPH. Nay, I know not: we shall be cursed with bell, book, and candle.

FAUST. How! bell, book, and candle,—candle, book, and bell,—
    Forward and backward, to curse Faustus to hell!    975
    Anon you shall hear a hog grunt, a calf bleat, and an ass bray,
    Because it is Saint Peter's holiday.

*Re-enter all the* FRIARS *to sing the Dirge.*

FIRST FRIAR. Come, brethren, let's about our business with good devotion.    979
    *They sing:*
*Cursed be he that stole away his Holiness' meat from the table!*
    *maledicat Dominus!* [64]
*Cursed be he that struck his Holiness a blow on the face!*
    *maledicat Dominus!*
*Cursed be he that took Friar Sandelo a blow on the pate!*
    *maledicat Dominus!*    985

[63] Beware.    [64] May the Lord curse him.

*Cursed be he that disturbeth our holy dirge!*
    *maledicat Dominus!*
*Cursed be he that took away his Holiness' wine!*
    *maledicat Dominus! Et omnes Sancti!* [65]
    *Amen!*    990

[MEPHISTOPHILIS *and* FAUSTUS *beat the* FRIARS, *and fling fireworks among them; and so exeunt.*

*Enter* CHORUS.

CHOR. When Faustus had with pleasure ta'en the view
    Of rarest things, and royal courts of kings,
    He stayed his course, and so returnéd home;
    Where such as bear his absence but with grief,
    I mean his friends and near'st companions,
    Did gratulate his safety with kind words, 996
    And in their conference of what befell,
    Touching his journey through the world and air,
    They put forth questions of astrology,
    Which Faustus answered with such learnéd skill    1000
    As they admired and wondered at his wit.
    Now is his fame spread forth in every land:
    Amongst the rest the Emperor is one,
    Carolus the Fifth, at whose palace now
    Faustus is feasted 'mongst his noblemen.
    What there he did, in trial of his art,    1006
    I leave untold; your eyes shall see performed.
    [*Exit.*

*Enter* ROBIN *the Ostler, with a book in his hand.*

ROBIN. Oh, this is admirable! here I ha' stolen one of Doctor Faustus' conjuring books, and, i'faith, I mean to search some circles for my own use. Now will I make all the maidens in our parish dance at my pleasure, stark naked before me; and so by that means I shall see more than e'er I felt or saw yet.    1015

*Enter* RALPH, *calling* ROBIN.

RALPH. Robin, prithee, come away; there's a gentleman tarries to have his horse, and he would have his things rubbed and made clean: he keeps such a chafing with my mistress about it; and she has set me to look thee out; prithee, come away.    1022

ROBIN. Keep out, keep out, or else you are blown up, you are dismembered, Ralph: keep out, for I am about a roaring piece of work.    1026

RALPH. Come, what doest thou with that same book? thou canst not read?

ROBIN. Yes, my master and mistress shall find

[65] And all the saints.

that I can read, he for his forehead, she for her private study; she's born to bear with me, or else my art fails.　1032

RALPH. Why, Robin, what book is that?

ROBIN. What book! why, the most intolerable book for conjuring that e'er was invented by any brimstone devil.

RALPH. Canst thou conjure with it?　1037

ROBIN. I can do all these things easily with it: first, I can make thee drunk with ippocras [66] at any tavern in Europe for nothing; that's one of my conjuring works.

RALPH. Our Master Parson says that's nothing.　1043

ROBIN. True, Ralph: and more, Ralph, if thou hast any mind to Nan Spit, our kitchenmaid, then turn her and wind her to thy own use, as often as thou wilt, and at midnight.　1049

RALPH. O brave Robin! shall I have Nan Spit, and to mine own use? On that condition I'll feed thy devil with horse-bread as long as he lives, of free cost.　1053

ROBIN. No more, sweet Ralph: let's go and make clean our boots, which lie foul upon our hands, and then to our conjuring in the devil's name.　[*Exeunt.* 1057

*Enter* ROBIN *and* RALPH *with a silver goblet.*

ROBIN. Come, Ralph: did not I tell thee, we were for ever made by this Doctor Faustus' book? *ecce, signum!* [67] here's a simple purchase [68] for horse-keepers: our horses shall eat no hay as long as this lasts.　1062

RALPH. But, Robin, here comes the vintner.

ROBIN. Hush! I'll gull him supernaturally.

*Enter* VINTNER.

Drawer, I hope all is paid; God be with you!—Come, Ralph.　1066

VINT. Soft, sir; a word with you. I must yet have a goblet paid from you, ere you go.

ROBIN. I a goblet, Ralph, I a goblet!—I scorn you; and you are but a, etc. [69] I a goblet! search me.　1072

VINT. I mean so, sir, with your favor.
　　　　　　　　　　　　　[*Searches* ROBIN.

ROBIN. How say you now?

VINT. I must say somewhat to your fellow.— You, sir!　1076

RALPH. Me, sir! me, sir! search your fill. [VINTNER *searches him.*] Now, sir, you may be ashamed to burden honest men with a matter of truth.　1080

VINT. Well, th' one of you hath this goblet about you.

ROBIN. You lie, drawer; 'tis afore me [*Aside*].

[66] Wine sweetened and spiced.　[67] Behold, the proof!　[68] A clear gain.
[69] The actor was expected to speak the abuse extemporaneously.

Sirrah you, I'll teach you to impeach honest men;—stand by;—I'll scour you for a goblet;—stand aside you had best, I charge you in the name of Belzebub.—Look to the goblet, Ralph [*Aside to* RALPH].　1089

VINT. What mean you, sirrah?

ROBIN. I'll tell you what I mean. [*Reads from a book*] *Sanctobulorum Periphrasticon*— nay, I'll tickle you, vintner.—Look to the goblet, Ralph [*Aside to* RALPH]. [*Reads*] *Polypragmos Belseborams framanto pacostiphos tostu, Mephistophilis, etc.*

*Enter* MEPHISTOPHILIS, *sets squibs at their backs, and then exit. They run about.*

VINT. O, *nomine Domini!* [70] what meanest thou, Robin? thou hast no goblet.　1099

RALPH. *Peccatum peccatorum!* [71]—Here's thy goblet, good vintner.
　　　[*Gives the goblet to* VINTNER, *who exit.*

ROBIN. *Misericordia pro nobis!* [72] what shall I do? Good devil, forgive me now, and I'll never rob thy library more.

*Re-enter* MEPHISTOPHILIS.

MEPH. Monarch of hell, under whose black survey　1105
Great potentates do kneel with awful fear,
Upon whose altars thousand souls do lie,
How am I vexéd with these villains' charms?
From Constantinople am I hither come,
Only for pleasure of these damnéd slaves.

ROBIN. How, from Constantinople! you have had a great journey: will you take sixpence in your purse to pay for your supper and be gone?　1114

MEPH. Well, villains, for your presumption, I transform thee into an ape, and thee into a dog; and so be gone!　[*Exit.*

ROBIN. How, into an ape! that's brave: I'll have fine sport with the boys; I'll get nuts and apples enow.　1120

RALPH. And I must be a dog.

ROBIN. I'faith, thy head will never be out of the pottage-pot.
　　　　　　　　　　　　　　　　[*Exeunt.*

*Enter* EMPEROR, FAUSTUS, *and a* KNIGHT, *with* ATTENDANTS.

EMP. Master Doctor Faustus, I have heard strange report of thy knowledge in the black art, how that none in my empire nor in the whole world can compare with thee for the rare effects of magic: they say thou hast a familiar spirit, by whom thou canst accomplish what thou list. This, therefore, is my request, that thou let me see some proof of thy skill, that mine eyes

[70] In the name of the Lord.　[71] Sin of sins.
[72] Mercy upon us.

may be witnesses to confirm what mine ears have heard reported: and here I swear to thee, by the honor of mine imperial crown, that, whatever thou doest, thou shalt be no ways prejudiced or endamaged.

KNIGHT. I'faith, he looks much like a conjurer. [*Aside.* 1140

FAUST. My gracious sovereign, though I must confess myself far inferior to the report men have published, and nothing answerable to the honor of your imperial majesty, yet, for that love and duty binds me thereunto, I am content to do whatsoever your majesty shall command me. 1147

EMP. Then, Doctor Faustus, mark what I shall say.

As I was sometime solitary set
Within my closet, sundry thoughts arose
About the honor of mine ancestors,
How they had won by prowess such exploits,
Got such riches, subdued so many kingdoms, 1154
As we that do succeed, or they that shall
Hereafter possess our throne, shall
(I fear me) ne'er attain to that degree
Of high renown and great authority:
Amongst which kings is Alexander the Great,
Chief spectacle of the world's pre-eminence, 1160
The bright shining of whose glorious acts
Lightens the world with his reflecting beams,
As when I hear but motion [73] made of him,
It grieves my soul I never saw the man:
If, therefore, thou, by cunning of thine art,
Canst raise this man from hollow vaults below, 1166
Where lies entombed this famous conqueror,
And bring with him his beauteous paramour,
Both in their right shapes, gesture, and attire
They used to wear during their time of life,
Thou shalt both satisfy my just desire 1171
And give me cause to praise thee whilst I live.

FAUST. My gracious lord, I am ready to accomplish your request, so far forth as by art and power of my spirit I am able to perform. 1176

KNIGHT. I'faith, that's just nothing at all. [*Aside.*

FAUST. But, if it like your grace, it is not in my ability to present before your eyes the true substantial bodies of those two deceased princes, which long since are consumed to dust. 1182

KNIGHT. Ay, marry, Master Doctor, now there's a sign of grace in you, when you will confess the truth. [*Aside.*

FAUST. But such spirits as can lively resemble Alexander and his paramour shall appear before your grace, in that manner that they best lived in, in their most flourishing

estate; which I doubt not shall sufficiently content your imperial majesty. 1192

EMP. Go to, Master Doctor; let me see them presently.

KNIGHT. Do you hear, Master Doctor? you bring Alexander and his paramour before the Emperor!

FAUST. How then, sir?

KNIGHT. I'faith, that's as true as Diana turned me to a stag. 1200

FAUST. No, sir; but, when Actaeon died, he left the horns for you.—Mephistophilis, be gone. [*Exit* MEPHISTOPHILIS.

KNIGHT. Nay, an you go to conjuring, I'll be gone. [*Exit.*

FAUST. I'll meet with you anon for interrupting me so.—Here they are, my gracious lord. 1208

*Re-enter* MEPHISTOPHILIS *with* SPIRITS *in the shapes of* ALEXANDER *and his* PARAMOUR.

EMP. Master Doctor, I heard this lady, while she lived, had a wart or mole in her neck: how shall I know whether it be so or no? 1212

FAUST. Your highness may boldly go and see.

EMP. Sure, these are no spirits, but the true substantial bodies of those two deceased princes. [*Exeunt* SPIRITS.

FAUST. Wilt please your highness now to send for the knight that was so pleasant with me here of late?

EMP. One of you call him forth. 1220
[*Exit* ATTENDANT.

*Re-enter the* KNIGHT *with a pair of horns on his head.*

How now, sir knight! why, I had thought thou hadst been a bachelor, but now I see thou hast a wife, that not only gives thee horns, but makes thee wear them. Feel on thy head. 1225

KNIGHT. Thou damnéd wretch and execrable dog,
Bred in the concave of some monstrous rock,
How dar'st thou thus abuse a gentleman?
Villain, I say, undo what thou hast done!

FAUST. Oh, not so fast, sir! there's no haste: but, good, are you remembered how you crossed me in my conference with the Emperor? I think I have met [74] with you for it. 1234

EMP. Good Master Doctor, at my entreaty release him: he hath done penance sufficient.

FAUST. My gracious lord, not so much for the injury he offered me here in your presence, as to delight you with some mirth, hath Faustus worthily requited this injurious knight; which being all I desire,

---

[73] Mention.

[74] I am even.

I am content to release him of his horns:—and, sir knight, hereafter speak well of scholars.—Mephistophilis, transform him straight. [MEPHISTOPHILIS *removes the horns.*]—Now, my good lord, having done my duty, I humbly take my leave.

EMP. Farewell, Master Doctor; yet, ere you go,                                                    1250
Expect from me a bounteous reward.
[*Exeunt* EMPEROR, KNIGHT, *and* ATTENDANTS.

FAUST. Now, Mephistophilis, the restless course
That time doth run with calm and silent foot,
Shortening my days and thread of vital life,
Calls for the payment of my latest years:
Therefore, sweet Mephistophilis, let us 1256
Make haste to Wertenberg.

MEPH. What, will you go on horse-back or on foot?

FAUST. Nay, till I am past this fair and pleasant green, I'll walk on foot.                          1260

*Enter a* HORSE-COURSER.[75]

HORSE-C. I have been all this day seeking one Master Fustian: mass, see where he is!—God save you, Master Doctor!

FAUST. What, horse-courser! you are well met.                                                        1265

HORSE-C. Do you hear, sir? I have brought you forty dollars for your horse.

FAUST. I cannot sell him so: if thou likest him for fifty, take him.

HORSE-C. Alas, sir, I have no more!—I pray you, speak for me.                                         1270

MEPH. I pray you, let him have him: he is an honest fellow, and he has a great charge, neither wife nor child.                        1274

FAUST. Well, come, give me your money [HORSE-COURSER *gives* FAUSTUS *the money*]: my boy will deliver him to you. But I must tell you one thing before you have him; ride him not into the water, at any hand.                                   1280

HORSE-C. Why, sir, will he not drink of all waters?

FAUST. O, yes, he will drink of all waters; but ride him not into the water; ride him over hedge or ditch, or where thou wilt, but not into the water.                           1286

HORSE-C. Well, sir.—Now am I made man forever: I'll not leave my horse for forty: if he had but the quality of hey-ding-ding, hey-ding-ding, I'd make a brave living on him: he has a buttock as slick as an eel [*Aside*].—Well, God b'wi'ye, sir: your boy will deliver him me: but, hark you, sir; if my horse be sick or ill at ease, if I bring his water to you, you'll tell me what it is?                                      1296

[75] Horse dealer.

FAUST. Away, you villain! what, dost think I am a horse-doctor?
[*Exit* HORSE-COURSER.
What art thou, Faustus, but a man condemned to die?
Thy fatal time doth draw to final end;  1300
Despair doth drive distrust unto my thoughts:
Confound these passions with a quiet sleep:
Tush, Christ did call the thief upon the Cross;                                          1303
Then rest thee, Faustus, quiet in conceit.
[*Sleeps in his chair.*

*Re-enter* HORSE-COURSER, *all wet, crying.*

HORSE-C. Alas, alas! Doctor Fustian, quotha? mass, Doctor Lopus [76] was never such a doctor: has given me a purgation, has purged me of forty dollars; I shall never see them more. But yet, like an ass as I was, I would not be ruled by him, for he bade me I should ride him into no water; now I, thinking my horse had had some rare quality that he would not have had me known of, I, like a venturous youth, rid him into the deep pond at the town's end. I was no sooner in the middle of the pond, but my horse vanished away, and I sat upon a bottle [77] of hay, never so near drowning in my life. But I'll seek out my doctor, and have my forty dollars again, or I'll make it the dearest horse!—Oh, yonder is his snipper-snapper. Do you hear? you hey-pass,[78] where's your master?                         1324

MEPH. Why, sir, what would you? you cannot speak with him.

HORSE-C. But I will speak with him.

MEPH. Why, he's fast asleep: come some other time.                                            1329

HORSE-C. I'll speak with him now, or I'll break his glass-windows about his ears.

MEPH. I tell thee, he has not slept this eight nights.

HORSE-C. An he have not slept this eight weeks, I'll speak with him.                        1335

MEPH. See, where he is, fast asleep.

HORSE-C. Ay, this is he.—God save you, Master Doctor, Master Doctor, Master Doctor Fustian! forty dollars, forty dollars for a bottle of hay!                                 1340

MEPH. Why, thou seest he hears thee not.

HORSE-C. So-ho, ho! so-ho, ho! [*Hollows in his ear.*] No, will you not wake? I'll make you wake ere I go. [*Pulls* FAUSTUS *by the leg, and pulls it away.*] Alas, I am undone! what shall I do?                          1346

FAUST. Oh, my leg, my leg!—Help, Meph-

[76] Roderigo Lopez, private physician to Queen Elizabeth, hanged in 1594 for conspiring to poison her.
[77] Bundle.          [78] Juggler.

istophilis! call the officers.—My leg, my
leg!

MEPH. Come, villain, to the constable.

HORSE-C. O Lord, sir, let me go, and I'll give
you forty dollars more! 1351

MEPH. Where be they?

HORSE-C. I have none about me: come to my
ostry,[79] and I'll give them you.

MEPH. Be gone quickly. 1355

[HORSE-COURSER *runs away.*

FAUST. What, is he gone? farewell he! Faustus
has his leg again, and the horse-courser, I
take it, a bottle of hay for his labor: well,
this trick shall cost him forty dollars
more. 1360

*Enter* WAGNER.

How now, Wagner! what's the news with
thee?

WAG. Sir, the Duke of Vanholt doth earnestly
entreat your company.

FAUST. The Duke of Vanholt! an honorable
gentleman, to whom I must be no nig-
gard of my cunning.—Come, Mephistophilis, let's away to him. [*Exeunt.* 1368

*Enter the* DUKE OF VANHOLT,
*the* DUCHESS, *and* FAUSTUS.

DUKE. Believe me, Master Doctor, this merriment hath much pleased me.

FAUST. My gracious lord, I am glad it contents
you so well.—But it may be, madam, you
take no delight in this. I have heard that
great-bellied women do long for some
dainties or other: what is it, madam?
tell me, and you shall have it. 1376

DUCHESS. Thanks, good Master Doctor: and,
for I see your courteous intent to pleasure me, I will not hide from you the
thing my heart desires; and, were it now
summer, as it is January and the dead
time of the winter, I would desire no
better meat than a dish of ripe grapes. 1383

FAUST. Alas, madam, that's nothing!—Mephistophilis, be gone. [*Exit* MEPHISTOPHI-
LIS.] Were it a greater thing than this,
so it would content you, you should have
it. 1388

*Re-enter* MEPHISTOPHILIS *with grapes.*

Here they be, madam: wilt please you taste
on them?

DUKE. Believe me, Master Doctor, this makes
me wonder above the rest, that being in
the dead time of winter and in the month
of January, how you should come by these
grapes. 1395

FAUST. If it like your grace, the year is divided

into two circles over the whole world,
that, when it is here winter with us, in
the contrary circle it is summer with
them, as in India, Saba, and farther countries in the east; and by means of a swift
spirit that I have, I had them brought
hither, as you see.—How do you like
them, madam? be they good?

DUCHESS. Believe me, Master Doctor, they be
the best grapes that e'er I tasted in my
life before. 1407

FAUST. I am glad they content you so, madam.

DUKE. Come, madam, let us in, where you
must well reward this learned man for
the great kindness he hath showed to
you.

DUCHESS. And so I will, my lord; and,
whilst I live, rest beholding for this
courtesy.

FAUST. I humbly thank your grace. 1416

DUKE. Come, Master Doctor, follow us, and
receive your reward. [*Exeunt.*

*Enter* WAGNER.

WAG. I think my master means to die shortly,
For he hath given to me all his goods: 1420
And yet, methinks, if that death were near,
He would not banquet, and carouse, and
swill
Amongst the students, as even now he doth,
Who are at supper with such belly-cheer
As Wagner ne'er beheld in all his life. 1425
See, where they come! belike the feast is
ended. [*Exit.*

*Enter* FAUSTUS *with two or three* SCHOLARS
*and* MEPHISTOPHILIS.

FIRST SCHOL. Master Doctor Faustus, since
our conference about fair ladies, which
was the beautifulest in all the world, we
have determined with ourselves that Helen
of Greece was the admirablest lady that
ever lived: therefore, Master Doctor, if
you will do us that favor, as to let us see
that peerless dame of Greece, whom all
the world admires for majesty, we should
think ourselves much beholding unto
you. 1437

FAUST. Gentlemen,
For that I know your friendship is unfeigned,
And Faustus' custom is not to deny 1440
The just requests of those that wish him
well
You shall behold that peerless dame of
Greece,
No otherways for pomp and majesty
Than when Sir Paris crossed the seas with
her,
And brought the spoils to rich Dardania.
Be silent then, for danger is in words. 1446

[79] Inn.

*Music sounds, and* HELEN *passeth over the
stage.*

SEC. SCHOL. Too simple is my wit to tell her
   praise,
Whom all the world admires for majesty.
THIRD SCHOL. No marvel though the angry
   Greeks pursued
With ten years' war the rape of such a
   queen,           1450
Whose heavenly beauty passeth all compare.
FIRST SCHOL. Since we have seen the pride of
   Nature's works,
And only paragon of excellence,
Let us depart; and for this glorious deed
Happy and blest be Faustus evermore! 1455
FAUST. Gentlemen, farewell: the same I wish
   to you.          [*Exeunt* SCHOLARS.

### Enter an OLD MAN.

OLD MAN. Ah, Doctor Faustus, that I might
   prevail
To guide thy steps unto the way of life,
By which sweet path thou mayst attain the
   goal
That shall conduct thee to celestial rest!
Break heart, drop blood, and mingle it with
   tears,           1461
Tears falling from repentant heaviness
Of thy most vile and loathsome filthiness,
The stench whereof corrupts the inward
   soul
With such flagitious crimes of heinous sin
As no commiseration may expel,    1466
But mercy, Faustus, of thy Savior sweet,
Whose blood alone must wash away thy
   guilt.
FAUST. Where art thou, Faustus? wretch, what
   hast thou done?
Damned art thou, Faustus, damned; despair
   and die!          1470
Hell calls for right, and with a roaring voice
Says, "Faustus, come; thine hour is almost
   come";
And Faustus now will come to do thee right.
   [MEPHISTOPHILIS *gives him a dagger.*
OLD MAN. Ah, stay, good Faustus, stay thy
   desperate steps!
I see an angel hovers o'er thy head,   1475
And, with a vial full of precious grace,
Offers to pour the same into thy soul:
Then call for mercy, and avoid despair.
FAUST. Ah, my sweet friend, I feel   1479
Thy words to comfort my distresséd soul!
Leave me a while to ponder on my sins.
OLD MAN. I go, sweet Faustus; but with heavy
   cheer,
Fearing the ruin of thy hopeless soul.
                [*Exit.*
FAUST. Accurséd Faustus, where is mercy now?
I do repent, and yet I do despair:   1485

Hell strives with grace for conquest in my
   breast:
What shall I do to shun the snares of death?
MEPH. Thou traitor, Faustus, I arrest thy soul
For disobedience to my sovereign lord: 1489
Revolt, or I'll in piece-meal tear thy flesh.
FAUST. Sweet Mephistophilis, entreat thy lord
To pardon my unjust presumption,
And with my blood again I will confirm
My former vow I made to Lucifer.
MEPH. Do it, then, quickly, with unfeignéd
   heart,          1495
Lest greater danger do attend thy drift.
FAUST. Torment, sweet friend, that base and
   crooked age,[80]
That durst dissuade me from thy Lucifer,
With greatest torments that our hell affords.
MEPH. His faith is great; I cannot touch his
   soul;          1500
But what I may afflict his body with
I will attempt, which is but little worth.
FAUST. One thing, good servant, let me crave
   of thee,
To glut the longing of my heart's desire,—
That I might have unto my paramour   1505
That heavenly Helen which I saw of late,
Whose sweet embracings may extinguish
   clean
Those thoughts that do dissuade me from my
   vow,
And keep mine oath I made to Lucifer.
MEPH. Faustus, this, or what else thou shalt
   desire,          1510
Shall be performed in twinkling of an eye.

### Re-enter HELEN.

FAUST. Was this the face that launched a
   thousand ships,
And burnt the topless towers of Ilium?—
Sweet Helen, make me immortal with a
   kiss.—          [*Kisses her.*
Her lips suck forth my soul: see, where it
   flies!          1515
Come, Helen, come, give me my soul again.
Here will I dwell, for heaven is in these lips,
And all is dross that is not Helena.
I will be Paris, and for love of thee,
Instead of Troy, shall Wertenberg be sacked;
And I will combat with weak Menelaus, 1521
And wear thy colors on my pluméd crest;
Yes, I will wound Achilles in the heel,
And then return to Helen for a kiss.
Oh, thou art fairer than the evening air 1525
Clad in the beauty of a thousand stars;
Brighter art thou than flaming Jupiter
When he appeared to hapless Semele;
More lovely than the monarch of the sky
In wanton Arethusa's azured arms;   1530
And none but thou shalt be my paramour!
                [*Exeunt.*

---

[80] The Old Man.

*Enter the* OLD MAN.

OLD MAN. Accurséd Faustus, miserable man,
That from thy soul exclud'st the grace of
heaven,
And fly'st the throne of his tribunal-seat!

*Enter* DEVILS.

Satan begins to sift me with his pride: 1535
As in this furnace God shall try my faith,
My faith, vile hell, shall triumph over thee.
Ambitious fiends, see how the heavens smile
At your repulse, and laugh your state to
scorn!
Hence, hell! for hence I fly unto my God.
[*Exeunt—on one side,* DEVILS; *on the other,*
OLD MAN.

*Enter* FAUSTUS, *with* SCHOLARS.

FAUST. Ah, gentlemen!                    1541
FIRST SCHOL. What ails Faustus?
FAUST. Ah, my sweet chamber-fellow, had I
lived with thee, then had I lived still! but
now I die eternally. Look, comes he not?
comes he not?                          1546
SEC. SCHOL. What means Faustus?
THIRD SCHOL. Belike he is grown into some
sickness by being over-solitary.
FIRST SCHOL. If it be so, we'll have physicians
to cure him.—'Tis but a surfeit; never
fear, man.                             1552
FAUST. A surfeit of deadly sin, that hath
damned both body and soul.
SEC. SCHOL. Yet, Faustus, look up to heaven;
remember God's mercies are infinite. 1556
FAUST. But Faustus' offense can ne'er be pardoned: the serpent that tempted Eve may
be saved, but not Faustus. Ah, gentlemen,
hear me with patience, and tremble not at
my speeches! Though my heart pants and
quivers to remember that I have been a
student here these thirty years, O would
I had never seen Wertenberg, never read
book! and what wonders I have done, all
Germany can witness, yea, all the world;
for which Faustus hath lost both Germany
and the world, yea, heaven itself, heaven,
the seat of God, the throne of the blessed,
the kingdom of joy; and must remain in
hell for ever, hell, ah, hell, for ever! Sweet
friends, what shall become of Faustus,
being in hell for ever?                1574
THIRD SCHOL. Yet, Faustus, call on God.
FAUST. On God, whom Faustus hath abjured!
on God, whom Faustus hath blasphemed!
Ah, my God, I would weep! but the devil
draws in my tears. Gush forth blood,
instead of tears! yea, life and soul! Oh, he
stays my tongue! I would lift up my hands;
but see, they hold them, they hold them!
ALL. Who, Faustus?                     1584

FAUST. Lucifer and Mephistophilis. Ah, gentlemen, I gave them my soul for my cunning!
ALL. God forbid!                        1588
FAUST. God forbade it, indeed; but Faustus
hath done it: for vain pleasure of twenty-
four years hath Faustus lost eternal joy
and felicity. I writ them a bill with mine
own blood: the date is expired; the time
will come, and he will fetch me.       1594
FIRST. SCHOL. Why did not Faustus tell us of
this before, that divines might have prayed
for thee?
FAUST. Oft have I thought to have done so;
but the devil threatened to tear me in
pieces, if I named God, to fetch both
body and soul, if I once gave ear to
divinity: and now 'tis too late. Gentlemen,
away, lest you perish with me.         1603
SEC. SCHOL. Oh, what shall we do to save
Faustus?
FAUST. Talk not of me, but save yourselves, and
depart.
THIRD SCHOL. God will strengthen me; I will
stay with Faustus.                     1609
FIRST SCHOL. Tempt not God, sweet friend;
but let us into the next room, and there
pray for him.
FAUST. Ay, pray for me, pray for me; and what
noise soever ye hear, come not unto me,
for nothing can rescue me.             1615
SEC. SCHOL. Pray thou, and we will pray that
God may have mercy upon thee.
FAUST. Gentlemen, farewell: if I live till morning, I'll visit you; if not, Faustus is gone
to hell.                               1620
ALL. Faustus, farewell.
[*Exeunt* SCHOLARS.—*The clock
strikes eleven.*

FAUST. Ah, Faustus,
Now hast thou but one bare hour to live,
And then thou must be damned perpetu-
ally!
Stand still, you ever-moving spheres of
heaven,                                1625
That time may cease, and midnight never
come;
Fair Nature's eye, rise, rise again, and make
Perpetual day; or let this hour be but
A year, a month, a week, a natural day,
That Faustus may repent and save his
soul!                                  1630
*O lente, lente currite, noctis equi!* [81]
The stars move still, time runs, the clock will
strike,
The devil will come, and Faustus must be
damned.
Oh, I'll leap up to my God!—Who pulls
me down?—
See, see, where Christ's blood streams in
the firmament!                         1635

[81] Run slowly, slowly, horses of night (Ovid,
*Amores,* i, 13).

One drop would save my soul, half a drop:
ah, my Christ!—
Ah, rend not my heart for naming of my
Christ!
Yet will I call on Him: O spare me,
Lucifer!—
Where is it now? 'tis gone: and see, where
God
Stretcheth out His arm and bends His ire-
ful brows!                          1640
Mountains and hills, come, come, and fall
on me,
And hide me from the heavy wrath of God!
No, no!
Then will I headlong run into the earth:
Earth, gape! O no, it will not harbor me!
You stars that reigned at my nativity, 1646
Whose influence hath allotted death and
hell,
Now draw up Faustus, like a foggy mist,
Into the entrails of yon laboring clouds,
That, when you vomit forth into the air, 1650
My limbs may issue from your smoky
mouths,
So that my soul may but ascend to heaven!
          [*The clock strikes the half-hour.*
Ah, half the hour is past! 'twill all be past
anon.
O God,                               1654
If Thou wilt not have mercy on my soul,
Yet for Christ's sake, whose blood hath
ransomed me,
Impose some end to my incessant pain;
Let Faustus live in hell a thousand years,
A hundred thousand, and at last be saved;
Oh, no end is limited to damnéd souls! 1660
Why wert thou not a creature wanting
soul?
Or why is this immortal that thou hast?
Ah, Pythagoras' metempsychosis, were that
true,
This soul should fly from me, and I be
changed

Unto some brutish beast! All beasts are
happy,                               1665
For, when they die,
Their souls are soon dissolved in elements;
But mine must live still to be plagued in
hell.
Curst be the parents that engendered me!
No, Faustus, curse thyself; curse Lucifer
That hath deprived thee of the joys of
heaven.                              1671
               [*The clock strikes twelve.*
Oh, it strikes, it strikes! Now, body, turn
to air,
Or Lucifer will bear thee quick to hell!
               [*Thunder and lightning.*
O soul, be changed into little water-drops,
And fall into the ocean—ne'er be found!
My God, my God, look not so fierce on me!

### Enter DEVILS.

Adders and serpents, let me breathe a
while!                               1677
Ugly hell, gape not! come not, Lucifer!
I'll burn my books!—Ah, Mephistophilis!
          [*Exeunt* DEVILS *with* FAUSTUS.

### Enter CHORUS.

CHOR. Cut is the branch that might have
grown full straight,                 1680
And burnéd is Apollo's laurel-bough,
That sometime grew within this learnéd
man.
Faustus is gone: regard his hellish fall,
Whose fiendful fortune may exhort the
wise.
Only to wonder at unlawful things,    1685
Whose deepness doth entice such forward
wits
To practice more than heavenly power per-
mits.                                 [*Exit.*

# Sir Philip Sidney

## 1554-1586

Sidney came of a distinguished family and was born at Penshurst on 30 November, 1554. King Philip of Spain, then in England, was one of his godfathers (whence the boy's name). In 1564 he entered Shrewsbury School, and in 1567 or 1568 proceeded to Christ Church, Oxford. It is probable that he studied also at Cambridge. In May, 1572, he went to the Continent, traveling first to Paris, where he witnessed the massacre of St. Bartholomew, and thence to Frankfort, where he spent about nine months with the humanist and diplomatist Hubert Languet. He went next (with Languet) to Vienna, penetrated Hungary, and then spent some months in Italy, returning to stay through a winter in Vienna, and then to journey on through the Low Countries to England in May, 1575. In July he was at Kenilworth when the Earl of Leicester received Queen Elizabeth there; and later in the summer, it is said, he first saw Stella (Penelope Devereux, daughter of the Earl of Essex), then aged about thirteen. Sidney's sonnets, Astrophel and Stella, were mostly written by 1581 (first published 1591, 1598). In 1577 he was sent as an ambassador to the Continent. In 1580 he was virtually banished from Elizabeth's court because of his protest against her project of marriage with Francis, Duke of Anjou (also known as Alençon); and at this time Sidney seems to have written the later and longer version of his pastoral romance, the Arcadia (published 1590, 1593). In the following year he sat in Parliament, and in 1583 Elizabeth knighted him. In the same year he married Frances, daughter of Sir Francis Walsingham, who bore him a daughter in 1585. The Defense of Poesy was probably begun in 1580, and finished in 1583 or 1584 (first published in 1595). In part a reply to Stephen Gosson's The School of Abuse (1579) and other attacks against drama and poetry, mostly on moral grounds, it so far exceeded them that it remains to this day one of the fairest monuments of English literary criticism. "In its mingling of gravity and gayety, of colloquialism and dignified, elevated speech, it is a true reflection of Sidney's character. His mind plays easily over the field which he is treating, and the enthusiasm of his personality fuses the seemingly incongruous elements. More than history or philosophy or any of the sciences, he maintains, poetry tends to elevate the whole man. Its delightful teaching leads us to virtuous action, the rational object of all learning. Sidney's love of beauty includes the beauty of a well-ordered life; all other beauty reaches but to dust. It is because, like Arnold, he believes that as time passes our race will find a surer and surer stay in poetry that he urges its claims in such unqualified terms. . . . His criticisms of contemporary literature missed the mark in some instances, but his book endures because in essence it is profoundly true, and because it is a true reflex of the author's versatile, highminded, gracious personality." (M. W. Wallace, Life of Sidney, p. 240.)

During the winter of 1584-1585 Sidney sat again in Parliament, and in the latter year he was appointed Governor of Flushing, assuming the office on 21 November. He thus went to play his part in the unwilling assistance which Elizabeth gave to the Dutch against Spain. Ten months later occurred the battle at Zutphen in which Sidney received a mortal wound. Instantly weakened, he was forced to retire, though still able to ride his horse. "In which sad progress," wrote Fulke Greville, "passing along by the rest of the army, where his uncle the general was, and being thirsty with excess of bleeding, he called for drink which was presently brought him; but as he was putting the bottle to his mouth, he saw a poor soldier carried along, who had eaten his last at the same feast, ghastly casting up his eyes at the bottle. Which Sir Philip perceiving, took it from his head before he drank, and delivered it to the poor man with these words, 'Thy necessity is *yet greater than mine.' And when he had pledged this poor soldier, he was presently carried to Arnheim." There he awaited death twenty-six days, until the end came on 17 October. Amidst universal mourning his body was conveyed to London and given a magnificent burial in old St. Paul's Cathedral. To contemporaries Sidney was the ideal embodiment of the virtues of the Renaissance gentleman and courtier; and this he has remained in the eyes of posterity.*

*The Complete Works of Sir Philip Sidney, ed. Albert Feuillerat (Cambridge, 1912–1926), contains the* Defense of Poesy *in vol. III; a good, fully annotated edition of the* Defense *alone is that edited by Albert S. Cook (Boston, 1890). For biography and interpretation, see Malcolm W. Wallace's Life of Sir Philip Sidney (Cambridge, 1915); Mona Wilson's Sir Philip Sidney (New York, 1950); and F. S. Boas' Sidney: His Life and Writings (London, 1955). Joel E. Spingarn summarizes the background of the* Defense *in his* History of Literary Criticism in the Renaissance *(New York, 1899); see also John Buxton,* Sir Philip Sidney and the English Renaissance *(London, 1954).*

## The Defense of Poesy [1]

### (1595)

WHEN the right virtuous Edward Wotton [2] and I were at the Emperor's [3] court together, we gave ourselves to learn horsemanship of John Pietro Pugliano, one that with great commendation had the place of an esquire in his stable; and he, according to the fertileness of the Italian wit, did not only afford us the demonstration of his practice, but sought to enrich our minds with the contemplations therein which he thought most precious. But with none I remember mine ears were at any time more loaden than when—either angered with slow payment, or moved with our learner-like admiration—he exercised his speech in the praise of his faculty. He said soldiers were the noblest estate of mankind, and horsemen the noblest of soldiers. He said they were the masters of war and ornaments of peace, speedy goers and strong abiders, triumphers both in camps and courts. Nay, to so unbelieved a

point he proceeded, as that no earthly thing bred such wonder to a prince as to be a good horseman; skill of government was but a *pedanteria* [4] in comparison. Then would he add certain praises, by telling what a peerless beast the horse was, the only serviceable courtier without flattery, the beast of most beauty, faithfulness, courage, and such more, that if I had not been a piece of a logician before I came to him, I think he would have persuaded me to have wished myself a horse. But thus much at least with his no few words he drave into me, that self-love is better than any gilding to make that seem gorgeous wherein ourselves be parties.

Wherein if Pugliano's strong affection and weak arguments will not satisfy you, I will give you a nearer example of myself, who, I know not by what mischance, in these my not old years and idlest times, having slipped into the title of a poet, am provoked to say something unto you in the defense of that my unelected vocation, which if I handle with more good will than good reasons, bear with me, since the scholar is to be pardoned that followeth the steps of his master. And yet I must say that, as I have just cause to make a pitiful defense of poor poetry, which from almost the highest estimation of learning is fallen to be the laughing-stock of children, so have I need to bring some more available proofs, since the former is by no man barred of his deserved credit, the silly [5] latter hath had even the names of philosophers used to the defacing of it, with great danger of civil war among the Muses.

And first, truly, to all them that, professing learning, inveigh against poetry, may justly be objected that they go very near to ungratefulness, to seek to deface that which, in the noblest nations and languages that are known, hath been the first light-giver to ignorance, and first nurse, whose milk by little and little enabled them to feed afterwards of tougher knowledges. And will they now play the hedgehog, that, being received into the den, drave out his host? Or rather the vipers, that with their birth kill their parents? Let learned Greece in any of her manifold sciences be able to show me one book before Musaeus, Homer, and Hesiod, all three nothing else but poets. Nay, let any history be brought that can say any writers were there before them, if they were not men of the same skill, as Orpheus, Linus, and some other are named, who, having

---

[1] In preparation of the text, A. S. Cook's modernization, based on both of the editions of 1595, was found useful.

[2] Later first Baron Wotton, half-brother to Sir Henry Wotton; lived 1548–1626. One of the pallbearers at Sidney's funeral.

[3] Maximilian II (1527–1576).

[4] Species of pedantry.    [5] Poor.

been the first of that country that made pens deliverers of their knowledge to their posterity, may justly challenge to be called their fathers in learning. For not only in time they had this priority—although in itself antiquity be venerable—but went before them as causes, to draw with their charming sweetness the wild untamed wits to an admiration of knowledge. So as Amphion was said to move stones with his poetry to build Thebes, and Orpheus to be listened to by beasts,—indeed stony and beastly people. So among the Romans were Livius Andronicus and Ennius; so in the Italian language the first that made it aspire to be a treasure-house of science were the poets Dante, Boccaccio, and Petrarch; so in our English were Gower and Chaucer, after whom, encouraged and delighted with their excellent foregoing, others have followed to beautify our mother tongue, as well in the same kind as in other arts.

This did so notably show itself, that the philosophers of Greece durst not a long time appear to the world but under the masks of poets. So Thales, Empedocles, and Parmenides sang their natural philosophy in verses; so did Pythagoras and Phocylides their moral counsels; so did Tyrtaeus in war matters, and Solon in matters of policy; or rather they, being poets, did exercise their delightful vein in those points of highest knowledge which before them lay hidden to the world. For that wise Solon was directly a poet it is manifest, having written in verse the notable fable of the Atlantic Island which was continued by Plato. And truly even Plato whosoever well considereth shall find that in the body of his work though the inside and strength were philosophy, the skin as it were and beauty depended most of poetry. For all standeth upon dialogues; wherein he feigneth many honest burgesses of Athens to speak of such matters that, if they had been set on the rack, they would never have confessed them; besides his poetical describing the circumstances of their meetings, as the well-ordering of a banquet, the delicacy of a walk,[6] with interlacing mere tales, as Gyges' Ring[7] and others, which who knoweth not to be flowers of poetry did never walk into Apollo's garden.

And even historiographers, although their lips sound of things done, and verity be written in their foreheads, have been glad to borrow both fashion and perchance weight of the poets. So Herodotus entitled his history by the name of the nine Muses; and both he and all the rest that followed him either stole or usurped of poetry their passionate describing of passions, the many particularities of battles which no man could affirm, or, if that be denied me, long orations put in the mouths of great kings and captains, which it is certain they never pronounced.

So that truly neither philosopher nor historiographer could at the first have entered into the gates of popular judgments, if they had not taken a great passport of poetry, which in all nations at this day, where learning flourisheth not, is plain to be seen; in all which they have some feeling of poetry. In Turkey, besides their lawgiving divines, they have no other writers but poets. In our neighbor country Ireland, where truly learning goeth very bare, yet are their poets held in a devout reverence. Even among the most barbarous and simple Indians, where no writing is, yet have they their poets, who make and sing songs (which they call *areytos* [8]), both of their ancestors' deeds and praises of their gods,—a sufficient probability that, if ever learning come among them, it must be by having their hard dull wits softened and sharpened with the sweet delights of poetry; for until they find a pleasure in the exercise of the mind, great promises of much knowledge will little persuade them that know not the fruits of knowledge. In Wales, the true remnant of the ancient Britons, as there are good authorities to show the long time they had poets which they called bards, so through all the conquests of Romans, Saxons, Danes, and Normans, some of whom did seek to ruin all memory of learning from among them, yet do their poets even to this day last; so as it is not more notable in soon beginning than in long continuing.

But since the authors of most of our sciences were the Romans, and before them the Greeks, let us a little stand upon their authorities, but even [9] so far as to see what names they have given unto this now scorned skill. Among the Romans a poet was called *vates*, which is as much as a diviner, foreseer, or prophet, as by his conjoined words, *vaticinium* and *vaticinari*, is manifest; so heavenly a title did that excellent people bestow upon this heart-ravishing knowledge. And so far were they carried into the admiration thereof, that they thought in the chanceable hitting upon any such verses great foretokens of their following fortunes

---

[6] *Symposium; Phaedrus.*
[7] *Republic*, II, 359–360.

[8] The native word was picked up by the Spaniards in the West Indies.
[9] Merely.

were placed; whereupon grew the word of *Sortes Virgilianae,* when by sudden opening Virgil's book they lighted upon some verse of his making. Whereof the *Histories of the Emperors' Lives* [10] are full: as of Albinus, the governor of our island, who in his childhood met with this verse,

*Arma amens capio, nec sat rationis in armis,* [11]

and in his age performed it. Although it were a very vain and godless superstition, as also it was to think that spirits were commanded by such verses—whereupon this word charms, derived of *carmina,* cometh—so yet serveth it to show the great reverence those wits were held in, and altogether not [12] without ground, since both the oracles of Delphos [13] and Sibylla's prophecies were wholly delivered in verses; for that same exquisite observing of number and measure in words, and that high-flying liberty of conceit [14] proper to the poet, did seem to have some divine force in it.

And may not I presume a little further to show the reasonableness of this word *vates,* and say that the holy David's Psalms are a divine poem? If I do, I shall not do it without the testimony of great learned men, both ancient and modern. But even the name of Psalms will speak for me, which, being interpreted, is nothing but Songs; then, that it is fully written in meter, as all learned Hebricians agree, although the rules be not yet fully found; lastly and principally, his handling his prophecy, which is merely poetical. For what else is the awaking his musical instruments, the often and free changing of persons, his notable prosopopoeias, [15] when he maketh you, as it were, see God coming in His majesty, his telling of the beasts' joyfulness and hills' leaping, but a heavenly poesy, wherein almost he showeth himself a passionate lover of that unspeakable and everlasting beauty to be seen by the eyes of the mind, only cleared by faith? But truly now having named him, I fear I seem to profane that holy name, applying it to poetry, which is among us thrown down to so ridiculous an estimation. But they that with quiet judgments will look a little deeper into it shall find the end and working of it such as, being rightly applied, deserveth not to be scourged out of the Church of God.

But now let us see how the Greeks named it and how they deemed of it. The Greeks called him ποιητήν, which name hath, as the most excellent, gone through other languages. It cometh of this word ποιεῖν, which is "to make"; wherein I know not whether by luck or wisdom we Englishmen have met with the Greeks in calling him a maker. [16] Which name how high and incomparable a title it is, I had rather were known by marking the scope of other sciences than by any partial allegation. There is no art delivered unto mankind that hath not the works of nature for his principal object, without which they could not consist, and on which they so depend as they become actors and players, as it were, of what nature will have set forth. So doth the astronomer look upon the stars and, by that he seeth, set down what order nature hath taken therein. So do the geometrician and arithmetician in their divers sorts of quantities. So doth the musician in times tell you which by nature agree, which not. The natural philosopher thereon hath his name, and the moral philosopher standeth upon the natural virtues, vices, and passions of man; and "follow nature," saith he, "therein, and thou shalt not err." The lawyer saith what men have determined, the historian what men have done. The grammarian speaketh only of the rules of speech, and the rhetorician and logician, considering what in nature will soonest prove and persuade, thereon give artificial rules, which still are compassed within the circle of a question, according to the proposed matter. The physician weigheth the nature of man's body, and the nature of things helpful or hurtful unto it. And the metaphysic, though it be in the second and abstract notions, and therefore be counted supernatural, yet doth he, indeed, build upon the depth of nature.

Only the poet, disdaining to be tied to any such subjection, lifted up with the vigor of his own invention, doth grow, in effect, into another nature, in making things either better than nature bringeth forth, or, quite anew, forms such as never were in nature, as the heroes, demi-gods, cyclops, chimeras, furies, and such like; so as he goeth hand in hand with nature, not enclosed within the narrow warrant of her gifts, but freely ranging within the zodiac of his own wit. Nature never set forth the earth in so rich tapestry as divers poets have done; neither with pleasant rivers, fruitful trees, sweet-smelling flowers, nor whatsoever else may make the too-much-loved earth

---

[10] The *Augustan Histories.*
[11] To arms I rush in frenzy,—not that good cause is shown for arms (*Aeneid,* II, 314).
[12] Not altogether.    [13] Delphi.
[14] Imaginative invention.    [15] Personifications.

[16] The word was used to signify a poet particularly in Scotland and by the Scottish Chaucerians.

more lovely; her world is brazen, the poets only deliver a golden.

But let those things alone, and go to man—for whom as the other things are, so it seemeth in him her uttermost cunning is employed—and know whether she have brought forth so true a lover as Theagenes,[17] so constant a friend as Pylades; so valiant a man as Orlando;[18] so right a prince as Xenophon's Cyrus; so excellent a man every way as Virgil's Aeneas? Neither let this be jestingly conceived, because the works of the one be essential, the other in imitation or fiction; for any understanding knoweth the skill of each artificer standeth in that idea, or fore-conceit of the work, and not in the work itself. And that the poet hath that idea is manifest, by delivering them forth in such excellency as he hath imagined them. Which delivering forth, also, is not wholly imaginative, as we are wont to say by[19] them that build castles in the air; but so far substantially it worketh, not only to make a Cyrus, which had been but a particular excellency, as nature might have done, but to bestow a Cyrus upon the world to make many Cyruses, if they will learn aright why and how that maker made him. Neither let it be deemed too saucy a comparison to balance the highest point of man's wit with the efficacy of nature; but rather give right honor to the Heavenly Maker of that maker, who, having made man to His own likeness, set him beyond and over all the works of that second nature. Which in nothing he showeth so much as in poetry, when with the force of a divine breath he bringeth things forth far surpassing her doings, with no small argument to the incredulous of that first accursed fall of Adam,—since our erected wit maketh us know what perfection is, and yet our infected will keepeth us from reaching unto it. But these arguments will by few be understood, and by fewer granted; thus much I hope will be given me, that the Greeks with some probability of reason gave him the name above all names of learning.

Now let us go to a more ordinary opening of him, that the truth may be the more palpable; and so, I hope, though we get not so unmatched a praise as the etymology of his names will grant, yet his very description, which no man will deny, shall not justly be barred from a principal commendation.

Poesy, therefore, is an art of imitation, for so Aristotle termeth it in his word μίμησις, that is to say, a representing, counterfeiting, or figuring forth; to speak metaphorically, a speaking picture, with this end,—to teach and delight.

Of this have been three general kinds. The chief, both in antiquity and excellency, were they that did imitate the inconceivable excellencies of God. Such were David in his Psalms; Solomon in his Song of Songs, in his Ecclesiastes and Proverbs; Moses and Deborah in their Hymns; and the writer of Job; which, beside other, the learned Emanuel Tremellius[20] and Franciscus Junius[21] do entitle the poetical part of the Scripture. Against these none will speak that hath the Holy Ghost in due holy reverence. In this kind, though in a full wrong divinity, were Orpheus, Amphion, Homer in his *Hymns*, and many other, both Greeks and Romans. And this poesy must be used by whosoever will follow St. James's counsel in singing psalms when they are merry;[22] and I know is used with the fruit of comfort by some, when, in sorrowful pangs of their death-bringing sins, they find the consolation of the never-leaving goodness.

The second kind is of them that deal with matters philosophical: either moral, as Tyrtaeus, Phocylides, and Cato;[23] or natural, as Lucretius and Virgil's *Georgics*; or astronomical, as Manilius and Pontanus;[24] or historical, as Lucan; which who mislike, the fault is in their judgment quite out of taste, and not in the sweet food of sweetly uttered knowledge.

But because this second sort is wrapped within the fold of the proposed subject, and takes not the free course of his own invention, whether they properly be poets or no let grammarians dispute, and go to the third, indeed right poets, of whom chiefly this question ariseth. Betwixt whom and these second is such a kind of difference as betwixt the meaner sort of painters, who counterfeit only such faces as are set before them, and the more excellent, who having no law but

[17] In the romance, *Ethiopic History*, by Heliodorus.
[18] Hero of Ariosto's *Orlando Furioso*.     [19] Of.

[20] Biblical scholar (1510–1580). A Jew of Ferrara, he was converted to Catholic Christianity, later became a Protestant, and lived for a time at Oxford.
[21] French Protestant (1545–1602); taught theology at Neustadt, Heidelberg, and Leyden.
[22] See James, 5:13.
[23] A certain Dionysius Cato who lived, perhaps, in the third century A.D. His moral distichs were widely popular in the Middle Age, and were still used in Elizabethan schools.
[24] Italian scholar of the Renaissance (1426–1503). Sidney refers to his *Urania*, an astronomical poem in five books.

wit, bestow that in colors upon you which is fittest for the eye to see,—as the constant though lamenting look of Lucretia,[25] when she punished in herself another's fault; wherein he painteth not Lucretia, whom he never saw, but painteth the outward beauty of such a virtue. For these third be they which most properly do imitate to teach and delight; and to imitate borrow nothing of what is, hath been, or shall be; but range, only reined with learned discretion, into the divine consideration of what may be and should be. These be they that, as the first and most noble sort may justly be termed *vates*, so these are waited on in the excellentest languages and best understandings with the foredescribed name of poets. For these, indeed, do merely make to imitate, and imitate both to delight and teach, and delight to move men to take that goodness in hand, which without delight they would fly as from a stranger; and teach to make them know that goodness whereunto they are moved:—which being the noblest scope to which ever any learning was directed, yet want there not idle tongues to bark at them.

These be subdivided into sundry more special denominations. The most notable be the heroic, lyric, tragic, comic, satiric, iambic, elegiac, pastoral, and certain others, some of these being termed according to the matter they deal with, some by the sort of verse they liked best to write in,—for indeed the greatest part of poets have appareled their poetical inventions in that numberous kind of writing which is called verse. Indeed but appareled, verse being but an ornament and no cause to poetry, since there have been many most excellent poets that never versified, and now swarm many versifiers that need never answer to the name of poets. For Xenophon, who did imitate so excellently as to give us *effigiem justi imperii*—the portraiture of a just empire under the name of Cyrus (as Cicero saith of him)—made therein an absolute heroical poem; so did Heliodorus in his sugared [26] invention of that picture of love in Theagenes and Chariclea; [27] and yet both these wrote in prose. Which I speak to show that it is not riming and versing that maketh a poet—no more than a long gown maketh an advocate, who, though he pleaded in armor, should be an advocate and no soldier—but it is that feigning notable images of virtues, vices, or what else, with that delightful teaching, which must be the right describing note to know a

poet by. Although indeed the senate of poets hath chosen verse as their fittest raiment, meaning, as in matter they passed all in all, so in manner to go beyond them; not speaking, table-talk fashion, or like men in a dream, words as they chanceably fall from the mouth, but peizing [28] each syllable of each word by just proportion, according to the dignity of the subject.

Now therefore it shall not be amiss, first to weigh this latter sort of poetry by his works, and then by his parts; and if in neither of these anatomies he be condemnable, I hope we shall obtain a more favorable sentence. This purifying of wit, this enriching of memory, enabling of judgment, and enlarging of conceit, which commonly we call learning, under what name soever it come forth or to what immediate end soever it be directed, the final end is to lead and draw us to as high a perfection as our degenerate souls, made worse by their clay lodgings, can be capable of. This, according to the inclination of man, bred many-formed impressions. For some that thought this felicity principally to be gotten by knowledge, and no knowledge to be so high or heavenly as acquaintance with the stars, gave themselves to astronomy; others, persuading themselves to be demigods if they knew the causes of things, became natural and supernatural philosophers. Some an admirable delight drew to music, and some the certainty of demonstration to the mathematics; but all, one and other, having this scope:—to know, and by knowledge to lift up the mind from the dungeon of the body to the enjoying his own divine essence. But when by the balance of experience it was found that the astronomer, looking to the stars, might fall into a ditch, that the inquiring philosopher might be blind in himself, and the mathematician might draw forth a straight line with a crooked heart; then lo! did proof, the over-ruler of opinions, make manifest, that all these are but serving sciences, which, as they have each a private end in themselves, so yet are they all directed to the highest end of the mistress-knowledge, by the Greeks called ἀρχιτεκτονικ ή,[29] which stands, as I think, in the knowledge of a man's self, in the ethic and politic consideration, with the end of well-doing, and not of well-knowing only:—even as the saddler's next end is to make a good saddle, but

[25] See Livy, i, 58.    [26] Charming.
[27] The *Ethiopic History*, referred to above.

[28] Poising, weighing.
[29] Fulke Greville calls this the "architectonical art."

his further end to serve a nobler faculty, which is horsemanship; so the horseman's to soldiery; and the soldier not only to have the skill, but to perform the practice of a soldier. So that the ending end of all earthly learning being virtuous action, those skills that most serve to bring forth that have a most just title to be princes over all the rest; wherein, if we can show, the poet is worthy to have it before any other competitors.

Among whom as principal challengers step forth the moral philosophers; whom, me thinketh, I see coming towards me with a sullen gravity, as though they could not abide vice by daylight; rudely clothed, for to witness outwardly their contempt of outward things; with books in their hands against glory, whereto they set their names; sophistically speaking against subtility; and angry with any man in whom they see the foul fault of anger. These men, casting largess as they go of definitions, divisions, and distinctions, with a scornful interrogative do soberly ask whether it be possible to find any path so ready to lead a man to virtue, as that which teacheth what virtue is, and teacheth it not only by delivering forth his very being, his causes and effects, but also by making known his enemy, vice, which must be destroyed, and his cumbersome servant, passion, which must be mastered; by showing the generalities that contain it, and the specialities that are derived from it; lastly, by plain setting down how it extendeth itself out of the limits of a man's own little world, to the government of families, and maintaining of public societies?

The historian scarcely giveth leisure to the moralist to say so much, but that he, loaden with old mouse-eaten records, authorizing himself for the most part upon other histories, whose greatest authorities are built upon the notable foundation of hearsay; having much ado to accord differing writers, and to pick truth out of partiality; better acquainted with a thousand years ago than with the present age, and yet better knowing how this world goeth than how his own wit runneth; curious for antiquities and inquisitive of novelties, a wonder to young folks and a tyrant in table-talk; denieth, in a great chafe, that any man for teaching of virtue and virtuous actions is comparable to him. "I am *testis temporum, lux veritatis, vita memoriae, magistra vitae, nuntia vetustatis.*[30] The philosopher," saith he,

"teacheth a disputative virtue, but I do an active. His virtue is excellent in the dangerless Academy of Plato, but mine showeth forth her honorable face in the battles of Marathon, Pharsalia, Poitiers, and Agincourt. He teacheth virtue by certain abstract considerations, but I only bid you follow the footing of them that have gone before you. Old-aged experience goeth beyond the fine-witted philosopher; but I give the experience of many ages. Lastly, if he make the songbook, I put the learner's hand to the lute; and if he be the guide, I am the light." Then would he allege you innumerable examples, confirming story by story, how much the wisest senators and princes have been directed by the credit of history, as Brutus, Alphonsus of Aragon[31]— and who not, if need be? At length the long line of their disputation maketh a point[32] in this,—that the one giveth the precept, and the other the example.

Now whom shall we find, since the question standeth for the highest form in the school of learning, to be moderator? Truly, as me seemeth, the poet; and if not a moderator, even the man that ought to carry the title from them both, and much more from all other serving sciences. Therefore compare we the poet with the historian and with the moral philosopher; and if he go beyond them both, no other human skill can match him. For as for the divine, with all reverence it is ever to be excepted, not only for having his scope as far beyond any of these as eternity exceedeth a moment, but even for passing each of these in themselves. And for the lawyer, though *Jus* be the daughter of Justice, and Justice the chief of virtues, yet because he seeketh to make men good rather *formidine poenae* than *virtutis amore*,[33] or, to say righter, doth not endeavor to make men good, but that their evil hurt not others, having no care, so he be a good citizen, how bad a man he be; therefore, as our wickedness maketh him necessary, and necessity maketh him honorable, so is he not in the deepest truth to stand in rank with these, who all endeavor to take naughtiness away, and plant goodness even in the secretest cabinet of our souls. And these four are all that any way deal in that consideration of men's manners, which being the supreme

---

[30] History, the evidence of time, the light of truth, the life of memory, the directress of life, the herald of antiquity (Cicero, *De Oratore,* II, ix, 36).

[31] Alphonso V of Aragon and I of Sicily (1416–1458).

[32] Cometh to an end.

[33] Rather from the fear of punishment than from the love of virtue (Horace, *Epistles,* I, xvi, 52–53).

knowledge, they that best breed it deserve the best commendation.

The philosopher therefore and the historian are they which would win the goal, the one by precept, the other by example; but both not having both, do both halt. For the philosopher, setting down with thorny arguments the bare rule, is so hard of utterance and so misty to be conceived that one that hath no other guide but him shall wade in him till he be old, before he shall find sufficient cause to be honest. For his knowledge standeth so upon the abstract and general that happy is that man who may understand him, and more happy that can apply what he doth understand. On the other side, the historian, wanting the precept, is so tied, not to what should be but to what is, to the particular truth of things and not to the general reason of things, that his example draweth no necessary consequence, and therefore a less fruitful doctrine.

Now doth the peerless poet perform both; for whatsoever the philosopher saith should be done, he giveth a perfect picture of it in some one by whom he presupposeth it was done, so as he coupleth the general notion with the particular example. A perfect picture, I say; for he yieldeth to the powers of the mind an image of that whereof the philosopher bestoweth but a wordish description, which doth neither strike, pierce, nor possess the sight of the soul so much as that other doth. For as, in outward things, to a man that had never seen an elephant or a rhinoceros, who should tell him most exquisitely all their shapes, color, bigness, and particular marks; or of a gorgeous palace, an architector,[34] with declaring the full beauties, might well make the hearer able to repeat, as it were by rote, all he had heard, yet should never satisfy his inward conceit with being witness to itself of a true lively [35] knowledge; but the same man, as soon as he might see those beasts well painted, or that house well in model, should straightways grow, without need of any description, to a judicial comprehending of them: so no doubt the philosopher, with his learned definitions, be it of virtues or vices, matters of public policy or private government, replenisheth the memory with many infallible grounds of wisdom, which notwithstanding lie dark before the imaginative and judging power, if they be not illuminated or figured forth by the speaking picture of poesy.

Tully [36] taketh much pains, and many times not without poetical helps, to make us know the force love of our country hath in us. Let us but hear old Anchises speaking in the midst of Troy's flames,[37] or see Ulysses, in the fullness of all Calypso's delights, bewail his absence from barren and beggarly Ithaca.[38] Anger, the Stoics said, was a short madness.[39] Let but Sophocles bring you Ajax on a stage, killing and whipping sheep and oxen, thinking them the army of Greeks, with their chieftains Agamemnon and Menelaus, and tell me if you have not a more familiar insight into anger, than finding in the schoolmen his genus and difference.[40] See whether wisdom and temperance in Ulysses and Diomedes, valor in Achilles, friendship in Nisus and Euryalus,[41] even to an ignorant man carry not an apparent shining. And, contrarily, the remorse of conscience in Oedipus; the soon-repenting pride of Agamemnon; [42] the self-devouring cruelty in his father Atreus; [43] the violence of ambition in the two Theban brothers; [44] the sour sweetness of revenge in Medea; [45] and, to fall lower, the Terentian Gnatho [46] and our Chaucer's Pandar [47] so expressed that we now use their names to signify their trades; and finally, all virtues, vices, and passions so in their own natural states laid to the view, that we seem not to hear of them, but clearly to see through them.

But even in the most excellent determination of goodness, what philosopher's counsel can so readily direct a prince, as the feigned Cyrus in Xenophon? Or a virtuous man in all fortunes, as Aeneas in Virgil? Or a whole commonwealth, as the way of Sir Thomas More's *Utopia*? I say the way, because where Sir Thomas More erred, it was the fault of the man, and not of the poet; for that way of patterning a commonwealth was most absolute, though he, perchance, hath not so absolutely performed it. For the question is, whether the feigned image of poesy, or the regular instruction of philosophy, hath the more force in

---

[34] Architect.    [35] Living.

[36] M. Tullius Cicero.    [37] *Aeneid*, II, 634–650.
[38] *Odyssey*, V, 149–158.
[39] Horace, *Epistles*, I, ii, 62; Seneca, *De Ira*, I, 1.
[40] In Sophocles's *Ajax*.
[41] *Aeneid*, IX, 176–182, 433–445.
[42] In Aeschylus's *Agamemnon*.
[43] *Ibid.*, ll. 1555–1580.
[44] Eteocles and Polynices, in Aeschylus's *Seven against Thebes*.
[45] In Euripides' *Medea*.
[46] In Terence's *Eunuch*.
[47] In Chaucer's *Troilus and Cressida*.

teaching. Wherein if the philosophers have more rightly showed themselves philosophers than the poets have attained to the high top of their profession,—as in truth,

*Mediocribus esse poetis*
*Non Dii, non homines, non concessere columnae,*—[48]

it is, I say again, not the fault of the art, but that by few men that art can be accomplished.

Certainly, even our Savior Christ could as well have given the moral commonplaces of uncharitableness and humbleness as the divine narration of Dives and Lazarus; or of disobedience and mercy, as that heavenly discourse of the lost child and the gracious father; but that his through-searching wisdom knew the estate of Dives burning in hell, and of Lazarus in Abraham's bosom, would more constantly, as it were, inhabit both the memory and judgment. Truly, for myself, meseems I see before mine eyes the lost child's disdainful prodigality, turned to envy a swine's dinner; which by the learned divines are thought not historical acts, but instructing parables.

For conclusion, I say the philosopher teacheth, but he teacheth obscurely, so as the learned only can understand him; that is to say, he teacheth them that are already taught. But the poet is the food for the tenderest stomachs; the poet is indeed the right popular philosopher. Whereof Aesop's tales give good proof; whose pretty allegories, stealing under the formal [49] tales of beasts, make many, more beastly than beasts, begin to hear the sound of virtue from those dumb speakers.

But now may it be alleged that if this imagining of matters be so fit for the imagination, then must the historian needs surpass, who bringeth you images of true matters, such as indeed were done, and not such as fantastically or falsely may be suggested to have been done. Truly, Aristotle himself, in his *Discourse of Poesy*, plainly determineth this question, saying that poetry is φιλοσοφώτερον and σπουδαιότερον, that is to say, it is more philosophical and more studiously serious than history. His reason is, because poesy dealeth with καθόλου, that is to say with the universal consideration, and the history with καθ' ἕκαστον, the particular. "Now," saith he, "the universal weighs what is fit to be said or done, either in likelihood or necessity—which the poesy considereth in his imposed names; and the particular only marketh whether Alcibiades did, or suffered, this or that": thus far Aristotle. Which reason of his, as all his, is most full of reason.

For, indeed, if the question were whether it were better to have a particular act truly or falsely set down, there is no doubt which is to be chosen, no more than whether you had rather have Vespasian's picture right as he was, or, at the painter's pleasure, nothing resembling. But if the question be for your own use and learning, whether it be better to have it set down as it should be or as it was, then certainly is more doctrinable [50] the feigned Cyrus in Xenophon than the true Cyrus in Justin; [51] and the feigned Aeneas in Virgil than the right Aeneas in Dares Phrygius; [52] as to a lady that desired to fashion her countenance to the best grace, a painter should more benefit her to portrait a most sweet face, writing Canidia upon it, than to paint Canidia as she was, who, Horace sweareth, was foul and ill-favored.[53]

If the poet do his part aright, he will show you in Tantalus, Atreus, and such like, nothing that is not to be shunned; in Cyrus, Aeneas, Ulysses, each thing to be followed. Where [54] the historian, bound to tell things as things were, cannot be liberal—without he will be poetical—of a perfect pattern; but, as in Alexander, or Scipio himself, show doings, some to be liked, some to be misliked; and then how will you discern what to follow but by your own discretion, which you had without reading Quintus Curtius? And whereas a man may say, though in universal consideration of doctrine the poet prevaileth, yet that the history, in his saying such a thing was done, doth warrant a man more in that he shall follow,—the answer is manifest: that if he stand upon that *was*, as if he should argue, because it rained yesterday therefore it should rain to-day, then indeed it hath some advantage to a gross conceit. But if he know an example only informs a conjectured likelihood,

---

[48] Mediocrity in poets is condemned by gods and men, and by booksellers too (Horace, *De Arte Poetica*, 372–373).
[49] Circumstantial.

[50] Instructive.
[51] Second century A.D. His history is an abridgment of an older one. His account of Cyrus (I, 4–8) probably comes ultimately from Herodotus.
[52] "An apocryphal history of the Trojan war passed current in the Middle Age under this name, and was regarded as the authentic account of an eyewitness and participant" (Cook). Sidney followed contemporaries in still assuming it to be authentic.
[53] See his *Epodes*, V, and *Satires*, I, viii.
[54] Whereas.

and so go by reason, the poet doth so far exceed him as he is to frame his example to that which is most reasonable, be it in warlike, politic, or private matters; where the historian in his bare *was* hath many times that which we call fortune to overrule the best wisdom. Many times he must tell events whereof he can yield no cause; or if he do, it must be poetically.

For, that a feigned example hath as much force to teach as a true example—for as for [10] to move, it is clear, since the feigned may be tuned to the highest key of passion—let us take one example wherein a poet and a historian do concur. Herodotus and Justin do both testify that Zopyrus, king Darius's faithful servant, seeing his master long resisted by the rebellious Babylonians, feigned himself in extreme disgrace of his king; for verifying of which he caused his own nose and ears to be cut off, and so flying to the Babylonians, was [20] received, and for his known valor so far credited, that he did find means to deliver them over to Darius. Much-like matter doth Livy record of Tarquinius and his son. Xenophon excellently feigneth such another stratagem, performed by Abradatas in Cyrus's behalf. Now would I fain know, if occasion be presented unto you to serve your prince by such an honest dissimulation, why do you not as well learn it of Xenophon's fiction as of the [30] other's verity? and, truly, so much the better, as you shall save your nose by the bargain; for Abradatas did not counterfeit so far.

So, then, the best of the historian is subject to the poet; for whatsoever action or faction, whatsoever counsel, policy, or war-stratagem the historian is bound to recite, that may the poet, if he list, with his imitation make his own, beautifying it both for further teaching and more delighting, as it pleaseth him; having [40] all, from Dante's Heaven to his Hell, under the authority of his pen. Which if I be asked what poets have done? so as I might well name some, yet say I, and say again, I speak of the art, and not of the artificer.

Now, to that which commonly is attributed to the praise of history, in respect of the notable learning is gotten by marking the success, as though therein a man should see virtue exalted and vice punished,—truly that com- [50] mendation is peculiar to poetry and far off from history. For, indeed, poetry ever setteth virtue so out in her best colors, making Fortune her well-waiting handmaid, that one must needs be enamored of her. Well may you see Ulysses in a storm and in other hard plights; but they are but exercises of patience and magnanimity,

to make them shine the more in the near following prosperity. And, of the contrary part, if evil men come to the stage, they ever go out—as the tragedy writer answered to one that misliked the show of such persons—so manacled as they little animate folks to follow them. But the historian, being captived to the truth of a foolish world, is many times a terror from well-doing, and an encouragement to unbridled wickedness. For see we not valiant Miltiades [55] rot in his fetters? The just Phocion [56] and the accomplished Socrates put to death like traitors? The cruel Severus [57] live prosperously? The excellent Severus [58] miserably murdered? Sylla and Marius dying in their beds? Pompey and Cicero slain then, when they would have thought exile a happiness? See we not virtuous Cato [59] driven to kill himself, and rebel Caesar so advanced that his name yet, after sixteen hundred years, lasteth in the highest honor? And mark but even Caesar's own words of the forenamed Sylla—who in that only did honestly, to put down his dishonest tyranny—*literas nescivit:* [60] as if want of learning caused him to do well. He meant it not by poetry, which, not content with earthly plagues, deviseth new punishments in hell for tyrants; nor yet by philosophy, which teacheth *occidendos esse;* [61] but, no doubt, by skill in history, for that indeed can afford you Cypselus, Periander,[62] Phalaris,[63] Dionysius,[64] and I know not how many more of the same kennel, that speed well enough in their abominable injustice or usurpation.

I conclude, therefore, that he excelleth history, not only in furnishing the mind with knowledge, but in setting it forward to that which deserveth to be called and accounted good; which setting forward, and moving to well-doing, indeed setteth the laurel crown upon the poet as victorious, not only of the historian, but over the philosopher, howsoever in teaching it may be questionable. For suppose it be granted—that which I suppose with great reason may be denied—that the philosopher, in respect of his methodical pro-

---

[55] The victor at Marathon. (Cf. Cicero, *Republic*, I, iii, 5.)
[56] See Plutarch's life of him.
[57] Septimius Severus (A.D. 193–211).
[58] Alexander Severus (A.D. 222–235).
[59] Cato of Utica.    [60] Was an ignorant fellow.
[61] That they are to be slain.
[62] Concerning both see Herodotus, V, 92.
[63] Tyrant of Agrigentum. (Cf. Cicero, *De Officiis*, II, vii, 26.)
[64] Tyrant of Syracuse. (Cf. Cicero, *Tusc. Disp.*, V, 20.)

ceeding, teach more perfectly than the poet, yet do I think that no man is so much φιλοφιλόσοφος [65] as to compare the philosopher in moving with the poet. And that moving is of a higher degree than teaching, it may by this appear, that it is well nigh both the cause and the effect of teaching; for who will be taught, if he be not moved with desire to be taught? And what so much good doth that teaching bring forth—I speak still of moral doctrine—as that it moveth one to do that which it doth teach? For, as Aristotle saith, it is not γνῶσις but πρᾶξις [66] must be the fruit; and how πρᾶξις can be without being moved to practise, it is no hard matter to consider. The philosopher showeth you the way; he informeth you of the particularities, as well of the tediousness of the way, as of the pleasant lodging you shall have when your journey is ended, as of the many by-turnings that may divert you from your way; but this is to no man but to him that will read him, and read him with attentive, studious painfulness; which constant desire whosoever hath in him, hath already passed half the hardness of the way, and therefore is beholding to the philosopher but for the other half. Nay, truly, learned men have learnedly thought that where once reason hath so much overmastered passion as that the mind hath a free desire to do well, the inward light each mind hath in itself is as good as a philosopher's book; since in nature we know it is well to do well, and what is well and what is evil, although not in the words of art which philosophers bestow upon us; for out of natural conceit the philosophers drew it. But to be moved to do that which we know, or to be moved with desire to know, *hoc opus, hic labor est*.[67]

Now therein of all sciences—I speak still of human and according to the human conceit—is our poet the monarch. For he doth not only show the way, but giveth so sweet a prospect into the way as will entice any man to enter into it. Nay, he doth, as if your journey should lie through a fair vineyard, at the very first give you a cluster of grapes, that full of that taste you may long to pass further. He beginneth not with obscure definitions, which must blur the margent with interpretations, and load the memory with doubtfulness. But he cometh to you with words set in delightful proportion, either accompanied with, or prepared for, the well-enchanting skill of music; and with a tale, forsooth, he cometh unto you, with a tale which holdeth children from play and old men from the chimney-corner, and, pretending no more, doth intend the winning of the mind from wickedness to virtue; even as the child is often brought to take most wholesome things by hiding them in such other as have a pleasant taste,—which, if one should begin to tell them the nature of the aloes or rhubarb they should receive, would sooner take their physic at their ears than at their mouth. So is it in men, most of which are childish in the best things, till they be cradled in their graves,—glad they will be to hear the tales of Hercules, Achilles, Cyrus, Aeneas; and, hearing them, must needs hear the right description of wisdom, valor, and justice; which, if they had been barely, that is to say philosophically, set out, they would swear they be brought to school again.

That imitation whereof poetry is hath the most conveniency to nature of all other; insomuch that, as Aristotle saith, those things which in themselves are horrible, as cruel battles, unnatural monsters, are made in poetical imitation delightful. Truly, I have known men that even with reading *Amadis de Gaule*, which, God knoweth, wanteth much of a perfect poesy, have found their hearts moved to the exercise of courtesy, liberality, and especially courage. Who readeth Aeneas carrying old Anchises on his back, that wisheth not it were his fortune to perform so excellent an act? Whom do not those words of Turnus move, the tale of Turnus having planted his image in the imagination:

> *Fugientem haec terra videbit?*
> *Usque adeone mori miserum est?* [68]

Where the philosophers, as they scorn to delight, so must they be content little to move—saving wrangling whether virtue be the chief or the only good, whether the contemplative or the active life do excel—which Plato and Boethius well knew, and therefore made Mistress Philosophy very often borrow the masking raiment of Poesy. For even those hardhearted evil men who think virtue a schoolname, and know no other good but *indulgere genio*,[69] and therefore despise the austere admonitions of the philosopher, and feel not the inward reason they stand upon, yet will be content to be

---

[65] A friend to the philosopher.
[66] Not knowledge but practise.
[67] This is the task, this is the struggle (*Aeneid*, VI, 129).

[68] Shall this land see Turnus a fugitive? Is it so passing hard to die? (*Aeneid*, XII, 645-646.)
[69] To give their genius free play (Persius, *Satires*, V, 151).

delighted, which is all the good-fellow poet seemeth to promise; and so steal to see the form of goodness—which seen, they cannot but love—ere themselves be aware, as if they took a medicine of cherries.

Infinite proofs of the strange effects of this poetical invention might be alleged; only two shall serve, which are so often remembered as I think all men know them. The one of Menenius Agrippa,[70] who, when the whole people of Rome had resolutely divided themselves from the senate, with apparent show of utter ruin, though he were, for that time, an excellent orator, came not among them upon trust either of figurative speeches or cunning insinuations, and much less with far-fet[71] maxims of philosophy, which, especially if they were Platonic, they must have learned geometry before they could well have conceived; but, forsooth, he behaves himself like a homely and familiar poet. He telleth them a tale, that there was a time when all the parts of the body made a mutinous conspiracy against the belly, which they thought devoured the fruits of each other's labor; they concluded they would let so unprofitable a spender starve. In the end, to be short—for the tale is notorious, and as notorious that it was a tale—with punishing the belly they plagued themselves. This, applied by him, wrought such effect in the people as I never read that ever words brought forth but then so sudden and so good an alteration; for upon reasonable conditions a perfect reconcilement ensued.

The other is of Nathan the prophet,[72] who, when the holy David had so far forsaken God as to confirm adultery with murder, when he was to do the tenderest office of a friend, in laying his own shame before his eyes,—sent by God to call again so chosen a servant, how doth he it but by telling of a man whose beloved lamb was ungratefully taken from his bosom? The application most divinely true, but the discourse itself feigned; which made David (I speak of the second and instrumental cause) as in a glass to see his own filthiness, as that heavenly Psalm of Mercy well testifieth.

By these, therefore, examples and reasons, I think it may be manifest that the poet with that same hand of delight doth draw the mind more effectually than any other art doth. And so a conclusion not unfitly ensueth: that as virtue is the most excellent resting-place for all worldly learning to make his end of, so poetry, being the most familiar to teach it, and most

princely to move towards it, in the most excellent work is the most excellent workman.

But I am content not only to decipher him by his works—although works in commendation or dispraise must ever hold a high authority—but more narrowly will examine his parts; so that, as in a man, though all together may carry a presence full of majesty and beauty, perchance in some one defectious piece we may find a blemish.

Now in his parts, kinds, or species, as you list to term them, it is to be noted that some poesies have coupled together two or three kinds,—as tragical and comical, whereupon is risen the tragi-comical; some, in the like manner, have mingled prose and verse, as Sannazaro[73] and Boethius;[74] some have mingled matters heroical and pastoral; but that cometh all to one in this question, for, if severed they be good, the conjunction cannot be hurtful. Therefore, perchance forgetting some, and leaving some as needless to be remembered, it shall not be amiss in a word to cite the special kinds, to see what faults may be found in the right use of them.

Is it then the pastoral poem which is misliked?—for perchance where the hedge is lowest they will soonest leap over. Is the poor pipe disdained, which sometimes out of Meliboeus' mouth can show the misery of people under hard lords and ravening soldiers, and again, by Tityrus, what blessedness is derived to them that lie lowest from the goodness of them that sit highest? sometimes, under the pretty tales of wolves and sheep, can include the whole considerations of wrongdoing and patience; sometimes show that contention for trifles can get but a trifling victory; where perchance a man may see that even Alexander and Darius, when they strave who should be cock of this world's dunghill, the benefit they got was that the after-livers may say:

*Haec memini et victum frustra contendere Thyrsim;*
*Ex illo Corydon, Corydon est tempore nobis.*[75]

Or is it the lamenting elegiac, which in a kind heart would move rather pity than blame; who bewaileth, with the great philosopher Heraclitus, the weakness of mankind and the wretchedness of the world; who surely is to be praised, either for compassionate accompany-

---

[70] See Livy, II, 32.    [71] Far-fetched.
[72] See II Samuel, 12.

[73] Neapolitan scholar and poet (1458–1530). Sidney refers to his *Arcadia*.
[74] In his *Consolation of Philosophy*.
[75] These verses I remember, and how the vanquished Thyrsis vainly strove; from that day it has been with us Corydon, none but Corydon (Virgil, *Eclogues*, VII, 69–70).

ing just causes of lamentation, or for rightly painting out how weak be the passions of woe-fulness?

Is it the bitter but wholesome iambic, who rubs the galled mind, in making shame the trumpet of villainy with bold and open cry-ing out against naughtiness?

Or the satiric? who

*Omne vafer vitium ridenti tangit amico;* [76]

who sportingly never leaveth till he make a man laugh at folly, and at length ashamed to laugh at himself, which he cannot avoid with-out avoiding the folly; who, while *circum praecordia ludit,* [77] giveth us to feel how many headaches a passionate life bringeth us to,—how, when all is done,

*Est Ulubris, animus si nos non deficit aequus.* [78]

No, perchance it is the comic; whom naughty play-makers and stage-keepers have justly made odious. To the argument of abuse I will answer after. Only thus much now is to be said, that the comedy is an imitation of the common errors of our life, which he represent-eth in the most ridiculous and scornful sort that may be, so as it is impossible that any beholder can be content to be such a one. Now, as in geometry the oblique must be known as well as the right, and in arithmetic the odd as well as the even; so in the actions of our life who seeth not the filthiness of evil wanteth a great foil to perceive the beauty of virtue. This doth the comedy handle so, in our private and domestical matters, as with hearing it we get, as it were, an experience what is to be looked for of a niggardly Demea, of a crafty Davus, of a flattering Gnatho, of a vain-glorious Thraso; [79] and not only to know what effects are to be expected, but to know who be such, by the signifying badge given them by the comedian. And little reason hath any man to say that men learn evil by seeing it so set out; since, as I said before, there is no man living but by the force truth hath in nature, no sooner seeth these men play their parts but wisheth them *in pistrinum,* [80] although perchance the sack of his own faults lie so behind his back

that he seeth not himself to dance the same measure,—whereto yet nothing can more open his eyes than to find his own actions contempt-ibly set forth.

So that the right use of comedy will, I think, by nobody be blamed, and much less of the high and excellent tragedy that openeth the greatest wounds, and showeth forth the ulcers that are covered with tissue; that maketh kings fear to be tyrants, and tyrants manifest their tyrannical humors; that with stirring the effects of admiration and commiseration teacheth the uncertainty of this world, and upon how weak foundations gilden roofs are builded; that maketh us know:

*Qui sceptra saevus duro imperio regit,*
*Timet timentes, metus in auctorem redit.* [81]

But how much it can move, Plutarch yieldeth a notable testimony of the abominable tyrant Alexander Pheraeus; [82] from whose eyes a trag-edy, well made and represented, drew abun-dance of tears, who without all pity had mur-dered infinite numbers, and some of his own blood; so as he that was not ashamed to make matters for tragedies, yet could not resist the sweet violence of a tragedy. And if it wrought no further good in him, it was that he, in despite of himself, withdrew himself from hearkening to that which might mollify his hardened heart. But it is not the tragedy they do mislike, for it were too absurd to cast out so excellent a representation of whatsoever is most worthy to be learned.

Is it the lyric that most displeaseth, who with his tuned lyre and well-accorded voice, giveth praise, the reward of virtue, to virtuous acts; who giveth moral precepts and natural problems; who sometimes raiseth up his voice to the height of the heavens, in singing the lauds of the immortal God? Certainly I must confess mine own barbarousness; I never heard the old song of Percy and Douglas that I found not my heart moved more than with a trumpet; and yet it is sung but by some blind crowder, [83] with no rougher voice than rude style; which being so evil appareled in the dust and cob-webs of that uncivil age, what would it work, trimmed in the gorgeous eloquence of Pindar? In Hungary I have seen it the manner at all feasts, and other such meetings, to have songs of their ancestors' valor, which that right sol-

---

[76] Cunningly probes every fault while making his friend laugh (Persius, *Sat.*, I, 116).

[77] He plays about the heart-strings (*ibid.*, 117).

[78] Even Ulubrae may be a happy place of abode, if we preserve a balanced mind. (The line cannot be translated without expanding it. Horace, *Epistles*, I, xi, 30.)

[79] All characters in the plays of Terence.

[80] In the mill (the place of punishment, as one learns from Plautus and Terence, for troublesome slaves).

[81] The savage tyrant who governs his peoples harshly fears those who fear him, and thus fear re-coils upon the author of fear (Seneca, *Oedipus*, 705–706).

[82] In his *Life of Pelopidas*, 29.

[83] Fiddler.

dier-like nation think the chiefest kindlers of brave courage. The incomparable Lacedaemonians did not only carry that kind of music ever with them to the field, but even at home as such songs were made, so were they all content to be singers of them; when the lusty men were to tell what they did, the old men what they had done, and the young men what they would do. And where a man may say that Pindar many times praiseth highly victories of small moment, matters rather of sport than virtue; as it may be answered it was the fault of the poet, and not of the poetry, so indeed the chief fault was in the time and custom of the Greeks, who set those toys at so high a price that Philip of Macedon reckoned a horse-race won at Olympus [84] among his three fearful felicities. But as the unimitable Pindar often did, so is that kind most capable and most fit to awake the thoughts from the sleep of idleness, to embrace honorable enterprises.

There rests the heroical, whose very name, I think, should daunt all backbiters. For by what conceit can a tongue be directed to speak evil of that which draweth with it no less champions than Achilles, Cyrus, Aeneas, Turnus, Tydeus,[85] [86] who doth not only teach and move to a truth, but teacheth and moveth to the most high and excellent truth; who maketh magnanimity and justice shine through all misty fearfulness and foggy desires; who, if the saying of Plato and Tully be true, that who could see virtue would be wonderfully ravished with the love of her beauty, this man setteth her out to make her more lovely, in her holiday apparel, to the eye of any that will deign not to disdain until they understand. But if anything be already said in the defense of sweet poetry, all concurreth to the maintaining the heroical, which is not only a kind, but the best and most accomplished kind of poetry. For, as the image of each action stirreth and instructeth the mind, so the lofty image of such worthies most inflameth the mind with desire to be worthy, and informs with counsel how to be worthy. Only let Aeneas be worn in the tablet of your memory, how he governeth himself in the ruin of his country; in the preserving his old father, and carrying away his religious ceremonies; in obeying the god's commandment to leave Dido, though not only all passionate kindness, but even the human consideration of virtuous gratefulness, would have craved other of him; how in storms, how in sports, how in war, how in peace, how a fugitive, how victorious, how besieged, how besieging, how to strangers, how to allies, how to enemies, how to his own; lastly, how in his inward self, and how in his outward government; and I think, in a mind most prejudiced with a prejudicating humor, he will be found in excellency fruitful—yea, even as Horace saith, *melius Chrysippo et Crantore*.[87] But truly I imagine it falleth out with these poet-whippers as with some good women who often are sick, but in faith they cannot tell where. So the name of poetry is odious to them, but neither his cause nor effects, neither the sum that contains him nor the particularities descending from him, give any fast handle to their carping dispraise.

Since, then, poetry is of all human learnings the most ancient and of most fatherly antiquity, as from whence other learnings have taken their beginnings; since it is so universal that no learned nation doth despise it, nor barbarous nation is without it; since both Roman and Greek gave divine names unto it, the one of "prophesying," the other of "making," and that indeed that name of "making" is fit for him, considering that whereas other arts retain themselves within their subject, and receive, as it were, their being from it, the poet only bringeth his own stuff, and doth not learn a conceit out of a matter, but maketh matter for a conceit; since neither his description nor his end containeth any evil, the thing described cannot be evil; since his effects be so good as to teach goodness, and delight the learners of it; since therein—namely in moral doctrine, the chief of all knowledges—he doth not only far pass the historian, but for instructing is well nigh comparable to the philosopher, and for moving leaveth him behind him; since the Holy Scripture, wherein there is no uncleanness, hath whole parts in it poetical, and that even our Savior Christ vouchsafed to use the flowers of it; since all his kinds are not only in their united forms, but in their several dissections fully commendable; I think, and think I think rightly, the laurel crown appointed for triumphant captains doth worthily, of all other learnings, honor the poet's triumph.

But because we have ears as well as tongues, and that the lightest reasons that may be will seem to weigh greatly if nothing be put in the counter-balance, let us hear, and, as well as we can, ponder, what objections be made against this art, which may be worthy either of yielding or answering. . . .

Before I give my pen a full stop, it shall be

---

[84] I. e., Olympia.     [85] See *Iliad*, IV.
[86] See Tasso's *Jerusalem Delivered*.

[87] Better than Chrysippus and Crantor (*Epistles*, I, ii, 4).

but a little more lost time to inquire why England, the mother of excellent minds, should be grown so hard a stepmother to poets; who certainly in wit ought to pass all others, since all only proceedeth from their wit, being indeed makers of themselves, not takers of others. . . .

But I that, before ever I durst aspire unto the dignity, am admitted into the company of the paper-blurrers, do find the very true cause of our wanting estimation is want of desert, taking upon us to be poets in despite of Pallas. Now wherein we want desert were a thank-worthy labor to express; but if I knew, I should have mended myself. But as I never desired the title, so have I neglected the means to come by it; only, overmastered by some thoughts, I yielded an inky tribute unto them. Marry, they that delight in poesy itself should seek to know what they do and how they do; and especially look themselves in an unflattering glass of reason, if they be inclinable unto it. For poesy must not be drawn by the ears, it must be gently led, or rather it must lead; which was partly the cause that made the ancient learned affirm it was a divine gift, and no human skill, since all other knowledges lie ready for any that hath strength of wit; a poet no industry can make if his own genius be not carried into it. And therefore is it an old proverb: *Orator fit, poeta nascitur.*[88] Yet confess I always that, as the fertilest ground must be manured, so must the highest-flying wit have a Daedalus to guide him. That Daedalus, they say, both in this and in other, hath three wings to bear itself up into the air of due commendation: that is, art, imitation, and exercise. But these, neither artificial rules nor imitative patterns, we much cumber ourselves withal. Exercise indeed we do, but that very fore-backwardly, for where we should exercise to know, we exercise as having known; and so is our brain delivered of much matter which never was begotten by knowledge. For there being two principal parts, matter to be expressed by words and words to express the matter, in neither we use art or imitation rightly. Our matter is *quodlibet*[89] indeed, though wrongly performing Ovid's verse,

*Quicquid condbar dicere, versus erat,*[90]

never marshaling it into any assured rank, that almost the readers cannot tell where to find themselves.

Chaucer, undoubtedly, did excellently in his *Troilus and Cressida*; of whom, truly, I know not whether to marvel more, either that he in that misty time could see so clearly, or that we in this clear age walk so stumblingly after him. Yet had he great wants, fit to be forgiven in so reverend antiquity. I account the *Mirror of Magistrates*[91] meetly furnished of beautiful parts; and in the Earl of Surrey's lyrics many things tasting of a noble birth, and worthy of a noble mind. The *Shepherd's Calendar*[92] hath much poetry in his eclogues indeed worthy the reading, if I be not deceived. That same framing of his style to an old rustic language I dare not allow, since neither Theocritus in Greek, Virgil in Latin, nor Sannazaro in Italian did affect it. Besides these, I do not remember to have seen but few (to speak boldly) printed that have poetical sinews in them. For proof whereof, let but most of the verses be put in prose, and then ask the meaning, and it will be found that one verse did but beget another, without ordering at the first what should be at the last; which becomes a confused mass of words, with a tinkling sound of rime, barely accompanied with reason.

Our tragedies and comedies not without cause cried out against, observing rules neither of honest civility nor of skilful poetry, excepting *Gorboduc*[93] (again I say of those that I have seen); which notwithstanding as it is full of stately speeches and well-sounding phrases, climbing to the height of Seneca's style, and as full of notable morality, which it doth most delightfully teach, and so obtain the very end of poesy; yet in truth it is very defectious in the circumstances, which grieveth me, because it might not remain as an exact model of all tragedies. For it is faulty both in place and time, the two necessary companions of all corporal actions. For where the stage should always represent but one place, and the uttermost time presupposed in it should be, both by Aristotle's precept and common reason, but one day; there is both many days and many places inartificially imagined.

But if it be so in *Gorboduc*, how much more in all the rest? where you shall have Asia of the one side, and Afric of the other, and so many other under-kingdoms that the player, when he cometh in, must ever begin with tell-

---

[88] The orator is made, the poet is born.
[89] Indifferent.
[90] Whatever I tried to express turned out to be poetry (quoted inexactly from *Tristia*, IV, x, 26).

[91] First published in 1559.
[92] By Edmund Spenser. It was dedicated to Sidney.
[93] By Thomas Sackville, Lord Buckhurst (1536–1608) and Thomas Norton (1532–1584). First published in 1565.

ing where he is, or else the tale will not be conceived. Now ye shall have three ladies walk to gather flowers, and then we must believe the stage to be a garden. By and by we hear news of shipwreck in the same place, and then we are to blame if we accept it not for a rock. Upon the back of that comes out a hideous monster with fire and smoke, and then the miserable beholders are bound to take it for a cave. While in the mean time two armies fly 10 in, represented with four swords and bucklers, and then what hard heart will not receive it for a pitched field?

Now of time they are much more liberal. For ordinary it is that two young princes [94] fall in love; after many traverses she is got with child, delivered of a fair boy; he is lost, groweth a man, falleth in love, and is ready to get another child,—and all this in two hours' space; which how absurd it is in sense even 20 sense may imagine, and art hath taught, and all ancient examples justified, and at this day the ordinary players in Italy will not err in. Yet will some bring in an example of *Eunuchus* [95] in Terence, that containeth matter of two days, yet far short of twenty years. True it is, and so was it to be played in two days, and so fitted to the time it set forth. And though Plautus have in one place done amiss, let us hit with him, and not miss with him. 30 But they will say, How then shall we set forth a story which containeth both many places and many times? And do they not know that a tragedy is tied to the laws of poesy, and not of history; not bound to follow the story, but having liberty either to feign a quite new matter, or to frame the history to the most tragical conveniency? Again, many things may be told which cannot be showed,—if they know the difference betwixt reporting and representing. 40 As for example, I may speak, though I am here, of Peru, and in speech digress from that to the description of Calicut; [96] but in action I cannot represent it without Pacolet's horse.[97] And so was the manner the ancients took, by some *nuntius* [98] to recount things done in former time or other place.

Lastly, if they will represent a history, they must not, as Horace saith, begin *ab ovo*,[99] but they must come to the principal point of that 50 one action which they will represent. By example this will be best expressed. I have a story of young Polydorus,[100] delivered for safety's sake, with great riches, by his father Priamus to Polymnestor, King of Thrace, in the Trojan war time. He, after some years, hearing the overthrow of Priamus, for to make the treasure his own murdereth the child; the body of the child is taken up by Hecuba; she, the same day, findeth a sleight to be revenged most cruelly of the tyrant. Where now would one of our tragedy-writers begin, but with the delivery of the child? Then should he sail over into Thrace, and so spend I know not how many years, and travel numbers of places. But where doth Euripides? Even with the finding of the body, leaving the rest to be told by the spirit of Polydorus. This needs no further to be enlarged; the dullest wit may conceive it.

But, besides these gross absurdities, how all their plays be neither right tragedies nor right comedies, mingling kings and clowns, not because the matter so carrieth it, but thrust in the clown by head and shoulders to play a part in majestical matters, with neither decency nor discretion; so as neither the admiration and commiseration, nor the right sportfulness, is by their mongrel tragi-comedy obtained. I know Apuleius did somewhat so,[101] but that is a thing recounted with space of time, not represented in one moment; and I know the ancients have one or two examples of tragi-comedies, as Plautus hath *Amphytrio*. But, if we mark them well, we shall find that they never, or very daintily, match hornpipes and funerals. So falleth it out that, having indeed no right comedy in that comical part of our tragedy, we have nothing but scurrility, unworthy of any chaste ears, or some extreme show of doltishness, indeed fit to lift up a loud laughter, and nothing else; where the whole tract of a comedy should be full of delight, as the tragedy should be still maintained in a well-raised admiration.

But our comedians think there is no delight without laughter, which is very wrong; for though laughter may come with delight, yet cometh it not of delight, as though delight should be the cause of laughter; but well may one thing breed both together. Nay, rather in themselves they have, as it were, a kind of contrariety. For delight we scarcely do, but in things that have a conveniency to ourselves, or to the general nature; laughter almost ever cometh of things most disproportioned to our-

---

[94] Title applied to both sexes.
[95] A slip. Sidney meant to refer to the *Heautontimoroumenos* of Terence.
[96] In India.
[97] In the romance of *Valentine and Orson*.
[98] Messenger.
[99] From the very beginning (*Satires*, I, iii, 6; also *De Arte Poetica*, 147).

[100] Euripides, *Hecuba*.
[101] In his *Metamorphoses*.

selves and nature. Delight hath a joy in it either permanent or present; laughter hath only a scornful tickling. For example, we are ravished with delight to see a fair woman, and yet are far from being moved to laughter. We laugh at deformed creatures, wherein certainly we cannot delight. We delight in good chances; we laugh at mischances. We delight to hear the happiness of our friends and country, at which he were worthy to be laughed at that would laugh. We shall, contrarily, laugh sometimes to find a matter quite mistaken and go down the hill against the bias, in the mouth of some such men, as for the respect of them one shall be heartily sorry he cannot choose but laugh, and so is rather pained than delighted with laughter. Yet deny I not but that they may go well together. For as in Alexander's picture well set out we delight without laughter, and in twenty mad antics we laugh without delight; so in Hercules, painted, with his great beard and furious countenance, in woman's attire, spinning at Omphale's commandment, it breedeth both delight and laughter; for the representing of so strange a power in love, procureth delight, and the scornfulness of the action stirreth laughter.

But I speak to this purpose, that all the end of the comical part be not upon such scornful matters as stir laughter only, but mixed with it that delightful teaching which is the end of poesy. And the great fault, even in that point of laughter, and forbidden plainly by Aristotle, is that they stir laughter in sinful things, which are rather execrable than ridiculous; or in miserable, which are rather to be pitied than scorned. For what is it to make folks gape at a wretched beggar or a beggarly clown, or, against law of hospitality, to jest at strangers because they speak not English so well as we do? what do we learn? since it is certain:

> *Nil habet infelix paupertas durius in se*
> *Quam quod ridiculos homines facit.*[102]

But rather a busy loving courtier; a heartless threatening Thraso; a self-wise-seeming schoolmaster; a wry-transformed traveler: these if we saw walk in stage-names, which we play naturally, therein were delightful laughter and teaching delightfulness,—as in the other, the tragedies of Buchanan do justly bring forth a divine admiration.

But I have lavished out too many words of this play-matter. I do it, because as they are excelling parts of poesy, so is there none so much used in England, and none can be more pitifully abused; which, like an unmannerly daughter, showing a bad education, causeth her mother Poesy's honesty to be called in question.

Other sorts of poetry almost have we none, but that lyrical kind of songs and sonnets, which, Lord if He gave us so good minds, how well it might be employed, and with how heavenly fruits both private and public, in singing the praises of the immortal beauty, the immortal goodness of that God who giveth us hands to write, and wits to conceive!—of which we might well want words, but never matter; of which we could turn our eyes to nothing, but we should ever have new-budding occasions.

But truly, many of such writings as come under the banner of unresistible love, if I were a mistress, would never persuade me they were in love; so coldly they apply fiery speeches, as men that had rather read lovers' writings, and so caught up certain swelling phrases—which hang together like a man which once told me the wind was at northwest and by south, because he would be sure to name winds enough—than that in truth they feel those passions, which easily, as I think, may be bewrayed by that same forcibleness, or *energia* (as the Greeks call it) of the writer. But let this be a sufficient, though short note, that we miss the right use of the material point of poesy.

Now for the outside of it, which is words, or (as I may term it) diction, it is even well worse, so is that honey-flowing matron eloquence appareled, or rather disguised, in a courtesan-like painted affectation: one time with so far-fet words, that many seem monsters—but must seem strangers—to any poor Englishman; another time with coursing of a letter, as if they were bound to follow the method of a dictionary; another time with figures and flowers extremely winter-starved.

But I would this fault were only peculiar to versifiers, and had not as large possession among prose-printers, and, which is to be marveled, among many scholars, and, which is to be pitied, among some preachers. Truly I could wish—if at least I might be so bold to wish in a thing beyond the reach of my capacity—the diligent imitators of Tully and Demosthenes (most worthy to be imitated) did not so much keep Nizolian [103] paper-books of their figures and phrases, as by attentive

---

[102] Poverty, bitter though it be, has no sharper pang than this, that it makes men ridiculous (Juvenal, *Satires*, III, 152-153).

[103] The Italian Marius Nizolius (1498-1566) compiled a Ciceronian lexicon.

translation, as it were devour them whole, and make them wholly theirs. For now they cast sugar and spice upon every dish that is served to the table; like those Indians, not content to wear ear-rings at the fit and natural place of the ears, but they will thrust jewels through their nose and lips, because they will be sure to be fine. Tully, when he was to drive out Catiline as it were with a thunderbolt of eloquence, often used that figure of repetition, as *Vivit. Vivit? Immo vero etiam in senatum venit*,[104] etc. Indeed, inflamed with a well-grounded rage, he would have his words, as it were, double out of his mouth; and so do that artificially which we see men in choler do naturally. And we, having noted the grace of those words, hale them in sometime to a familiar epistle, when it were too much choler to be choleric. How well store of *similiter* [105] cadences doth sound with the gravity of the pulpit, I would but invoke Demosthenes' soul to tell, who with a rare daintiness useth them. Truly they have made me think of the sophister that with too much subtility would prove two eggs three, and though he might be counted a sophister, had none for his labor. So these men bringing in such a kind of eloquence, well may they obtain an opinion of a seeming fineness, but persuade few,—which should be the end of their fineness.

Now for similitudes in certain printed discourses, I think all herbarists, all stories of beasts, fowls, and fishes are rifled up, that they may come in multitudes to wait upon any of our conceits, which certainly is as absurd a surfeit to the ears as is possible. For the force of a similitude not being to prove any thing to a contrary disputer, but only to explain to a willing hearer; when that is done, the rest is a most tedious prattling, rather overswaying the memory from the purpose whereto they were applied, than any whit informing the judgment, already either satisfied or by similitudes not to be satisfied.

For my part, I do not doubt, when Antonius and Crassus, the great forefathers of Cicero in eloquence, the one (as Cicero testifieth of them) pretended not to know art, the other not to set by it, because with a plain sensibleness they might win credit of popular ears, which credit is the nearest step to persuasion, which persuasion is the chief mark of oratory,—I do not doubt, I say, but that they used these knacks very sparingly; which who doth generally use any man may see

doth dance to his own music, and so be noted by the audience more careful to speak curiously than truly. Undoubtedly (at least to my opinion undoubtedly) I have found in divers small-learned courtiers a more sound style than in some professors of learning; of which I can guess no other cause, but that the courtier following that which by practice he findeth fittest to nature, therein, though he know it not, doth according to art, though not by art; where the other, using art to show art and not to hide art—as in these cases he should do—flieth from nature, and indeed abuseth art.

But what! me thinks I deserve to be pounded for straying from poetry to oratory. But both have such an affinity in the wordish consideration that I think this digression will make my meaning receive the fuller understanding:—which is not to take upon me to teach poets how they should do, but only, finding myself sick among the rest, to show some one or two spots of the common infection grown among the most part of writers; that, acknowledging ourselves somewhat awry, we may bend to the right use both of matter and manner: whereto our language giveth us great occasion, being, indeed, capable of any excellent exercising of it.

I know some will say it is a mingled language. And why not so much the better, taking the best of both the other? Another will say it wanteth grammar. Nay, truly, it hath that praise that it wanteth not grammar. For grammar it might have, but it needs it not; being so easy in itself, and so void of those cumbersome differences of cases, genders, moods, and tenses, which, I think, was a piece of the Tower of Babylon's curse, that a man should be put to school to learn his mother-tongue. But for the uttering sweetly and properly the conceits of the mind, which is the end of speech, that hath it equally with any other tongue in the world; and is particularly happy in compositions of two or three words together, near the Greek, far beyond the Latin,—which is one of the greatest beauties can be in a language.

Now of versifying there are two sorts, the one ancient, the other modern. The ancient marked the quantity of each syllable, and according to that framed his verse; the modern observing only number, with some regard of the accent, the chief life of it standeth in that like sounding of the words which we call rime. Whether of these be the more excellent would bear many speeches; the ancient no doubt more fit for music, both words and tune observing quantity; and more fit lively to ex-

---

[104] He lives. He lives? Yes, he comes even into the senate (Cicero, *Catiline*, I, 2).

[105] Similar.

press divers passions, by the low or lofty sound of the well-weighed syllable. The latter likewise with his rime striketh a certain music to the ear; and, in fine, since it doth delight, though by another way, it obtaineth the same purpose; there being in either, sweetness, and wanting in neither, majesty. Truly the English, before any other vulgar language I know, is fit for both sorts. For, for the ancient, the Italian is so full of vowels that it must ever be cumbered with elisions; the Dutch so, of the other side, with consonants, that they cannot yield the sweet sliding fit for a verse. The French in his whole language hath not one word that hath his accent in the last syllable saving two, called antepenultima, and little more hath the Spanish; and therefore very gracelessly may they use dactyls. The English is subject to none of these defects. Now for rime, though we do not observe quantity, yet we observe the accent very precisely, which other languages either cannot do, or will not do so absolutely. That caesura, or breathing-place in the midst of the verse, neither Italian nor Spanish have; the French and we never almost fail of.

Lastly, even the very rime itself the Italian cannot put in the last syllable, by the French named the masculine rime, but still in the next to the last, which the French call the female, or the next before that, which the Italians term *sdrucciola*. The example of the former is *buono:suono*; of the *sdrucciola* is *femina:semina*. The French, of the other side, hath both the male, as *bon:son*, and the female, as *plaise:taise*; but the *sdrucciola* he hath not. Where the English hath all three, as *due:true*, *father:rather*, *motion:potion*; with much more which might be said, but that already I find the triflingness of this discourse is much too much enlarged.

So that since the ever praiseworthy poesy is full of virtue-breeding delightfulness, and void of no gift that ought to be in the noble name of learning; since the blames laid against it are either false or feeble; since the cause why it is not esteemed in England is the fault of poet-apes, not poets; since, lastly, our tongue is most fit to honor poesy, and to be honored by poesy; I conjure you all that have had the evil luck to read this ink-wasting toy of mine, even in the name of the Nine Muses, no more to scorn the sacred mysteries of poesy; no more to laugh at the name of poets, as though they were next inheritors to fools; no more to jest at the reverend title of "a rimer"; but to believe, with Aristotle, that they were the an-

cient treasures of the Grecians' divinity; to believe, with Bembus, that they were first bringers-in of all civility; to believe, with Scaliger, that no philosopher's precepts can sooner make you an honest man than the reading of Virgil; to believe, with Clauserus, the translator of Cornutus, that it pleased the Heavenly Deity by Hesiod and Homer, under the veil of fables, to give us all knowledge, logic, rhetoric, philosophy natural and moral, and *quid non?* [106] to believe, with me, that there are many mysteries contained in poetry which of purpose were written darkly, lest by profane wits it should be abused; to believe, with Landino, [107] that they are so beloved of the gods that whatsoever they write proceeds of a divine fury; lastly, to believe themselves, when they tell you they will make you immortal by their verses.

Thus doing, your name shall flourish in the printers' shops. Thus doing, you shall be of kin to many a poetical preface. Thus doing, you shall be most fair, most rich, most wise, most all; you shall dwell upon superlatives. Thus doing, though you be *libertino patre natus*, [108] you shall suddenly grow *Herculea proles*, [109]

*Si quid mea carmina possunt.* [110]

Thus doing, your soul shall be placed with Dante's Beatrice or Virgil's Anchises.

But if—fie of such a but!—you be born so near the dull-making cataract of Nilus, that you cannot hear the planet-like music of poetry; if you have so earth-creeping a mind that it cannot lift itself up to look to the sky of poetry, or rather, by a certain rustical disdain, will become such a mome [111] as to be a Momus of poetry; then, though I will not wish unto you the ass's ears of Midas, nor to be driven by a poet's verses, as Bubonax [112] was, to hang himself; nor to be rimed to death, as is said to be done in Ireland; yet thus much curse I must send you in the behalf of all poets:—that while you live you live in love, and never get favor for lacking skill of a sonnet; and when you die, your memory die from the earth for want of an epitaph.

[106] What not?

[107] Florentine humanist (1424–1504).

[108] The son of a freedman (Horace, *Satires*, I, vi, 6).

[109] Herculean offspring.

[110] If my song can aught avail (*Aeneid*, IX, 446).

[111] Fool.

[112] "Sidney is referring to the tale of *Hippomax*, . . . of whom one story was that he satirized the statuary *Bupalus* so bitterly that he hanged himself. By some confusion . . . he has combined the two names" (Shuckburgh).

# Edmund Spenser

## 1552?-1599

The year of Spenser's birth is known only by inference from a sonnet which he wrote in 1593. His father was a man in humble circumstances and followed the trade of cloth-making in London. Spenser was sent to the Merchant Tailors' School, then newly founded under the direction of Richard Mulcaster, one of the most distinguished teachers of the time. Thence he proceeded in 1569 to Pembroke Hall, Cambridge, where he was a sizar, or undergraduate, some of whose expenses were paid in return for certain menial services. He took his B.A. in 1573 and his M.A. in 1576. At Cambridge Spenser formed a lasting friendship with Gabriel Harvey, a Fellow of Pembroke and later one of the notable figures of the University; there too, of course, he came under strong Puritan influences which also were lasting in their effects. When he left Cambridge Spenser may have gone for a time among his kinsmen in the north of England. In 1578 he was a secretary in the household of John Young, Bishop of Rochester. A year later he was back in London, in the household of Robert Dudley, Earl of Leicester, where he came to know and admire Leicester's nephew, Sir Philip Sidney. On 27 October, 1579, he married his first wife, Machabyas Childe. In 1579, too, Spenser published The Shepherd's Calendar, a series of twelve eclogues, in which he clearly announced himself as a significant new force in English poetry. But poetry, of course, brought in no money, and Spenser was at this time seeking public office. In 1580 he was successful in a manner which, it has generally been thought, was little to his taste. He went to Ireland as secretary to Lord Grey of Wilton, then Lord Deputy of Ireland. And in Ireland Spenser stayed, save for two lengthy visits to London, until within a month of his death. In 1589 he came to London with Sir Walter Ralegh, who had been in Ireland, to publish the first three books of The Faerie Queene in 1590; and five years later he again returned to England to oversee the publication (in 1596) of a new edition of The Faerie Queene, containing three additional books, and, in separate volumes, of his Four Hymns and Prothalamion. Spenser's career in Ireland was at once honorable and moderately successful. He filled several minor offices there, and in 1589 was granted an estate of some 3000 acres in the County of Cork. He found congenial friends in Ireland, and there he met and married his second wife, Elizabeth Boyle (1594). In 1598 there occurred an insurrection in Ireland in the course of which Spenser's castle of Kilcolman was pillaged and burned, he and his family escaping to Cork. In December he was sent thence to London with dispatches, and there he fell ill, and died on 13 January, 1599. He was buried in Westminster Abbey. According to tradition he died not only brokenhearted over the loss of a child in the burning of Kilcolman, but also in poverty.

Spenser is, as has been well said, "among the very greatest of our poets, but the significance of his poetry in the history of our literature is even greater than its intrinsic value. He recreated English prosody, giving back to our verse the fluidity and the grace that it had lost since the days of Chaucer, and extending the range of its achievement; he created English poetic diction, lifting it from anarchy and stiffness, daring greatly, but triumphing whether in the simple or the ornate, widening its scope, but at the same time never failing to give it ease and flexibility, so that language became to him a willing servant, and could voice the subtlest shades of mood or fancy. By means of this rich and varied style, fully expressive of his high seriousness, his spirituality, his inexhaustible sense of beauty, he has exercised a spell that has been potent for three centuries, and none has called so many poets to their vocation" (E. de Selincourt, Introduction to Spenser's Poetical Works, pp. xxxix–xl).

The Works of Edmund Spenser, ed. Edwin

Greenlaw, Charles G. Osgood, Frederick M. Padelford, and Ray Heffner (*Baltimore, 1932–1949*), *is a variorum edition, the object of which is to summarize Spenser scholarship, as well as to present the best text of his work. Alexander Judson's* Life of Edmund Spenser (*Baltimore, 1945*) *was prepared for this edition. The* Index (*Baltimore, 1957*) *is useful.*

*A compact volume of commentary is H. S. V. Jones's* Spenser Handbook (*New York, 1930*). *B. E. C. Davis,* Edmund Spenser, a Critical Study (*Cambridge, 1933*) *is valuable on the interpretative rather than on the biographical side. Outstanding studies are Emile Legouis,* Edmund Spenser (*New York, 1926*), *and William L. Renwick,* Edmund Spenser; an Essay on Renaissance Poetry (*London, 1925*). *For a study of* The Faerie Queene *as an epic, see E. M. W. Tillyard,* The English Epic and Its Background (*London, 1954*). *A useful introduction for the student approaching Spenser for the first time is Leicester Bradner,* Spenser and the Faerie Queene (*Chicago, 1948*).

# The Faerie Queene

## A LETTER OF THE AUTHOR'S,

*Expounding His Whole Intention in the Course of This Worke: Which, for that It Giveth Great Light to the Reader, for the Better Understanding Is Hereunto Annexed.*

To the Right Noble and Valorous Sir WALTER RALEGH, KNIGHT; Lord Wardein of the Stanneryes, and Her Majesties Liefetenaunt of the County of Cornewayll.

SIR, knowing how doubtfully all allegories may be construed, and this booke of mine, which I have entituled the *Faery Queene*, being a continued allegory, or darke conceit, I have thought good, as well for avoyding of gealous opinions and misconstructions, as also for your better light in reading thereof (being so by you commanded), to discover unto you the general intention and meaning, which in the whole course thereof I have fashioned, without expressing of any particular purposes, or by-accidents therein occasioned. The generall end therefore of all the booke is to fashion a gentleman or noble person in vertuous and gentle discipline: which for that I conceived shoulde be most plausible and pleasing, being coloured with an historicall fiction, the which the most part of men delight to read, rather for variety of matter than for profite of the ensample, I chose the historye of King Arthure, as most fitte for the excellency of his person, being made famous by many men's former workes, and also furthest from the daunger of envy, and suspition of present time. In which I have followed all the antique poets historicall: first Homer, who in the persons of Agamemnon and Ulysses hath ensampled a good governour and a vertuous man, the one in his Ilias, the other in his Odysseis; then Virgil, whose like intention was to doe in the person of Aeneas; after him Ariosto comprised them both in his Orlando: and lately Tasso dissevered them againe, and formed both parts in two persons, namely that part which they in philosophy call ethice, or vertues of a private man, coloured in his Rinaldo; the other named politice in his Godfredo. By ensample of which excellente poets, I labour to pourtraict in Arthure, before he was king, the image of a brave knight, perfected in the twelve private morall vertues, as Aristotle hath devised; the which is the purpose of these first twelve bookes: [1] which if I finde to be well accepted, I may be perhaps encoraged to frame the other part of polliticke vertues in his person, after that hee came to be king.

To some, I know, this methode will seeme displeasaunt, which had rather have good discipline delivered plainly in way of precepts, or sermoned at large, as they use, than thus clowdily enwrapped in allegoricall devices. But such, me seeme, should be satisfide with the use of these dayes, seeing all things accounted by their showes, and nothing esteemed of, that is not delightfull and pleasing to commune sence.[2] For this cause is Xenophon preferred before Plato, for that the one, in the exquisite depth of his judgement, formed a commune welth, such as it should be; but the other in the person of Cyrus, and the Persians, fashioned a governement, such as might best be: so much more profitable and gratious is doctrine by ensample, than by rule. So have I laboured to doe in the person of Arthure: whome I conceive, after his long education by Timon, to whom he was by Merlin delivered to be brought up, so soone as he was borne of the Lady Igrayne, to have seene in a dream or vision the Faery Queen,

---

[1] Of these Spenser completed only six, and a fragment probably designed for the seventh.

[2] I. e., the senses, in opposition to the reason.

with whose excellent beauty ravished, he awaking resolved to seeke her out; and so being by Merlin armed, and by Timon thoroughly instructed, he went to seeke her forth in Faerye Land. In that Faery Queene I meane glory in my generall intention, but in my particular I conceive the most excellent and glorious person of our soveraine the Queene, and her kingdome in Faery Land. And yet, in some places els, I doe otherwise shadow her. For considering she beareth two persons, the one of a most royall queene or empresse, the other of a most vertuous and beautifull lady, this latter part in some places I doe expresse in Belphoebe, fashioning her name according to your owne excellent conceipt of Cynthia (Phoebe and Cynthia being both names of Diana). So in the person of Prince Arthure I sette forth magnificence in particular, which vertue, for that (according to Aristotle and the rest) it is the perfection of all the rest, and conteineth in it them all, therefore in the whole course I mention the deedes of Arthure applyable to that vertue which I write of in that booke. But of the xii. other vertues, I make xii. other knights the patrones, for the more variety of the history: of which these three bookes contayn three.[3] The first of the Knight of the Redcrosse, in whome I expresse Holynes: The seconde of Sir Guyon, in whome I sette forth Temperaunce: The third of Britomartis, a lady knight, in whome I picture Chastity. But, because the beginning of the whole worke seemeth abrupte, and as depending upon other antecedents, it needs that ye know the occasion of these three knights severall adventures. For the methode of a poet historical is not such as of an historiographer. For an historiographer discourseth of affayres orderly as they were donne, accounting as well the times as the actions; but a poet thrusteth into the middest, even where it most concerneth him, and there recoursing to the thinges forepaste, and divining of thinges to come, maketh a pleasing analysis of all.

The beginning therefore of my history, if it were to be told by an historiographer, should be the twelfth booke, which is the last; where I devise that the Faery Queene kept her annuall feaste xii. dayes; upon which xii. severall dayes, the occasions of the xii. severall adventures hapned, which, being undertaken by xii. severall knights, are in these xii. books severally

handled and discoursed. The first was this. In the beginning of the feast, there presented himselfe a tall clownishe younge man, who, falling before the Queen of Faries, desired a boone (as the manner then was) which during that feast she might not refuse: which was that hee might have the atchievement of any adventure, which during that feaste should happen: that being graunted, he rested him on the floore, unfitte through his rusticity for a better place. Soone after entred a faire ladye in mourning weedes, riding on a white asse, with a dwarfe behind her leading a warlike steed, that bore the armes of a knight, and his speare in the dwarfes hand. Shee, falling before the Queene of Faeries, complayned that her father and mother, an ancient king and queene, had bene by an huge dragon many years shut up in a brasen castle, who thence suffred them not to yssew; and therefore besought the Faery Queene to assygne her some one of her knights to take on him that exployt. Presently that clownish person, upstarting, desired that adventure: whereat the Queene much wondering, and the lady much gaine-saying, yet he earnestly importuned his desire. In the end the lady told him, that unlesse that armour which she brought, would serve him (that is, the armour of a Christian man specified by Saint Paul, v. Ephes.[4]), that he could not succeed in that enterprise: which being forthwith put upon him with dewe furnitures thereunto, he seemed the goodliest man in al that company, and was well liked of the lady. And eftesoones taking on him knighthood, and mounting on that straunge courser, he went forth with her on that adventure: where beginneth the first booke, *viz.*,

A gentle knight was pricking on the playne, *etc.*

The second day there came in a palmer, bearing an infant with bloody hands, whose parents he complained to have bene slayn by an enchaunteresse called Acrasia; and therefore craved of the Faery Queene, to appoint him some knight to performe that adventure; which being assigned to Sir Guyon, he presently went forth with that same palmer: which is the beginning of the second booke and the whole subject thereof. The third day there came in a groome, who complained before the Faery Queene, that a vile enchaunter, called Busirane, had in hand a most faire lady, called Amoretta, whom he kept in most grievous torment, because she

[3] This letter was first published in the edition of 1590, which contained only the first three books.

[4] A mistake for "vi. Ephes."

would not yield him the pleasure of her body. Whereupon Sir Scudamour, the lover of that lady, presently tooke on him that adventure. But being unable to performe it by reason of the hard enchauntments, after long sorrow, in the end met with Britomartis, who succoured him, and reskewed his love.

But by occasion hereof many other adventures are intermedled, but rather as accidents then intendments: as the love of Britomart, the overthrow of Marinell, the misery of Florimell, the vertuousness of Belphoebe, the lasciviousness of Hellenora, and many the like.

Thus much, Sir, I have briefly overronne, to direct your understanding to the welhead of the history, that from thence gathering the whole intention of the conceit ye may, as in a handfull, gripe al the discourse, which otherwise may happily seeme tedious and confused. So, humbly craving the continuance of your honourable favour towards me, and th'eternall establishment of your happines, I humbly take leave.

23 January, 1589.

Yours most humbly affectionate,

Ed. Spenser.

# The First Booke of the Faerie Queene

## Contayning

### The Legende of the Knight of the Red Crosse, or of Holinesse

1

Lo I the man, whose Muse whilome did maske,
As time her taught, in lowly Shepheards weeds,[1]
Am now enforst a far unfitter taske,
For trumpets sterne to chaunge mine Oaten reeds,
And sing of Knights and Ladies gentle deeds; [5]
Whose prayses having slept in silence long,
Me, all too meane, the sacred Muse areeds
To blazon broad emongst her learnéd throng:
Fierce warres and faithfull loves shall moralize my song.

2

Helpe then, O holy Virgin chiefe of nine,[2] [10]
Thy weaker Novice to performe thy will,
Lay forth out of thine everlasting scryne
The antique rolles, which there lye hidden still,
Of Faerie knights and fairest *Tanaquill*,[3]

[1] In *The Shepherd's Calendar* (1579).
[2] Calliope, muse of heroic poetry; though according to some, Spenser means Clio, the muse of history.
[3] A British princess, representing Queen Elizabeth.

Whom that most noble Briton Prince[4] so long
Sought through the world, and suffered so much ill, [16]
That I must rue his undeservéd wrong:
O helpe thou my weake wit, and sharpen my dull tong.

3

And thou most dreaded impe of highest *Jove*,
Faire *Venus* sonne, that with thy cruell dart [20]
At that good knight so cunningly didst rove,
That glorious fire it kindled in his hart,
Lay now thy deadly Heben bow apart,
And with thy mother milde come to mine ayde:
Come both, and with you bring triumphant *Mart*, [25]
In loves and gentle jollities arrayed,
After his murdrous spoiles and bloudy rage allayd.

4

And with them eke, O Goddesse heavenly bright,[5]
Mirrour of grace and Majestie divine,
Great Lady of the greatest Isle, whose light [30]
Like *Phoebus* lampe throughout the world doth shine,
Shed thy faire beames into my feeble eyne,
And raise my thoughts too humble and too vile,
To thinke of that true glorious type of thine,
The argument of mine afflicted stile: [35]
The which to heare, vouchsafe, O dearest dred a-while.

## CANTO I

*The Patron of true Holinesse,*
*Foule Errour doth defeate:*
*Hypocrisie him to entrape,*
*Doth to his home entreate.*

1

A gentle knight was pricking on the plaine,
Y-cladd in mightie armes and silver shielde,
Wherein old dints of deepe wounds did remaine,
The cruell markes of many' a bloudy fielde;
Yet armes till that time did he never wield: [5]
His angry steede did chide his foming bitt,
As much disdayning to the curbe to yield:
Full jolly knight he seemd, and faire did sitt,
As one for knightly giusts and fierce encounters fitt.

2

But on his brest a bloudie Crosse he bore, [10]
The deare remembrance of his dying Lord,
For whose sweete sake that glorious badge he wore,
And dead as living ever him ador'd;
Upon his shield the like was also scor'd,

[4] Prince Arthur.    [5] Queen Elizabeth.

For soveraine hope, which in his helpe he had:
Right faithfull true he was in deede and
    word,                                        16
But of his cheere did seeme too solemne sad;
Yet nothing did he dread, but ever was ydrad.

### 3

Upon a great adventure he was bond,
That greatest *Gloriana* [6] to him gave,      20
That greatest Glorious Queene of *Faerie* lond,
To winne him worship, and her grace to have,
Which of all earthly things he most did crave;
And ever as he rode, his hart did earne
To prove his puissance in battell brave        25
Upon his foe, and his new force to learne;
Upon his foe, a Dragon horrible and stearne.[7]

### 4

A lovely Ladie [8] rode him faire beside,
Upon a lowly Asse more white then snow,
Yet she much whiter, but the same did hide [30]
Under a vele, that wimpled was full low,
And over all a blacke stole she did throw,
As one that inly mournd: so was she sad,
And heavie sat upon her palfrey slow;
Seeméd in heart some hidden care she had, [35]
And by her in a line a milke white lambe she
    lad.

### 5

So pure and innocent, as that same lambe,
She was in life and every vertuous lore,
And by descent from Royall lynage came
Of ancient Kings and Queenes, that had of
    yore                                         40
Their scepters stretcht from East to Westerne
    shore,
And all the world in their subjection held;
Till that infernall feend with foule uprore
Forwasted all their land, and them expeld:
Whom to avenge, she had this Knight from
    far compeld.                                 45

### 6

Behind her farre away a Dwarfe [9] did lag,
That lasie seemd in being ever last,
Or weariéd with bearing of her bag
Of needments at his backe. Thus as they past,
The day with cloudes was suddeine overcast, [50]
And angry *Jove* an hideous storme of raine
Did poure into his Lemans lap so fast,
That every wight to shrowd it did constrain,
And this fair couple eke to shroud themselves
    were fain.

### 7

Enforst to seeke some covert nigh at hand, [55]
A shadie grove not far away they spide,
That promist ayde the tempest to withstand:

Whose loftie trees yclad with sommers pride,
Did spred so broad, that heavens light did hide,
Not perceable with power of any starre:      60
And all within were pathes and alleies wide,
With footing worne, and leading inward farre:
Faire harbour that them seemes; so in they
    entred arre.

### 8

And foorth they passe, with pleasure forward
    led,
Joying to heare the birdes sweete harmony, 65
Which therein shrouded from the tempest
    dred,
Seemd in their song to scorne the cruell sky.
Much can they prayse the trees so straight and
    hy,
The sayling Pine, the Cedar proud and tall,
The vine-prop Elme, the Poplar never dry,[10] 70
The builder Oake, sole king of forrests all,
The Aspine good for staves, the Cypresse
    funerall.[11]

### 9

The Laurell, meed of mightie Conquerours
And Poets sage, the Firre that weepeth still,[12]
The Willow worne of forlorne Paramours, 75
The Eugh obedient to the benders will,
The Birch for shaftes, the Sallow for the mill,
The Mirrhe sweete bleeding in the bitter
    wound,[13]
The warlike Beech,[14] the Ash for nothing ill,
The fruitful Olive, and the Platane round, 80
The carver Holme, the Maple seeldom inward
    sound.

### 10

Led with delight, they thus beguile the way,
Untill the blustring storme is overblowne;
When weening to returne, whence they did
    stray,
They cannot finde that path, which first was
    showne,                                      85
But wander too and fro in wayes unknowne,
Furthest from end then, when they neerest
    weene,
That makes them doubt, their wits be not their
    owne:
So many pathes, so many turnings seene,
That which of them to take, in diverse doubt
    they been.                                   90

### 11

At last resolving forward still to fare,
Till that some end they finde or in or out,
That path they take, that beaten seemd most
    bare,
And like to lead the labyrinth about;

[6] Queen Elizabeth.
[7] The dragon typifies sin.
[8] Una, who typifies truth.
[9] Typifying prudence.

[10] Because it grows best in moist soil.
[11] Symbolic of death.    [12] It exudes resin.
[13] Myrrh is fragrant though bitter.
[14] "There is a tradition that the war chariots of
the ancients were made of beech" (Winstanley).

Which when by tract they hunted had through-
out,                                              95
At length it brought them to a hollow cave,
Amid the thickest woods. The Champion stout
Eftsoones dismounted from his courser brave,
And to the Dwarfe awhile his needlesse spere
he gave.

### 12

Be well aware, quoth then that Ladie milde, 100
Least suddaine mischiefe ye too rash provoke:
The danger hid, the place unknowne and wilde,
Breedes dreadfull doubts: Oft fire is without
smoke,
And perill without show: therefore your stroke
Sir knight with-hold, till further triall made.
Ah Ladie (said he) shame were to revoke 106
The forward footing for an hidden shade: 15
Vertue gives her selfe light, through darke-
nesse for to wade.

### 13

Yea but (quoth she) the perill of this place
I better wot then you, though now too late, 110
To wish you backe returne with foule disgrace,
Yet wisedome warnes, whilest foot is in the
gate,
To stay the steppe, ere forcéd to retrate.
This is the wandring wood, this *Errours den*,
A monster vile, whom God and man does hate:
Therefore I read beware. Fly fly (quoth then 116
The fearefull Dwarfe:) this is no place for
living men.

### 14

But full of fire and greedy hardiment,
The youthfull knight could not for ought be
staide,
But forth unto the darksome hole he went, 120
And lookéd in: his glistring armor made
A little glooming light, much like a shade,
By which he saw the ugly monster plaine,
Halfe like a serpent horribly displaide,
But th'other halfe did womans shape retaine,
Most lothsom, filthie, foule, and full of vile
disdaine.                                        126

### 15

And as she lay upon the durtie ground,
Her huge long taile her den all overspred,
Yet was in knots and many boughtes upwound,
Pointed with mortall sting. Of her there
bred                                             130
A thousand yong ones, which she dayly fed,
Sucking upon her poisonous dugs, eachone
Of sundry shapes, yet all ill favoréd:
Soone as that uncouth light upon them shone,
Into her mouth they crept, and suddain all
were gone.                                       135

15 It were a shame to turn back because of an
imagined danger.

### 16

Their dam upstart, out of her den effraide,
And rushéd forth, hurling her hideous taile
About her curséd head, whose folds displaid
Were stretcht now forth at length without
entraile.
She lookt about, and seeing one in mayle 140
Arméd to point, sought backe to turne againe;
For light she hated as the deadly bale,
Ay wont in desert darknesse to remaine,
Where plaine none might her see, nor she see
any plaine.

### 17

Which when the valiant Elfe 16 perceiv'd, he
lept                                             145
As Lyon fierce upon the flying pray,
And with his trenchand blade her boldly kept
From turning backe, and forcéd her to stay:
Therewith enrag'd she loudly gan to bray,
And turning fierce, her speckled taile ad-
vaunst,                                          150
Threatning her angry sting, him to dismay:
Who naught aghast, his mightie hand en-
haunst:
The stroke down from her head unto her
shoulder glaunst.

### 18

Much daunted with that dint, her sence was
dazd,
Yet kindling rage, her selfe she gathered round,
And all attonce her beastly body raizd      156
With doubled forces high above the ground:
Tho wrapping up her wrethed sterne arownd,
Lept fierce upon his shield, and her huge traine
All suddenly about his body wound,          160
That hand or foot to stirre he strove in vaine;
God helpe the man so wrapt in *Errours* end-
lesse traine.

### 19

His Lady sad to see his sore constraint,
Cride out, Now now Sir Knight, shew what
ye bee,
Add faith unto your force, and be not faint: 165
Strangle her, else she sure will strangle thee.
That when he heard, in great perplexitie,
His gall did grate for griefe and high disdaine,17
And knitting all his force got one hand free,
Wherewith he grypt her gorge with so great
paine,                                           170
That soone to loose her wicked bands did her
constraine.

### 20

Therewith she spewd out of her filthy maw
A floud of poyson horrible and blacke,

16 The Knight is so called because he is a fairy
knight.
17 His anger was kindled by his pain and great disgust.

Full of great lumpes of flesh and gobbets raw,
Which stunck so vildly, that it forst him
    slacke          175
His grasping hold, and from her turne him
    backe:
Her vomit full of bookes and papers was,[18]
With loathly frogs and toades, which eyes did
    lacke,
And creeping sought way in the weedy gras:
Her filthy parbreake all the place defiléd has.

21

As when old father *Nilus* gins to swell      181
With timely pride above the *Aegyptian* vale,
His fattie waves do fertile slime outwell,
And overflow each plaine and lowly dale:
But when his later spring gins to avale,     185
Huge heapes of mudd he leaves, wherein there
    breed
Ten thousand kindes of creatures, partly male
And partly female of his fruitfull seed;
Such ugly monstrous shapes elswhere may no
    man reed.

22

The same so sore annoyéd has the knight,  190
That welnigh chokéd with the deadly stinke,
His forces faile, ne can no longer fight.
Whose corage when the feend perceiv'd to
    shrinke,
She poured forth out of her hellish sinke    194
Her fruitfull curséd spawne of serpents small,
Deforméd monsters, fowle, and blacke as inke,
Which swarming all about his legs did crall,
And him encombred sore, but could not hurt
    at all.

23

As gentle Shepheard in sweete even-tide,
When ruddy *Phoebus* gins to welke in west, 200
High on an hill, his flocke to yewen wide,
Markes which do byte their hasty supper best;
A cloud of combrous gnattes do him molest,
All striving to infixe their feeble stings,
That from their noyance he no where can
    rest,          205
But with his clownish hands their tender wings
He brusheth oft, and oft doth mar their
    murmurings.

24

Thus ill bestedd, and fearefull more of shame,
Then of the certaine perill he stood in,
Halfe furious unto his foe he came,      210
Resolv'd in minde all suddenly to win,
Or soone to lose, before he once would lin;
And strooke at her with more then manly force,
That from her body full of filthie sin
He raft her hatefull head without remorse; 215
A streame of cole black bloud forth gushéd
    from her corse.

[18] The allusion is to pamphlets written by Catholics against Protestantism.

25

Her scattred brood, soone as their Parent deare
They saw so rudely falling to the ground,
Groning full deadly, all with troublous feare,
Gathred themselves about her body round, 220
Weening their wonted entrance to have found
At her wide mouth: but being there withstood
They flockéd all about her bleeding wound,
And suckéd up their dying mothers blood,
Making her death their life, and eke her hurt
    their good.          225

26

That detestable sight him much amazde,
To see th'unkindly Impes of heaven accurst,
Devoure their dam; on whom while so he gazd,
Having all satisfide their bloudy thurst,
Their bellies swolne he saw with fulnesse
    burst,          230
And bowels gushing forth: well worthy end
Of such as drunke her life, the which them
    nurst;
Now needeth him no lenger labour spend,
His foes have slaine themselves, with whom
    he should contend.         234

27

His Ladie seeing all, that chaunst, from farre
Approcht in hast to greet his victorie,
And said, Faire knight, borne under happy
    starre,
Who see your vanquisht foes before you lye:
Well worthy be you of that Armorie,[19]
Wherein ye have great glory wonne this day, 240
And proov'd your strength on a strong enimie,
Your first adventure: many such I pray,
And henceforth ever wish, that like succeed
    it may.

28

Then mounted he upon his Steede againe,
And with the Lady backward sought to wend;
That path he kept, which beaten was most
    plaine.          246
Ne ever would to any by-way bend,
But still did follow one unto the end,
The which at last out of the wood them
    brought.
So forward on his way (with God to frend) 250
He passéd forth, and new adventure sought;
Long way he travelléd, before he heard of
    ought.

29

At length they chaunst to meet upon the way
An agéd Sire,[20] in long blacke weedes yclad,
His feete all bare, his beard all hoarie gray, 255
And by his belt his booke he hanging had;
Sober he seemde, and very sagely sad,

[19] The armor of a Christian man.

[20] Archimago, a disguised enchanter, who typifies hypocrisy.

And to the ground his eyes were lowly bent,
Simple in shew, and voyde of malice bad,
And all the way he prayéd, as he went,     260
And often knockt his brest, as one that did
    repent.

### 30

He faire the knight saluted, louting low,
Who faire him quited, as that courteous was:
And after askéd him, if he did know
Of straunge adventures, which abroad did pas.
Ah my deare Sonne (quoth he) how should,
    alas,     266
Silly old man, that lives in hidden cell,
Bidding his beades all day for his trespas,
Tydings of warre and worldly trouble tell?
With holy father sits not with such things to
    mell.     270

### 31

But if of daunger which hereby doth dwell,
And homebred evill ye desire to heare,
Of a straunge man I can you tidings tell,
That wasteth all this countrey farre and neare.
Of such (said he) I chiefly do inquere,     275
And shall you well reward to shew the place,
In which that wicked wight his dayes doth
    weare
For to all knighthood it is foule disgrace,
That such a curséd creature lives so long a
    space.     279

### 32

Far hence (quoth he) in wastfull wildernesse
His dwelling is, by which no living wight
May ever passe, but thorough great distresse.
Now (sayd the Lady) draweth toward night,
And well I wote, that of your later fight
Ye all forwearied be: for what so strong,     285
But wanting rest will also want of might?
The Sunne that measures heaven all day long,
At night doth baite his steedes the *Ocean*
    waves emong.

### 33

Then with the Sunne take Sir, your timely rest,
And with new day new worke at once begin:     290
Untroubled night they say gives counsell best.
Right well Sir knight ye have advdiséd bin,
(Quoth then that aged man;) the way to win
Is wisely to advise: now day is spent;
Therefore with me ye may take up your In     295
For this same night. The knight was well
    content:
So with that godly father to his home they
    went.

### 34

A little lowly Hermitage it was,
Downe in a dale, hard by a forests side,
Far from resort of people, that did pas     300

In travell to and froe: a little wyde
There was an holy Chappell edifyde,
Wherein the Hermite dewly wont to say
His holy things each morne and eventyde:
Thereby a Christall streame did gently play,     305
Which from a sacred fountaine welléd forth
    alway.

### 35

Arrivéd there, the little house they fill,
Ne looke for entertainment, where none was:
Rest is their feast, and all things at their will;
The noblest mind the best contentment has.
With faire discourse the evening so they pas:
For that old man of pleasing wordes had
    store,     312
And well could file his tongue as smooth as
    glas;
He told of Saintes and Popes, and evermore
He strowd an *Ave-Mary* after and before.     315

### 36

The drouping Night thus creepeth on them
    fast,
And the sad humour loading their eye liddes,
As messenger of *Morpheus* on them cast
Sweet slombring deaw, the which to sleepe
    them biddes.
Unto their lodgings then his guestes he riddes:
Where when all drownd in deadly sleepe he
    findes,     321
He to his study goes, and there amiddes
His Magick bookes and artes of sundry kindes,
He seekes out mighty charmes, to trouble sleepy
    mindes.     324

### 37

Then choosing out few wordes most horrible,
(Let none them read) thereof did verses frame,
With which and other spelles like terrible,
He bad awake blacke *Plutoes* griesly Dame,[21]
And curséd heaven, and spake reprochfull
    shame
Of highest God, the Lord of life and light;     330
A bold bad man, that dar'd to call by name
Great *Gorgon*, Prince of darknesse and dead
    night,
At which *Cocytus* quakes, and *Styx* is put to
    flight.[22]

### 38

And forth he cald out of deepe darknesse dred
Legions of Sprights, the which like little flyes
Fluttring about his ever damnéd hed,     336
A-waite whereto their service he applyes,
To aide his friends, or fray his enimies:
Of those he chose out two, the falsest twoo,
And fittest for to forge true-seeming lyes;     340
The one of them he gave a message too,
The other by him selfe staide other worke to
    doo.

[21] Proserpine.     [22] Two rivers in Hades.

**39**

He making speedy way through sperséd ayre,
And through the world of waters wide and
    deepe,
To *Morpheus* house doth hastily repaire. 345
Amid the bowels of the earth full steepe,
And low, where dawning day doth never peepe,
His dwelling is; there *Tethys* [23] his wet bed
Doth ever wash, and *Cynthia* [24] still doth
    steepe
In silver deaw his ever-drouping hed,   350
Whiles sad Night over him her mantle black
    doth spred.

**40**

Whose double gates he findeth lockéd fast,
The one faire fram'd of burnisht Yvory,
The other all with silver overcast;
And wakefull dogges before them farre do lye,
Watching to banish Care their enimy,   356
Who oft is wont to trouble gentle Sleepe.
By them the Sprite doth passe in quietly,
And unto *Morpheus* comes, whom drownéd
    deepe
In drowsie fit he findes: of nothing he takes
    keepe.   360

**41**

And more, to lulle him in his slumber soft,
A trickling streame from high rocke tumbling
    downe
And ever-drizling raine upon the loft,
Mixt with a murmuring winde, much like the
    sowne
Of swarming Bees, did cast him in a swowne:
No other noyse, nor peoples troublous cryes, 366
As still are wont t'annoy the walléd towne,
Might there be heard: but carelesse Quiet lyes,
Wrapt in eternall silence farre from enemyes.

**42**

The messenger approching to him spake, 370
But his wast wordes returnd to him in vaine:
So sound he slept, that nought mought him
    awake.
Then rudely he him thrust, and pusht with
    paine,
Whereat he gan to stretch: but he againe 374
Shooke him so hard, that forcéd him to speake.
As one then in a dreame, whose dryer braine [25]
Is tost with troubled sights and fancies weake,
He mumbled soft, but would not all his silence
    breake.

**43**

The Sprite then gan more boldly him to wake,
And threatned unto him the dreaded name 380
Of *Hecate*: [26] whereat he gan to quake,

  [23] The ocean.     [24] The moon.
  [25] It was once supposed that the brain, when too
dry, gave rise to troubled dreams.
  [26] Goddess of Hades, the patroness of witches.

And lifting up his lumpish head, with blame
Halfe angry askéd him, for what he came.
Hither (quoth he) me *Archimago* sent,
He that the stubborne Sprites can wisely
    tame,   385
He bids thee to him send for his intent
A fit false dreame, that can delude the sleepers
    sent.

**44**

The God obayde, and calling forth straight way
A diverse dreame out of his prison darke,
Delivered it to him, and downe did lay   390
His heavie head, devoide of carefull carke,
Whose sences all were straight benumbd and
    starke.
He backe returning by the Yvorie dore,
Remounted up as light as chearefull Larke,
And on his litle winges the dreame he bore 395
In hast unto his Lord, where he him left afore.

**45**

Who all this while with charmes and hidden
    artes,
Had made a Lady of that other Spright,
And fram'd of liquid ayre her tender partes
So lively, and so like in all mens sight,   400
That weaker sence it could have ravisht quight:
The maker selfe for all his wondrous witt,
Was nigh beguiléd with so goodly sight:
Her all in white he clad, and over it
Cast a blacke stole, most like to seeme for *Una*
    fit.   405

**46**

Now when that ydle dreame was to him
    brought,
Unto that Elfin knight he bad him fly,
Where he slept soundly void of evill thought,
And with false shewes abuse his fantasy,
In sort as he him schooléd privily:   410
And that new creature borne without her dew,[27]
Full of the makers guile, with usage sly
He taught to imitate that Lady trew,
Whose semblance she did carrie under feignéd
    hew.

**47**

Thus well instructed, to their worke they hast,
And comming where the knight in slomber
    lay,   416
The one upon his hardy head him plast,
And made him dreame of loves and lustfull
    play,
That nigh his manly hart did melt away,
Bathéd in wanton blis and wicked joy:   420
Then seeméd him his Lady by him lay,
And to him playnd, how that false wingéd
    boy,[28]
Her chast hart had subdewd, to learne Dame
    pleasures toy.

  [27] Born unnaturally.     [28] Cupid.

### 48

And she her selfe of beautie soveraigne Queene,
*Faire Venus* seemde unto his bed to bring 425
Her, whom he waking evermore did weene,
To be the chastest flowre, that ay did spring
On earthly braunch, the daughter of a king,
Now a loose Leman to vile service bound:
And eke the *Graces* seeméd all to sing, 430
*Hymen Iö Hymen*,[29] dauncing all around,
Whilst freshest *Flora* [30] her with Yvie girlond
crownd.

### 49

In this great passion of unwonted lust,
Or wonted feare of doing ought amis,
He started up, as seeming to mistrust 435
Some secret ill, or hidden foe of his:
Lo there before his face his Lady is,
Under blake stole hyding her bayted hooke,
And as halfe blushing offred him to kis,
With gentle blandishment and lovely looke, 440
Most like that virgin true, which for her knight
him took.

### 50

All cleane dismayd to see so uncouth sight,
And halfe enragéd at her shamelesse guise,
He thought have slaine her in his fierce
despight:
But hasty heat tempring with sufferance wise,
He stayde his hand, and gan himselfe advise 446
To prove his sense, and tempt her faignéd
truth.
Wringing her hands in wemens pitteous wise,
Tho can she weepe, to stirre up gentle ruth,
Both for her noble bloud, and for her tender
youth. 450

### 51

And said, Ah Sir, my liege Lord and my love,
Shall I accuse the hidden cruell fate,
And mightie causes wrought in heaven above,
Or the blind God, that doth me thus amate,
For hopéd love to winne me certaine hate? 455
Yet thus perforce he bids me do, or die.
Die is my dew: yet rew my wretched state
You, whom my hard avenging destinie
Hath made judge of my life or death indif-
ferently.

### 52

Your owne deare sake forst me at first to
leave 460
My Fathers kingdome, There she stopt with
teares;
Her swollen hart her speach seemd to be-
reave,
And then againe begun, My weaker yeares
Captiv'd to fortune and frayle worldly feares,
Fly to your faith for succour and sure ayde: 465
Let me not dye in languor and long teares.

[29] Hymn to Hymen, god of marriage.
[30] Goddess of flowers.

Why Dame (quoth he) what hath ye thus
dismayd?
What frayes ye, that were wont to comfort me
affrayd?

### 53

Love of your selfe, she said, and deare con-
straint
Lets me not sleepe, but wast the wearie night
In secret anguish and unpittied plaint, 471
Whiles you in carelesse sleepe are drownéd
quight.
Her doubtfull words made that redoubted
knight
Suspect her truth: yet since no'untruth he
knew,
Her fawning love with foule disdainefull
spight 475
He would not shend, but said, Deare dame I
rew,
That for my sake unknowne such griefe unto
you grew.

### 54

Assure your selfe, it fell not all to ground;
For all so deare as life is to my hart,
I deeme your love, and hold me to you bound;
Ne let vaine feares procure your needlesse
smart, 481
Where cause is none, but to your rest depart.
Not all content, yet seemd she to appease
Her mournefull plaintes, beguiléd of her art,
And fed with words, that could not chuse but
please, 485
So slyding softly forth, she turnd as to her ease.

### 55

Long after lay he musing at her mood,
Much griev'd to thinke that gentle Dame so
light,
For whose defence he was to shed his blood.
At last dull wearinesse of former fight 490
Having yrockt asleepe his irkesome spright,
That troublous dreame gan freshly tosse his
braine,
With bowres, and beds, and Ladies deare de-
light:
But when he saw his labour all was vaine,
With that misforméd spright he backe re-
turnd againe. 495

### CANTO II

*The guilefull great Enchaunter parts*
*The Redcrosse Knight from Truth:*
*Into whose stead faire falshood steps,*
*And workes him wofull ruth.*

### 1

By this the Northerne wagoner [1] had set
His sevenfold teme [2] behind the stedfast
starre,[3]

[1] Boötes.   [2] Charles's Wain, or the Great Bear.
[3] The pole star.

That was in Ocean waves yet never wet,
But firme is fixt, and sendeth light from farre
To all, that in the wide deepe wandring arre: 5
And chearefull Chaunticlere with his note shrill
Had warnéd once, that *Phoebus* fiery carre
In hast was climbing up the Easterne hill,
Full envious that night so long his roome did
    fill.

### 2

When those accurséd messengers of hell,   10
That feigning dreame, and that faire-forgéd
    Spright
Came to their wicked maister, and gan tell
Their bootelesse paines, and ill succeeding
    night:
Who all in rage to see his skilfull might
Deluded so, gan threaten hellish paine   15
And sad *Proserpines* wrath, them to affright.
But when he saw his threatning was but vaine,
He cast about, and searcht his balefull bookes
    againe.

### 3

Eftsoones he tooke that miscreated faire,
And that false other Spright, on whom he spred
A seeming body of the subtile aire,   21
Like a young Squire, in loves and lusty-hed
His wanton dayes that ever loosely led,
Without regard of armes and dreaded fight:
Those two he tooke, and in a secret bed,   25
Covered with darknesse and misdeeming night,
Them both together laid, to joy in vaine de-
    light.

### 4

Forthwith he runnes with feignéd faithfull hast
Unto his guest, who after troublous sights
And dreames, gan now to take more sound re-
    past,   30
Whom suddenly he wakes with fearefull
    frights,
As one aghast with feends or damnéd sprights,
And to him cals, Rise rise unhappy Swaine,
That here wex old in sleepe, whiles wicked
    wights
Have knit themselves in *Venus* shamefull
    chaine;   35
Come see, where your false Lady doth her
    honour staine.

### 5

All in amaze he suddenly up start
With sword in hand, and with the old man
    went;
Who soone him brought into a secret part,
Where that false couple were full closely
    ment   40
In wanton lust and lewd embracément:
Which when he saw, he burnt with gealous fire,
The eye of reason was with rage yblent,
And would have slaine them in his furious ire,
But hardly was restreinéd of that agéd sire.   45

### 6

Returning to his bed in torment great,
And bitter anguish of his guiltie sight,
He could not rest, but did his stout heart eat,
And wast his inward gall with deepe despight,
Yrkesome of life, and too long lingring night.
At last faire *Hesperus* in highest skie   51
Had spent his lampe,[4] and brought forth dawn-
    ing light,
Then up he rose, and clad him hastily;
The Dwarfe him brought his steed: so both
    away do fly.

### 7

Now when the rosy-fingred Morning faire,   55
Weary of agéd *Tithones* saffron bed,
Had spred her purple robe through deawy aire,
And the high hils *Titan*[5] discoveréd,
The royall virgin shooke off drowsy-hed,
And rising forth out of her baser bowre,   60
Lookt for her knight, who far away was fled,
And for her Dwarfe, that wont to wait each
    houre;
Then gan she waile and weepe, to see that
    woefull stowre.

### 8

And after him she rode with so much speede
As her slow beast could make, but all in
    vaine;   65
For him so far had borne his light-foot steede,
Prickéd with wrath and fiery fierce disdaine,
That him to follow was but fruitlesse paine;
Yet she her weary limbes would never rest,
But every hill and dale, each wood and plaine   70
Did search, sore grievéd in her gentle brest,
He so ungently left her, whom she lovéd best.

### 9

But subtill *Archimago*, when his guests
He saw divided into double parts,
And *Una* wandring in woods and forrests,   75
Th'end of his drift, he praisd his divelish arts,
That had such might over true meaning harts;
Yet rests not so, but other meanes doth make,
How he may worke unto her further smarts:
For her he hated as the hissing snake,   80
And in her many troubles did most pleasure
    take.

### 10

He then devisde himselfe how to disguise;
For by his mightie science[6] he could take
As many formes and shapes in seeming wise,
As ever *Proteus*[7] to himselfe could make:   85
Sometime a fowle, sometime a fish in lake,
Now like a foxe, now like a dragon fell,
That of himselfe he oft for feare would quake,
And oft would flie away. O who can tell

---

[4] The morning star had yielded place to dawn.
[5] The sun.    [6] His magic.    [7] A sea-god.

The hidden power of herbes, and might of
　　Magicke spell?　　　　　　　　　　90

**11**

But now seemde best, the person to put on
Of that good knight, his late beguiléd guest:
In mighty armes he was yclad anon,
And silver shield: upon his coward brest
A bloudy crosse, and on his craven crest　　95
A bounch of haires discoulourd diversly:
Full jolly knight he seemde, and well addrest,
And when he sate upon his courser free,
*Saint George* himself ye would have deeméd
　　him to be.

**12**

But he the knight whose semblaunt he did
　　beare,　　　　　　　　　　　　　100
The true *Saint George* was wandred far away,
Still flying from his thoughts and gealous feare;
Will was his guide, and griefe led him astray.
At last him chaunst to meete upon the way
A faithlesse Sarazin [8] all arm'd to point,　105
In whose great shield was writ with letters gay
*Sans foy:* [9] full large of limbe and every joint
He was, and caréd not for God or man a point.

**13**

He had a faire companion of his way,
A goodly Lady [10] clad in scarlot red,　　110
Purfled with gold and pearle of rich assay,
And like a *Persian* mitre [11] on her hed.
She wore, with crownes and owches garnishéd,
The which her lavish lovers to her gave;
Her wanton palfrey all was overspred　　115
With tinsell trappings, woven like a wave,
Whose bridle rung with golden bels and bosses
　　brave.

**14**

With faire disport and courting dalliaunce
She intertainde her lover all the way:
But when she saw the knight his speare ad-
　　vaunce,　　　　　　　　　　　　120
She soone left off her mirth and wanton play,
And bad her knight addresse him to the fray:
His foe was nigh at hand. He, prickt with pride
And hope to winne his Ladies heart that day,
Forth spurréd fast: adowne his coursers side [125]
The red bloud trickling staind the way, as he
　　did ride.

**15**

The knight of the *Redcrosse* when him he
　　spide,
Spurring so hote with rage dispiteous,

---

[8] Used as a generic term for pagans.
[9] Faithless.
[10] Duessa, typifying falsehood, who calls herself
Fidessa. She probably represents Mary, Queen of
Scots—though it has also been suggested that she
represents Mary Tudor—and the Roman Catholic
Church.
[11] The papal crown is meant.

---

Gan fairely couch his speare, and towards ride:
Soone meete they both, both fell and furious,
That daunted with their forces hideous,　[131]
Their steeds do stagger, and amazéd stand,
And eke themselves too rudely rigorous,
Astonied with the stroke of their owne hand,
Do backe rebut, and each to other yeeldeth
　　land.　　　　　　　　　　　　135

**16**

As when two rams stird with ambitious pride,
Fight for the rule of the rich fleecéd flocke,
Their hornéd fronts so fierce on either side
Do meete, that with the terrour of the shocke
Astonied both, stand sencelesse as a blocke, [140]
Forgetfull of the hanging victory:
So stood these twaine, unmovéd as a rocke,
Both staring fierce, and holding idely
The broken reliques of their former cruelty. [12]

**17**

The *Sarazin* sore daunted with the buffe　[145]
Snatcheth his sword, and fiercely to him flies;
Who well it wards, and quyteth cuff with cuff:
Each others equall puissaunce envies,
And through their iron sides with cruell spies
Does seeke to perce: repining courage yields
No foote to foe. The flashing fier flies　[151]
As from a forge out of their burning shields,
And streames of purple bloud new dies the
　　verdant fields.

**18**

Curse on that Crosse (quoth then the *Sarazin*)
That keepes thy body from the bitter fit; [13] [155]
Dead long ygoe I wote thou haddest bin,
Had not that charme from thee forwarnéd it:
But yet I warne thee now assuréd sitt,
And hide thy head. Therewith upon his crest
With rigour so outrageous he smitt,　　160
That a large share it hewd out of the rest,
And glauncing downe his shield, from blame
　　him fairely blest.

**19**

Who thereat wondrous wroth, the sleeping
　　spark
Of native vertue gan eftsoones revive,
And at his haughtie helmet making mark,　165
So hugely stroke, that it the steele did rive,
And cleft his head. He tumbling downe alive,
With bloudy mouth his mother earth did kis,
Greeting his grave: his grudging ghost did strive
With the fraile flesh; at last it flitted is,　170
Whither the soules do fly of men, that live
　　amis.

**20**

The Lady when she saw her champion fall,
Like the old ruines of a broken towre,
Staid not to waile his woefull funerall,

---

[12] The broken shafts of their lances.
[13] Death.

But from him fled away with all her powre; 175
Who after her as hastily gan scowre,
Bidding the Dwarfe with him to bring away
The *Sarazins* shield, signe of the conqueroure.
Her soone he overtooke, and bad to stay,
For present cause was none of dread her to dis-
may.    180

**21**

She turning backe with ruefull countenaunce,
Cride, Mercy mercy Sir vouchsafe to show
On silly Dame, subject to hard mischaunce,
And to your mighty will. Her humblesse low
In so ritch weedes and seeming glorious show,
Did much emmove his stout heroïcke heart, 186
And said, Deare dame, your suddein overthrow
Much rueth me; but now put feare apart,
And tell, both who ye be, and who that tooke
your part.

**22**

Melting in teares, then gan she thus lament; 190
The wretched woman, whom unhappy howre
Hath now made thrall to your commandement,
Before that angry heavens list to lowre,
And fortune false betraide me to your powre,
Was (O what now availeth that I was!)    195
Borne the sole daughter of an Emperour,
He that the wide West under his rule has,
And high hath set his throne, where *Tiberis*
doth pas.[14]

**23**

He in the first flowre of my freshest age,
Betrothéd me unto the onely haire    200
Of a most mighty king, most rich and sage;
Was never Prince so faithfull and so faire,
Was never Prince so meeke and debonaire;
But ere my hopéd day of spousall shone.
My dearest Lord fell from high honours staire,
Into the hands of his accverséd fone,    206
And cruelly was slaine, that shall I ever mone.

**24**

His blesséd body spoild of lively breath,
Was afterward, I know not how, convaid
And from me hid: of whose most innocent
death    210
When tidings came to me unhappy maid,
O how great sorrow my sad soule assaid.
Then forth I went his woefull corse to find,
And many yeares throughout the world I straid,
A virgin widow, whose deepe wounded mind
With love, long time did languish as the
striken hind.    216

**25**

At last it chauncéd this proud *Sarazin*,
To meete me wandring, who perforce me led
With him away, but yet could never win

The Fort, that Ladies hold in soveraigne
dread.    220
There lies he now with foule dishonour dead,
Who whiles he liv'de, was calléd proud *Sans
foy*,
The eldest of three brethren, all three bred
Of one bad sire, whose youngest is *Sans joy*,[15]
And twixt them both was borne the bloudy
bold *Sans loy*.[16]    225

**26**

In this sad plight, friendlesse, unfortunate,
Now miserable I *Fidessa* dwell,
Craving of you in pitty of my state,
To do none ill, if please ye not do well.
He in great passion all this while did dwell, 230
More busying his quicke eyes, her face to view,
Then his dull eares, to heare what she did tell;
And said, faire Lady hart of flint would rew
The undeservéd woes and sorrowes, which ye
shew.

**27**

Henceforth in safe assuraunce may ye rest, 235
Having both found a new friend you to aid,
And lost an old foe, that did you molest:
Better new friend then an old foe is said.
With chaunge of cheare the seeming simple
maid
Let fall her eyen, as shamefast to the earth, 240
And yeelding soft, in that she nought gainsaid,
So forth they rode, he feining seemely merth,
And she coy lookes: so dainty they say maketh
derth.[17]

**28**

Long time they thus together traveiléd,
Till weary of their way, they came at last,    245
Where grew two goodly trees, that faire did
spred
Their armes abroad, with gray mosse overcast,
And their greene leaves trembling with every
blast,
Made a calme shadow far in compasse round:
The fearefull Shepheard often there aghast 250
Under them never sat, ne wont there sound
His mery oaten pipe, but shund th'unlucky
ground.

**29**

But this good knight soone as he them can spie,
For the coole shade him thither hastly got:
For golden *Phoebus* now ymounted hie,    255
From fiery wheeles of his faire chariot
Hurléd his beame so scorching cruell hot,
That living creature mote it not abide;
And his new Lady it enduréd not.
There they alight, in hope themselves to hide

[14] The Pope, at Rome, where the river Tiber
passes.

[15] Joyless.    [16] Lawless.
[17] The proverb, meaning that fastidiousness causes
scarcity, by a play on words is made to mean that
coyness causes desire.

From the fierce heat, and rest their weary limbs
  a tide.                                                   261

#### 30

Faire seemely pleasaunce each to other makes,
With goodly purposes there as they sit:
And in his falséd fancy he her takes
To be the fairest wight, that livéd yit;             265
Which to expresse, he bends his gentle wit,
And thinking of those braunches greene to
  frame
A girlond for her dainty forehead fit,
He pluckt a bough: out of whose rift there
  came
Small drops of gory bloud, that trickled downe
  the same.                                               270

#### 31

Therewith a piteous yelling voyce was heard,
Crying, O spare with guilty hands to teare
My tender sides in this rough rynd embard,
But fly, ah fly far hence away, for feare
Least to you hap, that happened to me heare,
And to this wretched Lady, my deare love,  276
O too deare love, love bought with death too
  deare.
Astond he stood, and up his haire did hove,
And with that suddein horror could no mem-
  ber move.

#### 32

At last whenas the dreadfull passion          280
Was overpast, and manhood well awake,
Yet musing at the straunge occasion,
And doubting much his sence, he thus be-
  spake;
What voyce of damnéd Ghost from *Limbo*
  lake,[18]                                                284
Or guilefull spright wandring in empty aire,
Both which fraile men do oftentimes mistake,
Sends to my doubtfull eares these speaches rare,
And ruefull plaints, me bidding guiltlesse bloud
  to spare?

#### 33

Then groning deepe, Nor damnéd Ghost
  (quoth he),
Nor guilefull sprite to thee these wordes doth
  speake,                                                  290
But once a man *Fradubio*,[19] now a tree,
Wretched man, wretched tree; whose nature
  weake,
A cruell witch her curséd will to wreake,
Hath thus transformd, and plast in open
  plaines,
Where *Boreas*[20] doth blow full bitter bleake,
And scorching Sunne does dry my secret
  vaines:                                                  296
For though a tree I seeme, yet cold and heat
  me paines.

[18] Hades.      [19] One of doubtful faith.
[20] The north wind.

#### 34

Say on *Fradubio* then, or man, or tree,
Quoth then the knight, by whose mischievous
  arts
Art thou misshapéd thus, as now I see?     300
He oft finds med'cine, who his griefe imparts;
But double griefs afflict concealing harts,
As raging flames who striveth to suppresse.
The author then (said he) of all my smarts,
Is one *Duessa* a false sorceresse,            305
That many errant knights hath brought to
  wretchednesse.

#### 35

In prime of youthly yeares, when corage hot
The fire of love and joy of chevalree
First kindled in my brest, it was my lot
To love this gentle Lady, whom ye see,     310
Now not a Lady, but a seeming tree;
With whom as once I rode accompanyde,
Me chauncéd of a knight encountred bee,
That had a like faire Lady by his syde,
Like a faire Lady, but did fowle *Duessa* hyde.

#### 36

Whose forgéd beauty he did take in hand,  316
All other Dames to have exceeded farre;
I in defence of mine did likewise stand,
Mine, that did then shine as the Morning
  starre:
So both to battell fierce arraungéd arre,   320
In which his harder fortune was to fall
Under my speare: such is the dye of warre:
His Lady left as a prise martiall,
Did yield her comely person, to be at my call.

#### 37

So doubly lov'd of Ladies unlike faire,       325
Th'one seeming such, the other such indeede,
One day in doubt I cast for to compare,
Whether in beauties glorie did exceede;
A Rosy girlond was the victors meede:
Both seemde to win, and both seemde won to
  bee,                                                     330
So hard the discord was to be agreede.
*Fraelissa*[21] was as faire, as faire mote bee,
And ever false *Duessa* seemde as faire as shee.

#### 38

The wicked witch now seeing all this while
The doubtfull ballaunce equally to sway,   335
What not by right, she cast to win by guile,
And by her hellish science raisd streightway
A foggy mist, that overcast the day,
And a dull blast, that breathing on her face,
Dimméd her former beauties shining ray,   340
And with foule ugly forme did her disgrace:
Then was she faire alone, when none was faire
  in place.

[21] Typifies such faith as is possible to a doubter.

### 39

Then cride she out, Fye, fye, deforméd wight,
Whose borrowed beautie now appeareth plaine
To have before bewitchéd all mens sight;    345
O leave her soone, or let her soone be slaine.
Her loathly visage viewing with disdaine,
Eftsoones I thought her such, as she me told,
And would have kild her; but with faignéd
    paine,
The false witch did my wrathfull hand with-
    hold;    350
So left her, where she now is turned to treen
    mould.

### 40

Thenceforth I tooke *Duessa* for my Dame,
And in the witch unweeting joyd long time,
Ne ever wist, but that she was the same,
Till on a day (that day is every Prime,    355
When Witches wont do penance for their
    crime)
I chaunst to see her in her proper hew,
Bathing her selfe in origane and thyme:
A filthy foule old woman I did vew,
That ever to have toucht her, I did deadly
    rew.    360

### 41

Her neather partes misshapen, monstruous,
Were hidd in water, that I could not see,
But they did seeme more foule and hideous,
Then womans shape man would beleeve to bee.
Thenceforth from her most beastly companie
I gan refraine, in minde to slip away,    366
Soone as appeard safe opportunitie:
For danger great, if not assur'd decay
I saw before mine eyes, if I were knowne to
    stray.

### 42

The divelish hag by chaunges of my cheare   370
Perceiv'd my thought, and drownd in sleepie
    night,
With wicked herbes and ointments did be-
    smeare
My bodie all, through charmes and magicke
    might,

That all my senses were bereavéd quight:
Then brought she me into this desert waste,   375
And by my wretched lovers side me pight,
Where now enclosd in wooden wals full faste,
Banisht from living wights, our wearie dayes we
    waste.

### 43

But how long time, said then the Elfin knight,
Are you in this misforméd house to dwell?   380
We may not chaunge (quoth he) this evil
    plight,
Till we be bathéd in a living well;
That is the terme prescribéd by the spell.
O how, said he, mote I that well out find,
That may restore you to your wonted well?   385
Time and suffiséd fates to former kynd
Shall us restore, none else from hence may us
    unbynd.

### 44

The false *Duessa*, now *Fidessa* hight,
Heard how in vaine *Fradubio* did lament,
And knew well all was true. But the good
    knight    390
Full of sad feare and ghastly dreriment,
When all this speech the living tree had spent,
The bleeding bough did thrust into the ground,
That from the bloud he might be innocent,
And with fresh clay did close the wooden
    wound:    395
Then turning to his Lady, dead with feare her
    found.

### 45

Her seeming dead he found with feignéd feare,
As all unweeting of that well she knew,
And paynd himselfe with busie care to reare
Her out of carelesse swowne. Her eylids
    blew    400
And dimméd sight with pale and deadly hew
At last she up gan lift: with trembling cheare
Her up he tooke, too simple and too trew,
And oft her kist. At length all passéd feare,
He set her on her steede, and forward forth did
    beare.    405

# Francis Bacon

## 1561 - 1626

Francis Bacon was a younger son of Sir Nicholas Bacon, lord keeper of the great seal under Queen Elizabeth. His mother was the sister-in-law of Lord Burghley, long Elizabeth's trusted adviser, so that it may fairly be said that Bacon was born a member of the governing class of England; and as one destined for public service he was brought up. In 1573 he went to Trinity College, Cambridge, staying there until the end of 1575. In 1576 he entered Gray's Inn to study the law, leaving in 1577, however, for two years' residence in France in the household of the English ambassador. The death of his father in 1579 left him to shift largely for himself, and he turned immediately to the law. He was admitted an utter barrister in 1582. In 1584 he entered Parliament and thus actively began his long political career. He persistently sought advancement through the friendship of the great—through Lord Burghley, then through the Earl of Essex, and then through Sir Robert Cecil, Burghley's son—and he sought to deserve friendship by his statesmanlike advice. His abilities were striking and his advice was good; yet the opening he wanted to a great career was long denied him. He was knighted in 1603, at the accession of James; in 1607 he was made solicitor-general, in 1613 attorney-general, in 1616 privy councilor, in 1617 lord keeper of the great seal, and in 1618 lord chancellor. In the same year he was created Baron Verulam, and in 1621 Viscount St. Alban. Later in 1621, however, came his sudden and complete downfall. He was impeached on the charge of bribery, confessed his guilt, and was sentenced by the House of Lords to a fine of £40,000 and to imprisonment in the Tower during the king's pleasure, while he was disabled from sitting in Parliament and from coming within the verge, i. e., within twelve miles, of the Court. The fine was immediately converted into a trust fund for Bacon's use and his imprisonment lasted only a few days; within a year, too, he

was allowed again to present himself at Court; but his exclusion from Parliament was not relaxed, and Bacon was politically a broken man. The remaining years of his life were devoted to study and writing. Born on 22 January, 1561, he died on 9 April, 1626.

Pope called Bacon "the wisest, brightest, meanest of mankind," and the line has stuck. Yet, while no one would for a moment contend that Bacon had either the elevation of character or the detachment of a saint, it is no less certain that he has suffered from grave misunderstanding. While not condoning his moral obtuseness, one should in justice remember that he simply suffered from the defects, as he enjoyed the advantages, of the clearly marked type of mind to which we owe the achievements of modern science. Morality is concerned with imperfectly realized ideals, it seeks to bend men to the commands of an invisible kingdom. Bacon, on the other hand, saw things and men as they are, and viewed his world as a field for the realization of human purposes.

In politics he undoubtedly wished to find a place for himself, and in this took, not a mean, but a common-sense view of his situation. No less clearly, however, he wanted to use his power when he obtained it for public ends, for furthering the greatness of his country and bettering the condition of its members. And for the achievement of his personal and public purposes he followed what, as things were in his day, was the only practicable method—the method of rising through favor of the great. If he was blind to the loss of dignity involved in seeking such favor, this was because his mind was centered on his end and because he judged means simply in relation to their probable efficacy. Again, in accepting gifts as a judge, Bacon merely followed the common custom of his day, and he was more scrupulous than other judges in that he appears not to have allowed the gifts to bias his judgments. If we may smile at the naïveté which blinded him to the enmities this was bound to arouse, still we cannot avoid agreement with his own statement. "I was," he said, "the justest judge that was in England these fifty years, but it was the justest sentence in Parliament that was these two hundred years."

When he was a young man Bacon wrote, in a letter hinting his desire for preferment, "I have as vast contemplative ends as I have moderate civil ends; for I have taken all knowledge to be my province." This was the second of the two related purposes of his life. A child of the Renaissance both in the vastness of his outlook and in his confidence in human powers, he saw the importance of knowledge in life as he understood it. And as he sought in public life an opportunity for the application of knowledge to the betterment of the condition of his country and its inhabitants, so he sought also to map out the field of knowledge and to elaborate a right method for its discovery. The former he attempted to achieve in The Advancement of Learning (1605) and, more fully, in the amplified Latin version of that book published in 1623. His imperfect formulation of scientific method is contained in his Novum Organum (1620). His fragmentary New Atlantis is a literary picture of the advantages to man which he saw in the pursuit of science. His History of Henry VII, one of the fruits of his retirement after 1621, is a masterly historical work which also occupies a deservedly high place in literature. But to most readers Bacon will always be known chiefly through his Essays, those "dispersed meditations," "set 10 down rather significantly than curiously," on which, in all probability, he never supposed that his fame would largely depend. Ten essays were published in 1597; in the second edition of 1612 they had grown to thirty-eight; and in the third edition of 1625 there were fifty-eight, while many of the earlier essays were amplified. They probably take their title from Montaigne's Essais (1580), though the two books have little in common save that both consist 20 of dispersed notes on life set down by a man of the world. Bacon's Essays introduced a new form into English literature; and they represent the man as he was, shrewd, incisive, somewhat hard, and yet on occasion finely imaginative.

The Works of Francis Bacon, ed. James Spedding, Robert L. Ellis, Douglas D. Heath, revised edition (New York, 1869), contains the Essays in vol. XII; a more up-to-date edition is 30 the volume Essays, Advancement of Learning, New Atlantis, and Other Pieces, ed. Richard F.

Jones (Garden City, 1937). For a sympathetic study of Bacon as a man see James Spedding, The Letters and Life of Francis Bacon, Including All his Occasional Works (London, 1861–1874); Lytton Strachey's Elizabeth and Essex, a Tragic History (New York, 1928) gives an effective and damaging portrait of the younger Bacon. The Philosophy of Francis Bacon by C. D. Broad (Cambridge, 1926) and The Philosophy of Francis Bacon by F. H. Anderson (Chicago, 1948) are useful. Two studies which deal with Bacon's intellectual importance are Basil Willey, The Seventeenth Century Background; Studies in the Thought of the Age in Relation to Poetry and Religion (London, 1934), and Richard F. Jones, Ancients and Moderns, a Study in the Background of the Battle of the Books (St. Louis, 1936).

# Essays or Counsels Civil and Moral

## 1.—OF TRUTH

"What is truth?" said jesting Pilate,[1] and would not stay for an answer. Certainly there be that delight in giddiness, and count it a bondage to fix a belief; affecting free-will in thinking, as well as in acting. And though the sects of philosophers of that kind be gone, yet there remain certain discoursing wits which are of the same veins, though there be not so much blood in them as was in those of the ancients. But it is not only the difficulty and labor which men take in finding out of truth, nor again that when it is found it imposeth upon men's thoughts, that doth bring lies in favor; but a natural though corrupt love of the lie itself. One of the later school of the Grecians examineth the matter, and is at a stand to think what should be in it that men should love lies; where neither they make for pleasure, as with poets; nor for advantage, as with the merchant; but for the lie's sake. But I cannot tell: this same truth is a naked and open daylight that doth not show the masques and mummeries and triumphs of the world half so stately and daintily as candle-lights. Truth may perhaps come to the price of a pearl, that showeth best by day; but it will not rise to the price of a diamond or carbuncle, that showeth best in varied lights. A mixture of a lie doth ever add pleasure. Doth any man doubt that if there were taken out of men's minds vain opinions, flattering hopes, false valuations, imagina-

[1] Cf. St. John, 18:38.

tions as one would, and the like, but it would leave the minds of a number of men poor shrunken things, full of melancholy and indisposition, and unpleasing to themselves? One of the fathers, in great severity, called poesy *vinum daemonum*,[2] because it filleth the imagination, and yet it is but with the shadow of a lie. But it is not the lie that passeth through the mind, but the lie that sinketh in and settleth in it, that doth the hurt, such as we spake of before. But howsoever these things are thus in men's depraved judgments and affections, yet truth, which only doth judge itself, teacheth that the inquiry of truth, which is the love-making or wooing of it, the knowledge of truth, which is the presence of it, and the belief of truth, which is the enjoying of it, is the sovereign good of human nature. The first creature of God, in the works of the days, was the light of the sense; the last was the light of reason; and his sabbath work, ever since, is the illumination of his Spirit. First he breathed light upon the face of the matter or chaos; then he breathed light into the face of man; and still he breatheth and inspireth light into the face of his chosen. The poet [3] that beautified the sect [4] that was otherwise inferior to the rest, saith yet excellently well: "It is a pleasure to stand upon the shore, and to see ships tossed upon the sea: a pleasure to stand in the window of a castle, and to see a battle and the adventures thereof below: but no pleasure is comparable to the standing upon the vantage ground of truth" (a hill not to be commanded, and where the air is always clear and serene), "and to see the errors, and wanderings, and mists, and tempests, in the vale below": so always that this prospect be with pity, and not with swelling or pride. Certainly, it is heaven upon earth to have a man's mind move in charity, rest in providence, and turn upon the poles of truth.

To pass from theological and philosophical truth to the truth of civil business: it will be acknowledged, even by those that practice it not, that clear and round [5] dealing is the honor of man's nature; and that mixture of falsehood is like alloy in coin of gold and silver, which may make the metal work the better, but it embaseth it. For these winding and crooked courses are the goings of the serpent; which goeth basely upon the belly, and not upon the feet. There is no vice that doth so cover a man with shame as to be found false and perfidious. And therefore Montaigne saith prettily, when he inquired the reason why the word of the lie should be such a disgrace and such an odious charge? saith he: "If it be well weighed, to say that a man lieth is as much to say as that he is brave towards God and a coward towards men." [6] For a lie faces God, and shrinks from man. Surely the wickedness of falsehood and breach of faith cannot possibly be so highly expressed, as in that it shall be the last peal to call the judgments of God upon the generations of men; it being foretold that when Christ cometh, "he shall not find faith upon the earth." [7]

### 6.—OF SIMULATION AND DISSIMULATION

DISSIMULATION is but a faint kind of policy or wisdom; for it asketh a strong wit and a strong heart to know when to tell truth, and to do it. Therefore it is the weaker sort of politics [1] that are the great dissemblers.

Tacitus saith: "Livia sorted well with the arts of her husband and dissimulation of her son"; [2] attributing arts or policy to Augustus, and dissimulation to Tiberius. And again, when Mucianus encourageth Vespasian to take arms against Vitellius, he saith: "We rise not against the piercing judgment of Augustus, nor the extreme caution or closeness of Tiberius." [3] These properties, of arts or policy and dissimulation or closeness, are indeed habits and faculties several and to be distinguished. For if a man have that penetration of judgment as he can discern what things are to be laid open, and what to be secreted, and what to be showed at half lights, and to whom, and when (which indeed are arts of state and arts of life, as Tacitus well calleth them), to him a habit of dissimulation is a hindrance and a poorness. But if a man cannot obtain to that judgment, then it is left to him, generally, to be close, and a dissembler. For where a man cannot choose or vary in particulars, there it is good to take the safest and wariest way in general; like the going softly by one that cannot well see. Certainly the ablest men that ever were have had all an openness and frankness of dealing, and a name of certainty and veracity; but then they were like horses well managed; for they could tell passing well when to stop or turn; and at

---

[2] Wine of devils. A phrase of similar meaning is used by Augustine (*Confessions*, I, xvi, 26).

[3] Lucretius. Bacon paraphrases a passage at the beginning of Bk. II of Lucretius's poem *On the Nature of Things*.

[4] The Epicureans.    [5] Straightforward.

[6] *Essays*, II, 18.    [7] St. Luke, 18:8.

[1] Politicians.    [2] *Annals*, V, 1.

[3] Tacitus, *Hist.*, II, 76.

such times when they thought the case indeed required dissimulation, if then they used it, it came to pass that the former opinion spread abroad of their good faith and clearness of dealing made them almost invisible.

There be three degrees of this hiding and veiling of a man's self. The first, closeness, reservation, and secrecy; when a man leaveth himself without observation, or without hold to be taken, what he is. The second, dissimu- 10 lation, in the negative; when a man lets fall signs and arguments, that he is not that he is. And the third, simulation, in the affirmative; when a man industriously and expressly feigns and pretends to be that he is not.

For the first of these, secrecy: it is indeed the virtue of a confessor; and assuredly the secret man heareth many confessions; for who will open himself to a blab or a babbler? But if a man be thought secret, it inviteth discovery; 20 as the more close air sucketh in the more open: and as in confession the revealing is not for worldly use, but for the ease of a man's heart, so secret men come to the knowledge of many things in that kind; while men rather discharge their minds than impart their minds. In few words, mysteries are due to secrecy. Besides (to say truth) nakedness is uncomely, as well in mind as body; and it addeth no small reverence to men's manners and actions, if they be 30 not altogether open. As for talkers and futile persons, they are commonly vain and credulous withal. For he that talketh what he knoweth will also talk what he knoweth not. Therefore set it down *that an habit of secrecy is both politic and moral.* And in this part, it is good that a man's face give his tongue leave to speak. For the discovery of a man's self by the tracts [4] of his countenance is a great weakness and betraying; by how much it is many 40 times more marked and believed than a man's words.

For the second, which is dissimulation: it followeth many times upon secrecy by a necessity; so that he that will be secret must be a dissembler in some degree. For men are too cunning to suffer a man to keep an indifferent [5] carriage between both, and to be secret, without swaying the balance on either side. They will so beset a man with questions, and draw 50 him on, and pick it out of him that, without an absurd silence, he must show an inclination one way; or if he do not, they will gather as much by his silence as by his speech. As for equivocations, or oraculous speeches, they cannot hold out long. So that no man can be

secret except he give himself a little scope of dissimulation; which is, as it were, but the skirts or train of secrecy.

But for the third degree, which is simulation and false profession: that I hold more culpable, and less politic; except it be in great and rare matters. And therefore a general custom of simulation (which is this last degree) is a vice, rising either of a natural falseness or fearfulness, or of a mind that hath some main faults, which because a man must needs disguise, it maketh him practice simulation in other things, lest his hand should be out of use.

The great advantages of simulation and dissimulation are three. First, to lay asleep opposition, and to surprise. For where a man's intentions are published, it is an alarm to call up all that are against them. The second is, to reserve to a man's self a fair retreat. For if a man engage himself by a manifest declaration, he must go through, or take a fall. The third is, the better to discover the mind of another. For to him that opens himself men will hardly show themselves adverse; but will (fair) [6] let him go on, and turn their freedom of speech to freedom of thought. And therefore it is a good shrewd proverb of the Spaniard, "Tell a lie and find a truth"; as if there were no way of discovery but by simulation. There be also three disadvantages to set it even. The first, that simulation and dissimulation commonly carry with them a show of fearfulness, which in any business doth spoil the feathers of round [7] flying up to the mark. The second, that it puzzleth and perplexeth the conceits [8] of many that perhaps would otherwise co-operate with him, and makes a man walk almost alone to his own ends. The third and greatest is, that it depriveth a man of one of the most principal instruments for action, which is trust and belief. The best composition and temperature [9] is to have openness in fame and opinion; secrecy in habit; dissimulation in seasonable use; and a power to feign, if there be no remedy.

### 7.—OF PARENTS AND CHILDREN

THE joys of parents are secret, and so are their griefs and fears: they cannot utter the one, nor they will not utter [1] the other. Children sweeten labors, but they make misfortunes more bitter; they increase the cares of life, but they mitigate the remembrance of death. The

---

[4] Features.　　　　[5] Impartial.

[6] Rather.　　　　　[7] I. e., swiftly.
[8] Thoughts.　　　　[9] Temperament.
[1] Nor will they utter.

perpetuity by generation is common to beasts; but memory, merit, and noble works are proper to men; and surely a man shall see the noblest works and foundations have proceeded from childless men, which have sought to express the images of their minds, where those of their bodies have failed; so the care of posterity is most in them that have no posterity. They that are the first raisers of their houses are most indulgent towards their children, beholding 10 them as the continuance not only of their kind but of their work, and so both children and creatures.

The difference in affection of parents towards their several children is many times unequal, and sometimes unworthy, especially in the mother; as Solomon saith: "A wise son rejoiceth the father, but an ungracious son shames the mother." [2] A man shall see, where there is a house full of children, one or two of 20 the eldest respected, and the youngest made wantons; but in the midst some that are as it were forgotten, who many times nevertheless prove the best. The illiberality of parents in allowance towards their children is an harmful error; makes them base; acquaints them with shifts; [3] makes them sort with mean company; and makes them surfeit more when they come to plenty: and therefore the proof is best when men keep their authority towards their chil- 30 dren, but not their purse. Men have a foolish manner (both parents and schoolmasters and servants) in creating and breeding an emulation between brothers during childhood, which many times sorteth to discord when they are men, and disturbeth families. The Italians make little difference between children and nephews or near kinsfolks; but so they be of the lump, they care not though they pass not through their own body. And, to say truth, in 40 nature it is much a like matter; insomuch that we see a nephew sometimes resembleth an uncle or a kinsman more than his own parents, as the blood happens. Let parents choose betimes the vocations and courses they mean their children should take, for then they are most flexible; and let them not too much apply themselves to the disposition of their children, as thinking they will take best to that which they have most mind to. It is true, that 50 if the affection or aptness of the children be extraordinary, then it is good not to cross it; but generally the precept is good, *Optimum elige, suave et facile illud faciet consuetudo.*[4]

[2] Proverbs, 10:1.          [3] Deceptions.
[4] Choose the best; habit will make it pleasant and easy. (Plutarch attributes this saying to Pythagoras.)

Younger brothers are commonly fortunate, but seldom or never where the elder are disinherited.

## 8.—OF MARRIAGE AND SINGLE LIFE

HE THAT hath wife and children hath given hostages to fortune; for they are impediments to great enterprises, either of virtue or mischief. Certainly, the best works, and of greatest merit for the public, have proceeded from the unmarried or childless men, which both in affection and means have married and endowed the public. Yet it were great reason that those that have children should have greatest care of future times; unto which they know they must transmit their dearest pledges. Some there are who though they lead a single life, yet their thoughts do end with themselves, and account future times impertinences. Nay, there are some other that account wife and children but as bills of charges. Nay more, there are some foolish rich covetous men that take a pride in having no children, because they may be thought so much the richer. For perhaps they have heard some talk: "Such an one is a great rich man," and another except to it: "Yea, but he hath a great charge of children"; as if it were an abatement to his riches. But the most ordinary cause of a single life is liberty; especially in certain self-pleasing and humorous [1] minds, which are so sensible of every restraint, as they will go near to think their girdles and garters to be bonds and shackles. Unmarried men are best friends, best masters, best servants, but not always best subjects; for they are light to run away; and almost all fugitives are of that condition. A single life doth well with churchmen; for charity will hardly water the ground where it must first fill a pool. It is indifferent for judges and magistrates; for if they be facile and corrupt, you shall have a servant five times worse than a wife. For soldiers, I find the generals commonly in their hortatives [2] put men in mind of their wives and children; and I think the despising of marriage amongst the Turks maketh the vulgar soldier more base. Certainly wife and children are a kind of discipline of humanity; and single men, though they be many times more charitable, because their means are less exhaust, [3] yet, on the other side, they are more cruel and hardhearted (good to make severe inquisitors), because their tenderness is not so oft called upon. Grave natures, led by custom, and therefore constant,

[1] Whimsical.          [2] Exhortations.
[3] Exhausted.

are commonly loving husbands; as was said of Ulysses, *Vetulam suam praetulit immortalitati.*[4] Chaste women are often proud and froward, as presuming upon the merit of their chastity. It is one of the best bonds both of chastity and obedience in the wife, if she think her husband wise; which she will never do if she find him jealous. Wives are young men's mistresses; companions for middle age; and old men's nurses. So as a man may have a quarrel[5] to marry when he will. But yet he was reputed one of the wise men, that made answer to the question, when a man should marry? "A young man not yet, an elder man not at all."[6] It is often seen that bad husbands have very good wives; whether it be that it raiseth the price of their husband's kindness when it comes, or that the wives take a pride in their patience. But this never fails, if the bad husbands were of their own choosing, against their friends' consent; for then they will be sure to make good their own folly.

## 10.—OF LOVE

THE stage is more beholding to love than the life of man. For as to the stage, love is ever matter of comedies, and now and then of tragedies; but in life it doth much mischief, sometimes like a siren, sometimes like a fury. You may observe that amongst all the great and worthy persons (whereof the memory remaineth, either ancient or recent) there is not one that hath been transported to the mad degree of love; which shows that great spirits and great business do keep out this weak passion. You must except, nevertheless, Marcus Antonius,[1] the half partner of the empire of Rome, and Appius Claudius,[2] the decemvir and lawgiver: whereof the former was indeed a voluptuous man, and inordinate; but the latter was an austere and wise man: and therefore it seems (though rarely) that love can find entrance not only into an open heart, but also into a heart well fortified, if watch be not well kept. It is a poor saying of Epicurus, *Satis magnum alter alteri theatrum sumus:*[3] as if man, made for the contemplation of heaven and all noble objects, should do nothing but kneel before a little idol, and make himself subject, though not of the mouth (as beasts are), yet of the

eye, which was given them for higher purposes. It is a strange thing to note the excess of this passion, and how it braves[4] the nature and value of things, by this, that the speaking in a perpetual hyperbole is comely in nothing but in love. Neither is it merely in the phrase; for whereas it hath been well said[5] that the arch-flatterer, with whom all the petty flatterers have intelligence, is a man's self, certainly the lover is more. For there was never proud man thought so absurdly well of himself as the lover doth of the person loved; and therefore it was well said: "That it is impossible to love and to be wise."[6] Neither doth this weakness appear to others only, and not to the party loved, but to the loved most of all, except the love be reciprocal. For it is a true rule, that love is ever rewarded either with the reciproque[7] or with an inward and secret contempt. By how much the more men ought to beware of this passion, which loseth not only other things, but itself. As for the other losses, the poet's relation doth well figure them: That he[8] that preferred Helena quitted the gifts of Juno and Pallas. For whosoever esteemeth too much of amorous affection quitteth both riches and wisdom. This passion hath his floods in the very times of weakness; which are great prosperity and great adversity (though this latter hath been less observed): both which times kindle love, and make it more fervent, and therefore show it to be the child of folly. They do best who, if they cannot but admit love, yet make it keep quarter,[9] and sever it wholly from their serious affairs and actions of life; for if it check[10] once with business, it troubleth men's fortunes, and maketh men that they can no ways be true to their own ends. I know not how, but martial men are given to love: I think it is but as they are given to wine; for perils commonly ask to be paid in pleasures. There is in man's nature a secret inclination and motion towards love of others, which, if it be not spent upon some one or a few, doth naturally spread itself towards many, and maketh men become humane and charitable; as it is seen sometime in friars. Nuptial love maketh mankind; friendly love perfecteth it; but wanton love corrupteth and embaseth it.

## 11.—OF GREAT PLACE

MEN in great places are thrice servants: servants of the sovereign or state; servants of fame;

---

[4] He preferred his aged wife to immortality (which had been offered him by Calypso).
[5] An excuse.
[6] The saying is ascribed by Plutarch to Thales, one of the "seven wise men" of Greece.
[1] Cleopatra's lover.      [2] The lover of Virginia.
[3] We are to one another an ample spectacle (quoted by Seneca, *Epistles,* I, vii, 11).

[4] Exaggerates.         [5] By Plutarch.
[6] By Publius Syrus.    [7] Returned affection.
[8] Paris.               [9] Keep within bounds.
[10] Interfere.

and servants of business. So as they have no freedom, neither in their persons, nor in their actions, nor in their times. It is a strange desire, to seek power and to lose liberty; or to seek power over others and to lose power over a man's self. The rising unto place is laborious, and by pains men come to greater pains; and it is sometimes base, and by indignities men come to dignities. The standing is slippery; and the regress is either a downfall, or at least an eclipse, which is a melancholy thing. *Cum non sis qui fueris, non esse cur velis vivere.*[1] Nay, retire men cannot when they would; neither will they when it were reason; but are impatient of privateness, even in age and sickness, which require the shadow:[2] like old townsmen, that will be still sitting at their street door, though thereby they offer age to scorn. Certainly, great persons had need to borrow other men's opinions to think themselves happy; for if they judge by their own feeling, they cannot find it: but if they think with themselves what other men think of them, and that other men would fain be as they are, then they are happy as it were by report, when perhaps they find the contrary within. For they are the first that find their own griefs, though they be the last that find their own faults. Certainly, men in great fortunes are strangers to themselves, and while they are in the puzzle of business they have no time to tend their health, either of body or mind. *Illi mors gravis incubat, qui notus nimis omnibus, ignotus moritur sibi.*[3] In place there is license to do good and evil; whereof the latter is a curse: for in evil the best condition is not to will, the second not to can.[4] But power to do good is the true and lawful end of aspiring. For good thoughts (though God accept them) yet towards men are little better than good dreams, except they be put in act; and that cannot be without power and place, as the vantage and commanding ground. Merit and good works is the end of man's motion; and conscience[5] of the same is the accomplishment of man's rest. For if a man can be partaker of God's theater, he shall likewise be partaker of God's rest. *Et conversus Deus ut aspiceret opera quae fecerunt manus suae, vidit quod omnia essent bona nimis;*[6] and then the Sabbath. In the discharge of thy place, set before thee the best examples; for imitation is a globe[7] of precepts. And after a time set before thee thine own example; and examine thyself strictly, whether thou didst not best at first. Neglect not also the examples of those that have carried themselves ill in the same place; not to set off thyself by taxing their memory, but to direct thyself what to avoid. Reform, therefore, without bravery[8] or scandal of former times and persons; but yet set it down to thyself as well to create good precedents as to follow them. Reduce things to the first institution, and observe wherein and how they have degenerate; but yet ask counsel of both times; of the ancient time, what is best; and of the latter time, what is fittest. Seek to make thy course regular, that men may know beforehand what they may expect; but be not too positive and peremptory; and express thyself well when thou digressest from thy rule. Preserve the right of thy place, but stir not questions of jurisdiction: and rather assume thy right in silence and *de facto*[9] than voice it with claims and challenges. Preserve likewise the rights of inferior places; and think it more honor to direct in chief than to be busy in all. Embrace and invite helps and advices touching the execution of thy place; and do not drive away such as bring thee information as meddlers, but accept of them in good part. The vices of authority are chiefly four: delays, corruption, roughness, and facility.[10] For delays: give easy access; keep times appointed; go through with that which is in hand; and interlace not business but of necessity. For corruption: do not only bind thine own hands or thy servants' hands from taking, but bind the hands of suitors also from offering. For integrity used doth the one; but integrity professed, and with a manifest detestation of bribery, doth the other. And avoid not only the fault, but the suspicion. Whosoever is found variable, and changeth manifestly without manifest cause, giveth suspicion of corruption. Therefore always when thou changest thine opinion or course, profess it plainly and declare it, together with the reasons that move thee to change; and do not think to steal[11] it. A servant or a favorite, if he be inward,[12] and no other apparent cause of esteem, is commonly thought but a by-way to close corruption. For roughness, it is a needless cause of discontent: severity breedeth fear, but roughness breedeth

---

[1] When you are no longer what you were, there is no reason why you should wish to keep on living (Cicero).

[2] Retirement.

[3] Sad is the fate of him who ends his days all too well known to others, but a stranger to himself (Seneca, *Thyestes*).

[4] To know.    [5] Consciousness.

[6] And God, turning back to look upon the works which his hands had made, saw that all were very good (Genesis, 1:31, quoted inexactly from the Vulgate).

[7] A complete or perfect body.    [8] Boast.

[9] As a matter of fact.    [10] Lack of firmness.

[11] Hide.    [12] Intimate.

hate. Even reproofs from authority ought to be grave, and not taunting. As for facility, it is worse than bribery. For bribes come but now and then; but if importunity or idle respects [13] lead a man, he shall never be without. As Solomon saith: "To respect persons is not good; for such a man will transgress for a piece of bread." [14] It is most true that was anciently spoken, "A place showeth the man": and it showeth some to the better, and some to the worse. *Omnium consensu capax imperii, nisi imperasset*,[15] saith Tacitus of Galba; but of Vespasian he saith, *Solus imperantium Vespasianus mutatus in melius:* [16] though the one was meant of sufficiency,[17] the other of manners and affection. It is an assured sign of a worthy and generous spirit, whom honor amends. For honor is, or should be, the place of virtue; and as in nature things move violently to their place, and calmly in their place; so virtue in ambition is violent, in authority settled and calm. All rising to great place is by a winding stair; and if there be factions, it is good to side a man's self whilst he is in the rising, and to balance himself when he is placed. Use the memory of thy predecessor fairly and tenderly; for if thou dost not, it is a debt will sure be paid when thou art gone. If thou have colleagues, respect them, and rather call them when they look not for it than exclude them when they have reason to look to be called. Be not too sensible or too remembering of thy place in conversation and private answers to suitors; but let it rather be said, "When he sits in place he is another man."

## 12.—OF BOLDNESS

IT IS a trivial grammar-school text, but yet worthy a wise man's consideration. Question was asked of Demosthenes, "What was the chief part of an orator?" he answered "Action": what next? "Action": what next again? "Action." He said it that knew it best, and had by nature himself no advantage in that he commended. A strange thing, that that part of an orator which is but superficial, and rather the virtue of a player, should be placed so high above those other noble parts of invention, elocution, and the rest; nay, almost alone, as if it were all in all. But the reason is plain. There is in human nature generally more of the

fool than of the wise; and therefore those faculties by which the foolish part of men's minds is taken are most potent. Wonderful like is the case of boldness in civil business: what first? "Boldness": what second and third? "Boldness." And yet boldness is a child of ignorance and baseness, far inferior to other parts. But nevertheless it doth fascinate and bind hand and foot those that are either shallow in judgment or weak in courage, which are the greatest part; yea, and prevaileth with wise men at weak times. Therefore we see it hath done wonders in popular [1] states, but with senates and princes less; and more ever upon the first entrance of bold persons into action than soon after; for boldness is an ill keeper of promise. Surely, as there are mountebanks for the natural body, so are there mountebanks for the politic body; men that undertake great cures, and perhaps have been lucky in two or three experiments, but want the grounds [2] of science, and therefore cannot hold out. Nay, you shall see a bold fellow many times do Mahomet's miracle. Mahomet made the people believe that he would call an hill to him, and from the top of it offer up his prayers for the observers of his law. The people assembled; Mahomet called the hill to come to him, again and again; and when the hill stood still, he was never a whit abashed, but said: "If the hill will not come to Mahomet, Mahomet will go to the hill." So these men, when they have promised great matters and failed most shamefully, yet (if they have the perfection of boldness) they will but slight it over, and make a turn, and no more ado. Certainly, to men of great judgment, bold persons are a sport to behold; nay, and to the vulgar also, boldness hath somewhat of the ridiculous. For if absurdity be the subject of laughter, doubt you not but great boldness is seldom without some absurdity. Especially it is a sport to see, when a bold fellow is out of countenance; for that puts his face into a most shrunken and wooden posture; as needs it must; for in bashfulness the spirits do a little go and come; but with bold men, upon like occasion, they stand at a stay; like a stale [3] at chess, where it is no mate, but yet the game cannot stir. But this last were fitter for a satire than for a serious observation. This is well to be weighed, that boldness is ever blind; for it seeth not dangers and inconveniences. Therefore it is ill in counsel, good in execution; so that the right use of bold persons

---

[13] Considerations.    [14] Proverbs, 28:21.
[15] All men would have thought him competent to rule if they had not seen him as a ruler.
[16] Of all the emperors Vespasian alone changed for the better.
[17] Ability.

[1] Democratic.    [2] Foundations.
[3] Stale-mate, where the king cannot move, save into check.

is, that they never command in chief, but be seconds, and under the direction of others. For in counsel it is good to see dangers; and in execution not to see them, except they be very great.

### 16.—OF ATHEISM

I HAD rather believe all the fables in the Legend,[1] and the Talmud, and the Alcoran,[2] than that this universal frame is without a mind. And therefore God never wrought miracle to convince [3] atheism, because his ordinary works convince it. It is true, that a little philosophy [4] inclineth man's mind to atheism; but depth in philosophy bringeth men's minds about to religion: for while the mind of man looketh upon second causes scattered, it may sometimes rest in them, and go no further; but when it beholdeth the chain of them, confederate and linked together, it must needs fly to Providence and Deity. Nay, even that school which is most accused of atheism doth most demonstrate religion; that is, the school of Leucippus and Democritus and Epicurus. For it is a thousand times more credible that four mutable elements and one immutable fifth essence, duly and eternally placed, need no God than that an army of infinite small portions or seeds unplaced should have produced this order and beauty without a divine marshal. The Scripture saith: "The fool hath said in his heart there is no God": [5] it is not said, "The fool hath thought in his heart"; so as he rather saith it by rote to himself, as that he would have, than that he can thoroughly believe it, or be persuaded of it. For none deny there is a God but those for whom it maketh that there were no God. It appeareth in nothing more that atheism is rather in the lip than in the heart of man than by this: that atheists will ever be talking of that their opinion, as if they fainted in it within themselves, and would be glad to be strengthened by the consent of others: nay more, you shall have atheists strive to get disciples, as it fareth with other sects: and, which is most of all, you shall have of them that will suffer for atheism, and not recant; whereas, if they did truly think that there were no such thing as God, why should they trouble themselves? Epicurus is charged that he did but dissemble for his credit's sake, when he affirmed there were blessed natures, but such as enjoyed themselves without having respect to the government of the world. Wherein they say he did temporize, though in secret he thought there was no God. But certainly he is traduced; for his words are noble and divine: *Non deos vulgi negare profanum, sed vulgi opiniones diis applicare profanum.*[6] Plato could have said no more. And although he had the confidence to deny the administration, he had not the power to deny the nature. The Indians of the West have names for their particular gods, though they have no name for God: as if the heathens should have had the names *Jupiter, Apollo, Mars, etc.,* but not the word *Deus;* which shows that even those barbarous people have the notion, though they have not the latitude and extent of it. So that against atheists the very savages take part with the very subtlest philosophers. The contemplative atheist is rare: a Diagoras, a Bion, a Lucian perhaps, and some others; and yet they seem to be more than they are, for that all that impugn a received religion, or superstition, are, by the adverse part, branded with the name of atheists. But the great atheists indeed are hypocrites; which are ever handling holy things, but without feeling; so as they must needs be cauterized in the end. The causes of atheism are: divisions in religion, if they be many; for any one main division addeth zeal to both sides, but many divisions introduce atheism. Another is, scandal of priests; when it is come to that which S. Bernard saith: *Non est jam dicere, ut populus, sic sacerdos; quia nec sic populus, ut sacerdos.*[7] A third is, custom of profane scoffing in holy matters, which doth by little and little deface the reverence of religion. And lastly, learned times, specially with peace and prosperity; for troubles and adversities do more bow men's minds to religion. They that deny a God destroy man's nobility; for certainly man is of kin to the beasts by his body; and if he be not of kin to God by his spirit, he is a base and ignoble creature. It destroys likewise magnanimity, and the raising of human nature; for take an example of a dog, and mark what a generosity and courage he will put on when he finds himself maintained by a man, who to him is in stead of a god, or *melior natura;*[8] which courage is manifestly such as that creature,

---

[1] The *Legenda Aurea,* a medieval collection of the lives of saints.

[2] Koran.  [3] Confute.

[4] Natural philosophy, or science.

[5] Psalms, 14:1, and 53:1.

[6] It is not impious to say that the gods of men do not exist; it is impious rather to apply to the gods the foolish notions of men (Diogenes Laertius).

[7] It can no longer be said, "As the people are so is the priest," because the people are not now like the priest (i. e., the priest is worse).

[8] Better nature.

without that confidence of a better nature than his own, could never attain. So man, when he resteth and assureth himself upon divine protection and favor, gathereth a force and faith which human nature in itself could not obtain. Therefore, as atheism is in all respects hateful, so in this, that it depriveth human nature of the means to exalt itself above human frailty. As it is in particular persons, so it is in nations: never was there such a state for magnanimity as Rome: of this state hear what Cicero saith: *Quam volumus licet, patres conscripti, nos amemus, tamen nec numero Hispanos, nec robore Gallos, nec calliditate Poenos, nec artibus Graecos, nec denique hoc ipso hujus gentis et terrae domestico nativoque sensu Italos ipsos et Latinos; sed pietate, ac religione, atque hac una sapientia, quod Deorum immortalium numine omnia regi gubernarique perspeximus, omnes gentes nationesque superavimus.*[9]

## 23.—OF WISDOM FOR A MAN'S SELF

An ant is a wise creature for itself, but it is a shrewd [1] thing in an orchard or garden. And certainly men that are great lovers of themselves waste the public. Divide with reason between self-love and society; and be so true to thyself as thou be not false to others, specially to thy king and country. It is a poor center of a man's actions, himself. It is right earth. For that only stands fast upon his own center; whereas all things that have affinity with the heavens move upon the center of another, which they benefit.[2] The referring of all to a man's self is more tolerable in a sovereign prince; because themselves are not only themselves, but their good and evil is at the peril of the public fortune. But it is a desperate evil in a servant to a prince, or a citizen in a republic. For whatsoever affairs pass such a man's hands, he crooketh them to his own ends; which must needs be often eccentric to [3] the ends

of his master or state. Therefore let princes, or states, choose such servants as have not this mark; except they mean their service should be made but the accessory. That which maketh the effect more pernicious is that all proportion is lost. It were disproportion enough for the servant's good to be preferred before the master's; but yet it is a greater extreme, when a little good of the servant shall carry things against a great good of the master's. And yet that is the case of bad officers, treasurers, ambassadors, generals, and other false and corrupt servants; which set a bias upon their bowl,[4] of their own petty ends and envies, to the overthrow of their master's great and important affairs. And for the most part, the good such servants receive is after the model of their own fortune; but the hurt they sell for that good is after the model of their master's fortune. And certainly it is the nature of extreme self-lovers, as they will set an house on fire, and it were but to roast their eggs; and yet these men many times hold credit with their masters, because their study is but to please them and profit themselves; and for either respect [5] they will abandon the good of their affairs.

Wisdom for a man's self is, in many branches thereof, a depraved thing. It is the wisdom of rats, that will be sure to leave a house somewhat before it fall. It is the wisdom of the fox, that thrusts out the badger who digged and made room for him. It is the wisdom of crocodiles, that shed tears when they would devour. But that which is specially to be noted is that those which (as Cicero says of Pompey) are *sui amantes sine rivali* [6] are many times unfortunate. And whereas they have all their time sacrificed to themselves, they become in the end themselves sacrifices to the inconstancy of fortune, whose wings they thought by their self-wisdom to have pinioned.

## 42.—OF YOUTH AND AGE

A man that is young in years may be old in hours, if he have lost no time. But that happeneth rarely. Generally, youth is like the first cogitations, not so wise as the second. For there is a youth in thoughts as well as in ages. And yet the invention of young men is more lively than that of the

[9] We may plume ourselves as we will, O senators, yet we have not conquered the Spaniards by force of numbers, nor the Gauls by superior might, nor the Carthaginians by strategy, nor the Greeks by our culture, nor lastly the Italians and Latins by the power of internal organization which is peculiar to this people and this land; but it is because of our devotion and our piety and, above all, our realization that human events are ruled and guided by the power of the immortal gods that we have conquered all nations and all peoples.

[1] Mischievous.

[2] Bacon writes in terms of the Ptolemaic astronomy, which he accepted, and according to which the earth is the center of the universe.

[3] Different from.

[4] Place a weight in one side of their ball in bowling.

[5] Consideration.

[6] Lovers of themselves without a rival.

old; and imaginations stream into their minds better, and, as it were, more divinely. Natures that have much heat, and great and violent desires and perturbations, are not ripe for action till they have passed the meridian of their years: as it was with Julius Caesar, and Septimius Severus. Of the latter of whom it is said, *Juventutem egit erroribus, imo furoribus, plenam.*[1] And yet he was the ablest emperor, almost, of all the list. But reposed natures may do well in youth. As it is seen in Augustus Caesar, Cosmus, Duke of Florence,[2] Gaston de Foix, and others. On the other side, heat and vivacity in age is an excellent composition for business. Young men are fitter to invent than to judge; fitter for execution than for counsel; and fitter for new projects than for settled business. For the experience of age, in things that fall within the compass of it, directeth them; but in new things, abuseth them. The errors of young men are the ruin of business; but the errors of aged men amount but to this, that more might have been done, or sooner. Young men, in the conduct and manage[3] of actions, embrace more than they can hold; stir more than they can quiet; fly to the end, without consideration of the means and degrees; pursue some few principles which they have chanced upon absurdly; care[4] not to innovate which draws unknown inconveniences; use extreme remedies at first; and, that which doubleth all errors, will not acknowledge or retract them, like an unready horse that will neither stop nor turn. Men of age object too much, consult too long, adventure too little, repent too soon, and seldom drive business home to the full period, but content themselves with a mediocrity of success. Certainly, it is good to compound employments of both; for that will be good for the present, because the virtues of either age may correct the defects of both; and good for succession, that young men may be learners, while men in age are actors; and, lastly, good for extern[5] accidents, because authority followeth old men, and favor and popularity youth. But for the moral part, perhaps youth will have the pre-eminence, as age hath for the politic. A certain rabbin, upon the text, "Your young men shall see visions, and your old men shall dream dreams,"[6] inferreth that young men are admitted nearer to God than old, because vision is a clearer revelation than a dream. And certainly, the more a man drinketh of the world, the more it intoxicateth; and age doth profit rather in the powers of understanding than in the virtues of the will and affections. There be some have an over-early ripeness in their years, which fadeth betimes. These are, first, such as have brittle wits, the edge whereof is soon turned; such as was Hermogenes the rhetorician, whose books are exceeding subtle, who afterwards waxed stupid. A second sort is of those that have some natural dispositions which have better grace in youth than in age; such as is a fluent and luxuriant speech, which becomes youth well, but not age; so Tully saith of Hortensius, *Idem manebat, neque idem decebat.*[7] The third is of such as take too high a strain at the first, and are magnanimous more than tract of years can uphold. As was Scipio Africanus, of whom Livy saith in effect, *Ultima primis cedebant.*[8]

## 47.—OF NEGOTIATING

IT IS generally better to deal by speech than by letter; and by the mediation of a third than by a man's self. Letters are good, when a man would draw an answer by letter back again; or when it may serve for a man's justification afterwards to produce his own letter; or where it may be danger to be interrupted, or heard by pieces. To deal in person is good, when a man's face breedeth regard, as commonly with inferiors; or in tender cases, where a man's eye upon the countenance of him with whom he speaketh may give him a direction how far to go; and generally, where a man will reserve to himself liberty either to disavow or to expound. In choice of instruments, it is better to choose men of a plainer sort, that are like to do that that is committed to them, and to report back again faithfully the success,[1] than those that are cunning to contrive out of other men's business somewhat to grace themselves, and will help the matter in report for satisfaction sake. Use also such persons as affect[2] the business wherein they are employed, for that quickeneth much; and such as are fit for the matter, as bold men for expostulation, fair-spoken men for persuasion, crafty men for inquiry and observation,

---

[1] He spent his youth in folly, nay, in madness (Spartianus).
[2] I. e., Cosimo de' Medici.    [3] Management.
[4] Hesitate.    [5] External.
[6] Joel, 2:28.

[7] He remained the same, but it was no longer becoming (Cicero).
[8] His latter days fell short of the first.
[1] Result.    [2] Are inclined to.

froward and absurd men for business that doth not well bear out itself. Use also such as have been lucky and prevailed before in things wherein you have employed them; for that breeds confidence, and they will strive to maintain their prescription.[3] It is better to sound a person, with whom one deals, afar off, than to fall upon the point at first; except you mean to surprise him by some short question. It is better dealing with men in appetite [4] than with those that are where they would be. If a man deal with another upon conditions, the start or first performance is all, which a man cannot reasonably demand, except either the nature of the thing be such which must go before; or else a man can persuade the other party that he shall still need him in some other thing; or else that he be counted the honester man. All practice [5] is to discover, or to work. Men discover themselves in trust; in passion; at unawares; and of necessity, when they would have somewhat done and cannot find an apt pretext. If you would work [6] any man, you must either know his nature and fashions, and so lead him; or his ends, and so persuade him; or his weakness and disadvantages, and so awe him; or those that have interest in him, and so govern him. In dealing with cunning persons, we must ever consider their ends, to interpret their speeches; and it is good to say little to them, and that which they least look for. In all negotiations of difficulty, a man may not look to sow and reap at once; but must prepare business, and so ripen it by degrees.

## 50.—OF STUDIES

STUDIES serve for delight, for ornament, and for ability. Their chief use for delight is in privateness and retiring; for ornament, is in discourse; and for ability, is in the judgment and disposition of business. For expert men can execute, and perhaps judge of particulars, one by one; but the general counsels, and the plots and marshaling of affairs come best from those that are learned. To spend too much time in studies is sloth; to use them too much for ornament is affectation; to make judgment wholly by their rules is the humor of a scholar. They perfect nature, and are perfected by experience; for natural abilities are like natural plants, that need pruning by study; and studies themselves do give forth directions too much at large, except they be bounded in by experience. Crafty men contemn studies; simple men admire them; and wise men use them: for they teach not their own use; but that is a wisdom without them and above them, won by observation. Read not to contradict and confute; nor to believe and take for granted; nor to find talk and discourse; but to weigh and consider. Some books are to be tasted, others to be swallowed, and some few to be chewed and digested: that is, some books are to be read only in parts; others to be read, but not curiously;[1] and some few to be read wholly, and with diligence and attention. Some books also may be read by deputy, and extracts made of them by others; but that would be only in the less important arguments, and the meaner sort of books; else distilled books are like common distilled waters, flashy [2] things. Reading maketh a full man; conference a ready man; and writing an exact man. And therefore, if a man write little, he had need have a great memory; if he confer little, he had need have a present wit; and if he read little, he had need have much cunning, to seem to know that he doth not. Histories make men wise; poets witty; the mathematics subtle; natural philosophy deep; moral grave; logic and rhetoric able to contend. *Abeunt studia in mores.*[3] Nay, there is no stond [4] or impediment in the wit, but may be wrought out by fit studies, like as diseases of the body may have appropriate exercises. Bowling is good for the stone and reins;[5] shooting for the lungs and breast; gentle walking for the stomach; riding for the head; and the like. So if a man's wit be wandering, let him study the mathematics; for in demonstrations, if his wit be called away never so little, he must begin again: if his wit be not apt to distinguish or find differences, let him study the schoolmen; for they are *cymini sectores:* [6] if he be not apt to beat over matters, and to call one thing to prove and illustrate another, let him study the lawyers' cases: so every defect of the mind may have a special receipt.

## 56.—OF JUDICATURE

JUDGES ought to remember that their office is *jus dicere*, and not *jus dare*; to interpret

---

[1] Not with great care.    [2] Insipid.
[3] Studies develop into manners (Ovid, *Heroides,* XV, 83).
[4] Hindrance.    [5] Kidneys.
[6] Splitters of cumin, i. e., hair-splitters.

[3] Reputation.    [4] Anxious to advance.
[5] Negotiation.    [6] Manage.

law, and not to make law, or give law. Else will it be like the authority claimed by the church of Rome; which, under pretext of exposition of Scripture, doth not stick [1] to add and alter, and to pronounce that which they do not find, and by show of antiquity to introduce novelty. Judges ought to be more learned than witty, more reverend than plausible, and more advised than confident. Above all things, integrity is their portion and proper virtue. "Cursed" (saith the law) "is he that removeth the land-mark." [2] The mislayer of a mere stone is to blame. But it is the unjust judge that is the capital remover of land-marks, when he defineth amiss of lands and property. One foul sentence doth more hurt than many foul examples. For these do but corrupt the stream; the other corrupteth the fountain. So saith Solomon: *Fons turbatus, et vena corrupta, est justus cadens in causa sua coram adversario*.[3] The office of judges may have reference unto the parties that sue; unto the advocates that plead; unto the clerks and ministers of justice underneath them; and to the sovereign or state above them.

First, for the causes or parties that sue. "There be" (saith the Scripture) "that turn judgment into wormwood";[4] and surely there be also that turn it into vinegar, for injustice maketh it bitter, and delays make it sour. The principal duty of a judge is to suppress force and fraud; whereof force is the more pernicious when it is open, and fraud when it is close and disguised. Add thereto contentious suits, which ought to be spewed out, as the surfeit of courts. A judge ought to prepare his way to a just sentence, as God useth to prepare his way, by raising valleys and taking down hills; so when there appeareth on either side an high hand, violent prosecution, cunning advantages taken, combination, power, great counsel, then is the virtue of a judge seen, to make inequality equal, that he may plant his judgment as upon an even ground. *Qui fortiter emungit, elicit sanguinem*,[5] and where the wine-press is hard wrought, it yields a harsh wine, that tastes of the grapestone. Judges must beware of hard constructions and strained inferences; for there is no worse torture than the torture of laws. Specially in case of laws penal, they ought to have care that that which was meant for terror be not turned into rigor; and that they bring not upon the people that shower whereof the Scripture speaketh, *Pluet super eos laqueos*:[6] for penal laws pressed are a *shower of snares* upon the people. Therefore let penal laws, if they have been sleepers of long, or if they be grown unfit for the present time, be by wise judges confined in the execution:

*Judicis officium est, ut res, ita tempora rerum, etc.*[7]

In causes of life and death, judges ought (as far as the law permitteth) in justice to remember mercy; and to cast a severe eye upon the example, but a merciful eye upon the person.

Secondly, for the advocates and counsel that plead. Patience and gravity of hearing is an essential part of justice; and an over-speaking judge is no well tuned cymbal. It is no grace to a judge first to find that which he might have heard in due time from the bar; or to show quickness of conceit in cutting off evidence or counsel too short; or to prevent information by questions, though pertinent. The parts of a judge in hearing are four: to direct the evidence; to moderate length, repetition, or impertinency of speech; to recapitulate, select, and collate the material points of that which hath been said; and to give the rule or sentence. Whatsoever is above these is too much; and proceedeth either of glory and willingness to speak or of impatience to hear, or of shortness of memory, or of want of a staid and equal attention. It is a strange thing to see that the boldness of advocates should prevail with judges; whereas they should imitate God, in whose seat they sit, who "represseth the presumptuous," and "giveth grace to the modest." [8] But it is more strange that judges should have noted favorites; which cannot but cause multiplication of fees, and suspicion of by-ways. There is due from the judge to the advocate some commendation and gracing, where causes are well handled and fair pleaded, especially towards the side which obtaineth not; for that upholds in the client the reputation of his counsel, and beats down in him the conceit [9] of his cause. There is likewise due to the public a civil reprehen-

---

[1] Hesitate.    [2] Deuteronomy, 27:17.
[3] As a troubled fountain and corrupted spring, so is the righteous man that must give way before his opponent (Proverbs, 25:26).
[4] Amos, 5:7.
[5] Hard pressure draws blood (Proverbs, 30:33).
[6] He will rain down snares upon them (Psalms, 11:6).
[7] The judge must consider the times as well as the circumstances of things (Ovid).
[8] St. James, 4:6.    [9] Opinion.

sion of advocates, where there appeareth cunning counsel, gross neglect, slight information, indiscreet pressing, or an overbold defense. And let not the counsel at the bar chop [10] with the judge, nor wind himself into the handling of the cause anew after the judge hath declared his sentence; but on the other side, let not the judge meet the cause half way, nor give occasion to the party to say his counsel or proofs were not heard.

Thirdly, for that that concerns clerks and ministers. The place of justice is an hallowed place; and therefore not only the bench, but the foot-pace [11] and precincts and purprise [12] thereof ought to be preserved without scandal and corruption. For certainly, "Grapes" (as the Scripture saith) "will not be gathered of thorns or thistles"; [13] neither can justice yield her fruit with sweetness amongst the briars and brambles of catching and polling [14] clerks and ministers. The attendance of courts is subject to four bad instruments. First, certain persons that are sowers of suits; which make the court swell, and the country pine. The second sort is of those that engage courts in quarrels of jurisdiction, and are not truly *amici curiae*, but *parasiti curiae*, [15] in puffing a court up beyond her bounds, for their own scraps and advantage. The third sort is of those that may be accounted the left hands of courts; persons that are full of nimble and sinister tricks and shifts, whereby they pervert the plain and direct courses of courts, and bring justice into oblique lines and labyrinths. And the fourth is the poller [16] and exacter of fees; which justifies the common resemblance of the courts of justice to the bush, whereunto while the sheep flies for defense in weather, he is sure to lose part of his fleece. On the other side, an ancient clerk, skillful in precedents, wary in proceeding, and understanding in the business of the court, is an excellent finger of a court, and doth many times point the way to the judge himself.

Fourthly, for that which may concern the sovereign and estate. Judges ought above all to remember the conclusion of the Roman Twelve Tables, *Salus populi suprema lex*; [17] and to know that laws, except they be in order to that end, are but things captious, and oracles not well inspired. Therefore it is an happy thing in a state when kings and states do often consult with judges; and again, when judges do often consult with the king and state: the one, when there is matter of law intervenient in business of state; the other, when there is some consideration of state intervenient in matter of law. For many times the things deduced to judgment may be *meum* and *tuum*, [18] when the reason and consequence thereof may trench to point of estate. [19] I call matter of estate not only the parts of sovereignty, but whatsoever introduceth any great alteration or dangerous precedent, or concerneth manifestly any great portion of people. And let no man weakly conceive that just laws and true policy have any antipathy; for they are like the spirits and sinews, that one moves with the other. Let judges also remember that Solomon's throne was supported by lions on both sides; let them be lions, but yet lions under the throne, being circumspect that they do not check or oppose any points of sovereignty. Let not judges also be so ignorant of their own right as to think there is not left to them, as a principal part of their office, a wise use and application of laws. For they may remember what the Apostle saith of a greater law than theirs: *Nos scimus quia lex bona est, modo quis ea utatur legitime.* [20]

## 57.—OF ANGER

To SEEK to extinguish anger utterly is but a bravery [1] of the Stoics. We have better oracles: "Be angry, but sin not. Let not the sun go down upon your anger." [2] Anger must be limited and confined, both in race and in time. We will first speak how the natural inclination and habit *to be angry* may be attempered and calmed. Secondly, how the particular motions of anger may be repressed, or at least refrained from doing mischief. Thirdly, how to raise anger, or appease anger, in another.

For the first: there is no other way but to meditate and ruminate well upon the effects of anger, how it troubles man's life. And the best time to do this is to look back upon anger when the fit is thoroughly over.

---

[10] Have words.
[11] Step on which the lawyer stands.
[12] Enclosure.     [13] St. Matthew, 7:16.
[14] Plundering.
[15] Friends of the court, but parasites of the court.
[16] Plunderer.
[17] The people's safety is the supreme law (Cicero, *Of Laws*, III, 3).

[18] Mine and thine.
[19] May extend to concern the state.
[20] We know that the law is good if a man use it lawfully (I Timothy, 1:8).
[1] Boast.     [2] Ephesians, 4:26.

Seneca saith well, "that anger is like ruin, which breaks itself upon that it falls." The Scripture exhorteth us "to possess our souls in patience." [3] Whosoever is out of patience, is out of possession of his soul. Men must not turn bees;

——*animasque in vulnere ponunt.*[4]

Anger is certainly a kind of baseness; as it appears well in the weakness of those sub- jects in whom it reigns, children, women, old folks, sick folks. Only men must beware that they carry their anger rather with scorn than with fear, so that they may seem rather to be above the injury than below it; which is a thing easily done, if a man will give law to himself in it.

For the second point: the causes and mo- tives of anger are chiefly three. First, to be too sensible of hurt; for no man is angry that feels not himself hurt, and therefore tender and delicate persons must needs be oft angry; they have so many things to trouble them which more robust natures have little sense of. The next is the apprehension and construc- tion of the injury offered to be, in the circum- stances thereof, full of contempt. For contempt is that which putteth an edge upon anger, as much or more than the hurt itself. And there- fore, when men are ingenious in picking out circumstances of contempt, they do kindle their anger much. Lastly, opinion of the touch [5] of a man's reputation, doth multiply and sharpen anger. Wherein the remedy is, that a man should have, as Consalvo was wont to say, *telam honoris crassiorem.*[6] But in all refrainings of anger, it is the best remedy to win time; and to make a man's self believe, that the opportunity of his revenge is not yet come, but that he foresees a time for it; and so to still himself in the mean time, and re- serve it.

To contain [7] anger from mischief, though it take hold of a man, there be two things whereof you must have special caution. The one, of extreme bitterness of words, especially if they be aculeate [8] and proper; for *communia maledicta* [9] are nothing so much; and again, that in anger a man reveal no secrets, for that makes him not fit for society. The other, that you do not peremptorily break off, in any business, in a fit of anger; but howsoever you show bitterness, do not act anything that is not revocable.

For raising and appeasing anger in an- other; it is done chiefly by choosing of times, when men are frowardest and worst disposed, to incense them. Again, by gathering (as was touched before) all that you can find out, to aggravate the contempt. And the two remedies are by the contraries. The former, to take good times, when first to relate to a man an angry business; for the first impression is much. And the other is to sever, as much as may be, the construction of the injury from the point of contempt, imputing it to misunderstanding, fear, passion, or what you will.

[3] St. Luke, 21:19.
[4] And spend their lives in stinging (Virgil, *Georgics*, IV, 238).
[5] Censure.

[6] A stout web of honor.   [7] Restrain.
[8] Stinging.   [9] General abuses.

# Lyric Poetry of the Sixteenth and Early Seventeenth Centuries

English lyric poetry of the sixteenth century is a new beginning, and has its sources not in older native literature, but in Italy. Late in the century Spenser went back to Chaucer, and to some extent in language, even more in the modulation and melody of his verse, continued and developed a national tradition, which he in turn handed on to Milton. The evidence for this is to be found, however, chiefly in Spenser's longer poems, The Shepherd's Calendar and The Faerie Queene, while much earlier in the century the course which the Elizabethan lyric was to take had been pretty clearly marked out by members of the Renaissance court of Henry VIII. The two chief poets of this earlier period were Sir Thomas Wyatt and Henry Howard, Earl of Surrey. And that a new thing had come into English poetry was made unmistakable when many of the poems written by Wyatt and Surrey, together with others by Grimald and by "uncertain authors," were gathered together and printed in Tottel's Miscellany (1557), the first of a series of collections of lyrics by various writers which appeared during the latter half of the sixteenth century. Full mastery of the new kind of poetry and complete freedom of expression hardly came before 1580; but their coming, when it did occur, was sudden, and for some fifteen or twenty years there was a veritable outburst of lyric song, gay, easy, rich, and musical, as remarkable for its spontaneity as for its frequent intensity, and perhaps even more remarkable for the great numbers who not only felt the lyrical impulse but were able to express it in a smooth and charming form. The more notable of the miscellanies into which many, though by no means all, of the lyrics of the period were collected were The Phoenix' Nest (1593), England's Helicon (1600), and the Davisons' Poetical Rhapsody (1602).

Of the various forms which the lyric took only one can be specifically mentioned here—the sonnet. Petrarch had not only written some of his greatest poetry in sonnet-form but had connected his sonnets in a sequence, so that in effect they told the story of his moods and feelings, above all of the course of his love, and of other things as they related themselves to that central theme. The sonnet-sequence made its way to England along with the rest, and became popular in the decade from 1590 to 1600. The most notable of the sequences were Sir Philip Sidney's Astrophel and Stella, Samuel Daniel's Delia, Michael Drayton's Idea, Spenser's Amoretti, and Shakespeare's Sonnets.

On the whole, the Elizabethan burst of song was as brief as it was splendid. Spontaneous expression quickly develops into more deliberate art, and so it was with the lyric in the closing years of the sixteenth century. Its exuberance became distasteful, its sweetness cloying, and Ben Jonson, lifting the same chastening voice of good sense in the lyric as in the drama, set the example of restraint, of greater attention to form, and of practice enlightened by study of the best models of classical Greek and Roman poetry. At the same time John Donne reacted harshly and powerfully from the sweetness and the conventional themes of the Petrarchians in their love-poetry. Probably literary historians have tended to make too much of the personal influence of Jonson and Donne. Perhaps they were not so much actually leaders of new movements in poetry as the earliest men to feel strongly, each in his own way, a pronounced change in the whole intellectual and emotional life of England which gathered force in the early years of the seventeenth century. One way of putting it is that a period of expansive, youthful feeling was succeeded by a period of doubt mixed with disillusionment. Certainly something like this took place, and the change made itself felt throughout literature, not merely within the little field of the lyric; yet it still remains useful within that field to remember that Jonson and Donne were the prophets of the new age. It should also be remembered, however, that some continued, as in every generation, to live in the past and to express the influences which for them were still potent, the most notable instance of this being the so-called school of *Spenserians who continued to echo their master until well into the troubled years of the middle of the seventeenth century.*

Tottel's Miscellany *has been thoroughly edited by Hyder E. Rollins (Cambridge, U. S. A., 1928); vol. II of this edition contains an abundance of scholarly material.* The Poems of Sir Thomas Wiat, *ed. A. K. Foxwell (London, 1913), and* The Poems of Henry Howard, Earl of Surrey, *ed. Frederick M. Padelford, revised edition (Seattle, 1928), may also be recommended.*

Norman Ault *has edited a useful anthology of* Elizabethan Lyrics *(London, 1949); Sir Sidney Lee's* Elizabethan Sonnets *(London, 1904) supplies the text of several sequences and an introduction which emphasizes the continental background for the poems written in this form. The most important Elizabethan miscellany,* England's Helicon, *has been edited by H. E. Rollins (Cambridge, U. S. A., 1935). Editions of individual Elizabethan poets, as well as studies devoted to them, are numerous. For Lyly's poetry see his* Complete Works, *ed. R. Warwick Bond (Oxford, 1902). The* Complete Works of Sir Philip Sidney, *ed. Albert Feuillerat (Cambridge, 1912–1926), and Mona Wilson's* Sir Philip Sidney *(New York, 1950) supply all that is needed to begin a study of that poet. Ralph M. Sargent's* At the Court of Queen Elizabeth; the Life and Lyrics of Sir Edward Dyer *(London, 1935) contains Dyer's poems and all that is known about him. The Poems of Sir Walter Ralegh are collected in Agnes M. C. Latham's editions (London, 1929–1951); Philip Edwards'* Sir Walter Raleigh *(London, 1953) and Hugh R. Williamson's* Sir Walter Raleigh *(London, 1951) are good studies. The* Life and Works of George Peele *is being edited by C. T. Prouty et al. (New Haven, 1952–    ). The most complete edition of* The Plays and Poems of Robert Greene *is the work of J. Churton Collins (Oxford, 1905). The* Works of Michael Drayton, *ed. J. William Hebel et al. (Oxford, 1931–1941), contains the complete text. The* Shakespeare Songs *have been edited by C. F. Tucker Brooke, with an introduction by Walter De La Mare (New York, 1929); the same editor has presented Shakespeare's* Sonnets, *arranged in a new order and accompanied by an acute introduction (New York, 1936); for informa-* tion on the life and background of Shakespeare *see Edmund K. Chambers,* William Shakespeare *(Oxford, 1930), and Marchette G. Chute's* Shakespeare of London *(New York, 1949).* Shakespeare's England; an Account of the Life & Manners of His Age *(Oxford, 1916) is an anthology of essays by experts, each dealing with a side of Elizabethan life which appears in Shakespeare's work. Thomas Campion's* Works *have been edited by Percival Vivian (Oxford, 1909). The monumental collected edition of Ben Jonson's complete works, ed. C. H. Herford, Percy Simpson, and Evelyn Simpson (Oxford, 1925–1952) also contains the best biography of Jonson.*

Metaphysical Lyrics & Poems of the Seventeenth Century, *ed. Sir Herbert J. C. Grierson (Oxford, 1921), is an excellent anthology with a valuable introduction. The definitive edition of* The Poems of John Donne *is edited by Sir Herbert J. C. Grierson (Oxford, 1912), but a more compact volume is the* Complete Poetry and Selected Prose, *ed. C. M. Coffin (New York, 1952);* A Garland for John Donne, 1631–1931, *ed. Theodore Spencer (Cambridge, U. S. A., 1931), contains essays of tribute by T. S. Eliot, Evelyn Simpson, Mario Praz, John Hayward, Mary P. Ramsay, John Sparrow, George Williamson, Theodore Spencer; George Williamson gives an artistic evaluation of seventeenth-century poetry in* The Donne Tradition; a Study in English Poetry from Donne to the Death of Cowley *(Cambridge, U. S. A., 1930), while Helen C. White's* Metaphysical Poets; a Study in Religious Experience *(New York, 1956) treats Donne, Herbert, Crashaw, Vaughan, and Traherne primarily as mystics. Three recent studies are D. Louthan,* The Poetry of Donne *(New York, 1951); K. W. Gransden,* John Donne *(London, 1954); and J. C. Hunt,* Donne's Poetry: Essays in Literary Analysis *(New Haven, 1954). The standard editions of the remaining poets in this section are as follows:* The Poetical Works of Robert Herrick, *ed. L. C. Martin (Oxford, 1956); The* Works of George Herbert, *ed. F. E. Hutchinson (Oxford, 1945);* The Poems of Edmund Waller, *ed. G. Thorn Drury (London, 1904); The* Works of Sir John Suckling in Prose and Verse, *ed. A. Hamilton Thompson (London, 1910);* The Poems of Richard Lovelace, *ed. C. H. Wilkinson (Oxford, 1930);* The Poems & Letters of Andrew Marvell, *ed. H. M. Margoliouth (Oxford, 1952); The* Works of Henry Vaughan, *ed. Leonard C. Martin (Oxford, 1958).*

# SIR THOMAS WYATT

### (1503–1542)

## The Lover for Shame-Fastness Hideth His Desire within His Faithful Heart

The long love that in my thought doth harbor,
And in my heart doth keep his residence,
Into my face presseth with bold pretense,
And therein campeth spreading his banner.
She that me learns to love and suffer,                    5
And wills that my trust and lust's negligence [1]
Be reined by reason, shame, and reverence,
With his hardiness takes displeasure.
Wherewithal [2] into the heart's forest he fleeth,
Leaving his enterprise with pain and cry,         10
And there him hideth, and not appeareth.
What may I do, when my master feareth?
But in the field with him to live and die?
For good is the life ending faithfully.

## The Wavering Lover Willeth, and Dreadeth, to Move His Desire

Such vain thought as wonted to mislead me
In desert hope, by well assuréd moan,
Makes me from company to live alone,
In following her whom reason bids me flee.
She flyeth as fast by gentle cruelty;              5
And after her my heart would fain be gone,
But arméd sighs my way do stop anon,
'Twixt hope and dread locking my liberty.
Yet as I guess, under disdainful brow
One beam of pity is in her cloudy look,           10
Which comforteth the mind, that erst for fear
    shook;
And therewithal bolded, I seek the way how
To utter the smart that I suffer within;
But such it is, I not [3] how to begin.

## The Lover Having Dreamed Enjoying of His Love, Complaineth That the Dream Is Not Either Longer or Truer

Unstable dream, according to the place,
Be steadfast once, or else at least be true.
By tasted sweetness make me not to rue
The sudden loss of thy false feignéd grace.
By good respect in such a dangerous case        5
Thou broughtst not her into this tossing mew,[4]
But madest my sprite [5] live, my care to renew.
My body in tempest her succor to embrace.
The body dead, the sprite had his desire;

Painless was th' one, the other in delight.     10
Why then, alas! did it not keep it right,
Returning to leap into the fire,
And where it was at wish, it could not remain?
Such mocks of dreams they turn to deadly pain!

## Description of the Contrarious Passions in a Lover

I find no peace, and all my war is done;
I fear and hope, I burn, and freeze like ice;
I fly above the wind, yet can I not arise;
And nought I have, and all the world I seize on,
That loseth nor locketh, holdeth me in prison,
And holdeth me not, yet can I scape no wise; [6]
Nor letteth me live, nor die, at my devise,[6]
And yet of death it giveth me occasion.
Without eye I see; and without tongue I
    plain.[7]
I desire to perish, and yet I ask health;       10
I love another, and thus I hate myself;
I feed me in sorrow, and laugh in all my pain.
Likewise displeaseth me both death and life,
And my delight is causer of this strife.

## The Lover Compareth His State to a Ship in Perilous Storm Tossed on the Sea

My galley chargéd with forgetfulness
Thorough sharp seas in winter nights doth pass,
'Tween rock and rock; and eke mine enemy,
    alas,
That is my lord, steerth with cruelness,
And every hour, a thought in readiness,         5
As though that death were light in such a case.
And endless wind doth tear the sail apace
Of forcéd sighs and trusty fearfulness.
A rain of tears, a cloud of dark disdain
Hath done the wearied cords great hinder-
    ance,                                        10
Wreathed with error, and eke with ignorance.
The stars be hid that led me to this pain;
Drownéd is reason that should me comfort,
And I remain despairing of the port.

## A Renouncing of Love

Farewell, Love, and all thy laws for ever!
Thy baited hooks shall tangle me no more:
Senec [8] and Plato call me from thy lore
To perfect wealth my wit for to endeavor.[9]
In blind error when I did perséver,             5
Thy sharp repulse, that pricketh aye so sore,
Hath taught me to set in trifles no store;
And 'scape forth, since liberty is lever [10]
Therefore, farewell! go trouble younger hearts,
And in me claim no more authority.              10

---

<sup></sup>
[1] Careless confidence.        [2] Whereupon.
[3] Know not.       [4] Cage.       [5] Spirit.

[6] Desire.        [7] Lament.        [8] Seneca.
[9] Exert.        [10] Preferable.

With idle youth go use thy property,
And thereon spend thy many brittle darts;
For hitherto though I have lost my time,
Me list no longer rotten boughs to climb.

## The Lover Sendeth Sighs to Moan His Suit

Go, burning sighs, unto the frozen heart
Go, break the ice which pity's painful dart
Might never pierce; and if mortal prayer
In heaven may be heard, at least I desire
That death or mercy be end of smart.     5
Take with thee pain, whereof I have my part,
And eke the flame from which I cannot start,
And leave me then in rest, I you require.
Go, burning sighs, fulfill that I desire,
I must go work, I see, by craft and art,     10
For truth and faith in her is laid apart:
Alas, I cannot therefore assail her
With pitiful complaint and scalding fire
That from my breast deceivably doth start.

## The Lover Complaineth the Unkindness of His Love

My lute, awake, perform the last
Labor that thou and I shall waste,
And end that I have now begun.
And when this song is sung and past,
My lute, be still, for I have done.     5

As to be heard where ear is none,
As lead to grave [11] in marble stone,
My song may pierce her heart as soon.
Should we then sigh, or sing, or moan?
No, no, my lute, for I have done.     10

The rocks do not so cruelly
Repulse the waves continually
As she my suit and affection;
So that I am past remedy,
Whereby my lute and I have done.     15

Proud of the spoil that thou hast got
Of simple hearts through Lovës shot,
By whom unkind thou hast them won,
Think not he hath his bow forgot,
Although my lute and I have done.     20

Vengeance shall fall on thy disdain
That makest but game on earnest pain.
Think not alone under the sun
Unquit to cause thy lovers plain,[12]
Although my lute and I have done.     25

Perchance thee lie withered and old,
The winter nights that are so cold,
Plaining in vain unto the moon;

Thy wishes then dare not be told.
Care then who list, for I have done.     30

And then may chance thee to repent
The time that thou hast lost and spent
To cause thy lovers sigh and swoon;
Then shalt thou know beauty but lent,
And wish and want, as I have done.     35

Now cease, my lute; this is the last
Labor that thou and I shall waste,
And ended is that we begun.
Now is the song both sung and past;
My lute, be still, for I have done.     40

## An Earnest Suit to His Unkind Mistress Not to Forsake Him

And wilt thou leave me thus?
Say nay, say nay, for shame!
To save thee from the blame
Of all my grief and grame.[13]
And wilt thou leave me thus?     5
Say nay! say nay!

And wilt thou leave me thus,
That hath loved thee so long
In wealth and woe among:
And is thy heart so strong     10
As for to leave me thus?
Say nay! say nay!

And wilt thou leave me thus,
That hath given thee my heart
Never for to depart,     15
Neither for pain nor smart:
And wilt thou leave me thus?
Say nay! say nay!

And wilt thou leave me thus,
And have no more pity     20
Of him that loveth thee?
Alas, thy cruelty!
And wilt thou leave me thus?
Say nay! say nay!

## The Lover Beseecheth His Mistress Not to Forget His Steadfast Faith and True Intent

Forget not yet the tried intent
Of such a truth as I have meant;
My great travail so gladly spent,
Forget not yet!

Forget not yet when first began     5
The weary life ye know, since when
The suit, the service none tell can;
Forget not yet!

[11] Engrave.     [12] To lament.     [13] Sorrow.

Forget not yet the great assays,
The cruel wrong, the scornful ways,     10
The painful patience in delays,
Forget not yet!

Forget not yet, forget not this,
How long ago hath been, and is,
The mind that never meant amiss—     15
Forget not yet!

Forget not then thine own approved,
The which so long hath thee so loved,
Whose steadfast faith yet never moved:
Forget not this!     20

## Of the Mean and Sure Estate [14]

### *Written to John Poins*

My mother's maids, when they did sew and
    spin,
They sung sometime a song of the field mouse
That, for because her livelod [15] was but thin,
Would needs go seek her townish sister's house.
She thought herself enduréd too much pain;   5
The stormy blasts her cave so sore did souse
That when the furrows swimméd with the rain,
She must lie cold and wet in sorry plight;
And worse than that, bare meat there did re-
    main
To comfort her when she her house had
    dight; [16]     10
Sometime a barley corn; sometime a bean,
For which she labored hard both day and night
In harvest time whilst she might go and glean;
And when her store was stroyéd [17] with the
    flood,
Then welaway! for she undone was clean.   15
Then was she fain to take, instead of food,
Sleep, if she might, her hunger to beguile.
    "My sister," quoth she, "hath a living good,
And hence from me she dwelleth not a mile;
In cold and storm she lieth warm and dry   20
In bed of down; the dirt doth not defile
Her tender foot; she laboreth not as I.
Richly she feedeth, and at the rich man's cost,
And for her meat she needs not crave nor cry.
By sea, by land, of delicates the most     25
Her cater [18] seeks and spareth for no peril,
She feedeth on boiled bacon, meat, and roast,
And hath thereof neither charge nor travail;
And, when she list, the liquor of the grape
Doth glad her heart till that her belly swell."  30
    And at this journey she maketh but a jape; [19]
So forth she goeth, trusting of all this wealth
With her sister her part so for to shape
That if she might keep herself in health,
To live a lady while her life doth last.     35

[14] This poem is based upon Horace, *Satires* II, 6.
It is not, of course, a lyric, but deserves inclusion
here to indicate the range of Wyatt's experiments.
   [15] Livelihood.     [16] Ordered.     [17] Destroyed.
   [18] Caterer.     [19] Jest.

And to the door now is she come by stealth,
And with her foot anon she scrapeth full fast.
Th' other, for fear, durst not well scarce appear,
Of every noise so was the wretch aghast.
At last she askéd softly who was there,     40
And in her language as well as she could.
"Peep!" quoth the other sister, "I am here."
"Peace," quoth the town mouse, "why speakest
    thou so loud?"
And by the hand she took her fair and well.
"Welcome," quoth she, "my sister, by the
    Rood!"     45
She feasted her, that joy it was to tell
The fare they had; they drank the wine so clear,
And, as to purpose now and then it fell,
She cheeréd her with "How, sister, what
    cheer!"
Amid this joy befell a sorry chance,     50
That, welaway! the stranger bought full dear
The fare she had, for, as she looked askance,
Under a stool she spied two steaming [20] eyes
In a round head with sharp ears. In France
Was never mouse so feared, for, though un-
    wise     55
Had not y-seen such a beast before,
Yet had nature taught her after her guise
To know her foe and dread him evermore.
The towny mouse fled, she knew whither to
    go;
Th'other had no shift, but wonders sore    60
Feared of her life. At home she wished her
    tho,[21]
And to the door, alas! as she did skip,
The heaven it would, lo! and eke her chance
    was so,
At the threshold her silly foot did trip;
And ere she might recover it again,     65
The traitor cat had caught her by the hip,
And made her there against her will remain,
That had forgot her poor surety and rest
For seeming wealth wherein she thought to
    reign.
Alas, my Poins, how men do seek the best   70
And find the worst by error as they stray!
And no marvel; when sight is so opprest,
And blinds the guide, anon out of the way
Goeth guide and all in seeking quiet life.
O wretched minds, there is no gold that may  75
Grant that you seek; no war, no peace, no strife.
No, no, although thy head were hooped with
    gold,
Sergeant with mace, halberd, sword, nor knife,
Cannot repulse the care that follow should.
Each kind of life hath with him his disease.  80
Live in delight even as thy lust would,
And thou shalt find, when lust doth most thee
    please,
It irketh straight, and by itself doth fade.
A small thing is it that may thy mind appease.
None of ye all there is that is so mad     85
To seek for grapes on brambles or on briars;

   [20] Gleaming.     [21] Then.

Nor none, I trow, that hath his wit so bad
To set his hay [22] for conies [23] over rivers,
Nor ye set not a drag-net for an hare;
And yet the thing that most is your desire   90
Ye do mis-seek with more travail and care.
Make plain thine heart, that it be not knotted
With hope or dread, and see thy will be bare
From all effects whom vice hath ever spotted.
Thyself content with that is thee assigned,   95
And use it well that is to thee allotted.
Then seek no more out [24] of thyself to find
The thing that thou hast sought so long before,
For thou shalt feel it sticking in thy mind.
Mad, if ye list to continue your sore,   100
Let present pass and gape on time to come,
And deep yourself in travail more and more.
  Henceforth, my Poins, this shall be all and
    some,
These wretched fools shall have naught else of
    me;
But to the great God and to his high dome,[25]
None other pain pray I for them to be,   106
But, when the rage doth lead them from the
    right,
That, looking backward, virtue they may see,
Even as she is so goodly fair and bright,
And whilst they clasp their lusts in arms across,
Grant them, good Lord, as thou mayst of thy
    might,   111
To fret inward for losing such a loss.

# HENRY HOWARD, EARL OF SURREY

## (1517?–1547)

## Description of Spring Wherein Each Thing Renews, Save Only the Lover

The soote [1] season that bud and bloom forth
    brings,
With green hath clad the hill and eke the vale;
The nightingale with feathers new she sings;
The turtle [2] to her make [3] hath told her tale:
Summer is come, for every spray now springs; 5
The hart hath hung his old head on the pale;
The buck in brake his winter coat he flings;
The fishes float with new repairéd scale;
The adder all her slough away she slings;
The swift swallow pursueth the flies smale;   10
The busy bee her honey now she mings.[4]
Winter is worn, that was the flowers' bale:
And thus I see among these pleasant things
Each care decays, and yet my sorrow springs!

[22] Snare.    [23] Rabbits.    [24] Outside.
[25] Judgment.
[1] Sweet.    [2] Turtle-dove.    [3] Mate.
[4] Mixes.

## Complaint of a Lover Rebuked

Love, that doth reign and live within my
    thought,
And build his seat within my captive breast,
Clad in the arms wherein with me he fought,
Oft in my face he doth his banner rest.
But she that taught me love and suffer pain, 5
My doubtful hope and eke my hot desire
With shamefast look to shadow and refrain,
Her smiling grace converteth straight to ire.
And coward Love then to the heart apace
Taketh his flight, where he doth lurk and plain
His purpose lost, and dare not show his face. 11
For my lord's guilt thus faultless bide I pain.
Yet from my lord shall not my foot remove;
Sweet is the death that taketh end by love.

## Vow to Love Faithfully Howsoever He Be Rewarded

Set me whereas the sun doth parch the green,
Or where his beams may not dissolve the ice;
In temperate heat, where he is felt and seen;
In presence prest of people, mad or wise;
Set me in high, or yet in low degree;   5
In longest night, or in the longest day;
In clearest sky, or where clouds thickest be;
In lusty youth, or when my hairs are gray:
Set me in heaven, in earth, or else in hell;
In hill, or dale, or in the foaming flood;   10
Thrall, or at large, alive whereso I dwell;
Sick or in health, in evil fame or good;
Hers will I be, and only with this thought
Content myself, although my chance be
    naught.

## Complaint of the Absence of Her Lover Being upon the Sea

O happy dames! that may embrace
The fruit of your delight;
Help to bewail the woeful case,
And eke the heavy plight,
Of me, that wonted to rejoice   5
The fortune of my pleasant choice:
Good ladies, help to fill my mourning voice.

In ship freight [5] with rememberance
Of thoughts and pleasures past,
He sails that hath in governance   10
My life, while it will last;
With scalding sighs, for lack of gale,
Furthering his hope, that is his sail,
Toward me, the sweet port of his avail.[6]

Alas, how oft in dreams I see   15
Those eyes that were my food;
Which sometime so delighted me,

[5] Freighted.    [6] Advantage.

That yet they do me good;
Wherewith I wake with his return,
Whose absent flame did make me burn:    20
But when I find the lack, Lord, how I mourn!

When other lovers in arms across
Rejoice their chief delight,
Drownéd in tears to mourn my loss,
I stand the bitter night    25
In my window, where I may see
Before the winds how the clouds flee:
Lo, what a mariner love hath made me!

And in green waves when the salt flood
Doth rise by rage of wind,    30
A thousand fancies in that mood
Assail my restless mind.
Alas, now drencheth [7] my sweet foe,
That with the spoil of my heart did go,
And left me; but, alas, why did he so?    35

And when the seas wax calm again
To chase from me annoy,
My doubtful hope doth cause me pain;
So dread cuts off my joy.
Thus is my wealth mingled with woe,    40
And of each thought a doubt doth grow;
Now he comes! Will he come? Alas, no, no!

## A Praise of His Love Wherein He Reproveth Them That Compare Their Ladies with His

Give place, ye lovers, here before
That spent your boasts and brags in vain;
My lady's beauty passeth more
The best of yours, I dare well sayn,[8]
Than doth the sun the candle light,    5
Or brightest day the darkest night.

And thereto hath a troth [9] as just
As had Penelope the fair;
For what she saith, ye may it trust
As it by writing sealéd were:    10
And virtues hath she many mo [10]
Than I with pen have skill to show.

I could rehearse, if that I would,
The whole effect of Nature's plaint,
When she had lost the perfect mold,    15
The like to whom she could not paint:
With wringing hands, how she did cry,
And what she said, I know it, I.

I know she swore with raging mind,
Her kingdom only set apart,    20
There was no loss by law of kind [11]
That could have gone so near her heart.
And this was chiefly all her pain:
She could not make the like again.

Sith [12] Nature thus gave her the praise,    25
To be the chiefest work she wrought;
In faith, methink, some better ways
On your behalf might well be sought
Than to compare, as ye have done,
To match the candle with the sun.    30

## The Means to Attain Happy Life [13]

Martial, the things that do attain
The happy life be these, I find:
The riches left, not got with pain;
The fruitful ground; the quiet mind;
The equal friend; no grudge, no strife;    5
No charge of rule, no governance;
Without disease, the healthful life;
The household of continuance;
The mean [14] diet, no delicate fare;
True wisdom joined with simpleness;    10
The night dischargéd of all care,
Where wine the wit may not oppress;
The faithful wife, without debate;
Such sleeps as may beguile the night:
Contented with thine own estate,    15
Ne wish for death, ne fear his might.

## Of the Death of Sir T[homas] W[yatt]

W. resteth here, that quick [15] could never rest;
Whose heavenly gifts, encreaséd by disdain,
And virtue sank the deeper in his breast;
Such profit he by envy could obtain.
A head where wisdom mysteries did frame;    5
Whose hammers beat still in that lively brain
As on a stithe [16] where that some work of fame
Was daily wrought to turn to Britain's gain.
A visage stern and mild, where both did grow,
Vice to condemn, in virtue to rejoice;    10
Amid great storms, whom grace assuréd so
To live upright and smile at fortune's choice.
A hand that taught what might be said in rime;
That reft [17] Chaucer the glory of his wit:
A mark, the which (unparfited,[18] for time)    15
Some may approach, but never none shall hit.
A tongue that served in foreign realms his king;
Whose courteous talk to virtue did enflame
Each noble heart; a worthy guide to bring
Our English youth by travail unto fame.    20
An eye whose judgment none affect [19] could
    blind,
Friends to allure, and foes to reconcile;
Whose piercing look did represent a mind
With virtue fraught, reposéd, void of guile.
A heart where dread was never so imprest    25

---

[7] Drowneth.    [8] Say.    [9] Faithfulness.
[10] More.    [11] Nature.

[12] Since.
[13] Translated from Martial's *Epigrams*, x, 47. The Latin poet is addressing a friend also named Martial.
[14] Moderate.    [15] Alive.    [16] Anvil.
[17] Took from.    [18] Unperfected.
[19] No affections.

To hide the thought that might the truth ad-
    vance;
In neither fortune lost, nor yet represt,
To swell in wealth, or yield unto mischance.
A valiant corse,[20] where force and beauty met;
Happy, alas, too happy, but for foes!    30
Lived, and ran the race that Nature set:
Of manhood's shape, where she the mold did
    lose.
But to the heavens that simple [21] soul is fled,
Which left with such as covet Christ to know
Witness of faith that never shall be dead,    35
Sent for our health, but not receivéd so.
Thus for our guilt, this jewel have we lost;
The earth his bones, the heavens possess his
    ghost!

# ANONYMOUS

## A Student at His Book [1]

A student at his book, so placed
That wealth he might have won,
From book to wife did fleet in haste,
From wealth to woe did run.
Now, who hath played a feater cast,[2]    5
Since juggling first begun?
In knitting of himself so fast,
Himself he hath undone.

## Back and Side Go Bare [3]

### Chorus

Back and side go bare, go bare;
    Both foot and hand go cold;
But, belly, God send thee good ale enough,
    Whether it be new or old.

I cannot eat but little meat,    5
    My stomach is not good;
But sure I think that I can drink
    With him that wears a hood.
Though I go bare, take ye no care,
    I am nothing a-cold;    10
I stuff my skin so full within
    Of jolly good ale and old.

I love no roast but a nutbrown toast,
    And a crab [4] laid in the fire;
A little bread shall do me stead,[5]    15
    Much bread I not desire.
No frost nor snow, no wind, I trow,
    Can hurt me if I would,

I am so wrapped and thoroughly lapped
    Of jolly good ale and old.    20

And Tib, my wife, that as her life
    Loveth well good ale to seek,
Full oft drinks she, till ye may see
    The tears run down her cheek.
Then doth she trowl [6] to me the bowl,    25
    Even as a maltworm should,
And saith, "Sweetheart, I have take my part
    Of this jolly good ale and old."

Now let them drink till they nod and wink,
    Even as good fellows should do;    30
They shall not miss to have the bliss
    Good ale doth bring men to.
And all poor souls that have scoured bowls,
    Or have them lustily trowled,
God save the lives of them and their wives, 35
    Whether they be young or old.

# JOHN LYLY

## (1553–1606)

### Apelles' Song [1]

Cupid and my Campaspe played
At cards for kisses; Cupid paid.
He stakes his quiver, bow, and arrows,
His mother's doves and team of sparrows;
Loses them too; then down he throws    5
The coral of his lip, the rose
Growing on's cheek (but none knows how);
With these, the crystal of his brow,
And then the dimple of his chin;
All these did my Campaspe win.    10
At last he set [2] her both his eyes;
She won, and Cupid blind did rise.
    O Love, has she done this to thee?
    What shall, alas! become of me?

## Spring's Welcome

What bird so sings, yet so does wail?
O 'tis the ravished nightingale.
"Jug, jug, jug, jug, tereu," she cries,
And still her woes at midnight rise.
Brave prick-song! who is 't now we hear?    5
None but the lark so shrill and clear;
Now at heaven's gates she claps her wings,
The morn not waking till she sings.
Hark, hark, with what a pretty throat
Poor robin redbreast tunes his note!    10
Hark how the jolly cuckoos sing,
"Cuckoo," to welcome in the spring!
"Cuckoo," to welcome in the spring!

---

[20] Body.    [21] I. e., incorruptible.
[1] One of the poems by "uncertain authors" in
Tottel's *Miscellany* (1557).
[2] A neater trick.
[3] From *Gammer Gurton's Needle* (written *c.*
1562).
[4] Apple.    [5] Be sufficient.

[6] Pass.
[1] This and the following song are both from *Campaspe* (1584). It is possible that the songs in Lyly's
plays are by another hand.
[2] Wagered.

# SIR PHILIP SIDNEY

## (1554–1586)

## Astrophel and Stella

### 1

Loving in truth, and fain in verse my love to
  show,
That she, dear she, might take some pleasure
  of my pain,—
Pleasure might cause her read, reading might
  make her know,
Knowledge might pity win, and pity grace
  obtain,—
I sought fit words to paint the blackest face of
  woe,                5
Studying inventions fine, her wits to entertain,
Oft turning others' leaves, to see if thence
  would flow
Some fresh and fruitful showers upon my sun-
  burnt brain.
But words came halting forth, wanting In-
  vention's stay;
Invention, Nature's child, fled step-dame
  Study's blows;           10
And others' feet still seemed but strangers' in
  my way.
Thus, great with child to speak, and helpless
  in my throes,
Biting my truant pen, beating myself for spite;
"Fool," said my Muse to me, "look in thy
  heart, and write."

### 15

You that do search for every purling spring
Which from the ribs of old Parnassus [1] flows,
And every flower, not sweet perhaps, which
  grows
Near thereabouts, into your poesy wring;
You that do dictionary's method bring     5
Into your rimes, running in rattling rows;
You that poor Petrarch's long deceaséd woes
With new-born sighs and denizened [2] wit do
  sing;
You take wrong ways; those far-fet [3] helps be
  such
As do bewray a want of inward touch, [4]    10
And sure, at length stolen goods do come to
  light:
But if, both for your love and skill, your name
You seek to nurse at fullest breasts of Fame,
Stella behold, and then begin to indite.

### 31

With how sad steps, O Moon, thou climb'st
  the skies!
How silently, and with how wan a face!

---

1 Abode of Apollo and the Muses.
2 Adopted, i. e., borrowed.     3 Far-fetched.
4 Emotion.

---

What, may it be that even in heavenly place
That busy archer his sharp arrows tries!
Sure, if that long-with-love-acquainted eyes [5]
Can judge of love, thou feel'st a lover's case;
I read it in thy looks; thy languished grace,
To me, that feel the like, thy state descries,
Then, even of fellowship, O Moon, tell me,
Is constant love deemed there but want of
  wit?          10
Are beauties there as proud as here they be?
Do they above love to be loved, and yet
Those lovers scorn whom that love doth pos-
  sess?
Do they call virtue there ungratefulness? [5]

### 39

Come, Sleep! O Sleep, the certain knot of
  peace,
The baiting-place of wit, the balm of woe,
The poor man's wealth, the prisoner's release,
Th' indifferent judge between the high and
  low;
With shield of proof shield me from out the
  press         5
Of those fierce darts Despair at me doth throw:
O make in me those civil wars to cease;
I will good tribute pay, if thou do so.
Take thou of me smooth pillows, sweetest bed,
A chamber deaf of noise and blind of light, [10]
A rosy garland and a weary head:
And if these things, as being thine by right,
Move not thy heavy grace, thou shalt in me,
Livelier than elsewhere, Stella's image see.

### 41

Having this day my horse, my hand, my lance
Guided so well that I obtained the prize,
Both by the judgment of the English eyes
And of some sent from that sweet enemy,
  France;
Horsemen my skill in horsemanship advance, [6]
Town folks my strength; a daintier judge ap-
  plies [6]
His praise to sleight which from good use doth
  rise;
Some lucky wits impute it but to chance;
Others, because of both sides I do take
My blood from them who did excel in this, [10]
Think Nature me a man-at-arms did make.
How far they shot awry! the true cause is,
Stella looked on, and from her heavenly face
Sent forth the beams which made so fair my
  race.

### 64

No more! My Dear, no more these counsels
  try!
O give my passions leave to run their race!
Let Fortune lay on me her worst disgrace!
Let folk o'ercharged with brain against me cry!
Let clouds bedim my face, break in mine eye!

---

5 Call ungratefulness a virtue.     6 Praise.

Let me no steps but of lost labor trace!    6
Let all the earth in scorn recount my case;
But do not will me from my love to fly!
I do not envy Aristotle's wit;
Nor do aspire to Caesar's bleeding fame;    10
Nor ought do care, though some above me sit;
Nor hope, nor wish another course to frame;
But that which once may win thy cruel heart.
Thou art my wit, and thou my virtue art.

### 95

Leave me, O Love, which reachest but to dust,
And thou, my mind, aspire to higher things!
Grow rich in that which never taketh rust:
Whatever fades, but fading pleasure brings.
Draw in thy beams, and humble all thy might    5
To that sweet yoke where lasting freedoms be;
Which breaks the clouds and open forth the
    light
That doth both shine and give us sight to see.
O take fast hold! let that light be thy guide
In this small course which birth draws out to
    death,    10
And think how evil becometh him to slide
Who seeketh Heaven, and comes of heavenly
    breath.
Then farewell, world! thy uttermost I see:
Eternal Love, maintain thy life in me!

### ELEVENTH SONG

"Who is it that this dark night
Underneath my window plaineth?"
It is one who from thy sight
Being, ah! exiled, disdaineth
Every other vulgar light.    5

"Why, alas! and are you he?
Be not yet those fancies changed?"
Dear, when you find change in me,
Though from me you be estranged,
Let my change to ruin be.    10

"Well, in absence this will die;
Leave to see, and leave to wonder."
Absence sure will help, if I
Can learn how myself to sunder
From what in my heart doth lie.    15

"But time will these thoughts remove;
Time doth work what no man knoweth."
Time doth as the subject prove;
With time still the affection groweth
In the faithful turtle-dove.    20

"What if we new beauties see?
Will not they stir new affection?"
I will think they pictures be,
(Image-like, of saint's perfection)
Poorly counterfeiting thee.    25

"But your reason's purest light
Bids you leave such minds to nourish."

Dear, do reason no such spite;
Never doth thy beauty flourish
More than in my reason's sight.    30

"But the wrongs Love bears will make
Love at length leave undertaking."
No, the more fools it do shake,
In the ground of so firm making,
Deeper still they drive the stake.    35

"Peace, I think that some give ear!
Come no more, lest I get anger!"
Bliss, I will my bliss forbear;
Fearing, sweet, you to endanger;
But my soul shall harbor there.    40

"Well, be gone! be gone, I say,
Lest that Argus' eyes [7] perceive you!"
O unjust is Fortune's sway,
Which can make me thus to leave you;
And from louts to run away.    45

## My True-Love Hath My Heart

My true-love hath my heart and I have his,
By just exchange one for the other given:
I hold his dear, and mine he cannot miss;
There never was a better bargain driven:
    My true-love hath my heart, and I have his.    5

His heart in me keeps him and me in one.
My heart in him his thoughts and senses guides:
He loves my heart, for once it was his own;
I cherish his because in me it bides:    9
    My true-love hath my heart, and I have his.

## My Sheep Are Thoughts [8]

My sheep are thoughts, which I both guide
    and serve;
Their pasture is fair hills of fruitless love;
On barren sweets they feed, and feeding sterve. [9]
I wail their lot, but will not other prove;
My sheep-hook is wan hope, which all up-
    holds;    5
My weeds, [10] desire, cut out in endless folds;
What wool my sheep shall bear, whilst thus
    they live,
In you it is, you must the judgment give.

## SIR  EDWARD  DYER

### (1550?–1607)

## My Mind to Me a Kingdom Is

My mind to me a kingdom is;
    Such present joys therein I find
That it excels all other bliss

---

[7] Argus had one hundred eyes.
[8] From Sidney's *Arcadia*.        [9] Starve.
[10] Clothes.

That earth affords or grows by kind: [1] 4
Though much I want which most would have,
Yet still my mind forbids to crave.

No princely pomp, no wealthy store,
 No force to win the victory,
No wily wit to salve a sore,
 No shape to feed a loving eye, 10
To none of these I yield as thrall:
For why? My mind doth serve for all.

I see how plenty surfeits oft,
 And hasty climbers soon do fall;
I see that those which are aloft 15
 Mishap doth threaten most of all;
They get with toil, they keep with fear:
Such cares my mind could never bear.

Content to live, this is my stay;
 I seek no more than may suffice; 20
I press to bear no haughty sway;
 Look, what I lack my mind supplies:
Lo, thus I triumph like a king,
Content with that my mind doth bring.

Some have too much, yet still do crave; 25
 I little have, and seek no more.
They are but poor, though much they have,
 And I am rich with little store:
They poor, I rich; they beg, I give;
They lack, I leave; they pine, I live. 30

I laugh not at another's loss;
 I grudge not at another's pain;
No worldly waves my mind can toss;
 My state at one doth still remain:
I fear no foe, I fawn no friend; 35
I loathe not life, nor dread my end.

Some weigh their pleasure by their lust,
 Their wisdom by their rage of will;
Their treasure is their only trust;
 A cloakèd craft their store of skill: 40
But all the pleasure that I find
Is to maintain a quiet mind.

My wealth is health and perfect ease;
 My conscience clear my chief defense;
I neither seek by bribes to please, 45
 Nor by deceit to breed offense:
Thus do I live; thus will I die;
Would all did so as well as I!

# SIR WALTER RALEGH

## (1552?–1618)

## His Pilgrimage

Give me my scallop-shell [1] of quiet,
 My staff of faith to walk upon,

[1] Nature.
[1] One of the badges of a pilgrim.

My scrip [2] of joy, immortal diet,
 My bottle of salvation,
My gown of glory, hope's true gage,[3] 5
And thus I'll take my pilgrimage.

Blood must be my body's balmer;
 No other balm will there be given;
Whilst my soul, like a quiet palmer,
 Traveleth towards the land of heaven, 10
Over the silver mountains,
Where spring the nectar fountains.
  There will I kiss
  The bowl of bliss,
And drink mine everlasting fill 15
Upon every milken hill.
My soul will be a-dry before;
But, after, it will thirst no more.

Then by that happy blissful day
 More peaceful pilgrims I shall see, 20
That have cast off their rags of clay,
 And walk appareled fresh like me.
  I'll take them first,
  To quench their thirst
And taste of nectar suckets,[4] 25
  At those clear wells
  Where sweetness dwells,
Drawn up by saints in crystal buckets.

And when our bottles and all we
 Are filled with immortality, 30
Then the blessèd paths we'll travel,
Strowed with rubies thick as gravel;
Ceilings of diamonds, sapphire floors,
High walls of coral, and pearly bowers.

 From thence to heaven's bribeless hall, 35
Where no corrupted voices brawl;
No conscience molten into gold;
No forged accuser bought or sold;
No cause deferred, no vain-spent journey;
For there Christ is the king's attorney, 40
Who pleads for all, without degrees,
And he hath angels [5] but no fees.

And when the grand twelve million jury
Of our sins, with direful fury,
Against our souls black verdicts give, 45
Christ pleads his death; and then we live.
 Be Thou my speaker, taintless pleader!
Unblotted lawyer! true proceeder!
Thou giv'st salvation, even for alms,
Not with a bribèd lawyer's palms. 50

 And this is mine eternal plea
To him that made heaven and earth and sea:
That, since my flesh must die so soon,
And want a head to dine next noon,
Just at the stroke, when my veins start and
 spread, 55
Set on my soul an everlasting head!

[2] Wallet.  [3] Pledge.  [4] Sweetmeats.
[5] Used with double meaning; it was also the name
of a coin.

Then am I ready, like a palmer fit,
To tread those blest paths, which before I writ.

# GEORGE PEELE

## (1558?–1597?)

## Cupid's Curse [1]

OENONE. Fair and fair, and twice so fair,
    As fair as any may be;
    The fairest shepherd on our green,
    A love for any lady.
PARIS.  Fair and fair, and twice so fair,    5
    As fair as any may be;
    Thy love is fair for thee alone,
    And for no other lady.
OEN.  My love is fair, my love is gay,
    As fresh as been the flowers in
      May,    10
    And of my love my roundelay,
    My merry, merry roundelay,
    Concludes with Cupid's curse,—
    "They that do change old love for
      new,
    Pray gods they change for worse!" 15
AMBO SIMUL.[2] They that do change, *etc.*
OEN.  Fair and fair, *etc.*
PAR.  Fair and fair, *etc.*
    Thy love is fair, *etc.*    19
OEN.  My love can pipe, my love can sing,
    My love can many a pretty thing,
    And of his lovely praises ring
    My merry, merry roundelays,
    Amen to Cupid's curse,—
    "They that do change," *etc.*    25
PAR.  They that do change, *etc.*
AMBO.  Fair and fair, *etc.*

## Harvestmen A-Singing [3]

All ye that lovely lovers be,
Pray you for me:
Lo, here we come a-sowing, a-sowing,
And sow sweet fruits of love;
In your sweet hearts well may it prove!    5
Lo, here we come a-reaping, a-reaping,
To reap our harvest-fruit!
And thus we pass the year so long,
And never be we mute.

# ROBERT GREENE

## (1560?–1592)

## Sweet Are the Thoughts That Savor of Content [1]

Sweet are the thoughts that savor of content:
  The quiet mind is richer than a crown;

[1] From the *Arraignment of Paris* (1584).
[2] Both together.
[3] From *The Old Wives' Tale* (c. 1590).
[1] From *The Farewell to Folly* (1591).

Sweet are the nights in careless slumber spent;
  The poor estate scorns fortune's angry frown:
Such sweet content, such minds, such sleep,
  such bliss,    5
Beggars enjoy, when princes oft do miss.

The homely house that harbors quiet rest;
  The cottage that affords no pride nor care;
The mean that 'grees with country music best;
  The sweet consort of mirth and music's fare;
Obscuréd life sets down a type of bliss:    11
A mind content both crown and kingdom is.

## Weep Not, My Wanton [2]

Weep not, my wanton; smile upon my knee;
When thou art old there's grief enough for
  thee.
    Mother's wag, pretty boy,
    Father's sorrow, father's joy;
    When thy father first did see    5
    Such a boy by him and me,
    He was glad, I was woe;
    Fortune changéd made him so;
    When he left his pretty boy
    Last his sorrow, first his joy.    10

Weep not, my wanton; smile upon my knee;
When thou art old there's grief enough for
  thee.
    Streaming tears that never stint,
    Like pearl-drops from a flint,
    Fell by course from his eyes,    15
    That one another's place supplies;
    Thus he grieved in every part,
    Tears of blood fell from his heart,
    When he left his pretty boy,
    Father's sorrow, father's joy.    20

Weep not, my wanton; smile upon my knee;
When thou art old there's grief enough for
  thee.
    The wanton smiled, father wept;
    Mother cried, baby leapt;
    More he crowed, more we cried;    25
    Nature could not sorrow hide:
    He must go, he must kiss
    Child and mother, baby bless,
    For he left his pretty boy,
    Father's sorrow, father's joy.    30
Weep not, my wanton; smile upon my knee;
When thou art old there's grief enough for
  thee.

# MICHAEL DRAYTON

## (1563–1631)

## To His Coy Love

I pray thee, leave, love me no more;
  Call home the heart you gave me!

[2] From *Menaphon* (1589). A wanton is a spoiled child.

I but in vain that saint adore
  That can but will not save me.
These poor half-kisses kill me quite—  5
  Was ever man thus servéd?
Amidst an ocean of delight
  For pleasure to be stervéd? [1]

Show me no more those snowy breasts
  With azure riverets branchéd,  10
Where, whilst mine eye with plenty feasts,
  Yet is my thirst not stanchéd;
O Tantalus, thy pains ne'er tell!
  By me thou art prevented: [2]
'Tis nothing to be plagued in hell,  15
  But thus in heaven tormented!

Clip [3] me no more in those dear arms,
  Nor thy life's comfort call me,
O these are but too powerful charms,
  And do but more enthral me!  20
But see how patient I am grown
  In all this coil [4] about thee:
Come, nice thing, let my heart alone,
  I cannot live without thee!

## Idea

### To the Reader of These Sonnets

Into these loves who but for passion looks,
At this first sight, here let him lay them by,
And seek elsewhere in turning other books
Which better may his labor satisfy.
No far-fetched sigh shall ever wound my breast;
Love from mine eye a tear shall never wring; [6]
Nor in "Ah me's!" my whining sonnets drest!
A libertine! fantasticly I sing!
My verse is the true image of my mind,
Ever in motion, still desiring change;  10
And as thus, to variety inclined,
So in all humors sportively I range!
My Muse is rightly of the English strain,
That cannot long one fashion entertain.

### 61

Since there's no help, come, let us kiss and part!
Nay, I have done; you get no more of me!
And I am glad, yea, glad with all my heart
That thus so cleanly I myself can free.
Shake hands for ever! Cancel all our vows!  5
And when we meet at any time again,
Be it not seen in either of our brows
That we one jot of former love retain!
Now at the last gasp of Love's latest breath,
When, his pulse failing, Passion speechless lies;
When Faith is kneeling by his bed of death,  11
And Innocence is closing up his eyes—
Now, if thou wouldst, when all have given him
  over,
From death to life thou might'st him yet re-
  cover!

[1] Starved.  [2] Anticipated.
[3] Embrace.  [4] Disturbance.

## Ode XI

### To the Virginian Voyage

You brave heroic minds,
Worthy your country's name,
  That honor still pursue;
  Go and subdue!
Whilst loitering hinds [5]  5
Lurk here at home with shame.

Britons, you stay too long;
Quickly aboard bestow you!
  And with a merry gale
  Swell your stretched sail,  10
With vows as strong
As the winds that blow you!

Your course securely steer,
West-and-by-south forth keep!
  Rocks, lee-shores, nor shoals,  15
  When Eolus [6] scowls,
You need not fear,
So absolute the deep.

And cheerfully at sea,
Success you still entice  20
  To get the pearl and gold;
  And ours to hold,
Virginia,
Earth's only Paradise;

Where Nature hath in store  25
Fowl, venison, and fish;
  And the fruitful'st soil,—
  Without your toil,
Three harvests more,
All greater than your wish.  30

And the ambitious vine
Crowns with his purple mass
  The cedar reaching high
  To kiss the sky,
The cypress, pine,  35
And useful sassafras.

To whom the Golden Age [7]
Still Nature's laws doth give:
  Nor other cares attend,
  But them to defend  40
From winter's rage,
That long there doth not live.

When as the luscious smell
Of that delicious land,
  Above the seas that flows,  45
  The clear wind throws,
Your hearts to swell,
Approaching the dear strand.

[5] Peasants.  [6] God of winds.
[7] A fabled period of peace and plenty.

In kenning [8] of the shore
(Thanks to God first given!)    50
  O you, the happiest men,
  Be frolic then!
Let cannons roar,
Frightening the wide heaven!

And in regions far    55
Such heroes bring ye forth
  As those from whom we came!
  And plant our name
Under that star
Not known unto our North!    60

And as there plenty grows
The laurel everywhere,
  Apollo's sacred tree,
  You may it see
A poet's brows    65
To crown, that may sing there.

Thy Voyages attend,
Industrious Hakluyt! [9]
  Whose reading shall inflame
  Men to seek fame,    70
And much commend
To after times thy wit.

# Ode XII

## To the Cambro-Britons and Their Harp His Ballad of Agincourt

Fair stood the wind for France,
When we our sails advance;
Nor now to prove our chance
  Longer will tarry;
But putting to the main,    5
At Caux, the mouth of Seine,
With all his martial train
  Landed King Harry.[10]

And taking many a fort,
Furnished in warlike sort,    10
Marcheth towards Agincourt [11]
  In happy hour;
Skirmishing day by day,
With those that stopped his way,
Where the French general lay    15
  With all his power.

Which, in his height of pride,
King Henry to deride,
His ransom to provide
  To the King sending;    20
Which he neglects the while,

[8] Recognition.

[9] Richard Hakluyt (1553–1616), compiler of a famous collection of narratives of Elizabethan voyages, first published in 1589.

[10] Henry V.

[11] The battle of Agincourt was fought on 25 October, 1415.

As from a nation vile,
Yet, with an angry smile,
  Their fall portending.

And turning to his men,    25
Quoth our brave Henry then:
"Though they to one be ten
  Be not amazéd!
Yet have we well begun:
Battles so bravely won    30
Have ever to the sun
  By Fame been raiséd!

"And for myself," quoth he,
"This my full rest shall be:
England ne'er mourn for me,    35
  Nor more esteem me!
Victor I will remain
Or on this earth lie slain;
Never shall she sustain
  Loss to redeem me!    40

"Poitiers and Crécy [12] tell,
When most their pride did swell,
Under our swords they fell.
  No less our skill is
Than when our grandsire great,    45
Claiming the regal seat,
By many a warlike feat
  Lopped the French lilies."

The Duke of York so dread
The eager vanward led;    50
With the main, Henry sped
  Amongst his henchmen;
Exeter had the rear,
A braver man not there!
O Lord, how hot they were    55
  On the false Frenchmen!

They now to fight are gone;
Armor on armor shone;
Drum now to drum did groan:
  To hear was wonder;    60
That, with the cries they make,
The very earth did shake;
Trumpet to trumpet spake;
  Thunder to thunder.

Well it thine age became,    65
O noble Erpingham,
Which didst the signal aim
  To our hid forces!
When, from a meadow by,
Like a storm suddenly,    70
The English archery
  Struck the French horses

With Spanish yew so strong;
Arrows a cloth-yard long,

[12] Victories of the English in France during the Hundred Years' War. The battle of Crécy took place on 26 August, 1346; that of Poitiers on 19 September, 1356.

That like to serpents stung,                                    75
  Piercing the weather.
None from his fellow starts;
But, playing manly parts,
And like true English hearts,
  Stuck close together.                                  80

When down their bows they threw,
And forth their bilboes [13] drew,
And on the French they flew:
  Not one was tardy.
Arms were from shoulders sent,                                  85
Scalps to the teeth were rent,
Down the French peasants went:
  Our men were hardy.

This while our noble King,
His broad sword brandishing,                                    90
Down the French host did ding,[14]
  As to o'erwhelm it.
And many a deep wound lent;
His arms with blood besprent,
And many a cruel dent                                           95
  Bruiséd his helmet.

Gloucester, that duke so good,
Next of the royal blood,
For famous England stood
  With his brave brother.                                 100
Clarence, in steel so bright,
Though but a maiden knight,
Yet in that furious fight
  Scarce such another!

Warwick in blood did wade;                                      105
Oxford, the foe invade,
And cruel slaughter made,
  Still as they ran up.
Suffolk his ax did ply;
Beaumont and Willoughby                                         110
Bare them right doughtily;
  Ferrers and Fanhope.

Upon Saint Crispin's Day
Fought was this noble fray,
Which Fame did not delay                                        115
  To England to carry.
O, when shall English men
With such acts fill a pen?
Or England breed again
  Such a King Harry?                                       120

# WILLIAM SHAKESPEARE

## (1564–1616)

### Sonnets

15

When I consider everything that grows
Holds in perfection but a little moment,

That this huge stage presenteth nought but
  shows
Whereon the stars in secret influence com-
  ment;
When I perceive that men as plants increase, 5
Cheeréd and checked e'en by the self-same sky,
Vaunt in their youthful sap, at height decrease,
And wear their brave state out of memory:
Then the conceit [1] of this inconstant stay
Sets you most rich in youth before my sight,   10
Where wasteful Time debateth [2] with decay,
To change your day of youth to sullied night;
  And all in war with Time for love of you,
  As he takes from you, I engraft you new.

18

Shall I compare thee to a summer's day?
Thou art more lovely and more temperate:
Rough winds do shake the darling buds of May,
And summer's lease hath all too short a date;
Sometime too hot the eye of heaven shines,   5
And often is his gold complexion dimmed;
And every fair from fair sometime declines,
By chance or nature's changing course un-
  trimmed:
But thy eternal summer shall not fade
Nor lose possession of that fair thou ow'st; [3] 10
Nor shall Death brag thou wand'rest in his
  shade,
When in eternal lines to time thou grow'st;[4]
  So long as men can breathe or eyes can see,
  So long lives this and this gives life to thee.

25

Let those who are in favor with their stars,
Of public honor and proud titles boast,
Whilst I, whom fortune of such triumph bars,
Unlooked for,[5] joy in that I honor most.
Great princes' favorites their fair leaves spread 5
But as the marigold at the sun's eye,
And in themselves their pride lies buriéd,
For at a frown they in their glory die.
The painful [6] warrior famouséd for worth,
After a thousand victories once foiled,          10
Is from the book of honor razéd forth,
And all the rest forgot for which he toiled.
  Then happy I, that love and am beloved
  Where I may not remove nor be removed.

29

When, in disgrace with Fortune and men's
  eyes,
I all alone beweep my outcast state,
And trouble deaf heaven with my bootless cries,
And look upon myself and curse my fate,
Wishing me like to one more rich in hope,      5
Featured like him, like him with friends pos-
  sessed,
Desiring this man's art, and that man's scope,

[1] Thought.        [2] Contends.
[3] Ownest.
[4] When you reach future times in my eternal lines.
[5] Unexpectedly.     [6] Suffering pain.

[13] Swords.        [14] Strike.

With what I most enjoy contented least.
Yet in these thoughts myself almost despising,
Haply I think on thee; and then my state,     10
Like to the lark at break of day arising
From sullen earth, sings hymns at heaven's gate;
  For thy sweet love remembered such wealth
    brings
  That then I scorn to change my state with
    kings.

### 30

When to the sessions of sweet silent thought
I summon up [7] remembrance of things past,
I sigh the lack of many a thing I sought,
And with old woes new wail my dear time's
    waste;
Then can I drown an eye, unused to flow,     5
For precious friends hid in death's dateless
    night,
And weep afresh love's long since canceled woe,
And moan th' expense [8] of many a vanished
    sight:
Then can I grieve at grievances foregone,
And heavily from woe to woe tell [9] o'er     10
The sad account of fore-bemoanéd moan,
Which I new pay as if not paid before.
  But if the while I think on thee, dear friend,
  All losses are restored and sorrows end.

### 31

Thy bosom is endearéd with all hearts
Which I by lacking have supposéd dead;
And there reigns love, and all love's loving
    parts,
And all those friends which I thought buriéd.
How many a holy and obsequious [10] tear     5
Hath dear religious love stol'n from mine eye
As interest of the dead, which now appear
But things removed that hidden in thee lie!
Thou art the grave where buried love doth live,
Hung with the trophies of my lovers gone,     10
Who all their parts of me to thee did give,
That due of many [11] now is thine alone.
  Their images I loved I view in thee,
  And thou, all they, hast all the all of me.

### 55

Not marble, nor the gilded monuments
Of princes, shall outlive this powerful rime;
But you shall shine more bright in these con-
    tents [12]
Than [13] unswept stone besmeared with sluttish
    time.
When wasteful war shall statues overturn,     5
And broils root out the work of masonry,
Nor Mars his sword nor war's quick fire shall
    burn
The living record of your memory.
'Gainst death and all-oblivious enmity

Shall you pace forth; your praise shall still find
    room,     10
Even in the eyes of all posterity
That wear this world out to the ending doom.
  So, till the judgment that [14] yourself arise,
  You live in this, and dwell in lovers' eyes.

### 57

Being your slave, what should I do but tend
Upon the hours and times of your desire?
I have no precious time at all to spend,
Nor services to do, till you require.
Nor dare I chide the world-without-end hour [5]
Whilst I, my sovereign, watch the clock for you,
Nor think the bitterness of absence sour
When you have bid your servant once adieu.
Nor dare I question with my jealous thought
Where you may be, or your affairs suppose,     10
But, like a sad slave, stay and think of nought
Save, where you are how happy you make those.
  So true a fool is love that in your will,[15]
  Though you do anything, he thinks no ill.

### 60

Like as the waves make towards the pebbled
    shore,
So do our minutes hasten to their end;
Each changing place with that which goes
    before,
In sequent toil all forwards do contend.
Nativity, once in the main of light,[16]     5
Crawls to maturity, wherewith being crowned,
Crooked [17] eclipses 'gainst his glory fight,
And Time that gave doth now his gift con-
    found.
Time doth transfix the flourish [18] set on youth
And delves the parallels [19] in beauty's brow,     10
Feeds on the rarities of nature's truth,
And nothing stands but for his scythe to mow;
  And yet to times in hope [20] my verse shall
    stand,
  Praising thy worth, despite his cruel hand.

### 64

When I have seen by Time's fell hand defaced
The rich proud cost of outworn buried age;
When sometime [21] lofty towers I see down-
    razed
And brass eternal slave to mortal rage;
When I have seen the hungry ocean gain     5
Advantage on the kingdom of the shore,
And the firm soil win of the watery main,
Increasing store with loss and loss with store;
When I have seen such interchange of state,
Or state [22] itself confounded to decay:     10

---

[14] When.
[15] The original text reads "Will," and perhaps a play was intended on Shakespeare's own first name.
[16] The sky.     [17] Malignant.
[18] Doth remove the garland.
[19] Parallels are, literally, trenches parallel with a fortification which is besieged.
[20] Future times.     [21] Once.     [22] Greatness.

[7] Summon up as in a court of justice.     [8] Cost.
[9] Count.     [10] Funereal.
[11] So that what belonged to many.
[12] In these verses.     [13] Than in.

Ruin hath taught me thus to ruminate,
That Time will come and take my love away.
  This thought is as a death, which cannot
    choose
  But weep to have that which it fears to lose.

### 71

No longer mourn for me when I am dead
Than you shall hear the surly sullen bell
Give warning to the world that I am fled
From this vile world, with vilest worms to
    dwell.
Nay, if you read this line, remember not    5
The hand that writ it; for I love you so
That I in your sweet thoughts would be forgot,
If thinking on me then should make you woe.
O, if, I say, you look upon this verse
When I perhaps compounded am with clay, 10
Do not so much as my poor name rehearse,
But let your love even with my life decay,
  Lest the wise world should look into your
    moan
  And mock you with me after I am gone.

### 73

That time of year thou mayst in me behold
When yellow leaves, or none, or few, do hang
Upon those boughs which shake against the
    cold,
Bare ruined choirs where late the sweet birds
    sang.
In me thou see'st the twilight of such day    5
As after sunset fadeth in the west,
Which by and by black night doth take away,
Death's second self, that seals up all in rest.
In me thou see'st the glowing of such fire
That on the ashes of his youth doth lie,    10
As the death-bed whereon it must expire,
Consumed with that which it was nourished
    by 23
  This thou perceiv'st, which makes thy love
    more strong,
  To love that well which thou must leave ere
    long.

### 90

Then hate me when thou wilt; if ever, now;
Now, while the world is bent my deeds to cross,
Join with the spite of fortune, make me bow,
And do not drop in for an after-loss:
Ah, do not, when my heart hath 'scaped this
    sorrow,                    5
Come in the rearward of a conquered woe;
Give not a windy night a rainy morrow,
To linger out a purposed overthrow.
If thou wilt leave me, do not leave me last,
When other petty griefs have done their spite,
But in the onset come; so shall I taste    11
At first the very worst of fortune's might,

23 Choked by the ashes of the wood by which it
was nourished.

And other strains 24 of woe, which now seem
    woe,
  Compared with loss of thee will not seem so.

### 94

They that have power to hurt and will do none,
That do not do the thing they most do show,
Who, moving others, are themselves as stone,
Unmovéd, cold, and to temptation slow,
They rightly do inherit heaven's graces    5
And husband nature's riches from expense;
They are the lords and owners of their faces,
Others but stewards of their excellence.25
The summer's flower is to the summer sweet,
Though to itself it only live and die;    10
But if that flower with base infection meet,
The basest weed outbraves his dignity:
  For sweetest things turn sourest by their
    deeds;
  Lilies that fester smell far worse than weeds.

### 97

How like a winter hath my absence been
From thee, the pleasure of the fleeting year!
What freezings have I felt, what dark days
    seen!
What old December's bareness everywhere!
And yet this time removed 26 was summer's
    time,                    5
The teeming autumn, big with rich increase,
Bearing the wanton burden of the prime,27
Like widowed wombs after their lords' decease.
Yet this abundant issue seemed to me
But hope of orphans 28 and unfathered fruit; 10
For summer and his pleasures wait on thee,
And, thou away, the very birds are mute;
  Or, if they sing, 'tis with so dull a cheer
  That leaves look pale, dreading the winter's
    near.

### 98

From you have I been absent in the spring,
When proud-pied 29 April, dressed in all his
    trim,
Hath put a spirit of youth in everything,
That heavy Saturn 30 laughed and leaped with
    him.
Yet nor the lays of birds nor the sweet smell 5
Of different flowers in 31 odor and in hue
Could make me any summer's story tell,32

24 Kinds.
25 Beautiful persons who are commanded by their
passions hold their beauty as stewards for the commanders, their passions, which are the real owners.
26 Time of my absence.
27 The children of the wanton spring.
28 Hope such as orphans bring.
29 Gaily colored.
30 Planet credited in astrology with producing a
sluggish and gloomy temperament in those born
under its influence.
31 Flowers different in.
32 Could make me tell a cheerful story; or, could
put me in harmony with the season.

Or from their proud lap pluck them where they
    grew;
Nor did I wonder at the lily's white,
Nor praise the deep vermilion in the rose; 10
They were but sweet, but figures of delight
Drawn after you, you pattern of all those.
    Yet seemed it winter still, and, you away,
    As with your shadow I with these did play.

### 106

When in the chronicle of wasted time
I see descriptions of the fairest wights,[33]
And beauty making beautiful old rime
In praise of ladies dead and lovely knights;
Then, in the blazon of sweet beauty's best, 5
Of hand, of foot, of lip, of eye, of brow,
I see their antique pen would have expressed
Even such a beauty as you master [34] now.
So all their praises are but prophecies
Of this our time, all you prefiguring; 10
And, for they looked but with divining eyes,
They had not skill enough your worth to sing:
    For we, which now behold these present
    days,
    Have eyes to wonder, but lack tongues to
    praise.

### 109

O, never say that I was false of heart,
Though absence seemed my flame to qualify.[35]
As easy might I from myself depart
As from my soul, which in thy breast doth lie.
That is my home of love; if I have ranged, 5
Like him that travels I return again,
Just to the time, not with the time ex-
    changed,[36]
So that myself bring water for my stain.
Never believe, though in my nature reigned
All frailties that besiege all kinds of blood,[37] 10
That it could so preposterously be stained
To leave for nothing all thy sum of good;
    For nothing this wide universe I call,
    Save thou, my rose; in it thou art my all.

### 110

Alas, 'tis true I have gone here and there
And made myself a motley to the view,[38]
Gored [39] mine own thoughts, sold cheap what
    is most dear,
Made old offenses of affections new;
Most true it is that I have looked on truth 5
Askance and strangely: but, by all above,
These blenches [40] gave my heart another youth,
And worse essays proved thee my best of love.
Now all is done, have what shall have no end:
Mine appetite I never more will grind [41] 10
On newer proof, to try an older friend,
A god in love, to whom I am confined.

Then give me welcome, next my heaven the
    best,
    Even to thy pure and most most loving
    breast.

### 111

O, for my sake do you with Fortune chide,
The guilty goddess of [42] my harmful deeds,
That did not better for my life provide
Than public means which public manners
    breeds.
Thence comes it that my name receives a
    brand, 5
And almost thence my nature is subdued
To what it works in, like the dyer's hand.
Pity me, then, and wish I were renewed;
Whilst, like a willing patient, I will drink
Potions of eisel [43] 'gainst my strong infec-
    tion; 10
No bitterness that I will bitter think,
Nor double penance, to correct correction.
    Pity me then, dear friend, and I assure ye
    Even that your pity is enough to cure me.

### 116

Let me not to the marriage of true minds
Admit impediments. Love is not love
Which alters when it alteration finds,
Or bends with the remover to remove.
O, no! it is an ever-fixéd mark 5
That looks on tempests and is never shaken;
It is the star to every wand'ring bark,
Whose worth's unknown, although his height
    be taken.
Love's not Time's fool,[44] though rosy lips and
    cheeks
Within his bending sickle's compass come; 10
Love alters not with his brief hours and weeks,
But bears it out even to the edge of doom.[45]
    If this be error and upon me proved,
    I never writ, nor no man ever loved.

### 129

Th' expense of spirit in a waste of shame
Is lust in action; [46] and till action, lust
Is perjured, murd'rous, bloody, full of blame,
Savage, extreme, rude, cruel, not to trust,
Enjoyed no sooner but despiséd straight, 5
Past reason hunted, and no sooner had,
Past reason hated, as a swallowed bait
On purpose laid to make the taker mad;
Mad in pursuit and in possession so;
Had, having, and in quest to have, extreme; 10
A bliss in proof,[47] and, proved, a very woe;
Before, a joy proposed; behind, a dream.
    All this the world well knows; yet none
    knows well

[33] People.    [34] Have.    [35] Moderate.
[36] Punctual, not altered by the time.
[37] Temperament.    [38] A public jester.
[39] Injured.    [40] Aberrations.    [41] Whet.

[42] Goddess guilty of.    [43] Vinegar.
[44] The sport of time.    [45] Doomsday.
[46] Lust in action is a shameful expenditure of
energy.
[47] In experience.

To shun the heaven that leads men to this
hell.

### 130

My mistress' eyes are nothing like the sun;
Coral is far more red than her lips' red;
If snow be white, why then her breasts are dun;
If hairs be wires, black wires grow on her head.
I have seen roses damasked, red and white, 5
But no such roses see I in her cheeks;
And in some perfumes is there more delight
Than in the breath that from my mistress
reeks.
I love to hear her speak, yet well I know
That music hath a far more pleasing sound; 10
I grant I never saw a goddess go; [48]
My mistress, when she walks, treads on the
ground:
　And yet, by heaven, I think my love as rare
　As any she belied with false compare.

### 146

Poor soul, the center of my sinful earth,[49]
Rebuke these rebel powers that thee array!
Why dost thou pine within and suffer dearth,
Painting thy outward walls so costly gay?
Why so large cost, having so short a lease, 5
Dost thou upon thy fading mansion spend?
Shall worms, inheritors of this excess,
Eat up thy charge? [50] Is this thy body's end?
Then, soul, live thou upon thy servant's loss,
And let that pine to aggravate [51] thy store; 10
Buy terms divine [52] in selling hours of dross;
Within be fed, without be rich no more;
　So shalt thou feed on Death,[53] that feeds
　　on men,
　And Death once dead, there's no more dying
　　then.

## SONGS FROM THE PLAYS
## When Daisies Pied [54]

When daisies pied and violets blue,
　And lady-smocks all silver-white,
And cuckoo-buds of yellow hue
　Do paint the meadows with delight,
The cuckoo then, on every tree, 5
Mocks married men; for thus sings he,
　　Cuckoo!
Cuckoo, cuckoo!—O word of fear,
Unpleasing to a married ear!

When shepherds pipe on oaten straws, 10
　And merry larks are plowmen's clocks,
When turtles [55] tread, and rooks, and daws,

And maidens bleach their summer smocks,
The cuckoo then, on every tree,
Mocks married men; for thus sings he, 15
　　Cuckoo!
Cuckoo, cuckoo!—O word of fear,
Unpleasing to a married ear!

## When Icicles Hang by the Wall

When icicles hang by the wall,
　And Dick the shepherd blows his nail,
And Tom bears logs into the hall,
　And milk comes frozen home in pail,
When blood is nipped and ways be foul, 5
Then nightly sings the staring owl,
"Tu-whit, tu-who!" a merry note,
While greasy Joan doth keel [56] the pot.

When all aloud the wind doth blow,
　And coughing drowns the parson's saw,[57] 10
And birds sit brooding in the snow,
　And Marian's nose looks red and raw,
When roasted crabs [58] hiss in the bowl,
Then nightly sings the staring owl,
"Tu-whit, tu-who!" a merry note, 15
While greasy Joan doth keel the pot.

## Who Is Sylvia? [59]

Who is Sylvia? what is she,
　That all our swains commend her?
Holy, fair, and wise is she;
　The heaven such grace did lend her,
That she might admiréd be. 5

Is she kind as she is fair?
　For beauty lives with kindness.
Love doth to her eyes repair
　To help him of his blindness,
And, being helped, inhabits there. 10

Then to Sylvia let us sing,
　That Sylvia is excelling;
She excels each mortal thing
　Upon the dull earth dwelling:
To her let us garlands bring. 15

## Tell Me, Where Is Fancy Bred [60]

Tell me, where is fancy bred,
Or in the heart, or in the head?
How begot, how nourished?
　　Reply, reply.
It is engendered in the eyes, 5
With gazing fed; and fancy dies
In the cradle where it lies:
Let us all ring fancy's knell;
I'll begin it,—Ding-dong, bell.
　　Ding, dong, bell. 10

---

　[48] Walk.　　　　　[49] My body.
　[50] The body on which so much has been spent.
　[51] Increase.　　　　[52] Eternity.
　[53] Consume the mortal elements.
　[54] This and the following song are from *Love's
Labor's Lost.*
　[55] Turtle-doves.

　[56] Skim.　　　[57] Discourse.　　　[58] Apples.
　[59] From *Two Gentlemen of Verona.*
　[60] From *The Merchant of Venice.*

## Under the Greenwood Tree [61]

Under the greenwood tree
Who loves to lie with me,
And turn his merry note
Unto the sweet bird's throat,
Come hither! come hither! come hither!     5
    Here shall he see
    No enemy
But winter and rough weather.

Who doth ambition shun
And loves to live i' the sun,     10
Seeking the food he eats
And pleased with what he gets,
Come hither! come hither! come hither!
    Here shall he see
    No enemy     15
But winter and rough weather.

## Blow, Blow, Thou Winter Wind

Blow, blow, thou winter wind!
Thou art not so unkind
As man's ingratitude;
Thy tooth is not so keen,
Because thou art not seen,     5
    Although thy breath be rude.
Heigh ho! sing, heigh ho! unto the green holly:
Most friendship is feigning, most loving mere
    folly:
       Then, heigh ho, the holly!
       This life is most jolly.     10

       Freeze, freeze, thou bitter sky!
       That dost not bite so nigh
         As benefits forgot;
Though thou the waters warp,[62]
    Thy sting is not so sharp     15
       As friend remembered not.
Heigh ho! sing, heigh ho! *etc.*

## Sigh No More [63]

Sigh no more, ladies, sigh no more!
    Men were deceivers ever,
One foot in sea and one on shore,
    To one thing constant never:
Then sigh not so, but let them go,     5
    And be you blithe and bonny,
Converting all your sounds of woe
    Into Hey nonny, nonny!

Sing no more ditties, sing no moe [64]
    Of dumps so dull and heavy!     10

[61] This and the following song are from *As You Like It.*
[62] Cause to shrink.
[63] From *Much Ado about Nothing.*     [64] More.

The fraud of men was ever so,
    Since summer first was leafy:
Then sigh not so, but let them go,
    And be you blithe and bonny,
Converting all your sounds of woe     15
    Into Hey nonny, nonny!

## O Mistress Mine [65]

O mistress mine, where are you roaming?
O stay and hear; your true love's coming,
    That can sing both high and low:
Trip no further, pretty sweeting;
Journeys end in lovers meeting,     5
    Every wise man's son doth know.

What is love? 't is not hereafter;
Present mirth hath present laughter;
    What's to come is still unsure:
In delay there lies no plenty;     10
Then come kiss me, sweet and twenty;
    Youth's a stuff will not endure.

## Take, O Take Those Lips Away [66]

Take, O take those lips away,
    That so sweetly were forsworn;
And those eyes, the break of day,
    Lights that do mislead the morn:
But my kisses bring again,     5
       Bring again;
Seals of love, but sealed in vain,
       Sealed in vain!

## Come, Thou Monarch of the Vine [67]

Come, thou monarch of the vine,
Plumpy Bacchus with pink eyne! [68]
In thy vats our cares be drowned,
With thy grapes our hairs be crowned!
Cup us, till the world go round,     5
Cup us, till the world go round!

## Hark, Hark! the Lark [69]

Hark, hark! the lark at heaven's gate sings,
    And Phoebus 'gins arise,
His steeds to water at those springs
    On chaliced flowers that lies;
And winking Mary-buds begin     5
    To ope their golden eyes:
With everything that pretty is,
    My lady sweet, arise!
       Arise, arise!

[65] From *Twelfth Night.*
[66] From *Measure for Measure.*
[67] From *Antony and Cleopatra.*     [68] Eyes.
[69] This and the following song are from *Cymbeline.*

## Fear No More the Heat o' the Sun

Fear no more the heat o' th' sun,
　Nor the furious winter's rages;
Thou thy worldly task hast done;
　Home art gone, and ta'en thy wages:
Golden lads and girls all must,　　　　　5
As chimney-sweepers, come to dust.

Fear no more the frown o' th' great;
　Thou art past the tyrant's stroke;
Care no more to clothe and eat;
　To thee the reed is as the oak:　　　10
The Scepter, Learning, Physic must
All follow this, and come to dust.

Fear no more the lightning-flash,
　Nor th' all-dreaded thunder-stone;
Fear not slander, censure rash;　　　　15
　Thou hast finished joy and moan:
All lovers young, all lovers must
Consign [70] to thee, and come to dust.

No exorciser harm thee!
　Nor no witchcraft charm thee!　　　20
Ghost unlaid forbear thee!
　Nothing ill come near thee!
Quiet consummation have;
And renownéd be thy grave!

## Full Fathom Five Thy Father Lies [71]

Full fathom five thy father lies:
　Of his bones are coral made;
Those are pearls that were his eyes;
　Nothing of him that doth fade
But doth suffer a sea-change　　　　　5
Into something rich and strange.
Sea-nymphs hourly ring his knell;
　　　　　Ding-dong!
Hark! now I hear them,—Ding-dong, bell!

# THOMAS CAMPION

## (1567–1619)

## Follow Thy Fair Sun

Follow thy fair sun, unhappy shadow,
　Though thou be black as night,
　And she made all of light;
Yet follow thy fair sun, unhappy shadow.

Follow her whose light thy light depriveth, 5
　Though here thou liest disgraced,
　And she in heaven is placed;
Yet follow her whose light the world reviveth.

Follow those pure beams whose beauty burneth,

[70] Agree.　　　[71] From *The Tempest.*

That so have scorchéd thee　　　　　10
　As thou still black must be,
Till her kind beams thy black to brightness
　turneth.

Follow her while yet her glory shineth:
　There comes a luckless night
　That will dim all her light;　　　　15
And this the black unhappy shade divineth.

Follow still, since so thy fates ordainéd;
　The Sun must have his shade,
　Till both at once do fade,
The Sun still proud, the shadow still dis-
　dainéd.　　　　　　　　　　　　20

## Follow Your Saint

Follow your saint, follow with accents sweet;
Haste you, sad notes; fall at her flying feet;
There, wrapt in cloud of sorrow, pity move,
And tell the ravisher of my soul I perish for
　her love:
But if she scorns my never-ceasing pain,　5
Then burst with sighing in her sight and ne'er
　return again.

All that I sung still to her praise did tend;
Still she was first; still she my songs did end.
Yet she my love and music both doth fly,
The music that her echo is and beauty's sym-
　pathy;　　　　　　　　　　　　10
Then let my notes pursue her scornful flight:
It shall suffice that they were breathed and
　died for her delight.

## There Is a Garden in Her Face

There is a garden in her face
　Where roses and white lilies grow;
A heavenly paradise is that place,
　Wherein all pleasant fruits do flow:
　　There cherries grow which none may
　　　buy　　　　　　　　　　　　5
　　Till "Cherry-ripe" themselves do cry.

Those cherries fairly do enclose
　Of orient pearl a double row,
Which when her lovely laughter shows,
　They look like rosebuds filled with snow; 10
　　Yet them nor peer nor prince can buy
　　Till "Cherry-ripe" themselves do cry.

Her eyes like angels watch them still;
　Her brows like bended bows do stand,
Threatening with piercing frowns to kill　15
　All that attempt, with eye or hand,
　　Those sacred cherries to come nigh
　　Till "Cherry-ripe" themselves do cry.

## When Thou Must Home

When thou must home to shades of under-
　ground,

And there arrived, a new admiréd guest,
The beauteous spirits do engirt thee round,
White Iöpe, blithe Helen, and the rest,
To hear the stories of thy finished love 5
From that smooth tongue whose music hell
    can move;

Then wilt thou speak of banqueting delights,
Of masques and revels which sweet youth did
    make,
Of tourneys and great challenges of knights,
And all these triumphs for thy beauty's sake: 10
When thou hast told these honors done to
    thee,
Then tell, O tell, how thou didst murder me.

## Now Winter Nights Enlarge

Now winter nights enlarge
The number of their hours;
And clouds their storms discharge
Upon the airy towers.
Let now the chimneys blaze, 5
And cups o'erflow with wine;
Let well-tuned words amaze
With harmony divine.
Now yellow waxen lights
Shall wait on honey love; 10
While youthful revels, masques, and courtly
    sights
Sleep's leaden spells remove.

This time doth well dispense
With lovers' long discourse;
Much speech hath some defense, 15
Though beauty no remorse.
All do not all things well:
Some measures comely tread,
Some knotted riddles tell,
Some poems smoothly read. 20
The summer hath his joys,
And winter his delights;
Though love and all his pleasures are but toys,
They shorten tedious nights.

## Rose-Cheeked Laura

Rose-cheeked Laura, come,
Sing thou smoothly with thy beauty's
Silent music, either other
    Sweetly gracing.

Lovely forms do flow 5
From consent [1] divinely framéd;
Heav'n is music, and thy beauty's
    Birth is heavenly.

These dull notes we sing
Discords need for helps to grace them; 10
Only beauty purely loving
    Knows no discord,

[1] Harmony.

But still moves delight,
Like clear springs renewed by flowing,
Ever perfect, ever in them- 15
    selves eternal.

## Never Love

Never love, unless you can
Bear with all the faults of man:
Men sometimes will jealous be,
Though but little cause they see,
    And hang the head, as discontent, 5
    And speak what straight they will repent.

Men that but one saint adore
Make a show of love to more:
Beauty must be scorned in none,
Though but truly served in one: 10
    For what is courtship but disguise?
    True hearts may have dissembling eyes.

Men, when their affairs require,
Must awhile themselves retire;
Sometimes hunt, and sometimes hawk, 15
And not ever sit and talk.
    If these and such like you can bear,
    Then like, and love, and never fear.

## Beauty Is but a Painted Hell

Beauty is but a painted hell;
    Aye me, aye me,
She wounds them that admire it;
She kills them that desire it;
    Give her pride but fuel, 5
    No fire is more cruel.

Pity from ev'ry heart is fled:
    Aye me, aye me,
Since false desire could borrow
Tears of dissembled sorrow, 10
    Constant vows turn truthless,
    Love cruel, Beauty ruthless.

Sorrow can laugh, and Fury sing:
    Aye me, aye me,
My raving griefs discover 15
I lived too true a lover;
    The first step to madness
    Is the excess of sadness.

## The Man of Life Upright

The man of life upright,
    Whose guiltless heart is free
From all dishonest deeds,
    Or thought of vanity;

The man whose silent days 5
    In harmless joys are spent,
Whom hopes cannot delude
    Nor sorrow discontent;

That man needs neither towers
   Nor armor for defense,      10
Nor secret vaults to fly
   From thunder's violence.

He only can behold
   With unaffrighted eyes
The horrors of the deep      15
   And terrors of the skies.

Thus, scorning all the cares
   That fate or fortune brings,
He makes the heav'n his book,
   His wisdom heav'nly things,      20

Good thoughts his only friends,
   His wealth a well-spent age,
The earth his sober inn
   And quiet pilgrimage.

# BEN JONSON

## (1573?–1637)

## Hymn to Diana

Queen and Huntress, chaste and fair,
   Now the sun is laid to sleep,
Seated in thy silver chair
   State in wonted manner keep:
     Hesperus [1] entreats thy light,     5
     Goddess excellently bright.

Earth, let not thy envious shade
   Dare itself to interpose;
Cynthia's shining orb was made
   Heaven to clear when day did close:     10
     Bless us then with wishéd sight,
     Goddess excellently bright.

Lay thy bow of pearl apart
   And thy crystal-shining quiver;
Give unto the flying hart     15
   Space to breathe, how short soever:
     Thou that mak'st a day of night,
     Goddess excellently bright.

## Song. To Celia [2]

Come, my Celia, let us prove,
While we may, the sports of love.
Time will not be ours for ever;
He, at length, our good will sever;
Spend not then his gifts in vain.     5
Suns that set may rise again;
But if once we lose this light,
'T is with us perpetual night.
Why should we defer our joys?
Fame and rumor are but toys.     10
Cannot we delude the eyes

[1] The evening star.
[2] An adaptation of Catullus (*Carmina*, v).

Of a few poor household spies?
Or his easier ears beguile,
Thus removéd by our wile?
'T is no sin love's fruits to steal;     15
But the sweet theft to reveal,
To be taken, to be seen,
These have crimes accounted been.

## To Celia

Drink to me only with thine eyes,
   And I will pledge with mine;
Or leave a kiss but in the cup,
   And I'll not look for wine.
The thirst that from the soul doth rise     5
   Doth ask a drink divine;
But might I of Jove's nectar sup,
   I would not change for [3] thine.

I sent thee late a rosy wreath,
   Not so much honoring thee     10
As giving it a hope that there
   It could not withered be.
But thou thereon didst only breathe,
   And sent'st it back to me;
Since when it grows, and smells, I swear,     15
   Not of itself, but thee.

## Song: That Women Are but Men's Shadows

Follow a shadow, it still flies you;
   Seem to fly it, it will pursue:
So court a mistress, she denies you;
   Let her alone, she will court you.
Say are not women truly, then,     5
Styled but the shadows of us men?

At morn and even shades are longest;
   At noon they are or short or none:
So men at weakest, they are strongest,
   But grant us perfect, they're not known.   10
Say are not women truly, then,
Styled but the shadows of us men?

## Still to Be Neat

Still to be neat, still to be drest,
As you were going to a feast;
Still to be powdered, still perfumed;—
Lady, it is to be presumed,
Though art's hid causes are not found,     5
All is not sweet, all is not sound.

Give me a look, give me a face,
That makes simplicity a grace;
Robes loosely flowing, hair as free:
Such sweet neglect more taketh me     10
Than all th' adulteries of art;
They strike mine eyes, but not my heart.

[3] From.

# Her Triumph

See the chariot at hand here of Love,
  Wherein my lady rideth!
Each that draws is a swan or a dove,
  And well the car Love guideth.
As she goes, all hearts do duty          5
  Unto her beauty;
And enamored, do wish, so they might
  But enjoy such a sight,
That they still were to run by her side,
Through swords, through seas, whither she   10
  would ride.

Do but look on her eyes: they do light
  All that Love's world compriseth!
Do but look on her hair: it is bright
  As Love's star when it riseth!
Do but mark: her forehead's smoother       15
  Than words that soothe her;
And from her arched brows, such a grace
  Sheds itself through the face
As alone there triumphs to the life
All the gain, all the good, of the elements'   20
  strife.

Have you seen but a bright lily grow
  Before rude hands have touched it?
Have you marked but the fall of the snow
  Before the soil hath smutched [4] it?
Have you felt the wool of the beaver?       25
  Or swan's down ever?
Or have smelt o' the bud of the briar?
  Or the nard in the fire?
Or have tasted the bag of the bee!
O so white! O so soft! O so sweet is she!    30

# An Ode

  High-spirited friend,
I send nor balms, nor corsives [5] to your wound;
  Your faith hath found
A gentler and more agile hand to tend
The cure of that which is but corporal,       5
And doubtful days, which were named critical,
  Have made their fairest flight,
  And now are out of sight.
Yet doth some wholesome physic for the mind
  Wrapt in this paper lie,                    10
Which in the taking if you misapply,
  You are unkind.

  Your covetous hand,
Happy in that fair honor it hath gained,
  Must now be reined.                         15
True valor doth her own renown command
In one full action; nor have you now more
To do than be a husband of that store.
  Think but how dear you bought
  This same which you have caught;            20

4 Dirtied.          5 A corrosive medicine.

Such thoughts will make you more in love with
  truth:
  'Tis wisdom, and that high,
For men to use their fortune reverently,
  Even in youth.

# A Song

O do not wanton with those eyes,
  Lest I be sick with seeing;
Nor cast them down, but let them rise,
  Lest shame destroy their being.

O be not angry with those fires,            5
  For then their threats will kill me;
Nor look too kind on my desires,
  For then my hopes will spill me.

O do not steep them in thy tears,
  For so will sorrow slay me;                10
Nor spread them as distract with fears;
  Mine own enough betray me.

# A Nymph's Passion

I love, and he loves me again,
  Yet dare I not tell who;
For if the nymphs should know my swain,
  I fear they'd love him too;
    Yet if he be not known,                  5
    The pleasure is as good as none,
For that's a narrow joy is but our own.

I'll tell, that if they be not glad,
  They yet may envy me;
But then if I grow jealous mad,             10
  And of them pitied be,
    It were a plague 'bove scorn,
    And yet it cannot be forborn,
Unless my heart would, as my thought, be torn.

He is, if they can find him, fair,          15
  And fresh and fragrant too,
As summer's sky, or purgéd air,
  And looks as lilies do
    That are this morning blown;
    Yet, yet I doubt he is not known,        20
And fear much more that more of him be
  shown.

But he hath eyes so round, and bright,
  As make away my doubt,
Where Love may all his torches light
  Though hate had put them out:              25
    But then, t' increase my fears,
    What nymph so'er his voice but hears
Will be my rival, though she have but ears.

I'll tell no more, and yet I love,
  And he loves me; yet no                    30
One unbecoming thought doth move
  From either heart, I know;
    But so exempt from blame,
    As it would be to each a fame,
If love or fear would let me tell his name. 35

## To the Memory of My Beloved Master William Shakespeare

To draw no envy, Shakespeare, on thy name,
Am I thus ample to thy book and fame;
While I confess thy writings to be such
As neither man, nor muse, can praise too much.
'T is true, and all men's suffrage.[6] But these ways      5
Were not the paths I meant unto thy praise;
For silliest ignorance on these may light,
Which, when it sounds at best, but echoes right;
Or blind affection, which doth ne'er advance
The truth, but gropes, and urgeth all by chance;      10
Or crafty malice might pretend this praise,
And think to ruin, where it seemed to raise.
These are as some infamous bawd or whore
Should praise a matron. What could hurt her more?
But thou art proof against them and, indeed, [15]
Above the ill fortune of them, or the need.
I therefore will begin. Soul of the age!
The applause, delight, the wonder of our stage!
My Shakespeare, rise! I will not lodge thee by
Chaucer, or Spenser, or bid Beaumont lie [20]
A little further, to make thee a room:
Thou art a monument without a tomb,
And art alive still while thy book doth live
And we have wits to read and praise to give.
That I not mix thee so, my brain excuses, [25]
I mean with great, but disproportioned muses;
For if I thought my judgment were of years,
I should commit thee surely with thy peers,
And tell how far thou didst our Lyly outshine,
Or sporting Kyd, or Marlowe's mighty line. [30]
And though thou hadst small Latin and less Greek,
From thence to honor thee I would not seek
For names; but call forth thundering Aeschylus,
Euripides, and Sophocles to us;
Pacuvius Accius,[7] him of Cordova[8] dead, [35]
To life again, to hear thy buskin[9] tread,
And shake a stage; or, when thy socks[10] were on,
Leave thee alone for the comparison
Of all that insolent Greece or haughty Rome
Sent forth, or since did from their ashes come.      40
Triumph, my Britain, thou hast one to show
To whom all scenes of Europe homage owe.
He was not of an age, but for all time!
And all the Muses still were in their prime
When, like Apollo, he came forth to warm [45]
Our ears, or like a Mercury to charm!

[6] Opinion.          [7] Roman tragic poet.
[8] Seneca the tragic poet.
[9] The high boot worn in classical times by actors
in tragedy.
[10] Light shoes worn in classical times by actors in
comedy.

Nature herself was proud of his designs
And joyed to wear the dressing of his lines!
Which were so richly spun, and woven so fit,
As, since, she will vouchsafe no other wit. [50]
The merry Greek, tart Aristophanes,
Neat Terence, witty Plautus, now not please;
But antiquated and deserted lie,
As they were not of Nature's family.
Yet must I not give Nature all; thy art, [55]
My gentle Shakespeare, must enjoy a part.
For though the poet's matter Nature be,
His art doth give the fashion; and that he
Who casts to write a living line must sweat,
(Such as thine are) and strike the second heat      60
Upon the Muses' anvil; turn the same
(And himself with it) that he thinks to frame,
Or, for the laurel, he may gain a scorn;
For a good poet's made, as well as born.
And such wert thou! Look how the father's face [65]
Lives in his issue; even so the race
Of Shakespeare's mind and manners brightly shines
In his well turnéd, and true filéd lines;
In each of which he seems to shake a lance,
As brandished at the eyes of ignorance. [70]
Sweet Swan of Avon! what a sight it were
To see thee in our waters yet appear,
And make those flights upon the banks of Thames,
That so did take Eliza, and our James![11]
But stay; I see thee in the hemisphere [75]
Advanced, and made a constellation there!
Shine forth, thou star of poets, and with rage
Or influence, chide or cheer the drooping stage,
Which, since thy flight from hence, hath mourned like night,
And despairs day, but for thy volume's light. [80]

## A Pindaric Ode

*To the Immortal Memory and Friendship
of that Noble Pair, Sir Lucius Cary and Sir
H. Morison* [12]

### I

#### THE STROPHE, OR TURN

Brave infant of Saguntum,[13] clear
Thy coming forth in that great year

[11] Queen Elizabeth and James I.
[12] Pindar was the greatest of Greek lyric poets.
This poem is modeled upon his odes in its stanzaic
structure, and to some extent in its style and tone.
Sir Lucius Cary, Viscount Falkland, was himself a
poet and the friend of men of letters, who visited
him freely at his country house near Oxford. He
married the sister of Sir Henry Morison. Morison
died in 1629, shortly before Jonson's ode was written.
[13] A city in Spain captured by Hannibal after a
painful siege (219 B.C.) The story told by Jonson is recorded by Pliny, *Natural History*, VII, iii.

When the prodigious Hannibal did crown
His rage with razing your immortal town.
     Thou looking then about,    5
     Ere thou were half got out,
Wise child, didst hastily return,
And mad'st thy mother's womb thine urn.
How summed [14] a circle didst thou leave man-
    kind
Of deepest lore, could we the center find!   10

## THE ANTISTROPHE, OR COUNTER-TURN

  Did wiser nature draw thee back
  From out the horror of that sack,
Where shame, faith, honor, and regard of right
Lay trampled on? the deeds of death and night
    Urged, hurried forth, and hurled   15
    Upon the affrighted world;
  Fire, famine, and fell fury met,
  And all on utmost ruin set:
As, could they but life's miseries foresee,
No doubt all infants would return like thee. 20

## THE EPODE, OR STAND

For what is life, if measured by the space,
    Not by the act?
Or maskéd man, if valued by his face
    Above his fact? [15]
    Here's one outlived his peers   25
    And told forth fourscore years;
He vexéd time, and busied the whole state,
  Troubled both foes and friends,
  But ever to no ends:
What did this stirrer but die late?   30
How well at twenty had he fallen or stood! [16]
For three of his four score he did no good.

## II

### THE STROPHE, OR TURN

  He entered well by virtuous parts,
  Got up, and thrived with honest arts,
He purchased friends, and fame, and honors
    then,
And had his noble name advanced with men;
    But weary of that flight,   5
    He stooped in all men's sight
  To sordid flatteries, acts of strife,
  And sunk in that dead sea of life,
So deep as he did then death's waters sup,
But that the cork of title buoyed him up.   10

### THE ANTISTROPHE, OR COUNTER-TURN

  Alas! but Morison fell young!
  He never fell,—thou fall'st, my tongue.
He stood a soldier to the last right end,
A perfect patriot and a noble friend;
    But most, a virtuous son.   15

[14] Complete.    [15] Deed.    [16] Stopped.

All offices were done
By him, so ample, full, and round,
In weight, in measure, number, sound,
As, though his age imperfect might appear,
His life was of humanity the sphere.[17]   20

## THE EPODE, OR STAND

Go now, and tell [18] our days summed up with
    fears,
    And make them years;
Produce thy mass of miseries on the stage,
    To swell thine age;
    Repeat of things a throng,   25
    To show thou hast been long,
  Not lived; for life doth her great actions spell
    By what was done and wrought
    In season, and so brought
  To light: her measures are, how well   30
Each syllabe answered, and was formed how
    fair;
These make the lines of life, and that's her air!

## III

### THE STROPHE, OR TURN

  It is not growing like a tree
  In bulk, doth make men better be;
Or standing long an oak, three hundred year,
To fall a log at last, dry, bald, and sear:
    A lily of a day   5
    Is fairer far in May,
  Although it fall and die that night;
  It was the plant and flower of light.
In small proportions we just beauties see;
And in short measures life may perfect be. 10

### THE ANTISTROPHE, OR COUNTER-TURN

  Call, noble Lucius, then, for wine,
  And let thy looks with gladness shine;
Accept this garland, plant it on thy head,
And think, nay know, thy Morison's now dead.
    He leaped the present age,   15
    Possest with holy rage,
  To see that bright eternal day,
  Of which we priests and poets say
Such truths as we expect for happy men;
And there he lives with memory and Ben   20

### THE EPODE, OR STAND

Jonson, who sung this of him, ere he went
    Himself to rest,
Or taste a part of that full joy he meant
    To have exprest,
    In this bright asterism; [19]   25
    Where it were friendship's schism,
  Were not his Lucius long with us to tarry,

[17] I. e., included all that humanity may achieve.
[18] Count.    [19] Constellation.

To separate these twi-
Lights, the Dioscuri; [20]
And keep the one half from his Harry.    30
But fate doth so altérnate the design,
Whilst that in heaven, this light on earth must
     shine.

### IV

#### THE STROPHE, OR TURN

And shine as you exalted are;
Two names of friendship, but one star:
Of hearts the union, and those not by chance
Made, or indenture, or leased out t' advance
     The profits for a time.    5
     No pleasures vain did chime
Of rimes, or riots, at your feasts,
Orgies of drink, or feigned protests;
But simple love of greatness and of good,
That knits brave minds and manners more than
     blood.    10

#### THE ANTISTROPHE, OR COUNTER-TURN

This made you first to know the why
You liked, then after to apply
That liking; and approach so one the t' other,
Till either grew a portion of the other;
     Each styléd by his end,    15
     The copy of his friend.
You lived to be the great sir-names
And titles by which all made claims
Unto the virtue: nothing perfect done,
But as a Cary or a Morison.    20

#### THE EPODE, OR STAND

And such a force the fair example had
     As they that saw
The good and durst not practice it, were glad
     That such a law
     Was left yet to mankind;    25
     Where they might read and find
Friendship, indeed, was written not in words;
     And with the heart, not pen,
     Of two so early men,
Whose lines her rolls were, and records; 30
Who, ere the first down blooméd on the chin,
Had sowed these fruits, and got the harvest in.

### Epitaph on Elizabeth, L. H.

Would'st thou hear what man can say
In a little? Reader, stay.

Underneath this stone doth lie
As much beauty as could die:
Which in life did harbor give    5
To more virtue than doth live.

[20] Castor and Pollux, children of Zeus.

If at all she had a fault,
Leave it buried in this vault.
One name was Elizabeth,
The other, let it sleep with death!    10
Fitter where it died to tell
Than that it lived at all. Farewell!

### Epitaph on Salathiel Pavy

Weep with me, all you that read
     This little story;
And know, for whom a tear you shed
     Death's self is sorry.
'T was a child that so did thrive    5
     In grace and feature
As heaven and nature seemed to strive
     Which owned the creature.
Years he numbered scarce thirteen
     When fates turned cruel;    10
Yet three filled zodiacs [21] had he been
     The stage's jewel,
And did act, what now we moan,
     Old men so duly
As, sooth, the Parcae [22] thought him one,    15
     He played so truly.
So, by error, to his fate
     They all consented;
But viewing him since, alas, too late!
     They have repented;    20
And have sought, to give new birth,
     In baths to steep him;
But being so much too good for earth,
     Heaven vows to keep him.

## JOHN DONNE
### (1573–1631)

### Song

Go and catch a falling star,
     Get with child a mandrake root,[1]
Tell me where all past years are,
     Or who cleft the devil's foot;
Teach me to hear mermaids singing,    5
Or to keep off envy's stinging,
          And find
          What wind
Serves to advance an honest mind.

If thou be'st born to strange sights,    10
     Things invisible to see,
Ride ten thousand days and nights
     Till age snow white hairs on thee;
Thou, when thou return'st, wilt tell me
All strange wonders that befell thee,    15
          And swear
          No where
Lives a woman true and fair.

[21] Full years.          [22] The Fates.
[1] This root has a shape somewhat like that of the
human body.

If thou find'st one, let me know;
  Such a pilgrimage were sweet.    20
Yet do not; I would not go,
  Though at next door we might meet.
Though she were true when you met her,
And last till you write your letter,
    Yet she          25
    Will be
False, ere I come, to two or three.

## The Indifferent

I can love both fair and brown;
Her whom abundance melts, and her whom
  want betrays;
Her who loves loneness best, and her who [2]
  masks and plays;
Her whom the country formed, and whom the
  town;
Her who believes, and her who tries;    5
Her who still weeps with spongy eyes,
And her who is dry cork and never cries.
I can love her, and her, and you, and you;
I can love any, so she be not true.

Will no other vice content you?    10
Will it not serve your turn to do as did your
  mothers?
Or have you all old vices spent and now would
  find out others?
Or doth a fear that men are true torment you?
O we are not, be not you so;
Let me—and do you—twenty know;    15
Rob me, but bind me not, and let me go.
Must I, who came to travel thorough you,
Grow your fixed subject, because you are true?

Venus heard me sigh this song;
And by love's sweetest part, variety, she swore
She heard not this till now; it should be so no
  more.    21
She went, examined, and returned ere long,
And said, "Alas! some two or three
Poor heretics in love there be,
Which think to stablish dangerous constancy.
But I have told them, 'Since you will be true, [26]
You shall be true to them who're false to
  you.' "

## The Canonization

For God's sake hold your tongue, and let me
  love,
  Or chide my palsy or my gout;
My five gray hairs or ruin'd fortune flout;
  With wealth your state, your mind with arts
    improve;
      Take you a course, get you a place,    5
      Observe his Honor or his Grace;
Or the king's real, or his stamped face

[2] Who loves.

Contemplate; what you will, approve,
  So you will let me love.

Alas, alas, who's injur'd by my love?    10
  What merchant's ships have my sighs
    drown'd?
Who says my tears have overflow'd his ground?
  When did my colds a forward spring remove?
    When did the heats which my veins fill
      Add one more to the plaguy bill? [3]  15
Soldiers find wars, and lawyers find out still
  Litigious men which quarrels move,
    Though she and I do love.

Call us what you will, we are made such by
  love;
  Call her one, me another fly,    20
We're tapers too and at our own cost die;
  And we in us find th'eagle and the dove. [4]
    The phoenix riddle [5] hath more wit
    By us: we two, being one, are it.
So to one neutral thing both sexes fit;    25
  We die and rise the same and prove
    Mysterious by this love.

We can die by it, if not live by love;
  And if unfit for tombs and hearse
Our legend be, it will be fit for verse;    30
  And if no piece of chronicle we prove,
    We'll build in sonnets pretty rooms.
    As well a well-wrought urn becomes
The greatest ashes, as half-acre tombs;
  And by these hymns all shall approve  35
  Us canonized for love,

And thus invoke us: "You whom reverend love
  Made one another's hermitage;
You to whom love was peace, that now is rage;
  Who did the whole world's soul contract,
  and drove    40
    Into the glasses of your eyes
    (So made such mirrors and such spies
That they did all to you epitomize)
  Countries, towns, courts: beg from above
  A pattern of your love!"    45

## Lovers' Infiniteness

If yet I have not all thy love,
Dear, I shall never have it all;
I cannot breathe one other sigh to move,
Nor can intreat one other tear to fall,
And all my treasure which should purchase
  thee,    5
Sighs, tears, and oaths, and letters, I have spent.
Yet no more can be due to me
Than at the bargain made was meant;
If then thy gift of love were partial,

[3] The official record of the number of those who
had died by the plague.
[4] The respective symbols of strength and purity.
[5] After living 500 or 1000 years the phoenix burned
itself to ashes and was reborn from the fire.

That some to me, some should to others fall, 10
  Dear, I shall never have thee all.

Or if then thou gavest me all,
All was but all which thou hadst then;
  But if in thy heart, since, there be or shall
New love created be by other men, 15
Which have their stocks entire, and can in tears,
In sighs, in oaths, and letters outbid me,
  This new love may beget new fears,
  For this love was not vowed by thee;
And yet it was, thy gift being general; 20
The ground, thy heart, is mine, whatever shall
  Grow there, dear; I should have it all.

Yet I would not have all yet;
  He that hath all can have no more,
And since my love doth every day admit 25
New growth, thou shouldst have new rewards in store;
Thou canst not every day give me thy heart;
If thou canst give it, then thou never gavest it:
Love's riddles are that, though thy heart depart,
It stays at home, and thou with losing savest it:
But we will have a way more liberal 31
Than changing hearts, to join them; so we shall
  Be one, and one another's all.

## Song

Sweetest love, I do not go
  For weariness of thee,
Nor in hope the world can show
  A fitter love for me;
    But since that I
Must die at last, 'tis best
To use myself in jest
  Thus by fain'd deaths to die.

Yesternight the sun went hence
  And yet is here today; 10
He hath no desire nor sense,
  Nor half so short a way.
    Then fear not me,
But believe that I shall make
Speedier journeys, since I take 15
  More wings and spurs than he.

O how feeble is man's power,
  That if good fortune fall
Cannot add another hour,
  Nor a lost hour recall! 20
    But come bad chance,
And we join to't our strength,
And we teach it art and length[6]
  Itself o'er us t'advance.

When thou sigh'st, thou sigh'st not wind, 25
  But sigh'st my soul away;
When thou weep'st, unkindly kind,

  [6] Endurance.

My life's blood doth decay.
    It cannot be
That thou lov'st me as thou say'st, 30
If in thine my life thou waste
  That art the best of me.

Let not thy divining heart
  Forethink me any ill;
Destiny may take thy part 35
  And may thy fears fulfil.
    But think that we
Are but turn'd aside to sleep;
They who one another keep
  Alive, ne'er parted be. 40

## The Dream

Dear love, for nothing less than thee
Would I have broke this happy dream;
    It was a theme
For reason, much too strong for fantasy.
Therefore thou waked'st me wisely; yet 5
My dream thou brok'st not, but continued'st it.
Thou art so true that thoughts of thee suffice
To make dreams truths and fables histories;
Enter these arms, for since thou thought'st it best
Not to dream all my dream, let's act the rest. 10

As lightning, or a taper's light,
Thine eyes, and not thine noise, waked me;
    Yet I thought thee—
For thou lov'st truth—an angel, at first sight;
But when I saw thou saw'st my heart, 15
And knew'st my thoughts beyond an angel's art,
When thou knew'st what I dreamt, when thou knew'st when
Excess of joy would wake me, and cam'st then,
I must confess it could not choose but be
Profane to think thee anything but thee. 20

Coming and staying showed thee thee,
But rising makes me doubt that now
    Thou art not thou.
That love is weak where fear's as strong as he;
'T is not all spirit pure and brave 25
If mixture it of fear, shame, honor have.
Perchance as torches, which must ready be,
Men light and put out, so thou deal'st with me.
Thou cam'st to kindle, go'st to come: then I
Will dream that hope again, but else would die.

## The Ecstasy

Where, like a pillow on a bed,
  A pregnant bank swelled up, to rest
The violet's reclining head,
  Sat we two, one another's best.
Our hands were firmly cemented 5
  With a fast balm, which thence did spring;

Our eye-beams twisted, and did thread
  Our eyes upon one double string;
So t' intergraft our hands as yet
  Was all the means to make us one,   10
And pictures in our eyes to get
  Was all our propagation.
As 'twixt two equal armies, fate
  Suspends uncertain victory,
Our souls (which to advance their state,   15
  Were gone out) hung 'twixt her and me.
And whil'st our souls negotiate there,
  We like sepulchral statues lay;
All day the same our postures were,
  And we said nothing all the day.   20
If any, so by love refined
  That he soul's language understood,
And by good love were grown all mind,
  Within convenient distance stood,
He (though he knew not which soul spake,   25
  Because both meant, both spake the same)
Might thence a new concoction take,
  And part far purer than he came.
This Ecstasy doth unperplex
  (We said) and tell us what we love;   30
We see by this it was not sex;
  We see we saw not what did move: [7]
But as all several souls contain
  Mixture of things, they know not what,
Love, these mixed souls, doth mix again,   35
  And makes both one, each this and that.
A single violet transplant,
  The strength, the color, and the size,
(All which before was poor, and scant)
  Redoubles still, and multiples.   40
When love with one another so
  Interinanimates two souls,
That abler soul, which thence doth flow,
  Defects of loneliness controls.
We then, who are this new soul, know   45
  Of what we are composed, and made,
For th' atomies of which we grow,
  Are souls, whom no change can invade.
But O alas, so long, so far
  Our bodies why do we forbear?   50
They're ours, though they're not we; we are
  The intelligences, they the sphere.[8]
We owe them thanks, because they thus
  Did us to us at first convey,
Yielded their forces, sense, to us,   55
  Nor are dross to us, but allay.[9]
On man heaven's influence works not so
  But that it first imprints the air;
So soul into the soul may flow,
  Though it to body first repair.   60
As our blood labors to beget
  Spirits as like souls as it can,
Because such fingers need to knit
  That subtle knot which makes us man:

So must pure lovers' souls descend   65
  T' affections, and to faculties,
Which sense may reach and apprehend;
  Else a great prince in prison lies.
T' our bodies turn we then, that so
  Weak men on love revealed may look;   70
Love's mysteries in souls do grow,
  But yet the body is his book.
And if some lover, such as we,
  Have heard this dialogue of one,
Let him still mark us: he shall see   75
  Small change when we're to bodies gone.

## The Funeral

Whoever comes to shroud me, do not harm
  Nor question much
That subtle wreath of hair [10] about mine arm:
The mystery, the sign you must not touch,
  For 'tis my outward soul,   5
Viceroy to that which, unto heav'n being
    gone,[11]
  Will leave this to control
And keep these limbs, her provinces, from dis-
    solution.

For if the sinewy thread my brain lets fall
  Through every part [12]   10
Can tie those parts, and make me one of all,
Those hairs which upward grew, and strength
    and art
  Have from a better brain,[13]
Can better do't; except she meant that I
  By this should know my pain,   15
As prisoners then are manacled when they're
    condemned to die.

Whate'er she meant by 't, bury it with me;
  For since I am
Love's martyr, it might breed idolatry
If into other hands these relics came;   20
  As 'twas humility
To afford to it all that a soul can do,
  So 'tis some bravery [14]
That, since you would have none of me, I bury
    some of you.

## Holy Sonnet

Death, be not proud, though some have calléd
    thee
Mighty and dreadful, for thou art not so;
For those whom thou think'st thou dost over-
    throw
Die not, poor Death; nor yet canst thou kill me.
From rest and sleep, which but thy picture be,

---

[7] We see now that we did not before know the true source of our love.
[8] The astronomical spheres were supposed to be moved by spirits known as intelligences.
[9] Alloy.

[10] Bracelet of the lady's hair.
[11] Viceroy to the inward, true soul which has departed from the body.
[12] Probably the soul.    [13] The lady's.
[14] Bravado.

Much pleasure; then from thee much more
   must flow;        6
And soonest our best men with thee do go—
Rest of their bones and souls' delivery!
Thou'rt slave to fate, chance, kings, and des-
   perate men,
And dost with poison, war, and sickness dwell;
And poppy or charms can make us sleep as
   well        11
And better than thy stroke. Why swell'st thou
   then?
One short sleep past, we wake eternally,
And Death shall be no more: Death, thou
   shalt die!

## A Hymn to God the Father

Wilt thou forgive that sin where I begun,
   Which was my sin, though it were done be-
   fore?  15
Wilt thou forgive that sin through which I run,
   And do run still, though still I do deplore?
When thou hast done, thou hast not done;  5
   For I have more.

Wilt thou forgive that sin which I have won
   Others to sin, and made my sins their door?
Wilt thou forgive that sin which I did shun
   A year or two, but wallowed in a score?  10
When thou hast done, thou has not done;
   For I have more.

I have a sin of fear, that when I've spun
   My last thread, I shall perish on the shore;
But swear by thyself that at my death thy
   Son        15
   Shall shine as he shines now and heretofore;
And having done that, thou hast done;
   I fear no more.

# ROBERT HERRICK

## (1591–1674)

## The Argument of His Book

I sing of brooks, of blossoms, birds, and bowers,
Of April, May, of June and July-flowers;
I sing of May-poles, hock-carts, wassails,
   wakes,[1]
Of bridegrooms, brides, and of their bridal
   cakes;
I write of youth, of love, and have access  5
By these to sing of cleanly wantonness;
I sing of dews, of rains, and, piece by piece,
Of balm, of oil, of spice, and ambergris;
I sing of times trans-shifting, and I write
How roses first came red and lilies white;  10
I write of groves, of twilights, and I sing
The court of Mab, and of the Fairy King;

[15] Original sin, derived from Adam and Eve.
[1] A hock-cart is the last cart drawn from the field
at harvest. Wassail is a drinking-bout. Wake is a
merry-making or fair held annually by a parish.

I write of hell; I sing (and ever shall)
Of heaven, and hope to have it after all.

## Upon the Loss of His Mistresses

I have lost, and lately, these
Many dainty mistresses:
Stately Julia, prime of all;
Sapho next, a principal;
Smooth Anthea, for a skin  5
White and heaven-like crystalline;
Sweet Electra; and the choice
Myrha, for the lute and voice.
Next Corinna, for her wit,
And the graceful use of it;  10
With Perilla: all are gone;
Only Herrick's left alone,
For to number sorrow by
Their departures hence, and die.

## Cherry-Ripe

Cherry-ripe, ripe, ripe, I cry,
Full and fair ones; come and buy!
If so be you ask me where
They do grow, I answer, there
Where my Julia's lips do smile;  5
There's the land, or cherry-isle,
Whose plantations fully show
All the year where cherries grow.

## Delight in Disorder

A sweet disorder in the dress
Kindles in clothes a wantonness.
A lawn about the shoulders thrown
Into a fine distraction;
An erring lace, which here and there  5
Enthralls the crimson stomacher,[2]
A cuff neglectful, and thereby
Ribbons to flow confusedly;
A winning wave (deserving note)
In the tempestuous petticoat;  10
A careless shoe-string, in whose tie
I see a wild civility;—
Do more bewitch me than when art
Is too precise in every part.

## Corinna's Going A-Maying

Get up, get up for shame; the blooming morn
Upon her wings presents the god unshorn.
   See how Aurora throws her fair
   Fresh-quilted colors through the air:
   Get up, sweet slug-a-bed, and see  5
   The dew bespangling herb and tree.
Each flower has wept and bowéd toward the
   east

[2] Front-piece of woman's dress.

Above an hour since: yet you not dressed;
  Nay! not so much as out of bed?
  When all the birds have matins said    10
  And sung their thankful hymns, 'tis sin,
  Nay, profanation, to keep in,
Whenas a thousand virgins on this day
Spring, sooner than the lark, to fetch in May.

Rise, and put on your foliage, and be seen    15
To come forth, like the spring-time, fresh and
    green,
  And sweet as Flora.[3] Take no care
  For jewels for your gown or hair:
  Fear not; the leaves will strew
  Gems in abundance upon you:    20
Besides, the childhood of the day has kept,
Against you come, some orient pearls unwept;
  Come and receive them while the light
  Hangs on the dew-locks of the night:
  And Titan [4] on the eastern hill    25
  Retires himself, or else stands still
Till you come forth. Wash, dress, be brief in
    praying:
Few beads [5] are best when once we go
  a-Maying.

Come, my Corinna, come; and coming mark
How each field turns a street, each street a
    park    30
  Made green and trimmed with trees; see how
  Devotion gives each house a bough
  Or branch: each porch, each door ere this
  An ark, a tabernacle is,
Made up of white-thorn, neatly interwove;    35
As if here were those cooler shades of love.
  Can such delights be in the street
  And open fields and we not see 't?
  Come, we'll abroad; and let's obey
  The proclamation made for May:    40
And sin no more, as we have done, by staying;
But, my Corinna, come, let's go a-Maying.

There's not a budding boy or girl this day
But is got up, and gone to bring in May.
  A deal of youth, ere this, is come    45
  Back, and with white-thorn laden home.
  Some have dispatched their cakes and cream
  Before that we have left to dream:
And some have wept, and wooed, and plighted
    troth,
And chose their priest, ere we can cast off
    sloth:    50
  Many a green-gown [6] has been given;
  Many a kiss, both odd and even;
  Many a glance too has been sent
  From out the eye, love's firmament;
Many a jest told of the keys betraying    55
This night, and locks picked, yet we're not
  a-Maying.

Come, let us go while we are in our prime;
And take the harmless folly of the time.
  We shall grow old apace, and die
  Before we know our liberty.    60
  Our life is short, and our days run
  As fast away as does the sun;
And, as a vapor or a drop of rain,
Once lost, can ne'er be found again,
  So when or you or I are made    65
  A fable, song, or fleeting shade,
  All love, all liking, all delight
  Lies drowned with us in endless night.
Then while time serves, and we are but decay-
    ing,
Come, my Corinna, come let's go a-Maying. 70

## To the Virgins to Make Much of Time

Gather ye rosebuds while ye may;
  Old Time is still a-flying;
And this same flower that smiles to-day
  To-morrow will be dying.

The glorious lamp of heaven, the sun,    5
  The higher he's a-getting,
The sooner will his race be run,
  And nearer he's to setting.

That age is best which is the first,
  When youth and blood are warmer;    10
But being spent, the worse and worst
  Times still succeed the former.

Then be not coy, but use your time,
  And while ye may, go marry;
For, having lost but once your prime,    15
  You may forever tarry.

## To Music, to Becalm His Fever

Charm me asleep, and melt me so
  With thy delicious numbers
That, being ravished, hence I go
  Away in easy slumbers.
Ease my sick head,    5
And make my bed,
  Thou power that canst sever
From me this ill;
And quickly still,
Though thou not kill,    10
  My fever.

Thou sweetly canst convert the same
  From a consuming fire
Into a gentle-licking flame,
  And make it thus expire.    15
Then make me weep
My pains asleep,
  And give me such reposes
That I, poor I,
May think, thereby,    20

---

[3] Goddess of flowers.    [4] The sun.
[5] Prayers.    [6] Many a tumble on the grass.

I live and die
  'Mongst roses.

Fall on me like a silent dew,
  Or like those maiden showers,
Which, by the peep of day, do strew   25
  A baptism o'er the flowers.
Melt, melt my pains
With thy soft strains,
  That having ease me given,
With full delight   30
I leave this light,
And take my flight
  For heaven.

## To Anthea, Who May Command Him Anything

Bid me to live, and I will live
  Thy protestant [7] to be:
Or bid me love, and I will give
  A loving heart to thee.

A heart as soft, a heart as kind,   5
  A heart as sound and free
As in the whole world thou canst find,
  That heart I'll give to thee.

Bid that heart stay, and it will stay,
  To honor thy decree:   10
Or bid it languish quite away,
  And 't shall do so for thee.

Bid me to weep, and I will weep,
  While I have eyes to see:
And having none, yet I will keep   15
  A heart to weep for thee.

Bid me despair, and I'll despair,
  Under that cypress tree:
Or bid me die, and I will dare
  E'en death, to die for thee.   20

Thou art my life, my love, my heart,
  The very eyes of me,
And hast command of every part,
  To live and die for thee.

## Upon a Child That Died

Here she lies, a pretty bud,
Lately made of flesh and blood:
Who as soon fell fast asleep,
As her little eyes did peep.
Give her strewings, but not stir   5
The earth that lightly covers her.

## To Daffodils

Fair Daffodils, we weep to see
  You haste away so soon;

[7] Suitor.

As yet the early rising sun
  Has not attained his noon.
    Stay, stay,   5
Until the hasting day
    Has run
But to the even-song;
And, having prayed together, we
  Will go with you along.   10

We have short time to stay as you;
  We have as short a spring;
As quick a growth to meet decay
  As you, or anything.
    We die   15
As your hours do, and dry
    Away,
Like to the summer's rain;
Or as the pearls of morning's dew,
  Ne'er to be found again.   20

## To Daisies, Not to Shut So Soon

Shut not so soon; the dull-eyed night
  Has not as yet begun
To make a seizure on the light,
  Or to seal up the sun.

No marigolds yet closéd are,   5
  No shadows great appear;
Nor doth the early shepherd's star
  Shine like a spangle here.

Stay but till my Julia close
  Her life-begetting eye;   10
And let the whole world then dispose
  Itself to live or die.

## To Enjoy the Time

While fates permit us, let's be merry:
Pass all we must the fatal ferry;
And this our life too whirls away
With the rotation of the day.

## His Winding-Sheet

Come thou, who are the wine and wit
  Of all I've writ;
The grace, the glory, and the best
  Piece of the rest.
Thou art of what I did intend   5
  The all and end;
And what was made, was made to meet
  Thee, thee, my sheet.
Come then, and be to my chaste side
  Both bed and bride.   10
We two as relics left will have
  One rest, one grave;
And, hugging close, we will not fear
  Lust ent'ring here,
Where all desires are dead, or cold   15
  As is the mold,

And all affections are forgot,
  Or trouble not.
Here, here the slaves and pris'ners be
  From shackles free,                                    20
And weeping widows, long oppressed,
  Do here find rest.
The wrongéd client ends his laws
  Here, and his cause;
Here those long suits of chancery lie          25
  Quiet, or die,
And all star-chamber bills [8] do cease,
  Or hold their peace.
Here needs no court for our request,
  Where all are best,                                    30
All wise, all equal, and all just,
  Alike i' th' dust;
Nor need we here to fear the frown
  Of court, or crown;
Where fortune bears no sway o'er things,     35
  There all are kings.
In this securer place we'll keep,
  As lulled asleep;
Or for a little time we'll lie,
  As robes laid by,                                       40
To be another day re-worn,—
  Turned, but not torn;
Or like old testaments engrossed,[9]
  Locked up, not lost:
And for a while lie here concealed,            45
  To be revealed
Next at that great Platonic year,[10]
  And then meet here.

## Art above Nature. To Julia

When I behold a forest spread
With silken trees upon thy head,
And when I see that other dress
Of flowers set in comeliness;
When I behold another grace                     5
In the ascent of curious lace,
Which like a pinnacle doth show
The top, and the top-gallant too;
Then, when I see thy tresses bound
Into an oval, square, or round,                  10
And knit in knots far more than I
Can tell by tongue, or true-love tie;
Next, when those lawny films I see
Play with a wild civility,
And all those airy silks to flow,                 15
Alluring me, and tempting so:
I must confess, mine eye and heart
Dotes less on nature than on art.

## The Primrose

Ask me why I send you here
This sweet infanta of the year?

[8] Bills handled by the court which originally sat in
the Star Chamber at Westminster.
[9] Collected.
[10] The year in which everything will return to its
original state.

Ask me why I send to you
This primrose, thus bepearled with dew?
  I will whisper to your ears,                        5
The sweets of love are mixed with tears.
  Ask me why this flower does show
So yellow-green, and sickly too?
  Ask me why the stalk is weak
And bending, yet it doth not break?          10
  I will answer, these discover
What fainting hopes are in a lover.

## The Night-Piece, to Julia

Her eyes the glow-worm lend thee;
The shooting stars attend thee;
  And the elves also,
  Whose little eyes glow
Like the sparks of fire, befriend thee.        5

No Will-o'-th'-Wisp mis-light thee,
Nor snake nor slow-worm bite thee;
  But on, on thy way,
  Not making a stay,
Since ghost there's none to affright thee.   10

Let not the dark thee cumber;
What though the moon does slumber?
  The stars of the night
  Will lend thee their light,
Like tapers clear without number.              15

Then, Julia, let me woo thee,
Thus, thus, to come unto me:
  And when I shall meet
  Thy silvery feet
My soul I'll pour into thee.                       20

## To Electra

I dare not ask a kiss;
  I dare not beg a smile;
Lest having that or this,
  I might grow proud the while.

No, no, the utmost share                          5
  Of my desire shall be
Only to kiss that air
  That lately kisséd thee.

## Upon Julia's Clothes

Whenas in silks my Julia goes,
Then, then (methinks) how sweetly flows
That liquefaction of her clothes.

Next, when I cast mine eyes and see
That brave vibration each way free;           5
O how that glittering taketh me!

## An Ode for Ben Jonson

        Ah, Ben!
      Say how or when
    Shall we, thy guests,

Meet at those lyric feasts,
        Made at the Sun            5
The Dog, the Triple Tun; [11]
Where we such clusters had,
As made us nobly wild, not mad?
And yet each verse of thine
Out-did the meat, out-did the frolic wine. 10

        My Ben!
        Or come again,
        Or send to us
Thy wit's great overplus;
        But teach us yet            15
        Wisely to husband it,
        Lest we that talent spend;
And having once brought to an end
        That precious stock, the store     19
Of such a wit the world should have no more.

## Comfort to a Youth That Had Lost His Love

What needs complaints,
When she a place
Has with the race
    Of saints?
In endless mirth,            5
She thinks not on
What's said or done
    In earth.
She sees no tears,
Or any tone            10
Of thy deep groan
    She hears;
Nor does she mind,
Or think on't now,
That ever thou            15
    Wast kind.
But changed above,
She likes not there,
As she did here,
    Thy love,            20
Forbear therefore,
And lull asleep
Thy woes, and weep
    No more.

## His Litany, to the Holy Spirit

In the hour of my distress,
When temptations me oppress,
And when I my sins confess,
    Sweet Spirit, comfort me!

When I lie within my bed,            5
Sick in heart, and sick in head,
And with doubts discomforted,
    Sweet Spirit, comfort me!

When the house doth sigh and weep,
And the world is drowned in sleep,      10

[11] Names of London taverns.

Yet mine eyes the watch do keep,
    Sweet Spirit, comfort me!

When the artless doctor sees
No one hope, but of his fees,
And his skill runs on the lees,            15
    Sweet Spirit, comfort me!

When his potion and his pill
Has or none or little skill,
Meet for nothing but to kill,
    Sweet Spirit, comfort me!            20

When the passing-bell doth toll,
And the furies in a shoal
Come to fright a parting soul,
    Sweet Spirit, comfort me!

When the tapers now burn blue,            25
And the comforters are few,
And that number more than true,
    Sweet Spirit, comfort me!

When the priest his last hath prayed,
And I nod to what is said,            30
'Cause my speech is now decayed,
    Sweet Spirit, comfort me!

When, God knows, I'm tossed about,
Either with despair or doubt,
Yet before the glass be out,            35
    Sweet Spirit, comfort me!

When the Tempter me pursu'th
With the sins of all my youth,
And half damns me with untruth,
    Sweet Spirit, comfort me!            40

When the flames and hellish cries
Fright mine ears and fright mine eyes,
And all terrors me surprise,
    Sweet Spirit, comfort me!

When the judgment is revealed,            45
And that opened which was sealed,
When to thee I have appealed,
    Sweet Spirit, comfort me!

## A Grace for a Child

Here, a little child, I stand,
Heaving up my either hand:
Cold as paddocks [12] though they be,
Here I lift them up to thee,
For a benison to fall            5
On our meat, and on us all. Amen.

# GEORGE HERBERT

(1593–1633)

## The Collar

I struck the board, and cried, "No more; I will abroad!

[12] Toads.

What! shall I ever sigh and pine?
My lines [1] and life are free; free as the road,
  Loose as the wind, as large as store.[2]
    Shall I be still in suit?       5
Have I no harvest but a thorn
To let me blood, and not restore
What I have lost with cordial fruit?
    Sure there was wine
Before my sighs did dry it; there was corn   10
  Before my tears did drown it;
Is the year only lost to me?
  Have I no bays to crown it,
No flowers, no garlands gay? all blasted,
    All wasted?           15
  Not so, my heart, but there is fruit,
    And thou hast hands.
Recover all thy sigh-blown age
On double pleasures; leave thy cold dispute
Of what is fit and not; forsake thy cage,    20
    Thy rope of sands
Which petty thoughts have made, and made
  to thee
Good cable, to enforce and draw,
    And be thy law,
While thou didst wink [3] and wouldst not
  see.            25
    Away! take heed;
    I will abroad.
Call in thy death's head there, tie up thy fears;
    He that forbears
    To suit and serve his need      30
    Deserves his load."
But as I raved, and grew more fierce and wild
    At every word,
  Methought I heard one calling, "Child";
    And I replied, "My Lord."     35

## Discipline

Throw away thy rod;
Throw away thy wrath:
    O my God,
Take the gentle path.

For my heart's desire          5
Unto thine is bent:
    I aspire
To a full consent.[4]

Not a word or look
I affect to own,           10
    But by book,
And thy book alone.

Though I fail, I weep;
Though I halt in pace,
    Yet I creep        15
To the throne of grace.

Then let wrath remove;
Love will do the deed:

[1] Appointed lot.      [2] An abundance.
[3] Blink, or perhaps sleep.      [4] Harmony.

For with love
Stony hearts will bleed.       20

Love is swift of foot;
Love's a man of war,
    And can shoot,
And can hit from far.

Who can scape his bow?      25
That which wrought on thee,
    Brought thee low,
Needs must work on me.

Throw away thy rod;
Though man frailties hath,      30
    Thou art God:
Throw away thy wrath.

## The Pulley

  When God at first made man,
Having a glass of blessing standing by,
  "Let us," said he, "pour on him all we can:
Let the world's riches, which disperséd lie,
  Contract into a span."        5

  So Strength first made a way;
Then Beauty flowed; then Wisdom, Honor,
  Pleasure.
  When almost all was out, God made a stay,
Perceiving that alone, of all his treasure,
  Rest in the bottom lay.       10

  "For if I should," said he,
"Bestow this jewel on my creature,
  He would adore my gifts instead of me,
And rest in Nature, not the God of Nature;
  So both should losers be.     15

  "Yet let him keep the rest,
But keep them with repining restlessness;
  Let him be rich and weary, that at least,
If goodness lead him not, yet weariness
  May toss him to my breast."     20

## Love

Love bade me welcome; yet my soul drew back,
  Guilty of dust and sin.
But quick-eyed Love, observing me grow slack
  From my first entrance in,
Drew nearer to me, sweetly questioning,     5
  If I lacked anything.

"A guest," I answered, "worthy to be here";
  Love said, "You shall be he."
"I, the unkind, ungrateful? Ah, my dear,
  I cannot look on thee!"       10
Love took my hand and smiling did reply,
  "Who made the eyes but I?"

"Truth, Lord; but I have marred them: let my
  shame

Go where it doth deserve."
"And know you not," says Love, "who bore the
   blame?"                          15
   "My dear, then I will serve."
"You must sit down," says Love, "and taste
   my meat."
   So I did sit and eat.

# EDMUND WALLER

## (1606–1687)

## Go, Lovely Rose!

Go, lovely rose!
Tell her that wastes her time and me,
   That now she knows,
   When I resemble her to thee,
How sweet and fair she seems to be.    5

Tell her that's young,
And shuns to have her graces spied,
   That hadst thou sprung
   In deserts, where no men abide,
Thou must have uncommended died.   10

Small is the worth
Of beauty from the light retired;
   Bid her come forth,
   Suffer herself to be desired,
And not blush so to be admired.   15

Then die! that she
The common fate of all things rare
   May read in thee;
   How small a part of time they share
That are so wondrous sweet and fair!   20

# SIR JOHN SUCKLING

## (1609–1642)

## A Doubt of Martyrdom

O for some honest lover's ghost,
   Some kind unbodied post
      Sent from the shades below!
      I strangely long to know
Whether [1] the noble chaplets wear,   5
Those that their mistress' scorn did bear
      Or those that were used kindly.

For whatso'er they tell us here
   To make those sufferings dear,
      'Twill there, I fear, be found   10
      That to the being crowned
T' have loved alone will not suffice,
Unless we also have been wise
      And have our loves enjoyed.

What posture can we think him in   15
   That, here unloved, again

[1] Which.

Departs, and 's thither gone
      Where each sits by his own?
Or how can that Elysium be
Where I my mistress still must see   20
      Circled in other's arms?

For there the judges all are just,
   And Sophonisba [2] must
      Be his whom she held dear,
      Not his who loved her here.   25
The sweet Philoclea,[3] since she died,
Lies by her Pirocles his side,
      Not by Amphialus.

Some bays, perchance, or myrtle bough
   For difference crowns the brow   30
      Of those kind souls that were
      The noble martyrs here;
And if that be the only odds
(As who can tell?) ye kinder gods,
      Give me the woman here!   35

## The Constant Lover

Out upon it, I have loved
   Three whole days together!
And am like to love three more,
   If it prove fair weather.

Time shalt molt away his wings   5
   Ere he shall discover
In the whole wide world again
   Such a constant lover.

But the spite on't is, no praise
   Is due at all to me:   10
Love with me had made no stays,
   Had it any been but she.

Had it any been but she,
   And that very face,
There had been at least ere this   15
   A dozen dozen in her place.

## Why So Pale and Wan?

Why so pale and wan, fond lover?
   Prithee, why so pale?
Will, when looking well can't move her,
   Looking ill prevail?
   Prithee, why so pale?   5

Why so dull and mute, young sinner?
   Prithee, why so mute?
Will, when speaking well can't win her,
   Saying nothing do 't?
   Prithee, why so mute?   10

[2] A Carthaginian. She was betrothed to a Numidian prince but married another; later, however, she married the Numidian when he conquered her husband.
[3] Philoclea and the two following are characters in Sir Philip Sidney's *Arcadia*.

Quit, quit for shame! This will not move;
 This cannot take her.
If of herself she will not love,
 Nothing can make her:
 The devil take her!      15

# RICHARD LOVELACE

## (1618–1658)

### To Althea, from Prison

When Love with unconfinéd wings
 Hovers within my gates,
And my divine Althea brings
 To whisper at the grates;
When I lie tangled in her hair      5
 And fettered to her eye,
The birds that wanton in the air
 Know no such liberty.

When flowing cups ran swiftly round
 With no allaying Thames,      10
Our careless heads with roses bound,
 Our hearts with loyal flames;
When thirsty grief in wine we steep,
 When healths and draughts go free,
Fishes that tipple in the deep      15
 Know no such liberty.

When, like committed [1] linnets, I
 With shriller throat will sing
The sweetness, mercy, majesty,
 And glories of my king;      20
When I shall voice aloud how good
 He is, how great should be,
Enlargéd winds, that curl the flood,
 Know no such liberty.

Stone walls do not a prison make,      25
 Nor iron bars a cage;
Minds innocent and quiet take
 That for an hermitage;
If I have freedom in my love
 And in my soul am free,      30
Angels alone, that soar above,
 Enjoy such liberty.

# ANDREW MARVELL

## (1621–1678)

### An Horatian Ode upon Crom-well's Return from Ireland

The forward youth that would appear
Must now forsake his muses dear,
 Nor in the shadows sing
 His numbers languishing:

'Tis time to leave the books in dust,      5
And oil the unused armor's rust,

[1] Confined.

Removing from the wall
The corselet of the hall.

So restless Cromwell would not cease
In the inglorious arts of peace,      10
 But through adventurous war
 Urgéd his active star;

And, like the three-forked lightning, first
Breaking the clouds where it was nursed,
 Did thorough his own side      15
 His fiery way divide,[1]

For 'tis all one to courage high,
The emulous, or enemy,
 And with such to enclose
 Is more than to oppose.      20

Then burning through the air he went,
And palaces and temples rent;
 And Caesar's [2] head at last
 Did through his laurels [3] blast.

'Tis madness to resist or blame      25
The face of angry heaven's flame;
 And if we would speak true,
 Much to the man is due

Who from his private gardens, where
He lived reservéd and austere,      30
 As if his highest plot
 To plant the bergamot,[4]

Could by industrious valor climb
To ruin the great work of Time,
 And cast the kingdoms old,      35
 Into another mold,

Though Justice against Fate complain,
And plead the ancient rights in vain;
 But those do hold or break,
 As men are strong or weak.      40

Nature, that hateth emptiness,
Allows of penetration less,
 And therefore must make room
 Where greater spirits come.

What field of all the civil war      45
Where his were not the deepest scar?
 And Hampton [5] shows what part
 He had of wiser art;

Where, twining subtle fears with hope,
He wove a net of such a scope      50

[1] The allusion is to differences which arose between the Puritan army and the Puritan parliament —differences which Cromwell forcibly resolved by bringing the army to London.
[2] Charles I's.   [3] Spite of his crown.
[4] A variety of pear.
[5] Hampton Court. Marvell shared the belief of other contemporaries (as the following lines show) that Cromwell tacitly abetted Charles I's flight from Hampton Court to Carisbrooke Castle.

That Charles himself might chase
To Caresbrooke's narrow case,

That thence the royal actor borne
The tragic scaffold might adorn,
   While round the arméd bands    55
   Did clap their bloody hands.

He [6] nothing common did, or mean,
Upon that memorable scene,
   But with his keener eye
   The ax's edge did try;    60

Nor called the gods with vulgar spite
To vindicate his helpless right,
   But bowed his comely head
   Down, as upon a bed.

This was that memorable hour    65
Which first assured the forcéd power;
   So, when they did design
   The capitol's first line,

A bleeding head, where they begun,
Did fright the architects to run; [7]    70
   And yet in that the state
   Foresaw its happy fate.

And now the Irish are ashamed
To see themselves in one year tamed;
   So much one man can do,    75
   That does both act and know.

They can affirm his praises best,
And have, though overcome, confessed
   How good he is, how just,
   And fit for highest trust;    80

Nor yet grown stiffer with command,
But still in the republic's hand,
   How fit he is to sway
   That can so well obey!

He to the Common's feet presents    85
A kingdom [8] for his first year's rents;
   And, what he may, forbears
   His fame, to make it theirs;

And has his sword and spoils ungirt,
To lay them at the public's skirt:    90
   So when the falcon high
   Falls heavy from the sky,

She, having killed, no more doth search,
But on the next green bough to perch;
   Where, when he first does lure,    95
   The falconer has her sure.

What may not then our isle presume,
While victory his crest does plume?

[6] Charles I.
[7] Pliny tells this story (*Natural History*, XXVIII, 4).
[8] Ireland.

What may not others fear,
If thus he crowns each year?    100

As Caesar he, ere long, to Gaul,
To Italy a Hannibal,
   And to all states not free
   Shall climacteric be.[9]

The Pict [10] no shelter now shall find    105
Within his parti-colored [11] mind,
   But, from this valor sad,[12]
   Shrink underneath the plaid;

Happy if in the tufted brake
The English hunter him mistake,    110
   Nor lay his hounds in [13] near
   The Caledonian deer.

But thou, the war's and Fortune's son,
March undefatigably on;
   And for the least effect,    115
   Still keep the sword erect;

Besides the force it has to fright
The spirits of the shady night,
   The same arts that did gain
   A power must it maintain.    120

## Bermudas [14]

Where the remote Bermudas ride,
In the ocean's bosom unespied,
From a small boat that rowed along
The listening winds received this song:

"What should we do but sing his praise    5
That led us through the watery maze,
Unto an isle so long unknown,
And yet far kinder than our own?
Where he the huge sea-monsters wracks,
That lift the deep upon their backs,    10
He lands us on a grassy stage,
Safe from the storms' and prelates' rage.
He gave us this eternal spring,
Which here enamels everything,
And sends the fowls to us in care,    15
On daily visits through the air;
He hangs in shades the orange bright,
Like golden lamps in a green night,
And does in the pomegranates close
Jewels more rich than Ormus [15] shows;    20
He makes the figs our mouths to meet,
And throws the melons at our feet,

[9] Shall be a dangerous menace.
[10] The Scot.
[11] I. e., fickle.    [12] Resolute; sober.
[13] Put his hounds on the scent.
[14] The Bermudas were settled early in the seventeenth century by Englishmen, who, like those who came to New England, sought to escape tyranny at home.
[15] An island in the Persian Gulf.

But apples [16] plants of such a price
No tree could ever bear them twice;
With cedars chosen by his hand     25
From Lebanon he stores the land,
And makes the hollow seas, that roar,
Proclaim the ambergris on shore;
He cast (of which we rather boast)
The Gospel's pearl upon our coast,     30
And in these rocks for us did frame
A temple, where to sound his name.
Oh! let our voice his praise exalt,
Till it arrive at heaven's vault,
Which, thence (perhaps) rebounding, may     35
Echo beyond the Mexique Bay."

Thus sung they, in the English boat,
A holy and a cheerful note,
And all the way, to guide their chime,
With falling oars they kept the time.     40

## To His Coy Mistress

Had we but world enough, and time,
This coyness, Lady, were no crime;
We would sit down and think which way
To walk and pass our long love's day.
Thou by the Indian Ganges' side     5
Shouldst rubies find; I by the tide
Of Humber would complain. I would
Love you ten years before the Flood,
And you should, if you please, refuse
Till the conversion of the Jews.     10
My vegetable love should grow
Vaster than empires, and more slow;
An hundred years should go to praise
Thine eyes and on thy forehead gaze;
Two hundred to adore each breast,     15
But thirty thousand to the rest;
An age at least to every part,
And the last age should show your heart.
For, Lady, you deserve this state,
Nor would I love at lower rate.     20
    But at my back I always hear
Time's wingéd chariot hurrying near;
And yonder all before us lie
Deserts of vast eternity.
Thy beauty shall no more be found,     25
Nor, in thy marble vault, shall sound
My echoing song; then worms shall try
That long preserved virginity,
And your quaint honor turn to dust,
And into ashes all my lust:     30
The grave's a fine and private place,
But none, I think, do there embrace.
    Now therefore, while the youthful hue
Sits on thy skin like morning dew,
And while thy willing soul transpires     35
At every pore with instant fires,
Now let us sport us while we may,
And now, like amorous birds of prey,
Rather at once our time devour

[16] Pineapples.

Than languish in his slow-chapt [17] power.  40
Let us roll all our strength and all
Our sweetness up into one ball,
And tear our pleasures with rough strife
Thorough the iron gates of life:
Thus, though we cannot make our sun     45
Stand still, yet we will make him run.

# HENRY VAUGHAN

## (1622–1695)

## The World [1]

I saw Eternity the other night,
Like a great ring of pure and endless [2] light,
    All calm as it was bright;
And round beneath it, Time, in hours, days,
    years,
        Driv'n by the spheres,     5
Like a vast shadow moved; in which the world
    And all her train were hurled.
The doting lover in his quaintest strain
    Did there complain;
Near him, his lute, his fancy, and his flights,
    Wit's four delights,     11
With gloves, and knots,[3] the silly snares of
    pleasure,
        Yet his dear treasure,
All scattered lay, while he his eyes did pour
    Upon a flower.     15

The darksome statesman, hung with weights
    and woe,
Like a thick midnight-fog, moved there so slow,
    He did not stay, nor go;
Condemning thoughts, like sad eclipses, scowl
    Upon his soul,     20
And clouds of crying witnesses without
    Pursued him with one shout.
Yet digged the mole, and lest his ways be
    found,
        Worked under ground,
Where he did clutch his prey; but one did see
    That policy: [4]     26
Churches and altars fed him; perjuries
    Were gnats and flies;
It rained about him blood and tears, but he
    Drank them as free.[5]     30

The fearful miser on a heap of rust
Sat pining all his life there, did scarce trust
    His own hands with the dust,
Yet would not place one piece above,[6] but lives
    In fear of thieves.     35

[17] Slow-devouring (a chap is a jaw).
[1] Vaughan printed I John, 2:16–17, at the end of
this poem.
[2] Endless not only in time but also, being a ring,
in space.
[3] Love-knots.          [4] Craft.
[5] As freely as if it had not rained blood and tears.
[6] In heaven.

Thousands there were as frantic as himself,
    And hugged each one his pelf;
The downright epicure placed heaven in sense,
    And scorned pretense;
While others, slipt into a wide excess,    40
    Said little less;
The weaker sort, slight, trivial wares enslave,
    Who think them brave;
And poor, despiséd Truth sat counting by
    Their victory.    45

Yet some, who all this while did weep and sing,
And sing and weep, soared up into the ring;
    But most would use no wing.
O fools, said I, thus to prefer dark night
    Before true light!    50
To live in grots and caves, and hate the day
    Because it shows the way,
The way, which from this dead and dark abode
    Leads up to God;
A way where you might tread the sun, and be  55
    More bright than he!
But, as I did their madness so discuss,
    One whispered thus,
"This ring the Bridegroom did for none provide
    But for his bride."    60

## The Retreat

Happy those early days, when I
Shined in my angel-infancy!
Before I understood this place
Appointed for my second race,
Or taught my soul to fancy aught    5
But a white, celestial thought;
When yet I had not walked above
A mile or two from my first love,
And looking back at that short space,
Could see a glimpse of his bright face;    10
When on some gilded cloud or flower
My gazing soul would dwell an hour,
And in those weaker glories spy
Some shadows of eternity;
Before I taught my tongue to wound    15
My conscience with a sinful sound,
Or had the black art to dispense,
A several sin to every sense,
But felt through all this fleshly dress
Bright shoots of everlastingness.    20
  O, how I long to travel back,
And tread again that ancient track,
That I might once more reach that plain,
Where first I felt my glorious train;
From whence th' enlightened spirit sees    25
That shady city of palm trees.[7]
But ah! my soul with too much stay
Is drunk, and staggers in the way!
Some men a forward motion love,
But I by backward steps would move;    30
And when this dust falls to the urn,
In that state I came, return.

[7] I. e., Jericho.

## Man

Weighing the steadfastness and state
    Of some mean things which here below
        reside,
Where birds like watchful clocks the noiseless
        date
    And intercourse of times divide,
Where bees at night get home and hive, and
        flowers    5
    Early, as well as late,
Rise with the sun, and set in the same bowers;

I would (said I) my God would give
The staidness of these things to man! for these
To his divine appointments ever cleave,    10
    And no new business breaks their peace;
The birds nor sow, nor reap, yet sup and dine;
    The flowers without clothes live,
Yet Solomon was never dressed so fine.

Man hath still either toys, or care;    15
He hath no root, nor to one place is tied,
But ever restless and irregular
    About this earth doth run and ride;
He knows he hath a home, but scarce knows
        where;
    He says it is so far    20
That he hath quite forgot how to go there.

He knocks at all doors, strays and roams,
Nay hath not so much wit as some stones [8]
        have
Which in the darkest nights point to their
        homes,
    By some hid sense their Maker gave;    25
Man is the shuttle, to whose winding quest
    And passage through these looms
God ordered motion, but ordained no rest.

## Ascension Hymn

They are all gone into the world of light!
    And I alone sit ling'ring here;
Their very memory is fair and bright,
    And my sad thoughts doth clear.

It glows and glitters in my cloudy breast    5
    Like stars upon some gloomy grove,
Or those faint beams in which this hill is drest,
    After the sun's remove.

I see them walking in an air of glory,
    Whose light doth trample on my days:    10
My days, which are at best but dull and hoary,
    Mere glimmering and decays.

O holy hope! and high humility,
    High as the heavens above!

[8] Loadstones.

These are your walks, and you have showed
  them me                                    15
To kindle my cold love.

Dear, beauteous death! the jewel of the just,
  Shining nowhere, but in the dark;
What mysteries do lie beyond thy dust;
  Could man outlook that mark!              20

He that hath found some fledged bird's nest
  may know
At first sight, if the bird be flown;
But what fair well [9] or grove he sings in now,
  That is to him unknown.

And yet, as angels in some brighter dreams [25]
  Call to the soul, when man doth sleep:
So some strange thoughts transcend our wonted
  themes,
  And into glory peep.

If a star were confined into a tomb,
  Her captive flames must needs burn there; [30]
But when the hand that locked her up gives
  room,
  She'll shine through all the sphere.

O Father of eternal life, and all
  Created glories under thee!
Resume [10] thy spirit from this world of thrall
  Into true liberty.                        36

Either disperse these mists, which blot and fill
  My perspective still as they pass,
Or else remove me hence unto that hill,
  Where I shall need no glass.              40

## The Waterfall

With what deep murmurs through time's silent
  stealth

[9] Spring or fountain.
[10] Take back to thyself.

Doth thy transparent, cool, and wat'ry wealth
  Here flowing fall,
  And chide, and call,
As if his liquid, loose retinue stayed        5
Ling'ring, and were of this steep place afraid;
  The common pass
  Where, clear as glass,
  All must descend
  Not to an end,                            10
But, quickened by this deep and rocky grave,
Rise to a longer course more bright and brave.

Dear stream! dear bank, where often I
Have sat, and pleased my pensive eye:
Why, since each drop of thy quick store [15]
Runs thither, whence it flowed before,
Should poor souls fear a shade or night,
Who came, sure, from a sea of light?
Or since those drops are all sent back
So sure to thee, that none doth lack,        20
Why should frail flesh doubt any more
That what God takes, he'll not restore?

O useful element and clear!
My sacred wash and cleanser here,
My first consigner unto those               25
Fountains of life, where the Lamb goes! [11]
What sublime truths, and wholesome
  themes,
Lodge in thy mystical, deep streams!—
Such as dull man can never find
Unless that Spirit lead his mind,           30
Which first upon thy face did move,
And hatched all with his quick'ning love.
As this loud brook's incessant fall
In streaming rings restagnates all
Which reach by course the bank, and then    35
Are no more seen, just so pass men.
O my invisible estate,
My glorious liberty, still late!
Thou art the channel my soul seeks,
Not this with cataracts and creeks.         40

[11] I. e., in baptism.

# Sir Thomas Browne

## 1605 - 1682

Sir Thomas Browne was born on 19 October, 1605. His father was a London textile dealer. Browne was sent to Winchester School in 1616, and in 1623 he went to Oxford. He took his B. A. in 1626, his M. A. in 1629, and little else is known about his Oxford years. In 1630 he began a period of travel and study on the Continent, going first to Montpellier, in the south of France, then famous for its medical school. He continued his medical studies at Padua, and then at Leyden, where it is thought he obtained a medical degree. In 1633 he returned to England and settled himself near Halifax. He was made doctor of medicine at Oxford in 1637. Soon after this he began to practice medicine at Norwich, where he remained until his death. He married, in 1641, Dorothy Mileham, "a lady of such symmetrical proportion to her worthy husband, both in the graces of her body and mind, that they seemed to come together by a kind of natural magnetism." About 1635 Browne had written, "at leisurable hours," for his "private exercise and satisfaction," his famous confession of faith, the Religio Medici. He apparently had no intention of publishing this, but allowed friends to read it in manuscript and to make copies of it; and thus, being admired, it came to be widely known (there are at least five manuscripts of the book extant, or were in the early nineteenth century). The result was that in 1642 an unauthorized edition was printed from one of these copies and so quickly sold out that a second edition was printed within a few months. This troubled Browne because the book was about so serious a subject as religion, and was now being much more widely read, and not only read but criticized, in a form very different from that in which it had actually been written. The copy which reached the press was, Browne wrote, "most depraved," as the result of successive transcriptions, and so in 1643 he published as a kind of duty the first authorized edition of the book. The general

scandal of his profession, Browne said, might help to persuade the world that he had no religion at all, but it was not so. On the contrary he was disposed rather to wish, if for anything, for more curious tests of his faith than Christianity afforded. "Methinks," he says, "there be not impossibilities enough in religion for an active faith; the deepest mysteries ours contains have not only been illustrated, but maintained, by syllogism and the rule of reason. I love to lose myself in a mystery, to pursue my reason to an O altitudo! 'Tis my solitary recreation to pose my apprehension with those involved enigmas and riddles of the Trinity, with Incarnation, and Resurrection." In this Browne told the simple truth; a touch of mystery fired his mind and sent it soaring on its speculative way. Whatever was odd or strange was food for him, and he became one of the most curiously learned men of any age. At the same time his wide reading helped him to clothe his grave meditations in a style which for richness and dignity is not surpassed even by any other of the great prose-writers of his own century.

Browne was a royalist, but lived through the Civil War without, apparently, being much disturbed by outward events. In 1646 he published an eminently characteristic book, his Pseudodoxia Epidemica or Enquiries into very many received Tenets and commonly presumed Truths, which examined prove but Vulgar and Common Errors. Some years later certain urns were unearthed in Norfolk, which were exactly the sort of thing to set his mind in motion, and the result was that he wrote and, in 1658, published Hydriotaphia; in this essay the qualities of his mind and of his personality are finely exhibited. Two other works, A Letter to a Friend and Christian Morals, were not published until after his death. In 1671 Browne was knighted, in consequence of the singular modesty of the then mayor of Norwich. Charles II was visiting Norwich and proposed to confer knighthood on the mayor, who declined it and begged that it be conferred instead on Browne, as the citizen of Norwich who most deserved the honor.

The Works of Sir Thomas Browne *have been well edited by Geoffrey Keynes (London, 1928–1931). For an able essay on Browne, see Sir Leslie Stephen,* Hours in a Library, Second Series *(London, 1876). Browne's intellectual position has been treated by Basil Willey in* The Seventeenth Century Background; Studies in the Thought of the Age in Relation to Poetry and Religion *(London, 1934).*

# Hydriotaphia, Urn-Burial

## CHAPTER V

Now since these dead bones [1] have already out-lasted the living one of Methuselah, and in a yard under ground, and thin walls of clay, out-worn all the strong and specious buildings above it, and quietly rested under the drums and tramplings of three conquests: what prince can promise such diuturnity [2] unto his relics, or might not gladly say,

*Sic ego componi versus in ossa velim?* [3]

Time, which antiquates antiquities, and hath an art to make dust of all things, hath yet spared these minor monuments.

In vain we hope to be known by open and visible conservatories,[4] when to be unknown was the means of their continuation, and obscurity their protection. If they died by violent hands, and were thrust into their urns, these bones become considerable, and some old philosophers would honor them, whose souls they conceived most pure, which were thus snatched from their bodies, and to retain a stronger propension unto them; whereas they weariedly left a languishing corpse, and with faint desires of re-union. If they fell by long and aged decay, yet wrapped up in the bundle of time, they fall into indistinction,[5] and make but one blot

---

[1] The bones in the urns found near Walsingham, in northern Norfolk, which caused Browne to write *Hydriotaphia.* The essay as a whole, of which the last chapter is here reprinted, is a general account of ancient burial customs. The funeral urns, which modern antiquaries regard as of Saxon origin, merely served to bring Browne's learning into play and to set his mind in motion.

[2] Lastingness.

[3] Thus I should wish to be buried when turned to bones (Tibullus, III, ii, 26).

[4] Repositories.  [5] Obscurity.

---

with infants. If we begin to die when we live, and long life be but a prolongation of death, our life is a sad composition; we live with death, and die not in a moment. How many pulses made up the life of Methuselah, were work for Archimedes: common counters sum up the life of Moses his man.[6] Our days become considerable, like petty sums, by minute accumulations; where numerous fractions make up but small round numbers; and our days of a span long, make not one little finger.

If the nearness of our last necessity brought a nearer conformity into it, there were a happiness in hoary hairs, and no calamity in half-senses. But the long habit of living indisposeth us for dying; when avarice makes us the sport of death, when even David grew politicly cruel and Solomon could hardly be said to be the wisest of men. But many are too early old, and before the date of age. Adversity stretcheth our days, misery makes Alemena's nights,[7] and time hath no wings unto it. But the most tedious being is that which can unwish itself, content to be nothing, or never to have been, which was beyond the malcontent of Job, who cursed not the day of his life, but his nativity; content to have so far been, as to have a title to future being, although he had lived here but in an hidden state of life, and as it were an abortion.

What song the Syrens sang, or what name Achilles assumed when he hid himself among women, though puzzling questions,[8] are not beyond all conjecture. What time the persons of these ossuaries entered the famous nations of the dead, and slept with princes and counselors, might admit a wide solution. But who were the proprietaries of these bones, or what bodies these ashes made up, were a question above antiquarism; not to be resolved by man, nor easily perhaps by spirits, except we consult the provincial guardians, or tutelary observators.[9] Had they made as good provision for their names, as they have done for their relics, they had not so grossly erred in the art of perpetuation. But to subsist in bones, and be but pyramidally [10] extant, is a fallacy in duration. Vain ashes which in the oblivion of names, persons, times, and sexes, have found unto themselves a fruit-

---

[6] The allusion is to Psalms, 90:10, where the normal life of man is said to be 70 years.

[7] One night as long as three (Browne's note).

[8] Browne says in a note that these are two of the three questions which Tiberius put to grammarians.

[9] Protecting spirits of the place.

[10] After the manner of a mummy.

less continuation, and only arise unto late posterity, as emblems of mortal vanities, antidotes against pride, vain-glory, and madding vices. Pagan vain-glories, which thought the world might last for ever, had encouragement for ambition; and, finding no Atropos [11] unto the immortality of their names, were never damped with the necessity of oblivion. Even old ambitions had the advantage of ours, in the attempts of their vain-glories, who acting early, and before the probable meridian of time,[12] have by this time found great accomplishment of their designs, whereby the ancient heroes have already out-lasted their monuments and mechanical preservations. But in this latter scene of time, we cannot expect such mummies unto our memories, when ambition may fear the prophecy of Elias, and Charles the Fifth can never hope to live within two Methuselahs of Hector.

And therefore, restless unquiet for the diuturnity of our memories unto present considerations seems a vanity almost out of date, and superannuated piece of folly. We cannot hope to live so long in our names as some have done in their persons. One face of Janus holds no proportion unto the other. 'Tis too late to be ambitious. The great mutations of the world are acted, or time may be too short for our designs. To extend our memories by monuments, whose death we daily pray for, and whose duration we cannot hope without injury to our expectations in the advent of the last day, were a contradiction to our beliefs. We whose generations are ordained in this setting part of time, are providentially taken off from such imaginations; and, being necessitated to eye the remaining particle of futurity, are naturally constituted unto thoughts of the next world, and cannot excusably decline the consideration of that duration which maketh pyramids pillars of snow, and all that's past a moment.

Circles and right lines limit and close all bodies, and the mortal right-lined circle [13] must conclude and shut up all. There is no antidote against the opium of time, which temporally considereth all things: our fathers find their graves in our short memories, and sadly tell us how we may be buried in our survivors. Gravestones tell truth scarce forty years. Generations pass while some trees stand, and old families last not three oaks. To be read by bare inscriptions like many in Gruter,[14] to hope for eternity by enigmatical epithets or first letters of our names, to be studied by antiquaries, who we were, and have new names given us like many of the mummies, are cold consolations unto the students of perpetuity, even by everlasting languages.

To be content that times to come should only know there was such a man, not caring whether they know more of him, was a frigid ambition in Cardan;[15] disparaging his horoscopical inclination and judgment of himself. Who cares to subsist like Hippocrates' patients, or Achilles' horses in Homer, under naked nominations, without deserts and noble acts, which are the balsam [16] of our memories, the *entelechia* [17] and soul of our subsistences? To be nameless in worthy deeds exceeds an infamous history. The Canaanitish woman lives more happily without a name than Herodias with one. And who had not rather been the good thief than Pilate?

But the iniquity of oblivion blindly scattereth her poppy, and deals with the memory of men without distinction to merit of perpetuity. Who can but pity the founder of the pyramids? Herostratus lives that burned the temple of Diana; he is almost lost that built it. Time hath spared the epitaph of Adrian's horse, confounded that of himself. In vain we compute our felicities by the advantage of our good names, since bad have equal durations, and Thersites is like to live as long as Agamemnon. Who knows whether the best of men be known, or whether there be not more remarkable persons forgot than any that stand remembered in the known account of time? Without the favor of the everlasting register, the first man had been as unknown as the last, and Methuselah's long life had been his only chronicle.

Oblivion is not to be hired. The greater part must be content to be as though they had not been, to be found in the register of God, not in the record of man. Twenty-seven names make up the first story,[18] and the recorded names ever since contain not one living century. The number of the dead long exceedeth all that shall live. The night of time far surpasseth the day, and who knows when was the equinox? Every hour

---

[11] One of the Fates. She cut the thread of life.
[12] Noon of the world's life.
[13] The Greek letter $\theta$, which stands for $\theta\acute{\alpha}\nu\alpha\tau\sigma\varsigma$, or death.

[14] A Dutch philologer.
[15] An Italian mathematician, physician, and philosopher.
[16] Preservative.    [17] Entelechy, actual existence.
[18] The time before the Flood.

adds unto that current arithmetic,[19] which scarce stands one moment. And since death must be the Lucina [20] of life, and even Pagans could doubt whether thus to live were to die; since our longest sun sets at right descensions, and makes but winter arches, and therefore it cannot be long before we lie down in darkness, and have our light in ashes; since the brother of death daily haunts us with dying mementos, and time, that grows old in itself, bids us hope no long duration;—diuturnity is a dream and folly of expectation.

Darkness and light divide the course of time, and oblivion shares with memory a great part even of our living beings; we slightly remember our felicities, and the smartest strokes of affliction leave but short smart upon us. Sense endureth no extremities, and sorrows destroy us or themselves. To weep into stones are fables. Afflictions induce callosities;[21] miseries are slippery, or fall like snow upon us, which notwithstanding is no unhappy stupidity. To be ignorant of evils to come, and forgetful of evils past, is a merciful provision in nature, whereby we digest the mixture of our few and evil days, and, our delivered senses not relapsing into cutting remembrances, our sorrows are not kept raw by the edge of repetitions. A great part of antiquity contented their hopes of subsistency with a transmigration of their souls,—a good way to continue their memories, while having the advantage of plural successions, they could not but act something remarkable in such variety of beings, and enjoying the fame of their passed selves, make accumulation of glory unto their last durations. Others, rather than be lost in the uncomfortable night of nothing, were content to recede into the common being, and make one particle of the public soul of all things, which was no more than to return into their unknown and divine original again. Egyptian ingenuity was more unsatisfied, contriving their bodies in sweet consistencies, to attend the return of their souls. But all was vanity, feeding the wind, and folly. The Egyptian mummies, which Cambyses or time hath spared, avarice now consumeth. Mummy is become merchandise,[22] Mizraim [23] cures wounds, and Pharaoh is sold for balsams.

In vain do individuals hope for immortality, or any patent from oblivion, in preservations below the moon; men have been deceived even in their flatteries above the sun, and studied conceits to perpetuate their names in heaven. The various cosmography of that part hath already varied the names of contrived constellations; Nimrod is lost in Orion, and Osyris in the Dog-star. While we look for incorruption in the heavens, we find they are but like the earth;—durable in their main bodies, alterable in their parts; whereof, beside comets and new stars, perspectives [24] begin to tell tales, and the spots that wander about the sun, with Phaëton's favor, would make clear conviction.

There is nothing strictly immortal but immortality. Whatever hath no beginning, may be confident of no end (all others have a dependent being and within the reach of destruction); which is the peculiar of that necessary Essence that cannot destroy itself; and the highest strain of omnipotency, to be so powerfully constituted as not to suffer even from the power of itself. But the sufficiency of Christian immortality frustrates all earthly glory, and the quality of either state after death makes a folly of posthumous memory. God who can only [25] destroy our souls, and had assured our resurrection, either of our bodies or names hath directly promised no duration. Wherein there is so much of chance, that the boldest expectants have found unhappy frustration; and to hold long subsistence, seems but a scape in oblivion.[26] But man is a noble animal, splendid in ashes, and pompous in the grave, solemnizing nativities and deaths with equal luster, nor omitting ceremonies of bravery in the infamy of his nature.

Life is a pure flame, and we live by an invisible sun within us. A small fire sufficeth for life; great flames seemed too little after death, while men vainly affected precious pyres, and to burn like Sardanapalus; but the wisdom of funeral laws found the folly of prodigal blazes, and reduced undoing fires unto the rule of sober obsequies, wherein few could be so mean as not to provide wood, pitch, a mourner, and an urn.

Five languages secured not the epitaph of Gordianus. The man of God lives longer without a tomb than any by one, invisibly interred by angels, and adjudged to obscurity, though not without some marks directing human discovery. Enoch and Elias, without either tomb

---

[19] That running account—i. e., continuously moving time.

[20] Goddess of childbirth.

[21] Cause insensibility.

[22] The substance of mummies was in use as a medicine in Browne's day and before.

[23] Hebrew name of Egypt.

[24] Telescopes.   [25] I. e., who only can.

[26] But a chance of escaping oblivion.

or burial, in an anomalous state of being, are the great examples of perpetuity, in their long and living memory, in strict account being still on this side death, and having a late part yet to act upon this stage of earth. If in the decretory term of the world,[27] we shall not all die but be changed, according to received translation, the last day will make but few graves; at least quick resurrections will anticipate lasting sepultures. Some graves will be opened before 'hey be quite closed, and Lazarus be no wonder. When many that feared to die shall groan that they can die but once, the dismal state is the second and living death, when life puts despair on the damned; when men shall wish the coverings of mountains, not of monuments, and annihilations shall be courted.

While some have studied monuments, others have studiously declined them, and some have been so vainly boisterous[28] that they durst not acknowledge their graves; wherein Alaricus seems most subtle, who had a river turned to hide his bones at the bottom. Even Sylla, that thought himself safe in his urn, could not prevent revenging tongues, and stones thrown at his monument. Happy are they whom privacy makes innocent, who deal so with men in this world that they are not afraid to meet them in the next; who, when they die, make no commotion among the dead, and are not touched with that poetical taunt of Isaiah.[29]

Pyramids, arches, obelisks, were but the irregularities of vain-glory, and wild enormities of ancient magnanimity. But the most magnanimous resolution rests in the Christian religion, which trampleth upon pride, and sits on the neck of ambition, humbly pursuing that infallible perpetuity unto which all others must diminish their diameters, and be poorly seen in angles of contingency.

Pious spirits who passed their days in raptures of futurity, made little more of this world than the world that was before it, while they lay obscure in the chaos of preordination, and night of their fore-beings. And if any have been so happy as truly to understand Christian annihilation, ecstasies, exolution, liquefaction, transformation, the kiss of the spouse, gustation of God, and ingression into the divine shadow,[30] they have already had an handsome anticipation of heaven; the glory of the world is surely over, and the earth in ashes unto them.

To subsist in lasting monuments, to live in their productions, to exist in their names and predicament of chimaeras,[31] was large satisfaction unto old expectations, and made one part of their Elysiums. But all this is nothing in the metaphysics of true belief. To live indeed, is to be again ourselves, which being not only an hope, but an evidence in noble believers, 'tis all one to lie in St. Innocents' church-yard, as in the sands of Egypt. Ready to be anything, in the ecstasy of being ever, and as content with six foot as the *moles* of Adrianus.[32]

*—tabesne cadavera solvat,*
*An rogus, haud refert.*[33]

[30] These terms are descriptive of the experiences of mystics.

[31] Condition of unfounded conceptions.

[32] The monument of Hadrian, now known in its altered form as the castle of St. Angelo.

[33] It matters not whether our bodies rot in the grave or are consumed by the funeral pyre (Lucan, *Pharsalia*, vii, 809–810).

---

[27] If at the day of judgment.    [28] Turbulent.
[29] Cf. Isaiah, 14:9, and following verses.

# Izaak Walton

## 1593 - 1683

Walton was born at Stafford on 9 August, 1593. Of his youth and education nothing is known—and indeed little enough is known of the whole course of his long life. He obeyed a text which he more than once used: "Study to be quiet, and to do your own business" (I Thessalonians, 4:11). He was in London by 1611, and in 1618 was admitted a "free brother" of the Ironmongers' Company. On 27 December, 1626, he married Rachel Floud of Canterbury, who died in 1640; in 1646 he married Anne Ken, a half-sister of Bishop Ken of Winchester, who bore him three children, of whom a daughter and a son survived him. Anne Walton died in 1662. George Morley, then Bishop of Worcester, later Bishop of Winchester, had appointed Walton his steward, and much of his time during his later years was spent at Farnham Castle, the bishop's residence. He died in his daughter's home in Winchester, 15 December, 1683.

Walton must have been from his youth interested in literature, and he must also have been, all his life, a reading man. He was besides, as everybody knows, a devoted fisherman. Guileless, simple, easy, charming, he had a genius for friendship, though—as his younger friend Charles Cotton said plainly—he was not everybody's friend: "My father Walton will be seen twice in no man's company he does not like, and likes none but such as he believes to be very honest men." Among these "very honest men" were Ben Jonson, Michael Drayton, John Hales of Eton, Henry King, Thomas Fuller, Sir Henry Wotton, and John Donne. And out of his friendships and "the contemplative man's recreation" issued Walton's unassuming and singularly perfect writings. His Life of Donne was published in 1640; eleven years later the Life of Wotton was published, and in 1653 appeared the first edition of The Compleat Angler. Walton modestly thought, "Most readers may receive so much pleasure or profit by it as may make it worthy the time of their perusal, if they be not very busy men." The Life of Hooker was first published in 1665, the Life of Herbert in 1670, and the Life of Bishop Sanderson in 1678.

Walton's writings have been conveniently gathered together in one volume, The Compleat Angler, The Lives of Donne, Wotton, Hooker, Herbert & Sanderson, with Love and Truth & Miscellaneous Writings, ed. Geoffrey Keynes (London, 1929). For Walton's life and personality see S. Martin, Isaak Walton and his Friends (London, 1904).

# The Compleat Angler,

*or*

## The Contemplative Man's Recreation

### CHAP. I

A Conference betwixt an ANGLER, a FALCONER, and a HUNTER, each commending his recreation

{ PISCATOR
{ VENATOR
{ AUCEPS [1]

PISC. You are well overtaken, Gentlemen! A good morning to you both; I have stretched my legs up Tottenham-hill to overtake you, hoping your business may occasion you towards Ware [2] this fine, fresh May morning.

VENAT. Sir, I, for my part, shall almost answer your hopes, for my purpose is to drink my morning's draught at the Thatched House in Hodsden; [3] and I think not to rest till I come thither, where I have appointed a friend or two to meet me: but for this Gentleman

[1] Angler, Hunter, Falconer.
[2] A market town about twenty miles north of London.
[3] Place on the road from London to Ware.

309

that you see with me, I know not how far he intends his journey; he came so lately into my company, that I have scarce had time to ask him the question.

AUCEPS. Sir, I shall by your favor bear you company as far as Theobalds, and there leave you; for then I turn up to a friend's house, who mews [4] a Hawk for me, which I now long to see.

VENAT. Sir, we are all so happy as to have a fine, fresh, cool morning; and I hope we shall each be the happier in the others' company. And, Gentlemen, that I may not lose yours, I shall either abate or amend my pace to enjoy it, knowing that (as the Italians say) Good company in a journey makes the way to seem the shorter.

AUCEPS. It may do so, Sir, with the help of good discourse, which, methinks, we may promise from you, that both look and speak so cheerfully: and for my part, I promise you, as an invitation to it, that I will be as free and openhearted as discretion will allow me to be with strangers.

VEN. And, Sir, I promise the like.

PISC. I am right glad to hear your answers, and, in confidence you speak the truth, I shall put on a boldness to ask you, Sir, whether business or pleasure caused you to be so early up, and walk so fast, for this other Gentleman hath declared he is going to see a Hawk, that a friend mews for him.

VEN. Sir, mine is a mixture of both, a little business and more pleasure; for I intend this day to do all my business, and then bestow another day or two in hunting the Otter, which a friend, that I go to meet, tells me is much pleasanter than any other chase whatsoever: howsoever, I mean to try it; for to-morrow morning we shall meet a pack of Otter-dogs of noble Mr. Sadler's, upon Amwell hill, who will be there so early, that they intend to prevent [5] the sun-rising.

PISC. Sir, my fortune has answered my desires, and my purpose is to bestow a day or two in helping to destroy some of those villainous vermin; for I hate them perfectly, because they love fish so well, or rather, because they destroy so much; indeed so much, that in my judgment all men that keep Otter-dogs ought to have pensions from the King, to encourage them to destroy the very breed of those base Otters, they do so much mischief.

VEN. But what say you to the Foxes of the Nation, would not you as willingly have them

destroyed? for doubtless they do as much mischief as Otters do.

PISC. Oh, Sir, if they do, it is not so much to me and my fraternity, as those base vermin the Otters do.

AUC. Why Sir, I pray, of what fraternity are you, that you are so angry with the poor Otter?

PISC. I am, Sir, a Brother of the Angle, and therefore an enemy to the Otter: for you are to note, that we Anglers all love one another, and therefore do I hate the Otter both for my own and for their sakes who are of my brotherhood.

VEN. And I am a lover of Hounds; I have followed many a pack of dogs many a mile, and heard many merry men make sport and scoff at Anglers.

AUC. And I profess myself a Falconer, and have heard many grave, serious men pity them, 'tis such a heavy, contemptible, dull recreation.

PISC. You know, Gentlemen, 'tis an easy thing to scoff at any Art or Recreation; a little wit mixed with ill nature, confidence, and malice, will do it; but though they often venture boldly, yet they are often caught, even in their own trap, according to that of Lucian, the father of the family of Scoffers.

Lucian, well skilled in scoffing, this hath writ,
Friend, that's your folly, which you think your wit:
This you vent oft, void both of wit and fear,
Meaning another, when yourself you jeer.

If to this you add what Solomon says of Scoffers, that they are abomination to mankind.[6] Let him that thinks fit be a Scoffer still; but I account them enemies to me, and to all that love virtue and Angling.

And for you that have heard many grave, serious men pity Anglers; let me tell you, Sir, there be many men that are by others taken to be serious, grave men, which we contemn and pity. Men that are taken to be grave, because Nature hath made them of a sour complexion, money-getting-men, men that spend all their time, first in getting, and next, in anxious care to keep it; men that are condemned to be rich, and then always busy or discontented: for these poor-rich-men, we Anglers pity them perfectly, and stand in no need to borrow their thoughts to think ourselves happy. No, no, Sir, we enjoy a contentedness above the reach of such dispositions, and as the learned and ingenuous Montaigne says, like himself, freely, "When my Cat and I entertain each other with mutual

---

[4] Confines during moulting.     [5] Anticipate.

[6] Proverbs, 24:9.

apish tricks (as playing with a garter) who knows but that I make my Cat more sport than she makes me? Shall I conclude her to be simple, that has her time to begin or refuse sportiveness as freely as I myself have? Nay, who knows but that it is a defect of my not understanding her language (for doubtless Cats talk and reason with one another) that we agree no better: and who knows but that she pities me for being no wiser, and laughs 10 and censures my folly, for making sport for her, when we play together?" [7]

Thus freely speaks Montaigne concerning Cats, and I hope I may take as great a liberty to blame any man, and laugh at him too, let him be never so serious, that hath not heard what Anglers can say in the justification of their Art and Recreation; which I may again tell you is so full of pleasure, that we need not borrow their thoughts, to think ourselves 20 happy.

VENAT. Sir, you have almost amazed me, for though I am no scoffer, yet I have, I pray let me speak it without offense, always looked upon Anglers as more patient and more simple men, than I fear I shall find you to be.

PISC. Sir, I hope you will not judge my earnestness to be impatience: and for my simplicity, if by that you mean a harmlessness, or that simplicity which was usually found in the 30 primitive Christians, who were, as most Anglers are, quiet men, and followers of peace; men that were so simply-wise, as not to sell their consciences to buy riches, and with them vexation and a fear to die, if you mean such simple men as lived in those times when there were fewer Lawyers; when men might have had a Lordship safely conveyed to them in a piece of parchment no bigger than your hand (though several sheets will not do it safely in 40 this wiser age); I say, Sir, if you take us Anglers to be such simple men as I have spoken of, then myself and those of my profession will be glad to be so understood: But if by simplicity you meant to express a general defect in those that profess and practice the excellent Art of Angling, I hope in time to disabuse you, and make the contrary appear so evidently, that if you will but have patience to hear me, I shall remove all the anticipations that dis- 50 course, or time, or prejudice, have possessed you with against that laudable and ancient art; for I know it is worthy the knowledge and practice of a wise man.

\*   \*   \*

[7] *Essays,* "Apology for Raymond Sebond."

## CHAP. IV [8]

*Observations of the nature and breeding of the Trout; and how to fish for him. And the Milkmaid's Song.*

PISC. The Trout is a fish highly valued both in this and foreign Nations: he may be justly said, (as the old Poet said of wine, and we English say of venison) to be a generous [9] fish: a fish that is so like the Buck that he also has his seasons; for it is observed, that he comes in and goes out of season with the Stag and Buck; Gesner [10] says, his name is of a German off-spring,[11] and says he is a fish that feeds clean and purely, in the swiftest streams, and on the hardest gravel; and that he may justly contend with all fresh-water-fish, as the Mullet may with all sea-fish, for precedency and daintiness of taste, and that being in right season, the most dainty palates have allowed precedency to him.

And before I go farther in my Discourse, let me tell you, that you are to observe, that as there be some barren Does, that are good in summer, so there be some barren Trouts that are good in winter, but there are not many that are so; for usually they be in their perfection in the month of May, and decline with the Buck. Now you are to take notice, that in several Countries, as in Germany and in other parts, compared to ours, fish do differ much in their bigness, and shape, and other ways, and so do Trouts; it is well known that in the Lake Leman (the Lake of Geneva) there are Trouts taken of three cubits long, as is affirmed by Gesner, a writer of good credit; and Mercator [12] says, the Trouts that are taken in the Lake of Geneva, are a great part of the merchandise of that famous city. And you are further to know, that there be certain waters that breed Trouts remarkable both for their number and smallness. I know a little brook in Kent, that breeds them to a number incredible, and you may take them twenty or forty in an hour, but none greater than about the size of a Gudgeon. There are also in divers

[8] Since Chapter I, a day has intervened during which Piscator has accompanied Venator in an otter hunt; and now on the third day Venator accompanies Piscator in his fishing.

[9] Of noble birth.

[10] Conrad Gesner (1516–1565), author of the *Historia Naturalis Animalium.*

[11] Origin.

[12] Gerard Mercator (1512–1594). Flemish geographer.

rivers, especially that relate to, or be near to the sea (as Winchester, or the Thames about Windsor) a little Trout called a Samlet or Skegger Trout (in both which places I have caught twenty or forty at a standing) that will bite as fast and as freely as Minnows; these be by some taken to be young Salmons, but in those waters they never grow to be bigger than a Herring.

There is also in Kent near to Canterbury, a Trout (called there a Fordidge Trout) a Trout (that bears the name of the town where it is usually caught) that is accounted the rarest of fish; many of them near the bigness of a Salmon, but known by their different color, and in their best season they cut very white; and none of these have been known to be caught with an Angle, unless it were one that was caught by Sir George Hastings (an excellent Angler, and now with God) and he hath told me, he thought that Trout bit not for hunger but wantonness; and it is the rather to be believed, because both he then, and many others before him, have been curious to search into their bellies, what the food was by which they lived; and have found out nothing by which they might satisfy their curiosity.

Concerning which you are to take notice, that it is reported by good authors, that there is a fish, that hath not any mouth, but lives by taking breath by the porings of her gills, and feeds and is nourished by no man knows what; and this may be believed of the Fordidge Trout, which (as it is said of the Stork, that he knows his season, so he) knows his times (I think almost his day) of coming into that river out of the sea, where he lives (and it is like, feeds) nine months of the year, and fasts three in the River of Fordidge. And you are to note, that the townsmen are very punctual in observing the very time of beginning to fish for them; and boast much that their river affords a Trout, that exceeds all others. And just so does Sussex boast of several fish; as namely, a Shelsey Cockle, a Chichester Lobster, an Arundel Mullet, and an Amerly Trout.

And now for some confirmation of the Fordidge Trout, you are to know that this Trout is thought to eat nothing in the fresh water; and it may be the better believed, because it is well known, that Swallows, which are not seen to fly in England for six months in the year, but about Michaelmas [13] leave us for a hotter climate; yet some of them that have been left behind their fellows, have been found (many thousands at a time) in hollow trees, where they have been observed to live and sleep out the whole winter without meat; and so Albertus [14] observes, that there is one kind of Frog that hath her mouth naturally shut up about the end of August, and that she lives so all the winter: and though it be strange to some, yet it is known to too many among us to be doubted.

And so much for these Fordidge trouts, which never afford an Angler sport, but either live their time of being in the fresh water, by their meat formerly gotten in the sea (not unlike the Swallow or Frog) or by the virtue of the fresh water only; or as the birds of Paradise, and the Chameleon are said to live by the sun and the air.

There is also in Northumberland a Trout called a Bull-trout, of a much greater length and bigness, than any in these Southern parts: and there are in many rivers that relate to the sea, Salmon-trouts, as much different from others, both in shape and in their spots, as we see sheep differ one from another in their shape and bigness, and in the fineness of their wool: and certainly, as some pastures do breed larger sheep, so do some rivers, by reason of the ground over which they run, breed larger Trouts.

Now the next thing that I will commend to your consideration is, that the Trout is of a more sudden growth than other fish: concerning which you are also to take notice, that he lives not so long as the Perch and divers other fishes do, as Sir Francis Bacon hath observed in his *History of Life and Death*.[15]

And next you are to take notice, that he is not like the Crocodile, which if he lives never so long, yet always thrives till his death: but 'tis not so with the Trout; for after he is come to his full growth, he declines in his body, but keeps his bigness or thrives only in his head till his death. And you are to know, that he will about (especially before) the time of his spawning, get almost miraculously through Weirs and Floodgates against the stream; even through such high and swift places as is almost incredible. Next, that the Trout usually spawns about October or November, but in some rivers a little sooner or later: which is the more observable, because most other fish spawn in the spring or summer, when the sun hath warmed both the earth and water, and made

[13] September 29.

[14] Albertus Magnus (d. 1280), whose observation Walton seems to have found in Edward Topsell's *Historie of Serpents* (1608).

[15] A part of the *History Naturall and Experimental*.

it fit for generation. And you are to note, that he continues many months out of season: for it may be observed of the Trout, that he is like the Buck or the Ox, that will not be fat in many months, though he go in the very same pastures that horses do, which will be fat in one month; and so you may observe, that most other fishes recover strength, and grow sooner fat, and in season than the Trout doth.

And next, you are to note, that till the sun gets to such a height as to warm the earth and the water, the Trout is sick and lean, and lousy, and unwholesome: for you shall in winter find him to have a big head, and then to be lank, and thin, and lean; at which time many of them have sticking on them Sugs, or Trout lice, which is a kind of a worm, in shape like a clove or pin with a big head, and sticks close to him and sucks his moisture; those, I think, the Trout breeds himself, and never thrives till he free himself from them, which is till warm weather comes; and then, as he grows stronger, he gets from the dead, still water, into the sharp streams, and the gravel, and there rubs off these worms or lice; and then, as he grows stronger, so he gets him into swifter and swifter streams, and there lies at the watch for any fly or Minnow, that comes near to him; and he especially loves the May-fly, which is bred of the Cod-worm, or Caddis; and these make the Trout bold and lusty, and he is usually fatter and better meat at the end of that month, than at any time of the year.

Now you are to know, that it is observed, that usually the best trouts are either red or yellow, though some (as the Fordidge Trout) be white and yet good; but that is not usual: and it is a note observable, that the female Trout hath usually a less head, and a deeper body than the male Trout; and is usually the better meat: and note that a hogback, and a little head to any fish, either Trout, Salmon, or other fish, is a sign that that fish is in season.

But yet you are to note, that as you see some Willows or palm-trees bud and blossom sooner than others do, so some Trouts be in rivers sooner in season; and as some Hollies or Oaks are longer before they cast their leaves, so are some Trouts, in some rivers, longer before they go out of season.

And you are to note, that there are several kinds of Trouts, though they all go under that general name; just as there be tame and wild Pigeons: and of tame, there be Cropers, Carriers, Runts, and too many to name, which all differ, and so do Trouts, in their bigness, shape, and color. The great Kentish Hens may be an instance, compared to other Hens; and doubtless there is a kind of small Trout, which will never thrive to be big, that breeds very many more than others do, that be of a larger size; which you may rather believe, if you consider, that the little Wren and Titmouse will have twenty young at a time, when usually the noble Hawk, or the Musical Throstle or Black-bird exceed not four or five.

And now I shall try my skill to catch a Trout, and at my next walking either this evening, or to-morrow morning, I will give you direction, how you yourself shall fish for him.

VENAT. Trust me, Master, I see now it is a harder matter to catch a Trout than a Chub: for I have put on patience, and followed you these two hours, and not seen a fish stir, neither at your Minnow nor your Worm.

PISC. Well, Scholar, you must endure worse luck sometime, or you will never make a good Angler. But what say you now? there is a Trout now, and a good one too, if I can but hold him, and two or three turns more will tire him: now you see he lies still, and the sleight is to land him: reach me that landing net. So, Sir, now he is mine own, what say you now? is not this worth all my labor and your patience?

VENAT. On my word, Master, this is a gallant Trout, what shall we do with him?

PISC. Marry, e'en eat him to supper: we'll go to my Hostess from whence we came; she told me, as I was going out of door, that my brother Peter, a good Angler and a cheerful companion, had sent word he would lodge there to-night, and bring a friend with him. My Hostess has two beds, and I know, you and I may have the best: we'll rejoice with my brother Peter and his friend, tell tales, or sing Ballads, or make a Catch,[16] or find some harmless sport to content us, and pass away a little time without offense to God or man.

VENAT. A match, good Master, let's go to that house for the linen looks white, and smells of lavender, and I long to lie in a pair of sheets that smell so: let's be going, good Master, for I am hungry again with fishing.

PISC. Nay, stay a little good Scholar, I caught my last Trout with a Worm, now I will put on a Minnow, and try a quarter of an hour about yonder trees for another, and so walk towards our lodging. Look you, Scholar, thereabout we shall have a bite presently, or not at all: have with you, Sir, on my word I have him! Oh, it is a great loggerheaded Chub; come, hang him upon that Willow-twig, and

[16] Song in which one singer catches up the words of another.

let's be going. But turn out of the way a little, Scholar, towards yonder high hedge; we'll sit whilst this shower falls so gently upon the teeming earth, and gives yet a sweeter smell to the lovely flowers that adorn these verdant meadows.

Look! under that broad Beech-tree, I sate down, when I was last this way a-fishing, and the birds in the adjoining grove seemed to have a friendly contention with an echo, whose dead 10 voice seemed to live in a hollow tree, near to the brow of that primrose-hill; there I sate viewing the silver streams glide silently towards their center, the tempestuous sea; yet, sometimes opposed by rugged roots, and pebble-stones, which broke their waves, and turned them into foam: and sometimes I beguiled time by viewing the harmless lambs, some leaping securely in the cool shade, whilst others sported themselves in the cheerful sun; and 20 saw others craving comfort from the swollen udders of their bleating dams. As I thus sate, these and other sights had so fully possessed my soul with content, that I thought as the Poet has happily expressed it:

I was for that time lifted above earth;
And possessed joys not promised in my birth.

As I left this place, and entered into the next field, a second pleasure entertained me, 'twas 30 a handsome Milkmaid that had cast away all care, and sung like a Nightingale: her voice was good, and the Ditty fitted for it; 'twas that smooth song, which was made by Kit. Marlowe, now at least fifty years ago: [17] and the Milkmaid's Mother sung an answer to it, which was made by Sir Walter Ralegh in his younger days.

They were old-fashioned Poetry, but choicely good, I think much better than the strong [18] 40 lines that are now in fashion in this critical age. Look yonder! on my word, yonder they both be a-milking again, I will give her the Chub, and persuade them to sing those two songs to us.

God speed you, good woman, I have been a-fishing, and am going to Bleak-Hall, to my bed, and having caught more fish than will sup myself and my friend, I will bestow this upon you and your Daughter; for I use to sell none.

MILK. Marry, God requite you, Sir, and 50 we'll eat it cheerfully: and if you come this way a-fishing two months hence, a grace of God

I'll give you a Sillybub [19] of new Verjuice in a new made Hay-cock, for it, and my Maudlin shall sing you one of her best Ballads, for she and I both love all Anglers, they be such honest, civil, quiet men; in the meantime will you drink a draught of Red-Cows milk, you shall have it freely.

PISC. No, I thank you, but I pray do us a courtesy that shall stand you and your daughter in nothing, and yet we will think ourselves still something in your debt: it is but to sing us a Song, that was sung by your daughter, when I last passed over this meadow, about eight or nine days since.

MILK. What Song was it, I pray? was it "Come, Shepherds, deck your herds," or "As at noon Dulcina rested," or "Phillida flouts me," or "Chevy Chase"? [20]

PISC. No, it is none of those: it is a Song that your daughter sung the first part, and you sung the answer to it.

MILK. Oh, I know it now, I learned the first part in my golden age, when I was about the age of my poor daughter; and the latter part, which indeed fits me best now, but two or three years ago, when the cares of the world began to take hold of me: but you shall, God willing, hear them both, and sung as well as we can, for we both love Anglers. Come, Maudlin, sing the first part to the Gentlemen, with a merry heart, and I'll sing the second, when you have done.

### THE MILKMAID'S SONG

Come live with me, and be my Love,
And we will all the pleasures prove
That valleys, groves, or hills, or fields,
Or woods, and steepy mountain yields.

Where we will sit upon the Rocks,
And see the Shepherds feed our flocks,
By shallow *Rivers*, to whose falls,
Melodious birds sing *Madrigals*.

And I will make thee beds of *Roses*,
And then a thousand fragrant Posies,
A Cap of flower, and a Kirtle,[21]
Embroidered all with leaves of myrtle.

A Gown made of the finest Wool
Which from our pretty Lambs we pull;
Slippers lined choicely for the cold,
With buckles of the purest gold.

A Belt of Straw, and Ivy-buds,
With Coral Clasps and Amber studs:
And if these pleasures may thee move,
Come live with me and be my Love.

---

[17] Marlowe had already been dead sixty years. His song, which the milkmaid sings, was first published over his name in *England's Helicon* (1600). Ralegh's satiric reply, sung by the milkmaid's mother, likewise appeared in that collection.

[18] Pointed.

[19] Drink of cream, curdled with some acidic admixture and then sweetened.

[20] All popular songs, the last the most famous of the ballads of the Scotch border.

[21] Skirt or outer petticoat.

Thy silver dishes for thy meat,
As precious as the Gods do eat,
Shall on an Ivory Table be
Prepared each day for thee and me.

The Shepherds' Swains shall dance and sing
For thy delight each May-morning:
If these delights thy mind may move,
Then live with me, and be my Love.

VENAT. Trust me, Master, it is a choice
Song, and sweetly sung by honest Maudlin. I
now see it was not without cause, that our
good Queen Elizabeth did so often wish herself
a Milkmaid all the month of May, because
they are not troubled with cares, but sing
sweetly all the day, and sleep securely all the
night: and without doubt, honest, innocent,
pretty Maudlin does so. I'll bestow Sir Thomas
Overbury's Milkmaid's wish upon her, That
she may die in the Spring, and have good store
of flowers stuck round about her winding
sheet.[22]

### THE MILKMAID'S MOTHER'S ANSWER

If all the world and Love were young,
And truth in every Shepherd's tongue,
These pretty pleasures might me move
To live with thee, and be thy Love.

But Time drives flocks from field to fold,
When Rivers rage, and rocks grow cold,
Then *Philomel* becometh dumb,
The Rest complains of care to come.

The flowers do fade, and wanton fields
To wayward Winter reckoning yields,
A honey tongue, a heart of gall,
Is fancy's spring, but sorrow's fall;

Thy gowns, thy shoes, thy beds of roses,
Thy cap, thy kirtle, and thy posies,
Soon break, soon wither, soon forgotten,
In folly ripe, in reason rotten.

Thy Belt of Straw, and Ivy-buds,
Thy Coral clasps, and Amber-studs,
All these in me no means can move
To come to thee, and be thy Love.

What should we talk of dainties then,
Of better meat than 's fit for men?
These are but vain: that's only good
Which God hath blest, and sent for food.

But could Youth last, and love still breed,
Had joys no date, nor age no need;
Then those delights my mind might move,
To live with thee, and be thy Love.

PISC. Well sung, good Woman, I thank you.
I'll give you another dish of fish one of these

[22] From Overbury's *Characters* (1615). The sketch of "A Fair and Happy Milkmaid," here quoted, is now thought to be the work of the dramatist, John Webster.

days; and then beg another song of you. Come, Scholar, let Maudlin alone: do not you offer to spoil her voice. Look, yonder comes mine Hostess, to call us to supper. How now? is my brother Peter come?

HOSTESS. Yes, and a friend with him, they are both glad to hear that you are in these parts, and long to see you, and are hungry, and long to be at supper.

## CHAP. VIII [23]

### *Observations of the Luce or Pike, with directions how to fish for him.*

PISC. The mighty Luce or Pike is taken to be the Tyrant (as the Salmon is the King) of the fresh waters. 'Tis not to be doubted, but that they are bred, some by generation, and some not: as namely, of a Weed called Pickerel-weed, unless learned Gesner be much mistaken; for he says, this weed and other glutinous matter, with the help of the sun's heat in some particular months, and some ponds apted for it by nature, do become Pikes. But doubtless divers Pikes are bred after this manner, or are brought into some ponds some other ways that is past man's finding out, of which we have daily testimonies.

Sir Francis Bacon, in his *History of Life and Death*, observes the Pike to be the longest lived of any fresh-water-fish, and yet he computes it to be not usually above forty years; and others think it to be not above ten years; and yet Gesner mentions a Pike taken in Swedeland in the year 1449 with a ring about his neck, declaring he was put into the pond by Frederick the second, more than two hundred years before he was last taken, as by the inscription of that ring (being Greek) was interpreted by the then Bishop of Worms. But of this no more, but that it is observed, that the old or very great Pikes have in them more of state than goodness; the smaller or middle sized Pikes being by the most and choicest palates observed to be the best meat; and contrary, the Eel is observed to be the better for age and bigness.

All Pikes that live long prove chargeable to their keepers, because their life is maintained by the death of so many other fish, even those of his own kind, which has made him by some writers to be called the Tyrant of the rivers, or the Fresh-water-wolf, by reason of his bold, greedy, devouring disposition; which is so keen,

[23] Piscator continues his explanations to Venator on the day following that of the milkmaid's song.

as Gesner relates, a man going to a pond (where it seems a Pike had devoured all the fish) to water his Mule, had a Pike bite his Mule by the lips; to which the Pike hung so fast, that the Mule drew him out of the water; and by that accident the owner of the Mule got the Pike. And the same Gesner observes, that a maid in Poland had a Pike bite her by the foot, as she was washing clothes in a pond. And I have heard the like of a woman in Kil- 10 lingworth Pond not far from Coventry. But I have been assured by my friend Mr. Segrave, of whom I spake to you formerly,[24] that keeps tame Otters, that he hath known a Pike in extreme hunger fight with one of his Otters for a Carp that the Otter had caught and was then bringing out of the water. I have told you who relates these things, and tell you they are persons of credit; and shall conclude this observation, by telling you what a wise man has 20 observed, It is a hard thing to persuade the belly, because it has no ears.

But if these relations be disbelieved, it is too evident to be doubted, that a Pike will devour a fish of his own kind, that shall be bigger than his belly or throat will receive, and swallow a part of him, and let the other part remain in his mouth till the swallowed part be digested, and then swallow that other part that was in his mouth, and so put it over by degrees; which 30 is not unlike the Ox and some other beasts, taking their meat not out of their mouth into their belly, but first into some place betwixt, and then chaw it, or digest it after, which is called Chewing the Cud. And doubtless Pikes will bite when they are not hungry, but as some think in very anger, when a tempting bait comes near to them.

And it is observed, that the Pike will eat venomous things (as some kind of Frogs are) 40 and yet live without being harmed by them: for, as some say, he has in him a natural Balsam or Antidote against all poison: and others, that he never eats the venomous Frog till he have first killed her, and then (as Ducks are observed to do to Frogs in spawning time, at which time some Frogs are observed to be venomous) so thoroughly washed her, by tumbling her up and down in the water, that he may devour her without danger. And Gesner affirms, 50 that a Polonian Gentleman, did faithfully assure him, he had seen two young Geese at one time in the belly of a Pike. And doubtless a Pike in his height of hunger will bite at and devour a dog that swims in a pond, and there have been examples of it, or the like; for as I

told you, The belly has no ears when hunger comes upon it.

The Pike is also observed to be a solitary, melancholy and a bold fish: melancholy, because he always swims or rests himself alone, and never swims in shoals or with company, as Roach and Dace, and most other fish do: and bold, because he fears not a shadow, or to see or be seen of anybody, as the Trout and Chub, and all other fish do.

And it is observed by Gesner, that the jawbones, and hearts, and galls of Pikes, are very medicinable for several diseases, or to stop blood, to abate fevers, to cure agues, to oppose or expel the infection of the plague, and to be many ways medicinable and useful for the good of Mankind; but he observes, that the biting of a Pike is venomous and hard to be cured.

And it is observed, that the Pike is a fish that breeds but once a year, and that other fish (as namely Loaches) do breed oftener: as we are certain tame Pigeons do almost every month, and yet the Hawk (a Bird of Prey, as the Pike is of Fish) breeds but once in twelve months: and you are to note, that his time of breeding or spawning is usually about the end of February, or somewhat later, in March, as the weather proves colder or warmer; and to note, that his manner of breeding is thus, a He and a She Pike will usually go together out of a river into some ditch or creek, and that there the Spawner casts her eggs, and the Milter [25] hovers over her all that time that she is casting her spawn, but touches her not.

I might say more of this, but it might be thought curiosity or worse, and shall therefore forbear it, and take up so much of your attention, as to tell you, that the best of Pikes are noted to be in rivers, next those in great ponds or meres, and the worst in small ponds.

But before I proceed further, I am to tell you that there is a great antipathy betwixt the Pike and some Frogs; and this may appear to the reader of Dubravius (a Bishop in Bohemia), who in his Book of Fish and Fishponds,[26] relates what, he says, he saw with his own eyes, and could not forbear to tell the reader. Which was:

As he and the Bishop Thurzo were walking by a large pond in Bohemia, they saw a Frog, when the Pike lay very sleepily and quiet by the shore side, leap upon his head, and the Frog having expressed malice or anger by his swollen cheeks and staring eyes, did stretch out his legs and embrace the Pike's head, and pres-

[24] In Chapter II, not included here.

[25] Male fish.

[26] Janus Dubravius Scala, *De Piscinis, etc.* (1559).

ently reached them to his eyes, tearing with them and his teeth those tender parts; the Pike moved with anguish, moves up and down the water, and rubs himself against weeds, and whatever he thought might quit him of his enemy; but all in vain, for the Frog did continue to ride triumphantly, and to bite and torment the Pike, till his strength failed, and then he sunk with the Pike to the bottom of the water; then presently the Frog appeared again at the top, and croaked, and seemed to rejoice like a Conqueror, and then presently retired to his secret hole. The Bishop, that had beheld the battle, called his fisherman to fetch his nets, and by all means to get the Pike that they might declare what had happened: and the Pike was drawn forth, and both his eyes eaten out, at which when they began to wonder, the Fisherman wished them to forbear, and assured them he was certain that Pikes were often so served.

I told this (which is to be read in the sixth chapter of the book of Dubravius), unto a friend, who replied, It was as improbable as to have the mouse scratch out the cat's eyes. But he did not consider, that there be fishing Frogs (which the Dalmatians call the Water-Devil) of which I might tell you as wonderful a story, but I shall tell you, that 'tis not to be doubted, but that there be some Frogs so fearful of the Water-snake, that, when they swim in a place in which they fear to meet with him, they get a reed across into their mouths, which if they two meet by accident, secures the frog from the strength and malice of the Snake, and note, that the frog swims the fastest.

And let me tell you, that as there be Water and Land-frogs, so there be Land and Water-Snakes. Concerning which take this observation, that the Land-snake breeds, and hatches her eggs, which become young snakes, in some old dunghill, or a like hot place; but the Water-snake, which is not venomous (and as I have been assured by a great observer of such secrets) does breed her young alive, which she does not then forsake, but bides with them, and in case of danger will take them all into her mouth and swim away from any apprehended danger, and then let them out again when she thinks all danger to be past; these be accidents that we Anglers sometimes see and often talk of.

But whither am I going? I had almost lost myself by remembering the Discourse of Dubravius. I will therefore stop here, and tell you according to my promise how to catch this fish.

His feeding is usually of fish or frogs, and sometimes a weed of his own called Pickerel-weed. Of which I told you some think some Pikes are bred; for they have observed, that where none have been put into ponds, yet they have there found many: and that there has been plenty of that weed in those ponds, and that that weed both breeds and feeds them; but whether those Pikes so bred will ever breed by generation as the others do, I shall leave to the disquisitions of men of more curiosity and leisure than I profess myself to have; and shall proceed to tell you that you may fish for a Pike, either with a ledger or a walking-bait; and you are to note, that I call that a ledger-bait, which is fixed, or made to rest in one certain place when you shall be absent; and I call that a walking-bait, which you take with you, and have ever in motion. Concerning which two, I shall give you this direction; that your ledger-bait is best to be a living bait, whether it be a fish or a frog; and that you may make them live the longer, you may, or indeed you must, take this course.

First, for your live bait of fish, a Roach or Dace is (I think) best and most tempting, and a Perch is the longest-lived on a hook, and having cut off his fin on his back, which may be done without hurting him, you must take your knife (which cannot be too sharp), and betwixt the head and the fin on the back, cut or make an incision, or such a scar, as you may put the arming wire of your hook into it, with as little bruising or hurting the fish as art and diligence will enable you to do; and so carrying your arming wire along his back, unto, or near the tail of your fish, betwixt the skin and the body of it, draw out that wire or arming of your hook at another scar near to his tail: then tie him about it with thread, but no harder than of necessity you must to prevent hurting the fish; and the better to avoid hurting the fish, some have a kind of probe to open the way, for the more easy entrance and passage of your wire or arming: but as for these, time, and a little experience will teach you better than I can by words; therefore I will for the present say no more of this, but come next to give you some directions, how to bait your hook with a frog.

VEN. But, good Master, did you not say even now, that some Frogs were venomous, and is it not dangerous to touch them?

PISC. Yes, but I will give you some rules or cautions concerning them: and first, you are to note, that there are two kinds of Frogs; that is to say (if I may so express myself), a flesh, and a fish-frog. By flesh-frogs, I mean frogs that breed and live on the land; and of these there be several sorts also and colors, some being peckled,[27] some greenish, some blackish, or brown: the green Frog, which is a small one, is, by Topsell taken to be venomous; and so is the padock, or Frog-padock, which usually keeps or breeds on the land, and is very large and bony, and big, especially the She frog of that kind; yet these will sometimes come into the water, but it is not often: and the land frogs are some of them observed by him, to breed by laying eggs: and others to breed of the slime and dust of the earth, and that in winter they turn to slime again, and that the next summer that very slime returns to be a living creature; this is the opinion of Pliny: And Cardanus undertakes to give a reason for the raining of Frogs: [28] but if it were in my power, it should rain none but water-Frogs, for those I think are not venomous, especially the right water-Frog, which about February or March breeds in ditches by slime, and blackish eggs in that slime: about which time of breeding the He and She frogs are observed to use divers somersaults, and to croak and make a noise, which the land-frog, or Padock-frog, never does. Now of these water-frogs, if you intend to fish with a frog for a Pike, you are to choose the yellowest that you can get, for that the Pike ever likes best. And thus use your frog, that he may continue long alive:

Put your hook into his mouth, which you may easily do from the middle of April till August, and then the frog's mouth grows up, and he continues so for at least six months without eating, but is sustained, none but he whose name is Wonderful, knows how: I say, put your hook, I mean the arming wire, through his mouth, and out at his gills, and then with a fine needle and silk sew the upper part of his leg with only one stitch to the arming wire of your hook, or tie the frog's leg above the upper joint, to the armed wire; and in so doing, use him as though you loved him, that is, harm him as little as you may possibly, that he may live the longer.

And now, having given you this direction for the baiting your ledger-hook with a live fish or frog, my next must be to tell you, how your hook thus baited must or may be used: and it is thus. Having fastened your hook to a line, which if it be not fourteen yards long, should not be less than twelve; you are to fasten that line to any bough near to a hole where a Pike is, or is likely to lie, or to have a haunt, and then wind your line on any forked stick, all your line, except half a yard of it or rather more, and split that forked stick with such a nick or notch at one end of it, as may keep the line from any more of it raveling from about the stick, than so much of it as you intended; and choose your forked stick to be of that bigness as may keep the fish or frog from pulling the forked stick under the water till the Pike bites, and then the Pike having pulled the line forth of the cleft or nick of that stick in which it was gently fastened, will have line enough to go to his hold and pouch the bait: and if you would have this ledger-bait to keep at a fixed place, undisturbed by wind or other accidents which may drive it to the shore side (for you are to note, that it is likeliest to catch a Pike in the midst of the water), then hang a small plummet of lead, a stone, or piece of tile, or a turf in a string, and cast it into the water, with the forked stick, to hang upon the ground, to be a kind of anchor to keep the forked stick from moving out of your intended place till the Pike come. This I take to be a very good way, to use so many ledger-baits as you intend to make trial of.

Or if you bait your hooks thus with live fish or frogs, and in a windy day, fasten them thus to a bough or bundle of straw, and by the help of that wind can get them to move cross a pond or mere, you are like to stand still on the shore and see sport, if there be any store of Pikes; or these live baits may make sport, being tied about the body or wings of a Goose or Duck, and she chased over a pond: and the like may be done with turning three or four live baits thus fastened to bladders, or boughs, or bottles of hay or flags,[29] to swim down a river, whilst you walk quietly alone on the shore, and are still in expectation of sport. The rest must be taught you by practice, for time will not allow me to say more of this kind of fishing with live baits.

And for your dead bait for a Pike, for that you may be taught by one day's going a-fishing with me, or any other body that fishes for him, for the baiting your hook with a dead Gudgeon or a Roach, and moving it up and down the water, is too easy a thing to take up any time to direct you to do it; and yet, because I cut you short in that, I will commute [30] for it, by telling you that that was told me for a secret; it is this:

Dissolve Gum of Ivy in Oil of Spike, and

---

[27] Speckled.
[28] Jerome Cardan (1501–1576) in *De Subtilitate* (1551).

[29] Bundles of hay or turf.          [30] Compound.

therewith anoint your dead bait for a Pike, and then cast it into a likely place, and when it has lain a short time at the bottom, draw it towards the top of the water and so up the stream, and it is more than likely that you have a Pike follow with more than common eagerness.

And some affirm, that any bait anointed with the marrow of the thigh-bone of an Heron is a great temptation to any fish.

These have not been tried by me, but told me by a friend of note, that pretended to do me a courtesy, but if this direction to catch a Pike thus, do you no good, yet I am certain this direction how to roast him when he is caught, is choicely good, for I have tried it, and it is somewhat the better for not being common; but with my direction you must take this caution, that your Pike must not be a small one, that is, it must be more than half a yard, and should be bigger.

First, open your Pike at the gills, and if need be, cut also a little slit towards the belly; out of these, take his guts, and keep his liver, which you are to shred very small with Thyme, Sweet-Marjoram, and a little Winter-savory; to these put some pickled Oysters, and some Anchovies, two or three, both these last whole (for the Anchovies will melt, and the Oysters should not); to these you must add also a pound of sweet butter, which you are to mix with the herbs that are shred, and let them all be well salted (if the Pike be more than a yard long, then you may put into these herbs more than a pound, or if he be less, then less Butter will suffice); these being thus mixed with a blade or two of Mace, must be put into the Pike's belly, and then his belly sewed up, as to keep all the Butter in his belly if it be possible, if not, then as much of it as you possibly can, but take not off the scales; then you are to thrust the spit through his mouth, out at his tail. And then with four or five or six split sticks, or very thin lathes, and a convenient quantity of Tape or Filleting, these lathes are to be

tied round about the Pike's body from his head to his tail, and the Tape tied somewhat thick to prevent his breaking or falling off from the spit; let him be roasted very leisurely, and often basted with Claret wine, and Anchovies, and butter mixed together, and also with what moisture falls from him into the pan: when you have roasted him sufficiently you are to hold under him (when you unwind or cut the Tape that ties him), such a dish as you propose to eat him out of; and let him fall into it with the sauce that is roasted in his belly, and by this means the Pike will be kept unbroken and complete: then, to the sauce which was within, and also in the pan, you are to add a fit quantity of the best Butter, and to squeeze the juice of three or four Oranges: lastly, you may either put into the Pike, with the Oysters, two cloves of Garlic, and take it whole out, when the Pike is cut off the spit, or, to give the sauce a hogo,[31] let the dish (into which you let the Pike fall) be rubbed with it: the using or not using of this Garlic is left to your discretion.

M. B.

This dish of meat is too good for any but Anglers or honest men; and I trust, you will prove both, and therefore I have trusted you with this secret.

Let me next tell you, that Gesner tells us there are no Pikes in Spain, and that the largest are in the Lake Thrasimene in Italy; and the next, if not equal to them, are the Pikes of England, and that in England, Lincolnshire boasteth to have the biggest. Just so doth Sussex boast of four sorts of fish; namely, an Arundel Mullet, a Chichester Lobster, a Shelsey Cockle, and an Amerly Trout.

But I will take up no more of your time with this relation, but proceed to give you some observations of the Carp, and how to angle for him.

[31] A strong flavor (*haut-goût*).

# John Milton

## 1608 - 1674

Milton was born in London on 9 December, 1608. His father was a scrivener or solicitor, and a convinced Puritan. There was indeed so much feeling behind his Puritanism as to have caused him to break with his family on this account, Milton's grandfather having been a Catholic recusant in the reign of Elizabeth. It should be remembered, however, that Puritanism had not yet become the narrow, ascetic, intolerant force that we generally associate with the name; and Milton, as a matter of fact, was brought up in an environment of cultivation in which music and poetry were ever-present realities. As a boy he attended St. Paul's School in London, and went thence to Christ's College, Cambridge, in 1625. There he remained for seven years, reading widely and deeply, laying the foundations of his immense learning, writing his first important poem, the ode On the Morning of Christ's Nativity (1629), and other shorter poems, and exhibiting already that spirit of independence which remained throughout his life a major characteristic. The immediate circumstances of Milton's trouble with his college tutor are obscure; but it is probable that his independent spirit had something to do with his temporary banishment from Cambridge in 1626 and his transference to another tutor on his return. In 1632 Milton left Cambridge and went to Horton, in Buckinghamshire, where his father had retired from his London business. Here he spent six years, perhaps the happiest of his life, continuing his studies with the conscious purpose of preparing himself for some great poetical achievement. For Milton was a dedicated spirit; from an early time aware of his great powers, he proceeded deliberately to make himself fit for the execution of his high purpose, the creation of a noble monument in verse. Many years later he expressed what was his abiding conviction from youth to old age: "He who would not be frustrate of his hope to write well hereafter in laudable things ought himself to be a true poem . . . not presuming to sing high praises of heroic men or famous cities unless he have in himself the experience and practice of all that which is praiseworthy." During the years at Horton, too, Milton not only read himself into the spirit of great poetry in ages past, but also wrote L'Allegro, Il Penseroso, Comus, and Lycidas. In 1638 he left England to travel southward to Italy, where he spent some months in pleasant intercourse with learned and cultivated men in several Italian cities, and had the opportunity of meeting Galileo—then old, blind, and in partial confinement at the hand of the Inquisition—at Florence.

Milton reached England in August, 1639, and proceeded to become a schoolmaster. His teaching was punctuated by the writing of controversial pamphlets, some of which won him appointment in 1649 as Latin Secretary in the Puritan government. He never made himself, however, the instrument of a party. His guiding star was liberty, and he was ready to turn against the Puritans themselves when they seemed to him in danger of deserting that principle for which, as he thought, they fundamentally stood. In 1641 and 1642 he wrote five pamphlets against episcopacy, or government of the church by bishops, fighting therein for religious liberty. In 1643 he began a series of pamphlets in which he contended passionately for easy divorce. The immediate occasion of these was his own unhappy marriage in that year, but the battle he waged was entirely consistent with his previously formed conviction that liberty was essential to human well-being. In 1644 he wrote his tract on liberal education, designed to principle the mind in virtue, "the only genuine source of political and individual liberty"; and also his Areopagitica, an eloquent defense of freedom of speech, in the course of which he uttered his celebrated praise of Spenser, "our sage and serious poet." After three years of work as Latin Secretary, Milton's devotion to his duties in the service of the Commonwealth caused his blindness, though he did not allow this to stop either his official work or his controversial writing, any more than he allowed it to prevent the later accomplishment of his purpose of writing a great poem. That purpose he never relinquished through all the central years of his life when the cause of liberty and public duty claimed his energy, and before the Restoration in 1660 he had begun the writing of Paradise Lost. There is no reason for thinking that either the theme or his execution of it in the poem was influenced by the decay of the Commonwealth and Charles II's return, bitter blows to Milton though both were. The theme was chosen, after long hesitation, simply on the ground that it was the most heroic in its proportions of all possible subjects. Milton suffered surprisingly little annoyance from the new government, and lived his remaining years quietly enough, save for disturbances within his family, at work upon various tasks, but chiefly Paradise Lost, Paradise Regained, and Samson Agonistes. The first was finished by the summer of 1665 and was published in 1667; Paradise Regained and Samson Agonistes appeared in 1671. Paradise Lost in the first edition has ten books; in the year of his death Milton published a second edition in which two of the original ten books were divided, making the twelve in which the poem has ever since been printed.

The "Columbia" Edition of The Works of John Milton, ed. Frank A. Patterson and others (New York, 1931–1938), represents an effort to establish a final text of both the poetry and prose. An excellent one-volume edition is John Milton: Complete Poems and Major Prose, edited by Merritt Y. Hughes (New York, 1957). James H. Hanford's Milton Handbook (New York, 1946) is a compact summary of scholarship on Milton. David Masson's Life of John Milton: Narrated in Connexion with the Political, Ecclesiastical, and Literary History of his time (London, 1877–1896) is a mine of information and a work still to be reckoned with; other important studies are Denis Saurat, Milton, Man and Thinker (New York, 1925), Eustace M. W. Tillyard, Milton (London, 1930), and J. Holly Hanford, John Milton, Englishman (New York, 1949). J. M. French is editing Life Records of John Milton (New Brunswick, N. J., 1949–    ). Among the scores of recent studies only a few can be mentioned: Arnold Stein's Answerable Style: Essays on Paradise Lost (Minneapolis, 1953) and Heroic Knowledge (Minneapolis, 1957);

H. F. Fletcher's Intellectual Development of John Milton (Urbana, Illinois, 1956); Rosemond Tuve's Images and Themes in Five Poems by Milton (Cambridge, U. S. A., 1957); and David Daiches' Milton (New York, 1957). In Cross Currents in English Literature of the XVIIth Century (London, 1929) Sir Herbert J. C. Grierson discusses the opposition between humanism and Puritanism as it appears in Milton and his age.

## On Time

Fly, envious Time, till thou run out thy race:
Call on the lazy leaden-stepping Hours,
Whose speed is but the heavy plummet's
    pace;[1]
And glut thyself with what thy womb devours,
Which is no more than what is false and vain, [5]
And merely mortal dross;
So little is our loss,
So little is thy gain!
For, when as each thing bad thou hast entombed,
And, last of all, thy greedy self consumed, [10]
Then long Eternity shall greet our bliss
With an individual kiss,
And Joy shall overtake us as a flood;
When everything that is sincerely good,
And perfectly divine, [15]
With Truth, and Peace, and Love, shall ever
    shine
About the supreme throne
Of him, to whose happy-making sight alone
When once our heavenly-guided soul shall
    climb,
Then, all this earthly grossness quit, [20]
Attired with stars we shall for ever sit,
    Triumphing over Death, and Chance, and
    thee, O Time!

## At a Solemn Music

Blest pair of Sirens, pledges of Heaven's joy,
Sphere-born harmonious sisters, Voice and
    Verse,
Wed your divine sounds, and mixed power
    employ,
Dead things with inbreathed sense able to
    pierce;
And to our high-raised fantasy present [5]
That undisturbéd song of pure consent,[2]
Aye sung before the sapphire-colored throne
To him that sits thereon,
With saintly shout and solemn jubilee;
Where the bright Seraphim in burning row [10]
Their loud uplifted angel-trumpets blow,
And the Cherubic host in thousand quires,[3]

[1] I. e., the gradual descent of the weights in a clock.
[2] Harmony.    [3] Choirs.

Touch their immortal harps of golden wires,
With those just Spirits that wear victorious
    palms,
Hymns devout and holy psalms            15
Singing everlastingly:
That we on Earth, with undiscording voice,
May rightly answer that melodious noise;
As once we did, till disproportioned sin
Jarred against nature's chime, and with harsh
    din                                  20
Broke the fair music that all creatures made
To their great Lord, whose love their motion
    swayed
In perfect diapason,[4] whilst they stood
In first obedience, and their state of good.
O, may we soon again renew that song,   25
And keep in tune with Heaven, till God ere
    long
To his celestial consort [5] us unite,
To live with him, and sing in endless morn of
    light!

## On Shakespeare

What needs my Shakespeare for his honored
    bones
The labor of an age in piléd stones?
Or that his hallowed relics should be hid
Under a star-ypointing pyramid?
Dear son of memory, great heir of fame,   5
What need'st thou such weak witness of thy
    name?
Thou in our wonder and astonishment
Has built thyself a livelong monument.
For whilst, to the shame of slow-endeavoring
    art,
Thy easy numbers flow, and that each heart 10
Hath from the leaves of thy unvalued [6] book
Those Delphic [7] lines with deep impression
    took,
Then thou, our fancy of itself bereaving,
Dost make us marble with too much conceiv-
    ing,
And so sepúlchered in such pomp dost lie  15
That kings for such a tomb would wish to die.

## L'Allegro

Hence, loathéd Melancholy,
    Of Cerberus and blackest Midnight born
In Stygian cave forlorn
    'Mongst horrid shapes, and shrieks, and
    sights unholy!
Find out some uncouth [1] cell,            5
    Where brooding Darkness spreads his jeal-
    ous wings,
And the night-raven sings;

There, under ebon [2] shades and low-browed
    rocks,
As ragged as thy locks,
    In dark Cimmerian desert [3] ever dwell.  10
But come, thou Goddess fair and free,
In heaven yclept [4] Euphrosyne,
And by men heart-easing Mirth;
    Whom lovely Venus, at a birth,
With two sister Graces more,               15
    To ivy-crownéd Bacchus bore:
Or whether (as some sager sing)
The frolic wind that breathes the spring,
Zephyr, with Aurora playing,
    As he met her once a-Maying,            20
There, on beds of violets blue,
    And fresh-blown roses washed in dew,
Filled her with thee, a daughter fair,
So buxom,[5] blithe, and debonair.
Haste thee, Nymph, and bring with thee    25
Jest, and youthful Jollity,
Quips and cranks [6] and wanton wiles,
Nods and becks and wreathéd smiles,
Such as hang on Hebe's cheek,
And love to live in dimple sleek;          30
Sport that wrinkled Care derides,
And Laughter holding both his sides.
Come, and trip it, as you go,
On the light fantastic toe;
And in thy right hand lead with thee       35
The mountain-nymph, sweet Liberty;
And, if I give thee honor due,
Mirth, admit me of thy crew,
To live with her, and live with thee,
In unreproved [7] pleasures free;          40
To hear the lark begin his flight,
And, singing, startle the dull night,
From his watch-tower in the skies,
Till the dappled dawn doth rise;
Then to come, in spite of sorrow,          45
And at my window bid good-morrow,
Through the sweet-briar or the vine,
Or the twisted eglantine;
While the cock, with lively din,
Scatters the rear of darkness thin;        50
And to the stack, or the barn-door,
Stoutly struts his dames before:
Oft listening how the hounds and horn
Cheerly rouse the slumbering morn,
From the side of some hoar hill,           55
Through the high wood echoing shrill:
Sometime walking, not unseen,
By hedgerow elms, on hillocks green,
Right against the eastern gate
Where the great Sun begins his state,      60
Robed in flames and amber light,
The clouds in thousand liveries dight; [8]
While the plowman, near at hand,

---

[4] Combination of notes or parts in harmonious
whole.
[5] Symphony.        [6] Invaluable.        [7] Inspired.
[1] Unknown, strange.

[2] Black.
[3] A mythical land involved in perpetual mist and
darkness (*Odyssey*, XI, 14).
[4] Called.        [5] Lively.
[6] Humorous turns of speech.
[7] Innocent.        [8] Adorned.

Whistles o'er the furrowed land,
And the milkmaid singeth blithe,                    65
And the mower whets his scythe,
And every shepherd tells his tale [9]
Under the hawthorn in the dale.
Straight mine eye hath caught new pleasures
Whilst the landscape round it measures:            70
Russet lawns, and fallows gray,
Where the nibbling flocks do stray,
Mountains on whose barren breast
The laboring clouds do often rest;
Meadows trim, with daisies pied;                   75
Shallow brooks, and rivers wide;
Towers and battlements it sees
Bosomed high in tufted trees,
Where perhaps some beauty lies,
The cynosure [10] of neighboring eyes.             80
Hard by a cottage chimney smokes
From betwixt two agéd oaks,
Where Corydon and Thyrsis [11] met
Are at their savory dinner set
Of herbs and other country messes,                 85
Which the neat-handed Phyllis dresses;
And then in haste her bower she leaves,
With Thestylis to bind the sheaves;
Or, if the earlier season lead,
To the tanned haycock in the mead.                 90
Sometimes, with secure [12] delight,
The upland hamlets will invite,
When the merry bells ring round,
And the jocund rebecks [13] sound
To many a youth and many a maid                    95
Dancing in the checkered shade,
And young and old come forth to play
On a sunshine holiday,
Till the livelong daylight fail:
Then to a spicy nut-brown ale,                     100
With stories told of many a feat,
How Faery Mab the junkets eat.
She was pinched and pulled, she said;
And he, by Friar's lantern [14] led,
Tells how the drudging goblin [15] sweat           105
To earn his cream-bowl duly set,
When in one night, ere glimpse of morn,
His shadowy flail hath threshed the corn
That ten day-laborers could not end;
Then lies him down, the lubber [16] fiend,         110
And, stretched out all the chimney's length,
Basks at the fire his hairy strength,
And crop-full out of doors he flings,
Ere the first cock his matin rings.
Thus done the tales, to bed they creep,            115
By whispering winds soon lulled asleep.
Towered cities please us then,
And the busy hum of men,
Where throngs of knights and barons bold,

---

[9] Counts his sheep.    [10] Center of attention.
[11] These and the two other names in following
lines are conventional names drawn from pastoral
poetry.
[12] Carefree.           [13] Fiddles.
[14] Will-o'-the-wisp.   [15] Robin Goodfellow.
[16] Clumsy.

In weeds [17] of peace, high triumphs hold, 120
With store of ladies, whose bright eyes
Rain influence, and judge the prize
Of wit or arms, while both contend
To win her grace whom all commend.
There let Hymen [18] oft appear                     125
In saffron robe, with taper clear,
And pomp, and feast, and revelry,
With mask and antique pageantry;
Such sights as youthful poets dream
On summer eves by haunted stream.                  130
Then to the well-trod stage anon,
If Jonson's learnéd sock [19] be on,
Or sweetest Shakespeare, Fancy's child,
Warble his native wood-notes wild.
And ever, against eating cares,                    135
Lap me in soft Lydian airs,
Married to immortal verse,
Such as the meeting soul may pierce,
In notes with many a winding bout [20]
Of linkéd sweetness long drawn out                 140
With wanton heed and giddy cunning,
The melting voice through mazes running,
Untwisting all the chains that tie
The hidden soul of harmony;
That Orpheus' self may heave his head              145
From golden slumber on a bed
Of heaped Elysian flowers, and hear
Such strains as would have won the ear
Of Pluto to have quite set free
His half-regained Eurydice.                        150
These delights if thou canst give,
Mirth, with thee I mean to live.

# Il Penseroso

Hence, vain deluding Joys,
    The brood of Folly without father bred!
How little you bested,[1]
    Or fill the fixéd mind with all your toys!
Dwell in some idle brain,                           5
    And fancies fond [2] with gaudy shapes possess,
As thick and numberless
    As the gay motes that people the sunbeam,
Or likest hovering dreams,
    The fickle pensioners of Morpheus' train. 10
But, hail! thou Goddess sage and holy!
Hail, divinest Melancholy!
Whose saintly visage is too bright
To hit the sense of human sight,
And therefore to our weaker view                   15
O'erlaid with black, staid Wisdom's hue;
Black, but such as in esteem
Prince Memnon's sister might beseem,
Or that starred Ethiop queen [3] that strove
To set her beauty's praise above                   20
The Sea-Nymphs, and their powers offended.

---

[17] Garments.           [18] God of marriage.
[19] The light shoe worn in classical times by actors
in comedy.
[20] Turn.
[1] Profit.              [2] Foolish.
[3] Cassiopeia, who was placed among the stars.

Yet thou art higher far descended:
Thee bright-haired Vesta long of yore
To solitary Saturn bore;
His daughter she; in Saturn's reign    25
Such mixture was not held a stain.
Oft in glimmering bowers and glades
He met her, and in secret shades
Of woody Ida's inmost grove,
Whilst yet there was no fear of Jove.    30
Come, pensive Nun, devout and pure,
Sober, steadfast, and demure,
All in a robe of darkest grain,[4]
Flowing with majestic train,
And sable stole of cypress lawn [5]    35
Over thy decent shoulders drawn.
Come; but keep thy wonted state,
With even step, and musing gait,
And looks commercing with the skies,
Thy rapt soul sitting in thine eyes:    40
There, held in holy passion still,
Forget thyself to marble, till
With a sad leaden downward cast
Thou fix them on the earth as fast.
And join with thee calm Peace and Quiet,    45
Spare Fast, that oft with gods doth diet,
And hears the Muses in a ring
Aye round about Jove's altar sing;
And add to these retiréd Leisure,
That in trim gardens takes his pleasure;    50
But, first and chiefest, with thee bring
Him that yon soars on golden wing,
Guiding the fiery-wheeléd throne,
The Cherub Contemplation;
And the mute Silence hist along,    55
'Less Philomel [6] will deign a song,
In her sweetest saddest plight,
Smoothing the rugged brow of Night,
While Cynthia [7] checks her dragon yoke
Gently o'er the accustomed oak.    60
Sweet bird, that shunn'st the noise of folly,
Most musical, most melancholy!
Thee, chauntress, oft the woods among
I woo, to hear thy even-song;
And, missing thee, I walk unseen    65
On the dry smooth-shaven green
To behold the wandering moon,
Riding near her highest noon,
Like one that had been led astray
Through the heaven's wide pathless way,    70
And oft, as if her head she bowed,
Stooping through a fleecy cloud.
Oft, on a plat of rising ground,
I hear the far-off curfew sound,
Over some wide-watered shore,    75
Swinging slow with sullen roar;
Or, if the air will not permit,
Some still removéd place will fit,
Where glowing embers through the room
Teach light to counterfeit a gloom,    80
Far from all resort of mirth,
Save the cricket on the hearth,

Or the bellman's [8] drowsy charm
To bless the doors from nightly harm.
Or let my lamp, at midnight hour,    85
Be seen in some high lonely tower,
Where I may oft outwatch the Bear,[9]
With thrice great Hermes,[10] or unsphere [11]
The spirit of Plato, to unfold
What worlds or what past regions hold    90
The immortal mind that hath forsook
Her mansion in this fleshly nook;
And of those demons that are found
In fire, air, flood, or underground,
Whose power hath a true consent [12]    95
With planet or with element.
Sometimes let gorgeous Tragedy
In sceptered pall come sweeping by,
Presenting Thebes, or Pelops' line,
Or the tale of Troy divine,    100
Or what (though rare) of later age
Ennobled hath the buskined [13] stage.
But, O sad Virgin! that thy power
Might raise Musaeus from his bower;
Or bid the soul of Orpheus sing    105
Such notes as, warbled to the string,
Drew iron tears down Pluto's cheek,
And made Hell grant what love did seek;
Or call up him [14] that left half-told
The story of Cambuscan bold,    110
Of Camball, and of Algarsife,
And who had Canace to wife,
That owned the virtuous ring and glass,
And of the wondrous horse of brass
On which the Tartar king did ride;    115
And if aught else great bards beside
In sage and solemn tunes have sung,
Of turneys, and of trophies hung,
Of forests, and enchantments drear,
Where more is meant than meets the ear.[15] 120
Thus, Night, oft see me in thy pale career,
Till civil-suited Morn appear,
Not tricked and frounced, as she was wont
With the Attic boy [16] to hunt,
But kerchiefed in a comely cloud,    125
While rocking winds are piping loud,
Or ushered with a shower still,
When the gust hath blown his fill,
Ending on the rustling leaves,
With minute-drops from off the eaves.    130
And, when the sun begins to fling
His flaring beams, me, Goddess, bring
To archéd walks of twilight groves,

[4] Color.          [5] A light crape.
[6] The nightingale.     [7] The moon.

[8] Watchman's.
[9] The Great Bear never sets in England, consequently he would have to sit up until dawn.
[10] Hermes Trismegistus, a fabled Egyptian ruler to whom were ascribed many books.
[11] Call his spirit from the sphere where it abides.
[12] Sympathy.
[13] Tragic (the buskin was the heavy boot worn by tragic actors in classical times).
[14] Chaucer (the allusion is to the uncompleted Squire's Tale).
[15] The allusion is probably to Spenser.
[16] Cephalus, loved by Aurora.

And shadows brown, that Sylvan loves,
Of pine, or monumental oak,    135
Where the rude ax with heavéd stroke
Was never heard the nymphs to daunt,
Or fright them from their hallowed haunt.
There, in close covert, by some brook,
Where no profaner eye may look,    140
Hide me from day's garish eye,
While the bee with honeyed thigh,
That at her flowery work doth sing,
And the waters murmuring,
With such consort as they keep,    145
Entice the dewy-feathered Sleep.
And let some strange mysterious dream
Wave at his wings, in airy stream
Of lively portraiture displayed,
Softly on my eyelids laid;    150
And, as I wake, sweet music breathe
Above, about, or underneath,
Sent by some Spirit to mortals good,
Or the unseen Genius of the wood.
But let my due feet never fail    155
To walk the studious cloister's pale,[17]
And love the high embowéd roof,
With antique pillars massy-proof,
And storied windows richly dight,[18]
Casting a dim religious light.    160
There let the pealing organ blow,
To the full-voiced quire below,
In service high and anthems clear,
As may with sweetness, through mine ear,
Dissolve me into ecstasies,    165
And bring all Heaven before mine eyes.
And may at last my weary age
Find out the peaceful hermitage,
The hairy gown and mossy cell,
Where I may sit and rightly spell [19]    170
Of every star that heaven doth shew,
And every herb that sips the dew,
Till old experience do attain
To something like prophetic strain.
These pleasures, Melancholy, give;    175
And I with thee will choose to live.

# Lycidas [1]

Yet once more, O ye laurels, and once more,
Ye myrtles brown, with ivy never sere,
I come to pluck your berries harsh and crude,
And with forced fingers rude
Shatter your leaves before the mellowing year.[2]

[17] Enclosure.
[18] Windows richly adorned with stories (from the Bible).
[19] Read.
[1] In this monody the author bewails a learned friend, unfortunately drowned in his passage from Chester on the Irish seas, 1637, and by occasion foretells the ruin of our corrupted clergy, then in their height (Milton's note). Milton's learned friend was Edward King of Christ's College, Cambridge.
[2] I. e., Milton was forced to break his resolution not to write until his powers were fully matured.

Bitter constraint and sad occasion dear    6
Compels me to disturb your season due;
For Lycidas [3] is dead, dead ere his prime,
Young Lycidas, and hath not left his peer.
Who would not sing for Lycidas? he knew 10
Himself to sing, and build the lofty rime.
He must not float upon his watery bier
Unwept, and welter to the parching wind,
Without the meed of some melodious tear.
Begin, then, Sisters of the sacred well [4]    15
That from beneath the seat of Jove doth spring;
Begin, and somewhat loudly sweep the string.
Hence with denial vain and coy excuse:
So may some gentle Muse
With lucky words favor *my* destined urn,    20
And as he passes turn,
And bid fair peace be to my sable shroud!
For we were nursed upon the self-same hill,
Fed the same flock, by fountain, shade, and rill;
Together both, ere the high lawns appeared 25
Under the opening eyelids of the Morn,
We drove a-field, and both together heard
What time the gray-fly winds her sultry horn,
Battening [5] our flocks with the fresh dews of night,
Oft till the star that rose at evening bright [6] 30
Toward heaven's descent had sloped his wester-
ing wheel.
Meanwhile the rural ditties were not mute;
Tempered to the oaten flute,
Rough Satyrs danced, and Fauns with cloven heel
From the glad sound would not be absent long;    35
And old Damoetas [7] loved to hear our song.
But, oh! the heavy change, now thou art gone,
Now thou art gone and never must return!
Thee, Shepherd, thee the woods and desert caves,
With wild thyme and the gadding vine o'er-grown,    40
And all their echoes, mourn.
The willows, and the hazel copses green,
Shall now no more be seen
Fanning their joyous leaves to thy soft lays.
As killing as the canker to the rose,    45
Or taint-worm to the weanling herds that graze,
Or frost to flowers, that their gay wardrobe wear,
When first the white-thorn blows;
Such, Lycidas, thy loss to shepherd's ear.
Where were ye, Nymphs, when the remorse-less deep    50
Closed o'er the head of your loved Lycidas?

[3] The name occurs in the seventh Idyll of Theocritus.
[4] Muses of the Pierian spring.    [5] Feeding.
[6] Hesperus, which appears at evening.
[7] A conventional name drawn from pastoral poetry. Probably some fellow or the master of Christ's College is meant.

For neither were ye playing on the steep
Where your old bards, the famous Druids, lie,
Nor on the shaggy top of Mona high,
Nor yet where Deva spreads her wizard stream.[8]
Ay me! I fondly [9] dream                              56
"Had ye been there," . . . for what could
    that have done?
What could the Muse [10] herself that Orpheus
    bore,
The Muse herself, for her enchanting son,
Whom universal nature did lament,                     60
When, by the rout that made the hideous roar,
His gory visage down the stream was sent,
Down the swift Hebrus to the Lesbian shore?
  Alas! what boots [11] it with uncessant care
To tend the homely, slighted, shepherd's trade,
And strictly meditate the thankless Muse?             66
Were it not better done, as others use,
To sport with Amaryllis in the shade,
Or with the tangles of Neaera's hair?
Fame is the spur that the clear spirit doth
    raise                                              70
(That last infirmity of noble mind)
To scorn delights and live laborious days;
But the fair guerdon when we hope to find,
And think to burst out into sudden blaze,
Comes the blind Fury [12] with the abhorréd
    shears,                                            75
And slits the thin-spun life. "But not the
    praise,"
Phoebus replied, and touched my trembling
    ears;
"Fame is no plant that grows on mortal soil,
Nor in the glistening foil [13]
Set off to the world, nor in broad rumor lies,    80
But lives and spreads aloft by those pure eyes
And perfect witness of all-judging Jove;
As he pronounces lastly on each deed,
Of so much fame in heaven expect thy meed."
  O fountain Arethuse, and thou honored
    flood,                                             85
Smooth-sliding Mincius, crowned with vocal
    reeds,
That strain I heard was of a higher mood.
But now my oat [14] proceeds,
And listens to the Herald of the Sea,
That came in Neptune's plea.                          90
He asked the waves, and asked the felon winds,
What hard mishap hath doomed this gentle
    swain?
And questioned every gust of rugged wings

That blows from off each beakéd promontory.
They knew not of his story;                           95
And sage Hippotades [15] their answer brings,
That not a blast was from his dungeon strayed:
The air was calm, and on the level brine
Sleek Panope [16] with all her sisters played.
It was that fatal [17] and perfidious bark,          100
Built in the eclipse, and rigged with curses
    dark,
That sunk so low that sacred head of thine.
  Next, Camus,[18] reverend sire, went footing
    slow,
His mantle hairy, and his bonnet sedge,
Inwrought with figures dim, and on the edge
Like to that sanguine flower inscribed with
    woe.[19]                                         106
"Ah! who hath reft," quoth he, "my dearest
    pledge?" [20]
Last came, and last did go,
The Pilot of the Galilean Lake; [21]
Two massy keys he bore of metals twain [22]         110
(The golden opes, the iron shuts amain [23]).
He shook his mitered locks, and stern be-
    spake:—
"How well could I have spared for thee, young
    swain,
Enow of such as, for their bellies' sake,
Creep, and intrude, and climb into the fold!        115
Of other care they little reckoning make
Than how to scramble at the shearers' feast,
And shove away the worthy bidden guest.
Blind mouths! that scarce themselves know
    how to hold
A sheep-hook, or have learned aught else the
    least                                            120
That to the faithful herdman's art belongs!
What recks [24] it them? What need they? They
    are sped; [25]
And, when they list, their lean and flashy songs
Grate on their scrannel [26] pipes of wretched
    straw;
The hungry sheep look up, and are not fed,          125
But, swoln with wind and the rank mist they
    draw,
Rot inwardly, and foul contagion spread;
Besides what the grim wolf with privy paw
Daily devours apace, and nothing said.
But that two-handed engine [27] at the door        130
Stands ready to smite once, and smite no
    more."
  Return, Alpheus; [28] the dread voice is past

---

[8] Neither on the Welsh hills, nor on Anglesea (Mona), nor along the river Dee: all places near the scene of King's shipwreck.
[9] Foolishly.
[10] Calliope. Orpheus was torn to pieces by Thracian women, and his head was thrown into the river Hebrus.
[11] Avails.
[12] Atropos, a Fate. Perhaps Milton here calls her a Fury because of his anger.
[13] Glittering setting of a gem.
[14] Shepherd's pipe.

[15] Aeolus, god of winds.
[16] One of the Nereids.          [17] Fated.
[18] The god of the Cam, the river at Cambridge.
[19] The hyacinth, whose leaves have certain markings, said by the ancients to be AI, AI (alas!), in mourning for Hyacinthus.
[20] Bereaved me of my dearest child.
[21] St. Peter.          [22] Cf. St. Matthew, 16:19.
[23] With force.          [24] Concerns.
[25] Provided for.          [26] Thin.
[27] Perhaps the ax of St. Matthew, 3:10, and St. Luke, 3:9.
[28] River of Arcadia, whose spirit loved Arethusa.

That shrunk thy streams; return, Sicilian Muse,
And call the vales, and bid them hither cast
Their bells and flowerets of a thousand hues.
Ye valleys low, where the mild whispers use [136]
Of shades, and wanton winds, and gushing
  brooks,
On whose fresh lap the swart star [29] sparely
  looks,
Throw hither all your quaint enameled eyes
That on the green turf suck the honeyed
  showers,                                    [140]
And purple all the ground with vernal flowers.
Bring the rathe [30] primrose that forsaken dies,
The tufted crow-toe, and pale jessamine,
The white pink, and the pansy freaked [31] with
  jet,
The growing violet,                          [145]
The musk rose, and the well-attired woodbine,
With cowslips wan that hang the pensive head,
And every flower that sad embroidery wears;
Bid amaranthus all his beauty shed,
And daffadillies fill their cups with tears,  [150]
To strew the laureate hearse where Lycid lies.
For so, to interpose a little ease,
Let our frail thoughts dally with false surmise,
Ay me! whilst thee the shores and sounding
  seas
Wash far away, where'er thy bones are hurled;
Whether beyond the stormy Hebrides,          [156]
Where thou perhaps under the whelming tide
Visit'st the bottom of the monstrous world; [32]
Or whether thou, to our moist vows denied,
Sleep'st by the fable of Bellerus old, [33]   [160]
Where the great Vision of the guarded
  mount [34]
Looks toward Namancos and Bayona's hold. [35]
Look homeward, Angel, [36] now, and melt with
  ruth: [37]
And, O ye dolphins, waft the hapless youth.
  Weep no more, woeful shepherds, weep no
  more,                                       [165]
For Lycidas, your sorrow, is not dead,
Sunk though he be beneath the watery floor.
So sinks the day-star in the ocean bed,
And yet anon repairs his drooping head,
And tricks [38] his beams, and with new-spangled
  ore [39]                                    [170]
Flames in the forehead of the morning sky:
So Lycidas sunk low, but mounted high,
Through the dear might of him that walked
  the waves,
Where, other groves and other streams along,
With nectar pure his oozy locks he laves, [175]
And hears the unexpressive [40] nuptial song,
In the blest kingdoms meek of joy and love.

[29] The dog-star, supposed to be injurious to plants.
[30] Early.          [31] Sprinkled.
[32] World of monsters.          [33] Land's End.
[34] St. Michael's Mount, near Land's End.
[35] In Spain, near Cape Finisterre.
[36] Either Lycidas or St. Michael.
[37] Pity.          [38] Adorns.          [39] Brightness.
[40] Inexpressible.

There entertain him all the Saints above,
In solemn troops, and sweet societies,
That sing, and singing in their glory move, [180]
And wipe the tears for ever from his eyes.
Now, Lycidas, the shepherds weep no more;
Henceforth thou art the Genius of the shore,
In thy large recompense, and shalt be good
To all that wander in that perilous flood. [185]
  Thus sang the uncouth swain to the oaks
    and rills,
While the still morn went out with sandals
    gray:
He touched the tender stops of various quills, [41]
With eager thought warbling his Doric lay: [42]
And now the sun had stretched out all the hills,
And now was dropped into the western bay. [191]
At last he rose, and twitched his mantle blue:
To-morrow to fresh woods, and pastures new.

# Sonnets [1]

## VII

How soon hath Time, the subtle thief of youth,
  Stolen on his wing my three-and-twentieth
    year!
  My hasting days fly on with full career,
  But my late spring no bud or blossom
    shew'th.
Perhaps my semblance might deceive the truth
  That I to manhood am arrived so near;     [6]
  And inward ripeness doth much less appear,
  That some more timely-happy spirits en-
    du'th.
Yet, be it less or more, or soon or slow,
  It shall be still in strictest measure even [10]
  To that same lot, however mean or high,
Toward which Time leads me, and the will of
    Heaven;
  All is, if I have grace to use it so,
  As ever in my great Task-Master's eye.

## VIII [2]

Captain or Colonel, or Knight in Arms,
  Whose chance on these defenseless doors
    may seize,
  If ever deed of honor did thee please,
  Guard them, and him within protect from
    harms:
He can requite thee, for he knows the charms [5]
  That call fame on such gentle acts as these;
  And he can spread thy name o'er lands and
    seas,
  Whatever clime the sun's bright circle
    warms.
Lift not thy spear against the Muses' bower:

[41] Reeds, i. e., pipes.          [42] Pastoral poem.
[1] The Sonnets are numbered as in H. C. Beeching's
edition.
[2] Written in the fall of 1642 when the army of
Charles I was advancing on London.

The great Emathian conqueror [3] bid spare [10]
The house of Pindarus, when temple and
    tower
Went to the ground; and the repeated air
Of sad Electra's poet [4] had the power
To save the Athenian walls from ruin bare.

### IX

Lady, that in the prime of earliest youth
    Wisely hast shunned the broad way and the
    green,
    And with those few art eminently seen
That labor up the hill of heavenly Truth,
The better part with Mary and with Ruth, [5]
    Chosen thou hast; and they that overween,
    And at thy growing virtues fret their spleen,
    No anger find in thee, but pity and ruth.
Thy care is fixed, and zealously attends
    To fill thy odorous lamp with deeds of light,
    And hope that reaps not shame. [5] Therefore
    be sure    [11]
Thou, when the Bridegroom with his feastful
    friends
    Passes to bliss at the mid-hour of night,
    Hast gained thy entrance, Virgin wise and
    pure.

### XI

A book was writ of late called *Tetrachordon*, [6]
    And woven close, both matter, form, and
    style;
    The subject new: it walked the town a while,
    Numbering good intellects; now seldom
    pored on.
Cries the stall-reader, "Bless us! what a word
    on    [5]
A title-page is this!"; and some in file
    Stand spelling false, while one might walk
    to Mile-
    End Green. Why, is it harder, sirs, than
    *Gordon*,
*Colkitto*, or *Macdonnel*, or *Galasp*? [7]
    Those rugged names to our like mouths grow
    sleek,    [10]
    That would have made Quintilian stare and
    gasp.
Thy age, like ours, O soul of Sir John Cheke, [8]
    Hated not learning worse than toad or asp,
    When thou taught'st Cambridge and King
    Edward Greek.

[3] Alexander the Great, when he sacked Thebes.
[4] Euripides.
[5] See the parable of the wise and foolish virgins
(St. Matthew, 25:6).
[6] One of Milton's pamphlets on divorce.
[7] Names of Scottish generals during the war of
1644–1645.
[8] English humanist of the mid-sixteenth century,
first professor of Greek at Cambridge and tutor of
Edward VI.

### XII

#### On the Same

I did but prompt the age to quit their clogs
    By the known rules of ancient liberty,
    When straight a barbarous noise environs
    me
Of owls and cuckoos, asses, apes, and dogs;
As when those hinds that were transformed to
    frogs    [5]
    Railed at Latona's twin-born progeny, [9]
    Which after held the Sun and Moon in fee.
    But this is got by casting pearl to hogs,
That bawl for freedom in their senseless mood,
    And still revolt when Truth would set them
    free.    [10]
    Licence they mean when they cry Liberty;
For who loves that must first be wise and good:
    But from that mark how far they rove we see,
    For all this waste of wealth and loss of blood.

### XV

#### On the Late Massacre in Piedmont [10]

Avenge, O Lord, thy slaughtered saints, whose
    bones
    Lie scattered on the Alpine mountains cold;
    Even them who kept thy truth so pure of old,
    When all our fathers worshiped stocks and
    stones,
Forget not: in thy book record their groans    [5]
    Who were thy sheep, and in their ancient
    fold
    Slain by the bloody Piemontese, that rolled
    Mother with infant down the rocks. Their
    moans
The vales redoubled to the hills, and they
    To heaven. Their martyred blood and ashes
    sow    [10]
    O'er all th' Italian fields, where still doth
    sway
The triple Tyrant; [11] that from these may grow
    A hundred fold, who, having learned thy way,
    Early may fly the Babylonian woe.

### XVI

When I consider how my light is spent
    Ere half my days in this dark world and wide,
    And that one talent [12] which is death to hide
    Lodged with me useless, though my soul
    more bent
To serve therewith my Maker, and present    [5]

[9] Apollo and Diana.
[10] In 1655 the Duke of Savoy subjected the Protestants of Piedmont to bitter persecution, cruelly killing a number of them.
[11] The pope. The Puritans identified Rome with
Babylon (cf. Revelation, 17:5).
[12] See the parable of the servant with whom one
talent (a sum of money) was left (St. Matthew,
25:26).

My true account, lest He returning chide,
"Doth God exact day-labor, light denied?"
I fondly ask. But Patience, to prevent
That murmur, soon replies, "God doth not
    need
Either man's work or his own gifts. Who
    best                   10
Bear his mild yoke, they serve him best.
    His state
Is kingly: thousands at his bidding speed,
    And post o'er land and ocean without rest;
    They also serve who only stand and wait."

### XVII

Lawrence, of virtuous father virtuous son,
    Now that the fields are dank, and ways are
        mire,
    Where shall we sometimes meet, and by the
        fire
    Help waste a sullen day, what may be won
From the hard season gaining? Time will run [5]
    On smoother, till Favonius [13] reinspire
    The frozen earth, and clothe in fresh attire
    The lily and rose, that neither sowed nor
        spun.
What neat repast shall feast us, light and
        choice,
    Of Attic taste, with wine, whence we may
        rise,                10
    To hear the lute well touched, or artful voice
Warble immortal notes and Tuscan air?
    He who of those delights can judge, and
        spare
    To interpose them oft, is not unwise.

### XVIII

Cyriack, whose grandsire [14] on the royal bench
    Of British Themis,[15] with no mean applause,
    Pronounced, and in his volumes taught, our
        laws,
    Which others at their bar so often wrench,
To-day deep thoughts resolve with me to drench
    In mirth that after no repenting draws;    6
    Let Euclid rest, and Archimedes pause,
    And what the Swede intend, and what the
        French.[16]
To measure life learn thou betimes, and know
    Towards solid good what leads the nearest
        way;                10
    For other things mild Heaven a time ordains,
And disapproves that care, though wise in show,
    That with superfluous burden loads the day,
    And, when God sends a cheerful hour, re-
        frains.

[13] The spring wind from the southwest.
[14] Sir Edward Coke.        [15] Goddess of justice.
[16] Charles X of Sweden was at war with Poland
and Russia, and Louis XIV was fighting the Spanish
in the Netherlands.

### XIX

Methought I saw my late espoused saint [17]
    Brought to me like Alcestis from the grave,
    Whom Jove's great son [18] to her glad hus-
        band gave,
    Rescued from Death by force, though pale
        and faint.
Mine, as whom washed from spot of childbed
        taint                5
    Purification in the Old Law [19] did save,
    And such as yet once more I trust to have
    Full sight of her in Heaven without restraint,
Came vested all in white, pure as her mind.
    Her face was veiled; yet to my fancied sight
    Love, sweetness, goodness, in her person
        shined            11
So clear as in no face with more delight.
    But, oh! as to embrace me she inclined,
    I waked, she fled, and day brought back my
        night.

# To the Lord
# General Cromwell
# May, 1652

### On the Proposals of Certain Ministers at the Committee for Propagation of the Gospel

Cromwell, our chief of men, who through a
    cloud
    Not of war only, but detractions rude,
    Guided by faith and matchless fortitude,
    To peace and truth thy glorious way hast
        plowed,
And on the neck of crowned Fortune proud [5]
    Hast reared God's trophies, and his work
        pursued,
    While Darwen stream, with blood of Scots
        imbrued,
    And Dunbar field, resounds thy praises loud,
And Worcester's laureate wreath: [20] yet much
        remains
    To conquer still; Peace hath her victories [10]
    No less renowned than War: new foes arise,
Threatening to bind our souls with secular
        chains.[21]
    Help us to save free conscience from the paw
    Of hireling wolves, whose Gospel is their
        maw.

[17] Catherine Woodcock, Milton's second wife, who
died in childbirth in February, 1658.
[18] Hercules.        [19] Leviticus, 12.
[20] Three victories of Cromwell over the Scotch,
respectively in 1648, 1650, and 1651.
[21] Government control. The proposals to which
Milton objected were that Puritan ministers be supported by the state.

# To Mr. Cyriack Skinner

## Upon His Blindness

Cyriack, this three years' day these eyes, though
    clear
  To outward view, of blemish or of spot,
  Bereft of light, their seeing have forgot;
Nor to their idle orbs doth sight appear
Of sun, or moon, or star, throughout the year,
  Or man, or woman. Yet I argue not      6
  Against Heaven's hand or will, nor bate a jot
Of heart or hope, but still bear up and steer
Right onward. What supports me, dost thou
    ask?
  The conscience, friend, to have lost them
    overplied      10
In Liberty's defense, my noble task,
Of which all Europe rings from side to side;
  This thought might lead me through the
    world's vain mask
  Content, though blind, had I no better
    guide.

# Paradise Lost

### THE VERSE

*The measure is English heroic verse without
rime, as that of Homer in Greek, and of Virgil
in Latin; rime being no necessary adjunct or
true ornament of poem or good verse, in longer
works especially, but the invention of a barbarous age to set off wretched matter and lame
meter; graced indeed since by the use of some
famous modern poets, carried away by custom,
but much to their own vexation, hindrance, and
constraint to express many things otherwise,
and for the most part worse, than else they
would have expressed them. Not without
cause therefore, some both Italian and Spanish
poets of prime note have rejected rime both
in longer and shorter works, as have long since
our best English tragedies; as a thing of itself,
to all judicious ears, trivial and of no true musical delight; which consists only in apt numbers, fit quantity of syllables, and the sense
variously drawn out from one verse into another; not in the jingling sound of like endings, a fault avoided by the learned ancients
both in poetry and all good oratory. This neglect then of rime so little is to be taken for a
defect, though it may seem so perhaps to vulgar readers, that it is rather to be esteemed an
example set, the first in English, of ancient liberty recovered to heroic poem, from the troublesome and modern bondage of riming.*

## BOOK I

### THE ARGUMENT

THIS *First Book proposes, first in brief, the
whole subject—Man's disobedience, and the
loss thereupon of Paradise, wherein he was
placed: then touches the prime cause of his
fall—the Serpent, or rather Satan in the Serpent; who, revolting from God, and drawing
to his side many legions of Angels, was, by the
command of God, driven out of Heaven, with
all his crew, into the great Deep. Which action
passed over, the Poem hastens into the midst
of things; presenting Satan, with his Angels,
now fallen into Hell—described here not in
the Center (for heaven and earth may be
supposed as yet not made, certainly not yet
accursed), but in a place of utter darkness, fit-
liest called Chaos. Here Satan, with his Angels
lying on the burning lake, thunderstruck and
astonished, after a certain space recovers, as
from confusion; calls up him who, next in order
of dignity, lay by him: they confer of their
miserable fall. Satan awakens all his legions,
who lay till then in the same manner confounded. They rise: their numbers; array of battle; their chief leaders named, according to the
idols known afterwards in Canaan and the
countries adjoining. To these Satan directs his
speech; comforts them with hope yet of regaining Heaven; but tells them, lastly, of a new
world and new kind of creature to be created,
according to an ancient prophecy, or report, in
Heaven—for that Angels were long before this
visible creation was the opinion of many ancient Fathers. To find out the truth of this
prophecy, and what to determine thereon, he
refers to a full council. What his associates
thence attempt. Pandemonium, the palace of
Satan, rises, suddenly built out of the Deep:
the infernal Peers there sit in council.*

Of man's first disobedience, and the fruit
Of that forbidden tree whose mortal taste
Brought death into the World, and all our woe,
With loss of Eden, till one greater Man
Restore us, and regain the blissful seat,    5
Sing, Heavenly Muse, that, on the secret top
Of Oreb, or of Sinai, didst inspire
That shepherd [1] who first taught the chosen
    seed
In the beginning how the heavens and earth
Rose out of Chaos: or, if Sion hill    10
Delight thee more, and Siloa's brook that
    flowed
Fast [2] by the oracle of God,[3] I thence
Invoke thy aid to my adventrous song,
That with no middle flight intends to soar
Above the Aonian mount,[4] while it pursues    15
Things unattempted yet in prose or rime.
And chiefly thou, O Spirit, that does prefer
Before all temples the upright heart and pure,
Instruct me, for thou know'st; thou from the
    first

[1] Moses.    [2] Close.
[3] The temple of Jerusalem.
[4] Helicon, home of the muses.

Wast present, and, with mighty wings outspread,  20
Dove-like sat'st brooding on the vast Abyss,
And mad'st it pregnant: what in me is dark
Illumine, what is low raise and support;
That, to the highth of this great argument,
I may assert [5] Eternal Providence,  25
And justify the ways of God to men.

Say first—for Heaven hides nothing from thy view,
Nor the deep tract of Hell—say first what cause
Moved our grand [6] Parents, in that happy state,
Favored of Heaven so highly, to fall off  30
From their Creator, and transgress his will
For [7] one restraint, lords of the World besides.
Who first seduced them to that foul revolt?

The infernal Serpent; he it was whose guile,
Stirred up with envy and revenge, deceived  35
The mother of mankind, what time his pride
Had cast him out from Heaven, with all his host
Of rebel Angels, by whose aid, aspiring
To set himself in glory above his peers,
He trusted to have equaled the Most High,  40
If he opposed, and, with ambitious aim
Against the throne and monarchy of God,
Raised impious war in Heaven and battle proud,
With vain attempt. Him the Almighty Power
Hurled headlong flaming from the ethereal sky,
With hideous ruin and combustion, down  46
To bottomless perdition, there to dwell
In adamantine chains and penal fire,
Who durst defy the Omnipotent to arms.[8]

Nine times the space that measure day and night  50
To mortal men, he, with his horrid crew,

[5] Vindicate.     [6] First.     [7] Because of.
[8] Milton's conception of the universe and of its relation to heaven and hell should be grasped at the outset. He follows the Ptolemaic system, according to which the earth is the center of the universe, about which the other bodies revolve. These (sun, moon, etc.) are supposed to be fastened in a series of hollow spheres, made of some transparent substance, which move around the earth as a common center. The hollow spheres were, in medieval and early modern times, supposed to be ten in number, the outermost being the *primum mobile*, or "first moved." Thus the starry universe has the form of a large globe, and it is suspended from the wall of heaven by a golden chain. Heaven is the region lying entirely outside the starry universe and immediately above it. Surrounding the universe and separated from heaven by a wall is chaos, the region of unformed, warring elements through which Satan and his host were hurled from heaven. At the bottom of this region of chaos is hell, the place of punishment prepared for Satan and his followers when they rebelled. Hell, then, is under the universe and is separated from it by a distance through chaos equal to the distance from the center of the earth to the *primum mobile* (see where Milton says the distance from heaven to hell is three times the radius of the universe).

Lay vanquished, rolling in the fiery gulf,
Confounded, though immortal. But his doom
Reserved him to more wrath; for now the thought
Both of lost happiness and lasting pain  55
Torments him: round he throws his baleful eyes,
That witnessed huge affliction and dismay,
Mixed with obdurate pride and steadfast hate.
At once, as far as Angels ken, he views
The dismal situation waste and wild.  60
A dungeon horrible, on all sides round,
As one great furnace flamed; yet from those flames
No light; but rather darkness visible
Served only to discover sights of woe,
Regions of sorrow, doleful shades, where peace
And rest can never dwell, hope never comes  66
That comes to all, but torture without end
Still urges, and a fiery deluge, fed
With ever-burning sulphur unconsumed.
Such place Eternal Justice had prepared  70
For those rebellious; here their prison ordained
In utter darkness, and their portion set,
As far removed from God and light of Heaven
As from the center thrice to the utmost pole.
Oh how unlike the place from whence they fell!  75
There the companions of his fall, o'erwhelmed
With floods and whirlwinds of tempestuous fire,
He soon discerns; and, weltering by his side,
One next himself in power, and next in crime,
Long after known in Palestine, and named  80
BEËLZEBUB. To whom the Arch-Enemy,
And thence in Heaven called SATAN,[9] with bold words
Breaking the horrid silence, thus began:—
"If thou beest he—but Oh how fallen! how changed
From him!—who, in the happy realms of light,
Clothed with transcendent brightness, didst outshine  86
Myriads, though bright—if he whom mutual league,
United thoughts and counsels, equal hope
And hazard in the glorious enterprise,
Joined with me once, now misery hath joined
In equal ruin; into what pit thou seest  91
From what highth fallen: so much the stronger proved
He with his thunder: and till then who knew
The force of those dire arms? Yet not for those,
Nor what the potent Victor in his rage  95
Can else inflict, do I repent, or change,
Though changed in outward luster, that fixed mind,
And high disdain from sense of injured merit,
That with the Mightiest raised me to contend,
And to the fierce contention brought along  100

[9] A Hebrew word meaning adversary.

Innumerable force of Spirits armed,
That durst dislike his reign, and, me preferring,
His utmost power with adverse power opposed
In dubious battle on the plains of Heaven,
And shook his throne. What though the field
    be lost?                          105
All is not lost—the unconquerable will,
And study of revenge, immortal hate,
And courage never to submit or yield;
And what is else not to be overcome?
That glory never shall his wrath or might   110
Extort from me. To bow and sue for grace
With suppliant knee, and deify his power
Who, from the terror of this arm, so late
Doubted [10] his empire—that were low indeed;
That were an ignominy and shame beneath
This downfall; since, by fate, the strength of
    Gods,                       116
And this empyreal substance, cannot fail;
Since, through experience of this great event,
In arms not worse, in foresight much advanced,
We may with more successful hope resolve 120
To wage by force or guile eternal war,
Irreconcilable to our grand Foe,
Who now triumphs, and in the excess of joy
Sole reigning holds the tyranny of Heaven."
    So spake the apostate Angel, though in
    pain,                         125
Vaunting aloud, but racked with deep despair;
And him thus answered soon his bold com-
    peer:—
    "O Prince, O Chief of many thronéd Powers
That led the embattled Seraphim to war
Under thy conduct, and, in dreadful deeds 130
Fearless, endangered Heaven's perpetual King,
And put to proof his high supremacy,
Whether upheld by strength, or chance, or
    fate,
Too well I see and rue the dire event
That, with sad overthrow and foul defeat, 135
Hath lost us Heaven, and all this mighty host
In horrible destruction laid thus low,
As far as Gods and Heavenly Essences
Can perish: for the mind and spirit remains
Invincible, and vigor soon returns,       140
Though all our glory extinct, and happy state
Here swallowed up in endless misery.
But what if he our Conqueror (whom I now
Of force believe almighty, since no less
Than such could have o'erpowered such force
    as ours)                    145
Have left us this our spirit and strength entire,
Strongly to suffer and support our pains,
That we may so suffice [11] his vengeful ire,
Or do him mightier service as his thralls
By right of war, whate'er his business be, 150
Here in the heart of Hell to work in fire,
Or do his errands in the gloomy Deep?
What can it then avail though yet we feel
Strength undiminished, or eternal being
To undergo eternal punishment?"    155

Whereto with speedy words the Arch-Fiend
    replied:—
"Fallen Cherub, to be weak is miserable,
Doing or suffering: but of this be sure—
To do ought good never will be our task,
But ever to do ill our sole delight,      160
As being the contrary to his high will
Whom we resist. If then his providence
Out of our evil seek to bring forth good,
Our labor must be to pervert that end,
And out of good still to find means of evil; 165
Which ofttimes may succeed so as perhaps
Shall grieve him, if I fail not,[12] and disturb
His inmost counsels from their destined aim.
But see! the angry Victor hath recalled
His ministers of vengeance and pursuit   170
Back to the gates of Heaven: the sulphurous
    hail,
Shot after us in storm, o'erblown hath laid
The fiery surge that from the precipice
Of Heaven received us falling; and the thunder,
Winged with red lightning and impetuous
    rage,                      175
Perhaps hath spent his shafts, and ceases now
To bellow through the vast and boundless
    Deep.
Let us not slip the occasion, whether scorn
Or satiate fury yield it from our Foe.
Seest thou yon dreary plain, forlorn and wild,
The seat of desolation, void of light,   181
Save what the glimmering of these livid flames
Casts pale and dreadful? Thither let us tend
From off the tossing of these fiery waves;
There rest, if any rest can harbor there;  185
And, re-assembling our afflicted powers,
Consult how we may henceforth most offend
Our enemy, our own loss how repair,
How overcome this dire calamity,
What reinforcement we may gain from hope,
If not, what resolution from despair."  191
    Thus Satan, talking to his nearest mate,
With head uplift above the wave, and eyes
That sparkling blazed; his other parts besides
Prone on the flood, extended long and large, 195
Lay floating many a rood, in bulk as huge
As whom the fables name of monstrous size,
Titanian or Earth-born, that warred on Jove,[13]
Briareos or Typhon, whom the den
By ancient Tarsus held, or that sea-beast  200
Leviathan, which God of all his works
Created hugest that swim the ocean-stream.
Him, haply slumbering on the Norway foam,
The pilot of some small night-foundered [14]
    skiff,
Deeming some island, oft, as seamen tell, 205
With fixéd anchor on his scaly rind,
Moors by his side under the lee, while night
Invests the sea, and wishéd morn delays.

[12] If I mistake not.

[13] The Titans warred on Uranus, the Giants (earth-born) on Jove (Zeus). Briareos was a Titan, Typhon a Giant.

[14] Overtaken by night and so brought to a stand.

[10] Feared for.                  [11] Satisfy.

So stretched out huge in length the Arch-Fiend
    lay,
Chained on the burning lake; nor ever thence
Had risen, or heaved his head, but that the
    will                      211
And high permission of all-ruling Heaven
Left him at large to his own dark designs,
That with reiterated crimes he might
Heap on himself damnation, while he sought
Evil to others, and enraged might see   216
How all his malice served but to bring forth
Infinite goodness, grace, and mercy, shown
On Man by him seduced, but on himself
Treble  confusion,  wrath,  and  vengeance
    poured.                          220
    Forthwith upright he rears from off the pool
His mighty stature; on each hand the flames
Driven backward slope their pointing spires,
    and, rolled
In billows, leave i'the midst a horrid vale.
Then with expanded wings he steers his flight
Aloft, incumbent on the dusky air,     226
That felt unusual weight; till on dry land
He lights—if it were land that ever burned
With solid, as the lake with liquid fire,
And such appeared in hue as when the force 230
Of subterranean wind transports a hill
Torn from Pelorus, or the shattered side
Of thundering Aetna, whose combustible
And fueled entrails, thence conceiving fire,
Sublimed with mineral fury, aid the winds, 235
And leave a singéd bottom all involved
With stench and smoke. Such resting found
    the sole
Of unblest feet. Him followed his next mate;
Both glorying to have scaped the Stygian flood
As gods, and by their own recovered strength,
Not by the sufferance of supernal power.  241
"Is this the region, this the soil, the clime,"
Said then the lost Archangel, "this the seat
That  we  must  change  for  Heaven?—this
    mournful gloom
For that celestial light? Be it so, since he   245
Who now is sovran can dispose and bid
What shall be right: farthest from him is best,
Whom  reason  hath  equaled,  force  hath  made
    supreme
Above his equals. Farewell, happy fields,   249
Where joy for ever dwells! Hail, horrors! hail,
Infernal World! and thou, profoundest Hell,
Receive thy new possessor—one who brings
A mind not to be changed by place or time.
The mind is its own place, and in itself
Can make a Heaven of Hell, a Hell of Heaven.
What matter where, if I be still the same,  256
And what I should be, all but less than [15] he
Whom thunder hath made greater? Here at
    least
We shall be free; the Almighty hath not built
Here for his envy, will not drive us hence:  260
Here we may reign secure; and, in my choice,

[15] I. e., only less than.

To reign is worth ambition, though in Hell:
Better to reign in Hell than serve in Heaven.
But wherefore let we then our faithful friends,
The associates and co-partners of our loss, 265
Lie thus astonished on the oblivious pool,[16]
And call them not to share with us their part
In this unhappy mansion, or once more
With rallied arms to try what may be yet
Regained in Heaven, or what more lost in
    Hell?"                     270
    So Satan spake; and him Beëlzebub
Thus  answered:—"Leader  of  those  armies
    bright
Which, but the Omnipotent, none could have
    foiled!
If once they hear that voice, their liveliest
    pledge
Of hope in fears and dangers—heard so oft 275
In worst extremes, and on the perilous edge
Of battle, when it raged, in all assaults
Their surest signal—they will soon resume
New courage and revive, though now they lie
Groveling and prostrate on yon lake of fire, 280
As we erewhile, astounded and amazed;
No wonder, fallen such a pernicious highth!"
    He  scarce  had  ceased  when  the  superior
    Fiend
Was moving toward the shore; his ponderous
    shield,
Ethereal temper, massy, large, and round,  285
Behind him cast. The broad circumference
Hung on his shoulders like the moon, whose
    orb
Through optic glass [17] the Tuscan artist views
At evening, from the top of Fesolé,
Or in Valdarno, to descry new lands,     290
Rivers, or mountains, in her spotty globe.
His spear—to equal which the tallest pine
Hewn on Norwegian hills, to be the mast
Of some great ammiral,[18] were but a wand—
He walked with, to support uneasy steps  295
Over the burning marl, not like those steps
On Heaven's azure; and the torrid clime
Smote on him sore besides, vaulted with fire.
Nathless [19] he so endured, till on the beach
Of that inflaméd sea he stood, and called  300
His legions—Angel Forms, who lay entranced
Thick as autumnal leaves that strow the brooks
In Vallombrosa,[20] where the Etrurian shades
High over-arched embower; or scattered sedge
Afloat, when with fierce winds Orion armed 305
Hath vexed the Red-Sea coast, whose waves
    o'erthrew
Busiris and his Memphian chivalry,[21]
While with perfidious hatred they pursued

[16] Lie thus thunderstruck on the benumbing pool.
[17] The telescope, greatly improved by Galileo (the Tuscan artist). Fiesole is a hill just outside of Florence; Val d'Arno, the valley in which Florence lies.
[18] Chief vessel in a fleet.      [19] Nevertheless.
[20] Eighteen miles from Florence.
[21] Busiris, Pharaoh; Memphian, Egyptian.

The sojourners of Goshen, who beheld
From the safe shore their floating carcases 310
And broken chariot-wheels. So thick bestrown,
Abject and lost, lay these, covering the flood,
Under amazement of their hideous change.
He called so loud that all the hollow deep
Of Hell resounded:—"Princes, Potentates, 315
Warriors, the Flower of Heaven—once yours;
    now lost,
If such astonishment as this can seize
Eternal Spirits! Or have ye chosen this place
After the toil of battle to repose
Your wearied virtue,[22] for the ease you find 320
To slumber here, as in the vales of Heaven?
Or in this abject posture have ye sworn
To adore the Conqueror, who now beholds
Cherub and Seraph rolling in the flood
With scattered arms and ensigns, till anon 325
His swift pursuers from Heaven-gates discern
The advantage, and, descending, tread us down
Thus drooping, or with linkéd thunderbolts
Transfix us to the bottom of this gulf?—
Awake, arise, or be for ever fallen!" 330
    They heard, and were abashed, and up they
        sprung
Upon the wing, as when men wont to watch
On duty sleeping found by whom they dread,
Rouse and bestir themselves ere well awake.
Nor did they not perceive [23] the evil plight 335
In which they were, or the fierce pains not feel;
Yet to their General's voice they soon obeyed
Innumerable. As when the potent rod
Of Amram's son,[24] in Egypt's evil day,
Waved round the coast, up-called a pitchy
    cloud 340
Of locusts, warping on the eastern wind,
That o'er the realm of impious Pharaoh hung
Like Night, and darkened all the land of Nile;
So numberless were those bad Angels seen
Hovering on wing under the cope of Hell, 345
'Twixt upper, nether, and surrounding fires;
Till, as a signal given, the uplifted spear
Of their great Sultan waving to direct
Their course, in even balance down they light
On the firm brimstone, and fill all the plain:
A multitude like which the populous North 351
Poured never from her frozen loins to pass
Rhene or the Danaw,[25] when her barbarous
    sons
Came like a deluge on the South, and spread
Beneath Gibraltar to the Libyan sands. 355
Forthwith, from every squadron and each band,
The heads and leaders thither haste where
    stood
Their great Commander—godlike Shapes, and
    Forms
Excelling human; princely Dignities;
And Powers that erst [26] in Heaven sat on
    thrones, 360

Though of their names in Heavenly records
    now
Be no memorial, blotted out and razed
By their rebellion from the Books of Life.
Nor had they yet among the sons of Eve
Got them new names, till, wandering o'er the
    earth, 365
Through God's high sufferance for the trial of
    man,
By falsities and lies the greatest part
Of mankind they corrupted to forsake
God their Creator, and the invisible
Glory of him that made them, to transform 370
Oft to the image of a brute, adorned
With gay religions full of pomp and gold,
And devils to adore for deities:
Then were they known to men by various
    names,
And various idols through the Heathen World.
    Say, Muse, their names then known, who
    first, who last, 376
Roused from the slumber on that fiery couch,
At their great Emperor's call, as next in worth
Came singly where he stood on the bare strand,
While the promiscuous crowd stood yet aloof.
    The chief were those who, from the pit of
        Hell 381
Roaming to seek their prey on Earth, durst fix
Their seats, long after, next the seat of God,
Their altars by his altar, gods adored
Among the nations round, and durst abide 385
Jehovah thundering out of Sion, throned
Between the Cherubim; yea, often placed
Within his sanctuary itself their shrines,
Abominations; and with curséd things
His holy rites and solemn feasts profaned, 390
And with their darkness durst affront his light.
First, *Moloch*, horrid king, besmeared with
    blood
Of human sacrifice, and parents' tears;
Though, for the noise of drums and timbrels
    loud,
Their children's cries unheard that passed
    through fire 395
To his grim idol. Him the Ammonite
Worshiped in Rabba and her watery plain,
In Argob and in Basan, to the stream
Of utmost Arnon. Nor content with such
Audacious neighborhood, the wisest heart 400
Of Solomon he led by fraud to build
His temple right against the temple of God
On that opprobrious hill,[27] and made his grove
The pleasant valley of Hinnom, Tophet thence
And black Gehenna called, the type of Hell. 405
Next *Chemos*, the obscene dread of Moab's
    sons,
From Aroar to Nebo and the wild
Of southmost Abarim; in Hesebon
And Horonaim, Seon's realm, beyond
The flowery dale of Sibma clad with vines, 410

[22] Courage.    [23] Nor did they fail to perceive.
[24] Aaron.    [25] Rhine or the Danube.
[26] Formerly.

[27] The Mount of Olives, later called the Mount of
Offense.

And Elealé to the Asphaltic Pool: [28]
Peor his other name, when he enticed
Israel in Sittim on their march from Nile,
To do him wanton rites, which cost them woe.
Yet thence his lustful orgies he enlarged     415
Even to that hill of scandal, by the grove
Of Moloch homicide, lust hard by hate,
Till good Josiah drove them thence to Hell.
With these came they who, from the bordering
    flood
Of old Euphrates to the brook that parts     420
Egypt from Syrian ground, had general names
Of *Baälim* and *Ashtaroth*—those male,
These feminine. For spirits, when they please,
Can either sex assume, or both; so soft
And uncompounded is their essence pure,     425
Not tied or manacled with joint or limb,
Nor founded on the brittle strength of bones,
Like cumbrous flesh; but, in what shape they
    choose,
Dilated or condensed, bright or obscure,
Can execute their aery purposes,     430
And works of love or enmity fulfill.
For those the race of Israel oft forsook
Their Living Strength, and unfrequented left
His righteous altar, bowing lowly down     434
To bestial gods; for which their heads, as low
Bowed down in battle, sunk before the spear
Of despicable foes. With these in troop
Came *Astoreth*, whom the Phoenicians called
Astarté, queen of heaven, with crescent horns;
To whose bright image nightly by the moon
Sidonian virgins paid their vows and songs; [441]
In Sion also not unsung, where stood
Her temple on the offensive mountain, built
By that uxorious king [29] whose heart, though
    large,
Beguiled by fair idolatresses, fell     445
To idols foul. *Thammuz* came next behind,
Whose annual wound in Lebanon allured
The Syrian damsels to lament his fate
In amorous ditties all a summer's day,     449
While smooth Adonis [30] from his native rock
Ran purple to the sea, supposed with blood,
Of Thammuz yearly wounded: the love-tale
Infected Sion's daughters with like heat,
Whose wanton passions in the sacred porch
Ezekiel saw, when, by the vision led,     455
His eye surveyed the dark idolatries
Of alienated Judah. Next came one
Who mourned in earnest, when the captive ark
Maimed his brute image, head and hands
    lopped off,
In his own temple, on the grunsel [31] edge,     460
Where he fell flat and shamed his worshipers:
*Dagon* his name, sea-monster, upward man
And downward fish; yet had his temple high
Reared in Azotus, dreaded through the coast
Of Palestine, in Gath and Ascalon,     465

And Accaron and Gaza's frontier bounds.
Him followed *Rimmon*, whose delightful seat
Was fair Damascus, on the fertile banks
Of Abbana and Pharphar, lucid streams.
He also against the house of God was bold: [470]
A leper [32] once he lost, and gained a king—
Ahaz, his sottish conqueror, whom he drew
God's altar to disparage and displace
For one of Syrian mode, whereon to burn
His odious offerings, and adore the gods     475
Whom he had vanquished. After these ap-
    peared
A crew who, under names of old renown—
*Osiris, Isis, Orus,* and their train—
With monstrous shapes and sorceries abused
Fanatic Egypt and her priests to seek     480
Their wandering gods disguised in brutish
    forms
Rather than human. Nor did Israel scape
The infection, when their borrowed gold [33]
    composed
The calf in Oreb; and the rebel king [34]
Doubled that sin in Bethel and in Dan,     485
Likening his Maker to the grazéd ox—
Jehovah, who, in one night, when he [35] passed
From Egypt marching, equaled [36] with one
    stroke
Both her first-born and all her bleating gods.
*Belial* came last; than whom a Spirit more lewd
Fell not from Heaven, or more gross to love [491]
Vice for itself. To him no temple stood
Or altar smoked; yet who more oft than he
In temples and at altars, when the priest
Turns atheist, as did Eli's sons, who filled     495
With lust and violence the house of God?
In courts and palaces he also reigns,
And in luxurious cities, where the noise
Of riot ascends above their loftiest towers,
And injury and outrage; and, when night     500
Darkens the streets, then wander forth the sons
Of Belial, flown [37] with insolence and wine.
Witness the streets of Sodom, and that night
In Gibeah, when the hospitable door
Exposed a matron, to avoid worse rape.     505
    These were the prime in order and in might:
The rest were long to tell; though far renowned
The Ionian gods—of Javan's issue held
Gods, yet confessed later than Heaven and
    Earth,
Their boasted parents;—*Titan,* Heaven's first-
    born,     510
With his enormous brood, and birthright seized
By younger *Saturn:* he from mightier Jove,
His own and Rhea's son, like measure found;
So *Jove* usurping reigned. These, first in Crete
And Ida known, thence on the snowy top     515
Of cold Olympus ruled the middle air,
Their highest heaven; or on the Delphian cliff,
Or in Dodona, and through all the bounds

---

[28] The Dead Sea.     [29] Solomon.
[30] A river in Phoenicia whose waters are colored
by the soil through which it flows.
[31] Threshold.

[32] Naaman.
[33] "Borrowed" from the Egyptians.
[34] Jeroboam.     [35] I. e., Israel.
[36] Struck down.     [37] Flushed.

Of Doric land; or who with Saturn old
Fled over Adria to the Hesperian fields,    520
And o'er the Celtic roamed the utmost Isles.
    All these and more came flocking; but with
        looks
Downcast and damp; [38] yet such wherein ap-
        peared
Obscure some glimpse of joy to have found
        their Chief
Not in despair, to have found themselves not
        lost    525
In loss itself; which on his countenance cast
Like doubtful hue. But he, his wonted pride
Soon recollecting,[39] with high words, that bore
Semblance of worth, not substance, gently
        raised
Their fainting courage, and dispelled their
        fears:    530
Then straight commands that, at the warlike
        sound
Of trumpets loud and clarions, be upreared
His mighty standard. That proud honor
        claimed
Azazel as his right, a Cherub tall:
Who forthwith from the glittering staff un-
        furled    535
The imperial ensign; which, full high advanced,
Shone like a meteor streaming to the wind,
With gems and golden luster rich emblazed,
Seraphic arms and trophies; all the while
Sonorous metal blowing martial sounds:    540
At which the universal host up-sent
A shout that tore Hell's concave, and beyond
Frighted the reign of Chaos and old Night.
All in a moment through the gloom were seen
Ten thousand banners rise into the air,    545
With orient [40] colors waving: with them rose
A forest huge of spears; and thronging helms
Appeared, and serried shields in thick array
Of depth immeasurable. Anon they move
In perfect phalanx to the Dorian mood [41]    550
Of flutes and soft recorders [42]—such as raised
To highth of noblest temper heroes old
Arming to battle, and instead of rage
Deliberate valor breathed, firm, and un-
        moved [43]
With dread of death to flight or foul retreat;
Nor wanting power to mitigate and swage [44]
With solemn touches troubled thoughts, and
        chase    557
Anguish and doubt and fear and sorrow and
        pain
From mortal or immortal minds. Thus they,
Breathing united force with fixéd thought,    560
Moved on in silence to soft pipes that charmed
Their painful steps o'er the burnt soil. And
        now
Advanced in view they stand—a horrid [45] front

Of dreadful length and dazzling arms, in guise
Of warriors old, with ordered spear and shield,
Awaiting what command their mighty Chief [56]
Had to impose. He through the arméd files
Darts his experienced eye, and soon traverse [46]
The whole battalion views—their order due,
Their visages and stature as of gods;    570
Their number last he sums. And now his heart
Distends with pride, and, hardening in his
        strength,
Glories: for never, since created Man,[47]
Met such embodied force as, named with these
Could merit more than that small infantry [57]
Warred on by cranes [48]—though all the giant
        brood
Of Phlegra with the heroic race were joined
That fought at Thebes and Ilium, on each side
Mixed with auxiliar gods; and what resounds
In fable or romance of Uther's son [49]    580
Begirt with British and Armoric [50] knights;
And all who since, baptized or infidel,
Jousted in Aspramont, or Montalban,
Damasco, or Marocco, or Trebisond,
Or whom Biserta sent from Afric shore    585
When Charlemagne with all his peerage fell
By Fontarabbia. Thus far these beyond
Compare of mortal prowess, yet observed [51]
Their dread Commander. He, above the rest
In shape and gesture proudly eminent,    590
Stood like a tower. His form had yet not lost
All her original brightness, nor appeared
Less than Archangel ruined, and the excess
Of glory obscured: as when the sun new-risen
Looks through the horizontal misty air    595
Shorn of his beams, or from behind the moon,
In dim eclipse, disastrous twilight sheds
On half the nations, and with fear of change
Perplexes monarchs. Darkened so, yet shone
Above them all the Archangel: but his face [60]
Deep scars of thunder had intrenched, and care
Sat on his faded cheek, but under brows
Of dauntless courage, and considerate [52] pride
Waiting revenge. Cruel his eye, but cast
Signs of remorse and passion,[53] to behold [605]
The fellows of his crime, the followers rather
(Far other once beheld in bliss), condemned
For ever now to have their lot in pain—
Millions of Spirits for his fault amerced [54]
Of Heaven, and from eternal splendors flung
For his revolt—yet faithful how they stood,    611
Their glory withered; as, when heaven's fire
Hath scathed [55] the forest oaks or mountain
        pines,
With singéd top their stately growth, though
        bare,
Stands on the blasted heath. He now prepared
To speak; whereat their doubled ranks they
        bend    616

[38] Depressed.    [39] Regaining.    [40] Bright.
[41] It was grave, or even stern, in character—suitable for soldiers.
[42] A kind of flute.    [43] Immovable.
[44] Assuage.    [45] Bristling.

[46] Across.    [47] Since man's creation.
[48] The Pygmies (*Iliad*, III, 5).
[49] King Arthur.    [50] Breton.    [51] Obeyed.
[52] Thoughtful.    [53] Pity and strong emotion.
[54] Punished by loss.    [55] Injured.

From wing to wing, and half enclose him round
With all his peers: Attention held them mute.
Thrice he assayed, and thrice, in spite of scorn,
Tears, such as angels weep, burst forth: at last    620
Words interwove with sighs found out their way:—
   "O myriads of immortal Spirits! O Powers
Matchless, but with the Almighty!—and that strife
Was not inglorious, though the event [56] was dire,
As this place testifies, and this dire change,    625
Hateful to utter. But what power of mind,
Foreseeing or presaging, from the depth
Of knowledge past or present, could have feared
How such united force of gods, how such
As stood like these, could ever know repulse?
For who can yet believe, though after loss,    631
That all these puissant legions, whose exile
Hath emptied Heaven, shall fail to re-ascend,
Self-raised, and re-possess their native seat?
For me, be witness all the host of Heaven,    635
If counsels different, or danger shunned
By me, have lost our hopes. But he who reigns
Monarch in Heaven till then as one secure
Sat on his throne, upheld by old repute,
Consent or custom, and his regal state    640
Put forth at full, but still his strength concealed—
Which tempted our attempt, and wrought our fall.
Henceforth his might we know, and know our own,
So as not either to provoke, or dread
New war provoked: our better part remains    645
To work in close design, by fraud or guile,
What force effected not; that he no less
At length from us may find, who overcomes
By force hath overcome but half his foe.
Space may produce new Worlds; whereof so rife    650
There went a fame in Heaven that he ere long
Intended to create, and therein plant
A generation whom his choice regard
Should favor equal to the Sons of Heaven.
Thither, if but to pry, shall be perhaps    655
Our first eruption—thither, or elsewhere;
For this infernal pit shall never hold
Celestial Spirits in bondage, nor the Abyss
Long under darkness cover. But these thoughts
Full counsel must mature. Peace is despaired;
For who can think submission? War, then, war    661
Open or understood,[57] must be resolved."
   He spake; and, to confirm his words, outflew
Millions of flaming swords, drawn from the thighs
Of mighty Cherubim; the sudden blaze    665
Far round illumined Hell. Highly they raged

Against the Highest, and fierce with graspéd arms
Clashed on their sounding shields the din of war,
Hurling defiance toward the vault of Heaven.
   There stood a hill not far, whose grisly top
Belched fire and rolling smoke; the rest entire
Shone with a glossy scurf—undoubted sign [672]
That in his womb was hid metallic ore,
The work of sulphur.[58] Thither, winged with speed,
A numerous brigad hastened: as when bands [675]
Of pioneers, with spade and pickax armed,
Forerun the royal camp, to trench a field,
Or cast a rampart. Mammon led them on—
Mammon, the least erected Spirit that fell
From Heaven; for even in Heaven his looks and thoughts    680
Were always downward bent, admiring more
The riches of Heaven's pavement, trodden gold,
Than aught divine or holy else enjoyed
In vision beatific. By him first
Men also, and by his suggestion taught,    685
Ransacked the center,[59] and with impious hands
Rifled the bowels of their mother earth
For treasures better hid. Soon had his crew
Opened into the hill a spacious wound,
And digged out ribs [60] of gold. Let none admire [61]    690
That riches grow in Hell; that soil may best
Deserve the precious bane. And here let those
Who boast in mortal things, and wondering tell
Of Babel, and the works of Memphian kings,[62]
Learn how their greatest monuments of fame
And strength, and art, are easily outdone [696]
By Spirits reprobate, and in an hour
What in an age they, with incessant toil
And hands innumerable, scarce perform.
Nigh on the plain, in many cells prepared, [700]
That underneath had veins of liquid fire
Sluiced from the lake, a second multitude
With wondrous art founded [63] the massy ore,
Severing each kind, and scummed the bullion-dross.
A third as soon had formed within the ground
A various mold, and from the boiling cells [706]
By strange conveyance filled each hollow nook;
As in an organ, from one blast of wind,
To many a row of pipes the sound-board breathes.
Anon out of the earth a fabric huge    710
Rose like an exhalation, with the sound
Of dulcet symphonies and voices sweet—
Built like a temple, where pilasters round
Were set, and Doric pillars overlaid [64]
With golden architrave; nor did there want [715]

[58] Sulphur was formerly believed to be the formative element of metals.
[59] The earth.    [60] Bars.    [61] Wonder.
[62] The pyramids.    [63] Melted.
[64] Surmounted.

[56] Result.    [57] Not openly declared.

Cornice or frieze, with bossy [65] sculptures graven;
The roof was fretted [66] gold. Not Babylon
Nor great Alcairo such magnificence
Equaled in all their glories, to enshrine
Belus or Serapis their gods, or seat          720
Their kings, when Egypt with Assyria strove
In wealth and luxury. The ascending pile
Stood fixed her stately highth; and straight the doors,
Opening their brazen folds, discover, wide
Within, her ample spaces o'er the smooth 725
And level pavement: from the archéd roof,
Pendent by subtle magic, many a row
Of starry lamps and blazing cressets, fed
With naphtha and asphaltus, yielded light
As from a sky. The hasty multitude          730
Admiring entered; and the work some praise,
And some the architect. His hand was known
In Heaven by many a towered structure high,
Where sceptered Angels held their residence,
And sat as Princes, whom the supreme King 735
Exalted to such power, and gave to rule,
Each in his hierarchy, the Orders bright.
Nor was his name unheard or unadored
In ancient Greece; and in Ausonian land [67]
Men called him Mulciber; and how he fell 740
From Heaven they fabled, thrown by angry Jove
Sheer o'er the crystal battlements: from morn
To noon he fell, from noon to dewy eve,
A summer's day, and with the setting sun
Dropped from the zenith, like a falling star, 745
On Lemnos, the Aegæan isle. Thus they relate,
Erring; for he with this rebellious rout
Fell long before; nor aught availed him now
To have built in Heaven high towers; nor did he scape
By all his engines, [68] but was headlong sent, 750
With his industrious crew, to build in Hell.
   Meanwhile the wingéd heralds, by command
Of sovran power, with awful ceremony
And trumpet's sound, throughout the host proclaim
A solemn council forthwith to be held      755
At Pandemonium, [69] the high capital
Of Satan and his peers. Their summons called
From every band and squaréd regiment
By place or choice the worthiest: they anon came          760
With hundreds and with thousands trooping
Attended. All access was thronged; the gates
And porches wide, but chief the spacious hall
(Though like a covered field, where champions bold
Wont ride in armed, and at the soldan's [70] chair
Defied the best of paynim [71] chivalry      765
To mortal combat, or career with lance),

Thick swarmed, both on the ground and in the air,
Brushed with the hiss of rustling wings. As bees
In spring-time, when the Sun with Taurus [72] rides,
Pour forth their populous youth about the hive          770
In clusters; they among fresh dews and flowers
Fly to and fro, or on the smoothéd plank,
The suburb of their straw-built citadel,
New rubbed with balm, expatiate, [73] and confer [74]
Their state-affairs: so thick the aery crowd 775
Swarmed and were straitened; till, the signal given,
Behold a wonder! They but now who seemed
In bigness to surpass earth's giant sons,
Now less than smallest dwarfs, in narrow room
Throng numberless—like that pygmean race [78]
Beyond the Indian mount; or faery elves,
Whose midnight revels, by a forest-side
Or fountain, some belated peasant sees,
Or dreams he sees, while overhead the Moon
Sits arbitress, [75] and nearer to the earth      785
Wheels her pale course: they, on their mirth and dance
Intent, with jocund music charm his ear;
At once with joy and fear his heart rebounds.
Thus incorporeal Spirits to smallest forms
Reduced their shapes immense, and were at large,          790
Though without number still, amidst the hall
Of that infernal court. But far within,
And in their own dimensions like themselves,
The great Seraphic Lords and Cherubim
In close recess [76] and secret conclave sat, 795
A thousand demi-gods on golden seats,
Frequent [77] and full. After short silence then,
And summons read, the great consult [78] began.

## BOOK II

### THE ARGUMENT

THE *consultation begun, Satan debates whether another battle be to be hazarded for the recovery of Heaven: some advise it, others dissuade. A third proposal is preferred, mentioned before by Satan—to search the truth of that prophecy or tradition in Heaven concerning another world, and another kind of creature, equal, or not much inferior, to themselves, about this time to be created. Their doubt who shall be sent on this difficult search: Satan, their chief, undertakes alone the voyage; is honored and applauded. The council thus ended, the rest betake them several ways and to several employments, as their inclinations lead them, to*

[65] Projecting.
[66] Checkered; or adorned with embossed designs.
[67] Italy.          [68] Contrivances.
[69] Abode of all demons.          [70] Sultan's.
[71] Pagan.

[72] Sign of the zodiac (the time is 19 April to 20 May).
[73] Walk abroad.          [74] Discuss.          [75] Witness.
[76] Retirement.          [77] Numerous.
[78] Consultation.

*entertain the time till Satan return. He passes on his journey to Hell-gates; finds them shut, and who sat there to guard them; by whom at length they are opened, and discover to him the great gulf between Hell and Heaven. With what difficulty he passes through, directed by Chaos, the Power of that place, to the sight of this new World which he sought.*

High on a throne of royal state, which far
Outshone the wealth of Ormus [1] and of Ind,
Or where the gorgeous East with richest hand
Showers on her kings barbaric pearl and gold,
Satan exalted sat, by merit raised     5
To that bad eminence; and, from despair
Thus high uplifted beyond hope, aspires
Beyond thus high, insatiate to pursue
Vain war with Heaven; and, by success [2] un-
    taught,
His proud imaginations thus displayed:— 10
  "Powers and Dominions, Deities of
    Heaven!—
For, since no deep within her gulf can hold
Immortal vigor, though oppressed and fallen,
I give not Heaven for lost: from this descent
Celestial Virtues rising will appear     15
More glorious and more dread than from no
    fall,
And trust themselves to fear no second fate!—
Me though just right, and the fixed laws of
    Heaven,
Did first create your leader—next, free choice,
With what besides in council or in fight     20
Hath been achieved of merit—yet this loss,
Thus far at least recovered, hath much more
Established in a safe, unenvied throne,
Yielded with full consent. The happier state
In Heaven, which follows dignity, might draw
Envy from each inferior; but who here     26
Will envy whom the highest place exposes
Foremost to stand against the Thunderer's aim
Your bulwark, and condemns to greatest share
Of endless pain? Where there is, then, no
    good     30
For which to strive, no strife can grow up there
From faction: for none sure will claim in Hell
Precedence; none whose portion is so small
Of present pain that with ambitious mind
Will covet more! With this advantage, then, 35
To union, and firm faith, and firm accord,
More than can be in Heaven, we now return
To claim our just inheritance of old,
Surer to prosper than prosperity
Could have assured us; and by what best way, 40
Whether of open war or covert guile,
We now debate. Who can advise may speak."
  He ceased; and next him Moloch, sceptered
    king,
Stood up—the strongest and the fiercest Spirit
That fought in Heaven, now fiercer by despair.
His trust was with the Eternal to be deemed 46

Equal in strength, and rather than be less
Cared not to be at all; with that care lost
Went all his fear: of God, or Hell, or worse,
He recked [3] not, and these words thereafter
    spake:—     50
  "My sentence is for open war. Of wiles,
More unexpert,[4] I boast not: them let those
Contrive who need, or when they need; not
    now.
For, while they sit contriving, shall the rest—
Millions that stand in arms, and longing wait 55
The signal to ascend—sit lingering here,
Heaven's fugitives, and for their dwelling-place
Accept this dark opprobrious den of shame,
The prison of his tyranny who reigns
By our delay? No! let us rather choose,     60
Armed with Hell-flames and fury, all at once
O'er Heaven's high towers to force resistless
    way,
Turning our tortures into horrid arms
Against the Torturer; when, to meet the noise
Of his almighty engine, he shall hear     65
Infernal thunder, and, for lightning, see
Black fire and horror shot with equal rage
Among his Angels, and his throne itself
Mixed with Tartarean [5] sulphur and strange
    fire,
His own invented torments. But perhaps     70
The way seems difficult, and steep to scale
With upright wing against a higher foe!
Let such bethink them, if the sleepy drench
Of that forgetful lake benumb not still,
That in our proper [6] motion we ascend     75
Up to our native seat; descent and fall
To us is adverse. Who but felt of late,
When the fierce foe hung on our broken rear
Insulting, and pursued us through the Deep,
With what compulsion and laborious flight 80
We sunk thus low? The ascent is easy, then;
The event [7] is feared! Should we again provoke
Our stronger, some worse way his wrath may
    find
To our destruction, if there be in Hell
Fear to be worse destroyed! What can be worse
Than to dwell here, driven out from bliss,
    condemned     86
In this abhorréd deep to utter woe!
Where pain of unextinguishable fire
Must exercise [8] us without hope of end
The vassals of his anger, when the scourge 90
Inexorably, and the torturing hour,
Calls us to penance? More destroyed than thus,
We should be quite abolished, and expire.
What fear we then? what doubt we to incense
His utmost ire? which, to the highth enraged,
Will either quite consume us, and reduce     96
To nothing this essential [9]—happier far
Than miserable to have eternal being!—
Or, if our substance be indeed divine,

[1] An island in the Persian Gulf.
[2] Experience.
[3] Cared.     [4] Inexperienced.     [5] Infernal.
[6] Natural.     [7] Its result.     [8] Torment.
[9] Substance (adjective for substantive, as frequently with Milton).

And cannot cease to be, we are at worst    100
On this side nothing; and by proof we feel
Our power sufficient to disturb his Heaven
And with perpetual inroads to alarm,
Though inaccessible, his fatal throne:
Which, if not victory, is yet revenge."    105
    He ended frowning, and his look de-
        nounced [10]
Desperate revenge, and battle dangerous
To less than gods. On the other side up rose
Belial, in act more graceful and humane.
A fairer person lost not Heaven; he seemed [110]
For dignity composed, and high exploit.
But all was false and hollow; though his tongue
Dropped manna, and could make the worse
        appear
The better reason, to perplex and dash
Maturest counsels: for his thoughts were low—
To vice industrious, but to nobler deeds    116
Timorous and slothful. Yet he pleased the ear,
And with persuasive accent thus began:—
    "I should be much for open war, O Peers,
As not behind in hate, if what was urged [120]
Main reason to persuade immediate war
Did not dissuade me most, and seem to cast
Ominous conjecture on the whole success;
When he who most excels in fact [11] of arms,
In what he counsels and in what excels    125
Mistrustful, grounds his courage on despair
And utter dissolution, as the scope
Of all his aim, after some dire revenge.
First, what revenge? The towers of Heaven are
        filled
With arméd watch, that render all access [130]
Impregnable: oft on the bordering Deep
Encamp their legions, or with obscure wing
Scout far and wide into the realm of Night,
Scorning surprise. Or, could we break our way
By force, and at our heels all Hell should rise
With blackest insurrection to confound    136
Heaven's purest light, yet our great Enemy,
All incorruptible, would on his throne
Sit unpolluted, and the ethereal mold,[12]
Incapable of stain, would soon expel    140
Her mischief, and purge off the baser fire,
Victorious. Thus repulsed, our final hope
Is flat despair: we must exasperate
The Almighty Victor to spend all his rage;
And that must end us; that must be our cure—
To be no more. Sad cure! for who would
        lose,    146
Though full of pain, this intellectual being,
Those thoughts that wander through eternity,
To perish rather, swallowed up and lost
In the wide womb of uncreated Night,    150
Devoid of sense and motion? And who knows,
Let this be good, whether our angry Foe
Can give it, or will ever? How he can
Is doubtful; that he never will is sure.
Will he, so wise, let loose at once his ire,    155
Belike [13] through impotence or unaware,

To give his enemies their wish, and end
Them in his anger whom his anger saves
To punish endless? 'Wherefore cease we, then?'
Say they who counsel war; 'we are decreed, [160]
Reserved, and destined to eternal woe;
Whatever doing, what can we suffer more,
What can we suffer worse?' Is this, then,
        worst—
Thus sitting, thus consulting, thus in arms?
What when we fled amain, pursued and strook
With Heaven's afflicting thunder, and be-
        sought    166
The Deep to shelter us? This Hell then seemed
A refuge from those wounds. Or when we lay
Chained on the burning lake? That sure was
        worse.
What if the breath that kindled those grim
        fires,    170
Awaked, should blow them into sevenfold rage
And plunge us in the flames; or from above
Should intermitted vengeance arm again
His red right hand to plague us? What if all
Her stores were opened, and this firmament [175]
Of Hell should spout her cataracts of fire,
Impendent horrors, threatening hideous fall
One day upon our heads; while we perhaps,
Designing or exhorting glorious war
Caught in a fiery tempest, shall be hurled, [180]
Each on his rock transfixed, the sport and prey
Of racking whirlwinds, or for ever sunk
Under yon boiling ocean, wrapped in chains,
There to converse with everlasting groans,
Unrespited, unpitied, unreprieved,    185
Ages of hopeless end? This would be worse.
War, therefore, open or concealed, alike
My voice dissuades; for what can force or guile
With him, or who deceive his mind, whose eye
Views all things at one view? He from Heaven's
        highth    190
All these our motions vain sees and derides,
Not more almighty to resist our might
Than wise to frustrate all our plots and wiles.
Shall we, then, live thus vile—the race of
        Heaven
Thus trampled, thus expelled, to suffer here [195]
Chains and these torments? Better these than
        worse,
By my advice; since fate inevitable
Subdues us, and omnipotent decree,
The Victor's will. To suffer, as to do,
Our strength is equal; nor the law unjust [200]
That so ordains. This was at first resolved,
If we were wise, against so great a foe
Contending, and so doubtful what might fall.
I laugh when those who at the spear are bold
And venturous, if that fail them, shrink, and
        fear    205
What yet they know must follow—to endure
Exile, or ignominy, or bonds, or pain,
The sentence of their conqueror. This is now
Our doom; which if we can sustain and bear,
Our Supreme Foe in time may much remit [210]
His anger, and perhaps, thus far removed,

[10] Indicated.        [11] Deeds.        [12] Substance.
[13] Probably.

Not mind us not offending, satisfied
With what is punished; whence these raging
fires
Will slacken, if his breath stir not their flames.
Our purer essence then will overcome        215
Their noxious vapor; or, inured, not feel;
Or, changed at length, and to the place con-
formed
In temper and in nature, will receive
Familiar the fierce heat; and, void of pain,
This horror will grow mild, this darkness light;
Besides what hope the never-ending flight 221
Of future days may bring, what chance, what
change
Worth waiting—since our present lot appears
For happy though but ill, for ill not worst,[14]
If we procure not to ourselves more woe." 225
 Thus Belial, with words clothed in reason's
garb,
Counseled ignoble ease and peaceful sloth,
Not peace; and after him thus Mammon
spake:—
"Either to disenthrone the King of Heaven
We war, if war be best, or to regain        230
Our own right lost. Him to unthrone we then
May hope, when everlasting Fate shall yield
To fickle Chance, and Chaos judge the strife.
The former, vain to hope, argues as vain
The latter; for what place can be for us     235
Within Heaven's bound, unless Heaven's Lord
Supreme
We overpower? Suppose he should relent,
And publish grace to all, on promise made
Of new subjection; with what eyes could we
Stand in his presence humble, and receive 240
Strict laws imposed, to celebrate his throne
With warbled hymns, and to his Godhead sing
Forced Halleluiahs, while he lordly sits
Our envied sovran, and his altar breathes
Ambrosial odors and ambrosial flowers,      245
Our servile offerings? This must be our task
In Heaven, this our delight. How wearisome
Eternity so spent in worship paid
To whom we hate! Let us not then pursue,
By force impossible, by leave obtained       250
Unacceptable, though in Heaven, our state
Of splendid vassalage; but rather seek
Our own good from ourselves, and from our
own
Live to ourselves, though in this vast recess,
Free and to none accountable, preferring 255
Hard liberty before the easy yoke
Of servile pomp. Our greatness will appear
Then most conspicuous when great things of
small,
Useful of hurtful, prosperous of adverse,
We can create, and in what place soe'er    260
Thrive under evil, and work ease out of pain
Through labor and endurance. This deep world
Of darkness do we dread? How oft amidst

Thick clouds and dark doth Heaven's all-
ruling Sire
Choose to reside, his glory unobscured,      265
And with the majesty of darkness round
Covers his throne, from whence deep thunders
roar,
Mustering their rage, and Heaven resembles
Hell!
As he our darkness, cannot we his light
Imitate when we please? This desert soil 270
Wants not her hidden luster, gems and gold;
Nor want we skill or art from whence to raise
Magnificence; and what can Heaven show
more?
Our torments also may, in length of time,
Become our elements, these piercing fires 275
As soft as now severe, our temper changed
Into their temper; which must needs remove
The sensible [15] of pain. All things invite
To peaceful counsels, and the settled state
Of order, how in safety best we may          280
Compose our present evils, with regard
Of what we are and where, dismissing quite
All thoughts of war. Ye have what I advise."
 He scarce had finished, when such murmur
filled
The assembly as when hollow rocks retain 285
The sound of blustering winds, which all night
long
Had roused the sea, now with hoarse cadence
lull
Seafaring men o'erwatched,[16] whose bark by
chance,
Or pinnace, anchors in a craggy bay
After the tempest. Such applause was heard 290
As Mammon ended, and his sentence pleased,
Advising peace: for such another field [17]
They dreaded worse than Hell; so much the
fear
Of thunder and the sword of Michaël
Wrought still within them; and no less de-
sire                                          295
To found this nether empire, which might rise,
By policy and long process of time,
In emulation opposite to Heaven.
Which  when  Beëlzebub  perceived—than
whom,
Satan except, none higher sat—with grave 300
Aspect he rose, and in his rising seemed
A pillar of state. Deep on his front engraven
Deliberation sat, and public care;
And princely counsel in his face yet shone,
Majestic, though in ruin. Sage he stood,     305
With Atlantean shoulders,[18] fit to bear
The weight of mightiest monarchies; his look
Drew audience and attention still as night
Or summer's noontide air, while thus he
spake:—

[15] Sense.        [16] Wearied with watching.
[17] Battle.
[18] Shoulders like those of Atlas, who supported the
columns on which the heavens rest.

[14] Since our present lot appears ill, indeed, compared with happiness, yet not so bad as it might be.

"Thrones and Imperial Powers, Offspring of
 Heaven,      310
Ethereal Virtues! or these titles now
Must we renounce, and, changing style, be
 called
Princes of Hell? for so the popular vote
Inclines—here to continue, and build up here
A growing empire; doubtless! while we dream,
And know not that the King of Heaven hath
 doomed      316
This place our dungeon—not our safe retreat
Beyond his potent arm, to live exempt
From Heaven's high jurisdiction, in new league
Banded against his throne, but to remain 320
In strictest bondage, though thus far removed,
Under the inevitable curb, reserved
His captive multitude. For He, be sure,
In highth or depth, still first and last will reign
Sole king, and of his kingdom lose no part 325
By our revolt, but over Hell extend
His empire, and with iron scepter rule
Us here, as with his golden those in Heaven.
What sit we then projecting peace and war?
War hath determined [19] us and foiled with loss
Irreparable; terms of peace yet none  331
Vouchsafed or sought; for what peace will be
 given
To us enslaved, but custody severe,
And stripes and arbitrary punishment
Inflicted? and what peace can we return, 335
But, to [20] our power, hostility and hate,
Untamed reluctance, and revenge, though slow,
Yet ever plotting how the Conqueror least
May reap his conquest, and may least rejoice
In doing what we most in suffering feel? 340
Nor will occasion want, nor shall we need
With dangerous expedition to invade
Heaven, whose high walls fear no assault or
 siege,
Or ambush from the Deep. What if we find
Some easier enterprise? There is a place  345
(If ancient and prophetic fame [21] in Heaven
Err not)—another World, the happy seat
Of some new race, called Man, about this time
To be created like to us, though less
In power and excellence, but favored more 350
Of him who rules above; so was his will
Pronounced among the gods, and by an oath
That shook Heaven's whole circumference con-
 firmed.
Thither let us bend all our thoughts, to learn
What creatures there inhabit, of what mold
Or substance, how endued, and what their
 power.      356
And where their weakness: how attempted best
By force or subtlety. Though Heaven be shut,
And Heaven's high Arbitrator sit secure
In his own strength, this place may lie exposed,
The utmost border of his kingdom, left  361
To their defense who hold it: here, perhaps,
Some advantageous act may be achieved

By sudden onset—either with Hell-fire
To waste his whole creation, or possess  365
All as our own, and drive, as we are driven,
The puny habitants; or, if not drive,
Seduce them to our party, that their God
May prove their foe, and with repenting hand
Abolish his own works. This would surpass 370
Common revenge, and interrupt his joy
In our confusion, and our joy upraise
In his disturbance; when his darling sons,
Hurled headlong to partake with us, shall curse
Their frail original, and faded bliss—  375
Faded so soon! Advise [22] if this be worth
Attempting, or to sit in darkness here
Hatching vain empires." Thus Beëlzebub
Pleaded his devilish counsel—first devised
By Satan, and in part proposed: for whence, 380
But from the author of all ill, could spring
So deep a malice, to confound the race
Of mankind in one root, and Earth with Hell
To mingle and involve, done all to spite
The great Creator? But their spite still serves
His glory to augment. The bold design 386
Pleased highly those Infernal States,[23] and joy
Sparkled in all their eyes: with full assent
They vote: whereat his speech he thus re-
 news:—
"Well have ye judged, well ended long debate,
Synod of Gods, and, like to what ye are, 391
Great things resolved, which from the lowest
 deep
Will once more lift us up, in spite of fate,
Nearer our ancient seat—perhaps in view
Of those bright confines, whence, with neigh-
 boring arms,      395
And opportune excursion, we may chance
Re-enter Heaven; or else in some mild zone
Dwell, not unvisited of Heaven's fair light,
Secure, and at the brightening orient beam
Purge off this gloom: the soft delicious air, 400
To heal the scar of these corrosive fires,
Shall breathe her balm. But, first, whom shall
 we send
In search of this new World? whom shall we
 find
Sufficient? who shall tempt [24] with wandering
 feet
The dark, unbottomed, infinite Abyss,  405
And through the palpable obscure [25] find out
His uncouth [26] way, or spread his aery flight,
Upborne with indefatigable wings
Over the vast Abrupt,[27] ere he arrive
The happy Isle? What strength, what art, can
 then      410
Suffice, or what evasion bear him safe,
Through the strict senteries and stations thick
Of angels watching round? Here he had need
All circumspection: and we now no less
Choice [28] in our suffrage; for on whom we send
The weight of all, and our last hope, relies." 416

[19] Undone.    [20] To the limit of.    [21] Report.

[22] Consider.    [23] Councilors.    [24] Try.
[25] Obscurity.    [26] Unknown.
[27] The region of chaos.    [28] Care.

This said, he sat; and expectation held
His look suspense,[29] awaiting who appeared
To second, or oppose, or undertake
The perilous attempt. But all sat mute,     420
Pondering the danger with deep thoughts; and
     each
In other's countenance read his own dismay,
Astonished. None among the choice and prime
Of those Heaven-warring champions could be
     found
So hardy as to proffer or accept,     425
Alone, the dreadful voyage; till, at last,
Satan, whom now transcendent glory raised
Above his fellows, with monarchal pride
Conscious of highest worth, unmoved thus
     spake:—
"O Progeny of Heaven! Empyreal Thrones!
With reason hath deep silence and demur [30] [431]
Seized us, though undismayed. Long is the way
And hard, that out of Hell leads up to Light;
Our prison strong, this huge convex of fire,
Outrageous to devour, immures us round [435]
Ninefold; and gates of burning adamant,
Barred over us, prohibit all egress.
These passed, if any pass, the void profound
Of unessential [31] Night receives him next,
Wide-gaping, and with utter loss of being [440]
Threatens him, plunged in that abortive [32] gulf.
If thence he scape, into whatever world,
Or unknown region, what remains [33] him less
Than unknown dangers, and as hard escape?
But I should ill become this throne, O Peers,
And this imperial sovranty, adorned     446
With splendor, armed with power, if aught
     proposed
And judged of public moment in the shape
Of difficulty or danger, could deter
Me from attempting. Wherefore do I assume
These royalties, and not refuse to reign,     451
Refusing to accept as great a share
Of hazard as of honor, due alike
To him who reigns, and so much to him due
Of hazard more as he above the rest     455
High honored sits? Go, therefore, mighty
     Powers,
Terror of Heaven, though fallen: intend [34] at
     home,
While here shall be our home, what best may
     ease
The present misery, and render Hell
More tolerable; if there be cure or charm [460]
To respite, or deceive,[35] or slack the pain
Of this ill mansion: intermit no watch
Against a wakeful foe, while I abroad
Through all the coasts of dark destruction seek
Deliverance for us all. This enterprise     465
None shall partake with me." Thus saying, rose
The Monarch, and prevented all reply;
Prudent lest, from his resolution raised,[36]

Others among the chief might offer now,
Certain to be refused, what erst they feared, [470]
And, so refused, might in opinion stand
His rivals, winning cheap the high repute
Which he through hazard huge must earn.
     But they
Dreaded not more the adventure than his voice
Forbidding; and at once with him they rose. [475]
Their rising all at once was as the sound
Of thunder heard remote. Towards him they
     bend
With awful reverence prone, and as a God
Extol him equal to the Highest in Heaven.
Nor failed they to express how much they
     praised     [480]
That for the general safety he despised
His own: for neither do the Spirits damned
Lose all their virtue; lest bad men should boast
Their specious deeds on earth, which glory
     excites,
Or close [37] ambition varnished o'er with zeal.
Thus they their doubtful consultations dark
Ended, rejoicing in their matchless Chief: [487]
As, when from mountain-tops the dusky clouds
Ascending, while the North-wind sleeps, o'er-
     spread
Heaven's cheerful face, the louring element [490]
Scowls o'er the darkened landscape snow or
     shower,
If chance the radiant sun, with farewell sweet,
Extend his evening beam, the fields revive,
The birds their notes renew, and bleating herds
Attest their joy, that hill and valley rings. [495]
O shame to men! Devil with devil damned
Firm concord holds; men only disagree
Of creatures rational, though under hope
Of heavenly grace, and, God proclaiming peace,
Yet live in hatred, enmity, and strife     500
Among themselves, and levy cruel wars
Wasting the earth, each other to destroy:
As if (which might induce us to accord)
Man had not hellish foes enow [38] besides,
That day and night for his destruction wait! [505]
    The Stygian council thus dissolved; and forth
In order came the grand Infernal Peers:
Midst came their mighty Paramount,[39] and
     seemed
Alone the antagonist of Heaven, nor less
Than Hell's dread Emperor, with pomp
     supreme,     510
And god-like imitated state: him round
A globe of fiery Seraphim enclosed
With bright emblazonry, and horrent [40] arms.
Then of their session ended they bid cry
With trumpet's regal sound the great result: [515]
Toward the four winds four speedy Cherubim
Put to their mouths the sounding alchemy,[41]
By herald's voice explained; [42] the hollow
     Abyss

[29] In suspense.          [30] Hesitancy.
[31] Void of being.          [32] Dangerous.
[33] Awaits.     [34] Consider.     [35] Divert us from.
[36] Lest, encouraged by his bravery.

[37] Secret.          [38] Enough.          [39] Chief.
[40] Bristling.          [41] Trumpets.
[42] I. e., the herald states the meaning of the trumpet blasts.

Heard far and wide, and all the host of Hell
With deafening shout returned them loud
    acclaim.      520
Thence more at ease their minds, and some-
    what raised
By false presumptuous hope, the rangéd Powers
Disband; and, wandering, each his several way
Pursues, as inclination or sad choice
Leads him perplexed, where he may likeliest
    find      525
Truce to his restless thoughts, and entertain
The irksome hours, till his great Chief return.
Part on the plain, or in the air sublime,
Upon the wing or in swift race contend,
As at the Olympian games or Pythian fields; 530
Part curb their fiery steeds, or shun the goal
With rapid wheels, or fronted brigads form:
As when, to warn proud cities, war appears
Waged in the troubled sky, and armies rush
To battle in the clouds; before each van   535
Prick [43] forth the aery knights, and couch their
    spears,
Till thickest legions close; with feats of arms
From either end of heaven the welkin [44] burns.
Others, with vast Typhoean rage, more fell,
Rend up both rocks and hills, and ride the air
In whirlwind; Hell scarce holds the wild up-
    roar:     541
As when Alcides,[45] from Oechalia crowned
With conquest, felt the envenomed robe, and
    tore
Through pain up by the roots Thessalian pines,
And Lichas from the top of Oeta threw   545
Into the Euboic sea. Others, more mild,
Retreated in a silent valley, sing
With notes angelical to many a harp
Their own heroic deeds, and hapless fall
By doom of battle, and complain that Fate 550
Free Virtue should enthrall to Force or Chance.
Their song was partial; but the harmony
(What could it less when Spirits immortal
    sing?)
Suspended Hell, and took with ravishment
The throning audience. In discourse more
    sweet     555
(For Eloquence the Soul, Song charms the
    Sense)
Others apart sat on a hill retired,
In thoughts more elevate, and reasoned high
Of Providence, Foreknowledge, Will, and
    Fate—
Fixed fate, free will, foreknowledge absolute,
And found no end, in wandering mazes lost. 561
Of good and evil much they argued then,
Of happiness and final misery,
Passion and apathy, and glory and shame:
Vain wisdom all, and false philosophy!— 565
Yet, with a pleasing sorcery, could charm
Pain for a while or anguish, and excite

    [43] Ride.        [44] Sky.
  [45] Hercules. The robe is the poisoned shirt which
his wife obtained from the centaur Nessus and sent
to him by his servant Lichas.

Fallacious hope, or arm the obduréd breast
With stubborn patience as with triple steel.
Another part, in squadrons and gross [46] bands,
On bold adventure to discover wide   571
That dismal world, if any clime perhaps
Might yield them easier habitation, bend
Four ways their flying march, along the banks
Of four infernal rivers, that disgorge   575
Into the burning lake their baleful streams—
Abhorréd Styx, the flood of deadly hate;
Sad Acheron of sorrow, black and deep;
Cocytus, named of lamentation loud
Heard on the rueful stream; fierce Phlege-
    ton,     580
Whose waves of torrent fire inflame with rage.
Far off from these, a slow and silent stream,
Lethe, the river of oblivion, rolls
Her watery labyrinth, whereof who drinks
Forthwith his former state and being forgets—
Forgets both joy and grief, pleasure and pain.
Beyond this flood a frozen continent   587
Lies dark and wild, beat with perpetual storms
Of whirlwind and dire hail, which on firm land
Thaws not, but gathers heap, and ruin seems
Of ancient pile; all else deep snow and ice, 591
A gulf profound as that Serbonian bog
Betwixt Damiata and Mount Casius old,[47]
Where armies whole have sunk: the parching
    air
Burns frore,[48] and cold performs the effect of
    fire.     595
Thither, by harpy-footed Furies haled,
At certain revolutions all the damned
Are brought; and feel by turns the bitter change
Of fierce extremes, extremes by change more
    fierce,
From beds of raging fire to starve in ice   600
Their soft ethereal warmth, and there to pine
Immovable, infixed, and frozen round
Periods of time—thence hurried back to fire.
They ferry over this Lethean sound
Both to and fro, their sorrow to augment, 605
And wish and struggle, as they pass, to reach
The tempting stream, with one small drop to
    lose
In sweet forgetfulness all pain and woe,
All in one moment, and so near the brink;
But Fate withstands, and, to oppose the at-
    tempt,     610
Medusa with Gorgonian terror guards
The ford, and of itself the water flies
All taste of living wight,[49] as once it fled
The lip of Tantalus. Thus roving on
In confused march forlorn, the adventurous
    bands,     615
With shuddering horror pale, and eyes aghast,
Viewed first [50] their lamentable lot, and found
No rest. Through many a dark and dreary vale
They passed, and many a region dolorous,
O'er many a frozen, many a fiery Alp,   620

  [46] Large.    [47] I. e., in Egypt.    [48] Frozen.
  [49] Living being.    [50] Viewed for the first time.

Rocks, caves, lakes, fens, bogs, dens, and shades
    of death—
A universe of death, which God by curse
Created evil, for evil only good;
Where all life dies, death lives, and Nature
    breeds,
Perverse, all monstrous, all prodigious things,
Abominable, inutterable, and worse    626
Than fables yet have feigned or fear conceived,
Gorgons, and Hydras, and Chimaeras dire.
   Meanwhile the Adversary of God and Man,
Satan, with thoughts inflamed of highest de-
    sign,    630
Puts on swift wings, and toward the gates of
    Hell
Explores his solitary flight: sometimes
He scours the right hand coast, sometimes the
    left;
Now shaves with level wing the deep, then
    soars
Up to the fiery concave towering high.    635
As when far off at sea a fleet descried
Hangs in the clouds, by equinoctial winds
Close sailing from Bengala, or the isles
Of Ternate and Tidore,[51] whence merchants
    bring
Their spicy drugs; they on the trading flood,    640
Through the wide Ethiopian to the Cape,[52]
Ply stemming nightly toward the pole:[53] so
    seemed
Far off the flying Fiend. At last appear
Hell-bounds, high reaching to the horrid roof,
And thrice threefold the gates; three folds were
    brass,    645
Three iron, three of adamantine rock,
Impenetrable, impaled with circling fire,
Yet unconsumed. Before the gates there sat
On either side a formidable Shape,
The one seemed woman to the waist, and fair,
But ended foul in many a scaly fold,    651
Voluminous and vast—a serpent armed
With mortal sting. About her middle round
A cry[54] of Hell-hounds never-ceasing barked
With wide Cerberean mouths full loud, and
    rung    655
A hideous peal; yet, when they list, would
    creep,
If aught disturbed their noise, into her womb,
And kennel there; yet there still barked and
    howled
Within unseen. Far less abhorred[55] than these
Vexed Scylla, bathing in the sea that parts    660
Calabria from the hoarse Trinacrian shore;[56]
Nor uglier follow the night-hag, when, called
In secret, riding through the air she comes,
Lured with the smell of infant blood, to dance

[51] Two of the Moluccas.
[52] Through the Indian Ocean to the Cape of Good
Hope.
[53] The South Pole.
[54] Pack.
[55] Less to be abhorred.
[56] The sea between Italy and Sicily.

With Lapland witches,[57] while the laboring
    moon    665
Eclipses at their charms. The other Shape—
If shape it might be called that shape had none
Distinguishable in member, joint, or limb;
Or substance might be called that shadow
    seemed,
For each seemed either—black it stood as
    Night,    670
Fierce as ten Furies, terrible as Hell,
And shook a dreadful dart: what seemed his
    head
The likeness of a kingly crown had on.
Satan was now at hand, and from his seat
The monster moving onward came as fast    675
With horrid strides; Hell trembled as he strode.
The undaunted Fiend what this might be ad-
    mired[58]—
Admired, not feared (God and his Son except,
Created thing naught valued he nor shunned),
And with disdainful look thus first began:—    680
   "Whence and what art thou, execrable
    Shape,
That dar'st, though grim and terrible, advance
Thy miscreated front athwart my way
To yonder gates? Through them I mean to
    pass,
That be assured, without leave asked of thee.
Retire; or taste thy folly, and learn by proof,    686
Hell-born, not to contend with Spirits of
    Heaven."
   To whom the Goblin,[59] full of wrath, re-
    plied:—
"Art thou that Traitor-Angel, art thou he,
Who first broke peace in Heaven and faith, till
    then    690
Unbroken, and in proud rebellious arms
Drew after him the third part of Heaven's sons,
Conjured[60] against the Highest—for which
    both thou
And they, outcast from God, are here con-
    demned
To waste eternal days in woe and pain?    695
And reckon'st thou thyself with Spirits of
    Heaven,
Hell-doomed, and breath'st defiance here and
    scorn,
Where I reign king, and, to enrage thee more,
Thy king and lord? Back to thy punishment,
False fugitive; and to thy speed add wings,    700
Lest with a whip of scorpions I pursue
Thy lingering, or with one stroke of this dart
Strange horror seize thee, and pangs unfelt be-
    fore."
   So spake the grisly Terror, and in shape,    704
So speaking and so threatening, grew tenfold
More dreadful and deform. On the other side,
Incensed with indignation, Satan stood
Unterrified, and like a comet burned,

[57] Lapland was believed to be a favorite home of
witches.
[58] Wondered.    [59] I. e., demon, or fiend.
[60] Banded by oath.

That fires the length of Ophiuchus [61] huge
In the arctic sky, and from his horrid hair    710
Shakes pestilence and war. Each at the head
Leveled his deadly aim; their fatal hands
No second stroke intend; and such a frown
Each cast at the other as when two black clouds,
With heaven's artillery fraught, come rattling on    715
Over the Caspian—then stand front to front
Hovering a space, till winds the signal blow
To join their dark encounter in mid-air.
So frowned the mighty combatants that Hell
Grew darker at their frown; so matched they stood;    720
For never but once more was either like
To meet so great a foe.[62] And now great deeds
Had been achieved, whereof all Hell had rung,
Had not the snaky Sorceress, that sat
Fast by Hell-gate and kept the fatal key,    725
Risen, and with hideous outcry rushed between.
"O father, what intends thy hand," she cried,
"Against thy only son? What fury, O son,
Possesses thee to bend that mortal dart
Against thy father's head? And know'st for whom; [63]    730
For him who sits above, and laughs the while
At thee, ordained his drudge to execute
Whate'er his wrath, which he calls justice, bids—
His wrath, which one day will destroy ye both!"
She spake, and at her words the hellish Pest    735
Forbore: then these to her Satan returned:—
"So strange thy outcry, and thy words so strange
Thou interposest, that my sudden hand,
Prevented, spares to tell thee yet by deeds
What it intends, till first I know of thee    740
What thing thou art, thus double-formed, and why,
In this infernal vale first met, thou call'st
Me father, and that phantasm call'st my son.
I know thee not, nor ever saw till now
Sight more detestable than him and thee." 745
To whom thus the Portress of Hell-gate replied:—
"Hast thou forgot me, then; and do I seem
Now in thine eye so foul?—once deemed so fair
In Heaven, when at the assembly, and in sight
Of all the Seraphim with thee combined    750
In bold conspiracy against Heaven's King,
All on a sudden miserable pain
Surprised thee, dim thine eyes and dizzy swum
In darkness, while thy head flames thick and fast

Threw forth, till on the left side opening wide,    755
Likest to thee in shape and countenance bright,
Then shining heavenly fair, a goddess armed,
Out of thy head I sprung. Amazement seized
All the host of Heaven; back they recoiled afraid
At first, and called me *Sin*, and for a sign    760
Portentous held me; but, familiar grown,
I pleased, and with attractive graces won
The most averse—thee chiefly, who, full oft
Thyself in me thy perfect image viewing,
Becam'st enamored; and such joy thou took'st
With me in secret that my womb conceived 766
A growing burden. Meanwhile war arose,
And fields were fought in Heaven: wherein remained
(For what could else?) to our Almighty Foe
Clear victory; to our part loss and rout    770
Through all the Empyrean. Down they fell,
Driven headlong from the pitch of Heaven, down
Into this Deep; and in the general fall
I also: at which time this powerful key
Into my hands was given, with charge to keep
These gates for ever shut, which none can pass    776
Without my opening. Pensive here I sat
Alone; but long I sat not, till my womb,
Pregnant by thee, and now excessive grown,
Prodigious motion felt and rueful throes.    780
At last this odious offspring whom thou seest,
Thine own begotten, breaking violent way,
Tore through my entrails, that, with fear and pain
Distorted, all my nether shape thus grew
Transformed: but he my inbred enemy    785
Forth issued, brandishing his fatal dart,
Made to destroy. I fled, and cried out *Death!*
Hell trembled at the hideous name, and sighed
From all her caves, and back resounded *Death!*
I fled; but he pursued (though more, it seems,
Inflamed with lust than rage), and, swifter far,    791
Me overtook, his mother, all dismayed,
And, in embraces forcible and foul
Engendering with me, of that rape begot
These yelling monsters, that with ceaseless cry
Surround me, as thou saw'st—hourly conceived    796
And hourly born, with sorrow infinite
To me; for, when they list, into the womb
That bred them they return, and howl, and gnaw    799
My bowels, their repast; then, bursting forth
Afresh, with conscious terrors vex me round,
That rest or intermission none I find.
Before mine eyes in opposition sits
Grim Death, my son and foe, who sets them on,
And me, his parent, would full soon devour 805
For want of other prey, but that he knows
His end with mine involved, and knows that I

---

[61] A large constellation.
[62] Christ (cf. I Corinthians, 25:26, and Hebrews, 2:14).
[63] I. e., and though thou knowest for whom.

Should prove a bitter morsel, and his bane,
Whenever that shall be: so Fate pronounced.
But thou, O father, I forewarn thee, shun 810
His deadly arrow; neither vainly hope
To be invulnerable in those bright arms,
Though tempered heavenly; for that mortal dint,[64]
Save he who reigns above, none can resist."
  She finished; and the subtle Fiend his lore
Soon learned, now milder, and thus answered
    smooth:— 816
  "Dear daughter—since thou claim'st me for
    thy sire,
And my fair son here show'st me, the dear
    pledge
Of dalliance had with thee in Heaven, and joys
Then sweet, now sad to mention, through dire
    change 820
Befallen us unforeseen, unthought-of—know,
I come no enemy, but to set free
From out this dark and dismal house of pain
Both him and thee, and all the Heavenly host
Of Spirits that, in our just pretenses [65] armed,
Fell with us from on high. From them I go 826
This uncouth [66] errand sole, and one for all
Myself expose, with lonely steps to tread
The unfounded [67] Deep, and through the void
    immense
To search, with wandering quest, a place fore-
    told 830
Should be—and, by concurring signs, ere now
Created vast and round—a place of bliss
In the purlieus [68] of Heaven; and therein
    placed
A race of upstart creatures, to supply
Perhaps our vacant room, though more re-
    moved, 835
Lest Heaven, surcharged with potent multi-
    tude,
Might hap to move new broils. Be this, or
    aught
Than this more secret, now designed, I haste
To know; and, this once known, shall soon re-
    turn,
And bring ye to the place where thou and
    Death 840
Shall dwell at ease, and up and down unseen
Wing silently the buxom [69] air, embalmed
With odors. There ye shall be fed and filled
Immeasurably; all things shall be your prey."
  He ceased; for both seemed highly pleased,
    and Death 845
Grinned horrible a ghastly smile, to hear
His famine should be filled, and blessed his
    maw
Destined to that good hour. No less rejoiced
His mother bad, and thus bespake her sire:—
  "The key of this infernal Pit, by due 850
And by command of Heaven's all-powerful
    king,

I keep, by him forbidden to unlock
These adamantine gates; against all force
Death ready stands to interpose his dart,
Fearless to be o'ermatched by living might. 855
But what owe I to his commands above,
Who hates me, and hath hither thrust me
    down
Into this gloom of Tartarus profound,
To sit in hateful office here confined,
Inhabitant of Heaven and heavenly born 860
Here in perpetual agony and pain,
With terrors and with clamors compassed
    round
Of mine own brood, that on my bowels feed?
Thou art my father, thou my author, thou
My being gav'st me; whom should I obey 865
But thee? whom follow? Thou wilt bring me
    soon
To that new world of light and bliss, among
The gods who live at ease, where I shall reign
At thy right hand voluptuous, as beseems
Thy daughter and thy darling, without end."
  Thus saying, from her side the fatal key, 871
Sad instrument of all our woe, she took;
And, towards the gate rolling her bestial train,
Forthwith the huge portcullis [70] high up-drew,
Which, but herself, not all the Stygian Powers
Could once have moved; then in the key-hole
    turns 876
The intricate wards,[71] and every bolt and bar
Of massy iron or solid rock with ease
Unfastens. On a sudden open fly,
With impetuous recoil and jarring sound, 880
The infernal doors, and on their hinges grate
Harsh thunder, that the lowest bottom shook
Of Erebus. She opened; but to shut
Excelled her power: the gates wide open stood,
That with extended wings a bannered host,
Under spread ensigns marching, might pass
    through 886
With horse and chariots ranked in loose array;
So wide they stood, and like a furnace-mouth
Cast forth redounding [72] smoke and ruddy
    flame.
Before their eyes in sudden view appear 890
The secrets of the hoary Deep—a dark
Illimitable ocean, without bound,
Without dimension; where length, breadth,
    and highth,
And time, and place, are lost; where eldest
    Night
And Chaos, ancestors of Nature, hold 895
Eternal anarchy, amidst the noise
Of endless wars, and by confusion stand.
For Hot, Cold, Moist, and Dry, [73] four cham-
    pions fierce,
Strive here for mastery, and to battle bring
Their embryon atoms: they around the flag 900

[64] Blow.     [65] Claims.     [66] Unknown, strange.
[67] Without foundation.     [68] Suburbs.
[69] Yielding.

[70] Heavy grating sliding up and down in grooves
placed at sides of gateway.
[71] Notches and projections in key and lock.
[72] Rolling in billows.
[73] The four humors of medieval medicine.

Of each his faction, in their several clans,
Light-armed or heavy, sharp, smooth, swift, or
  slow,
Swarm populous, unnumbered as the sands
Of Barca or Cyrene's [74] torrid soil,
Levied to side with warring winds, and poise
Their lighter wings. To whom these most ad-
  here                                           906
He rules a moment: Chaos umpire sits,
And by decision more embroils the fray
By which he reigns: next him, high arbiter,
Chance governs all. Into this wild Abyss,   910
The womb of Nature, and perhaps her grave,
Of neither Sea, nor Shore, nor Air, nor Fire,[75]
But all these in their pregnant causes mixed
Confusedly, and which thus must ever fight,
Unless the Almighty Maker them ordain   915
His dark materials to create more worlds—
Into this wild Abyss the wary Fiend
Stood on the brink of Hell and looked a while,
Pondering his voyage; for no narrow frith [76]
He had to cross. Nor was his ear less pealed 920
With noises loud and ruinous (to compare
Great things with small) than when Bellona [77]
  storms
With all her battering engines, bent to raze
Some capital city; or less than if this frame
Of Heaven were falling, and these elements 925
In mutiny had from her axle torn
The steadfast Earth. At last his sail-broad
  vans [78]
He spread for flight, and, in the surging smoke
Uplifted, spurns the ground; thence many a
  league,
As in a cloudy chair, ascending rides      930
Audacious; but, that seat soon failing, meets
A vast vacuity. All unawares,
Fluttering his pennons vain, plumb-down he
  drops
Ten thousand fathom deep, and to this hour
Down had been falling, had not, by ill
  chance,                                    935
The strong rebuff of some tumultuous cloud,
Instinct with fire and niter, hurried him
As many miles aloft. That fury stayed—
Quenched in a boggy Syrtis,[79] neither sea,
Nor good dry land—nigh foundered, on he
  fares,                                     940
Treading the crude consistence, half on foot,
Half flying; behoves him now both oar and sail.
As when a gryphon through the wilderness
With wingèd course, o'er hill or moory dale,
Pursues the Arimaspian,[80] who by stealth  945

Had from his wakeful custody purloined
The guarded gold; so eagerly the Fiend
O'er bog or steep, through strait, rough, dense,
  or rare,
With head, hands, wings, or feet, pursues his
  way,
And swims, or sinks, or wades, or creeps, or flies.
At length a universal hubbub wild          951
Of stunning sounds, and voices all confused,
Borne through the hollow dark, assaults his ear
With loudest vehemence. Thither he plies
Undaunted, to meet there whatever Power  955
Or Spirit of the nethermost Abyss
Might in that noise reside, of whom to ask
Which way the nearest coast of darkness lies
Bordering on light; when straight behold the
  throne
Of *Chaos,* and his dark pavilion spread      960
Wide on the wasteful Deep! With him en-
  throned
Sat sable-vested *Night,* eldest of things,
The consort of his reign; and by them stood
Orcus and Ades, and the dreaded name
Of Demogorgon; Rumor next, and Chance, 965
And Tumult, and Confusion, all embroiled,
And Discord with a thousand various mouths.
    To whom Satan, turning boldly, thus:—"Ye
      Powers
And Spirits of this nethermost Abyss,
Chaos and ancient Night, I come no spy      970
With purpose to explore or to disturb
The secrets of your realm; but, by constraint
Wandering this darksome desert, as my way
Lies through your spacious empire up to light,
Alone and without guide, half lost, I seek, 975
What readiest path leads where your gloomy
  bounds
Confine with Heaven; or, if some other place,
From your dominion won, the Ethereal King
Possesses lately, thither to arrive
I travel this profound. Direct my course:  980
Directed, no mean recompense it brings
To your behoof,[81] if I that region lost,
All usurpation thence expelled, reduce
To her original darkness and your sway
(Which is my present journey [82]), and once
  more                                       985
Erect the standard there of ancient Night.
Yours be the advantage all, mine the revenge!"
    Thus Satan; and him thus the Anarch old,
With faltering speech and visage incomposed,
Answered:—"I know thee, stranger, who thou
  art—                                       990
That mighty leading Angel, who of late
Made head against Heaven's King, though
  overthrown.
I saw and heard; for such a numerous host
Fled not in silence through the frighted Deep,
With ruin upon ruin, rout on rout,          995
Confusion worse confounded; and Heav'n
  Gates

---

[74] Cities of north Africa.
[75] The four elements of the older physical science.
[76] Arm of the sea.        [77] Goddess of war.
[78] Wings.
[79] The Syrtes were two quicksands off the north
coast of Africa.
[80] The Arimaspians were a one-eyed people of
Scythia who, according to ancient writers, were continually fighting the griffins for the sake of the gold
guarded by the latter.

[81] Advantage.              [82] Work.

Poured out by millions her victorious bands
Pursuing. I upon my frontiers here
Keep residence; if all I can will serve
That little which is left so to defend, 1000
Encroached on still through our intestine broils
Weakening the scepter of old Night: first, Hell,
Your dungeon, stretching far and wide be-
    neath,
Now lately Heaven and Earth, another world
Hung o'er my realm, linked in a golden chain
To that side Heaven from whence your legions
    fell! 1006
If that way be your walk, you have not far;
So much the nearer danger. Go, and speed;
Havoc, and spoil, and ruin, are my gain."

He ceased; and Satan stayed not to reply, 1010
But, glad that now his sea should find a shore,
With fresh alacrity and force renewed
Springs upward, like a pyramid of fire,
Into the wild expanse, and through the shock
Of fighting elements, on all sides round 1015
Environed, wins his way; harder beset
And more endangered than when Argo [83]
    passed
Through Bosporus betwixt the justling rocks,[84]
Or when Ulysses on the larboard shunned
Charybdis, and by the other whirlpool steered.
So he with difficulty and labor hard 1021
Moved on. With difficulty and labor he;
But, he once passed, soon after, when Man fell,
Strange alteration! Sin and Death amain,[85]
Following his track (such was the will of
    Heaven) 1025
Paved after him a broad and beaten way
Over the dark Abyss, whose boiling gulf
Tamely endured a bridge of wondrous length,
From Hell continued, reaching the utmost
    Orb [86]
Of this frail World; by which the Spirits per-
    verse 1030
With easy intercourse pass to and fro
To tempt or punish mortals, except whom
God and good Angels guard by special grace.

But now at last the sacred influence
Of light appears, and from the walls of Heaven
Shoots far into the bosom of dim Night 1036
A glimmering dawn. Here Nature first begins
Her farthest verge, and Chaos to retire,
As from her outmost works, a broken foe,
With tumult less and with less hostile din; 1040
That [87] Satan with less toil, and now with ease,
Wafts on the calmer wave by dubious light,
And, like a weather-beaten vessel, holds [88]
Gladly the port, though shrouds and tackle
    torn;

[83] The boat in which Jason went to Colchis for the golden fleece.
[84] The Symplegades, at the entrance of the Black Sea.
[85] In great haste.
[86] The outermost of the concentric spheres surrounding the earth.
[87] So that.    [88] Makes for.

Or in the emptier waste, resembling air, 1045
Weighs his spread wings, at leisure to behold
Far off the empyreal Heaven, extended wide
In circuit, undetermined square or round,
With opal towers and battlements adorned
Of living sapphire, once his native seat, 1050
And, fast by, hanging in a golden chain,
This pendent World, in bigness as a star
Of smallest magnitude close by the moon.
Thither, full fraught with mischievous revenge,
Accursed, and in a curséd hour, he hies. 1055

## BOOK III

### THE ARGUMENT

GOD, *sitting on his throne, sees Satan flying towards this World, then newly created; shows him to the Son, who sat at his right hand; foretells the success of Satan in perverting mankind; clears his own justice and wisdom from all imputation, having created Man free, and able enough to have withstood his Tempt-er; yet declares his purpose of grace towards him, in regard he fell not of his own malice, as did Satan, but by him seduced. The Son of God renders praises to his Father for the manifestation of his gracious purpose towards Man: but God again declares that grace cannot be extended towards Man without the satisfac-tion of divine justice; Man hath offended the majesty of God by aspiring to Godhead, and therefore, with all his progeny, devoted to death, must die, unless some one can be found sufficient to answer for his offence, and undergo his punishment. The Son of God freely offers himself a ransom for Man: the Father accepts him, ordains his incarnation, pronounces his exaltation above all Names in Heaven and Earth; commands all the Angels to adore him. They obey, and, hymning to their harps in full choir, celebrate the Father and the Son. Mean-while Satan alights upon the bare convex of this World's outermost orb; where wandering he finds a place since called the Limbo of Van-ity; what persons and things fly up thither: thence comes to the gate of Heaven, described ascending by stairs, and the waters above the firmament that flow about it. His passage thence to the orb of the Sun: he finds there Uriel, the regent of that orb, but first changes himself into the shape of a meaner Angel, and, pretending a zealous desire to behold the new Creation, and Man whom God had placed here, inquires of him the place of his habita-tion, and is directed: alights first on Mount Niphates.*

## BOOK IV

### THE ARGUMENT

SATAN, *now in prospect of Eden, and nigh the place where he must now attempt the bold* enterprise which he undertook alone against God and Man, falls into many doubts with himself, and many passions—fear, envy, and despair; but at length confirms himself in evil; journeys on to Paradise, whose outward prospect and situation is described; overleaps the bounds; sits, in the shape of a cormorant, on the Tree of Life, as highest in the Garden, to look about him. The Garden described; Satan's first sight of Adam and Eve; his wonder at their excellent form and happy state, but with resolution to work their fall; overhears their discourse; thence gathers that the Tree of Knowledge was forbidden them to eat of under penalty of death, and thereon intends to found his temptation by seducing them to transgress; then leaves them a while, to know further of their state by some other means. Meanwhile Uriel, descending on a sunbeam, warns Gabriel, who had in charge the gate of Paradise, that some evil Spirit has escaped the Deep, and passed at noon by his Sphere, in the shape of a good Angel, down to Paradise, discovered after by his furious gestures in the mount. Gabriel promises to find him ere morning. Night coming on, Adam and Eve discourse of going to their rest; their bower described; the evening worship. Gabriel, drawing forth his bands of night-watch to walk the rounds of Paradise, appoints two strong Angels to Adam's bower, lest the evil Spirit should be there doing some harm to Adam or Eve sleeping; there they find him at the ear of Eve, tempting her in a dream, and bring him, though unwilling, to Gabriel; by whom questioned, he scornfully answers; prepares resistance; but, hindered by a sign from Heaven, flies out of Paradise.

## BOOK V

### THE ARGUMENT

MORNING approached, Eve relates to Adam her troublesome dream; he likes it not, yet comforts her. They come forth to their day labors: their Morning Hymn at the door of their Bower. God, to render Man inexcusable, sends Raphael to admonish him of his obedience, of his free estate, of his enemy near at hand;— who he is, and why his enemy, and whatever else may avail Adam to know. Raphael comes down to Paradise; his appearance described, his coming discerned by Adam afar off, sitting at the door of his Bower; he goes out to meet him, brings him to his lodge, entertains him with the choicest fruits of Paradise, got together by Eve; their discourse at table: Raphael performs his message, minds Adam of his state and of his enemy; relates at Adam's request who that enemy is, and how he came to be so, beginning from his first revolt in Heaven, and the occasion thereof; how he drew his Legions after

him to the parts of the North, and there incited them to rebel with him, persuading all but only Abdiel, a Seraph, who in argument dissuades and opposes him, then forsakes him.

## BOOK VI

### THE ARGUMENT

RAPHAEL continues to relate how Michael and Gabriel were sent forth to battle against Satan and his Angels. The first fight described: Satan and his Powers retire under Night; he calls a council, invents devilish engines, which in the second day's fight put Michael and his Angels to some disorder; but they, at length pulling up mountains, overwhelmed both the force and machines of Satan. Yet the tumult not so ending, God on the third day sends Messiah, his Son, for whom he had reserved the glory of that victory: He, in the Power of his Father coming to the place, and causing all his Legions to stand still on either side, with his chariot and thunder driving into the midst of his enemies, pursues them, unable to resist, towards the wall of Heaven; which opening, they leap down with horror and confusion into the place of punishment prepared for them in the Deep. Messiah returns with triumph to his Father.

## BOOK VII

### THE ARGUMENT

RAPHAEL at the request of Adam relates how and wherefore this world was first created; that God, after the expelling of Satan and his Angels out of Heaven, declared his pleasure to create another World and other Creatures to dwell therein; sends his Son with glory and attendance of Angels to perform the work of Creation in six days: the Angels celebrate with hymns the performance thereof, and his reascension into Heaven.

## BOOK VIII

### THE ARGUMENT

ADAM inquires concerning celestial motions, is doubtfully answered, and exhorted to search rather things more worthy of knowledge. Adam assents, and, still desirous to detain Raphael, relates to him what he remembered since his own creation, his placing in Paradise, his talk with God concerning solitude and fit society, his first meeting and nuptials with Eve, his discourse with the Angel thereupon; who after admonitions repeated departs.

# BOOK IX

## THE ARGUMENT

SATAN, *having compassed the Earth, with meditated guile returns as a mist by night into Paradise; enters into the Serpent sleeping. Adam and Eve in the morning go forth to their labors, which Eve proposes to divide in several places, each laboring apart: Adam consents not, alleging the danger lest that enemy of whom they were forewarned should attempt her found alone. Eve, loath to be thought not circumspect or firm enough, urges her going apart, the rather desirous to make trial of her strength; Adam at last yields. The Serpent finds her alone: his subtle approach, first gazing, then speaking, with much flattery extolling Eve above all other creatures. Eve, wondering to hear the Serpent speak, asks how he attained to human speech and such understanding not till now; the Serpent answers that by tasting of a certain tree in the Garden he attained both to speech and reason, till then void of both. Eve requires him to bring her to that tree, and finds it to be the Tree of Knowledge forbidden: the Serpent, now grown bolder with many wiles and arguments, induces her at length to eat. She, pleased with the taste, deliberates a while whether to impart thereof to Adam or not; at last brings him of the fruit; relates what persuaded her to eat thereof. Adam, at first amazed, but perceiving her lost, resolves, through vehemence of love, to perish with her, and, extenuating the trespass, eats also of the fruit. The effect thereof in them both; they seek to cover their nakedness; then fall to variance and accusation of one another.*

# BOOK X

## THE ARGUMENT

MAN's *transgression known, the guardian Angels forsake Paradise, and return up to Heaven to approve their vigilance, and are approved; God declaring that the entrance of Satan could not be by them prevented. He sends his Son to judge the transgressors; who descends, and gives sentence accordingly; then, in pity, clothes them both, and reascends. Sin and Death, sitting till then at the gates of Hell, by wondrous sympathy feeling the success of Satan in this new world, and the sin of man there committed, resolve to sit no longer confined in Hell, but to follow Satan, their sire, up to the place of man: to make the way easier from Hell to this world to and fro, they pave a broad highway or bridge over Chaos, according to the track that Satan first made; then, preparing for earth, they meet him, proud of his success, returning to Hell; their mutual gratula-*

*tion. Satan arrives at Pandemonium; in full assembly relates, with boasting, his success against man; instead of applause is entertained with a general hiss by all his audience, transformed, with himself also, suddenly into Serpents, according to his doom given in Paradise; then, deluded with a show of the Forbidden Tree springing up before them, they, greedily reaching to take of the fruit, chew dust and bitter ashes. The proceedings of Sin and Death: God foretells the final victory of his Son over them, and the renewing of all things; but, for the present, commands his Angels to make several alterations in the heavens and elements. Adam, more and more perceiving his fallen condition, heavily bewails, rejects the condolement of Eve; she persists, and at length appeases him: then, to evade the curse likely to fall on their offspring, proposes to Adam violent ways; which he approves not, but, conceiving better hope, puts her in mind of the late promise made them, that her seed should be revenged on the Serpent, and exhorts her, with him, to seek peace of the offended Deity by repentance and supplication.*

# BOOK XI

## THE ARGUMENT

THE *Son of God presents to his Father the prayers of our first Parents, now repenting, and intercedes for them. God accepts them, but declares that they must no longer abide in Paradise; sends Michael with a Band of Cherubim to dispossess them, but first to reveal to Adam future things: Michael's coming down. Adam shows to Eve certain ominous signs; he discerns Michael's approach; goes out to meet him: the Angel denounces*[1] *their departure. Eve's lamentation. Adam pleads, but submits: the Angel leads him up to a high hill; sets before him in vision what shall happen till the Flood.*

# BOOK XII

## THE ARGUMENT

THE *Angel Michael continues from the Flood to relate what shall succeed; then, in the mention of Abraham, comes by degrees to explain who that Seed of the Woman shall be, which was promised Adam and Eve in the Fall: his Incarnation, Death, Resurrection, the Ascension; the state of the Church till his second Coming. Adam, greatly satisfied and recomforted by these relations and promises, descends the hill with Michael; wakens Eve, who all this while had slept, but with gentle dreams composed to quietness of mind and submission. Michael in either hand leads them out of Para-*

[1] Proclaims.

dise, the fiery Sword waving behind them, and the Cherubim taking their stations to guard the Place.

# Areopagitica [1]

### A Speech for the Liberty of Unlicensed Printing

#### TO THE PARLIAMENT OF ENGLAND

This is true liberty, when free-born men,
Having to advise the public, may speak free;
Which he who can and will deserves high praise,
Who neither can nor will may hold his peace.
What can be juster in a state than this?

Euripides, *The Suppliants*

THEY who to states and governors of the Commonwealth direct their speech, High Court of Parliament, or wanting such access in a private condition, write that which they foresee may advance the public good, I suppose them as at the beginning of no mean endeavor not a little altered [2] and moved inwardly in their minds, some with doubt of what will be the success, others with fear of what will be the censure; [3] some with hope, others with confidence of what they have to speak. And me perhaps each of these dispositions, as the subject was whereon I entered, may have at other times variously affected; and likely might in these foremost expressions now also disclose which of them swayed most, but that the very attempt of this address thus made, and the thought of whom it hath recourse to, hath got the power within me to a passion far more welcome than incidental to a preface. Which though I stay not to confess ere any ask, I shall be blameless, if it be no other than the joy and gratulation which it brings to all who wish and promote their country's liberty; whereof this whole discourse proposed will be a certain testimony, if not a trophy.[4] For this is not the liberty which we can hope, that no grievance should arise in the Commonwealth; that let no man in this world expect; but when complaints are freely heard, deeply considered, and speedily reformed, then is the utmost bound of civil liberty attained that wise men look for. To which if I now manifest by the very sound of this which I shall utter that we are already in good part arrived, and yet from such a steep disadvantage of tyranny and superstition grounded into our principles as was beyond the manhood of a Roman recovery,[5] it will be attributed first, as is most due, to the strong assistance of God, our deliverer, next to your faithful guidance and undaunted wisdom, Lords and Commons of England. Neither is it in God's esteem the diminution of his glory when honorable things are spoken of good men and worthy magistrates; which if I now first should begin to do, after so fair a progress of your laudable deeds and such a long obligement upon the whole realm to your indefatigable virtues, I might be justly reckoned among the tardiest and the unwillingest of them that praise ye. Nevertheless there being three principal things without which all praising is but courtship [6] and flattery: first, when that only is praised which is solidly worth praise; next, when greatest likelihoods are brought that such things are truly and really in those persons to whom they are ascribed: the other, when he who praises, by showing that such his actual persuasion is of whom he writes, can demonstrate that he flatters not. The former two of these I have heretofore endeavored, rescuing the employment from him who went about to impair your merits with a trivial and malignant encomium; [7] the latter, as belonging chiefly to mine own acquittal, that whom I so extolled I did not flatter, hath been reserved opportunely to this occasion. For he who freely magnifies what hath been nobly done, and fears not to declare as freely what might be done better, gives ye the best covenant of his fidelity, and that his loyalest affection and his hope waits on your proceedings. His highest praising is not flattery, and his plainest advice is a kind of praising; for though I should affirm and hold by argument that it would fare better with truth, with learning, and the Commonwealth, if one of your published orders, which I should name, were called in, yet at the same time it could not but much redound to the luster of your mild and equal government whenas private persons are hereby animated to think ye better pleased with public advice than

---

[1] The title is borrowed from the Areopagitic Oration of Isocrates, addressed to the Areopagus, or Great Council of Athens, and like Milton's work intended to be read rather than heard.
[2] Disturbed.          [3] Judgment.
[4] Even though unsuccessful.

[5] The recovery of Rome from her many disasters.
[6] Fawning of courtiers.
[7] Bishop Joseph Hall in his *Humble Remonstrance* to Parliament against the abolition of episcopacy, against which Milton wrote his *Apology for Smectymnuus.*

other statists have been delighted heretofore with public flattery. And men will then see what difference there is between the magnanimity of a triennial parliament, and that jealous haughtiness of prelates and cabin [8] counsellors that usurped of late, whenas they shall observe ye in the midst of your victories and successes more gently brooking written exceptions against a voted order than other courts, which had produced nothing worth memory but the weak ostentation of wealth, would have endured the least signified dislike at any sudden proclamation. If I should thus far presume upon the meek demeanor of your civil and gentle greatness, Lords and Commons, as what your published order hath directly said, that to gainsay, I might defend myself with ease, if any should accuse me of being new or insolent, did they but know how much better I find ye esteem it to imitate the old and elegant humanity of Greece than the barbaric pride of a Hunnish and Norwegian stateliness. And out of those ages to whose polite wisdom and letters we owe that we are not yet Goths and Jutlanders I could name him [9] who from his private house wrote that discourse to the Parliament of Athens that persuades them to change the form of democracy which was then established. Such honor was done in those days to men who professed the study of wisdom and eloquence, not only in their own country but in other lands, that cities and signories heard them gladly and with great respect, if they had aught in public to admonish the state. Thus did Dion Prusaeus, a stranger and a private orator, counsel the Rhodians against a former edict; and I abound with other like examples, which to set here would be superfluous. But if from the industry of a life wholly dedicated to studious labors, and those natural endowments haply not the worst for two and fifty degrees of northern latitude, so much must be derogated as to count me not equal to any of those who had this privilege, I would obtain to be thought not so inferior as yourselves are superior to the most of them who received their counsel; and how far you excel them, be assured, Lords and Commons, there can no greater testimony appear than when your prudent spirit acknowledges and obeys the voice of reason, from what quarter soever it be heard speaking, and renders ye as willing to repeal any act of your own setting forth as any set forth by your predecessors.

If ye be thus resolved, as it were injury to think ye were not, I know not what should withold me from presenting ye with a fit instance wherein to show both that love of truth which ye eminently profess, and that uprightness of your judgment which is not wont to be partial to yourselves, by judging over again that order [10] which ye have ordained to regulate printing: "that no book, pamphlet, or paper shall be henceforth printed unless the same be first approved and licensed by such, or at least one of such, as shall be thereto appointed." For that part which preserves justly every man's copy [11] to himself, or provides for the poor, I touch not, only wish they be not made pretences to abuse and persecute honest and painful [12] men who offend not in either of these particulars. But that other clause of licensing books, which we thought had died with his brother quadragesimal and matrimonial [13] when the prelates expired, I shall now attend with such a homily as shall lay before ye: first, the inventors of it to be those whom ye will be loath to own; next, what is to be thought in general of reading, whatever sort the books be, and that this Order avails nothing to the suppressing of scandalous, seditious, and libellous books, which were mainly intended to be suppressed; last, that it will be primely to the discouragement of all learning and the stop of truth, not only by disexercising and blunting our abilities in what we know already, but by hindering and cropping the discovery that might be yet further made both in religious and civil wisdom.

I deny not but that it is of greatest concernment in the Church and Commonwealth to have a vigilant eye how books demean themselves as well as men, and thereafter to confine, imprison, and do sharpest justice on them as malefactors. For books are not absolutely dead things, but do contain a potency of life in them to be as active as that soul was whose progeny they are; nay, they do preserve as in a vial the purest efficacy and extraction of that living intellect that bred them. I know they are as lively and as vigorously productive as those fabulous dragon's teeth,[14] and, being sown up and down, may chance to spring up armed men.

---

[8] Cabinet.  [9] Isocrates.

[10] Of June 14, 1643.  [11] Copyright.
[12] Painstaking.
[13] Ecclesiastical licenses for eating forbidden foods in Lent and for marriage.
[14] Which, when sown, sprang up as armed men in the legends of both Jason and Cadmus.

And yet on the other hand, unless wariness be used, as good almost kill a man as kill a good book; who kills a man kills a reasonable creature, God's image; but he who destroys a good book kills reason itself, kills the image of God, as it were, in the eye. Many a man lives a burden to the earth; but a good book is the precious life-blood of a master-spirit, embalmed and treasured up on purpose to a life beyond life. 'Tis true, no age can restore a life, whereof perhaps there is no great loss; and revolutions of ages do not oft recover the loss of a rejected truth, for the want of which whole nations fare the worse. We should be wary therefore what persecution we raise against the living labors of public men, how we spill that seasoned life of man preserved and stored up in books; since we see a kind of homicide may be thus committed, sometimes a martyrdom, and if it extend to the whole impression, a kind of massacre, whereof the execution ends not in the slaying of an elemental life, but strikes at that ethereal and fifth essence,[15] the breath of reason itself, slays an immortality rather than a life. But lest I should be condemned of introducing licence, while I oppose licensing, I refuse not the pains to be so much historical as will serve to show what hath been done by ancient and famous commonwealths against this disorder, till the very time that this project of licensing crept out of the Inquisition, was catched up by our prelates, and hath caught some of our presbyters.

In Athens, where books and wits were ever busier than in any other part of Greece, I find but only two sorts of writings which the magistrate cared to take notice of: those either blasphemous and atheistical, or libellous. Thus the books of Protagoras [16] were by the judges of Areopagus commanded to be burnt, and himself banished the territory for a discourse begun with his confessing not to know whether there were gods, or whether not. And against defaming it was decreed that none should be traduced by name, as was the manner of *Vetus Comoedia*,[17] whereby we may guess how they censured libelling. And this course was quick enough, as Cicero writes, to quell both the

desperate wits of other atheists and the open way of defaming, as the event showed. Of other sects and opinions, though tending to voluptuousness and the denying of divine providence, they took no heed. Therefore we do not read that either Epicurus, or that libertine school of Cyrene, or what the Cynic impudence uttered,[18] was ever questioned by the laws. Neither is it recorded that the writings of those old comedians [19] were suppressed, though the acting of them were forbid; and that Plato commended the reading of Aristophanes, the loosest of them all, to his royal scholar, Dionysius, is commonly known, and may be excused, if holy Chrysostom,[20] as is reported, nightly studied so much the same author and had the art to cleanse a scurrilous vehemence into the style of a rousing sermon. That other leading city of Greece, Lacedaemon, considering that Lycurgus, their law-giver, was so addicted to elegant learning as to have been the first that brought out of Ionia the scattered works of Homer, and sent the poet Thales from Crete to prepare and mollify the Spartan surliness with his smooth songs and odes, the better to plant among them law and civility, it is to be wondered how museless and unbookish they were, minding nought but the feats of war. There needed no licensing of books among them, for they disliked all but their own Laconic apophthegms, and took a slight occasion to chase Archilochus out of their city, perhaps for composing in a higher strain than their own soldierly ballads and roundels could reach to; or if it were for his broad verses, they were not therein so cautious but they were as dissolute in their promiscuous conversing; whence Euripides affirms in *Andromache* that their women were all unchaste. Thus much may give us light after what sort books were prohibited among the Greeks. The Romans also, for many ages trained up only to a military roughness, resembling most the Lacedaemonian guise, knew of learning little but what their twelve tables and the Pontific College with their augurs and flamens [21] taught them in religion and law, so unacquainted with other learning that when

---

[15] Fifth or spiritual essence, as opposed to the four elements, the material essences.

[16] The first of the Greek Sophists (B.C. 480–c. 411).

[17] The early Greek comedy, of which Aristophanes was the chief representative.

[18] Epicurus (B.C. 342–270) believed that happiness was the highest good; the school of Cyrene in northern Africa gave the pre-eminence to pleasure; and the Cynic philosophers made a point of impudently flouting human pretensions.

[19] Writers of comedies.

[20] St. Chrysostom (A.D. 347–407), Bishop of Constantinople.

[21] Various orders of priests in pagan Rome.

Carneades and Critolaus, with the Stoic Diogenes coming ambassadors to Rome, took thereby occasion to give the city a taste of their philosophy, they were suspected for seducers by no less a man than Cato, the censor, who moved it in the Senate to dismiss them speedily and to banish all such Attic babblers out of Italy. But Scipio and others of the noblest senators withstood him and his old Sabine austerity; honored and admired the 10 men; and the censor himself at last in his old age fell to the study of that whereof before he was so scrupulous. And yet at the same time Naevius and Plautus, the first Latin comedians, had filled the city with all the borrowed scenes of Menander and Philemon.[22] Then began to be considered there also what was to be done to libellous books and authors; for Naevius was quickly cast into prison for his unbridled pen, and released by the trib- 20 unes upon his recantation. We read also that libels were burnt, and the makers punished by Augustus. The like severity no doubt was used if aught were impiously written against their esteemed gods. Except in these two points, how the world went in books the magistrate kept no reckoning. And therefore Lucretius without impeachment versifies his Epicurism to Memmius, and had the honor to be set forth the second 30 time by Cicero, so great a father of the Commonwealth, although himself disputes against that opinion in his own writings. Nor was the satirical sharpness or naked plainness of Lucilius, or Catullus, or Flaccus[23] by any order prohibited. And for matters of state, the story of Titus Livius, though it extolled that part which Pompey held, was not therefore suppressed by Octavius Caesar of the other faction. But that Naso[24] was by him 40 banished in his old age for the wanton poems of his youth was but a mere covert[25] of state over some secret cause; and besides, the books were neither banished nor called in. From hence we shall meet with little else but tyranny in the Roman Empire, that we may not marvel if not so often bad as good books were silenced. I shall therefore deem to have been large enough in producing what among the ancients was punishable to write, save 50 only which all other arguments were free to treat on.

By this time the emperors were become Christians, whose discipline in this point I do not find to have been more severe than what was formerly in practice. The books of those whom they took to be grand heretics were examined, refuted, and condemned in the general councils, and not till then were prohibited or burnt by authority of the emperor. As for the writings of heathen authors, unless they were plain invectives against Christianity, as those of Porphyrius and Proclus,[26] they met with no interdict that can be cited till about the year 400 in a Carthaginian council, wherein bishops themselves were forbid to read the books of gentiles,[27] but heresies they might read; while others long before them on the contrary scrupled more the books of heretics than of gentiles. And that the primitive councils and bishops were wont only to declare what books were not commendable, passing no further but leaving it to each one's conscience to read or to lay by, till after the year 800 is observed already by Padre Paolo, the great unmasker of the Trentine Council.[28] After which time the popes of Rome, engrossing what they pleased of political rule into their own hands, extended their dominion over men's eyes, as they had before over their judgments, burning and prohibiting to be read what they fancied not, yet sparing in their censures, and the books not many which they so dealt with; till Martin V[29] by his bull not only prohibited, but was the first that excommunicated the reading of heretical books; for about that time Wicliffe and Huss, growing terrible, were they who first drove the Papal Court to a stricter policy of prohibiting. Which course Leo X[30] and his successors followed, until the Council of Trent and the Spanish Inquisition, engendering together, brought forth, or perfected those catalogues and expurging indexes that rake through the entrails of many an old good author, with a violation worse than any could be offered to his tomb. Nor did they stay in matters heretical, but any subject that was not to their palate they either condemned in a prohibition, or had it straight into the new purgatory of an index. To fill up the measure of encroachment their last invention was to ordain that no book, pamphlet, or paper should be printed (as if St. Peter

[26] Neoplatonic philosophers of the fourth and fifth centuries A.D.

[27] Pagans.

[28] Fra Paolo Sarpi, a Venetian scholar of the late sixteenth century, whose best known work was a history of the Catholic Council of Trent.

[29] Pope, 1417–1431.    [30] Pope, 1513–1521.

[22] Two leading writers of "new," or later, Greek comedy.

[23] Horace.    [24] Ovid.    [25] Pretext.

had bequeathed them the keys of the press also out of Paradise) unless it were approved and licensed under the hands of two or three glutton friars. For example:

"Let the Chancellor Cini be pleased to see if in this present work be contained aught that may withstand the printing.
Vincent Rabatta Vicar of Florence."
"I have seen this present work, and find nothing athwart the Catholic faith and good manners: in witness whereof I have given, etc.
Niccolò Cini Chancellor of Florence."
"Attending the precedent relation, it is allowed that this present work of Davanzati may be printed.
Vincent Rabatta, etc."
"It may be printed, 15 July.
Friar Simon Mompei d'Amelia Chancellor of the holy office in Florence." [31]

Sure they have a conceit, if he of the bottomless pit had not long since broke prison, that this quadruple exorcism would bar him down. I fear their next design will be to get into their custody the licensing of that which they say Claudius intended, but went not through with.[32] Vouchsafe to see another of their forms, the Roman stamp:

"*Imprimatur*,[33] if it seem good to the reverend Master of the Holy Palace,
Belcastro, vicegerent."
"*Imprimatur*.
Friar Niccolò Rodolphi Master of the Holy Palace."

Sometimes five *imprimaturs* are seen together dialogue-wise in the piazza of one title-page, complimenting and ducking each to other with their shaven reverences, whether the author, who stands by in perplexity at the foot of his epistle, shall to the press or to the sponge. These are the pretty responsories, these are the dear antiphonies that so bewitched of late our prelates and their chaplains with the goodly echo they made; and besotted us to the gay imitation of a lordly *imprimatur*, one from Lambeth House, another from the west end of Paul's,[34] so apishly Romanizing that the word of command still was set down in Latin, as if the learned, grammatical pen that wrote it would cast no ink without Latin,

or perhaps, as they thought, because no vulgar tongue was worthy to express the pure conceit of an *imprimatur*; but rather, as I hope, for that our English, the language of men ever famous and foremost in the achievements of liberty, will not easily find servile letters enow to spell such a dictatory presumption English. And thus ye have the inventors and the original of book-licensing ripped up, and drawn as lineally as any pedigree. We have it not, that can be heard of, from any ancient state, or polity, or church, nor by any statute left us by our ancestors elder or later; nor from the modern custom of any reformed city or church abroad; but from the most Anti-Christian Council and the most tyrannous Inquisition that ever inquired. Till then books were ever as freely admitted into the world as any other birth; the issue of the brain was no more stifled than the issue of the womb; no envious Juno sate cross-legged [35] over the nativity of any man's intellectual offspring; but if it proved a monster, who denies but that it was justly burnt, or sunk into the sea. But that a book, in worse condition than a peccant soul, should be to stand before a jury ere it be born to the world, and undergo yet in darkness the judgment of Radamanth and his colleagues [36] ere it can pass the ferry backward into light, was never heard before till that mysterious iniquity, provoked and troubled at the first entrance of reformation, sought out new limboes and new hells wherein they might include our books also within the number of their damned. And this was the rare morsel so officiously snatched up, and so ill-favoredly imitated by our inquisiturient [37] bishops and the attendant Minorities [38] their chaplains. That ye like not now these most certain authors of this licensing order, and that all sinister intention was far distant from your thoughts when ye were importuned the passing it, all men who know the integrity of your actions, and how ye honor truth, will clear ye readily.

But some will say, "What though the inventors were bad? the thing for all that may be good." It may so; yet if that thing be no such deep invention, but obvious and easy for any man to light on, and yet best and wisest commonwealths through all ages and occasions have forborne to use it, and falsest

[31] This example of licensing is taken from Bernardo Davanzati Bostichi's *Scisma d'Inghilterra*, published at Florence in 1638, probably during Milton's visit in that city.
[32] "*Quo veniam daret flatum crepitumque ventris in convivio emittendi. Sueton. in Claudio*" (Milton's note).
[33] Let it be printed.
[34] One from the London house of the Archbishop of Canterbury, another from the house of the Bishop of London.
[35] Juno put a curse.
[36] Radamanth and the other judges of Hades.
[37] Desirous of being inquisitors.
[38] Franciscan friars.

seducers and oppressors of men were the first who took it up, and to no other purpose but to obstruct and hinder the first approach of reformation; I am of those who believe, it will be a harder alchemy than Lullius [39] ever knew to sublimate any good use out of such an invention. Yet this only is what I request to gain from this reason, that it may be held a dangerous and suspicious fruit, as certainly it deserves, for the tree that bore it, until I can dissect one by one the properties it has. But I have first to finish, as was propounded, what is to be thought in general of reading books, whatever sort they be, and whether be more the benefit or the harm that thence proceeds.

Not to insist upon the examples of Moses, Daniel, and Paul, who were skilful in all the learning of the Egyptians, Chaldeans, and Greeks, which could not probably be without reading their books of all sorts, in Paul especially, who thought it no defilement to insert into holy Scripture the sentences of three Greek poets, and one of them a tragedian,[40] the question was, notwithstanding, sometimes controverted among the primitive doctors, but with great odds on that side which affirmed it both lawful and profitable, as was then evidently perceived when Julian,[41] the Apostate and subtlest enemy to our faith, made a decree forbidding Christians the study of heathen learning; for, said he, they wound us with our own weapons, and with our own arts and sciences they overcome us. And indeed the Christians were put so to their shifts by this crafty means, and so much in danger to decline into all ignorance, that the two Appollinarii were fain, as a man may say, to coin all the seven liberal sciences [42] out of the Bible, reducing it into divers forms of orations, poems, dialogues, even to the calculating of a new Christian grammar. But, saith the historian Socrates,[43] the providence of God provided better than the industry of Appollinarius and his son, by taking away that illiterate law with the life of him who devised it. So great an injury they then held it to be deprived of Hellenic learning, and thought it a persecution more undermining and secretly decaying the Church than the open cruelty of Decius or Diocletian. And perhaps it was the same politic drift that the Devil whipped St. Jerome in a lenten dream for reading Cicero; or else it was a phantasm bred by the fever which had then seized him.[44] For had an angel been his discipliner, unless it were for dwelling too much upon Ciceronianisms, and had chastised the reading, not the vanity, it had been plainly partial; first, to correct him for grave Cicero and not for scurril Plautus, whom he confesses to have been reading not long before; next, to correct him only and let so many more ancient fathers wax old in those pleasant and florid studies without the lash of such a tutoring apparition, insomuch that Basil teaches how some good use may be made of *Margites,* a sportful poem, not now extant, writ by Homer; and why not then of *Morgante,*[45] an Italian romance much to the same purpose? But if it be agreed we shall be tried by visions, there is a vision recorded by Eusebius [46] far ancienter than this tale of Jerome to the nun Eustochium, and besides has nothing of a fever in it. Dionysius Alexandrinus was about the year 240 a person of great name in the Church for piety and learning, who had wont to avail himself much against heretics by being conversant in their books, until a certain presbyter laid it scrupulously to his conscience how he durst venture himself among those defiling volumes. The worthy man, loath to give offence, fell into a new debate with himself what was to be thought; when suddenly a vision sent from God (it is his own epistle that so avers it) confirmed him in these words: "Read any books whatever come to thy hands, for thou art sufficient both to judge aright, and to examine each matter." To this revelation he assented the sooner, as he confesses, because it was answerable to that of the Apostle to the Thessalonians: "Prove all things; hold fast that which is good." And he might have added another remarkable saying of the same author: "To the pure all things are pure," not only meats and drinks, but all kind of knowledge whether of good or evil; the knowledge cannot defile, nor consequently the books, if the will and conscience

[39] Raymond Lully (1234–1315), alchemist.

[40] Euripides, from whom Paul is supposed to have taken I Corinthians, 15:33.

[41] Roman emperor and leader of a movement to return to paganism (A.D. 331–363).

[42] Grammar, logic, rhetoric, arithmetic, music, geometry, and astronomy.

[43] Flourished in the fifth century A.D.

[44] St. Jerome (A.D. *c.* 345–420) in a letter to the nun Eustochium ascribes the dream to the Devil.

[45] The *Morgante Maggiore* of Luigi Pulci (1431–1487).

[46] Bishop of Caesarea at the beginning of the fourth century A.D.

be not defiled. For books are as meats and viands are, some of good, some of evil substance; and yet God in that unapocryphal [47] vision said without exception, "Rise Peter, kill and eat," leaving the choice to each man's discretion. Wholesome meats to a vitiated stomach differ little or nothing from unwholesome; and best books to a naughty mind are not unappliable to occasions of evil. Bad meats will scarce breed good nourishment in the healthiest concoction; but herein the difference is of bad books that they to a discreet and judicious reader serve in many respects to discover, to confute, to forewarn, and to illustrate. Whereof what better witness can ye expect I should produce than one of your own now sitting in Parliament, the chief of learned men reputed in this land, Mr. Selden? [48] whose volume of natural and national laws proves, not only by great authorities brought together, but by exquisite reasons and theorems almost mathematically demonstrative, that all opinions, yea errors, known, read, and collected, are of main service and assistance toward the speedy attainment of what is truest. I conceive therefore that when God did enlarge the universal diet of man's body, saving ever the rules of temperance, he then also, as before, left arbitrary the dieting and repasting of our minds, as wherein every mature man might have to exercise his own leading capacity. How great a virtue is temperance, how much of moment through the whole life of man! yet God commits the managing so great a trust, without particular law or prescription, wholly to the demeanor [49] of every grown man. And therefore, when he himself tabled the Jews from heaven, that omer which was every man's daily portion of manna is computed to have been more than might have well sufficed the heartiest feeder thrice as many meals. For those actions which enter into a man rather than issue out of him, and therefore defile not, God uses not to captivate under a perpetual childhood of prescription, but trusts him with the gift of reason to be his own chooser; there were but little work left for preaching if law and compulsion should grow so fast upon those things which heretofore were governed only by exhortation. Solomon informs us that much reading is a weariness to the flesh, but neither

he nor other inspired author tells us that such or such reading is unlawful; yet certainly had God thought good to limit us herein, it had been much more expedient to have told us what was unlawful than what was wearisome. As for the burning of those Ephesian books by St. Paul's converts, 'tis replied the books were magic: the Syriac so renders them. It was a private act, a voluntary act, and leaves us to a voluntary imitation; the men in remorse burnt those books which were their own; the magistrate by this example is not appointed; these men practised the books; another might perhaps have read them in some sort usefully. Good and evil we know in the field of this world grow up together almost inseparably; and the knowledge of good is so involved and interwoven with the knowledge of evil, and in so many cunning resemblances hardly to be discerned, that those confused seeds which were imposed on Psyche as an incessant labor to cull out and sort asunder were not more intermixed.[50] It was from out the rind of one apple tasted that the knowledge of good and evil as two twins cleaving together leaped forth into the world. And perhaps this is that doom which Adam fell into of knowing good and evil, that is to say, of knowing good by evil. As therefore the state of man now is, what wisdom can there be to choose, what continence to forbear without the knowledge of evil? He that can apprehend and consider vice with all her baits and seeming pleasures, and yet abstain, and yet distinguish, and yet prefer that which is truly better, he is the true wayfaring [51] Christian. I cannot praise a fugitive and cloistered virtue, unexercised and unbreathed, that never sallies out and sees her adversary, but slinks out of the race where that immortal garland is to be run for not without dust and heat. Assuredly we bring not innocence into the world; we bring impurity much rather; that which purifies us is trial, and trial is by what is contrary. That virtue therefore which is but a youngling in the contemplation of evil, and knows not the utmost that vice promises to her followers, and rejects it, is but a blank virtue, not a pure; her whiteness is but an excremental [52] whiteness. Which was the reason why our sage and serious poet Spenser, whom I dare

---

[47] In the Bible (Acts, 10:9–16).

[48] John Selden (1584–1654), author of *De Jure Naturali et Gentium* (1640).

[49] Management.

[50] The story is told in *The Golden Ass* of Apuleius.

[51] In one copy of the *Areopagitica* Milton himself corrected "wayfaring" to "warfaring."

[52] External.

be known to think a better teacher than Scotus or Aquinas,[53] describing true temperance under the person of Guyon,[54] brings him in with his palmer through the cave of Mammon and the bower of earthly bliss, that he might see and know, and yet abstain. Since therefore the knowledge and survey of vice is in this world so necessary to the constituting of human virtue, and the scanning of error to the confirmation of truth, how can we more safely and with less danger scout into the regions of sin and falsity than by reading all manner of tractates, and hearing all manner of reason? And this is the benefit which may be had of books promiscuously read. But of the harm that may result hence three kinds are usually reckoned. First is feared the infection that may spread; but then all human learning and controversy in religious points must remove out of the world, yea the Bible itself; for that ofttimes relates blasphemy not nicely, it describes the carnal sense of wicked men not unelegantly, it brings in holiest men passionately murmuring against providence through all the arguments of Epicurus; in other great disputes it answers dubiously and darkly to the common reader; and ask a Talmudist what ails the modesty of his marginal *keri*, that Moses and all the prophets cannot persuade him to pronounce the textual *chetiv*.[55] For these causes we all know the Bible itself put by the Papist into the first rank of prohibited books. The ancientest Fathers must be next removed, as Clement of Alexandria and that Eusebian book of evangelic preparation, transmitting our ears through a hoard of heathenish obscenities to receive the Gospel. Who finds not that Irenaeus, Epiphanius, Jerome, and others discover more heresies than they well confute, and that oft for heresy which is the truer opinion. Nor boots it to say for these and all the heathen writers of greatest infection, if it must be thought so, with whom is bound up the life of human learning, that they writ in an unknown tongue, so long as we are sure those languages are known as well to the worst of men, who are both most able and most diligent to instil the poison they suck, first into the courts of princes, acquainting them with the choicest delights and criticisms of sin; as perhaps did that Petronius whom Nero called his arbiter, the master of his revels, and that notorious ribald of Arezzo, dreaded and yet dear to the Italian courtiers.[56] I name not him for posterity's sake whom Harry VIII named in merriment his Vicar of Hell.[57] By which compendious way all the contagion that foreign books can infuse will find a passage to the people far easier and shorter than an Indian voyage, though it could be sailed either by the north of Cataio [58] eastward, or of Canada westward, while our Spanish licensing gags the English press never so severely. But on the other side, that infection which is from books of controversy in religion is more doubtful and dangerous to the learned than to the ignorant; and yet those books must be permitted untouched by the licenser. It will be hard to instance where any ignorant man hath been ever seduced by papistical book in English, unless it were commended and expounded to him by some of that clergy: and indeed all such tractates, whether false or true, are as the prophecy of Isaiah was to the eunuch, not to be understood without a guide. But of our priests and doctors how many have been corrupted by studying the comments of Jesuits and Sorbonists,[59] and how fast they could transfuse that corruption into the people, our experience is both late and sad. It is not forgot since the acute and distinct [60] Arminius [61] was perverted merely by the perusing of a nameless discourse written at Delft, which at first he took in hand to confute. Seeing therefore that those books, and those in great abundance which are likeliest to taint both life and doctrine, cannot be suppressed without the fall of learning and of all ability in disputation, and that these books of either sort are most and soonest catching to the learned, from whom to the common people whatever is heretical or dissolute may quickly be conveyed, and that evil manners are as perfectly learnt without books a thousand other ways which cannot be stopped, and evil doctrine not with books can propagate, except a teacher guide, which

---

[53] Duns Scotus and St. Thomas Aquinas, the greatest medieval philosophers.

[54] Hero of the second book of the *Faerie Queene*.

[55] The original text of the *Talmud*, or great compilation of Jewish laws; the *keri* are marginal annotations.

[56] Petronius Arbiter, author of the *Satyricon*, and Pietro Aretino (1492–1557), the "Scourge of Princes."

[57] Perhaps the poet John Skelton.    [58] Cathay.

[59] Scholars of the Sorbonne, the great theological school in Paris.

[60] Clear-headed.

[61] Dutch theologian, converted to an anti-Calvinistic position.

he might also do without writing, and so beyond prohibiting, I am not able to unfold how this cautelous [62] enterprise of licensing can be exempted from the number of vain and impossible attempts. And he who were pleasantly disposed could not well avoid to liken it to the exploit of that gallant man who thought to pound up the crows by shutting his park gate. Besides another inconvenience: if learned men be the first receivers out of books and dispreaders both of vice and error, how shall the licensers themselves be confided in, unless we can confer upon them, or they assume to themselves above all others in the land, the grace of infallibility and uncorruptedness? And again, if it be true that a wise man like a good refiner can gather gold out of the drossiest volume, and that a fool will be a fool with the best book, yea or without book, there is no reason that we should deprive a wise man of any advantage to his wisdom, while we seek to restrain from a fool that which being restrained will be no hindrance to his folly. For if there should be so much exactness always used to keep that from him which is unfit for his reading, we should in the judgment of Aristotle not only, but of Solomon and of our Savior, not vouchsafe him good precepts, and by consequence not willingly admit him to good books, as being certain that a wise man will make better use of an idle pamphlet than a fool will do of sacred Scripture. 'Tis next alleged we must not expose ourselves to temptations without necessity, and next to that not employ our time in vain things. To both these objections one answer will serve, out of the grounds already laid, that to all men such books are not temptations nor vanities, but useful drugs and materials wherewith to temper and compose effective and strong medicines, which man's life cannot want.[63] The rest, as children and childish men, who have not the art to qualify and prepare these working minerals, well may be exhorted to forbear, but hindered forcibly they cannot be by all the licensing that Sainted Inquisition could ever yet contrive. Which is what I promised to deliver next: that this order of licensing conduces nothing to the end for which it was framed; and hath almost prevented [64] me by being clear already while thus much hath been explaining. See the ingenuity [65] of Truth, who, when she gets a free and willing hand, opens herself faster than the pace of method and discourse can overtake her. It was the task which I began with, to shew that no nation or well instituted state, if they valued books at all, did ever use this way of licensing; and it might be answered that this is a piece of prudence lately discovered. To which I return that, as it was a thing slight and obvious to think on, so if it had been difficult to find out, there wanted not among them long since who suggested such a course; which they not following, leave us a pattern of their judgment, that it was not the not knowing but the not approving which was the cause of their not using it. Plato, a man of high authority indeed, but least of all for his commonwealth, in the book of his laws, which no city ever yet received, fed his fancy with making many edicts to his airy burgomasters, which they who otherwise admire him wish had been rather buried and excused in the genial cups of an Academic night-sitting. By which laws he seems to tolerate no kind of learning but by unalterable decree, consisting most of practical traditions, to the attainment whereof a library of smaller bulk than his own dialogues would be abundant; and there also enacts that no poet should so much as read to any private man what he had written, until the judges and law-keepers had seen it and allowed it. But that Plato meant this law peculiarly to that commonwealth which he had imagined, and to no other, is evident. Why was he not else a law-giver to himself, but a transgressor and to be expelled by his own magistrates, both for the wanton epigrams and dialogues which he made, and his perpetual reading of Sophron Mimus [66] and Aristophanes, books of grossest infamy, and also for commending the latter of them, though he were the malicious libeller of his chief friends, to be read by the tyrant Dionysius, who had little need of such trash to spend his time on? but that he knew this licensing of poems had reference and dependence to many other provisoes there set down in his fancied republic, which in this world could have no place; and so neither he himself, nor any magistrate or city ever imitated that course, which taken apart from those other collateral injunctions must needs be vain and fruitless. For if they fell upon one kind of strictness, unless their care were equal to regulate all other things of like aptness to corrupt the mind, that single endeavor they knew would be but

[62] Dangerous.
[63] Do without.
[64] Forestalled.
[65] Ingenuousness.
[66] Writer of coarse farces (fifth century B.C.).

a fond labor, to shut and fortify one gate against corruption, and be necessitated to leave others round about wide open. If we think to regulate printing, thereby to rectify manners, we must regulate all recreations and pastimes, all that is delightful to man. No music must be heard, no song be set or sung but what is grave and Doric.[67] There must be licensing dancers that no gesture, motion, or deportment be taught our youth but what by their allowance shall be thought honest; for such Plato was provided of. It will ask more than the work of twenty licensers to examine all the lutes, the violins, and the guitars in every house; they must not be suffered to prattle as they do, but must be licensed what they may say. And who shall silence all the airs and madrigals that whisper softness in chambers? The windows also and the balconies must be thought on. There are shrewd [68] books with dangerous frontispieces set to sale; who shall prohibit them? shall twenty licensers? The villages also must have their visitors to inquire what lectures the bagpipe and the rebeck [69] reads even to the ballatry, and the gamut of every municipal fiddler, for these are the countryman's *Arcadias,* and his Montemayors.[70] Next, what more national corruption, for which England hears ill [71] abroad, than household gluttony? who shall be the rectors of our daily rioting? and what shall be done to inhibit the multitudes that frequent those houses where drunkenness is sold and harbored? Our garments also should be referred to the licensing of some more sober work-masters to see them cut into a less wanton garb. Who shall regulate all the mixed conversation of our youth, male and female together, as is the fashion of this country? who shall still appoint what shall be discoursed, what presumed, and no further? Lastly, who shall forbid and separate all idle resort, all evil company? These things will be, and must be; but how they shall be least hurtful, how least enticing, herein consists the grave and governing wisdom of a state. To sequester out of the world into Atlantic and Utopian polities,[72] which never can be drawn into use, will not mend our condition,

but to ordain wisely as in this world of evil, in the midst whereof God hath placed us unavoidably. Nor is it Plato's licensing of books will do this, which necessarily pulls along with it so many other kinds of licensing as will make us all both ridiculous and weary, and yet frustrate; but those unwritten, or at least unconstraining laws of virtuous education, religious and civil nurture, which Plato there mentions as the bonds and ligaments of the commonwealth, the pillars and the sustainers of every written statute, these they be which will bear chief sway in such matters as these, when all licensing will be easily eluded. Impunity and remissness for certain are the bane of a commonwealth; but here the great art lies to discern in what the law is to bid restraint and punishment, and in what things persuasion only is to work. If every action which is good or evil in man at ripe years were to be under pittance,[73] and prescription, and compulsion, what were virtue but a name? what praise could be then due to well-doing? what gramercy to be sober, just, or continent? Many there be that complain of divine providence for suffering Adam to transgress: foolish tongues! When God gave him reason, he gave him freedom to choose, for reason is but choosing; he had been else a mere artificial Adam, such an Adam as he is in the motions.[74] We ourselves esteem not of that obedience, or love, or gift, which is of force: God therefore left him free, set before him a provoking object, ever almost in his eyes herein consisted his merit, herein the right of his reward, the praise of his abstinence. Wherefore did he create passions within us, pleasures round about us, but that these rightly tempered are the very ingredients of virtue? They are not skilful considerers of human things who imagine to remove sin by removing the matter of sin; for, besides that it is a huge heap increasing under the very act of diminishing, though some part of it may for a time be withdrawn from some persons, it cannot from all in such a universal thing as books are; and when this is done, yet the sin remains entire. Though ye take from a covetous man all his treasure, he has yet one jewel left; ye cannot bereave him of his covetousness. Banish all objects of lust; shut up all youth into the severest discipline that can be exercised in any hermitage; ye cannot make them chaste that came not thither so: such great care and wisdom is

---

[67] Of a martial character.
[68] Malicious.      [69] Fiddle.
[70] Pastoral entertainments like the *Arcadia* of Sir Philip Sidney or the *Diana* of the Portuguese poet, Jorge de Montemayor (*c.* 1520–1562).
[71] Is ill spoken of.
[72] Ideal states like the New Atlantis of Bacon and the Utopia of More.

[73] A system of allowances.      [74] Puppet-shows.

required to the right managing of this point. Suppose we could expel sin by this means; look how much we thus expel of sin, so much we expel of virtue, for the matter of them both is the same; remove that, and ye remove them both alike. This justifies the high providence of God, who though he commands us temperance, justice, continence, yet pours out before us even to a profuseness all desirable things, and gives us minds that can wander beyond all limit and satiety. Why should we then affect a rigor contrary to the manner of God and of nature, by abridging or scanting those means, which books freely permitted are, both to the trial of virtue and the exercise of truth? It would be better done to learn that the law must needs be frivolous which goes to restrain things, uncertainly and yet equally working to good and to evil. And were I the chooser, a dram of well-doing should be preferred before many times as much the forcible hindrance of evil-doing. For God sure esteems the growth and completing of one virtuous person more than the restraint of ten vicious. And albeit whatever thing we hear or see, sitting, walking, travelling, or conversing may be fitly called our book, and is of the same effect that writings are, yet, grant the things to be prohibited were only books, it appears that this order hitherto is far insufficient to the end which it intends. Do we not see, not once or oftener but weekly, that continued court libel [75] against the Parliament and city printed, as the wet sheets can witness, and dispersed among us for all that licensing can do? yet this is the prime service, a man would think, wherein this order should give proof of itself. If it were executed, you'll say. But certain, if execution be remiss or blindfold now, and in this particular, what will it be hereafter, and in other books? If then the order shall not be vain and frustrate, behold a new labor, Lords and Commons; ye must repeal and proscribe all scandalous and unlicensed books already printed and divulged, after ye have drawn them up into a list that all may know which are condemned and which not, and ordain that no foreign books be delivered out of custody till they have been read over. This office will require the whole time of not a few overseers, and those no vulgar men. There be also books which are partly useful and excellent, partly culpable and

pernicious; this work will ask as many more officials, to make expurgations and expunctions that the commonwealth of learning be not damnified.[76] In fine, when the multitude of books increase upon their hands, ye must be fain to catalogue all those printers who are found frequently offending, and forbid the importation of their whole suspected typography. In a word, that this your order may be exact and not deficient, ye must reform it perfectly according to the model of Trent and Seville,[77] which I know ye abhor to do. Yet though ye should condescend [78] to this, which God forbid, the order still would be but fruitless and defective to that end whereto ye meant it. If to prevent sects and schisms, who is so unread or so uncatechised in story [79] that hath not heard of many sects refusing books as a hindrance and preserving their doctrine unmixed for many ages, only by unwritten traditions. The Christian faith (for that was once a schism) is not unknown to have spread all over Asia ere any gospel or epistle was seen in writing. If the amendment of manners be aimed at, look into Italy and Spain, whether those places be one scruple the better, the honester, the wiser, the chaster, since all the inquisitional rigor that hath been executed upon books.

Another reason whereby to make it plain that this order will miss the end it seeks, consider by the quality which ought to be in every licenser. It cannot be denied but that he who is made judge to sit upon the birth or death of books, whether they may be wafted into this world or not, had need to be a man above the common measure, both studious, learned, and judicious; there may be else no mean mistakes in the censure of what is passable or not, which is also no mean injury. If he be of such worth as behoves him, there cannot be a more tedious and unpleasing journey-work,[80] a greater loss of time levied upon his head, than to be made the perpetual reader of unchosen books and pamphlets, ofttimes huge volumes. There is no book that is acceptable unless at certain seasons; but to be enjoined the reading of that at all times, and in a hand scarce legible, whereof three pages would not down at any time in the fairest print, is an imposition which I cannot believe

[75] The weekly Royalist paper, the *Mercurius Aulicus.*

[76] Made to suffer injury.
[77] The Council of Trent and the Inquisition of Seville.
[78] Give consent to.    [79] History.
[80] Day-laborer's work.

how he that values time and his own studies, or is but of a sensible [81] nostril, should be able to endure. In this one thing I crave leave of the present licensers to be pardoned for so thinking, who doubtless took this office up, looking on it through their obedience to the Parliament, whose command perhaps made all things seem easy and unlaborious to them; but that this short trial hath wearied them out already their own expressions and excuses to them who make so many journeys to solicit their license are testimony enough. Seeing therefore those who now possess the employment by all evident signs wish themselves well rid of it, and that no man of worth, none that is not a plain unthrift of his own hours, is ever likely to succeed them, except he mean to put himself to the salary of a press-corrector, we may easily foresee what kind of licensers we are to expect hereafter, either ignorant, imperious, and remiss, or basely pecuniary. This is what I had to show wherein this order cannot conduce to that end whereof it bears the intention.

I lastly proceed from the no good it can do to the manifest hurt it causes in being, first, the greatest discouragement and affront that can be offered to learning and to learned men. It was the complaint and lamentation of prelates, upon every least breath of a motion to remove pluralities and distribute more equally church revenues, that then all learning would be forever dashed and discouraged. But as for that opinion, I never found cause to think that the tenth part of learning stood or fell with the clergy; nor could I ever but hold it for a sordid and unworthy speech of any churchman who had a competency left him. If therefore ye be loath to dishearten utterly and discontent, not the mercenary crew of false pretenders to learning, but the free and ingenuous sort of such as evidently were born to study, and love learning for itself, not for lucre or any other end but the service of God and of truth, and perhaps that lasting fame and perpetuity of praise which God and good men have consented shall be the reward of those whose published labors advance the good of mankind; then know that so far to distrust the judgment and the honesty of one who hath but a common repute in learning, and never yet offended, as not to count him fit to print his mind without a tutor and examiner, lest he should drop a schism or something of corruption, is the greatest displeasure and indignity to a free and knowing spirit that can be put

upon him. What advantage is it to be a man over it is to be a boy at school, if we have only escaped the ferule to come under the fescue [82] of an *imprimatur?* if serious and elaborate writings, as if they were no more than the theme of a grammar-lad under his pedagogue, must not be uttered without the cursory eyes of a temporizing and extemporizing licenser. He who is not trusted with his own actions, his drift not being known to be evil, and standing to the hazard of law and penalty, has no great argument to think himself reputed in the commonwealth wherein he was born for other than a fool or a foreigner. When a man writes to the world, he summons up all his reason and deliberation to assist him; he searches, meditates, is industrious, and likely consults and confers with his judicious friends; after all which done he takes himself to be informed in what he writes as well as any that writ before him; if in this the most consummate act of his fidelity and ripeness, no years, no industry, no former proof of his abilities can bring him to that state of maturity as not to be still mistrusted and suspected, unless he carry all his considerate diligence, all his midnight watchings, and expense of Palladian [83] oil, to the hasty view of an unleisured licenser, perhaps much his younger, perhaps far his inferior in judgment, perhaps one who never knew the labor of book-writing, and if he be not repulsed, or slighted, must appear in print like a puny [84] with his guardian, and his censor's hand on the back of his title to be his bail and surety that he is no idiot or seducer, it cannot be but a dishonor and derogation to the author, to the book, to the privilege and dignity of learning. And what if the author shall be one so copious of fancy as to have many things well worth the adding come into his mind after licensing, while the book is yet under the press, which not seldom happens to the best and diligentest writers, and that perhaps a dozen times in one book. The printer dares not go beyond his licensed copy; so often then must the author trudge to his leave-giver that those his new insertions may be viewed; and many a jaunt will be made ere that licenser, for it must be the same man, can either be found, or found at leisure; meanwhile either the press must stand still, which is no small damage, or the author lose his accuratest thoughts, and send the book forth worse than he had made it, which to a diligent writer is

---

[81] Sensitive.

[82] Escaped the rod to come under the pointer.
[83] Learned (concerning Pallas Athene).
[84] Minor.

the greatest melancholy and vexation that can befall. And how can a man teach with authority, which is the life of teaching, how can he be a doctor in his book as he ought to be, or else had better be silent, whenas all he teaches, all he delivers, is but under the tuition, under the correction of his patriarchal licenser to blot or alter what precisely accords not with the hide-bound humor which he calls his judgment? When every acute reader upon the first sight of a pedantic license will be ready with these like words to ding [85] the book a quoit's distance from him, I hate a pupil teacher; I endure not an instructor that comes to me under the wardship of an overseeing fist. I know nothing of the licenser but that I have his own hand here for his arrogance; who shall warrant me his judgment? "The state, sir," replies the stationer, but has a quick return, "The state shall be my governors, but not my critics; they may be mistaken in the choice of a licenser as easily as this licenser may be mistaken in an author; this is some common stuff." And he might add from Sir Francis Bacon that such authorized books are but the language of the times.[86] For though a licenser should happen to be judicious more than ordinary, which will be a great jeopardy of the next succession,[87] yet his very office and his commission enjoins him to let pass nothing but what is vulgarly received already. Nay, which is more lamentable, if the work of any deceased author, though never so famous in his lifetime, and even to this day, come to their hands for license to be printed or reprinted, if there be found in his book one sentence of a venturous edge, uttered in the height of zeal, and who knows whether it might not be the dictate of a divine spirit, yet not suiting with every low decrepit humor of their own, though it were Knox himself, the reformer of a kingdom that spake it, they will not pardon him their dash; the sense of that great man shall to all posterity be lost for the fearfulness or the presumptuous rashness of a perfunctory licenser. And to what an author this violence hath been lately done, and in what book of greatest consequence to be faithfully published, I could now instance, but shall forbear till a more convenient season. Yet if these things be not resented seriously and timely by them who have the remedy in their power, but that such iron molds [88] as these shall have authority to gnaw out the choicest periods of exquisitest books and to commit such a treacherous fraud against the orphan remainders of worthiest men after death, the more sorrow will belong to that hapless race of men whose misfortune it is to have understanding. Henceforth let no man care to learn, or care to be more than worldly wise; for certainly in higher matters to be ignorant and slothful, to be a common steadfast dunce will be the only pleasant life, and only in request.

And as it is a particular disesteem of every knowing person alive, and most injurious to the written labors and monuments of the dead, so to me it seems an undervaluing and vilifying of the whole nation. I cannot set so light by all the invention, the art, the wit, the grave and solid judgment which is in England, as that it can be comprehended in any twenty capacities how good soever, much less that it should not pass except their superintendence be over it, except it be sifted and strained with their strainers, that it should be uncurrent without their manual stamp. Truth and understanding are not such wares as to be monopolized and traded in by tickets and statutes and standards. We must not think to make a staple commodity of all the knowledge in the land, to mark and license it like our broad-cloth and our woolpacks. What is it but a servitude like that imposed by the Philistines, not to be allowed the sharpening of our own axes and colters, but we must repair from all quarters to twenty licensing forges. Had any one written and divulged erroneous things and scandalous to honest life, misusing and forfeiting the esteem had of his reason among men, if after conviction this only censure were adjudged him, that he should never henceforth write but what were first examined by an appointed officer, whose hand should be annexed to pass his credit for him that now he might be safely read, it could not be apprehended less than a disgraceful punishment. Whence to include the whole nation, and those that never yet thus offended, under such a diffident and suspectful prohibition may plainly be understood what a disparagement it is. So much the more whenas debtors and delinquents may walk abroad without a keeper, but inoffensive books must not stir forth without a visible jailer in their title. Nor is it to the common people less than a reproach; for if we be so jealous over them as that we dare not trust them with an English pamphlet, what do we but censure

---

[85] Throw.

[86] See Bacon's *Advertisement Touching the Controversies in the Church of England.*

[87] Which will make it hard to find a worthy successor.

[88] Rusts.

them for a giddy, vicious, and ungrounded people, in such a sick and weak estate of faith and discretion as to be able to take nothing down but through the pipe [89] of a licenser? That this is care or love of them we cannot pretend, whenas in those Popish places where the laity are most hated and despised the same strictness is used over them. Wisdom we cannot call it, because it stops but one breach of license, nor that neither; whenas those corruptions which it seeks to prevent break in faster at other doors which cannot be shut.

And in conclusion it reflects to the disrepute of our ministers also, of whose labors we should hope better, and of the proficiency which their flock reaps by them, than that after all this light of the Gospel which is, and is to be, and all this continual preaching, they should be still frequented with such an unprincipled, unedified, and laic rabble as that the whiff of every new pamphlet should stagger them out of their catechism and Christian walking. This may have much reason to discourage the ministers when such a low conceit is had of all their exhortations and the benefiting of their hearers as that they are not thought fit to be turned loose to three sheets of paper without a licenser, that all the sermons, all the lectures preached, printed, vented in such numbers and such volumes as have now well-nigh made all other books unsalable, should not be armor enough against one single *enchiridion*,[90] without the castle St. Angelo [91] of an *imprimatur*.

And lest some should persuade ye, Lords and Commons, that these arguments of learned men's discouragement at this your order are mere flourishes and not real, I could recount what I have seen and heard in other countries, where this kind of inquisition tyrannizes; when I have sat among their learned men, for that honor I had, and been counted happy to be born in such a place of philosophic freedom as they supposed England was, while themselves did nothing but bemoan the servile condition into which learning amongst them was brought, that this was it which had damped the glory of Italian wits, that nothing had been there written now these many years but flattery and fustian. There it was that I found and visited the famous Galileo grown old,[92] a prisoner to the Inquisition for thinking in astronomy otherwise than the Franciscan and Dominican licensers thought. And though I knew that England then was groaning loudest under the prelatical yoke, nevertheless I took it as a pledge of future happiness that other nations were so persuaded of her liberty. Yet was it beyond my hope that those worthies were then breathing in her air who should be her leaders to such a deliverance as shall never be forgotten by any revolution of time that this world hath to finish. When that was once begun, it was as little in my fear that what words of complaint I heard among learned men of other parts uttered against the Inquisition, the same I should hear by as learned men at home uttered in time of Parliament against an order of licensing; and that so generally that when I had disclosed myself a companion of their discontent, I might say, if without envy, that he whom an honest quaestorship had endeared to the Sicilians,[93] was not more by them importuned against Verres than the favorable opinion which I had among many who honor ye, and are known and respected by ye, loaded me with entreaties and persuasions that I would not despair to lay together that which just reason should bring into my mind toward the removal of an undeserved thraldom upon learning. That this is not therefore the disburdening of a particular fancy, but the common grievance of all those who had prepared their minds and studies above the vulgar pitch to advance truth in others, and from others to entertain it, thus much may satisfy. And in their name I shall for neither friend nor foe conceal what the general murmur is: that if it come to inquisitioning again and licensing, and that we are so timorous of ourselves and so suspicious of all men as to fear each book and the shaking of every leaf before we know what the contents are, if some who but of late were little better than silenced from preaching shall come now to silence us from reading except what they please, it cannot be guessed what is intended by some but a second tyranny over learning, and will soon put it out of controversy that bishops and presbyters are the same to us both name and thing. That those evils of prelaty which before from five or six and twenty sees were distributively charged upon the whole people will now light wholly upon learning is not obscure to us; whenas now the pastor of a small, unlearned parish on the sudden shall be exalted archbishop over a large diocese of books, and yet not remove but keep his other cure too, a mystical pluralist. He who but of late cried down the sole ordination of every novice bachelor of art, and denied sole jurisdic-

[89] Tube used to feed patients.
[90] Handbook.    [91] Papal fortress in Rome.
[92] Near Florence in 1638, when Galileo was 74.
[93] Cicero.

tion over the simplest parishioner, shall now at home in his private chair assume both these over worthiest and excellentest books and ablest authors that write them. This is not, ye covenants and protestations that we have made, this is not to put down prelaty; this is but to chop an episcopacy; this is but to translate the palace metropolitan [94] from one kind of dominion into another; this is but an old canonical sleight of commuting our penance. To startle thus betimes at a mere unlicensed pamphlet will after a while be afraid of every conventicle, and a while after will make a conventicle of every Christian meeting. But I am certain that a state governed by the rules of justice and fortitude, or a church built and founded upon the rock of faith and true knowledge, cannot be so pusillanimous. While things are not yet constituted in religion that freedom of writing should be restrained by a discipline imitated from the prelates, and learned by them from the Inquisition, to shut us up all again into the breast of a licenser must needs give cause of doubt and discouragement to all learned and religious men. Who cannot but discern the fineness of this politic drift and who are the contrivers? that while bishops were to be baited [95] down, then all presses might be open; it was the people's birthright and privilege in time of Parliament; it was the breaking forth of light. But now the bishops abrogated and voided out of the Church, as if our reformation sought no more but to make room for others into their seats under another name, the episcopal arts begin to bud again; the cruse of truth must run no more oil; liberty of printing must be enthralled again under a prelatical commission of twenty, the privilege of the people nullified; and which is worse, the freedom of learning must groan again, and to her old fetters: all this the Parliament yet sitting, although their own late arguments and defences against the prelates might remember them that this obstructing violence meets for the most part with an event utterly opposite to the end which it drives at. Instead of suppressing sects and schisms, it raises them and invests them with a reputation. *"The punishing of wits enhances their authority,"* saith the Viscount St. Albans,[96] *"and a forbidden writing is thought to be a certain spark of truth that flies up in the faces of them who seek to tread it out."* This order therefore may prove a nursing mother to sects, but I shall easily show

how it will be a step-dame to Truth, and first by disenabling us to the maintenance of what is known already.

Well knows he who uses to consider, that our faith and knowledge thrives by exercise, as well as our limbs and complexion. Truth is compared in Scripture to a streaming fountain; if her waters flow not in a perpetual progression, they sicken into a muddy pool of conformity and tradition. A man may be a heretic in the truth; and if he believe things only because his pastor says so, or the assembly so determines, without knowing other reason, though his belief be true, yet the very truth he holds becomes his heresy. There is not any burden that some would gladlier post off to another than the charge and care of their religion. There be, who knows not that there be of Protestants and professors [97] who live and die in as arrant an implicit faith as any lay Papist of Loretto? A wealthy man addicted to his pleasure and to his profits finds religion to be a traffic so entangled and of so many piddling accounts that of all mysteries [98] he cannot skill to keep a stock going upon that trade. What should he do? fain he would have the name to be religious; fain he would bear up with his neighbors in that. What does he therefore but resolves to give over toiling and to find himself out some factor to whose care and credit he may commit the whole managing of his religious affairs? some divine of note and estimation that must be. To him he adheres, resigns the whole warehouse of his religion, with all the locks and keys, into his custody; and indeed makes the very person of that man his religion; esteems his associating with him a sufficient evidence and commendatory of his own piety; so that a man may say his religion is now no more within himself, but is become a dividual [99] movable and goes and comes near him according as that good man frequents the house. He entertains him, gives him gifts, feasts him, lodges him; his religion comes home at night, prays, is liberally supped, and sumptuously laid to sleep, rises, is saluted; and after the malmsey or some well-spiced brewage, and better breakfasted than he whose morning appetite would have gladly fed on green figs between Bethany and Jerusalem, his religion walks abroad at eight, and leaves his kind entertainer in the shop trading all day without his religion.

Another sort there be who when they hear

---

[94] Lambeth Palace, standing for the Archbishopric of Canterbury.

[95] Hunted.          [96] Francis Bacon.

[97] Those who make open profession of their religion, particularly Puritans.

[98] Trades.          [99] Dividable.

that all things shall be ordered, all things regulated and settled, nothing written but what passes through the custom-house of certain publicans[100] that have the tonnaging and the poundaging of all free-spoken truth, will straight give themselves up into your hands, make 'em and cut 'em out what religion ye please. There be delights, there be recreations and jolly pastimes that will fetch the day about from sun to sun, and rock the tedious year as in a delightful dream. What need they torture their heads with that which others have taken so strictly and so unalterably into their own purveying? These are the fruits which a dull ease and cessation of our knowledge will bring forth among the people. How goodly and how to be wished were such an obedient unanimity as this? what a fine conformity would it starch us all into? doubtless a staunch and solid piece of framework, as any January could freeze together.

Nor much better will be the consequence even among the clergy themselves. It is no new thing, never heard of before, for a parochial minister, who has his reward and is at his Hercules' pillars[101] in a warm benefice, to be easily inclinable, if he have nothing else that may rouse up his studies, to finish his circuit in an English concordance and a topic folio, the gatherings and savings of a sober graduateship, a harmony and a catena,[102] treading the constant round of certain common doctrinal heads, attended with their uses, motives, marks, and means; out of which as out of an alphabet or sol-fa[103] by forming and transforming, joining and disjoining variously a little bookcraft, and two hours' meditation might furnish him unspeakably to the performance of more than a weekly charge of sermoning, not to reckon up the infinite helps of interliniaries, breviaries, synopses, and other loitering gear. But as for the multitude of sermons ready printed and piled up on every text that is not difficult, our London trading St. Thomas in his vestry, and add to boot St. Martin and St. Hugh, have not within their hallowed limits more vendible ware of all sorts ready made; so that penury he never need fear of pulpit provision, having where so plenteously to refresh his magazine. But if his rear and flanks be not impaled, if his back door be not secured by the rigid licenser, but that a bold book may now and then issue

forth and give the assault to some of his old collections in their trenches, it will concern him then to keep waking, to stand in watch, to set good guards and sentinels about his received opinions, to walk the round and counter-round with his fellow-inspectors, fearing lest any of his flock be seduced, who also then would be better instructed, better exercised and disciplined. And God send that the fear of this diligence which must then be used do not make us affect the laziness of a licensing church.

For if we be sure we are in the right, and do not hold the truth guiltily, which becomes not if we ourselves condemn not our own weak and frivolous teaching, and the people for an untaught and irreligious gadding rout, what can be more fair than when a man judicious, learned, and of a conscience, for aught we know, as good as theirs that taught us what we know, shall not privily from house to house, which is more dangerous, but openly by writing publish to the world what his opinion is, what his reasons, and wherefore that which is now thought cannot be sound? Christ urged it as wherewith to justify himself that he preached in public; yet writing is more public than preaching, and more easy to refutation, if need be, there being so many whose business and profession merely it is, to be the champions of truth; which if they neglect, what can be imputed but their sloth or inability?

Thus much we are hindered and disinured[104] by this course of licensing toward the true knowledge of what we seem to know. For how much it hurts and hinders the licensers themselves in the calling of their ministry more than any secular employment, if they will discharge that office as they ought, so that of necessity they must neglect either the one duty or the other, I insist not, because it is a particular, but leave it to their own conscience how they will decide it there.

There is yet, behind of what I purposed to lay open, the incredible loss and detriment that this plot of licensing puts us to; more than if some enemy at sea should stop up all our havens and ports and creeks, it hinders and retards the importation of our richest merchandise, truth. Nay, it was first established and put in practice by Anti-Christian malice and mystery on set purpose to extinguish, if it were possible, the light of reformation and to settle falsehood, little differing from that policy wherewith the Turk upholds his Alcoran by the prohibition of printing. 'Tis not denied, but gladly confessed, we are to send our thanks

[100] Tax-collectors.
[101] Has reached the height of his expectations.
[102] A synopsis of the four Gospels and a series of extracts from the Church Fathers.
[103] Musical gamut.

[104] Made unaccustomed.

and vows to heaven, louder than most of nations, for that great measure of truth which we enjoy, especially in those main points between us and the Pope, with his appurtenances, the prelates; but he who thinks we are to pitch our tent here, and have attained the utmost prospect of reformation that the mortal glass wherein we contemplate can show us till we come to beatific vision, that man by this very opinion declares that he is yet far short of truth.

Truth indeed came once into the world with her divine master, and was a perfect shape most glorious to look on; but when he ascended, and his apostles after him were laid asleep, then straight arose a wicked race of deceivers who, as that story goes of the Egyptian Typhon with his conspirators, how they dealt with the good Osiris, took the virgin Truth, hewed her lovely form into a thousand pieces, and scattered them to the four winds. From that time ever since the said friends of Truth, such as durst appear, imitating the careful[105] search that Isis made for the mangled body of Osiris, went up and down gathering up limb by limb still as they could find them. We have not yet found them all, Lords and Commons, nor ever shall do till her master's second coming; he shall bring together every joint and member, and shall mold them into an immortal feature of loveliness and perfection. Suffer not these licensing prohibitions to stand at every place of opportunity, forbidding and disturbing them that continue seeking, that continue to do our obsequies to the torn body of our martyred saint. We boast our light; but if we look not wisely on the sun itself, it smites us into darkness. Who can discern those planets that are oft combust,[106] and those stars of brightest magnitude that rise and set with the sun, until the opposite motion of their orbs bring them to such a place in the firmament where they may be seen evening or morning? The light which we have gained was given us, not to be ever staring on, but by it to discover onward things more remote from our knowledge. It is not the unfrocking of a priest, the unmitering of a bishop, and the removing him from off the presbyterian shoulders that will make us a happy nation; no, if other things as great in the church and in the rule of life both economical[107] and political be not looked into and reformed, we have looked so long upon the

blaze that Zuinglius and Calvin[108] hath beaconed up to us that we are stark blind. There be who perpetually complain of schisms and sects, and make it such a calamity that any man dissents from their maxims. 'Tis their own pride and ignorance which causes the disturbing, who neither will hear with meekness nor can convince, yet all must be suppressed which is not found in their syntagma.[109] They are the troublers; they are the dividers of unity, who neglect and permit not others to unite those dissevered pieces which are yet wanting to the body of Truth. To be still searching what we know not by what we know, still closing up truth to truth as we find it (for all her body is homogeneal[110] and proportional), this is the golden rule in theology as well as in arithmetic, and makes up the best harmony in a church, not the forced and outward union of cold, and neutral, and inwardly divided minds.

Lords and Commons of England, consider what nation it is whereof ye are and whereof ye are the governors: a nation not slow and dull, but of a quick, ingenious, and piercing spirit, acute to invent, subtle and sinewy to discourse, not beneath the reach of any point the highest that human capacity can soar to. Therefore the studies of learning in her deepest sciences have been so ancient and so eminent among us that writers of good antiquity and ablest judgment have been persuaded that even the school of Pythagoras and the Persian wisdom took beginning from the old philosophy of this island. And that wise and civil Roman, Julius Agricola, who governed once here for Caesar,[111] preferred the natural wits of Britain before the labored studies of the French. Nor is it for nothing that the grave and frugal Transylvanian sends out yearly from as far as the mountainous borders of Russia, and beyond the Hercynian wilderness,[112] not their youth, but their staid men to learn our language and our theologic arts. Yet that which is above all this, the favor and the love of heaven, we have great argument to think in a peculiar manner propitious and propending towards us. Why else was this nation chosen before any other, that out of her as out of Sion should be proclaimed and sounded forth the first tidings and trumpet of reformation to all Europe. And

[105] Sorrowful.
[106] So near the sun as to be invisible.
[107] Concerning private management.

[108] Swiss and French reformers of the sixteenth century.
[109] Personal collections of beliefs.
[110] Homogeneous.
[111] For the emperors Vespasian, Titus, and Domitian.
[112] The forests of southern Germany.

had it not been the obstinate perverseness of our prelates against the divine and admirable spirit of Wicliffe, to suppress him as a schismatic and innovator, perhaps neither the Bohemian Huss and Jerome, no, nor the name of Luther or of Calvin had been ever known; the glory of reforming all our neighbors had been completely ours. But now, as our obdurate clergy have with violence demeaned the matter, we are become hitherto the latest 10 and the backwardest scholars, of whom God offered to have made us the teachers. Now once again by all concurrence of signs and by the general instinct of holy and devout men, as they daily and solemnly express their thoughts, God is decreeing to begin some new and great period in his Church, even to the reforming of reformation itself; what does he then but reveal himself to his servants and, as his manner is, first to his Englishmen? I say, 20 as his manner is, first to us, though we mark not the method of his counsels and are unworthy. Behold now this vast city, a city of refuge, the mansion house of liberty, encompassed and surrounded with his protection; the shop of war hath not there more anvils and hammers waking, to fashion out the plates and instruments of armed justice in defence of beleaguered truth, than there be pens and heads there, sitting by their studious lamps, 30 musing, searching, revolving new notions and ideas wherewith to present, as with their homage and their fealty, the approaching reformation; others as fast reading, trying all things, assenting to the force of reason and convincement. What could a man require more from a nation so pliant and so prone to seek after knowledge? What wants there to such towardly [113] and pregnant soil but wise and faithful laborers, to make a knowing people, a 40 nation of prophets, of sages, and of worthies? We reckon more than five months yet to harvest; there need not be five weeks; had we but eyes to lift up, the fields are white already. Where there is much desire to learn, there of necessity will be much arguing, much writing, many opinions; for opinion in good men is but knowledge in the making. Under these fantastic terrors of sect and schism we wrong the earnest and zealous thirst after knowledge and 50 understanding which God hath stirred up in this city. What some lament of we rather should rejoice at, should rather praise this pious forwardness among men to reassume the ill-deputed care of their religion into their own

hands again. A little generous prudence, a little forbearance of one another, and some grain of charity might win all these diligences to join and unite into one general and brotherly search after truth, could we but forego this prelatical tradition of crowding free consciences and Christian liberties into canons and precepts of men. I doubt not, if some great and worthy stranger should come among us, wise to discern the mold and temper of a people, and how to govern it, observing the high hopes and aims, the diligent alacrity of our extended thoughts and reasonings in the pursuance of truth and freedom, but that he would cry out as Pyrrhus [114] did, admiring the Roman docility and courage, "if such were my Epirots, I would not despair the greatest design that could be attempted to make a church or kingdom happy." Yet these are the men cried out against for schismatics and sectaries, as if, while the Temple of the Lord was building, some cutting, some squaring the marble, others hewing the cedars, there should be a sort of irrational men who could not consider there must be many schisms and many dissections made in the quarry and in the timber, ere the house of God can be built. And when every stone is laid artfully together, it cannot be united into a continuity, it can but be contiguous in this world; neither can every piece of the building be of one form; nay, rather the perfection consists in this, that out of many moderate varieties and brotherly dissimilitudes that are not vastly disproportional arises the goodly and the graceful symmetry that commends the whole pile and structure. Let us therefore be more considerate builders, more wise in spiritual architecture, when great reformation is expected. For now the time seems come wherein Moses, the great prophet, may sit in heaven rejoicing to see that memorable and glorious wish of his fulfilled, when not only our seventy elders but all the Lord's people are become prophets. No marvel then though some men, and some good men too perhaps, but young in goodness, as Joshua then was, envy them. They fret, and out of their own weakness are in agony lest these divisions and sub-divisions will undo us. The adversary again applauds and waits the hour: "When they have branched themselves out," saith he, "small enough into parties and partitions, then will be our time." Fool! he sees not the firm root out of which we all grow, though into branches; nor will beware until he see our small

[113] Easily cultivated.

[114] King of Epirus (B.C. 318–272).

divided maniples cutting through at every angle of his ill-united and unwieldy brigade. And that we are to hope better of all these supposed sects and schisms, and that we shall not need that solicitude, honest perhaps though over-timorous, of them that vex in this behalf, but shall laugh in the end at those malicious applauders of our differences, I have these reasons to persuade me.

First, when a city shall be as it were besieged and blocked about, her navigable river infested, inroads and incursions round, defiance and battle oft rumored to be marching up even to her walls and suburb trenches, that then the people, or the greater part, more than at other times wholly taken up with the study of highest and most important matters to be reformed, should be disputing, reasoning, reading, inventing, discoursing, even to a rarity and admiration, things not before discoursed or written of, argues first a singular good will, contentedness and confidence in your prudent foresight and safe government, Lords and Commons; and from thence derives itself to a gallant bravery and well-grounded contempt of their enemies, as if there were no small number of as great spirits among us as his was who when Rome was nigh besieged by Hannibal, being in the city, bought that piece of ground at no cheap rate whereon Hannibal himself encamped his own regiment. Next it is a lively and cheerful presage of our happy success and victory. For as in a body, when the blood is fresh, the spirits pure and vigorous, not only to vital but to rational faculties, and those in the acutest and the pertest [115] operations of wit and subtlety, it argues in what good plight and constitution the body is; so when the cheerfulness of the people is so sprightly up as that it has, not only wherewith to guard well its own freedom and safety, but to spare and to bestow upon the solidest and sublimest points of controversy and new invention, it betokens us not degenerated nor drooping to a fatal decay, but casting off the old and wrinkled skin of corruption to outlive these pangs and wax young again, entering the glorious ways of truth and prosperous virtue destined to become great and honorable in these latter ages. Methinks I see in my mind a noble and puissant nation rousing herself like a strong man after sleep, and shaking her invincible locks. Methinks I see her as an eagle mewing [116] her mighty youth and kindling her undazzled eyes at the full mid-day beam, purging and unscaling her long-abused sight at the fountain itself of heavenly radiance;

[115] Liveliest.          [116] Renewing.

while the whole noise of timorous and flocking birds, with those also that love the twilight, flutter about, amazed at what she means, and in their envious gabble would prognosticate a year of sects and schisms.

What should ye do then, should ye suppress all this flowery crop of knowledge and new light sprung up and yet springing daily in this city; should ye set an oligarchy of twenty engrossers [117] over it, to bring a famine upon our minds again, when we shall know nothing but what is measured to us by their bushel? Believe it, Lords and Commons, they who counsel ye to such a suppressing do as good as bid ye suppress yourselves; and I will soon show how. If it be desired to know the immediate cause of all this free writing and free speaking, there cannot be assigned a truer than your own mild, and free, and humane government; it is the liberty, Lords and Commons, which your own valorous and happy counsels have purchased us, liberty which is the nurse of all great wits; this is that which hath rarefied and enlightened our spirits like the influence of heaven; this is that which hath enfranchised, enlarged, and lifted up our apprehensions degrees above themselves. Ye cannot make us now less capable, less knowing, less eagerly pursuing of the truth, unless ye first make yourselves, that made us so, less the lovers, less the founders of our true liberty. We can grow ignorant again, brutish, formal, and slavish, as ye found us; but you then must first become that which ye cannot be, oppressive, arbitrary, and tyrannous, as they were from whom ye have freed us. That our hearts are now more capacious, our thoughts more erected to the search and expectation of greatest and exactest things is the issue of your own virtue propagated in us; ye cannot suppress that unless ye reinforce an abrogated and merciless law that fathers may dispatch at will their own children. And who shall then stick closest to ye and excite others? not he who takes up arms for coat and conduct [118] and his four nobles of Danegelt.[119] Although I dispraise not the defence of just immunities, yet love my peace better, if that [120] were all. Give me the liberty to know, to utter, and to argue freely according to conscience, above all liberties.

[117] Monopolizers.
[118] Takes up arms to resist taxation for clothing and transporting troops.
[119] Originally, a land-tax for protection against Danish raids; here, referring to the ship-money which Charles I had exacted, supposedly to afford naval protection.
[120] Immunity from taxation.

What would be best advised then, if it be found so hurtful and so unequal to suppress opinions for the newness, or the unsuitableness to a customary acceptance, will not be my task to say; I only shall repeat what I have learned from one of your own honorable number, a right noble and pious lord, who, had he not sacrificed his life and fortunes to the Church and Commonwealth, we had not now missed and bewailed a worthy and undoubted patron of this argument. Ye know him I am sure; yet I for honor's sake, and may it be eternal to him, shall name him the Lord Brooke.[121] He, writing of episcopacy, and by the way treating of sects and schisms, left ye his vote, or rather now the last words of his dying charge, which I know will ever be of dear and honored regard with ye, so full of meekness and breathing charity that next to his last testament, who bequeathed love and peace to his disciples, I cannot call to mind where I have read or heard words more mild and peaceful. He there exhorts us to hear with patience and humility those, however they be miscalled, that desire to live purely, in such a use of God's ordinances as the best guidance of their conscience gives them, and to tolerate them, though in some disconformity to ourselves. The book itself will tell us more at large, being published to the world and dedicated to the Parliament by him who both for his life and for his death deserves that what advice he left be not laid by without perusal.

And now the time in special is by privilege to write and speak what may help to the further discussing of matters in agitation. The Temple of Janus with his two controversal faces might now not unsignificantly be set open. And though all the winds of doctrine were let loose to play upon the earth, so Truth be in the field, we do injuriously by licensing and prohibiting to misdoubt her strength. Let her and Falsehood grapple; who ever knew Truth put to the worse in a free and open encounter. Her confuting is the best and surest suppressing. He who hears what praying there is for light and clearer knowledge to be sent down among us would think of other matters to be constituted beyond the discipline of Geneva, framed and fabricked already to our hands. Yet when the new light which we beg for shines in upon us, there be who envy and oppose if it come not first in at their casements. What a collusion is this, whenas

we are exhorted by the wise man [122] to use diligence, to seek for wisdom as for hidden treasures early and late, that another order shall enjoin us to know nothing but by statute. When a man hath been laboring the hardest labor in the deep mines of knowledge, hath furnished out his findings in all their equipage, drawn forth his reasons as it were a battle ranged, scattered and defeated all objections in his way, calls out his adversary into the plain, offers him the advantage of wind and sun, if he please, only that he may try the matter by dint of argument, for his opponents then to skulk, to lay ambushments, to keep a narrow bridge of licensing where the challenger should pass, though it be valor enough in soldiership, is but weakness and cowardice in the wars of Truth. For who knows not that Truth is strong next to the Almighty; she needs no policies, nor stratagems, nor licensings to make her victorious; those are the shifts and the defences that Error uses against her power; give her but room, and do not bind her when she sleeps, for then she speaks not true, as the old Proteus did, who spake oracles only when he was caught and bound, but then rather she turns herself into all shapes except her own, and perhaps tunes her voice according to the time, as Micaiah did before Ahab, until she be adjured into her own likeness. Yet is it not impossible that she may have more shapes than one. What else is all that rank of things indifferent wherein Truth may be on this side, or on the other, without being unlike herself. What but a vain shadow else is the abolition of those ordinances, that hand-writing nailed to the cross? what great purchase is this Christian liberty which Paul so often boasts of? His doctrine is that he who eats or eats not, regards a day, or regards it not, may do either to the Lord. How many other things might be tolerated in peace and left to conscience, had we but charity, and were it not the chief stronghold of our hypocrisy to be ever judging one another. I fear yet this iron yoke of outward conformity hath left a slavish print upon our necks; the ghost of a linen decency [123] yet haunts us. We stumble and are impatient at the least dividing of one visible congregation from another, though it be not in fundamentals; and through our forwardness to suppress and our backwardness to recover any en-

---

[121] Robert Greville (1607–1643), author of *A Discourse on Episcopacy.*

[122] Christ (St. Matthew, 13:44).

[123] The controversy over ecclesiastical vestments.

thralled piece of truth out of the gripe [124] of custom we care not to keep truth separated from truth, which is the fiercest rent and disunion of all. We do not see that while we still affect by all means a rigid external formality, we may as soon fall again into a gross conforming stupidity, a stark and dead congealment of wood and hay and stubble forced and frozen together, which is more to the sudden degenerating of a church than many sub-dichotomies [125] of petty schisms. Not that I can think well of every light separation, or that all in a church is to be expected gold and silver and precious stones; it is not possible for man to sever the wheat from the tares, the good fish from the other fry; that must be the angel's ministry at the end of mortal things. Yet if all cannot be of one mind, as who looks they should be? this doubtless is more wholesome, more prudent, and more Christian that many be tolerated rather than all compelled. I mean not tolerated Popery and open superstition, which as it extirpates all religions and civil supremacies, so itself should be extirpate, provided first that all charitable and compassionate means be used to win and regain the weak and the misled; that also which is impious or evil absolutely either against faith or manners no law can possibly permit, that intends not to unlaw itself; but those neighboring differences, or rather indifferences, are what I speak of, whether in some point of doctrine or of discipline which though they may be many, yet need not interrupt the unity of spirit, if we could but find among us the bond of peace. In the meanwhile if any one would write and bring his helpful hand to the slow-moving reformation which we labor under, if truth have spoken to him before others, or but seemed at least to speak, who hath so bejesuited us that we should trouble that man with asking license to do so worthy a deed? and not consider this, that if it come to prohibiting, there is not aught more likely to be prohibited than truth itself; whose first appearance to our eyes, bleared and dimmed with prejudice and custom, is more unsightly and unplausible than many errors, even as the person is of many a great man slight and contemptible to see to. And what do they tell us vainly of new opinions, when this very opinion of theirs, that none must be heard but whom they like, is the worst and newest opinion of all others, and is the chief cause why sects

and schisms do so much abound, and true knowledge is kept at distance from us, besides yet a greater danger which is in it? For when God shakes a kingdom with strong and healthful commotions to a general reforming, 'tis not untrue that many sectaries and false teachers are then busiest in seducing; but yet more true it is that God then raises to his own work men of rare abilities and more than common industry not only to look back and revise what hath been taught heretofore, but to gain further and go on some new enlightened steps in the discovery of truth. For such is the order of God's enlightening his Church, to dispense and deal out by degrees his beam, so as our earthly eyes may best sustain it. Neither is God appointed and confined where and out of what place these his chosen shall be first heard to speak; for he sees not as man sees, chooses not as man chooses, lest we should devote ourselves again to set places, and assemblies, and outward callings of men, planting our faith one while in the old convocation house, and another while in the chapel at Westminster; [126] when all the faith and religion that shall be there canonized is not sufficient without plain convincement and the charity of patient instruction to supple [127] the least bruise of conscience, to edify the meanest Christian who desires to walk in the spirit and not in the letter of human trust, for all the number of voices that can be there made; no, though Harry VII himself there, [128] with all his liege tombs about him, should lend them voices from the dead to swell their number. And if the men be erroneous who appear to be the leading schismatics, what withholds us but our sloth, our self-will and distrust in the right cause, that we do not give them gentle meetings and gentle dismissions, that we debate not and examine the matter thoroughly with liberal and frequent audience, if not for their sakes, yet for our own? seeing no man who hath tasted learning but will confess the many ways of profiting by those who not contented with stale receipts are able to manage and set forth new positions to the world. And were they but as the dust and cinders of our feet, so long as in that notion they may yet serve to

[124] Grip.    [125] Minute divisions.

[126] One while in the place where the clergy of the Church of England assembled, and another in the place where the Presbyterian Church held its meetings when it became the state religion in 1643.

[127] Soften.

[128] Henry VII is buried in the chapel at Westminster.

polish and brighten the armory of truth, even for that respect they were not utterly to be cast away. But if they be of those whom God hath fitted for the special use of these times with eminent and ample gifts, and those perhaps neither among the priests nor among the pharisees, and we in the haste of a precipitant zeal shall make no distinction but resolve to stop their mouths, because we fear they come with new and dangerous opinions, as we commonly forejudge them ere we understand them, no less than woe to us, while thinking thus to defend the Gospel, we are found the persecutors.

There have been not a few since the beginning of this Parliament, both of the presbytery and others, who by their unlicensed books to the contempt of an *imprimatur* first broke that triple ice clung about our hearts and taught the people to see day; I hope that none of those were the persuaders to renew upon us this bondage which they themselves have wrought so much good by contemning. But if neither the check that Moses gave to young Joshua, nor the countermand which our Savior gave to young John, who was so ready to prohibit those whom he thought unlicensed, be not enough to admonish our elders how unacceptable to God their testy mood of prohibiting is; if neither their own remembrance what evil hath abounded in the Church by this let [129] of licensing, and what good they themselves have begun by transgressing it, be not enough but that they will persuade and execute the most Dominican part of the Inquisition over us, and are already with one foot in the stirrup so active at suppressing; it would be no unequal distribution in the first place to suppress the suppressors themselves, whom the change of their condition hath puffed up more than their late experience of harder times hath made wise.

And as for regulating the press, let no man think to have the honor of advising ye better than yourselves have done in that order published next before this, that no book be printed unless the printer's and the author's name, or at least the printer's, be registered. Those which otherwise come forth, if they be found mischievous and libellous, the fire

and the executioner will be the timeliest and the most effectual remedy that man's prevention can use. For this authentic Spanish policy of licensing books, if I have said aught, will prove the most unlicensed book itself within a short while; and was the immediate image of a Star-Chamber decree [130] to that purpose made in those very times when that court did the rest of those her pious works for which she is now fallen from the stars with Lucifer. Whereby ye may guess what kind of state prudence, what love of the people, what care of religion or good manners there was at the contriving, although with singular hypocrisy it pretended to bind books to their good behavior. And how it got the upper hand of your precedent order so well constituted before, if we may believe those men whose profession gives them cause to inquire most, it may be doubted there was in it the fraud of some old patentees and monopolizers in the trade of book-selling; who under pretence of the poor in their company not to be defrauded and the just retaining of each man his several copy, which God forbid should be gainsaid, brought divers glossing colors to the House, which were indeed but colors and serving to no end except it be to exercise a superiority over their neighbors, men who do not therefore labor in an honest profession to which learning is indebted, that they should be made other men's vassals. Another end is thought was aimed at by some of them in procuring by petition this order, that having power in their hands, malignant books might the easier escape abroad, as the event shows. But of these sophisms and elenches [131] of merchandise I skill not. This I know, that errors in a good government and in a bad are equally almost incident; for what magistrate may not be misinformed, and much the sooner, if liberty of printing be reduced into the power of a few; but to redress willingly and speedily what hath been erred, and in highest authority to esteem a plain advertisement more than others have done a sumptuous bribe is a virtue (honored Lords and Commons) answerable to your highest actions, and whereof none can participate but greatest and wisest men.

[129] Hindrance.

[130] A decree by the royal court of the Star Chamber, abolished in 1641.
[131] Fallacious arguments.

# THE RESTORATION AND THE EIGHTEENTH CENTURY, 1660-1784

Upon the death of Oliver Cromwell in 1658 it rapidly became clear that the Puritan Commonwealth was a failure. Oliver named his son Richard as his successor, but Richard had none of his father's overmastering strength of character, and was forced to abdicate within less than a year after he had become Protector. It now became clear that Oliver's personal ability, or genius, had alone kept the Commonwealth together for even a few years, and that there was no one capable of taking Oliver's place.

Royalists were ready with the only practical solution that presented itself—the recall of Charles I's son from across the waters. Thus royal government was restored through the return, in 1660, of Charles II. Charles had been sent abroad for safety in 1645. An exile for nearly fifteen years, he had spent the greater part of that time in France, surrounded by a considerable number of loyal Englishmen. Life had not been easy for the royal exile, and he was very glad to come home.

## CHARLES II AND HIS INFLUENCE

Charles II was not without characteristic Stuart ambitions and beliefs. He, like his father and grandfather, wanted to become an absolute ruler, and he also wanted to bring the country back to Catholicism. He had, however, learned some lessons. Providence had at length given him a position of great wealth and of the highest dignity, and he was resolved to enjoy the gift to the utmost and not on any account to allow it to be snatched away. Besides, he was easygoing, and always ready to sacrifice business for pleasure. Hence, when op-

position to one or another of his designs became stiff, he would abandon his plan rather than fight for it.

Charles's court was notorious for the open and gross immorality which flourished there. The court, moreover, was still the center of the nation's life. The moral standards, the manners, the tastes and interests, the dress, the household furniture, the whole order and setting of life brought in by the king exerted an influence stronger than we today can easily imagine, not only upon London but upon the nation at large. Charles himself might complain that a king forced to consult his parliament was a king only in name, but that name was majestic, as a humorous example may show: One Sunday in the Chapel Royal the preacher of the day stopped in his sermon to cry out to the sleeping Earl of Lauderdale, "My lord, my lord, you snore so loud you will wake the king!"

Charles had a genuine, persistent interest in chemistry, and maintained a laboratory in his palace; indeed, he had an active interest in the whole realm of science, and a surprising fund of practical knowledge. In addition, Charles inherited his father's love of the painter's art. He tried to gather again the pictures Charles I had collected, and which had been dispersed under the Commonwealth; he specially cherished the paintings of Raphael, Titian, and Holbein. He was also a liberal patron of living artists, and kept half a dozen of them busy. Music too he loved, and he drew to his court the best English and some of the best foreign masters of that art. From France he brought gilt mirrors and furniture and colorful clothes. Paris in the middle of the seventeenth century had become the brilliant center of all European culture, art, and polished elegance, and Charles introduced into England every new thing Paris could boast of, until the stream of refinements gathered a momentum of its own and no longer needed royal encouragement. To give one example, trifling enough in itself, in the summer of 1669 four thousand gilt mirrors were sent from Paris to supply the London trade.

Much more important than mirrors was good breeding. When Charles returned he found England a country of boors, rough in their play, always jeering at anything strange, stiff and awkward in manner, and much inclined to be ill-tempered. Charles set a very different standard, which had an immediate and permanent influence. His conception of a gentleman was, "to be easy himself and to make everybody else so." It can be expressed in ten words, but it would be difficult in as many pages to explain all that this new ideal meant and to outline its bearings upon English life and letters for the next hundred years and more. Without this change in manners, the flood of other French influences could have had but little effect; with it, everything hung together, and the total effect we can see fairly reflected in the new prose and poetry of the time.

## CONTINUITY OF RENAISSANCE TRADITION

Before we turn to the new prose and poetry, however, we must understand that there were elements of continuity in English artistic and intellectual life through the seventeenth century no less important than the changes we see. Charles II's scientific interests, for example, represented nothing new or foreign, for from the early years of the century scientific investigation had been actively carried on in England. Similarly, modes of thought which were to prevail in the new age go back to Bacon, and to the rationalism which we have seen growing in the work of Anglican divines of the first half of the century.

Literature of the Restoration and the eighteenth century also has its roots in England, going back chiefly to Ben Jonson and his followers. Restoration comedy, for example, owes much to several courtly dramatists who were of Jonson's school. This element of continuity can be seen most distinctly in some of the lyrical poetry of the Restoration period, but it is present everywhere, and is unmistakable once we begin to look closely for it. As the

eighteenth century advances, moreover, we find poets looking back to Spenser and even more to Milton as their teachers and sources of inspiration. There is abundant evidence, then, that men of the Restoration and the eighteenth century did not think of themselves as having broken with the Elizabethan or Renaissance tradition.

On the contrary, they thought of themselves as continuing this tradition and building upon it, or advancing from it. They were, within limits, quite right. This is the first thing concerning this new period which we must get clearly fixed in mind. We have seen that the revival of classical studies was, for literature, a central part of that very complex movement of change called the Renaissance. The revival at first took strongest hold, as we might expect, upon a few scholars, and then spread slowly outward. The consequence was that Elizabethan literature was rather humanistic than classical. It expressed primarily the spirit of the age: the new confidence in human powers, the new conviction of the dignity and worth of earthly human nature, and the new desire to match the cultural achievements of the ancient pre-Christian world. Most Elizabethan writers were not deeply read in ancient literature, but they were emphatically men of the Renaissance. With Ben Jonson, however, literature began to be more genuinely classical in form and spirit. As poets became more intimately and appreciatively acquainted with classical writers, they became more critical, and better able to use what they were learning, in verse which was not less English for being smooth, polished, and carefully modulated.

## THE HEROIC COUPLET

To aim at clarity, ease, and steady control, without sacrifice of interest, strength, or depth, may be accepted as a classical standard. And in the new age Sir John Denham and Edmund Waller were given most credit for showing the way to a kind of verse which could meet this standard. Actually the thing aimed at was the "closed couplet," as it is called, in which a complete general statement is made with neatness and point:

Know then thyself, presume not God to scan;
The proper study of Mankind is Man.

Alexander Pope is the author of this familiar example; his rimed couplets have never been excelled or equalled in English. John Dryden bridges the long distance between Denham and Pope. Dryden used the rimed couplet for many

purposes, including narrative and heroic poetry, heroic drama, argument, and satire. He
used it in these varied ways with unfailing
energy, and did more than anyone else to fix
it, for several generations, as the dominant
form of English verse. It soon came to be
regarded as the one form of verse suited to
heroic poetry, and for this reason it is often
called the "heroic couplet."

### FRENCH INFLUENCE

If we are to reach a genuine understanding
of the Restoration and the eighteenth century, we must attempt to distinguish those
changes which were mainly caused by the
continuous operation of Renaissance impulses
from other changes which were really caused
by the religious and political strife of the seventeenth century. It was at one time generally
believed that the new characteristics of Restoration literature were largely the result of
French influences brought in by Charles II
and those loyal Englishmen who shared his
years of exile. As has already been said, the
French did exert a strong influence upon the
English people in the years following the
Restoration; and this influence extended beyond gilt mirrors and the like to literature, and
was certainly important in the field of literature. Nevertheless, we cannot really be sure
that any important difference between Elizabethan literature and that of the Restoration
can be traced to influences from France felt
after 1660. The fact is that French influence
in the later seventeenth century really worked,
not to alter, but to reinforce an already-present
tendency towards critical and orderly restraint.
In addition, French influence had begun to be
important a whole generation before 1660, and
in this earlier period also reinforced Renaissance impulses which had already been felt in
England.

The earlier period of French influence is
centered about the interminable prose romance
*Astrée*, by Honoré d'Urfé. This book not only
initiated a vogue, becoming the father of a
family of seventeenth century heroic romances
popular in both France and England, but had
a wide influence. It elaborated an "heroic"
theme which had a genuine contemporary interest, and thus it seemed for a while to answer
the need of men who were trying to create a
modern literature in the light of classical example. *Astrée* and the other heroic romances
thus became a major influence in the creation of the heroic drama of the Restoration,

which was in fact simply a refashioning in
dramatic form of the stuff of these romances.
Nor did their influence stop here; for they
exerted a controlling effect on Restoration
comedy, and they also had a determining effect upon the novel of the eighteenth century.

### INFLUENCE OF THE FRENCH
### CLASSICAL CRITICS

The most important new influence from
France felt in the 1660's and 1670's, and later,
came from the French classical critics, and
above all from Boileau's treatise on the art of
poetry. The authority of the French critics
stood very high in England, and their discourses encouraged thought about literary aims
and methods, and helped to give precision to
such thought. At the same time, the development of literary criticism in England was encouraged. This was good, but even more wholesome was the appearance of a new critical attitude. Dryden's critical essays are written on
a conversational level; they are not pronounced
from on high, but are genial discussions, such
as cultivated gentlemen with a natural and
intelligent concern for the arts might be expected to participate in. This is a change, like
much else we find in the Restoration and
eighteenth century, which is a perfectly appropriate fulfillment of Renaissance humanism; but it is not a change for which any
English criticism before the Restoration prepares the way.

### ENGLISH STILL DIVIDED
### AFTER THE RESTORATION

Though England as a whole welcomed the
return of Charles II, the Puritans were by no
means disposed to abandon their religious convictions. The result was that they were forced
into the position of outcasts, living a submerged life of their own. This would have been
bad enough, for both sides, had the country
been divided into only two camps; but it was
really divided into a number of separate elements. The Puritans, as we have seen, had split
up into various sects, and in addition there
were the Roman Catholics. The loss of unity
which had begun as the Reformation was thus
continued and the growth of provincial narrowness and exclusiveness encouraged. Everybody
was the weaker for it, and everybody tended,
of course, to be blind to his own deficiencies
and keenly aware of the failings of those outside his immediate circle. Inasmuch as the

royal court remained the unchallenged center of all cultivated life, writers gathered around it and wrote for the courtly circle; but this meant that Restoration literature was written not only for a small and aristocratic public, but also for a public that no longer fairly represented the nation as the court had represented it in the sixteenth century.

## EMERGENCE OF THE SATIRIC SPIRIT

Further, the opinion held at the court was that Puritanism had degenerated into hypocrisy. We may be just as sure that this opinion did not represent the whole truth as that there was some truth in it—enough truth to give courtiers the feeling that they were on solid ground in refusing to be hypocrites themselves. Thus there was an element of serious conviction underlying the bold outspoken worldliness and irreligion of the Restoration court. This anti-Puritan attitude was brilliantly and wittily expressed very soon after Charles's return by Samuel Butler in *Hudibras*, published in 1662. Butler was one of the earliest to exhibit in literature the changed temper of the Restoration period; and readers of *Hudibras* are at once struck forcibly by the poem's spirit of contemptuous hatred, mirrored in its rough and ready style, its witty forced rimes, and its mock-heroic scheme. Butler is impelled by an indignant sense of the vice and folly of mankind, and holds up the Puritans as a special example. His method is that of ridicule. Inspired by *Don Quixote*, in which Cervantes had made the outworn conventions and ideals of chivalry ridiculous by burlesquing them, Butler writes a burlesque poem in which he parodies the persons, aims, and activities of the Puritans. This is his way of getting underneath appearances to reality. He wants to convince us that beneath their pretended saintliness the Puritans were really a crackbrained, opinionated, stubbornly perverse lot, and hypocritical to boot.

And though *Hudibras* is a burlesque in form, it is satirical in aim. Butler is above all conscious of the divided state of the nation; he is obsessed by that cruel fact, and cannot get by it or outside of it to any positive universal truths. He is caught up in the strife of parties, and forced to become a party man himself, who attacks his opponents by merciless decision. He is reduced by the pressure of events from any optimistic consideration of what man might be or should be, to a disillusioned recognition of what men actually are, too often, too generally—a vicious compound of "hypocrisy and nonsense." And by the spectacle he is impelled to satire.

## SATIRE AND IRONY DEFINED

Satire may be defined as a kind of writing, in verse or prose, in which vice, folly, and even individual human beings are held up to ridicule. Satirical verse is not the highest kind of poetry, but we ought not to make the mistake of denying that it is poetry at all. As Butler, Dryden, and Pope use it, verse satire is not wholly intellectual argument which merely happens to be given metrical form; it is a true and passionately imagined *embodiment* of a critical attitude, and hence is true poetry.

The most effective of satirical methods, if it is well used, is irony. Nevertheless, there are readers who dislike it and complain against it. They take a poem or essay in good faith, and are gradually bewildered as they begin to suspect that the author cannot mean what he is saying. And of course this is just what the ironist aims at. Irony can be defined as the assertion of the opposite of what one actually means. The ironist explodes some plausible fallacy or hidden vice by taking it at its apparent value and then drawing out the logical consequences. These are so obviously absurd that we are forced to see that the fallacy is a fallacy and the vice really vicious. The great master of irony is Swift; he has been excelled by no one, ancient or modern. It is not his irony, however, that makes Swift so well loved —it is his warmth and loyalty and friendship, his playful but deeply rooted and noble human sympathy, and the unique flight of his imagination in *Gulliver's Travels*, where he has succeeded in giving biting pictures of humanity an outer form perennially delightful to children, who do not suspect the underlying satire.

## SATIRE AND THE HUMANISTIC TRADITION

Perhaps we ought to be most grateful to the satirists of the half century and more after 1660 for their demonstration that it is possible to be serious, even profound, and devotedly on the side of the angels, without being solemn, labored, fanatical, or obscure. It may seem odd in Butler's case and in the case of most satirists to say that they are "on the side of the angels"; but at any rate they are on the side of reason and sweetness and light, and the positive ideal of the eighteenth-century satirists was a cultivated and developed humanity, intelligent enough to put first things first and tolerant enough to live together in a friendly way. Butler was no more favorable to the immorality of Restoration society than he was to Puritan fanaticism and hypocrisy. The truth is that Butler, Swift, and the other satirists were campaigning for sanity. And in this they were carrying on the program of Renaissance humanism.

Nevertheless, we have only to repeat the word—sanity—to realize that the new aim represents a shrinkage of Renaissance optimism. We are helped to see how great the shrinkage was when we discover that in the varied wealth of Elizabethan literature satire remained a minor and almost alien element. It was not until after 1660 that classical satire found a real welcome in England; and it then for two generations assumed a foremost place not only because it was written with genius and was eagerly received but also because it had no effective competition. In short, the times were such that satire could be written effectively; and no one with outstanding genius for higher forms of literature appeared.

## "ENTHUSIASM" REPLACED BY DISILLUSIONED COMMON SENSE

The reasons for this change of temper, and this shrinkage, are to be found in the fact that Protestant individualism, in itself not a bad thing, had been perverted into the doctrine of "private inspiration." This is simply another name for absolute confidence in the individual's own inward, non-rational conviction that what he happens to believe is the whole truth and nothing but the truth. And this kind of Protestantism had had its chance in the years of the Puritan Commonwealth, and had failed. Private inspiration had been proved a failure, a dangerous thing. Here we have the explanation of the widespread hatred felt in the eighteenth century for what the men of that time called "enthusiasm." The enthusiastic person is one who is carried away, carried out of himself, by an inward conviction of the worth of something. This is not rational behavior; it is a species of "possession" closing the ears of its victim to argument. The English came to fear it and hate it; what they needed and longed for was plain unoriginal common sense.

## GROWTH OF THE SCIENTIFIC SPIRIT AND ITS INFLUENCES

At this point another element which had been an integral part of the Renaissance, and which had, with Francis Bacon, begun to take a separate line of its own in England, entered in to reinforce distrust of the inspired imagination. This was the growth of the scientific spirit. It was of the essence of this spirit to reject not only the authority of tradition but also the power of man's intuition, and to rely exclusively on methodical observation. What was wanted was knowledge: not a strong inward conviction of knowledge, but knowledge which could be proved. Such a demand limited the knowledge sought to that which the eye could see, or the hand touch. It thus tended to transform and limit the conception of knowledge. And it immediately began to rob poetry of serious justification. The Renaissance poet had set up to be, at his highest, an inspired teacher of mankind. His claim to inspiration had been challenged and ridiculed by religious enthusiasts who had in turn themselves discredited their own claim to inspiration. Serious men would henceforth know better than to look to poets, or to any literary folk, for the discovery of truth. Poets could still write about truth in pleasing form; and they could continue to make delightful contributions, of a merely decorative or ornamental kind, to the enjoyment of leisure. This role, however, was a sadly shrunken one for the inheritors of the proud Renaissance tradition. And it was no comfort that the claims of religion were undergoing an exactly similar deflation.

## NEW EMPHASIS ON CONTROL OVER NATURAL WORLD

This rise of science in the seventeenth century caused a shift in emphasis from man to his material environment, just as rapidly as the progress of science enabled men to command and use nature, or material resources, for their own purposes. Thus the progress of civilization came to be thought of in terms of improved agriculture, improved transport, increased production, and the like; and human welfare began to be measured in terms of available power, or material wealth. The underlying assumption was that man was by nature a good and civilized being, and that the ills of life arose from an insufficient command over the means to physical well-being and to enjoyment.

## RATIONALISM AND THE PRESCRIPTION TO "FOLLOW NATURE"

This new view had been foreshadowed from the beginning in the writings of Bacon. It was later called utilitarianism, and also, when sentimentalized, humanitarianism. It began to make itself felt as early as the end of the seventeenth century in a demand for education directed not so much to self-knowledge and self-development as to "practical subjects"—a demand which has been steadily growing ever since. The educational shift—for better, for worse, very slowly accomplished—illustrates clearly the nature of the change which was taking place. Considered broadly, it was a change from humanism to rationalism.

And in literature this meant that a writer was to aim, not at originality, but at the perfect expression of what was received for universal truth, rationally or scientifically determined. This was what the eighteenth century man of letters had in mind when he agreed that his chief rule was to "follow Nature." The "nature" he had in mind was the nature of the universe or of its many parts as these can be discovered by scientific observation and rational deduction, and expressed in scientific laws. In other words, it was accepted that the universe throughout is a rationally ordered structure, and that it should be so treated in literature.

## THE DRAMATIC UNITIES

It was only natural that this rationalistic attitude should cause the critics to seek "rational" laws for literature itself. They were convinced that there were such laws, exactly as there were laws of motion awaiting discovery. In their sphere they wanted to substitute knowledge for stupid hit-or-miss methods, or for a blind following of tradition. We should especially notice, however, that in proportion as the practice of literary art was reduced to rule, the task of the writer was a problem of conformity, and not of origination.

The most famous of the "rules" is that of the three dramatic unities, of time, place, and action. Aristotle, the father of dramatic criticism, had insisted only on the unity of action: the limiting of the play to one main plot. He had added that "tragedy endeavors, as far as possible, to confine itself to a single revolution of the sun, or but slightly to exceed this limit." About unity of place he had said nothing at all. Critics of the Renaissance, therefore, who insisted on all three unities, were departing from Aristotle. Actually, they were starting a movement towards a set of artistic standards based, not on tradition, but on rationalism.

## POETIC DICTION

One of the other rules of the time is that concerning diction. It was generally held that a writer should avoid technical terms, colloquialisms, words not fully domesticated (such as French phrases or turns of speech), and, in general, any words which might distract attention from what was being said because they seemed inappropriate in the context. This is a special development of the Renaissance doctrine of "decorum." It led to a decided preference for general and often abstract expressions instead of concrete words, and so opened the way to some absurdities, especially from mediocre or poor writers. Erasmus Darwin at the end of the century, in his anxiety not to call a spade a spade, called it a

Metallic Blade, wedded to ligneous Rod.

Fortunately many poets were not willing to go so far to avoid calling something by its name.

## RESTORATION DRAMA

One extreme almost inevitably produces another. And the cynical worldliness and immorality of the Restoration court and its devotion to French elegance and polish were produced directly by the Puritans' extreme of moral and cultural repression. It was natural that a principal part of the effort to restore the worldliness which Puritanism had sought to banish should center in the stage. The glories of the English drama were to be revived, with much help from French and classical standards. But nothing great in art can be made to order. Tragedies were written and the heroic drama ran its brief course, to demonstrate that demand could not create supply. The best tragedy that was composed in full obedience to so-called classical standards was Dryden's *All for Love*. It is a more than respectable achievement, all the more interesting because it is a rewriting of Shakespeare's *Anthony and Cleopatra*. Dryden had unfailing energy and an active mind, and he shared the Renaissance ambition to write in a heroic way. But neither Dryden nor the Restoration court had anything at all of the true heroic temper, and *All for Love*, like Dryden's other serious plays, has false notes and no sublimity.

Restoration society found its true expression in comedy—the comedy of manners, as it is called. The characteristics of this comedy are its wit and fashionable banter, its moral cynicism descending at times to the grossest brutality and license of speech, with action to match, its almost exclusive concern with adulterous intrigue, and its restriction of its field of representation to aristocratic society. In this field some masterpieces of a kind were written by such playwrights as Sir George Etherege, William Wycherley, William Congreve, and Sir John Vanbrugh. Congreve was the most distinguished of all the Restoration dramatists, and no English writer has excelled him in the portrayal of polished manners, or in his achievement of a prose flawless for its purpose, along with perfect unity of tone.

The lack of morality in these comedies, however, cannot be ignored. It caused a descent into animalism where all true and genuine human feeling was lost. And it is at bottom the sense of this great loss which makes us conclude that Restoration society was hollow and decadent and that its comedy is empty and sterile, no matter how brilliant in execution.

### JOHN BUNYAN'S ACHIEVEMENT OF UNIVERSALITY

We must not go too far, however, in pointing out characteristics of the Restoration period as though the society of that period were unified, the writers alike. For despite the most unfavorable conditions, not only did Milton go on triumphantly to complete *Paradise Lost* after the Restoration, but also to write *Paradise Regained* and *Samson Agonistes*. We think of Milton, quite properly, as really belonging to and surviving from an earlier time; but we ought to remember that he was not crushed or essentially changed by the Restoration. And after Milton there followed John Bunyan. With every disadvantage from surrounding conditions and also from personal circumstances, Bunyan somehow contrived to write several books which are classics of English literature, above all *The Pilgrim's Progress*. In *The Pilgrim's Progress* Bunyan has gone, as it were, through personal feeling and experience to universality, and has produced a nar-

rative which can give something of both pleasure and heightened understanding to every kind of reader, young or old, learned or unlearned, in any country of the world, of whatever faith or creed. He succeeded in making what he had learned a true work of art by, not just saying it, but *embodying* it in the persons and lives of real men and women. But though it must be emphasized that Bunyan did rise above seventeenth century Puritanism to a conception of life which is true to human experience everywhere, it is also true that he spoke for a very large number of his contemporaries who were not much longer to remain silent before the worldly spectacle of Restoration society.

### THE REVOLUTION OF 1688–89—AND ITS CONSEQUENCES

Charles II died in 1685, and was succeeded by his brother, James II, also a Roman Catholic. Even so, he might have kept the throne as Charles had done if, in the summer of 1688, his second wife, herself a Roman Catholic, had not borne him a son. His first wife had been a Protestant, and by her he had had two daughters, Mary and Anne, who had survived. Both of these daughters had remained Protestants. Thus until the son was born, Mary was James's heir, and the future seemed secure for Protestantism. But with a Catholic Prince of Wales all was suddenly changed.

A few years before Charles II's death, the country had become divided over the question of a Catholic successor, and the party names, Whig and Tory, had come into use—the former designating those, chiefly men of the middle class with a sprinkling of powerful country families, who were opposed to the accession of James II; and Tory designating those who believed in a strict succession of royalty. The Whigs were so strengthened by the prospect of a Catholic successor to James II that, at the end of 1688, they took the bold step of calling upon Mary's husband, a Dutch prince, William of Orange, to rescue the country. When William landed in England, it immediately became clear that the country approved of this solution, and James II fled to France. A second revolution had taken place, with practically no fighting.

This revolution of 1688–89 had consequences of the utmost importance. William and Mary became joint sovereigns in the latter year upon their acceptance of terms laid down by Parliament. For centuries the English people had been moving uncertainly in the direction of limiting kingly power. Now it was recognized that if the Parliament could make a king, it could also unmake him; and henceforth the people of the realm through Parliament were in a genuine sense their own rulers. Within a few years after the revolution, party government in the modern sense was firmly established, as were freedom of the press and a wide measure of religious tolerance.

Queen Mary died childless in 1694, and William reigned alone until his death in 1702. He was succeeded by Mary's younger sister, Anne. She had seventeen children; all of them died in infancy but one, and he died at the age of eleven before Anne became queen. Hence at her death in 1714 there was some threat of trouble from James Edward Stuart, son of James II. Parliament, however, had settled succession to the throne upon a Protestant German prince—George, Elector of Hanover, who was a great-grandson of James I of England, and he took possession without difficulty. His descendants have reigned over England ever since, although they have changed their name to Windsor.

Throughout the eighteenth century the country steadily grew in wealth and power, expanded in commerce and empire. And satisfaction with this "progress" and with existing social, intellectual, and cultural conditions was on the whole dominant until about the time of the French Revolution. Hence arises the picture often painted of the eighteenth century as a happy time, with peace and prosperity at home, with Common Sense holding the reins—a time of "rest and refreshment" when cultivation had reached a level leaving nothing more to be desired, and men could begin to look back with tolerance at all the ages of Gothic barbarism which had preceded their own enlightened era, and could even begin to find some amusement in poking about among the Gothic ruins.

## THE "VIRTUOSO" AND THE "MAN OF TASTE"

There is truth in this picture, enough truth to help us to understand why the "virtuoso" and the "man of taste" flourished in the eighteenth century, and why men of that time tended to be complacent. The "virtuoso" was the man who had nothing more important to do than to indulge in idle miscellaneous curiosity. He was a "collector," the early representative of a type still very familiar. He

might collect anything. There was the man who prided himself, if we are to believe contemporary report, on possession of a bottle containing water which "was formerly an icicle on the crags of Caucasus," and of "a snail that has crawled upon the Wall of China"; also the man who had acquired Pontius Pilate's wife's chambermaid's sister's hat. These are satirical exaggerations, because common sense was quick to perceive in the collector's activities an opportunity for effective ridicule. The "virtuoso," however, was sometimes also a "man of taste," and might collect paintings, or build and adorn a great house in the country, or spend a fortune in remodelling the landscape around his house in accordance with new standards of gardening which began to be fashionable at the very beginning of the eighteenth century. The "man of taste" was an idle man too, who, regarding all vital or troublesome questions as settled for the best, could indulge himself in the solution of nice problems of fit adornment.

We owe a great deal to both of these types. Modern historical research, archaeology, and natural history are indebted to the "virtuoso"; and the "man of taste" has left us the furniture of Chippendale and Hepplewhite, the china of Wedgwood, Georgian architecture and interior decoration, and modern landscape gardening. We ought not to underestimate these debts in forming our own conception and estimate of the eighteenth century. Nevertheless, the picture they suggest is something less than a half-truth concerning the age. We begin to see how much it leaves out as soon as we ask ourselves whether Swift, for example, was full of complacent optimism. We know that he was, instead, through the greater part of his life, burning with indignant rage against all he saw around him of human folly and stupidity, pedantry, corruption, empty pride, and senseless conflict. Nor are Swift's the only writings of the time which show us that under the splendid decorative surface of the eighteenth century there were turbulent cross-currents which were forcing thought in new directions and men of letters into new paths.

## THE BIRTH OF JOURNALISM: GOVERNMENT BY ORGANIZED PUBLIC OPINION

To understand this significant aspect of the times we have to remember that the Civil War of the second quarter of the seventeenth century had been an attempt to settle by force political and religious conflicts of opinion and principle which could not be thus settled. It had been preceded by a flood of argument, and the resort to arms had only intensified and embittered this verbal warfare. In the hundreds of pamphlets and printed addresses of the 1640's and 1650's some have seen the birth of journalism in England. And certainly it seems with the Restoration to have been assumed that the publication of officially doctored news was one necessary political activity. The revolution of 1688–89 carried this development several steps further. The emergence with the revolution of party government meant that henceforth England was more and more to be ruled by organized public opinion. Thus it became a practical necessity for party leaders to try to sway public opinion by employing skillful writers who were ready to give versions of public affairs favorable to the party hiring them and unfavorable to the opposed party. At the same time other developments were making the control of public opinion through the printed word more practical than it would have been in any earlier period. The reading public was growing in size quite rapidly; and the new readers were members of the middle class who were becoming prosperous through the increase in commerce. As they acquired property they grew in importance, and as they grew in importance the policies of government became more important to them. Throughout the eighteenth century the transition from aristocratic government by the wealthy landholders to middle class government by the merchants and industrialists was under way. The rising middle class was, on the whole, earnest, orderly, thrifty, ambitious, pious, and anxious for education and information.

The other major change at the beginning of the eighteenth century which gave journalism a much enlarged field was the amazing growth in London of coffee-houses and clubs. The first coffee-house was opened in London shortly after the Restoration, and by 1700 or soon after there were about three thousand of them. The coffee-houses were places where men gathered with their friends to smoke and drink, read the latest pamphlets and the news of the day, and discuss whatever interested them. They were comfortable lounging places, where free and easy discussion with congenial friends could be enjoyed at all times—and the more satisfactorily because women were wholly excluded. They were places of escape from uncomfortable lodgings, nagging wives, loneliness, troublesome business, or whatever men wanted to escape from. They became specialized, in that one house got to be known as a gathering place for Whigs, another for Tories, another for men of letters, and so on. And public opinion on all kinds of questions—political, religious, literary—came to be formed in the coffee-houses and to be spread abroad from them. In this the growing journalism of the time played a crucial part, as we have much evidence to show that the coffee-house politicians and critics depended upon the journalists for topics of discussion and also very often for the substance of their talk.

## DANIEL DEFOE

The first writer of importance who was produced by these new conditions was Daniel Defoe, the author of *Robinson Crusoe*. He was one of the most rapid and prolific writers the world has ever seen, and he was the journalist in everything he wrote. He wrote voluminously for party leaders who would pay him, turning out news, propaganda, and argument; but he also saw that the new middle-class reading public would eagerly buy any exciting book that could be regarded as a source of useful or improving information. His most famous books were written to satisfy this new demand. *Robinson Crusoe* pretends to be an historical narrative, and does have objective fact as its starting point. But Defoe found it easier, quicker, and more effective for his purpose to leave fact behind, once he had begun, and to rely on his imagination for the development of his narratives. He was always very careful, however, to preserve the air of a simple reporter of actual events narrated just as they had taken place. Robinson Crusoe is the ideal middle-class individualist, with every admirable quality the middle-class reader might envy, and would like to see in a man successfully making his own way against the most extraordinary obstacles. The English novel is one of the gifts of the rising middle class to literature, and we trace its ancestry from *The Pilgrim's Progress* through *Robinson Crusoe* to Samuel Richardson, who actually created it.

Before we discuss the novel, however, we must notice that the development of journalism brought into being a new kind of literature in the opening years of the eighteenth century. For nine years Defoe published *The Review*—a journal which combined brief news-reports with brief discussions of public questions. This suggested to Richard Steele the possibility of carrying such a journal outside of the field of politics into the broad realm of cultural standards—manners, social customs, morals, literary taste. This was the origin of the famous *Tatler*, which in turn became the father of a very numerous family, from *The Spectator* through Dr. Johnson's *Rambler* and *Idler* to Goldsmith's *Citizen of the World*, and beyond.

## *The Spectator:* JOSEPH ADDISON

Steele was a very talented as well as a lovable man; yet the greatest of his services to letters was the opportunity he gave in *The Tatler* to his friend Joseph Addison. Addison found in the informal periodical essay exactly the right medium for the full exercise of his powers and the perfect development of his genius. And it was he, chiefly in *The Spectator*, who established the vogue of the periodical essay so firmly that almost every eighteenth century man of letters had to try his hand at it. Addison discussed every type of problem with exquisite politeness and unfailing clarity. He aimed with unqualified success to be understood by everybody, including frivolous and empty-headed ladies of fashion, and to make his discussions interesting to everybody; and he hammered tirelessly at his critical objective—the creation of an enlightened, tolerant, well-balanced body of public opinion. Addison's attacks upon intolerance, upon pedantry, upon false wit, and his steady good-humored advocacy of humanity, reasonableness, moderation, and common sense seem pertinent even today.

### REVOLT AGAINST MORAL INSENSIBILITY

Addison's journalistic crusade was pertinent in his own day, also. A spirit of calculating and corrupt selfishness appeared to be spreading through society. Restoration comedy at its best was representation of complete moral bankruptcy among the aristocracy—moral bankruptcy accompanied, however, by every evidence of social refinement and intellectual acuteness. The spectacle was regarded with horror by a large part of the nation. In the 1690's there was a concerted effort to combat the influences spreading out from aristocratic circles by the establishment of societies for the reformation of manners. And in 1698 Jeremy Collier published his famous *Short View of the Immorality and Profaneness of the English*

*Stage,* which Dryden met by a frank confession of guilt, and other dramatists by some very lame defenses. Collier was not a Puritan, but a "high church" Anglican clergyman. He was on the side of intelligence and cultivation, but clearheaded enough to see that moral insensibility masquerading under the reputable name of rational enlightenment was leading the nation towards disaster. Steele attempted in the early years of the eighteenth century to write comedies of manners coated over with moral sentiments, but without notable success. And though the stage itself flourished through the eighteenth century because of such great performers as David Garrick, dramatic creation lost its vitality because others did not succeed even as well as Steele in plausibly mixing immoral intrigue and moral sentiment.

### ADDISON'S ATTEMPTS TO REUNITE SOCIETY

The situation, then, which Addison confronted was this: On the one side was refinement, educated taste, and cultivation, united with a lack of morals against which a large part of the nation was revolting with great violence. On the other side was the rising middle class, which tended to be narrowly moral and was unrefined and relatively uneducated. At the same time society was torn by violent political differences between Whig and Tory. The complete breakdown of civilized social existence seemed to be threatened. The middle class might be the backbone of the nation, but it was extremely desirable to get it organically connected with the head. Addison's task was one of reconciliation. The form of essay suggested by Defoe, created by Steele, and perfected by Addison may be described as a kind of genial sermon, addressed to people who did want to be improved and who liked to be amused at the same time. Addison provided amusement lavishly, but his serious aim was the noble one of reconciling differences. He tried to reunite moral sensibility and cultivation. He wanted to bring together warring individuals into a real society.

### SHAFTESBURY AND DEISM

Addison did not get much further with the problem of morality than an implication that moral behavior was a matter of good taste as well as of good sense. Such a view was elaborated also by the third Earl of Shaftesbury, the grandson of Dryden's "Achitophel." Shaftesbury, like most men of his time, was a rationalist. He praised tolerance and attacked fanaticism, and even wrote a defense of satire as the most effective touchstone for exposing folly and vice. But he struck out on his own in his conception of reason. He thought the good taste which enables us to recognize beauty to be a direct intuition of good and evil—the good being identical with the beautiful, the evil with the ugly—which he declared to be something ultimate and absolute. Furthermore, the fellow-feeling or sympathy which causes us to be unhappy in the presence of suffering or misery he declared to be an evidence of our inborn regard for the interests of others. It is because of something basic in human nature itself that we instinctively feel satisfaction in the presence of others who are well and happy, and find our own well-being is best served when we are promoting the general welfare. Not every man feels this way, to be sure, but he who does not is "unnatural" or inwardly deformed.

Here we see what Shaftesbury is driving at: Human nature, unless deformed or diseased, is good. Man is naturally good. According to historic Christianity, on the other hand, man had been created good, but as a consequence of the fall of Adam and Eve human nature had been corrupted. According to the Christian view, then, all men born of human parents are brought forth in sin and are in their own nature evil. Shaftesbury, however, is full of the optimism, and confidence in the worth of earthly human nature, which we have seen to be characteristic of Renaissance humanism. And his thinking brings him to the conclusion that man is naturally good, here and now, and that his goodness is to be seen in his consideration for the interests of others. Shaftesbury was led on to declare, on the principle that man has in himself in some degree all the qualities which the universe exhibits in a greater degree, that the universe, considered as a whole, is perfect, partaking of the nature of its Creator, the all-perfect Deity. This is what Pope set out to say in his *Essay on Man*. The famous last words of Epistle I of this *Essay*, "Whatever is, is right," mean that since the universe as a whole is perfect, the parts considered separately are imperfect, but still are such parts as are required to make up, together, the perfect whole.

The kind of thought represented by Shaftesbury is called deistical. It developed from the acceptance of rationalism, and became completely independent of historic Christianity and in some respects contradictory of it.

Shaftesbury and other deists considered it wise to conform outwardly to the Church of England; but actually the whole current of philosophical thought and rational theology was carrying clergymen and laymen alike away from any real belief in Christianity as a divine revelation. This we shall have reason to recall as we proceed into the next age. At present we must notice that just as Bunyan's work shows a powerful current of truly religious and Christian conviction flowing under the surface in the Restoration era, so in the first half of the eighteenth century the work of William Law shows us the same thing continuing. Law is best known for a devotional book, *A Serious Call to a Devout and Holy Life*, published in 1729, which was eagerly and widely read. John Wesley regarded this book as a prime source of the Methodist revival of religion which shortly after began under Wesley's leadership and, in the mid-eighteenth century, swept the country.

## CULTIVATION OF SENSIBILITY

Shaftesbury's work was destined to have repercussions which would have astonished and disgusted him, had he lived to witness the dazzling apparition of Jean-Jacques Rousseau later in the century and the outbreak of the French Revolution. As was said above, Shaftesbury was on the side of balanced good sense. And in his moral theory, though he tried to swing free of the doctrine that the useful is good, he did not in fact succeed. His ethical system is basically, as much as any other rationalist's, a calculation in terms of self-interest. We have seen how Shaftesbury contended that moral feeling was *natural* to man, however, and how as a consequence the unfeeling or unsympathetic man was thought of as a deformed or diseased person. The reaction against brutal callousness more and more took form as a cultivation of the emotions. It began to be a sign of refinement, even of genuine humanity, to have feelings. Tears, sighs, and groans began to be fashionable, and, in time, even fainting fits among members of the tender sex. The rising tide of sensibility produced, quite naturally, a rising interest in the inward workings of the sensitive heart, and, generally, in the springs of personality.

## SAMUEL RICHARDSON: *Pamela*

Perhaps no one guessed how absorbing this new interest could be until it was gratified in 1740 by the publication of Samuel Richardson's *Pamela, or Virtue Rewarded*. Richardson was a mousy little printer, precise, fussy, perfectly conventional, very religious, industrious, and prosperous. Eighteenth century printers were sometimes editors also, and Richardson not only made indexes for some books he printed but wrote dedicatory letters capably. At the age of fifty he was asked by some booksellers to compile a volume of model letters for the use of maidservants, sailors, countrymen, and the like, who occasionally had to write but did not know how to go about it. Richardson accepted the task, and in due time published *Letters Written to and for Particular Friends, On the Most Important Occasions, Directing not only the Requisite Style and Forms to be Observed in Writing Familiar Letters; But how to Think and Act Justly and Prudently, in the Common Concerns of Human Life* (1741). Richardson was, like most of his contemporaries, a moralist, and he could not let this opportunity slip without doing his bit for the moral improvement of those who might use the book. *Pamela* happened to be written because Richardson became so interested in one group of model letters that he laid aside the booksellers' job in order to expand those dealing with a not uncommon problem confronting maidservants in great eighteenth century houses—the attempts of young masters in those households to seduce them. Thus by accident the first full-fledged English novel was produced. In so far as it was the result of literary influence, the book expressed a reaction against the "vain," "empty," highflying heroic romances of the seventeenth century. It brought fiction down to earth and reality, for the sake of moral betterment.

Pamela is a very pretty young maidservant, whose virtue is assailed by the wealthy young Mr. B——. The story is told in a series of letters: how Pamela repels Mr. B—— with disgust, how in time she falls in love with him, in spite of his villainy, but keeps her head, and how thus she finally succeeds in making him marry her—the reward for her virtue. There is a good deal of action, but the interest is centered in character portrayal achieved through Pamela's own minute self-analysis and detailed record of all her feelings in every circumstance in which she is involved. In his two later, and longer, novels, *Clarissa Harlowe* and *The History of Sir Charles Grandison*, Richardson had the same aim and stuck to the same method, of telling the story through a series of letters written by the characters to one another. It is an awkward way of telling a story, and not many of Richardson's successors have adopted it. Yet it does lend itself admirably to the purpose of building up gradually, through many small touches, a portrait of inward character, seen through all its minutest workings, until a reader feels that he knows one of Richardson's heroines far better than he can ever know anyone in actual life.

## "NOVEL" AND "ROMANCE" DEFINED

Richardson came to regard himself as the founder of an entirely new species of writing, and he was substantially right. Moreover, he was phenomenally successful. He was the one man of the eighteenth century who wrote a book which instantly broke through all barriers and divisions and was devoured literally by everybody. How are we to define the novel, which from his day to ours has been the most popular kind of imaginative literature? The word "romance," used to denote a type of fiction, has kept the meaning which became attached to it in the beginning. It was first used to designate narratives of strange adventure. In the early medieval romances the interest was centered in the action itself, and the characters were interesting only because of what they did. As those for whom the romances were written became more mature, the center of interest shifted from action to presentation of inward character.

This gives us the key to the meaning of "novel." The novel requires a certain amplitude of treatment. It must have a plot in order that the characters may be seen not only in action but in conflict which serves to reveal them; but the action is subordinated to the representation of character, and perhaps, though not necessarily, of character developing through experience. And finally, the novel is realistic, or is a transcript of real life in the real world of our own experience. On the other hand, as early as the end of the fifteenth century "romance" had come to be used as a synonym for "lie," obviously because the writers of medieval romances had not paid much attention to reality or truth. And the words "romance" and "romantic" have kept something of this meaning ever since.

## SENTIMENTALISM: LAURENCE STERNE

Dr. Johnson said, "If you were to read Richardson for the story, your impatience would be so much fretted that you would hang yourself. But you must read him for the sentiment, and consider the story as only giving the occasion to the sentiment." This was perfectly sound advice, but advice that most of Richardson's contemporary readers did not need. The novelist wonderfully gratified the rising tide of sensibility by drawing out the sentiment with loving exhaustiveness, until the emotions of readers were not only touched, but frayed. And they loved it. Richardson was helping to produce a brood of sentimentalists; though it must be said, for his credit, that they would certainly have appeared without his help. Sentimentalism may be defined as the love and cultivation of emotion for its own sake. The sentimentalist seeks occasion for pity, for tears, because he *enjoys* being emotionally stirred; and when he has become thus unbalanced almost any occasion will suffice for his purpose. This is well illustrated in the work of Richardson's younger contemporary, Laurence Sterne, author of *Tristram Shandy* and *A Sentimental Journey through France and Italy*. Sterne is, beyond all his monkey tricks and elaborate absurdities, at the same time a master at portraying character; but he is also a sentimentalist who shows the worst lengths to which this trivial and in the end unmeaning emotionalism could go.

### HENRY FIELDING: *Tom Jones*

What Henry Fielding would have thought of Sterne's sentimentalism, had he lived to read *Tristram Shandy* and the *Sentimental Journey*, would probably be unprintable, though certainly his judgment would have been tempered by a genial appreciation of Sterne's sophisticated artistry and disarming good nature. Fielding died in 1754, six years before *Tristram* began to appear. He had lived hard and worked incessantly, as playwright and essayist and poet, when Richardson's *Pamela* appeared. That book disgusted him, and caused him to write a parody in which he ruthlessly exposed what he took to be the real bearing and tendency of *Pamela*, and laughed at Richardson's pious pretension to the name of moralist. He entitled the book, *An Apology for the Life of Mrs. Shamela Andrews, in which the Many Notorious Falsehoods and Misrepresentations of a Book Called* Pamela *are Exposed and Refuted; and All the Matchless Arts of that Young Politician Set in a True and Just Light.* But this witty and devastating skit did not exhaust Fielding's satirical impulse. He went on to mock at *Pamela* in a book giving the alleged history of her brother, Joseph An-

drews, a virtuous young serving-man whose mistress tries to tempt him into misconduct. In *Joseph Andrews*, however, Fielding was carried far beyond his first intention, and produced a novel which could stand on its own feet by virtue of its portrayal of the lovable Parson Adams and its pictures of English country life. Having thus discovered his powers, Fielding went on to write *Tom Jones*, a comic epic in prose as he called it, and perhaps still the greatest of all English novels.

Though *Tom Jones* has imperfections obvious enough to present-day readers, it still holds a supreme place because Fielding had something important and sound to communicate and saw it with the great artist's eye—*embodied* to the life in full-blooded characters. Fielding is incomparably vivid; he makes us see with delight what he saw with delight, converts us, and carries us triumphantly with him over the English countryside, through all manner of escapades, into London and out again, until we not only catch the perfect flavor of the eighteenth century but feel the glow of a hearty, healthy life which is simply and soundly human, and independent of time or place. Fielding does not see everything; he does not carry us quite to the heights or to the depths of life, as Shakespeare does; he is like his own century in preferring the broad level space between extremes; but this after all is the center, and Fielding is completely at home in it. Probably the secret of Fielding's genius lies in his directness and his confident sanity. He comes straight out with what he sees and feels, and shows us everything without hesitation or fear. Thackeray in his Preface to *Pendennis* said the right thing about Fielding: "Since the author of *Tom Jones* was buried, no writer of fiction among us has been permitted to depict to his utmost power A MAN."

Fielding did it, against the background of the time—the intellectual as well as the social background. And the historical student finds in *Tom Jones* a simple clear-cut picture of the difficulty with which the eighteenth century was wrestling. Fielding recognized the evils of utilitarianism and sentimentalism; he portrayed each in *Tom Jones*, but he himself steered clear of both. He presented an example of morality based on sentiment without the slightest trace of sentimentalism, and arranged himself on the side of the rising belief in the natural goodness of earthly human nature. But his greatness as a novelist remains secure whatever may be our estimate of eighteenth century problems or beliefs, because he did see and portray human nature as it is, without omission, honestly and fairly.

## THE PERIOD AS A WHOLE

The century and a quarter which we have been surveying was dominated, in the field of letters, by three men: Dryden, and then Pope, and finally Dr. Johnson. And from the beginning of the English Renaissance to the end of the nineteenth century two influences are constantly present in English literature—that of the classics and that of the Bible. The kind of influence exerted by the classics, however, varied greatly from one generation to another, because classically educated men took from the varied wealth of the ancient world what they could understand and use, and this was a varying quantity.

If we try to generalize about the age, we may come nearest the truth if we say it was a time when newly emancipated reason got into the saddle and attempted the control of the whole domain of life. Men hopefully laid the foundations of a "science" of literary creation, of a "science" of morals, as well as of the science of physical phenomena. But reason overreached herself, was perplexed by unforeseen consequences of her activity, and then began to dissolve under critical scrutiny. Meanwhile distrusted emotion began to say something on her own account, first by way of satire, but then more rebelliously and alarmingly by claiming to represent what was good in human nature. Reason had made this exclusive claim, had been given her opportunity, and was showing herself unable to sustain it. As we have said before, when false oppositions are set up, indefensible extremes are encouraged. Against a one-sided rationalism, there grew up the hardy weed of sentimentalism.

As the century advanced, men tended increasingly to withdraw themselves from problems they did not know how to solve, and found that they could live contentedly without solving them. The day of the professional author was dawning, and men were beginning, not to lead, but to follow the taste of the reading public. The fierce political differences of the early years of the century had died away. There was no serious concern about religion. Methodism might be exciting the lower classes, but their devotion was more amusing than disturbing to men of the polite world. The spirit of dilettantism was growing, and along with it a new interest in people. Great ambitions, high hopes, heroic achievement—these were becoming legendary. A bad time for literature, we are tempted to say, and many have said it. Certainly it was a bad time for the grander kinds of literature. But it was not an unfruitful time. It was in these placid days that Dr. Johnson talked freely and magnificently with the tireless Boswell at his side, and so sat for a literary portrait that has never been rivaled. And it was in these days that Gray and Horace Walpole and Cowper and others wrote innumerable letters which form a priceless addition to English literature. It was in these days, too, that England's greatest historian, Edward Gibbon, composed the stately paragraphs which trace out *The Decline and Fall of the Roman Empire*. We have much reason for gratitude when we really consider what the last quarter-century of this period has left us. Other literature, before and after this quiet time, we read with astonishment, with awe, with deeply stirred emotions; but of the companionable authors with whom we can live pleasantly, and who can give us day after day, year in year out, a never-failing yet serene delight, some of the best lived in the latter part of the "excellent and indispensable eighteenth century."

# Samuel Pepys

## 1633-1703

Samuel Pepys was born in London on 23 February, 1633. His father, a poor tailor, had migrated thither from the region of the fens, or bogs, north of Cambridge; Samuel, who inherited the strong natural instincts of a fens-man, was brought up in an urban world of lower middle-class Puritanism. He received most of his early education at St. Paul's School in London, a foundation which displayed, among others, the sensible motto: Aut doce, aut disce, aut discede—"Teach, or learn, or get out." The schoolboy also enjoyed the more questionable advantage of living in the capital during the stormy years of the Civil War; on 30 January, 1649, when he was fifteen, young Pepys saw the beheading of Charles I and re-marked that, were he to preach on the event, his text would be: "The memory of the wicked shall rot." A year later he was admitted to Mag-dalen College, Cambridge, as a sizar, i. e., a scholar whose expenses were paid in return for certain menial duties. Before he received the B. A. degree in 1653 he showed that in spite of his Puritan upbringing he was not averse to drink and boon companionship. In 1655, once more back in London, he married Elizabeth St. Michel, the fifteen-year-old daughter of a pen-niless Huguenot gentleman. Although the young couple undoubtedly felt a real affection for each other, their life together was fre-quently made unhappy by jealousy on both sides; in 1668, only a year before Elizabeth's death, they were finally reconciled as a result of their most serious quarrel. In the beginning, moreover, Pepys was a poor man, who had to be contented with a position little better than that of an upper servant in the household of a well-to-do cousin, Edward Montagu. This con-nection eventually proved to be a fortunate one, for Montagu, a naval official of the Common-wealth, was one of the men most influential in procuring the Restoration of Charles II; in the spring of 1660 he was appointed admiral of the fleet which brought the new king over from the Continent, and he was subsequently made Earl of Sandwich. Pepys, who had been Montagu's secretary on the voyage, was now advanced to the post of Clerk of the Acts for the Navy Office; from this time on he was among the most loyal supporters of the Stuart cause. His new position at first interested him only as a source of profit and prestige; of marine affairs he was almost completely ignorant; but as soon as his curiosity had been aroused, he set out to learn all that was to be known about the Navy. Before long his bourgeois love of order, thor-oughness, and discipline came into conflict with a corrupt and inefficient administration; unfortunately, a Clerk of the Acts could effect only minor reforms. The Plague (1665), the Fire of London (1666), and the success of the Dutch in destroying a large part of the English fleet in the dockyards along the Medway (1667) were national disasters which placed the government in a difficult position; Pepys, now recognized to be the most able member of the Navy Office, faced and defeated Parlia-mentary criticism of that department in 1669. Four years later his worth was rewarded by advancement to the important post of Secre-tary to the Admiralty; with the backing of his immediate superior, the Duke of York, he was now able to reform the Navy. He not only es-tablished military convoys for trading vessels and an efficient system of victualing the fleet; he was also responsible for building thirty new men-of-war; and he made so radical and per-manent an improvement in the discipline re-quired of naval officers that he may be called the founder of the British Civil Service. In 1679, after the discovery of the "Popish Plot," he was falsely accused of being a Papist and a traitor, compelled to resign his position, and for a short time even imprisoned in the Tower; his Whig enemies later dropped the case with-out allowing him to establish his innocence. Another political shift, however, restored him to the Admiralty in 1684, with a salary equivalent to £20,000 in modern money; a year later, when the Duke of York ascended the throne as James II, Pepys reached the brief climax of his career. Although the fleet had been badly neglected during the period when he was out of office, it was quickly rehabilitated through his own energy and the special interest of the king in naval affairs. By 1688 the finances and discipline of the service were so well established that from now on, the Navy was the right hand of national greatness. But in 1688 the Glorious Revolution compelled James to flee the country; and early in the next year, upon the accession of William and Mary, Pepys laid down the secretaryship for ever. The remainder of his life was passed in learned retirement. His Memoirs of the Royal Navy, for which he had long been collecting material, appeared in 1690. When he died in 1703, he left a select and valuable library which, in accordance with his instructions, eventually came into the possession of Magdalene College, Cambridge.

The most valuable part of this Bibliotheca Pepysiana, as it is called, is the manuscript journal which Pepys kept for a period of almost ten years, from 1660 to 1669. It consists of about 3000 pages, written in a seventeenth-century form of shorthand which he doubtless used, not only to save time, but also to prevent the contents from being read. The Diary was discontinued in 1669 because Pepys was suffering from an acute eye trouble which made it almost impossible for him to write shorthand. In 1660 he may have begun to keep a minute record of his actions with the idea of securing [10] an alibi during the political troubles of the period; soon, however, his chief motive can only have been the satisfaction he took in describing, without restraint, exactly what he had done and seen and thought. The personality which he thus uncovers has been variously interpreted. After the first and very fragmentary publication of the Diary in 1825, Coleridge remarked that Pepys was a "pollard," or stunted, man; and Lowell once referred to him [20] as a naïve and humorless Philistine. More recent critics, who are better acquainted with both the Diary and the facts of his life, are not so inclined to emphasize his limitations. With a middle-class respect for virtue and piety he combined the instinct to confess the most unpalatable truths; if he frequently displayed a narrow, hard-headed selfishness, he was also a faithful and charming friend; his genius as a practical administrator was mingled with a keen artistic sensibility—witness his love of music and his gift for literary expression. It is

precisely because his nature was neither simple nor commonplace that Pepys can tell us so much about himself and about his world.

The best edition of the Diary is still that edited by Henry B. Wheatley (London, 1893–1899), but in many passages it omits or modifies what Pepys actually wrote. H. T. Heath has edited Letters of Pepys and His Family Circle (Oxford, 1955). Arthur Bryant's Samuel Pepys (Cambridge, 1933–1938) is an outstanding biography, important for its interpretation of Pepys as a public servant as well as a domestic personality. Bryant is also the author of an interesting study of the life of the time, The England of Charles II (London, 1934). Thomas Babington Macaulay's History of England from the Accession of James the Second (London, 1848–1861) is the standard, although not an unbiased, political account of the period in which Pepys was a public figure.

## Passages from *The Diary*

### I

22 MAY, 1660.[1] Up very early, and now beginning to be settled in my wits again, I went about setting down my last four days' observations this morning. After that, was trimmed by a barber that has not trimmed me yet, my Spaniard being on shore. News brought that the two Dukes [2] are coming on board, which, by and by, they did, in a Dutch boat, the Duke of York in yellow trimmings, the Duke of Gloucester in gray and red. My Lord [3] went in a boat to meet them, the Captain, myself, and others, standing at the entering port. So soon as they were entered we shot the guns off round the fleet. After that they went to view the ship all over, and were most exceedingly pleased with it. They seem to be both very fine gentlemen. After that done, upon the quarter-deck table, under the awning, the Duke of York, and my Lord, Mr. Coventry, and I, spent an hour at allotting to every ship their service, in their return to England; which having done, they went to dinner, where the table was very full: the two Dukes at the upper end, my Lord Opdam next on one side, and my Lord on the other. Two guns given to every

[1] At this time Pepys was aboard ship off the coast of Holland, serving as secretary to the commander of the English fleet sent to bring Charles II back to England at the beginning of the Restoration era.
[2] Brothers of the new king. The Duke of York later became James II.
[3] Sir Edward Montagu, commander of the expedition.

man while he was drinking the King's health, and so likewise to the Dukes' health. I took down Monsieur d'Esquier to the great cabin below, and dined with him in state alone with only one or two friends of his. All dinner the harper belonging to Captain Sparling played to the Dukes. After dinner, the Dukes and my Lord to see the Vice and Rear-Admirals, and I in a boat after them. After that done, they made to the shore in the Dutch boat that brought them, and I got into the boat with them; but the shore was so full of people to expect their coming, as that it was as black (which otherwise is white sand), as every one could stand by another. When we came near the shore, my Lord left them and came into his own boat, and General Penn[4] and I with him; my Lord being very well pleased with this day's work. By the time we came on board again, news is sent us that the King is on shore; so my Lord fired all his guns round twice, and all the fleet after him, which in the end fell into disorder, which seemed very handsome. The gun over against my cabin I fired myself to the King, which was the first time that he had been saluted by his own ships since this change; but holding my head too much over the gun, I had almost spoiled my right eye. Nothing in the world but going of guns almost all this day. In the evening we began to remove cabins; I to the carpenter's cabin, and Dr. Clerke with me, who came on board this afternoon, having been twice ducked in the sea to-day coming from shore, and Mr. North and John Pickering the like. Many of the King's servants came on board to-night; and so many Dutch of all sorts came to see the ship till it was quite dark, that we could not pass by one another, which was a great trouble to us all. This afternoon Mr. Downing[5] (who was knighted yesterday by the King) was here on board, and had a ship for his passage into England, with his lady and servants. By the same token he called me to him when I was going to write the order, to tell me that I must write him Sir G. Downing. My Lord lay in the roundhouse to-night. This evening I was late writing a French letter myself by my Lord's order to Monsieur Krag, Ambassador *de Denmarke à la Haye*,[6] which my Lord signed in bed. After that I to bed, and the Doctor, and sleep well.

23rd. The Doctor and I waked very merry, only my eye was very red and ill in the morning from yesterday's hurt. In the morning came infinity of people on board from the King to go along with him. My Lord, Mr. Crew, and others, go on shore to meet the King as he comes off from shore, where Sir R. Stayner bringing His Majesty into the boat, I hear that His Majesty did with a great deal of affection kiss my Lord upon his first meeting. The King, with the two Dukes and Queen of Bohemia, Princess Royal, and Prince of Orange,[7] came on board, where I in their coming in kissed the King's, Queen's, and Princess's hands, having done the other before. Infinite shooting off of the guns, and that in a disorder on purpose, which was better than if it had been otherwise. All day nothing but Lords and persons of honor on board, that we were exceeding full. Dined in a great deal of state, the Royal company by themselves in the coach,[8] which was a blessed sight to see. I dined with Dr. Clerke, Dr. Quartermaine, and Mr. Darcy in my cabin. This morning Mr. Lucy came on board, to whom and his company of the King's Guard in another ship my Lord did give three dozen of bottles of wine. He made friends between Mr. Pierce and me. After dinner the King and Duke altered the name of some of the ships, viz., the *Naseby* into *Charles*; the *Richard*, *James*; the *Speaker*, *Mary*; the *Dunbar* (which was not in company with us), the *Henry*; *Winsby*, *Happy Return*; *Wakefield*, *Richmond*; *Lambert*, the *Henrietta*; *Cheriton*, the *Speedwell*; *Bradford*, the *Success*.[9] That done, the Queen, Princess Royal, and Prince of Orange, took leave of the King, and the Duke of York went on board the *London*, and the Duke of Gloucester, the *Swiftsure*. Which done, we weighed anchor, and with a fresh gale and most happy weather we set sail for England. All the afternoon the King walked here and there, up and down (quite contrary to what I thought him to have been), very active and stirring. Upon the quarter-deck he fell into discourse of his escape from Worcester,[10] where it made me ready to weep to hear the stories that he told of his difficulties that he had passed through, as his traveling four days and three nights on foot, every step up to his knees in dirt, with nothing but a green

---

[4] Admiral William Penn, father of the founder of Pennsylvania.

[5] One of the principal negotiators for the return of Charles.

[6] Ambassador of Denmark to The Hague.

[7] The aunt, sister, and nephew of the King.

[8] Apartment in the stern of a man-of-war.

[9] Thus the names of various Roundhead leaders and victories were exchanged for Royalist or for traditional names of ships in the English fleet.

[10] The last stand of the Royalists against Cromwell's army (1651).

coat and a pair of country breeches on, and a pair of country shoes that made him so sore all over his feet, that he could scarce stir. Yet he was forced to run away from a miller and other company, that took them for rogues. His sitting at table at one place, where the master of the house, that had not seen him in eight years, did know him, but kept it private; when at the same table there was one that had been of his own regiment at Worcester, could not know him, but made him drink the King's health, and said that the King was at least four fingers higher than he. At another place he was by some servants of the house made to drink, that they might know him not to be a Roundhead, which they swore he was. In another place at his inn, the master of the house, as the King was standing with his hands upon the back of a chair by the fire-side, kneeled down and kissed his hand, privately, saying, that he would not ask him who he was, but bid God bless him whither he was going. Then the difficulty of getting a boat to get into France, where he was fain to plot with the master thereof to keep his design from the four men and a boy (which was all his ship's company), and so got to Fécamp in France. At Rouen he looked so poorly, that the people went into the rooms before he went away to see whether he had not stole something or other. In the evening I went up to my Lord to write letters for England, which we sent away with word of our coming, by Mr. Edw. Pickering. The King supped alone in the coach; after that I got a dish, and we four supped in my cabin, as at noon. About bed-time my Lord Bartlett [11] (who I had offered my service to before) sent for me to get him a bed, who with much ado I did get to bed to my Lord Middlesex in the great cabin below, but I was cruelly troubled before I could dispose of him, and quit myself of him. So to my cabin again, where the company still was, and were talking more of the King's difficulties; as how he was fain to eat a piece of bread and cheese out of a poor boy's pocket; how, at a Catholic house, he was fain to lie in the priest's hole a good while in the house for his privacy. After that our company broke up, and the Doctor and I to bed. We have all the Lords Commissioners on board us, and many others. Under sail all night, and most glorious weather.

24th. Up, and make myself as fine as I could, with the linen stockings on and wide canons [12] that I bought the other day at Hague.

Extraordinary press of noble company, and great mirth all the day. There dined with me in my cabin (that is, the carpenter's) Dr. Earle and Mr. Holles, the King's Chaplains, Dr. Scarborough, Dr. Quartermaine, and Dr. Clerke, Physicians, Mr. Darcy, and Mr. Fox (both very fine gentlemen), the King's servants, where we had brave discourse. Walking upon the decks, where persons of honor all the afternoon, among others, Thomas Killigrew [13] (a merry droll, but a gentleman of great esteem with the King), who told us many merry stories: one, how he wrote a letter three or four days ago to the Princess Royal, about a Queen Dowager of Judea and Palestine, that was at The Hague *incognita*, that made love to the King, *etc.*, which was Mr. Cary (a courtier's) wife that had been a nun, who are all married to Jesus. At supper the three Drs. of Physic again at my cabin; where I put Dr. Scarborough in mind of what I heard him say about the use of the eyes, which he owned, that children do, in every day's experience, look several ways with both their eyes, till custom teaches them otherwise. And that we do now see but with one eye, our eyes looking in parallel lines. After this discourse I was called to write a pass for my Lord Mandeville to take up horses to London, which I wrote in the King's name, and carried it to him to sign, which was the first and only one that ever he signed in the ship *Charles*. To bed, coming in sight of land a little before night.

25th. By the morning we were come close to the land, and everybody made ready to get on shore. The King and the two Dukes did eat their breakfast before they went, and there being set some ship's diet before them, only to show them the manner of the ship's diet, they eat of nothing else but pease and pork, and boiled beef. I had Mr. Darcy in my cabin and Dr. Clerke, who eat with me, told me how the King had given £50 to Mr. Shepley for my Lord's servants, and £500 among the officers and common men of the ship. I spoke with the Duke of York about business, who called me Pepys by name, and upon my desire did promise me his future favor. Great expectation of the King's making some Knights, but there was none. About noon (though the brigantine that Beale made was there ready to carry him) yet he would go in my Lord's barge with the two Dukes. Our Captain steered, and my Lord went along bare with him. I went, and Mr. Mansell, and one of the King's footmen, with

---

[11] Mistake for Lord Berkeley.
[12] Ornaments for the legs.
[13] A well-known wit of the time (1612–1683).

a dog that the King loved, (which [dirted] [14] the boat, which made us laugh, and methink that a King and all that belonged to him are but just as others are), in a boat by ourselves, and so got on shore when the King did, who was received by General Monk [15] with all imaginable love and respect at his entrance upon the land of Dover. Infinite the crowd of people and the horsemen, citizens, and noblemen of all sorts. The Mayor of the town came and gave him his white staff, the badge of his place, which the King did give him again. The Mayor also presented him from the town a very rich Bible, which he took and said it was the thing that he loved above all things in the world. A canopy was provided for him to stand under, which he did, and talked awhile with General Monk and others, and so into a stately coach there set for him, and so away through the town towards Canterbury, without making any stay at Dover. The shouting and joy expressed by all is past imagination. Seeing that my Lord did not stir out of his barge, I got into a boat, and so into his barge, whither Mr. John Crew stepped, and spoke a word or two to my Lord, and so returned, we back to the ship, and going did see a man almost drowned that fell out of his boat into the sea, but with much ado was got out. My Lord almost transported with joy that he had done all this without any the least blur or obstruction in the world, that could give an offense to any, and with the great honor he thought it would be to him. Being overtook by the brigantine, my Lord and we went out of our barge into it, and so went on board with Sir W. Batten and the Vice and Rear-Admirals. At night my Lord supped and Mr. Thomas Crew with Captain Stokes, I supped with the Captain, who told me what the King had given us. My Lord returned late, and at his coming did give me order to cause the mark to be gilded, and a Crown and C. R. to be made at the head of the coach table, where the King to-day with his own hand did mark his height, which accordingly I caused the painter to do, and is now done as is to be seen.

II

13 OCTOBER, 1660. To my Lord's in the morning, where I met with Captain Cuttance,

but my Lord not being up I went out to Charing Cross, to see Major-general Harrison [16] hanged, drawn, and quartered; which was done there, he looking as cheerful as any man could do in that condition. He was presently cut down, and his head and heart shown to the people, at which there was great shouts of joy. It is said, that he said that he was sure to come shortly at the right hand of Christ to judge them that now had judged him; and that his wife do expect his coming again. Thus it was my chance to see the King beheaded at Whitehall, and to see the first blood shed in revenge for the blood of the King at Charing Cross. From thence to my Lord's, and took Captain Cuttance and Mr. Shepley to the Sun Tavern, and did give them some oysters. After that I went by water home, where I was angry with my wife for her things lying about, and in my passion kicked the little fine basket, which I bought her in Holland, and broke it, which troubled me after I had done it. Within all the afternoon setting up shelves in my study. At night to bed.

14th (Lord's day). Early to my Lord's, in my way meeting with Dr. Fairbrother, who walked with me to my father's [17] back again, and there we drank my morning draft, my father having gone to church and my mother asleep in bed. Here he caused me to put my hand among a great many honorable hands to a paper or certificate in his behalf. To Whitehall chapel, where one Dr. Croft made an indifferent sermon, and after it an anthem, ill sung, which made the King laugh. Here I first did see the Princess Royal since she came into England. Here I also observed, how the Duke of York and Mrs. Palmer [18] did talk to one another very wantonly through the hangings that parts the King's closet and the closet where the ladies sit. To my Lord's, where I found my wife, and she and I did dine with my Lady (my Lord dining with my Lord Chamberlain), who did treat my wife with a good deal of respect. In the evening we went home through the rain by water in a sculler, having borrowed some coats of Mr. Shepley. So home, wet and dirty, and to bed.

15th. Office all the morning. My wife and I by water; I landed her at Whitefriars, she went to my father's to dinner, it being my father's wedding day, there being a very

---

[14] Here and elsewhere in the selections from *The Diary* brackets indicate changes by Pepys's editor, Henry B. Wheatley.

[15] General of the Commonwealth instrumental in bringing about the return of the Stuarts; created Duke of Albemarle by Charles II.

[16] General Thomas Harrison, signer of the warrant for the execution of Charles I in 1649.

[17] John Pepys, tailor (1601–1680).

[18] Mistress of Charles II, later made Countess of Castlemaine and Duchess of Cleveland.

great dinner, and only the Fenners and Joyces there. This morning Mr. Carew [19] was hanged and quartered at Charing Cross; but his quarters, by a great favor, are not to be hanged up. I was forced to go to my Lord's to get him to meet the officers of the Navy this afternoon, and so could not go along with her, but I missed my Lord, who was this day upon the bench at the Sessions house. So I dined there, and went to Whitehall, where I met with Sir W. Batten and Penn, who with the Comptroller, Treasurer, and Mr. Coventry (at his chamber) made up a list of such ships as are fit to be kept out for the winter guard, and the rest to be paid off by the Parliament when they can get money, which I doubt will not be a great while. That done, I took coach, and called my wife at my father's, and so homewards, calling at Thos. Pepys [20] the turner's for some things that we wanted. And so home, where I fell to read *The Fruitless Precaution* (a book formerly recommended by Dr. Clerke at sea to me), which I read in bed till I had made an end of it, and do find it the best writ tale that ever I read in my life. After that done to sleep, which I did not very well do, because that my wife having a stopping in her nose she snored much, which I never did hear her do before.

## III

### CORONATION DAY

23 APRIL, 1661. About 4 I rose and got to the Abbey, where I followed Sir J. Denham,[21] the Surveyor, with some company that he was leading in. And with much ado, by the favor of Mr. Cooper, his man, did get up into a great scaffold across the North end of the Abbey, where with a great deal of patience I sat from past 4 till 11 before the King came in. And a great pleasure it was to see the Abbey raised in the middle, all covered with red, and a throne (that is a chair) and footstool on the top of it; and all the officers of all kinds, so much as the very fiddlers, in red vests. At last comes in the dean and prebends of Westminster, with the bishops (many of them in cloth of gold copes), and after them the nobility, all in their Parliament robes, which was a most magnificent sight. Then the Duke, and the King with a scepter (carried by my Lord Sandwich) and sword and mond [22] before him, and the crown too. The King in his robes, bareheaded, which was very fine. And after all had placed themselves, there was a sermon and the service; and then in the choir at the high altar, the King passed through all the ceremonies of the coronation, which to my great grief I and most in the Abbey could not see. The crown being put upon his head, a great shout begun, and he came forth to the throne, and there passed more ceremonies: as taking the oath, and having things read to him by the Bishop; and his lords (who put on their caps as soon as the King put on his crown) and bishops come, and kneeled before him. And three times the King at Arms went to the three open places on the scaffold, and proclaimed, that if any one could show any reason why Charles Stuart should not be King of England, that now he should come and speak. And a General Pardon also was read by the Lord Chancellor, and medals flung up and down by my Lord Cornwallis, of silver, but I could not come by any. But so great a noise that I could make but little of the music; and indeed, it was lost to everybody. But I had so great a lust to . . . [23] that I went out a little while before the King had done all his ceremonies, and went round the Abbey to Westminster Hall, all the way within rails, and 10,000 people, with the ground covered with blue cloth; and scaffolds all the way. Into the Hall I got, where it was very fine with hangings and scaffolds one upon another full of brave ladies; and my wife in one little one, on the right hand. Here I stayed walking up and down, and at last upon one of the side stalls I stood and saw the King come in with all the persons (but the soldiers) that were yesterday in the cavalcade; and a most pleasant sight it was to see them in their several robes. And the King came in with his crown on, and his scepter in his hand, under a canopy borne up by six silver staves, carried by Barons of the Cinque Ports,[24] and little bells at every end. And after a long time, he got up to the farther end, and all set themselves down at their several tables;

---

[19] John Carew, who had signed the death warrant of Charles I.

[20] A cousin.

[21] A well-known poet (1615–1669).

[22] Orb of gold, topped by a cross set with jewels.

[23] Apparently a word or words omitted by Wheatley.

[24] Members of Parliament for five (later seven) ports of the southeastern coast which enjoyed special privileges.

and that was also a brave sight: and the King's first course carried up by the Knights of the Bath. And many fine ceremonies there was of the Heralds leading up people before him, and bowing; and my Lord Albemarle's going to the kitchen and eat a bit of the first dish that was to go to the King's table. But, above all, was these three Lords, Northumberland, and Suffolk, and the Duke of Ormond,[25] coming before the courses on [10] horseback, and staying so all dinner-time, and at last to bring up [Dymock] the King's Champion, all in armor on horseback, with his spear and target carried before him. And a Herald proclaims "That if any dare deny Charles Stuart to be lawful King of England, here was a Champion that would fight with him"; and with these words, the Champion flings down his gauntlet, and all this he do three times in his going up to- [20] wards the King's table. At last when he is come, the King drinks to him, and then sends him the cup which is of gold, and he drinks it off, and then rides back again with the cup in his hand. I went from table to table to see the bishops and all others at their dinner, and was infinitely pleased with it. And at the lords' table, I met with William Howe, and he spoke to my Lord for me, and he did give me four rabbits and a pullet, and so I [30] got it and Mr. Creed and I got Mr. Michell to give us some bread, and so we at a stall eat it, as everybody else did what they could get. I took a great deal of pleasure to go up and down, and look upon the ladies, and to hear the music of all sorts, but above all, the 24 violins. About six at night they had dined, and I went up to my wife, and there met with a pretty lady (Mrs. Frankleyn, a Doctor's wife, a friend of Mr. Bowyer's), [40] and kissed them both, and by and by took them down to Mr. Bowyer's. And strange it is to think, that these two days have held up fair till now that all is done, and the King gone out of the Hall; and then it fell a-raining and thundering and lightening as I have not seen it do for some years: which people did take great notice of; God's blessing of the work of these two days, which is a foolery to take too much notice of such things. I ob- [50] served little disorder in all this, but only the King's footmen had got hold of the canopy, and would keep it from the Barons of the Cinque Ports, which they endeavored to force from them again, but could not do it till my

Lord Duke of Albemarle caused it to be put into Sir R. Pye's hand till to-morrow to be decided. At Mr. Bowyer's; a great deal of company, some I knew, others I did not. Here we stayed upon the leads [26] and below till it was late, expecting to see the fire-works, but they were not performed to-night: only the City [27] had a light like a glory round about it with bonfires. At last I went to King Street, and there sent Crockford to my father's and my house, to tell them I could not come home to-night, because of the dirt, and a coach could not be had. And so after drinking a pot of ale alone at Mrs. Harper's I returned to Mr. Bowyer's, and after a little stay more I took my wife and Mrs. Frankleyn (who I proffered the civility of lying with my wife at Mrs. Hunt's to-night) to Axe Yard, in which at the further end there were three great bonfires, and a great many great gallants, men and women; and they laid hold of us, and would have us drink the King's health upon our knees, kneeling upon a fagot, which we all did, they drinking to us one after another. Which we thought a strange frolic; but these gallants continued thus a great while, and I wondered to see how the ladies did tipple. At last I sent my wife and her bedfellow to bed, and Mr. Hunt and I went in with Mr. Thornbury (who did give the company all their wine, he being yeoman of the wine-cellar to the King) to his house; and there, with his wife and two of his sisters, and some gallant sparks that were there, we drank the King's health, and nothing else, till one of the gentlemen fell down stark drunk, and there lay spewing; and I went to my Lord's pretty well. But no sooner a-bed with Mr. Shepley but my head began to hum, and I to vomit, and if ever I was foxed it was now, which I cannot say yet, because I fell asleep and slept till morning. Only when I waked I found myself wet with my spewing. Thus did the day end with joy everywhere; and blessed be God, I have not heard of any mischance to anybody through it all, but only to Serjt. Glynne, whose horse fell upon him yesterday, and is like to kill him, which people do please themselves to see how just God is to punish the rogue at [50] such a time as this; he being now one of the King's Serjeants, and rode in the cavalcade with Maynard,[28] to whom people wish the

---

[25] Respectively Lord High Constable, acting Earl Marshal, and acting Lord High Steward of England.

[26] On the roof.

[27] The small inner section of London included within the ancient boundaries.

[28] Glynne and Maynard, although eminent under the government of Cromwell, had now contrived to win recognition as King's serjeants, lawyers by royal patent.

same fortune. There was also this night in King Street, [a woman] had her eye put out by a boy's flinging a firebrand into the coach. Now, after all this, I can say that, besides the pleasure of the sight of these glorious things, I may now shut my eyes against any other objects, nor for the future trouble myself to see things of state and show, as being sure never to see the like again in this world.

## IV

14 AUGUST, 1666. (Thanksgiving [29] day.) Up, and comes Mr. Foley and his man, with a box of a great variety of carpenter's and joiner's tools, which I had bespoke, to me, which please me mightily; but I will have more. Then I abroad down to the Old Swan, and there I called and kissed Betty Michell, and would have got her to go with me to Westminster, but I find her a little colder than she used to be, methought, which did a little molest me. So I away not pleased, and to Whitehall, where I find them at Chapel, and met with Povy, and he and I together, who tells me how mad my letter makes my Lord Peterborough, and what a furious letter he hath writ to me in answer, though it is not come yet. This did trouble me; for though there be no reason, yet to have a nobleman's mouth open against a man may do a man hurt; so I endeavored to have found him out and spoke with him, but could not. So to the chapel and heard a piece of the Dean of Westminster's sermon, and a special good anthem before the King, after a sermon, and then home by coach with Captain Cocke, who is in pain about his hemp, of which he says he hath brought great quantities, and would gladly be upon good terms with us for it, wherein I promise to assist him. So we 'light at the 'Change, where, after a small turn or two, taking no pleasure nowadays to be there, because of answering questions that would be asked there which I cannot answer; so home and dined, and after dinner, with my wife and Mercer to the Bear-garden [30] where I have not been, I think, of many years, and saw some good sport of the bull's tossing of the dogs: one into the very boxes. But it is a very rude and nasty pleasure. We had a great many hectors in the same box with us (and one very fine went into the pit, and played his dog for a wager, which was a

strange sport for a gentleman), where they drank wine, and drank Mercer's health first, which I pledged with my hat off; and who should be in the house but Mr. Pierce the surgeon, who saw us and spoke to us. Thence home, well enough satisfied, however, with the variety of this afternoon's exercise; and so I to my chamber, till in the evening our company come to supper. We had invited to a venison pasty Mr. Batelier and his sister Mary, Mrs. Mercer,[31] her daughter Anne, Mr. Le Brun, and W. Hewer; [32] and so we supped, and very merry. And then about nine o'clock to Mrs. Mercer's gate, where the fire and boys expected us, and her son had provided abundance of serpents [33] and rockets; and there mighty merry (my Lady Penn and Pegg going thither with us, and Nan Wright), till about twelve at night, flinging our fireworks, and burning one another and the people over the way. And at last our businesses being most spent, we into Mrs. Mercer's, and there mighty merry, smutting one another with candle grease and soot, till most of us were like devils. And that being done, then we broke up, and to my house; and there I made them drink, and upstairs we went, and then fell into dancing (W. Batelier dancing well), and dressing, him and I and one Mr. Banister (who with his wife come over also with us) like women; and Mercer put on a suit of Tom's, like a boy, and mighty mirth we had, and Mercer danced a jig; and Nan Wright and my wife and Pegg Penn put on periwigs. Thus we spent till three or four in the morning, mighty merry; and then parted, and to bed.

## V

2 SEPTEMBER, 1666 (Lord's day). Some of our maids sitting up late last night to get things ready against our feast to-day, Jane called us up about three in the morning, to tell us of a great fire they saw in the City. So I rose and slipped on my night-gown, and went to her window, and thought it to be on the back-side of Mark Lane at the farthest; but, being unused to such fires as followed, I thought it far enough off; and so went to bed again and to sleep. About seven rose again to dress myself, and there looked out at the window, and saw the fire not so much as it was and further off. So to my closet

[29] Thanksgiving for a late victory over the Dutch.
[30] A theater for animal combats on the south side of the Thames.

[31] Mother of Mary Mercer, Mrs. Pepys's servant.
[32] Pepys's chief clerk.
[33] Firework that burns with a serpentine motion or flame.

to set things to rights after yesterday's cleaning. By and by Jane comes and tells me that she hears that above 300 houses have been burned down to-night by the fire we saw, and that it is now burning down all Fish Street, by London Bridge. So I made myself ready presently, and walked to the Tower, and there got up upon one of the high places, Sir J. Robinson's little son going up with me; and there I did see the houses at that end of the bridge all on fire, and an infinite great fire on this and the other side the end of the bridge; which, among other people, did trouble me for poor little Michell and our Sarah on the bridge. So down, with my heart full of trouble, to the Lieutenant of the Tower, who tells me that it begun this morning in the King's baker's house in Pudding Lane, and that it hath burned St. Magnus's Church and most part of Fish Street already. So I down to the water-side, and there got a boat and through bridge, and there saw a lamentable fire. Poor Michell's house, as far as the Old Swan, already burned that way, and the fire running further, that in a very little time it got as far as the Steelyard, while I was there. Everybody endeavoring to remove their goods, and flinging into the river or bringing them into lighters that lay off; poor people staying in their houses as long as till the very fire touched them, and then running into boats, or clambering from one pair of stairs by the waterside to another. And among other things, the poor pigeons, I perceive, were loath to leave their houses, but hovered about the windows and balconies till they some of them burned their wings, and fell down. Having stayed, and in an hour's time seen the fire rage every way, and nobody, to my sight, endeavoring to quench it, but to remove their goods, and leave all to the fire, and having seen it get as far as the Steelyard, and the wind mighty high and driving it into the City; and everything, after so long a drought, proving combustible, even the very stones of churches, and among other things the poor steeple by which pretty Mrs. —— lives, and whereof my old schoolfellow Elborough is parson, taken fire in the very top, and there burned till it fell down: I to Whitehall (with a gentleman with me who desired to go off from the Tower, to see the fire, in my boat); to Whitehall, and there up to the King's closet in the Chapel, where people come about me, and I did give them an account dismayed them all, and word was carried in to the King. So I was called for, and did tell the King and Duke of York what I saw, and that unless His Majesty did command houses to be pulled down nothing could stop the fire. They seemed much troubled, and the King commanded me to go to my Lord Mayor for him, and command him to spare no houses, but to pull down before the fire every way. The Duke of York bid me tell him that if he would have any more soldiers he shall; and so did my Lord Arlington [34] afterwards, as a great secret. Here meeting with Captain Cocke, I in his coach, which he lent me, and Creed with me to Paul's, and there walked along Watling Street, as well as I could, every creature coming away loaden with goods to save, and here and there sick people carried away in beds. Extraordinary good goods carried in carts and on backs. At last met my Lord Mayor in Canning Street, like a man spent, with a handkercher about his neck. To the King's message he cried, like a fainting woman, "Lord! what can I do? I am spent: people will not obey me. I have been pulling down houses; but the fire overtakes us faster than we can do it." That he needed no more soldiers; and that, for himself, he must go and refresh himself, having been up all night. So he left me, and I him, and walked home, seeing people all almost distracted, and no manner of means used to quench the fire. The houses, too, so very thick thereabouts, and full of matter for burning, as pitch and tar, in Thames Street; and warehouses of oil, and wines, and brandy, and other things. Here I saw Mr. Isaac Houblon, the handsome man, prettily dressed and dirty, at his door at Dowgate, receiving some of his brothers' things, whose houses were on fire; and, as he says, have been removed twice already; and he doubts (as it soon proved) that they must be in a little time removed from his house also, which was a sad consideration. And to see the churches all filling with goods by people who themselves should have been quietly there at this time. By this time it was about twelve o'clock; and so home, and there find my guests, which was Mr. Wood and his wife Barbary Sheldon, and also Mr. Moone: she mighty fine, and her husband, for aught I see, a likely man. But Mr. Moone's design and mine, which was to look over my closet and please him with the sight thereof, which he hath long desired, was wholly disappointed; for we were in great trouble and

[34] Secretary of State.

disturbance at this fire, not knowing what to think of it. However, we had an extraordinary good dinner, and as merry as at this time we could be. While at dinner Mrs. Batelier come to inquire after Mr. Wolfe and Stanes (who, it seems, are related to them), whose houses in Fish Street are all burned, and they in a sad condition. She would not stay in the fright. Soon as dined, I and Moone away, and walked through the City, the streets full of nothing but people and horses and carts loaden with goods, ready to run over one another, and removing goods from one burned house to another. They now removing out of Canning Street (which received goods in the morning) into Lombard Street, and further; and among others I now saw my little goldsmith, Stokes, receiving some friend's goods, whose house itself was burned the day after. We parted at Paul's; he home, and I to Paul's Wharf, where I had appointed a boat to attend me, and took in Mr. Carcasse and his brother, whom I met in the street, and carried them below and above bridge to and again to see the fire, which was now got further, both below and above, and no likelihood of stopping it. Met with the King and Duke of York in their barge, and with them to Queenhithe, and there called Sir Richard Browne to them. Their order was only to pull down houses apace, and so below bridge at the water-side; but little was or could be done, the fire coming upon them so fast. Good hopes there was of stopping it at the Three Cranes above, and at Buttolph's Wharf below bridge, if care be used; but the wind carries it into the City, so as we know not by the water-side what it do there. River full of lighters and boats taking in goods, and good goods swimming in the water, and only I observed that hardly one lighter or boat in three that had the goods of a house in, but there was a pair of virginals [35] in it. Having seen as much as I could now, I away to Whitehall by appointment, and there walked to St. James's Park, and there met my wife and Creed and Wood and his wife, and walked to my boat; and there upon the water again, and to the fire up and down, it still increasing, and the wind great. So near the fire as we could for smoke; and all over the Thames, with one's face in the wind, you were almost burned with a shower of firedrops. This is very true; so as houses were burned by these drops and flakes of fire,

three or four, nay, five or six houses, one from another. When we could endure no more upon the water, we to a little alehouse on the Bankside, over against the Three Cranes, and there stayed till it was dark almost, and saw the fire grow; and, as it grew darker, appeared more and more, and in corners and upon steeples, and between churches and houses, as far as we could see up the hill of the City, in a most horrid malicious bloody flame, not like the fine flame of an ordinary fire. Barbary and her husband away before us. We stayed till, it being darkish, we saw the fire as only one entire arch of fire from this to the other side the bridge, and in a bow up the hill for an arch of above a mile long: it made me weep to see it. The churches, houses, and all on fire and flaming at once; and a horrid noise the flames made, and the cracking of houses at their ruin. So home with a sad heart, and there find everybody discoursing and lamenting the fire; and poor Tom Hater come with some few of his goods saved out of his house, which is burned upon Fish Street Hill. I invited him to lie at my house, and did receive his goods, but was deceived in his lying there, the news coming every moment of the growth of the fire; so as we were forced to begin to pack up our own goods, and prepare for their removal; and did by moonshine (it being brave dry, and moonshine, and warm weather) carry much of my goods into the garden, and Mr. Hater and I did remove my money and iron chests into my cellar, as thinking that the safest place. And got my bags of gold into my office, ready to carry away, and my chief papers of accounts also there, and my tallies into a box by themselves. So great was our fear, as Sir W. Batten hath carts come out of the country to fetch away his goods this night. We did put Mr. Hater, poor man, to bed a little; but he got but very little rest, so much noise being in my house, taking down of goods.

3rd. About four o'clock in the morning, my Lady Batten sent me a cart to carry away all my money, and plate, and best things, tc Sir W. Rider's at Bethnal Green. Which I did, riding myself in my night-gown in the cart; and, Lord! to see how the streets and the highways are crowded with people running and riding, and getting of carts at any rate to fetch away things. I find Sir W. Rider tired with being called up all night, and receiving things from several friends. His house full of goods, and much of Sir W.

[35] A spinet-like musical instrument.

Batten's and Sir W. Penn's. I am eased at my heart to have my treasure so well secured. Then home, with much ado to find a way, nor any sleep all this night to me nor my poor wife. But then and all this day she and I, and all my people laboring to get away the rest of our things, and did get Mr. Tooker to get me a lighter to take them in, and we did carry them (myself some) over Tower Hill, which was by this time full of people's goods, bringing their goods thither; and down to the lighter, which lay at the next quay, above the Tower Dock. And here was my neighbor's wife, Mrs. ——, with her pretty child, and some few of her things, which I did willingly give way to be saved with mine; but there was no passing with anything through the postern, the crowd was so great. The Duke of York come this day by the office, and spoke to us, and did ride with his guard up and down the City to keep all quiet (he being now General, and having the care of all). This day, Mercer being not at home, but against her mistress's order gone to her mother's, and my wife going thither to speak with W. Hewer, met her there, and was angry; and her mother saying that she was not a 'prentice girl, to ask leave every time she goes abroad, my wife with good reason was angry, and, when she came home, bid her be gone again. And so she went away, which troubled me, but yet less than it would, because of the condition we are in, fear of coming into in a little time of being less able to keep one in her quality. At night lay down a little upon a quilt of W. Hewer's in the office, all my own things being packed up or gone; and after me my poor wife did the like, we having fed upon the remains of yesterday's dinner, having no fire nor dishes, nor any opportunity of dressing anything.

4th. Up by break of day to get away the remainder of my things; which I did by a lighter at the Iron gate: and my hands so few, that it was the afternoon before we could get them all away. Sir W. Penn and I to Tower Street, and there met the fire burning three or four doors beyond Mr. Howell's, whose goods, poor man, his trays, and dishes, shovels, &c., were flung all along Tower Street in the kennels, and people working therewith from one end to the other; the fire coming on in that narrow street, on both sides, with infinite fury. Sir W. Batten not knowing how to remove his wine, did dig a pit in the garden, and laid it in there; and I took the opportunity of laying all the papers of my office that I could not otherwise dispose of. And in the evening Sir W. Penn and I did dig another, and put our wine in it; and I my Parmesan cheese, as well as my wine and some other things. The Duke of York was at the office this day, at Sir W. Penn's; but I happened not to be within. This afternoon, sitting melancholy with Sir W. Penn in our garden, and thinking of the certain burning of this office, without extraordinary means, I did propose for the sending up of all our workmen from Woolwich and Deptford yards [36] (none whereof yet appeared); and to write to Sir W. Coventry to have the Duke of York's permission to pull down houses, rather than lose this office, which would much hinder the King's business. So Sir W. Penn he went down this night, in order to the sending them up to-morrow morning; and I wrote to Sir W. Coventry about the business, but received no answer. This night Mrs. Turner (who, poor woman, was removing her goods all this day, good goods into the garden, and knows not how to dispose of them); and her husband supped with my wife and I at night, in the office, upon a shoulder of mutton from the cook's, without any napkin or anything, in a sad manner, but were merry. Only now and then walking into the garden, and saw how horridly the sky looks, all on a fire in the night, was enough to put us out of our wits; and, indeed, it was extremely dreadful, for it looks just as if it was at us, and the whole heaven on fire. I after supper walked in the dark down to Tower Street, and there saw it all on fire, at the Trinity House on that side, and the Dolphin Tavern on this side, which was very near us; and the fire with extraordinary vehemence. Now begins the practice of blowing up of houses in Tower Street, those next the Tower, which at first did frighten people more than anything; but it stopped the fire where it was done, it bringing down the houses to the ground in the same places they stood, and then it was easy to quench what little fire was in it, though it kindled nothing almost. W. Hewer this day went to see how his mother did, and comes late home, telling us how he hath been forced to remove her to Islington, her house in Pye Corner being burned; so that the fire is got so far that way, and all the Old Bailey, and was running down to Fleet Street; and Paul's is burned, and all Cheapside. I wrote to my

---

[36] Workmen at the naval yards.

father this night, but the post-house being burned, the letter could not go.

5th. I lay down in the office again upon W. Hewer's quilt, being mighty weary, and sore in my feet with going till I was hardly able to stand. About two in the morning my wife calls me up and tells me of new cries of fire, it being come to Barking Church, which is the bottom of our lane. I up, and finding it so, resolved presently to take her away, and did, and took my gold, which was about £2,350, W. Hewer, and Jane, down by Poundy's boat to Woolwich; but, Lord! what a sad sight it was by moon-light to see the whole City almost on fire, that you might see it plain at Woolwich, as if you were by it. There, when I come, I find the gates shut, but no guard kept at all, which troubled me, because of discourse now begun, that there is plot in it, and that the French had done it. I got the gates open, and to Mr. Sheldon's, where I locked up my gold, and charged my wife and W. Hewer never to leave the room without one of them in it, night or day. So back again, by the way seeing my goods well in the lighters at Deptford, and watched well by people. Home, and whereas I expected to have seen our house on fire, it being now about seven o'clock, it was not. But to the fire, and there find greater hopes than I expected; for my confidence of finding our Office on fire was such, that I durst not ask anybody how it was with us, till I come and saw it not burned. But going to the fire, I find by the blowing up of houses, and the great help given by the workmen out of the King's yards, sent up by Sir W. Penn, there is a good stop given to it, as well as at Mark Lane end as ours; it having only burned the dial of Barking Church, and part of the porch, and was there quenched. I up to the top of Barking steeple, and there saw the saddest sight of desolation that I ever saw; everywhere great fires, oil-cellars, and brimstone, and other things burning. I became afeard to stay there long, and therefore down again as fast as I could, the fire being spread as far as I could see it; and to Sir W. Penn's, and there eat a piece of cold meat, having eaten nothing since Sunday, but the remains of Sunday's dinner. Here I met with Mr. Young and Whistler; and having removed all my things, and received good hopes that the fire at our end is stopped, they and I walked into the town, and find Fenchurch Street, Gracious Street, and Lombard Street all in dust. The Exchange a sad sight,

nothing standing there, of all the statues or pillars, but Sir Thomas Gresham's picture [37] in the corner. Walked into Moorfields (our feet ready to burn, walking through the town among the hot coals), and find that full of people, and poor wretches carrying their goods there, and everybody keeping his goods together by themselves (and a great blessing it is to them that it is fair weather for them to keep abroad night and day); drank there, and paid twopence for a plain penny loaf. Thence homeward, having passed through Cheapside and Newgate Market, all burned, and seen Anthony Joyce's house in fire. And took up (which I keep by me) a piece of glass of Mercers' Chapel in the street, where much more was, so melted and buckled with the heat of the fire like parchment. I also did see a poor cat taken out of a hole in the chimney, joining to the wall of the Exchange, with the hair all burned off the body, and yet alive. So home at night, and find there good hopes of saving our office; but great endeavors of watching all night, and having men ready; and so we lodged them in the office, and had drink and bread and cheese for them. And lay down and slept a good night about midnight, though when I rose I heard that there had been a great alarm of French and Dutch being risen, which proved nothing. But it is a strange thing to see how long this time did look since Sunday, having been always full of variety of actions, and little sleep, that it looked like a week or more, and I had forgot almost the day of the week.

6th. Up about five o'clock, and there met Mr. Gauden at the gate of the office (I intending to go out, as I used, every now and then to-day, to see how the fire is) to call our men to Bishop's Gate, where no fire had yet been near, and there is now one broke out: which did give great grounds to people, and to me too, to think that there is some kind of plot in this (on which many by this time have been taken, and it hath been dangerous for any stranger to walk in the streets), but I went with the men, and we did put it out in a little time; so that that was well again. It was pretty to see how hard the women did work in the kennels,[38] sweeping of water; but then they would scold for drink, and be as drunk as devils. I saw good butts of sugar broke open in the street, and people

[37] Statue (Gresham was the Elizabethan founder of the Royal Exchange).
[38] Gutters.

go and take handsfull out, and put into beer, and drink it. And now all being pretty well, I took boat, and over to Southwark, and took boat on the other side the bridge, and so to Westminster, thinking to shift myself, being all in dirt from top to bottom; but could not there find any place to buy a shirt or pair of gloves, Westminster Hall being full of people's goods, those in Westminster hav- ing removed all their goods, and the Ex- chequer money put into vessels to carry to Nonsuch; [39] but to the Swan, and there was trimmed; and then to Whitehall, but saw nobody; and so home. A sad sight to see how the river looks: no houses nor church near it, to the Temple, where it stopped. At home, did go with Sir W. Batten, and our neighbor, Knightly (who, with one more, was the only man of any fashion left in all the neighborhood thereabouts, they all re- moving their goods and leaving their houses to the mercy of the fire), to Sir R. Ford's, and there dined in an earthen platter—a fried breast of mutton; a great many of us, but very merry, and indeed as good a meal, though as ugly a one, as ever I had in my life. Thence down to Deptford, and there with great satis- faction landed all my goods at Sir G. Carteret's safe, and nothing missed I could see, or hurt. This being done to my great content, I home, and to Sir W. Batten's, and there with Sir R. Ford, Mr. Knightly, and one Withers, a pro- fessed lying rogue, supped well, and mighty merry, and our fears over. From them to the office, and there slept with the office full of laborers, who talked, and slept, and walked all night long there. But strange it was to see Clothworkers' Hall on fire these three days and nights in one body of flame, it being the cellar full of oil.

### VI

5 OCTOBER, 1667. . . . And I to my tailor's, and there took up my wife and Willet,[40] who stayed there for me, and to the Duke of York's playhouse, but the house so full, it being a new play, *The Coffee House*,[41] that we could not get in, and so to the King's house: and there, going in, met with Knepp,[42] and she took us up into the tiring-rooms: and to the women's shift, where Nell [43] was

dressing herself, and was all unready, and is very pretty, prettier than I thought. And so walked all up and down the house above, and then below into the scene-room, and there sat down, and she gave us fruit: and here I read the questions to Knepp, while she answered me, through all her part of *Flora's Vagaries* which was acted to-day. But, Lord! to see how they were both painted would make a man mad, and did make me loath them; and what base company of men comes among them, and how lewdly they talk! and how poor the men are in clothes, and yet what a show they make on the stage by candle-light, is very observable. But to see how Nell cursed, for having so few people in the pit, was pretty; the other house carrying away all the people at the new play, and is said, nowadays, to have generally most company, as being better play- ers. By and by into the pit, and there saw the play, which is pretty good, but my belly was full of what I had seen in the house, and so, after the play done, away home, and there to the writing my letters, and so home to supper and to bed.

### VII

5 DECEMBER, 1668. Up, after a little talk with my wife, which troubled me, she being ever since our late difference mighty watch- ful of sleep and dreams, and will not be per- suaded but I do dream of Deb.,[44] and do tell me that I speak in my dreams and that this night I did cry, Huzzy, and it must be she, and now and then I start otherwise than I used to do, she says, which I know not, for I do not know that I dream of her more than usual, though I cannot deny that my thoughts waking do run now and then against my will and judgment upon her, for that only is want- ing to undo me, being now in every other thing as to my mind most happy, and may still be so but for my own fault, if I be catched loving anybody but my wife again. So up and to the office, and at noon to din- ner, and thence to office, where late, mighty busy, and dispatching much business, settling papers in my own office, and so home to sup- per, and to bed. No news stirring, but that my Lord of Ormond is likely to go to Ire- land again, which do show that the Duke of Buckingham [45] do not rule all so absolutely; and that, however, we shall speedily have

[39] A place more than ten miles southwest of Lon- don.

[40] Deborah Willet, Mrs. Pepys's servant.

[41] A comedy by Thomas St. Serfe, printed 1668.

[42] Mrs. Knepp, a well-known actress.

[43] Nell Gwynn, actress and one-time mistress of Charles II.

[44] Deborah Willet, her servant.

[45] George Villiers, second Duke of Buckingham, the Zimri of Dryden's *Absalom and Achitophel*.

more changes in the Navy: and it is certain that the Nonconformists [46] do now preach openly in houses, in many places, and among others the house that was heretofore Sir G. Carteret's, in Leadenhall Street, and have ready access to the King. And now the great dispute is, whether this Parliament or another; and my great design, if I continue in the Navy, is to get myself to be a Parliament man.

6th (Lord's day). Up, and with my wife to church; which pleases me mightily, I being full of fear that she would never go to church again, after she had declared to me that she was a Roman Catholic. But though I do verily think she fears God, and is truly and sincerely righteous, yet I do see she is not so strictly so a Catholic as not to go to church with me, which pleases me mightily. Here Mills made a lazy sermon, upon Moses's

[46] Protestants outside the Church of England.

meekness, and so home, and my wife and I alone to dinner, and then she to read a little book concerning speech in general,[47] a translation late out of French, a most excellent piece as ever I read, proving a soul in man, and all the ways and secrets by which nature teaches speech in man, which do please me most infinitely to read. By and by my wife to church, and I to my Office to complete my Journal for the last three days, and so home to my chamber to settle some papers, and so to spend the evening with my wife and W. Hewer talking over the business of the Office, and particularly my own Office, how I will make it, and it will become, in a little time, an Office of ease, and not slavery, as it hath for so many years been. So to supper, and to bed.

[47] William Holder, *Elements of Speech* (1669).

# John Bunyan

## 1628–1688

The Bunyan family was settled in Bedford-shire from at least the end of the twelfth century. Bunyan's grandfather was a "petty chapman," or small retail trader. Thomas, his father, called himself a "brazier";—he made and mended pots and kettles, but did not belong to the more or less disreputable tribe of wandering tinkers. Bunyan carried on the same trade. His father married three times, and John, the first child of his second wife, was born at the village of Elstow, about a mile south of the town of Bedford, in November, 1628. His baptism was recorded on 30 November. As a child he had some schooling, learning to read and to write, probably at Elstow. In 1644 he became a soldier in the Commonwealth army, fighting against his king until July, 1647. Towards the close of 1648 or the beginning of 1649 he married. No record of his marriage remains, and the name of his wife is not known; but she came of a godly family, and, though she brought little else, she contributed to the new household two books inherited from her father—The Plain Man's Pathway to Heaven and The Practice of Piety. Her own devout conversation and the former of these books combined to send Bunyan off on that quest of the spirit of religious certitude and for the right pathway to salvation which ended by making him a nonconformist preacher, a writer for edification, —and something that he himself never suspected and would not have desired—one of the great figures in the annals of English literature. Sensitive, highly strung, vividly imaginative, he came to manhood at a time of general religious excitement, and could scarcely in any event have escaped its influence. His long and agonized conflict with himself and final victory he described years later in a book which (though not trustworthy as a record of fact) is a classic of spiritual autobiography: Grace Abounding to the Chief of Sinners: or, A Brief and Faithful Relation of the Exceeding Mercy of God in Christ to his Poor Servant, John Bunyan;

Wherein is particularly showed the manner of his conversion, his sight and trouble for sin, his dreadful temptations, also how he despaired of God's mercy, and how the Lord at length through Christ did deliver him from all the guilt and terror that lay upon him. Whereunto is added a brief relation of his call to the work of the ministry, of his temptations therein, as also what he hath met with in prison. All which was written by his own hand there, and now published for the support of the weak and tempted people of God (1666).

This was not Bunyan's first book; it was in fact his twelfth publication. In 1653 he had joined a nonconformist body which met in St. John's Church, at Bedford, and he had moved there in 1655. Soon thereafter he lost his wife, who had borne him four children. About the same time he was made a deacon, and in 1656 he published (at Newport Pagnell, where he had been stationed while in the army) his first book, Some Gospel Truths Opened, written in confutation of the Quakers. In the following year his calling as a preacher was formally recognized, and his fame began to spread. In 1658 he published his third book, A Few Sighs from Hell, or the Groans of a Damned Soul. Probably late in 1659 he married a second time. In the next year, after the accession of Charles II, steps were taken to restore the Church of England to her former position, and Bunyan's preaching at public assemblies became illegal. He determined, however, to persist, and was accordingly arrested on 12 November at the hamlet of Lower Samsell by Harlington (about 13 miles south of Bedford). He was imprisoned for the next 12 years, with the exception, probably, of a brief interval in 1666. While in jail he made long tagged laces to support his family. During part of this period he was allowed much freedom, was often present at church meetings in Bedford, and even went to "see Christians in London." In 1672, following Charles's Declaration of Indulgence, he was

*pardoned, but was again imprisoned in 1675;
—and it was during this period of confinement
that he wrote the first part of* The Pilgrim's
Progress *(published in 1678). Thereafter,
though he continued to be active in preaching, and ran some risks, he escaped molestation.* The Life and Death of Mr. Badman *was
published in 1680,* The Holy War *in 1682,
and the second part of* The Pilgrim's Progress
*in 1684. In 1688 he was caught in a severe
storm while riding to London after aiding in
the reconciliation of a father and son. He
came down with a severe cold followed by a
fever, and died on 31 August. He was buried
in Bunhill Fields, Finsbury.*

*In all, Bunyan wrote 60 books and tracts. It
is thought that no fewer than 100,000 copies of*
The Pilgrim's Progress *were sold before his
death; and during the first century of the
book's existence 33 editions of Part I were published, and 59 editions of Parts I and II together. There are said to be versions of the
book in no less than 108 languages and dialects.
No book has had a comparable circulation save
the Bible. And on the Bible, almost alone,
Bunyan was nourished, and its language and
rhythms mingle pleasantly with the homelier
speech of the seventeenth-century English
countryside in his great allegory of the spiritual
life. Bunyan was no poet, but he chose to tell
in verse the genesis of his book, and one may
best learn from his own words one reason for
its enduring vitality:*

"When at the first I took my pen in hand
Thus for to write, I did not understand
That I at all should make a little Book
In such a mode. Nay, I had undertook
To make another; which when almost done,
Before I was aware, I this begun;
. . . . . but yet I did not think
To show to all the world my pen and ink
In such a mode. I only thought to make
I knew not what; nor did I undertake
Thereby to please my neighbor. No, not I,
I did it mine own self to gratify."

*When he had been humanized by a full experi-
ence of life, knowing the workings of the human heart and mind as few in any age are
given to know them, he wrote this book, not of
set purpose nor expressly for the improvement
of mankind, but almost in his own despite—
just because it so "gratified" him to dramatize
the spiritual conflict within the soul's dark
habitation. And thus was one of the world's
few great books born.*

*The best edition of* The Pilgrim's Progress
*is that edited by James B. Wharey (Oxford,
1928). The standard biography is still John*

*Brown's* John Bunyan (1628–1688), His Life,
Times, and Work, *rev. Frank M. Harrison
(London, 1928); and a useful general study
is Roger Sharrock's* John Bunyan *(London,
1954). Barbara Wall has translated an important study by Henri Talon,* John Bunyan: the
Man and His Works *(Cambridge, U. S. A.,
1951).*

## Passages from
## *The Pilgrim's Progress*

*From This World to That Which Is to
Come: Delivered Under the Similitude of a
Dream*

### THE FIRST PART (1678)

#### I

As I walked through the wilderness of this
world, I lighted on a certain place where was
a Den, and I laid me down in that place to
sleep: and as I slept I dreamed a dream. I
dreamed, and behold, I saw a man clothed
with rags, standing in a certain place, with
his face from his own house, a book in his
hand, and a great burden upon his back. I
looked, and saw him open the book, and read
therein; and, as he read, he wept, and trembled; and, not being able longer to contain,
he brake out with a lamentable cry, saying,
What shall I do?

In this plight, therefore, he went home and
refrained himself as long as he could, that his
wife and children should not perceive his distress; but he could not be silent long, because
that his trouble increased. Wherefore at
length he brake his mind to his wife and
children; and thus he began to talk to them:
O my dear wife, said he, and you the children
of my bowels, I, your dear friend, am in myself undone by reason of a burden that lieth
hard upon me; moreover, I am for certain
informed that this our city will be burned
with fire from heaven; in which fearful overthrow, both myself, with thee my wife, and
you my sweet babes, shall miserably come to
ruin, except (the which yet I see not) some
way of escape can be found, whereby we may
be delivered. At this his relations were sore
amazed; not for that they believed that what
he had said to them was true, but because
they thought that some frenzy distemper
had got into his head; therefore, it drawing
towards night, and they hoping that sleep
might settle his brains, with all haste they

got him to bed. But the night was as troublesome to him as the day; wherefore, instead of sleeping, he spent it in sighs and tears. So, when the morning was come, they would know how he did. He told them, Worse and worse: he also set to talking to them again; but they began to be hardened. They also thought to drive away his distemper by harsh and surly carriages to him; sometimes they would deride, sometimes they would chide, and some- 10 times they would quite neglect him. Wherefore he began to retire himself to his chamber, to pray for and pity them, and also to condole his own misery; he would also walk solitary in the fields, sometimes reading, and sometimes praying: and thus for some days he spent his time.

Now, I saw, upon a time, when he was walking in the fields, that he was, as he was wont, reading in his book, and greatly distressed in 20 his mind; and, as he read, he burst out, as he had done before, crying, What shall I do to be saved?

I saw also that he looked this way and that way, as if he would run; yet he stood still, because, as I perceived, he could not tell which way to go. I looked then, and saw a man named *Evangelist* coming to him, and asked, Wherefore dost thou cry?

He answered, Sir, I perceive by the book 30 in my hand, that I am condemned to die, and after that to come to judgment; and I find that I am not willing to do the first, nor able to do the second.

Then said *Evangelist*, Why not willing to die, since this life is attended with so many evils? The man answered, Because I fear that this burden that is upon my back will sink me lower than the grave, and I shall fall into Tophet. And, Sir, if I be not fit to go to prison, 40 I am not fit to go to judgment, and from thence to execution; and the thoughts of these things make me cry.

Then said *Evangelist*, If this be thy condition, why standest thou still? He answered, Because I know not whither to go. Then he gave him a parchment roll, and there was written within, Fly from the wrath to come.

The man, therefore, read it, and looking upon *Evangelist* very carefully, said, Whither 50 must I fly? Then said *Evangelist*, pointing with his finger over a very wide field, Do you see yonder wicket-gate? The man said, No. Then said the other, Do you see yonder shining light? He said, I think I do. Then said *Evangelist*, Keep that light in your eye, and go up directly thereto: so shalt thou see the gate; at which, when thou knockest, it shall be told thee what thou shalt do. So I saw in my dream that the man began to run. Now, he had not run far from his own door, but his wife and children, perceiving it, began to cry after him to return; but the man put his fingers in his ears, and ran on, crying, Life! life! eternal life! So he looked not behind him, but fled towards the middle of the plain.

The neighbors also came out to see him run; and, as he ran, some mocked, others threatened, and some cried after him to return; and, among those that did so, there were two that resolved to fetch him back by force. The name of the one was *Obstinate*, and the name of the other *Pliable*. Now, by this time, the man was got a good distance from them; but, however, they were resolved to pursue him, which they did, and in a little time they overtook him. Then said the man, Neighbors, wherefore are you come? They said, To persuade you to go back with us. But he said, That can by no means be; you dwell, said he, in the *City of Destruction*, the place also where I was born: I see it to be so; and, dying there, sooner or later, you will sink lower than the grave, into a place that burns with fire and brimstone: be content, good neighbors, and go along with me.

OBST. What! said *Obstinate*, and leave our friends and our comforts behind us?

CHR. Yes, said *Christian*, for that was his name, because that ALL which you shall forsake is not worthy to be compared with a little of that, that I am seeking to enjoy; and, if you will go along with me, and hold it, you shall fare as I myself; for there, where I go, is enough and to spare. Come away, and prove my words.

OBST. What are the things you seek, since you leave all the world to find them?

CHR. I seek an inheritance incorruptible, undefiled, and that fadeth away, and it is laid up in heaven, and safe there, to be bestowed, at the time appointed, on them that diligently seek it. Read it so, if you will, in my book.

OBST. Tush! said *Obstinate*, away with your book; will you go back with us or no?

CHR. No, not I, said the other, because I have laid my hand to the plow.

OBST. Come, then, neighbor *Pliable*, let us turn again, and go home without him; there is a company of these crazed-headed coxcombs, that, when they take a fancy by the end, are wiser in their own eyes than seven men that can render a reason.

PLI. Then said *Pliable*, Don't revile; if what the good *Christian* says is true, the things he looks after are better than ours: my heart inclines to go with my neighbor.

OBST. What! more fools still? Be ruled by me, go back; who knows whither such a brain-sick fellow will lead you? Go back, go back, and be wise.

CHR. Nay, but do thou come with thy neighbor, *Pliable*; there are such things to be had 10 which I spoke of, and many more glories besides. If you believe not me, read here in this book; and for the truth of what is expressed therein, behold, all is confirmed by the blood of Him that made it.

PLI. Well, neighbor *Obstinate*, saith *Pliable*, I begin to come to a point; I intend to go along with this good man, and to cast in my lot with him: but, my good companion, do you know the way to this desired place? 20

CHR. I am directed by a man, whose name is *Evangelist*, to speed me to a little gate that is before us, where we shall receive instructions about the way.

PLI. Come, then, good neighbor, let us be going. Then they went both together.

OBST. And I will go back to my place, said *Obstinate*; I will be no companion of such misled, fantastical fellows.

Now I saw in my dream, that when *Obsti-* 30 *nate* was gone back, *Christian* and *Pliable* went talking over the plain; and thus they began their discourse.

CHR. Come, neighbor *Pliable*, how do you do? I am glad you are persuaded to go along with me. Had even *Obstinate* himself but felt what I have felt of the powers and terrors of what is yet unseen, he would not thus lightly have given us the back.

PLI. Come, neighbor *Christian*, since there 40 is none but us two here, tell me now further what the things are, and how to be enjoyed, whither we are going.

CHR. I can better conceive of them with my mind, than speak of them with my tongue: but yet, since you are desirous to know, I will read of them in my book.

PLI. And do you think that the words of your book are certainly true?

CHR. Yes, verily; for it was made by Him 50 that cannot lie.

PLI. Well said; what things are they?

CHR. There is an endless kingdom to be inhabited, and everlasting life to be given us, that we may inhabit that kingdom for ever.

PLI. Well said; and what else?

CHR. There are crowns of glory to be given

us, and garments that will make us shine like the sun in the firmament of heaven.

PLI. This is very pleasant; and what else?

CHR. There shall be no more crying, nor sorrow: for He that is owner of the place will wipe all tears from our eyes.

PLI. And what company shall we have there?

CHR. There we shall be with seraphims and cherubims, creatures that will dazzle your eyes to look on them. There also you shall meet with thousands and ten thousands that have gone before us to that place; none of them are hurtful, but loving and holy; every one walking in the sight of God, and standing in his presence with acceptance for ever. In a word, there we shall see the elders with their golden crowns, there we shall see the holy virgins with their golden harps, there we shall see men that by the world were cut in pieces, burnt in flames, eaten of beasts, drowned in the seas, for the love that they bear to the Lord of the place; all well, and clothed with immortality as with a garment.

PLI. The hearing of this is enough to ravish one's heart. But are these things to be enjoyed? How shall we get to be sharers thereof?

CHR. The Lord, the Governor of the country, hath recorded that in this book; the substance of which is, If we be truly willing to 30 have it, he will bestow it upon us freely.

PLI. Well, my good companion, glad am I to hear of these things: come on, let us mend our pace.

CHR. I cannot go so fast as I would, by reason of this burden that is on my back.

Now I saw in my dream, that just as they had ended this talk they drew near to a very miry slough, that was in the midst of the plain; and they, being heedless, did both fall suddenly into the bog. The name of the slough was *Despond*. Here, therefore, they wallowed for a time, being grievously bedaubed with dirt; and *Christian*, because of the burden that was on his back, began to sink in the mire.

PLI. Then said *Pliable*, Ah! neighbor *Christian*, where are you now?

CHR. Truly, said *Christian*, I do not know.

PLI. At that *Pliable* began to be offended, and angrily said to his fellow, Is this the hap- 50 piness you have told me all this while of? If we have such ill speed at our first setting out, what may we expect betwixt this and our journey's end? May I get out again with my life, you shall possess the brave country alone for me. And, with that, he gave a desperate struggle or two, and got out of the mire on that side of the slough which was next to his own house: so away he went, and *Christian* saw him no more.

Wherefore *Christian* was left to tumble in the *Slough of Despond* alone: but still he endeavored to struggle to that side of the slough that was further from his own house, and next to the wicket-gate; the which he did, but could not get out, because of the burden that was upon his back: but I beheld in my dream, that a man came to him, whose name was *Help*, 10 and asked him, What he did there?

CHR. Sir, said *Christian*, I was bid go this way by a man called *Evangelist*, who directed me also to yonder gate, that I might escape the wrath to come; and as I was going thither I fell in here.

HELP. But why did you not look for the steps?

CHR. Fear followed me so hard, that I fled the next way, and fell in. 20

HELP. Then said he, Give me thy hand: so he gave him his hand, and he drew him out, and set him upon sound ground, and bid him go on his way.

Then I stepped to him that plucked him out, and said, Sir, wherefore, since over this place is the way from the *City of Destruction* to yonder gate, is it that this plat[1] is not mended, that poor travelers might go thither with more security? And he said unto me, 30 This miry slough is such a place as cannot be mended; it is the descent whither the scum and filth that attends conviction for sin doth continually run, and therefore it was called the *Slough of Despond*; for still, as the sinner is awakened about his lost condition, there ariseth in his soul many fears, and doubts, and discouraging apprehensions, which all of them get together, and settle in this place. And this is the reason of the badness of this ground. 40

It is not the pleasure of the King that this place should remain so bad. His laborers also have, by the direction of His Majesty's surveyors, been for above these sixteen hundred years employed about this patch of ground, if perhaps it might have been mended: yea, and to my knowledge, said he, here have been swallowed up at least twenty thousand cartloads, yea, millions of wholesome instructions, that have at all seasons been brought from all 50 places of the King's dominions, and they that can tell, say they are the best materials to make good ground of the place; if so be, it might have been mended, but it is the *Slough of*

_____
[1] Plot of ground.

*Despond* still, and so will be when they have done what they can.

True, there are, by the direction of the Lawgiver, certain good and substantial steps, placed even through the very midst of this slough; but at such time as this place doth much spew out its filth, as it doth against change of weather, these steps are hardly seen; or, if they be, men, through the dizziness of their heads, step beside, and then they are bemired to purpose, notwithstanding the steps be there; but the ground is good when they are once got in at the gate.

Now, I saw in my dream, that by this time *Pliable* was got home to his house, so his neighbors came to visit him; and some of them called him wise man for coming back, and some called him fool for hazarding himself with *Christian*: others again did mock at his cowardliness; saying, Surely, since you began to venture, I would not have been so base to have given out for a few difficulties. So *Pliable* sat sneaking among them. But at last he got more confidence, and then they all turned their tales, and began to deride poor *Christian* behind his back. And thus much concerning *Pliable*.

Now, as *Christian* was walking solitarily by himself, he espied one afar off, come crossing over the field to meet him; and their hap was to meet just as they were crossing the way of each other. The gentleman's name that met him was Mr. *Worldly Wiseman*; he dwelt in the town of *Carnal Policy*, a very great town, and also hard by from whence *Christian* came. This man, then, meeting with *Christian*, and having some inkling of him—for *Christian's* setting forth from the *City of Destruction* was much noised abroad, not only in the town where he dwelt, but also it began to be the town talk in some other places—Master *Worldly Wiseman*, therefore, having some guess of him, by beholding his laborious going, by observing his sighs and groans, and the like, began thus to enter into some talk with *Christian*.

WORLD. How now, good fellow, whither away after this burdened manner?

CHR. A burdened manner, indeed, as ever, I think, poor creature had! And whereas you ask me, Whither away? I tell you, Sir, I am going to yonder wicket-gate before me; for there, as I am informed, I shall be put into a way to be rid of my heavy burden.

WORLD. Hast thou a wife and children?

CHR. Yes; but I am so laden with this burden that I cannot take that pleasure in them as formerly; methinks I am as if I had none.

WORLD. Wilt thou hearken to me if I give thee counsel?

CHR. If it be good, I will; for I stand in need of good counsel.

WORLD. I would advise thee, then, that thou with all speed get thyself rid of thy burden; for thou wilt never be settled in thy mind till then; nor canst thou enjoy the benefits of the blessing which God hath bestowed upon thee till then.

CHR. That is that which I seek for, even to be rid of this heavy burden; but get it off myself, I cannot; nor is there any man in our country that can take it off my shoulders; therefore am I going this way, as I told you, that I may be rid of my burden.

WORLD. Who bid you go this way to be rid of your burden?

CHR. A man that appeared to me to be a very great and honorable person; his name, as I remember, is *Evangelist.*

WORLD. I beshrew him for his counsel! there is not a more dangerous and troublesome way in the world than is that unto which he hath directed thee; and that thou shalt find, if thou will be ruled by his counsel. Thou hast met with something, as I perceive already; for I see the dirt of the *Slough of Despond* is upon thee; but that slough is the beginning of the sorrows that do attend those that go on in that way. Hear me, I am older than thou; thou art like to meet with, in the way which thou goest, wearisomeness, painfulness, hunger, perils, nakedness, sword, lions, dragons, darkness, and, in a word, death, and what not! These things are certainly true, having been confirmed by many testimonies. And should a man so carelessly cast away himself, by giving heed to a stranger?

CHR. Why, Sir, this burden upon my back is more terrible to me than are all these things which you have mentioned; nay, methinks I care not what I meet with in the way, if so be I can also meet with deliverance from my burden.

WORLD. How camest thou by the burden at first?

CHR. By reading this book in my hand.

WORLD. I thought so; and it is happened unto thee as to other weak men, who, meddling with things too high for them, do suddenly fall into thy distractions; which distractions do not only unman men, as thine, I perceive, has done thee, but they run them upon desperate ventures to obtain they know not what.

CHR. I know what I would obtain; it is ease for my heavy burden.

## II

Then he went on till he came to the house of the *Interpreter,* where he knocked over and over; at last one came to the door, and asked who was there.

CHR. Sir, here is a traveler, who was bid by an acquaintance of the good-man of this house to call here for my profit; I would therefore speak with the master of the house. So he called for the master of the house, who, after a little time, came to *Christian,* and asked him what he would have.

CHR. Sir, said *Christian,* I am a man that am come from the *City of Destruction,* and am going to the Mount *Zion;* and I was told by the man that stands at the gate, at the head of this way, that if I called here, you would show me excellent things, such as would be an help to me in my journey.

INTER. Then said the *Interpreter,* Come in; I will show that which will be profitable to thee. So he commanded his man to light the candle, and bid *Christian* follow him: so he had him into a private room, and bid his man open a door; the which when he had done, *Christian* saw the picture of a very grave person hang up against the wall; and this was the fashion of it. It had eyes lifted up to heaven, the best of books in his hand, the law of truth was written upon its lips, the world was behind his back. It stood as if it pleaded with men, and a crown of gold did hang over its head.

CHR. Then said *Christian,* What meaneth this?

INTER. The man whose picture this is, is one of a thousand; he can beget children, travail in birth with children, and nurse them himself when they are born. And whereas thou seest him with his eyes lift up to heaven, the best of books in his hand, and the law of truth writ on his lips, it is to show thee that his work is to know and unfold dark things to sinners; even as also thou seest him stand as if he pleaded with men: and whereas thou seest the world as cast behind him, and that a crown hangs over his head, that is to show thee that slighting and despising the things that are present, for the love that he hath to his Master's service, he is sure in the world that comes next to have glory for his reward. Now, said the *Interpreter,* I have showed thee this picture first, because the man whose picture this is, is the only man whom the Lord of the place whither thou art going, hath authorized to be thy guide in all difficult places thou mayest meet with in the way; wherefore, take good heed to what I have showed thee, and bear well in thy mind what thou hast seen, lest in thy journey thou meet with some that pretend to lead thee right, but their way goes down to death.

Then he took him by the hand, and led him into a very large parlor that was full of dust, because never swept; the which after he had reviewed a little while, the *Interpreter* called for a man to sweep. Now, when he began to sweep, the dust began so abundantly to fly about, that *Christian* had almost therewith been choked. Then said the *Interpreter* to a damsel that stood by, Bring hither water, and sprinkle the room; the which, when she had 20 done, it was swept and cleansed with pleasure.

CHR. Then said *Christian*, What means this?

INTER. The *Interpreter* answered, This parlor is the heart of a man that was never sanctified by the sweet grace of the gospel; the dust is his original sin and inward corruptions, that have defiled the whole man. He that began to sweep at first, is the *Law*; but she that brought water, and did sprinkle it, is the *Gospel*. Now, 30 whereas thou sawest, that so soon as the first began to sweep, the dust did so fly about that the room by him could not be cleansed, but that thou wast almost choked therewith; this is to show thee, that the law, instead of cleansing the heart (by its working) from sin, doth revive, put strength into, and increase it in the soul, even as it doth discover and forbid it, for it doth not give power to subdue.

Again, as thou sawest the damsel sprinkle 40 the room with water, upon which it was cleansed with pleasure; this is to show thee, that when the gospel comes in the sweet and precious influences thereof to the heart, then, I say, even as thou sawest the damsel lay the dust by sprinkling the floor with water, so is sin vanquished and subdued, and the soul made clean through the faith of it, and consequently fit for the King of glory to inhabit.

I saw, moreover, in my dream, that the 50 *Interpreter* took him by the hand, and had him into a little room, where sat two little children, each one in his chair. The name of the eldest was *Passion*, and the name of the other *Patience*. *Passion* seemed to be much discontented; but *Patience* was very quiet. Then *Christian* asked, What is the reason of the discontent of *Passion?* The *Interpreter* answered, The Governor of them would have him stay for his best things till the beginning of the next year; but he will have all now: but *Patience* is willing to wait.

Then I saw that one came to *Passion*, and brought him a bag of treasure, and poured it down at his feet, the which he took up and rejoiced therein, and withal laughed *Patience* to 10 scorn. But I beheld but a while, and he had lavished all away, and had nothing left him but rags.

CHR. Then said *Christian* to the *Interpreter*, Expound this matter more fully to me.

INTER. So he said, These two lads are figures: *Passion*, of the men of this world; and *Patience*, of the men of that which is to come; for as here thou seest, *Passion* will have all now this year, that is to say, in this world; so 20 are the men of this world, they must have all their good things now, they cannot stay till next year, that is until the next world, for their portion of good. That proverb, "A bird in the hand is worth two in the bush," is of more authority with them than are all the Divine testimonies of the good of the world to come. But as thou sawest that he had quickly lavished all away, and had presently left him nothing but rags; so will it be with all such men at the end 30 of this world.

CHR. Then said *Christian*, Now I see that *Patience* has the best wisdom, and that upon many accounts. First, because he stays for the best things. Second, and also because he will have the glory of his, when the other had nothing but rags.

INTER. Nay, you may add another, to wit, the glory of the next world will never wear out; but these are suddenly gone. Therefore 40 *Passion* had not so much reason to laugh at *Patience*, because he had his good things first, as *Patience* will have to laugh at *Passion*, because he had his best things last; for first must give place to last, because last must have his time to come; but last gives place to nothing; for there is not another to succeed. He, therefore, that hath his portion first, must needs have a time to spend it; but he that has his portion last, must have it lastingly; therefore 50 it is said of Dives, In thy lifetime thou receivedst thy good things, and likewise Lazarus evil things; but now he is comforted, and thou art tormented.

CHR. Then I perceive 'tis not best to covet things that are now, but to wait for things to come.

INTER. You say the truth: For the things

that are seen are temporal; but the things which are not seen are eternal. But though this be so, yet since things present and our fleshly appetite are such near neighbors one to another; and again, because things to come, and carnal sense, are such strangers one to another; therefore it is that the first of these so suddenly fall into amity, and that distance is so continually between the second.

Then I saw in my dream that the *Inter-* preter took *Christian* by the hand, and led him into a place where was a fire burning against a wall, and one standing by it, always casting much water upon it, to quench it; yet did the fire burn higher and hotter.

Then said *Christian*, What means this?

The *Interpreter* answered, This fire is the work of grace that is wrought in the heart; he that casts water upon it, to extinguish and put it out, is the Devil; but in that thou seest the fire notwithstanding burn higher and hotter, thou shalt also see the reason of that. So he had him about to the backside of the wall, where he saw a man with a vessel of oil in his hand, of the which he did also continually cast, but secretly, into the fire.

Then said *Christian*, What means this?

The *Interpreter* answered, This is Christ, who continually, with the oil of his grace, maintains the work already begun in the heart: by the means of which, notwithstanding what the devil can do, the souls of his people prove gracious still. And in that thou sawest that the man stood behind the wall to maintain the fire, this is to teach thee that it is hard for the tempted to see how this work of grace is maintained in the soul.

I saw also, that the *Interpreter* took him again by the hand, and led him into a pleasant place, where was builded a stately palace, beautiful to behold; at the sight of which *Christian* was greatly delighted. He saw also, upon the top thereof, certain persons walking, who were clothed all in gold.

Then said *Christian*, May we go in thither?

Then the *Interpreter* took him, and led him up towards the door of the palace; and behold, at the door stood a great company of men, as desirous to go in, but durst not. There also sat a man at a little distance from the door, at a table-side, with a book and his inkhorn before him, to take the name of him that should enter therein; he saw also, that in the doorway stood many men in armor to keep it, being resolved to do to the men that would enter what hurt and mischief they could. Now was *Christian* somewhat in amaze. At last, when every man

started back for fear of the armed men, *Christian* saw a man of a very stout countenance come up to the man that sat there to write, saying, Set down my name, Sir: the which when he had done, he saw the man draw his sword, and put an helmet upon his head, and rush toward the door upon the armed men, who laid upon him with deadly force; but the man, not at all discouraged, fell to cutting and hacking most fiercely. So after he had received and given many wounds to those that attempted to keep him out, he cut his way through them all, and pressed forward into the palace, at which there was a pleasant voice heard from those that were within, even of those that walked upon the top of the palace, saying—

> Come in, come in;
> Eternal glory thou shalt win.

So he went in, and was clothed with such garments as they. Then *Christian* smiled and said, I think verily I know the meaning of this.

Now, said *Christian*, let me go hence. Nay, stay, said the *Interpreter*, till I have showed thee a little more, and after that thou shalt go on thy way. So he took him by the hand again, and led him into a very dark room, where there sat a man in an iron cage.

Now the man, to look on, seemed very sad; he sat with his eyes looking down to the ground, his hands folded together, and he sighed as if he would break his heart. Then said *Christian*, What means this? At which the *Interpreter* bid him talk with the man.

Then said *Christian* to the man, What art thou? The man answered, I am what I was not once.

CHR. What wast thou once?

MAN. The man said, I was once a fair and flourishing professor,[2] both in mine own eyes, and also in the eyes of others; I once was, as I thought, fair for the *Celestial City*, and had then even joy at the thoughts that I should get thither.

CHR. Well, but what art thou now?

MAN. I am now a man of despair, and am shut up in it, as in this iron cage. I cannot get out. Oh, now I cannot!

CHR. But how camest thou in this condition?

MAN. I left off to watch and be sober; I laid the reins upon the neck of my lusts; I sinned against the light of the Word and the goodness of God; I have grieved the Spirit, and he is gone; I tempted the devil, and he is come to me; I have provoked God to anger, and he has

[2] Professing Christian.

left me: I have so hardened my heart, that I cannot repent.

Then said *Christian* to the *Interpreter*, But is there no hopes for such a man as this? Ask him, said the *Interpreter*.

CHR. Then said *Christian*, Is there no hope, but you must be kept in the iron cage of despair?

MAN. No, none at all.

CHR. Why, the Son of the Blessed is very 10 pitiful.

MAN. I have crucified him to myself afresh; I have despised his person; I have despised his righteousness; I have counted his blood an unholy thing; I have done despite to the Spirit of grace. Therefore I have shut myself out of all the promises, and there now remains to me nothing but threatenings, dreadful threatenings, faithful threatenings, of certain judgment and fiery indignation, which shall devour me as 20 an adversary.

CHR. For what did you bring yourself into this condition?

MAN. For the lusts, pleasures, and profits of this world; in the enjoyment of which I did then promise myself much delight; but now every one of those things also bite me, and gnaw me like a burning worm.

CHR. But canst thou not now repent and turn?

MAN. God hath denied me repentance. His Word gives me no encouragement to believe; yea, himself hath shut me up in this iron cage; nor can all the men in the world let me out. O eternity, eternity! how shall I grapple with the misery that I must meet with in eternity!

INTER. Then said the *Interpreter* to *Christian*, Let this man's misery be remembered by thee, and be an everlasting caution to thee. 40

CHR. Well, said *Christian*, this is fearful! God help me to watch and be sober, and to pray that I may shun the cause of this man's misery! Sir, is it not time for me to go on my way now?

INTER. Tarry till I shall show thee one thing more, and then thou shalt go on thy way.

So he took *Christian* by the hand again, and led him into a chamber, where there was one rising out of bed; and as he put on his 50 raiment he shook and trembled. Then said *Christian*, Why doth this man thus tremble? The *Interpreter* then bid him tell to *Christian* the reason of his so doing. So he began and said, This night, as I was in my sleep, I dreamed, and behold the heavens grew exceed-

ing black; also it thundered and lightened in most fearful wise, that it put me into an agony; so I looked up in my dream, and saw the clouds rack at an unusual rate, upon which I heard a great sound of a trumpet, and saw also a man sit upon a cloud, attended with the thousands of heaven; they were all in flaming fire: also the heavens were in a burning flame. I heard then a voice saying, Arise, ye dead, and come to judgment; and with that the rocks rent, the graves opened, and the dead that were therein came forth. Some of them were exceeding glad, and looked upward; and some sought to hide themselves under the mountains. Then I saw the man that sat upon the cloud open the book, and bid the world draw near. Yet there was, by reason of a fierce flame that issued out and came before him, a convenient distance betwixt him and them, as betwixt the judge and the prisoners at the bar. I heard it also proclaimed to them that attended on the man that sat on the cloud, Gather together the tares, the chaff, and stubble, and cast them into the burning lake. And with that, the bottomless pit opened, just whereabout I stood; out of the mouth of which there came, in an abundant manner, smoke and coals of fire, with hideous noises. It was also said to the same persons, Gather my wheat into the garner. And with that I saw many catched up and carried away into the clouds, but I was left behind. I also sought to hide myself, but I could not, for the man that sat upon the cloud still kept his eye upon me; my sins also came into my mind; and my conscience did accuse me on every side. Upon this I awaked from my sleep.

CHR. But what is it that made you so afraid of this sight?

MAN. Why, I thought that the day of judgment was come, and that I was not ready for it: but this frighted me most, that the angels gathered up several, and left me behind; also the pit of hell opened her mouth just where I stood. My conscience, too, afflicted me; and, as I thought, the Judge had always his eye upon me, showing indignation in his countenance.

Then said the *Interpreter* to *Christian*, Hast thou considered all these things?

CHR. Yes, and they put me in hope and 50 fear.

INTER. Well, keep all things so in thy mind that they may be as a goad in thy sides, to prick thee forward in the way thou must go. Then *Christian* began to gird up his loins, and to address himself to his journey. Then said the *Interpreter*, The Comforter be always with thee, good *Christian,* to guide thee in the way that leads to the City.

So *Christian* went on his way, saying—

Here I have seen things rare and profitable;
Things pleasant, dreadful, things to make me stable
In what I have began to take in hand;
Then let me think on them and understand
Wherefore they showed me were, and let me be
Thankful, O good *Interpreter,* to thee.

Now I saw in my dream, that the highway 10 up which *Christian* was to go, was fenced on either side with a wall, and that wall was called *Salvation.* Up this way, therefore, did burdened *Christian* run, but not without great difficulty, because of the load on his back.

He ran thus till he came at a place somewhat ascending, and upon that place stood a cross, and a little below, in the bottom, a sepulcher. So I saw in my dream, that just as *Christian* came up with the cross, his burden 20 loosed from off his shoulders, and fell from off his back, and began to tumble, and so continued to do, till it came to the mouth of the sepulcher, where it fell in, and I saw it no more.

Then was *Christian* glad and lightsome, and said, with a merry heart, He hath given me rest by his sorrow, and life by his death. Then he stood still awhile to look and wonder; for it was very surprising to him, that the sight of the cross should thus ease him of his burden. 30 He looked therefore, and looked again, even till the springs that were in his head sent the waters down his cheeks. Now, as he stood looking and weeping, behold three Shining Ones came to him and saluted him with, Peace be unto thee. So the first said to him, Thy sins be forgiven thee; the second stripped him of his rags, and clothed him with change of raiment; the third also set a mark in his forehead, and gave him a roll with a seal upon 40 it, which he bade him look on as he ran, and that he should give it in at the *Celestial Gate.*

### III

So he went on, and *Apollyon* met him. Now the monster was hideous to behold; he was clothed with scales, like a fish (and they are his pride); he had wings like a dragon, feet like a bear, and out of his belly came fire and 50 smoke, and his mouth was as the mouth of a lion. When he was come up to *Christian,* he beheld him with a disdainful countenance, and thus began to question with him.

APOL. Whence come you? and whither are you bound?

CHR. I am come from the *City of Destruction,* which is the place of all evil, and am going to the *City of Zion.*

APOL. By this I perceive thou art one of my subjects, for all that country is mine, and I am the prince and god of it. How is it, then, that thou hast run away from thy king? Were it not that I hope thou mayest do me more service, I would strike thee now, at one blow, to the ground.

CHR. I was born, indeed, in your dominions, but your service was hard, and your wages such as a man could not live on, for the wages of sin is death; therefore, when I was come to years, I did, as other considerate persons do, look out, if, perhaps, I might mend myself.

APOL. There is no prince that will thus lightly lose his subjects, neither will I as yet lose thee; but since thou complainest of thy service and wages, be content to go back: what our country will afford, I do here promise to give thee.

CHR. But I have let myself to another, even to the King of princes; and how can I, with fairness, go back with thee?

APOL. Thou hast done in this, according to the proverb, "Change a bad for a worse"; but it is ordinary for those that have professed themselves his servants, after a while to give him the slip, and return again to me. Do thou so too, and all shall be well.

CHR. I have given him my faith, and sworn my allegiance to him; how, then, can I go back from this, and not be hanged as a traitor?

APOL. Thou didst the same by me, and yet I am willing to pass by all, if now thou wilt yet turn again and go back.

CHR. What I promised thee was in my nonage;[3] and, besides, I count that the Prince under whose banner now I stand is able to absolve me; yea, and to pardon also what I did as to my compliance with thee; and besides, O thou destroying *Apollyon!* to speak truth, I like his service, his wages, his servants, his government, his company, and country, better than thine; and, therefore, leave off to persuade me further; I am his servant, and I will follow him.

APOL. Consider, again, when thou art in cool blood, what thou art like to meet with in the way that thou goest. Thou knowest that, for the most part, his servants come to an ill end, because they are transgressors against me and my way. How many of them have been put to shameful death! and, besides, thou

---

[3] Immaturity.

countest his service better than mine, whereas he never came yet from the place where he is to deliver any that served him out of their hands; but as for me, how many times, as all the world very well knows, have I delivered, either by power, or fraud, those that have faithfully served me, from him and his, though taken by them; and so I will deliver thee.

CHR. His forbearing at present to deliver them is on purpose to try their love, whether 10 they will cleave to him to the end; and as for the ill end thou sayest they come to, that is most glorious in their account; for, for present deliverance, they do not much expect it, for they stay for their glory, and then they shall have it when their Prince comes in his and the glory of the angels.

APOL. Thou hast already been unfaithful in thy service to him; and how dost thou think to receive wages of him? 20

CHR. Wherein, O Apollyon! have I been unfaithful to him?

APOL. Thou didst faint at first setting out, when thou wast almost choked in the *Gulf of Despond*; thou didst attempt wrong ways to be rid of thy burden, whereas thou shouldst have stayed till thy Prince had taken it off; thou didst sinfully sleep and lose thy choice things; thou wast, also, almost persuaded to go back at the sight of the lions; and when 30 thou talkest of thy journey, and of what thou hast heard and seen, thou art inwardly desirous of vain-glory in all that thou sayest or doest.

CHR. All this is true, and much more which thou hast left out; but the Prince whom I serve and honor is merciful, and ready to forgive; but, besides, these infirmities possessed me in thy country, for there I sucked them in; and I have groaned under them, being sorry for them, and have obtained pardon of my Prince. 40

APOL. Then *Apollyon* broke out into a grievous rage, saying, I am an enemy to this Prince; I hate his person, his laws, and people; I am come out on purpose to withstand thee.

CHR. *Apollyon*, beware what you do; for I am in the King's highway, the way of holiness; therefore take heed to yourself.

APOL. Then *Apollyon* straddled quite over the whole breadth of the way, and said, I am void of fear in this matter: prepare thyself to 50 die; for I swear by my infernal den, that thou shalt go no further; here will I spill thy soul.

And with that he threw a flaming dart at his breast; but *Christian* had a shield in his hand, with which he caught it, and so prevented the danger of that.

Then did *Christian* draw, for he saw it was time to bestir him; and *Apollyon* as fast made at him, throwing darts as thick as hail; by the which, notwithstanding all that *Christian* could do to avoid it, *Apollyon* wounded him in his head, his hand, and foot. This made *Christian* give a little back; *Apollyon*, therefore, followed his work amain, and *Christian* again took courage, and resisted as manfully as he could. This sore combat lasted for above half a day, even till *Christian* was almost quite spent; for you must know that *Christian*, by reason of his wounds, must needs grow weaker and weaker.

Then *Apollyon*, espying his opportunity, began to gather up close to *Christian*, and wrestling with him, gave him a dreadful fall; and with that *Christian's* sword flew out of his hand. Then said *Apollyon*, I am sure of thee now. And with that he had almost pressed him 20 to death, so that *Christian* began to despair of life; but as God would have it, while *Apollyon* was fetching his last blow, thereby to make a full end of this good man, *Christian* nimbly stretched out his hand for his sword, and caught it, saying, Rejoice not against me, O mine enemy; when I fall I shall arise; and with that gave him a deadly thrust, which made him give back, as one that had received his mortal wound. *Christian* perceiving that, 30 made at him again, saying, Nay, in all these things we are more than conquerors through him that loved us. And with that *Apollyon* spread forth his dragon's wings, and sped him away, that *Christian* saw him no more.

In this combat no man can imagine, unless he had seen and heard as I did, what yelling and hideous roaring *Apollyon* made all the time of the fight—he spake like a dragon; and, on the other side, what sighs and groans burst 40 from *Christian's* heart. I never saw him all the while give so much as one pleasant look, till he perceived he had wounded *Apollyon* with his two-edged sword; then, indeed, he did smile, and look upward; but it was the dreadfulest sight that ever I saw.

So when the battle was over, *Christian* said, I will here give thanks to him that delivered me out of the mouth of the lion, to him that did help me against *Apollyon*. And so he did, saying—

Great Beelzebub, the captain of this fiend,
Designed my ruin; therefore to this end
He sent him harnessed out: and he with rage
That hellish was, did fiercely me engage.
But blessed Michael helpéd me, and I,
By dint of sword, did quickly make him fly.
Therefore to him let me give lasting praise,
And thanks, and bless his holy name always.

Then there came to him an hand, with some of the leaves of the tree of life, the which *Christian* took, and applied to the wounds that he had received in the battle, and was healed immediately. He also sat down in that place to eat bread, and to drink of the bottle that was given him a little before; so, being refreshed, he addressed himself to his journey, with his sword drawn in his hand; for he said, I know not but some other enemy may be at hand. But he met with no other affront from *Apollyon* quite through this valley.

Now, at the end of this valley was another, called the *Valley of the Shadow of Death*, and *Christian* must needs go through it, because the way to the *Celestial City* lay through the midst of it. Now, this valley is a very solitary place. The prophet Jeremiah thus describes it:—A wilderness, a land of deserts and of pits, a land of drought, and of the shadow of death, a land that no man (but a Christian) passeth through, and where no man dwelt.

Now here *Christian* was worse put to it than in his fight with *Apollyon*, as by the sequel you shall see.

I saw then in my dream, that when *Christian* was got on the borders of the *Shadow of Death*, there met him two men, children of them that brought up an evil report of the good land, making haste to go back; to whom *Christian* spake as follows:—

CHR. Whither are you going?

MEN. They said, Back! back! and we would have you do so too, if either life or peace is prized by you.

CHR. Why, what's the matter? said *Christian*.

MEN. Matter! said they; we were going that way as you are going, and went as far as we durst; and indeed we were almost past coming back; for had we gone a little further, we had not been here to bring the news to thee.

CHR. But what have you met with? said *Christian*.

MEN. Why, we were almost in the *Valley of the Shadow of Death*; but that, by good hap, we looked before us, and saw the danger before we came to it.

CHR. But what have you seen? said *Christian*.

MEN. Seen! Why, the Valley itself, which is as dark as pitch; we also saw there the hob-goblins, satyrs, and dragons of the pit; we heard also in that Valley a continual howling and yelling, as of a people under unutterable misery, who were sat down in affliction and irons; and over that Valley hangs the discour-aging clouds of confusion. Death also doth always spread his wings over it. In a word, it is every whit dreadful, being utterly without order.

CHR. Then, said *Christian*, I perceive not yet, by what you have said, but that this is my way to the desired heaven.

MEN. Be it thy way; we will not choose it for ours. So they parted, and *Christian* went on his way, but still with his sword drawn in his hand, for fear lest he should be assaulted.

I saw then in my dream, so far as this valley reached, there was on the right hand a very deep ditch; that ditch is it into which the blind hath led the blind in all ages, and have both there miserably perished. Again, behold, on the left hand, there was a very dangerous quag, into which, if even a good man falls, he finds no bottom for his foot to stand on. Into this quag King David once did fall, and had no doubt there been smothered, had not He that is able plucked him out.

The pathway was here also exceeding narrow, and therefore good *Christian* was the more put to it; for when he sought, in the dark, to shun the ditch on the one hand, he was ready to tip over into the mire on the other; also when he sought to escape the mire, without great carefulness he would be ready to fall into the ditch. Thus he went on, and I heard him here sigh bitterly; for, besides the danger mentioned above, the pathway was here so dark, that ofttimes, when he lift up his foot to go forward, he knew not where or upon what he should set it next.

About the midst of this valley, I perceived the mouth of hell to be, and it stood also hard by the way-side. Now, thought *Christian*, what shall I do? And ever and anon the flame and smoke would come out in such abundance, with sparks and hideous noises (things that cared not for *Christian's* sword, as did *Apollyon* before), that he was forced to put up his sword, and betake himself to another weapon called *all-prayer*. So he cried, in my hearing, O Lord, I beseech thee, deliver my soul! Thus he went on a great while, yet still the flames would be reaching towards him. Also he heard doleful voices, and rushings to and fro, so that sometimes he thought he should be torn in pieces, or trodden down like mire in the streets. This frightful sight was seen, and these dreadful noises were heard by him for several miles together; and, coming to a place where he thought he heard a company of fiends coming forward to meet him, he stopped, and began to muse what he had best to do. Sometimes he had half a thought to go back; then again he thought he might be half way through the valley; he remembered also how he had already vanquished many a danger, and that the danger of going back might be much more than for to go forward; so he resolved to go on. Yet the fiends seemed to come nearer and nearer; but when they were come even almost at him, he cried out with a most vehement voice, I will walk in the strength of the Lord God!—so 10 they gave back, and came no further.

One thing I would not let slip; I took notice that now poor *Christian* was so confounded, that he did not know his own voice; and thus I perceived it. Just when he was come over against the mouth of the burning pit, one of the wicked ones got behind him, and stepped up softly to him, and whisperingly suggested many grievous blasphemies to him, which he verily thought had proceeded from his own 20 mind. This put *Christian* more to it than anything that he met with before, even to think that he should now blaspheme him that he loved so much before; yet, if he could have helped it, he would not have done it; but he had not the discretion neither to stop his ears, nor to know from whence these blasphemies came.

When *Christian* had traveled in this disconsolate condition some considerable time, 30 he thought he heard the voice of a man, going before him, saying, Though I walk through the valley of the shadow of death, I will fear none ill, for thou art with me.

Then was he glad.

## IV

Then I saw in my dream, that when they [4] were got out the wilderness, they presently 40 saw a town before them, and the name of that town is *Vanity*; and at the town there is a fair kept, called *Vanity Fair:* it is kept all the year long; it beareth the name of *Vanity Fair*, because the town where it is kept is lighter than vanity; and also because all that is there sold, or that cometh thither, is vanity. As is the saying of the wise, all that cometh is vanity.

This fair is no new-erected business, but a thing of ancient standing; I will show you the 50 original of it.

Almost five thousand years agone, there were pilgrims walking to the *Celestial City*,

---

[4] Shortly after he had passed through the *Valley of the Shadow of Death*, *Christian* met *Faithful*, journeying likewise towards the *Celestial City*, and they went on together.

---

as these two honest persons are: and *Beelzebub, Apollyon*, and *Legion*, with their companions, perceiving by the path that the pilgrims made, that their way to the city lay through this town of *Vanity*, they contrived here to set up a fair; a fair wherein should be sold all sorts of vanity, and that it should last all the year long: therefore at this fair are all such merchandise sold, as houses, lands, trades, places, honors, preferments, titles, countries, kingdoms, lusts, pleasures, and delights of all sorts, as whores, bawds, wives, husbands, children, masters, servants, lives, blood, bodies, souls, silver, gold, pearls, precious stones, and what not.

And, moreover, at this fair there is at all times to be seen jugglings, cheats, games, plays, fools, apes, knaves, and rogues, and that of every kind.

Here are to be seen, too, and that for nothing, thefts, murders, adulteries, false swearers, and that of a blood-red color.

And, as in other fairs of less moment, there are several rows and streets, under their proper names, where such wares are vended; so here likewise you have the proper places, rows, streets (*viz.*, countries and kingdoms), where the wares of this fair are soonest to be found. Here is the *Britain Row*, the *French Row*, the *Italian Row*, the *Spanish Row*, the *German Row*, where several sorts of vanities are to be sold. But, as in other fairs, some one commodity is as the chief of all the fair, so the ware of *Rome* and her merchandise is greatly promoted in this fair; only our *English* nation, with some others, have taken a dislike thereat.

Now, as I said, the way to the *Celestial City* lies just through this town where this lusty fair is kept; and he that will go to the city, and yet not go through this town, must needs go out of the world. The Prince of princes himself, when here, went through this town to his own country, and that upon a fair day too; yea, and as I think, it was *Beelzebub*, the chief lord of this fair, that invited him to buy of his vanities; yea, would have made him lord of the fair, would he but have done him reverence as he went through the town. Yea, because he was such a person of honor, *Beelzebub* had him 50 from street to street, and showed him all the kingdoms of the world in a little time, that he might, if possible, allure that Blessed One to cheapen and buy some of his vanities; but he had no mind to the merchandise, and therefore left the town, without laying out so much as one farthing upon these vanities. This fair, therefore, is an ancient thing, of long standing, and a very great fair. Now these pilgrims, as I said, must needs go through this fair. Well, so they did: but, behold, even as they entered into the fair, all the people in the fair were moved, and the town itself as it were in a hubbub about them; and that for several reasons: for—

*First*, the Pilgrims were clothed with such kind of raiment as was diverse from the raiment of any that traded in that fair. The 10 people, therefore, of the fair, made a great gazing upon them: some said they were fools, some they were bedlams, and some they were outlandish men.

*Secondly*, And as they wondered at their apparel, so they did likewise at their speech; for few could understand what they said; they naturally spoke the language of Canaan, but they that kept the fair were the men of this world; so that, from one end of the fair to the 20 other, they seemed barbarians each to the other.

*Thirdly*, But that which did not a little amuse the merchandisers was, that these pilgrims set very light by all their wares; they cared not so much as to look upon them; and if they called upon them to buy, they would put their fingers in their ears, and cry, Turn away mine eyes from beholding vanity, and look upwards, signifying that their trade and 30 traffic was in heaven.

One chanced mockingly, beholding the carriages of the men, to say unto them, What will ye buy? But they, looking gravely upon him, said, We buy the truth. At that there was an occasion taken to despise the men the more; some mocking, some taunting, some speaking reproachfully, and some calling upon others to smite them. At last things came to an hubbub and great stir in the fair, insomuch that all 40 order was confounded. Now was word presently brought to the great one of the fair, who quickly came down, and deputed some of his most trusty friends to take these men into examination, about whom the fair was almost overturned. So the men were brought to examination; and they that sat upon them, asked them whence they came, whither they went, and what they did there, in such an unusual garb? The men told them that they were pil- 50 grims and strangers in the world, and that they were going to their own country, which was the heavenly *Jerusalem*, and that they had given no occasion to the the men of the town, nor yet to the merchandisers, thus to abuse them, and to let [5] them in their journey, except it was for

[5] Hinder.

that, when one asked them what they would buy, they said they would buy the truth. But they that were appointed to examine them did not believe them to be any other than bedlams and mad, or else such as came to put all things into a confusion in the fair. Therefore they took them and beat them, and besmeared them with dirt, and then put them into the cage, that they might be made a spectacle to all the men of the fair.

There, therefore, they lay for some time, and were made the objects of any man's sport, or malice, or revenge, the great one of the fair laughing still at all that befell them. But the men being patient, and not rendering railing for railing, but contrariwise, blessing, and giving good words for bad, and kindness for injuries done, some men in the fair that were more observing, and less prejudiced than the rest, began to check and blame the baser sort for their continual abuses done by them to the men; they, therefore, in angry manner, let fly at them again, counting them as bad as the men in the cage, and telling them that they seemed confederates, and should be made partakers of their misfortunes. The other replied that, for aught they could see, the men were quiet, and sober, and intended nobody any harm; and that there were many that traded in their fair that were more worthy to be put into the cage, yea, and pillory too, than were the men that they had abused. Thus, after divers words had passed on both sides, the men behaving themselves all the while very wisely and soberly before them, they fell to some blows among themselves, and did harm one to another. Then were these two poor men brought before their examiners again, and there charged as being guilty of the late hubbub that had been in the fair. So they beat them pitifully, and hanged irons upon them, and led them in chains up and down the fair, for an example and a terror to others, lest any should speak in their behalf, or join themselves unto them. But *Christian* and *Faithful* behaved themselves yet more wisely, and received the ignominy and shame that was cast upon them with so much meekness and patience, that it won to their side, though but few in comparison of the rest, several of the men in the fair. This put the other party yet into a greater rage, insomuch that they concluded the death of these two men. Wherefore they threatened, that neither the cage nor irons should serve their turn, but that they should die, for the abuse they had done, and for deluding the men of the fair.

Then were they remanded to the cage again, until further order should be taken with them. So they put them in, and made their feet fast in the stocks.

Here, therefore, they called again to mind what they had heard from their faithful friend *Evangelist*, and were the more confirmed in their way and sufferings by what he told them would happen to them. They also now comforted each other, that whose lot it was to suffer, even he should have the best on't; therefore each man secretly wished that he might have that preferment: but committing themselves to the all-wise dispose of Him that ruleth all things, with much content, they abode in the condition in which they were, until they should be otherwise disposed of.

Then a convenient time being appointed, they brought them forth to their trial, in order to their condemnation. When the time was come, they were brought before their enemies and arraigned. The judge's name was Lord *Hate-good*. Their indictment was one and the same in substance, though somewhat varying in form, the contents whereof was this:—

That they were enemies to and disturbers of their trade; that they had made commotions and divisions in the town, and had won a party to their own most dangerous opinions, in contempt of the law of their prince.

Then *Faithful* began to answer, that he had only set himself against that which hath set itself against Him that is higher than the highest. And, said he, as for disturbance, I make none, being myself a man of peace; the parties that were won to us, were won by beholding our truth and innocence, and they are only turned from the worse to the better. And as to the king you talk of, since he is *Beelzebub*, the enemy of our Lord, I defy him and all his angels.

Then proclamation was made, that they that had aught to say for their lord the king against the prisoner at the bar, should forthwith appear and give in their evidence. So there came in three witnesses, to wit, *Envy*, *Superstition*, and *Pickthank*.[6] They were then asked, if they knew the prisoner at the bar; and what they had to say for their lord the king against him.

Then stood forth *Envy*, and said to this effect: My Lord, I have known this man a long time, and will attest upon my oath before this honorable bench that he is—

JUDGE. Hold! Give him his oath. So they sware him. Then he said—

⁶ Flatterer.

ENVY. My Lord, this man, notwithstanding his plausible name, is one of the vilest men in our country. He neither regardeth prince nor people, law nor custom; but doth all that he can to possess all men with certain of his disloyal notions, which he in the general calls principles of faith and holiness. And, in particular, I heard him once myself affirm that Christianity and the customs of our town of *Vanity* were diametrically opposite, and could not be reconciled. By which saying, my Lord, he doth at once not only condemn all our laudable doings, but us in the doing of them.

JUDGE. Then did the Judge say unto him, Hast thou any more to say?

ENVY. My Lord, I could say much more, only I would not be tedious to the court. Yet, if need be, when the other gentlemen have given in their evidence, rather than anything shall be wanting that will dispatch him, I will enlarge my testimony against him. So he was bid to stand by.

Then they called *Superstition*, and bid him look upon the prisoner. They also asked, what he could say for their lord the king against him. Then they sware him; so he began.

SUPER. My Lord, I have no great acquaintance with this man, nor do I desire to have farther knowledge of him; however, this I know, that he is a very pestilent fellow, from some discourse that, the other day, I had with him in this town; for then, talking with him, I heard him say, that our religion was nought, and such by which a man could by no means please God. Which saying of his, my Lord, your Lordship very well knows, what necessarily thence will follow, to wit, that we still do worship in vain, are yet in our sins, and finally shall be damned; and this is that which I have to say.

Then was *Pickthank* sworn, and bid say what he knew, in behalf of their lord the king, against the prisoner at the bar.

PICK. My Lord, and you gentlemen all, This fellow I have known of a long time, and have heard him speak things that ought not to be spoke; for he hath railed on our noble prince *Beelzebub*, and hath spoken contemptible of his honorable friends, whose names are the Lord *Old Man*, the Lord *Carnal Delight*, the Lord *Luxurious*, the Lord *Desire of Vain Glory*, my old Lord *Lechery*, Sir *Having Greedy*, with all the rest of our nobility; and he hath said, moreover, That if all men were of his mind, if possible, there is not one of these noblemen should have any longer a being in this town. Besides, he hath not been afraid to rail on you, my Lord, who are now appointed to be his judge, calling you an ungodly villain, with many other such like villifying terms, with which he hath bespattered most of the gentry of our town.

When this *Pickthank* had told his tale, the Judge directed his speech to the prisoner at the bar, saying, Thou runagate, heretic, and traitor, hast thou heard what these honest gentlemen have witnessed against thee?

FAITH. May I speak a few words in my own defense?

JUDGE. Sirrah! sirrah! thou deservest to live no longer, but to be slain immediately upon the place; yet, that all men may see our gentleness towards thee, let us hear what thou, vile runagate, hast to say.

FAITH. 1. I say, then, in answer to what Mr. *Envy* hath spoken, I never said aught but this, That what rule, or laws, or custom, or people, were flat against the Word of God, are diametrically opposite to Christianity. If I have said amiss in this, convince me of my error, and I am ready here before you to make my recantation.

2. As to the second, to wit, Mr. *Superstition*, and his charge against me, I said only this, That in the worship of God there is required a Divine faith; but there can be no Divine faith without a Divine revelation of the will of God. Therefore, whatever is thrust into the worship of God that is not agreeable to Divine revelation, cannot be done but by a human faith, which faith will not be profitable to eternal life.

3. As to what Mr. *Pickthank* hath said, I say (avoiding terms, as that I am said to rail, and the like) that the prince of this town, with all the rabblement, his attendants, by this gentleman named, are more fit for being in hell, than in this town and country: and so, the Lord have mercy upon me!

Then the Judge called to the jury (who all this while stood by, to hear and observe): Gentlemen of the jury, you see this man about whom so great an uproar hath been made in this town. You have also heard what these worthy gentlemen have witnessed against him. Also you have heard his reply and confession. It lieth now in your breast to hang him or save his life; but yet I think meet to instruct you in our law.

There was an Act made in the days of Pharaoh the Great, servant to our prince, that lest those of a contrary religion should multiply and grow too strong for him, their males should be thrown into the river. There was an Act also made in the days of Nebuchadnezzar the Great, another of his servants, that whoever would not fall down and worship his golden image, should be thrown into a fiery furnace. There was also an Act made in the days of Darius, that whoso, for some time, called upon any god but him, should be cast into the lions' den. Now the substance of these laws this rebel has broken, not only in thought (which is not to be borne), but also in word and deed, which must therefore needs be intolerable.

For that of Pharaoh, his law was made upon supposition, to prevent mischief, no crime yet being apparent; but here is a crime apparent. For the second and third, you see he disputeth against our religion; and for the treason he hath confessed, he deserveth to die the death.

Then went the jury out, whose names were, Mr. *Blind-man*, Mr. *No-good*, Mr. *Malice*, Mr. *Love-lust*, Mr. *Live-loose*, Mr. *Heady*, Mr. *High-mind*,[7] Mr. *Enmity*, Mr. *Liar*, Mr. *Cruelty*, Mr. *Hate-light*, and Mr. *Implacable*; who every one gave in his private verdict against him among themselves, and afterwards unanimously concluded to bring him in guilty before the Judge. And first, among themselves, Mr. *Blind-man*, the foreman, said, I see clearly that this man is a heretic. Then said Mr. *No-good*, Away with such a fellow from the earth. Ay, said Mr. *Malice*, for I hate the very looks of him. Then said Mr. *Love-lust*, I could never endure him. Nor I, said Mr. *Live-loose*, for he would always be condemning my way. Hang him, hang him, said Mr. *Heady*. A sorry scrub, said Mr. *High-mind*. My heart riseth against him, said Mr. *Enmity*. He is a rogue, said Mr. *Liar*. Hanging is too good for him, said Mr. *Cruelty*. Let's dispatch him out of the way, said Mr. *Hate-light*. Then said Mr. *Implacable*, Might I have all the world given me, I could not be reconciled to him; therefore, let us forthwith bring him in guilty of death. And so they did; therefore he was presently condemned to be had from the place where he was, to the place from whence he came, and there to be put to the most cruel death that could be invented.

They, therefore, brought him out, to do with him according to their law; and, first, they scourged him, then they buffeted him, then they lanced his flesh with knives; after that, they stoned him with stones, then pricked him with their swords; and, last of all, they

[7] Arrogance.

burned him to ashes at the stake. Thus came *Faithful* to his end.

Now I saw that there stood behind the multitude a chariot and a couple of horses, waiting for *Faithful*, who (so soon as his adversaries had dispatched him) was taken up into it, and straightway was carried up through the clouds, with sound of trumpet, the nearest way to the *Celestial Gate*.

But as for *Christian*, he had some respite, and was remanded back to prison. So he there remained for a space; but He that overrules all things, having the power of their rage in his own hand, so wrought it about, that *Christian* for that time escaped them, and went his way.

### V

Now there was, not far from the place where they[8] lay, a castle called *Doubting Castle*, the owner whereof was *Giant Despair*; and it was in his grounds they were now sleeping: wherefore he, getting up in the morning early, and walking up and down in his fields, caught *Christian* and *Hopeful* asleep in his grounds. Then, with a grim and surly voice, he bid them awake; and asked them whence they were, and what they did in his grounds. They told him they were pilgrims, and that they had lost their way. Then said the Giant, You have this night trespassed on me, by trampling in and lying on my ground, and therefore you must go along with me. So they were forced to go, because he was stronger than they. They also had but little to say, for they knew themselves in a fault. The Giant, therefore, drove them before him, and put them into his castle, into a very dark dungeon, nasty and stinking to the spirits of these two men. Here, then, they lay from Wednesday morning till Saturday night, without one bit of bread, or drop of drink, or light, or any to ask how they did; they were, therefore, here in evil case, and were far from friends and acquaintance. Now in this place *Christian* had double sorrow, because 'twas through his unadvised counsel that they were brought into this distress.

Now, *Giant Despair* had a wife, and her name was *Diffidence*. So when he was gone to bed, he told his wife what he had done; to wit, that he had taken a couple of prisoners and cast them into his dungeon, for trespassing on his grounds. Then he asked her also what he had best to do further to them. So she asked what they were, whence they came, and whither they were bound; and he told her. Then she counseled him that when he arose in the morning he should beat them without mercy. So, when he arose, he getteth him a grievous crab-tree cudgel, and goes down into the dungeon to them, and there first falls to rating of them as if they were dogs, although they gave him never a word of distaste. Then he falls upon them, and beats them fearfully, in such sort that they were not able to help themselves, or to turn them upon the floor. This done, he withdraws and leaves them, there to condole their misery and to mourn under their distress. So all that day they spent the time in nothing but sighs and bitter lamentations. The next night, she, talking with her husband about them further, and understanding that they were yet alive, did advise him to counsel them to make away themselves. So when morning was come, he goes to them in a surly manner as before, and perceiving them to be very sore with the stripes that he had given them the day before, he told them, that since they were never like to come out of that place, their only way would be forthwith to make an end of themselves, either with knife, halter, or poison, for why, said he, should you choose life, seeing it is attended with so much bitterness? But they desired him to let them go. With that he looked ugly upon them, and, rushing to them, had doubtless made an end of them himself, but that he fell into one of his fits (for he sometimes, in sunshiny weather, fell into fits), and lost for a time the use of his hand; wherefore he withdrew, and left them as before, to consider what to do. Then did the prisoners consult between themselves whether 'twas best to take his counsel or no; and thus they began to discourse:—

CHR. Brother, said *Christian*, what shall we do? The life that we now live is miserable. For my part I know not whether is best, to live thus, or to die out of hand. My soul chooseth strangling rather than life, and the grave is more easy for me than this dungeon. Shall we be ruled by the Giant?

HOPE. Indeed, our present condition is

[8] At his escape from *Vanity Fair*, "*Christian* went not forth alone, for there was one whose name was *Hopeful* (being so made by the beholding of *Christian* and *Faithful* in their words and behavior, in their sufferings at the *Fair*), who joined himself unto him."

dreadful, and death would be far more welcome to me than thus for ever to abide; but yet, let us consider, the Lord of the country to which we are going hath said, Thou shalt do no murder: no, not to another man's person; much more, then, are we forbidden to take his counsel to kill ourselves. Besides, he that kills another, can but commit murder upon his body; but for one to kill himself is to kill body and soul at once. And, moreover, my brother, thou talkest of ease in the grave; but hast thou forgotten the hell, whither for certain the murderers go? For no murderer hath eternal life, *etc*. And let us consider, again, that all the law is not in the hand of *Giant Despair*. Others, so far as I can understand, have been taken by him, as well as we; and yet have escaped out of his hand. Who knows, but that God that made the world may cause that *Giant Despair* may die? or that, at some time or other, he may forget to lock us in? or but he may, in a short time, have another of his fits before us, and may lose the use of his limbs? and if ever that should come to pass again, for my part, I am resolved to pluck up the heart of a man, and to try my utmost to get from under his hand. I was a fool that I did not try to do it before; but, however, my brother, let us be patient, and endure a while. The time may come that may give us a happy release; but let us not be our own murderers. With these words *Hopeful* at present did moderate the mind of his brother; so they continued together (in the dark) that day, in their sad and doleful condition.

Well, towards evening, the Giant goes down into the dungeon again, to see if his prisoners had taken his counsel; but when he came there he found them alive; and truly, alive was all; for now, what for want of bread and water, and by reason of the wounds they received when he beat them, they could do little but breathe. But, I say, he found them alive; at which he fell into a grievous rage, and told them that, seeing they had disobeyed his counsel, it should be worse with them than if they had never been born.

At this they trembled greatly, and I think that *Christian* fell into a swoon; but, coming a little to himself again, they renewed their discourse about the Giant's counsel; and whether yet they had best take it or no. Now *Christian* again seemed to be for doing it, but *Hopeful* made his second reply as followeth:—

HOPE. My brother, said he, rememberest thou not how valiant thou hast been heretofore? *Apollyon* could not crush thee, nor could all that thou didst hear, or see, or feel, in the *Valley of the Shadow of Death*. What hardship, terror, and amazement hast thou already gone through! And art thou now nothing but fears? Thou seest that I am in the dungeon with thee, a far weaker man by nature than thou art; also, this Giant has wounded me as well as thee, and hath also cut off the bread and water from my mouth; and with that I mourn without the light. But let's exercise a little more patience; remember how thou playedest the man at *Vanity Fair*, and wast neither afraid of the chain or cage, nor yet of bloody death. Wherefore let us (at least to avoid the shame, that becomes not a Christian to be found in) bear up with patience as well as we can.

Now, night being come again, and the Giant and his wife being in bed, she asked him concerning the prisoners, and if they had taken his counsel. To which he replied, They are sturdy rogues, they choose rather to bear all hardship, than to make away themselves. Then she said, Take them into the castle-yard to-morrow, and show them the bones and skulls of those that thou hast already dispatched, and make them believe, ere a week comes to an end, thou also wilt tear them in pieces, as thou hast done their fellows before them.

So when the morning was come, the Giant goes to them again, and takes them into the castle-yard, and shows them, as his wife had bidden him. These, said he, were pilgrims as you are, once, and they trespassed in my grounds, as you have done; and when I thought fit, I tore them in pieces, and so, within ten days, I will do you. Get you down into your den again; and with that he beat them all the way thither. They lay, therefore, all day on Saturday in a lamentable case, as before. Now, when night was come, and when Mrs. *Diffidence* and her husband, the Giant, were got to bed, they began to renew their discourse of their prisoners; and withal the old Giant wondered, that he could neither by his blows nor his counsel bring them to an end. And with that his wife replied, I fear, said she, that they live in hopes that some will come to relieve them, or that they have picklocks about them, by the means of which they hope to escape. And sayest thou so, my dear? said the Giant; I will, therefore, search them in the morning.

Well, on Saturday, about midnight, they

began to pray, and continued in prayer till almost break of day.

Now, a little before it was day, good *Christian*, as one half amazed, brake out in this passionate speech:—What a fool, quoth he, am I, thus to lie in a stinking dungeon, when I may as well walk at liberty! I have a key in my bosom, called *Promise*, that will, I am persuaded, open any lock in *Doubting Castle*. Then said *Hopeful*, That's good news, good brother; pluck it out of thy bosom, and try.

Then *Christian* pulled it out of his bosom, and began to try at the dungeon door, whose bolt (as he turned the key) gave back, and the door flew open with ease, and *Christian* and *Hopeful* both came out. Then he went to the outward door that leads into the castle-yard, and, with his key, opened that door also. After, he went to the iron gate, for that must be opened too; but that lock went damnable hard, yet the key did open it. Then they thrust open the gate to make their escape with speed, but that gate, as it opened, made such a cracking, that it waked *Giant Despair*, who, hastily rising to pursue his prisoners, felt his limbs to fail, for his fits took him again, so that he could by no means go after them. Then they went on, and came to the King's highway, and so were safe, because they were out of his jurisdiction.

## VI

They went then till they came to the *Delectable Mountains*, which mountains belong to the Lord of that hill of which we have spoken before; so they went up to the mountains, to behold the gardens and orchards, the vineyards and fountains of water; where also they drank and washed themselves, and did freely eat of the vineyards. Now there were on the tops of these mountains Shepherds feeding their flocks, and they stood by the highway side. The Pilgrims therefore went to them, and leaning upon their staves (as is common with weary pilgrims when they stand to talk with any by the way), they asked, Whose *Delectable Mountains* are these? And whose be the sheep that feed upon them?

SHEP. These mountains are *Immanuel's Land*, and they are within sight of His city; and the sheep also are His, and He laid down His life for them.

CHR. Is this the way to the *Celestial City*?

SHEP. You are just in your way.

CHR. How far is it thither?

SHEP. Too far for any but those that shall get thither indeed.

CHR. Is the way safe or dangerous?

SHEP. Safe for those for whom it is to be safe; but transgressors shall fall therein.

# John Dryden

## 1631 - 1700

Dryden was born on 9 August, 1631, at Ald-winkle, a Northamptonshire village. His parents belonged to good families which had been conspicuous for their Puritanism. Dryden was sent to Westminster School, in London, and in 1650 entered Trinity College, Cambridge. Like Milton, Dryden did not escape trouble with his college authorities. He took his B. A. in 1654. His first notable poem was Heroic Stanzas consecrated to the Memory of his Highness Oliver Cromwell, written in 1658. It is significant of much in Dryden's life and character that two years later, in Astraea Redux, he was among the first to celebrate the return of Charles II. If he changed, Dr. Johnson said, he changed with the nation; but it is also true that Dryden as a working man of letters was dependent for his livelihood upon the favor of the great. This was an influence constantly determining what he should write, and how he should write, and it was undeniably harmful to him as a poet.

Dryden was dramatist as well as poet, but here too his need drove him into close dependence on the taste of his day. The serious plays of the Restoration were heroic tragedies, sensational in plot, sentimental in conception, and more or less classical in form. The more notable of Dryden's heroic plays are The Indian Emperor (1665), Tyrannic Love (1669), The Conquest of Granada (in two parts, 1670–1672), and Aurengzebe (1675). All of these were written in rimed couplets, a practice which Dryden defended in his Essay of Dramatic Poesy (1668). In All for Love (1678), however, Dryden returned to blank verse. Some of his comedies are The Rival Ladies (1664), Sir Martin Mar-All (1667), Marriage à la Mode (1672), and The Spanish Friar (1681).

In 1670 Dryden attained office, being made historiographer-royal and poet laureate, and some years later he was made collector of customs for the port of London, posts which to some extent relieved his financial burdens until the Revolution of 1688, when he lost all his offices and was again reduced to the necessity of earning his living by his pen. The satires for which Dryden is best known as a poet were written in 1681 and 1682—Absalom and Achitophel, Mac Flecknoe, and The Medal. In 1682 he also published his defense of the Church of England, Religio Laici. In 1686 he became a Roman Catholic, and in the following year published a defense of his new faith in the form of a beast-fable, The Hind and the Panther. The latter part of the seventeenth century was little favorable to lyric poetry, nor did Dryden attempt to write much in that kind, though his ode, Alexander's Feast, written in 1697, is a brilliant performance. One can hardly escape astonishment at the range of Dryden's power, successfully exerted despite the handicaps of his circumstances and character. In panegyric and satire, in comedy and heroic play and tragedy, in criticism and translation—in all these he excelled; and as England's greatest and most fully representative man of letters in the latter years of the seventeenth century he amply deserved the dictatorship of literature which he attained in his old age.

The poems have been newly edited by James Kinsley: The Poems of John Dryden (Oxford, 1958). Another edition, partially completed, is Works of John Dryden, edited by E. N. Hooker and H. T. Swedenberg, Jr. (Berkeley, 1956–     ). The literary side of Dryden has been well treated by Mark Van Doren in Dryden: a Study of His Poetry (New York, 1946), by T. S. Eliot in John Dryden, the Poet, the Dramatist, the Critic (New York, 1932), and by D. Nichol Smith in Dryden (Cambridge, 1950). In his Intellectual Milieu of John Dryden (Ann Arbor, 1956) Louis I. Bredvold has placed the emphasis on the skeptical and conservative side of Dryden's creed. For a short but provocative study see Bonamy Dobrée, "Milton and Dryden: A Comparison and Contrast in Poetic Ideas and Poetic Method," Journal of English Literary History, III (1936), 83–100.

# Mac Flecknoe

*or,*

## A Satire upon the True-Blue-Protestant Poet T. S.[1]

(1682)

All human things are subject to decay,
And when fate summons, monarchs must obey.
This Flecknoe[2] found, who, like Augustus, young
Was called to empire, and had governed long;
In prose and verse was owned, without dispute,                5
Through all the realms of Nonsense absolute.
This aged prince, now flourishing in peace,
And bless'd with issue of a large increase;
Worn out with business, did at length debate
To settle the succession of the State;          10
And, pond'ring which of all his sons was fit
To reign, and wage immortal war with wit,
Cried: " 'T is resolved; for nature pleads, that he
Should rule, who most resembles me.
Sh—— alone my perfect image bears,          15
Mature in dullness from his tender years:
Sh—— alone, of all my sons, is he
Who stands confirmed in full stupidity.
The rest to some faint meaning make pretense,
But Sh—— never deviates into sense.          20
Some beams of wit on other souls may fall,
Strike through, and make a lucid interval;
But Sh——'s genuine night admits no ray,
His rising fogs prevail upon the day.
Besides, his goodly fabric fills the eye,          25
And seems designed for thoughtless majesty;
Thoughtless as monarch oaks that shade the plain,
And, spread in solemn state, supinely reign.
Heywood and Shirley[3] were but types of thee,
Thou last great prophet of tautology.          30
Even I, a dunce of more renown than they,
Was sent before but to prepare thy way;
And, coarsely clad in Norwich drugget, came
To teach the nations in thy greater name.
My warbling lute, the lute I whilom strung,          35

[1] Dryden published *The Medal* in the spring of 1682. One of the answers to it was *The Medal of John Bayes*, by Thomas Shadwell. Dryden and Shadwell had once been friends, but Shadwell was a strong Whig, the two were now enemies, and Shadwell's poem was savagely abusive. *Mac Flecknoe* was Dryden's reply.

[2] Flecknoe died in 1678. He was a Roman Catholic priest before the restoration of Charles II. At one time he was entertained at Lisbon by King John of Portugal.

[3] Thomas Heywood and James Shirley, both dramatists of the early seventeenth century.

When to King John of Portugal I sung,
Was but the prelude to that glorious day,
When thou on silver Thames didst cut thy way,
With well-timed oars before the royal barge,
Swelled with the pride of thy celestial charge;
And big with hymn, commander of a host,          41
The like was ne'er in Epsom blankets tossed.[4]
Methinks I see the new Arion[5] sail,
The lute still trembling underneath thy nail.
At thy well-sharpened thumb from shore to shore          45
The treble squeaks for fear, the basses roar;
Echoes from Pissing Alley Sh—— call,
And Sh—— they resound from Aston Hall.
About thy boat the little fishes throng,
As at the morning toast that floats along.          50
Sometimes, as prince of thy harmonious band,
Thou wield'st thy papers in thy threshing hand.
St. André's[6] feet ne'er kept more equal time,
Not e'en the feet of thy own *Psyche's*[7] rime;
Though they in number as in sense excel:          55
So just, so like tautology, they fell,
That, pale with envy, Singleton[8] forswore
The lute and sword, which he in triumph bore,
And vow'd he ne'er would act Villerius[9] more."
Here stopped the good old sire, and wept for joy          60
In silent raptures of the hopeful boy.
All arguments, but most his plays, persuade,
That for anointed dullness he was made.
    Close to the walls which fair Augusta[10] bind
(The fair Augusta much to fears inclined),          65
An ancient fabric raised t' inform the sight,
There stood of yore, and Barbican it hight:
A watchtower once; but now, so fate ordains,
Of all the pile an empty name remains.
From its old ruins brothel-houses rise,          70
Scenes of lewd loves, and of polluted joys,
Where their vast courts the mother-strumpets keep,
And, undisturbed by watch, in silence sleep.
Near these a Nursery[11] erects its head,
Where queens are formed, and future heroes bred;          75
Where unfledged actors learn to laugh and cry,
Where infant punks their tender voices try,
And little Maximins[12] the gods defy.

[4] A play of Shadwell's was entitled *Epsom Wells;* tossing in a blanket is also the punishment given a character in Shadwell's *The Virtuoso.*
[5] A Greek musician of the eighth century B.C. Shadwell was a musician as well as a poet.
[6] A French dancing-master.
[7] An opera in rime by Shadwell.
[8] A singer of the day.
[9] A character in Davenant's *Siege of Rhodes.*
[10] London, at the time fearful of the King and Roman Catholicism.
[11] A theater for the training of young actors.
[12] The name of the chief character in Dryden's *Tyrannic Love.*

Great Fletcher never treads in buskins here,
Nor greater Jonson dares in socks appear;  80
But gentle Simkin [13] just reception finds
Amidst this monument of vanished minds:
Pure clinches [14] the suburbian Muse affords,
And Panton waging harmless war with words.
Here Flecknoe, as a place to fame well known,
Ambitiously designed his Sh——'s throne;  86
For ancient Dekker [15] prophesied long since,
That in this pile should reign a mighty
    prince,
Born for a scourge of wit, and flail of
    sense;
To whom true dullness should some *Psyches*
    owe,  90
But worlds of *Misers* from his pen should
    flow;
*Humorists* and hypocrites it should produce,
Whole Raymond families, and tribes of
    Bruce.[16]
    Now Empress Fame had published the re-
    nown
Of Sh——'s coronation through the town.  95
Roused by report of Fame, the nations meet,
From near Bunhill, and distant Watling Street.
No Persian carpets spread th' imperial way,
But scattered limbs of mangled poets lay;
From dusty shops neglected authors come,  100

Martyrs of pies, and relics of the bum.
Much Heywood, Shirley, Ogleby [17] there lay,
But loads of Sh—— almost choked the way.
Bilked stationers for yeomen stood prepared,
And Herringman [18] was captain of the guard.
The hoary prince in majesty appeared,  106
High on a throne of his own labors reared.
At his right hand our young Ascanius sate,
Rome's other hope, and pillar of the State.
His brows thick fogs, instead of glories, grace,
And lambent dullness played around his face.
As Hannibal did to the altars come,  112
Sworn by his sire a mortal foe to Rome;
So Sh—— swore, nor should his vow be vain,
That he till death true dullness would maintain;
And, in his father's right, and realm's defense,
Ne'er to have peace with wit, nor truce with
    sense.  117
The king himself the sacred unction made,
As king by office, and as priest by trade.
In his sinister hand, instead of ball,  120
He placed a mighty mug of potent ale;
*Love's Kingdom* [19] to his right he did convey,

[13] A clown.
[14] Puns. Panton is said to have been a celebrated punster.
[15] Thomas Dekker, the dramatist of the early seventeenth century, author of *The Shoemakers' Holiday.*
[16] *The Miser* and *The Humorists* are plays by Shadwell. Raymond is a character in the latter, Bruce a character in Shadwell's *The Virtuoso.*
[17] Ogleby had been a dancing-master and had afterwards translated Homer, Virgil, and Aesop, besides writing other poems.
[18] A London publisher.  [19] A play by Flecknoe.

At once his scepter, and his rule of sway;
Whose righteous lore the prince had practiced
    young,
And from whose loins recorded *Psyche* sprung.
His temples, last, with poppies were o'er-
    spread,  126
That nodding seemed to consecrate his head.
Just at that point of time, if fame not lie,
On his left hand twelve reverend owls did fly.
So Romulus, 't is sung, by Tiber's brook,  130
Presage of sway from twice six vultures took.
Th' admiring throng loud acclamations make,
And omens of his future empire take.
The sire then shook the honors of his head,
And from his brows damps of oblivion shed [135]
Full on the filial dullness: long he stood,
Repelling from his breast the raging god;
At length burst out in this prophetic mood:
    "Heavens bless my son, from Ireland let him
    reign
To far Barbadoes on the western main;  140
Of his dominion may no end be known,
And greater than his father's be his throne;
Beyond *Love's Kingdom* let him stretch his
    pen!"
He paused, and all the people cried, "Amen."
Then thus continued he: "My son, advance [145]
Still in new impudence, new ignorance.
Success let others teach, learn thou from me
Pangs without birth, and fruitless industry.
Let *Virtuosos* in five years be writ;
Yet not one thought accuse thy toil of wit. [150]
Let gentle George [20] in triumph tread the stage,
Make Dorimant betray, and Loveit rage;
Let Cully, Cockwood, Fopling, charm the pit,
And in their folly show the writer's wit.
Yet still thy fools shall stand in thy defense, [155]
And justify their author's want of sense.
Let 'em be all by thy own model made
Of dullness, and desire no foreign aid;
That they to future ages may be known,
Not copies drawn, but issue of thy own.  160
Nay, let thy men of wit too be the same,
All full of thee, and differing but in name.
But let no alien S—dl—y [21] interpose,
To lard with wit thy hungry *Epsom* prose.
And when false flowers of rhetoric thou wouldst
    cull,  165
Trust nature, do not labor to be dull;
But write thy best, and top; and, in each line,
Sir Formal's [22] oratory will be thine:
Sir Formal, though unsought, attends thy quill,
And does thy northern dedications [23] fill. [170]

[20] Sir George Etherege. The names in the two following lines are those of characters in Etherege's plays.
[21] Sir Charles Sedley, who had written the prologue for Shadwell's *Epsom Wells*, and who probably, as Dryden suggests, gave Shadwell other assistance.
[22] Sir Formal Trifle is a character in Shadwell's *Virtuoso.*
[23] An allusion to Shadwell's dedication of various books to the Duke of Newcastle and members of his family.

Nor let false friends seduce thy mind to fame,
By arrogating Jonson's hostile name.[24]
Let father Flecknoe fire thy mind with praise,
And uncle Ogleby thy envy raise.
Thou art my blood, where Jonson has no
    part:
What share have we in nature, or in art? [176]
Where did his wit on learning fix a brand,
And rail at arts he did not understand?
Where made he love in Prince Nicander's [25]
    vein,
Or swept the dust in *Psyche's* humble strain?
Where sold he bargains, 'whip-stitch, kiss my
    arse,' [26]              181
Promised a play and dwindled to a farce?
When did his Muse from Fletcher scenes
    purloin,
As thou whole Eth'rege dost transfuse to thine?
But so transfused as oil in water's flow,   185
His always floats above, thine sinks below.
This is thy province, this thy wondrous way,
New humors to invent for each new play:
This is that boasted bias of thy mind,
By which one way, to dullness, 't is inclined; [190]
Which makes thy writings lean on one side
    still,
And, in all changes, that way bends thy will.
Nor let thy mountain-belly make pretense
Of likeness; thine's a tympany of sense.
A tun of man in thy large bulk is writ,   195
But sure thou 'rt but a kilderkin [27] of wit.
Like mine, thy gentle numbers freely creep;
Thy tragic Muse gives smiles, thy comic sleep.
With whate'er gall thou sett'st thyself to write,
Thy inoffensive satires never bite.   200
In thy felonious heart though venom lies,
It does but touch thy Irish pen, and dies.
Thy genius calls thee not to purchase fame
In keen iambics, but mild anagram.
Leave writing plays, and choose for thy com-
    mand   205
Some peaceful province in acrostic land.
There thou may'st wings display the altars raise,
And torture one poor word ten thousand ways.
Or, if thou wouldst thy diff'rent talents suit,
Set thy own songs, and sing them to thy lute."
He said: but his last words were scarcely
    heard;   211
For Bruce and Longvil had a trap pre-
    pared,[28]
And down they sent the yet declaiming bard.
Sinking he left his drugget robe behind,
Borne upwards by a subterranean wind.   215
The mantle fell to the young prophet's part,
With double portion of his father's art.

---

[24] Shadwell frequently eulogized Jonson and professed to imitate him.
[25] A character in Shadwell's *Psyche.*
[26] Such phrases are used by Sir Samuel Hearty in
Shadwell's *Virtuoso.*
[27] The fourth part of a tun.
[28] These characters thus make Sir Formal Trifle
disappear in Shadwell's *Virtuoso.*

# A Song for St. Cecilia's Day [1]

## (1687)

### I

From harmony, from heav'nly harmony
    This universal frame began:
      When Nature underneath a heap
        Of jarring atoms lay,
      And could not heave her head,   5
The tuneful voice was heard from high:
    "Arise, ye more than dead."
Then cold, and hot, and moist, and dry,
In order to their stations leap,
    And Music's pow'r obey.   10
From harmony, from heav'nly harmony
    This universal frame began:
    From harmony to harmony
Through all the compass of the notes it ran,
The diapason closing full in Man.   15

### II

What passion cannot Music raise and quell!
    When Jubal [2] struck the corded shell,
    His list'ning brethren stood around,
    And, wond'ring, on their faces fell
    To worship that celestial sound.   20
Less than a god they thought there could not
    dwell
    Within the hollow of that shell
    That spoke so sweetly and so well.
What passion cannot Music raise and quell!

### III

The Trumpet's loud clangor   25
    Excites us to arms,
With shrill notes of anger,
    And mortal alarms.
The double double double beat
    Of the thund'ring Drum   30
Cries: "Hark! the foes come;
Charge, charge, 't is too late to retreat."

### IV

The soft complaining Flute
In dying notes discovers
The woes of hopeless lovers,   35
Whose dirge is whispered by the warbling Lute.

### V

Sharp Violins proclaim
Their jealous pangs, and desperation,

---

[1] St. Cecilia is said to have invented the organ,
and was canonized as the patron saint of music.
A musical society was organized in London in 1683
for the celebration of St. Cecilia's day, 22 November, and each year an ode, composed for the occasion, was sung. This and the following poem
were written by Dryden for this purpose.
[2] See Genesis, 4:21.

Fury, frantic indignation,
Depth of pains, and height of passion,     40
    For the fair, disdainful dame.

### VI

    But O! what art can teach,
    What human voice can reach,
The sacred Organ's praise?
    Notes inspiring holy love,     45
Notes that wing their heav'nly ways
    To mend the choirs above.

### VII

Orpheus could lead the savage race;
And trees unrooted left their place,
    Sequacious of[3] the lyre;     50
But right Cecilia raised the wonder high'r:
When to her Organ vocal breath was giv'n,
An angel heard, and straight appeared,
    Mistaking earth for heav'n.

### GRAND CHORUS

As from the pow'r of sacred lays     55
    The spheres began to move,
And sung the great Creator's praise
    To all the blest above;
So, when the last and dreadful hour
This crumbling pageant shall devour,     60
The Trumpet shall be heard on high,
The dead shall live, the living die,
And Music shall untune the sky.

# Alexander's Feast

*or,*

## The Power of Music

### AN ODE IN HONOR OF
### ST. CECILIA'S DAY

### (1697)

### I

'T was at the royal feast, for Persia won
    By Philip's warlike son:[1]
    Aloft in awful state
    The godlike hero sate
        On his imperial throne:     5
    His valiant peers were placed around;
Their brows with roses and with myrtles bound
    (So should desert in arms be crowned).
The lovely Thais, by his side,
Sate like a blooming Eastern bride     10
In flow'r of youth and beauty's pride.

[3] Following.
[1] Alexander the Great.

Happy, happy, happy pair!
None but the brave,
None but the brave,
None but the brave deserves the fair.[15]

### CHORUS

Happy, happy, happy pair!
None but the brave,
None but the brave,
None but the brave deserves the fair.

### II

Timotheus,[2] placed on high     20
    Amid the tuneful choir,
    With flying fingers touched the lyre:
The trembling notes ascend the sky,
        And heav'nly joys inspire.
The song began from Jove,     25
Who left his blissful seats above
(Such is the power of mighty love).
A dragon's fiery form belied the god:
Sublime on radiant spires[3] he rode,
        When he to fair Olympia pressed;     30
        And while he sought her snowy breast:
Then, round her slender waist he curled,
And stamped an image of himself, a sov'reign
        of the world.
The list'ning crowd admire the lofty sound;
"A present deity," they shout around;     35
"A present deity," the vaulted roofs rebound:
        With ravished ears
        The monarch hears,
        Assumes the god,
        Affects to nod,     40
And seems to shake the spheres.

### CHORUS

        With ravished ears
        The monarch hears,
        Assumes the god,
        Affects to nod,     45
And seems to shake the spheres.

### III

The praise of Bacchus then the sweet musician
        sung,
    Of Bacchus ever fair and ever young:
        The jolly god in triumph comes;
        Sound the trumpets; beat the drums;     50
        Flushed with a purple grace
        He shows his honest face:
Now give the hautboys breath; he comes, he
        comes.
        Bacchus, ever fair and young,
        Drinking joys did first ordain;     55
        Bacchus' blessings are a treasure.

[2] A Boeotian musician, a favorite of Alexander.
[3] Spirals.

Drinking is the soldier's pleasure:
    Rich the treasure,
    Sweet the pleasure,
Sweet is pleasure after pain.    60

### CHORUS

Bacchus' blessings are a treasure,
Drinking is the soldier's pleasure:
    Rich the treasure,
    Sweet the pleasure,
Sweet is pleasure after pain.    65

### IV

Soothed with the sound, the king grew vain;
Fought all his battles o'er again;
And thrice he routed all his foes; and thrice he
    slew the slain.
The master saw the madness rise;
His glowing cheeks, his ardent eyes;    70
And, while he heav'n and earth defied,
Changed his hand, and checked his pride.
    He chose a mournful Muse,
    Soft pity to infuse:
He sung Darius [4] great and good,    75
    By too severe a fate,
Fallen, fallen, fallen, fallen,
    Fallen from his high estate,
    And welt'ring in his blood;
Deserted, at his utmost need,    80
By those his former bounty fed;
On the bare earth exposed he lies,
With not a friend to close his eyes.
With downcast looks the joyless victor sate,
    Revolving in his altered soul    85
    The various turns of chance below;
And, now and then, a sigh he stole;
And tears began to flow.

### CHORUS

Revolving in his altered soul
    The various turns of chance below;    90
And, now and then, a sigh he stole;
And tears began to flow.

### V

The mighty master smiled, to see
That love was in the next degree:
'Twas but a kindred sound to move,    95
For pity melts the mind to love.
    Softly sweet, in Lydian measures,
    Soon he soothed his soul to pleasures.
"War," he sung, "is toil and trouble;
Honor, but an empty bubble;    100
    Never ending, still beginning,
    Fighting still, and still destroying;
    If the world be worth thy winning,
    Think, O think it worth enjoying;

[4] The Persian monarch conquered by Alexander.

Lovely Thais sits beside thee,    105
    Take the good the gods provide thee."
The many rend the skies with loud applause;
So Love was crowned, but Music won the cause.
The prince, unable to conceal his pain,
    Gazed on the fair    110
    Who caused his care,
And sighed and looked, sighed and looked,
Sighed and looked, and sighed again:
At length, with love and wine at once op-
    pressed,
The vanquished victor sunk upon her breast. 115

### CHORUS

The prince, unable to conceal his pain,
    Gazed on the fair
    Who caused his care,
And sighed and looked, sighed and looked,
Sighed and looked, and sighed again:    120
At length, with love and wine at once op-
    pressed,
The vanquished victor sunk upon her breast.

### VI

Now strike the golden lyre again:
A louder yet, and yet a louder strain.
Break his bands of sleep asunder,    125
And rouse him, like a rattling peal of thunder.
    Hark, hark, the horrid sound
    Has raised up his head:
    As awaked from the dead,
    And amazed, he stares around.    130
"Revenge, revenge!" Timotheus cries,
    "See the Furies arise!
    See the snakes that they rear,
    How they hiss in their hair,
And the sparkles that flash from their eyes!
    Behold a ghastly band,    136
    Each a torch in his hand!
Those are Grecian ghosts, that in battle were
    slain,
    And unburied remain
    Inglorious on the plain:    140
    Give the vengeance due
    To the valiant crew.
Behold how they toss their torches on high,
    How they point to the Persian abodes,
And glitt'ring temples of their hostile gods!"
The princes applaud, with a furious joy;    146
And the king seized a flambeau with zeal to
    destroy;
    Thais led the way,
    To light him to his prey,
And, like another Helen, fired another Troy.

### CHORUS

And the king seized a flambeau with zeal to
    destroy;    151
    Thais led the way,

To light him to his prey,
And like another Helen, fired another Troy.

### VII

Thus, long ago,                                   155
Ere heaving bellows learned to blow,
While organs yet were mute;
Timotheus, to his breathing flute,
And sounding lyre,
Could swell the soul to rage, or kindle soft   10
    desire.                                 160
At last, divine Cecilia came,
Inventress of the vocal frame; [5]
The sweet enthusiast, from her sacred store,
Enlarged the former narrow bounds,
And added length to solemn sounds,          165
With nature's mother wit, and arts unknown
    before.
Let old Timotheus yield the prize,
Or both divide the crown;
He raised a mortal to the skies;             20
She drew an angel down.                      170

### GRAND CHORUS

At last, divine Cecilia came,
Inventress of the vocal frame;
The sweet enthusiast, from her sacred store,
Enlarged the former narrow bounds,
And added length to solemn sounds,          175
With nature's mother wit, and arts unknown
    before.                                30
Let old Timotheus yield the prize,
Or both divide the crown;
He raised a mortal to the skies;
She drew an angel down.                      180

## Preface to the *Fables* [1]

### (1700)

'Tis with a Poet, as with a man who designs to build, and is very exact, as he sup-  40
poses, in casting up the cost beforehand; but,

---

[5] I. e., organ.

[1] Full title: *Fables Ancient and Modern; translated into verse, from Homer, Ovid, Boccace, and
Chaucer; with Original Poems. The Preface,* "addressed to the Duke of Ormond, is a piece of work
of which it is hard to speak except in some such
terms as those which Dryden himself employs in it
when he has to write about Chaucer. . . . [It] is
more full of life than anything else in Dryden's
prose; . . . while nothing, either in prose or verse,
brings out more admirably or to better advantage
the qualities of Dryden as the great English man
of letters. For this is what he was, rather than
essentially a poet; his genius is one that commands
both vehicles of expression, it is not one that is
specially inclined to verse; and the free movement
of his mind and speech is scarcely less wonderful in
a prose tract like this *Preface* than in the verse of
*Absalom and Achitophel*" (W. P. Ker).

generally speaking, he is mistaken in his
account, and reckons short of the expense he
first intended. He alters his mind as the
work proceeds, and will have this or that convenience more, of which he had not thought
when he began. So has it happened to me; I
have built a house, where I intended but a
lodge; yet with better success than a certain
nobleman,[2] who, beginning with a dog-kennel,
never lived to finish the palace he had contrived.

From translating the first of Homer's
*Iliads* (which I intended as an essay to the
whole work), I proceeded to the translation
of the twelfth book of Ovid's *Metamorphoses,* because it contains, among other
things, the causes, the beginning, and ending,
of the Trojan war. Here I ought in reason
to have stopped; but the speeches of Ajax and
Ulysses lying next in my way, I could not
balk 'em. When I had compassed them, I
was so taken with the former part of the
fifteenth book (which is the masterpiece of
the whole *Metamorphoses*), that I enjoined
myself the pleasing task of rendering it into
English. And now I found, by the number
of my verses, that they began to swell into a
little volume; which gave me an occasion of
looking backward on some beauties of my
author, in his former books: there occurred
to me the *Hunting of the Boar, Cinyras and
Myrrha,* the good-natured story of *Baucis
and Philemon,* with the rest, which I hope I
have translated closely enough, and given
them the same turn of verse which they had
in the original; and this, I may say, without
vanity, is not the talent of every poet. He
who has arrived the nearest to it, is the ingenious and learned Sandys,[3] the best versifier of the former age; if I may properly call
it by that name, which was the former part of
this concluding century. For Spenser and
Fairfax [4] both flourished in the reign of
Queen Elizabeth; great masters in our language, and who saw much further into the
beauties of our numbers than those who immediately followed them. Milton was the poetical son of Spenser, and Mr. Waller of
Fairfax; for we have our lineal descents and
clans as well as other families. Spenser
more than once insinuates that the soul of

---

[2] The Duke of Buckingham (Zimri in *Absalom
and Achitophel*).

[3] George Sandys (1578–1644), who translated
Ovid's *Metamorphoses.*

[4] Edward Fairfax (died 1635) published his translation of Tasso's *Godfrey of Bulloign, or the Recovery of Jerusalem* in 1600.

Chaucer was transfused into his body;[5] and that he was begotten by him two hundred years after his decease. Milton has acknowledged to me, that Spenser was his original; and many besides myself have heard our famous Waller own that he derived the harmony of his numbers from *Godfrey of Bulloign*, which was turned into English by Mr. Fairfax.

But to return: having done with Ovid for this time, it came into my mind that our old English poet, Chaucer, in many things resembled him, and that with no disadvantage on the side of the modern author, as I shall endeavor to prove when I compare them; and as I am, and always have been, studious to promote the honor of my native country, so I soon resolved to put their merits to the trial, by turning some of the *Canterbury Tales* into our language, as it is now refined; for by this means, both the poets being set in the same light, and dressed in the same English habit, story to be compared with story, a certain judgment may be made betwixt them by the reader, without obtruding my opinion on him. Or, if I seem partial to my countryman and predecessor in the laurel, the friends of antiquity are not few; and, besides many of the learned, Ovid has almost all the beaux, and the whole fair sex, his declared patrons. Perhaps I have assumed somewhat more to myself than they allow me, because I have adventured to sum up the evidence; but the readers are the jury, and their privilege remains entire, to decide according to the merits of the cause; or, if they please, to bring it to another hearing before some other court. In the mean time, to follow the thread of my discourse (as thoughts, according to Mr. Hobbes,[6] have always some connection), so from Chaucer I was led to think on Boccaccio, who was not only his contemporary, but also pursued the same studies; wrote novels in prose, and many works in verse; particularly is said to have invented the octave rime, or stanza of eight lines, which ever since has been maintained by the practice of all Italian writers who are, or at least assume the title of, heroic poets. He and Chaucer, among other things, had this in common, that they refined their mother-tongues; but with this difference, that Dante had begun to file their language, at least in verse, before the time of

[5] See *Faerie Queene*, Bk. IV, 2, 34.
[6] Thomas Hobbes (1588–1679). The reference is to Pt. I, Chap. 3, of the *Leviathan*.

Boccaccio, who likewise received no little help from his master Petrarch; but the reformation of their prose was wholly owing to Boccaccio himself, who is yet the standard of purity in the Italian tongue, though many of his phrases are become obsolete, as in process of time it must needs happen. Chaucer (as you have formerly been told by our learned Mr. Rymer[7]) first adorned and amplified our barren tongue from the Provençal, which was then the most polished of all the modern languages; but this subject has been copiously treated by that great critic, who deserves no little commendation from us his countrymen. For these reasons of time, and resemblance of genius, in Chaucer and Boccaccio, I resolved to join them in my present work; to which I have added some original papers of my own, which whether they are equal or inferior to my other poems, an author is the most improper judge; and therefore I leave them wholly to the mercy of the reader. I will hope the best, that they will not be condemned; but if they should, I have the excuse of an old gentleman, who, mounting on horseback before some ladies, when I was present, got up somewhat heavily, but desired of the fair spectators that they would count fourscore and eight before they judged him. By the mercy of God, I am already come within twenty years of his number; a cripple in my limbs, but what decays are in my mind the reader must determine. I think myself as vigorous as ever in the faculties of my soul, excepting only my memory, which is not impaired to any great degree; and if I lose not more of it, I have no great reason to complain. What judgment I had, increases rather than diminishes; and thoughts, such as they are, come crowding in so fast upon me that my only difficulty is to choose or to reject, to run them into verse, or

[7] Thomas Rymer (1641–1713), author of *The Tragedies of the Last Age* (1678) and of *A Short View of Tragedy* (1693). It is in the latter that Rymer puts forward his notion that Chaucer belongs to the "Provençal School": "They who attempted verse in English, down till Chaucer's time, made an heavy pudder, and are always miserably put to 't for a word to clink; which commonly fall so awkward and unexpectedly as dropping from the clouds by some machine or miracle. Chaucer found an Herculean labor on his hands; and did perform to admiration. He seizes all Provençal, French, and Latin that came in his way, gives them a new garb and livery, and mingles them amongst our English: turns out English, gouty or superannuated, to place in their room the foreigners fit for service, trained and accustomed to poetical discipline."

to give them the other harmony of prose: I have so long studied and practiced both, that they are grown into a habit, and become familiar to me. In short, though I may lawfully plead some part of the old gentleman's excuse, yet I will reserve it till I think I have greater need, and ask no grains of allowance for the faults of this my present work, but those which are given of course to human frailty. I will not trouble my reader with [10] the shortness of time in which I writ it, or the several intervals of sickness. They who think too well of their own performances are apt to boast in their prefaces how little time their works have cost them, and what other business of more importance interfered; but the reader will be as apt to ask the question, why they allowed not a longer time to make their works more perfect? and why they had so despicable an opinion of their judges as to [20] thrust their indigested stuff upon them, as if they deserved no better?

With this account of my present undertaking, I conclude the first part of this discourse: in the second part, as at a second sitting, though I alter not the draft, I must touch the same features over again, and change the dead-coloring [8] of the whole. In general I will only say, that I have written nothing which savors of immorality or pro- [30] faneness; at least, I am not conscious to myself of any such intention. If there happen to be found an irreverent expression, or a thought too wanton, they are crept into my verses through my inadvertency; if the searchers find any in the cargo, let them be staved [9] or forfeited, like counterbanded goods; at least, let their authors be answerable for them, as being but imported merchandise, and not of my own manufacture. [40] On the other side, I have endeavored to choose such fables, both ancient and modern, as contain in each of them some instructive moral; which I could prove by induction, but the way is tedious, and they leap foremost into sight, without the reader's trouble of looking after them. I wish I could affirm, with a safe conscience, that I had taken the same care in all my former writings; for it must be owned, that supposing verses are [50] never so beautiful or pleasing, yet, if they contain anything which shocks religion or good manners, they are at best what Horace

says of good numbers without good sense, *Versus inopes rerum, nugaeque canorae*.[10] Thus far, I hope, I am right in court, without renouncing to my other right of self-defense, where I have been wrongfully accused, and my sense wire-drawn into blasphemy or bawdry, as it has often been by a religious lawyer,[11] in a late pleading against the stage; in which he mixes truth with falsehood, and has not forgotten the old rule of calumniating strongly, that something may remain.

I resume the thread of my discourse with the first of my translations, which was the first *Iliad* of Homer. If it shall please God to give me longer life, and moderate health, my intentions are to translate the whole *Ilias*; provided still that I meet with those encouragements from the public which may [20] enable me to proceed in my undertaking with some cheerfulness. And this I dare assure the world beforehand, that I have found, by trial, Homer a more pleasing task than Virgil, though I say not the translation will be less laborious; for the Grecian is more according to my genius than the Latin poet. In the works of the two authors we may read their manners, and natural inclinations, which are wholly different. Virgil was of a [30] quiet, sedate temper; Homer was violent, impetuous, and full of fire. The chief talent of Virgil was propriety of thoughts, and ornament of words: Homer was rapid in his thoughts, and took all the liberties, both of numbers and of expressions, which his language, and the age in which he lived, allowed him. Homer's invention was more copious, Virgil's more confined; so that if Homer had not led the way, it was not in [40] Virgil to have begun heroic poetry; for nothing can be more evident than that the Roman poem is but the second part of the *Ilias*; a continuation of the same story, and the persons already formed. The manners of Aeneas are those of Hector, superadded to those which Homer gave him. The adventures of Ulysses in the *Odysseis* are imitated in the first six books of Virgil's *Aeneis*; and though the accidents are not the same (which [50] would have argued him of a servile copying, and total barrenness of invention), yet the

---

[8] First coat of paint applied to a canvas.

[9] Destroyed, as contraband hogsheads were, by breaking holes in them.

[10] Verses lacking substance, and melodious trumpery (*De Arte Poetica*, 322).

[11] Jeremy Collier (1650–1726), in his *Short View of the Immorality and Profaneness of the English Stage* (1698).

seas were the same in which both the heroes wandered; and Dido cannot be denied to be the poetical daughter of Calypso. The six latter books of Virgil's poem are the four-and-twenty *Iliads* contracted; a quarrel occasioned by a lady, a single combat, battles fought, and a town besieged. I say not this in derogation to Virgil, neither do I contradict anything which I have formerly said in his just praise; for his episodes are almost wholly of his own invention, and the form which he has given to the telling makes the tale his own, even though the original story had been the same. But this proves, however, that Homer taught Virgil to design; and if invention be the first virtue of an epic poet, then the Latin poem can only be allowed the second place. Mr. Hobbes, in the preface to his own bald translation of the *Ilias* (studying poetry as he did mathematics, when it was too late), Mr. Hobbes, I say, begins the praise of Homer where he should have ended it. He tells us that the first beauty of an epic poem consists in diction; that is, in the choice of words, and harmony of numbers. Now the words are the coloring of the work, which, in the order of nature, is last to be considered. The design, the disposition, the manners, and the thoughts, are all before it: where any of those are wanting or imperfect, so much wants or is imperfect in the imitation of human life, which is in the very definition of a poem. Words, indeed, like glaring colors, are the first beauties that arise and strike the sight; but, if the draft be false or lame, the figures ill disposed, the manners obscure or inconsistent, or the thoughts unnatural, then the finest colors are but daubing, and the piece is a beautiful monster at the best. Neither Virgil nor Homer were deficient in any of the former beauties; but in this last, which is expression, the Roman poet is at least equal to the Grecian, as I have said elsewhere; supplying the poverty of his language by his musical ear, and by his diligence.

But to return: our two great poets being so different in their tempers, one choleric and sanguine, the other phlegmatic and melancholic; that which makes them excel in their several ways is, that each of them has followed his own natural inclination, as well in forming the design, as in the execution of it. The very heroes show their authors: Achilles is hot, impatient, revengeful—

*Impiger, iracundus, inexorabilis, acer, etc.,*[12]

[12] Impatient, fiery, ruthless, keen (Horace, *De Arte Poetica*, 121).

Aeneas patient, considerate, careful of his people, and merciful to his enemies; ever submissive to the will of heaven—

*quo fata trahunt retrahuntque, sequamur.*[13]

I could please myself with enlarging on this subject, but am forced to defer it to a fitter time. From all I have said, I will only draw this inference, that the action of Homer, being more full of vigor than that of Virgil, according to the temper of the writer, is of consequence more pleasing to the reader. One warms you by degrees; the other sets you on fire all at once, and never intermits his heat. 'Tis the same difference which Longinus makes betwixt the effects of eloquence in Demosthenes and Tully;[14] one persuades, the other commands. You never cool while you read Homer, even not in the second book (a graceful flattery to his countrymen); but he hastens from the ships, and concludes not that book till he has made you an amends by the violent playing of a new machine.[15] From thence he hurries on his action with variety of events, and ends it in less compass than two months. This vehemence of his, I confess, is more suitable to my temper; and, therefore, I have translated his first book with greater pleasure than any part of Virgil; but it was not a pleasure without pains. The continual agitations of the spirits must needs be a weakening of any constitution, especially in age; and many pauses are required for refreshment betwixt the heats; the *Iliad* of itself being a third part longer than all Virgil's works together.

This is what I thought needful in this place to say of Homer. I proceed to Ovid and Chaucer, considering the former only in relation to the latter. With Ovid ended the golden age of the Roman tongue; from Chaucer the purity of the English tongue began. The manners of the poets were not unlike. Both of them were well-bred, well-natured, amorous, and libertine, at least in their writings; it may be, also in their lives. Their studies were the same, philosophy and philology.[16] Both of them were knowing in astronomy; of which Ovid's books of the *Roman Feasts*, and Chaucer's *Treatise of the*

[13] Whither the Fates, in their ebb and flow, draw us, let us follow (Virgil, *Aeneid*, V, 709).

[14] M. Tullius Cicero.

[15] This is a slip. The dream of Agamemnon (referred to at the end of the sentence) *precedes* the catalogue of the ships in Bk. II.

[16] The word here denotes all studies connected with literature.

*Astrolabe,* are sufficient witnesses. But Chaucer was likewise an astrologer, as were Virgil, Horace, Persius, and Manilius. Both writ with wonderful facility and clearness; neither were great inventors: for Ovid only copied the Grecian fables, and most of Chaucer's stories were taken from his Italian contemporaries, or their predecessors. Boccaccio his *Decameron* was first published, and from thence our Englishman has borrowed many of his *Canterbury Tales:* [17] yet that of *Palamon and Arcite* was written, in all probability, by some Italian wit, in a former age, as I shall prove hereafter. The tale of *Griselda* was the invention of Petrarch; by him sent to Boccaccio,[18] from whom it came to Chaucer. *Troilus and Cressida* was also written by a Lombard author,[19] but much amplified by our English translator, as well as beautified; the genius of our countrymen, in general, being rather to improve an invention than to invent themselves, as is evident not only in our poetry, but in many of our manufactures. I find I have anticipated already, and taken up from Boccaccio before I come to him: but there is so much less behind; and I am of the temper of most kings, who love to be in debt, are all for present money, no matter how they pay it afterwards: besides, the nature of a preface is rambling, never wholly out of the way, nor in it. This I have learned from the practice of honest Montaigne, and return at my pleasure to Ovid and Chaucer, of whom I have little more to say.

Both of them built on the inventions of other men; yet since Chaucer had something of his own, as *The Wife of Bath's Tale, The Cock and the Fox,*[20] which I have translated, and some others, I may justly give our countryman the precedence in that part; since I can remember nothing of Ovid which was wholly his. Both of them understood the manners;

[17] "In all probability, Chaucer was unacquainted with" the *Decameron* (R. K. Root, *The Poetry of Chaucer*).

[18] "What Petrarch sent to Boccaccio was a Latin version of Boccaccio's story of Griselda in the *Decameron*" (W. P. Ker). Chaucer took the tale from Petrarch's version.

[19] The *Filostrato,* by Boccaccio, was Chaucer's immediate source. Dryden was misled by Chaucer's reference to one Lollius as his authority. This Lollius seems to be the *Maxime Lolli* of Horace's Second *Epistle* (Bk. I). Chaucer, probably, saw the first verse without its context, and mistakenly inferred that "Lollius was the name of a writer on the Trojan war" (Skeat).

[20] Chaucer invented neither of these tales. Both contain traditional matter—though Chaucer's immediate sources remain still unknown, and are probably lost.

under which name I comprehend the passions, and, in a larger sense, the descriptions of persons, and their very habits. For an example, I see Baucis and Philemon as perfectly before me, as if some ancient painter had drawn them; and all the Pilgrims in the *Canterbury Tales,* their humors, their features, and the very dress, as distinctly as if I had supped with them at the *Tabard* in Southwark. Yet even there, too, the figures of Chaucer are much more lively, and set in a better light; which though I have not time to prove, yet I appeal to the reader, and am sure he will clear me from partiality. The thoughts and words remain to be considered, in the comparison of the two poets, and I have saved myself one-half of the labor, by owning that Ovid lived when the Roman tongue was in its meridian; Chaucer, in the dawning of our language: therefore that part of the comparison stands not on an equal foot, any more than the diction of Ennius and Ovid, or of Chaucer and our present English. The words are given up, as a post not to be defended in our poet, because he wanted the modern art of fortifying. The thoughts remain to be considered; and they are to be measured only by their propriety; that is, as they flow more or less naturally from the persons described, on such and such occasions. The vulgar judges, which are nine parts in ten of all nations, who call conceits and jingles wit, who see Ovid full of them, and Chaucer altogether without them, will think me little less than mad for preferring the Englishman to the Roman. Yet, with their leave, I must presume to say that the things they admire are only glittering trifles, and so far from being witty, that in a serious poem they are nauseous, because they are unnatural. Would any man, who is ready to die for love, describe his passion like Narcissus? Would he think of *inopem me copia fecit,*[21] and a dozen more of such expressions, poured on the neck of one another, and signifying all the same thing? If this were wit, was this a time to be witty, when the poor wretch was in the agony of death? This is just John Littlewit, in *Bartholomew Fair,*[22] who had a conceit (as he tells you) left him in his misery; a miserable conceit. On these occasions the poet should endeavor to raise pity; but, instead of this, Ovid is tickling you to laugh. Virgil never made use of such machines when he was moving you to com-

[21] My very riches have made me poor (Ovid, *Metamorphoses,* III, 466).

[22] By Ben Jonson. Dryden's memory betrays him, not as to Jonson's intention, but as to Littlewit's words.

miserate the death of Dido: he would not destroy what he was building. Chaucer makes Arcite violent in his love, and unjust in the pursuit of it; yet, when he came to die, he made him think more reasonably: he repents not of his love, for that had altered his character; but acknowledges the injustice of his proceedings, and resigns Emilia to Palamon. What would Ovid have done on this occasion? He would certainly have made Arcite witty on [10] his deathbed; he had complained he was further off from possession, by being so near, and a thousand such boyisms, which Chaucer rejected as below the dignity of the subject. They who think otherwise, would, by the same reason, prefer Lucan and Ovid to Homer and Virgil, and Martial to all four of them. As for the turn of words, in which Ovid particularly excels all poets, they are sometimes a fault, and sometimes a beauty, as they are used properly [20] or improperly; but in strong passions always to be shunned, because passions are serious, and will admit no playing. The French have a high value for them; and, I confess, they are often what they call delicate, when they are introduced with judgment; but Chaucer writ with more simplicity, and followed Nature more closely than to use them. I have thus far, to the best of my knowledge, been an upright judge betwixt the parties in competition, not [30] meddling with the design nor the disposition of it; because the design was not their own; and in the disposing of it they were equal. It remains that I say somewhat of Chaucer in particular.

In the first place, as he is the father of English poetry, so I hold him in the same degree of veneration as the Grecians held Homer, or the Romans Virgil. He is a perpetual fountain of good sense; learned in all sciences; and, [40] therefore, speaks properly on all subjects. As he knew what to say, so he knows also when to leave off; a continence which is practiced by few writers, and scarcely by any of the ancients, excepting Virgil and Horace. One of our late great poets [23] is sunk in his reputation, because he could never forgive [24] any conceit which came in his way; but swept like a drag-net, great and small. There was plenty enough, but the dishes were ill sorted; whole pyramids of [50] sweetmeats for boys and women, but little of solid meat for men. All this proceeded not from any want of knowledge, but of judgment. Neither did he want that in discerning the beauties and faults of other poets, but only

indulged himself in the luxury of writing; and perhaps knew it was a fault, but hoped the reader would not find it. For this reason, though he must always be thought a great poet, he is no longer esteemed a good writer; and for ten impressions which his works have had in so many successive years, yet at present a hundred books are scarcely purchased once a twelvemonth; for, as my last Lord Rochester said, though somewhat profanely, "Not being of God, he could not stand."

Chaucer followed Nature everywhere, but was never so bold to go beyond her; and there is a great difference of being *poeta* and *nimis poeta*, if we may believe Catullus,[25] as much as betwixt a modest behavior and affectation. The verse of Chaucer, I confess, is not harmonious to us; but 'tis like the eloquence of one whom Tacitus commends, it was *auribus istius temporis accommodata:* [26] they who lived with him, and some time after him, thought it musical; and it continues so, even in our judgment, if compared with the numbers of Lidgate and Gower, his contemporaries: there is the rude sweetness of a Scotch tune in it, which is natural and pleasing, though not perfect. 'Tis true, I cannot go so far as he who published the last edition of him; [27] for he would make us believe the fault is in our ears, and that there were really ten syllables in a verse where we find but nine: but this opinion is not worth confuting; 'tis so gross and obvious an error, that common sense (which is a rule in everything but matters of Faith and Revelation) must convince the reader, that equality of numbers, in every verse which we call *heroic,* was either not known, or not always practiced, in Chaucer's age. It were an easy matter to produce some thousands of his verses, which are lame for want of half a foot, and sometimes a whole one, and which no pronunciation can make otherwise. We can only say, that he lived in the infancy of our poetry, and that nothing is brought to perfection at the first. We must be children before we grow men. There was an Ennius, and in process of time a Lucilius,

[25] Another slip. The man "too much a poet" is admonished by Martial, *Epigrams,* III, 44.

[26] Well suited to the taste of that time (*De Oratoribus,* 21, where, however, Tacitus has *auribus judicum,* "to the taste of a law-court").

[27] Thomas Speght, 1598. This edition was reprinted with additions in 1602, and again reprinted in 1687. As everybody now knows, Speght was right;—though it should be remembered in Dryden's favor that the text of Chaucer was very imperfectly printed in Speght's edition, and that the principles of Chaucerian pronunciation were unknown in the seventeenth century.

[23] Abraham Cowley (1618–1667).
[24] Give up.

and a Lucretius, before Virgil and Horace; even after Chaucer there was a Spenser, a Harrington,[28] a Fairfax, before Waller and Denham [29] were in being; and our numbers were in their nonage till these last appeared. I need say little of his parentage, life, and fortunes; they are to be found at large in all the editions of his works. He was employed abroad, and favored, by Edward the Third, Richard the Second, and Henry the Fourth, and was poet, as I suppose, to all three of them. In Richard's time, I doubt, he was a little dipped in the rebellion of the Commons; and being brother-in-law to John of Gaunt, it was no wonder if he followed the fortunes of that family; and was well with Henry the Fourth when he had deposed his predecessor. Neither is it to be admired, that Henry, who was a wise as well as a valiant prince, who claimed by succession, and was sensible that his title was not sound, but was rightfully in Mortimer, who had married the heir of York; it was not to be admired, I say, if that great politician should be pleased to have the greatest Wit of those times in his interest, and to be the trumpet of his praises. Augustus had given him the example, by the advice of Maecenas, who recommended Virgil and Horace to him; whose praises helped to make him popular while he was alive, and after his death have made him precious to posterity. As for the religion of our poet, he seems to have some little bias towards the opinions of Wyclif, after John of Gaunt his patron; somewhat of which appears in the tale of *Piers Plowman*: [30] yet I cannot blame him for inveighing so sharply against the vices of the clergy in his age: their pride, their ambition, their pomp, their avarice, their worldly interest, deserved the lashes which he gave them, both in that, and in most of his *Canterbury Tales*. Neither has his contemporary Boccaccio spared them: yet both those poets lived in much esteem with good and holy men in orders; for the scandal which is given by particular priests reflects not on the sacred function. Chaucer's Monk, his Canon, and his Friar, took not from the character of his Good Parson. A satirical poet is the check of the laymen on bad priests. We are only to take care, that we involve not the innocent with the guilty

in the same condemnation. The good cannot be too much honored, nor the bad too coarsely used; for the corruption of the best becomes the worst. When a clergyman is whipped, his gown is first taken off, by which the dignity of his order is secured. If he be wrongfully accused, he has his action of slander; and 'tis at the poet's peril if he transgress the law. But they will tell us that all kind of satire, though never so well deserved by particular priests, yet brings the whole order into contempt. Is then the peerage of England anything dishonored when a peer suffers for his treason? If he be libeled, or any way defamed, he has his *scandalum magnatum* [31] to punish the offender. They who use this kind of argument, seem to be conscious to themselves of somewhat which has deserved the poet's lash, and are less concerned for their public capacity than for their private; at least there is pride at the bottom of their reasoning. If the faults of men in orders are only to be judged among themselves, they are all in some sort parties; for, since they say the honor of their order is concerned in every member of it, how can we be sure that they will be impartial judges? How far I may be allowed to speak my opinion in this case, I know not; but I am sure a dispute of this nature caused mischief in abundance betwixt a King of England and an Archbishop of Canterbury; [32] one standing up for the laws of his land, and the other for the honor (as he called it) of God's Church; which ended in the murder of the prelate, and in the whipping of His Majesty from post to pillar for his penance. The learned and ingenious Dr. Drake [33] has saved me the labor of inquiring into the esteem and reverence which the priests have had of old; and I would rather extend than diminish any part of it: yet I must needs say that when a priest provokes me without any occasion given him, I have no reason, unless it be the charity of a Christian, to forgive him: *prior laesit* [34] is justification sufficient in the civil law. If I answer him in his own language, self-defense I am sure must be allowed me; and if I carry it further, even to a sharp recrimination, somewhat may be indulged to human frailty. Yet my resentment has not wrought so far but that I have followed Chaucer, in his character of a holy man, and have enlarged on that sub-

[28] Sir John Harrington (1561–1612), whose translation of Ariosto's *Orlando Furioso* was published in 1591.

[29] Sir John Denham (1618–1669).

[30] That is, the *Plowman's Tale*, which Dryden found in Speght's edition. It was not, however, written by Chaucer, but by the unknown author of the *Plowman's Creed*.

[31] The offense of defaming magnates of the realm.

[32] Henry II and Thomas à Becket.

[33] James Drake (1667–1707) wrote an answer to Jeremy Collier, *The Ancient and Modern Stages Reviewed*, 1699.

[34] He gave the provocation (Terence, *Eunuchus*, Prologue 6).

ject with some pleasure; reserving to myself the right, if I shall think fit hereafter, to describe another sort of priests, such as are more easily to be found than the Good Parson; such as have given the last blow to Christianity in this age, by a practice so contrary to their doctrine. But this will keep cold till another time. In the meanwhile, I take up Chaucer where I left him.

He must have been a man of a most won- 10 derful comprehensive nature, because, as it has been truly observed of him, he has taken into the compass of his *Canterbury Tales* the various manners and humors (as we now call them) of the whole English nation, in his age. Not a single character has escaped him. All his pilgrims are severally distinguished from each other; and not only in their inclinations, but in their very physiognomies and persons. Baptista Porta [35] could not have described their 20 natures better than by the marks which the poet gives them. The matter and manner of their tales, and of their telling, are so suited to their different educations, humors, and callings, that each of them would be improper in any other mouth. Even the grave and serious characters are distinguished by their several sorts of gravity: their discourses are such as belong to their age, their calling, and their breeding; such as are becoming of them, and of them 30 only. Some of his persons are vicious, and some virtuous; some are unlearned, or (as Chaucer calls them) lewd, and some are learned. Even the ribaldry of the low characters is different: the Reeve, the Miller, and the Cook, are several men, and distinguished from each other as much as the mincing Lady-Prioress and the broad-speaking, gap-toothed Wife of Bath. But enough of this; there is such a variety of game springing up before me that I am distracted in 40 my choice, and know not which to follow. 'Tis sufficient to say, according to the proverb, that "Here is God's plenty." We have our forefathers and great-grand-dames all before us, as they were in Chaucer's days: their general characters are still remaining in mankind, and even in England, though they are called by other names than those of Monks, and Friars, and Canons, and Lady Abbesses, and Nuns; for mankind is ever the same, and nothing lost 50 out of Nature, though everything is altered. May I have leave to do myself the justice (since my enemies will do me none, and are so far from granting me to be a good poet, that they will not allow me so much as to be a Christian,

or a moral man), may I have leave, I say, to inform my reader, that I have confined my choice to such tales of Chaucer as savor nothing of immodesty. If I had desired more to please than to instruct, the Reeve, the Miller, the Shipman, the Merchant, the Sumner, and, above all, the Wife of Bath, in the *Prologue* to her *Tale*, would have procured me as many friends and readers as there are beaux and ladies of pleasure in the town. But I will no more offend against good manners: I am sensible as I ought to be of the scandal I have given by my loose writings; and make what reparation I am able, by this public acknowledgment. If anything of this nature, or of profaneness, be crept into these poems, I am so far from defending it, that I disown it. *Totum hoc indictum volo.*[36] Chaucer makes another manner of apology for his broad speaking, and Boccaccio makes the like; but I will follow neither of them. Our countryman, in the end of his Characters, before the *Canterbury Tales*, thus excuses the ribaldry, which is very gross in many of his novels:—

> But firste, I pray you, of your courtesy,
> That ye ne arrete it not my villany,
> Though that I plainly speak in this mattere,
> To tellen you her words, and eke her chere:
> Ne though I speak her words properly,
> For this ye knowen as well as I,
> Who shall tellen a tale after a man,
> He mote rehearse as nye as ever he can:
> Everich word of it ben in his charge,
> All speke he, never so rudely, ne large:
> Or else he mote tellen his tale untrue,
> Or feine things, or find words new:
> He may not spare, altho he were his brother,
> He mote as wel say o word as another.
> Crist spake himself ful broad in holy Writ,
> And well I wote no villany is it,
> Eke Plato saith, who so can him rede,
> The words mote been cousin to the dede.

Yet if a man should have inquired of Boccaccio or of Chaucer, what need they had of introducing such characters, where obscene words were proper in their mouths, but very indecent to be heard; I know not what answer they could have made; for that reason, such tales shall be left untold by me. You have here a specimen of Chaucer's language, which is so obsolete, that his sense is scarce to be understood; and you have likewise more than one example of his unequal numbers, which were mentioned before. Yet many of his verses consist of ten syllables, and the words not much behind our present English: as for example, these two lines, in the description of the Carpenter's young wife:—

---

[35] A famous Italian physiognomist (1538–1615).

[36] I wish this wholly unsaid.

Wincing she was, as is a jolly colt,
Long as a mast, and upright as a bolt.[87]

I have almost done with Chaucer, when I have answered some objections relating to my present work. I find some people are offended that I have turned these tales into modern English; because they think them unworthy of my pains, and look on Chaucer as a dry, old-fashioned wit, not worth reviving. I have often heard the late Earl of Leicester say, that Mr. Cowley himself was of that opinion; who, having read him over at my Lord's request declared he had no taste of him. I dare not advance my opinion against the judgment of so great an author; but I think it fair, however, to leave the decision to the public. Mr. Cowley was too modest to set up for a dictator; and being shocked perhaps with his old style, never examined into the depth of his good sense. Chaucer, I confess, is a rough diamond, and must first be polished, ere he shines. I deny not likewise, that, living in our early days of poetry, he writes not always of a piece; but sometimes mingles trivial things with those of greater moment. Sometimes also, though not often, he runs riot, like Ovid, and knows not when he has said enough. But there are more great wits besides Chaucer, whose fault is their excess of conceits, and those ill sorted. An author is not to write all he can, but only all he ought. Having observed this redundancy in Chaucer (as it is an easy matter for a man of ordinary parts to find a fault in one of greater), I have not tied myself to a literal translation; but have often omitted what I judged unnecessary, or not of dignity enough to appear in the company of better thoughts. I have presumed further, in some places, and added somewhat of my own where I thought my author was deficient, and had not given his thoughts their true luster, for want of words in the beginning of our language. And to this I was the more emboldened, because (if I may be permitted to say it of myself) I found I had a soul congenial to his, and that I had been conversant in the same studies. Another poet, in another age, may take the same liberty with my writings; if at least they live long enough to deserve correction. It was also necessary sometimes to restore the sense of Chaucer, which was lost or mangled in the errors of the press. Let this example suffice at present: in the story of *Palamon and Arcite*, where the temple of Diana is described, you find these verses in all the editions of our author:—

There saw I Danè turned unto a tree,
I mean not the goddess Diane,
But Venus daughter, which that hight Danè.[38]

Which, after a little consideration, I knew was to be reformed into this sense, that Daphne, the daughter of Peneus, was turned into a tree. I durst not make thus bold with Ovid, lest some future Milbourne [39] should arise, and say, I varied from my author, because I understood him not.

But there are other judges, who think I ought not to have translated Chaucer into English, out of a quite contrary notion: they suppose there is a certain veneration due to his old language; and that it is little less than profanation and sacrilege to alter it. They are farther of opinion, that somewhat of his good sense will suffer in this transfusion, and much of the beauty of his thoughts will infallibly be lost, which appear with more grace in their old habit. Of this opinion was that excellent person, whom I mentioned, the late Earl of Leicester, who valued Chaucer as much as Mr. Cowley despised him. My Lord dissuaded me from this attempt (for I was thinking of it some years before his death), and his authority prevailed so far with me as to defer my undertaking while he lived, in deference to him; yet my reason was not convinced with what he urged against it. If the first end of a writer be to be understood, then, as his language grows obsolete, his thoughts must grow obscure:—

*Multa renascentur, quae nunc cecidere; cadentque*
*Quae nunc sunt in honore vocabula, si volet usus,*
*Quem penes arbitrium est et jus et norma loquendi.*[40]

When an ancient word, for its sound and significancy, deserves to be revived, I have that reasonable veneration for antiquity to restore it. All beyond this is superstition. Words are not like landmarks, so sacred as never to be removed; customs are changed, and even statutes are silently repealed, when the reason ceases for which they were enacted. As for the other part of the argument, that his thoughts will lose of their original beauty by the innovation of words; in the first place, not only their beauty, but their being is lost, where they

[87] *The Miller's Tale*, II, 77–78.

[38] *The Knight's Tale*, ll. 1204–1206.
[39] Luke Milbourne (1649–1720), author of *Notes on Dryden's Virgil*, 1698.
[40] . . . Words long faded may again revive,
And words may fade now blooming and alive,
If usage wills it so, to whom belongs
The rule, the law, the government of tongues.
(Horace, *De Arte Poetica*, ll. 70–72; Conington's translation. In the first line *nunc* should be *jam*.)

are no longer understood, which is the present case. I grant that something must be lost in all transfusion, that is, in all translations; but the sense will remain, which would otherwise be lost, or at least be maimed, when it is scarce intelligible, and that but to a few. How few are there, who can read Chaucer, so as to understand him perfectly? And if imperfectly, then with less profit, and no pleasure. It is not for the use of some old Saxon friends [41] that I have taken these pains with him: let them neglect my version, because they have no need of it. I made it for their sakes who understand sense and poetry as well as they, when that poetry and sense is put into words which they understand. I will go farther, and dare to add, that what beauties I lose in some places, I give to others which had them not originally: but in this I may be partial to myself; let the reader judge, and I submit to his decision. Yet I think I have just occasion to complain of them who, because they understand Chaucer, would deprive the greater part of their countrymen of the same advantage, and hoard him up, as misers do their grandam gold, only to look on it themselves, and hinder others from making use of it. In sum, I seriously protest that no man ever had, or can have, a greater veneration for Chaucer than myself. I have translated some part of his works, only that I might perpetuate his memory, or at least refresh it, amongst my countrymen. If I have altered him anywhere for the better, I must at the same time acknowledge that I could have done nothing without him. *Facile est inventis addere* [42] is no great commendation; and I am not so vain to think I have deserved a greater. I will conclude what I have to say of him singly, with this one remark: A lady of my acquaintance, who keeps a kind of correspondence with some authors of the fair sex in France, has been informed by them, that Mademoiselle de Scudéry,[43] who is as old as Sibyl, and inspired like her by the same God of Poetry, is at this time translating Chaucer into modern French. From which I gather that he has been formerly translated into the old Provençal; [44] for how she should come to understand old English, I know not. But the matter of fact being true, it makes me think that there is something in it like fatality; that, after certain periods of time, the fame and memory of great wits should be renewed, as Chaucer is both in France and England. If this be wholly chance, 'tis extraordinary; and I dare not call it more, for fear of being taxed with superstition.

Boccaccio comes last to be considered, who, living in the same age with Chaucer, had the same genius, and followed the same studies. Both writ novels, and each of them cultivated his mother-tongue. But the greatest resemblance of our two modern authors being in their familiar style, and pleasing way of relating comical adventures, I may pass it over, because I have translated nothing from Boccaccio of that nature. In the serious part of poetry, the advantage is wholly on Chaucer's side; for though the Englishman has borrowed many tales from the Italian, yet it appears that those of Boccaccio were not generally of his own making, but taken from authors of former ages, and by him only modeled; so that what there was of invention, in either of them, may be judged equal. But Chaucer has refined on Boccaccio, and has mended the stories which he has borrowed, in his way of telling; though prose allows more liberty of thought, and the expression is more easy when unconfined by numbers. Our countryman carries weight, and yet wins the race at disadvantage. I desire not the reader should take my word; and, therefore, I will set two of their discourses, on the same subject, in the same light, for every man to judge betwixt them. I translated Chaucer first, and, amongst the rest, pitched on *The Wife of Bath's Tale*; not daring, as I have said, to adventure on her *Prologue*, because 'tis too licentious. There Chaucer introduces an old woman, of mean parentage, whom a youthful knight, of noble blood, was forced to marry, and consequently loathed her. The crone being in bed with him on the wedding-night, and finding his aversion, endeavors to win his affection by reason, and speaks a good word for herself (as who could blame her?), in hope to mollify the sullen bridegroom. She takes her topics from the benefits of poverty, the advantages of old age and ugliness, the vanity of youth, and the silly pride of ancestry and titles, without inherent virtue, which is the true nobility. When I had closed Chaucer, I returned to Ovid, and translated some more of his fables; and, by this time, had so far forgotten *The Wife of Bath's Tale* that, when I took up Boccaccio, unawares I fell on the same argument, of preferring virtue to nobility

[41] That is, friends acquainted with very early English, the study of which was making progress at this time, through the industry of several antiquaries.

[42] It is easy to make additions to inventions.

[43] Madeleine de Scudéry (1607–1701), poet and author of huge romances (*Artamenes, Clelia, Cleopatra*) which live now only in the histories.

[44] Here, as earlier in the *Preface*, Dryden supposes Provençal to be identical with early French.

of blood and titles, in the story of *Sigismonda;* which I had certainly avoided, for the resemblance of the two discourses, if my memory had not failed me. Let the reader weigh them both; and, if he thinks me partial to Chaucer, 'tis in him to right Boccaccio.

I prefer, in our countryman, far above all his other stories, the noble poem of *Palamon and Arcite,* which is of the epic kind, and perhaps not much inferior to the *Ilias,* or the *Aeneis.* The story is more pleasing than either of them, the manners as perfect, the diction as poetical, the learning as deep and various, and the disposition full as artful: only it includes a greater length of time, as taking up seven years at least; but Aristotle has left undecided the duration of the action; which yet is easily reduced into the compass of a year, by a narration of what preceded the return of Palamon to Athens. I had thought, for the honor of our narration, and more particularly for his, whose laurel, though unworthy, I have worn after him, that this story was of English growth, and Chaucer's own: but I was undeceived by Boccaccio; for, casually looking on the end of his seventh *Giornata,*[45] I found Dioneo (under which name he shadows himself), and Fiammetta (who represents his mistress, the natural daughter of Robert, King of Naples), of whom these words are spoken: *Dioneo e Fiammetta gran pezza cantarono insieme d'Arcita, e di Palemone;* [46] by which it appears that this story was written before the time of Boccaccio; but the name of its author being wholly lost, Chaucer is now become an original; and I question not but the poem has received many beauties, by passing through his noble hands. Besides this tale, there is another of his own invention, after the manner of the Provençals, called *The Flower and the Leaf,*[47] with which I was so particularly pleased, both for the invention and the moral, that I cannot hinder myself from recommending it to the reader.

As a corollary to this preface, in which I have done justice to others, I owe somewhat to myself; not that I think it worth my time to enter the lists with one M——, and one B——,[48] but barely to take notice that such

men there are, who have written scurrilously against me, without any provocation. M——, who is in orders, pretends, amongst the rest, this quarrel to me, that I have fallen foul on priesthood: if I have, I am only to ask pardon of good priests, and am afraid his part of the reparation will come to little. Let him be satisfied, that he shall not be able to force himself upon me for an adversary. I contemn him too much to enter into competition with him. His own translations of Virgil have answered his criticisms on mine. If (as they say, he has declared in print), he prefers the version of Ogilby to mine, the world has made him the same compliment; for 'tis agreed, on all hands, that he writes even below Ogilby. That, you will say, is not easily to be done; but what cannot M—— bring about? I am satisfied, however, that, while he and I live together, I shall not be thought the worst poet of the age. It looks as if I had desired him underhand to write so ill against me; but upon my honest word I have not bribed him to do me this service, and am wholly guiltless of his pamphlet. 'Tis true, I should be glad if I could persuade him to continue his good offices, and write such another critique on anything of mine; for I find, by experience, he has a great stroke with the reader, when he condemns any of my poems, to make the world have a better opinion of them. He has taken some pains with my poetry; but nobody will be persuaded to take the same with his. If I had taken to the Church, as he affirms, but which was never in my thoughts, I should have had more sense, if not more grace, than to have turned myself out of my benefice, by writing libels on my parishioners. But his account of my manners and my principles are of a piece with his cavils and his poetry; and so I have done with him for ever.

As for the City Bard, or Knight Physician, I hear his quarrel to me is, that I was the author of *Absalom and Achitophel,* which, he thinks, is a little hard on his fanatic patrons in London.

But I will deal the more civilly with his two poems, because nothing ill is to be spoken of the dead; and therefore peace be to the *manes* of his *Arthurs.* I will only say that it was not for this noble Knight that I drew the plan of an epic poem on King Arthur, in my preface to the translation of Juvenal. The Guardian Angels of kingdoms were machines too ponderous for him to manage; and therefore he rejected them, as Dares did the whirlbats [49]

---

[45] Day (in the *Decameron*).

[46] Dioneo and Fiammetta sang together a great while of Arcite and Palamon. (Dryden did not know Boccaccio's *Teseide,* the immediate source of *The Knight's Tale.*)

[47] It has now been shown that Chaucer did not write this.

[48] Milbourne; and Sir Richard Blackmore (died 1729), author of *Prince Arthur* (1695), *King Arthur* (1697), and other poetical pieces.

[49] Coverings worn by boxers on their hands.

of Eryx when they were thrown before him by Entellus:[50] yet from that preface, he plainly took his hint; for he began immediately upon the story, though he had the baseness not to acknowledge his benefactor, but instead of it, to traduce me in a libel.

I shall say the less of Mr. Collier, because in many things he has taxed me justly; and I have pleaded guilty to all thoughts and expressions of mine, which can be truly argued of ob- [10] scenity, profaneness, or immorality, and retract them. If he be my enemy, let him triumph; if he be my friend, as I have given him no personal occasion to be otherwise, he will be glad of my repentance. It becomes me not to draw my pen in the defense of a bad cause, when I have so often drawn it for a good one. Yet it were not difficult to prove that in many places he has perverted my meaning by his glosses, and interpreted my words into blasphemy and [20] bawdry, of which they were not guilty. Besides that, he is too much given to horse-play in his raillery, and comes to battle like a dictator from the plow. I will not say, "The zeal of God's house has eaten him up"; but I am sure it has devoured some part of his good manners and civility. It might also be doubted, whether it were altogether zeal which prompted him to this rough manner of proceeding; perhaps, it became not one of his function to rake into [30] the rubbish of ancient and modern plays: a divine might have employed his pains to better purpose, than in the nastiness of Plautus and Aristophanes, whose examples, as they excuse not me, so it might be possibly supposed that he read them not without some pleasure. They

[50] Cf. *Aeneid*, V, 400.

who have written commentaries on those poets, or on Horace, Juvenal, and Martial, have explained some vices, which, without their interpretation, had been unknown to modern times. Neither has he judged impartially betwixt the former age and us. There is more bawdry in one play of Fletcher's, called *The Custom of the Country*, than in all ours together. Yet this has been often acted on the stage, in my remembrance. Are the times so much more reformed now, than they were five-and-twenty years ago? If they are, I congratulate the amendment of our morals. But I am not to prejudice the cause of my fellow poets, though I abandon my own defense: they have some of them answered for themselves; and neither they nor I can think Mr. Collier so formidable an enemy that we should shun him. He has lost ground, at the latter end of the day, by pursuing his point too far, like the Prince of Condé, at the battle of Senneph:[51] from immoral plays to no plays, *ab abusu ad usum, non valet consequentia.*[52] But, being a party, I am not to erect myself into a judge. As for the rest of those who have written against me, they are such scoundrels, that they deserve not the least notice to be taken of them. B—— and M—— are only distinguished from the crowd by being remembered to their infamy:——

> . . . *Demetri, teque, Tigelli,*
> *Discipulorum inter jubeo plorare cathedras.*[53]

[51] At this battle (11 August, 1674) Condé attacked the rearguard of the Prince of Orange, then in retreat between Charleroi and Mons.

[52] The argument from abuse against use is weak.

[53] Demetrius, and you, Tigellius, go weep amidst your pupils' chairs (Horace, *Satires*, I, x, 90–91. Horace has *discipularum*).

# Lyric Poetry of the Restoration

The Restoration poets may with some justice be said to have inherited the lyric tradition of the earlier seventeenth century. They did not, however, inherit the whole of that tradition, nor did the surviving elements remain unchanged. By 1660 the Spenserian school had virtually disappeared, and that of Donne was on the wane. Devotional poetry of an imaginative and personal character could still be written by a man like Thomas Traherne; but if his lyrics are compared with those of George Herbert, it is apparent that a decisive change has taken place. Traherne was an obscure Welsh clergyman, a childlike and highly gifted mystic, who contributed nothing to the main literary currents of his time. His work remained in manuscript until the beginning of the twentieth century; and even his most appealing poems betray, in their lack of self-assurance and in their failure to express his inspiration fully, how little he relied upon the achievements of his predecessors and contemporaries. Far more typical of the ecclesiastical life of the period was Henry Aldrich, Doctor of Divinity, Dean of Christ Church, Oxford, at one time Vice-Chancellor of the University: a scholar whose wide interests embraced logic, mathematics, and classical literature, as well as architecture and music, and whose sincere piety was no bar to the composition of such verses as "The Five Reasons for Drinking" and a Latin rendering of Congreve's song, "A Soldier and a Sailor."

But the most compact and important group of Restoration lyric poets were in a very real sense the inheritors of an earlier tradition: Sir George Etherege, the Earl of Dorset, Sir Charles Sedley, and the Earl of Rochester brought to the court of Charles II much of the spirit and technique of the poetry written at the court of Charles I. Distinguished men of letters from the Cavalier period—for example, Edmund Waller and Sir William Davenant—were not only alive in 1660 but personally connected with the newer writers; and Dorset supplied a link with a still remoter past, since he was a great-great-grandson of that Thomas Sackville who had been eminent both as a poet and as a courtier in the reign of Queen Elizabeth. The court lyrics of the Restoration are, in fact, the last fruit of an aristocratic tradition which had first appeared in the lyrics of Wyatt and Surrey a century and a half before.

One of the distinguishing marks of this tradition is an indifference to publication. The poems of Etherege and Dorset and Sedley and Rochester were intended, at least originally, for circulation in manuscript; Dorset's indeed have never been adequately collected and printed. The best of their lyrics, on the other hand, are also marked by poetic skill of a high order, even though they may have been written in great haste: how much they owe to Cavalier models is revealed by the delicate phrasing and the exquisite naturalness of their lines. The themes which they set forth may appear to be a new departure since they are occasionally, and in the case of Rochester far more than occasionally, licentious; but it is well to remember that not all the love poetry written at the court of Charles I had been idealistic. The view which the aristocratic tradition took of love, its most important subject, had undergone a steady development from the first. Petrarchian imitation, as well as other influences, had led to the idealizing of woman; but this very interest caused in turn a closer and closer study of her actual qualities. The court poets of the Restoration, while they preserved an attitude of deferential gallantry, were also students of certain, if not all, sides of feminine character: woman as woman assumes a new prominence in their lyrics. At the same time their realistic view of her completed, rather than violated, the courtly ideal. If they are frequently cynical, there has never been a cynicism better-humored or more graceful than theirs.

William Kerr has edited a convenient anthology, Restoration Verse, 1660–1715 (London, 1930). H. M. Margoliouth has edited The Works of Thomas Traherne (Oxford, 1958); Helen C. White's Metaphysical Poets (New York, 1956) contains an evaluation of Traherne. The Dramatic Works of Sir George Etherege are edited with an authoritative introduction by H. F. B. Brett-Smith (Oxford, 1927), but Etherege's few poems are accessible only in the earlier Works, edited by A. W. Verity (1888); in the first of his Essays in Biography, 1680–1726 (London, 1925) Bonamy Dobrée gives a spirited study of Etherege's last years. Vivian de Sola Pinto, the editor of The Poetical and Dramatic Works of Sir Charles Sedley (London, 1928), has also written the most complete account of the poet, Sir Charles Sedley, 1639–1701, A Study in the Life and Literature of the Restoration (London, 1927). The Collected Works of John Wilmot, Earl of Rochester have been edited by John Hayward (London, 1926) and the Poems by Vivian de Sola Pinto (London, 1953). A shrewd commentary on Rochester and his times appears in the last of three essays in Kenneth B. Murdock's Sun at Noon (New York, 1939). The standard edition of The Complete Works of William Congreve is that edited by Montague Summers (London, 1923).

# SIR GEORGE ETHEREGE

## (1635?–1691)

## To Chloris

Chloris, 'tis not in our power
To say how long our love will last:
It may be, we within this hour
May lose those joys we now may taste.
  The blessèd that immortal be    5
  From change in love are only free.

And though you now immortal seem,
Such is th'exactness of your fame:
Those that your beauty so esteem,
Will find it cannot last the same:    10
  Love from mine eyes has stol'n my fire,
  As apt to waste, and to expire.

Then since we mortal Lovers are,
Let's question not how long 'twill last;
But while we love let us take care,    15
Each minute be with pleasure past:
  It were a madness, to deny
  To live, because w'are sure to die.

Fear not, though love and beauty fail,
My reason shall my heart direct:    20

Your kindness now will then prevail,
And passion turn into respect:
  Chloris, at worst, you'll in the end
  But change your Lover for a Friend.

# THOMAS TRAHERNE

## (1636?–1674)

## Wonder

How like an Angel came I down!
  How bright are all things here!
When first among his Works I did appear
  O how their Glory me did crown!
The World resembled his *Eternity*,    5
  In which my Soul did walk;
  And ev'ry thing that I did see,
    Did with me talk.

The skies in their magnificence,
  The lively, lovely air;    10
O how divine, how soft, how sweet, how fair!
  The stars did entertain my sense,
And all the Works of God so bright and pure,
  So rich and great did seem,
  As if they ever must endure,    15
    In my esteem.

A native health and innocence
  Within my bones did grow,
And while my God did all his Glories show,
  I felt a vigor in my sense    20
That was all Spirit. I within did flow
  With seas of life, like wine;
  I nothing in the World did know,
    But 'twas Divine.

Harsh ragged objects were concealed,    25
  Oppressions, tears and cries,
Sins, griefs, complaints, dissensions, weeping eyes,
  Were hid: and only things revealed,
Which Heavenly Spirits, and the Angels prize.
  The state of innocence    30
  And bliss, not trades and poverties,
    Did fill my sense.

The streets were paved with golden stones,
  The boys and girls were mine,
O how did all their lovely faces shine!    35
  The sons of men all holy ones,
In joy, and beauty, then appeared to me,
  And ev'ry thing which here I found,
  While like an Angel I did see,
    Adorned the ground.    40

Rich diamond and pearl and gold
  In ev'ry place was seen;
Rare splendors, yellow, blue, red, white and green,
  Mine eyes did ev'rywhere behold.

Great Wonders clothed with Glory did appear,
    Amazement was my bliss.      46
That and my wealth met ev'rywhere:
    No joy to this!

Cursed and devised proprieties,
    With envy, avarice      50
And fraud, those fiends that spoil even Paradise,
    Fled from the splendor of mine eyes.
And so did hedges, ditches, limits, bounds,
    I dreamed not aught of those,
But wandered over all men's grounds,    55
    And found repose.

Proprieties themselves were mine,
    And hedges ornaments;
Walls, boxes, coffers, and their rich contents
    Did not divide my joys, but all combine.  60
Clothes, ribbons, jewels, laces, I esteemed
    My joys by others worn;
For me they all to wear them seemed
    When I was born.

## Shadows in the Water

In unexperienced infancy
Many a sweet mistake doth lie:
Mistake though false, intending true;
A *Seeming* somewhat more than *View*;
    That doth instruct the mind      5
    In things that lie behind,
And many secrets to us show
Which afterwards we come to know.

Thus did I by the water's brink
Another world beneath me think;    10
And while the lofty spacious skies
Reversèd there abused mine eyes,
    I fancied other feet
    Came mine to touch or meet;
As by some puddle I did play    15
Another world within it lay.

Beneath the water people drowned,
Yet with another Heaven crowned,
In spacious regions seemed to go
As freely moving to and fro:    20
    In bright and open space
    I saw their very face;
Eyes, hands, and feet they had like mine;
Another sun did with them shine.

'Twas strange that people there should walk,
And yet I could not hear them talk:    26
That through a little wat'ry chink,
Which one dry ox or horse might drink,
    We other worlds should see,
    Yet not admitted be;    30
And other confines there behold
Of light and darkness, heat and cold.

I called them oft, but called in vain;
No speeches we could entertain:
Yet did I there expect to find    35
Some other world, to please my mind.

I plainly saw by these
    A new Antipodes,
Whom, though they were so plainly seen,
A film kept off that stood between.    40

By walking men's reversèd feet
I chanced another world to meet;
Though it did not to view exceed
A phantasm, 'tis a world indeed,
    Where skies beneath us shine,    45
    And earth by art divine
Another face presents below,
Where people's feet against ours go.

Within the regions of the air,
Compassed about with heav'ns fair,    50
Great tracts of land there may be found
Enriched with fields and fertile ground;
    Where many num'rous hosts,
    In those far distant coasts,
For other great and glorious ends,    55
Inhabit, my yet unknown friends.

O ye that stand upon the brink,
Whom I so near me, through the chink,
With wonder see: What faces there,
Whose feet, whose bodies, do ye wear?    60
    I my companions see
    In you, another me.
They seemèd others, but are we;
Our second selves those shadows be.

Look how far off those lower skies    65
Extend themselves! scarce with mine eyes
I can them reach. O ye my friends,
What *Secret* borders on those ends?
    Are lofty heavens hurled
    'Bout your inferior world?    70
Are ye the representatives
Of other people's distant lives?

Of all the playmates which I knew
That here I do the image view
In other selves; what can it mean?    75
But that below the purling stream
    Some unknown joys there be
    Laid up in store for me;
To which I shall, when that thin skin
Is broken, be admitted in.    80

# CHARLES SACKVILLE, EARL OF DORSET

## (1638–1706)

## Song, Written at Sea,

### *In the First Dutch War, 1665, the Night before an Engagement* [1]

To all you ladies now at land
    We men at sea indite;

[1] The poem may have been written as early as the end of 1664 and later given this title to suggest that it was written on the eve of the English naval victory of 3 June, 1665.

But first would have you understand
  How hard it is to write;
The Muses now, and Neptune too,     5
We must implore to write to you,
  With a fa, la, la, la, la.

For though the Muses should prove kind,
  And fill our empty brain;
Yet if rough Neptune rouse the wind,    10
  To wave the azure main,
Our paper, pen, and ink, and we,
Roll up and down our ships at sea,
  With a fa, la, la, la, la.

Then, if we write not by each post,    15
  Think not we are unkind;
Nor yet conclude our ships are lost
  By Dutchmen, or by wind:
Our tears we'll send a speedier way,
The tide shall bring 'em twice a day,    20
  With a fa, la, la, la, la.

The king with wonder, and surprise,
  Will swear the seas grow bold;
Because the tides will higher rise,
  Than e'er they used of old:    25
But let him know it is our tears
Bring floods of grief to Whitehall stairs.
  With a fa, la, la, la, la.

Should foggy Opdam [2] chance to know
  Our sad and dismal story;    30
The Dutch would scorn so weak a foe,
  And quit their fort at Goree:
For what resistance can they find
From men who've left their hearts behind!
  With a fa, la, la, la, la.    35

Let wind and weather do its worst,
  Be you to us but kind;
Let Dutchmen vapor, Spaniards curse,
  No sorrow we shall find:
'Tis then no matter how things go,    40
Or who's our friend, or who's our foe.
  With a fa, la, la, la, la.

To pass our tedious hours away,
  We throw a merry main; [3]
Or else at serious ombre [4] play;    45
  But, why should we in vain
Each other's ruin thus pursue?
We were undone when we left you.
  With a fa, la, la, la, la.

But now our fears tempestuous grow,    50
  And cast our hopes away;
Whilst you, regardless of our woe,
  Sit careless at a play:
Perhaps permit some happier man

[2] Jacob van Wassenaer, Baron d'Opdam, admiral of the Dutch fleet.
[3] Number to be thrown for in games of dice.
[4] Game of cards, usually played by three people.

To kiss your hand, or flirt your fan.    55
  With a fa, la, la, la, la.

When any mournful tune you hear,
  That dies in ev'ry note;
As if it sighed with each man's care,
  For being so remote;    60
Think then how often love we've made
To you, when all those tunes were played.
  With a fa, la, la, la, la.

In justice you cannot refuse,
  To think of our distress;    65
When we for hopes of honor lose
  Our certain happiness;
All those designs are but to prove
Ourselves more worthy of your love.
  With a fa, la, la, la, la.    70

And now we've told you all our loves,
  And likewise all our fears;
In hopes this declaration moves
  Some pity from your tears:
Let's hear of no inconstancy,    75
We have too much of that at sea.
  With a fa, la, la, la, la.

## Song

Dorinda's sparkling wit, and eyes,
  United, cast too fierce a light,
Which blazes high, but quickly dies,
  Pains not the heart, but hurts the sight.

Love is a calmer, gentler joy,    5
  Smooth are his looks, and soft his pace;
Her Cupid is a blackguard boy,
  That runs his link [5] full in your face.

# SIR CHARLES SEDLEY

## (1639?–1701)

## Song

Not *Celia*, that I juster am
  Or better than the rest,
For I would change each hour like them,
  Were not my heart at rest.

But I am tied to very thee,    5
  By every thought I have;
Thy face I only care to see,
  Thy heart I only crave.

All that in woman is adored,
  In thy dear self I find,    10
For the whole sex can but afford,
  The handsome and the kind.

Why then should I seek farther store,
  And still make love anew;

[5] Torch.

When change itself can give no more, 15
  'Tis easy to be true.

## Song

Love still has something of the sea,
  From whence his Mother rose; [1]
No time his slaves from doubt can free,
  Nor give their thoughts repose:

They are becalmed in clearest days, 5
  And in rough weather tost;
They wither under cold delays,
  Or are in tempests lost.

One while they seem to touch the port,
  Then straight into the main, 10
Some angry wind in cruel sport
  The vessel drives again.

At first disdain and pride they fear,
  Which if they chance to 'scape,
Rivals and falsehood soon appear 15
  In a more dreadful shape.

By such degrees to joy they come,
  And are so long withstood,
So slowly they receive the sum,
  It hardly does them good. 20

'Tis cruel to prolong a pain,
  And to defer a joy;
Believe me, gentle *Celemene*
  Offends the wingéd boy.

An hundred thousand oaths your fears 25
  Perhaps would not remove;
And if I gazed a thousand years
  I could no deeper love.

## HENRY ALDRICH

### (1647–1710)

## A Catch

If all be true that I do think
There are Five Reasons we should drink;
Good wine, a friend, or being dry,
Or lest we should be by and by;
Or any other reason why. 5

## JOHN WILMOT,
## EARL OF ROCHESTER

### (1647–1680)

## The Mistress

### A Song

An age in her embraces past,
  Would seem a winter's day;

[1] Venus, according to one myth, was born from the sea.

Where life and light with envious haste,
  Are torn and snatched away.

But, oh! how slowly minutes roll, 5
  When absent from her eyes,
That fed my love, which is my soul;
  It languishes and dies.

For then no more a soul but shade,
  It mournfully does move; 10
And haunts my breast, by absence made
  The living tomb of love.

You wiser men despise me not,
  Whose love-sick fancy raves,
On shades of souls, and Heav'n knows what; 15
  Short ages live in graves.

Whene'er those wounding eyes, so full
  Of sweetness, you did see;
Had you not been profoundly dull,
  You had gone mad like me. 20

Nor censure us, you who perceive
  My best belov'd and me,
Sigh and lament, complain and grieve;
  You think we disagree.

Alas! 'tis sacred jealousy, 25
  Love raised to an extreme;
The only proof 'twixt them and me,
  We love, and do not dream.

Fantastic fancies fondly move;
  And in frail joys believe, 30
Taking false pleasure for true love;
  But pain can ne'er deceive.

Kind jealous doubts, tormenting fears,
  And anxious cares, when past,
Prove our hearts' treasure fixed and dear, 35
  And make us blest at last.

## Love and Life

### A Song

All my past life is mine no more,
  The flying hours are gone:
Like transitory dreams giv'n o'er,
Whose images are kept in store,
  By memory alone. 5

The time that is to come is not;
  How can it then be mine?
The present moment's all my lot;
And that, as fast as it is got,
  *Phyllis*, is only thine. 10

Then talk not of inconstancy,
  False hearts, and broken vows;
If I, by miracle, can be
This live-long minute true to thee,
  'Tis all that Heav'n allows. 15

## Upon His Leaving His Mistress

'Tis not that I am weary grown
Of being yours, and yours alone:
But with what face can I incline,
To damn you to be only mine?
You, whom some kinder Pow'r did fashion,    5
By merit, and by inclination,
The joy at least of a whole nation.

Let meaner spirits of your sex,
With humble aims their thoughts perplex:
And boast, if, by their arts they can    10
Contrive to make one happy man.
While, moved by an impartial sense,
Favors, like Nature, you dispense,
With universal influence.

See the kind seed-receiving earth,    15
To every grain affords a birth:
On her no show'rs unwelcome fall,
Her willing womb retains 'em all.
And shall my Caelia be confined?
No, live up to thy mighty mind;    20
And be the mistress of mankind.

## Upon Nothing

Nothing! thou elder brother ev'n to shade,
Thou hadst a being ere the world was made,
And (well fixt) art alone, of ending not afraid.

Ere time and place were, time and place were
    not,
When primitive Nothing something straight
    begot,    5
Then all proceeded from the great united—
    What.

Something the gen'ral attribute of all,
Severed from thee, its sole original,
Into thy boundless self must undistinguished
    fall.

Yet something did thy mighty pow'r command,
And from thy fruitful emptiness's hand,    11
Snatched men, beasts, birds, fire, air, and land.

Matter, the wickedst off-spring of thy race,
By Form assisted, flew from thy embrace,
And Rebel Light obscured thy reverend dusky
    face.    15

With Form, and Matter, Time and Place did
    join,
Body, thy foe, with thee did leagues combine,
To spoil thy peaceful realm, and ruin all thy
    line.

But turn-coat Time assists the foe in vain,
And, bribed by thee, assists thy short-lived
    reign,    20

And to thy hungry womb drives back thy slaves
    again.

Though mysteries are barred from laic eyes,
And the Divine alone, with warrant, pries
Into thy bosom, where the Truth in private lies.

Yet this of thee the wise may freely say,    25
Thou from the Virtuous nothing tak'st away,
And to be part with thee the Wicked wisely
    pray.

Great Negative, how vainly would the Wise
Inquire, define, distinguish, teach, devise,
Didst thou not stand to point their dull phi-
    losophies?    30

Is, or is not, the two great ends of Fate,
And, true or false, the subject of debate,
That perfect, or destroy, the vast designs of
    Fate.

When they have racked the Politician's breast,
Within thy bosom must securely rest,    35
And, when reduced to thee, are least unsafe
    and best.

But, Nothing, why does Something still permit,
That sacred Monarchs should at council sit,
With persons highly thought, at best, for noth-
    ing fit.

Whilst weighty Something modestly abstains,
From Princes' coffers, and from Statesmen's
    brains,    41
And nothing there like stately Nothing reigns.

Nothing, who dwell'st with fools in grave dis-
    guise,
For whom they reverend shapes and forms de-
    vise,
Lawn sleeves and furs and gowns, when they
    like thee look wise.    45

French truth, Dutch prowess, British policy,
Hibernian learning, Scotch civility,
Spaniards' dispatch, Danes' wit, are mainly
    seen in thee.

The great man's gratitude to his best friend,
King's promises, Whore's vows, towards thee
    they bend,    50
Flow swiftly into thee, and in thee ever end.

## The King's Epitaph

Here lies a great and mighty King,
    Whose promise none relies on;
He never said a foolish thing,
    Nor ever did a wise one.

# WILLIAM CONGREVE

## (1670–1729)

## Song [1]

A Soldier, and a Sailor,
A Tinker, and a Tailor,
Had once a doubtful strife, Sir,
To make a maid a wife, Sir,
    Whose name was Buxom *Joan.*   5
For now the time was ended,
When she no more intended,
To lick her lips at men, Sir,
And gnaw the sheets in vain, Sir,
    And lie o' nights alone.   10

[1] From the end of Act III of Congreve's *Love for
Love* (1695). It is quite possible that the dramatist
merely shortened a popular broadside ballad of the
time in order to secure a suitable song for his play.
(Cf. D. Crane Taylor, *William Congreve*, pp. 77–
79.)

The Soldier swore like thunder,
He loved her more than plunder;
And showed her many a scar, Sir,
That he had brought from far, Sir,
    With fighting for her sake.   15
The Tailor thought to please her,
With off'ring her his measure.
The Tinker too with mettle,
Said he could mend her kettle,
    And stop up ev'ry leak.   20

But while these three were prating,
The Sailor slyly waiting,
Thought if it came about, Sir:
That they should all fall out, Sir:
    He then might play his part.   25
And just e'en as he meant, Sir,
To loggerheads they went, Sir,
And then he let fly at her,
A shot 'twixt wind and water,
    That won this Fair Maid's heart.   30

# Joseph Addison
## 1672 - 1719

### and

# Richard Steele
## 1672 - 1729

Addison was born at Milston, Wiltshire, on 1 May, 1672. His father was a clergyman, and the boy was brought up in a cultivated environment. He was sent to the Charterhouse School in London and then to Queen's College, Oxford. At Oxford he distinguished himself both as a scholar and as a writer of smooth English and Latin verse, and he won a fellowship at Magdalen College which he held until 1699. His Latin poem on the peace of Ryswick, together with his general ability as a man of letters, won him a pension from the Whigs, who wished to secure his continued support. This enabled him to spend four years in travel and study on the Continent. Immediately on his return in 1704 he was asked to write a poem celebrating Marlborough's victory at Blenheim. He produced The Campaign, which was at once successful and which ensured his political position. He was somewhat reserved and cautious in temperament, yet nevertheless became intimate with many of the "wits" of the day. He wrote three plays which would hardly be remembered now were it not that one of them, Cato, which was put on the stage in 1713, attained a remarkable but artificial success. It had a long run, not because of its dramatic interest or power, but because it was believed to contain good Whig doctrine. When the Whigs returned to power in 1714, Addison was made Chief Secretary for Ireland. Later he became Commissioner for Trade and the Colonies, and finally Secretary of State in 1717. After he had held this post for only a few months he resigned it, chiefly because of ill-health. He died on 17 June, 1719, and was buried in Westminster Abbey.

Richard Steele was born in Dublin in March, 1672. He was sent to Charterhouse, where he became acquainted with Addison; and like Addison he went up to Oxford. He entered Christ Church, at Oxford, in 1690, but left without a degree to become a soldier. His career in the army was not without irregularities, but he rose to a captaincy by 1700. In the following year he began writing for the theater, his first play being The Funeral, or Grief à la Mode. In 1703 The Lying Lover was produced at Drury Lane, and in 1705 The Tender Husband. In these plays Steele attempted to reform the taste of the day; he proved successfully that a comedy could be genuinely amusing without descending to ribaldry and the exhibition of gross immorality, and thus he foreshadowed one of the prominent aims of later work which he and Addison were to do together. In 1707 Steele was appointed Gazetteer, a post which he lost in 1710. In 1713 he sat in Parliament for Stockbridge, but in the following spring was expelled from the House of Commons for uttering seditious sentiments—a charge without real foundation, the vote on which served to show, not Steele's guilt, but simply the solid Tory majority in the House. On the accession of George I in the fall of 1714 Steele was rewarded for his support of the Hanoverian succession by the gift of several offices, and in 1715 he was again elected to Parliament, and was knighted. He also became in that year the Patentee, or manager, of Drury Lane Theater. In spite, however, of these and other turns of fortune in his favor, Steele, owing to his reckless expenditures, was never out of financial difficulties, and his difficulties of this sort grew worse as he grew older. In the fall of 1723 he left London for Bath, then lived for a time at Hereford, and finally retired to Carmarthen in Wales—all this being done in pursuit of an arrangement designed to aid his creditors. At Carmarthen he died on 1 September, 1729, and was buried there in St. Peter's Church.

Both Steele and Addison are remembered

*today for their two periodicals, the* Tatler *and
the* Spectator. *While Steele was editing the*
Gazette, *an official government paper, he conceived the idea of a livelier periodical than that
organ, and in 1709 began the* Tatler. *Addison
soon joined him in writing for it, and the paper
ran successfully until they stopped it in January, 1711, in order a few months later to begin the* Spectator *on a somewhat different plan.
The* Spectator *was issued daily until 6 December, 1712, reaching a total of 555 numbers. The
purposes of Steele and Addison are indicated
by themselves in numbers of the two papers
printed below. Briefly, their most general aim
was the reformation of manners, and to this
end they freely employed good-humored satire.
Their style was marked by simplicity, as the
content of their papers was marked by common
sense. Of the two writers Addison was easily
the superior, his style exhibiting a fine urbanity
and quiet distinction which Steele could not
attain. Addison, too, extended the* Spectator's
*reforming activities to the sphere of taste, and
made effective attacks on pedantry which have
not yet lost either their force or their applica-
bility. It should be remembered, however, that
the whole design was of Steele's invention, and
that Steele's reputation has suffered in a sense
unfairly from the constant comparison of his
essays with those of Addison.*

*Both the* Tatler *and the* Spectator *have been
ably edited by George A. Aitken (London,
1898–1899 and 1898). A standard critical and
biographical essay on Addison is Samuel Johnson's, in* The Lives of the English Poets, *ed.
George B. Hill (Oxford, 1905), vol. II; a valuable brief study of Addison's life appears in
Bonamy Dobrée's* Essays in Biography, *1680–
1726 (London, 1925). An excellent modern
biography is Peter Smithers'* Life of Joseph
Addison *(Oxford, 1954). For the life of Steele
see Willard Connely,* Sir Richard Steele *(New
York, 1934).*

## The Tatler

NO. 1. TUESDAY, 12 APRIL, 1709.
[STEELE.]

*Quicquid agunt homines——
nostri est farrago libelli.*[1]
—Juv. Sat. i. 85, 86.

THOUGH the other papers, which are published for the use of the good people of
England, have certainly very wholesome ef-

fects, and are laudable in their particular
kinds, they do not seem to come up to the
main design of such narrations, which, I
humbly presume, should be principally intended for the use of politic persons, who are
so public-spirited as to neglect their own
affairs to look into transactions of state.
Now these gentlemen, for the most part, being persons of strong zeal, and weak intellects, it is both a charitable and necessary
work to offer something, whereby such
worthy and well-affected members of the
commonwealth may be instructed, after their
reading, what to think; which shall be the
end and purpose of this my paper, wherein I
shall, from time to time, report and consider
all matters of what kind soever that shall occur to me, and publish such my advices and
reflections every Tuesday, Thursday, and
Saturday in the week, for the convenience of
the post. I resolve to have something which
may be of entertainment to the fair sex, in
honor of whom I have invented the title of
this paper. I therefore earnestly desire all persons, without distinction, to take it in for
the present *gratis*, and hereafter at the price
of one penny, forbidding all hawkers to take
more for it at their peril. And I desire all
persons to consider, that I am at a very great
charge for proper materials for this work, as
well as that, before I resolved upon it, I had
settled a correspondence in all parts of the
known and knowing world. And forasmuch
as this globe is not trodden upon by mere
drudges of business only, but that men of
spirit and genius are justly to be esteemed as
considerable agents in it, we shall not, upon
a dearth of news, present you with musty
foreign edicts, and dull proclamations, but
shall divide our relation of the passages
which occur in action or discourse throughout this town, as well as elsewhere, under
such dates of places as may prepare you for
the matter you are to expect in the following
manner.

All accounts of gallantry, pleasure, and entertainment, shall be under the article of
White's Chocolate-house; poetry under that
of Will's Coffee-house; Learning, under the
title of Grecian; foreign and domestic news,
you will have from St. James's Coffee-house;[2]

[1] Whate'er men do, or say, or think, or dream,
Our motley paper seizes for its theme. (Pope.)

[2] These famous institutions occupied an important place in London life in the late seventeenth and
early eighteenth centuries, serving as informal clubs
and as centers of social, political, and literary influence. Steele indicates in a general way the kinds of
people who frequented the four he mentions.

and what else I have to offer on any other subject shall be dated from my own Apartment.

I once more desire my reader to consider, that as I cannot keep an ingenious man to go daily to Will's under two-pence each day, merely for his charges; to White's under sixpence; nor to the Grecian, without allowing him some plain Spanish,[3] to be as able as others at the learned table; and that a good observer cannot speak with even Kidney[4] at St. James's without clean linen; I say, these considerations will, I hope, make all persons willing to comply with my humble request (when my *gratis* stock is exhausted) of a penny apiece; especially since they are sure of some proper amusement, and that it is impossible for me to want means to entertain them, having, besides the force of my own parts, the power of divination, and that I can, by casting a figure, tell you all that will happen before it comes to pass.

But this last faculty I shall use very sparingly, and speak but of few things until they are passed, for fear of divulging matters which may offend our superiors.

## NO. 25. TUESDAY, 7 JUNE, 1709.
### [STEELE.]

A LETTER from a young lady, written in the most passionate terms, wherein she laments the misfortune of a gentleman, her lover, who was lately wounded in a duel, has turned my thoughts to that subject, and inclined me to examine into the causes which precipitate men into so fatal a folly. And as it has been proposed to treat of subjects of gallantry in the article from hence,[5] and no one point in nature is more proper to be considered by the company who frequent this place than that of duels, it is worth our consideration to examine into this chimerical groundless humor, and to lay every other thought aside, until we have stripped it of all its false pretenses to credit and reputation amongst men.

But I must confess, when I consider what I am going about, and run over in my imagination all the endless crowd of men of honor who will be offended at such a discourse; I am undertaking, methinks, a work worthy an invulnerable hero in romance, rather than a private gentleman with a single rapier: but as I am pretty well acquainted by great opportunities with the nature of man, and know of a truth that all men fight against their will, the danger vanishes, and resolution rises upon this subject. For this reason, I shall talk very freely on a custom which all men wish exploded, though no man has courage enough to resist it.

But there is one unintelligible word, which I fear will extremely perplex my dissertation, and I confess to you I find very hard to explain, which is the term "satisfaction." An honest country gentleman had the misfortune to fall into company with two or three modern men of honor, where he happened to be very ill-treated; and one of the company, being conscious of his offense, sends a note to him in the morning, and tells him, he was ready to give him satisfaction. "This is fine doing," says the plain fellow; "last night he sent me away cursedly out of humor, and this morning he fancies it would be a satisfaction to be run through the body."

As the matter at present stands, it is not to do handsome actions denominates a man of honor; it is enough if he dares to defend ill ones. Thus you often see a common sharper in competition with a gentleman of the first rank; though all mankind is convinced, that a fighting gamester is only a pickpocket with the courage of an highwayman. One cannot with any patience reflect on the unaccountable jumble of persons and things in this town and nation, which occasions very frequently, that a brave man falls by a hand below that of a common hangman, and yet his executioner escapes the clutches of the hangman for doing it. I shall therefore hereafter consider, how the bravest men in other ages and nations have behaved themselves upon such incidents as we decide by combat; and show, from their practice, that this resentment neither has its foundation from true reason or solid fame; but is an imposture, made of cowardice, falsehood, and want of understanding. For this work, a good history of quarrels would be very edifying to the public, and I apply myself to the town for particulars and circumstances within their knowledge, which may serve to embellish the dissertation with proper cuts.[6] Most of the quarrels I have ever known, have proceeded from some valiant coxcomb's persisting in the wrong, to defend some prevailing folly, and preserve himself from the ingenuousness of owning a mistake.

By this means it is called "giving a man satisfaction," to urge your offense against

---

[3] Wine.    [4] One of the waiters at St. James's.
[5] This number of the *Tatler* is dated from White's Chocolate-House.
[6] Illustrations.

him with your sword; which puts me in mind of Peter's order to the keeper, in *The Tale of a Tub*.[7] "If you neglect to do all this, damn you and your generation for ever: and so we bid you heartily farewell." If the contradiction in the very terms of one of our challenges were as well explained and turned into downright English, would it not run after this manner?

"Sir,

"Your extraordinary behavior last night, and the liberty you were pleased to take with me, makes me this morning give you this, to tell you, because you are an ill-bred puppy, I will meet you in Hyde Park, an hour hence; and because you want both breeding and humanity, I desire you would come with a pistol in your hand, on horseback, and endeavor to shoot me through the head, to teach you more manners. If you fail of doing me this pleasure, I shall say, you are a rascal, on every post in town: and so, sir, if you will not injure me more, I shall never forgive what you have done already. Pray, sir, do not fail of getting everything ready; and you will infinitely oblige, sir, your most obedient humble servant, *etc*."

## NO. 85. TUESDAY, 25 OCTOBER, 1709. [STEELE.]

My brother Tranquillus, who is a man of business, came to me this morning into my study, and after very many civil expressions in return for what good offices I had done him, told me, "he desired to carry his wife, my sister, that very morning, to his own house." I readily told him, "I would wait upon him," without asking why he was so impatient to rob us of his good company. He went out of my chamber, and I thought seemed to have a little heaviness upon him, which gave me some disquiet. Soon after my sister came to me, with a very matron-like air, and most sedate satisfaction in her looks, which spoke her very much at ease; but the traces of her countenance seemed to discover that she had been lately in a passion, and that air of content to flow from a certain triumph upon some advantage obtained. She no sooner sat down by me, but I perceived she was one of those ladies who begin to be managers within the time of their being brides. Without letting her speak, which I saw she had a mighty inclination to do, I said, "Here has been your husband, who tells me he has a mind to go home this

[7] By Jonathan Swift.

very morning, and I have consented to it." "It is well," said she, "for you must know—" "Nay, Jenny," said I. "I beg your pardon, for it is you must know— You are to understand, that now is the time to fix or alienate your husband's heart for ever; and I fear you have been a little indiscreet in your expressions or behavior towards him, even here in my house." "There has," says she, "been some words; but I will be judged by you if he was not in the wrong; nay I need not be judged by anybody, for he gave it up himself, and said not a word when he saw me grow passionate, but, 'Madam, you are perfectly in the right of it'; as you shall judge—" "Nay, Madam," said I, "I am judge already, and tell you that you are perfectly in the wrong of it; for if it was a matter of importance, I know he has better sense than you; if a trifle, you know what I told you on your wedding-day, that you were to be above little provocations." She knows very well I can be sour upon occasion, therefore gave me leave to go on.

"Sister," said I, "I will not enter into the dispute between you, which I find his prudence put an end to before it came to extremity; but charge you to have a care of the first quarrel, as you tender your happiness; for then it is that the mind will reflect harshly upon every circumstance that has ever passed between you. If such an accident is ever to happen, which I hope never will, be sure to keep to the circumstance before you; make no allusions to what is passed, or conclusions referring to what is to come: do not show a hoard of matter for dissension in your breast: but, if it is necessary, lay before him the thing as you understand it, candidly, without being ashamed of acknowledging an error, or proud of being in the right. If a young couple be not careful in this point, they will get into a habit of wrangling: and when to displease is thought of no consequence, to please is always of as little moment. There is a play, Jenny, I have formerly been at when I was a student: we got into a dark corner with a porringer of brandy, and threw raisins into it, then set it on fire. My chamber-fellow and I diverted ourselves with the sport of venturing our fingers for the raisins; and the wantonness of the thing was to see each other look like a demon, as we burned ourselves, and snatched out the fruit. This fantastical mirth was called Snap-Dragon. You may go into many a family, where you see the man and wife at this sport; every word at their table alludes to some passage between themselves; and you see by the paleness and emotion in their countenances, that it is for your sake, and not their own, that they forbear playing out the whole game in burning each other's fingers. In this case, the whole purpose of life is inverted, and the ambition turns upon a certain contention who shall contradict best, and not upon an inclination to excel in kindnesses and good offices. Therefore, dear Jenny, re- 10 member me, and avoid Snap-Dragon."

"I thank you, brother," said she, "but you do not know how he loves me; I find I can do anything with him." "If you can so, why should you desire to do anything but please him? but I have a word or two more before you go out of the room; for I see you do not like the subject I am upon: let nothing provoke you to fall upon an imperfection he cannot help; for, if he has a resenting spirit, 20 he will think your aversion as immovable as the imperfection with which you upbraid him. But, above all, dear Jenny, be careful of one thing, and you will be something more than woman; that is, a levity you are almost all guilty of, which is, to take a pleasure in your power to give pain. It is even in a mistress an argument of meanness of spirit, but in a wife it is injustice and ingratitude. When a sensible man once observes this in a woman, 30 he must have a very great, or very little spirit, to overlook it. A woman ought, therefore, to consider very often, how few men there are who will regard a meditated offense as a weakness of temper."

I was going on in my confabulation, when Tranquillus entered. She cast all her eyes upon him with much shame and confusion, mixed with great complacency and love, and went up to him. He took her in his arms, 40 and looked so many soft things at one glance, that I could see he was glad I had been talking to her, sorry she had been troubled, and angry at himself that he could not disguise the concern he was in an hour before. After which he says to me, with an air awkward enough, but, methought, not unbecoming, "I have altered my mind, brother; we will live upon you a day or two longer." I replied, "That is what I have been persuading Jenny 50 to ask you, but she is resolved never to contradict your inclination, and refused me."

We were going on in that way which one hardly knows how to express; as when two people mean the same thing in a nice case, but come at it by talking as distantly from it as they can; when very opportunely came in upon us an honest inconsiderable fellow Tim Dapper, a gentleman well known to us both. Tim is one of those who are very necessary, by being very inconsiderable. Tim dropped in at an incident when we knew not how to fall into either a grave or a merry way. My sister took this occasion to make off, and Dapper gave us an account of all the company he has been in to-day, who was and was not at home where he visited. This Tim is the head of a species; he is a little out of his element in this town; but he is a relation of Tranquillus, and his neighbor in the country, which is the true place of residence for this species. The habit of a Dapper, when he is at home, is a light broadcloth, with calamanco [8] or red waistcoat and breeches; and it is remarkable that their wigs seldom hide the collar of their coats. They have always a peculiar spring in their arms, a wriggle in their bodies, and a trip in their gait. All which motions they express at once in their drinking, bowing, or saluting ladies; for a distant imitation of a forward fop, and a resolution to overtop him in his way, are the distinguishing marks of a Dapper. These under-characters of men, are parts of the sociable world by no means to be neglected: they are like pegs in a building; they make no figure in it, but hold the structure together, and are as absolutely necessary as the pillars and columns. I am sure we found it so this morning; for Tranquillus and I should, perhaps, have looked cold at each other the whole day, but Dapper fell in with his brisk way, shook us both by the hand, rallied the bride, mistook the acceptance he met with amongst us for extraordinary perfection in himself, and heartily pleased, and was pleased all the while he stayed. His company left us all in good humor, and we were not such fools as to let it sink, before we confirmed it by great cheerfulness and openness in our carriage the whole evening.

## NO. 132. SATURDAY, 11 FEBRUARY, 1710.

[STEELE.]

*Habeo senectuti magnam gratiam, quae mihi sermonis aviditatem auxit, potionis et cibi sustulit.* [9]
—TULL. *de Sen.*

AFTER having applied my mind with more than ordinary attention to my studies, it is

---

[8] A woolen material.

[9] I owe much gratitude to old age, which has sharpened my appetite for conversation and dulled my appetite for food and drink (Cicero, *De Senectute*).

my usual custom to relax and unbend it in the conversation of such, as are rather easy than shining companions. This I find particularly necessary for me before I retire to rest, in order to draw my slumbers upon me by degrees, and fall asleep insensibly. This is the particular use I make of a set of heavy honest men, with whom I have passed many hours with much indolence, though not with great pleasure. Their conversation is a kind of preparative for sleep; it takes the mind down from its abstractions, leads it into the familiar traces of thought, and lulls it into that state of tranquillity which is the condition of a thinking man, when he is but half awake. After this, my reader will not be surprised to hear the account, which I am about to give of a club of my own contemporaries, among whom I pass two or three hours every evening. This I look upon as taking my first nap before I go to bed. The truth of it is, I should think myself unjust to posterity, as well as to the society at the Trumpet, of which I am a member, did not I in some part of my writings give an account of the persons among whom I have passed almost a sixth part of my time for these last forty years. Our club consisted originally of fifteen; but, partly by the severity of the law in arbitrary times, and partly by the natural effects of old age, we are at present reduced to a third part of that number: in which, however, we hear this consolation, that the best company is said to consist of five persons. I must confess, besides the aforementioned benefit which I meet with in the conversation of this select society, I am not the less pleased with the company, in that I find myself the greatest wit among them, and am heard as their oracle in all points of learning and difficulty.

Sir Jeoffry Notch, who is the oldest of the club, has been in possession of the right-hand chair time out of mind, and is the only man among us that has the liberty of stirring the fire. This our foreman is a gentleman of an ancient family, that came to a great estate some years before he had discretion, and run it out in hounds, horses, and cock-fighting; for which reason he looks upon himself as an honest, worthy gentleman, who has had misfortunes in the world, and calls every thriving man a pitiful upstart.

Major Matchlock is the next senior, who served in the last civil wars, and has all the battles by heart. He does not think any action in Europe worth talking of since the fight of Marston Moor; and every night tells us of his having been knocked off his horse at the rising of the London apprentices; for which he is in great esteem among us.

Honest old Dick Reptile is the third of our society. He is a good-natured indolent man, who speaks little himself, but laughs at our jokes; and brings his young nephew along with him, a youth of eighteen years old, to show him good company, and give him a taste of the world. This young fellow sits generally silent; but whenever he opens his mouth, or laughs at anything that passes, he is constantly told by his uncle, after a jocular manner, "Ay, ay, Jack, you young men think us fools; but we old men know you are."

The greatest wit of our company, next to myself, is a Bencher of the neighboring Inn,[10] who in his youth frequented the ordinaries about Charing Cross, and pretends to have been intimate with Jack Ogle. He has about ten distichs of *Hudibras* without book, and never leaves the club until he has applied them all. If any modern wit be mentioned, or any town-frolic spoken of, he shakes his head at the dullness of the present age, and tells us a story of Jack Ogle.

For my own part, I am esteemed among them, because they see I am something respected by others; though at the same time I understand by their behavior, that I am considered by them as a man of a great deal of learning, but no knowledge of the world; insomuch, that the Major sometimes, in the height of his military pride, calls me the Philosopher: and Sir Jeoffrey, no longer ago than last night, upon a dispute what day of the month it was then in Holland, pulled his pipe out of his mouth, and cried, "What does the scholar say to it?"

Our club meets precisely at *six o'clock in the evening*; but I did not come last night until half an hour after seven, by which means I escaped the battle of Naseby, which the Major usually begins at about three-quarters after six: I found also, that my good friend the Bencher had already spent three of his distichs; and only waited an opportunity to hear a sermon spoken of, that he might introduce the couplet where "a stick" rimes to "ecclesiastic." At my entrance into the room, they were naming a red petticoat and a cloak, by which I found that the Bencher had been diverting them with a story of Jack Ogle.

I had no sooner taken my seat, but Sir Jeoffrey, to show his good-will towards me,

[10] A senior member of one of the London legal colleges.

gave me a pipe of his own tobacco, and stirred up the fire. I look upon it as a point of morality, to be obliged by those who endeavor to oblige me; and therefore, in requital for his kindness, and to set the conversation a-going, I took the best occasion I could to put him upon telling us the story of old Gantlett, which he always does with very particular concern. He traced up his descent on both sides for several generations, describing [10] his diet and manner of life, with his several battles, and particularly that in which he fell. This Gantlett was a gamecock, upon whose head the knight, in his youth, had won five hundred pounds, and lost two thousand. This naturally set the Major upon the account of Edge Hill fight, and ended in a duel of Jack Ogle's.

Old Reptile was extremely attentive to all that was said, though it was the same he had [20] heard every night for these twenty years, and, upon all occasions, winked upon his nephew to mind what passed.

This may suffice to give the world a taste of our innocent conversation, which we spun out until about ten of the clock, when my maid came with a lantern to light me home. I could not but reflect with myself, as I was going out, upon the talkative humor of old men, and the little figure which that part of [30] life makes in one who cannot employ his natural propensity in discourses which would make him venerable. I must own, it makes me very melancholy in company, when I hear a young man begin a story; and have often observed, that one of a quarter of an hour long in a man of five-and-twenty, gathers circumstances every time he tells it, until it grows into a long Canterbury tale of two hours by the time he is threescore. [40]

The only way of avoiding such a trifling and frivolous old age, is to lay up in our way to it such stores of knowledge and observation, as may make us useful and agreeable in our declining years. The mind of man in a long life will become a magazine of wisdom or folly, and will consequently discharge itself in something impertinent or improving. For which reason, as there is nothing more ridiculous than an old trifling story-teller, so [50] there is nothing more venerable, than one who has turned his experience to the entertainment and advantage of mankind.

In short, we, who are in the last stage of life, and are apt to indulge ourselves in talk, ought to consider, if what we speak be worth being heard, and endeavor to make our discourse like that of Nestor, which Homer compares to the flowing of honey for its sweetness.

I am afraid I shall be thought guilty of this excess I am speaking of, when I cannot conclude without observing, that Milton certainly thought of this passage in Homer, when, in his description of an eloquent spirit, he says, "His tongue dropped manna." [11]

## NO. 158. THURSDAY, 13 APRIL, 1710.
### [ADDISON.]

*Faciunt nae intelligendo, ut nihil intelligant.*[12]
— Ter.

Tom Folio is a broker in learning, employed to get together good editions, and stock the libraries of great men. There is not a sale of books begins until Tom Folio is seen at the door. There is not an auction where his name is not heard, and that too in the very nick of time, in the critical moment, before the last decisive stroke of the hammer. There is not a subscription goes forward in which Tom is not privy to the first rough draught of the proposals; nor a catalogue printed, that doth not come to him wet from the press. He is an universal scholar, so far as the title-page of all authors; knows the manuscripts in which they were discovered, the editions through which they have passed, with the praises or censures which they have received from the several members of the learned world. He has a greater esteem for Aldus and Elzevir,[13] than for Virgil and Horace. If you talk of Herodotus, he breaks out into panegyric upon Harry Stephens.[14] He thinks he gives you an account of an author, when he tells you the subject he treats of, the name of the editor, and the year in which it was printed. Or if you draw him into farther particulars, he cries up the goodness of the paper, extols the diligence of the corrector, and is transported with the beauty of the letter. This he looks upon to be sound learning, and substantial criticism. As for those who talk of the fineness of style, and the justness of thought, or describe the brightness of any particular passages; nay, though they themselves write in the genius and spirit of the author they admire; Tom looks upon them as

[11] Said of Belial, *Paradise Lost*, II, 112–113.
[12] While they pretend to know more than others, they really know nothing (Terence, *Andr.*, Prol., 17).
[13] Famous publishers of books.
[14] Henri Estienne, a sixteenth-century editor of and apologist for Herodotus.

men of superficial learning, and flashy parts.

I had yesterday morning a visit from this learned *idiot*, for *that* is the light in which I consider every pedant, when I discovered in him some little touches of the coxcomb, which I had not before observed. Being very full of the figure which he makes in the republic of letters, and wonderfully satisfied with his great stock of knowledge, he gave me broad intimations, that he did not believe in all points as his forefathers had done. He then communicated to me a thought of a certain author upon a passage of Virgil's account of the dead, which I made the subject of a late paper. This thought hath taken very much among men of Tom's pitch and understanding, though universally exploded by all that know how to construe Virgil, or have any relish of antiquity. Not to trouble my reader with it, I found, upon the whole, that Tom did not believe a future state of rewards and punishments, because Aeneas, at his leaving the empire of the dead, passed through the gate of ivory, and not through that of horn. Knowing that Tom had not sense enough to give up an opinion which he had once received, that I might avoid wrangling, I told him "that Virgil possibly had his oversights as well as another author." "Ah! Mr. Bickerstaff," [15] says he, "you would have another opinion of him, if you would read him in Daniel Heinsius's edition. I have perused him myself several times in that edition," continued he; "and after the strictest and most malicious examination, could find but two faults in him; one of them is in the Aeneids, where there are two commas instead of a parenthesis; and another in the third Georgic, where you may find a semicolon turned upside down." "Perhaps," said I, "these were not Virgil's faults, but those of the transcriber." "I do not design it," says Tom, "as a reflection on Virgil; on the contrary, I know that all the manuscripts declaim against such a punctuation. Oh! Mr. Bickerstaff," says he, "what would a man give to see one simile of Virgil writ in his own hand?" I asked him which was the simile he meant; but was answered, any simile in Virgil. He then told me all the secret history in the commonwealth of learning; of modern pieces that had the names of ancient authors annexed to them; of all the books that were

now writing or printing in the several parts of Europe; of many amendments which are made, and not yet published, and a thousand other particulars, which I would not have my memory burdened with for a Vatican.

At length, being fully persuaded that I thoroughly admired him, and looked upon him as a prodigy of learning, he took his leave. I know several of Tom's class, who are professed admirers of Tasso, without understanding a word of Italian: and one in particular, that carries a *Pastor Fido* [16] in his pocket, in which, I am sure, he is acquainted with no other beauty but the clearness of the character.

There is another kind of pedant, who, with all Tom Folio's impertinences, hath greater superstructures and embellishments of Greek and Latin; and is still more insupportable than the other, in the same degree as he is more learned. Of this kind very often are editors, commentators, interpreters, scholiasts, and critics; and, in short, all men of deep learning without common sense. These persons set a greater value on themselves for having found out the meaning of a passage in Greek, than upon the author for having written it; nay, will allow the passage itself not to have any beauty in it, at the same time that they would be considered as the greatest men of the age, for having interpreted it. They will look with contempt on the most beautiful poems that have been composed by any of their contemporaries; but will lock themselves up in their studies for a twelvemonth together, to correct, publish, and expound such trifles of antiquity, as a modern author would be contemned for. Men of the strictest morals, severest lives, and gravest professions, will write volumes upon an idle sonnet, that is originally in Greek or Latin; give editions of the most immoral authors; and spin out whole pages upon the various readings of a lewd expression. All that can be said in excuse for them is, that their works sufficiently show they have no taste of their authors; and that what they do in this kind, is out of their great learning, and not out of any levity or lasciviousness of temper.

A pedant of this nature is wonderfully well described in six lines of Boileau, with which I shall conclude his character:

*Un Pédant enyvré de sa vaine science,*
*Tout herissé de Grec, tout bouffi d'arrogance;*
*Et qui de mille auteurs retenus mot pour mot,*
*Dans sa tête entassés n'a souvent fait qu'un sot,*
*Croit qu'un livre fait tout, et que sans Aristote*
*La raison ne voit goute, et le bon sens radote.*

[15] The *Tatler* papers, it was pretended, were written by Isaac Bickerstaff, a fictitious astrologer invented several years before by Swift for the purpose of making fun of one Partridge, an astrologer who published predictions much after the manner of the old-fashioned almanac still occasionally to be met with.

[16] Italian pastoral drama of the late sixteenth century by G. B. Guarini.

Brim-full of learning see that pedant stride,
Bristling with horrid Greek, and puffed with pride!
A thousand authors he in vain has read,
And with their maxims stuffed his empty head;
And thinks that, without Aristotle's rule,
Reason is blind, and common sense a fool.

## The Spectator

### NO. 1. THURSDAY, 1 MARCH, 1711.
[ADDISON.]

*Non fumum ex fulgore, sed ex fumo dare lucem
Cogitat, ut speciosa dehinc miracula promat.*[1]
                                        HORACE.

I HAVE observed that a reader seldom peruses a book with pleasure till he knows whether the writer of it be a black or a fair man, of a mild or choleric disposition, married or a bachelor, with other particulars of the like nature that conduce very much to the right understanding of an author. To gratify this curiosity, which is so natural to a reader, I design this paper and my next as prefatory discourses to my following writings, and shall give some account in them of the several persons that are engaged in this work. As the chief trouble of compiling, digesting, and correcting will fall to my share, I must do myself the justice to open the work with my own history. I was born to a small hereditary estate, which, according to the tradition of the village where it lies, was bounded by the same hedges and ditches in William the Conqueror's time that it is at present, and has been delivered down from father to son whole and entire, without the loss or acquisition of a single field or meadow, during the space of six hundred years. There runs a story in the family, that my mother dreamed that she was brought to bed of a judge: whether this might proceed from a lawsuit which was then depending in the family, or my father's being a justice of the peace, I cannot determine; for I am not so vain as to think it presaged any dignity that I should arrive at in my future life, though that was the interpretation which the neighborhood put upon it. The gravity of my behavior at my very first appearance in the world seemed to favor my mother's dream: for, as she has often told me, I threw away my rattle before I was two months old, and would not make use of my coral till they had taken away the bells from it.

As for the rest of my infancy, there being nothing in it remarkable, I shall pass it over in silence. I find that, during my nonage, I had the reputation of a very sullen youth, but was always a favorite of my schoolmaster, who used to say *that my parts were solid and would wear well.* I had not been long at the University before I distinguished myself by a most profound silence; for during the space of eight years, excepting in the public exercises of the college, I scarce uttered the quantity of an hundred words; and indeed do not remember that I ever spoke three sentences together in my whole life. Whilst I was in this learned body, I applied myself with so much diligence to my studies that there are very few celebrated books, either in the learned or the modern tongues, which I am not acquainted with.

Upon the death of my father I was resolved to travel into foreign countries, and therefore left the University with the character of an odd, unaccountable fellow, that had a great deal of learning if I would but show it. An insatiable thirst after knowledge carried me into all the countries of Europe in which there was anything new or strange to be seen; nay, to such a degree was my curiosity raised, that having read the controversies of some great men concerning the antiquities of Egypt, I made a voyage to Grand Cairo, on purpose to take the measure of a pyramid; and as soon as I had set myself right in that particular, returned to my native country with great satisfaction.

I have passed my latter years in this city, where I am frequently seen in most public places, though there are not above half a dozen of my select friends that know me; of whom my next paper shall give a more particular account. There is no place of general sort wherein I do not often make my appearance; sometimes I am seen thrusting my head into a round of politicians at Will's, and listening with great attention to the narratives that are made in those little circular audiences. Sometimes I smoke a pipe at Child's, and whilst I seem attentive to nothing but *The Postman,* overhear the conversation of every table in the room. I appear on Sunday nights at St. James's Coffeehouse, and sometimes join the little committee of politics in the Inner room, as one who comes there to hear and improve. My face is likewise very well known at the Grecian, the Cocoa-Tree, and in the theaters both of Drury Lane and the Hay-Market. I have been taken for a merchant upon the Exchange for above these ten years, and sometimes pass for a Jew in the assembly of stockjobbers at Jonathan's. In

---

[1] Not smoke from fire his object is to bring,
  But fire from smoke, a very different thing.
(*Art of Poetry,* 143–144; Conington's translation.)

short, wherever I see a cluster of people, I always mix with them, though I never open my lips but in my own club.

Thus I live in the world rather as a SPECTATOR of mankind than as one of the species; by which means I have made myself a speculative statesman, soldier, merchant, and artisan, without ever meddling with any practical part in life. I am very well versed in the theory of an husband or a father, and can discern the errors in the economy, business, and diversion of others better than those who are engaged in them; as standersby discover blots which are apt to escape those who are in the game. I never espoused any party with violence, and am resolved to observe an exact neutrality between the Whigs and Tories, unless I shall be forced to declare myself by the hostilities of either side. In short, I have acted in all the parts of my life as a looker-on, which is the character I intend to preserve in this paper.

I have given the reader just so much of my history and character as to let him see I am not altogether unqualified for the business I have undertaken. As for other particulars in my life and adventures, I shall insert them in following papers as I shall see occasion. In the meantime, when I consider how much I have seen, read, and heard, I began to blame my own taciturnity: and since I have neither time nor inclination to communicate the fullness of my heart in speech, I am resolved to do it in writing, and to print myself out, if possible, before I die. I have been often told by my friends that it is a pity so many useful discoveries which I have made, should be in the possession of a silent man. For this reason, therefore, I shall publish a sheetful of thoughts every morning for the benefit of my contemporaries; and if I can in any way contribute to the diversion or improvement of the country in which I live, I shall leave it, when I am summoned out of it, with the secret satisfaction of thinking that I have not lived in vain.

There are three very material points which I have not spoken to in this paper, and which, for several important reasons, I must keep to myself, at least for some time: I mean, an account of my name, my age, and my lodgings. I must confess, I would gratify my reader in anything that is reasonable; but, as for these three particulars, though I am sensible they might tend very much to the embellishment of my paper, I cannot yet come to a resolution of communicating them to the public. They would indeed draw me out of that obscurity which I have enjoyed for many years, and expose me in public places to several salutes and civilities which have been always very disagreeable to me; for the greatest pain I can suffer is the being talked to and being stared at. It is for this reason, likewise, that I keep my complexion and dress as very great secrets, though it is not impossible but I may make discoveries of both in the progress of the work I have undertaken.

After having been thus particular upon myself, I shall in to-morrow's paper give an account of those gentlemen who are concerned with me in this work; for, as I have before intimated, a plan of it is laid and concerted (as all other matters of importance are) in a club. However, as my friends have engaged me to stand in the front, those who have a mind to correspond with me may direct their letters *To The Spectator, at Mr. Buckley's, in Little Britain*. For I must further acquaint the reader that, though our club meets only on Tuesdays and Thursdays, we have appointed a committee to sit every night for the inspection of all such papers as may contribute to the advancement of the public weal.

### NO. 2. FRIDAY, 2 MARCH, 1711.

[STEELE.]

——*Haec alii sex
Vel plures uno conclamant ore.*[2]
—JUVENAL.

THE first of our society is a gentleman of Worcestershire, of ancient descent, a baronet, his name Sir Roger de Coverly. His great-grandfather was inventor of that famous country-dance which is called after him. All who know that shire are very well acquainted with the parts and merits of Sir Roger. He is a gentleman that is very singular in his behavior, but his singularities proceed from his good sense, and are contradictions to the manners of the world only as he thinks the world is in the wrong. However, this humor creates him no enemies, for he does nothing with sourness of obstinacy; and his being unconfined to modes and forms, makes him but the readier and more capable to please and oblige all who know him. When he is in town, he lives in Soho Square. It is said he keeps himself a bachelor by reason he was crossed in love by a perverse, beautiful widow of the next county to him. Before this disappointment, Sir Roger was what you call a fine gentleman, had

[2] Six others and more cry out with one voice (*Satires*, VII, 167).

often supped with my Lord Rochester and Sir George Etherege,[3] fought a duel upon his first coming to town, and kicked Bully Dawson in a public coffee-house for calling him "youngster." But being ill-used by the above-mentioned widow, he was very serious for a year and a half; and though, his temper being naturally jovial, he at last got over it, he grew careless of himself, and never dressed afterward. He continues to wear a coat and doublet 10 of the same cut that were in fashion at the time of his repulse, which, in his merry humors, he tells us, has been in and out twelve times since he first wore it. 'Tis said Sir Roger grew humble in his desires after he had forgot this cruel beauty; but this is looked upon by his friends rather as matter of raillery than truth. He is now in his fifty-sixth year, cheerful, gay, and hearty; keeps a good house in both town and country; a great lover of mankind; but 20 there is such a mirthful cast in his behavior that he is rather beloved than esteemed. His tenants grow rich, his servants look satisfied, all the young women profess love to him, and the young men are glad of his company; when he comes into a house he calls the servants by their names, and talks all the way up stairs to a visit. I must not omit that Sir Roger is a justice of the quorum; that he fills the chair at a quarter-session with great abilities; and, three 30 months ago, gained universal applause by explaining a passage in the Game Act.

The gentleman next in esteem and authority among us is another bachelor, who is a member of the Inner Temple; a man of great probity, wit, and understanding; but he has chosen his place of residence rather to obey the direction of an old humorsome father, than in pursuit of his own inclinations. He was placed there to study the laws of the land, and 40 is the most learned of any of the house in those of the stage. Aristotle and Longinus are much better understood by him than Littleton or Coke.[4] The father sends up, every post, questions relating to marriage-articles, leases, and tenures, in the neighborhood; all which questions he agrees with an attorney to answer and take care of in the lump. He is studying the passions themselves, when he should be inquiring into the debates among men which arise 50 from them. He knows the argument of each of the orations of Demosthenes and Tully,[5] but not one case in the reports of our own courts.

No one ever took him for a fool, but none, except his intimate friends, know he has a great deal of wit. This turn makes him at once both disinterested and agreeable; as few of his thoughts are drawn from business, they are most of them fit for conversation. His taste of books is a little too just for the age he lives in; he has read all, but approves of very few. His familiarity with the customs, manners, actions, and writings of the ancients makes him a very delicate observer of what occurs to him in the present world. He is an excellent critic, and the time of the play is his hour of business; exactly at five he passes through New Inn, crosses through Russell Court, and takes a turn at Will's till the play begins; he has his shoes rubbed and his periwig powdered at the barber's as you go into the Rose. It is for the good of the audience when he is at a play, for 20 the actors have an ambition to please him.

The person of next consideration is Sir Andrew Freeport, a merchant of great eminence in the city of London, a person of indefatigable industry, strong reason, and great experience. His notions of trade are noble and generous, and (as every rich man has usually some sly way of jesting which would make no great figure were he not a rich man) he calls the sea the British Common. He is acquainted 30 with commerce in all its parts, and will tell you that it is a stupid and barbarous way to extend dominion by arms; for true power is to be got by arts and industry. He will often argue that if this part of our trade were well cultivated, we should gain from one nation; and if another, from another. I have heard him prove that diligence makes more lasting acquisitions than valor, and that sloth has ruined more nations than the sword. He abounds in several 40 frugal maxims, among which the greatest favorite is, "A penny saved is a penny got." A general trader of good sense is pleasanter company than a general scholar; and Sir Andrew having a natural unaffected eloquence, the perspicuity of his discourse gives the same pleasure that wit would in another man. He has made his fortunes himself, and says that England may be richer than other kingdoms by as plain methods as he himself is richer than other men; 50 though at the same time I can say this of him, that there is not a point in the compass but blows home a ship in which he is an owner.

Next to Sir Andrew in the club-room sits Captain Sentry, a gentleman of great courage, good understanding, but invincible modesty. He is one of those that deserve very well, but are very awkward at putting their talents within

[3] Men of letters during the Restoration period, a generation earlier.

[4] Outstanding English legal authorities.

[5] Cicero.

the observation of such as should take notice of them. He was some years a captain, and behaved himself with great gallantry in several engagements and at several sieges; but having a small estate of his own, and being next heir to Sir Roger, he has quitted a way of life in which no man can rise suitably to his merit who is not something of a courtier as well as a soldier. I have heard him often lament that in a profession where merit is placed in so conspicuous a 10 view, impudence should get the better of modesty. When he has talked to this purpose I never heard him make a sour expression, but frankly confess that he left the world because he was not fit for it. A strict honesty and an even, regular behavior are in themselves obstacles to him that must press through crowds who endeavor at the same end with himself,— the favor of a commander. He will, however, in this way of talk, excuse generals for not dis- 20 posing according to men's desert, or inquiring into it, "For," says he, "that great man who has a mind to help me, has as many to break through to come at me as I have to come at him"; therefore he will conclude that the man who would make a figure, especially in a military way, must get over all false modesty, and assist his patron against the importunity of other pretenders by a proper assurance in his own vindication. He says it is a civil cowardice 30 to be backward in asserting what you ought to expect, as it is a military fear to be slow in attacking when it is your duty. With this candor does the gentleman speak of himself and others. The same frankness runs through all his conversation. The military part of his life has furnished him with many adventures, in the relation of which he is very agreeable to the company; for he is never overbearing, though accustomed to command men in the 40 utmost degree below him; nor ever too obsequious from an habit of obeying men highly above him.

But that our society may not appear a set of humorists unacquainted with the gallantries and pleasures of the age, we have among us the gallant Will Honeycomb, a gentleman who, according to his years, should be in the decline of his life, but having ever been very careful of his person, and always had a very 50 easy fortune, time has made but very little impression either by wrinkles on his forehead or traces in his brain. His person is well turned and of a good height. He is very ready at that sort of discourse with which men usually entertain women. He has all his life dressed very well, and remembers habits as others do

men. He can smile when one speaks to him, and laughs easily. He knows the history of every mode, and can inform you from which of the French king's wenches our wives and daughters had this manner of curling their hair, that way of placing their hoods; whose frailty was covered by such a sort of petticoat, and whose vanity to show her foot made that part of the dress so short in such a year. In a word, all his conversation and knowledge has been in the female world. As other men of his age will take notice to you what such a minister said upon such and such an occasion, he will tell you when the Duke of Monmouth danced at court such a woman was then smitten, another was taken with him at the head of his troop in the Park. In all these important relations, he has ever about the same time received a kind glance or a blow of a fan from some celebrated beauty, mother of the present Lord Such-a-one. If you speak of a young commoner that said a lively thing in the House, he starts up: "He has good blood in his veins; Tom Mirabell, the rogue, cheated me in that affair; that young fellow's mother used me more like a dog than any woman I ever made advances to." This way of talking of his very much enlivens the conversation among us of a more sedate turn; and I find there is not one of the company but myself, who rarely speak at all, but speaks of him as of that sort of man who is usually called a well-bred, fine gentleman. To conclude his character, where women are not concerned, he is an honest, worthy man.

I cannot tell whether I am to account him whom I am next to speak of as one of our company, for he visits us but seldom; but when he does, it adds to every man else a new enjoyment of himself. He is a clergyman, a very philosophic man, of general learning, great sanctity of life, and the most exact good breeding. He has the misfortune to be of a very weak constitution, and consequently cannot accept of such cares and business as preferments in his function would oblige him to; he is therefore among divines what a chamber-counselor is among lawyers. The probity of his mind and the integrity of his life create him followers, as being eloquent or loud advances others. He seldom introduces the subject he speaks upon; but we are so far gone in years that he observes, when he is among us, an earnestness to have him fall on some divine topic, which he always treats with much authority, as one who has no interest in this world, as one who is hastening to the object of all his wishes and conceives hope from his decays and infirmities. These are my ordinary companions.

## NO. 10. MONDAY, 12 MARCH, 1711.
### [ADDISON.]

*Non aliter quam qui adverso vix flumine lembum*
*Remigiis subigit, si brachia forte remisit,*
*Atque illum in praeceps prono rapit alveus amni.*[6]
　　　　　　　　　　　　　　　　VIRG.

IT IS with much satisfaction that I hear this great city inquiring day by day after these my papers, and receiving my morning lectures with a becoming seriousness and attention. My publisher tells me that there are already three thousand of them distributed every day. So that if I allow twenty readers to every paper, which I look upon as a modest computation, I may reckon about three-score thousand disciples in London and Westminster, who I hope will take care to distinguish themselves from the thoughtless herd of their ignorant and unattentive brethren. Since I have raised to myself so great an audience, I shall spare no pains to make their instruction agreeable, and their diversion useful. For which reasons I shall endeavor to enliven morality with wit, and to temper wit with morality, that my readers may, if possible, both ways find their account in the speculation of the day. And to the end that their virtue and discretion may not be short, transient, intermitting starts of thought, I have resolved to refresh their memories from day to day, till I have recovered them out of that desperate state of vice and folly into which the age is fallen. The mind that lies fallow but a single day, sprouts up in follies that are only to be killed by a constant and assiduous culture. It was said of Socrates, that he brought philosophy down from heaven, to inhabit among men; and I shall be ambitious to have it said of me, that I have brought philosophy out of closets and libraries, schools and colleges, to dwell in clubs and assemblies, at tea-tables and in coffee-houses.

I would therefore in a very particular manner recommend these my speculations to all well-regulated families, that set apart an hour in every morning for tea and bread and butter; and would earnestly advise them for their good to order this paper to be punctually served up, and to be looked upon as a part of the tea-equipage.

Sir Francis Bacon observes, that a well

[6] Like a man whose oars can barely force the boat upstream, and if he relaxes his arms the current carries it headlong down the river (*Georgics*, I, 201).

written book, compared with its rivals and antagonists, is like Moses' serpent, that immediately swallowed up and devoured those of the Egyptians. I shall not be so vain as to think, that where *The Spectator* appears, the other public prints will vanish; but shall leave it to my reader's consideration, whether, is it not much better to be let into the knowledge of one's self, than to hear what passes in Muscovy or Poland; and to amuse ourselves with such writings as tend to the wearing out of ignorance, passion, and prejudice, than such as naturally conduce to inflame hatreds, and make enmities irreconcilable?

In the next place, I would recommend this paper to the daily perusal of those gentlemen whom I cannot but consider as my good brothers and allies, I mean the fraternity of spectators, who live in the world without having anything to do in it; and either by the affluence of their fortunes, or laziness of their dispositions, have no other business with the rest of mankind, but to look upon them. Under this class of men are comprehended all contemplative tradesmen, titular physicians, fellows of the Royal Society, Templars that are not given to be contentious, and statesmen that are out of business; in short, every one that considers the world as a theater, and desires to form a right judgment of those who are the actors on it.

There is another set of men that I must likewise lay a claim to, whom I have lately called the blanks of society, as being altogether unfurnished with ideas, till the business and conversation of the day has supplied them. I have often considered these poor souls with an eye of great commiseration, when I have heard them asking the first man they have met with, whether there was any news stirring? and by that means gathering together materials for thinking. These needy persons do not know what to talk of, till about twelve o'clock in the morning; for by that time they are pretty good judges of the weather, know which way the wind sits, and whether the Dutch mail be come in. As they lie at the mercy of the first man they meet, and are grave or impertinent all the day long, according to the notions which they have imbibed in the morning, I would earnestly entreat them not to stir out of their chambers till they have read this paper, and do promise them that I will daily instil into them such sound and wholesome sentiments, as shall have a good effect on their conversation for the ensuing twelve hours.

But there are none to whom this paper will be more useful, than to the female world.

I have often thought there has not been sufficient pains taken in finding out proper employments and diversions for the fair ones. Their amusements seem contrived for them, rather as they are women, than as they are reasonable creatures; and are more adapted to the sex than to the species. The toilet is their great scene of business, and the right adjusting of their hair the principal employment of their lives. The sorting of a suit of ribbons is reckoned a very good morning's work; and if they make an excursion to a mercer's or a toy-shop, so great a fatigue makes them unfit for anything else all the day after. Their more serious occupations are sewing and embroidery, and their greatest drudgery the preparation of jellies and sweetmeats. This, I say, is the state of ordinary women; though I know there are multitudes of those of a more elevated life and conversation, that move in an exalted sphere of knowledge and virtue, that join all the beauties of the mind to the ornaments of dress, and inspire a kind of awe and respect, as well as love, into their male beholder. I hope to increase the number of these by publishing this daily paper, which I shall always endeavor to make an innocent if not an improving entertainment, and by that means at least divert the minds of my female readers from greater trifles. At the same time, as I would fain give some finishing touches to those which are already the most beautiful pieces in human nature, I shall endeavor to point out all those imperfections that are the blemishes, as well as those virtues which are the embellishments of the sex. In the meanwhile I hope these my gentle readers, who have so much time on their hands, will not grudge throwing away a quarter of an hour in a day on this paper, since they may do it without any hindrance to business.

I know several of my friends and well-wishers are in great pain for me, lest I should not be able to keep up the spirit of a paper which I oblige myself to furnish every day; but to make them easy in this particular, I will promise them faithfully to give it over as soon as I grow dull. This I know will be matter of great raillery to the small wits; who will frequently put me in mind of my promise, desire me to keep my word, assure me that it is high time to give over, with many other little pleasantries of the like nature, which men of a little smart genius cannot forbear throwing out against their best friends, when they have such a handle given them of being witty. But let them remember that I do hereby enter my caveat against this piece of raillery.

## NO. 81. SATURDAY, 2 JUNE, 1711.
### [ADDISON.]

*Qualis ubi audito venantum murmure tigris*
*Horruit in maculas—*[7]
                                        —STATIUS.

ABOUT the middle of last winter I went to see an opera at the theater in the Haymarket, where I could not but take notice of two parties of very fine women, that had placed themselves in the opposite side-boxes, and seemed drawn up in a kind of battle array one against another. After a short survey of them, I found they were patched differently; the faces on one hand being spotted on the right side of the forehead, and those upon the other on the left. I quickly perceived that they cast hostile glances upon one another; and that their patches were placed in those different situations, as party-signals to distinguish friends from foes. In the middle boxes, between these two opposite bodies, were several ladies who patched indifferently on both sides of their faces, and seemed to sit there with no other intention but to see the opera. Upon inquiry I found that the body of Amazons on my right hand, were Whigs, and those on my left, Tories; and that those who had placed themselves in the middle boxes were a neutral party, whose faces had not yet declared themselves. These last, however, as I afterwards found, diminished daily, and took their party with one side or the other; insomuch that I observed in several of them, the patches, which were before dispersed equally, are now all gone over to the Whig or Tory side of the face. The censorious say, that the men, whose hearts are aimed at, are very often the occasions that one part of the face is thus dishonored, and lies under a kind of disgrace, while the other is so much set off and adorned by the owner; and that the patches turn to the right or to the left, according to the principles of the man who is most in favor. But whatever may be the motives of a few fantastical coquettes, who do not patch for the public good so much as for their own private advantage, it is certain, that there are several women of honor who patch out

---

[7] Like the tigress when, at the sound of the hunters, spots appear upon her skin (*Theb.*, II, 128).

of principle, and with an eye to the interest of their country. Nay, I am informed that some of them adhere so steadfastly to their party, and are so far from sacrificing their zeal for the public to their passion for any particular person, that in a late draft of marriage articles a lady has stipulated with her husband, that, whatever his opinions are, she shall be at liberty to patch on which side she pleases.

I must here take notice, that Rosalinda, a famous Whig partisan, has most unfortunately a very beautiful mole on the Tory part of her forehead; which being very conspicuous, has occasioned many mistakes, and given a handle to her enemies to misrepresent her face, as though it had revolted from the Whig interest. But, whatever this natural patch may seem to intimate, it is well-known that her notions of government are still the same. This unlucky mole, however, has misled several coxcombs; and like the hanging out of false colors, made some of them converse with Rosalinda in what they thought the spirit of her party, when on a sudden she has given them an unexpected fire, that has sunk them all at once. If Rosalinda is unfortunate in her mole, Nigranilla is as unhappy in a pimple, which forces her, against her inclinations, to patch on the Whig side.

I am told that many virtuous matrons, who formerly have been taught to believe that this artificial spotting of the face was unlawful, are now reconciled by a zeal for their cause, to what they could not be prompted by a concern for their beauty. This way of declaring war upon one another, puts me in mind of what is reported of the tigress, that several spots rise in her skin when she is angry, or as Mr. Cowley has imitated the verses that stands as the motto on this paper,

——She swells with angry pride,
And calls forth all her spots on ev'ry side.[8]

When I was in the theater the time abovementioned, I had the curiosity to count the patches on both sides, and found the Tory patches to be about twenty stronger than the Whig; but to make amends for this small inequality, I the next morning found the whole puppet-show filled with faces spotted after the Whiggish manner. Whether or no the ladies had retreated hither in order to rally their forces I cannot tell; but the next night they came in so great a body to the opera, that they outnumbered the enemy.

This account of party patches will, I am

afraid, appear improbable to those who live at a distance from the fashionable world; but as it is a distinction of a very singular nature, and what perhaps may never meet with a parallel, I think I should not have discharged the office of a faithful Spectator had I not recorded it.

I have, in former papers, endeavored to expose this party-rage in women, as it only serves to aggravate the hatreds and animosities that reign among men, and in a great measure deprive the fair sex of those peculiar charms with which nature has endowed them.

When the Romans and Sabines were at war, and just upon the point of giving battle, the women, who were allied to both of them, interposed with so many tears and entreaties, that they prevented the mutual slaughter which threatened both parties, and united them together in a firm and lasting peace.

I would recommend this noble example to our British ladies, at a time when their country is torn with so many unnatural divisions, that if they continue, it will be a misfortune to be born in it. The Greeks thought it so improper for women to interest themselves in competitions and contentions, that for this reason, among others, they forbade them, under pain of death, to be present at the Olympic games, notwithstanding these were the public diversions of all Greece.

As our English women excel those of all nations in beauty, they should endeavor to outshine them in all other accomplishments proper to the sex, and to distinguish themselves as tender mothers, and faithful wives, rather than as furious partisans. Female virtues are of a domestic turn. The family is the proper province for private women to shine in. If they must be showing their zeal for the public, let it not be against those who are perhaps of the same family, or at least of the same religion or nation, but against those who are the open, professed, undoubted enemies of their faith, liberty, and country. When the Romans were pressed with a foreign enemy, the ladies voluntarily contributed all their rings and jewels to assist the government under a public exigence, which appeared so laudable an action in the eyes of their countrymen, that from thenceforth it was permitted by a law to pronounce public orations at the funeral of a woman in praise of the deceased person, which till that time was peculiar to men. Would our English ladies instead of sticking on a patch against those of their own country, show themselves so truly public-spirited as to sacrifice every one he

⁸ *Davideis,* III, 403–404.

necklace against the common enemy, what decrees ought not to be made in favor of them?

Since I am recollecting upon this subject such passages as occur to my memory out of ancient authors, I cannot omit a sentence in the celebrated funeral oration of Pericles, which he made in honor of those brave Athenians that were slain in a fight with the Lacedaemonians. After having addressed himself to the several ranks and orders of his countrymen, and shown them how they should behave themselves in the public cause, he turns to the female part of his audience: "And as for you (says he) I shall advise you in very few words: Aspire only to those virtues that are peculiar to your sex; follow your natural modesty, and think it your greatest commendation not to be talked of one way or other." [9]

## NO. 112. MONDAY, 9 JULY, 1711.
### [ADDISON.]

'Αθανάτους μὲν πρῶτα θεοὺς, νόμῳ ὡς διάκειται, Τίμα.[10]
—PYTHAGORAS.

I AM always very well pleased with a country Sunday, and think, if keeping holy the seventh day were only a human institution, it would be the best method that could have been thought of for the polishing and civilizing of mankind. It is certain the country people would soon degenerate into a kind of savages and barbarians were there not such frequent returns of a stated time, in which the whole village meet together with their best faces, and in their cleanliest habits, to converse with one another upon indifferent subjects, hear their duties explained to them, and join together in adoration of the Supreme Being. Sunday clears away the rust of the whole week, not only as it refreshes in their minds the notions of religion, but as it puts both the sexes upon appearing in their most agreeable forms, and exerting all such qualities as are apt to give them a figure in the eye of the village. A country fellow distinguishes himself as much in the churchyard as a citizen does upon the 'Change, the whole parish politics being generally discussed in that place either after sermon or before the bell rings.

My friend Sir Roger, being a good churchman, has beautified the inside of his church with several texts of his own choosing; he has likewise given a handsome pulpit-cloth, and railed in the communion-table at his own expense. He has often told me that, at his coming to his estate, he found his parishioners very irregular; and that, in order to make them kneel and join in the responses, he gave every one of them a hassock and a common-prayer-book, and at the same time employed an itinerant singing-master, who goes about the country for that purpose, to instruct them rightly in the tunes of the Psalms; upon which they now very much value themselves, and indeed outdo most of the country churches that I have ever heard.

As Sir Roger is landlord to the whole congregation, he keeps them in very good order, and will suffer nobody to sleep in it besides himself; for, if by chance he has been surprised into a short nap at sermon, upon recovering out of it he stands up and looks about him, and, if he sees anybody else nodding, either wakes them himself, or sends his servant to them. Several other of the old knight's particularities break out upon these occasions; sometimes he will be lengthening out a verse in the Singing-Psalms half a minute after the rest of the congregation have done with it; sometimes, when he is pleased with the matter of his devotion, he pronounces "Amen" three or four times to the same prayer; and sometimes stands up when everybody else is upon their knees, to count the congregation, or see if any of his tenants are missing.

I was yesterday very much surprised to hear my old friend, in the midst of the service, calling out to one John Matthews to mind what he was about, and not disturb the congregation. This John Matthews, it seems, is remarkable for being an idle fellow, and at that time was kicking his heels for his diversion. This authority of the knight, though exerted in that odd manner which accompanies him in all circumstances of life, has a very good effect upon the parish, who are not polite enough to see anything ridiculous in his behavior; besides that the general good sense and worthiness of his character makes his friends observe these little singularities as foils that rather set off than blemish his good qualities.

As soon as the sermon is finished, nobody presumes to stir till Sir Roger is gone out of the church. The knight walks down from his seat in the chancel between a double row of his tenants, that stand bowing to him on each side, and every now and then inquires how such an one's wife, or mother, or son, or father do, whom he does not see at church,—which is understood as a secret reprimand to the person that is absent.

[9] Thucydides, II, xlv.
[10] First reverence the immortal gods, as custom decrees (*Carmina Aurea*, 1–2).

The chaplain has often told me that, upon a catechizing day, when Sir Roger had been pleased with a boy that answers well, he has ordered a Bible to be given him next day for his encouragement, and sometimes accompanies it with a flitch of bacon to his mother. Sir Roger has likewise added five pounds a year to the clerk's place; and, that he may encourage the young fellows to make themselves perfect in the church service, has 10 promised, upon the death of the present incumbent, who is very old, to bestow it according to merit.

The fair understanding between Sir Roger and his chaplain, and their mutual concurrence in doing good, is the more remarkable because the very next village is famous for the differences and contentions that rise between the parson and the squire, who live in a perpetual state of war. The parson is always 20 preaching at the squire, and the squire, to be revenged on the parson, never comes to church. The squire has made all his tenants atheists and tithe-stealers; while the parson instructs them every Sunday in the dignity of his order, and insinuates to them in almost every sermon that he is a better man than his patron. In short, matters are come to such an extremity that the squire has not said his prayers either in public or private this half year; and that the 30 parson threatens him, if he does not mend his manners, to pray for him in the face of the whole congregation.

Feuds of this nature, though too frequent in the country, are very fatal to the ordinary people, who are so used to be dazzled with riches that they pay as much deference to the understanding of a man of an estate as of a man of learning; and are very hardly brought to regard any truth, how important soever it 40 may be, that is preached to them, when they know there are several men of five hundred a year who do not believe it.

NO. 122. FRIDAY, 20 JULY, 1711.
[ADDISON.]

*Comes jucundus in via pro vehiculo est.[11]*
—PUBL. SYR.

A MAN'S first care should be to avoid the 50 reproaches of his own heart; his next, to escape the censures of the world. If the last interferes with the former, it ought to be entirely neglected; but otherwise there cannot be a greater satisfaction to an honest mind than to see those approbations which it gives

[11] A pleasant comrade on a journey is as good as a carriage (Publilius Syrus, *Fragments*).

itself seconded by the applauses of the public. A man is more sure of his conduct when the verdict which he passes upon his own behavior is thus warranted and confirmed by the opinion of all that know him.

My worthy friend Sir Roger is one of those who is not only at peace with himself but beloved and esteemed by all about him. He receives a suitable tribute for his universal 10 benevolence to mankind in the returns of affection and good-will which are paid him by every one that lives within his neighborhood. I lately met with two or three odd instances of that general respect which is shown to the good old knight. He would needs carry Will Wimble and myself with him to the county assizes. As we were upon the road, Will Wimble joined a couple of plain men who rid before us, and conversed with them for 20 some time, during which my friend Sir Roger acquainted me with their characters.

"The first of them," says he, "that has a spaniel by his side, is a yeoman of about an hundred pounds a year, an honest man. He is just within the Game Act, and qualified to kill an hare or a pheasant. He knocks down a dinner with his gun twice or thrice a week; and by that means lives much cheaper than those who have not so good an estate as himself. He would be a good neighbor if he did 30 not destroy so many partridges; in short he is a very sensible man, shoots flying, and has been several times foreman of the petty-jury.

"The other that rides along with him is Tom Touchy, a fellow famous for taking the law of everybody. There is not one in the town where he lives that he has not sued for a quarter-sessions. The rogue had once the impudence to go to law with the widow. His head is full of costs, damages, and ejectments; he 40 plagued a couple of honest gentlemen so long for a trespass in breaking one of his hedges, till he was forced to sell the ground it enclosed to defray the charges of the prosecution. His father left him four-score pounds a year, but he has cast and been cast so often that he is not now worth thirty. I suppose he is going upon the old business of the willow tree."

As Sir Roger was giving me this account 50 of Tom Touchy, Will Wimble and his two companions stopped short till we came up to them. After having paid their respects to Sir Roger, Will told him that Mr. Touchy and he must appeal to him upon a dispute that arose between them. Will, it seems, had been giving his fellow-traveler an account of his angling one day in such a hole; when Tom

Touchy, instead of hearing out his story, told him that Mr. Such-an-one, if he pleased, might take the law of him for fishing in that part of the river. My friend Sir Roger heard them both, upon a round trot; and, after having paused some time, told them, with the air of a man who would not give his judgment rashly, *that much might be said on both sides.* They were neither of them dissatisfied with the knight's determination, because neither of them found himself in the wrong by it. Upon which we made the best of our way to the assizes.

The court was sat before Sir Roger came; but notwithstanding all the justices had taken their places upon the bench, they made room for the old knight at the head of them; who, for his reputation in the country, took occasion to whisper in the judge's ear that he was glad his lordship had met with so much good weather in his circuit. I was listening to the proceeding of the court with much attention, and infinitely pleased with that great appearance and solemnity which so properly accompanies such a public administration of our laws, when, after about an hour's sitting, I observed, to my great surprise, in the midst of a trial, that my friend Sir Roger was getting up to speak. I was in some pain for him, till I found he had acquitted himself of two or three sentences, with a look of much business and great intrepidity.

Upon his first rising the court was hushed, and a general whisper ran among the country people that Sir Roger was up. The speech he made was so little to the purpose that I shall not trouble my readers with an account of it; and I believe was not so much designed by the knight himself to inform the court, as to give him a figure in my eye, and keep up his credit in the country.

I was highly delighted, when the court rose, to see the gentlemen of the country gathering about my old friend, and striving who should compliment him most; at the same time that the ordinary people gazed upon him at a distance, not a little admiring his courage that was not afraid to speak to the judge.

In our return home we met with a very odd accident, which I cannot forbear relating, because it shows how desirous all who know Sir Roger are of giving him marks of their esteem. When we were arrived upon the verge of his estate, we stopped at a little inn to rest ourselves and our horses. The man of the house had, it seems, been formerly a servant in the knight's family; and, to do honor to his old master, had some time since,

unknown to Sir Roger, put him up in a signpost before the door; so that the knight's head had hung out upon the road about a week before he himself knew anything of the matter. As soon as Sir Roger was acquainted with it, finding that his servant's indiscretion proceeded wholly from affection and goodwill, he only told him that he had made him too high a compliment; and when the fellow seemed to think that could hardly be, added, with a more decisive look, that it was too great an honor for any man under a duke; but told him at the same time that it might be altered with a very few touches, and that he himself would be at the charge of it. Accordingly they got a painter, by the knight's directions, to add a pair of whiskers to the face, and by a little aggravation to the features to change it into Saracen's Head. I should not have known this story had not the innkeeper, upon Sir Roger's alighting, told him in my hearing that his honor's head was brought back last night with the alterations that he had ordered to be made in it. Upon this, my friend, with his usual cheerfulness, related the particulars above mentioned, and ordered the head to be brought into the room. I could not forbear discovering greater expressions of mirth than ordinary upon the appearance of this monstrous face, under which, notwithstanding it was made to frown and stare in a most extraordinary manner, I could still discover a distant resemblance of my old friend. Sir Roger, upon seeing me laugh, desired me to tell him truly if I thought it possible for people to know him in that disguise. I at first kept my usual silence; but upon the knight's conjuring me to tell him whether it was not still more like himself than a Saracen, I composed my countenance in the best manner I could, and replied that much might be said on both sides.

These several adventures, with the knight's behavior in them, gave me as pleasant a day as ever I met with in any of my travels.

## NO. 159. SATURDAY, 1 SEPTEMBER, 1711.

[ADDISON.]

*—Omnem, quae nunc obducta tuenti Mortales habetat visus tibi, et humida circum Caligat, nubem eripiam—*[12]

—VIRG.

WHEN I was at Grand Cairo, I picked up several Oriental manuscripts, which I have

[12] All the cloud which, drawn across your eyes, now dulls your mortal vision and shrouds you in mist, I shall snatch away (*Aeneid*, II, 604–606).

still by me. Among others I met with one entitled The Visions of Mirza, which I have read over with great pleasure. I intend to give it to the public when I have no other entertainment for them; and shall begin with the first vision, which I have translated word for word as follows:—

"On the fifth day of the moon, which according to the custom of my forefathers I always keep holy, after having washed myself, and offered up my morning devotions, I ascended the high hills of Bagdad, in order to pass the rest of the day in meditation and prayer. As I was here airing myself on the tops of the mountains, I fell into a profound contemplation on the vanity of human life; and passing from one thought to another, 'Surely,' said I, 'man is but a shadow, and life a dream.' Whilst I was thus musing, I cast my eyes towards the summit of a rock that was not far from me, where I discovered one in the habit of a shepherd, with a musical instrument in his hand. As I looked upon him he applied it to his lips, and began to play upon it. The sound of it was exceedingly sweet, and wrought into a variety of tunes that were inexpressibly melodious, and altogether different from anything I had ever heard. They put me in mind of those heavenly airs that are played to the departed souls of good men upon their first arrival in Paradise, to wear out the impressions of their last agonies, and qualify them for the pleasures of that happy place. My heart melted away in secret raptures.

"I had been often told that the rock before me was the haunt of a Genius; [13] and that several had been entertained with music who had passed by it, but never heard that the musician had before made himself visible. When he had raised my thoughts by those transporting airs which he played to taste the pleasures of his conversation, as I looked upon him like one astonished, he beckoned to me, and by the waving of his hand directed me to approach the place where he sat. I drew near with that reverence which is due to a superior nature; and as my heart was entirely subdued by the captivating strains I had heard, I fell down at his feet and wept. The Genius smiled upon me with a look of compassion and affability that familiarized him to my imagination, and at once dispelled all the fears and apprehensions with which I approached him. He lifted me from the ground, and taking me by the hand, 'Mirza,' said he,

[13] Spirit.

'I have heard thee in thy soliloquies; follow me.'

"He then led me to the highest pinnacle of the rock, and placing me on the top of it, 'Cast thy eyes eastward,' said he, 'and tell me what thou seest.' 'I see,' said I, 'a huge valley, and a prodigious tide of water rolling through it.' 'The valley that thou seest,' said he, 'is the Vale of Misery, and the tide of water that thou seest is part of the great Tide of Eternity.' 'What is the reason,' said I, 'that the tide I see rises out of a thick mist at one end, and again loses itself in a thick mist at the other?' 'What thou seest,' said he, 'is that portion of eternity which is called time, measured out by the sun, and reaching from the beginning of the world to its consummation. Examine now,' said he, 'this sea that is bounded with darkness at both ends, and tell me what thou discoverest in it.' 'I see a bridge,' said I, 'standing in the midst of the tide.' 'The bridge thou seest,' said he, 'is Human Life: consider it attentively.' Upon a more leisurely survey of it, I found that it consisted of three-score and ten entire arches, with several broken arches, which added to those that were entire, made up the number about a hundred. As I was counting the arches, the Genius told me that this bridge consisted at first of a thousand arches; but that a great flood swept away the rest, and left the bridge in the ruinous condition I now beheld it. 'But tell me farther,' said he, 'what thou discoverest on it.' 'I see multitudes of people passing over it,' said I, 'and a black cloud hanging on each end of it.' As I looked more attentively, I saw several of the passengers dropping through the bridge into the great tide that flowed underneath it; and upon farther examination, perceived there were innumerable trap-doors that lay concealed in the bridge, which the passengers no sooner trod upon, but they fell through them into the tide, and immediately disappeared. These hidden pitfalls were set very thick at the entrance of the bridge, so that throngs of people no sooner broke through the cloud, but many of them fell into them. They grew thinner towards the middle, but multiplied and lay closer together towards the end of the arches that were entire.

"There were indeed some persons, but their number was very small, that continued a kind of hobbling march on the broken arches, but fell through one after another, being quite tired and spent with so long a walk.

"I passed some time in the contemplation

of this wonderful structure, and the great variety of objects which it presented. My heart was filled with a deep melancholy to see several dropping unexpectedly in the midst of mirth and jollity, and catching at everything that stood by them to save themselves. Some were looking up towards the heavens in a thoughtful posture, and in the midst of a speculation stumbled and fell out of sight. Multitudes were very busy in the pursuit of bubbles that glittered in their eyes and danced before them; but often when they thought themselves within the reach of them, their footing failed and down they sunk. In this confusion of objects, I observed some with scimitars in their hands, and others with urinals, who ran to and fro upon the bridge, thrusting several persons on trap-doors which did not seem to lie in their way, and which they might have escaped had they not been thus forced upon them.

"The Genius seeing me indulge myself on this melancholy prospect, told me I had dwelt long enough upon it. 'Take thine eyes off the bridge,' said he, 'and tell me if thou yet seest anything thou dost not comprehend.' Upon looking up, 'What mean,' said I, 'those great flights of birds that are perpetually hovering about the bridge, and settling upon it from time to time? I see vultures, harpies, ravens, cormorants, and among many other feathered creatures several little winged boys, that perch in great numbers upon the middle arches.' 'These,' said the Genius, 'are Envy, Avarice, Superstition, Despair, Love, with the like cares and passions that infest human life.'

"I here fetched a deep sigh. 'Alas,' said I, 'Man was made in vain! how is he given away to misery and mortality! tortured in life, and swallowed up in death!' The Genius being moved with compassion towards me, bid me quit so uncomfortable a prospect. 'Look no more,' said he, 'on man in the first stage of his existence, in his setting out for eternity; but cast thine eye on that thick mist into which the tide bears the several generations of mortals that fall into it.' I directed my sight as I was ordered, and (whether or no the good Genius strengthened it with any supernatural force, or dissipated part of the mist that was before too thick for the eye to penetrate) I saw the valley opening at the farther end, and spreading forth into an immense ocean, that had a huge rock of adamant running through the midst of it, and dividing it into two equal parts. The clouds still rested on one half of it, insomuch that I could discover nothing in it; but the other appeared to me a vast ocean planted with innumerable islands, that were covered with fruits and flowers, and interwoven with a thousand little shining seas that ran among them. I could see persons dressed in glorious habits with garlands upon their heads, passing among the trees, lying down by the sides of fountains, or resting on beds of flowers; and could hear a confused harmony of singing birds, falling waters, human voices and musical instruments. Gladness grew in me upon the discovery of so delightful a scene. I wished for the wings of an eagle, that I might fly away to those happy seats; but the Genius told me there was no passage to them, except through the gates of death that I saw opening every moment upon the bridge. 'The islands,' said he, 'that lie so fresh and green before thee, and with which the whole face of the ocean appears spotted as far as thou canst see, are more in number than the sands on the seashore: there are myriads of islands behind those which thou here discoverest, reaching farther than thine eye, or even thine imagination can extend itself. These are the mansions of good men after death, who, according to the degree and kinds of virtue in which they excelled, are distributed among these several islands, which abound with pleasures of different kinds and degrees, suitable to the relishes and perfections of those who are settled in them: every island is a paradise accommodated to its respective inhabitants. Are not these, O Mirza, habitations worth contending for? Does life appear miserable that gives thee opportunities of earning such a reward? Is death to be feared that will convey thee to so happy an existence? Think not man was made in vain, who has such an eternity reserved for him.' I gazed with inexpressible pleasure on these happy islands. At length, said I, 'Show me now, I beseech thee, the secrets that lie hid under those dark clouds which cover the ocean on the other side of the rock of adamant.' The Genius making me no answer, I turned me about to address myself to him a second time, but I found that he had left me; I then turned again to the vision which I had been so long contemplating; but instead of the rolling tide, the arched bridge, and the happy islands, I saw nothing but the long hollow valley of Bagdad, with oxen, sheep, and camels grazing upon the sides of it."

NO. 323. TUESDAY, 11 MARCH, 1712.

[ADDISON.]

*Modo vir, modo femina.*[14]

—OVID.

THE Journal with which I presented my readers on Tuesday last,[15] has brought me in several letters with accounts of many private lives cast into that form. I have the Rake's Journal, the Sot's Journal, the Whoremaster's Journal, and among several others a very curious piece, entitled, The Journal of a Mohock.[16] By these instances I find that the intention of my last Tuesday's paper has been mistaken by many of my readers. I did not design so much to expose vice as idleness, and aimed at those persons who pass away their time rather in trifles and impertinence, than in crimes and immoralities. Offenses of this later kind are not to be dallied with, or treated in so ludicrous a manner. In short, my journal only holds up folly to the light, and shows the disagreeableness of such actions as are indifferent in themselves, and blamable only as they proceed from creatures endowed with reason.

My following correspondent, who calls herself Clarinda, is such a journalist as I require: she seems by her letter to be placed in a modish state of indifference between vice and virtue, and to be susceptible of either, were there proper pains taken with her. Had her journal been filled with gallantries, or such occurrences as had shown her wholly divested of her natural innocence, notwithstanding it might have been more pleasing to the generality of readers, I should not have published it; but as it is only the picture of a life filled with a fashionable kind of gayety and laziness, I shall set down five days of it, as I have received it from the hand of my correspondent.

Dear Mr. Spectator,

You having set your readers an exercise in one of your last week's papers, I have performed mine according to your orders, and herewith send it you enclosed. You must know, Mr. Spectator, that I am a maiden lady of good fortune, who have had several matches offered me for these ten years last past, and have at present warm applications made to me by a very pretty fellow. As I am at my own disposal, I come up to town every winter, and pass my time after the manner you will find in the following journal, which I began to write upon the very day after your *Spectator* upon that subject.

TUESDAY *night.* Could not go to sleep till one in the morning for thinking of my journal.

WEDNESDAY. *From Eight till Ten.* Drank two dishes of chocolate in bed, and fell asleep after them.

*From Ten to Eleven.* Eat a slice of bread and butter, drank a dish of bohea,[17] read *The Spectator.*

*From Eleven to One.* At my toilette, tried a new head.[18] Gave orders for Veny to be combed and washed. Mem. I look best in blue.

*From One till half an hour after Two.* Drove to the Change. Cheapened a couple of fans.

*Till Four.* At dinner. Mem. Mr. Froth passed by in his new liveries.

*From Four to Six.* Dressed, paid a visit to old Lady Blithe and her sister, having before heard they were gone out of town that day.

*From Six to Eleven.* At basset. Mem. Never set again upon the ace of diamonds.

THURSDAY. *From Eleven at night to Eight in the morning.* Dreamed that I punted to Mr. Froth.

*From Eight to Ten.* Chocolate. Read two acts in *Aurenzebe* [19] a-bed.

*From Ten to Eleven.* Tea-table. Sent to borrow Lady Faddle's Cupid for Veny. Read the play-bills. Received a letter from Mr. Froth. Mem. Locked it up in my strong box.

*Rest of the morning.* Fontange,[20] the tirewoman, her account of my Lady Blithe's wash. Broke a tooth in my little tortoise-shell comb. Sent Frank to know how my Lady Hectic rested after her monkey's leaping out at window. Looked pale. Fontange tells me my glass is not true. Dressed by Three.

*From Three to Four.* Dinner cold before I sat down.

---

[14] Sometimes a man, sometimes a woman (*Metamorphoses*, IV, 280).

[15] *Spectator* No. 317. The journal was that of a "sober citizen," "of greater consequence in his own thoughts than in the eye of the world."

[16] The name given to the ruffians and thieves who infested London and terrorized many at night. They had formerly been called "Hectors."

[17] Tea.    [18] I. e., head-dress.

[19] Heroic play by Dryden.

[20] Mlle. de Fontange introduced a new type of head-dress which was fashionable among English-women at the end of the seventeenth century.

*From Four to Eleven.* Saw company. Mr. Froth's opinion of Milton. His account of the Mohocks. His fancy for a pincushion. Picture in the lid of his snuff-box. Old Lady Faddle promises me her woman to cut my hair. Lost five guineas at crimp.

*Twelve a clock at night.* Went to bed.

FRIDAY. *Eight in the morning.* A-bed. Read over all Mr. Froth's letters. Cupid and Veny.

*Ten a clock.* Stayed within all day, not at home.

*From Ten to Twelve.* In conference with my mantua-maker. Sorted a suit of ribands. Broke my blue china cup.

*From Twelve to One.* Shut myself up in my chamber, practiced Lady Betty Modley's skuttle.

*One in the afternoon.* Called for my flowered handkerchief. Worked half a violet leaf in it. Eyes ached and head out of order. Threw by my work, and read over the remaining part of *Aurenzebe.*

*From Three to Four.* Dined.

*From Four to Twelve.* Changed my mind, dressed, went abroad, and played at crimp till midnight. Found Mrs. Spitely at home. Conversation: Mrs. Brilliant's necklace false stones. Old Lady Loveday going to be married to a young fellow that is not worth a groat. Miss Prue gone into the country. Tom Townley has red hair. Mem. Mrs. Spitely whispered in my ear that she had something to tell me about Mr. Froth; I am sure it is not true.

*Between Twelve and One.* Dreamed that Mr. Froth lay at my feet, and called me Indamora.[21]

SATURDAY. Rose at eight a clock in the morning. Sat down to my toilette.

*From Eight to Nine.* Shifted a patch for half an hour before I could determine it. Fixed it above my left eyebrow.

*From Nine to Twelve.* Drank my tea, and dressed.

*From Twelve to Two.* At Chapel. A great deal of good company. Mem. The third air in the new opera. Lady Blithe dressed frightfully.

*From Three to Four.* Dined. Mrs. Kitty called upon me to go to the opera before I was risen from table.

*From dinner to Six.* Drank tea. Turned off a footman for being rude to Veny.

*Six a clock.* Went to the opera. I did not see Mr. Froth till the beginning of the second act. Mr. Froth talked to a gentleman in a black wig. Bowed to a lady in the front box. Mr. Froth and his friend clapped Nicolini[22] in the third act. Mr. Froth cried out *Ancora.*[23] Mr. Froth led me to my chair. I think he squeezed my hand.

*Eleven at night.* Went to bed. Melancholy dreams. Methought Nicolini said he was Mr. Froth.

SUNDAY. Indisposed.

MONDAY. *Eight a clock.* Waked by Miss Kitty. *Aurenzebe* lay upon the chair by me. Kitty repeated without book the eight best lines in the play. Went in our mobs to the dumb man, according to appointment. Told me that my lover's name began with a G. Mem. The conjurer was within a letter of Mr. Froth's name, etc.

Upon looking back into this my journal, I find that I am at a loss to know whether I pass my time well or ill; and indeed never thought of considering how I did it, before I perused your speculation upon that subject. I scarce find a single action in these five days that I can thoroughly approve of, except the working upon the violet leaf, which I am resolved to finish the first day I am at leisure. As for Mr. Froth and Veny, I did not think they took up so much of my time and thoughts, as I find they do upon my journal. The latter of them I will turn off if you insist upon it; and if Mr. Froth does not bring matters to a conclusion very suddenly, I will not let my life run away in a dream.

> Your humble servant,
> Clarinda.

To resume one of the morals of my first paper, and to confirm Clarinda in her good inclinations, I would have her consider what a pretty figure she would make among posterity, were the history of her whole life published like these five days of it. I shall conclude my paper with an epitaph written by an uncertain author[24] on Sir Philip Sidney's sister, a lady who seems to have been of a temper very much different from that of Clarinda. The last

[21] The "Captive Queen" in Dryden's *Aureng-Zebe.*

[22] Nicolino Grimaldi, a famous Italian singer, who came to England in 1708.

[23] I. e., Encore.

[24] The poem (of which Addison quotes only the first half) has been generally ascribed to Ben Jonson, but in recent years has been claimed for William Browne of Tavistock.

thought of it is so very noble, that I dare say my reader will pardon the quotation.

ON THE COUNTESS DOWAGER OF PEMBROKE

Underneath this marble hearse
Lies the subject of all verse,
Sidney's sister, Pembroke's mother;
Death, ere thou hast killed another,
Fair and learn'd and good as she,
Time shall throw a dart at thee.

## NO. 377. TUESDAY, 13 MAY, 1712.
### [ADDISON.]

*Quid quisque vitet, nunquam homini satis
Cautum est in horas.*[25]
—HOR.

LOVE was the mother of poetry, and still produces, among the most ignorant and barbarous, a thousand imaginary distresses and poetical complaints. It makes a footman talk like Oroondates,[26] and converts a brutal rustic into a gentle swain. The most ordinary plebian or mechanic in love bleeds and pines away with a certain elegance and tenderness of sentiments which this passion naturally inspires.

These inward languishings of a mind infected with this softness have given birth to a phrase which is made use of by all the melting tribe, from the highest to the lowest, I mean that of *dying for love*.

Romances, which owe their very being to this passion, are full of these metaphorical deaths. Heroes and heroines, knights, squires, and damsels, are all of them in a dying condition. There is the same kind of mortality in our modern tragedies, where every one gasps, faints, bleeds, and dies. Many of the poets, to describe the execution which is done by this passion, represent the fair sex as Basilisks that destroy with their eyes; but I think Mr. Cowley has with great justness of thought compared a beautiful woman to a porcupine, that sends an arrow from every part.

I have often thought, that there is no way so effectual for the cure of this general infirmity, as a man's reflecting upon the motives that produce it. When the passion proceeds from the sense of any virtue or perfection in the person beloved, I would by no means discourage it; but if a man considers that all his heavy complaints of wounds and deaths rise from some little affectations of coquetry, which are improved into charms by his own fond imagination, the very laying before himself the cause of his distemper may be sufficient to effect the cure of it.

It is in this view that I have looked over the several bundles of letters which I have received from dying people, and composed out of them the following bill of mortality, which I shall lay before my reader without any further preface, as hoping that it may be useful to him in discovering those several places where there is most danger, and those fatal arts which are made use of to destroy the heedless and unwary.

*Lysander*, slain at a puppet-show on the 3rd of September.

*Thyrsis*, shot from a casement in Pickadilly.

*T.S.*, wounded by Zelinda's scarlet stocking as she was stepping out of a coach.

*Will. Simple*, smitten at the opera by the glance of an eye that was aimed at one who stood by him.

*Tho. Vainlove*, lost his life at a ball.

*Tim. Tattle*, killed by the tap of a fan on his left shoulder by Coquetilla, as he was talking carelessly with her in a bow-window.

*Sir Simon Softly*, murdered at the playhouse in Drury Lane by a frown.

*Philander*, mortally wounded by Cleora, as she was adjusting her tucker.

*Ralph Gapely, Esq.*, hit by a random shot at the ring.

*F. R.*, caught his death upon the water, April the 31st.

*W. W.*, killed by an unknown hand, that was playing, with the glove off, upon the side of the front box in Drury Lane.

*Sir Christopher Crazy, Bar.*, hurt by the brush of a whalebone petticoat.

*Sylvius*, shot through the sticks of a fan at St. James's Church.

*Damon*, struck through the heart by a diamond necklace.

*Thomas Trusty, Francis Goosequill, William Meanwell, Edward Callow, Esqrs.*, standing in a row, fell all four at the same time by an ogle of the Widow Trapland.

*Tom Rattle*, chancing to tread upon a lady's tail as he came out of the play-house, she turned full upon him, and laid him dead upon the spot.

*Dick Tastewell*, slain by a blush from the Queen's box in the third act of the *Trip to the Jubilee*.

---

[25] The dangers of the hour! no thought
    We give them.
(Horace, *Odes*, II, xiii, 13–14; Conington's translation.)
[26] A character in de Scudéry's romance of *Artamène ou le Grand Cyrus*.

*Samuel Felt*, Haberdasher, wounded in his walk to Islington by Mrs. Susannah Crossstitch, as she was clambering over a stile.

*R. F. T., W. S. I., M. P.*, etc., put to death in the last birthday massacre.

*Roger Blinko*, cut off in the twenty-first year of his age by a white-wash.

*Musidorus*, slain by an arrow that flew out of a dimple in Belinda's left cheek.

*Ned Courtly*, presenting Flavia with her glove (which she had dropped on purpose) she received it, and took away his life with a curtsy.

*John Gosselin*, having received a slight hurt from a pair of blue eyes, as he was making his escape was dispatched by a smile.

*Strephon*, killed by Clarinda as she looked down into the pit.

*Charles Careless*, shot flying by a girl of fifteen who unexpectedly popped her head upon him out of a coach.

*Josiah Wither*, aged threescore and three, sent to his long home by Elizabeth Jettwell, spinster.

*Jack Freelave*, murdered by Melissa in her hair.

*William Wiseaker, Gent.*, drowned in a flood of tears by Moll Common.

*John Pleadwell, Esq.*, of the Middle Temple, barrister at law, assassinated in his chambers the sixth instant by Kitty Sly, who pretended to come to him for his advice.

# Jonathan Swift

## 1667-1745

One of the things Swift was heard to say to himself in his dreadful last days was "I am what I am; I am what I am." This has been difficult for many, particularly for comfortable people, to believe, and Swift has often been explained away. Yet he lives on, not merely in the minds and hearts of children who, by a consummate irony, find Lilliput amusing, but as a man speaking to men. For Swift, by virtue of a simplicity of outlook which has its parallel only in the lives and words of a few of the world's great religious figures, attained an insight into human folly which pierces the hearts of men by its profound truth. Uneasily men may squirm, attempting to minimize or to disregard his words, but they do not succeed; for in the end they cannot deny that beneath his coarseness and exaggeration, beneath the contemporary trappings in which he clothed his thought, and beneath his grotesque imaginings, Swift was essentially right. He wrote satirically in accordance with his own bent and the temper of his age, but he does not live simply as the prose counterpart of Pope; not alone for his mastery of satire, nor for its unexampled fierceness, nor yet for the downright plainness and directness and daemonic force of his speech does he live, but because he was what he was, beneath all else a noble personality, deeply sensitive to the confused splendor and misery of humankind.

The first blow of adverse fortune which Swift had to endure came with his birth, for he always considered it an indignity that, though his parents were English, he happened to be born in Ireland, which he hated. He was born on 30 November, 1667, in Dublin. His father had died a short time before his birth, leaving his mother practically destitute. As a consequence he was dependent through his early years on the charity of an uncle—a kind of dependence which was inevitably galling to him, though there is no evidence that his uncle treated him worse than victims of charity are generally treated. In 1673 he was sent to Kil-

kenny School; in 1681 he proceeded to Trinity College, Dublin, from which he was graduated in 1685, with a poor academic record. In 1689 he was employed as an amanuensis and secretary by Sir William Temple, a kinsman and a man now largely forgotten, though of great note in his day. Temple was a man of the world and had been a diplomat; he was on intimate terms with many of the great and influential people of the time, and he was a smooth and polished writer. There can be no doubt that he did much for Swift, whose association with him lasted, with several interruptions, until Temple's death in 1699. Through his employer's influence Swift was in 1692 admitted an M. A. at Oxford, and in 1694 he took holy orders. He had earlier considered this method of making a living, but had refused to take the step as long as he could not at least say that he had other alternatives and so had not entered the priesthood simply for the sake of income. It was during Swift's stay with Temple that he experimented until he learned how to write and what he could best do. He began apparently with poems, but was told by Dryden that he would never be a poet—a blunt verdict which may have been wrong and which Swift never forgave, although he acted on it and thereafter devoted himself chiefly to prose. It was a result, too, of a controversy in which Temple had been involved over the relative merits of the ancients and the moderns that Swift wrote one of his most effective satirical pamphlets, The Battle of the Books, chiefly composed in 1697. And it was while he was living with Temple that he first met Esther Johnson, the Stella of the famous Journal; he remained her devoted friend, in spite of passing attachments to other women, and in spite of Hester Vanhomrigh's love for him, until Stella's death in 1728. It has been maintained that Swift was secretly married to Stella, and the truth about this cannot be determined. It is not, however, a matter of very great impor-

*tance, it being sufficiently plain that only the ceremony is in question, the relations between the two having been simply those of close friends. In 1699 Swift returned to Ireland and in the following year was made Vicar of Laracor. He became attached to the place and did much to improve the living, though he never remained there very long at a time. From 1701, indeed, until 1714 he was much in England. He returned in the first instance to present to the government certain grievances of the Irish clergy; but, particularly after the publication of A Tale of a Tub and The Battle of the Books in 1704, it was recognized that he would make a powerful political writer and both Whigs and Tories made bids for his support. In the end he threw himself in with the Tories and for several years worked hard and brilliantly for them. His reward, however, was not the bishopric he desired and thought he deserved, nor even a lesser post in England, but the Deanery of St. Patrick's Cathedral, in Dublin. Thus, to his bitter* 10 *disappointment, was Swift's exile perpetuated, and after 1714—save for two visits to England in 1726 and 1727—he remained in Ireland until his death. He never ceased to hate Ireland, but in the course of time he was moved by the wretched condition of the island and the character of English misrule to write indignantly in support of Irish causes, as, for example, in the* Drapier's Letters. Gulliver's Travels into several remote Nations of the World— 20 *unquestionably Swift's greatest and most fully representative book—was also written during these years, and published in 1726. It comprises four voyages, all intended "to vex the world rather than divert it." During the last years of his life Swift became hopelessly mad. He died on 19 October, 1745, and was buried in his own cathedral.*

*For the text of Swift's more important works see* The Prose Works of Jonathan Swift, *ed. Herbert Davis (Oxford, 1939–1959), and* The Poems of Jonathan Swift, *ed. Harold H. Williams (Oxford, 1958). Carl Van Doren's* Swift *(New York, 1930) and J. M. Murry's* Swift: a Critical Biography *(London, 1954) are useful studies of Swift, the man. The comments of Arthur E. Case in his introduction to* Gulliver's Travels *(New York, 1938) and in* Four Essays on Gulliver's Travels *(Princeton, 1945) should prove helpful to the student. Herbert Davis's* The Satire of Swift *(New York, 1947) and W. B. Ewald's* The Masks of Swift *(Oxford, 1954) point up the complexity of Swift. For one aspect of Swift's thought G. B. Harrison's "Jonathan Swift" may be recommended, in*

The Social and Political Ideas of Some English Thinkers of the Augustan Age, A. D. 1650–1750, *ed. F. J. C. Hearnshaw (London, 1928); but the best general commentary is Ricardo B. Quintana's* Mind and Art of Jonathan Swift *(New York, 1953). Finally, Quintana's* Swift —an Introduction *(Oxford, 1955) is an excellent synthesis.*

## The Spider and the Bee [1]

THINGS were at this crisis, when a material accident fell out. For, upon the highest corner of a large window, there dwelt a certain spider, swollen up to the first magnitude by the destruction of infinite numbers of flies, whose spoils lay scattered before the gates of his palace, like human bones before the cave of some giant. The avenues to his castle were guarded with turnpikes and palisadoes, all after the modern way of fortification.[2] After you had passed several courts, you came to the center, wherein you might behold the constable himself in his own lodgings, which had windows fronting to each avenue, and ports to sally out, upon all occasions of prey or defense. In this mansion he had for some time dwelt in peace and plenty, without danger to his person by swallows from above, or to his palace, by brooms from below; when it was the pleasure of fortune to conduct thither a wandering bee, to whose curiosity a broken pane in the glass had discovered itself, and in he went; where, expatiating a while, he at last happened to alight upon one of the outward walls of the spider's citadel; which, yielding to the unequal weight, sunk down to the very foundation. Thrice he endeavored to force his passage, and thrice the center shook. The spider within,

---

[1] This well-known passage occurs near the beginning of *The Battle of the Books* (published 1704), Swift's contribution to the so-called Quarrel of the Ancients and the Moderns. The party of the ancients, to which he belonged through his connection with Sir William Temple, had used *Aesop's Fables* and the *Epistles of Phalaris* as evidence that modern writing was not superior to the ancient. Unfortunately the leaders of the opposite party, William Wotton and Richard Bentley, keeper of the Royal Library, had been able to prove that both *Fables* and *Epistles* were spurious works of late origin. Swift replies, not with scholarship, but with a mock-epic description of a battle among the books in the Royal Library; and his central theme is cunningly introduced in the guise of a quarrel between a spider and a bee in the same place.

[2] "Fortification was one of the arts, upon the improvement of which the argument in favor of the moderns was founded by their advocates" (Scott).

feeling the terrible convulsion, supposed at first that nature was approaching to her final dissolution; or else, that Beelzebub,[3] with all his legions, was come to revenge the death of many thousands of his subjects, whom his enemy had slain and devoured. However, he at length valiantly resolved to issue forth, and meet his fate. Meanwhile the bee had acquitted himself of his toils, and, posted securely at some distance, was employed in cleansing his wings, and disengaging them from the ragged remnants of the cobweb. By this time the spider was adventured out, when, beholding the chasms, and ruins, and dilapidations of his fortress, he was very near at his wit's end; he stormed and swore like a madman, and swelled till he was ready to burst. At length, casting his eye upon the bee, and wisely gathering causes from events (for they knew each other by sight): "A plague split you," said he, "for a giddy son of a whore. Is it you, with a vengeance, that have made this litter here? Could not you look before you, and be damned? Do you think I have nothing else to do (in the devil's name) but to mend and repair after your arse?"— "Good words, friend," said the bee (having now pruned himself, and being disposed to droll), "I'll give you my hand and word to come near your kennel no more; I was never in such a confounded pickle since I was born."— "Sirrah," replied the spider, "if it were not for breaking an old custom in our family, never to stir abroad against an enemy, I should come and teach you better manners."—"I pray, have patience," said the bee, "or you will spend your substance, and, for aught I see, you may stand in need of it all, towards the repair of your house."—"Rogue, rogue," replied the spider, "yet, methinks you should have more respect to a person, whom all the world allows to be so much your betters."—"By my troth," said the bee, "the comparison will amount to a very good jest, and you will do me a favor to let me know the reasons that all the world is pleased to use in so hopeful a dispute." At this the spider, having swelled himself into the size and posture of a disputant, began his argument in the true spirit of controversy, with a resolution to be heartily scurrilous and angry, to urge on his own reasons, without the least regard to the answers or objections of his opposite, and fully predetermined in his mind against all conviction.

"Not to disparage myself," said he, "by the comparison with such a rascal, what art thou

but a vagabond without house or home, without stock or inheritance? Born to no possession of your own, but a pair of wings and a drone-pipe. Your livelihood is an universal plunder upon nature; a freebooter over fields and gardens; and, for the sake of stealing, will rob a nettle as readily as a violet. Whereas I am a domestic animal, furnished with a native stock within myself. This large castle (to show my improvements in the mathematics) is all built with my own hands, and the materials extracted altogether out of my own person."

"I am glad," answered the bee, "to hear you grant at least that I am come honestly by my wings and my voice; for then, it seems, I am obliged to Heaven alone for my flights and my music; and Providence would never have bestowed on me two such gifts, without designing them for the noblest ends. I visit indeed all the flowers and blossoms of the field and the garden; but whatever I collect from thence, enriches myself, without the least injury to their beauty, their smell, or their taste. Now, for you and your skill in architecture, and other mathematics, I have little to say: in that building of yours there might, for aught I know, have been labor and method enough; but, by woeful experience for us both, 'tis too plain, the materials are naught, and I hope you will henceforth take warning, and consider duration and matter, as well as method and art. You boast, indeed, of being obliged to no other creature, but of drawing and spinning out all from yourself; that is to say, if we may judge of the liquor in the vessel by what issues out, you possess a good plentiful store of dirt and poison in your breast; and, though I would by no means lessen or disparage your genuine stock of either, yet, I doubt you are somewhat obliged, for an increase of both, to a little foreign assistance. Your inherent portion of dirt does not fail of acquisitions, by sweepings exhaled from below; and one insect furnishes you with a share of poison to destroy another. So that, in short, the question comes all to this— Whether is the nobler being of the two, that which, by a lazy contemplation of four inches round, by an overweening pride, which feeding and engendering on itself, turns all into excrement and venom, producing nothing at all, but flybane and a cobweb; or that which, by an universal range, with long search, much study, true judgment, and distinction of things, brings home honey and wax."

This dispute was managed with such eagerness, clamor, and warmth, that the two parties of books, in arms below, stood silent a while,

[3] "Supposed to be the tutelar deity of the flies" (Scott).

waiting in suspense what would be the issue, which was not long undetermined: For the bee, grown impatient at so much loss of time, fled straight away to a bed of roses, without looking for a reply, and left the spider, like an orator, collected in himself, and just prepared to burst out.

It happened upon this emergency, that Aesop broke silence first. He had been of late most barbarously treated by a strange [10] effect of the regent's [4] humanity, who had tore off his title-page, sorely defaced one half of his leaves, and chained him fast among a shelf of Moderns. Where, soon discovering how high the quarrel was like to proceed, he tried all his arts, and turned himself to a thousand forms. At length, in the borrowed shape of an ass, the regent mistook him for a Modern; by which means he had time and opportunity to escape to the Ancients, just [20] when the spider and the bee were entering into their contest, to which he gave his attention with a world of pleasure; and when it was ended, swore in the loudest key, that in all his life he had never known two cases so parallel and adapt to each other, as that in the window, and this upon the shelves. "The disputants," said he, "have admirably managed the dispute between them, have taken in the full strength of all that is to be said on both sides, and ex- [30] hausted the substance of every argument *pro* and *con*. It is but to adjust the reasonings of both to the present quarrel, then to compare and apply the labors and fruits of each, as the bee has learnedly deduced them, and we shall find the conclusion fall plain and close upon the Moderns and us. For, pray, gentlemen, was ever anything so modern as the spider in his air, his turns, and his paradoxes? He argues in the behalf of you his brethren and himself, [40] with many boastings of his native stock and great genius; that he spins and spits wholly from himself, and scorns to own any obligation or assistance from without. Then he displays to you his great skill in architecture, and improvement in the mathematics. To all this the bee, as an advocate, retained by us the Ancients, thinks fit to answer—that, if one may judge of the great genius or inventions of the Moderns by what they have produced, you will [50] hardly have countenance to bear you out, in boasting of either. Erect your schemes with as much method and skill as you please; yet if the materials be nothing but dirt, spun out of your own entrails (the guts of modern brains) the edifice will conclude at last in a cobweb, the

[4] The librarian, Richard Bentley.

duration of which, like that of other spiders' webs, may be imputed to their being forgotten, or neglected, or hid in a corner. For anything else of genuine that the Moderns may pretend to, I cannot recollect; unless it be a large vein of wrangling and satire, much of a nature and substance with the spider's poison; which, however, they pretend to spit wholly out of themselves, is improved by the same arts, by feeding [10] upon the insects and vermin of the age. As for us the Ancients, we are content, with the bee, to pretend to nothing of our own, beyond our wings and our voice, that is to say, our flights and our language. For the rest, whatever we have got, has been by infinite labor and search, and ranging through every corner of nature; the difference is, that, instead of dirt and poison, we have rather chosen to fill our hives with honey and wax, thus furnishing mankind with [20] the two noblest of things, which are sweetness and light."

# An Argument to Prove That the Abolishing of Christianity in England

*May, As Things Now Stand, Be Attended with Some Inconveniences, and Perhaps Not Produce Those Many Good Effects Proposed Thereby.*

WRITTEN IN THE YEAR 1708.

I AM very sensible what a weakness and presumption it is, to reason against the general humor and disposition of the world. I remember it was with great justice, and a due regard to the freedom both of the public and the press, forbidden upon several penalties to write, or discourse, or lay wagers against the Union,[1] even before it was confirmed by parliament, because that was looked upon as a design, to oppose the current of the people, which, besides the folly of it, is a manifest breach of the fundamental law that makes this majority of opinion the voice of God. In like manner, and for the very same reasons, it may perhaps be neither safe nor prudent to argue against the abolishing of Christianity, at a [50] juncture when all parties seem so unanimously determined upon the point, as we cannot but allow from their actions, their discourses, and their writings. However, I know not how, whether from the affection of singularity, or the perverseness of human nature, but so it

[1] The parliamentary union of England and Scotland (1707).

unhappily falls out, that I cannot be entirely of this opinion. Nay, though I were sure an order were issued out for my immediate prosecution by the Attorney-General, I should still confess that in the present posture of our affairs at home or abroad, I do not yet see the absolute necessity of extirpating the Christian religion from among us.

This perhaps may appear too great a paradox even for our wise and paradoxical age to endure; therefore I shall handle it with all tenderness, and with the utmost deference to that great and profound majority which is of another sentiment.

And yet the curious may please to observe, how much the genius of a nation is liable to alter in half an age. I have heard it affirmed for certain by some very old people, that the contrary opinion was even in their memories as much in vogue as the other is now; and, that a project for the abolishing of Christianity would then have appeared as singular, and been thought as absurd, as it would be at this time to write or discourse in its defense.

Therefore I freely own that all appearances are against me. The system of the Gospel, after the fate of other systems, is generally antiquated and exploded; and the mass or body of the common people, among whom it seems to have had its latest credit, are now grown as much ashamed of it as their betters; opinions, like fashions, always descending from those of quality to the middle sort, and thence to the vulgar, where at length they are dropped and vanish.

But here I would not be mistaken, and must therefore be so bold as to borrow a distinction from the writers on the other side, when they make a difference betwixt nominal and real Trinitarians.[2] I hope no reader imagines me so weak to stand up in the defense of real Christianity, such as used in primitive times (if we may believe the authors of those ages) to have an influence upon men's belief and actions: to offer at the restoring of that would indeed be a wild project; it would be to dig up foundations; to destroy at one blow all the wit, and half the learning of the kingdom; to break the entire frame and constitution of things; to ruin trade, extinguish arts and sciences with the professors of them; in short, to turn our courts, exchanges, and shops into deserts; and would be full as absurd as the proposal of Horace,[3] where he advises the Romans

[2] Between believers in the nominal and in the real nature of the Trinity.

[3] *Epodes,* xvi.

all in a body to leave their city, and seek a new seat in some remote part of the world, by way of a cure for the corruption of their manners.

Therefore I think this caution was in itself altogether unnecessary (which I have inserted only to prevent all possibility of caviling), since every candid reader will easily understand my discourse to be intended only in defense of nominal Christianity; the other having been for some time wholly laid aside by general consent, as utterly inconsistent with all our present schemes of wealth and power.

But why we should therefore cast off the name and title of Christian, although the general opinion and resolution be so violent for it, I confess I cannot (with submission) apprehend the consequence necessary. However, since the undertakers propose such wonderful advantages to the nation by this project, and advance many plausible objections against the system of Christianity, I shall briefly consider the strength of both, fairly allow them their greatest weight, and offer such answers as I think most reasonable. After which I will beg leave to show what inconveniences may possibly happen by such an innovation, in the present posture of our affairs.

*First,* One great advantage proposed by the abolishing of Christianity is, that it would very much enlarge and establish liberty of conscience, that great bulwark of our nation, and of the Protestant Religion, which is still too much limited by priestcraft, notwithstanding all the good intentions of the legislature, as we have lately found by a severe instance. For it is confidently reported, that two young gentlemen of real hopes, bright wit, and profound judgment, who upon a thorough examination of causes and effects, and by the mere force of natural abilities, without the least tincture of learning, have made a discovery, that there was no God, and generously communicating their thoughts for the good of the public, were some time ago, by an unparalleled severity, and upon I know not what obsolete law, broke[4] for blasphemy. And as it hath been wisely observed, if persecution once begins, no man alive knows how far it may reach, or where it will end.

In answer to all which, with deference to wiser judgments, I think this rather shows the necessity of a nominal religion among us. Great wits love to be free with the highest objects; and if they cannot be allowed a God to revile or renounce, they will speak evil of dignities, abuse the government, and reflect upon the

[4] *I. e.,* tortured.

ministry; which I am sure few will deny to be of much more pernicious consequence, according to the saying of Tiberius, *Deorum offensa diis curae*.[5] As to the particular fact related, I think it is not fair to argue from one instance, perhaps another cannot be produced; yet (to the comfort of all those who may be apprehensive of persecution) blasphemy we know is freely spoken a million of times in every coffeehouse and tavern, or wherever else good company meet. It must be allowed indeed, that to break an English free-born officer only for blasphemy, was, to speak the gentlest of such an action, a very high strain of absolute power. Little can be said in excuse for the general; perhaps he was afraid it might give offense to the allies, among whom, for aught we know, it may be the custom of the country to believe a God. But if he argued, as some have done, upon a mistaken principle, that an officer who is guilty of speaking blasphemy, may some time or other proceed so far as to raise a mutiny, the consequence is by no means to be admitted; for, surely the commander of an English army is like to be but ill obeyed, whose soldiers fear and reverence him as little as they do a Deity.

It is further objected against the Gospel System, that it obliges men to the belief of things too difficult for freethinkers, and such who have shaken off the prejudices that usually cling to a confined education. To which I answer, that men should be cautious how they raise objections which reflect upon the wisdom of the nation. Is not everybody freely allowed to believe whatever he pleases, and to publish his belief to the world whenever he thinks fit, especially if it serves to strengthen the party which is in the right? Would any indifferent foreigner, who should read the trumpery lately written by Asgil, Tindal, Toland, Coward,[6] and forty more, imagine the Gospel to be our rule of faith, and to be confirmed by parliaments? Does any man either believe, or say he believes, or desire to have it thought that he says he believes one syllable of the matter? And is any man worse received upon that score, or does he find his want of nominal faith a disadvantage to him in the pursuit of any civil or military employment? What if there be an old dormant statute or two against him, are they not now obsolete, to a de-

gree, that Empsom and Dudley[7] themselves if they were now alive, would find it impossible to put them in execution?

It is likewise urged, that there are, by computation, in this kingdom, above ten thousand parsons, whose revenues added to those of my lords the bishops, would suffice to maintain at least two hundred young gentlemen of wit and pleasure, and freethinking, enemies to priestcraft, narrow principles, pedantry, and prejudices; who might be an ornament to the Court and Town: and then, again, so great a number of able [bodied][8] divines might be a recruit to our fleet and armies. This indeed appears to be a consideration of some weight: but then, on the other side, several things deserve to be considered likewise: as, first, whether it may not be thought necessary that in certain tracts of country, like what we call parishes, there should be one man at least of abilities to read and write. Then it seems a wrong computation, that the revenues of the Church throughout this island would be large enough to maintain two hundred young gentlemen, or even half that number, after the present refined way of living; that is, to allow each of them such a rent, as in the modern form of speech, would make them easy. But still there is in this project a greater mischief behind; and we ought to beware of the woman's folly, who killed the hen that every morning laid her a golden egg. For, pray what would become of the race of men in the next age, if we had nothing to trust to besides the scrofulous, consumptive productions, furnished by our men of wit and pleasure, when, having squandered away their vigor, health and estates, they are forced by some disagreeable marriage to piece up their broken fortunes, and entail rottenness and politeness on their posterity? Now, here are ten thousand persons reduced by the wise regulations of Henry VIII,[9] to the necessity of a low diet, and moderate exercise, who are the only great restorers of our breed, without which the nation would in an age or two become one great hospital. Another advantage proposed by the abolishing of Christianity, is the clear gain of one day in seven, which is now entirely lost, and consequently the kingdom one seventh less considerable in trade, business, and pleasure; besides the loss to the public of so many stately structures now in the hands of the Clergy, which might be converted into playhouses, ex-

---

[5] Let the gods take care of their own offences (Tacitus, *Annals*, I, lxxiii).

[6] These were deists, who believed that religion derived its authority from human reason and not from divine revelation.

[7] Tyrannous officers of the crown in the reign of Henry VII.

[8] Brackets in the original edition.

[9] His seizures of church revenues.

changes, market-houses, common dormitories, and other public edifices.

I hope I shall be forgiven a hard word, if I call this a perfect cavil. I readily own there hath been an old custom time out of mind, for people to assemble in the churches every Sunday, and that shops are still frequently shut, in order as it is conceived, to preserve the memory of that ancient practice, but how this can prove a hindrance to business or pleasure, 10 is hard to imagine. What if the men of pleasure are forced one day in the week, to game at home instead of the chocolate-house? Are not the taverns and coffee houses open? Can there be a more convenient season for taking a dose of physic? Are fewer claps got upon Sunday than other days? Is not that the chief day for traders to sum up the accounts of the week, and for lawyers to prepare their briefs? But I would fain know how it can be pretended that 20 the churches are misapplied? Where are more appointments and rendezvouzes of gallantry? Where more care to appear in the foremost box with greater advantage of dress? Where more meetings for business? Where more bargains driven of all sorts? And where so many conveniences or enticements to sleep?

There is one advantage greater than any of the foregoing, proposed by the abolishing of Christianity: that it will utterly extinguish 30 parties among us, by removing those factitious distinctions of High and Low Church, of Whig and Tory, Presbyterian and Church of England, which are now so many mutual clogs upon public proceedings, and art apt to prefer the gratifying themselves, or depressing their adversaries, before the most important interest of the state.

I confess, if it were certain that so great an advantage would redound to the nation by this 40 expedient, I would submit and be silent. But will any man say, that if the words *whoring, drinking, cheating, lying, stealing,* were by act of parliament ejected out of the English tongue and dictionaries, we should all awake next morning chaste and temperate, honest and just, and lovers of truth? Is this a fair consequence? Or, if the physicians would forbid us to pronounce the words *pox, gout, rheumatism* and *stone,* would that expedient 50 serve like so many talismans to destroy the diseases themselves? Are party and faction rooted in men's hearts no deeper than phrases borrowed from religion, or founded upon no firmer principles? And is our language so poor that we cannot find other terms to express them? Are *envy, pride, avarice* and *ambition*

such ill nomenclators, that they cannot furnish appellations for their owners? Will not *heyducks*[10] and *mamalukes, mandarins* and *pashas,* or any other words formed at pleasure, serve to distinguish those who are in the ministry from others who would be in it if they could? What, for instance, is easier than to vary the form of speech, and instead of the word *church,* make it a question in politics, whether the Monument be in danger? Because religion was nearest at hand to furnish a few convenient phrases, is our invention so barren, we can find no other? Suppose, for argument sake, that the Tories favored Margarita, the Whigs Mrs. Tofts, and the Trimmers Valentini,[11] would not *Margaritians, Toftians* and *Valentinians* be very tolerable marks of distinction? The *Prasini* and *Veniti,*[12] two most virulent factions in Italy, began (if I remember right) by a distinction of colors in ribbons, which we might do with as good a grace about the dignity of the blue and the green, and would serve as properly to divide the Court, the Parliament, and the Kingdom between them, as any terms of art whatsoever, borrowed from religion. And therefore I think there is little force in this objection against Christianity, or prospect of so great an advantage as is proposed in the abolishing of it.

'Tis again objected, as a very absurd ridiculous custom, that a set of men should be suffered, much less employed and hired, to bawl one day in seven against the lawfulness of those methods most in use toward the pursuit of greatness, riches and pleasure, which are the constant practice of all men alive on the other six. But this objection is, I think, a little unworthy so refined an age as ours. Let us argue this matter calmly: I appeal to the breast of any polite freethinker, whether in the pursuit of gratifying a predominant passion, he hath not always felt a wonderful incitement, by reflecting it was a thing forbidden; and therefore we see, in order to cultivate this taste, the wisdom of the nation hath taken special care, that the ladies should be furnished with prohibited silks, and the men with prohibited wine. And indeed it were to be wished, that some other prohibitions were promoted, in 50 order to improve the pleasures of the town; which, for want of such expedients, begin

---

[10] Slavic name for foot-soldiers or members of a noble's retinue.

[11] Margarita, Mrs. Tofts, and Valentini were famous opera singers. The Trimmers were the political party who believed in compromise.

[12] Rival parties in the Roman chariot races.

already, as I am told, to flag and grow languid, giving way daily to cruel inroads from the spleen.

'Tis likewise proposed as a great advantage to the public, that if we once discard the system of the Gospel, all religion will of course be banished forever; and consequently, along with it, those grievous prejudices of education, which under the names of *virtue, conscience, honor, justice,* and the like, are so apt to disturb the peace of human minds, and the notions whereof are so hard to be eradicated by right reason or freethinking, sometimes during the whole course of our lives.

Here first, I observe how difficult it is to get rid of a phrase, which the world is once grown fond of, though the occasion that first produced it, be entirely taken away. For some years past, if a man had but an ill-favored nose, the deep-thinkers of the age would some way or other contrive to impute the cause to the prejudice of his education. From this fountain are said to be derived all our foolish notions of justice, piety, love of our country, all our opinions of God, or a future state, Heaven, Hell, and the like: and there might formerly perhaps have been some pretense for this charge. But so effectual care hath been taken to remove those prejudices, by an entire change in the methods of education, that (with honor I mention it to our polite innovators) the young gentlemen who are now on the scene, seem to have not the least tincture left of those infusions, or string of those weeds; and, by consequence, the reason for abolishing nominal Christianity upon that pretext, is wholly ceased.

For the rest, it may perhaps admit a controversy, whether the banishing all notions of religion whatsoever, would be convenient for the vulgar. Not that I am in the least of opinion with those who hold religion to have been the invention of politicians, to keep the lower part of the world in awe by the fear of invisible powers; unless mankind were then very different from what it is now: for I look upon the mass or body of our people here in England, to be as freethinkers, that is to say, as stanch unbelievers, as any of the highest rank. But I conceive some scattered notions about a superior power to be of singular use for the common people, as furnishing excellent materials to keep children quiet when they grow peevish, and providing topics of amusement in a tedious winter-night.

Lastly, 'tis proposed as a singular advantage, that the abolishing of Christianity will very much contribute to the uniting of Protestants, by enlarging the terms of communion so as to take in all sorts of dissenters, who are now shut out of the pale upon account of a few ceremonies which all sides confess to be things indifferent: that this alone will effectually answer the great ends of a scheme for comprehension, by opening a large noble gate, at which all bodies may enter; whereas the chaffering with dissenters, and dodging about this or t'other ceremony, is but like opening a few wickets, and leaving them at jar, by which no more than one can get in at a time, and that, not without stooping, and sideling, and squeezing his body.

To all this I answer; that there is one darling inclination of mankind, which usually affects to be a retainer to religion, though she be neither its parent, its godmother, nor its friend; I mean the spirit of opposition, that lived long before Christianity, and can easily subsist without it. Let us, for instance, examine wherein the opposition of sectaries among us consists, we shall find Christianity to have no share in it at all. Does the Gospel anywhere prescribe a starched, squeezed countenance, a stiff, formal gait, a singularity of manners and habit, or any affected forms and modes of speech different from the reasonable part of mankind? Yet, if Christianity did not lend its name to stand in the gap, and to employ or divert these humors, they must of necessity be spent in contraventions to the laws of the land, and disturbance of the public peace. There is a portion of enthusiasm assigned to every nation, which, if it hath not proper objects to work on, will burst out, and set all into a flame. If the quiet of a state can be bought by only flinging men and a few ceremonies to devour, it is a purchase no wise man would refuse. Let the mastiffs amuse themselves about a sheep's skin stuffed with hay, provided it will keep them from worrying the flock. The institution of convents abroad, seems in one point a strain of great wisdom, there being few irregularities in human passions, which may not have recourse to vent themselves in some of those orders, which are so many retreats for the speculative, the melancholy, the proud, the silent, the politic and the morose, to spend themselves, and evaporate the noxious particles; for each of whom we in this island are forced to provide a several sect of religion, to keep them quiet: and whenever Christianity shall be abolished, the legislature must find some other expedient to employ and entertain them. For what imports it how large a gate you open, if there will be always left a number who place a pride and a merit in not coming in?

Having thus considered the most important objections against Christianity, and the chief advantages proposed by the abolishing thereof; I shall now with equal deference and submission to wiser judgments as before, proceed to mention a few inconveniences that may happen, if the Gospel should be repealed; which perhaps the projectors may not have sufficiently considered.

And first, I am very sensible how much the gentlemen of wit and pleasure are apt to murmur, and be choqued [13] at the sight of so many daggled-tail parsons, that happen to fall in their way, and offend their eyes; but at the same time, these wise reformers do not consider what an advantage and felicity it is, for great wits to be always provided with objects of scorn and contempt, in order to exercise and improve their talents, and divert their spleen from falling on each other or on themselves; especially when all this may be done without the least imaginable danger to their persons.

And to urge another argument of a parallel nature: if Christianity were once abolished, how would the freethinkers, the strong reasoners, and the men of profound learning, be able to find another subject so calculated in all points whereon to display their abilities? What wonderful productions of wit should we be deprived of, from those whose genius by continual practice hath been wholly turned upon raillery and invectives against religion, and would therefore never be able to shine or distinguish themselves upon any other subject! We are daily complaining of the great decline of wit among us, and would we take away the greatest, perhaps the only topic we have left? Who would ever have suspected Asgil for a wit, or Toland for a philosopher, if the inexhaustible stock of Christianity had not been at hand to provide them with materials? What other subject, through all art or nature, could have produced Tindal for a profound author, or furnished him with readers? It is the wise choice of the subject that alone adorns and distinguishes the writer. For, had a hundred such pens as these been employed on the side of religion, they would have immediately sunk into silence and oblivion.

Nor do I think it wholly groundless, or my fears altogether imaginary, that the abolishing of Christianity may perhaps bring the Church into danger, or at least put the senate to the

trouble of another securing vote. I desire I may not be mistaken; I am far from presuming to affirm or think that the Church is in danger at present, or as things now stand; but we know not how soon it may be so when the Christian religion is repealed. As plausible as this project seems, there may a dangerous design lurk under it: nothing can be more notorious, than that the Atheists, Deists, Socinians,[14] Antitrinitarians, and other subdivisions of freethinkers, are persons of little zeal for the present ecclesiastical establishment: their declared opinion is for repealing the Sacramental Test; [15] they are very indifferent with regard to ceremonies; nor do they hold the *jus divinum* [16] of Episcopacy. Therefore they may be intended as one politic step towards altering the constitution of the Church established, and setting up Presbytery in the stead, which I leave to be further considered by those at the helm.

In the last place, I think nothing can be more plain, than that by this expedient, we shall run into the evil we chiefly pretend to avoid; and that the abolishment of the Christian religion will be the readiest course we can take to introduce popery. And I am the more inclined to this opinion, because we know it has been the constant practice of the Jesuits to send over emissaries, with instructions to personate themselves members of the several prevailing sects among us. So it is recorded, that they have at sundry times appeared in the guise of Presbyterians, Anabaptists, Independents and Quakers, according as any of these were most in credit; so, since the fashion hath been taken up of exploding religion, the popish missionaries have not been wanting to mix with the freethinkers; among whom, Toland, the great oracle of the Antichristians, is an Irish priest, the son of an Irish priest; and the most learned and ingenious author of a book called *The Rights of the Christian Church*,[17] was in a proper juncture reconciled to the Romish faith, whose true son, as appears by a hundred passages in his treatise, he still continues. Perhaps I could add some others to the number; but the fact is beyond dispute, and the reasoning they proceed by is right: for, supposing Christianity to be extinguished, the people will never be at ease till they find out some other method of worship; which will as infallibly produce superstition, as this will end in popery.

And therefore, if notwithstanding all I have

[13] Shocked.

[14] A sect which denied the divinity of Christ.
[15] The law requiring all holders of office under the crown to take communion in the Anglican Church.
[16] Divine right.    [17] Dr. Matthew Tindal.

said, it still be thought necessary to have a bill brought in for repealing Christianity, I would humbly offer an amendment; that instead of the word, *Christianity*, may be put *religion in general;* which I conceive will much better answer all the good ends proposed by the projectors of it. For, as long as we leave in being a God and his providence, with all the necessary consequences which curious and inquisitive men will be apt to draw from such premises, we do not strike at the root of the evil, though we should ever so effectually annihilate the present scheme of the Gospel; for, of what use is freedom of thought, if it will not produce freedom of action, which is the sole end, how remote soever in appearance, of all objections against Christianity? And therefore, the freethinkers consider it as a sort of edifice, wherein all the parts have such a mutual dependence on each other, that if you happen to pull out one single nail, the whole fabric must fall to the ground. This was happily expressed by him who had heard of a text brought for proof of the Trinity, which in an ancient manuscript was differently read; he thereupon immediately took the hint, and by a sudden deduction of a long *sorites*,[18] most logically concluded; "Why, if it be as you say, I may safely whore and drink on, and defy the parson." From which, and many the like instances easy to be produced, I think nothing can be more manifest, than that the quarrel is not against any particular points of hard digestion in the Christian system, but against religion in general; which, by laying restraints on human nature, is supposed the great enemy to the freedom of thought and action.

Upon the whole, if it shall still be thought for the benefit of Church and State, that Christianity be abolished; I conceive however, it may be more convenient to defer the execution to a time of peace, and not venture in this conjecture to disoblige our allies, who, as it falls out, are all Christians, and many of them, by the prejudices of their education, so bigoted, as to place a sort of pride in the appellation. If upon being rejected by them, we are to trust to an alliance with the Turk, we shall find ourselves much deceived: for, as he is too remote, and generally engaged in war with the Persian emperor, so his people would be more scandalized at our infidelity, than our Christian neighbors. For they[19] are not only strict observers of religious worship, but what is worse, believe a God; which is more than is required

of us even while we preserve the name of Christians.

To conclude: Whatever some may think of the great advantages to trade by this favorite scheme, I do very much apprehend, that in six months' time after the act is passed for the extirpation of the Gospel, the Bank, and East-India Stock, may fall at least one *per cent.* And since that is fifty times more than ever the wisdom of our age thought fit to venture for the preservation of Christianity, there is no reason we should be at so great a loss, merely for the sake of destroying it.

## Gulliver's Travels

### (1726)

#### THE PUBLISHER TO THE READER

THE author of these Travels, Mr. Lemuel Gulliver, is my ancient and intimate friend; there is likewise some relation between us by the mother's side. About three years ago, Mr. Gulliver growing weary of the concourse of curious people coming to him at his house in Redriff, made a small purchase of land, with a convenient house, near Newark, in Nottinghamshire, his native country; where he now lives retired, yet in good esteem among his neighbors.

Although Mr. Gulliver was born in Nottinghamshire, where his father dwelt, yet I have heard him say his family came from Oxfordshire; to confirm which, I have observed in the churchyard at Banbury, in that county, several tombs and monuments of the Gullivers.

Before he quitted Redriff, he left the custody of the following papers in my hands, with the liberty to dispose of them as I should think fit. I have carefully perused them three times: the style is very plain and simple; and the only fault I find is, that the author, after the manner of travelers, is a little too circumstantial. There is an air of truth apparent through the whole; and indeed the author was so distinguished for his veracity, that it became a sort of proverb among his neighbors at Redriff, when any one affirmed a thing, to say it was as true as if Mr. Gulliver had spoke it.

By the advice of several worthy persons, to whom, with the author's permission, I communicated these papers, I now venture to send them into the world, hoping they may be at least, for some time, a better entertainment to our young noblemen, than the common scribbles of politics and party.

[18] Chain of propositions in logic.
[19] The Turks.

This volume would have been at least twice as large, if I had not made bold to strike out innumerable passages relating to the winds and tides, as well as to the variations and bearings in the several voyages; together with the minute descriptions of the management of the ship in storms, in the style of sailors: likewise the account of longitudes and latitudes; wherein I have reason to apprehend that Mr. Gulliver may be a little dissatisfied: but I was resolved to fit the work as much as possible to the general capacity of readers. However, if my own ignorance in sea-affairs shall have led me to commit some mistakes, I alone am answerable for them: and if any traveler hath a curiosity to see the whole work at large, as it came from the hand of the author, I will be ready to gratify him.

As for any further particulars relating to the author, the reader will receive satisfaction from the first pages of the book.

RICHARD SYMPSON.

## PART I

### A Voyage to Lilliput [1]

#### CHAPTER I

*The Author Gives Some Account of Himself and Family, His First Inducements to Travel. He Is Shipwrecked, and Swims for His Life, Gets Safe on Shore in the Country of* Lilliput, *Is Made a Prisoner, and Is Carried up Country.*

MY FATHER had a small estate in Nottinghamshire; I was the third of five sons. He sent me to Emanuel College in Cambridge, at fourteen years old, where I resided three years, and applied myself close to my studies; but the charge of maintaining me (although I had a very scanty allowance) being too great for a narrow fortune, I was bound apprentice to Mr. James Bates, an eminent surgeon in London, with whom I continued four years; and my father now and then sending me small sums of money, I laid them out in learning navigation, and other parts of the mathematics, useful to those who intend to travel, as I always believed it would be some time or other my fortune to do. When I left Mr. Bates, I went down to my father; where, by the assistance of him and my uncle John, and some other relations, I got forty pounds, and a promise of thirty pounds a year

[1] Lilliput means "little fellow."

to maintain me at Leyden: there I studied physic two years and seven months, knowing it would be useful in long voyages.

Soon after my return from Leyden, I was recommended by my good master, Mr. Bates, to be surgeon to the *Swallow,* Captain Abraham Pannell, commander; with whom I continued three years and a half, making a voyage or two into the Levant, and some other parts. When I came back, I resolved to settle in London, to which Mr. Bates, my master, encouraged me, and by him I was recommended to several patients. I took part of a small house in the Old Jury; and being advised to alter my condition, I married Mrs. Mary Burton, second daughter to Mr. Edmund Burton, hosier, in Newgate-Street, with whom I received four hundred pounds for a portion.

But, my good master Bates dying in two years after, and I having few friends, my business began to fail; for my conscience would not suffer me to imitate the bad practice of too many among my brethren. Having therefore consulted with my wife, and some of my acquaintance, I determined to go again to sea. I was surgeon successively in two ships, and made several voyages, for six years, to the East and West Indies, by which I got some addition to my fortune. My hours of leisure I spent in reading the best authors, ancient and modern, being always provided with a good number of books; and when I was ashore, in observing the manners and dispositions of the people, as well as learning their language, wherein I had a great facility by the strength of my memory.

The last of these voyages not proving very fortunate, I grew weary of the sea, and intended to stay at home with my wife and family. I removed from the Old Jury to Fetter-Lane, and from thence to Wapping, hoping to get business among the sailors; but it would not turn to account. After three years' expectation that things would mend, I accepted an advantageous offer from Captain William Prichard, master of the *Antelope,* who was making a voyage to the South Sea. We set sail from Bristol, May 4, 1699, and our voyage at first was very prosperous.

It would not be proper, for some reasons, to trouble the reader with the particulars of our adventures in those seas; let it suffice to inform him, that in our passage from thence to the East Indies, we were driven by a violent storm to the north-west of Van

Diemen's Land.² By an observation, we found ourselves in the latitude of 30 degrees 2 minutes south. Twelve of our crew were dead by immoderate labor, and ill food, the rest were in a very weak condition. On the fifth of November, which was the beginning of summer in those parts, the weather being very hazy, the seamen spied a rock, within half a cable's length of the ship; but the wind was so strong, that we were driven directly upon it, and immediately split. Six of the crew, of whom I was one, having let down the boat into the sea, made a shift to get clear of the ship, and the rock. We rowed, by my computation, about three leagues, till we were able to work no longer, being already spent with labor while we were in the ship. We therefore trusted ourselves to the mercy of the waves, and in about half an hour the boat was overset by a sudden flurry from the north. What became of my companions in the boat, as well as of those who escaped on the rock, or were left in the vessel, I cannot tell; but conclude they were all lost. For my own part, I swam as fortune directed me, and was pushed forward by wind and tide. I often let my legs drop, and could feel no bottom: but when I was almost gone, and able to struggle no longer, I found myself within my depth; and by this time the storm was much abated. The declivity was so small, that I walked near a mile before I got to the shore, which I conjectured was about eight o'clock in the evening. I then advanced forward near half a mile, but could not discover any sign of houses or inhabitants; at least I was in so weak a condition, that I did not observe them. I was extremely tired, and with that, and the heat of the weather, and about half a pint of brandy that I drank as I left the ship, I found myself much inclined to sleep. I lay down on the grass, which was very short and soft, where I slept sounder than ever I remember to have done in my life; and, as I reckoned, above nine hours; for when I awaked, it was just day-light. I attempted to rise, but was not able to stir: for as I happened to lie on my back, I found my arms and legs were strongly fastened on each side to the ground; and my hair, which was long and thick, tied down in the same manner. I like-

² Perhaps Tasmania is meant, or a part of New Zealand. The latitude mentioned in the next sentence would indicate that Swift meant Australia, were it not for the fact that western Australia was very vaguely known in the early eighteenth century.

wise felt several slender ligatures across my body, from my arm-pits to my thighs. I could only look upwards, the sun began to grow hot, and the light offended my eyes. I heard a confused noise about me, but in the posture I lay, could see nothing except the sky. In a little time I felt something alive moving on my left leg, which advancing gently forward over my breast, came almost up to my chin; when bending my eyes downwards as much as I could, I perceived it to be a human creature not six inches high, with a bow and arrow in his hands, and a quiver at his back. In the mean time, I felt at least forty more of the same kind (as I conjectured) following the first. I was in the utmost astonishment, and roared so loud, that they all ran back in a fright; and some of them as I was afterwards told, were hurt with the falls they got by leaping from my sides upon the ground. However, they soon returned, and one of them, who ventured so far as to get a full sight of my face, lifting up his hands and eyes by way of admiration, cried out in a shrill, but distinct voice, *Hekinah degul*: the others repeated the same words several times, but then I knew not what they meant. I lay all this while, as the reader may believe, in great uneasiness: at length, struggling to get loose, I had the fortune to break the strings, and wrench out the pegs that fastened my left arm to the ground; for, by lifting it up to my face, I discovered the methods they had taken to bind me, and at the same time with a violent pull, which gave me excessive pain, I a little loosened the strings that tied down my hair on the left side, so that I was just able to turn my head about two inches. But the creatures ran off a second time, before I could seize them; whereupon there was a great shout in a very shrill accent, and after it ceased, I heard one of them cry aloud *Tolgo phonac*; when in an instant I felt above an hundred arrows discharged on my left hand, which pricked me like so many needles; and besides, they shot another flight into the air, as we do bombs in Europe, whereof many, I suppose, fell on my body (though I felt them not), and some on my face, which I immediately covered with my left hand. When this shower of arrows was over, I fell a groaning with grief and pain, and then striving again to get loose, they discharged another volley larger than the first, and some of them attempted with spears to stick me in the sides; but, by good luck, I had on a buff jerkin, which they could not pierce. I thought it the most prudent method to lie still, and my design was to continue so till night, when, my left hand being already loose, I could easily free myself: and as for the inhabitants, I had reason to believe I might be a match for the greatest armies they could bring against me, if they were all of the same size with him that I saw. But fortune disposed otherwise of me. When the people observed I was quiet, they discharged no more arrows; but, by the noise I heard, I knew their numbers increased; and about four yards from me, over-against my right ear, I heard a knocking for above an hour, like that of people at work; when turning my head that way, as well as the pegs and strings would permit me, I saw a stage erected, about a foot and a half from the ground, capable of holding four of the inhabitants, with two or three ladders to mount it: from whence one of them, who seemed to be a person of quality, made me a long speech, whereof I understood not one syllable. But I should have mentioned, that before the principal person began his oration, he cried out three times, *Langro dehul san* (these words and the former were afterwards repeated and explained to me). Whereupon immediately about fifty of the inhabitants came and cut the strings that fastened the left side of my head, which gave me the liberty of turning it to the right, and of observing the person and gesture of him that was to speak. He appeared to be of a middle age, and taller than any of the other three who attended him, whereof one was a page that held up his train, and seemed to be somewhat longer than my middle finger; the other two stood one on each side to support him. He acted every part of an orator, and I could observe many periods of threatenings, and others of promises, pity, and kindness. I answered in a few words, but in the most submissive manner, lifting up my left hand, and both my eyes to the sun, as calling him for a witness; and being almost famished with hunger, having not eaten a morsel for some hours before I left the ship, I found the demands of nature so strong upon me, that I could not forbear showing my impatience (perhaps against the strict rules of decency) by putting my finger frequently on my mouth to signify that I wanted food. The *Hurgo* (for so they call a great lord, as I afterwards learned) understood me very well. He descended

from the stage, and commanded that several ladders should be applied to my sides, on which above an hundred of the inhabitants mounted and walked towards my mouth, laden with baskets full of meat, which had been provided and sent thither by the King's orders, upon the first intelligence he received of me. I observed there was the flesh of several animals, but could not distinguish them by the taste. There were shoulders, legs, and loins, shaped like those of mutton, and very well dressed, but smaller than the wings of a lark. I ate them by two or three at a mouthful, and took three loaves at a time, about the bigness of musket bullets. They supplied me as fast as they could, showing a thousand marks of wonder and astonishment at my bulk and appetite. I then made another sign that I wanted drink. They found by my eating, that a small quantity would not suffice me: and being a most ingenious people, they slung up with great dexterity one of their largest hogsheads, then rolled it towards my hand, and beat out the top; I drank it off at a draught, which I might well do, for it did not hold half a pint, and tasted like a small wine of Burgundy, but much more delicious. They brought me a second hogshead, which I drank in the same manner, and made signs for more, but they had none to give me. When I had performed these wonders, they shouted for joy, and danced upon my breast, repeating several times as they did at first, *Hekinah degul*. They made me a sign that I should throw down the two hogsheads, but first warning the people below to stand out of the way, crying aloud, *Borach mivola,* and when they saw the vessels in the air, there was an universal shout of *Hekinah degul*. I confess I was often tempted while they were passing backwards and forwards on my body, to seize forty or fifty of the first that came in my reach, and dash them against the ground. But the remembrance of what I had felt, which probably might not be the worst they could do, and the promise of honor I made them, for so I interpreted my submissive behavior, soon drove out these imaginations. Besides, I now considered myself as bound by the laws of hospitality to a people who had treated me with so much expense and magnificence. However, in my thoughts, I could not sufficiently wonder at the intrepidity of these diminutive mortals, who durst venture to mount and walk upon my body, while one of my hands was at liberty, without trembling at the very sight of so prodigious a creature as I must appear to them. After some time, when they observed that I made no more demands for meat, there appeared before me a person of high rank from his Imperial Majesty. His Excellency, having mounted on the small of my right leg, advanced forwards up to my face, with about a dozen of his retinue. And producing his credentials under the Signet Royal, which he 10 applied close to my eyes, spoke about ten minutes, without any signs of anger, but with a kind of determinate resolution; often pointing forwards, which, as I afterwards found, was towards the capital city, about half a mile distant, whither it was agreed by his Majesty in council that I must be conveyed. I answered in few words, but to no purpose, and made a sign with my hand that was loose, putting it to the other (but over his Excel- 20 lency's head for fear of hurting him or his train), and then to my own head and body, to signify that I desired my liberty. It appeared that he understood me well enough, for he shook his head by way of disapprobation, and held his hand in a posture to show that I must be carried as a prisoner. However, he made other signs to let me understand that I should have meat and drink enough, and very good treatment. Where- 30 upon I once more thought of attempting to break my bonds; but again, when I felt the smart of their arrows, upon my face and hands, which were all in blisters, and many of the darts still sticking in them, and observing likewise that the number of my enemies increased, I gave tokens to let them know that they might do with me what they pleased. Upon this, the *Hurgo* and his train withdrew, with much civility and cheerful 40 countenances. Soon after I heard a general shout, with frequent repetitions of the words, *Peplom selan,* and I felt great numbers of people on my left side relaxing the cords to such a degree, that I was able to turn upon my right, and to ease myself with making water; which I very plentifully did, to the great astonishment of the people, who conjecturing by my motions what I was going to do, immediately opened to the right and 50 left on that side to avoid the torrent which fell with such noise and violence from me. But before this, they had daubed my face and both my hands with a sort of ointment very pleasant to the smell, which in a few minutes removed all the smart of their arrows. These circumstances, added to the refreshment I had

received by their victuals and drink, which were very nourishing, disposed me to sleep. I slept about eight hours, as I was afterwards assured; and it was no wonder, for the physicians, by the Emperor's order, had mingled a sleepy potion in the hogshead of wine.

It seems that upon the first moment I was discovered sleeping on the ground after my landing, the Emperor had early notice of it by an express; and determined in council that I should be tied in the manner I have related (which was done in the night while I slept), that plenty of meat and drink should be sent to me, and a machine prepared to carry me to the capital city.

This resolution perhaps may appear very bold and dangerous, and I am confident would not be imitated by any prince in Europe on the like occasion; however, in my opinion, it was extremely prudent, as well as generous: for supposing these people had endeavored to kill me with their spears and arrows while I was asleep, I should certainly have awaked with the first sense of smart, which might so far have roused my rage and strength, as to have enabled me to break the strings wherewith I was tied; after which, as they were not able to make resistance, so they could expect no mercy.

These people are most excellent mathematicians, and arrived to a great perfection in mechanics, by the countenance and encouragement of the Emperor, who is a renowned patron of learning. This prince hath several machines fixed on wheels, for the carriage of trees and other great weights. He often builds his largest men of war, whereof some are nine foot long, in the woods where the timber grows, and has them carried on these engines three or four hundred yards to the sea. Five hundred carpenters and engineers were immediately set at work to prepare the greatest engine they had. It was a frame of wood raised three inches from the ground, about seven foot long and four wide, moving upon twenty-two wheels. The shout I heard was upon the arrival of this engine, which it seems set out in four hours after my landing. It was brought parallel to me as I lay. But the principal difficulty was to raise and place me in this vehicle. Eighty poles, each of one foot high, were erected for this purpose, and very strong cords of the bigness of packthread were fastened by hooks to many bandages, which the workmen had girt round my neck, my hands, my body, and my legs. Nine hundred of the strongest men were employed to draw up these cords by many pulleys fastened on the poles, and thus, in less than three hours, I was raised and slung into the engine, and there tied fast. All this I was told, for, while the whole operation was performing, I lay in a profound sleep, by the force of that soporiferous medicine infused into my liquor. Fifteen hundred of the Emperor's largest horses, each about four inches and a half high, were employed to draw 10 me towards the metropolis, which, as I said, was half a mile distant.

About four hours after we began our journey, I awaked by a very ridiculous accident; for the carriage being stopped a while to adjust something that was out of order, two or three of the young natives had the curiosity to see how I looked when I was asleep; they climbed up into the engine, and advancing very softly to my face, one of 20 them, an officer in the guards, put the sharp end of his half-pike a good way up into my left nostril, which tickled my nose like a straw, and made me sneeze violently: whereupon they stole off unperceived, and it was three weeks before I knew the cause of my awakening so suddenly. We made a long march the remaining part of that day, and rested at night with five hundred guards on each side of me, half with torches, and half 30 with bows and arrows, ready to shoot me if I should offer to stir. The next morning at sun-rise we continued our march, and arrived within two hundred yards of the city gates about noon. The Emperor, and all his court, came out to meet us; but his great officers would by no means suffer his Majesty to endanger his person by mounting on my body.

At the place where the carriage stopped, there stood an ancient temple, esteemed to 40 be the largest in the whole kingdom; which having been polluted some years before by an unnatural murder, was, according to the zeal of those people, looked upon as profane, and therefore had been applied to common uses, and all the ornaments and furniture carried away. In this edifice it was determined I should lodge. The great gate fronting to the north was about four foot high, and almost two foot wide, through which I could easily 50 creep. On each side of the gate was a small window not above six inches from the ground: into that on the left side, the King's smiths conveyed fourscore and eleven chains, like those that hang to a lady's watch in Europe, and almost as large, which were locked to my left leg with six and thirty pad-

locks. Over-against this temple, on t'other side of the great highway, at twenty foot distance, there was a turret at least five foot high. Here the Emperor ascended, with many principal lords of his court, to have an opportunity of viewing me, as I was told, for I could not see them. It was reckoned that above an hundred thousand inhabitants came out of the town upon the same errand; and, in spite of my guards, I believe there could not be fewer than ten thousand at several times, who mounted my body by the help of ladders. But a proclamation was soon issued to forbid it upon pain of death. When the workmen found it was impossible for me to break loose, they cut all the strings that bound me; whereupon I rose up, with as melancholy a disposition as ever I had in my life. But the noise and astonishment of the people at seeing me rise and walk, are not to be expressed. The chains that held my left leg were about two yards long, and gave me not only the liberty of walking backwards and forwards in a semicircle; but, being fixed within four inches of the gate, allowed me to creep in, and lie at my full length in the temple.

## CHAPTER II

*The Emperor of Lilliput, Attended by Several of the Nobility, Comes to See the Author in His Confinement. The Emperor's Person and Habit Described. Learned Men Appointed to Teach the Author Their Language. He Gains Favor by His Mild Disposition. His Pockets Are Searched, and His Sword and Pistols Taken from Him.*

WHEN I found myself on my feet, I looked about me, and must confess I never beheld a more entertaining prospect. The country round appeared like a continued garden, and the inclosed fields, which were generally forty foot square, resembled so many beds of flowers. These fields were intermingled with woods of half a stang,[3] and the tallest trees, as I could judge, appeared to be seven foot high. I viewed the town on my left hand, which looked like the painted scene of a city in a theater.

I had been for some hours extremely pressed by the necessities of nature; which was no wonder, it being almost two days since I had last disburdened myself. I was under great difficulties between urgency and

_____

[3] I. e., half a square rod.

shame. The best expedient I could think on, was to creep into my house, which I accordingly did; and shutting the gate after me, I went as far as the length of my chain would suffer, and discharged my body of that uneasy load. But this was the only time I was ever guilty of so uncleanly an action; for which I cannot but hope the candid reader will give some allowance, after he hath maturely and impartially considered my case, and the distress I was in. From this time my constant practice was, as soon as I rose, to perform that business in open air, at the full extent of my chain, and due care was taken every morning before company came, that the offensive matter should be carried off in wheel-barrows, by two servants appointed for that purpose. I would not have dwelt so long upon a circumstance, that perhaps at first sight may appear not very momentous, if I had not thought it necessary to justify my character in point of cleanliness to the world; which I am told some of my maligners have been pleased, upon this and other occasions, to call in question.

When this adventure was at an end, I came back out of my house, having occasion for fresh air. The Emperor was already descended from the tower, and advancing on horseback towards me, which had like to have cost him dear; for the beast, though very well trained, yet wholly unused to such a sight, which appeared as if a mountain moved before him, reared up on his hinder feet: but that prince, who is an excellent horseman, kept his seat, till his attendants ran in, and held the bridle, while his Majesty had time to dismount. When he alighted, he surveyed me round with great admiration, but kept beyond the length of my chain. He ordered his cooks and butlers, who were already prepared, to give me victuals and drink, which they pushed forward in a sort of vehicles upon wheels, till I could reach them. I took these vehicles, and soon emptied them all; twenty of them were filled with meat, and ten with liquor; each of the former afforded me two or three good mouthfuls, and I emptied the liquor of ten vessels, which was contained in earthen vials, into one vehicle, drinking it off at a draught; and so I did with the rest. The Empress, and young Princes of the blood of both sexes, attended by many ladies, sat at some distance in their chairs; but upon the accident that happened to the Emperor's horse, they alighted, and came near his person, which I am now going to describe. He is taller by almost the breadth of my nail, than any of his court; which alone is enough to strike an awe into the beholders. His features are strong and masculine, with an Austrian lip and arched nose, his complexion olive, his countenance erect, his body and limbs well proportioned, all his motions graceful, and his deportment majestic. He was then past his prime, being twenty-eight years and three-quarters old, of which he had reigned about seven, in great felicity, and generally victorious. For the better convenience of beholding him, I lay on my side, so that my face was parallel to his, and he stood but three yards off: however, I have had him since many times in my hand, and therefore cannot be deceived in the description. His dress was very plain and simple, and the fashion of it between the Asiatic and the European: but he had on his head a light helmet of gold, adorned with jewels, and a plume on the crest. He held his sword drawn in his hand, to defend himself, if I should happen to break loose; it was almost three inches long, the hilt and scabbard were gold enriched with diamonds. His voice was shrill, but very clear and articulate, and I could distinctly hear it when I stood up. The ladies and courtiers were all most magnificently clad, so that the spot they stood upon seemed to resemble a petticoat spread on the ground, embroidered with figures of gold and silver. His Imperial Majesty spoke often to me, and I returned answers, but neither of us could understand a syllable. There were several of his priests and lawyers present (as I conjectured by their habits) who were commanded to address themselves to me, and I spoke to them in as many languages as I had the least smattering of, which were High and Low Dutch, Latin, French, Spanish, Italian, and Lingua Franca;[4] but all to no purpose. After about two hours the court retired, and I was left with a strong guard, to prevent the impertinence, and probably the malice of the rabble, who were very impatient to crowd about me as near as they durst, and some of them had the impudence to shoot their arrows at me as I sat on the ground by the door of my house, whereof one very narrowly missed my left eye. But the colonel ordered six of the ringleaders to be seized, and thought no punish-

[4] The mixed language used in communication between European travelers and the Greeks and others at the eastern end of the Mediterranean.

ment so proper as to deliver them bound into my hands, which some of his soldiers accordingly did, pushing them forwards with the butt-ends of their pikes into my reach; I took them all in my right hand, put five of them into my coat-pocket, and as to the sixth, I made a countenance as if I would eat him alive. The poor man squalled terribly, and the colonel and his officers were in much pain, especially when they saw me take out my pen-knife: but I soon put them out of fear: for, looking mildly, and immediately cutting the strings he was bound with, I set him gently on the ground, and away he ran. I treated the rest in the same manner, taking them one by one out of my pocket, and I observed both the soldiers and people were highly obliged at this mark of my clemency, which was represented very much to my advantage at court.

Towards night I got with some difficulty into my house, where I lay on the ground, and continued to do so about a fortnight; during which time the Emperor gave orders to have a bed prepared for me. Six hundred beds of the common measure were brought in carriages, and worked up in my house; an hundred and fifty of their beds sewn together made up the breadth and length, and these were four double, which however kept me but very indifferently from the hardness of the floor, that was of smooth stone. By the same computation they provided me with sheets, blankets, and coverlets, tolerable enough for one who had been so long inured to hardships as I.

As the news of my arrival spread through the kingdom, it brought prodigious numbers of rich, idle, and curious people to see me; so that the villages were almost emptied, and great neglect of tillage and household affairs must have ensued, if his Imperial Majesty had not provided, by several proclamations and orders of state, against this inconveniency. He directed that those who had already beheld me should return home, and not presume to come within fifty yards of my house without license from the court; whereby the secretaries of state got considerable fees.

In the mean time, the Emperor held frequent councils to debate what course should be taken with me; and I was afterwards assured by a particular friend, a person of great quality, who was looked upon to be as much in the secret as any, that the court was under many difficulties concerning me.

They apprehended my breaking loose, that my diet would be very expensive, and might cause a famine. Sometimes they determined to starve me, or at least to shoot me in the face and hands with poisoned arrows, which would soon dispatch me; but again they considered, that the stench of so large a carcass might produce a plague in the metropolis, and probably spread through the whole kingdom. In the midst of these consultations, several officers of the army went to the door of the great council-chamber; and two of them being admitted, gave an account of my behavior to the six criminals abovementioned, which made so favorable an impression in the breast of his Majesty and the whole board, in my behalf, that an Imperial Commission was issued out, obliging all the villages nine hundred yards round the city, to deliver in every morning six beeves, forty sheep, and other victuals for my sustenance; together with a proportionable quantity of bread, and wine, and other liquors; for the due payment of which his Majesty gave assignments upon his treasury. For this prince lives chiefly upon his own demesnes, seldom, except upon great occasions, raising any subsidies upon his subjects, who are bound to attend him in his wars at their own expense. An establishment was also made of six hundred persons to be my domestics, who had board-wages allowed for their maintenance, and tents built for them very conveniently on each side of my door. It was likewise ordered, that three hundred tailors should make me a suit of clothes after the fashion of the country: that six of his Majesty's greatest scholars should be employed to instruct me in their language: and, lastly, that the Emperor's horses, and those of the nobility, and troops of guards, should be frequently exercised in my sight, to accustom themselves to me. All these orders were duly put in execution, and in about three weeks I made a great progress in learning their language; during which time, the Emperor frequently honored me with his visits, and was pleased to assist my masters in teaching me. We began already to converse together in some sort; and the first words I learned were to express my desire that he would please give me my liberty, which I every day repeated on my knees. His answer, as I could comprehend it, was, that this must be a work of time, not to be thought on without the advice of his council, and that first I must *Lumos kelmin pesso desmar lon*

*Emposo*; that is, swear a peace with him and his kingdom. However, that I should be used with all kindness; and he advised me to acquire, by my patience and discreet behavior, the good opinion of himself and his subjects. He desired I would not take it ill, if he gave orders to certain proper officers to search me; for probably I might carry about me several weapons, which must needs be dangerous things, if they answered the bulk of so prodigious a person. I said, his Majesty should be satisfied, for I was ready to strip myself, and turn up my pockets before him. This I delivered part in words, and part in signs. He replied, that by the laws of the kingdom I must be searched by two of his officers; that he knew this could not be done without my consent and assistance; that he had so good an opinion of my generosity and justice, as to trust their persons in my hands: that whatever they took from me should be returned when I left the country, or paid for at the rate which I would set upon them. I took up the two officers in my hands, put them first into my coat-pockets, and then into every other pocket about me, except my two fobs, and another secret-pocket which I had no mind should be searched, wherein I had some little necessaries that were of no consequence to any but myself. In one of my fobs there was a silver watch, and in the other a small quantity of gold in a purse. These gentlemen, having pen, ink, and paper about them, made an exact inventory of everything they saw; and when they had done, desired I would set them down, that they might deliver it to the Emperor. This inventory I afterwards translated into English, and is word for word as follows:

*Imprimis*, In the right coat-pocket of the Great Man-Mountain (for so I interpret the words *Quinbus Flestrin*) after the strictest search, we found only one great piece of coarse cloth, large enough to be a foot-cloth for your Majesty's chief room of state. In the left pocket we saw a huge silver chest, with a cover of the same metal, which we, the searchers, were not able to lift. We desired it should be opened, and one of us stepping into it, found himself up to the mid leg in a sort of dust, some part whereof flying up to our faces, set us both a sneezing for several times together. In his right waistcoat-pocket we found a prodigious bundle of white thin substances, folded one over another, about the bigness of three men, tied with a strong cable, and marked with black figures, which we humbly conceive to be writings, every letter almost half as large as the palm of our hands. In the left there was a sort of engine, from the back of which were extended twenty long poles, resembling the palisadoes before your Majesty's court; wherewith we conjecture the Man-Mountain combs his head; for we did not always trouble him with questions, because we found it a great difficulty to make him understand us. In the large pocket on the right side of his middle cover (so I translate the word *ranfulo*, by which they meant my breeches) we saw a hollow pillar of iron, about the length of a man, fastened to a strong piece of timber, larger than the pillar; and upon one side of the pillar were huge pieces of iron sticking out, cut into strange figures, which we know not what to make of. In the left pocket, another engine of the same kind. In the smaller pocket on the right side, were several round flat pieces of white and red metal, of different bulk; some of the white, which seemed to be silver, were so large and heavy, that my comrade and I could hardly lift them. In the left pocket were two black pillars irregularly shaped: we could not, without difficulty, reach the top of them as we stood at the bottom of his pocket. One of them was covered, and seemed all of a piece: but at the upper end of the other, there appeared a white round substance, about twice the bigness of our heads. Within each of these was enclosed a prodigious plate of steel; which, by our orders, we obliged him to show us, because we apprehended they might be dangerous engines. He took them out of their cases, and told us, that in his own country his practice was to shave his beard with one of these, and cut his meat with the other. There were two pockets which we could not enter: these he called his fobs; they were two large slits cut into the top of his middle cover, but squeezed close by the pressure of his belly. Out of the right fob hung a great silver chain, with a wonderful kind of engine at the bottom. We directed him to draw out whatever was fastened to that chain; which appeared to be a globe, half silver, and half of some transparent metal; for, on the transparent side, we saw certain strange figures circularly drawn, and thought we could touch them, till we found our fingers stopped by that lucid substance. He put this engine to our ears, which made an incessant noise like that of a water-mill. And we conjecture it is either some unknown animal, or the god that he worships; but we are more inclined to the latter opinion, because he assured us (if we understood him right, for he expressed himself very imperfectly), that he seldom did anything without consulting it. He called it his oracle, and said it pointed out the time for every action of his life. From the left fob he took out a net almost large enough for a fisherman, but contrived to open and shut like a purse, and served him for the same use: we found therein several massy pieces of yellow metal, which, if they be real gold, must be of immense value.

Having thus, in obedience to your Majesty's commands, diligently searched all his pockets, we observed a girdle about his waist made of the hide of some prodigious animal; from which, on the left side, hung a sword of the length of five men; and on the right, a bag or pouch divided into two cells, each cell capable of holding three of your Majesty's subjects. In one of these cells were several globes or balls of a most ponderous metal, about the bigness of our heads, and requiring a strong hand to lift them: the other cell contained a heap of certain black grains, but of no great bulk or weight, for we could hold above fifty of them in the palms of our hands.

This is an exact inventory of what we found about the body of the Man-Mountain, who used us with great civility, and due respect to your Majesty's Commission. Signed and sealed on the fourth day of the eighty-ninth moon of your Majesty's auspicious reign.

Clefrin Frelock, Marsi Frelock.

When this inventory was read over to the Emperor, he directed me, although in very gentle terms, to deliver up the several particulars. He first called for my scimitar, which I took out, scabbard and all. In the mean time he ordered three thousand of his choicest troops (who then attended him) to surround me at a distance, with their bows and arrows just ready to discharge: but I did not observe it, for my eyes were wholly fixed upon his Majesty. He then desired me to draw my scimitar, which, although it had got some rust by the sea-water, was in most parts exceeding bright. I did so, and immediately all the troops gave a shout between terror and surprise; for the sun shone clear, and the reflection dazzled their eyes, as I waved the scimitar to and fro in my hand. His Majesty, who is a most magnanimous prince, was less daunted than I could expect; he ordered me to return it into the scabbard, and cast it on the ground as gently as I could, about six foot from the end of my chain. The next thing he demanded, was one of the hollow iron pillars, by which he meant my pocket-pistols. I drew it out, and at his desire, as well as I could, expressed to him the use of it; and charging it only with powder, which, by the closeness of my pouch, happened to escape wetting in the sea (an inconvenience against which all prudent mariners take special care to provide), I first cautioned the Emperor not to be afraid, and then I let it off in the air. The astonishment here was much greater than at the sight of my scimitar. Hundreds fell down, as if they had been struck dead; and even the Emperor, although he stood his ground, could not recover himself in some time. I delivered up both my pistols in the same manner as I had done my scimitar, and then my pouch of powder and bullets; begging him that the former might be kept from fire, for it would kindle with the smallest spark, and blow up his imperial palace into the air. I likewise delivered up my watch, which the Emperor was very curious to see, and commanded two of his tallest yeomen of the guards to bear it on a pole upon their shoulders, as draymen in England do a barrel of ale. He was amazed at the continual noise it made, and the motion of the minute-hand, which he could easily discern; for their sight is much more acute than ours: and asked the opinions of his learned men about him, which were various and remote,[5] as the reader may well imagine without my repeating; although indeed I could not very perfectly understand them. I then gave up my silver and copper money, my purse, with nine large pieces of gold, and some smaller ones; my knife and razor, my comb and silver snuff-box, my handkerchief and journal-book. My scimitar, pistols, and pouch, were conveyed in carriages to his Majesty's stores; but the rest of my goods were returned to me.

I had, as I before observed, one private pocket which escaped their search, wherein there was a pair of spectacles (which I sometimes use for the weakness of my eyes), a pocket perspective,[6] and several other little conveniences; which being of no consequence to the Emperor, I did not think myself bound

⁵ Recondite.        ⁶ Telescope.

in honor to discover, and I apprehended they might be lost or spoiled if I ventured them out of my possession.

## CHAPTER III

*The Author Diverts the Emperor, and His Nobility of Both Sexes, in a Very Uncommon Manner. The Diversions of the Court of Lilliput Described. The Author Has His Liberty Granted Him upon Certain Conditions.*

MY GENTLENESS and good behavior had gained so far on the Emperor and his court, and indeed upon the army and people in general, that I began to conceive hopes of getting my liberty in a short time. I took all possible methods to cultivate this favorable disposition. The natives came by degrees to be less apprehensive of any danger from me. I would sometimes lie down, and let five or six of them dance on my hand. And at last the boys and girls would venture to come and play at hide and seek in my hair. I had now made a good progress in understanding and speaking their language. The Emperor had a mind one day to entertain me with several of the country shows, wherein they exceed all nations I have known, both for dexterity and magnificence. I was diverted with none so much as that of the ropedancers, performed upon a slender white thread, extended about two foot, and twelve inches from the ground. Upon which I shall desire liberty, with the reader's patience, to enlarge a little.

This diversion is only practiced by those persons who are candidates for great employments, and high favor, at court.[7] They are trained in this art from their youth, and are not always of noble birth, or liberal education. When a great office is vacant, either by death or disgrace (which often happens), five or six of those candidates petition the Emperor to entertain his Majesty and the court with a dance on the rope, and whoever jumps the highest without falling succeeds in the office. Very often the chief ministers themselves are commanded to show their skill, and to convince the Emperor that they have not lost their faculty. Flimnap,[8] the Treasurer, is allowed to cut a caper on the straight rope, at least an inch higher than any other lord in the whole empire. I have seen him do the summerset several times together upon a trencher fixed on the rope, which is no thicker than a common packthread in England. My friend Reldresal, principal Secretary for Private Affairs, is, in my opinion, if I am not partial, the second after the Treasurer; the rest of the great officers are much upon a par.

These diversions are often attended with fatal accidents, whereof great numbers are on record. I myself have seen two or three candidates break a limb. But the danger is much greater when the ministers themselves are commanded to show their dexterity; for, by contending to excel themselves and their fellows, they strain so far, that there is hardly one of them who hath not received a fall, and some of them two or three. I was assured that a year or two before my arrival, Flimnap would have infallibly broke his neck, if one of the King's cushions, that accidentally lay on the ground, had not weakened the force of his fall.

There is likewise another diversion, which is only shown before the Emperor and Empress, and first minister, upon particular occasions. The Emperor lays on the table three fine silken threads of six inches long.[9] One is blue, the other red, and the third green. These threads are proposed as prizes for those persons whom the Emperor hath a mind to distinguish by a peculiar mark of his favor. The ceremony is performed in his Majesty's great chamber of state, where the candidates are to undergo a trial of dexterity very different from the former, and such as I have not observed the least resemblance of in any other country of the old or the new world. The Emperor holds a stick in his hands, both ends parallel to the horizon, while the candidates advancing one by one, sometimes leap over the stick, sometimes creep under it backwards and forwards several times, according as the stick is advanced or depressed. Sometimes the Emperor holds one end of the stick, and his first minister the other; sometimes the minister has it entirely to himself. Whoever performs his part with most agility, and holds out the longest in leaping and creeping, is rewarded with the blue-colored silk; the red is given to the next, and the green to the

---

[7] Swift, of course, has the English court in mind.

[8] Sir Robert Walpole, a Whig. One should remember, however, that the analogies with English affairs cannot be pushed too far.

[9] The ribbons of the Garter, the Thistle, and the Bath.

third, which they all wear girt twice round about the middle; and you see few great persons about this court, who are not adorned with one of these girdles.

The horses of the army, and those of the royal stables, having been daily led before me, were no longer shy, but would come up to my very feet without starting. The riders would leap them over my hand as I held it on the ground, and one of the Emperor's 10 huntsmen, upon a large courser, took my foot, shoe and all; which was indeed a prodigious leap. I had the good fortune to divert the Emperor one day after a very extraordinary manner. I desired he would order several sticks of two foot high, and the thickness of an ordinary cane, to be brought me; whereupon his Majesty commanded the master of his woods to give directions accordingly; and the next morning 20 six woodsmen arrived with as many carriages, drawn by eight horses to each. I took nine of these sticks, fixing them firmly in the ground in a quadrangular figure, two foot and a half square. I took four other sticks, and tied them parallel at each corner, about two foot from the ground; then I fastened my handkerchief to the nine sticks that stood erect, and extended it on all sides, till it was tight as the top of a drum; and the four paral- 30 lel sticks rising about five inches higher than the handkerchief, served as ledges on each side. When I had finished my work, I desired the Emperor to let a troop of his best horse, twenty-four in number, come and exercise upon this plain. His Majesty approved of the proposal, and I took them up, one by one, in my hands, ready mounted and armed, with the proper officers to exercise them. As soon as they got into order, 40 they divided into two parties, performed mock skirmishes, discharged blunt arrows, drew their swords, fled and pursued, attacked and retired, and in short discovered the best military discipline I ever beheld. The parallel sticks secured them and their horses from falling over the stage; and the Emperor was so much delighted that he ordered this entertainment to be repeated several days, and once was pleased to be 50 lifted up and give the word of command; and, with great difficulty, persuaded even the Empress herself to let me hold her in her close chair within two yards of the stage, from whence she was able to take a full view of the whole performance. It was my good fortune that no ill accident happened

in these entertainments, only once a fiery horse, that belonged to one of the captains, pawing with his hoof, struck a hole in my handkerchief, and his foot slipping, he overthrew his rider and himself; but I immediately relieved them both, and covering the hole with one hand, I set down the troop with the other, in the same manner as I took them up. The horse that fell was strained in the left shoulder, but the rider got no hurt, and I repaired my handkerchief as well as I could; however, I would not trust to the strength of it any more in such dangerous enterprises.

About two or three days before I was set at liberty, as I was entertaining the court with these kind of feats, there arrived an express to inform his Majesty, that some of his subjects riding near the place where I was first taken up, had seen a great black substance lying on the ground, very oddly shaped, extending its edges round as wide as his Majesty's bedchamber, and rising up in the middle as high as a man; that it was no living creature, as they at first apprehended, for it lay on the grass without motion, and some of them had walked round it several times: that by mounting upon each other's shoulders, they had got to the top, which was flat and even, and stamping upon it they found it was hollow within; that they humbly conceived it might be something belonging to the Man-Mountain; and if his Majesty pleased, they would undertake to bring it with only five horses. I presently knew what they meant, and was glad at heart to receive this intelligence. It seems upon my first reaching the shore after our ship-wreck, I was in such confusion, that before I came to the place where I went to sleep, my hat, which I had fastened with a string to my head while I was rowing, and had stuck on all the time I was swimming, fell off after I came to land; the string, as I conjecture, breaking by some accident which I never observed, but thought my hat had been lost at sea. I entreated his Imperial Majesty to give orders it might be brought to me as soon as possible, describing to him the use and the nature of it: and the next day the wagoners arrived with it, but not in a very good condition; they had bored two holes in the brim, within an inch and half of the edge, and fastened two hooks in the holes; these hooks were tied by a long cord to the harness, and thus my hat was dragged along for above half an English mile; but the ground in that country being extremely smooth and level, it received less damage than I expected.

Two days after this adventure, the Emperor having ordered that part of his army which quarters in and about his metropolis to be in readiness, took a fancy of diverting himself in a very singular manner. He desired I would stand like a Colossus, with my legs as far asunder as I conveniently could. He then commanded his General (who was an old experienced leader, and a great patron of mine) to draw up the troops in close order, and march 10 them under me; the foot by twenty-four in a breast, and the horse by sixteen, with drums beating, colors flying, and pikes advanced. This body consisted of three thousand foot, and a thousand horse. His Majesty gave orders, upon pain of death, that every soldier in his march should observe the strictest decency with regard to my person; which, however, could not prevent some of the younger officers from turning up their eyes as they passed under me. And, 20 to confess the truth, my breeches were at that time in so ill a condition, that they afforded some opportunities for laughter and admiration.

I had sent so many memorials and petitions for my liberty, that his Majesty at length mentioned the matter, first in the cabinet, and then in a full council; where it was opposed by none, except Skyresh Bolgolam, who was pleased, without any provocation, to be my mortal enemy. But it was carried against 30 him by the whole board, and confirmed by the Emperor. That minister was *Galbet*, or Admiral of the Realm, very much in his master's confidence, and a person well versed in affairs, but of a morose and sour complexion. However, he was at length persuaded to comply; but prevailed that the articles and conditions upon which I should be set free, and to which I must swear, should be drawn up by himself. These articles were brought to me by Skyresh Bolgo- 40 lam in person, attended by two undersecretaries, and several persons of distinction. After they were read, I was demanded to swear to the performance of them; first in the manner of my own country, and afterwards in the method prescribed by their laws; which was to hold my right foot in my left hand, to place the middle finger of my right hand on the crown of my head, and my thumb on the tip of my right ear. But because the reader may 50 be curious to have some idea of the style and manner of expression peculiar to that people, as well as to know the articles upon which I recovered my liberty, I have made a translation of the whole instrument word for word, as near as I was able, which I here offer to the public.

GOLBASTO MOMAREM EVLAME GURDILO SHEFIN MULLY ULLY GUE, most mighty Emperor of Lilliput, delight and terror of the universe, whose dominions extend five thousand *blustrugs* (about twelve mile in circumference) to the extremities of the globe; monarch of all monarchs, taller than the sons of men; whose feet press down to the center, and whose head strikes against the sun; at whose nod the princes of the earth shake their knees; pleasant as the spring, comfortable as the summer, fruitful as autumn, dreadful as winter. His most sublime Majesty proposeth to the Man-Mountain, lately arrived to our celestial dominions, the following articles, which by a solemn oath he shall be obliged to perform.

First, The Man-Mountain shall not depart from our dominions, without our license under our great seal.

2d, He shall not presume to come into our metropolis, without our express order; at which time, the inhabitants shall have two hours' warning to keep within their doors.

3rd, The said Man-Mountain shall confine his walks to our principal high-roads, and not offer to walk or lie down in a meadow or field of corn.

4th, As he walks the said roads, he shall take the utmost care not to trample upon the bodies of any of our loving subjects, their horses, or carriages, nor take any of our subjects into his hands, without their own consent.

5th, If an express requires extraordinary dispatch, the Man-Mountain shall be obliged to carry in his pocket the messenger and horse a six days' journey once in every moon, and return the said messenger back (if so required) safe to our Imperial Presence.

6th, He shall be our ally against our enemies in the Island of Blefuscu,[10] and do his utmost to destroy their fleet, which is now preparing to invade us.

7th, That the said Man-Mountain shall, at his times of leisure, be aiding and assisting our workmen, in helping to raise certain great stones, towards covering the wall of the principal park, and other our royal buildings.

8th, That the said Man-Mountain shall, in two moons' time, deliver in an exact survey of the circumference of our dominions by a computation of his own paces round the coast.

[10] This country probably represents France under Louis XIV.

Lastly, That upon his solemn oath to observe all the above articles, the said Man-Mountain shall have a daily allowance of meat and drink sufficient for the support of 1728 of our subjects, with free access to our Royal Person, and other marks of our favor. Given at our Palace at Belfaborac the twelfth day of the ninety-first moon of our reign.

I swore and subscribed to these articles with 10 great cheerfulness and content, although some of them were not so honorable as I could have wished; which proceeded wholly from the malice of Skyresh Bolgolam, the High-Admiral: whereupon my chains were immediately unlocked, and I was at full liberty; the Emperor himself in person did me the honor to be by at the whole ceremony. I made my acknowledgments by prostrating myself at his Majesty's feet: but he commanded me to rise; and after 20 many gracious expressions, which, to avoid the censure of vanity, I shall not repeat, he added, that he hoped I should prove a useful servant, and well deserve all the favors he had already conferred upon me, or might do for the future.

The reader may please to observe, that in the last article for the recovery of my liberty, the Emperor stipulates to allow me a quantity of meat and drink sufficient for the support of 1728 Lilliputians. Some time after, asking a 30 friend at court how they came to fix on that determinate number; he told me that his Majesty's mathematicians, having taken the height of my body by the help of a quadrant, and finding it to exceed theirs in the proportion of twelve to one, they concluded from the similarity of their bodies, that mine must contain at least 1728 of theirs, and consequently would require as much food as was necessary to support that number of Lilliputians. By which, the 40 reader may conceive an idea of the ingenuity of that people, as well as the prudent and exact economy of so great a prince.

### CHAPTER IV

*Mildendo, the Metropolis of Lilliput, Described, together with the Emperor's Palace. A Conversation between the Author and a Principal Secretary, concerning the Affairs of* 50 *That Empire. The Author's Offer to Serve the Emperor in His Wars.*

THE first request I made after I had obtained my liberty, was, that I might have license to see Mildendo, the metropolis; which the Emperor easily granted me, but with a special charge to do no hurt either to the inhabitants or their houses. The people had notice by proclamation of my design to visit the town. The wall which encompassed it, is two foot and an half high, and at least eleven inches broad, so that a coach and horses may be driven very safely round it; and it is flanked with strong towers at ten foot distance. I stepped over the great Western Gate, and passed very gently, and sideling through the two principal streets, only in my short waistcoat, for fear of damaging the roofs and eaves of the houses with the skirts of my coat. I walked with the utmost circumspection, to avoid treading on any stragglers, that might remain in the streets, although the orders were very strict, that all people should keep in their houses, at their own peril. The garret windows and tops of houses were so crowded with spectators, that I thought in all my travels I had not seen a more populous place. The city is an exact square, each side of the wall being five hundred foot long. The two great streets, which run cross and divide it into four quarters, are five foot wide. The lanes and alleys, which I could not enter, but only viewed them as I passed, are from twelve to eighteen inches. The town is capable of holding five hundred thousand souls. The houses are from three to five stories. The shops and markets well provided.

The Emperor's palace is in the center of the city, where the two great streets meet. It is enclosed by a wall of two foot high, and twenty foot distant from the buildings. I had his Majesty's permission to step over this wall; and the space being so wide between that and the palace, I could easily view it on every side. The outward court is a square of forty foot, and includes two other courts: in the inmost are the royal apartments, which I was very desirous to see, but found it extremely difficult; for the great gates, from one square into another, were but eighteen inches high, and seven inches wide. Now the buildings of the outer court were at least five foot high, and it was impossible for me to stride over them without infinite damage to the pile, though the walls were strongly built of hewn stone, and four inches thick. At the same time the Emperor had a great desire that I should see the magnificence of his palace; but this I was not able to do till three days after, which I spent in cutting down with my knife some of the largest trees in the royal park, about an hundred yards distant from the city. Of these trees I made two stools, each about three foot high, and strong enough to bear my weight. The people having received notice a second time, I went again through the city to the palace, with my two stools in my hands. When I came to the side of the outer court, I stood upon one stool, and took the other in my hand: this I lifted over the roof, and gently set it down on the space between the first and second court, which was eight foot wide. I then stepped over the buildings very conveniently from one stool to the other, and drew up the first after me with 10 a hooked stick. By this contrivance I got into the inmost court; and lying down upon my side, I applied my face to the windows of the middle stories, which were left open on purpose, and discovered the most splendid apartments that can be imagined. There I saw the Empress and the young Princes, in their several lodgings, with their chief attendants about them. Her Imperial Majesty [11] was pleased to smile very graciously upon me, and gave me out 20 of the window her hand to kiss.

But I shall not anticipate the reader with farther descriptions of this kind, because I reserve them for a greater work, which is now almost ready for the press, containing a general description of this empire, from its first erection, through a long series of Princes, with a particular account of their wars and politics, laws, learning, and religion: their plants and animals, their peculiar manners and customs, 30 with other matters very curious and useful; my chief design at present being only to relate such events and transactions as happened to the public, or to myself, during a residence of about nine months in that empire.

One morning, about a fortnight after I had obtained my liberty, Reldresal, principal Secretary (as they style him) of Private Affairs, came to my house attended only by one servant. He ordered his coach to wait at a distance, 40 and desired I would give him an hour's audience; which I readily consented to, on account of his quality and personal merits, as well as the many good offices he had done me during my solicitations at court. I offered to lie down, that he might the more conveniently reach my ear; but he chose rather to let me hold him in my hand during our conversation. He began with compliments on my liberty; said he might pretend to some merit in it: but, however, 50 added, that if it had not been for the present situation of things at court, perhaps I might not have obtained it so soon. For, said he, as flourishing a condition as we may appear to be in to foreigners, we labor under two mighty evils; a violent faction at home, and the danger

[11] Probably Queen Anne.

of an invasion by a most potent enemy from abroad. As to the first, you are to understand, that for about seventy moons past there have been two struggling parties in this empire, under the names of *Tramecksan* and *Slamecksan*, from the high and low heels on their shoes,[12] by which they distinguish themselves. It is alleged indeed, that the high heels are most agreeable to our ancient constitution; but, however this be, his Majesty hath determined to make use of only low heels in the administration of the government, and all offices in the gift of the Crown, as you cannot but observe; and particularly, that his Majesty's Imperial heels are lower at least by a *drurr* than any of his court (*drurr* is a measure about the fourteenth part of an inch). The animosities between these two parties run so high, that they will neither eat nor drink, nor talk with each other. We compute the *Tramecksan*, or High-Heels, to exceed us in number; but the power is wholly on our side. We apprehend his Imperial Highness, the Heir to the Crown, to have some tendency towards the High-Heels; [13] at least we can plainly discover one of his heels higher than the other, which gives him a hobble in his gait. Now, in the midst of these intestine disquiets, we are threatened with an invasion from the Island of Blefuscu, which is the other great empire of the universe, almost as large and powerful as this of his Majesty. For as to what we have heard you affirm, that there are other kingdoms and states in the world inhabited by human creatures as large as yourself, our philosophers are in much doubt, and would rather conjecture that you dropped from the moon, or one of the stars; because it is certain, that an hundred mortals of your bulk would, in a short time, destroy all the fruits and cattle of his Majesty's dominions. Besides, our histories of six thousand moons make no mention of any other regions, than the two great empires of Lilliput and Blefuscu. Which two mighty powers have, as I was going to tell you, been engaged in a most obstinate war for six and thirty moons past. It began upon the following occasion. It is allowed on all hands, that the primitive way of breaking eggs before we eat them, was upon the larger end: but his present Majesty's grandfather, while he was a boy going to eat an egg,

[12] This and what follows is a satire upon party government, but it is a mistake to suppose, from Swift's terms, that it refers specially to the High and Low Church parties in England.

[13] This probably refers to intrigues of the Prince of Wales (later George II) directed against his father's policies.

and breaking it according to the ancient practice, happened to cut one of his fingers. Whereupon the Emperor his father published an edict, commanding all his subjects, upon great penalties, to break the smaller end of their eggs.[14] The people so highly resented this law, that our histories tell us there have been six rebellions raised on that account; wherein one Emperor lost his life, and another his crown. These civil commotions were constantly fomented by the monarchs of Blefuscu; and when they were quelled, the exiles always fled for refuge to that empire. It is computed, that eleven thousand persons have, at several times, suffered death, rather than submit to break their eggs at the smaller end. Many hundred large volumes have been published upon this controversy: but the books of the Big-Endians have been long forbidden, and the whole party rendered incapable by law of holding employments. During the course of these troubles, the Emperors of Blefuscu did frequently expostulate by their ambassadors, accusing us of making a schism in religion, by offending against a fundamental doctrine of our great prophet Lustrog, in the fifty-fourth chapter of the Blundecral (which is their Alcoran). This, however, is thought to be a mere strain upon the text: for the words are these; *That all true believers break their eggs at the convenient end:* and which is the convenient end, seems, in my humble opinion, to be left to every man's conscience, or at least in the power of the chief magistrate to determine. Now the Big-Endian exiles have found so much credit in the Emperor of Blefuscu's court, and so much private assistance and encouragement from their party here at home, that a bloody war has been carried on between the two empires for six and thirty moons with various success; during which time we have lost forty capital ships, and a much greater number of smaller vessels, together with thirty thousand of our best seamen and soldiers; and the damage received by the enemy is reckoned to be somewhat greater than ours. However, they have now equipped a numerous fleet, and are

[14] This controversy is usually said to refer to the troubles between Catholics and Protestants in England, and no doubt correctly; though the full force of the satire is lost, here and elsewhere in the book, if we tend to think of it as having only, or even chiefly, a particular application. The Little-Endians are explained to be the Protestants, the Big-Endians the Catholics. The Emperor's grandfather is thus Henry VIII and, in the next sentence, the Emperor who lost his life is Charles I, he who lost his crown James II. France (Blefuscu), of course, encouraged the English Catholics.

just preparing to make a descent upon us; and his Imperial Majesty, placing great confidence in your valor and strength, has commanded me to lay this account of his affairs before you.

I desired the Secretary to present my humble duty to the Emperor, and to let him know, that I thought it would not become me, who was a foreigner, to interfere with parties; but I was ready, with the hazard of my life, to defend his person and state against all invaders.

## CHAPTER V

*The Author, by an Extraordinary Stratagem, Prevents an Invasion. A High Title of Honor Is Conferred upon Him. Ambassadors Arrive from the Emperor of Blefuscu, and Sue for Peace. The Emperor's Apartment on Fire by an Accident; the Author Instrumental in Saving the Rest of the Palace.*

THE Empire of Blefuscu is an island situated to the north north-east side of Lilliput, from whence it is parted only by a channel of eight hundred yards wide. I had not yet seen it, and upon this notice of an intended invasion, I avoided appearing on that side of the coast, for fear of being discovered by some of the enemy's ships, who had received no intelligence of me, all intercourse between the two empires having been strictly forbidden during the war, upon pain of death, and an embargo laid by our Emperor upon all vessels whatsoever. I communicated to his Majesty a project I had formed of seizing the enemy's whole fleet: which, as our scouts assured us, lay at anchor in the harbor ready to sail with the first fair wind. I consulted the most experienced seamen, upon the depth of the channel, which they had often plumbed, who told me, that in the middle at high-water it was seventy *glumgluffs* deep, which is about six foot of European measure; and the rest of it fifty *glumgluffs* at most. I walked towards the northeast coast over against Blefuscu; and lying down behind a hillock, took out my small pocket perspective-glass, and viewed the enemy's fleet at anchor, consisting of about fifty men of war, and a great number of transports: I then came back to my house, and gave order (for which I had a warrant) for a great quantity of the strongest cable and bars of iron. The cable was about as thick as packthread, and the bars of the length and size of a knitting-needle. I trebled the cable to make it stronger, and for the same reason I twisted three of the iron bars together, binding the extremities into a hook. Having thus fixed fifty hooks to as many cables, I went back to the north-east coast, and putting off my coat, shoes, and stockings, walked into the sea in my leathern jerkin, about half an hour before high water. I waded with what haste I could, and swam in the middle about thirty yards till I felt ground; I arrived at the fleet in less than half an hour. The enemy was so frighted when they saw me, that they leaped out of their ships, and swam to shore, where there could not be fewer than thirty thousand souls. I then took my tackling, and fastening a hook to the hole at the prow of each, I tied all the cords together at the end. While I was thus employed, the enemy discharged several thousand arrows, many of which stuck in my hands and face; and besides the excessive smart, gave me much disturbance in my work. My greatest apprehension was for my eyes, which I should have infallibly lost, if I had not suddenly thought of an expedient. I kept among other little necessaries a pair of spectacles in a private pocket, which, as I observed before, had scaped the Emperor's searchers. These I took out and fastened as strongly as I could upon my nose, and thus armed went on boldly with my work in spite of the enemy's arrows, many of which struck against the glasses of my spectacles, but without any other effect, further than a little to discompose them. I had now fastened all the hooks, and taking the knot in my hand, began to pull; but not a ship would stir, for they were all too fast held by their anchors, so that the boldest part of my enterprise remained. I therefore let go the cord, and leaving the hooks fixed to the ships, I resolutely cut with my knife the cables that fastened the anchors, receiving about two hundred shots in my face and hands; then I took up the knotted end of the cables, to which my hooks were tied, and with great ease drew fifty of the enemy's largest men of war after me.

The Blefuscudians, who had not the least imagination of what I intended, were at first confounded with astonishment. They had seen me cut the cables, and thought my design was only to let the ships run adrift, or fall foul on each other: but when they perceived the whole fleet moving in order, and saw me pulling at the end, they set up such a scream of grief and despair, that it is almost impossible to describe or conceive. When I had got out of danger, I stopped awhile to pick out the arrows that stuck in my hands and face; and rubbed on some of the same ointment that was given me at my first arrival, as I have formerly mentioned. I then took off my spectacles, and waiting about an hour, till the tide was a little fallen, I waded through the middle with my cargo, and arrived safe at the royal port of Lilliput.

The Emperor and his whole court stood on the shore, expecting the issue of this great adventure. They saw the ships move forward in a large half-moon, but could not discern me, who was up to my breast in water. When I advanced in the middle of the channel, they were yet in more pain, because I was under water to my neck. The Emperor concluded me to be drowned, and that the enemy's fleet was approaching in a hostile manner: but he was soon eased of his fears, for the channel growing shallower every step I made, I came in a short time within hearing, and holding up the end of the cable by which the fleet was fastened, I cried in a loud voice, *Long live the most puissant Emperor of Lilliput!* This great prince received me at my landing with all possible encomiums, and created me a *Nardac* upon the spot, which is the highest title of honor among them.

His Majesty desired I would take some other opportunity of bringing all the rest of his enemy's ships into his ports. And so unmeasurable is the ambition of princes, that he seemed to think of nothing less than reducing the whole empire of Blefuscu into a province, and governing it by a viceroy; of destroying the Big-Endian exiles, and compelling the people to break the smaller end of their eggs, by which he would remain the sole monarch of the whole world. But I endeavored to divert him from this design, by many arguments drawn from the topics [15] of policy as well as justice; and I plainly protested, that I would never be an instrument of bringing a free and brave people into slavery. And when the matter was debated in council, the wisest part of the ministry were of my opinion.

This open bold declaration of mine was so opposite to the schemes and politics of his Imperial Majesty, that he could never forgive it; he mentioned it in a very artful manner at council, where I was told that some of the wisest appeared, at least by their silence, to be of my opinion; but others, who were my secret enemies, could not forbear some expressions, which by a side-wind reflected on me. And from this time began an intrigue between his Majesty and a junto of ministers maliciously bent against me, which broke out in less than

[15] Principles.

two months, and had like to have ended in my utter destruction. Of so little weight are the greatest services to princes, when put into the balance with a refusal to gratify their wishes.

About three weeks after this exploit, there arrived a solemn embassy from Blefuscu, with humble offers of a peace; which was soon concluded upon conditions very advantageous to our Emperor, wherewith I shall not trouble the reader. There were six ambassadors, with a train of about five hundred persons, and their entry was very magnificent, suitable to the grandeur of their master, and the importance of their business. When their treaty was finished, wherein I did them several good offices by the credit I now had, or at least appeared to have at court, their Excellencies, who were privately told how much I had been their friend, made me a visit in form. They began with many compliments upon my valor and generosity, invited me to that kingdom in the Emperor their master's name, and desired me to show them some proofs of my prodigious strength, of which they had heard so many wonders; wherein I readily obliged them, but shall not trouble the reader with the particulars.

When I had for some time entertained their Excellencies, to their infinite satisfaction and surprise, I desired they would do me the honor to present my most humble respects to the Emperor their master, the renown of whose virtues had so justly filled the whole world with admiration, and whose royal person I resolved to attend before I returned to my own country: accordingly, the next time I had the honor to see our Emperor, I desired his general license to wait on the Blefuscudian monarch, which he was pleased to grant me, as I could perceive, in a very cold manner; but could not guess the reason, till I had a whisper from a certain person that Flimnap and Bolgolam had represented my intercourse with those ambassadors as a mark of disaffection, from which I am sure my heart was wholly free. And this was the first time I began to conceive some imperfect idea of courts and ministers.

It is to be observed, that these ambassadors spoke to me by an interpreter, the languages of both empires differing as much from each other as any two in Europe, and each nation priding itself upon the antiquity, beauty, and energy of their own tongues, with an avowed contempt for that of their neighbor; yet our Emperor, standing upon the advantage he had got by the seizure of their fleet, obliged them to deliver their credentials, and make their speech in the Lilliputian tongue. And

it must be confessed, that from the great intercourse of trade and commerce between both realms, from the continual reception of exiles, which is mutual among them, and from the custom in each empire to send their young nobility and richer gentry to the other, in order to polish themselves by seeing the world, and understanding men and manners; there are few persons of distinction, or merchants, or seamen, who dwell in the maritime parts, but what can hold conversation in both tongues; as I found some weeks after, when I went to pay my respects to the Emperor of Blefuscu, which in the midst of great misfortunes, through the malice of my enemies, proved a very happy adventure to me, as I shall relate in its proper place.

The reader may remember, that when I signed those articles upon which I recovered my liberty, there were some which I disliked upon account of their being too servile, neither could anything but an extreme necessity have forced me to submit. But being now a *Nardac* of the highest rank in that empire, such offices were looked upon as below my dignity, and the Emperor (to do him justice) never once mentioned them to me. However, it was not long before I had an opportunity of doing his Majesty, at least, as I then thought, a most signal service. I was alarmed at midnight with the cries of many hundred people at my door; by which being suddenly awaked, I was in some kind of terror. I heard the word *burglum* repeated incessantly: several of the Emperor's court, making their way through the crowd, entreated me to come immediately to the palace, where her Imperial Majesty's apartment was on fire, by the carelessness of a maid of honor, who fell asleep while she was reading a romance. I got up in an instant; and orders being given to clear the way before me, and it being likewise a moonshine night, I made a shift to get to the Palace without trampling on any of the people. I found they had already applied ladders to the walls of the apartment, and were well provided with buckets, but the water was at some distance. These buckets were about the size of a large thimble, and the poor people supplied me with them as fast as they could; but the flame was so violent that they did little good. I might easily have stifled it with my coat, which I unfortunately left behind me for haste, and came away only in my leathern jerkin. The case seemed wholly desperate and deplorable; and this magnificent palace would have infallibly been burned down to the ground, if, by a presence of mind, unusual to me, I had not suddenly thought of an expedient. I had the evening before drunk plentifully of a most delicious wine, called *glimigrim* (the Blefuscudians call it *flunec*, but ours is esteemed the better sort), which is very diuretic. By the luckiest chance in the world, I had not discharged myself of any part of it. The heat I had contracted by coming very near the flames, and by laboring to quench them, made the wine begin to operate by urine; which I voided in such a quantity, and applied so well to the proper places, that in three minutes the fire was wholly extinguished, and the rest of that noble pile, which had cost so many ages in erecting, preserved from destruction.

It was now day-light, and I returned to my house without waiting to congratulate with the Emperor: because, although I had done a very eminent piece of service, yet I could not tell how his Majesty might resent the manner by which I had performed it: for, by the fundamental laws of the realm, it is capital in any person, of what quality soever, to make water within the precincts of the palace. But I was a little comforted by a message from his Majesty, that he would give orders to the Grand Justiciary for passing my pardon in form; which, however, I could not obtain. And I was privately assured, that the Empress, conceiving the greatest abhorrence of what I had done, removed to the most distant side of the court, firmly resolved that those buildings should never be repaired for her use: and, in the presence of her chief confidents could not forbear vowing revenge.[16]

### CHAPTER VI

*Of the Inhabitants of* Lilliput; *Their Learning, Laws, and Customs, the Manner of Educating Their Children. The Author's Way of Living in That Country. His Vindication of a Great Lady.*

ALTHOUGH I intend to leave the description of this empire to a particular treatise, yet in the mean time I am content to gratify the curious reader with some general ideas. As the common size of the natives is somewhat under six inches high, so there is an exact proportion in all other animals, as well as plants and trees: for instance, the tallest horses and oxen are between four and five inches in height, the sheep an inch and a half, more or less: their geese

about the bigness of a sparrow, and so the several gradations downwards till you come to the smallest, which, to my sight, were almost invisible; but nature hath adapted the eyes of the Lilliputians to all objects proper for their view: they see with great exactness, but at no great distance. And to show the sharpness of their sight towards objects that are near, I have been much pleased with observing a cook pulling a lark, which was not so large as a common fly; and a young girl threading an invisible needle with invisible silk. Their tallest trees are about seven foot high: I mean some of those in the great royal park, the tops whereof I could but just reach with my fist clinched. The other vegetables are in the same proportion; but this I leave to the reader's imagination.

I shall say but little at present of their learning, which for many ages hath flourished in all its branches among them: but their manner of writing is very peculiar, being neither from the left to the right, like the Europeans; nor from the right to the left, like the Arabians; nor from up to down, like the Chinese; nor from down to up, like the Cascagians; but aslant from one corner of the paper to the other, like ladies in England.

They bury their dead with their heads directly downwards, because they hold an opinion, that in eleven thousand moons they are all to rise again, in which period the earth (which they conceive to be flat) will turn upside down, and by this means they shall, at their resurrection, be found ready standing on their feet. The learned among them confess the absurdity of this doctrine, but the practice still continues, in compliance to the vulgar.

There are some laws and customs in this empire very peculiar; and if they were not so directly contrary to those of my own dear country, I should be tempted to say a little in their justification. It is only to be wished, that they were as well executed. The first I shall mention, relates to informers. All crimes against the state are punished here with the utmost severity; but if the person accused maketh his innocence plainly to appear upon his trial, the accuser is immediately put to an ignominious death; and out of his goods or lands, the innocent person is quadruply recompensed for the loss of his time, for the danger he underwent, for the hardship of his imprisonment, and for all the charges he hath been at in making his defense. Or, if that fund be deficient, it is largely supplied by the Crown. The Emperor does also confer on him some public mark of his favor, and proclamation is

---

[16] This episode may have reference to Swift's failure to obtain a bishopric because of his authorship of *A Tale of a Tub.*

made of his innocence through the whole city.

They look upon fraud as a greater crime than theft, and therefore seldom fail to punish it with death; for they allege, that care and vigilance, with a very common understanding, may preserve a man's goods from thieves, but honesty has no fence against superior cunning; and since it is necessary that there should be a perpetual intercourse of buying and selling, and dealing upon credit, where fraud is permitted and connived at, or hath no law to punish it, the honest dealer is always undone, and the knave gets the advantage. I remember when I was once interceding with the Emperor for a criminal who had wronged his master of a great sum of money, which he had received by order, and ran away with; and happening to tell his Majesty, by way of extenuation, that it was only a breach of trust; the Emperor thought it monstrous in me to offer, as a defense, the greatest aggravation of the crime: and truly I had little to say in return, farther than the common answer, that different nations had different customs; for, I confess, I was heartily ashamed.

Although we usually call reward and punishment the two hinges upon which all government turns, yet I could never observe this maxim to be put in practice by any nation except that of Lilliput. Whoever can there bring sufficient proof that he hath strictly observed the laws of his country for seventy-three moons, hath a claim to certain privileges, according to his quality and condition of life, with a proportionable sum of money out of a fund appropriated for that use: he likewise acquires the title of *Snilpall*, or Legal, which is added to his name, but does not descend to his posterity. And these people thought it a prodigious defect of policy among us, when I told them that our laws were enforced only by penalties, without any mention of reward. It is upon this account that the image of Justice, in their courts of judicature, is formed with six eyes, two before, as many behind, and on each side one, to signify circumspection; with a bag of gold open in her right hand, and a sword sheathed in her left, to show she is more disposed to reward than to punish.

In choosing persons for all employments, they have more regard to good morals than to great abilities; for, since government is necessary to mankind, they believe that the common size of human understandings is fitted to some station or other, and that Providence never intended to make the management of public affairs a mystery, to be comprehended only by a few persons of sublime genius, of which there seldom are three born in an age: but they suppose truth, justice, temperance, and the like, to be in every man's power; the practice of which virtues, assisted by experience and a good intention, would qualify any man for the service of his country, except where a course of study is required. But they thought the want of moral virtues was so far from being supplied by superior endowments of the mind, that employments could never be put into such dangerous hands as those of persons so qualified; and at least, that the mistakes committed by ignorance in a virtuous disposition, would never be of such fatal consequence to the public weal, as the practices of a man whose inclinations led him to be corrupt, and had great abilities to manage, and multiply, and defend his corruptions.

In like manner, the disbelief of a Divine Providence renders a man uncapable of holding any public station; for, since kings avow themselves to be the deputies of Providence, the Lilliputians think nothing can be more absurd than for a prince to employ such men as disown the authority under which he acts.

In relating these and the following laws, I would only be understood to mean the original institutions, and not the most scandalous corruptions into which these people are fallen by the degenerate nature of man. For as to that infamous practice of acquiring great employments by dancing on the ropes, or badges of favor and distinction by leaping over sticks and creeping under them, the reader is to observe, that they were first introduced by the grandfather of the Emperor now reigning, and grew to the present height, by the gradual increase of party and faction.

Ingratitude is among them a capital crime, as we read it to have been in some other countries: for they reason thus, that whoever makes ill returns to his benefactor, must needs be a common enemy to the rest of mankind, from whom he hath received no obligation, and therefore such a man is not fit to live.

Their notions relating to the duties of parents and children differ extremely from ours. For, since the conjunction of male and female is founded upon the great law of nature, in order to propagate and continue the species, the Lilliputians will needs have it, that men and women are joined together like other animals, by the motives of concupiscence; and that their tenderness towards their young proceeds from the like natural principle: for which reason they will never allow, that a child is under any obligation to his father for begetting him, or to his mother for bringing him into the world, which, considering the miseries of human life, was neither a benefit in itself, nor intended so by his parents, whose thoughts in their love-encounters were otherwise employed. Upon these, and the like reasonings, their opinion is, that parents are the last of all others to be trusted with the education of their own children; and therefore they have in every town public nurseries, where all parents, except cottagers and laborers, are obliged to send their infants of both sexes to be reared and educated when they come to the age of twenty moons, at which time they are supposed to have some rudiments of docility. These schools are of several kinds, suited to different qualities, and to both sexes. They have certain professors well skilled in preparing children for such a condition of life as befits the rank of their parents, and their own capacities as well as inclinations. I shall first say something of the male nurseries, and then of the female.

The nurseries for males of noble or eminent birth, are provided with grave and learned professors, and their several deputies. The clothes and food of the children are plain and simple. They are bred up in the principles of honor, justice, courage, modesty, clemency, religion, and love of their country; they are always employed in some business, except in the times of eating and sleeping, which are very short, and two hours for diversions, consisting of bodily exercises. They are dressed by men till four years of age, and then are obliged to dress themselves, although their quality be ever so great; and the women attendants, who are aged proportionably to ours at fifty, perform only the most menial offices. They are never suffered to converse with servants, but go together in small or greater numbers to take their diversions, and always in the presence of a professor, or one of his deputies; whereby they avoid those early bad impressions of folly and vice to which our children are subject. Their parents are suffered to see them only twice a year; the visit is to last but an hour. They are allowed to kiss the child at meeting and parting; but a professor, who always stands by on these occasions, will not suffer them to whisper, or use any fondling expressions, or bring any presents of toys, sweetmeats, and the like.

The pension from each family for the education and entertainment of a child, upon failure of due payment, is levied by the Emperor's officers.

The nurseries for children of ordinary gentlemen, merchants, traders, and handicrafts, are managed proportionably after the same manner; only those designed for trades, are put out apprentices at eleven years old, whereas those of persons of quality continue in their exercises till fifteen, which answers to one and twenty with us: but the confinement is gradually lessened for the last three years.

In the female nurseries, the young girls of quality are educated much like the males, only they are dressed by orderly servants of their own sex; but always in the presence of a professor or deputy, till they come to dress themselves, which is at five years old. And if it be found that these nurses ever presume to entertain the girl with frightful or foolish stories, or the common follies practiced by chambermaids among us, they are publicly whipped thrice about the city, imprisoned for a year, and banished for life to the most desolate part of the country. Thus the young ladies there are as much ashamed of being cowards and fools, as the men, and despise all personal ornaments beyond decency and cleanliness: neither did I perceive any difference in their education, made by their difference of sex, only that the the exercises of the females were not altogether so robust; and that some rules were given them relating to domestic life, and a smaller compass of learning was enjoined them: for their maxim is, that among people of quality, a wife should be always a reasonable and agreeable companion, because she cannot always be young. When the girls are twelve years old, which among them is the marriageable age, their parents or guardians take them home, with great expressions of gratitude to the professors, and seldom without tears of the young lady and her companions.

In the nurseries of females of the meaner sort, the children are instructed in all kinds of works proper for their sex, and their several degrees: those intended for apprentices, are dismissed at seven years old, the rest are kept to eleven.

The meaner families who have children at these nurseries, are obliged, besides their annual pension, which is as low as possible, to return to the steward of the nursery a small monthly share of their gettings, to be a portion for the child; and therefore all parents are limited in their expenses by the law. For the Lilliputians think nothing can be more unjust, than for people, in subservience to their own appetites, to bring children into the world, and leave the burden of supporting them on the public. As to persons of quality, they give security to appropriate a certain sum for each child, suitable to their condition; and these funds are always managed with good husbandry, and the most exact justice.

The cottagers and laborers keep their children at home, their business being only to till and cultivate the earth, and therefore their education is of little consequence to the public; but the old and diseased among them are supported by hospitals: for begging is a trade unknown in this empire.

And here it may perhaps divert the curious reader, to give some account of my domestic, and my manner of living in this country, during a residence of nine months and thirteen days. Having a head mechanically turned, and being likewise forced by necessity, I had made for myself a table and chair convenient enough, out of the largest trees in the royal park. Two hundred sempstresses were employed to make me shirts, and linen for my bed and table, all of the strongest and coarsest kind they could get; which, however, they were forced to quilt together in several folds, for the thickest was some degrees finer than lawn. Their linen was usually three inches wide, and three foot make a piece. The sempstresses took my measure as I lay on the ground, one standing at my neck, and another at my mid-leg, with a strong cord extended, that each held by the end, while the third measured the length of the cord with a rule of an inch long. Then they measured my right thumb, and desired no more; for by a mathematical computation, that twice round the thumb is once round the wrist, and so on to the neck and the waist, and by the help of my old shirt, which I displayed on the ground before them for a pattern, they fitted me exactly. Three hundred tailors were employed in the same manner to make me clothes; but they had another contrivance for taking my measure. I kneeled down, and they raised a ladder from the ground to my neck; upon this ladder one of them mounted, and let fall a plumbline from my collar to the floor, which just answered the length of my coat: but my waist and arms I measured myself. When my clothes were finished, which was done in my house, (for the largest of theirs would not have been able to hold them) they looked like the patchwork made by the ladies in England, only that mine were all of a color.

I had three hundred cooks to dress my victuals, in little convenient huts built about my house, where they and their families lived, and prepared me two dishes apiece. I took up twenty waiters in my hand, and placed them on the table: an hundred more attended below on the ground, some with dishes of meat, and some with barrels of wine, and other liquors, slung on their shoulders; all which the waiters above drew up as I wanted, in a very ingenious manner, by certain cords, as we draw the bucket up a well in Europe. A dish of their meat was a good mouthful, and a barrel of their liquor a reasonable draught. Their mutton yields to ours, but their beef is excellent. I have had a sirloin so large, that I have been forced to make three bites of it; but this is rare. My servants were astonished to see me eat it bones and all, as in our country we do the leg of a lark. Their geese and turkeys I usually ate at a mouthful, and I must confess they far exceed ours. Of their smaller fowl I could take up twenty or thirty at the end of my knife.

One day his Imperial Majesty, being informed of my way of living, desired that himself and his Royal Consort, with the young Princes of the blood of both sexes, might have the happiness (as he was pleased to call it) of dining with me. They came accordingly, and I placed them in chairs of state on my table, just over against me, with their guards about them. Flimnap, the Lord High Treasurer, attended there likewise with his white staff; and I observed he often looked on me with a sour countenance, which I would not seem to regard, but ate more than usual, in honor to my dear country, as well as to fill the court with admiration. I have some private reasons to believe, that this visit from his Majesty gave Flimnap an opportunity of doing me ill offices to his master. That minister had always been my secret enemy, though he outwardly caressed me more than was usual to the moroseness of his nature. He represented to the Emperor the low condition of his treasury; that he was forced to take up money at great discount; that exchequer bills would not circulate under nine *per cent.* below par; that in short I had cost his Majesty above a million and a half of *sprugs* (their greatest gold coin, about the bigness of a spangle); and upon the whole, that it would be advisable in the Emperor to take the first fair occasion of dismissing me.

I am here obliged to vindicate the reputation of an excellent lady, who was an innocent sufferer upon my account. The Treasurer took a fancy to be jealous of his wife, from the malice of some evil tongues, who informed him that her Grace had taken a violent affection for my person; and the court-scandal ran for some time, that she once came privately to my lodging. This I solemnly declare to be a most infamous falsehood, without any grounds, farther than that her Grace was pleased to treat me with all innocent marks of freedom and friendship. I own she came often to my house, but always publicly, nor ever without three more in the coach, who were usually her sister and young daughter, and some particular acquaintance; but this was common to many other ladies of the court. And I still appeal to my servants round, whether they at any time saw a coach at my door without knowing what persons were in it. On those occasions, when a servant had given me notice, my custom was to go immediately to the door; and, after paying my respects, to take up the coach and two horses very carefully in my hands (for, if there were six horses, the postillion always unharnessed four), and place them on a table, where I had fixed a moveable rim quite round, of five inches high, to prevent accidents. And I have often had four coaches and horses at once on my table full of company, while I sat in my chair leaning my face towards them; and when I was engaged with one set, the coachmen would gently drive the others round my table. I have passed many an afternoon very agreeably in these conversations. But I defy the Treasurer, or his two informers (I will name them, and let them make their best of it) Clustril and Drunlo, to prove that any person ever came to me *incognito*, except the secretary Reldresal, who was sent by express command of his Imperial Majesty, as I have before related. I should not have dwelt so long upon this particular, if it had not been a point wherein the reputation of a great lady is so nearly concerned, to say nothing of my own; though I then had the honor to be a *Nardac*, which the Treasurer himself is not; for all the world knows he is only a *Clumglum*, a title inferior by one degree, as that of a Marquis is to a Duke in England, although I allow he preceded me in right of his post. These false informations, which I afterwards came to the knowledge of, by an accident not proper to mention, made Flimnap, the Treasurer, show his lady for some time an ill countenance, and me a worse; and although he were at last undeceived and reconciled to her, yet I lost all credit with him, and found my interest decline very fast with the Emperor himself, who was indeed too much governed by that favorite.

## CHAPTER VII

*The Author, Being Informed of a Design to Accuse Him of High Treason, Makes His Escape to* Blefuscu. *His Reception There.*

BEFORE I proceed to give an account of my leaving this kingdom, it may be proper to inform the reader of a private intrigue which had been for two months forming against me.

I had been hitherto all my life a stranger to courts, for which I was unqualified by the meanness of my condition. I had indeed heard and read enough of the dispositions of great princes and ministers; but never expected to have found such terrible effects of them in so remote a country, governed, as I thought, by very different maxims from those in Europe.

When I was just preparing to pay my attendance on the Emperor of Blefuscu, a considerable person at court (to whom I had been very serviceable at a time when he lay under the highest displeasure of his Imperial Majesty) came to my house very privately at night in a close chair, and without sending his name, desired admittance. The chairmen were dismissed; I put the chair, with his Lordship in it, into my coat-pocket: and giving orders to a trusty servant to say I was indisposed and gone to sleep, I fastened the door of my house, placed the chair on the table, according to my usual custom, and sat down by it. After the common salutations were over, observing his Lordship's countenance full of concern, and inquiring into the reason, he desired I would hear him with patience in a matter that highly concerned my honor and my life. His speech was to the following effect, for I took notes of it as soon as he left me.

You are to know, said he, that several Committees of Council have been lately called in the most private manner on your account; and it is but two days since his Majesty came to a full resolution.

You are very sensible that Skyresh Bolgolam (*Galbet*, or High-Admiral) hath been your mortal enemy almost ever since your arrival. His original reasons I know not; but his hatred is much increased since your great success against Blefuscu, by which his glory, as Admiral, is obscured. This Lord, in conjunction with Flimnap the High-Treasurer, whose enmity against you is notorious on account of his lady, Limtoc the General, Lalcon the Chamberlain, and Balmuff the Grand Justiciary, have prepared articles of impeachment against you, for treason, and other capital crimes.

This preface made me so impatient, being conscious of my own merits and innocence, that I was going to interrupt; when he entreated me to be silent, and thus proceeded.

Out of gratitude for the favors you have done me, I procured information of the whole proceedings, and a copy of the articles, wherein 10 I venture my head for your service.

### Articles of Impeachment against Quinbus Flestrin (the Man-Mountain)

#### ARTICLE I

Whereas, by a statute made in the reign of his Imperial Majesty Calin Deffar Plune, it is enacted, that whoever shall make water within the precincts of the royal palace, shall be liable to the pains and penalties of high treason; notwithstanding, the said Quinbus Flestrin, in open breach of the said law, 20 under color of extinguishing the fire kindled in the apartment of his Majesty's most dear Imperial Consort, did maliciously, traitorously, and devilishly, by discharge of his urine, put out the said fire kindled in the said apartment, lying and being within the precincts of the said royal palace, against the statute in that case provided, *etc.*, against the duty, *etc.*

#### ARTICLE II

That the said Quinbus Flestrin having brought the imperial fleet of Blefuscu into the royal port, and being afterwards commanded by his Imperial 30 Majesty to seize all the other ships of the said empire of Blefuscu, and reduce that empire to a province, to be governed by a viceroy from hence, and to destroy and put to death not only all the Big-Endian exiles, but likewise all the people of that empire, who would not immediately forsake the Big-Endian heresy: He, the said Flestrin, like a false traitor against his most Auspicious, Serene, Imperial Majesty, did petition to be excused from the said service, upon pretense of unwillingness to force the consciences, or destroy the liberties and lives of an innocent people.

#### ARTICLE III

That, whereas certain ambassadors arrived from the court of Blefuscu, to sue for peace in his Majesty's court: He, the said Flestrin, did, like a false traitor, aid, abet, comfort, and divert the said ambassadors, although he knew them to be servants to a Prince who was lately an open enemy to his Imperial Majesty, and in open war against his said Majesty.

#### ARTICLE IV

That the said Quinbus Flestrin, contrary to the 50 duty of a faithful subject, is now preparing to make a voyage to the court and empire of Blefuscu, for which he hath received only verbal license from his Imperial Majesty; and under color of the said license, doth falsely and traitorously intend to take the said voyage, and thereby to aid, comfort, and abet the Emperor of Blefuscu, so late an enemy, and in open war with his Imperial Majesty aforesaid.

There are some other articles, but these are the most important, of which I have read you an abstract.

In the several debates upon this impeachment, it must be confessed that his Majesty gave many marks of his great lenity, often urging the services you had done him, and endeavoring to extenuate your crimes. The Treasurer and Admiral insisted that you 10 should be put to the most painful and ignominious death, by setting fire on your house at night, and the General was to attend with twenty thousand men armed with poisoned arrows to shoot you on the face and hands. Some of your servants were to have private orders to strew a poisonous juice on your shirts, which would soon make you tear your own flesh, and die in the utmost torture. The General came into the same opinion; so 20 that for a long time there was a majority against you. But his Majesty resolving, if possible, to spare your life, at last brought off the Chamberlain.

Upon this incident, Reldresal, principal Secretary for Private Affairs, who always approved himself your true friend, was commanded by the Emperor to deliver his opinion, which he accordingly did; and therein justified the good thoughts you have of him. He allowed 30 your crimes to be great, but that still there was room for mercy, the most commendable virtue in a prince, and for which his Majesty was so justly celebrated. He said, the friendship between you and him was so well known to the world, that perhaps the most honorable board might think him partial: however, in obedience to the command he had received, he would freely offer his sentiments. That if his Majesty, in consideration of your 40 services, and pursuant to his own merciful disposition, would please to spare your life, and only give orders to put out both your eyes, he humbly conceived, that by this expedient, justice might in some measure be satisfied, and all the world would applaud the lenity of the Emperor, as well as the fair and generous proceedings of those who have the honor to be his counselors. That the loss of your eyes would be no impediment to your 50 bodily strength, by which you might still be useful to his Majesty. That blindness is an addition to courage, by concealing dangers from us; that the fear you had for your eyes, was the greatest difficulty in bringing over the enemy's fleet, and it would be sufficient for you to see by the eyes of the ministers, since the greatest princes do no more.

This proposal was received with the utmost disapprobation by the whole board. Bolgolam, the Admiral, could not preserve his temper; but rising up in fury, said, he wondered how the Secretary durst presume to give his opinion for preserving the life of a traitor: that the services you had performed, were, by all true reasons of state, the great aggravation of your crimes; that you, who were able to extinguish the fire, by discharge of urine in her Majesty's apartment (which he mentioned with horror), might, at another time, raise an inundation by the same means, to drown the whole palace; and the same strength which enabled you to bring over the enemy's fleet, might serve, upon the first discontent, to carry it back: that he had good reasons to think you were a Big-Endian in your heart; and as treason begins in the heart, before it appears in overt acts, so he accused you as a traitor on that account, and therefore insisted you should be put to death.

The Treasurer was of the same opinion; he showed to what straits his Majesty's revenue was reduced by the charge of maintaining you, which would soon grow insupportable: that the Secretary's expedient of putting out your eyes was so far from being a remedy against this evil, that it would probably increase it, as it is manifest from the common practice of blinding some kind of fowl, after which they fed the faster, and grew sooner fat: that his sacred Majesty and the Council, who are your judges, were in their own consciences fully convinced of your guilt, which was a sufficient argument to condemn you to death, without the formal proofs required by the strict letter of the law.

But his Imperial Majesty, fully determined against capital punishment, was graciously pleased to say, that since the Council thought the loss of your eyes too easy a censure, some other may be inflicted hereafter. And your friend the Secretary humbly desiring to be heard again, in answer to what the Treasurer had objected concerning the great charge his Majesty was at in maintaining you, said, that his Excellency, who had the sole disposal of the Emperor's revenue, might easily provide against that evil, by gradually lessening your establishment; by which, for want of sufficient food, you would grow weak and faint, and lose your appetite, and consequently decay and consume in a few months; neither would the stench of your carcass be then so dangerous, when it should become more than half diminished; and immediately upon your death, five or six thousand of his Majesty's subjects might, in two or three days, cut your flesh from your bones, take it away by cartloads, and bury it in distant parts to prevent infection, leaving the skeleton as a monument of admiration to posterity.

Thus by the great friendship of the Secretary, the whole affair was compromised. It was strictly enjoined, that the project of starving you by degrees should be kept a secret, but the sentence of putting out your eyes was entered on the books; none dissenting except Bolgolam the Admiral, who, being a creature of the Empress, was perpetually instigated by her Majesty to insist upon your death, she having borne perpetual malice against you, on account of that infamous and illegal method you took to extinguish the fire in her apartment.

In three days your friend the Secretary will be directed to come to your house, and read before you the articles of impeachment; and then to signify the great lenity and favor of his Majesty and Council, whereby you are only condemned to the loss of your eyes, which his Majesty doth not question you will gratefully and humbly submit to; and twenty of his Majesty's surgeons will attend, in order to see the operation well performed, by discharging very sharp-pointed arrows into the balls of your eyes, as you lie on the ground.

I leave to your prudence what measures you will take; and to avoid suspicion, I must immediately return in as private a manner as I came.

His Lordship did so, and I remained alone, under many doubts and perplexities of mind.

It was a custom introduced by this prince and his ministry (very different, as I have been assured, from the practices of former times), that after the court had decreed any cruel execution, either to gratify the monarch's resentment, or the malice of a favorite, the Emperor always made a speech to his whole Council, expressing his great lenity and tenderness, as qualities known and confessed by all the world. This speech was immediately published through the kingdom; nor did anything terrify the people so much as those encomiums on his Majesty's mercy; because it was observed, that the more these praises were enlarged and insisted on, the more inhuman was the punishment, and the sufferer more innocent. And as to myself, I must confess, having never been designed for a courtier either by my birth or education, I was so ill a judge of things, that I could not discover the lenity and favor of his sentence, but conceived it (perhaps erroneously) rather to be rigorous than gentle. I sometimes thought of standing my trial, for although I could not deny the facts alleged in the several articles, yet I hoped they would admit of some extenuations. But having in my life perused many state-trials, which I ever observed to terminate as the judges thought fit to direct, I durst not rely on so dangerous a decision, in so critical a juncture, and against such powerful enemies. Once I was strongly bent upon resistance, for while I had liberty, the whole strength of that empire could hardly subdue me, and I might easily with stones pelt the metropolis to pieces; but I soon rejected that project with horror, by remembering the oath I had made to the Emperor, the favors I received from him, and the high title of *Nardac* he conferred upon me. Neither had I so soon learned the gratitude of courtiers, to persuade myself that his Majesty's present severities acquitted me of all past obligations.

At last I fixed upon a resolution, for which it is probable I may incur some censure, and not unjustly; for I confess I owe the preserving my eyes, and consequently my liberty, to my own great rashness and want of experience: because if I had then known the nature of princes and ministers, which I have since observed in many other courts, and their methods of treating criminals less obnoxious than myself, I should with great alacrity and readiness have submitted to so easy a punishment. But hurried on by the precipitancy of youth, and having his Imperial Majesty's licence to pay my attendance upon the Emperor of Blefuscu, I took this opportunity, before the three days were elapsed, to send a letter to my friend the Secretary, signifying my resolution of setting out that morning for Blefuscu pursuant to the leave I had got; and without waiting for an answer, I went to that side of the island where our fleet lay. I seized a large man of war, tied a cable to the prow, and, lifting up the anchors, I stripped myself, put my clothes (together with my coverlet, which I brought under my arm) into the vessel, and drawing it after me between wading and swimming, arrived at the royal port of Blefuscu, where the people had long expected me: they lent me two guides to direct me to the capital city, which is of the same name. I held them in my hands till I came within two hundred yards of the gate, and desired them to signify my arrival to one of the secretaries, and let

him know, I there waited his Majesty's command. I had an answer in about an hour, that his Majesty, attended by the Royal Family, and great officers of the court, was coming out to receive me. I advanced a hundred yards. The Emperor and his train alighted from their horses, the Empress and ladies from their coaches, and I did not perceive they were in any fright or concern. I lay on the ground to kiss his Majesty's and the Empress's hands. I told his Majesty, that I was come according to my promise, and with the license of the Emperor my master, to have the honor of seeing so mighty a monarch, and to offer him any service in my power, consistent with my duty to my own prince; not mentioning a word of my disgrace, because I had hitherto no regular information of it, and might suppose myself wholly ignorant of any such design; neither could I reasonably conceive that the Emperor would discover the secret while I was out of his power: wherein, however, it soon appeared I was deceived.

I shall not trouble the reader with the particular account of my reception at this court, which was suitable to the generosity of so great a prince; nor of the difficulties I was in for want of a house and bed, being forced to lie on the ground, wrapped up in my coverlet.

## CHAPTER VIII

*The Author, by a Lucky Accident, Finds Means to Leave* Blefuscu: *and, after Some Difficulties, Returns Safe to His Native Country.*

THREE days after my arrival, walking out of curiosity to the north-east coast of the island, I observed, about half a league off, in the sea, somewhat that looked like a boat overturned. I pulled off my shoes and stockings, and wading two or three hundred yards, I found the object to approach nearer by force of the tide; and then plainly saw it to be a real boat, which I suppose might, by some tempest, have been driven from a ship; whereupon I returned immediately towards the city, and desired his Imperial Majesty to lend me twenty of the tallest vessels he had left after the loss of his fleet, and three thousand seamen under the command of his Vice-Admiral. This fleet sailed round, while I went back the shortest way to the coast where I first discovered the boat; I found the tide had driven it still nearer. The seamen were all provided with cordage, which I had beforehand twisted to a sufficient strength. When the ships came up, I stripped myself, and waded till I came within an hundred yards of the boat, after which I was forced to swim till I got up to it. The seamen threw me the end of the cord, which I fastened to a hole in the fore-part of the boat, and the other end to a man of war; but I found all my labor to little purpose; for being out of my depth, I was not able to work. In this necessity, I was forced to swim behind, and push the boat forwards as often as I could, with one of my hands; and the tide favoring me, I advanced so far, that I could just hold up my chin and feel the ground. I rested two or three minutes, and then gave the boat another shove, and so on till the sea was no higher than my arm-pits; and now the most laborious part being over, I took out my other cables, which were stowed in one of the ships, and fastening them first to the boat, and then to nine of the vessels which attended me; the wind being favorable, the seamen towed, and I shoved till we arrived within forty yards of the shore; and waiting till the tide was out, I got dry to the boat, and by the assistance of two thousand men, with ropes and engines, I made a shift to turn it on its bottom, and found it was but little damaged.

I shall not trouble the reader with the difficulties I was under by the help of certain paddles, which cost me ten days making, to get my boat to the royal port of Blefuscu, where a mighty concourse of people appeared upon my arrival, full of wonder at the sight of so prodigious a vessel. I told the Emperor that my good fortune had thrown this boat in my way, to carry me to some place from whence I might return into my native country, and begged his Majesty's orders for getting materials to fit it up, together with his license to depart; which, after some kind of expostulations, he was pleased to grant.

I did very much wonder, in all this time, not to have heard of any express relating to me from our Emperor to the court of Blefuscu. But I was afterwards given privately to understand, that his Imperial Majesty, never imagining I had the least notice of his designs, believed I was only gone to Blefuscu in performance of my promise, according to the license he had given me, which was well known at our court, and would return in a few days when that ceremony was ended. But he was at last in pain at my long absence; and after consulting with the Treasurer, and the rest of that cabal, a person of quality was dispatched with a copy of the articles against me. This envoy had instructions to represent to the monarch of Blefuscu, the great lenity of his master, who was content to punish me no farther than with the loss of my eyes; that I had fled from justice, and if I did not return in two hours, I should be deprived of my title of *Nardac*, and declared a traitor. The envoy further added, that in order to maintain the peace and amity between both empires, his master expected that his brother of Blefuscu would give orders to have me sent back to Lilliput, bound hand and foot, to be punished as a traitor.

The Emperor of Blefuscu having taken three days to consult, returned an answer consisting of many civilities and excuses. He said, that as for sending me bound, his brother knew it was impossible; that although I had deprived him of his fleet, yet he owed great obligations to me for many good offices I had done him in making the peace. That, however, both their Majesties would soon be made easy; for I had found a prodigious vessel on the shore, able to carry me on the sea, which he had given order to fit up with my own assistance and direction and he hoped in a few weeks both empires would be freed from so insupportable an incumbrance.

With this answer the envoy returned to Lilliput, and the monarch of Blefuscu related to me all that had passed; offering me at the same time (but under the strictest confidence) his gracious protection, if I would continue in his service; wherein although I believed him sincere, yet I resolved never more to put any confidence in princes or ministers, where I could possibly avoid it; and therefore, with all due acknowledgments for his favorable intentions, I humbly begged to be excused. I told him, that since fortune, whether good or evil, had thrown a vessel in my way, I was resolved to venture myself in the ocean, rather than be an occasion of difference between two such mighty monarchs. Neither did I find the Emperor at all displeased; and I discovered by a certain accident, that he was very glad of my resolution, and so were most of his ministers.

These considerations moved me to hasten my departure somewhat sooner than I intended; to which the court, impatient to have me gone, very readily contributed. Five hundred workmen were employed to make two sails to my boat, according to my directions, by quilting thirteen fold of their strongest linen together. I was at the pains of making ropes and cables, by twisting ten, twenty, or thirty of the thickest and strongest of theirs. A great stone that I happened to find, after a long search, by the sea-shore, served me for an anchor. I had the tallow of three hundred cows for greasing my boat, and other uses. I was at incredible pains in cutting down some of the largest timber-trees for oars and masts, wherein 10 I was, however, much assisted by his Majesty's ship-carpenters, who helped me in smoothing them, after I had done the rough work.

In about a month, when all was prepared, I sent to receive his Majesty's commands, and take my leave. The Emperor and Royal Family came out of the palace; I lay down on my face to kiss his hand, which he very graciously gave me: so did the Empress and young Princes of the blood. His 20 Majesty presented me with fifty purses of two hundred *sprugs* apiece, together with his picture at full length, which I put immediately into one of my gloves, to keep it from being hurt. The ceremonies at my departure were too many to trouble the reader with at this time.

I stored the boat with the carcasses of an hundred oxen, and three hundred sheep, with bread and drink proportionable, and as 30 much meat ready dressed as four hundred cooks could provide. I took with me six cows and two bulls alive, with as many ewes and rams, intending to carry them into my own country, and propagate the breed. And to feed them on board, I had a good bundle of hay, and a bag of corn. I would gladly have taken a dozen of the natives, but this was a thing the Emperor would by no means permit; and besides a diligent search into my pockets, 40 his Majesty engaged my honor not to carry away any of his subjects, although with their own consent and desire.

Having thus prepared all things as well as I was able, I set sail on the twenty-fourth day of September, 1701, at six in the morning; and when I had gone about four leagues to the northward, the wind being at southeast, at six in the evening I descried a small island about half a league to the north-west. I 50 advanced forward, and cast anchor on the lee-side of the island, which seemed to be uninhabited. I then took some refreshment, and went to my rest. I slept well, and as I conjectured at least six hours, for I found the day broke in two hours after I awaked. It was a clear night. I ate my

breakfast before the sun was up; and heaving anchor, the wind being favorable, I steered the same course that I had done the day before, wherein I was directed by my pocket-compass. My intention was to reach, if possible, one of those islands, which I had reason to believe lay to the north-east of Van Diemen's Land. I discovered nothing all that day, but upon the next, about three in the afternoon, when I had by my computation made twenty-four leagues from Blefuscu, I descried a sail steering to the south-east; my course was due east. I hailed her, but could get no answer; yet I found I gained upon her, for the wind slackened. I made all the sail I could, and in half an hour she spied me, then hung out her ancient, and discharged a gun. It is not easy to express the joy I was in upon the unexpected hope of once 20 more seeing my beloved country, and the dear pledges I had left in it. The ship slackened her sails, and I came up with her between five and six in the evening, September 26; but my heart leaped within me to see her English colors. I put my cows and sheep into my coat-pockets, and got on board with all my little cargo of provisions. The vessel was an English merchantman returning from Japan by the North and South Seas; the Captain, Mr. John Biddel of Deptford, a very civil man, and an excellent sailor. We were now in the latitude of 30 degrees south; there were about fifty men in the ship; and here I met an old comrade of mine, one Peter Williams, who gave me a good character to the Captain. This gentleman treated me with kindness, and desired I would let him know what place I came from last, and whither I was bound; which I did in a few 40 words, but he thought I was raving, and that the dangers I underwent had disturbed my head; whereupon I took my black cattle and sheep out of my pocket, which, after great astonishment, clearly convinced him of my veracity. I then showed him the gold given me by the Emperor of Blefuscu, together with his Majesty's picture at full length, and some other rarities of that country. I gave him two purses of two hundred *sprugs* each, 50 and promised, when we arrived in England, to make him a present of a cow and a sheep big with young.

I shall not trouble the reader with a particular account of this voyage, which was very prosperous for the most part. We arrived in the Downs on the 13th of April, 1702. I had only one misfortune, that the rats on board carried away one of my sheep; I found her bones in a hole, picked clean from the flesh. The rest of my cattle I got safe on shore, and set them a grazing in a bowling-green at Greenwich, where the fineness of the grass made them feed very heartily, though I had always feared the contrary: neither could I possibly have preserved them in so long a voyage, if the Captain had not allowed me some of his best biscuit, which, rubbed to 10 powder, and mingled with water, was their constant food. The short time I continued in England, I made a considerable profit by showing my cattle to many persons of quality, and others: and before I began my second voyage, I sold them for six hundred pounds. Since my last return, I find the breed is considerably increased, especially the sheep; which I hope will prove much to the advantage of the woolen manufacture, by the fineness of the fleeces. 20

I stayed but two months with my wife and family; for my insatiable desire of seeing foreign countries would suffer me to continue no longer. I left fifteen hundred pounds with my wife, and fixed her in a good house at Redriff. My remaining stock I carried with me, part in money, and part in goods, in hopes to improve my fortunes. My eldest uncle John had left me an estate in land, near Epping, of about thirty pounds a year; and I 30 had a long lease of the Black Bull in Fetter-Lane, which yielded me as much more; so that I was not in any danger of leaving my family upon the parish. My son Johnny, named so after his uncle, was at the Grammar School, and a towardly child. My daughter Betty (who is now well married, and has children) was then at her needle-work. I took leave of my wife, and boy and girl, with tears on both sides, and went on board the *Adventure*, a merchant- 40 ship of three hundred tons, bound for Surat, Captain John Nicholas, of Liverpool, Commander. But my account of this voyage must be referred to the second part of my Travels.

# A Description of a City Shower

## (OCTOBER, 1710)

Careful observers may foretell the hour,
(By sure prognostics) when to dread a show'r.
While rain depends, the pensive cat gives o'er
Her frolics, and pursues her tail no more.
Returning home at night, you'll find the sink 5
Strike your offended sense with double stink.
If you be wise, then, go not far to dine:

You'll spend in coach-hire more than save in
  wine.
A coming show'r your shooting corns presage,
Old aches throb, your hollow tooth will rage. 10
Saunt'ring in coffeehouse is Dulman seen;
He damns the climate, and complains of
  spleen.
  Meanwhile the South, rising with dabbled
    wings,
A sable cloud athwart the welkin flings,
That swill'd more liquor than it could contain,
And, like a drunkard, gives it up again. 16
Brisk Susan whips her linen from the rope,
While the first drizzling show'r is borne aslope;
Such is that sprinkling which some careless
  quean
Flirts on you from her mop, but not so clean:
You fly, invoke the gods; then, turning, stop 21
To rail; she singing, still whirls on her mop.
Not yet the dust had shunn'd th'unequal strife,
But, aided by the wind, fought still for life,
And wafted with its foe by violent gust, 25
'Twas doubtful which was rain, and which was
  dust.
Ah! where must needy poet seek for aid,
When dust and rain at once his coat invade?
His only coat, where dust confused with rain,
Roughen the nap, and leave a mingled stain. 30
  Now in contiguous drops the flood comes
    down,
Threat'ning with deluge this *devoted* town.
To shops in crowds the daggled females fly,
Pretend to cheapen goods, but nothing buy.
The Templar[1] spruce, while every spout's
  abroach, 35
Stays till 'tis fair, yet seems to call a coach.
The tucked-up sempstress walks with hasty
  strides,
While streams run down her oiled umbrella's
  sides.
Here various kinds, by various fortunes led,
Commence acquaintance underneath a shed. 40
Triumphant Tories, and desponding Whigs,
Forget their feuds, and join to save their wigs.
Boxed in a chair the beau impatient sits,
While spouts run clattering o'er the roof by fits,
And ever and anon with frightful din 45
The leather sounds; he trembles from within.
So when Troy chairmen bore the wooden steed,
Pregnant with Greeks impatient to be freed,
(Those bully Greeks, who, as the moderns do,
Instead of paying chairmen, run them through)
Laoco'n struck the outside with his spear, 51
And each imprisoned hero quaked for fear.
  Now from all parts the swelling kennels[2]
    flow,
And bear their trophies with them as they go:
Filth of all hues and odors, seem to tell 55

---

[1] Legal student, attending one of the London Inns of Court which occupied land once belonging to the Knights Templars.
[2] Gutters.

What street they sailed from, by their sight and
  smell.
They, as each torrent drives with rapid force,
From Smithfield or St. Pulchre's shape their
  course,
And in huge confluent join at Snowhill ridge,
Fall from the conduit prone to Holborn bridge
Sweepings from butchers' stalls, dung, guts, and
  blood,                                              61
Drowned puppies, stinking sprats, all drenched
  in mud,
Dead cats, and turnip-tops, come tumbling
  down the flood.

## On the Day of Judgment

With a whirl of thought oppressed,
I sink from reverie to rest.
An horrid vision seized my head;

I saw the graves give up their dead!
Jove, armed with terrors, burst the skies,          5
And thunder roars and lightning flies!
Amazed, confused, its fate unknown,
The world stands trembling at his throne!
While each pale sinner hangs his head,
Jove, nodding, shook the heav'ns, and said:        10
"Offending race of human kind,
By nature, reason, learning, blind;
You who, through frailty, stepped aside;
And you, who never fell—*through pride*:
You who in different sects were shammed,           15
And come to see each other damned;
(So some folks told you, but they knew
No more of Jove's designs than you;)
The world's mad business now is o'er,
And I resent these pranks no more.                 20
I to such blockheads set my wit!
I damn such fools!—Go, go, you're bit."

# Alexander Pope

## 1688 - 1744

What Dryden was in the latter part of the seventeenth century Pope became in the first half of the eighteenth—the foremost man of letters of the age and the acknowledged arbiter of literary taste. He was born in the year of the Revolution, on 21 May. His father was a London merchant and a Roman Catholic. The latter fact colored Pope's whole life, because for many years after the Revolution Catholics suffered oppressive disabilities, both social and legal, which marked them as a class apart from the rest of the nation and almost forced them to live in an atmosphere of suspicion, intrigue, and evasion of the law. Among other things, they were debarred from the universities, they were burdened with heavy taxes, and they could hold no public offices. Pope, moreover, always refused to change his religion, although the heaviest inducements were held before him from time to time, and although, too, his adherence to Catholicism was merely formal, the result rather of filial piety than of personal conviction. It is doubtful, however, if Pope would have been able to attend one of the universities, even had his parents been Church-of-England people, for from his birth he was deformed and delicate in health. In his Epistle to Arbuthnot he called his life one long disease, which was scarcely an exaggeration; there must have been hardly a day when he was free from pain, and his face was lined and contorted from his intense sufferings. His education was largely got through his own eager and wide reading in classical and English poetry, with the result that his scholarship always remained seriously defective and that he had no methodical training save such as was administered by his father in the correction of his youthful verses. He was a precocious boy, and determined at an early age to be a poet. At an early age, too, he succeeded in attracting the interest of several men of taste and cultivation, at least one of whom, William Walsh, deserves to be mentioned in any account of Pope. For "knowing

Walsh," whether he exerted a decisive influence or not, marked out precisely the direction in which Pope was to travel. "He used to encourage me much," Pope in later years wrote to a friend, "and used to tell me there was one way left of excelling: for though we had several great poets, we never had any one great poet that was correct; and he desired me to make that my study and aim." Pope did so; and in correctness of form, in clarity, pointed wit, polish, studied concision, smoothness, and metrical precision, Pope excelled remarkably, as is witnessed, for example, by the number of familiar sayings he has given to the English-speaking world, and as no one who reads more than a few pages of his poetry needs to be told.

Pope's Pastorals were his first published poems, printed in 1709, but written, as he always claimed, when he was only sixteen years old. They were followed by his Essay on Criticism in 1711 and by his Rape of the Lock, in its earlier form, in 1712. These poems made his reputation immediately, placing him by general consent at the head of living poets. He was not, however, too well off and could not expect, on account of his Catholicism, either public office or a pension, the usual rewards bestowed on successful and useful men of letters by the government in his day. Consequently Pope had to find some new way of securing an income, and he found it. In 1713 he issued proposals for a translation of the Iliad, inviting immediate subscriptions in support of the project. Warm friends helped him with enthusiasm to secure subscriptions, a publisher offered him a large sum for the right of publication, and, as the combined result of his reputation and of his persistent hard work with the translation, Pope managed to clear over £5000 on the work, and later made another large sum when, with the help of assistants, he translated the Odyssey. Such profits from literary work were unprecedented, and they were sufficient to enable him to buy a country house with a small estate at Twickenham and to live there comfortably through the remainder of his life, independent of private patronage or the favor of public men.

The Essay on Criticism, *though didactic in character, had shown Pope's gift as a satirist, and his greatest success came in that field, particularly in the* Dunciad *and in the poems collected under the title,* Satires and Epistles. *His satire was never, like Dryden's, political; and though in* The Rape of the Lock *his ridicule was general, he chiefly devoted himself to personal attacks. In this he was biting, even venomous, and he has often been blamed for the number and virulence of his enmities, for his spitefulness, and for his treachery. Yet despite all blemishes and all limitations Pope remains an arresting figure in his own right, besides embodying more completely than any of his contemporaries the classicism of his age.*

The Works of Alexander Pope *are edited by John W. Croker, Whitwell Elwin, and William J. Courthope (London, 1871–1879); Volume V is a detailed biography by Courthope. The Twickenham Edition of the Poems, under the general editorship of J. Butt, has been partially completed (New Haven, 1939– ). George Sherburn has edited* The Correspondence *(Oxford, 1956) and a convenient volume of selections,* The Best of Pope *(New York, 1929). Sherburn is also the author of a standard work on* The Early Career of Alexander Pope *(Oxford, 1934). Biographies include the subjective* Alexander Pope *by Edith Sitwell (New York, 1930);* New Light on Pope *by Norman Ault (London, 1949); and* Alexander Pope *by Bonamy Dobrée (London, 1951). Among the many critical studies are Austin Warren,* Alexander Pope as Critic and Humanist *(Princeton, 1929); Geoffrey Tillotson,* On the Poetry of Pope *(Oxford, 1950); and Douglas Knight,* Pope and the Heroic Tradition *(New Haven, 1951). An interesting collection of studies appears in* Pope and His Contemporaries: Essays Presented to George Sherburn *(Oxford, 1949).*

## Ode on Solitude [1]

Happy the man whose wish and care
     A few paternal acres bound,

[1] According to Pope himself this poem was written when he was only twelve years old, in 1700. Pope's statements about the dates of his earlier works are unreliable, and it seems unlikely that this one can be true. In any case, however, this is in all probability the earliest poem by Pope which has been preserved.

Content to breathe his native air
     In his own ground.

Whose herds with milk, whose fields with
     bread,                                         5
Whose flocks supply him with attire,
Whose trees in summer yield him shade,
     In winter fire.

Bless'd, who can unconcern'dly find
     Hours, days, and years slide soft away,   10
In health of body, peace of mind,
     Quiet by day,

Sound sleep by night; study and ease
     Together mixed; sweet recreation;
And Innocence, which most does please,        15
     With meditation.

Thus let me live, unseen, unknown,
     Thus unlamented let me die;
Steal from the world, and not a stone
     Tell where I lie.                          20

## An Essay on Criticism [2]

### CONTENTS

#### PART I

*Introduction. That 'tis as great a fault to judge ill, as to write ill, and a more dangerous one to the public, v. 1. That a true Taste is as rare to be found, as a true Genius, v. 9 to 18. That most men are born with some Taste, but spoiled by false Education, v. 19 to 25. The multitude of Critics, and causes of them, v. 26 to 45. That we are to study our own Taste, and know the Limits of it, v. 46 to 67. Nature the best guide of Judgment, v. 68 to 87. Improved by Art and Rules, which are but methodized Nature, 88. Rules derived from the Practice of the Ancient Poets, v. id. to 110. That therefore the Ancients are necessary to be studied, by a Critic, particularly Homer and Virgil, v. 120 to 138. Of Licenses, and the use of them by the Ancients, v. 140 to 180. Reverence due to the Ancients, and praise of them, v. 181, etc.*

#### PART II. VER. 201, etc.

*Causes hindering a true Judgment. 1. Pride, v. 208. 2. Imperfect Learning, v. 215. 3. Judging by parts, and not by the whole, v. 233 to 288. Critics in Wit, Language, Versification, only, v. 288, 305, 399, etc. 4. Being too hard to please, or too apt to admire, v. 384. 5. Partiality —too much Love to a Sect—to the Ancients or Moderns, v. 394. 6. Prejudice or Prevention, v. 408. 7. Singularity, v. 424. 8. Inconstancy, v. 430. 9. Party Spirit, v. 452, etc. 10. Envy, v.*

[2] Pope began to write the *Essay* perhaps as early as 1707. It was finished in 1709, and published in 1711.

466. *Against Envy, and in praise of Good-nature, v. 508, etc. When Severity is chiefly to be used by Critics, v. 526, etc.*

### PART III. VER. 560, *etc.*

*Rules for the Conduct of Manners in a Critic.* 1. *Candor, v. 563. Modesty, v. 566. Good breeding, v. 572. Sincerity, and Freedom of advice, v. 578. 2. When one's Counsel is to be restrained, v. 584. Character of an incorrigible Poet, v. 600. And of an impertinent Critic, v. 610, etc. Character of a good Critic, v. 629. The History of Criticism, and Characters of the best Critics, Aristotle, v. 645. Horace, v. 653. Dionysius, v. 665. Petronius, v. 667. Quintilian, v. 670. Longinus, v. 675. Of the Decay of Criticism, and its Revival. Erasmus, v. 693. Vida, v. 705. Boileau, v. 714. Lord Roscommon, etc., v. 725. Conclusion.*

### PART I

'Tis hard to say, if greater want of skill
Appear in writing or in judging ill;
But, of the two, less dang'rous is th' offense
To tire our patience, than mislead our sense.
Some few in that, but numbers err in this,    5
Ten censure wrong for one who writes amiss;
A fool might once himself alone expose,
Now one in verse makes many more in prose.
    'Tis with our judgments as our watches, none
Go just alike, yet each believes his own.    10
In Poets as true genius is but rare,
True Taste as seldom is the Critic's share;
Both must alike from Heav'n derive their light,
These born to judge, as well as those to write.
Let such teach others who themselves excel, 15
And censure freely who have written well.
Authors are partial to their wit, 'tis true,
But are not Critics to their judgment too?
    Yet if we look more closely, we shall find
Most have the seeds of judgment in their mind:
Nature affords at least a glimm'ring light;    21
The lines, though touched but faintly, are
    drawn right.
But as the slightest sketch, if justly traced,
Is by ill-coloring but the more disgraced,
So by false learning is good sense defaced;
Some are bewildered in the maze of schools, 26
And some made coxcombs Nature meant but
    fools.
In search of wit these lose their common sense,
And then turn Critics in their own defense:
Each burns alike, who can, or cannot write, 30
Or with a Rival's, or an Eunuch's spite.
All fools have still an itching to deride,
And fain would be upon the laughing side.
If Maevius[3] scribble in Apollo's spite,
There are who judge still worse than he can
    write.    35
    Some have at first for Wits, then Poets
    passed,

[3] A Roman poet of no ability, whose name has been preserved by Virgil and Horace.

Turned Critics next, and proved plain fools at
    last.
Some neither can for Wits nor Critics pass,
As heavy mules are neither horse nor ass.
Those half-learn'd witlings, num'rous in our
    isle,    40
As half-formed insects on the banks of Nile;
Unfinished things, one knows not what to call,
Their generation's so equivocal:
To tell 'em, would a hundred tongues require,
Or one vain wit's, that might a hundred tire. 45
    But you who seek to give and merit fame,
And justly bear a Critic's noble name,
Be sure yourself and your own reach to know,
How far your genius, taste, and learning go;
Launch not beyond your depth, but be discreet,
And mark that point where sense and dullness
    meet.    51
Nature to all things fixed the limits fit,
And wisely curbed proud man's pretending wit.
As on the land while here the ocean gains,
In other parts it leaves wide sandy plains;    55
Thus in the soul while memory prevails,
The solid pow'r of understanding fails;
Where beams of warm imagination play,
The memory's soft figures melt away.
One science only will one genius fit;    60
So vast is art, so narrow human wit:
Not only bounded to peculiar arts,
But oft in those confined to single parts.
Like kings we lose the conquests gained before,
By vain ambition still to make them more;    65
Each might his sev'ral province well command,
Would all but stoop to what they understand.
    First follow Nature, and your judgment
    frame
By her just standard, which is still the same:
Unerring Nature, still divinely bright,    70
One clear, unchanged, and universal light,
Life, force, and beauty, must to all impart,
At once the source, and end, and test of Art.
Art from that fund each just supply provides,
Works without show, and without pomp pre-
    sides:    75
In some fair body thus th' informing soul
With spirits feeds, with vigor fills the whole,
Each motion guides, and ev'ry nerve sustains;
Itself unseen, but in th' effects, remains.
Some, to whom Heav'n in wit has been pro-
    fuse,    80
Want as much more, to turn it to its use;
For wit and judgment often are at strife,
Though meant each other's aid, like man and
    wife.
'Tis more to guide, than spur the Muse's steed;
Restrain his fury, than provoke his speed;    85
The wingéd courser, like a gen'rous horse,
Shows most true mettle when you check his
    course.
    Those Rules of old discovered, not devised,
Are Nature still, but Nature methodized;
Nature, like liberty, is but restrained    90
By the same laws which first herself ordained.

Hear how learn'd Greece her useful rules in-
dites,
When to repress, and when indulge our flights:
High on Parnassus' top her sons she showed,
And pointed out those arduous paths they trod;
Held from afar, aloft, th' immortal prize,      96
And urged the rest by equal steps to rise.
Just precepts thus from great examples giv'n,
She drew from them what they derived from
Heav'n.
The gen'rous Critic fanned the Poet's fire,    100
And taught the world with reason to admire.
Then Criticism the Muse's handmaid proved,
To dress her charms, and make her more be-
loved:
But following wits from that intention strayed,
Who could not win the mistress, wooed the
maid;                                           105
Against the Poets their own arms they turned,
Sure to hate most the men from whom they
learned.
So modern 'Pothecaries, taught the art
By Doctors' bills to play the Doctor's part,
Bold in the practice of mistaken rules,        110
Prescribe, apply, and call their masters fools.
Some on the leaves of ancient authors prey,
Nor time nor moths e'er spoiled so much as
they.
Some dryly plain, without invention's aid,
Write dull receipts how poems may be made.
These leave the sense, their learning to dis-
play,                                           116
And those explain the meaning quite away.
  You then whose judgment the right course
would steer,
Know well each Ancient's proper character;
His fable,[4] subject, scope in ev'ry page;    120
Religion, Country, genius of his Age:
Without all these at once before your eyes,
Cavil you may, but never criticize.
Be Homer's works your study and delight,
Read them by day, and meditate by night;       125
Thence form your judgment, thence your max-
ims bring,
And trace the Muses upward to their spring.
Still with itself compared, his text peruse;
And let your comment be the Mantuan Muse.[5]
  When first young Maro[5] in his boundless
mind                                            130
A work t' outlast immortal Rome designed,
Perhaps he seemed above the critic's law,
And but from nature's fountains scorned to
draw:
But when t' examine every part he came,        134
Nature and Homer were, he found, the same.
Convinced, amazed, he checks the bold de-
sign;
And rules as strict his labored work confine,
As if the Stagirite[6] o'erlooked each line.
Learn hence for ancient rules a just esteem;

[4] Story.          [5] Virgil.
[6] Aristotle.

To copy nature is to copy them.               140
  Some beauties yet no Precepts can declare,
For there's a happiness as well as care.
Music resembles Poetry, in each
Are nameless graces which no methods teach,
And which a master-hand alone can reach.
If, where the rules not far enough extend      146
(Since rules were made but to promote their
end),
Some lucky License answer to the full
Th' intent proposed, that License is a rule.
Thus Pegasus, a nearer way to take,            150
May boldly deviate from the common track;
From vulgar bounds with brave disorder part,
And snatch a grace beyond the reach of art,
Which without passing through the judgment,
gains
The heart, and all its end at once attains.    155
In prospects thus, some objects please our
eyes,
Which out of nature's common order rise,
The shapeless rock, or hanging precipice.
Great wits sometimes may gloriously offend,
And rise to faults true Critics dare not mend.
But though the Ancients thus their rules in-
vade                                            161
(As Kings dispense with laws themselves have
made),
Moderns, beware! or if you must offend
Against the precept, ne'er transgress its End;
Let it be seldom, and compelled by need;       165
And have, at least, their precedent to plead.
The Critic else proceeds without remorse,
Seizes your fame, and puts his laws in force.
  I know there are, to whose presumptuous
thoughts
Those freer beauties, e'en in them, seem faults.
Some figures monstrous and mis-shaped ap-
pear,                                           171
Considered singly, or beheld too near,
Which, but proportioned to their light, or
place,
Due distance reconciles to form and grace.
A prudent chief not always must display        175
His powers in equal ranks, and fair array.
But with th' occasion and the place comply,
Conceal his force, nay seem sometimes to fly.
Those oft are stratagems which error seem,
Nor is it Homer nods, but we that dream.       180
  Still green with bays each ancient Altar
stands,
Above the reach of sacrilegious hands;
Secure from Flames, from Envy's fiercer rage,
Destructive War, and all-involving Age.
See, from each clime the learn'd their incense
bring!                                          185
Hear, in all tongues consenting paeans ring!
In praise so just let ev'ry voice be joined,
And fill the gen'ral chorus of mankind.
Hail, Bards triumphant! born in happier days;
Immortal heirs of universal praise!            190
Whose honors with increase of ages grow,
As streams roll down, enlarging as they flow;

Nations unborn your mighty names shall sound,
And worlds applaud that must not yet be
    found!
Oh may some spark of your celestial fire,    195
The last, the meanest of your sons inspire
(That on weak wings, from far, pursues your
    flights;
Glows while he reads, but trembles as he
    writes),
To teach vain Wits a science little known,
T' admire superior sense, and doubt their
    own!    200

### PART II

Of all the Causes which conspire to blind
Man's erring judgment, and misguide the mind,
What the weak head with strongest bias rules,
Is Pride, the never-failing voice of fools.
Whatever nature has in worth denied,    205
She gives in large recruits of needful pride;
For as in bodies, thus in souls, we find
What wants in blood and spirits, swelled with
    wind:
Pride, where wit fails, steps in to our defense,
And fills up all the mighty Void of sense.    210
If once right reason drives that cloud away,
Truth breaks upon us with resistless day.
Trust not yourself; but your defects to know,
Make use of ev'ry friend—and ev'ry foe.
    A little learning is a dang'rous thing;    215
Drink deep, or taste not the Pierian spring.[7]
There shallow draughts intoxicate the brain,
And drinking largely sobers us again.
Fired at first sight with what the Muse imparts,
In fearless youth we tempt the heights of Arts,
While from the bounded level of our mind    221
Short views we take, nor see the lengths be-
    hind;
But more advanced, behold with strange sur-
    prise
New distant scenes of endless science rise!
So pleased at first the tow'ring Alps we try,    225
Mount o'er the vales, and seem to tread the
    sky,
Th' eternal snows appear already past,
And the first clouds and mountains seem the
    last;
But, those attained, we tremble to survey
The growing labors of the lengthened way,    230
Th' increasing prospect tires our wand'ring
    eyes,
Hills peep o'er hills, and Alps on Alps arise!
    A perfect Judge will read each work of Wit
With the same spirit that its author writ:
Survey the Whole, nor seek slight faults to
    find    235
Where nature moves, and rapture warms the
    mind;
Nor lose, for that malignant dull delight,
The gen'rous pleasure to be charmed with Wit.
But in such lays as neither ebb, nor flow,

[7] Pieria was said to be the birthplace of the muses.

Correctly cold, and regularly low,    240
That, shunning faults, one quiet tenor keep,
We cannot blame indeed—but we may sleep.
In wit, as nature, what affects our hearts
Is not th' exactness of peculiar parts;
'Tis not a lip, or eye, we beauty call,    245
But the joint force and full result of all.
Thus when we view some well-proportioned
    dome
(The world's just wonder, and e'en thine, O
    Rome![8]),
No single parts unequally surprise,
All comes united to th' admiring eyes;    250
No monstrous height, or breadth, or length ap-
    pear;
The Whole at once is bold and regular.
    Whoever thinks a faultless piece to see,
Thinks what ne'er was, nor is, nor e'er shall be.
In every work regard the writer's End,    255
Since none can compass more than they in-
    tend;
And if the means be just, the conduct true,
Applause, in spite of trivial faults, is due;
As men of breeding, sometimes men of wit,
T' avoid great errors, must the less commit:    260
Neglect the rules each verbal Critic lays,
For not to know some trifles is a praise.
Most Critics, fond of some subservient art,
Still make the Whole depend upon a Part:
They talk of principles, but notions prize,    265
And all to one loved Folly sacrifice.
    Once on a time, La Mancha's Knight,[9] they
    say,
A certain bard encount'ring on the way,
Discoursed in terms as just, with looks as sage,
As e'er could Dennis [10] of the Grecian stage;
Concluding all were desp'rate sots and fools,    271
Who durst depart from Aristotle's rules.
Our Author, happy in a judge so nice,
Produced his Play, and begged the Knight's ad-
    vice;
Made him observe the subject, and the plot,    275
The manners, passions, unities; what not?
All which, exact to rule, were brought about,
Were but a Combat in the lists left out.
"What! leave the Combat out?" exclaims the
    Knight;
Yes, or we must renounce the Stagirite.    280
"Not so, by Heav'n" (he answers in a rage),
"Knights, squires, and steeds, must enter on the
    stage."
So vast a throng the stage can ne'er contain.
"Then build a new, or act it in a plain."
    Thus Critics, of less judgment than caprice,
Curious, not knowing, not exact but nice,    286
Form short Ideas; and offend in arts
(As most in manners) by a love to parts.
    Some to Conceit alone their taste confine,
And glitt'ring thoughts struck out at ev'ry line;

[8] St. Peter's.    [9] Don Quixote.
[10] John Dennis, critic and playwright contemporary
with Pope.

Pleased with a work where nothing's just or
   fit; 291
One glaring Chaos and wild heap of wit.
Poets like painters, thus, unskilled to trace
The naked nature and the living grace,
With gold and jewels cover ev'ry part, 295
And hide with ornaments their want of art.
True Wit is Nature to advantage dressed,
What oft was thought, but ne'er so well ex-
   pressed;
Something, whose truth convinced at sight we
   find,
That gives us back the image of our mind. 300
As shades more sweetly recommend the light,
So modest plainness sets off sprightly wit.
For works may have more wit than does 'em
   good,
As bodies perish through excess of blood.
  Others for Language all their care express,
And value books, as women men, for Dress: 306
Their praise is still—the Style is excellent:
The sense, they humbly take upon content.
Words are like leaves; and where they most
   abound,
Much fruit of sense beneath is rarely found, 310
False Eloquence, like the prismatic glass,
Its gaudy colors spreads on ev'ry place;
The face of Nature we no more survey,
All glares alike, without distinction gay:
But true expression, like th' unchanging ⎫
   Sun, 315 ⎬
Clears and improves whate'er it shines upon, ⎪
It gilds all objects, but it alters none. ⎭
Expression is the dress of thought, and still
Appears more decent, as more suitable;
A vile conceit in pompous words expressed, 320
Is like a clown in regal purple dressed:
For diff'rent styles with diff'rent subjects sort,
As sev'ral garbs with country, town, and court.
Some by old words to fame have made pre-
   tense,
Ancients in phrase, mere moderns in their
   sense; 325
Such labored nothings, in so strange a style,
Amaze th' unlearn'd, and make the learned
   smile.
Unlucky, as Fungoso [11] in the play, ⎫
These sparks with awkward vanity display ⎬
What the fine gentleman wore yesterday; ⎭
And but so mimic ancient wits at best, 331
As apes our grandsires, in their doublets dressed.
In words, as fashions, the same rule will hold;
Alike fantastic, if too new, or old:
Be not the first by whom the new are tried, 335
Nor yet the last to lay the old aside.
  But most by Numbers judge a Poet's song;
And smooth or rough, with them is right or
   wrong:
In the bright Muse though thousand charms
   conspire,
Her voice is all these tuneful fools admire; 340

[11] A character in Ben Jonson's *Every Man out of
His Humor.*

Who haunt Parnassus but to please their ear, ⎫
Not mend their minds; as some to Church ⎬
   repair, ⎭
Not for the doctrine, but the music there.
These equal syllables alone require,
Though oft the ear the open vowels tire; 345
While expletives their feeble aid do join;
And ten low words oft creep in one dull line:
While they ring round the same unvaried
   chimes,
With sure returns of still expected rimes;
Where'er you find "the cooling western
   breeze," 350
In the next line, it "whispers through the
   trees";
If crystal streams "with pleasing murmurs
   creep,"
The reader's threatened (not in vain) with
   "sleep";
Then, at the last and only couplet fraught
With some unmeaning thing they call a
   thought, 355
A needless Alexandrine ends the song
That, like a wounded snake, drags its slow
   length along.
Leave such to tune their own dull rimes, and
   know
What's roundly smooth or languishingly slow;
And praise the easy vigor of a line, 360
Where Denham's strength, and Waller's sweet-
   ness join.[12]
True ease in writing comes from art, not
   chance,
As those move easiest who have learned to
   dance.
'T is not enough no harshness gives offense,
The sound must seem an echo to the sense:
Soft is the strain when Zephyr gently blows, 366
And the smooth stream in smoother numbers
   flows;
But when loud surges lash the sounding shore,
The hoarse, rough verse should like the torrent
   roar:
When Ajax strives some rock's vast weight to
   throw, 370
The line too labors, and the words move slow;
Not so, when swift Camilla scours the plain,
Flies o'er th' unbending corn, and skims along
   the main.
Hear how Timotheus' varied lays surprise,
And bid alternate passions fall and rise! [13] 375
While, at each change, the son of Libyan Jove
Now burns with glory, and then melts with
   love,
Now his fierce eyes with sparkling fury glow,
Now sighs steal out, and tears begin to flow:
Persians and Greeks like turns of nature found,

[12] Both poets of the mid-seventeenth century, long
highly praised as the "fathers" of the plain style
and the closed couplet which Dryden developed and
Pope perfected.
[13] The reference in these and the following lines
is to Dryden's *Alexander's Feast.*

And the world's victor stood subdued by
   Sound!    381
The pow'r of Music all our hearts allow,
And what Timotheus was, is Dryden now.

   Avoid Extremes; and shun the fault of such,
Who still are pleased too little or too much. 385
At ev'ry trifle scorn to take offense,
That always shows great pride, or little sense;
Those heads, as stomachs, are not sure the best,
Which nauseate all, and nothing can digest.
Yet let not each gay Turn thy rapture move;
For fools admire, but men of sense approve:
As things seem large which we through mists
   descry,    392
Dullness is ever apt to magnify.

   Some foreign writers, some our own despise;
The Ancients only, or the Moderns prize. 395
Thus Wit, like Faith, by each man is applied
To one small sect, and all are damned beside.
Meanly they seek the blessing to confine,
And force that sun but on a part to shine,
Which not alone the southern wit sublimes, 400
But ripens spirits in cold northern climes;
Which from the first has shone on ages past,
Enlights the present, and shall warm the last;
Though each may feel increases and decays,
And see now clearer and now darker days. 405
Regard not then if Wit be old or new,
But blame the false, and value still the true.

   Some ne'er advance a Judgment of their own,
But catch the spreading notion of the Town;
They reason and conclude by precedent, 410
And own stale nonsense which they ne'er in-
   vent.
Some judge of authors' names, not works, and
   then
Nor praise nor blame the writings, but the men.
Of all this servile herd the worst is he
That in proud dullness joins with Quality, 415
A constant Critic at the great man's board,
To fetch and carry nonsense for my Lord.
What woeful stuff this madrigal would be,
In some starved hackney sonneteer, or me!
But let a Lord once own the happy lines, 420
How the wit brightens! how the style refines!
Before his sacred name flies ev'ry fault,
And each exalted stanza teems with thought!

   The Vulgar thus through Imitation err;
As oft the Learn'd by being singular; 425
So much they scorn the crowd, that if the
   throng
By chance go right, they purposely go wrong;
So Schismatics the plain believers quit,
And are but damned for having too much wit.
Some praise at morning what they blame at
   night;    430
But always think the last opinion right.
A Muse by these is like a mistress used,
This hour she's idolized, the next abused;
While their weak heads like towns unfortified,
'Twixt sense and nonsense daily change their
   side.    435
Ask them the cause; they're wiser still, they say;

And still to-morrow's wiser than to-day.
We think our fathers fools, so wise we grow,
Our wiser sons, no doubt, will think us so.
Once School-divines this zealous isle o'er-
   spread;    440
Who knew most Sentences,[14] was deepest read;
Faith, Gospel, all, seemed made to be disputed,
And none had sense enough to be confuted:
Scotists and Thomists,[15] now, in peace remain,
Amidst their kindred cobwebs in Duck-lane.
If Faith itself has different dresses worn, 446
What wonder modes in Wit should take their
   turn?
Oft', leaving what is natural and fit,
The current folly proves the ready wit;
And authors think their reputation safe, 450
Which lives as long as fools are pleased to
   laugh.

   Some valuing those of their own side or
   mind,
Still make themselves the measure of mankind:
Fondly we think we honor merit then,
When we but praise ourselves in other men. 455
Parties in Wit attend on those of State,
And public faction doubles private hate.
Pride, Malice, Folly, against Dryden rose,
In various shapes of Parsons, Critics, Beaus;
But sense survived, when merry jests were
   past;    460
For rising merit will buoy up at last.
Might he return, and bless once more our eyes,
New Blackmores and new Milbourns must
   arise:[16]
Nay should great Homer lift his awful head,
Zoilus[17] again would start up from the dead.
Envy will merit, as its shade, pursue; 466
But like a shadow, proves the substance true;
For envied Wit, like Sol eclipsed, makes known
Th' opposing body's grossness, not its own,
When first that sun too powerful beams dis-
   plays,    470
It draws up vapors which obscure its rays;
But e'en those clouds at last adorn its way,
Reflect new glories, and augment the day.

   Be thou the first true merit to befriend;
His praise is lost, who stays till all commend.
Short is the date, alas, of modern rimes, 476
And 't is but just to let them live betimes.
No longer now that golden age appears,
When Patriarch-wits survived a thousand years:
Now length of Fame (our second life) is lost,
And bare threescore is all e'en that can boast;
Our sons their fathers' failing language see, 482

[14] The reference is to the *Book of Sentences* of
Peter Lombard.

[15] Followers of Duns Scotus and St. Thomas
Aquinas, scholastic philosophers of the thirteenth
century. Duck Lane was a London street where
second-hand books were formerly sold.

[16] Blackmore was a physician and a dull poet, Milbourne a clergyman; both attacked Dryden.

[17] Greek critic (fourth century, B.C.) who attacked Homer.

And such as Chaucer is, shall Dryden be.
So when the faithful pencil has designed
Some bright Idea of the master's mind,    485
Where a new world leaps out at his command,
And ready Nature waits upon his hand;
When the ripe colors soften and unite,
And sweetly melt into just shade and light;
When mellowing years their full perfection
    give,    490
And each bold figure just begins to live,
The treach'rous colors the fair art betray,
And all the bright creation fades away!
    Unhappy Wit, like most mistaken things,
Atones not for that envy which it brings.    495
In youth alone its empty praise we boast,
But soon the short-lived vanity is lost:
Like some fair flow'r the early spring supplies,
That gaily blooms, but e'en in blooming dies.
What is this Wit, which must our cares em-
    ploy?    500
The owner's wife, that other men enjoy;
Then most our trouble still when most ad-
    mired,
And still the more we give, the more required;
Whose fame with pains we guard, but lose with
    ease,
Sure some to vex, but never all to please;    505
'Tis what the vicious fear, the virtuous shun,
By fools 'tis hated, and by knaves undone!
    If Wit so much from Ign'rance undergo,
Ah, let not Learning too commence its foe!
Of old, those met rewards who could excel,    510
And such were praised who but endeavored
    well:
Though triumphs were to gen'rals only due,
Crowns were reserved to grace the soldiers too.
Now, they who reach Parnassus' lofty crown,
Employ their pains to spurn some others down;    516
And while self-love each jealous writer rules,
Contending wits become the sport of fools:
But still the worst with most regret commend,
For each ill Author is as bad a Friend.
To what base ends, and by what abject ways,
Are mortals urged through sacred lust of praise!
Ah ne'er so dire a thirst of glory boast,    522
Nor in the Critic let the Man be lost.
Good-nature and good-sense must ever join;
To err is human, to forgive, divine.    525
    But if in noble minds some dregs remain
Not yet purged off, of spleen and sour disdain;
Discharge that rage on more provoking crimes,
Nor fear a dearth in these flagitious times.
No pardon vile Obscenity should find,    530
Though wit and art conspire to move your
    mind;
But Dullness with Obscenity must prove
As shameful sure as Impotence in love.
In the fat age of pleasure, wealth, and ease
Sprung the rank weed, and thrived with large
    increase:    535
When love was all an easy Monarch's care; [18]

[18] During the reign of Charles II.

Seldom at council, never in a war:
Jilts ruled the state, and statesmen farces writ;
Nay wits had pensions, and young Lords had
    wit:
The Fair sate panting at a Courtier's play,    540
And not a Mask [19] went unimproved away:
The modest fan was lifted up no more,
And Virgins smiled at what they blushed be-
    fore.
The following license of a Foreign reign [20]
Did all the dregs of bold Socinus [21] drain;    545
Then unbelieving priests reformed the nation,
And taught more pleasant methods of salvation;
Where Heav'n's free subjects might their rights
    dispute,
Lest God himself should seem too absolute:
Pulpits their sacred satire learned to spare,    550
And Vice admired [22] to find a flatt'rer there!
Encouraged thus, Wit's Titans braved the skies,
And the press groaned with licensed blasphe-
    mies.
These monsters, Critics! with your darts engage,
Here point your thunder, and exhaust your
    rage!    555
Yet shun their fault, who, scandalously nice,
Will needs mistake an author into vice;
All seems infected that th' infected spy,
As all looks yellow to the jaundiced eye.

## PART III

    Learn then what Morals Critics ought to
    show,    560
For 'tis but half a Judge's task, to know.
'Tis not enough, taste, judgment, learning,
    join;
In all you speak, let truth and candor shine:
That not alone what to your sense is due
All may allow; but seek your friendship too.    565
    Be silent always when you doubt your sense;
And speak, though sure, with seeming diffi-
    dence:
Some positive, persisting fops we know,
Who, if once wrong, will needs be always so;
But you, with pleasure own your errors past,    570
And make each day a Critic on the last.
    'Tis not enough, your counsel still be true;
Blunt truths more mischief than nice false-
    hoods do;
Men must be taught as if you taught them not,
And things unknown proposed as things forgot.
Without Good Breeding, truth is disapproved;
That only makes superior sense beloved.    577
    Be niggards of advice on no pretense;
For the worst avarice is that of sense.
With mean complacence ne'er betray your
    trust,    580

[19] I. e., woman wearing a mask.
[20] The reign of William and Mary.
[21] The name of two Italians of the sixteenth century who revived Arianism and may be regarded as
forerunners of modern Unitarianism.
[22] Wondered.

Nor be so civil as to prove unjust.
Fear not the anger of the wise to raise;
Those best can bear reproof, who merit praise.
  'Twere well might critics still this freedom
    take,
But Appius [23] reddens at each word you speak,
And stares, tremendous, with a threat'ning eye,
Like some fierce Tyrant in old tapestry.   587
Fear most to tax an Honorable fool,
Whose right it is, uncensured, to be dull;
Such, without wit, are Poets when they please
As without learning they can take Degrees. 591
Leave dang'rous truths to unsuccessful Satires,
And flattery to fulsome Dedicators,
Whom, when they praise, the world believes
    no more,
Than when they promise to give scribbling o'er.
'Tis best sometimes your censure to restrain, 596
And charitably let the dull be vain:
Your silence there is better than your spite,
For who can rail so long as they can write!
Still humming on, their drowsy course they
    keep,         600
And lashed so long, like tops, are lashed asleep.
False steps but help them to renew the race,
As, after stumbling, Jades will mend their pace.
What crowds of these, impenitently bold,
In sounds and jingling syllables grown old, 605
Still run on Poets, in a raging vein,
E'en to the dregs and squeezings of the brain,
Strain out the last dull droppings of their sense,
And rime with all the rage of Impotence.
  Such shameless Bards we have; and yet 'tis
    true,         610
There are as mad abandoned Critics too.
The bookful blockhead, ignorantly read,
With loads of learnéd lumber in his head,
With his own tongue still edifies his ears,
And always list'ning to himself appears.   615
All books he reads, and all he reads assails,
From Dryden's Fables down to Durfey's [24]
    Tales.
With him, most authors steal their works, or
    buy;
Garth did not write his own Dispensary.[25]
Name a new Play, and he's the Poet's friend,
Nay showed his faults—but when would Poets
    mend?         621
No place so sacred from such fops is barred,
Nor is Paul's church more safe than Paul's
    churchyard:
Nay, fly to Altars; there they'll talk you dead:
For Fools rush in where Angels fear to tread. 625
Distrustful sense with modest caution speaks, ⎤
It still looks home, and short excursions   ⎟
    makes;              ⎬
But rattling nonsense in full volleys breaks, ⎟
And never shocked, and never turned aside, ⎦

Bursts out, resistless, with a thund'ring tide.
  But where's the man, who counsel can
    bestow,         631
Still pleased to teach, and yet not proud to
    know?
Unbiassed, or by favor, or by spite;
Not dully prepossessed, nor blindly right;
Though learn'd, well-bred; and though well-
    bred, sincere,     635
Modestly bold, and humanly severe;
Who to a friend his faults can freely show,
And gladly praise the merit of a foe?
Bless'd with a taste exact, yet unconfined;
A knowledge both of books and human kind:
Gen'rous converse; a soul exempt from pride;
And love to praise, with reason on his side? 642
  Such once were Critics; such the happy few,
Athens and Rome in better ages knew.
The mighty Stagirite first left the shore,   645
Spread all his sails, and durst the deeps ex-
    plore:
He steered securely, and discovered far,
Led by the light of the Maeonian Star.[26]
Poets, a race long unconfined, and free,
Still fond and proud of savage liberty,   650
Received his laws; and stood convinced 'twas
    fit,
Who conquered Nature, should preside o'er
    Wit.
  Horace still charms with graceful negligence,
And without method talks us into sense,
Will, like a friend, familiarly convey   655
The truest notions in the easiest way.
He, who supreme in judgment, as in wit,
Might boldly censure, as he boldly writ,
Yet judged with coolness, though he sung with
    fire;
His Precepts teach but what his works inspire.
Our Critics take a contrary extreme,   661
They judge with fury, but they write with
    fle'me: [27]
Nor suffers Horace more in wrong Translations
By Wits, than Critics in as wrong Quotations.
  See Dionysius [28] Homer's thoughts refine, 665
And call new beauties forth from every line!
  Fancy and art in gay Petronius please,
The scholar's learning, with the courtier's ease.
  In grave Quintilian's copious work, we find
The justest rules, and clearest method joined:
Thus useful arms in magazines we place, 671
All ranged in order, and disposed with grace,
But less to please the eye, than arm the hand,
Still fit for use, and ready at command.
  Thee, bold Longinus! all the Nine [29] inspire,
And bless their Critic with a Poet's fire.   676
An ardent Judge, who zealous in his trust,
With warmth gives sentence, yet is always just;
Whose own example strengthens all his laws;
And is himself that great Sublime he draws. 680
  Thus long succeeding Critics justly reigned,

---

[23] I. e., John Dennis. The name was taken from
his tragedy, *Appius and Virginia*.
[24] Scurrilous writer (1653–1723).
[25] Samuel Garth's *Dispensary* (1699), a burlesque
poem on apothecaries.

[26] Homer.       [27] Phlegm, i. e., dullness.
[28] Dionysius of Halicarnassus, Greek critic.
[29] The muses.

License repressed, and useful laws ordained.
Learning and Rome alike in empire grew;
And Arts still followed where her Eagles flew;
From the same foes, at last, both felt their
　　doom,　　　　　　　　　　　　　　685
And the same age saw Learning fall, and Rome.
With Tyranny, then Superstition joined,
As that the body, this enslaved the mind;
Much was believed, but little understood,
And to be dull was construed to be good; 690
A second deluge Learning thus o'er-run,
And the Monks finished what the Goths begun.

　　At length Erasmus, that great injured name
(The glory of the Priesthood, and the
　　shame!),[30]
Stemmed the wild torrent of a barb'rous age, 695
And drove those holy Vandals off the stage.

　　But see! each Muse, in Leo's [31] golden days,
Starts from her trance, and trims her withered
　　bays,
Rome's ancient Genius, o'er its ruins spread,
Shakes off the dust, and rears his rev'rend head.
Then Sculpture and her sister-arts revive; 701
Stones leaped to form, and rocks began to
　　live;
With sweeter notes each rising Temple rung;
A Raphael painted, and a Vida [32] sung.
Immortal Vida: on whose honored brow 705
The Poet's bays and Critic's ivy grow:
Cremona now shall ever boast thy name,
As next in place to Mantua, next in fame!

　　But soon by impious arms from Latium
　　chased,
Their ancient bounds the banished Muses
　　passed;　　　　　　　　　　　　　710
Thence Arts o'er all the northern world ad-
　　vance,
But Critic-learning flourished most in France:
The rules a nation, born to serve, obeys;
And Boileau still in right of Horace sways.
But we, brave Britons, foreign laws despised,
And kept unconquered, and uncivilized; 716
Fierce for the liberties of wit, and bold,
We still defied the Romans, as of old.
Yet some there were, among the sounder few
Of those who less presumed, and better knew,
Who durst assert the juster ancient cause, 721
And here restored Wit's fundamental laws.
Such was the Muse, whose rules and practice
　　tell,
"Nature's chief Master-piece is writing well."
Such was Roscommon,[33] not more learn'd than
　　good,　　　　　　　　　　　　725
With manners gen'rous as his noble blood;
To him the wit of Greece and Rome was
　　known,
And ev'ry author's merit, but his own.

[30] Though himself a monk, Erasmus attacked the narrowness of monastic life.
[31] Leo X.
[32] Girolamo Vida (1489–1566), author of a Latin critical poem, *De Arte Poetica*.
[33] Wentworth Dillon, Earl of Roscommon.

Such late was Walsh [34]—the Muse's judge and
　　friend,
Who justly knew to blame or to commend: 730
To failings mild, but zealous for desert;
The clearest head, and the sincerest heart.
This humble praise, lamented shade! receive,
This praise at least a grateful Muse may give:
The Muse, whose early voice you taught to sing,
Prescribed her heights, and pruned her tender
　　wing　　　　　　　　　　　　736
(Her guide now lost), no more attempts to
　　rise,
But in low numbers short excursions tries:
Content, if hence th' unlearn'd their wants may
　　view,
The learn'd reflect on what before they knew:
Careless of censure, nor too fond of fame; 741
Still pleased to praise, yet not afraid to blame,
Averse alike to flatter, or offend;
Not free from faults, nor yet too vain to mend.

# The Rape of the Lock [1]

## An Heroi-Comical Poem

*Nolueram, Belinda, tuos violare capillos;*
*Sed juvat, hoc precibus me tribuisse tuis.*[2]
　　　　　　　　　　　　　　MART.

### TO MRS. ARABELLA FERMOR

*Madam,*
　*It will be in vain to deny that I have some re-
gard for this piece, since I dedicate it to You.
Yet you may bear me witness, it was intended
only to divert a few young Ladies, who have
good sense and good humor enough to laugh
not only at their sex's little unguarded follies,
but at their own. But as it was communicated
with the air of a Secret, it soon found its way
into the world. An imperfect copy having been
offered to a Bookseller, you had the good nature
for my sake to consent to the publication of one
more correct: This I was forced to, before I had
executed half my design, for the Machinery was
entirely wanting to complete it.*
　*The Machinery, Madam, is a term invented*

[34] See the introductory account of Pope above.
[1] First published in 1712, but rewritten and published in its present form in 1714. The occasion of
the poem was as follows: Lord Petre had in a moment of fun cut off a lock of Miss Arabella Fermor's
hair. Miss Fermor became angry, the families of
both took up the quarrel, and serious consequences
seemed likely to follow. At this point a common
friend, Mr. John Caryll, suggested to Pope that he
write a poem to make a jest of the whole affair.
The result was the earlier version of the *Rape of the
Lock*, which is said to have succeeded in its immediate purpose.
[2] I did not want, Belinda, to do violence to your
lock, but I am glad to yield this gift to your entreaties (Martial, *Epigrams*, xii, 84; Pope alters the
name).

by the Critics, to signify that part which the
Deities, Angels, or Demons are made to act in a
Poem: For the ancient Poets are in one respect
like many modern Ladies: let an action be never
so trivial in itself, they always make it appear of
the utmost importance. These Machines I determined to raise on a very new and odd foundation, the Rosicrucian doctrine of Spirits.

I know how disagreeable it is to make use of
hard words before a Lady; but 'tis so much the
concern of a Poet to have his works understood,
and particularly by your Sex, that you must give
me leave to explain two or three difficult terms.

The Rosicrucians are a people I must bring
you acquainted with. The best account I know
of them is in a French book called Le Comte
de Gabalis, which both in its title and size is
so like a Novel, that many of the Fair Sex have
read it for one by mistake. According to these
Gentlemen, the four Elements are inhabited
by Spirits, which they call Sylphs, Gnomes,
Nymphs, and Salamanders. The Gnomes or
Demons of Earth delight in mischief; but the
Sylphs, whose habitation is in the Air, are the
best-conditioned creatures imaginable. For,
they say, any mortals may enjoy the most intimate familiarities with these gentle Spirits,
upon a condition very easy to all true Adepts,
an inviolate preservation of Chastity.

As to the following Cantos, all the passages
of them are as fabulous as the Vision at the
beginning, or the Transformation at the end
(except the loss of your Hair, which I always
mention with reverence). The Human persons
are as fictitious as the airy ones; and the
character of Belinda, as it is now managed, resembles you in nothing but in Beauty.

If this Poem had as many Graces as there are
in your Person, or in your Mind, yet I could
never hope it should pass through the world
half so Uncensured as You have done. But let
its fortune be what it will, mine is happy
enough, to have given me this occasion of assuring you that I am, with the truest esteem,
Madam,

    Your most obedient, Humble Servant,

                    A. Pope.

## CANTO I

What dire offense from am'rous causes springs,
What mighty contests rise from trivial things,
I sing—This verse to Caryl, Muse! is due:
This, e'en Belinda may vouchsafe to view:
Slight is the subject, but not so the praise,   5
If She inspire, and He approve my lays.
  Say what strange motive, Goddess! could
    compel
A well-bred Lord t' assault a gentle Belle?
O say what stranger cause, yet unexplored,
Could make a gentle Belle reject a Lord?   10
In tasks so bold, can little men engage,
And in soft bosoms dwells such mighty Rage?

Sol through white curtains shot a tim'rous
  ray,
And oped those eyes that must eclipse the day:
Now lap-dogs give themselves the rousing
  shake,   15
And sleepless lovers, just at twelve, awake:
Thrice rung the bell, the slipper knocked the
  ground,[3]
And the pressed watch returned a silver sound.
Belinda still her downy pillow pressed,
Her guardian Sylph prolonged the balmy rest:
'Twas He had summoned to her silent bed  21
The morning-dream that hovered o'er her head;
A youth more glitt'ring than a Birth-night [4]
  Beau
(That e'en in slumber caused her cheek to
  glow),
Seemed to her ear his winning lips to lay,   25
And thus in whispers said, or seemed to say:
  "Fairest of mortals, thou distinguished care
Of thousand bright Inhabitants of Air!
If e'er one vision touched thy infant thought,
Of all the Nurse and all the Priest have taught;
Of airy Elves by moonlight shadows seen,  31
The silver token, and the circled green,
Or virgins visited by Angel-pow'rs,
With golden crowns and wreaths of heav'nly
  flow'rs;
Hear and believe! thy own importance know,  35
Nor bound thy narrow views to things below.
Some secret truths, from learnèd pride con-
  cealed,
To Maids alone and Children are revealed:
What though no credit doubting Wits may
  give?
The Fair and Innocent shall still believe.   40
Know, then, unnumbered Spirits round thee
  fly,
The light Militia of the lower sky:
These, though unseen, are ever on the wing,
Hang o'er the Box, and hover round the Ring.[5]
Think what an equipage thou hast in Air,   45
And view with scorn two Pages and a Chair.
As now your own, our beings were of old,
And once enclosed in Woman's beauteous
  mold;
Thence, by a soft transition, we repair
From earthly Vehicles to these of air.   50
Think not, when Woman's transient breath is
  fled,
That all her vanities at once are dead;
Succeeding vanities she still regards,
And though she plays no more, o'erlooks the
  cards.
Her joy in gilded Chariots, when alive,   55
And love of Ombre, after death survive.
For when the Fair in all their pride expire,
To their first Elements their Souls retire:
The Sprites of fiery Termagants in Flame

[3] To call her maid, who had not come when the
bell was rung.

[4] Dressed for the king's birthday entertainment.

[5] Drive in Hyde Park.

Mount up, and take a Salamander's name. 60
Soft yielding minds to Water gilde away,
And sip, with Nymphs, their elemental Tea.
The graver Prude sinks downward to a Gnome,
In search of mischief still on Earth to roam.
The light Coquettes in Sylphs aloft repair, 65
And sport and flutter in the fields of Air.
    "Know further yet; whoever fair and chaste
Rejects mankind, is by some Sylph embraced:
For Spirits, freed from mortal laws, with ease
Assume what sexes and what shapes they
    please 6               70
What guards the purity of melting Maids,
In courtly balls, and midnight masquerades,
Safe from the treach'rous friend, the daring
    spark,
The lance by day, the whisper in the dark,
When kind occasion prompts their warm
    desires,                75
When music softens, and when dancing fires?
'Tis but their Sylph, the wise Celestials know,
Though Honor is the word with Men below.
    "Some nymphs there are, too conscious of
    their face,
For life predestined to the Gnomes' embrace,
These swell their prospects and exalt their
    pride,                81
When offers are disdained, and love denied:
Then gay Ideas crowd the vacant brain,
While Peers, and Dukes, and all their sweeping
    train,
And Garters, Stars, and Coronets appear, 85
And in soft sounds, Your Grace salutes their
    ear.
'Tis these that early taint the female soul,
Instruct the eyes of young Coquettes to roll,
Teach Infant-cheeks a bidden blush to know,
And little hearts to flutter at a Beau. 90
    "Oft, when the world imagine women stray,
The Sylphs through mystic mazes guide their
    way,
Through all the giddy circle they pursue,
And old impertinence expel by new.
What tender maid but must a victim fall 95
To one man's treat, but for another's ball?
When Florio speaks what virgin could with-
    stand,
If gentle Damon did not squeeze her hand?
With varying vanities, from ev'ry part,
They shift the moving Toyshop of their heart;
Where wigs with wigs, with sword-knots sword-
    knots strive,                101
Beaux banish beaux, and coaches coaches drive.
This erring mortals Levity may call;
Oh blind to truth! the Sylphs contrive it all.
    "Of these am I, who thy protection claim,
A watchful sprite, and Ariel is my name. 106
Late, as I ranged the crystal wilds of air,
In the clear Mirror of thy ruling Star
I saw, alas! some dread event impend,
Ere to the main this morning sun descend, 110

But heav'n reveals not what, or how, or where:
Warned by the Sylph, oh pious maid, beware!
This to disclose is all thy guardian can:
Beware of all, but most beware of Man!"
    He said; when Shock, who thought she slept
    too long,                115
Leaped up, and waked his mistress with his
    tongue.
'Twas then, Belinda, if report say true,
Thy eyes first opened on a Billet-doux;
Wounds, Charms, and Ardors were no sooner
    read,
But all the Vision vanished from thy head. 120
    And now, unveiled, the Toilet stands dis-
    played,
Each silver Vase in mystic order laid.
First, robed in white, the Nymph intent adores,
With head uncovered, the Cosmetic pow'rs.
A heav'nly image in the glass appears, 125
To that she bends, to that her eyes she rears;
Th' inferior Priestess,7 at her altar's side,
Trembling begins the sacred rites of Pride.
Unnumbered treasures ope at once, and here
The various off'rings of the world appear; 130
From each she nicely culls with curious toil,
And decks the Goddess with the glitt'ring spoil.
This casket India's glowing gems unlocks,
And all Arabia breathes from yonder box.
The Tortoise here and Elephant unite, 135
Transformed to combs, the speckled, and the
    white.
Here files of pins extend their shining rows,
Puffs, Powders, Patches, Bibles, Billet-doux.
Now awful Beauty put on all its arms;
The fair each moment rises in her charms, 140
Repairs her smiles, awakens ev'ry grace,
And calls forth all the wonders of her face;
Sees by degrees a purer blush arise,
And keener lightnings quicken in her eyes.
The busy Sylphs surround their darling care, 145
These set the head, and those divide the hair,
Some fold the sleeve, whilst others plait the
    gown;
And Betty's praised for labors not her own.

## CANTO II

Not with more glories, in th' ethereal plain,
The Sun first rises o'er the purple main,
Than, issuing forth, the rival of his beams
Launched on the bosom of the silver Thames.
Fair Nymphs, and well-dressed Youths around
    her shone,                5
But ev'ry eye was fixed on her alone.
On her white breast a sparkling Cross she wore,
Which Jews might kiss, and Infidels adore.
Her lively looks a sprightly mind disclose,
Quick as her eyes, and as unfixed as those: 10
Favors to none, to all she smiles extends;
Oft she rejects, but never once offends.
Bright as the sun, her eyes the gazers strike,

---

6 Cf. *Paradise Lost*, I, 423–431.

7 Betty, the maid.

And, like the sun, they shine on all alike.
Yet graceful ease, and sweetness void of pride,
Might hide her faults, if Belles had faults to
    hide: 16
If to her share some female errors fall,
Look on her face, and you'll forget 'em all.
  This Nymph, to the destruction of mankind,
Nourished two Locks which graceful hung be-
    hind 20
In equal curls, and well conspired to deck
With shining ringlets the smooth iv'ry neck.
Love in these labyrinths his slaves detains,
And mighty hearts are held in slender chains.
With hairy springes we the birds betray, 25
Slight lines of hair surprise the finny prey,
Fair tresses man's imperial race ensnare,
And beauty draws us with a single hair.
  Th' advent'rous Baron the bright locks ad-
    mired;
He saw, he wished, and to the prize aspired. 30
Resolved to win, he meditates the way,
By force to ravish, or by fraud betray;
For when success a Lover's toil attends,
Few ask, if fraud or force attained his ends.
  For this, ere Phoebus rose, he had implored
Propitious heav'n, and every pow'r adored, 36
But chiefly Love—to Love an Altar built,
Of twelve vast French Romances, neatly gilt.
There lay three garters, half a pair of gloves;
And all the trophies of his former loves; 40
With tender Billet-doux he lights the pyre,
And breathes three am'rous sighs to raise the
    fire.
Then prostrate falls, and begs with ardent eyes
Soon to obtain, and long possess the prize:
The pow'rs gave ear, and granted half his
    pray'r, 45
The rest, the winds dispersed in empty air.
  But now secure the painted vessel glides,
The sun-beams trembling on the floating tides:
While melting music steals upon the sky,
And softened sounds along the waters die; 50
Smooth flow the waves, the Zephyrs gently play,
Belinda smiled, and all the world was gay.
All but the Sylph—with careful thoughts op-
    pressed,
Th' impending woe sat heavy on his breast.
He summons straight his Denizens of air; 55
The lucid squadrons round the sails repair:
Soft o'er the shrouds aërial whispers breathe,
That seemed but Zephyrs to the train beneath.
Some to the sun their insect-wings unfold,
Waft on the breeze, or sink in clouds of gold; 60
Transparent forms, too fine for mortal sight,
Their fluid bodies half dissolved in light,
Loose to the wind their airy garments flew,
Thin glitt'ring textures of the filmy dew,
Dipped in the richest tincture of the skies, 65
Where light disports in ever-mingling dyes,
While ev'ry beam new transient colors flings,
Colors that change whene'er they wave their
    wings.
Amid the circle, on the gilded mast,

Superior by the head, was Ariel placed; 70
His purple pinions op'ning to the sun,
He raised his azure wand, and thus begun:
  "Ye Sylphs and Sylphids, to your chief give
    ear!
Fays, Fairies, Genii, Elves, and Demons, hear!
Ye know the spheres and various tasks assigned
By laws eternal to th' aërial kind. 76
Some in the fields of purest ether play,
And bask and whiten in the blaze of day.
Some guide the course of wand'ring orbs on
    high,
Or roll the planets through the boundless sky.
Some less refined, beneath the moon's pale
    light 81
Pursue the stars that shoot athwart the night,
Or suck the mists in grosser air below,
Or dip their pinions in the painted bow,
Or brew fierce tempests on the wintry main, 85
Or o'er the glebe distil the kindly rain.
Others on earth o'er human race preside,
Watch all their ways, and all their actions
    guide:
Of these the chief the care of Nations own,
And guard with Arms divine the British
    Throne. 90
  "Our humbler province is to tend the Fair,
Not a less pleasing, though less glorious care;
To save the powder from too rude a gale,
Nor let th' imprisoned essences exhale;
To draw fresh colors from the vernal flow'rs; 95
To steal from rainbows e'er they drop in show'rs
A brighter wash; to curl their waving hairs,
Assist their blushes, and inspire their airs;
Nay oft, in dreams, invention we bestow,
To change a Flounce, or add a Furbelow. 100
  "This day, black Omens threat the brightest
    Fair,
That e'er deserved a watchful spirit's care;
Some dire disaster, or by force, or slight;
But what, or where, the fates have wrapped in
    night.
Whether the nymph shall break Diana's law,
Or some frail China jar receive a flaw; 106
Or stain her honor or her new brocade;
Forget her pray'rs, or miss a masquerade;
Or lose her heart, or necklace, at a ball;
Or whether Heav'n has doomed that Shock
    must fall. 110
Haste, then, ye spirits! to your charge repair:
The flutt'ring fan be Zephyretta's care;
The drops [8] to thee, Brillante, we consign;
And, Momentilla, let the watch be thine;
Do thou, Crispissa, tend her fav'rite Lock; 115
Ariel himself shall be the guard of Shock.
  "To fifty chosen Sylphs, of special note,
We trust th' important charge, the Petticoat:
Oft have we known that seven-fold fence to
    fail,
Though stiff with hoops, and armed with ribs
    of whale; 120

[8] Earrings.

Form a strong line about the silver bound,
And guard the wide circumference around.
    "Whatever spirit, careless of his charge,
His post neglects, or leaves the fair at large,
Shall feel sharp vengeance soon o'ertake his
    sins,    125
Be stopped in vials, or transfixed with pins;
Or plunged in lakes of bitter washes lie,
Or wedged whole ages in a bodkin's eye:
Gums and Pomatums shall his flight restrain,
While clogged he beats his silken wings in vain;
Or Alum styptics with contracting pow'r    131
Shrink his thin essence like a riveled [9] flow'r:
Or, as Ixion fixed, the wretch shall feel
The giddy motion of the whirling Mill,
In fumes of burning Chocolate shall glow,    135
And tremble at the sea that froths below!"
    He spoke; the spirits from the sails descend;
Some, orb in orb, around the nymph extend;
Some thread the mazy ringlets of her hair;
Some hang upon the pendants of her ear:    140
With beating hearts the dire event they wait,
Anxious, and trembling for the birth of Fate.

## CANTO III

Close by those meads, for ever crowned with
    flow'rs,
Where Thames with pride surveys his rising
    tow'rs,
There stands a structure of majestic frame,[10]
Which from the neighb'ring Hampton takes its
    name.
Here Britain's statesmen oft the fall foredoom
Of foreign Tyrants and of Nymphs at home;    6
Here thou, great Anna! whom three realms
    obey,
Dost sometimes counsel take—and sometimes
    Tea.
Hither the heroes and the nymphs resort,
To taste awhile the pleasures of a Court;    10
In various talk th' instructive hours they passed,
Who gave the ball, or paid the visit last;
One speaks the glory of the British Queen,
And one describes a charming Indian screen;
A third interprets motions, looks, and eyes;    15
At ev'ry word a reputation dies.
Snuff, or the fan, supply each pause of chat,
With singing, laughing, ogling, and all that.
    Meanwhile, declining from the noon of day,
The sun obliquely shoots his burning ray;    20
The hungry Judges soon the sentence sign,
And wretches hang that jurymen may dine;
The merchant from th' Exchange returns in
    peace,
And the long labors of the Toilet cease.
Belinda now, whom thirst of fame invites,    25
Burns to encounter two advent'rous Knights,
At Ombre [11] singly to decide their doom;

[9] Shrunken.
[10] Hampton Court, a royal palace.
[11] A game of cards, of Spanish origin, usually
played by three people. Each player received nine

And swells her breast with conquests yet to
    come.
Straight the three bands prepare in arms to join,
Each band the number of the sacred nine.    30
Soon as she spreads her hand, th' aërial guard
Descend, and sit on each important card:
First Ariel perched upon a Matadore,
Then each, according to the rank they bore;
For Sylphs, yet mindful of their ancient race,    35
Are, as when women, wondrous fond of place.
    Behold, four Kings in majesty revered,
With hoary whiskers and a forky beard;
And four fair Queens whose hands sustain a
    flow'r,
Th' expressive emblem of their softer pow'r;    40
Four Knaves in garbs succinct, a trusty band,
Caps on their heads, and halberts in their hand;
And particolored troops, a shining train,
Draw forth to combat on the velvet plain.
    The skillful Nymph reviews her force with
    care:    45
"Let Spades be trumps!" she said, and trumps
    they were.
    Now move to war her sable Matadores,
In show like leaders of the swarthy Moors.
Spadillio first, unconquerable Lord!
Led off two captive trumps, and swept the
    board.    50
As many more Manillio forced to yield,
And marched a victor from the verdant field.
Him Basto followed, but his fate more hard
Gained but one trump and one plebeian card.
With his broad saber next, a chief in years,    55
The hoary Majesty of Spades appears,
Puts forth one manly leg, to sight revealed,
The rest, his many-colored robe concealed.
The rebel Knave, who dares his prince engage,
Proves the just victim of his royal rage.    60
E'en mighty Pam,[12] that Kings and Queens
    o'erthrew
And mowed down armies in the fights of Lu,
Sad chance of war! now destitute of aid,
Falls undistinguished by the victor spade!
    Thus far both armies to Belinda yield;    65
Now to the Baron fate inclines the field.
His warlike Amazon her host invades,
Th' imperial consort of the crown of Spades.
The Club's black Tyrant first her victim died,
Spite of his haughty mien, and barb'rous pride:
What boots the regal circle on his head,    71
His giant limbs, in state unwieldy spread;
That long behind he trails his pompous robe,
And, of all monarchs, only grasps the globe?

cards. The one who declared the trump became the
"ombre" and played against the other two. If one
of these took more tricks than the "ombre" the
latter was defeated, which was called "codille."
The three highest cards were called "matadores."
They were, in the order of their value, "Spadillio"
(ace of spades), "Manillio" (when trumps were
black, the two of trumps; when red, the seven of
trumps), and "Basto" (ace of clubs).
[12] Knave of clubs, highest card in the game of loo.

The Baron now his Diamonds pours apace;
Th' embroidered King who shows but half his
   face,       76
And his refulgent Queen, with pow'rs com-
   bined
Of broken troops an easy conquest find.
Clubs, Diamonds, Hearts, in wild disorder seen,
With throngs promiscuous strew the level
   green.      80
Thus when dispersed a routed army runs,
Of Asia's troops, and Afric's sable sons,
With like confusion different nations fly,
Of various habit, and of various dye,
The pierced battalions dis-united fall,    85
In heaps on heaps; one fate o'erwhelms them
   all.
    The Knave of Diamonds tries his wily arts,
And wins (oh shameful chance!) the Queen of
   Hearts.
At this, the blood the virgin's cheek forsook,
A livid paleness spreads o'er all her look;    90
She sees, and trembles at th' approaching ill,
Just in the jaws of ruin, and Codille.
And now (as oft in some distempered State)
On one nice Trick depends the gen'ral fate.
An Ace of Hearts steps forth: The King un-
   seen      95
Lurked in her hand, and mourned his captive
   Queen:
He springs to Vengeance with an eager pace,
And falls like thunder on the prostrate Ace.
The nymph exulting fills with shouts the sky;
The walls, the woods, and long canals reply. 100
    O thoughtless mortals! ever blind to fate,
Too soon dejected, and too soon elate.
Sudden, these honors shall be snatched away,
And cursed for ever this victorious day.
    For lo! the board with cups and spoons is
   crowned,     105
The berries [13] crackle, and the mill turns round;
On shining Altars of Japan they raise
The silver lamp; the fiery spirits blaze:
From silver spouts the grateful liquors glide,
While China's earth receives the smoking
   tide:
At once they gratify their scent and taste, 111
And frequent cups prolong the rich repast.
Straight hover round the Fair her airy band;
Some, as she sipped, the fuming liquor fanned,
Some o'er her lap their careful plumes dis-
   played,     115
Trembling, and conscious of the rich brocade.
Coffee (which makes the politician wise,
And see through all things with his half-shut
   eyes),
Sent up in vapors to the Baron's brain
New Stratagems, the radiant Lock to gain. 120
Ah cease, rash youth! desist ere 't is too late,
Fear the just Gods, and think of Scylla's Fate!
Changed to a bird, and sent to flit in air,
She dearly pays for Nisus' injured hair!

[13] Coffee beans.

But when to mischief mortals bend their
   will,     125
How soon they find fit instruments of ill!
Just then, Clarissa drew with tempting grace
A two-edged weapon from her shining case:
So Ladies in Romance assist their Knight,
Present the spear, and arm him for the fight.
He takes the gift with rev'rence, and extends
The little engine on his fingers' ends;    132
This just behind Belinda's neck he spread,
As o'er the fragrant steams she bends her head.
Swift to the Lock a thousand Sprites repair, 135
A thousand wings, by turns, blow back the hair;
And thrice they twitched the diamond in her
   ear;
Thrice she looked back, and thrice the foe drew
   near.
Just in that instant, anxious Ariel sought
The close recesses of the Virgin's thought; 140
As on the nosegay in her breast reclined,
He watched th' Ideas rising in her mind,
Sudden he viewed, in spite of all her art,
An earthly Lover lurking at her heart.
Amazed, confused, he found his pow'r expired,
Resigned to fate, and with a sigh retired. 146
    The Peer now spreads the glitt'ring Forfex
   wide,
T' enclose the Lock; now joins it, to divide.
E'en then, before the fatal engine closed,
A wretched Sylph too fondly interposed;    150
Fate urged the shears, and cut the Sylph in
   twain
(But airy substance soon unites again),
The meeting points the sacred hair dissever
From the fair head, for ever, and for ever!
    Then flashed the living lightning from her
   eyes,     155
And screams of horror rend th' affrighted skies.
Not louder shrieks to pitying heav'n are cast,
When husbands, or when lap-dogs breathe
   their last;
Or when rich China vessels fall'n from high,
In glitt'ring dust and painted fragments lie! 160
    Let wreaths of triumph now my temples
   twine
(The victor cried) the glorious Prize is mine!
While fish in streams, or birds delight in air,
Or in a coach and six the British Fair,
As long as Atalantis [14] shall be read,    165
Or the small pillow grace a Lady's bed,
While visits shall be paid on solemn days,
When num'rous wax-lights in bright order
   blaze,
While nymphs take treats, or assignations give,
So long my honor, name, and praise shall live!
What Time would spare, from Steel receives its
   date,     171
And monuments, like men, submit to fate!
Steel could the labor of the Gods destroy,
And strike to dust th' imperial towers of Troy;

[14] *The New Atalantis* by Mrs. Manley (published
in 1709), a voluminous work which chronicled contemporary scandal.

Steel could the works of mortal pride con-
    found,                                      175
And hew triumphal arches to the ground.
What wonder then, fair nymph! thy hairs
    should feel,
The conqu'ring force of unresisted steel?

## CANTO IV

But anxious cares the pensive nymph op-
    pressed,
And secret passions labored in her breast.
Not youthful kings in battle seized alive,
Not scornful virgins who their charms survive,
Not ardent lovers robbed of all their bliss,     5
Not ancient ladies when refused a kiss,
Not tyrants fierce that unrepenting die,
Not Cynthia when her manteau's pinned awry,
E'er felt such rage, resentment, and despair,
As thou, sad Virgin! for thy ravished Hair. 10
    For, that sad moment, when the Sylphs with-
        drew
And Ariel weeping from Belinda flew,
Umbriel, a dusky, melancholy sprite,
As ever sullied the fair face of light,
Down to the central earth, his proper scene, 15
Repaired to search the gloomy Cave of
    Spleen.15
Swift on his sooty pinions flits the Gnome,
And in a vapor reached the dismal dome.
No cheerful breeze this sullen region knows,
The dreaded East is all the wind that blows. 20
Here in a grotto, sheltered close from air,
And screened in shades from day's detested
    glare,
She sighs for ever on her pensive bed,
Pain at her side, and Megrim 16 at her head.
    Two handmaids wait the throne: alike in
        place,                                   25
But diff'ring far in figure and in face.
Here stood Ill-nature like an ancient maid,
Her wrinkled form in black and white arrayed;
With store of pray'rs, for mornings, nights, and
    noons,
Her hand is filled; her bosom with lampoons. 30
    There Affectation, with a sickly mien,
Shows in her cheek the roses of eighteen,
Practiced to lisp, and hang the head aside,
Faints into airs, and languishes with pride,
On the rich quilt sinks with becoming woe, 35
Wrapped in a gown, for sickness, and for show.
The fair ones feel such maladies as these,
When each new night-dress gives a new disease.
    A constant Vapor o'er the palace flies;
Strange phantoms rising as the mists arise; 40
Dreadful, as hermit's dreams in haunted shades,
Or bright, as visions of expiring maids.
Now glaring fiends, and snakes on rolling spires,

15 Low spirits, or ill temper.
16 Headache, but the word was used in the early
eighteenth century (as was "vapors") for what we
should call "the blues."

Pale specters, gaping tombs, and purple fires:
Now lakes of liquid gold, Elysian scenes,     45
And crystal domes, and angels in machines.17
    Unnumbered throngs on every side are seen,
Of bodies changed to various forms by Spleen.
Here living Tea-pots stand, one arm held out,
One bent; the handle this, and that the
    spout:                                      50
A Pipkin 18 there, like Homer's Tripod walks;
Here sighs a Jar, and there a Goose-pie talks;
Men prove with child, as powerful fancy works,
And maids turned bottles, call aloud for corks.
Safe passed the Gnome through this fantastic
    band,                                       55
A branch of healing Spleenwort in his hand.
Then thus addressed the pow'r: "Hail, way-
    ward Queen!
Who rule the sex of fifty from fifteen:
Parent of vapors and of female wit,
Who give th' hysteric, or poetic fit,          60
On various tempers act by various ways,
Make some take physic, others scribble plays;
Who cause the proud their visits to delay,
And send the godly in a pet to pray.
A nymph there is, that all thy pow'r disdains, 65
And thousands more in equal mirth maintains.
But oh! if e'er thy Gnome could spoil a grace,
Or raise a pimple on a beauteous face,
Like Citron-waters matrons' cheeks inflame,
Or change complexions at a losing game;       70
If e'er with airy horns I planted heads,
Or rumpled petticoats, or tumbled beds,
Or caused suspicion when no soul was rude,
Or discomposed the head-dress of a Prude,
Or e'er to costive lap-dog gave disease,       75
Which not the tears of brightest eyes could
    ease:
Hear me, and touch Belinda with chagrin,
That single act gives half the world the spleen."
    The Goddess with a discontented air
Seems to reject him, though she grants his
    pray'r.                                     80
A wondrous Bag with both her hands she binds,
Like that where once Ulysses held the winds;
There she collects the force of female lungs,
Sighs, sobs, and passions, and the war of
    tongues.
A Vial next she fills with fainting fears,      85
Soft sorrows, melting griefs, and flowing tears.
The Gnome rejoicing bears her gifts away,
Spreads his black wings, and slowly mounts to
    day.
    Sunk in Thalestris' 19 arms the nymph he
        found,
Her eyes dejected and her hair unbound.        90
Full o'er their heads the swelling bag he rent,
And all the Furies issued at the vent.

17 The "*deus ex machina.*"
18 A small jar. "Homer's tripod" is one of the self-
moving tripods made by Vulcan, described in the
*Iliad* (XVIII, 373–277).
19 A friend of Belinda's, said to be a Mrs. Morley.

Belinda burns with more than mortal ire,
And fierce Thalestris fans the rising fire.
"O wretched maid!" she spread her hands, and
  cried               95
(While Hampton's echoes, "Wretched maid!"
  replied),
"Was it for this you took such constant care
The bodkin, comb, and essence to prepare?
For this your locks in paper durance bound,
For this with tort'ring irons wreathed around?
For this with fillets strained your tender
  head,              101
And bravely bore the double loads of lead? [20]
Gods! shall the ravisher display your hair,
While the Fops envy, and the Ladies stare!
Honor forbid! at whose unrivaled shrine    105
Ease, pleasure, virtue, all our sex resign.
Methinks already I your tears survey,
Already hear the horrid things they say,
Already see you a degraded toast,[21]
And all your honor in a whisper lost!    110
How shall I, then, your helpless fame defend?
'Twill then be infamy to seem your friend!
And shall this prize, th' inestimable prize,
Exposed through crystal to the gazing eyes,
And heightened by the diamond's circling rays,
On that rapacious hand for ever blaze?    116
Sooner shall grass in Hyde-park Circus grow,
And wits take lodgings in the sound of Bow; [22]
Sooner let earth, air, sea, to Chaos fall,
Men, monkeys, lap-dogs, parrots, perish all!" 120
  She said; then raging to Sir Plume [23] repairs,
And bids her Beau demand the precious hairs:
(Sir Plume of amber snuff-box justly vain,
And the nice conduct of a clouded [24] cane)
With earnest eyes, and round unthinking face,
He first the snuff-box opened, then the case,126
And thus broke out—"My Lord, why, what the
  devil?
Z—ds! damn the lock! 'fore Gad, you must be
  civil!
Plague on 't! 'tis past a jest—nay prithee, pox!
Give her the hair"—he spoke, and rapped his
  box.           130
  "It grieves me much" (replied the Peer
  again)
"Who speaks so well should ever speak in vain.
But by this Lock, this sacred Lock I swear
(Which never more shall join its parted hair;
Which never more its honors shall renew,    135
Clipped from the lovely head where late it
  grew),
That while my nostrils draw the vital air,

This hand, which won it, shall for ever wear."
He spoke, and speaking, in proud triumph
  spread
The long-contended honors of her head.    140
  But Umbriel, hateful Gnome! forbears not
  so;
He breaks the Vial whence the sorrows flow.
Then see! the nymph in beauteous grief ap-
  pears,
Her eyes half-languishing, half-drowned in
  tears;
On her heaved bosom hung her drooping head,
Which, with a sigh, she raised; and thus she
  said:           146
  "For ever cursed be this detested day,
Which snatched my best, my fav'rite curl
  away!
Happy! ah, ten times happy had I been,
If Hampton Court these eyes had never seen!
Yet am not I the first mistaken maid,    151
By love of Courts to num'rous ills betrayed.
O had I rather un-admired remained
In some lone isle, or distant Northern land;
Where the gilt Chariot never marks the way,
Where none learn Ombre, none e'er taste
  Bohea! [25]    156
There kept my charms concealed from mortal
  eye,
Like roses, that in deserts bloom and die.
What moved my mind with youthful Lords to
  roam?
O had I stayed, and said my pray'rs at home!
'T was this, the morning omens seemed to
  tell,    161
Thrice from my trembling hand the patch-
  box [26] fell;
The tott'ring Chine shook without a wind,
Nay, Poll sat mute, and Shock was most un-
  kind!
A Sylph too warned me of the threats of fate,
In mystic visions, now believed too late!    166
See the poor remnants of these slighted hairs!
My hands shall rend what e'en thy rapine
  spares:
These in two sable ringlets taught to break,
Once gave new beauties to the snowy neck; 170
The sister-lock now sits uncouth, alone,
And in its fellow's fate foresees its own;
Uncurled it hangs, the fatal shears demands,
And tempts once more thy sacrilegious hands.
O hadst thou, cruel! been content to seize    175
Hairs less in sight, or any hairs but these!"

## CANTO V

She said: the pitying audience melt in tears.
But Fate and Jove had stopped the Baron's
  ears.
In vain Thalestris with reproach assails,

[20] Fastenings for curl-papers.

[21] A slang term for a woman whose health was drunk by her admirers.

[22] The bells of the Church of St. Mary le Bow, in Cheapside, an unfashionable quarter of the city.

[23] Sir George Brown, brother of Mrs. Morley. He is said to have threatened Pope with violence for the picture of him which follows.

[24] Covered with cloudy markings.

[25] Tea.

[26] Box which held patches of sticking plaster for the face.

For who can move when fair Belinda fails?
Not half so fixed the Trojan [27] could remain, 5
While Anna begged and Dido raged in vain.
Then grave Clarissa graceful waved her fan;
Silence ensued, and thus the nymph began:
    "Say why are Beauties praised and honored
        most,
The wise man's passion, and the vain man's
        toast?    10
Why decked with all that land and sea afford,
Why Angels called, and Angel-like adored?
Why round our coaches crowd the white-gloved
        Beaux,
Why bows the side-box from its inmost rows;
How vain are all these glories, all our pains, 15
Unless good sense preserve what beauty gains;
That men may say, when we the front-box
        grace:
'Behold the first in virtue as in face!'
Oh! if to dance all night, and dress all day,
Charmed the small-pox, or chased old age
        away;    20
Who would not scorn what housewife's cares
        produce,
Or who would learn one earthly thing of use?
To patch, nay ogle, might become a Saint,
Nor could it sure be such a sin to paint.
But since, alas! frail beauty must decay,    25
Curled or uncurled, since Locks will turn to
        gray;
Since painted, or not painted, all shall fade,
And she who scorns a man, must die a maid;
What then remains but well our pow'r to use,
And keep good-humor still whate'er we lose 30
And trust me, dear! good-humor can prevail,
When airs, and flights, and screams, and scold-
        ing fail.
Beauties in vain their pretty eyes may roll;
Charms strike the sight, but merit wins the
        soul."
    So spoke the Dame, but no applause ensued;
Belinda frowned, Thalestris called her Prude. 36
"To arms, to arms!" the fierce Virago cries,
And swift as lightning to the combat flies.
All side in parties, and begin th' attack;
Fans clap, silks rustle, and tough whalebones
        crack;    40
Heroes' and Heroines' shouts confus'dly rise,
And bass, and treble voices strike the skies.
No common weapons in their hands are found,
Like Gods they fight, nor dread a mortal
        wound.
    So when bold Homer makes the Gods en-
        gage,    45
And heav'nly breasts with human passions rage;
'Gainst Pallas, Mars; Latona, Hermes arms;
And all Olympus rings with loud alarms:
Jove's thunder roars, heav'n trembles all around,
Blue Neptune storms, the bellowing deeps re-
        sound:    50
Earth shakes her nodding tow'rs, the ground
        gives way,

[27] Aeneas.

And the pale ghosts start at the flash of day!
    Triumphant Umbriel on a sconce's height
Clapped his glad wings, and sat to view the
        fight:
Propped on the bodkin spears, the Sprites sur-
        vey    55
The growing combat, or assist the fray.
    While through the press enraged Thalestris
        flies,
And scatters death around from both her eyes,
A Beau and Witling perished in the throng,
One died in metaphor, and one in song.    60
"O cruel nymph! a living death I bear,"
Cried Dapperwit, and sunk beside his chair.
A mournful glance Sir Fopling upwards cast,
"Those eyes are made so killing"—was his last.
Thus on Maeander's flowery margin lies    65
Th' expiring Swan, and as he sings he dies.
    When bold Sir Plume had drawn Clarissa
        down,
Chloe stepped in, and killed him with a frown;
She smiled to see the doughty hero slain,
But at her smile, the Beau revived again.    70
    Now Jove suspends his golden scales in air,
Weighs the Men's wits against the Lady's hair;
The doubtful beam long nods from side to side;
At length the wits mount up, the hairs subside.
    See, fierce Belinda on the Baron flies,    75
With more than usual lightning in her eyes:
Nor feared the Chief th' unequal fight to try,
Who sought no more than on his foe to die.
But this bold Lord with manly strength endued,
She with one finger and a thumb subdued:    80
Just where the breath of life his nostrils drew,
A charge of Snuff the wily virgin threw;
The Gnomes direct, to ev'ry atom just,
The pungent grains of titillating dust.
Sudden, with starting tears each eye o'erflows,
And the high dome re-echoes to his nose.    86
"Now meet thy fate," incensed Belinda cried,
And drew a deadly bodkin from her side.
(The same, his ancient personage to deck,
Her great great grandsire wore about his neck,
In three seal-rings; which after, melted down,
Formed a vast buckle for his widow's gown: 92
Her infant grandame's whistle next it grew,
The bells she jingled, and the whistle blew;
Then in a bodkin graced her mother's hairs, 95
Which long she wore, and now Belinda wears.)
    "Boast not my fall" (he cried) "insulting
        foe!
Thou by some other shalt be laid as low,
Nor think, to die dejects my lofty mind:
All that I dread is leaving you behind!    100
Rather than so, ah, let me still survive,
And burn in Cupid's flame—but burn alive."
    "Restore the Lock!" she cries; and all around
"Restore the Lock!" the vaulted roofs rebound.
Not fierce Othello in so loud a strain    105
Roared for the handkerchief that caused his
        pain.
But see how oft ambitious aims are crossed,
And chiefs contend 'till all the prize is lost!

The Lock, obtained with guilt, and kept with
    pain,
In every place is sought, but sought in vain: 110
With such a prize no mortal must be bless'd,
So heav'n decrees! with heav'n who can contest?
  Some thought it mounted to the Lunar
    sphere,
Since all things lost on earth are treasured there.
There Heroes' wits are kept in pond'rous
    vases,                                                            115
And beaux' in snuff-boxes and tweezer-cases.
There broken vows and death-bed alms are
    found,
And lovers' hearts with ends of riband bound,
The courtier's promises, and sick man's pray'rs,
The smiles of harlots, and the tears of heirs, 120
Cages for gnats, and chains to yoke a flea,
Dried butterflies, and tomes of casuistry.
  But trust the Muse—she saw it upward rise,
Though marked by none but quick, poetic eyes
(So Rome's great founder 28 to the heav'ns
    withdrew,                                                       125
To Proculus alone confessed in view);
A sudden Star, it shot through liquid air,
And drew behind a radiant trail of hair.
Not Berenice's 29 Locks first rose so bright,
The heav'ns bespangling with disheveled light.
The Sylphs behold it kindling as it flies,      131
And pleased pursue its progress through the
    skies.
  This the Beau monde shall from the Mall 30
    survey,
And hail with music its propitious ray.
This the bless'd Lover shall for Venus take, 135
And send up vows from Rosamonda's lake.31
This Partridge 32 soon shall view in cloudless
    skies,
When next he looks through Galileo's eyes;
And hence th' egregious wizard shall foredoom
The fate of Louis, and the fall of Rome.33  140
  Then cease, bright Nymph! to mourn thy
    ravished hair,
Which adds new glory to the shining sphere!
Not all the tresses that fair head can boast,
Shall draw such envy as the Lock you lost.
For, after all the murders of your eye,          145
When, after millions slain, yourself shall die:
When those fair suns shall set, as set they must,
And all those tresses shall be laid in dust,
This Lock, the Muse shall consecrate to fame,
And 'midst the stars inscribe Belinda's name.

28 Romulus (the legend Pope alludes to is to be
found in Livy, I, xvi).
29 An Egyptian queen who dedicated a lock of hair
for her husband's safe return from war. It was said
to have become a constellation.
30 Upper side of St. James's Park, London.
31 A pond in St. James's Park.
32 An astrologer who published predictions. Swift
made fun of him in his Bickerstaff papers, foretelling
his death, and later pretending that the astrologer
had duly died at the appointed time.
33 Louis XIV and the Papacy.

# An Essay on Man [1]

## To H. St. John Lord Bolingbroke

### ARGUMENT OF EPISTLE I

### Of the Nature and State of Man, with Respect to the Universe.

*Of Man in the abstract. I. That we can judge
only with regard to our own system, being ignorant of the relations of systems and things,
v. 17, etc. II. That Man is not to be deemed
imperfect, but a Being suited to his place and
rank in the creation, agreeable to the general
Order of things, and conformable to Ends and
Relations to him unknown, v. 35, etc. III. That
it is partly upon his ignorance of future events,
and partly upon the hope of a future state, that
all his happiness in the present depends, v. 77,
etc. IV. The pride of aiming at more knowledge, and pretending to more Perfection, the
cause of Man's error and misery. The impiety
of putting himself in the place of God, and
judging of the fitness or unfitness, perfection or
imperfection, justice or injustice of his dispen-
sations, v. 109, etc. V. The absurdity of con-
ceiting himself the final cause of the creation,
or expecting that perfection in the moral world,
which is not in the natural, v. 131, etc. VI. The
unreasonableness of his complaints against
Providence, while on the one hand he demands
the Perfections of the Angels, and on the other
the bodily qualifications of the Brutes; though,
to possess any of the sensitive faculties in a
higher degree, would render him miserable,
v. 173, etc. VII. That throughout the whole
visible world, an universal order and gradation
in the sensual and mental faculties is observed,
which causes a subordination of creature to
creature, and of all creatures to Man. The
gradations of sense, instinct, thought, reflection, reason; that Reason alone countervails all
the other faculties, v. 207. VIII. How much
further this order and subordination of living
creatures may extend, above and below us;
were any part of which broken, not that part
only, but the whole connected creation must
be destroyed, v. 233. IX. The extravagance,
madness, and pride of such a desire, v. 250.*

1 The first epistle, all that is here printed, was
written in 1732, though the complete work (four
epistles) was not finished and published until 1734.
The *Essay* purports to be a philosophical poem, an
aim characteristic of the age. Pope, however, had
not a philosophic mind, and the interest of the poem
lies in its detached sayings. It has even been claimed
that Pope merely put into verse material given him
by Lord Bolingbroke, his "guide, philosopher, and
friend," to whom the poem is addressed. Though
this can hardly be true, at least in the literal sense
of the words, doubtless the matter of the poem was
a subject of frequent discussion between the two.

X. *The consequence of all, the absolute sub-*
*mission due to Providence, both as to our pres-*
*ent and future state, v. 281, etc. to the end.*

### EPISTLE I

Awake, my St. John! leave all meaner things
To low ambition, and the pride of Kings.
Let us (since Life can little more supply
Than just to look about us and to die)
Expatiate [2] free o'er all this scene of Man;     5
A mighty maze! but not without a plan; [3]
A Wild, where weeds and flow'rs promiscuous
    shoot;
Or Garden, tempting with forbidden fruit.
Together let us beat [4] this ample field,
Try what the open, what the covert yield;     10
The latent tracts, the giddy heights, explore
Of all who blindly creep, or sightless soar;
Eye Nature's walks, shoot Folly as it flies,
And catch the Manners living as they rise;
Laugh where we must, be candid where we
    can;     15
But vindicate the ways of God to Man.
**I.** Say first, of God above, or Man below,
What can we reason, but from what we know?
Of Man, what see we but his station here,
From which to reason, or to which refer?     20
Through worlds unnumbered though the God
    be known,
'T is ours to trace him only in our own.
He, who through vast immensity can pierce,
See worlds on worlds compose one universe,
Observe how system into system runs,     25
What other planets circle other suns,
What varied Being peoples ev'ry star,
May tell why Heav'n has made us as we are.
But of this frame the bearings, and the ties,
The strong connections, nice dependencies,     30
Gradations just, has thy pervading soul
Looked through? or can a part contain the
    whole?
    Is the great chain, that draws all to agree,
And drawn supports, upheld by God, or thee?
**II.** Presumptuous Man! the reason wouldst
    thou find,     35
Why formed so weak, so little, and so blind?
First, if thou canst, the harder reason guess,
Why formed no weaker, blinder, and no less?
Ask of thy mother earth, why oaks are made
Taller or stronger than the weeds they shade?
Or ask of yonder argent fields above,     41
Why Jove's satellites are less than Jove?
    Of Systems possible, if 'tis confessed
That Wisdom infinite must form the best,
Where all must full or not coherent be,     45

[2] Wander.

[3] This line in the original editions stood,

"A mighty maze of walks without a plan;"

and it has been remarked (by Lowell) that "perhaps
this came nearer Pope's real opinion than the verse
he substituted for it."

[4] Scour, as in hunting game.

And all that rises, rise in due degree;
Then, in the scale of reas'ning life, 'tis plain,
There must be, somewhere, such a rank as
    Man:
And all the question (wrangle e'er so long)
Is only this, if God has placed him wrong?     50
    Respecting Man, whatever wrong we call,
May, must be right, as relative to all.
In human works, though labored on with pain,
A thousand movements scarce one purpose
    gain;
In God's, one single can its end produce;     55
Yet serves to second too some other use.
So Man, who here seems principal alone,
Perhaps acts second to some sphere unknown,
Touches some wheel, or verges to some goal:
'Tis but a part we see, and not a whole.     60
    When the proud steed shall know why Man
    restrains
His fiery course, or drives him o'er the plains:
When the dull Ox, why now he breaks the
    clod,
Is now a victim, and now Egypt's God:
Then shall Man's pride and dullness compre-
    hend     65
His actions', passions', being's, use and end;
Why doing, suff'ring, checked, impelled; and
    why
This hour a slave, the next a deity.
    Then say not Man's imperfect, Heav'n in
    fault;
Say rather, Man's as perfect as he ought:     70
His knowledge measured to his state and place;
His time a moment, and a point his space.
If to be perfect in a certain sphere,
What matter, soon or late, or here or there?
The bless'd to-day is as completely so,     75
As who began a thousand years ago.
**III.** Heav'n from all creatures hides the book
    of Fate,
All but the page prescribed, their present state:
From brutes what men, from men what spirits
    know:
Or who could suffer Being here below?     80
The lamb thy riot dooms to bleed to-day,
Had he thy Reason, would he skip and play?
Pleased to the last, he crops the flow'ry food,
And licks the hand just raised to shed his blood.
O blindness to the future! kindly giv'n,     85
That each may fill the circle marked by Heav'n:
Who sees with equal eye, as God of all,
A hero perish, or a sparrow fall,
Atoms or systems into ruin hurled,
And now a bubble burst, and now a world.     90
    Hope humbly then; with trembling pinions
    soar;
Wait the great teacher Death: and God adore.
What future bliss, he gives not thee to know,
But gives that Hope to be thy blessing now.
Hope springs eternal in the human breast:     95
Man never Is, but always To be bless'd:
The soul, uneasy and confined from home,
Rests and expatiates in a life to come.

Lo, the poor Indian! whose untutored mind
Sees God in clouds, or hears him in the wind:
His soul proud Science never taught to stray 101
Far as the solar walk, or milky way;
Yet simple Nature to his hope has giv'n,
Behind the cloud-topped hill, an humbler
    heav'n;
Some safer world in depth of woods embraced,
Some happier island in the wat'ry waste,    106
Where slaves once more their native land be-
    hold,
No fiends torment, no Christians thirst for gold.
To Be, contents his natural desire,
He asks no Angel's wing, no Seraph's fire;    110
But thinks, admitted to that equal 5 sky,
His faithful dog shall bear him company.
IV.    Go, wiser thou! and, in thy scale of sense,
Weigh thy Opinion against Providence;
Call imperfection what thou fanci'st such,    115
Say, here he gives too little, there too much:
Destroy all Creatures for thy sport or gust,6
Yet cry, If Man's unhappy, God's unjust;
If Man alone engross not Heav'n's high care,
Alone made perfect here, immortal there:    120
Snatch from his hand the balance and the rod,
Re-judge his justice, be the God of God.
In Pride, in reas'ning Pride, our error lies;
All quit their sphere, and rush into the skies.
Pride still is aiming at the bless'd abodes,    125
Men would be Angels, Angels would be Gods
Aspiring to be Gods, if Angels fell,
Aspiring to be Angels, Men rebel:
And who but wishes to invert the laws
Of Order, sins against th' Eternal Cause.    130
V.    Ask for what end the heav'nly bodies shine,
Earth for whose use? Pride answers, " 'Tis for
    mine:
For me kind Nature wakes her genial Pow'r,
Suckles each herb, and spreads out ev'ry flow'r;
Annual for me, the grape, the rose renew    135
The juice nectareous, and the balmy dew;
For me, the mine a thousand treasures brings;
For me, health gushes from a thousand springs;
Seas roll to waft me, suns to light me rise;
My foot-stool earth, my canopy the skies."    140
    But errs not Nature from his gracious end,
From burning suns when livid deaths descend,
When earthquakes swallow, or when tempests
    sweep
Towns to one grave, whole nations to the deep?
"No," ('tis replied) "the first Almighty Cause
Acts not by partial, but by gen'ral laws;    146
Th' exceptions few; some change since all be-
    gan:
And what created perfect?"—Why then Man?
If the great end be human Happiness,
Then Nature deviates; and can Man do less?    150
As much that end a constant course requires
Of show'rs and sun-shine, as of Man's desires;
As much eternal springs and cloudless skies,
As Men for ever temp'rate, calm, and wise.

If plagues or earthquakes break not Heav'n's
    design,    155
Why then a Borgia, or a Catiline?
Who knows but he, whose hand the lightning
    forms,
Who heaves old Ocean, and who wings the
    storms;
Pours fierce Ambition in a Caesar's mind,
Or turns young Ammon,7 loose to scourge man-
    kind?    160
From pride, from pride, our very reas'ning
    springs;
Account for moral as for nat'ral things:
Why charge we Heav'n in those, in these ac-
    quit?
In both, to reason right is to submit.
    Better for Us, perhaps, it might appear,    165
Were there all harmony, all virtue here;
That never air or ocean felt the wind;
That never passion discomposed the mind.
But all subsists by elemental strife;
And Passions are the elements of Life.    170
The gen'ral Order, since the whole began
Is kept in Nature, and is kept in Man.
VI.    What would this Man? Now upward will
    he soar,
And, little less than Angel, would be more;
Now looking downwards, just as grieved ap-
    pears    175
To want the strength of bulls, the fur of bears.
Made for his use all creatures if he call,
Say what their use, had he the pow'rs of all?
Nature to these, without profusion, kind,
The proper organs, proper pow'rs assign'd;    180
Each seeming want compensated of course,
Here with degrees of swiftness, there of force;
All in exact proportion to the state;
Nothing to add, and nothing to abate.
Each beast, each insect, happy in its own:    185
Is Heav'n unkind to Man, and Man alone?
Shall he alone, whom rational we call,
Be pleased with nothing, if not bless'd with all?
    The bliss of Man (could Pride that blessing
    find)
Is not to act or think beyond mankind;    190
No pow'rs of body or of soul to share,
But what his nature and his state can bear.
Why has not Man a microscopic eye?
For this plain reason, Man is not a Fly.
Say what the use, were finer optics giv'n,    195
T' inspect a mite, not comprehend the heav'n?
Or touch, if tremblingly alive all o'er,
To smart and agonize at every pore?
Or quick effluvia darting through the brain,
Die of a rose in aromatic pain?    200
If Nature thundered in his op'ning ears,
And stunned him with the music of the spheres,
How would he wish that Heav'n had left him
    still
The whisp'ring Zephyr, and the purling rill?
Who finds not Providence all good and wise,

7 Alexander the Great, who allowed himself to be
called the son of Jupiter Ammon.

5 Impartial.        6 Pleasure.

Alike in what it gives, and what denies? 206
**VII.**  Far as Creation's ample range extends,
The scale of sensual,[8] mental pow'rs ascends:
Mark how it mounts, to Man's imperial race,
From the green myriads in the peopled grass:
What modes of sight betwixt each wide ex-
    treme,                                      211
The mole's dim curtain, and the lynx's beam:
Of smell, the headlong lioness between,
And hound sagacious on the tainted green:
Of hearing, from the life that fills the Flood,
To that which warbles through the vernal
    wood:                                       216
The spider's touch, how exquisitely fine!
Feels at each thread, and lives along the line:
In the nice bee, what sense so subtly true
From pois'nous herbs extracts the healing dew?
How Instinct varies in the grov'ling swine, 221
Compared, half-reas'ning elephant, with thine!
'Twixt that, and Reason, what a nice barrier,
For ever sep'rate, yet for ever near!
Remembrance and Reflection how allied; 225
What thin partitions Sense from Thought di-
    vide:
And Middle natures, how they long to join,
Yet never pass th' insuperable line!
Without this just gradation, could they be
Subjected, these to those, or all to thee? 230
The pow'rs of all subdued by thee alone,
Is not thy Reason all these pow'rs in one?
**VIII.**  See, through this air, this ocean, and
    this earth,
All matter quick, and bursting into birth.
Above, how high progressive life may go! 235
Around, how wide! how deep extend below!
Vast chain of Being! which from God began,
Natures ethereal, human, angel, man,
Beast, bird, fish, insect, what no eye can see,
No glass can reach; from Infinite to thee, 240
From thee to Nothing.—On superior pow'rs
Were we to press, inferior might on ours:
Or in the full creation leave a void,
Where, one step broken, the great scale's de-
    stroyed:
From Nature's chain whatever link you strike,
Tenth or ten-thousandth, breaks the chain
    alike.                                      246
And, if each system in gradation roll
Alike essential to th' amazing Whole,
The least confusion but in one, not all
That system only, but the Whole must fall. 250
Let Earth unbalanced from her orbit fly,
Planets and Suns run lawless through the sky;
Let ruling Angels from their spheres be hurled,
Being on Being wrecked, and world on world;
Heav'n's whole foundations to their center nod,
And Nature tremble to the throne of God. 256
All this dread Order break—for whom? for
    thee?
Vile worm!—O Madness! Pride! Impiety!
**IX.**  What if the foot, ordained the dust to
    tread,

[8] Sensory.

Or hand, to toil, aspired to be the head? 260
What if the head, the eye, or ear repined
To serve mere engines to the ruling Mind?
Just as absurd for any part to claim
To be another, in this gen'ral frame:
Just as absurd, to mourn the tasks or pains, 265
The great directing Mind of all ordains.
  All are but parts of one stupendous whole,
Whose body Nature is, and God the soul;
That, changed through all, and yet in all the
    same;
Great in the earth, as in th' ethereal frame; 270
Warms in the sun, refreshes in the breeze,
Glows in the stars, and blossoms in the trees,
Lives through all life, extends through all ex-
    tent,
Spreads undivided, operates unspent;
Breathes in our soul, informs our mortal part,
As full, as perfect, in a hair as heart: 276
As full, as perfect, in vile Man that mourns,
As the rapt Seraph that adores and burns:
To him no high, no low, no great, no small;
He fills, he bounds, connects, and equals all. 280
**X.**  Cease then, nor Order Imperfection name:
Our proper bliss depends on what we blame.
Know thy own point: This kind, this due degree
Of blindness, weakness, Heav'n bestows on
    thee.
Submit.—In this, or any other sphere, 285
Secure to be as bless'd as thou canst bear:
Safe in the hand of one disposing Pow'r,
Or in the natal, or the mortal hour.
All Nature is but Art, unknown to thee;
All Chance, Direction, which thou canst not
    see;                                        290
All Discord, Harmony not understood;
All partial Evil, universal Good:
And, spite of Pride, in erring Reason's spite,
One truth is clear, *Whatever is, is right.*

## Epistle to Dr. Arbuthnot [1]

### *Advertisement to the First Publication of*
### *This EPISTLE*

THIS *paper is a sort of bill of complaint, begun many years since, and drawn up by*

[1] Pope indicates, in the "Advertisement" here
printed, the purpose of this *Epistle*, but his statement concerning the time of its composition cannot
be taken literally. A few passages were written
earlier than 1734 (the portraits of Addison and
Bufo, and the reference to his mother), but the
*Epistle* as a whole dates from this year, or from
1735. Its immediate occasion was the abusive attack
on Pope contained in the two poems he mentions in
the "Advertisement." The first of these is said to
have been written by Lady Mary Wortley Montagu
and Lord John Hervey together; the second was
written by Hervey. Dr. John Arbuthnot was both
physician and man of letters, and Pope's close
friend until his death in 1735, only a short time
after the publication of the *Epistle.* The poem is
cast in the form of a dialogue between Pope himself
and Arbuthnot.

snatches, as the several occasions offered. I had no thoughts of publishing it, till it pleased some Persons of Rank and Fortune (the Authors of Verses to the Imitator of Horace, and of an Epistle to a Doctor of Divinity from a Nobleman of Hampton Court) to attack, in a very extraordinary manner, not only my Writings (of which, being public, the Public is judge), but my Person, Morals, and Family, whereof, to those who know me not, a truer information may be requisite. Being divided between the necessity to say something of myself, and my own laziness to undertake so awkward a task, I thought it the shortest way to put the last hand to this Epistle. If it have anything pleasing, it will be that by which I am most desirous to please, the Truth and the Sentiment; and if anything offensive, it will be only to those I am least sorry to offend, the vicious or the ungenerous.

Many will know their own pictures in it, there being not a circumstance but what is true; but I have, for the most part, spared their Names, and they may escape being laughed at, if they please.

I would have some of them know, it was owing to the request of the learned and candid Friend to whom it is inscribed, that I make not as free use of theirs as they have done of mine. However, I shall have this advantage, and honor, on my side, that whereas, by their proceeding, any abuse may be directed at any man, no injury can possibly be done by mine, since a nameless character can never be found out, but by its truth and likeness. P.

P.   Shut, shut the door, good John![2] fatigued, I said,
Tie up the knocker, say I'm sick, I'm dead.
The Dog-star rages! nay 'tis past a doubt,
All Bedlam, or Parnassus, is let out:
Fire in each eye, and papers in each hand, [5]
They rave, recite, and madden round the land.

What walls can guard me, or what shade can hide?
They pierce my thickets, through my Grot[3] they glide;
By land, by water, they renew the charge;
They stop the chariot, and they board the barge. [10]
No place is sacred, not the Church is free;
E'en Sunday shines no Sabbath-day to me;
Then from the Mint[4] walks forth the Man of rime,
Happy to catch me just at Dinner-time.

[2] John Searl, Pope's body-servant.
[3] An artificial grotto that formed a passage-way under a road which ran through Pope's grounds at Twickenham. This grotto and its ornamentation gave Pope a particular pleasure.
[4] A district in London where debtors could not be arrested; nor could they be arrested anywhere on Sundays.

Is there a Parson, much bemused in beer, [15]
A maudlin Poetess, a riming Peer,
A Clerk,[5] foredoomed his father's soul to cross,
Who pens a Stanza, when he should engross?
Is there, who, locked from ink and paper, scrawls
With desp'rate charcoal round his darkened walls? [20]
All fly to Twit'nam,[6] and in humble strain
Apply to me, to keep them mad or vain.
Arthur,[7] whose giddy son neglects the Laws,
Imputes to me and my damned works the cause:
Poor Cornus[8] sees his frantic wife elope, [25]
And curses Wit, and Poetry, and Pope.

Friend to my Life (which did not you prolong,
The world had wanted many an idle song)
What Drop or Nostrum can this plague remove?
Or which must end me, a Fool's wrath or love?
A dire dilemma! either way I'm sped,[9] [31]
If foes, they write, if friends, they read me dead.
Seized and tied down to judge, how wretched I!
Who can't be silent, and who will not lie.
To laugh, were want of goodness and of grace,
And to be grave, exceeds all Pow'r of face. [36]
I sit with sad civility, I read
With honest anguish, and an aching head;
And drop at last, but in unwilling ears,
This saving counsel, "Keep your piece nine years."[10] [40]

"Nine years!" cries he, who high in Drury-Lane,
Lulled by soft Zephyrs through the broken pane,
Rimes ere he wakes, and prints before Term ends,[11]
Obliged by hunger, and request of friends:
"The piece, you think, is incorrect? why, take it, [45]
I'm all submission, what you'd have it, make it."

Three things another's modest wishes bound,
My Friendship, and a Prologue, and ten pound.
Pitholeon sends to me: "You know his Grace,
I want a Patron; ask him for a Place." [50]
Pitholeon libeled me—"but here's a letter
Informs you, Sir, 'twas when he knew no better.
Dare you refuse him? Curll[12] invites to dine,
He'll write a Journal, or he'll turn Divine."

Bless me! a packet.—" 'Tis a stranger sues, [55]
A Virgin Tragedy, an Orphan Muse."
If I dislike it, "Furies, death and rage!"
If I approve, "Commend it to the Stage."

[5] Law clerk.
[6] Twickenham, where Pope lived.
[7] Arthur Moore, a politician.
[8] Robert, Lord Walpole.   [9] Done for.
[10] Horace's advice in his *Art of Poetry* (line 388).
[11] I. e., before the season is over.
[12] A piratical publisher and an enemy of Pope.

There (thank my stars) my whole Commission
   ends,
The Play'rs and I are, luckily, no friends.    60
Fired that the house reject him, " 'Sdeath I'll
   print it,
And shame the fools—Your Int'rest, Sir, with
   Lintot!" [13]
Lintot, dull rogue! will think your price too
   much:
"Not, Sir, if you revise it, and retouch."
All my demurs but double his Attacks;    65
At last he whispers, "Do; and we go snacks."
Glad of a quarrel, straight I clap the door,
Sir, let me see your works and you no more.

'Tis sung, when Midas' Ears began to spring
(Midas, a sacred person and a king),    70
His very Minister who spied them first,
(Some say his Queen) was forced to speak, or
   burst.
And is not mine, my friend, a sorer case,
When ev'ry coxcomb perks them in my face?
A.   Good friend, forbear! you deal in dang'rous
   things.    75
I'd never name Queens, Ministers, or Kings; [14]
Keep close to Ears, and those let asses prick;
'Tis nothing— P.   Nothing? if they bite and
   kick?
Out with it, *Dunciad!* let the secret pass,
That secret to each fool, that he's an Ass:    80
The truth once told (and wherefore should we
   lie?)
The Queen of Midas slept, and so may I.
   You think this cruel? take it for a rule,
No creature smarts so little as a fool.
Let peals of laughter, Codrus! round thee break,
Thou unconcerned canst hear the mighty
   crack:
Pit, Box, and gall'ry in convulsions hurled,    87
Thou stand'st unshook amidst a bursting world.
Who shames a Scribbler? break one cobweb
   through,
He spins the slight, self-pleasing thread anew:
Destroy his fib or sophistry, in vain,    91
The creature's at his dirty work again,
Throned in the center of his thin designs,
Proud of a vast extent of flimsy lines!
Whom have I hurt? has Poet yet, or Peer,    95
Lost the arched eye-brow, or Parnassian sneer?
And has not Colley [15] still his Lord and Whore?
His butchers Henley? his freemasons Moore?
Does not the table Bavius still admit?
Still to one Bishop Philips [16] seem a wit?    100
Still Sappho [17]— A.   Hold! for God's sake—
   you'll offend,
No Names!—be calm!—learn prudence of a
   friend!
I too could write, and I am twice as tall;

But foes like these— P.   One Flatt'rer's worse
   than all.
Of all mad creatures, if the learn'd are right,
It is the slaver kills, and not the bite.    106
A fool quite angry is quite innocent:
Alas! 'tis ten times worse when they *repent.*
   One dedicates in high heroic prose,
And ridicules beyond a hundred foes:    110
One from all Grubstreet will my fame defend,
And, more abusive, calls himself my friend.
This prints my *Letters,* that expects a bribe,
And others roar aloud, "Subscribe, subscribe."
   There are, who to my person pay their court:
I cough like Horace, and, though lean, am
   short,    116
Ammon's great son [18] one shoulder had too
   high,
Such Ovid's nose, and "Sir! you have an Eye"—
Go on, obliging creatures, make me see
All that disgraced my Betters, met in me.    120
Say for my comfort, languishing in bed,
"Just so immortal Maro [19] held his head:"
And when I die, be sure you let me know
Great Homer died three thousand years ago.
   Why did I write? what sin to me unknown
Dipped me in ink, my parents', or my own? [126]
As yet a child, nor yet a fool to fame,
I lisped in numbers, for the numbers came.
I left no calling for this idle trade,
No duty broke, no father disobeyed.    130
The Muse but served to ease some friend, not
   Wife,
To help me through this long disease, my Life,
To second, Arbuthnot! thy Art and Care,
And teach the Being you preserved, to bear.
   But why then publish? Granville [20] the
   polite,    135
And knowing Walsh,[21] would tell me I could
   write;
Well-natured Garth [22] inflamed with early
   praise;
And Congreve loved, and Swift endured my
   lays;
The courtly Talbot, Somers, Sheffield,[23] read;
E'en mitered Rochester [24] would nod the head,
And St. John's self [25] (great Dryden's friends
   before)    141
With open arms received one Poet more.
Happy my studies, when by these approved!
Happier their author, when by these beloved!
From these the world will judge of men and
   books,    145
Not from the Burnets, Oldmixons, and
   Cookes.[26]

[13] Another publisher, who published much of
Pope's work.
[14] A glance at Queen Caroline, Walpole, and
George II.
[15] Colley Cibber.       [16] Ambrose Philips.
[17] Lady Mary Wortley Montagu.

[18] Alexander the Great.          [19] Virgil.
[20] George Granville, Lord Lansdowne.
[21] See introductory account of Pope above.
[22] Samuel Garth, physician and man of letters.
[23] All statesmen and patrons of letters.
[24] Francis Atterbury, Bishop of Rochester.
[25] Lord Bolingbroke, to whom Pope's *Essay on
Man* is dedicated.
[26] Authors of secret and scandalous history (Pope's
note).

Soft were my numbers; who could take offense,
While pure Description held the place of Sense?
Like gentle Fanny's [27] was my flow'ry theme,
A painted mistress, or a purling stream.     150
Yet then did Gildon draw his venal quill;—
I wished the man a dinner, and sat still.
Yet then did Dennis [28] rave in furious fret;
I never answered,—I was not in debt.
If want provoked, or madness made them print,
I waged no war with Bedlam or the Mint. 156
    Did some more sober Critic come abroad;
If wrong, I smiled; if right, I kissed the rod.
Pains, reading, study, are their just pretense,
And all they want is spirit, taste, and sense. 160
Commas and points they set exactly right,
And 'twere a sin to rob them of their mite.
Yet ne'er one sprig of laurel graced these ribalds,
From slashing Bentley down to pidling Tibalds: [29]
Each wight, who reads not, and but scans and spells,     165
Each Word-catcher, that lives on syllables,
E'en such small Critics some regard may claim,
Preserved in Milton's or in Shakespeare's name.
Pretty! in amber to observe the forms
Of hairs, or straws, or dirt, or grubs, or worms!
The things, we know, are neither rich nor rare,
But wonder how the devil they got there. 172
    Were others angry: I excused them too;
Well might they rage, I gave them but their due.
A man's true merit 'tis not hard to find;     175
But each man's secret standard in his mind,
That Casting-weight pride adds to emptiness,
This, who can gratify? for who can guess?
The Bard [30] whom pilfered Pastorals renown,
Who turns a Persian tale for half a Crown, 180
Just writes to make his barrenness appear,
And strains, from hard-bound brains, eight lines a year;
He, who still wanting, though he lives on theft,
Steals much, spends little, yet has nothing left:
And He, who now to sense, now nonsense leaning,     185
Means not, but blunders round about a meaning:
And He, whose fustian's so sublimely bad,
It is not Poetry, but prose run mad:
All these, my modest Satire bade translate,
And owned that nine such Poets made a Tate.[31]     190
How did they fume, and stamp, and roar, and chafe!

And swear, not Addison himself was safe.
    Peace to all such! but were there One whose fires
True Genius kindles, and fair Fame inspires;
Bless'd with each talent and each art to please,
And born to write, converse, and live with ease:
Should such a man, too fond to rule alone, [197]
Bear, like the Turk, no brother near the throne,
View him with scornful, yet with jealous eyes,
And hate for arts that caused himself to rise; [200]
Damn with faint praise, assent with civil leer,
And without sneering, teach the rest to sneer;
Willing to wound, and yet afraid to strike,
Just hint a fault, and hesitate dislike;
Alike reserved to blame, or to commend,     205
A tim'rous foe, and a suspicious friend;
Dreading e'en fools, by Flatterers besieged,
And so obliging, that he ne'er obliged;
Like Cato, give his little Senate laws,
And sit attentive to his own applause;     210
White Wits and Templars [32] ev'ry sentence raise,
And wonder with a foolish face of praise:——
Who but must laugh, if such a man there be?
Who would not weep, if Atticus [33] were he?
    What though my Name stood rubric [34] on the walls     215
Or plastered posts, with claps,[35] in capitals?
Or smoking forth, a hundred hawkers' load,
On wings of winds came flying all abroad?
I sought no homage from the Race that write;
I kept, like Asian Monarchs, from their sight:
Poems I heeded (now be-rimed so long)     221
No more than thou, great George! a birthday song.
I ne'er with wits or witlings passed my days,
To spread about the itch of verse and praise;
Nor like a puppy, daggled through the town, 225
To fetch and carry sing-song up and down;
Nor at Rehearsals sweat, and mouthed, and cried,
With handkerchief and orange at my side;
But sick of fops, and poetry, and prate,
To Bufo,[36] left the whole Castalian state. 230
    Proud as Apollo on his forkéd hill,[37]
Sat full-blown Bufo, puffed by ev'ry quill;
Fed with soft Dedication all day long,
Horace and he went hand in hand in song.
His Library (where busts of Poets dead     235
And a true Pindar stood without a head),
Received of wits an undistinguished race,

---

[27] John, Lord Hervey.
[28] Gildon and Dennis were critics of the day.
[29] Bentley was a famous classical scholar who published an edition of *Paradise Lost*; Theobald a scholar and editor of Shakespeare.
[30] Ambrose Philips.
[31] Nahum Tate, at the time poet laureate.

[32] Legal student, attending one of the London Inns of Court which occupied land once belonging to the Knights Templars.
[33] Addison.
[34] The reference is to Lintot's practice of posting on the walls of his shop the titles of new books in red letters.
[35] Posters.
[36] Probably the Earl of Halifax (the following portrait is said to have been intended, when first written, for Bubb Doddington).
[37] The cleft summit of Parnassus.

Who first his judgment asked, and then a
    place:
Much they extolled his pictures, much his seat,
And flattered ev'ry day, and some days eat: 240
Till grown more frugal in his riper days,
He paid some bards with port, and some with
    praise:
To some a dry rehearsal saw assigned,
And others (harder still) he paid in kind.
Dryden alone (what wonder?) came not nigh,
Dryden alone escaped this judging eye:    246
But still the Great have kindness in reserve,
He helped to bury whom he helped to starve.

    May some choice patron bless each gray goose
    quill!
May ev'ry Bavius have his Bufo still!    250
So, when a Statesman wants a day's defense,
Or Envy holds a whole week's war with Sense,
Or simple pride for flatt'ry makes demands,
May dunce by dunce be whistled off my hands!
Bless'd be the Great! for those they take away,
And those they left me; for they left me Gay; 38
Left me to see neglected Genius bloom,    257
Neglected die, and tell it on his tomb:
Of all thy blameless life the sole return
My Verse, and Queensb'ry weeping o'er thy
    urn.    260

    Oh, let me live my own, and die so too!
(To live and die is all I have to do)
Maintain a Poet's dignity and ease,
And see what friends, and read what books I
    please;
Above a Patron, though I condescend    265
Sometimes to call a minister my friend.
I was not born for Courts or great affairs;
I pay my debts, believe, and say my pray'rs;
Can sleep without a Poem in my head;
Nor know, if Dennis be alive or dead.    270

    Why am I asked what next shall see the
    light?
Heav'ns! was I born for nothing but to write?
Has Life no joys for me? or (to be grave)
Have I no friend to serve, no soul to save?
"I found him close with Swift"—"Indeed? no
    doubt"    275
(Cries prating Balbus), "something will come
    out."
'Tis all in vain, deny it as I will.
"No, such a Genius never can lie still;"
And then for mine obligingly mistakes    279
The first Lampoon Sir Will or Bubo 39 makes.
Poor guiltless I! and can I choose but smile,
When ev'ry Coxcomb knows me by my Style?

    Cursed be the verse, how well soe'er it flow,
That tends to make one worthy man my foe,
Give Virtue scandal, Innocence a fear,    285
Or from the soft-eyed Virgin steal a tear!
But he who hurts a harmless neighbor's peace,
Insults fall'n worth, or Beauty in distress,
Who loves a Lie, lame slander helps about,

38 John Gay, the poet (1685–1732).
39 Sir William Yonge and Bubb Doddington.

Who writes a Libel, or who copies out:    290
That Fop, whose pride affects a patron's name,
Yet absent, wounds an author's honest fame:
Who can your merit selfishly approve,
And show the sense of it without the love;
Who has the vanity to call you friend,    295
Yet wants the honor, injured, to defend;
Who tells whate'er you think, whate'er you say,
And, if he lie not, must at least betray:
Who to the Dean, and silver bell can swear,
And sees at Canons 40 what was never there;
Who reads, but with a lust to misapply,    301
Make Satire a Lampoon, and Fiction, Lie.
A lash like mine no honest man shall dread,
But all such babbling blockheads in his stead.

    Let Sporus 41 tremble—A. What? that
    thing of silk,    305
Sporus, that mere white curd of Ass's milk!
Satire or sense, alas! can Sporus feel?
Who breaks a butterfly upon a wheel?
P. Yet let me flap this bug with gilded wings,
This painted child of dirt, that stinks and
    stings;    310
Whose buzz the witty and the fair annoys,
Yet wit ne'er tastes, and beauty ne'er enjoys:
So well-bred spaniels civilly delight
In mumbling of the game they dare not bite.
Eternal smiles his emptiness betray,    315
As shallow streams run dimpling all the way.
Whether in florid impotence he speaks,
And, as the prompter breathes, the puppet
    squeaks;
Or at the ear of Eve,42 familiar Toad,
Half froth, half venom, spits himself abroad, 320
In puns, or politics, or tales, or lies,
Or spite, or smut, or rimes, or blasphemies.
His wit all see-saw, between that and this,
Now high, now low, now master up, now
    miss,
And he himself one vile Antithesis.    325
Amphibious thing! that acting either part,
The trifling head or the corrupted heart,
Fop at the toilet, flatt'rer at the board,
Now trips a Lady, and now struts a Lord.
Eve's tempter thus the Rabbins have expressed,
A Cherub's face, a reptile all the rest;    331
Beauty that shocks you, parts that none will
    trust;
Wit that can creep, and pride that licks the
    dust.

    Not Fortune's worshiper, nor fashion's fool,
Not Lucre's madman, nor Ambition's tool, 335
Not proud, nor servile;—be one Poet's praise,
That, if he pleased, he pleased by manly ways:
That Flatt'ry, e'en to Kings, he held a shame,

40 Estate of the Duke of Chandos, which Pope was
supposed to have satirized in the fourth of his *Moral
Essays.*
41 Lord Hervey, whom ill health forced to drink
ass's milk.
42 Queen Caroline. Cf. *Paradise Lost*, IV, 799–
809.

And thought a Lie in verse or prose the same.
That not in Fancy's maze he wandered long,
But stooped to Truth, and moralized his song:
That not for Fame, but Virtue's better end, 342
He stood the furious foe, the timid friend,
The damning critic, half approving wit,
The coxcomb hit, or fearing to be hit; 345
Laughed at the loss of friends he never had,
The dull, the proud, the wicked, and the mad;
The distant threats of vengeance on his head,
The blow unfelt, the tear he never shed;
The tale revived, the lie so oft o'erthrown, 350
Th' imputed trash, and dullness not his own;
The morals blackened when the writings 'scape,
The libeled person, and the pictured shape;
Abuse, on all he loved, or loved him, spread,
A friend in exile, or a father dead; 355
The whisper, that to greatness still too near,
Perhaps, yet vibrates on his Sov'reign's ear:—
Welcome for thee, fair Virtue! all the past;
For thee, fair Virtue! welcome e'en the last!
    A.  But why insult the poor, affront the
        great? 360
P.  A knave's a knave, to me, in ev'ry state:
Alike my scorn, if he succeed or fail.
Sporus at court, or Japhet 43 in a jail,
A hireling scribbler, or a hireling peer,
Knight of the post corrupt, or of the shire; 365
If on a Pillory, or near a Throne,
He gain his Prince's ear, or lose his own.
    Yet soft by nature, more a dupe than wit,
Sappho can tell you how this man was bit;
This dreaded Sat'rist Dennis will confess 370
Foe to his pride, but friend to his distress:
So humble, he has knocked at Tibbald's door,
Has drunk with Cibber, nay has rimed for
    Moore.
Full ten years slandered, did he once reply?
Three thousand suns went down on Wel-
    sted's 44 lie. 375
To please a Mistress one aspersed his life;
He lashed him not, but let her be his wife.
Let Budgell 45 charge low Grubstreet on his
    quill,
And write whate'er he pleased, except his Will;

43 Japhet Crooke, a forger.
44 A hack-writer of the day.
45 Budgell was charged with forging a will, to his
own profit.

Let the two Curlls 46 of Town and Court, abuse
His father, mother, body, soul and muse.   381
Yet why? that Father held it for a rule,
It was a sin to call our neighbor fool;
That harmless Mother thought no wife a
    whore:
Hear this, and spare his family, James Moore!
Unspotted names, and memorable long!   386
If there be force in Virtue, or in Song.
    Of gentle blood (part shed in Honor's cause,
While yet in Britain Honor had applause)
Each  parent  sprung—  A.  What  fortune,
    pray?— P.   Their own,   390
And better got, than Bestia's from the throne.
Born to no Pride, inheriting no Strife,
Nor marrying Discord in a noble wife,47
Stranger to civil and religious rage,
The good man walked innoxious through his
    age. 395
Nor Courts he saw, no suits would ever try,
Nor dared an Oath, nor hazarded a Lie.
Unlearn'd, he knew no schoolman's subtle art,
No language, but the language of the heart.
By Nature honest, by Experience wise,   400
Healthy by temp'rance, and by exercise;
His life, though long, to sickness past unknown,
His death was instant, and without a groan.
O grant me, thus to live, and thus to die!
Who sprung from Kings shall know less joy
    than I. 405
    O Friend! may each domestic bliss be thine!
Be no unpleasing Melancholy mine:
Me, let the tender office long engage,
To rock the cradle of reposing Age,
With lenient arts extend a Mother's breadth,
Make Languor smile, and smooth the bed of
    Death, 411
Explore the thought, explain the asking eye,
And keep a while one parent from the sky!
On cares like these if length of days attend,
May Heav'n, to bless those days, preserve my
    friend, 415
Preserve him social, cheerful and serene,
And just as rich as when he served a Queen.48
A.   Whether that blessing be denied or giv'n,
Thus far was right, the rest belongs to Heav'n.

46 The bookseller and Lord Hervey.
47 Alluding to Addison's marriage with the Countess of Warwick.
48 Arbuthnot had been physician to Queen Anne.

Thomas Gray

1716-1771

Gray was born in Cornhill, London, on 26 December, 1716. When he was about eleven years old he was sent to Eton, where he formed close friendships with Horace Walpole, Richard West, whose early death in 1742 caused him deep grief, and Thomas Ashton. In 1734 he entered Peterhouse, Cambridge. He made but few acquaintances there, his life-long habit of reserve already asserting itself, and he left Cambridge in 1738 without taking a degree, because of his hatred of mathematics. In 1739 he went with Horace Walpole to travel on the Continent, and they spent some months together very agreeably, though in Italy there arose a difference between them which caused them to part company, Gray returning home alone in the summer of 1741. He spent about a year living with his mother at Stoke Poges, and then in 1742 returned to Peterhouse. He made some efforts to study the law, and was given the bachelor's degree in law in 1743, but he never took any steps looking to active practice. Instead, he settled down to a life of study at Cambridge, where he remained, save for one interruption, through the rest of his life. In consequence of some disturbance by undergraduates he moved from Peterhouse to Pembroke in 1756, and in a life outwardly so quiet as his this was a great event. When the British Museum was opened in 1759 he took lodgings in London and remained there two years, studying manuscripts and old books in the Museum. He is said to have become one of the most learned men in Europe in his time, his studies including classical literature, history, modern languages and literatures, architecture, botany, and music. He made extensive collections and notes for a history of English poetry, but gave over his design when he learned that Thomas Warton was engaged on the same subject. His few poems he wrote slowly and with difficulty, and he had no ambition for fame. He was occupied with the famous Elegy for about eight years before he completed it, and then was induced to publish it in 1751 only when he learned that a mutilated copy was about to be printed without his permission. Nevertheless, the few poems he published in 1753 and 1757 won him immediate recognition, and he was offered the post of poet laureate in the latter year. This he refused without hesitation, regarding it, in view of the character of recent incumbents, as a questionable honor, and as one in any case for which he did not care. In 1768 he was made a professor of modern history at Cambridge, a post which in his day did not necessarily carry any duties with it; and, though he planned to deliver some lectures, he never did so. Gray died on 30 July, 1771, and he was buried at Stoke Poges, by the side of his mother.

Gray's poems are almost as few in number as those of his contemporary, Collins, and like Collins's they are characterized by an exquisite sense of form. Gray's fastidious classicism of style and form issued from qualities of temperament which were reënforced by his close study of the Greeks and, among English poets, of Milton and Dryden. His antiquarianism, which found expression in the Bard and in his Norse and other Welsh poems, together with admiration which he felt for rugged natural scenery, has caused him to be regarded as a forerunner of the romantic poets of the early nineteenth century. This to a certain extent he was, but he was "romantic" in only a very partial and external sense.

The Poems of Gray and Collins have most recently been edited by Austin L. Poole (London, 1937), and the Correspondence of Thomas Gray by Paget Toynbee and Leonard Whibley (Oxford, 1935). In addition to the biographical material supplied by the Correspondence the life by R. W. Ketton Cremer, Gray: a Biography (Cambridge, 1955), may be recommended. A more limited side of Gray is investigated by William P. Jones in Thomas Gray, Scholar; the True Tragedy of an

Eighteenth-Century Gentleman (*Cambridge, U. S. A., 1937*). *Matthew Arnold's well-known essay on Gray appears in* Essays in Criticism, Second Series (*London, 1888*).

## Ode on the Death of a Favorite Cat

### Drowned in a Tub of Gold Fishes [1]

'Twas on a lofty vase's side,
Where China's gayest art had dyed
   The azure flowers, that blow;
Demurest of the tabby kind,
The pensive Selima reclined,      5
   Gazed on the lake below.

Her conscious tail her joy declared;
The fair round face, the snowy beard,
   The velvet of her paws,
Her coat, that with the tortoise vies,   10
Her ears of jet, and emerald eyes,
   She saw; and purred applause.

Still had she gazed; but 'midst the tide
Two angel forms were seen to glide,
   The Genii of the stream:      15
Their scaly armor's Tyrian hue
Through richest purple to the view
   Betrayed a golden gleam:

The hapless Nymph with wonder saw:
A whisker first and then a claw,   20
   With many an ardent wish,
She stretched in vain to reach the prize.
What female heart can gold despise?
   What Cat's averse to fish?

Presumptuous Maid! with looks intent   25
Again she stretched, again she bent,
   Nor knew the gulf between.
(Malignant Fate sat by, and smiled)
The slipp'ry verge her feet beguiled,
   She tumbled headlong in.   30

Eight times emerging from the flood
She mewed to ev'ry wat'ry God,
   Some speedy aid to send.
No Dolphin came, no Nereid stirred:
Nor cruel Tom, nor Susan heard.   35
   A Fav'rite has no friend!

From hence, ye Beauties, undeceived,
Know, one false step is ne'er retrieved,
   And be with caution bold.
Not all that tempts your wand'ring eyes   40
And heedless hearts, is lawful prize;
   Nor all, that glisters, gold.

[1] Written early in 1747; first published in 1748. The cat belonged to Gray's friend, Horace Walpole.

## Ode on a Distant Prospect of Eton College [1]

*Ἄνθρωπος· ἱκανὴ πρόφασις εἰς τὸ δυστυχεῖν.*[2]
—MENANDER.

Ye distant spires, ye antique towers,
   That crown the wat'ry glade,
Where grateful Science still adores
   Her Henry's [3] holy Shade;
And ye, that from the stately brow   5
Of Windsor's [4] heights th' expanse below
   Of grove, of lawn, of mead survey,
Whose turf, whose shade, whose flowers among
Wanders the hoary Thames along
   His silver-winding way.   10

Ah happy hills, ah pleasing shade,
   Ah fields beloved in vain,
Where once my careless childhood strayed,
   A stranger yet to pain!
I feel the gales, that from ye blow,   15
A momentary bliss bestow,
   As waving fresh their gladsome wing,
My weary soul they seem to sooth,
And, redolent of joy and youth,
   To breathe a second spring.   20

Say, Father Thames, for thou hast seen
   Full many a sprightly race
Disporting on thy margent green
   The paths of pleasure trace,
Who foremost now delight to cleave   25
With pliant arm thy glassy wave?
   The captive linnet which enthrall?
What idle progeny succeed
To chase the rolling circle's speed,[5]
   Or urge the flying ball?   30

While some on earnest business bent
   Their murm'ring labors ply
'Gainst graver hours, that bring constraint
   To sweeten liberty:
Some bold adventurers disdain   35
The limits of their little reign,
   And unknown regions dare descry:
Still as they run they look behind,
They hear a voice in every wind,
   And snatch a fearful joy.   40

Gay hope is theirs by fancy fed,
   Less pleasing when possessed;
The tear forgot as soon as shed,
   The sunshine of the breast:
Theirs buxom health of rosy hue,   45
Wild wit, invention ever-new,
   And lively cheer of vigor born;

[1] Written in 1742; first published in 1747.
[2] A human being: sufficient cause for misery.
[3] Henry VI, founder of Eton College (1440).
[4] Windsor Castle, a royal palace near Eton.
[5] Roll the hoop.

The thoughtless day, the easy night,
The spirits pure, the slumbers light,
    That fly th' approach of morn.                    50

Alas, regardless of their doom,
    The little victims play!
No sense have they of ills to come,
    Nor care beyond to-day:
Yet see how all around 'em wait                      55
The Ministers of human fate,
    And black Misfortune's baleful train!
Ah, show them where in ambush stand
To seize their prey the murd'rous band!
    Ah, tell them, they are men!                      60

These shall the fury Passions tear,
    The vultures of the mind,
Disdainful Anger, pallid Fear,
    And Shame that skulks behind;
Or pining Love shall waste their youth,              65
Or Jealousy with rankling tooth,
    That inly gnaws the secret heart,
And Envy wan, and faded Care,
Grim-visaged comfortless Despair,
    And Sorrow's piercing dart.                       70

Ambition this shall tempt to rise,
    Then whirl the wretch from high,
To bitter Scorn a sacrifice,
    And grinning Infamy.
The stings of Falsehood those shall try,             75
And hard Unkindness' altered eye,
    That mocks the tear it forced to flow;
And keen Remorse with blood defiled,
And moody Madness laughing wild
    Amid severest woe.                                80

Lo, in the vale of years beneath
    A grisly troop are seen,
The painful family of Death,
    More hideous than their Queen:
This racks the joints, this fires the veins,         85
That every laboring sinew strains,
    Those in the deeper vitals rage:
Lo, Poverty, to fill the band,
That numbs the soul with icy hand,
    And slow-consuming Age.                           90

To each his suff'rings: all are men,
    Condemned alike to groan;
The tender for another's pain,
    Th' unfeeling for his own.
Yet ah! why should they know their fate?             95
Since sorrow never comes too late,
    And happiness too swiftly flies.
Thought would destroy their paradise.
No more; where ignorance is bliss,
    'Tis folly to be wise.                            100

# Hymn to Adversity [1]

——Ζῆνα
τὸν φρονεῖν βροτοὺς ὁδώ-
σαντα, τῷ πάθει μαθάν
θέντα κυρίως ἔχειν.[2]
    —Aeschylus, *Agamemnon.*

Daughter of Jove, relentless Power,
Thou Tamer of the human breast,
Whose iron scourge and tort'ring hour,
The Bad affright, afflict the Best!
Bound in thy adamantine chain               5
The Proud are taught to taste of pain,
And purple Tyrants vainly groan
With pangs unfelt before, unpitied and alone.

When first thy Sire to send on earth
Virtue, his darling Child, designed,         10
To thee he gave the heav'nly Birth,
And bade to form her infant mind.
Stern rugged Nurse! thy rigid lore
With patience many a year she bore:
What sorrow was, thou bad'st her know,       15
And from her own she learned to melt at others'
    woe.

Scared at thy frown terrific, fly
Self-pleasing Folly's idle brood,
Wild Laughter, Noise, and thoughtless Joy,
And leave us leisure to be good.            20
Light they disperse, and with them go
The summer Friend, the flatt'ring Foe;
By vain Prosperity received,
To her they vow their truth, and are again be-
    lieved.

Wisdom in sable garb arrayed                 25
Immersed in rapt'rous thought profound,
And Melancholy, silent maid
With leaden eye, that loves the ground,
Still on thy solemn steps attend:
Warm Charity, the gen'ral Friend,            30
With Justice to herself severe,
And Pity dropping soft the sadly-pleasing tear.

Oh, gently on thy Suppliant's head,
Dread Goddess, lay thy chast'ning hand!
Not in thy Gorgon terrors clad,[3]           35
Nor circled with the vengeful Band
(As by the Impious thou art seen)
With thund'ring voice, and threat'ning mien,
With screaming Horror's funeral cry,
Despair, and fell Disease, and ghastly Pov-
    erty.                                    40

[1] Written in 1742; first published in 1753.
[2] Zeus has set men on the way to wisdom and decreed that they shall learn through suffering (lines
167–171).
[3] Gorgon means dreadful; the reference is to the
image on the shield of Pallas Athene. In the next
line "the vengeful Band" are the Furies.

Thy form benign, O Goddess, wear,
Thy milder influence impart,
Thy philosophic Train be there
To soften, not to wound my heart,
The gen'rous spark extinct revive, 45
Teach me to love and to forgive,
Exact my own defects to scan,
What others are, to feel, and know myself a
   Man.

## The Progress of Poesy [1]

### A *Pindaric Ode*

Φωνᾶντα συνετοῖσιν· ἐς
Δὲ τὸ πᾶν ἑρμηνέων χατίζει.[2]
    —PINDAR, *Olymp. II.*

#### I. STROPHE

Awake, Aeolian lyre,[3] awake,
And give to rapture all thy trembling strings.
From Helicon's harmonious springs
A thousand rills their mazy progress take:
The laughing flowers, that round them blow, 5
Drink life and fragrance as they flow.
Now the rich stream of music winds along
Deep, majestic, smooth, and strong,
Through verdant vales, and Ceres' golden
   reign:[4]
Now rolling down the steep amain, 10
Headlong, impetuous, see it pour:
The rocks, and nodding groves rebellow to the
   roar.

#### ANTISTROPHE

Oh! Sovereign of the willing soul,
Parent of sweet and solemn-breathing airs,
Enchanting shell![5] the sullen Cares, 15
And frantic Passions hear thy soft control.
On Thracia's hills the Lord of War,[6]
Has curbed the fury of his car,
And dropped his thirsty lance at thy command.
Perching on the sceptered hand 20
Of Jove, thy magic lulls the feathered king[7]
With ruffled plumes, and flagging wing:
Quenched in dark clouds of slumber lie
The terror of his beak, the lightnings of his eye.

#### EPODE

Thee the voice, the dance, obey, 25
Tempered to thy warbled lay.
O'er Idalia's[8] velvet-green

[1] Written in 1754; first published in 1757.
[2] A voice intelligible to the wise, but one that
needs interpreters for the rabble (lines 153–154).
[3] The lyre of Pindar.
[4] Fields over which Ceres reigns.
[5] The lyre was said to have been made first by
Hermes from a tortoise shell.
[6] Mars. Thrace was thought to be his favorite
abode.
[7] The eagle.
[8] A town in Cyprus containing a temple to Venus,
or Cytherea, as she was sometimes called.

The rosy-crownéd Loves are seen
On Cytherea's day
With antic Sports, and blue-eyed Pleasures, 30
Frisking light in frolic measures;
Now pursuing, now retreating,
Now in circling troops they meet:
To brisk notes in cadence beating
Glance their many-twinkling feet. 35
Slow melting strains their Queen's approach de-
   clare:
Where'er she turns the Graces homage pay.
With arms sublime, that float upon the air,
In gliding state she wins her easy way:
O'er her warm cheek, and rising bosom, move 40
The bloom of Young Desire, the purple light
   of Love.

#### II. STROPHE

Man's feeble race what Ills await,
Labor and Penury, the racks of Pain,
Disease, and Sorrow's weeping train,
And Death, sad refuge from the storms of Fate!
The fond complaint, my Song, disprove, 46
And justify the laws of Jove.
Say, has he giv'n in vain the heav'nly Muse?
Night, and all her sickly dews,
Her Specters wan, and Birds of boding cry, 50
He gives to range the dreary sky:
Till down the eastern cliffs afar
Hyperion's march[9] they spy, and glitt'ring
   shafts of war.

#### ANTISTROPHE

In climes beyond the solar road,
Where shaggy forms o'er ice-built mountains
   roam, 55
The Muse has broke the twilight-gloom
To cheer the shiv'ring Native's dull abode.
And oft, beneath the od'rous shade
Of Chili's boundless forests laid,
She deigns to hear the savage Youth repeat 60
In loose numbers wildly sweet
Their feather-cinctured Chiefs, and dusky
   Loves.
Her track, where'er the Goddess roves,
Glory pursue, and generous Shame,
Th' unconquerable Mind, and Freedom's holy
   flame. 65

#### EPODE

Woods, that wave o'er Delphi's steep,
Isles, that crown th' Aegean deep,
Fields, that cool Ilissus[10] laves,
Or where Maeander's[11] amber waves
In lingering Lab'rinths creep, 70
How do your tuneful Echoes languish,
Mute, but to the voice of Anguish?
Where each old poetic Mountain
Inspiration breathed around:
Ev'ry shade and hallowed Fountain 75

[9] The sunrise.
[10] A stream flowing through Athens.
[11] A river in Asia Minor.

Murmured deep a solemn sound:
Till the sad Nine in Greece's evil hour
Left their Parnassus for the Latian plains.
Alike they scorn the pomp of tyrant-Power,
And coward Vice, that revels in her chains. 80
When Latium had her lofty spirit lost,
They sought, O Albion! next thy sea-encircled
　　coast.[12]

### III. STROPHE

Far from the sun and summer-gale,
In thy green lap was Nature's Darling[13] laid,
What time, where lucid Avon strayed, 85
To Him the mighty Mother did unveil
Her awful face: The dauntless Child
Stretched forth his little arms, and smiled.
This pencil take (she said) whose colors clear
Richly paint the vernal year: 90
Thine too these golden keys, immortal Boy!
This can unlock the gates of Joy;
Of Horror that, and thrilling Fears,
Or ope the sacred source of sympathetic Tears.

### ANTISTROPHE

Nor second He,[14] that rode sublime 95
Upon the seraph-wings of Ecstasy,
The secrets of th' Abyss to spy.
He passed the flaming bounds of Place and
　　Time:
The living Throne, the sapphire-blaze,
Where Angels tremble, while they gaze, 100
He saw; but blasted with excess of light,
Closed his eyes in endless night.
Behold, where Dryden's less presumptuous car,
Wide o'er the fields of Glory bear
Two Coursers of ethereal race, 105
With necks in thunder clothed, and long-
　　resounding pace.

### EPODE

Hark, his hands the lyre explore!
Bright-eyed Fancy hovering o'er
Scatters from her pictured urn
Thoughts that breathe, and words that burn.
But ah! 'tis heard no more—— 111
Oh! Lyre divine, what daring Spirit
Wakes thee now? though he inherit
Nor the pride, nor ample pinion,
That the Theban Eagle bear[15] 115

[12] Gray's note on this epode is as follows: Progress of poetry from Greece to Italy, and from Italy
to England. Chaucer was not unacquainted with
the writings of Dante or of Petrarch. The Earl of
Surrey and Sir Tho. Wyatt had traveled in Italy
[Gray is wrong about Surrey, who was never in
Italy, though he spent some time in France], and
formed their taste there; Spenser imitated the Italian
writers; Milton improved on them: but this school
expired soon after the Restoration, and a new one
arose on the French model, which has subsisted ever
since.

[13] Shakespeare.　　　　[14] Milton.
[15] Pindar compares himself to that bird, and his
enemies to ravens that croak and clamor in vain

Sailing with supreme dominion
Through the azure deep of air:
Yet oft before his infant eyes would run
Such forms, as glitter in the Muse's ray
With orient hues, unborrowed of the Sun: 120
Yet shall he mount, and keep his distant way
Beyond the limits of a vulgar fate,
Beneath the Good how far—but far above the
　　Great.

# The Bard[1]

## A Pindaric Ode

### ADVERTISEMENT

*The following Ode is founded on a Tradi-
tion current in Wales, that Edward the First,
when he completed the conquest of that country, ordered all the Bards that fell into his
hands to be put to death.[2]*

### I. STROPHE

"Ruin seize thee, ruthless King!
Confusion on thy banners wait,
Though fanned by Conquest's crimson wing
They mock the air with idle state.
Helm, nor Hauberk's twisted mail, 5
Nor even thy virtues, Tyrant, shall avail
To save thy secret soul from nightly fears,
From Cambria's[3] curse, from Cambria's tears!"
Such were the sounds, that o'er the crested
　　pride
Of the first Edward scattered wild dismay, 10
As down the steep of Snowdon's[4] shaggy side
He wound with toilsome march his long array.
Stout Glo'ster[5] stood aghast in speechless
　　trance;
To arms! cried Mortimer,[6] and couched his
　　quiv'ring lance.

### ANTISTROPHE

On a rock, whose haughty brow 15
Frowns o'er old Conway's foaming flood,
Robed in the sable garb of woe,
With haggard eyes the Poet stood;

below, while it pursues its flight, regardless of their
noise (Gray's note).
[1] Begun in 1754 and finished in 1757, when it was
first published.
[2] This tradition has no foundation in fact. Edward I reigned from 1272 to 1307.
[3] Wales.
[4] A name given by the Saxons to that mountainous
tract which the Welsh themselves call *Craigian-
eryri:* it included all the highlands of Carnarvonshire and Merionethshire, as far east as the river
Conway (Gray's note).
[5] Gilbert de Clare, surnamed the Red, Earl of
Gloucester and Hertford, son-in-law to King Edward (Gray's note).
[6] Edmond de Mortimer, Lord of Wigmore. They
were both Lords-Marchers, whose lands lay on the
borders of Wales, and probably accompanied the
king in this expedition (Gray's note).

(Loose his beard, and hoary hair
Streamed, like a meteor, to the troubled air) [20]
And with a Master's hand, and Prophet's fire,
Struck the deep sorrows of his lyre.
"Hark, how each giant-oak, and desert cave,
Sighs to the torrent's awful voice beneath!
O'er thee, O King! their hundred arms they
wave,                                        [25]
Revenge on thee in hoarser murmurs breathe;
Vocal no more, since Cambria's fatal day,
To high-born Hoel's harp, or soft Llewellyn's
lay.

### EPODE

"Cold is Cadwallo's tongue,
That hushed the stormy main:                  [30]
Brave Urien sleeps upon his craggy bed:
Mountains, ye mourn in vain
Modred, whose magic song
Made huge Plinlimmon [7] bow his cloud-topped
head.
On dreary Arvon's shore they lie,[8]          [35]
Smeared with gore, and ghastly pale:
Far, far aloof th' affrighted ravens sail;
The famished Eagle screams, and passes by.
Dear lost companions of my tuneful art,
Dear, as the light that visits these sad eyes, [40]
Dear, as the ruddy drops that warm my heart,
Ye died amidst your dying country's cries—
No more I weep. They do not sleep.
On yonder cliffs, a grisly band,
I see them sit, they linger yet,              [45]
Avengers of their native land:
With me in dreadful harmony they join,
And weave with bloody hands the tissue of thy
line.

### II. STROPHE

"Weave the warp, and weave the woof,
The winding-sheet of Edward's race.           [50]
Give ample room, and verge enough
The characters of hell to trace.
Mark the year, and mark the night,
When Severn shall re-echo with affright
The shrieks of death, through Berkeley's roofs
that ring,                                    [55]
Shrieks of an agonizing King! [9]
She-Wolf [10] of France, with unrelenting fangs,
That tear'st the bowels of thy mangled Mate,
From thee be born, who o'er thy country
hangs [11]
The scourge of Heav'n. What Terrors round
him wait!                                     [60]
Amazement in his van, with Flight combined,
And sorrow's faded form, and solitude behind.

[7] A mountain in Wales.
[8] The shores of Carnarvonshire opposite to the isle
of Anglesey (Gray's note).
[9] Edward II, murdered in Berkeley Castle, 1327.
[10] Isabel of France, Edward II's adulterous queen
(Gray's note).
[11] Edward III. The reference is to his triumphs in
France.

### ANTISTROPHE

"'Mighty Victor, mighty Lord,
Low on his funeral couch he lies!
No pitying heart, no eye, afford              [65]
A tear to grace his obsequies.
Is the sable Warrior [12] fled?
Thy son is gone. He rests among the Dead.
The Swarm, that in thy noon-tide beam were
born?
Gone to salute the rising Morn.               [70]
Fair laughs [13] the Morn, and soft the Zephyr
blows,
While proudly riding o'er the azure realm
In gallant trim the gilded Vessel goes;
Youth on the prow, and Pleasure at the helm;
Regardless of the sweeping Whirlwind's sway,
That, hushed in grim repose, expects his eve-
ning prey.                                    [76]

### EPODE

"'Fill high the sparkling bowl,
The rich repast prepare,
Reft of a crown, he yet may share the feast:
Close by the regal chair                      [80]
Fell Thirst and Famine scowl
A baleful smile upon their baffled Guest.
Heard ye the din of battle bray,
Lance to lance, and horse to horse?
Long Years of havoc [14] urge their destined
course,                                       [85]
And through the kindred squadrons mow their
way.
Ye Towers of Julius,[15] London's lasting shame,
With many a foul and midnight murder fed,
Revere his Consort's [16] faith, his Father's [17]
fame,
And spare the meek Usurper's [18] holy head.  [90]
Above, below, the rose,[19] of snow,
Twined with her blushing foe, we spread:
The bristled Boar [20] in infant gore
Wallows beneath the thorny shade.
Now, Brothers, bending o'er th' accursèd
loom                                          [95]
Stamp we our vengeance deep, and ratify his
doom.

### III. STROPHE

"'Edward, lo! to sudden fate
(Weave we the woof. The thread is spun.)

[12] The Black Prince.
[13] These lines describe the reign of Richard II and
(in the epode) his death by starvation.
[14] The Wars of the Roses.
[15] The Tower of London. The oldest part of that
structure is vulgarly attributed to Julius Caesar
(Gray's note).
[16] Margaret of Anjou.      [17] Henry V.
[18] Henry VI, who was "very near being canonized"
(Gray).
[19] The white and red roses, devices of York and
Lancaster (Gray).
[20] The silver boar was the device of Richard III
(Gray). The "infant gore" is that of the murdered
princes.

Half of thy heart we consecrate.
(The web is wove. The work is done.)' 100
Stay, O stay! nor thus forlorn
Leave me unblessed, unpitied, here to mourn:
In yon bright track, that fires the western skies,
They melt, they vanish from my eyes.
But oh! what solemn scenes on Snowdon's
   height 105
Descending slow their glitt'ring skirts unroll?
Visions of glory, spare my aching sight,
Ye unborn Ages, crowd not on my soul!
No more our long-lost Arthur we bewail.
All-hail, ye genuine Kings,[21] Britannia's Issue,
   hail! 110

### ANTISTROPHE

"Girt with many a Baron bold
Sublime their starry fronts they rear;
And gorgeous Dames, and Statesmen old
In bearded majesty, appear.
In the midst a Form divine! [22] 115
Her eye proclaims her of the Briton-Line;
Her lion-port, her awe-commanding face,
Attempered sweet to virgin grace.
What strings symphonious tremble in the air,
What strains of vocal transport round her play!
Hear from the grave, great Taliessin, hear: [21]
They breathe a soul to animate thy clay.
Bright Rapture calls, and soaring, as she sings,
Waves in the eye of Heav'n her many-colored
   wings.

### EPODE

"The verse adorn again 125
Fierce War, and faithful Love,
And Truth severe, by fairy Fiction dressed.[23]
In buskined measures move
Pale Grief, and pleasing Pain,
With Horror, Tyrant of the throbbing breast.[24]
A Voice, as of the Cherub-Choir, 131
Gales from blooming Eden bear; [25]
And distant warblings lessen on my ear,
That lost in long futurity expire.[26]
Fond impious Man, think'st thou, yon san-
   guine cloud, 135
Raised by thy breath, has quenched the Orb of
   day?
To-morrow he repairs the golden flood,
And warms the nations with redoubled ray.
Enough for me: With joy I see
The different doom our Fates assign. 140
Be thine Despair, and sceptered Care,
To triumph, and to die, are mine."

[21] Both Merlin and Taliessin [Cymric bard, sixth century] had prophesied that the Welsh should regain their sovereignty over this island, which seemed to be accomplished in the House of Tudor [beginning with Henry VII] (Gray).
[22] Queen Elizabeth.
[23] The reference is to Spenser's *Faerie Queene*.
[24] Shakespeare.     [25] Milton.
[26] The succession of poets after Milton's time (Gray).

He spoke, and headlong from the mountain's
   height
Deep in the roaring tide he plunged to endless
   night.

# The Fatal Sisters

### *An Ode* [1]

### PREFACE

*In the Eleventh Century Sigurd, Earl of the Orkney Islands, went with a fleet of ships and a considerable body of troops into Ireland, to the assistance of Sictryg with the silken beard, who was then making war on his father-in-law Brian, King of Dublin: the Earl and all his forces were cut to pieces, and Sictryg was in danger of a total defeat; but the enemy had a greater loss by the death of Brian, their King, who fell in action. On Christmas day (the day of the battle), a Native of Caithness in Scotland saw at a distance a number of persons on horseback riding full speed towards a hill, and seeming to enter into it. Curiosity led him to follow them, till looking through an opening in the rocks he saw twelve gigantic figures resembling women: they were all employed about a loom; and as they wove, they sung the following dreadful Song; which when they had finished, they tore the web into twelve pieces, and (each taking her portion) galloped Six to the North and as many to the South.*

Now the storm begins to lower
(Haste, the loom of Hell prepare),
Iron-sleet of arrowy shower
Hurtles in the darkened air.

Glitt'ring lances are the loom, 5
Where the dusky warp we strain,
Weaving many a Soldier's doom,
Orkney's woe, and Randver's bane.

See the grisly texture grow
('Tis of human entrails made),
And the weights, that play below, 10
Each a gasping Warrior's head.

[1] Written in 1761; first published in 1768. Gray made this version from a Latin translation of an Old Norse poem. The original text, with an English prose translation, is to be found in Vigfusson and Powell's *Corpus Poeticum Boreale*, I, 281–283. The prose which precedes and follows the poem Gray embodied in the Preface printed above. The event which it celebrates is the Battle of Clontarf, fought 23 April (not on Chirstmas day, as Gray says), 1014. Sictryg, it may be noted, was King of Dublin; Brian, King of Ireland. Brian was Sictryg's stepfather, which may be what Gray means when he says "father-in-law." The "gigantic figures resembling women" are the Valkyries, who in the poem are represented as weaving the web of battle.

Shafts for shuttles, dipped in gore,
Shoot the trembling cords along.
Sword, that once a Monarch bore,    15
Keep the tissue close and strong.

Mista black, terrific Maid,
Sangrida, and Hilda [2] see,
Join the wayward work to aid:
'Tis the woof of victory.    20

Ere the ruddy sun be set,
Pikes must shiver, javelins sing,
Blade with clattering buckler meet,
Hauberk crash, and helmet ring.

(Weave the crimson web of war)    25
Let us go, and let us fly,
Where our Friends the conflict share,
Where they triumph, where they die.

As the paths of fate we tread,
Wading through th' ensanguined field:    30
Gondula, and Geira, spread
O'er the youthful King [3] your shield.

We the reins to slaughter give,
Ours to kill, and ours to spare:
Spite of danger he shall live.    35
(Weave the crimson web of war.)

They, whom once the desert-beach
Pent within its bleak domain,
Soon their ample sway shall stretch
O'er the plenty of the plain.    40

Low the dauntless Earl is laid,
Gored with many a gaping wound:
Fate demands a nobler head;
Soon a King [4] shall bite the ground.

Long his loss shall Eirin [5] weep,    45
Ne'er again his likeness see;
Long her strains in sorrow steep,
Strains of Immortality!

Horror covers all the heath,
Clouds of carnage blot the sun.    50
Sisters, weave the web of death;
Sisters, cease, the work is done.

Hail the task, and hail the hands!
Songs of joy and triumph sing!
Joy to the victorious bands;    55
Triumph to the younger King.

Mortal, thou that hear'st the tale,
Learn the tenor of our song.
Scotland, through each winding vale
Far and wide the notes prolong.    60

[2] These are names of Valkyries, as are also the
names in the third stanza below.
[3] Sictryg.    [4] Brian.    [5] Ireland.

Sisters, hence with spurs of speed:
Each her thundering falchion [6] wield;
Each bestride her sable steed.
Hurry, hurry to the field.

# Elegy

### Written in a Country Church-Yard [1]

The Curfew tolls the knell of parting day,
    The lowing herd wind slowly o'er the lea,
The plowman homeward plods his weary way,
    And leaves the world to darkness and to me.

Now fades the glimmering landscape on the
        sight,    5
    And all the air a solemn stillness holds,
Save where the beetle wheels his droning flight,
    And drowsy tinklings lull the distant folds;

Save that from yonder ivy-mantled tower
    The moping owl does to the moon com-
        plain    10
Of such, as wand'ring near her secret bower,
    Molest her ancient solitary reign.

Beneath those rugged elms, that yew-tree's
        shade,
    Where heaves the turf in many a mold'ring
        heap,
Each in his narrow cell for ever laid,    15
    The rude Forefathers of the hamlet sleep.

The breezy call of incense-breathing Morn,
    The swallow twitt'ring from the straw-built
        shed,
The cock's shrill clarion, or the echoing horn,
    No more shall rouse them from their lowly
        bed.    20

For them no more the blazing hearth shall
        burn,
    Or busy housewife ply her evening care:
No children run to lisp their sire's return,
    Or climb his knees the envied kiss to share.

Oft did the harvest to their sickle yield,    25
    Their furrow oft the stubborn glebe has
        broke;
How jocund did they drive their team afield!
    How bowed the woods beneath their sturdy
        stroke!

Let not Ambition mock their useful toil,
    Their homely joys, and destiny obscure;    30
Nor Grandeur hear with a disdainful smile,
    The short and simple annals of the poor.

The boast of heraldry, the pomp of pow'r,
    And all that beauty, all that wealth e'er gave,
Awaits alike th' inevitable hour.    35
    The paths of glory lead but to the grave.

[6] Short sword.
[1] Completed in 1750; first published in 1751.

Nor you, ye Proud, impute to These the fault,
   If Mem'ry o'er their Tomb no Trophies raise,
Where through the long-drawn aisle and
   fretted vault
The pealing anthem swells the note of
   praise.       40

Can storied [2] urn or animated bust
   Back to its mansion call the fleeting breath?
Can Honor's voice provoke the silent dust,
   Or Flatt'ry sooth the dull cold ear of Death?

Perhaps in this neglected spot is laid    45
   Some heart once pregnant with celestial fire;
Hands, that the rod of empire might have
   swayed,
   Or waked to ecstasy the living lyre.

But Knowledge to their eyes her ample page
   Rich with the spoils of time did ne'er un-
     roll;     50
Chill Penury repressed their noble rage,
   And froze the genial [3] current of the soul.

Full many a gem of purest ray serene,
   The dark unfathomed caves of ocean bear:
Full many a flower is born to blush unseen,  55
   And waste its sweetness on the desert air.

Some village-Hampden,[4] that with dauntless
   breast
The little Tyrant of his fields withstood;
Some mute inglorious Milton here may rest,
   Some Cromwell guiltless of his country's
     blood.     60

Th' applause of list'ning senates to command,
   The threats of pain and ruin to despise,
To scatter plenty o'er a smiling land,
   And read their hist'ry in a nation's eyes,

Their lot forbade: nor circumscribed alone  65
   Their growing virtues, but their crimes con-
     fined;
Forbade to wade through slaughter to a throne,
   And shut the gates of mercy on mankind,

The struggling pangs of conscious truth to hide,
   To quench the blushes of ingenuous shame,
Or heap the shrine of Luxury and Pride   71
   With incense kindled at the Muse's flame.

Far from the madding crowd's ignoble strife,
   Their sober wishes never learned to stray;
Along the cool sequestered vale of life   75
   They kept the noiseless tenor of their way.

Yet e'en these bones from insult to protect
   Some frail memorial still erected nigh,

[2] Inscribed.         [3] Enlivening.
[4] John Hampden, who in 1636 refused to pay the
ship-money demanded by Charles I.

With uncouth rimes and shapeless sculpture
   decked,
   Implores the passing tribute of a sigh.   80

Their name, their years, spelt by th' unlettered
   muse,
   The place of fame and elegy supply:
And many a holy text around she strews,
   That teach the rustic moralist to die.

For who to dumb Forgetfulness a prey,   85
   This pleasing anxious being e'er resigned,
Left the warm precincts of the cheerful day,
   Nor cast one longing ling'ring look behind?

On some fond breast the parting soul relies,
   Some pious drops the closing eye requires; 90
E'en from the tomb the voice of Nature cries,
   E'en in our Ashes live their wonted Fires.

For thee, who mindful of th' unhonored Dead
   Dost in these lines their artless tale relate;
If chance, by lonely contemplation led,   95
   Some kindred Spirit shall inquire thy fate,

Haply some hoary-headed Swain may say,
   "Oft have we seen him at the peep of dawn
Brushing with hasty steps the dews away
   To meet the sun upon the upland lawn. 100

"There at the foot of yonder nodding beech
   That wreathes its old fantastic roots so high,
His listless length at noontide would he stretch,
   And pore upon the brook that babbles by.

"Hard by yon wood, now smiling as in scorn,
   Mutt'ring his wayward fancies he would
     rove,    106
Now drooping, woeful wan, like one forlorn,
   Or crazed with care, or crossed in hopeless
     love.

"One morn I missed him on the customed hill,
   Along the heath and near his fav'rite tree; 110
Another came; nor yet beside the rill,
   Nor up the lawn, nor at the wood was he;

"The next with dirges due in sad array
   Slow through the church-way path we saw
     him borne.
Approach and read (for thou can'st read) the
   lay,    115
   Graved on the stone beneath yon agéd
     thorn."

### THE EPITAPH

*Here rests his head upon the lap of Earth*
   *A Youth to Fortune and to Fame unknown.*
*Fair Science [5] frowned not on his humble birth,*
   *And Melancholy marked him for her own.*

[5] Learning.

Large was his bounty, and his soul sincere, [121]
   Heav'n did a recompense as largely send:
He gave to Mis'ry all he had, a tear,
   He gained from Heav'n ('twas all he wished)
     a friend.

No farther seek his merits to disclose, [125]
   Or draw his frailties from their dread abode
(There they alike in trembling hope repose),
   The bosom of his Father and his God.

# Sonnet

## On the Death of Richard West [1]

In vain to me the smiling Mornings shine,
   And redd'ning Phoebus lifts his golden Fire:
The Birds in vain their amorous Descant [2] join;
   Or cheerful Fields resume their green Attire:
These Ears, alas! for other Notes repine,   5
   A different Object do these Eyes require.
My lonely Anguish melts no Heart, but mine;
   And in my Breast the imperfect Joys expire.
Yet Morning smiles the busy Race to cheer,

[1] Written in 1742; first published in 1775.
[2] Melody.

And new-born Pleasure brings to happier
   Men:                 10
The Fields to all their wonted Tribute bear;
   To warm their little Loves the Birds com-
     plain;
I fruitless mourn to him that cannot hear,
   And weep the more, because I weep in vain.

# Sketch of His Own Character [3]

Too poor for a bribe, and too proud to impor-
   tune;
He had not the method of making a fortune;
Could love, and could hate, so was thought
   somewhat odd;
No very great wit, he believed in a God.
A Post or a Pension he did not desire,   5
But left Church and State to Charles Town-
   shend and Squire.[4]

[3] Written in 1761; first published in 1775.
[4] Townshend was Chancellor of the Exchequer in
1767; he was a politician, orator, and man of the
world. Samuel Squire was a fellow of St. John's
College, Cambridge; in 1761 he was Bishop of St.
David's.

# Samuel Johnson

## 1709 - 1784

Johnson's father was a bookseller doing business in Lichfield, and there Johnson was born on 18 September, 1709. There was little money in the family, and his struggle with poverty began almost with his birth. The one fortunate circumstance of his youth was the fact that he had the freedom of his father's shop; his early education was got largely from wide reading in the books which the people of Lichfield did not buy. In 1728 Johnson entered Pembroke College, Oxford, but was able to remain there only fourteen months. He then did not know where to turn for a living. He took a position in a school, but such were schools in that time that after a few months "he relinquished a situation which all his life long he recollected with the strongest aversion, and even a degree of horror." He next made unsuccessful attempts to obtain appointment to headmasterships, and almost equally unsuccessful attempts to earn money by literary hackwork. When he was twenty-six he married Mrs. Porter, a widow who was many years older than himself, whom he regarded with true and undiminished affection until her death in 1752, and the loss of whom he did not cease to lament until his own death. With a little money which his wife had, Johnson opened a school at Edial, near Lichfield—a school which was never attended by more than three pupils and which he soon abandoned. Other efforts having failed, he now determined to try his fortune in London, whither he went in the company of one of his three former pupils, David Garrick, who was to become the greatest of English actors.

Johnson found employment in the capital, managing to make a bare living, often enough to do little better than escape starvation, by means of hackwriting for the booksellers. In 1738 he published London, a satirical poem, imitated from Juvenal after the manner of Pope's imitations of Horace, which won him immediate recognition from the best judges of the day, including Pope himself, but which brought him very little money. Gradually he became known, but could not cease struggling, by means of all kinds of literary work that offered, for a bare subsistence. In 1745 he projected a new edition of Shakespeare, but did not actually publish it until 1765. In 1747 he announced his plan for what was his greatest work, though a work which has now little more than historical interest and one whose value it is not entirely easy for us to grasp. This was his Dictionary of the English Language, which it took him and his assistants eight years of hard work to complete. Meanwhile Johnson had published The Vanity of Human Wishes in 1749, had seen his classical tragedy, Irene, acted with little success, and had published two series of periodical essays, The Rambler (1750–1752) and The Adventurer (1753). A third series, The Idler, was written from 1758 to 1760. Early in 1759 occurred the death of his mother, and it was to meet the expenses of her illness and death that he wrote Rasselas. His need was urgent, and he wrote the tale within the space of a single week or, at the most, if we are to accept O. F. Emerson's criticism of Boswell's account, within a period of ten days—a period during which he was distracted by fears and sorrow and was expecting daily to hear the news of his mother's death. Though Johnson all his life had a pronounced tendency to indolence, his mind could on occasion work, as this instance proves, with astonishing rapidity. In 1762, two years after the accession of George III, however, his long struggle with poverty ceased. The Tories at that time returned to power; and Johnson, who was strongly attached to their party, was granted a pension of £300, which was sufficient to make him fairly comfortable through the remainder of his life. From this time until within a few years of the end of his life, he wrote but little. These years after 1762 were the years of his famous talk. It was in 1763 that he met Boswell, who was to record it all in the greatest of English biographies, and it was in 1764 that the Club (later called the Literary Club) was founded, which brought together at once some of Johnson's closest friends and a remarkable group of the men of that age whose names time has not obliterated—Sir Joshua Reynolds, Edmund Burke, Garrick, Boswell, Goldsmith, Charles James Fox, Thomas and Joseph Warton, Edward Gibbon, and others, including R. B. Sheridan and Bishop Percy. These were the happiest years of Johnson's life, and at the close they were crowned by a great achievement. In the late 1770's a group of booksellers planned to issue a collection of the works of the English poets, and Johnson undertook to write biographical and critical notices of those included in the series. The result was his Lives of the Poets, which contains some of his best and easiest writing, and which, as a monument of the man and of his type of criticism, is of lasting interest and importance.

Johnson's fame remains secure, as secure as that of any man in the annals of English literature. As a writer, he has had the curious fate to be overshadowed by his own biography, but the day has now happily passed when one can think that one sufficiently knows Johnson from the pages of Boswell. The man, truly enough, was greater than any of his works; yet those works have a vitality which Johnson's enemies have belittled in vain. In them still lives a man "who cared passionately for truth and nothing at all for novelty." And one must go to the writer, as well as to the talker, if one is to understand what Sir Joshua Reynolds gratefully said of his friend: "I acknowledge the highest obligations to him. He may be said to have formed my mind, and to have brushed from it a great deal of rubbish. . . . He qualified my mind to think justly."

A new collected edition of Johnson's Works is being edited by Allen T. Hazen et al. (New Haven, 1958–  ); of The Lives of the English Poets there is an excellent separate edition, ed. George B. Hill (Oxford, 1905); London and The Vanity of Human Wishes have been published in a volume with an introduction by T. S. Eliot (London, 1930). The Poems have been edited by D. N. Smith and E. L. McAdam (Oxford, 1941), and the Letters by R. W. Chapman (Oxford, 1952). The Critical Opinions of Samuel Johnson have been gathered together in a convenient form by J. E. Brown (Princeton, 1926). The most important biographical account is, naturally, Boswell's Life of Johnson together with Boswell's Journal of a Tour of the Hebrides and Johnson's Diary of a Journey into North Wales, ed. George B. Hill, rev. L. F. Powell (Oxford, 1934–1950). Joseph W. Krutch's Samuel Johnson (New York, 1944), Walter J. Bate's The Achievement of Johnson (New York, 1955), and T. S. Eliot's "Johnson as Critic and Poet" in his On Poetry and Poets (London, 1957), are valuable studies. The background of the period is thoroughly covered in the collection of essays, Johnson's England; an Account of the Life and Manners of His Age, ed. A. S. Turberville (Oxford, 1933).

# The Vanity of Human Wishes
## In Imitation of the Tenth Satire of Juvenal

Let Observation with extensive view
Survey mankind, from China to Peru;
Remark each anxious toil, each eager strife,
And watch the busy scenes of crowded life;
Then say how hope and fear, desire and hate,
O'erspread with snares the clouded maze of fate,                                6
Where wav'ring man, betrayed by vent'rous pride
To chase the dreary paths without a guide,
As treach'rous phantoms in the mist delude,
Shuns fancied ills, or chases airy [1] good;        10
How rarely reason guides the stubborn choice,
Rules the bold hand, or prompts the suppliant voice,
How Nations sink, by darling schemes oppressed,
When vengeance listens to the fool's request.
Fate wings with ev'ry wish th'afflictive dart, 15
Each gift of nature and each grace of art;
With fatal heat impetuous courage glows,
With fatal sweetness elocution flows,
Impeachment stops the speaker's pow'rful breath,
And restless fire precipitates on death.        20
  But, scarce observed, the knowing and the bold
Fall in the gen'ral massacre of gold;
Wide wasting pest! that rages unconfined,
And crowds with crimes the records of mankind;
For gold his sword the hireling ruffian draws, 25
For gold the hireling judge distorts the laws;
Wealth heaped on wealth, not truth nor safety buys,
The dangers gather as the treasures rise.
  Let Hist'ry tell where rival kings command,
And dubious title shakes the madded land, 30
When statutes glean the refuse of the sword,[2]

[1] Unreal.
[2] Statutes execute those spared by war.

How much more safe the vassal than the lord:
Low skulks the hind beneath the rage of power,
And leaves the wealthy traitor in the Tower,
Untouched his cottage, and his slumbers sound,
Though Confiscation's vultures hover round. 36
　The needy traveller, serene and gay,
Walks the wild heath, and sings his toil away.
Does envy seize thee? crush th'upbraiding joy,
Increase his riches, and his peace destroy;　40
Now fears in dire vicissitude invade,
The rustling brake alarms, and quiv'ring shade,
Nor light nor darkness bring his pain relief,
One shows the plunder, and one hides the thief.
　Yet still one gen'ral cry the skies assails,　45
And gain and grandeur load the tainted gales:
Few know the toiling statesman's fear or care,
Th'insidious rival and the gaping heir.
Once more, Democritus,[3] arise on earth,
With cheerful wisdom and instructive mirth,
See motley life in modern trappings dressed,
And feed with varied fools th'eternal jest:　52
Thou who could'st laugh where want enchained
　caprice,
Toil crushed conceit,[4] and man was of a piece;
Where wealth unloved without a mourner died;
And scarce a sycophant was fed by pride;　56
Where ne'er was known the form of mock
　debate,[5]
Or seen a new-made mayor's unwieldy state;
Where change of fav'rites made no change of
　laws,
And senates heard before they judged a cause;
How would'st thou shake at Britain's modish
　tribe,　61
Dart the quick taunt, and edge the piercing
　gibe?
Attentive truth and nature to descry,
And pierce each scene with philosophic eye,
To thee were solemn toys, or empty show,　65
The robes of pleasure and the veils of woe:
All aid the farce, and all thy mirth maintain,
Whose joys are causeless, or whose griefs are
　vain.
　Such was the scorn that filled the sage's
　mind,
Renewed at ev'ry glance on human kind;　70
How just that scorn ere yet thy voice declare,
Search ev'ry state, and canvass ev'ry pray'r.
　Unnumbered suppliants crowd Preferment's
　gate,
Athirst for wealth, and burning to be great;
Delusive Fortune hears th'incessant call,　75
They mount, they shine, evaporate, and fall.
On ev'ry stage the foes of peace attend,
Hate dogs their flight, and insult mocks their
　end.
Love ends with hope, the sinking statesman's
　door

[3] The laughing philosopher, a Greek of the fifth
century B.C.
[4] Empty opinion.
[5] Parliamentary debate that was unnecessary since
the government had already made up its mind.

Pours in the morning worshipper no more;　80
For growing names the weekly scribbler lies,
To growing wealth the dedicator flies;
From ev'ry room descends the painted face,
That hung the bright palladium [6] of the place;
And, smoked in kitchens, or in auctions sold,　85
To better features yields the frame of gold;
For now no more we trace in ev'ry line
Heroic worth, benevolence divine:
The form distorted justifies the fall,
And detestation rids th'indignant wall.　90
　But will not Britain hear the last appeal,
Sign her foes' doom, or guard her fav'rites' zeal?
Through Freedom's sons no more remonstrance
　rings,
Degrading nobles and controlling kings;
Our supple tribes repress their patriot throats,　95
And ask no questions but the price of votes;
With weekly libels and septennial ale,[7]
Their wish is full to riot and to rail.
　In full-blown dignity see Wolsey [8] stand,
Law in his voice, and fortune in his hand;　100
To him, the church, the realm, their pow'rs
　consign,
Through him the rays of regal bounty shine,
Turned by his nod the stream of honor flows,
His smile alone security bestows:
Still to new heights his restless wishes tow'r,　105
Claim leads to claim, and pow'r advances
　pow'r;
Till conquest unresisted ceased to please,
And rights submitted left him none to seize.
At length his sov'reign frowns—the train of
　state
Mark the keen glance, and watch the sign to
　hate.　110
Where'er he turns, he meets a stranger's eye,
His suppliants scorn him, and his followers fly;
Now drops at once the pride of awful state,
The golden canopy, the glitt'ring plate,
The regal palace, the luxurious board,　115
The liv'ried army, and the menial lord.
With age, with cares, with maladies oppressed,
He seeks the refuge of monastic rest.
Grief aids disease, remembered folly stings,
And his last sighs reproach the faith of kings.
　Speak thou, whose thoughts at humble peace
　repine,　121
Shall Wolsey's wealth, with Wolsey's end, be
　thine?
Or liv'st thou now, with safer pride content,
The wisest justice on the banks of Trent?
For, why did Wolsey, near the steeps of fate,
On weak foundations raise th'enormous weight?
Why but to sink beneath misfortune's blow,　127
With louder ruin to the gulfs below?

[6] Protective image.
[7] Ale dispersed during the parliamentary elections
which had to be held every seven years.
[8] Cardinal Wolsey (c. 1471–1530), chief minister
to Henry VIII. After losing the king's favor, he
retired and died in a monastery shortly before he
was to be executed.

What gave great Villiers [9] to th'assassin's
　　knife,
And fixed disease on Harley's [10] closing life?
What murdered Wentworth,[11] and what exiled
　　Hyde,[12]　　　　　　　　　　　　　131
By kings protected, and to kings allied?
What but their wish indulged in courts to
　　shine,
And pow'r too great to keep, or to resign?

When first the college rolls receive his name,
The young enthusiast quits his ease for fame;
Through all his veins the fever of renown [137]
Burns from the strong contagion of the gown;
O'er Bodley's dome [13] his future labors spread,
And Bacon's mansion [14] trembles o'er his head.
Are these thy views? Proceed, illustrious youth,
And Virtue guard thee to the throne of
　　Truth!　　　　　　　　　　　　　142
Yet, should thy soul indulge the gen'rous heat
Till captive Science yields her last retreat;
Should reason guide thee with her brightest ray,
And pour on misty Doubt resistless day; [146]
Should no false kindness lure to loose delight,
Nor praise relax, nor difficulty fright;
Should tempting Novelty thy cell refrain,
And Sloth effuse her opiate fumes in vain; [150]
Should Beauty blunt on fops her fatal dart,
Nor claim the triumph of a lettered heart;
Should no disease thy torpid veins invade,
Nor Melancholy's phantoms haunt thy shade;
Yet hope not life from grief or danger free, [155]
Nor think the doom of man reversed for thee:
Deign on the passing world to turn thine eyes,
And pause awhile from Letters to be wise;
There mark what ills the scholar's life assail,
Toil, envy, want, the patron, and the gaol. [160]
See nations, slowly wise and meanly just,
To buried merit raise the tardy bust.
If dreams yet flatter, once again attend;
Here Lydiat's life, and Galileo's, end.[15]

　　Nor deem, when Learning her vast prize
　　　bestows,　　　　　　　　　　165

[9] George Villiers, first Duke of Buckingham, favorite of James I and Charles I, slain by an assassin in 1628.
[10] Robert Harley, first Earl of Oxford, leader of the Tories during the reign of Queen Anne, but impeached in 1717.
[11] Sir Thomas Wentworth, first Earl of Strafford, the adviser of Charles I, executed by a bill of Parliament in 1641.
[12] Edward Hyde, first Earl of Clarendon, the adviser of Charles II and author of the great *History of the Rebellion*. He was exiled in 1667; previously his daughter had married the Duke of York, who later became James II.
[13] The Bodleian Library at Oxford.
[14] A cell in an old tower at Oxford, said to have been built by Roger Bacon in the thirteenth century.
[15] Lydiat (1572–1646) was an English mathematician who died in misery after having been imprisoned by the Roundheads; Galileo (1564–1642) spent the end of his life in blindness and as the prisoner of the Inquisition.

The glitt'ring eminence exempt from foes;
See, when the vulgar 'scape, despised or awed,
Rebellion's vengeful talons seize on Laud.[16]
From meaner minds, though smaller fines
　　content,
The plundered palace, or sequestered rent; [170]
Marked out for dang'rous parts, he meets the
　　shock,
And fatal Learning leads him to the block:
Around his tomb let Art and Genius weep,
But hear his death, ye blockheads, hear and
　　sleep.
　　The festal blazes, the triumphal show, [175]
The ravished standard, and the captive foe,
The senate's thanks, the Gazette's pompous
　　tale,
With force resistless o'er the brave prevail.
Such bribes the rapid Greek o'er Asia whirled,
For such the steady Romans shook the world;
For such in distant lands the Britons shine, [181]
And stain with blood the Danube or the
　　Rhine; [17]
This pow'r has praise, that virtue scarce can
　　warm
Till Fame supplies the universal charm.
Yet Reason frowns on War's unequal game, [185]
Where wasted nations raise a single name;
And mortgaged states their grandsires' wreaths
　　regret,
From age to age in everlasting debt;
Wreaths which at last the dear-bought right
　　convey
To rust on medals, or on stones decay. [190]
　　On what foundation stands the warrior's
　　　pride,
How just his hopes, let Swedish Charles [18] decide;
A frame of adamant, a soul of fire,
No dangers fright him, and no labors tire;
O'er love, o'er fear, extends his wide domain,
Unconquered lord of pleasure and of pain; [196]
No joys to him pacific sceptres yield,
War sounds the trump, he rushes to the field;
Behold surrounding kings their pow'rs combine,
And one capitulate, and one resign; [19]　[200]
Peace courts his hand, but spreads her charms
　　in vain;
"Think nothing gained," he cries, "till nought
　　remain,
On Moscow's walls till Gothic standards fly,
And all be mine beneath the polar sky."
The march begins in military state, [205]
And nations on his eye suspended wait;

[16] William Laud (1573–1645), Archbishop of Canterbury and one of the strongest opponents of the Puritans. His palace was plundered, his rents sequestered; and in the end he was executed by his enemies.
[17] References to the brilliant campaigns of the Duke of Marlborough in 1702–1704.
[18] Charles XII of Sweden (1682–1718).
[19] Respectively Charles IV of Denmark and August II of Poland.

Stern Famine guards the solitary coast,
And Winter barricades the realms of Frost;
He comes, nor want nor cold his course delay;—
Hide, blushing Glory, hide Pultowa's day: [20] 210
The vanquished hero leaves his broken bands,
And shows his miseries in distant lands;
Condemned a needy suppliant to wait,
While ladies interpose, and slaves debate.
But did not Chance at length the error mend?
Did no subverted empire mark his end?     216
Did rival monarchs give the fatal wound?
Or hostile millions press him to the ground?
His fall was destined to a barren strand,
A petty fortress, and a dubious hand; [21]     220
He left the name at which the world grew pale,
To point a moral, or adorn a tale.
All times their scenes of pompous woes afford,
From Persia's tyrant to Bavaria's lord.
In gay hostility and barb'rous pride,     225
With half mankind embattled at his side,
Great Xerxes [22] comes to seize the certain prey,
And starves exhausted regions in his way;
Attendant Flatt'ry counts his myriads o'er,
Till counted myriads soothe his pride no more;
Fresh praise is tried till madness fires his mind,
The waves he lashes, and enchains the wind; [23]
New pow'rs are claimed, new pow'rs are still
    bestowed,
Till rude resistance lops the spreading god;
The daring Greeks deride the martial show, 235
And heap their valleys with the gaudy foe;
Th'insulted sea with humbler thought he gains,
A single skiff to speed his flight remains;
Th'incumbered oar scarce leaves the dreaded
    coast
Through purple billows and a floating host. 240
    The bold Bavarian,[23] in a luckless hour,
Tries the dread summits of a Caesarean pow'r,
With unexpected legions bursts away,
And sees defenseless realms receive his sway;
Short sway! fair Austria spreads her mournful
    charms,     245
The queen, the beauty, sets the world in arms;
From hill to hill the beacon's rousing blaze
Spreads wide the hope of plunder and of praise;
The fierce Croatian, and the wild Hussar,[24]
With all the sons of ravage crowd the war; 250
The baffled prince, in honor's flatt'ring bloom

Of hasty greatness, finds the fatal doom,
His foes' derision, and his subjects' blame,
And steals to death from anguish and from
    shame.
    Enlarge my life with multitude of days! 255
In health, in sickness, thus the suppliant prays;
Hides from himself his state, and shuns to
    know,
That life protracted is protracted woe.
Time hovers o'er, impatient to destroy,
And shuts up all the passages of joy:     260
In vain their gifts the bounteous seasons pour,
The fruit autumnal, and the vernal flow'r;
With listless eyes the dotard views the store,
He views, and wonders that they please no
    more.
Now pall the tasteless meats, and joyless wines,
And Luxury with sighs her slave resigns.     266
Approach, ye minstrels, try the soothing strain,
Diffuse the tuneful lenitives of pain:
No sounds, alas! would teach th'impervious ear,
Though dancing mountains witnessed Orpheus
    near;     270
Nor lute nor lyre his feeble pow'rs attend,
Nor sweeter music of a virtuous friend;
But everlasting dictates crowd his tongue,
Perversely grave, or positively wrong.
The still returning tale, and ling'ring jest, 275
Perplex the fawning niece and pampered guest,
While growing hopes scarce awe the gath'ring
    sneer,
And scarce a legacy can bribe to hear;
The watchful guests still hint the last offense;
The daughter's petulance, the son's expense, 280
Improve his heady rage with treach'rous skill,
And mould his passions till they make his will.
    Unnumbered maladies his joints invade,
Lay siege to life, and press the dire blockade;
But unextinguished Av'rice still remains,     285
And dreaded losses aggravate his pains;
He turns, with anxious heart and crippled
    hands,
His bonds of debt, and mortgages of lands;
Or views his coffers with suspicious eyes,
Unlocks his gold, and counts it till he dies. 290
    But grant, the virtues of a temp'rate prime
Bless with an age exempt from scorn and crime;
An age that melts with unperceived decay,
And glides in modest innocence away;
Whose peaceful day Benevolence endears, 295
Whose night congratulating Conscience cheers;
The gen'ral fav'rite as the gen'ral friend:
Such age there is, and who shall wish its end?
    Yet ev'n on this her load Misfortune flings,
To press the weary minutes' flagging wings; 300
New sorrow rises as the day returns,
A sister sickens, or a daughter mourns.
Now kindred Merit fills the sable bier,
Now lacerated Friendship claims a tear;
Year chases year, decay pursues decay,     305
Still drops some joy from with'ring life away;
New forms arise, and diff'rent views engage,
Superfluous lags the vet'ran on the stage,

[20] The battle of Pultowa on July 9, 1709, after which the defeated Charles sought refuge in Turkey.

[21] Charles was slain, it is not known by whom, while besieging a small place on the coast of Norway.

[22] King of Persia 485–465 B.C. The naval battle of Salamis, to which Johnson alludes, took place in 480 B.C.

[23] Charles Albert, Elector of Bavaria, whose attempt to gain the crown of the Holy Roman Empire led to the struggle with Queen Maria Theresa which is known as the War of the Austrian Succession (1740–1748). The Elector died in disgrace in 1745.

[24] Originally a Hungarian light cavalryman.

Till pitying Nature signs the last release,
And bids afflicted worth retire to peace.   310
  But few there are whom hours like these
      await,
Who set unclouded in the gulfs of Fate.
From Lydia's monarch [25] should the search
      descend,
By Solon cautioned to regard his end,
In life's last scene what prodigies surprise,   315
Fears of the brave, and follies of the wise!
From Marlb'rough's eyes the streams of dotage
      flow,
And Swift expires a driv'ler and a show.[26]
  The teeming mother anxious for her race,
Begs for each birth the fortune of a face;   320
Yet Vane [27] could tell what ills from beauty
      spring;
And Sedley [28] cursed the form that pleased a
      king.
Ye nymphs of rosy lips and radiant eyes,
Whom Pleasure keeps too busy to be wise;
Whom joys with soft varieties invite,   325
By day the frolic, and the dance by night;
Who frown with vanity, who smile with art,
And ask the latest fashion of the heart;
What care, what rules, your heedless charms
      shall save,
Each nymph your rival, and each youth your
      slave?   330
Against your fame with fondness hate com-
      bines,
The rival batters, and the lover mines.
With distant voice neglected Virtue calls,
Less heard and less, the faint remonstrance
      falls;
Tired with contempt, she quits the slipp'ry
      reign,   335
And Pride and Prudence take her seat in vain.
In crowd at once, where none the pass defend,
The harmless freedom and the private friend.
The guardians yield, by force superior plied:
To int'rest, Prudence: and to Flatt'ry, Pride.   340
Here Beauty falls betrayed, despised, distressed,
And hissing infamy proclaims the rest.
  Where then shall Hope and Fear their ob-
      jects find?
Must dull suspense corrupt the stagnant
      mind?
Must helpless man, in ignorance sedate,   345
Roll darkling down the torrent of his fate?
Must no dislike alarm, no wishes rise,
No cries invoke the mercies of the skies?
Enquirer, cease; petitions yet remain
Which Heav'n may hear, nor deem Religion
      vain.   350
Still raise for good the supplicating voice,

[25] Croesus.
[26] Allusions to the paralytic strokes suffered by
Marlborough and to Swift's madness.
[27] Anne Vane, mistress of Frederick, Prince of
Wales, son of George II and father of George III.
[28] Catherine Sedley, Countess of Dorchester, mistress of James II.

But leave to Heav'n the measure and the
      choice.
Safe in his pow'r whose eyes discern afar
The secret ambush of a specious pray'r;
Implore his aid, in his decisions rest,   355
Secure, whate'er he gives, he gives the best.
Yet, when the sense of sacred presence fires,
And strong devotion to the skies aspires,
Pour forth thy fervors for a healthful mind,
Obedient passions, and a will resigned;   360
For love, which scarce collective man can fill;
For patience, sov'reign o'er transmuted ill;
For faith, that, panting for a happier seat,
Counts death kind Nature's signal of retreat.
These goods for man the laws of Heav'n or-
      dain,   365
These goods he grants, who grants the pow'r to
      gain;
With these celestial Wisdom calms the mind,
And makes the happiness she does not find.

## *The Rambler*

### NO. 50. SATURDAY, 8
### SEPTEMBER, 1750.

*Credebant hoc grande nefas, et morte piandum,*
*Si juvenis vetulo non assurrexerat, atque*
*Barbato cuicunque puer, licet ipse videret*
*Plura domi fraga, et majores glandis acervos.*
                    —JUVENAL.[1]

And had not men the hoary head revered,
And boys paid rev'rence when a man appeared,
Both must have died, though richer skids they wore,
And saw more heaps of acorns in their store.
                    —CREECH.

  I HAVE always thought it the business of
those who turn their speculations upon the
living world, to commend the virtues, as well
as to expose the faults of their contemporaries,
and to confute a false as well as to support a
just accusation; not only because it is peculiarly
the business of a monitor to keep his own reputation untainted, lest those who can once
charge him with partiality, should indulge
themselves afterwards in disbelieving him at 10
pleasure; but because he may find real crimes
sufficient to give full employment to caution or
repentance, without distracting the mind by
needless scruples and vain solicitudes.
  There are certain fixed and stated reproaches
that one part of mankind has in all ages thrown
upon another, which are regularly transmitted
through continued successions, and which he
that has once suffered them is certain to use
with the same undistinguishing vehemence, 20

[1] *Satires*, XIII, 54–57. In the 2nd line *atque*
should be *et si*. Often Johnson's quotations are
somewhat inexact, but these unimportant slips will
not be noted here.

when he has changed his station, and gained the prescriptive right of inflicting on others what he had formerly endured himself.

To these hereditary imputations, of which no man sees the justice, till it becomes his interest to see it, very little regard is to be shown; since it does not appear that they are produced by ratiocination or inquiry, but received implicitly, or caught by a kind of instantaneous contagion, and supported rather by willingness to credit, than ability to prove, them.

It has been always the practice of those who are desirous to believe themselves made venerable by length of time, to censure the new-comers into life, for want of respect to gray hairs and sage experience, for heady confidence in their own understandings, for hasty conclusions upon partial views, for disregard of counsels, which their fathers and grandsires are ready to afford them, and a rebellious impatience of that subordination to which youth is condemned by nature, as necessary to its security from evils into which it would be otherwise precipitated, by the rashness of passion, and the blindness of ignorance.

Every old man complains of the growing depravity of the world, of the petulance and insolence of the rising generation. He recounts the decency and regularity of former times, and celebrates the discipline and sobriety of the age in which his youth was passed; a happy age, which is now no more to be expected, since confusion has broken in upon the world and thrown down all the boundaries of civility and reverence.

It is not sufficiently considered how much he assumes who dares to claim the privilege of complaining; for as every man has, in his own opinion, a full share of the miseries of life, he is inclined to consider all clamorous uneasiness, as a proof of impatience rather than of affliction, and to ask, What merit has this man to show, by which he has acquired a right to repine at the distributions of nature? Or, why does he imagine that exemptions should be granted him from the general condition of man? We find ourselves excited rather to captiousness than pity, and instead of being in haste to soothe his complaints by sympathy and tenderness, we inquire, whether the pain be proportionate to the lamentation; and whether, supposing the affliction real, it is not the effect of vice and folly, rather than calamity.

The querulousness and indignation which *is* observed so often to disfigure the last scene of life, naturally leads us to inquiries like these. For surely it will be thought at the first view of things, that if age be thus contemned and ridiculed, insulted and neglected, the crime must at least be equal on either part. They who have had opportunities of establishing their authority over minds ductile and unresisting, they who have been the protectors of helplessness, and the instructors of ignorance, and who yet retain in their own hands the power of wealth, and the dignity of command, must defeat their influence by their own misconduct, and make use of all these advantages with very little skill, if they cannot secure to themselves an appearance of respect, and ward off open mockery, and declared contempt.

The general story of mankind will evince, that lawful and settled authority is very seldom resisted when it is well employed. Gross corruption, or evident imbecility, is necessary to the suppression of that reverence with which the majority of mankind look upon their governors, and on those whom they see surrounded by splendor, and fortified by power. For though men are drawn by their passions into forgetfulness of invisible rewards and punishments, yet they are easily kept obedient to those who have temporal dominion in their hands, till their veneration is dissipated by such wickedness and folly as can neither be defended nor concealed.

It may, therefore, very reasonably be suspected that the old draw upon themselves the greatest part of those insults which they so much lament, and that age is rarely despised but when it is contemptible. If men imagine that excess of debauchery can be made reverend by time, that knowledge is the consequence of long life, however idly or thoughtlessly employed, that priority of birth will supply the want of steadiness or honesty, can it raise much wonder that their hopes are disappointed, and that they see their posterity rather willing to trust their own eyes in their progress into life, than enlist themselves under guides who have lost their way?

There are indeed, many truths which time necessarily and certainly teaches, and which might, by those who have learned them from experience, be communicated to their successors at a cheaper rate; but dictates, though liberally enough bestowed, are generally without effect, the teacher gains few proselytes by instruction which his own behavior contradicts; and young men miss the benefit of counsel, because they are not very ready to believe that those who fall below them in practice, can much excel them in theory. Thus the progress of knowledge is retarded, the world is kept long in the same state, and every new race is to gain the prudence of their predecessors by committing and redressing the same miscarriages.

To secure to the old that influence which they are willing to claim, and which might so much contribute to the improvement of the arts of life, it is absolutely necessary that they give themselves up to the duties of declining years; and contentedly resign to youth its levity, its pleasures, its frolics, and its fopperies. It is a hopeless endeavor to unite the contrarieties of spring and winter; it is unjust to claim the privileges of age, and retain the playthings of childhood. The young always form magnificent ideas of the wisdom and gravity of men, whom they consider as placed at a distance from them in the ranks of existence, and naturally look on those whom they find trifling with long beards, with contempt and indignation, like that which women feel at the effeminacy of men. If dotards will contend with boys in those performances in which boys must always excel them; if they will dress crippled limbs in embroidery, endeavor at gayety with faltering voices, and darken assemblies of pleasure with the ghastliness of disease, they may well expect those who find their diversions obstructed will hoot them away; and that if they descend to competition with youth, they must bear the insolence of successful rivals.

*Lusisti satis, edisti satis atque bibisti:*
*Tempus abire tibi est.*[2]

You've had your share of mirth, of meat and drink;
'Tis time to quit the scene—'tis time to think.
—ELPHINSTON.

Another vice of age, by which the rising generation may be alienated from it, is severity and censoriousness, that gives no allowance to the failings of early life, that expects artfulness[3] from childhood, and constancy from youth, that is peremptory in every command, and inexorable to every failure. There are many who live merely to hinder happiness, and whose descendants can only tell of long life, that it produces suspicion, malignity, peevishness, and persecution; and yet even these tyrants can talk of the ingratitude of the age, curse their heirs for impatience, and wonder that young men cannot take pleasure in their father's company.

He that would pass the latter part of life with honor and decency, must, when he is young, consider that he shall one day be old; and remember, when he is old, that he has once been young. In youth, he must lay up knowledge for his support, when his powers of acting shall forsake him; and in age forbear to animadvert with rigor on faults which experience only can correct.

## NO. 59. TUESDAY, 9 OCTOBER, 1750.

*Est aliquid fatale malum per verba levare:*
  *Hoc querulam Prognen Halcyonenque facit.*
*Hoc erat, in solo quare Paeantius antro*
  *Voce fatigaret Lemnia saxa sua.*
*Strangulat inclusus dolor, atque exaestuat intus;*
  *Cogitur et vires multiplicare suas.*
                        —OVID.[4]

Complaining oft gives respite to our grief;
From hence the wretched Progne sought relief,
Hence the Paeantian chief his fate deplores,
And vents his sorrow to Lemnian shores;
In vain by secrecy we would assuage
Our cares; concealed they gather tenfold rage.
                        —F. LEWIS.

IT IS common to distinguish men by the names of animals which they are supposed to resemble. Thus a hero is frequently termed a lion, and a statesman a fox, an extortioner gains the appellation of vulture, and a fop the title of monkey. There is also among the various anomalies of character, which a survey of the world exhibits, a species of beings in human form, which may be properly marked out as the screech-owls of mankind.

These screech-owls seem to be settled in an opinion that the great business of life is to complain, and that they were born for no other purpose than to disturb the happiness of others, to lessen the little comforts, and shorten the short pleasures of our condition, by painful remembrances of the past, or melancholy prognostics of the future; their only care is to crush the rising hope, to damp the kindling transport, and allay the golden hours of gayety with the hateful dross of grief and suspicion.

To those whose weakness of spirits, or timidity of temper, subjects them to impressions from others, and who are to suffer by fascination, and catch the contagion of misery, it is extremely unhappy to live within the compass of a screech-owl's voice; for it will often fill their ears in the hour of dejection, terrify them with apprehensions, which their own thoughts would never have produced, and sadden, by intruded sorrows, the day which might have been passed in amusements or in business; it

---

[2] Horace, *Epistles*, II, ii, 214–215.     [3] Skill.

[4] *Tristia*, V, i, 59–64.

will burden the heart with unnecessary discontents, and weaken for a time that love of life which is necessary to the vigorous prosecution of any undertaking.

Though I have, like the rest of mankind, many failings and weaknesses, I have not yet, by either friends or enemies, been charged with superstition; I never count the company which I enter, and I look at the new moon indifferently over either shoulder. I have, like most other philosophers, often heard the cuckoo without money in my pocket, and have been sometimes reproached as foolhardy for not turning down my eyes when a raven flew over my head. I never go home abruptly because a snake crosses my way, nor have any particular dread of a climacterical year;[5] yet I confess that, with all my scorn of old women, and their tales, I consider it as an unhappy day when I happen to be greeted, in the morning, by Suspirius the screech-owl.

I have now known Suspirius fifty-eight years and four months, and have never yet passed an hour with him in which he has not made some attack upon my quiet. When we were first acquainted, his great topic was the misery of youth without riches; and whenever we walked out together, he solaced me with a long enumeration of pleasures, which, as they were beyond the reach of my fortune, were without the verge of my desires, and which I should never have considered as the objects of a wish, had not his unseasonable representations placed them in my sight.

Another of his topics is the neglect of merit, with which he never fails to amuse[6] every man whom he sees not eminently fortunate. If he meets with a young officer, he always informs him of gentlemen whose personal courage is unquestioned, and whose military skill qualifies them to command armies, that have, notwithstanding all their merit, grown old with subaltern commissions. For a genius in the church, he is always provided with a curacy for life. The lawyer he informs of many men of great parts and deep study, who have never had an opportunity to speak in the courts: And meeting Serenus the physician, "Ah, doctor," says he, "what, a-foot still, when so many blockheads are rattling in their char-

iots? I told you seven years ago that you would never meet with encouragement, and I hope you will now take more notice, when I tell you that your Greek, and your diligence, and your honesty, will never enable you to live like yonder apothecary, who prescribes to his own shop, and laughs at the physician."

Suspirius has, in his time, intercepted fifteen authors in their way to the stage; persuaded nine and thirty merchants to retire from a prosperous trade for fear of bankruptcy, broke off an hundred and thirteen matches by prognostications of unhappiness, and enabled the smallpox to kill nineteen ladies, by perpetual alarm of the loss of beauty.

Whenever my evil stars bring us together, he never fails to represent to me the folly of my pursuits, and informs me that we are much older than when we began our acquaintance, that the infirmities of decrepitude are coming fast upon me, that whatever I now get, I shall enjoy but a little time, that fame is to a man tottering on the edge of the grave of very little importance, and that the time is at hand when I ought to look for no other pleasures than a good dinner and an easy chair.

Thus he goes on in his unharmonious strain, displaying present miseries, and foreboding more, νυκτικόραξ ᾄδει θανατηφόρον,[7] every syllable is loaded with misfortune, and death is always brought nearer to the view. Yet, what always raises my resentment and indignation, I do not perceive that his mournful meditations have much effect upon himself. He talks and has long talked of calamities, without discovering otherwise than by the tone of his voice, that he feels any of the evils which he bewails or threatens, but has the same habit of uttering lamentations, as others of telling stories, and falls into expressions of condolence for past, or apprehension of future mischiefs, as all men studious of their ease have recourse to those subjects upon which they can most fluently or copiously discourse.

It is reported of the Sybarites,[8] that they destroyed all their cocks, that they might dream out their morning dreams without disturbance. Though I would not so far promote effeminacy as to propose the Sybarites for an example, yet since there is no man so corrupt or foolish, but something useful may be learned

---

[5] "Certain observable years are supposed to be attended with some considerable change in the body; as the 7th year; the 21st, made up of three times seven; the 49th, made up of seven times seven; the 63rd, being nine times seven; and the 81st, which is nine times nine; which two last are called the grand climacterics." (Johnson's *Dictionary*.)

[6] To engage the attention of.

[7] The night-raven's song bodes death. (*Greek Anthology*, XI, Satirical Epigrams, 186. In one of his sleepless nights Johnson turned this epigram into Latin verse.)

[8] Inhabitants of Sybaris in southern Italy, known for their love of luxury.

from him, I could wish that, in imitation of a people not often to be copied, some regulations might be made to exclude screech-owls from all company, as the enemies of mankind, and confine them to some proper receptacle, where they may mingle sighs at leisure, and thicken the gloom of one another.

"Thou prophet of evil," says Homer's Agamemnon, "thou never foretellest me good, but the joy of thy heart is to predict misfortunes." [9] Whoever is of the same temper, might there find the means of indulging his thoughts, and improving his vein of denunciation, and the flock of screech-owls might hoot together without injury to the rest of the world.

Yet, though I have so little kindness for this dark generation, I am very far from intending to debar the soft and tender mind from the privilege of complaining, when the sigh arises from the desire not of giving pain, but of gaining ease. To hear complaints with patience, even when complaints are vain, is one of the duties of friendship; and though it must be allowed that he suffers most like a hero that hides his grief in silence,

*Spem vultu simulat, premit altum corde dolorem,* [10]

His outward smiles concealed his inward smart.
—DRYDEN.

yet it cannot be denied, that he who complains acts like a man, like a social being, who looks for help from his fellow-creatures. Pity is to many of the unhappy a source of comfort in hopeless distresses, as it contributes to recommend them to themselves, by proving that they have not lost the regard of others; and heaven seems to indicate the duty even of barren compassion, by inclining us to weep for evils which we cannot remedy.

## NO. 137. TUESDAY, 9 JULY, 1751.

*Dum vitant stulti vitia, in contraria currunt.*
—HORACE. [11]

—— Whilst fools one vice condemn,
They run into the opposite extreme.
—CREECH.

THAT wonder is the effect of ignorance, has been often observed. The awful stillness of attention, with which the mind is overspread at the first view of an unexpected effect, ceases when we have leisure to disentangle complications and investigate causes. Wonder is a pause of reason, a sudden cessation of the mental progress, which lasts only while the understanding is fixed upon some single idea, and is at an end when it recovers force enough to divide the object into its parts, or mark the intermediate gradations from the first agent to the last consequence.

It may be remarked with equal truth, that ignorance is often the effect of wonder. It is common for those who have never accustomed themselves to the labor of inquiry, nor invigorated their confidence by conquests over difficulty, to sleep in the gloomy quiescence of astonishment, without any effort to animate inquiry or dispel obscurity. What they cannot immediately conceive, they consider as too high to be reached, or too extensive to be comprehended; they therefore content themselves with the gaze of folly, forbear to attempt what they have no hopes of performing, and resign the pleasure of rational contemplation to more pertinacious study of more active faculties.

Among the productions of mechanic art, many are of a form so different from that of their first materials, and many consist of parts so numerous and so nicely adapted to each other, that it is not possible to view them without amazement. But when we enter the shops of artificers, observe the various tools by which every operation is facilitated, and trace the progress of a manufacture through the different hands, that, in succession to each other, contribute to its perfection, we soon discover that every single man has an easy task, and that the extremes, however remote, of natural rudeness and artificial elegance, are joined by a regular concatenation of effects, of which every one is introduced by that which precedes it, and equally introduces that which is to follow.

The same is the state of intellectual and manual performances. Long calculations or complex diagrams affright the timorous and unexperienced from a second view; but if we have skill sufficient to analyze them into simple principles, it will be discovered that our fear was groundless. *Divide and Conquer,* is a principle equally just in science as in policy. Complication is a species of confederacy which, while it continues united, bids defiance to the most active and vigorous intellect; but of which every member is separately weak, and which may therefore be quickly subdued, if it can once be broken.

The chief art of learning, as Locke has observed, is to attempt but little at a time. [12]

---

[9] *Iliad,* I, 106.  [10] *Aeneid,* I, 209.
[11] *Satires,* I, ii, 34.

[12] See *Some Thoughts concerning Education,* Sect. 160, Writing.

The widest excursions of the mind are made by short flights frequently repeated; the most lofty fabrics of science are formed by the continued accumulation of single propositions.

It often happens, whatever be the cause, that impatience of labor, or dread of miscarriage, seizes those who are most distinguished for quickness of apprehension; and that they who might with greatest reason promise themselves victory, are least willing to hazard the encounter. This diffidence, where the attention is not laid asleep by laziness, or dissipated by pleasures, can arise only from confused and general views, such as negligence snatches in haste, or from the disappointment of the first hopes formed by arrogance without reflection. To expect that the intricacies of science will be pierced by a careless glance, or the eminences of fame ascended without labor, is to expect a particular privilege, a power denied to the rest of mankind; but to suppose that the maze is inscrutable to diligence, or the heights inaccessible to perseverance, is to submit tamely to the tyranny of fancy, and enchain the mind in voluntary shackles.

It is the proper ambition of the heroes in literature to enlarge the boundaries of knowledge by discovering and conquering new regions of the intellectual world. To the success of such undertakings perhaps some degree of fortuitous happiness is necessary, which no man can promise or procure to himself; and therefore doubt and irresolution may be forgiven in him that ventures into the unexplored abysses of truth, and attempts to find his way through the fluctuations of uncertainty, and the conflicts of contradiction. But when nothing more is required than to pursue a path already beaten, and to trample obstacles which others have demolished, why should any man so much distrust his own intellect as to imagine himself unequal to the attempt?

It were to be wished that they who devote their lives to study would at once believe nothing too great for their attainment, and consider nothing as too little for their regard; that they would extend their notice alike to science and to life; and unite some knowledge of the present world to their acquaintance with past ages and remote events.

Nothing has so much exposed men of learning to contempt and ridicule, as their ignorance of things which are known to all but themselves. Those who have been taught to consider the institutions of the schools [13] as giving the last perfection to human abilities, are surprised to see men wrinkled with study, yet wanting to be instructed in the minute circumstances of propriety, or the necessary forms of daily transaction; and quickly shake off their reverence for modes of education which they find to produce no ability above the rest of mankind.

"Books," says Bacon, "can never teach the use of books." [14] The student must learn by commerce with mankind to reduce his speculations to practice, and accommodate his knowledge to the purposes of life.

It is too common for those who have been bred to scholastic professions, and passed much of their time in academies where nothing but learning confers honors, to disregard every other qualification, and to imagine that they shall find mankind ready to pay homage to their knowledge, and to crowd about them for instruction. They therefore step out from their cells into the open world with all the confidence of authority and dignity of importance; they look round about them at once with ignorance and scorn on a race of beings to whom they are equally unknown and equally contemptible, but whose manners they must imitate, and with whose opinions they must comply, if they desire to pass their time happily among them.

To lessen that disdain with which scholars are inclined to look on the common business of the world, and the unwillingness with which they condescend to learn what is not to be found in any system of philosophy, it may be necessary to consider that though admiration is excited by abstruse researches and remote discoveries, yet pleasure is not given, nor affection conciliated, but by softer accomplishments, and qualities more easily communicable to those about us. He that can only converse upon questions about which only a small part of mankind has knowledge sufficient to make them curious, must lose his days in unsocial silence, and live in the crowd of life without a companion. He that can be only useful on great occasions may die without exerting his abilities, and stand a helpless spectator of a thousand vexations which fret away happiness, and which nothing is required to remove but a little dexterity of conduct and readiness of expedients.

No degree of knowledge attainable by man is able to set him above the want of hourly assistance, or to extinguish the desire of fond

---

[13] I. e., of the university.

[14] See *Essays*, "Of Studies" ("They teach not their own use").

endearments, and tender officiousness; [15] and therefore, no one should think it unnecessary to learn those arts by which friendship may be gained. Kindness is preserved by a constant reciprocation of benefits or interchange of pleasures; but such benefits only can be bestowed, as others are capable to receive, and such pleasures only imparted, as others are qualified to enjoy.

By this descent from the pinnacles of art no honor will be lost; for the condescensions of learning are always overpaid by gratitude. An elevated genius employed in little things, appears, to use the simile of Longinus, like the sun in his evening declination, he remits his splendor but retains his magnitude, and pleases more though he dazzles less.

### NO. 191. TUESDAY, 14 JANUARY, 1752.

*Cereus in vitium flecti, monitoribus asper.*
— Horace.[16]

The youth——
Yielding like wax, th' impressive folly bears;
Rough to reproof, and slow to future cares.
— Francis.

#### TO THE RAMBLER

Dear Mr. Rambler:

I have been four days confined to my chamber by a cold, which has already kept me from three plays, nine sales, five shows, and six card-tables, and put me seventeen visits behindhand; and the doctor tells my mamma, that if I fret and cry, it will settle in my head, and I shall not be fit to be seen these six weeks. But, dear Mr. Rambler, how can I help it? At this very time Melissa is dancing with the prettiest gentleman; she will breakfast with him tomorrow, and then run to two auctions, and hear compliments, and have presents; then she will be dressed, and visit, and get a ticket to the play; then go to cards and win, and come home with two flambeaux before her chair. Dear Mr. Rambler, who can bear it?

My aunt has just brought me a bundle of your papers for my amusement. She says, you are a philosopher, and will teach me to moderate my desires, and look upon the world with indifference. But, dear sir, I do not wish, nor intend, to moderate my desires, nor can I think it proper to look upon the world with indifference, till the world looks with indifference on me. I have been forced, however, to sit

this morning a whole quarter of an hour with your paper before my face; but just as my aunt came in, Phyllida had brought me a letter from Mr. Trip, which I put within the leaves; and read about "absence" and "inconsolableness," and "ardor," and "irresistible passion," and "eternal constancy," while my aunt imagined that I was puzzling myself with your philosophy, and often cried out, when she saw me look confused, "If there is any word that you do not understand, child, I will explain it."

Dear soul! How old people that think themselves wise may be imposed upon! But it is fit that they should take their turn, for I am sure, while they can keep poor girls close in the nursery, they tyrannize over us in a very shameful manner, and fill our imaginations with tales of terror, only to make us live in quiet subjection, and fancy that we can never be safe but by their protection.

I have a mamma and two aunts, who have all been formerly celebrated for wit and beauty, and are still generally admired by those that value themselves upon their understanding, and love to talk of vice and virtue, nature and simplicity, and beauty and propriety; but if there was not some hope of meeting me, scarcely a creature would come near them that wears a fashionable coat. These ladies, Mr. Rambler, have had me under their government fifteen years and a half, and have all that time been endeavoring to deceive me by such representations of life as I now find not to be true; but I know not whether I ought to impute them to ignorance or malice, as it is possible the world may be much changed since they mingled in general conversation.

Being desirous that I should love books, they told me that nothing but knowledge could make me an agreeable companion to men of sense, or qualify me to distinguish the superficial glitter of vanity from the solid merit of understanding; and that a habit of reading would enable me to fill up the vacuities of life without the help of silly or dangerous amusements, and preserve me from the snares of idleness and the inroads of temptation.

But their principal intention was to make me afraid of men; in which they succeeded so well for a time, that I durst not look in their faces, or be left alone with them in a parlor; for they made me fancy that no man ever spoke but to deceive, or looked but to allure; that the girl who suffered him that had once squeezed her hand, to approach her a second time, was on the brink of ruin; and that she who answered a billet, without consulting her

---

[15] Readiness in doing good offices.
[16] *De Arte Poetica,* 163.

relations, gave love such power over her that she would certainly become either poor or infamous.

From the time that my leading-strings were taken off, I scarce heard any mention of my beauty but from the milliner, the mantua-maker, and my own maid; for my mamma never said more, when she heard me commended, but "The girl is very well," and then endeavored to divert my attention by some inquiry after my needle, or my book.

It is now three months since I have been suffered to pay and receive visits, to dance at public assemblies, to have a place kept for me in the boxes, and to play at Lady Racket's rout;[17] and you may easily imagine what I think of those who have so long cheated me with false expectations, disturbed me with fictitious terrors, and concealed from me all that I have found to make the happiness of woman.

I am so far from perceiving the usefulness or necessity of books, that if I had not dropped all pretensions to learning, I should have lost Mr. Trip, whom I once frighted into another box, by retailing some of Dryden's remarks upon a tragedy; for Mr. Trip declares that he hates nothing like hard words, and, I am sure, there is not a better partner to be found; his very walk is a dance. I have talked once or twice among ladies about principles and ideas, but they put their fans before their faces, and told me I was too wise for them, who for their part never pretended to read anything but the play-bill, and then asked me the price of my best head.[18]

Those vacancies of time which are to be filled up with books I have never yet obtained; for, consider, Mr. Rambler, I go to bed late, and therefore cannot rise early; as soon as I am up, I dress for the gardens; then walk in the park; then always go to some sale or show, or entertainment at the little theater; then must be dressed for dinner; then must pay my visits; then walk in the park; then hurry to the play; and from thence to the card-table. This is the general course of the day, when there happens nothing extraordinary; but sometimes I ramble into the country, and come back again to a ball; sometimes I am engaged for a whole day and part of the night. If, at any time, I can gain an hour by not being at home, I have so many things to do, so many orders to give to the milliner, so many alterations to make in my clothes, so many visitants' names to read over, so many invitations to accept or refuse, so many cards to write, and so many fashions to consider, that I am lost in confusion, forced at last to let in company or step into my chair, and leave half my affairs to the direction of my maid.

This is the round of my day; and when shall I either stop my course, or so change it as to want a book? I suppose it cannot be imagined, that any of these diversions will soon be at an end. There will always be gardens, and a park, and auctions, and shows, and playhouses, and cards; visits will always be paid, and clothes always be worn; and how can I have time unemployed upon my hands?

But I am most at a loss to guess for what purpose they related such tragic stories of the cruelty, perfidy, and artifices of men, who, if they ever were so malicious and destructive, have certainly now reformed their manners. I have not, since my entrance into the world, found one who does not profess himself devoted to my service, and ready to live or die as I shall command him. They are so far from intending to hurt me, that their only contention is, who shall be allowed most closely to attend, and most frequently to treat me. When different places of entertainment or schemes of pleasure are mentioned, I can see the eye sparkle and the cheeks glow of him whose proposals obtain my approbation; he then leads me off in triumph, adores my condescension, and congratulates himself that he has lived to the hour of felicity. Are these, Mr. Rambler, creatures to be feared? Is it likely that any injury will be done me by those who can enjoy life only while I favor them with my presence?

As little reason can I yet find to suspect them of stratagems and fraud. When I play at cards, they never take advantage of my mistakes, nor exact from me a rigorous observation of the game. Even Mr. Shuffle, a grave gentleman, who has daughters older than myself, plays with me so negligently that I am sometimes inclined to believe he loses his money by design, and yet he is so fond of play, that he says he will one day take me to his house in the country, that we may try by ourselves who can conquer. I have not yet promised him; but when the town grows a little empty, I shall think upon it, for I want some trinkets, like Letitia's, to my watch. I do not doubt my luck, but must study some means of amusing[19] my relations.

For all these distinctions I find myself indebted to that beauty which I was never suffered to hear praised, and of which, therefore,

17 Large evening assembly.
18 I. e., head-dress.
19 Of distracting the attention of.

I did not before know the full value. The concealment was certainly an intentional fraud, for my aunts have eyes like other people, and I am every day told that nothing but blindness can escape the influence of my charms. Their whole account of that world which they pretend to know so well has been only one fiction entangled with another; and though the modes of life oblige me to continue some appearances of respect, I cannot think that they, who have 10 been so clearly detected in ignorance or imposture, have any right to the esteem, veneration, or obedience of,

Sir, Yours,<br>Bellaria.

## The Idler

### NO. 16. SATURDAY, 29 JULY, 1758.

I PAID a visit yesterday to my old friend 20 Ned Drugget, at his country lodgings. Ned began trade with a very small fortune; he took a small house in an obscure street, and for some years dealt only in remnants. Knowing that *light gains make a heavy purse*, he was content with moderate profit; having observed or heard the effects of civility, he bowed down to the counter-edge at the entrance and departure of every customer, listened without impatience to the objections of the ignorant, and 30 refused without resentment the offers of the penurious. His only recreation was to stand at his own door and look into the street. His dinner was sent him from a neighboring alehouse, and he opened and shut the shop at a certain hour with his own hands.

His reputation soon extended from one end of the street to the other; and Mr. Drugget's exemplary conduct was recommended by every master to his apprentice, and by every father 40 to his son. Ned was not only considered as a thriving trader, but as a man of elegance and politeness, for he was remarkably neat in his dress, and would wear his coat threadbare without spotting it; his hat was always brushed, his shoes glossy, his wig nicely curled, and his stockings without a wrinkle. With such qualifications it was not very difficult for him to gain the heart of Miss Comfit, the only daughter of Mr. Comfit the confectioner. 50

Ned is one of those whose happiness marriage has increased. His wife had the same disposition with himself; and his method of life was very little changed, except that he dismissed the lodgers from the first floor,[1] and took the whole house into his own hands.

[1] I. e., the first floor above the ground-floor.

He had already, by his parsimony, accumulated a considerable sum, to which the fortune of his wife was now added. From this time he began to grasp at greater acquisitions, and was always ready, with money in his hand, to pick up the refuse of a sale, or to buy the stock of a trader who retired from business. He soon added his parlor to his shop, and was obliged a few months afterwards to hire a warehouse.

He had now a shop splendidly and copiously furnished with everything that time had injured, or fashion had degraded, with fragments of tissues, odd yards of brocade, vast bales of faded silk, and innumerable boxes of antiquated ribbons. His shop was soon celebrated through all quarters of the town, and frequented by every form of ostentatious poverty. Every maid, whose misfortune it was to be taller than her lady, matched [2] her gown at Mr. Drugget's; and many a maiden, who had passed a winter with her aunt in London, dazzled the rustics, at her return, with cheap finery which Drugget had supplied. His shop was often visited in a morning by ladies who left their coaches in the next street, and crept through the alley in linen gowns. Drugget knows the rank of his customers by their bashfulness; and, when he finds them unwilling to be seen, invites them upstairs, or retires with them to the back window.

I rejoiced at the increasing prosperity of my friend, and imagined, that as he grew rich, he was growing happy. His mind has partaken the enlargement of his fortune. When I stepped in for the first five years, I was welcomed only with a shake of the hand; in the next period of his life, he beckoned across the way for a pot of beer; but for six years past, he invites me to dinner; and if he bespeaks me the day before, never fails to regale me with a fillet of veal.

His riches neither made him uncivil nor negligent; he rose at the same hour, attended with the same assiduity, and bowed with the same gentleness. But for some years he has been much inclined to talk of the fatigues of business, and the confinement of a shop, and to wish that he had been so happy as to have renewed his uncle's lease of a farm, that he might have lived without noise and hurry, in a pure air, in the artless society of honest villagers, and the contemplation of the works of nature.

I soon discovered the cause of my friend's philosophy. He thought himself grown rich

[2] I. e., shopped for; found one there which (in this instance) accorded with her height.

enough to have a lodging in the country, like the mercers on Ludgate Hill, and was resolved to enjoy himself in the decline of life. This was a revolution not to be made suddenly. He talked three years of the pleasures of the country, but passed every night over his own shop. But at last he resolved to be happy, and hired a lodging in the country, that he may steal some hours in the week from business; for, says he, *when a man advances in life, he loves to enter-* 10 *tain himself sometimes with his own thoughts.*

I was invited to this seat of quiet and contemplation among those whom Mr. Drugget considers as his most reputable friends, and desires to make the first witnesses of his elevation to the highest dignities of a shopkeeper. I found him at Islington, in a room which overlooked the high road, amusing himself with looking through the window, which the clouds of dust would not suffer him to open. He em- 20 braced me, told me I was welcome into the country, and asked me, if I did not feel myself refreshed. He then desired that dinner might be hastened, for fresh air always sharpened his appetite, and ordered me a toast and a glass of wine after my walk. He told me much of the pleasure he found in retirement, and wondered what had kept him so long out of the country. After dinner, company came in, and Mr. Drugget again repeated the praises of the 30 country, recommended the pleasures of meditation, and told them, that he had been all the morning at the window, counting the carriages as they passed before him.

### NO. 19. SATURDAY, 19 AUGUST, 1758.

SOME of those ancient sages that have exercised their abilities in the inquiry after the 40 *supreme good*, have been of opinion, that the highest degree of earthly happiness is quiet; a calm repose both of mind and body undisturbed by the sight of folly or the noise of business, the tumults of public commotion, or the agitations of private interest; a state in which the mind has no other employment but to observe and regulate her own motions, to trace thought from thought, combine one image with another, raise systems of science 50 and form theories of virtue.

To the scheme of these solitary speculatists, it has been justly objected, that if they are happy, they are happy only by being useless. That mankind is one vast republic, where every individual receives many benefits from the labors of others, which, by laboring in his

turn for others, he is obliged to repay; and that where the united efforts of all are not able to exempt all from misery, none have a right to withdraw from their task of vigilance, or to be indulged in idle wisdom, or solitary pleasures.

It is common for controvertists, in the heat of disputation, to add one position to another till they reach the extremities of knowledge, where truth and falsehood lose their distinction. Their admirers follow them to the brink of absurdity, and then start back from each side towards the middle point. So it has happened in this great disquisition. Many perceive alike the force of the contrary arguments, find quiet shameful, and business dangerous, and therefore pass their lives between them, in bustle without business, and negligence without quiet.

Among the principal names of this moderate set is that great philosopher Jack Whirler,[3] whose business keeps him in perpetual motion, and whose motion always eludes his business; who is always to do what he never does, who cannot stand still because he is wanted in another place, and who is wanted in many places because he stays in none.

Jack has more business than he can conveniently transact in one house; he has therefore one habitation near Bow Church, and another about a mile distant. By this ingenious distribution of himself between two houses, Jack has contrived to be found at neither. Jack's trade is extensive, and he has many dealers; his conversation is sprightly, and he has many companions; his disposition is kind, and he has many friends. Jack neither forbears pleasure for business, nor omits business for pleasure, but is equally invisible to his friends and his customers; to him that comes with an invitation to a club, and to him that waits to settle an account.

When you call at his house, his clerk tells you, that Mr. Whirler was just stepped out, but will be at home exactly at two; you wait at a coffee-house till two, and then find that he has been at home, and is gone out again, but left word that he should be at the Half Moon Tavern at seven, where he hopes to meet you. At seven you go to the tavern. At eight in comes Mr. Whirler to tell you that he is glad to see you, and only begs leave to run for a few minutes to a gentleman that lives near the Exchange, from whom he will return before supper can be ready. Away he

[3] It is said that John Newbury, a bookseller (and one of the publishers of the collected edition of *The Idler*), was the original of Whirler.

runs to the Exchange, to tell those who are waiting for him, that he must beg them to defer the business till to-morrow, because his time is come at the Half Moon.

Jack's cheerfulness and civility rank him among those whose presence never gives pain, and whom all receive with fondness and caresses. He calls often on his friends, to tell them, that he will come again to-morrow; on the morrow he comes again, to tell them how 10 an unexpected summons hurries him away. When he enters a house, his first declaration is, that he cannot sit down; and so short are his visits, that he seldom appears to have come for any other reason but to say, He must go.

The dogs of Egypt, when thirst brings them to the Nile, are said to run as they drink for fear of the crocodiles. Jack Whirler always dines at full speed. He enters, finds the family at table, sits familiarly down, and fills his 20 plate; but while the first morsel is in his mouth, hears the clock strike, and rises; then goes to another house, sits down again, recollects another engagement; has only time to taste the soup, makes a short excuse to the company, and continues through another street his desultory dinner.

But, overwhelmed as he is with business, his chief desire is to have still more. Every new proposal takes possession of his thoughts; he 30 soon balances probabilities, engages in the project, brings it almost to completion, and then forsakes it for another, which he catches with some alacrity, urges with the same vehemence, and abandons with the same coldness.

Every man may be observed to have a certain strain of lamentation, some peculiar theme of complaint on which he dwells in his moments of dejection. Jack's topic of sorrow is 40 the want of time. Many an excellent design languishes in empty theory for want of time. For the omission of any civilities, want of time is his plea to others; for the neglect of any affairs, want of time is his excuse to himself. That he wants time, he sincerely believes; for he once pined away many months with a lingering distemper, for want of time to attend his health.

Thus Jack Whirler lives in perpetual fatigue 50 without proportionate advantage, because he does not consider that no man can see all with his own eyes, or do all with his own hands; that whoever is engaged in multiplicity of business, must transact much by substitution, and leave something to hazard: and that he who attempts to do all, will waste his life in doing little.

## NO. 48. SATURDAY, 17 MARCH, 1759.

THERE is no kind of idleness by which we are so easily seduced, as that which dignifies itself by the appearance of business, and, by making the loiterer imagine that he has something to do which must not be neglected, keeps him in perpetual agitation, and hurries him rapidly from place to place.

He that sits still, or reposes himself upon a couch, no more deceives himself than he deceives others; he knows that he is doing nothing, and has no other solace of his insignificance than the resolution, which the lazy hourly make, of changing his mode of life.

To do nothing every man is ashamed: and to do much almost every man is unwilling or afraid. Innumerable expedients have therefore been invented to produce motion without labor, and employment without solicitude. The greater part of those whom the kindness of fortune has left to their own direction, and whom want does not keep chained to the counter or the plow, play throughout life with the shadows of business, and know not at last what they have been doing.

These imitators of action are of all denominations. Some are seen at every auction without intention to purchase; others appear punctually at the Exchange, though they are known there only by their faces. Some are always making parties to visit collections for which they have no taste; and some neglect every pleasure and every duty to hear questions, in which they have no interest, debated in parliament.

These men never appear more ridiculous than in the distress which they imagine themselves to feel, from some accidental interruption of those empty pursuits. A tiger newly imprisoned is indeed more formidable, but not more angry, than Jack Tulip withheld from a florist's feast, or Tom Distich hindered from seeing the first representation of a play.

As political affairs are the highest and most extensive of temporal concerns, the mimic of a politician is more busy and important than any other trifler. Monsieur le Noir, a man who, without property or importance in any corner of the earth, has, in the present confusion of the world, declared himself a steady adherent to the French, is made miserable by a wind that keeps back the packetboat, and still more miserable by every account of a Malouin privateer [4] caught in his cruise; he knows well that

---

[4] A privateer of St. Malo.

nothing can be done or said by him which can produce any effect but that of laughter, that he can neither hasten nor retard good or evil, that his joys and sorrows have scarcely any partakers; yet such is his zeal, and such his curiosity, that he would run barefooted to Gravesend, for the sake of knowing first that the English had lost a tender, and would ride out to meet every mail from the continent if he might be permitted to open it.

Learning is generally confessed to be desirable, and there are some who fancy themselves always busy in acquiring it. Of these ambulatory students, one of the most busy is my friend Tom Restless.[5]

Tom has long had a mind to be a man of knowledge, but he does not care to spend much time among authors; for he is of opinion that few books deserve the labor of perusal, that they give the mind an unfashionable cast, and destroy that freedom of thought and easiness of manners indispensably requisite to acceptance in the world. Tom has therefore found another way to wisdom. When he rises he goes into a coffee-house, where he creeps so near to men whom he takes to be reasoners as to hear their discourse, and endeavors to remember something which, when it has been strained through Tom's head, is so near to nothing, that what it once was cannot be discovered. This he carries round from friend to friend through a circle of visits, till, hearing what each says upon the question, he becomes able at dinner to say a little himself; and, as every great genius relaxes himself among his inferiors, meets with some who wonder how so young a man can talk so wisely.

At night he has a new feast prepared for his intellects; he always runs to a disputing society, or a speaking club, where he half hears what, if he had heard the whole, he would but half understand; goes home pleased with the consciousness of a day well spent, lies down full of ideas, and rises in the morning empty as before.

## NO. 60. SATURDAY, 9 JUNE, 1759.

CRITICISM is a study by which men grow important and formidable at a very small ex-

[5] Johnson said that Restless was meant for Thomas Tyers, son of the founder of Vauxhall Gardens. He was "bred to the law; but, having a handsome fortune, vivacity of temper, and eccentricity of mind, he could not confine himself to the regularity of practice. He therefore ran about the world with a pleasant carelessness, amusing everybody by his desultory conversation" (Boswell, *Life of Johnson*).

pense. The power of invention has been conferred by nature upon few, and the labor of learning those sciences which may by mere labor be obtained is too great to be willingly endured; but every man can exert such judgment as he has upon the works of others; and he whom nature has made weak, and idleness keeps ignorant, may yet support his vanity by the name of a Critic.

I hope it will give comfort to great numbers who are passing through the world in obscurity, when I inform them how easily distinction may be obtained. All the other powers of literature are coy and haughty, they must be long courted, and at last are not always gained; but Criticism is a goddess easy of access and forward of advance, who will meet the slow, and encourage the timorous; the want of meaning she supplies with words, and the want of spirit she recompenses with malignity.

This profession has one recommendation peculiar to itself, that it gives vent to malignity without real mischief. No genius was ever blasted by the breath of critics. The poison, which, if confined, would have burst the heart, fumes away in empty hisses, and malice is set at ease with very little danger to merit. The Critic is the only man whose triumph is without another's pain, and whose greatness does not rise upon another's ruin.

To a study at once so easy and so reputable, so malicious and so harmless, it cannot be necessary to invite my readers by a long or labored exhortation; it is sufficient, since all would be Critics if they could, to show by one eminent example that all can be critics if they will.

Dick Minim, after the common course of puerile studies, in which he was no great proficient, was put an apprentice to a brewer, with whom he had lived two years, when his uncle died in the city, and left him a large fortune in the stocks. Dick had for six months before used the company of the lower players, of whom he had learned to scorn a trade, and, being now at liberty to follow his genius, he resolved to be a man of wit and humor. That he might be properly initiated in his new character, he frequented the coffee-houses near the theaters, where he listened very diligently, day after day, to those who talked of language and sentiments, and unities and catastrophes, till by slow degrees he began to think that he understood something of the stage, and hoped in time to talk himself.

But he did not trust so much to natural

sagacity as wholly to neglect the help of books. When the theaters were shut, he retired to Richmond with a few select writers,[6] whose opinions he impressed upon his memory by unwearied diligence; and, when he returned with other wits to the town, was able to tell, in very proper phrases, that the chief business of art is to copy nature; that a perfect writer is not to be expected, because genius decays as judgment increases; that the great art is the art of blotting; and that, according to the rule of Horace, every piece should be kept nine years.

Of the great authors he now began to display the characters, laying down as an universal position, that all had beauties and defects. His opinion was, that Shakespeare, committing himself wholly to the impulse of nature, wanted that correctness which learning would have given him; and that Jonson, trusting to learning, did not sufficiently cast his eye on nature. He blamed the *stanza* of Spenser, and could not bear the *hexameters* of Sidney. Denham and Waller he held the first reformers of English numbers; and thought that if Waller could have obtained the strength of Denham, or Denham the sweetness of Waller, there had been nothing wanting to complete a poet. He often expressed his commiseration of Dryden's poverty, and his indignation at the age which suffered him to write for bread; he repeated with rapture the first lines of *All for Love*, but wondered at the corruption of taste which could bear anything so unnatural as riming tragedies. In Otway he found uncommon powers of moving the passions, but was disgusted by his general negligence, and blamed him for making a conspirator his hero; and never concluded his disquisition, without remarking how happily the sound of the clock is made to alarm the audience. Southern[7] would have been his favorite, but that he mixes comic with tragic scenes, intercepts the natural course of the passions, and fills the mind with a wild confusion of mirth and melancholy. The versification of Rowe he thought too melodious for the stage, and too little varied in different passions. He made it the great fault of Congreve, that all his persons were wits, and that he always wrote with more art than nature. He considered *Cato* rather as a poem than a play, and allowed Addison to be the complete master of allegory and grave humor,

but paid no great deference to him as a critic. He thought the chief merit of Prior was in his easy tales and lighter poems, though he allowed that his *Solomon* had many noble sentiments elegantly expressed. In Swift he discovered an inimitable vein of irony, and an easiness which all would hope and few would attain. Pope he was declined to degrade from a poet to a versifier, and thought his numbers rather luscious than sweet. He often lamented the neglect of *Phaedra and Hippolitus*,[8] and wished to see the stage under better regulations.

These assertions passed commonly uncontradicted; and if now and then an opponent started up, he was quickly repressed by the suffrages of the company, and Minim went away from every dispute with elation of heart and increase of confidence.

He now grew conscious of his abilities, and began to talk of the present state of dramatic poetry; wondered what was become of the comic genius which supplied our ancestors with wit and pleasantry, and why no writer could be found that durst now venture beyond a farce. He saw no reason for thinking that the vein of humor was exhausted, since we live in a country where liberty suffers every character to spread itself to its utmost bulk, and which therefore produces more originals than all the rest of the world together. Of tragedy he concluded business to be the soul, and yet often hinted that love predominates too much upon the modern stage.

He was now an acknowledged critic, and had his own seat in a coffee-house, and headed a party in the pit. Minim has more vanity than ill-nature, and seldom desires to do much mischief; he will perhaps murmur a little in the ear of him that sits next him, but endeavors to influence the audience to favor, by clapping when an actor exclaims "Ye gods!" or laments the misery of his country.

By degrees he was admitted to rehearsals, and many of his friends are of opinion that our present poets are indebted to him for their happiest thoughts; by his contrivance the bell was rung twice in *Barbarossa*,[9] and by his persuasion the author of *Cleone*[10] concluded his

---

[6] The opinions which follow come from these writers—from Pope chiefly, but also from Collins's *Epistle to Hanmer*, from Dryden, from Addison, and from Joseph Warton.

[7] Thomas Southerne (1660–1746).

[8] A tragedy by Edmund Smith (1672–1710), which pleased Addison, but not the public.

[9] A tragedy by Dr. John Brown (1715–1766).

[10] A tragedy by Robert Dodsley (1703–1764). "Mr. Langton, when a very young man," read this play to Johnson. At the end of an act, Johnson said: "Come, let's have some more, let's go into the slaughter-house again, Lanky. But I am afraid there is more blood than brains" (Boswell, *Life of Johnson*).

play without a couplet; for what can be more absurd, said Minim, than that part of a play should be rimed, and part written in blank verse? and by what acquisition of faculties is the speaker, who never could find rimes before, enabled to rime at the conclusion of an act?

He is the great investigator of hidden beauties, and is particularly delighted when he finds *the sound an echo to the sense.* He has read all our poets with particular attention to this deli- [10] cacy of versification, and wonders at the supineness with which their works have been hitherto perused, so that no man has found the sound of a drum in this distich:

> When pulpit, drum ecclesiastic,
> Was beat with fist instead of a stick; [11]

and that the wonderful lines upon honor and a bubble have hitherto passed without notice:

> Honor is like the glassy bubble,
> Which cost philosophers such trouble; [20]
> Where, one part cracked, the whole does fly,
> And wits are cracked to find out why. [12]

In these verses, says Minim, we have two striking accommodations of the sound to the sense. It is impossible to utter the two lines emphatically without an act like that which they describe; *bubble* and *trouble* causing a momentary inflation of the cheeks by the retention of the breath, which is afterwards forcibly [30] emitted, as in the practice of *blowing bubbles.* But the greatest excellence is in the third line, which is *cracked* in the middle to express a crack, and then shivers into monosyllables. Yet has this diamond laid neglected with common stones, and among the innumerable admirers of *Hudibras* the observation of this superlative passage has been reserved for the sagacity of Minim.

## NO. 61. SATURDAY, 15 JUNE, 1759.

MR. MINIM had now advanced himself to the zenith of critical reputation; when he was in the pit, every eye in the boxes was fixed upon him; when he entered his coffee-house, he was surrounded by circles of candidates, who passed their novitiate of literature under his tuition; his opinion was asked by all who had no opinion of their own, and yet loved to [50] debate and decide; and no composition was supposed to pass in safety to posterity, till it had been secured by Minim's approbation.

[11] Samuel Butler's *Hudibras*, I, i, 11–12.
[12] *Ibid.*, II, ii, 385–388. The "bubble" (Prince Rupert's drop) of which Butler speaks is made of glass, and the "philosophers" whom it puzzled were the members of the Royal Society.

Minim professes great admiration of the wisdom and munificence by which the academies of the continent were raised; and often wishes for some standard of taste, for some tribunal, to which merit may appeal from caprice, prejudice, and malignity. He has formed a plan for an academy of criticism, where every work of imagination may be read before it is printed, and which shall authorita- [10] tively direct the theaters what pieces to receive or reject, to exclude or to revive.

Such an institution would, in Dick's opinion, spread the fame of English literature over Europe, and make London the metropolis of elegance and politeness, the place to which the learned and ingenious of all countries would repair for instruction and improvement, where nothing would any longer be applauded or endured that was not conformed to the [20] nicest rules, and finished with the highest elegance.

Till some happy conjunction of the planets shall dispose our princes or ministers to make themselves immortal by such an academy, Minim contents himself to preside four nights in a week in a critical society selected by himself, where he is heard without contradiction, and whence his judgment is disseminated through the great vulgar and the small. [13]

When he is placed in the chair of criticism, he declares loudly for the noble simplicity of our ancestors, in opposition to the petty refinements, and ornamental luxuriance. Sometimes he is sunk in despair, and perceives false delicacy daily gaining ground, and sometimes brightens his countenance with a gleam of hope, and predicts the revival of the true sublime. He then fulminates his loudest censures against the monkish barbarity of rime; wonders [40] how beings that pretend to reason can be pleased with one line always ending like another; tells how unjustly and unnaturally sense is sacrificed to sound; how often the best thoughts are mangled by the necessity of confining or extending them to the dimensions of a couplet; and rejoices that genius has, in our days, shaken off the shackles which had encumbered it so long. Yet he allows that rime may sometimes be borne, if the lines be often [50] broken, and the pauses judiciously diversified.

From blank verse he makes an easy transition to Milton, whom he produces as an example of the slow advance of lasting reputation. Milton is the only writer in whose books

[13] See Abraham Cowley, *Several Discourses by Way of Essays, in Verse and Prose*, 6. Of Greatness (at end, imitation of Horace, *Odes*, III, i, 2).

Minim can read for ever without weariness. What cause it is that exempts this pleasure from satiety he has long and diligently inquired, and believes it to consist in the perpetual variation of the numbers, by which the ear is gratified and the attention awakened. The lines that are commonly thought rugged and unmusical, he conceives to have been written to temper the melodious luxury of the rest, or to express things by a proper cadence: for he scarcely finds a verse that has not this favorite beauty; he declares that he could shiver in a hot-house when he reads that

The ground
Burns frore, and cold performs th' effect of fire; [14]

and that, when Milton bewails his blindness, the verse,

So thick a drop serene has quenched these orbs, [15]

has, he knows not how, something that strikes him with an obscure sensation like that which he fancies would be felt from the sound of darkness.

Minim is not so confident of his rules of judgment as not very eagerly to catch new light from the name of the author. He is commonly so prudent as to spare those whom he cannot resist, unless, as will sometimes happen, he finds the public combined against them. But a fresh pretender to fame he is strongly inclined to censure, till his own honor requires that he commend him. Till he knows the success of a composition, he intrenches himself in general terms; there are some new thoughts and beautiful passages, but there is likewise much which he would have advised the author to expunge. He has several favorite epithets, of which he has never settled the meaning, but which are very commodiously applied to books which he has not read, or cannot understand. One is *manly*, another is *dry*, another *stiff*, and another *flimsy*; sometimes he discovers delicacy of style, and sometimes meets with *strange expressions*.

He is never so great, or so happy, as when a youth of promising parts is brought to receive his directions for the prosecution of his studies. He then puts on a very serious air; he advises the pupil to read none but the best authors, and, when he finds one congenial to his own mind, to study his beauties, but avoid his faults; and, when he sits down to write, to consider how his favorite author would think at the present time on the present occasion. He exhorts him to catch those moments when he finds his thoughts expanded and his genius exalted, but to take care lest imagination hurry him beyond the bounds of nature. He holds diligence the mother of success; yet enjoins him, with great earnestness, not to read more than he can digest, and not to confuse his mind by pursuing studies of contrary tendencies. He tells him, that every man has his genius, and that Cicero could never be a poet. The boy retires illuminated, resolves to follow his genius, and to think how Milton would have thought: and Minim feasts upon his own beneficence till another day brings another pupil.

# Lives of the English Poets

## PASSAGES FROM *THE LIFE OF MILTON* [1]

HE TOOK both the usual degrees, that of bachelor in 1628, and that of master in 1632; but he left the university with no kindness for its institution, alienated either by the injudicious severity of his governors, or his own captious perverseness. The cause cannot now be known, but the effect appears in his writings. His scheme of education, inscribed to Hartlib,[2] supersedes all academical instruction, being intended to comprise the whole time which men usually spend in literature, from their entrance upon grammar "till they proceed, as it is called, masters of arts." And in his discourse *On the likeliest Way to Remove Hirelings out of the Church* he ingeniously proposes that "the profits of the lands forfeited by the act for superstitious uses, should be applied to such academies all over the land, where languages and arts may be taught together; so that youth may be at once brought up to a competency of learning and an honest trade, by which means such of them as had the gift, being enabled to support themselves (without tithes) by the latter, may, by the help of the former, become worthy preachers."

One of his objections to academical education, as it was then conducted, is that men designed for orders in the church were permitted to act plays, "writhing and unboning

---

[14] *Paradise Lost*, II, 594–595.
[15] *Ibid.*, III, 25.

[1] The first thirteen paragraphs dealing with Milton's life before he left Cambridge University, are omitted from the present abridgment.
[2] *Of Education*, a letter addressed to Samuel Hartlib (1644).

their clergy limbs to all the antic and dishonest gestures of Trincalos,[3] buffoons, and bawds, prostituting the shame of that ministry which they had, or were near having, to the eyes of courtiers and court-ladies, their grooms and mademoiselles."[4]

This is sufficiently peevish in a man who, when he mentions his exile from the college, relates, with great luxuriance, the compensation which the pleasures of the theater afford him. Plays were therefore only criminal when they were acted by academics.

He went to the university with a design of entering into the church, but in time altered his mind; for he declared that whoever became a clergyman must "subscribe slave, and take an oath withal which, unless he took with a conscience that could retch, he must straight perjure himself. He thought it better to prefer a blameless silence before the office of speaking, bought and begun with servitude and forswearing."[5]

These expressions are, I find, applied to the subscription of the Articles;[6] but it seems more probable that they relate to canonical obedience. I know not any of the Articles which seem to thwart his opinions; but the thoughts of obedience, whether canonical or civil, raised his indignation.

His unwillingness to engage in the ministry, perhaps not yet advanced to a settled resolution of declining it, appears in a letter to one of his friends[7] who had reproved his suspended and dilatory life, which he seems to have imputed to an insatiable curiosity and fantastic luxury of various knowledge. To this he writes a cool and plausible answer, in which he endeavors to persuade him that the delay proceeds not from the delights of desultory study, but from the desire of obtaining more fitness for his task; and that he goes on, "not taking thought of being late, so it give advantage to be more fit."

When he left the university, he returned to his father, then residing at Horton in Buckinghamshire, with whom he lived five years; in which time he is said to have read all the Greek and Latin writers. With what

limitations this universality is to be understood, who shall inform us?

It might be supposed that he who read so much should have done nothing else; but Milton found time to write the masque of *Comus*, which was presented to Ludlow, then the residence of the Lord President of Wales,[8] in 1634; and had the honor of being acted by the Earl of Bridgewater's sons and daughter. The fiction is derived from Homer's *Circe*; but we never can refuse to any modern the liberty of borrowing from Homer:

> ——*a quo ceu fonte perenni*
> *Vatum Pieriis ora rigantur aquis.*[9]

His next production was *Lycidas*, an elegy written in 1637 on the death of Mr. King,[10] the son of Sir John King, secretary for Ireland in the time of Elizabeth, James, and Charles. King was much a favorite at Cambridge, and many of the wits joined to do honor to his memory. Milton's acquaintance with the Italian writers may be discovered by a mixture of longer and shorter verses, according to the rules of Tuscan poetry, and his malignity to the church by some lines which are interpreted as threatening its extermination.

He is supposed about this time to have written his *Arcades*; for while he lived at Horton he used sometimes to steal from his studies a few days, which he spent at Harefield, the house of the Countess Dowager of Derby,[11] where the *Arcades* made part of a dramatic entertainment.

He began now to grow weary of the country, and had some purpose of taking chambers in the Inns of Court,[12] when the death of his mother set him at liberty to travel, for which he obtained his father's consent and Sir Henry Wotton's directions, with the celebrated precept of prudence, *i pensieri stretti, ed il viso sciolto,* "thoughts close, and looks loose."[13]

In 1638 he left England, and went first to Paris; where, by the favor of Lord Scudamore, he had the opportunity of visiting

[8] John Egerton, first Earl of Bridgewater.

[9] From whom as from an ever-flowing fountain the mouths of poets are moistened by the muses' waters (Ovid, *Amores*, III, ix, 25).

[10] Edward King, a fellow student of Milton's at Christ's College, Cambridge.

[11] Alice Spenser, who had been celebrated by Edmund Spenser in her youth and was the grandmother of the three children who performed in *Comus*.

[12] The legal colleges in London.

[13] In Wotton's letter (13 April, 1638), prefixed to *Comus* in 1645.

[3] Trincalo was a character in Thomas Tomkis's *Albumazar*, a play acted before James I at Cambridge in 1615.

[4] From the *Apology for Smectymnuus* (1642).

[5] From *The Reason of Church Government Urged against Prelaty* (1642).

[6] Assent to the Thirty-nine Articles of the Anglican Church.

[7] A letter probably written in 1632. The name of the friend is unknown.

Grotius,[14] then residing at the French court as ambassador from Christina of Sweden. From Paris he hasted into Italy, of which he had with particular diligence studied the language and literature, and, though he seems to have intended a very quick perambulation of the country, stayed two months at Florence; where he found his way into the academies, and produced his compositions with such applause as appears to have exalted him in his own opinion, and confirmed him in the hope that "by labor and intense study, which," says he, "I take to be my portion in this life, joined with a strong propensity of nature," he might "leave something so written to aftertimes as they should not willingly let it die." [15]

It appears, in all his writings, that he had the usual concomitant of great abilities, a lofty and steady confidence in himself, perhaps not without some contempt of others; for scarcely any man ever wrote so much, and praised so few. Of his praise he was very frugal, as he set its value high, and considered his mention of a name as a security against the waste of time and a certain preservative from oblivion.

At Florence he could not indeed complain that his merit wanted distinction. Carlo Dati presented him with an encomiastic inscription, in the tumid lapidary style;[16] and Francini wrote him an ode, of which the first stanza is only empty noise; the rest are perhaps too diffuse on common topics, but the last is natural and beautiful.

From Florence he went to Siena, and from Siena to Rome, where he was again received with kindness by the learned and the great. Holstenius, the keeper of the Vatican Library, who had resided three years at Oxford, introduced him to Cardinal Barberini; and he, at a musical entertainment, waited for him at the door, and led him by the hand into the assembly. Here Selvaggi praised him in a distich, and Salsilli in a tetrastich: [17] neither of them of much value. The Italians were gainers by this literary commerce; for the encomiums with which Milton repaid Salsilli, though not secure against a stern grammarian, turn the balance indisputably in Milton's favor.

Of these Italian testimonies, poor as they are, he was proud enough to publish them before his poems; though he says he cannot be suspected but to have known that they were said *"non tam de se quàm supra se."* [18]

At Rome, as at Florence, he stayed only two months; a time indeed sufficient, if he desired only to ramble with an explainer of its antiquities, or to view palaces and count pictures, but certainly too short for the contemplation of learning, policy, or manners.

From Rome, he passed on to Naples, in company of a hermit, a companion from whom little could be expected; yet to him Milton owed his introduction to Manso, Marquis of Villa, who had been before the patron of Tasso. Manso was enough delighted with his accomplishments to honor him with a sorry distich, in which he commends him for everything but his religion; and Milton, in return, addressed him in a Latin poem [19] which must have raised an high opinion of English elegance and literature.

His purpose was now to have visited Sicily and Greece; but, hearing of the differences between the king and parliament, he thought it proper to hasten home rather than pass his life in foreign amusements while his countrymen were contending for their rights. He therefore came back to Rome, though the merchants informed him of plots laid against him by the Jesuits for the liberty of his conversations on religion. He had sense enough to judge that there was no danger, and therefore kept on his way, and acted as before, neither obtruding nor shunning controversy. He had perhaps given some offence by visiting Galileo,[20] then a prisoner in the Inquisition for philosophical heresy; and at Naples he was told by Manso that, by his declarations on religious questions, he had excluded himself from some distinctions which he should otherwise have paid him. But such conduct, though it did not please, was yet sufficiently safe; and Milton stayed two months more at Rome, and went on to Florence without molestation.

From Florence he visited Lucca. He afterwards went to Venice; and having sent away a collection of music and other books, traveled to Geneva, which he probably considered as the metropolis of orthodoxy.[21]

[14] Hugo Grotius (1583–1645), the Dutch poet, scholar, and statesman.
[15] From *The Reason of Church Government Urged against Prelaty* (1642).
[16] The style of monumental inscriptions.
[17] A distich is a couplet; a tetrastich, a stanza of four lines.
[18] Not so much about as above his real character (words before Latin section in Milton's *Poems*, 1645).
[19] The *Mansus*, written in 1639.
[20] Galileo Galilei (1564–1642). Cf. *Paradise Lost*, I, 286–291.
[21] Since it was the seat of Calvinism.

Here he reposed as in a congenial element, and became acquainted with John Diodati and Frederick Spanheim, two learned professors of divinity. From Geneva he passed through France, and came home, after an absence of a year and three months.

At his return he heard of the death of his friend Charles Diodati,[22] a man whom it is reasonable to suppose of great merit since he was thought by Milton worthy of a poem, entitled *Epitaphium Damonis*, written with the common but childish imitation of pastoral life.

He now hired a lodging at the house of one Russel, a tailor, in St. Bride's Church-yard, and undertook the education of John and Edward Phillips, his sister's sons. Finding his rooms too little, he took a house and garden in Aldersgate Street, which was not then so much out of the world as it is now, and chose his dwelling at the upper end of a passage that he might avoid the noise of the street. Here he received more boys, to be boarded and instructed.

Let not our veneration for Milton forbid us to look with some degree of merriment on great promises and small performance, on the man who hastens home because his countrymen are contending for their liberty, and, when he reaches the scene of action, vapors away his patriotism in a private boarding-school. This is the period of his life from which all his biographers seem inclined to shrink. They are unwilling that Milton should be degraded to a schoolmaster; but, since it cannot be denied that he taught boys, one finds out that he taught for nothing, and another that his motive was only zeal for the propagation of learning and virtue; and all tell what they do not know to be true, only to excuse an act which no wise man will consider as in itself disgraceful. His father was alive; his allowance was not ample; and he supplied its deficiencies by an honest and useful employment.

It is told that in the art of education he performed wonders; and a formidable list is given of the authors, Greek and Latin, that were read in Aldersgate Street by youth between ten and fifteen or sixteen years of age. Those who tell or receive these stories should consider that nobody can be taught faster than he can learn. The speed of the horseman must be limited by the power of his horse. Every man that has ever undertaken

to instruct others can tell what slow advances he has been able to make, and how much patience it requires to recall vagrant inattention, to stimulate sluggish indifference, and to rectify absurd misapprehension.

The purpose of Milton, as it seems, was to teach something more solid than the common literature of schools, by reading those authors that treat of physical subjects, such as the Georgic[23] and astronomical treatises of the ancients. This was a scheme of improvement which seems to have busied many literary projectors of that age. Cowley,[24] who had more means than Milton of knowing what was wanting to the embellishments of life, formed the same plan of education in his imaginary college.

But the truth is that the knowledge of external nature, and the sciences which that knowledge requires or includes, are not the great or the frequent business of the human mind. Whether we provide for action or conversation, whether we wish to be useful or pleasing, the first requisite is the religious and moral knowledge of right and wrong; the next is an acquaintance with the history of mankind, and with those examples which may be said to embody truth, and prove by events the reasonableness of opinions. Prudence and justice are virtues and excellences of all times and of all places; we are perpetually moralists, but we are geometricians only by chance. Our intercourse with intellectual nature is necessary; our speculations upon matter are voluntary, and at leisure. Physiological learning[25] is of such rare emergence that one man may know another half his life without being able to estimate his skill in hydrostatics or astronomy; but his moral and prudential character immediately appears.

Those authors, therefore, are to be read at schools that supply most axioms of prudence, most principles of moral truth, and most materials for conversation; and these purposes are best served by poets, orators, and historians.

Let me not be censured for this digression as pedantic or paradoxical; for if I have Milton against me, I have Socrates on my side. It was his labor to turn philosophy from the study of nature to speculations upon life; but the innovators whom I oppose are turning off attention from life to nature.

[22] Schoolfellow of Milton's and nephew of John Diodati. He had died a year before Milton's return.

[23] Agricultural.

[24] Abraham Cowley (1618–1667), poet. Johnson refers to his tract, *A Proposition for the Advancement of Experimental Philosophy* (1661).

[25] Knowledge of natural science.

They seem to think that we are placed here to watch the growth of plants, or the motions of the stars. Socrates was rather of opinion that what we had to learn was how to do good and avoid evil.

Ὅττι τοι ἐν μεγάροισι κακόν τ' ἀγαθόν τε τέτυκται.[26]

Of institutions we may judge by their effects. From this wonder-working academy I do not know that there ever proceeded any man very eminent for knowledge; its only genuine product, I believe, is a small history of poetry, written in Latin by his nephew, Phillips,[27] of which perhaps none of my readers has ever heard.

That in his school, as in everything else which he undertook, he labored with great diligence there is no reason for doubting. One part of his method deserves general imitation. He was careful to instruct his scholars in religion. Every Sunday was spent upon theology, of which he dictated a short system, gathered from the writers that were then fashionable in the Dutch universities.

He set his pupils an example of hard study and spare diet; only now and then he allowed himself to pass a day of festivity and indulgence with some gay gentlemen of Gray's Inn.[28]

He now began to engage in the controversies of the times, and lent his breath to blow the flames of contention. In 1641 he published a treatise *Of Reformation* in two books, against the Established Church, being willing to help the Puritans, who were, he says, "inferior to the prelates in learning."[29]

*       *       *

His next[30] work was *The Reason of Church Government urged against Prelacy, by Mr. John Milton*, 1642. In this book he discovers, not with ostentatious exultation, but with calm confidence, his high opinion of his own powers; and promises to undertake something, he yet knows not what, that may be of use and honor to his country. "This," says he, "is not to be obtained but by devout prayer to that Eternal Spirit that can enrich with all utterance and knowledge, and sends

out his Seraphim with the hallowed fire of his altar, to touch and purify the lips of whom he pleases. To this must be added industrious and select reading, steady observation, and insight into all seemly and generous arts and affairs; till which in some measure be compassed, I refuse not to sustain this expectation." From a promise like this, at once fervid, pious, and rational, might be expected the *Paradise Lost*.

He published the same year two more pamphlets upon the same question. To one of his antagonists, who affirms that he was "vomited out of the university," he answers in general terms: "The fellows of the college wherein I spent some years, at my parting, after I had taken two degrees, as the manner is, signified many times how much better it would content them that I should stay.—As for the common approbation or dislike of that place, as now it is, that I should esteem or disesteem myself the more for that, too simple is the answerer, if he think to obtain with me. Of small practice were the physician who could not judge, by what she and her sister have of long time vomited, that the worser stuff she strongly keeps in her stomach, but the better she is ever kecking[31] at, and is queasy; she vomits now out of sickness; but before it be well with her, she must vomit by strong physic. The university, in the time of her better health, and my younger judgment, I never greatly admired, but now much less."[32]

This is surely the language of a man who thinks that he has been injured. He proceeds to describe the course of his conduct and the train of his thoughts; and, because he has been suspected of incontinence, gives an account of his own purity: "That if I be justly charged," says he, "with this crime, it may come upon me with tenfold shame."

The style of his piece is rough, and such perhaps was that of his antagonist. This roughness he justifies by great examples in a long digression. Sometimes he tries to be humorous: "Lest I should take him for some chaplain in hand, some squire of the body to his prelate, one who serves not at the altar only but at the court-cupboard,[33] he will bestow on us a pretty model of himself; and sets me out half a dozen phthisical mottoes, wherever he had them, hopping short in the

---

[26] What good, what ill
Hath in thine house befallen.
(*Odyssey*, IV, 392; Cowper's translation.)

[27] Probably Edward Phillips, author of *Tractatulus de Carmine Dramatico* (1670).

[28] One of the London legal colleges.

[29] Milton actually says they were inferior in eloquence (*Defensio Secunda*, 1654).

[30] Next after *Of Prelatical Episcopacy* (1641).

[31] Making a noise as if about to vomit.

[32] Both this and the two following quotations are from the *Apology for Smectymnuus* (1642).

[33] Sideboard on which plates were displayed.

measure of convulsion fits; in which labor the agony of his wit having escaped narrowly, instead of well-sized periods, he greets us with a quantity of thumb-ring posies.[34]— And thus ends this section, or rather dissection, of himself." Such is the controversial merriment of Milton; his gloomy seriousness is yet more offensive. Such is his malignity "that hell grows darker at his frown." [35]

His father, after Reading was taken by Essex,[36] came to reside in his house; and his school increased. At Whitsuntide in his thirty-fifth year he married Mary, the daughter of Mr. Powell, a justice of the peace in Oxfordshire. He brought her to town with him, and expected all the advantages of a conjugal life. The lady, however, seems not much to have delighted in the pleasures of spare diet and hard study; for, as Phillips relates, "having for a month led a philosophical life, after having been used at home to a great house and much company and joviality, her friends, possibly by her own desire, made earnest suit to have her company the remaining part of the summer; which was granted, upon a promise of her return at Michaelmas."

Milton was too busy to much miss his wife; he pursued his studies, and now and then visited the Lady Margaret Leigh, whom he has mentioned in one of his sonnets. At last Michaelmas arrived; but the lady had no inclination to return to the sullen gloom of her husband's habitation, and therefore very willingly forgot her promise. He sent her a letter, but had no answer; he sent more with the same success. It could be alleged that letters miscarry; he therefore despatched a messenger, being by this time too angry to go himself. His messenger was sent back with some contempt. The family of the lady were Cavaliers.

In a man whose opinion of his own merit was like Milton's, less provocation than this might have raised violent resentment. Milton soon determined to repudiate her for disobedience; and, being one of those who could easily find arguments to justify inclination, published (in 1644) [37] *The Doctrine and Discipline of Divorce*, which was followed by *The Judgment of Martin Bucer* concerning

*Divorce*, and the next year his *Tetrachordon*, *Expositions upon the Four Chief Places of Scripture Which Treat of Marriage.*

This innovation was opposed, as might be expected, by the clergy, who, then holding their famous assembly at Westminster, procured that the author should be called before the Lords; "but that house," says Wood,[38] "whether approving the doctrine or not favoring his accusers, did soon dismiss him."

There seems not to have been much written against him, nor anything by any writer of eminence. The antagonist that appeared is styled by him "a serving man turned solicitor." [39] Howell [40] in his letters mentions the new doctrine with contempt; and it was, I suppose, thought more worthy of derision than of confutation. He complains of this neglect in two sonnets,[41] of which the first is contemptible, and the second not excellent.

From this time it is observed that he became an enemy to the Presbyterians, whom he had favored before. He that changes his party by his humor is not more virtuous than he that changes it by his interest; he loves himself rather than truth.

His wife and her relations now found that Milton was not an unresisting sufferer of injuries; and perceiving that he had begun to put his doctrine in practice by courting a young woman of great accomplishments, the daughter of one Dr. Davis, who was, however, not ready to comply, they resolved to endeavor a reunion. He went sometimes to the house of one Blackborough, his relation, in the lane of St. Martin's-le-Grand, and at one of his usual visits was surprised to see his wife come from another room and implore forgiveness on her knees. He resisted her intreaties for a while; "but partly," says Phillips,[42] "his own generous nature, more inclinable to reconciliation than to perseverance in anger or revenge, and partly the strong intercession of friends on both sides, soon brought him to an act of oblivion and a firm league of peace." It were injurious to omit that Milton afterwards received her father and her brothers in his own house when they were distressed, with other Royalists.

[34] Mottoes.
[35] *Paradise Lost*, II, 719–720.
[36] The third Earl of Essex (1591–1646), general of the parliamentary army.
[37] The first of the three tracts was published in 1643, the second in 1644, and third in 1645.

[38] Anthony à Wood in *Athenae Oxonienses* (1691–1692).
[39] In *Colasterion* (1645).
[40] James Howell (1596–1666), author of *Epistolae Ho-elianae.*
[41] Sonnets XI and XII in the present collection.
[42] Edward Phillips, in the preface to Milton's *Letters of State* (1694).

He published about the same time [43] his *Areopagitica, a Speech of Mr. John Milton for the Liberty of Unlicensed Printing.* The danger of such unbounded liberty and the danger of bounding it have produced a problem in the science of government which human understanding seems hitherto unable to solve. If nothing may be published but what civil authority shall have previously approved, power must always be the standard of truth; if every dreamer of innovations may propagate his projects, there can be no settlement; if every murmurer at government may diffuse discontent, there can be no peace; and if every sceptic in theology may teach his follies, there can be no religion. The remedy against these evils is to punish the authors, for it is yet allowed that every society may punish, though not prevent, the publication of opinions which that society shall think pernicious; but this punishment, though it may crush the author, promotes the book; and it seems not more reasonable to leave the right of printing unrestrained because writers may be afterwards censured than it would be to sleep with doors unbolted because by our laws we can hang a thief.

But whatever were his engagements, civil or domestic, poetry was never long out of his thoughts.

\* \* \*

Being now forty-seven years old,[44] and seeing himself disencumbered from external interruptions, he seems to have recollected his former purposes, and to have resumed three great works which he had planned for his future employment: an epic poem, the history of his country, and a dictionary of the Latin tongue.

To collect a dictionary seems a work of all others least practicable in a state of blindness, because it depends upon perpetual and minute inspection and collation. Nor would Milton probably have begun it after he had lost his eyes; but, having had it always before him, he continued it, says Phillips, "almost to his dying day; but the papers were so discomposed and deficient that they could not be fitted for the press." The compilers of the Latin dictionary printed at Cambridge had the use of those collections in three folios; but what was their fate afterwards is not known.

To compile a history from various authors, when they can only be consulted by other eyes, is not easy nor possible but with more skilful and attentive help than can be commonly obtained; and it was probably the difficulty of consulting and comparing that stopped Milton's narrative at the Conquest, a period at which affairs were not yet very intricate, nor authors very numerous.

For the subject of his epic poem, after much deliberation, "long choosing, and beginning late," [45] he fixed upon *Paradise Lost,* a design so comprehensive that it could be justified only by success. He had once designed to celebrate King Arthur, as he hints in his verses to Mansus; but "Arthur was reserved," says Fenton,[46] "to another destiny."

It appears, by some sketches of poetical projects left in manuscript and to be seen in a library [47] at Cambridge, that he had digested his thoughts on this subject into one of those wild dramas which were anciently called mysteries; [48] and Phillips had seen what he terms part of a tragedy, beginning with the first ten lines of Satan's address to the sun. These mysteries consist of allegorical persons, such as Justice, Mercy, Faith. Of the tragedy or mystery of *Paradise Lost* there are two plans:

| THE PERSONS | THE PERSONS |
|---|---|
| MICHAEL. | MOSES. |
| CHORUS OF ANGELS. | DIVINE JUSTICE, WISDOM, HEAVENLY LOVE. |
| HEAVENLY LOVE. | |
| LUCIFER. | THE EVENING STAR, HESPERUS. |
| ADAM, } with the | |
| EVE, } Serpent. | CHORUS OF ANGELS. |
| CONSCIENCE. | LUCIFER. |
| DEATH. | ADAM. |
| LABOR, | EVE. |
| SICKNESS, | CONSCIENCE. |
| DISCONTENT, } Mutes. | LABOR, |
| IGNORANCE, | SICKNESS, |
| with others; | DISCONTENT, |
| FAITH. | IGNORANCE, } Mutes. |
| HOPE. | FEAR, |
| CHARITY. | DEATH; |
| | FAITH. |
| | HOPE. |
| | CHARITY. |

[45] *Paradise Lost,* IX, 26.
[46] Elijah Fenton (1683–1730). He alludes to the notorious *Prince Arthur* (1695) of Sir Richard Blackmore.
[47] Library of Trinity College.
[48] Miracle-plays.

[43] In 1644.
[44] In 1656, about four years after Milton had become totally blind.

## PARADISE LOST

### THE PERSONS

#### ACT I

Moses προλογίζει,[49] recounting how he assumed his true body; that it corrupts not, because it is with God in the mount; declares the like of Enoch and Elijah; besides the purity of the place, that certain pure winds, dews, and clouds preserve it from corruption; whence exhorts to the sight of God; tells they cannot see Adam in the state of innocence, by reason of their sin.

JUSTICE,  
MERCY, } debating what should become of man,  
WISDOM, } if he fall.  
CHORUS OF ANGELS singing a hymn of the Creation.

#### ACT II

HEAVENLY LOVE.  
EVENING STAR.  
CHORUS sing the marriage-song and describe Paradise.

#### ACT III

LUCIFER contriving ADAM's ruin.  
CHORUS fears for ADAM, and relates LUCIFER's rebellion and fall.

#### ACT IV

ADAM, } fallen.  
EVE, }  
CONSCIENCE cites them to God's examination.  
CHORUS bewails, and tells the good ADAM has lost.

#### ACT V

ADAM and EVE driven out of Paradise.  
———————— presented by an angel with  
LABOR, GRIEF, HATRED, ENVY, WAR,  
  FAMINE, PESTILENCE, SICKNESS, } Mutes.  
  DISCONTENT, IGNORANCE, FEAR,  
  DEATH,  
To whom he gives their names. Likewise WINTER, HEAT, TEMPEST, *etc.*  
FAITH,  
HOPE, } comfort him and instruct him.  
CHARITY,  
CHORUS briefly concludes.

Such was his first design, which could have produced only an allegory, or mystery. The following sketch seems to have attained more maturity:

### ADAM UNPARADISED

The angel GABRIEL, either descending or entering, showing, since this globe was created, his frequency as much on earth as in heaven; describes Paradise. Next, the CHORUS, showing the reason of his coming to keep his watch in Paradise, after

LUCIFER's rebellion, by command from God; and withal expressing his desire to see and know more concerning this excellent new creature, man. The angel GABRIEL, as by his name signifying a prince of power, tracing Paradise with a more free office, passes by the station of the CHORUS, and, desired by them, relates what he knew of man, as the creation of EVE, with their love and marriage. After this LUCIFER appears; after his overthrow, bemoans himself, seeks revenge on man. The CHORUS prepare resistance at his first approach. At last, after discourse of enmity on either side, he departs; whereat the CHORUS sings of the battle and victory in heaven, against him and his accomplices, as before, after the first act, was sung a hymn of the creation. Here again may appear LUCIFER, relating and insulting in what he had done to the destruction of man. Man next, and EVE having by this time been seduced by the SERPENT, appears confusedly covered with leaves. CONSCIENCE, in a shape,[50] accuses him; JUSTICE cites him to the place whither Jehovah called for him. In the meanwhile the CHORUS entertains the stage, and is informed by some angel the manner of the Fall. Here the CHORUS bewails ADAM's fall; ADAM then and EVE return; accuse one another; but especially ADAM lays the blame to his wife; is stubborn in his offence. JUSTICE appears, reasons with him, convinces him. The CHORUS admonisheth ADAM, and bids him beware LUCIFER's example of impenitence. The ANGEL is sent to banish them out of Paradise, but before causes to pass before his eyes, in shapes, a masque of all the evils of this life and world. He is humbled, relents, despairs: at last appears MERCY, comforts him, promises the Messiah; then calls in FAITH, HOPE, and CHARITY; instructs him; he repents, gives God the glory, submits to his penalty. The CHORUS briefly concludes. Compare this with the former draught.

These are very imperfect rudiments of *Paradise Lost*; but it is pleasant to see great works in their seminal state, pregnant with latent possibilities of excellence; nor could there be any more delightful entertainment than to trace their gradual growth and expansion, and to observe how they are sometimes suddenly advanced by accidental hints, and sometimes slowly improved by steady 10 meditation.

Invention is almost the only literary labor which blindness cannot obstruct, and therefore he naturally solaced his solitude by the indulgence of his fancy, and the melody of his numbers. He had done what he knew to be necessarily previous to poetical excellence; he had made himself acquainted with "seemly arts and affairs";[51] his comprehension was extended by various knowledge, and his memory 20 stored with intellectual treasures. He was skillful in many languages, and had by reading and composition attained the full mastery of his own. He would have wanted

———————————

[49] Delivers a prologue.

[50] Suitable costume and make-up.  
[51] From *The Reason of Church Government.*

little help from books, had he retained the power of perusing them.

* * *

He was now busied by *Paradise Lost*. Whence he drew the original design has been variously conjectured by men who cannot bear to think themselves ignorant of that which, at last, neither diligence nor sagacity can discover. Some find the hint in an Italian tragedy. Voltaire [52] tells a wild and unauthorized story of a farce seen by Milton in Italy, which opened thus: "Let the rainbow be the fiddlestick of the fiddle of heaven." It has been already shown that the first conception was a tragedy or mystery, not of a narrative but a dramatic work, which he is supposed to have begun to reduce to its present form about the time (1655) when he finished his dispute with the defenders of the king.

He long before had promised to adorn his native country by some great performance, while he had yet perhaps no settled design, and was stimulated only by such expectations as naturally arose from the survey of his attainments and the consciousness of his powers. What he should undertake it was difficult to determine. He was "long choosing, and began late."

While he was obliged to divide his time between his private studies and affairs of state, his poetical labor must have been often interrupted; and perhaps he did little more in that busy time, than construct the narrative, adjust the episodes, proportion the parts, accumulate images and sentiments, and treasure in his memory, or preserve in writing, such hints as books or meditation would supply. Nothing particular is known of his intellectual operations while he was a statesman; for, having every help and accommodation at hand, he had no need of uncommon expedients.

Being driven from all public stations, he is yet too great not to be traced by curiosity to his retirement; where he has been found by Mr. Richardson,[53] the fondest of his admirers, sitting "before his door in a grey coat of coarse cloth, in warm sultry weather, to enjoy the fresh air, and so, as well as in his own room, receiving the visits of people of distinguished parts as well as quality." His visitors of high quality must now be imagined to be few; but men of parts might reasonably court the conversation of a man so generally illustrious that foreigners are reported by Wood to have visited the house in Bread Street where he was born.

According to another account, he was seen in a small house, "neatly enough dressed in black clothes, sitting in a room hung with rusty green; pale but not cadaverous, with chalkstones [54] in his hands. He said that if it were not for the gout, his blindness would be tolerable."

In the intervals of his pain, being made unable to use the common exercises, he used to swing in a chair, and sometimes played upon an organ.

He was now confessedly and visibly employed upon his poem, of which the progress might be noted by those with whom he was familiar; for he was obliged, when he had composed as many lines as his memory would conveniently retain, to employ some friend in writing them, having, at least for part of the time, no regular attendant. This gave opportunity to observations and reports.

Mr. Phillips observes that there was a very remarkable circumstance in the composure of *Paradise Lost*, "which I have a particular reason," says he, "to remember; for whereas I had the perusal of it from the very beginning, for some years, as I went from time to time to visit him, in parcels of ten, twenty, or thirty verses at a time (which, being written by whatever hand came next, might possibly want correction as to the orthography and pointing [55]), having as the summer came on not been showed any for a considerable while, and desiring the reason thereof, was answered that his vein never happily flowed but from the autumnal equinox to the vernal; and that whatever he attempted at other times was never to his satisfaction, though he courted his fancy never so much; so that, in all the years he was about this poem, he may be said to have spent half his time therein."

Upon this relation Toland [56] remarks that in his opinion Phillips has mistaken the time of the year; for Milton in his elegies declares that with the advance of the spring he feels the increase of his poetical force, *"redeunt in carmina vires."* [57] To this it is answered that Phillips could hardly mistake time so well

---

[52] In his *Essai sur la Poésie Épique*. The "farce" is G. B. Andreini's religious drama, the *Adamo* (1613).

[53] Jonathan Richardson, author of *Explanatory Notes and Remarks on Paradise Lost* (1734).

[54] Concretions of hard matter in the joints, an evidence of gout.

[55] Punctuation.

[56] John Toland in his life of Milton (1698).

[57] My powers of song return (Elegy V, 5).

marked; and it may be added that Milton might find different times of the year favorable to different parts of life. Mr. Richardson conceives it impossible that "such a work should be suspended for six months, or for one. It may go on faster or slower, but it must go on." By what necessity it must continually go on, or why it might not be laid aside and resumed, it is not easy to discover.

This dependence of the soul upon the seasons, those temporary and periodical ebbs and flows of intellect, may, I suppose, justly be derided as the fumes of vain imagination. *Sapiens dominabitur astris.*[58] The author that thinks himself weatherbound will find, with a little help from hellebore,[59] that he is only idle or exhausted. But while this notion has possession of the head, it produces the inability which it supposes. Our powers owe much of their energy to our hopes; *possunt quia posse videntur.*[60] When success seems attainable, diligence is enforced; but when it is admitted that the faculties are suppressed by a cross wind or a cloudy sky, the day is given up without resistance; for who can contend with the course of nature?

From such prepossessions Milton seems not to have been free. There prevailed in his time an opinion that the world was in its decay, and that we have had the misfortune to be produced in the decrepitude of nature. It was suspected that the whole creation languished, that neither trees nor animals had the height or bulk of their predecessors, and that everything was daily sinking by gradual diminution. Milton appears to suspect that souls partake of the general degeneracy, and is not without some fear that his book is to be written in "an age too late" for heroic poesy.[61]

Another opinion wanders about the world, and sometimes finds reception among wise men, an opinion that restrains the operations of the mind to particular regions, and supposes that a luckless mortal may be born in a degree of latitude too high or too low for wisdom or for wit. From this fancy, wild as it is, he had not wholly cleared his head when he feared lest the "climate" of his country might be "too cold" for flights of imagination.

Into a mind already occupied by such fancies another not more reasonable might easily find its way. He that could fear lest his genius had fallen upon too old a world, or too chill a climate, might consistently magnify to himself the influence of the seasons, and believe his faculties to be vigorous only half the year.

His submission to the seasons was at least more reasonable than his dread of decaying nature, or a frigid zone, for general causes must operate uniformly in a general abatement of mental power; if less could be performed by the writer, less likewise would content the judges of his work. Among this lagging race of frosty grovelers he might still have risen into eminence by producing something which "they should not willingly let die."[62] However inferior to the heroes who were born in better ages, he might still be great among his contemporaries, with the hope of growing every day greater in the dwindle of posterity. He might still be the giant of the pygmies, the one-eyed monarch of the blind.

Of his artifices of study, or particular hours of composition, we have little account, and there was perhaps little to be told. Richardson, who seems to have been very diligent in his inquiries, but discovers always a wish to find Milton discriminated from other men, relates that "he would sometimes lie awake whole nights, but not a verse could he make; and on a sudden his poetical faculty would rush upon him with an *impetus* or *oestrum*,[63] and his daughter was immediately called to secure what came. At other times he would dictate perhaps forty lines in a breath, and then reduce them to half the number."

These bursts of lights and involutions of darkness, these transient and involuntary excursions and retrocessions of invention, having some appearance of deviation from the common train of nature, are eagerly caught by the lovers of a wonder. Yet something of this inequality happens to every man in every mode of exertion, manual or mental. The mechanic cannot handle his hammer and his file at all times with equal dexterity; there are hours, he knows not why, when his hand is out. By Mr. Richardson's relation, casually conveyed, much regard cannot be claimed. That in his intellectual hour Milton called

[58] The wise man will rule the stars (an adage attributed to the astronomer Ptolemy).
[59] A plant from which was derived a cure for mental diseases.
[60] They are able because they seem to be able.
[61] This fear and that discussed in the following paragraph seem to be derived from *The Reason of Church Government.*

[62] From *The Reason of Church Government.*
[63] Impulse or inspiration.

for his daughter "to secure what came" may be questioned; for unluckily it happens to be known that his daughters were never taught to write; nor would he have been obliged, as is universally confessed, to have employed any casual visitor in disburthening his memory, if his daughter could have performed the office.

The story of reducing his exuberance has been told of other authors, and, though doubtless true of every fertile and copious mind, seems to have been gratuitously transferred to Milton.

What he has told us, and we cannot now know more, is that he composed much of his poem in the night and morning, I suppose before his mind was disturbed with common business; and that he poured out with great fluency his "unpremeditated verse." [64] Versification, free, like his, from the distresses of rime, must by a work so long be made prompt and habitual; and, when his thoughts were once adjusted, the words would come at his command.

\* \* \*

The slow sale and tardy reputation of this poem [65] have been always mentioned as evidences of neglected merit, and of the uncertainty of literary fame; and inquiries have been made, and conjectures offered, about the causes of its long obscurity and late reception. But has the case been truly stated? Have not lamentation and wonder been lavished on an evil that was never felt?

That in the reigns of Charles and James the *Paradise Lost* received no public acclamations is readily confessed. Wit and literature were on the side of the court; and who that solicited favor or fashion would venture to praise the defender of the regicides? All that he himself could think his due, from "evil tongues" in "evil days," [66] was that reverential silence which was generously preserved. But it cannot be inferred that his poem was not read, or not, however unwillingly, admired.

The sale, if it be considered, will justify the public. Those who have no power to judge of past times but by their own should always doubt their conclusions. The call for books was not in Milton's age what it is in the present. To read was not then a general amusement; neither traders, nor often gentlemen, thought themselves disgraced by ignorance. The women had not then aspired to literature, nor was every house supplied with a closet of knowledge. Those, indeed, who professed learning, were not less learned than at any other time; but of that middle race of students who read for pleasure or accomplishment, and who buy the numerous products of modern typography, the number was then comparatively small. To prove the paucity of readers it may be sufficient to remark that the nation had been satisfied from 1623 to 1664, that is forty-one years, with only two editions of the works of Shakespeare,[67] which probably did not together make one thousand copies.

The sale of thirteen hundred copies in two years, in opposition to so much recent enmity, and to a style of versification new to all and disgusting to many, was an uncommon example of the prevalence of genius. The demand did not immediately increase; for many more readers than were supplied at first the nation did not afford. Only three thousand were sold in eleven years, for it forced its way without assistance; its admirers did not dare to publish their opinion, and the opportunities now given of attracting notice by advertisements were then very few; the means of proclaiming the publication of new books have been produced by that general literature which now pervades the nation through all its ranks.

But the reputation and price of the copy still advanced till the Revolution [68] put an end to the secrecy of love, and *Paradise Lost* broke into open view with sufficient security of kind reception.

Fancy can hardly forbear to conjecture with what temper Milton surveyed the silent progress of his work, and marked his reputation stealing its way in a kind of subterraneous current through fear and silence. I cannot but conceive him calm and confident, little disappointed, not at all dejected, relying on his own merit with steady consciousness, and waiting without impatience the vicissitudes of opinion, and the impartiality of a future generation.

\* \* \*

Milton has the reputation of having been in his youth eminently beautiful, so as to have been called the lady of his college. His hair, which was of a light brown, parted at the foretop and hung down upon his shoulders, according to the picture which he has given of Adam. He was, however, not of the

[64] *Paradise Lost*, IX, 21–24.
[65] *Paradise Lost*.
[66] *Paradise Lost*, VII, 26.
[67] There were editions in 1623, 1632, and 1664.
[68] The Glorious Revolution of 1688.

heroic stature, but rather below the middle size, according to Mr. Richardson, who mentions him as having narrowly escaped from being "short and thick." He was vigorous, and active, and delighted in the exercise of the sword, in which he is related to have been eminently skilful. His weapon was, I believe, not the rapier, but the back-sword,[69] of which he recommends the use in his book on education.

His eyes are said never to have been bright; but, if he was a dexterous fencer, they must have been once quick.

His domestic habits, so far as they are known, were those of a severe student. He drank little strong drink of any kind, and fed without excess in quantity, and in his earlier years without delicacy of choice. In his youth he studied late at night; but afterwards changed his hours, and rested in bed from nine to four in the summer, and five in the winter. The course of his day was best known after he was blind. When he first rose, he heard a chapter in the Hebrew Bible, and then studied till twelve; then took some exercise for an hour; then dined; then played on the organ, and sang or heard another sing; then studied to six; then entertained his visitors till eight; then supped, and, after a pipe of tobacco and a glass of water, went to bed.

So is his life described; but this even tenor appears attainable only in colleges. He that lives in the world will sometimes have the succession of his practice broken and confused. Visitors, of whom Milton is represented to have had great numbers, will come and stay unseasonably; business, of which every man has some, must be done when others will do it.

When he did not care to rise early, he had something read to him by his bedside; perhaps at this time his daughters were employed. He composed much in the morning, and dictated in the day, sitting obliquely in an elbow-chair, with his leg thrown over the arm.

Fortune appears not to have had much of his care. In the civil wars he lent his personal estate to the parliament; but when, after the contest was decided, he solicited repayment, he met not only with neglect but "sharp rebuke," and, having tried both himself and his friends, was given up to poverty and hopeless indignation, till he showed how able he was to do greater service. He was then made Latin secretary, with two hundred pounds

a-year, and had a thousand pounds for his *Defence of the People*.[70] His widow, who, after his death, retired to Nantwich in Cheshire, and died about 1729, is said to have reported that he lost two thousand pounds by entrusting it to a scrivener; and that, in the general depredation upon the church, he had grasped an estate of about sixty pounds a year belonging to Westminster Abbey, which, like other sharers of the plunder of rebellion, he was afterwards obliged to return. Two thousand pounds which he had placed in the Excise Office were also lost. There is yet no reason to believe that he was ever reduced to indigence. His wants, being few, were competently supplied. He sold his library before his death, and left his family fifteen hundred pounds, on which his widow laid hold, and only gave one hundred to each of his daughters.

His literature was unquestionably great. He read all the languages which are considered either as learned or polite: Hebrew, with its two dialects, Greek, Latin, Italian, French, and Spanish. In Latin his skill was such as places him in the first rank of writers and critics; and he appears to have cultivated Italian with uncommon diligence. The books in which his daughter, who used to read to him, represented him as most delighting, after Homer, which he could almost repeat, were Ovid's *Metamorphoses* and Euripides. His Euripides is, by Mr. Cradock's kindness, now in my hands; the margin is sometimes noted, but I have found nothing remarkable.

Of the English poets he set most value upon Spenser, Shakespeare, and Cowley. Spenser was apparently his favorite; Shakespeare he may easily be supposed to like, with every other skilful reader; but I should not have expected that Cowley, whose ideas of excellence were different from his own, would have had much of his approbation. His character of Dryden, who sometimes visited him, was that he was a good rimist but no poet.

His theological opinions are said to have been first Calvinistical; and afterwards, perhaps when he began to hate the Presbyterians, to have tended towards Arminianism.[71] In the mixed questions of theology and government he never thinks that he can recede far enough from popery, or prelacy; but what Baudius says of Erasmus seems applicable to him: "*magis habuit quod fugeret quam quod*

---

[69] Sword with only one cutting edge.

[70] The *Pro Populo Anglicano Defensio* (1651), written to defend the execution of Charles I.

[71] The anti-Calvinistic doctrines of James Arminius, the Dutch theologian.

*sequeretur.*" [72] He had determined rather what to condemn than what to approve. He has not associated himself with any denomination of Protestants; we know rather what he was not than what he was. He was not of the Church of Rome; he was not of the Church of England.

To be of no church is dangerous. Religion, of which the rewards are distant, and which is animated only by faith and hope, will glide by degrees out of the mind, unless it be invigorated and reimpressed by external ordinances, by stated calls to worship and the salutary influence of example. Milton, who appears to have had full conviction of the truth of Christianity, and to have regarded the Holy Scriptures with the profoundest veneration, to have been untainted by any heretical peculiarity of opinion, and to have lived in a confirmed belief of the immediate and occasional agency of Providence, yet grew old without any visible worship. In the distribution of his hours there was no hour of prayer, either solitary or with his household; omitting public prayers, he omitted all.

Of this omission the reason has been sought, upon a supposition which ought never to be made, that men live with their own approbation, and justify their conduct to themselves. Prayer certainly was not thought superfluous by him who represents our first parents as praying acceptably in the state of innocence, and efficaciously after their fall. That he lived without prayer can hardly be affirmed; his studies and meditations were an habitual prayer. The neglect of it in his family was probably a fault for which he condemned himself, and which he intended to correct, but that death, as too often happens, intercepted his reformation.

His political notions were those of an acrimonious and surly republican, for which it is not known that he gave any better reason than "a popular government was the most frugal; for the trappings of a monarchy would set up an ordinary commonwealth." [73] It is surely very shallow policy that supposes money to be the chief good; and even this, without considering that the support and expense of a court is, for the most part, only a particular kind of traffic by which money is circulated without any national impoverishment.

Milton's republicanism was, I am afraid, founded in an envious hatred of greatness, and a sullen desire of independence; in petulance impatient of control, and pride disdainful of

superiority. He hated monarchs in the state, and prelates in the church; for he hated all whom he was required to obey. It is to be suspected that his predominant desire was to destroy rather than establish, and that he felt not so much the love of liberty as repugnance to authority.

It has been observed that they who most loudly clamor for liberty do not most liberally grant it. What we know of Milton's character in domestic relations is that he was severe and arbitrary. His family consisted of women; and there appears in his books something like a Turkish contempt of females, as subordinate and inferior beings. That his own daughters might not break the ranks, he suffered them to be depressed by a mean and penurious education. He thought woman made only for obedience, and man only for rebellion.

\*    \*    \*

In the examination of Milton's poetical works I shall pay so much regard to time as to begin with his juvenile productions. For his early pieces he seems to have had a degree of fondness not very laudable; what he has once written he resolves to preserve, and gives to the public an unfinished poem [74] which he broke off because he was "nothing satisfied with what he had done," supposing his readers less nice than himself. These preludes to his future labors are in Italian, Latin, and English. Of the Italian I cannot pretend to speak as a critic; but I have heard them commended by a man well qualified to decide their merit. The Latin pieces are lusciously elegant; but the delight which they afford is rather by the exquisite imitation of the ancient writers, by the purity of the diction and the harmony of the numbers, than by any power of invention or vigor of sentiment. They are not all of equal value; the elegies excell the odes; and some of the exercises on Gunpowder Treason might have been spared.

The English poems, though they make no promises of *Paradise Lost*, have this evidence of genius, that they have a cast original and unborrowed. But their peculiarity is not excellence; if they differ from the verses of others, they differ for the worse; for they are too often distinguished by repulsive harshness; the combinations of words are new, but they are not pleasing; the rimes and epithets seem to be laboriously sought, and violently applied.

That in the early parts of his life he wrote

[72] He knew what to avoid rather than what to follow.
[73] Remark of Milton's reported in Toland's life.

[74] "The Passion." Johnson quotes from Milton's note at the end of the poem.

with much care appears from his manuscripts, happily preserved at Cambridge, in which many of his smaller works are found as they were first written, with the subsequent corrections. Such relics show how excellence is acquired; what we hope ever to do with ease, we must learn first to do with diligence.

Those who admire the beauties of this great poet sometimes force their own judgment into false approbation of his little pieces, and prevail upon themselves to think that admirable which is only singular. All that short compositions can commonly attain is neatness and elegance. Milton never learned the art of doing little things with grace; he overlooked the milder excellence of suavity and softness; he was a lion that had no skill "in dandling the kid." [75]

One of the poems on which much praise has been bestowed is *Lycidas*, of which the diction is harsh, the rimes uncertain, and the numbers unpleasing. What beauty there is we must therefore seek in the sentiments and images. It is not to be considered as the effusion of real passion; for passion runs not after remote allusions and obscure opinions. Passion plucks no berries from the myrtle and ivy, nor calls upon Arethuse and Mincius, nor tells of rough "satyrs" and "fauns with cloven heel." Where there is leisure for fiction there is little grief.

In this poem there is no nature, for there is no truth; there is no art, for there is nothing new. Its form is that of a pastoral, easy, vulgar, and therefore disgusting: whatever images it can supply are long ago exhausted; and its inherent improbability always forces dissatisfaction on the mind. When Cowley tells of Hervey [76] that they studied together, it is easy to suppose how much he must miss the companion of his labors and the partner of his discoveries; but what image of tenderness can be excited by these lines?

We drove afield, and both together heard
What time the grey fly winds her sultry horn,
Battening our flocks with the fresh dews of night. [77]

We know that they never drove afield, and that they had no flocks to batten; [78] and though it be allowed that the representation may be allegorical, the true meaning is so uncertain and remote that it is never sought because it cannot be known when it is found.

Among the flocks, and copses, and flowers appear the heathen deities, Jove and Phoebus, Neptune and Aeolus, with a long train of mythological imagery, such as a college [79] easily supplies. Nothing can less display knowledge, or less exercise invention, than to tell how a shepherd has lost his companion, and must now feed his flocks alone, without any judge of his skill in piping; and how one god asks another god what is become of Lycidas, and how neither god can tell. He who thus grieves will excite no sympathy; he who thus praises will confer no honor.

This poem has yet a grosser fault. With these trifling fictions are mingled the most awful and sacred truths, such as ought never to be polluted with such irreverent combinations. The shepherd likewise is now a feeder of sheep, and afterwards an ecclesiastical pastor, a superintendent of a Christian flock. Such equivocations are always unskilful; but here they are indecent, and at least approach to impiety, of which, however, I believe the writer not to have been conscious.

Such is the power of reputation justly acquired that its blaze drives away the eye from nice examination. Surely no man could have fancied that he read *Lycidas* with pleasure, had he not known its author.

Of the two pieces, *L'Allegro* and *Il Penseroso*, I believe opinion is uniform; every man that reads them reads them with pleasure. The author's design is not, what Theobald [80] has remarked, merely to show how objects derive their colors from the mind, by representing the operation of the same things upon the gay and the melancholy temper, or upon the same man as he is differently disposed; but rather how, among the successive variety of appearances, every disposition of mind takes hold on those by which it may be gratified.

The cheerful man hears the lark in the morning; the pensive man hears the nightingale in the evening. The cheerful man sees the cock strut, and hears the horn and hounds echo in the wood; then walks "not unseen" to observe the glory of the rising sun, or listen to the singing milk-maid, and view the labors of the plowman and the mower; then casts his eyes about him over scenes of smiling plenty, and looks up to the distant tower, the residence of some fair inhabitants; thus he pursues rural gaiety through a day of labor or of play, and delights himself at night with the fanciful narratives of superstitious ignorance.

[75] *Paradise Lost*, IV, 343.
[76] In his poem "On the Death of Mr. William Hervey."
[77] *Lycidas*, 27–29.    [78] Fatten.

[79] A college education.
[80] Lewis Theobald (1688–1744), the editor of Shakespeare.

The pensive man at one time walks "unseen" to muse at midnight, and at another hears the sullen curfew. If the weather drives him home, he sits in a room lighted only by "glowing embers"; or by a lonely lamp outwatches the North Star, to discover the habitation of separate souls, and varies the shades of meditation by contemplating the magnificent or pathetic scenes of tragic and epic poetry. When the morning comes, a morning gloomy with rain and wind, he walks into the dark, trackless woods, falls asleep by some murmuring water, and with melancholy enthusiasm expects some dream of prognostication, or some music played by aërial performers.

Both mirth and melancholy are solitary, silent inhabitants of the breast that neither receive nor transmit communication; no mention is therefore made of a philosophical friend, or a pleasant companion. The seriousness does not arise from any participation of calamity, nor the gaiety from the pleasures of the bottle.

The man of cheerfulness, having exhausted the country, tries what "towered cities" will afford, and mingles with scenes of splendor, gay assemblies, and nuptial festivities; but he mingles a mere spectator, as, when the learned comedies of Jonson, or the wild dramas of Shakespeare, are exhibited, he attends the theater.

The pensive man never loses himself in crowds, but walks the cloister, or frequents the cathedral. Milton probably had not yet forsaken the church.

Both his characters delight in music; but he seems to think that cheerful notes would have obtained from Pluto a complete dismission of Eurydice,[81] of whom solemn sounds only procured a conditional release.

For the old age of cheerfulness he makes no provision; but melancholy he conducts with great dignity to the close of life. His cheerfulness is without levity, and his pensiveness without asperity.

Through these two poems the images are properly selected and nicely distinguished; but the colors of the diction seem not sufficiently discriminated. I know not whether the characters are kept sufficiently apart. No mirth can, indeed, be found in his melancholy; but I am afraid that I always meet some melancholy in his mirth. They are two noble efforts of imagination.

The greatest of his juvenile performances is the masque of *Comus*, in which may very plainly be discovered the dawn or twilight of *Paradise Lost*. Milton appears to have formed very early that system of diction and mode of verse which his maturer judgment approved, and from which he never endeavored nor desired to deviate.

Nor does *Comus* afford only a specimen of his language; it exhibits likewise his power of description and his vigor of sentiment, employed in the praise and defence of virtue. A work more truly poetical is rarely found; allusions, images, and descriptive epithets embellish almost every period with lavish decoration. As a series of lines, therefore, it may be considered as worthy of all the admiration with which the votaries have received it.

As a drama it is deficient. The action is not probable. A masque, in those parts where supernatural intervention is admitted, must indeed be given up to all the freaks of imagination; but, so far as the action is merely human, it ought to be reasonable; which can hardly be said of the conduct of the two brothers, who, when their sister sinks with fatigue in a pathless wilderness, wander both away together in search of berries too far to find their way back, and leave a helpless lady to all the sadness and danger of solitude. This, however, is a defect overbalanced by its convenience.

What deserves more reprehension is that the prologue spoken in the wild wood by the attendant spirit is addressed to the audience, a mode of communication so contrary to the nature of dramatic representation that no precedents can support it.

The discourse of the spirit is too long, an objection that may be made to almost all the following speeches; they have not the sprightliness of a dialogue animated by reciprocal contention, but seem rather declamations deliberately composed, and formally repeated, on a moral question. The auditor therefore listens as to a lecture, without passion, without anxiety.

The song of Comus has airiness and jollity; but, what may recommend Milton's morals as well as his poetry, the invitations to pleasure are so general that they excite no distinct images of corrupt enjoyment, and take no dangerous hold on the fancy.

The following soliloquies of Comus and the lady are elegant but tedious. The song must owe much to the voice, if it ever can delight. At last the brothers enter with too much tranquillity; and when they have feared lest their sister should be in danger, and hoped that she is not in danger, the elder makes a

---

[81] She was almost rescued from the nether world by the music of her husband, Orpheus.

speech in praise of chastity, and the younger finds how fine it is to be a philosopher.

Then descends the spirit in form of a shepherd; and the brother, instead of being in haste to ask his help, praises his singing, and inquires his business in that place. It is remarkable that at this interview the brother is taken with a short fit of riming. The spirit relates that the lady is in the power of Comus; the brother moralises again; and the spirit makes a long 10 narration, of no use because it is false, and therefore unsuitable to a good being.

In all these parts the language is poetical, and the sentiments are generous; but there is something wanting to allure attention.

The dispute between the lady and Comus is the most animated and affecting scene of the drama, and wants nothing but a brisker reciprocation of objections and replies to invite attention, and detain it. 20

The songs are vigorous, and full of imagery; but they are harsh in their diction, and not very musical in their numbers.

Throughout the whole the figures are too bold, and the language too luxuriant for dialogue. It is a drama in the epic style, inelegantly splendid, and tediously instructive.

The sonnets were written in different parts of Milton's life, upon different occasions. They deserve not any particular criticism; for of the 30 best it can only be said that they are not bad; and perhaps only the eighth and the twenty-first [82] are truly entitled to this slender commendation. The fabric of a sonnet, however adapted to the Italian language, has never succeeded in ours, which, having greater variety of termination, requires the rimes to be often changed.

Those little pieces may be despatched without much anxiety; a greater work calls for 40 greater care. I am now to examine *Paradise Lost*, a poem which, considered with respect to design, may claim the first place, and with respect to performance the second, among the productions of the human mind.

By the general consent of critics the first praise of genius is due to the writer of an epic poem, as it requires an assemblage of all the powers which are singly sufficient for other compositions. Poetry is the art of uniting pleas- 50 ure with truth by calling imagination to the help of reason. Epic poetry undertakes to teach the most important truths by the most pleasing precepts, and therefore relates some great event in the most affecting manner. History must

supply the writer with the rudiments of narration, which he must improve and exalt by a nobler art, must animate by dramatic energy, and diversify by retrospection and anticipation; morality must teach him the exact bounds, and different shades, of vice and virtue; from policy and the practice of life he has to learn the discriminations of character and the tendency of the passions, either single or combined; and physiology must supply him with illustrations and images. To put these materials to poetical use is required an imagination capable of painting nature, and realizing fiction. Nor is he yet a poet till he has attained the whole extension of his language, distinguished all the delicacies of phrase and all the colors of words, and learned to adjust their different sounds to all the varieties of metrical modulation.

Bossu [83] is of opinion that the poet's first work is to find a moral, which his fable [84] is afterwards to illustrate and establish. This seems to have been the process only of Milton; the moral of other poems is incidental and consequent; in Milton's only it is essential and intrinsic. His purpose was the most useful and the most arduous: "to vindicate the ways of God to man," [85] to show the reasonableness of religion and the necessity of obedience to the divine law.

To convey this moral there must be a fable, a narration artfully constructed, so as to excite curiosity and surprise expectation. In this part of his work Milton must be confessed to have equaled every other poet. He has involved in his account of the Fall of Man the events which preceded, and those that were to follow it; he has interwoven the whole system of theology with such propriety that every part appears to be necessary; and scarcely any recital is wished shorter for the sake of quickening the progress of the main action.

The subject of an epic poem is naturally an event of great importance. That of Milton is not the destruction of a city, the conduct of a colony, or the foundation of an empire. His subject is the fate of worlds, the revolutions of heaven and of earth; rebellion against the Supreme King, raised by the highest order of created beings; the overthrow of their host, and the punishment of their crimes; the creation of a new race of reasonable creatures; their original happiness and innocence, their for-

[82] Sonnets VIII and XVIII in the present collection.

[83] René le Bossu (1631–1689) in his *Traité du Poème Épique*.
[84] Story.
[85] *Paradise Lost*, I, 26.

feiture of immortality, and their restoration to hope and peace.

Great events can be hastened or retarded only by persons of elevated dignity. Before the greatness displayed in Milton's poem all other greatness shrinks away. The weakest of his agents are the highest and noblest of human beings, the original parents of mankind; with whose actions the elements consented; [86] on whose rectitude, or deviation of will, depended the state of terrestrial nature, and the condition of all the future inhabitants of the globe.

Of the other agents in the poem the chief are such as it is irreverence to name on slight occasions. The rest are lower powers,

> ——of which the least could wield
> Those elements, and arm him with the force
> Of all their regions; [87]

powers which only the control of Omnipotence restrains from laying creation waste, and filling the vast expanse of space with ruin and confusion. To display the motives and actions of beings thus superior, so far as human reason can examine them, or human imagination represent them, is the task which this mighty poet has undertaken and performed.

In the examination of epic poems much speculation is commonly employed upon the characters. The characters in the *Paradise Lost* which admit of examination are those of angels and of man, of angels good and evil, of man in his innocent and sinful state.

Among the angels, the virtue of Raphael is mild and placid, of easy condescension and free communication; that of Michael is regal and lofty and, as may seem, attentive to the dignity of his own nature. Abdiel and Gabriel appear occasionally, and act as every incident requires; the solitary fidelity of Abdiel is very amiably painted.

Of the evil angels the characters are more diversified. To Satan, as Addison observes, such sentiments are given as suit "the most exalted and most depraved being." [88] Milton has been censured by Clarke [89] for the impiety which sometimes breaks from Satan's mouth; for there are thoughts, as he justly remarks, which no observation of character can justify, because no good man would willingly permit them to pass, however transiently, through his own mind. To make Satan speak as a rebel, without any such expressions as might taint the reader's imagination, was indeed one of the great difficulties in Milton's undertaking,

and I cannot but think that he has extricated himself with great happiness. There is in Satan's speeches little that can give pain to a pious ear. The language of rebellion cannot be the same with that of obedience. The malignity of Satan foams in haughtiness and obstinacy; but his expressions are commonly general, and no otherwise offensive than as they are wicked.

The other chiefs of the celestial rebellion are very judiciously discriminated in the first and second books; and the ferocious character of Moloch appears, both in the battle and the council, with exact consistency.

To Adam and to Eve are given, during their innocence, such sentiments as innocence can generate and utter. Their love is pure benevolence and mutual veneration; their repasts are without luxury, and their diligence without toil. Their addresses to their Maker have little more than the voice of admiration and gratitude. Fruition left them nothing to ask, and innocence left them nothing to fear.

But with guilt enter distrust and discord, mutual accusation, and stubborn self-defence; they regard each other with alienated minds, and dread their Creator as the avenger of their transgression. At last they seek shelter in his mercy, soften to repentance, and melt in supplication. Both before and after the Fall the superiority of Adam is diligently sustained.

Of the probable and the marvelous, two parts of a vulgar epic poem which immerge the critic in deep consideration, the *Paradise Lost* requires little to be said. It contains the history of a miracle, of creation and redemption; it displays the power and the mercy of the Supreme Being; the probable therefore is marvelous, and the marvelous is probable. The substance of the narrative is truth; and as truth allows no choice, it is, like necessity, superior to rule. To the accidental or adventitious parts, as to everything human, some slight exceptions may be made. But the main fabric is immovably supported.

It is justly remarked by Addison that this poem has, by the nature of its subject, the advantage above all others that it is universally and perpetually interesting.[90] All mankind will, through all ages, bear the same relation to Adam and to Eve, and must partake of that good and evil which extend to themselves.

Of the machinery, so called from θεὸς ἀπὸ μηχανῆς,[91] by which is meant the occasional

---

[86] Sympathized.     [87] *Paradise Lost*, VI, 221–223.
[88] *Spectator*, no. 303.
[89] John Clarke in *An Essay upon Study*.

[90] *Spectator*, no. 273.
[91] *Deus ex machina*, an artificial solution of difficulties (Aristotle, *Poetics*, xv, 7).

interposition of supernatural power, another fertile topic of critical remarks, here is no room to speak, because everything is done under the immediate and visible direction of Heaven; but the rule is so far observed that no part of the action could have been accomplished by any other means.

Of episodes I think there are only two, contained in Raphael's relation of the war in heaven, and Michael's prophetic account of the changes to happen in this world. Both are closely connected with the great action; one was necessary to Adam as a warning, the other as a consolation.

To the completeness or integrity of the design nothing can be objected; it has distinctly and clearly what Aristotle requires, a beginning, a middle, and an end. There is perhaps no poem of the same length from which so little can be taken without apparent mutilation. Here are no funeral games, nor is there any long description of a shield. The short digressions at the beginning of the third, seventh, and ninth books, might doubtless be spared; but superfluities so beautiful who would take away? or who does not wish that the author of the *Iliad* had gratified succeeding ages with a little knowledge of himself? Perhaps no passages are more frequently or more attentively read than those extrinsic paragraphs; and, since the end of poetry is pleasure, that cannot be unpoetical with which all are pleased.

The questions whether the action of the poem be strictly one, whether the poem can be properly termed heroic, and who is the hero, are raised by such readers as draw their principles of judgment rather from books than from reason. Milton, though he entitled *Paradise Lost* only a "poem," yet calls it himself "heroic song." Dryden [92] petulantly and indecently denies the heroism of Adam because he was overcome; but there is no reason why the hero should not be unfortunate, except established practice, since success and virtue do not go necessarily together. Cato is the hero of Lucan; but Lucan's authority will not be suffered by Quintilian to decide. However, if success be necessary, Adam's deceiver was at last crushed; Adam was restored to his Maker's favor, and therefore may securely resume his human rank.

After the scheme and fabric of the poem must be considered its component parts, the sentiments and the diction.

The sentiments, as expressive of manners, or appropriated to characters, are for the greater part unexceptionally just.

Splendid passages, containing lessons of morality or precepts of prudence, occur seldom. Such is the original formation of this poem that as it admits no human manners till the Fall, it can give little assistance to human conduct. Its end is to raise the thoughts above sublunary cares or pleasures. Yet the praise of that fortitude with which Abdiel maintained his singularity of virtue against the scorn of multitudes may be accommodated to all times; and Raphael's reproof of Adam's curiosity after the planetary motions, with the answer returned by Adam, may be confidently opposed to any rule of life which any poet has delivered.

The thoughts which are occasionally called forth in the progress are such as could only be produced by an imagination in the highest degree fervid and active, to which materials were supplied by incessant study and unlimited curiosity. The heat of Milton's mind may be said to sublimate his learning, to throw off into his work the spirit of science, unmingled with its grosser parts.

He had considered creation in its whole extent, and his descriptions are therefore learned. He had accustomed his imagination to unrestrained indulgence, and his conceptions therefore were extensive. The characteristic quality of his poem is sublimity. He sometimes descends to the elegant, but his element is the great. He can occasionally invest himself with grace; but his natural port is gigantic loftiness. He can please when pleasure is required; but it is his peculiar power to astonish.

He seems to have been well acquainted with his own genius, and to know what it was that nature had bestowed upon him more bountifully than upon others, the power of displaying the vast, illuminating the splendid, enforcing the awful, darkening the gloomy, and aggravating the dreadful; he therefore chose a subject on which too much could not be said, on which he might tire his fancy without the censure of extravagance.

The appearances of nature, and the occurrences of life, did not satiate his appetite of greatness. To paint things as they are requires a minute attention, and employs the memory rather than the fancy. Milton's delight was to sport in the wide regions of possibility; reality was a scene too narrow for his mind. He sent his faculties out upon discovery, into worlds where only imagination can travel, and delighted to form new modes of existence, and furnish sentiment and action to superior be-

[92] In his *Essay on Satire* (1692).

ings, to trace the counsels of hell, or accompany the choirs of heaven.

But he could not be always in other worlds; he must sometimes revisit earth; and tell of things visible and known. When he cannot raise wonder by the sublimity of his mind, he gives delight by its fertility.

Whatever be his subject, he never fails to fill the imagination. But his images and descriptions of the scenes or operations of nature do not seem to be always copied from original form, nor to have the freshness, raciness, and energy of immediate observation. He saw nature, as Dryden expresses it, "through the spectacles of books," [93] and on most occasions calls learning to his assistance. The garden of Eden brings to his mind the vale of Enna, where Proserpine was gathering flowers. Satan makes his way through fighting elements, like Argo between the Cyanean rocks, or Ulysses between the two Sicilian whirlpools, when he shunned Charybdis on the larboard. The mythological allusions have been justly censured as not being always used with notice of their vanity; but they contribute variety to the narration, and produce an alternate exercise of the memory and the fancy.

His similes are less numerous, and more various, than those of his predecessors. But he does not confine himself within the limits of rigorous comparison; his great excellence is amplitude, and he expands the adventitious image beyond the dimensions which the occasion required. Thus, comparing the shield of Satan to the orb of the moon, he crowds the imagination with the discovery of the telescope, and all the wonders which the telescope discovers.

Of his moral sentiments it is hardly praise to affirm that they excell those of all other poets; for this superiority he was indebted to his acquaintance with the sacred writings. The ancient epic poets, wanting the light of revelation, were very unskilful teachers of virtue; their principal characters may be great, but they are not amiable. The reader may rise from their works with a greater degree of active or passive fortitude, and sometimes of prudence; but he will be able to carry away few precepts of justice, and none of mercy.

From the Italian writers it appears that the advantages of even Christian knowledge may be possessed in vain. Ariosto's pravity [94] is generally known; and though the *Deliverance of Jerusalem* [95] may be considered as a sacred subject, the poet has been very sparing of moral instruction.

In Milton every line breathes sanctity of thought, and purity of manners, except when the train of the narration requires the introduction of the rebellious spirits; and even they are compelled to acknowledge their subjection to God in such a manner as excites reverence, and confirms piety.

Of human beings there are but two; but those two are the parents of mankind, venerable before their fall for dignity and innocence, and amiable after it for repentance and submission. In their first state their affection is tender without weakness, and their piety sublime without presumption. When they have sinned, they show how discord begins in mutual frailty, and how it ought to cease in mutual forbearance; how confidence of the divine favor is forfeited by sin, and how hope of pardon may be obtained by penitence and prayer. A state of innocence we can only conceive, if indeed, in our present misery, it be possible to conceive it; but the sentiments and worship proper to a fallen and offending being we have all to learn, as we have all to practise.

The poet, whatever be done, is always great. Our progenitors in their first state conversed with angels; even when folly and sin had degraded them, they had not in their humiliation "the port of mean suitors"; [96] and they rise again to reverential regard when we find that their prayers were heard.

As human passions did not enter the world before the Fall, there is in the *Paradise Lost* little opportunity for the pathetic; but what little there is has not been lost. That passion which is peculiar to rational nature, the anguish arising from the consciousness of transgression, and the horrors attending the sense of the divine displeasure, are very justly described and forcibly impressed. But the passions are moved only on one occasion; sublimity is the general and prevailing quality in this poem, sublimity variously modified, sometimes descriptive, sometimes argumentative.

The defects and faults of *Paradise Lost*, for faults and defects every work of man must have, it is the business of impartial criticism to discover. As, in displaying the excellence of Milton, I have not made long quotations, because of selecting beauties there had been no end, I shall in the same general manner men-

[93] In the *Essay on Dramatic Poesy* (1668). Dryden applies the phrase to Shakespeare.
[94] The immorality of Ariosto (in his *Orlando Furioso*).
[95] The *Gerusalemme Liberata* of Tasso.
[96] *Paradise Lost*, XI, 8–9.

tion that which seems to deserve censure; for what Englishman can take delight in transcribing passages which, if they lessen the reputation of Milton, diminish in some degree the honor of our country?

The generality of my scheme does not admit the frequent notice of verbal inaccuracies; which Bentley,[97] perhaps better skilled in grammar than in poetry, has often found, though he sometimes made them, and which he imputed to the obtrusions of a reviser whom the author's blindness obliged him to employ,—a supposition rash and groundless, if he thought it true, and vile and pernicious, if, as is said, he in private allowed it to be false.

The plan of *Paradise Lost* has this inconvenience, that it comprises neither human actions nor human manners. The man and woman who act and suffer, are in a state which no other man or woman can ever know. The reader finds no transaction in which he can be engaged, beholds no condition in which he can by any effort of imagination place himself; he has, therefore, little natural curiosity or sympathy.

We all, indeed, feel the effects of Adam's disobedience; we all sin like Adam, and like him must all bewail our offences; we have restless and insidious enemies in the fallen angels, and in the blessed spirits we have guardians and friends; in the redemption of mankind we hope to be included; in the description of heaven and hell we are surely interested, as we are all to reside hereafter either in the regions of horror or of bliss.

But these truths are too important to be new; they have been taught to our infancy; they have mingled with our solitary thoughts and familiar conversation, and are habitually interwoven with the whole texture of life. Being therefore not new, they raise no unaccustomed emotion in the mind; what we knew before we cannot learn; what is not unexpected cannot surprise.

Of the ideas suggested by these awful scenes, from some we recede with reverence, except when stated hours require their association; and from others we shrink with horror, or admit them only as salutary inflictions, as counterpoises to our interests and passions. Such images rather obstruct the career of fancy than incite it.

Pleasure and terror are indeed the genuine sources of poetry; but poetical pleasure must be such as human imagination can at least

conceive, and poetical terror such as human strength and fortitude may combat. The good and evil of eternity are too ponderous for the wings of wit; the mind sinks under them in passive helplessness, content with calm belief and humble adoration.

Known truths, however, may take a different appearance, and be conveyed to the mind by a new train of intermediate images. This Milton has undertaken, and performed with pregnancy and vigor of mind peculiar to himself. Whoever considers the few radical positions [98] which the Scriptures afforded him will wonder by what energetic operation he expanded them to such extent, and ramified them to so much variety, restrained as he was by religious reverence from licentiousness of fiction.[99]

Here is a full display of the united force of study and genius, of a great accumulation of materials with judgment to digest, and fancy to combine them: Milton was able to select from nature or from story, from ancient fable or from modern science, whatever could illustrate or adorn his thoughts. An accumulation of knowledge impregnated his mind, fermented by study and exalted by imagination.

It has been therefore said, without an indecent hyperbole, by one of his encomiasts, that in reading *Paradise Lost* we read a book of universal knowledge.

But original deficience cannot be supplied. The want of human interest is always felt. *Paradise Lost* is one of the books which the reader admires and lays down, and forgets to take up again. None ever wished it longer than it is. Its perusal is a duty rather than a pleasure. We read Milton for instruction, retire harassed and overburdened, and look elsewhere for recreation; we desert our master, and seek for companions.

Another inconvenience of Milton's design is that it requires the description of what cannot be described, the agency of spirits. He saw that immateriality supplied no images, and that he could not show angels acting but by instruments of action; he therefore invested them with form and matter. This, being necessary, was therefore defensible; and he should have secured the consistency of his system by keeping immateriality out of sight, and enticing his reader to drop it from his thoughts. But he has unhappily perplexed his poetry with his philosophy. His infernal and celestial powers are sometimes pure spirit, and sometimes animated body. When Satan walks with

[97] Richard Bentley (1682–1742), editor and emendator of *Paradise Lost*.

[98] Original statements.
[99] Freedom in handling the story.

his lance upon the "burning marl," he has a body; when, in his passage between hell and the new world, he is in danger of sinking in the vacuity, and is supported by a gust of rising vapors, he has a body; when he animates the toad, he seems to be mere spirit, that can penetrate matter at pleasure; when he "starts up in his own shape," he has at least a determined form; and when he is brought before Gabriel, he has "a spear and a shield," which he had the power of hiding in the toad, though the arms of the contending angels are evidently material.

The vulgar inhabitants of Pandaemonium, being "incorporeal spirits," are "at large, though without number," in a limited space; yet in the battle, when they were overwhelmed by mountains, their armor hurt them, "crushed in upon their substance, now grown gross by sinning." This likewise happened to the uncorrupted angels, who were overthrown the "sooner for their arms, for unarmed they might easily as spirits have evaded by contraction or remove." Even as spirits they are hardly spiritual, for "contraction" and "remove" are images of matter; but if they could have escaped without their armor, they might have escaped from it, and left only the empty cover to be battered. Uriel, when he rides on a sunbeam, is material; Satan is material when he is afraid of the prowess of Adam.

The confusion of spirit and matter which pervades the whole narration of the war of heaven fills it with incongruity; and the book in which it is related [100] is, I believe, the favorite of children, and gradually neglected as knowledge is increased.

After the operation of immaterial agents, which cannot be explained, may be considered that of allegorical persons, which have no real existence. To exalt causes into agents, to invest abstract ideas with form, and animate them with activity, has always been the right of poetry. But such airy beings are, for the most part, suffered only to do their natural office, and retire. Thus Fame tells a tale, and Victory hovers over a general, or perches on a standard; but Fame and Victory can do no more. To give them any real employment, or ascribe to them any material agency, is to make them allegorical no longer, but to shock the mind by ascribing effects to nonentity. In the *Prometheus* of Aeschylus we see Violence and Strength, and in the *Alcestis* of Euripides we see Death, brought upon the stage, all as active persons of the drama; but no precedents can justify absurdity.

Milton's allegory of Sin and Death is undoubtedly faulty. Sin is indeed the mother of Death, and may be allowed to be the portress of hell; but when they stop the journey of Satan, a journey described as real, and when Death offers him battle, the allegory is broken. That Sin and Death should have shown the way to hell might have been allowed; but they cannot facilitate the passage by building a bridge, because the difficulty of Satan's passage is described as real and sensible, and the bridge ought to be only figurative. The hell assigned to the rebellious spirits is described as not less local than the residence of man. It is placed in some distant part of space, separated from the regions of harmony and order by a chaotic waste and an unoccupied vacuity; but Sin and Death worked up a "mole of aggravated soil," cemented with asphaltus, a work too bulky for ideal architects.

This unskilful allegory appears to me one of the greatest faults of the poem; and to this there was no temptation but the author's opinion of its beauty.

To the conduct of the narrative some objections may be made. Satan is with great expectation brought before Gabriel in Paradise, and is suffered to go away unmolested. The creation of man is represented as the consequence of the vacuity left in heaven by the expulsion of the rebels; yet Satan mentions it as a report "rife in heaven" before his departure.

To find sentiments for the state of innocence was very difficult; and something of anticipation perhaps is now and then discovered. Adam's discourse of dreams seems not to be the speculation of a new-created being. I know not whether his answer to the angel's reproof for curiosity does not want something of propriety; it is the speech of a man acquainted with many other men. Some philosophical notions, especially when the philosophy is false, might have been better omitted. The angel, in a comparison, speaks of "timorous deer" before deer were yet timorous, and before Adam could understand the comparison.

Dryden remarks that Milton has some flats among his elevations.[101] This is only to say that all the parts are not equal. In every work one part must be for the sake of others; a palace must have passages; a poem must have transitions. It is no more to be required that

---

[100] Book VI.

[101] In the *Essay on Satire* (1692).

wit should always be blazing than that the sun should always stand at noon. In a great work there is a vicissitude of luminous and opaque parts, as there is in the world a succession of day and night. Milton, when he has expatiated in the sky, may be allowed sometimes to revisit earth; for what other author ever soared so high, or sustained his flight so long?

Milton, being well versed in the Italian poets, appears to have borrowed often from them; and, as every man catches something from his companions, his desire of imitating Ariosto's levity [102] has disgraced his work with the Paradise of Fools, a fiction not in itself ill-imagined, but too ludicrous for its place.

His play on words, in which he delights too often; his equivocations, which Bentley endeavors to defend by the example of the ancients; his unnecessary and ungraceful use of terms of art, it is not necessary to mention, because they are easily remarked, and generally censured, and at last bear so little proportion to the whole that they scarcely deserve the attention of a critic.

Such are the faults of that wonderful performance *Paradise Lost*; which he who can put in balance with its beauties must be considered not as nice but as dull, as less to be censured for want of candor than pitied for want of sensibility.

Of *Paradise Regained* the general judgment seems now to be right, that it is in many parts elegant and everywhere instructive. It was not to be supposed that the writer of *Paradise Lost* could ever write without great effusions of fancy, and exalted precepts of wisdom. The basis of *Paradise Regained* is narrow; a dialogue without action can never please like an union of the narrative and dramatic powers. Had this poem been written not by Milton, but by some imitator, it would have claimed and received universal praise.

If *Paradise Regained* has been too much depreciated, *Samson Agonistes* has in requital been too much admired. It could only be by long prejudice and the bigotry of learning that Milton could prefer the ancient tragedies, with their encumbrance of a chorus, to the exhibitions of the French and English stages; and it is only by a blind confidence in the reputation of Milton that a drama can be praised in which the intermediate parts have neither cause nor consequence, neither hasten nor retard the catastrophe.

In this tragedy are, however, many particular beauties, many just sentiments and striking lines; but it wants that power of attracting the attention which a well-connected plan produces.

Milton would not have excelled in dramatic writing; he knew human nature only in the gross, and had never studied the shades of character, nor the combinations of concurring, or the perplexity of contending passions. He had read much, and knew what books could teach; but had mingled little in the world, and was deficient in the knowledge which experience must confer.

Through all his greater works there prevails an uniform peculiarity of diction, a mode and cast of expression which bears little resemblance to that of any former writer, and which is so far removed from common use that an unlearned reader, when he first opens his book, finds himself surprised by a new language.

This novelty has been, by those who can find nothing wrong in Milton, imputed to his laborious endeavors after words suitable to the grandeur of his ideas. "Our language," says Addison, "sunk under him." [103] But the truth is that, both in prose and verse, he had formed his style by a perverse and pedantic principle. He was desirous to use English words with a foreign idiom. This in all his prose is discovered and condemned, for there judgment operates freely, neither softened by the beauty, nor awed by the dignity of his thoughts, but such is the power of his poetry that his call is obeyed without resistance, the reader feels himself in captivity to a higher and a nobler mind, and criticism sinks in admiration.

Milton's style was not modified by his subject; what is shown with greater extent in *Paradise Lost* may be found in *Comus*. One source of his peculiarity was his familiarity with the Tuscan poets; the disposition of his words is, I think, frequently Italian, perhaps sometimes combined with other tongues. Of him, at last, may be said what Jonson says of Spenser, that "he wrote no language," [104] but has formed what Butler calls a "Babylonish dialect," [105] in itself harsh and barbarous, but made by exalted genius and extensive learning the vehicle of so much instruction and so much pleasure that, like other lovers, we find grace in its deformity.

Whatever be the faults of his diction, he cannot want the praise of copiousness and variety; he was master of his language in its

---

[102] In the *Orlando Furioso*, XXXIV.

[103] *Spectator*, no. 297.    [104] In *Discoveries*.
[105] *Hudibras*, I, i, 89.

full extent, and has selected the melodious words with such diligence that from his book alone the art of English poetry might be learned.

After his diction, something must be said of his versification. The measure, he says, "is the English heroic verse without rime." [106] Of this mode he had many examples among the Italians, and some in his own country. The Earl of Surrey is said to have translated one of Virgil's books without rime; and, besides our tragedies, a few short poems had appeared in blank verse, particularly one tending to reconcile the nation to Raleigh's wild attempt upon Guiana, and probably written by Raleigh himself. These petty performances cannot be supposed to have much influenced Milton, who more probably took his hint from Trissino's *Italia Liberata,* and, finding blank verse easier than rime, was desirous of persuading himself that it is better.

"Rime," he says, and says truly, "is no necessary adjunct of true poetry." [106] But, perhaps, of poetry as a mental operation meter or music is no necessary adjunct; it is, however, by the music of meter that poetry has been discriminated in all languages; and in languages melodiously constructed with a due proportion of long and short syllables, meter is sufficient. But one language cannot communicate its rules to another; where meter is scanty and imperfect, some help is necessary. The music of the English heroic [107] line strikes the ear so faintly that it is easily lost, unless all the syllables of every line co-operate together; this co-operation can be only obtained by the preservation of every verse unmingled with another, as a distinct system of sounds; and this distinctness is obtained and preserved by the artifice of rime. The variety of pauses, so much boasted by the lovers of blank verse, changes the measures of an English poet to the periods of a declaimer; and there are only a few skilful and happy readers of Milton who enable their audience to perceive where the lines end or begin. "Blank verse," said an ingenious critic, [108] "seems to be verse only to the eye."

Poetry may subsist without rime, but English poetry will not often please; nor can rime ever be safely spared but where the subject is able to support itself. Blank verse makes some approach to that which is called the lapidary style, has neither the easiness of prose nor the melody of numbers, and therefore tires by long continuance. Of the Italian writers without rime, whom Milton alleges as precedents, not one is popular; what reason could urge in its defence has been confuted by the ear.

But, whatever be the advantage of rime, I cannot prevail on myself to wish that Milton had been a rimer, for I cannot wish his work to be other than it is; yet, like other heroes, he is to be admired rather than imitated. He that thinks himself capable of astonishing may write blank verse; but those that hope only to please must condescend to rime.

The highest praise of genius is original invention. Milton cannot be said to have contrived the structure of an epic poem, and therefore owes reverence to that vigor and amplitude of mind to which all generations must be indebted for the art of poetical narration, for the texture of the fable, the variation of incidents, the interposition of dialogue, and all the stratagems that surprise and enchain attention. But, of all the borrowers from Homer, Milton is perhaps the least indebted. He was naturally a thinker for himself, confident of his own abilities, and disdainful of help or hindrance; he did not refuse admission to the thoughts or images of his predecessors, but he did not seek them. From his contemporaries he neither courted nor received support; there is in his writings nothing by which the pride of other authors might be gratified, or favor gained, no exchange of praise, nor solicitation of support. His great works were performed under discountenance, and in blindness, but difficulties vanished at his touch; he was born for whatever is arduous; and his work is not the greatest of heroic poems, only because it is not the first.

## On the Death of Mr. Robert Levet, a Practicer in Physic [1]

Condemned to Hope's delusive mine,
 As on we toil from day to day,
By sudden blasts, or slow decline,
 Our social comforts drop away.

[106] "The Verse," at the beginning of *Paradise Lost.*
[107] Iambic pentameter.
[108] A Mr. Lock of Norbury Park, Surrey.

[1] Levett died on 17 January, 1782. Johnson wrote this poem in the same year. It was published in the *Gentleman's Magazine,* August, 1783. Boswell says: "[He was] an obscure practicer in physic amongst the lower people. . . . It appears from Johnson's diary that their acquaintance commenced about the year 1746." For many years Levett "had an apartment in his house, or his chambers, and waited upon him every morning, through the whole course of his late and tedious breakfast. He was of a strange, grotesque appearance, stiff and formal in his manner, and seldom said a word while any company was present."

Well tried through many a varying year,    5
  See Levet to the grave descend,
Officious,[2] innocent, sincere,
  Of every friendless name the friend.

Yet still he fills affection's eye,
  Obscurely wise and coarsely kind;    10
Nor lettered arrogance deny
  Thy praise to merit unrefined.

When fainting nature called for aid,
  And hovering death prepared the blow,
His vigorous remedy displayed    15
  The power of art without the show.

In misery's darkest cavern known,
  His useful care was ever nigh,
Where hopeless anguish poured his groan,
  And lonely want retired to die.    20

  [2] Ready in doing good offices.

No summons mocked by chill delay,
  No petty gain disdained by pride;
The modest wants of every day
  The toil of every day supplied.

His virtues walked their narrow round,    25
  Nor made a pause, nor left a void;
And sure th' Eternal master found
  The single talent well employed.[3]

The busy day—the peaceful night,
  Unfelt, uncounted, glided by;    30
His frame was firm—his powers were bright,
  Though now his *eightieth* year was nigh.

Then with no fiery throbbing pain,
  No cold gradations of decay,
Death broke at once the vital chain,    35
  And freed his soul the nearest way.

  [3] An allusion to the parable of the servant to whom one talent (sum of money) was entrusted (St. Matthew, 25:24–28).

# James Boswell

## 1740 - 1795

Boswell's parents were both members of distinguished and ancient Scottish families. His father, Alexander Boswell, was an able lawyer and judge and, moreover, the master of Auchinleck, in Ayrshire—an estate conferred by James IV upon his ancestor, Thomas Boswell, in 1504. James was born at Edinburgh on 29 October, 1740. He was educated privately and at the Edinburgh High School, proceeding thence to Edinburgh University. His father designed him for the law, and to pursue that study he went to Glasgow in November, 1759, "where he also attended the lectures of Dr. Adam Smith on moral philosophy and rhetoric." James's own inclination was not for the law, however, but for the army, and for a characteristic reason. He discovered in soldiers "an animation and relish of existence" unequaled except, perhaps, amongst actors; and he also "had acquired, from reading and conversation, an almost enthusiastic notion of the felicity of London"—a notion which experience did not disappoint. Hence he "was now earnest to have a commission as an officer of the Guards," in order at once to gratify his love of London and of the most animated society. Early in 1760 his father took him to the metropolis, apparently yielding to martial ardor, but continuing to press the claims of the law. After a year, a commission not being obtained, Boswell returned to Edinburgh and legal studies. But he was again in London in the autumn of 1762, still trying to obtain a commission. In the following spring, on 16 May, he was introduced to Dr. Johnson. During the summer he finally agreed to follow the law and in August, 1763, left for Utrecht to continue his studies. In the summer of 1764 he was in Berlin, and thereafter in Switzerland, where he contrived to meet both Rousseau and Voltaire. Thence he journeyed to Italy, where he managed to renew his acquaintance with John Wilkes, then a political exile, and whence he traveled to Corsica, armed with an introduction from Rousseau to

General Paoli. He returned to England in February, 1766, and became an advocate at the Scottish bar in the same year. On 25 November, 1769, he married his cousin Margaret Montgomery. He was already the father of two natural children. His wife bore him four sons (two of whom died in infancy) and three daughters.

In 1772 Boswell was again in London, and saw much of Johnson. From this time, indeed, he was with him as much as possible, spending long periods in London in 1773, 1775, 1776, 1778, 1779, 1781, 1783, and 1784. He was kept in Scotland by lack of money—of which he never had enough to free him from embarrassments—in 1774, 1780, and 1782. In April, 1773, he was elected a member of the Literary Club, despite some opposition. In August of the same year Johnson went to Scotland and journeyed with Boswell to the Hebrides. In 1776 they also visited Lichfield and other places together. It has been calculated that, in all, Boswell saw Johnson on 276 days. Meanwhile he had begun in 1775 to keep terms at the Inner Temple, and in 1786 (two years after Johnson's death) he was called to the English bar. In 1788 he was in London, and in the following year took a house there. And in London he died, on 19 May, 1795.

Boswell began writing very early, publishing in 1760 a pamphlet which "is a rather strained imitation of the style of Sterne," with whom he had been intimate in London during his first visit. Other minor publications followed rapidly, including in 1761 An Ode to Tragedy which Boswell gaily dedicated to himself, and in 1763 a series of letters "which is the first considerable example of his life-long willingness to be indiscreet provided thereby he could be interesting." (F. A. Pottle, Literary Career of Boswell.) Through many years he contributed steadily and voluminously to periodicals; and one series of his essays, numbering 70— originally published in the London Magazine,

*1777–1783—has been reprinted* (The Hypochondriack, *edited by Margery Bailey, 2 vols., 1928). The mass of his publications is in fact very large, though only three of his books give him any claim to remembrance: An Account of Corsica (1768); The Journal of a Tour to the Hebrides with Samuel Johnson, LL. D. (1785); The Life of Samuel Johnson, LL.D. (1791). It is for the last, of course, that he is remembered; because, as Macaulay has splendidly and* 10 *truly said: "Homer is not more decidedly the first of heroic poets, Shakespeare is not more decidedly the first of dramatists, Demosthenes is not more decidedly the first of orators, than Boswell is the first of biographers. He has no second. He has distanced all his competitors so decidedly that it is not worth while to place them. Eclipse is first, and the rest nowhere."*

*The great biography has been reissued in Boswell's Life of Johnson together with Bos-* 20 *well's Journal of a Tour to the Hebrides and Johnson's Diary of a Journey into North Wales, ed. George B. Hill, rev. L. F. Powell (Oxford, 1934–1950). Private Papers of James Boswell from Malahide Castle, ed. Geoffrey Scott and Frederick A. Pottle (Mount Vernon, New York, 1928–1934) were published privately in 18 volumes; since then additional discoveries of Boswell papers have been made, and a new edition of over thirty volumes, The Private* 30 *Papers, edited by F. A. Pottle and others (New York, 1950–    ), has begun to appear. Biographies of Boswell written before the new material was available are of course severely limited, and no biography has yet tried to encompass the material now known. James Boswell, a Short Life by D. B. Wyndham Lewis (London, 1952) is a lively book which makes no claim to definitive thoroughness.*

# Passages from
## *The Life of Samuel Johnson, LL.D.*
### (1791)

#### THE DICTIONARY (1747–1756)

THE year 1747 is distinguished as the epoch when Johnson's arduous and important work, his DICTIONARY OF THE ENGLISH LANGUAGE was announced to the world, by the publica- 50 tion of its *Plan* or *Prospectus*.

How long this immense undertaking had been the object of his contemplation, I do not know. I once asked him by what means he had attained to that astonishing knowledge of our language, by which he was enabled to realize a design of such extent, and accumu-

lated difficulty. He told me, that "it was not the effect of particular study; but that it had grown up in his mind insensibly." I have been informed by Mr. James Dodsley, that several years before this period, when Johnson was one day sitting in his brother Robert's shop, he heard his brother suggest to him, that a Dictionary of the English Language would be a work that would be well received by the public; that Johnson seemed at first to catch at the proposition, but, after a pause, said, in his abrupt decisive manner, "I believe I shall not undertake it." That he, however, had bestowed much thought upon the subject, before he published his *Plan*, is evident from the enlarged, clear, and accurate views which it exhibits; and we find him mentioning in that tract, that many of the writers whose testimonies were to be produced as authorities, were selected by Pope; which proves that he had been furnished, probably by Mr. Robert Dodsley, with whatever hints that eminent poet had contributed towards a great literary project, that had been the subject of important consideration in a former reign.

The booksellers who contracted with Johnson, single and unaided, for the execution of a work, which in other countries has not been effected but by the co-operating exertions of many, were Mr. Robert Dodsley, Mr. Charles Hitch, Mr. Andrew Millar, the two Messieurs Longman, and the two Messieurs Knapton. The price stipulated was fifteen hundred and seventy-five pounds.

The *Plan* was addressed to Philip Dormer, Earl of Chesterfield, then one of his Majesty's Principal Secretaries of State; a nobleman who was very ambitious of literary distinction, and who, upon being informed of 40 the design, had expressed himself in terms very favorable to its success. There is, perhaps in everything of any consequence, a secret history which it would be amusing to know, could we have it authentically communicated. Johnson told me, "Sir, the way in which the *Plan* of my *Dictionary* came to be inscribed to Lord Chesterfield, was this: I had neglected to write it by the time appointed. Dodsley suggested a desire to have 50 it addressed to Lord Chesterfield. I laid hold of this as a pretext for delay, that it might be better done, and let Dodsley have his desire. I said to my friend, Dr. Bathurst, 'Now if any good comes of my addressing to Lord Chesterfield, it will be ascribed to deep policy, when, in fact, it was only a casual excuse for laziness.'" * * *

Dr. Adams found him one day busy at his *Dictionary*, when the following dialogue ensued. "ADAMS. This is a great work, Sir. How are you to get all the etymologies? JOHNSON. Why, Sir, here is a shelf with Junius, and Skinner,[1] and others; and there is a Welsh gentleman who has published a collection of Welsh proverbs, who will help me with the Welsh. ADAMS. But, Sir, how can you do this in three years? JOHNSON. Sir, I have no doubt that I can do it in three years. ADAMS. But the French Academy, which consists of forty members, took forty years to compile their Dictionary. JOHNSON. Sir, thus it is. This is the proportion. Let me see; forty times forty is sixteen hundred. As three to sixteen hundred, so is the proportion of an Englishman to a Frenchman." With so much ease and pleasantry could he talk of that prodigious labor which he had undertaken to execute. * * *

For the mechanical part he employed, as he told me, six amanuenses; and let it be remembered by the natives of North-Britain,[2] to whom he is supposed to have been so hostile, that five of them were of that country. * * *

1754: AETAT. 45.] * * * The *Dictionary*, we may believe, afforded Johnson full occupation this year. As it approached to its conclusion, he probably worked with redoubled vigor, as seamen increase their exertion and alacrity when they have a near prospect of their haven.

Lord Chesterfield, to whom Johnson had paid the high compliment of addressing to his Lordship the *Plan* of his *Dictionary*, had behaved to him in such a manner as to excite his contempt and indignation. The world has been for many years amused with a story confidently told, and as confidently repeated with additional circumstances, that a sudden disgust was taken by Johnson upon occasion of his having been one day kept long in waiting in his Lordship's antechamber, for which the reason assigned was, that he had company with him; and that at last, when the door opened, out walked Colley Cibber;[3] and that Johnson was so violently provoked when he found for whom he had been so long excluded, that he went away in a passion, and never would return. I remember having mentioned this story to George Lord Lyttelton, who told me, he was very intimate with Lord Chesterfield; and holding it as a

well-known truth, defended Lord Chesterfield, by saying, that "Cibber, who had been introduced familiarly by the back-stairs, had probably not been there above ten minutes." It may seem strange even to entertain a doubt concerning a story so long and so widely current, and thus implicitly adopted, if not sanctioned, by the authority which I have mentioned; but Johnson himself assured me that there was not the least foundation for it. He told me that there never was any particular incident which produced a quarrel between Lord Chesterfield and him; but that his Lordship's continued neglect was the reason why he resolved to have no connection with him. When the *Dictionary* was upon the eve of publication, Lord Chesterfield, who, it is said, had flattered himself with expectations that Johnson would dedicate the work to him, attempted, in a courtly manner, to soothe, and insinuate himself with the Sage, conscious, as it should seem, of the cold indifference with which he had treated its learned author; and further attempted to conciliate him, by writing two papers in *The World*, in recommendation of the work; and it must be confessed, that they contain some studied compliments, so finely turned, that if there had been no previous offense, it is probable that Johnson would have been highly delighted. Praise, in general, was pleasing to him; but by praise from a man of rank and elegant accomplishments, he was peculiarly gratified. * * *

This courtly device failed of its effect. Johnson, who thought that "all was false and hollow," despised the honeyed words, and was even indignant that Lord Chesterfield should, for a moment, imagine that he could be the dupe of such an artifice. His expression to me concerning Lord Chesterfield, upon this occasion, was, "Sir, after making great professions, he had, for many years, taken no notice of me; but when my *Dictionary* was coming out, he fell a scribbling in *The World* about it. Upon which, I wrote him a letter expressed in civil terms, but such as might show him that I did not mind what he said or wrote, and that I had done with him."

This is that celebrated letter of which so much has been said, and about which curiosity has been so long excited, without being gratified. I for many years solicited Johnson to favor me with a copy of it, that so excellent a composition might not be lost to posterity. He delayed from time to time to give it me; till at last in 1781, when we were on a visit at

---

[1] Previous lexicographers.     [2] Scotland.
[3] Dramatist and Poet Laureate. Cibber was held in general contempt.

Mr. Dilly's, at Southill in Bedfordshire, he was pleased to dictate it to me from memory. He afterwards found among his papers a copy of it, which he had dictated to Mr. Baretti, with its title and corrections, in his own handwriting. This he gave to Mr. Langton; adding that if it were to come into print, he wished it to be from that copy. By Mr. Langton's kindness, I am enabled to enrich my work with a perfect transcript of what the world has so eagerly desired to see.

### To the Right Honorable the Earl of Chesterfield.

February 7, 1755.

MY LORD, I have been lately informed, by the proprietor of *The World*, that two papers, in which my Dictionary is recommended to the public, were written by your Lordship. To be so distinguished, is an honor, which, being very little accustomed to favors from the great, I know not well how to receive, or in what terms to acknowledge.

When, upon some slight encouragement, I first visited your Lordship, I was overpowered, like the rest of mankind, by the enchantment of your address; and could not forbear to wish that I might boast myself *Le vainqueur du vainqueur de la terre;*[4] —that I might obtain that regard for which I saw the world contending; but I found my attendance so little encouraged, that neither pride nor modesty would suffer me to continue it. When I had once addressed your Lordship in public, I had exhausted all the art of pleasing which a retired and uncourtly scholar can possess. I had done all that I could; and no man is well pleased to have his all neglected, be it ever so little.

Seven years, my Lord, have now passed, since I waited in your outward rooms, or was repulsed from your door; during which time I have been pushing on my work through difficulties, of which it is useless to complain, and have brought it, at last, to the verge of publication, without one act of assistance, one word of encouragement, or one smile of favor. Such treatment I did not expect, for I never had a Patron before.

The shepherd in Virgil grew at last acquainted with Love, and found him a native of the rocks.[5]

Is not a Patron, my Lord, one who looks with unconcern on a man struggling for life in the water, and, when he has reached ground, encumbers him with help? The notice which you have been pleased to take of my labors, had it been early, had been kind; but it has been delayed till I am indifferent, and cannot enjoy it; till I am solitary,[6] and cannot impart it; till I am known, and do not want it. I hope it is no very cynical asperity not to confess obligations where no benefit has been received, or to be unwilling that the Public should consider me as owing that to a Patron, which Providence has enabled me to do for myself.

Having carried on my work thus far with so little obligation to any favorer of learning, I shall not be disappointed though I should conclude it, if less be possible, with less; for I have been long wakened from that dream of hope, in which I once boasted myself with so much exultation, my Lord, your Lordship's most humble, most obedient servant,

Sam. Johnson.

\* \* \*

The *Dictionary*, with a *Grammar and History of the English Language*, being now at length published, in two volumes folio, the world contemplated with wonder so stupendous a work achieved by one man, while other countries had thought such undertakings fit only for whole academies. Vast as his powers were, I cannot but think that his imagination deceived him, when he supposed that by constant application he might have performed the task in three years. \* \* \*

The extensive reading which was absolutely necessary for the accumulation of authorities, and which alone may account for Johnson's retentive mind being enriched with a very large and various store of knowledge and imagery, must have occupied several years. The Preface furnishes an eminent instance of a double talent, of which Johnson was fully conscious. Sir Joshua Reynolds heard him say, "There are two things which I am confident I can do very well: one is an introduction to any literary work, stating what it is to contain, and how it should be executed in the most perfect manner; the other is a conclusion, showing from various causes why the execution has not been equal to what the author promised to himself and to the public." \* \* \*

A few of his definitions must be admitted to be erroneous. Thus, *Windward* and *Leeward*, though directly of opposite meaning, are defined identically the same way; as to which inconsiderable specks it is enough to observe, that his Preface announces that he was aware there might be many such in so immense a work; nor was he at all disconcerted when an instance was pointed out to him. A lady once asked him how he came to define *Pastern* the *knee* of a horse: instead of making an elaborate defense, as she expected, he at once answered, "Ignorance, Madame, pure ignorance." His definition of *Network*[7] has been often quoted with sportive malignity, as obscuring a thing in itself very plain. But to these frivolous censures no other answer is necessary than that with which we are furnished by his own Preface. \* \* \*

---

[4] The conqueror of the conqueror of the earth (Boileau, *L'Art Poétique*, III, 272).

[5] *Eclogues*, VIII, 43.

[6] Johnson's wife had died on 17 March, 1752.

[7] "Anything reticulated or decussated, at equal distances, with interstices between the intersections."

His introducing his own opinions, and even prejudices, under general definitions of words, while at the same time the original meaning of the words is not explained, as his *Tory, Whig, Pension, Oats, Excise*,[8] and a few more, cannot be fully defended, and must be placed to the account of capricious and humorous indulgence. Talking to me upon this subject when we were at Ashbourne in 1777, he mentioned a still stronger instance of the predominance of his private feelings in the composition of this work, than any now to be found in it. "You know, Sir, Lord Gower forsook the old Jacobite interest. When I came to the word *Renegado*, after telling that it meant 'one who deserts to the enemy, a revolter,' I added, *Sometimes we say a* GOWER. Thus it went to the press; but the printer had more wit than I, and struck it out."

Let it, however, be remembered, that this indulgence does not display itself only in sarcasm towards others, but sometimes in playful allusion to the notions commonly entertained of his own laborious task. Thus: "*Grubstreet*, the name of a street in London, much inhabited by writers of small histories, *dictionaries*, and temporary poems; whence any mean production is called *Grubstreet*."—"*Lexicographer*, a writer of dictionaries, a *harmless drudge*." * * *

He had spent, during the progress of the work, the money for which he had contracted to write his *Dictionary*. We have seen that the reward of his labor was only fifteen hundred and seventy-five pounds; and when the expense of amanuenses and paper, and other articles are deducted, his clear profit was very inconsiderable. I once said to him, "I am sorry, Sir, you did not get more for your *Dictionary*." His answer was, "I am sorry, too. But it was very well. The booksellers are generous, liberal-minded men." He, upon all occasions, did ample justice to their character in this respect. He considered them as the patrons of literature; and, indeed, although they have eventually been considerable gainers by his *Dictionary*, it is to them that we

[8] *Tory*: "One who adheres to the ancient constitution of the state, and the apostolical hierarchy of the Church of England; opposed to a whig." *Whig*: "The name of a faction." *Pension*: "An allowance made to any one without an equivalent. In England it is generally understood to mean pay given to a state hireling for treason to his country." *Oats*: "A grain which in England is generally given to horses, but in Scotland supports the people." *Excise*: "A hateful tax levied upon commodities, and adjudged not by the common judges of property, but wretches hired by those to whom Excise is paid."

owe its having been undertaken and carried through at the risk of great expense, for they were not absolutely sure of being indemnified.

## CHRISTOPHER SMART (1763)

CONCERNING this unfortunate poet, Christopher Smart, who was confined in a madhouse, he had, at another time, the following conversation with Dr. Burney:—BURNEY. "How does poor Smart do, Sir; is he likely to recover?" JOHNSON. "It seems as if his mind had ceased to struggle with the disease; for he grows fat upon it." BURNEY. "Perhaps, Sir, that may be from want of exercise." JOHNSON. "No, Sir; he has partly as much exercise as he used to have, for he digs in the garden. Indeed, before his confinement, he used for exercise to walk to the ale-house; but he was *carried* back again. I did not think he ought to be shut up. His infirmities were not noxious to society. He insisted on people praying with him; and I'd as lief pray with Kit Smart as any one else. Another charge was, that he did not love clean linen; and I have no passion for it."—Johnson continued. "Mankind have a great aversion to intellectual labor; but even supposing knowledge to be easily attainable, more people would be content to be ignorant than would take even a little trouble to acquire it."

## THE SOCIAL ORDER (1763)

I DESCRIBED to him an impudent fellow from Scotland, who affected to be a savage, and railed at all establishing systems. JOHNSON. "There is nothing surprising in this, Sir. He wants to make himself conspicuous. He would tumble in a hog-sty, as long as you looked at him and called to him to come out. But let him alone, never mind him, and he'll soon give it over."

I added, that the same person maintained that there was no distinction between virtue and vice. JOHNSON. "Why, Sir, if the fellow does not think as he speaks, he is lying; and I see not what honor he can propose to himself from having the character of a liar. But if he does really think that there is no distinction between virtue and vice, why, Sir, when he leaves our houses let us count our spoons." * * *

He recommended to me to keep a journal of my life, full and unreserved. He said it would be a very good exercise, and would yield me great satisfaction when the particulars were faded from my remembrance. I was uncommonly fortunate in having had a previous coincidence of opinion with him upon this subject, for I had kept such a journal for some time; and it was no small pleasure to me to have this to tell him, and to receive his approbation. He counseled me to keep it private, and said I might surely have a friend who would burn it in case of my death. From this habit I have been enabled to give the world so many anecdotes, which would otherwise have been lost to posterity. I mentioned that I was afraid I put into my journal too many little incidents. JOHNSON. "There is nothing, Sir, too little for so little a creature as man. It is by studying little things that we attain the great art of having as little misery and as much happiness as possible."

Next morning Mr. Dempster happened to call on me, and was so much struck even with the imperfect account which I gave him of Dr. Johnson's conversation, that to his honor be it recorded, when I complained that drinking port and sitting up late with him affected my nerves for some time after, he said, "One had better be palsied at eighteen than not to keep company with such a man."

On Tuesday, July 18, I found tall Sir Thomas Robinson sitting with Johnson. Sir Thomas said, that the King of Prussia valued himself upon three things;—upon being a hero, a musician, and an author. JOHNSON. "Pretty well, Sir, for one man. As to his being an author, I have not looked at his poetry; but his prose is poor stuff. He writes just as you might suppose Voltaire's footboy to do, who has been his amanuensis. He has such parts as the valet might have, and about as much of the coloring of the style as might be got by transcribing his works." When I was at Ferney, I repeated this to Voltaire, in order to reconcile him somewhat to Johnson, whom he, in affecting the English mode of expression, had previously characterized as "a superstitious dog"; but after hearing such a criticism on Frederick the Great, with whom he was then on bad terms, he exclaimed, "An honest fellow!" * * *

Mr. Levet[9] this day showed me Dr. Johnson's library, which was contained in two garrets over his Chambers, where Lintot, son of the celebrated bookseller of that name, had formerly his warehouse. I found a number of good books, but very dusty and in great confusion. The floor was strewed with manuscript leaves, in Johnson's own handwriting, which I beheld with a degree of veneration, supposing they perhaps might contain portions of *The Rambler* or of *Rasselas*. I observed an apparatus for chemical experiments, of which Johnson was all his life very fond. The place seemed to be very favorable for retirement and meditation. Johnson told me that he went up thither without mentioning it to his servant, when he wanted to study, secure from interruption; for he would not allow his servant to say he was not at home when he really was. "A servant's strict regard for truth (said he), must be weakened by such a practice. A philosopher may know that it is merely a form of denial; but few servants are such nice distinguishers. If I accustom a servant to tell a lie for *me*, have I not reason to apprehend that he will tell many lies for *himself*?" * * *

Mr. Temple,[10] now vicar of St. Gluvias, Cornwall, who had been my intimate friend for many years, had at this time chambers in Farrar's Buildings, at the bottom of Inner Temple Lane, which he kindly lent me upon my quitting my lodgings, he being to return to Trinity Hall, Cambridge. I found them particularly convenient for me, as they were so near Dr. Johnson's.

On Wednesday, July 20, Dr. Johnson, Mr. Dempster, and my uncle Dr. Boswell, who happened to be now in London, supped with me at these chambers. JOHNSON. "Pity is not natural to man. Children are always cruel. Savages are always cruel. Pity is acquired and improved by the cultivation of reason. We may have uneasy sensations from seeing a creature in distress, without pity; for we have not pity unless we wish to relieve them. When I am on my way to dine with a friend, and finding it late, have bid the coachman make haste, if I happen to attend when he whips his horses, I may feel unpleasantly that the animals are put to pain, but I do not wish him to desist. No, Sir, I wish him to drive on." * * *

Rousseau's treatise on the inequality of mankind was at this time a fashionable topic. It gave rise to an observation by Mr. Dempster, that the advantages of fortune and rank were nothing to a wise man, who ought to value only merit. JOHNSON. "If man were a savage, living in the woods by himself, this might be true; but in civilized society we all depend upon each other, and our happiness is

[9] See Johnson's poem on his death and the note concerning him, printed at the end of the selections from Johnson in this volume.

[10] William Johnston Temple (1739-1796).

very much owing to the good opinion of mankind. Now, Sir, in civilized society, external advantages make us more respected. A man with a good coat upon his back meets with a better reception than he who has a bad one. Sir, you may analyze this, and say what is there in it? But that will avail you nothing, for it is a part of a general system. Pound St. Paul's Church into atoms, and consider any single atom; it is, to be sure, good for nothing: but, put all these atoms together, and you have St. Paul's Church. So it is with human felicity, which is made up of many ingredients, each of which may be shown to be very insignificant. In civilized society, personal merit will not serve you so much as money will. Sir, you may make the experiment. Go into the street, and give one man a lecture on morality, and another a shilling, and see which will respect you most. If you wish only to support nature, Sir William Petty [11] fixes your allowance at three pounds a year; but as times are much altered, let us call it six pounds. This sum will fill your belly, shelter you from the weather, and even get you a strong lasting coat, supposing it to be made of good bull's hide. Now, Sir, all beyond this is artificial, and is desired in order to obtain a greater degree of respect from our fellow-creatures. And, Sir, if six hundred pounds a year procure a man more consequence, and, of course, more happiness than six pounds a year, the same proportion will hold as to six thousand, and so on as far as opulence can be carried. Perhaps he who has a large fortune may not be so happy as he who has a small one; but that must proceed from other causes than from his having the large fortune: for, *caeteris paribus*,[12] he who is rich in a civilized society, must be happier than he who is poor; as riches, if properly used (and it is a man's own fault if they are not), must be productive of the highest advantages. Money, to be sure, of itself is of no use, for its only use is to part with it. Rousseau, and all those who deal in paradoxes, are led away by a childish desire of novelty. When I was a boy, I used always to choose the wrong side of a debate, because most ingenious things, that is to say, most new things, could be said upon it. Sir, there is nothing for which you may not muster up more plausible arguments, than those which are urged

[11] Author of a *Treatise on Taxes* (1662), and *The Multiplication of Mankind* (1682).

[12] Other things being equal.

against wealth and other external advantages. Why, now, there is stealing; why should it be thought a crime? When we consider by what unjust methods property has been often acquired, and that what was unjustly got it must be unjust to keep, where is the harm in one man's taking the property of another from him? Besides, Sir, when we consider the bad use that many people make of their property, and how much better use the thief may make of it, it may be defended as a very allowable practice. Yet, Sir, the experience of mankind has discovered stealing to be so very bad a thing, that they make no scruple to hang a man for it. When I was running about this town a very poor fellow, I was a great arguer for the advantages of poverty; but I was, at the same time, very sorry to be poor. Sir, all the arguments which are brought to represent poverty as no evil, show it to be evidently a great evil. You never find people laboring to convince you that you may live very happily upon a plentiful fortune.—So you hear people talking how miserable a King must be; and yet they all wish to be in his place."

It was suggested that Kings must be unhappy, because they are deprived of the greatest of all satisfactions, easy and unreserved society. JOHNSON. "That is an illfounded notion. Being a King does not exclude a man from such society. Great Kings have always been social. The King of Prussia, the only great King at present, is very social. Charles the Second, the last King of England who was a man of parts, was social; and our Henrys and Edwards were all social."

Mr. Dempster having endeavored to maintain that intrinsic merit *ought* to make the only distinction amongst mankind. JOHNSON. "Why, Sir, mankind have found that this cannot be. How shall we determine the proportion of intrinsic merit? Were that to be the only distinction amongst mankind, we should soon quarrel about the degrees of it. Were all distinctions abolished, the strongest would not long acquiesce, but would endeavor to obtain a superiority by their bodily strength. But, Sir, as subordination is very necessary for society, and contentions for superiority very dangerous, mankind, that is to say, all civilized nations, have settled it upon a plain invariable principle. A man is born to hereditary rank; or his being appointed to certain offices, gives him a certain rank. Subordination tends greatly to human happiness. Were we all upon an equality, we should have no other enjoyment that mere animal pleasure." * * *

He took care to guard himself against any possible suspicion that his settled principles of reverence for rank and respect for wealth were at all owing to mean or interested motives; for he asserted his own independence as a literary man. "No man (said he) who ever lived by literature, has lived more independently than I have done."

### YOUNG PEOPLE (1763)

"Sir, I love the acquaintance of young people; because, in the first place, I don't like to think myself growing old. In the next place, young acquaintances must last longest, if they do last; and then, Sir, young men have more virtue than old men: they have more generous sentiments in every respect. I love the young dogs of this age: they have more wit and humor and knowledge of life than we had; but then the dogs are not so good scholars. Sir, in my early years I read very hard. It is a sad reflection, but a true one, that I knew almost as much at eighteen as I do now. My judgment, to be sure, was not so good; but I had all the facts. I remember very well, when I was at Oxford, an old gentleman said to me, 'Young man, ply your book diligently now, and acquire a stock of knowledge; for when years come upon you, you will find that poring upon books will be but an irksome task.'"

### A WOMAN'S PREACHING (1763)

Next day, Sunday, July 31, I told him I had been that morning at a meeting of the people called Quakers, where I had heard a woman preach. Johnson. "Sir, a woman's preaching is like a dog's walking on his hinder legs. It is not done well; but you are surprised to find it done at all."

### GEORGE III (1767)

In February, 1767, there happened one of the most remarkable incidents of Johnson's life, which gratified his monarchical enthusiasm, and which he loved to relate with all its circumstances, when requested by his friends. This was his being honored by a private conversation with his Majesty, in the library at the Queen's house. He had frequently visited those splendid rooms and noble collection of books, which he used to say was more numerous and curious than he supposed

any person could have made in the time which the King had employed. Mr. Barnard, the librarian, took care that he should have every accommodation that could contribute to his ease and convenience, while indulging his literary taste in that place; so that he had here a very agreeable resource at leisure hours.

His Majesty having been informed of his occasional visits, was pleased to signify a desire that he should be told when Dr. Johnson came next to the library. Accordingly, the next time that Johnson did come, as soon as he was fairly engaged with a book, on which, while he sat by the fire, he seemed quite intent, Mr. Barnard stole round to the apartment where the King was, and, in obedience to his Majesty's commands, mentioned that Dr. Johnson was then in the library. His Majesty said he was at leisure, and would go to him; upon which Mr. Barnard took one of the candles that stood on the King's table, and lighted his Majesty through a suite of rooms, till they came to a private door into the library, of which his Majesty had the key. Being entered, Mr. Barnard stepped forward hastily to Dr. Johnson, who was still in a profound study, and whispered him, "Sir, here is the King," Johnson started up, and stood still. His Majesty approached him, and at once was courteously easy.

His Majesty began by observing, that he understood he came sometimes to the library; and then mentioning his having heard that the Doctor had been lately at Oxford, asked him if he was not fond of going thither. To which Johnson answered, that he was indeed fond of going to Oxford sometimes, but was likewise glad to come back again. The King then asked him what they were doing at Oxford. Johnson answered, he could not much commend their diligence, but that in some respects they were mended, for they had put their press under better regulations, and were at that time printing Polybius. He was then asked whether there were better libraries at Oxford or Cambridge. He answered, he believed the Bodleian was larger than any they had at Cambridge; at the same time adding, "I hope, whether we have more books or not than they have at Cambridge, we shall make as good use of them as they do." Being asked whether All-Souls or Christ-Church library was the largest, he answered, "All-Souls library is the largest we have, except the Bodleian." "Aye (said the King), that is the public library."

His Majesty inquired if he was then writing anything. He answered, he was not, for he had pretty well told the world what he knew, and must now read to acquire more knowledge. The King, as it should seem with a view to urge him to rely on his own stores as an original writer, and to continue his labors, then said "I do not think you borrow much from anybody." Johnson said, he thought he had already done his part as a writer. "I should have thought so too (said the King), if you had not written so well."—Johnson observed to me, upon this, that "No man could have paid a handsomer compliment; and it was fit for a King to pay. It was decisive." When asked by another friend, at Sir Joshua Reynolds's, whether he made any reply to this high compliment, he answered, "No, Sir. When the King had said it, it was to be so. It was not for me to bandy civilities with my Sovereign." Perhaps no man who had spent his whole life in courts could have shown a more nice and dignified sense of true politeness, than Johnson did in this instance.

His Majesty having observed to him that he supposed he must have read a great deal; Johnson answered, that he thought more than he read; that he had read a great deal in the early part of his life, but having fallen into ill health, he had not been able to read much, compared with others: for instance, he said he had not read much, compared with Dr. Warburton. Upon which the King said, that he heard Dr. Warburton [13] was a man of such general knowledge that you could scarce talk with him on any subject on which he was not qualified to speak; and that his learning resembled Garrick's acting, in its universality. His Majesty then talked of the controversy between Warburton and Lowth, which he seemed to have read, and asked Johnson what he thought of it. Johnson answered, "Warburton has most general, most scholastic learning; Lowth is the more correct scholar. I do not know which of them calls names best." The King was pleased to say he was of the same opinion; adding, "You do not think, then, Dr. Johnson, that there was much argument in the case." Johnson said, he did not think there was. "Why truly (said the King), when once it comes to calling names, argument is pretty well at an end."

## CRITICISM (1769)

Mrs. Montagu, a lady distinguished for having written an Essay on Shakespeare, being mentioned; Reynolds. "I think that essay does her honor." Johnson. "Yes, Sir; it does *her* honor, but it would do nobody else honor. I have, indeed, not read it all. But when I take up the end of a web, and find it packthread, I do not expect, by looking further, to find embroidery. Sir, I will venture to say, there is not one sentence of true criticism in her book." Garrick. "But, Sir, surely it shows how much Voltaire has mistaken Shakespeare, which nobody else has done." Johnson. "Sir, nobody else has thought it worth while. And what merit is there in that? You may as well praise a schoolmaster for whipping a boy who has construed ill. No, Sir, there is no real criticism in it: none showing the beauty of thought, as formed on the workings of the human heart."

The admirers of this Essay may be offended at the slighting manner in which Johnson spoke of it; but let it be remembered, that he gave his honest opinion unbiased by any prejudice, or any proud jealousy of a woman intruding herself into the chair of criticism; for Sir Joshua Reynolds has told me, that when the Essay first came out, and it was not known who had written it, Johnson wondered how Sir Joshua could like it. At this time Sir Joshua himself had received no information concerning the author, except being assured by one of our most eminent literati, that it was clear its author did not know the Greek tragedies in the original. One day at Sir Joshua's table, when it was related that Mrs. Montagu, in an excess of compliment to the author of a modern tragedy, had exclaimed, "I tremble for Shakespeare"; Johnson said, "When Shakespeare has got —— for his rival, and Mrs. Montagu for his defender, he is in a poor state indeed."

Johnson proceeded: "The Scotchman [14] has taken the right method in his *Elements of Criticism*. I do not mean that he has taught us anything; but he has told us old things in a new way." Murphy. "He seems to have read a great deal of French criticism, and wants to make it his own; as if he had been for years anatomizing the heart of man, and peeping into every cranny of it." Goldsmith. "It is easier to write that book, than to read it." Johnson. "We have an example

---

[13] William Warburton (1698–1779), Bishop of Gloucester, author of *The Divine Legation of Moses*, and editor of Pope's works.

[14] Henry Home, Lord Kames (1696–1782).

of true criticism in Burke's *Essay on the Sublime and Beautiful*; and, if I recollect, there is also Du Bos; and Bouhours, who shows all beauty to depend on truth. There is no great merit in telling how many plays have ghosts in them, and how this Ghost is better than that. You must show how terror is impressed on the human heart. In the description of night in *Macbeth*, the beetle and the bat detract from the general idea of darkness,— inspissated gloom."

## SYMPATHY (1769)

TALKING of our feeling for the distresses of others;—JOHNSON. "Why, Sir, there is much noise made about it, but it is greatly exaggerated. No, Sir, we have a certain degree of feeling to prompt us to do good: more than that, Providence does not intend. It would be misery to no purpose." BOSWELL. "But suppose now, Sir, that one of your intimate friends were apprehended for an offense for which he might be hanged." JOHNSON. "I should do what I could to bail him, and give him any other assistance; but if he were once fairly hanged, I should not suffer." BOSWELL. "Would you eat your dinner that day, Sir?" JOHNSON. "Yes, Sir; and eat it as if he were eating it with me. Why, there's Baretti, who is to be tried for his life tomorrow; friends have risen up for him on every side; yet if he should be hanged, none of them will eat a slice of plum-pudding the less. Sir, that sympathetic feeling goes a very little way in depressing the mind."

I told him that I had dined lately at Foote's, who showed me a letter which he had received from Tom Davies, telling him that he had not been able to sleep from the concern which he felt on account of "This sad affair of Baretti," begging of him to try if he could suggest anything that might be of service; and, at the same time, recommending to him an industrious young man who kept a pickleshop. JOHNSON. "Ay, Sir, here you have a specimen of human sympathy; a friend hanged, and a cucumber pickled. We know not whether Baretti or the pickle-man has kept Davies from sleep; nor does he know himself. And as to his not sleeping, Sir; Tom Davies is a very great man; Tom has been upon the stage, and knows how to do those things. I have not been upon the stage, and cannot do those things." BOSWELL. "I have often blamed myself, Sir, for not feeling for others as sensibly as many say they do." JOHNSON. "Sir, don't be

duped by them any more. You will find these very feeling people are not very ready to do you good. They *pay* you by *feeling*."

## GOOD BEINGS (1772)

I TALKED of the recent expulsion of six students from the University of Oxford, who were methodists and would not desist from publicly praying and exhorting. JOHNSON. "Sir, that expulsion was extremely just and proper. What have they to do at an University who are not willing to be taught, but will presume to teach? Where is religion to be learned but at an University? Sir, they were examined, and found to be mighty ignorant fellows." BOSWELL. "But, was it not hard, Sir, to expell them, for I am told they were good beings?" JOHNSON. "I believe they might be good beings; but they were not fit to be in the University of Oxford. A cow is a very good animal in the field; but we turn her out of a garden." Lord Elibank used to repeat this as an illustration uncommonly happy.

## READING (1773)

ON MONDAY, April 19, he called on me with Mrs. Williams, in Mr. Strahan's coach, and carried me out to dine with Mr. Elphinston, at his academy at Kensington. A printer having acquired a fortune sufficient to keep his coach, was a good topic for the credit of literature. Mrs. Williams said, that another printer, Mr. Hamilton, had not waited so long as Mr. Strahan, but had kept his coach several years sooner. JOHNSON. "He was in the right. Life is short. The sooner that a man begins to enjoy his wealth the better."

Mr. Elphinston talked of a new book that was much admired, and asked Dr. Johnson if he had read it. JOHNSON. "I have looked into it." "What (said Elphinston), have you not read it through?" Johnson, offended at being thus pressed, and so obliged to own his cursory mode of reading, answered tartly, "No, Sir, do *you* read books *through*?"

## OSSIAN (1775)

*Mr. Boswell to Dr. Johnson*

Edinburgh, Feb. 2, 1775.
. . . . As TO Macpherson,[15] I am anxious to have from yourself a full and pointed account of what

[15] James Macpherson (1736–1796) had in 1760 begun publishing what he claimed were translations of ancient poetry composed in the Gaelic (or Erse) tongue by Ossian. These "translations" (it is now

has passed between you and him. It is confidently told here, that before your book came out he sent to you, to let you know that he understood you meant to deny the authenticity of Ossian's poems; that the originals were in his possession; that you might have inspection of them, and might take the evidence of people skilled in the Erse language; and that he hoped, after this fair offer, you would not be so uncandid as to assert that he had refused reasonable proof. That you paid no regard to his message, but published your strong attack upon him; and then he wrote a letter to you, in such terms as he thought suited to one who had not acted as a man of veracity. * * *

### To James Boswell, Esq.

My dear Boswell,—I am surprised that, knowing as you do the disposition of your countrymen to tell lies in favor of each other,[16] you can be at all affected by any reports that circulate among them. Macpherson never in his life offered me a sight of any original or of any evidence of any kind; but thought only of intimidating me by noise and threats, till my last answer—that I would not be deterred from detecting what I thought a cheat, by the menaces of a ruffian—put an end to our correspondence.

The state of the question is this. He, and Dr. Blair, whom I consider as deceived, say, that he copied the poem from old manuscripts. His copies, if he had them, and I believe them to have none, are nothing. Where are the manuscripts? They can be shown if they exist, but they were never shown. *De non existentibus et non apparentibus*, says our law, *eadem est ratio.*[17] No man has a claim to credit upon his own word, when better evidence, if he had it, may be easily produced. But, so far as we can find, the Erse language was never written till very lately for the purposes of religion. A nation that cannot write, or a language that was never written, has no manuscripts.

But whatever he has he never offered to show. If old manuscripts should now be mentioned, I should, unless there were more evidence than can be easily had, suppose them another proof of Scotch conspiracy in national falsehood.

Do not censure the expression; you know it to be true. * * *

My compliments to Madam and Veronica.[18]

I am, Sir, Your most humble servant,
Sam. Johnson.

*February 7, 1775.*

What words were used by Mr. Macpherson in his letter to the venerable Sage, I have never heard; but they are generally said to have been of a nature very different from the language of literary contest. Dr. John-

son's answer appeared in the newspapers of the day, and has since been frequently republished; but not with perfect accuracy. I give it as dictated to me by himself, written down in his presence, and authenticated by a note in his own handwriting, "This, I think, is a true copy."

Mr. James Macpherson,—I received your foolish and impudent letter. Any violence offered me I shall do my best to repel; and what I cannot do for myself, the law shall do for me. I hope I shall never be deterred from detecting what I think a cheat, by the menaces of a ruffian.

What would you have me retract? I thought your book an imposture; I think it an imposture still. For this opinion I have given my reasons to the public, which I here dare you to refute. Your rage I defy. Your abilities, since your Homer, are not so formidable; and what I hear of your morals, inclines me to pay regard not to what you shall say, but to what you shall prove. You may print this if you will.
Sam. Johnson.

Mr. Macpherson little knew the character of Dr. Johnson, if he supposed that he could be easily intimidated; for no man was ever more remarkable for personal courage. He had, indeed, an awful dread of death, or rather, "of something after death"; and what rational man, who seriously thinks of quitting all that he has ever known, and going into a new and unknown state of being, can be without that dread? But his fear was from reflection; his courage natural. His fear, in that one instance, was the result of philosophical and religious consideration. He feared death, but he feared nothing else, not even what might occasion death. Many instances of his resolution may be mentioned. One day, at Mr. Beauclerk's house in the country, when two large dogs were fighting, he went up to them, and beat them till they separated; and at another time, when told of the danger there was that a gun might burst if charged with many balls, he put in six or seven, and fired it off against a wall. Mr. Langton told me, that when they were swimming together near Oxford, he cautioned Dr. Johnson against a pool, which was reckoned particularly dangerous; upon which Johnson directly swam into it. He told me himself that one night he was attacked in the street by four men, to whom he would not yield, but kept them all at bay, till the watch came up, and carried both him and them to the round-house. In the playhouse at Lichfield, as Mr. Garrick informed me, Johnson having for a moment quitted a chair which was placed for him between the side-scenes, a gentleman took possession of it, and when

---

agreed they were forgeries) were eagerly accepted in Scotland, were popular on the Continent, and occupy an important place in the rise of Romanticism. Macpherson's prose translation of the *Iliad* of Homer was published in 1773.

[16] My friend has, in this letter, relied upon my testimony, with a confidence, of which the ground has escaped my recollection (Boswell's note).

[17] Reasoning is identical, says our law, concerning the nonexistent and concerning the invisible.

[18] Boswell's wife and daughter.

Johnson on his return civilly demanded his seat, rudely refused to give it up; upon which Johnson laid hold of it, and tossed him and the chair into the pit. Foote, who so successfully revived the old comedy, by exhibiting living characters, had resolved to imitate Johnson on the stage, expecting great profits from his ridicule of so celebrated a man. Johnson being informed of his intention, and being at dinner at Mr. Thomas Davies's the bookseller, from whom I had the story, he asked Mr. Davies "what was the common price of an oak stick"; and being answered six-pence, "Why then, Sir (said he), give me leave to send your servant to purchase me a shilling one. I'll have a double quantity; for I am told Foote means to *take me off*, as he calls it, and I am determined the fellow shall not do it with impunity." Davies took care to acquaint Foote of this, which effectually checked the wantonness of the mimic. Mr. Macpherson's menaces made Johnson provide himself with the same implement of defense; and had he been attacked, I have no doubt that, old as he was, he would have made his corporal prowess be felt as much as his intellectual.

## THE IRISH (1775)

My much-valued friend Dr. Barnard, now Bishop of Killaloe, having once expressed to him an apprehension, that if he should visit Ireland he might treat the people of that country more unfavorably than he had done the Scotch, he answered, with strong pointed double-edged wit, "Sir, you have no reason to be afraid of me. The Irish are not in a conspiracy to cheat the world by false representations of the merits of their countrymen. No, Sir; the Irish are a fair people;—they never speak well of one another."

## THE INDISTINCT RELATER (1775)

I visited him by appointment in the evening, and we drank tea with Mrs. Williams.[19] He told me that he had been in the company of a gentleman whose extraordinary travels had been much the subject of conversation. But I found that he had not listened to him with that full confidence, without which there is little satisfaction in the society of travelers. I was curious to hear what opinion so able a judge as Johnson had formed of

[19] A blind and aged woman of letters whom Johnson supported as a member of his household.

his abilities, and I asked if he was not a man of sense. Johnson. "Why, Sir, he is not a distinct relater; and I should say, he is neither abounding nor deficient in sense. I did not perceive any superiority of understanding." Boswell. "But will you not allow him a nobleness of resolution, in penetrating into distant regions?" Johnson. "That, Sir, is not to the present purpose. We are talking of his sense. A fighting cock has a nobleness of resolution."

## A GOOD THING (1775)

No more of his conversation for some days appears in my journal, except that when a gentleman told him he had bought a suit of lace for his lady, he said, "Well, Sir, you have done a good thing and a wise thing." "I have done a good thing (said the gentleman), but I do not know that I have done a wise thing." Johnson. "Yes, Sir; no money is better spent than what is laid out for domestic satisfaction. A man is pleased that his wife is dressed as well as other people; and a wife is pleased that she is dressed."

## THE FELICITY OF ENGLAND IN ITS TAVERNS (1776)

We dined at an excellent inn at Chapel House, where he expatiated on the felicity of England in its taverns and inns, and triumphed over the French for not having, in any perfection, the tavern life. "There is no private house (said he), in which people can enjoy themselves so well, as at a capital tavern. Let there be ever so great plenty of good things, ever so much grandeur, ever so much elegance, ever so much desire that everybody should be easy; in the nature of things it cannot be: there must always be some degree of care and anxiety. The master of the house is anxious to entertain his guests; the guests are anxious to be agreeable to him: and no man, but a very impudent dog indeed, can as freely command what is in another man's house, as if it were his own. Whereas, at a tavern, there is a general freedom from anxiety. You are sure you are welcome: and the more noise you make, the more trouble you give, the more good things you call for, the welcomer you are. No servants will attend you with the alacrity which waiters do, who are incited by the prospect of an immediate reward in proportion as they please. No, Sir; there is nothing which has yet been contrived by man, by which so much happiness is produced as by a good tavern or inn." [20] He then repeated, with great emotion, Shenstone's lines:—

> Whoe'er has traveled life's dull round,
> Where'er his stages may have been,
> May sigh to think he still has found
> The warmest welcome at an inn.

## MARRIAGE (1776)

WHEN he again talked of Mrs. Careless tonight, he seemed to have had his affection revived; for he said, "If I had married her, it might have been as happy for me." BOSWELL. "Pray, Sir, do you not suppose that there are fifty women in the world, with any one of whom a man may be as happy, as with any one woman in particular?" JOHNSON. "Ay, Sir, fifty thousand." BOSWELL. "Then, Sir, you are not of opinion with some who imagine that certain men and certain women are made for each other; and that they cannot be happy if they miss their counterparts?" JOHNSON. "To be sure not, Sir. I believe marriages would in general be as happy, and often more so, if they were all made by the Lord Chancellor, upon a due consideration of characters and circumstances, without the parties having any choice in the matter."

## THE REVIEWS (1776)

"THE Monthly Reviewers (said he) are not Deists; [21] but they are Christians with as little Christianity as may be; and are for pulling down all establishments. The Critical Reviewers are for supporting the constitution both in church and state. The Critical Reviewers, I believe, often review without reading the books through; but lay hold of a topic, and write chiefly from their own minds. The Monthly Reviewers are duller men, and are glad to read the books through."

## JOHN WILKES (1776)

MY DESIRE of being acquainted with celebrated men of every description had made me, much about the same time, obtain an introduction to Dr. Samuel Johnson and to John Wilkes, Esq.[22] Two men more different could perhaps not be selected out of all mankind. They had even attacked one another with some asperity in their writings; yet I lived in habits of friendship with both. I could fully relish the excellence of each; for I have ever delighted in that intellectual chemistry, which can separate good qualities from evil in the same person.

Sir John Pringle, "mine own friend and my Father's friend," between whom and Dr. Johnson I in vain wished to establish an acquaintance, as I respected and lived in intimacy with both of them, observed to me once, very ingeniously, "It is not in friendship as in mathematics, where two things, each equal to a third, are equal between themselves. You agree with Johnson as a middle quality, and you agree with me as a middle quality; but Johnson and I should not agree." Sir John was not sufficiently flexible; so I desisted; knowing, indeed, that the repulsion was equally strong on the part of Johnson; who, I know not from what cause, unless his being a Scotchman, had formed a very erroneous opinion of Sir John. But I conceived an irresistible wish, if possible, to bring Dr. Johnson and Mr. Wilkes together. How to manage it, was a nice and difficult matter.

My worthy booksellers and friends, Messieurs Dilly in the Poultry, at whose hospitable and well-covered table I have seen a greater number of literary men, than at any other, except that of Sir Joshua Reynolds, had invited me to meet Mr. Wilkes and some more gentlemen on Wednesday, May 15. "Pray (said I), let us have Dr. Johnson."—

---

[20] Sir John Hawkins has preserved very few *Memorabilia* of Johnson. There is, however, to be found, in his bulky tome, a very excellent one upon this subject:—"In contradiction to those, who, having a wife and children, prefer domestic enjoyments to those which a tavern affords, I have heard him assert, *that a tavern chair was the throne of human felicity.*—'As soon,' said he, 'as I enter the door of a tavern, I experience an oblivion of care, and a freedom from solicitude: when I am seated, I find the master courteous, and the servants obsequious to my call; anxious to know and ready to supply my wants: wine there exhilarates my spirits, and prompts me to free conversation and an interchange of discourse with those whom I most love. I dogmatize and am contradicted, and in this conflict of opinions and sentiments I find delight'" (Boswell's note).

[21] One who believes in God on the testimony of reason, not a revelation.

[22] Demagogue and man of loose life (1727–1797); editor of the political periodical *The North Briton,* for one number of which he suffered a brief imprisonment which helped to make him popular. Later he was outlawed, but in 1768 returned to England and was elected to Parliament for Middlesex. He was then imprisoned and in 1769 expelled from Parliament. He was several times reëlected, but each time declared ineligible. In 1774 he became lord mayor of London, and, again elected to Parliament, he was now allowed to sit, and remained a member until 1790.

"What, with Mr. Wilkes? not for the world (said Mr. Edward Dilly): Dr. Johnson would never forgive me."—"Come (said I), if you'll let me negotiate for you, I will be answerable that all shall go well." DILLY. "Nay, if you will take it upon you, I am sure I shall be very happy to see them both here."

Notwithstanding the high veneration which I entertained for Dr. Johnson, I was sensible that he was sometimes a little actuated by the 10 spirit of contradiction, and by means of that I hoped I should gain my point. I was persuaded that if I had come upon him with a direct proposal, "Sir, will you dine in company with Jack Wilkes?" he would have flown into a passion, and would probably have answered, "Dine with Jack Wilkes, Sir! I'd as soon dine with Jack Ketch." [23] I therefore, while we were sitting quietly by ourselves at his house in an evening, took occasion to 20 open my plan thus:—"Mr. Dilly, Sir, sends his respectful compliments to you, and would be happy if you would do him the honor to dine with him on Wednesday next along with me, as I must soon go to Scotland." JOHNSON. "Sir, I am obliged to Mr. Dilly. I will wait upon him—" BOSWELL. "Provided, Sir, I suppose, that the company which he is to have, is agreeable to you." JOHNSON. "What do you mean, Sir? What do you take me for? Do you 30 think I am so ignorant of the world as to imagine that I am to prescribe to a gentleman what company he is to have at his table?" BOSWELL. "I beg your pardon, Sir, for wishing to prevent you from meeting people whom you might not like. Perhaps he may have some of what he calls his patriotic friends with him." JOHNSON. "Well, Sir, and what then? What care I for his *patriotic friends*? Poh!" BOSWELL. "I should not be surprised to find Jack Wilkes 40 there." JOHNSON. "And if Jack Wilkes *should* be there, what is that to *me*, Sir? My dear friend, let us have no more of this. I am sorry to be angry with you; but really it is treating me strangely to talk to me as if I could not meet any company whatever, occasionally." BOSWELL. "Pray forgive me, Sir: I meant well. But you shall meet whoever comes, for me." Thus I secured him, and told Dilly that he would find him very well pleased to be one of 50 his guests on the day appointed.

Upon the much-expected Wednesday, I called on him about half an hour before dinner, as I often did when we were to dine out to-

gether, to see that he was ready in time, and to accompany him. I found him buffeting his books, as upon a former occasion, covered with dust, and making no preparation for going abroad. "How is this, Sir? (said I). Don't you recollect that you are to dine at Mr. Dilly's?" JOHNSON. "Sir, I did not think of going to Dilly's: it went out of my head. I have ordered dinner at home with Mrs. Williams." BOS-WELL. "But, my dear Sir, you know you were engaged to Mr. Dilly, and I told him so. He will expect you, and will be much disappointed if you don't come." JOHNSON. "You must talk to Mrs. Williams about this."

Here was a sad dilemma. I feared that what I was so confident I had secured would yet be frustrated. He had accustomed himself to show Mrs. Williams such a degree of humane attention, as frequently imposed some restraint upon him; and I knew that if she should be obstinate, he would not stir. I hastened down stairs to the blind lady's room, and told her I was in great uneasiness, for Dr. Johnson had engaged to me to dine this day at Mr. Dilly's, but that he had told me he had forgotten his engagement, and had ordered dinner at home. "Yes, Sir (said she, pretty peevishly), Dr. Johnson is to dine at home."—"Madam (said I), his respect for you is such, that I know he will not leave you unless you absolutely desire it. But as you have so much of his company, I hope you will be good enough to forgo it for a day; as Mr. Dilly is a very worthy man, has frequently had agreeable parties at his house for Dr. Johnson, and will be vexed if the Doctor neglects him to-day. And then, Madam, be pleased to consider my situation; I carried the message, and I assured Mr. Dilly that Dr. Johnson was to come, and no doubt he has made a dinner, and invited a company, and boasted of the honor he expected to have. I shall be quite disgraced if the Doctor is not there." She gradually softened to my solicitations, which were certainly as earnest as most entreaties to ladies upon any occasion, and was graciously pleased to empower me to tell Dr. Johnson, "That all things considered, she thought he should certainly go." I flew back to him, still in dust, and careless of what should be the event, "indifferent in his choice to go or stay"; but as soon as I had announced to him Mrs. Williams's consent, he roared, "Frank,[24] a clean shirt," and was very soon dressed. When I had him fairly seated in a hackney-coach with me, I exulted as much as a fortune-hunter who has

---

[23] An executioner of the seventeenth century, notorious for his barbarity.

[24] Francis Barber, Johnson's negro servant.

got an heiress into a post-chaise with him to set out for Gretna Green.[25]

When we entered Mr. Dilly's drawing room, he found himself in the midst of a company he did not know. I kept myself snug and silent, watching how he would conduct himself. I observed him whispering to Mr. Dilly, "Who is that gentleman, Sir?"—"Mr. Arthur Lee."—JOHNSON. "Too, too, too" (under his breath), which was one of his habitual mutterings. Mr. Arthur Lee could not but be very obnoxious to Johnson, for he was not only a *patriot* but an *American*. He was afterwards minister from the United States at the court of Madrid. "And who is the gentleman in lace?"—"Mr. Wilkes, Sir." This information confounded him still more; he had some difficulty to restrain himself, and taking up a book, sat down upon a window-seat and read, or at least kept his eye upon it intently for some time, till he composed himself. His feelings, I dare say, were awkward enough. But he no doubt recollected his having rated me for supposing that he could be at all disconcerted by any company, and he, therefore, resolutely set himself to behave quite as an easy man of the world, who could adapt himself at once to the disposition and manners of those whom he might chance to meet.

The cheering sound of "Dinner is upon the table," dissolved his reverie, and we *all* sat down without any symptom of ill humor. There were present, beside Mr. Wilkes, and Mr. Arthur Lee, who was an old companion of mine when he studied physic at Edinburgh, Mr. (now Sir John) Miller, Dr. Lettsom, and Mr. Slater the druggist. Mr. Wilkes placed himself next to Dr. Johnson, and behaved to him with so much attention and politeness, that he gained upon him insensibly. No man ate more heartily than Johnson, or loved better what was nice and delicate. Mr. Wilkes was very assiduous in helping him to some fine veal. "Pray give me leave, Sir:—It is better here—A little of the brown—Some fat, Sir—A little of the stuffing—Some gravy—Let me have the pleasure of giving you some butter—Allow me to recommend a squeeze of this orange;—or the lemon, perhaps, may have more zest."—"Sir, Sir, I am obliged to you, Sir," cried Johnson, bowing, and turning his head to him with a look for some time of "surly virtue," but, in a short while, of complacency.

Foote being mentioned, Johnson said, "He is not a good mimic." One of the company added, "A merry Andrew, a buffoon." JOHNSON. "But he has wit too, and is not deficient in ideas, or in fertility and variety of imagery, and not empty of reading; he has knowledge enough to fill up his part. One species of wit he has in an eminent degree, that of escape. You drive him into a corner with both hands; but he's gone, Sir, when you think you have got him—like an animal that jumps over your head. Then he has a great range for wit; he never lets truth stand between him and a jest, and he is sometimes mighty coarse. Garrick is under many restraints from which Foote is free." WILKES. "Garrick's wit is more like Lord Chesterfield's." JOHNSON. "The first time I was in company with Foote was at Fitzherbert's. Having no good opinion of the fellow, I was resolved not to be pleased; and it is very difficult to please a man against his will. I went on eating my dinner pretty sullenly, affecting not to mind him. But the dog was so very comical, that I was obliged to lay down my knife and fork, throw myself back upon my chair, and fairly laugh it out. No, Sir, he was irresistible. He upon one occasion experienced, in an extraordinary degree, the efficacy of his powers of entertaining. Amongst the many and various modes which he tried of getting money, he became a partner with a small-beer brewer, and he was to have a share of the profits for procuring customers amongst his numerous acquaintance. Fitzherbert was one who took his small-beer; but it was so bad that the servants resolved not to drink it. They were at some loss how to notify their resolution, being afraid of offending their master, who they knew liked Foote much as a companion. At last they fixed upon a little black boy, who was rather a favorite, to be their deputy, and deliver their remonstrance; and having invested him with the whole authority of the kitchen, he was to inform Mr. Fitzherbert, in all their names, upon a certain day, that they would drink Foote's small-beer no longer. On that day Foote happened to dine at Fitzherbert's, and this boy served at table; he was so delighted with Foote's stories, and merriment, and grimace, that when he went down stairs, he told them, 'This is the finest man I have ever seen. I will not deliver your message. I will drink his small-beer.'"

Somebody observed that Garrick could not have done this. WILKES. "Garrick would have made the small-beer still smaller. He is now leaving the stage; but he will play *Scrub* [26] all

[25] The Scotch town, just over the border from England, where run-away marriages were made.

[26] A servant in George Farquhar's *Beaux' Stratagem*.

his life." I knew that Johnson would let nobody attack Garrick but himself, as Garrick
once said to me, and I had heard him praise
his liberality; so to bring out his commendation
of his celebrated pupil, I said, loudly, "I have
heard Garrick is liberal." JOHNSON. "Yes, Sir,
I know that Garrick has given away more
money than any man in England that I am
acquainted with, and that not from ostentatious views. Garrick was very poor when he 10
began life; so when he came to have money, he
probably was very unskillful in giving away,
and saved when he should not. But Garrick
began to be liberal as soon as he could; and I
am of opinion, the reputation of avarice which
he has had, has been very lucky for him, and
prevented his having many enemies. You despise a man for avarice, but do not hate him.
Garrick might have been much better attacked
for living with more splendor than is suitable 20
to a player: if they had had the wit to have
assaulted him in that quarter, they might have
galled him more. But they have kept clamor-
ing about his avarice, which has rescued him
from much obloquy and envy."

Talking of the great difficulty of obtaining
authentic information for biography, Johnson
told us, "When I was a young fellow I wanted
to write the *Life of Dryden*, and in order to
get materials, I applied to the only two per- 30
sons then alive who had seen him; these were
old Swinney, and old Cibber. Swinney's information was no more than this, 'That at Will's
coffee-house Dryden had a particular chair for
himself, which was set by the fire in winter,
and was then called his winter-chair; and that
it was carried out for him to the balcony in
summer, and was then called his summer-chair.'
Cibber could tell no more but 'That he remembered him a decent old man, arbiter of critical 40
disputes at Will's.' You are to consider that
Cibber was then at a great distance from Dryden, had perhaps one leg only in the room, and
durst not draw in the other." BOSWELL. "Yet
Cibber was a man of observation?" JOHNSON.
"I think not." BOSWELL. "You will allow his
*Apology* to be well done." JOHNSON. "Very well
done, to be sure, Sir. That book is a striking
proof of the justice of Pope's remark:

Each might his several province well command,
Would all but stoop to what they understand." [27]

BOSWELL. "And his plays are good." JOHNSON.
"Yes; but that was his trade; *l'esprit du corps*:
he had been all his life among players and
play-writers. I wondered that he had so little

to say in conversation, for he had kept the best
company, and learned all that can be got by
the ear. He abused Pindar to me, and then
showed me an Ode of his own, with an absurd
couplet, making a linnet soar on an eagle's
wing. I told him that when the ancients made
a simile, they always made it like something
real."

Mr. Wilkes remarked, that "among all the
bold flights of Shakespeare's imagination, the
boldest was making Birnam Wood march to
Dunsinane; creating a wood where there never
was a shrub; a wood in Scotland! ha! ha! ha!"
And he also observed, that "the clannish
slavery of the Highlands of Scotland was the
single exception to Milton's remark of 'The
Mountain Nymph, sweet Liberty,' [28] being
worshiped in all hilly countries."—"When I
was at Inverary (said he) on a visit to my old
friend, Archibald, Duke of Argyle, his depend-
ents congratulated me on being such a favorite
of his Grace. I said, 'It is then, gentlemen, truly
lucky for me; for if I had displeased the Duke,
and he had wished it, there is not a Campbell
among you but would have been ready to bring
John Wilkes's head to him in a charger. It
would have been only

Off with his head! So much for Aylesbury.'

I was then member for Aylesbury." * * *

Mr. Arthur Lee mentioned some Scotch
who had taken possession of a barren part of
America, and wondered why they should choose
it. JOHNSON. "Why, Sir, all barrenness is comparative. The *Scotch* would not know it to be
barren." BOSWELL. "Come, come, he is flattering the English. You have now been in Scotland, Sir, and say if you did not see meat and
drink enough there." JOHNSON. "Why yes, Sir;
meat and drink enough to give the inhabitants
sufficient strength to run away from home."
All these quick and lively sallies were said
sportively, quite in jest, and with a smile,
which showed that he meant only wit. Upon
this topic he and Mr. Wilkes could perfectly
assimilate; here was a bond of union between
them, and I was conscious that as both of
them had visited Caledonia, both were fully
satisfied of the strange narrow ignorance of
those who imagine that it is a land of famine.
But they amused themselves with persevering
in the old jokes. When I claimed a supcriority
for Scotland over England in one respect, that
no man can be arrested there for a debt merely
because another swears it against him; but there
must first be the judgment of a court of law

---

[27] *Essay on Criticism*, I, 66–67.

[28] *L'Allegro*, 36.

ascertaining its justice; and that a seizure of the person, before judgment is obtained, can take place only if his creditor should swear that he is about to fly from the country, or, as it is technically expressed, is *in meditatione fugae*: WILKES. "That, I should think, may be safely sworn of all the Scotch nation." JOHNSON. (to Mr. Wilkes) "You must know, Sir, I lately took my friend Boswell and showed him genuine civilized life in an English provincial town. I turned him loose at Lichfield, my native city, that he might see for once real civility: for you know he lives among savages in Scotland, and among rakes in London." WILKES. "Except when he is with grave, sober, decent people like you and me." JOHNSON. (smiling) "And we ashamed of him."

### A BAD STYLE OF POETRY (1777)

HE OBSERVED, that a gentleman of eminence in literature had got into a bad style of poetry of late. "He puts (said he) a very common thing in a strange dress till he does not know it himself, and thinks other people do not know it." BOSWELL. "That is owing to his being so much versant in old English poetry." JOHN-SON. "What is that to the purpose, Sir? If I say a man is drunk, and you tell me it is owing to his taking much drink, the matter is not mended. No, Sir, —— [29] has taken to an odd mode. For example, he'd write thus:

> Hermit hoar, in solemn cell,
> Wearing out life's evening gray.

*Gray evening* is common enough; but *evening gray* he'd think fine.—Stay;—we'll make out the stanza:

> Hermit hoar, in solemn cell,
> Wearing out life's evening gray;
> Smite thy bosom, sage, and tell,
> What is bliss? and which the way?"

BOSWELL. "But why smite his bosom, Sir?" JOHNSON. "Why, to show he was in earnest" (smiling).—He at an after period added the following stanza:

> Thus I spoke; and speaking sighed;
> —Scarce repressed the starting tears;—
> When the smiling sage replied—
> —Come, my lad, and drink some beer.

### HAPPINESS (1777)

IN OUR way, Johnson strongly expressed his love of driving fast in a post-chaise. "If (said he) I had no duties, and no reference to fu-

turity, I would spend my life in driving briskly in a post-chaise with a pretty woman; but she should be one who could understand me, and would add something to the conversation."

### LONDON (1777)

WE ENTERED seriously upon a question of much importance to me, which Johnson was pleased to consider with friendly attention. I had long complained to him that I felt myself discontented in Scotland, as too narrow a sphere, and that I wished to make my chief residence in London, the great scene of ambition, instruction, and amusement: a scene, which was to me, comparatively speaking, a heaven upon earth. JOHNSON. "Why, Sir, I never knew any one who had such a *gust* for London as you have: and I cannot blame you for your wish to live there: yet, Sir, were I in your father's place, I should not consent to your settling there; for I have the old feudal notions, and I should be afraid that Auchinleck would be deserted, as you would soon find it more desirable to have a countryseat in a better climate." * * *

I suggested a doubt, that if I were to reside in London, the exquisite zest with which I relished it in occasional visits might go off, and I might grow tired of it. JOHNSON. "Why, Sir, you find no man, at all intellectual, who is willing to leave London. No, Sir, when a man is tired of London, he is tired of life; for there is in London all that life can afford."

### OLIVER EDWARDS (1778)

AND now I am to give a pretty full account of one of the most curious incidents in Johnson's life, of which he himself has made the following minute on this day: "In my return from church, I was accosted by Edwards, an old fellow-collegian, who had not seen me since 1729. He knew me, and asked if I remembered one Edwards; I did not at first recollect the name, but gradually as we walked along, recovered it, and told him a conversation that had passed at an ale-house between us. My purpose is to continue our acquaintance."

It was in Butcher Row that this meeting happened. Mr. Edwards, who was a decent-looking elderly man in gray clothes, and a wig of many curls, accosted Johnson with familiar confidence, knowing who he was, while Johnson returned his salutation with a courteous formality, as to a stranger. But as soon as Edwards had brought to his recollection their having

---

[29] Thomas Warton (1728–1790).

been at Pembroke College together nine-and-forty years ago, he seemed much pleased, asked where he lived, and said he should be glad to see him in Bolt Court. EDWARDS. "Ah, Sir! we are old men now." JOHNSON. (who never liked to think of being old), "Don't let us discourage one another." EDWARDS. "Why, Doctor, you look stout and hearty, I am happy to see you so; for the newspapers told us you were very ill." JOHNSON. "Ay, Sir, they are al- 10 ways telling lies of *us old fellows*."

Wishing to be present at more of so singular a conversation as that between two fellow-collegians, who had lived forty years in London without ever having chanced to meet, I whispered to Mr. Edwards that Dr. Johnson was going home, and that he had better accompany him now. So Edwards walked along with us, I eagerly assisting to keep up the conversation. Mr. Edwards informed Dr. Johnson that he 20 had practiced long as a solicitor in Chancery, but that he now lived in the country upon a little farm, about sixty acres, just by Stevenage in Hertfordshire, and that he came to London (to Barnard's Inn, No. 6), generally twice a week. Johnson appearing to me in a reverie, Mr. Edwards addressed himself to me, and expatiated on the pleasure of living in the country. BOSWELL. "I have no notion of this, Sir. What you have to entertain you, is, I 30 think, exhausted in half an hour." EDWARDS. "What? don't you love to have hope realized? I see my grass, and my corn, and my trees growing. Now, for instance, I am curious to see if this frost has not nipped my fruit-trees." JOHNSON. (who we did not imagine was attending) "You find, Sir, you have fears as well as hopes."—So well did he see the whole, when another saw but the half of a subject.

When we got to Dr. Johnson's house, and 40 were seated in his library, the dialogue went on admirably. EDWARDS. "Sir, I remember you would not let us say *prodigious* at College. For even then, Sir (turning to me), he was delicate in language, and we all feared him." [30] JOHNSON. (to Edwards) "From your having practiced the law long, Sir, I presume you must be rich." EDWARDS. "No, Sir; I got a good deal of money; but I had a number of poor relations to whom I gave a great part of 50 it." JOHNSON. "Sir, you have been rich in the most valuable sense of the word." EDWARDS.

[30] Johnson said to me afterwards, "Sir, they respected me for my literature; and yet it was not great but by comparison. Sir, it is amazing how little literature there is in the world" (Boswell's note).

"But I shall not die rich." JOHNSON. "Nay, sure, Sir, it is better to *live* rich than to *die* rich." EDWARDS. "I wish I had continued at College." JOHNSON. "Why do you wish that, Sir?" EDWARDS. "Because I think I should have had a much easier life than mine has been. I should have been a parson, and had a good living, like Bloxam and several others, and lived comfortably." JOHNSON. "Sir, the life of a parson, of a conscientious clergyman, is not easy. I have always considered a clergyman as the father of a larger family than he is able to maintain. I would rather have Chancery suits upon my hands than the cure of souls. No, Sir, I do not envy a clergyman's life as an easy life, nor do I envy the clergyman who makes it an easy life." Here taking himself up all of a sudden, he exclaimed, "O! Mr. Edwards! I'll convince you that I recollect you. Do you remember our drinking together at an ale-house near Pembroke gate? At that time, you told me of the Eton boy, who, when verses on our SAVIOR's turning water into wine were prescribed as an exercise, brought up a single line, which was highly admired,—

*Vidit et erubuit lympha pudica* DEUM,[31]

and I told you of another fine line in Camden's *Remains*, an eulogy upon one of our Kings, who was succeeded by his son, a prince of equal merit:—

*Mira cano, Sol occubuit, nox nulla secuta est.*" [32]

EDWARDS. "You are a philosopher, Dr. Johnson. I have tried too in my time to be a philosopher; but, I don't know how, cheerfulness was always breaking in."—Mr. Burke, Sir Joshua Reynolds, Mr. Courtenay, Mr. Malone, and, indeed, all the eminent men to whom I have mentioned this, have thought it an exquisite trait of character. The truth is, that philosophy, like religion, is too generally supposed to be hard and severe, at least so grave as to exclude all gayety.

EDWARDS. "I have been twice married, Doctor. You, I suppose, have never known what it was to have a wife." JOHNSON. "Sir, I have known what it was to have a wife, and (in a solemn, tender, faltering tone) I have known

[31] The line is really lifted (as the "Mr. Malone" of the next paragraph later discovered) from an epigram, on the miracle of the water turned into wine, by Richard Crashaw: "The modest spring has seen her God and blushed."

[32] Camden says that some ascribe this line, written to "honor King Henry II, then departed, and King Richard succeeding," to Giraldus Cambrensis: "I sing of wonders, the Sun has set, yet no night has followed."

what it was to *lose a wife*.—It had almost broke my heart."

EDWARDS. "How do you live, Sir? For my part, I must have my regular meals, and a glass of good wine. I find I require it." JOHNSON. "I now drink no wine, Sir. Early in life I drank wine: for many years I drank none. I then for some years drank a great deal." EDWARDS. "Some hogsheads, I warrant you." JOHNSON. "I then had a severe illness, and left it off, and I have never begun it again. I never felt any difference upon myself from eating one thing rather than another, nor from one kind of weather rather than another. There are people, I believe, who feel a difference; but I am not one of them. And as to regular meals, I have fasted from the Sunday's dinner to the Tuesday's dinner, without any inconvenience. I believe it is best to eat just as one is hungry: but a man who is in business, or a man who has a family, must have stated meals. I am a straggler. I may leave this town and go to Grand Cairo, without being missed here or observed there." EDWARDS. "Don't you eat supper, Sir?" JOHNSON. "No, Sir." EDWARDS. "For my part, now, I consider supper as a turnpike through which one must pass, in order to get to bed."

JOHNSON. "You are a lawyer, Mr. Edwards. Lawyers know life practically. A bookish man should always have them to converse with. They have what he wants." EDWARDS. "I am grown old: I am sixty-five." JOHNSON. "I shall be sixty-eight next birthday. Come, Sir, drink water, and put in for a hundred." * * *

This interview confirmed my opinion of Johnson's most humane and benevolent heart. His cordial and placid behavior to an old fellow-collegian, a man so different from himself; and his telling him that he would go down to his farm and visit him, showed a kindness of disposition very rare at an advanced age. He observed, "how wonderful it was that they had both been in London forty years, without having ever once met, and both walkers in the street too!" Mr. Edwards, when going away, again recurred to his consciousness of senility, and looking full in Johnson's face, said to him, "You'll find in Dr. Young,

O my coevals! remnants of yourselves."[33]

Johnson did not relish this at all; but shook his head with impatience. Edwards walked off, seemingly highly pleased with the honor of having been thus noticed by Dr. Johnson. When he was gone, I said to Johnson, I

[33] *Night Thoughts,* IV, 109.

thought him but a weak man. JOHNSON. "Why, yes, Sir. Here is a man who has passed through life without experience: yet I would rather have him with me than a more sensible man who will not talk readily. This man is always willing to say what he has to say." Yet Dr. Johnson had himself by no means that willingness which he praised so much, and I think so justly; for who has not felt the painful effect of the dreary void, when there is a total silence in a company, for any length of time; or, which is as bad, or perhaps worse, when the conversation is with difficulty kept up by a perpetual effort?

Johnson once observed to me, "Tom Tyers described me the best: 'Sir (said he), you are like a ghost: you never speak till you are spoken to.'"

## BAD MANAGEMENT (1778)

ON MONDAY, April 20, I found him at home in the morning. We talked of a gentleman who we apprehended was gradually involving his circumstances by bad management. JOHNSON. "Wasting a fortune is evaporation by a thousand imperceptible means. If it were a stream, they'd stop it. You must speak to him. It is really miserable. Were he a gamester, it could be said he had hopes of winning. Were he a bankrupt in trade, he might have grown rich; but he has neither spirit to spend nor resolution to spare. He does not spend fast enough to have pleasure from it. He has the crime of prodigality, and the wretchedness of parsimony. If a man is killed in a duel, he is killed as many a one has been killed; but it is a sad thing for a man to lie down and die; to bleed to death, because he has not fortitude enough to sear the wound, or even to stitch it up." I cannot but pause a moment to admire the fecundity of fancy, and choice of language, which in this instance, and, indeed, on almost all occasions, he displayed. It was well observed by Dr. Percy, now Bishop of Dromore, "The conversation of Johnson is strong and clear, and may be compared to an antique statue, where every vein and muscle is distinct and bold. Ordinary conversation resembles an inferior cast."

## THE FIRST WHIG (1778)

BOSWELL. "I drank chocolate, Sir, this morning with Mr. Eld; and, to my no small surprise, found him to be a *Staffordshire Whig,* a being which I did not believe had existed."

JOHNSON. "Sir, there are rascals in all countries." BOSWELL. "Eld said, a Tory was a creature generated between a non-juring parson and one's grandmother." JOHNSON. "And I have always said, the first Whig was the Devil." BOSWELL. "He certainly was, Sir. The Devil was impatient of subordination; he was the first who resisted power:—

Better to reign in Hell, than serve in Heaven."[34]

### KINDNESS (1783)

JOHNSON'S love of little children, which he discovered upon all occasions, calling them "pretty dears," and giving them sweetmeats, was an undoubted proof of the real humanity and gentleness of his disposition.

His uncommon kindness to his servants, and serious concern, not only for their comfort in this world, but their happiness in the next, was another unquestionable evidence of what all, who were intimately acquainted with him, knew to be true.

Nor would it be just, under this head, to omit the fondness which he showed for animals which he had taken under his protection. I never shall forget the indulgence with which he treated Hodge, his cat: for whom he himself used to go out and buy oysters, lest the servants having that trouble should take a dislike to the poor creature. I am, unluckily, one of those who have an antipathy to a cat, so that I am uneasy when in the room with one; and I own, I frequently suffered a good deal from the presence of this same Hodge. I recollect him one day scrambling up Dr. Johnson's breast, apparently with much satisfaction, while my friend smiling and half-whistling, rubbed down his back, and pulled him by the tail; and when I observed he was a fine cat, saying, "Why yes, Sir, but I have had cats whom I liked better than this"; and then as if perceiving Hodge to be out of countenance, adding, "but he is a very fine cat, a very fine cat indeed."

This reminds me of the ludicrous account

[34] *Paradise Lost*, I, 263.

which he gave Mr. Langton, of the despicable state of a young Gentleman of good family. "Sir, when I heard of him last, he was running about town shooting cats." And then in a sort of kindly reverie, he bethought himself of his own favorite cat, and said, "But Hodge shan't be shot; no, no, Hodge shall not be shot."

### CANT (1783)

BOSWELL. "I wish much to be in Parliament, Sir." JOHNSON. "Why, Sir, unless you come resolved to support any administration, you would be the worse for being in Parliament, because you would be obliged to live more expensively." BOSWELL. "Perhaps, Sir, I should be the less happy for being in Parliament. I never would sell my note, and I should be vexed if things went wrong." JOHNSON. "That's cant, Sir. It would not vex you more in the House, than in the gallery: public affairs vex no man." BOSWELL. "Have not they vexed yourself a little, Sir? Have not you been vexed by all the turbulence of this reign, and by that absurd vote of the House of Commons, 'That the influence of the Crown has increased, is increasing, and ought to be diminished?'" JOHNSON. "Sir, I have never slept an hour less, nor eat an ounce less meat. I would have knocked the factious dogs on the head, to be sure; but I was not *vexed*." BOSWELL. "I declare, Sir, upon my honor, I did imagine I was vexed, and took a pride in it; but it *was*, perhaps, cant; for I own I neither ate less, nor slept less." JOHNSON. "My dear friend, clear your *mind* of cant. You may *talk* as other people do: you may say to a man, 'Sir, I am your most humble servant.' You are *not* his most humble servant. You may say, 'These are bad times; it is a melancholy thing to be reserved to such times.' You don't mind the times. You tell a man, 'I am sorry you had such bad weather the last day of your journey, and were so much wet.' You don't care sixpence whether he is wet or dry. You may *talk* in this manner; it is a mode of talking in Society: but don't *think* foolishly."

# Oliver Goldsmith

## 1728-1774

Goldsmith's family was of English origin, but had long been settled in Ireland when he was born there on 10 November, 1728. His father was a clergyman and farmer, with a small income and a large family. Oliver has sketched the elder Goldsmith's character in the narrative of the Man in Black in The Citizen of the World, and it is said that all members of the family were "equally generous, credulous, simple," and improvident. The greater part of Oliver's boyhood was passed in the village of Lissoy, where he was given some rather irregular instruction, and whence he proceeded in 1744 to Trinity College, Dublin. There he was entered as a poor scholar, or "sizar," a position humiliating to one of his sensitiveness of temper. He was also unfortunate in having a tutor who delighted in two subjects which Goldsmith detested—logic and mathematics—and who was apparently rather brutal besides. In addition, Goldsmith's awkwardness, ungainly appearance, and mental unreadiness—not to speak of his infractions of collegiate rules—all made against his academic success. He did, however, manage to obtain the degree of B. A. in 1749. His relatives wanted him to become a clergyman, and he unwillingly undertook to prepare himself for ordination; but when he presented himself to Bishop Synge of Elphin he was rejected because, according to tradition, he was wearing a pair of flaming scarlet breeches. A period of uncertain groping for a career followed, until finally, early in 1753, Goldsmith reached Edinburgh to study medicine. There he attended some lectures, and then went to Leyden to continue his studies. From Leyden he presently set out "with one shirt in his pocket and a devout reliance on Providence," as Sir Walter Scott says, to travel through Europe on foot. By one means or another he succeeded in procuring subsistence as he walked through Flanders, France, Germany, Switzerland, and Italy, learning much which he afterwards put to lit-

erary use. Early in 1756 he was back again in England, living miserably in London, and trying with little or no success to earn a bare living by various occupations. By 1760 he had drifted into hackwriting for the booksellers, and this he continued until his death on 4 April, 1774.

Goldsmith was the master of an easy, finished style—he touched no branch of literature that he did not adorn, wrote Dr. Johnson in the Latin epitaph inscribed on his monument in Westminster Abbey—and, despite his irregular habits, the booksellers found him a profitable servant. He compiled histories of Rome, Greece, and England, A History of the Earth and Animated Nature, and many another work which cannot even be mentioned here. Of the Animated Nature Dr. Johnson said: "He is now writing a Natural History, and will make it as interesting as a Persian tale." It has been estimated that in the later years of his life Goldsmith's income from literary work may have been as high as £800 a year. He never learned, however, how to control his expenditures; as his income rose so did his debts, with the result that he was never free from financial difficulties, and at the time of his death owed not less than £2000. "Was ever poet," asked Dr. Johnson, "so trusted before?"

Much of Goldsmith's writing was ephemeral and perished with his age, yet he contrived to give lasting interest to a surprising variety of work, and is still remembered as essayist (The Citizen of the World, 1760–1761), as poet (The Traveler, 1764; The Deserted Village, 1770; Retaliation, 1774), as novelist (The Vicar of Wakefield, 1766), and as playwright (The Good-Natured Man, 1768; She Stoops to Conquer, 1773). Probably he took greater care with his poems than with anything else, as we know that he wrote them very slowly and spent much time in revising them. The Vicar of Wakefield, on the other hand, he never revised, although it was not published until several *years after it was written. It was, he explained, already paid for, so that there was no need to take further trouble with it. Yet, as Scott says, "we read* The Vicar of Wakefield *in youth and in age. We return to it again and again, and bless the memory of an author who contrives so well to reconcile us to human nature." Keen observation lay always behind Goldsmith's quiet satire, to give substance to this happy reconciliation; but it is his exquisite good humor which his readers remember best and longest. "Who," asked Thackeray, "of the millions whom he has amused, does not love him? To be the most beloved of English writers, what a title that is for a man!"*

*Goldsmith's* Citizen of the World *has been edited by Austin Dobson (London, 1891); the poems, the plays, and* The Vicar of Wakefield *are available in* Selected Works of Oliver Goldsmith, *edited by Richard Garnett (Cambridge, U. S. A., 1951).* The Collected Letters *were edited by Katherine C. Balderston (Cambridge, 1928). A study by William Freeman,* Oliver Goldsmith *(London, 1951), and a critical biography by Ralph M. Wardle,* Oliver Goldsmith *(Lawrence, Kansas, 1957), help to balance the lack of attention given to study of Goldsmith in the first half of the century.*

# The Citizen of the World [1]

*or,*

*Letters from a Chinese Philosopher, Residing in London, to His Friends in the East*

### LETTER XIII

*From Lien Chi Altangi to Fum Hoam, First President of the Ceremonial Academy at Pekin, in China*

#### AN ACCOUNT OF
#### WESTMINSTER ABBEY

I am just returned from Westminster Abbey, the place of sepulture for the philosophers, heroes, and kings of England. What a gloom

[1] These essays first appeared in a newspaper, *The Public Ledger,* in 1760–1761, and were then collected and published (with some changes and additions) in 1762. Goldsmith's device of writing over the name of an imaginary Asiatic was not of his own invention. He had before him the example of Montesquieu, of Voltaire, and of other French writers, and also, closer at hand, of Horace Walpole's very popular *Letter from Xo Ho, a Chinese Philosopher at London, to his Friend Lien-Chi, at Peking* (1757).

do monumental inscriptions, and all the venerable remains of deceased merit inspire! Imagine a temple marked with the hand of antiquity, solemn as religious awe, adorned with all the magnificence of barbarous profusion, dim windows, fretted pillars, long colonnades, and dark ceilings. Think, then, what were my sensations at being introduced to such a scene. I stood in the midst of the temple, and threw my eyes round on the walls, filled with the statues, the inscriptions, and the monuments of the dead.

Alas! I said to myself, how does pride attend the puny child of dust even to the grave! Even humble as I am, I possess more consequence in the present scene than the greatest hero of them all: they have toiled for an hour to gain a transient immortality, and are at length retired to the grave, where they have no attendant but the worm, none to flatter but the epitaph.

As I was indulging such reflections, a gentleman dressed in black, perceiving me to be a stranger, came up, entered into conversation, and politely offered to be my instructor and guide through the temple. "If any monument," said he, "should particularly excite your curiosity, I shall endeavor to satisfy your demands." I accepted, with thanks, the gentleman's offer, adding, that "I was come to observe the policy, the wisdom, and the justice of the English, in conferring rewards upon deceased merit. If adulation like this," continued I, "be properly conducted, as it can no ways injure those who are flattered, so it may be a glorious incentive to those who are now capable of enjoying it. It is the duty of every good government to turn this monumental pride to its own advantage; to become strong in the aggregate from the weakness of the individual. If none but the truly great have a place in this awful repository, a temple like this will give the finest lessons of morality, and be a strong incentive to true ambition. I am told that none have a place here but characters of the most distinguished merit." The man in black seemed impatient at my observations, so I discontinued my remarks, and we walked on together to take a view of every particular monument in order as it lay.

As the eye is naturally caught by the finest objects, I could not avoid being particularly curious about one monument, which appeared more beautiful than the rest: "That," said I to my guide, "I take to be the tomb of some very great man. By the peculiar excellence of the workmanship, and the magnificence of the design, this must be a trophy raised to the memory of some king who has saved his country from ruin, or lawgiver who has reduced his fellow-citizens from anarchy into just subjection."—"It is not requisite," replied my companion, smiling, "to have such qualifications in order to have a very fine monument here; more humble abilities will suffice."—"What, I suppose, then, the gaining two or three battles, or the taking half a score towns, is thought a sufficient qualification?"—"Gaining battles, or taking towns," replied the man in black, "may be of service; but a gentleman may have a very fine monument here without ever seeing a battle or a siege."—"This, then, is the monument of some poet, I presume—of one whose wit has gained him immortality?"—"No, Sir," replied my guide, "the gentleman who lies here never made verses; and as for wit, he despised it in others, because he had none himself."— "Pray tell me, then, in a word," said I, peevishly, "what is the great man who lies here particularly remarkable for?"—"Remarkable, Sir?" said my companion; "why, Sir, the gentleman that lies here is remarkable, very remarkable—for a tomb in Westminster Abbey."— "But, head of my Ancestors! how has he got here? I fancy he could never bribe the guardians of the temple to give him a place: should he not be ashamed to be seen among company where even moderate merit would look like infamy?"—"I suppose," replied the man in black, "the gentleman was rich, and his friends, as is usual in such a case, told him he was great. He readily believed them; the guardians of the temple, as they got by the self-delusion, were ready to believe him too; so he paid his money for a fine monument; and the workman, as you see, has made him one of the most beautiful. Think not, however, that this gentleman is singular in his desire of being buried among the great; there are several others in the temple, who, hated and shunned by the great while alive, have come here, fully resolved to keep them company now they are dead."

As we walked along to a particular part of the temple, "There," says the gentleman, pointing with his finger, "that is the Poet's Corner; there you see the monuments of Shakespeare, and Milton, and Prior, and Drayton."—"Drayton!" I replied; "I never heard of him before; but I have been told of one Pope—is he there?"—"It is time enough," replied my guide, "these hundred years; he is not long dead; people have not done hating him yet."—"Strange," cried I; "can any be found to hate a man whose life was wholly spent in entertaining and instructing his fellow-

creatures?"—"Yes," says my guide, "they hate him for that very reason. There are a set of men called answerers of books, who take upon them to watch the republic of letters, and distribute reputation by the sheet; they somewhat resemble the eunuchs in a seraglio, who are incapable of giving pleasure themselves, and hinder those that would. These answerers have no other employment but to cry out Dunce and Scribbler; to praise the dead, and revile the living; to grant a man of confessed abilities some small share of merit; to applaud twenty blockheads in order to gain the reputation of candor; and to revile the moral character of the man whose writings they cannot injure. Such wretches are kept in pay by some mercenary bookseller, or, more frequently, the bookseller himself takes this dirty work off their hands, as all that is required is to be very abusive and very dull. Every poet of any genius is sure to find such enemies; he feels, though he seems to despise their malice; they make him miserable here, and in the pursuit of empty fame, at last he gains solid anxiety."

"Has this been the case with every poet I see here?" cried I. "Yes, with every mother's son of them," replied he, "except he happened to be born a mandarin. If he has much money, he may buy reputation from your book-answerers, as well as a monument from the guardians of the temple."

"But are there not some men of distinguished taste, as in China, who are willing to patronize men of merit, and soften the rancor of malevolent dullness?"

"I own there are many," replied the man in black; "but, alas! Sir, the book-answerers crowd about them, and call themselves the writers of books; and the patron is too indolent to distinguish: thus poets are kept at a distance, while their enemies eat up all their rewards at the mandarin's table."

Leaving this part of the temple, we made up to an iron gate, through which my companion told me we were to pass, in order to see the monuments of the kings. Accordingly, I marched up without further ceremony, and was going to enter, when a person, who held the gate in his hand, told me I must pay first. I was surprised at such a demand; and asked the man, whether the people of England kept a *show*—whether the paltry sum he demanded was not a national reproach?—whether it was not more to the honor of the country to let their magnificence, or their antiquities, be openly seen, than thus meanly to tax a curiosity which tended to their own honor? "As for your questions," replied the gate-keeper, "to be sure they may be very right, because I don't understand them; but, as for that there three-pence, I farm it from one—who rents it from another—who hires it from a third—who leases it from the guardians of the temple,—and we all must live." I expected, upon paying here, to see something extraordinary, since what I had seen for nothing filled me with so much surprise: but in this I was disappointed; there was little more within than black coffins, rusty armor, tattered standards, and some few slovenly figures in wax. I was sorry I had paid, but I comforted myself by considering it would be my last payment. A person attended us, who, without once blushing, told a hundred lies: he talked of a lady who died by pricking her finger;[2] of a king with a golden head,[3] and twenty such pieces of absurdity. "Look ye there, gentleman," says he, pointing to an old oak chair, "there's a curiosity for ye; in that chair the kings of England were crowned: you see also a stone underneath, and that stone is Jacob's pillow." I could see no curiosity either in the oak chair or the stone: could I, indeed, behold one of the old kings of England seated in this, or Jacob's head laid upon the other, there might be something curious in the sight; but in the present case, there was no more reason for my surprise, than if I should pick a stone from their streets, and call it a curiosity, merely because one of the kings happened to tread upon it as he passed in the procession.

From hence our conductor led us through several dark walks and winding ways, uttering lies, talking to himself, and flourishing a wand which he held in his hand. He reminded me of the black magicians of Kobi.[4] After we had been almost fatigued with a variety of objects, he at last desired me to consider attentively a certain suit of armor, which seemed to show nothing remarkable. "This armor," said he, "belonged to General Monk."[5]—"Very surprising that a general should wear armor!"—"And pray," added he, "observe this cap; this is General Monk's cap."—"Very strange, indeed, very strange, that a general should have a cap also! Pray, friend, what might this cap have cost originally?"—"That, Sir," says he, "I don't know; but this cap is all the wages I

[2] Lady Elizabeth Russell. Her tomb is in the chapel of St. Edmund.
[3] The head (of the figure of Henry V, chapel of St. Edward) was of silver, but it had disappeared before the close of the sixteenth century.
[4] Or Gobi, the desert of central Asia.
[5] George Monk (1608–1670), parliamentary general in the Civil Wars.

have for my trouble."—"A very small recompense, truly," said I. "Not so very small," replied he, "for every gentleman puts some money into it, and I spend the money." "What—more money! still more money!"—"Every gentleman gives something, Sir."—"I'll give thee nothing," returned I; "the guardians of the temple should pay you your wages, friend, and not permit you to squeeze thus from every spectator. When we pay our money at the door to see a show, we never give more as we are going out. Sure, the guardians of the temple can never think they get enough. Show me the gate; if I stay longer I may probably meet with more of those ecclesiastical beggars."

Thus leaving the temple precipitately, I returned to my lodgings, in order to ruminate over what was great, and to despise what was mean, in the occurrences of the day.

## LETTER XXI

### *To the Same*

#### THE CHINESE GOES TO SEE A PLAY

The English are as fond of seeing plays acted as the Chinese; but there is a vast difference in the manner of conducting them. We play our pieces in the open air, the English theirs under cover; we act by daylight, they by the blaze of torches. One of our plays continues eight or ten days successively; an English piece seldom takes up above four hours of the representation.

My companion in black, with whom I am now beginning to contract an intimacy, introduced me a few nights ago to the playhouse, where we placed ourselves conveniently at the foot of the stage. As the curtain was not drawn before my arrival, I had an opportunity of observing the behavior of the spectators, and indulging those reflections which novelty generally inspires.

The rich in general were placed in the lowest seats, and the poor rose above them in degrees proportioned to their poverty. The order of precedence seemed here inverted; those who were undermost all the day, now enjoyed a temporary eminence, and became masters of the ceremonies. It was they who called for the music, indulging every noisy freedom, and testifying all the insolence of beggary in exaltation.

They who held the middle region seemed not so riotous as those above them, nor yet so tame as those below: to judge by their looks, many of them seemed strangers there as well as myself. They were chiefly employed, during this period of expectation, in eating oranges, reading the story of the play, or making assignations.

Those who sat in the lowest rows, which are called the pit, seemed to consider themselves as judges of the merit of the poet and the performers; they were assembled partly to be amused, and partly to show their taste; appearing to labor under that restraint which 10 an affectation of superior discernment generally produces. My companion, however, informed me, that not one in a hundred of them knew even the first principles of criticism; that they assumed the right of being censors because there was none to contradict their pretensions; and that every man who now called himself a connoisseur, became such to all intents and purposes.

Those who sat in the boxes appeared in the 20 most unhappy situation of all. The rest of the audience came merely for their own amusement; these, rather to furnish out a part of the entertainment themselves. I could not avoid considering them as acting parts in dumb show—not a courtesy or nod, that was not all the result of art; not a look nor a smile that was not designed for murder. Gentlemen and ladies ogled each other through spectacles; for, my companion observed, that blindness was of 30 late become fashionable; all affected indifference and ease, while their hearts at the same time burned for conquest. Upon the whole, the lights, the music, the ladies in their gayest dresses, the men with cheerfulness and expectation in their looks, all conspired to make a most agreeable picture, and to fill a heart that sympathizes at human happiness with inexpressible serenity.

The expected time for the play to begin at 40 last arrived; the curtain was drawn, and the actors came on. A woman, who personated a queen, came in curtseying to the audience, who clapped their hands upon her appearance. Clapping of hands is, it seems, the manner of applauding in England; the manner is absurd, but every country, you know, has its peculiar absurdities. I was equally surprised, however, at the submission of the actress, who should have considered herself 50 as a queen, as at the little discernment of the audience who gave her such marks of applause before she attempted to deserve them. Preliminaries between her and the audience being thus adjusted, the dialogue was supported between her and a most hopeful youth, who acted the part of her confidant. They

both appeared in extreme distress, for it seems the queen had lost a child some fifteen years before, and still kept its dear resemblance next her heart, while her kind companion bore a part in her sorrows.

Her lamentations grew loud; comfort is offered, but she detests the very sound: she bids them preach comfort to the winds. Upon this her husband comes in, who, seeing the queen so much afflicted, can himself hardly refrain from tears, or avoid partaking in the soft distress. After thus grieving through three scenes, the curtain dropped for the first act.

"Truly," said I to my companion, "these kings and queens are very much disturbed at no very great misfortune: certain I am, were people of humbler stations to act in this manner, they would be thought divested of common sense." I had scarcely finished this observation, when the curtain rose, and the king came on in a violent passion. His wife had, it seems, refused his proffered tenderness, had spurned his royal embrace, and he seemed resolved not to survive her fierce disdain. After he had thus fretted, and the queen had fretted through the second act, the curtain was let down once more.

"Now," says my companion, "you perceive the king to be a man of spirit; he feels at every pore: one of your phlegmatic sons of clay would have given the queen her own way, and let her come to herself by degrees; but the king is for immediate tenderness, or instant death: death and tenderness are leading passions of every modern buskined [6] hero, this moment they embrace, and the next stab, mixing daggers and kisses in every period."

I was going to second his remarks, when my attention was engrossed by a new object; a man came in balancing a straw upon his nose, and the audience were clapping their hands in all the raptures of applause. "To what purpose," cried I, "does this unmeaning figure make his appearance? is he a part of the plot?"—"Unmeaning do you call him?" replied my friend in black; "this is one of the most important characters of the whole play; nothing pleases the people more than seeing a straw balanced: there is a good deal of meaning in the straw: there is something suited to every apprehension in the sight; and a fellow possessed of talents like these is sure of making his fortune."

The third act now began with an actor who came to inform us that he was the villain of the play, and intended to show strange things

⁶ Tragic.

before all was over. He was joined by another who seemed as much disposed for mischief as he: their intrigues continued through this whole division. "If that be a villain," said I, "he must be a very stupid one to tell his secrets without being asked; such soliloquies of late are never admitted in China."

The noise of clapping interrupted me once more; a child of six years old was learning to dance on the stage, which gave the ladies and mandarins infinite satisfaction. "I am sorry," said I, "to see the pretty creature so early learning so very bad a trade; dancing being, I presume, as contemptible here as in China."— "Quite the reverse," interrupted my companion; "dancing is a very reputable and genteel employment here; men have a greater chance for encouragement from the merit of their heels than their heads. One who jumps up and flourishes his toes three times before he comes to the ground, may have three hundred a year; he who flourishes them four times, gets four hundred; but he who arrives at five is inestimable, and may demand what salary he thinks proper. The female dancers, too, are valued for this sort of jumping and crossing; and it is a cant word amongst them, that she deserves most who shows highest. But the fourth act is begun; let us be attentive."

In the fourth act the queen finds her long lost child, now grown up into a youth of smart parts and great qualifications; wherefore she wisely considers that the crown will fit his head better than that of her husband, whom she knows to be a driveler. The king discovers her design, and here comes on the deep distress: he loves the queen, and he loves the kingdom; he resolves, therefore, in order to possess both, that her son must die. The queen exclaims at his barbarity, is frantic with rage, and at length, overcome with sorrow, falls into a fit; upon which the curtain drops, and the act is concluded.

"Observe the art of the poet," cries my companion. "When the queen can say no more, she falls into a fit. While thus her eyes are shut, while she is supported in the arms of Abigail, what horrors do we not fancy! We feel it in every nerve: take my word for it, that fits are the true *aposiopesis* [7] of modern tragedy."

The fifth act began, and a busy piece it was. Scenes shifting, trumpets sounding, mobs hallooing, carpets spreading, guards bustling from one door to another; gods, demons, daggers, racks, and ratsbane. But whether the

[7] Sudden breaking-off in the middle of a speech.

king was killed, or the queen was drowned, or the son was poisoned, I have absolutely forgotten.

When the play was over, I could not avoid observing that the persons of the drama appeared in as much distress in the first act as the last. "How is it possible," said I, "to sympathize with them through five long acts? Pity is but a short-lived passion. I hate to hear an actor mouthing trifles. Neither startings, strainings, nor attitudes, affect me, unless there be cause: after I have been once or twice deceived by those unmeaning alarms, my heart sleeps in peace, probably unaffected by the principal distress. There should be one great passion aimed at by the actor as well as the poet; all the rest should be subordinate, and only contribute to make that the greater; if the actor, therefore, exclaims upon every occasion, in the tones of despair, he attempts to move us too soon; he anticipates the blow, he ceases to affect, though he gains our applause."

I scarce perceived that the audience were almost all departed; wherefore, mixing with the crowd, my companion and I got into the street, where, essaying a hundred obstacles from coach-wheels and palanquin poles, like birds in their flight through the branches of a forest, after various turnings, we both at length got home in safety. Adieu.

## LETTER XXXIII

### To the Same

#### THE MANNER OF WRITING AMONG THE CHINESE—THE EASTERN TALES OF MAGAZINES, ETC., RIDICULED

I AM disgusted, O Fum Hoam, even to sickness disgusted. Is it possible to bear the presumption of those islanders, when they pretend to instruct me in the ceremonies of China! They lay it down as a maxim, that every person who comes from thence must express himself in metaphor, swear by Alla, rail against wine, and behave, and talk, and write, like a Turk or Persian. They make no distinction between our elegant manners, and the voluptuous barbarities of our Eastern neighbors. Wherever I come, I raise either diffidence or astonishment: some fancy me no Chinese, because I am formed more like a man than a monster; and others wonder to find one born five thousand miles from England, endued with common sense.

"Strange," say they, "that a man who has received his education at such a distance from London, should have common sense; to be born out of England, and yet have common sense! Impossible! He must be some Englishman in disguise; his very visage has nothing of the true exotic barbarity."

I yesterday received an invitation from a lady of distinction, who, it seems, had collected all her knowledge of Eastern manners from fictions every day propagated here, under the titles of Eastern Tales and Oriental Histories. She received me very politely, but seemed to wonder that I neglected bringing opium and a tobacco-box: when chairs were drawn for the rest of the company, I was assigned my place on a cushion on the floor. It was in vain that I protested the Chinese used chairs as in Europe; she understood decorums too well to entertain me with the ordinary civilities.

I had scarce been seated according to her directions, when the footman was ordered to pin a napkin under my chin: this I protested against, as being no way Chinese; however, the whole company, who, it seems, were a club of connoisseurs, gave it unanimously against me, and the napkin was pinned accordingly.

It was impossible to be angry with people, who seemed to err only from an excess of politeness, and I sat contented, expecting their importunities were now at an end; but as soon as ever dinner was served, the lady demanded, whether I was for a plate of bear's claws, or a slice of birds' nests. As these were dishes with which I was utterly unacquainted, I was desirous of eating only what I knew, and therefore begged to be helped from a piece of beef that lay on the side-table: my request at once disconcerted the whole company. A Chinese eat beef! that could never be: there was no local propriety in Chinese beef, whatever there might be in Chinese pheasant. "Sir," said my entertainer, "I think I have some reason to fancy myself a judge of these matters; in short, the Chinese never eat beef; so that I must be permitted to recommend the pilaw.[8] There was never better dressed at Pekin; the saffron and rice were well boiled, and the spices in perfection.

I had no sooner begun to eat what was laid before me, than I found the whole company as much astonished as before: it seems I made no use of my chop-sticks. A grave gentleman, whom I take to be an author, harangued very learnedly (as the company seemed to think) upon the use which was made of them in China. He entered into a long argument with himself about their first introduction, without once appealing to me, who might be supposed best capable of silencing the inquiry. As the gentleman therefore took my silence for a mark of his own superior sagacity, he was resolved to pursue the triumph: he talked of our cities, mountains, and animals, as familiarly as if he had been born in Quamsi, but as erroneously as if a native of the moon. He attempted to prove that I had nothing of the true Chinese cut in my visage; showed that my cheek-bones should have been higher, and my forehead broader. In short, he almost reasoned me out of my country, and effectually persuaded the rest of the company to be of his opinion.

I was going to expose his mistakes, when it was insisted, that I had nothing of the true Eastern manner in my delivery. "This gentleman's conversation," says one of the ladies, who was a great reader, "is like our own,— mere chit-chat and common sense: there is nothing like sense in the true Eastern style, where nothing more is required but sublimity. Oh! for a history of Aboulfaouris, the grand voyager, of genii, magicians, rocks, bags of bullets, giants, and enchanters, where all is great, obscure, magnificent, and unintelligible!"— "I have written many a sheet of Eastern tale myself," interrupts the author, "and I defy the severest critic to say but that I have stuck close to the true manner. I have compared a lady's chin to the snow upon the mountains of Bomek; a soldier's sword to the clouds that obscure the face of heaven. If riches are mentioned, I compare them to the flocks that graze the verdant Tefflis; if poverty, to the mists that veil the brow of Mount Baku. I have used *thee* and *thou* upon all occasions; I have described fallen stars, and splitting mountains, not forgetting the little houris, who make a pretty figure in every description. But you shall hear how I generally begin—'Eben-ben-bolo, who was the son of Ban, was born on the foggy summits of Benderabassi. His beard was whiter than the feathers which veil the breast of the penguin; his eyes were like the eyes of doves when washed by the dews of the morning; his hair, which hung like the willow weeping over the glassy stream, was so beautiful that it seemed to reflect its own brightness; and his feet were as the feet of a wild deer which fleeth to

[8] An oriental dish of rice with meat, spices, etc.

the tops of the mountains.' There, there is the true Eastern taste for you; every advance made towards sense, is only a deviation from sound. Eastern tales should always be sonorous, lofty, musical, and unmeaning."

I could not avoid smiling, to hear a native of England attempt to instruct me in the true Eastern idiom; and after he looked round some time for applause, I presumed to ask him, whether he had ever traveled into the East? to which he replied in the negative. I demanded whether he understood Chinese, or Arabic? to which he also answered as before. "Then how, Sir," said I, "can you pretend to determine upon the Eastern style, who are entirely unacquainted with the Eastern writings? Take, Sir, the word of one who is professedly a Chinese, and who is actually acquainted with the Arabian writers, that what is palmed upon you daily for an imitation of Eastern writing, no way resembles their manner, either in sentiment or diction. In the East, similes are seldom used, and metaphors almost wholly unknown; but in China particularly, the very reverse of what you allude to takes place: a cool phlegmatic method of writing prevails there. The writers of that country, ever more assiduous to instruct than to please, address rather the judgment than the fancy. Unlike many authors of Europe who have no consideration of the reader's time, they generally leave more to be understood than they express.

"Besides, Sir, you must not expect from an inhabitant of China the same ignorance, the same unlettered simplicity, that you find in a Turk, Persian, or native of Peru. The Chinese are versed in the sciences as well as you, and are masters of several arts unknown to the people of Europe. Many of them are instructed not only in their own national learning, but are perfectly well acquainted with the languages and learning of the West. If my word in such a case is not to be taken, consult your own travelers on this head, who affirm, that the scholars of Pekin and Siam sustain theological theses in Latin. 'The college of Masprend, which is but a league from Siam,' says one of your travelers, 'came in a body to salute our ambassador. Nothing gave me more sincere pleasure, than to behold a number of priests, venerable both from age and modesty, followed by a number of youths of all nations, Chinese, Japanese, Tonquinese, of Cochin China, Pegu, and Siam, all willing to pay their respects in the most polite manner imaginable. A Cochin Chinese made an ex-

cellent Latin oration upon this occasion; he was succeeded and even outdone by a student of Tonquin, who was as well skilled in the Western learning as any scholar of Paris.' Now, Sir, if youths who never stirred from home are so perfectly skilled in your laws and learning, surely more must be expected from one like me, who have traveled so many thousand miles, who have conversed familiarly for several years with the English factors established at Canton, and the missionaries sent us from every part of Europe. The unaffected of every country nearly resemble each other, and a page of our Confucius and of your Tillotson [9] have scarce any material difference. Paltry affectation, strained allusions, and disgusting finery, are easily attained by those who choose to wear them: and they are but too frequently the badges of ignorance or of stupidity, whenever it would endeavor to please."

I was proceeding in my discourse, when, looking round, I perceived the company no way attentive to what I attempted, with so much earnestness, to enforce. One lady was whispering her that sat next, another was studying the merits of a fan, a third began to yawn, and the author himself fell fast asleep. I thought it, therefore, high time to make a retreat, nor did the company seem to show any regret at my preparations for departure: even the lady who had invited me, with the most mortifying insensibility, saw me seize my hat, and arise from my cushion; nor was I invited to repeat my visit, because it was found that I aimed at appearing rather a reasonable creature, than an outlandish idiot. Adieu.

### LETTER LI

#### To the Same

#### A BOOKSELLER'S VISIT TO THE CHINESE

As I was yesterday seated at breakfast over a pensive dish of tea, my meditations were interrupted by my old friend and companion, who introduced a stranger, dressed pretty much like himself. The gentleman made several apologies for his visit, begged of me to impute his intrusion to the sincerity of his respect, and the warmth of his curiosity.

As I am very suspicious of my company when I find them very civil without any apparent reason, I answered the stranger's

---

[9] John Tillotson (1630–1694), Archbishop of Canterbury, whose sermons were used as models of a lucid prose style.

caresses at first with reserve; which my friend perceiving, instantly let me into my visitant's trade and character, asking Mr. Fudge, whether he had lately published anything new. I now conjectured that my guest was no other than a bookseller, and his answer confirmed my suspicions.

"Excuse me, Sir," says he, "it is not the season; books have their time as well as cucumbers. I would no more bring out a new work in summer than I would sell pork in the dog days. Nothing in my way goes off in summer, except very light goods indeed. A review, a magazine, or a Sessions paper,[10] may amuse a summer reader; but all our stock of value we reserve for a spring and winter trade." "I must confess, Sir," says I, "a curiosity to know what you call a valuable stock, which can only bear a winter perusal."—"Sir," replied the bookseller, "it is not my way to cry up my own goods; but, without exaggeration, I will venture to show with any of the trade: my books at least have the peculiar advantage of being always new; and it is my way to clear off my old to the trunk-makers every season. I have ten new title-pages now about me, which only want books to be added to make them the finest things in nature. Others may pretend to direct the vulgar; but that is not my way; I always let the vulgar direct me; wherever popular clamor arises, I always echo the million. For instance, should the people in general say that such a man is a rogue, I instantly give orders to set him down in print a villain; thus every man buys the book, not to learn new sentiments, but to have the pleasure of seeing his own reflected."—"But, Sir," interrupted I, "you speak as if you yourself wrote the books you publish; may I be so bold as to ask a sight of some of those intended publications which are shortly to surprise the world?"—"As to that, Sir," replied the talkative bookseller, "I only draw out the plans myself; and though I am very cautious of communicating them to any, yet, as in the end I have a favor to ask, you shall see a few of them. Here, Sir, here they are; diamonds of the first water, I assure you. *Imprimis,* a Translation of several Medical precepts for the use of such physicians as do not understand Latin. *Item,* the Young Clergyman's art of placing patches regularly, with a Dissertation on the different manners of smiling without distorting the face. *Item,* the whole Art of Love made perfectly easy, by a broker of 'Change Alley. *Item,* the proper manner of

10 List of cases put down for trial.

Cutting blacklead pencils, and making crayons, by the Right Hon. the Earl of ——. *Item,* the Muster-master-general, or the review of reviews."—"Sir," cried I, interrupting him, "my curiosity, with regard to title-pages, is satisfied; I should be glad to see some longer manuscript, a history, or an epic poem."— "Bless me!" cries the man of industry, "now you speak of an epic poem, you shall see an excellent farce. Here it is; dip into it where you will, it will be found replete with true modern humor. Strokes, Sir; it is filled with strokes of wit and satire in every line."—"Do you call these dashes of the pen strokes," replied I, "for I must confess I can see no other?"—"And pray, Sir," returned he, "what do you call them? Do you see anything good now-a-days, that is not filled with strokes— and dashes?—Sir, a well placed dash makes half the wit of our writers of modern humor. I bought a piece last season that had no other merit upon earth than nine hundred and ninety-five breaks, seventy-two ha-ha's, three good things, and a garter. And yet it played off, and bounced, and cracked, and made more sport than a firework." [11]—"I fancy, then, Sir, you were a considerable gainer?"—"It must be owned the piece did pay; but, upon the whole, I cannot much boast of last winter's success; I gained by two murders; but then I lost by an ill-timed charity sermon. I was a considerable sufferer by my Direct Road to an Estate, but the Infernal Guide brought me up again. Ah, Sir, that was a piece touched off by the hand of a master; filled with good things from one end to the other. The author had nothing but the jest in view; no dull moral lurking beneath, nor ill-natured satire to sour the reader's good-humor; he wisely considered that moral and humor at the same time were quite overdoing the business."—"To what purpose was the book then published?" cried I.—"Sir, the book was published in order to be sold; and no book sold better, except the criticisms upon it, which came out soon after: of all kinds of writing, that goes off best at present; and I generally fasten a criticism upon every selling book that is published.

"I once had an author who never left the least opening for the critics: close was the word; always very right and very dull; ever on the safe side of an argument; yet, with all his qualifications, incapable of coming into favor. I soon perceived that his bent was

11 Here Goldsmith is probably satirizing Laurence Sterne's *Tristram Shandy,* which had begun to appear shortly before this.

for criticism; and, as he was good for nothing else, supplied him with pens and paper, and planted him, at the beginning of every month, as a censor on the works of others. In short, I found him a treasure; no merit could escape him; but what is most remarkable of all, he ever wrote best and bitterest when drunk." "But are there not some works," interrupted I, "that, from the very manner of their com-position, must be exempt from criticism; par- 10 ticularly such as profess to disregard its laws?" —"There is no work whatsoever but he can criticize," replied the bookseller; "even though you wrote in Chinese, he would have a pluck at you. Suppose you should take it into your head to publish a book, let it be a volume of Chinese letters, for instance; write how you will, he shall show the world you could have written better. Should you, with the most local exactness, stick to the manners and customs of 20 the country from whence you come; should you confine yourself to the narrow limits of East-ern knowledge, and be perfectly simple, and perfectly natural, he has then the strongest reason to exclaim. He may, with a sneer, send you back to China for readers. He may ob-serve that after the first or second letter, the iteration of the same simplicity is insupportably tedious. But the worst of all is, the public, in such a case, will anticipate his censures, and 30 leave you, with all your uninstructive sim-plicity, to be mauled at discretion."

"Yes," cried I, "but in order to avoid his indignation, and, what I should fear more, that of the public, I would, in such a case, write with all the knowledge I was master of. As I am not possessed of much learning, at least I would not suppress what little I had; nor would I appear more stupid than nature made me."—"Here, then," cries the book- 40 seller, "we should have you entirely in our power; unnatural, un-Eastern, quite out of character, erroneously sensible, would be the whole cry. Sir, we should then hunt you down like a rat."—"Head of my father!" said I, "sure there are but two ways; the door must either be shut or it must be open. I must either be natural or unnatural."—"Be what you will, we shall criticize you," returned the bookseller, "and prove you a dunce in spite of 50 your teeth. But, Sir, it is time that I should come to business. I have just now in the press a history of China; and if you will but put your name to it as the author, I shall repay the obligation with gratitude."—"What, Sir!" replied I, "put my name to a work which I have not written? Never, while I retain a proper respect for the public and myself." The

bluntness of my reply quite abated the ardor of the bookseller's conversation; and, after about half an hour's disagreeable reserve, he, with some ceremony, took his leave, and withdrew. Adieu.

## LETTER LXVII

### *To Hingpo, a Slave in Persia*

### THE FOLLY OF ATTEMPTING TO LEARN WISDOM BY BEING RECLUSE

Books, my son, while they teach us to re-spect the interests of others, often make us unmindful of our own; while they instruct the youthful reader to grasp at social happi-ness, he grows miserable in detail, and, at-tentive to universal harmony, often forgets that he himself has a part to sustain in the concert. I dislike, therefore, the philosopher, who describes the inconveniences of life in such pleasing colors that the pupil grows enamored of distress, longs to try the charms of poverty, meets it without dread, nor fears its in-conveniences till he severely feels them.

A youth who has thus spent his life among books, new to the world, and unacquainted with man but by philosophic information, may be considered as a being whose mind is filled with the vulgar errors of the wise; ut-terly unqualified for a journey through life, yet confident of his own skill in the direction, he sets out with confidence, blunders on with vanity, and finds himself at last undone.

He first has learned from books, and then lays it down as a maxim, that all mankind are virtuous or vicious in excess; and he has been long taught to detest vice, and love virtue: warm, therefore in attachments, and stead-fast in enmity, he treats every creature as a friend or foe; expects from those he loves unerring integrity, and consigns his enemies to the reproach of wanting every virtue. On this principle he proceeds; and here begin his disappointments. Upon a closer inspection of human nature he perceives that he should have moderated his friendship, and softened his severity; for he often finds the excellencies of one part of mankind clouded with vice, and the faults of the other brightened with vir-tue; he finds no character so sanctified that has not its failings, none so infamous but has somewhat to attract our esteem; he beholds impiety in lawn,[12] and fidelity in fetters.

He now, therefore, but too late, perceives that his regards should have been more cool,

[12] The sleeves of a bishop are made of lawn.

and his hatred less violent; that the truly wise seldom court romantic friendships with the good, and avoid, if possible, the resentment even of the wicked: every moment gives him fresh instances that the bonds of friendship are broken if drawn too closely, and that those whom he has treated with disrespect more than retaliate the injury; at length, therefore, he is obliged to confess that he has declared war upon the vicious half of mankind, without being able to form an alliance among the virtuous to espouse his quarrel.

Our book-taught philosopher, however, is now too far advanced to recede; and though poverty be the just consequence of the many enemies his conduct has created, yet he is resolved to meet it without shrinking. Philosophers have described poverty in most charming colors, and even his vanity is touched in thinking that he shall show the world, in himself, one more example of patience, fortitude, and resignation. "Come, then, O Poverty! for what is there in thee dreadful to the WISE? Temperance, Health, and Frugality walk in thy train; Cheerfulness and Liberty are ever thy companions. Shall any be ashamed of thee, of whom Cincinnatus was not ashamed? The running brook, the herbs of the field, can amply satisfy nature; man wants but little, nor that little long.[13] Come, then, O Poverty, while kings stand by, and gaze with admiration at the true philosopher's resignation!"

The goddess appears; for Poverty ever comes at the call; but, alas! he finds her by no means the charming figure books and his warm imagination had painted. As when an Eastern bride, whom her friends and relations had long described as a model of perfection, pays her first visit, the longing bridegroom lifts the veil to see a face he had never seen before; but instead of a countenance blazing with beauty like the sun, he beholds deformity shooting icicles to his heart: such appears Poverty to her new entertainer; all the fabric of enthusiasm is at once demolished, and a thousand miseries rise up on its ruins, while Contempt, with pointing finger, is foremost in the hideous procession.

The poor man now finds that he can get no kings to look at him while he is eating; he finds that in proportion as he grows poor, the world turns its back upon him, and gives him leave to act the philosopher in all the majesty of solitude. It might be agreeable enough to play the philosopher while we are conscious that mankind are spectators: but what signifies wearing the mask of sturdy contentment, and

mounting the stage of restraint, when not one creature will assist at the exhibition! Thus is he forsaken of men, while his fortitude wants the satisfaction even of self-applause: for either he does not feel his present calamities, and that is natural insensibility; or he disguises his feelings, and that is dissimulation.

Spleen now begins to take up the man: not distinguishing in his resentments, he regards all mankind with detestation, and commencing man-hater, seeks solitude to be at liberty to rail.

It has been said, that he who retires to solitude is either a beast or an angel.[14] The censure is too severe, and the praise unmerited; the discontented being, who retires from society, is generally some good-natured man, who has begun life without experience, and knew not how to gain it in his intercourse with mankind. Adieu.

## LETTER LXXXVI

### *To Fum Hoam*

#### THE RACES OF NEWMARKET RIDICULED. DESCRIPTION OF A CART RACE

OF ALL the places of amusement where gentlemen and ladies are entertained, I have not been yet to visit Newmarket. This, I am told, is a large field, where, upon certain occasions, three or four horses are brought together, then set a-running, and that horse which runs fastest wins the wager.

This is reckoned a very polite and fashionable amusement here, much more followed by the nobility than partridge fighting at Java, or paper kites in Madagascar. Several of the great here, I am told, understand as much of farriery as their grooms; and a horse, with any share of merit, can never want a patron among the nobility.

We have a description of this entertainment almost every day in some of the gazettes, as for instance: "On such a day the Give and Take Plate was run for between his Grace's Crab, his Lordship's Periwinkle, and 'Squire Smacken's Slamerkin. All rode their own horses. There was the greatest concourse of nobility that has been known here for several seasons. The odds were in favor of Crab in the beginning; but Slamerkin, after the first heat, seemed to have the match hollow: however, it was soon seen that Periwinkle improved in wind, which at last turned out accordingly; Crab was run to a standstill, Slamerkin was knocked up, and

---

[13] Lifted from Young's *Night Thoughts*, IV, 9.

[14] See Aristotle, *Politics*, I, ii (1253a, 2–4).

Periwinkle was brought in with universal applause." Thus, you see, Periwinkle received universal applause, and, no doubt, his lordship came in for some share of that praise which was so liberally bestowed upon Periwinkle. Sun of China! how glorious must the senator appear in his cap and leather breeches, his whip crossed in his mouth, and thus coming to the goal, amongst the shouts of grooms, jockeys, pimps, stable-bred dukes, and degraded generals!

From the description of this princely amusement, now transcribed, and from the great veneration I have for the characters of its principal promoters, I make no doubt but I shall look upon a horse-race with becoming reverence, predisposed as I am by a similar amusement, of which I have lately been a spectator; for just now I happened to have an opportunity of being present at a cart race.

Whether this contention between three carts of different parishes was promoted by a subscription among the nobility, or whether the grand jury, in council assembled, had gloriously combined to encourage plaustral[15] merit, I cannot take upon me to determine; but certain it is, the whole was conducted with the utmost regularity and decorum, and the company, which made a brilliant appearance, were universally of opinion, that the sport was high, the running fine, and the riders influenced by no bribe.

It was run on the road from London, to a village called Brentford, between a turnip-cart, a dust-cart, and a dung-cart; each of the owners condescending to mount, and be his own driver. The odds, at starting, were Dust against Dung, five to four; but, after half a mile's going, the knowing ones found themselves all on the wrong side, and it was Turnip against the field, brass to silver.

Soon, however, the contest became more doubtful; Turnip indeed kept the way, but it was perceived that Dung had better bottom. The road re-echoed with the shouts of the spectators—"Dung against Turnip! Turnip against Dung!" was now the universal cry; neck and neck; one rode lighter, but the other had more judgment. I could not but particularly observe the ardor with which the fair sex espoused the cause of the different riders on this occasion; one was charmed with the unwashed beauties of Dung; another was captivated with the patibulary[16] aspect of Turnip;

[15] Pertaining to a cart or wagon. (The word was apparently introduced into English by Goldsmith.)
[16] Gallows-like.

while, in the meantime, unfortunate gloomy Dust, who came whipping behind, was cheered by the encouragement of some, and pity of all.

The contention now continued for some time, without a possibility of determining to whom victory designed the prize. The winning post appeared in view, and he who drove the turnip-cart assured himself of success; and successful he might have been, had his horse been as ambitious as he; but, upon approaching a turn from the road, which led homewards, the horse fairly stood still, and refused to move a foot farther. The dung-cart had scarce time to enjoy this temporary triumph, when it was pitched headlong into a ditch by the way-side, and the rider left to wallow in congenial mud. Dust, in the meantime, soon came up, and not being far from the post, came in, amidst the shouts and acclamations of all the spectators, and greatly caressed by all the quality of Brentford. Fortune was kind only to one, who ought to have been favorable to all; each had peculiar merit, each labored hard to earn the prize, and each richly deserved the cart he drove.

I do not know whether this description may not have anticipated that which I intended giving of Newmarket. I am told, there is little else to be seen even there. There may be some minute differences in the dress of the spectators, but none at all in their understandings: the quality of Brentford are as remarkable for politeness and delicacy as the breeders of Newmarket. The quality of Brentford drive their own carts, and the honorable fraternity of Newmarket ride their own horses. In short, the matches in one place are as rational as those in the other; and it is more than probable that turnips, dust, and dung, are all that can be found to furnish out description in either.

Forgive me, my friend; but a person like me, bred up in a philosophic seclusion, is apt to regard perhaps with too much asperity, those occurrences which sink man below his station in nature, and diminish the intrinsic value of humanity. Adieu.

## LETTER CVI

### To the Same

#### FUNERAL ELEGIES WRITTEN UPON THE GREAT RIDICULED. A SPECIMEN OF ONE

It was formerly the custom here, when men of distinction died, for their surviving acquaintance to throw each a slight present into the grave. Several things of little value were made use of for that purpose,—perfumes, relics, spices, bitter herbs, camomile, wormwood, and verses. This custom, however, is almost discontinued, and nothing but verses alone are now lavished on such occasions; an oblation which they suppose may be interred with the dead, without any injury to the living.

Upon the death of the great, therefore, the poets and undertakers are sure of employment. While one provides the long cloak, black staff, and mourning coach, the other produces the pastoral or elegy, the monody or apotheosis. The nobility need be under no apprehensions, but die as fast as they think proper; the poet and undertaker are ready to supply them; these can find metaphorical tears and family escutcheons at an hour's warning; and when the one has soberly laid the body in the grave, the other is ready to fix it figuratively among the stars.

There are several ways of being poetically sorrowful on such occasions. The bard is now some pensive youth of science, who sits deploring among the tombs; again, he is Thyrsis, complaining in a circle of harmless sheep. Now Britannia sits upon her own shore, and gives a loose to maternal tenderness; at another time, Parnassus, even the mountain Parnassus, gives way to sorrow, and is bathed in tears of distress.

But the most usual manner is this: Damon meets Menalcas, who has got a most gloomy countenance. The shepherd asks his friend, whence that look of distress? To which the other replies, that Pollio is no more. "If that be the case, then," cries Damon, "let us retire to yonder bower at some distance off, where the cypress and the jessamine add fragrance to the breeze; and let us weep alternately for Pollio, the friend of shepherds, and the patron of every muse."—"Ah!" returns his fellow shepherd, "what think you rather of that grotto by the fountain side? the murmuring stream will help to assist our complaints, and a nightingale on a neighboring tree will join her voice to the concert!" When the place is thus settled, they begin: the brook stands still to hear their lamentations; the cows forget to graze; and the very tigers start from the forest with sympathetic concern. By the tombs of our ancestors, my dear Fum, I am quite unaffected in all this distress: the whole is liquid laudanum to my spirits; and a tiger of common sensibility has twenty times more tenderness than I.

But though I could never weep with the complaining shepherd, yet I am sometimes induced to pity the poet, whose trade is thus to make demigods and heroes for a dinner. There is not in nature a more dismal figure than a man who sits down to premeditated flattery: every stanza he writes tacitly reproaches the meanness of his occupation, till, at last, his stupidity becomes more stupid, and his dullness more diminutive.

I am amazed, therefore, that none have yet found out the secret of flattering the worthless, and yet of preserving a safe conscience. I have often wished for some method, by which a man might do himself and his deceased patron justice, without being under the hateful reproach of self-conviction. After long lucubration, I have hit upon such an expedient; and send you the specimen of a poem upon the decease of a great man, in which the flattery is perfectly fine, and yet the poet perfectly innocent.

ON THE DEATH OF THE RIGHT
HONORABLE ——

Ye Muses, pour the pitying tear
  For Pollio snatched away;
Oh, had he lived another year!
  —*He had not died to-day.*

Oh, were he born to bless mankind,
  In virtuous times of yore,
Heroes themselves had fall'n behind!
  —*Whene'er he went before.*

How sad the groves and plains appear,
  And sympathetic sheep;
E'en pitying hills would drop a tear!
  —*If hills could learn to weep.*

His bounty in exalted strain
  Each bard may well display;
Since none implored relief in vain!
  —*That went relieved away.*

And hark! I hear the tuneful throng
  His obsequies forbid;
He still shall live, shall live as long
  —*As ever dead man did.*

## Stanzas on Woman [1]

When lovely woman stoops to folly,
  And finds, too late, that men betray,
What charm can soothe her melancholy,
  What art can wash her guilt away?

The only art her guilt to cover,          5
  To hide her shame from every eye,
To give repentance to her lover,
  And wring his bosom, is—to die.

[1] From *The Vicar of Wakefield* (1766), chap. 24.

# The Deserted Village

## (1770)

### To Sir Joshua Reynolds

Dear Sir,—I can have no expectations, in an address of this kind, either to add to your reputation, or to establish my own. You can gain nothing from my admiration, as I am ignorant of that art in which you are said to 10 excel; and I may lose much by the severity of your judgment, as few have a juster taste in poetry than you. Setting interest, therefore, aside, to which I never paid much attention, I must be indulged at present in following my affections. The only dedication I ever made was to my brother, because I loved him better than most other men. He is since dead. Permit me to inscribe this Poem to you.

How far you may be pleased with the versi- 20 fication and mere mechanical parts of this attempt, I don't pretend to inquire; but I know you will object (and indeed several of our best and wisest friends concur in the opinion), that the depopulation it deplores is nowhere to be seen, and the disorders it laments are only to be found in the poet's own imagination. To this I can scarce make any other answer, than that I sincerely believe what I have written; that I have taken all possible pains, in 30 my country excursions, for these four or five years past, to be certain of what I allege; and that all my views and inquiries have led me to believe those miseries real, which I here attempt to display. But this is not the place to enter into an inquiry whether the country be depopulating or not: the discussion would take up much room, and I should prove myself, at best, an indifferent politician, to tire the reader with a long preface, when I want his unfatigued 40 attention to a long poem.

In regretting the depopulation of the country, I inveigh against the increase of our luxuries; and here also I expect the shout of modern politicians against me. For twenty or thirty years past, it has been the fashion to consider luxury as one of the greatest national advantages; and all the wisdom of antiquity in that particular as erroneous. Still, however, I must remain a professed ancient on that head, 50 and continue to think those luxuries prejudicial to states by which so many vices are introduced, and so many kingdoms have been undone. Indeed, so much has been poured out of late on the other side of the question, that, merely for the sake of novelty and variety, one would sometimes wish to be in the right.

I am, dear sir, your sincere friend, and ardent admirer,

Oliver Goldsmith.

Sweet Auburn! [1] loveliest village of the plain,
Where health and plenty cheered the laboring
  swain,
Where smiling Spring its earliest visit paid,
And parting Summer's lingering blooms delayed:
Dear lovely bowers of innocence and ease,    5
Seats of my youth, when every sport could
  please:
How often have I loitered o'er thy green,
Where humble happiness endeared each scene!
How often have I paused on every charm,
The sheltered cot, the cultivated farm,    10
The never-failing brook, the busy mill,
The decent church that topped the neighboring
  hill;
The hawthorn bush, with seats beneath the
  shade,
For talking age and whispering lovers made!
How often have I blessed the coming day,    15
When toil, remitting, lent its turn to play,
And all the village train, from labor free,
Led up their sports beneath the spreading tree!
While many a pastime circled in the shade,
The young contending as the old surveyed;    20
And many a gambol frolicked o'er the ground,
And sleights of art and feats of strength went
  round;
And still, as each repeated pleasure tired,
Succeeding sports the mirthful band inspired—
The dancing pair that simply [2] sought renown,
By holding out to tire each other down;    26
The swain mistrustless of his smutted face,
While secret laughter tittered round the place;
The bashful virgin's side-long looks of love;
The matron's glance, that would those looks
  reprove.    30
These were thy charms, sweet village! sports
  like these,
With sweet succession, taught e'en toil to
  please;
These round thy bowers their cheerful influence shed;
These were thy charms—but all these charms
  are fled.
  Sweet smiling village, loveliest of the lawn,
Thy sports are fled, and all thy charms withdrawn;    36
Amidst thy bowers the tyrant's hand is seen,
And Desolation saddens all thy green:
One only master grasps the whole domain, [3]

---

[1] It is practically certain that Goldsmith had Lissoy in mind (which has changed its name to Auburn), though this has been disputed.

[2] In a simple way.

[3] Landlords were empowered by the Enclosure Acts (of which there were 700 between 1760 and 1774)

And half a tillage stints thy smiling plain. 40
No more thy glassy brook reflects the day,
But, choked with sedges, works its weedy way;
Along thy glades, a solitary guest,
The hollow-sounding bittern guards its nest:
Amidst thy desert walks the lapwing flies, 45
And tires their echoes with unvaried cries:
Sunk are thy bowers in shapeless ruin all,
And the long grass o'ertops the mouldering
wall;
And, trembling, shrinking from the spoiler's
hand,
Far, far away thy children leave the land. 50
Ill fares the land, to hastening ills a prey,
Where wealth accumulates, and men decay,
Princes and lords may flourish, or may fade;
A breath can make them, as a breath has made:
But a bold peasantry, their country's pride, 55
When once destroyed, can never be supplied.
　A time there was, ere England's griefs be-
gan,
When every rood of ground maintained its
man;
For him light Labor spread her wholesome
store,
Just gave what life required, but gave no more:
His best companions, Innocence and Health; 61
And his best riches, ignorance of wealth.
　But times are altered: Trade's unfeeling train
Usurp the land, and dispossess the swain;
Along the lawn, where scattered hamlets rose,
Unwieldy wealth and cumbrous pomp repose;
And every want to opulence allied, 67
And every pang that folly pays to pride.
Those gentle hours that plenty bade to bloom,
Those calm desires that asked but little room,
Those healthful sports that graced the peaceful
scene, 71
Lived in each look, and brightened all the
green—
These, far departing, seek a kinder shore,
And rural mirth and manners are no more.
　Sweet Auburn! parent of the blissful hour, 75
Thy glades forlorn confess the tyrant's power.
Here, as I take my solitary rounds,
Amidst thy tangling walks and ruined grounds,
And, many a year elapsed, return to view
Where once the cottage stood, the hawthorn
grew— 80
Remembrance wakes with all her busy train,
Swells at my breast, and turns the past to pain.
　In all my wanderings round this world of
care,
In all my griefs—and God has given my
share—
I still had hopes, my latest hours to crown, 85
Amidst these humble bowers to lay me down;
To husband out life's taper at the close,
And keep the flame from wasting by repose:
I still had hopes, for pride attends us still,

Amidst the swains to show my book-learn'd
skill, 90
Around my fire an evening group to draw,
And tell of all I felt, and all I saw;
And, as a hare, whom hounds and horns
pursue,
Pants to the place from whence at first she
flew,
I still had hopes, my long vexations past, 95
Here to return—and die at home at last.
　O blest retirement, friend to life's decline,
Retreats from care, that never must be mine,
How happy he who crowns, in shades like these,
A youth of labor with an age of ease; 100
Who quits a world where strong temptations
try,
And, since 'tis hard to combat, learns to fly!
For him no wretches, born to work and weep,
Explore the mine, or tempt the dangerous deep;
No surly porter stands, in guilty state, 105
To spurn imploring famine from the gate;
But on he moves to meet his latter end,
Angels around befriending virtue's friend;
Bends to the grave with unperceived decay,
While resignation gently slopes the way; 110
And, all his prospects brightening to the last,
His heaven commences ere the world be past!
　Sweet was the sound, when oft, at evening's
close,
Up yonder hill the village murmur rose.
There, as I passed with careless [4] steps and
slow, 115
The mingled notes came softened from below;
The swain responsive as the milkmaid sung,
The sober herd that lowed to meet their young;
The noisy geese that gabbled o'er the pool,
The playful children just let loose from school;
The watch-dog's voice that bayed the whisper-
ing wind, 121
And the loud laugh that spoke the vacant [5]
mind;—
These all in sweet confusion sought the shade,
And filled each pause the nightingale had made.
But now the sounds of population fail, 125
No cheerful murmurs fluctuate in the gale,
No busy steps the grass-grown footway tread,
For all the bloomy flush of life is fled—
All but yon widowed, solitary thing,
That feebly bends beside the plashy spring; 130
She, wretched matron—forced, in age, for
bread,
To strip the brook with mantling cresses spread,
To pick her wintry faggot from the thorn,
To seek her nightly shed, and weep till morn,—
She only left of all the harmless train, 135
The sad historian of the pensive plain.
　Near yonder copse, where once the garden
smiled,
And still where many a garden-flower grows
wild,

to enclose common land, for the improvement of
their estates. This often involved ejectments.

[4] Care-free.
[5] Untroubled, perhaps, rather than stupid.

There, where a few torn shrubs the place dis-
close,
The village preacher's [6] modest mansion rose.
A man he was to all the country dear,    141
And passing rich with forty pounds a year.
Remote from towns he ran his godly race,
Nor e'er had changed, nor wished to change,
his place;
Unpracticed he to fawn, or seek for power [145]
By doctrines fashioned to the varying hour;
Far other aims his heart had learned to prize,
More skilled to raise the wretched than to rise.
His house was known to all the vagrant train;
He chid their wanderings, but relieved their
pain;    150
The long-remembered beggar was his guest,
Whose beard descending swept his aged breast;
The ruined spendthrift, now no longer proud,
Claimed kindred there, and had his claims
allowed;
The broken soldier, kindly bade to stay,    155
Sat by his fire, and talked the night away;—
Wept o'er his wounds, or, tales of sorrow done,
Shouldered his crutch, and showed how fields
were won.
Pleased with his guests, the good man learned
to glow,
And quite forgot their vices in their woe;    160
Careless their merits or their faults to scan,
His pity gave ere charity began.
Thus to relieve the wretched was his pride,
And e'en his failings leaned to virtue's side;
But in his duty prompt at every call,    165
He watched and wept, he prayed and felt for
all;
And, as a bird each fond endearment tries,
To tempt its new-fledged offspring to the skies,
He tried each art, reproved each dull delay,
Allured to brighter worlds, and led the way. [170]
Beside the bed where parting life was laid,
And sorrow, guilt, and pain, by turns dismayed,
The reverend champion stood. At his control,
Despair and anguish fled the struggling soul;
Comfort came down the trembling wretch to
raise,    175
And his last faltering accents whispered praise.
At church, with meek and unaffected grace,
His looks adorned the venerable place;
Truth from his lips prevailed with double sway,
And fools, who came to scoff, remained to pray.
The service past, around the pious man    181
With steady zeal, each honest rustic ran;
E'en children followed, with endearing wile,
And plucked his gown, to share the good man's
smile;
His ready smile a parent's warmth expressed; [185]
Their welfare pleased him, and their cares
distressed:
To them his heart, his love, his griefs were
given,
But all his serious thoughts had rest in heaven.

[6] Probably Goldsmith had both 'his father and his
brother, Henry, in mind in describing the preacher.

As some tall cliff that lifts its awful form,
Swells from the vale, and midway leaves the
storm,    190
Though round its breast the rolling clouds are
spread,
Eternal sunshine settles on its head.
Beside yon straggling fence that skirts the
way,
With blossomed furze unprofitably gay,
There, in his noisy mansion, skilled to rule, [195]
The village master taught his little school.
A man severe he was, and stern to view;
I knew him well, and every truant knew:
Well had the boding tremblers learned to trace
The day's disasters in his morning face;    200
Full well they laughed with counterfeited glee
At all his jokes, for many a joke had he;
Full well the busy whisper, circling round,
Conveyed the dismal tidings when he frowned.
Yet he was kind, or if severe in aught,    205
The love he bore to learning was in fault.
The village all declared how much he knew;
'Twas certain he could write, and cipher too;
Lands he could measure, terms and tides
presage,
And e'en the story ran that he could gauge. [210]
In arguing, too, the parson owned his skill,
For e'en though vanquished, he could argue
still;
While words of learned length and thundering
sound
Amazed the gazing rustics ranged around;
And still they gazed, and still the wonder grew,
That one small head could carry all he knew.
But past is all his fame;—the very spot    217
Where many a time he triumphed, is forgot.
Near yonder thorn, that lifts its head on
high,
Where once the sign-post caught the passing
eye,    220
Low lies that house where nut-brown drafts
inspired,
Where gray-beard mirth and smiling toil re-
tired,
Where village statesmen talked with looks
profound,
And news much older than their ale went
round.
Imagination fondly stoops to trace    225
The parlor splendors of that festive place;
The whitewashed wall, the nicely-sanded floor,
The varnished clock that clicked behind the
door,
The chest, contrived a double debt to pay,
A bed by night, a chest of drawers by day, 230
The pictures placed for ornament and use,
The twelve good rules,[7] the royal game of
goose,[8]

[7] These rules were said to have been found in the
study of Charles I after his death. Printed on a
card, they were hung on the wall.
[8] Played with dice on a board divided into com-
partments.

The hearth, except when winter chilled the
   day,
With aspen boughs, and flowers, and fennel,
   gay;—
While broken tea-cups, wisely kept for show,
Ranged o'er the chimney, glistened in a row. 236
   Vain transitory splendors! could not all
Reprieve the tottering mansion from its fall?
Obscure it sinks, nor shall it more impart
An hour's importance to the poor man's heart.
Thither no more the peasant shall repair, 241
To sweet oblivion of his daily care;
No more the farmer's news, the barber's tale,
No more the woodman's ballad shall prevail;
No more the smith his dusky brow shall clear,
Relax his ponderous strength, and lean to
   hear; 246
The host himself no longer shall be found
Careful to see the mantling bliss go round;
Nor the coy maid, half willing to be pressed,
Shall kiss the cup to pass it to the rest. 250
   Yes! let the rich deride, the proud disdain,
These simple blessings of the lowly train;
To me more dear, congenial to my heart,
One native charm, than all the gloss of art.
Spontaneous joys, where nature has its play, 255
The soul adopts, and owns their first-born sway;
Lightly they frolic o'er the vacant mind,
Unenvied, unmolested, unconfined:
But the long pomp, the midnight masquerade,
With all the freaks of wanton wealth arrayed,
In these, ere triflers half their wish obtain, 261
The toiling pleasure sickens into pain;
And, e'en while Fashion's brightest arts decoy,
The heart distrusting asks, if this be joy.
   Ye friends to truth, ye statesmen, who sur-
   vey 265
The rich man's joys increase, the poor's decay,
'Tis yours to judge how wide the limits stand
Between a splendid and a happy land.
Proud swells the tide with loads of freighted
   ore,
And shouting Folly hails them from her shore;
Hoards, e'en beyond the miser's wish, abound,
And rich men flock from all the world around.
Yet count our gains. This wealth is but a
   name 273
That leaves our useful products still the same.
Not so the loss. The man of wealth and pride
Takes up a space that many poor supplied; 276
Space for his lake, his park's extended bounds,
Space for his horses, equipage, and hounds;
The robe that wraps his limbs in silken sloth,
Has robbed the neighboring fields of half their
   growth; 280
His seat, where solitary sports are seen,
Indignant spurns the cottage from the green;
Around the world each needful product flies,
For all the luxuries the world supplies;
While thus the land, adorned for pleasure all,
In barren splendor feebly waits the fall. 286
   As some fair female, unadorned and plain,
Secure to please while youth confirms her reign,

Slights every borrowed charm that dress sup-
   plies,
Nor shares with art the triumph of her eyes; 290
But when those charms are past, for charms are
   frail,
When time advances, and when lovers fail,
She then shines forth, solicitous to bless,
In all the glaring impotence of dress:
Thus fares the land by luxury betrayed; 295
In nature's simplest charms at first arrayed;—
But verging to decline, its splendors rise,
Its vistas strike, its palaces surprise;
While, scourged by famine, from the smiling
   land
The mournful peasant leads his humble band;
And while he sinks, without one arm to save,
The country blooms—a garden and a grave! 302
   Where, then, ah! where shall poverty reside,
To 'scape the pressure of contiguous pride?
If to some common's fenceless limits strayed,
He drives his flock to pick the scanty blade, 306
Those fenceless fields the sons of wealth divide,
And e'en the bare-worn common is denied.
   If to the city sped—what waits him there?
To see profusion that he must not share; 310
To see ten thousand baneful arts combined
To pamper luxury and thin mankind;
To see those joys the sons of pleasure know
Extorted from his fellow-creature's woe:
Here while the courtier glitters in brocade, 315
There the pale artist [9] plies the sickly trade;
Here while the proud their long-drawn pomps
   display,
There the black gibbet glooms beside the way:
The dome where Pleasure holds her midnight
   reign,
Here, richly decked, admits the gorgeous train;
Tumultuous grandeur crowds the blazing
   square, 321
The rattling chariots clash, the torches glare.
Sure scenes like these no troubles e'er annoy!
Sure these denote one universal joy!—
Are these thy serious thoughts?—ah, turn thine
   eyes 325
Where the poor houseless shivering female lies:
She once, perhaps, in village plenty blessed,
Has wept at tales of innocence distressed;
Her modest looks the cottage might adorn,
Sweet as the primrose peeps beneath the thorn:
Now lost to all, her friends, her virtue, fled, 331
Near her betrayer's door she lays her head,
And, pinched with cold, and shrinking from
   the shower,
With heavy heart deplores that luckless hour,
When idly first, ambitious of the town, 335
She left her wheel, and robes of country brown.
   Do thine, sweet Auburn, thine, the loveliest
   train,
Do thy fair tribes participate her pain?
E'en now, perhaps, by cold and hunger led,
At proud men's doors they ask a little bread! 340
   Ah, no. To distant climes, a dreary scene,

[9] Craftsman.

Where half the convex world intrudes between,
Through torrid tracts with fainting steps they
    go,
Where wild Altama [10] murmurs to their woe.
Far different there from all that charmed be-
    fore,                                                    345
The various terrors of that horrid shore;
Those blazing suns that dart a downward ray,
And fiercely shed intolerable day;
Those matted woods where birds forget to sing,
But silent bats in drowsy clusters cling;        350
Those poisonous fields, with rank luxuriance
    crowned,
Where the dark scorpion gathers death around;
Where at each step the stranger fears to wake
The rattling terrors of the vengeful snake;
Where crouching tigers [11] wait their hapless
    prey,                                                    355
And savage men more murderous still than
    they:
While oft in whirls the mad tornado flies,
Mingling the ravaged landscape with the skies.
Far different these from every former scene,
The cooling brook, the grassy-vested green, 360
The breezy covert of the warbling grove,
That only sheltered thefts of harmless love.

    Good Heaven! what sorrows gloomed that
    parting day,
That called them from their native walks away;
When the poor exiles, every pleasure past, 365
Hung round their bowers, and fondly looked
    their last,
And took a long farewell, and wished in vain,
For seats like these beyond the western main;
And shuddering still to face the distant deep,
Returned and wept, and still returned to weep!
The good old sire the first prepared to go 371
To new-found worlds, and wept for others' woe;
But for himself, in conscious virtue brave,
He only wished for worlds beyond the grave.
His lovely daughter, lovelier in her tears,    375
The fond companion of his helpless years,
Silent went next, neglectful of her charms,
And left a lover's for a father's arms.
With louder plaints the mother spoke her woes,
And blessed the cot where every pleasure rose,
And kissed her thoughtless babes with many
    a tear,                                                 381
And clasped them close, in sorrow doubly dear;
Whilst her fond husband strove to lend relief
In all the silent manliness of grief.

    O Luxury, thou cursed by Heaven's decree,

How ill exchanged are things like these for
    thee!                                                    386
How do thy potions, with insidious joy,
Diffuse their pleasures only to destroy!
Kingdoms by thee to sickly greatness grown,
Boast of a florid vigor not their own;          390
At every draft more large and large they grow,
A bloated mass of rank unwieldy woe;
Till sapped their strength, and every part un-
    sound,
Down, down they sink, and spread a ruin
    round.
E'en now the devastation is begun,              395
And half the business of destruction done;
E'en now, methinks, as pondering here I stand,
I see the rural Virtues leave the land.
Down where yon anchoring vessel spreads the
    sail
That idly waiting flaps with every gale,        400
Downward they move, a melancholy band,
Pass from the shore, and darken all the strand;
Contented Toil, and hospitable Care,
And kind connubial Tenderness are there;
And Piety with wishes placed above,             405
And steady Loyalty, and faithful Love.

    And thou, sweet Poetry, thou loveliest maid,
Still first to fly where sensual joys invade!
Unfit, in these degenerate times of shame,
To catch the heart, or strike for honest fame;
Dear charming nymph, neglected and decried,
My shame in crowds, my solitary pride;          412
Thou source of all my bliss and all my woe,
That found'st me poor at first, and keep'st me
    so;
Thou guide by which the nobler arts excel, 415
Thou nurse of every virtue, fare thee well!
Farewell! and oh! where'er thy voice be tried,
On Torno's [12] cliffs, or Pambamarca's [13] side,
Whether where equinoctial [14] fervors glow,
Or winter wraps the polar world in snow, 420
Still let thy voice, prevailing over time,
Redress the rigors of th'inclement clime;
Aid slighted Truth with thy persuasive strain;
Teach erring man to spurn the rage of gain;
Teach him that states, of native strength
    possessed,                                              425
Though very poor, may still be very blest;
That Trade's proud empire hastes to swift
    decay,
As ocean sweeps the labored mole away;
While self-dependent power can time defy,
As rocks resist the billows and the sky.[15]    430

---

[10] Altamaha, a river in Georgia.
[11] Goldsmith had not yet become the historian of
Animated Nature; but Noah Webster later called
the jaguar "the American tiger."

[12] Tornea, Gulf of Bothnia, Sweden.
[13] Mountain in Ecuador.    [14] Equatorial.
[15] According to Boswell, Dr. Johnson wrote the
last four lines.

# V

# THE ROMANTIC REAC-
# TION AND TRIUMPH,
# 1784-1837

No important literary change takes place overnight. We are not to suppose that a reaction against eighteenth-century standards occurred instantly upon the death of Dr. Johnson in 1784. The rise of Romanticism was a gradual development. But the year in which Dr. Johnson died offers itself as a convenient point of division because Johnson was the last of the three acknowledged rulers of the literary world of England who successively "reigned" in the years from 1660 to 1784. (The earlier two had been Dryden and Pope.) Dr. Johnson shared the literary faith of the eighteenth century—for example, its reliance on common sense and distrust of the free imagination—and hence threw the massive weight of his judgments nearly always on the side of accepted standards. Thus as long as he lived, the forces of rebellion against eighteenth-century rules had a powerful foe, and the unity of the period from 1660 to 1784 was substantially maintained.

## THE "ROMANTIC" AND THE
## ROMANTIC MOVEMENT

That unity was before Johnson's death persistently challenged, and after Johnson's death destroyed, by a rising group of "romantic" writers. "Romantic" means simply the kind of thing which the unimaginative and balanced mind rejects as a contradiction of common sense or of rational knowledge. Anything which takes us beyond the bounds of accustomed experience, and makes us feel that life can be an adventurous encounter with the unknown; anything which breaks the prison bars of supposed necessity, and brings it home to us that

life is a mystery and that we are surrounded by mysteries; any vision which causes us even momentarily to suspend our usual skepticism and disbelief is "romantic."

The Romantic Movement was not the expression in literature of a change in outlook which the English nation underwent, or even of a change which overtook a certain class. It was not a social or political movement. It was a personal, and in a sense private, reaction against the inhuman mechanistic philosophy of the Restoration and eighteenth century. Its importance arises from the fact that it gave freedom of development and expression, as well as inspiration, to half a dozen men of remarkable genius who, with others possessed of real though slighter gifts, in the space of a few years enriched English literature immeasurably. In so doing, moreover, certain of the romantic writers kept men awake to the fact that the spirit or soul has its own needs distinct from those of the body. Romanticism, in short, gave new life not only to the artistic impulse, but also to spiritual aspiration and religious faith.

## THE BEGINNINGS OF ROMANTICISM:
## INTEREST IN THE MIDDLE AGES

One of the earliest achievements of awakened sensibility in the eighteenth century was the stimulation of interest in the Middle Ages, and especially in the old heroic poetry of the Germanic and Celtic peoples. This interest was gratified astonishingly by a Scottish school teacher, James Macpherson, who in the 1760's published several volumes which he said were translations of early Celtic poems discovered by him in the Highlands. Though most of these "poems of Ossian" were forgeries, they were immediately popular. Thomas Gray was enraptured, and declared them to be "full of nature and noble wild imagination." Macpherson's earliest readers had already begun to think in a sentimental way about the virtues of primitive people living simple lives amidst unspoiled natural scenery; and Macpherson gave them just what they wanted. He made no attempt at a faithful representation of early Celtic life or even of early Celtic poetry. Using the language and cadences of the English Bible, and deriving from Homer some hints concerning heroic life and character, he made a series of fancy pictures, representing ancient Northern life, not as it was but as his readers wanted to imagine it. His heroes are elaborately polite, full of tender feeling, generous, and brave; the scenic background of the poems is appropriately elemental and awe-inspiring. Macpherson, in short, succeeded in being both "noble" and "wild," and succeeded so well that his "translations" became a major influence in awakening romantic feeling.

Another series of forgeries, the *Rowley Poems* of Thomas Chatterton, had a temporary vogue for much the same reasons. Chatterton was hailed as "the marvelous boy," and not unjustly, because all his poetry was written while he was in his teens. Made desperate by poverty, he poisoned himself with arsenic in his eighteenth year. His early miserable death has kept his name alive, but not his poetry.

Chatterton's "wild" inventions were modeled chiefly on the traditional ballads collected by Bishop Thomas Percy and published in three volumes in 1765 as *Reliques of Ancient English Poetry*. Though Percy's collection did not cause the sensation that the Ossianic poems did, interest in the old English and Scottish ballads has never waned from Percy's time to ours. The ballads not only helped to awaken romantic feeling but served as a direct inspiration to Coleridge and Keats, and later to Tennyson, Swinburne, and Rossetti.

### GOTHIC TALES OF TERROR

Another early manifestation of English romanticism was the "Gothic" tale of mystery and terror. In these tales medieval settings serve as an excuse for sensational action. The earliest of them was written by Horace Walpole and was entitled *The Castle of Otranto* (1764). The species reached its peak in *The Mysteries of Udolpho* (1794) of Mrs. Anne Radcliffe and in *The Monk* (1796) of Matthew Gregory

Lewis. The first requirement for this kind of fiction was a setting distant in time or place, which by its strangeness could make almost anything seem plausible: horrible conspiracies, fiendish kidnapings or murders, cruel tortures, ghosts and spirits, and, in general, whatever might make the fascinated reader's hair stand on end. In his *History of the Caliph Vathek* (1786), William Beckford proved that an oriental setting could be just as effective as the medieval ones.

Though several of them can still be read with pleasure, this crop of "thrillers," taken as a whole, seems absurd and trivial. Yet the "Gothic" tales have real historical importance. In them the creative imagination was set free; and this in itself was important. Moreover, these tales presented a world in which the passions ruled and excitement prevailed, and so prepared the way for Walter Scott; and in addition they did something to nourish a growing love of the picturesque.

### GROWTH OF INTEREST IN WILD NATURAL SCENERY

Thomas Gray was as ready to welcome a "noble wild" scene as a "noble wild imagination," and for the same reason. He found such a scene pleasurably stimulating to poetic emotion, primarily to the feeling of awe. This was a discovery, but Gray soon had company. At first, appreciation of natural scenery was very like the dawning interest in things "Gothic," in that nature's theatrical aspects were sought and admired. Admirers of the Middle Ages were thrilled by towering battlements, dungeons, secret passages and the like; and now "the sounding cataract," "the tall rock, the mountains, and the deep and gloomy wood" were also found to be thrilling. But gradually the entertainment derived from such scenery was transformed. The eighteenth-century Englishman was full of sentiment, and presently he began to attribute to nature qualities suggested by his own feelings when in the presence of lofty crags, sylvan dells, banks of wooded hills, and the like. In such moments it seemed to him that he was lifted out of his ordinary cares, above life's trivialities, and not only breathed a purer air but was himself purified in spirit. Thus began to dawn a conviction that somehow nature spoke to man directly through the feelings; and, what was more, that the closer man's contact with nature the closer he would come to true wisdom.

## GROWING BELIEF IN MAN'S NATURAL GOODNESS: HUMANITARIANISM

The transition just outlined from the search for amusement and thrills to the search for wisdom and truth was vitally important. But it was not brought about exclusively through devotion to picturesque scenery. Along with the new conception of nature there was developing a new conception of man. And though we must separate these conceptions from each other in order to look at them one by one, we must remember that actually the new interest in the Middle Ages, the new conception of nature, and the new conception of man all went together and helped one another forward to the full romantic outlook.

The keystone of the new conception of man was simply the belief that man is by nature good. The first steps in the establishment of this belief had been taken in England by the deistical philosopher Shaftesbury in his *Characteristics* (1711). The doctrine of man's natural goodness can be stated in a few words: Man is born with a good nature; his instinctive sympathies and impulses guide him in the right directions, toward moral goodness and also toward personal happiness; he has, in addition, the powers needed to carry out his impulses. Therefore man can, in his present life on earth, fulfill his nature and enjoy a perfectly happy existence. All that is needed to this end is that men should *just be themselves,* unafraid, trusting their spontaneous impulses.

This doctrine immeasurably sharpened the contrast between what should be and what is. If men are born good, why do most men behave badly and live miserably? The answer which suggested itself was that men themselves could not be held responsible for their evil acts—environment was the responsible agent. Thus if environmental influences could be changed an ideal existence for all would follow.

At this point the new confidence that nature and society might be controlled to the good of humanity came into play. Social ills in particular became the subject of anxious consideration. Awakened moral sensibility expressed itself in sympathy for the unfortunate and in the determination to aid them. The helpless foundling, deposited on the doorstep and left to its fate, the highwayman, the burglar, and the murderer began to be regarded as the victims of an ill-organized society. And since society itself was the real criminal, the murderer as much as the foundling deserved pity and aid rather than punishment. Such pity and aid began to be offered in the middle and later years of the eighteenth century by a new species of being—the philanthropist or friend of mankind.

Thus humanitarianism appeared. It was in effect a new religion, based on faith in man's natural goodness and on the confident belief that humanity could be virtuous and happy. The humanitarian spirit showed itself most notably in the late eighteenth century, in efforts to reform English prisons and to abolish slavery. These and other efforts, however, barely scratched the surface of what was seen to be needed. It became apparent, indeed, that for the perfect reformation of society nothing less than a revolution would suffice.

## EFFECTS OF THE FRENCH REVOLUTION IN ENGLAND

The American Revolution had been welcomed by some liberty-loving Englishmen as a triumphant assertion of human rights against the oppressor, even though the tyrant overthrown in this instance was their own king. When, a few years afterwards, the French Revolution came, it was welcomed on the same ground. The French, it was supposed, were at last striking for the freedom which Englishmen had enjoyed for a century, and of course they deserved success. Upon some the impression made was far stronger. The response of many idealistic young men can best be seen from what Wordsworth wrote about his own feeling and faith at the time in his autobiographical poem, *The Prelude.* "In the People," he says, "was my trust." As a youth he had seen only the golden side of human nature and had been ready to fight, "even to the death," to support his confidence in the virtues of simple, lowly people.

He says of his feelings,

O pleasant exercise of hope and joy!
For mighty were the auxiliars which then stood
Upon our side, us who were strong in love!
Bliss was it in that dawn to be alive,
But to be young was very Heaven! O times,
In which the meager, stale, forbidding ways
Of custom, law, and statute, took at once
The attraction of a country in romance!

In these lines we have a classic expression of the joyous hope which the French Revolution aroused in the minds of some young men. They were ready to welcome with feverish excitement just such an uprising, yet until the Revolution burst upon them they had not really believed that so good a thing could happen. At one blow the Revolution transformed romantic visions into waking reality. All that the soaring spirit wanted to believe, and all that men of the world cynically disbelieved, was true! "Time was ready to set all things right"; and "the multitude, so long oppressed," had overnight gained the power to become all that human nature ought to be.

This was the first impression. There followed a period of dismay, anger, and almost inexpressible disappointment as Wordsworth and other glad young men saw that, after all, the revolution in France was not bringing about the reformation of humanity. The revolutionary leaders presently became "oppressors in their turn," and "changed a war of self-defense" to "one of conquest, losing sight of all which they had struggled for." Bitterly disillusioned, Wordsworth, Coleridge, and others had to readjust their outlook as best they could. The very great majority of Englishmen were thrown into political conservatism because of their horror at the bloody excesses of the French Terror and at the appearance of military tyranny under Napoleon. Wordsworth and Coleridge went with this majority, yet preserved unshaken their romantic faith in man. Thus it became their problem to justify that faith philosophically and poetically in ways consistent with social and political conservatism.

The effect of the French Revolution on English romanticism does not, however, end here. The Revolution was the most profound upheaval which Europe had experienced since the Protestant Reformation in the sixteenth century, and it left permanent marks. Nothing, indeed, could be quite the same after it, as time was to show.

## JOHN WESLEY AND METHODISM

The Methodist revival of religion was, in effect, a reaction against scientific rationalism, and as such it pointed unmistakably toward the growth of romanticism. It is not likely that the Methodist revival had an important connection with the romantic literary revival of the 1790's and the early nineteenth century; nevertheless, some knowledge of it is indispensable for our purposes. The Romantic Movement was the literary expression of a general reaction against eighteenth-century "enlightenment" and standardization, which extended

beyond literature and embraced the whole of life. Some of those who participated in the literary movement did not fully understand its bearings, though they gave their aid in liberating the human spirit from one or another form of tyrannical repression. Today it is possible to see the meaning of the whole reaction, as well as the need for it, more clearly than could some of the participants; but we can, of course, only do so by looking at all of its aspects. When we attempt this, we discover that it was indeed an advance on several fronts, unplanned, apparently disconnected, yet having a common object.

Practically speaking, the Methodist church is the creation of one man, John Wesley, probably the most extraordinary Englishman of the whole eighteenth century. Not even Wesley, however, could have succeeded in bringing about a great revival of religion had his work not met a vital need. In England rationalism had gone far to destroy Christianity by sweeping away its personal and historical elements, and putting in their place a body of abstract doctrine which appealed not at all to the hearts and souls of the people. The consequence was that educated people and fashionable people either were not Christians or were Christians only in name, and that ignorant people were becoming not only irreligious but brutal.

There were exceptions to this rule. Christianity was being kept alive in England; but it was carrying on an underground existence. It lived on outside the Anglican Church in societies of Presbyterians, Baptists, Quakers, and the like, and also in the homes of a few Anglicans. These groups were small, obscure, and weak. The population of England, moreover, was both growing and shifting, and in the 1740's there were thousands of Englishmen who had no opportunity even to hear Christian teaching of any kind.

These, briefly, were the conditions amidst which John Wesley appeared. He was born in 1703, into a family where undiluted Christianity remained a living force; nevertheless, he was slow in making up his mind to a life of religious ministry, and he was not finally converted to what he conceived to be the state of a Christian until he was thirty-five. Before that he had been drawn into methodical religious observances, partly formal and partly the performance of good works. He was affected by the rising wave of sentimentalism, and promised to be an early ornament of the new humanitarianism. He became convinced, however, that neither ceremonial observances nor good works were enough. The mark of a Christian, he concluded, was to be seen in one thing only: the assurance of the individual that he had experienced a direct act of supernatural grace in being born again of the Holy Spirit at some time following his first or natural birth.

Wesley believed that the natural man was made, by the New Birth or conversion, a saint, and must act like a saint. Wesley himself did. And by the power of his saintliness he brought thousands to do likewise.

For us the important thing in the Methodist Awakening is the doctrine of the New Birth, and the fact that living belief in it spread rapidly over England, and was not confined to one sect or to one class. The doctrine of the New Birth shattered, for believers, the conception of a self-contained universe of mechanical law, and made the mystery, indeed the miracle, of divine grace once again a living reality. Wesley thus revived among his followers the sense that life's real issues and rewards are not confined to earth but are spread out to eternity. Beyond this he brought back into life unexpected possibilities through the operations of divine grace, and the consciousness of mystery permeating life. Further, he reasserted the rights of direct individual experience against formalism, and taught men to trust their own intuitions and to back them against all odds.

The most significant feature of the romantic reaction was the renewed conviction that human nature contains an element which expresses itself in sure intuitions, through the passions, and that such intuitions are to be trusted in preference to any conclusions of the mere reasoning intellect. At the point of sharpest opposition, then, to scientific rationalism, Wesley and the romantic writers were united. But the application of this conviction, to Wesley and his followers, was simply and narrowly religious. The early Methodists were "enthusiasts," in the eighteenth-century sense of the word, but they did not carry their "enthusiasm" into the realms of philosophy, poetry, or fiction.

## WILLIAM COWPER

Cowper is sometimes said to link rising religious awakening with rising romanticism, for he wrote many hymns, some of them beautiful and all full of sincere feeling. Besides this, he was haunted through the greater part of his

life by desperate religious fears, and resorted to various methods to distract his attention and keep himself busy. The composition of poetry was one of these methods.

Cowper was a cultivated gentleman, sensitive, kindly, observant, reflective, who loved simplicity and quiet. He was in touch with his times, and felt complete sympathy with the new humanitarianism. Like many another who enjoyed English freedom, too, he applauded the first efforts of the French to shake off ancient tyranny. In addition, he loved country scenes and hated the sophistication and corruption of cities. Thus his poetry brings one agreeably into contact with some of the feelings and thoughts which were leading on to Romanticism. He was not carried off his feet, however, by any of the doctrines of Romanticism. These he encountered with an alert critical eye.

Cowper's moderation and balance can be seen especially well in the quality of his humanitarianism. He was capable of strong feeling, and had a horror of needless suffering inflicted on man or beast. This horror arose from sympathetic kindliness. It was direct and personal. But Cowper did not accept the sharp opposition between reason and sentiment which had long been accepted both by rationalists and by sentimentalists. His eyes were not closed by excess of feeling. He was not led on from humanitarian sympathy to believe that spontaneous sentiment was humanity's one and sufficient source of wisdom. And this means, precisely, that he was a humanitarian without being romantic.

## GEORGE CRABBE

The fact that there is no necessary connection between humanitarianism and Romanticism can be seen even more clearly in the work of Cowper's younger contemporary, George Crabbe. Crabbe won the attention of the public by his treatment of the theme he knew best from personal experience—the miseries and degradation of the simple life according to nature.

Goldsmith had professed to treat the same theme in *The Deserted Village*; but the part of this poem on which Goldsmith had lavished his care and skill, and the part which has stuck in the minds of readers, is that describing the former idyllic existence of the villagers. Goldsmith, with no thought of abandoning the poetic style, the manners, or the balanced good sense of the eighteenth century, had thrown himself into the oncoming current of sentimentalism and had drawn a romantically "idealistic" picture of the beauty and goodness of village life, before the coming of the land-grabbing oppressor. His essential point was that until then, contentment and the simple natural virtues had flourished upon poverty.

Crabbe wrote his first notable poem, *The Village* (1783), in conscious reaction against such falsehood. Rustic life as he knew it was full of wretchedness and vice; and elemental human nature as he knew it was hard, selfish, calculating, sordid. Indignantly he sought to discredit poetic "idealism" by picturing country life as it actually was, and showing the real effects of simplicity and poverty. He was moved by pity, and we can see the difference between pity and sentimentalism in the difference between his *Village* and Goldsmith's. He felt that if the lot of poor country folk was ever to be bettered, the public must be aroused by methods of unsparing realism and so be made, in effect, to share its wretchedness. From beginning to end Crabbe was consistently humanitarian and consistently unromantic.

## ROBERT BURNS

With Burns, we come to something different. Burns was born five years later than Crabbe, and died thirty-six years earlier. He was a peasant, and knew the life of poor country folk as intimately as Crabbe and at approximately the same time. Mostly self-educated, he studied not only English literature, but also the popular poetry of his own Scotland, and in the latter he found the inspiration of a technique which set free his full powers. The songs he then wrote, using his native Scots dialect, really sing themselves, and appear to be the spontaneous overflow of simple emotion with a universal appeal. Such expressiveness, we feel, must come straight from the heart; and in fact Burns did learn to express his own personality and sentiments perfectly, not alone in song, but also in satire and realistic tale. Though verses of the kind he wrote were traditional in Scotland, he made the form his own. In its homeliness, raciness, and informality, it offered a startling contrast to the abstract and comparatively cold formal diction regarded at the time as the correct language of poetry.

Thus Burns found himself master of a style which implied revolt from accepted standards; and at the same time he learned to trust himself, and to consult his own feelings and reactions for his themes. His reactions were clearcut and his feelings intense even when not deep or lasting. He was eminently the kind of man who throws himself heart and soul, impulsively, into the face of any kind of danger, into a desperate love-affair, into a forlorn cause; who may do things he is bound to be sorry for, and who may equally, the next moment, stand forth a hero. The chief difference, then, between him and Crabbe was one of temper. Crabbe was disillusioned, pessimistic, steady, persistent, and objective. Burns was joyful, optimistic, sentimental when not passionate, frank, convivial, and unstable. He was quickly plunged into depths of grief or remorse, but as quickly rose again on a new wave of hopeful feeling. He was, indeed, an "enthusiast," which is to say that he possessed the romantic temper.

Burns as well as Crabbe read Goldsmith's *Deserted Village*, but Burns accepted it with delight, and wrote his own version of idyllic peasant life in *The Cotter's Saturday Night.* It is quite true that in this poem, and in general in his treatment of "honest poverty," he had a basis of experience materially different from Crabbe's. The Scottish peasant often had a conscious integrity, a spirit of independence and self-reliance, and an iron will which promoted a stiff reaction to hardship. Nevertheless, Burns "idealized" his picture, under the influence of sentimentalism.

Although Burns was steeped in two literatures, and learned his art from one and drew his ideas from the other, it is true that he was significantly original. He took up pretty sentiments and charged them with passion which transformed them; he broke with established conventions and wrote the better poetry for it. He not only praised freedom, but also did a great deal, poetically, in its cause. In all this he pointed more directly than anyone before him to Romanticism.

## WILLIAM BLAKE

There was a contemporary of Burns, unknown to the public, living obscurely on the outermost borders of the literary and artistic worlds, who showed in his convictions and work almost everything that was to enter into the Romantic Movement, and almost everything that was to issue from it to our own day. This extraordinary genius was William Blake. He exerted no literary influence on those of his own time. English romanticism would have taken exactly the same course had he never lived. Yet in the historical study of the movement he is of great importance, both because he puts its fundamental character in a bright light, and also just because he was an isolated figure. This isolation compels us to infer that the Romantic Movement was something bound to come, if not through one man or a group, then through another.

Blake was a mystic. The mystic believes that he has made direct contact with ultimate or absolute reality which leaves behind all our earthly distinctions and rises above our limitations. But no mystic can put directly into words the truth he has learned, because speech partakes of our human limitations. Hence the mystic's vision can only be hinted at or suggested in one way or another.

The upshot of Blake's message was simply that energy, spontaneous energy, is life and truth and goodness—is divine. He was supremely confident of this because he had seen it, in mystical visions. He imagined that the prophets Isaiah and Ezekiel were dining with him and that he asked them how they had dared "so roundly to assert that God spoke to them." Isaiah answered, Blake tells us, that he never literally saw or heard God, but that his "senses discovered the infinite in everything," and since he was firmly persuaded that the voice of honest indignation was the voice of God, he felt justified in asserting that God had spoken to him. Then Blake asked the prophet, "Does a firm persuasion that a thing is so, make it so?" And Isaiah replied, "All poets believe that it does, and in ages of imagination this firm persuasion removed mountains; but many are not capable of a firm persuasion of anything."

Here we have the secret of Blake's confidence. A "firm persuasion" was enough. Whatever was real and true for him *must* be Truth Itself. And, since it was Truth, it must be equally truth for everybody else. Hence those who did not agree must be fools, idiots, outrageous demons, cunning knaves, pale priests, insolent reasoners, or sneaking reptiles. (These are his own descriptive terms for those who differed from him.)

From these premises Blake concluded that every impulse, every stir of imprisoned energy, should be carried into instant action without regard to consequences. Everything spontaneous he held to be good, and all calculations bad. The promptings of energy, he said, were the promptings of genius; and to give one's genius scope one had only to let one's self

go, with perfect trustfulness. Hence the man who is all impulse rises above the limits of earthly existence, and partakes of the happiness of the heavenly or infinite world. If this does not seem to make sense, Blake's reply is that you are lacking in faith. A firm persuasion that a thing is so makes it so.

Here at one bound we are within the guarded portals of romance, the land of dreams, the land of the heart's desire. True wisdom is to know that nothing is impossible, and that each of us can live, and does live, in whatever kind of world he chooses. The inspired man chooses eternal beauty and loveliness, and does really create what he chooses, in poetry, painting, music, or some handicraft. He is the true alchemist, changing lifeless sounds or inert matter into golden living forms of timeless perfection.

Although most of his poetry is not timeless—much of it is unintelligible or lacking in substance—Blake did write some poetry of imperishable loveliness. There is only a little of it, but what we have is precious. His successful poems are lyrics; and, like other romantic writers a few years later, he went back for inspiration to the great Elizabethan age.

Blake may fairly be called a sublime crank. Looking at him we can see instantly what is meant when we are told that the romantic temper is unqualifiedly individualistic, that it turns men's eyes inward upon themselves, and that it relies on "firm persuasion" as its standard of truth. The romantic reaction was a many-sided rebellion against restrictions that had come to seem arbitrary. The rebels broke their chains and walked about, celebrating the goodness of freedom. Blake shows us some of the rewards of freedom, and equally shows us its perils. Freedom to be utterly one's self should, of course, encourage the virtue of sincerity; but neither this nor any other good personal quality is in itself enough. The experiments of Blake, in fact, come sadly close to suggesting that uninhibited freedom may finally issue in gibberish.

Freedom, then, is rather a door opened to opportunity than an end in itself; and the high importance of the Romantic Movement arises from the significant uses made of freedom by the great men who converted the romantic reaction into a romantic triumph. To them we now turn, and first to Wordsworth, who stands earliest in time as he stands first in importance.

## WILLIAM WORDSWORTH

*Lyrical Ballads, with a Few Other Poems* was published in 1798. No one, except perhaps its two authors, regarded the book's appearance as an epoch-making event. Reviewers were on the whole unfavorable, and the general public was scarcely aware of the book's existence. Yet this volume contained *The Ancient Mariner* and three other poems by Coleridge, and the rest of the poems in it were written by Wordsworth! The public of 1798 need not be harshly condemned for its failure to recognize the worth of *Lyrical Ballads*. The book's contents were, certainly, remarkable, but the book would never have attained its present historical position had its authors not gone on to become the two greatest figures in the English Romantic Movement. And Wordsworth himself realized that those who attempt something new must, if they are to succeed, slowly educate readers and thus in time create their own public. His poems were a deliberate challenge to existing standards and so invited controversy. Critical condemnation, when it came, did not unsettle him. In 1800 he republished his poems with additions, and introduced them with a Preface in which he explained and defended his aims. He felt compelled, the Preface tells us, to attack the artificiality of eighteenth-century poetic style and also the sensational extravagance of the popular fiction of the 1790's. He wanted to bring in a kind of poetry which should be simple, natural, and direct, as the old ballads were, and which should express the universal passions of humanity in the language of real men. Controversy hinged chiefly on this matter of the language proper to poetry; and Coleridge, though he fully shared Wordsworth's desire for simplicity, naturalness, and directness, felt that Wordsworth had pushed too far his demand for the language actually spoken by men, and had in fact in his poems practiced better than he preached. Coleridge published his own account of the origin of *Lyrical Ballads* and his own opinions on the subject of poetic diction in his *Biographia Literaria* (1817).

William Wordsworth from childhood was formed by impressions of extraordinary intensity received from the world of nature, from "the sounding cataract, the tall rock, the mountain, and the deep and gloomy wood." Out of these impressions arose the conviction that he was a "dedicated spirit," and his later thought and work were centered in the effort to explore and set forth poetically the meaning of the revelation that had come to him through "nature and the language of the sense." The revelation came before he had any sort of contact with eighteenth-century philosophical thought or with the romantic reaction. When he reached manhood he found that natural scenery could no longer give him the supreme joy, or mood of mystical insight, that formerly it had. At the same time he encountered skeptical philosophy, which made him ask whether he had been the victim of a delusion. He did not think so; he had not embraced a theory which might be exploded, but had undergone a transforming experience which nothing could wipe out or explain away. Henceforth he sought to understand life in terms of that experience, welcoming help from any likely quarter, turning from some sources that failed him to others, but remaining true to his early impressions.

One of these impressions he recorded in the earliest version of *The Prelude*:

I love a public road: few sights there are
That please me more; such object hath had power
O'er my imagination since the dawn
Of childhood, when its disappearing line,
Seen daily afar off, on one bare steep
Beyond the limits which my feet had trod
Was like a guide into eternity,
At least to things unknown and without bound.

His love arose from the suggestion of guidance into eternity, but his imagination did not, like Blake's, leap ahead to construct symbolic representations of things unknown and without bound. He held fast to the road and to his own feelings, and tried resolutely to pierce the mystery of this and other responses produced in him by the surrounding world. He came to see reality as something half-created, half-perceived; not just an object seen, lying wholly outside of the perceiving mind, but a union of mind and object in which each actively brought something to the whole. Reality thus conceived was alive with feeling, and perception was not a dispassionate intellectual act, but an induced mood which on occasion rose into mystical ecstasy.

Wordsworth was convinced that Reality is a poetical mood of rapture which all may experience. The poet is the man exceptionally gifted with the shaping power of imagination which enables him to translate the mood into words and rhythms which we recognize as saying for us what we could not have expressed for ourselves, and even what we could not have felt distinctly without his guidance. Poetry, Wordsworth logically says, is "the breath and finer spirit of all knowledge." The poet, then, is a teacher, and a teacher of the highest knowledge—which is wisdom, or the key to fullness of life. We gain fullness of life in so far as, with the poet's help, we learn for ourselves that Reality is not something objectively given, existing independently of us, to be discovered through the senses, but is *a state of feeling created through the union of man and his surrounding world.*

In trying to give form to the wisdom revealed to him, Wordsworth gathered into his poetry a great deal from the romantic reaction as it has been reviewed in this chapter. Like others before him and contemporary with him, he backed the individual and "enthusiasm" against common sense, turning from the abstract or general to the concrete or even the unique, from the external to the inward or subjective, from the seen to the unseen, from the mechanical to the dynamic, and philosophically, from scientific rationalism to romantic faith in human goodness. In these and other ways he remains typical of his age; but he swings free of the limitations of time sufficiently to be regarded by many today as the greatest of English poets after Shakespeare and Milton. And he does so despite serious personal limitations. Many in his own lifetime and since have been unable to restrain amusement or annoyance at certain peculiarities of this "dedicated spirit," and particularly at his self-importance. Moreover, his poetry is markedly uneven, is very limited in range, and makes rather heavy demands on readers.

Nevertheless, Wordsworth out-tops even the most brilliant and attractive of his contemporaries. And the fundamental reason is that he inspires confidence, and actually does reveal to others what was revealed to him. Wordsworth was himself extraordinarily awake to the mysterious harmonies between man and nature, to the beauties of personal character, to the golden (not the merely gilded) opportunities of freedom, to the grandeur of manly independence, individual and national, to the real values of earthly life. He did not merely see them, he *felt* them, and drew strength and joy from them. He did not, for joy and strength, fly off on the wings of fancy to any Utopia, but kept his eyes fixed upon this very world of our daily lives and found it filled with goodness and beauty. And what Wordsworth found, and what he was, he communicates to his readers with unique directness and fullness, "from everyday forms educing the

unknown and the uncommon." No other poet of modern times makes us feel with equal force that "a good book is the precious lifeblood of a master-spirit" ordained to a life beyond life. Wordsworth achieves this because we find, after we have discarded all in him that belongs only to an age now dead and gone, that he did penetrate to imperishable truths of human nature. Time has justified his brave confidence that he was dedicated to the part of a teacher, and it is as a source of one solid kind of wisdom that he securely lives. Faith in our human nature has never been easy, but Wordsworth, even today, can give us unchallengeable grounds for it and can make it live again.

## COLERIDGE AND ROMANTIC CRITICISM

Coleridge and Wordsworth, as has been said above, began their real work together in *Lyrical Ballads,* and they must always be spoken of together. Neither of them could have accomplished what he did without the friendship and stimulus of the other. But for the most part their fields of activity were different. Coleridge wrote a few poems supremely good of their kind; but of these one was only a short fragment ("Kubla Khan") and another, *Christabel,* was never completed. No praise is too high for these poems; nevertheless, Coleridge's own first wish was to be a philosopher, and his chief work was done in the field of criticism—philosophical, religious, political, and literary.

Inevitably, the romantic reaction brought in a new criticism along with a new imaginative literature; Coleridge was the founder of romantic criticism. In considering his work we must first understand the nature of the problem he faced. The conflict between Romanticism and the eighteenth century was at bottom one between two philosophies or "wisdoms"—the wisdom to be gained from dispassionate observation through the senses and generalization therefrom, and the wisdom to be gained from our emotional responses to life. Criticism is judgment, and judgment is impossible without standards. Whatever the value of the effort made in England in the seventeenth and eighteenth centuries to formulate rational standards, the romantic writers were bound to attack those standards and, indeed, the effort itself. If emotional responses, direct intuitions, were really a source of wisdom and beauty, writers needed freedom to express them in whatever form and style seemed best for the particular goal in view. Further, if direct intuition was the foundation of a sonnet or an ode, its only appeal was to the reader's intuitional appreciation. Hence a criticism founded on intuition, to replace the objective method of eighteenth-century criticism, was a basic need of the Romantic Movement.

Coleridge was perfectly confident that it was possible to construct on a basis of intuition an idealistic philosophy which would afford sound critical standards. He was encouraged in this belief by the new literature and philosophy coming into existence by the end of the eighteenth century in Germany. There, largely under the influence of English sentimental writers and critics of rationalism, Romanticism was already flourishing, and developing a new philosophy. And there Coleridge went in 1798, with Wordsworth and Wordsworth's sister Dorothy, to learn something about the new wisdom. He came back in the following year with a competent knowledge of German and with a good many volumes of German philosophy. Coleridge did a great deal to open the eyes of Englishmen to German romantic literature, criticism, and philosophy; and in his own critical and philosophical writings and lectures he prepared the way for the decisive influence in the nineteenth century of German idealism on English thought, besides opening up a new era in literary criticism.

Nothing like an examination of Coleridge's philosophy is possible here. It is necessary, however, to show how he attempted to lay a solid philosophical foundation for romantic criticism. First, he tried to prove that by direct intuition we are in contact with eternal truths, the same always and for all men, or at least for all good men. Imagination he then defined as the power to give organic form and substance to that which is revealed to the poet or artist intuitionally. This is a power of true creation. The poet is not, as men of the eighteenth century supposed, a craftsman skillfully working according to rule. He is a god-like creator, and the form of his work issues as naturally and inevitably out of his moral intuition as the form of a tree issues out of its nature. It follows that when we are confronted by a work of true creative genius we cannot judge it by an external standard. There is no one right way of constructing a tragedy, or a comedy, or any other work of art. Every true work of art is unique and has the one form it can have to express what it does express.

Coleridge's great example was Shakespeare.

To read him was to recognize, directly or intuitively, that here was a supreme creative genius. Hence his plays must have the one form right in every way for their purpose. Consequently the critic's business was to study him reverently. He could not be judged by any established standard, because the only standard applicable was implicit in his unique inspiration which dictated the form and style of the plays. Shakespeare, by the very nature of creative genius, was a law unto himself. What the critic could do was to discover the law inherent in the plays and explain Shakespeare's perfect adaptation of means to ends. This is the nature of Coleridge's own criticism of Shakespeare, and the method is applied not only to the plays but also to the characters appearing in them. The characters, in other words, are regarded as having a life of their own, as if they were real human beings, impelled by the motives of real persons, and not by a playwright's practical needs.

The net outcome was that the work of the critic was to be confined to interpretation and appreciation. All of the romantic critics lavished attention on Shakespeare, whose plays seemed providentially adapted to the new method of treatment. The consequence, however, was something which has since been called Shakespeare idolatry.

But though Coleridge encouraged an attitude toward imaginative writers which was really uncritical and was bound to provoke a reaction in time, he also did much that was needed and fruitful. In particular, he deserves gratitude for his contention that there is an organic relation between form and meaning in works of art. In addition, he contributed materially to that revival of interest in older English literature which was a marked characteristic of the Romantic Movement and has remained one of its permanent legacies. And thus also he led the way towards another new thing, the rise of what is called the historical method in criticism. In this method it is considered that an institution is a product of what we now call evolution, and that it cannot be understood except in the light of its history.

Coleridge not only encouraged uncritical reverence for imaginative writers, but also encouraged a chaotic diversity of critical evaluations based on emotional responses. He justified impressively the "right" of the man of genius to artistic freedom. He exerted an influence which was to deepen and enrich later criticism when he insisted that the critic must endeavor to enter sympathetically into the mind and heart of the poet or artist and, in effect, re-create interpretatively the work of art under discussion. But time alone, not Coleridge or anyone else, could show whether or not such a treatment of literature would reveal a common intuitive wisdom holding free men together in a "natural" society. Coleridge himself could only help to liberate emotion, and hope for the best. Time, however, quickly showed that when critics were encouraged to rely on their instinctive responses they differed, just as imaginative writers also differed. And time quickly showed, in addition, that when critics were turned to writing about literature in terms of their own responses, or "reactions," they would begin to use literature as a point of departure for writing about themselves.

## HAZLITT, LAMB, AND DE QUINCEY

The trend towards the subjective in literary criticism is seen clearly in the essays of William Hazlitt, the most important of the romantic critics after Coleridge. Hazlitt declaimed against the indulgence of eccentricity but indulged his own, and believed, too, that we come closest to ideal truth in extreme individual embodiments. Hence he was always searching for and marking the *characteristic* trait or style, and so laying bare the peculiar, differentiating, personal qualities in literature and art. His approach to his subject was of course also personal, through the emotions. His essays are a chronicle of loves and hates; and, as we should expect from this, he wrote best about his contemporaries, though he also wrote about older literature, and inevitably about Shakespeare. He discusses Shakespeare's characters in the romantic way, as if they were people. Throughout, one finds that Hazlitt's criticism is personal in some fashion. This has the very real advantage that it adds variety, liveliness, and human interest to his essays, and gives criticism in his hands a literary importance and a life of its own which critical writings previously had not attained. The advantage arises, however, from Hazlitt's success in making criticism a means of self-expression, and thus to some extent a kind of creative writing. The result, too, is that the criticism of literature and art merges, not only into the criticism of life, but into the frankly personal essay.

What Hazlitt inaugurated, Charles Lamb delightfully completed. The difference between the two is strictly one of degree. Both continually express themselves, whatever their subject of discourse. Both consult their feelings and instinctive responses without regard for tradition or social standards. And both engage our interest because we are glad to know them personally, aside from what they have to tell us about the ignorance of the learned, or the fear of death, or disagreeable people, or chimney sweepers, or roast pig; or, on subjects literary, wit and humor, or the prose style of the poets, or Restoration drama. Hazlitt significantly entitled one of his volumes *Table Talk*. And we are in fact, when we read him, really listening to the conversation of a talented man, eminently worth knowing, whose like we shall never meet face to face, or outside his own books.

Lamb's supreme advantage over Hazlitt is that the same thing is true of him, with the addition that to know him is to love him. It should be no recommendation of a critic that the first word on the lips of every reader who attempts to characterize him is "whimsical," but what reader of Lamb cares? We love Lamb precisely on account of his unique personality, and would not for the world have him other than he is.

No more would we have De Quincey other than he is, though for a very different reason. De Quincey irresistibly prompts one to exclaim that he is a museum-piece; one could not have believed humanity capable of producing a "specimen" so rare—at once so curious, so remote, so highly individualized, and so typically romantic. He was at his best when writing about himself, and he developed, for this purpose, a prose style which is the principal basis of his fame. It is almost musical, in that its expressiveness seems to arise out of pure sound and rhythm, independently of words and their meanings. What can be thus expressed is a mood, a state of the emotions; and this is usually accomplished by lyric poetry. De Quincey was typically romantic here, in breaking down the distinction between prose and verse, and also in going back for inspiration to some of the seventeenth-century masters of learned eloquence, such as Jeremy Taylor and Sir Thomas Browne. Like Lamb, too, he was capable of impish tricks. His papers "On Murder Considered as One of the Fine Arts" are his best known examples. In the second of these, speaking as a connoisseur to a man desirous of becoming his servant, who, however, was reputed to have dabbled a little in murder, he said:

If once a man indulges himself in murder, very soon he comes to think little of robbing, and from robbing he comes next to drinking and Sabbath-breaking, and from that to incivility and procrastination. Once begun upon this downward path, you never know where you are to stop. Many a man dated his ruin from some murder or other that perhaps he thought little of at the time.

De Quincey's life is no longer the mystery it was to his contemporaries, but increased knowledge has not served to make him seem less extraordinary. He was in many respects closer to our common humanity than used to be supposed, but he was also just as wayward as we would infer when we learn that, having stayed at a dinner-party one night beyond the hour when he was safe from seizure for debt, he remained in the house of his host for a whole year. Waywardness, no doubt, was really one side of De Quincey's unique and splendid genius; nevertheless, it is not, any more than whimsicality, a characteristic appropriate to a critic. But the romantic critics did not wrestle with the thorny problem of social standards. It was not in them to fight against what John Stuart Mill called "the natural tendency of mankind to anarchy." They themselves were individualists and did not care, as Hazlitt said, to tire readers or puzzle themselves "with pedantic rules and pragmatical formulas of criticism that can do no good to anybody." None of them perceived that though genius may indeed require freedom, criticism must somehow work in terms of standards, or suffer extinction.

Yet this does not mean that the romantic critics failed. The best of them—those here under discussion—are people worth knowing; and, in revealing themselves frankly in personal talk, often not even pretending to be critical, they have given us a new kind of literature which we would not be without and would not have other than it is. Many would unhesitatingly declare that if they have done this only at the sacrifice of what is properly called criticism, so much the worse for criticism. But, even strictly as critics, they accomplished much which leaves posterity in their debt. They opened up the riches of English literature before 1680, which, with the exception of Shakespeare's plays, had been condemned and neglected; and in the case of Shakespeare, though they went to extremes, they did bring about a better understanding of his greatness. They also broadened the literary outlook by bringing the new literature and philosophy of Germany to England.

These in themselves were considerable and lasting achievements. But the romantic critics did more; they deepened criticism, made it flexible, and made it broadly significant by joining the discussion of literature with the discussion of life. Finally, they placed some critical standards on the scrap heap where they belonged, and though they failed to place criticism on a new foundation, they did stimulate interest in literature and continue still to do so. If we are on our guard, and do not expect to find accuracy, sound judgment, or even criticism in the full sense of the word, we can still find in the romantic critics something invaluable and rare: we can find personal friends to whom literature is an absorbing delight, not a thing set apart, but something inseparably bound up with life, and indeed a complete expression and concentration of life at its richest and best. After all else has been said about the romantic critics, everyone who reads them knows that they loved literature. Hence they remain their own best advocates; for we can still feel the freshness, the glow and ardor, of their discoveries and of their absorption in the life of the imagination.

## SIR WALTER SCOTT

At the beginning of the nineteenth century no one saw that Wordsworth and Coleridge were turning the romantic reaction into a romantic triumph. While the authors of *Lyrical Ballads* were being reproved by critics and were still unknown to most readers, the earliest popular triumphs in the romantic way of writing were achieved by Walter Scott.

Born in Edinburgh, Scott came from a distinguished family of the once unruly border country—the picturesque hilly region just north of the boundary between Scotland and England. He was bred to the law, and from early manhood practically to the end of his life was a court officer and also a county sheriff. Furthermore, even after he had become successful and famous as a writer, he looked upon literature as almost a side-issue, placing it far below the life of action. In later life his hero was no man of letters, but Wellington, the conqueror of Napoleon. And he took more pleasure in the building of Abbotsford, and in the gradual increase of his land around it, than in his literary successes.

As a youth Scott was set upon a long course of reading by an illness which kept him inactive. Without method but with eager interest he read every kind of fiction, from the French heroic romances of the seventeenth century down to the tales of terror and sentiment of his own time. He then "began, by degrees, to seek in histories, memoirs, voyages, and travels, and the like, events nearly as wonderful as those which were the work of imagination, with the additional advantage that they were at least in a great measure true." In periods when activity was possible, he learned from one of his early friends the joys of antiquarianism, and particularly the pleasure to be got from collecting popular ballads of the border country which had been transmitted orally from one generation to another. In his ballad hunts, too, he became intimately acquainted with the country and with many a strongly marked local character. Always sociable, he was able to meet every kind of person on his own ground; and instinctively his keen eye took in every trait of individuality. As he grew older he became acquainted with some of the new romantic literature of Germany, and was attracted but not overwhelmed by it.

Briefly this is the foundation of Scott's great career. He became sufficiently an antiquarian to edit the ballads he collected, and published them under the title, *The Minstrelsy of the Scottish Border* (1802–1803). Then, filled with the old traditional narratives, he wrote some new ballads, and out of one of these attempts grew *The Lay of the Last Minstrel* (1805), a metrical romance based on a border legend concerning a feud of the mid-sixteenth century. It was immediately so successful that he was bound to write other metrical romances; *Marmion* followed in 1808, and *The Lady of the Lake* in 1810. Still others appeared in the next couple of years, but in 1812 Lord Byron published the first two cantos of *Childe Harold's Pilgrimage*, and in the following year the first two of his romantic tales of the orient, *The Bride of Abydos* and *The Giaur*; and it became clear at once that Scott was outdistanced. His younger rival, whatever the defects of his poems, was better able to excite a thrilling interest in "strange fits of passion." By comparison Scott seemed pale. But he had tasted blood, in the form of popular success, and was already counting heavily on the money which it had appeared he could earn from writing. Hence he determined not to be thrust aside without a struggle. As early as 1805 he had written a couple of chapters of an attempt at a novel, and several years later he had again been fiddling with it, but had been discouraged by friends who thought it dull. He now pulled out the manuscript and began to work in earnest. The result was *Waverley*, which was published anonymously in 1814. It is a romantic tale centered about the Stuart rebellion of 1745.

The book's success was instantaneous, and left no room for doubt that in the novel Scott had found a better medium for his genius than he had had in the metrical romance. From this first triumph he went on to produce *Guy Mannering* (1815), *The Antiquary* (1816), *The Heart of Midlothian* (1818), *Ivanhoe* (1820), *Kenilworth* (1821), and in all some twenty novels between 1814 and 1825. These were identified on their title-pages only as "by the author of *Waverley*"; and "the Great Unknown," as he came to be called, did not publicly admit his authorship until 1827.

The Great Unknown was amused by mystification, but he had other reasons for anonymity. It gave him a valuable freedom. He was forced to write rapidly for money because, in spite of the great success of his novels, his expenses continued to outrun his income, and he was always gambling on his future capacity to earn still more. He did not want to cheapen his name, or appear to be a mere publisher's hack, and he was almost certainly right in thinking that the public would absorb more books by the Great Unknown than they would have welcomed under the name of Walter Scott, antiquarian, poet, and Clerk of Session of Edinburgh. The fact, too, that he was a responsible officer of a law court had something to do with the matter. It was not beneath the position he held to appear as a critic or a poet, but when *Waverley* appeared, novel-writing was an undignified, if not disreputable, kind of activity.

The art of prose fiction had had a bad name at the beginning of the eighteenth century. Defoe had smuggled his tales of adventure into the homes of decent people on the pretense that they were edifying histories. Richardson towards the middle of the century had appeared as a grave moralist with a mission to banish false and corrupting romances in favor of sober truth. He, Fielding, Smollett, and even Sterne with all his fantastic whimsies, had together lifted the novel to great heights as a flexible medium for the interpretation of life and character, with a field as broad as the whole of English society. They had won their success as realists, or as portrayers of character and manners. But Fanny Burney's *Evelina* (1778) had been the last considerable achievement of the eighteenth-century school of novelists. And meanwhile popular craving for the marvelous, the sensational, the crudely sentimental thing, had begun to be fed by the new

Gothic romances discussed earlier in this chapter. In the years from about 1790 to about 1810 many trivial and childish, though by no means always innocent, tales of sentiment or terror were devoured by an eager public. They provided coarse food for the imagination, but to some thousands of readers they seemed better than nothing.

What Scott accomplished under the cover of anonymity was an organic union of romance and realism. He used most of the stage properties of the lesser writers whom he followed, and gave readers their fill of strange and colorful pageantry, dangerous escapes, resounding battles, picturesque scenes, magic, and indeed every kind of thrill save that to be got from the presentation of passionate love. But in his hands the setting and trappings of romance ceased to be stage properties. He carried his readers to distant scenes, not to give them a cheap escape from reality, but to drive home the truth that the present is continuous with the past, that society is an organic growth, that people are interdependent and the product in a large measure of environing conditions, and that reverence for tradition is the cornerstone of culture. Scott's own reverence for the past did not save him from inaccuracies, but in general he succeeded admirably in creating true and right pictures of past social conditions and in catching the temper and outlook of the periods he dealt with.

But Scott never lost sight of the fact that whatever serious purposes his revival of the past might serve, he was writing to entertain. He had stories to tell, of which history was only the scene; and exciting stories he told, with moving power, because he saw to it that the actors should be real personalities, capable of engaging the affections. His characters are not puppets who exist for the sake of the action. He had an inexhaustible interest in people, and brought to the creation of his actors a wealth of realistic observation which enabled him to make them live as genuine personalities. In this part of his work he kept his feet firmly on the ground, and we see all his practical shrewdness, his direct confrontation of reality, and his frank delighted acceptance of people as they are and life as it has to be lived.

Scott, then, rehabilitated the novel as a serious form of art, extended its range indefinitely and impressed on the minds of thousands some of the simpler articles of romantic belief. His romanticism consists essentially in his optimistic faith in human nature and in "firm persuasions," and in his attempted projection of an "ideal" world—his own "inner world of dream and memory"—into "the world of facts." This in his novels he did under the disguise of history, and so became the originator of the modern historical novel which flourished for half a century or more after his death, in England, in the United States, and all over Europe; and everywhere it helped to enlarge the field of men's sympathetic comprehension and also to inspire patriotic loyalties founded upon the supposedly heroic past.

## LORD BYRON

Byron, in driving Scott from poetry to prose, was an unconscious benefactor, because, as was said above, Scott's genius did not have full scope in his metrical romances. The younger poet, however, could say everything he had to say in verse of one kind of another, with unfailing verve and superb effect; and presently his fashionable successes in England were followed by international renown. The English lord was accepted everywhere as the classic personification of the new romantic spirit; or rather what was so accepted was his own magnificent, reckless dramatization of himself in the role. He appeared undisguised in *Childe Harold*, and thinly disguised in tales of passion with exotic settings, and in poetic dramas, of which the "satanic" *Manfred* and *Cain* are the most impressive examples. He was well endowed by nature and upbringing for the role, and did his best to live up to it.

Byron's was the role of the proud and noble spirit, who has tasted all the pleasures and glories of life, has found them empty and mankind despicable, and has contemptuously withdrawn himself from society. He remains in the world but not of it. He is an outlaw, self-sentenced to a station *above* the world. He is remorseful over darkly hinted crimes, yet at the same time defiantly scornful of those who venture to condemn him. This seeming contradiction arises from the conviction that though he is guilty of the blackest sin, still, he *is* what he is. Born under a fatal star, he does act consistently his destined part, and is superior in honesty to the weaklings, turncoats, hypocrites, and pious snufflers who band themselves together to set the tone of respectable society. To be disreputable in the eyes of a set of canting "pillars of society" is true glory and true honor. He therefore stands above all social judgment, and is the champion of Liberty. Beyond this point he is not a little confused. Goethe said that when Byron paused to reflect he seemed to be only a child; and in truth he does often appear to be rather a volcanic force of nature than a man capable of reason, and it is impossible to harmonize all the ideals about himself and about his loyalties which he entertained.

In one of the later cantos of *Don Juan*, Byron said that he "was born for opposition" and verily believed that if kings were overthrown he would become "an ultra-royalist in loyalty." It is tempting to make this a key to Byron—to say that romantic liberation simply gave scope to a full-blown contrariness, now impish, now satanic. And without doubt this does explain much in his personal life and in his poetry, yet not the most important things. For Byron, underneath his morbid desire to pluck forbidden fruit, underneath his childish vanity, false heroics, and shallow sentimentalism, did have integrity and a large capacity for right feeling. He had a soul not only of generous kindness, but of sanity.

Scott once referred to his poem *Rokeby* as a "pseudo-romance of pseudo-chivalry." Byron was capable of a similar detachment, could stand off and poke fun at his romantic pseudo-self, and managed in this and other ways to keep a firm hold on objective reality. He was never quite seduced into slavery, whether to a person, to his own dramatization of himself, to a cause, or to some "better world" existing only in the realm of imagination. As a result he grew and matured through experience. And finally, throwing off the disguises with which he had thrilled himself and others, he wrote those satirical masterpieces which constitute his surest claim to immortality—*Beppo*, *The Vision of Judgment*, and *Don Juan*.

## PERCY BYSSHE SHELLEY

Both Byron and his younger contemporary Shelley did nearly all that was humanly possible to justify the worst fears of those who felt that an ordered society, whatever its defects, was a safer basis for civilized life than romantic freedom and individualism. The picture of Shelley drawn by an English critic is not a pretty one: He was "an unfilial son, a professed atheist, unhonored by his school, rejected by his university, an adulterer, and the deserter, if not the murderer of his wife—the avowed enemy of all constituted power, in state, church, and family—advocate, it was reported, of a polygamous and godless Arcadia."

Now of course such a representation is open to question. It is by no means completely true

of Byron that he lived in the conviction that he was right, and the world wrong, but this is strictly and unqualifiedly true of Shelley. And he did not merely talk; he had the courage of his convictions, and attempted to live what he believed, or to believe what he lived. "At the moment of doing a thing," said Mary Shelley, he "always thought himself right." But this is an understatement; he *knew* he was right, and never admitted that he could have been wrong, whatever the consequences of his acts. Such a man, we feel, must have been something more or less than human—he must have been a monster, or a saint. There have been very few, from his day to ours, who could regard him with indifference or could think of him in any middle position between these extremes.

Obviously in Shelley, then, Romanticism reaches a climax, in the sense that we do not find, even in Blake, a stronger inward assurance at work, and that we do not find, even in Byron, a rebellious spirit making so strong an impact on the world. It is true that upon men of his own time Byron made the stronger impression—Byron and Scott being the only romantic writers who won immediate fame. But while Shelley's fame had been of relatively slow growth and his influence more confined than Byron's, or Scott's, he has today apostles who appear to regard him almost as a messiah; and nothing like this is now true of any of the other English romantic writers.

Shelley lives, both because his poetical gifts enabled him to give perfect expression to the lyrical rapture he felt when contemplating the world of his imagination, and, perhaps even more, because his visionary world was a direct outgrowth from social and personal discontents which disturb humanity as deeply today as they did in the late eighteenth century and throughout the nineteenth century. The motive-force which roused Shelley was love. If we ask, not unnaturally, love of what? it appears that Shelley's final answer was Love Itself, just Love. It appeared to him that the real power which controls all things, animate and inanimate, was a universal sympathy, or the principle of Love itself.

Shelley accepted the doctrine of natural goodness and believed human nature capable of perfection. What was needed for progress towards perfection was freedom—freedom to follow our naturally good natures. Hence priests, kings, and indeed all agents of constituted authority were wicked monsters who should be trampled under foot. Here he was inconsistent. He firmly insisted that he was against all violence, even for the sake of free-dom or reform, and desired slow peaceful change. Yet in fact, he was enthusiastic over every armed revolt that occurred in Europe. He was logical and thorough in carrying his demand for personal freedom to the utmost lengths, advocating in effect the abolition of marriage, and also the abolition of poverty. This most desirable change was to be brought about by destroying the existing social system, based on selfishness, and replacing it by one based on brotherly love. Meanwhile, he be-lieved that those in need had a right to any surplus of goods held by others.

Shelley appeals particularly, of course, to youthful enthusiasts who have not yet learned from experience that good intentions will not suffice to reform human nature or the social structure. But by many he has been accepted as a saint of modern humanitarianism because they feel that it is inspiring and heartening to see a man cherishing absolute faith in hu-manity.

At the close of his high-flying, romantic *Defense of Poetry* Shelley exclaimed, "Poets are the unacknowledged legislators of the world," and expressed a revealing wish rather than a truth. But this and similar statements are primarily interesting because they show how he was, in his way, animated by the con-viction which we have already seen at work in Blake, Wordsworth, and Coleridge—the con-viction that the poetic imagination can dis-cover ultimate truth inaccessible to the mere reasoning intellect.

## JOHN KEATS

Keats's life was even briefer than Shelley's, and falls within the span of Shelley's just as Shelley's in turn falls within the span of By-ron's. But his life was not too short for growth and change, and at the time of his death, early in his twenty-sixth year, he was not only discontented with the poetry he had written, but was forming new designs of the highest promise. It is therefore hard to discuss him critically. The critic sees change and growth in the poetry Keats did write, and equally in his letters; and finds that his critical and reflective powers were constantly outrunning his poetical performance. Justice, then, pushes the critic forward, and causes him to qualify what he must say of the poetry by reference to the letters, and to qualify what he must say of the letters by consideration of what Keats would

have achieved, or at any rate would have be-come, had he not died in early manhood.

Nevertheless, whatever Keats was becoming, he did write certain imperishable poems; and those poems had a determining influence upon the course of English poetry during the re-mainder of the nineteenth century.

Keats discovered himself poetically through the excitement he felt when reading Spenser's *Faerie Queene* and Chapman's translation of Homer. He was transported on fairy wings to other worlds; magic casements were opened, through which he saw the glories of chivalry and the gods and goddesses of the ancient heroic age, shining in a light that never was on land or sea. And to his wondering mind the fable of old poets seemed more real than any of the signs or sounds of his own contemporary London. His brain "new-stuffed with triumphs gay of old romance," he bent himself to the study of poetic words and images, impressions of seeing, hearing, feeling, and even smelling; intoxicating himself with their sensuous charm, and in effect losing himself delightedly in golden realms. He began to love words and images for their own sake, with the pure crafts-man's pleasure in the materials of his craft, and he continued his reading with the eye of a craftsman. He went on from Spenser and Chap-man to other Elizabethan writers, and, above all, to Shakespeare. He also read Milton and, from his contemporaries, Wordsworth. He was soaking himself in figurative and sensuous lan-guage, and asking himself what it was to be a poet.

Keats admired particularly in Shakespeare the dramatic imagination which enabled him so to enter into his characters that he seems to lose his own identity and become for the moment now this one, now that one. Keats, however, does not enter into the characters who appear in his own poems, but only into the at-mosphere surrounding them. And even here his range is limited. Distance lent enchantment to his view, and his settings were medieval or Greek, far off enough to permit the free en-trance of magic, of the supernatural, and of nameless graces—far off enough, in a word, to set free an imagination eager for sensuous beauty but able to see it only beyond the hori-zon.

Keats fought shy of committing himself to any new positive view of man's nature or des-tiny because he wanted to keep himself free, disinterested, impartially receptive to sugges-tions of beauty upon which his imagination might work creatively. The consequence was, however, that when he had to find something to say *through* the mythological or other machinery in which he delighted, he was at a loss.

Keats was genuinely concerned over Truth, but it is significant that, in the famous concluding lines of the "Ode on a Grecian Urn" as well as in earlier writings, Beauty always comes first. And, furthermore, the formulas "Beauty must be Truth" and "Beauty is Truth" encouraged Keats to drift into a kind of romanticism which is a retreat from the hard, ugly world of objective fact to a dream-world where the imagination is free to create a species of beauty sufficient unto itself. Such a retreat ends in the view that life is one thing, and art another; and from this view springs the doctrine of art for art's sake. Keats was not alone and not earliest in planting the seeds from which, in England, this doctrine was later to grow. They are clearly present in Blake; and Coleridge, in *Christabel* and "Kubla Khan," gave as much encouragement as Keats to the separation of art and life.

Those who study Keats's letters are convinced that his influence in the nineteenth century rested upon misunderstanding; and they are right to this extent, that he did grow dissatisfied with his work and did feel, at the time of his death, that his name had only been "writ in water." But the misunderstanding for which the nineteenth century is blamed is not really a misunderstanding of his poems as they are. It is something quite different; it is a failure to take into account his changing aims and hopes, and consequently a failure to understand Keats himself. The study of his development is interesting and illuminating. Nevertheless, we today, like men of the last century, remember Keats for what he wrote, and not because he came to feel that his poems betrayed immaturity. Even *Lamia*, moreover, and *Isabella*, *The Eve of St. Agnes*, *La Belle Dame sans Merci*, and *The Eve of St. Mark* are not in the least immature; they are unsurpassed masterpieces of one kind of romantic literature. And the "kind" to which they belong was bound to appear; escape on the wings of imagination is the most obvious of retorts to the tyranny of brute fact.

The trouble with the literature of escape is that it is insubstantial, and that it may easily become trivial, or even unintelligible. Gradually and uncertainly, Keats perceived that he could no longer devote himself to visionary glimpses of the land of faery. Self-knowledge became a knowledge of a division between his own art and his own life. He became conscious of an insufficiency, for the needs of life, in the contemplation of "cold pastorals" or other cold dreams of timeless perfection; and it was this inward conflict which gave vitality to the series of great odes he wrote in 1819.

## ROMANTIC LITERATURE AND THE NATIONAL LIFE

It was said at the beginning of this chapter that though the dominant literature of the early nineteenth century was romantic, the age itself was not. The Romantic writers were a small minority engaged in rebellion, and though several of them gained enormous popularity, none of them had any great immediate effect on the national life or thought. It is, indeed, by no means always true—at any rate not true in any simple or obvious sense—that literature expresses the spirit of the age in which it is written. Of course it always has a relation of some kind to contemporary conditions, but that relation may be, as in this instance, one of reaction and revolt which makes an impression but does not convince. And in the romantic era it is not even true that all of the significant and still living literature of the time is romantic.

## JANE AUSTEN

It is important to recall that Jane Austen wrote her famous novels in the very midst of the romantic age. *Sense and Sensibility*, *Pride and Prejudice*, *Mansfield Park*, *Emma*, *Northanger Abbey*, and *Persuasion* were all published between 1811 and 1818, and Jane Austen was at work on them from about 1795 until within less than a year of her death in 1817. She lived in a small world which was perfectly formed, in the sense that its ways seemed fixed, its life settled, and its people predictable. Its center was the country town, and its inhabitants the provincial and rural gentry. Jane Austen knew this small world, in which she was born and brought up, inside and out. What was more, she liked it thoroughly, just as it was, and saw it just as it was. Her novels are a singularly clear reflection of her own world, constructed with the most discriminating and delicate art. Her characters are minutely and sympathetically observed, and at first sight it might appear that all one gets is observation from the outside—and someone might add, observation of people without much to be discovered inside. But Jane Austen did penetrate within her characters; and it is one of the signs of her genius that she got beyond the portrayal of manners and built up fully rounded persons by showing them as acted upon, and acting upon, one another.

One could carry this description further, but the further one went the more insistent would become the question, How did Jane Austen manage to make the commonplace activities of a small set of very ordinary comfortable people interesting? The answer brings in her reading; for of course she read constantly. The two writers of serious literature who meant most to her were Dr. Johnson and Cowper. Apparently next came Goldsmith and Crabbe, and Scott. The books she read constantly were the latest novels from the circulating library. She read older novels too, particularly Richardson's, Fanny Burney's, and Maria Edgeworth's. Her debt to Fanny Burney is large, and historically she carries on the eighteenth-century tradition of the novel of manners as she received it from *Evelina*. But her direct stimulus came from the short-lived novels of the circulating library. It was these which suggested her way of dealing with the apparently commonplace, if not dull, matter of her own observation, and which consequently give us the answer to our question, How did she make her little country world interesting?

We have noticed that popular fiction was not in good repute at the beginning of the nineteenth century. Thrillers were the order of the day, and in them, as we have seen, readers were transported to imaginary worlds where the most sensational events were continually enacted in an atmosphere of frightful agitation. Jane Austen read these romances with delight because she found them hilariously funny. She did not need the warning which Walter Scott himself addressed to a correspondent, telling her that "the world we actually live in is not that of poetry and romance." She knew what kind of world we actually live in: and in the light of the "thrilling" unrealities of shoddy romance her perceptions of its solid and enduring interest were quickened and heightened and sharpened. She began as a mere girl to write burlesque tales in which she made fun of the absurdities of romantic tales. From this beginning she went on in her mature work to satirize what Scott in a candid moment would have called the pseudo-romantic view of life, with its overwrought emotionalism, its senti-

mentalism, its fanciful medievalism, and its sensationalism. It is this satirical undercurrent which fills her novels with humor, and which gives sharpness, importance, and endless interest to her characters and their lives.

## THE INDUSTRIAL REVOLUTION

For those engaged in historical study Jane Austen has this value as a witness: She may be taken as the accomplished representative of the prevailing temper of her generation. Englishmen by and large in the romantic era felt as they had through most of the eighteenth century, that their country was a good and comfortable place to live in; and they were not torn by romantic discontents. Scott and Byron were, as has been said, the only romantic writers who, following in the wake of the writers of "Gothic" and sentimental romances which have been discussed, achieved widespread popularity among their contemporaries; and they obviously did so because they gratified in a superior way an already existing popular taste for exciting entertainment. The progress of the French Revolution confirmed the average Englishman in his feeling of satisfaction with things as they were, and made him anxious only to keep them as they were.

But the effort to keep steady in a changing world is one thing, and the effort to keep change itself from occurring is another—is, indeed, bound to be wholly unsuccessful. Changes were taking place in England in these years, even more momentous than the long struggle against Napoleon, and a quite new economic and social order which had not been designed or foreseen by anybody was coming into existence. This great internal change is called the Industrial Revolution. It was brought about by the discovery of the steam engine, perfected by the Scotchman, James Watt, in the later years of the eighteenth century. Watt's engine made it possible to use steam power in industry, which brought about mass production of consumable goods in factories, at a great saving in labor, and caused the rapid decay of home industry. Thus England was transformed from an agricultural into an industrial country, and a new era began, not only in English economic and social organization, but also in English thought and literature.

# William Blake

## 1757 - 1827

William Blake was born on 28 November, 1757, in London, where his father, James Blake, kept a hosier's shop. He received an elementary education, but the circumstances of his family made it necessary that he should early learn some trade. His father, perceiving that the boy's tastes ran in that direction, sent him at the age of ten to a teacher of drawing. Four years later he apprenticed him to the engraver Basire, with whom Blake remained until he was twenty. Then for a short time he was a member of the antique class of the Royal Academy, after which he set up as an engraver on his own account. The course of Blake's life was outwardly uneventful. In August, 1782, he married Catherine Boucher, the daughter of a Richmond market-gardener. She was entirely uneducated—when she married she could not even read or write—but she proved a true helpmate to Blake, sustaining him with unshaken devotion throughout his life, and enabling him, despite their poverty, to do his own unrewarded work as artist and poet. In 1800 William Hayley was at work on a biography of his friend the poet Cowper, and he invited Blake to engrave the illustrations for this work. Blake accepted the invitation, and he and his wife removed from London to Felpham, and lived in the country near Hayley for several years. Save for this period, however, Blake's life was passed in London, where he worked in obscurity until his death on 12 August, 1827. His small earnings came chiefly from his work as an engraver, though he had a few friends who purchased his drawings and paintings. Among his more notable achievements were his series of designs for Young's Night Thoughts, for Blair's Grave, for the Book of Job, for Dante's Divine Comedy, and the recently discovered designs for Gray's poems. Blake was, however, a poet as well as an artist, and to this fact we owe the existence of a series of books unique in the history of literature. For he himself published—if "publishing" it can be called—all of his poems save those which remained in manuscript and those in his earliest volume (Poetical Sketches, 1783). He inscribed the text, together with accompanying decorative designs, upon metal plates, to which he then applied acid which ate away the remaining surface. He thus obtained plates, similar in character to modern stereotype plates, from which he printed in the color which was to form the groundwork of the resulting page, and these pages were then tinted by hand, either by himself or by his wife. In this way Blake literally made his own books, and they were singularly beautiful. The process was, of course, both slow and expensive, and buyers were few, so that only a few copies of each of his books were made—copies which have become almost priceless. In this way were produced the two series of lyrics on which Blake's reputation as a poet now chiefly rests, Songs of Innocence (1789) and Songs of Experience (1794), as well as the longer poems, prophetic books, as he called them, in which he more directly expounded his peculiar system of thought in a symbolic language which is so much his own creation as to remain almost unintelligible.

Fortunately one does not need to understand Blake's intricate and obscure symbolism in order to appreciate his shorter lyrics. Yet one should realize that Blake was a confident rebel against all the conventions of organized society. Quiet and blameless as was his outward life, still, in theory he permitted no concessions which might impair complete freedom of thought and action. In the name of freedom he made war alike upon civil law and the rational intellect, believing that the natural impulses of the human heart would lead us to better lives than external compulsion, and that the imagination is a surer guide to truth than reason or common sense. Blake was so confident of the truth of his intuitions that they took on sensible form and appeared to him as visions from the eternal, spiritual world from *which, as he believed, we are more or less cut off by earthly life. "I assert, for myself, that I do not behold the outward creation, and that to me it is hindrance and not action. 'What!' it will be questioned, 'when the sun rises, do you not see a round disk of fire somewhat like a guinea?' Oh! no, no! I see an innumerable company of the heavenly host crying, 'Holy, holy, holy is the Lord God Almighty!' I question not my corporeal eye any more than I would question a window concerning a sight. I look through it, and not with it." Much of Blake's thought, no doubt, is the fruit, developing in an unusually positive personality, of his early acquaintance with the writings of Emanuel Swedenborg and of ideas imbibed in the days when he was associating, in the rooms of the bookseller Johnson, with Tom Paine and others sympathetic to the French Revolution. Blake became, indeed, the embodiment of practically everything that was contradictory to the spirit of the eighteenth century, and so foreshadowed much that was to be characteristic of the romantic movement. As the champion of the imagination against the reason he exclaimed, "To generalize is to be an idiot. To particularize is the great distinction of merit." And again he asserted, "Mere enthusiasm is the all in all." It is little wonder that some, like Southey and Crabb Robinson, thought him mad. Yet the latter wrote, in his Reminiscences: "There is something in the madness of this man which interests me more than the sanity of Lord Byron or Walter Scott!"*

*The best edition of* The Writings of William Blake *is that of Geoffrey Keynes including the complete writings with all the variant readings (London, 1957); several of the illuminated books are available in facsimile editions. Mona Wilson's* Life of Blake *(London, 1948), Bernard Blackstone's* English Blake *(Cambridge, 1949), and H. M. Margoliouth's* Blake *(Oxford, 1951) represent a variety of general approaches; more specialized are Northrop Frye's* Fearful Symmetry *(Princeton, 1947), Mark Shorer's* William Blake: the Politics of Vision *(New York, 1946), and Stanley Gardner's* Infinity on the Anvil *(Oxford, 1954). Useful studies of the philosophy underlying Blake's poetry are J. Foster Damon,* William Blake, His Philosophy and Symbols *(Boston, 1924), and Milton O. Percival,* William Blake's Circle of Destiny *(New York, 1938). Basil de Selincourt's* William Blake *(London, 1909) is still a sound introduction, including appreciative treatment of the poet's artistic work, with many illustrations.*

# To Winter [1]

"O winter! bar thine adamantine doors:
The north is thine; there hast thou built thy dark
Deep-founded habitation. Shake not thy roofs,
Nor bend thy pillars with thine iron car."

He hears me not, but o'er the yawning deep    5
Rides heavy; his storms are unchained, sheathéd
In ribbéd steel; I dare not lift mine eyes,
For he hath reared his scepter o'er the world.

Lo! now the direful monster, whose skin clings
To his strong bones, strides o'er the groaning rocks:    10
He withers all in silence, and in his hand
Unclothes the earth, and freezes up frail life.

He takes his seat upon the cliffs,—the mariner
Cries in vain. Poor little wretch, that deal'st
With storms!—till heaven smiles, and the monster    15
Is driv'n yelling to his caves beneath mount Hecla.[2]

## Song [3]

How sweet I roamed from field to field
And tasted all the summer's pride,
Till I the Prince of Love beheld
Who in the sunny beams did glide!

He showed me lilies for my hair,    5
And blushing roses for my brow;
He led me through his gardens fair
Where all his golden pleasures grow.

With sweet May dews my wings were wet,
And Phœbus fired my vocal rage;    10
He caught me in his silken net,
And shut me in his golden cage.

He loves to sit and hear me sing,
Then, laughing, sports and plays with me;
Then stretches out my golden wing,    15
And mocks my loss of liberty.

## Song

My silks and fine array,
My smiles and languished air,
By love are driv'n away;
And mournful lean Despair
Brings me yew to deck my grave;    5
Such end true lovers have.

[1] This and the four following poems are from *Poetical Sketches*, 1783.
[2] In southwestern Iceland.
[3] This poem is said to have been written before Blake was fourteen.

His face is fair as heav'n
When springing buds unfold;
O why to him was't giv'n
Whose heart is wintry cold?    10
His breast is love's all-worshiped tomb,
Where all love's pilgrims come.

Bring me an ax and spade,
Bring me a winding-sheet;
When I my grave have made    15
Let winds and tempests beat:
Then down I'll lie as cold as clay.
True love doth pass away!

## Mad Song

The wild winds weep,
And the night is a-cold;
Come hither, Sleep,
And my griefs unfold:
But lo! the morning peeps    5
Over the eastern steeps,
And the rustling beds of dawn
The earth do scorn.

Lo! to the vault
Of pavéd heaven,    10
With sorrow fraught
My notes are driven:
They strike the ear of night,
Make weep the eyes of day;
They make mad the roaring winds,    15
And with tempests play.

Like a fiend in a cloud,
With howling woe
After night I do crowd,
And with night will go;    20
I turn my back to the east
From whence comforts have increased;
For light doth seize my brain
With frantic pain.

## To the Muses

Whether on Ida's shady brow,
Or in the chambers of the East,
The chambers of the sun, that now
From ancient melody have ceased;

Whether in Heaven ye wander fair,    5
Or the green corners of the earth,
Or the blue regions of the air
Where the melodious winds have birth;

Whether on crystal rocks ye rove,
Beneath the bosom of the sea    10
Wand'ring in many a coral grove,
Fair Nine, forsaking Poetry!

How have you left the ancient love
That bards of old enjoyed in you!
The languid strings do scarcely move!    15
The sound is forced, the notes are few!

## Song from An Island in the Moon [4]

Hear then the pride and knowledge of a sailor!
His sprit sail, fore sail, main sail, and his mizen.
A poor frail man—God wot! I know none
   frailer,
I know no greater sinner than John Taylor.

## Introduction to Songs of Innocence [5]

Piping down the valleys wild,
Piping songs of pleasant glee,
On a cloud I saw a child,
And he laughing said to me:

"Pipe a song about a Lamb!"    5
So I piped with merry cheer.
"Piper, pipe that song again;"
So I piped: he wept to hear.

"Drop thy pipe, thy happy pipe;
Sing thy songs of happy cheer:"    10
So I sang the same again,
While he wept with joy to hear.

"Piper, sit thee down and write
In a book, that all may read."
So he vanished from my sight,    15
And I plucked a hollow reed,

And I made a rural pen,
And I stained the water clear,
And I wrote my happy songs
Every child may joy to hear.    20

## The Lamb

Little Lamb, who made thee?
  Dost thou know who made thee?
Gave thee life, and bid thee feed,
By the stream and o'er the mead;
Gave thee clothing of delight,    5
Softest clothing, woolly, bright;
Gave thee such a tender voice,
Making all the vales rejoice?
  Little Lamb, who made thee?
  Dost thou know who made thee?    10

  Little Lamb, I'll tell thee,
  Little Lamb, I'll tell thee:
He is calléd by thy name,
For He calls Himself a Lamb,
He is meek, and He is mild;    15
He became a little child.

[4] *An Island in the Moon* is a satirical sketch which
Blake never completed. It was written probably in
1784, or shortly thereafter. It was first printed in
full by E. J. Ellis in *The Real Blake*, 1907.
[5] This and the five following poems are from *Songs
of Innocence*, 1789.

I a child, and thou a lamb,
We are calléd by His name.
  Little Lamb, God bless thee!
  Little Lamb, God bless thee!                20

## Infant Joy

"I have no name:
I am but two days old."
What shall I call thee?
"I happy am,
Joy is my name."                             5
Sweet joy befall thee!

Pretty Joy!
Sweet Joy, but two days old.
Sweet joy I call thee:
Thou dost smile,                             10
I sing the while,
Sweet joy befall thee!

## The Little Black Boy

My mother bore me in the southern wild,
And I am black, but O! my soul is white;
White as an angel is the English child,
But I am black, as if bereaved of light.

My mother taught me underneath a tree,      5
And, sitting down before the heat of day,
She took me on her lap and kisséd me,
And, pointing to the east, began to say:

"Look on the rising sun,—there God does live,
And gives His light, and gives His heat away; 10
And flowers and trees and beasts and men re-
  ceive
Comfort in morning, joy in the noonday.

"And we are put on earth a little space,
That we may learn to bear the beams of love;
And these black bodies and this sunburnt face
Is but a cloud, and like a shady grove.      16

"For when our souls have learned the heat to
  bear,
The cloud will vanish; we shall hear His voice,
Saying: 'Come out from the grove, My love and
  care,
And round My golden tent like lambs rejoice.' "                                   20

Thus did my mother say, and kisséd me;
And thus I say to little English boy.
When I from black and he from white cloud
  free,
And round the tent of God like lambs we joy,

I'll shade him from the heat, till he can bear 25
To lean in joy upon our Father's knee;
And then I'll stand and stroke his silver hair,
And be like him, and he will then love me.

## A Cradle Song

Sweet dreams, form a shade
O'er my lovely infant's head;
Sweet dreams of pleasant streams
By happy, silent, moony beams.

Sweet sleep, with soft down                  5
Weave thy brows an infant crown.
Sweet sleep, Angel mild,
Hover o'er my happy child.

Sweet smiles, in the night
Hover over my delight;                       10
Sweet smiles, mother's smiles,
All the livelong night beguiles.

Sweet moans, dovelike sighs,
Chase not slumber from thy eyes.
Sweet moans, sweeter smiles,                 15
All the dovelike moans beguiles.

Sleep, sleep, happy child,
All creation slept and smiled;
Sleep, sleep, happy sleep,
While o'er thee thy mother weep.             20

Sweet babe, in thy face
Holy image I can trace.
Sweet babe, once like thee,
Thy Maker lay and wept for me,

Wept for me, for thee, for all,              25
When He was an infant small.
Thou His image ever see,
Heavenly face that smiles on thee,

Smiles on thee, on me, on all;
Who became an infant small.                  30
Infant smiles are His own smiles;
Heaven and earth to peace beguiles.

## The Divine Image

To Mercy, Pity, Peace, and Love
All pray in their distress;
And to these virtues of delight
Return their thankfulness.

For Mercy, Pity, Peace, and Love             5
Is God, our Father dear,
And Mercy, Pity, Peace, and Love
Is man, His child and care.

For Mercy has a human heart,
Pity a human face,                           10
And Love, the human form divine,
And Peace, the human dress.

Then every man, of every clime,
That prays in his distress,

Prays to the human form divine, 15
Love, Mercy, Pity, Peace.

And all must love the human form,
In heathen, Turk, or Jew;
Where Mercy, Love, and Pity dwell
There God is dwelling too. 20

## The Fly [6]

Little Fly,
Thy summer's play
My thoughtless hand
Has brushed away.

Am not I 5
A fly like thee?
Or art not thou
A man like me?

For I dance,
And drink, and sing, 10
Till some blind hand
Shall brush my wing.

If thought is life
And strength and breath,
And the want 15
Of thought is death;

Then am I
A happy fly,
If I live
Or if I die. 20

## The Tiger

Tiger! Tiger! burning bright
In the forests of the night,
What immortal hand or eye
Could frame thy fearful symmetry?

In what distant deeps or skies 5
Burnt the fire of thine eyes?
On what wings dare he aspire?
What the hand dare seize the fire?

And what shoulder, and what art,
Could twist the sinews of thy heart? 10
And when thy heart began to beat,
What dread hand? and what dread feet?

What the hammer? what the chain?
In what furnace was thy brain?
What the anvil? what dread grasp 15
Dare its deadly terrors clasp?

When the stars threw down their spears,
And watered heaven with their tears,
Did he smile his work to see?
Did he who made the Lamb make thee? 20

[6] This and the four following poems are from
*Songs of Experience*, 1794.

Tiger! Tiger! burning bright
In the forests of the night,
What immortal hand or eye
Dare frame thy fearful symmetry?

## The Clod and the Pebble

"Love seeketh not itself to please,
Nor for itself hath any care,
But for another gives its ease,
And builds a Heaven in Hell's despair."

So sung a little Clod of Clay, 5
Trodden with the cattle's feet,
But a Pebble of the brook
Warbled out these meters meet:

"Love seeketh only Self to please,
To bind another to its delight, 10
Joys in another's loss of ease,
And builds a Hell in Heaven's despite."

## A Little Boy Lost

"Nought loves another as itself,
Nor venerates another so,
Nor is it possible to Thought
A greater than itself to know:

"And, Father, how can I love you 5
Or any of my brothers more?
I love you like the little bird
That picks up crumbs around the door."

The Priest sat by and heard the child,
In trembling zeal he seized his hair: 10
He led him by his little coat,
And all admired the priestly care.

And standing on the altar high,
"Lo! what a fiend is here," said he,
"One who sets reason up for judge 15
Of our most holy Mystery."

The weeping child could not be heard,
The weeping parents wept in vain;
They stripped him to his little shirt,
And bound him in an iron chain; 20

And burned him in a holy place,
Where many had been burned before:
The weeping parents wept in vain.
Are such things done on Albion's shore?

## Infant Sorrow

My mother groaned, my father wept,
Into the dangerous world I leapt;
Helpless, naked, piping loud,
Like a fiend hid in a cloud.

Struggling in my father's hands, 5
Striving against my swaddling-bands,

Bound and weary, I thought best
To sulk upon my mother's breast.

## Stanzas from *Milton* [7]

And did those feet in ancient time
  Walk upon England's mountains green?
And was the holy Lamb of God
  On England's pleasant pastures seen?

And did the Countenance Divine     5
  Shine forth upon our clouded hills?

[7] *Milton*, one of Blake's "prophetic books," was begun at some time between 1800 and 1803, though the plates from which it was printed were not completed until 1808 or 1809.

And was Jerusalem builded here
  Among these dark Satanic Mills? [8]

Bring me my bow of burning gold!
  Bring me my arrows of desire!     10
Bring me my spear! O clouds, unfold!
  Bring me my chariot of fire!

I will not cease from mental fight,
  Nor shall my sword sleep in my hand,
Till we have built Jerusalem     15
  In England's green and pleasant land.

[8] Either the figurative mills of learning or the real mills of the industrial revolution.

# Robert Burns

## 1759-1796

The parents of Burns both came of yeoman stock. His father began life as a gardener and was later a small farmer, renting his land and toiling hard to wrest from it a bare living for himself and his family. Burns was born in the parish of Alloway, in Ayrshire, Scotland, on 25 January, 1759, in a small clay cottage which his father had built with his own hands. He was the oldest of seven children, all of whom, as fast as they grew sufficiently to do anything useful, had to share the hard, incessant labors of the farm. His father moved to Mount Oliphant in 1766, and then to a somewhat better farm at Lochlie in 1777, where the family remained until the death of the father in 1784. On these farms Burns grew to manhood, toiling like a galley slave, as he said, and yet managing to get the rudiments of an education and to do—for one in his circumstances at least—much reading. In a letter written in 1787 he says, "Though it cost the schoolmaster some thrashings, I made an excellent English scholar; and by the time I was ten or eleven years of age I was a critic in substantives, verbs, and particles. In my infant and boyish days, too, I owe much to an old woman who resided in the family, remarkable for her ignorance, credulity, and superstition. She had, I suppose, the largest collection in the country of tales and songs concerning devils, ghosts, fairies, brownies, witches, warlocks, spunkies, kelpies, elf-candles, dead-lights, wraiths, apparitions, cantraips, giants, enchanted towers, dragons and other trumpery. This cultivated the latent seeds of poetry; but had so strong an effect on my imagination that to this hour, in my nocturnal rambles, I sometimes keep a sharp lookout in suspicious places. . . . The first two books I ever read in private, and which gave me more pleasure than any two books I ever read since, were The Life of Hannibal and The History of Sir William Wallace. . . . What I know of ancient story was gathered from Salmon's and Guthrie's Geographical Grammars; and the ideas I had formed of modern manners of literature and criticism I got from the Spectator. These, with Pope's works, some plays of Shakespeare, Tull and Dickson On Agriculture, the Pantheon, Locke's Essay on the Human Understanding, Stackhouse's History of the Bible, Justice's British Gardener's Directory, Boyle's Lectures, Allan Ramsay's works, Taylor's Scripture Doctrine of Original Sin, A Select Collection of English Songs, and Hervey's Meditations, had formed the whole of my reading [when sixteen years old]. The collection of songs was my vade mecum. I pored over them, driving my cart or walking to labor, song by song, verse by verse, carefully noting the true, tender, or sublime from affectation and fustian. I am convinced I owe to this practice much of my critic-craft, such as it is. . . . The addition of two more authors to my library gave me great pleasure: Sterne and Mackenzie—Tristram Shandy and The Man of Feeling—were my bosom favorites. Poesy was still a darling walk for my mind, but it was only indulged in according to the humor of the hour. I had usually half a dozen or more pieces on hand; I took up one or other, as it suited the momentary tone of the mind, and dismissed the work as it bordered on fatigue. My passions, when once lighted up, raged like so many devils till they got vent in rime; and then the conning over my verses, like a spell, soothed all into quiet."

In 1781 Burns left the farm at Lochlie to try flax-dressing at Irvine. He did not prosper at this, but did learn the bad habits of companions he found in the town. He was a man of turbulent passions and weak will; and if his life was a life of song, he tended from this time more and more to unite with song the other two members of the famous triad. One of his friends at Irvine was a certain Richard Brown, who, said Burns, "was the only man I ever saw who was a greater fool than myself when Woman was the presiding star." After the death of their father in 1784 Burns and his brother Gilbert took Mossgiel farm, several miles from Lochlie. In the same year, too, Burns met Jean Armour, who later bore him a child, and whom he finally married in 1788. Things going badly on the farm, Burns resolved to emigrate to Jamaica; and it was in order to obtain money for his passage that he published a volume of his poems at Kilmarnock in 1786. The edition was soon sold, and its success led him to remain and bring out a second edition at Edinburgh in the following year. Burns was in that city through the winters of 1786–1787 and 1787–1788. There also his poems succeeded, netting him a profit of some £500, and attracting much social attention to himself. The latter was at first pleasing to him, but probably did him more harm than good, as he was disappointed in the hope of getting any substantial help from his new acquaintances and soon discovered that he was merely the object of a temporary curiosity. In 1788 he took a farm at Ellisland—chosen, it has been said, rather with a poet's than a farmer's eye—and settled there with Jean Armour. He found it impossible, however, to make a living from the land, and in 1789 took a position in the excise. In 1791 he gave up the farm and moved to the near-by town of Dumfries. During these years Burns wrote less and less as he drank more and more. He died, wrecked in both health and reputation by his habits, on 21 July, 1796.

Death came to Burns as a friend. His life was ruined, and his work as a poet was done. Principal Shairp has said, "At the basis of all his power lay absolute truthfulness, intense reality, truthfulness to the objects which he saw, truthfulness to himself as the seer of them." This the failures of his life did not prevent, and this, doubtless, is the secret of the permanence of his fame. His intensity and his truthfulness have made him for all time one of the greatest of lyric poets.

The standard edition is The Poetry of Robert Burns, ed. William E. Henley and Thomas F. Henderson (Edinburgh, 1896–1897); this also contains Henley's acute "Essay on the Life, Genius and Achievement of Burns." Burns's letters have been excellently edited by J. DeLancey Ferguson (2 vols., Oxford, 1931). The Life of Robert Burns has been recorded by Catharine Carswell (London, 1930) and by F. B. Snyder (New York, 1932); biographical emphasis is dominant also in DeLancey Ferguson's Pride and Passion: Robert Burns (New York, 1939) and G. F. O. Smith's The Man

Robert Burns (Toronto, 1940). Two well known studies by countrymen of the poet are Thomas Carlyle's "Burns," in vol. II of Critical and Miscellaneous Essays, and Robert Louis Stevenson's "Some Aspects of Robert Burns," in Familiar Studies of Men and Books. Of interpretations written in this century, the most useful is David Daiches' Robert Burns (New York, 1952).

## Mary Morison [1]

O Mary, at thy window be,
　It is the wished, the trysted hour!
Those smiles and glances let me see,
　That make the miser's treasure poor:
How blithely wad I bide the stoure,[2]　　5
　A weary slave frae sun to sun,
Could I the rich reward secure,
　The lovely Mary Morison.

Yestreen,[3] when to the trembling string
　The dance gaed [4] thro' the lighted ha',　10
To thee my fancy took its wing,
　I sat, but neither heard nor saw:
Tho' this was fair, and that was braw,[5]
　And yon the toast of a' the town,
I sighed, and said amang them a',　　15
　"Ye are na Mary Morison."

O Mary, canst thou wreck his peace,
　Wha for thy sake wad gladly die?
Or canst thou break that heart of his,
　Whase only faut is loving thee?　　20
If love for love thou wilt na gie,[6]
　At least be pity to me shown!
A thought ungentle canna be
　The thought o' Mary Morison.

## Epistle to John Lapraik, an Old Scottish Bard [1]

While briers an' woodbines budding green,
An' paitricks scraichin' loud [2] at e'en,
An' morning poussie whiddin' [3] seen,
　　Inspire my Muse,
This freedom, in an unknown frien',　　5
　　I pray excuse.

[1] Written in 1780 or 1781. From a statement by Gilbert Burns it has been inferred (perhaps wrongly) that the subject of this song was Elison Begbie.
[2] Would I bear the struggle.　[3] Last night.
[4] Went.　[5] Fine, handsome.　[6] Not give.
[1] Written in the spring of 1785. Lapraik (1727–1807) was an Ayrshire poet who, until he lost all his means in 1772, possessed an estate near Muirkirk. Burns addressed two other epistles to him, both also written in 1785. The song referred to in the third stanza is Lapraik's When I Upon Thy Bosom Lean.
[2] Partridges calling.　[3] The hare scudding.

On Fasten-een [4] we had a rockin',[5]
To ca' the crack [6] and weave our stockin';
And there was muckle [7] fun and jokin',
    Ye need na doubt;        10
At length we had a hearty yokin' [8]
    At "sang about." [9]

There was ae [10] sang, amang the rest,
Aboon [11] them a' it pleased me best,
That some kind husband had addressed    15
    To some sweet wife:
It thirled [12] the heart-strings thro' the breast,
    A' to the life.

I've scarce heard ought described sae weel,
What gen'rous, manly bosoms feel;        20
Thought I "Can this be Pope, or Steele,
    Or Beattie's wark?"
They tauld me 'twas an odd kind chiel [13]
    About Muirkirk.

It pat me fidgin' fain [14] to heart,    25
And sae about him there I spiered; [15]
Then a' that kenned [16] him round declared
    He had ingine,[17]
That nane excelled it, few cam near't,
    It was sae fine.    30

That, set him to a pint of ale,
An' either douce [18] or merry tale,
Or rimes an' sangs he'd made himsel,
    Or witty catches,[19]
'Tween Inverness and Teviotdale,    35
    He had few matches.

Then up I gat, an' swoor an aith,[20]
Tho' I should pawn my pleugh and graith,[21]
Or die a cadger pownie's [22] death,
    At some dyke-back,[23]    40
A pint an' gill I'd gie them baith
    To hear your crack.[24]

But, first an' foremost, I should tell,
Amaist [25] as soon as I could spell,
I to the crambo-jingle [26] fell;    45
    Tho' rude an' rough,
Yet crooning to a body's sel,
    Does weel eneugh.

I am nae poet, in a sense,
But just a rimer, like, by chance,    50

An' hae to learning nae pretense,
    Yet what the matter?
Whene'er my Muse does on me glance,
    I jingle at her.

Your critic-folk may cock their nose,    55
And say "How can you e'er propose,
You wha ken hardly verse frae prose,
    To mak a sang?"
But, by your leaves, my learned foes,
    Ye're maybe wrang.    60

What's a' your jargon o' your schools.
Your Latin names for horns [27] an' stools;
If honest nature made you fools,
    What sairs [28] your grammars?
Ye'd better ta'en up spades and shools,[29]    65
    Or knappin'-hammers.[30]

A set o' dull conceited hashes [31]
Confuse their brains in college classes!
They gang [32] in stirks,[33] and come out asses,
    Plain truth to speak;    70
An' syne [34] they think to climb Parnassus
    By dint o' Greek!

Gie me ae spark o' nature's fire,
    That's a' the learning I desire;
Then tho' I drudge thro' dub [35] an' mire    75
    At pleugh or cart,
My Muse, though hamely in attire,
    May touch the heart.

O for a spunk [36] o' Allan's [37] glee,
Or Fergusson's,[38] the bauld an' slee,[39]    80
Or bright Lapraik's, my friend to be,
    If I can hit it!
That would be lear [40] eneugh for me,
    If I could get it.

Now, sir, if ye hae friends enow,    85
Tho' real friends, I b'lieve, are few,
Yet, if your catalogue be fou,[41]
    I'se no [42] insist,
But gif ye want ae friend that's true,
    I'm on your list.    90

I winna blaw [43] about mysel,
As ill I like my fauts to tell;
But friends, an' folks that wish me well,
    They sometimes roose [44] me;
Tho' I maun [45] own, as mony still    95
    As far abuse me.

[4] Evening before Lent.    [5] Social meeting.
[6] To have a chat.    [7] Much.    [8] Set-to.
[9] I. e., each in turn sang a song.    [10] One.
[11] Above.    [12] Thrilled.    [13] Chap.
[14] Made me tingle with pleasure.    [15] Asked.
[16] Knew.    [17] Genius.    [18] Sober.
[19] Three-part songs, each sung in turn.
[20] Swore an oath.    [21] Plow and harness.
[22] Peddler's pony's.    [23] Behind a fence.
[24] Talk.    [25] Almost.
[26] Riming (Crambo is a game in which one has to supply a rime to a word given by another).

[27] Ink-horns (?).    [28] Serves.    [29] Shovels.
[30] Hammers for breaking stone.    [31] Fools.
[32] Go.    [33] Young bullocks.    [34] Then.
[35] Puddle.    [36] Spark.
[37] Allan Ramsay (1686–1738).
[38] Robert Ferguson (1750–1774).
[39] The bold and clever.    [40] Learning.
[41] Full.    [42] I'll not.    [43] I will not brag.
[44] Praise.    [45] Must.

There's ae wee faut they whiles [46] lay to me,
I like the lasses—Gude [47] forgie me!
For mony a plack [48] they wheedle frae [49] me,
    At dance or fair;    100
Maybe some ither thing they gie me
    They weel can spare.

But Mauchline [50] race, or Mauchline fair,
I should be proud to meet you there;
We'se gie ae night's discharge to care,    105
    If we forgather,
An' hae a swap [51] o' rimin'-ware
    Wi' ane anither.

The four-gill chap, we'se gar [52] him clatter,
An' kirsen [53] him wi' reekin [54] water;    110
Syne we'll sit down an' tak our whitter,[55]
    To cheer our heart;
An' faith, we'se be acquainted better
    Before we part.

Awa, ye selfish warly [56] race,    115
Wha think that havins,[57] sense, an' grace,
E'en love an' friendship, should give place
    To catch-the-plack! [58]
I dinna [59] like to see your face,
    Nor hear your crack.    120

But ye whom social pleasure charms,
Whose hearts the tide of kindness warms
Who hold your being on the terms,
    "Each aid the others,"
Come to my bowl, come to my arms,    125
    My friends, my brothers!

But to conclude my lang epistle,
As my auld pen's worn to the gristle;
Twa lines frae you wad gar me fissle,[60]
    Who am, most fervent,    130
While I can either sing, or whistle,
    Your friend and servant.

# To a Louse [1]

### On Seeing One on a Lady's Bonnet at Church

Ha! wh'are ye gaun, ye crowlin' ferlie! [2]
Your impudence protects you sairly: [3]
I canna say but ye strunt [4] rarely,
    Owre gauze and lace;

Tho' faith! I fear ye dine but sparely    5
    On sic a place.

Ye ugly, creepin', blastit wonner,[5]
Detested, shunned by saunt an' sinner!
How dare ye set your fit [6] upon her,
    Sae fine a lady?    10
Gae somewhere else, and seek your dinner
    On some poor body.

Swith,[7] in some beggar's haffet squattle; [8]
There ye may creep, and sprawl, and sprattle [9]
Wi'ither kindred jumping cattle,    15
    In shoals and nations;
Where horn nor bane [10] ne'er dare unsettle
    Your thick plantations.

Now haud [11] ye there, ye're out o' sight,
Below the fatt'rels,[12] snug an' tight;    20
Na, faith ye yet! ye'll no be right
    Till ye've got on it,
The very tapmost tow'ring height
    O' Miss's bonnet.

My sooth! right bauld ye set your nose out,    25
As plump and gray as onie grozet; [13]
O for some rank mercurial rozet,[14]
    Or fell red smeddum! [15]
I'd gie you sic a hearty dose o't,
    Wad dress your droddum! [16]    30

I wad na been surprised to spy
You on an auld wife's flannen toy; [17]
Or aiblins [18] some bit duddie [19] boy,
    On's wyliecoat; [20]
But Miss's fine Lunardi! [21] fie,    35
    How daur ye do't?

O Jenny, dinna toss your head,
An' set your beauties a' abread! [22]
Ye little ken what curséd speed
    The blastie's makin'! [23]    40
Thae [24] winks and finger-ends, I dread,
    Are notice takin'!

O wad some Pow'r the giftie [25] gie us
To see oursels as others see us!
It wad frae mony a blunder free us,    45
    And foolish notion:
What airs in dress an' gait wad lea'e us,
    And e'en devotion!

---

[46] Sometimes.    [47] God.
[48] Scotch coin of small value.    [49] From.
[50] This town is not far from Mossgiel Farm. It is the town where Burns married Jean Armour.
[51] An exchange.
[52] The four-gill cup, we'll make.    [53] Christen.
[54] Steaming.    [55] Draught.    [56] Worldly.
[57] Manners.    [58] The hunt for coin.
[59] Do not.    [60] Make me tingle.
[1] Written in 1786.    [2] Crawling wonder.
[3] Greatly.    [4] Strut.

[5] Blasted wonder.    [6] Foot.
[7] Quick, i. e., "Off with you!"
[8] Temples sprawl.    [9] Struggle.
[10] Comb nor poison.    [11] Hold.
[12] Ribbon-ends.    [13] Gooseberry.    [14] Rosin.
[15] Powder.    [16] Breech.
[17] Flannel head-dress.    [18] Maybe.
[19] Small ragged.    [20] Flannel vest.
[21] Bonnet, named after Lunardi, an aeronaut.
[22] Abroad.    [23] The blasted creature is making.
[24] Those.    [25] Small gift.

# To a Mouse [1]

## On Turning Her Up in Her Nest with the Plow

Wee, sleekit,[2] cow'rin', tim'rous beastie,
O what a panic's in thy breastie!
Thou need na start awa sae hasty,
    Wi' bickering brattle! [3]
I wad be laith [4] to rin an' chase thee   5
    Wi' murd'ring pattle! [5]

I'm truly sorry man's dominion
Has broken nature's social union,
An' justifies that ill opinion
    Which makes thee startle   10
At me, thy poor earth-born companion,
    An' fellow-mortal!

I doubt na, whyles,[6] but thou may thieve;
What then? poor beastie, thou maun live!
A daimen-icker in a thrave [7]   15
    'S a sma' request:
I'll get a blessin' wi' the lave,[8]
    And never miss't!

Thy wee bit housie, too, in ruin!
Its silly wa's the win's are strewin'!   20
An' naething, now, to big [9] a new ane,
    O' foggage green! [10]
An' bleak December's winds ensuin',
    Baith snell [11] an' keen!

Thou saw the fields laid bare and waste,   25
An' weary winter comin' fast,
An' cozie here, beneath the blast,
    Thou thought to dwell,
Till crash! the cruel coulter [12] past
    Out-thro' thy cell.   30

That wee bit heap o' leaves an' stibble
Has cost thee mony a weary nibble!
Now thou's turned out, for a' thy trouble,
    But house or hald,[13]
To thole [14] the winter's sleety dribble,   35
    An' cranreuch [15] cauld!

But, Mousie, thou art no thy lane,[16]
In proving foresight may be vain:
The best laid schemes o' mice an' men
    Gang aft a-gley,[17]   40
An' lea'e us nought but grief an' pain
    For promised joy.

[1] Written in November, 1785.   [2] Sleek.
[3] Hurrying scamper.   [4] Loath.
[5] Plow-spade.   [6] Sometimes.
[7] An odd ear in 24 sheaves.
[8] With what's left.   [9] Build.
[10] Coarse grass.   [11] Both bitter.
[12] Cutter on plow to cut the sward.
[13] Without house or abode.   [14] Endure.
[15] Hoar-frost.   [16] Not alone.
[17] Go often astray.

Still thou art blest compared wi' me!
The present only toucheth thee:
But oh! I backward cast my e'e   45
    On prospects drear!
An' forward tho' I canna see,
    I guess an' fear!

# To a Mountain Daisy [1]

## On Turning One Down with the Plow

Wee modest crimson-tippéd flow'r,
Thou's met me in an evil hour;
For I maun crush amang the stoure [2]
    Thy slender stem:
To spare thee now is past my pow'r,   5
    Thou bonnie gem.

Alas! it's no thy neibor sweet,
The bonnie lark, companion meet,
Bending thee 'mang the dewy weet
    Wi' spreckled breast,   10
When upward springing, blithe, to greet
    The purpling east.

Cauld blew the bitter-biting north
Upon thy early humble birth;
Yet cheerfully thou glinted forth   15
    Amid the storm,
Scarce reared above the parent-earth
    Thy tender form.

The flaunting flow'rs our gardens yield
High shelt'ring woods and wa's [3] maun shield,
But thou, beneath the random bield [4]   21
    O' clod or stane,
Adorns the histie stibble-field,[5]
    Unseen, alane.

There, in thy scanty mantle clad,   25
Thy snawy bosom sun-ward spread,
Thou lifts thy unassuming head
    In humble guise;
But now the share uptears thy bed,
    And low thou lies!   30

Such is the fate of artless maid,
Sweet flow'ret of the rural shade,
By love's simplicity betrayed,
    And guileless trust,
Till she like thee, all soiled, is laid   35
    Low i' the dust.

Such is the fate of simple bard,
On life's rough ocean luckless starred:
Unskillful he to note the card
    Of prudent lore,   40
Till billows rage, and gales blow hard,
    And whelm him o'er!

[1] Written in April, 1786.   [2] Dust.
[3] Walls.   [4] Shelter.   [5] Bare stubble-field.

Such fate to suffering worth is giv'n,
Who long with wants and woes has striv'n,
By human pride or cunning driv'n　　45
　　To mis'ry's brink,
Till wrenched of ev'ry stay but Heav'n,
　　He, ruined, sink!

E'en thou who mourn'st the Daisy's fate,
That fate is thine—no distant date;　　50
Stern Ruin's plowshare drives elate
　　Full on thy bloom,
Till crushed beneath the furrow's weight
　　Shall be thy doom!

## The Cotter's Saturday Night [1]

My loved, my honored, much respected friend!
　　No mercenary bard his homage pays:
With honest pride I scorn each selfish end,
　　My dearest meed a friend's esteem and
　　praise:
To you I sing, in simple Scottish lays,　　5
The lowly train in life's sequestered scene;
　　The native feelings strong, the guileless
　　ways;
What Aiken in a cottage would have been—
Ah! tho' his worth unknown, far happier there,
　　I ween.

November chill blaws loud wi' angry sough; [2] [10]
　　The short'ning winter-day is near a close;
The miry beasts retreating frae the pleugh;
　　The black'ning trains o' craws [3] to their re-
　　pose:
The toil-worn Cotter [4] frae his labor goes,
This night his weekly moil is at an end,　　15
　　Collects his spades, his mattocks, and his
　　hoes,
Hoping the morn in ease and rest to spend,
And weary, o'er the moor, his course does
　　hameward bend.

At length his lonely cot appears in view,
　　Beneath the shelter of an agéd tree;　　20
Th' expectant wee-things, toddlin', stacher [5]
　　through
　　To meet their Dad, wi' flichterin' [6] noise an'
　　glee.
His wee bit ingle, [7] blinkin bonnilie, [8]
His clean hearth-stane, his thrifty wifie's smile,

The lisping infant prattling on his knee,　　25
Does a' his weary kiaugh [9] and care beguile,
An' makes him quite forget his labor an' his
　　toil.

Belyve, [10] the elder bairns [11] come drapping in,
　　At service out, amang the farmers roun';
Some ca' [12] the pleugh, some herd, some tentie
　　rin [13]　　30
　　A cannie [14] errand to a neibor town: [15]
Their eldest hope, their Jenny, woman-grown,
In youthfu' bloom, love sparkling in her e'e,
　　Comes hame, perhaps to shew a braw [16] new
　　gown,
Or deposite her sair-won penny-fee, [17]　　35
To help her parents dear, if they in hardship be.

With joy unfeigned brothers and sisters meet,
　　An' each for other's weelfare kindly spiers: [18]
The social hours, swift-winged, unnoticed fleet;
　　Each tells the uncos [19] that he sees or hears;
The parents, partial, eye their hopeful
　　years;　　41
Anticipation forward points the view.
　　The mother, wi' her needle an' her sheers,
Gars auld claes look amaist [20] as weel's the new;
The father mixes a' wi' admonition due.　　45

Their master's an' their mistress's command,
　　The younkers a' are warnéd to obey;
An' mind their labors wi' an eydent [21] hand,
　　An' ne'er, tho' out o' sight, to jauk [22] or play:
"And O! be sure to fear the Lord alway,　　50
An' mind your duty, duly, morn an' night!
　　Lest in temptation's path ye gang astray,
Implore His counsel and assisting might:
They never sought in vain that sought the Lord
　　aright!"

But hark! a rap comes gently to the door;　　55
　　Jenny, wha kens the meaning o' the same,
Tells how a neibor lad cam o'er the moor,
　　To do some errands, and convoy her hame.
The wily mother sees the conscious flame
Sparkle in Jenny's e'e, and flush her cheek;　　60
　　Wi' heart-struck anxious care, inquires his
　　name,
While Jenny hafflins [23] is afraid to speak;
Weel pleased the mother hears it's nae wild
　　worthless rake.

Wi' kindly welcome, Jenny brings him ben; [24]
　　A strappin' youth; he takes the mother's eye;
Blithe Jenny sees the visit's no ill ta'en;　　66
　　The father cracks [25] of horses, pleughs, and
　　kye. [26]

---

[1] Written in November, 1785, or shortly thereafter. Burns used as a motto for this poem a stanza
from Gray's *Elegy* ("Let not Ambition mock their
useful toil," etc.), and addressed it to Robert Aiken
(1739–1807), an Ayrshire solicitor. Aiken subscribed
for 105 copies of the Kilmarnock edition of Burns's
poems. The Spenserian stanza Burns borrowed, not
from Spenser, whom he had not yet read at this
time, but from Beattie, Shenstone, and Thomson.
　[2] Wail.　　　　[3] Crows.
　[4] Cottager, peasant occupying a small holding.
　[5] Totter.　　[6] Fluttering.　[7] Fire-place.
[8] Shining prettily.

[9] Worry.　　　　[10] Soon.　　　[11] Children.
[12] Drive.　　　[13] Heedful run.　　[14] Quiet.
[15] Farm-house, with its surrounding buildings.
[16] Fine.　　[17] Hard-earned wages.　　[18] Asks.
[19] Strange things.
[20] Makes old clothes look almost.　　[21] Diligent.
[22] Trifle.　　[23] Partly.　　[24] In.
[25] Talks.　　[26] Cows.

The youngster's artless heart o'erflows wi'
    joy,
But blate and laithfu',[27] scarce can weel be-
    have;
    The mother, wi' a woman's wiles, can spy [70]
What makes the youth sae bashfu' an' sae
    grave;
Weel-pleased to think her bairn's respected like
    the lave.[28]

O happy love! where love like this is found;
    O heart-felt raptures! bliss beyond compare!
I've pacéd much this weary mortal round, [75]
    And sage experience bids me this declare—
    "If Heaven a draught of heavenly pleasure
    spare,
One cordial in this melancholy vale,
'Tis when a youthful, loving, modest pair
In other's arms breathe out the tender tale, [80]
Beneath the milk-white thorn that scents the
    evening gale."

Is there, in human form, that bears a heart—
    A wretch, a villain, lost to love and truth—
That can, with studied, sly, ensnaring art,
    Betray sweet Jenny's unsuspecting youth? [85]
    Curse on his perjured arts, dissembling
    smooth!
Are honor, virtue, conscience, all exiled?
    Is there no pity, no relenting ruth,
Points to the parents fondling o'er their child?
Then paints the ruined maid, and their distrac-
    tion wild? [90]

But now the supper crowns their simple board,
    The halesome parritch,[29] chief of Scotia's
    food:
The sowpe [30] their only hawkie [31] does afford,
    That 'yont the hallan [32] snugly chows her
    cood;
    The dame brings forth in complimental
    mood, [95]
To grace the lad, her weel-hain'd kebbuck,
    fell; [33]
And aft he's pressed, and aft he ca's it good;
The frugal wifie, garrulous, will tell
How 'twas a towmond [34] auld sin' lint was i'
    the bell.[35]

The cheerfu' supper done, wi' serious face [100]
    They round the ingle form a circle wide;
The sire turns o'er, wi' patriarchal grace,
    The big ha'-Bible,[36] ance his father's pride:
    His bonnet rev'rently is laid aside,

His lyart haffets [37] wearing thin an' bare; [105]
    Those strains that once did sweet in Zion
    glide—
He wales [38] a portion with judicious care,
And "Let us worship God!" he says with sol-
    emn air.

They chant their artless notes in simple guise;
    They tune their hearts, by far the noblest
    aim: [110]
Perhaps *Dundee's* wild warbling measures rise,
    Or plaintive *Martyrs*, worthy of the name;
    Or noble *Elgin* [39] beets [40] the heav'nward
    flame,
The sweetest far of Scotia's holy lays:
    Compared with these, Italian trills are tame;
The tickled ears no heartfelt raptures raise; [116]
Nae unison hae they with our Creator's praise.

The priest-like father reads the sacred page,
    How Abram was the friend of God on high;
Or Moses bade eternal warfare wage [120]
    With Amalek's ungracious progeny;
    Or how the royal bard [41] did groaning lie
Beneath the stroke of Heaven's avenging ire;
    Or Job's pathetic plaint, and wailing cry;
Or rapt Isaiah's wild seraphic fire; [125]
Or other holy seers that tune the sacred lyre.

Perhaps the Christian volume is the theme,
    How guiltless blood for guilty man was shed;
How He who bore in Heaven the second name
    Had not on earth whereon to lay His head;
    How His first followers and servants sped; [131]
The precepts sage they wrote to many a land:
    How he,[42] who lone in Patmos banishéd,
Saw in the sun a mighty angel stand,
And heard great Bab'lon's doom pronounced
    by Heaven's command. [135]

Then kneeling down to Heaven's Eternal King
    The saint, the father, and the husband prays:
Hope "springs exulting on triumphant wing" [43]
    That thus they all shall meet in future days:
    There ever bask in uncreated rays, [140]
No more to sigh, or shed the bitter tear,
    Together hymning their Creator's praise,
In such society, yet still more dear;
While circling Time moves round in an eternal
    sphere.

Compared with this, how poor Religion's pride,
    In all the pomp of method and of art, [146]
When men display to congregations wide
    Devotion's every grace, except the heart!
    The Power, incensed, the pageant will de-
    sert,
The pompous strain, the sacerdotal stole; [150]
    But haply, in some cottage far apart,

---

[27] Shy and bashful.      [28] Rest.
[29] Wholesome porridge.      [30] Milk.
[31] Cow.      [32] Beyond the wall.
[33] Her well-saved cheese, ripe.
[34] Twelve-month.      [35] Since flax was in flower.
[36] Hall-Bible ("So called from its original use in
the noble's hall, wherein the whole household assembled for religious services."—Henley and Henderson).

[37] Gray side-locks.      [38] Chooses.
[39] All sacred melodies.      [40] Fans.
[41] King David.      [42] John.
[43] Pope, *Windsor Forest*, l. 112, inexactly quoted.

May hear, well pleased, the language of the
　　soul;
And in His Book of Life the inmates poor en-
　　roll.

Then homeward all take off their several way;
　　The youngling cottagers retire to rest: 155
The parent-pair their secret homage pay,
　　And proffer up to Heav'n the warm request,
　　That He who stills the raven's clamorous
　　　　nest,
And decks the lily fair in flowery pride,
　　Would, in the way His wisdom sees the best,
For them and for their little ones provide; 161
　　But chiefly in their hearts with grace divine
　　　　preside.

From scenes like these old Scotia's grandeur
　　springs,
　　That makes her loved at home, revered
　　　　abroad:
Princes and lords are but the breath of kings,
　　"An honest man's the noblest work of
　　　　God;" 44　　　　　166
　　And certes, in fair virtue's heavenly road,
The cottage leaves the palace far behind;
　　What is a lordling's pomp? a cumbrous load,
Disguising oft the wretch of human kind, 170
Studied in arts of hell, in wickedness refined!

O Scotia! my dear, my native soil!
　　For whom my warmest wish to Heaven is
　　　　sent!
Long may thy hardy sons of rustic toil
　　Be blest with health, and peace, and sweet
　　　　content! 175
　　And O may Heaven their simple lives pre-
　　　　vent
From luxury's contagion, weak and vile;
　　Then, howe'er crowns and coronets be rent,
A virtuous populace may rise the while,
And stand a wall of fire around their much-
　　loved isle. 180

O Thou! who poured the patriotic tide
　　That streamed thro' Wallace's 45 undaunted
　　　　heart,
Who dared to nobly stem tyrannic pride,
　　Or nobly die—the second glorious part,
　　(The patriot's God, peculiarly thou art, 185
His friend, inspirer, guardian, and reward!)
　　O never, never, Scotia's realm desert;
But still the patriot, and the patriot-bard,
In bright succession raise, her ornament and
　　guard!

44 Pope, *Essay on Man*, Epistle IV, 1. 248.
45 William Wallace (1274?–1305), the Scottish
national hero. Burns wrote in a letter: "The story
of Wallace poured a Scottish prejudice into my
veins which will boil along there till the floodgates
of life shut in eternal rest."

# Address to the Deil [1]

O Thou! whatever title suit thee,
Auld Hornie, Satan, Nick, or Clootie,[2]
Wha in yon cavern grim an' sootie,
　　　　Closed under hatches,
Spairges [3] about the brunstane cootie,[4] 5
　　　　To scaud [5] poor wretches!

Hear me, auld Hangie,[6] for a wee,[7]
An' let poor damnéd bodies be;
I'm sure sma' pleasure it can gie,
　　　　E'en to a deil, 10
To skelp [8] an' scaud poor dogs like me,
　　　　An' hear us squeal!

Great is thy pow'r, an' great thy fame:
Far kenned an' noted is thy name;
An', tho' yon lowin heugh's [9] thy hame, 15
　　　　Thou travels far;
An' faith! thou's neither lag [10] nor lame,
　　　　Nor blate nor scaur.[11]

Whyles [12] rangin' like a roarin' lion
For prey, a' holes an' corners tryin'; 20
Whyles on the strong-winged tempest flyin',
　　　　Tirlin' the kirks; [13]
Whyles, in the human bosom pryin',
　　　　Unseen thou lurks.

I've heard my reverend grannie say, 25
In lanely glens ye like to stray;
Or, where auld ruined castles gray
　　　　Nod to the moon,
Ye fright the nightly wand'rer's way,
　　　　Wi' eldritch croon.[14] 30

When twilight did my grannie summon
To say her pray'rs, douce,[15] honest woman!
Aft yont [16] the dyke she's heard you bum-
　　min',[17]
　　　　Wi' eerie drone; [18]
Or, rustlin', thro' the boortrees [19] comin', 35
　　　　Wi' heavy groan.

Ae dreary windy winter night
The stars shot down wi' sklentin' [20] light,

1 Written at Mossgiel towards the end of 1785.
Burns used for a motto 11. 128–9 of *Paradise Lost*,
Bk. I:
　　"O Prince, O Chief of many thronéd Powers
　　That led the embattled Seraphim to war."
2 Little hoof.　　　　　3 Splashes.
4 Brimstone tub.　　　　5 Scald.
6 Old hangman.　　　　7 For a minute.
8 Spank.　　　　　　　9 Flaming hollow.
10 Backward.　　　　11 Not bashful nor timid.
12 Sometimes.　　　　13 Uncovering the churches.
14 Hideous groan.　　15 Grave.　　16 Beyond.
17 Humming.　　　　18 With unearthly sound.
19 Elder bushes.　　　20 Slanting.

Wi' you mysel I gat a fright
    Ayont the lough; [21]    40
Ye like a rash-buss [22] stood in sight
    Wi' waving sough. [23]

The cudgel in my nieve [24] did shake,
Each bristled hair stood like a stake,
When wi' an eldritch, stoor [25] "quaick,
    quaick,"    45
    Amang the springs,
Awa ye squattered like a drake
    On whistlin' wings.

Let warlocks [26] grim, an' withered hags,
Tell how wi' you on ragweed nags [27]    50
They skim the muirs, [28] an' dizzy crags
    Wi' wicked speed;
And in kirk-yards renew their leagues
    Owre howkit [29] dead.

Thence country wives, wi' toil an' pain,    55
May plunge an' plunge the kirn [30] in vain;
For oh! the yellow treasure's taen
    By witchin' skill;
An' dawtit twal-pint Hawkie's gane
    As yell's the bill. [31]    60

Thence mystic knots mak great abuse
On young guidmen, [32] fond, keen, an' crouse; [33]
When the best wark-lume [34] i' the house,
    By cantrip [35] wit,
Is instant made no worth a louse,    65
    Just at the bit. [36]

When thowes [37] dissolve the snawy hoord,
An' float the jinglin' icy-boord, [38]
Then water-kelpies [39] haunt the foord,
    By your direction,    70
An' 'nighted trav'lers are allured
    To their destruction.

An' aft your moss-traversing spunkies [40]
Decoy the wight that late an' drunk is:
The bleezin, [41] curst, mischievous monkies    75
    Delude his eyes,
Till in some miry slough he sunk is,
    Ne'er mair to rise.

When masons' mystic word an' grip
In storms an' tempests raise you up,    80

[21] Beyond the pond.    [22] Bush of rushes.
[23] Moan.    [24] Fist.
[25] With an hideous, harsh.    [26] Wizards.
[27] Ragwort stems;—the witch's steed, more usually a broomstick.
[28] Moors.    [29] Over dug-up.    [30] Churn.
[31] And the petted twelve-pint cow has gone as dry as the bull. (A Scottish pint is rather more than a quart.)
[32] Husbands.    [33] Bold.    [34] Tool.
[35] Magic.    [36] Just when most needed.
[37] Thaws.    [38] Surface of ice.
[39] Water-spirits, usually in the form of horses.
[40] Bog-traversing will-o'-the-wisps.    [41] Blazing.

Some cock or cat your rage maun stop, [42]
    Or, strange to tell!
The youngest brither ye wad whip
    Aff straught to hell.

Lang syne, [43] in Eden's bonnie yard,    85
When youthfu' lovers first were paired,
And all the soul of love they shared,
    The raptured hour,
Sweet on the fragrant flow'ry swaird,
    In shady bow'r;    90

Then you, ye auld snick-drawing [44] dog!
Ye cam to Paradise incog,
An' played on man a cursèd brogue, [45]
    (Black be you fa'! [46])
An' gied the infant warld a shog, [47]    95
    'Maist ruined a'.

D'ye mind that day, when in a bizz, [48]
Wi' reekit [49] duds, an' reestit gizz, [50]
Ye did present your smoutie [51] phiz
    'Mang better folk,    100
An' sklented [52] on the man of Uz [53]
    Your spitefu' joke?

An' how ye gat him i' your thrall,
An' brak him out o' house an' hal',
While scabs an' blotches did him gall    105
    Wi' bitter claw,
An' lows'd [54] his ill-tongued wicked scawl, [55]
    Was warst ava? [56]

But a' your doings to rehearse,
Your wily snares an' fechtin' [57] fierce,    110
Sin' that day Michael did you pierce,
    Down to this time,
Wad ding a' Lallan tongue, or Erse, [58]
    In prose or rime.

An' now, auld Cloots, I ken ye're thinkin',    115
A certain Bardie's rantin', drinkin',
Some luckless hour will send him linkin'[59]
    To your black pit;
But faith! he'll turn a corner jinkin', [60]
    An' cheat you yet.    120

But fare you weel, auld Nickie-ben!
O wad ye tak a thought an' men'!
Ye aiblins [61] might—I dinna ken—
    Still hae a stake: [62]
I'm wae [63] to think upo' yon den,    125
    E'en for your sake!

[42] I. e., by being offered as a sacrifice.
[43] Long since.    [44] Intruding.    [45] Trick.
[46] Lot.    [47] Shock.    [48] Bustling haste.
[49] Smoky.    [50] Scorched wig.    [51] Smutty.
[52] Squinted.    [53] Job.    [54] Loosed.
[55] Scold.    [56] Of all.    [57] Fighting.
[58] Would surpass a Lowland tongue or Gaelic.
[59] Hurrying.    [60] Dodging.    [61] Perhaps.
[62] Have something to gain.    [63] Sad.

## A Bard's Epitaph [1]

Is there a whim-inspiréd fool,
Owre fast for thought, owre hot for rule,
Owre blate [2] to seek, owre proud to snool,[3]
    Let him draw near;
And owre this grassy heap sing dool,[4]    5
    And drap a tear.

Is there a bard of rustic song,
Who, noteless, steals the crowds among,
That weekly this aréa throng,
    O, pass not by!    10
But, with a frater-feeling strong,
    Here heave a sigh.

Is there a man whose judgment clear,
Can others teach the course to steer,
Yet runs, himself, life's mad career,    15
    Wild as the wave;
Here pause—and, thro' the starting tear,
    Survey this grave.

The poor inhabitant below
Was quick to learn and wise to know,    20
And keenly felt the friendly glow,
    And softer flame;
But thoughtless follies laid him low,
    And stained his name!

Reader, attend! whether thy soul    25
Soars fancy flights beyond the pole,
Or darkling grubs this earthly hole,
    In low pursuit;
Know prudent cautious self-control
    Is wisdom's root.

## Address to the Unco Guid,[1] or the Rigidly Righteous [2]

    My son, these maxims make a rule,
      And lump them aye thegither:
    The rigid righteous is a fool,
    The rigid wise anither:
    The cleanest corn that e'er was dight,[3]
    May hae some pyles o' caff in,[4]
    So ne'er a fellow-creature slight
    For random fits o' daffin.[5]
        —Solomon (Eccles., 7:16).

O ye wha are sae guid yoursel,
    Sae pious and sae holy,
Ye've nought to do but mark and tell
    Your neibor's fauts and folly!
Whase life is like a weel-gaun [6] mill,    5
    Supplied wi' store o' water:
The heapéd happer's [7] ebbing still,
    And still the clap [8] plays clatter:

[1] Written in 1786.    [2] Modest.
[3] Cringe.    [4] Woe.
[1] Uncommonly good.    [2] Written in 1786.
[3] Winnowed.    [4] Grains of chaff in it.
[5] Larking.    [6] Well-going.
[7] Hopper.    [8] Clapper.

Hear me, ye venerable core,[9]
    As counsel for poor mortals,    10
That frequent pass douce [10] Wisdom's door
    For glaikit [11] Folly's portals;
I, for their thoughtless careless sakes,
    Would here propone [12] defenses,—
Their donsie [13] tricks, their black mistakes,    15
    Their failings and mischances.

Ye see your state wi' theirs compared,
    And shudder at the niffer; [14]
But cast a moment's fair regard—
    What maks the mighty differ?    20
Discount what scant occasion gave,
    That purity ye pride in,
And (what's aft mair than a' the lave [15])
    Your better art o' hidin'.

Think, when your castigated pulse    25
    Gies now and then a wallop,
What ragings must his veins convulse,
    That still eternal gallop!
Wi' wind and tide fair i' your tail,
    Right on ye scud your sea-way;    30
But in the teeth o' baith to sail,
    It makes an unco leeway.

See Social Life and Glee sit down,
    All joyous and unthinking,
Till, quite transmogrified,[16] they're grown    35
    Debauchery and Drinking:
O would they stay to calculate
    Th' eternal consequences;
Or—your more dreaded hell to state—
    Damnation of expenses!    40

Ye high, exalted, virtuous Dames,
    Tied up in godly laces,
Before ye gie poor Frailty names,
    Suppose a change o' cases;
A dear loved lad, convenience snug,    45
    A treacherous inclination—
But, let me whisper i' your lug,[17]
    Ye're aiblins [18] nae temptation.

Then gently scan your brother man,
    Still gentler sister woman;    50
Tho' they may gang a kennin [19] wrang,
    To step aside is human.
One point must still be greatly dark,
    The moving why they do it;
And just as lamely can ye mark    55
    How far perhaps they rue it.

Who made the heart, 'tis He alone
    Decidedly can try us;
He knows each chord, its various tone,
    Each spring, its various bias.    60

[9] Company.    [10] Staid.    [11] Giddy.
[12] Propose.    [13] Restive.    [14] Exchange.
[15] Rest.    [16] Transformed.    [17] Ear.
[18] Perhaps.    [19] Trifle.

Then at the balance let's be mute,
  We never can adjust it;
What's done we partly may compute,
  But know not what's resisted.

## John Anderson My Jo [1]

John Anderson my jo,[2] John,
  When we were first acquent,
Your locks were like the raven,
  Your bonnie brow was brent; [3]
But now your brow is beld,[4] John,          5
  Your locks are like the snow;
But blessings on your frosty pow,[5]
  John Anderson, my jo.

John Anderson my jo, John,
  We clamb the hill thegither;                10
And mony a canty [6] day, John,
  We've had wi' ane anither:
Now we maun totter down, John,
  And hand in hand we'll go,
And sleep thegither at the foot,              15
  John Anderson, my jo.

## The Lovely Lass of Inverness [7]

The lovely lass o' Inverness,
  Nae joy nor pleasure can she see;
For e'en and morn she cries, alas!
  And aye the saut [8] tear blin's her e'e:
"Drumossie [9] moor, Drumossie day,           5
  A faefu' day it was to me;
For there I lost my father dear,
  My father dear, and brethren three.

"Their winding-sheet the bluidy [10] clay,
  Their graves are growing green to see;      10
And by them lies the dearest lad
  That ever blest a woman's e'e!
Now wae to thee, thou cruel lord,[11]
  A bluidy man I trow [12] thou be;
For mony a heart thou hast made sair,[13]     15
  That ne'er did wrang [14] to thine or thee."

## A Red, Red Rose [15]

My love is like a red, red rose
  That's newly sprung in June:
My love is like the melodie
  That's sweetly played in tune.

So fair art thou, my bonnie lass,             5
  So deep in love am I:
And I will love thee still, my dear,
  Till a' the seas gang [16] dry.

Till a' the seas gang dry, my dear,
  And the rocks melt wi' the sun:             10
And I will love thee still, my dear,
  While the sands o' life shall run.

And fare thee weel, my only love,
  And fare thee weel awhile!
And I will come again, my love,               15
  Tho' it were ten thousand mile.

## Auld Lang Syne [17]

Should auld acquaintance be forgot,
  And never brought to min'?
Should auld acquaintance be forgot,
  And auld lang syne? [18]

### CHORUS

For auld lang syne, my dear,                  5
  For auld lang syne,
We'll tak a cup o' kindness yet,
  For auld lang syne.

And surely ye'll be your pint-stowp,[19]
  And surely I'll be mine;                    10
And we'll tak a cup o' kindness yet
  For auld lang syne.

We twa hae run about the braes,[20]
  And pu'd [21] the gowans [22] fine,
But we've wandered mony a weary foot          15
  Sin' auld lang syne.

We twa hae paidled i' the burn,[23]
  From morning sun till dine; [24]
But seas between us braid hae roared
  Sin' auld lang syne.                        20

And there's a hand, my trusty fiere,[25]
  And gie's a hand o' thine;
And we'll tak a right guid-willie waught,[26]
  For auld lang syne.

## Tam Glen [27]

My heart is breaking, dear Tittie,[28]
  Some counsel unto me come len',
To anger them a' is a pity;
  But what will I do wi' Tam Glen?

I'm thinking, wi' sic a braw [29] fellow,      5
  In poortith [30] I might mak a fen'; [31]
What care I in riches to wallow,
  If I maunna [32] marry Tam Glen?

---

[1] Written in 1788 or 1789.          [2] Sweetheart.
[3] Smooth.        [4] Bald.        [5] Head.
[6] Jolly.        [7] Written in 1794.        [8] Salt.
[9] I. e., Culloden. The poem commemorates the
Battle of Culloden, fought on 16 April, 1746.
[10] Bloody.        [11] William, Duke of Cumberland.
[12] Believe.        [13] Sore.        [14] Wrong.
[15] Written probably in 1794.        [16] Go.

[17] Written in 1788.        [18] I. e., old times.
[19] Pay for your three-pint measure.
[20] Hill-sides.        [21] Pulled.        [22] Daisies.
[23] Paddled in the brook.        [24] Dinner-time.
[25] Comrade.        [26] Hearty good-will draught.
[27] Written in 1788 or 1789.        [28] Sister.
[29] Such a fine.        [30] Poverty.        [31] Shift.
[32] Must not.

There's Lowrie the laird o' Dumeller,
  "Guid-day to you," brute! he comes ben: [33]
He brags and he blaws o' his siller,     11
  But when will he dance like Tam Glen?

My minnie [34] does constantly deave [35] me,
  And bids me beware o' young men;
They flatter, she says, to deceive me;    15
  But wha can think sae o' Tam Glen?

My daddie says, gin [36] I'll forsake him,
  He'll gie me guid hunder marks [37] ten:
But, if it's ordained I maun take him,
  O wha will I get but Tam Glen?    20

Yestreen at the Valentines' dealing,[38]
  My heart to my mou gied a sten: [39]
For thrice I drew ane without failing,
  And thrice it was written, Tam Glen.

The last Halloween I was waukin'    25
  My droukit sark-sleeve,[40] as ye ken;
His likeness cam up the house stalkin'—
  And the very gray breeks [41] o' Tam Glen!

Come, counsel, dear Tittie, don't tarry;
  I'll gie you my bonnie black hen,    30
Gif ye will advise me to marry
  The lad I lo'e dearly, Tam Glen.

# Willie Brewed a Peck o' Maut [42]

O Willie brewed a peck o' maut,
  And Rob and Allan cam to see;
Three blither hearts, that lee-lang [43] night,
  Ye wad na found in Christendie.

[33] In.     [34] Mother.     [35] Deafen.     [36] If.
[37] Coins worth slightly more than 26 cents each.
[38] The custom was for the men and girls to pair off by drawing slips of paper with names written on them.
[39] To my mouth gave a spring.
[40] Was watching my drenched shirt-sleeve. ("You go out, one or more—for this is a social spell—to a south-running spring, or rivulet, where 'three lairds' lands meet,' and dip your left shirt-sleeve. Go to bed in sight of a fire, and hang your wet sleeve before it to dry. Lie awake; and, some time near midnight, an apparition, having the exact figure of the grand object in question [your future husband], will come and turn the sleeve, as if to dry the other side of it"—Burns's note to *Halloween*, stanza 24, l. 7).
[41] Breeches.
[42] Written in 1789. "The air is Masterton's; the song mine. The occasion of it was this:—Mr. Wm. Nicol of the High School, Edinburgh, during the autumn vacation being at Moffat, honest Allan (who was at that time on a visit to Dalswinton) and I went to pay Nicol a visit. We had such a joyous meeting that Mr. Masterton and I agreed, each in our own way, that we should celebrate the business" (Burns's note). Allan Masterton was appointed writing-master in the Edinburgh High School in the fall of 1789.
[43] Live-long.

## CHORUS

We are na fou,[44] we're no that fou,    5
  But just a drappie [45] in our e'e;
The cock may craw, the day may daw,
  And aye we'll taste the barley bree.[46]

Here are we met, three merry boys,
  Three merry boys, I trow, are we;    10
And mony a night we've merry been,
  And mony mae we hope to be!

It is the moon, I ken her horn,
  That's blinkin' in the lift [47] sae hie;
She shines sae bright to wyle [48] us hame,    15
  But, by my sooth! she'll wait a wee.

Wha first shall rise to gang awa,
  A cuckold, coward loun [49] is he!
Wha first beside his chair shall fa',
  He is the king among us three!    20

# To Mary in Heaven [50]

Thou lingring star, with lessening ray,
  That lov'st to greet the early morn,
Again thou usherest in the day
  My Mary from my soul was torn.
O Mary! dear departed shade!    5
  Where is thy place of blissful rest?
Seest thou thy lover lowly laid?
  Hear'st thou the groans that rend his breast?

That sacred hour can I forget?
  Can I forget the hallowed grove,    10
Where by the winding Ayr we met,
  To live one day of parting love?
Eternity will not efface
  Those records dear of transports past;
Thy image at our last embrace—    15
  Ah! little thought we 'twas our last!

Ayr gurgling kissed his pebbled shore,
  O'erhung with wild woods, thickening green;

[44] Full.     [45] Small drop.     [46] Barley-brew.
[47] Sky.     [48] Entice.     [49] Rogue.
[50] Written in the fall of 1789. Mary Campbell, the subject of this poem, is generally supposed to have died in the fall of 1788, though about her, her relations with Burns, and the time of her death there is some uncertainty. Burns wrote the following note about *My Highland Lassie, O*: "My 'Highland Lassie' was a warm-hearted, charming young creature as ever blessed a man with generous love. After a pretty long tract of the most ardent reciprocal attachment we met by appointment on the second Sunday of May, in a sequestered spot by the banks of Ayr, where we spent the day in taking farewell, before she should embark for the West Highlands to arrange matters for our projected change of life. At the close of the autumn following she crossed the sea to meet me at Greenock, where she had scarce landed when she was seized with a malignant fever, which hurried my dear girl to the grave in a few days, before I could even hear of her illness."

The fragrant birch, and hawthorn hoar,
　Twined amorous round the raptured scene.
The flowers sprang wanton to be pressed, 21
　The birds sang love on ev'ry spray;
Till too, too soon, the glowing west
　Proclaimed the speed of wingéd day.

Still o'er these scenes my memory wakes, 25
　And fondly broods with miser care!
Time but the impression deeper makes,
　As streams their channels deeper wear.
My Mary, dear departed shade!
　Where is thy place of blissful rest? 30
Seest thou thy lover lowly laid?
　Hear'st thou the groans that rend his breast?

## Sweet Afton [51]

Flow gently, sweet Afton, among thy green
　braes,[52]
Flow gently, I'll sing thee a song in thy praise;
My Mary's asleep by the murmuring stream,
Flow gently, sweet Afton, disturb not her
　dream.

Thou stock-dove whose echo resounds through
　the glen, 5
Ye wild whistling blackbirds in yon thorny den,
Thou green-crested lapwing, thy screaming
　forbear,
I charge you disturb not my slumbering fair.

How lofty, sweet Afton, thy neighboring hills,
Far marked with the courses of clear winding
　rills; 10
There daily I wander as noon rises high,
My flocks and my Mary's sweet cot in my eye.

How pleasant thy banks and green valleys
　below,
Where wild in the woodlands the primroses
　blow;
There oft as mild ev'ning weeps over the lea, 15
The sweet-scented birk [53] shades my Mary and
　me.

Thy crystal stream, Afton, how lovely it glides,
And winds by the cot where my Mary resides;
How wanton thy waters her snowy feet lave,
As gathering sweet flow'rets she stems thy clear
　wave. 20

Flow gently, sweet Afton, among thy green
　braes,
Flow gently, sweet river, the theme of my lays;

[51] Written, probably, early in 1789. There have
been attempts to connect Mary Campbell with this
poem, but Burns probably had no special person
in mind. He stated that the poem was written as
a compliment to the "small river Afton that flows
into Nith, near New Cummock, which has some
charming, wild, romantic scenery on its banks."
　[52] Slopes.　　　[53] Birch.

My Mary's asleep by the murmuring stream,
Flow gently, sweet Afton, disturb not her
　dream.

## Tam o' Shanter [1]

### A *Tale*

When chapman billies [2] leave the street,
And drouthy [3] neibors neibors meet,
As market-days are wearing late,
An' folk begin to tak the gate; [4]
While we sit bousing at the nappy,[5]　　5
An' getting fou and unco [6] happy,
We think na on the lang Scots miles,[7]
The mosses, waters, slaps,[8] and styles,
That lie between us and our hame,
Where sits our sulky sullen dame,　　10
Gathering her brows like gathering storm,
Nursing her wrath to keep it warm.
　This truth fand honest Tam o' Shanter,
As he frae Ayr ae night did canter—
(Auld Ayr, wham ne'er a town surpasses　15
For honest men and bonnie lasses).
　O Tam! hadst thou but been sae wise
As ta'en thy ain wife Kate's advice!
She tauld thee weel thou was a skellum,[9]
A bletherin',[10] blusterin', drunken blellum; [11]
That frae November till October,　　21
Ae market-day thou was na sober;
That ilka melder [12] wi' the miller
Thou sat as lang as thou had siller;
That every naig was ca'd [13] a shoe on,　25
The smith and thee gat roarin' fou on;
That at the Lord's house, even on Sunday,

[1] Written in 1790. Alloway Kirk is less than a
mile south of Burns's birthplace. It fell into disuse
after the annexation of the parish of Alloway to
that of Ayr in 1690, and, when Burns wrote, it
had long been ruinous. The old bridge over the
Doon, which dates from the fifteenth century, stands
about 200 yards to the south of the church. Burns
had from his childhood heard witch-stories relating
to Alloway Kirk, and *Tam o' Shanter* is based on
one of them. It is said that Burns probably drew
the suggestion of his hero from the character and
adventures of Douglas Graham (1739–1811), a
farmer noted for his convivial habits, and tenant
of the farm of Shanter on the Carrick shore (Henley
and Henderson, I, 437). Burns wrote to Mrs. Dun-
lop in 1791: "I look on *Tam o' Shanter* to be my
standard performance in the poetical line. 'Tis true
both the one [his new-born son] and the other discover a spice of roguish waggery that might perhaps
be as well spared; but then they also show, in my
opinion, a force of genius and a finishing polish
that I despair of ever excelling."
　[2] Peddler fellows.　　[3] Thirsty.　　[4] Road.
　[5] Drinking ale.
　[6] Getting full (drunk) and very.
　[7] The Scottish mile was about an eighth longer
than the English mile.
　[8] The bogs, pools, gaps (in fences).
　[9] Good-for-nothing.　　[10] Chattering.
　[11] Babbler.　　[12] Every meal-grinding.
　[13] Driven.

Thou drank wi' Kirkton Jean till Monday.
She prophesied that, late or soon,
Thou would be found deep drowned in Doon;
Or catched wi' warlocks in the mirk [14]                31
By Alloway's auld haunted kirk.

    Ah, gentle dames! it gars me greet [15]
To think how mony counsels sweet,
How mony lengthened sage advices,          35
The husband frae the wife despises!

    But to our tale: Ae market night,
Tam had got planted unco right,
Fast by an ingle, bleezing finely,
Wi' reaming swats,[16] that drank divinely;    40
And at his elbow, Souter [17] Johnny,
His ancient, trusty, drouthy crony;
Tam lo'ed him like a very brither;
They had been fou for weeks thegither.
The night drave on wi' sangs and clatter,     45
And aye the ale was growing better:
The landlady and Tam grew gracious,
Wi' favors secret, sweet, and precious;
The souter tauld his queerest stories;
The landlord's laugh was ready chorus:        50
The storm without might rair and rustle,
Tam did na mind the storm a whistle.

    Care, mad to see a man sae happy,
E'en drowned himsel amang the nappy.
As bees flee hame wi' lades o' treasure,       55
The minutes winged their way wi' pleasure;
Kings may be bless'd, but Tam was glorious,
O'er a' the ills o' life victorious!

    But pleasures are like poppies spread—
You seize the flow'r, its bloom is shed;       60
Or like the snow falls in the river—
A moment white, then melts for ever;
Or like the borealis race,
That flit ere you can point their place;
Or like the rainbow's lovely form             65
Evanishing amid the storm.
Nae man can tether time nor tide;
The hour approaches Tam maun [18] ride;
That hour, o' night's black arch the keystane,
That dreary hour, he mounts his beast in;     70
And sic a night he taks the road in,
As ne'er poor sinner was abroad in.

    The wind blew as 'twad blawn its last;
The rattling show'rs rose on the blast;
The speedy gleams the darkness swallowed;     75
Loud, deep, and lang, the thunder bellowed:
That night, a child might understand,
The Deil had business on his hand.

    Weel mounted on his gray mare, Meg,
A better never lifted leg,                     80
Tam skelpit [19] on thro' dub [20] and mire,
Despising wind, and rain, and fire;
Whiles [21] holding fast his gude blue bonnet;
Whiles crooning o'er some auld Scots sonnet; [22]
Whiles glow'ring round wi' prudent cares,     85
Lest bogles [23] catch him unawares.

Kirk-Alloway was drawing nigh,
Whare ghaists and houlets [24] nightly cry.
    By this time he was cross the ford,
Where in the snaw the chapman smoor'd; [25]
And past the birks and meikle stane,[26]       91
Where drunken Charlie brak's neck-bane;
And thro' the whins,[27] and by the cairn,[28]
Where hunters fand the murdered bairn; [29]
And near the thorn, aboon [30] the well,        95
Where Mungo's mither hanged hersel.
Before him Doon pours all his floods;
The doubling storm roars thro' the woods;
The lightnings flash from pole to pole;
Near and more near the thunders roll:          100
When, glimmering thro' the groaning trees,
Kirk-Alloway seem'd in a bleeze;
Thro' ilka bore [31] the beams were glancing;
And loud resounded mirth and dancing.

    Inspiring bold John Barleycorn!              105
What dangers thou canst make us scorn!
Wi' tippenny,[32] we fear nae evil;
Wi' usquebae,[33] we'll face the devil!
The swats sae reamed in Tammie's noddle,
Fair play, he cared na deils a boddle! [34]     110
But Maggie stood right sair astonished,
Till, by the heel and hand admonished,
She ventured forward on the light;
And, vow! Tam saw an unco [35] sight!

    Warlocks and witches in a dance!            115
Nae cotillion brent new [36] frae France,
But hornpipes, jigs, strathspeys, and reels,[37]
Put life and mettle in their heels.
A winnock-bunker [38] in the east,
There sat auld Nick, in shape o' beast—        120
A touzie tyke,[39] black, grim, and large!
To gie them music was his charge:
He screwed the pipes and gart them skirl,[40]
Till roof and rafters a' did dirl.[41]
Coffins stood round like open presses,         125
That shawed the dead in their last dresses;
And by some devilish cantrip [42] sleight
Each in its cauld hand held a light,
By which heroic Tam was able
To note upon the haly [43] table               130
A murderer's banes in gibbet-airns; [44]
Twa span-lang, wee, unchristened bairns;
A thief new-cutted frae the rape,[45]
Ki' his last gasp his gab [46] did gape;
Five tomahawks, wi' blude red rusted;          135
Five scymitars, wi' murder crusted;
A garter, which a babe had strangled;
A knife, a father's throat had mangled,
Whom his ain son o' life bereft—
The gray hairs yet stack to the heft;          140

---

[14] Wizards in the dark.    [15] Makes me weep.
[16] Foaming new ale.    [17] Shoemaker.
[18] Must.   [19] Clattered.   [20] Puddle.
[21] Now.   [22] Song.   [23] Bogies.

[24] Ghosts and owls.    [25] Peddler smothered.
[26] Birches and big stone.    [27] Furze.
[28] Pile of stones.   [29] Child.   [30] Above.
[31] Every chink.   [32] Ale.   [33] Whisky.
[34] Copper.   [35] Wonderful.   [36] Brand-new.
[37] Names of Scottish dances.   [38] Window-seat.
[39] Shaggy dog.   [40] Made them squeal.
[41] Ring.   [42] Magic.   [43] Holy.
[44] Bones in gibbet-irons.   [45] Rope.   [46] Mouth.

Wi' mair of horrible and awfu',
Which even to name wad be unlawfu'.

As Tammie glowred,[47] amazed, and curious,
The mirth and fun grew fast and furious:
The piper loud and louder blew;    145
The dancers quick and quicker flew;
They reeled, they set, they crossed, they
    cleekit,[48]
Till ilka carlin swat and reekit,[49]
And coost her duddies to the wark,[50]
And linkit at it in her sark! [51]    150

Now Tam, O Tam! had thae been queans,[52]
A' plump and strapping in their teens;
Their sarks, instead o' creeshie flannen,[53]
Been snaw-white seventeen hunder linen! [54]
Thir breeks [55] o' mine, my only pair,    155
That ance were plush, o' gude blue hair,
I wad hae gi'en them off my hurdies,[56]
For ae blink o' the bonnie burdies.[57]

But withered beldams, auld and droll,
Rigwoodie [58] hags wad spean [59] a foal,    160
Louping and flinging on a crummock,[60]
I wonder didna turn thy stomach.

But Tam kent [61] what was what fu' braw-
    lie: [62]
There was ae winsome wench and walie [63]
That night enlisted in the core,[64]    165
Lang after kent on Carrick shore!
(For mony a beast to dead she shot,
And perished mony a bonnie boat,
And shook baith meikle corn and bear,[65]
And kept the country-side in fear.)    170
Her cutty [66] sark, o' Paisley harn,[67]
That while a lassie she had worn,
In longitude tho' sorely scanty,
It was her best, and she was vauntie.[68]
Ah! little kent thy reverend grannie    175
That sark she coft [69] for her wee Nannie
Wi' twa pund Scots [70] ('twas a' her riches)
Wad ever graced a dance of witches!

But here my muse her wing maun cour; [71]
Sic flights are far beyond her pow'r—    180
To sing how Nannie lap and flang [72]
(A souple jade she was, and strang);
And how Tam stood, like ane bewitched,
And thought his very e'en enriched;
Even Satan glowred, and fidged [73] fu' fain,   185

And hotched [74] and blew wi' might and main:
Till first ae caper, syne anither,
Tam tint [75] his reason a' thegither,
And roars out, "Weel done, Cutty-sark!"
And in an instant all was dark!    190
And scarcely had he Maggie rallied,
When out the hellish legion sallied.

As bees bizz out wi' angry fyke [76]
When plundering herds [77] assail their byke,[78]
As open pussie's mortal foes [79]    195
When, pop! she starts before their nose,
As eager runs the market-crowd,
When "Catch the thief!" resounds aloud,
So Maggie runs; the witches follow,
Wi' mony an eldritch skriech [80] and hollow.

Ah, Tam! ah, Tam! thou'll get thy fairin'! [81]
In hell they'll roast thee like a herrin'!   202
In vain thy Kate awaits thy comin'!
Kate soon will be a woefu' woman!
Now do thy speedy utmost, Meg,    205
And win the key-stane o' the brig: [82]
There at them thou thy tail may toss,
A running stream they darena cross,
But ere the key-stane she could make,
The fient [83] a tail she had to shake!    210
For Nannie, far before the rest,
Hard upon noble Maggie pressed,
And flew at Tam wi' furious ettle; [84]
But little wist [85] she Maggie's mettle!
Ae spring brought off her master hale,   215
But left behind her ain gray tail:
The carlin claught [86] her by the rump,
And left poor Maggie scarce a stump.

Now, wha this tale o' truth shall read,
Each man and mother's son, take heed;   220
Whene'er to drink you are inclined,
Or cutty-sarks run in your mind,
Think! ye may buy the joys o'er dear;
Remember Tam o' Shanter's mare.

## Ye Flowery Banks o' Bonnie Doon [1]

Ye flowery banks o' bonnie Doon,
   How can ye blume sae fair?
How can ye chant, ye little birds,
   And I sae fu' o' care?

Thou'll break my heart, thou bonnie bird,   5
   That sings upon the bough;

[47] Stared.     [48] Linked themselves.
[49] Till every old woman sweat and steamed.
[50] And cast off her clothes to the work.
[51] And tripped at it in her shirt.
[52] Had these been young women.
[53] Greasy flannel.
[54] I. e., fine linen, with 1700 threads to a width.
[55] These breeches.    [56] Hips.
[57] Maidens.    [58] *Probably* ancient, or lean.
[59] Wean (from disgust).
[60] Leaping and kicking on a staff.    [61] Knew.
[62] Full well.    [63] Choice.    [64] Company.
[65] Much wheat and barley.    [66] Short.
[67] Coarse linen.    [68] Proud.    [69] Bought.
[70] A pound Scots was only about 40 cents.
[71] Must stoop.    [72] Leaped and kicked.
[73] Fidgeted.

[74] Jerked.    [75] Lost.    [76] Fret.
[77] Herders of cattle.    [78] Hive.
[79] As the hare's mortal foes begin to bark.
[80] Unearthly screech.
[81] Literally, a present from a fair, but the word came to be used ironically (as it is here) for a beating.
[82] Bridge. "It is a well-known fact that witches, or any evil spirits, have no power to follow a poor wight any farther than the middle of the next running stream" (Burns's note).
[83] Devil.    [84] Aim.    [85] Knew.
[86] Seized.
[1] Written probably in 1791.

Thou minds me o' the happy days,
　　When my fause luve was true.

Thou'll break my heart, thou bonnie bird,
　　That sings beside thy mate;　　　　10
For sae I sat, and sae I sang,
　　And wist [2] na o' my fate.

Aft hae I roved by bonnie Doon,
　　To see the woodbine twine,
And ilka [3] bird sang o' its love,　　15
　　And sae did I o' mine.

Wi' lightsome heart I pu'd a rose
　　Frae off its thorny tree:
And my fause luver staw [4] my rose,
　　But left the thorn wi' me.　　　　20

## Ae Fond Kiss [5]

Ae fond kiss, and then we sever!
Ae fareweel, alas, for ever!
Deep in heart-wrung tears I'll pledge thee,
Warring sighs and groans I'll wage [6] thee.
Who shall say that fortune grieves him　　5
While the star of hope she leaves him?
Me, nae cheerfu' twinkle lights me,
Dark despair around benights me.

I'll ne'er blame my partial fancy,
Naething could resist my Nancy;　　　10
But to see her was to love her,
Love but her, and love for ever.
Had we never loved sae kindly,
Had we never loved sae blindly,
Never met—or never parted—　　　15
We had ne'er been broken-hearted.

Fare thee weel, thou first and fairest!
Fare thee weel, thou best and dearest!
Thine be ilka [7] joy and treasure,
Peace, enjoyment, love, and pleasure.　　20
Ae fond kiss, and then we sever;
Ae fareweel, alas, for ever!
Deep in heart-wrung tears I'll pledge thee,
Warring sighs and groans I'll wage thee.

## Duncan Gray [8]

Duncan Gray came here to woo,
　　　Ha, ha, the wooing o't,
On blithe Yule night [9] when we were fou,[10]
　　　Ha, ha, the wooing o't.
Maggie coost [11] her head fu' heigh,　　5

Looked asklent and unco skeigh [12]
Gart [13] poor Duncan stand abeigh; [14]
　　　Ha, ha, the wooing o't.

Duncan fleeched,[15] and Duncan prayed;
　　　Ha, ha, the wooing o't,　　　10
Meg was deaf as Ailsa Craig,[16]
　　　Ha, ha, the wooing o't.
Duncan sighed baith out and in,
Grat [17] his e'en baith bleer't and blin',
Spak o' lowpin o'er a linn; [18]　　15
　　　Ha, ha, the wooing o't.

Time and chance are but a tide,
　　　Ha, ha, the wooing o't,
Slighted love is sair to bide,[19]
　　　Ha, ha, the wooing o't.　　　20
Shall I, like a fool, quoth he,
For a haughty hizzie [20] die?
She may gae to—France for me!
　　　Ha, ha, the wooing o't.

How it comes let doctors tell,　　　25
　　　Ha, ha, the wooing o't,
Meg grew sick as he grew hale,
　　　Ha, ha, the wooing o't.
Something in her bosom wrings;
For relief a sigh she brings;　　　30
And O, her e'en they spak sic [21] things!
　　　Ha, ha, the wooing o't.

Duncan was a lad o' grace,
　　　Ha, ha, the wooing o't,
Maggie's was a piteous case,　　　35
　　　Ha, ha, the wooing o't.
Duncan couldna be her death,
Swelling pity smoored [22] his wrath;
Now they're crouse and cantie [23] baith!
　　　Ha, ha, the wooing o't.　　　40

## Highland Mary [24]

Ye banks and braes [25] and streams around
　　The castle o' Montgomery,
Green be your woods, and fair your flowers,
　　Your waters never drumlie! [26]
There summer first unfauld her robes,　　5
　　And there the langest tarry;
For there I took the last fareweel
　　O' my sweet Highland Mary.

How sweetly bloomed the gay green birk,[27]
　　How rich the hawthorn's blossom,　　10

[12] Askance and very disdainful.　　　[13] Made.
[14] Off.　　　　　[15] Wheedled.
[16] A rocky islet in the Firth of Clyde, frequented by screaming sea-fowl.
[17] Wept.　　　[18] Leaping over a waterfall.
[19] Hard to endure.　　　[20] Young woman.
[21] Such.　　　[22] Smothered.
[23] Brisk and cheerful.
[24] Written in 1792. Concerning Mary Campbell, the subject of this song, see footnote on *To Mary in Heaven.*
[25] Slopes.　　　[26] Turbid.　　　[27] Birch.

[2] Knew.　　　[3] Every.　　　[4] Stole.
[5] Written in 1791.　　[6] Pledge.　　[7] Every.
[8] Written in 1792. The second or (as Henley and Henderson say) drawing-room set. Of the tune Burns wrote: "*Duncan Gray* is that kind of light-horse gallop of an air which precludes sentiment. The ludicrous is its ruling feature."
[9] Christmas Eve.　　　[10] Drunk.　　　[11] Cast.

As underneath their fragrant shade
    I clasped her to my bosom!
The golden hours on angel wings
    Flew o'er me and my dearie;
For dear to me as light and life      15
    Was my sweet Highland Mary.

Wi' mony a vow, and locked embrace,
    Our parting was fu' tender;
And, pledging aft to meet again,
    We tore oursels asunder;      20
But oh! fell death's untimely frost,
    That nipped my flower sae early!
Now green's the sod, and cauld's the clay,
    That wraps my Highland Mary!

O pale, pale now, those rosy lips,      25
    I aft have kissed sae fondly!
And closed for aye the sparkling glance,
    That dwelt on me sae kindly!
And mold'ring now in silent dust,
    That heart that lo'ed me dearly!      30
But still within my bosom's core
    Shall live my Highland Mary.

## Scots Wha Hae [28]

Scots, wha hae wi' Wallace bled,
Scots, wham Bruce has aften led,
Welcome to your gory bed,
    Or to victorie.

Now's the day, and now's the hour;      5
See the front o' battle lour!
See approach proud Edward's power—
    Chains and slaverie!

Wha will be a traitor knave?
Wha can fill a coward's grave?      10
Wha sae base as be a slave?
    Let him turn and flee!

Wha for Scotland's king and law
Freedom's sword will strongly draw,
Freeman stand, or freeman fa'?      15
    Let him follow me!

[28] Written in 1793. There was a tradition that the air *Hey Tutti Taitti* was Robert Bruce's march at Bannockburn. Burns wrote: "This thought, in my solitary wanderings, roused me to a pitch of enthusiasm on the theme of liberty and independence, which I threw into a kind of Scottish ode, fitted to the air, that one might suppose to be the gallant royal Scot's address to his heroic followers on that eventful morning." The Battle of Bannockburn was fought on 24 June, 1314. The Scots under Bruce won a victory over Edward II and the English which secured the independence of Scotland until the union of the kingdoms in 1603. In the same letter from which the above sentence is quoted Burns also indicated that the French Revolution was in his mind when he was writing the poem.

By oppression's woes and pains!
By your sons in servile chains!
We will drain our dearest veins,
    But they shall be free!      20

Lay the proud usurpers low!
Tyrants fall in every foe!
Liberty's in every blow!
    Let us do or die!

## Is There for Honest Poverty [29]

Is there, for honest poverty,
    That hangs his head, and a' that?
The coward-slave, we pass him by,
    We dare be poor for a' that!
      For a' that, and a' that,      5
      Our toils obscure, and a' that,
      The rank is but the guinea stamp;
      The man's the gowd [30] for a' that.

What tho' on hamely fare we dine,
    Wear hodden-gray,[31] and a' that?      10
Gie fools their silks, and knaves their wine,
    A man's a man for a' that.
      For a' that, and a' that,
      Their tinsel show, and a' that,
      The honest man, tho' e'er sae poor,      15
      Is king o' men for a' that.

Ye see yon birkie,[32] ca'd a lord,
    Wha struts, and stares, and a' that;
Tho' hundreds worship at his word,
    He's but a coof [33] for a' that:      20
      For a' that, and a' that,
      His ribband, star, and a' that,
      The man of independent mind,
      He looks and laughs at a' that.

A prince can mak a belted knight,      25
    A marquis, duke, and a' that;
But an honest man's aboon [34] his might,
    Guid faith he mauna fa [35] that!
      For a' that, and a' that,
      Their dignities, and a' that,      30
      The pith o' sense, and pride o' worth,
      Are higher rank than a' that.

Then let us pray that come it may,
    As come it will for a' that,
That sense and worth, o'er a' the earth,      35
    Shall bear the gree [36] and a' that;
      For a' that, and a' that,
      It's comin' yet for a' that,
      That man to man, the world o'er,
      Shall brithers be for a' that.      40

[29] Written in 1793 or 1794.    [30] Gold.
[31] Coarse gray woolen cloth.    [32] Fellow.
[33] Fool.    [34] Above.
[35] Must not lay claim to.    [36] Have the prize.

## O, Wert Thou in the Cauld Blast [37]

O, wert thou in the cauld blast
  On yonder lea, on yonder lea,
My plaidie to the angry airt,[38]
  I'd shelter thee, I'd shelter thee.
Or did misfortune's bitter storms     5

[37] Written in 1796, during Burns's last illness, in honor of Jessie Lewars, who did much for him and his family at that time.
[38] Quarter.

Around thee blaw, around thee blaw,
Thy bield [39] should be my bosom,
  To share it a', to share it a'.

Or were I in the wildest waste,
  Sae black and bare, sae black and bare,    10
The desert were a paradise,
  If thou wert there, if thou wert there.
Or were I monarch o' the globe,
  Wi' thee to reign, wi' thee to reign,
The brightest jewel in my crown    15
  Wad be my queen, wad be my queen.

[39] Shelter.

# William Wordsworth

## 1770 - 1850

Wordsworth was born at Cockermouth in the county of Cumberland on 7 April, 1770. His early life was one of simplicity, almost of poverty, amid picturesque rural surroundings. His mother died when he was eight years old, and his father five years later. He attended the grammar school of Hawkshead, living as a boarder in the village, and thence passed in 1787 to St. John's College, Cambridge, two of his uncles providing the means necessary for his university education. He took his B. A. in 1791. Wordsworth was never a great reader, and he did not distinguish himself as a student. There may even have been a degree of wildness in his life during these years which it is still not usual to associate with the "Daddy Wordsworth"—to use Edward FitzGerald's phrase—perpetuated by the poet's earlier biographers. It is evident at any rate that, as he himself later said, he "was not for that hour, nor for that place," and that, while his strictly intellectual training was pursued somewhat listlessly at Cambridge, his heart was roused to fresh life in his vacations spent in the northern country known as the Lake District and, in the summer of 1790, in a walking tour through France and Switzerland. After he left Cambridge he spent some months in London and then went to France, where he remained until the beginning of 1793. There he was in close association with members of the revolutionary party, and at the same time he fell in love with a member of a royalist family, Marie-Anne Vallon, some four or five years his senior, who bore him a daughter in December, 1792. Reason exists for believing that Wordsworth later intended to marry the mother of his daughter, but he did not do so. On the other hand, as Professor G. M. Harper has said, "whatever from a legal point of view, may have been the nature of the connection between Wordsworth and Marie-Anne Vallon, it was openly acknowledged and its consequences were hon-

orably endured" (Wordsworth's French Daughter, p. 12).

Soon after his return to England in 1793 Wordsworth published An Evening Walk and Descriptive Sketches, and presently he became, at least partly by way of reaction from the excesses of the French Revolution, a disciple of William Godwin, who for a time was regarded as the leader of English liberalism. His period of full allegiance to Godwin was, however, short, and also unhappy. He did not, in fact, really find himself until he became acquainted with Samuel Taylor Coleridge. In 1797 he went to live near Coleridge in Somersetshire. Coleridge was "one of those minds which startle other minds out of the ordinariness which so easily besets most men, and besets at fitful intervals even genius" (H. W. Garrod, Wordsworth, p. 139). By the beginning of his intimacy with Coleridge Wordsworth had finally wrung himself completely free of "that strong disease," as he calls it, of Godwinism, and it was during the years of his close association with Coleridge—that is to say, for about nine years following 1797—that he wrote practically all of his greatest poetry. In 1798 the two poets published Lyrical Ballads (the volume contained four poems by Coleridge). In 1798 and 1799 a large part of The Prelude, Wordsworth's long autobiographical poem, was written, and it was finished in 1805. In this period the fragment of The Recluse was written (1800) and part of The Excursion, including the episode concerning Margaret (1799). And at the end of this period was published Poems in Two Volumes (1807). This sums up the best of Wordsworth's poetry, and after 1807 he began to settle more and more deeply into that ordinariness to which he was, perhaps, naturally more prone than other men of equally great gifts.

Since 1795, when he had received a small legacy from Raisley Calvert which had freed *him from dependence on his other relatives, Wordsworth had been living with his sister Dorothy—who also exerted a strong influence upon him. In 1798 Wordsworth and Dorothy and Coleridge had gone to spend some time in Germany; and in 1799 the Wordsworths took Dove Cottage, Grasmere, where they remained nine years. In 1802 Wordsworth married Mary Hutchinson. In 1813 he was given a government post, a sinecure, which greatly increased his income and enabled him to move to Rydal Mount, where he remained until his death. In the year following his appointment he published* The Excursion, *and in 1815* The White Doe of Rylstone, Laodamia, *and other poems. In 1836–1837 a collected edition of his poems was published, in six volumes. In 1843 he was made poet laureate, in succession to Southey. He died on 23 April, 1850.*

In the note concerning his Ode, Intimations of Immortality from Recollections of Early Childhood, which Wordsworth dictated to Miss Isabella Fenwick, he spoke of a difficulty he had had in childhood in admitting "the notion of death as a state applicable to my own being." This arose, he went on to say, "from a sense of the indomitableness of the Spirit within me," and from this it came about that "I was often unable to think of external things as having external existence, and I communed with all that I saw as something not apart from, but inherent in, my own immaterial nature. Many times while going to school have I grasped at a wall or tree to recall myself from this abyss of idealism to the reality. At that time I was afraid of such processes. In later periods of life I have deplored, as we have all reason to do, a subjugation of an opposite character. . . . . To that dream-like vividness and splendor which invest objects of sight in childhood, every one, I believe, if he would look back, could bear testimony." It is hardly too much to say that this passage contains the key to Wordsworth's poetry. In his youth Wordsworth's animal sensibilities were strong. The life of the eye and ear was more to him than to other men. And while his richest and most vivid experiences came to him through the senses, at the same time they often carried him beyond sense to visions of an eternity not beyond the reach of man. From this Wordsworth inferred the natural goodness of the senses, and thus he was prepared for the influence of Rousseau and the French Revolution. To this faith in the life of the senses he returned after his period of subjection to Godwin, and in this faith much of his great poetry

*was written. In his great period he also attacked, with Coleridge's help, the question how one was to maintain one's spiritual life as one grew older and the impressions of the senses became less piercingly vivid. To this question he found answers—we may read them in* The Character of the Happy Warrior *and the* Ode to Duty—*but evidently no answer that enabled him to maintain his own life on the exalted level of his great decade.*

The Lyrical Ballads of 1798 mark, as is usually said, a new epoch in the history of English literature;—they definitely usher in the romantic movement. Among other things it is notable that these poems are largely concerned with the experiences of humble people living in the country and that their style has a simplicity and directness which marks a deliberate break with the artificial poetic diction of the eighteenth century. But the latter characteristic is not really separable from the substance of Wordsworth's poetry. What he wrote came from the depths of the man, and his style when at its best is simply the result of his effort to deal faithfully with his experience.

The best one-volume edition of his writings is The Poetical Works of William Wordsworth, ed. Thomas Hutchinson and Ernest de Selincourt (Oxford, 1950); the standard text is the Poetical Works of William Wordsworth, ed. Ernest de Selincourt and Helen Darbishire (Oxford, 1940–1949; 1952– ). The letters of William and Dorothy Wordsworth have been definitively edited by Ernest de Selincourt (6 vols., Oxford, 1935–1939). Professor de Selincourt's edition of The Prelude, revised by Helen Darbishire (Oxford, 1959), presents early manuscript versions of the poem, together with the text published in 1850. Wordsworth's Literary Criticism has been conveniently edited by Nowell Smith (Oxford, 1905). An indispensable companion to Wordsworth studies is The Journals of Dorothy Wordsworth, ed. Ernest de Selincourt (New York, 1941). The first volume of Mary Moorman's extremely able William Wordsworth, a Biography (Oxford, 1957) covers the period 1770–1803; the projected second volume will complete the life. Meanwhile George McLean Harper's William Wordsworth, His Life, Works, and Influence, preferably the two-volume edition (London, 1916), may be used, supplemented by Edith C. Batho's The Later Wordsworth (Cambridge, 1933). There have been many studies and interpretations; the centenary of the poet's death in particular stimulated dozens of publications. Only a few

can be mentioned: H. W. Garrod's Wordsworth: Lectures and Essays (*Oxford*, 1927);
*Helen Darbshire's* The Poet Wordsworth (*Oxford*, 1950); *Lascelles Abercrombie's* The Art
of Wordsworth (*Oxford*, 1952); F. G. *Marsh's*
Wordsworth's Imagery: a Study in Poetic Vision (*New Haven*, 1952); *and Herschel
Margoliouth's* Wordsworth and Coleridge,
1795–1834 (*Oxford*, 1953).

## Preface to the Second Edition of Lyrical Ballads [1]

The first Volume of these Poems has already been submitted to general perusal. It
was published as an experiment, which, I
hoped, might be of some use to ascertain how
far, by fitting to metrical arrangement a
selection of the real language of men in a state
of vivid sensation, that sort of pleasure and
that quantity of pleasure may be imparted,
which a Poet may rationally endeavor to impart.

I had formed no very inaccurate estimate
of the probable effect of those Poems: I flattered myself that they who should be pleased
with them would read them with more than
common pleasure: and, on the other hand, I
was well aware, that by those who should
dislike them they would be read with more
than common dislike. The result has differed from my expectation in this only, that
a greater number have been pleased than I
ventured to hope I should please.

Several of my Friends are anxious for the
success of these Poems, from a belief that, if
the views with which they were composed
were indeed realized, a class of Poetry would
be produced, well adapted to interest mankind
permanently, and not unimportant in the
quality and in the multiplicity of its moral
relations: and on this account they have advised me to prefix a systematic defense of
the theory upon which the Poems were
written. But I was unwilling to undertake
the task, knowing that on this occasion the
reader would look coldly upon my arguments, since I might be suspected of having
been principally influenced by the selfish and
foolish hope of *reasoning* him into an approbation of these particular Poems: and I was
still more unwilling to undertake the task,
because adequately to display the opinions,

and fully to enforce the arguments, would
require a space wholly disproportionate to a
preface. For, to treat the subject with the
clearness and coherence of which it is susceptible, it would be necessary to give a full
account of the present state of the public
taste in this country, and to determine how
far this taste is healthy or depraved; which,
again, could not be determined without pointing out in what manner language and the
human mind act and re-act on each other,
and without retracing the revolutions, not of
literature alone, but likewise of society itself. I have therefore altogether declined
to enter regularly upon this defense; yet I
am sensible that there would be something
like impropriety in abruptly obtruding upon
the Public, without a few words of introduction, Poems so materially different from
those upon which general approbation is at
present bestowed.

It is supposed that by the act of writing in
verse an Author makes a formal engagement
that he will gratify certain known habits of
association; that he not only thus apprises
the Reader that certain classes of ideas and
expressions will be found in his book, but
that others will be carefully excluded. This
exponent or symbol held forth by metrical
language must in different eras of literature
have excited very different expectations: for
example, in the age of Catullus, Terence, and
Lucretius, and that of Statius or Claudian; [2]
and in our own country, in the age of Shakespeare and Beaumont and Fletcher, and that
of Donne and Cowley, or Dryden, or Pope.
I will not take upon me to determine the exact import of the promise which, by the act
of writing in verse, an Author in the present
day makes to his reader; but it will undoubtedly appear to many persons that I have not
fulfilled the terms of an engagement thus
voluntarily contracted. They who have been
accustomed to the gaudiness and inane
phraseology of many modern writers, if they
persist in reading this book to its conclusion,
will, no doubt, frequently have to struggle
with feelings of strangeness and awkwardness: they will look round for poetry, and
will be induced to inquire by what species of
courtesy these attempts can be permitted to
assume that title. I hope, therefore, the
reader will not censure me for attempting to
state what I have proposed to myself to per-

---

[1] The second edition of the *Lyrical Ballads*, with
additions, was published in two volumes in 1800.
The Preface which was then added was later revised
and enlarged, and is here printed in its final form.

[2] The first three belong to the great period of
Latin poetry, the latter two to a later age comparatively barren of high achievement.

form; and also (as far as the limits of a preface will permit) to explain some of the chief reasons which have determined me in the choice of my purpose: that at least he may be spared any unpleasant feeling of disappointment, and that I myself may be protected from one of the most dishonorable accusations which can be brought against an Author; namely, that of an indolence which prevents him from endeavoring to ascertain what is his duty, or, when his duty is ascertained, prevents him from performing it.

The principal object, then, proposed in these Poems, was to choose incidents and situations from common life, and to relate or describe them throughout, as far as was possible, in a selection of language really used by men, and, at the same time, to throw over them a certain coloring of imagination, whereby ordinary things should be presented to the mind in an unusual aspect; and further, and above all, to make these incidents and situations interesting by tracing in them, truly though not ostentatiously, the primary laws of our nature: chiefly, as far as regards the manner in which we associate ideas in a state of excitement. Humble and rustic life was generally chosen, because in that condition the essential passions of the heart find a better soil in which they can attain their maturity, are less under restraint, and speak a plainer and more emphatic language; because in that condition of life our elementary feelings co-exist in a state of greater simplicity, and, consequently, may be more accurately contemplated, and more forcibly communicated; because the manners of rural life germinate from those elementary feelings, and, from the necessary character of rural occupations, are more easily comprehended, and are more durable; and, lastly, because in that condition the passions of men are incorporated with the beautiful and permanent forms of nature. The language, too, of these men has been adopted (purified indeed from what appear to be its real defects, from all lasting and rational causes of dislike or disgust), because such men hourly communicate with the best objects from which the best part of language is originally derived; and because, from their rank in society and the sameness and narrow circle of their intercourse, being less under the influence of social vanity, they convey their feelings and notions in simple and unelaborated expressions. Accordingly, such a language, arising out of repeated experience and regular feelings, is a more permanent, and a far more philosophical language, than that which is frequently substituted for it by Poets, who think that they are conferring honor upon themselves and their art in proportion as they separate themselves from the sympathies of men, and indulge in arbitrary and capricious habits of expression, in order to furnish food for fickle tastes and fickle appetites of their own creation.[3]

I cannot, however, be insensible to the present outcry against the triviality and meanness, both of thought and language, which some of my contemporaries have occasionally introduced into their metrical compositions; and I acknowledge that this defect, where it exists, is more dishonorable to the Writer's own character than false refinement or arbitrary innovation, though I should contend at the same time that it is far less pernicious in the sum of its consequences. From such verses the Poems in these volumes will be found distinguished at least by one mark of difference, that each of them has a worthy *purpose*. Not that I always began to write with a distinct purpose formally conceived, but habits of meditation have, I trust, so prompted and regulated my feelings, that my descriptions of such objects as strongly excite those feelings will be found to carry along with them a *purpose*. If this opinion be erroneous, I can have little right to the name of a Poet. For all good poetry is the spontaneous overflow of powerful feelings: and though this be true, Poems to which any value can be attached were never produced on any variety of subjects but by a man who, being possessed of more than usual organic sensibility, had also thought long and deeply. For our continued influxes of feeling are modified and directed by our thoughts, which are indeed the representatives of all our past feelings; and as, by contemplating the relation of these general representatives to each other, we discover what is really important to men, so, by the repetition and continuance of this act, our feelings will be connected with important subjects, till at length, if we be originally possessed of much sensibility, such habits of mind will be produced that, by obeying blindly and mechanically the impulses of those habits, we shall describe objects, and utter sentiments,

[3] It is worth while here to observe that the affecting parts of Chaucer are almost always expressed in language pure and universally intelligible even to this day (Wordsworth's note).

of such a nature, and in such connection with each other, that the understanding of the Reader must necessarily be in some degree enlightened, and his affection strengthened and purified.

It has been said that each of these Poems has a purpose. Another circumstance must be mentioned which distinguishes these Poems from the popular Poetry of the day; it is this, that the feeling therein developed gives im- portance to the action and situation, and not the action and situation to the feeling.

A sense of false modesty shall not prevent me from asserting that the Reader's attention is pointed to this mark of distinction, far less for the sake of these particular Poems than from the general importance of the subject. The subject is indeed important! For the human mind is capable of being excited with- out the application of gross and violent stimu- lants; and he must have a very faint percep- tion of its beauty and dignity who does not know this, and who does not further know that one being is elevated above another in proportion as he possesses this capability. It has therefore appeared to me, that to en- deavor to produce or enlarge this capability is one of the best services in which, at any period, a Writer can be engaged; but this service, excellent at all times, is especially so at the present day. For a multitude of causes, unknown to former times, are now acting with a combined force to blunt the discriminating powers of the mind, and, un- fitting it for all voluntary exertion, to re- duce it to a state of almost savage torpor. The most effective of these causes are the great national events which are daily taking place, and the increasing accumulation of men in cities, where the uniformity of their occupations produces a craving for extraor- dinary incident which the rapid communica- tion of intelligence hourly gratifies. To this tendency of life and manners the literature and theatrical exhibitions of the country have conformed themselves. The invaluable works of our elder writers, I had almost said the works of Shakespeare and Milton, are driven into neglect by frantic novels, sickly and stupid German Tragedies, and deluges of idle and extravagant stories in verse.— When I think upon this degrading thirst after outrageous stimulation, I am almost ashamed to have spoken of the feeble en- deavor made in these volumes to counteract it; and, reflecting upon the magnitude of the general evil, I should be oppressed with no

dishonorable melancholy, had I not a deep impression of certain inherent and indestruct- ible qualities of the human mind, and like- wise of certain powers in the great and per- manent objects that act upon it, which are equally inherent and indestructible; and were there not added to this impression a belief that the time is approaching when the evil will be systematically opposed by men of greater powers, and with far more distin- guished success.

Having dwelt thus long on the subjects and aim of these Poems, I shall request the Reader's permission to apprise him of a few circumstances relating to their *style*, in order, among other reasons, that he may not censure me for not having performed what I never attempted. The Reader will find that per- sonifications of abstract ideas rarely occur in these volumes, and are utterly rejected as an ordinary device to elevate the style and raise it above prose. My purpose was to imitate, and, as far as is possible, to adopt the very language of men; and assuredly such per- sonifications do not make any natural or regu- lar part of that language. They are, indeed, a figure of speech occasionally prompted by passion, and I have made use of them as such; but have endeavored utterly to reject them as a mechanical device of style, or as a family language which Writers in meter seem to lay claim to by prescription. I have wished to keep the Reader in the company of flesh and blood, persuaded that by so doing I shall interest him. Others who pursue a different track will interest him likewise; I do not interfere with their claim, but wish to prefer a claim of my own. There will also be found in these volumes little of what is usually called poetic diction; as much pains has been taken to avoid it as is ordinarily taken to produce it; this has been done for the reason already alleged, to bring my lan- guage near to the language of men; and fur- ther, because the pleasure which I have pro- posed to myself to impart is of a kind very different from that which is supposed by many persons to be the proper object of poetry. Without being culpably particular, I do not know how to give my Reader a more exact notion of the style in which it was my wish and intention to write, than by inform- ing him that I have at all times endeavored to look steadily at my subject; consequently there is, I hope, in these Poems little false- hood of description, and my ideas are ex- pressed in language fitted to their respective importance. Something must have been gained by this practice, as it is friendly to one property of all good poetry, namely, good sense: but it has necessarily cut me off from a large portion of phrases and figures of speech which from father to son have long been regarded as the common inheritance of Poets. I have also thought it expedient to restrict myself still further, having abstained from the use of many expressions, in them- [10] selves proper and beautiful, but which have been foolishly repeated by bad Poets, till such feelings of disgust are connected with them as it is scarcely possible by any art of association to overpower.

If in a poem there should be found a series of lines, or even a single line, in which the language, though naturally arranged, and according to the strict laws of meter, does not differ from that of prose, there is a [20] numerous class of critics, who, when they stumble upon these prosaisms, as they call them, imagine that they have made a notable discovery, and exult over the Poet as over a man ignorant of his own profession. Now these men would establish a canon of criticism which the Reader will conclude he must utterly reject, if he wishes to be pleased with these volumes. And it would be a most easy task to prove to him that not only the lan- [30] guage of a large portion of every good poem, even of the most elevated character, must necessarily, except with reference to the meter, in no respect differ from that of good prose, but likewise that some of the most interesting parts of the best poems will be found to be strictly the language of prose when prose is well written. The truth of this assertion might be demonstrated by innumerable passages from almost all the poetical [40] writings, even of Milton himself. To illustrate the subject in a general manner, I will here adduce a short composition of Gray, who was at the head of those who, by their reasonings, have attempted to widen the space of separation betwixt Prose and Metrical composition,[4] and was more than any other man curiously elaborate in the structure of his own poetic diction.

> In vain to me the smiling morning shine,
> And reddening Phoebus lifts his golden fire;
> The birds in vain their amorous descant join,
> Or cheerful fields resume their green attire;
> These ears, alas! for other notes repine;

[4] "The language of the age is never the language of poetry": letter from Thomas Gray to Richard West, 8 April, 1742.

> *A different object do these eyes require;*
> *My lonely anguish melts no heart but mine;*
> *And in my breast the imperfect joys expire;*
> Yet morning smiles the busy race to cheer,
> And new-born pleasure brings to happier men;
> The fields to all their wonted tribute bear;
> To warm their little loves the birds complain.
> *I fruitless mourn to him that cannot hear,*
> *And weep the more because I weep in vain.*[5]

It will easily be perceived, that the only part of this Sonnet which is of any value is the lines printed in Italics; it is equally obvious that, except in the rime and in the use of the single word "fruitless" for fruitlessly, which is so far a defect, the language of these lines does in no respect differ from that of prose.

By the foregoing quotation it has been shown that the language of Prose may yet be well adapted to Poetry; and it was previously asserted that a large portion of the language of every good poem can in no respect differ from that of good Prose. We will go further. It may be safely affirmed that there neither is, nor can be, any *essential* difference between the language of prose and metrical composition. We are fond of tracing the resemblance between Poetry and Painting, and, accordingly, we call them Sisters: but where shall we find bonds of connection sufficiently strict to typify the affinity betwixt metrical and prose composition? They both speak by and to the same organs; the bodies in which both of them are clothed may be said to be of the same substance, their affections are kindred, and almost identical, not necessarily differing even in degree; Poetry[6] sheds no tears "such as Angels weep," but natural and human tears; she can boast of no celestial ichor[7] that distinguishes her vital juices from those of Prose; the same human blood circulates through the veins of them both.

If it be affirmed that rime and metrical arrangement of themselves constitute a dis-

[5] Gray's *Sonnet on the Death of Richard West.*
[6] I here use the word "Poetry" (though against my own judgment) as opposed to the word Prose, and synonymous with metrical composition. But much confusion has been introduced into criticism by this contradistinction of Poetry and Prose, instead of the more philosophical one of Poetry and Matter of Fact, or Science. The only strict antithesis to Prose is Meter; nor is this, in truth, a *strict* antithesis, because lines and passages of meter so naturally occur in writing prose, that it would be scarcely possible to avoid them, even were it desirable (Wordsworth's note).
[7] An ethereal fluid that flows in the veins of the gods.

tinction which overturns what has just been said on the strict affinity of metrical language with that of Prose, and paves the way for other artificial distinctions which the mind voluntarily admits, I answer that the language of such Poetry as is here recommended is, as far as is possible, a selection of the language really spoken by men; that this selection, wherever it is made with true taste and feeling, will of itself form a distinction far greater than would at first be imagined, and will entirely separate the composition from the vulgarity and meanness of ordinary life; and, if meter be superadded thereto, I believe that a dissimilitude will be produced altogether sufficient for the gratification of a rational mind. What other distinction would we have? Whence is it to come? And where is it to exist? Not, surely, where the Poet speaks through the mouths of his characters: it cannot be necessary here, either for elevation of style, or any of its supposed ornaments; for, if the Poet's subject be judiciously chosen, it will naturally, and upon fit occasion, lead him to passions, the language of which, if selected truly and judiciously, must necessarily be dignified and variegated, and alive with metaphors and figures. I forbear to speak of an incongruity which would shock the intelligent Reader, should the Poet interweave any foreign splendor of his own with that which the passion naturally suggests: it is sufficient to say that such addition is unnecessary. And, surely, it is more probable that those passages, which with propriety abound with metaphors and figures, will have their due effect if, upon other occasions where the passions are of a milder character, the style also be subdued and temperate.

But, as the pleasure which I hope to give by the Poems now presented to the Reader must depend entirely on just notions upon this subject, and as it is in itself of high importance to our taste and moral feelings, I cannot content myself with these detached remarks. And if, in what I am about to say, it shall appear to some that my labor is unnecessary, and that I am like a man fighting a battle without enemies, such persons may be reminded that, whatever be the language outwardly holden by men, a practical faith in the opinions which I am wishing to establish is almost unknown. If my conclusions are admitted, and carried as far as they must be carried if admitted at all, our judgments concerning the works of the great-est Poets, both ancient and modern, will be far different from what they are at present, both when we praise and when we censure: and our moral feelings influencing and influenced by these judgments will, I believe, be corrected and purified.

Taking up the subject, then, upon general grounds, let me ask, what is meant by the word Poet? What is a Poet? To whom does he address himself? And what language is to be expected from him?—He is a man speaking to men: a man, it is true, endowed with more lively sensibility, more enthusiasm and tenderness, who has a greater knowledge of human nature, and a more comprehensive soul, than are supposed to be common among mankind; a man pleased with his own passions and volitions, and who rejoices more than other men in the spirit of life that is in him; delighting to contemplate similar volitions and passions as manifested in the goings-on of the Universe, and habitually impelled to create them where he does not find them. To these qualities he has added a disposition to be affected more than any other men by absent things as if they were present; an ability of conjuring up in himself passions, which are indeed far from being the same as those produced by real events, yet (especially in those parts of the general sympathy which are pleasing and delightful) do more nearly resemble the passions produced by real events than anything which, from the motions of their own minds merely, other men are accustomed to feel in themselves:— whence, and from practice, he has acquired a greater readiness and power in expressing what he thinks and feels, and especially those thoughts and feelings which, by his own choice, or from the structure of his own mind, arise in him without immediate external excitement.

But whatever portion of this faculty we may suppose even the greatest Poet to possess, there cannot be a doubt that the language which it will suggest to him must often, in liveliness and truth, fall short of that which is uttered by men in real life under the actual pressure of those passions, certain shadows of which the Poet thus produces, or feels to be produced, in himself.

However exalted a notion we would wish to cherish of the character of a Poet, it is obvious that, while he describes and imitates passions, his employment is in some degree mechanical compared with the freedom and power of real and substantial action and suffering. So that it will be the wish of the Poet to bring his feelings near to those of the persons whose feelings he describes, nay, for short spaces of time, perhaps, to let himself slip into an entire delusion, and even confound and identify his own feelings with theirs; modifying only the language which is thus suggested to him by a consideration that he describes for a particular purpose, that of giving pleasure. Here, then, he will apply the principle of selection which has been already insisted upon. He will depend upon this for removing what would otherwise be painful or disgusting in the passion; he will feel that there is no necessity to trick out or to elevate nature: and the more industriously he applies this principle the deeper will be his faith that no words, which *his* fancy or imagination can suggest, will be to be compared with those which are the emanations of reality and truth.

But it may be said by those who do not object to the general spirit of these remarks, that, as it is impossible for the Poet to produce upon all occasions language as exquisitely fitted for the passion as that which the real passion itself suggests, it is proper that he should consider himself as in the situation of a translator, who does not scruple to substitute excellences of another kind for those which are unattainable by him; and endeavors occasionally to surpass his original, in order to make some amends for the general inferiority to which he feels he must submit. But this would be to encourage idleness and unmanly despair. Further, it is the language of men who speak of what they do not understand; who talk of Poetry, as of a matter of amusement and idle pleasure; who will converse with us as gravely about a *taste* for Poetry, as they express it, as if it were a thing as indifferent as a taste for rope-dancing, or Frontiniac or Sherry. Aristotle, I have been told, has said that Poetry is the most philosophic of all writing: [8] it is so: its object is truth, not individual and local, but general and operative; not standing upon external testimony, but carried alive into the heart by passion; truth which is its own testimony, which gives competence and confidence to the tribunal to which it appeals, and receives them from the same tribunal. Poetry is the image of man and nature. The

[8] "Poetry is a more philosophical and a higher thing than history; for poetry tends to express the universal, history the particular" (Aristotle, *Poetics,* IX, 3).

obstacles which stand in the way of the fidelity of the Biographer and Historian, and of their consequent utility, are incalculably greater than those which are to be encountered by the Poet who comprehends the dignity of his art. The Poet writes under one restriction only, namely, the necessity of giving immediate pleasure to a human Being possessed of that information which may be expected from him, not as a lawyer, a physician, a mariner, an astronomer, or a natural philosopher, but as a Man. Except this one restriction, there is no object standing between the Poet and the image of things; between this, and the Biographer and Historian, there are a thousand.

Nor let this necessity of producing immediate pleasure be considered as a degradation of the Poet's art. It is far otherwise. It is an acknowledgment of the beauty of the universe, an acknowledgment the more sincere because not formal, but indirect; it is a task light and easy to him who looks at the world in the spirit of love: further, it is a homage paid to the native and naked dignity of man, to the grand elementary principle of pleasure, by which he knows, and feels, and lives, and moves. We have no sympathy but what is propagated by pleasure: I would not be misunderstood; but wherever we sympathize with pain, it will be found that the sympathy is produced and carried on by subtle combinations with pleasure. We have no knowledge, that is, no general principles drawn from the contemplation of particular facts, but what has been built up by pleasure, and exists in us by pleasure alone. The Man of science, the Chemist and Mathematician, whatever difficulties and disgusts they may have had to struggle with, know and feel this. However painful may be the objects with which the Anatomist's knowledge is connected, he feels that his knowledge is pleasure; and where he has no pleasure he has no knowledge. What then does the Poet? He considers man and the objects that surround him as acting and re-acting upon each other, so as to produce an infinite complexity of pain and pleasure; he considers man in his own nature and in his ordinary life as contemplating this with a certain quantity of immediate knowledge, with certain convictions, intuitions, and deductions, which from habit acquire the quality of intuitions; he considers him as looking upon this complex scene of ideas and sensations, and finding everywhere objects that immediately excite in him sympathies which, from the necessities of his nature, are accompanied by an overbalance of enjoyment.

To this knowledge which all men carry about with them, and to these sympathies in which, without any other discipline than that of our daily life, we are fitted to take delight, the Poet principally directs his attention. He considers man and nature as essentially adapted to each other, and the mind of man 10 as naturally the mirror of the fairest and most interesting properties of nature. And thus the Poet, prompted by this feeling of pleasure, which accompanies him through the whole course of his studies, converses with general nature, with affections akin to those which, through labor and length of time, the Man of science has raised up in himself, by conversing with those particular parts of nature which are the objects of his studies. 20 The knowledge both of the Poet and the Man of science is pleasure; but the knowledge of the one cleaves to us as a necessary part of our existence, or natural and un-alienable inheritance; the other is a personal and individual acquisition, slow to come to us, and by no habitual and direct sympathy connecting us with our fellow-beings. The Man of science seeks truth as a remote and unknown benefactor; he cherishes and loves 30 it in his solitude: the Poet, singing a song in which all human beings join with him, re-joices in the presence of truth as our visible friend and hourly companion. Poetry is the breath and finer spirit of all knowledge; it is the impassioned expression which is in the countenance of all Science. Emphatically may it be said of the Poet, as Shakespeare hath said of man, "that he looks before and after." [9] He is the rock of defense 40 for human nature; an upholder and pre-server, carrying everywhere with him rela-tionship and love. In spite of difference of soil and climate, of language and manners, of laws and customs: in spite of things silently gone out of mind, and things vio-lently destroyed; the Poet binds together by passion and knowledge the vast empire of human society, as it is spread over the whole earth and over all time. The objects of the 50 Poet's thoughts are everywhere; though the eyes and senses of man are, it is true, his favorite guides, yet he will follow whereso-ever he can find an atmosphere of sensation in which to move his wings. Poetry is the first and last of all knowledge—it is as im-

[9] *Hamlet,* IV, iv, 37.

mortal as the heart of man. If the labors of Men of science should ever create any ma-terial revolution, direct or indirect, in our condition, and in the impressions which we habitually receive, the Poet will sleep then no more than at present; he will be ready to follow the steps of the Man of science, not only in those general indirect effects, but he will be at his side, carrying sensation into the midst of the objects of the science itself. The remotest discoveries of the Chemist, the Botanist, or Mineralogist, will be as proper objects of the Poet's art as any upon which it can be employed, if the time should ever come when these things shall be familiar to us, and the relations under which they are contemplated by the followers of these re-spective sciences shall be manifestly and palpa-bly material to us as enjoying and suffering beings. If the time should ever come when what is now called science, thus familiarized to men, shall be ready to put on, as it were, a form of flesh and blood, the Poet will lend his divine spirit to aid the transfiguration, and will welcome the Being thus produced as a dear and genuine inmate of the household of man. —It is not, then, to be supposed that any one, who holds that sublime notion of Poetry which I have attempted to convey, will break in upon the sanctity and truth of his pictures by transitory and accidental ornaments, and en-deavor to excite admiration of himself by arts, the necessity of which must manifestly depend upon the assumed meanness of his subject.

What has been thus far said applies to Poetry in general, but especially to those parts of compositions where the Poet speaks through the mouths of his characters; and upon this point it appears to authorize the conclusion that there are few persons of good sense who would not allow that the dramatic parts of composition are defective in propor-tion as they deviate from the real language of nature, and are colored by a diction of the Poet's own, either peculiar to him as an indi-vidual Poet or belonging simply to Poets in general; to a body of men who, from the cir-cumstance of their compositions being in meter, it is expected will employ a particular language.

It is not, then, in the dramatic parts of composition that we look for this distinction of language; but still it may be proper and necessary where the Poet speaks to us in his own person and character. To this I answer by referring the Reader to the description be-fore given of a Poet. Among the quali-

ties there enumerated as principally con-
ducing to form a Poet, is implied nothing
differing in kind from other men, but only
in degree. The sum of what was said is,
that the Poet is chiefly distinguished from
other men by a greater promptness to think
and feel without immediate external excitement, and a greater power in expressing such
thoughts and feelings as are produced in him
in that manner. But these passions and 10
thoughts and feelings are the general passions and thoughts and feelings of men.
And with what are they connected? Undoubtedly with our moral sentiments and
animal sensations, and with the causes which
excite these; with the operations of the elements, and the appearances of the visible
universe; with storm and sunshine, with the
revolutions of the seasons, with cold and
heat, with loss of friends and kindred, with 20
injuries and resentments, gratitude and hope,
with fear and sorrow. These, and the like,
are the sensations and objects which the
Poet describes, as they are the sensations of
other men and the objects which interest
them. The Poet thinks and feels in the spirit
of human passions. How, then, can his language differ in any material degree from that
of all other men who feel vividly and see
clearly? It might be *proved* that it is im- 30
possible. But supposing that this were not
the case, the Poet might then be allowed
to use a peculiar language when expressing
his feelings for his own gratification, or that
of men like himself. But Poets do not write
for Poets alone, but for men. Unless, therefore, we are advocates for that admiration
which subsists upon ignorance, and that
pleasure which arises from hearing what we
do not understand, the Poet must descend 40
from this supposed height; and, in order to
excite rational sympathy, he must express
himself as other men express themselves.
To this it may be added, that while he is
only selecting from the real language of men,
or, which amounts to the same thing, composing accurately in the spirit of such selection, he is treading upon safe ground, and
we know what we are to expect from him.
Our feelings are the same with respect to 50
meter; for, as it may be proper to remind
the Reader, the distinction of meter is regular and uniform, and not, like that which is
produced by what is usually called "poetic
diction," arbitrary, and subject to infinite
caprices upon which no calculation whatever
can be made. In the one case, the Reader

is utterly at the mercy of the Poet, respecting
what imagery or diction he may choose to
connect with the passion; whereas, in the
other, the meter obeys certain laws, to which
the Poet and Reader both willingly submit
because they are certain, and because no interference is made by them with the passion
but such as the concurring testimony of ages
has shown to heighten and improve the
pleasure which co-exists with it.

It will now be proper to answer an obvious
question, namely, Why, professing these
opinions, have I written in verse? To this,
in addition to such answer as is included in
what has been already said, I reply, in the
first place, Because, however I may have restricted myself, there is still left open to me
what confessedly constitutes the most valuable object of all writing, whether in prose or
verse; the great and universal passions of
men, the most general and interesting of
their occupations, and the entire world of nature before me—to supply endless combinations of forms and imagery. Now, supposing
for a moment that whatever is interesting
in these objects may be as vividly described in prose, why should I be condemned for attempting to superadd to such
description the charm which, by the consent
of all nations, is acknowledged to exist in
metrical language? To this, by such as are
yet unconvinced, it may be answered that a
very small part of the pleasure given by
Poetry depends upon the meter, and that it is
injudicious to write in meter, unless it be accompanied with the other artificial distinctions of style with which meter is usually
accompanied, and that, by such deviation,
more will be lost from the shock which will
thereby be given to the Reader's associations
than will be counter-balanced by any pleasure
which he can derive from the general power
of numbers. In answer to those who still
contend for the necessity of accompanying
meter with certain appropriate colors of style
in order to the accomplishment of its appropriate end, and who also, in my opinion,
greatly underrate the power of meter in itself, it might, perhaps, as far as relates to
these Volumes, have been almost sufficient
to observe, that poems are extant, written
upon more humble subjects, and in a still
more naked and simple style, which have
continued to give pleasure from generation
to generation. Now, if nakedness and
simplicity be a defect, the fact here mentioned affords a strong presumption that

poems somewhat less naked and simple are capable of affording pleasure at the present day; and, what I wished *chiefly* to attempt, at present, was to justify myself for having written under the impression of this belief. But various causes might be pointed out why, when the style is manly, and the subject of some importance, words metrically arranged will long continue to impart such a pleasure to mankind as he who proves the extent of that pleasure will be desirous to impart. The end of poetry is to produce excitement in co-existence with an overbalance of pleasure; but, by the supposition, excitement is an unusual and irregular state of the mind; ideas and feelings do not, in that state, succeed each other in accustomed order. If the words, however, by which this excitement is produced be in themselves powerful, or the images and feelings have an undue proportion of pain connected with them, there is some danger that the excitement may be carried beyond its proper bounds. Now the co-presence of something regular, something to which the mind has been accustomed in various moods and in a less excited state, cannot but have great efficacy in tempering and restraining the passion by an intertexture of ordinary feeling, and of feeling not strictly and necessarily connected with the passion. This is unquestionably true; and hence, though the opinion will at first appear paradoxical, from the tendency of meter to divest language, in a certain degree, of its reality, and thus to throw a sort of half-consciousness of unsubstantial existence over the whole composition, there can be little doubt but that more pathetic situations and sentiments, that is, those which have a greater proportion of pain connected with them, may be endured in metrical composition, especially in rime, than in prose. The meter of the old ballads is very artless, yet they contain many passages which would illustrate this opinion; and, I hope, if the following poems be attentively perused, similar instances will be found in them. This opinion may be further illustrated by appealing to the Reader's own experience of the reluctance with which he comes to the reperusal of the distressful parts of *Clarissa Harlowe*, or the *Gamester*;[10] while Shakespeare's writings, in the most pathetic scenes, never act upon us, as pathetic, beyond the bounds of pleasure—an effect which, in a

much greater degree than might at first be imagined, is to be ascribed to small, but continual and regular impulses of pleasurable surprise from the metrical arrangement.—On the other hand (what it must be allowed will much more frequently happen), if the Poet's words should be incommensurate with the passion, and inadequate to raise the Reader to a height of desirable excitement, then (unless the Poet's choice of his meter has been grossly injudicious), in the feelings of pleasure which the Reader has been accustomed to connect with meter in general, and in the feeling, whether cheerful or melancholy, which he has been accustomed to connect with that particular movement of meter, there will be found something which will greatly contribute to impart passion to the words, and to effect the complex end which the Poet proposes to himself.

If I had undertaken a *systematic* defense of the theory here maintained, it would have been my duty to develop the various causes upon which the pleasure received from metrical language depends. Among the chief of these causes is to be reckoned a principle which must be well known to those who have made any of the Arts the object of accurate reflection; namely, the pleasure which the mind derives from the perception of similitude in dissimilitude. This principle is the great spring of the activity of our minds, and their chief feeder. From this principle the direction of the sexual appetite, and all the passions connected with it, take their origin: it is the life of our ordinary conversation; and upon the accuracy with which similitude in dissimilitude, and dissimilitude in similitude, are perceived, depend our taste and our moral feelings. It would not be a useless employment to apply this principle to the consideration of meter, and to show that meter is hence enabled to afford much pleasure, and to point out in what manner that pleasure is produced. But my limits will not permit me to enter upon this subject, and I must content myself with a general summary.

I have said that poetry is the spontaneous overflow of powerful feelings; it takes its origin from emotion recollected in tranquillity; the emotion is contemplated till, by a species of re-action, the tranquillity gradually disappears, and an emotion, kindred to that which was before the subject of contemplation, is gradually produced, and does itself actually exist in the mind. In this mood successful composition generally begins, and in a mood similar to this it is carried on; but the emotion, of whatever kind, and in whatever degree, from various

[10] The former a novel by Samuel Richardson, published in 1748; the latter a tragedy by Edward Moore, published in 1753.

causes, is qualified by various pleasures, so that in describing any passions whatsoever, which are voluntarily described, the mind will, upon the whole, be in a state of enjoyment. If Nature be thus cautious to preserve in a state of enjoyment a being so employed, the Poet ought to profit by the lesson held forth to him, and ought especially to take care that, whatever passions he communicates to his Reader, those passions, if his Reader's mind be sound and 10 vigorous, should always be accompanied with an over-balance of pleasure. Now the music of harmonious metrical language, the sense of difficulty overcome, and the blind association of pleasure which has been previously received from works of rime or meter of the same or similar construction, an indistinct perception perpetually renewed of language closely resembling that of real life, and yet, in the circumstance of meter, differing from it so widely—all 20 these imperceptibly make up a complex feeling of delight, which is of the most important use in tempering the painful feeling always found intermingled with powerful descriptions of the deeper passions. This effect is always produced in pathetic and impassioned poetry; while, in lighter compositions, the ease and gracefulness with which the Poet manages his numbers are themselves confessedly a principal source of the gratification of the Reader. All that it is *neces-* 30 *sary* to say, however, upon this subject, may be effected by affirming, what few persons will deny, that of two descriptions, either of passions, manners, or characters, each of them equally well executed, the one in prose and the other in verse, the verse will be read a hundred times where the prose is read once.

Having thus explained a few of my reasons for writing in verse, and why I have chosen subjects from common life, and endeavored to 40 bring my language near to the real language of men, if I have been too minute in pleading my own cause, I have at the same time been treating a subject of general interest; and for this reason a few words shall be added with reference solely to these particular poems, and to some defects which will probably be found in them. I am sensible that my associations must have sometimes been particular instead of general, and that, consequently, giving to 50 things a false importance, I may have sometimes written upon unworthy subjects; but I am less apprehensive on this account, than that my language may frequently have suffered from those arbitrary connections of feelings and ideas with particular words and phrases from which no man can altogether protect himself.

Hence I have no doubt that, in some instances, feelings, even of the ludicrous, may be given to my Readers by expressions which appeared to me tender and pathetic. Such faulty expressions, were I convinced they were faulty at present, and that they must necessarily continue to be so, I would willingly take all reasonable pains to correct. But it is dangerous to make these alterations on the simple authority of a few individuals, or even of certain classes of men; for where the understanding of an author is not convinced, or his feelings altered, this cannot be done without great injury to himself: for his own feelings are his stay and support; and, if he set them aside in one instance, he may be induced to repeat this act till his mind shall lose all confidence in itself, and become utterly debilitated. To this it may be added that the critic ought never to forget 20 that he is himself exposed to the same errors as the Poet, and, perhaps, in a much greater degree: for there can be no presumption in saying of most readers that it is not probable they will be so well acquainted with the various stages of meaning through which words have passed, or with the fickleness of stability of the relations of particular ideas to each other; and, above all, since they are so much less interested in the subject, they may decide lightly and 30 carelessly.

Long as the reader has been detained, I hope he will permit me to caution him against a mode of false criticism which has been applied to poetry, in which the language closely resembles that of life and nature. Such verses have been triumphed over in parodies, of which Dr. Johnson's stanza is a fair specimen:—

> I put my hat upon my head,
> And walked into the Strand,
> And there I met another man
> Whose hat was in his hand.

Immediately under these lines let us place one of the most justly-admired stanzas of the *Babes in the Wood*.[11]

> These pretty Babes with hand in hand
> Went wandering up and down;
> But never more they saw the Man
> Approaching from the Town.

In both these stanzas the words, and the order of the words, in no respect differ from the most unimpassioned conversation. There are words in both, for example, "the Strand," and "the Town," connected with none but the most familiar ideas; yet the one stanza we admit as admirable, and the other as a fair exam-

[11] A popular ballad of the sixteenth century.

ple of the superlatively contemptible. Whence arises this difference? Not from the meter, not from the language, not from the order of the words; but the *matter* expressed in Dr. Johnson's stanza is contemptible. The proper method of treating trivial and simple verses, to which Dr. Johnson's stanza would be a fair parallelism, is not to say, this is a bad kind of poetry, or, this is not poetry; but, this wants sense; it is neither interesting in itself, nor can lead to anything interesting; the images neither originate in that sane state of feeling which arises out of thought, nor can excite thought or feeling in the Reader. This is the only sensible manner of dealing with such verses. Why trouble yourself about the species till you have previously decided upon the genus? Why take pains to prove that an ape is not a Newton, when it is self-evident that he is not a man?

One request I must make of my Reader, which is, that in judging these Poems he would decide by his own feelings genuinely, and not by reflection upon what will probably be the judgment of others. How common is it to hear a person say, I myself do not object to this style of composition, or this or that expression, but to such and such classes of people it will appear mean or ludicrous! This mode of criticism, so destructive of all sound unadulterated judgment, is almost universal: let the Reader then abide, independently, by his own feelings, and, if he finds himself affected, let him not suffer such conjectures to interfere with his pleasure.

If an Author, by any single composition, has impressed us with respect for his talents, it is useful to consider this as affording a presumption that on other occasions where we have been displeased he, nevertheless, may not have written ill or absurdly; and further, to give him so much credit for this one composition as may induce us to review what has displeased us with more care than we should otherwise have bestowed upon it. This is not only an act of justice, but, in our decisions upon poetry especially, may conduce, in a high degree, to the improvement of our own taste: for an *accurate* taste in poetry, and in all the other arts, as Sir Joshua Reynolds has observed, is an *acquired* talent, which can only be produced by thought and a long-continued intercourse with the best models of composition. This is mentioned, not with so ridiculous a purpose as to prevent the most inexperienced Reader from judging for himself (I have already said that I wish him to judge for himself), but merely to temper the rashness of decision, and to suggest that, if Poetry be a subject on which much time has not been bestowed, the judgment may be erroneous; and that, in many cases, it necessarily will be so.

Nothing would, I know, have so effectually contributed to further the end which I have in view, as to have shown of what kind the pleasure is, and how that pleasure is produced, which is confessedly produced by metrical composition essentially different from that which I have here endeavored to recommend: for the Reader will say that he has been pleased by such composition; and what more can be done for him? The power of any art is limited; and he will suspect that, if it be proposed to furnish him with new friends, that can be only upon condition of his abandoning his old friends. Besides, as I have said, the Reader is himself conscious of the pleasure which he has received from such composition, composition to which he has peculiarly attached the endearing name of Poetry; and all men feel an habitual gratitude, and something of an honorable bigotry, for the objects which have long continued to please them: we not only wish to be pleased, but to be pleased in that particular way in which we have been accustomed to be pleased. There is in these feelings enough to resist a host of arguments; and I should be the less able to combat them successfully, as I am willing to allow that, in order entirely to enjoy the Poetry which I am recommending, it would be necessary to give up much of what is ordinarily enjoyed. But would my limits have permitted me to point out how this pleasure is produced, many obstacles might have been removed, and the Reader assisted in perceiving that the powers of language are not so limited as he may suppose; and that it is possible for poetry to give other enjoyments, of a purer, more lasting, and more exquisite nature. This part of the subject has not been altogether neglected, but it has not been so much my present aim to prove that the interest excited by some other kinds of poetry is less vivid, and less worthy of the nobler powers of the mind, as to offer reasons for presuming that if my purpose were fulfilled, a species of poetry would be produced which is genuine poetry; in its nature well adapted to interest mankind permanently, and likewise important in the multiplicity and quality of its moral relations.

From what has been said, and from a perusal of the Poems, the Reader will be able clearly to perceive the object which I

had in view: he will determine how far it has
been attained, and, what is a much more important question, whether it be worth attaining: and upon the decision of these two questions will rest my claim to the approbation of
the Public.

## Lines

*Left upon a Seat in a Yew-Tree, Which
Stands near the Lake of Esthwaite, on a
Desolate Part of the Shore, Commanding
a Beautiful Prospect* [1]

Nay, Traveler! rest. This lonely Yew-tree stands
Far from all human dwelling: what if here
No sparkling rivulet spread the verdant herb?
What if the bee love not these barren boughs?
Yet, if the wind breathe soft, the curling waves,
That break against the shore, shall lull thy
mind                                                6
By one soft impulse saved from vacancy.
                              Who he was
That piled these stones and with the mossy sod
First covered, and here taught this agèd Tree 10
With its dark arms to form a circling bower,
I well remember.—He was one who owned
No common soul. In youth by science nursed,
And led by nature into a wild scene
Of lofty hopes, he to the world went forth 15
A favored Being, knowing no desire
Which genius did not hallow; 'gainst the taint
Of dissolute tongues, and jealousy, and hate,
And scorn,—against all enemies prepared,
All but neglect. The world, for so it thought, 20
Owed him no service; wherefore he at once
With indignation turned himself away,
And with the food of pride sustained his soul
In solitude.—Stranger! these bloomy boughs
Had charms for him; and here he loved to sit,
His only visitants a straggling sheep,        26
The stone-chat, or the glancing sand-piper:
And on these barren rocks, with fern and heath,
And juniper and thistle, sprinkled o'er,
Fixing his downcast eye, he many an hour 30
A morbid pleasure nourished, tracing here
An emblem of his own unfruitful life:
And, lifting up his head, he then would gaze
On the more distant scene,—how lovely 'tis
Thou seest,—and he would gaze till it became
Far lovelier, and his heart could not sustain 36
The beauty, still more beauteous! Nor that
time,
When nature had subdued him to herself,
Would he forget those Beings to whose minds,
Warm from the labors of benevolence,      40
The world, and human life, appeared a scene
Of kindred loveliness: then he would sigh,
Inly disturbed, to think that others felt

What he must never feel: and so, lost Man!
On visionary views would fancy feed,       45
Till his eye streamed with tears. In this deep
vale
He died,—this seat his only monument.
   If Thou be one whose heart the holy forms
Of young imagination have kept pure,
Stranger! henceforth be warned; and know that
pride,                                        50
Howe'er disguised in its own majesty,
Is littleness; that he who feels contempt
For any living thing, hath faculties
Which he has never used; that thought with
him
Is in its infancy. The man whose eye       55
Is ever on himself doth look on one,
The least of Nature's works, one who might
move
The wise man to that scorn which wisdom
holds
Unlawful, ever. O be wiser, Thou!
Instructed that true knowledge leads to love; 60
True dignity abides with him alone
Who, in the silent hour of inward thought,
Can still suspect, and still revere himself,
In lowliness of heart.

## We Are Seven [1]

——A simple Child,
That lightly draws its breath,
And feels its life in every limb,
What should it know of death? [2]

I met a little cottage Girl:                    5
She was eight years old, she said;
Her hair was thick with many a curl
That clustered round her head.

She had a rustic, woodland air,
And she was wildly clad:                     10
Her eyes were fair, and very fair;
—Her beauty made me glad.

"Sisters and brothers, little Maid,
How many may you be?"
"How many? Seven in all," she said,         15
And wondering looked at me.

"And where are they? I pray you tell."
She answered, "Seven are we;
And two of us at Conway dwell,
And two are gone to sea.                     20

"Two of us in the church-yard lie,
My sister and my brother;
And, in the church-yard cottage, I
Dwell near them with my mother."

"You say that two at Conway dwell,          25
And two are gone to sea,

[1] Begun in 1787; completed in 1795; published
in 1798.

[1] Composed in 1798; published in the same year.
[2] This stanza was written by Coleridge.

Yet ye are seven!—I pray you tell,
Sweet Maid, how this may be."

Then did the little Maid reply,
"Seven boys and girls are we;    30
Two of us in the church-yard lie,
Beneath the church-yard tree."

"You run about, my little Maid,
Your limbs they are alive;
If two are in the church-yard laid,    35
Then ye are only five."

"Their graves are green, they may be seen,"
The little Maid replied,
"Twelve steps or more from my mother's door,
And they are side by side.    40

"My stockings there I often knit,
My kerchief there I hem;
And there upon the ground I sit,
And sing a song to them.

"And often after sunset, Sir,    45
When it is light and fair,
I take my little porringer,
And eat my supper there.

"The first that died was sister Jane;
In bed she moaning lay,    50
Till God released her of her pain;
And then she went away.

"So in the church-yard she was laid;
And, when the grass was dry,
Together round her grave we played,    55
My brother John and I.

"And when the ground was white with snow,
And I could run and slide,
My brother John was forced to go,
And he lies by her side."    60

"How many are you, then," said I,
"If they two are in heaven?"
Quick was the little Maid's reply,
"O Master! we are seven."

"But they are dead; those two are dead!    65
Their spirits are in heaven!"
'T was throwing words away; for still
The little Maid would have her will,
And said, "Nay, we are seven!"

## Lines Written in Early Spring [1]

I heard a thousand blended notes,
While in a grove I sat reclined,
In that sweet mood when pleasant thoughts
Bring sad thoughts to the mind.

[1] Written and published in 1798.

To her fair works did Nature link    5
The human soul that through me ran;
And much it grieved my heart to think
What man has made of man.

Through primrose tufts, in that green bower
The periwinkle trailed its wreaths;    10
And 'tis my faith that every flower
Enjoys the air it breathes.

The birds around me hopped and played,
Their thoughts I cannot measure:—
But the least motion which they made,    15
It seemed a thrill of pleasure.

The budding twigs spread out their fan,
To catch the breezy air;
And I must think, do all I can,
That there was pleasure there.    20

If this belief from heaven be sent,
If such be Nature's holy plan,
Have I not reason to lament
What man has made of man?

## Expostulation and Reply [2]

"Why, William, on that old gray stone,
Thus for the length of half a day,
Why, William, sit you thus alone,
And dream your time away?

"Where are your books?—that light bequeathed    5
To Beings else forlorn and blind!
Up! up! and drink the spirit breathed
From dead men to their kind.

"You look round on your Mother Earth,
As if she for no purpose bore you;    10
As if you were her first-born birth,
And none had lived before you!"

One morning thus, by Esthwaite lake,
When life was sweet, I knew not why,
To me my good friend Matthew spake,    15
And thus I made reply:

"The eye—it cannot choose but see;
We cannot bid the ear be still;
Our bodies feel, where'er they be,
Against or with our will.    20

"Nor less I deem that there are Powers
Which of themselves our minds impress;
That we can feed this mind of ours
In a wise passiveness.

"Think you, 'mid all this mighty sum    25
Of things for ever speaking,
That nothing of itself will come,
But we must still be seeking?

[2] Written and published in 1798.

"—Then ask not wherefore, here, alone,
Conversing as I may,                        30
I sit upon this old gray stone,
And dream my time away."

## The Tables Turned [3]

### An Evening Scene on the Same Subject

Up! up! my Friend, and quit your books;
Or surely you'll grow double:
Up! up! my Friend, and clear your looks;
Why all this toil and trouble?

The sun, above the mountain's head,          5
A freshening luster mellow
Through all the long green fields has spread,
His first sweet evening yellow.

Books! 'tis a dull and endless strife:
Come, hear the woodland linnet,             10
How sweet his music! on my life,
There's more of wisdom in it.

And hark! how blithe the throstle sings!
He, too, is no mean preacher:
Come forth into the light of things,        15
Let Nature be your Teacher.

She has a world of ready wealth,
Our minds and hearts to bless—
Spontaneous wisdom breathed by health,
Truth breathed by cheerfulness.             20

One impulse from a vernal wood
May teach you more of man,
Of moral evil and of good,
Than all the sages can.

Sweet is the lore which Nature brings;      25
Our meddling intellect
Mis-shapes the beauteous forms of things:—
We murder to dissect.

Enough of Science and of Art;
Close up those barren leaves;               30
Come forth, and bring with you a heart
That watches and receives.

## Lines

### Composed a Few Miles above Tintern Abbey, on Revisiting the Banks of the Wye during a Tour. July 13, 1798 [1]

Five years have passed; five summers, with the
     length
Of five long winters! and again I hear

[3] Written and published in 1798.
[1] Published in 1798. "No poem of mine was composed under circumstances more pleasant for me to remember than this. I began it upon leaving Tintern, after crossing the Wye, and concluded it just as I was entering Bristol in the evening, after a ramble

These waters, rolling from their mountain-
     springs
With a soft inland murmur.—Once again
Do I behold these steep and lofty cliffs,    5
That on a wild secluded scene impress
Thoughts of more deep seclusion; and connect
The landscape with the quiet of the sky.
The day is come when I again repose
Here, under this dark sycamore, and view     10
These plots of cottage-ground, these orchard-
     tufts,
Which at this season, with their unripe fruits,
Are clad in one green hue, and lose themselves
'Mid groves and copses. Once again I see
These hedge-rows, hardly hedge-rows, little
     lines                                   15
Of sportive wood run wild: these pastoral farms,
Green to the very door; and wreaths of smoke
Sent up, in silence, from among the trees!
With some uncertain notice, as might seem
Of vagrant dwellers in the houseless woods    20
Or of some Hermit's cave, where by his fire
The hermit sits alone.
                        These beauteous forms,
Through a long absence, have not been to me
As is a landscape to a blind man's eye:
But oft, in lonely rooms, and 'mid the din   25
Of towns and cities, I have owed to them
In hours of weariness, sensations sweet,
Felt in the blood, and felt along the heart;
And passing even into my purer mind,
With tranquil restoration:—feelings too      30
Of unremembered pleasure: such, perhaps,
As have no slight or trivial influence
On that best portion of a good man's life,
His little, nameless, unremembered acts
Of kindness and of love. Nor less, I trust,  35
To them I may have owed another gift,
Of aspect more sublime; that blessed mood,
In which the burthen of the mystery,
In which the heavy and the weary weight
Of all this unintelligible world,            40
Is lightened:—that serene and blessed mood,
In which the affections gently lead us on,—
Until, the breath of this corporeal frame
And even the motion of our human blood
Almost suspended, we are laid asleep         45
In body, and become a living soul:
While with an eye made quiet by the power
Of harmony, and the deep power of joy,
We see into the life of things.
                              If this
Be but a vain belief, yet, oh! how oft—      50
In darkness and amid the many shapes
Of joyless daylight; when the fretful stir
Unprofitable, and the fever of the world,
Have hung upon the beatings of my heart—

of four or five days, with my sister. Not a line of it was altered, and not any part of it written down till I reached Bristol" (Wordsworth, *Fenwick Note*). This great poem is of the utmost importance for understanding the influence Wordsworth felt from nature.

How oft, in spirit, have I turned to thee,  55
O sylvan Wye! thou wanderer through the
woods,
How often has my spirit turned to thee!
    And now, with gleams of half-extinguished
    thought,
With many recognitions dim and faint,
And somewhat of a sad perplexity,  60
The picture of the mind revives again:
While here I stand, not only with the sense
Of present pleasure, but with pleasing thoughts
That in this moment there is life and food
For future years. And so I dare to hope,  65
Though changed, no doubt, from what I was
    when first
I came among these hills; when like a roe
I bounded o'er the mountains, by the sides
Of the deep rivers, and the lonely streams,
Wherever nature led: more like a man  70
Flying from something that he dreads, than one
Who sought the thing he loved. For nature
    then
(The coarser pleasures of my boyish days,
And their glad animal movements all gone by)
To me was all in all.—I cannot paint  75
What then I was. The sounding cataract
Haunted me like a passion; the tall rock,
The mountain, and the deep and gloomy wood,
Their colors and their forms, were then to me
An appetite; a feeling and a love,  80
That had no need of a remoter charm,
By thought supplied, nor any interest
Unborrowed from the eye.—That time is past,
And all its aching joys are now no more,
And all its dizzy raptures. Not for this  85
Faint I, nor mourn nor murmur; other gifts
Have followed; for such loss, I would believe,
Abundant recompense. For I have learned
To look on nature, not as in the hour
Of thoughtless youth; but hearing oftentimes  90
The still, sad music of humanity,
Nor harsh nor grating, though of ample power
To chasten and subdue. And I have felt
A presence that disturbs me with the joy
Of elevated thoughts; a sense sublime  95
Of something far more deeply interfused,
Whose dwelling is the light of setting suns,
And the round ocean and the living air,
And the blue sky, and in the mind of man;
A motion and a spirit, that impels  100
All thinking things, all objects of all thought,
And rolls through all things. Therefore am I
    still
A lover of the meadows and the woods,
And mountains; and of all that we behold
From this green earth; of all the mighty world
Of eye, and ear,—both what they half create,
And what perceive; well pleased to recognize  107
In nature and the language of the sense,
The anchor of my purest thoughts, the nurse,
The guide, the guardian of my heart, and soul
Of all my moral being.
                        Nor perchance,  111

If I were not thus taught, should I the more
Suffer my genial spirits to decay:
For thou art with me here upon the banks
Of this fair river; thou my dearest Friend,  115
My dear, dear Friend; [2] and in thy voice I catch
The language of my former heart, and read
My former pleasures in the shooting lights
Of thy wild eyes. Oh! yet a little while
May I behold in thee what I was once,  120
My dear, dear Sister! and this prayer I make,
Knowing that Nature never did betray
The heart that loved her; 'tis her privilege,
Through all the years of this our life, to lead
From joy to joy: for she can so inform  125
The mind that is within us, so impress
With quietness and beauty, and so feed
With lofty thoughts, that neither evil tongues,
Rash judgments, nor the sneers of selfish men,
Nor greetings where no kindness is, nor all  130
The dreary intercourse of daily life,
Shall e'er prevail against us, or disturb
Our cheerful faith, that all which we behold
Is full of blessings. Therefore let the moon
Shine on thee in thy solitary walk;  135
And let the misty mountain-winds be free
To blow against thee: and, in after years,
When these wild ecstasies shall be matured
Into a sober pleasure; when thy mind
Shall be a mansion for all lovely forms,  140
Thy memory be as a dwelling-place
For all sweet sounds and harmonies; oh! then,
If solitude, or fear, or pain, or grief,
Should be thy portion, with what healing
    thoughts
Of tender joy wilt thou remember me,  145
And these my exhortations! Nor, perchance—
If I should be where I no more can hear
Thy voice, nor catch from thy wild eyes these
    gleams
Of past existence—wilt thou then forget
That on the banks of this delightful stream  150
We stood together; and that I, so long
A worshiper of Nature, hither came
Unwearied in that service: rather say
With warmer love—oh! with far deeper zeal
Of holier love. Nor wilt thou then forget,  155
That after many wanderings, many years
Of absence, these steep woods and lofty cliffs,
And this green pastoral landscape, were to me
More dear, both for themselves and for thy
    sake!

## Strange Fits of Passion
## Have I Known [1]

Strange fits of passion have I known:
And I will dare to tell,

[2] Dorothy Wordsworth.
[1] Written in 1799; published in 1800. This poem
and the following four form a group known as the
"Lucy Poems." If Lucy was a real woman, there
seems to be little likelihood that she will ever be
identified.

But in the Lover's ear alone,
  What once to me befell.

When she I loved looked every day    5
Fresh as a rose in June,
I to her cottage bent my way,
  Beneath an evening-moon.

Upon the moon I fixed my eye,
  All over the wide lea;    10
With quickening pace my horse drew nigh
  Those paths so dear to me.

And now we reached the orchard-plot;
  And, as we climbed the hill,
The sinking moon to Lucy's cot    15
  Came near, and nearer still.

In one of those sweet dreams I slept,
  Kind nature's gentlest boon!
And all the while my eyes I kept
  On the descending moon.    20

My horse moved on; hoof after hoof
  He raised, and never stopped:
When down behind the cottage roof,
  At once, the bright moon dropped.

What fond and wayward thoughts will slide
Into a Lover's head!    26
"O mercy!" to myself I cried,
  "If Lucy should be dead!"

## She Dwelt among the Untrodden Ways [2]

She dwelt among the untrodden ways
  Beside the springs of Dove,
A Maid whom there were none to praise
  And very few to love:

A violet by a mossy stone    5
  Half hidden from the eye!
—Fair as a star, when only one
  Is shining in the sky.

She lived unknown, and few could know
  When Lucy ceased to be;    10
But she is in her grave, and, oh,
  The difference to me!

## I Traveled among Unknown Men [3]

I traveled among unknown men,
  In lands beyond the sea;
Nor, England! did I know till then
  What love I bore to thee.

[2] Written in 1799; published in 1800.
[3] Written in 1799; published in 1807.

'Tis past, that melancholy dream!    5
  Nor will I quit thy shore
A second time; for still I seem
  To love thee more and more.

Among thy mountains did I feel
  The joy of my desire;    10
And she I cherished turned her wheel
  Beside an English fire.

Thy mornings showed, thy nights concealed
  The bowers where Lucy played;
And thine too is the last green field    15
  That Lucy's eyes surveyed.

## Three Years She Grew in Sun and Shower [4]

Three years she grew in sun and shower,
Then Nature said, "A lovelier flower
On earth was never sown;
This Child I to myself will take;
She shall be mine, and I will make    5
A Lady of my own.

"Myself will to my darling be
Both law and impulse: and with me
The Girl, in rock and plain,
In earth and heaven, in glade and bower,    10
Shall feel an overseeing power
To kindle or restrain.

"She shall be sportive as the fawn
That wild with glee across the lawn,
Or up the mountain springs;    15
And hers shall be the breathing balm,
And hers the silence and the calm
Of mute insensate things.

"The floating clouds their state shall lend
To her; for her the willow bend;    20
Nor shall she fail to see
Even in the motions of the Storm
Grace that shall mold the Maiden's form
By silent sympathy.

"The stars of midnight shall be dear    25
To her; and she shall lean her ear
In many a secret place
Where rivulets dance their wayward round,
And beauty born of murmuring sound
Shall pass into her face.    30

"And vital feelings of delight
Shall rear her form to stately height,
Her virgin bosom swell;
Such thoughts to Lucy I will give
While she and I together live    35
Here in this happy dell."

Thus Nature spake—The work was done—
How soon my Lucy's race was run!

[4] Written in 1799; published in 1800.

She died, and left to me
This heath, this calm, and quiet scene; 40
The memory of what has been,
And never more will be.

## A Slumber Did My Spirit Seal [5]

A slumber did my spirit seal;
 I had no human fears:
She seemed a thing that could not feel
 The touch of earthly years.

No motion has she now, no force; 5
 She neither hears nor sees;
Rolled round in earth's diurnal course,
 With rocks, and stones, and trees.

## Lucy Gray

### *or*

### Solitude [1]

Oft I had heard of Lucy Gray:
And, when I crossed the wild,
I chanced to see at break of day
The solitary child.

No mate, no comrade Lucy knew; 5
She dwelt on a wide moor,
—The sweetest thing that ever grew
Beside a human door!

You yet may spy the fawn at play,
The hare upon the green; 10
But the sweet face of Lucy Gray
Will never more be seen.

"To-night will be a stormy night—
You to the town must go;
And take a lantern, Child, to light 15
Your mother through the snow."

"That, Father! will I gladly do:
'Tis scarcely afternoon—
The minster-clock has just struck two,
And yonder is the moon!" 20

At this the Father raised his hook,
And snapped a faggot-band;
He plied his work;—and Lucy took
The lantern in her hand.

Not blither is the mountain roe: 25
With many a wanton stroke
Her feet disperse the powdery snow,
That rises up like smoke.

The storm came on before its time:
She wandered up and down; 30
And many a hill did Lucy climb:
But never reached the town.

[5] Written in 1799; published in 1800.
[1] Written in 1799; published in 1800.

The wretched parents all that night
Went shouting far and wide;
But there was neither sound nor sight 35
To serve them for a guide.

At day-break on a hill they stood
That overlooked the moor;
And thence they saw the bridge of wood,
A furlong from their door. 40

They wept—and, turning homeward, cried,
"In heaven we all shall meet;"
—When in the snow the mother spied
The print of Lucy's feet.

Then downwards from the steep hill's edge 45
They tracked the footmarks small;
And through the broken hawthorn hedge,
And by the long stone-wall;

And then an open field they crossed:
The marks were still the same; 50
They tracked them on, nor ever lost;
And to the bridge they came.

They followed from the snowy bank
Those footmarks, one by one,
Into the middle of the plank; 55
And further there were none!

—Yet some maintain that to this day
She is a living child;
That you may see sweet Lucy Gray
Upon the lonesome wild. 60

O'er rough and smooth she trips along,
And never looks behind;
And sings a solitary song
That whistles in the wind.

## Michael [1]

### A Pastoral Poem

If from the public way you turn your steps
Up the tumultuous brook of Greenhead Ghyll,[2]

[1] Written and published in 1800. "Written at
Town-end, Grasmere, about the same time as *The
Brothers*. The Sheepfold, on which so much of
the poem turns, remains, or rather the ruins of it.
The character and circumstances of Luke were taken
from a family to whom had belonged, many years
before, the house we lived in at Town-end, along
with some fields and woodlands on the eastern shore
of Grasmere. The name of the Evening Star was
not in fact given to this house, but to another on
the same side of the valley, more to the north"
(Wordsworth, *Fenwick Note*). Most of *Michael*,
as the journal of Dorothy Wordsworth reveals, was
actually written in the sheepfold. Wordsworth wrote
to a friend: "I have attempted to give a picture of
a man, of strong mind and lively sensibility, agitated
by two of the most powerful affections of the human
heart: the parental affection and the love of property (*landed* property), including the feelings of inheritance, home, and personal and family independence."

[2] A ravine with a stream running through it.

You will suppose that with an upright path
Your feet must struggle; in such bold ascent
The pastoral mountains front you, face to face.
But, courage! for around that boisterous brook 6
The mountains have all opened out them-
selves,
And made a hidden valley of their own.
No habitation can be seen; but they
Who journey thither find themselves alone 10
With a few sheep, with rocks and stones, and
kites
That overhead are sailing in the sky.
It is in truth an utter solitude;
Nor should I have made mention of this Dell
But for one object which you might pass by, 15
Might see and notice not. Beside the brook
Appears a straggling heap of unhewn stones!
And to that simple object appertains
A story—unenriched with strange events,
Yet not unfit, I deem, for the fireside,          20
Or for the summer shade. It was the first
Of those domestic tales that spake to me
Of shepherds, dwellers in the valleys, men
Whom I already loved; not verily
For their own sakes, but for the fields and hills
Where was their occupation and abode.       26
And hence this Tale, while I was yet a Boy
Careless of books, yet having felt the power
Of Nature, by the gentle agency
Of natural objects, led me on to feel          30
For passions that were not my own, and think
(At random and imperfectly indeed)
On man, the heart of man, and human life.
Therefore, although it be a history
Homely and rude, I will relate the same      35
For the delight of a few natural hearts;
And, with yet fonder feeling, for the sake
Of youthful Poets, who among these hills
Will be my second self when I am gone.

Upon the forest-side in Grasmere Vale       40
There dwelt a Shepherd, Michael was his name;
An old man, stout of heart, and strong of limb.
His bodily frame had been from youth to age
Of an unusual strength: his mind was keen,
Intense, and frugal, apt for all affairs,        45
And in his shepherd's calling he was prompt
And watchful more than ordinary men.
Hence had he learned the meaning of all winds,
Of blasts of every tone; and oftentimes,
When others heeded not, He heard the South
Make subterraneous music, like the noise    51
Of bagpipers on distant Highland hills.
The Shepherd, at such warning, of his flock
Bethought him, and he to himself would say,
"The winds are now devising work for me!" 55
And, truly, at all times, the storm, that drives
The traveler to a shelter, summoned him
Up to the mountains: he had been alone
Amid the heart of many thousand mists,
That came to him, and left him, on the
heights.                                          60
So lived he till his eightieth year was past.

And grossly that man errs, who should suppose
That the green valleys, and the streams and
rocks,
Were things indifferent to the Shepherd's
thoughts.
Fields, where with cheerful spirits he had
breathed                                          65
The common air; hills, which with vigorous
step
He had so often climbed; which had impressed
So many incidents upon his mind
Of hardship, skill or courage, joy or fear;
Which, like a book, preserved the memory   70
Of the dumb animals, whom he had saved,
Had fed or sheltered, linking to such acts
The certainty of honorable gain;
Those fields, those hills—what could they less?
had laid
Strong hold on his affections, were to him   75
A pleasurable feeling of blind love,
The pleasure which there is in life itself.
His days had not been passed in singleness.
His Helpmate was a comely matron, old—
Though younger than himself full twenty years.
She was a woman of a stirring life,            81
Whose heart was in her house: two wheels she
had
Of antique form; this large, for spinning wool;
That small, for flax; and if one wheel had rest
It was because the other was at work.        85
The Pair had but one inmate in their house,
An only Child, who had been born to them
When Michael, telling o'er his years, began
To deem that he was old,—in shepherd's
phrase,
With one foot in the grave. This only Son,   90
With two brave sheep-dogs tried in many a
storm,
The one of an inestimable worth,
Made all their household. I may truly say,
That they were as a proverb in the vale
For endless industry. When day was gone,   95
And from their occupations out of doors
The Son and Father were come home, even
then,
Their labor did not cease; unless when all
Turned to the cleanly supper-board, and there,
Each with a mess of potage and skimmed milk,
Sat round the basket piled with oaten cakes, 101
And their plain home-made cheese. Yet when
the meal
Was ended, Luke (for so the Son was named)
And his old Father both betook themselves
To such convenient work as might employ  105
Their hands by the fireside; perhaps to card
Wool for the Housewife's spindle, or repair
Some injury done to sickle, flail, or scythe,
Or other implement of house or field.
    Down from the ceiling, by the chimney's
edge,                                            110
That in our ancient uncouth country style
With huge and black projection overbrowed
Large space beneath, as duly as the light

Of day grew dim the Housewife hung a lamp;
An agéd utensil, which had performed      115
Service beyond all others of its kind.
Early at evening did it burn—and late,
Surviving comrade of uncounted hours,
Which, going by from year to year, had found,
And left, the couple neither gay perhaps      120
Nor cheerful, yet with objects and with hopes,
Living a life of eager industry.
And now, when Luke had reached his eight-
      eenth year,
There by the light of this old lamp they sat,
Father and Son, while far into the night      125
The Housewife plied her own peculiar work,
Making the cottage through the silent hours
Murmur as with the sound of summer flies.
This light was famous in its neighborhood,
And was a public symbol of the life      130
That thrifty Pair had lived. For, as it chanced,
Their cottage on a plot of rising ground
Stood single, with large prospect, north and
      south,
High into Easedale,[3] up to Dunmail-Raise,[4]
And westward to the village near the lake;      135
And from this constant light, so regular
And so far seen, the House itself, by all
Who dwelt within the limits of the vale,
Both old and young, was named the *Evening
      Star.*
      Thus living on through such a length of
      years,      140
The Shepherd, if he loved himself, must needs
Have loved his Helpmate; but to Michael's
      heart
This son of his old age was yet more dear—
Less from instinctive tenderness, the same
Fond spirit that blindly works in the blood of
      all—      145
Than that a child, more than all other gifts
That earth can offer to declining man,
Brings hope with it, and forward-looking
      thoughts,
And stirrings of inquietude, when they
By tendency of nature needs must fail.      150
Exceeding was the love he bare to him,
His heart and his heart's joy! For oftentimes
Old Michael, while he was a babe in arms,
Had done him female service, not alone
For pastime and delight, as is the use      155
Of fathers, but with patient mind enforced
To acts of tenderness; and he had rocked
His cradle, as with a woman's gentle hand.
      And, in a later time, ere yet the Boy
Had put on boy's attire, did Michael love,      160
Albeit of a stern unbending mind,
To have the Young-one in his sight, when he
Wrought in the field, or on his shepherd's stool
Sat with a fettered sheep before him stretched
Under the large old oak, that near his door      165
Stood single, and, from matchless depth of
      shade,

[3] Near Grasmere.
[4] The pass on the way from Grasmere to Keswick.

Chosen for the Shearer's covert from the sun,
Thence in our rustic dialect was called
The *Clipping Tree,* a name which yet it bears.
There, while they two were sitting in the
      shade,      170
With others round them, earnest all and blithe,
Would Michael exercise his heart with looks
Of fond correction and reproof bestowed
Upon the Child, if he disturbed the sheep
By catching at their legs, or with his shouts
Scared them, while they lay still beneath the
      shears.      176
      And when by Heaven's good grace the boy
      grew up
A healthy Lad, and carried in his cheek
Two steady roses that were five years old;
Then Michael from a winter coppice cut      180
With his own hand a sapling, which he hooped
With iron, making it throughout in all
Due requisites a perfect shepherd's staff,
And gave it to the Boy; wherewith equipped
He as a watchman oftentimes was placed      185
At gate or gap, to stem or turn the flock;
And, to his office prematurely called,
There stood the urchin, as you will divine,
Something between a hindrance and a help;
And for this cause not always, I believe,      190
Receiving from his Father hire of praise;
Though nought was left undone which staff, or
      voice,
Or looks, or threatening gestures, could per-
      form.
      But soon as Luke, full ten years old, could
      stand
Against the mountain blasts; and to the
      heights,      195
Not fearing toil, nor length of weary ways,
He with his Father daily went, and they
Were as companions, why should I relate
That objects which the Shepherd loved before
Were dearer now? that from the Boy there
      came      200
Feelings and emanations—things which were
Light to the sun and music to the wind;
And that the old Man's heart seemed born
      again?
      Thus in his Father's sight the Boy grew up:
And now, when he had reached his eighteenth
      year,      205
He was his comfort and his daily hope.
      While in this sort the simple household lived
From day to day, to Michael's ear there came
Distressful tidings. Long before the time
Of which I speak, the Shepherd had been
      bound      210
In surety for his brother's son, a man
Of an industrious life, and ample means;
But unforeseen misfortunes suddenly
Had pressed upon him; and old Michael now
Was summoned to discharge the forfeiture,      215
A grievous penalty, but little less
Than half his substance. This unlooked-for
      claim,

At the first hearing, for a moment took
More hope out of his life than he supposed
That any old man ever could have lost.    220
As soon as he had armed himself with strength
To look his trouble in the face, it seemed
The Shepherd's sole resource to sell at once
A portion of his patrimonial fields.
Such was his first resolve; he thought again, 225
And his heart failed him. "Isabel," said he,
Two evenings after he had heard the news,
"I have been toiling more than seventy years,
And in the open sunshine of God's love
Have we all lived; yet if these fields of ours 230
Should pass into a stranger's hand, I think
That I could not lie quiet in my grave.
Our lot is a hard lot; the sun himself
Has scarcely been more diligent than I;
And I have lived to be a fool at last    235
To my own family. An evil man
That was, and made an evil choice, if he
Were false to us; and if he were not false,
There are ten thousand to whom loss like
    this
Had been no sorrow. I forgive him;—but    240
'Twere better to be dumb than to talk thus.

    "When I began, my purpose was to speak
Of remedies and of a cheerful hope.
Our Luke shall leave us, Isabel; the land
Shall not go from us, and it shall be free;    245
He shall possess it, free as is the wind
That passes over it. We have, thou know'st,
Another kinsman—he will be our friend
In this distress. He is a prosperous man,
Thriving in trade—and Luke to him shall go,
And with his kinsman's help and his own
    thrift    251
He quickly will repair this loss, and then
He may return to us. If here he stay,
What can be done? Where every one is poor,
What can be gained?"
            At this the old Man paused,    255
And Isabel sat silent, for her mind
Was busy, looking back into past times.
There's Richard Bateman, thought she to her-
    self,
He was a parish-boy—at the church-door
They made a gathering for him, shillings,
    pence,    260
And halfpennies, wherewith the neighbors
    bought
A basket, which they filled with peddler's
    wares;
And, with this basket on his arm, the lad
Went up to London, found a master there,
Who, out of many, chose the trusty boy    265
To go and overlook his merchandise
Beyond the seas; where he grew wondrous rich,
And left estates and monies to the poor.
And, at his birthplace, built a chapel, floored
With marble which he sent from foreign
    lands.    270
These thoughts, and many others of like sort,
Passed quickly through the mind of Isabel,

And her face brightened. The old Man was
    glad,
And thus resumed:—"Well, Isabel! this
    scheme
These two days has been meat and drink to
    me.    275
Far more than we have lost is left us yet.
—We have enough—I wish indeed that I
Were younger;—but this hope is a good hope.
—Make ready Luke's best garments, of the best
Buy for him more, and let us send him forth 280
To-morrow, or the next day, or to-night:
—If he *could* go, the Boy should go to-night."
    Here Michael ceased, and to the fields went
    forth
With a light heart. The Housewife for five days
Was restless morn and night, and all day
    long    285
Wrought on with her best fingers to prepare
Things needful for the journey of her son.
But Isabel was glad when Sunday came
To stop her in her work: for, when she lay
By Michael's side, she through the last two
    nights    290
Heard him, how he was troubled in his sleep:
And when they rose at morning she could see
That all his hopes were gone. That day at noon,
She said to Luke, while they two by themselves
Were sitting at the door, "Thou must not go:
We have no other Child but thee to lose— 296
None to remember—do not go away,
For if thou leave thy Father he will die."
The Youth made answer with a jocund voice;
And Isabel, when she had told her fears,    300
Recovered heart. That evening her best fare
Did she bring forth, and all together sat
Like happy people round a Christmas fire.
    With daylight Isabel resumed her work;
And all the ensuing week the house appeared
As cheerful as a grove in Spring: at length 306
The expected letter from their kinsman came.
With kind assurances that he would do
His utmost for the welfare of the Boy;
To which, requests were added, that forthwith
He might be sent to him. Ten times or more 311
The letter was read over; Isabel
Went forth to show it to the neighbors round;
Nor was there at that time on English land
A prouder heart than Luke's. When Isabel 315
Had to her house returned, the old Man said,
"He shall depart to-morrow." To this word
The Housewife answered, talking much of
    things
Which, if at such short notice he should go,
Would surely be forgotten. But at length 320
She gave consent, and Michael was at ease.
    Near the tumultuous brook of Greenhead
    Ghyll,
In that deep valley, Michael had designed
To build a Sheepfold; and, before he heard
The tidings of his melancholy loss,    325
For this same purpose he had gathered up
A heap of stones, which by the streamlet's edge

Lay thrown together, ready for the work.
With Luke that evening thitherward he
    walked:
And soon as they had reached the place he
    stopped,        330
And thus the old Man spake to him:—"My
    Son,
To-morrow thou wilt leave me: with full heart
I look upon thee, for thou art the same
That wert a promise to me ere thy birth,
And all thy life hast been my daily joy.    335
I will relate to thee some little part
Of our two histories; 'twill do thee good
When thou art from me, even if I should touch
On things thou canst not know of.——After
    thou
First cam'st into the world—as oft befalls    340
To new-born infants—thou didst sleep away
Two days, and blessings from thy Father's
    tongue
Then fell upon thee. Day by day passed on,
And still I loved thee with increasing love.
Never to living ear came sweeter sounds    345
Than when I heard thee by our own fireside
First uttering, without words, a natural tune;
While thou, a feeding babe, didst in thy joy
Sing at thy Mother's breast. Month followed
    month,
And in the open fields my life was passed    350
And on the mountains; else I think that thou
Hadst been brought up upon thy Father's
    knees.
But we were playmates, Luke: among these
    hills,
As well thou knowest, in us the old and young
Have played together, nor with me didst thou
Lack any pleasure which a boy can know."    356
Luke had a manly heart; but at these words
He sobbed aloud. The old Man grasped his
    hand,
And said, "Nay, do not take it so—I see
That these are things of which I need not
    speak.    360
—Even to the utmost I have been to thee
A kind and a good Father: and herein
I but repay a gift which I myself
Received at others' hands; for, though now old
Beyond the common life of man, I still    365
Remember them who loved me in my youth.
Both of them sleep together: here they lived,
As all their Forefathers had done; and when
At length their time was come, they were not
    loath
To give their bodies to the family mold.    370
I wished that thou should'st live the life they
    lived:
But, 'tis a long time to look back, my Son,
And see so little gain from threescore years.
These fields were burthened when they came to
    me;
Till I was forty years of age, not more    375
Than half of my inheritance was mine.
I toiled and toiled; God blessed me in my work,

And till these three weeks past the land was
    free.
—It looks as if it never could endure
Another Master. Heaven forgive me, Luke,    380
If I judge ill for thee, but it seems good
That thou should'st go."
                At this the old Man paused;
Then, pointing to the stones near which they
    stood,
Thus, after a short silence, he resumed:
"This was a work for us; and now, my Son,    385
It is a work for me. But, lay one stone—
Here, lay it for me, Luke, with thine own
    hands.
Nay, Boy, be of good hope;—we both may live
To see a better day. At eighty-four
I still am strong and hale;—do thou thy part;
I will do mine.—I will begin again    391
With many tasks that were resigned to thee:
Up to the heights, and in among the storms,
Will I without thee go again, and do
All works which I was wont to do alone,    395
Before I knew thy face.—Heaven bless thee,
    Boy!
Thy heart these two weeks has been beating
    fast
With many hopes; it should be so—yes—yes—
I knew that thou could'st never have a wish
To leave me, Luke: thou hast been bound to
    me    400
Only by links of love: when thou art gone,
What will be left to us!—But, I forget
My purposes. Lay now the corner-stone,
As I requested; and hereafter, Luke,
When thou art gone away, should evil men    405
Be thy companions, think of me, my Son,
And of this moment; hither turn thy thoughts,
And God will strengthen thee: amid all fear
And all temptation, Luke, I pray that thou
May'st bear in mind the life thy Fathers lived,
Who, being innocent, did for that cause    411
Bestir them in good deeds. Now, fare thee
    well—
When thou return'st, thou in this place wilt see
A work which is not here: a covenant
'Twill be between us; but, whatever fate    415
Befall thee, I shall love thee to the last,
And bear thy memory with me to the grave."
    The Shepherd ended here; and Luke stooped
    down,
And, as his Father had requested, laid
The first stone of the Sheepfold. At the
    sight    420
The old Man's grief broke from him; to his
    heart
He pressed his Son, he kisséd him and wept:
And to the house together they returned.
—Hushed was that House in peace, or seeming
    peace,
Ere the night fell:—with morrow's dawn the
    Boy    425
Began his journey, and when he had reached
The public way, he put on a bold face;

And all the neighbors, as he passed their doors,
Came forth with wishes and with farewell
    prayers,
That followed him till he was out of sight. 430
  A good report did from their Kinsman come,
Of Luke and his well-doing: and the Boy
Wrote loving letters, full of wondrous news,
Which, as the Housewife phrased it, were
    throughout
"The prettiest letters that were ever seen." 435
Both parents read them with rejoicing hearts.
So, many months passed on: and once again
The Shepherd went about his daily work
With confident and cheerful thoughts; and
    now
Sometimes when he could find a leisure hour
He to that valley took his way, and there 441
Wrought at the Sheepfold. Meantime Luke be-
    gan
To slacken in his duty; and, at length,
He in the dissolute city gave himself
To evil courses: ignominy and shame 445
Fell on him, so that he was driven at last
To seek a hiding-place beyond the seas.
  There is a comfort in the strength of love;
'Twill make a thing endurable, which else
Would overset the brain, or break the heart:
I have conversed with more than one who
    well 451
Remember the old Man, and what he was
Years after he had heard this heavy news.
His bodily frame had been from youth to age
Of an unusual strength. Among the rocks 455
He went, and still looked up to sun and cloud,
And listened to the wind; and, as before,
Performed all kinds of labor for his sheep,
And for the land, his small inheritance.
And to that hollow dell from time to time 460
Did he repair, to build the Fold, of which
His flock had need. 'Tis not forgotten yet
The pity which was then in every heart
For the old Man—and 'tis believed by all
That many and many a day he thither went, 465
And never lifted up a single stone.
  There, by the Sheepfold, sometimes was he
    seen
Sitting alone, or with his faithful Dog,
Then old, beside him, lying at his feet.
The length of full seven years, from time to
    time, 470
He at the building of this Sheepfold wrought,
And left the work unfinished when he died.
Three years, or little more, did Isabel
Survive her Husband: at her death the estate
Was sold, and went into a stranger's hand. 475
The Cottage which was named the *Evening*
    *Star*
Is gone—the plowshare has been through the
    ground
On which it stood; great changes have been
    wrought
In all the neighborhood:—yet the oak is left
That grew beside their door; and the remains
Of the unfinished Sheepfold may be seen 481

Beside the boisterous brook of Greenhead
    Ghyll.

# To a Young Lady

### *Who Had Been Reproached for Taking Long Walks in the Country* [1]

Dear Child of Nature, let them rail!
—There is a nest in a green dale,
A harbor and a hold;
Where thou, a Wife and Friend, shalt see
Thy own heart-stirring days, and be    5
A light to young and old.

There, healthy as a shepherd boy,
And treading among flowers of joy
Which at no season fade,
Thou, while thy babes around thee cling,  10
Shalt show us how divine a thing
A Woman may be made.

Thy thoughts and feelings shall not die,
Nor leave thee, when gray hairs are nigh,
A melancholy slave;    15
But an old age serene and bright,
And lovely as a Lapland night,
Shall lead thee to thy grave.

# Alice Fell

### *or*

### *Poverty* [2]

The post-boy drove with fierce career,
For threatening clouds the moon had drowned;
When, as we hurried on, my ear
Was smitten with a startling sound.

As if the wind blew many ways,    5
I heard the sound,—and more and more;
It seemed to follow with the chaise,
And still I heard it as before.

At length I to the boy called out;
He stopped his horses at the word,    10
But neither cry, nor voice, nor shout,
Nor aught else like it, could be heard.

The boy then smacked his whip, and fast
The horses scampered through the rain;
But, hearing soon upon the blast    15
The cry, I bade him halt again.

Forthwith alighting on the ground,
"Whence comes," said I, "this piteous moan?"
And there a little Girl I found,
Sitting behind the chaise, alone.    20

"My cloak!" no other word she spake,
But loud and bitterly she wept,

[1] Written perhaps in 1801; printed in the *Morning Post*, 1802, and in the *Poems* of 1807.
[2] Written in 1802; published in 1807.

As if her innocent heart would break;
And down from off her seat she leapt.

"What ails you, child?"—she sobbed, "Look
          here!" 25
I saw it in the wheel entangled
A weather-beaten rag as e'er
From any garden scare-crow dangled.

There, twisted between nave and spoke,
It hung, nor could at once be freed; 30
But our joint pains unloosed the cloak,
A miserable rag indeed!

"And whither are you going, child,
To-night along these lonesome ways?"
"To Durham," answered she, half wild— 35
"Then come with me into the chaise."

Insensible to all relief
Sat the poor girl, and forth did send
Sob after sob, as if her grief
Could never, never have an end. 40

"My child, in Durham do you dwell?"
She checked herself in her distress,
And said, "My name is Alice Fell;
I'm fatherless and motherless.

"And I to Durham, Sir, belong." 45
Again, as if the thought would choke
Her very heart, her grief grew strong;
And all was for her tattered cloak!

The chaise drove on; our journey's end
Was nigh; and, sitting by my side, 50
As if she had lost her only friend
She wept, nor would be pacified.

Up to the tavern-door we post;
Of Alice and her grief I told;
And I gave money to the host, 55
To buy a new cloak for the old.

"And let it be of duffel [3] gray,
As warm a cloak as man can sell!"
Proud creature was she the next day,
The little orphan, Alice Fell! 60

## To the Cuckoo [4]

O blithe New-comer! I have heard,
I hear thee and rejoice.
O Cuckoo! shall I call thee Bird,
Or but a wandering Voice?

While I am lying on the grass 5
Thy twofold shout I hear,
From hill to hill it seems to pass,
At once far off, and near.

[3] Coarse woolen cloth with thick nap.
[4] Written in 1802; published in 1807.

Though babbling only to the Vale,
Of sunshine and of flowers, 10
Thou bringest unto me a tale
Of visionary hours.

Thrice welcome, darling of the Spring!
Even yet thou art to me
No bird, but an invisible thing, 15
A voice, a mystery;

The same whom in my school-boy days
I listened to; that Cry
Which made me look a thousand ways
In bush, and tree, and sky. 20

To seek thee did I often rove
Through woods and on the green;
And thou wert still a hope, a love;
Still longed for, never seen.

And I can listen to thee yet; 25
Can lie upon the plain
And listen, till I do beget
That golden time again.

O blesséd Bird! the earth we pace
Again appears to be 30
An unsubstantial, faery place;
That is fit home for Thee!

## My Heart Leaps Up [5]

My heart leaps up when I behold
          A rainbow in the sky:
So was it when my life began;
So is it now I am a man;
So be it when I shall grow old, 5
          Or let me die!
The Child is father of the Man;
And I could wish my days to be
Bound each to each by natural piety.

## Resolution and Independence [1]

### I

There was a roaring in the wind all night;
The rain came heavily and fell in floods;
But now the sun is rising calm and bright;
The birds are singing in the distant woods;

[5] Written in 1802; published in 1807. Wordsworth wrote this poem immediately before beginning the *Ode on Intimations of Immortality*; and in early editions the last three lines of it appeared as a motto at the head of the longer poem.

[1] Written in 1802; published in 1807. "Written at Town-end, Grasmere. This old Man I met a few hundred yards from my cottage; and the account of him is taken from his own mouth. I was in the state of feeling described in the beginning of the poem, while crossing over Barton Fell from Mr. Clarkson's, at the foot of Ullswater, towards Askham. The image of the hare I then observed on the ridge of the Fell" (Wordsworth, *Fenwick Note*).

Over his own sweet voice the Stock-dove broods;
The Jay makes answer as the Magpie chatters; [6]
And all the air is filled with pleasant noise of
    waters.

## II

All things that love the sun are out of doors;
The sky rejoices in the morning's birth;
The grass is bright with rain-drops;—on the
    moors    10
The hare is running races in her mirth;
And with her feet she from the plashy earth
Raises a mist; that, glittering in the sun,
Runs with her all the way, wherever she doth
    run.

## III

I was a Traveler then upon the moor,    15
I saw the hare that raced about with joy;
I heard the woods and distant waters roar;
Or heard them not, as happy as a boy:
The pleasant season did my heart employ:
My old remembrances went from me wholly;
And all the ways of men, so vain and melan-
    choly.    21

## IV

But, as it sometimes chanceth, from the might
Of joy in the minds that can no further go,
As high as we have mounted in delight
In our dejection do we sink as low;    25
To me that morning did it happen so;
And fears and fancies thick upon me came;
Dim sadness—and blind thoughts, I knew not,
    nor could name.

## V

I heard the sky-lark warbling in the sky;
And I bethought me of the playful hare:    30
Even such a happy Child of earth am I;
Even as these blissful creatures do I fare;
Far from the world I walk, and from all care;
But there may come another day to me—
Solitude, pain of heart, distress, and poverty. 35

## VI

My whole life I have lived in pleasant thought,
As if life's business were a summer mood;
As if all needful things would come unsought
To genial faith, still rich in genial good;
But how can He expect that others should    40
Build for him, sow for him, and at his call
Love him, who for himself will take no heed at
    all?

## VII

I thought of Chatterton,[2] the marvelous Boy,
The sleepless Soul that perished in his pride;
Of Him [3] who walked in glory and in joy    45
Following his plow, along the mountainside:

[2] Thomas Chatterton (1752–1770), who died by
his own hand.
[3] Robert Burns.

By our own spirits are we deified:
We Poets in our youth begin in gladness;
But thereof come in the end despondency and
    madness.

## VIII

Now, whether it were by peculiar grace,    50
A leading from above, a something given,
Yet it befell that, in this lonely place,
When I with these untoward thoughts had
    striven,
Beside a pool bare to the eye of heaven
I saw a Man before me unawares:    55
The oldest man he seemed that ever wore gray
    hairs.

## IX

As a huge stone is sometimes seen to lie
Couched on the bald top of an eminence;
Wonder to all who do the same espy,
By what means it could thither come, and
    whence;    60
So that it seems a thing endued with sense:
Like a sea-beast crawled forth, that on a shelf
Of rock or sand reposeth, there to sun itself;

## X

Such seemed this Man, not all alive nor dead,
Nor all asleep—in his extreme old age:—    65
His body was bent double, feet and head
Coming together in life's pilgrimage;
As if some dire constraint of pain, or rage
Of sickness felt by him in times long past,
A more than human weight upon his frame had
    cast.    70

## XI

Himself he propped, limbs, body, and pale face,
Upon a long gray staff of shaven wood:
And, still as I drew near with gentle pace,
Upon the margin of that moorish flood
Motionless as a cloud the old Man stood,    75
That heareth not the loud winds when they call
And moveth all together, if it move at all.

## XII

At length, himself unsettling, he the pond
Stirred with his staff, and fixedly he did look
Upon the muddy water, which he conned,    80
As if he had been reading in a book:
And now a stranger's privilege I took;
And, drawing to his side, to him did say,
"This morning gives us promise of a glorious
    day."

## XIII

A gentle answer did the old Man make,    85
In courteous speech which forth he slowly drew:
And him with further words I thus bespake,
"What occupation do you there pursue?
This is a lonesome place for one like you."
Ere he replied, a flash of mild surprise    90
Broke from the sable orbs of his yet-vivid eyes,

### XIV

His words came feebly, from a feeble chest,
But each in solemn order followed each,
With something of a lofty utterance dressed—
Choice word and measured phrase, above the
    reach           95
Of ordinary men; a stately speech;
Such as grave Livers do in Scotland use,
Religious men, who give to God and man their
    dues.

### XV

He told, that to these waters he had come
To gather leeches, being old and poor:   100
Employment hazardous and wearisome!
And he had many hardships to endure:
From pond to pond he roamed, from moor to
    moor;
Housing, with God's good help, by choice or
    chance,
And in this way he gained an honest main-
    tenance.         105

### XVI

The old Man still stood talking by my side;
But now his voice to me was like a stream
Scarce heard; nor word from word could I di-
    vide;
And the whole body of the Man did seem
Like one whom I had met with in a dream; 110
Or like a man from some far region sent
To give me human strength, by apt admonish-
    ment.

### XVII

My former thoughts returned: the fear that
    kills;
And hope that is unwilling to be fed;
Cold, pain, and labor, and all fleshly ills;  115
And mighty Poets in their misery dead.
—Perplexed, and longing to be comforted,
My question eagerly did I renew,
"How is it that you live, and what is it you
    do?"

### XVIII

He with a smile did then his words repeat; 120
And said, that, gathering leeches, far and wide
He traveled; stirring thus above his feet
The waters of the pools where they abide.
"Once I could meet with them on every side;
But they have dwindled long by slow decay; 125
Yet still I persevere, and find them where I
    may."

### XIX

While he was talking thus, the lonely place,
The old Man's shape, and speech—all troubled
    me:
In my mind's eye I seemed to see him pace
About the weary moors continually,   130
Wandering about alone and silently.

While I these thoughts within myself pursued,
He, having made a pause, the same discourse
    renewed.

### XX

And soon with this he other matter blended,
Cheerfully uttered, with demeanor kind,   135
But stately in the main; and, when he ended,
I could have laughed myself to scorn to find
In that decrepit Man so firm a mind.
"God," said I, "be my help and stay secure;
I'll think of the Leech-gatherer on the lonely
    moor!"        140

# To the Daisy [1]

Bright Flower! whose home is everywhere,
Bold in maternal Nature's care,
And all the long year through the heir
    Of joy and sorrow;
Methinks that there abides in thee   5
Some concord with humanity,
Given to no other flower I see
    The forest thorough!

Is it that Man is soon depressed?
A thoughtless Thing! who, once unbless'd,  10
Does little on his memory rest,
    Or on his reason,
And Thou wouldst teach him how to find
A shelter under every wind,
A hope for times that are unkind   15
    And every season?

Thou wander'st the wide world about,
Unchecked by pride or scrupulous doubt,
With friends to greet thee, or without,
    Yet pleased and willing;   20
Meek, yielding to the occasion's call,
And all things suffering from all,
Thy function apostolical
    In peace fulfilling.

# Composed upon Westminster Bridge, September 3, 1802 [2]

Earth has not anything to show more fair;
Dull would he be of soul who could pass by
A sight so touching in its majesty:
This City now doth, like a garment, wear
The beauty of the morning; silent, bare,   5
Ships, towers, domes, theaters, and temples lie
Open unto the fields, and to the sky;
All bright and glittering in the smokeless air.
Never did sun more beautifully steep
In his first splendor, valley, rock, or hill;  10
Ne'er saw I, never felt, a calm so deep!
The river glideth at his own sweet will:
Dear God! the very houses seem asleep;
And all that mighty heart is lying still!

[1] Written in 1802; published in 1807.
[2] Really written on 31 July, 1802; published in
1807.

# It Is a Beauteous Evening, Calm and Free [3]

It is a beauteous evening, calm and free,
The holy time is quiet as a Nun
Breathless with adoration; the broad sun
Is sinking down in its tranquillity;
The gentleness of heaven broods o'er the Sea: 5
Listen! the mighty Being is awake,
And doth with his eternal motion make
A sound like thunder—everlastingly.
Dear Child! [4] dear Girl! that walkest with me
    here,
If thou appear untouched by solemn thought, 10
Thy nature is not therefore less divine:
Thou liest in Abraham's bosom all the year,
And worship'st at the Temple's inner shrine,
God being with thee when we know it not.

# Composed by the Seaside, Near Calais, August, 1802 [5]

Fair Star of evening, Splendor of the west,
Star of my Country!—on the horizon's brink
Thou hangest, stooping, as might seem, to sink
On England's bosom, yet well pleased to rest,
Meanwhile, and be to her a glorious crest 5
Conspicuous to the Nations. Thou, I think,
Shouldst be my Country's emblem; and
    shouldst wink,
Bright Star! with laughter on her banners,
    dressed
In thy fresh beauty. There! that dusky spot
Beneath thee, that is England; there she lies. 10
Blessings be on you both! one hope, one lot,
One life, one glory!—I, with many a fear
For my dear Country, many heartfelt sighs,
Among men who do not love her, linger here.

# On the Extinction of the Venetian Republic [6]

Once did She hold the gorgeous east in fee;
And was the safeguard of the west: the worth
Of Venice did not fall below her birth,
Venice, the eldest Child of Liberty.
She was a maiden City, bright and free; 5
No guile seduced, no force could violate;
And, when she took unto herself a Mate,
She must espouse the everlasting Sea.[7]

And what if she had seen those glories fade,
Those titles vanish, and that strength decay; 10
Yet shall some tribute of regret be paid
When her long life hath reached its final day:
Men are we, and must grieve when even the
    Shade
Of that which once was great is passed away.

# To Toussaint L'Ouverture [8]

Toussaint, the most unhappy man of men!
Whether the whistling Rustic tend his plow
Within thy hearing, or thy head be now
Pillowed in some deep dungeon's earless den;—
O miserable Chieftain! where and when    5
Wilt thou find patience? Yet die not; do thou
Wear rather in thy bonds a cheerful brow:
Though fallen thyself, never to rise again,
Live, and take comfort. Thou hast left behind
Powers that will work for thee; air, earth, and
    skies;    10
There's not a breathing of the common wind
That will forget thee; thou hast great allies;
Thy friends are exultations, agonies,
And love, and man's unconquerable mind.

# September, 1802. Near Dover [9]

Inland, within a hollow vale, I stood;
And saw, while sea was calm and air was clear,
The coast of France—the coast of France how
    near!
Drawn almost into frightful neighborhood.
I shrunk; for verily the barrier flood    5
Was like a lake, or river bright and fair,
A span of waters; yet what power is there!
What mightiness for evil and for good!
Even so doth God protect us if we be
Virtuous and wise. Winds blow, and waters
    roll,    10
Strength to the brave, and Power, and Deity;
Yet in themselves are nothing! One decree
Spake laws to *them*, and said that by the soul
Only, the Nations shall be great and free.

# Written in London, September, 1802 [10]

O friend! I know not which way I must look
For comfort, being, as I am, oppressed,
To think that now our life is only dressed

and the Adriatic, in which the Doge threw a ring
into the sea.

[3] Written in August, 1802; published in 1807.
[4] Wordsworth's French daughter, Caroline.
[5] Published in 1807.
[6] Written in 1802; published in 1807. In the
thirteenth century Venice controlled a portion of
the Eastern Empire, and for a long time protected
Western Europe from the Turks. The city was
founded in the fifth century and had been independent for more than a thousand years when it
was conquered by Napoleon in 1797, and its territory divided between Austria and France.
[7] An allusion to the annual ceremony, dating from
the twelfth century, of marriage between Venice

[8] Written probably in August, 1802; published in
the *Morning Post* in 1803 and in the *Poems* of
1807. Toussaint was governor of St. Domingo and
leader of the African slaves freed by decree of the
French Convention in 1794. When Napoleon published an edict reëstablishing slavery in St. Domingo,
Toussaint offered resistance, was arrested and sent
to France in June, 1802, and there died in prison
in April, 1803.
[9] Published in 1807.    [10] Published in 1807.

For show; mean handy-work of craftsman, cook,
Or groom!—We must run glittering like a brook　5
In the open sunshine, or we are unbless'd:
The wealthiest man among us is the best:
No grandeur now in nature or in book
Delights us. Rapine, avarice, expense,
This is idolatry; and these we adore:　10
Plain living and high thinking are no more:
The homely beauty of the good old cause
Is gone; our peace, our fearful innocence,
And pure religion breathing household laws.

## London, 1802 [11]

Milton! thou shouldst be living at this hour:
England hath need of thee: she is a fen
Of stagnant waters: altar, sword, and pen,
Fireside, the heroic wealth of hall and bower,
Have forfeited their ancient English dower　5
Of inward happiness. We are selfish men;
Oh! raise us up, return to us again;
And give us manners, virtue, freedom, power.
Thy soul was like a Star, and dwelt apart;
Thou hadst a voice whose sound was like the sea:　10
Pure as the naked heavens, majestic, free,
So didst thou travel on life's common way,
In cheerful godliness; and yet thy heart
The lowliest duties on herself did lay.

## Great Men Have Been among Us [12]

Great men have been among us; hands that penned
And tongues that uttered wisdom—better none:
The later Sidney, Marvel, Harrington,
Young Vane,[13] and others who called Milton friend.
These moralists could act and comprehend:　5
They knew how genuine glory was put on;
Taught us how rightfully a nation shone
In splendor: what strength was, that would not bend
But in magnanimous meekness. France, 'tis strange,
Hath brought forth no such souls as we had then.　10
Perpetual emptiness! unceasing change!
No single volume paramount, no code,
No master spirit, no determined road;
But equally a want of books and men!

[11] Written in September, 1802; published in 1807.
[12] Written in September, 1802; published in 1807.
[13] Algernon Sidney (1622?–1683), Andrew Marvell (1621–1678), James Harrington (1611–1677), and Sir Henry Vane (1612–1662).

## It Is Not to Be Thought Of [14]

It is not to be thought of that the Flood
Of British freedom, which, to the open sea
Of the world's praise, from dark antiquity
Hath flowed, "with pomp of waters, unwithstood," [15]
Roused though it be full often to a mood　5
Which spurns the check of salutary bands,
That this most famous Stream in bogs and sands
Should perish; and to evil and to good
Be lost for ever. In our halls is hung
Armory of the invincible Knights of old:　10
We must be free or die, who speak the tongue
That Shakespeare spake; the faith and morals hold
Which Milton held.—In everything we are sprung
Of Earth's first blood, have titles manifold.

## When I Have Borne in Memory [16]

When I have borne in memory what has tamed
Great Nations, how ennobling thoughts depart
When men change swords for ledgers, and desert
The student's bower for gold, some fears unnamed
I had, my Country!—am I to be blamed?　5
Now, when I think of thee, and what thou art,
Verily, in the bottom of my heart,
Of those unfilial fears I am ashamed.
For dearly must we prize thee; we who find
In thee a bulwark for the cause of men:　10
And I by my affection was beguiled:
What wonder if a Poet now and then,
Among the many movements of his mind,
Felt for thee as a lover or a child!

## She Was a Phantom of Delight [1]

She was a Phantom of delight
When first she gleamed upon my sight;
A lovely Apparition, sent
To be a moment's ornament;
Her eyes as stars of Twilight fair;　5
Like Twilight's, too, her dusky hair;
But all things else about her drawn
From May-time and the cheerful Dawn;
A dancing Shape, an Image gay,
To haunt, to startle, and waylay.　10

[14] Written in 1802 or 1803; published in the latter year in the *Morning Post* and in the *Poems* of 1807.
[15] Samuel Daniel, *Civil War*, Bk. II, Stanza 7.
[16] Written in 1802 or 1803; published in the latter year in the *Morning Post* and in the *Poems* of 1807.
[1] Written in 1804; published in 1807. The subject of this poem is Mary Hutchinson, Wordsworth's wife.

I saw her upon nearer view,
A Spirit, yet a Woman too!
Her household motions light and free,
And steps of virgin-liberty;
A countenance in which did meet     15
Sweet records, promises as sweet;
A Creature not too bright or good
For human nature's daily food;
For transient sorrows, simple wiles,
Praise, blame, love, kisses, tears, and smiles.     20

And now I see with eye serene
The very pulse of the machine;
A Being breathing thoughtful breath,
A Traveler between life and death;
The reason firm, the temperate will,     25
Endurance, foresight, strength, and skill;
A perfect Woman, nobly planned,
To warn, to comfort, and command;
And yet a Spirit still, and bright
With something of angelic light.     30

## The Solitary Reaper [2]

Behold her, single in the field,
Yon solitary Highland Lass!
Reaping and singing by herself;
Stop here, or gently pass!
Alone she cuts and binds the grain,     5
And sings a melancholy strain;
O listen! for the Vale profound
Is overflowing with the sound.

No Nightingale did ever chaunt
More welcome notes to weary bands     10
Of travelers in some shady haunt,
Among Arabian sands:
A voice so thrilling ne'er was heard
In spring-time from the Cuckoo-bird,
Breaking the silence of the seas     15
Among the farthest Hebrides.

Will no one tell me what she sings?—
Perhaps the plaintive numbers flow
For old, unhappy, far-off things,
And battles long ago:     20
Or is it some more humble lay,
Familiar matter of to-day?
Some natural sorrow, loss, or pain,
That has been, and may be again?

Whate'er the theme, the Maiden sang     25
As if her song could have no ending;
I saw her singing at her work,
And o'er the sickle bending;—
I listened, motionless and still;
And, as I mounted up the hill     30
The music in my heart I bore,
Long after it was heard no more.

[2] Written between 1803 and 1805; published in 1807.

# I Wandered Lonely As a Cloud [1]

I wandered lonely as a cloud
That floats on high o'er vales and hills,
When all at once I saw a crowd,
A host, of golden daffodils;
Beside the lake, beneath the trees,     5
Fluttering and dancing in the breeze.

Continuous as the stars that shine
And twinkle on the milky way,
They stretched in never-ending line
Along the margin of a bay:     10
Ten thousand saw I at a glance,
Tossing their heads in sprightly dance.

The waves beside them danced; but they
Out-did the sparkling waves in glee:
A poet could not but be gay,     15
In such a jocund company:
I gazed—and gazed—but little thought
What wealth the show to me had brought:

For oft, when on my couch I lie
In vacant or in pensive mood,     20
They flash upon that inward eye
Which is the bliss of solitude; [2]
And then my heart with pleasure fills,
And dances with the daffodils.

# Elegiac Stanzas

*Suggested by a Picture of Peele Castle,
in a Storm, Painted by Sir George
Beaumont* [1]

I was thy neighbor once, thou rugged Pile!
Four summer weeks I dwelt in sight of thee: [2]
I saw thee every day; and all the while
Thy Form was sleeping on a glassy sea.

So pure the sky, so quiet was the air!     5
So like, so very like, was day to day!
Whene'er I looked, thy Image still was there;
It trembled, but it never passed away.

[1] Written in 1804; published in 1807. "The two best lines in it are by Mary. The daffodils grew, and still grow, on the margin of Ullswater, and probably may be seen to this day as beautiful in the month of March, nodding their golden heads beside the dancing and foaming waves" (Wordsworth, *Fenwick Note*).
[2] This and the preceding line are those by "Mary": Mrs. Wordsworth.
[1] Written in 1805; published in 1807. The Peele Castle here referred to (there are two) is in Lancashire. Wordsworth's friend Beaumont painted two pictures of the Castle, one of them intended for Mrs. Wordsworth.
[2] A reference to a visit paid by Wordsworth during a college vacation to his cousin, Mrs. Barker, who lived at Rampside, not far from Peele Castle.

How perfect was the calm! it seemed no sleep;
No mood, which season takes away, or brings:
I could have fancied that the mighty Deep  11
Was even the gentlest of all gentle Things.

Ah! then, if mine had been the Painter's hand,
To express what then I saw; and add the gleam,
The light that never was, on sea or land,  15
The consecration, and the Poet's dream;

I would have planted thee, thou hoary Pile
Amid a world how different from this!
Beside a sea that could not cease to smile;
On tranquil land, beneath a sky of bliss.  20

Thou shouldst have seemed a treasure-house
      divine
Of peaceful years; a chronicle of heaven;—
Of all the sunbeams that did ever shine
The very sweetest had to thee been given.

A Picture had it been of lasting ease,  25
Elysian quiet, without toil or strife;
No motion but the moving tide, a breeze,
Or merely silent Nature's breathing life.

Such, in the fond illusion of my heart,
Such Picture would I at that time have
      made:  30
And seen the soul of truth in every part,
A steadfast peace that might not be betrayed.

So once it would have been,—'tis so no more;
I have submitted to a new control:
A power is gone, which nothing can restore;  35
A deep distress hath humanized my Soul.[3]

Not for a moment could I now behold
A smiling sea, and be what I have been:
The feeling of my loss will ne'er be old;
This, which I know, I speak with mind serene.

Then, Beaumont, Friend! who would have been
      the Friend,  41
If he had lived, of Him whom I deplore,
This work, of thine I blame not, but commend;
This sea in anger, and that dismal shore.

O 'tis a passionate Work!—yet wise and well,
Well chosen is the spirit that is here;  46
That Hulk which labors in the deadly swell,
This rueful sky, this pageantry of fear!

And this huge Castle, standing here sublime,
I love to see the look with which it braves,  50
Cased in the unfeeling armor of old time,
The lightning, the fierce wind, and trampling
      waves.

[3] Wordsworth's brother, Captain John Wordsworth, went down with his ship, an East Indiaman,
off the Bill of Portland on 5 February, 1805.

Farewell, farewell the heart that lives alone,
Housed in a dream, at distance from the Kind!
Such happiness, wherever it be known,  55
Is to be pitied; for 'tis surely blind.

But welcome fortitude, and patient cheer,
And frequent sights of what is to be borne!
Such sights, or worse, as are before me here.—
Not without hope we suffer and we mourn.  60

## Ode to Duty [1]

Stern Daughter of the Voice of God!
O Duty! if that name thou love
Who art a light to guide, a rod
To check the erring, and reprove;
Thou, who art victory and law  5
When empty terrors overawe;
From vain temptations dost set free;
And calm'st the weary strife of frail humanity!

There are who ask not if thine eye
Be on them; who, in love and truth,  10
Where no misgiving is, rely
Upon the genial sense of youth:
Glad Hearts! without reproach or blot;
Who do thy work, and know it not:
Oh! if through confidence misplaced  15
They fail, thy saving arms, dread Power! around
      them cast.

Serene will be our days and bright,
And happy will our nature be,
When love is an unerring light,
And joy its own security.  20
And they a blissful course may hold
Even now, who, not unwisely bold,
Live in the spirit of this creed;
Yet seek thy firm support, according to their
      need.

I, loving freedom, and untried;  25
No sport of every random gust,
Yet being to myself a guide,
Too blindly have reposed my trust:
And oft, when in my heart was heard
Thy timely mandate, I deferred  30
The task, in smoother walks to stray;
But thee I now would serve more strictly, if I
      may.

Through no disturbance of my soul,
Or strong compunction in me wrought,
I supplicate for thy control;  35
But in the quietness of thought:
Me this unchartered freedom tires;
I feel the weight of chance-desires:

[1] Written in 1805; published in 1807. "This ode
is on the model of Gray's *Ode to Adversity*" (Wordsworth, *Fenwick Note*).

My hopes no more must change their name,
I long for a repose that ever is the same.[2]     40

Stern Lawgiver! yet thou dost wear
The Godhead's most benignant grace;
Nor know we anything so fair
As is the smile upon thy face:
Flowers laugh before thee on their beds     45
And fragrance in thy footing treads;
Thou dost preserve the stars from wrong;
And the most ancient heavens, through Thee,
      are fresh and strong.

To humbler functions, awful Power!
I call thee: I myself commend     50
Unto thy guidance from this hour;
Oh, let my weakness have an end!
Give unto me, made lowly wise,
The spirit of self-sacrifice;
The confidence of reason give;     55
And in the light of truth thy Bondman let me
      live!

## Character of the Happy Warrior [1]

Who is the happy Warrior? Who is he
That every man in arms should wish to be?
—It is the generous Spirit, who, when brought

[2] In the edition of 1807 a stanza here followed
which was omitted in all later editions:
      Yet not the less would I throughout
      Still act according to the voice
      Of my own wish; and feel past doubt
      That my submissiveness was choice:
      Not seeking in the school of pride
      For "precepts over dignified,"
      Denial and restraint I prize
      No farther than they breed a second Will more
         wise.
[1] Written in December, 1805, or January, 1806;
published in 1807. "The course of the great war
with the French naturally fixed one's attention upon
the military character, and, to the honor of our
country, there were many illustrious instances of
the qualities that constitute its highest excellence.
Lord Nelson carried most of the virtues that the
trials he was exposed to in his department of the
service necessarily call forth and sustain, if they
do not produce the contrary vices. But his public
life was stained with one great crime, so that though
many passages of these lines were suggested by what
was generally known as excellent in his conduct, I
have not been able to connect his name with the
poem as I could wish, or even to think of him
with satisfaction in reference to the idea of what
a warrior ought to be. . . . I will add that many
elements of the character here portrayed were found
in my brother John, who perished by shipwreck"
(Wordsworth, *Fenwick Note*). But in 1807, forty
years earlier, Wordsworth had connected Nelson's
name with this poem, in the following note: "The
above Verses were written soon after tidings had
been received of the death of Lord Nelson, which
event directed the Author's thoughts to the subject.
His respect for the memory of his great fellow-
countryman induces him to mention this; though

Among the tasks of real life, hath wrought
Upon the plan that pleased his boyish thought:
Whose high endeavors are an inward light     6
That makes the path before him always bright:
Who, with a natural instinct to discern
What knowledge can perform, is diligent to
      learn;
Abides by this resolve, and stops not there,     10
But makes his moral being his prime care;
Who, doomed to go in company with Pain,
And Fear, and Bloodshed, miserable train!
Turns his necessity to glorious gain;
In face of these doth exercise a power     15
Which is our human nature's highest dower;
Controls them and subdues, transmutes, be-
      reaves
Of their bad influence, and their good receives:
By objects, which might force the soul to abate
Her feeling, rendered more compassionate;     20
Is placable—because occasions rise
So often that demand such sacrifice;
More skillful in self-knowledge, even more pure,
As tempted more; more able to endure,
As more exposed to suffering and distress;     25
Thence, also, more alive to tenderness.
—'Tis he whose law is reason; who depends
Upon that law as on the best of friends;
Whence, in a state where men are tempted still
To evil for a guard against worse ill,     30
And what in quality or act is best
Doth seldom on a right foundation rest,
He labors good on good to fix, and owes
To virtue every triumph that he knows:
—Who, if he rise to station of command,     35
Rises by open means; and there will stand
On honorable terms, or else retire,
And in himself possess his own desire;
Who comprehends his trust, and to the same
Keeps faithful with a singleness of aim;     40
And therefore does not stoop, nor lie in wait
For wealth, or honors, or for worldly state;
Whom they must follow; on whose head must
      fall,
Like showers of manna, if they come at all:
Whose powers shed round him in the common
      strife,     45
Or mild concerns of ordinary life,
A constant influence, a peculiar grace;
But who, if he be called upon to face
Some awful moment to which Heaven has
      joined
Great issues, good or bad for human kind,     50
Is happy as a Lover; and attired
With sudden brightness, like a Man inspired;
And, through the heat of conflict, keeps the
      law
In calmness made, and sees what he foresaw;
Or if an unexpected call succeed,     55
Come when it will, is equal to the need:
—He who, though thus endued as with a sense

he is well aware that the Verses must suffer from
any connection in the reader's mind with a name so
illustrious."

And faculty for storm and turbulence,
Is yet a Soul whose master-bias leans
To homefelt pleasures and to gentle scenes; 60
Sweet images! which, wheresoe'er he be,
Are at his heart; and such fidelity
It is his darling passion to approve;
More brave for this, that he hath much to
    love:—
'Tis, finally, the Man, who, lifted high,   65
Conspicuous object in a Nation's eye,
Or left unthought-of in obscurity,—
Who, with a toward or untoward lot,
Prosperous or adverse, to his wish or not—
Plays, in the many games of life, that one 70
Where what he most doth value must be won:
Whom neither shape of danger can dismay,
Nor thought of tender happiness betray;
Who, not content that former worth stand fast,
Looks forward, persevering to the last,   75
From well to better, daily self-surpassed:
Who, whether praise of him must walk the
    earth
For ever, and to noble deeds give birth,
Or he must fall, to sleep without his fame,
And leave a dead unprofitable name—   80
Finds comfort in himself and in his cause;
And, while the mortal mist is gathering, draws
His breath in confidence of Heaven's applause:
This is the Happy Warrior; this is He
That every Man in arms should wish to be. 85

## A Complaint [1]

There is a change—and I am poor;
Your love hath been, not long ago,
A fountain at my fond heart's door,
Whose only business was to flow;
And flow it did; not taking heed   5
Of its own bounty, or my need.

What happy moments did I count!
Bless'd was I then all bliss above!
Now, for that consecrated fount
Of murmuring, sparkling, living love,   10
What have I? shall I dare to tell?
A comfortless and hidden well.

A well of love—it may be deep—
I trust it is,—and never dry:
What matter? if the waters sleep   15
In silence and obscurity.
—Such change, and at the very door
Of my fond heart, hath made me poor.

## Nuns Fret Not at Their Convent's Narrow Room [2]

Nuns fret not at their convent's narrow room;
And hermits are contented with their cells;

[1] Written in 1806; published in 1807. "Suggested by a change in the manner of a friend" (Wordsworth, *Fenwick Note*). The friend was probably Coleridge.
[2] Published in 1807.

And students with their pensive citadels; [3]
Maids at the wheel, the weaver at his loom,
Sit blithe and happy; bees that soar for bloom, [5]
High as the highest Peak of Furness-fells,[4]
Will murmur by the hour in foxglove bells:
In truth the prison, into which we doom
Ourselves, no prison is: and hence for me,
In sundry moods, 'twas pastime to be bound 10
Within the Sonnet's scanty plot of ground;
Pleased if some Souls (for such there needs
    must be)
Who have felt the weight of too much liberty,
Should find brief solace there, as I have found.

## Personal Talk [5]

### I

I am not One who much or oft delight
To season my fireside with personal talk,—
Of friends, who live within an easy walk,
Or neighbors, daily, weekly, in my sight:
And, for my chance-acquaintance, ladies bright,
Sons, mothers, maidens withering on the stalk,
These all wear out of me, like Forms, with
    chalk   7
Painted on rich men's floors, for one feast-
    night.
Better than such discourse doth silence long,
Long, barren silence, square with my desire; 10
To sit without emotion, hope, or aim,
In the loved presence of my cottage-fire,
And listen to the flapping of the flame,
Or kettle whispering its faint undersong.

### II

"Yet life," you say, "is life; we have seen and
    see,
And with a living pleasure we describe;
And fits of sprightly malice do but bribe
The languid mind into activity.
Sound sense, and love itself, and mirth and
    glee   5
Are fostered by the comment and the gibe."
Even be it so; yet still among your tribe,
Our daily world's true Worldings, rank not me!
Children are bless'd, and powerful; their world
    lies
More justly balanced; partly at their feet,   10
And part far from them:—sweetest melodies
Are those that are by distance made more sweet;
Whose mind is but the mind of his own eyes,
He is a Slave; the meanest we can meet!

### III

Wings have we,—and as far as we can go,
We may find pleasure: wilderness and wood,
Blank ocean and mere sky, support that mood
Which with the lofty sanctifies the low.

[3] Retreats secure for uninterrupted thought.
[4] The hill country east of the Duddon, south of the Brathay, and west of Windermere.
[5] Published in 1807.

Dreams, books, are each a world; and books, we
    know, [5]
Are a substantial world, both pure and good:
Round these, with tendrils strong as flesh and
    : blood,
Our pastime and our happiness will grow.
There find I personal themes, a plenteous store,
Matter wherein right voluble I am, [10]
To which I listen with a ready ear;
Two shall be named, pre-eminently dear,—
The gentle Lady married to the Moor; [6]
And heavenly Una with her milk-white Lamb.[7]

### IV

Nor can I not believe but that hereby
Great gains are mine; for thus I live remote
From evil-speaking; rancor, never sought,
Comes to me not; malignant truth, or lie.
Hence have I genial seasons, hence have I [5]
Smooth passions, smooth discourse, and joyous
    thought:
And thus from day to day my little boat
Rocks in its harbor, lodging peaceably.
Blessings be with them—and eternal praise,
Who gave us nobler loves, and nobler cares—
The Poets, who on earth have made us heirs [11]
Of truth and pure delight by heavenly lays!
Oh! might my name be numbered among
    theirs,
Then gladly would I end my mortal days.

## The World Is Too Much
## with Us [8]

The world is too much with us; late and soon,
Getting and spending, we lay waste our powers:
Little we see in Nature that is ours;
We have given our hearts away, a sordid boon!
The Sea that bares her bosom to the moon; [5]
The winds that will be howling at all hours,
And are up-gathered now like sleeping flowers;
For this, for everything, we are out of tune;
It moves us not.—Great God I'd rather be
A Pagan suckled in a creed outworn; [10]
So might I, standing on this pleasant lea,
Have glimpses that would make me less forlorn;
Have sight of Proteus rising from the sea;
Or hear old Triton blow his wreathéd horn.

## Ode

*Intimations of Immortality from Recol-
lections of Early Childhood* [1]

### I

There was a time when meadow, grove, and
    stream,

[6] Desdemona, in *Othello*.
[7] Spenser, *Faerie Queene*, Bk. I.
[8] Published in 1807.
[1] Written in the years from 1803, or possibly 1802,
to 1806; published in 1807. Concerning the mean-

The earth, and every common sight,
      To me did seem
    Apparelled in celestial light,
The glory and the freshness of a dream. [5]
It is not now as it hath been of yore;—
      Turn wheresoe'er I may,
      By night or day,
The things which I have seen I now can see
    no more.

### II

    The Rainbow comes and goes, [10]
    And lovely is the Rose,
    The Moon doth with delight
Look round her when the heavens are bare,
    Waters on a starry night
    Are beautiful and fair; [15]
  The sunshine is a glorious birth;
  But yet I know, where'er I go,
That there hath passed away a glory from the
    earth.

### III

Now, while the birds thus sing a joyous song,
  And while the young lambs bound [20]
    As to the tabor's [2] sound,
To me alone there came a thought of grief:
A timely utterance gave that thought relief,
    And I again am strong:
The cataracts blow their trumpets from the
    steep; [25]
Nor more shall grief of mine the season
    wrong; [3]
I hear the Echoes through the mountains
    throng,
The Winds come to me from the fields of sleep,
    And all the earth is gay;
    Land and sea [30]
  Give themselves up to jollity,
    And with the heart of May
Doth every Beast keep holiday;—
    Thou Child of Joy,
Shout round me, let me hear thy shouts, thou
    happy Shepherd-boy! [35]

### IV

Ye blessed Creatures, I have heard the call
  Ye to each other make; I see
The heavens laugh with you in your jubilee;
    My heart is at your festival,
    My head hath its coronal,[4] [40]
The fullness of your bliss, I feel—I feel it all.
  Oh evil day! if I were sullen
  While Earth herself is adorning

ing of this poem see the introductory note to Words-
worth's poems, above, where part of the *Fenwick
Note* to the *Ode* is quoted.
  The Child is father of the Man;
  And I could wish my days to be
  Bound each to each by natural piety.
[2] Small drum.     [3] I. e., by lack of sympathy.
[4] Garland.

This sweet May-morning,
And the Children are culling          45
    On every side,
In a thousand valleys far and wide,
Fresh flowers; while the sun shines warm,
And the Babe leaps up on his Mother's arm:—
    I hear, I hear, with joy I hear!          50
—But there's a Tree, of many, one,
A single Field which I have looked upon,
Both of them speak of something that is gone:
    The Pansy at my feet
    Doth the same tale repeat:          55
Whither is fled the visionary gleam?
Where is it now, the glory and the dream?

### v

Our birth is but a sleep and a forgetting:
The Soul that rises with us, our life's Star,
    Hath had elsewhere its setting,          60
    And cometh from afar:
    Not in entire forgetfulness,
    And not in utter nakedness,
But trailing clouds of glory do we come
    From God, who is our home:          65
Heaven lies about us in our infancy!
Shades of the prison-house begin to close
    Upon the growing Boy,
But He beholds the light, and whence it flows,
    He sees it in his joy;          70
The Youth, who daily farther from the east
    Must travel, still is Nature's Priest,
    And by the vision splendid
    Is on his way attended;
At length the Man perceives it die away,          75
And fade into the light of common day.

### VI

Earth fills her lap with pleasures of her own;
Yearnings she hath in her own natural kind,
And, even with something of a Mother's mind,
    And no unworthy aim,          80
    The homely Nurse doth all she can
To make her Foster-child, her Inmate Man,
    Forget the glories he hath known,
And that imperial palace whence he came.

### VII

Behold the Child among his new-born blisses,
A six years' Darling of a pigmy size!          86
See, where 'mid work of his own hand he lies,
Fretted by sallies of his mother's kisses,
With light upon him from his father's eyes!
See, at his feet, some little plan or chart,          90
Some fragment from his dream of human life,
Shaped by himself with newly-learned art;
    A wedding or a festival,
    A mourning or a funeral;
        And this hath now his heart,          95
    And unto this he frames his song:
        Then will he fit his tongue
To dialogues of business, love, or strife;
    But it will not be long

Ere this be thrown aside,          100
    And with new joy and pride
The little Actor cons another part;
Filling from time to time his "humorous
    stage" [5]
With all the Persons, down to palsied Age,
That Life brings with her in her equipage;          105
    As if his whole vocation
    Were endless imitation.

### VIII

Thou, whose exterior semblance doth belie
    Thy Soul's immensity;
Thou best Philosopher, who yet dost keep          110
Thy heritage, thou Eye among the blind,
That, deaf and silent, read'st the eternal deep,
Haunted for ever by the eternal mind,—
    Mighty Prophet! Seer bless'd!
    On whom those truths do rest,          115
Which we are toiling all our lives to find,
In darkness lost, the darkness of the grave;
Thou, over whom thy Immortality
Broods like the Day, a Master o'er a Slave,
A Presence which is not to be put by;          120
Thou little Child, yet glorious in the might
Of heaven-born freedom on thy being's height,
Why with such earnest pains dost thou provoke
The years to bring the inevitable yoke,
Thus blindly with thy blessedness at strife?          125
Full soon thy Soul shall have her earthly freight,
And custom lie upon thee with a weight,
Heavy as frost, and deep almost as life!

### IX

    O joy! that in our embers
    Is something that doth live,          130
    That nature yet remembers
    What was so fugitive!
The thought of our past years in me doth
    breed
Perpetual benediction: not indeed
For that which is most worthy to be bless'd—
Delight and liberty, the simple creed          136
Of Childhood, whether busy or at rest,
With new-fledged hope still fluttering in his
    breast:—
    Not for these I raise
        The song of thanks and praise;          140
    But for those obstinate questionings
    Of sense and outward things,
    Fallings from us, vanishings;
    Blank misgivings of a Creature
Moving about in worlds not realized,          145
High instincts before which our mortal Nature
Did tremble like a guilty Thing surprised:
        But for those first affections,
        Those shadowy recollections,
    Which, be they what they may,          150

[5] Moody stage. The allusion in these lines is to
the speech beginning "All the world's a stage," in
*As You Like It*, II, vii, 139–166.

Are yet the fountain light of all our day,
Are yet a master light of all our seeing;
  Uphold us, cherish, and have power to make
Our noisy years seem moments in the being
Of the eternal Silence: truths that wake, 155
    To perish never;
Which neither listlessness, nor mad endeavor,
    Nor Man nor Boy,
Nor all that is at enmity with joy,
Can utterly abolish or destroy! 160
    Hence in a season of calm weather
      Though inland far we be,
Our Souls have sight of that immortal sea
    Which brought us hither,
      Can in a moment travel thither, 165
And see the Children sport upon the shore,
And hear the mighty waters rolling evermore.

### X

Then sing, ye Birds, sing, sing a joyous song!
    And let the young Lambs bound
    As to the tabor's sound! 170
We in thought will join your throng,
  Ye that pipe and ye that play,
  Ye that through your hearts to-day
  Feel the gladness of the May!
What though the radiance which was once so
    bright 175
Be now for ever taken from my sight,
  Though nothing can bring back the hour
Of splendor in the grass, of glory in the flower;
    We will grieve not, rather find
    Strength in what remains behind; 180
    In the primal sympathy
      Which having been must ever be;
    In the soothing thoughts that spring
    Out of human suffering;
    In the faith that looks through [6] death, 185
In years that bring the philosophic mind.

### XI

And O, ye Fountains, Meadows, Hills, and
    Groves,
Forebode not any severing of our loves!
Yet in my heart of hearts I feel your might;
I only have relinquished one delight 190
To live beneath your more habitual sway.
I love the Brooks which down their channels
    fret,
Even more than when I tripped lightly as they;
The innocent brightness of a new-born Day
    Is lovely yet; 195
The Clouds that gather round the setting sun
Do take a sober coloring from an eye
That hath kept watch o'er man's mortality;
Another race hath been, and other palms are
    won.
Thanks to the human heart by which we live,
Thanks to its tenderness, its joys, and fears, 201
To me the meanest flower that blows can give
Thoughts that do often lie too deep for tears.

[6] Beyond.

## After-Thought, Appended to *The River Duddon* [1]

I thought of Thee, my partner and my guide,
As being passed away.—Vain sympathies!
For, backward, Duddon, as I cast my eyes,
I see what was, and is, and will abide;
Still glides the Stream, and shall for ever glide,
The Form remains, the Function never dies, [6]
While we, the brave, the mighty, and the wise,
We Men, who in our morn of youth defied
The elements, must vanish,—be it so!
Enough, if something from our hands have
    power 10
To live, and act, and serve the future hour,
And if, as toward the silent tomb we go,
Through love, through hope, and faith's
    transcendent dower,
We feel that we are greater than we know.

## Mutability [2]

From low to high doth dissolution climb,
And sink from high to low, along a scale
Of awful notes, whose concord shall not fail;
A musical but melancholy chime,
Which they can hear who meddle not with
    crime, 5
Nor avarice, nor over-anxious care.
Truth fails not; but her outward forms that
    bear
The longest date do melt like frosty rime,
That in the morning whitened hill and plain
And is no more; drop like the tower sublime
Of yesterday, which royally did wear 11
His crown of weeds, but could not even sustain
Some casual shout that broke the silent air,
Or the unimaginable touch of Time.

## Inside of King's College Chapel, Cambridge [3]

Tax not the royal Saint with vain expense,
With ill-matched aims the Architect who
    planned—
Albeit laboring for a scanty band
Of white robed Scholars only—this immense
And glorious Work of fine intelligence! 5
Give all thou canst; high Heaven rejects the
    lore

[1] Published in 1820. This is the final sonnet of a
series entitled *The River Duddon*. This stream rises
on the borders of Westmoreland, Cumberland, and
Lancashire, and flows between the latter two counties
into the Irish Sea.

[2] This and the three following sonnets are from
*Ecclesiastical Sonnets*, published in 1822. Most of
the sonnets in the series were written in 1821.

[3] The College was founded (in 1441) and the
chapel built by Henry VI, who was never actually
canonized but who was worshiped as a martyr and
saint. The scholars for whom the Chapel was built
were clerks of St. Nicholas.

Of nicely-calculated less or more;
So deemed the man who fashioned for the
sense
These lofty pillars, spread that branching roof
Self-poised, and scooped into ten thousand
cells,                                      10
Where light and shade repose, where music
dwells
Lingering—and wandering on as loath to die;
Like thoughts whose very sweetness yieldeth
proof
That they were born for immortality.

## The Same

What awful pérspective! while from our sight
With gradual stealth the lateral windows hide
Their Portraitures, their stone-work glimmers,
dyed
In the soft checkerings of a sleepy light.
Martyr, or King, or sainted Eremite,          5
Whoe'er ye be, that thus, yourselves unseen,
Imbue your prison-bars with solemn sheen,
Shine on, until ye fade with coming Night!—
But, from the arms of silence—list! O list!
The music bursteth into second life;          10
The notes luxuriate, every stone is kissed
By sound, or ghost of sound, in mazy strife;
Heart-thrilling strains, that cast, before the eye
Of the devout, a veil of ecstasy!

## Continued

They dreamt not of a perishable home
Who thus could build. Be mine, in hours of fear
Or groveling thought, to seek a refuge here;
Or through the aisles of Westminster [4] to
roam:
Where bubbles burst, and folly's dancing foam
Melts, if it cross the threshold; where the
wreath                                      6
Of awe-struck wisdom droops: or let my path
Lead to that younger Pile,[5] whose sky-like dome
Hath typified by reach of daring art
Infinity's embrace; whose guardian crest,    10
The silent Cross, among the stars shall spread
As now, when She hath also seen her breast
Filled with mementos, satiate with its part
Of grateful England's overflowing Dead.

## To ——— [6]

O dearer far than light and life are dear,
Full oft our human foresight I deplore;
Trembling, through my unworthiness, with fear
That friends, by death disjoined, may meet no
more!

[4] Westminster Abbey.
[5] St. Paul's Cathedral, built in the seventeenth
century by Sir Christopher Wren.
[6] Written in 1824; published in 1827. Addressed
to Mrs. Wordsworth.

Misgivings, hard to vanquish or control,      5
Mix with the day, and cross the hour of rest;
While all the future, for thy purer soul,
With "sober certainties" [7] of love is bless'd.

That sigh of thine, not meant for human ear,
Tells that these words thy humbleness offend;
Yet bear me up—else faltering in the rear [11]
Of a steep march: support me to the end.

Peace settles where the intellect is meek,
And Love is dutiful in thought and deed;
Through Thee communion with that Love I
seek:                                       15
The faith Heaven strengthens where *he* molds
the Creed.

## To a Skylark [8]

Ethereal minstrel! pilgrim of the sky!
Dost thou despise the earth where cares
abound?
Or, while the wings aspire, are heart and eye
Both with thy nest upon the dewy ground?
Thy nest which thou canst drop into at will,  5
Those quivering wings composed, that music
still!

Leave to the nightingale her shady wood;
A privacy of glorious light is thine;
Whence thou dost pour upon the world a flood
Of harmony, with instinct more divine;       10
Type of the wise who soar, but never roam;
True to the kindred points of Heaven and
Home!

## Scorn Not the Sonnet [9]

Scorn not the Sonnet; Critic, you have frowned,
Mindless of its just honors; with this key
Shakespeare unlocked his heart; the melody
Of this small lute gave ease to Petrarch's
wound; [10]
A thousand times this pipe did Tasso [11] sound;
With it Camöens [12] soothed in exile's grief; 6
The Sonnet glittered a gay myrtle leaf
Amid the cypress with which Dante crowned
His visionary brow: a glow-worm lamp,
It cheered mild Spenser, called from Faery-
land                                        10
To struggle through dark ways; and, when a
damp
Fell round the path of Milton, in his hand
The Thing became a trumpet; whence he blew
Soul-animating strains—alas, too few!

[7] *Comus,* l. 264.
[8] Written in 1825; published in 1827.
[9] Published in 1827.
[10] Italian humanist and poet (1304–1374), who
wrote a series of love sonnets to Laura.
[11] Italian poet (1544–1595).
[12] Portuguese poet (1524–1580).

## If This Great World of Joy and Pain [1]

If this great world of joy and pain
Revolve in one sure track;

[1] Written in 1833; published in 1835.

If freedom, set, will rise again,
And virtue, flown, come back;
Woe to the purblind crew who fill
The heart with each day's care;
Nor gain, from past or future, skill
To bear, and to forbear!

# Samuel Taylor Coleridge

## 1772-1834

Coleridge, the son of a clergyman of the Church of England, was born at Ottery St. Mary, in Devonshire, on 21 October, 1772. His early childhood clearly foreshadowed his later development. "I read," he says, speaking of his boyhood, "every book that came in my way without distinction; and my father was fond of me, and used to take me on his knee, and hold long conversations with me. I remember, when eight years old, walking with him one winter's evening from a farmer's house, a mile from Ottery; and he then told me the names of the stars, and how Jupiter was a thousand times larger than our world, and that the other twinkling stars were suns that had worlds rolling round them; and when I came home he showed me how they rolled round. I heard him with a profound delight and admiration, but without the least mixture of wonder or incredulity. For from my early reading of fairy tales and about genii, and the like, my mind had been habituated to the Vast; and I never regarded my senses in any way as the criteria of my belief. I regulated all my creeds by my conceptions, not by my sight, even at that age." Coleridge, in other words, was born with a sense of immaterial reality, and this he never lost. From 1782 until 1790 he was at Christ's Hospital, where he began his lifelong friendship with Charles Lamb. And as Lamb later sketched his schoolfellow we see still the same Coleridge who as a boy of eight regulated his creeds by his conceptions, not by his sight: "Come back into memory, like as thou wert in the dayspring of thy fancies, with hope like a fiery column before thee—the dark pillar not yet turned—Samuel Taylor Coleridge—Logician, Metaphysician, Bard!—How have I seen the casual passer through the Cloisters stand still, entranced with admiration . . . to hear thee unfold, in thy deep and sweet intonations, the mysteries of Jamblichus, or Plotinus (for even in those years thou waxedst not pale at such philosophic draughts), or reciting Homer

in his Greek, or Pindar—while the walls of the old Gray Friars re-echoed to the accents of the inspired charity-boy!" From Christ's Hospital Coleridge proceeded to Jesus College, Cambridge. There he became a radical in politics and displayed ardor for the French Revolution, continued to read everything he could lay hands on, accumulated debts, and suffered disappointment in love. Then after two years of Cambridge he suddenly enlisted in a regiment of dragoons, but found inside of four months that a soldier's life was not for him. Consequently he went back to Cambridge, but began also to plan, with Robert Southey, then a student at Oxford, the foundation of an ideal community along the banks of the Susquehanna in America. The plan, of course, fell through, but it did result in the marriage of Coleridge and Southey to the two Miss Frickers, who were to have been fellow-members of the American Pantisocracy. Coleridge's marriage proved unhappy. His would have been a difficult nature in any household, and it was doubtless the more so in one ill-provided with money. In later years he lived apart from his wife and children.

In 1795 Coleridge met Wordsworth, and at subsequent meetings each made a profound impression on the other. In 1797 they were much together, and there opened for both of them the period when their greatest poetry was written. In his Biographia Literaria Coleridge has written of these early days of friendship, and, at the same time, in his discussion of Wordsworth's poetry and poetical theory, has left us the best example we have of his critical genius and methods. He has also told how Wordsworth and he coöperated in writing the Lyrical Ballads. As he says, Wordsworth's industry proved greater than his, so that the book appeared in 1798 with only four poems by Coleridge—though one of these was The Ancient Mariner, sufficiently notable for its quality to make up for many failures in in-

*dustry. In the same year Coleridge and Words-worth went to Germany, the former to study philosophy, and to find in German Transcen-dentalism the confirmation of much of his own earlier thought. Philosophy and religion had always been major interests with Cole-ridge, and after 1800 his attention was more and more absorbed into the effort to lay a solid philosophic foundation for Christian be-lief. In the early years of the new century, how-ever, he became the victim of opium, which in the course of time so undermined his health that he grew unfit for prolonged and steady work. To the end of his life he never ceased forming vast projects, and he apparently con-tinued to believe that he was at least making progress towards the completion of his great philosophic reconstitution of Christianity; but neither this—the most famous unwritten book in English literature, as it has been called— nor other books ever saw the light. Some things were written, the essays composing* The Friend *(1809–1810), many articles for newspapers,* The Statesman's Manual *(1816), the Bio-graphia Literaria (1817),* Aids to Reflection *(1825),* On the Constitution of the Church and State *(1830), and* The Confessions of an Inquiring Spirit *(not published until 1840), but these were fragments only in comparison with what Coleridge thought he could do.*

*In 1816 Coleridge was taken into the house-hold of Dr. James Gillman of Highgate, and there he continued to live until his death on 25 July, 1834. Under Gillman's care he was par-tially cured of the opium habit, and his last years were years of comparative peace. They were also years in which Coleridge was re-garded as little less than an oracle by a group of younger disciples who gathered round him at Highgate to hear his copious floods of ex-traordinary talk.*

The Complete Poetical Works of Samuel Taylor Coleridge *have been edited by Ernest Hartley Coleridge (Oxford, 1912), and the* Biographia Literaria *by J. Shawcross (Oxford, 1907). No complete edition of Coleridge's prose has been published, but Coleridge's* Shakespearean Criticism *has been collected and elaborately edited by T. M. Raysor (2 vols., Cambridge, Mass., 1930), and the same editor has also published Coleridge's* Miscel-laneous Criticism *(Cambridge, Mass., 1936). An admirable selection from the whole range of Coleridge's writings—poetry, political jour-nalism, notes, literary criticism, theological and philosophical fragments, table talk, and letters —is to be found in* Coleridge: Select Poetry *and Prose, ed. Stephen Potter (London, 1950). Volumes I and II of the six-volume* Collected Letters *(Oxford, 1956–   ) have appeared, under the editorship of E. L. Griggs. Volume I of* The Notebooks of Samuel Taylor Coleridge, *ed. Kathleen Coburn (New York, 1957–   ), includes valuable material from 1794 to 1804; a total of eleven volumes is projected. Sir Ed-mund K. Chambers has written a succinct biography,* Samuel Taylor Coleridge *(Oxford, 1950); and there has appeared the first volume of a much fuller account, Lawrence Hanson's* Life of Samuel Taylor Coleridge: The Early Years *(London, 1938). The process by which Coleridge's imagination converted his reading into poetry has been thoroughly studied by John L. Lowes in* The Road to Xanadu *(Bos-ton, 1930). I. A. Richards has notably ex-pounded the poet's aesthetic theories in* Cole-ridge on Imagination *(London, 1950). Help-ful studies include* Coleridge as Philosopher, *by John H. Muirhead (London, 1930),* Cole-ridge and S. T. C., *by Stephen Potter (London, 1935),* Samuel Taylor Coleridge, *by Hugh I'A. Fausset (London, 1936),* Strange Seas of Thought, *by N. P. Stallknecht (Durham, N. C., 1945), and* Coleridge, *by Humphry House (London, 1953).*

# Kubla Khan [1]

In Xanadu did Kubla Khan
A stately pleasure-dome decree:
Where Alph, the sacred river, ran
Through caverns measureless to man
  Down to a sunless sea.     5

[1] Written in 1797 or 1798; published in 1816. In a preface (written in the third person) Coleridge explains its composition: "In consequence of a slight indisposition an anodyne had been prescribed, from the effects of which he fell asleep in his chair at the moment that he was reading the following sentence, or words of the same substance, in *Pur-chas's Pilgrimage:* 'Here the Khan Kubla com-manded a palace to be built, and a stately garden thereunto. And thus ten miles of fertile ground were enclosed with a wall.' The author continued for about three hours in a profound sleep, at least of the external senses, during which time he has the most vivid confidence that he could not have com-posed less than from two to three hundred lines; . . . On awaking he appeared to himself to have a distinct recollection of the whole, and, taking his pen, ink, and paper, instantly and eagerly wrote down the lines that are here preserved. At this mo-ment he was unfortunately called out by a person on business . . . and detained by him above an hour, and on his return to his room found, to his no small surprise and mortification, that though he still retained some vague and dim recollection of the general purport of the vision, yet, with the ex-ception of some eight or ten scattered lines and

So twice five miles of fertile ground
With walls and towers were girdled round:
And here were gardens bright with sinuous rills
Where blossomed many an incense-bearing
tree,
And here were forests ancient as the hills, 10
Enfolding sunny spots of greenery.

But oh! that deep romantic chasm which
slanted
Down the green hill athwart a cedarn cover!
A savage place! as holy and enchanted
As e'er beneath a waning moon was haunted
By woman wailing for her demon-lover!    16
And from this chasm, with ceaseless turmoil
seething,
As if this earth in fast thick pants were
breathing,
A mighty fountain momently was forced,
Amid whose swift half-intermitted burst    20
Huge fragments vaulted like rebounding hail,
Or chaffy grain beneath the thresher's flail:
And 'mid these dancing rocks at once and ever
It flung up momently the sacred river.
Five miles meandering with a mazy motion 25
Through wood and dale the sacred river ran,
Then reached the caverns measureless to man,
And sank in tumult to a lifeless ocean:
And 'mid this tumult Kubla heard from far
Ancestral voices prophesying war!    30
    The shadow of the dome of pleasure
    Floated midway on the waves;
    Where was heard the mingled measure
    From the fountain and the caves.
It was a miracle of rare device,    35
A sunny pleasure-dome with caves of ice!

    A damsel with a dulcimer
    In a vision once I saw:
    It was an Abyssinian maid,
    And on her dulcimer she played,    40
    Singing of Mount Abora.²
    Could I revive within me
    Her symphony and song,
    To such a deep delight 'twould win me,
That with music loud and long,    45
I would build that dome in air,
That sunny dome! those caves of ice!
And all who heard should see them there,
And all should cry, Beware! Beware!
His flashing eyes, his floating hair!    50
Weave a circle round him thrice,

images, all the rest had passed away." Kubla Khan
lived in the thirteenth century and was the founder
of the Mongol dynasty in China. Khan, sometimes
written Cham, is equivalent to "King." Xanadu
(the form is Zaindu in *Purchas*) is a region in
Tartary.
    ² Professor Lane Cooper has suggested that this
is a variant of Amara, the name of a mountain in
Abyssinia on which, according to tradition, there
was a terrestrial paradise like that of the Khan
Kubla.

And close your eyes with holy dread,
For he on honey-dew hath fed,
And drunk the milk of Paradise.

# The Rime of the Ancient Mariner ¹

## In Seven Parts

*Facile credo, plures esse Naturas invisibiles
quam visibiles in revum universitate. Sed horum
omnium familiam quis nobis enarrabit, et
gradus et cognationes et discrimina et singulo-
rum munera? Quid agunt? quae loca habitant?
Harum rerum notitiam semper ambivit in-
genium humanum, nunquam attigit. Juvat, interea, non diffiteor, quandoque in animo, tan-
quam in tabula, majoris et melioris mundi
imaginem contemplari: ne mens assuefacta
hodiernae vitae minutiis se contrahat nimis et
tota subsidat in pusillas cogitationes. Sede
veritati interea invigilandum est, modusque
servandus, ut certa ab incertis, diem a nocte,
distinguamus.*

T. BURNET: ARCHAEOL. PHIL., p. 68.

### ARGUMENT

*How a Ship having passed the Line ² was driven
by storm to the cold Country towards the
South Pole; and how from thence she made*

¹ Written 1797–1798; published 1798. Many
changes were made for the 2nd edition of the *Lyrical Ballads*, 1800. The marginal gloss was added in
1815–1816, and was first published in *Sibylline
Leaves*, 1817, when, also, the poem first appeared
under Coleridge's name. In 1843 Wordsworth said
that "much the greatest part of the story was Mr.
Coleridge's invention," but that he had made certain suggestions, including the killing of the albatross
as the crime which was wanted, to bring upon the
Mariner the spectral persecution. Then and previously Wordsworth also said that he had contributed
a few lines to the poem; and he told Alexander
Dyce, in 1835 or 1836, that he had written one
complete stanza (ll. 13–16).
    The Latin motto from Thomas Burnet's *Archae-
ologiae Philosophicae* has been translated by Herbert Bates: "I find it easy to believe that in the
universe the visible beings are outnumbered by the
invisible. But who shall tell us the nature common
to these, their rank, their kindreds, the signs by
which they are distinguished, the gifts in which
they excel? What is their task? Where is their
abode? Close to full knowledge of these wonders,
the mind of man has ever circled, nor ever attained
the center. Meanwhile, I trust, it will give us profit
to contemplate in the mind, as in a picture, the
image of this other world, greater than ours and
better, lest our minds, becoming wont to the petty
details of daily life, be narrowed overmuch, and sink
to paltry thoughts. We must, meanwhile, keep
watch, with vigilance, toward truth, preserving temperance of judgment, that we distinguish things
certain from things uncertain, day from night."
    ² Equator.

*her course to the tropical Latitude of the
Great Pacific Ocean; and of the strange
things that befell; and in what manner the
Ancyent Marinere came back to his own
Country.*

## PART I

*An ancient Mariner
meeteth three Gal-
lants bidden to a
wedding-feast, and
detaineth one.*

It is an ancient Mariner,
And he stoppeth one of three.
"By thy long gray beard and glittering eye,
Now wherefore stopp'st thou me?

"The Bridegroom's doors are opened wide, 5
And I am next of kin;
The guests are met, the feast is set:
May'st hear the merry din."

He holds him with his skinny hand,
"There was a ship," quoth he. 10
"Hold off! unhand me, gray-beard loon!"
Eftsoons [3] his hand dropped he.

*The Wedding-Guest
is spellbound by the
eye of the old sea-
faring man, and con-
strained to hear his
tale.*

He holds him with his glittering eye—
The Wedding-Guest stood still,
And listens like a three years' child: 15
The Mariner hath his will.

The Wedding-Guest sat on a stone:
He cannot choose but hear;
And thus spake on that ancient man,
The bright-eyed Mariner. 20

"The ship was cheered, the harbor cleared,
Merrily did we drop
Below the kirk, below the hill,
Below the lighthouse top.

*The Mariner tells how
the ship sailed south-
ward with a good
wind and fair weather
till it reached the
Line.*

"The sun came up upon the left, 25
Out of the sea came he!
And he shone bright, and on the right
Went down into the sea.

"Higher and higher every day,
Till over the mast at noon—" 30
The Wedding-Guest here beat his breast,
For he heard the loud bassoon.

*The Wedding-Guest
heareth the bridal
music; but the
Mariner continueth
his tale.*

The bride hath paced into the hall,
Red as a rose is she;
Nodding their heads before her goes 35
The merry minstrelsy.

The Wedding-Guest he beat his breast,
Yet he cannot choose but hear;
And thus spake on that ancient man,
The bright-eyed Mariner. 40

*The ship driven by a
storm toward the south
pole.*

"And now the Storm-blast came, and he
Was tyrannous and strong:
He struck with his o'ertaking wings,
And chased us south along.

[3] At once.

"With sloping masts and dipping prow,     45
As who pursued with yell and blow
Still treads the shadow of his foe,
And forward bends his head,
The ship drove fast, loud roared the blast,
And southward aye we fled.     50

"And now there came both mist and snow,
And it grew wondrous cold:
And ice, mast-high, came floating by,
As green as emerald.

*The land of ice, and*
*of fearful sounds*
*where no living*
*thing was to be seen.*

"And through the drifts the snowy clifts     55
Did send a dismal sheen:
Nor shapes of men nor beasts we ken—
The ice was all between.

"The ice was here, the ice was there,
The ice was all around:     60
It cracked and growled, and roared and howled,
Like noises in a swound! [4]

*Till a great sea-bird,*
*called the Albatross,*
*came through the*
*snow-fog, and was*
*received with great*
*joy and hospitality.*

"At length did cross an Albatross,
Thorough the fog it came;
As if it had been a Christian soul,     65
We hailed it in God's name.

"It ate the food it ne'er had eat,
And round and round it flew.
The ice did split with a thunder-fit;
The helmsman steered us through!     70

*And lo! the Albatross*
*proveth a bird of good*
*omen, and followeth*
*the ship as it returned*
*northward through fog*
*and floating ice.*

"And a good south wind sprung up behind;
The Albatross did follow,
And every day, for food or play,
Came to the mariner's hollo!

*In mist or cloud, on mast or shroud,*     75
It perched for vespers nine;
Whiles all the night, through fog-smoke white,
Glimmered the white moon-shine."

*The ancient Mariner*
*inhospitably killeth the*
*pious bird of good*
*omen.*

"God save thee, ancient Mariner!
From the fiends, that plague thee thus!—     80
Why look'st thou so?"—"With my cross-bow
I shot the Albatross!"

## PART II

"The Sun now rose upon the right:
Out of the sea came he,
Still hid in mist, and on the left     85
Went down into the sea.

"And the good south wind still blew behind,
But no sweet bird did follow,
Nor any day for food or play
Came to the mariner's hollo!     90

*His shipmates cry out*
*against the ancient*
*Mariner, for killing*
*the bird of good luck.*

"And I had done a hellish thing,
And it would work 'em woe:
For all averred, I had killed the bird

[4] Swoon.

That made the breeze to blow.
Ah wretch! said they, the bird to slay,                95
That made the breeze to blow!

*But when the fog
cleared off they justify
the same, and thus
make themselves ac-
complices in the
crime.*

"Nor dim nor red, like God's own head,
The glorious Sun uprist:
Then all averred, I had killed the bird
That brought the fog and mist.                         100
'Twas right, said they, such birds to slay,
That bring the fog and mist.

*The fair breeze con-
tinues; the ship enters
the Pacific Ocean, and
sails northward, even
till it reaches the Line.*

"The fair breeze blew, the white foam flew,
The furrow followed free;
We were the first that ever burst
Into that silent sea.                                  105

*The ship hath been
suddenly becalmed.*

"Down dropped the breeze, the sails dropped
        down,
'Twas sad as sad could be;
And we did speak only to break
The silence of the sea!                                110

"All in a hot and copper sky,
The bloody Sun, at noon,
Right up above the mast did stand,
No bigger than the Moon.

"Day after day, day after day,                         115
We stuck, nor breath nor motion;
As idle as a painted ship
Upon a painted ocean.

*And the Albatross be-
gins to be avenged.*

"Water, water, everywhere,
And all the boards did shrink;                         120
Water, water, everywhere,
Nor any drop to drink.

"The very deep did rot: O Christ!
That ever this should be!
Yea, slimy things did crawl with legs                  125
Upon the slimy sea.

"About, about, in reel and rout
The death-fires danced at night;
The water, like a witch's oils,
Burned green, and blue and white.                      130

*A Spirit had followed
them; one of the in-
visible inhabitants of
this planet, neither de-
parted souls nor
angels; concerning
whom the learned
Jew, Josephus, and the
Platonic Constanti-
nopolitan, Michael
Psellus, may be con-
sulted. They are very
numerous, and there is
no climate or element
without one or more.*

"And some in dreams assured were
Of the Spirit that plagued us so;
Nine fathom deep he had followed us
From the land of mist and snow.

"And every tongue, through utter drought, 135
Was withered at the root;
We could not speak, no more than if
We had been choked with soot.

*The shipmates, in
their sore distress,
would fain throw the
whole guilt on the
ancient Mariner: in
sign whereof they
hang the dead sea-bird
round his neck.*

"Ah! well-a-day! what evil looks
Had I from old and young!                              140
Instead of the cross, the Albatross
About my neck was hung.

## PART III

"There passed a weary time. Each throat
Was parched, and glazed each eye.

*The ancient Mariner beholdeth a sign in the element afar off.*

A weary time! a weary time!　　　　145
How glazed each weary eye,
When looking westward, I beheld
A something in the sky.

"At first it seemed a little speck,
And then it seemed a mist;　　　　150
It moved and moved, and took at last
A certain shape, I wist.[5]

"A speck, a mist, a shape, I wist!
And still it neared and neared:
As if it dodged a water-sprite,　　　155
It plunged and tacked and veered.

*At its nearer approach, it seemeth him to be a ship; and at a dear ransom he freeth his speech from the bonds of thirst.*

"With throats unslaked, with black lips baked,
We could nor laugh nor wail;
Through utter drought all dumb we stood!
I bit my arm, I sucked the blood,　　　160
And cried, A sail! a sail!

"With throats unslaked, with black lips baked,
Agape they heard me call:

*A flash of joy;*

Gramercy! they for joy did grin,[6]
And all at once their breath drew in,　　　165
As they were drinking all.

*And horror follows. For can it be a ship that comes onward without wind or tide?*

"See! see! (I cried) she tacks no more!
Hither to work us weal;
Without a breeze, without a tide,
She steadies with upright keel!　　　170

"The western wave was all aflame,
The day was well nigh done!
Almost upon the western wave
Rested the broad bright Sun;
When that strange shape drove suddenly　175
Betwixt us and the Sun.

*It seemeth him but the skeleton of a ship.*

"And straight the Sun was flecked with bars,
(Heaven's Mother send us grace!)
As if through a dungeon-grate he peered
With broad and burning face.　　　180

"Alas! (thought I, and my heart beat loud)
How fast she nears and nears!
Are those *her* sails that glance in the Sun,
Like restless gossameres?

*And its ribs are seen as bars on the face of the setting Sun. The Specter-Woman and her Death-mate, and no other on board the skeleton-ship.*

"Are those *her* ribs through which the Sun　185
Did peer, as through a grate?
And is that Woman all her crew?
Is that a Death? and are there two?
Is death that woman's mate?

[5] Knew.

[6] "I took the thought of *grinning for joy* . . . from my companion's remark to me, when we had climbed to the top of Plinlimmon, and were nearly dead with thirst. We could not speak from the constriction, till we found a little puddle under a stone. He said to me, 'You grinned like an idiot!' He had done the same" (Coleridge, *Table Talk*, 31 May, 1830).

*Like vessel, like crew!*

"Her lips were red, *her* looks were free,　190
Her locks were yellow as gold:
Her skin was as white as leprosy,
The Nightmare Life-in-Death was she,
Who thicks man's blood with cold.

*Death and Life-in-Death have diced for the ship's crew, and she (the latter) winneth the ancient Mariner.*

"The naked hulk alongside came,　195
And the twain were casting dice;
'The game is done! I've won, I've won!'
Quoth she, and whistles thrice.

*No twilight within the courts of the Sun.*

"The Sun's rim dips; the stars rush out:
At one stride comes the dark;　200
With far-heard whisper, o'er the sea,
Off shot the specter-bark.

*At the rising of the Moon,*

"We listened and looked sideways up!
Fear at my heart, as at a cup,
My life-blood seemed to sip!　205
The stars were dim, and thick the night,
The steersman's face by his lamp gleamed white;
From the sails the dew did drip—
Till clomb above the eastern bar
The hornéd Moon with one bright star　210
Within the nether tip.

*One after another,*

"One after one, by the star-dogged Moon,
Too quick for groan or sigh,
Each turned his face with a ghastly pang,
And cursed me with his eye.　215

*His shipmates drop down dead.*

"Four times fifty living men
(And I heard nor sigh nor groan),
With heavy thump, a lifeless lump,
They dropped down one by one.

*But Life-in-Death begins her work on the ancient Mariner.*

"The souls did from their bodies fly—　220
They fled to bliss or woe!
And every soul, it passed me by,
Like the whizz of my cross-bow!"

## PART IV

*The Wedding-Guest feareth that a Spirit is talking to him.*

"I fear thee, ancient Mariner!
I fear thy skinny hand!　225
And thou art long, and lank, and brown,
As is the ribbed sea-sand.[7]

*But the ancient Mariner assureth him of his bodily life, and proceedeth to relate his horrible penance.*

"I fear thee and thy glittering eye,
And thy skinny hand, so brown."—
"Fear not, fear not, thou Wedding-Guest!　230
This body dropped not down.

"Alone, alone, all, all alone,
Alone on a wide wide sea!
And never a saint took pity on
My soul in agony.　235

*He despiseth the creatures of the calm.*

"The many men, so beautiful!
And they all dead did lie:

---

[7] The last two lines of this stanza were contributed by Wordsworth.

And a thousand thousand slimy things
Lived on; and so did I.

*And envieth that they should live, and so many lie dead.*

"I looked upon the rotting sea,          240
And drew my eyes away;
I looked upon the rotting deck,
And there the dead men lay.

"I looked to heaven, and tried to pray;
But or ever a prayer had gushed,          245
A wicked whisper came, and made
My heart as dry as dust.

"I closed my lids, and kept them close,
And the balls like pulses beat;
For the sky and the sea, and the sea and the sky,
Lay like a load on my weary eye,          251
And the dead were at my feet.

*But the curse liveth for him in the eye of the dead men.*

"The cold sweat melted from their limbs,
Nor rot nor reek did they:
The look with which they looked on me          255
Had never passed away.

"An orphan's curse would drag to hell
A spirit from on high;
But oh! more horrible than that
Is the curse in a dead man's eye!          260
Seven days, seven nights, I saw that curse,
And yet I could not die.

*In his loneliness and fixedness he yearneth towards the journeying Moon, and the stars that still sojourn, yet still move onward; and everywhere the blue sky belongs to them, and is their appointed rest, and their native country and their own natural homes, which they enter unannounced, as lords that are certainly expected, and yet there is a silent joy at their arrival.*

"The moving Moon went up the sky,
And nowhere did abide:
Softly she was going up,          265
And a star or two beside—

"Her beams bemocked the sultry main,
Like April hoar-frost spread;
But where the ship's huge shadow lay,
The charméd water burned alway          270
A still and awful red.

*By the light of the Moon he beholdeth God's creatures of the great calm.*

"Beyond the shadow of the ship,
I watched the water-snakes:
They moved in tracks of shining white,
And when they reared, the elfish light          275
Fell off in hoary flakes.

"Within the shadow of the ship
I watched their rich attire:
Blue, glossy green, and velvet black,
They coiled and swam; and every track          280
Was a flash of golden fire.

*Their beauty and their happiness.*

*He blesseth them in his heart.*

"O happy living things! no tongue
Their beauty might declare:
A spring of love gushed from my heart,
And I blessed them unaware;          285
Sure my kind saint took pity on me,
And I blessed them unaware.

*The spell begins to break.*

"The selfsame moment I could pray;
And from my neck so free

The Albatross fell off, and sank                                    290
Like lead into the sea."

## PART V

"Oh sleep! it is a gentle thing,
Beloved from pole to pole!
To Mary Queen the praise be given!
She sent the gentle sleep from Heaven,              295
That slid into my soul.

*By grace of the holy*
*Mother, the ancient*
*Mariner is refreshed*
*with rain.*

"The silly [8] buckets on the deck,
That had so long remained,
I dreamt that they were filled with dew;
And when I awoke, it rained.                        300

"My lips were wet, my throat was cold,
My garments all were dank;
Sure I had drunken in my dreams,
And still my body drank.

"I moved, and could not feel my limbs:             305
I was so light—almost
I thought that I had died in sleep,
And was a blessed ghost.

*He heareth sounds*
*and seeth strange*
*sights and commotions*
*in the sky and the*
*element.*

"And soon I heard a roaring wind:
It did not come anear;                             310
But with its sound it shook the sails,
That were so thin and sere.

"The upper air burst into life!
And a hundred fire-flags sheen,[9]
To and fro they were hurried about!                315
And to and fro, and in and out,
The wan stars danced between.

"And the coming wind did roar more loud,
And the sails did sigh like sedge; [10]
And the rain poured down from one black cloud;
The Moon was at its edge.                          321

"The thick black cloud was cleft, and still
The Moon was at its side:
Like waters shot from some high crag,
The lightning fell with never a jag,               325
A river steep and wide.

*The bodies of the*
*ship's crew are in-*
*spired, and the ship*
*moves on;*

"The loud wind never reached the ship,
Yet now the ship moved on!
Beneath the lightning and the Moon
The dead men gave a groan.                         330

"They groaned, they stirred, they all uprose,
Nor spake, nor moved their eyes;
It had been strange, even in a dream,
To have seen those dead men rise.

[8] What meaning Coleridge intended the word to
have here it is not easy to say. The buckets were
not fulfilling the purpose for which they were made:
perhaps he meant that this made them look "silly."
[9] Bright.                    [10] Swamp-grass.

"The helmsman steered, the ship moved on;
Yet never a breeze up blew;                        336
The mariners all 'gan work the ropes,
Where they were wont to do;
They raised their limbs like lifeless tools—
We were a ghastly crew.                            340

"The body of my brother's son
Stood by me, knee to knee:
The body and I pulled at one rope,
But he said nought to me."

*But not by the souls*
*of the men, nor by*
*demons of earth or*
*middle air, but by a*
*blessed troop of*
*angelic spirits, sent*
*down by the invoca-*
*tion of the guardian*
*saint.*

"I fear thee, ancient Mariner!"                    345
"Be calm, thou Wedding-Guest!
'Twas not those souls that fled in pain,
Which to their corses came again,
But a troop of spirits blest:

"For when it dawned—they dropped their
        arms,                                       350
And clustered round the mast;
Sweet sounds rose slowly through their mouths,
And from their bodies passed.

"Around, around, flew each sweet sound,
Then darted to the Sun;                             355
Slowly the sounds come back again,
Now mixed, now one by one.

"Sometimes a-dropping from the sky
I heard the sky-lark sing;
Sometimes all little birds that are,               360
How they seemed to fill the sea and air
With their sweet jargoning!

"And now 'twas like all instruments,
Now like a lonely flute;
And now it is an angel's song,                     365
That makes the heavens be mute.

"It ceased; yet still the sails made on
A pleasant noise till noon,
A noise like of a hidden brook
In the leafy month of June,                         370
That to the sleeping woods all night
Singeth a quiet tune.

"Till noon we quietly sailed on,
Yet never a breeze did breathe:
Slowly and smoothly went the ship,                 375
Moved onward from beneath.

*The lonesome Spirit*
*from the south-pole*
*carries on the ship*
*as far as the Line, in*
*obedience to the an-*
*gelic troop, but still*
*requireth vengeance.*

"Under the keel nine fathom deep,
From the land of mist and snow,
The spirit slid; and it was he
That made the ship to go.                           380
The sails at noon left off their tune,
And the ship stood still also.

"The Sun, right up above the mast,
Had fixed her to the ocean;
But in a minute she 'gan stir,                     385
With a short uneasy motion—

Backwards and forwards half her length,
With a short uneasy motion.

"Then like a pawing horse let go,
She made a sudden bound:                                    390
It flung the blood into my head,
And I fell down in a swound.

*The Polar Spirit's*
*fellow-demons, the in-*
*visible inhabitants of*
*the element, take part*
*in his wrong; and two*
*of them relate one to*
*the other, that penance*
*long and heavy for*
*the ancient Mariner*
*hath been accorded to*
*the Polar Spirit, who*
*returneth southward.*

"How long in that same fit I lay,
I have not to declare,
But ere my living life returned,                           395
I heard, and in my soul discerned
Two voices in the air.

" 'Is it he?' quoth one, 'is this the man?
By Him who died on cross,
With his cruel bow he laid full low                        400
The harmless Albatross.

" 'The spirit who bideth by himself
In the land of mist and snow,
He loved the bird that loved the man
Who shot him with his bow.'                                405

"The other was a softer voice,
As soft as honey-dew;
Quoth he, 'The man hath penance done,
And penance more will do.'

## PART VI

### First Voice

" 'But tell me, tell me! speak again                       410
Thy soft response renewing—
What makes that ship drive on so fast?
What is the ocean doing?'

### Second Voice

" 'Still as a slave before his lord,
The ocean hath no blast;                                   415
His great bright eye most silently
Up to the Moon is cast—

" 'If he may know which way to go;
For she guides him, smooth or grim.
See, brother, see! how graciously                          420
She looketh down on him.'

### First Voice

" 'But why drives on that ship so fast,
Without or wave or wind?'

### Second Voice

*The Mariner hath*
*been cast into a*
*trance; for the*
*angelic power causeth*
*the vessel to drive*
*northward faster than*
*human life could en-*
*dure.*

" 'The air is cut away before,
And closes from behind.'                                   425

" 'Fly, brother, fly! more high, more high!
Or we shall be belated:
For slow and slow that ship will go,
When the Mariner's trance is abated.'

"I woke, and we were sailing on                            430
As in a gentle weather:

*The supernatural motion is retarded; the Mariner awakes, and his penance begins anew.*

'Twas night, calm night, the moon was high;
The dead men stood together.

"All stood together on the deck,
For a charnel-dungeon fitter:                                    435
All fixed on me their stony eyes,
That in the Moon did glitter.

"The pang, the curse, with which they died,
Had never passed away:
I could not draw my eyes from theirs,                           440
Nor turn them up to pray.

*The curse is finally expiated.*

"And now this spell was snapped: once more
I viewed the ocean green,
And looked far forth, yet little saw
Of what had else been seen—                                     445

"Like one, that on a lonesome road
Doth walk in fear and dread,
And having once turned round, walks on,
And turns no more his head;
Because he knows, a frightful fiend                             450
Doth close behind him tread.

"But soon there breathed a wind on me,
Nor sound nor motion made:
Its path was not upon the sea,
In ripple or in shade.                                          455

"It raised my hair, it fanned my cheek
Like a meadow-gale of spring—
It mingled strangely with my fears,
Yet it felt like a welcoming.

"Swiftly, swiftly flew the ship,                                460
Yet she sailed softly too:
Sweetly, sweetly blew the breeze—
On me alone it blew.

*And the ancient Mariner beholdeth his native country.*

"Oh! dream of joy! is this indeed
The light-house top I see?                                      465
Is this the hill? is this the kirk?
Is this mine own countree?

"We drifted o'er the harbor-bar,
And I with sobs did pray—
O let me be awake, my God!                                      470
Or let me sleep alway.

"The harbor-bay was clear as glass,
So smoothly it was strewn!
And on the bay the moonlight lay,
And the shadow of the Moon.                                     475

"The rock shone bright, the kirk no less,
That stands above the rock:
The moonlight steeped in silentness
The steady weathercock.

"And the bay was white with silent light,                       480
Till, rising from the same,

*The angelic spirits*
*leave the dead bodies,*

Full many shapes, that shadows were,
In crimson colors came.

*And appear in their*
*own forms of light.*

"A little distance from the prow
Those crimson shadows were:                      485
I turned my eyes upon the deck—
Oh, Christ! what saw I there!

"Each corse lay flat, lifeless and flat,
And, by the holy rood! [11]
A man all light, a seraph-man,                   490
On every corse there stood.

"This seraph-band, each waved his hand:
It was a heavenly sight!
They stood as signals to the land,
Each one a lovely light;                          495

"This seraph-band, each waved his hand,
No voice did they impart—
No voice; but oh! the silence sank
Like music on my heart.

"But soon I heard the dash of oars,              500
I heard the Pilot's cheer;
My head was turned perforce away,
And I saw a boat appear.

"The Pilot and the Pilot's boy,
I heard them coming fast:                         505
Dear Lord in Heaven! it was a joy
The dead men could not blast.

"I saw a third—I heard his voice:
It is the Hermit good!
He singeth loud his godly hymns                   510
That he makes in the wood.
He'll shrieve my soul,[12] he'll wash away
The Albatross's blood.

### PART VII

*The Hermit of the*
*Wood,*

"This Hermit good lives in that wood
Which slopes down to the sea.                     515
How loudly his sweet voice he rears!
He loves to talk with marineres
That come from a far countree.

"He kneels at morn, and noon, and eve—
He hath a cushion plump:                          520
It is the moss that wholly hides
The rotted old oak-stump.

"The skiff-boat neared: I heard them talk,
'Why, this is strange, I trow!
Where are those lights so many and fair,          525
That signal made but now?'

*Approacheth the ship*
*with wonder.*

" 'Strange, by my faith!' the Hermit said—
'And they answered not our cheer!

[11] Cross.
[12] Hear my confession, assign penance, and absolve
me.

The planks look [13] warped! and see those sails,
How thin they are and sere!                                    530
I never saw aught like to them,
Unless perchance it were

" 'Brown skeletons of leaves that lag
My forest-brook along;
When the ivy-tod [14] is heavy with snow,         535
And the owlet whoops to the wolf below,
That eats the she-wolf's young.'

" 'Dear Lord! it hath a fiendish look—
(The Pilot made reply)
I am a-feared'—'Push on, push on!'                  540
Said the Hermit cheerily.

"The boat came closer to the ship,
But I nor spake nor stirred;
The boat came close beneath the ship,
And straight a sound was heard.                      545

*The ship suddenly sinketh.*

"Under the water it rumbled on,
Still louder and more dread:
It reached the ship, it split the bay;
The ship went down like lead.

*The ancient Mariner is saved in the Pilot's boat.*

"Stunned by that loud and dreadful sound,    550
Which sky and ocean smote,
Like one that hath been seven days drowned,
My body lay afloat;
But swift as dreams, myself I found
Within the Pilot's boat.                                    555

"Upon the whirl, where sank the ship,
The boat spun round and round;
And all was still, save that the hill
Was telling of the sound.

"I moved my lips—the Pilot shrieked,          560
And fell down in a fit;
The holy Hermit raised his eyes,
And prayed where he did sit.

"I took the oars: the Pilot's boy,
Who now doth crazy go,                                  565
Laughed loud and long, and all the while
His eyes went to and fro.
'Ha! ha!' quoth he, 'full plain I see,
The Devil knows how to row.'

"And now, all in my own countree,             570
I stood on the firm land!
The Hermit stepped forth from the boat,
And scarcely he could stand.

*The ancient Mariner earnestly entreateth the Hermit to shrieve him; and the penance of life falls on him.*

" 'O shrieve me, shrieve me, holy man!'
The Hermit crossed his brow,                         575
'Say quick,' quoth he, 'I bid thee say—
What manner of man art thou?'

---

[13] In the edition of 1828 this was changed to "looked," which was kept in the editions of 1829 and 1834.
[14] Ivy-bush.

"Forthwith this frame of mine was wrenched
With a woeful agony,
Which forced me to begin my tale;            580
And then it left me free.

*And ever and anon throughout his future life an agony constraineth him to travel from land to land,*
"Since then at an uncertain hour,
That agony returns;
And till my ghastly tale is told,
This heart within me burns.                  585

"I pass, like night, from land to land;
I have strange power of speech;
That moment that his face I see,
I know the man that must hear me:
To him my tale I teach.                       590

"What loud uproar bursts from that door!
The wedding-guests are there;
But in the garden-bower the bride
And bride-maids singing are;
And hark the little vesper bell,              595
Which biddeth me to prayer!

"O Wedding-Guest! this soul hath been
Alone on a wide, wide sea:
So lonely 'twas, that God himself
Scarce seeméd there to be.                    600

"O sweeter than the marriage-feast,
'Tis sweeter far to me,
To walk together to the kirk
With a goodly company!—

"To walk together to the kirk,               605
And all together pray,
While each to his great Father bends,
Old men, and babes, and loving friends,
And youths and maidens gay!

*And to teach by his own example love and reverence to all things that God made and loveth.*
"Farewell, farewell! but this I tell         610
To thee, thou Wedding-Guest!
He prayeth well, who loveth well
Both man and bird and beast.

"He prayeth best, who loveth best
All things both great and small;             615
For the dear God who loveth us,
He made and loveth all."

The Mariner, whose eye is bright,
Whose beard with age is hoar,
Is gone: and now the Wedding-Guest          620
Turned from the bridegroom's door.

He went like one that hath been stunned,
And is of sense forlorn: [15]
A sadder and a wiser man,
He rose the morrow morn.[16]                 625

[15] Deprived.

[16] "Mrs. Barbauld once told me that she admired *The Ancient Mariner* very much, but that there were two faults in it—it was improbable, and had no moral. As for the probability, I owned that

# Christabel [1]

## PART THE FIRST

'Tis the middle of night by the castle clock,
And the owls have awakened the crowing cock,
Tu—whit!—— Tu—whoo!
And hark, again! the crowing cock,
How drowsily it crew.     5

Sir Leoline, the Baron rich,
Hath a toothless mastiff bitch;
From her kennel beneath the rock
She maketh answer to the clock,
Four for the quarters, and twelve for the hour;
Ever and aye, by shine and shower,     11
Sixteen short howls, not over loud;
Some say, she sees my lady's shroud.

Is the night chilly and dark?
The night is chilly, but not dark.     15
The thin gray cloud is spread on high,
It covers but not hides the sky.
The moon is behind, and at the full;
And yet she looks both small and dull.
The night is chill, the cloud is gray:     20
'Tis a month before the month of May,
And the Spring comes slowly up this way.

The lovely lady, Christabel,
Whom her father loves so well,
What makes her in the wood so late,     25
A furlong from the castle gate?
She had dreams all yesternight
Of her own betrothéd knight;
And she in the midnight wood will pray
For the weal of her lover that's far away.     30

She stole along, she nothing spoke,
The sighs she heaved were soft and low,
And naught was green upon the oak
But moss and rarest mistletoe:
She kneels beneath the huge oak tree,     35
And in silence prayeth she.

The lady sprang up suddenly,
The lovely lady, Christabel!

that might admit some question; but as to the want
of a moral, I told her that in my own judgment the
poem had too much; and that the only, or chief
fault, if I might say so, was the obtrusion of the
moral sentiment so openly on the reader as a principle or cause of action in a work of such pure imagination. It ought to have had no more moral than
the *Arabian Nights'* tale of the merchant's sitting
down to eat dates by the side of a well, and throwing the shells aside, and lo! a genie starts up, and
says he *must* kill the aforesaid merchant, *because*
one of the date shells had, it seems, put out the eye
of the genie's son" (Coleridge, *Table Talk*, 31 May,
1830).
  [1] The first part was written in 1797, the second in
1800, and the conclusion to the second part perhaps
in 1801. Published in 1816.

It moaned as near, as near can be,
But what it is she cannot tell.—     40
On the other side it seems to be,
Of the huge, broad-breasted, old oak tree.

The night is chill; the forest bare;
Is it the wind that moaneth bleak?
There is not wind enough in the air     45
To move away the ringlet curl
From the lovely lady's cheek—
There is not wind enough to twirl
The one red leaf, the last of its clan,
That dances as often as dance it can,     50
Hanging so light, and hanging so high,
On the topmost twig that looks up at the sky.

Hush, beating heart of Christabel!
Jesu, Maria, shield her well!
She folded her arms beneath her cloak,     55
And stole to the other side of the oak.
    What sees she there?

There she sees a damsel bright,
Dressed in a silken robe of white,
That shadowy in the moonlight shone:     60
The neck that made that white robe wan.
Her stately neck, and arms were bare;
Her blue-veined feet unsandaled were;
And wildly glittered here and there
The gems entangled in her hair.     65
I guess, 'twas frightful there to see
A lady so richly clad as she—
Beautiful exceedingly!

"Mary mother, save me now!"
Said Christabel; "and who art thou?"     70
The lady strange made answer meet,
And her voice was faint and sweet:—
"Have pity on my sore distress,
I scarce can speak for weariness:
Stretch forth thy hand, and have no fear!"     75
Said Christabel, "How camest thou here?"
And the lady, whose voice was faint and sweet,
Did thus pursue her answer meet:—

"My sire is of a noble line,
And my name is Geraldine:     80
Five warriors seized me yestermorn,
Me, even me, a maid forlorn:
They choked my cries with force and fright,
And tied me on a palfrey white.
The palfrey was as fleet as wind,     85
And they rode furiously behind.
They spurred amain, their steeds were white:
And once we crossed the shade of night
As sure as Heaven shall rescue me,
I have no thought what men they be;     90
Nor do I know how long it is
(For I have lain entranced, I wis [2])
Since one, the tallest of the five,
Took me from the palfrey's back,

  [2] Think.

A weary woman, scarce alive.                              95
Some muttered words his comrades spoke:
He swore they would return with haste;
He placed me underneath this oak;
Whither they went I cannot tell—
I thought I heard, some minutes past;                    100
Sounds as of a castle bell.
Stretch forth thy hand," thus ended she,
"And help a wretched maid to flee."

Then Christabel stretched forth her hand,
And comforted fair Geraldine:                            105
"O well, bright dame! may you command
The service of Sir Leoline;
And gladly our stout chivalry
Will he send forth, and friends withal,
To guide and guard you safe and free                     110
Home to your noble father's hall."

She rose: and forth with steps they passed
That strove to be, and were not, fast.
Her gracious stars the lady bless'd,
And thus spake on sweet Christabel:                      115
"All our household are at rest,
The hall as silent as the cell;
Sir Leoline is weak in health,
And may not well awakened be,
But we will move as if in stealth;                       120
And I beseech your courtesy,
This night, to share your couch with me."

They crossed the moat, and Christabel
Took the key that fitted well;
A little door she opened straight,                       125
All in the middle of the gate;
The gate that was ironed within and without,
Where an army in battle array had marched
        out.
The lady sank, belike through pain,
And Christabel with might and main                       130
Lifted her up, a weary weight,
Over the threshold of the gate: [3]
Then the lady rose again,
And moved, as she were not in pain.

So free from danger, free from fear,                     135
They crossed the court: right glad they were.
And Christabel devoutly cried
To the lady by her side,
"Praise we the Virgin all divine,
Who hath rescued thee from thy distress!"                140
"Alas, alas!" said Geraldine,
"I cannot speak for weariness."
So free from danger, free from fear,
They crossed the court: right glad they were.

Outside her kennel, the mastiff old                      145
Lay fast asleep, in moonshine cold.

The mastiff old did not awake,
Yet she an angry moan did make! [4]
And what can ail the mastiff bitch?
Never till now she uttered yell                          150
Beneath the eye of Christabel.
Perhaps it is the owlet's scritch:
For what can ail the mastiff bitch?

They passed the hall, that echoes still,
Pass as lightly as you will!                             155
The brands were flat, the brands were dying,
Amid their own white ashes lying;
But when the lady passed, there came
A tongue of light, a fit of flame;
And Christabel saw the lady's eye,                       160
And nothing else saw she thereby,
Save the boss of the shield of Sir Leoline tall,
Which hung in a murky old niche in the wall.
"O softly tread," said Christabel,
"My father seldom sleepeth well."                        165

Sweet Christabel her feet doth bare,
And jealous of the listening air
They steal their way from stair to stair,
Now in glimmer, and now in gloom,
And now they pass the Baron's room,                      170
As still as death, with stifled breath!
And now have reached her chamber door;
And now doth Geraldine press down
The rushes of the chamber floor.

The moon shines dim in the open air,                     175
And not a moonbeam enters here.
But they without its light can see
The chamber carved so curiously,
Carved with figures strange and sweet,
All made out of the carver's brain,                      180
For a lady's chamber meet:
The lamp with twofold silver chain
Is fastened to an angel's feet.

The silver lamp burns dead and dim;
But Christabel the lamp will trim.                        185
She trimmed the lamp, and made it bright,
And left it swinging to and fro,
While Geraldine, in wretched plight,
Sank down upon the floor below.
"O weary lady, Geraldine,                                190
I pray you, drink this cordial wine!
It is a wine of virtuous powers;
My mother made it of wild flowers."

"And will your mother pity me,
Who am a maiden most forlorn?"                            195
Christabel answered—"Woe is me!
She died the hour that I was born.
I have heard the gray-haired friar tell
How on her death-bed she did say,
That she should hear the castle-bell                     200

[3] The first intimation of Geraldine's real nature.
It was formerly believed that evil spirits could not
cross a Christian threshold. In the following stanza,
again, Geraldine refuses to join in giving thanks to
the Virgin Mary.

[4] Animals were formerly supposed to have a sense
which warned them of the presence of spirits. In
the following stanza even the fire feels Geraldine's
presence.

Strike twelve upon my wedding-day.
O mother dear! that thou wert here!"
"I would," said Geraldine, "she were!"
But soon with altered voice, said she—
"Off, wandering mother! Peak and pine!     205
I have power to bid thee flee."
Alas! what ails poor Geraldine?
Why stares she with unsettled eye?
Can she the bodiless dead espy?
And why with hollow voice cries she,     210
"Off, woman, off! this hour is mine—
Though thou her guardian spirit be,
Off, woman, off! 'tis given to me."

Then Christabel knelt by the lady's side,
And raised to heaven her eyes so blue—     215
"Alas!" said she, "this ghastly ride—
Dear lady! it hath wildered you!"
The lady wiped her moist cold brow,
And faintly said, " 'Tis over now!"

Again the wild-flower wine she drank:     220
Her fair large eyes 'gan glitter bright,
And from the floor whereon she sank,
The lofty lady stood upright:
She was most beautiful to see,
Like a lady of a far countree.     225

And thus the lofty lady spake—
"All they who live in the upper sky,
Do love you, holy Christabel!
And you love them, and for their sake
And for the good which me befell,     230
Even I in my degree will try,
Fair maiden, to requite you well.
But now unrobe yourself; for I
Must pray, ere yet in bed I lie."

Quoth Christabel, "So let it be!"     235
And as the lady bade, did she.
Her gentle limbs did she undress,
And lay down in her loveliness.

But through her brain of weal and woe
So many thoughts moved to and fro,     240
That vain it were her lids to close;
So half-way from the bed she rose,
And on her elbow did recline
To look at the lady Geraldine.

Beneath the lamp the lady bowed,     245
And slowly rolled her eyes around;
Then drawing in her breath aloud,
Like one that shuddered, she unbound
The cincture from beneath her breast:
Her silken robe, and inner vest,     250
Dropped to her feet, and full in view,
Behold! her bosom and half her side—
A sight to dream of, not to tell!
O shield her! shield sweet Christabel!

Yet Geraldine nor speaks nor stirs;     255
Ah! what a stricken look was hers!

Deep from within she seems half-way
To lift some weight with sick assay,
And eyes the maid and seeks delay;
Then suddenly, as one defied,     260
Collects herself in scorn and pride,
And lay down by the Maiden's side!—
And in her arms the maid she took,
    Ah well-a-day!
And with low voice and doleful look     265
These words did say:
"In the touch of this bosom there worketh a
    spell,
Which is lord of thy utterance, Christabel!
Thou knowest to-night, and wilt know tomor-
    row,
This mark of my shame, this seal of my sor-
    row;     270
    But vainly thou warrest,
        For this is alone in
    Thy power to declare,
        That in the dim forest
    Thou heard'st a low moaning,     275
And found'st a bright lady, surpassingly fair;
And didst bring her home with thee in love
    and in charity,
To shield her and shelter her from the damp
    air."

THE CONCLUSION TO PART THE FIRST

It was a lovely sight to see
The lady Christabel, when she
Was praying at the old oak tree.
        Amid the jaggéd shadows
        Of mossy leafless boughs,     5
        Kneeling in the moonlight,
        To make her gentle vows;
Her slender palms together pressed,
Heaving sometimes on her breast;
Her face resigned to bliss or bale—     10
Her face, oh call it fair not pale,
And both blue eyes more bright than clear,
Each about to have a tear.

With open eyes (ah woe is me!)
Asleep, and dreaming fearfully,     15
Fearfully dreaming, yet, I wis,
Dreaming that alone, which is—
O sorrow and shame! Can this be she,
The lady, who knelt at the old oak tree?
And lo! the worker of these harms,     20
That holds the maiden in her arms,
Seems to slumber still and mild
As a mother with her child.

A star hath set, a star hath risen,
O Geraldine! since arms of thine     25
Have been the lovely lady's prison.
O Geraldine! one hour was thine—
Thou'st had thy will! By tairn [5] and rill,
The night-birds all that hour were still.
But now they are jubilant anew,     30

---

[5] I. e., tarn, small mountain pool or lake.

From cliff and tower, tu—whoo! tu—whoo!
Tu—whoo! tu—whoo! from wood and fell! [6]

And see! the lady Christabel
Gathers herself from out her trance;
Her limbs relax, her countenance            35
Grows sad and soft; the smooth thin lids
Close o'er her eyes; and tears she sheds—
Large tears that leave the lashes bright!
And oft the while she seems to smile
As infants at a sudden light!               40

Yea, she doth smile, and she doth weep,
Like a youthful hermitess,
Beauteous in a wilderness,
Who, praying always, prays in sleep.
And, if she move unquietly,                 45
Perchance, 'tis but the blood so free
Comes back and tingles in her feet.
No doubt, she hath a vision sweet.
What if her guardian spirit 'twere,
What if she knew her mother near?           50
But this she knows, in joys and woes,
That saints will aid if men will call:
For the blue sky bends over all!

### PART THE SECOND

Each matin bell, the Baron saith,
Knells us back to a world of death.
These words Sir Leoline first said,
When he rose and found his lady dead:
These words Sir Leoline will say            5
Many a morn to his dying day!

And hence the custom and law began
That still at dawn the sacristan,
Who duly pulls the heavy bell,
Five and forty beads must tell              10
Between each stroke—a warning knell,
Which not a soul can choose but hear
From Bratha Head to Wyndermere. [7]

Saith Bracy the bard, "So let it knell!
And let the drowsy sacristan                15
Still count as slowly as he can!
There is no lack of such, I ween,
As well fill up the space between.
In Langdale Pike and Witch's Lair,
And Dungeon-ghyll [8] so foully rent,        20
With ropes of rock and bells of air
Three sinful sextons' ghosts are pent,
Who all give back, one after t'other,
The death-note to their living brother;
And oft too, by the knell offended,         25
Just as their one! two! three! is ended,
The devil mocks the doleful tale
With a merry peal from Borodale."

[6] Mountain.
[7] From the source of the river Brathay to Lake
Windermere, into which it flows. These and the
places subsequently mentioned are all in the Lake
Country.
[8] A ghyll is a ravine containing a stream.

The air is still! through mist and cloud
That merry peal comes ringing loud;         30
And Geraldine shakes off her dread,
And rises lightly from the bed,
Puts on her silken vestments white,
And tricks her hair in lovely plight, [9]
And nothing doubting of her spell           35
Awakens the lady Christabel.
"Sleep you, sweet lady Christabel?
I trust that you have rested well."

And Christabel awoke and spied
The same who lay down by her side           40
O rather say, the same whom she
Raised up beneath the old oak tree!
Nay, fairer yet! and yet more fair!
For she belike hath drunken deep
Of all the blessedness of sleep!            45
And while she spake, her looks, her air
Such gentle thankfulness declare,
That (so it seemed) her girded vests
Grew tight beneath her heaving breasts.
"Sure I have sinned!" said Christabel,      50
"Now heaven be praised if all be well!"
And in low faltering tones, yet sweet,
Did she the lofty lady greet
With such perplexity of mind
As dreams too lively leave behind.          55

So quickly she rose, and quickly arrayed
Her maiden limbs, and having prayed
That He, who on the cross did groan,
Might wash away her sins unknown,
She forthwith led fair Geraldine            60
To meet her sire, Sir Leoline.

The lovely maid and the lady tall
Are pacing both into the hall,
And pacing on through page and groom,
Enter the Baron's presence-room.            65

The Baron rose, and while he pressed
His gentle daughter to his breast,
With cheerful wonder in his eyes
The lady Geraldine espies,
And gave such welcome to the same,          70
As might beseem so bright a dame!

But when he heard the lady's tale,
And when she told her father's name,
Why waxed Sir Leoline so pale,
Murmuring o'er the name again,              75
Lord Roland de Vaux of Tryermaine?

Alas! they had been friends in youth;
But whispering tongues can poison truth;
And constancy lives in realms above;
And life is thorny; and youth is vain;      80
And to be wroth with one we love
Doth work like madness in the brain.
And thus it chanced, as I divine,

[9] Plait.

With Roland and Sir Leoline.
Each spake words of high disdain 85
And insult to his heart's best brother:
They parted—ne'er to meet again!
But never either found another
To free the hollow heart from paining—
They stood aloof, the scars remaining, 90
Like cliffs which had been rent asunder;
A dreary sea now flows between:
But neither heat, nor frost, nor thunder,
Shall wholly do away, I ween,
The marks of that which once hath been. 95

Sir Leoline, a moment's space,
Stood gazing on the damsel's face:
And the youthful Lord of Tryermaine
Came back upon his heart again.
O then the Baron forgot his age, 100
His noble heart swelled high with rage;
He swore by the wounds in Jesu's side
He would proclaim it far and wide,
With trump and solemn heraldry,
That they, who thus had wronged the dame, 105
Were base as spotted infamy!
"And if they dare deny the same,
My herald shall appoint a week,
And let the recreant traitors seek
My tourney court—that there and then 110
I may dislodge their reptile souls
From the bodies and forms of men!"
He spake: his eye in lightning rolls!
For the lady was ruthlessly seized; and he kenned
In the beautiful lady the child of his friend! 115

And now the tears were on his face,
And fondly in his arms he took
Fair Geraldine, who met the embrace,
Prolonging it with joyous look.
Which when she viewed, a vision fell 120
Upon the soul of Christabel,
The vision of fear, the touch and pain!
She shrunk and shuddered, and saw again—
(Ah, woe is me! Was it for thee,
Thou gentle maid! such sights to see?) 125

Again she saw that bosom old,
Again she felt that bosom cold,
And drew in her breath with a hissing sound:
Whereat the Knight turned wildly round,
And nothing saw, but his own sweet maid 130
With eyes upraised, as one that prayed.

The touch, the sight, had passed away,
And in its stead that vision bless'd,
Which comforted her after-rest,
While in the lady's arms she lay, 135
Had put a rapture in her breast,
And on her lips and o'er her eyes
Spread smiles like light!
　　　　With new surprise,
"What ails then my belovéd child?"
The Baron said.—His daughter mild 140

Made answer, "All will yet be well!"
I ween, she had no power to tell
Aught else: so mighty was the spell.

Yet he who saw this Geraldine
Had deemed her sure a thing divine. 145
Such sorrow with such grace she blended,
As if she feared she had offended
Sweet Christabel, that gentle maid!
And with such lowly tones she prayed
She might be sent without delay 150
Home to her father's mansion.
　　　　　　　　"Nay!
Nay, by my soul!" said Leoline.
"Ho! Bracy the bard, the charge be thine!
Go thou, with music sweet and loud,
And take two steeds with trappings proud, 155
And take the youth whom thou lov'st best
To bear thy harp, and learn thy song,
And clothe you both in solemn vest,
And over the mountains haste along,
Lest wandering folk, that are abroad, 160
Detain you on the valley road.

"And when he has crossed the Irthing flood,
My merry bard! he hastes, he hastes
Up Knorren Moor, through Halegarth Wood,
And reaches soon that castle good 165
Which stands and threatens Scotland's wastes.

"Bard Bracy! bard Bracy! your horses are fleet,
Ye must ride up the hall, your music so sweet,
More loud than your horses' echoing feet!
And loud and loud to Lord Roland call, 170
Thy daughter is safe in Langdale hall!
Thy beautiful daughter is safe and free—
Sir Leoline greets thee thus through me.
He bids thee come without delay
With all thy numerous array 175
And take thy lovely daughter home:
And he will meet thee on the way
With all his numerous array
White with their panting palfreys' foam:
And, by mine honor! I will say, 180
That I repent me of the day
When I spake words of fierce disdain
To Roland de Vaux of Tryermaine!—
—For since that evil hour hath flown,—
Many a summer's sun hath shone; 185
Yet ne'er found I a friend again
Like Roland de Vaux of Tryermaine."

The lady fell, and clasped his knees,
Her face upraised, her eyes o'erflowing;
And Bracy replied, with faltering voice, 190
His gracious hail on all bestowing:
"Thy words, thou sire of Christabel,
Are sweeter than my harp can tell;
Yet might I gain a boon of thee,
This day my journey should not be; 195
So strange a dream hath come to me,
That I had vowed with music loud
To clear yon wood from thing unbless'd,

Warned by a vision in my rest!
For in my sleep I saw that dove,                          200
That gentle bird, whom thou dost love,
And call'st by thy own daughter's name—
Sir Leoline! I saw the same,
Fluttering, and uttering fearful moan,
Among the green herbs in the forest alone. 205
Which when I saw and when I heard,
I wondered what might ail the bird;
For nothing near it could I see,
Save the grass and green herbs underneath the
    old tree.

"And in my dream methought I went          210
To search out what might there be found;
And what the sweet bird's trouble meant,
That thus lay fluttering on the ground.
I went and peered, and could descry
No cause for her distressful cry;                          215
But yet for her dear lady's sake
I stooped, methought, the dove to take,
When lo! I saw a bright green snake
Coiled around its wings and neck.
Green as the herbs on which it couched,      220
Close by the dove's its head it crouched;
And with the dove it heaves and stirs,
Swelling its neck as she swelled hers!
I woke; it was the midnight hour,
The clock was echoing in the tower;            225
But though my slumber was gone by,
This dream it would not pass away—
It seems to live upon my eye!
And thence I vowed this self-same day
With music strong and saintly song              230
To wander through the forest bare,
Lest aught unholy loiter there."

Thus Bracy said: the Baron, the while,
Half-listening heard him with a smile;
Then turned to Lady Geraldine,                    235
His eyes made up of wonder and love;
And said in courtly accents fine,
"Sweet maid, Lord Roland's beauteous dove,
With arms more strong than harp or song,
Thy sire and I will crush the snake!"            240
He kissed her forehead as he spake,
And Geraldine in maiden wise
Casting down her large bright eyes,
With blushing cheek and courtesy fine
She turned her from Sir Leoline;                  245
Softly gathering up her train,
That o'er her right arm fell again;
And folded her arms across her chest,
And couched her head upon her breast,
And looked askance at Christabel—             250
Jesu, Maria, shield her well!

A snake's small eye blinks dull and shy;
And the lady's eyes they shrunk in her head,
Each shrunk up to a serpent's eye,
And with somewhat of malice, and more of
    dread,                                                          255
At Christabel she looked askance!—

One moment—and the sight was fled!
But Christabel in dizzy trance
Stumbling on the unsteady ground
Shuddered aloud, with a hissing sound;        260
And Geraldine again turned round,
And like a thing that sought relief,
Full of wonder and full of grief,
She rolled her large bright eyes divine
Wildly on Sir Leoline.                                    265

The maid, alas! her thoughts are gone,
She nothing sees—no sight but one!
The maid, devoid of guile and sin,
I know not how, in fearful wise,
So deeply had she drunken in                        270
That look, those shrunken serpent eyes,
That all her features were resigned
To this sole image in her mind:
And passively did imitate
That look of dull and treacherous hate!        275
And thus she stood, in dizzy trance,
Still picturing that look askance
With forced unconscious sympathy
Full before her father's view——
As far as such a look could be                        280
In eyes so innocent and blue!

And when the trance was o'er, the maid
Paused awhile, and inly prayed:
Then falling at the Baron's feet,
"By my mother's soul do I entreat                  285
That thou this woman send away!"
She said: and more she could not say:
For what she knew she could not tell,
O'er-mastered by the mighty spell.

Why is thy cheek so wan and wild,              290
Sir Leoline? Thy only child
Lies at thy feet, thy joy, thy pride,
So fair, so innocent, so mild;
The same, for whom thy lady died!
O, by the pangs of her dear mother              295
Think thou no evil of thy child!
For her, and thee, and for no other,
She prayed the moment ere she died:
Prayed that the babe for whom she died,
Might prove her dear lord's joy and pride! 300
    That prayer her deadly pangs beguiled,
        Sir Leoline!
    And wouldst thou wrong thy only child,
        Her child and thine?

Within the Baron's heart and brain
If thoughts like these had any share,
They only swelled his rage and pain,            305
And did but work confusion there.
His heart was cleft with pain and rage,
His cheeks they quivered, his eyes were wild,
Dishonored thus in his old age;
Dishonored by his only child,                        310
And all his hospitality
To the wronged daughter of his friend
By more than woman's jealousy

Brought thus to a disgraceful end—
He rolled his eye with stern regard          315
Upon the gentle minstrel bard,
And said in tones abrupt, austere—
"Why, Bracy! dost thou loiter here?
I bade thee hence!" The bard obeyed;
And turning from his own sweet maid,          320
The agéd knight, Sir Leoline,
Led forth the lady Geraldine!

#### THE CONCLUSION TO PART THE SECOND

A little child, a limber elf,
Singing, dancing to itself,
A fairy thing with red round cheeks,
That always finds, and never seeks,
Makes such a vision to the sight          5
As fills a father's eyes with light;
And pleasures flow in so thick and fast
Upon his heart, that he at last
Must needs express his love's excess
With words of unmeant bitterness.          10
Perhaps 'tis pretty to force together
Thoughts so all unlike each other;
To mutter and mock a broken charm,
To dally with wrong that does no harm.
Perhaps 'tis tender too and pretty          15
At each wild word to feel within
A sweet recoil of love and pity.
And what, if in a world of sin
(O sorrow and shame should this be true!)
Such giddiness of heart and brain          20
Comes seldom save from rage and pain,
So talks as it's most used to do.[10]

[10] Coleridge never finished *Christabel*, though he more than once insisted that he had "the whole plan entire from beginning to end" in his mind. James Gillman states that Coleridge outlined to his friends the conclusion of the story as follows: "The following relation was to have occupied a third and fourth canto, and to have closed the tale. Over the mountains, the Bard, as directed by Sir Leoline, hastes with his disciple; but in consequence of one of those inundations supposed to be common to this country, the spot only where the castle once stood is discovered—the edifice itself being washed away. He determines to return. Geraldine, being acquainted with all that is passing, like the weird sisters in Macbeth, vanishes. Reappearing, however, she awaits the return of the Bard, exciting in the meantime, by her wily arts, all the anger she could rouse in the Baron's breast, as well as that jealousy of which he is described to have been susceptible. The old Bard and the youth at length arrive, and therefore she can no longer personate the character of Geraldine, the daughter of Lord Roland de Vaux, but changes her appearance to that of the accepted though absent lover of Christabel. Now ensues a courtship most distressing to Christabel, who feels, she knows not why, great disgust for her once favored knight. This coldness is very painful to the Baron, who has no more conception than herself of the supernatural transformation. She at last yields to her father's entreaties, and consents to approach the altar with this hated suitor. The real lover, returning, enters at this moment, and produces the ring which she had once given him in sign of her

# Dejection: An Ode

### Written April 4, 1802

> Late, late yestreen I saw the new Moon,
> With the old Moon in her arms;
> And I fear, I fear, my Master dear!
> We shall have a deadly storm.
>                    *Ballad of Sir Patrick Spence.*

#### I

Well! If the Bard was weather-wise, who made
  The grand old ballad of Sir Patrick Spence,
    This night, so tranquil now, will not go hence
Unroused by winds, that ply a busier trade
Than those which mold yon cloud in lazy
    flakes,          5
Or the dull sobbing draft, that moans and rakes
    Upon the strings of this Aeolian lute,[1]
    Which better far were mute.
  For lo! the New-moon winter-bright!
  And overspread with phantom light,          10
  (With swimming phantom light o'erspread
  But rimmed and circled by a silver thread)
I see the old Moon in her lap, foretelling
  The coming-on of rain and squally blast.
And oh! that even now the gust were swelling,
  And the slant night-shower driving loud and
    fast!          16
Those sounds which oft have raised me, whilst
    they awed,
    And sent my soul abroad,
Might now perhaps their wonted impulse give,
Might startle this dull pain, and make it move
    and live!          20

#### II

A grief without a pang, void, dark, and drear,
  A stifled, drowsy, unimpassioned grief,
  Which finds no natural outlet, no relief,
    In word, or sigh, or tear—
O Lady![2] in this wan and heartless mood,          25
To other thoughts by yonder throstle wooed,
  All this long eve, so balmy and serene,
Have I been gazing on the western sky,
  And its peculiar tint of yellow green:
And still I gaze—and with how blank an eye!          30
And those thin clouds above, in flakes and bars,
That give away their motion to the stars;
Those stars, that glide behind them or between,
Now sparkling, now bedimmed, but always
    seen:

betrothment. Thus defeated, the supernatural being Geraldine disappears. As predicted, the castle bell tolls, the mother's voice is heard, and, to the exceeding great joy of the parties, the rightful marriage takes place, after which follows a reconciliation and explanation between the father and daughter."

[1] An Aeolian harp, a stringed instrument which produced musical sounds when touched by the wind.

[2] "Oh Lady" reads "O William" in manuscript, since the poem was originally offered to Wordsworth on the occasion of his marriage.

Yon crescent Moon, as fixed as if it grew    35
In its own cloudless, starless lake of blue;
I see them all so excellently fair,
I see, not feel, how beautiful they are!

### III

My genial spirits fail;
    And what can these avail    40
To lift the smothering weight from off my
    breast?
    It were a vain endeavor,
    Though I should gaze for ever
On that green light that lingers in the west:
I may not hope from outward forms to win    45
The passion and the life, whose fountains are
    within.

### IV

O Lady! we receive but what we give,
And in our life alone does Nature live:
Ours is her wedding-garment, ours her shroud!
    And would we aught behold, of higher
        worth,    50
Than that inanimate cold world allowed
To the poor loveless ever-anxious crowd,
    Ah! from the soul itself must issue forth
A light, a glory, a fair luminous cloud
    Enveloping the Earth—    55
And from the soul itself must there be sent
    A sweet and potent voice, of its own birth,
Of all sweet sounds the life and element!

### V

O pure of heart! thou need'st not ask of me
What this strong music in the soul may be!    60
What, and wherein it doth exist,
This light, this glory, this fair luminous mist,
This beautiful and beauty-making power.
    Joy, virtuous Lady! Joy that ne'er was given,
Save to the pure, and in their purest hour,    65
Life, and Life's effluence, cloud at once and
    shower,
Joy, Lady! is the spirit and the power,
Which, wedding Nature to us, gives in dower
    A new Earth and new Heaven,
Undreamt of by the sensual and the proud—    70
Joy is the sweet, Joy the luminous cloud—
    We in ourselves rejoice!
And thence flows all that charms or ear or
    sight,
    All melodies the echoes of that voice,
All colors a suffusion from that light.    75

### VI

There was a time when, though my path was
    rough,
    This joy within me dallied with distress,
And all misfortunes were but as the stuff
    Whence Fancy made me dreams of happi-
        ness:
For Hope grew round me, like the twining vine,
And fruits, and foliage, not my own, seemed
    mine.    81

But now afflictions bow me down to earth:
Nor care I that they rob me of my mirth;
    But oh! each visitation
Suspends what nature gave me at my birth,    85
    My shaping spirit of Imagination.
For not to think of what I needs must feel
    But to be still and patient, all I can;
And haply by abstruse research to steal
    From my own nature all the natural man—
    This was my sole resource, my only plan:    91
Till that which suits a part infects the whole,
And now is almost grown the habit of my soul.

### VII

Hence, viper thoughts, that coil around my
    mind,
    Reality's dark dream!    95
I turn from you, and listen to the wind,
    Which long has raved unnoticed. What a
        scream
Of agony by torture lengthened out
That lute sent forth! Thou Wind, that rav'st
    without,
Bare crag, or mountain-tairn, or blasted
    tree,    100
Or pine-grove whither woodman never clomb,
Or lonely house, long held the witches' home,
    Methinks were fitter instruments for thee,
Mad Lutanist! who in this month of showers,
Of dark-brown gardens, and of peeping flowers,
Mak'st Devils' yule, with worse than wintry
    song,    106
The blossoms, buds, and timorous leaves
    among.
    Thou actor, perfect in all tragic sounds!
Thou mighty Poet, e'en to frenzy bold!
    What tell'st thou now about?    110
    'Tis of the rushing of an host in rout,
    With groans of trampled men, with smarting
        wounds—
At once they groan with pain, and shudder with
    the cold!
But hush! there is a pause of deepest silence!
    And all that noise, as of a rushing crowd,    115
With groans, and tremulous shudderings—all
    is over—
    It tells another tale, with sounds less deep
        and loud!
    A tale of less affright,
    And tempered with delight,
As Otway's[3] self had framed the tender lay,—    121
    'Tis of a little child
    Upon a lonesome wild,
Not far from home, but she hath lost her way:
And now moans low in bitter grief and fear,
And now screams loud, and hopes to make her
    mother hear.    125

[3] Thomas Otway (1652–1685), the dramatist. In
the original version the allusion was made, not to
Otway, but to Wordsworth, whose *Lucy Gray* seems
to be described in the lines that follow.

VIII

'Tis midnight, but small thoughts have I of
    sleep:
Full seldom may my friend such vigils keep!
Visit her, gentle Sleep! with wings of healing,
    And may this storm be but a mountain-birth,
May all the stars hang bright above her dwell-
    ing, 130
    Silent as though they watched the sleeping
        Earth!
      With light heart may she rise,
      Gay fancy, cheerful eyes,
Joy lift her spirit, joy attune her voice;
To her may all things live, from pole to pole,
Their life the eddying of her living soul! 135
    O simple spirit, guided from above,
Dear Lady! friend devoutest of my choice,
Thus mayest thou ever, evermore rejoice.

## Youth and Age [1]

Verse, a breeze mid blossoms straying,
Where Hope clung feeding, like a bee—
Both were mine! Life went a-maying
    With Nature, Hope, and Poesy,
      When I was young! 5

When I was young?—Ah, woeful When!
Ah! for the change 'twixt Now and Then!
This breathing house not built with hands,
This body that does me grievous wrong,
O'er aery cliffs and glittering sands, 10
How lightly then it flashed along:—
Like those trim skiffs, unknown of yore,
On winding lakes and rivers wide,
That ask no aid of sail or oar,
That fear no spite of wind or tide! 15
Nought cared this body for wind or weather
When Youth and I lived in't together.

Flowers are lovely; Love is flower-like;
Friendship is a sheltering tree;
O! the joys, that came down shower-like, 20
Of Friendship, Love, and Liberty,
      Ere I was old!

Ere I was old? Ah woeful Ere,
Which tells me, Youth's no longer here!
O Youth! for years so many and sweet, 25
'Tis known, that Thou and I were one,
I'll think it but a fond conceit—
It cannot be that Thou art gone!
Thy vesper-bell hath not yet tolled:—
And thou wert aye a masker bold! 30
What strange disguise hast now put on,
To make believe, that thou art gone?
I see these locks in silvery slips,
This drooping gait, this altered size:
But Spring-tide blossoms on thy lips, 35

[1] Begun in 1823; first printed (without the last
eleven lines) in 1828. The last eleven lines were
written, and published as a separate poem, in 1832.

And tears take sunshine from thine eyes!
Life is but thought: so think I will
That Youth and I are house-mates still.

Dew-drops are the gems of morning,
But the tears of mournful eve! 40
Where no hope is, life's a warning
That only serves to make us grieve,
        When we are old:

That only serves to make us grieve
With oft and tedious taking-leave, 45
Like some poor nigh-related guest,
That may not rudely be dismissed;
Yet hath outstayed his welcome while,
And tells the jest without the smile.

## Work without Hope [2]

### Lines Composed 21st February, 1825

All Nature seems at work. Slugs leave their
    lair—
The bees are stirring—birds are on the wing—
And Winter slumbering in the open air,
Wears on his smiling face a dream of Spring!
And I the while, the sole unbusy thing, 5
Nor honey make, nor pair, nor build, nor sing.

    Yet well I ken the banks where amaranths
      blow,
Have traced the fount whence streams of nectar
      flow.
Bloom, O ye amaranths! bloom for whom ye
      may,
For me ye bloom not! Glide, rich streams,
      away! 10
With lips unbrightened, wreathless brow, I
      stroll:
And would you learn the spells that drowse my
      soul?
Work without Hope draws nectar in a sieve,
And Hope without an object cannot live.

## Biographia Literaria;

*or*

## Biographical Sketches of My Literary Life and Opinions (1817)

### CHAPTER I

It HAS been my lot to have had my name
introduced both in conversation, and in print,
more frequently than I find it easy to explain,
whether I consider the fewness, unimpor-
tance, and limited circulation of my writings,
or the retirement and distance in which I
have lived, both from the literary and political world. Most often it has been connected with some charge which I could not

[2] First printed in 1828.

acknowledge, or some principle which I had never entertained. Nevertheless, had I had no other motive or incitement, the reader would not have been troubled with this exculpation. What my additional purposes were, will be seen in the following pages. It will be found that the least of what I have written concerns myself personally. I have used the narration chiefly for the purpose of giving a continuity to the work, in part for the sake of the miscellaneous reflections suggested to me by particular events, but still more as introductory to the statement of my principles in Politics, Religion, and Philosophy, and an application of the rules, deduced from philosophical principles, to poetry and criticism. But of the objects which I proposed to myself, it was not the least important to effect, as far as possible, a settlement of the long continued controversy concerning the true nature of poetic diction; and at the same time to define with the utmost impartiality the real *poetic* character of the poet [1] by whose writings this controversy was first kindled, and has been since fueled and fanned.

In 1794,[2] when I had barely passed the verge of manhood, I published a small volume of juvenile poems. They were received with a degree of favor which, young as I was, I well know was bestowed on them not so much for any positive merit, as because they were considered buds of hope, and promises of better works to come. The critics of that day, the most flattering, equally with the severest, concurred in objecting to them obscurity, a general turgidness of diction, and a profusion of new coined double epithets. The first is the fault which a writer is the least able to detect in his own composition: and my mind was not then sufficiently disciplined to receive the authority of others, as a substitute for my own conviction. Satisfied that the thoughts, such as they were, could not have been expressed otherwise, or at least more perspicuously, I forgot to inquire, whether the thoughts themselves did not demand a degree of attention unsuitable to the nature and objects of poetry. This remark, however, applies chiefly, though not exclusively, to the *Religious Musings*. The remainder of the charge I admitted to its full extent, and not without sincere acknowledgments both to my private and public censors for their friendly admonitions. In the after editions, I pruned the double epithets with no sparing hand, and used my best efforts to tame the swell and glitter both of thought and diction; though in truth, these parasite plants of youthful poetry had insinuated themselves into my longer poems with such intricacy of union, that I was often obliged to omit disentangling the weed, from the fear of snapping the flower. From that period to the date of the present work I have published nothing, with my name, which could by any possibility have come before the board of anonymous criticism. Even the three or four poems printed with the works of a friend,[3] as far as they were censured at all, were charged with the same or similar defects, though I am persuaded not with equal justice—with an excess of ornament, in addition to strained and elaborate diction.[4] May I be permitted to add, that, even at the early period of my juvenile poems, I saw and admitted the superiority of an austerer and more natural style, with an insight not less clear than I at present possess. My judgment was stronger than were my powers of realizing its dictates; and the faults of my language, though indeed partly owing to a wrong choice of subjects, and the desire of giving a poetic coloring to abstract and metaphysical truths, in which a new world then seemed to open upon me, did yet, in part likewise, originate in unfeigned diffidence of my own comparative talent.— During several years of my youth and early manhood, I reverenced those who had reintroduced the manly simplicity of the Greek, and of our own elder poets, with such enthusiasm as made the hope seem presumptuous of writing successfully in the same style. Perhaps a similar process has happened to others; but my earliest poems were marked by an ease and simplicity, which I have studied, perhaps with inferior success, to impress on my later compositions.

At school I enjoyed the inestimable advantage of a very sensible, though at the

---

[1] Wordsworth.

[2] A slip—really the spring of 1796. Coleridge's memory was treacherous, and there are other inaccuracies in the *Biographia Literaria*.

[3] Printed with Wordsworth's poems in *Lyrical Ballads*, 1798. Coleridge's poems in the volume were: *The Rime of the Ancient Mariner; The Nightingale, a Conversation Poem; The Foster-Mother's Tale;* and *The Dungeon*.

[4] See the criticisms on the *Ancient Mariner*, in the *Monthly* and *Critical Reviews* of the first volume of the *Lyrical Ballads* (Coleridge's note).

same time, a very severe master. He [5] early molded my taste to the preference of Demosthenes to Cicero, of Homer and Theocritus to Virgil, and again of Virgil to Ovid. He habituated me to compare Lucretius (in such extracts as I then read), Terence, and above all the chaster poems of Catullus, not only with the Roman poets of the, so called, silver and brazen ages; but with even those of the Augustan era: and on grounds of plain sense and universal logic to see and assert the superiority of the former in the truth and nativeness both of their thoughts and diction. At the same time that we were studying the Greek tragic poets, he made us read Shakespeare and Milton as lessons: and they were the lessons too, which required most time and trouble to *bring up*, so as to escape his censure. I learned from him that poetry, even that of the loftiest and, seemingly, that of the wildest odes, had a logic of its own, as severe as that of science; and more difficult, because more subtle, more complex, and dependent on more, and more fugitive causes. In the truly great poets, he would say, there is a reason assignable, not only for every word, but for the position of every word; and I well remember that, availing himself of the synonyms to the Homer of Didymus, he made us attempt to show, with regard to each, why it would not have answered the same purpose; and wherein consisted the peculiar fitness of the word in the original text.

In our own English compositions (at least for the last three years of our school education), he showed no mercy to phrase, metaphor, or image, unsupported by a sound sense, or where the same sense might have been conveyed with equal force and dignity in plainer words. *Lute*, *harp*, and *lyre*, *Muse*, *Muses*, and *inspirations*, *Pegasus*, *Parnassus*, and *Hippocrene* were all an abomination to him. In fancy I can almost hear him now, exclaiming "Harp? Harp? Lyre? Pen and ink, boy, you mean! Muse, boy, Muse? Your nurse's daughter, you mean! Pierian spring? Oh aye! the cloister-pump, I suppose!" Nay certain introductions, similes, and examples, were placed by name on a list of interdiction. Among the similes, there was, I remember, that of the manchineel fruit,[6] as suiting equally well with too many subjects; in which however it yielded the palm at once to the example of Alexander and Clytus, which was equally good and apt, whatever might be the theme. Was it ambition? Alexander and Clytus!—Flattery? Alexander and Clytus!—anger—drunkenness—pride—friendship—ingratitude—late repentance? Still, still Alexander and Clytus! At length, the praises of agriculture having been exemplified in the sagacious observation that, had Alexander been holding the plow, he would not have run his friend Clytus through with a spear, this tried and serviceable old friend was banished by public edict in *saecula saeculorum*.[7] I have sometimes ventured to think that a list of this kind, or an *index expurgatorius* [8] of certain well-known and ever-returning phrases, both introductory, and transitional, including a large assortment of modest egoisms, and flattering illeisms,[9] *etc.*, *etc.*, might be hung up in our Law-Courts, and both Houses of Parliament, with great advantage to the public, as an important saving of national time, an incalculable relief to his Majesty's ministers, but above all, as insuring the thanks of country attorneys, and their clients, who have private bills to carry through the House.

Be this as it may, there was one custom of our master's which I cannot pass over in silence, because I think it imitable and worthy of imitation. He would often permit our exercises, under some pretext of want of time, to accumulate, till each lad had four or five to be looked over. Then placing the whole number abreast on his desk, he would ask the writer, why this or that sentence might not have found as appropriate a place under this or that other thesis: and if no satisfying answer could be returned, and two faults of the same kind were found in one exercise, the irrevocable verdict followed, the exercise was torn up, and another on the same subject to be produced, in addition to the tasks of the day. The reader will, I trust, excuse this tribute of recollection to a man whose severities, even now, not seldom furnish the dreams, by which the blind

[5] The Rev. James Bowyer, many years Head Master of the Grammar School, Christ's Hospital (Coleridge's note).

[6] The manchineel is a West Indian tree with poisonous milky sap and acrid fruit.

[7] Forever.

[8] List of prohibitions (as here used).

[9] Excessive use of the pronoun *he*, with reference either to another or to one's self in the 3rd person. Coleridge used this word also in *The Friend*, but apparently no one else has ever used it.

fancy would fain interpret to the mind the painful sensations of distempered sleep; but neither lessen nor dim the deep sense of my moral and intellectual obligations. He sent us to the University excellent Latin and Greek scholars, and tolerable Hebraists. Yet our classical knowledge was the least of the good gifts which we derived from his zealous and conscientious tutorage. He is now gone to his final reward, full of years, and full of honors, even of those honors which were dearest to his heart, as gratefully bestowed by that school, and still binding him to the interests of that school, in which he had been himself educated, and to which during his whole life he was a dedicated thing.

\* \* \*

## CHAPTER IV

\* \* \* During the last year of my residence at Cambridge, I became acquainted with Mr. Wordsworth's first publication [1] entitled *Descriptive Sketches*; and seldom, if ever, was the emergence of an original poetic genius above the literary horizon more evidently announced. In the form, style, and manner of the whole poem, and in the structure of the particular lines and periods, there is an harshness and acerbity connected and combined with words and images all a-glow, which might recall those products of the vegetable world, where gorgeous blossoms rise out of the hard and thorny rind and shell, within which the rich fruit was elaborating. The language was not only peculiar and strong, but at times knotty and contorted, as by its own impatient strength; while the novelty and struggling crowd of images, acting in conjunction with the difficulties of the style, demanded always a greater closeness of attention, than poetry— at all events, than descriptive poetry—has a right to claim. It not seldom therefore justified the complaint of obscurity. In the following extract I have sometimes fancied that I saw an emblem of the poem itself, and of the author's genius as it was then displayed.—

'Tis storm; and hid in mist from hour to hour,
All day the floods a deepening murmur pour;
The sky is veiled, and every cheerful sight:
Dark is the region as with coming night;
And yet what frequent bursts of overpowering light!
Triumphant on the bosom of the storm,
Glances the fire-clad eagle's wheeling form;

[1] Actually Wordsworth's second publication.

Eastward, in long perspective glittering, shine
The wood-crowned cliffs that o'er the lake recline;
Wide o'er the Alps a hundred streams unfold,
At once to pillars turned that flame with gold;
Behind his sail the peasant strives to shun
The west, that burns like one dilated sun,
Where in a mighty crucible expire
The mountains, glowing hot, like coals of fire.

The poetic Psyche, in its process to full development, undergoes as many changes as its Greek namesake, the butterfly.[2] And it is remarkable how soon genius clears and purifies itself from the faults and errors of its earliest products; faults which, in its earliest compositions, are the more obtrusive and confluent, because as heterogeneous elements, which had only a temporary use, they constitute the very ferment, by which themselves are carried off. Or we may compare them to some diseases, which must work on the humors, and be thrown out on the surface, in order to secure the patient from their future recurrence. I was in my twenty-fourth year, when I had the happiness of knowing Mr. Wordsworth personally, and while memory lasts, I shall hardly forget the sudden effect produced on my mind, by his recitation of a manuscript poem, which still remains unpublished, but of which the stanza and tone of style were the same as those of *The Female Vagrant*, as originally printed in the first volume of the *Lyrical Ballads*. There was here no mark of strained thought, or forced diction, no crowd or turbulence of imagery; and, as the poet hath himself well described in his *Lines on revisiting the Wye*,[3] manly reflection and human associations had given both variety, and an additional interest to natural objects, which, in the passion and appetite of the first love, they had seemed to him neither to need nor permit. The occasional obscurities, which had risen from an imperfect control over the resources of his native language, had

[2] The fact that, in Greek, Psyche is the common name for the soul and the butterfly, is thus alluded to in the following stanzas from an unpublished poem of the author:

"The Butterfly the ancient Grecians made
The soul's fair emblem, and its only name—
But of the soul, escaped the slavish trade
Of mortal life! For in this earthly frame
Ours is the reptile's lot, much toil, much blame,
Manifold motions making little speed,
And to deform and kill the things whereon we feed."

(Coleridge's note.)

[3] I. e., *Lines Composed a Few Miles above Tintern Abbey*.

almost wholly disappeared, together with that worse defect of arbitrary and illogical phrases, at once hackneyed and fantastic, which hold so distinguished a place in the *technique* of ordinary poetry, and will, more or less, alloy the earlier poems of the truest genius, unless the attention has been specifically directed to their worthlessness and incongruity.[4] I did not perceive anything particular in the mere style of the poem alluded to during its recitation, except indeed such difference as was not separable from the thought and manner; and the Spenserian stanza, which always, more or less, recalls to the reader's mind Spenser's own style, would doubtless have authorized, in my then opinion, a more frequent descent to the phrases of ordinary life, than could without an ill effect have been hazarded in the heroic couplet. It was not, however, the freedom from false taste, whether as to common defects, or to those more properly his own, which made so unusual an impression on my feelings immediately, and subsequently on my judgment. It was the union of deep feeling with profound thought; the fine balance of truth in observing, with the imaginative faculty in modifying, the objects observed; and above all the original gift of spreading the tone, the atmosphere, and with it the depth and height of the ideal world around forms, incidents, and situations, of which, for the common view, custom had bedimmed all the luster, had dried up the sparkle and the dew drops. "To find no contradiction in the union of old and new; to contemplate the ANCIENT of days and all his works with feelings as fresh, as if all had then sprang forth at the first creative fiat; characterizes the mind that feels the riddle

[4] Mr. Wordsworth, even in his two earliest, *The Evening Walk* and the *Descriptive Sketches*, is more free from this latter defect than most of the young poets his contemporaries. It may however be exemplified, together with the harsh and obscure construction, in which he more often offended, in the following lines:—

" 'Mid stormy vapors ever driving by,
Where ospreys, cormorants, and herons cry;
Where hardly given the hopeless waste to cheer,
Denied the bread of life the foodful ear,
Dwindles the pear on autumn's latest spray,
And *apple sickens* pale in summer's ray;
Ev'n here content has fixed her smiling reign
With independence, child of high disdain."

I hope, I need not say, that I have quoted these lines for no other purpose than to make my meaning fully understood. It is to be regretted that Mr. Wordsworth has not republished these two poems entire (Coleridge's note).

of the world, and may help to unravel it. To carry on the feelings of childhood into the powers of manhood; to combine the child's sense of wonder and novelty with the appearances, which every day for perhaps forty years had rendered familiar;

'With sun and moon and stars throughout the year,
And man and woman';

this is the character and privilege of genius, and one of the marks which distinguish genius from talents. And therefore is it the prime merit of genius and its most unequivocal mode of manifestation, so to represent familiar objects as to awaken in the minds of others a kindred feeling concerning them and that freshness of sensation which is the constant accompaniment of mental, no less than of bodily, convalescence. Who has not a thousand times seen snow fall on water? Who has not watched it with a new feeling, from the time that he has read Burns's comparison of sensual pleasure

'To snow that falls upon a river
A moment white—then gone for ever'![5]

In poems, equally as in philosophic disquisitions, genius produces the strongest impressions of novelty, while it rescues the most admitted truths from the impotence caused by the very circumstance of their universal admission. Truths of all others the most awful and mysterious, yet being at the same time of universal interest, are too often considered as *so* true, that they lose all the life and efficiency of truth, and lie bed-ridden in the dormitory of the soul, side by side with the most despised and exploded errors." [6]

This excellence, which in all Mr. Wordsworth's writings is more or less predominant, and which constitutes the character of his mind, I no sooner felt, that I sought to understand. Repeated meditations led me first to suspect—and a more intimate analysis of the human faculties, their appropriate marks, functions, and effects, matured my conjecture into full conviction—that Fancy and Imagination were two distinct and widely different faculties, instead of being, according to the general belief, either two names with one meaning, or, at furthest, the lower and higher degree of one and the same power. It is not, I own, easy to conceive a more opposite translation of the

[5] See *Tam O'Shanter*, ll. 59ff.
[6] Quoted (with omissions) from *The Friend*, No. 5. In a note Coleridge justifies quoting from an already-published work of his own.

Greek *phantasia* than the Latin *imaginatio;* but it is equally true that in all societies there exists an instinct of growth, a certain collective, unconscious good sense working progressively to desynonymize those words originally of the same meaning, which the conflux of dialects supplied to the more homogeneous languages, as the Greek and German: and which the same cause, joined with accidents of translation from original works of different countries, occasion in mixed languages like our own. The first and most important point to be proved is, that two conceptions perfectly distinct are confused under one and the same word, and —this done—to appropriate that word exclusively to one meaning, and the synonym, should there be one, to the other. But if— as will be often the case in the arts and sciences—no synonym exists, we must either invent or borrow a word. In the present instance the appropriation has already begun, and been legitimated in the derivative adjective: Milton had a highly *imaginative,* Cowley a very *fanciful* mind. If therefore I should succeed in establishing the actual existences of two faculties generally different, the nomenclature would be at once determined. To the faculty by which I had characterized Milton, we should confine the term *imagination;* while the other would be contra-distinguished as *fancy.* Now were it once fully ascertained, that this division is no less grounded in nature than that of delirium from mania, or Otway's

Lutes, lobsters, seas of milk, and ships of amber,[7]

from Shakespeare's

What! have his daughters brought him to this pass?[8]

or from the preceding apostrophe to the elements; the theory of the fine arts, and of poetry in particular, could not, I thought, but derive some additional and important light. It would in its immediate effects furnish a torch of guidance to the philosophical critic; and ultimately to the poet himself. In energetic minds, truth soon changes by domestication into power; and from directing in the discrimination and appraisal of the product, becomes influencive in the production. To admire on principle, is the only way to imitate without loss of originality.  * * *

[7] *Venice Preserved,* Act V. Otway wrote "laurels," *not* "lobsters."
[8] *Lear,* III, iv. 65.

## CHAPTER XIV

DURING the first year that Mr. Wordsworth and I were neighbors, our conversations turned frequently on the two cardinal points of poetry, the power of exciting the sympathy of the reader by a faithful adherence to the truth of nature, and the power of giving the interest of novelty by the modifying colors of imagination. The sudden charm, which accidents of light and shade, which moon-light or sunset diffused over a known and familiar landscape, appeared to represent the practicability of combining both. These are the poetry of nature. The thought suggested itself—to which of us I do not recollect—that a series of poems might be composed of two sorts. In the one, the incidents and agents were to be, in part at least, supernatural; and the excellence aimed at was to consist in the interesting of the affections by the dramatic truth of such emotions, as would naturally accompany such situations, supposing them real. And real in this sense they have been to every human being who, from whatever source of delusion, has at any time believed himself under supernatural agency. For the second class, subjects were to be chosen from ordinary life; the characters and incidents were to be such as will be found in every village and its vicinity, where there is a meditative and feeling mind to seek after them, or to notice them, when they present themselves.

In this idea originated the plan of the *Lyrical Ballads*; in which it was agreed that my endeavors should be directed to persons and characters supernatural, or at least romantic; yet so as to transfer from our inward nature a human interest and a semblance of truth sufficient to procure for these shadows of imagination that willing suspension of disbelief for the moment, which constitutes poetic faith. Mr. Wordsworth, on the other hand, was to propose to himself as his object, to give the charm of novelty to things of every day, and to excite a feeling analogous to the supernatural, by awakening the mind's attention from the lethargy of custom, and directing it to the loveliness and the wonders of the world before us; an inexhaustible treasure, but for which, in consequence of the film of familiarity and selfish solicitude, we have eyes, yet see not, ears that hear not, and hearts that neither feel nor understand.

With this view I wrote *The Ancient Mar-*

*iner,* and was preparing among other poems, *The Dark Ladie,* and the *Christabel,* in which I should have more nearly realized my ideal than I had done in my first attempt. But Mr. Wordsworth's industry had proved so much more successful, and the number of his poems so much greater, that my compositions, instead of forming a balance, appeared rather an interpolation of heterogeneous matter. Mr. Wordsworth added two or three poems written 10 in his own character, in the impassioned, lofty, and sustained diction which is characteristic of his genius. In this form the *Lyrical Ballads* were published; and were presented by him, as an experiment, whether subjects, which from their nature rejected the usual ornaments and extra-colloquial style of poems in general, might not be so managed in the language of ordinary life as to produce the pleasurable interest, which it is the peculiar business of poetry to 20 impart. To the second edition he added a preface of considerable length; in which, notwithstanding some passages of apparently a contrary import, he was understood to contend for the extension of this style to poetry of all kinds, and to reject as vicious and indefensible all phrases and forms of style that were not included in what he (unfortunately, I think, adopting an equivocal expression) called the language of real life. From this preface, pre- 30 fixed to poems in which it was impossible to deny the presence of original genius, however mistaken its direction might be deemed, arose the whole long-continued controversy. For from the conjunction of perceived power with supposed heresy I explain the inveteracy and in some instances, I grieve to say, the acrimonious passions, with which the controversy has been conducted by the assailants.

Had Mr. Wordsworth's poems been the 40 silly, the childish things, which they were for a long time described as being: had they been really distinguished from the compositions of other poets merely by meanness of language and inanity of thought; had they indeed contained nothing more than what is found in the parodies and pretended imitations of them; they must have sunk at once, a dead weight, into the slough of oblivion, and have dragged the preface along with them. But year after 50 year increased the number of Mr. Wordsworth's admirers. They were found, too, not in the lower classes of the reading public, but chiefly among young men of strong sensibility and meditative minds; and their admiration (inflamed perhaps in some degree by opposi-

tion) was distinguished by its intensity, I might almost say, by its religious fervor. These facts, and the intellectual energy of the author, which was more or less consciously felt, where it was outwardly and even boisterously denied, meeting with sentiments of aversion to his opinions, and of alarm at their consequences, produced an eddy of criticism, which would of itself have borne up the poems by the violence with which it whirled them round and round. With many parts of this preface in the sense attributed to them and which the words undoubtedly seem to authorize, I never concurred; but on the contrary objected to them as erroneous in principle, and as contradictory (in appearance at least) both to other parts of the same preface, and to the author's own practice in the greater part of the poems themselves. Mr. Wordsworth in his recent collection has, I find, degraded this prefatory disquisition to the end of his second volume, to be read or not at the reader's choice. But he has not, as far as I can discover, announced any change in his poetic creed. At all events, considering it as the source of a controversy, in which I have been honored more than I deserve by the frequent conjunction of my name with his, I think it expedient to declare once for all, in what points I coincide with his opinions, and in what points I altogether differ. But in order to render myself intelligible I must previously, in as few words as possible, explain my views, first, of a Poem; and secondly, of Poetry itself, in kind, and in essence.

The office of philosophical disquisition consists in just distinction; while it is the privilege of the philosopher to preserve himself constantly aware that distinction is not division. In order to obtain adequate notions of any truth, we must intellectually separate its distinguishable parts; and this is the technical process of philosophy. But having so done, we must then restore them in our conceptions to the unity in which they actually co-exist; and this is the result of philosophy. A poem contains the same elements as a prose composition; the difference therefore must consist in a different combination of them, in consequence of a different object being proposed. According to the difference of the object will be the difference of the combination. It is possible that the object may be merely to facilitate the recollection of any given facts or observations by artificial arrangement; and the composition will be a poem, merely because it is distinguished from prose by meter, or by rime, or by both conjointly. In this, the lowest sense, a man might attribute the name of a poem to the well-known enumeration of the days in the several months:

> Thirty days hath September,
> April, June, and November, etc.,

and others of the same class and purpose. And as a particular pleasure is found in anticipating the recurrence of sounds and quantities, all compositions that have this charm super-added, whatever be their contents, *may* be entitled poems.

So much for the superficial form. A difference of object and contents supplies an additional ground of distinction. The immediate purpose may be the communication of truths; either of truth absolute and demonstrable, as in works of science; or of facts experienced and recorded, as in history. Pleasure, and that of the highest and most permanent kind, may result from the attainment of the end; but it is not itself the immediate end. In other works the communication of pleasure may be the immediate purpose; and though truth, either moral or intellectual, ought to be the ultimate end, yet this will distinguish the character of the author, not the class to which the work belongs. Blest indeed is that state of society, in which the immediate purpose would be baffled by the perversion of the proper ultimate end; in which no charm of diction or imagery could exempt the *Bathyllus* even of an Anacreon, or the *Alexis* of Virgil, from disgust and aversion!

But the communication of pleasure may be the immediate object of a work not metrically composed; and that object may have been in a high degree attained, as in novels and romances. Would then the mere superaddition of meter, with or without rime, entitle these to the name of poems? The answer is, that nothing can permanently please, which does not contain in itself the reason why it is so, and not otherwise. If meter be superadded, all other parts must be made consonant with it. They must be such, as to justify the perpetual and distinct attention to each part, which an exact correspondent recurrence of accent and sound are calculated to excite. The final definition then, so deduced, may be thus worded: A poem is that species of composition, which is opposed to works of science, by proposing for its *immediate* object pleasure not truth; and from all other species—having *this* ob-

ject in common with it—it is discriminated by proposing to itself such delight from the *whole*, as is compatible with a distinct gratification from each component *part*.

Controversy is not seldom excited in consequence of the disputants attaching each a different meaning to the same word; and in few instances has this been more striking than in disputes concerning the present subject. If a man chooses to call every composition a poem which is rime, or measure, or both, I must leave his opinion uncontroverted. The distinction is at least competent to characterize the writer's intention. If it were subjoined, that the whole is likewise entertaining or affecting, as a tale, or as a series of interesting reflections, I of course admit this as another fit ingredient of a poem, and an additional merit. But if the definition sought for be that of a *legitimate* poem, I answer, it must be one, the parts of which mutually support and explain each other; all in their proportion harmonizing with, and supporting the purpose and known influences of metrical arrangement. The philosophic critics of all ages coincide with the ultimate judgment of all countries, in equally denying the praises of a just poem, on the one hand, to a series of striking lines or distiches, each of which, absorbing the whole attention of the reader to itself, disjoins it from its context, and makes it a separate whole, instead of an harmonizing part; and on the other hand, to an unsustained composition, from which the reader collects rapidly the general result unattracted by the component parts. The reader should be carried forward, not merely or chiefly by the mechanical impulse of curiosity, or by a restless desire to arrive at the final solution; but by the pleasurable activity of mind excited by the attractions of the journey itself. Like the motion of a serpent, which the Egyptians made the emblem of intellectual power; or like the path of sound through the air;—at every step he pauses and half recedes, and from the retrogressive movement collects the force which again carries him onward. *Praecipitandus est liber spiritus,*[1] says Petronius most happily. The epithet, *liber,* here balances the preceding verb; and it is not easy to conceive more meaning condensed in fewer words.

But if this should be admitted as a satis-

---

[1] A free spirit must be urged forward (from the *Satyricon,* according to H. N. Coleridge's edition of 1847).

factory character of a poem, we have still to seek for a definition of poetry. The writings of Plato, and Bishop Taylor,[2] and the *Theoria Sacra* of Burnet,[3] furnish undeniable proofs that poetry of the highest kind may exist without meter, and even without the contra-distinguishing objects of a poem. The first chapter of Isaiah—indeed a very large portion of the whole book—is poetry in the most emphatic sense; yet it would be not less irrational than strange to assert, that pleasure, and not truth was the immediate object of the prophet. In short, whatever specific import we attach to the word, Poetry, there will be found involved in it, as a necessary consequence, that a poem of any length neither can be, or ought to be, all poetry. Yet if an harmonious whole is to be produced, the remaining parts must be preserved *in keeping* with the poetry; and this can be no otherwise effected than by such a studied selection and artificial arrangement as will partake of *one*, though not a *peculiar* property of poetry. And this again can be no other than the property of exciting a more continuous and equal attention than the language of prose aims at, whether colloquial or written.

My own conclusions on the nature of poetry, in the strictest use of the word, have been in part anticipated in the preceding disquisition on the Fancy and Imagination. What is poetry? is so nearly the same question with, What is a poet? that the answer to the one is involved in the solution of the other. For it is a distinction resulting from the poetic genius itself, which sustains and modifies the images, thoughts, and emotions of the poet's own mind.

The poet, described in ideal perfection, brings the whole soul of man into activity, with the subordination of its faculties to each other according to their relative worth and dignity. He diffuses a tone and spirit of unity, that blends, and (as it were) *fuses*, each into each, by that synthetic and magical power, to which we have exclusively appropriated the name of Imagination. This power, first put in action by the will and understanding, and retained under their irremissive, though gentle and unnoticed, control (*laxis effertur habenis*)[4] reveals itself

in the balance or reconciliation of opposite or discordant qualities: of sameness, with difference; of the general with the concrete; the idea with the image; the individual with the representative; the sense of novelty and freshness with old and familiar objects; a more than usual state of emotion with more than usual order; judgment ever awake and steady self-possession with enthusiasm and feeling profound or vehement; and while it blends and harmonizes the natural and the artificial, still subordinates art to nature; the manner to the matter; and our admiration of the poet to our sympathy with the poetry. "Doubtless," as Sir John Davies observes of the soul—and his words may with slight alteration be applied, and even more appropriately, to the poetic Imagination—

Doubtless this could not be, but that she turns
　Bodies to spirit by sublimation strange,
As fire converts to fire the things it burns,
　As we our food into our nature change.

From their gross matter she abstracts their forms,
　And draws a kind of quintessence from things;
Which to her proper nature she transforms,
　To bear them light on her celestial wings.

Thus does she, when from individual states
　She doth abstract the universal kinds;
Which then re-clothed in divers names and fates
　Steal access through our senses to our minds.[5]

Finally, Good Sense is the Body of poetic genius, Fancy its Drapery, Motion its Life, and Imagination the Soul that is everywhere, and in each; and forms all into one graceful and intelligent whole.

## CHAPTER XVII

As far then as Mr. Wordsworth in his preface contended, and most ably contended, for a reformation in our poetic diction, as far as he has evinced the truth of passion, and the *dramatic* propriety of those figures and metaphors in the original poets, which, stripped of their justifying reasons, and converted into mere artifices of connection or ornament, constitute the characteristic falsity in the poetic style of the moderns; and as far as he has, with equal acuteness and clearness, pointed out the process by which this change was effected, and the resemblances between that state into which the reader's

---

[2] Jeremy Taylor (1613–1667).

[3] Bishop Thomas Burnet (1635–1715), whose *Telluris Theoria Sacra* (1681–1689; English translation, 1684–1689) was a fanciful theory of the earth's structure. Wordsworth also knew the book.

[4] Driven with loosened reins.

[5] *Nosce Teipsum* (1599), Of the Soul of Man and the Immortality Thereof, Stanzas 8–10 of the section entitled "That it cannot be a Body." Coleridge has made numerous changes from Davies' text.

mind is thrown by the pleasurable confusion of thought from an unaccustomed train of words and images; and that state which is induced by the natural language of impassioned feeling; he undertook a useful task, and deserves all praise, both for the attempt and for the execution. The provocations to this remonstrance in behalf of truth and nature were still of perpetual recurrence before and after the publication of this preface. I cannot likewise but add, that the comparison of such poems of merit, as have been given to the public within the last ten or twelve years, with the majority of those produced previously to the appearance of that preface, leave no doubt on my mind, that Mr. Wordsworth is fully justified in believing his efforts to have been by no means ineffectual. Not only in the verses of those who have professed their admiration of his genius, but even of those who have distinguished themselves by hostility to his theory, and depreciation of his writings, are the impressions of his principles plainly visible. It is possible that with these principles others may have been blended, which are not equally evident; and some which are unsteady and subvertible from the narrowness or imperfection of their basis. But it is more than possible that these errors of defect or exaggeration, by kindling and feeding the controversy, may have conduced not only to the wider propagation of the accompanying truths, but that, by their frequent presentation to the mind in an excited state, they may have won for them a more permanent and practical result. A man will borrow a part from his opponent the more easily, if he feels himself justified in continuing to reject a part. While there remain important points in which he can still feel himself in the right, in which he still finds firm footing for continued resistance, he will gradually adopt those opinions which were the least remote from his own convictions, as not less congruous with his own theory than that which he reprobates. In like manner with a kind of instinctive prudence, he will abandon by little and little his weakest posts, till at length he seems to forget that they had ever belonged to him, or affects to consider them at most as accidental and "petty annexments," the removal of which leaves the citadel unhurt and unendangered.

My own differences from certain supposed parts of Mr. Wordsworth's theory ground themselves on the assumption that his words had been rightly interpreted, as purporting that the proper diction for poetry in general consists altogether in a language taken, with due exceptions, from the mouths of men in real life, a language which actually constitutes the natural conversation of men under the influence of natural feelings. My objection is, first, that in *any* sense this rule is applicable only to *certain* classes of poetry; secondly, that even to these classes it is not applicable, except in such a sense as hath never by any one (as far as I know or have read) been denied or doubted; and lastly, that as far as, and in that degree in which it is *practicable*, yet as a *rule* it is useless, if not injurious, and therefore either need not, or ought not to be practiced. The poet informs his reader that he had generally chosen *low and rustic* life; but not *as* low and rustic, or in order to repeat that pleasure of doubtful moral effect, which persons of elevated rank and of superior refinement oftentimes derive from a happy imitation of the rude unpolished manners and discourse of their inferiors. For the pleasure so derived may be traced to three exciting causes. The first is the naturalness, in *fact*, of the things represented. The second is the apparent naturalness of the representation, as raised and qualified by an imperceptible infusion of the author's own knowledge and talent, which infusion does, indeed, constitute it an imitation as distinguished from a mere copy. The third cause may be found in the reader's conscious feeling of his superiority awakened by the contrast presented to him; even as for the same purpose the kings and great barons of yore retained, sometimes actual clowns and fools, but more frequently shrewd and witty fellows in that character. These, however, were not Mr. Wordsworth's objects. *He* chose low and rustic life, "because in that condition the essential passions of the heart find a better soil, in which they can attain their maturity, are less under restraint, and speak a plainer and more emphatic language; because in that condition of life our elementary feelings coexist in a state of greater simplicity, and consequently may be more accurately contemplated, and more forcibly communicated; because the manners of rural life germinate from those elementary feelings; and from the necessary character of rural occupations are more easily comprehended, and are more durable; and lastly, because in that condition the passions of men are incorporated with the beautiful and permanent forms of nature." [1]

Now it is clear to me, that in the most interesting of the poems, in which the author is more or less dramatic, as *The Brothers, Michael, Ruth, The Mad Mother,* etc., the persons introduced are by no means taken from low or rustic life in the common acceptation of those words; and it is not less clear that the sentiments and language, as far as they can be conceived to have been really transferred from the minds and conversation of such persons, are attributable to causes and circumstances not necessarily connected with "their occupations and abode." The thoughts, feelings, language, and manners of the shepherd-farmers in the vales of Cumberland and Westmoreland, as far as they are actually adopted in those poems, may be accounted for from causes, which will and do produce the same results in every state of life, whether in town or country. As the two principal I rank that Independence, which raises a man above servitude, or daily toil for the profit of others, yet not above the necessity of industry and a frugal simplicity of domestic life; and the accompanying unambitious, but solid and religious, Education, which has rendered few books familiar, but the Bible, and the Liturgy or Hymn book. To this latter cause, indeed, which is so far accidental, that it is the blessing of particular countries and a particular age, not the product of particular places or employments, the poet owes the show of probability that his personages might really feel, think, and talk with any tolerable resemblance to his representation. It is an excellent remark of Dr. Henry More's, that "a man of confined education, but of good parts, by constant reading of the Bible will naturally form a more winning and commanding rhetoric than those that are learned: the intermixture of tongues and of artificial phrases debasing *their* style." [2]

It is, moreover, to be considered that to the formation of healthy feelings, and a reflecting mind, negations involve impediments not less formidable than sophistication and vicious intermixture. I am convinced, that for the human soul to prosper in rustic life a certain vantage-ground is prerequisite. It is not every man that is likely to be improved by a country life or by country labors. Education, or original sensibility, or both, must pre-exist, if the changes, forms, and incidents of nature are to prove a sufficient stimulant. And where these are not sufficient, the mind contracts and hardens by want of stimulants: and the man becomes selfish, sensual, gross, and hard-hearted. Let the management of the Poor Laws in Liverpool, Manchester, or Bristol be compared with the ordinary dispensation of the poor rates in agricultural villages, where the farmers are the overseers and guardians of the poor. If my own experience have not been particularly unfortunate, as well as that of the many respectable country clergymen with whom I have conversed on the subject, the result would engender more than scepticism concerning the desirable influences of low and rustic life in and for itself. Whatever may be concluded on the other side, from the stronger local attachments and enterprising spirit of the Swiss, and other mountaineers, applies to a particular mode of pastoral life, under forms of property that permit and beget manners truly republican, not to rustic life in general, or to the absence of artificial cultivation. On the contrary the mountaineers, whose manners have been so often eulogized, are in general better educated and greater readers than men of equal rank elsewhere. But where this is not the case, as among the peasantry of North Wales, the ancient mountains, with all their terrors and all their glories, are pictures to the blind, and music to the deaf.

I should not have entered so much into detail upon this passage, but here seems to be the point, to which all the lines of difference converge as to their source and center— I mean, as far as, and in whatever respect, my poetic creed *does* differ from the doctrines promulgated in this preface.—I adopt with full faith, the principle of Aristotle,[3] that poetry, as poetry, is essentially *ideal*, that it avoids and excludes all *accident*; that its apparent individualities of rank, character, or occupation must be representative of a class; and that the persons of poetry must be clothed with generic attributes, with the common attributes of the class: not with such as one gifted individual might possibly possess, but such as from his situation it is most probable before-hand that he would possess. If

---

[1] Preface to *Lyrical Ballads.*

[2] *Enthusiasmus Triumphatus,* Sec. XXXV (Coleridge's note). More (1614–1687) was one of the group known as the Cambridge Platonists. This book was published in 1656. Its sub-title is: "A Discourse of the Nature, Causes, Kinds, and Cure of Enthusiasm."

[3] In the *Poetics,* IX, 1–4.

my premises are right and my deductions legitimate, it follows that there can be no poetic medium between the swains of Theocritus and those of an imaginary golden age.

The characters of the vicar and the shepherd-mariner in the poem of *The Brothers*, that of the shepherd of Green-head Ghyll in the *Michael*, have all the verisimilitude and representative quality that the purposes of poetry can require. They are 10 persons of a known and abiding class, and their manners and sentiments the natural product of circumstances common to the class. Take Michael for instance:

An old man stout of heart, and strong of limb,
His bodily frame had been from youth to age
Of an unusual strength: his mind was keen,
Intense, and frugal, apt for all affairs,
And in his shepherd's calling he was prompt
And watchful more than ordinary men.
Hence he had learned the meaning of all winds, 20
Of blasts of every tone; and oftentimes
When others heeded not, he heard the South
Make subterraneous music, like the noise
Of bagpipers on distant Highland hills.
The Shepherd, at such warning, of his flock
Bethought him, and he to himself would say,
"The winds are now devising work for me!"
And truly, at all times, the storm, that drives
The traveler to a shelter, summoned him
Up to the mountains: he had been alone
Amid the heart of many thousand mists,
That came to him and left him on the heights. 30
So lived he, until his eightieth year was past.
And grossly that man errs, who should suppose
That the green valleys, and the streams and rocks,
Were things indifferent to the Shepherd's thoughts.
Fields, where with cheerful spirits he had breathed
The common air; the hills, which he so oft
Had climbed with vigorous steps; which had impressed
So many incidents upon his mind
Of hardship, skill or courage, joy or fear;
Which, like a book, preserved the memory
Of the dumb animals, whom he had saved, 40
Had fed or sheltered, linking to such acts,
So grateful in themselves, the certainty
Of honorable gain; these fields, these hills
Which were his living being, even more
Than his own blood—what could they less? had laid
Strong hold on his affections, were to him
A pleasurable feeling of blind love,
The pleasure which there is in life itself.

On the other hand, in the poems which are pitched at a lower note, as the *Harry Gill*, 50 and *The Idiot Boy*, the feelings are those of human nature in general; though the poet has judiciously laid the scene in the country, in order to place himself in the vicinity of interesting images, without the necessity of ascribing a sentimental perception of their beauty to the persons of his drama. In *The*

*Idiot Boy*, indeed, the mother's character is not so much a real and native product of a "situation where the essential passions of the heart find a better soil, in which they can attain their maturity and speak a plainer and more emphatic language," as it is an impersonation of an instinct abandoned by judgment. Hence the two following charges seem to me not wholly groundless: at least, they are the only plausible objections, which I have heard to that fine poem. The one is, that the author has not, in the poem itself, taken sufficient care to preclude from the reader's fancy the disgusting images of ordinary morbid idiocy, which yet it was by no means his intention to represent. He was even by the "burr, burr, burr," uncounteracted by any preceding description of the boy's beauty, assisted in recalling them. The other is, that the idiocy of 20 the boy is so evenly balanced by the folly of the mother, as to present to the general reader rather a laughable burlesque on the blindness of anile [4] dotage, than an analytic display of maternal affection in its ordinary workings.

In *The Thorn*, the poet himself acknowledges in a note the necessity of an introductory poem, in which he should have portrayed the character of the person from whom the words of the poem are supposed to proceed: 30 a superstitious man moderately imaginative, of slow faculties and deep feelings, "a captain of a small trading vessel, for example, who, being past the middle age of life, had retired upon an annuity, or small independent income, to some village or country town of which he was not a native, or in which he had not been accustomed to live. Such men having nothing to do become credulous and talkative from indolence." But in a poem, 40 still more in a lyric poem—and the Nurse in Shakespeare's *Romeo and Juliet* alone prevents me from extending the remark even to dramatic poetry, if indeed the Nurse itself can be deemed altogether a case in point—it is not possible to imitate truly a dull and garrulous discourser, without repeating the effects of dullness and garrulity. However this may be, I dare assert that the parts—and these form the far larger portion of the whole 50 —which might as well or still better have proceeded from the poet's own imagination, and have been spoken in his own character, are those which have given, and which will continue to give, universal delight; and that the passages exclusively appropriate to the supposed narrator, such as the last couplet of the

[4] Old-womanish.

third stanza;[5] the seven last lines of the tenth;[6] and the five following stanzas, with the exception of the four admirable lines at the commencement of the fourteenth, are felt by many unprejudiced and unsophisticated hearts, as sudden and unpleasant sinkings from the height to which the poet had previously lifted them, and to which he again re-elevates both himself and his reader.

If then I am compelled to doubt the theory by which the choice of characters was to be directed, not only *a priori,* from grounds of reason, but both from the few instances in which the poet himself need be supposed to have been governed by it, and from the comparative inferiority of those instances; still more must I hesitate in my assent to the sentence which immediately follows the former citation; and which I can neither admit as particular fact, or as general rule. "The language, too, of these men is adopted (purified indeed from what appear to be its real defects, from all lasting and rational causes of dislike or disgust) because such men hourly communicate with the best objects from which the best part of language is originally derived; and because, from their rank in society and the sameness and narrow circle of their intercourse, being less under the action of social vanity, they convey their feelings and notions in simple and unelaborated expressions." To this I reply; that a rustic's language, purified from all provincialism and grossness, and so far reconstructed as to be made consistent with the rules of grammar—which are in essence no other than the laws of universal logic, applied to psychological materials—will not differ from the language of any other man of common sense, however learned or refined he may be, except as far as the notions, which the rustic has to convey, are fewer and more indiscriminate. This will become still clearer, if we add the consideration—equally important though less obvious—that the rustic, from the more imperfect development of his faculties, and from the lower state of their cultivation, aims almost solely to convey insulated facts, either those of his scanty experience or his traditional belief; while the educated man chiefly seeks to discover and express those connections of things, or those relative bearings of fact to fact, from which some more or less general law is deducible. For facts are valuable to a wise man, chiefly as they lead to the discovery of the indwelling law, which is the true being of things, the sole solution of their modes of existence, and in the knowledge of which consists our dignity and our power.

As little can I agree with the assertion, that from the objects with which the rustic hourly communicates the best part of language is formed. For first, if to communicate with an object implies such an acquaintance with it as renders it capable of being discriminately reflected on, the distinct knowledge of an uneducated rustic would furnish a very scanty vocabulary. The few things and modes of action requisite for his bodily conveniences would alone be individualized; while all the rest of nature would be expressed by a small number of confused general terms. Secondly, I deny that the words and combinations of words derived from the objects, with which the rustic is familiar, whether with distinct or confused knowledge, can be justly said to form the best part of language. It is more than probable that many classes of the brute creation possess discriminating sounds, by which they can convey to each other notices of such objects as concern their food, shelter, or safety. Yet we hesitate to call the aggregate of such sounds a language, otherwise than metaphorically. The best part of human language, properly so called, is derived from reflection on the acts of the mind itself. It is formed by a voluntary appropriation of fixed symbols to internal acts, to processes and results of imagination, the greater part of which have no place in the consciousness of uneducated man; though in civilized society, by imitation and passive remembrance of what they hear from their religious instructors and other superiors, the most uneducated share in the harvest which they neither sowed, nor reaped. If the history of the phrases in hourly currency among our peasants were traced, a person not previously aware of the fact would be surprised at finding so large a number, which three or four centuries ago were the exclusive property of the universities

5 "I've measured it from side to side:
'Tis three feet long, and two feet wide."

6 "Nay, rack your brain—'tis all in vain,
I'll tell you everything I know;
But to the Thorn, and to the Pond
Which is a little step beyond,
I wish that you would go:
Perhaps, when you are at the place,
You something of her tale may trace."

(Coleridge also quotes the stanzas next mentioned, but these two passages sufficiently illustrate his criticism.)

and the schools; and, at the commencement of the Reformation, had been transferred from the school to the pulpit, and thus gradually passed into common life. The extreme difficulty, and often the impossibility, of finding words for the simplest moral and intellectual processes of the languages of uncivilized tribes has proved perhaps the weightiest obstacle to the progress of our most zealous and adroit missionaries. Yet these tribes are surrounded by the same nature as our peasants are; but in still more impressive forms; and they are, moreover, obliged to particularize many more of them. When, therefore, Mr. Wordsworth adds, "accordingly, such a language"—meaning, as before, the language of rustic life purified from provincialism—"arising out of repeated experience and regular feelings, is a more permanent, and a far more philosophical language, than that which is frequently substituted for it by Poets, who think they are conferring honor upon themselves and their art in proportion as they indulge in arbitrary and capricious habits of expression"; it may be answered, that the language, which he has in view, can be attributed to rustics with no greater right, than the style of Hooker [7] or Bacon to Tom Brown [8] or Sir Roger L'Estrange.[9] Doubtless, if what is peculiar to each were omitted in each, the result must needs be the same. Further, that the poet, who uses an illogical diction, or a style fitted to excite only the low and changeable pleasure of wonder by means of groundless novelty, substitutes a language of folly and vanity, not for that of the rustic, but for that of good sense and natural feeling.

Here let me be permitted to remind the reader that the positions which I controvert are contained in the sentences—"a selection of the real language of men";—"the language of these men" (*i.e.*, men in low and rustic life) "I propose to myself to imitate, and, as far as is possible, to adopt the very language of men." "Between the language of prose and that of metrical composition, there neither is, nor can be, any essential difference." It is against these exclusively that my opposition is directed.

I object, in the very first instance, to an equivocation in the use of the word "real." Every man's language varies, according to the extent of his knowledge, the activity of his faculties, and the depth or quickness of his feelings. Every man's language has, first, its individualities; secondly, the common properties of the class to which he belongs; and thirdly, words and phrases of universal use. The language of Hooker, Bacon, Bishop Taylor, and Burke differs from the common language of the learned class only by the superior number and novelty of the thoughts and relations which they had to convey. The language of Algernon Sidney [10] differs not at all from that which every well-educated gentleman would wish to write, and (with due allowances for the undeliberateness, and less connected train, of thinking natural and proper to conversation) such as he would wish to talk. Neither one nor the other differ half as much from the general language of cultivated society, as the language of Mr. Wordsworth's homeliest composition differs from that of a common peasant. For "real" therefore, we must substitute ordinary, or *lingua communis.*[11] And this, we have proved, is no more to be found in the phraseology of low and rustic life than in that of any other class. Omit the peculiarities of each and the result of course must be common to all. And assuredly the omissions and changes to be made in the language of rustics, before it could be transferred to any species of poem, except the drama or other professed imitation, are at least as numerous and weighty, as would be required in adapting to the same purpose the ordinary language of tradesmen and manufacturers. Not to mention, that the language so highly extolled by Mr. Wordsworth varies in every county, nay in every village, according to the accidental character of the clergyman, the existence or nonexistence of schools; or even, perhaps, as the exciseman, publican, or barber happen to be, or not to be, zealous politicians, and readers of the weekly newspaper *pro bono publico.*[12] Anterior to cultivation the *lingua communis* of every country, as Dante has well observed, exists everywhere in parts, and nowhere as a whole.

---

[7] Richard Hooker (1554?–1600), author of the treatise *Of the Laws of Ecclesiastical Polity.*

[8] Born 1663, died 1704; translator of the *Comical Romance* of Scarron, and author of many burlesque pieces in prose and verse.

[9] Born *c.* 1617, died 1705; journalist, pamphleteer, author of controversial works remarkable chiefly for their scurrility.

[10] Born *c.* 1622, beheaded for alleged treason 1683. He was active on the Puritan side in the Civil War, held office under Cromwell, and was an able political theorist, advocating the republican form of government.

[11] Common tongue.

[12] For the public good.

Neither is the case rendered at all more tenable by the addition of the words, "in a state of excitement." For the nature of a man's words, where he is strongly affected by joy, grief, or anger, must necessarily depend on the number and quality of the general truths, conceptions and images, and of the words expressing them, with which his mind had been previously stored. For the property of passion is not to create; but to set in increased activity. At least, whatever new connections of thoughts or images, or —which is equally, if not more than equally, the appropriate effect of strong excitement— whatever generalizations of truth or experience the heat of passions may produce; yet the terms of their conveyance must have pre-existed in his former conversations, and are only collected and crowded together by the unusual stimulation. It is indeed very possible to adopt in a poem the unmeaning repetitions, habitual phrases, and other blank counters, which an unfurnished or confused understanding interposes at short intervals, in order to keep hold of his subject, which is still slipping from him, and to give him time for recollection; or, in mere aid of vacancy, as in the scanty companies of a country stage the same player pops backwards and forwards, in order to prevent the appearance of empty spaces, in the procession of Macbeth, or Henry VIII. But what assistance to the poet, or ornament to the poem, these can supply, I am at a loss to conjecture. Nothing assuredly can differ either in origin or in mode more widely from the *apparent* tautologies of intense and turbulent feeling, in which the passion is greater and of longer endurance than to be exhausted or satisfied by a single representation of the image or incident exciting it. Such repetitions I admit to be a beauty of the highest kind; as illustrated by Mr. Wordsworth himself from the song of Deborah. "At her feet he bowed, he fell, he lay down: at her feet he bowed, he fell: where he bowed, there he fell down dead." [13]

### CHAPTER XVIII

I conclude, therefore, that the attempt is impracticable; and that, were it not impracticable, it would still be useless. For the very power of making the selection implies the previous possession of the language selected. Or where can the poet have lived?

[13] Judges, 5:27.

And by what rules could he direct his choice, which would not have enabled him to select and arrange his words by the light of his own judgment? We do not adopt the language of a class by the mere adoption of such words exclusively, as that class would use, or at least understand; but likewise by following the *order*, in which the words of such men are wont to succeed each other. Now this order, in the intercourse of uneducated men, is distinguished from the diction of their superiors in knowledge and power, by the greater disjunction and separation in the component parts of that, whatever it be, which they wish to communicate. There is a want of that prospectiveness of mind, that surview, which enables a man to foresee the whole of what he is to convey, appertaining to any one point; and by this means so to subordinate and arrange the different parts according to their relative importance, as to convey it at once, and as an organized whole.

Now I will take the first stanza on which I have chanced to open, in the *Lyrical Ballads*. It is one the most simple and the least peculiar in its language.

> In distant countries have I been,
> And yet I have not often seen
> A healthy man, a man full grown,
> Weep in the public roads, alone.
> But such a one, on English ground,
> And in the broad highway, I met;
> Along the broad highway he came,
> His cheeks with tears were wet:
> Sturdy he seemed, though he was sad;
> And in his arms a lamb he had.[1]

The words here are doubtless such as are current in all ranks of life; and of course not less so in the hamlet and cottage than in the shop, manufactory, college, or palace. But is this the *order*, in which the rustic would have placed the words? I am grievously deceived, if the following less compact mode of commencing the same tale be not a far more faithful copy. "I have been in a many parts, far and near, and I don't know that I ever saw before a man crying by himself in the public road; a grown man I mean, that was neither sick nor hurt," *etc., etc.* But when I turn to the following stanza in *The Thorn*:

> At all times of the day and night
> This wretched woman thither goes;
> And she is known to every star,
> And every wind that blows:
> And there, beside the Thorn, she sits,

[1] This is the first stanza of Wordsworth's poem, *The Last of the Flock.*

> When the blue day-light's in the skies,
> And when the whirlwind's on the hill,
> Or frosty air is keen and still,
> And to herself she cries,
> Oh misery! Oh misery!
> Oh woe is me! Oh misery!

and compare this with the language of ordinary men; or with that which I can conceive at all likely to proceed, in real life, from such a narrator, as is supposed in the note to the poem; compare it either in the succession of the images or of the sentences; I am reminded of the sublime prayer and hymn of praise, which Milton, in opposition to an established liturgy, presents as a fair specimen of common extemporary devotion, and such as we might expect to hear from every self-inspired minister of a conventicle! And I reflect with delight, how little a mere theory, though of his own workmanship, interferes with the processes of genuine imagination in a man of true poetic genius, who possesses, as Mr. Wordsworth, if ever man did, most assuredly does possess,

> The Vision and the Faculty divine.[2]

[2] Wordsworth, *Excursion*, I, 79.

# Charles Lamb
## 1775-1834

Lamb's father was a clerk and confidential servant of a barrister, and lived with his family in rooms in the Inner Temple, London, where Charles Lamb was born on 10 February, 1775, the youngest of seven children. Of these only two others survived childhood—John and Mary, who were respectively twelve and ten years older than Charles. In the Temple Lamb passed the first seven years of his life, and then, through the fortunate interest of one of the governors of Christ's Hospital, was admitted to that school, where he remained until he was fourteen. This was the sum of his formal education, which included a very fair knowledge of Latin and some knowledge of Greek. At Christ's Hospital, too, he formed several lasting friendships, perhaps the closest and certainly the most significant being that with Coleridge. Lamb was never blind to Coleridge's faults, small and large—he described him as an "archangel, a little damaged"—but, like most of Coleridge's other friends, he was deeply impressed by him; and when Coleridge died he wrote: "I feel how great a part he was of me. His great and dear spirit haunts me. I cannot think a thought, I cannot make a criticism on men or books, without an ineffectual turning and reference to him. He was the proof and touchstone of all my cogitations." After leaving Christ's Hospital Lamb obtained a minor post in the South Sea House, where his brother John was employed. A couple of years later, in 1792, he became a clerk in the employ of the East India Company—a position in which he faithfully served until 1825, when the directors of the company retired him on a pension. Thus Lamb's life was passed in London. In his childhood and youth he made occasional visits into the country in Hertfordshire, where his grandmother was housekeeper at Blakesware, a country home of the Plumer family; and there, possibly in the near-by village of Widford, he saw and fell in love with the "fair Alice" of Dream Children, whom he could not

marry. Later in life, too, he spent some of his brief vacations in the country, but to London he always returned with joy—"London," as he wrote to a Cambridge friend, "whose dirtiest drab-frequented alley, and her lowest-bowing tradesman, I would not exchange for Skiddaw, Helvellyn, James, Walter, and the parson into the bargain. O! her lamps of a night! her rich goldsmiths, print-shops, toy-shops, mercers, hardware men, pastry-cooks, St. Paul's Church-Yard, the Strand, Exeter Change, Charing Cross, with the man upon a black horse! These are thy gods, O London! Ain't you mightily moped on the banks of the Cam? Had you not better come and set up here? You can't think what a difference. All the streets and pavements are pure gold, I warrant you. At least, I know an alchemy that turns her mud into that metal —a mind that loves to be at home in crowds."

Yet life in his beloved London was in one respect a never-ending tragedy to Lamb. There was a strain of insanity in his family which attacked him in the winter of 1795–1796. After it was over he could be merry enough about it, as he could so fortunately be merry over almost everything else. "My life," he wrote Coleridge, "has been somewhat diversified of late. The six weeks that finished last year and began this, your very humble servant spent very agreeably in a mad-house at Hoxton. I am got somewhat rational now, and don't bite any one. But mad I was!" Insanity never attacked Lamb again; but in September, 1796, his sister Mary suddenly became mad and, in Lamb's presence, stabbed their mother to death and wounded their father. Although she later recovered her sanity, she was still subject to recurrent fits of madness, and Lamb sacrificed his life to her welfare, becoming responsible for her and caring for her tenderly until his own death on 27 December, 1834.

In the earlier years of their life together the two were poor, and it was in the hope of increasing their income that Lamb published A

747

Tale of Rosamund Gray *in 1798. This, however, brought in very little money, and Lamb next attempted to write plays; but he could not get his tragedy,* John Woodvil, *accepted by any theatrical manager, while his comedy,* Mr. H., *was hissed down as a failure on the first, and only, night of its performance at Drury Lane, Lamb himself joining in the hisses. Several years later William Godwin commissioned the Lambs to write a book for children, and this was immediately successful upon its publication in 1807. It was the* Tales from Shakespeare, *in which Mary did the comedies and Charles the tragedies. In the following year Lamb published his* Specimens of English Dramatic Poets Contemporary with Shakespeare, 10 *which was a not unimportant manifesto of the English romantic movement, and in which Lamb finely exhibited his powers as a critic. But his most fully characteristic work was yet to come. This was the series of* Essays of Elia *contributed to the* London Magazine *in 1820–1822 and published as a book in 1823. A second series was published as the* Last Essays of Elia *in 1833. In these essays Lamb wrote at his ease in a style more intimately personal 20 than had been usual with essayists before his day, and on topics which he freely chose for himself. No analysis is likely to succeed in disentangling their charms; for one reader it may lie chiefly in their quaint bookish flavor derived from Lamb's wide reading in seventeenth-century literature, for another it may lie in their vein of sensibility at once delicate and tender, and for still another it may lie in Lamb's odd, irrepressible humor. Yet the majority of Lamb's readers are probably content not to ask such questions, but simply to read and enjoy.*

*E. V. Lucas is the editor of both* The Works of Charles and Mary Lamb *(7 vols., London, 1903–1905) and* The Letters of Charles Lamb, to Which Are Added Those of His Sister, Mary Lamb *(3 vols., London, 1935). Lucas is also the author of the standard* Life of Charles Lamb *in two volumes (London, 1921). A shorter biography is that by Alfred C. Ward,* The Frolic and the Gentle; a Centenary Study of Charles Lamb *(London, 1934); and Edmund Blunden has given an affectionate portrait in* Charles Lamb and His Contemporaries *(Cambridge, 1933). E. C. Johnson's* Lamb Always Elia *(London, 1935) contends that the essayist was not a thwarted man of action, but realized his potentialities in his writing. None of these books, however, has displaced Alfred Ainger's* Charles Lamb *("Eng-*

*lish Men of Letters" series, 1882) as a sound and admirable introduction to the study of Elia.*

# The Two Races of Men [1]

THE human species, according to the best theory I can form of it, is composed of two distinct races, *the men who borrow,* and *the men who lend.* To these two original diversities may be reduced all those impertinent classifications of Gothic and Celtic tribes, white men, black men, red men. All the dwellers upon earth, "Parthians, and Medes, and Elamites," [2] flock hither, and do naturally fall in with one or other of these primary distinctions. The infinite superiority of the former, which I choose to designate as the *great race,* is discernible in their figure, port, and a certain instinctive sovereignty. The latter are born degraded. "He shall serve his brethren." [3] There is something in the air of one of this cast, lean and suspicious; contrasting with the open, trusting, generous manners of the other.

Observe who have been the greatest borrowers of all ages—Alcibiades [4]—Falstaff—Sir Richard Steele—our late incomparable Brinsley [5]—what a family likeness in all four!

What a careless, even deportment hath your borrower! what rosy gills! what a beautiful reliance on Providence doth he manifest—taking no more thought than lilies! [6] What contempt for money—accounting it (yours and mine especially) no better than

---

[1] The first four of the essays here printed come from *Elia* (1823), the fifth from *The Last Essays of Elia* (1833). All of them were published in the *London Magazine* before being collected into books. Elia was the name of an Italian who had been a clerk in the South Sea House when Lamb was there (before 1792). Lamb explained why he began using this pseudonym in a letter to the publisher of the *London Magazine* concerning *The South Sea House* (the earliest of the Elia essays): "Having a brother now there, and doubting how he might relish certain descriptions in it, I clapped down the name of Elia to it, which passed off pretty well, for Elia himself added the function of an author to that of a scrivener, like myself. I went the other day (not having seen him [Elia] for a year) to laugh over with him at my usurpation of his name, and found him, alas! no more than a name, for he died of consumption eleven months ago, and I knew not of it. So the name has fairly devolved on me, I think; and 'tis all he has left me."

[2] Acts, 2:9.        [3] Genesis, 9:25.
[4] Athenian general, B.C. 450–404.
[5] Richard Brinsley Sheridan (1751–1816), playwright and wit.
[6] St. Matthew, 6:28.

dross! What a liberal confounding of those pedantic distinctions of *meum* and *tuum!* [7] or rather, what a noble simplification of language (beyond Tooke [8]), resolving these supposed opposites into one clear, intelligible pronoun adjective!—What near approaches doth he make to the primitive *community* [9]— to the extent of one-half of the principle at least!—

He is the true taxer who "calleth all the world up to be taxed"; [10] and the distance is as vast between him and *one of us*, as subsisted betwixt the Augustan Majesty and the poorest obolary Jew [11] that paid it tributepittance at Jerusalem!—His exactions, too, have such a cheerful, voluntary air! So far removed from your sour parochial or stategatherers—those ink-horn varlets, who carry their want of welcome in their faces! He cometh to you with a smile, and troubleth you with no receipt; confining himself to no set season. Every day is his Candlemas,[12] or his Feast of Holy Michael. He applieth the *lene tormentum* [13] of a pleasant look to your purse—which to that gentle warmth expands her silken leaves, as naturally as the cloak of the traveler, for which sun and wind contended! He is the true Propontic [14] which never ebbeth! The sea which taketh handsomely at each man's hand. In vain the victim, whom he delighteth to honor, struggles with destiny; he is in the net. Lend therefore cheerfully, O man ordained to lend—that thou lose not in the end, with thy worldly penny, the reversion promised. Combine not preposterously in thine own person the penalties of Lazarus and of Dives! [15]—but, when thou seest the proper authority coming, meet it smilingly, as it were half-way. Come, a handsome sacrifice! See how light *he* makes of it! Strain not courtesies with a noble enemy.

Reflections like the foregoing were forced upon my mind by the death of my old friend, Ralph Bigod,[16] Esq., who departed this life on Wednesday evening; dying, as he had lived, without much trouble. He boasted himself a descendant from mighty ancestors of that name, who heretofore held ducal dignities in this realm. In his actions and sentiments he belied not the stock to which he pretended. Early in life he found himself invested with ample revenues; which, with that noble disinterestedness which I have noticed as inherent in men of the *great race*, he took almost immediate measures entirely to dissipate and bring to nothing: for there is something revolting in the idea of a king holding a private purse; and the thoughts of Bigod were all regal. Thus furnished, by the very act of disfurnishment; getting rid of the cumbersome luggage of riches, more apt (as one sings)

To slacken virtue, and abate her edge,
Than prompt her to do aught may merit praise,[17]

he set forth, like some Alexander, upon his great enterprise, "borrowing and to borrow!"

In his periegesis,[18] or triumphant progress throughout this island, it has been calculated that he laid a tithe [19] part of the inhabitants under contribution. I reject this estimate as greatly exaggerated:—but having had the honor of accompanying my friend divers times, in his perambulations about this vast city, I own I was greatly struck at first with the prodigious number of faces we met, who claimed a sort of respectful acquaintance with us. He was one day so obliging as to explain the phenomenon. It seems, these were his tributaries; feeders of his exchequer; gentlemen, his good friends (as he was pleased to express himself), to whom he had occasionally been beholden for a loan. Their multitudes did in no way disconcert him. He rather took a pride in numbering them; and, with Comus, seemed pleased to be "stocked with so fair a herd."

With such sources, it was a wonder how he contrived to keep his treasury always empty. He did it by force of an aphorism, which he had often in his mouth, that "money kept longer than three days stinks." So he made use of it while it was fresh. A good part he drank away (for he was an excellent toss-pot), some he gave away, the rest he threw away, literally tossing and hurling it violently from him—as boys do burrs, or as if it had been infectious,—into ponds, or ditches, or deep holes,—inscrutable cavities of the earth;—or he would bury it (where he

---

[7] Mine and thine.

[8] John Horne Tooke (1736–1812), politician and philologer, who published his philological theories in *The Diversions of Purley.*

[9] I. e., communism.          [10] St. Luke, 2:1.

[11] I. e., between the Emperor Augustus and the Jew who paid an obolus (about 3 cents).

[12] 2nd February, a quarter-day, for the payment of rents, in Scotland. Michaelmas, 29 September, is an English quarter-day.

[13] Gentle stimulus.

[14] The Sea of Marmora, which has no tides.

[15] St. Luke, 16:19–31.

[16] I. e., John Fenwick, a friend of the Lambs who was usually in financial difficulties.

[17] *Paradise Regained*, II, 455–6.

[18] Journey round.          [19] Tenth.

would never seek it again) by a river's side under some bank, which (he would facetiously observe) paid no interest—but out away from him it must go peremptorily, as Hagar's offspring[20] into the wilderness, while it was sweet. He never missed it. The streams were perennial which fed his fisc.[21] When new supplies became necessary, the first person that had the felicity to fall in with him, friend or stranger, was sure to contribute to the deficiency. For Bigod had an *undeniable* way with him. He had a cheerful, open exterior, a quick jovial eye, a bald forehead, just touched with gray (*cana fides*[22]). He anticipated no excuse, and found none. And, waiving for a while my theory as to the *great race*, I would put it to the most untheorizing reader, who may at times have disposable coin in his pocket, whether it is not more repugnant to the kindliness of his nature to refuse such a one as I am describing, than to say *no* to a poor petitionary rogue (your bastard borrower), who, by his mumping visnomy,[23] tells you that he expects nothing better; and, therefore, whose preconceived notions and expectations you do in reality so much less shock in the refusal.

When I think of this man; his fiery glow of heart; his swell of feeling; how magnificent, how *ideal* he was; how great at the midnight hour; and when I compare with him the companions with whom I have associated since, I grudge the saving of a few idle ducats,[24] and think that I am fallen into the society of *lenders*, and *little men*.

To one like Elia, whose treasures are rather cased in leather covers than closed in iron coffers, there is a class of alienators[25] more formidable than that which I have touched upon; I mean your *borrowers of books*—those mutilators of collections, spoilers of the symmetry of shelves, and creators of odd volumes. There is Comberbatch,[26] matchless in his depredations!

That foul gap in the bottom shelf facing you, like a great eye-tooth knocked out— (you are now with me in my little back study in Bloomsbury,[27] reader!)——with the huge Switzer-like[28] tomes on each side (like the Guildhall giants,[29] in their reformed posture, guardant of nothing) once held the tallest of my folios, *Opera Bonaventurae*,[30] choice and massy divinity, to which its two supporters (school[31] divinity also, but of a lesser caliber—Bellarmine,[32] and Holy Thomas[33]), showed but as dwarfs,—itself an Ascapart![34] —*that* Comberbatch abstracted upon the faith of a theory he holds, which is more easy, I confess, for me to suffer by than to refute, namely, that "the title to property in a book (my Bonaventure, for instance), is in exact ratio to the claimant's powers of understanding and appreciating the same." Should he go on acting upon this theory, which of our shelves is safe?

The slight vacuum in the left-hand case— two shelves from the ceiling—scarcely distinguishable but by the quick eye of a loser ——was whilom the commodious resting-place of Browne on Urn Burial.[35] C. will hardly allege that he knows more about that treatise than I do, who introduced it to him, and was indeed the first (of the moderns) to discover its beauties—but so have I known a foolish lover to praise his mistress in the presence of a rival more qualified to carry her off than himself.—Just below, Dodsley's dramas[36] want their fourth volume, where Vittoria Corombona is! The remainder nine are as distasteful as Priam's refuse sons, when the Fates *borrowed* Hector. Here stood the Anatomy of Melancholy,[37] in sober state.—There loitered the Complete Angler,[38] quiet as in life, by some stream side.—In yonder nook, John Buncle,[39] a widower-volume, with "eyes closed," mourns his ravished mate.

One justice I must do my friend, that if he sometimes, like the sea, sweeps away a treasure, at another time, sea-like, he throws up as rich an equivalent to match it. I have a small under-collection of this nature (my friend's

---

[20] Ishmael (Genesis, 21:9).    [21] Purse.
[22] The gray hair of honor. *Cf. Aeneid*, I, 292.
[23] Begging physiognomy.
[24] Coins; originally, Italian coins.
[25] Takers of others' property.
[26] Coleridge, who when he enlisted in a regiment of dragoons assumed the name of Silas Titus Comberback.
[27] A section of London in which Lamb was *not* living when he wrote this.

[28] I. e., very large.
[29] Gog and Magog, Biblical giants whose statues are in the London Guildhall.
[30] The Works of St. Bonaventura.
[31] Scholastic.    [32] Italian cardinal (1542–1621).
[33] St. Thomas Aquinas, 1227–1274.
[34] A giant thirty feet in height. He appears in *Bevis of Hampton*.
[35] Sir Thomas Browne's *Hydriotaphia, or Urn-Burial*.
[36] Robert Dodsley (1703–1764) edited a collection of plays, among which was John Webster's *The White Devil, or Vittoria Corombona* (1612).
[37] By Robert Burton (1577–1640).
[38] By Izaak Walton (1593–1683).
[39] By Thomas Amory (1691?–1788).

gatherings in his various calls), picked up, he has forgotten at what odd places, and deposited with as little memory at mine. I take in these orphans, the twice-deserted. These proselytes of the gate are welcome as the true Hebrews. There they stand in conjunction; natives, and naturalized. The latter seem as little disposed to inquire out their true lineage as I am.—I charge no warehouse-room for these deodands,[40] nor shall ever put myself to the un-gentlemanly trouble of advertising a sale of them to pay expenses.

To lose a volume to C. carries some sense and meaning in it. You are sure that he will make one hearty meal on your viands, if he can give no account of the platter after it. But what moved thee, wayward, spiteful K.,[41] to be so importunate to carry off with thee, in spite of tears and adjurations to thee to forbear, the Letters of that princely woman, the thrice noble Margaret Newcastle? [42]—knowing at the time, and knowing that I knew also, thou most assuredly wouldst never turn over one leaf of the illustrious folio:—what but the mere spirit of contradiction, and childish love of getting the better of thy friend?—Then, worst cut of all! to transport it with thee to the Gallican land—

Unworthy land to harbor such a sweetness,
A virtue in which all ennobling thoughts dwelt,
Pure thoughts, kind thoughts, high thoughts, her
    sex's wonder!

——hadst thou not thy play-books, and books of jests and fancies, about thee, to keep thee merry, even as thou keepest all companies with thy quips and mirthful tales?—Child of the Green-room, it was unkindly done of thee. Thy wife, too, that part-French, better-part-English-woman!—that *she* could fix upon no other treatise to bear away in kindly token of remembering us, than the works of Fulke Greville, Lord Brook [43]—of which no Frenchman, nor woman of France, Italy, or England, was ever by nature constituted to comprehend a tittle! *Was there not Zimmerman* [44] *on Solitude?*

Reader, if haply thou art blessed with a moderate collection, be shy of showing it; or if thy heart overfloweth to lend them, lend thy books; but let it be to such a one as S. T. C. —he will return them (generally anticipating the time appointed) with usury; enriched with annotations, tripling their value. I have had experience. Many are these precious MSS. of his—(in *matter* oftentimes, and almost in *quantity* not infrequently, vying with the originals)—in no very clerkly hand—legible in my Daniel; [45] in old Burton; in Sir Thomas Browne; and those obstruser cogitations of the Greville, now, alas! wandering in Pagan lands. ——I counsel thee, shut not thy heart, nor thy library, against S. T. C.

# Dream-Children; A Reverie [1]

CHILDREN love to listen to stories about their elders, when *they* were children; to stretch their imagination to the conception of a traditionary great-uncle or grandame, whom they never saw. It was in this spirit that my little ones crept about me the other evening to hear about their great-grandmother Field, who lived in a great house in Norfolk [2] (a hundred times bigger than that in which they and papa lived) which had been the scene—so at least it was generally believed in that part of the country— of the tragic incidents which they had lately become familiar with from the ballad of the Children in the Wood.[3] Certain it is that the whole story of the children and their cruel uncle was to be seen fairly carved out in wood upon the chimney-piece of the great hall, the whole story down to the Robin Redbreasts,[4] till a foolish rich person pulled it down to set up a marble one of modern invention in its stead, with no story upon it. Here Alice put out one of her dear mother's looks, too tender to be called upbraiding. Then I went on to say how religious and how good their great-grandmother Field was, how beloved and respected by everybody, though she was not indeed the mistress of this great house, but had only the charge of it (and yet in some respects she might be said to be the mistress of it too)

[40] In English law a thing which, having caused the death of a person, was forfeited to the Crown for pious uses.

[41] James Kenney (1780–1849), a dramatist, at this time living in France.

[42] The first Duchess of Newcastle (1624–1673).

[43] Lived 1554–1628, the friend and biographer of Sir Philip Sidney.

[44] Johann Georg von Zimmermann (1728–1795), a Swiss physician.

[45] Samuel Daniel (1562–1619).

[1] Lamb's brother John died on 26 October, 1821, and Lamb is believed to have begun this essay shortly afterwards, in a mood of reminiscence and reverie.

[2] The house is Blakesware, really in Hertfordshire, where Mary Field, Lamb's grandmother, was housekeeper.

[3] The scene of this legend is the county of Norfolk, a fact which may have induced Lamb to choose Norfolk in seeking to disguise the identity of Blakesware.

[4] Which, at the close of the ballad, cover with leaves the bodies of the murdered children.

committed to her by the owner, who preferred living in a newer and more fashionable mansion which he had purchased somewhere in the adjoining county; but still she lived in it in a manner as if it had been her own, and kept up the dignity of the great house in a sort while she lived, which afterwards came to decay, and was nearly pulled down, and all its old ornaments stripped and carried away to the owner's other house, where they were set 10 up, and looked as awkward as if some one were to carry away the old tombs they had seen lately at the Abbey, and stick them up in Lady C.'s tawdry gilt drawing-room. Here John smiled, as much as to say, "that would be foolish indeed." And then I told how, when she came to die, her funeral was attended by a concourse of all the poor, and some of the gentry too, of the neighborhood for many miles round, to show their respect for her memory, 20 because she had been such a good and religious woman; so good indeed that she knew all the Psaltery[5] by heart, ay, and a great part of the Testament besides. Here little Alice spread her hands. Then I told what a tall, upright, graceful person their great-grandmother Field once was; and how in her youth she was esteemed the best dancer—here Alice's little right foot played an involuntary movement, till upon my looking grave, it desisted—the best 30 dancer, I was saying, in the county, till a cruel disease, called a cancer, came, and bowed her down with pain; but it could never bend her good spirits, or make them stoop, but they were still upright, because she was so good and religious. Then I told how she was used to sleep by herself in a lone chamber of the great lone house; and how she believed that an apparition of two infants was to be seen at midnight gliding up 40 and down the great staircase near where she slept, but she said "those innocents would do her no harm"; and how frightened I used to be, though in those days I had my maid to sleep with me, because I was never half so good or religious as she—and yet I never saw the infants. Here John expanded all his eyebrows and tried to look courageous. Then I told how good she was to all her grandchildren, having us to the great house in the 50 holidays, where I in particular used to spend many hours by myself, in gazing upon the old busts of the Twelve Caesars,[6] that had been Emperors of Rome, till the old marble

heads would seem to live again, or I to be turned into marble with them; how I never could be tired with roaming about that huge mansion, with its vast empty rooms, with their worn-out hangings, fluttering tapestry, and carved oaken panels, with the gilding almost rubbed out—sometimes in the spacious old-fashioned gardens, which I had almost to myself, unless when now and then a solitary gardening man would cross me—and how the nectarines and peaches hung upon the walls, without my ever offering to pluck them, because they were forbidden fruit, unless now and then,—and because I had more pleasure in strolling about among the old melancholy-looking yew trees, or the firs, and picking up the red berries, and the fir apples,[7] which were good for nothing but to look at—or in lying about upon the fresh grass, with all the fine garden smells around me—or basking in the orangery, till I could almost fancy myself ripening too along with the oranges and the limes in that grateful warmth—or in watching the dace that darted to and fro in the fish-pond, at the bottom of the garden, with here and there a great sulky pike hanging midway down the water in silent state, as if it mocked at their impertinent friskings,—I had more pleasure in these busy-idle diversions than in all the sweet flavors of peaches, nectarines, oranges, and such like common baits of children. Here John slily deposited back upon the plate a bunch of grapes, which, not unobserved by Alice, he had meditated dividing with her, and both seemed willing to relinquish them for the present as irrelevant. Then in somewhat a more heightened tone, I told how, though their great-grandmother Field loved all her grandchildren, yet in an especial manner she might be said to love their uncle, John L——,[8] because he was so handsome and spirited a youth, and a king to the rest of us; and, instead of moping about in solitary corners, like some of us, he would mount the most mettlesome horse he could get, when but an imp no bigger than themselves, and make it carry him half over the county in a morning, and join the hunters when there were any out—and yet he loved the old great house and gardens too, but had too much spirit to be always pent up within their boundaries—and how their uncle grew up to man's estate as brave as he was handsome, to the admiration of everybody, but of their great-grandmother Field most espe-

---

[5] Psalter, the Book of Psalms.

[6] The Roman Emperors from Julius Caesar to Domitian.

[7] Fir cones.          [8] Lamb's brother.

cially; and how he used to carry me upon his back when I was a lame-footed boy—for he was a good bit older than me—many a mile when I could not walk for pain;—and how in after life he became lame-footed too, and I did not always (I fear) make allowances enough for him when he was impatient, and in pain, nor remember sufficiently how considerate he had been to me when I was lame-footed; and how when he died, though he had not been dead an hour, it seemed as if he had died a great while ago, such a distance there is betwixt life and death; and how I bore his death as I thought pretty well at first, but afterwards it haunted and haunted me; and though I did not cry or take it to heart as some do, and as I think he would have done if I had died, yet I missed him all day long, and knew not till then how much I had loved him. I missed his kindness, and I missed his crossness, and wished him to be alive again, to be quarreling with him (for we quarreled sometimes), rather than not have him again, and was as uneasy without him, as he their poor uncle must have been when the doctor took off his limb.[9] Here the children fell a crying, and asked if their little mourning which they had on was not for uncle John, and they looked up, and prayed me not to go on about their uncle, but to tell them some stories about their pretty dead mother. Then I told how for seven long years, in hope sometimes, sometimes in despair, yet persisting ever, I courted the fair Alice W——n;[10] and, as much as children could understand, I explained to them what coyness, and difficulty, and denial meant in maidens—when suddenly, turning to Alice, the soul of the first Alice looked out at her eyes with such a reality of re-presentment, that I became in doubt which of them stood there before me, or whose that bright hair was; and while I stood gazing, both the children gradually grew fainter to my view, receding, and still receding till nothing at last but two mournful features were seen in the uttermost distance, which, without speech, strangely impressed upon me the effects of speech; "We are not of Alice, nor of thee, nor are we children at all. The children of Alice call Bartrum [11] father. We are nothing; less than nothing, and dreams. We are only what might have been, and must wait upon the tedious shores of Lethe [12] millions of ages before we have existence, and a name" —and immediately awaking, I found myself quietly seated in my bachelor armchair, where I had fallen asleep, with the faithful Bridget [13] unchanged by my side—but John L. (or James Elia) was gone for ever.

## The Praise of Chimney-Sweepers

I LIKE to meet a sweep—understand me— not a grown sweeper—old chimney-sweepers are by no means attractive—but one of those tender novices, blooming through their first nigritude,[1] the maternal washings not quite effaced from the cheek—such as come forth with the dawn, or somewhat earlier, with their little professional notes sounding like the *peep peep* of a young sparrow; or liker to the matin lark should I pronounce them, in their aerial ascents not seldom anticipating the sun-rise?

I have a kindly yearning toward these dim specks—poor blots—innocent blacknesses——

I reverence these young Africans of our own growth—these almost clergy imps, who sport their cloth [2] without assumption; and from their little pulpits (the tops of chimneys), in the nipping air of a December morning, preach a lesson of patience to mankind.

When a child, what a mysterious pleasure it was to witness their operation! to see a chit no bigger than one's self enter, one knew not by what process, into what seemed the *fauces Averni* [3]—to pursue him in imagination, as he went sounding on through so many dark stifling caverns, horrid shades!— to shudder with the idea that "now, surely, he must be lost for ever!"—to revive at hearing his feeble shout of discovered daylight—and then (O fullness of delight) run-

[9] This, as far as is known, did not actually happen.
[10] According to a key Lamb made for a fellow clerk at the East India House this name is Alice Winterton, but Lamb adds that the name is feigned. It has been suggested that Lamb means Ann Simmons, of Blenheims, near Blakesware, but Mr. E. V. Lucas thinks that "that Alice W——n was more an abstraction around which now and then to group tender imaginings of what might have been than any tangible figure."

[11] Ann Simmons married a Mr. Bartrum, or Bartram, a London pawnbroker.
[12] The river of forgetfulness, in Hades. In the *Aeneid* (VI, 703–751) Virgil tells how the soul, after many ages and after drinking of this river, returns to earth in a new body.
[13] Lamb's sister Mary, although in the *Essays of Elia* Bridget is spoken of as a cousin.
[1] Blackness.    [2] The dress of their calling.
[3] The jaws of Hell (*Aeneid*, VI, 201).

ning out of doors, to come just in time to see the sable phenomenon emerge in safety, the brandished weapon of his art victorious like some flag waved over a conquered citadel! I seem to remember having been told that a bad sweep was once left in a stack with his brush, to indicate which way the wind blew. It was an awful spectacle certainly; not much unlike the old stage direction in Macbeth,[4] where the "Apparition of a child crowned with a tree in his hand rises."

Reader, if thou meetest one of these small gentry in thy early rambles, it is good to give him a penny. It is better to give him twopence. If it be starving weather, and to the proper troubles of his hard occupation, a pair of kibed [5] heels (no unusual accompaniment) be superadded, the demand on thy humanity will surely rise to a tester.[6]

There is a composition, the ground-work of which I have understood to be the sweet wood 'yclept [7] sassafras. This wood boiled down to a kind of tea, and tempered with an infusion of milk and sugar, hath to some tastes a delicacy beyond the China luxury. I know not how thy palate may relish it; for myself, with every deference to the judicious Mr. Read, who hath time out of mind kept open a shop (the only one he avers in London) for the vending of this "wholesome and pleasant beverage, on the south side of Fleet Street, as thou approachest Bridge Street—*the only Salopian house*," [8]—I have never yet ventured to dip my own particular lip in a basin of his commended ingredients —a cautious premonition to the olfactories constantly whispering to me that my stomach must infallibly, with all due courtesy, decline it. Yet I have seen palates, otherwise not uninstructed in dietetical elegances, sup it up with avidity.

I know not by what particular conformation of the organ it happens, but I have always found that this composition is surprisingly gratifying to the palate of a young chimney-sweeper—whether the oily particles (sassafras is slightly oleaginous) do attenuate and soften the fuliginous [9] concretions, which are sometimes found (in dissections) to adhere to the roof of the mouth in these unfledged practitioners; or whether Nature, sensible that she had mingled too much of

bitter wood [10] in the lot of these raw victims, caused to grow out of the earth her sassafras for a sweet lenitive [11]—but so it is, that no possible taste or odor to the senses of a young chimney-sweeper can convey a delicate excitement comparable to this mixture. Being penniless, they will yet hang their black heads over the ascending steam, to gratify one sense if possible, seemingly no less pleased than those domestic animals— cats—when they purr over a new-found sprig of valerian.[12] There is something more in these sympathies than philosophy can inculcate.

Now albeit Mr. Read boasteth, not without reason, that his is the *only Salopian house*; yet be it known to thee, reader—if thou art one who keepest what are called good hours, thou art haply ignorant of the fact—he hath a race of industrious imitators, who from stalls, and under open sky, dispense the same savory mess to humbler customers, at that dead time of the dawn, when (as extremes meet) the rake, reeling home from his midnight cups, and the hard-handed artisan leaving his bed to resume the premature labors of the day, jostle, not unfrequently to the manifest disconcerting of the former, for the honors of the pavement. It is the time when, in summer, between the expired and the not yet relumined kitchen fires, the kennels of our fair metropolis give forth their least satisfactory odors. The rake, who wisheth to dissipate his o'er-night vapors in more grateful coffee, curses the ungenial fume, as he passeth; but the artisan stops to taste, and blesses the fragrant breakfast.

This is *Saloop*—the precocious herb-woman's darling—the delight of the early gardener, who transports his smoking cabbages by break of day from Hammersmith to Covent Garden's famed piazzas [13]—the delight, and, oh I fear, too often the envy, of the unpennied sweep. Him shouldest thou haply encounter, with his dim visage pendent over the grateful steam, regale him with a sumptuous basin (it will cost thee but three halfpennies) and a slice of delicate bread and butter (an added halfpenny)—so may thy culinary fires, eased of the o'er-charged secretions from thy worse-placed hospitalities, curl up a lighter volume to the welkin [14]

---

[4] Act IV, sc. i.  [5] Afflicted with chilblains.
[6] Sixpence.  [7] Called.
[8] Saloop was the name of this beverage, whence salopian.
[9] Sooty.

[10] Wormwood.  [11] Softener of pain.
[12] Or catnip.
[13] I. e., to London's fruit and flower market.
[14] Sky.

—so may the descending soot never taint thy costly well-ingredienced soups—nor the odious cry, quick-reaching from street to street, of the *fired chimney*, invite the rattling engines from ten adjacent parishes, to disturb for a casual scintillation[15] thy peace and pocket!

I am by nature extremely susceptible of street affronts; the jeers and taunts of the populace; the low-bred triumph they display over the casual trip, or splashed stocking, of a gentleman. Yet can I endure the jocularity of a young sweep with something more than forgiveness.—In the last winter but one, pacing along Cheapside with my accustomed precipitation when I walk westward, a treacherous slide brought me upon my back in an instant. I scrambled up with pain and shame enough—yet outwardly trying to face it down, as if nothing had happened—when the roguish grin of one of these young wits encountered me. There he stood, pointing me out with his dusky finger to the mob, and to a poor woman (I suppose his mother) in particular, till the tears for the exquisiteness of the fun (so he thought it) worked themselves out at the corners of his poor red eyes, red from many a previous weeping, and soot-inflamed, yet twinkling through all with such a joy, snatched out of desolation, that Hogarth—but Hogarth has got him already (how could he miss him?) in the March to Finchley, grinning at the pie-man—there he stood, as he stands in the picture, irremovable, as if the jest was to last for ever—with such a maximum of glee, and minimum of mischief, in his mirth—for the grin of a genuine sweep hath absolutely no malice in it—that I could have been content, if the honor of a gentleman might endure it, to have remained his butt and his mockery till midnight.

I am by theory obdurate to the seductiveness of what are called a fine set of teeth. Every pair of rosy lips (the ladies must pardon me) is a casket, presumably holding such jewels; but, methinks, they should take leave to "air" them as frugally as possible. The fine lady, or fine gentleman, who show me their teeth, show me bones. Yet must I confess, that from the mouth of a true sweep a display (even to ostentation) of those white and shining ossifications, strikes me as an agreeable anomaly in manners, and

an allowable piece of foppery. It is, as when

A sable cloud
Turns forth her silver lining on the night.[16]

It is like some remnant of gentry not quite extinct; a badge of better days; a hint of nobility:—and, doubtless, under the obscuring darkness and double night of their forlorn disguisement, oftentimes lurketh good blood, and gentle conditions, derived from lost ancestry, and a lapsed pedigree. The premature apprenticements of these tender victims give but too much encouragement, I fear, to clandestine, and almost infantile abductions; the seeds of civility and true courtesy, so often discernible in these young grafts (not otherwise to be accounted for), plainly hint at some forced adoptions; many noble Rachels[17] mourning for their children, even in our days, countenance the fact; the tales of fairy-spiriting may shadow a lamentable verity, and the recovery of the young Montagu[18] be but a solitary instance of good fortune, out of many irreparable and hopeless *defiliations*.[19]

In one of the state-beds at Arundel Castle,[20] a few years since—under a ducal canopy—(that seat of the Howards is an object of curiosity to visitors, chiefly for its beds, in which the late duke was especially a connoisseur)—encircled with curtains of delicatest crimson, with starry coronets inwoven—folded between a pair of sheets whiter and softer than the lap where Venus lulled Ascanius[21]—was discovered by chance, after all methods of search had failed, at noon-day, fast asleep, a lost chimney-sweeper. The little creature, having somehow confounded his passage among the intricacies of those lordly chimneys, by some unknown aperture had alighted upon this magnificent chamber; and, tired with his tedious explorations, was unable to resist the delicious invitement to repose which he there saw exhibited; so, creeping between the sheets very quietly, laid his black head upon the pillow, and slept like a young Howard.

Such is the account given to the visitors

[15] Eruption of sparks.
[16] Milton, *Comus*, 221-2.
[17] Jeremiah, 31:15.
[18] Edward Wortley Montagu (1713–1776), son of Lady Mary Wortley Montagu, several times ran away from Westminster School and on one of these occasions became for a time a chimney-sweeper.
[19] Losses of sons.
[20] The Sussex seat of the Dukes of Norfolk.
[21] Ascanius was the son of Aeneas, whose mother was Venus.

at the Castle.—But I cannot help seeming to perceive a confirmation of what I have just hinted at in this story. A high instinct was at work in the case, or I am mistaken. Is it probable that a poor child of that description, with whatever weariness he might be visited, would have ventured, under such a penalty as he would be taught to expect, to uncover the sheets of a Duke's bed, and de- 10 liberately to lay himself down between them, when the rug, or the carpet, presented an obvious couch, still far above his pretentions— is this probable, I would ask, if the great power of nature, which I contend for, had not been manifested within him, prompting to the adventure? Doubtless this young nobleman (for such my mind misgives me that he must be) was allured by some memory, not amounting to full consciousness, of his condition in infancy, when he was used 20 to be lapped by his mother, or his nurse, in just such sheets as he there found, into which he was but now creeping back as into his proper *incunabula*,[22] and resting-place.—By no other theory than by this sentiment of a pre-existent state (as I may call it), can I explain a deed so venturous, and, indeed, upon any other system, so indecorous, in this tender, but unseasonable, sleeper.

My pleasant friend JEM WHITE [23] was so 30 impressed with a belief of metamorphoses like this frequently taking place, that in some sort to reverse the wrongs of fortune in these poor changelings, he instituted an annual feast of chimney-sweepers, at which it was his pleasure to officiate as host and waiter. It was a solemn supper held in Smithfield, upon the yearly return of the fair of St. Bartholomew.[24] Cards were issued a week before to the master-sweeps in and 40 about the metropolis, confining the invitation to their younger fry. Now and then an elderly stripling would get in among us and be good-naturedly winked at; but our main body were infantry. One unfortunate wight, indeed, who relying upon his dusky suit, had intruded himself into our party, but by tokens was providentially discovered in time to be no chimney-sweeper (all is not soot which looks so), was quoited [25] out of the 50 presence with universal indignation, as not

[22] Cradle.
[23] James White (1775–1820), author of *Original Letters of Sir John Falstaff* (1796). He was a school-fellow of Lamb at Christ's Hospital.
[24] Held at Smithfield on 3 September until its abolition in the middle of the nineteenth century.
[25] Hurled.

having on the wedding garment; [26] but in general the greatest harmony prevailed. The place chosen was a convenient spot among the pens, at the north side of the fair, not so far distant as to be impervious to the agreeable hubbub of that vanity; [27] but remote enough not to be obvious to the interruption of every gaping spectator in it. The guests assembled about seven. In those little temporary parlors three tables were spread with napery, not so fine as substantial, and at every board a comely hostess presided with her pan of hissing sausages. The nostrils of the young rogues dilated at the savor. JAMES WHITE, as head waiter, had charge of the first table; and myself, with our trusty companion BIGOD [28] ordinarily ministered to the other two. There was clambering and jostling, you may be sure, who should get at the first table—for Rochester [29] in his maddest days could not have done the humors of the scene with more spirit than my friend. After some general expression of thanks for the honor the company had done him, his inaugural ceremony was to clasp the greasy waist of old dame Ursula [30] (the fattest of the three), that stood frying and fretting, half-blessing, half-cursing "the gentleman," and imprint upon her chaste lips a tender salute, whereat the universal host would set up a shout that tore the concave, while hundreds of grinning teeth startled the night with their brightness.[31] O it was a pleasure to see the sable younkers [32] lick in the unctuous meat, with *his* more unctuous sayings—how he would fit the tit-bits to the puny mouths, reserving the lengthier links for the seniors—how he would intercept a morsel even in the jaws of some young desperado, declaring it "must to the pan again to be browned, for it was not fit for a gentleman's eating"—how he would recommend this slice of white bread, or that piece of kissing-crust,[33] to a tender juvenile, advising them all to have a care of cracking their teeth, which were their best

[26] I. e., the garb of a sweep. See St. Matthew, 22:11.
[27] The word is used in allusion to Bunyan's Vanity Fair in *The Pilgrim's Progress*.
[28] John Fenwick, who is also mentioned in *The Two Races of Men*.
[29] The Earl of Rochester (1647–1680), a notorious rake.
[30] Lamb took this name from a character in Ben Jonson's *Bartholomew Fair*.
[31] Cf. *Paradise Lost*, I, 541.    [32] Youngsters.
[33] The soft part of a loaf's crust, where loaves have touched each other in baking.

patrimony,—how genteelly he would deal about the small ale, as if it were wine, naming the brewer, and protesting, if it were not good he should lose their custom, with a special recommendation to wipe the lip before drinking. Then we had our toasts—"The King,"—the "Cloth," [34]—which, whether they understood or not, was equally diverting and flattering;—and for a crowning sentiment, which never failed, "May the Brush super- 10 sede the Laurel!" [35] All these, and fifty other fancies, which were rather felt than comprehended by his guests, would he utter, standing upon tables, and prefacing every sentiment with a "Gentlemen, give me leave to propose so and so," which was a prodigious comfort to those young orphans; every now and then stuffing into his mouth (for it did not do to be squeamish on these occasions) indiscriminate pieces of those reek- 20 ing sausages, which pleased them mightily, and was the savoriest part, you may believe, of the entertainment.

> Golden lads and lasses must,
> As chimney-sweepers, come to dust—[36]

JAMES WHITE is extinct, and with him these suppers have long ceased. He carried away with him half the fun of the world when he died—of my world at least. His 30 old clients look for him among the pens; and, missing him, reproach the altered feast of St. Bartholomew, and the glory of Smithfield departed for ever.

## A Dissertation upon Roast Pig

MANKIND, says a Chinese manuscript, which my friend M.[1] was obliging enough to read and explain to me, for the first seventy 40 thousand ages ate their meat raw, clawing or biting it from the living animal, just as they do in Abyssinia to this day. This period is not obscurely hinted at by their great Confucius [2] in the second chapter of his Mundane Mutations, where he designates a kind of golden age by the term Cho-fang,

literally the Cook's holiday. The manuscript goes on to say, that the art of roasting, or rather broiling (which I take to be the elder brother) was accidentally discovered in the manner following. The swine-herd, Ho-ti, having gone out into the woods one morning, as his manner was, to collect mast [3] for his hogs, left his cottage in the care of his eldest son Bo-bo, a great lubberly boy, 10 who being fond of playing with fire, as younkers of his age commonly are, let some sparks escape into a bundle of straw, which kindling quickly, spread the conflagration over every part of their poor mansion, till it was reduced to ashes. Together with the cottage (a sorry antediluvian makeshift of a building, you may think it), what was of much more importance, a fine litter of new-farrowed [4] pigs, no less than nine in number, 20 perished. China pigs have been esteemed a luxury all over the East from the remotest periods that we read of. Bo-bo was in utmost consternation, as you may think, not so much for the sake of the tenement, which his father and he could easily build up again with a few dry branches, and the labor of an hour or two, at any time, as for the loss of the pigs. While he was thinking what he should say to his father, and wringing his 30 hands over the smoking remnants of one of these untimely sufferers, an odor assailed his nostrils, unlike any scent which he had before experienced. What could it proceed from?—not from the burned cottage—he had smelt that smell before—indeed this was by no means the first accident of the kind which had occurred through the negligence of this unlucky young fire-brand. Much less did it resemble that of any known 40 herb, weed, or flower. A premonitory moistening at the same time overflowed his nether lip. He knew not what to think. He next stooped down to feel the pig, if there were any signs of life in it. He burned his fingers, and to cool them he applied them in his booby fashion to his mouth. Some of the crumbs of the scorched skin had come away with his fingers, and for the first time in his life (in the world's life indeed, for before him 50 no man had known it) he tasted—*crackling!* Again he felt and fumbled at the pig. It did not burn him so much now, still he licked his fingers from a sort of habit. The truth at length broke into his slow understanding, that it was the pig that smelt so, and the pig that tasted so delicious; and,

[34] I. e., the profession of chimney-sweepers.
[35] The brush is taken to be emblematic of the chimney-sweeper, as the laurel is emblematic of the poet.
[36] *Cymbeline*, IV, ii, 262–3.
[1] Thomas Manning (1772–1840), who spent some years in China. The central idea of this essay is a commonplace, but there is no reason for doubting Lamb's statement, here and in a letter to Bernard Barton, that he heard it from Manning.
[2] Chinese philosopher of the sixth century B.C. The reference is of Lamb's invention.
[3] Beech nuts.　　[4] Newly born.

surrendering himself up to the newborn pleasure, he fell to tearing up whole handfuls of the scorched skin with the flesh next it, and was cramming it down his throat in his beastly fashion, when his sire entered amid the smoking rafters, armed with retributory cudgel, and finding how affairs stood, began to rain blows upon the young rogue's shoulders, as thick as hailstones, which Bo-bo heeded not any more than if they had been flies. The tickling pleasure which he experienced in his lower regions, had rendered him quite callous to any inconveniences he might feel in those remote quarters. His father might lay on, but he could not beat him from his pig, till he had fairly made an end of it, when, becoming a little more sensible of his situation, something like the following dialogue ensued.

"You graceless whelp, what have you got there devouring? Is it not enough that you have burned me down three houses with your dog's tricks, and be hanged to you, but you must be eating fire, and I know not what—what have you got there, I say?"

"O, father, the pig, the pig, do come and taste how nice the burnt pig eats."

The ears of Ho-ti tingled with horror. He cursed his son, and he cursed himself that ever he should beget a son that should eat burnt pig.

Bo-bo, whose scent was wonderfully sharpened since morning, soon raked out another pig, and fairly rending it asunder, thrust the lesser half by main force into the fists of Ho-ti, still shouting out "Eat, eat, eat the burnt pig, father, only taste—O Lord,"—with suchlike barbarous ejaculations, cramming all the while as if he would choke.

Ho-ti trembled in every joint while he grasped the abominable thing, wavering whether he should not put his son to death for an unnatural young monster, when the crackling scorching his fingers, as it had done his son's, and applying the same remedy to them, he in his turn tasted some of its flavor, which, make what sour mouths he would for a pretense, proved not altogether displeasing to him. In conclusion (for the manuscript here is a little tedious), both father and son fairly sat down to the mess, and never left off till they had despatched all that remained of the litter.

Bo-bo was strictly enjoined not to let the secret escape, for the neighbors would certainly have stoned them for a couple of abominable wretches, who could think of improving upon the good meat which God had sent them. Nevertheless, strange stories got about. It was observed that Ho-ti's cottage was burned down now more frequently than ever. Nothing but fires from this time forward. Some would break out in broad day, others in the night-time. As often as the sow farrowed, so sure was the house of Ho-ti to be in a blaze; and Ho-ti himself, which was the more remarkable, instead of chastising his son, seemed to grow more indulgent to him than ever. At length they were watched, the terrible mystery discovered, and father and son summoned to take their trial at Pekin, then an inconsiderable assize town.[5] Evidence was given, the obnoxious food itself produced in court, and verdict about to be pronounced, when the foreman of the jury begged that some of the burnt pig, of which the culprits stood accused, might be handed into the box. He handled it, and they all handled it, and burning their fingers, as Bo-bo and his father had done before them, and nature prompting to each of them the same remedy, against the face of all the facts, and the clearest charge which judge had ever given,—to the surprise of the whole court, townsfolk, strangers, reporters, and all present—without leaving the box, or any manner of consultation whatever, they brought in a simultaneous verdict of Not Guilty.

The judge, who was a shrewd fellow, winked at the manifest iniquity of the decision: and, when the court was dismissed, went privily, and bought up all the pigs that could be had for love or money. In a few days his Lordship's town house was observed to be on fire. The thing took wing, and now there was nothing to be seen but fires in every direction. Fuel and pigs grew enormously dear all over the district. The insurance offices one and all shut up shop. People built slighter and slighter every day, until it was feared that the very science of architecture would in no long time be lost to the world. Thus this custom of firing the houses continued, till in process of time, says my manuscript, a sage arose, like our Locke,[6] who made a discovery, that the flesh of swine, or indeed of any other animal, might be cooked (*burnt*, as they called it) without the necessity of consuming a whole house to dress it. Then first began the rude form

[5] In England the county town in which sessions of a superior court are held.

[6] English philosopher (1632–1704).

of a gridiron. Roasting by the string, or spit, came in a century or two later, I forget in whose dynasty. By such slow degrees, concludes the manuscript, do the most useful, and seemingly the most obvious arts, make their way among mankind.——

Without placing too implicit faith in the account above given, it must be agreed, that if a worthy pretext for so dangerous an experiment as setting houses on fire (especially in these days) could be assigned in favor of any culinary object, that pretext and excuse might be found in ROAST PIG.

Of all the delicacies in the whole *mundus edibilis*,[7] I will maintain it to be the most delicate—*princeps obsoniorum*.[8]

I speak not of your grown porkers—things between pig and pork—those hobbydehoys [9] —but a young and tender suckling—under a moon old—guiltless as yet of the sty—with no original speck of the *amor immunditiae*,[10] the hereditary failing of the first parent, yet manifest—his voice as yet not broken, but something between a childish treble, and a grumble—the mild forerunner, or *praeludium*,[11] of a grunt.

*He must be roasted.* I am not ignorant that our ancestors ate them seethed, or boiled—but what a sacrifice of the exterior tegument! [12]

There is no flavor comparable, I will contend, to that of the crisp, tawny, well-watched, not over-roasted, *crackling*, as it is well called —the very teeth are invited to their share of the pleasure at this banquet in overcoming the coy, brittle resistance—with the adhesive oleaginous—O call it not fat—but an indefinable sweetness growing up to it—the tender blossoming of fat—fat cropped in the bud—taken in the shoot—in the first innocence—the cream and quintessence of the child-pig's yet pure food——the lean, no lean, but a kind of animal manna [13] or, rather, fat and lean (if it must be so), so blended and running into each other, that both together make but one ambrosian [14] result, or common substance.

Behold him, while he is doing [15]—it seemeth rather a refreshing warmth, than a scorching heat, that he is so passive to. How equally he twirleth round the string! [16]—Now he is just done. To see the extreme sensibility of that tender age, he hath wept out his pretty eyes—radiant jellies—shooting stars—— [17]

See him in the dish, his second cradle, how meek he lieth!—wouldst thou have had this innocent grow up to the grossness and indocility which too often accompany maturer swinehood? Ten to one he would have proved a glutton, a sloven, an obstinate, disagreeable animal—wallowing in all manner of filthy conversation [18]—from these sins he is happily snatched away—

> Ere sin could blight, or sorrow fade,
> Death came with timely care—[19]

his memory is odoriferous—no clown curseth, while his stomach half rejecteth, the rank bacon—no coalheaver bolteth him in reeking sausages—he hath a fair sepulcher in the grateful stomach of the judicious epicure—and for such a tomb might be content to die.

He is the best of sapors.[20] Pine-apple is great. She is indeed almost too transcendent—a delight, if not sinful, yet so like to sinning, that really a tender-conscienced person would do well to pause—too ravishing for mortal taste, she woundeth and excoriateth [21] the lips that approach her—like lovers' kisses, she biteth—she is a pleasure bordering on pain from the fierceness and insanity of her relish—but she stoppeth at the palate—she meddleth not with the appetite [22]—and the coarsest hunger might barter her consistently for a mutton chop.

Pig—let me speak his praise—is no less provocative of the appetite, than he is satisfactory to the criticalness of the censorious palate. The strong man may batten [23] on him, and the weakling refuseth not his mild juices.

Unlike to mankind's mixed characters, a bundle of virtues and vices, inexplicably intertwisted, and not to be unraveled without hazard, he is—good throughout. No part of him is better or worse than another. He helpeth, as far as his little means extend, all around. He is the least envious [24] of banquets. He is all neighbors' fare.

I am one of those who freely and ungrudg-

---

[7] World of eatables.   [8] King of daintics.

[9] Youths between boys and men.

[10] Love of dirt.   [11] Prelude.   [12] Skin.

[13] Animal food sent from heaven. Concerning manna see Exodus, 16:14–15.

[14] In Greek mythology ambrosia was the food of the gods.

[15] Being cooked.

[16] By which he hangs while roasting.

[17] It was once believed that shooting stars left jellies where they fell.

[18] Ways of life.

[19] Coleridge, *Epitaph on an Infant.*

[20] Flavors.   [21] Takes the skin off.

[22] I. e., she gratifies the taste but does not satisfy the stomach.

[23] Feed.

[24] I. e., he gives no guest cause to envy another, for "he is—good throughout."

ingly impart a share of the good things of this life which fall to their lot (few as mine are in this kind) to a friend. I protest I take as great an interest in my friend's pleasures, his relishes, and proper satisfactions, as in mine own. "Presents," I often say, "endear Absents." Hares, pheasants, partridges, snipes, barn-door chickens (those "tame villatic fowl"[25]), capons, plovers, brawn,[26] barrels of oysters, I dispense as freely as I receive them. I love to taste them, as it were, upon the tongue of my friend. But a stop must be put somewhere. One would not, like Lear, "give everything."[27] I make my stand upon pig. Methinks it is an ingratitude to the Giver of all good flavors, to extra-domiciliate, or send out of the house, slightingly (under pretext of friendship, or I know not what), a blessing so particularly adapted, predestined, I may say, to my individual palate——It argues an insensibility.

I remember a touch of conscience in this kind at school. My good old aunt,[28] who never parted from me at the end of a holiday without stuffing a sweetmeat, or some nice thing, into my pocket, had dismissed me one evening with a smoking plum-cake, fresh from the oven. In my way to school (it was over London Bridge) a gray-headed old beggar saluted me (I have no doubt at this time of day that he was a counterfeit). I had no pence to console him with, and in the vanity of self-denial, and the very coxcombry of charity, school-boy-like, I made him a present of—the whole cake! I walked on a little, buoyed up, as one is on such occasions, with a sweet soothing of self-satisfaction; but before I had got to the end of the bridge, my better feelings returned, and I burst into tears, thinking how ungrateful I had been to my good aunt, to go and give her good gift away to a stranger that I had never seen before, and who might be a bad man for aught I knew; and then I thought of the pleasure my aunt would be taking in thinking that I—I myself, and not another—would eat her nice cake—and what should I say to her the next time I saw her— how naughty I was to part with her pretty present—and the odor of that spicy cake came back upon my recollection, and the pleasure and the curiosity I had taken in seeing her make it, and her joy when she sent it to the oven, and how disappointed she would feel that I had never had a bit of it in my mouth

at last—and I blamed my impertinent spirit of alms-giving, and out-of-place hypocrisy of goodness, and above all I wished never to see the face again of that insidious, good-for-nothing, old gray impostor.

Our ancestors were nice[29] in their method of sacrificing these tender victims. We read of pigs whipped to death with something of a shock, as we hear of any other obsolete custom. The age of discipline is gone by, or it would be curious to inquire (in a philosophical light merely) what effect this process might have towards intenerating and dulcifying[30] a substance, naturally so mild and dulcet as the flesh of young pigs. It looks like refining a violet.[31] Yet we should be cautious, while we condemn the inhumanity, how we censure the wisdom of the practice. It might impart a gusto——

I remember an hypothesis, argued upon by the young students, when I was at St. Omer's,[32] and maintained with much learning and pleasantry on both sides, "Whether, supposing that the flavor of a pig who obtained his death by whipping (*per flagellationem extremam*) superadded a pleasure upon the palate of a man more intense than any possible suffering we can conceive in the animal, is man justified in using that method of putting the animal to death?" I forget the decision.

His sauce should be considered. Decidedly, a few bread crumbs, done up with his liver and brains, and a dash of mild sage. But, banish, dear Mrs. Cook, I beseech you, the whole onion tribe. Barbecue[33] your whole hogs to your palate, steep them in shalots,[34] stuff them out with plantations of the rank and guilty garlic; you cannot poison them, or make them stronger than they are—but consider, he is a weakling—a flower.

## The Superannuated Man [1]

*Sera tamen respexit*
*Libertas.*[2]            VIRGIL.
A *clerk* I was in London gay.
            O'KEEFE.[3]

IF PERADVENTURE, Reader, it has been thy lot to waste the golden years of thy life—

[25] Milton, *Samson Agonistes*, l. 1695.
[26] Boar's meat.        [27] *King Lear*, II, iv, 253.
[28] Probably Sarah Lamb, whom Lamb called Aunt Hetty.

[29] Discriminating.        [30] Making tender and sweet.
[31] Cf. *King John*, IV, ii, 10–12.
[32] A Jesuit college for English youths, in France. Lamb, of course, was never there.
[33] To roast whole.        [34] Small onions.
[1] Lamb disguises his real employment, but in other respects this essay is substantially a record of fact.
[2] Liberty, though late, nevertheless visited me (from the first *Eclogue*, l. 27).
[3] John O'Keeffe (1747–1833), a writer of farces

thy shining youth—in the irksome confinement of an office; to have thy prison days prolonged through middle age down to decrepitude and silver hairs, without hope of release or respite; to have lived to forget that there are such things as holidays, or to remember them but as the prerogatives of childhood; then, and then only, will you be able to appreciate my deliverance.

It is now six and thirty years since I took my seat at the desk in Mincing Lane. Melancholy was the transition at fourteen from the abundant playtime, and the frequently intervening vacations of school days, to the eight, nine, and sometimes ten hours' a-day attendance at a counting-house. But time partially reconciles us to anything. I gradually became content—doggedly content, as wild animals in cages.

It is true I had my Sundays to myself; but Sundays, admirable as the institution of them is for purposes of worship, are for that very reason the very worst adapted for days of unbending and recreation. In particular, there is a gloom for me attendant upon a city Sunday, a weight in the air. I miss the cheerful cries of London, the music, and the ballad-singers—the buzz and stirring murmur of the streets. Those eternal bells depress me. The closed shops repel me. Prints, pictures, all the glittering and endless succession of knacks and gewgaws, and ostentatiously displayed wares of tradesmen, which make a weekday saunter through the less busy parts of the metropolis so delightful—are shut out. No book-stalls deliciously to idle over—No busy faces to recreate the idle man who contemplates them ever passing by—the very face of business a charm by contrast to his temporary relaxation from it. Nothing to be seen but unhappy countenances—or half-happy at best—of emancipated 'prentices and little tradesfolks, with here and there a servant maid that has got leave to go out, who, slaving all the week, with the habit has lost almost the capacity of enjoying a free hour; and livelily expressing the hollowness of a day's pleasuring. The very strollers in the fields on that day looked anything but comfortable.

But besides Sundays I had a day at Easter, and a day at Christmas, with a full week in the summer to go and air myself in my native fields of Hertfordshire.[4] This last was a great in-

dulgence; and the prospect of its recurrence, I believe, alone kept me up through the year, and made my durance tolerable. But when the week came round, did the glittering phantom of the distance keep touch with me? or rather was it not a series of seven uneasy days, spent in restless pursuit of pleasure, and a wearisome anxiety to find out how to make the most of them? Where was the quiet, where the promised rest? Before I had a taste of it, it was vanished. I was at the desk again, counting upon the fifty-one tedious weeks that must intervene before such another snatch would come. Still the prospect of its coming threw something of an illumination upon the darker side of my captivity. Without it, as I have said, I could scarcely have sustained my thraldom.

Independently of the rigors of attendance, I have ever been haunted with a sense (perhaps a mere caprice) of incapacity for business. This, during my latter years, had increased to such a degree that it was visible in all the lines of my countenance. My health and my good spirits flagged. I had perpetually a dread of some crisis, to which I should be found unequal. Besides my daylight servitude, I served over again all night in my sleep, and would awake with terrors of imaginary false entries, errors in my accounts, and the like. I was fifty years of age, and no prospect of emancipation presented itself. I had grown to my desk, as it were; and the wood had entered into my soul.

My fellows in the office would sometimes rally me upon the trouble legible in my countenance; but I did not know that it had raised the suspicions of any of my employers, when on the 5th of last month, a day ever to be remembered by me, L——, the junior partner in the firm, calling me on one side, directly taxed me with my bad looks, and frankly inquired the cause of them. So taxed, I honestly made confession of my infirmity, and added that I was afraid I should eventually be obliged to resign his service. He spoke some words of course to hearten me, and there the matter rested. A whole week I remained laboring under the impression that I had acted imprudently in my disclosure; that I had foolishly given a handle against myself, and had been anticipating my own dismissal. A week passed in this manner, the most anxious one, I verily believe in my whole life, when on the evening of the 12th of April, just as I was about quit-

and comic operas. The song has also been attributed to George Colman.

[4] An exaggeration, as Lamb was born and brought up in London, though his mother and grandmother were natives of Hertfordshire.

ting my desk to go home (it might be about eight o'clock) I received an awful summons to attend the presence of the whole assembled firm in the formidable back parlor. I thought, now my time is surely come, I have done for myself, I am going to be told that they have no longer occasion for me. L——, I could see, smiled at the terror I was in, which was a little relief to me,—when to my utter astonishment B——, the eldest partner, began a 10 formal harangue to me on the length of my services, my very meritorious conduct during the whole of the time (the deuce, thought I, how did he find out that? I protest I never had the confidence to think as much). He went on to descant [5] on the expediency of retiring at a certain time of life (how my heart panted!) and asking me a few questions as to the amount of my own property, of which I have a little, ended with a proposal, to which his 20 three partners nodded a grave assent, that I should accept from the house, which I had served so well, a pension for life to the amount of two-thirds of my accustomed salary [6]—a magnificent offer! I do not know what I answered between surprise and gratitude, but it was understood that I accepted their proposal, and I was told that I was free from that hour to leave their service. I stammered out a bow, and at just ten minutes after eight I went home 30 —for ever. This noble benefit—gratitude forbids me to conceal their names—I owe to the kindness of the most munificent firm in the world—the house of Boldero, Merryweather, Bosanquet, and Lacy.[7]

### *Esto Perpetua!* [8]

For the first day or two I felt stunned, overwhelmed. I could only apprehend my felicity; I was too confused to taste it sincerely. 40 I wandered about, thinking I was happy, and knowing that I was not. I was in the condition of a prisoner in the Old Bastile, suddenly let loose after a forty years' confinement. I could scarce trust myself with myself. It was like passing out of Time into Eternity—for it is a sort of Eternity for a man to have his Time all to himself. It seemed to me that I had more time on my hands than I could ever manage. From a poor man, poor in Time, I was sud- 50 denly lifted up into a vast revenue; I could see

no end of my possessions; I wanted some steward, or judicious bailiff, to manage my estates in Time for me. And here let me caution persons grown old in active business, not lightly, nor without weighing their own resources, to forgo their customary employment all at once, for there may be danger in it. I feel it by myself, but I know that my resources are sufficient; and now that those first giddy raptures have subsided, I have a quiet home-feeling of the blessedness of my condition. I am in no hurry. Having all holidays, I am as though I had none. If Time hung heavy upon me, I could walk it away; but I do *not* walk all day long, as I used to do in those old transient holidays, thirty miles a day, to make the most of them. If Time were troublesome, I could read it away, but I do *not* read in that violent measure, with which, having no Time my own but candlelight Time, I used to weary out my head and eye-sight in by-gone winters. I walk, read, or scribble (as now) just when the fit seizes me. I no longer hunt after pleasure; I let it come to me. I am like the man

——That's born, and has his years come to him, In some green desert.[9]

"Years," you will say; "what is this superannuated simpleton calculating upon? He has already told us he is past fifty."

I have indeed lived nominally fifty years, but deduct out of them the hours which I have lived to other people, and not to myself, and you will find me still a young fellow. For *that* is the only true Time, which a man can properly call his own, that which he has all to himself; the rest, though in some sense he may be said to live it, is other people's time, not his. The remnant of my poor days, long or short, is at least multiplied for me threefold. My ten next years, if I stretch so far, will be as long as any preceding thirty. 'Tis a fair rule-of-three sum.

Among the strange fantasies which beset me at the commencement of my freedom, and of which all traces are not yet gone, one was, that a vast tract of time had intervened since I quitted the Counting House. I could not conceive of it as an affair of yesterday. The partners, and the clerks with whom I had for so many years, and for so many hours in each day of the year, been so closely associated—being suddenly removed from them—they seemed as dead to me. There is a fine passage, which may serve to illustrate

---

[5] To discourse at large.

[6] Lamb's salary was £730 the year. He was granted a pension of £450.

[7] Fictitious names, of course, standing for the directors of the East India Company.

[8] May it be eternal.

[9] Thomas Middleton, *Mayor of Queenborough,* I, i, 102–3.

this fancy, in a Tragedy [10] by Sir Robert Howard, speaking of a friend's death:—

——'Twas but just now he went away;
I have not since had time to shed a tear;
And yet the distance does the same appear
As if he had been a thousand years from me,
Time takes no measure in Eternity.

To dissipate this awkward feeling, I have been fain to go among them once or twice since; to visit my old desk-fellows—my co-brethren of the quill—that I had left below in the state militant. Not all the kindness with which they received me could quite re-store to me that pleasant familiarity, which I had heretofore enjoyed among them. We cracked some of our old jokes, but methought they went off but faintly. My old desk; the peg where I hung my hat, were appro-priated to another. I knew it must be, but I could not take it kindly. D——l take me if I did not feel some remorse—beast, if I had not,—at quitting my old compeers, the faithful partners of my toils for six and thirty years, that smoothed for me with their jokes and conundrums the ruggedness of my professional road. Had it been so rugged then after all? or was I a coward simply? Well, it is too late to repent; and I also know that these suggestions are a common fallacy of the mind on such occa-sions. But my heart smote me. I had violently broken the bands betwixt us. It was at least not courteous. I shall be some time before I get quite reconciled to the sep-aration. Farewell, old cronies, yet not for long, for again and again I will come among ye, if I shall have your leave. Farewell, Ch——, dry, sarcastic, and friendly! Do——, mild, slow to move, and gentlemanly! Pl——,[11] officious to do, and to volunteer, good services!—and thou, thou dreary pile, fit mansion for a Gresham or a Whittington [12] of old, stately House of Merchants; with thy labyrinthine pas-sages, and light-excluding, pent-up offices, where candles for one half the year supplied the place of the sun's light; unhealthy contributor to my weal, stern foster of my living, fare-well! In thee remain, and not in the obscure collection of some wandering bookseller, my "works!" [13] There let them rest, as I do from

my labors, piled on thy massy shelves, more MSS. in folio than ever Aquinas left, and full as useful! My mantle I bequeath among ye.

A fortnight has passed since the date of my first communication. At that period I was approaching to tranquillity, but had not reached it. I boasted of a calm indeed, but it was comparative only. Something of the first flutter was left; an unsettling sense of novelty; the dazzle to weak eyes of unac-customed light. I missed my old chains, for-sooth, as if they had been some necessary part of my apparel. I was a poor Car-thusian,[14] from strict cellular discipline sud-denly by some revolution returned upon the world. I am now as if I had never been other than my own master. It is natural to me to go where I please, to do what I please. I find myself at eleven o'clock in the day in Bond Street, and it seems to me that I have been sauntering there at that very hour for years past. I digress into Soho, to explore a book-stall. Methinks I have been thirty years a collector. There is nothing strange nor new in it. I find myself before a fine pic-ture in the morning. Was it ever otherwise? What is become of Fish Street Hill? Where is Fenchurch Street? Stones of old Mincing Lane which I have worn with my daily pil-grimage for six and thirty years, to the foot-steps of what toil-worn clerk are your ever-lasting flints now vocal? I indent the gayer flags of Pall Mall. It is 'Change time, and I am strangely among the Elgin marbles.[15] It was no hyperbole when I ventured to compare the change in my condition to a passing into another world. Time stands still in a manner to me. I have lost all distinction of season. I do not know the day of the week, or of the month. Each day used to be individually felt by me in its reference to the foreign post days; in its distance from, or propinquity to the next Sunday. I had my Wednesday feelings, my Saturday nights' sensations. The genius of each day was upon me distinctly during the whole of it, affecting my appetite, spirits, *etc.* The phantom of the next day, with the dreary five to follow, sat as a load upon my poor Sabbath recreations. What charm has washed the Ethiop white?—What is gone of Black Monday? All days are the same. Sun-day itself—that unfortunate failure of a

[10] *The Vestal Virgin, or the Roman Ladies.* Howard was Dryden's brother-in-law and lived 1626–1698.

[11] These are thought to be John Chambers, Henry Dodwell, and W. D. Plumely.

[12] Sir Thomas Gresham and Sir Richard Whitting-ton.

[13] I. e., the ledgers which Lamb had filled with

accounts. The 1570 edition of the works of St. Thomas Aquinas filled 17 folio volumes.

[14] I. e., a monk.

[15] They were brought to the British Museum in 1816.

holiday as it too often proved, what with my sense of its fugitiveness, and over-care to get the greatest quantity of pleasure out of it— is melted down into a week day. I can spare to go to church now, without grudging the huge cantle [16] which it used to seem to cut out of the holiday. I have Time for everything. I can visit a sick friend. I can interrupt the man of much occupation when he is busiest. I can insult over him with an invitation to take a day's pleasure with me to Windsor this fine May-morning. It is Lucretian pleasure [17] to behold the poor drudges, whom I have left behind in the world, carking and caring; like horses in a mill, drudging on in the same eternal round —and what is it all for? A man can never have too much Time to himself, nor too little to do. Had I a little son, I would christen him NOTHING-TO-DO; he should do nothing. Man, I verily believe, is out of his element as long as he is operative. I am altogether

for the life contemplative. Will no kindly earthquake come and swallow up those accursed cotton mills? Take me that lumber of a desk there, and bowl it down

As low as to the fiends.[18]

I am no longer —— ——, clerk to the firm of, *etc.* I am Retired Leisure. I am to be met with in trim gardens. I am already come to be known by my vacant face and careless gesture, perambulating at no fixed pace nor with any settled purpose. I walk about; not to and from. They tell me, certain *cum dignitate* [19] air, that has been buried so long with my other good parts, has begun to shoot forth in my person. I grow into gentility perceptibly. When I take up a newspaper it is to read the state of the opera. *Opus operatum est.*[20] I have done all that I came into this world to do. I have worked taskwork, and have the rest of the day to myself.

[16] Slice.

[17] The allusion is to a famous passage at the beginning of Bk. II of Lucretius's *On the Nature of Things.* There is a paraphrase of the passage in Bacon's essay *Of Truth.*

[18] *Hamlet*, II, ii, 519.

[19] The allusion is to the phrase *otium cum dignitate*, ease with dignity.

[20] The work has been completed.

# George Noel Gordon, Lord Byron

## 1788 - 1824

One with Byron's ancestry could scarcely have escaped a passionate temperament and a turbulent life; Byron had both. His father, John Byron, was a "dazzlingly handsome and very dissipated guardsman" who came of a family many members of which had led wild lives. In his younger days he had eloped with and later married the Marchioness of Carmarthen, and on her death, shortly after the birth of their daughter Augusta, he had returned to England, badly in debt and avowedly on the lookout for a "Golden Dolly," to use Byron's phrase. He found her in the person of Catherine Gordon of Gight, whom he married in 1784 and then impoverished in the course of paying off his accumulated debts. She was a Scotch girl, not without intelligence, but provincial, capricious, and violent-tempered. "She is very amiable at a distance," her husband later wrote to his sister, "but I defy you and all the Apostles to live with her two months, for if anybody could live with her, it was me." To such parents Byron was born, in London, on 22 January, 1788. A little over three years later his father died in France, at the age of thirty-six, and Byron was left to be brought up solely by his mother. The two lived in Aberdeen until he was ten years old, the boy getting the beginnings of an education there, and witnessing many a scene of violence caused by his mother's temper. In 1798 he became Lord Byron on the death of his grand-uncle at Newstead Abbey. He immediately grew worried because he could discern no change in his appearance now that he was a lord, and he long remained too conscious and too proud of his title. The estate which came to him with his peerage was in bad condition; and, though it yielded much more money than his mother had had even before her marriage, Byron was seldom free from financial difficulties, which were sometimes acute.

In the summer of 1798 Byron and his mother traveled south to Nottingham, and there and in the following year at London ineffectual efforts were made to cure the boy of the lameness with which he had been born. From 1801 to 1805 he was at Harrow, whence he proceeded to Trinity College, Cambridge. There his career was, if not spectacular on a large scale, at least not without excitements and the beginnings of dissipation, love, and poetry. A volume of his poems (Fugitive Pieces) was privately printed in 1806, but all save two copies were destroyed by the author because one of the poems was harshly criticized for its viciousness. Hours of Idleness was published in 1807, and was seized on for castigation by the Edinburgh Review. This attack is chiefly notable because it aroused Byron's anger and led him to retaliate in an effective and immediately successful satire, English Bards and Scotch Reviewers (1809). Meanwhile he had left Cambridge in the summer of 1808 with an M. A. and had taken up residence at Newstead Abbey. In the spring of 1809 he took his seat in the House of Lords, and later in the same year he left England for his Albanian tour, which lasted until 1811. On 3 May, 1810, he swam the Hellespont in one hour and ten minutes, an event which he is said never afterwards to have allowed his friends to forget.

In 1812, the year after his return to England, Byron published the first two cantos of Childe Harold's Pilgrimage and immediately found himself famous. Romantic interest in both the man and his poem became intense, and he was the social sensation of London. Sir Walter Scott had been finding the English public ready for the romantic tale in verse, and Byron now proceeded to outdo Scott—or at least for the time being to make him seem tame and spiritless by comparison—in what he had made his own field. With a rapid succession of exciting oriental tales (The Giaour, 1813; The Bride of Abydos, 1813; The Corsair, 1814; Lara, 1814) he kept up or even increased the interest which

Childe Harold *had aroused. He was beginning to achieve a more than British, a European renown when, at the height of his dazzling fame, he married Miss Anna Isabella Milbanke in January, 1815. In the following December a child, Augusta Ada, was born, and a little over a month afterwards Lady Byron left her husband, never to return. The marriage had proved a miserable failure. It is doubtful if any woman could have retained Byron's wholehearted allegiance for long; certainly, at any rate, none did. He could not do without women or with them, and in this he was at least true to the attitude he took towards the whole life of the world in which he found himself. Moreover, Lady Byron's nature was of an unlikely sort to touch his feelings, while he was almost from the first extraordinarily brutal in his behavior towards her. She had, indeed, from many of his actions, come to doubt his sanity. Immediately after the separation ugly rumors about its crowning cause began to spread through society, and Byron suddenly found himself ostracized by the world— a world, he felt, at least no better than he was —which had recently paid lavish homage to him as its brightest star. Towards the end of April, 1816, he left England, to spend the remainder of his life on the Continent.*

*Byron went first to Geneva, where he spent some months and met Shelley for the first time. Each made a strong impression on the other, and their friendship then, and later in Italy, was important for both of them. During this summer Byron took up* Childe Harold *again, and wrote the third canto. He also wrote* The Prisoner of Chillon *at this time and began* Manfred. *In the fall of 1816 he went down into Italy and settled at Venice. There he finished* Manfred, *wrote* The Lament of Tasso *(both in 1817),* Beppo, *and the fourth canto of* Childe Harold's Pilgrimage *(both in 1818). In 1819 he moved to Ravenna in order to be near the Countess Guiccioli, a young Italian girl with an aged husband. The latter at times gave Byron uncomfortable moments, but in the end proved dangerous to his pocketbook rather than to his person. In the same year the opening cantos of* Don Juan, *Byron's greatest poem, were published, and further portions continued to appear until 1824. In following years Byron wrote a number of dramatic poems—* Cain, Sardanapalus, *and* The Two Foscari *were published in 1821—and his satire,* The Vision of Judgment *(1822). At the same time he was growing restless in Italy. He had been interested in the cause of Italian freedom, but his interest now began to ebb with the failure of some enterprises which he had tried to assist, and his interest in the Guiccioli was also ebbing. He had some thoughts of going to "Bolivar's country," but finally decided to aid the Greeks in their fight against the Turks for independence. He sailed from Genoa in July, 1823, and proceeded to devote both his time and his money to the Greek cause, despite discouragement, hardships, and increasing illness. Finally he succumbed to a fever at Missolonghi, and died there on 19 April, 1824. Nothing, it has been said, so well became his life as the manner of its ending; and the man died, as he had lived and written, in a way that stirred the feeling and fired the imagination of Europe.*

*Byron in a sense courted rivalry with Napoleon in the romantic age when giants walked the earth, and he holds the stage securely still. Not preëminently a lyric poet in an age of great lyrics, he yet had a largeness and force which gave weight to his disillusioned re-action from the European society and politics of his day, and keep alive the poems in which he voiced it. "You have so many 'divine' poems," he exclaimed to his publisher, "is it nothing to have written a human one?" And while other poets were among the clouds, or at least among the mountains, Byron kept his station in the world and wrote, in* Don Juan, *the great epic of modern life.*

*The standard edition of Byron's* Works *is one in thirteen volumes (London, 1898–1904), in which the Poetry is edited by Ernest Hartley Coleridge and the Letters and Journals by Rowland E. Prothero (Lord Ernle). Two additional volumes of letters, edited by John Murray, appeared in 1922 under the title* Lord Byron's Correspondence. *Truman Steffan and Willis W. Pratt have completed a variorum edition of* Don Juan *(Austin, Texas, 1957) in four volumes, including a new critical study of the poem and a volume of notes. Paul Elmer More's fine edition in the Cambridge series notwithstanding, the best one-volume selection for use is now the Reynard Library* Byron: Selections from Poetry, Letters and Journals *(London, 1950), edited by Peter Quennell. Peter Quennell has also edited* Byron, a Self-Portrait: Letters and Diaries, 1798–1824 *(London, 1950) and has written* Byron: the Years of Fame *(London, 1935) and* Byron in Italy *(London, 1941). Studies of other periods in the poet's life include W. A. Borst's* Lord Byron's First Pilgrimage *(New Haven, 1948) and Sir Harold Nicolson's* Byron: The Last

Journey (*London,* 1940). *Ethel Colburn Mayne's biography is a good basic life:* Byron (*New York,* 1924). *More recent is* Byron: a Biography (*New York,* 1957) *by Leslie A. Marchand.*

# Childe Harold's Pilgrimage [1]

## CANTO III

*Afin que cette application vous forçât de penser à autre chose; il n'y a en vérité de remède que celui-là et le temps.*[2]

Lettre du Roi de Prusse à D'Alembert, Sept. 7, 1776.

### 1

Is thy face thy mother's, my fair child!
ADA! sole daughter of my house and heart?[3]
When last I saw thy young blue eyes they
   smiled,
And then we parted,—not as now we part,
But with a hope.—
         Awaking with a start,  5
The waters heave around me; and on high
The winds lift up their voices: I depart,
Whither I know not, but the hour's gone by,
When Albion's lessening shores could grieve
   or glad mine eye.

### 2

Once more upon the waters! yet once
   more!  10
And the waves bound beneath me as a steed
That knows his rider. Welcome to their roar!
Swift be their guidance, wheresoe'er it lead!
Though the strained mast should quiver as a
   reed,
And the rent canvas fluttering strew the
   gale,  15
Still must I on; for I am as a weed,

[1] The first two cantos of *Childe Harold* were published in 1812. They tell of the travels of a disillusioned young man through Portugal, Spain, Albania, and Greece—what he saw and what he felt. Byron did not at the time continue the poem, but took it up again after his final departure from England in the spring of 1816. Canto III was written in Switzerland in May and June, 1816, and was published in the same year. Substantially the third and fourth cantos form a distinct poem. An external connection with the earlier cantos is maintained, but in the intervening years Byron had experienced much and suffered much, and now he speaks almost without disguise in his own person. The present canto tells of Byron's journey through Belgium and up the Rhine into Switzerland, description being mingled with reflective passages inspired by the scenes through which he passed.

[2] So that this employment may force you to think of something else; there is in truth no remedy save that and time.

[3] Byron never saw his daughter after she was five weeks old.

Flung from the rock, on Ocean's foam to
   sail
Where'er the surge may sweep, the tempest's
   breath prevail.

### 3

In my youth's summer I did sing of One,[4]
The wandering outlaw of his own dark mind;
Again I seize the theme, then but begun,  21
And bear it with me, as the rushing wind
Bears the cloud onwards: in that Tale I find
The furrows of long thought, and dried-up
   tears,
Which, ebbing, leave a sterile track behind,
O'er which all heavily the journeying years  26
Plod the last sands of life,—where not a flower
   appears.

### 4

Since my young days of passion—joy, or
   pain,
Perchance my heart and harp have lost a
   string,
And both may jar: it may be, that in vain  30
I would essay as I have sung to sing.
Yet, though a dreary strain, to this I cling,
So that it wean me from the weary dream
Of selfish grief or gladness—so it fling
Forgetfulness around me—it shall seem   35
To me, though to none else, a not ungrateful
   theme.

### 5

He, who grown agéd in this world of woe,
In deeds, not years, piercing the depths of
   life,
So that no wonder waits him; nor below
Can love or sorrow, fame, ambition, strife,  40
Cut to his heart again with the keen knife
Of silent, sharp endurance: he can tell
Why thought seeks refuge in lone caves, yet
   rife
With airy images, and shapes which dwell
Still unimpaired, though old, in the soul's
   haunted cell.  45

### 6

'Tis to create, and in creating live
A being more intense that we endow
With form our fancy, gaining as we give
The life we image, even as I do now.
What am I? Nothing: but not so art thou,
Soul of my thought! with whom I traverse
   earth,  51
Invisible but gazing, as I glow
Mixed with thy spirit, blended with thy birth,
And feeling still with thee in my crushed feel-
   ings' dearth.

### 7

Yet must I think less wildly:—I *have*
   thought  55

[4] I. e., Childe Harold.

Too long and darkly, till my brain became,
In its own eddy boiling and o'erwrought,
A whirling gulf of phantasy and flame:
And thus, untaught in youth my heart to
    tame,
My springs of life were poisoned. 'Tis too
    late!                                        60
Yet am I changed; though still enough the
    same
In strength to bear what time cannot abate,
And feed on bitter fruits without accusing Fate.

8

Something too much of this:—but now 'tis
    past,
And the spell closes with its silent seal.    65
Long absent HAROLD re-appears at last;
He of the breast which fain no more would
    feel,
Wrung with the wounds which kill not, but
    ne'er heal;
Yet Time, who changes all, had altered him
In soul and aspect as in age: years steal  70
Fire from the mind as vigor from the limb;
And life's enchanted cup but sparkles near the
    brim.

9

His had been quaffed too quickly, and he
    found
The dregs were wormwood; but he filled
    again,
And from a purer fount, on holier ground,
And deemed its spring perpetual; but in
    vain!                                        76
Still round him clung invisibly a chain
Which galled for ever, fettering though
    unseen,
And heavy though it clanked not; worn with
    pain,
Which pined although it spoke not, and
    grew keen,                                   80
Entering with every step he took through many
    a scene.

10

Secure in guarded coldness, he had mixed
Again in fancied safety with his kind,
And deemed his spirit now so firmly fixed
And sheathed with an invulnerable mind, 85
That, if no joy, no sorrow lurked behind;
And he, as one, might 'midst the many stand
Unheeded, searching through the crowd to
    find
Fit speculation; such as in strange land
He found in wonder-works of God and Nature's
    hand.                                        90

11

But who can view the ripened rose, nor seek
To wear it? who can curiously behold
The smoothness and the sheen of beauty's
    cheek,

Nor feel the heart can never all grow old?
Who can contemplate Fame through clouds
    unfold                                       95
The star which rises o'er her steep, nor
    climb?
Harold, once more within the vortex, rolled
On with the giddy circle, chasing Time,
Yet with a nobler aim than in his youth's fond
    prime.

12

But soon he knew himself the most unfit 100
Of men to herd with Man; with whom he
    held
Little in common; untaught to submit
His thoughts to others, though his soul was
    quelled
In youth by his own thoughts; still uncom-
    pelled,
He would not yield dominion of his mind 105
To spirits against whom his own rebelled;
Proud though in desolation; which could find
A life within itself, to breathe without man-
    kind.

13

Where rose the mountains, there to him
    were friends,
Where rolled the ocean, thereon was his
    home,                                        110
Where a blue sky, and glowing clime, ex-
    tends,
He had the passion and the power to roam;
The desert, forest, cavern, breaker's foam,
Were unto him companionship; they spake
A mutual language, clearer than the tome 115
Of his land's tongue, which he would oft
    forsake
For Nature's pages glassed by sunbeams on the
    lake.

14

Like the Chaldean, he could watch the stars,
Till he had peopled them with beings bright
As their own beams; and earth, and earth-
    born jars,                                   120
And human frailties, were forgotten quite:
Could he have kept his spirit to that flight
He had been happy; but this clay will sink
Its spark immortal, envying it the light
To which it mounts, as if to break the link
That keeps us from yon heaven which woos us
    to its brink.                               126

15

But in Man's dwellings he became a thing
Restless and worn, and stern and wearisome,
Drooped as a wild-born falcon with clipped
    wing,
To whom the boundless air alone were home:
Then came his fit again, which to o'ercome,
As eagerly the barred-up bird will beat    132
His breast and beak against his wiry dome

Till the blood tinge his plumage, so the heat
Of his impeded soul would through his bosom
eat. 135

### 16

Self-exiled Harold wanders forth again,
With nought of hope left, but with less of
gloom,
The very knowledge that he lived in vain,
That all was over on this side the tomb,
Had made Despair a smilingness assume, 140
Which, though 'twere wild,—as on the
plundered wreck
When mariners would madly meet their
doom
With draughts intemperate on the sinking
deck,—
Did yet inspire a cheer, which he forbore to
check.

### 17

Stop!—for thy tread is on an Empire's dust!
An Earthquake's spoil is sepulchered be-
low! 146
Is the spot marked with no colossal bust?
Nor column trophied for triumphal show?
None; but *the moral's truth* tells simpler so.
As the ground was before, thus let it be;—
How that red rain hath made the harvest
grow! 151
And is this all the world has gained by thee,
Thou first and last of fields! king-making
Victory?

### 18

And Harold stands upon this place of skulls,
The grave of France, the deadly Water-
loo! 155
How in an hour the power which gave an-
nuls
Its gifts, transferring fame as fleeting too!
In "pride of place" here last the eagle [5] flew,
Then tore with bloody talon the rent plain,
Pierced by the shaft of banded nations
through; 160
Ambition's life and labors all were vain;
He wears the shattered links of the world's
broken chain.

### 19

Fit retribution! Gaul may champ the bit
And foam in fetters;—but is Earth more
free?
Did nations combat to make *One* submit; 165
Or league to teach all kings true sovereignty?
What! shall reviving Thraldom again be
The patched-up idol of enlightened days?
Shall we, who struck the Lion down, shall
we
Pay the Wolf homage? proffering lowly
gaze 170

[5] Napoleon. "*Pride of place* is a term of falconry,
meaning the highest pitch of flight" (Byron's note).

And servile knees to thrones? No; *prove* before
ye praise!

### 20

If not, o'er one fallen despot boast no more!
In vain fair cheeks were furrowed with hot
tears
For Europe's flowers long rooted up before
The trampler of her vineyards; in vain, years
Of death, depopulation, bondage, fears, 176
Have all been borne, and broken by the
accord
Of roused-up millions; all that most endears
Glory, is when the myrtle wreathes a sword
Such as Harmodius [6] drew on Athens' tyrant
lord. 180

### 21

There was a sound of revelry by night,
And Belgium's capital had gathered then
Her Beauty and her Chivalry, and bright
The lamps shone o'er fair women and brave
men;
A thousand hearts beat happily; and when 185
Music arose with its voluptuous swell,
Soft eyes looked love to eyes which spake
again,
And all went merry as a marriage bell;
But hush! hark! a deep sound strikes like a
rising knell!

### 22

Did ye not hear it?—No; 'twas but the wind,
Or the car rattling o'er the stony street; 191
On with the dance! let joy be unconfined;
No sleep till morn, when Youth and Pleasure
meet
To chase the glowing Hours with flying
feet—
But hark!—that heavy sound breaks in once
more, 195
As if the clouds its echo would repeat;
And nearer, clearer, deadlier than before!
Arm! Arm! it is—it is—the cannon's opening
roar!

### 23

Within a windowed niche of that high hall
Sat Brunswick's fated chieftain; [7] he did
hear 200
That sound the first amidst the festival,
And caught its tone with Death's prophetic
ear;
And when they smiled because he deemed
it near,
His heart more truly knew that peal too well

[6] Harmodius and Aristogiton, concealing their
swords in branches of myrtle during a religious festival, slew Hipparchus, who with his brother Hippias
tyrannically ruled Athens. After their death and the
later banishment of Hippias the two were praised as
martyred patriots.
[7] Frederick William, Duke of Brunswick.

Which stretched his father on a bloody bier,
And roused the vengeance blood alone could
    quell;                                                206
He rushed into the field, and, foremost fighting,
    fell.

### 24

Ah! then and there was hurrying to and fro,
And gathering tears, and tremblings of
    distress,
And cheeks all pale, which but an hour ago
Blushed at the praise of their own loveli-
    ness;                                                211
And there were sudden partings, such as
    press
The life from out young hearts, and choking
    sighs
Which ne'er might be repeated; who could
    guess
If ever more should meet those mutual eyes,
Since upon night so sweet such awful morn
    could rise!                                          216

### 25

And there was mounting in hot haste; the
    steed,
The mustering squadron, and the clattering
    car,
Went pouring forward with impetuous speed,
And swiftly forming in the ranks of war; 220
And the deep thunder peal on peal afar;
And near, the beat of the alarming drum
Roused up the soldier ere the morning star;
While thronged the citizens with terror
    dumb,
Or whispering, with white lips—"The foe! they
    come! they come!"                                   225

### 26

And wild and high the "Cameron's gather-
    ing" [8] rose!
The war-note of Lochiel, which Albyn's hills
Have heard, and heard, too, have her Saxon
    foes:—
How in the noon of night that pibroch
    thrills,
Savage and shrill! But with the breath which
    fills                                               230
Their mountain-pipe, so fill the mountain-
    eers
With the fierce native daring which instills
The stirring memory of a thousand years,
And Evan's, Donald's fame rings in each
    clansman's ears!

### 27

And Ardennes waves above them her green
    leaves,                                             235
Dewy with nature's tear-drops as they pass,
Grieving, if aught inanimate e'er grieves,

[8] The gathering-cry of the clan Cameron. The
chief of the clan was called Lochiel because this
was the name of his estate.

Over the unreturning brave,—alas!
Ere evening to be trodden like the grass
Which now beneath them, but above shall
    grow                                               240
In its next verdure, when this fiery mass
Of living valor, rolling on the foe
And burning with high hope shall molder cold
    and low.

### 28

Last noon beheld them full of lusty life,
Last eve in Beauty's circle proudly gay, 245
The midnight brought the signal-sound of
    strife,
The morn the marshaling in arms,—the day
Battle's magnificently stern array!
The thunder-clouds close o'er it, which when
    rent
The earth is covered thick with other clay,
Which her own clay shall cover, heaped and
    pent,                                              251
Rider and horse,—friend, foe,—in one red
    burial blent!

### 29

Their praise is hymned by loftier harps than
    mine:
Yet one I would select from that proud
    throng,
Partly because they blend me with his line,
And partly that I did his sire some wrong, 256
And partly that bright names will hallow
    song;
And his was of the bravest, and when
    showered
The death-bolts deadliest the thinned files
    along,
Even where the thickest of war's tempest
    lowered,                                           260
They reached no nobler breast than thine,
    young gallant Howard! [9]

### 30

There have been tears and breaking hearts
    for thee,
And mine were nothing had I such to give;
But when I stood beneath the fresh green
    tree,
Which living waves where thou didst cease
    to live,                                           265
And saw around me the wide field revive
With fruits and fertile promise, and the
    Spring
Came forth her work of gladness to contrive,
With all her reckless birds upon the wing,
I turned from all she brought to those she
    could not bring.                                   270

[9] Major Frederick Howard, Byron's second cousin.
His father, the Earl of Carlisle, was Byron's guardian.
Byron had given a satirical sketch of him in *English
Bards and Scotch Reviewers.*

31

I turned to thee, to thousands, of whom
  each
And one as all a ghastly gap did make
In his own kind and kindred, whom to teach
Forgetfulness were mercy for their sake;
The Archangel's trump, not Glory's, must
  awake        275
Those whom they thirst for; though the
  sound of Fame
May for a moment soothe, it cannot slake
The fever of vain longing, and the name
So honored but assumes a stronger, bitterer
  claim.

32

They mourn, but smile at length; and,
  smiling, mourn;     280
The tree will wither long before it fall;
The hull drives on, though mast and sail be
  torn;
The roof-tree sinks, but molders on the hall
In massy hoariness; the ruined wall
Stands when its wind-worn battlements are
  gone;     285
The bars survive the captive they enthrall;
The day drags through, though storms keep
  out the sun;
And thus the heart will break, yet brokenly
  live on:

33

Even as a broken mirror, which the glass
In every fragment multiplies; and makes 290
A thousand images of one that was,
The same, and still the more, the more it
  breaks;
And thus the heart will do which not for-
  sakes,
Living in shattered guise; and still, and cold,
And bloodless, with its sleepless sorrow
  aches,     295
Yet withers on till all without is old,
Showing no visible sign, for such things are
  untold.

34

There is a very life in our despair,
Vitality of poison,—a quick root
Which feeds these deadly branches; for it
  were     300
As nothing did we die; but Life will suit
Itself to Sorrow's most detested fruit,
Like to the apples on the Dead Sea's shore,
All ashes to the taste: Did man compute
Existence by enjoyment, and count o'er 305
Such hours 'gainst years of life,—say, would he
  name threescore?

35

The Psalmist numbered out the years of
  man:

They are enough; and if thy tale be *true*,
Thou, who didst grudge him even that fleet-
  ing span,
More than enough, thou fatal Waterloo! 310
Millions of tongues record thee, and anew
Their children's lips shall echo them, and
  say—
"Here, where the sword united nations drew,
Our countrymen were warring on that day!"
And this is much—and all—which will not pass
  away.     315

36

There sunk the greatest, nor the worst of
  men,[10]
Whose spirit, antithetically mixed,
One moment of the mightiest, and again
On little objects with like firmness fixed;
Extreme in all things! hadst thou been
  betwixt,     320
Thy throne had still been thine, or never
  been;
For daring made thy rise as fall: thou seek'st
Even now to re-assume the imperial mien,
And shake again the world, the Thunderer of
  the scene!

37

Conqueror and captive of the earth art thou!
She trembles at thee still, and thy wild name
Was ne'er more bruited in men's minds than
  now     327
That thou art nothing, save the jest of Fame,
Who wooed thee once, thy vassal, and be-
  came
The flatterer of thy fierceness, till thou wert
A god unto thyself; nor less the same 331
To the astounded kingdoms all inert,
Who deemed thee for a time whate'er thou
  didst assert.

38

Oh, more or less than man—in high or low,
Battling with nations, flying from the field;
Now making monarchs' necks thy footstool,
  now     336
More than thy meanest soldier taught to
  yield;
An empire thou couldst crush, command,
  rebuild,
But govern not thy pettiest passion, nor,
However deeply in men's spirits skilled, 340
Look through thine own, nor curb the lust
  of war,
Nor learn that tempted Fate will leave the
  loftiest star.

39

Yet well thy soul hath brooked the turning
  tide
With that untaught innate philosophy,

[10] Napoleon.

Which, be it wisdom, coldness, or deep
pride,                                        345
Is gall and wormwood to an enemy.
When the whole host of hatred stood hard
by,
To watch and mock thee shrinking, thou
hast smiled
With a sedate and all-enduring eye;—
When Fortune fled her spoiled and favorite
child,                                        350
He stood unbowed beneath the ills upon him
piled.

### 40

Sager than in thy fortunes; for in them
Ambition steeled thee on too far to show
That just habitual scorn, which could con-
temn
Men and their thoughts; 'twas wise to feel,
not so                                        355
To wear it ever on thy lip and brow,
And spurn the instruments thou wert to use
Till they were turned unto thine overthrow:
'Tis but a worthless world to win or lose;
So hath it proved to thee, and all such lot who
choose.                                       360

### 41

If, like a tower upon a headland rock,
Thou hadst been made to stand or fall alone,
Such scorn of man had helped to brave the
shock;
But men's thoughts were the steps which
paved thy throne,
*Their* admiration thy best weapon shone; 365
The part of Philip's son [11] was thine, not
then
(Unless aside thy purple had been thrown)
Like stern Diogenes to mock at men;
For sceptered cynics earth were far too wide a
den.

### 42

But quiet to quick bosoms is a hell,          370
And *there* hath been thy bane; there is a fire
And motion of the soul which will not dwell
In its own narrow being, but aspire
Beyond the fitting medium of desire;
And, but once kindled, quenchless evermore,
Preys upon high adventure, nor can tire 376
Of aught but rest; a fever at the core,
Fatal to him who bears, to all who ever bore.

### 43

This makes the madmen who have made
men mad
By their contagion: Conquerors and Kings,
Founders of sects and systems, to whom add
Sophists, Bards, Statesmen, all unquiet
things                                        382
Which stir too strongly the soul's secret
springs,

[11] Alexander the Great.

And are themselves the fools to those they
fool;
Envied, yet how unenviable! what stings 385
Are theirs! One breast laid open were a
school
Which would unteach mankind the lust to
shine or rule:

### 44

Their breath is agitation, and their life
A storm whereon they ride, to sink at last,
And yet so nursed and bigoted to strife, 390
That should their days, surviving perils past,
Melt to calm twilight, they feel overcast
With sorrow and supineness, and so die;
Even as a flame unfed, which runs to waste
With its own flickering, or a sword laid by,
Which eats into itself, and rusts ingloriously.

### 45

He who ascends to mountain-tops, shall
find                                          397
The loftiest peaks most wrapped in clouds
and snow;
He who surpasses or subdues mankind,
Must look down on the hate of those be-
low.                                          400
Though high *above* the sun of glory glow,
And far *beneath* the earth and ocean spread,
*Round* him are icy rocks, and loudly blow
Contending tempests on his naked head,
And thus reward the toils which to those sum-
mits led.                                     405

### 46

Away with these! true Wisdom's world will
be
Within its own creation, or in thine,
Maternal Nature! for who teems like thee,
Thus on the banks of thy majestic Rhine?
There Harold gazes on a work divine,         410
A blending of all beauties; streams and dells,
Fruit, foliage, crag, wood, cornfield, moun-
tain, vine,
And chiefless castles breathing stern farewells
From gray but leafy walls, where Ruin greenly
dwells.

### 47

And there they stand, as stands a lofty mind,
Worn, but unstooping to the baser crowd, 416
All tenantless, save to the crannying wind,
Or holding dark communion with the cloud.
There was a day when they were young and
proud;
Banners on high, and battles passed below;
But they who fought are in a bloody shroud,
And those which waved are shredless dust
ere now,                                      422
And the bleak battlements shall bear no future
blow.

### 48

Beneath these battlements, within those
walls,
Power dwelt amidst her passions; in proud
state                                                        425
Each robber chief upheld his arméd halls,
Doing his evil will, nor less elate
Than mightier heroes of a longer date.
What want these outlaws conquerors should
have
But history's purchased page to call them
great?                                                      430
A wider space, an ornamented grave?
Their hopes were not less warm, their souls
were full as brave.

### 49

In their baronial feuds and single fields,
What deeds of prowess unrecorded died!
And Love, which lent a blazon to their
shields,                                                     435
With emblems well devised by amorous
pride,
Through all the mail of iron hearts would
glide;
But still their flame was fierceness, and drew
on
Keen contest and destruction near allied,
And many a tower for some fair mischief
won,                                                         440
Saw the discolored Rhine beneath its ruin run.

### 50

But Thou, exulting and abounding river!
Making thy waves a blessing as they flow
Through banks whose beauty would endure
for ever
Could man but leave thy bright creation so,
Nor its fair promise from the surface mow   446
With the sharp scythe of conflict,—then
to see
Thy valley of sweet waters, were to know
Earth paved like Heaven; and to seem such
to me,
Even now what wants thy stream?—that it
should Lethe [12] be.                                        450

### 51

A thousand battles have assailed thy banks,
But these and half their fame have passed
away,
And Slaughter heaped on high his weltering
ranks;
Their very graves are gone, and what are
they?
Thy tide washed down the blood of yester-
day,                                                          455
And all was stainless, and on thy clear stream

[12] The river of forgetfulness. Were it Lethe, Byron
could drink of it and forget the past, his own included.

Glassed, with its dancing light, the sunny
ray;
But o'er the blackened memory's blighting
dream
Thy waves would vainly roll, all sweeping as
they seem.

### 52

Thus Harold inly said, and passed along, 460
Yet not insensible to all which here
Awoke the jocund birds to early song
In glens which might have made even exile
dear:
Though on his brow were graven lines
austere,
And tranquil sternness, which had ta'en the
place                                                        465
Of feelings fiercer far but less severe,
Joy was not always absent from his face,
But o'er it in such scenes would steal with
transient trace.

### 53

Nor was all love shut from him, though his
days
Of passion had consumed themselves to
dust.                                                        470
It is in vain that we would coldly gaze
On such as smile upon us; the heart must
Leap kindly back to kindness, though dis-
gust
Hath weaned it from all worldings: thus he
felt,
For there was soft remembrance, and sweet
trust                                                        475
In one fond breast,[13] to which his own would
melt,
And in its tenderer hour on that his bosom
dwelt.

### 54

And he had learned to love,—I know not
why,
For this in such as him seems strange of
mood,—
The helpless looks of blooming infancy, 480
Even in its earliest nurture; what subdued,
To change like this, a mind so far imbued
With scorn of man, it little boots to know,
But thus it was; and though in solitude
Small power the nipped affections have to
grow,                                                        485
In him this glowed when all beside had ceased
to glow.

### 55

And there was one soft breast, as hath been
said,
Which unto his was bound by stronger ties
Than the church links withal; and, though
unwed,

[13] In that of Byron's half-sister Augusta.

*That* love was pure, and, far above disguise,
Had stood the test of mortal enmities   491
Still undivided, and cemented more
By peril, dreaded most in female eyes;
But this was firm, and from a foreign shore
Well to that heart might his these absent greet-
    ings pour!      495

### I

The castled crag of Drachenfels [14]
Frowns o'er the wide and winding Rhine,
Whose breast of waters broadly swells
Between the banks which bear the vine,
And hills all rich with blossomed trees,  500
And fields which promise corn and wine,
And scattered cities crowning these,
Whose far white walls along them shine,
Have strewed a scene, which I should see
With double joy wert *thou* with me.   505

### II

And peasant girls, with deep blue eyes,
And hands which offer early flowers,
Walk smiling o'er this paradise;
Above, the frequent feudal towers
Through green leaves lift their walls of gray;
And many a rock which steeply lowers,   511
And noble arch in proud decay,
Look o'er this vale of vintage-bowers;
But one thing want these banks of Rhine,—
Thy gentle hand to clasp in mine!   515

### III

I send the lilies given to me;
Though long before thy hand they touch,
I know that they must withered be,
But yet reject them not as such;
For I have cherished them as dear,   520
Because they yet may meet thine eye,
And guide thy soul to mine even here,
When thou behold'st them drooping nigh,
And know'st them gathered by the Rhine,
And offered from my heart to thine!   525

### IV

The river nobly foams and flows,
The charm of this enchanted ground,
And all its thousand turns disclose
Some fresher beauty's varying round:
The haughtiest breast its wish might bound
Through life to dwell delighted here;   531
Nor could on earth a spot be found
To nature and to me so dear,
Could thy dear eyes in following mine
Still sweeten more these banks of Rhine!  535

### 56

By Coblentz, on a rise of gentle ground,
There is a small and simple pyramid,
Crowning the summit of the verdant mound;

[14] Dragon Rock. One of the Siebengebirge (Seven
Mountains) on the right bank of the Rhine between
Remagen and Bonn.

Beneath its base are heroes' ashes hid,
Our enemy's—but let not that forbid   540
Honor to Marceau! [15] o'er whose early tomb
Tears, big tears, gushed from the rough
    soldier's lid,
Lamenting and yet envying such a doom,
Falling for France, whose rights he battled to
    resume.

### 57

Brief, brave, and glorious was his young
    career,—   545
His mourners were two hosts, his friends and
    foes;
And fitly may the stranger lingering here
Pray for his gallant spirit's bright repose;
For he was Freedom's champion, one of
    those,
The few in number, who had not o'er-
    stepped   550
The charter to chastise which she bestows
On such as wield her weapons; he had kept
The whiteness of his soul, and thus men o'er
    him wept.

### 58

Here Ehrenbreitstein, [16] with her shattered
    wall
Black with the miner's blast, upon her height
Yet shows of what she was, when shell and
    ball   556
Rebounding idly on her strength did light:
A tower of victory! from whence the flight
Of baffled foes was watched along the plain:
But Peace destroyed what War could never
    blight,   560
And laid those proud roofs bare to Summer's
    rain—
On which the iron shower for years had poured
    in vain.

### 59

Adieu to thee, fair Rhine! How long de-
    lighted
The stranger fain would linger on his way!
Thine is a scene alike where souls united  565
Or lonely Contemplation thus might stray;
And could the ceaseless vultures cease to
    prey
On self-condemning bosoms, it were here,
Where Nature, nor too somber nor too gay,
Wild but not rude, awful yet not austere,  570
Is to the mellow Earth as Autumn to the year.

### 60

Adieu to thee again! a vain adieu!
There can be no farewell to scene like thine;
The mind is colored by thy every hue;

[15] Soldier of revolutionary France who fell in battle in 1796, at the age of twenty-seven.
[16] A fortress on the Rhine opposite the mouth of
the Moselle. The French captured it in 1799 and
later destroyed it.

And if reluctantly the eyes resign  575
Their cherished gaze upon thee, lovely
  Rhine!
'Tis with the thankful glance of parting
  praise;
More mighty spots may rise, more glaring
  shine,
But none unite in one attaching maze
The brilliant, fair, and soft,—the glories of old
  days.  580

### 61

The negligently grand, the fruitful bloom
Of coming ripeness, the white city's sheen,
The rolling stream, the precipice's gloom,
The forest's growth, and Gothic walls be-
  tween,
The wild rocks shaped as they had turrets
  been,  585
In mockery of man's art; and these withal
A race of faces happy as the scene,
Whose fertile bounties here extend to all,
Still springing o'er thy banks, though Empires
  near them fall.

### 62

But these recede. Above me are the Alps,  590
The palaces of Nature, whose vast walls
Have pinnacled in clouds their snowy scalps,
And throned Eternity in icy halls
Of cold sublimity, where forms and falls
The avalanche—the thunderbolt of snow!
All that expands the spirit, yet appalls,  596
Gather around these summits, as to show
How Earth may pierce to Heaven, yet leave
  vain man below.

### 63

But ere these matchless heights I dare to
  scan,
There is a spot should not be passed in
  vain,—  600
Morat! [17] the proud, the patriot field! where
  man
May gaze on ghastly trophies of the slain,
Nor blush for those who conquered on that
  plain;
Here Burgundy bequeathed his tombless
  host,
A bony heap, through ages to remain,  605
Themselves their monument;—the Stygian
  coast
Unsepulchered they roamed, and shrieked each
  wandering ghost.

### 64

While Waterloo with Cannæ's [18] carnage
  vies,

---

[17] Name of a town and lake east of Neufchâtel;
the scene of a Swiss victory over Charles the Bold,
Duke of Burgundy, in 1476.
[18] Scene of a Roman defeat by Hannibal in the
Second Punic War.

---

Morat and Marathon twin names shall stand;
They were true Glory's stainless victories,  610
Won by the unambitious heart and hand
Of a proud, brotherly, and civic band,
All unbought champions in no princely cause
Of vice-entailed Corruption; they no land
Doomed to bewail the blasphemy of laws  615
Making kings' rights divine, by some Dra-
conic [19] clause.

### 65

By a lone wall a lonelier column rears
A gray and grief-worn aspect of old days;
'Tis the last remnant of the wreck of years,
And looks as with the wild-bewildered gaze
Of one to stone converted by amaze,  621
Yet still with consciousness; and there it
  stands
Making a marvel that it not decays,
When the coeval pride of human hands,
Leveled Adventicum,[20] hath strewed her sub-
ject lands.  625

### 66

And there—oh! sweet and sacred be the
  name!—
Julia [21]—the daughter, the devoted—gave
Her youth to Heaven; her heart, beneath a
  claim
Nearest to Heaven's, broke o'er a father's
  grave.
Justice is sworn 'gainst tears, and hers would
  crave  630
The life she lived in; but the judge was just,
And then she died on him she could not save.
Their tomb was simple, and without a bust,
And held within their urn one mind, one heart,
  one dust.

### 67

But these are deeds which should not pass
  away,  635
And names that must not wither, though the
  earth
Forgets her empires with a just decay,
The enslavers and the enslaved, their death
  and birth;
The high, the mountain-majesty of worth
Should be, and shall, survivor of its woe,  640
And from its immortality look forth
In the sun's face, like yonder Alpine snow,
Imperishably pure beyond all things below.

---

[19] Draco was an Athenian, said to have been the
first to draw up a code of laws. This code has become proverbial for its severity.
[20] Near Morat, capital of the Roman colony of
Helvetia.
[21] Julia Alpinula, a young Aventian priestess, died
soon after a vain endeavor to save her father, condemned to death as a traitor by Aulus Caecina
(Byron's note).

68

Lake Leman [22] woos me with its crystal face,
The mirror where the stars and mountains
    view                                    645
The stillness of their aspect in each trace
Its clear depth yields of their far height and
    hue:
There is too much of man here, to look
    through
With a fit mind the might which I behold;
But soon in me shall Loneliness renew  650
Thoughts hid, but not less cherished than of
    old,
Ere mingling with the herd had penned me in
    their fold.

69

To fly from, need not be to hate, mankind:
All are not fit with them to stir and toil,
Nor is it discontent to keep the mind    655
Deep in its fountain, lest it overboil
In the hot throng, where we become the
    spoil
Of our infection, till too late and long
We may deplore and struggle with the coil,[23]
In wretched interchange of wrong for wrong
Midst a contentious world, striving where none
    are strong.                            661

70

There, in a moment we may plunge our
    years
In fatal penitence, and in the blight
Of our own soul turn all our blood to tears,
And color things to come with hues of
    Night;                                 665
The race of life becomes a hopeless flight
To those that walk in darkness: on the sea
The boldest steer but where their ports
    invite;
But there are wanderers o'er Eternity
Whose bark drives on and on, and anchored
    ne'er shall be.                        670

71

Is it not better, then, to be alone,
And love Earth only for its earthly sake?
By the blue rushing of the arrowy Rhone,
Or the pure bosom of its nursing lake,
Which feeds it as a mother who doth make
A fair but froward infant her own care,  676
Kissing its cries away as these awake;—
Is it not better thus our lives to wear,
Than join the crushing crowd, doomed to
    inflict or bear?

72

I live not in myself, but I become      680
Portion of that around me; and to me
High mountains are a feeling, but the hum

Of human cities torture: I can see
Nothing to loathe in nature, save to be
A link reluctant in a fleshly chain,     685
Classed among creatures, when the soul can
    flee,
And with the sky, the peak, the heaving
    plain
Of ocean, or the stars, mingle, and not in vain.

73

And thus I am absorbed, and this is life:
I look upon the peopled desert past,     690
As on a place of agony and strife,
Where, for some sin, to sorrow I was cast,
To act and suffer, but remount at last
With a fresh pinion; which I feel to spring,
Though young, yet waxing vigorous as the
    blast                                  695
Which it would cope with, on delighted
    wing,
Spurning the clay-cold bonds which round our
    being cling.

74

And when, at length, the mind shall be all
    free
From what it hates in this degraded form,
Reft of its carnal life, save what shall be  700
Existent happier in the fly and worm,—
When elements to elements conform,
And dust is as it should be, shall I not
Feel all I see, less dazzling, but more warm?
The bodiless thought? the Spirit of each
    spot?                                  705
Of which, even now, I share at times the im-
    mortal lot?

75

Are not the mountains, waves, and skies, a
    part
Of me and of my soul, as I of them?
Is not the love of these deep in my heart
With a pure passion? should I not contemn
All objects, if compared with these? and
    stem                                   711
A tide of suffering, rather than forgo
Such feelings for the hard and worldly
    phlegm
Of those whose eyes are only turned below,
Gazing upon the ground, with thoughts which
    dare not glow?                        715

76

But this is not my theme; and I return
To that which is immediate, and require
Those who find contemplation in the urn,[24]
To look on One,[25] whose dust was once all
    fire,
A native of the land where I respire     720
The clear air for a while—a passing guest,

[22] The Lake of Geneva.          [23] Trouble.

[24] Which contains the ashes of the dead.
[25] Jean Jacques Rousseau (1712–1778). He was
born at Geneva and spent his earliest years there.

Where he became a being,—whose desire
Was to be glorious; 'twas a foolish quest,
The which to gain and keep, he sacrificed all
    rest.

### 77

Here the self-torturing sophist, wild Rous-
    seau,     725
The apostle of affliction, he who threw
Enchantment over passion, and from woe
Wrung overwhelming eloquence, first drew
The breath which made him wretched; yet
    he knew
How to make madness beautiful, and cast
O'er erring deeds and thoughts a heavenly
    hue     731
Of words, like sunbeams, dazzling as they
    passed
The eyes, which o'er them shed tears feelingly
    and fast.

### 78

His love was passion's essence:—as a tree
On fire by lightning, with ethereal flame 735
Kindled he was, and blasted; for to be
Thus, and enamored, were in him the same.
But his was not the love of living dame,
Nor of the dead who rise upon our dreams,
But of ideal beauty, which became     740
In him existence, and o'erflowing teems
Along his burning page, distempered though
    it seems.

### 79

*This* breathed itself to life in Julie,[26] *this*
Invested her with all that's wild and sweet;
This hallowed, too, the memorable kiss     745
Which every morn his fevered lip would
    greet,
From hers, who but with friendship his
    would meet; [27]
But to that gentle touch through brain and
    breast
Flashed the thrilled spirit's love-devouring
    heat;
In that absorbing sigh perchance more
    bless'd     750
Than vulgar minds may be with all they seek
    possessed.

### 80

His life was one long war with self-sought
    foes,
Or friends by him self-banished; for his mind
Had grown Suspicion's sanctuary, and chose,
For its own cruel sacrifice, the kind,     755

[26] Heroine of Rousseau's novel, *Julie, ou la nou-
velle Héloïse.*

[27] This refers to the account in his *Confessions* of
his passion for the Comtesse d'Houdetot, and his
long walk every morning, for the sake of the single
kiss which was the common salutation of French
acquaintance (Byron's note).

'Gainst whom he raged with fury strange and
    blind.
But he was frensied,—wherefore, who may
    know?
Since cause might be which skill could never
    find;
But he was frensied by disease or woe,
To that worst pitch of all, which wears a
    reasoning show.     760

### 81

For then he was inspired, and from him
    came,
As from the Pythian's mystic cave of yore,
Those oracles which set the world in flame,
Nor ceased to burn till kingdoms were no
    more:
Did he not this for France? which lay be-
    fore     765
Bowed to the inborn tyranny of years?
Broken and trembling to the yoke she bore,
Till by the voice of him and his compeers
Roused up to too much wrath, which follows
    o'ergrown fears?

### 82

They made themselves a fearful monument!
The wreck of old opinions—things which
    grew,     771
Breathed from the birth of time: the veil
    they rent,
And what behind it lay, all earth shall view.
But good with ill they also overthrew,
Leaving but ruins, wherewith to rebuild 775
Upon the same foundation, and renew
Dungeons and thrones, which the same hour
    refilled,
As heretofore, because ambition was self-willed.

### 83

But this will not endure, nor be endured!
Mankind have felt their strength, and made
    it felt.     780
They might have used it better, but, allured
By their new vigor, sternly have they dealt
On one another; pity ceased to melt
With her once natural charities. But they,
Who in oppression's darkness caved had
    dwelt,     785
They were not eagles, nourished with the
    day;
What marvel then, at times, if they mistook
    their prey?

### 84

What deep wounds ever closed without a
    scar?
The heart's bleed longest, and but heal to
    wear
That which disfigures it; and they who war
With their own hopes, and have been van-
    quished, bear     791
Silence, but not submission: in his lair

Fixed Passion holds his breath, until the hour
Which shall atone for years; none need de-
    spair:
It came, it cometh, and will come,—the
    power                                       795
To punish or forgive—in *one* we shall be slower.

### 85

Clear, placid Leman! thy contrasted lake,
With the wild world I dwelt in, is a thing
Which warns me, with its stillness, to for-
    sake
Earth's troubled waters for a purer spring. 800
This quiet sail is as a noiseless wing
To waft me from distraction; once I loved
Torn ocean's roar, but thy soft murmuring
Sounds sweet as if a Sister's voice reproved,
That I with stern delights should e'er have been
    so moved.                                  805

### 86

It is the hush of night, and all between
Thy margin and the mountains, dusk, yet
    clear,
Mellowed and mingling, yet distinctly seen,
Save darkened Jura, whose capped heights
    appear
Precipitously steep; and drawing near,  810
There breathes a living fragrance from the
    shore,
Of flowers yet fresh with childhood; on the
    ear
Drops the light drip of the suspended oar,
Or chirps the grasshopper one good-night carol
    more.

### 87

He is an evening reveler, who makes  815
His life an infancy, and sings his fill;
At intervals, some bird from out the brakes
Starts into voice a moment, then is still.
There seems a floating whisper on the hill,
But that is fancy, for the starlight dews 820
All silently their tears of love instill,
Weeping themselves away, till they infuse
Deep into Nature's breast the spirit of her hues.

### 88

Ye stars! which are the poetry of heaven!
If in your bright leaves we would read the
    fate                                        825
Of men and empires,—'tis to be forgiven,
That in our aspirations to be great,
Our destinies o'erleap their mortal state,
And claim a kindred with you; for ye are
A beauty and a mystery, and create  830
In us such love and reverence from afar,
That fortune, fame, power, life, have named
    themselves a star.

### 89

All heaven and earth are still—though not
    in sleep,

But breathless, as we grow when feeling most;
And silent, as we stand in thoughts too
    deep:—                                     835
All heaven and earth are still: From the high
    host
Of stars, to the lulled lake and mountain-
    coast,
All is concentered in a life intense,
Where not a beam, nor air, nor leaf is lost,
But hath a part of being, and a sense  840
Of that which is of all Creator and defense.

### 90

Then stirs the feeling infinite, so felt
In solitude, where we are *least* alone;
A truth, which through our being then doth
    melt,
And purifies from self: it is a tone,  845
The soul and source of music, which makes
    known
Eternal harmony, and sheds a charm
Like to the fabled Cytherea's zone,[28]
Binding all things with beauty;—'twould
    disarm
The specter Death, had he substantial power to
    harm.                                      850

### 91

Not vainly did the early Persian make
His altar the high places, and the peak
Of earth-o'ergazing mountains, and thus take
A fit and unwalled temple, there to seek
The Spirit, in whose honor shrines are weak,
Upreared of human hands. Come, and com-
    pare                                        856
Columns and idol-dwellings, Goth or Greek,
With Nature's realms of worship, earth and
    air,
Nor fix on fond abodes to circumscribe thy
    pray'r!

### 92

The sky is changed!—and such a change!
    Oh night,                                  860
And storm, and darkness, ye are wondrous
    strong,
Yet lovely in your strength, as is the light
Of a dark eye in woman! Far along,
From peak to peak, the rattling crags among
Leaps the live thunder! Not from one lone
    cloud,                                      865
But every mountain now hath found a
    tongue,
And Jura answers, through her misty shroud,
Back to the joyous Alps, who call to her aloud!

### 93

And this is in the night:—Most glorious
    night!
Thou wert not sent for slumber! let me be 870
A sharer in thy fierce and far delight,—

[28] Aphrodite's girdle, which attracted love to its
wearer.

A portion of the tempest and of thee!
How the lit lake shines, a phosphoric sea,
And the big rain comes dancing to the earth!
And now again 'tis black,—and now, the glee       875
Of the loud hills shakes with its mountain-mirth,
As if they did rejoice o'er a young earthquake's birth.

#### 94

Now, where the swift Rhone cleaves his way between
Heights which appear as lovers who have parted
In hate, whose mining depths so intervene
That they can meet no more, though broken-hearted;       881
Though in their souls, which thus each other thwarted,
Love was the very root of the fond rage
Which blighted their life's bloom, and then departed:
Itself expired, but leaving them an age       885
Of years all winters,—war within themselves to wage.

#### 95

Now, where the quick Rhone thus hath cleft his way,
The mightiest of the storms hath ta'en his stand:
For here, not one, but many, make their play,
And fling their thunder-bolts from hand to hand,       890
Flashing and cast around; of all the band,
The brightest through these parted hills hath forked
His lightnings,—as if he did understand,
That in such gaps as desolation worked,
There the hot shaft should blast whatever therein lurked.       895

#### 96

Sky, mountains, river, winds, lake, lightnings! ye!
With night, and clouds, and thunder, and a soul
To make these felt and feeling, well may be
Things that have made me watchful; the far roll
Of your departing voices, is the knoll [29]       900
Of what in me is sleepless,—if I rest.
But where of ye, O tempests! is the goal?
Are ye like those within the human breast?
Or do ye find, at length, like eagles, some high nest?

#### 97

Could I embody and unbosom now       905
That which is most within me,—could I wreak

[29] Knell.

My thoughts upon expression, and thus throw
Soul, heart, mind, passions, feelings, strong or weak,
All that I would have sought, and all I seek,
Bear, know, feel, and yet breathe—into *one* word,       910
And that one word were Lightning, I would speak;
But as it is, I live and die unheard,
With a most voiceless thought, sheathing it as a sword.

#### 98

The morn is up again, the dewy morn,
With breath all incense, and with cheek all bloom,       915
Laughing the clouds away with playful scorn,
And living as if earth contained no tomb,—
And glowing into day: we may resume
The march of our existence: and thus I,
Still on thy shores, fair Leman! may find room       920
And food for meditation, nor pass by
Much, that may give us pause, if pondered fittingly.

#### 99

Clarens! [30] sweet Clarens, birthplace of deep Love!
Thine air is the young breath of passionate thought;
Thy trees take root in Love; the snows above
The very Glaciers have his colors caught,       926
And sun-set into rose-hues sees them wrought
By rays which sleep there lovingly: the rocks,
The permanent crags, tell here of Love, who sought
In them a refuge from the worldly shocks,       930
Which stir and sting the soul with hope that woos, then mocks.

#### 100

Clarens! by heavenly feet thy paths are trod,—
Undying Love's, who here ascends a throne
To which the steps are mountains; where the god
Is a pervading life and light,—so shown       935
Not on those summits solely, nor alone
In the still cave and forest; o'er the flower
His eye is sparkling, and his breath hath blown,
His soft and summer breath, whose tender power
Passes the strength of storms in their most desolate hour.       940

#### 101

All things are here of *him*; from the black pines,

[30] Village on the Lake of Geneva, the scene of meetings of the lovers in Rousseau's *Julie*.

Which are his shade on high, and the loud
    roar
Of torrents, where he listeneth, to the vines
Which slope his green path downward to the
    shore,
Where the bowed waters meet him, and
    adore,           945
Kissing his feet with murmurs; and the wood,
The covert of old trees, with trunks all hoar,
But light leaves, young as joy, stands where
    it stood,
Offering to him, and his, a populous solitude.

102

A populous solitude of bees and birds   950
And fairy-formed and many-colored things,
Who worship him with notes more sweet
    than words,
And innocently open their glad wings,
Fearless and full of life: the gush of springs,
And fall of lofty fountains, and the bend 955
Of stirring branches, and the bud which
    brings
The swiftest thought of beauty, here extend,
Mingling, and made by Love, unto one mighty
    end.

103

He who hath loved not, here would learn
    that lore,
And make his heart a spirit; he who knows
That tender mystery, will love the more; 961
For this is Love's recess, where vain men's
    woes,
And the world's waste, have driven him far
    from those,
For 'tis his nature to advance or die;
He stands not still, but or decays, or grows
Into a boundless blessing, which may vie 966
With the immortal lights, in its eternity!

104

'Twas not for fiction chose Rousseau this
    spot,
Peopling it with affections; but he found
It was the scene which Passion must allot 970
To the mind's purified beings; 'twas the
    ground
Where early Love his Psyche's zone un-
    bound,
And hallowed it with loveliness: 'tis lone,
And wonderful, and deep, and hath a sound,
And sense, and sight of sweetness; here the
    Rhone      975
Hath spread himself a couch, the Alps have
    reared a throne.

105

Lausanne! and Ferney! [31] ye have been the
    abodes

[31] In the former Gibbon had lived, in the latter
Voltaire.

Of names which unto you bequeathed a
    name;
Mortals, who sought and found, by dan-
    gerous roads,
A path to perpetuity of fame:      980
They were gigantic minds, and their steep
    aim
Was, Titan-like, on daring doubts to pile
Thoughts which should call down thunder,
    and the flame
Of Heaven again assailed, if Heaven the
    while
On man and man's research could deign do
    more than smile.      985

106

The one [32] was fire and fickleness, a child
Most mutable in wishes, but in mind
A wit as various,—gay, grave, sage, or wild,—
Historian, bard, philosopher, combined;
He multiplied himself among mankind, 990
The Proteus of their talents: But his own
Breathed most in ridicule,—which, as the
    wind,
Blew where it listed, laying all things
    prone,—
Now to o'erthrow a fool, and now to shake a
    throne.

107

The other, deep and slow, exhausting
    thought,      995
And hiving wisdom with each studious year,
In meditation dwelt, with learning wrought,
And shaped his weapon with an edge severe,
Sapping a solemn creed with solemn sneer;
The lord of irony,—that master-spell,  1000
Which stung his foes to wrath, which grew
    from fear,
And doomed him to the zealot's ready Hell,
Which answers to all doubts so eloquently well.

108

Yet, peace be with their ashes,—for by them,
If merited, the penalty is paid;      1005
It is not ours to judge,—far less condemn;
The hour must come when such things shall
    be made
Known unto all, or hope and dread allayed
By slumber, on one pillow, in the dust,
Which, thus much we are sure, must lie
    decayed,      1010
And when it shall revive, as is our trust,
'Twill be to be forgiven, or suffer what is just.

109

But let me quit man's works, again to read
His Maker's, spread around me, and suspend
This page, which from my reveries I feed,
Until it seems prolonging without end. 1016
The clouds above me to the white Alps tend,

[32] Voltaire.

And I must pierce them, and survey whate'er
May be permitted, as my steps I bend
To their most great and growing region,
 where                                      1020
The earth to her embrace compels the powers
 of air.

### 110

Italia, too! Italia! looking on thee,
Full flashes on the soul the light of ages,
Since the fierce Carthaginian almost won
 thee,
To the last halo of the chiefs and sages   1025
Who glorify thy consecrated pages;
Thou wert the throne and grave of empires;
 still,
The fount at which the panting mind as-
 suages
Her thirst of knowledge, quaffing there her
 fill,
Flows from the eternal source of Rome's im-
 perial hill.                               1030

### 111

Thus far have I proceeded in a theme
Renewed with no kind auspices:—to feel
We are not what we have been, and to deem
We are not what we should be, and to steel
The heart against itself; and to conceal,   1035
With a proud caution, love, or hate, or
 aught,—
Passion or feeling, purpose, grief, or zeal,—
Which is the tyrant spirit of our thought,
Is a stern task of soul:—No matter,—it is
 taught.

### 112

And for these words, thus woven into
 song,                                       1040
It may be that they are a harmless wile,—
The coloring of the scenes which fleet along,
Which I would seize, in passing, to beguile
My breast, or that of others, for a while.
Fame is the thirst of youth, but I am not    1045
So young as to regard men's frown or smile,
As loss or guerdon of a glorious lot;
I stood and stand alone,— remembered or for-
 got.

### 113

I have not loved the world, nor the world me;
I have not flattered its rank breath, nor
 bowed                                       1050
To its idolatries a patient knee,
Nor coined my cheek to smiles, nor cried
 aloud
In worship of an echo; in the crowd
They could not deem me one of such; I
 stood
Among them, but not of them; in a shroud
Of thoughts which were not their thoughts,
 and still could,                            1056

Had I not filed [33] my mind, which thus itself
 subdued.

### 114

I have not loved the world, nor the world
 me,—
But let us part fair foes; I do believe,
Though I have found them not, that there
 may be                                      1060
Words which are things, hopes which will
 not deceive,
And virtues which are merciful, nor weave
Snares for the failing; I would also deem
O'er others' griefs that some sincerely grieve;
That two, or one, are almost what they
 seem,                                       1065
That goodness is no name, and happiness no
 dream.

### 115

My daughter! with thy name this song be-
 gun;
My daughter! with thy name thus much
 shall end;
I see thee not, I hear thee not, but none
Can be so wrapped in thee; thou art the
 friend                                      1070
To whom the shadows of far years extend:
Albeit my brow thou never shouldst behold,
My voice shall with thy future visions blend,
And reach into thy heart, when mine is cold,
A token and a tone, even from thy father's
 mold.                                       1075

### 116

To aid thy mind's development, to watch
Thy dawn of little joys, to sit and see
Almost thy very growth, to view thee catch
Knowledge of objects,—wonders yet to thee!
To hold thee lightly on a gentle knee,       1080
And print on thy soft cheek a parent's kiss,—
This, it should seem, was not reserved for
 me;
Yet this was in my nature: as it is,
I know not what is there, yet something like to
 this.

### 117

Yet, though dull Hate as duty should be
 taught,                                     1085
I know that thou wilt love me; though my
 name
Should be shut from thee, as a spell still
 fraught
With desolation, and broken claim:
Though the grave closed between us,—'twere
 the same,
I know that thou wilt love me; though to
 drain                                       1090
My blood from out thy being were an aim,
And an attainment,—all would be in vain,—

[33] Defiled.

Still thou wouldst love me, still that more than
    life retain.

### 118

The child of love, though born in bitterness,
And nurtured in convulsion! Of thy sire [1095]
These were the elements, and thine no less.
As yet such are around thee, but thy fire
Shall be more tempered, and thy hope far
    higher.
Sweet be thy cradled slumbers! O'er the sea
And from the mountains where I now re-
    spire, [1100]
Fain would I waft such blessing upon thee,
As, with a sigh, I deem thou might'st have
    been to me!

## Maid of Athens, Ere We Part [1]

*Ζωή μου, σᾶς ἀγαπῶ.* [2]

Maid of Athens, ere we part,
Give, oh give me back my heart!
Or, since that has left my breast,
Keep it now, and take the rest!     5
Hear my vow before I go,
*Ζωή μου, σᾶς ἀγαπῶ.*

By those tresses unconfined,
Wooed by each Aegean wind;
By those lids whose jetty fringe
Kiss thy soft cheeks' blooming tinge;     10
By those wild eyes like the roe,
*Ζωή μου, σᾶς ἀγαπῶ.*

By that lip I long to taste;
By that zone-encircled waist;
By all the token-flowers that tell     15
What words can never speak so well;
By love's alternate joy and woe,
*Ζωή μου, σᾶς ἀγαπῶ.*

Maid of Athens! I am gone:
Think of me, sweet! when alone.     20
Though I fly to Istambol, [3]
Athens holds my heart and soul:
Can I cease to love thee? No!
*Ζωή μου, σᾶς ἀγαπῶ.*

## She Walks in Beauty [4]

### I

She walks in beauty, like the night
    Of cloudless climes and starry skies;
And all that's best of dark and bright
    Meet in her aspect and her eyes:
Thus mellowed to that tender light     5
    Which heaven to gaudy day denies.

[1] Written at Athens in 1810, published in 1812.
Supposed to have been addressed to Theresa Macri,
with whose mother Byron lodged while in Athens.
    [2] My life, I love you.     [3] Constantinople.
    [4] Written in 1814; published in 1815.

### II

One shade the more, one ray the less,
    Had half impaired the nameless grace
Which waves in every raven tress,
    Or softly lightens o'er her face;     10
Where thoughts serenely sweet express
    How pure, how dear their dwelling-place.

### III

And on that cheek, and o'er that brow,
    So soft, so calm, yet eloquent,
The smiles that win, the tints that glow,     15
    But tell of days in goodness spent,
A mind at peace with all below,
    A heart whose love is innocent!

## The Destruction of Sennacherib [5]

### I

The Assyrian came down like the wolf on the
    fold,
And his cohorts were gleaming in purple and
    gold;
And the sheen of their spears was like stars on
    the sea,
When the blue wave rolls nightly on deep
    Galilee.

### II

Like the leaves of the forest when Summer is
    green,     5
That host with their banners at sunset were
    seen:
Like the leaves of the forest when Autumn hath
    blown,
That host on the morrow lay withered and
    strown.

### III

For the Angel of Death spread his wings on the
    blast,
And breathed in the face of the foe as he
    passed;     10
And the eyes of the sleepers waxed deadly and
    chill,
And their hearts but once heaved, and for ever
    grew still!

### IV

And there lay the steed with his nostril all wide,
But through it there rolled not the breath of
    his pride;
And the foam of his gasping lay white on the
    turf,     15
And cold as the spray of the rock-beating surf.

### V

And there lay the rider distorted and pale,
With the dew on his brow, and the rust on his
    mail:

[5] Written and published in 1815. See 2 Kings
xviii–xix.

And the tents were all silent, the banners alone,
The lances unlifted, the trumpet unblown. 20

VI

And the widows of Ashur [6] are loud in their
wail,
And the idols are broke in the temple of Baal;
And the might of the Gentile, unsmote by the
sword,
Hath melted like snow in the glance of the
Lord!

## When We Two Parted [7]

When we two parted
In silence and tears,
Half broken-hearted
To sever for years,
Pale grew thy cheek and cold,      5
Colder thy kiss;
Truly that hour foretold
Sorrow to this.

The dew of the morning
Sunk chill on my brow—      10
It felt like the warning
Of what I feel now.
Thy vows are all broken,
And light is thy fame:
I hear thy name spoken,      15
And share in its shame.

They name thee before me,
A knell to mine ear;
A shudder comes o'er me—
Why wert thou so dear?      20
They know not I knew thee,
Who knew thee too well:—
Long, long shall I rue thee,
Too deeply to tell.

In secret we met—      25
In silence I grieve,
That thy heart could forget,
Thy spirit deceive.
If I should meet thee
After long years,      30
How should I greet thee?—
With silence and tears.

## Stanzas for Music [8]

There's not a joy the world can give like that it
takes away,
When the glow of early thought declines in
feeling's dull decay;
'Tis not on youth's smooth cheek the blush
alone, which fades so fast,
But the tender bloom of heart is gone, ere
youth itself be past.

[6] Assyria.
[7] Written in 1808; published in 1816.
[8] Written in 1815; published in 1816.

Then the few whose spirits float above the
wreck of happiness      5
Are driven o'er the shoals of guilt or ocean of
excess:
The magnet of their course is gone, or only
points in vain
The shore to which their shivered sail shall
never stretch again.

Then the mortal coldness of the soul like death
itself comes down;
It cannot feel for others' woes, it dare not
dream its own;      10
That heavy chill has frozen o'er the fountain of
our tears,
And though the eye may sparkle still, 'tis where
the ice appears.

Though wit may flash from fluent lips, and
mirth distract the breast,
Through midnight hours that yield no more
their former hope of rest;
'Tis but as ivy-leaves around the ruined turret
wreath,      15
All green and wildly fresh without, but worn
and gray beneath.

Oh could I feel as I have felt,—or be what I
have been,
Or weep as I could once have wept o'er many
a vanished scene;
As springs in deserts found seem sweet, all
brackish though they be,
So, midst the withered waste of life, those tears
would flow to me.      20

## Stanzas for Music [9]

There be none of Beauty's daughters
With a magic like thee;
And like music on the waters
Is thy sweet voice to me:
When, as if its sound were causing      5
The charméd ocean's pausing,
The waves lie still and gleaming,
And the lulled winds seem dreaming:

And the midnight moon is weaving
Her bright chain o'er the deep;      10
Whose breast is gently heaving,
As an infant's asleep:
So the spirit bows before thee,
To listen and adore thee;
With a full but soft emotion,      15
Like the swell of Summer's ocean.

## Sonnet on Chillon [10]

Eternal Spirit of the chainless Mind!
Brightest in dungeons, Liberty! thou art,

[9] Written and published in 1816.
[10] This and the following poem were written in
June, 1816, immediately after a visit with Shelley
to the Castle of Chillon; published in the same
year. The Castle is on the shore of the Lake of
Geneva at the end farthest from the city of Geneva.

For there thy habitation is the heart—
The heart which love of thee alone can bind;
And when thy sons to fetters are consigned—
    To fetters, and the damp vault's dayless
        gloom,                                         6
    Their country conquers with their martyr-
        dom,
And Freedom's fame finds wings on every wind.
Chillon! thy prison is a holy place,
    And thy sad floor an altar—for 'twas trod, 10
Until his very steps have left a trace
    Worn, as if thy cold pavement were a sod,
By Bonnivard! [11] May none those marks efface!
For they appeal from tyranny to God.


# The Prisoner of Chillon

### I

My hair is gray, but not with years,
    Nor grew it white
    In a single night,
As men's have grown from sudden fears:
My limbs are bowed, though not with toil, 5
    But rusted with a vile repose,
For they have been a dungeon's spoil,
    And mine has been the fate of those
To whom the goodly earth and air
Are banned, and barred—forbidden fare:    10
But this was for my father's faith
I suffered chains and courted death;
That father perished at the stake
For tenets he would not forsake;
And for the same his lineal race        15
In darkness found a dwelling-place;
We were seven—who now are one.
    Six in youth, and one in age,
Finished as they had begun,
    Proud of Persecution's rage;          20
One in fire, and two in field,
Their belief with blood have sealed,
Dying as their father died,
For the God their foes denied;
Three were in a dungeon cast,           25
Of whom this wreck is left the last.

### II

There are seven pillars of Gothic mold,
In Chillon's dungeons deep and old,
There are seven columns, massy and gray,
Dim with a dull imprisoned ray,         30
A sunbeam which hath lost its way,
And through the crevice and the cleft
Of the thick wall is fallen and left;

[11] A Swiss republican (1493–1570) who aided the Genevese in an attempt to free their city from the rule of the Duke of Savoy. He was imprisoned for six years at Chillon, four of which were spent in the cell Byron describes. At the time when Byron wrote his poem he knew little or nothing of the actual history of Bonnivard, so that Byron's "Prisoner" is largely an imaginary character.

Creeping o'er the floor so damp,
Like a marsh's meteor lamp:              35
And in each pillar there is a ring,
    And in each ring there is a chain;
That iron is a cankering thing,
    For in these limbs its teeth remain,
With marks that will not wear away,     40
Till I have done with this new day,
Which now is painful to these eyes,
Which have not seen the sun so rise
For years—I cannot count them o'er,
I lost their long and heavy score,      45
When my last brother drooped and died,
And I lay living by his side.

### III

They chained us each to a column stone,
And we were three—yet, each alone;
We could not move a single pace,        50
We could not see each other's face,
But with that pale and livid light
That made us strangers in our sight:
And thus together—yet apart,
Fettered in hand, but joined in heart,  55
'Twas still some solace, in the dearth
Of the pure elements of earth,
To hearken to each other's speech,
And each turn comforter to each
With some new hope, or legend old,      60
Or song heroically bold;
But even these at length grew cold.
Our voices took a dreary tone,
An echo of the dungeon stone,
    A grating sound, not full and free,  65
    As they of yore were wont to be:
    It might be fancy, but to me
They never sounded like our own.

### IV

I was the eldest of the three,
    And to uphold and cheer the rest     70
    I ought to do—and did my best—
And each did well in his degree.
    The youngest, whom my father loved,
Because our mother's brow was given
To him, with eyes as blue as heaven—    75
    For him my soul was sorely moved;
And truly might it be distressed
To see such bird in such a nest;
For he was beautiful as day—
    (When day was beautiful to me        80
    As to young eagles, being free)—
    A polar day, which will not see
A sunset till its summer's gone,
    Its sleepless summer of long light,
The snow-clad offspring of the sun;     85
    And thus he was as pure and bright,
And in his natural spirit gay,
With tears for nought but others' ills,
And then they flowed like mountain rills,
Unless he could assuage the woe         90
Which he abhorred to view below.

V

The other was as pure of mind,
But formed to combat with his kind;
Strong in his frame, and of a mood
Which 'gainst the world in war had stood, 95
And perished in the foremost rank
    With joy:—but not in chains to pine:
His spirit withered with their clank,
    I saw it silently decline—
    And so perchance in sooth did mine: 100
But yet I forced it on to cheer
Those relics of a home so dear.
He was a hunter of the hills,
    Had followed there the deer and wolf;
    To him this dungeon was a gulf, 105
And fettered feet the worst of ills.

VI

Lake Leman lies by Chillon's walls:
A thousand feet in depth below
Its massy waters meet and flow;
Thus much the fathom-line was sent 110
From Chillon's snow-white battlement,
    Which round about the wave enthralls:
A double dungeon wall and wave
Have made—and like a living grave
Below the surface of the lake 115
The dark vault lies wherein we lay:
We heard it ripple night and day;
    Sounding o'er our heads it knocked;
And I have felt the winter's spray
Wash through the bars when winds were high
And wanton in the happy sky; 121
    And then the very rock hath rocked,
    And I have felt it shake, unshocked,
Because I could have smiled to see
The death that would have set me free. 125

VII

I said my nearer brother pined,
I said his mighty heart declined,
He loathed and put away his food;
It was not that 'twas coarse and rude,
For we were used to hunter's fare, 130
And for the like had little care:
The milk drawn from the mountain goat
Was changed for water from the moat,
Our bread was such as captives' tears
Have moistened many a thousand years, 135
Since man first pent his fellow men
Like brutes within an iron den;
But what were these to us or him?
These wasted not his heart or limb;
My brother's soul was of that mold 140
Which in a palace had grown cold,
Had his free breathing been denied
The range of the steep mountain's side;
But why delay the truth?—he died.
I saw, and could not hold his head, 145
Nor reach his dying hand—nor dead,—
Though hard I strove, but strove in vain,
To rend and gnash my bonds in twain.

He died, and they unlocked his chain,
And scooped for him a shallow grave 150
Even from the cold earth of our cave,
I begged them as a boon to lay
His corse in dust whereon the day
Might shine—it was a foolish thought,
But then within my brain it wrought, 155
That even in death his freeborn breast
In such a dungeon could not rest.
I might have spared my idle prayer—
They coldly laughed, and laid him there:
The flat and turfless earth above 160
The being we so much did love;
His empty chain above it leant,
Such murder's fitting monument!

VIII

But he, the favorite and the flower,
Most cherished since his natal hour, 165
His mother's image in fair face,
The infant love of all his race,
His martyred father's dearest thought,
My latest care, for whom I sought
To hoard my life, that his might be 170
Less wretched now, and one day free;
He, too, who yet had held untired
A spirit natural or inspired—
He, too, was struck, and day by day
Was withered on the stalk away. 175
Oh, God! it is a fearful thing
To see the human soul take wing
In any shape, in any mood:
I've seen it rushing forth in blood,
I've seen it on the breaking ocean 180
Strive with a swoll'n convulsive motion,
I've seen the sick and ghastly bed
Of sin delirious with its dread;
But these were horrors—this was woe
Unmixed with such—but sure and slow: 185
He faded, and so calm and meek,
So softly worn, so sweetly weak,
So tearless, yet so tender, kind,
And grieved for those he left behind;
With all the while a cheek whose bloom 190
Was as a mockery of the tomb,
Whose tints as gently sunk away
As a departing rainbow's ray;
An eye of most transparent light,
That almost made the dungeon bright, 195
And not a word of murmur, not
A groan o'er his untimely lot,—
A little talk of better days,
A little hope my own to raise,
For I was sunk in silence—lost 200
In this last loss, of all the most;
And then the sighs he would suppress
Of fainting nature's feebleness,
More slowly drawn, grew less and less:
I listened, but I could not hear; 205
I called, for I was wild with fear;
I knew 'twas hopeless, but my dread
Would not be thus admonishéd;
I called, and thought I heard a sound—

I burst my chain with one strong bound,   210
And rushed to him:—I found him not,
*I* only stirred in this black spot,
*I* only lived, *I* only drew
The accursèd breath of dungeon-dew;
The last, the sole, the dearest link   215
Between me and the eternal brink,
Which bound me to my failing race,
Was broken in this fatal place.
One on the earth, and one beneath—
My brothers—both had ceased to breathe:   220
I took that hand which lay so still,
Alas! my own was full as chill;
I had not strength to stir, or strive,
But felt that I was still alive—
A frantic feeling, when we know   225
That what we love shall ne'er be so.

  I know not why
  I could not die,
I had no earthly hope but faith,
And that forbade a selfish death.   230

### IX

What next befell me then and there
  I know not well—I never knew—
First came the loss of light, and air,
  And then of darkness too:
I had no thought, no feeling—none—   235
Among the stones I stood a stone,
And was, scarce conscious what I wist,
As shrubless crags within the mist;
For all was blank, and bleak, and gray;
It was not night, it was not day;   240
It was not even the dungeon-light
So hateful to my heavy sight,
But vacancy absorbing space,
And fixedness without a place;
There were no stars, no earth, no time,   245
No cheek, no change, no good, no crime,
But silence, and a stirless breath
Which neither was of life nor death;
A sea of stagnant idleness,
Blind, boundless, mute, and motionless!   250

### X

A light broke in upon my brain,—
  It was the carol of a bird;
It ceased, and then it came again,
  The sweetest song ear ever heard,
And mine was thankful till my eyes   255
Ran over with the glad surprise,
And they that moment could not see
I was the mate of misery;
But then by dull degrees came back
My senses to their wonted track;   260
I saw the dungeon walls and floor
Close slowly round me as before,
I saw the glimmer of the sun
Creeping as it before had done,
But through the crevice where it came   265
That bird was perched, as fond and tame,
  And tamer than upon the tree;
A lovely bird, with azure wings,

And song that said a thousand things,
  And seemed to say them all for me!   270
I never saw its like before,
I ne'er shall see its likeness more:
It seemed like me to want a mate,
But was not half so desolate,
And it was come to love me when   275
None lived to love me so again,
And cheering from my dungeon's brink,
Had brought me back to feel and think.
I know not if it late were free,
  Or broke its cage to perch on mine,   280
But knowing well captivity,
  Sweet bird! I could not wish for thine!
Or if it were, in wingèd guise,
A visitant from Paradise;
For—Heaven forgive that thought! the while   285
Which made me both to weep and smile—
I sometimes deemed that it might be
My brother's soul come down to me;
But then at last away it flew,
And then 'twas mortal well I knew,   290
For he would never thus have flown,
And left me twice so doubly lone,
Lone as the corse within its shroud,
Lone as a solitary cloud,—
  A single cloud on a sunny day,   295
While all the rest of heaven is clear,
A frown upon the atmosphere,
That hath no business to appear
  When skies are blue, and earth is gay.

### XI

A kind of change came in my fate,   300
My keepers grew compassionate;
I know not what had made them so,
They were inured to sights of woe,
But so it was:—my broken chain
With links unfastened did remain,   305
And it was liberty to stride
Along my cell from side to side,
And up and down, and then athwart,
And tread it over every part;
And round the pillars one by one,   310
Returning where my walk begun,
Avoiding only, as I trod,
My brothers' graves without a sod;
For if I thought with heedless tread
My step profaned their lowly bed,   315
My breath came gaspingly and thick,
And my crushed heart felt blind and sick.

### XII

I made a footing in the wall,
  It was not therefrom to escape,
For I had buried one and all   320
  Who loved me in a human shape;
And the whole earth would henceforth be
A wider prison unto me:
No child, no sire, no kin had I,
No partner in my misery;   325
I thought of this, and I was glad,

For thought of them had [1] made me mad;
But I was curious to ascend
To my barred windows, and to bend
Once more, upon the mountains high,    330
The quiet of a loving eye.

### XIII

I saw them, and they were the same,
They were not changed like me in frame;
I saw their thousand years of snow
On high—their wide long lake below,    335
And the blue Rhone in fullest flow;
I heard the torrents leap and gush
O'er channeled rock and broken bush;
I saw the white-walled distant town,
And whiter sails go skimming down;    340
And then there was a little isle,
Which in my very face did smile,
    The only one in view;
A small green isle, it seemed no more,
Scarce broader than my dungeon floor,    345
But in it there were three tall trees,
And o'er it blew the mountain breeze,
And by it there were waters flowing,
And on it there were young flowers growing,
    Of gentle breath and hue.    350
The fish swam by the castle wall,
And they seemed joyous each and all:
The eagle rode the rising blast,
Methought he never flew so fast
As then to me he seemed to fly;    355
And then new tears came in my eye,
And I felt troubled—and would fain
I had not left my recent chain;
And when I did descend again,
The darkness of my dim abode    360
Fell on me as a heavy load;
It was as is a new-dug grave,
Closing o'er one we sought to save,—
And yet my glance, too much oppressed,
Had almost need of such a rest.    365

### XIV

It might be months, or years, or days,
    I kept no count, I took no note,
I had no hope my eyes to raise,
    And clear them of their dreary mote;
At last men came to set me free;    370
    I asked not why, and recked not where;
It was at length the same to me,
Fettered or fetterless to be,
    I learned to love despair.
And thus when they appeared at last,    375
And all my bonds aside were cast,
These heavy walls to me had grown
A hermitage—and all my own!
And half I felt as they were come
To tear me from a second home:    380
With spiders I had friendship made,
And watched them in their sullen trade,
Had seen the mice by moonlight play,

[1] Would have.

And why should I feel less than they?
We were all inmates of one place,    385
And I, the monarch of each race,
Had power to kill—yet, strange to tell!
In quiet we had learned to dwell;
My very chains and I grew friends,
So much a long communion tends    390
To make us what we are:—even I
Regained my freedom with a sigh.

## To Thomas Moore [1]

My boat is on the shore,
    And my bark is on the sea;
But, before I go, Tom Moore,
    Here's a double health to thee!

Here's a sigh to those who love me,    5
    And a smile to those who hate;
And, whatever sky's above me,
    Here's a heart for every fate.

Though the Ocean roar around me,
    Yet it still shall bear me on;    10
Though a desert shall surround me,
    It hath springs that may be won.

Were 't the last drop in the well,
    As I gasped upon the brink,
Ere my fainting spirit fell,    15
    'Tis to thee that I would drink.

With that water, as this wine,
    The libation I would pour
Should be—peace with thine and mine,
    And a health to thee, Tom Moore.    20

## So We'll Go No More A-Roving [2]

So we'll go no more a-roving
    So late into the night,
Though the heart be still as loving,
    And the moon be still as bright.

For the sword outwears its sheath,    5
    And the soul wears out the breast,
And the heart must pause to breathe,
    And Love itself have rest.

Though the night was made for loving,
    And the day returns too soon,    10
Yet we'll go no more a-roving
    By the light of the moon.

[1] Written in 1817 (the first stanza in 1816); published in 1821. This poem and the two following ones were all sent in letters to Thomas Moore (1779–1852), Irish poet and wit, and Byron's friend and biographer.
[2] Written in 1817; published in 1830.

## To Thomas Moore [3]

What are you doing now,
  Oh Thomas Moore?
What are you doing now,
  Oh Thomas Moore?
Sighing or suing now,     5
Riming or wooing now,
Billing or cooing now,
  Which, Thomas Moore?

But the Carnival's coming,
  Oh Thomas Moore!     10
The Carnival's coming,
  Oh Thomas Moore!
Masking and humming,
Fifing and drumming,
Guitarring and strumming,     15
  Oh Thomas Moore!

## Don Juan [1]

### CANTO III

#### The Isles of Greece

##### I

The isles of Greece, the isles of Greece!
  Where burning Sappho loved and sung,

[3] Written in December, 1816, and published in 1830.

[1] Written at intervals from 1818 to 1823 and published in 1819–1824, save for a fragment—the unfinished seventeenth canto—published in 1903. Byron took the name of his hero from a Spanish traditional story concerning the libertinism of one Don Juan Tenorio. But he took little more than the name, practically disregarding both the original Spanish dramatization of the story and the later French and Italian adaptations. When he had finished the first canto Byron wrote to Moore that his new poem was "meant to be a little quietly facetious upon everything." It was that—and more. For, as Byron went on, the work grew upon him and developed into a satirical picture of European aristocracy and politics. When he had completed the fifth canto he wrote to Murray, his publisher: "The 5th is so far from being the last of *D. J.* that it is hardly the beginning. I meant to take him the tour of Europe, with a proper mixture of siege, battle, and adventure, and to make him finish as Anacharsis Cloots in the French Revolution [who was executed in 1794]. To how many cantos this may extend, I know not, nor whether (even if I live) I shall complete it; but this was my notion: I meant to have him a Cavalier Servente in Italy, and a cause for a divorce in England, and a Sentimental 'Werther-faced man' in Germany, so as to show the different ridicules of the society in each of those countries, and to have displayed him gradually *gâté* and *blasé* [growing tainted and dulled] as he grew older, as is natural. But I had not quite fixed whether to make him end in Hell, or in an unhappy marriage, not knowing which would be the severest. The Spanish tradition says

Where grew the arts of war and peace,
  Where Delos rose, and Phoebus sprung! [2]
Eternal summer gilds them yet,     5
  But all, except their sun, is set.

##### II

The Scian and the Teian muse,[3]
  The hero's harp, the lover's lute,
Have found the fame your shores refuse:
  Their place of birth alone is mute     10
To sounds which echo further west
Than your sires' "Islands of the Blest." [4]

##### III

The mountains look on Marathon [5]—
  And Marathon looks on the sea;
And musing there an hour alone,     15
  I dreamed that Greece might still be free;
For standing on the Persians' grave,
I could not deem myself a slave.

##### IV

A king [6] sat on the rocky brow
  Which looks o'er sea-born Salamis;     20
And ships, by thousands, lay below,
  And men in nations;—all were his!
He counted them at break of day—
And when the sun set where were they?

##### V

And where are they? and where art thou,     25
  My country? On thy voiceless shore
The heroic lay is tuneless now—
  The heroic bosom beats no more!
And must thy lyre, so long divine,
Degenerate into hands like mine?     30

##### VI

'Tis something, in the dearth of fame,
  Though linked among a fettered race,
To feel at least a patriot's shame,
  Even as I sing, suffuse my face;

Hell: but it is probably only an Allegory of the other state." In pursuance of this sufficiently elastic plan Byron wrote sixteen cantos, and had begun a seventeenth before he died, leaving the poem unfinished. The passages from the third and fourth cantos here printed are not sufficient to give any fair idea of the variety, the buoyancy, the largeness and force, and the human truth of *Don Juan.* They are justly famous passages, however, and within their limits may at least serve to illustrate some of the salient characteristics of the poem.

[2] Delos was said to have risen from the waves of the Aegean and to have been the birthplace of Phoebus Apollo.

[3] Homer, said to have been born on the island of Scio, and Anacreon, in Teos, Asia Minor.

[4] Mythical islands said to lie in the "Western Ocean," where those favored of the gods dwelt in happiness after death.

[5] The plain where the Greeks under Miltiades defeated the Persians (B.C. 490).

[6] Xerxes, King of Persia, whose fleet was defeated by the Greeks in the battle of Salamis (B.C. 480).

For what is left the poet here? 35
For Greeks a blush—for Greece a tear.

### VII

Must *we* but weep o'er days more blest?
   Must *we* but blush?—Our fathers bled.
Earth! render back from out thy breast
   A remnant of our Spartan dead! 40
Of the three hundred grant but three,
To make a new Thermopylae! [7]

### VIII

What, silent still? and silent all?
   Ah! no;—the voices of the dead
Sound like a distant torrent's fall, 45
   And answer, "Let one living head,
But one arise,—we come, we come!"
'Tis but the living who are dumb.

### IX

In vain—in vain: strike other chords;
   Fill high the cup with Samian wine! [8] 50
Leave battles to the Turkish hordes,
   And shed the blood of Scio's vine!
Hark! rising to the ignoble call—
How answers each bold Bacchanal!

### X

You have the Pyrrhic dance as yet; 55
   Where is the Pyrrhic phalanx gone? [9]
Of two such lessons, why forget
   The nobler and the manlier one?
You have the letters Cadmus [10] gave—
Think ye he meant them for a slave? 60

### XI

Fill high the bowl with Samian wine!
   We will not think of themes like these!
It made Anacreon's song divine:
   He served—but served Polycrates—
A tyrant; but our masters then 65
Were still, at least, our countrymen.

### XII

The tyrant of the Chersonese
   Was freedom's best and bravest friend;
*That* tyrant was Miltiades!
   Oh! that the present hour would lend 70
Another despot of the kind!
Such chains as his were sure to bind.

### XIII

Fill high the bowl with Samian wine!
   On Suli's rock, and Parga's shore, [11]

[7] The mountain pass where three hundred Spartans
heroically opposed the advance of Xerxes' army
(B.C. 480).
[8] Anacreon, the poet of love and wine, lived at
Samos.
[9] The former an ancient war dance, the latter a
military formation used by Pyrrhus.
[10] A legendary figure reputed to have introduced
the alphabet into Greece from Phoenicia.
[11] Places in Albania.

Exists the remnant of a line 75
   Such as the Doric mothers bore;
And there, perhaps, some seed is sown,
   The Heracleidan blood [12] might own.

### XIV

Trust not for freedom to the Franks—
   They have a king who buys and sells; 80
In native swords, and native ranks,
   The only hope of courage dwells:
But Turkish force, and Latin fraud,
Would break your shield, however broad.

### XV

Fill high the bowl with Samian wine! 85
   Our virgins dance beneath the shade—
I see their glorious black eyes shine;
   But gazing on each glowing maid,
My own the burning tear-drop laves,
To think such breasts must suckle slaves. 90

### XVI

Place me on Sunium's marbled steep, [13]
   Where nothing, save the waves and I,
May hear our mutual murmurs sweep;
   There, swan-like, let me sing and die:
A land of slaves shall ne'er be mine— 95
Dash down yon cup of Samian wine!

### 87

Thus sung, or would, or could, or should have
      sung,
   The modern Greek, in tolerable verse; [14]
If not like Orpheus quite, when Greece was
      young,
   Yet in these times he might have done much
      worse: 100
His strain displayed some feeling—right or
      wrong;
   And feeling, in a poet, is the source
Of others' feeling; but they are such liars,
And take all colors—like the hands of dyers.

### 88

But words are things, and a small drop of
      ink, 105
   Falling like dew, upon a thought, produces
That which makes thousands, perhaps millions,
      think; 107
   'Tis strange, the shortest letter which man
      uses
Instead of speech, may form a lasting link

[12] The blood of Hercules.
[13] The promontory of Sunium, at the southern extremity of Attica.
[14] Juan, surviving shipwreck, had found himself on
an island where lived Haidée, the daughter of a
pirate, Lambro, who then was at sea. Juan and
Haidée had fallen in love with each other and, supposing Lambro dead, were expending his treasures
in feasting and revelry. One of Haidée's retinue
was a poet, who is described in stanzas immediately
preceding *The Isles of Greece*, and who "thus sung,
or would, or could, or should have sung."

Of ages; to what straits old Time reduces 110
Frail man, when paper—even a rag like this,
Survives himself, his tomb, and all that's his!

#### 89

And when his bones are dust, his grave a blank,
   His station, generation, even his nation,
Become a thing, or nothing, save to rank    115
   In chronological commemoration,
Some dull MS. oblivion long has sank,
   Or graven stone found in a barrack's station
In digging the foundation of a closet,
May turn his name up, as a rare deposit.    120

#### 90

And glory long has made the sages smile;
   'Tis something, nothing, words, illusion,
      wind—
Depending more upon the historian's style
   Than on the name a person leaves behind:
Troy owes to Homer what whist owes to
      Hoyle: 15                               125
   The present century was growing blind
To the great Marlborough's skill in giving
      knocks,
Until his late Life by Archdeacon Coxe.16

#### 91

Milton's the prince of poets—so we say;
   A little heavy, but no less divine:        130
An independent being in his day—
   Learned, pious, temperate in love and wine;
But his life falling into Johnson's way,17
   We're told this great high priest of all the
      Nine 18
Was whipped at college—a harsh sire—odd
      spouse,                                 135
For the first Mrs. Milton left his house.

#### 92

All these are, *certes*, entertaining facts,
   Like Shakespeare's stealing deer, Lord
      Bacon's bribes;
Like Titus' 19 youth, and Caesar's earliest acts;
   Like Burns (whom Doctor Currie well de-
      scribes);                              140
Like Cromwell's pranks;—but although truth
      exacts
   These amiable descriptions from the scribes,
As most essential to their hero's story,
They do not much contribute to his glory.

#### 93

All are not moralists, like Southey, when  145
   He prated to the world of "Pantisocracy"; 20

---

15 Edmund Hoyle (1672–1769).
16 William Coxe (1747–1828), published his *Life*
of the victor of Blenheim in 1817–1819.
17 When Johnson was writing his *Lives of the
English Poets.*
18 The Nine Muses.
19 Titus Vespasianus, who as a youth learned the
art of forgery.
20 See the introductory note prefixed to Coleridge's

Or Wordsworth unexcised, unhired, who then
   Seasoned his peddler poems with democracy;
Or Coleridge, long before his flighty pen
   Let to the Morning Post its aristocracy; 150
When he and Southey, following the same
      path,
Espoused two partners (milliners of Bath).

#### 94

Such names at present cut a convict figure,
   The very Botany Bay 21 in moral geography;
Their loyal treason, renegado rigor,          155
   Are good manure for their more bare biog-
      raphy;
Wordsworth's last quarto, by the way, is bigger
   Than any since the birthday of typography;
A drowsy, frowsy poem, called the "Excur-
      sion,"
Writ in a manner which is my aversion.     160

#### 95

He there builds up a formidable dyke
   Between his own and others' intellect;
But Wordsworth's poem, and his followers,
      like
   Joanna Southcote's Shiloh 22 and her sect,
Are things which in this century don't strike
   The public mind,—so few are the elect; 166
And the new births of both their stale vir-
      ginities
Have proved but dropsies, taken for divinities.

#### 96

But let me to my story: I must own,
   If I have any fault, it is digression,      170
Leaving my people to proceed alone,
   While I soliloquize beyond expression:
But these are my addresses from the throne,
   Which put off business to the ensuing ses-
      sion:
Forgetting each omission is a loss to        175
The world, not quite so great as Ariosto.

#### 97

I know that what our neighbors call *"lon-
      gueurs,"* 23
   (We've not so good a *word,* but have the
      thing,
In that complete perfection which insures
   An epic from Bob Southey every spring—)
Form not the true temptation which allures 181
   The reader; but 'twould not be hard to bring
Some fine examples of the *epopée,*24
To prove its grand ingredient is *ennui.*

---

poems, above. Southey, Wordsworth, and Coleridge all were believers in democracy in their youth
but became more conservative in their views as they
grew older.
21 Australian penal colony.
22 She had prophesied that on 19 October, 1814,
she would give birth to a second Shilo, or Messiah.
This she failed to do, and shortly afterwards she
died of dropsy.
23 Tedious things.          24 Epic poem.

## 98

We learn from Horace, "Homer sometimes
  sleeps"; [25]                                    185
  We feel without him,—Wordsworth some-
  times wakes,—
To show with what complacency he creeps,
  With his dear "*Wagoners*," around his lakes.
He wishes for "a boat" to sail the deeps—
  Of ocean?—No, of air; and then he makes
Another outcry for "a little boat," [26]          191
And drivels seas to set it well afloat.

## 99

If he must fain sweep o'er the ethereal plain,
  And Pegasus runs restive in his "Wagon,"
Could he not beg the loan of Charles's
  Wain? [27]                                       195
  Or pray Medea for a single dragon?
Or if, too classic for his vulgar brain,
  He feared his neck to venture such a nag on,
And he must needs mount nearer to the moon,
Could not the blockhead ask for a balloon? [20]   200

## 100

"Peddlers," [28] and "Boats," and "Wagons"!
  Oh! ye shades
Of Pope and Dryden, are we come to this?
That trash of such sort not alone evades
  Contempt, but from the bathos' vast abyss
Floats scumlike uppermost, and these Jack
  Cades [29]                                       205
Of sense and song above your graves may
  hiss—
The "little boatman" and his "Peter Bell"
Can sneer at him who drew "Achitophel!"

## 101

T' our tale.—The feast was over, the slaves
  gone,
  The dwarfs and dancing girls had all re-
  tired;                                           210
The Arab lore and poet's song were done,
  And every sound of revelry expired,
The lady and her lover, left alone,
  The rosy flood of twilight's sky admired;—
Ave Maria! o'er the earth and sea,               215
That heavenliest hour of Heaven is worthiest
  thee!

## 102

Ave Maria! blessèd be the hour!
  The time, the clime, the spot, where I so oft

[25] *Ars Poetica*, l. 359.
[26] See the opening stanza of *Peter Bell. The
Wagoner* was a narrative poem of Wordsworth's,
dealing with the inhabitants and landscape of the
English Lake Country.
[27] Charles's wagon, the constellation also known as
the Dipper.
[28] One of the most important figures in Wordsworth's *Excursion* is a peddler.
[29] Jack Cade was the leader of a popular rebellion
in the fifteenth century.

Have felt that moment in its fullest power
  Sink o'er the earth, so beautiful and soft, 220
While swung the deep bell in the distant tower,
  Or the faint dying day-hymn stole aloft,
And not a breath crept through the rosy air,
And yet the forest leaves seemed stirred with
  prayer.

## 103

Ave Maria! 'tis the hour of prayer!               225
  Ave Maria! 'tis the hour of love!
Ave Maria! may our spirits dare
  Look up to thine and to thy Son's above!
Ave Maria! oh that face so fair!
  Those downcast eyes beneath the Almighty
  Dove—                                            230
What though 'tis but a pictured image?—
  strike—
That painting is no idol,—'tis too like.

## 104

Some kinder casuists are pleased to say,
  In nameless print—that I have no devotion;
But set those persons down with me to pray, 235
  And you shall see who has the properest
  notion
Of getting into heaven the shortest way;
  My altars are the mountains and the ocean,
Earth, air, stars,—all that springs from the great
  Whole,
Who hath produced, and will receive the soul.

## 105

Sweet hour of twilight!—in the solitude          240
  Of the pine forest, and the silent shore
Which bounds Ravenna's immemorial wood,
  Rooted where once the Adrian wave flowed
  o'er,
To where the last Caesarean fortress stood,      245
  Evergreen forest! which Boccaccio's lore
And Dryden's lay [30] made haunted ground to
  me,
How have I loved the twilight hour and thee!

## 106

The shrill cicalas, people of the pine,
  Making their summer lives one ceaseless
  song,                                            250
Were the sole echoes, save my steed's and
  mine,
  And vesper bell's that rose the boughs along;
The specter huntsman of Onesti's [31] line,
  His hell-dogs, and their chase, and the fair
  throng
Which learned from this example not to fly       255
From a true lover,—shadowed my mind's eye.

## 107

Oh, Hesperus! thou bringest all good things—
  Home to the weary, to the hungry cheer,

[30] Dryden's *Theodore and Honoria* is an adaptation
of the eighth tale of the fifth day of Boccaccio's
*Decameron*.
[31] Dryden's Theodore is Boccaccio's Onesti.

To the young bird the parent's brooding wings,
　The welcome stall to the o'erlabored steer;
Whate'er of peace about our hearthstone
　clings,　　　　　　　　　　　　　　261
　Whate'er our household gods protect of dear,
Are gathered round us by thy look of rest;
Thou bring'st the child, too, to the mother's
　breast.

### 108

Soft hour! which wakes the wish and melts the
　heart　　　　　　　　　　　　　265
Of those who sail the seas, on the first day
When they from their sweet friends are torn
　apart;
　Or fills with love the pilgrim on his way
As the far bell of vesper makes him start,
　Seeming to weep the dying day's decay; 270
Is this a fancy which our reason scorns?
Ah! surely nothing dies but something mourns!

## CANTO IV

### 12

"Whom the gods love die young" was said of
　yore,[32]
　And many deaths do they escape by this:
The death of friends, and that which slays even
　more—
　The death of friendship, love, youth, all that
　is,
Except, mere breath; and since the silent shore 5
　Awaits at last even those who longest miss
The old archer's shafts, perhaps the early grave
Which men weep over may be meant to save.

### 13

Haidée and Juan thought not of the dead.
　The heavens, and earth, and air, seemed
　made for them:　　　　　　　　10
They found no fault with Time, save that he
　fled;
　They saw not in themselves aught to con-
　demn;
Each was the other's mirror, and but read
　Joy sparkling in their dark eyes like a gem,
And knew such brightness was but the reflec-
　tion　　　　　　　　　　　　15
Of their exchanging glances of affection.

### 14

The gentle pressure, and the thrilling touch,
　The least glance better understood than
　words,
Which still said all, and ne'er could say too
　much;
　A language, too, but like to that of birds, 20
Known but to them, at least appearing such
　As but to lovers a true sense affords;

──────────
[32] The statement is found among the fragments of
Menander, in Plautus's *Bacchides*, IV, vii, 18–19,
and elsewhere.

Sweet playful phrases, which would seem
　absurd
To those who have ceased to hear such, or ne'er
　heard.

### 15

All these were theirs, for they were children
　still,　　　　　　　　　　　　25
　And children still they should have ever been;
They were not made in the real world to fill
　A busy character in the dull scene,
But like two beings born from out a rill,
　A nymph and her belovéd, all unseen　30
To pass their lives in fountains and on flowers,
And never know the weight of human hours.

### 16

Moons changing had rolled on, and changeless
　found
　Those their bright rise had lighted to such
　joys
As rarely they beheld throughout their round;
　And these were not of the vain kind which
　cloys,　　　　　　　　　　　36
For theirs were buoyant spirits, never bound
　By the mere senses; and that which destroys
Most love, possession, unto them appeared
A thing which each endearment more en-
　deared.　　　　　　　　　　　40

### 17

Oh beautiful! and rare as beautiful!
　But theirs was love in which the mind de-
　lights
To lose itself, when the old world grows dull,
　And we are sick of its hack sounds and sights,
Intrigues, adventures of the common school,
　Its petty passions, marriages, and flights, 46
Where Hymen's torch but brands one strum-
　pet more,
Whose husband only knows her not a whore.

### 18

Hard words—harsh truth! a truth which many
　know.
　Enough.—The faithful and the fairy pair, 50
Who never found a single hour too slow,
　What was it made them thus exempt from
　care?
Young innate feelings all have felt below,
　Which perish in the rest, but in them were
Inherent—what we mortals call romantic, 55
And always envy, though we deem it frantic.

### 19

This is in others a factitious state,
　An opium dream of too much youth and
　reading,
But was in them their nature or their fate:
　No novels e'er had set their young hearts
　bleeding,　　　　　　　　　　60
For Haidée's knowledge was by no means great,
　And Juan was a boy of saintly breeding;

So that there was no reason for their loves
More than for those of nightingales or doves.

### 20

They gazed upon the sunset; 'tis an hour   65
  Dear unto all, but dearest to *their* eyes,
For it had made them what they were: the
  power
  Of love had first o'erwhelmed them from
  such skies,
When happiness had been their only dower,
  And twilight saw them linked in passion's
  ties;   70
Charmed with each other, all things charmed
  that brought
The past still welcome as the present thought.

### 21

I know not why, but in that hour to-night,
  Even as they gazed, a sudden tremor came,
And swept, as 'twere, across their hearts' delight,
  Like the wind o'er a harp-string, or a flame,   76
When one is shook in sound, and one in sight.
  And thus some boding flashed through either
  frame,
And called from Juan's breast a faint low sigh,
While one new tear arose in Haidée's eye.   80

### 22

That large black prophet eye seemed to dilate
  And follow far the disappearing sun,
As if their last day of a happy date
  With his broad, bright, and dropping orb
  were gone.
Juan gazed on her as to ask his fate—   85
  He felt a grief, but knowing cause for none,
His glance inquired of hers for some excuse
For feelings causeless, or at least abstruse.

### 23

She turned to him, and smiled, but in that sort
  Which makes not others smile; then turned
  aside:   90
Whatever feeling shook her, it seemed short,
  And mastered by her wisdom or her pride;
When Juan spoke, too—it might be in sport—
  Of this their mutual feeling, she replied—
"If it should be so,—but—it cannot be—   95
Or I at least shall not survive to see."

### 24

Juan would question further, but she pressed
  His lips to hers, and silenced them with this,
And then dismissed the omen from her breast,
  Defying augury with that fond kiss;   100
And no doubt of all methods 'tis the best:
  Some people prefer wine—'tis not amiss;
I have tried both; so those who would a part
  take
May choose between the headache and the
  heartache.

### 25

One of the two, according to your choice,   105
  Woman or wine, you'll have to undergo;
Both maladies are taxes on our joys:
  But which to choose, I really hardly know;
And if I had to give a casting voice,   109
  For both sides I could many reasons show,
And then decide, without great wrong to either,
It were much better to have both than neither.

### 26

Juan and Haidée gazed upon each other
  With swimming looks of speechless tender-
  ness,
Which mixed all feelings, friend, child, lover,
  brother;   115
  All that the best can mingle and express
When two pure hearts are poured in one an-
  other,
  And love too much, and yet cannot love less;
But almost sanctify the sweet excess
By the immortal wish and power to bless.   120

### 27

Mixed in each other's arms, and heart in heart,
  Why did they not then die?—they had lived
  too long
Should an hour come to bid them breathe
  apart;
  Years could but bring them cruel things or
  wrong;
The world was not for them, nor the world's
  art   125
  For beings passionate as Sappho's song;
Love was born *with* them, *in* them, so intense,
It was their very spirit—not a sense.

### 28

They should have lived together deep in woods,
  Unseen as sings the nightingale; they were   130
Unfit to mix in these thick solitudes
  Called social, haunts of hate, and vice, and
  care;
How lonely every freeborn creature broods!
  The sweetest song-birds nestle in a pair;
The eagle soars alone; the gull and crow   135
Flock o'er their carrion, just like men below.

### 29

Now pillowed cheek to cheek, in loving sleep,
  Haidée and Juan their siesta took,
A gentle slumber, but it was not deep,
  For ever and anon a something shook   140
Juan, and shuddering o'er his frame would
  creep;
  And Haidée's sweet lips murmured like a
  brook
A wordless music, and her face so fair
Stirred with her dream, as rose-leaves with the
  air.

30

Or as the stirring of a deep clear stream    145
  Within an Alpine hollow, when the wind
Walks o'er it, was she shaken by the dream,
  The mystical usurper of the mind—
O'erpowering us to be whate'er may seem
    Good to the soul which we no more can
    bind:    150
Strange state of being! (for 'tis still to be)
Senseless to feel, and with sealed eyes to see.

31

She dreamed of being alone on the sea-shore,
  Chained to a rock; she knew not how, but
  stir
She could not from the spot, and the loud roar
  Grew, and each wave rose roughly, threaten-
    ing her;    156
And o'er her upper lip they seemed to pour,
  Until she sobbed for breath, and soon they
  were
Foaming o'er her lone head, so fierce and
  high—
Each broke to drown her, yet she could not
  die.    160

32

Anon—she was released, and then she strayed
  O'er the sharp shingles with her bleeding
  feet,
And stumbled almost every step she made;
  And something rolled before her in a sheet,
Which she must still pursue howe'er afraid:    165
  'Twas white and indistinct, nor stopped to
  meet
Her glance nor grasp, for still she gazed and
  grasped,
And ran, but it escaped her as she clasped.

33

The dream changed:—in a cave she stood, its
  walls
  Were hung with marble icicles; the work    170
Of ages on its water-fretted halls,
  Where waves might wash, and seals might
  breed and lurk;
Her hair was dripping, and the very balls
  Of her black eyes seemed turned to tears, and
  mirk
The sharp rocks looked below each drop they
  caught,    175
Which froze to marble as it fell,—she thought.

34

And wet, and cold, and lifeless at her feet,
  Pale as the foam that frothed on his dead
  brow,
Which she essayed in vain to clear (how sweet
  Were once her cares, how idle seemed they
  now!),    180
Lay Juan, nor could aught renew the beat

Of his quenched heart; and the sea dirges
  low
Rang in her sad ears like a mermaid's song,
And that brief dream appeared a life too long.

35

And gazing on the dead, she thought his face
  Faded, or altered into something new—    186
Like to her father's features, till each trace
  More like and like to Lambro's aspect grew—
With all his keen worn look and Grecian grace;
  And starting, she awoke, and what to view?
Oh! Powers of Heaven! what dark eye meets
  she there?    191
'Tis—'tis her father's—fixed upon the pair!

36

Then shrieking, she arose, and shrieking fell,
  With joy and sorrow, hope and fear, to see
Him whom she deemed a habitant where dwell
  The ocean-buried, risen from death, to be    196
Perchance the death of one she loved too well:
  Dear as her father had been to Haidée,
It was a moment of that awful kind——
I have seen such—but must not call to mind.

37

Up Juan sprang to Haidée's bitter shriek,    201
  And caught her falling, and from off the wall
Snatched down his saber, in hot haste to wreak
  Vengeance on him who was the cause of all:
Then Lambro, who till now forebore to speak,
  Smiled scornfully, and said, "Within my
  call,    206
A thousand scimitars await the word;
Put up, young man, put up your silly sword."

38

And Haidée clung around him; "Juan, 'tis—
  'Tis Lambro—'tis my father! Kneel with
  me—    210
He will forgive us—yes—it must be—yes.
  Oh! dearest father, in this agony
Of pleasure and of pain—even while I kiss
  Thy garment's hem with transport, can it be
That doubt should mingle with my filial
  joy?    215
Deal with me as thou wilt, but spare this boy."

39

High and inscrutable the old man stood,
  Calm in his voice, and calm within his eye—
Not always signs with him of calmest mood:
  He looked upon her, but gave no reply;    220
Then turned to Juan, in whose cheek the blood
  Oft came and went, as there resolved to die;
In arms, at least, he stood, in act to spring
On the first foe whom Lambro's call might
  bring.

40

"Young man, your sword"; so Lambro once
  more said:    225

Juan replied, "Not while this arm is free."
The old man's cheek grew pale, but not with
    dread,
    And drawing from his belt a pistol, he
Replied, "Your blood be then on your own
    head."
Then looked close at the flint, as if to see 230
'Twas fresh—for he had lately used the lock—
And next proceeded quietly to cock.

### 41

It has a strange quick jar upon the ear,
    That cocking of a pistol, when you know
A moment more will bring the sight to bear 235
    Upon your person, twelve yards off, or so;
A gentlemanly distance, not too near,
    If you have got a former friend for foe;
But after being fired at once or twice,
The ear becomes more Irish, and less nice. 240

### 42

Lambro presented, and one instant more
    Had stopped this Canto, and Don Juan's
    breath,
When Haidée threw herself her boy before;
    Stern as her sire: "On me," she cried, "let
    death
Descend—the fault is mine; this fatal shore 245
    He found—but sought not. I have pledged
    my faith;
I love him—I will die with him: I knew
Your nature's firmness—know your daughter's
    too."

### 43

A minute past, and she had been all tears,
    And tenderness, and infancy; but now    250
She stood as one who championed human
    fears—
Pale, statue-like, and stern, she wooed the
    blow;
And tall beyond her sex, and their compeers,
    She drew up to her height, as if to show
A fairer mark; and with a fixed eye scanned 255
Her father's face—but never stopped his hand.

### 44

He gazed on her, and she on him; 'twas strange
    How like they looked! the expression was the
    same;
Serenely savage, with a little change
    In the large dark eye's mutual-darted flame;
For she, too, was as one who could avenge, 261
    If cause should be—a lioness, though tame.
Her father's blood before her father's face
Boiled up, and proved her truly of his race.

### 45

I said they were alike, their features and    265
    Their stature, differing but in sex and years:
Even to the delicacy of their hand
There was resemblance, such as true blood
    wears;

And now to see them, thus divided, stand
    In fixed ferocity, when joyous tears    270
And sweet sensations should have welcomed
    both,
Shows what the passions are in their full
    growth.

### 46

The father paused a moment, then withdrew
    His weapon, and replaced it; but stood still,
And looking on her, as to look her through, 275
    "Not I," he said, "have sought this stranger's
    ill;
Not I have made this desolation: few
    Would bear such outrage, and forbear to kill;
But I must do my duty—how thou hast
Done thine, the present vouches for the past.

### 47

"Let him disarm, or, by my father's head, 281
    His own shall roll before you like a ball!"
He raised his whistle as the word he said,
    And blew; another answered to the call,
And rushing in disorderly, though led,    285
    And armed from boot to turban, one and all,
Some twenty of his train came, rank on rank;
He gave the word, "Arrest or slay the Frank."

### 48

Then, with a sudden movement, he withdrew
    His daughter; while compressed within his
    clasp,    290
'Twixt her and Juan interposed the crew;
    In vain she struggled in her father's grasp—
His arms were like a serpent's coil: then flew
    Upon their prey, as darts an angry asp,
The file of pirates—save the foremost, who 295
Had fallen, with his right shoulder half cut
    through.

### 49

The second had his cheek laid open; but
    The third, a wary, cool old sworder, took
The blows upon his cutlass, and then put    299
    His own well in; so well, ere you could look,
His man was floored, and helpless at his foot,
    With the blood running like a little brook
From two smart saber gashes, deep and red—
One on the arm, the other on the head.

### 50

And then they bound him where he fell, and
    bore    305
    Juan from the apartment; with a sign
Old Lambro bade them take him to the shore,
    Where lay some ships which were to sail at
    nine.
They laid him in a boat, and plied the oar
    Until they reached some galliots,[33] placed in
    line;    310
On board of one of these, and under hatches,

[33] Small swift galleys.

They stowed him, with strict orders to the
watches.

### 51

The world is full of strange vicissitudes,
  And here was one exceedingly unpleasant:
A gentleman so rich in the world's goods,    315
  Handsome and young, enjoying all the present,
Just at the very time when he least broods
  On such a thing, is suddenly to sea sent,
Wounded and chained, so that he cannot move,
And all because a lady fell in love.    320

### 52

Here I must leave him, for I grow pathetic,
  Moved by the Chinese nymph of tears, green
    tea!
Than whom Cassandra was not more prophetic;
  For if my pure libations exceed three,
I feel my heart become so sympathetic,    325
  That I must have recourse to black Bohea: [34]
'Tis pity wine should be so deleterious,
For tea and coffee leave us much more serious,

### 53

Unless when qualified with thee, Cogniac! [35]
  Sweet Naïad of the Phlegethontic rill! [36] 330
Ah! why the liver wilt thou thus attack,
  And make, like other nymphs, thy lovers ill?
I would take refuge in weak punch, but *rack*
  (In each sense [37] of the word), whene'er I fill
My mild and midnight beakers to the brim, [335]
Wakes me next morning with its synonym.

### 54

I leave Don Juan for the present, safe—
  Not sound, poor fellow, but severely
    wounded;
Yet could his corporal pangs amount to half
  Of those with which his Haidée's bosom
    bounded!    340
She was not one to weep, and rave, and chafe,
  And then give way, subdued because sur-
    rounded;
Her mother was a Moorish maid from Fez,[38]
Where all is Eden, or a wilderness.

### 55

There the large olive rains its amber store    345
  In marble fonts; there grain, and flour, and
    fruit,
Gush from the earth until the land runs o'er;
  But there, too, many a poison-tree has root,
And midnight listens to the lion's roar,

[34] Another variety of tea.
[35] French brandy made from wine produced near
the town of Cognac.
[36] Phlegethon: a river of Hades containing fire instead of water.
[37] I. e., "punch" and "suffering."
[38] In Morocco.

And long, long deserts scorch the camel's
    foot,    350
Or heaving whelm the helpless caravan;
And as the soil is, so the heart of man.

### 56

Afric is all the sun's, and as her earth
  Her human clay is kindled; full of power
For good or evil, burning from its birth,    355
  The Moorish blood partakes the planet's
    hour,
And like the soil beneath it will bring forth:
  Beauty and love were Haidée's mother's
    dower;
But her large dark eye showed deep Passion's
    force,
Though sleeping like a lion near a source.    360

### 57

Her daughter, tempered with a milder ray,
  Like summer clouds all silvery, smooth, and
    fair,
Till slowly charged with thunder they display
  Terror to earth, and tempest to the air,
Had held till now her soft and milky way;    365
  But overwrought with passion and despair,
The fire burst forth from her Numidian veins,
Even as the Simoom [39] sweeps the blasted
    plains.

### 58

The last sight which she saw was Juan's gore,
  And he himself o'ermastered and cut down;
His blood was running on the very floor    371
  Where late he trod, her beautiful, her own;
Thus much she viewed an instant and no
    more,—
  Her struggles ceased with one convulsive
    groan;
On her sire's arm, which until now scarce held
Her writhing, fell she like a cedar felled.    376

### 59

A vein had burst, and her sweet lips' pure dyes
  Were dabbled with the deep blood which ran
    o'er;
And her head drooped, as when the lily lies
  O'ercharged with rain: her summoned hand-
    maids bore    380
Their lady to her couch with gushing eyes;
  Of herbs and cordials they produced their
    store,
But she defied all means they could employ,
Like one life could not hold, nor death destroy.

### 60

Days lay she in that state unchanged, though
    chill—    385
  With nothing livid, still her lips were red;
She had no pulse, but death seemed absent still;
  No hideous sign proclaimed her surely dead;
Corruption came not in each mind to kill

[39] A dry, hot, violent, dust-laden wind.

All hope; to look upon her sweet face bred
New thoughts of life, for it seemed full of
   soul— 391
She had so much, earth could not claim the
   whole.

### 61

The ruling passion, such as marble shows
   When exquisitely chiseled, still lay there,
But fixed as marble's unchanged aspect throws
   O'er the fair Venus, but for ever fair; 396
O'er the Laocoön's all eternal throes,
   And ever-dying Gladiator's air,
Their energy like life forms all their fame,
Yet looks not life, for they are still the same. 400

### 62

She woke at length, but not as sleepers wake,
   Rather the dead, for life seemed something
   new,
A strange sensation which she must partake
   Perforce, since whatsoever met her view
Struck not on memory, though a heavy ache 405
   Lay at her heart, whose earliest beat still true
Brought back the sense of pain without the
   cause,
For, for a while, the furies made a pause.

### 63

She looked on many a face with vacant eye,
   On many a token without knowing what; 410
She saw them watch her without asking why,
   And recked not who around her pillow sat;
Not speechless, though she spoke not; not a
   sigh
   Relieved her thoughts; dull silence and quick
   chat
Were tried in vain by those who served; she
   gave 415
No sign, save breath, of having left the grave.

### 64

Her handmaids tended, but she heeded not;
   Her father watched, she turned her eyes
   away;
She recognized no being, and no spot,
   However dear or cherished in their day; 420
They changed from room to room, but all for-
   got,
   Gentle, but without memory she lay;
At length those eyes, which they would fain be
   weaning
Back to old thoughts, waxed full of fearful
   meaning.

### 65

And then a slave bethought her of a harp; 425
   The harper came, and tuned his instrument;
At the first notes, irregular and sharp,
   On him her flashing eyes a moment bent,
Then to the wall she turned as if to warp
   Her thoughts from sorrow through her heart
   re-sent; 430

And he began a long low island-song
Of ancient days, ere tyranny grew strong.

### 66

Anon her thin wan fingers beat the wall
   In time to his old tune; he changed the
   theme,
And sung of love; the fierce name struck
   through all 435
   Her recollection; on her flashed the dream
Of what she was, and is, if ye could call
   To be so being; in a gushing stream
The tears rushed forth from her o'erclouded
   brain,
Like mountain mists at length dissolved in rain.

### 67

Short solace, vain relief!—thought came too
   quick, 441
   And whirled her brain to madness; she arose
As one who ne'er had dwelt among the sick,
   And flew at all she met, as on her foes;
But no one ever heard her speak or shriek, 445
   Although her paroxysm drew towards its
   close;—
Hers was a frenzy which disdained to rave,
Even when they smote her, in the hope to save.

### 68

Yet she betrayed at times a gleam of sense;
   Nothing could make her meet her father's
   face, 450
Though on all other things with looks intense
   She gazed, but none she ever could retrace;
Food she refused, and raiment; no pretense
   Availed for either; neither change of place,
Nor time, nor skill, nor remedy, could give her
Senses to sleep—the power seemed gone for
   ever. 456

### 69

Twelve days and night she withered thus; at
   last,
   Without a groan, or sigh, or glance, to show
A parting pang, the spirit from her passed:
   And they who watched her nearest could not
   know 460
The very instant, till the change that cast
   Her sweet face into shadow, dull and slow,
Glazed o'er her eyes—the beautiful, the black—
Oh! to possess such luster—and then lack!

### 70

She died, but not alone; she held, within, 465
   A second principle of life, which might
Have dawned a fair and sinless child of sin;
   But closed its little being without light,
And went down to the grave unborn, wherein
   Blossom and bough lie withered with one
   blight; 470
In vain the dews of Heaven descend above
The bleeding flower and blasted fruit of love.

### 71

Thus lived—thus died she; never more on her
  Shall sorrow light, or shame. She was not
    made
Through years or moons the inner weight to
    bear,                                    475
  Which colder hearts endure till they are laid
By age in earth: her days and pleasures were
  Brief, but delightful—such as had not stayed
Long with her destiny; but she sleeps well
By the sea-shore, whereon she loved to dwell.

### 72

That isle is now all desolate and bare,       481
  Its dwellings down, its tenants passed away;
None but her own and father's grave is there,
  And nothing outward tells of human clay;
Ye could not know where lies a thing so fair,
  No stone is there to show, no tongue to
    say,                                     486
What was; no dirge, except the hollow sea's,
Mourns o'er the beauty of the Cyclades.[40]

### 73

But many a Greek maid in a loving song
  Sighs o'er her name; and many an islander
With her sire's story makes the night less
    long;                                    491
  Valor was his, and beauty dwelt with her;
If she loved rashly, her life paid for wrong—
  A heavy price must all pay who thus err,
In some shape; let none think to fly the danger,
For soon or late Love is his own avenger.   496

## On This Day I Complete
## My Thirty-Sixth Year [1]

'Tis time this heart should be unmoved,
  Since others it hath ceased to move:
Yet, though I cannot be beloved,
    Still let me love!

[40] A group of islands in the Aegean, lying south-
east of Attica.
[1] Written at Missolonghi on 22 January, 1824;
published in the same year.

My days are in the yellow leaf;              5
  The flowers and fruits of love are gone;
The worm, the canker, and the grief
    Are mine alone!

The fire that on my bosom preys
  Is lone as some volcanic isle;             10
No torch is kindled at its blaze—
    A funeral pile.

The hope, the fear, the jealous care,
  The exalted portion of the pain
And power of love, I cannot share,           15
    But wear the chain.

But 'tis not *thus*—and 'tis not *here*—
  Such thoughts should shake my soul, nor
    *now*,
Where glory decks the hero's bier,
    Or binds his brow.                       20

The sword, the banner, and the field,
  Glory and Greece, around me see!
The Spartan, borne upon his shield,[2]
    Was not more free.

Awake! (not Greece—she *is* awake!)          25
  Awake, my spirit! Think through *whom*
Thy life-blood tracks its parent lake,
    And then strike home!

Tread those reviving passions down,
  Unworthy manhood!—unto thee               30
Indifferent should the smile or frown
    Of beauty be.

If thou regrett'st thy youth, *why live?*
  The land of honorable death
Is here:—up to the field, and give          35
    Away thy breath!

Seek out—less often sought than found—
  A soldier's grave, for thee the best;
Then look around, and choose thy ground,
    And take thy rest.                        40

[2] Wounded or slain Spartans were borne from the
field upon their shields.

# Percy Bysshe Shelley

## 1792-1822

Shelley was born at Field Place, near Horsham, in Sussex, on 4 August, 1792, the eldest of the six children of Sir Timothy and Elizabeth Shelley. His childhood was sheltered and happy until, at the age of ten, he was placed in a school at Brentford, where his remarkable beauty and appearance of gentleness tempted his school-fellows to bully and torment him. There is reason for believing that his days here and later at Eton, where he was in residence from 1804 until 1810, were by no means wholly unhappy, and he made some friends at Eton. Nevertheless, he neither understood nor was understood by his school-fellows, and the strangeness of his temperament was more in evidence than his talents, with the result that he suffered much. A school-contemporary wrote, "I have seen him surrounded, hooted, baited like a maddened bull, and at this distance of time I seem to hear ringing in my ears the cry which Shelley was wont to utter in his paroxysm of revengeful anger." Imaginative, sensitive, overwrought, largely unguided, Shelley in effect retired as much as possible from the external world to one of his own. There he dreamed his own dreams, pursued studies not admitted to the curriculum, and read strange books—among them William Godwin's Political Justice. In the spring of 1810 he entered University College, Oxford. Here, of course, he had greater freedom than at Eton, and no wise guidance to direct his thoughts and activities, no critics even to stiffen with substance his eager scientific and philosophic inquiries. The result was that Shelley, already converted to Godwin's gospel of reason, after some study of Locke and Hume wrote a pamphlet on The Necessity of Atheism, grounding his conclusion on the contention that all knowledge must come through the senses. This pamphlet he proceeded to circulate among bishops, heads of colleges, and others, with the consequence that, about eleven months after his coming to Oxford, he was ex-

pelled. The event not unnaturally caused difficulties with his father, who was a kindly, well-intentioned country gentleman, not without his perceptions—as is shown by a sentence from a letter to his solicitor, "This misguided young man courts persecution, and which to him would be a favor"—but totally unfitted to deal amicably with such a son. It was impossible that either should understand the other, and from this time Shelley's personal relations with his father practically ceased, though after a short interval Sir Timothy agreed to give him a small allowance. In August, 1811, Shelley eloped with Harriet Westbrook, the daughter of a well-to-do coffee-house keeper—an event which completed Shelley's estrangement from his father. He was nineteen at the time, and the girl sixteen. He had made her a convert to his political and philosophical radicalism, and he felt for her a master's enthusiasm for a willing disciple, and perhaps something more. She was in love with him, and made him believe that by marrying her he could rescue her from the tyranny exercised by her father.

A part of Shelley's strangeness was his habit of acting fully and immediately upon his convictions, whatever they were; and, in spite of experience, he believed that other people needed only to be told the saving truth in order to act on it. After his marriage he spent several years in wandering about, going to Ireland and to various places in England, attempting to advance the cause of freedom and of emancipation from outworn institutions by scattering incendiary literature among the people he met. During this period he learned that William Godwin was still alive and immediately got into communication with him, flattering him as the author of all his beliefs. In the spring of 1814 Shelley became definitely estranged from his wife, and the two finally separated in May. She had borne him one child and was about to bear him another. He, however, had *fallen violently in love with Godwin's daughter Mary, and it was in accordance with the principles of all three that the existence of his wife should be no bar to his union with another; Godwin, Shelley, and Mary believed that marriage was an iniquitous institution, since love as well as everything else should be completely free. Accordingly in July, 1814, Shelley and Mary began living together. They were married, however, two years later, after Harriet had drowned herself in the Serpentine. It is not clear how far Shelley is to be blamed for his wife's suicide, but it is clear enough that his habit of acting instantly on his convictions was a force which no ordinary considerations of humanity towards others could have stopped. In 1814 he had gone to France with Mary Godwin; in 1816 he was in Switzerland, and during that summer spent much time with Byron there; in 1818 he again left England, this time not to return. The remaining years of his life were spent in Italy. He was at Naples and Venice in 1818 and 1819, at Rome in the latter year and in 1820, and at Pisa from 1820 until 1822. He was drowned while sailing in the Bay of Lerici on 8 July, 1822. When his body was found later, washed up on the shore, he had a volume of Sophocles in one pocket and a volume of Keats in another—the latter open with its covers turned back, as if he had suddenly thrust it there when the waters threatened to engulf him.*

*When Shelley went to Italy he had already written much prose and poetry, but nearly all his greatest work was done during the last four years of his life. Then the fire of conviction which had intensely burned in him since boyhood broke forth into poetry which, for its union of metrical skill, ethereal imagination, and passionate ardor, has no equal in English literature. Much of this poetry, like much of the poet's life, is concerned with a Godwinian attack on the institutions which have given form to European society. But it is well to remember that some of Shelley's wisest critics consider him a follower, not only of Godwin, but of Plato. Although his debt to the revolutionary doctrines of his time is large and specific, he also responds to an older teaching: the belief that happiness is obtainable through spiritual regeneration. Shelley did not believe that men, or any class of men, are perfect; he came, in fact, to recognize that there is deep-seated evil in the human heart; but he held to his conviction that we are right to hope for a conversion to better things. It is this hope which makes* Prometheus Unbound *a noble poem; and all of Shelley's finest poems have a relevant nobility.*

The Complete Works of Shelley *have been edited by Roger Ingpen and Walter E. Peck (10 vols., London, 1926–1930). This edition includes, in the last three volumes, Shelley's letters, with the exception of those discovered and edited by Leslie Hotson, in* Shelley's Lost Letters to Harriet *(Boston, 1930), and by Walter Sidney Scott in* New Shelley Letters *(New Haven, 1949). Probably the best one-volume edition of Shelley's* Complete Poetical Works *is that edited by T. Hutchinson, with Introduction and Bibliographical Notes by Benjamin P. Kurtz ("Oxford Standard Editions," 1933). The* Selected Poetry, Prose and Letters *(London, 1951), edited by A. S. B. Glover, shares the usefulness and convenience of the other Reynard Library editions. The best biography is by Newman I. White:* Shelley *(London, 1947) in two volumes. Among the many specialized biographical studies only a few can be listed: K. N. Cameron's* The Young Shelley *(New York, 1950), Newman I. White's* The Examination of the Shelley Legend *(Philadelphia, 1951), and Ivan Roe's* Shelley, the Last Phase *(London, 1953). H. N. Brailsford's* Shelley, Godwin, and Their Circle *("Home University Library") is a good introduction; as is also, in a different kind, Carl H. Grabo's* Magic Plant; the Growth of Shelley's Thought *(Chapel Hill, 1936). Grabo's* A Newton Among Poets *(Chapel Hill, 1930) is also valuable. A. Clutton-Brock's* Shelley: The Man and the Poet *(London, 1910), and Mrs. Olwen Ward Campbell's* Shelley and the Unromantics *(London, 1924) are both readable, interesting, and valuable books. More recent critical studies include Carlos Baker's* Shelley's Major Poetry *(New Haven, 1948), A. M. Hughes's* The Nascent Mind of Shelley *(Oxford, 1947), and Richard Fogle's* The Imagery of Keats and Shelley *(Chapel Hill, 1949).*

## Hymn to Intellectual Beauty [1]

### I

The awful shadow of some unseen Power
  Floats though unseen among us,—visiting
  This various world with as inconstant wing

[1] Written probably in Switzerland in the summer of 1816; published in the *Examiner* (edited by Leigh Hunt), January, 1817. By intellectual beauty Shelley means an immaterial form or archetype which is beauty itself. When we contemplate beautiful objects we get some notion, but only a partial, incomplete notion, of what beauty itself must be; for

As summer winds that creep from flower to
    flower,—
Like moonbeams that behind some piny moun-
        tain shower,                               5
        It visits with inconstant glance
        Each human heart and countenance;
Like hues and harmonies of evening,—
        Like clouds in starlight widely spread,—
        Like memory of music fled,—        10
        Like aught that for its grace may be
Dear, and yet dearer for its mystery.

### II

Spirit of BEAUTY, that dost consecrate
    With thine own hues all thou dost shine
        upon
    Of human thought or form,—where art thou
        gone?                                      15
Why dost thou pass away and leave our state,
This dim vast vale of tears, vacant and desolate?
        Ask why the sunlight not for ever
        Weaves rainbows o'er yon mountain-
        river,
Why aught should fail and fade that once is
        shown,                                     20
        Why fear and dream and death and
        birth
        Cast on the daylight of this earth
        Such gloom,—why man has such a
        scope
For love and hate, despondency and hope?

### III

No voice from some sublimer world hath
    ever                                           25
    To sage or poet these responses given—
    Therefore the names of Demon, Ghost, and
        Heaven,
Remain the records of their vain endeavor,
Frail spells—whose uttered charm might not
        avail to sever,
        From all we hear and all we see,    30
        Doubt, chance, and mutability.
Thy light alone—like mist o'er mountains
        driven,
        Or music by the night-wind sent
        Through strings of some still instru-
        ment,

material objects, no matter how beautiful, always
contain some flaws and are subject to change and
decay. It is only when we are carried beyond the
incomplete beauty of material objects that we are
able to contemplate the idea of beauty itself. The
conception is Platonic and the best commentary on
this and other poems by Shelley is the speech of
Diotima in Plato's *Symposium.* Shelley's Platonism, however, is frequently, if not always, combined with essentially modern ideas which are its
negative. This is illustrated in the present poem
by Shelley's hope that the spirit of beauty, could
it be more securely possessed by men, would throw
them back on themselves in a sudden access of universal brotherly love.

        Or moonlight on a midnight stream,   35
Gives grace and truth to life's unquiet dream.

### IV

Love, Hope, and Self-esteem, like clouds de-
    part
    And come, for some uncertain moments lent.
    Man were immortal, and omnipotent,
Didst thou, unknown and awful as thou art,  40
Keep with thy glorious train firm state within
        his heart.
        Thou messenger of sympathies,
        That wax and wane in lovers' eyes—
Thou—that to human thought art nourish-
        ment,
        Like darkness to a dying flame!      45
        Depart not as thy shadow came,
        Depart not—lest the grave should be,
Like life and fear, a dark reality.

### V

While yet a boy I sought for ghosts, and sped
    Through many a listening chamber, cave and
        ruin,                                      50
    And starlight wood, with fearful steps pur-
        suing
Hopes of high talk with the departed dead.
I called on poisonous names with which our
        youth is fed;
        I was not heard—I saw them not—
        When musing deeply on the lot        55
Of life, at that sweet time when winds are
        wooing
        All vital things that wake to bring
        News of birds and blossoming,—
        Sudden, thy shadow fell on me;
I shrieked, and clasped my hands in ecstasy!  60

### VI

I vowed that I would dedicate my powers
    To thee and thine—have I not kept the vow?
    With beating heart and streaming eyes, even
        now
I call the phantoms of a thousand hours
Each from his voiceless grave: they have in
        visioned bowers                            65
        Of studious zeal or love's delight
        Outwatched with me the envious
        night—
They know that never joy illumed my brow
        Unlinked with hope that thou wouldst
        free
        This world from its dark slavery,    70
        That thou—O awful LOVELINESS,
Wouldst give whate'er these words cannot ex-
        press.

### VII

The day becomes more solemn and serene
    When noon is past—there is a harmony
In autumn, and a luster in its sky,            75
Which through the summer is not heard or
        seen,

As if it could not be, as if it had not been!
  Thus let thy power, which like the truth
  Of nature on my passive youth
Descended, to my onward life supply      80
  Its calm—to one who worships thee,
  And every form containing thee,
  Whom, SPIRIT fair, thy spells did bind
To fear himself, and love all human kind.

## Ozymandias [1]

I met a traveler from an antique land
Who said: Two vast and trunkless legs of stone
Stand in the desert. Near them, on the sand,
Half sunk, a shattered visage lies, whose frown,
And wrinkled lip, and sneer of cold command, [5]
Tell that its sculptor well those passions read
Which yet survive, stamped on these lifeless
    things,
The hand that mocked them, and the heart that
    fed: [2]
And on the pedestal these words appear:
"My name is Ozymandias, King of Kings:      10
Look on my works, ye Mighty, and despair!"
Nothing beside remains. Round the decay
Of that colossal wreck, boundless and bare
The lone and level sands stretch far away.

## Stanzas

### Written in Dejection, near Naples [3]

#### I

The sun is warm, the sky is clear,
  The waves are dancing fast and bright,
Blue isles and snowy mountains wear
  The purple noon's transparent might,
  The breath of the moist earth is light, [5]
  Around its unexpanded buds;
  Like many a voice of one delight,
  The winds, the birds, the ocean floods,
The City's voice itself, is soft like Solitude's.

#### II

I see the Deep's untrampled floor      10
  With green and purple seaweeds strown;
I see the waves upon the shore,
  Like light dissolved in star-showers,
      thrown:
  I sit upon the sands alone,—
  The lightning of the noontide ocean      15
  Is flashing round me, and a tone
  Arises from its measured motion,
How sweet! did any heart now share in my
    emotion.

#### III

Alas! I have nor hope nor health,
  Nor peace within nor calm around,      20
Nor that content surpassing wealth
  The sage in meditation found,
  And walked with inward glory crowned—
Nor fame, nor power, nor love, nor leisure.
  Others I see whom these surround—      25
Smiling they live, and call life pleasure;—
To me that cup has been dealt in another meas-
    ure.

#### IV

Yet now despair itself is mild,
  Even as the winds and waters are;
I could lie down like a tired child,      30
  And weep away the life of care
  Which I have borne and yet must bear,
  Till death like sleep might steal on me,
  And I might feel in the warm air
My cheek grow cold, and hear the sea      35
Breathe o'er my dying brain its last monotony.

#### V

Some might lament that I were cold,
  As I, when this sweet day is gone,
Which my lost heart, too soon grown old,
  Insults with this untimely moan;      40
  They might lament—for I am one
Whom men love not,—and yet regret,
  Unlike this day, which, when the sun
Shall on its stainless glory set,
Will linger, though enjoyed, like joy in mem-
    ory yet. [4]      45

## England in 1819 [5]

An old, mad, blind, despised, and dying
    king,— [6]
Princes, the dregs of their dull race, who flow
Through public scorn,—mud from a muddy
    spring,—
Rulers who neither see, nor feel, nor know,
But leech-like to their fainting country cling, [5]
Till they drop, blind in blood, without a
    blow,—
A people starved and stabbed in the untilled
    field,—
An army, which liberticide and prey
Makes as a two-edged sword to all who wield,—
Golden and sanguine laws which tempt and
    slay;      10
Religion Christless, Godless—a book sealed;

---

[1] Published in the *Examiner*, January, 1818.
[2] The hand, i. e., of the sculptor, and the heart of Ozymandias.
[3] Said by Mrs. Shelley to have been written in December, 1818; published in 1824.

[4] This stanza may be paraphrased: Some might lament my death, as I shall lament the passing of this sweet day;—they might lament, but not with joy, such as will surround the memory of this day.
[5] First published in 1839; presumably written in 1819.
[6] George III.

A Senate,—Time's worst statute unre-
    pealed,—[7]
Are graves, from which a glorious Phantom [8]
    may
Burst, to illumine our tempestuous day.

# Ode to the West Wind [1]

### I

O Wild West Wind, thou breath of Autumn's
    being,
Thou, from whose unseen presence the leaves
    dead
Are driven, like ghosts from an enchanter flee-
    ing,

Yellow, and black, and pale, and hectic red,
Pestilence-stricken multitudes: O thou,    5
Who chariotest to their dark wintry bed

The wingéd seeds, where they lie cold and low,
Each like a corpse within its grave, until
Thine azure sister of the Spring shall blow

Her clarion o'er the dreaming earth, and fill  10
(Driving sweet buds like flocks to feed in air)
With living hues and odors plain and hill:

Wild Spirit, which art moving everywhere;
Destroyer and preserver; hear, oh, hear!

### II

Thou on whose stream, 'mid the steep sky's
    commotion,                                 15
Loose clouds like earth's decaying leaves are
    shed,
Shook from the tangled boughs of Heaven and
    Ocean,

Angels of rain and lightning: there are spread
On the blue surface of thine aëry surge,
Like the bright hair uplifted from the head  20

[7] The law imposing civil disabilities on Roman
Catholics.
[8] Liberty.
[1] Written in 1819; published in 1820. "This poem
was conceived and chiefly written in a wood that
skirts the Arno, near Florence, and on a day when
that tempestuous wind, whose temperature is at
once mild and animating, was collecting the vapors
which pour down the autumnal rains. They began,
as I foresaw, at sunset with a violent tempest of
hail and rain, attended by that magnificent thunder
and lightning peculiar to the Cisalpine regions.
The phenomenon alluded to at the conclusion of the
third stanza is well known to naturalists. The
vegetation at the bottom of the sea, of rivers, and
of lakes, sympathizes with that of the land in the
change of seasons, and is consequently influenced by
the winds which announce it" (Shelley's note).

Of some fierce Maenad,[2] even the dim verge
Of the horizon to the zenith's height,
The locks of the approaching storm. Thou dirge

Of the dying year, to which this closing night
Will be the dome of a vast sepulcher,        25
Vaulted with all thy congregated might

Of vapors, from whose solid atmosphere
Black rain, and fire, and hail will burst: oh,
    hear!

### III

Thou who didst waken from his summer dreams
The blue Mediterranean, where he lay,        30
Lulled by the coil of his crystálline streams,

Beside a pumice isle in Baiae's bay,[3]
And saw in sleep old palaces and towers
Quivering within the wave's intenser day,

All overgrown with azure moss and flowers    35
So sweet, the sense faints picturing them! Thou
For whose path the Atlantic's level powers

Cleave themselves into chasms, while far below
The sea-blooms and the oozy woods which wear
The sapless foliage of the ocean, know        40

Thy voice, and suddenly grow gray with fear,
And tremble and despoil themselves: oh, hear!

### IV

If I were a dead leaf thou mightest bear;
If I were a swift cloud to fly with thee;
A wave to pant beneath thy power, and share  45

The impulse of thy strength, only less free
Than thou, O uncontrollable! If even
I were as in my boyhood, and could be

The comrade of thy wanderings over Heaven,
As then, when to outstrip thy skyey speed    50
Scarce seemed a vision; I would ne'er have
    striven

As thus with thee in prayer in my sore need.
Oh, lift me as a wave, a leaf, a cloud!
I fall upon the thorns of life! I bleed!

A heavy weight of hours has chained and
    bowed                                      55
One too like thee: tameless, and swift, and
    proud.

### V

Make me thy lyre, even as the forest is:
What if my leaves are falling like its own!
The tumult of thy mighty harmonies

Will take from both a deep, autumnal tone,   60
Sweet though in sadness. Be thou, Spirit fierce,
My spirit! Be thou me, impetuous one!

[2] Female attendant upon Bacchus.
[3] In Campania, Italy.

Drive my dead thoughts over the universe
Like withered leaves to quicken a new birth!
And, by the incantation of this verse,    65

Scatter, as from an unextinguished hearth
Ashes and sparks, my words among mankind!
Be through my lips to unawakened earth

The trumpet of a prophecy! O, Wind,
If Winter comes, can Spring be far behind?  70

## The Indian Serenade [1]

### I

I arise from dreams of thee
In the first sweet sleep of night,
When the winds are breathing low,
And the stars are shining bright:
I arise from dreams of thee,    5
And a spirit in my feet
Hath led me—who knows how?
To thy chamber window, Sweet!

### II

The wandering airs they faint
On the dark, the silent stream—    10
The Champak [2] odors fail
Like sweet thoughts in a dream;
The nightingale's complaint,
It dies upon her heart;—
As I must on thine,    15
Oh, belovéd as thou art!

### III

O lift me from the grass!
I die! I faint! I fail!
Let thy love in kisses rain
On my lips and eyelids pale.    20
My cheek is cold and white, alas!
My heart beats loud and fast;—
Oh! press it to thine own again,
Where it will break at last.

## Love's Philosophy [3]

### I

The fountains mingle with the river
  And the rivers with the Ocean,
The winds of Heaven mix for ever
  With a sweet emotion;
Nothing in the world is single;    5
  All things by a law divine
In one spirit meet and mingle.
  Why not I with thine?—

### II

See the mountains kiss high Heaven
  And the waves clasp one another;    10
No sister-flower would be forgiven

[1] Written in 1819; published in *The Liberal*, 1822.
[2] An East Indian tree related to the magnolia.
[3] Written in 1819 and published by Hunt in *The Indicator* in the same year.

If it disdained its brother;
And the sunlight clasps the earth
  And the moonbeams kiss the sea:
What is all this sweet work worth    15
  If thou kiss not me?

## Prometheus Unbound
### Song of Asia [1]

My soul is an enchanted boat,
  Which, like a sleeping swan, doth float
Upon the silver waves of thy sweet singing;
  And thine doth like an angel sit
  Beside a helm conducting it,    5
Whilst all the winds with melody are ringing.
  It seems to float ever, for ever,
  Upon that many-winding river,
  Between mountains, woods, abysses,
  A paradise of wildernesses!    10
Till, like one in slumber bound,
Borne to the ocean, I float down, around,
Into a sea profound, of ever-spreading sound:

  Meanwhile thy spirit lifts its pinions
  In music's most serene dominions;    15
Catching the winds that fan that happy heaven.
  And we sail on, away, afar,
  Without a course, without a star,
But, by the instinct of sweet music driven;
  Till through Elysian garden islets    20
  By thee, most beautiful of pilots,
  Where never mortal pinnace glided,
  The boat of my desire is guided:
Realm where the air we breathe is love,
Which in the winds and on the waves doth    25
  move,
Harmonizing this earth with what we feel
  above.

  We have passed Age's icy caves,
  And Manhood's dark and tossing waves,
And Youth's smooth ocean, smiling to betray:
  Beyond the glassy gulfs we flee    30
  Of shadow-peopled Infancy,
Through Death and Birth, to a diviner day;
  A paradise of vaulted bowers,
  Lit by downward-gazing flowers,
  And watery paths that wind between    35
  Wildernesses calm and green,
Peopled by shapes too bright to see,
And rest, having beheld; somewhat like thee;
Which walk upon the sea, and chant melodi-
  ously!

### Song of Demogorgon [2]

This is the day, which down the void abysm
At the Earth-born's spell yawns for Heaven's
  despotism,

[1] Act II, scene v, ll. 72–110. Asia is a nymph of the ocean; she also symbolizes earthly love, and is ultimately married to the Titan, Prometheus. Here she is replying to a song sung by an invisible spirit.
[2] Act IV, ll. 554–578. Demogorgon is the embodi-

And Conquest is dragged captive through the
deep:
Love, from its awful throne of patient power
In the wise heart, from the last giddy hour   5
  Of dread endurance, from the slippery, steep,
And narrow verge of crag-like agony, springs
And folds over the world its healing wings.

Gentleness, Virtue, Wisdom, and Endurance,
These are the seals of that most firm assurance
  Which bars the pit over Destruction's
  strength;   11
And if, with infirm hand, Eternity,
Mother of many acts and hours, should free
  The serpent that would clasp her with his
  length;
These are the spells by which to reassume   15
An empire o'er the disentangled doom.

To suffer woes which Hope thinks infinite;
To forgive wrongs darker than death or night;
  To defy Power, which seems omnipotent;
To love, and bear; to hope till Hope creates   20
From its own wreck the thing it contemplates;
  Neither to change, nor falter, nor repent;
This, like thy glory, Titan,[3] is to be
Good, great, and joyous, beautiful and free;
This is alone Life, Joy, Empire, and Victory.   25

# The Cloud [1]

I bring fresh showers for the thirsting flowers,
  From the seas and the streams;
I bear light shade for the leaves when laid
  In their noonday dreams.
From my wings are shaken the dews that waken
  The sweet buds every one,   6
When rocked to rest on their mother's breast,
  As she dances about the sun.
I wield the flail of the lashing hail,
  And whiten the green plains under,   10
And then again I dissolve it in rain,
  And laugh as I pass in thunder.

I sift the snow on the mountains below,
  And their great pines groan aghast;
And all the night 'tis my pillow white,   15
  While I sleep in the arms of the blast.
Sublime on the towers of my skyey bowers,
  Lightning my pilot sits;
In a cavern under is fettered the thunder,
  It struggles and howls at fits;   20
Over earth and ocean, with gentle motion,
  This pilot is guiding me,
Lured by the love of the genii that move
  In the depths of the purple sea;
Over the rills, and the crags, and the hills,   25
  Over the lakes and the plains,

ment of that eternal force which Shelley believed
would in the end overthrow all tyrannies and redeem the universe.
[3] Prometheus.
[1] Written and published in 1820.

Wherever he dream, under mountain or
stream,
  The Spirit he loves remains;
And I all the while bask in Heaven's blue smile,
  Whilst he is dissolving in rains.   30

The sanguine Sunrise, with his meteor eyes,
  And his burning plumes outspread,
Leaps on the back of my sailing rack,
  When the morning star shines dead;
As on the jag of a mountain crag,   35
  Which an earthquake rocks and swings,
An eagle alit one moment may sit
  In the light of its golden wings.
And when Sunset may breathe, from the lit sea
beneath,
  Its ardors of rest and of love,   40
And the crimson pall of eve may fall
  From the depth of Heaven above,
With wings folded I rest, on mine aëry nest,
  As still as a brooding dove.

That orbéd maiden with white fire laden,   45
  Whom mortals call the Moon,
Glides glimmering o'er my fleece-like floor,
  By the midnight breezes strewn;
And wherever the beat of her unseen feet,
  Which only the angels hear,   50
May have broken the woof of my tent's thin
roof,
  The stars peep behind her and peer;
And I laugh to see them whirl and flee,
  Like a swarm of golden bees,
When I widen the rent in my wind-built tent,
  Till the calm rivers, lakes, and seas,   56
Like strips of the sky fallen through me on
high,
  Are each paved with the moon and these.[2]

I bind the Sun's throne with a burning zone,
  And the Moon's with a girdle of pearl;   60
The volcanoes are dim, and the stars reel and
swim,
  When the whirlwinds my banner unfurl.
From cape to cape, with a bridge-like shape,
  Over a torrent sea,
Sunbeam-proof, I hang like a roof,—   65
  The mountains its columns be.
The triumphal arch through which I march
  With hurricane, fire, and snow,
When the Powers of the air are chained to my
chair,
  Is the million-colored bow;   70
The sphere-fire above its soft colors wove,
  While the moist Earth was laughing below.

I am the daughter of Earth and Water,
  And the nursling of the Sky;
I pass through the pores of the ocean and
shores;   75
  I change, but I cannot die.
For after the rain when with never a stain
[2] The stars.

The pavilion of Heaven is bare,
And the winds and sunbeams with their con-
    vex gleams
Build up the blue dome of air,     80
I silently laugh at my own cenotaph,[3]
And out of the caverns of rain,
Like a child from the womb, like a ghost from
    the tomb,
I arise and unbuild it again.

## To a Skylark [1]

Hail to thee, blithe Spirit!
    Bird thou never wert,
That from Heaven, or near it,
    Pourest thy full heart
In profuse strains of unpremeditated art.    5

Higher still and higher
    From the earth thou springest
Like a cloud of fire;
    The blue deep thou wingest,
And singing still dost soar, and soaring ever
    singest.    10

In the golden lightning
    Of the sunken sun,
O'er which clouds are bright'ning,
    Thou dost float and run;
Like an unbodied joy whose race is just be-
    gun.    15

The pale purple even
    Melts around thy flight:
Like a star of Heaven,
    In the broad daylight
Thou art unseen, but yet I hear thy shrill
    delight,    20

Keen as are the arrows
    Of that silver sphere,
Whose intense lamp narrows
    In the white dawn clear
Until we hardly see—we feel that it is there.   25

All the earth and air
    With thy voice is loud,
As, when night is bare,
    From one lonely cloud
The moon rains out her beams, and Heaven is
    overflowed.    30

What thou art we know not;
    What is most like thee?
From rainbow clouds there flow not
    Drops so bright to see
As from thy presence showers a rain of melody.

[3] I. e., the blue dome of air. A cenotaph is an
empty tomb, or a monument erected in honor of one
buried elsewhere.
[1] Written at Leghorn in 1820 and published in the
same year.

Like a Poet hidden
    In the light of thought,
Singing hymns unbidden,
    Till the world is wrought
To sympathy with hopes and fears it heeded
    not:    40

Like a high-born maiden
    In a palace-tower,
Soothing her love-laden
    Soul in secret hour
With music sweet as love, which overflows her
    bower:    45

Like a glow-worm golden
    In a dell of dew,
Scattering unbeholden
    Its aërial hue
Among the flowers and grass, which screen it
    from the view!    50

Like a rose embowered
    In its own green leaves,
By warm winds deflowered,
    Till the scent it gives
Makes faint with too much sweet those heavy-
    wingéd thieves:    55

Sound of vernal showers
    On the twinkling grass,
Rain-awakened flowers,
    All that ever was
Joyous, and clear, and fresh, thy music doth
    surpass:    60

Teach us, Sprite or Bird,
    What sweet thoughts are thine:
I have never heard
    Praise of love or wine
That panted forth a flood of rapture so divine.

Chorus Hymeneal,
    Or triumphal chant,    66
Matched with thine would be all
    But an empty vaunt,
A thing wherein we feel there is some hidden
    want.    70

What objects are the fountains
    Of thy happy strain?
What fields, or waves, or mountains?
    What shapes of sky or plain?
What love of thine own kind? what ignorance
    of pain?    75

With thy clear keen joyance
    Languor cannot be:
Shadow of annoyance
    Never came near thee:
Thou lovest—but ne'er knew love's sad satiety.

Waking or asleep,    81
    Thou of death must deem

Things more true and deep
    Than we mortals dream,
Or how could thy notes flow in such a crystal
    stream?                                85

We look before and after,
    And pine for what is not:
Our sincerest laughter
    With some pain is fraught;
Our sweetest songs are those that tell of saddest
    thought.                               90

Yet if we could scorn
    Hate, and pride, and fear;
If we were things born
    Not to shed a tear,
I know not how thy joy we ever should come
    near.                                  95

Better than all measures
    Of delightful sound,
Better than all treasures
    That in books are found,
Thy skill to poet were, thou scorner of the
    ground!                               100

Teach me half the gladness
    That thy brain must know,
Such harmonious madness
    From my lips would flow
The world should listen then—as I am listen-
    ing now.                              105

# Ode to Liberty [1]

### I

A glorious people vibrated again
    The lightning of the nations: Liberty
From heart to heart, from tower to tower, o'er
    Spain,
Scattering contagious fire into the sky,
Gleamed. My soul spurned the chains of its
    dismay,                                5
    And in the rapid plumes of song
    Clothed itself, sublime and strong
(As a young eagle soars the morning clouds
    among),
Hovering in verse o'er its accustomed prey;
Till from its station in the Heaven of fame
The Spirit's whirlwind rapped it, and the
    ray                                   11
Of the remotest sphere of living flame
Which paves the void was from behind it flung,

[1] Written early in 1820 and published in the same
year. The motto is from *Childe Harold*, IV, Stanza
98. The occasion of the poem was an uprising
against absolutist government in Spain, which occurred early in 1820 and at the time appeared to be
triumphing in Madrid.
Yet, Freedom, yet, thy banner, torn but flying,
Streams like a thunder-storm against the wind.
                                        —BYRON.

As foam from a ship's swiftness, when there
    came
A voice out of the deep: I will record the
    same.                                 15

### II

"The Sun and the serenest Moon sprang forth:
    The burning stars of the abyss were hurled
Into the depths of Heaven. The daedal [2]
    earth,
    That island in the ocean of the world,
Hung in its cloud of all-sustaining air:        20
    But this divinest universe
    Was yet a chaos and a curse,
For thou [3] wert not: but, power from worst
    producing worse,
    The spirit of the beasts was kindled there,
    And of the birds, and of the watery forms,
    And there was war among them, and despair
    Within them, raging without truce or
    terms:                                27
The bosom of their violated nurse
Groaned, for beasts warred on beasts, and
    worms on worms,
And men on men; each heart was as a hell
    of storms.                            30

### III

"Man, the imperial shape, then multiplied
    His generations under the pavilion
Of the Sun's throne: palace and pyramid,
    Temple and prison, to many a swarming
    million
Were, as to mountain-wolves their raggéd caves.
    This human living multitude              36
    Was savage, cunning, blind, and rude,
For thou wert not; but o'er the populous soli-
    tude,
    Like one fierce cloud over a waste of waves,
    Hung Tyranny; beneath, sat deified       40
    The sister-pest, [4] congregator of slaves;
    Into the shadow of her pinions wide
Anarchs and priests, who feed on gold and
    blood
Till with the stain their inmost souls are
    dyed,
Drove the astonished herds of men from
    every side.                           45

### IV

"The nodding promontories, and blue isles,
    And cloud-like mountains, and dividuous [5]
    waves
Of Greece, basked glorious in the open smiles
    Of favoring Heaven: from their enchanted
    caves
Prophetic echoes flung dim melody.              50
    On the unapprehensive wild,
    The vine, the corn, the olive mild,
Grew savage yet, to human use unreconciled;

[2] Curiously contrived or variously adorned.
[3] Liberty.     [4] I. e., religion.
[5] Dividing.

And, like unfolded flowers beneath the sea,
　Like the man's thought dark in the in-
　　fant's brain,　　　　　　　55
Like aught that is which wraps what is to be,
　Art's deathless dreams lay veiled by many
　　a vein
Of Parian stone; and, yet a speechless child,
Verse murmured, and Philosophy did strain
　Her lidless eyes for thee; when o'er the
　　Aegean main　　　　　　60

### V

"Athens arose: a city such as vision
Builds from the purple crags and silver towers
Of battlemented cloud, as in derision
Of kingliest masonry: the ocean-floors
Pave it; the evening sky pavilions it;　　65
　Its portals are inhabited
　By thunder-zonéd winds, each head
Within its cloudy wings with sun-fire gar-
　　landed,—
　A divine work! Athens, diviner yet,
　　Gleamed with its crest of columns, on the
　　　will　　　　　　　　70
Of man, as on a mount of diamond, set; [6]
For thou wert, and thine all-creative skill
Peopled, with forms that mock the eternal dead
In marble immortality, that hill [7]
Which was thine earliest throne and latest
　　oracle.　　　　　　　75

### VI

"Within the surface of Time's fleeting river
　Its wrinkled image lies, as then it lay
Immovably unquiet, and for ever
　It trembles, but it cannot pass away!
The voices of thy bards and sages thunder [80]
　With an earth-awakening blast
　Through the caverns of the past
(Religion veils her eyes; Oppression shrinks
　　aghast):
　A wingéd sound of joy, and love, and won-
　　der,
　Which soars where Expectation never flew,
Rending the veil of space and time asunder!
　One ocean feeds the clouds, and streams,
　　and dew;　　　　　　87
One Sun illumines Heaven; one Spirit vast
With life and love makes chaos ever new,
As Athens doth the world with thy delight
　　renew.　　　　　　　90

### VII

"Then Rome was, and from thy deep bosom
　　fairest,
Like a wolf-cub from a Cadmaean Maenad,[8]

[6] I. e., Athens was a state based on the will of its citizens.
[7] The Acropolis.
[8] See Euripides, *Bacchae*, ll. 699–700. The Cadmaean Maenads are Theban followers of Bacchus, and are described by Euripides as nursing young wolves.

She drew the milk of greatness, though thy
　　dearest [9]
From that Elysian food was yet unweanéd;
And many a deed of terrible uprightness　[95]
　By thy sweet love was sanctified;
　And in thy smile, and by thy side,
Saintly Camillus [10] lived, and firm Atilius [11]
　　died.
　But when tears stained thy robe of vestal
　　whiteness,
　And gold profaned thy Capitolian throne,
　Thou didst desert, with spirit-wingéd light-
　　ness,　　　　　　　101
　The senate of the tyrants: they sunk prone
Slaves of one tyrant: Palatinus [12] sighed
Faint echoes of Ionian song; that tone
Thou didst delay to hear, lamenting to dis-
　　own.　　　　　　　105

### VIII

"From what Hyrcanian [13] glen or frozen hill,
　Or piny promontory of the Arctic main,
Or utmost islet inaccessible,
　Didst thou lament the ruin of thy reign,
Teaching the woods and waves, and desert
　　rocks,　　　　　　　110
　And every Naiad's ice-cold urn,
　To talk in echoes sad and stern
Of that sublimest lore which man had dared
　　unlearn?
　For neither didst thou watch the wizard
　　flocks
　Of the Scald's [14] dreams, nor haunt the
　　Druid's sleep.　　　　115
What if the tears rained through thy shat-
　　tered locks
　Were quickly dried? for thou didst groan,
　　not weep,
When from its sea of death, to kill and burn,
　The Galilean serpent [15] forth did creep,
　And made thy world an undistinguishable
　　heap.　　　　　　　120

### IX

"A thousand years the Earth cried, 'Where art
　　thou?'
And then the shadow of thy cunning fell
On Saxon Alfred's [16] olive-cinctured brow:
　And many a warrior-peopled citadel,
Like rocks which fire lifts out of the flat deep,
　Arose in sacred Italy,　　　126

[9] Athens.
[10] A hero of republican Rome who defeated the Gauls under Brennus in 390 B.C.
[11] Generally called Regulus. He was captured by the Carthaginians but dissuaded the Senate from concluding a peace that would have saved his life (B.C. 250).
[12] One of the seven hills of Rome, on which was the residence of Augustus and later emperors.
[13] Hyrcania was a region at the southeastern corner of the Caspian Sea.
[14] A skald was a Scandinavian poet.
[15] Christianity.　　　[16] Alfred the Great.

Frowning o'er the tempestuous sea
Of kings, and priests, and slaves, in tower-
    crowned majesty;
  That multitudinous anarchy did sweep
    And burst around their walls, like idle
      foam,            130
Whilst from the human spirit's deepest deep
  Strange melody with love and awe struck
    dumb
Dissonant arms; and Art, which cannot die,
  With divine wand traced on our earthly
    home
  Fit imagery to pave Heaven's everlasting
    dome.           135

### X

"Thou huntress swifter than the Moon! thou
    terror
  Of the world's wolves! thou bearer of the
    quiver,
Whose sunlike shafts pierce tempest-wingéd
    Error,
  As light may pierce the clouds when they
    dissever
In the calm regions of the orient day!    140
    Luther caught thy wakening glance;
    Like lightning, from his leaden lance
Reflected, it dissolved the visions of the trance
  In which, as in a tomb, the nations lay;
    And England's prophets hailed thee as
      their queen,        145
  In songs whose music cannot pass away,
    Though it must flow for ever: not unseen
Before the spirit-sighted countenance
  Of Milton didst thou pass, from the sad
    scene
  Beyond whose night he saw, with a dejected
    mien.          150

### XI

"The eager hours and unreluctant years
  As on a dawn-illumined mountain stood,
Trampling to silence their loud hopes and
    fears,
  Darkening each other with their multitude,
And cried aloud, 'Liberty!' Indignation    155
    Answered Pity from her cave;
    Death grew pale within the grave,
And Desolation howled to the destroyer, Save!
  When like Heaven's Sun girt by the exhala-
    tion
  Of its own glorious light, thou didst arise,
Chasing thy foes from nation unto nation 161
    Like shadows: as if day had cloven the
    skies
At dreaming midnight o'er the western wave,
  Men started, staggering with a glad surprise,
  Under the lightnings of thine unfamiliar
    eyes.          165

### XII

"Thou Heaven of earth! what spells could pall
    thee then

In ominous eclipse? a thousand years
Bred from the slime of deep Oppression's den,
  Dyed all thy liquid light with blood and
    tears,
Till thy sweet stars could weep the stain away;
  How like Bacchanals of blood      171
    Round France, the ghastly vintage, stood
Destruction's sceptered slaves, and Folly's
    mitered brood!
  When one,[17] like them, but mightier far than
    they,
    The Anarch of thine own bewildered
      powers,        175
  Rose: armies mingled in obscure array,
    Like clouds with clouds, darkening the
      sacred bowers
Of serene Heaven. He, by the past pursued,
  Rests with those dead, but unforgotten hours,
  Whose ghosts scare victor kings in their
    ancestral towers.       180

### XIII

"England yet sleeps: was she not called of old?
  Spain calls her now, as with its thrilling
    thunder
Vesuvius wakens Aetna, and the cold
  Snow-crags by its reply are cloven in sunder:
O'er the lit waves every Aeolian isle [18]    185
    From Pithecusa to Pelorus
    Howls, and leaps, and glares in chorus:
They cry, 'Be dim; ye lamps of Heaven sus-
    pended o'er us!'
  Her [19] chains are threads of gold, she need
    but smile
    And they dissolve; but Spain's were links
      of steel,        190
  Till bit to dust by virtue's keenest file.
    Twins of a single destiny! appeal
To the eternal years enthroned before us
  In the dim West; impress us from a seal,
  All ye have thought and done! Time cannot
    dare conceal.       195

### XIV

"Tomb of Arminius [20] render up thy dead
  Till, like a standard from a watch-tower's
    staff,
His soul may stream over the tyrant's head;
  Thy victory shall be his epitaph,
Wild Bacchanal of truth's mysterious wine, 200
    King-deluded Germany,
    His dead spirit lives in thee.
Why do we fear or hope? thou art already
    free!
  And thou, lost Paradise of this divine

---

[17] Napoleon.

[18] A group of islands northeast of Sicily. Pithe-
cusa is an island outside the Bay of Naples, and
Pelorus is a promontory northeast of Sicily.

[19] England's.

[20] He preserved the freedom of Germany in A.D. 9
by preventing the advance of the Romans beyond
the Rhine.

And glorious world! thou flowery wilder-
    ness!                                    205
Thou island of eternity! thou shrine
    Where Desolation, clothed with loveliness,
Worships the thing thou wert! O Italy,
Gather thy blood into thy heart; repress
The beasts who make their dens thy sacred
    palaces.                                 210

xv

"Oh, that the free would stamp the impious
    name
Of KING into the dust! or write it there,
So that this blot upon the page of fame
Were as a serpent's path, which the light air
Erases, and the flat sands close behind!    215
    Ye the oracle have heard:
    Lift the victory-flashing sword,
And cut the snaky knots of this foul gordian 21
    word,
    Which, weak itself as stubble, yet can bind
    Into a mass, irrefragably firm,          220
The axes and the rods which awe mankind;
    The sound has poison in it, 'tis the sperm
Of what makes life foul, cankerous, and ab-
    horred;
    Disdain not thou, at thine appointed term,
    To set thine arméd heel on this reluctant
    worm.                                    225

xvi

"Oh, that the wise from their bright minds
    would kindle
Such lamps within the dome of this dim
    world,
That the pale name of PRIEST might shrink
    and dwindle
Into the hell from which it first was hurled,
A scoff of impious pride from fiends impure; 230
    Till human thoughts might kneel alone,
    Each before the judgment-throne
Of its own aweless soul, or of the Power un-
    known!
    Oh, that the words which make the thoughts
    obscure
    From which they spring, as clouds of
    glimmering dew                           235
From a white lake blot Heaven's blue por-
    traiture,
    Were stripped of their thin masks and
    various hue
And frowns and smiles and splendors not their
    own,
    Till in the nakedness of false and true
    They stand before their Lord, each to receive
    its due!                                 240

xvii

"He who taught man to vanquish whatsoever
    Can be between the cradle and the grave

21 Intricate.

Crowned him the King of Life. Oh, vain
    endeavor!
If on his own high will, a willing slave,
He has enthroned the oppression and the
    oppressor.                               245
    What if earth can clothe and feed
    Amplest millions at their need,
And power in thought be as the tree within
    the seed?
    Or what if Art, an ardent intercessor,
    Driving on fiery wings to Nature's throne,
Checks the great mother stooping to caress
    her,                                     251
    And cries: 'Give me, thy child, dominion
Over all height and depth'? if Life can breed
    New wants, and wealth from those who toil
    and groan,
    Rend of thy gifts and hers a thousandfold
    for one!                                 255

xviii

"Come thou, but lead out of the inmost cave
Of man's deep spirit, as the morning-star
Beckons the Sun from the Eoan wave,22
    Wisdom. I hear the pennons of her car
Self-moving, like cloud charioted by flame; 260
    Come she not, and come ye not,
    Rulers of eternal thought,
To judge, with solemn truth, life's ill-appor-
    tioned lot?
    Blind Love, and equal Justice, and the Fame
    Of what has been, the Hope of what will
    be?                                      265
O Liberty! if such could be thy name
    Wert thou disjoined from these, or they
    from thee:
If thine or theirs were treasures to be bought
    By blood or tears, have not the wise and free
    Wept tears, and blood like tears?"—The
    solemn harmony                           270

xix

Paused, and the Spirit of that mighty singing
    To its abyss was suddenly withdrawn;
Then, as a wild swan, when sublimely winging
    Its path athwart the thunder-smoke of dawn,
Sinks headlong through the aërial golden light
    On the heavy-sounding plain,             276
    When the bolt has pierced its brain;
As summer clouds dissolve, unburthened of
    their rain;
    As a far taper fades with fading night,
    As a brief insect dies with dying day,— 280
My song, its pinions disarrayed of might,
    Drooped; o'er it closed the echoes far away
Of the great voice which did its flight sustain,
    As waves which lately paved his watery way
Hiss round a drowner's head in their tem-
    pestuous play.                           285

22 The wave of dawn.

# Ode to Naples [1]

### EPODE I a

I stood within the City disinterred; [2]
  And heard the autumnal leaves like light
    footfalls
Of spirit passing through the streets; and heard
  The Mountain's [3] slumberous voice at in-
    tervals
    Thrill through those roofless halls;    5
The oracular thunder penetrating shook
  The listening soul in my suspended blood;
I felt that Earth out of her deep heart spoke—
  I felt, but heard not:—through white
    columns glowed
    The isle-sustaining ocean-flood,   10
A plane of light between two heavens of azure!
Around me gleamed many a bright sepulcher
Of whose pure beauty, Time, as if his pleasure
Were to spare Death, had never made erasure;
  But every living lineament was clear   15
As in the sculptor's thought; and there
The wreaths of stony myrtle, ivy, and pine,
  Like winter leaves o'ergrown by molded snow,
  Seemed only not to move and grow
Because the crystal silence of the air   20
  Weighed on their life; even as the Power
    divine
  Which then lulled all things, brooded upon
    mine.

### EPODE II a

    Then gentle winds arose
    With many a mingled close
Of wild Aeolian sound, and mountain-odors
    keen;   25
    And where the Baian ocean
    Welters with airlike motion,
Within, above, around its bowers of starry
    green,
  Moving the sea-flowers in those purple caves,
    Even as the ever stormless atmosphere 30
    Floats o'er the Elysian realm,
  It bore me, like an Angel, o'er the waves
    Of sunlight, whose swift pinnace of dewy
    air
    No storm can overwhelm.
  I sailed, where ever flows   35
    Under the calm Serene
    A spirit of deep emotion

From the unknown graves
  Of the dead Kings of Melody. [4]
Shadowy Aornos [5] darkened o'er the helm  40
  The horizontal aether; Heaven stripped bare
Its depth over Elysium, where the prow
Made the invisible water white as snow;
From that Typhaean mount, Inarime, [6]
  There streamed a sunbright vapor, like the
    standard   45
    Of some ethereal host;
    Whilst from all the coast,
  Louder and louder, gathering round, there
    wandered
Over the oracular woods and divine sea
Prophesyings which grew articulate—   50
They seize me—I must speak them!—be they
    fate!

### STROPHE I

Naples! thou Heart of men which ever pantest
  Naked, beneath the lidless eye of Heaven!
Elysian City, which to calm enchantest
  The mutinous air and sea! they round thee,
    even   55
  As sleep round Love, are driven!
Metropolis of a ruined Paradise
  Long lost, late won, and yet but half re-
    gained!
Bright Altar of the bloodless sacrifice,
  Which arméd Victory offers up unstained 60
To Love, the flower-enchained!
Thou which wert once, and then didst cease to
    be,
Now art, and henceforth ever shalt be, free,
  If Hope, and Truth, and Justice can avail,—
    Hail, hail, all hail!   65

### STROPHE II

  Thou youngest giant birth
  Which from the groaning earth
Leap'st, clothed in armor of impenetrable scale!
  Last of the Intercessors!
  Who 'gainst the Crowned Transgressors
Pleadest before God's love! Arrayed in Wis-
    dom's mail,   71
    Wave thy lightning lance in mirth
    Nor let thy high heart fail,
Though from their hundred gates the leagued
    Oppressors
    With hurried legions move!   75
    Hail, hail, all hail!

### ANTISTROPHE I a

What though Cimmerian Anarchs [7] dare
    blaspheme
  Freedom and thee? thy shield is as a mirror

---

[1] Written in August, 1820; published in 1824.
"The author has connected many recollections of
his visit to Pompeii and Baiae with the enthusiasm
excited by the intelligence of the proclamation of a
Constitutional Government at Naples. This has
given a tinge of picturesque and descriptive imagery
to the introductory Epodes which depicture these
scenes, and some of the majestic feelings permanently connected with the scene of this animating
event" (Shelley's note).

[2] Pompeii.       [3] Vesuvius.

[4] Homer and Virgil (Shelley's note).
[5] Hades.
[6] An island northwest of the Bay of Naples containing a volcanic mountain under which Typhon
was said to be buried.
[7] The Cimmerians, according to legend, dwelt in a
northern land of perpetual darkness.

To make their blind slaves see, and with fierce
    gleam
  To turn his hungry sword upon the wearer; 80
    A new Actaeon's [8] error
Shall theirs have been—devoured by their own
    hounds!
Be thou like the imperial Basilisk [9]
Killing thy foe with unapparent wounds!
  Gaze on Oppression, till at that dread risk
Aghast she pass from the Earth's disk:    86
Fear not, but gaze—for freemen mightier grow,
And slaves more feeble, gazing on their foe:—
  If Hope, and Truth, and Justice may avail,
    Thou shalt be great—All hail!     90

### ANTISTROPHE II α

  From Freedom's form divine,
  From Nature's inmost shrine,
Strip every impious gawd, rend Error veil by
    veil;
    O'er Ruin desolate,
    O'er Falsehood's fallen state,     95
Sit thou sublime, unawed; be the Destroyer
    pale!
    And equal laws be thine,
    And wingéd words let sail,
Freighted with truth even from the throne of
    God:
    That wealth, surviving fate,     100
    Be thine.—All hail!

### ANTISTROPHE I β

Didst thou not start to hear Spain's thrilling
    paean
  From land to land re-echoed solemnly,
Till silence became music? From the Aeaean [10]
    To the cold Alps, eternal Italy     105
    Starts to hear thine! The Sea
Which paves the desert streets of Venice laughs
In light and music; widowed Genoa wan
By moonlight spells ancestral epitaphs,
  Murmuring, "Where is Doria?" [11] fair Mi-
    lan,     110
    Within whose veins long ran
The viper's [12] palsying venom, lifts her heel
To bruise his head. The signal and the seal
  (If Hope and Truth and Justice can avail)
  Art thou of all these hopes.—O hail!    115

### ANTISTROPHE II β

  Florence! beneath the sun,
  Of cities fairest one,
Blushes within her bower for Freedom's ex-
    pectation:

[8] Actaeon was devoured by his own hounds after
he had seen Artemis bathing.
[9] A monster who could slay by merely looking at
its victim.
[10] The island of Circe (Shelley's note).
[11] Andrea Doria, an admiral who victoriously
fought, early in the sixteenth century, for the independence of Genoa.
[12] The viper was the armorial device of the Vis-
conti, tyrants of Milan (Shelley's note).

  From eyes of quenchless hope
  Rome tears the priestly cope,     120
As ruling once by power, so now by admira-
    tion,—
    An athlete stripped to run
    From a remoter station
For the high prize lost on Philippi's shore: [13]
  As then Hope, Truth, and Justice did avail,
  So now may Fraud and Wrong! O hail! [126]

### EPODE I β

Hear ye the march as of the Earth-born
    Forms [14]
  Arrayed against the ever-living Gods?
The crash and darkness of a thousand storms
  Bursting their inaccessible abodes     130
    Of crags and thunder-clouds?
See ye the banners blazoned to the day,
  Inwrought with emblems of barbaric pride?
Dissonant threats kill Silence far away,
  The serene Heaven which wraps our Eden
    wide     135
    With iron light is dyed;
The Anarchs of the North [15] lead forth their
    legions
  Like Chaos o'er creation, uncreating;
An hundred tribes nourished on strange re-
    ligions
And lawless slaveries,—down the aërial regions
    Of the white Alps, desolating,     141
    Famished wolves that bide no waiting,
Blotting the glowing footsteps of old glory,
Trampling our columned cities into dust,
    Their dull and savage lust     145
On Beauty's corse to sickness satiating—
They come! The fields they tread look black
    and hoary
With fire—from their red feet the streams run
    gory!

### EPODE II β

  Great Spirit, deepest Love!
  Which rulest and dost move     150
All things which live and are, within the Italian
    shore;
    Who spreadest Heaven around it,
    Whose woods, rocks, waves, surround it;
Who sittest in thy star, o'er Ocean's western
    floor;
Spirit of beauty! at whose soft command [155]
  The sunbeams and the showers distil its
    foison [16]
    From the Earth's bosom chill;
Oh, bid those beams be each a blinding brand
  Of lightning! bid those showers be dews of
    poison!
    Bid the Earth's plenty kill!     160

[13] Brutus and Cassius at Philippi fought vainly for
republican Rome against Octavius (42 B.C.).
[14] The Titans, sons of Earth, who warred on the
gods.
[15] Austria and other countries.
[16] Plentiful harvest.

Bid thy bright Heaven above,
Whilst light and darkness bound it,
Be their tomb who planned
To make it ours and thine!
Or, with thine harmonizing ardors fill    165
And raise thy sons, as o'er the prone horizon
Thy lamp feeds every twilight wave with fire—
Be man's high hope and unextinct desire
The instrument to work thy will divine!
Then clouds from sunbeams, antelopes from
    leopards,    170
    And frowns and fears from thee,
    Would not more swiftly flee
Than Celtic wolves from the Ausonian [17]
    shepherds.—
Whatever, Spirit, from thy starry shrine
    Thou yieldest or withholdest, oh, let be [175]
    This city of thy worship ever free!

## Sonnet [1]

Ye hasten to the grave! What seek ye there,
Ye restless thoughts and busy purposes
Of the idle brain, which the world's livery
    wear?
O thou quick heart, which pantest to possess
All that pale Expectation feigneth fair!    5
Thou vainly curious mind which wouldest guess
Whence thou didst come, and whither thou
    must go,
And all that never yet was known would
    know—
Oh, whither hasten ye, that thus ye press,
With such swift feet life's green and pleasant
    path,    10
Seeking, alike from happiness and woe,
A refuge in the cavern of gray death?
O heart, and mind, and thoughts! what thing
    do you
Hope to inherit in the grave below?

## Good-Night [2]

### I

Good-night? ah! no; the hour is ill
    Which severs those it should unite;
Let us remain together still,
    Then it will be *good* night.

### II

How can I call the lone night good,    5
    Though thy sweet wishes wing its flight?
Be it not said, thought, understood—
    Then it will be—*good* night.

### III

To hearts which near each other move
    From evening close to morning light,    10

[17] Italian.
[1] Written in 1820; published by Leigh Hunt in 1823.
[2] Written in 1820; published by Hunt in 1822.

The night is good; because, my love,
    They never *say* good-night.

## To Night [3]

### I

Swiftly walk o'er the western wave,
    Spirit of Night!
Out of the misty eastern cave,
Where, all the long and lone daylight,
Thou wovest dreams of joy and fear,    5
Which make thee terrible and dear,—
    Swift be thy flight!

### II

Wrap thy form in a mantle gray,
    Star-inwrought!
Blind with thine hair the eyes of Day;    10
Kiss her until she be wearied out,
Then wander o'er city, and sea, and land,
Touching all with thine opiate wand—
    Come, long-sought!

### III

When I arose and saw the dawn,    15
    I sighed for thee;
When light rode high, and the dew was gone,
And noon lay heavy on flower and tree,
And the weary Day turned to his rest,
Lingering like an unloved guest,    20
    I sighed for thee.

### IV

Thy brother Death came, and cried,
    Wouldst thou me?
Thy sweet child Sleep, the filmy-eyed,
Murmured like a noontide bee,    25
Shall I nestle near thy side?
Wouldst thou me?—And I replied,
    No, not thee!

### V

Death will come when thou art dead,
    Soon, too soon—    30
Sleep will come when thou art fled;
Of neither would I ask the boon
I ask of thee, belovéd Night—
Swift be thine approaching flight,
    Come soon, soon!    35

## Time [4]

Unfathomable Sea! whose waves are years,
    Ocean of Time, whose waters of deep woe
Are brackish with the salt of human tears!
    Thou shoreless flood, which in thy ebb and
        flow

[3] Written in 1821; published in 1824.
[4] Written in 1821; published in 1824.

Claspest the limits of mortality,                              5
And sick of prey, yet howling on for more,
Vomitest thy wrecks on its inhospitable shore;
Treacherous in calm, and terrible in storm,
    Who shall put forth on thee,
    Unfathomable Sea?                                          10

## To ——— [5]

Music, when soft voices die,
Vibrates in the memory—
Odors, when sweet violets sicken,
Live within the sense they quicken.

Rose leaves, when the rose is dead,                            5
Are heaped for the belovéd's bed;
And so thy thoughts, when thou art gone,
Love itself shall slumber on.

## Song [6]

### I

Rarely, rarely, comest thou,
    Spirit of Delight!
Wherefore hast thou left me now
    Many a day and night?
Many a weary night and day                                     5
'Tis since thou art fled away.

### II

How shall ever one like me
    Win thee back again?
With the joyous and the free
    Thou wilt scoff at pain.                                   10
Spirit false! thou has forgot
All but those who need thee not.

### III

As a lizard with the shade
    Of a trembling leaf,
Thou with sorrow art dismayed;                                 15
    Even the sighs of grief
Reproach thee, that thou art not near,
And reproach thou wilt not hear.

### IV

Let me set my mournful ditty
    To a merry measure;                                        20
Thou wilt never come for pity,
    Thou wilt come for pleasure;
Pity then will cut away
Those cruel wings, and thou wilt stay.

### V

I love all that thou lovest,                                   25
    Spirit of Delight!

[5] Written in 1821; published in 1824.
[6] Written in 1821; published in 1824.

The fresh Earth in new leaves dressed,
    And the starry night;
Autumn evening, and the morn
When the golden mists are born.                                30

### VI

I love snow, and all the forms
    Of the radiant frost;
I love waves, and winds, and storms,
    Everything almost
Which is Nature's, and may be                                  35
Untainted by man's misery.

### VII

I love tranquil solitude,
    And such society
As is quiet, wise, and good;
    Between thee and me                                        40
What difference? but thou dost possess
The things I seek, not love them less.

### VIII

I love Love—though he has wings,
    And like light can flee,
But above all other things,                                    45
    Spirit, I love thee—
Thou art love and life! Oh, come,
Make once more my heart thy home.

## Mutability [7]

### I

The flower that smiles to-day
    To-morrow dies;
All that we wish to stay
    Tempts and then flies.
What is this world's delight?                                  5
Lightning that mocks the night,
    Brief even as bright.

### II

Virtue, how frail it is!
    Friendship how rare!
Love, how it sells poor bliss                                  10
    For proud despair!
But we, though soon they fall,
Survive their joy, and all
    Which ours we call.

### III

Whilst skies are blue and bright,                              15
    Whilst flowers are gay,
Whilst eyes that change ere night
    Make glad the day;
Whilst yet the calm hours creep,
Dream thou—and from thy sleep                                  20
    Then wake to weep.

[7] Written in 1821; published in 1824.

## Political Greatness [8]

Nor happiness, nor majesty, nor fame,
Nor peace, nor strength, nor skill in arms or
    arts,
Shepherd those herds whom tyranny makes
    tame;
Verse echoes not one beating of their hearts,
History is but the shadow of their shame, 5
Art veils her glass, or from the pageant starts
As to oblivion their blind millions fleet,
Staining that Heaven with obscene imagery
Of their own likeness. What are numbers knit
By force or custom? Man who man would be, 10
Must rule the empire of himself; in it
Must be supreme, establishing his throne
On vanquished will, quelling the anarchy
Of hopes and fears, being himself alone.

## A Lament [9]

### I

O world! O life! O time!
On whose last steps I climb,
   Trembling at that where I had stood be-
     fore;
When will return the glory of your prime?
   No more—Oh, never more! 5

### II

Out of the day and night
A joy has taken flight;
   Fresh spring, and summer, and winter hoar,
Move my faint heart with grief, but with de-
    light
   No more—Oh, never more! 10

## To ——— [10]

### I

One word is too often profaned
   For me to profane it,
One feeling too falsely disdained
   For thee to disdain it;
One hope is too like despair 5
   For prudence to smother,
And pity from thee more dear
   Than that from another.

### II

I can give not what men call love,
   But wilt thou accept not 10
The worship the heart lifts above
   And the Heavens reject not,—
The desire of the moth for the star,
   Of the night for the morrow,
The devotion to something afar 15
   From the sphere of our sorrow?

[8] Written in 1821; published in 1824.
[9] Written in 1821; published in 1824.
[10] Written in 1821; published in 1824.

## Adonais [1]

### An Elegy on the Death of John Keats, Author of Endymion, Hyperion, Etc.

Ἀστὴρ πρὶν μὲν ἔλαμπες ἐνὶ ζωοῖσιν Ἐῶος. νῦν δὲ
θανὼν λάμπεις Ἕσπερος ἐν φθιμένοις.
                 —PLATO. [2]

### PREFACE

Φάρμακον ἦλθε, Βίων, ποτὶ σὸν στόμα, φάρμακον εἶδες.
πῶς τευ τοῖς χείλεσσι ποτέδραμε, κοὐκ ἐγλυκάνθη;
τίς δὲ βροτὸς τοσσοῦτον ἀνάμερος, ἢ κεράσαι τοι,
ἢ δοῦναι λαλέοντι τὸ φάρμακον; ἔκφυγεν ᾠδάν.
        —MOSCHUS, EPITAPH. BION. [3]

IT IS my intention to subjoin to the London
edition of this poem a criticism upon the
claims of its lamented object to be classed
among the writers of the highest genius who
have adorned our age. My known repugnance to the narrow principles of taste on
which several of his earlier compositions
were modeled proves at least that I am an
impartial judge. I consider the fragment
of *Hyperion* as second to nothing that was
ever produced by a writer of the same years.
   John Keats died at Rome of a consump-

[1] Written at Pisa during the early days of June,
1821, and published at Pisa in the middle of July in
the same year. Part of the edition was sent to be
sold in London, but there was, during Shelley's lifetime, no London edition such as is mentioned in the
first sentence of the Preface. When he wrote the
Preface Shelley did not know the exact time of
Keats's death. He shared, too, the incorrect impression current at the time that adverse criticism had
brought about Keats's illness. (Concerning this see
the introductory note to Keats's poems, below.)
Keats and Shelley had met each other at the house
of Leigh Hunt, but had never seen much of each
other. *Adonais* is not the result of a feeling of
warm personal friendship so much as of Shelley's
recognition of the similarity between his own life
and that of Keats. While the poem was in progress
he wrote: "I have been engaged these last days in
composing a poem on the death of Keats, which will
shortly be finished. . . . It is a highly wrought *piece
of art*, and perhaps better in point of composition
than anything I have written." The poem is modeled on the Greek pastoral elegy, and Shelley is particularly indebted to Bion's *Lament for Adonis* and
Moschus's *Elegy on the Death of Bion*.
  [2] Thou wert the morning star among the living,
    Ere thy fair light had fled;—
  Now, having died, thou art as Hesperus, giving
    New splendor to the dead.
             (Shelley's translation.)
  [3] Poison came, Bion, to thy mouth—thou didst
know poison. To such lips as thine did it come,
and was not sweetened? What mortal was so cruel
that could mix poison for thee, or who could give
thee the venom that heard thy voice? Surely he
had no music in his soul (Lang's translation).

tion, in his twenty-fourth year, on the——
of—— 1821; and was buried in the romantic
and lonely cemetery of the Protestants in
that city, under the pyramid which is the tomb
of Cestius, and the massy walls and towers,
now mouldering and desolate, which formed
the circuit of ancient Rome. The cemetery is
an open space among the ruins, covered in
winter with violets and daisies. It might make
one in love with death, to think that one 10
should be buried in so sweet a place.

The genius of the lamented person to
whose memory I have dedicated these unworthy verses was not less delicate and fragile
than it was beautiful; and where canker-
worms abound, what wonder if its young
flower was blighted in the bud? The savage
criticism on his *Endymion*, which appeared
in the *Quarterly Review*, produced the most
violent effect on his susceptible mind; the 20
agitation thus originated ended in the rup-
ture of a blood-vessel in the lungs; a rapid
consumption ensued, and the succeeding acknowledgments from more candid critics of
the true greatness of his powers were ineffectual to heal the wound thus wantonly inflicted.

It may be well said that these wretched
men know not what they do. They scatter
their insults and their slanders without heed
as to whether the poisoned shaft lights on a 30
heart made callous by many blows or one
like Keats's composed of more penetrable
stuff. One of their associates is, to my
knowledge, a most base and unprincipled
calumniator. As to *Endymion*, was it a
poem, whatever might be its defects, to be
treated contemptuously by those who had
celebrated, with various degrees of complacency and panegyric, *Paris*, and *Woman*,
and a *Syrian Tale*, and Mrs. Lefanu, and 40
Mr. Barrett, and Mr. Howard Payne, and
a long list of the illustrious obscure? Are
these the men who in their venal good nature
presumed to draw a parallel between the Rev.
Mr. Milman and Lord Byron? What gnat
did they strain at here, after having swallowed
all those camels? Against what woman taken
in adultery dares the foremost of these literary
prostitutes to cast his opprobrious stone? Miserable man! you, one of the meanest, have 50
wantonly defaced one of the noblest specimens
of the workmanship of God. Nor shall it be
your excuse, that, murderer as you are, you have
spoken daggers, but used none.

The circumstances of the closing scene of
poor Keats's life were not made known to
me until the *Elegy* was ready for the press.

I am given to understand that the wound
which his sensitive spirit had received from
the criticism of *Endymion* was exasperated
by the bitter sense of unrequited benefits;
the poor fellow seems to have been hooted
from the stage of life, no less by those on
whom he had wasted the promise of his
genius, than those on whom he had lavished
his fortune and his care. He was accompanied to Rome, and attended in his last
illness by Mr. Severn, a young artist of the
highest promise, who, I have been informed,
"almost risked his own life, and sacrificed
every prospect to unwearied attendance upon
his dying friend." Had I known these circumstances before the completion of my poem,
I should have been tempted to add my feeble
tribute of applause to the more solid recompense which the virtuous man finds in the
recollection of his own motives. Mr. Severn
can dispense with a reward from "such stuff as
dreams are made of." His conduct is a golden
augury of the success of his future career—may
the unextinguished Spirit of his illustrious
friend animate the creations of his pencil, and
plead against Oblivion for his name!

1

I weep for Adonais—he is dead!
Oh, weep for Adonais! though our tears
Thaw not the frost which binds so dear a
    head!
And thou, sad Hour, selected from all years
To mourn our loss, rouse thy obscure
    compeers,
And teach them thine own sorrow, say:
    "With me                                    6
Died Adonais; till the Future dares
Forget the Past, his fate and fame shall be
An echo and a light unto eternity!"

2

Where wert thou, mighty Mother, when he
    lay,                                        10
When thy Son lay, pierced by the shaft which
    flies
In darkness? where was lorn Urania [4]
When Adonais died? With veiléd eyes,
'Mid listening Echoes, in her Paradise
She sat, while one, with soft enamored
    breath,                                     15
Rekindled all the fading melodies,
With which, like flowers that mock the corse
    beneath,
He had adorned and hid the coming bulk of
    Death.

---

[4] The heavenly muse, to whom Milton appeals in
*Paradise Lost*; or, more probably, the Uranian Aphrodite, spirit of heavenly love.

### 3

Oh, weep for Adonais—he is dead!
Wake, melancholy Mother, wake and weep!
Yet wherefore? Quench within their burning
    bed                        21
Thy fiery tears, and let thy loud heart keep,
Like his, a mute and uncomplaining sleep;
For he is gone, where all things wise and fair
Descend;—oh, dream not that the amorous
    Deep                        25
Will yet restore him to the vital air;
Death feeds on his mute voice, and laughs at
    our despair.

### 4

Most musical of mourners, weep again!
Lament anew, Urania!—he [5] died,
Who was the Sire of an immortal strain, 30
Blind, old, and lonely, when his country's
    pride,
The priest, the slave, and the liberticide,
Trampled and mocked with many a loathéd
    rite
Of lust and blood; he went, unterrified,
Into the gulf of death; but his clear Sprite
Yet reigns o'er the earth; the third [6] among the
    sons of light.              36

### 5

Most musical of mourners, weep anew!
Not all to that bright station dared to climb;
And happier they their happiness who knew,
Whose tapers yet burn through that night of
    time                       40
In which suns perished; others more sublime,
Struck by the envious wrath of man or god,
Have sunk, extinct in their refulgent prime;
And some yet live, treading the thorny road,
Which leads, through toil and hate, to Fame's
    serene abode.           45

### 6

But now, thy youngest, dearest one, has
    perished—
The nursling of thy widowhood, who grew,
Like a pale flower by some sad maiden
    cherished,
And fed with true-love tears, instead of dew;
Most musical of mourners, weep anew! 50
Thy extreme hope, the loveliest and the last,
The bloom, whose petals, nipped before they
    blew,
Died on the promise of the fruit, is waste;
The broken lily lies—the storm is overpast.

### 7

To that high Capital,[7] where kingly Death 55
Keeps his pale court in beauty and decay,

[5] Milton.
[6] The first and second, if one may judge from
Shelley's *Defense of Poetry*, were Homer and Dante.
[7] Rome.

He came; and bought, with price of purest
    breath,
A grave among the eternal.—Come away!
Haste, while the vault of blue Italian day
Is yet his fitting charnel-roof! while still 60
He lies, as if in dewy sleep he lay;
Awake him not! surely he takes his fill
Of deep and liquid rest, forgetful of all ill.

### 8

He will awake no more, oh, never more!—
Within the twilight chamber spreads apace
The shadow of white Death, and at the
    door                     66
Invisible Corruption waits to trace
His extreme way to her dim dwelling-place;
The eternal Hunger sits, but pity and awe
Soothe her pale rage, nor dares she to deface
So fair a prey, till darkness, and the law 71
Of change, shall o'er his sleep the mortal cur-
    tain draw.

### 9

Oh, weep for Adonais!—The quick Dreams,
The passion-wingéd Ministers of thought,
Who were his flocks, whom near the living
    streams                 75
Of his young spirit he fed, and whom he
    taught
The love which was its music, wander not,—
Wander no more, from kindling brain to
    brain,
But droop there, whence they sprung; and
    mourn their lot
Round the cold heart, where, after their
    sweet pain,           80
They ne'er will gather strength, or find a home
    again.

### 10

And one with trembling hands clasps his
    cold head,
And fans him with her moonlight wings, and
    cries;
"Our love, our hope, our sorrow, is not dead;
See, on the silken fringe of his faint eyes, 85
Like dew upon a sleeping flower, there lies
A tear some Dream has loosened from his
    brain."
Lost Angel of a ruined Paradise!
She knew not 'twas her own; as with no stain
She faded, like a cloud which had outwept its
    rain.                   90

### 11

One from a lucid urn of starry dew
Washed his light limbs as if embalming
    them;
Another clipped her profuse locks, and threw
The wreath upon him, like an anadem,[8]
Which frozen tears instead of pearls begem;
Another in her willful grief would break 96

[8] Garland.

Her bow and wingéd reeds, as if to stem
A greater loss with one which was more weak;
And dull the barbéd fire against his frozen
cheek.

### 12

Another Splendor on his mouth alit,          100
That mouth, whence it was wont to draw
the breath
Which gave it strength to pierce the guarded
wit,
And pass into the panting heart beneath
With lightning and with music: the damp
death
Quenched its caress upon his icy lips;        105
And, as a dying meteor stains a wreath
Of moonlight vapor, which the cold night
clips,[9]
It flushed through his pale limbs, and passed
to its eclipse.

### 13

And others came . . . . Desires and Adora-
tions,
Wingéd Persuasions and veiled Destinies, 110
Splendors, and Glooms, and glimmering In-
carnations
Of hopes and fears, and twilight Phantasies;
And Sorrow, with her family of Sighs,
And Pleasure, blind with tears, led by the
gleam
Of her own dying smile instead of eyes,  115
Came in slow pomp;—the moving pomp
might seem
Like pageantry of mist on an autumnal stream.

### 14

All he had loved, and molded into thought,
From shape, and hue, and odor, and sweet
sound,
Lamented Adonais. Morning sought       120
Her eastern watch-tower, and her hair un-
bound,
Wet with the tears which should adorn the
ground,
Dimmed the aërial eyes that kindle day;
Afar the melancholy thunder moaned,
Pale Ocean in unquiet slumber lay,        125
And the wild Winds flew round, sobbing in
their dismay.

### 15

Lost Echo sits amid the voiceless mountains,
And feeds her grief with his remembered lay,
And will no more reply to winds or fountains,
Or amorous birds perched on the young
green spray,                                 130
Or herdsman's horn, or bell at closing day;
Since she can mimic not his lips, more dear

Than those for whose disdain she pined
away [10]
Into a shadow of all sounds:—a drear
Murmur, between their songs, is all the wood-
men hear.                                   135

### 16

Grief made the young Spring wild, and she
threw down
Her kindling buds, as if she Autumn were,
Or they dead leaves; since her delight is
flown,
For whom should she have waked the sullen
year?
To Phoebus was not Hyacinth [11] so dear 140
Nor to himself Narcissus,[12] as to both
Thou, Adonais: wan they stand and sere
Amid the faint companions of their youth,
With dew all turned to tears; odor, to sighing
ruth.

### 17

Thy spirit's sister, the lorn nightingale   145
Mourns not her mate with such melodious
pain;
Not so the eagle, who like thee could scale
Heaven, and could nourish in the sun's do-
main
Her mighty youth with morning, doth com-
plain,
Soaring and screaming round her empty
nest,                                        150
As Albion wails for thee: the curse of Cain
Light on his head who pierced thy innocent
breast,[13]
And scared the angel soul that was its earthly
guest!

### 18

Ah, woe is me! Winter is come and gone,
But grief returns with the revolving year; 155
The airs and streams renew their joyous tone;
The ants, the bees, the swallows reappear;
Fresh leaves and flowers deck the dead Sea-
sons' bier;
The amorous birds now pair in every brake,
And build their mossy homes in field and
brere; [14]                                  160
And the green lizard, and the golden snake,
Like unimprisoned flames, out of their trance
awake.

[10] Than those of Narcissus, because of whose disdain she pined away, etc.
[11] A youth loved by Apollo, who changed him,
when he died, into a flower.
[12] After disdaining Echo and other nymphs, Narcissus was punished by falling in love with his own
reflected image. At his death he was changed into
a flower.
[13] J. W. Croker, the author of the anonymous
paper on *Endymion* in the *Quarterly Review* which
Shelley and other contemporaries believed to have
been the proximate cause of Keats's death.
[14] Brier.

[9] Embraces.

### 19

Through wood and stream and field and hill
and Ocean
A quickening life from the Earth's heart has
burst
As it has ever done, with change and mo-
tion, 165
From the great morning of the world when
first
God dawned on Chaos; in its stream im-
mersed,
The lamps of Heaven flash with a softer
light;
All baser things pant with life's sacred thirst;
Diffuse themselves; and spend in love's de-
light, 170
The beauty and the joy of their renewéd might.

### 20

The leprous corpse, touched by this spirit
tender,
Exhales itself in flowers of gentle breath;
Like incarnations of the stars, when splendor
Is changed to fragrance, they illumine death
And mock the merry worm that wakes be-
neath; 176
Nought we know, dies. Shall that alone
which knows
Be as a sword consumed before the sheath
By sightless [15] lightning?—the intense atom
glows
A moment, then is quenched in a most cold
repose. 180

### 21

Alas! that all we loved of him should be,
But for our grief, as if it had not been,
And grief itself be mortal! Woe is me!
Whence are we, and why are we? of what
scene
The actors or spectators? Great and mean 185
Meet massed in death, who lends what life
must borrow.
As long as skies are blue, and fields are green,
Evening must usher night, night urge the
morrow,
Month follow month with woe, and year wake
year to sorrow.

### 22

*He* will awake no more, oh, never more! 190
"Wake thou," cried Misery, "childless
Mother, rise
Out of thy sleep, and slake, in thy heart's
core,
A wound more fierce than his, with tears and
sighs."
And all the Dreams that watched Urania's
eyes,
And all the Echoes whom their sister's song

Had held in holy silence, cried: "Arise!" 196
Swift as a Thought by the snake Memory
stung,
From her ambrosial rest the fading Splendor
sprung.

### 23

She rose like an autumnal Night, that springs
Out of the East, and follows wild and drear
The golden Day, which, on eternal wings, 201
Even as a ghost abandoning a bier,
Had left the Earth a corpse. Sorrow and fear
So struck, so roused, so rapped Urania;
So saddened round her like an atmosphere
Of stormy mist; so swept her on her way 206
Even to the mournful place where Adonais lay.

### 24

Out of her secret Paradise she sped,
Through camps and cities rough with stone,
and steel,
And human hearts, which to her aery tread
Yielding not, wounded the invisible 211
Palms of her tender feet where'er they fell:
And barbéd tongues, and thoughts more
sharp than they,
Rent the soft Form, they never could repel,
Whose sacred blood, like the young tears of
May, 215
Paved with eternal flowers that undeserving
way.

### 25

In the death-chamber for a moment Death,
Shamed by the presence of that living Might,
Blushed to annihilation, and the breath
Revisited those lips, and Life's pale light 220
Flashed through those limbs, so late her dear
delight.
"Leave me not wild and drear and comfort-
less,
As silent lightning leaves the starless night!
Leave me not!" cried Urania: her distress
Roused Death: Death rose and smiled, and met
her vain caress. 225

### 26

"Stay yet awhile! speak to me once again;
Kiss me, so long but as a kiss may live;
And in my heartless breast and burning brain
That word, that kiss, shall all thoughts else
survive,
With food of saddest memory kept alive, 230
Now thou art dead, as if it were a part
Of thee, my Adonais! I would give
All that I am to be as thou now art!
But I am chained to Time, and cannot thence
depart!

### 27

"O gentle child, beautiful as thou wert, 235
Why didst thou leave the trodden paths of
men

Too soon, and with weak hands though
　　mighty heart
Dare the unpastured dragon [16] in his den?
Defenseless as thou wert, oh, where was then
Wisdom the mirrored shield, or scorn the
　　spear?　　　　　　　　　　　　　　240
Or hadst thou waited the full cycle, when
Thy spirit should have filled its crescent
　　sphere,
The monsters of life's waste had fled from thee
　　like deer.

28

"The herded wolves, bold only to pursue; 244
The obscene ravens, clamorous o'er the dead;
The vultures to the conqueror's banner true
Who feed where Desolation first has fed,
And whose wings rain contagion;—how they
　　fled,
When, like Apollo, from his golden bow
The Pythian of the age [17] one arrow sped  250
And smiled!—The spoilers tempt no second
　　blow,
They fawn on the proud feet that spurn them
　　lying low.

29

"The sun comes forth, and many reptiles
　　spawn;
He sets, and each ephemeral insect then
Is gathered into death without a dawn,  255
And the immortal stars awake again;
So it is in the world of living men:
A godlike mind soars forth, in its delight
Making earth bare and veiling heaven, and
　　when
It sinks, the swarms that dimmed or shared
　　its light  260
Leave to its kindred lamps the spirit's awful
　　night."

30

Thus ceased she: and the mountain shep-
　　herds came,
Their garlands sere, their magic mantles rent;
The Pilgrim of Eternity,[18] whose fame
Over his living head like Heaven is bent,  265
An early but enduring monument,
Came, veiling all the lightnings of his song
In sorrow; from her wilds Ierne sent
The sweetest lyrist of her saddest wrong,[19]
And Love taught Grief to fall like music from
　　his tongue.　　　　　　　　　　　270

31

Midst others of less note, came one frail
　　Form,[20]
A phantom among men; companionless
As the last cloud of an expiring storm
Whose thunder is its knell; he, as I guess,
Had gazed on Nature's naked loveliness, 275
Actaeon-like,[21] and now he fled astray
With feeble steps o'er the world's wilderness,
And his own thoughts, along that rugged
　　way,
Pursued, like raging hounds, their father and
　　their prey.

32

A pardlike [22] Spirit beautiful and swift— 280
A Love in desolation masked;—a Power
Girt round with weakness;—it can scarce up-
　　lift
The weight of the superincumbent hour;
It is a dying lamp, a falling shower,
A breaking billow;—even whilst we speak
Is it not broken? On the withering flower 286
The killing sun smiles brightly: on a cheek
The life can burn in blood, even while the
　　heart may break.

33

His head was bound with pansies overblown,
And faded violets, white, and pied, and
　　blue;　　　　　　　　　　　　　290
And a light spear topped with a cypress cone,
Round whose rude shaft dark ivy-tresses grew
Yet dripping with the forest's noonday dew,
Vibrated, as the ever-beating heart
Shook the weak hand that grasped it; of that
　　crew　　　　　　　　　　　　　295
He came the last, neglected and apart;
A herd-abandoned deer struck by the hunter's
　　dart.

34

All stood aloof, and at his partial [23] moan
Smiled through their tears; well knew that
　　gentle band
Who in another's fate now wept his own, 300
As in the accents of an unknown land
He sung new sorrow; sad Urania scanned
The Stranger's mien, and murmured: "Who
　　art thou?"
He answered not, but with a sudden hand
Made bare his branded and ensanguined
　　brow,　　　　　　　　　　　　305
Which was like Cain's or Christ's—oh! that it
　　should be so!

---

[16] The world of men.
[17] Apollo was called the Pythian because he slew
the Python. Shelley here applies the epithet to
Byron, who attacked the reviewers in his satirical
poem *English Bards and Scotch Reviewers.*
[18] Byron; so called because of *Childe Harold's Pilgrimage.* Cf. III, 70, 8, of *Childe Harold.*
[19] I. e., Ireland sent Thomas Moore.

[20] Shelley.
[21] Actaeon was torn to pieces by his own hounds
after he had seen Artemis bathing.
[22] Leopard-like.　　　　　　　[23] Fond.

### 35

What softer voice is hushed over the dead?
Athwart what brow is that dark mantle thrown?
What form leans sadly o'er the white death-bed,
In mockery of monumental stone, 310
The heavy heart heaving without a moan?
If it be He,[24] who, gentlest of the wise,
Taught, soothed, loved, honored the departed one,
Let me not vex, with inharmonious sighs,
The silence of that heart's accepted sacrifice.

### 36

Our Adonais has drunk poison—oh! 316
What deaf and viperous murderer could crown
Life's early cup with such a draught of woe?
The nameless worm [25] would now itself disown:
It felt, yet could escape, the magic tone 320
Whose prelude held all envy, hate, and wrong,
But what was howling in one breast alone,
Silent with expectation of the song,
Whose master's hand is cold, whose silver lyre unstrung.

### 37

Live thou, whose infamy is not thy fame! 325
Live! fear no heavier chastisement from me,
Thou noteless blot on a remembered name!
But be thyself, and know thyself to be!
And ever at thy season be thou free
To spill the venom when thy fangs o'erflow:
Remorse and Self-contempt shall cling to thee; 331
Hot Shame shall burn upon thy secret brow,
And like a beaten hound tremble thou shalt—as now.

### 38

Nor let us weep that our delight is fled
Far from these carrion kites that scream below; 335
He wakes or sleeps with the enduring dead;
Thou canst not soar where he is sitting now.—
Dust to the dust! but the pure spirit shall flow
Back to the burning fountain whence it came,
A portion of the Eternal, which must glow
Through time and change, unquenchably the same, 341
Whilst the cold embers choke the sordid hearth of shame.

[24] Leigh Hunt.
[25] The *Quarterly* reviewer; see note to stanza 17 above.

### 39

Peace, peace! he is not dead, he doth not sleep—
He hath awakened from the dream of life—
'Tis we, who lost in stormy vision, keep 345
With phantoms an unprofitable strife,
And in mad trance, strike with our spirit's knife
Invulnerable nothings.— We decay
Like corpses in a charnel; fear and grief
Convulse us and consume us day by day, 350
And cold hopes swarm like worms within our living clay.

### 40

He has outsoared the shadow of our night;
Envy and calumny and hate and pain,
And that unrest which men miscall delight,
Can touch him not and torture not again; 355
From the contagion of the world's slow stain
He is secure, and now can never mourn
A heart grown cold, a head grown gray in vain;
Nor, when the spirit's self has ceased to burn,
With sparkless ashes load an unlamented urn.

### 41

He lives, he wakes—'tis Death is dead, not he; 361
Mourn not for Adonais.—Thou young Dawn,
Turn all thy dew to splendor, for from thee
The spirit thou lamentest is not gone;
Ye caverns and ye forests, cease to moan! 365
Cease, ye faint flowers and fountains, and thou Air,
Which like a mourning veil thy scarf hadst thrown
O'er the abandoned Earth, now leave it bare
Even to the joyous stars which smile on its despair!

### 42

He is made one with Nature: there is heard
His voice in all her music, from the moan 371
Of thunder, to the song of night's sweet bird;
He is a presence to be felt and known
In darkness and in light, from herb and stone,
Spreading itself where'er that Power may move 375
Which has withdrawn his being to its own;
Which wields the world with never-wearied love,
Sustains it from beneath, and kindles it above.

### 43

He is a portion of the loveliness
Which once he made more lovely: he doth bear 380
His part, while the one Spirit's plastic stress

Sweeps through the dull dense world, compelling there,
All new successions to the forms they wear;
Torturing th' unwilling dross that checks its flight
To its own likeness, as each mass may bear;                385
And bursting in its beauty and its might
From trees and beasts and men into the Heaven's light.

### 44

The splendors of the firmament of time
May be eclipsed, but are extinguished not;
Like stars to their appointed height they climb,                390
And death is a low mist which cannot blot
The brightness it may veil. When lofty thought
Lifts a young heart above its mortal lair,
And love and life contend in it, for what
Shall be its earthly doom, the dead live there
And move like winds of light on dark and stormy air.                396

### 45

The inheritors of unfulfilled renown
Rose from their thrones, built beyond mortal thought,
Far in the Unapparent. Chatterton [26]
Rose pale,—his solemn agony had not                400
Yet faded from him; Sidney,[27] as he fought
And as he fell and as he lived and loved
Sublimely mild, a Spirit without spot,
Arose; and Lucan,[28] by his death approved:
Oblivion as they rose shrank like a thing reproved.                405

### 46

And many more, whose names on Earth are dark,
But whose transmitted effluence cannot die
So long as fire outlives the parent spark,
Rose, robed in dazzling immortality.
"Thou art become as one of us," they cry, 410
"It was for thee yon kingless sphere has long
Swung blind in unascended majesty,
Silent alone amid an Heaven of Song.
Assume thy wingéd throne, thou Vesper [29] of our throng!"

### 47

Who mourns for Adonais? Oh, come forth,
Fond wretch! and know thyself and him aright.                416

[26] Thomas Chatterton (1752–1770), who died by his own hand.
[27] Sir Philip Sidney (1554–1586), who died from a wound received in battle.
[28] Roman poet (A.D. 39–65), who committed suicide to escape execution commanded by Nero.
[29] Evening star.

Clasp with thy panting soul the pendulous Earth;
As from a center, dart thy spirit's light
Beyond all worlds, until its spacious might
Satiate the void circumference: then shrink
Even to a point within our day and night; 421
And keep thy heart light lest it make thee sink
When hope has kindled hope, and lured thee to the brink.

### 48

Or go to Rome, which is the sepulcher,
Oh, not of him, but of our joy: 'tis nought
That ages, empires, and religions there                426
Lie buried in the ravage they have wrought;
For such as he can lend,—they borrow not
Glory from those who made the world their prey;
And he is gathered to the kings of thought
Who waged contention with their time's decay,                431
And of the past are all that cannot pass away.

### 49

Go thou to Rome,—at once the Paradise,
The grave, the city, and the wilderness;
And where its wrecks like shattered mountains rise,                435
And flowering weeds, and fragrant copses dress
The bones of Desolation's nakedness
Pass, till the spirit of the spot shall lead
Thy footsteps to a slope of green access
Where, like an infant's smile, over the dead
A light of laughing flowers along the grass is spread;                441

### 50

And gray walls molder round, on which dull Time
Feeds, like slow fire upon a hoary brand;
And one keen pyramid [30] with wedge sublime,
Pavilioning the dust of him who planned 445
This refuge for his memory, doth stand
Like flame transformed to marble; and beneath,
A field is spread, on which a newer band
Have pitched in Heaven's smile their camp of death,
Welcoming him we lose with scarce extinguished breath.                450

### 51

Here pause: these graves are all too young as yet
To have outgrown the sorrow which consigned
Its charge to each; and if the seal is set,
Here, on one fountain of a mourning mind,

[30] The tomb of Cestius, overlooking the Protestant Cemetery in which Keats is buried.

Break it not thou! too surely shalt thou
   find     455
Thine own well full, if thou returnest home,
Of tears and gall. From the world's bitter
   wind
Seek shelter in the shadow of the tomb.
What Adonais is, why fear we to become?

### 52

The One remains, the many change and pass;
Heaven's light forever shines, Earth's shad-
   ows fly;     461
Life, like a dome of many-colored glass,
Stains the white radiance of Eternity,
Until Death tramples it to fragments.—Die,
If thou wouldst be with that which thou dost
   seek!     465
Follow where all is fled!—Rome's azure sky,
Flowers, ruins, statues, music, words, are
   weak
The glory they transfuse [31] with fitting truth
   to speak.

### 53

Why linger, why turn back, why shrink, my
   Heart?
Thy hopes are gone before: from all things
   here     470
They have departed; thou shouldst now de-
   part!
A light is passed from the revolving year,
And man, and woman; and what still is dear
Attracts to crush, repels to make thee wither.
The soft sky smiles,—the low wind whispers
   near:     475
'Tis Adonais calls! oh, hasten thither,
No more let Life divide what Death can join
   together.

### 54

That Light whose smile kindles the Universe,
That Beauty in which all things work and
   move,
That Benediction which the eclipsing Curse
Of birth can quench not, that sustaining
   Love     481
Which through the web of being blindly
   wove
By man and beast and earth and air and sea,
Burns bright or dim, as each are mirrors of
The fire for which all thirst; now beams on
   me,     485
Consuming the last clouds of cold mortality.

### 55

The breath whose might I have invoked in
   song
Descends on me; my spirit's bark is driven,
Far from the shore, far from the trembling
   throng
Whose sails were never to the tempest
   given;     490

[31] Instill.

The massy earth and spheréd skies are riven!
I am borne darkly, fearfully, afar;
Whilst, burning through the inmost veil of
   Heaven,
The soul of Adonais, like a star,
Beacons from the abode where the Eternal
   are.     495

# Hellas [1]

### The Final Chorus

The world's great age begins anew,
   The golden years return,
The earth doth like a snake renew
   Her winter weeds outworn:
Heaven smiles, and faiths and empires gleam, [5]
Like wrecks of a dissolving dream.

A brighter Hellas rears its mountains
   From waves serener far;
A new Peneus [2] rolls his fountains
   Against the morning star.     10
Where fairer Tempes [3] bloom, there sleep
Young Cyclads [4] on a sunnier deep.

A loftier Argo [5] cleaves the main,
   Fraught with a later prize;
Another Orpheus sings again,     15
   And loves, and weeps, and dies.
A new Ulysses leaves once more
Calypso [6] for his native shore.

Oh, write no more the tale of Troy,
   If earth Death's scroll must be!     20
Nor mix with Laian [7] rage the joy
   Which dawns upon the free:
Although a subtler Sphinx renew
Riddles of death Thebes never knew.

Another Athens shall arise,     25
   And to remoter time
Bequeath, like sunset to the skies,
   The splendor of its prime;

[1] A lyrical drama, written in the autumn of 1821
and published in the spring of 1822; inspired by the
Greek war for independence, which Shelley thinks
of as ushering in a new Golden Age which will surpass the ancient glories of Greece. The opening
of the Final Chorus is reminiscent of Virgil's fourth
Eclogue.
   [2] A river of Thessaly.
   [3] The valley through which the Peneus flows.
   [4] The Cyclades, islands in the Aegean Sea.
   [5] The ship of Jason, in which the Golden Fleece
was carried.
   [6] The nymph who vainly sought to keep Ulysses on
her island with her, though she promised him immortality if he would remain.
   [7] The family of Laius, king of Thebes, was pursued by dreadful misfortunes. The son of Laius was
Oedipus, who freed Thebes from the affliction of
the Sphinx by answering her riddle correctly, but
who unwittingly killed his father and married his
mother.

And leave, if nought so bright may live,
All earth can take or Heaven can give.        30

Saturn and Love their long repose
    Shall burst,[8] more bright and good
Than all who fell, than One who rose,
    Than many unsubdued:
Not gold, not blood, their altar dowers,      35
But votive tears and symbol flowers.

Oh, cease! must hate and death return?
    Cease! must men kill and die?
Cease! drain not to its dregs the urn
    Of bitter prophecy.                       40
The world is weary of the past,
Oh, might it die or rest at last!

# Lines: "When the Lamp Is Shattered" [1]

### I

When the lamp is shattered
The light in the dust lies dead—

[8] Saturn and Love were among the deities of a real or imaginary state of innocence and happiness. *All* those *who fell*, or the Gods of Greece, Asia, and Egypt; the *One who rose*, or Jesus Christ, at whose appearance the idols of the Pagan World were amerced of their worship; and *the many unsubdued*, or the monstrous objects of the idolatry of China, India, the Antarctic islands, and the native tribes of America, certainly have reigned over the understandings of men in conjunction or in succession, during periods in which all we know of evil has been in a state of portentous, and, until the revival of learning, perpetually increasing, activity. The Grecian gods seem indeed to have been personally more innocent, although it cannot be said, that as far as temperance and chastity are concerned, they gave so edifying an example as their successor. The sublime human character of Jesus Christ was deformed by an imputed identification with a Power, who tempted, betrayed, and punished the innocent beings who were called into existence by His sole will; and for the period of a thousand years, the spirit of this most just, wise, and benevolent of men has been propitiated with myriads of hecatombs of those who approached the nearest to His innocence and wisdom, sacrificed under every aggravation of atrocity and variety of torture. The horrors of the Mexican, the Peruvian, and the Indian superstitions are well known (Shelley's note).
[1] Written in 1822; published in 1824.

When the cloud is scattered
The rainbow's glory is shed.
    When the lute is broken,                  5
Sweet tones are remembered not;
    When the lips have spoken,
Loved accents are soon forgot.

### II

As music and splendor
Survive not the lamp and the lute,            10
    The heart's echoes render
No song when the spirit is mute:—
    No song but sad dirges,
Like the wind through a ruined cell,
    Or the mournful surges                    15
That ring the dead seaman's knell.

### III

When the hearts have once mingled
Love first leaves the well-built nest;
    The weak one is singled
To endure what it once possessed.            20
    O Love! who bewailest
The frailty of all things here,
    Why choose you the frailest
For your cradle, your home, and your bier?

### IV

Its passions will rock thee                   25
As the storms rock the ravens on high;
    Bright reason will mock thee,
Like the sun from a wintry sky.
    From thy nest every rafter
Will rot, and thine eagle home               30
    Leave thee naked to laughter,
When leaves fall and cold winds come.

# A Dirge [1]

Rough wind, that moanest loud
    Grief too sad for song;
Wild wind, when sullen cloud
    Knells all the night long;
Sad storm, whose tears are vain,              5
Bare woods, whose branches strain,
Deep caves and dreary main,—
    Wail, for the world's wrong!

[1] Written in 1822; published in 1824.

# John Keats

## 1795-1821

Keats's father was stable-keeper at the Swan and Hoop Inn, Finsbury Pavement, London. He had married the daughter of the proprietor, and Keats was born there on 31 October, 1795. In 1803 the boy was sent to a good private school kept by the Rev. J. Clarke at Enfield. Here he attracted the attention of the junior master, Charles Cowden Clarke, and a relationship sprang up which extended beyond his period at the school and was of great use to him. Clarke later said that Keats, although during his last years at school an eager reader of history, fiction, and books of mythology, was also a sturdy, active youngster and a favorite amongst his school-fellows. In 1804 his father was killed by a fall from his horse, and in 1810 his mother died of a consumption. Keats's guardians at once removed him from school and apprenticed him to a surgeon. His passion for reading did not leave him in his new work and surroundings, and he kept in touch with the Clarkes. It was in 1812 or 1813 that Cowden Clarke introduced him to the works of Spenser, reading to him Spenser's Epithalamion and lending him The Faerie Queene. A couple of years later it was also Clarke who introduced him to Chapman's Homer, which inspired the famous sonnet. Meanwhile Keats had in 1814 broken his apprenticeship and had gone to London to study medicine. Soon after this he began to write poetry, though continuing his medical studies. In 1816, through the instrumentality of Clarke, he met Leigh Hunt, who communicated his zeal for liberty to Keats and also gave his poetry enthusiastic encouragement. Directly or indirectly through Hunt, Keats became acquainted with Benjamin Haydon—an artist who helped the poet to appreciate Greek sculpture—with Shelley, Horace Smith, Hazlitt, Wordsworth, and others.

In 1817 Keats published his first volume, Poems, a volume which on the whole showed much immaturity and which was harshly criti-cized. This, however, hardly discouraged him, for his own critical faculty was developing and he saw many of his faults as clearly as did his critics. In 1816 when he had come of age he had determined to abandon medicine for poetry, and there is no sign that he ever wavered concerning the rightness of this decision. In 1818 he published Endymion. He was dissatisfied with it, but felt that it was as good a poem as he could then write, and that it was better to put it out of his reach by publication than to attempt to mend it. In a preface he said as much:—any reader of the poem "must soon perceive great inexperience, immaturity, and every error denoting a feverish attempt, rather than a deed accomplished." But despite this admission the poem was greeted with extreme abuse by the critics—abuse so extreme that at the time it was reputed to have been a cause of Keats's early death. This, as we now know, it was not. Keats's reaction to criticism can only be described as fine and manly. As for hostile critics, he wrote to his publisher several months after the appearance of the poem, "I begin to get a little acquainted with my own strength and weakness. Praise or blame has but a momentary effect on the man whose love of beauty in the abstract makes him a severe critic on his own works. My own domestic criticism has given me pain without comparison beyond what Blackwood or the Quarterly could possibly inflict—and also when I feel I am right, no external praise can give me such a glow as my own solitary reperception and ratification of what is fine. J. S. [the writer of a letter about the poem to the Morning Chronicle] is perfectly right in regard to the slip-shod Endymion. That it is so is no fault of mine. No! —though it may sound a little paradoxical. It is as good as I had power to make it—by myself. Had I been nervous about its being a perfect piece, and with that view asked advice, and trembled over every page, it would not have been written; for it is not in my nature to fum-

*ble—I will write independently.—I have written independently* without judgment. *I may write independently, and* with judgment, *hereafter. The Genius of Poetry must work out its own salvation in a man: it cannot be matured by law and precept, but by sensation and watchfulness in itself. That which is creative must create itself. In Endymion I leaped headlong into the sea, and thereby have become better acquainted with the soundings, the quicksands, and the rocks, than if I had stayed upon the green shore, and piped a silly pipe, and took tea and comfortable advice."*

Already, indeed, before Endymion was published Keats was at work upon Isabella in the attempt to do something better. In the summer of 1818 he went with his friend Charles Brown on a walking tour through the Lake country to Scotland. After about six weeks of tramping he was compelled to return to London on account of throat trouble which had developed. This was the first warning sign of the illness which was to cut his life short. In the fall of the same year he met Fanny Brawne, a girl with whom he fell deeply in love. He was also during the fall of this year in constant attendance at the bedside of his brother Tom, who died of consumption in December. Early in 1819 Keats was at work on Hyperion and The Eve of St. Agnes, and during the spring and fall he wrote the greater number of his finest poems. In February, 1820, it became unmistakable that he had consumption. During the spring he saw the 1820 volume of his poems through the press, but from that time forward he was, and felt himself to be, a doomed man. His condition continually grew worse, and at the end of the summer he was warned that it would be fatal to him to spend another winter in England. He sailed for Naples in September, stayed there until November, and then went to Rome. He was, however, too ill for the Italian climate materially to help him, and he died on 23 February, 1821.

It has been remarked that, while Shelley wrote nearly all his greatest poetry in the period between his twenty-sixth year and the time of his death, Keats died at twenty-five, nor had he been a precocious youth. And yet, while Coleridge and Shelley were also pioneers in the nineteenth-century development of poetry, Sir Herbert Grierson has said that "Keats has been, without any exception, the greatest influence in English poetry for a whole century. To his example and inspiration are due all the wonderful sensuous felicity, the splendor of exotic phrasing and harmony of Tennyson's 1842 volumes; the bold and varied experiments of Browning's Bells and Pomegranates; the curious subtleties of The Blessed Damozel and The House of Life; The Defense of Guinevere and The Earthly Paradise; Poems and Ballads and Atalanta in Calydon. If poetry be first and last a sensuous pleasure, then Keats and his successors are the greatest of our poets since Spenser, and the Marlowe of Hero and Leander, the Shakespeare of Venus and Adonis and the 'sugared sonnets'; as virtuosi of phrase and harmonies perhaps greater even than these." (Warton Lect. XI, Brit. Acad.). Of course poetry is not first and last a sensuous pleasure, but it is a part of Keats's greatness that, although he began his work wishing only to mirror in poetry the fine flower of exquisite sensation, he rapidly outgrew his starting-point and was unmistakably approaching a rich maturity when death cut him down. He "is a great poet, first of all because he had the supreme sensitiveness of a poet's imagination, and caught up the beauty about him as a lake takes color and shadow from the sky, partly because he was a born artist and studied with constant devotion the technique of his art, but also because he had a mind and spirit bent on applying to his art the searching test of hard thought and vital experience. We only read Keats aright when we learn from his own lips that he wrote, not for art's sake only, but for the sake of truth and for the sake of life" (E. de Selincourt, Warton Lect. XII, Brit. Acad.).

The best edition of The Complete Works of John Keats is edited by H. Buxton Forman (5 vols., Glasgow, 1900–1901). This contains Keats's letters which, however, have been reedited with additions by Maurice Buxton Forman (Oxford, 1952). One of the two best editions of Keats's Poems is edited by E. de Selincourt (London, 1926); the other is edited by H. W. Garrod: The Poetical Works of John Keats (Oxford, 1958). The best biography is Sidney Colvin's John Keats: His Life and Poetry, His Friends, Critics, and After-Fame (New York, 1925). The much longer John Keats by Amy Lowell (Boston, 1925) is almost more interesting for its author than for its subject; still it is valuable. Other biographical studies include H. W. Garrod's Keats (Oxford, 1939), and Robert Gittings' John Keats: the Living Year, Sept., 1818–Sept., 1819 (Cambridge, U. S. A., 1954). Elucidations and critical studies have multiplied of late years. Those most likely to be useful are The

Mind of John Keats, *by Clarence DeWitt Thorpe (New York, 1926);* The Evolution of Keats's Poetry, *by C. L. Finney (Cambridge, U. S. A., 1936);* The Stylistic Development of Keats, *by Warner Bate (Oxford, 1945);* John Keats' Fancy, *by James Caldwell (Ithaca, N. Y., 1945);* The Mystery of Keats *(London, 1949) and* Keats *(London, 1955), by J. M. Murry; and* The Finer Tone: Keats's Major Poems, *by E. R. Wasserman (Baltimore, 1953).*

## Sonnet [1]

Keen, fitful gusts are whisp'ring here and there
  Among the bushes, half leafless and dry;
  The stars look very cold about the sky,
And I have many miles on foot to fare;
Yet feel I little of the cold bleak air,    5
  Or of the dead leaves rustling drearily,
  Or of those silver lamps that burn on high,
Or of the distance from home's pleasant lair:
For I am brimful of the friendliness
  That in a little cottage I have found;   10
Of fair-haired Milton's eloquent distress,
  And all his love for gentle Lycid [2] drowned;
Of lovely Laura [3] in her light green dress,
  And faithful Petrarch gloriously crowned.

## On First Looking into Chapman's Homer [4]

Much have I traveled in the realms of gold,
  And many goodly states and kingdoms seen;
  Round many western islands have I been
Which bards in fealty to Apollo hold.
Oft of one wide expanse had I been told,   5
  That deep-browed Homer ruled as his demesne:
  Yet did I never breathe its pure serene
Till I heard Chapman [5] speak out loud and bold:
Then felt I like some watcher of the skies
  When a new planet swims into his ken;   10
Or like stout Cortez [6] when with eagle eyes
  He stared at the Pacific—and all his men
Looked at each other with a wild surmise—
  Silent, upon a peak in Darien.

[1] Written in 1816 after a visit to Leigh Hunt's cottage at Hampstead; published in 1817.
[2] *Lycidas.*
[3] The lady whose name Petrarch immortalized in the sonnets which record his love for her.
[4] Written in 1815; published in 1817.
[5] George Chapman (1559?-1634) published his translations of the *Iliad* and *Odyssey* 1598-1616.
[6] Either a conscious alteration or a slip, as it was really Balboa who discovered the Pacific.

## Endymion [1]

### BOOK I

#### Hymn to Pan

O thou, whose mighty palace roof doth hang
From jaggéd trunks, and overshadoweth
Eternal whispers, glooms, the birth, life, death
Of unseen flowers in heavy peacefulness;
Who lov'st to see the hamadryads [2] dress   5
Their ruffled locks where meeting hazels darken;
And through whole solemn hours dost sit, and hearken
The dreary melody of bedded reeds—
In desolate places, where dank moisture breeds
The pipy hemlock [3] to strange overgrowth,   10
Bethinking thee, how melancholy loath
Thou wast to lose fair Syrinx [4]—do thou now,
By thy love's milky brow!
By all the trembling mazes that she ran,
Hear us, great Pan!   15

O thou, for whose soul-soothing quiet, turtles [5]
Passion their voices cooingly 'mong myrtles,
What time thou wanderest at eventide
Through sunny meadows, that outskirt the side
Of thine enmosséd realms: O thou, to whom [20]
Broad-leaved fig-trees even now foredoom
Their ripened fruitage; yellow-girted bees
Their golden honeycombs; our village leas
Their fairest-blossomed beans and poppied corn; [6]
The chuckling linnet its five young unborn, [25]
To sing for thee; low-creeping strawberries
Their summer coolness; pent-up butterflies [7]
Their freckled wings; yea, the fresh-budding year
All its completions—be quickly near,
By every wind that nods the mountain pine, [30]
O forester divine!

Thou, to whom every faun and satyr flies
For willing service; whether to surprise
The squatted hare while in half-sleeping fit;
Or upward ragged precipices flit   35
To save poor lambkins from the eagle's maw;
Or by mysterious enticement draw

[1] Published in 1818. The *Hymn to Pan* forms ll. 232-306 of Bk. I and was written in the early summer of 1817. It is sung by those at the festival of Latmian shepherds with which *Endymion* opens.
[2] Tree-nymphs.
[3] A poisonous European plant with a hollow stem, like a pipe.
[4] A nymph who fled from Pan and, when she sought refuge in a river, was changed into a reed.
[5] Turtle-doves.
[6] Wheat intermingled with poppies.
[7] Chrysalises.

Bewildered shepherds to their path again;
Or to tread breathless round the frothy main,
And gather up all fancifulest shells          40
For thee to tumble into Naiads' cells,[8]
And, being hidden, laugh at their out-peeping;
Or to delight thee with fantastic leaping,
The while they pelt each other on the crown
With silvery oak-apples, and fir-cones brown—
By all the echoes that about thee ring,          46
Hear us, O satyr king!

   O Hearkener to the loud-clapping shears,
While ever and anon to his shorn peers
A ram goes bleating: Winder of the horn,          50
When snouted wild-boars routing tender corn
Anger our huntsmen: Breather round our farms,
To keep off mildews, and all weather harms:
Strange ministrant of undescribéd sounds,
That come a-swooning over hollow grounds,          55
And wither drearily on barren moors:
Dread opener of the mysterious doors
Leading to universal knowledge—see,
Great son of Dryope,
The many that are come to pay their vows          60
With leaves about their brows!

   Be still the unimaginable lodge
For solitary thinkings; such as dodge
Conception to the very bourn [9] of heaven,          64
Then leave the naked brain: be still the leaven
That, spreading in this dull and clodded earth,
Gives it a touch ethereal—a new birth:
Be still a symbol of immensity;
A firmament reflected in a sea;
An element filling the space between;          70
An unknown—but no more: we humbly screen
With uplift hands or foreheads, lowly bending,
And giving out a shout most heaven-rending,
Conjure thee to receive our humble Paean,[10]
Upon thy Mount Lycean! [11]

## BOOK IV

### Song of the Indian Maid [12]

O Sorrow,
Why dost borrow
The natural hue of health, from vermeil [13]
   lips?—
   To give maiden blushes
   To the white rose bushes?          5
Or is 't thy dew hand the daisy tips?

  [8] The dwelling-places of nymphs of fresh-water streams.
  [9] Boundary.      [10] Hymn of praise.
  [11] Pan was born on Lycaeus, a mountain in Arcadia.
  [12] This song, or hymn, forms ll. 146–290 of Bk. IV. It was written in the autumn of 1817. Endymion, while searching vainly for Cynthia, whom he loves, finds in the forest an Indian maiden who is bewailing the loss of her lover and the emptiness of her soul without love.
  [13] Vermilion.

O Sorrow,
Why dost borrow
The lustrous passion from a falcon-eye?—
   To give the glow-worm light?          10
   Or, on a moonless night,
To tinge, on siren shores, the salt sea-spry? [14]

O Sorrow,
Why dost borrow
The mellow ditties from a mourning tongue?—
   To give at evening pale          16
   Unto the nightingale,
That thou mayst listen the cold dews among?

O Sorrow,
Why dost borrow          20
Heart's lightness from the merriment of
   May?—
   A lover would not tread
   A cowslip on the head,
Though he should dance from eve till peep of
   day—
   Nor any drooping flower          25
   Held sacred for thy bower,
Wherever he may sport himself and play.

To Sorrow
   I bade good morrow,
And thought to leave her far away behind;          30
   But cheerly, cheerly,
   She loves me dearly;
She is so constant to me, and so kind:
   I would deceive her
   And so leave her,          35
But ah! she is so constant and so kind.

Beneath my palm-trees, by the river side,
I sat a-weeping: in the whole world wide
There was no one to ask me why I wept—
   And so I kept          40
Brimming the water-lily cups with tears
   Cold as my fears.

Beneath my palm-trees, by the river side,
I sat a-weeping: what enamored bride,
Cheated by shadowy wooer from the clouds,          44
   But hides and shrouds
Beneath dark palm-trees by a river side?

And as I sat, over the light blue hills
There came a noise of revelers: the rills
Into the wide stream came of purple hue—          50
   'Twas Bacchus and his crew! [15]
The earnest trumpet spake, and silver thrills
From kissing cymbals made a merry din—
   'Twas Bacchus and his kin!
Like to a moving vintage down they came,          55

  [14] Sea-spray.
  [15] The following description of the progress of Bacchus is inspired by Titian's *Bacchus and Ariadne*, a picture which is now in the National Gallery, London.

Crowned with green leaves, and faces all on
    flame;
All madly dancing through the pleasant valley,
    To scare thee, Melancholy!
O then, O then, thou wast a simple name!
And I forgot thee, as the berried holly     60
By shepherds is forgotten, when, in June,
Tall chestnuts keep away the sun and moon:—
    I rushed into the folly!

Within his car, aloft, young Bacchus stood,
Trifling his ivy-dart,[16] in dancing mood,     65
    With sidelong laughing;
And little rills of crimson wine imbrued
His plump white arms, and shoulders, enough
    white
    For Venus' pearly bite;
And near him rode Silenus [17] on his ass,     70
Pelted with flowers as he on did pass
    Tipsily quaffing.

Whence came ye, merry Damsels! whence
    came ye,
So many, and so many, and such glee?
Why have ye left your bowers desolate,     75
    Your lutes, and gentler fate?
"We follow Bacchus! Bacchus on the wing,
    A-conquering!
Bacchus, young Bacchus! good or ill betide,
We dance before him thorough kingdoms
    wide:—     80
Come hither, lady fair, and joinéd be
    To our wild minstrelsy!"

Whence came ye, jolly Satyrs! whence came ye,
So many, and so many, and such glee?
Why have ye left your forest haunts, why left
    Your nuts in oak-tree cleft?—     86
"For wine, for wine we left our kernel tree;
For wine we left our heath, and yellow brooms,
    And cold mushrooms;
For wine we follow Bacchus through the earth;
Great god of breathless cups and chirping
    mirth!—     91
Come hither, lady fair, and joinéd be
    To our mad minstrelsy!"

Over wide streams and mountains great we
    went,
And, save when Bacchus kept his ivy tent,     95
Onward the tiger and the leopard pants,
    With Asian elephants:
Onward these myriads—with song and dance,
With zebras striped, and sleek Arabians' prance,
Web-footed alligators, crocodiles,     100
Bearing upon their scaly backs, in files,
Plump infant laughers mimicking the coil
Of seamen, and stout galley-rowers' toil:
With toying oars and silken sails they glide,
    Nor care for wind and tide.     105

[16] Playing with his thyrsus, or wand, which he
always carried.
[17] The foster-father of Bacchus.

Mounted on panthers' furs and lions' manes,
From rear to van they scour about the plains;
A three days' journey in a moment done:
And always, at the rising of the sun,
About the wilds they hunt with spear and horn,
    On spleenful unicorn.     111

I saw Osirian [18] Egypt kneel adown
    Before the vine-wreath crown!
I saw parched Abyssinia rouse and sing
    To the silver cymbals' ring!     115
I saw the whelming vintage hotly pierce
    Old Tartary the fierce!
The kings of Ind their jewel-scepters vail,[19]
And from their treasures scatter pearléd hail;
Great Brahma from his mystic heaven groans,
    And all his priesthood moans,     121
Before young Bacchus' eye-wink turning pale.—
Into these regions came I, following him,
Sick-hearted, weary—so I took a whim
To stray away into these forests drear,     125
    Alone, without a peer:
And I have told thee all thou mayest hear.

    Young stranger!
    I've been a ranger
In search of pleasure throughout every clime;
    Alas, 'tis not for me!     131
    Bewitched I sure must be,
To lose in grieving all my maiden prime.

    Come then, Sorrow,
    Sweetest Sorrow!     135
Like an own babe I nurse thee on my breast:
    I thought to leave thee,
    And deceive thee,
But now of all the world I love thee best.

    There is not one,     140
    No, no, not one
But thee to comfort a poor lonely maid;
    Thou art her mother,
    And her brother,
Her playmate, and her wooer in the shade. [145]

## Sonnet [1]

When I have fears that I may cease to be
    Before my pen has gleaned my teeming
    brain,
Before high-piléd books, in charact'ry,[2]
    Hold like rich garners the full-ripened grain;
When I behold, upon the night's starred face, [5]
    Huge cloudy symbols of a high romance,
And think that I may never live to trace

[18] According to Keats's authority (Lemprière)
Osiris, a god worshiped by the Egyptians, corre-
sponded to the Greek god Bacchus.
[19] Bend down.
[1] Written before 31 January, 1818; published in
1848.
[2] Writing.

Their shadows, with the magic hand of
    chance;
And when I feel, fair creature of an hour,
    That I shall never look upon thee more,  10
Never have relish in the faery power
    Of unreflecting love;—then on the shore
Of the wide world I stand alone, and think,
Till Love and Fame to nothingness do sink.

## Fragment of an Ode to Maia, Written on May Day, 1818 [3]

Mother of Hermes! and still youthful Maia!
    May I sing to thee
As thou wast hymnéd on the shores of Baiae? [4]
    Or may I woo thee
In earlier Sicilian? or thy smiles  5
Seek as they once were sought, in Grecian isles,
By bards who died content on pleasant sward,
Leaving great verse unto a little clan?
O, give me their old vigor, and unheard
Save of the quiet primrose, and the span  10
    Of heaven and few ears,
Rounded by thee, my song should die away
    Content as theirs,
Rich in the simple worship of a day.

## Stanzas [5]

In a drear-nighted December,
Too happy, happy tree,
Thy branches ne'er remember
Their green felicity:
The north cannot undo them,  5
With a sleety whistle through them;
Nor frozen thrawings glue them
From budding at the prime.

In a drear-nighted December,
Too happy, happy brook,  10
Thy bubblings ne'er remember
Apollo's summer look;
But with a sweet forgetting,
They stay their crystal fretting,
Never, never petting  15
About the frozen time.

Ah! would 'twere so with many
A gentle girl and boy!
But were there ever any
Writhed not at passéd joy?  20
To know the change and feel it,

[3] Published in 1848. Maia was the eldest and most
beautiful of the seven sisters known as the Pleiads,
and was a goddess of the spring.

[4] Baiae, near Naples, was famous for its situation
and baths, and many wealthy Romans had country
houses there. Keats thinks of the cult of Maia as
extending from Roman times back to the days when
Greek colonies were planted in Sicily and further
back to earlier days in the Greek islands.

[5] Written in 1817 or 1818; published in 1829.

When there is none to heal it,
Nor numbéd sense to steel it,
Was never said in rime.

## Fancy [1]

Ever let the Fancy roam,
Pleasure never is at home:
At a touch sweet Pleasure melteth,
Like to bubbles when rain pelteth;
Then let wingéd Fancy wander  5
Through the thought still spread beyond her:
Open wide the mind's cage-door,
She'll dart forth, and cloudward soar.
O sweet Fancy! let her loose;
Summer's joys are spoilt by use,  10
And the enjoying of the Spring
Fades as does its blossoming:
Autumn's red-lipped fruitage too,
Blushing through the mist and dew,
Cloys with tasting: What do then?  15
Sit thee by the ingle, [2] when
The sear faggot blazes bright,
Spirit of a winter's night;
When the soundless earth is muffled,
And the cakéd snow is shuffled  20
From the plowboy's heavy shoon; [3]
When the Night doth meet the Noon
In a dark conspiracy
To banish Even from her sky.
Sit thee there, and send abroad,  25
With a mind self-overawed,
Fancy, high-commissioned:—send her!
She has vassals to attend her:
She will bring, in spite of frost,
Beauties that the earth hath lost;  30
She will bring thee, all together,
All delights of summer weather;
All the buds and bells of May,
From dewy sward or thorny spray;
All the heapéd Autumn's wealth,  35
With a still, mysterious stealth:
She will mix these pleasures up
Like three fit wines in a cup,
And thou shalt quaff it:—thou shalt hear
Distant harvest-carols clear;  40
Rustle of the reapéd corn;
Sweet birds antheming the morn:
And, in the same moment—hark!
'Tis the early April lark,
Or the rooks, with busy caw,  45
Foraging for sticks and straw.
Thou shalt, at one glance, behold
The daisy and the marigold;
White-plumed lilies, and the first
Hedge-grown primrose that hath burst;  50
Shaded hyacinth, alway
Sapphire queen of the mid-May;
And every leaf, and every flower
Pearléd with the self-same shower.
Thou shalt see the field-mouse peep  55

[1] Written in 1818; published in 1820.
[2] Fireside.    [3] Shoes.

Meager from its célléd sleep;
And the snake all winter-thin
Cast on sunny bank its skin;
Freckled nest eggs thou shalt see
Hatching in the hawthorn-tree,         60
When the hen-bird's wing doth rest
Quiet on her mossy nest;
Then the hurry and alarm
When the bee-hive casts [4] its swarm;
Acorns ripe down-pattering,          65
While the autumn breezes sing.

Oh, sweet Fancy! let her loose;
Everything is spoilt by use:
Where's the cheek that doth not fade,
Too much gazed at? Where's the maid      70
Whose lip mature is ever new?
Where's the eye, however blue,
Doth not weary? Where's the face
One would meet in every place?
Where's the voice, however soft,        75
One would hear so very oft?
At a touch sweet Pleasure melteth
Like to bubbles when rain pelteth.
Let, then, wingéd Fancy find
Thee a mistress to thy mind:          80
Dulcet-eyed as Ceres' daughter,[5]
Ere the God of Torment taught her
How to frown and how to chide;
With a waist and with a side
White as Hebe's,[6] when her zone      85
Slipped its golden clasp, and down
Fell her kirtle to her feet,
While she held the goblet sweet,
And Jove grew languid.—Break the mesh
Of the Fancy's silken leash;         90
Quickly break her prison-string,
And such joys as these she'll bring.
Let the wingéd Fancy roam,
Pleasure never is at home.

## Ode [1]

Bards of Passion and of Mirth,
Ye have left your souls on earth!
Have ye souls in heaven too,
Double-lived in regions new?
Yes, and those of heaven commune       5
With the spheres of sun and moon;
With the noise of fountains wond'rous,
And the parle [2] of voices thund'rous;
With the whisper of heaven's trees

  [4] Emits.
  [5] Proserpine, who became the queen of Pluto,
king of the underworld of shades.
  [6] Jove's cup-bearer.
  [1] Written in 1818; published in 1820. Keats wrote
this in his copy of the plays of Beaumont and
Fletcher, on the blank page preceding the tragi-
comedy entitled *The Fair Maid of the Inn.* The
poem was, therefore, if not addressed to Beaumont
and Fletcher, at least inspired by thought of their
work.
  [2] Speech.

And one another, in soft ease         10
Seated on Elysian lawns
Browsed by none but Dian's fawns;
Underneath large blue-bells tented,
Where the daisies are rose-scented,
And the rose herself has got         15
Perfume which on earth is not;
Where the nightingale doth sing
Not a senseless, trancéd thing,
But divine, melodious truth;
Philosophic numbers smooth;          20
Tales and golden histories
Of heaven and its mysteries.

Thus ye live on high, and then
On the earth ye live again;
And the souls ye left behind you      25
Teach us, here, the way to find you,
Where your other souls are joying
Never slumbered, never cloying.
Here, your earth-born souls still speak
To mortals, of their little week;     30
Of their sorrows and delights;
Of their passions and their spites;
Of their glory and their shame;
What doth strengthen and what maim.
Thus ye teach us, every day,          35
Wisdom, though fled far away.

Bards of Passion and of Mirth,
Ye have left your souls on earth!
Ye have souls in heaven too,
Double-lived in regions new!          40

## Lines on the Mermaid Tavern [3]

Souls of poets dead and gone,
What Elysium have ye known,
Happy field or mossy cavern,
Choicer than the Mermaid Tavern?
Have ye tippled drink more fine        5
Than mine host's Canary wine?
Or are fruits of Paradise
Sweeter than those dainty pies
Of venison? O generous food!
Dressed as though bold Robin Hood     10
Would, with his maid Marian,
Sup and bowse [4] from horn and can.

I have heard that on a day
Mine host's sign-board flew away,
Nobody knew whither, till            15
An Astrologer's old quill
To a sheepskin gave the story,—
Said he saw you in your glory,
Underneath a new-old sign
Sipping beverage divine,             20

  [3] Written in 1818; published in 1820. The Mermaid Tavern, in Bread Street, Cheapside, was the
favorite meeting-place of the chief men of letters
at the close of the sixteenth century and in the early
seventeenth.
  [4] Drink.

And pledging with contented smack
The Mermaid in the Zodiac.[5]

Souls of poets dead and gone,
What Elysium have ye known,
Happy field or mossy cavern,          25
Choicer than the Mermaid Tavern?

## Robin Hood [1]

### To a Friend

No! those days are gone away,
And their hours are old and gray,
And their minutes buried all
Under the down-trodden pall
Of the leaves of many years:          5
Many times have Winter's shears,
Frozen North, and chilling East,
Sounded tempests to the feast
Of the forest's whispering fleeces,[2]
Since men knew nor rent nor leases.   10

No, the bugle sounds no more,
And the twanging bow no more;
Silent is the ivory[3] shrill
Past the heath and up the hill;
There is no mid-forest laugh,          15
Where lone Echo gives the half
To some wight, amazed to hear
Jesting, deep in forest drear.

On the fairest time of June
You may go, with sun or moon,          20
Or the seven stars to light you,
Or the polar ray to right you;[4]
But you never may behold
Little John, or Robin bold:
Never one, of all the clan,            25
Thrumming on an empty can
Some old hunting ditty, while
He doth his green way beguile
To fair hostess Merriment,
Down beside the pasture Trent,[5]      30
For he left the merry tale,
Messenger for spicy ale.

Gone, the merry morris[6] din;
Gone, the song of Gamelyn;[7]
Gone, the tough-belted outlaw          35
Idling in the "grenè shawe";[8]

[5] I. e., in the heavens.
[1] Written early in 1818; published in 1820. The
friend was John Hamilton Reynolds.
[2] Leaves.          [3] Whistle.
[4] Or with Charles's Wain (the Dipper), or the
North Star as your guide.
[5] The fields about the River Trent, which runs by
Sherwood Forest.
[6] An outdoor dance in costume generally danced
by five men and a boy who impersonated Maid
Marian.
[7] Name of the hero of a tale of outlawry formerly
attributed to Chaucer.
[8] Green wood.

All are gone away and past!
And if Robin should be cast
Sudden from his turféd grave,
And if Marian should have              40
Once again her forest days,
She would weep, and he would craze;
He would swear, for all his oaks,
Fall'n beneath the dock-yard strokes,
Have rotted on the briny seas;         45
She would weep that her wild bees
Sang not to her—strange! that honey
Can't be got without hard money!

So it is; yet let us sing
Honor to the old bow-string!           50
Honor to the bugle-horn!
Honor to the woods unshorn!
Honor to the Lincoln green![9]
Honor to the archer keen!
Honor to tight little John,             55
And the horse he rode upon!
Honor to bold Robin Hood,
Sleeping in the underwood!
Honor to Maid Marian,
And to all the Sherwood clan!           60
Though their days have hurried by
Let us two a burden try.

## The Eve of St. Agnes [1]

St. Agnes' Eve—ah, bitter chill it was!
The owl, for all his feathers, was a-cold;
The hare limped trembling throug the frozen
    grass,
And silent was the flock in woolly fold;
Numb were the Beadsman's[2] fingers while
    he told                             5
His rosary, and while his frosted breath,
Like pious incense from a censer old,
Seemed taking flight for heaven without a
    death,
Past the sweet Virgin's picture, while his prayer
    he saith.

His prayer he saith, this patient, holy man; 10
Then takes his lamp, and riseth from his
    knees,
And back returneth, meager, barefoot, wan,
Along the chapel aisle by slow degrees:
The sculptured dead, on each side, seem to
    freeze,
Emprisoned in black, purgatorial rails:  15

[9] Green cloth dyed at Lincoln.
[1] Written early in 1819; published in 1820. The
Eve of St. Agnes is 20 January. The subject may
have been suggested to Keats by a passage in Burton's *Anatomy of Melancholy* (III, ii, 3, i), or by a
popular pamphlet called *Mother Bunches Closet
Newly Broken Open*, or merely by the words of a
friend who had heard of the superstition that a girl
who fasted on St. Agnes's Eve would dream of her
future husband.
[2] Man paid to pray for his benefactor.

Knights, ladies, praying in dumb orat'ries,[3]
He passeth by; and his weak spirit fails
To think how they may ache in icy hoods and
   mails.

Northward he turneth through a little door,
And scarce three steps, ere Music's golden
   tongue                 20
Flattered to tears this agéd man and poor.
But no—already had his death-bell rung;
The joys of all his life were said and sung;
His was harsh penance on St. Agnes' Eve:
Another way he went, and soon among 25
Rough ashes sat he for his soul's reprieve,
And all night kept awake, for sinners' sake to
   grieve.

That ancient Beadsman heard the prelude
   soft;
And so it chanced, for many a door was wide,
From hurry to and fro. Soon, up aloft,    30
The silver, snarling trumpets 'gan to chide:
The level chambers, ready with their pride,
Were glowing to receive a thousand guests:
The carvéd angels, ever eager-eyed,
Stared, where upon their heads the cornice
   rests,                 35
With hair blown back, and wings put crosswise
   on their breasts.

At length burst in the argent revelry,
With plume, tiara, and all rich array,
Numerous as shadows haunting fairily
The brain, new-stuffed, in youth, with
   triumphs gay          40
Of old romance. These let us wish away,
And turn, sole-thoughted, to one Lady there,
Whose heart had brooded, all that wintry
   day,
On love, and winged St. Agnes' saintly care,
As she had heard old dames full many times
   declare.              45

They told her how, upon St. Agnes' Eve,
Young virgins might have visions of delight,
And soft adorings from their loves receive
Upon the honeyed middle of the night,
If ceremonies due they did aright;     50
As, supperless to bed they must retire,
And couch supine their beauties, lily white;
Nor look behind, nor sideways, but require [4]
Of Heaven with upward eyes for all that they
   desire.[5]

Full of this whim was thoughtful Madeline:
The music, yearning like a God in pain, 56
She scarcely heard: her maiden eyes divine,

Fixed on the floor, saw many a sweeping
   train
Pass by—she heeded not at all: in vain
Came many a tiptoe, amorous cavalier,    60
And back retired; not cooled by high disdain,
But she saw not: her heart was otherwhere;
She sighed for Agnes' dreams, the sweetest of
   the year.

She danced along with vague, regardless eyes,
Anxious her lips, her breathing quick and
   short:              65
The hallowed hour was near at hand: she
   sighs
Amid the timbrels, and the thronged resort
Of whisperers in anger or in sport;
'Mid looks of love, defiance, hate, and scorn,
Hoodwinked with fairy fancy; all amort,[6] 70
Save to St. Agnes and her lambs unshorn,[7]
And all the bliss to be before to-morrow morn.

So, purposing each moment to retire,
She lingered still. Meantime, across the
   moors,
Had come young Porphyro,[8] with heart on
   fire              75
For Madeline. Beside the portal doors,
Buttressed from moonlight, stands he, and
   implores
All saints to give him sight of Madeline,
But for one moment in the tedious hours,
That he might gaze and worship all unseen;
Perchance speak, kneel, touch, kiss—in sooth
   such things have been.        81

He ventures in: let no buzzed whisper tell;
All eyes be muffled, or a hundred swords
Will storm his heart, Love's fev'rous citadel:
For him, those chambers held barbarian
   hordes,              85
Hyena foeman, and hot-blooded lords,
Whose very dogs would execrations howl
Against his lineage; not one breast affords
Him any mercy in that mansion foul,

an understanding of what happens later, but apparently omitted from the printed text to satisfy the scruples of the poet's friends:

'Twas said her future lord would there appear
Offering as sacrifice—all in the dream—
Delicious food even to her lips brought near:
Viands and wine and fruit and sugared cream,
To touch her palate with the fine extreme
Of relish: then soft music heard; and then
More pleasures followed in a dizzy stream
Palpable almost: then to wake again
Warm in the virgin morn, no weeping Magdalen.

[6] Deadened.

[7] St. Agnes was always pictured with lambs. On the anniversary of her martyrdom two lambs are blessed, then shorn, and the wool is spun and woven by nuns.

[8] The hero, as one of Keats's manuscripts reveals, was originally named Lionel.

[3] Oratories, small chapel for prayer. The adjective is transferred from the statues to the place.

[4] Request.

[5] At this point one of the original manuscripts of the poem contains the following stanza, helpful to

Save one old beldame, weak in body and in
soul.                                        90

Ah, happy chance! the agéd creature came
Shuffling along with ivory-headed wand,
To where he stood, hid from the torch's
flame,
Behind a broad hall-pillar, far beyond
The sound of merriment and chorus bland. 95
He startled her; but soon she knew his face,
And grasped his fingers in her palsied hand,
Saying, "Mercy, Porphyro! hie thee from
this place;
They are all here to-night, the whole blood-
thirsty race!

"Get hence! get hence! there's dwarfish
Hildebrand;                                 100
He had a fever late, and in the fit
He curséd thee and thine, both house and
land:
Then there's that old Lord Maurice, not a
whit
More tame for his gray hairs—Alas me! flit!
Flit like a ghost away."—"Ah, Gossip dear,
We're safe enough; here in this arm-chair
sit,                                        106
And tell me how"—"Good saints! not here,
not here;
Follow me, child, or else these stones will be
thy bier."

He followed through a lowly archéd way, 109
Brushing the cobwebs with his lofty plume,
And as she muttered "Well-a—well-a-day!"
He found him in a little moonlight room,
Pale, latticed, chill, and silent as a tomb.
"Now tell me where is Madeline," said he,
"O tell me, Angela, by the holy loom    115
Which none but secret sisterhood may see,
When they St. Agnes' wool are weaving
piously."

"St. Agnes! Ah! it is St. Agnes' Eve—
Yet men will murder upon holy days:
Thou must hold water in a witch's sieve,[9] 120
And be liege-lord of all the Elves and Fays
To venture so: it fills me with amaze
To see thee, Porphyro!—St. Agnes' Eve!
God's help! my lady fair the conjurer plays
This very night: good angels her deceive! 125
But let me laugh awhile,—I've mickle [10] time
to grieve."

Feebly she laugheth in the languid moon,
While Porphyro upon her face doth look,
Like puzzled urchin on an agéd crone
Who keepeth closed a wondrous riddle-
book,                                       130
As spectacled she sits in chimney nook.

[9] Supposed to be a sign of supernatural power.
[10] Much.

But soon his eyes grew brilliant, when she
told
His lady's purpose; and he scarce could brook
Tears, at the thought of those enchantments
cold,
And Madeline asleep in lap of legends old. 135

Sudden a thought came like a full-blown
rose,
Flushing his brow, and in his painéd heart
Made purple riot: then doth he propose
A stratagem, that makes the beldame start:
"A cruel man and impious thou art:     140
Sweet lady! let her pray, and sleep, and
dream
Alone with her good angels, far apart
From wicked men like thee. Go, go! I deem
Thou canst not surely be the same that thou
didst seem."                              144

"I will not harm her, by all saints I swear,"
Quoth Porphyro: "O may I ne'er find grace
When my weak voice shall whisper its last
prayer,
If one of her soft ringlets I displace,
Or look with ruffian passion in her face.
Good Angela, believe me, by these tears, 150
Or I will, even in a moment's space,
Awake, with horrid shout, my foemen's ears,
And beard them, though they be more fanged
than wolves and bears."

"Ah! why wilt thou affright a feeble soul?
A poor, weak, palsy-stricken, churchyard
thing,                                      155
Whose passing-bell may ere the midnight
toll;
Whose prayers for thee, each morn and
evening,
Were never missed." Thus plaining, doth she
bring
A gentler speech from burning Porphyro;
So woeful, and of such deep sorrowing, 160
That Angela gives promise she will do
Whatever he shall wish, betide her weal or woe.

Which was, to lead him, in close secrecy,
Even to Madeline's chamber, and there hide
Him in a closet, of such privacy     165
That he might see her beauty unespied,
And win perhaps that night a peerless bride,
While legioned fairies paced the coverlet,
And pale enchantment held her sleepy-eyed.
Never on such a night have lovers met, 170
Since Merlin paid his Demon all the mon-
strous debt.[11]

"It shall be as thou wishest," said the Dame:
"All cates [12] and dainties shall be stored there

[11] According to one legend Merlin's father was a
demon, so that his "debt" to the demon was his
existence. He paid this when Vivien destroyed him
by means of a spell which he himself had taught her.
[12] Provisions.

Quickly on this feast-night: by the tambour-
frame [13]
Her own lute thou wilt see: no time to spare,
For I am slow and feeble, and scarce dare [176]
On such a catering trust my dizzy head.
Wait here, my child, with patience; kneel in
prayer
The while. Ah! thou must needs the lady
wed,
Or may I never leave my grave among the
dead." [180]

So saying, she hobbled off with busy fear.
The lover's endless minutes slowly passed;
The dame returned, and whispered in his
ear
To follow her; with agéd eyes aghast
From fright of dim espial. Safe at last, [185]
Through many a dusky gallery, they gain
The maiden's chamber, silken, hushed, and
chaste;
Where Porphyro took covert, pleased amain.
His poor guide hurried back with agues in her
brain.

Her faltering hand upon the balustrade, [190]
Old Angela was feeling for the stair,
When Madeline, St. Agnes' charméd-maid,
Rose, like a missioned spirit, unaware:
With silver taper's light, and pious care,
She turned, and down the agéd gossip led [195]
To a safe level matting. Now prepare,
Young Porphyro, for gazing on that bed;
She comes, she comes again, like ring-dove
frayed [14] and fled.

Out went the taper as she hurried in;
Its little smoke, in pallid moonshine, died:
She closed the door, she panted, all akin [201]
To spirits of the air, and visions wide:
No uttered syllable, or, woe betide!
But to her heart, her heart was voluble,
Paining with eloquence her balmy side; [205]
As though a tongueless nightingale should
swell
Her throat in vain, and die, heart-stifled, in her
dell.

A casement high and triple-arched there was,
All garlanded with carven imag'ries,
Of fruits and flowers, and bunches of knot-
grass, [210]
And diamonded with panes of quaint device,
Innumerable of stains and splendid dyes,
As are the tiger-moth's deep-damasked wings;
And in the midst, 'mong thousand heraldries,
And twilight saints, and dim emblazonings,
A shielded scutcheon blushed with blood of
queens and kings. [216]

Full on this casement shone the wintry
moon,

[13] Double hoops for holding embroidery.
[14] Frightened.

And threw warm gules [15] on Madeline's fair
breast,
As down she knelt for Heaven's grace and
boon;
Rose-bloom fell on her hands, together
pressed, [220]
And on her silver cross soft amethyst,
And on her hair a glory, like a saint:
She seemed a splendid angel, newly dressed,
Save wings, for heaven:—Porphyro grew
faint:
She knelt, so pure a thing, so free from mortal
taint. [225]

Anon his heart revives: her vespers done,
Of all its wreathéd pearls her hair she frees;
Unclasps her warméd jewels one by one;
Loosens her fragrant bodice; by degrees
Her rich attire creeps rustling to her knees:
Half-hidden, like a mermaid in sea-weed, [231]
Pensive awhile she dreams awake, and sees,
In fancy, fair St. Agnes in her bed,
But dares not look behind, or all the charm is
fled.

Soon, trembling in her soft and chilly nest,
In sort of wakeful swoon, perplexed she lay,
Until the poppied warmth of sleep op-
pressed [237]
Her soothéd limbs, and soul fatigued away;
Flown, like a thought, until the morrow-
day;
Blissfully havened both from joy and pain;
Clasped like a missal where swart Paynims
pray; [16] [241]
Blinded alike from sunshine and from rain,
As though a rose should shut, and be a bud
again.

Stol'n to this paradise, and so entranced,
Porphyro gazed upon her empty dress, [245]
And listened to her breathing, if it chanced
To wake into a slumberous tenderness;
Which when he heard, that minute did he
bless,
And breathed himself: then from the closet
crept,
Noiseless as fear in a wide wilderness, [250]
And over the hushed carpet, silent, stepped,
And 'tween the curtains peeped, where lo!
—how fast she slept!

Then by the bedside, where the faded moon
Made a dim, silver twilight, soft he set
A table, and, half anguished, threw there-
on [255]
A cloth of woven crimson, gold, and jet:—
O for some drowsy Morphean amulet! [17]

[15] Blood-red (heraldic term).
[16] As tightly closed as a Christian prayer-book in
a pagan land. (Keats originally wrote, "Shut like
a missal," etc.)
[17] Charm. Morpheus was the god of sleep.

The boisterous, midnight, festive clarion,
The kettle-drum, and far-heard clarinet,
Affray his ears, though but in dying tone:—
The hall-door shuts again, and all the noise is
    gone.    261

And still she slept an azure-lidded sleep,
In blanchéd linen, smooth, and lavendered,
While he from forth the closet brought a
    heap
Of candied apple, quince, and plum, and
    gourd;    265
With jellies soother [18] than the creamy curd,
And lucent syrops, tinct [19] with cinnamon;
Manna and dates, in argosy [20] transferred
From Fez; and spicéd dainties, every one, 269
From silken Samarcand to cedared Lebanon.

These delicates he heaped with glowing hand
On golden dishes and in baskets bright
Of wreathéd silver: sumptuous they stand
In the retiréd quiet of the night,    274
Filling the chilly room with perfume light.—
"And now, my love, my seraph fair, awake!
Thou art my heaven, and I thine eremite:[21]
Open thine eyes, for meek St. Agnes' sake,
Or I shall drowse beside thee, so my soul doth
    ache."

Thus whispering, his warm, unnervéd arm
Sank in her pillow. Shaded was her dream 281
By the dusk curtains:—'twas a midnight
    charm
Impossible to melt as icéd stream:
The lustrous salvers in the moonlight gleam;
Broad golden fringe upon the carpet lies: 285
It seemed he never, never could redeem
From such a steadfast spell his lady's eyes;
So mused awhile, entoiled in wooféd phan-
    tasies.[22]

Awakening up, he took her hollow lute,—
Tumultuous,—and, in chords that tenderest
    be,    290
He played an ancient ditty, long since mute,
In Provence called "La belle dame sans
    mercy": [23]
Close to her ear touching the melody;—
Where disturbed, she uttered a soft moan:
He ceased—she panted quick—and suddenly
Her blue affrayéd eyes wide open shone: 296
Upon his knees he sank, pale as smooth-
    sculptured stone.

[18] Softer.    [19] Flavored.    [20] Merchant-ship.
[21] Literally, hermit—i. e., here, consecrated servant.
[22] Fancies mingled together as are woven threads.
[23] The Beautiful Lady without Pity. The poem
is not of Provençal origin, but is by Alain Chartier,
court poet of Charles II of France. An English
translation of it was attributed to Chaucer, and
thus Keats happened to see the title.

Her eyes were open, but she still beheld,
Now wide awake, the vision of her sleep:
There was a painful change, that nigh ex-
    pelled    300
The blisses of her dream so pure and deep,
At which fair Madeline began to weep,
And moan forth witless words with many a
    sigh,
While still her gaze on Porphyro would keep;
Who knelt, with joinéd hands and piteous
    eye,    305
Fearing to move or speak, she looked so dream-
    ingly.

"Ah Porphyro!" said she, "but even now
Thy voice was at sweet tremble in mine ear,
Made tunable with every sweetest vow;
And those sad eyes were spiritual and clear:
How changed thou art! how pallid, chill, and
    drear!    311
Give me that voice again, my Porphyro,
Those looks immortal, those complainings
    dear!
Oh leave me not in this eternal woe,
For if thou diest, my Love, I know not where
    to go."    315

Beyond a mortal man impassioned far
At these voluptuous accents, he arose,
Ethereal, flushed, and like a throbbing star
Seen 'mid the sapphire heaven's deep repose;
Into her dream he melted, as the rose    320
Blendeth its odor with the violet,—[24]
Solution sweet: meantime the frost-wind
    blows
Like Love's alarum, pattering the sharp sleet
Against the window-panes; St. Agnes' moon
    hath set.

'Tis dark: quick pattereth the flaw-blown
    sleet:    325
"This is no dream, my bride, my Madeline!"
'Tis dark: the icéd gusts still rave and beat:
"No dream, alas! alas! and woe is mine!
Porphyro will leave me here to fade and pine.
Cruel! what traitor could thee hither bring?
I curse not, for my heart is lost in thine, 331
Though thou forsakest a deceivéd thing;—
A dove forlorn and lost with sick unprunéd
    wing."

"My Madeline! sweet dreamer! lovely bride!
Say, may I be for aye thy vassal blest? 335
Thy beauty's shield, heart-shaped and
    vermeil-dyed?
Ah, silver shrine, here will I take my rest
After so many hours of toil and quest,

[24] At this point some three stanzas, now lost, were
omitted from the printed text on the advice of
Keats's friends lest they "render the poem unfit
for ladies." Keats, though he yielded, said that
he did not want ladies to read his poetry, and that
he wrote for men.

A famished pilgrim,—saved by miracle.
Though I have found, I will not rob thy
   nest,        340
Saving of thy sweet self; if thou think'st well
To trust, fair Madeline, to no rude infidel.

"Hark! 'tis an elfin storm from fairy land,
Of haggard seeming, but a boon indeed:
Arise—arise! the morning is at hand;—345
The bloated wassailers will never heed;—
Let us away, my love, with happy speed;
There are no ears to hear, or eyes to see,—
Drowned all in Rhenish and the sleepy mead.
Awake! arise! my love,[25] and fearless be, 350
For o'er the southern moors I have a home for
   thee."

She hurried at his words, beset with fears,
For there were sleeping dragons all around,
At glaring watch, perhaps, with ready
   spears—
Down the wide stairs a darkling way they
   found;      355
In all the house was heard no human sound.
A chain-drooped lamp was flickering by each
   door;
The arras, rich with horseman, hawk, and
   hound,
Fluttered in the besieging wind's uproar;
And the long carpets rose along the gusty floor.

They glide, like phantoms, into the wide
   hall;      361
Like phantoms to the iron porch they glide;
Where lay the Porter, in uneasy sprawl,
With a huge empty flagon by his side:
The wakeful bloodhound rose, and shook his
   hide,      365
But his sagacious eye an inmate owns:[26]
By one, and one, the bolts full easy slide:—
The chains lie silent on the footworn stones;
The key turns, and the door upon its hinges
   groans.

And they are gone: ay, ages long ago 370
These lovers fled away into the storm.
That night the Baron dreamed of many a
   woe,
And all his warrior-guests, with shade and
   form
Of witch, and demon, and large coffin-worm,
Were long be-nightmared. Angela the old 375
Died palsy-twitched, with meager face de-
   form;
The Beadsman, after thousand aves told,
For aye unsought-for slept among his ashes
   cold.

[25] For "Awake! arise! my love" Keats originally
wrote, "Put on warm clothing, sweet."
[26] Recognizes.

# To Sleep [1]

O soft embalmer of the still midnight!
   Shutting, with careful fingers and benign,
Our gloom-pleased eyes, embowered from the
   light,
   Enshaded in forgetfulness divine;
O soothest Sleep! if so it please thee, close, 5
   In midst of this thine hymn, my willing eyes,
Or wait the amen, ere thy poppy throws
   Around my bed its lulling charities;
   Then save me, or the passéd day will shine
Upon my pillow, breeding many woes;   10
   Save me from curious conscience, that still
   lords
Its strength for darkness, burrowing like a mole;
   Turn the key deftly in the oiléd wards,[2]
And seal the hushéd casket of my soul.

# La Belle Dame Sans Merci [3]

O what can ail thee, knight-at-arms,
   Alone and palely loitering?
The sedge has withered from the lake,
   And no birds sing.

O what can ail thee, knight-of-arms,   5
   So haggard and so woe-begone?
The squirrel's granary is full,
   And the harvest's done.

I see a lily on thy brow
   With anguish moist and fever dew,   10
And on thy cheeks a fading rose
   Fast withereth too.

I met a lady in the meads,
   Full beautiful—a faery's child,
Her hair was long, her foot was light,   15
   And her eyes were wild.

I made a garland for her head,
   And bracelets too, and fragrant zone; [4]
She looked at me as she did love,
   And made sweet moan.   20

I set her on my pacing steed
   And nothing else saw all day long,
For sidelong would she bend, and sing
   A faery's song.

She found me roots of relish sweet,   25
   And honey wild, and manna dew,

[1] Written in 1819; published in 1848 (an early
draft was published in America, in the *Dial*, in
1843).
[2] Ridges on the inside of a lock.
[3] Written in the spring of 1819; published (by
Leigh Hunt in the *Indicator*) in 1820. Two versions of the poem exist, the earlier of which is here
printed. Keats owes the title—but nothing more
than the title—to a poem by Alain Chartier.
[4] Girdle.

And sure in language strange she said—
    "I love thee true!"

She took me to her elfin grot,
    And there she wept and sighed full sore, 30
And there I shut her wild, wild eyes
    With kisses four.

And there she lulléd me asleep,
    And there I dreamed—ah, woe betide!
The latest dream I ever dreamed          35
    On the cold hill side.

I saw pale kings, and princes too,
    Pale warriors, death-pale were they all;
They cried—"La Belle Dame sans Merci
    Thee hath in thrall!"                40

I saw their starved lips in the gloam,
    With horrid warning gapéd wide,
And I awoke and found me here,
    On the cold hill's side.

And this is why I sojourn here,         45
    Alone and palely loitering,
Though the sedge is withered from the lake,
    And no birds sing.

## Two Sonnets on Fame [5]

### I

Fame, like a wayward girl, will still be coy
    To those who woo her with too slavish knees,
But makes surrender to some thoughtless boy,
    And dotes the more upon a heart at ease;
She is a Gypsy will not speak to those      5
    Who have not learned to be content with-
        out her;
A Jilt, whose ear was never whispered close,
    Who thinks they scandal her who talk about
        her;
A very Gypsy is she, Nilus-born,[6]
    Sister-in-law to jealous Potiphar;          10
Ye love-sick Bards! repay her scorn for scorn;
    Ye Artists lovelorn! madmen that ye are!
Make your best bow to her and bid adieu,
Then, if she likes it, she will follow you.

### II

"You cannot eat your cake and have it too."—
*Proverb.*

How fevered is the man, who cannot look
    Upon his mortal days with temperate blood,
Who vexes all the leaves of his life's book,
    And robs his fair name of its maidenhood;
It is as if the rose should pluck herself,      5
    Or the ripe plum finger its misty bloom,
As if a Naiad, like a meddling elf,

[5] Both sonnets were written in 1819 and published in 1848.
[6] Gypsies were formerly supposed to come from Egypt.

Should darken her pure grot with muddy
        gloom;
But the rose leaves herself upon the brier,
    For winds to kiss and grateful bees to feed, 10
And the ripe plum still wears its dim attire;
    The undisturbéd lake has crystal space;
Why then should man, teasing the world for
        grace,
Spoil his salvation for a fierce miscreed? [7]

## Ode to a Nightingale [1]

My heart aches, and a drowsy numbness pains
    My sense, as though of hemlock [2] I had
        drunk,
Or emptied some dull opiate to the drains
    One minute past, and Lethe-wards had sunk:
'Tis not through envy of thy happy lot,      5
    But being too happy in thine happiness,—
        That thou, light-wingéd Dryad [3] of the
            trees,
            In some melodious plot
    Of beechen green, and shadows numberless,
        Singest of summer in full-throated ease. 10

O for a draught of vintage! that hath been
    Cooled a long age in the deep-delvéd earth,
Tasting of Flora [4] and the country-green,
    Dance, and Provençal song, and sunburnt
        mirth!
O for a beaker full of the warm South,       15
    Full of the true, the blushful Hippocrene,[5]
        With beaded bubbles winking at the brim,
            And purple-stainéd mouth;
    That I might drink, and leave the world
        unseen,
        And with thee fade away into the forest
            dim:                             20

Fade far away, disolve, and quite forget
    What thou among the leaves hast never
        known,
The weariness, the fever, and the fret
    Here, where men sit and hear each other
        groan;
Where palsy shakes a few, sad, last gray
        hairs,                               25
    Where youth grows pale, and specter-thin,
        and dies;
        Where but to think is to be full of sorrow
            And leaden-eyed despairs;
    Where beauty cannot keep her lustrous eyes,
        Or new Love pine at them beyond to-
            morrow.

Away! away! for I will fly to thee,          31
    Not charioted by Bacchus and his pards,[6]

[7] Mistaken creed.
[1] Written in May, 1819; published in 1820.
[2] A poison.          [3] Tree-nymph.
[4] Goddess of flowers.
[5] Spring of the Muses on Mount Helicon.
[6] Leopards.

But on the viewless [7] wings of Poesy,
  Though the dull brain perplexes and retards:
Already with thee! tender is the night,     35
    And haply the Queen-Moon is on her throne,
      Clustered around by all her starry Fays;
      But here there is no light,
    Save what from heaven is with the breezes
      blown
      Through verdurous glooms and winding
        mossy ways.    40

I cannot see what flowers are at my feet,
  Nor what soft incense hangs upon the
    boughs,
But, in embalméd darkness, guess each sweet
  Wherewith the seasonable month endows
The grass, the thicket, and the fruit-tree wild;
  White hawthorn, and the pastoral eglan-
    tine;      46
    Fast-fading violets covered up in leaves;
    And mid-May's eldest child,
The coming musk-rose, full of dewy wine,
  The murmurous haunt of flies on summer
    eves.      50

Darkling I listen; and, for many a time
  I have been half in love with easeful Death,
Called him soft names in many a muséd rime,
  To take into the air my quiet breath,—
Now more than ever seems it rich to die,    55
  To cease upon the midnight with no pain,
    While thou art pouring forth thy soul
      abroad
      In such an ecstasy!
    Still wouldst thou sing, and I have ears in
      vain—
      To thy high requiem become a sod.    60

Thou wast not born for death, immortal Bird!
  No hungry generations tread thee down;
The voice I hear this passing night was heard
  In ancient days by emperor and clown: [8]
Perhaps the self-same song that found a path  65
  Through the sad heart of Ruth,[9] when, sick
    for home,
    She stood in tears amid the alien corn;
    The same that oft-times hath
Charmed magic casements, opening on the
    foam
    Of perilous seas, in faery lands forlorn.  70

Forlorn! the very word is like a bell
  To toll me back from thee to my sole self.
Adieu! the fancy cannot cheat so well
  As she is famed to do, deceiving elf.
Adieu! adieu! thy plaintive anthem fades    75
  Past the near meadows, over the still stream,
    Up the hill-side; and now 'tis buried deep
    In the next valley-glades:
    Was it a vision, or a waking dream?
    Fled is that music:—do I wake or sleep?  80

[7] Invisible.     [8] Peasant.     [9] See Ruth, 2.

# Ode on a Grecian Urn [1]

Thou still unravished bride of quietness,
  Thou foster-child of silence and slow time,
Sylvan historian, who canst thus express
  A flowery tale more sweetly than our rime:
What leaf-fringed legend haunts about thy
    shape     5
  Of deities or mortals, or of both,
    In Tempe or the dales of Arcady? [2]
  What men or gods are these? What maidens
    loath?
What mad pursuit? What struggle to escape?
  What pipes and timbrels? What wild ec-
    stasy?      10

Heard melodies are sweet, but those unheard
  Are sweeter; therefore, ye soft pipes, play on;
Not to the sensual ear, but, more endeared,
  Pipe to the spirit ditties of no tone:
Fair youth, beneath the trees, thou canst not
    leave      15
  Thy song, nor ever can those trees be bare;
    Bold Lover, never, never canst thou kiss,
Though winning near the goal—yet, do not
    grieve;
    She cannot fade, though thou hast not thy
      bliss,
  For ever wilt thou love, and she be fair!    20

Ah, happy, happy boughs! that cannot shed
  Your leaves, nor ever bid the Spring adieu;
And, happy melodist, unweariéd,
  For ever piping songs for ever new;
More happy love! more happy, happy love!  25
  For ever warm and still to be enjoyed,
    For ever panting and for ever young;
All breathing human passion far above,
  That leaves a heart high-sorrowful and
    cloyed,
    A burning forehead, and a parching
    tongue.      30

Who are these coming to the sacrifice?
  To what green altar, O mysterious priest,
Lead'st thou that heifer lowing at the skies,
  And all her silken flanks with garlands
    dressed?
What little town by river or sea-shore,    35
  Or mountain-built with peaceful citadel,
    Is emptied of this folk, this pious morn?
And, little town, thy streets for evermore
  Will silent be; and not a soul to tell
    Why thou art desolate, can e'er return.  40

O Attic shape! Fair attitude! with brede [3]
  Of marble men and maidens overwrought,

[1] Written in February or March, 1819; published
in 1820.
[2] Tempe is a valley in Thessaly, Arcadia a mountainous region in the Peloponnese.
[3] Embroidery.

With forest branches and the trodden weed;
　Thou, silent form, dost tease us out of
　　thought
As doth eternity: Cold Pastoral!　　　45
　When old age shall this generation waste,
　　Thou shalt remain, in midst of other woe
Than ours, a friend to man, to whom thou
　　say'st,
　"Beauty is truth, truth beauty,"—that is all
　Ye know on earth, and all ye need to
　　know.　　　50

# Ode to Psyche [1]

O goddess! hear these tuneless numbers wrung
　By sweet enforcement and remembrance
　　dear,
And pardon that thy secrets should be sung
　Even into thine own soft-conchéd [2] ear:
Surely I dreamed to-day, or did I see　　5
　The wingéd Psyche with awakened eyes?
I wandered in a forest thoughtlessly,
　And, on the sudden, fainting with surprise,
Saw two fair creatures, couchéd side by side
　In deepest grass, beneath the whispering
　　roof　　　10
Of leaves and trembled blossoms, where there
　　ran
　A brooklet, scarce espied:

'Mid hushed, cool-rooted flowers, fragrant-eyed,
　Blue, silver-white, and budded Tyrian, [3]
They lay calm-breathing, on the bedded grass;
　Their arms embracéd, and their pinions
　　too;　　　16
　Their lips touched not, but had not bade
　　adieu,
As if disjoinéd by soft-handed slumber,
And ready still past kisses to outnumber
　At tender eye-drawn of aurorean love:　20
　The wingéd boy I knew; [4]
But who wast thou, O happy, happy dove?
　His Psyche true!

O latest-born and loveliest vision far
　Of all Olympus' faded hierarchy!　　25
Fairer than Phoebe's sapphire-regioned star, [5]

[1] Written in the spring of 1819; published in
1820. Keats wrote in a letter, "You must recollect
that Psyche was not embodied as a goddess before
the time of Apuleius the Platonist, who lived after
the Augustan age, and consequently the goddess
was never worshiped or sacrificed to with any of
the ancient fervor, and perhaps never thought of
in the old religion—I am more orthodox than to
let a heathen goddess be so neglected." In the same
letter he said that this poem was the first with
which he had taken "even moderate pains."
[2] Shaped like a shell.　　　[3] Crimson or purple.
[4] Cupid. The story of Cupid and Psyche may be
read in Walter Pater's translation of Apuleius's
version of it (in *Marius the Epicurean*) or in Robert Bridges' poem, *Eros and Psyche*.
[5] The moon. Phoebe is Artemis.

Or Vesper, amorous glow-worm of the sky; [6]
Fairer than these, though temple thou hast
　　none,
　Nor altar heaped with flowers;
Nor Virgin-choir to make delicious moan　30
　Upon the midnight hours;
No voice, no lute, no pipe, no incense sweet
　From chain-swung censer teeming;
No shrine, no grove, no oracle, no heat
　Of pale-mouthed prophet dreaming.　　35

O brightest! though too late for antique vows,
　Too, too late for the fond believing lyre,
When holy were the haunted forest boughs,
　Holy the air, the water, and the fire;
Yet even in these days so far retired　　40
　From happy pieties, thy lucent fans, [7]
　Fluttering among the faint Olympians,
I see, and sing, by my own eyes inspired.
So let me be thy choir, and make a moan
　Upon the midnight hours;　　45
Thy voice, thy lute, thy pipe, thy incense sweet
　From swingéd censer teeming;
Thy shrine, thy grove, thy oracle, thy heat
　Of pale-mouthed prophet dreaming.

Yes, I will be thy priest, and build a fane [8]　50
　In some untrodden region of my mind,
Where branchéd thoughts, new-grown with
　　pleasant pain,
　Instead of pines shall murmur in the wind:
Far, far around shall those dark-clustered trees
　Fledge the wild-ridged mountains steep by
　　steep;　　55
And there by zephyrs, streams, and birds, and
　　bees,
　The moss-lain Dryads shall be lulled to sleep;
And in the midst of this wide quietness
A rosy sanctuary will I dress
With the wreathed trellis of a working brain, [60]
　With buds, and bells, and stars without a
　　name,
With all the gardener Fancy e'er could feign,
　Who breeding flowers, will never breed the
　　same;
And there shall be for thee all soft delight
　That shadowy thought can win,　　65
A bright torch, and a casement ope at night,
　To let the warm Love in!

# To Autumn [1]

Season of mists and mellow fruitfulness,
　Close bosom-friend of the maturing sun;
Conspiring with him how to load and bless
　With fruit the vines that round the thatch-
　　eaves run;
To bend with apples the mossed cottage-trees, 5
　And fill all fruit with ripeness to the core;
　To swell the gourd, and plump the hazel
　　shells

[6] The Evening Star, Venus.
[7] Translucent wings.　　　[8] Temple.
[1] Written in September, 1819; published in 1820.

With a sweet kernel; to set budding more,
And still more, later flowers for the bees,
Until they think warm days will never cease, 10
    For Summer has o'er-brimmed their
        clammy cells.

Who hath not seen thee oft amid thy store?
  Sometimes whoever seeks abroad may find
Thee sitting careless on a granary floor,
  Thy hair soft-lifted by the winnowing wind;
Or on a half-reaped furrow sound asleep, 16
    Drowsed with the fumes of poppies, while
        thy hook
    Spares the next swath and all its twinéd
        flowers;
And sometimes like a gleaner thou dost keep
  Steady thy laden head across a brook;   20
  Or by a cider-press, with patient look,
    Thou watchest the last oozings, hours by
        hours.

Where are the songs of Spring? Ay, where are
    they?
  Think not of them, thou hast thy music too,
While barréd clouds bloom the soft dying day,
  And touch the stubble-plains with rosy
        hue;       26
Then in a wailful choir, the small gnats mourn
  Among the river sallows,[2] borne aloft
    Or sinking as the light wind lives or dies;
And full-grown lambs loud bleat from hilly
    bourn;[3]        30
    Hedge-crickets[4] sing; and now with treble
        soft
    The redbreast whistles from a garden-croft;[5]
    And gathering swallows twitter in the
        skies.

# Ode on Melancholy [1]

No, no, go not to Lethe,[2] neither twist
  Wolf's-bane, tight-rooted, for its poisonous
    wine;
Nor suffer thy pale forehead to be kissed
  By nightshade, ruby grape of Proserpine;[3]
Make not your rosary of yew-berries,     5
  Nor let the beetle, nor the death-moth be
    Your mournful Psyche,[4] nor the downy
        owl
A partner in your sorrow's mysteries;
  For shade to shade will come too drowsily,
    And drown the wakeful anguish of the
        soul.     10

[2] Willows.
[3] Literally, boundary, but the word can also mean,
as here, domain.
[4] Grasshoppers.        [5] Garden-enclosure.
[1] Written in the spring of 1819; published in 1820.
[2] River of forgetfulness, in Hades.
[3] Queen of the lower world.
[4] The soul. Psyche was sometimes represented as
a butterfly. Do not, says Keats, let insects who symbolize death represent your mournful soul.

But when the melancholy fit shall fall
  Sudden from heaven like a weeping cloud,
That fosters the droop-headed flowers all,
  And hides the green hill in an April shroud;
Then glut thy sorrow on a morning rose,   15
  Or on the rainbow of the salt sand-wave,
    Or on the wealth of globéd peonies;
Or if thy mistress some rich anger shows,
  Emprison her soft hand, and let her rave,
    And feed deep, deep upon her peerless
        eyes.    20

She[5] dwells with Beauty—Beauty that must
    die;
  And Joy, whose hand is ever at his lips
Bidding adieu; and aching Pleasure nigh,
  Turning to poison while the bee-mouth sips:
Ay, in the very temple of Delight    25
  Veiled Melancholy has her sovran shrine,
    Though seen of none save him whose
        strenuous tongue
Can burst Joy's grape against his palate fine:
His soul shall taste the sadness of her might,
    And be among her cloudy trophies
        hung.    30

# Lamia [1]

## PART I

Upon a time, before the faery broods
Drove Nymph and Satyr from the prosperous
  woods,

[5] Melancholy.
[1] Written in 1819 (finished apparently by 5 September); published in 1820. In a note appended to
the poem on its first publication Keats gave his
source, as follows: "Philostratus in his fourth book
*de Vita Apollonii* [concerning the life of Apollo-
nius], hath a memorable instance in this kind, which
I may not omit, of one Menippus Lycius, a young
man twenty-five years of age, that going betwixt
Cenchreas and Corinth, met such a phantasm in the
habit of a fair gentlewoman, which taking him by
the hand, carried him home to her house, in the suburbs of Corinth, and told him she was a Phoenician
by birth, and if he would tarry with her, he should
hear her sing and play, and drink such wine as never
any drank, and no man should molest him; but she,
being fair and lovely, would live and die with him,
that was fair and lovely to behold. The young man,
a philosopher, otherwise staid and discreet, able to
moderate his passions, though not this of love, tarried with her a while to his great content, and at
last married her, to whose wedding, amongst other
guests, came Apollonius; who, by some probable
conjectures, found her out to be a serpent, a lamia;
and that all her furniture was, like Tantalus' gold,
described by Homer, no substance but mere illusions. When she saw herself described, she wept,
and desired Apollonius to be silent, but he would not
be moved, and thereupon she, plate, house, and all
that was in it, vanished in an instant: many thousands took notice of this fact, for it was done in the
midst of Greece" (Burton's *Anatomy of Melancholy*, III, ii, 1, i).

Before King Oberon's bright diadem,
Scepter, and mantle, clasped with dewy gem,
Frighted away the Dryads and the Fauns    5
From rushes green, and brakes, and cow-slipped
    lawns,
The ever-smitten Hermes empty left
His golden throne, bent warm on amorous
    theft:
From high Olympus had he stolen light,
On this side of Jove's clouds, to escape the
    sight                                    10
Of his great summoner, and made retreat
Into a forest on the shores of Crete.
For somewhere in that sacred island dwelt
A nymph to whom all hooféd Satyrs knelt;
At whose white feet the languid Tritons
    poured                                   15
Pearls, while on land they withered and adored.
Fast by the springs where she to bathe was
    wont,
And in those meads where sometime she might
    haunt,
Were strewn rich gifts, unknown to any Muse,
Though Fancy's casket were unlocked to
    choose.                                  20
Ah, what a world of love was at her feet!
So Hermes thought, and a celestial heat
Burned from his wingéd heels to either ear,
That, from a whiteness as the lily clear,
Blushed into roses 'mid his golden hair,     25
Fallen in jealous curls about his shoulders bare.

From vale to vale, from wood to wood, he
    flew,
Breathing upon the flowers his passion new,
And wound with many a river to its head,
To find where this sweet nymph prepared her
    secret bed:                             30
In vain; the sweet nymph might nowhere be
    found,
And so he rested on the lonely ground,
Pensive, and full of painful jealousies
Of the Wood-Gods, and even the very trees.
There as he stood, he heard a mournful voice,
Such as, once heard, in gentle heart destroys 36
All pain but pity; thus the lone voice spake:
"When from this wreathéd tomb shall I awake?
When move in a sweet body fit for life,
And love, and pleasure, and the ruddy strife 40
Of hearts and lips? Ah, miserable me!"
The God, dove-footed, glided silently
Round bush and tree, soft-brushing in his speed
The taller grasses and full-flowering weed,
Until he found a palpitating snake,          45
Bright and cirque-couchant,[2] in a dusky brake.

She was a gordian [3] shape of dazzling hue.
Vermilion-spotted, golden, green, and blue;
Striped like a zebra, freckled like a pard,
Eyed like a peacock, and all crimson-barred; 50
And full of silver moons, that, as she breathed,

[2] Lying coiled.          [3] Knotted.

Dissolved, or brighter shone, or interwreathed
Their lusters with the gloomier tapestries—
So rainbow-sided, touched with miseries,
She seemed, at once, some penanced lady elf.
Some demon's mistress, or the demon's self. 56
Upon her crest she wore a wannish fire
Sprinkled with stars, like Ariadne's tiar: [4]
Her head was serpent, but ah, bitter-sweet!
She had a woman's mouth with all its pearls
    complete;                              60
For her eyes—what could such eyes do there
But weep and weep, that they were born so
    fair,
As Proserpine still weeps for her Sicilian air?
Her throat was serpent, but the words she spake
Came, as though bubbling honey, for Love's
    sake,                                  65
And thus; while Hermes on his pinions lay,
Like a stooped falcon ere he takes his prey:

    "Fair Hermes, crowned with feathers, flutter-
        ing light,
I had a splendid dream of thee last night:
I saw thee sitting, on a throne of gold,      70
Among the Gods, upon Olympus old,
The only sad one; for thou didst not hear
The soft, lute-fingered Muses chaunting clear,
Nor even Apollo when he sang alone,
Deaf to his throbbing throat's long, long melo-
    dious moan.                            75
I dreamed I saw thee, robed in purple flakes,
Break amorous through the clouds, as morning
    breaks,
And, swiftly as a bright Phoebean dart,[5]
Strike for the Cretan isle; and here thou art!
Too gentle Hermes, hast thou found the
    maid?"                                 80
Whereat the star of Lethe [6] not delayed
His rosy eloquence, and thus inquired:
"Thou smooth-lipped serpent, surely high-
    inspired!
Thou beauteous wreath, with melancholy eyes,
Possess whatever bliss thou canst devise,     85
Telling me only where my nymph is fled—
Where she doth breathe!" "Bright planet, thou
    hast said,"
Returned the snake, "but seal with oaths, fair
    God!"
"I swear," said Hermes, "by my serpent rod,
And by thine eyes, and by thy starry crown!" 90
Light flew his earnest words, among the blos-
    soms blown.
Then thus again the brilliance feminine:
"Too frail of heart! for this lost nymph of
    thine,
Free as the air, invisibly she strays
About these thornless wilds; her pleasant days
She tastes unseen; unseen her nimble feet  96

[4] Bacchus gave Ariadne a tiara, or crown, of seven
stars which after her death became a constellation.
[5] As one of Phoebus Apollo's arrows.
[6] Hermes is so called because it was one of his
duties to lead the souls of the dead to Hades.

Leave traces in the grass and flowers sweet:
From weary tendrils and bowed branches green
She plucks the fruit unseen, she bathes unseen:
And by my power is her beauty veiled    100
To keep it unaffronted, unassailed
By the love-glances of unlovely eyes,
Of Satyrs, Fauns, and bleared Silenus'[7] sighs.
Pale grew her immortality, for woe
Of all these lovers, and she grievéd so    105
I took compassion on her, bade her steep
Her hair in weïrd syrops, that would keep
Her loveliness invisible, yet free
To wander as she loves, in liberty.
If thou wilt, as thou swearest, grant my boon!"
Thou shalt behold her, Hermes, thou alone, 110
Then, once again, the charméd God began
An oath, and through the serpent's ears it ran
Warm, tremulous, devout, psalterian.[8]
Ravished, she lifted her Circean head,    115
Blushed a live damask, and swift-lisping said,
"I was a woman, let me have once more
A woman's shape, and charming as before.
I love a youth of Corinth—O the bliss!
Give me my woman's form, and place me
   where he is.    120
Stoop, Hermes, let me breathe upon thy brow,
And thou shalt see thy sweet nymph even
   now."
The God on half-shut feathers sank serene,
She breathed upon his eyes, and swift was seen
Of both the guarded nymph near-smiling on
   the green.    125
It was no dream; or say a dream it was,
Real are the dreams of Gods, and smoothly pass
Their pleasures in a long immortal dream.
One warm, flushed moment, hovering, it might
   seem,
Dashed by the wood-nymph's beauty, so he
   burned;    130
Then, lighting on the printless verdure, turned
To the swooned serpent, and with languid arm,
Delicate, put to proof the lithe Caducean
   charm.[9]
So done, upon the nymph his eyes he bent
Full of adoring tears and blandishment,    135
And towards her stepped: she, like a moon in
   wane,
Faded before him, cowered, nor could restrain
Her fearful sobs, self-folding like a flower
That faints into itself at evening hour:
But the God fostering her chilléd hand,    140
She felt the warmth, her eyelids opened bland,
And, like new flowers at morning song of bees,
Bloomed, and gave up her honey to the lees.
Into the green-recesséd woods they flew;
Nor grew they pale, as mortal lovers do.    145

   Left to herself, the serpent now began
To change; her elfin blood in madness ran;

Her mouth foamed, and the grass, therewith
   besprent,[10]
Withered at dew so sweet and virulent;
Her eyes in torture fixed, and anguish drear, 150
Hot, glazed, and wide, with lid-lashes all sear,
Flashed phosphor and sharp sparks, without
   one cooling tear.
The colors all inflamed throughout her train,
She writhed about, convulsed with scarlet pain:
A deep volcanian yellow took the place    155
Of all her milder-moonéd body's grace;
And, as the lava ravishes the mead,
Spoiled all her silver mail, and golden brede:[11]
Made gloom all her frecklings, streaks and bars,
Eclipsed her crescents, and licked up her stars:
So that, in moments few, she was undressed 161
Of all her sapphires, greens, and amethyst,
And rubious-argent: of all these bereft,
Nothing but pain and ugliness were left.
Still shone her crown; that vanished, also she
Melted and disappeared as suddenly;    166
And in the air, her new voice luting soft,
Cried, "Lycius! gentle Lycius!"—Borne aloft
With the bright mists about the mountains
   hoar
These words dissolved: Crete's forests heard no
   more.    170

   Whither fled Lamia, now a lady bright,
A full-born beauty new and exquisite?
She fled into that valley they pass o'er
Who go to Corinth from Cenchreas' shore;
And rested at the foot of those wild hills,    175
The rugged founts of the Peraean rills,
And of that other ridge whose barren back
Stretches, with all its mist and cloudy rack,
South-westward to Cleone. There she stood,
About a young bird's flutter from a wood, 180
Fair, on a sloping green of mossy tread,
By a clear pool, wherein she passionéd
To see herself escaped from so sore ills,
While her robes flaunted with the daffodils.

   Ah, happy Lycius!—for she was a maid 185
More beautiful than ever twisted braid,
Or sighed, or blushed, or on spring-flowered lea
Spread a green girtle to the minstrelsy:
A virgin purest lipped, yet in the lore
Of love deep learnéd to the red heart's core: 190
Not one hour old, yet of sciential brain
To unperplex bliss from its neighbor pain;
Define their pettish limits, and estrange
Their points of contact, and swift counter-
   change;
Intrigue with the specious chaos,[12] and dispart
Its most ambiguous atoms with sure art;    196
As though in Cupid's college she had spent
Sweet days a lovely graduate, still unshent,[13]
And kept his rosy terms in idle languishment.

---

[7] Foster-father of Bacchus.
[8] Musical.
[9] Caduceus was the name of Hermes' wand.

[10] Sprinkled.    [11] Embroidery.
[12] The fair-appearing confusion of joy and pain.
[13] Yet unreproached.

Why this fair creature chose so faerily    200
By the wayside to linger, we shall see;
But first 'tis fit to tell how she could muse
And dream, when in the serpent prison-house,
Of all she list, strange or magnificent:
How, ever, where she willed her spirit went; 205
Whether to faint Elysium, or where
Down through tress-lifting waves the Nereids [14]
fair
Wind into Thetis' bower by many a pearly
stair;
Or where God Bacchus drains his cups divine,
Stretched out, at ease, beneath a glutinous
pine;    210
Or where in Pluto's gardens palatine [15]
Mulciber's columns gleam in far piazzian line.[16]
And sometimes into cities she would send
Her dream, with feast and rioting to blend;
And once, while among mortals dreaming thus,
She saw the young Corinthian Lycius    216
Charioting foremost in the envious race,
Like a young Jove with calm uneager face,
And fell into a swooning love of him.
Now on the moth-time of that evening dim 220
He would return that way, as well she knew,
To Corinth from the shore; for freshly blew
The eastern soft-wind, and his galley now
Grated the quay-stones with her brazen prow
In port Cenchreas, from Egina isle    225
Fresh anchored; whither he had been awhile
To sacrifice to Jove, whose temple there
Waits with high marble doors for blood and in-
cense rare.
Jove heard his vows, and bettered his desire;
For by some freakful chance he made retire 230
From his companions, and set forth to walk,
Perhaps grown wearied of their Corinth talk:
Over the solitary hills he fared,
Thoughtless at first, but ere eve's star appeared
His phantasy was lost, where reason fades, 235
In the calmed twilight of Platonic shades.[17]
Lamia beheld him coming, near, more near—
Close to her passing, in indifference drear,
His silent sandals swept the mossy green;
So neighbored to him, and yet so unseen,    240
She stood: he passed, shut up in mysteries,
His mind wrapped like his mantle, while her
eyes
Followed his steps, and her neck regal white
Turned—syllabling thus: "Ah, Lycius bright,
And will you leave me on the hills alone? 245
Lycius, look back! and be some pity shown."
He did; not with cold wonder, fearingly,
But Orpheus-like at an Eurydice; [18]

[14] Sea-nymphs, sisters of Thetis.
[15] Palatial.
[16] Vulcan's columns gleam, forming covered walks.
[17] His thoughtless fancies disappeared while he
considered the mysteries of Plato's philosophy.
[18] Orpheus succeeded in winning back his wife
Eurydice from the world of shades on condition that
as they returned to the world he would not look
back to see her following him. He, however, so

For so delicious were the words she sung,
It seemed he had loved them a whole summer
long.    250
And soon his eyes had drunk her beauty up,
Leaving no drop in the bewildering cup,
And still the cup was full,—while he, afraid
Lest she should vanish ere his lip had paid
Due adoration, thus began to adore;    255
Her soft look growing coy, she saw his chain so
sure:
"Leave thee alone! Look back! Ah, Goddess,
see
Whether my eyes can ever turn from thee!
For pity do not this sad heart belie—
Even as thou vanishest so I shall die.    260
Stay! though a Naiad of the rivers, stay!
To thy far wishes will thy streams obey:
Stay! though the greenest woods be thy do-
main,
Alone they can drink up the morning rain;
Though a descended Pleiad,[19] will not one 265
Of thine harmonious sisters keep in tune
Thy spheres, and as thy silver proxy shine?
So sweetly to these ravished ears of mine
Came thy sweet greeting, that if thou shouldst
fade,
Thy memory will waste me to a shade:—    270
For pity do not melt!" "If I should stay,"
Said Lamia, "here, upon this floor of clay,
And pain my steps upon these flowers too
rough,
What canst thou say or do of charm enough
To dull the nice remembrance of my home? 275
Thou canst not ask me with thee here to roam
Over these hills and vales, where no joy is,—
Empty of immortality and bliss!
Thou art a scholar, Lycius, and must know
That finer spirits cannot breathe below    280
In human climes, and live. Alas! poor youth,
What taste of purer air hast thou to soothe
My essence? What serener palaces,
Where I may all my many senses please,
And by mysterious sleights a hundred thirsts
appease?    285
It cannot be—adieu!" So said, she rose
Tiptoe, with white arms spread. He, sick to lose
The amorous promise of her lone complain,
Swooned, murmuring of love, and pale with
pain.
The cruel lady, without any show    290
Of sorrow for her tender favorite's woe,
But rather, if her eyes could brighter be,
With brighter eyes and slow amenity,
Put her new lips to his, and gave afresh
The life she had so tangled in her mesh:    295
And as he from one trance was wakening
Into another, she began to sing,—

loved her that he could not forbear looking back—
whereupon she vanished and returned to Hades.
[19] The Pleiads were seven sisters, changed into the
constellation. The concentric spheres which, according to the old astronomy, surrounded the earth,
were supposed to make music as they revolved.

Happy in beauty, life, and love, and every-
thing,—
A song of love, too sweet for earthly lyres,
While, like held breath, the stars drew in their
panting fires.                                          300
And then she whispered in such trembling tone
As those who, safe together met alone
For the first time through many anguished
days,
Use other speech than looks; bidding him raise
His drooping head, and clear his soul of doubt,
For that she was a woman, and without    306
Any more subtle fluid in her veins
Than throbbing blood, and that the self-same
pains
Inhabited her frail-strung heart as his.
And next she wondered how his eyes could
miss                                                    310
Her face so long in Corinth, where, she said,
She dwelt but half retired, and there had led
Days happy as the gold coin could invent
Without the aid of love; yet in content,
Till she saw him, as once she passed him by, 315
Where 'gainst a column he leaned thoughtfully
At Venus' temple porch, 'mid baskets heaped
Of amorous herbs and flowers, newly reaped
Late on that eve, as 'twas the night before
The Adonian feast; [20] whereof she saw no more,
But wept alone those days,—for why should she
adore?                                                  321
Lycius from death awoke into amaze
To see her still, and singing so sweet lays;
Then from amaze into delight he fell
To hear her whisper woman's lore so well; 325
And every word she spake enticed him on
To unperplexed delight and pleasure known.
Let the mad poets say whate'er they please
Of the sweets of Faeries, Peris,[21] Goddesses,
There is not such a treat among them all— 330
Haunters of cavern, lake, and waterfall—
As a real woman, lineal indeed
From Pyrrha's pebbles [22] or old Adam's seed.
Thus gentle Lamia judged, and judged aright,
That Lycius could not love in half a fright, 335
So threw the goddess off, and won his heart
More pleasantly by playing woman's part,
With no more awe than what her beauty gave,
That, while it smote, still guaranteed to save.
Lycius to all made eloquent reply,             340
Marrying to every word a twin-born sigh;
And last, pointing to Corinth, asked her sweet,
If 'twas too far that night for her soft feet.
The way was short, for Lamia's eagerness
Made, by a spell, the triple league decrease 345
To a few paces; not at all surmised

By blinded Lycius, so in her comprised.
They passed the city gates, he knew not how,
So noiseless, and he never thought to know.

As men talk in a dream, so Corinth all,    350
Throughout her palaces imperial,
And all her populous streets and temples lewd,
Muttered, like tempest in the distance brewed,
To the wide-spreaded night above her towers.
Men, women, rich and poor, in the cool
hours,                                                  355
Shuffled their sandals o'er the pavement white,
Companioned or alone; while many a light
Flared, here and there, from wealthy festivals,
And threw their moving shadows on the walls,
Or found them clustered in the corniced shade
Of some arched temple door or dusky colon-
nade.                                                   361

Muffling his face, of greeting friends in fear,
Her fingers he pressed hard, as one came near
With curled gray beard, sharp eyes, and smooth
bald crown,                                             364
Slow-stepped, and robed in philosophic gown:
Lycius shrank closer, as they met and passed,
Into his mantle, adding wings to haste,
While hurried Lamia trembled. "Ah," said he,
"Why do you shudder, love, so ruefully?
Why does your tender palm dissolve in
dew?"—                                                  370
"I'm wearied," said fair Lamia: "tell me who
Is that old man? I cannot bring to mind
His features:—Lycius! wherefore did you blind
Yourself with his quick eyes?" Lycius replied,
"'Tis Apollonius sage, my trusty guide    375
And good instructor; but to-night he seems
The ghost of folly haunting my sweet dreams."

While yet he spake they had arrived before
A pillared porch, with lofty portal door,
Where hung a silver lamp, whose phosphor
glow                                                    380
Reflected in the slabbéd steps below,
Mild as a star in water; for so new
And so unsullied was the marble's hue,
So through the crystal polish, liquid fine,
Ran the dark veins, that none but feet divine
Could e'er have touched there. Sounds
Aeolian [23]                                            386
Breathed from the hinges, as the ample span
Of the wide doors disclosed a place unknown
Some time to any, but those two alone,
And a few Persian mutes, who that same year
Were seen about the markets: none knew
where                                                   391
They could inhabit; the most curious
Were foiled, who watched to trace them to
their house:
And but the flitter-wingéd verse [24] must tell,
For truth's sake, what woe afterwards befell, 395

[20] Festival in honor of Adonis. He was a beautiful youth loved by Venus. When he was killed by
a wild boar she had him carried to Elysium.
[21] A Peri is, according to Persian fable, one descended from the fallen angels.
[22] After the flood Pyrrha and Deucalion, according to legend, cast stones behind them which sprang
up human beings, and so they re-peopled the world.

[23] Musical sounds.
[24] The verse winging its way like a bird.

'Twould humor many a heart to leave them
    thus
Shut from the busy world of more incredulous.

## PART II

Love in a hut, with water and a crust,
Is—Love, forgive us!—cinders, ashes, dust;
Love in a palace is perhaps at last
More grievous torment than a hermit's fast:—
That is a doubtful tale from faery land,    5
Hard for the non-elect to understand.
Had Lycius lived to hand his story down,
He might have given the moral a fresh frown,
Or clenched it quite: but too short was their
    bliss
To breed distrust and hate, that make the soft
    voice hiss.    10
Besides, there, nightly, with terrific glare,
Love, jealous grown of so complete a pair,
Hovered and buzzed his wings, with fearful
    roar,
Above the lintel of their chamber door,
And down the passage cast a glow upon the
    floor.    15

For all this came a ruin: side by side
They were enthronéd, in the eventide,
Upon a couch, near to a curtaining
Whose airy texture, from a golden string,
Floated into the room, and let appear    20
Unveiled the summer heaven, blue and clear,
Betwixt two marble shafts:—there they re-
    posed,
Where use had made it sweet, with eyelids
    closed,
Saving a tithe which love still open kept,
That they might see each other while they al-
    most slept;    25
When from the slope side of a suburb hill,
Deafening the swallow's twitter, came a thrill
Of trumpets—Lycius started—the sounds fled,
But left a thought, a buzzing in his head.
For the first time, since first he harbored in    30
That purple-linéd palace of sweet sin,
His spirit passed beyond its golden bourn [1]
Into the noisy world almost forsworn.
The lady, ever watchful, penetrant,
Saw this with pain, so arguing a want    35
Of something more, more than her empery
Of joys; and she began to moan and sigh
Because he mused beyond her, knowing well
That but a moment's thought is passion's pass-
    ing bell.
"Why do you sigh, fair creature?" whispered
    he:    40
"Why do you think?" returned she tenderly:
"You have deserted me; where am I now?
Not in your heart while care weighs on your
    brow:
No, no, you have dismissed me, and I go

[1] Domain.

From your breast houseless: ay, it must be so."
He answered, bending to her open eyes,    46
Where he was mirrored small in paradise,
"My silver planet, both of eve and morn!
Why will you plead yourself so sad forlorn,
While I am striving how to fill my heart    50
With deeper crimson and a double smart?
How to entangle, trammel up, and snare
Your soul in mine, and labyrinth you there
Like the hid scent in an unbudded rose?
Ay, a sweet kiss—you see your mighty woes.    55
My thoughts! shall I unveil them? Listen then!
What mortal hath a prize, that other men
May be confounded and abashed withal,
But lets it sometimes pace abroad majestical,
And triumph, as in thee I should rejoice    60
Amid the hoarse alarm of Corinth's voice.
Let my foes choke, and my friends shout afar,
While through the throngéd streets your bridal
    car
Wheels round its dazzling spokes." The lady's
    cheek
Trembled; she nothing said, but, pale and
    meek,    65
Arose and knelt before him, wept a rain
Of sorrows at his words; at last with pain
Beseeching him, the while his hand she wrung,
To change his purpose. He thereat was stung,
Perverse, with stronger fancy to reclaim    70
Her wild and timid nature to his aim;
Besides, for all his love, in self despite,
Against his better self, he took delight
Luxurious in her sorrows, soft and new.
His passion, cruel grown, took on a hue    75
Fierce and sanguineous as 'twas possible
In one whose brow had no dark veins to swell.
Fine was the mitigated fury, like
Apollo's presence when in act to strike
The serpent—Ha, the serpent! certes, she    80
Was none. She burned, she loved the tyranny,
And, all subdued, consented to the hour
When to the bridal he should lead his par-
    amour.
Whispering in midnight silence, said the
    youth,
"Sure some sweet name thou hast, though, by
    my truth,    85
I have not asked it, ever thinking thee
Not mortal, but of heavenly progeny,
As still I do. Hast any mortal name,
Fit appellation for this dazzling frame?
Or friends or kinsfolk on the citied earth,    90
To share our marriage feast and nuptial mirth?"
"I have no friends," said Lamia, "no, not one;
My presence in wide Corinth hardly known:
My parents' bones are in their dusty urns    94
Sepulchered, where no kindled incense burns,
Seeing all their luckless race are dead save me,
And I neglect the holy rite for thee.
Even as you list invite your many guests;
But if, as now it seems, your vision rests
With any pleasure on me, do not bid    100
Old Apollonius—from him keep me hid."

Lycius, perplexed at words so blind and blank,
Made close inquiry; from whose touch she
    shrank,
Feigning a sleep; and he to the dull shade
Of deep sleep in a moment was betrayed. 105

It was the custom then to bring away
The bride from home at blushing shut of day,
Veiled, in a chariot, heralded along
By strewn flowers, torches, and a marriage song,
With other pageants: but this fair unknown 110
Had not a friend. So being left alone
(Lycius was gone to summon all his kin),
And knowing surely she could never win
His foolish heart from its mad pompousness,
She set herself, high-thoughted, how to dress
The misery in fit magnificence. 116
She did so, but 'tis doubtful how and whence
Came, and who were her subtle servitors.
About the halls, and to and from the doors,
There was a noise of wings, till in short space
The glowing banquet-room shone with wide-
    archéd grace. 121
A haunting music, sole perhaps and lone
Supportress of the faery-roof, made moan
Throughout, as fearful the whole charm might
    fade.
Fresh carvéd cedar, mimicking a glade 125
Of palm and plantain, met from either side,
High in the midst, in honor of the bride:
Two palms and then two plantains, and so on,
From either side their stems branched one to
    one
All down the aisléd place; and beneath all 130
There ran a stream of lamps straight on from
    wall to wall.
So canopied, lay an untasted feast
Teeming with odors. Lamia, regal dressed,
Silently paced about, and as she went,
In pale contented sort of discontent, 135
Missioned her viewless servants to enrich
The fretted splendor of each nook and niche.
Between the tree-stems, marbled plain at first,
Came jasper panels; then anon there burst
Forth creeping imagery of slighter trees, 140
And with the larger wove in small intricacies.
Approving all, she faded at self-will,
And shut the chamber up, close, hushed and
    still,
Complete and ready for the revels rude,
When dreadful guests would come to spoil her
    solitude. 145

The day appeared, and all the gossip rout.
O senseless Lycius! Madman! wherefore flout
The silent-blessing fate, warm cloistered hours,
And show to common eyes these secret bowers?
The herd approached; each guest, with busy
    brain, 150
Arriving at the portal, gazed amain,
And entered marveling: for they knew the
    street,
Remembered it from childhood all complete

Without a gap, yet ne'er before had seen
That royal porch, that high-built fair de-
    mesne; [2] 155
So in they hurried all, mazed, curious and keen;
Save one, who looked thereon with eye severe,
And with calm-planted steps walked in austere;
'Twas Apollonius: something too he laughed,
As though some knotty problem, that had
    daft [3] 160
His patient thought, had now begun to thaw
And solve and melt: 'twas just as he foresaw.

He met within the murmurous vestibule
His young disciple. " 'Tis no common rule,
Lycius," said he, "for uninvited guest 165
To force himself upon you, and infest
With an unbidden presence the bright throng
Of younger friends; yet must I do this wrong,
And you forgive me." Lycius blushed, and led
The old man through the inner doors broad-
    spread; 170
With reconciling words and courteous mien
Turning into sweet milk the sophist's spleen.

Of wealthy luster was the banquet-room,
Filled with pervading brilliance and perfume:
Before each lucid panel fuming stood 175
A censer fed with myrrh and spicéd wood,
Each by a sacred tripod held aloft,
Whose slender feet wide-swerved upon the soft
Wool-wooféd carpets: fifty wreaths of smoke
From fifty censers their light voyage took 180
To the high roof, still mimicked as they rose
Along the mirrored walls by twin-clouds odor-
    ous.
Twelve sphéred tables by silk seats insphered,
High as the level of a man's breast reared
On libbard's [4] paws, upheld the heavy gold 185
Of cups and goblets, and the store thrice told
Of Ceres' horn,[5] and, in huge vessels, wine
Come from the gloomy tun [6] with merry shine.
Thus loaded with a feast the tables stood,
Each shrining in the midst the image of a God.

When in an antechamber every guest 191
Had felt the cold full sponge to pleasure
    pressed,
By ministering slaves, upon his hands and feet,
And fragrant oils with ceremony meet 194
Poured on his hair, they all moved to the feast
In white robes, and themselves in order placed
Around the silken couches, wondering
Whence all this mighty cost and blaze of
    wealth could spring.

Soft went the music the soft air along,
While fluent Greek a voweled under-song 200
Kept up among the guests, discoursing low
At first, for scarcely was the wine at flow;

---

[2] Dwelling.    [3] Eluded.    [4] Leopard's.
[5] Ceres was the goddess of harvests. The horn
was symbolic of plenty.
    [6] Cask.

But when the happy vintage touched their
    brains,
Louder they talk, and louder come the strains
Of powerful instruments:—the gorgeous dyes,
The space, the splendor of the draperies,    206
The roof of awful richness, nectarous cheer,
Beautiful slaves, and Lamia's self, appear,
Now, when the wine has done its rosy deed,
And every soul from human trammels freed,
No more so strange; for merry wine, sweet
    wine,    211
Will make Elysian shades not too fair, too di-
    vine.
Soon was God Bacchus at meridian height;
Flushed were their cheeks, and bright eyes
    double bright;
Garlands of every green and every scent    215
From vales deflowered or forest-trees branch-
    rent,
In baskets of bright osiered gold [7] were brought,
High as the handles heaped, to suit the thought
Of every guest; that each, as he did please,
Might fancy-fit his brows, silk-pillowed at his
    ease.    220

What wreath for Lamia? What for Lycius?
What for the sage, old Apollonius?
Upon her aching forehead be there hung
The leaves of willow [8] and of adder's tongue;
And for the youth, quick, let us strip for him
The thyrsus,[9] that his watching eyes may
    swim    226
Into forgetfulness; and, for the sage,
Let spear-grass and the spiteful thistle wage
War on his temples. Do not all charms fly
At the mere touch of cold philosophy?    230
There was an awful rainbow once in heaven:
We know her woof, her texture; she is given
In the dull catalogue of common things.
Philosophy will clip an Angel's wings,
Conquer all mysteries by rule and line,    235
Empty the haunted air and gnoméd mine—
Unweave a rainbow, as it erewhile made
The tender-personed Lamia melt into a shade.

By her glad Lycius sitting, in chief place,
Scarce saw in all the room another face,    240
Till, checking his love trance, a cup he took
Full brimmed, and opposite sent forth a look
Cross the broad table, to beseech a glance
From his old teacher's wrinkled countenance,
And pledge him. The bald-head philosopher
Had fixed his eye, without a twinkle or stir, 246
Full on the alarméd beauty of the bride,
Brow-beating her fair form and troubling her
    sweet pride.
Lycius then pressed her hand, with devout
    touch,

[7] Baskets of woven gold.
[8] The weeping-willow, symbolic of grief. "Adder's
tongue" is the popular name for a certain variety
of fern.
[9] A rod wreathed with ivy, the staff of Bacchus.

As pale it lay upon the rosy couch:    250
'Twas icy, and the cold ran through his veins;
Then sudden it grew hot, and all the pains
Of an unnatural heat shot to his heart.
"Lamia, what means this? Wherefore dost thou
    start?
Know'st thou that man?" Poor Lamia answered
    not.    255
He gazed into her eyes, and not a jot
Owned they the lovelorn piteous appeal:
More, more he gazed: his human senses reel:
Some hungry spell that loveliness absorbs;
There was no recognition in those orbs.    260
"Lamia!" he cried—and no soft-toned reply.
The many heard, and the loud revelry
Grew hush; the stately music no more breathes;
The myrtle sickened in a thousand wreaths.
By faint degrees, voice, lute, and pleasure
    ceased;    265
A deadly silence step by step increased
Until it seemed a horrid presence there,
And not a man but felt the terror in his hair.
"Lamia!" he shrieked; and nothing but the
    shriek
With its sad echo did the silence break.    270
"Begone, foul dream!" he cried, gazing again
In the bride's face, where now no azure vein
Wandered on fair-spaced temples, no soft
    bloom
Misted the cheek, no passion to illume
The deep-recesséd vision:—all was blight;    275
Lamia, no longer fair, there sat, a deadly white.
"Shut, shut those juggling eyes, thou ruthless
    man!
Turn them aside, wretch! or the righteous ban
Of all the Gods, whose dreadful images
Here represent their shadowy presences,    280
May pierce them on the sudden with the thorn
Of painful blindness; leaving thee forlorn,
In trembling dotage to the feeblest fright
Of conscience, for their long-offended might,
For all thine impious proud-heart sophistries,
Unlawful magic, and enticing lies.    286
Corinthians! look upon that gray-beard wretch!
Mark how, possessed, his lashless eyelids stretch
Around his demon eyes! Corinthians, see!
My sweet bride withers at their potency."    290
"Fool!" said the sophist, in an undertone
Gruff with contempt; which a death-nighing
    moan
From Lycius answered, as, heart-struck and lost,
He sank supine beside the aching ghost.
"Fool! Fool!" repeated he, while his eyes still
Relented not, nor moved; "from every ill    296
Of life have I preserved thee to this day,
And shall I see thee made a serpent's prey?"
Then Lamia breathed death-breath; the soph-
    ist's eye,    299
Like a sharp spear, went through her utterly,
Keen, cruel, perceant,[10] stinging: she, as well
As her weak hand could any meaning tell,

[10] Piercing.

Motioned him to be silent; vainly so;
He looked and looked again a level—No!
"A serpent!" echoed he; no sooner said,      305
Than with a frightful scream she vanishéd;
And Lycius' arms were empty of delight,
As were his limbs of life, from that same night.
On the high couch he lay—his friends came round—
Supported him; no pulse or breath they found,
And in its marriage robe the heavy body wound.      311

## Sonnet [1]

Bright star! would I were steadfast as thou art—

[1] Believed to have been written in March, 1819; published in 1848. This was formerly thought to have been the last poem written by Keats, as he wrote the later (and until recently the only known)

Not in lone splendor hung aloft the night,
And watching, with eternal lids apart,
   Like Nature's patient, sleepless Eremite,[2]
The moving waters at their priestlike task      5
   Of pure ablution round earth's human shores,
Or gazing on the new soft fallen mask
   Of snow upon the mountains and the moors—
No—yet still steadfast, still unchangeable,
   Pillowed upon my fair love's ripening breast,
To feel for ever its soft fall and swell,      11
   Awake for ever in a sweet unrest,
Still, still to hear her tender-taken breath,
And so live ever—or else swoon to death.

version of the sonnet after he had embarked for Italy, in September, 1820. This he wrote on a blank page, facing *A Lover's Complaint*, in a folio volume of Shakespeare which he gave to Severn, who accompanied him on his journey.
[2] Hermit.

# Thomas De Quincey

## 1785-1859

De Quincey was born in Manchester, where his father was a merchant, on 15 August, 1785. Of his father, who died when Thomas was still a child, he never saw anything; and of his mother, who showed no signs of really understanding him, one is tempted to say he saw too much. He was a frail child, and in his earliest days, as in his later ones, he lived the life of a solitary. In 1796 his mother moved to Bath and placed Thomas at school there. Later he was sent to Winkfield School, in Wiltshire. He showed astonishing precocity, and at fifteen was ready to enter Oxford. Instead, however, he was sent to Manchester Grammar School to mark time for three years, so that he might gain a scholarship at Brasenose College. He strongly rebelled against this waste of time: "I ask," he wrote to his mother, "whether a person can be happy, or even simply easy, who is in a situation which deprives him of health, of society, of amusement, of liberty, of congeniality of pursuits, and which, to complete the precious picture, admits of no variety." But his pleas were met with denial, so that in the end, in desperation, he ran away. His experiences he describes in his Confessions. In the spring of 1803 he was discovered by friends, brought home, and finally allowed to go to Oxford, where he entered Worcester College because of the smallness of his allowance. He came to be known in Oxford "as a strange being who associated with no one." He says himself: "For the first two years I compute that I did not utter one hundred words." It was at this time that he began the use of opium, though the first period of his great excesses did not come until his twenty-ninth year. At Oxford he extended his acquaintance with the Greek and Latin classics, studied Hebrew and German, and read widely in English literature. But he took no degree. Being displeased with the conduct of his examinations, in particular at not being allowed to answer questions in

Greek, he simply disappeared, as he later did more than once on other occasions.

During several years after he left Oxford De Quincey led a rather wandering existence, becoming acquainted at one place or another with a number of literary people, among them Lamb, Coleridge, Wordsworth, and Southey. Wordsworth he regarded with peculiar veneration, and in 1809 he settled at Grasmere in the Lake Country in order to be near the Wordsworths. In 1816 he married Margaret Simpson, the daughter of a Westmoreland dalesman. However unsuited to him De Quincey's wife was—and it is practically impossible to imagine any woman who would have made him a suitable wife—she at least may be said to have put him in the way of beginning his literary career. For soon after his marriage he found his money exhausted, and he was compelled to turn from the reading of German literature and philosophy to productive work. It was in this way that he came to write, in 1821, the Confessions of an English Opium-Eater for the London Magazine. The work immediately aroused wide and keen interest, and De Quincey thereafter always found periodicals open for all that he could write. About 1830 he removed to Edinburgh, and maintained a home there for his family throughout the remainder of his life. He often even lived with his family, though he kept separate lodgings for himself in Edinburgh, and kept rooms for some years also in Glasgow, and perhaps elsewhere, for he was always likely to disappear suddenly for indefinite periods. The years of his worst opium-excesses were 1813, 1817, 1823, and 1844. After 1844, however, though he continued to drink laudanum until his death, he managed to keep the quantity within a moderate compass. During all this time he wrote voluminously for periodicals, though besides the Confessions he composed only two extended works, his romance, Klosterheim (1839), and his Logic of Political Economy (1844). *Though we hear less of them in his later years, he frequently suffered from what he called "pecuniary embarrassments," not so much because his income was insufficient as because he was incapable of taking care of his money. He died in Edinburgh on 8 December, 1859.*

*De Quincey was, like Coleridge and Lamb, widely read in the great English prose writers of the first half of the seventeenth century, and this is one secret of the richness and majesty of his style. His biographer, A. H. Japp, has indicated the qualities of his mind which we find united in the* Confessions: *"De Quincey himself, in descanting on the dream-faculty, says, 'Habitually to dream magnificently, a man must have a constitutional determination to reverie.' In that sentence he announces the true law of all literature that comes under the order of pure fantasy. But in his case, in spite of the strength of the dream-element, we cannot proceed far till we discover that his determination to reverie was but the extreme projection of one phase of a phenomenal nature balancing its opposite. . . . He was skilled in the exercises of the analytic understanding—a logician exacting and precise—else his dreaming had never gained for him the eminence it has gained. Surely it is calculated to strike the most casual reader on a perusal of . . . the* Confessions, *that his power of following up sensational effects and tracing with absolute exactness the most delicately varying shades of experience, and recording them with conscientious precision, were as noticeable as were the dreams to which they served to give effect."*

*The standard edition of De Quincey's Collected Writings is edited by David Masson (14 vols., Edinburgh, 1889–1890; and later reprinted). The* Selected Writings *of De Quincey, ed. Philip Van Doren Stern (New York, 1937), is a useful volume. A number of good biographies have appeared: H. A. Eaton's* Thomas De Quincey *(Oxford, 1936) supplies a great deal of biographical material, while Edward Sackville-West's* A Flame in Sunlight; the Life and Work of Thomas De Quincey *(London, 1936) makes a more critical approach to the essayist.* De Quincey, *by Malcolm Elwin (London, 1935), is a much briefer sketch.* De Quincey: a Portrait, *by J. C. Metcalf (Cambridge, U. S. A., 1940), is a well-balanced study. Interpretations and stylistic studies include J. H. Fowler's* De Quincey as Literary Critic *(Oxford, 1922), J. E. Jordan's* Thomas De Quincey, Literary Critic *(Berkeley,*

*1952), and S. K. Proctor's* Thomas De Quincey's Theory of Literature *(Ann Arbor, 1943).*

## Passages from

# Confessions of an English Opium-Eater [1]

## I

I have often been asked how I came to be a regular opium-eater; and have suffered, very unjustly, in the opinion of my acquaintance, from being reputed to have brought upon myself all the sufferings which I shall have to record, by a long course of indulgence in this practice purely for the sake of creating an artificial state of pleasurable excitement. This, however, is a misrepresentation of my case. True it is, that for nearly ten years I did occasionally take opium for the sake of the exquisite pleasure it gave me; but, so long as I took it with this view, I was effectually protected from all material bad consequences by the necessity of interposing long intervals between the several acts of indulgence, in order to renew the pleasurable sensations. It was not for the purpose of creating pleasure, but of mitigating pain in the severest degree, that I first began to use opium as an article of daily diet. In the twenty-eighth year of my age, a most painful affection of the stomach, which I had first experienced about ten years before, attacked me in great strength. This affection had originally been caused by extremities of hunger, suffered in my boyish days. During the season of hope and redundant happiness which succeeded (that is, from eighteen to twenty-four) it had slumbered: for the three following years it had revived at intervals; and now, under unfavorable circumstances, from depression of spirits, it attacked me with a violence that yielded to no remedies but opium. As the youthful sufferings which first produced this derangement of the stomach were interesting in themselves and in the circumstances that attended them, I shall here briefly retrace them.

My father died when I was about seven years old, and left me to the care of four guardians. I was sent to various schools, great and small; and was very early distin-

[1] The *Confessions* were first published as a book in 1822. In 1856 De Quincey published, as part of a collected edition of his works, a greatly enlarged version. The text used in these selections is that of 1822, which has been generally preferred by critics and which there is some reason for believing that De Quincey himself preferred. Words inside square brackets replace dashes in the original edition.

guished for my classical attainments, especially for my knowledge of Greek. At thirteen I wrote Greek with ease; and at fifteen my command of that language was so great that I not only composed Greek verses in lyric meters, but could converse in Greek fluently, and without embarrassment—an accomplishment which I have not since met with in any scholar of my times, and which, in my case, was owing to the practice of daily 10 reading off the newspapers into the best Greek I could furnish *extempore*; for the necessity of ransacking my memory and invention for all sorts and combinations of periphrastic expressions, as equivalents for modern ideas, images, relations of things, *etc.*, gave me a compass of diction which would never have been called out by a dull translation of moral essays, *etc.* "That boy," said one of my masters, pointing the attention 20 of a stranger to me, "that boy could harangue an Athenian mob better than you or I could address an English one." He who honored me with this eulogy was a scholar, "and a ripe and good one," [2] and, of all my tutors, was the only one whom I loved or reverenced. Unfortunately for me (and, as I afterwards learned, to this worthy man's great indignation), I was transferred to the care, first of a blockhead, [3] who was in a perpetual panic lest I should 30 expose his ignorance; and, finally, to that of a respectable scholar, [4] at the head of a great school on an ancient foundation. This man had been appointed to his situation by [Brasenose] College, Oxford; and was a sound, well-built scholar, but (like most men whom I have known from that college) coarse, clumsy, and inelegant. A miserable contrast he presented, in my eyes, to the Etonian brilliancy of my favorite master; and, besides, he could not dis- 40 guise from my hourly notice the poverty and meagerness of his understanding. It is a bad thing for a boy to be, and know himself, far beyond his tutors, whether in knowledge or in power of mind. This was the case, so far as regarded knowledge at least, not with myself only; for the two boys who jointly with myself composed the first form were better Grecians than the headmaster, though not more elegant scholars, nor at all more accustomed to 50 sacrifice to the graces. When I first entered, I remember that we read Sophocles; and it was a constant matter of triumph to us, the learned

triumvirate of the first form, to see our "Archididascalus" [5] (as he loved to be called) conning our lesson before we went up, and laying a regular train, with lexicon and grammar, for blowing up and blasting (as it were) any difficulties he found in the choruses; whilst *we* never condescended to open our books until the moment of going up, and were generally employed in writing epigrams upon his wig, or some such important matter. My two class-fellows were poor, and dependent for their future prospects at the university on the recommendation of the head-master; but I, who had a small patrimonial property, the income of which was sufficient to support me at college, wished to be sent thither immediately. I made earnest representations on the subject to my guardians but all to no purpose. One, who was more reasonable, and had more knowledge of the world than the rest, lived at a distance; two of the other three resigned all their authority into the hands of the fourth; and this fourth, [6] with whom I had to negotiate, was a worthy man in his way, but haughty, obstinate, and intolerant of all opposition to his will. After a certain number of letters and personal interviews, I found that I had nothing to hope for, not even a compromise of the matter, from my guardian: unconditional submission was what he demanded; and I prepared myself, therefore, for other measures. Summer was now coming on with hasty steps, and my seventeenth birthday was fast approaching; after which day I had sworn within myself that I would no longer be numbered amongst school-boys. Money being what I chiefly wanted, I wrote to a woman of high rank, [7] who, though young herself, had known me from a child, and had latterly treated me with great distinction, requesting that she would "lend" me five guineas. [8] For upwards of a week no answer came; and I was beginning to despond, when, at length, a servant put into my hands a double letter, with a coronet on the seal. The letter was kind and obliging; the fair writer was on the sea-coast, and in that way the delay had arisen; she enclosed double of what I had asked, and good-naturedly hinted that if I should *never* repay her it would not absolutely 50 ruin her. Now, then, I was prepared for my scheme: ten guineas, added to about two which

---

[2] Cf. *Henry VIII*, IV, ii, 51–52. The master was a Mr. Morgan, of Bath Grammar School.

[3] Mr. Spencer, of Winkfield School.

[4] Mr. Lawson, of Manchester Grammar School.

[5] Head-master (Greek).

[6] The Rev. Samuel Hall, at one time De Quincey's tutor.

[7] Lady Carbery, a young friend of Mrs. De Quincey's, about ten years older than De Quincey.

[8] About $25.

I had remaining from my pocket money, seemed to me sufficient for an indefinite length of time; and at that happy age, if no *definite* boundary can be assigned to one's power, the spirit of hope and pleasure makes it virtually infinite.

It is a just remark of Dr. Johnson's [9] (and, what cannot often be said of his remarks, it is a very feeling one) that we never do anything consciously for the last time (of things, that is, which we have long been in the habit of doing), without sadness of heart. This truth I felt deeply when I came to leave [Manchester], a place which I did not love, and where I had not been happy. On the evening before I left [Manchester] for ever, I grieved when the ancient and lofty school-room resounded with the evening service, performed for the last time in my hearing; and at night, when the muster-roll of names was called over, and mine (as usual) was called first, I stepped forward, and, passing the head-master, who was standing by, I bowed to him, and looked earnestly in his face, thinking to myself, "He is old and infirm, and in this world I shall not see him again." I was right; I never *did* see him again, nor ever shall. He looked at me complacently, smiled good-naturedly, returned my saluation (or rather my valediction), and we parted (though he knew it not) for ever. I could not reverence him intellectually; but he had been uniformly kind to me, and had allowed me many indulgences; and I grieved at the thought of the mortification I should inflict upon him.

The morning came, which was to launch me into the world, and from which my whole succeeding life has, in many important points, taken its coloring. I lodged in the head-master's house, and had been allowed, from my first entrance, the indulgence of a private room, which I used both as a sleeping room and as a study. At half after three I rose, and gazed with deep emotion at the ancient towers of [the Collegiate Church], "dressed in earliest light," and beginning to crimson with the radiant luster of a cloudless July morning. I was firm and immovable in my purpose, but yet agitated by anticipation of uncertain danger and troubles; and if I could have foreseen the hurricane and perfect hail-storm of affliction which soon fell upon me, well might I have been agitated. To this agitation the deep peace of the morning presented an affecting contrast, and in some degree a medicine. The

silence was more profound than that of midnight: and to me the silence of a summer morning is more touching than all other silence, because, the light being broad and strong, as that of noon-day at other seasons of the year, it seems to differ from perfect day chiefly because man is not yet abroad; and thus the peace of nature, and of the innocent creatures of God, seems to be secure and deep, only so long as the presence of man, and his restless and unquiet spirit, are not there to trouble its sanctity. I dressed myself, took my hat and gloves, and lingered a little in the room. For the last year and a half this room had been my "pensive citadel": [10] here I had read and studied through all the hours of night; and, though true it was that for the latter part of this time I, who was framed for love and gentle affections, had lost my gayety and happiness, during the strife and fever of contention with my guardian; yet, on the other hand, as a boy so passionately fond of books, and dedicated to intellectual pursuits, I could not fail to have enjoyed many happy hours in the midst of general dejection. I wept as I looked round on the chair, hearth, writing-table, and other familiar objects, knowing too certainly that I looked upon them for the last time. Whilst I write this, it is eighteen years ago; and yet, at this moment, I see distinctly, as if it were yesterday, the lineaments and expressions of the object on which I fixed my parting gaze; it was a picture of the lovely ――,[11] which hung over the mantle-piece, the eyes and mouth of which were so beautiful, and the whole countenance so radiant with benignity and divine tranquillity, that I had a thousand times laid down my pen, or my book, to gather consolation from it, as a devotee from his patron saint. Whilst I was yet gazing upon it, the deep tones of [the Collegiate Church] clock proclaimed that it was four o'clock. I went up to the picture, kissed it, and then gently walked out, and closed the door for ever!

\*　　\*　　\*

So blended and intertwisted in this life are occasions of laughter and of tears, that I cannot yet recall, without smiling, an incident which occurred at that time, and which had nearly put a stop to the immediate execution of my plan. I had a trunk of immense weight;

---

[9] In the *Idler*, No. 103, with which the periodical ended.

[10] From Wordsworth's sonnet, *Nuns Fret not at their Convent's Narrow Room*, l. 3.

[11] It was really a portrait of an unknown lady, according to a tradition in the school a copy from Vandyke.

for, besides my clothes, it contained nearly all my library. The difficulty was to get this removed to a carrier's: my room was at an aërial elevation in the house, and (what was worse) the staircase which communicated with this angle of the building was accessible only by a gallery, which passed the head-master's chamber-door. I was a favorite with all the servants; and knowing that any of them would screen me, and act confidentially, I communi- [10] cated my embarrassment to a groom of the head-master's. The groom swore he would do anything I wished; and, when the time arrived, went upstairs to bring the trunk down. This I feared was beyond the strength of any one man: however, the groom was a man

> Of Atlantean shoulders, fit to bear
> The weight of mightiest monarchies; [12]

and had a back as spacious as Salisbury Plain.[13] [20] Accordingly he persisted in bringing down the trunk alone, whilst I stood waiting at the foot of the last flight, in anxiety for the event. For some time I heard him descending with slow and firm steps; but, unfortunately, from his trepidation, as he drew near the dangerous quarter, within a few steps of the gallery, his foot slipped; and the mighty burden, falling from his shoulders, gained such increase of impetus at each step of the descent, that, on [30] reaching the bottom, it tumbled, or rather leaped, right across, with the noise of twenty devils, against the very bedroom door of the Archididascalus. My first thought was, that all was lost; and that my only chance for executing a retreat was to sacrifice my baggage. However, on reflection, I determined to abide the issue. The groom was in the utmost alarm, both on his own account and on mine: but, in spite of this, so irresistibly had the sense of [40] the ludicrous, in this unhappy *contretemps*,[14] taken possession of his fancy, that he sang out a long, loud, and canorous [15] peal of laughter, that might have awakened the Seven Sleepers.[16] At the sound of this resonant merriment, within the very ears of insulted authority, I could not myself forbear joining in it: subdued to this, not so much by the unhappy *étourderie* [17] of the trunk, as by the effect it had upon the groom. We both expected, as a [50]

matter of course, that Dr. [Lawson] [18] would sally out of his room; for, in general, if but a mouse stirred, he sprang out like a mastiff from his kennel. Strange to say, however, on this occasion, when the noise of laughter had ceased, no sound, or rustling even, was to be heard in the bedroom. Dr. [Lawson] had a painful complaint, which, sometimes keeping him awake, made his sleep, perhaps, when it did come, the deeper. Gathering courage from the silence, the groom hoisted his burden again, and accomplished the remainder of his descent without accident. I waited until I saw the trunk placed on a wheelbarrow, and on its road to the carrier's: then, "with Providence my guide," [19] I set off on foot, carrying a small parcel, with some articles of dress, under my arm: a favorite English poet in one pocket; and a small 12mo. volume, containing about nine plays of Euripides, in the other.

It had been my intention, originally, to proceed to Westmoreland, both from the love I bore to that county, and on other personal accounts.[20] Accident, however, gave a different direction to my wanderings, and I bent my steps towards North Wales.[21]

## II

Soon after this,[22] I contrived, by means which I must omit for want of room,[23] to transfer myself to London. And now began the latter and fiercer stage of my long sufferings; without using a disproportionate expression, I might say, of my agony. For I now suffered, for upwards of sixteen weeks, the physical anguish of hunger in various degrees of intensity; but as bitter, perhaps, as ever any human being can have suffered who has survived it. I would not needlessly harass my reader's feelings by a detail of all that I endured; for extremities such as these, under any circumstances of heaviest misconduct or guilt, cannot be contemplated, even in description, without a rueful pity that is painful to the

---

[18] De Quincey explained in the edition of 1856 that he had created him a doctor in order "to evade too close an approach to the realities of the case, and consequently to personalities" which might have displeased others.
[19] Cf. the last four lines of *Paradise Lost.*
[20] He wished to see Wordsworth.
[21] De Quincey actually went first to Chester, where he saw some members of his family, and then journeyed into Wales.
[22] After a period of some days spent in Wales.
[23] He borrowed twelve guineas (about $60) from two lawyers whom he encountered in the Snowdon district.

---

[12] Milton, *Paradise Lost*, II, 306–7.
[13] In Wiltshire.    [14] Accident.    [15] Ringing.
[16] Christian youths of Ephesus who, according to legend, hid themselves in a cave during the persecution under Decius (A.D. 249–251) and slept there for several hundred years.
[17] Blunder.

natural goodness of the human heart. Let it suffice, at least on this occasion, to say that a few fragments of bread from the breakfast-table of one individual [24] (who supposed me to be ill, but did not know of my being in utter want), and these at uncertain intervals, constituted my whole support. During the former part of my sufferings (that is, generally in Wales, and always for the first two months in London), I was houseless, and very seldom slept under a roof. To this constant exposure to the open air I ascribe it mainly that I did not sink under my torments. Latterly, however, when colder and more inclement weather came on, and when, from the length of my sufferings, I had begun to sink into a more languishing condition, it was, no doubt, fortunate for me that the same person to whose breakfast-table I had access allowed me to sleep in a large, unoccupied house, of which he was tenant. Unoccupied, I call it, for there was no household or establishment in it; nor any furniture, indeed, except a table and a few chairs. But I found, on taking possession of my new quarters, that the house already contained one single inmate, a poor, friendless child, apparently ten years old; but she seemed hunger-bitten; and sufferings of that sort often make children look older than they are. From this forlorn child I learned that she had slept and lived there alone for some time before I came; and great joy the poor creature expressed, when she found that I was in future to be her companion through the hours of darkness. The house was large; and, from the want of furniture, the noise of the rats made a prodigious echoing on the spacious staircase and hall; and, amidst the real fleshly ills of cold, and, I fear, hunger, the forsaken child had found leisure to suffer still more (it appeared) from the self-created one of ghosts. I promised her protection against all ghosts whatsoever; but, alas! I could offer her no other assistance. We lay upon the floor, with a bundle of cursed law papers for a pillow, but with no other covering than a sort of large horseman's cloak; afterwards, however, we discovered, in a garret, an old sofa-cover, a small piece of rug, and some fragments of other articles, which added a

little to our warmth. The poor child crept close to me for warmth, and for security against her ghostly enemies. When I was not more than usually ill, I took her into my arms, so that, in general, she was tolerably warm, and often slept when I could not; for, during the last two months of my sufferings, I slept much in the daytime, and was apt to fall into transient dozing at all hours. But my sleep distressed me more than my watching; for, besides the tumultuousness of my dreams (which were only not so awful as those which I shall have to describe hereafter as produced by opium) my sleep was never more than what is called *dog-sleep*; so that I could hear myself moaning, and was often, as it seemed to me, awakened suddenly by my own voice; and, about this time, a hideous sensation began to haunt me as soon as I fell into a slumber, which has since returned upon me, at different periods of my life, namely, a sort of twitching (I know not where, but apparently about the region of the stomach), which compelled me violently to throw out my feet for the sake of relieving it. This sensation coming on as soon as I began to sleep, and the effort to relieve it constantly awaking me, at length I slept only from exhaustion; and, from increasing weakness (as I said before), I was constantly falling asleep, and constantly awaking. Meantime, the master of the house sometimes came in upon us suddenly, and very early; sometimes not till ten o'clock; sometimes not at all. He was in constant fear of bailiffs; improving on the plan of Cromwell, every night he slept in a different quarter of London; [25] and I observed that he never failed to examine, through a private window, the appearance of those who knocked at the door, before he would allow it to be opened. He breakfasted alone; indeed, his tea equipage would hardly have admitted of his hazarding an invitation to a second person, any more than the quantity of esculent *matériel*,[26] which, for the most part, was little more than a roll, or a few biscuits, which he had bought on his road from the place where he had slept. Or, if he *had* asked a party, as I once learnedly and facetiously observed to him, the several members of it must have *stood* in the relation to each other (not *sat* in any

[24] This was a Mr. Brunell, or Brown, to whom De Quincey had been referred by a money-lender named Dell. As De Quincey explains in a later passage of the *Confessions*, "he was one of those anomalous practitioners in lower departments of the law, who—what shall I say?—who, on prudential reasons, or from necessity, deny themselves all indulgence in the luxury of too delicate a conscience."

[25] De Quincey had perhaps read in Clarendon's *History of the Rebellion*, Bk. XV, the story that Cromwell became apprehensive of danger after the dissolution of his last Parliament, and "rarely lodged two nights together in one chamber, but had many furnished and prepared, to which his own key conveyed him."

[26] Edible substance.

relation whatever) of succession, as the meta-physicians have it, and not of coexistence; in the relation of the parts of time, and not of the parts of space. During his breakfast, I generally contrived a reason for lounging in; and, with an air of as much indifference as I could assume, took up such fragments as he had left,—sometimes, indeed, there were none at all. In doing this, I committed no robbery except upon the man himself, who was thus 10 obliged (I believe), now and then, to send out at noon for an extra biscuit; for, as to the poor child, *she* was never admitted into his study (if I may give that name to his chief de-pository of parchments, law writings, *etc.*); that room was to her the Bluebeard room of the house, being regularly locked on his departure to dinner, about six o'clock, which usually was his final departure for the night. Whether this child was an illegitimate daughter of Mr. 20 [Brunell], or only a servant, I could not ascer-tain; she did not herself know; but certainly she was treated altogether as a menial servant. No sooner did Mr. [Brunell] make his appear-ance, than she went below stairs, brushed his shoes, coat, *etc.*; and, except when she was summoned to run an errand, she never emerged from the dismal Tartarus of the kitchens, *etc.*, to the upper air, until my welcome knock at night called up her little trembling footsteps to 30 the front door. Of her life during the daytime, however, I knew little but what I gathered from her own account at night; for, as soon as the hours of business commenced, I saw that my absence would be acceptable; and, in general, therefore, I went off and sat in the parks, or elsewhere, until night-fall.

### III

Whether desperate or not, however, the issue of the struggle of 1813 was what I have 40 mentioned;[27] and from this date the reader is to consider me as a regular and confirmed opium-eater, of whom to ask whether on any particular day he had or had not taken opium,

---

[27] The section from which this passage is taken is preceded by one entitled "The Pleasures of Opium." In it De Quincey tells how he began taking opium when he was at Oxford—though he made his first purchase of it from a druggist in London—in 1804. He then goes on to state that he had continued to take a small quantity once a week until 1813, but that in this year he had suffered from "a most ap-palling irritation of the stomach" from which he had been able to find no relief except in daily doses of opium, and that his subsequent efforts to break off the habit had been unavailing.

would be to ask whether his lungs had per-formed respiration, or the heart fulfilled its functions. You understand now, reader, what I am; and you are by this time aware, that no old gentleman, "with a snow-white beard," will have any chance of persuading me to surrender "the little golden receptacle of the pernicious drug."[28] No; I give notice to all, whether moralists or surgeons, that, whatever be their pretensions and skill in their respective lines of practice, they must not hope for any coun-tenance from me, if they think to begin by any savage proposition for a Lent or Ramadan [29] of abstinence from opium. This, then, being all fully understood between us, we shall in future sail before the wind. Now, then, reader, from 1813, where all this time we have been sitting down and loitering, rise up, if you please, and walk forward about three years more. Now draw up the curtain, and you shall see me in a new character.

If any man, poor or rich, were to say that he would tell us what had been the happiest day in his life, and the why and the where-fore, I suppose that we should all cry out, Hear him! hear him! As to the happiest *day,* that must be very difficult for any wise man to name; because any event, that could occupy so distinguished a place in a man's retrospect of his life, or be entitled to have shed a special felicity on any one day, ought to be of such an enduring character as that (accidents apart) it should have continued to shed the same felicity, or one not distinguishably less, on many years together. To the happiest *lus-trum*,[30] however, or even to the happiest *year,* it may be allowed to any man to point without discountenance from wisdom. This year, in my case, reader, was the one which we have now reached; though it stood, I confess, as a paren-thesis between years of a gloomier character. It was a year of brilliant water (to speak after the manner of jewelers), set, as it were, and insulated, in the gloom and cloudy melancholy of opium. Strange as it may sound, I had a little before this time descended suddenly, and without any considerable effort, from three hundred and twenty grains of opium (that is,

---

[28] A reference to a preceding note in which De Quincey warns his readers not to believe statements about the harmful effects of opium made by Thomas Hope in a novel entitled *Anastasius* (published in 1819).

[29] Ninth month of the Mahometan year, each day of which is observed as a fast from dawn until sun-set.

[30] Period of five years.

eight [31] thousand drops of laudanum) per day, to forty grains, or one-eighth part. Instantaneously, and as if by magic, the cloud of profoundest melancholy which rested upon my brain, like some black vapors that I have seen roll away from the summits of mountains, drew off in one day ($\nu\nu\chi\theta\eta\mu\epsilon\rho\sigma\nu$ [32]); passed off with its murky banners as simultaneously as a ship that has been stranded, and is floated off by a spring tide,—

That moveth altogether, if it move at all.[33]

Now, then, I was again happy: I now took only one thousand drops of laudanum per day —and what was that? A latter spring had come to close up the season of youth: my brain performed its functions as healthily as ever before. I read Kant [34] again, and again I understood him, or fancied that I did. Again my feelings of pleasure expanded themselves to all around me; and if any man from Oxford or Cambridge, or from neither, had been announced to me in my unpretending cottage, I should have welcomed him with as sumptuous a reception as so poor a man could offer. Whatever else was wanting to a wise man's happiness, of laudanum I would have given him as much as he wished, and in a golden cup. And, by the way, now that I speak of giving laudanum away, I remember, about this time, a little incident, which I mention, because, trifling as it was, the reader will soon meet it again in my dreams, which it influenced more fearfully than could be imagined. One day a Malay knocked at my door. What business a Malay could have to transact amongst English mountains, I cannot conjecture; but possibly he was on his road to a seaport about forty miles distant.

The servant who opened the door to him was a young girl [35] born and bred amongst the mountains, who had never seen an Asiatic dress of any sort: his turban, therefore, confounded her not a little; and as it turned out that his attainments in English were exactly of the same extent as hers in the Malay there seemed to be an impassable gulf fixed between all communication of ideas, if either party had happened to possess any. In this dilemma, the girl, recollecting the reputed learning of her master (and, doubtless, giving me credit for a knowledge of all the languages of the earth, besides, perhaps, a few of the lunar ones), came and gave me to understand that there was a sort of demon below, whom she clearly imagined that my art could exorcise from the house. I did not immediately go down; but when I did, the group which presented itself, arranged as it was by accident, though not very elaborate, took hold of my fancy and my eye in a way that none of the statuesque attitudes exhibited in the ballets at the opera-house, though so ostentatiously complex, had ever done. In a cottage kitchen, but paneled on the wall with dark wood that from age and rubbing resembled oak, and looking more like a rustic hall of entrance than a kitchen, stood the Malay, his turban and loose trousers of dingy white relieved upon the dark paneling; he had placed himself nearer to the girl than she seemed to relish, though her native spirit of mountain intrepidity contended with the feeling of simple awe which her countenance expressed, as she gazed upon the tiger-cat before her. And a more striking picture there could not be imagined than the beautiful English face of the girl, and its exquisite fairness, together with her erect and independent attitude, contrasted with the sallow and bilious skin of the Malay, enameled or veneered with mahogany by marine air, his small, fierce, restless eyes, thin lips, slavish gestures, and adorations. Half hidden by the ferocious-looking Malay was a little child from a neighboring cottage, who had crept in after him, and was now in the act of reverting its head and gazing upwards at the turban and the fiery eyes beneath it, whilst with one hand he caught at the dress of the young woman for protection.

My knowledge of the oriental tongues is

[31] I here reckon twenty-five drops of laudanum as equivalent to one grain of opium, which, I believe, is the common estimate. However, as both may be considered variable quantities (the crude opium varying much in strength, and the tincture still more), I suppose that no infinitesimal accuracy can be had in such a calculation. Tea-spoons vary as much in size as opium in strength. Small ones hold about one hundred drops: so that eight thousand drops are about eighty times a tea-spoonful. The reader sees how much I kept within Doctor Buchan's indulgent allowance. (De Quincey's note. The allusion is to a pirated edition of Buchan's *Domestic Medicine* which De Quincey had seen, in which "the Doctor was made to say—'Be particularly careful never to take above 25 *ounces* of laudanum at once'; the true reading being probably 25 *drops*, which are held equal to about one grain of crude opium.")

[32] A night and a day.

[33] Wordsworth's *Resolution and Independence*.

[34] Immanuel Kant (1724–1804), the difficulty of whose writings has become proverbial.

[35] She was Barbara Lewthwaite, named in Wordsworth's *The Pet Lamb*.

not remarkably extensive, being, indeed, confined to two words,—the Arabic word for barley, and the Turkish for opium (madjoon), which I have learned from *Anastasius*. And, as I had neither a Malay dictionary, nor even Adelung's *Mithridates*,[36] which might have helped me to a few words, I addressed him in some lines from the *Iliad*, considering that, of such languages as I possessed, Greek, in point of longitude, came geographically nearest to an oriental one. He worshiped me in a most devout manner, and replied in what I suppose was Malay. In this way I saved my reputation with my neighbors, for the Malay had no means of betraying the secret. He lay down upon the floor for about an hour, and then pursued his journey. On his departure, I presented him with a piece of opium. To him, as an orientalist, I concluded that opium must be familiar; and the expression of his face convinced me that it was. Nevertheless, I was struck with some little consternation when I saw him suddenly raise his hand to his mouth, and (in the school-boy phrase) bolt the whole, divided into three pieces, at one mouthful. The quantity was enough to kill three dragoons and their horses, and I felt some alarm for the poor creature; but what could be done? I had given him the opium in compassion for his solitary life, on recollecting that, if he had traveled on foot from London, it must be nearly three weeks since he could have exchanged a thought with any human being. I could not think of violating the laws of hospitality by having him seized and drenched with an emetic, and thus frightening him into a notion that we were going to sacrifice him to some English idol. No; there was clearly no help for it. He took his leave, and for some days I felt anxious; but, as I never heard of any Malay being found dead, I became convinced that he was used [37] to opium, and that

I must have done him the service I designed, by giving him one night of respite from the pains of wandering.

This incident I have digressed to mention, because this Malay (partly from the picturesque exhibition he assisted to frame, partly from the anxiety I connected with his image for some days) fastened afterwards upon my dreams, and brought other Malays with him worse than himself, that ran "amuck" [38] at me, and led me into a world of troubles.—But to quit this episode, and to return to my intercalary [39] year of happiness. I have said already, that on a subject so important to us all as happiness, we should listen with pleasure to any man's experience or experiments, even though he were but a plowboy, who cannot be supposed to have plowed very deep in such an intractable soil as that of human pains and pleasures, or to have conducted his researches upon any very enlightened principles. But I, who have taken happiness, both in a solid and a liquid shape, both boiled and unboiled, both East India and Turkey—who have conducted my experiments upon this interesting subject with a sort of galvanic battery—and have, for the general benefit of the world, inoculated myself, as it were, with the poison of eight thousand drops of laudanum per day (just for the same reason as a French surgeon inoculated himself lately with cancer—an English one, twenty years ago, with plague—and a third, I know not of what nation,[40] with hydrophobia), *I*, it will be admitted, must surely know what happiness is, if anybody does. And therefore I will here lay down an analysis of happiness; and, as the most interesting mode of communicating it, I will give it, not didactically, but wrapped up and involved in a picture of one evening, as I spent every evening during the intercalary year when laudanum, though taken daily, was to me no more than the elixir of pleasure. This done, I shall quit the subject of happiness altogether, and pass to a very different one—the *pains of opium*.

[36] A work on oriental languages named from the king of Pontus who, according to tradition, could speak the 22 dialects of his kingdom. The author was J. C. Adelung (1732–1806), a German philologer.

[37] This, however, is not a necessary conclusion; the varieties of effect produced by opium on different constitutions are infinite. A London magistrate (Harriott's *Struggles through Life*, vol. iii, p. 391, third edition) has recorded that on the first occasion of his trying laudanum for the gout, he took *forty* drops; the next night *sixty*, and on the fifth night *eighty*, without any effect whatever; and this at an advanced age. I have an anecdote from a country surgeon, however, which sinks Mr. Harriott's case into a trifle; and, in my projected medical treatise on opium, which I will publish, provided the College of

Surgeons will pay me for enlightening their benighted understandings upon this subject, I will relate it; but it is far too good a story to be published gratis (De Quincey's note).

[38] See the common accounts, in any Eastern traveler or voyager, of the frantic excesses committed by Malays who have taken opium, or are reduced to desperation by ill luck at gambling (De Quincey's note).

[39] Interpolated.

[40] He also was English—a surgeon of Brighton—as De Quincey states in the edition of 1856.

Let there be a cottage, standing in a valley, eighteen miles from any town;[41] no spacious valley, but about two miles long by three-quarters of a mile in average width—the benefit of which provision is, that all the families resident within its circuit will compose, as it were, one larger household, personally familiar to your eye, and more or less interesting to your affections. Let the mountains be real mountains, between three and four thousand feet high, and the cottage a real cottage, not (as a witty author has it) "a cottage with a double coach-house";[42] let it be, in fact (for I must abide by the actual scene), a white cottage, embowered with flowering shrubs, so chosen as to unfold a succession of flowers upon the walls, and clustering around the windows, through all the months of spring, summer, and autumn—beginning, in fact, with May roses, and ending with jasmine. Let it, however, *not* be spring, nor summer, nor autumn —but winter, in his sternest shape. This is a most important point in the science of happiness. And I am surprised to see people overlook it, and think it matter of congratulation that winter is going, or, if coming, is not likely to be a severe one. On the contrary, I put up a petition annually for as much snow, hail, frost, or storm of one kind or other as the skies can possibly afford us. Surely everybody is aware of the divine pleasures which attend a winter fireside—candles at four o'clock, warm hearth-rugs, tea, a fair tea-maker, shutters closed, curtains flowing in ample draperies on the floor, whilst the wind and rain are raging audibly without,

And at the doors and windows seem to call,
As heaven and earth they would together mell;
Yet the least entrance find they none at all;
Whence sweeter grows our rest secure in massy hall.
                              *Castle of Indolence.*[43]

All these are items in the description of a winter evening which must surely be familiar to everybody born in a high latitude. And it is evident that most of these delicacies, like ice-cream, require a very low temperature of the atmosphere to produce them: they are fruits which cannot be ripened without weather stormy or inclement, in some way or other. I am not "*particular*," as people say, whether it be snow, or black frost, or wind so strong that (as Mr. [Anti-Slavery Clarkson] says) "you may lean your back against it like a post." I can put up even with rain, provided that it rains cats and dogs; but something of the sort I must have; and, if I have it not, I think myself in a manner ill used: for why am I called on to pay so heavily for winter, in coals, and candles, and various privations that will occur even to gentlemen, if I am not to have the article good of its kind? No: a Canadian winter for my money: or a Russian one, where every man is but a co-proprietor with the north wind in the fee-simple[44] of his own ears. Indeed, so great an epicure am I in this matter, that I cannot relish a winter night fully, if it be much past St. Thomas's day,[45] and have degenerated into disgusting tendencies to vernal appearances;—no, it must be divided by a thick wall of dark nights from all return of light and sunshine. From the latter weeks of October to Christmas-eve, therefore, is the period during which happiness is in season, which, in my judgment, enters the room with the tea-tray; for tea, though ridiculed by those who are naturally of coarse nerves, or are become so from wine-drinking, and are not susceptible of influence from so refined a stimulant, will always be the favorite beverage of the intellectual; and, for my part, I would have joined Dr. Johnson in a *bellum*

[41] The cottage and the valley concerned in this description were not imaginary: the valley was the lovely one, *in those days,* of Grasmere; and the cottage was occupied for more than twenty years by myself, as immediate successor, in the year 1809, to Wordsworth. Looking to the limitation here laid down—*viz., in those days*—the reader will inquire in what way *Time* can have affected the beauty of Grasmere. Do the Westmoreland valleys turn grayheaded? O reader! this is a painful memento for some of us! Thirty years ago, a gang of Vandals (nameless, I thank heaven, to me), for the sake of building a mail-coach road that never would be wanted, carried, at a cost of £3000 to the defrauded parish, a horrid causeway of sheer granite masonry, for three-quarters of a mile, right through the loveliest succession of secret forest dells and sly recesses of the lake, margined by unrivaled ferns, amongst which was the *Osmunda regalis.* This sequestered angle of Grasmere is described by Wordsworth, as it unveiled itself on a September morning, in the exquisite poems on the "Naming of Places." From this also—*viz.,* this spot of ground, and this magnificent crest (the *Osmunda*)—was suggested that unique line, the finest independent line through all the records of verse,

"Or lady of the lake,
Sole-sitting by the shores of old romance."

Rightly, therefore, did I introduce this limitation. The Grasmere before and after this outrage were two different vales (De Quincey's note in the edition of 1856. The poem quoted from is IV in the *Poems on the Naming of Places*).
[42] Coleridge, in *The Devil's Thoughts.*

[43] By James Thomson. Canto I, stanza 43, quoted inexactly.
[44] I. e., absolute ownership.          [45] 21 December.

*internecinum* [46] against Jonas Hanway, or any other impious person who should presume to disparage it. But here, to save myself the trouble of too much verbal description, I will introduce a painter, and give him directions for the rest of the picture. Painters do not like white cottages, unless a good deal weather-stained, but, as the reader now understands that it is a winter night, his services will not be required except for the inside of the house. 10

Paint me, then, a room seventeen feet by twelve, and not more than seven and a half feet high. This, reader, is somewhat ambitiously styled, in my family, the drawing-room; but being contrived "a double debt to pay," [47] it is also, and more justly, termed the library, for it happens that books are the only article of property in which I am richer than my neighbors. Of these I have about five thousand, collected gradually since my eighteenth year. 20 Therefore, painter, put as many as you can into this room. Make it populous with books; and, furthermore, paint me a good fire, and furniture plain and modest, befitting the unpretending cottage of a scholar. And near the fire paint me a tea-table; and (as it is clear that no creature can come to see one, such a stormy night) place only two cups and saucers on the tea-tray; and, if you know how to paint such a thing symbolically, or otherwise, paint 30 me an eternal tea-pot—eternal *à parte ante* and *à parte post;* [48] for I usually drink tea from eight o'clock at night to four o'clock in the morning. And, as it is very unpleasant to make tea, or to pour it out for one's self, paint me a lovely young woman, sitting at the table. Paint her arms like Aurora's, and her smiles like Hebe's;—but no, dear M[argaret], [49] not even in jest let me insinuate that thy power to illuminate my cottage rests upon a tenure so 40 perishable as mere personal beauty; or that the witchcraft of angelic smiles lies within the empire of any earthly pencil. Pass, then, my good painter, to something more within its power; and the next article brought forward should naturally be myself—a picture of the Opium-eater, with his "little golden receptacle

of the pernicious drug" lying beside him on the table. As to the opium, I have no objection to see a picture of *that,* though I would rather see the original; you may paint it, if you choose; but I apprize you that no "little" receptacle would, even in 1816, answer *my* purpose, who was at a distance from the "stately Pantheon," [50] and all druggists (mortal or otherwise). No: you may as well paint the real receptacle, which was not of gold, but of glass, and as much like a wine-decanter as possible. Into this you may put a quart of ruby-colored laudanum; that, and a book of German metaphysics placed by its side, will sufficiently attest my being in the neighborhood; but as to myself, there I demur. I admit that, naturally, I ought to occupy the foreground of the picture; that being the hero of the piece, or (if you choose) the criminal at the bar, my body should be had into court. This 20 seems reasonable; but why should I confess, on this point, to a painter? or why confess at all? If the public (into whose private ear I am confidentially whispering my confessions, and not into any painter's) should chance to have framed some agreeable picture for itself of the Opium-eater's exterior—should have ascribed to him, romantically, an elegant person, or a handsome face, why should I barbarously tear from it so pleasing a delusion— 30 pleasing both to the public and to me? No: paint me, if at all, according to your own fancy; and, as a painter's fancy should teem with beautiful creations, I cannot fail, in that way, to be a gainer. And now, reader, we have run through all the ten categories of my condition, as it stood about 1816–1817, up to the middle of which latter year I judge myself to have been a happy man; and the elements of that happiness I have endeavored to place 40 before you, in the above sketch of the interior of a scholar's library, in a cottage among the mountains, on a stormy winter evening.

But now farewell, a long farewell, to happiness, winter or summer! farewell to smiles and laughter! farewell to peace of mind! farewell to hope and to tranquil dreams, and to the blessed consolations of sleep! For more than three years and a half I am summoned 50 away from these, I am now arrived at an Iliad of woes: [51] for I have now to record

### THE PAINS OF OPIUM.

[46] War to the death. Hanway, said to have been "the first man who ventured to walk the streets of London with an umbrella over his head," wrote an *Essay on Tea* (1756) which Dr. Johnson attacked in a review. Hanway angrily replied, and Dr. Johnson persisted in his defense of tea in a reply to the reply.

[47] Goldsmith, *The Deserted Village*, l. 229.

[48] From the times before and from the times to come.

[49] De Quincey's wife.

[50] A London concert hall, called stately by Wordsworth, near which was the druggist's shop in which De Quincey first purchased opium in 1804.

[51] The allusion is to the opening lines of the *Iliad.*

## IV

I now pass [52] to what is the main subject of these latter confessions, to the history and journal of what took place in my dreams; for these were the immediate and proximate cause of my acutest suffering.

The first notice I had of any important change going on in this part of my physical economy, was from the reawakening of a state of eye generally incident to childhood, or exalted states of irritability. I know not whether my reader is aware that many children, perhaps most, have a power of painting, as it were, upon the darkness, all sorts of phantoms: in some that power is simply a mechanic affection [53] of the eye; others have a voluntary or a semi-voluntary power to dismiss or to summon them; or, as a child once said to me when I questioned him on this matter, "I can tell them to go, and they go; but sometimes they come when I don't tell them to come." Whereupon I told him that he had almost as unlimited a command over apparitions as a Roman centurion over his soldiers.—In the middle of 1817, I think it was, that this faculty became positively distressing to me: at night, when I lay awake in bed, vast processions passed along in mournful pomp; friezes of never-ending stories, that to my feelings were as sad and solemn as if they were stories drawn from times before Oedipus or Priam, before Tyre, before Memphis. And, at the same time, a corresponding change took place in my dreams; a theater seemed suddenly opened and lighted up within my brain, which presented, nightly, spectacles of more than earthly splendor. And the four following facts may be mentioned, as noticeable at this time:

1. That, as the creative state of the eye increased, a sympathy seemed to arise between the waking and the dreaming states of the brain in one point—that whatsoever I happened to call up and to trace by a voluntary act upon the darkness was very apt to transfer itself to my dreams; so that I feared to exercise this faculty; for, as Midas turned all things to gold, that yet baffled his hopes and defrauded his human desires, so whatsoever things capable of being visually represented I did but think of in the darkness, immediately shaped themselves into phantoms of the eye; and, by a process apparently no less inevitable, when thus once traced in faint and visionary colors, like writings in sympathetic ink, they were drawn out, by the fierce chemistry of my dreams, into insufferable splendor that fretted my heart.

2. For this, and all other changes in my dreams, were accompanied by deep-seated anxiety and gloomy melancholy, such as are wholly incommunicable by words. I seemed every night to descend—not metaphorically, but literally to descend—into chasms and sunless abysses, depths below depths, from which it seemed hopeless that I could ever reascend. Nor did I, by waking, feel that I *had* reascended. This I do not dwell upon; because the state of gloom which attended these gorgeous spectacles, amounting at least to utter darkness, as of some suicidal despondency, cannot be approached by words.

3. The sense of space, and in the end the sense of time, were both powerfully affected. Buildings, landscapes, *etc.*, were exhibited in proportions so vast as the bodily eye is not fitted to receive. Space swelled, and was amplified to an extent of unutterable infinity. This, however, did not disturb me so much as the vast expansion of time. I sometimes seemed to have lived for seventy or one hundred years in one night; nay, sometimes had feelings representative of a millennium, passed in that time, or, however, of a duration far beyond the limits of any human experience.

4. The minutest incidents of childhood, or forgotten scenes of later years, were often revived. I could not be said to recollect them; for if I had been told of them when waking, I should not have been able to acknowledge them as parts of my past experience. But placed as they were before me, in dreams like intuitions, and clothed in all their evanescent circumstances and accompanying feelings, I *recognized* them instantaneously. I was once told by a near relative of mine, [54] that having in her childhood fallen into a river, and being on the very verge of death but for the critical assistance which reached her, she saw in a moment her whole life, in its minutest incidents, arrayed before her simultaneously as in a mirror; and she had a faculty developed as suddenly for comprehending the whole and every part. This, from some opium experiences of mine, I can believe; I have, indeed, seen the same thing asserted twice in modern books,

[52] After statements showing the intellectual torpor to which the excessive use of opium reduced him.

[53] Property.

[54] It is said that the relative was De Quincey's mother.

and accompanied by a remark which I am convinced is true, namely, that the dread book of account which the Scriptures speak of [55] is, in fact, the mind itself of each individual. Of this, at least, I feel assured, that there is no such thing as *forgetting* possible to the mind; a thousand accidents may and will interpose a veil between our present consciousness and the secret inscriptions on the mind; accidents of the same sort will also rend away this veil; but alike, whether veiled or unveiled, the inscription remains for ever; just as the stars seem to withdraw before the common light of day, whereas, in fact, we all know that it is the light which is drawn over them as a veil, and that they are waiting to be revealed, when the obscuring daylight shall have withdrawn.

Having noticed these four facts as memorably distinguishing my dreams from those of health, I shall now cite a case illustrative of the first fact; and shall then cite any others that I remember, either in their chronological order, or any other that may give them more effect as pictures to the reader.

I had been in youth, and even since, for occasional amusement, a great reader of Livy, whom I confess that I prefer, both for style and matter, to any other of the Roman historians; and I had often felt as most solemn and appalling sounds, and most emphatically representative of the majesty of the Roman people, the two words so often occurring in Livy— *Consul Romanus*; especially when the consul is introduced in his military character. I mean to say, that the words king, sultan, regent, *etc.*, or any other titles of those who embody in their own persons the collective majesty of a great people, had less power over my reverential feelings. I had also, though no great reader of history, made myself minutely and critically familiar with one period of English history, namely, the period of the Parliamentary War, having been attracted by the moral grandeur of some who figured in that day, and by the many interesting memoirs which survive those unquiet times. Both these parts of my lighter reading, having furnished me often with matter of reflection, now furnished me with matter for my dreams. Often I used to see, after painting upon the blank darkness a sort of rehearsal whilst waking, a crowd of ladies, and perhaps a festival, and dances. And I heard it said, or I said to myself, "These are English ladies from the unhappy times of Charles I. These are the wives and the daughters of those who met in peace, and sat at the same tables, and were allied by marriage or by blood; and yet, after a certain day in August, 1642,[56] never smiled upon each other again, nor met but in the field of battle; and at Marston Moor, at Newbury, or at Naseby, cut asunder all ties of love by the cruel saber, and washed away in blood the memory of ancient friendship." The ladies danced, and looked as lovely as the court of George IV. Yet I knew, even in my dream, that they had been in the grave for nearly two centuries. This pageant would suddenly dissolve; and, at a clapping of hands, would be heard the heart-quaking sound of *Consul Romanus*; and immediately came "sweeping by," in gorgeous paludaments,[57] Paulus, or Marius [58] girt round by a company of centurions, with the crimson tunic [59] hoisted on a spear, and followed by the *alalagmos* [60] of the Roman legions.

Many years ago, when I was looking over Piranesi's [61] *Antiquities of Rome*, Mr. Coleridge, who was standing by, described to me a set of plates by that artist, called his *Dreams*, and which record the scenery of his own visions during the delirium of a fever: some of them (I describe only from memory of Mr. Coleridge's account) representing vast Gothic halls; on the floor of which stood all sorts of engines and machinery, wheels, cables, pulleys, levers, catapults, *etc.*, *etc.*, expressive of enormous power put forth, and resistance overcome. Creeping along the sides of the walls, you perceived a staircase; and upon it, groping his way upwards, was Piranesi himself. Follow the stairs a little further, and you perceive it come to a sudden, abrupt termination, without any balustrade, and allowing no step onwards to him who had reached the extremity, except into the depths below. Whatever is to become of poor Piranesi, you suppose, at least, that his labors must in some way terminate here. But raise your eyes, and

---

[55] Cf. Revelation, 20:12.

[56] Charles I's standard, which gave the signal for the actual beginning of the English Civil War, was raised at Nottingham on 22 August, 1642.

[57] Military cloaks, worn by generals and their principal officers.

[58] Lucius Aemilius Paulus (died 160 B.C.), and Caius Marius (died 86 B.C.).

[59] The signal which announced a day of battle (De Quincey's note, edition of 1856).

[60] A word expressing collectively the gathering of the Roman war-cries—*Alála*, *Alála* (De Quincey's note, edition of 1856). Greek ἀλαλή means war-cry.

[61] Italian engraver (died 1778). Piranesi never published a set of plates entitled *Dreams*, though some of his engravings depict imaginary edifices.

behold a second flight of stairs still higher; on which again Piranesi is perceived, but this time standing on the very brink of the abyss. Again elevate your eye, and a still more aërial flight of stairs is beheld; and again is poor Piranesi busy on his aspiring labors; and so on, until the unfinished stairs and Piranesi both are lost in the upper gloom of the hall. With the same power of endless growth and self-reproduction did my architecture proceed in dreams. In the early stage of my malady, the splendors of my dreams were indeed chiefly architectural; and I beheld such pomp of cities and palaces as was never yet beheld by the waking eye, unless in the clouds. From a great modern poet I cite part of a passage which describes, as an appearance actually beheld in the clouds, what in many of its circumstances I saw frequently in sleep:

> The appearance, instantaneously disclosed
> Was of a mighty city—boldly say
> A wilderness of building, sinking far
> And self-withdrawn into a wondrous depth,
> Far sinking into splendor—without end!
> Fabric it seemed of diamond, and of gold,
> With alabaster domes, and silver spires,
> And blazing terrace upon terrace, high
> Uplifted; here, serene pavilions bright,
> In avenues disposed; there towers begirt
> With battlements that on their restless fronts
> Bore stars—illumination of all gems!
> By earthly nature had the effect been wrought
> Upon the dark materials of the storm
> Now pacified; on them, and on the coves,
> And mountain-steeps and summits, whereunto
> The vapors had receded—taking there
> Their station under a cerulean sky, etc.[62]

The sublime circumstance—"battlements that on their *restless* fronts bore stars"—might have been copied from my architectural dreams, for it often occurred. We hear it reported of Dryden, and of Fuseli [63] in modern times, that they thought proper to eat raw meat for the sake of obtaining splendid dreams: how much better, for such a purpose, to have eaten opium, which yet I do not remember that any poet is recorded to have done, except the dramatist Shadwell; [64] and in ancient days, Homer is, I think, rightly reputed to have known the virtues of opium.[65]

To my architecture succeeded dreams of lakes and silvery expanses of water: these haunted me so much, that I feared (though possibly it will appear ludicrous to a medical man) that some dropsical state or tendency of the brain might thus be making itself (to use a metaphysical word) *objective*,[66] and the sentient organ *project* itself as its own object. For two months I suffered greatly in my head—a part of my bodily structure which had hitherto been so clear from all touch or taint of weakness (physically, I mean) that I used to say of it, as the last Lord Orford [67] said of his stomach, that it seemed likely to survive the rest of my person. Till now I had never felt headache even, or any the slightest pain, except rheumatic pains caused by my own folly. However, I got over this attack, though it must have been verging on something very dangerous.

The waters now changed their character— from translucent lakes, shining like mirrors, they now became seas and oceans. And now came a tremendous change, which, unfolding itself slowly like a scroll, through many months, promised an abiding torment; and, in fact, never left me until the winding up of my case. Hitherto the human face had mixed often in my dreams, but not despotically, nor with any special power of tormenting. But now that which I have called the tyranny of the human face began to unfold itself. Perhaps some part of my London life might be answerable for this.

---

[62] Wordsworth, *The Excursion*, Bk. II, ll. 834–851. De Quincey explains, in the edition of 1856, why he did not in the first instance name Wordsworth: "The year in which I wrote and published these *Confessions* was 1821; and at that time the name of Wordsworth, though beginning to emerge from the dark cloud of scorn and contumely which had hitherto overshadowed it, was yet most imperfectly established. Not until ten years later was his greatness cheerfully and generally acknowledged. I, therefore, as the very earliest (without one exception) of all who came forward, in the beginning of his career, to honor and welcome him, shrank with disgust from making any sentence of mine the occasion for an explosion of vulgar malice against him. But the grandeur of the passage here cited inevitably spoke for itself; and he that would have been most scornful on hearing the name of the poet coupled with this epithet of 'great' could not but find his malice intercepted, and himself cheated into cordial admiration, by the splendor of the verses."

[63] John Henry Fuseli (1741–1825), an artist of Swiss extraction who passed most of his life in England.

[64] Thomas Shadwell (1640–1692), Dryden's Mac Flecknoe.

[65] The opinion is based on a passage in the *Odyssey*, Bk. IV, where Helen is represented as giving Telemachus a potion which made him oblivious of his sorrows.

[66] This word, so nearly unintelligible in 1821, so intensely scholastic, and, consequently, when surrounded by familiar and vernacular words, so apparently pedantic, yet, on the other hand, so indispensable to accurate thinking, and to *wide* thinking, has since 1821 become too common to need any apology (De Quincey's note, edition of 1856).

[67] Horace Walpole (1717–1797).

Be that as it may, now it was that upon the rocking waters of the ocean the human face began to appear; the sea appeared paved with innumerable faces, upturned to the heavens; faces, imploring, wrathful, despairing, surged upwards by thousands, by myriads, by generations, by centuries: my agitation was infinite, my mind tossed, and surged with the ocean.

*May*, 1818.—The Malay had been a fearful enemy for months. I have been every night, through his means, transported into Asiatic scenes. I know not whether others share in my feelings on this point; but I have often thought that if I were compelled to forgo England, and to live in China, and among the Chinese manners and modes of life and scenery, I should go mad. The causes of my horror lie deep, and some of them must be common to others. Southern Asia, in general, is the seat of awful images and associations. As the cradle of the human race, it would alone have a dim and reverential feeling connected with it. But there are other reasons. No man can pretend that the wild, barbarous, and capricious superstitions of Africa, or of savage tribes elsewhere, affect him in the way that he is affected by the ancient, monumental, cruel, and elaborate religions of Indostan, *etc.* The mere antiquity of Asiatic things, of their institutions, histories, modes of faith, *etc.*, is so impressive, that to me the vast age of the race and name overpowers the sense of youth in the individual. A young Chinese seems to me an antediluvian man renewed. Even Englishmen, though not bred in any knowledge of such institutions, cannot but shudder at the mystic sublimity of *castes* that have flowed apart, and refused to mix, through such immemorial tracts of time; nor can any man fail to be awed by the names of the Ganges, or the Euphrates. It contributes much to these feelings that Southern Asia is, and has been for thousands of years, the part of the earth most swarming with human life, the great *officina gentium*.[68] Man is a weed in those regions. The vast empires, also, into which the enormous population of Asia has always been cast, give a further sublimity to the feelings associated with all oriental names or images. In China, over and above what it has in common with the rest of Southern Asia, I am terrified by the modes of life, by the manners, and the barrier of utter abhorrence, and want of sympathy, placed between us by feelings deeper than I can analyze. I could sooner live with lunatics, or brute animals. All

[68] Workshop of races.

this, and much more than I can say, or have time to say, the reader must enter into, before he can comprehend the unimaginable horror which these dreams of oriental imagery, and mythological tortures, impressed upon me. Under the connecting feeling of tropical heat and vertical sunlights, I brought together all creatures, birds, beasts, reptiles, all trees and plants, usages and appearances, that are found in all tropical regions, and assembled them together in China or Indostan. From kindred feelings, I soon brought Egypt and all her gods under the same law. I was stared at, hooted at, grinned at, chattered at, by monkeys, by paroquets, by cockatoos. I ran into pagodas, and was fixed, for centuries, at the summit, or in secret rooms: I was the idol; I was the priest; I was worshiped; I was sacrificed. I fled from the wrath of Brama [69] through all the forests of Asia: Vishnu hated me; Seeva laid wait for me. I came suddenly upon Isis and Osiris; [70] I had done a deed, they said, which the ibis and the crocodile [71] trembled at. I was buried for a thousand years in stone coffins, with mummies and sphinxes, in narrow chambers at the heart of eternal pyramids. I was kissed, with cancerous kisses, by crocodiles; and laid, confounded with all unutterable slimy things, amongst reeds and Nilotic mud.[72]

I thus give the reader some slight abstraction of my oriental dreams, which always filled me with such amazement at the monstrous scenery, that horror seemed absorbed, for a while, in sheer astonishment. Sooner or later came a reflux of feeling that swallowed up the astonishment, and left me, not so much in terror, as in hatred and abomination of what I saw. Over every form, and threat, and punishment, and dim sightless incarceration, brooded a sense of eternity and infinity that drove me into an oppression as of madness. Into these dreams only, it was, with one or two slight exceptions, that any circumstances of physical horror entered. All before had been moral and spiritual terrors. But here the main agents were ugly birds, or snakes, or crocodiles, especially the last. The cursed crocodile became to me the object of more horror than almost all the rest. I was compelled to live with him; and (as was always the case, almost, in my dreams) for cen-

[69] Brahma, Vishnu, and Siva compose the Trinity of the Hindu religion of Brahmanism.

[70] Female and male deities, sister and brother, in Egyptian mythology.

[71] Both sacred animals to the Egyptians.

[72] I. e., mud of the Nile.

turies. I escaped sometimes, and found myself in Chinese houses with cane tables, *etc.* All the feet of the tables, sofas, *etc.*, soon became instinct with life: the abominable head of the crocodile, and his leering eyes, looked out at me, multiplied into a thousand repetitions; and I stood loathing and fascinated. And so often did this hideous reptile haunt my dreams, that many times the very same dream was broken up in the very same way: I heard gen- 10 tle voices speaking to me (I hear everything when I am sleeping), and instantly I awoke: it was broad noon, and my children were standing, hand in hand, at my bedside; come to show me their colored shoes, or new frocks, or to let me see them dressed for going out. I protest that so awful was the transition from the damned crocodile, and the other unutterable monsters and abortions of my dreams, to the sight of innocent *human* natures and of in- 20 fancy, that, in the mighty and sudden revulsion of mind, I wept, and could not forbear it, as I kissed their faces.

## V

As a final specimen, I cite one of a different character, from 1820.

The dream commenced with a music which now I often heard in dreams—a music of 30 preparation and of awakening suspense; a music like the opening of the Coronation Anthem, and which, like *that*, gave the feeling of a vast march, of infinite cavalcades filing off, and the tread of innumerable armies. The morning was come of a mighty day—a day of crisis and of final hope for human nature, then suffering some mysterious eclipse, and laboring in some dread extremity. Somewhere, I knew not where—somehow, I knew 40 not how—by some beings, I knew not whom —a battle, a strife, an agony, was conducting— was evolving like a great drama, or piece of music; with which my sympathy was the more insupportable from my confusion as to its place, its cause, its nature, and its possible issue. I, as is usual in dreams (where, of necessity, we make ourselves central to every movement), had the power, and yet had not the power, to decide it. I had the power, if I could raise 50 myself, to will it; and yet again had not the power, for the weight of twenty Atlantics was upon me, or the oppression of inexpiable guilt. "Deeper than ever plummet sounded," [73] I lay inactive. Then, like a chorus, the passion deepened. Some greater interest was at stake;

[73] Cf. *The Tempest*, V, i, 56.

some mightier cause than ever yet the sword had pleaded, or trumpet had proclaimed. Then came sudden alarms; hurryings to and fro; trepidations of innumerable fugitives, I knew not whether from the good cause or the bad; darkness and lights; tempest and human faces; and at last, with the sense that all was lost, female forms, and the features that were worth all the world to me, and but a moment allowed—and clasped hands, and heart-breaking partings, and then—everlasting farewells! and, with a sigh, such as the caves of hell sighed when the incestuous mother uttered the abhorred name of death,[74] the sound was reverberated—everlasting farewells! and again, and yet again reverberated—everlasting farewells!

And I awoke in struggles, and cried aloud —"I will sleep no more!"

## Suspiria De Profundis

### *Being a Sequel to "The Confessions of an English Opium-Eater"* [1]

#### LEVANA AND OUR LADIES OF SORROW

Oftentimes at Oxford I saw Levana in my dreams. I knew her by her Roman symbols. Who is Levana? Reader, that do not pretend to have leisure for very much scholarship, you will not be angry with me for telling you. Levana was the Roman goddess that performed for the new-born infant the earliest office of ennobling kindness—typical, by its mode, of that grandeur which belongs to man everywhere, and of that benignity in powers invisible which even in pagan worlds sometimes descends to sustain it. At the very moment of birth, just as the infant tasted for the first time the atmosphere of our troubled planet, it was laid on the ground. *That* might bear different interpretations. But immediately, lest so grand a creature should grovel there for more than one instant, either the paternal hand, as proxy of the goddess Levana, or some near kinsman, as proxy for the father, raised it upright, bade it look erect as the king of all this world, and presented its forehead to the stars, saying, perhaps, in his heart. "Behold what is greater than yourselves!" This symbolic act represented the function of Levana. And that mysterious lady, who never revealed her face (except to me in dreams), but always acted

[74] Cf. *Paradise Lost*, Bk. II, l. 746 and following lines.

[1] The title means Breathings, or Sighs, from the Depths. *Levana* was first published in the June, 1845, issue of *Blackwood's Magazine*.

by delegation, had her name from the Latin verb (as still it is the Italian verb) *levare,* to raise aloft.

This is the explanation of Levana. And hence it has arisen that some people have understood by Levana the tutelary power that controls the education of the nursery. She, that would not suffer at his birth even a prefigurative or mimic degradation for her awful ward, far less could be supposed to suffer the real degradation attaching to the non-development of his powers. She therefore watches over human education. Now, the word *edŭco,* with the penultimate short, was derived (by a process often exemplified in the crystallization of languages) from the word *edūco,* with the penultimate long. Whatsoever *edūces,* or develops, *educates.* By the education of Levana, therefore, is meant— not the poor machinery that moves by spelling-books and grammars, but that mighty system of central forces hidden in the deep bosom of human life, which by passion, by strife, by temptation, by the energies of resistance, works for ever upon children—resting not day or night, any more than the mighty wheel of day and night themselves, whose moments, like restless spokes, are glimmering [2] for ever as they revolve.

If, then, *these* are the ministries by which Levana works, how profoundly must she reverence the agencies of grief! But you, reader, think that children generally are not liable to grief such as mine. There are two senses in the word *generally*—the sense of Euclid, where it means *universally* (or in the whole extent of the *genus*), and a foolish sense of this word, where it means *usually.* Now, I am far from saying that children universally are capable of grief like mine. But there are more than you ever heard of who die of grief in this island of ours. I will tell you a common case. The rules

of Eton require that a boy on the *foundation* [3] should be there twelve years: he is superannuated at eighteen, consequently he must come at six. Children torn away from mothers and sisters at that age not unfrequently die. I speak of what I know. The complaint is not entered by the registrar as grief, but *that* it is. Grief of that sort, and at that age, has killed more than ever have been counted amongst its martyrs.

Therefore it is that Levana often communes with the powers that shake man's heart; therefore it is that she dotes upon grief. "These ladies," said I softly to myself, on seeing the ministers with whom Levana was conversing, "these are the Sorrows, and they are three in number, as the *Graces* are three, who dress man's life with beauty; the *Parcae* [4] are three, who weave the dark arras [5] of man's life in their mysterious loom always with colors sad in part, sometimes angry with tragic crimson and black; the *Furies* are three, who visit with retributions called from the other side of the grave offenses that walk upon this; and once even the *Muses* were but three, who fit the harp, the trumpet, or the lute, to the great burdens of man's impassioned creations. These are the Sorrows, all three of whom I know." The last words I say *now*; but in Oxford I said, "one of whom I know, and the others too surely I *shall* know." For already, in my fervent youth, I saw (dimly relieved upon the dark background of my dreams) the imperfect lineaments of the awful Sisters.

These Sisters—by what name shall we call them? If I say simply, "The Sorrows," there will be a chance of mistaking the term; it might be understood of individual sorrow— separate cases of sorrow—whereas I want a term expressing the mighty abstractions that incarnate themselves in all individual sufferings of man's heart, and I wish to have these abstractions presented as impersonations—that is, as clothed with human attributes of life, and with functions pointing to flesh. Let us call them, therefore, *Our Ladies of Sorrow.*

I know them thoroughly, and have walked in all their kingdoms. Three sisters they are, of one mysterious household; and their paths are wide apart; but of their dominion there is no end. Them I saw often conversing

---

[2] As I have never allowed myself to covet any man's ox nor his ass, nor anything that is his, still less would it become a philosopher to covet other people's images or metaphors. Here, therefore, I restore to Mr. Wordsworth this fine image of the revolving wheel and the glimmering spokes, as applied by him to the flying successions of day and night. I borrowed it for one moment in order to point my own sentence; which being done, the reader is witness that I now pay it back instantly by a note made for that sole purpose. On the same principle I often borrow their seals from young ladies, when closing my letters, because there is sure to be some tender sentiment upon them about "memory," or "hope," or "roses," or "reunion," and my correspondent must be a sad brute who is not touched by the eloquence of the seal, even if his taste is so bad that he remains deaf to mine (De Quincey's note).

[3] I. e., holding a scholarship, provided for in the college's original endowment.

[4] The Fates.

[5] Tapestry, originally tapestry made at Arras, France.

with Levana, and sometimes about myself. Do they talk, then? O no! Mighty phantoms like these disdain the infirmities of language. They may utter voices through the organs of man when they dwell in human hearts, but amongst themselves is no voice nor sound; eternal silence reigns in *their* kingdoms. They spoke not as they talked with Levana; they whispered not; they sang not; though often-times methought they *might* have sung: for I upon earth had heard their mysteries often-times deciphered by harp and timbrel, by dulcimer and organ. Like God, whose servants they are, they utter their pleasure not by sounds that perish, or by words that go astray, but by signs in heaven, by changes on earth, by pulses in secret rivers, heraldries painted on darkness, and hieroglyphics written on the tablets of the brain. *They* wheeled in mazes; *I* spelled the steps. *They* telegraphed from afar; *I* read the signals. *They* conspired together; and on the mirrors of darkness *my* eye traced the plots. *Theirs* were the symbols; *mine* are the words.

What is it the Sisters are? What is it that they do? Let me describe their form and their presence, if form it were that still fluctuated in its outline, or presence it were that for ever advanced to the front or for ever receded amongst shades.

The eldest of the three is named *Mater Lachrymarum*, Our Lady of Tears. She it is that night and day raves and moans, calling for vanished faces. She stood in Rama, where a voice was heard of lamentation—Rachel weeping for her children, and refusing to be comforted.[6] She it was that stood in Bethlehem on the night when Herod's sword swept its nurseries of Innocents, and the little feet were stiffened for ever which, heard at times as they trotted along floors overhead, woke pulses of love in household hearts that were not un-marked in heaven. Her eyes are sweet and subtle, wild and sleepy, by turns; oftentimes rising to the clouds, oftentimes challenging the heavens. She wears a diadem round her head. And I knew by childish memories that she could go abroad upon the winds, when she heard the sobbing of litanies, or the thun-dering of organs, and when she beheld the mustering of summer clouds. This Sister, the elder, it is that carries keys more than papal at her girdle, which open every cottage and every palace. She, to my knowledge, sat all last sum-mer by the bedside of the blind beggar, him that so often and so gladly I talked with,

whose pious daughter, eight years old, with the sunny countenance, resisted the temptations of play and village mirth, to travel all day long on dusty roads with her afflicted father. For this did God send her a great reward. In the spring-time of the year, and whilst yet her own spring was budding, He recalled her to him-self. But her blind father mourns for ever over *her*; still he dreams at midnight that the little guiding hand is locked within his own; and still he wakens to a darkness that is *now* within a second and a deeper darkness. This *Mater Lachrymarum* also has been sitting all this winter of 1844–5 within the bedchamber of the Czar, bringing before his eyes a daughter (not less pious) that vanished to God not less suddenly, and left behind her a darkness not less profound.[7] By the power of the keys it is that Our Lady of Tears glides, a ghostly in-truder, into the chambers of sleepless men, sleepless women, sleepless children, from Ganges to the Nile, from Nile to Mississippi. And her, because she is the first-born of her house, and has the widest empire, let us honor with the title of "Madonna."

The second Sister is called *Mater Sus-piriorum*, Our Lady of Sighs. She never scales the clouds, nor walks abroad upon the winds. She wears no diadem. And her eyes, if they were ever seen, would be neither sweet nor subtle; no man could read their story; they would be found filled with perishing dreams, and with wrecks of forgotten delirium. But she raises not her eyes; her head, on which sits a dilapidated turban, droops for ever, for ever fastens on the dust. She weeps not. She groans not. But she sighs inaudibly at intervals. Her sister, Madonna, is oftentimes stormy and frantic, raging in the highest against heaven, and demanding back her darlings. But Our Lady of Sighs never clamors, never defies, dreams not of rebellious aspirations. She is humble to abjectness. Hers is the meekness that belongs to the hopeless. Murmur she may, but it is in her sleep. Whisper she may, but it is to herself in the twilight. Mutter she does at times, but it is in solitary places that are desolate as she is desolate, in ruined cities, and when the sun has gone down to his rest. This Sister is the visitor of the Pariah, of the Jew, of the bondsman to the oar in the Mediter-ranean galleys; of the English criminal in Nor-folk Island,[8] blotted out from the books of re-

[6] See Jeremiah, 31:15, and St. Matthew, 2:18.

[7] The Princess Alexandra, third daughter of the Czar Nicholas, died in August, 1844.
[8] In the southern Pacific, east of Australia; for-merly used by England as a penal settlement.

membrance in sweet far-off England; of the baffled penitent reverting his eyes for ever upon a solitary grave, which to him seems the altar overthrown of some past and bloody sacrifice, on which altar no oblations can now be availing, whether towards pardon that he might implore, or towards reparation that he might attempt. Every slave that at noonday looks up to the tropical sun with timid reproach, as he points with one hand to the earth, our general mother, but for *him* a stepmother, as he points with the other hand to the Bible, our general teacher, but against *him* sealed and sequestered; [9] every woman sitting in darkness, without love to shelter her head, or hope to illumine her solitude, because the heaven-born instincts kindling in her nature germs of holy affections, which God implanted in her womanly bosom, having been stifled by social necessities, now burn sullenly to waste, like sepulchral lamps amongst the ancients; every nun defrauded of her unreturning May-time by wicked kinsman, whom God will judge; every captive in every dungeon; all that are betrayed, and all that are rejected; outcasts by traditionary law, and children of *hereditary* disgrace—all these walk with Our Lady of Sighs. She also carries a key, but she needs it little. For her kingdom is chiefly amongst the tents of Shem,[10] and the houseless vagrant of every clime. Yet in the very highest ranks of man she finds chapels of her own; and even in glorious England there are some that, to the world, carry their heads as proudly as the reindeer, who yet secretly have received her mark upon their foreheads.

But the third Sister, who is also the youngest——! Hush! whisper whilst we talk of *her!* Her kingdom is not large, or else no flesh should live; but within that kingdom all power is hers. Her head, turreted like that of Cybele,[11] rises almost beyond the reach of sight. She droops not; and her eyes, rising so high, *might* be hidden by distance. But, being what they are, they cannot be hidden; through the treble veil of crape which she wears the fierce light of a blazing misery, that rests not

for matins or for vespers,[12] for noon of day or noon of night, for ebbing or for flowing tide, may be read from the very ground. She is the defier of God. She also is the mother of lunacies, and the suggestress of suicides. Deep lie the roots of her power; but narrow is the nation that she rules. For she can approach only those in whom a profound nature has been upheaved by central convulsions; in whom the heart trembles and the brain rocks under conspiracies of tempest from without and tempest from within. Madonna moves with uncertain steps, fast or slow, but still with tragic grace. Our Lady of Sighs creeps timidly and stealthily. But this youngest Sister moves with incalculable motions, bounding, and with a tiger's leaps. She carries no key; for, though coming rarely amongst men, she storms all doors at which she is permitted to enter at all. And *her* name is *Mater Tenebrarum*—Our Lady of Darkness.

These were the *Semnai Theai* or Sublime Goddesses,[13] these were the *Eumenides* or Gracious Ladies (so called by antiquity in shuddering propitiation) of my Oxford dreams. Madonna spoke. She spoke by her mysterious hand. Touching my head, she beckoned to Our Lady of Sighs; and *what* she spoke, translated out of the signs which (except in dreams) no man reads, was this:

"Lo! here is he whom in childhood I dedicated to my altars. This is he that once I made my darling. Him I led astray, him I beguiled; and from heaven I stole away his young heart to mine. Through me did he become idolatrous; and through me it was, by languishing desires, that he worshiped the worm, and prayed to the wormy grave. Holy was the grave to him; lovely was its darkness; saintly its corruption. Him, this young idolator, I have seasoned for thee, dear gentle Sister of Sighs! Do thou take him now to *thy* heart, and season him for our dreadful sister. And thou,"—turning to the *Mater Tenebrarum*, she said—"wicked sister, that temptest and hatest, do thou take him from *her*. See that thy scepter lie heavy on his head. Suffer not woman and her tenderness to sit near him in his darkness. Banish the frailties of hope, wither the relenting of love, scorch

[9] This, the reader will be aware, applies chiefly to the cotton and tobacco States of North America; but not to them only: on which account I have not scrupled to figure the sun, which looks down upon slavery, as *tropical,*—no matter if strictly within the tropics, or simply so near to them as to produce a similar climate (De Quincey's note).

[10] See Genesis, 9:27.

[11] Nature goddess of the peoples of Asia Minor, She was pictured wearing a turreted diadem.

[12] For the religious offices of early morning or evening.

[13] The word σεμνος is usually rendered *venerable* in dictionaries—not a very flattering epithet for females. But I am disposed to think that it comes nearest to our idea of the *sublime*—as near as a Greek word *could* come (De Quincey's note).

the fountains of tears, curse him as only *thou* canst curse. So shall he be accomplished in the furnace, so shall he see the things that ought *not* to be seen, sights that are abominable, and secrets that are unutterable. So shall he read elder truths, sad truths, grand truths, fearful truths. So shall he rise again *before* he dies. And so shall our commission be accomplished which from God we had—to plague his heart until we had unfolded the capacities of his spirit." [14]

[14] The reader who wishes at all to understand the course of these Confessions ought not to pass over this dream-legend. There is no great wonder that a vision which occupied my waking thoughts in those years should reappear in my dreams. It was, in fact, a legend recurring in sleep, most of which I had myself silently written or sculptured in my daylight reveries. But its importance to the present Confessions is this, that it rehearses or prefigures their course. This FIRST part belongs to Madonna. The THIRD belongs to the "Mater Suspiriorum," and will be entitled *The Pariah Worlds*. The FOURTH, which terminates the work, belongs to the "Mater Tenebrarum," and will be entitled *The Kingdom of Darkness*. As to the SECOND, it is an interpolation requisite to the effect of the others, and will be explained in its proper place (De Quincey's note). The plan here somewhat vaguely outlined was never completed by De Quincey.

# THE VICTORIAN ERA AND AFTER, 1837-1914

In 1837 Alexandrina Victoria, the daughter of the fourth son of George III, succeeded her uncle, William IV, on the English throne. She was then eighteen years old, and she reigned over the British Isles and the overseas empire until her death in 1901. She has given her name to an era of extraordinary development and expansion, but the word "Victorian" signifies above all a certain outlook and moral standard which the queen shared with the vast majority of her subjects during most of her reign. That moral outlook, furthermore, is the key to an orderly understanding of Victorian literature; for every writer in this era was strongly influenced by Victorianism, either by way of attraction or by way of repulsion. Hence we must clearly define Victorianism. In so doing, we may begin with the queen herself.

Victoria was not a remarkable person. Even as a young girl she had no beauty, though she was not without the charm which youth in itself gives, and she did have a clear musical voice. She was short, less than five feet in height, and as she grew older she became dumpy; but she is said to have been always graceful and dignified. She was an accomplished horse-woman, and was fond of dancing and of games. She was "modern" in her love of fresh air. Her intelligence was middling. She had an exceptional memory, but otherwise her mental powers were those of the man in the street. Her artistic sense, too, was as little developed as that of the man in the street, who is notoriously comfortable in tasteless and even ugly surroundings. She had a lively sense of the importance of her position, and took her responsibilities seriously; but her

limitations can be judged from the fact that she never understood the social problems which were acute throughout her reign.

At the start, Victoria received invaluable instruction in the duties of her position from Viscount Melbourne, who was prime minister when she became queen. In 1840 she married her cousin Albert, the son of the Duke of Saxe-Coburg-Gotha, who was both keen and resourceful. He became a useful adviser, and she regarded him with feeling approaching reverence, though she was not at all disposed to share her sovereignty with him. After his early death, from typhoid fever, in 1861, she virtually retired from public life for about ten years. During these years she became unpopular. After 1871, however, she grew popular again; and from about 1880 until the close of her reign she was fairly worshiped. In these years she was regarded as the living symbol of empire, though at the same time her actual power diminished.

From even so brief a sketch as this it is evident that Victoria was not a great dominating personality, bound to leave a mark on the nineteenth century. Her character was representative rather than masterful. She happened to possess the mind and outlook of the middle class, at a time when that class, which had been slowly rising in importance for several generations, had finally attained a commanding position in the state. She was not a mere personification of the middle class; she herself, for example, was not really prudish. But she did share some limitations of the new middle class. She upheld its narrow formal morality, its emphasis on the domestic virtues, its notion that many facts of life could be disposed of by shutting the eyes to them and not mentioning them, and its new standard, which was "respectability." She imposed severe rules on her court, but not on the nation, because the rules were for the most part already accepted by the nation. It cannot be said that anybody imposed them on the nation; they arose out of new conditions.

## EXPANSION OF INDUSTRY

It was said in the preceding chapter that the development of English life has continued, without any real break, from about the middle of the eighteenth century to the present, and that this continuous development has been determined by the progress of scientific discovery and by the applications of science in industry. It was also said that a revolutionary change in the processes of industry, brought about by the harnessing of steam power and by a succession of mechanical inventions, was well under way in the early years of the nineteenth century. The result was the rapid transformation of England from an agricultural to an industrial country, with much accompanying hardship and distress felt by laborers who found their work taken away from them by machines, and even by those who found employment under the new system, whether as machine tenders or as miners of coal and of iron ore. The change was inevitable and impersonal. The initial cost of power-driven machinery was large, but the efficiency of the machinery was such that cloth and other commodities could be produced far more cheaply than by hand labor. The machine, therefore, could, in a real sense, dictate its own terms, and in fact it became the master both of its owners and of its attendants. Only if its conditions were met would it yield a profit, but the profits it could yield were enormous; because, throughout the nineteenth century, there seemed to be no limit to the world-wide demand for cheap consumable goods.

The market was capable of apparently endless expansion for several reasons. The population of the western world was increasing with extraordinary rapidity in the nineteenth century. Wealth also was increasing, and many hundreds of thousands of families came into the market for increased purchases of necessities, and for comforts and luxuries, as quickly as old necessities or new comforts could be manufactured cheaply. Improved and cheapened transportation, in addition, helped to widen the market as much as cheap produc-

tion. With the appearance of railways and steamships the manufactured goods of England spread out over the whole world; for England was first in the field of industrial development, and scarcely began to feel the competition of other countries until toward the end of the nineteenth century.

One consequence was that money came rolling in. England prospered as never before. The flag followed trade to protect British interests, and the overseas empire grew as commerce expanded. Optimistic confidence rose high. After long ages of snail-like growth, the human race was finally entering into an era of magnificent progress and plenty, with God's own Englishmen directing everything and bringing the blessings of civilization to all the world.

## THE PLIGHT OF LABORERS

Although the ascendancy of the machine was lifting England to a proud height as the wealthiest, strongest, and largest empire the world has ever known, it was at the same time producing misery. The hardship, already mentioned, which was brought about by the shift from home industry to the urban factory was not a small thing. But it was small in comparison with the appalling working conditions, in factories and in mines, to which laborers were subjected, and in comparison with the wretched living quarters in which the slaves of the new mechanized industry were housed. As long as the market for manufactured goods was expanding in the nineteenth century, labor-saving machinery did not really save labor; on the contrary, it increased the demand for laborers. The individual whose work was taken away from him by the machine was, it is true, faced with ruin and starvation, and repeatedly such persons took the desperate step of trying to smash up the hated machine. Presently, however, the increased demand for the machine-made article necessitated more and more machines, with the result that there was again employment, not only for the man whose former work had vanished, but also for his wife, and his children. The far more serious trouble was that work in factory and in mine, when it was found, was so ill-paid, so confining, so ruinous to health and character, and often so monotonous and mechanical, that industrial workers were reduced to a state of misery impossible to describe in general terms. It seems unbelievable that human beings could have existed under such conditions as, for instance, young boys in coal mines were subjected to. It seems unbelievable that any men, for any purpose, could have associated themselves with enterprises which subjected their fellow creatures—not only men and women, but very young children—to such suffering as was for many years almost universal.

The machine itself was the key to the complex Victorian social problem; owner and employee alike followed its law. The machine owed its power entirely to the cheapness of its products, and all costs, including the cost of labor, had to be kept as low as possible. Moreover, there was a theory abroad which seemed to fit the facts and which was supposed to be, not a theory, but a branch of science. Economists regarded it as self-evident that the nature of business enterprise was to buy in the cheapest market and sell in the dearest. Labor was the laborer's commodity, that which he had to sell. In theory, the workingman was free to fix a price for his services and to try to get it. In theory, he was free to refuse his services unless he did receive his price—or for that matter, to refuse his services at any price. But actually the laborer was helpless, and had to accept whatever was offered, or become a pauper, or starve. Employers found labor plentiful at wages far below the level of decent living, with workdays of twelve hours or even more, in factories ill-lighted, unventilated, unsafe, and only less unsanitary than the dark holes in which families of workers were huddled together for sleep, feeding, and the debauchery in which many sought forgetfulness of their troubles. Hence any employer who offered higher wages or better conditions than his competitors simply invited bankruptcy, as was demonstrated in a few cases. The truth is that the machine imposed conditions which no individual could resist, and offered rewards which no society could resist.

### MACHINE-MADE MEN AND MORALS

We find, then, at the beginning of the Victorian era, a situation in which commercial shrewdness had become the essential quality needed for rising in the world. We find also a situation which was sharply dividing the nation in half, or which was, as Carlyle and Disraeli said, creating two nations, the rich and the poor. The former had no past, and the latter seemed to have no future. Both "nations" were bred from the slums of the manufacturing towns, and within the space of a few years were beginning to dominate English life.

The new poor were worse off than if they had been slaves, because nobody was, even in theory, responsible for them. They were, as fully as the machines they tended, instruments of production; and to them the individualistic doctrine of *laissez-faire* was a cruel mockery. They were a brutalized herd, rapidly multiplying, utterly helpless and unimportant individually, and socially important only as a necessary evil for the sake of cheap goods.

The new rich were without taste—and they were tasteless in ways almost too appalling to be believed, save by those who have themselves seen Victorian domestic architecture, Victorian furniture and bric-a-brac, Victorian wallpaper, pictures and picture frames, carpets, and window draperies. The Victorians really felt proud of their hideous flowered carpets, heavy plush draperies, haircloth sofas and chairs, moderator lamps, over-mantels, ornate metal bedsteads, marble-topped tables, and antimacassars. These, and houses to hold them which were the worst monstrosities in the whole history of architecture, were what they toiled for, and spent large sums on. They felt, quite rightly, that a new age had dawned. The ugly Victorian fireplace really did throw out far more heat than its eighteenth-century predecessor. The moderator lamp really did give more and better light than its predecessors. These and other improvements encouraged the notion that the newest things made by the latest processes were the best. Those who had them were progressive and had something to boast of.

The truth is that the new rich had really no connection with the past and no standards except those afforded by a narrow religion. They did inherit the Wesleyan-Evangelical tradition of the preceding generation; and, what is more, many of them were sincerely as well as seemingly religious. But the otherworldliness of the great religious revival of the eighteenth-century was radically inconsistent with conditions which now made commercial shrewdness the first necessity for success in life, and which were causing civilization to be identified with bathtubs, spring cushions for chairs, patented ventilators, and all kinds of improved gadgets. Therefore religion was revised.

The revision was not, of course, carried out deliberately or consciously, but it was thorough. The man of business discovered that certain virtues, heartily endorsed by Christian teachers, were profitable. He was much more likely to succeed in the battle of commerce if he took life seriously and kept himself unspotted by the sinful pleasures of the worldly. Abstinence from all forms of gambling, cautious moderation in drink if not teetotalism, and perfect fidelity to a lawful wife were restrictions which had their immediate reward. They really promoted health and wealth. So also the conviction that life was not an opportunity for enjoyment, but a solemn responsibility imposed by the Lord of Righteousness, encouraged whole-souled application to work. The cause of commerce was the cause of progressive civilization. Hence its earnest prosecution was a duty, in the performance of which a man could piously feel that he was justifying his existence.

It is not easy to describe this or any form of self-delusion without the suspicion of irony. The fallacy is always obvious to everyone except those who are themselves guilty of it. The famous Victorian compromise under discussion is an example of hypocrisy. Yet historically it is a fact that many adopted this compromise in the sincere conviction that religion and their kind of worldliness were not inconsistent. They engaged in religious observances with zeal. The Victorian Sunday, indeed, has become notorious because of the strictness with which every form of non-religious activity was prohibited. It is true enough that the man of business who was almost fiercely religious all day on Sunday spent his energies, throughout the rest of the week, in the service of self-interest. But he was not guilty of the kind of inconsistency of which he has often been accused. For out of the compromise he had made there had come a new standard of conduct which he followed equally on Sundays and weekdays. His aim was simply to be irreproachable at all times in the eyes of his associates.

So phrased, this aim looks its best; but even at its best it was negative, and was, besides, impossible of achievement. To try to be irreproachable was to have to ask continually, "What would Mrs. Grundy say?" That formidable censor became the unseen tyrant of the Victorian era. In practice, her rule required men to reduce themselves to a norm of conventionality which banished individual taste and thought and action, and made them colorless units in a society standardized by scandalmongers, and gossips, or in general, by the scum of the earth. She made most biological

facts unmentionable, and, as an acute critic has said, thus inevitably made hypocrisy the one vice allowed to be respectable.

## RESPECTABILITY

Nothing is wholly new, and doubtless there have been hypocrites in all ages. Nevertheless, the Victorian era is the only one known to history in which the subhuman standard of "respectability" made a nation of hypocrites. Even though an appreciable number of Victorian manufacturers and merchants were men of sound integrity both in their private lives and in their business dealings, they could not redeem competitive trade from an element of ambiguity which seemed to be bound up with its very nature and which spread corruption throughout the new ruling class. Men might say that in the development of manufacture and trade they were serving the cause of the national welfare, and that in conquering new markets abroad they were spreading the benefits of civilization among benighted peoples, and they might in both cases speak truly; yet at the same time they were reaping enormous profits from these services, and were growing rich while the poor were being reduced to a lower-than-animal level of existence.

We can, therefore, see an affinity between the Victorian man of business and the sham standard of respectability. We can see, too, that in so far as men appeared to satisfy this standard, they lost individuality and became standardized products of the industrial system. Thus the machine dehumanized both its slaves and their masters. Civilization was no longer thought of as the fruit of self-discipline, self-development, personal maturity, and hard-won wisdom. Not this kind of triumph over nature was now wanted, but the transformation of the material environment. In short the march of civilization was to be measured by the march of industry. The whole change seems to be summed up in two sentences from the prospectus of the Rochdale Pioneers:

> The objects of this Society are the moral and intellectual advancement of its members. It provides them with groceries, butcher's meat, drapery goods, clothes and clogs.

The definition of "Victorianism" cannot be so neatly compressed into a few words, though essentially the word signifies the outlook and moral standard of the newly risen industrial class. Hence it has been identified particularly with respectability and hypocrisy, with abject conventionality, with prudery, and with materialistic worldliness. It might be called the spirit of pretense trying to sanctify itself by pious sentiment. But whatever else it was, it was a triumph of mechanics over man, of means over ends, of the herd over individuality, of vulgarity over taste, and of fear over honesty—all in the name of magnificent progress towards a democratic millennium.

## MACAULAY AND CARLYLE

We could not have a clearer illustration of the two-faced nature of the Victorian age than that afforded by the contrast between the two essayists and historians, Macaulay and Carlyle.

Macaulay, in his inadequate essay on Bacon, did at least contrive to reveal himself and some part of his own age when he wrote: "An acre in Middlesex is better than a principality in Utopia." He was an amiable materialist without knowing it. He thought all religious opinions to be basically unreasonable, but was Victorian in the skill with which he veiled this side of his worldliness. He was certainly not a conscious hypocrite. He was courageous, generous, high-principled, and personally independent. He was, too, incessantly and prodigiously active; and indeed his activity enables us to understand both his fame and his limitations. We hear of his impressiveness as a speaker in Parliament; and every reader of his essays or of his *History* has admired his ability to organize and dispose the material at his command. That material was usually vast because he read a great deal and apparently remembered everything he read. *But he never stopped to think.*

Macaulay appears to have been born with his mind already made up; and it was made up to accept the goodness of Whig liberalism and of industrial "progress." The inventions, the improvements, the growing trade, the hideous new cities of the midlands—none of these things suggested any question or doubt to him. He accepted them all unhesitatingly, enthusiastically, almost reverently, as evidences of the growth of civilization and the march of progress, led appropriately by Englishmen. Although Macaulay was dazzled by material development and physical growth, and considered that statistical evidence was a complete proof of magnificent human progress, he did not look through rose-colored spectacles. He based himself on fact; and the facts which impressed him were truly impressive. There *was* growth, there *was* improvement, there *was*

a sudden tremendous progress to see and record. But there were two sides to the picture, and to one side he was blind. Macaulay never dreamed that the men of his age who were making England the home of a triumphant, vulgar materialism were sacrificing humanity, their own and that of their workers, in the process.

His fellow historian, Carlyle, however, beheld the sacrifice with fierce indignation; and poured out in torrents his contemptuous hatred of the new tyranny of the machine. He hated the impersonality of the machine, and saw that his contemporaries were fooling themselves in fancying that it was an efficient servant. He saw, earlier than most men, that it was really a master, leading all England down to its own subhuman level of standardization. He was not content to look only at the material results of growing industry; he looked also at the processes, and was filled with pitying rage. When one sees the little children laboring for said, "inhaling at every breath a quantity of sixteen hours a day in Lancashire factories, he *fuzz*, falling asleep over their wheels, and roused again by the lash of thongs over their backs, or by the slap of 'billy-rollers' over their little crowns, one pauses with a kind of amazed horror, to ask if this be Earth, the place of Hope, or Tophet, where hope never comes!"

Whatever the gains, they were purchased too dearly at such a rate. And yet, he realized, the sheer inhumanity of machine production was not the worst evil the system brought in. The deadly thing was the corruption of individualism, fostered by the economists of the day and enforced by the machine.

Carlyle had extraordinary literary gifts, deep true feeling, piercing insight, and integrity. But just because he saw further and more truly than others, and was passionately determined to tell all that was in his heart without compromise or hindrance, he was unable to ally himself with any practical cause or existing movement or party, and was even unable in the end to offer his followers a clear-cut program. The English nation was destroying itself through unleashed selfishness and the confusion of means with ends—*that* he could see, and attack; and he could see also that men must be brought back to first principles. Like Coleridge he went to the German romantic philosophers for wisdom. He became convinced that the darkness of misunderstanding, unbelief, and despair in which men's souls were imprisoned could only be pierced by the living example, sympathy, and leadership of heroic characters capable of inspiring confidence because they were worthy of it. Thus he believed that every man has within him a spark of divinity, small and flickering in the vast majority, but burning brightly in a few men of incorruptible honesty. The latter were the natural aristocracy of the race, born to lead and rule the weak majority, who under true leadership could rise to great heights of self-sacrificing devotion and work, but who without such leadership could only destroy themselves and society and civilization. This society was founded on personal responsibility—the responsibility of the governor to the governed, and of the governed to the just governor.

The trouble, from the practical point of view, with Carlyle's gospel of social reform was that there was nothing in his own age to which it could be attached. Carlyle stood alone. He was emancipated from Christianity, and from every existing group or interest, because he saw fatal misdirection or falsehood wherever he turned.

This is worth dwelling on, because the more one thinks about Carlyle's search for wisdom, the more clearly one sees in him the pattern of later Victorian thought. The literature of the age, whatever form it took, became increasingly a protest, or a series of differing protests, against "Victorianism," and a series of attempts to find some way of stamping it out, as if it were a disease. And Carlyle is typical of those who were to follow him, who could see and denounce the disease, who could see some kind of cure, but who could not follow old methods and could not find successful new ones. To this generalization, however, there is an important exception.

### NEWMAN AND THE OXFORD MOVEMENT

In the 1830's a small group of Oxford men tried to revive the conception of the Church which had been held by seventeenth-century Anglican divines. This "Oxford Movement" was led by John Henry Newman. He was a man of truly heroic proportions, clear-headed, sincere, bold, uncompromising, and persistent; with a genius for persuasive utterance which made an indelible impression on all who heard him. What he and his companions set out to do was to remind their generation that the spiritual faith of Christians was founded, not on the subjective experience of individuals, but on an historical revelation. To them the clergy of the Church of England were not

primarily moral teachers, but were priests holding a supernatural office, without whose mediation the bridge between earth and Heaven could not be crossed. The campaign of the Oxford men was conducted partly through a series of *Tracts for the Times*. Ninety tracts were published between 1833 and 1841, of which Newman wrote twenty-four. Newman saw men getting nowhere by trying moderately to hold the balance between extremes in each of which they could see something desirable—trying in other words, to make the best of both worlds. Boldly he took the course of combating worldliness by cleaving to other-worldliness. But the Church of England misunderstood him, and severely condemned him, thinking that he was a Roman Catholic who was trying to destroy the Church of England. He was in effect, as he felt, driven out of the Church. Finally he did, after painful deliberation, enter the Roman Catholic Church, and for some years he practically disappeared from public view. After the publication of his *Apologia pro Vita Sua* he became again famous, and did much to bring Englishmen into friendly relations with the Roman Catholic Church. Time was to show that both his Anglican career and his conversion to the Roman Catholic Church were to have a permanent influence. He exerted, however, no direct influence on Victorian literature until towards the very end of the century. Not Newman, but Carlyle, is typical of the successive waves of reaction against Victorianism which were to give us a great part of the literature of this era.

### TENNYSON AND BROWNING

Beginning, as we have, with Macaulay, Carlyle, and Newman, we see that one change which came with the 1830's was the predominance of prose. The poetic impulse which made the romantic age a great period in English poetry could not last. The Victorian age gave us much significant and beautiful poetry, but no poet of the first rank. Victorian life, Victorian people, and Victorian achievements were all unpoetical, and could give satisfaction only to unpoetical observers.

Of the poets that the Victorian age did produce, the most important are Tennyson and Browning. Tennyson was a born poet and mystic on the defensive. As a craftsman he was superb. In boyhood he had idolized Byron, but Keats was the romantic poet to whom he was closest in talent and from whom he learned most.

Tennyson's art was entirely deliberate and conscious. He disciplined himself to subordinate the flow of beautiful sound to his predetermined purpose. He never conquered entirely his tendency to write too much, to elaborate details, or even to drag them in, for their own sake, and to lose the sense of what he was saying in pleasing sound and richly decorated language. He did fight against this tendency, however.

For Tennyson wanted to be something more than a "perfect" artist for art's sake; he wanted to turn his art to a high purpose. He wanted, like Spenser, like Milton, like Wordsworth, to be a great teacher and a source of wisdom. He knew that if he was to be more than an exquisite minor poet, if he was to write not simply for the pleasure of other poets as a pure artist, but for the world at large, he must concern himself with the world's interests and problems, and have something important, and wise, to say.

The trouble was that he did not have the inner confidence, the piercing insight, the prophetic inspiration, or whatever it takes to fill the role. He was not content to trust himself, for better, for worse. Instead, he sought to learn from the world and to adjust himself to the needs of the time. What was the most advanced opinion concerning religious faith? What seemed to be suggested as a next step in social progress? What was the meaning of industrial development? What attitude towards it ought one to take? What kind of example ought to be placed before the British people in the field of morals? These were not so much Tennyson's questions as questions of the age; and we discover him, as he asks, and conscientiously prepares answers, saying what the occasion seems to demand. Men of science spoke admiringly of his knowledge of their discoveries; naturalists wondered at the exactness of his observation; the earliest advocates of women's rights had scarcely opened their mouths when, lo, he was with them. He was one of the first to ride on a steam railway, and immediately got this new sign of progress into a poem. And so he continued—Alfred always up and coming, Alfred first on the spot.

His own age generously repaid him for his effort to become its spiritual voice. Today, however, though poets may look upon his subtle and elaborate craftsmanship with admiring wonder, others will look at him regretfully as one who did not fulfill his promise.

In contrast to Tennyson's uncertainty, we find Robert Browning full of exuberant confidence. Besides this, Browning was hearty, cheerful, and radiantly optimistic. The famous song from *Pippa Passes* may be accepted as an expression both of Browning's conviction and of the buoyancy with which he held it:

> The year's at the spring
> And day's at the morn;
> Morning's at seven;
> The hillside's dew-pearled;
> The lark's on the wing;
> The snail's on the thorn;
> God's in his heaven—
> All's right with the world!

Browning does not hide, much less deny, the fact of evil, widely flourishing in the world. Indeed, he emphasizes it. But from all his instances he draws the same conclusion: this world is the proving ground of virtue. Souls are made and developed by strife; without deficiency there would be no spur to effort for betterment. That we endeavor strenuously and fail is of no significance, because striving itself is the important thing. It is important not for its own sake, but as giving opportunity for the growth, through activity, of the spirit of love within us. Love is the spiritual principle animating all things—the soul of man, the earth, the universe. Thus, Browning triumphantly concluded, "All's right with the world." And he went further. The student of English literature is inevitably struck by the fact that Browning reaches exactly the same point that Alexander Pope reached under the guidance of Shaftesbury and other deists, when he declared, in his *Essay on Man*, that "Whatever is, is right." And if Pope's optimism was frivolous and shallow, so was Browning's.

But Browning was thought to be profound, partly because his style was difficult, and partly because he did have a subtle and curious mind. His style is not so difficult for us as it was for his earliest readers. The difficulties mostly arise, not from complexity of thought, but simply from incomplete or crabbed expression. Browning was an accomplished craftsman, able to write almost any kind of verse with brilliancy and ease, but he habitually wrote without much regard for the limitations of readers. Hence he sometimes presented riddles to the public; and intellectual or curiously learned people felt pleased with themselves when they had unraveled them. Not unnaturally, too, after they had worked hard for it, they felt they had got hold of something "choice." In reality, of course, Browning's style was a weakness.

The famous Browning gallery of dramatic

portraits is something different. It is a triumph. By these studies of character, of personalities revealed in crucial action or sketched perfectly in their own words, Browning lives, and deserves to live long. Most of them are not spoiled, many of them are not obviously touched, by the philosophy which inspired or justified them. They can be enjoyed without it, fortunately, and every one of them enlarges or enriches our understanding of human nature. A great part of the enduring strength and interest of English literature, from Chaucer, through Shakespeare, through the eighteenth-century novelists (of whom Jane Austen is properly one), comes from its wealth of living persons drawn with matchless penetration and vigor. Browning is one of the glories of this tradition, and he added to it not only a varied group of personalities of unfailing human interest, but also a distinctive method of portraiture, prophetic of the so-called psychological studies of character which later in the century were to give added interest to the novel.

## WRITING AS A FORM OF BUSINESS

Browning himself, indeed, was almost a novelist in verse; and the fact suggests again what has already been said, that the Victorian age was not favorable to poetry, and placed those who would be poets in false positions, or else gave them tasks too difficult for human powers. One important reason was that writing was becoming a business.

The reading public was increasing rapidly in size as the eighteenth century drew to a close, and continued to grow as the nineteenth century advanced, until it embraced practically the whole population of such countries as England and the United States. The provision of reading matter for the growing market at the same time became a business like any other, with possibilities of considerable profit. And those possibilities could most certainly be realized by the publishers who followed popular taste.

The rise of a cheap press with the spread of reading, and the appearance of popular magazines and inexpensive newspapers, had been hopefully regarded by the friends of democracy. With the means now available, the multitude would be eager, it was thought, to fill its head with sound knowledge and to cultivate its taste by familiarity with the best literature. And in fact a few publishers acted on this confident prediction, and a few of those who

did prospered. But, in general, literature sought the level of the multitude, instead of the multitude rising to the level of literature; no one for a long time has spoken, without ribald laughter, of the educational value of the newspaper or the cheap magazine or popular fiction. There have been, of course, some exceptions to the rule; we have seen that Walter Scott was an early one. They made commercial writing profitable by supplying a sound article, with no sacrifice of the enjoyment which readers had been deriving from shoddy romances. But too few followed his example.

The pressure of the commercial market was for entertainment, and for fiction as the form of literary entertainment requiring the least effort from readers. Mere poetry began to seem high-falutin—the kind of thing only a wild-eyed, long-haired eccentric would waste his time on. The practical thing in verse was a simple narrative or song flowing with obvious sentiment, with enough pathos to bring up a sympathetic moisture in the reader's eyes. It was Tennyson's effort to reach a satisfactory adjustment with this situation that drove him into falsity.

## CHARLES DICKENS

The first writer of fiction after Scott who proved able to meet the new conditions just discussed, and to triumph over them, was Dickens. He was the most popular writer of the nineteenth century; and in spite of his many faults he can still today give more instant and irresistible pleasure to readers than any other writer of that century. Dickens's characters are *alive*, as are few others in all literature, and have a simple, yet rich and full humanity. These characters were created with delight—Mrs. Sarah Gamp, Mr. Pecksniff, Uriah Heep, Mr. Micawber, Fagin, Bill Sikes and the Artful Dodger, the Cheeryble brothers, Harold Skimpole, Mrs. Jellyby, the Reverend Mr. Chadband, Thomas Gradgrind, Scrooge, Mr. and Mrs. Boffin, the Veneerings, Little Nell, Dick Swiveller, and Sam Weller, not to mention Mr. Pickwick himself or any of the others who gave their names to titles of the novels. Their creator laughed with them, cried with them, felt and acted with them, lived out their parts in his own person. It is not enough to say that he imagined them vividly. He was full of cheerful energy, confidence, humor, and instinctively humane feeling, with an unique power to project his own full-blooded vitality into his creations. Most of

Dickens's characters are drawn from the lower middle class or from the ranks of working people or, in a few cases, from the underworld. In general the scenes of his novels are depressing, or would be if we were actually placed in them ourselves, and often they are worse than depressing. We know what the real Mrs. Gamp must have been like, and the real Mr. Pecksniff. They must have been unbearable. How, then, did Dickens recommend such people and their surroundings to his own generation? And why are they still interesting today?

He took them as they were, and did not hide what they were. In fact he often emphasized their essential traits until his characters became classic types, definite, monumental, immortal. This is one part of the answer to our questions. Dickens's genius enabled him to give his characters broadly representative qualities which give them a human interest not only independent of time or place, but independent as well of the merely ugly or painful, elements of personality which, in real life, would often make it impossible for us to see anything else in them. Mrs. Gamp, Mr. Pecksniff, Mr. Micawber, and all the rest are ideal portraits, just as is Shakespeare's Falstaff. They differ from everyday reality only in being more real, more richly, intensely, and amusingly human than their originals. The secret of Dickens's achievement lies in this—his power of idealization. The world seen through his eyes is transformed by his own heartiness, kindliness, and humor. It is transformed, yet in his masterpieces it is not essentially falsified.

This is why Dickens's characters instantly fixed themselves in the hearts and minds of the whole reading public when they were created, and why they have a perennial life and universal appeal. It matters not how distant and strange the England of a hundred years ago may become. Dickens has seen to it that his world will always be vivid and fresh, and in no need of historical explanation. Nor do we go to Dickens for the sake of history. We go to him for enjoyment of a kind sufficiently rare and hearty that for our own sakes we ought not to miss it; and when we have gone to him, we find our own humanity enlarged and refreshed.

Yet Dickens, aside from his genius, was emphatically a man of his own age. He accepted Victorian prudery, for example, quite as artists of other ages have accepted other conventions, and simply worked within it, and found he was not really hampered by it. And he cordially agreed with his readers that literature should have a moral purpose. He was, generally speaking, one with his readers; and it was this rather than any deliberate calculation which enabled him to give them what they wanted.

Dickens did not accept his own age uncritically; he hated hypocrisy in all its forms, and religious fanaticism, special privilege, the law's delays, and a good deal else which he attacked satirically in his novels. On the whole he stood with the reforming radicals of the 1830's and 1840's, and shared their belief in progress and their indifference to the past. He shared also their confused outlook, attacking on grounds of humanity those who permitted social injustice to flourish, but also attacking, as the friend of liberty, those who attempted to reform by processes of governmental control. In later years he was influenced by Carlyle, who did nothing to help him out of his dilemma. Critics nowadays say that he got beyond his depth in meddling with economic and political problems, but the truth is that the problems of the age in these fields were beyond everybody's depth. And Dickens at any rate was always on the side of goodness, honor, justice, mercy—those values which, in so far as they can be kept aloft in a hostile world, make the difference between civilized humanity and brutish existence.

Dickens's first great book was *The Posthumous Papers of the Pickwick Club* (1836–1837). Of his novels the following should certainly be mentioned: *Oliver Twist* (1837–1838), *David Copperfield* (1849–1850), *Bleak House* (1852–1853), *Hard Times* (1854), *A Tale of Two Cities* (1859), *Great Expectations* (1860–1861), and the much shorter *A Christmas Carol in Prose* (1843).

### THACKERAY AND TROLLOPE

Dickens was not alone in writing novels in the interest of reform. He began earliest, with *Oliver Twist*, but he soon had company. Benjamin Disraeli's *Sybil* (1845) was devoted to the problem of social injustice. Mrs. Elizabeth Cleghorn Gaskell, who lived in the industrial city of Manchester, wrote from first-hand observation of the wretchedness of the factory-workers in *Mary Barton* (1848) and in other novels. Charles Kingsley, the Anglican clergyman whose false accusation caused Newman to write the *Apologia pro Vita Sua*, attacked the evils of sweated labor and other wrongs against the working classes in *Alton Locke*

(1850). Charlotte Brontë pictured at length the troubles of industrial workers in *Shirley* (1849). And there were others, all showing that by the middle of the century the English were becoming deeply concerned over the inhumanity of industrial "progress."

From the literary point of view, however, it is significant that Mrs. Gaskell is remembered, not for her novels of reform, but for her delightful idyl of village life, *Cranford* (1853), and for her classic *Life of Charlotte Brontë* (1857). And Charlotte Brontë is remembered, not as a chronicler of evils arising from industrialism, but as the author of *Jane Eyre* (1847), a novel which proved, as did Emily Brontë's *Wuthering Heights* (1847), that romantic passion and rebellion were still alive in England. It is significant also that William Makepeace Thackeray made no contribution to the literature of reform. Dickens and Thackeray are markedly different in many ways which promptly strike the eye, and this obscures the fact that they have important resemblances also. Both were thorough Victorians, and honestly democratic, yet socially snobs, while they ridiculed snobbery in others. Both, furthermore, were nourished by the literature of the eighteenth century. Thackeray's reading was much wider than that of Dickens, yet the writers of that time from whom he learned most—Addison, Fielding, and Goldsmith—are among those who also nourished Dickens's mind and imagination. And both novelists carried on in their own time the work of their eighteenth-century predecessors in the humorous, satirical, and yet sympathetic portrayal of manners and character, with a great deal of moralizing and of sentimentalism.

Here the resemblances between the two end. They were as different in background, upbringing, and manner as were the fields to which they devoted their work. Dickens was self-made and almost uneducated. He worked his way up to fame from a shoe-blacking factory where he was employed as a boy, and the social scene he depicts is mostly that which he knew first hand in his boyhood and youth. Thackeray's early life was very like that of Arthur Pendennis, in the novel called *The History of Pendennis* (1848–1850), except that Thackeray came of an Anglo-Indian family in easy circumstances, was born in India, and was sent back to England at the age of six for his education, which included some years at Cambridge. Like Pendennis, he entered the Temple to study the law, but soon began to use his natural gift for writing in order to fill an empty purse.

Thackeray's writings are exceedingly large in volume and miscellaneous in character. As a professional man of letters he wrote reviews, parodies, ballads and other verse both humorous and pathetic, art criticism, journalistic correspondence, satirical burlesques, lectures on English writers and sovereigns of the eighteenth century, essays, Christmas books, tales, and finally, the great novels on which his enduring fame rests. *Pendennis* has already been mentioned. The others are: *Vanity Fair* (1847–1848), *Henry Esmond* (1852), *The Newcomes* (1853–1855), and *The Virginians* (1857–1859). *Vanity Fair*, *Pendennis*, and *The Newcomes* are contemporary: the society pictured is that of the upper middle class and of the aristocracy, which Thackeray knew, inside and out, from his own observation. The other two novels are historical. All of the novels are deliberately unromantic.

Though he saw through and disliked pretense and hypocrisy and selfish materialism, as a thinker he was superficial and easy-going. His moral outlook can almost be summed up in some such imagined statement as this: "Alas, my dears, we live in a topsy-turvy world, where the wicked flourish at the expense of the virtuous; and, what is more, where the wicked are lively, clever, and interesting and the virtuous are inactive, dull, and boring. Yet wickedness is ugly, and virtue, of course, is beautiful—never more beautiful than when in distress. Come, let us shed a tear for distressed virtue."

We value Thackeray for his extraordinary penetration and skill in characterization. He created a large group of persons who rise above their Victorian surroundings and loom before us as classic types, to be found in every generation and in every community. "Once created," he said, "they lead me, and I follow where they direct. I have no idea where it all comes from. I have never seen the people I describe, nor heard the conversations I put down. I am often astonished myself to read it when I have got it on paper." Thackeray, in other words, worked by a kind of instinct, which we may call a genius for the creation of living character in some of its perennial aspects. And this is the source both of his strength and of his weakness in his novels. The characters live, as few imagined characters ever have lived, and we know them completely as we cannot really know anyone in daily life; yet at the same time Thackeray is never in control of the progress of his tales, and often fails to grasp the full meaning of the drama wherein they play their parts.

Thackeray, shortly before his death in 1863, was the first editor of *The Cornhill Magazine.* Among his contributors was Anthony Trollope (1815–1882), already known as the author of several of the novels in the series which eventually was called "The Chronicles of Barsetshire." It is not possible here to do more than mention him, but he must be mentioned because, of all the novelists of the mid-Victorian time, he most faithfully portrayed the manners and life of well-to-do people of the middle class. He was probably as successful as Thackeray in picturing enduring types, and he had some of Jane Austen's ability to make commonplace people interesting. He was a capable workman, and his novels today are not only eminently readable, but ring true. Finally, just as Jane Austen shows us solid people going contentedly about their own business scarcely touched by the fervors of romanticism, so Trollope shows us other members of the same class a half-century later, busy with their own affairs, amusements, gossip, match-making, and the like, and mostly untouched by the great causes and changes which loom large on the page of history. A student does well to remember that while Carlyle was thundering against the age, and social reform was becoming a burning issue, Trollope's Bishop Proudie was troubled by a different kind of problem, and was praying to God to "save him from being glad that his wife was dead."

### THE WIDENING FIELD OF SCIENCE:
### THE DOCTRINE OF EVOLUTION

The Victorian compromise which gave the appearance of stability to English society in the middle years of the nineteenth century was only a temporary makeshift; Victorians were gradually compelled to recognize that no amount of personal respectability could resolve conflicts between self-interest and social interest. They were also compelled, by the end of the 1850's, to face the fact that the traditional religion which had served them as a basis for their moral standards was being shattered by the progress of science.

Through the pressure of new conditions and of humanitarian sentiment a peaceful democratic revolution was brought about in England. Sympathy and compassion for the industrial workers, reinforced by fear of the large new class which was arising, caused many important political and social reforms. More important than the reforms themselves, however, was the direction of the revolution of which they were a part; for every social reform was secured only by the sacrifice of some measure of personal liberty and only through the assumption, on the part of Government, of added power. Government was both centralized and strengthened, and its sphere was immensely extended. At the same time the laborer lost independence by binding himself with his fellows in unions, wherein all were pledged to act together. The laborer made this sacrifice eagerly, of course, because he gained by it; neverthless, he lost something valuable, whether or not he felt the loss. The whole movement was a march from individualism toward collectivism.

The sciences of geology and biology in the middle years of the nineteenth century brought on another revolution—a revolution in belief which undermined Christianity and for many persons destroyed the validity of all religious faith. Sir Charles Lyell's *Principles of Geology* (1830–1833) and Robert Chambers' *Vestiges of the Natural History of Creation* (1844) prepared the way for the book that touched off the fireworks, Charles Darwin's *The Origin of Species* (1859).

*The Origin of Species* presented a picture of the earth and of all the life upon its surface as a gradual evolution, or development, from a simple undifferentiated beginning, proceeding in accordance with natural laws, which adequately account for everything, without any necessity for acts of special creation.

Darwin and Genesis could not be reconciled. Those who accepted Darwin's evidence as conclusive had to set down the Bible's story of the creation as a fable. In addition, Darwin placed man among the animals, and in so doing seemed to destroy not only the hope of immortality but all of the values and moral standards derived from Christianity. It would be difficult to exaggerate the effect of the doctrine of evolution. *The Origin of Species* caused a profound shock, especially to the thousands of Englishmen who believed that the whole Bible was the direct word of God, and therefore literally true throughout. A bitter and long-drawn-out controversy followed, in which the champions of orthodox religious belief did everything they could in a losing battle to discredit evolution. Darwin did not fight for his theory, but had a determined, skillful, and eloquent supporter in Thomas Henry Huxley (1825–1895), who engaged not only in popular exposition of the doctrine, but also in much destructive criticism of the Bible and of Christianity, and in attempts to formulate a new view of life based on science.

The attitude and outlook which we have called Victorian did not, of course, break asunder instantly under the impact of Darwinian evolution. Victorian respectability, prudery, and ugliness continued their course. But the unity of outlook and purpose which had been the strength of Victorianism could no longer be maintained. No English writer, in prose or verse, has spoken to the whole nation in the later nineteenth century or in the twentieth as Dickens and Thackeray did before 1860. Victorian earnestness persisted for some years despite increasing division, but it could not, and did not, hold out indefinitely before the spectacle of a dozen different prophets expounding a dozen conflicting "truths." As disunion and conflict appeared, a vein of sheer nonsense showed up in English literature as a relief from the perplexity of the times. The masters of nonsense were the painter, Edward Lear (1812–1888), and the mathematician, Charles Lutwidge Dodgson (1832–1898), known to all the world as "Lewis Carroll." Lear's fame as a writer of nonsense verse which delighted grown people as well as children followed the appearance of his *Nonsense Songs and Stories* and his *More Nonsense Songs* in 1871 and 1872. "Lewis Carroll's" *Alice in Wonderland* was published in 1865, and *Through the Looking Glass* followed in 1871. Another master of nonsense, which in this case was not unmixed with satire, was Sir William Schwenk Gilbert (1836–1911). His lasting fame was won by the series of comic operas for which music was composed by Sir Arthur Sullivan (1842–1900). They include the popular *H.M.S. Pinafore* (1878), *The Pirates of Penzance* (1879), and *The Mikado* (1885).

## SPENCER AND ARNOLD

It is scarcely possible to make any general statement concerning the combined effect of scientific discovery and of historical criticism of the Bible. Some people were depressed and alarmed, others rejoiced, and still others soberly addressed themselves to the task of re-orientation. Those who rejoiced did so because they welcomed the personal freedom promised in the threatened destruction of Victorian standards or because they saw in the continuing advance of knowledge fresh evidence of the progress of humanity towards perfection.

Of the perfectionists the most important was Herbert Spencer (1820–1903). The keynote of the many volumes of his "Synthetic Philosophy" is the alleged "law" of nature whereby man, *of necessity,* progressed towards perfection. His optimistic view of man as by nature a progressive animal became the leading article in the belief of a growing number in the later nineteenth century who found in humanitarianism a new religion.

The immediate effect, however, of the unsettlement, if not destruction, of traditional belief, as we see it in the literature of the eighteen-sixties, seventies, and eighties, was not one of relief and optimistic exultation. There is no evidence that Matthew Arnold, for example, was seriously disturbed by any of the implications of the doctrine of evolution. It might or might not be true that man was descended from some tree-dwelling ape-like creature, but the truth, whatever it was, did not strike him as of the first importance. It did not alter what man had become—a moral being with spiritual aspirations and a noble human history. He saw in history, religion, and art (more particularly in literature) the evidence of man's success in establishing life on a human level which answered to his abiding nature and distinctive capacities, with brutality always threatening the achievement, yet somehow kept down.

The loss of Christian faith in his own day seemed to him a calamity because he regarded Christianity as a "translation" into terms which men could understand of eternal truths which could not be allowed to perish. Men had grounded their faith in a book, which was coming to be understood as a human record, subject to error, written in the terms of the credulities, the ignorance, of the times when the book was made. They had made claims for that book which it was impossible that any book should sustain. Discovering this, they were now in danger of throwing away both the book and the truth which it imperfectly expressed. Indeed, a generation was growing up ignorant of history and indifferent to it, and was being asked to contemplate with pride the new railways, the new steamships, all the new conveniences of life, and the freedom of Englishmen to say whatever they pleased, as if such things were the real achievements of civilization. Arnold saw these things for what they were. He labeled them all "machinery." By this he meant that they were means, not ends, and that judgment concerning them must depend on what they were used for. Liberty itself was to be valued in terms of its use. He saw the approach of a barbaric anarchy in which people were growing wild like weeds. He saw that into the hands of these raw and ignorant people were being placed instruments of incalculable power, not only all of the fruits of applied science in which his century was uniquely productive, but the control of the state itself.

Accordingly, Arnold felt that the state must assume both the position of positive moral leadership and the responsibility for education which formerly the church had held. The kind of education he wanted was liberal or human-istic in character. He wanted to open the eyes of youth to what man has been and can be, to the enduring values of life as discerned and illustrated by the genius of the race, and thus to form cultivated persons, capable them-selves of seeing life steadily and of seeing it whole. The aim, in a word, was culture, to be got by maintaining continuity between the past and the present.

Arnold himself has weathered the passage of time more successfully than any of his con-temporaries. Others were more brilliant in var-ious ways, but he saw more clearly than any of them the real problems of the age of democ-racy. He wrote a series of meditative poems which speak with the accents of reality, and classically express the moods of a spiritual being condemned to live in an age which mistakes bustling activity for achievement, gadgets for progress, distraction for happiness, and mate-rialism for wisdom. He could not, however, rest satisfied with a passive role, and he discovered an outlet for his full powers when he turned to criticism for which he was unusually quali-fied and which he rightly felt the age most needed.

## GEORGE ELIOT

The first novelist of power after Trollope was Mary Ann Evans (1819–1880), who used the pseudonym "George Eliot." She was a learned woman of extremely serious interests who, had she been born a man or had she been born in a later generation, would in all probability have become a scholar, or perhaps a moral philosopher. As it was, after translating a German life of Christ and another German theological work, and after writing critical articles for *The Westminster Review*, she turned to fiction, when in her late thirties, for the sake of money. It seemed clear from her first attempts (*Scenes of Clerical Life*, 1858) that she had a genius for it, and she won great fame from *Adam Bede* (1859) *The Mill on the Floss* (1860), and *Silas Marner* (1861). Enthusiastic readers have compared her with Thackeray to his disadvantage, but they have been forced to limit the comparison to her early novels and tales, just mentioned. For in her later novels George Eliot became a source of weariness and finally of boredom. And to-day, whatever critics may say in her honor, she is no longer read.

Moreover, we can easily see why, even though it may be agreed that present-day readers miss something genuine and fine in neglecting her. She was a deeply religious person; and like Matthew Arnold, the poet Arthur Hugh Clough, and the critic Leslie Stephen, she felt compelled to give up tradi-tional Christian faith. However, she set to work with much earnestness to try to build new and independent foundations, chiefly psycho-logical, for the morality she had learned in the Church, and still cherished.

## GEORGE MEREDITH

We see evidences of the unsettlement and perplexities of the times in both the novels and the poems of George Meredith (1828–1909). He had extraordinary abilities. His novels spar-kle with wit, which often rises to the plane of wisdom and demonstrates the penetrating quality of his insight. He was not only brilliant but profound in characterization. Probably no reader of *The Egoist* (1879) has left it with-out feeling that he has been in the presence of genius. Yet every reader also feels that Mere-dith's reach exceeded his grasp, and this—in spite of Browning's contrary opinion—is a fatal disadvantage, at least in a writer. He gave up Christianity more easily than George Eliot, and clearly saw that this entailed not only a new outlook on life but also a new and differ-ent morality. Since man was now seen to be a product of natural forces, he made Nature his god, addressed the earth as our great Mother, and sought to show that all is well with us when we allow Nature to have free play, but that we come to grief when we disregard Na-ture or pit ourselves against her.

He himself came to grief, however, when he tried to be buoyantly natural. His mind was incisive, ironical, disillusioned, and detached; he stood aloof from common humanity in con-scious superiority. And since his professed be-lief was so at odds with his own nature, he seems always to be reaching for a lucidity he could not achieve. Not only was the public becoming divided; the divided self was beginning to appear.

## SAMUEL BUTLER

To Samuel Butler (1835–1902) his emancipation from Christianity had the effect of a pleasurable release from intolerable bondage. He was irreverent, skeptical, and self-confident. Mockery of whatever the world believed or esteemed was his delight, and he gaily attacked scholars, men of science, moralists, churches, tradition—everything. His practice was systematically to turn everything upside down, and then to develop the inverted sentiment, thought, or theory in essay or treatise if he saw in it a possibility of shocking the public and if he felt he could make out a case for it. For example, he took Pope's line, "An honest man's the noblest work of God," and transformed it into "An honest God's the noblest work of man." This expressed his belief that men have created their gods by use of imagination, and in so doing have created idealized images of themselves.

He had only a fraction of the abilities of such a writer as Meredith, but he reached at one bound, with an undivided self, the subversive attitude and wittily shocking style which was to become the fashion in the next generation, and which is still regarded in some quarters as the essence of the modern emancipated spirit. Hence a few of his books, especially the Utopian novel *Erewhon* (1872) and *The Way of All Flesh* (1903), are still extremely interesting and still much read.

## THOMAS HARDY

The truest and finest artist of this period was Thomas Hardy (1840–1928), who also perceived more clearly than any of his slightly older contemporaries the real drift and meaning of the knowledge recently gained concerning the earth's past and concerning the natural history of man. There was only one word for it. That word was Disillusion. If the new knowledge and all its plain implications were to be accepted, man was stripped bare of every ground for optimistic faith, of every comforting hope, of every aspiration which for many centuries had given meaning and worth to earthly life. Life was transformed into a riddle whose solution was impossible, and there was but too much reason to fear that in fact the riddle

was meaningless. Human reason itself now appeared to be only a power we have of making plausible excuses for believing and doing what we are instinctively compelled to do—a power, in other words, of self-justification, or of giving a good appearance to a bad business.

To such a desolating revelation there were only two possible reactions. One, by a species of accident, was classically expressed for the modern English-speaking world by Edward FitzGerald in his paraphrase of the *Rubáiyát* of Omar Khayyám (first published, oddly enough, in the same year as *The Origin of Species,* 1859). The counsels of Omar were those of despair, rationalized. Sink yourself, he advised, in forgetfulness, in the pleasant oblivion of instinctive enjoyments, breathing the odor of the rose, cooling your parched throat with draughts of wine; and cease from bothering your head over silly questions about yesterday and tomorrow:

> Ah, take the cash, and let the credit go,
> Nor heed the rumble of a distant drum.

The other possibility was to face despair steadily, with calm resignation, without cringing, without bitterness, but with no pretense that reality was one whit nearer "the heart's desire" than all human experience has shown it to be. This was Hardy's way, and in a half-dozen of his novels and in much of his poetry he transformed his somber vision of life into enduring art. The world has agreed that he showed his power much more fully and effectively in his novels than in his verse. Indeed, in his power to depict the beauty of the Dorsetshire settings of his novels, and to connect those settings intimately and completely with the characters and fortunes of his actors, he not only achieved unity of atmosphere but proved himself to be one of the supreme imaginative artists of modern times. Finally, in comparison with his perfect integrity, the well-meant but futile rationalizations of his contemporaries and of some of his successors seem like the whistling of boys in the dark to keep their courage up.

## JOHN RUSKIN

The first volume of Ruskin's *Modern Painters* appeared in 1843. In this work Ruskin set out to defend the art of J. M. W. Turner (1775–1851), who had been attacked by the critics of the day, and to correct the appalling state of ignorance in England concerning the nature of art, its place in life, and the conditions under which art could be expected to flourish.

The prevalent notion was that art was decoration, hence a luxury; and possession of a work of art, accordingly, was a sign that one could afford luxuries. A man would build a home and furnish it for comfort, and then add "art" here and there to the extent that he could, or wished to show that he could. This viewpoint, in conjunction with other factors mentioned earlier in this chapter, produced the most hideous buildings and house-furnishings in the history of the western world, and paintings which were imitative and lifeless.

Ruskin's studies and meditation brought him to the conviction that art is great only as it succeeds in revealing aspects of God, and can be expected only from a man who is good, sincere, and happy—who is, in other words, in a right relation to God, and able to perceive the Divinity shining out of God's earth and God's creatures. The artist must, of course, have an artist's keen eye, and be master of brush or chisel; but no amount of technical ability and training can suffice without the nobility and integrity which enable the artist to see "the beauty of holiness" in concrete earthly form. The mere imitation of natural objects is contemptible. The artist must see *through* the object and give *that* vision form. Thus Ruskin was led to see that great art could not be expected from the England of the mid-nineteenth century because the kind of life fostered by industrialism was wholly adverse to the appearance of true artists and of a public able to appreciate them if they did appear. He was led to attack the age for its Mammon-worship and to try to pulverize the political economists who, he thought, were encouraging the notion that the pursuit of wealth was the prime purpose of life. He vehemently assailed the materialism of the age, its social injustice, and its subjection of the workman to the conditions of profit-making. And, like Carlyle, he looked back to the Middle Ages as a time when conditions had been good. He praised Gothic architecture as the noble expression of sincere faith, produced by men who took pride in their work, and who worked, not for gain, but for the sake of giving appropriate, and hence beautiful, expression to their vision of divinity. Likewise he praised the medieval organization of society. Though not many paid any serious heed to his specific suggestions concerning social reform, during his later years he finally gained great fame and an enormous public. Wider and wider agreement with his condemnation of industrial society was felt, and he came to be regarded with reverent awe as an arbiter of taste; but sober people dismissed him as a fantastic dreamer in his constructive plans for a better social order. It is a remarkable fact, however, that what he really proposed was a paternalistic government, with a large measure of state-capitalism, government-made work for the unemployed, old-age pensions, universal education, vocational guidance and training, fixed minimum wages in all fields of employment, and a good deal else which has a prophetic appearance.

## ROSSETTI AND THE PRE-RAPHAELITE BROTHERHOOD

In the late 1840's a group of young painters and poets formed the Pre-Raphaelite Brotherhood, in a return to the naïve simplicity of medieval painters of the age before Raphael. Their leader was Dante Gabriel Rossetti, who succeeded better as a poet than as a painter, and illustrated their principles as fully in his verse as in his paintings.

W. B. Yeats has said that Rossetti did not care whether the earth moved around the sun or the sun moved around the earth. There was a great deal else that Rossetti did not care about. He did not so much revolt from the conventions and standards of the Victorians as simply turn his back to them, to step into the sensuous, romantic other-world of Keats. The Victorians could revel in ugliness and in all their earnest employments, and go their own way. Their works were no concern of his. In a world where everything seemed to be questionable if not already questioned, he felt free to devote himself wholly to beauty for beauty's sake, that being the one thing entirely real to him.

## SWINBURNE AND WILLIAM MORRIS

As we have noticed before, extremes provoke extremes; and Rossetti's implied criticism of Victorianism was taken up by others and carried still further. Swinburne presently claimed the liberty to pursue beauty for beauty's sake in a manner outrageously shocking to Victorian moral feeling. Ruskin, however, though he deplored Swinburne's moral "corruption," said, when he was asked to protest against Swinburne's *Poems and Ballads* in 1866, "He is infinitely above me in all knowledge and power, and I should no more think of advising or criticizing him than of venturing to do it to Turner if he were alive again." Ruskin meant that Swinburne had the divine fire of creative genius and perfect mastery of a medium for its expression, and that this placed his work above criticism, as something to be accepted for the sake of his music and integral feeling.

Also influenced by Rossetti was William Morris (1834–1896). He was a born craftsman, and was instinctively sympathetic to Ruskin's assertion that all work should be done in the spirit of the craftsman who loved his materials, respected them and their uses, and took pride in honest workmanship. Thus he set about making well-designed and soundly built furniture, good fabrics, wallpapers, finely printed books, stained glass, tapestries, and wrought metal pieces. In all this he was trying, under Ruskin's inspiration, to bring art and life together again, as they had been united in the Middle Ages. And the art which appealed to him and influenced all his work was medieval. He was influenced not only as a craftsman by Ruskin; he also, as a consequence of Ruskin's teaching and Carlyle's, became a socialist. His socialism found literary expression principally in two prose works, *A Dream of John Ball* (1888) and a Utopian novel, *News from Nowhere* (1890).

## WALTER PATER, THE AESTHETIC MOVEMENT, AND NATURALISTIC FICTION

The legacy of the Romantic Movement in the Victorian era was carried by Carlyle, as we have just seen, to Ruskin. Rossetti then went back to Keats. And Rossetti and Swinburne between them rescued Blake from oblivion, and made him a strong influence on poets of the next generation. Through all these writers, beginning with Blake, there is an unmistakable, though not deliberate or conscious, drift towards the doctrine of art for art's sake.

One young person who became interested in this doctrine and then convinced, and who happened to be both an Oxford scholar and a fastidious writer, was Walter Pater. He believed that absolute truth was a will-o'-the-wisp —or that it lay in the disillusioned conclusion that nothing endures. What, then, is real? Nothing, Pater replied, except the momentary pleasures we receive through the senses. These are immediate and genuine, and while they last are real, at least to ourselves. What, then, is wisdom? Wisdom, he replied, consists in

living as pleasurably as one can during the short time that the phosphorus, lime, carbon, water, and other substances of which a man consists hold together. There are, he added, differences in pleasures; some are more exquisite and intense than others, and it is these which best enable us to make the most of our time. And "of such wisdom," he concluded, "the poetic passion, the desire of beauty, the love of art for its own sake, has most," because art frankly proposes "to give nothing but the highest quality to your moments as they pass, and simply for those moments' sake."

So Pater ended the celebrated "Conclusion" to his *Studies in the History of the Renaissance*. His counsel, like that of FitzGerald's Omar, was the fruit of disillusion, but it was welcomed by readers still younger than he as authorization for a joyful release from the whole stuffy Victorian outlook and attitude. Pater himself was austere, almost priest-like, a high-minded man. By publishing his meditations, however, he became the rather unwilling and troubled leader of the so-called aesthetic movement of the late nineteenth century. Oscar Wilde was the most prominent figure in that movement because he did everything humanly possible, by dress, manner, conversation, and printed work, to flaunt before the world his emancipation from all conventions; and then, with dramatic suddenness, he met in his prison sentence what the conventional world thought to be his just fate. Wilde, however, was only one of many who all welcomed the doctrine of art for its own sake because it gave complete freedom to the artist to treat any subject he pleased in any way he pleased. And it was inevitable that the first effort of these emancipated artists should be the eager exploration of just those aspects of life to which the Victorians had closed their eyes. Thus the final act of rebellion against Victorianism was an outburst of naughtiness—an orgy of unashamed and impudent literary and artistic treatment of forbidden subjects.

Wilde was the playwright of this aesthetic movement. Also part of the movement were the poet Ernest Dowson, the critic Arthur Symons, and the artist Aubrey Beardsley. *The Yellow Book*, which was from 1894 to 1897 the almost official organ of the movement, is as notable for its Beardsley illustrations as for any of its literary contributions.

Closely related to the aesthetic movement, yet distinct from it, is "naturalism." It stems from Flaubert's *Madame Bovary* (1856), which combines realism and aestheticism, and was developed in France by Emile Zola (1840–1902), whose novels depict life's most cruel, debased, brutal aspects. In England the foremost representative of Zolaesque naturalism in the 1880's was George Moore (1852–1933), whose *Mummer's Wife* (1884) and *Esther Waters* (1894), though they do not reach Zola's level of intensity, are impressive novels.

## ROMANCE AND IMPERIALISM

As we traverse the years after 1860, the impression derived from literature is that English life was disintegrating under the influence of disillusion. The old earnestness, confidence, and hearty enjoyment, all preserved magnificently in the pages of Dickens, were gone. In their place had come pessimism, decadence, immoralism, morbidity, and disunion. If we should look further, at the realistic novels of George Gissing (1857–1903) for example, our impression that the human spirit was disheartened and faltering would be deepened.

Yet at the same time the outward condition of the English seemed more fortunate than that of any other people at any period of history. A century of unexampled material prosperity had made the nation wealthy beyond even Macaulay's rosiest anticipations. The British flag had followed trade to every corner of the world, and an empire had been created beside which that of Rome looked small, and on which the sun never set. At home, though much remained to be done, much had been achieved in the correction of social injustice; and England, while clinging to the forms of ancient usage, was becoming in reality the most democratic country on earth.

The explanation of this difference between literature and life is to be found partly in what has already in this chapter been called the ambiguous character of Victorian expansion. England was raised to the very pinnacle of earthly power and greatness, but this end was accomplished by means which could appeal to no imagination or generous feeling. On the contrary, the means of mass-production, the things produced, and the methods of their distribution were all repellent to high-minded people. "Things were in the saddle, and rode mankind." On top of this, the science which had put things in the saddle had gone on to place man among the animals in a godless and perhaps meaningless world. There was unescapable reason for disillusion and for a feeling of helplessness in the face of blind forces. There were, however, a few voices raised toward the end of the century to show that the spirit of disillusion was not yet by any means universal. Robert Louis Stevenson spoke out for the joy of adventure and manly daring, and bade men see themselves once more in the mirror of bold human action and indomitable spirit triumphing over difficulties, instead of morbidly analyzing themselves and paralyzing their wills by self-pity. And though he wrote only for boys in *Treasure Island*, he showed himself a true inheritor of Walter Scott in his romances entitled *Kidnapped*, *The Master of Ballantrae*, and *Catriona*.

Stevenson won a large public in his own day, and he is likely to be read longer than any of his contemporaries. Rudyard Kipling won an even larger public in the early part of his career, and he also is likely to be read longer than many of his and Stevenson's contemporaries, though from the first he provoked hostility in some quarters, and through the latter half of his life was condemned by every self-appointed spokesman for the welfare of mankind. Kipling was not, as a young man, a refined artist, and he perhaps never became a really masterly craftsman. But it must be added that he had superb energy and a ready command of humor, pathos, tenderness, and surprise, and an unusual power to catch the authentic flavor of certain types. His ballads concerning soldiers have had an universal appeal, and have been as popular among the soldiers themselves as elsewhere. Why, then, has it been long the fashion to condemn him? The reason is political. Kipling perceived a romantic glory in the far-flung empire and made himself an ardent "booster" of imperialism at a time when it was being more and more questioned by liberals. In so doing he not only took an unfashionable stand for "Law, Order, Duty an' Restraint, Obedience, Discipline," but also seemed to some people to be playing directly into the hands of those few who, they thought, were using imperialism to exploit mankind.

## DIVERSITY IN POETIC EXPRESSION

Three poets who were very widely read in the dozen years or so before the first World War were Kipling, A. E. Housman, and John Masefield. The popularity of Kipling and of Masefield is easy to understand. They both wrote to tell a story or sing a song of broad, elemental human appeal. And they both wanted to get away from literary language and delighted in the colloquialism. Both of them managed to be direct, vivid, and forceful. Masefield found an effective way in which to tell a good story, and used it half a dozen times, with minor variations, after the sensational success of *The Everlasting Mercy*. The popularity of A. E. Housman rests on significantly different grounds. Housman was full of that pessimistic sense of the futility of life which we have seen growing in the literature of the late nineteenth century, and he seemed to give compressed and classic expression to it. Obviously he was popular because an ever larger number of readers shared his outlook.

But none of these poets was "typical" of the poetry of his time, nor could any poet have been. We have discussed poets representing extremes as sharply opposed as can be imagined: and in addition practically every possible position between those extremes was being held by some poet or group of poets. The net result, in other words, of that increasing diversity of opinion and practice whose course we have been tracing, was that finally a kind of literary and intellectual freedom was being achieved wherein everyone was at liberty to think what he pleased and to write as he pleased, and could be sure of an audience.

Still another of the diverse sources of distinguished poetic expression was Roman Catholicism. Francis Thompson's *Hound of Heaven* was no isolated achievement, but the forerunner of a new stream of Catholic English literature. The poetic style of Gerard Manly Hopkins continues to influence world poetry. Among other distinguished Catholic writers were Alice Meynell, G. K. Chesterton, and Hilaire Belloc.

### THE NOVEL FROM 1890 TO 1914

The novel remained the most popular form of literary art throughout this period, though the poems of Kipling and Masefield probably reached as large a public. The principal novelists who achieved fame in these years were Joseph Conrad (1857–1924), Herbert George Wells (1866–1946), Arnold Bennett (1867–1931), and John Galsworthy (1867–1933).

Conrad's position in English literature is unique. He was a Pole, born in the part of Poland held by Russia in the mid-nineteenth century. His education was French, and he could not even speak English until he was in his early twenties. He had an inborn love for the sea, and as a young man joined an English ship and worked his way up until he obtained his master's certificate in 1885. Ten years later his health was so impaired that he had to give

up the sea. He completed a novel on which he had been desultorily working, was surprised to find a publisher for it, and found at the same time that he had a new profession. The novel was *Almayer's Folly* (1895). It was followed by a long succession of books, mostly sea tales, including *The Nigger of the Narcissus* (1897), *Lord Jim* (1900), *Typhoon* (1903), *Nostromo* (1904), *The Secret Agent* (1907), *Under Western Eyes* (1911), *Victory* (1915), and *The Arrow of Gold* (1919).

Conrad thought of himself as a pure artist, aiming only at perfection of form and fidelity in portraiture. He loved methods of indirection, which seemed to him true to the inconclusiveness and indefiniteness of our knowledge of human beings, and which helped to emphasize his sense of the mystery of life. At the same time he was interested, not in action for its own sake, but in traits of character, in states of emotion, and especially in the tortuous ways in which impressions alter men. He was much preoccupied with misery; he felt that men's lives are formed, and often malformed, by forces which we cannot control and do not even understand; and consequently he was deeply and darkly pessimistic.

H. G. Wells, like Dickens, made his own way up from the lower middle class. As a youth he was apprenticed to a druggist, and later became a clerk in a dry-goods shop, but he contrived to attend classes in the University of London and to enter journalism. He is the great literary representative of all those in recent times who have been thrilled by the progress of science and of invention, and have fancied there is nothing that man cannot accomplish by setting his mind to it. At the beginning of his career he experimented with and helped to develop science fiction as a form, describing the end of the earth (*The Time Machine*, 1895), an invasion from Mars (*The War of the Worlds*, 1898), and other fantastic events. In these books he showed unusual creative power, great vigor, and remarkable originality. From them he went on to depict real people in the contemporary world, with equal vigor, a keen eye for comedy, and much feeling. His novels include *Tono-Bungay* (1909), *The History of Mr. Polly* (1910), *The New Machiavelli* (1911), and *Mr. Britling Sees It Through* (1916).

Arnold Bennett during most of his life, while strongly influenced by the French naturalists— the de Goncourts, Zola, and de Maupassant— felt that a flawless technique and a "courageous facing of the truth" were essential to the novelist. "What was not precise, factual and contemporary," said Henry James, "could not enter into his consciousness." In his later years, on the other hand, he openly admired Dickens, whose work had influenced his own *Buried Alive* (1908) and *Riceyman Steps* (1923). His other most famous works are *The Old Wives' Tale* (1908), and the three novels of his trilogy, *Clayhanger* (1910), *Hilda Lessways* (1911), and *These Twain* (1916).

John Galsworthy's general theme is the disintegration of English society, and the powerlessness of the individual to stay a process which is really a failure of energy, of grasp, of constructive imagination, of will, of moral passion; and which has a startling resemblance to the decay of old age, the approach of death. His most important and impressive work is comprised in *The Forsyte Saga* (1922), a series of three novels, of which the earliest is *The Man of Property* (1906). The *Saga* was continued in *A Modern Comedy* (1929) and *End of the Chapter* (1934), each made up of three novels. In these novels he recounts the history

of a family in its several branches from 1886 to 1932, against the background of England's passage from mid-Victorian stability and prosperity to the perplexities, unsettlement, divisions, and decline of the years after the first World War.

Three other writers of the period, perhaps best known for essays and for unusual works partaking of their highly individual personalities, are generally thought of as part of the Wells-Bennett-Galsworthy generation. Sir Max Beerbohm (1872–1956) drew cartoons and caricatures, and wrote essays and the novel *Zuleika Dobson* (1911), a satiric but humorous *tour de force* about a girl and her conquest of Oxford University undergraduates. Hilaire Belloc (1870–1953) wrote essays, criticism, and penetrating social and economic studies that are at the same time highly literary (*The Road*, 1924, is an example). G. K. Chesterton (1894–1936) wrote religious, literary and biographical studies, a highly readable autobiography and the extremely popular Father Brown detective stories.

# Thomas Carlyle

## 1795 - 1881

Carlyle was born at Ecclefechan, Dumfries-shire, Scotland, on 4 December, 1795. His father was a stone-mason and a man of highly unusual character. "More remarkable man than my father," the son wrote, "I have never met in my journey through life; sterling sincerity in thought, word, and deed, most quiet, but capable of blazing into whirlwinds when needful, and such a flash of just insight and natural eloquence and emphasis, true to every feature of it, as I have never known in any other. . . . None of us will ever forget that bold, glowing style of his, flowing free from the untutored soul, full of metaphor, though he knew not what metaphor was, with all manner of potent words which he appropriated and applied with surprising accuracy." This characterization of his father helps us to see how Carlyle came to be the man he was, for sincerity was the touch-stone by which the son later tried the world's great men, and the son's burning yet strug-gling utterance was clearly the development of a heritage. As a boy Carlyle received his first training in the village of his birth, and there showed such mental aptitude that his parents sent him to the Annan Grammar School in 1805. As he continued to show parts above the usual, his parents hoped that he might qualify himself for the ministry of the Scottish Kirk, and so in the fall of 1809 he walked the eighty miles from Ecclefechan to Edinburgh to enter the University. There he continued, as at An-nan, to read widely, but with little or no guidance; he later called Edinburgh "the worst of all hitherto discovered universities," which means, as has been said, that he found no Fichte there to pierce the deep springs of idealism in his nature. Full self-discovery was only to come later, after painful enough wan-derings. In 1814 he left the University and be-came the mathematical teacher at Annan Grammar School. Two years later he was ap-pointed master of a school in Kirkcaldy, a posi-tion which he held until the fall of 1818.

Meanwhile doubts had been growing in him about entrance into the ministry, and he had finally determined in 1817 that he could not do it—a decision severely disappointing to his parents but one which they accepted without remonstrance. After leaving Kirkcaldy Carlyle spent some time in Edinburgh, doing some writ-ing and attempting to study the law; but the law too he found impossible as a career. And while he was thus uncertain about his future he was suffering physical anguish from dys-pepsia, a curse which never left him, and spiritual anguish from the confused state of his beliefs. Unable to accept the simple Christianity of his mother, or any miracu-lously revealed religion, he yet reacted against the "mechanical philosophy" of the eighteenth century. He accepted the destructive work of Hume and Gibbon, whom he had been reading, but not their explicit or implied con-structions—yet he knew of nothing with which to fill the void. It was at this juncture that he began the study of German, and presently found answers to his questions in the works of the transcendentalists, particularly in Jean Paul Richter and Fichte. In 1822 he began doing some writing for periodicals about his German discoveries, and from that year until 1824 he held a position as tutor in the Buller family. Meanwhile in 1821 he had met Jane Baillie Welsh, a brilliant girl to whom he was deeply attracted and whom he later married in 1826.

By this time Carlyle was definitely com-mitted to literature as a career. He and his wife lived in Edinburgh until 1828, when they moved to Craigenputtock, a farm-house in Dumfriesshire, fifteen miles from anywhere. The loneliness of the place was disagreeable to Mrs. Carlyle; but the two lived there for six years, save for visits to London—when Carlyle became acquainted with John Stuart Mill and other men of letters—and to Edinburgh. Dur-ing the earlier years of this period Carlyle fairly found himself, and managed to express in *Sartor Resartus* the chief ideas on which his later writings depended. In 1834 he moved to London and took the house in Cheyne Row, Chelsea, in which he lived throughout the remainder of his life. He was now at work upon his history of *The French Revolution*. Composition was always extraordinarily difficult for him, and while work was in progress he lived in anguish and despair. Mrs. Carlyle spoke, when a later work was being written, about living in "the valley of the shadow of Cromwell." But, as if this were not enough, when the first volume of *The French Revolution* was finished Carlyle suffered an additional grievous blow. He lent the manuscript of the volume to J. S. Mill, who lent it to Mrs. Taylor, whose maid burned it up. Carlyle had no notes, he was shattered by the pains the volume had cost him, he was hoping in despair only somehow to get the work done, whether it should be good or bad, and he was writing, besides, against time, as he had practically no money and was staking everything on this book. All that was fine in his nature, however, appeared in the gentleness with which he treated Mill; and, after several months of ineffectual effort, he heroically set to work and rewrote his volume. In January, 1837, the work was finished, and was published that year. Carlyle said to his wife, "I know not whether this book is worth anything, nor what the world will do with it, or misdo, or entirely forbear to do, as is likeliest; but this I could tell the world: You have not had for a hundred years any book that comes more direct and flamingly from the heart of a living man. Do what you like with it, you." The world bought, and read, and praised, and Carlyle's position as a writer was secure from this time. In the years from 1837 to 1840 he delivered several courses of lectures in London, one of which, *On Heroes, Hero-Worship, and the Heroic in History*, has been probably his most widely read book. During these years, he was also occupied in applying his ideas to contemporary political and social questions. He published *Chartism* in 1840 and *Past and Present* in 1843. In 1845 he published *Oliver Cromwell's Letters and Speeches*, in 1850 the *Latter-Day Pamphlets*, and in 1851 *The Life of John Sterling*. (Sterling was a disciple of Coleridge and a man of singularly winning personality who, before his untimely death, had attracted the interest and friendship of Carlyle.) From 1851 until 1865 he was at work upon his *History of Frederick the Great*, which was published in six volumes, 1858-

1865. In the latter year he was elected Lord Rector of Edinburgh University, where he delivered his inaugural address in April, 1866, less than three weeks before the sudden death of Mrs. Carlyle. His marriage had been, as is now known, one in name only; the domestic scene had often been stormy; and Mrs. Carlyle's death awoke in her husband bitter remorse for the wrongs which he began to feel he had done her. The remaining years of his life were full of honors from the outer world, full of sadness welling up from the world within. He died on 5 February, 1881, and was buried at Ecclefechan.

*Sartor Resartus* is the most fully expressive of Carlyle's writings, and it contains all the ideas which he variously developed in his other works. They are not many. "Belief in human freedom and in the 'infinite nature of Duty,' as the basis of religion; belief in the rule of the few wise and strong over the many weak and foolish, as the basis of government; belief in mutual sympathy, as the basis of society; belief in a spiritual interpretation of natural appearances, as the basis of philosophy; and, above all, belief in sincerity as the condition of all knowledge—these are the foundations upon which Carlyle built, and they will all be found well and truly laid in Sartor" (P. C. Parr, Introd. to Sartor, *p. v.*).

Carlyle's *Works* have been published in many editions; perhaps the best is the "Centenary Edition," ed. H. D. Traill (31 vols., London, 1897-1901). A good text of *Sartor Resartus* has been edited with an informative introduction and notes by Charles F. Harrold (New York, 1937). A convenient single volume is Carlyle, *Selected Works, Reminiscences and Letters*, edited by Julian Symons (Cambridge, U.S.A., 1957). James Anthony Froude's *Thomas Carlyle* (London, 1882-1884) is inaccurate in detail but illuminating and a classic. David A. Wilson has written the fullest of more recent accounts, *The Life of Carlyle* (London, 1923-1934). For a general interpretation L. Cazamian's *Carlyle*, trans. E. K. Brown (New York, 1932), and Emory Neff's *Carlyle* (New York, 1932), may be recommended. Julian Symons's *Carlyle: the Life and Ideas of a Prophet* (London, 1952) combines biographical and critical approaches. Valuable studies of special aspects of Carlyle are: Frederick W. Roe, *The Social Philosophy of Carlyle and Ruskin* (New York, 1921); Charles F. Harrold, *Carlyle and German Thought: 1819-1834* (New Haven, 1934); and G. J. Calder, *The Writing of Past and*

*Present:* a Study of Carlyle's Manuscripts (*New Haven,* 1949).

## Sartor Resartus [1]

### BOOK II

#### CHAPTER VII

#### *The Everlasting No*

Under the strange nebulous envelopment, wherein our Professor has now shrouded himself, no doubt but his spiritual nature is nevertheless progressive, and growing: for how can the "Son of Time," in any case, stand still? We behold him, through those dim years, in a state of crisis, of transition: his mad Pilgrimings, and general solution into aimless Discontinuity, what is all this but a mad Fermentation; wherefrom, the fiercer it is, the clearer product will one day evolve itself?

Such transitions are ever full of pain: thus the Eagle when he molts is sickly; and, to attain his new beak, must harshly dash-off the old one upon rocks. What Stoicism soever our Wanderer, in his individual acts and motions, may affect, it is clear that there is a hot fever of anarchy and misery raging within; coruscations of which flash out: as, indeed, how could there be other? Have we not seen him disappointed, bemocked of Destiny, through long years? All that the young heart might desire and pray for has been denied; nay, as in the last worst instance, offered and then snatched away. Ever an "excellent Passivity"; but of useful, reasonable Activity, essential to the former as Food to Hunger, nothing granted: till at length, in this wild Pilgrimage, he must forcibly seize for himself an Activity, though useless, unreasonable. Alas, his cup of bitterness, which had been filling drop by drop, ever since that first "ruddy morning" in the Hinterschlag Gymnasium,[2] was at the very lip; and then with that poisondrop, of the Towgood-and-Blumine business,[3] it runs over, and even hisses over in a deluge of foam.

[1] First written in the fall of 1830; then revised and enlarged in the months from February until August, 1831. Printed in *Fraser's Magazine,* 1833–1834. First published as a book in America (Boston), 1836; first English edition, 1838. The title means, "the tailor patched." Diogenes Teufelsdröckh, author of the philosophy of clothes, is the tailor; Carlyle does the patching as his editor.

[2] The Smite-behind Grammar-School. Teufelsdröckh had seen a little dog, to whose tail the boys had tied a tin kettle, rush by on that morning, a symbol of what he himself was to suffer at the school.

[3] Towgood was a worldly young English friend

He himself says once, with more justice than originality: "Man is, properly speaking, based upon Hope, he has no other possession but Hope; this world of his is emphatically the 'Place of Hope.'" What, then, was our Professor's possession? We see him, for the present, quite shut-out from Hope; looking not into the golden orient, but vaguely all round into a dim copper firmament, pregnant with earthquake and tornado.

Alas, shut-out from Hope, in a deeper sense than we yet dream of! For, as he wanders wearisomely through this world, he has now lost all tidings of another and higher. Full of religion, or at least of religiosity, as our Friend has since exhibited himself, he hides not that, in those days, he was wholly irreligious: "Doubt had darkened into Unbelief," says he; "shade after shade goes grimly over your soul, till you have the fixed, starless, Tartarean black."[4] To such readers as have reflected, what can be called reflecting, on man's life, and happily discovered, in contradiction to much Profit-and-Loss Philosophy, speculative and practical, that Soul is *not* synonymous with Stomach; who understand, therefore, in our Friend's words, "that, for man's well-being, Faith is properly the one thing needful; how, with it, Martyrs, otherwise weak, can cheerfully endure the shame and the cross; and without it, Worldlings puke-up their sick existence, by suicide, in the midst of luxury": to such it will be clear that, for a pure moral nature, the loss of his religious Belief was the loss of everything. Unhappy young man! All wounds, the crush of long-continued Destitution, the stab of false Friendship and of false Love, all wounds in thy so genial heart, would have healed again, had not its life-warmth been withdrawn. Well might he exclaim, in his wild way: "Is there no God, then; but at best an absentee God, sitting idle, ever since the first Sabbath, at the outside of his Universe, and *seeing* it go? Has the word Duty no meaning; is what we call Duty no divine Messenger and Guide, but a false earthly Phantasm, made-up of Desire and Fear, of emanations from the Gallows and from Doctor Graham's Celestial-Bed?[5] Happiness of an approving Conscience! Did not Paul of Tarsus, whom admiring men have since

of Teufelsdröckh, who married Blumine, the young lady whom Teufelsdröckh loved.

[4] Gloomy as Tartarus, the inner region of Hell.

[5] An elaborate bed supposed to cure sterility in married people, invented by the notorious quack doctor, James Graham (1745–94).

named Saint, feel that *he* was 'the chief of sinners'; [6] and Nero of Rome, jocund in spirit (*wohlgemuth*), spend much of his time in fiddling? Foolish Wordmonger and Motive-grinder,[7] who in thy Logic-mill hast an earthly mechanism for the Godlike itself, and wouldst fain grind me out Virtue from the husks of Pleasure,—I tell thee, Nay! To the unregenerate Prometheus Vinctus [8] of a man, it is ever the bitterest aggravation of his wretchedness that he is conscious of Virtue, that he feels himself the victim not of suffering only, but of injustice. What then? Is the heroic inspiration we name Virtue but some Passion; some bubble of the blood, bubbling in the direction others *profit* by? I know not: only this I know, If what thou namest Happiness be our true aim, then are we all astray. With Stupidity and sound Digestion man may front much. But what, in these dull unimaginative days, are the terrors of Conscience to the diseases of the Liver! Not on Morality, but on Cookery, let us build our stronghold: there brandishing our frying-pan, as censer, let us offer sweet incense to the Devil, and live at ease on the fat things *he* has provided for his Elect!"

Thus has the bewildered Wanderer to stand, as so many have done, shouting question after question into the Sibyl-cave of Destiny, and receive no Answer but an Echo. It is all a grim Desert, this once-fair world of his; wherein is heard only the howling of wild-beasts, or the shrieks of despairing, hate-filled men; and no Pillar of Cloud by day, and no Pillar of Fire by night,[9] any longer guides the Pilgrim. To such length has the spirit of Inquiry carried him. "But what boots it (*was thut's*)?" cries he: "it is but the common lot in this era. Not having come to spiritual majority prior to the *Siècle de Louis Quinze*,[10] and not being born purely a Loghead (*Dummkopf*), thou hadst no other outlook. The whole world is, like thee, sold to Unbelief; their old Temples of the Godhead, which for long have not been rainproof, crumble down; and men ask now: where is the Godhead; our eyes never saw him?"

Pitiful enough were it, for all these wild utterances, to call our Diogenes wicked. Unprofitable servants as we all are, perhaps at no era of his life was he more decisively the Servant of Goodness, the Servant of God, than even now when doubting God's existence. "One circumstance I note," says he: "after all the nameless woe that Inquiry, which for me, what it is not always, was genuine Love of Truth, had wrought me, I nevertheless still loved Truth, and would bate no jot of my allegiance to her. 'Truth!' I cried, 'though the Heavens crush me for following her: no Falsehood! though a whole celestial Lubberland were the price of Apostasy." In conduct it was the same. Had a divine Messenger from the clouds, or miraculous Handwriting on the wall, convincingly proclaimed to me *This thou shalt do*, with what passionate readiness, as I often thought, would I have done it, had it been leaping into the infernal Fire. Thus, in spite of all Motive-grinders, and Mechanical Profit-and-Loss Philosophies, with the sick ophthalmia and hallucination they had brought on, was the Infinite nature of Duty [11] still dimly present to me: living without God in the world, of God's light I was not utterly bereft; if my as yet sealed eyes, with their unspeakable longing, could nowhere see Him, nevertheless in in my heart He was present, and His heaven-written Law still stood legible and sacred there."

Meanwhile, under all these tribulations, and temporal and spiritual destitutions, what must the Wanderer, in his silent soul, have endured! "The painfullest feeling," writes he, "is that of your own Feebleness (*Unkraft*); ever, as the English Milton says, to be weak is the true misery.[12] And yet of your Strength there is and can be no clear feeling, save by what you have prospered in, by what you have done. Between vague wavering Capability and fixed indubitable Performance, what a difference! A certain inarticulate Self-consciousness dwells dimly in us; which only our Works can render articulate and decisively discernible. Our Works are the mirror wherein the spirit first sees its natural lineaments. Hence, too, the folly of that impossible Precept, *Know thy-*

---

[6] I Timothy, 1:15.

[7] An allusion to utilitarian philosophers like Jeremy Bentham (1748-1832), who believed that pleasure was the proper reward for virtue.

[8] Prometheus Bound, the title of Aeschylus's drama, representing the conflict of audacious genius with Fate.

[9] Cf. Exodus, 13:21.

[10] The age of Louis XV; i. e., the Age of Reason.

[11] That is, that duty is to be performed, not from considerations of reward and punishment—from space-time considerations—but from a conviction of the non-temporal, non-spatial (or absolute) good in performing it; also that the results of duty performed or neglected go on through endless time and infinite space (Charles F. Harrold).

[12] *Paradise Lost*, I, 157.

self; [13] till it be translated into this partially possible one, *Know what thou canst work at.*

"But for me, so strangely unprosperous had I been, the net-result of my Workings amounted as yet simply to—Nothing. How then could I believe in my Strength, when there was as yet no mirror to see it in? Ever did this agitating, yet, as I now perceive, quite frivolous question, remain to me insolu- 10 ble: Hast thou a certain Faculty, a certain Worth, such even as the most have not; or art thou the completest Dullard of these mod- ern times? Alas, the fearful Unbelief is un- belief in yourself; and how could I believe? Had not my first, last Faith in myself, when even to me the Heavens seemed laid open, and I dared to love, been all-too cruelly belied? The speculative Mystery of Life grew ever more mysterious to me: neither in the practi- cal Mystery had I made the slightest progress, 20 but been everywhere buffeted, foiled, and con- temptuously cast out. A feeble unit in the mid- dle of a threatening Infinitude, I seemed to have nothing given me but eyes, whereby to discern my own wretchedness. Invisible yet impenetrable walls, as of Enchantment, divided me from all living: was there, in the wide world, any true bosom I could press trustfully to mine? O Heaven, No, there was none! I kept a lock upon my lips: why should I speak 30 much with that shifting variety of so-called Friends, in whose withered, vain and too- hungry souls Friendship was but an incredi- ble tradition? In such cases, your resource is to talk little, and that little mostly from the Newspapers. Now when I look back, it was a strange isolation I then lived in. The men and women around me, even speaking with me, were but Figures; I had, practically, forgotten that they were alive, that they were not merely 40 automatic. In the midst of their crowded streets and assemblages, I walked solitary; and (except as it was my own heart, not another's, that I kept devouring) savage also, as the tiger in his jungle. Some comfort it would have been, could I, like a Faust, have fancied my- self tempted and tormented of the Devil; for a Hell, as I imagine, without Life, though only diabolic Life, were more frightful: but in our age of Down-pulling and Disbelief, the 50 very Devil has been pulled down, you cannot so much as believe in a Devil. To me the Universe was all void of Life, of Purpose, of Volition, even of Hostility: it was one huge,

dead, immeasurable Steam-engine, rolling on, in its dead indifference, to grind me limb from limb. O, the vast, gloomy, solitary Golgotha, and Mill of Death! Why was the Living ban- ished thither companionless, conscious? Why, if there is no Devil; nay, unless the Devil is your God?"

A prey incessantly to such corrosions, might not, moreover, as the worst aggravation to them, the iron constitution even of a Teufelsdröckh threaten to fail? We conjecture that he has known sickness; and, in spite of his loco- motive habits, perhaps sickness of the chronic sort. Hear this, for example: "How beautiful to die of broken-heart, on Paper! Quite another thing in practice; every window of your Feel- ing, even of your Intellect, as it were, begrimed and mud-bespattered, so that no pure ray can enter; a whole Drugshop in your inwards; the fordone soul drowning slowly in quagmires of Disgust!"

Putting all which external and internal miseries together, may we not find in the fol- lowing sentences, quite in our Professor's still vein, significance enough? "From Suicide a certain aftershine (*Nachschein*) of Christi- anity withheld me: perhaps also a certain in- dolence of character; for, was not that a remedy I had at any time within reach? Often, how- ever, was there a question present to me: Should some one now, at the turning of that corner, blow thee suddenly out of Space, into the other World, or other No-world, by pistol- shot,—how were it? On which ground, too, I often, in sea-storms and sieged cities and other death-scenes, exhibited an imperturba- bility, which passed, falsely enough, for cour- age."

"So had it lasted," concludes the Wan- derer, "so had it lasted, as in bitter protracted Death-agony, through long years. The heart within me, unvisited by any heavenly dew- drop was smoldering in sulphurous, slow-con- suming fire. Almost since earliest memory I had shed no tear; or once only when I, mur- muring half-audibly, recited Faust's Death- song, that wild *Selig der den er im Siegesglanze findet* (Happy whom *he* finds in Battle's splendor),[14] and thought that of this last Friend even I was not forsaken, that Destiny itself could not doom me not to die. Having no hope, neither had I any definite fear, were it of Man or of Devil: nay, I often felt as if it might be solacing, could the Arch-Devil him- self, though in Tartarean terrors, but rise to

---

[13] A maxim attributed to Solon, Socrates, Thales, etc.; inscribed over the portico of the temple at Delphi.

[14] Adapted from Goethe's *Faust*, I, iv, 1573–1576.

me, that I might tell him a little of my mind. And yet, strangely enough, I lived in a continual, indefinite, pining fear; tremulous, pusillanimous, apprehensive of I knew not what; it seemed as if all things in the Heavens above and the Earth beneath would hurt me; as if the Heavens and the Earth were but boundless jaws of a devouring monster, wherein I, palpitating, waited to be devoured.

"Full of such humor, and perhaps the miserablest man in the whole French Capital or Suburbs, was I, one sultry Dog-day, after much perambulation, toiling along the dirty little *Rue Saint-Thomas de l'Enfer*,[15] among civic rubbish enough, in a close atmosphere, and over pavements hot as Nebuchadnezzar's Furnace;[16] whereby doubtless my spirits were little cheered; when, all at once, there rose a Thought in me, and I asked myself: 'What *art* thou afraid of? Wherefore, like a coward, dost thou forever pip and whimper, and go cowering and trembling? Despicable biped! what is the sum-total of the worst that lies before thee? Death? Well, Death; and say the pangs of Tophet too, and all that the Devil and Man may, will or can do against thee! Hast thou not a heart; canst thou not suffer whatsoever it be; and, as a Child of Freedom, though outcast, trample Tophet itself under thy feet, while it consumes thee? Let it come, then; I will meet it and defy it!' And as I so thought, there rushed like a stream of fire over my whole soul; and I shook base Fear away from me forever. I was strong, of unknown strength; a spirit, almost a god. Ever from that time, the temper of my misery was changed: not Fear or whining Sorrow was it, but Indignation and grim fire-eyed Defiance.

"Thus had the EVERLASTING No (*das ewige Nein*) pealed authoritatively through all the recesses of my Being, of my ME; and then was it that my whole ME stood up, in native God-created majesty, and with emphasis recorded its Protest. Such a Protest, the most important transaction in Life, may that same Indignation and Defiance, in a psychological point of view, be fitly called. The Everlasting No had said: 'Behold, thou art fatherless, outcast, and the Universe is mine (the Devil's)'; to which my whole Me now made answer: 'I am not thine, but Free, and forever hate thee!'

"It is from this hour that I incline to date my Spiritual Newbirth, or Baphometic Fire-

baptism;[17] perhaps I directly thereupon began to be a Man."

## CHAPTER VIII
### *Center of Indifference*

Though, after this "Baphometic Firebaptism" of his, our Wanderer signifies that his Unrest was but increased; as, indeed, "Indignation and Defiance," especially against things in general, are not the most peaceable inmates; yet can the Psychologist surmise that it was no longer a quite hopeless Unrest; that henceforth it had at least a fixed center to revolve round. For the fire-baptized soul, long so scathed and thunder-riven, here feels its own Freedom, which feeling is its Baphometic Baptism: the citadel of its whole kingdom it has thus gained by assault, and will keep inexpugnable; outwards from which the remaining dominions, not indeed without hard battling, will doubtless by degrees be conquered and pacificated. Under another figure, we might say, if in that great moment, in the *Rue Saint-Thomas de l'Enfer*, the old inward Satanic School[1] was not yet thrown out of doors, it received peremptory judicial notice to quit;—whereby, for the rest, its howl-chantings, Ernulphus-cursings,[2] and rebellious gnashings of teeth, might, in the meanwhile, become only the more tumultuous, and difficult to keep secret.

Accordingly, if we scrutinize these Pilgrimings well, there is perhaps discernible henceforth a certain incipient method in their madness. Not wholly as a Specter does Teufelsdröckh now storm through the world; at worst as a specter-fighting Man, nay who will one day be a Specter-queller. If pilgriming restlessly to so many "Saints' Wells,"[3] and ever without quenching of his thirst, he nevertheless finds little secular wells, whereby from time to time some alleviation is ministered. In a word, he is now, if not ceasing, yet intermitting to "eat his own heart"; and clutches round him out-

---

[17] A baptism of sudden, flame-like spiritual understanding (from Baffometus, an outcast who will receive such a baptism, in the novel of Zacharias Werner, *Die Söhne des Thals*; Baphomet was originally the name of an idol).

[1] I. e., the psychological equivalent of the so-called Satanic School of English poetry: Byron, Shelley, and their followers.

[2] Ernulf was a medieval bishop of Rochester, whose curse is given in Sterne's *Tristram Shandy*, III, chapter xi.

[3] Wells dedicated to saints, whose patronage was supposed to give medicinal properties to the water.

---

[15] St. Thomas-of-Hell Street. Carlyle admitted that he himself had had Teufelsdröckh's experience, in Leith Walk, Edinburgh.

[16] Daniel, 3:19.

wardly on the NOT-ME for wholesomer food. Does not the following glimpse exhibit him in a much more natural state?

"Towns also and Cities, especially the ancient, I failed not to look upon with interest. How beautiful to see thereby, as through a long vista, into the remote Time; to have, as it were, an actual section of almost the earliest Past brought safe into the Present, and set before your eyes! There, in that old City, was a live 10 ember of Culinary Fire put down, say only two-thousand years ago; and there, burning more or less triumphantly, with such fuel as the region yielded, it has burnt, and still burns, and thou thyself seest the very smoke thereof. Ah! and the far more mysterious live ember of Vital Fire was then also put down there; and still miraculously burns and spreads; and the smoke and ashes thereof (in these Judgment-Halls and Churchyards), and its bellows- 20 engines (in these Churches), thou still seest; and its flame, looking out from every kind countenance, and every hateful one, still warms thee or scorches thee.

"Of Man's Activity and Attainment the chief results are aeriform, mystic, and preserved in Tradition only: such are his Forms of Government, with the Authority they rest on; his Customs, or Fashions both of Cloth-habits and of Soul-habits; much more his 30 collective stock of Handicrafts, the whole Faculty he has acquired of manipulating Nature: all these things, as indispensable and priceless as they are, cannot in any way be fixed under lock and key, but must flit, spirit-like, on impalpable vehicles, from Father to Son; if you demand sight of them, they are nowhere to be met with. Visible Plowmen and Hammermen there have been, ever from Cain and Tubalcain[4] downwards; but where does 40 your accumulated Agricultural, Metallurgic, and other Manufacturing SKILL lie ware-housed? It transmits itself on the atmospheric air, on the sun's rays (by Hearing and by Vision); it is a thing aeriform, impalpable, of quite spiritual sort. In like manner, ask me not, Where are the LAWS; where is the GOV-ERNMENT? In vain wilt thou go to Schönbrunn, to Downing Street, to the Palais Bourbon:[5] thou findest nothing there but brick or stone 50

houses, and some bundles of Papers tied with tape. Where, then, is that same cunningly-devised almighty GOVERNMENT of theirs to be laid hands on? Everywhere, yet nowhere: seen only in its works, this too is a thing aeriform, invisible; or if you will, mystic and miraculous. So spiritual (*geistig*) is our whole daily Life: all that we do springs out of Mystery, Spirit, invisible Force; only like a little Cloud-image, or Armida's Palace,[6] air-built, does the Actual body itself forth from the great mystic Deep.

"Visible and tangible products of the Past, again, I reckon-up to the extent of three. Cities, with their Cabinets and Arsenals; then tilled Fields, to either or to both of which divisions Roads with their Bridges, may belong; and thirdly—Books. In which third truly, the last invented, lies a worth far surpassing that of the two others. Wondrous indeed is the virtue of a true Book. Not like a dead city of stones, yearly crumbling, yearly needing repair; more like a tilled field, but then a spiritual field: like a spiritual tree, let me rather say, it stands from year to year, and from age to age (we have Books that already number some hundred-and-fifty human ages); and yearly comes its new produce of leaves (Commentaries, Deductions, Philosophical, Political Systems; or were it only Sermons, Pamphlets, Journalistic Essays), every one of which is talismanic and thaumaturgic, for it can persuade men. O thou art able to write a Book, which once in the two centuries or oftener there is a man gifted to do, envy not him whom they name City-builder, and inexpressibly pity him whom they name Conqueror or City-burner! Thou too art a Conqueror and Victor; but of the true sort, namely over the Devil: thou too hast built what will outlast all marble and metal, and be a wonder-bringing City of the Mind, a Temple and Seminary and Prophetic Mount, whereto all kindreds of the Earth will pilgrim. —Fool! why journeyest thou wearisomely, in thy antiquarian fervor, to gaze on the stone pyramids of Geeza, or the clay ones of Sacchara?[7] These stand there, as I can tell thee, idle and inert, looking over the Desert, foolishly enough, for the last three-thousand years: but canst thou not open thy Hebrew BIBLE, then, or even Luther's Version[8] thereof?"

---

[4] See Genesis, 4:1–22.
[5] Respectively, to the palace in Vienna where many early nineteenth-century treaties were signed, to the residence of the English Prime Minister in London, and to the building in Paris where the French Chamber of Deputies met.

[6] The palace of an enchantress in Tasso's *Jerusalem Delivered*.
[7] The Pyramids of Ghizeh and Sakkara, near Cairo in Egypt.
[8] Luther's German translation of the Bible (1534–1535).

No less satisfactory is his sudden appearance not in Battle, yet on some Battle-field; which, we soon gather, must be that of Wagram; so that here, for once, is a certain approximation to distinctiveness of date. Omitting much, let us impart what follows:

"Horrible enough! A whole Marchfeld [9] strewed with shell-splinters, cannon-shot, ruined tumbrels, and dead men and horses; stragglers still remaining not so much as buried. And those red mold heaps: ay, there lie the Shells of Men, out of which all the Life and Virtue has been blown; and now are they swept together, and crammed-down out of sight, like blown Egg-shells!—Did Nature, when she bade the Donau bring down his mold-cargoes from the Carinthian and Carpathian Heights, and spread them out here into the softest, richest level,—intend thee, O Marchfeld, for a corn-bearing Nursery, whereon her children might be nursed; or for a Cockpit, wherein they might the more commodiously be throttled and tattered? Were thy three broad Highways, meeting here from the ends of Europe, made for Ammunition-wagons, then? Were thy Wagrams and Stillfrieds but so many ready-built Casemates,[10] wherein the house of Hapsburg might batter with artillery, and with artillery be battered? König Ottokar, amid yonder hillocks, dies under Rodolf's truncheon; here Kaiser Franz falls a-swoon under Napoleon's: within which five centuries, to omit the others, how has thy breast, fair Plain, been defaced and defiled! The greensward is torn-up and trampled-down; man's fond care of it, his fruit-trees, hedge-rows, and pleasant dwellings, blown away with gunpowder; and the kind seedfield lies a desolate, hideous Place of Sculls.—Nevertheless, Nature is at work; neither shall these Powder-Devilkins with their utmost devilry gainsay her: but all that gore and carnage will be shrouded-in, absorbed into manure; and next year the Marchfeld will be green, nay greener. Thrifty unwearied Nature, ever out of our great waste educing some little profit of thy own,—how dost thou, from the very carcass of the Killer, bring Life for the Living!

"What, speaking in quite unofficial language, is the net-purport and upshot of war? To my own knowledge, for example, there dwell and toil, in the British village of Dumdrudge,[11] usually some five-hundred souls. From these, by certain 'Natural Enemies' of the French, there are successively selected, during the French war, say thirty able-bodied men: Dumdrudge, at her own expense, has suckled and nursed them: she has, not without difficulty and sorrow, fed them up to manhood, and even trained them to crafts, so that one can weave, another build, another hammer, and the weakest can stand under thirty stone avoirdupois. Nevertheless, amid much weeping and swearing, they are selected; all dressed in red; and shipped away, at the public charges, some two-thousand miles, or say only to the south of Spain; [12] and fed there till wanted. And now to that same spot, in the south of Spain, are thirty similar French artisans, from a French Dumdrudge, in like manner wending: till at length, after infinite effort, the two parties come into actual juxtaposition; and Thirty stands fronting Thirty, each with a gun in his hand. Straightway the word 'Fire!' is given: and they blow the souls out of one another; and in place of sixty brisk useful craftsmen, the world has sixty dead carcasses, which it must bury, and anew shed tears for. Had these men any quarrel? Busy as the Devil is, not the smallest! They lived far enough apart; were the entirest strangers; nay, in so wide a Universe, there was even, unconsciously, by Commerce, some mutual helpfulness between them. How then? Simpleton! their Governors had fallen-out; and, instead of shooting one another, had the cunning to make these poor blockheads shoot.—Alas, so is it in Deutschland, and hitherto in all other lands; still as of old, 'what devilry soever Kings do, the Greeks must pay the piper!' [13]—In that fiction of the English Smollett,[14] it is true, the final Cessation of War is perhaps prophetically shadowed forth; where the two Natural Enemies, in person, take each a Tobacco-pipe, filled with Brimstone; light the same, and smoke in one another's faces, till the weaker gives in: but from such predicted Peace-Era, what blood-filled trenches, and contentious centuries, may still divide us!"

Thus can the Professor, at least in lucid intervals, look away from his own sorrows, over the many-colored world, and pertinently

[9] A plain near Vienna, north of the Danube (Donau), where Ottokar, King of Bohemia, was slain by Rudolph of Hapsburg in the battle of Stillfried (or Stielfried) in 1278. In 1809, at Wagram in the same plain, Napoleon conquered the Hapsburgs.

[10] Fortress chambers.

[11] Name invented by Carlyle for the typical English village of the time.

[12] To fight in the Peninsular War, 1808–1814.

[13] A free adaptation of Horace, *Epistles*, I, ii, 14.

[14] The Scottish novelist, Tobias Smollett (1721–1771), in *The Adventures of Ferdinand Count Fathom* (chapter xli).

enough note what is passing there. We may remark, indeed, that for the matter of spiritual culture, if for nothing else, perhaps few periods of his life were richer than this. Internally, there is the most momentous instructive Course of Practical Philosophy, with Experiments, going on; towards the right comprehension of which his Peripatetic [15] habits, favorable to Meditation, might help him rather than hinder. Externally, again, as he wanders to and fro, there are, if for the longing heart little substance, yet for the seeing eye sights enough: in these so boundless Travels of his, granting that the Satanic School was even partially kept down, what an incredible knowledge of our Planet, and its Inhabitants and their Works, that is to say, of all knowable things, might not Teufelsdröckh acquire!

"I have read in most Public Libraries," says he, "including those of Constantinople and Samarcand: in most Colleges, except the Chinese Mandarin ones, I have studied, or seen that there was no studying. Unknown Languages have I oftenest gathered from their natural repertory, the Air, by my organ of Hearing; Statistics, Geographics, Topographics came, through the Eye, almost of their own accord. The ways of Man, how he seeks food, and warmth, and protection for himself, in most regions, are ocularly known to me. Like the great Hadrian,[16] I meted-out much of the terraqueous Globe with a pair of Compasses that belonged to myself only.

"Of great Scenes why speak? Three summer days, I lingered reflecting, and even composing (*dichtete*), by the Pine-chasms of Vaucluse;[17] and in that clear Lakelet moistened my bread. I have sat under the Palm-trees of Tadmor;[18] smoked a pipe among the ruins of Babylon. The great Wall of China I have seen; and can testify that it is of gray brick, coped and covered with granite, and shows only second-rate masonry.—Great Events, also, have not I witnessed? Kings sweated-down (*ausgemergelt*) into Berlin-and-Milan Customhouse-Officers; the World well won, and the World well lost; oftener than once a hundred-thousand individuals shot (by each other) in one day. All kin-

dreds and peoples and nations dashed together, and shifted and shoveled into heaps, that they might ferment there, and in time unite. The birth pangs of Democracy,[19] wherewith convulsed Europe was groaning in cries that reached Heaven, could not escape me.

"For great Men I have ever had the warmest predilection; and can perhaps boast that few such in this era have wholly escaped me. Great Men are the inspired (speaking and acting) Texts of that divine BOOK OF REVELATION, whereof a Chapter is completed from epoch to epoch, and by some named HISTORY; to which inspired Texts your numerous talented men, and your innumerable untalented men, are the better or worse exegetic Commentaries, and wagonload of too-stupid, heretical or orthodox, weekly Sermons. For my study, the inspired Texts themselves! Thus did not I, in very early days, having disguised me as tavern-waiter, stand behind the field-chairs, under that shady Tree at Treisnitz [20] by the Jena Highway; waiting upon the great Schiller and greater Goethe; and hearing what I have not forgotten. For——"

——But at this point the Editor recalls his principle of caution, some time ago laid down, and must suppress much. Let not the sacredness of Laureled, still more, of Crowned Heads, be tampered with. Should we, at a future day, find circumstances altered, and the time come for Publication, then may these glimpses into the privacy of the Illustrious be conceded; which for the present were little better than treacherous, perhaps traitorous Eavesdroppings. Of Lord Byron, therefore, of Pope Pius, Emperor Tarakwang,[21] and the "White Waterroses" (Chinese Carbonari [22]) with their mysteries, no notice here! Of Napoleon himself we shall only, glancing from afar, remark that Teufelsdröckh's relation to him seems to have been of very varied character. At first we find our poor Professor on the point of being shot as a spy; then taken into private conversation, even pinched on the ear, yet presented with no money; at last indignantly dismissed, almost thrown out of doors, as an "Ideologist." "He himself," says the Professor, "was among the completest Ideologists, at least Ideopraxists: [23] in the Idea (*in der Idee*) he lived, moved and

---

[15] Itinerant. The followers of Aristotle were known as Peripatetics because his lectures were delivered on the walk.

[16] Emperor Hadrian (76–138) spent most of his reign traveling throughout the Roman Empire. The pair of compasses with which Teufelsdröckh similarly measures the globe are his two legs.

[17] A valley in southern France, famous as the home of Petrarch.

[18] Otherwise known as Palmyra, the City of Palms.

[19] Probably an allusion to the famous Three Days' Revolution in Paris, July 27–29, 1830, in which Charles X was overthrown.

[20] Triesnitz, near Jena in Germany.

[21] Pope Pius VII (Pope from 1800 to 1823) and the Chinese Emperor Tao Kuang (1781–1850).

[22] Secret revolutionaries.

[23] Those who put ideas into practice.

fought. The man was a Divine Missionary, though unconscious of it; and preached, through the cannon's throat, that great doctrine, *La carrière ouverte aux talens* [24] (The Tools to him that can handle them), which is our ultimate Political Evangel, wherein alone can liberty lie. Madly enough he preached, it is true, as Enthusiasts and first Missionaries are wont, with imperfect utterance, amid much frothy rant; yet as articulately perhaps as the case admitted. Or call him, if you will, an American Backwoodsman, who had to fell unpenetrated forests, and battle with innumerable wolves, and did not entirely forbear strong liquor, rioting, and even theft; whom, notwithstanding, the peaceful Sower will follow, and, as he cuts the boundless harvest, bless."

More legitimate and decisively authentic is Teufelsdröckh's appearance and emergence (we know not well whence) in the solitude of the North Cape, on that June Midnight. He has a "light-blue Spanish cloak" hanging round him, as his "most commodious, principal, indeed sole upper-garment"; and stands there, on the World-promontory, looking over the infinite Brine, like a little blue Belfry (as we figure), now motionless indeed, yet ready, if stirred, to ring quaintest changes.

"Silence as of death," writes he; "for Midnight, even in the Arctic latitudes, has its character: nothing but the granite cliffs ruddy-tinged, the peaceable gurgle of that slow-heaving Polar Ocean, over which in the utmost North the great Sun hangs low and lazy, as if he too were slumbering. Yet is his cloud-couch wrought of crimson and cloth-of-gold; yet does his light stream over the mirror of waters, like a tremulous fire-pillar, shooting downwards to the abyss, and hide itself under my feet. In such moments, Solitude also is invaluable; for who would speak, or be looked on, when behind him lies all Europe and Africa, fast asleep, except the watchmen; and before him the silent Immensity, and Palace of the Eternal, whereof our Sun is but a porch-lamp?

"Nevertheless, in this solemn moment comes a man, or monster, scrambling from among the rock-hollows; and, shaggy, huge as the Hyperborean [25] Bear, hails me in Russian speech: most probably, therefore, a Russian Smuggler. With courteous brevity, I signify my indifference to contraband trade, my humane intentions, yet strong wish to be private. In vain: the monster, counting doubtless on his superior stature, and minded to make sport for himself, or perhaps profit, were it with murder, continues to advance; ever assailing me with his importunate train-oil [26] breath; and now has advanced, till we stand both on the verge of the rock, the deep Sea rippling greedily down below. What argument will avail? On the thick Hyperborean, cherubic reasoning, seraphic eloquence were lost. Prepared for such extremity, I, deftly enough, whisk aside one step; draw out, from my interior reservoirs, a sufficient Birmingham Horse-pistol, and say, 'Be so obliging as retire, Friend (*Er ziehe sich zurück, Freund*), and with promptitude!' This logic even the Hyperborean understands: fast enough, with apologetic, petitionary growl, he sidles off; and, except for suicidal as well as homicidal purposes, need not return.

"Such I hold to be the genuine use of Gunpowder: that it makes all men alike tall. Nay, if thou be cooler, cleverer than I, if thou have more *Mind*, though all but no *Body* whatever, then canst thou kill me first, and art the taller. Hereby, at last, is the Goliath powerless, and the David resistless; savage Animalism is nothing, inventive Spiritualism is all.

"With respect to Duels, indeed, I have my own ideas. Few things, in this so surprising world, strike me with more surprise. Two little visual Spectra of men, hovering with insecure enough cohesion in the midst of the UNFATH-OMABLE, and to dissolve therein, at any rate, very soon,—make pause at the distance of twelve paces asunder; whirl round; and, simultaneously by the cunningest mechanism, explode one another into Dissolution; and offhand become Air, and Non-extant! Deuce on it (*verdammt*), the little spitfires!—Nay, I think with old Hugo von Trimberg: [27] 'God must needs laugh outright, could such a thing be, to see his wondrous Manikins here below.'"

But amid these specialties, let us not forget the great generality, which is our chief quest here: How prospered the inner man of Teufelsdröckh under so much outward shifting? Does Legion [28] still lurk in him, though repressed; or has he exorcised that Devil's Brood? We can answer that the symptoms continue promising. Experience is the grand spiritual Doctor; and with him Teufelsdröckh has been long a patient, swallowing many a bitter bolus.[29] Unless our poor Friend belong to the numerous class

---

[24] Careers open to talents.    [25] Northern.

[26] Whale oil.
[27] Medieval moralist and poet (1260–1309).
[28] Cf. St. Mark, 5:9; St. Luke, 8:30.
[29] Large pill.

of Incurables, which seems not likely, some cure will doubtless be effected. We should rather say that Legion, or the Satanic School, was now pretty well extirpated and cast out, but next to nothing introduced in its room; whereby the heart remains, for the while, in a quiet but no comfortable state.

"At length, after so much roasting," thus writes our Autobiographer, "I was what you might name calcined. Pray only that it be not rather, as is the more frequent issue, reduced to a *caput-mortuum!* [30] But in any case, by mere dint of practice, I had grown familiar with many things. Wretchedness was still wretched; but I could now partly see through it, and despise it. Which highest mortal, in this inane Existence, had I not found a Shadow-hunter, or Shadow-hunted; and, when I looked through his brave garnitures, miserable enough? Thy wishes have all been sniffed aside, thought I: but what, had they even been all granted! Did not the Boy Alexander weep because he had not two Planets to conquer; or a whole Solar System; or after that, a whole Universe? *Ach Gott,*[31] when I gazed into these Stars, have they not looked-down on me as if with pity, from their serene spaces; like Eyes glistening with heavenly tears over the little lot of man! Thousands of human generations, all as noisy as our own, have been swallowed-up of Time, and there remains no wreck [32] of them any more; and Arcturus and Orion and Sirius and the Pleiades are still shining in their courses, clear and young, as when the Shepherd first noted them in the plain of Shinar.[33] Pshaw! what is this paltry little Dog-cage [34] of an Earth; what art thou that sittest whining there? Thou art still Nothing, Nobody: true; but who, then, is Something, Somebody? For thee the Family of Man has no use; it rejects thee; thou art wholly as a dissevered limb: so be it; perhaps it is better so!"

Too-heavy-laden Teufelsdröckh! Yet surely his bands are loosening; one day he will hurl the burden far from him, and bound forth free and with a second youth.

"This," says our Professor, "was the CENTER OF INDIFFERENCE I had now reached; through which whoso travels from the Negative Pole to the Positive must necessarily pass."

---

[30] Literally, a death's head; also, a worthless residue.

[31] Good Heavens!     [32] Wrack, ruin.

[33] Where the Tower of Babel was built (Genesis, 11:1–9).

[34] A wheel-like cage in which a dog was placed to turn the jack of a turnspit, and so roast the meat.

## CHAPTER IX

### The Everlasting Yea

"Temptations in the Wilderness!" [1] exclaims Teufelsdröckh: "Have we not all to be tried with such? Not so easily can the old Adam, lodged in us by birth, be dispossessed. Our Life is compassed round with Necessity; yet is the meaning of Life itself no other than Freedom, than Voluntary Force: thus have we a warfare; in the beginning, especially, a hard-fought battle. For the God-given mandate, *Work thou in Welldoing,* lies mysteriously written, in Promethean [2] Prophetic Characters, in our hearts; and leaves us no rest, night or day, till it be deciphered and obeyed; till it burn forth, in our conduct, a visible, acted Gospel of Freedom. And as the clay-given mandate, *Eat thou and be filled,* at the same time persuasively proclaims itself through every nerve,—must not there be a confusion, a contest, before the better Influence can become the upper?

"To me nothing seems more natural than the Son of Man, when such God-given mandate first prophetically stirs within him, and the Clay must now be vanquished or vanquish, —should be carried of the spirit into grim Solitudes, and there fronting the Tempter do grimmest battle with him; defiantly setting him at naught, till he yield and fly. Name it as we choose: with or without visible Devil, whether in the natural Desert of rocks and sands, or in the populous moral Desert of selfishness and baseness,—to such Temptation are we all called. Unhappy if we are not! Unhappy if we are but Half-men, in whom that divine hand-writing has never blazed forth, all-subduing, in true sun-splendor; but quivers dubiously amid meaner lights: or smolders, in dull pain, in darkness, under earthly vapors!—Our Wilderness is the wide World in an Atheistic Century; our Forty Days are long years of suffering and fasting: nevertheless, to these also comes an end. Yes, to me also was given, if not Victory, yet the consciousness of Battle, and the resolve to persevere therein while life or faculty is left. To me also, entangled in the enchanted forests, demon-peopled, doleful of sight and of sound, it was given, after weariest wanderings, to work out my way into the higher sunlight slopes—of that Mountain [3] which has no summit, or whose summit is in Heaven only!"

---

[1] St. Matthew, 4:1.

[2] Fire-bearing. Prometheus brought fire to men.

[3] Symbol of spiritual insight.

He says elsewhere, under a less ambitious figure; as figures are, once for all, natural to him: "Has not thy Life been that of most sufficient men (*tüchtigen Männer*) thou hast known in this generation? An outflush of foolish young Enthusiasm, like the first fallow-crop, wherein are as many weeds as valuable herbs: this all parched away, under the Droughts of practical and spiritual Unbelief, as Disappointment, in thought and act, often-repeated gave rise to Doubt, and Doubt gradually settled into Denial! If I have had a second-crop, and now see the perennial greensward, and sit under umbrageous cedars, which defy all Drought (and Doubt); herein too, be the Heavens praised, I am not without examples, and even exemplars."

So that, for Teufelsdröckh also, there has been a "glorious revolution": [4] these mad shadow-hunting and shadow-hunted Pilgrimings of his were but some purifying "Temptation in the Wilderness," before his apostolic work (such as it was) could begin; which Temptation is now happily over, and the Devil once more worsted! Was "that high moment in the *Rue de l'Enfer*," then, properly the turning-point of the battle; when the Fiend said, *Worship me, or be torn in shreds*; and was answered valiantly with an *Apage Satana?* [5]—singular Teufelsdröckh, would thou hadst told thy singular story in plain words! But it is fruitless to look there, in those Paper-bags, for such. Nothing but innuendoes, figurative crotchets: a typical Shadow, fitfully wavering, prophetico-satiric; no clear logical Picture. "How paint to the sensual eye," asks he once, "What passes in the Holy-of-Holies of Man's Soul; in what words, known to these profane times, speak even afar-off of the unspeakable?" We ask in turn: Why perplex these times, profane as they are, with needless obscurity, by omission and by commission? Not mystical only is our Professor, but whimsical; and involves himself, now more than ever, in eye-bewildering *chiaroscuro*.[6] Successive glimpses, here faithfully imparted, our more gifted readers must endeavor to combine for their own behoof.

He says: "The hot Harmattan wind [7] had raged itself out; its howl went silent within me; and the long-deafened soul could now hear. I paused in my wild wanderings; and sat me down to wait, and consider; for it was as if the hour of change drew nigh. I seemed to surrender, to renounce utterly, and say: Fly, then, false shadows of Hope; I will chase you no more, I will believe you no more. And ye too, haggard specters of Fear, I care not for you; ye too are all shadows and a lie. Let me rest here: for I am way-weary and life-weary; I will rest here, were it but to die: to die or to live is alike to me; alike insignificant."
—And again: "Here, then, as I lay in that CENTER OF INDIFFERENCE; cast, doubtless by benignant upper Influence, into a healing sleep, the heavy dreams rolled gradually away, and I awoke to a new Heaven and a new Earth.[8] The first preliminary moral Act, Annihilation of Self (*Selbst-tödtung*), had been happily accomplished; and my mind's eyes were now unsealed, and its hands ungyved." [9]

Might we not also conjecture that the following passage refers to his Locality, during this same "healing sleep"; that his Pilgrim-staff lies cast aside here, on "the high table-land"; and indeed that the repose is already taking wholesome effect on him? If it were not that the tone, in some parts, has more of riancy,[10] even of levity, than we could have expected! However, in Teufelsdröckh, there is always the strangest Dualism: light dancing, with guitar-music, will be going on in the fore-court, while by fits from within comes the faint whimpering of woe and wail. We transcribe the piece entire.

"Beautiful it was to sit there, as in my skyey Tent, musing and meditating; on the high table-land, in front of the Mountains; over me, as roof, the azure Dome, and around me, for walls, four azure-flowing curtains,—namely, of the Four azure Winds, on whose bottom-fringes also I have seen gilding. And then to fancy the fair Castles that stood sheltered in these Mountain hollows; with their green flower-lawns, and white dames and damosels, lovely enough: or better still, the straw-roofed Cottages, wherein stood many a Mother baking bread, with her children round her:—all hidden and protectingly folded-up in the valley-folds; yet there and alive, as sure as if I beheld them. Or to see, as well as fancy, the nine Towns and Villages, that lay round my mountain-seat, which, in still weather, were wont to speak to me (by their steeple-bells) with metal tongue: and, in almost all weather, proclaimed their vitality by repeated Smoke-clouds; whereon, as on a culinary horologe,[11] I might

---

[4] Name generally given to the revolution which in 1688 replaced James II with William III and Mary II.

[5] Get thee hence, Satan! (Matthew, 4:8-10).

[6] Light and shade.

[7] Dry, dust-laden wind, at certain seasons blowing along the Atlantic coast of Africa from the interior.

[8] Cf. Revelation, 21:1.    [9] Unfettered.

[10] Laughableness.    [11] Clock.

read the hour of the day. For it was the smoke of cookery, as kind housewives at morning, midday, eventide, were boiling their husbands' kettles; and ever a blue pillar rose up into the air, successively or simultaneously, from each of the nine, saying, as plainly as smoke could say: Such and such a meal is getting ready here. Not uninteresting! For you have the whole Borough, with all its love-makings and scandal-mongerings, contentions and content-ments, as in miniature, and could cover it all with your hat.—If, in my wide Wayfarings, I had learned to look into the business of the World in its details, here perhaps was the place for combining it into general proposi-tions, and deducing inferences therefrom.

"Often also could I see the black Tempest marching in anger through the Distance: round some Schreckhorn,[12] as yet grim-blue, would the eddying vapor gather, and there tumul-tuously eddy, and flow down like a mad witch's hair; till, after a space, it vanished, and, in the clear sunbeam, your Schreckhorn stood smiling grim-white, for the vapor had held snow. How thou fermentest and elaboratest, in thy great fermenting-vat and laboratory of an Atmos-phere, of a World, O Nature!—Or what is Na-ture? Ha! why do I not name thee GOD? Art not thou the 'Living Garment of God'? O Heavens, is it, in very deed, HE, then, that ever speaks through thee; that lives and loves in thee, that lives and loves in me?

"Fore-shadows, call them rather fore-splendors, of that Truth, and Beginning of Truths, fell mysteriously over my soul. Sweeter than Dayspring to the Ship-wrecked in Nova Zembla;[13] ah, like the mother's voice to her little child that strays bewildered, weep-ing, in unknown tumults; like soft streamings of celestial music to my too-exasperated heart, came that Evangel. The Universe is not dead and demoniacal, a charnel-house with specters; but godlike, and my Father's!

"With other eyes, too, could I now look upon my fellow man: with an infinite Love, an infinite Pity. Poor, wandering, wayward man! Art thou not tired, and beaten with stripes, even as I am? Ever, whether thou bear the royal mantle or the beggar's gabardine, art thou not so weary, so heavy-laden; and thy Bed of Rest is but a Grave. O my Brother, my Brother, why cannot I shelter thee in my bosom, and wipe away all tears from thy eyes! —Truly, the din of many-voiced Life, which,

in this solitude, with the mind's organ, I could hear, was no longer a maddening discord, but a melting one; like inarticulate cries, and sob-bings of a dumb creature, which in the ear of Heaven are prayers. The poor Earth, with her poor joys, was now my needy Mother, not my cruel Stepdame; Man, with his so mad Wants and so mean Endeavors, had become the dearer to me; and even for his sufferings and his sins, I now first named him Brother. Thus was I standing in the porch of that 'Sanctuary of Sorrow';[14] by strange, steep ways had I too been guided thither; and ere long its sacred gates would open, and the 'Divine Depth of Sorrow'[15] lie disclosed to me."

The Professor says, he here first got eye on the Knot that had been strangling him, and straightway could unfasten it, and was free. "A vain interminable controversy," writes he, "touching what is at present called Origin of Evil, or some such thing, arises in every soul, since the beginning of the world; and in every soul, that would pass from idle Suffering into actual Endeavoring, must first be put an end to. The most, in our time, have to go content with a simple, incomplete enough Suppression of this controversy; to a few some Solution of it is indispensable. In every new era, too, such Solution comes-out in different terms; and ever the Solution of the last era has become obso-lete, and is found unserviceable. For it is man's nature to change his Dialect from century to century; he cannot help it though he would. The authentic *Church-Catechism* of our pres-ent century has not yet fallen into my hands: meanwhile, for my own private behoof, I at-tempt to elucidate the matter so. Man's Un-happiness, as I construe, comes of his Great-ness; it is because there is an Infinite in him, which with all his cunning he cannot quite bury under the Finite. Will the whole Finance Ministers and Upholsterers and Confectioners of modern Europe undertake, in joint-stock company, to make one Shoeblack HAPPY? They cannot accomplish it, above an hour or two: for the Shoeblack also has a Soul quite other than his Stomach; and would require, if you consider it, for his permanent satisfaction and saturation, simply this allotment, no more, and no less: *God's infinite Universe altogether to himself,* therein to enjoy infinitely, and fill

---

[12] Peak of Terror. One of the principal summits of the Bernese Alps, in Switzerland.

[13] Island in the Arctic Ocean north of Russia.

[14] The name of the hall into which Wilhelm Meis-ter is to be taken to view the remaining murals representing the life of Christ; used here to denote a state of soul, later the state of the whole world (Charles F. Harrold).

[15] Christ's sorrow.

every wish as fast as it rose. Oceans of Hochheimer,[16] a Throat like that of Ophiuchus: [17] speak not of them; to the infinite Shoeblack they are as nothing. No sooner is your ocean filled, than he grumbles that it might have been of better vintage. Try him with half of a Universe, of an Omnipotence, he sets to quarreling with the proprietor of the other half, and declares himself the most maltreated of men.— Always there is a black spot in our sunshine: it is even, as I said, the *Shadow of Ourselves.*

"But the whim we have of Happiness is somewhat thus. By certain valuations, and averages, of our own striking, we come upon some sort of average terrestrial lot; this we fancy belongs to us by nature, and of indefeasible right. It is simple payment of our wages, of our deserts; requires neither thanks nor complaint; only such *overplus* as there may be do we account Happiness; any *deficit* again is Misery. Now consider that we have the valuation of our own deserts ourselves, and what a fund of Self-conceit there is in each of us,—do you wonder that the balance should so often dip the wrong way, and many a Blockhead cry: See there, what a payment; was ever worthy gentleman so used!—I tell thee, Blockhead, it all comes of thy Vanity; of what thou *fanciest* those same deserts of thine to be. Fancy that thou deservest to be hanged (as is most likely), thou wilt feel it happiness to be only shot: fancy that thou deservest to be hanged in a hair-halter, it will be a luxury to die in hemp.

"So true is it, what I then said, that *the Fraction of Life can be increased in value not so much by increasing your Numerator as by lessening your Denominator.* Nay, unless my Algebra deceive me, *Unity* itself divided by *Zero* will give *Infinity.* Make thy claim of wages a zero, then; thou hast the world under thy feet. Well did the Wisest of our time write: 'It is only with Renunciation (*Entsagen*) that Life, properly speaking, can be said to begin.' [18]

"I asked myself: What is this that, ever since earliest years, thou hast been fretting and fuming, and lamenting and self-tormenting, on account of? Say it in a word: is it not because thou art not HAPPY? Because the THOU (sweet gentleman) is not sufficiently honored, nourished, soft-bedded, and lovingly cared-for?

Foolish soul! What Act of Legislature was there that *thou* shouldst be Happy? A little while ago thou hadst no right to *be* at all. What if thou wert born and predestined not to be Happy, but to be Unhappy! Art thou nothing other than a Vulture, then, that fliest through the Universe seeking after somewhat to *eat*; and shrieking dolefully because carrion enough is not given thee? Close thy *Byron;* open thy *Goethe.*"

"*Esleuchtet mir ein,*[19] I see a glimpse of it!" cries he elsewhere: "there is in man a HIGHER than Love of Happiness: he can do without Happiness, and instead thereof find Blessedness! Was it not to preach-forth this same HIGHER that sages and martyrs, the Poet and the Priest, in all times, have spoken and suffered; bearing testimony, through life and through death, of the Godlike that is in Man, and how in the Godlike only has he Strength and Freedom? Which God-inspired Doctrine art thou also honored to be taught; O Heavens! and broken with manifold merciful Afflictions, even till thou become contrite, and learn it! O, thank thy Destiny for these; thankfully bear what yet remain: thou hadst need of them; the Self in thee needed to be annihilated. By benignant fever-paroxysms is Life rooting out the deep-seated chronic Disease, and triumphs over Death. On the roaring billows of Time, thou art not engulfed, but borne aloft into the azure of Eternity. Love not Pleasure; love God. This is the EVERLASTING YEA, wherein all contradiction is solved: wherein whoso walks and works, it is well with him."

And again: "Small is it that thou canst trample the Earth with its injuries under thy feet, as old Greek Zeno [20] trained thee: thou canst love the Earth while it injures thee, and even because it injures thee; for this a Greater than Zeno was needed, and he too was sent. Knowest thou that '*Worship of Sorrow*'? The Temple thereof, founded some eighteen centuries ago, now lies in ruins, overgrown with jungle, the habitation of doleful creatures: [21] nevertheless, venture forward; in a low crypt, arched out of falling fragments, thou findest the Altar still there, and its sacred Lamp perennially burning."

Without pretending to comment on which strange utterances, the Editor will only remark, that there lies beside them much of a still more questionable character; unsuited to the general

---

[16] A Rhine wine from Hochheim near Mainz.

[17] Evidently the throat of the serpent in the constellation of Ophiuchus.

[18] Adapted, rather than quoted, from Goethe's *Wilhelm Meister.*

[19] An exclamation of Wilhelm Meister's.

[20] A Greek Stoic philosopher of the third century B.C.

[21] Cf. Isaiah, 13:21.

apprehension; nay wherein he himself does not see his way. Nebulous disquisitions on Religion, yet not without bursts of splendor; on the "perennial continuance of Inspiration"; on Prophecy; that there are "true Priests, as well as Baal-Priests,[22] in our own day": with more of the like sort. We select some fractions, by way of finish to this farrago.

"Cease, my much respected Herr von Voltaire,"[23] thus apostrophizes the Professor: "shut thy sweet voice; for the task appointed thee seems finished. Sufficiently hast thou demonstrated this proposition, considerable or otherwise: That the Mythus[24] of the Christian Religion looks not in the eighteenth century as it did in the eighth. Alas, were thy six-and-thirty quartos, and the six-and-thirty thousand other quartos and folios, and flying sheets or reams, printed before and since on the same subject, all needed to convince us of so little! But what next? Wilt thou help us to embody the divine Spirit of that Religion in a new Mythus, in a new vehicle and vesture, that our Souls, otherwise too like perishing, may live? What! thou hast no faculty in that kind? Only a torch for burning, no hammer for building? Take our thanks, then, and——thyself away.

"Meanwhile what are antiquated Mythuses to me? Or is the God present, felt in my own heart, a thing which Herr von Voltaire will dispute out of me; or dispute into me? To the '*Worship of Sorrow*' ascribe what origin and genesis thou pleasest, *has* not that Worship originated, and been generated; is it not *here*? Feel it in thy heart, and then say whether it is of God! This is Belief; all else is Opinion,—for which latter whoso will, let him worry and be worried."

"Neither," observes he elsewhere, "shall ye tear-out one another's eyes, struggling over 'Plenary Inspiration,'[25] and such-like: try rather to get a little even Partial Inspiration, each of you for himself. ONE BIBLE I know, of whose Plenary Inspiration doubt is not so much as possible; nay with my own eyes I saw the God's-Hand writing it: thereof all other Bibles are but Leaves,—say, in Picture-Writing to assist the weaker faculty."

Or, to give the wearied reader relief, and bring it to an end, let him take the following perhaps more intelligible passage:

"To me, in this our life," says the Professor, "which is an internecine warfare with the Time-spirit, other warfare seems questionable. Hast thou in any way a Contention with thy brother, I advise thee, think well what the meaning thereof is. If thou gauge it to the bottom, it is simply this: 'Fellow, see! thou art taking more than thy share of Happiness in the world, something from *my* share: which, by the Heavens, thou shalt not; nay I will fight thee rather.'—Alas, and the whole lot to be divided is such a beggarly matter, truly a 'feast of shells,' for the substance has been spilled out: not enough to quench one Appetite; and the collective human species clutching at them! —Can we not, in all such cases, rather say: 'Take it, thou too-ravenous individual; take that pitiful additional fraction of a share, which I reckoned mine, but which thou so wantest; take it with a blessing: would to Heaven I had enough for thee!'—If Fichte's *Wissenschaftslehre*[26] be, 'to a certain extent, Applied Christianity,' surely to a still greater extent, so is this. We have here not a Whole Duty of Man,[27] yet a Half Duty, namely the Passive half: could we but do it, as we can demonstrate it!

"But indeed Conviction, were it never so excellent, is worthless till it convert itself into Conduct. Nay properly Conviction is not possible till then; inasmuch as all Speculation is by nature endless, formless, a vortex amid vortices: only by a felt indubitable certainty of Experience does it find any center to revolve round, and so fashion itself into a system. Most true is it, as a wise man teaches us, that 'Doubt of any sort cannot be removed except by Action.'[28] On which ground, too, let him who gropes painfully in darkness or uncertain light, and prays vehemently that the dawn may ripen into day, lay this other precept well to heart, which to me was of invaluable service: '*Do the Duty which lies nearest thee*,' which thou

---

[22] False priests.

[23] François Marie Arouet (1694–1778), who for Carlyle typifies the skepticism of the eighteenth century.

[24] Myth.

[25] The theological doctrine of plenary inspiration, against which Voltaire was particularly violent, regards supernatural inspiration as extending to all subjects dealt with in the Bible, and therefore to be accepted as true and authoritative. Carlyle regarded Voltaire's attack as beside the point, since "Christianity, the worship of Sorrow," does not rest upon "miracles" and other "evidences," but has its verification "in mysterious, ineffaceable characters . . . written in the purest nature of man" (Charles F. Harrold).

[26] The Doctrine of Knowledge of the German philosopher, Johann Gottlieb Fichte (1762–1814).

[27] The title of an anonymous devotional work first published in 1658.

[28] This and the quotation in the following sentence are from Goethe's *Wilhelm Meister*.

knowest to be a Duty! Thy second Duty will already have become clearer.

"May we not say, however, that the hour of Spiritual Enfranchisement is even this: When your Ideal World, wherein the whole man has been dimly struggling and inexpressibly languishing to work, becomes revealed, and thrown open; and you discover, with amazement enough, like the Lothario in *Wilhelm Meister*, that your 'America is here or nowhere'? The Situation that has not its Duty, its Ideal, was never yet occupied by man. Yes here, in this poor, miserable, hampered, despicable Actual, wherein thou even now standest, here or nowhere is thy Ideal: work it out therefrom; and working, believe, live, be free. Fool! the Ideal is in thyself, the impediment too is in thyself: thy Condition is but the stuff thou art to shape that same Ideal out of: what matters whether such stuff be of this sort or that, so the Form thou give it be heroic, be poetic? O thou that pinest in the imprisonment of the Actual, and criest bitterly to the gods for a kingdom wherein to rule and create, know this of a truth: the thing thou seekest is already with thee, 'here or nowhere,' couldst thou only see!

"But it is with man's Soul as it was with Nature: the beginning of Creation is—Light.[29] Till the eye have vision, the whole members are in bonds. Divine moment, when over the tempest-tossed Soul, as once over the wild-weltering Chaos, it is spoken: Let there be Light! Ever to the greatest that has felt such moment, is it not miraculous and God-announcing; even as, under simpler figures, to the simplest and least. The mad primeval Discord is hushed; the rudely-jumbled conflicting elements bind themselves into separate Firmaments: deep silent rock-foundations are built beneath; and the skyey vault with its everlasting Luminaries above: instead of a dark wasteful Chaos, we have a blooming, fertile, heaven-encompassed World.

"I too could now say to myself: Be no longer a Chaos, but a World, or even Worldkin. Produce! Produce! Were it but the pitifullest infinitesimal fraction of a Product, produce it, in God's name! 'Tis the utmost thou hast in thee: out with it, then. Up, up! Whatsoever thy hand findeth to do, do it with thy whole might. Work while it is called Today; for the Night cometh, wherein no man can work." [30]

[29] Cf. Genesis, 1:3.
[30] Cf. Ecclesiastes, 9:10; John, 9:4.

## BOOK III

### CHAPTER IX

#### *Circumspective*

Here, then, arises the so momentous question: Have many British Readers actually arrived with us at the new promised country; is the Philosophy of Clothes now at last opening around them? Long and adventurous has the journey been: from those outmost vulgar, palpable Woolen Hulls of Man; through his wondrous Flesh-Garments, and his wondrous Social Garnitures; inwards to the Garments of his very Soul's Soul, to Time and Space themselves! And now does the spiritual, eternal Essence of Man, and of Mankind, bared of such wrappages, begin in any measure to reveal itself? Can many readers discern, as through a glass darkly, in huge wavering outlines, some primeval rudiments of Man's Being, what is changeable divided from what is unchangeable? Does that Earth-Spirit's speech in *Faust*,—

'Tis thus at the roaring Loom of Time I ply,
And weave for God the Garment thou seest Him by; [1]

or that other thousand-times repeated speech of the Magician, Shakespeare,—

And like the baseless fabric of this vision,
The cloudcapt Towers, the gorgeous Palaces,
The solemn Temples, the great Globe itself,
And all which it inherit, shall dissolve;
And like this unsubstantial pageant faded,
Leave not a wrack behind; [2]

begin to have some meaning for us? In a word, do we at length stand safe in the far region of Poetic Creation and Palingenesia, where that Phoenix Death-Birth of Human Society, and of all Human Things, appears possible, is seen to be inevitable?

Along this most insufficient, unheard-of Bridge, which the Editor, by Heaven's bless-

[1] Goethe's *Faust*, I, 508–509. The whole passage, as quoted by Carlyle elsewhere in *Sartor*, is:

"In Being's floods, in Action's storm,
I walk and work, above, beneath,
Work and weave in endless motion!
Birth and Death,
An infinite ocean;
A seizing and giving
The fire of Living:
'Tis thus at the roaring Loom of Time I ply,
And weave for God the Garment thou seest Him by."
(Spoken by the Earth-Spirit.)
[2] *Tempest*, IV, i, 151–156.

ing, has now seen himself enabled to conclude if not complete, it cannot be his sober calculation, but only his fond hope, that many have traveled without accident. No firm arch, overspanning the Impassable with paved highway, could the Editor construct; only, as was said,[3] some zigzag series of rafts floating tumultuously thereon. Alas, and the leaps from raft to raft were too often of a breakneck character; the darkness, the nature of the element, all was against us!

Nevertheless, may not here and there one of a thousand, provided with a discursiveness of intellect rare in our day, have cleared the passage, in spite of all? Happy few! little band of Friends! be welcome, be of courage. By degrees, the eye grows accustomed to its new Whereabout; the hand can stretch itself forth to work there: it is in this grand and indeed highest work of Palingenesia that ye shall labor, each according to ability. New laborers will arrive; new Bridges will be built; nay, may not our own poor rope-and-raft Bridge, in your passings and repassings, be mended in many a point, till it grow quite firm, passable even for the halt?

Meanwhile, of the innumerable multitude that started with us, joyous and full of hope, where now is the innumerable remainder, whom we see no longer by our side? The most have recoiled, and stand gazing afar off, in unsympathetic astonishment, at our career: not a few, pressing forward with more courage, have missed footing, or leaped short; and now swim weltering in the Chaos-flood, some towards this shore, some towards that. To these also a helping hand should be held out; at least some word of encouragement be said.

Or, to speak without metaphor, with which mode of utterance Teufelsdröckh unhappily has somewhat infected us,—can it be hidden from the Editor that many a British Reader sits reading quite bewildered in head, and afflicted rather than instructed by the present Work? Yes, long ago has many a British Reader been, as now, demanding with something like a snarl: Whereto does all this lead; or what use is in it?

In the way of replenishing thy purse, or otherwise aiding thy digestive faculty, O British Reader, it leads to nothing, and there is no use in it; but rather the reverse, for it costs thee somewhat. Nevertheless, if through this unpromising Horn-gate,[4] Teufelsdröckh,

and we by means of him, have led thee into the true Land of Dreams; and through the Clothes-screen, as through a magical *Pierre-Pertuis*,[5] thou lookest, even for moments, into the region of the Wonderful, and seest and feelest that thy daily life is girt with Wonder, and based on Wonder, and thy very blankets and breeches are Miracles,—then art thou profited beyond money's worth; and hast a thankfulness towards our Professor; nay, perhaps in many a literary Tea-circle wilt open thy kind lips, and audibly express that same.

Nay, further, art thou not too perhaps by this time made aware that all Symbols are properly Clothes; that all Forms whereby Spirit manifests itself to sense, whether outwardly or in the imagination, are Clothes; and thus not only the parchment Magna Charta,[6] which a Tailor was nigh cutting into measures, but the Pomp and Authority of Law, the sacredness of Majesty, and all inferior Worships (Worthships) are properly a Vesture and Raiment; and the Thirty-nine Articles [7] themselves are articles of wearing-apparel (for the Religious Idea)? In which case, must it not also be admitted that this Science of Clothes is a high one, and may with infinitely deeper study on thy part yield richer fruit: that it takes scientific rank beside Codification,[8] and Political Economy, and the Theory of the British Constitution; nay rather, from its prophetic height looks down on all these, as on so many weaving-shops and spinning-mills, where the Vestures which *it* has to fashion, and consecrate and distribute, are, too often by haggard hungry operatives [9] who see no farther than their nose, mechanically woven and spun?

But omitting all this, much more all that concerns Natural Supernaturalism, and indeed whatever has reference to the Ulterior or Transcendental portion of the Science, or bears never so remotely on that promised Volume of the *Palingenesie der menschlichen Gesellschaft* (Newbirth of Society),—we humbly

[3] In Bk. I, chap. xi, "Prospective."

[4] See *Aeneid*, VI, 893ff.

[5] In the Bernese Alps; a natural opening in the rock between Tayannes and Sancboz.

[6] The Charter granted by King John at Runnymede, 15 June, 1215. The story Carlyle alludes to is that Sir Robert Cotton (1571–1631), the antiquary, one day found his tailor about to cut up the charter. Cotton bought the document, which is now in the British Museum.

[7] Articles of belief, in the Anglican Church.

[8] The process of reducing laws to a systematic body. The allusion is to Bentham, whose Utilitarianism was at the time dominant in English thought and a force in practical politics.

[9] Workers.

suggest that no province of Clothes-Philosophy, even the lowest, is without its direct value, but that innumerable inferences of a practical nature may be drawn therefrom. To say nothing of those pregnant considerations, ethical, political, symbolical, which crowd on the Clothes-Philosopher from the very threshold of his Science; nothing even of those "architectural ideas," [10] which, as we have seen, lurk at the bottom of all Modes, and will one day, better unfolding themselves, lead to important revolutions,—let us glance for a moment, and with the faintest light of Clothes-Philosophy, on what may be called the Habilatory Class of our fellowmen. Here too overlooking, where so much were to be looked on, the million spinners, weavers, fullers, dyers, washers, and wringers, that puddle and muddle in their dark recesses, to make us Clothes, and die that we may live,—let us but turn the reader's attention upon two small divisions of mankind, who, like moths, may be regarded as Cloth-animals, creatures that live, move, and have their being in Cloth: we mean, Dandies [11] and Tailors.

In regard to both which small divisions it may be asserted without scruple, that the public feeling, unenlightened by Philosophy, is at fault; and even that the dictates of humanity are violated. As will perhaps abundantly appear to readers of the two following Chapters.

## CHAPTER X
### The Dandiacal Body

First, touching Dandies, let us consider, with some scientific strictness, what a Dandy specially is. A Dandy is a Clothes-wearing Man, a Man whose trade, office, and existence consists in the wearing of Clothes. Every faculty of his soul, spirit, purse, and person is heroically consecrated to this one object, the wearing of Clothes wisely and well: so that as others dress to live, he lives to dress. The all-importance of Clothes, which a German Professor, of unequaled learning and acumen, writes his enormous Volume to demonstrate, has sprung up in the intellect of the Dandy without effort, like an instinct of genius; he is inspired with Cloth, a Poet of Cloth. What Teufelsdröckh would call a "Divine Idea of Cloth" is born with him; and this, like other such Ideas, will express itself outwardly, or wring his heart asunder with unutterable throes.

But, like a generous, creative enthusiast, he fearlessly makes his Idea an Action; shows himself in peculiar guise to mankind; walks forth, a witness and living Martyr to the eternal worth of Clothes. We called him a Poet: is not his body the (stuffed) parchment-skin whereon he writes, with cunning Huddersfield [1] dyes, a Sonnet to his mistress' eyebrow? [2] Say, rather, an Epos, and *Clotha Virumque cano*,[3] to the whole world, in Macaronic verses,[4] which he that runs may read. Nay, if you grant, what seems to be admissible, that the Dandy has a Thinking-principle in him, and some notions of Time and Space, is there not in this Life-devotedness to Cloth, in this so willing sacrifice of the Immortal to the Perishable, something (though in reverse order) of that blending and identification of Eternity with Time, which, as we have seen, constitutes the Prophetic character?

And now, for all this perennial Martyrdom, and Poesy, and even Prophecy, what is it that the Dandy asks in return? Solely, we may say, that you would recognize his existence; would admit him to be a living object; or even failing this, a visual object, or thing that will reflect rays of light. Your silver or your gold (beyond what the niggardly Law has already secured him) he solicits not; simply the glance of your eyes. Understand his mystic significance, or altogether miss and misinterpret it; do but look at him, and he is contented.

---

[10] "Neither in tailoring nor in legislating does man proceed by mere Accident, but the hand is ever guided on by mysterious operations of the mind. In all his Modes, and habilatory endeavors, an Architectural Idea will be found lurking; his Body and the Cloth are the site and materials whereon and whereby his beautiful edifice, of a Person, is to be built. Whether he flow gracefully out in folded mantles, based on light sandals; tower-up in high head-gear, from amid peaks, spangles, and bell-girdles; swell-out in starched ruffs, buckram stuffings, and monstrous tuberosities; or girth himself into separate sections, and front the world an Agglomeration of four limbs,—will depend on the nature of such architectural Idea: whether Grecian, Gothic, Later-Gothic or altogether Modern, and Parisian or Anglo-dandiacal" (*Sartor*, Bk. I, ch. v).

[11] The period of the dandies in London society was from about 1813 to 1830.

[1] A town famous for the production of woolen goods.

[2] *As You Like It*, II, vii, 147–149:
"And then the lover
Sighing like a furnace, with a woeful ballad
Made to his mistress' eyebrow."

[3] The first line of the *Aeneid* begins, *Arma virumque cano*.

[4] Verses written in a mixture of Latin and vernacular words. Macaroni was also a name applied to English dandies in the latter half of the eighteenth century.

May we not well cry shame on an ungrateful world, which refuses even this poor boon; which will waste its optic faculty on dried Crocodiles, and Siamese Twins; and over the domestic wonderful wonder of wonders, a live Dandy, glance with hasty indifference, and a scarcely concealed contempt! Him no Zoologist classes among the Mammalia, no Anatomist dissects with care: when did we see any injected Preparation of the Dandy in our Museums; any specimen of him preserved in spirits? Lord Herringbone may dress himself in a snuff-brown suit, with snuff-brown shirt and shoes: it skills [5] not; the undiscerning public, occupied with grosser wants, passes by regardless on the other side.

The age of Curiosity, like that of Chivalry, is indeed, properly speaking, gone. Yet perhaps only gone to sleep: for here arises the Clothes-Philosophy to resuscitate, strangely enough, both the one and the other! Should sound views of this Science come to prevail, the essential nature of the British Dandy, and the mystic significance that lies in him, cannot always remain hidden under laughable and lamentable hallucination. The following long Extract from Professor Teufelsdröckh may set the matter, if not in its true light, yet in the way towards such. It is to be regretted, however, that here, as so often elsewhere, the Professor's keen philosophic perspicacity is somewhat marred by a certain mixture of almost owlish purblindness, or else of some perverse, ineffectual, ironic tendency; our readers shall judge which:

"In these distracted times," writes he, "when the Religious Principle, driven out of most Churches, either lies unseen in the hearts of good men, looking and longing and silently working there towards some new Revelation; or else wanders homeless over the world, like a disembodied soul seeking its terrestrial organization,—into how many strange shapes, of Superstition and Fanaticism, does it not tentatively and errantly cast itself! The higher Enthusiasm of man's nature is for the while without Exponent; yet does it continue indestructible, unweariedly active, and work blindly in the great chaotic deep: thus Sect after Sect, and Church after Church, bodies itself forth, and melts again into new metamorphosis.

"Chiefly is this observable in England, which, as the wealthiest and worst-instructed of European nations, offers precisely the elements (of Heat, namely, and of Darkness), in which such moon-calves and monstrosities are best generated. Among the newer Sects of that country, one of the most notable, and closely connected with our present subject, is that of the *Dandies*; concerning which, what little information I have been able to procure may fitly stand here.

"It is true, certain of the English Journalists, men generally without sense for the Religious Principle, or judgment for its manifestations, speak, in their brief enigmatic notices, as if this were perhaps rather a Secular Sect, and not a Religious one; nevertheless, to the psychologic eye its devotional and even sacrificial character plainly enough reveals itself. Whether it belongs to the class of Fetish-worships, or of Hero-worships or Polytheisms, or to what other class, may in the present state of our intelligence remain undecided (*schweben*). A certain touch of Manicheism,[6] not indeed in the Gnostic [7] shape, is discernible enough: also (for human Error walks in a cycle, and reappears at intervals) a not-inconsiderable resemblance to that Superstition of the Athos Monks,[8] who by fasting from all nourishment, and looking intensely for a length of time into their own navels, came to discern therein the true Apocalypse of Nature, and Heaven Unveiled. To my own surmise, it appears as if this Dandiacal Sect were but a new modification, adapted to the new time, of that primeval Superstition, *Self-worship*; which Zerdusht,[9] Quangfoutchee,[10] Mohammed and others, strove rather to subordinate and restrain than to eradicate; and which only in the purer forms of Religion has been altogether rejected. Wherefore, if any one chooses to name it revived Ahrimanism,[11] or a new figure of Demonworship, I have, so far as is yet visible, no objection.

"For the rest, these people, animated with the zeal of a new Sect, display courage and perseverance, and what force there is in man's nature, though never so enslaved. They affect great purity and separatism; distinguish

---

[5] Matters.

[6] Recognition of two opposed powers in the world, manifesting themselves variously as light and darkness, good and evil, spirit and matter; so named from Mani, or Manes, a Persian.

[7] Because the Gnostics stressed the impurity of matter and the degradation of the body and so would have condemned the creed of the dandy.

[8] Mount Athos is in Macedonia. Monasteries have been there from earliest Christian times.

[9] Zarathustra, or Zoroaster, founder of the Persian religion which is called by his name.

[10] Confucius, an ethical teacher rather than the founder of a religion.

[11] Ahriman was the principle of darkness and evil in the dualism of Zoroaster.

themselves by a particular costume (whereof some notices were given in the earlier part of this Volume); likewise, so far as possible, by a particular speech (apparently some broken *Lingua-franca*,[12] or English-French); and, on the whole, strive to maintain a true Nazarene [13] deportment, and keep themselves unspotted from the world.

"They have their Temples, whereof the chief, as the Jewish Temple did, stands in 10 their metropolis; and is named *Almack's*,[14] a word of uncertain etymology. They worship principally by night; and have their High-priests and Highpriestesses, who, however, do not continue for life. The rites, by some supposed to be of the Menadic [15] sort, or perhaps with an Eleusinian [16] or Cabiric [17] character, are held strictly secret. Nor are Sacred Books wanting to the Sect; these they call *Fashionable Novels*: however, the Canon is not completed, 20 and some are canonical and others not.

"Of such Sacred Books I, not without expense, procured myself some samples; and in hope of true insight, and with the zeal which beseems an Inquirer into Clothes, set to interpret and study them. But wholly to no purpose: that tough faculty of reading, for which the world will not refuse me credit, was here for the first time foiled and set at naught. In vain that I summoned my whole energies 30 (*mich weidlich anstrenge*), and did my very utmost; at the end of some short space, I was uniformly seized with not so much  what I can call a drumming in my ears, as a kind of infinite, unsufferable, Jew's-harping and scrannel-piping [18] there; to which the frightfullest species of Magnetic [19] Sleep soon supervened. And if I strove to shake this way, and absolutely would not yield, there came a hitherto unfelt sensation, as of *Delirium Tremens*, and 40 a melting into total deliquium: [20] till at last, by order of the Doctor, dreading ruin to my

whole intellectual and bodily faculties, and a general breaking-up of the constitution, I reluctantly but determinedly forbore. Was there some miracle at work here; like those Fire-balls, and supernal and infernal prodigies, which, in the case of the Jewish Mysteries, have also more than once scared-back the Alien? Be this as it may, such failure on my part, after best efforts, must excuse the imperfection of this sketch; altogether incomplete, yet the completest I could give of a Sect too singular to be omitted.

"Loving my own life and senses as I do, no power shall induce me, as a private individual, to open another *Fashionable Novel*. But luckily, in this dilemma, comes a hand from the clouds; whereby if not victory, deliverance is held out to me. Round one of those Book-packages, which the *Stillschweigen'sche Buchhandlung* [21] is in the habit of importing from England, come, as is usual, various waste printed-sheets (*Maculaturblätter*), by way of interior wrappage: into these the Clothes-Philosopher, with a certain Mohammedan reverence even for waste-paper,[22] where curious knowledge will sometimes hover, disdains not to cast his eye. Readers may judge of his astonishment when on such a defaced stray-sheet, probably the outcast fraction of some English Periodical, such as they name *Magazine*, appears something like a Dissertation on this very subject of *Fashionable Novels!* It sets out, indeed, chiefly from a Secular point of view; directing itself, not without asperity, against some to me unknown individual named *Pelham*,[23] who seems to be a Mystagogue, and leading Teacher and Preacher of the Sect; so that, what indeed otherwise was not to be expected in such a fugitive fragmentary sheet, the true secret, the Religious physiognomy and physiology of the Dandiacal Body, is nowise laid fully open there. Nevertheless scattered lights do from time to time sparkle out, whereby I have endeavored to profit. Nay, in one passage selected from the Prophecies, or Mythic Theogonies,[24] or whatever they are (for the style seems very mixed) of this Mystagogue, I find what appears to be a

[12] A bastard or hybrid language used by European travelers in the lands at the eastern end of the Mediterranean. Carlyle uses the term in allusion to the habit, fashionable at the time, of using many French terms in English speech.

[13] Native of Nazareth. Carlyle has probably confused the word with Nazarite, the name applied to a Jew living under certain strict vows.

[14] A famous club, or suite of assembly rooms, where fashionable people gathered.

[15] Belonging to the Maenads, female attendants on Bacchus.

[16] The Eleusinian mysteries were celebrated at Eleusis in Attica.

[17] The Cabiri were deities worshiped chiefly in Samothrace.

[18] See Milton, *Lycidas*, l. 124.      [19] Hypnotic.

[20] Liquefaction.

[21] Bookshop.

[22] "It is the custom of the Mahometans, if they see any printed or written paper on the ground, to take it up and lay it aside carefully, as not knowing but it may contain some piece of their Alcoran" —*Spectator*, No. 85 (MacMechan).

[23] The title of a novel by Bulwer Lytton, published 1828. Passages resembling those which here follow may be found particularly in Chapters 44 and 46.

[24] Genealogies of the gods.

Confession of Faith, or Whole Duty of Man, according to the tenets of that Sect. Which Confession or Whole Duty, therefore, as proceeding from a source so authentic, I shall here arrange under Seven distinct Articles, and in very abridged shape lay before the German world; therewith taking leave of this matter. Observe also, that to avoid possibility of error, I, as far as may be, quote literally from the Original:

### Articles of Faith

1. Coats should have nothing of the triangle about them; at the same time, wrinkles behind should be carefully avoided.
2. The collar is a very important point: it should be low behind, and slightly rolled.
3. No license of fashion can allow a man of delicate taste to adopt the posterial luxuriance of a Hottentot.
4. There is safety in a swallow-tail.
5. The good sense of a gentleman is nowhere more finely developed than in his rings.
6. It is permitted to mankind, under certain restrictions, to wear white waistcoats.
7. The trousers must be exceedingly tight across the hips.

"All which Propositions I, for the present, content myself with modestly but peremptorily and irrevocably denying.

"In strange contrast with this Dandiacal Body stands another British Sect, originally, as I understand, of Ireland, where its chief seat still is; but known also in the main Island, and indeed everywhere rapidly spreading. As this Sect has hitherto emitted no Canonical Books, it remains to me in the same state of obscurity as the Dandiacal, which has published Books that the unassisted human faculties are inadequate to read. The members appear to be designated by a considerable diversity of names, according to their various places of establishment: in England they are generally called the *Drudge* Sect; also, unphilosophically enough, the *White Negroes*; and, chiefly in scorn by those of other communions, the *Ragged-Beggar* Sect. In Scotland, again, I find them entitled *Hallanshakers*,[25] or the *Stook of Duds* Sect; any individual communicant is named *Stook of Duds* (that is, Shock of Rags), in allusion, doubtless, to their professional Costume. While in Ireland, which, as mentioned, is their grandparent hive, they go by a perplexing multiplicity of designations, such as *Bogtrotters, Redshanks, Ribbonmen, Cottiers, Peep-of-Day Boys, Babes of the Wood, Rockites, Poor-Slaves:*[26] which last, however,

[25] Sturdy beggars.

[26] All names given to the poor and rebellious Irish in the early nineteenth century.

seems to be the primary and generic name; whereto, probably enough, the others are only subsidiary species, or slight varieties; or, at most, propagated offsets from the parent stem, whose minute subdivisions, and shades of difference, it were here loss of time to dwell on. Enough for us to understand, what seems indubitable, that the original Sect is that of the *Poor-Slaves*; whose doctrines, practices, and fundamental characteristics pervade and animate the whole Body, howsoever denominated or outwardly diversified.

"The precise speculative tenets of this Brotherhood: how the Universe, and Man, and Man's Life, picture themselves to the mind of an Irish Poor-Slave; with what feelings and opinions he looks forward on the Future, round on the Present, back on the Past, it were extremely difficult to specify. Something Monastic there appears to be in their Constitution: we find them bound by the two Monastic Vows, of Poverty and Obedience; which Vows, especially the former, it is said, they observe with great strictness; nay, as I have understood it, they are pledged, and be it by any solemn Nazarene ordination or not, irrevocably consecrated thereto, even *before* birth. That the third Monastic Vow, of Chastity, is rigidly enforced among them, I find no ground to conjecture.

"Furthermore, they appear to imitate the Dandiacal Sect in their grand principal of wearing a peculiar Costume. Of which Irish Poor-Slave Costume no description will indeed be found in the present Volume; for this reason, that by the imperfect organ of Language it did not seem describable. Their raiment consists of innumerable skirts, lappets,[27] and irregular wings, of all cloths and of all colors; through the labyrinthic intricacies of which their bodies are introduced by some unknown process. It is fastened together by a multiplex combination of buttons, thrums,[28] and skewers; to which frequently is added a girdle of leather, of hempen or even of straw rope, round the loins. To straw rope, indeed, they seem partial, and often wear it by way of sandals. In head-dress they affect a certain freedom: hats with partial brim, without crown, or with only a loose, hinged, or valve crown; in the former case, they sometimes invert the hat, and wear it brim uppermost, like a University-cap, with what view is unknown.

"The name Poor-Slaves seems to indicate a Slavonic, Polish, or Russian origin: not so, however, the interior essence and spirit of

[27] Folds.        [28] Loose threads.

their Superstition, which rather displays a Teutonic or Druidical character. One might fancy them worshipers of Hertha,[29] or the Earth: for they dig and affectionately work continually in her bosom; or else, shut-up in private Oratories,[30] meditate and manipulate the substances derived from her; seldom looking-up towards the Heavenly Luminaries, and then with comparative indifference. Like the Druids, on the other hand, they live in dark dwellings; often even breaking their glass-windows, where they find such, and stuffing them up with pieces of raiment, or other opaque substances, till the fit obscurity is restored. Again, like all followers of Nature-Worship, they are liable to outbreakings of an enthusiasm rising to ferocity; and burn men, if not in wicker idols, yet in sod cottages.

"In respect of diet, they have also their observances. All Poor-Slaves are Rhizophagous (or Root-eaters); a few are Ichthyophagous,[31] and use Salted Herrings: other animal food they abstain from; except indeed, with perhaps some strange inverted fragment of a Brahminical feeling, such animals as die a natural death.[32] Their universal sustenance is the root named Potato, cooked by fire alone; and generally without condiment or relish of any kind, save an unknown condiment named *Point*, into the meaning of which I have vainly inquired; the victual *Potatoes-and-Point*[33] not appearing, at least not with specific accuracy of description, in any European Cookery-Book whatever. For drink, they use, with an almost epigrammatic counterpoise of taste, Milk, which is the mildest of liquors, and *Potheen*,[34] which is the fiercest. This latter I have tasted, as well as the English *Blue-Ruin*, and the Scotch *Whisky*, analogous fluids used by the Sect in those countries: it evidently contains some form of alcohol, in the highest state of concentration, though disguised with acrid oils; and is, on the whole, the most pungent substance known to me,—indeed, a perfect liquid fire. In all their Religious Solemnities, Potheen is said to be an indispensable requisite, and largely consumed.

"An Irish Traveler, of perhaps common veracity, who presents himself under the to me unmeaning title of *The late John Bernard*, offers the following sketch[35] of a domestic establishment, the inmates whereof, though such is not stated expressly, appear to have been of that Faith. Thereby shall my German readers now behold an Irish Poor-Slave, as it were with their own eyes; and even see him at meat. Moreover, in the so precious waste-paper sheet above mentioned, I have found some corresponding picture of a Dandiacal Household, painted by the same Dandiacal Mystagogue, or Theogonist: this also, by way of counterpart and contrast, the world shall look into.

"First, therefore, of the Poor-Slave, who appears likewise to have been a species of Innkeeper. I quote from the original:

### POOR-SLAVE HOUSEHOLD

The furniture of this Caravansera consisted of a large iron Pot, two oaken Tables, two Benches, two Chairs, and a Potheen Noggin.[36] There was a Loft above (attainable by a ladder), upon which the inmates slept; and the space below was divided by a hurdle into two Apartments; the one for their cow and pig, the other for themselves and guests. On entering the house we discovered the family, eleven in number, at dinner: the father sitting at the top, the mother at the bottom, the children on each side, of a large oaken Board, which was scooped-out in the middle, like a trough, to receive the contents of their Pot of Potatoes. Little holes were cut at equal distances to contain Salt; and a bowl of Milk stood on the table: all the luxuries of meat and beer, bread, knives, and dishes were dispensed with.

The Poor-Slave himself our Traveler found, as he says, broad-backed, black-browed, of great personal strength, and mouth from ear to ear. His Wife was a sun-browned but well-featured woman; and his young ones, bare and chubby, had the appetite of ravens. Of their Philosophical or Religious tenets or observances, no notice or hint.

"But now, secondly, of the Dandiacal Household; in which, truly, that often-mentional Mystagogue and inspired Penman himself has his abode:

### DANDIACAL HOUSEHOLD

A Dressing-room splendidly furnished; violet-colored curtains, chairs and ottomans of the same hue. Two full-length Mirrors are placed, one on each side of a table, which supports the luxuries of the Toilet. Several Bottles of Perfumes, arranged in a peculiar fashion, stand upon a smaller table of mother-of-pearl: opposite to these are placed

---

[29] Germanic goddess of fertility, mentioned by Tacitus.
[30] I. e., factories.     [31] Fish-eating.
[32] The Brahmins do not permit themselves to kill any animals or insects.
[33] I. e., potatoes and nothing besides; bacon or herring, if there was any, being simply pointed at, not eaten, because there was not enough to go round.
[34] "Moonshine" whisky.

[35] Condensed from several paragraphs (Vol. I, pp. 348–350) in *Retrospections of the Stage* by John Bernard, published in 1830.
[36] Small mug.

the appurtenances of Lavation richly wrought in frosted silver. A Wardrobe of Buhl [37] is on the left; the doors of which, being partly open, discover a profusion of Clothes; Shoes of a singularly small size monopolize the lower shelves. Fronting the wardrobe a door ajar gives some slight glimpse of a Bathroom. Folding-doors in the background.—Enter the Author [our Theogonist in person] obsequiously preceded by a French Valet, in white silk Jacket and cambric Apron.[38]

"Such are the two Sects which, at this moment, divide the more unsettled portion of the British People; and agitate that ever-vexed country. To the eye of the political Seer, their mutual relation, pregnant with the elements of discord and hostility, is far from consoling. These two principals of Dandiacal Self-worship or Demon-worship, and Poor-Slavish or Drudgical Earth-worship, or whatever that same Drudgism may be, do as yet indeed manifest themselves under distant and nowise considerable shapes: nevertheless, in their roots and subterranean ramifications, they extend through the entire structure of Society, and work unweariedly in the secret depths of English national Existence; striving to separate and isolate it into two contradictory, uncommunicating masses.

"In numbers, and even individual strength, the Poor-Slaves or Drudges, it would seem, are hourly increasing. The Dandiacal, again, is by nature no proselytizing Sect; but it boasts of great hereditary resources, and is strong by union; whereas the Drudges, split into parties, have as yet no rallying-point; or at best only co-operate by means of partial secret affiliations. If, indeed, there were to arise a *Communion of Drudges*, as there is already a Communion of Saints, what strangest effects would follow therefrom! Dandyism as yet affects to look-down on Drudgism: but perhaps the hour of trial, when it will be practically seen which ought to look down, and which up, is not so distant.

"To me it seems probable that the two Sects will one day part England between them; each recruiting itself from the intermediate ranks, till there be none left to enlist on either side. Those Dandiacal Manicheans, with the host of Dandyizing Christians, will form one body: the Drudges, gathering round them whosoever is Drudgical, be he Christian or Infidel Pagan; sweeping-up likewise all manner of Utilitarians, Radicals, refractory Potwallopers,[39] and so forth, into their general mass, will form another. I could liken Dandyism and Drudgism to two bottomless boiling Whirlpools that had broken-out on opposite quarters of the firm land: as yet they appear only disquieted, foolishly bubbling wells, which man's art might cover-in; yet mark them, their diameter is daily widening: they are hollow Cones that boil-up from the infinite Deep, over which your firm land is but a thin crust or rind! Thus daily is the intermediate land crumbling-in, daily the empire of the two Buchan-Bullers [40] extending; till now there is but a foot-plank, a mere film of Land between them; this too is washed away: and then—we have the true Hell of Waters, and Noah's Deluge is outdeluged!

"Or better, I might call them two boundless, and indeed unexampled Electric Machines (turned by the 'Machinery of Society'), with batteries of opposite quality; Drudgism the Negative, Dandyism the Positive: one attracts hourly towards it and appropriates all the Positive Electricity of the nation (namely, the Money thereof); the other is equally busy with the Negative (that is to say the Hunger), which is equally potent. Hitherto you see only partial transient sparkles and sputters: but wait a little, till the entire nation is in an electric state; till your whole vital Electricity, no longer healthfully Neutral, is cut into two isolated portions of Positive and Negative (of Money and of Hunger); and stands there bottled-up in two World-Batteries! The stirring of a child's finger brings the two together; and then—What then? The Earth is but shivered into impalpable smoke by that Doom's-thunderpeal; the Sun misses one of his Planets in Space, and thenceforth there are no eclipses of the Moon.—Or better still, I might liken"——

Oh! enough, enough of likenings and similitudes; in excess of which, truly, it is hard to say whether Teufelsdröckh or ourselves sin the more.

We have often blamed him for a habit of wire-drawing and over-refining; from of old we have been familiar with his tendency to

[37] Cabinetwork inlaid with tortoise-shell or metal.

[38] Quoted, with a few minor changes, from the introduction to Bulwer Lytton's novel, *The Disowned* (1828).

[39] One who boils a pot, i. e., who prepares his own food. The name was applied to a certain class of voters in England before the passage of the Reform Bill of 1832—those who had resided in a borough for six months and had not been given poor-relief for twelve.

[40] The name of a well, or whirlpool enclosed in a rocky recess, six miles south of Peterhead on the Aberdeenshire coast.

Mysticism and Religiosity, whereby in everything he was still scenting-out Religion: but never perhaps did these amaurosis-suffusions [41] so cloud and distort his otherwise most piercing vision, as in this of the *Dandiacal Body!* Or was there something of intended satire; is the Professor and Seer not quite the blinkard he affects to be? Of an ordinary mortal we should have decisively answered in the affirmative; but with a Teufelsdröckh there ever hovers some shade of doubt. In the meanwhile, if satire were actually intended, the case is little better. There are not wanting men who will answer: Does your Professor take us for simpletons? His irony has overshot itself; we see through it, and perhaps through him.

## CHAPTER XI

### *Tailors*

Thus, however, has our first Practical Inference from the Clothes-Philosophy, that which respects Dandies, been sufficiently drawn; and we come now to the second, concerning Tailors. On this latter our opinion happily quite coincides with that of Teufelsdröckh himself, as expressed in the concluding page of his Volume, to whom, therefore, we willingly give place. Let him speak his own last words, in his own way:

"Upwards of a century," says he, "must elapse, and still the bleeding fight of Freedom be fought, whoso is noblest perishing in the van, and thrones be hurled on altars like Pelion on Ossa,[1] and the Moloch [2] of Iniquity have his victims, and the Michael of Justice his martyrs, before Tailors can be admitted to their true prerogatives of manhood, and this last wound of suffering Humanity be closed.

"If aught in the history of the world's blindness could surprise us, here might we indeed pause and wonder. An idea has gone abroad, and fixed itself down into a widespreading rooted error, that Tailors are a distinct species in Physiology, not Men, but fractional Parts of a Man.[3] Call any one a *Schneider* (Cutter, Tailor), is it not, in our dislocated, hoodwinked, and indeed delirious condition of Society, equivalent to defying his perpetual fellest enmity? The epithet

*schneidermässig* (tailor-like) betokens an otherwise unapproachable degree of pusillanimity: we introduce a *Tailor's-Melancholy*,[4] more opprobrious than any Leprosy, into our Books of Medicine; and fable I know not what of his generating it by living on Cabbage. Why should I speak of Hans Sachs [5] (himself a Shoemaker, or kind of Leather-Tailor), with his *Schneider mit dem Panier?* [6] Why of Shakespeare, in his *Taming of the Shrew*, and elsewhere? Does it not stand on record that the English Queen Elizabeth, receiving a deputation of Eighteen Tailors, addressed them with a 'Good morning, gentlemen both!' Did not the same virago boast that she had a Cavalry Regiment, whereof neither horse nor man could be injured; her Regiment, namely, of Tailors on Mares? Thus everywhere is the falsehood taken for granted, and acted on as an indisputable fact.

"Nevertheless, need I put the question to any Physiologist, whether it is disputable or not? Seems it not at least presumable, that, under his Clothes, the Tailor has bones and viscera, and other muscles than the sartorius? [7] Which function of manhood is the Tailor not conjectured to perform? Can he not arrest for debt? Is he not in most countries a tax-paying animal?

"To no reader of this Volume can it be doubtful which conviction is mine. Nay if the fruit of these long vigils, and almost preternatural Inquiries, is not to perish utterly, the world will have approximated towards a higher Truth; and the doctrine, which Swift,[8] with the keen forecast of genius, dimly anticipated, will stand revealed in clear light: that the Tailor is not only a Man, but something of a Creator or Divinity. Of Franklin it was said, that 'he snatched the Thunder from Heaven and the Scepter from Kings':[9] but which is greater, I would ask, he that lends, or he that snatches? For, looking away from individual cases, and how a Man is by the Tailor new-created into a Nobleman, and clothed not only with Wool but with Dignity and a Mystic Dominion,—is not the fair

[41] Amaurosis is a form of blindness.

[1] Mountains in Thessaly, the former of which the Titans were fabled to have piled on the latter in an effort to reach the abode of the gods.

[2] God of the Ammonites who was worshiped with human sacrifices.

[3] According to a proverb of uncertain origin, "nine tailors make a man."

[4] See Lamb's essay *On the Melancholy of Tailors*. Lamb discusses the influence of cabbage.

[5] German poet and Meistersinger (1494–1576).

[6] Tailor with the Flag. In his song of this title Sachs tells how a tailor was frightened in a dream by a flag made of cloth he had stolen.

[7] A long muscle in the thigh.

[8] See *A Tale of a Tub*, Sec. II. This probably suggested to Carlyle the idea of writing a philosophy of clothes.

[9] The remark is ascribed to Turgot.

fabric of Society itself, with all its royal mantles and pontifical stoles, whereby, from nakedness and dismemberment, we are organized into Polities, into nations, and a whole co-operating Mankind, the creation, as has here been often irrefragably evinced, of the Tailor alone? —What too are all Poets and moral Teachers, but a species of Metaphorical Tailors? Touching with high Guild the greatest living Guild-brother has triumphantly asked us: 'Nay 10 if thou wilt have it, who but the Poet first made Gods for men; brought them down to us; and raised us up to them?' [10]

"And this is he, whom sitting downcast, on the hard basis of his Shopboard, the world treats with contumely, as the ninth part of a man! Look up, thou much-injured one, look up with the kindling eye of hope, and prophetic bodings of a noble better time. Too long hast thou sat there, on crossed legs, 20 wearing thy ankle-joints to horn; like some sacred Anchorite, or Catholic Fakir, doing penance, drawing down Heaven's richest blessings, for a world that scoffed at thee. Be of hope! Already streaks of blue peer through our clouds; the thick gloom of Ignorance is rolling asunder, and it will be Day. Mankind will repay with interest their long-accumulated debt: the Anchorite that was scoffed at will be worshiped; the Fraction will become not an Integer 30 only, but a Square and Cube. With astonishment the world will recognize that the Tailor is its Hierophant and Hierarch, or even its God.

"As I stood in the Mosque of St. Sophia,[11]

[10] From Goethe's *Wilhelm Meister*.
[11] In Constantinople.

and looked upon these Four-and-Twenty Tailors, sewing and embroidering that rich Cloth, which the Sultan sends yearly for the Caaba of Mecca,[12] I thought within myself: How many other Unholies has your covering Art made holy, besides this Arabian Whinstone!

"Still more touching was it when, turning the corner of a lane, in the Scottish Town of Edinburgh, I came upon a Signpost, whereon stood written that such and such a one was 'Breeches-Maker to his Majesty'; and stood painted the Effigies of a Pair of Leather Breeches, and between the knees these memorable words, SIC ITUR AD ASTRA.[13] Was not this the martyr prison-speech of a Tailor sighing indeed in bonds, yet sighing towards deliverance, and prophetically appealing to a better day? A day of justice, when the worth of 20 Breeches would be revealed to man, and the Scissors become forever venerable.

"Neither, perhaps, may I now say, has his appeal been altogether in vain. It was in this high moment, when the soul, rent, as it were, and shed asunder, is open to inspiring influence, that I first conceived this Work on Clothes: the greatest I can ever hope to do; which has already, after long retardations, occupied, and will yet occupy, so large a section 30 of my Life; and of which the Primary and simpler Portion may here find its conclusion."

[12] The Caaba is a square building in the mosque at Mecca. In its northwest corner a black stone is let into the wall ("this Arabian whinstone") which is supposed to have been the original god of the natives of Mecca. This stone is an object of veneration for all Mahometans.
[13] Thus one goes to the stars—i. e., this is the way to immortality (*Aeneid*, IX, 641).

# John Henry, Cardinal Newman

## 1801-1890

Newman was born in London on 21 February, 1801. His father was a banker and a man of cultivated interests; his mother a descendant of French Huguenots who had come to England after the revocation of the Edict of Nantes (1685). In his childhood he received religious training which may be described as a "modified Calvinism," and from an early time he was familiar with the Authorized Version of the Bible, but there is nothing in his ancestry or training which accounts for the strong sense of immaterial reality which he had even as a boy, and which contained the germs of his later development. As a child, he tells us, "I used to wish the Arabian Tales were true; my imagination ran on unknown influences, on magical powers, and talismans. . . . I thought life might be a dream, or I an Angel, and all this world a deception, my fellow-angels by a playful device concealing themselves from me, and deceiving me with the semblance of a material world." This was not a mere passing fancy with him, but an early manifestation of a conviction of immaterial reality which was later strengthened by such apparently diverse influences as the tales of Sir Walter Scott and the theological treatises of Thomas Scott, and which, deepened after his experience of "conversion" at fifteen, remained his abiding possession. He says that his religious studies at fifteen and in the years immediately following aided "in isolating me from the objects which surrounded me, in confirming me in my mistrust of the reality of material phenomena, and making me rest in the thought of two and two only supreme and luminously self-evident beings, myself and my Creator."

Newman received his secondary education at a school in Ealing, and went thence to Trinity College, Oxford, in 1816. He received his B.A. in 1820. In 1822 he was elected a Fellow of Oriel College, and two years later he was ordained a deacon in the Church of England. In 1825 he was ordained a priest and in the following year became one of the tutors of his college. About this time he also preached his first university sermon, and in 1828 he became vicar of St. Mary's Church, Oxford. This remained his outward position for a number of years. Newman's nature was closely akin to Coleridge's and Carlyle's. He heard the same inner voice that they heard, telling him of truths beyond the ken of rationalists and scientists. In his case this experience took the form of a living sense of the truth of Christianity very different from the largely formal professions of faith then usual in the Anglican Church outside of the evangelical party. Newman, moreover, saw with remarkable clearness the character and strength of the forces which were to oppose Christianity in the nineteenth century, and he consecrated his life to warfare against liberalism, as he called it, or rationalism. For this purpose he deemed it essential that the Anglican Church should be aroused from its lethargy and awakened to a full sense of the unbroken Christian tradition which it claimed to represent. This was the starting-point of the Oxford Movement, of which Newman was the leading spirit. He held that the "campaign" actually began with a sermon preached by John Keble in Oxford in 1833, a sermon in which an anti-clerical act of Parliament was termed an act of national apostasy. Keble's attack was quickly followed by the first of the famous series of ninety Tracts for the Times. In these pamphlets as well as in other ways Newman and his associates sought to emphasize the Catholic doctrines of the Anglican Church and to demonstrate that that Church was really the modern representative of Christianity as it had existed in earlier days before the degeneracy and corruption of the Roman Church had brought about the Reformation. In the course of his studies, however, Newman gradually became convinced that, despite the corruption and idolatry of Rome, the English Reformation had been an act of *schism; and at the same time he had it forcibly borne in upon him that the Anglican Church would not follow him in his conclusion. The result was that in 1845 Newman himself went over to the Roman Catholic Church. He had by this time become a national figure whose every movement was watched with deep interest and fear, and it is hardly too much to say that for a time the fate of the Church of England seemed to hang upon his actions.*

*In the early eighteen-fifties there was a movement on foot to establish a Catholic University in Dublin. In 1852, as a means of preparation for this, Newman delivered in Dublin a course of lectures* On the Scope and Nature of University Education, *later published with other papers as* The Idea of a University. *These lectures well illustrate the felicity of his prose style and have, in addition, been generally recognized as a classic statement of the meaning of a liberal education. From 1854 until 1858 Newman was Rector of the new Catholic University, but the enterprise was in the end a failure. His career in the Catholic Church was in fact outwardly a series of disappointments until late in his life, because he was misunderstood and distrusted by some of his ecclesiastical superiors. In addition he was, in the years after 1845, regarded with dislike by Englishmen in general because of the effort they felt he had made to destroy the Anglican Church. But in 1864 he was attacked by Charles Kingsley— "a popular writer, more remarkable for vigorous writing than vigorous thought"—who pub-*

10 *lished an assertion that Newman had countenanced falsehood on the part of the Roman clergy. The latter immediately took advantage of this opportunity both to clear his name and to explain to the English public the development of his religious opinions. This he did in his* Apologia pro Vita Sua, *a justly famous book written with transparent candor and sincerity. In his old age Newman received honors both from England and from Rome which indicate the position he had attained as the greatest English religious leader of the nineteenth cen-*

20 *tury. In 1877 he was elected an Honorary Fellow of Trinity College, Oxford, and in 1879 was created a cardinal of the Roman Catholic Church. He died on 11 August, 1890.*

*The late C. F. Harrold began an edition now in process,* Works of John Henry Newman *(New York, 1947–   ). A convenient single volume is* Newman, Prose and Poetry, *edited by Geoffrey Tillotson (London, 1957). The standard biography is* The Life and Letters of John Henry Cardinal Newman *by Wilfrid Ward (2*

*vols., London, 1912), which, however, does not supersede the earlier* Letters and Correspondence of J. H. Newman during His Life in the English Church, *ed. Anne Mozley (2 vols., London, 1891). More recent biographies include J. Lewis May's* Cardinal Newman, a Study *(London, 1929), Frank Leslie Cross's* John Henry Newman *(London, 1933), John Moody's* John Henry Newman *(New York, 1945), and R. E. G. George's* The Life of Newman *(London, 1948). Paul Elmer More includes an acute interpretation of Newman in his* Shelburne Essays, Eighth Series *(Boston, 1913). Other interpretations include C. F. Harrold's* Newman: an Expository and Critical Study of his Mind, Thought, and Art *(New York, 1945), Sean O'Faolain's* Newman's Way *(New York, 1952), and A. D. Culler's* The Imperial Intellect: a Study of Newman's Educational Ideal *(New Haven, 1955).*

## The Idea of a University
### DISCOURSE VI [1]

*Liberal Knowledge Viewed in Relation to Learning*

It were well if the English, like the Greek language, possessed some definite word to express, simply and generally, intellectual proficiency or perfection, such as "health," as used with reference to the animal frame, and "virtue," with reference to our moral nature. I am not able to find such a term;—talent, ability, genius, belong distinctly to the raw material, which is the subject-matter, not to that excellence which is the result of exercise and training. When we turn, indeed, to the particular kinds of intellectual perfection, words are forthcoming for our purpose, as, for instance, judgment, taste, and skill; yet even these belong, for the most part, to powers or habits bearing upon practice or upon art, and not to any perfect condition of the intellect, considered in itself. Wisdom, again, which is a more comprehensive word than any other, certainly has a direct relation to conduct and to human life. Knowledge, indeed, and science express purely intellectual ideas, but still not a state or habit of the intellect; for knowledge, in its ordinary sense, is but one of its circum-

[1] The two Discourses here printed are given the numbers by which they are generally referred to, but they are taken from the revised edition of 1859 (where they are differently numbered), not from the first edition of 1852. They are reprinted with the permission of Messrs. Longmans, Green and Company, Newman's authorized publishers.

stances, denoting a possession or a faculty; and science has been appropriated to the subject-matter of the intellect, instead of belonging at present, as it ought to do, to the intellect itself. The consequence is that, on an occasion like this, many words are necessary, in order, first, to bring out and convey what surely is no difficult idea in itself—that of the cultivation of the intellect as an end; next, in order to recommend what surely is no unreasonable object; and lastly, to describe and make the mind realize the particular perfection in which that object consists. Every one knows practically what are the constituents of health or virtue; and every one recognizes health and virtue as ends to be pursued; it is otherwise with intellectual excellence, and this must be my excuse, if I seem to any one to be bestowing a good deal of labor on a preliminary matter.

In default of a recognized term, I have called the perfection or virtue of the intellect by the name of philosophy, philosophical knowledge, enlargement of mind, or illumination; terms which are not uncommonly given to it by writers of this day: but, whatever name we bestow on it, it is, I believe, as a matter of history, the business of a university to make this intellectual culture its direct scope, or to employ itself in the education of the intellect—just as the work of a hospital lies in healing the sick or wounded; of a riding or fencing school, or of a gymnasium, in exercising the limbs; of an almshouse, in aiding and solacing the old; of an orphanage, in protecting innocence; of a penitentiary, in restoring the guilty. I say a university, taken in its bare idea, and before we view it as an instrument of the Church, has this object and this mission; it contemplates neither moral impression nor mechanical production; it professes to exercise the mind neither in art nor in duty; its function is intellectual culture: here it may leave its scholars, and it has done its work when it has done as much as this. It educates the intellect to reason well in all matters, to reach out towards truth, and to grasp it.

This, I said in my foregoing Discourse, was the object of a university, viewed in itself, and apart from the Catholic Church, or from the state, or from any other power which may use it; and I illustrated this in various ways. I said that the intellect must have an excellence of its own, for there was nothing which had not its specific good; that the word "educate" would not be used of intellectual culture, as it is used, had not the intellect had an end of its own; that, had it not such an end, there would be

no meaning in calling certain intellectual exercises "liberal," in contrast with "useful," as is commonly done; that the very notion of a philosophical temper implied it, for it threw us back upon research and system as ends in themselves, distinct from effects and works of any kind; that a philosophical scheme of knowledge, or system of sciences, could not, from the nature of the case, issue in any one definite art or pursuit, as its end; and that, on the other hand, the discovery and contemplation of truth, to which research and systematizing led, were surely sufficient ends, though nothing beyond them were added, and that they had ever been accounted sufficient by mankind.

Here then I take up the subject; and having determined that the cultivation of the intellect is an end distinct and sufficient in itself, and that, so far as words go it is an enlargement or illumination, I proceed to inquire what this mental breadth, or power, or light, or philosophy consists in. A hospital heals a broken limb or cures a fever; what does an institution effect, which professes the health, not of the body, not of the soul, but of the intellect? What is this good, which in former times, as well as our own, has been found worth the notice, the appropriation, of the Catholic Church?

I have then to investigate, in the Discourses which follow, those qualities and characteristics of the intellect in which its cultivation issues or rather consists; and, with a view of assisting myself in this undertaking, I shall recur to certain questions which have already been touched upon. These questions are three: *viz.,* the relation of intellectual culture, first, to *mere* knowledge; secondly, to *professional* knowledge; and thirdly, to *religious* knowledge. In other words, are *acquirements* and *attainments* the scope of a university education? or *expertness in particular arts and pursuits?* or *moral and religious proficiency?* or something besides these three? These questions I shall examine in succession, with the purpose I have mentioned; and I hope to be excused if, in this anxious undertaking, I am led to repeat what, either in these Discourses or elsewhere, I have already put upon paper. And first, of *mere knowledge,* or learning, and its connection with intellectual illumination or philosophy.

I suppose the *primâ-facie* [2] view which the public at large would take of a university, considered as a place of education, is nothing

²  Superficial.

more or less than a place for acquiring a great deal of knowledge on a great many subjects. Memory is one of the first developed of the mental faculties; a boy's business when he goes to school is to learn, that is, to store up things in his memory. For some years his intellect is little more than an instrument for taking in facts, or a receptacle for storing them; he welcomes them as fast as they come to him; he lives on what is without; he has his eyes ever about him; he has a lively susceptibility of impressions; he imbibes information of every kind; and little does he make his own in a true sense of the word, living rather upon his neighbors all around him. He has opinions, religious, political, and literary, and, for a boy, is very positive in them and sure about them; but he gets them from his schoolfellows, or his masters, or his parents, as the case may be. Such as he is in his other relations, such also is he in his school exercises; his mind is observant, sharp, ready, retentive; he is almost passive in the acquisition of knowledge. I say this in no disparagement of the idea of a clever boy. Geography, chronology, history, language, natural history, he heaps up the matter of these studies as treasures for a future day. It is the seven years of plenty with him: he gathers in by handfuls, like the Egyptians, without counting; and though, as time goes on, there is exercise for his argumentative powers in the elements of mathematics, and for his taste in the poets and orators, still, while at school, or at least, till quite the last years of his time, he acquires, and little more; and when he is leaving for the university, he is mainly the creature of foreign influences and circumstances, and made up of accidents, homogeneous or not, as the case may be. Moreover, the moral habits, which are a boy's praise, encourage and assist this result; that is, diligence, assiduity, regularity, dispatch, persevering application; for these are the direct conditions of acquisition, and naturally lead to it. Acquirements, again, are emphatically producible, and at a moment; they are a something to show, both for master and scholar; an audience, even though ignorant themselves of the subjects of an examination, can comprehend when questions are answered and when they are not. Here again is a reason why mental culture should in the minds of men be identified with the acquisition of knowledge.

The same notion possesses the public mind, when it passes on from the thought of a school to that of a university: and with the best of reasons so far as this, that there is no true culture without acquirements, and that philosophy presupposes knowledge. It requires a great deal of reading, or a wide range of information, to warrant us in putting forth our opinions on any serious subject; and without such learning the most original mind may be able indeed to dazzle, to amuse, to refute, to perplex, but not to come to any useful result or any trustworthy conclusion. There are indeed persons who profess a different view of the matter, and even act upon it. Every now and then you will find a person of vigorous or fertile mind, who relies upon his own resources, despises all former authors, and gives the world, with the utmost fearlessness, his views upon religion, or history, or any other popular subject. And his works may sell for a while; he may get a name in his day; but this will be all. His readers are sure to find in the long run that his doctrines are mere theories, and not the expression of facts, that they are chaff instead of bread, and then his popularity drops as suddenly as it rose.

Knowledge, then, is the indispensable condition of expansion of mind, and the instrument of attaining to it; this cannot be denied, it is ever to be insisted on; I begin with it as a first principle; however, the very truth of it carries men too far, and confirms to them the notion that it is the whole of it. A narrow mind is thought to be that which contains little knowledge; and an enlarged mind, that which holds a deal; and what seems to put the matter beyond dispute is, the fact of the number of studies which are pursued in a university, by its very profession. Lectures are given on every kind of subject; examinations are held; prizes awarded. There are moral, metaphysical, physical professors; professors of languages, of history, of mathematics, of experimental science. Lists of questions are published, wonderful for their range and depth, variety and difficulty; treatises are written, which carry upon their very face the evidence of extensive reading or multifarious information; what then is wanted for mental culture to a person of large reading and scientific attainments? what is grasp of mind but acquirement? where shall philosophical repose be found, but in the consciousness and enjoyment of large intellectual possessions?

And yet this notion is, I conceive, a mistake, and my present business is to show that it is one, and that the end of a liberal education is not mere knowledge, or knowledge considered in its *matter*; and I shall best attain my object by actually setting down some cases, which will be generally granted to be instances of the process of enlightenment or enlargement of mind, and others which are not, and thus, by the comparison, you will be able to judge for yourselves, gentlemen, whether knowledge, that is, acquirement, is after all the real principle of the enlargement, or whether that principle is not rather something beyond it.

For instance, let a person, whose experience has hitherto been confined to the more calm and unpretending scenery of these islands, whether here [3] or in England, go for the first time into parts where physical nature puts on her wilder and more awful forms, whether at home or abroad, as into mountainous districts; or let one, who has ever lived in a quiet village, go for the first time to a great metropolis—then I suppose he will have a sensation which perhaps he never had before. He has a feeling not in addition or increase of former feelings, but of something different in its nature. He will perhaps be borne forward, and find for a time that he has lost his bearings. He has made a certain progress, and he has a consciousness of mental enlargement; he does not stand where he did, he has a new center, and a range of thoughts to which he was before a stranger.

Again, the view of the heavens which the telescope opens upon us, if allowed to fill and possess the mind, may almost whirl it round and make it dizzy. It brings in a flood of ideas, and is rightly called an intellectual enlargement, whatever is meant by the term.

And so again, the sight of beasts of prey and other foreign animals, their strangeness, the originality (if I may use the term) of their forms and gestures and habits and their variety and independence of each other, throw us out of ourselves into another creation, and as if under another Creator, if I may so express the temptation which may come on the mind. We seem to have new faculties, or a new exercise for our faculties, by this addition to our knowledge; like a prisoner who, having been accustomed to wear manacles or fetters, suddenly finds his arms and legs free.

Hence physical science generally, in all its departments, as bringing before us the exuberant riches and resources, yet the orderly course, of the universe, elevates and excites the student, and at first, I may say, almost takes away his breath, while in time it exercises a tranquilizing influence upon him.

Again, the study of history is said to enlarge and enlighten the mind, and why? because, as I conceive, it gives it a power of judging of passing events, and of all events, and a con-

scious superiority over them which before it did not possess.

And in like manner, what is called seeing the world, entering into active life, going into society, traveling, gaining acquaintance with the various classes of the community, coming into contact with the principles and modes of thought of various parties, interests, and races, their views, aims, habits, and manners, their religious creeds and forms of worship—gaining experience how various yet how alike men are, how low-minded, how bad, how opposed, yet how confident in their opinions; all this exerts a perceptible influence upon the mind, which it is impossible to mistake, be it good or be it bad, and is popularly called its enlargement.

And then again, the first time the mind comes across the arguments and speculations of unbelievers, and feels what a novel light they cast upon what he has hitherto accounted sacred; and still more, if it gives in to them and embraces them, and throws off as so much prejudice what it has hitherto held, and, as if waking from a dream, begins to realize to its imagination that there is now no such thing as law and the transgression of law, that sin is a phantom, and punishment a bugbear, that it is free to sin, free to enjoy the world and the flesh; and still further, when it does enjoy them, and reflects that it may think and hold just what it will, that "the world is all before it where to choose," [4] and what system to build up as its own private persuasion; when this torrent of bad thoughts rushes over and inundates it, who will deny that the fruit of the tree of knowledge, or what the mind takes for knowledge, has made it one of the gods, with a sense of expansion and elevation—an intoxication in reality, still, so far as the subjective state of the mind goes, an illumination? Hence the fanaticism of individuals or nations, who suddenly cast off their Maker. Their eyes are opened, and, like the judgment-stricken king in the tragedy, [5] they see two suns, and a magic universe, out of which they look back upon their former state of faith and innocence with a sort of contempt and indignation, as if they were then but fools, and the dupes of imposture.

On the other hand, religion has its own enlargement, and an enlargement, not of tumult, but of peace. It is often remarked of uneducated persons, who have hitherto thought little of the unseen world, that, on their turning to

---

[3] In Ireland.

[4] *Paradise Lost,* XII, 646.

[5] Pentheus of Thebes, in the *Bacchae* of Euripides. Pentheus speaks of seeming to see two suns in l. 918.

God, looking into themselves, regulating their hearts, reforming their conduct, and meditating on death and judgment, heaven and hell, they seem to become, in point of intellect, different beings from what they were. Before, they took things as they came, and thought no more of one thing than another. But now every event has a meaning; they have their own estimate of whatever happens to them; they are mindful of times and seasons, and compare the present with the past; and the world, no longer dull, monotonous, unprofitable, and hopeless, is a various and complicated drama, with parts and an object, and an awful moral.

Now from these instances, to which many more might be added, it is plain, first, that the communication of knowledge certainly is either a condition or the means of that sense of enlargement or enlightenment, of which at this day we hear so much in certain quarters: this cannot be denied; but next, it is equally plain, that such communication is not the whole of the process. The enlargement consists, not merely in the passive reception into the mind of a number of ideas hitherto unknown to it, but in the mind's energetic and simultaneous action upon and towards and among those new ideas, which are rushing in upon it. It is the action of a formative power, reducing to order and meaning the matter of our acquirements; it is a making the objects of our knowledge subjectively our own, or, to use a familiar word, it is a digestion of what we receive, into the substance of our previous state of thought; and without this no enlargement is said to follow. There is no enlargement, unless there be a comparison of ideas one with another, as they come before the mind, and a systematizing of them. We feel our minds to be growing and expanding *then*, when we not only learn, but refer what we learn to what we know already. It is not a mere addition to our knowledge which is the illumination; but the locomotion, the movement onwards, of that mental center, to which both what we know and what we are learning, the accumulating mass of our acquirements, gravitates. And therefore a truly great intellect, and recognized to be such by the common opinion of mankind, such as the intellect of Aristotle, or of St. Thomas,[6] or of Newton, or of Goethe (I purposely take instances within and without the Catholic pale, when I would speak of the intellect as such), is one which takes a connected view of old and new, past and present, far and near, and which has an insight into the

[6] Aquinas (*c.* 1225–1274).

influence of all these one on another; without which there is no whole, and no center. It possesses the knowledge, not only of things, but also of their mutual and true relations; knowledge, not merely considered as acquirement, but as philosophy.

Accordingly, when this analytical, distributive, harmonizing process is away, the mind experiences no enlargement, and is not reckoned as enlightened or comprehensive, whatever it may add to its knowledge. For instance, a great memory, as I have already said, does not make a philosopher, any more than a dictionary can be called a grammar. There are men who embrace in their minds a vast multitude of ideas, but with little sensibility about their real relations towards each other. These may be antiquarians, annalists, naturalists; they may be learned in the law; they may be versed in statistics; they are most useful in their own place; I should shrink from speaking disrespectfully of them; still, there is nothing in such attainments to guarantee the absence of narrowness of mind. If they are nothing more than well-read men, or men of information, they have not what specially deserves the name of culture of mind, or fulfills the type of liberal education.

In like manner we sometimes fall in with persons who have seen much of the world, and of the men who, in their day, have played a conspicuous part in it, but who generalize nothing, and have no observation, in the true sense of the word. They abound in information in detail, curious and entertaining, about men and things; and, having lived under the influence of no very clear or settled principles, religious or political, they speak of every one and everything, only as so many phenomena, which are complete in themselves, and lead to nothing, not discussing them, or teaching any truth, or instructing the hearer, but simply talking. No one would say that these persons, well informed as they are, had attained to any great culture of intellect or to philosophy.

The case is the same still more strikingly where the persons in question are beyond dispute men of inferior powers and deficient education. Perhaps they have been much in foreign countries, and they receive, in a passive, otiose, unfruitful way, the various facts which are forced upon them there. Seafaring men, for example, range from one end of the earth to the other; but the multiplicity of external objects which they have encountered forms no symmetrical and consistent picture upon their imagination; they see the tapestry of human life as it were on the wrong side, and it tells no story. They sleep, and they rise up, and they find themselves now in Europe, now in Asia; they see visions of great cities and wild regions; they are in the marts of commerce or amid the islands of the South; they gaze on Pompey's Pillar [7] or on the Andes; and nothing which meets them carries them forward or backward to any idea beyond itself. Nothing has a drift or relation; nothing has a history or a promise. Everything stands by itself, and comes and goes in its turn, like the shifting scenes of a show, which leave the spectator where he was. Perhaps you are near such a man on a particular occasion, and expect him to be shocked or perplexed at something which occurs; but one thing is much the same to him as another, or, if he is perplexed, it is as not knowing what to say, whether it is right to admire, or to ridicule, or to disapprove, while conscious that some expression of opinion is expected from him; for in fact he has no standard of judgment at all, and no landmarks to guide him to a conclusion. Such is mere acquisition, and, I repeat, no one would dream of calling it philosophy.

Instances such as these confirm, by the contrast, the conclusion I have already drawn from those which preceded them. That only is true enlargement of mind which is the power of viewing many things at once as one whole, of referring them severally to their true place in the universal system, of understanding their respective values, and determining their mutual dependence. Thus is that form of universal knowledge, of which I have on a former occasion spoken, set up in the individual intellect, and constitutes its perfection. Possessed of this real illumination, the mind never views any part of the extended subject-matter of knowledge without recollecting that it is but a part, or without the associations which spring from this recollection. It makes everything in some sort lead to everything else; it would communicate the image of the whole to every separate portion, till that whole becomes in imagination like a spirit, everywhere pervading and penetrating its component parts, and giving them one definite meaning. Just as our bodily organs, when mentioned, recall their function in the body, as the word "creation" suggests the Creator, and "subjects" a sovereign, so, in the mind of the philosopher, as we are abstractedly conceiving of him, the elements of the physical and moral world, sciences, arts, pursuits, ranks,

offices, events, opinions, individualities, are all viewed as one, with correlative functions, and as gradually by successive combinations converging, one and all, to the true center.

To have even a portion of this illuminative reason and true philosophy is the highest state to which nature can aspire, in the way of intellect; it puts the mind above the influences of chance and necessity, above anxiety, suspense, tumult, and superstition, which are the portion of the many. Men, whose minds are possessed with some one object, take exaggerated views of its importance, are feverish in the pursuit of it, make it the measure of things which are utterly foreign to it, and are startled and despond if it happens to fail them. They are ever in alarm or in transport. Those on the other hand who have no object or principle whatever to hold by, lose their way, every step they take. They are thrown out, and do not know what to think or say, at every fresh juncture; they have no view of persons, or occurrences, or facts, which come suddenly upon them, and they hang upon the opinion of others, for want of internal resources. But the intellect, which has been disciplined to the perfection of its powers, which knows, and thinks while it knows, which has learned to leaven the dense mass of facts and events with the elastic force of reason, such an intellect cannot be partial, cannot be exclusive, cannot be impetuous, cannot be at a loss, cannot but be patient, collected, and majestically calm, because it discerns the end in every beginning, the origin in every end, the law in every interruption, the limit in each delay; because it ever knows where it stands, and how its path lies from one point to another. It is the τετράγωνος of the Peripatetic,[8] and has the *nil admirari* [9] of the Stoic—

*Felix qui potuit rerum cognoscere causas,*
*Atque metus omnes, et inexorabile fatum*
*Subjecit pedibus, strepitumque Acherontis avari.* [10]

There are men who, when in difficulties, originate at the moment vast ideas or dazzling projects; who, under the influence of excitement, are able to cast a light, almost as if from inspiration, on a subject or course of action which comes before them; who have a sudden

---

[7] Near Alexandria.

[8] The four-square man of Aristotle (see *Nicomachean Ethics*, I, x, 11), who was called the Peripatetic because, according to tradition, he walked about in the Lyceum while lecturing to his pupils.

[9] To wonder at nothing (Horace, *Epistles*, I, vi, 1).

[10] Happy is he who is able to know the sequences of things, and thus triumphs over all fear, and inexorable fate, and the roar of greedy Acheron (Virgil, *Georgics*, II, 490–492).

presence of mind equal to any emergency, rising with the occasion, and an undaunted magnanimous bearing, and an energy and keenness which is but made intense by opposition. This is genius, this is heroism; it is the exhibition of a natural gift, which no culture can teach, at which no institution can aim; here, on the contrary, we are concerned, not with mere nature, but with training and teaching. That perfection of the intellect, which is the result of education, and its *beau ideal*, to be imparted to individuals in their respective measures, is the clear, calm, accurate vision and comprehension of all things, as far as the finite mind can embrace them, each in its place, and with its own characteristics upon it. It is almost prophetic from its knowledge of history; it is almost heart-searching from its knowledge of human nature; it has almost supernatural charity from its freedom from littleness and prejudice; it has almost the repose of faith, because nothing can startle it; it has almost the beauty and harmony of heavenly contemplation, so intimate is it with the eternal order of things and the music of the spheres.

And now, if I may take for granted that the true and adequate end of intellectual training and of a university is not learning or acquirement, but rather, is thought or reason exercised upon knowledge, or what may be called philosophy, I shall be in a position to explain the various mistakes which at the present day beset the subject of university education.

I say then, if we would improve the intellect, first of all, we must ascend: we cannot gain real knowledge on a level; we must generalize, we must reduce to method, we must have a grasp of principles, and group and shape our acquisitions by them. It matters not whether our field of operation be wide or limited; in every case, to command it, is to mount above it. Who has not felt the irritation of mind and impatience created by a deep, rich country, visited for the first time, with winding lanes, and high hedges, and green steeps, and tangled woods, and everything smiling indeed, but in a maze? The same feeling comes upon us in a strange city, when we have no map of its streets. Hence you hear of practiced travelers, when they first come into a place, mounting some high hill or church tower, by way of reconnoitering its neighborhood. In like manner you must be above your knowledge, gentlemen, not under it, or it will oppress you; and the more you have of it the greater will be the load. The learning of a Salmasius [11] or a Burman, [12] unless you are its master, will be your tyrant. *Imperat aut servit*; [13] if you can wield it with a strong arm, it is a great weapon; otherwise,

> *Vis consili expers*
> *Mole ruit sua.* [14]

You will be overwhelmed, like Tarpeia, [15] by the heavy wealth which you have exacted from tributary generations.

Instances abound; there are authors who are as pointless as they are inexhaustible in their literary resources. They measure knowledge by bulk, as it lies in the rude block, without symmetry, without design. How many commentators are there on the Classics, how many on Holy Scripture, from whom we rise up, wondering at the learning which has passed before us, and wondering why it passed! How many writers are there of ecclesiastical history, such as Mosheim or Du Pin, [16] who, breaking up their subject into details, destroy its life, and defraud us of the whole by their anxiety about the parts! The sermons, again, of the English divines in the seventeenth century, how often are they mere repertories of miscellaneous and officious learning! Of course Catholics also may read without thinking; and in their case, equally as with Protestants, it holds good, that that knowledge of theirs is unworthy of the name, knowledge which they have not thought through, and thought out. Such readers are only possessed by their knowledge, and not possessed of it; nay, in matter of fact they are often even carried away by it, without any volition of their own. Recollect, the memory can tyrannize as well as the imagination. Derangement, I believe, has been considered as a loss of control over the sequence of ideas. The mind, once set in motion, is henceforth deprived of the power of initiation, and becomes the victim of a train of associations, one thought suggesting another, in the way of cause and effect, as if by a mechanical process, or some physical

[11] Dutch classical scholar (1588–1653), professor at Leyden.

[12] Also a Dutch scholar (1668–1741), professor at Utrecht and Leyden.

[13] It either commands or serves (said of money, Horace, *Epistles*, I, x, 48).

[14] Force without discretion falls of its own weight (Horace, *Odes*, III, iv, 65).

[15] She betrayed the Roman citadel on the Capitoline Hill to the Sabines, in return for what they wore on their arms. What she wanted was their bracelets, but instead they cast their shields on her and crushed her to death.

[16] The former a German Protestant (1694–1755), the latter a Frenchman (1782–1865).

necessity. No one, who has had experience of men of studious habits, but must recognize the existence of a parallel phenomenon in the case of those who have over-stimulated the memory. In such persons reason acts almost as feebly and as impotently as in the madman; once fairly started on any subject whatever, they have no power of self-control; they passively endure the succession of impulses which are evolved out of the original exciting cause; they are passed on from one idea to another and go steadily forward, plodding along one line of thought in spite of the amplest concessions of the hearer, or wandering from it in endless digression in spite of his remonstrances. Now, if, as is very certain, no one would envy the madman the glow and originality of his conceptions, why must we extol the cultivation of that intellect, which is the prey, not indeed of barren fancies but of barren facts, of random intrusions from without, though not of morbid imaginations from within? And in thus speaking, I am not denying that a strong and ready memory is in itself a real treasure; I am not disparaging a well-stored mind, though it be nothing besides, provided it be sober, any more than I would despise a bookseller's shop: it is of great value to others, even when not so to the owner. Nor am I banishing, far from it, the possessors of deep and multifarious learning from my ideal university; they adorn it in the eyes of men; I do but say that they constitute no type of the results at which it aims; that it is no great gain to the intellect to have enlarged the memory at the expense of faculties which are indisputably higher.

Nor indeed am I supposing that there is any great danger, at least in this day, of over-education; the danger is on the other side. I will tell you, gentlemen, what has been the practical error of the last twenty years—not to load the memory of the student with a mass of undigested knowledge, but to attempt so much that nothing has been really effected, to teach so many things, that nothing has properly been learned at all. It has been the error of distracting and enfeebling the mind by an unmeaning profusion of subjects; of implying that a smattering in a dozen branches of study was not shallowness, which it really is, but enlargement; of considering an acquaintance with the learned names of things and persons, and the possession of clever duodecimos, and attendance on eloquent lecturers, and membership with scientific institutions, and the sight of the experiments of a platform and the specimens of a museum, that all this was not dissipation of mind, but progress. All things now are to be learned at once, not first one thing, then another, not one well but many badly. Learning is to be without exertion, without attention, without toil; without grounding, without advance, without finishing. There is to be nothing individual in it; and this, forsooth, is the wonder of the age. What the steam-engine does with matter, the printing-press is to do with mind; it is to act mechanically, and the population is to be passively, almost unconsciously enlightened, by the mere multiplication and dissemination of volumes. Whether it be the schoolboy, or the schoolgirl, or the youth at college, or the mechanic in the town, or the politician in the senate, all have been the victims in one way or other of this most preposterous and pernicious of delusions. Wise men have lifted up their voices in vain; and at length, lest their own institutions should be outshone and should disappear in the folly of the hour, they have been obliged, as far as was conscientiously possible, to humor a spirit which they could not withstand, and make temporizing concessions at which they could not but inwardly smile.

Now I must guard, gentlemen, against any possible misconception of my meaning. Let me frankly declare then, that I have no fear at all of the education of the people: the more education they have the better, so that it is really education. Next, as to the cheap publication of scientific and literary works, which is now in vogue, I consider it a great advantage, convenience, and gain; that is, to those to whom education has given a capacity for using them. Further, I consider such innocent recreations as science and literature are able to furnish will be a very fit occupation of the thoughts and the leisure of young persons, and may be made the means of keeping them from bad employments and bad companions. Moreover, as to that superficial acquaintance with chemistry, and geology, and astronomy, and political economy, and modern history, and biography, and other branches of knowledge, which periodical literature and occasional lectures and scientific institutions diffuse through the community, I think it a graceful accomplishment, and a suitable, nay, in this day a necessary accomplishment, in the case of educated men. Nor, lastly, am I disparaging or discouraging the thorough acquisition of any one of these studies, or denying that, as far as it goes, such thorough acquisition is a real education of the mind. All I say is, call things by their right names, and do not confuse together ideas which are essentially different. A thorough knowledge of one science and a superficial acquaintance with many, are not the same thing; a smattering of a hundred things or a memory for detail, is not a philosophical or comprehensive view. Recreations are not education; accomplishments are not education. Do not say, the people must be educated, when, after all, you only mean amused, refreshed, soothed, put into good spirits and good humor, or kept from vicious excesses. I do not say that such amusements, such occupations of mind, are not a great gain; but they are not education. You may as well call drawing and fencing education, as a general knowledge of botany or conchology. Stuffing birds or playing stringed instruments is an elegant pastime, and a resource to the idle, but it is not education; it does not form or cultivate the intellect. Education is a high word; it is the preparation for knowledge, and it is the imparting of knowledge in proportion to that preparation. We require intellectual eyes to know withal, as bodily eyes for sight. We need both objects and organs intellectual; we cannot gain them without setting about it; we cannot gain them in our sleep or by haphazard. The best telescope does not dispense with eyes; the printing-press or the lecture room will assist us greatly, but we must be true to ourselves, we must be parties in the work. A university is, according to the usual designation, an *alma mater*, knowing her children one by one, not a foundry, or a mint, or a treadmill.

I protest to you, gentlemen, that if I had to choose between a so-called university which dispensed with residence and tutorial superintendence, and gave its degrees to any person who passed an examination in a wide range of subjects, and a university which had no professors or examinations at all, but merely brought a number of young men together for three or four years, and then sent them away as the University of Oxford is said to have done some sixty years since, if I were asked which of these two methods was the better discipline of the intellect—mind, I do not say which is *morally* the better, for it is plain that compulsory study must be a good and idleness an intolerable mischief—but if I must determine which of the two courses was the more successful in training, molding, enlarging the mind, which sent out men the more fitted for their secular duties, which produced better public men, men of the world, men whose names would descend to posterity, I have no hesitation in giving the preference to that university which did nothing, over that which exacted of its members an acquaintance with every science under the sun. And, paradox as this may seem, still if results be the test of systems, the influence of the public schools and colleges of England, in the course of the last century, at least will bear out one side of the contrast as I have drawn it. What would come, on the other hand, of the ideal systems of education which have fascinated the imagination of this age, could they ever take effect, and whether they would not produce a generation frivolous, narrow-minded, and resourceless, intellectually considered, is a fair subject for debate, but so far is certain, that the universities and scholastic establishments to which I refer, and which did little more than bring together first boys and then youths in large numbers, these institutions, with miserable deformities on the side of morals, with a hollow profession of Christianity, and a heathen code of ethics—I say, at least they can boast of a succession of heroes and statesmen, of literary men and philosophers, of men conspicuous for great natural virtues, for habits of business, for knowledge of life, for practical judgment, for cultivated tastes, for accomplishments, who have made England what it is—able to subdue the earth, able to domineer over Catholics.

How is this to be explained? I suppose as follows: When a multitude of young persons, keen, open-hearted, sympathetic, and observant, as young persons are, come together and freely mix with each other, they are sure to learn one from another, even if there be no one to teach them; the conversation of all is a series of lectures to each, and they gain for themselves new ideas and views, fresh matter of thought, and distinct principles for judging and acting, day by day. An infant has to learn the meaning of the information which its senses convey to it, and this seems to be its employment. It fancies all that the eye presents to it to be close to it, till it actually learns the contrary, and thus by practice does it ascertain the relations and uses of those first elements of knowledge which are necessary for its animal existence. A parallel teaching is necessary for our social being, and it is secured by a large school or a college, and this effect may be fairly called in its own department an enlargement of mind. It is seeing the world on a small field with little trouble; for the pupils or students come from very different places, and with widely different notions, and there is much to generalize, much to adjust, much to eliminate, there are inter-relations to be defined, and conventional rules to be established, in the process, by which the whole assemblage is molded together, and gains one tone and one character. Let it be clearly understood, I repeat it, that I am not taking into account moral or religious considerations; I am but saying that that youthful community will constitute a whole, it will embody a specific idea, it will represent a doctrine, it will administer a code 10 of conduct, and it will furnish principles of thought and action. It will give birth to a living teaching, which in course of time will take the shape of a self-perpetuating tradition, or a *genius loci*,[17] as it is sometimes called, which haunts the home where it has been born, and which imbues and forms, more or less, and one by one, every individual who is successively brought under its shadow. Thus it is that, independent of direct instruction on the part of 20 superiors, there is a sort of self-education in the academic institutions of protestant England; a characteristic tone of thought, a recognized standard of judgment is found in them, which, as developed in the individual who is submitted to it, becomes a twofold source of strength to him, both from the distinct stamp it impresses on his mind, and from the bond of union which it creates between him and others —effects which are shared by the authorities 30 of the place, for they themselves have been educated in it, and at all times are exposed to the influence of its moral atmosphere. Here then is a real teaching, whatever be its standards and principles, true or false; and it at least tends towards cultivation of the intellect; it at least recognizes that knowledge is something more than a sort of passive reception of scraps and details; it is a something, and it does a something, which never will issue from the 40 most strenuous efforts of a set of teachers, with no mutual sympathies and no intercommunion, of a set of examiners with no opinions which they dare profess, and with no common principles, who are teaching or questioning a set of youths who do not know them, and do not know each other, on a large number of subjects, different in kind, and connected by no wide philosophy, three times a week, or three times a year, or once in three years, in chill lecture- 50 rooms or on a pompous anniversary.

Nay, self-education in any shape, in the most restricted sense, is preferable to a system of teaching which, professing so much, really does so little for the mind. Shut your college gates against the votary of knowledge, throw

[17] Spirit of the place.

him back upon the searchings and the efforts of his own mind; he will gain by being spared an entrance into your Babel. Few indeed there are who can dispense with the stimulus and support of instructors, or will do anything at all, if left to themselves. And fewer still (though such great minds are to be found) who will not, from such unassisted attempts, contract a self-reliance and a self-esteem, which are not only moral evils, but serious hindrances to the attainment of truth. And next to none, perhaps, or none, who will not be reminded from time to time of the disadvantage under which they lie, by their imperfect grounding, by the breaks, deficiencies, and irregularities of their knowledge, by the eccentricity of opinion and the confusion of principle which they exhibit. They will be too often ignorant of what every one knows and takes for granted, of that multitude of small truths which fall upon the mind like dust, impalpable and ever accumulating; they may be unable to converse, they may argue perversely, they may pride themselves on their worst paradoxes or their grossest truisms, they may be full of their own mode of viewing things, unwilling to be put out of their way, slow to enter into the minds of others;—but, with these and whatever other liabilities upon their heads, they are likely to have more thought, more mind, more philosophy, more true enlargement, than those earnest but ill-used persons who are forced to load their minds with a score of subjects against an examination, who have too much on their hands to indulge themselves in thinking or investigation, who devour premise and conclusion together with indiscriminate greediness, who hold whole sciences on faith, and commit demonstrations to memory, and who too often, as might be expected, when their period of education is passed, throw up all they have learned in disgust, having gained nothing really by their anxious labors, except perhaps the habit of application.

Yet such is the better specimen of the fruit of that ambitious system which has of late years been making way among us: for its result on ordinary minds, and on the common run of students, is less satisfactory still; they leave their place of education simply dissipated and relaxed by the multiplicity of subjects, which they have never really mastered, and so shallow as not even to know their shallowness. How much better, I say, is it for the active and thoughtful intellect, where such is to be found, to eschew the college and the university altogether, than to submit to a drudgery so ignoble, a mockery so contumelious! How much more profitable for the independent mind, after the mere rudiments of education, to range through a library at random, taking down books as they meet him, and pursuing the trains of thought which his mother wit suggests! How much healthier to wander into the fields, and there with the exiled prince to find "tongues in the trees, books in the running brooks!" [18] How much more genuine an education is that of the poor boy in the poem [19]—a poem, whether in conception or in execution, one of the most touching in our language—who, not in the wide world, but ranging day by day around his widowed mother's home, "a dexterous gleaner" in a narrow field, and with only such slender outfit

"as the village school and books a few
Supplied,"

contrived from the beach, and the quay, and the fisher's boat, and the inn's fireside, and the tradesman's shop, and the shepherd's walk, and the smuggler's hut, and the mossy moor, and the screaming gulls, and the restless waves, to fashion for himself a philosophy and a poetry of his own!

But in a large subject I am exceeding my necessary limits. Gentlemen, I must conclude abruptly; and postpone any summing up of my argument, should that be necessary, to another day.

## DISCOURSE VII

### Liberal Knowledge Viewed in Relation to Professional

I have been insisting, in my two preceding Discourses, first, on the cultivation of the intellect, as an end which may reasonably be pursued for its own sake; and next, on the nature of that cultivation, or what that cultivation consists in. Truth of whatever kind is the proper object of the intellect; its cultivation then lies in fitting it to apprehend and contemplate truth. Now the intellect in its present state, with exceptions which need not here be specified, does not discern truth intuitively, or as a whole. We know, not by a direct

[18] See *As You Like It*, II, i, 16.
[19] Crabbe's *Tales of the Hall* [Book IV]. This Poem, let me say, I read on its first publication, above thirty years ago, with extreme delight, and have never lost my love of it; and on taking it up lately found I was even more touched by it than heretofore. A work which can please in youth and age seems to fulfill (in logical language) the *accidental definition* of a Classic (Newman's note).

and simple vision, not at a glance, but, as it were, by piecemeal and accumulation, by a mental process, by going round an object, by the comparison, the combination, the mutual correction, the continual adaptation, of many partial notions, by the joint application and concentration upon it of many faculties and exercises of mind. Such a union and concert of the intellectual powers, such an enlargement and development, such a comprehensiveness, is necessarily a matter of training. And again, such a training is a matter of rule; it is not mere application, however exemplary, which introduces the mind to truth, nor the reading many books, nor the getting up many subjects, nor the witnessing many experiments, nor the attending many lectures. All this is short of enough; a man may have done it all, yet be lingering in the vestibule of knowledge: he may not realize what his mouth utters; he may not see with his mental eye what confronts him; he may have no grasp of things as they are; or at least he may have no power at all of advancing one step forward of himself, in consequence of what he has already acquired, no power of discriminating between truth and falsehood, of sifting out the grains of truth from the mass, of arranging things according to their real value, and, if I may use the phrase, of building up ideas. Such a power is the result of a scientific formation of mind; it is an acquired faculty of judgment, of clear-sightedness, of sagacity, of wisdom, of philosophical reach of mind, and of intellectual self-possession and repose—qualities which do not come of mere acquirement. The bodily eye, the organ for apprehending material objects, is provided by nature; the eye of the mind, of which the object is truth, is the work of discipline and habit.

This process of training, by which the intellect, instead of being formed or sacrificed to some particular or accidental purpose, some specific trade or profession, or study or science, is disciplined for its own sake, for the perception of its own proper object, and for its own highest culture, is called liberal education; and though there is no one in whom it is carried as far as is conceivable, or whose intellect would be a pattern of what intellects should be made, yet there is scarcely any one but may gain an idea of what real training is, and at least look towards it, and make its true scope and result, not something else, his standard of excellence; and numbers there are who may submit themselves to it, and secure it to themselves in good measure. And to set forth the right standard, and to train according to it, and to help forward all students towards it according to their various capacities, this I conceive to be the business of a university. . . .

To-day I have confined myself to saying that that training of the intellect, which is best for the individual himself, best enables him to discharge his duties to society. The philosopher, indeed, and the man of the world differ in their very notion, but the methods by which [10] they are respectively formed are pretty much the same. The philosopher has the same command of matters of thought, which the true citizen and gentleman has of matters of business and conduct. If then a practical end must be assigned to a university course, I say it is that of training good members of society. Its art is the art of social life, and its end is fitness for the world. It neither confines its views to particular professions on the one hand, [20] nor creates heroes or inspires genius on the other. Works indeed of genius fall under no art; heroic minds come under no rule; a university is not a birthplace of poets or of immortal authors, of founders of schools, leaders of colonies, or conquerors of nations. It does not promise a generation of Aristotles or Newtons, of Napoleons or Washingtons, of Raphaels or Shakespeares, though such miracles of nature it has before now contained within [30] its precincts. Nor is it content on the other hand with forming the critic or the experimentalist, the economist or the engineer, though such too it includes within its scope. But a university training is the great ordinary means to a great but ordinary end; it aims at raising the intellectual tone of society, at cultivating the public mind, at purifying the national taste, at supplying true principles to popular enthusiasm and fixed aims to popular aspiration, at [40] giving enlargement and sobriety to the ideas of

the age, at facilitating the exercise of political power, and refining the intercourse of private life. It is the education which gives a man a clear conscious view of his own opinions and judgments, a truth in developing them, an eloquence in expressing them, and a force in urging them. It teaches him to see things as they are, to go right to the point, to disentangle a skein of thought, to detect what is sophistical, and to discard what is irrelevant. It prepares him to fill any post with credit, and to master any subject with facility. It shows him how to accommodate himself to others, how to throw himself into their state of mind, how to bring before them his own, how to influence them, how to come to an understanding with them, how to bear with them. He is at home in any society, he has common ground with every class; he knows when to speak and when to be silent; he is able to converse, he is able to listen; he can ask a question pertinently, and gain a lesson seasonably, when he has nothing to impart himself; he is ever ready, yet never in the way; he is a pleasant companion, and a comrade you can depend upon; he knows when to be serious and when to trifle, and he has a sure tact which enables him to trifle with gracefulness and to be serious with effect. He has the repose of a mind which lives in itself, while it lives in the world, and which has resources for its happiness at home when it cannot go abroad. He has a gift which serves him in public, and supports him in retirement, without which good fortune is but vulgar, and with which failure and disappointment have a charm. The art which tends to make a man all this, is in the object which it pursues as useful as the art of wealth or the art of health, though it is less susceptible of method, and less tangible, less certain, less complete in its result.

# Edward FitzGerald

## 1809-1883

FitzGerald's father was John Purcell, the son of a wealthy Irish doctor, who had married his first cousin, Mary Francis FitzGerald, and who, on the death of her father, took the name and arms of FitzGerald. Edward was the seventh of their eight children, and was born at Bredfield House, near Woodbridge, Suffolk, on 31 March, 1809. In 1821 he was sent to King Edward the Sixth's Grammar School at Bury St. Edmonds. He entered Trinity College, Cambridge, in 1826, and took his degree in 1830. At school had begun what was to be a life-long friendship with James Spedding, the editor, biographer, and wholehearted defender of Francis Bacon. At Cambridge a similar friendship with Thackeray was formed. The Tennysons, Charles, Frederic, and Alfred, were also college contemporaries, but he did not know them until later. The greater part of Fitz-Gerald's life was passed in the county of his birth. He was not pressed by his family to enter any profession, and apparently never even thought of doing so. He had an allowance from his father until the latter's bankruptcy, and thereafter from his mother—her estates not being involved—until her death, after which he enjoyed a large income. For some of his relatives he felt a true affection, but got along well with all of them by dint of meeting them very seldom. At Cambridge he had formed large plans for literary work; but after his departure he drifted promptly into a vague, easy, indeterminate way of life which lasted, not entirely to his content, yet not without its sufficient rewards, until his death. In 1837, feeling a need for a place of his own, he took a thatched lodge on property belonging to his family. "Here, with Shakespeare's bust in a recess, with a cat, a dog, and a parrot called 'Beauty Bob,' he began what he called a very pleasant Robinson Crusoe sort of life. He was waited upon by an old couple, John Faiers, a laborer on the estate, a Waterloo veteran, and Mrs. Faiers, a red-armed, vain, and snuff-taking lady, with a flower-trimmed bonnet. FitzGerald installed his books and pictures in the cottage. The place was a scene of desperate confusion. There were books everywhere; pictures on easels; music, pipes, sticks lying on tables or on the piano. A barrel of beer provided the means of simple conviviality. Here FitzGerald would sit, unkempt and unshaven, in dressing-gown and slippers, or moon about in the garden. He strolled about the neighborhood, calling on his friends; sometimes, but rarely, he went to church, noting the toadstools that grew in the chancel; and led a thoroughly indolent life," though still with dreams of literary achievement.

This picture, drawn by A. C. Benson, is typical, and may stand for FitzGerald's way of life from this time on, though as he grew older he grew somewhat more eccentric, withdrew himself further and further from the world and society, and became more convinced than ever of the futility of earthly existence—without, however, losing his interest in literature and in his own occasional and modest achievements, and without ceasing to carry on correspondence with dear friends. The two closest to him at the time of Benson's picture were George Crabbe, son of the poet (who liked his father for everything except his poetry), and Bernard Barton, a Quaker poet of Woodbridge and friend of Charles Lamb. When Barton died, FitzGerald undertook to see that his daughter, Lucy, was provided for, and ended by marrying her (November, 1856). It was, as he seems himself to have suspected, a wretchedly mistaken venture; and after a few months the two separated, without ill-feeling, Lucy receiving through the remainder of her life a liberal allowance from him. Meanwhile FitzGerald had published Euphranor (1851), a dialogue in the Platonic manner, in which he sought to define the well-balanced man; Polonius: A Collection of Wise Saws and Modern Instances (1852); and Six Dramas of Calderon Freely Translated

(1853). *The last was the only book which he published with his own name attached to it— and he did so in this instance only to help distinguish his book from another volume of translations from Calderon which was published almost simultaneously. His modesty, his detachment, his concern for the work rather than for his own reputation, all contributed to his determined anonymity; but, in addition, he had an actual dislike for his own name. He had "some unpleasant associations with it," he said. Later he printed other translations— all, like the one upon which his fame now securely rests, free adaptations rather than faithful renderings, aimed to catch the spirit rather than the letter, in a form pleasing to English readers. He owed his acquaintance with Persian literature to his friend E. B. Cowell, later a professor at Cambridge, and found the quatrains of Omar Khayyám peculiarly congenial to his own temper—so much so, in fact, that he drifted almost unawares into the attempt to make an English poem of them. The first edition of the* Rubáiyát *was printed in 1859. Other editions, much changed, appeared in 1868, 1872, and 1879.*

*During all these years FitzGerald's quiet life went on with little change. Very rarely he saw friends from a distance. Carlyle had visited him in 1855, and had never afterwards lost touch with this "lonely, shy, kind-hearted man," as he called him. In 1876 Tennyson visited him, and on this occasion his host told the great man that it would have been better for his reputation had he ceased to write poetry after 1842—but their old friendship was not broken. FitzGerald was then living in his own house, Little Grange, which he had owned since 1864, but which he apparently objected to occupying—as he was only forced to inhabit it after he had been ejected from lodgings in Woodbridge, and had found other lodgings uncomfortable. The reason for his ejection was characteristic. His landlord, named Berry, became engaged to a widow. FitzGerald did not like the impending change, and remarked that "old Berry would now have to be called 'Old Gooseberry.'" The widow heard of this, and punished the offender by compelling his ejection. He had still some years to live, dying suddenly on 14 June, 1883, while on a visit to the grandson of the poet Crabbe, at Merton Rectory, in Norfolk. In 1889 his friend W. Aldis Wright published FitzGerald's* Letters and Literary Remains *in three volumes, and thus gave him a new claim to remembrance; —for, if he very properly remains best known for his singularly happy rendering of the* Rubáiyát, *he has become only less well known as one of the most delightful letter-writers England has had.*

*The Variorum and Definitive Edition of the Poetical and Prose Writings of Edward FitzGerald is edited by George Bentham and includes an Introduction by Edmund Gosse (7 vols., New York, 1902–1903). Most of the published letters may be found in the following volumes:* Letters and Literary Remains of Edward FitzGerald, *ed. William Aldis Wright (London, 1889; the letters were reprinted separately with additions in 2 vols., 1894);* Letters of Edward FitzGerald to Fanny Kemble, 1871– 1883, *ed. William Aldis Wright (London, 1895); and* More Letters of Edward FitzGerald *(London, 1901). Arthur C. Benson's* Edward FitzGerald *(London, 1905) and Alfred M. Terhune's* The Life of Fitzgerald *(New Haven, 1947) are useful biographies.*

# Rubáiyát of Omar Khayyám [1]

## (1859)

### I

Wake! For the Sun, who scattered into flight
The Stars before him from the field of Night,
   Drives Night along with them from heav'n,
    and strikes
The Sultán's turret with a shaft of light.

### II

Before the phantom of False Morning [2] died,   5
Methought a Voice within the Tavern cried:
   "When all the temple is prepared within,
Why nods the drowsy worshiper outside?"

[1] The poem is here printed in its final form (4th ed., 1879). Omar Khayyám lived during the last half of the 11th century and the earlier years of the 12th. He was a philosopher and a man of science, and during the later years of his life was the astronomer-royal at the court of the Turkish sultan then ruling in Persia. He aided at this time in reforming the calendar. His extant quatrains are about 1200 in number, though not all of these may really come from his hand. Those qualified to judge say that FitzGerald's poem reproduces very exactly the spirit of Omar's verse; but it is not, in the sense of the word now usual, a translation. Great liberties are taken in rearranging, combining, compressing, and omitting Omar's quatrains, so as to permit the composition of an English poem of moderate length having the connection between its parts, the organic structure, which Western readers expect.

[2] A transient light on the horizon about an hour before the true dawn; a well-known phenomenon in the East. (FitzGerald.)

### III

And, as the cock crew, those who stood before
The Tavern shouted: "Open, then, the door! [10]
You know how little while we have to stay,
And, once departed, may return no more."

### IV

Now the New Year [3] reviving old desires,
The thoughtful soul to solitude retires,
Where the WHITE HAND OF MOSES [4] on the
bough 15
Puts out, and Jesus from the ground suspires.[5]

### V

Iram [6] indeed is gone with all his Rose,
And Jamshyd's Sev'n-ringed Cup [7] where no
one knows:
But still a ruby kindles in the vine,
And many a garden by the water blows. 20

### VI

And David's lips are locked; but in divine
High-piping Pehlevi,[8] with "Wine! Wine!
Wine!
Red Wine!"—the Nightingale cries to the
Rose
That sallow cheek of hers to incarnadine.

### VII

Come, fill the cup, and in the fire of spring 25
Your winter-garment of repentance fling:
The Bird of Time has but a little way
To flutter—and the Bird is on the wing.

### VIII

Whether at Naishápúr or Babylon,
Whether the Cup with sweet or bitter run, 30
The Wine of Life keeps oozing drop by
drop,
The Leaves of Life keep falling one by one.

### IX

Each morn a thousand roses brings, you say:
Yes, but where leaves the rose of yesterday?
And this first summer month that brings the
rose 35
Shall take Jamshyd and Kaikobád away.

[3] Beginning on 21 March.
[4] See Exodus, iv, 6. (The expression here denotes the white blossoms of the spring.)
[5] Breathes. (The Persians conceived the healing power of Jesus to reside in his breath.)
[6] A royal garden now sunk somewhere in the sands of Arabia. (FitzGerald.)
[7] It was typical of the 7 heavens, 7 planets, 7 seas, *etc.*, and was a divining cup. (FitzGerald.) Jamshyd: an ancient legendary king of Persia.
[8] The old heroic Sanskrit of Persia. (FitzGerald.) The people's language changes with the generations, while the nightingale's song remains ever the same.

### X

Well, let it take them! What have we to do
With Kaikobád the Great, or Kaikhosrú?
Let Zál and Rustum [9] bluster as they will,
Or Hátim call to supper—heed not you. 40

### XI

With me along the strip of herbage strown
That just divides the desert from the sown,
Where name of Slave and Sultán is forgot—
And peace to Mahmúd [10] on his golden throne!

### XII

A book of verses underneath the bough, 45
A jug of wine, a loaf of bread—and Thou
Beside me singing in the wilderness—
Oh, wilderness were Paradise enow!

### XIII

Some for the glories of this world; and some
Sigh for the Prophet's [11] Paradise to come; 50
Ah, take the cash, and let the credit go,
Nor heed the rumble of a distant drum! [12]

### XIV

Look to the blowing Rose about us—"Lo,
Laughing," she says, "into the world I blow,
At once the silken tassel of my purse 55
Tear, and its treasure [13] on the garden throw."

### XV

And those who husbanded the golden grain,
And those who flung it to the winds like rain,
Alike to no such aureate earth are turned
As, buried once, men want dug up again. 60

### XVI

The worldly hope men set their hearts upon
Turns ashes—or it prospers; and anon,
Like snow upon the desert's dusty face,
Lighting a little hour or two—is gone.

### XVII

Think, in this battered Caravanserai 65
Whose portals are altérnate Night and Day,
How Sultán after Sultán with his pomp
Abode his destined hour, and went his way.

### XVIII

They say the lion and the lizard keep
The Courts where Jamshyd gloried and drank
deep: 70
And Bahrám,[14] that great Hunter—the wild ass

[9] The Hercules of Persia. Zál was his father. Hátim, a well-known type of oriental generosity (FitzGerald).
[10] The earliest ruler of Persia to call himself sultan (c. 975).
[11] Mahomet's.
[12] Beaten outside a palace (FitzGerald).
[13] The rose's golden center (FitzGerald).
[14] A Sassanid ruler of Persia, who sank in a swamp while hunting.

Stamps o'er his head, but cannot break his
    sleep.

#### XIX

I sometimes think that never blows so red
The rose as where some buried Caesar bled;
    That every hyacinth the garden wears     75
Dropped in her lap from some once lovely head.

#### XX

And this reviving herb whose tender green
Fledges [15] the river-lip on which we lean—
    Ah, lean upon it lightly! for who knows
From what once lovely lip it springs unseen! [80]

#### XXI

Ah, my Belovéd, fill the cup that clears
To-day of past regrets and future fears:
    To-*morrow!*—Why, to-morrow I may be
Myself with yesterday's Sev'n Thousand
    Years.[16]

#### XXII

For some we loved, the loveliest and the best [85]
That from his vintage rolling Time hath
    pressed,
    Have drunk their Cup a round or two before,
And one by one crept silently to rest.

#### XXIII

And we that now make merry in the room
They left, and Summer dresses in new bloom,
    Ourselves, must we beneath the couch of
        earth     91
Descend—ourselves to make a couch—for
    whom?

#### XXIV

Ah, make the most of what we yet may spend,
Before we too into the dust descend:
    Dust into dust, and under dust to lie,     95
Sans [17] wine, sans song, sans singer, and—sans
    end!

#### XXV

Alike for those who for To-day prepare,
And those that after some To-morrow stare,
    A Muezzín [18] from the Tower of Darkness
        cries,
"Fools! your reward is neither here nor there."

#### XXVI

Why, all the Saints and Sages who dis-
    cussed     101
Of the Two Worlds so wisely—they are thrust
    Like foolish prophets forth: their words to
        scorn
Are scattered, and their mouths are stopped
    with dust.

[15] Adorns as with feathers.
[16] A thousand years to each planet (FitzGerald).
[17] Without.
[18] One who calls Mahometans to prayer.

#### XXVII

Myself when young did eagerly frequent     105
Doctor and saint, and heard great argument
    About it and about: but evermore
Came out by the same door where in I went.

#### XXVIII

With them the seed of Wisdom did I sow,
And with mine own hand wrought to make it
    grow;     110
    And this was all the harvest that I reaped:
"I came like water, and like wind I go."

#### XXIX

Into this Universe, and *Why* not knowing
Nor *Whence,* like water willy-nilly flowing;
    And out of it, as wind along the waste,     115
I know not *Whither,* willy-nilly blowing.

#### XXX

What, without asking, hither hurried *Whence?*
And, without asking, *Whither* hurried hence?
    Oh, many a cup of this forbidden wine
Must drown the memory of that insolence! [120]

#### XXXI

Up from Earth's center through the Seventh
    Gate
I rose, and on the throne of Saturn [19] sate,
    And many a knot unraveled by the road,
But not the Master-knot of Human Fate.

#### XXXII

There was the door to which I found no key;
There was the veil through which I might not
    see:     126
    Some little talk awhile of Me and Thee [20]
There was—and then no more of Thee and
    Me.

#### XXXIII

Earth could not answer; nor the seas that
    mourn
In flowing purple, of their Lord forlorn;     130
    Nor rolling Heaven, with all his Signs re-
        vealed
And hidden by the sleeve of Night and Morn.

#### XXXIV

Then of the Thee in Me who works behind
The Veil, I lifted up my hands to find
    A lamp amid the Darkness; and I heard, [135]
As from Without: "The Me within Thee
    blind!"

#### XXXV

Then to the lip of this poor earthen urn
I learned, the Secret of my Life to learn:
    And lip to lip it murmured: "While you live,

[19] Lord of the seventh heaven (FitzGerald).
[20] Some dividual existence or personality distinct
from the Whole (FitzGerald).

Drink!—for, once dead, you never shall re-
    turn."                                    140

#### XXXVI

I think the vessel, that with fugitive
Articulation answered, once did live,
    And drink; and ah! the passive lip I kissed,
How many kisses might it take—and give!

#### XXXVII

For I remember stopping by the way    145
To watch a Potter thumping his wet Clay:
    And with its all-obliterated tongue
It murmured: "Gently, Brother, gently,
    pray!" 21

#### XXXVIII

And has not such a story from of old
Down Man's successive generations rolled 150
    Of such a clod of saturated earth
Cast by the Maker into human mold?

#### XXXIX

And not a drop that from our cups we throw
For Earth to drink of,22 but may steal below
    To quench the fire of anguish in some eye 155
There hidden—far beneath, and long ago.

#### XL

As then the Tulip, for her morning sup
Of heav'nly vintage, from the soil looks up,
    Do you devoutly do the like, till Heav'n
To Earth invert you—like an empty Cup.    160

#### XLI

Perplexed no more with Human or Divine,
To-morrow's tangle to the winds resign,
    And lose your fingers in the tresses of
The cypress-slender minister of wine.

#### XLII

And if the wine you drink, the lip you press,
End in what All begins and ends in—Yes:  166
    Think then you are To-day what Yesterday
You were—To-morrow you shall not be less.

#### XLIII

So when that Angel of the Darker Drink
At last shall find you by the river-brink,    170
    And, offering his cup, invite your soul
Forth to your lips to quaff—you shall not
    shrink.

#### XLIV

Why, if the Soul can fling the dust aside,
And naked on the air of Heaven ride,

21 The clay from which the bowl is made was once
man (FitzGerald).
22 The custom of throwing a little wine on the
ground before drinking still continues in Persia, and
perhaps generally in the East (FitzGerald).

Were't not a shame—were't not a shame for
    him                                        175
In this clay carcase crippled to abide?

#### XLV

'Tis but a tent where takes his one day's rest
A sultán to the realm of Death addressed:
    The Sultán rises, and the dark Ferrásh 23
Strikes and prepares it for another Guest.    180

#### XLVI

And fear not lest Existence closing your
Account, and mine, should know the like no
    more:
    The Eternal Sákí 24 from that bowl has
        poured
Millions of bubbles like us, and will pour.

#### XLVII

When You and I behind the Veil are past, 185
Oh, but the long, long while the World shall
    last,
    Which of our coming and departure heeds
As the Sea's self should heed a pebble-cast.

#### XLVIII

A moment's halt—a momentary taste
Of BEING from the Well amid the Waste—  190
    And lo! the phantom Caravan has reached
The NOTHING it set out from . . . Oh, make
    haste!

#### XLIX

Would you that spangle of Existence spend
About THE SECRET—quick about it, Friend!
    A hair perhaps divides the False and True—
And upon what, prithee, may life depend? 196

#### L

A hair perhaps divides the False and True:
Yes; and a single Alif 25 were the clue—
    Could you but find it—to the Treasure-
        house,
And peradventure to THE MASTER too;    200

#### LI

Whose secret Presence, through Creation's
    veins
Running, quicksilver-like eludes your pains;
    Taking all shapes from Máh to Máhi; 26 and
They change and perish all—but He remains;

#### LII

A moment guessed—then back behind the fold
Immersed of darkness round the Drama rolled
    Which, for the pastime of Eternity,    207
He doth Himself contrive, enact, behold.

23 Servant.                    24 Wine-bearer.
25 Letter A, represented by a single stroke.
26 From Fish to Moon (FitzGerald).

### LIII

But if in vain, down on the stubborn floor
Of Earth, and up to Heav'n's unopening door,
   You gaze *To-day*, while You are You—how
     then     211
To-morrow, when You shall be You no more?

### LIV

Waste not your hour; nor, in the vain pursuit
Of This and That endeavor and dispute:
   Better be jocund with the fruitful grape 215
Than sadden after none, or bitter, fruit.

### LV

You know, my Friends, with what a brave
   carouse
I made a second marriage in my house;
   Divorced old barren Reason from my bed,
And took the Daughter of the Vine to spouse.

### LVI

For "Is" and "Is-not" though with rule and
   line,     221
And "Up-and-down" by Logic, I define,
   Of all that one should care to fathom, I
Was never deep in anything but—Wine.

### LVII

Ah, but my Computations, people say,   225
Reduced the Year to better reckoning?—Nay,
   'Twas only striking from the Calendar
Unborn To-morrow, and dead Yesterday.

### LVIII

And lately, by the Tavern Door agape,
Came shining through the dusk an Angel
   Shape     230
   Bearing a vessel on his shoulder; and
He bid me taste of it; and 'twas—the Grape!

### LIX

The Grape that can with Logic absolute
The two-and-seventy jarring sects [27] confute,
   The sovereign Alchemist that in a trice 235
Life's leaden metal into gold transmute;

### LX

The mighty Mahmúd, Allah-breathing Lord,
That all the misbelieving and black horde [28]
   Of Fears and Sorrows that infest the Soul
Scatters before him with his whirlwind sword.

### LXI

Why, be this Juice the growth of God, who
   dare     241
Blaspheme the twisted tendril as a snare?
   A blessing, we should use it, should we not?
And if a curse—why, then, Who set it there?

[27] The 72 religions supposed to divide the world (FitzGerald).

[28] Alluding to Sultan Mahmúd's conquest of India and its dark people (FitzGerald).

### LXII

I must abjure the balm of life, I must,   245
Scared by some After-reckoning ta'en on trust,
   Or lured with hope of some diviner drink
To fill the Cup—when crumbled into dust!

### LXIII

Oh, threats of Hell and hopes of Paradise!
One thing at least is certain,—*This* Life flies;
   One thing is certain and the rest is lies; 251
The flower that once has blown for ever dies.

### LXIV

Strange, is it not? that of the myriads who
Before us passed the door of Darkness through,
   Not one returns to tell us of the Road, 255
Which to discover we must travel too.

### LXV

The revelations of Devout and Learn'd
Who rose before us, and as prophets burned,
   Are all but stories which, awoke from sleep,
They told their comrades, and to sleep re-
     turned.     260

### LXVI

I sent my Soul through the Invisible,
Some letter of that After-life to spell:
   And by and by my Soul returned to me,
And answered, "I myself am Heav'n and
     Hell"—

### LXVII

Heav'n but the vision of fulfilled desire,   265
And Hell the shadow from a soul on fire,
   Cast on the Darkness into which Ourselves,
So late emerged from, shall so soon expire.

### LXVIII

We are no other than a moving row
Of magic shadow-shapes that come and go 270
   Round with the Sun-illumined Lantern held
In midnight by the Master of the Show;

### LXIX

But helpless Pieces of the game He plays
Upon this checker-board of nights and days;
   Hither and thither moves, and checks, and
     slays,     275
And one by one back in the closet lays.

### LXX

The ball no question makes of Ayes and Noes,
But here or there, as strikes the player, goes;
   And He that tossed you down into the field,
*He* knows about it all—HE knows—HE knows!

### LXXI

The Moving Finger writes; and, having writ, 231
Moves on: nor all your piety nor wit
   Shall lure it back to cancel half a line;
Nor all your tears wash out a word of it.

### LXXII

And that inverted bowl they call the Sky, 285
Whereunder crawling cooped we live and die,
   Lift not your hands to *It* for help—for *It*
As impotently moves as you or I.

### LXXIII

With Earth's first clay they did the last man
   knead,
And there of the last harvest sowed the seed; 290
   And the first morning of Creation wrote
What the last dawn of reckoning shall read.

### LXXIV

YESTERDAY *This* Day's Madness did prepare,
TO-MORROW's silence, triumph, or despair:
   Drink! for you know not whence you came,
      nor why;                               295
Drink! for you know not why you go, nor
   where.

### LXXV

I tell you this:—When, started from the goal,
Over the flaming shoulders of the Foal
   Of Heav'n, Parwín and Mushtarí [29] they
      flung,
In my predestined plot of Dust and Soul 300

### LXXVI

The Vine had struck a fiber; which about
If clings my Being—let the Dervish flout:
   Of my base metal may be filed a key
That shall unlock the Door he howls without.

### LXXVII

And this I know: whether the one True Light
Kindle to Love, or wrath-consume me quite, 306
   One flash of It within the Tavern caught
Better than in the Temple lost outright.

### LXXVIII

What! out of senseless Nothing to provoke
A conscious Something to resent the yoke 310
   Of unpermitted pleasure, under pain
Of everlasting penalties, if broke!

### LXXIX

What! from his helpless creature be repaid
Pure gold for what he lent him dross-allayed—
   Sue for a debt he never did contract,      315
And cannot answer—Oh, the sorry trade!

### LXXX

Oh Thou, who didst with pitfall and with gin [30]
Beset the road I was to wander in,
   Thou wilt not with predestined evil round
Enmesh, and then impute my fall to sin! 320

[29] The Pleiads and Jupiter (FitzGerald).
[30] Snare.

### LXXXI

Oh Thou, who Man of baser Earth didst make,
And ev'n with Paradise devise the Snake:
   For all the sin wherewith the face of Man
Is blackened—Man's forgiveness give—and
   take!

\* \* \*

### LXXXII

As under cover of departing day           325
Slunk hunger-stricken Ramazán [31] away,
   Once more within the Potter's house alone
I stood, surrounded by the shapes of clay:

### LXXXIII

Shapes of all sorts and sizes, great and small,
That stood along the floor and by the wall; 330
   And some loquacious vessels were; and some
Listened perhaps, but never talked at all.

### LXXXIV

Said one among them: "Surely not in vain
My substance of the common earth was ta'en
   And to this figure molded, to be broke, 335
Or trampled back to shapeless earth again."

### LXXXV

Then said a second: "Ne'er a peevish boy
Would break the bowl from which he drank in
   joy;
   And He that with his hand the vessel made
Will surely not in after wrath destroy."   340

### LXXXVI

After a momentary silence spake
Some vessel of a more ungainly make:
   "They sneer at me for leaning all awry—
What! did the hand, then, of the Potter
   shake?"

### LXXXVII

Whereat some one of the loquacious lot— 345
I think a Súfi [32] pipkin—waxing hot:
   "All this of Pot and Potter—Tell me, then,
Who is the Potter, pray, and who the Pot?"

### LXXXVIII

"Why," said another, "some there are who tell
Of one who threatens he will toss to Hell 350
   The luckless Pots he marred in making—
      Pish!
He's a Good Fellow, and 'twill all be well."

### LXXXIX

"Well," murmured one, "let whoso make or
   buy,
My clay with long oblivion is gone dry:
   But fill me with the old familiar Juice,   355
Methinks I might recover by and by."

[31] The month for fasting.          [32] A pantheist.

### XC

So while the vessels one by one were speaking,
The little Moon [33] looked in that all were seek-
   ing;
   And then they jogged each other: "Brother!
      Brother!
Now for the Porter's shoulder-knot [34] a-creak-
   ing!"                                           360

\*      \*      \*

### XCI

Ah, with the Grape my fading life provide;
And wash the body whence the life has died,
   And lay me, shrouded in the living Leaf,
By some not unfrequented garden-side—

### XCII

That ev'n my buried ashes such a snare        365
Of vintage shall fling up into the air
   As not a True-believer passing by
But shall be overtaken unaware.

### XCIII

Indeed, the Idols I have loved so long
Have done my credit in this World much
      wrong:                                      370
   Have drowned my glory in a shallow cup,
And sold my reputation for a song.

### XCIV

Indeed, indeed, repentance oft before
I swore—but was I sober when I swore?
   And then, and then came Spring, and rose-
      in-hand                                     375
My threadbare penitence apieces tore.

### XCV

And much as Wine has played the Infidel,
And robbed me of my robe of Honor—Well,
   I wonder often what the vintners buy
One half so precious as the stuff they sell.  380

[33] Signalizing the end of Ramazán.
[34] Used for carrying jars of wine.

### XCVI

Yet ah, that Spring should vanish with the
      rose!
That Youth's sweet-scented manuscript should
      close!
   The nightingale that in the branches sang,
Ah whence, and whither flown again, who
      knows!

### XCVII

Would but the Desert of the Fountain yield
One glimpse—if dimly, yet indeed, revealed—
   To which the fainting Traveler might
      spring,                                     387
As springs the trampled herbage of the field!

### XCVIII

Would but some wingéd angel, ere too late,
Arrest the yet unfolded Roll of Fate,         390
   And make the stern Recorder otherwise
Enregister, or quite obliterate!

### XCIX

Ah Love! could you and I with Him conspire
To grasp this sorry Scheme of Things entire,
   Would not we shatter it to bits—and then
Remold it nearer to the Heart's desire!       396

\*      \*      \*

### C

Yon rising Moon that looks for us again—
How oft hereafter will she wax and wane;
   How oft hereafter rising look for us
Through this same garden—and for *one* in
      vain!                                       400

### CI

And when like her, oh Sákí, you shall pass
Among the guests star-scattered on the grass,
   And in your joyous errand reach the spot
Where I made one—turn down an empty
      glass!

TAMAM [35]

[35] The end.

# Alfred, Lord Tennyson

## 1809 - 1892

Tennyson's father was a clergyman, and his mother the daughter of a clergyman. To them were born twelve children, one of whom died in infancy. Their fourth child was Alfred, who was born at Somersby, in Lincolnshire, on 6 August, 1809. Somersby was at that time a village of less than a hundred inhabitants, and the children of the Rev. George Tennyson had a country upbringing. The rectory and the garden, the surrounding fen country, and the Lincolnshire farmers—all these made a deep impression upon Alfred and remained abiding influences upon which later experiences were, so to say, grafted. When he was eight years old he was sent to the grammar school at Louth, about ten miles north of Somersby. There he spent more than three years, miserable years which he hated at the time and hated afterwards in memory so deeply that he would never revisit the school. It is said that he was bullied both by a brutal schoolmaster and by his schoolfellows. At the end of this period he went back to Somersby and completed his preparation for the university under his father's guidance. At the same time he was writing poetry, had indeed been writing more or less poetry from early childhood. "The first poetry that moved me," he later said, "was my own at five years old." To this influence others succeeded, that of Scott, and then Byron's. When Byron died in 1824, Tennyson later said, "I thought everything was over and finished for every one —that nothing else mattered. I remember I walked out alone and carved 'Byron is dead' into the sandstone." And in 1827 Tennyson published with his brother Charles his first volume, Poems by Two Brothers. Early in the following year the two brothers went up to Cambridge, where they entered Trinity College. Tennyson probably never felt quite at home in Cambridge; yet the friendships he made there had a deep influence upon him. He became a member of a group known as "The Apostles," a band "of Platonico-Wordsworthian-Cole-ridgean-anti-utilitarians," as one of their number afterwards called them; and these morally earnest, theologically liberal young men did much to convince Tennyson that as a poet it was his office not merely to give pleasure to his readers but to become the spiritual guide of his age. Moreover, one of the "Apostles" was Arthur Henry Hallam, son of the historian, who became Tennyson's closest friend, with results that markedly colored both his life and his poetry. Meanwhile poetry continued to be written. In 1829 Tennyson won the Chancellor's Medal with a blank-verse piece called Timbuctoo, and in 1830 he published his second volume, Poems Chiefly Lyrical. In 1831 he left Cambridge without a degree. In December, 1832 (the volume is dated 1833), he published more verse, under the title Poems. This volume and that of 1830 contained some of the works by which Tennyson is still best known, but there were few to perceive that a great poet had made his appearance. Not only so, but, at least partly because of injudicious praise given the Poems by Hallam and other young friends, this volume was seized on for destruction by Lockhart, who published a merciless attack on it in the Quarterly Review. Tennyson was always extremely sensitive to criticism, and in his later years would never tolerate it even from his closest friends. So severely wounded was he by Lockhart's article that he did not publish another volume for ten years—years spent in study, writing, and the careful revision of those of his earlier poems which he wished to republish.

In September, 1833, Hallam died suddenly in Vienna, causing Tennyson the greatest sorrow of his life. He almost immediately began writing the "Elegies" which gradually grew in number until they were finally published under the title In Memoriam A. H. H. in 1850. Eight years before, in 1842, he had published English Idyls, which had at once been recognized as an important volume and had given him a secure *place in the world of letters. In 1845 he had been granted a pension, and in 1847 he had published* The Princess. *At length in 1850 he felt able to marry Emily Sellwood, to whom he had been engaged for some thirteen years. In the same years he was appointed, in succession to Wordsworth, poet laureate. His position as the great poet of the age was now secure, and during the remainder of his long life all, or nearly all, that he wrote contributed to the steady growth of his almost fabulous reputation amongst his contemporaries. Shortly after his marriage he acquired Farringford, on the Isle of Wight. In 1852 was published the* Ode on the Death of the Duke of Wellington, *in 1855* Maud, *and in 1859 the first group of* Idyls of the King. *More* Idyls *were published in 1869 and in 1872. In 1864* Enoch Arden *was published. Shortly before 1870 Tennyson built Aldworth, near Haslemere, in Surrey, and thenceforth his time was divided between his new home and Farringford. In 1875 he published* Queen Mary, *the first of some half-dozen plays which he wrote. In January, 1884, he was created Baron of Aldworth and Farringford, an honor which he is said to have accepted reluctantly and only "for the sake of literature," but an honor, too, which not unfairly indicates the exalted position he had attained in the eyes of the whole English-speaking world. He was by this time an old man, but he continued to the last to write and publish poetry which not only maintained but even added to his reputation. He died on 6 October, 1892, and was buried in Westminster Abbey.*

*Tennyson was in a peculiar sense the poet of his age. In his pages we read its littleness and its greatness—its religious doubts and insecure faith, its moral primness, its muddled politics, its ugly all-enveloping industrialism, its confidence in human progress and in the worth of individual endeavor, its pride of achievement, its active sense of a great past to be lived up to, and its noble—if perhaps too emotional and thoughtless—patriotism. Yet at the same time Tennyson was curiously different from his age. One who knows only the legendary Tennyson comes with some surprise on Sir Edmund Gosse's description of him as "a gaunt, black, touzled man, rough in speech, brooding like an old gypsy over his inch of clay pipe stuffed with shag and sucking in port wine with gusto"—a description confirmed by Carlyle's portrait: "A fine, large-featured, dim-eyed, bronze-colored, shaggy-headed man is Alfred: dusty, smoky, free and easy: who swims, outwardly and inwardly, with great composure in an articulate element as of tranquil chaos and tobacco smoke; great now and then when he does emerge; a most restful, brotherly, solid-hearted man." The truth is that Tennyson's was a complex, if not divided, nature. He was a great public and civic figure, the almost official Victorian guide through life's mazes, but he was also a serious, subtle, painstaking craftsman in verse; and he was at bottom a heavy-hearted mystic, anxious to be alone with his moods, and never perhaps so truly himself as in the purely lyric portions of his poetry.*

*The standard authorized edition of Tennyson's* Poems *is one annotated by Tennyson himself and edited by his son Hallam, Lord Tennyson (9 vols., London, 1898–1899; and later reprinted). The single-volume edition in the Oxford Standard Authors series has been expanded:* The Poetical Works, Including the Dramas *(Oxford, 1953). Hallam, Lord Tennyson's memoir of his father (London, 1897), is a standard biography; much more useful, however, is Sir Charles Tennyson's* Alfred Tennyson *(London, 1949). Thomas R. Lounsbury's* Life and Times of Tennyson *(New Haven, 1915) is valuable for the period from 1809 to 1850. In his* Tennyson, Aspects of His Life, Character and Poetry *(New York, 1923) Harold G. Nicolson emphasizes Tennyson's importance as a lyric rather than as a didactic poet. A. C. Bradley's* Commentary on Tennyson's In Memoriam *(London, 1915) and Morton Luce's* Handbook to the Works of Alfred Lord Tennyson *(London, 1910) are standard works of reference. Interpretations include Cleanth Brooks's "The Motivation of Tennyson's Weeper" in* The Well Wrought Urn *(New York, 1947), E. D. H. Johnson's* The Alien Vision of Victorian Poetry: Sources of the Poetic Imagination in Tennyson, Browning and Arnold *(Princeton, 1952), and E. B. Mattes's* "In Memoriam": the Way of a Soul *(New York, 1951). For Tennyson's intellectual background see D. C. Somervell,* English Thought in the Nineteenth Century *(London, 1929).*

# The Poet [1]

The poet in a golden clime was born,
  With golden stars above;
Dowered with the hate of hate, the scorn of
    scorn,
  The love of love.

[1] Published in 1830. Tennyson frequently revised his poems as they were reprinted in successive editions, but the dates appended to those here printed are in general simply those of first publication.

He saw through life and death, through good
    and ill,                                5
He saw through his own soul.
The marvel of the everlasting will,
    An open scroll,

Before him lay; with echoing feet he threaded
    The secretest walks of fame:          10
The viewless [2] arrows of his thoughts were
    headed
    And winged with flame,

Like Indians reeds blown from his silver tongue,
    And of so fierce a flight,
From Calpe [3] unto Caucasus they sung,     15
    Filling with light

And vagrant melodies the winds which bore
    Them earthward till they lit;
Then, like the arrow-seeds of the field flower,
    The fruitful wit                       20

Cleaving took root and springing forth anew
    Where'er they fell, behold,
Like to the mother plant in semblance, grew
    A flower all gold,

And bravely furnished all abroad to fling    25
    The wingèd shafts of truth,
To throng with stately blooms the breathing
    spring
    Of Hope and Youth.

So many minds did gird their orbs with beams,
    Though one did fling the fire;        30
Heaven flowed upon the soul in many dreams
    Of high desire.

Thus truth was multiplied on truth, the world
    Like one great garden showed,
And through the wreaths of floating dark
    upcurled,                             35
    Rare sunrise flowed.

And Freedom reared in that august sunrise
    Her beautiful bold brow,
When rites and forms before his burning eyes
    Melted like snow.                     40

There was no blood upon her maiden robes
    Sunned by those orient skies;
But round about the circles of the globes
    Of her keen eyes

And in her raiment's hem was traced in flame
    WISDOM, a name to shake              46
All evil dreams of power—a sacred name.
    And when she spake,

Her words did gather thunder as they ran,
    And as the lightning to the thunder   50

[2] Invisible.     [3] Gibraltar.

Which follows it, riving the spirit of man,
    Making earth wonder,

So was their meaning to her words. No sword
    Of wrath her right arm whirled,
But one poor poet's scroll, and with *his* word [55]
    She shook the world.

# The Lady of Shalott [1]

## PART I

On either side the river lie
Long fields of barley and of rye,
That clothe the wold [2] and meet the sky;
And through the field the road runs by
    To many-towered Camelot; [3]        5
And up and down the people go,
Gazing where the lilies blow
Round an island there below,
    The island of Shalott. [4]

Willows whiten, aspens quiver,               10
Little breezes dusk and shiver
Through the wave that runs for ever
By the island in the river
    Flowing down to Camelot.
Four gray walls, and four gray towers,       15
Overlook a space of flowers,
And the silent isle imbowers
    The Lady of Shalott.

By the margin, willow-veiled,
Slide the heavy barges trailed               20
By slow horses; and unhailed
The shallop flitteth silken-sailed
    Skimming down to Camelot:
But who hath seen her wave her hand?
Or at the casement seen her stand?           25
Or is she known in all the land,
    The Lady of Shalott?

Only reapers, reaping early
In among the bearded barley,
Hear a song that echoes cheerly              30
From the river winding clearly,
    Down to towered Camelot;
And by the moon the reaper weary,
Piling sheaves in uplands airy,
Listening, whispers " 'Tis the fairy         35
    Lady of Shalott."

[1] Published in 1832. Tennyson's earliest handling
of a theme from Arthurian legend. When he later
wrote *Lancelot and Elaine* he adopted a different
version of the story he tells here.
  [2] Open country.
  [3] The legendary city where King Arthur held his
court, commonly supposed to be in Cornwall.
  [4] In Malory (*Morte d'Arthur*, Bk. XVIII) this
word is Astolat. An Italian version of the story of
Elaine is said to have suggested Tennyson's poem,
which would account for the form Shalott.

## PART II

There she weaves by night and day
A magic web with colors gay.
She has heard a whisper say,
A curse is on her if she stay　　　40
　　　To look down to Camelot.
She knows not what the curse may be,
And so she weaveth steadily,
And little other care hath she,
　　　The Lady of Shalott.　　　45

And moving through a mirror clear
That hangs before her all the year,
Shadows of the world appear.
There she sees the highway near
　　　Winding down to Camelot;　　　50
There the river eddy whirls,
And there the surly village-churls,
And the red cloaks of market girls,
　　　Pass onward from Shalott.

Sometimes a troop of damsels glad,　　　55
An abbot on an ambling pad,[5]
Sometimes a curly shepherd-lad,
Or long-haired page in crimson clad,
　　　Goes by to towered Camelot;
And sometimes through the mirror blue　　　60
The knights come riding two and two:
She hath no loyal knight and true,
　　　The Lady of Shalott.

But in her web she still delights
To weave the mirror's magic sights,　　　65
For often through the silent nights
A funeral, with plumes and lights
　　　And music, went to Camelot;
Or when the moon was overhead,
Came two young lovers lately wed:　　　70
"I am half sick of shadows," said
　　　The Lady of Shalott.

## PART III

A bow-shot from her bower-eaves,
He rode between the barley-sheaves,
The sun came dazzling through the leaves,　75
And flamed upon the brazen greaves
　　　Of bold Sir Lancelot.
A red-cross knight for ever kneeled
To a lady in his shield,
That sparkled on the yellow field,　　　80
　　　Beside remote Shalott.

The gemmy bridle glittered free,
Like to some branch of stars we see
Hung in the golden Galaxy.[6]
The bridle bells rang merrily　　　85
　　　As he rode down to Camelot;
And from his blazoned baldric slung

---

[5] Easy-paced horse.　　　[6] The Milky Way.

A mighty silver bugle hung,
And as he rode his armor rung,
　　　Beside remote Shalott.　　　90

All in the blue unclouded weather
Thick-jeweled shone the saddle-leather,
The helmet and the helmet-feather
Burned like one burning flame together,
　　　As he rode down to Camelot;　　　95
As often through the purple night,
Below the starry clusters bright,
Some bearded meteor, trailing light,
　　　Moves over still Shalott.

His broad clear brow in sunlight glowed;　100
On burnished hooves his war-horse trode;
From underneath his helmet flowed
His coal-black curls as on he rode,
　　　As he rode down to Camelot.
From the bank and from the river　　　105
He flashed into the crystal mirror,
"Tirra lirra," by the river
　　　Sang Sir Lancelot.

She left the web, she left the loom,
She made three paces through the room,　110
She saw the water-lily bloom,
She saw the helmet and the plume,
　　　She looked down to Camelot.
Out flew the web and floated wide;
The mirror cracked from side to side;　115
"The curse is come upon me," cried
　　　The Lady of Shalott.

## PART IV

In the stormy east-wind straining,
The pale yellow woods were waning,
The broad stream in his banks complaining, 120
Heavily the low sky raining
　　　Over towered Camelot;
Down she came and found a boat
Beneath a willow left afloat,
And round about the prow she wrote　　　125
　　　*The Lady of Shalott.*

And down the river's dim expanse
Like some bold seër in a trance,
Seeing all his own mischance—
With a glassy countenance　　　130
　　　Did she look to Camelot.
And at the closing of the day
She loosed the chain, and down she lay;
The broad stream bore her far away,
　　　The Lady of Shalott.　　　135

Lying, robed in snowy white
That loosely flew to left and right—
The leaves upon her falling light—
Through the noises of the night
　　　She floated down to Camelot;　　　140
And as the boat-head wound along
The willowy hills and fields among,

They heard her singing her last song,
    The Lady of Shalott.

Heard a carol, mournful, holy,      145
Chanted loudly, chanted lowly,
Till her blood was frozen slowly,
And her eyes were darkened wholly,
    Turned to towered Camelot.
For ere she reached upon the tide      150
The first house by the water-side,
Singing in her song she died,
    The Lady of Shalott.

Under tower and balcony,
By garden-wall and gallery,      155
A gleaming shape she floated by,
Dead-pale between the houses high,
    Silent into Camelot.
Out upon the wharfs they came,
Knight and burgher, lord and dame,      160
And round the prow they read her name,
    *The Lady of Shalott.*

Who is this? and what is here?
And in the lighted palace near
Died the sound of royal cheer;      165
And they crossed themselves for fear,
    All the knights at Camelot:
But Lancelot mused a little space;
He said, "She has a lovely face;
God in his mercy lend her grace,      170
    The Lady of Shalott."

# Oenone [1]

There lies a vale in Ida, lovelier
Than all the valleys of Ionian hills.
The swimming vapor slopes athwart the glen,
Puts forth an arm, and creeps from pine to pine,
And loiters, slowly drawn. On either hand      5
The lawns and meadow-ledges midway down
Hang rich in flowers, and far below them roars
The long brook falling through the cloven
    ravine
In cataract after cataract to the sea.
Behind the valley topmost Gargarus      10

---

[1] Published in 1832. Oenone was the daughter of a river-god, and the wife of Paris, son of King Priam of Troy. Paris was asked to judge which of the three goddesses, Hera, Pallas Athena, and Aphrodite, was the fairest, and each tried to influence his judgment in her own favor by offering him a reward. Aphrodite said she would give him the most beautiful of women for a wife, whereupon Paris immediately judged her the fairest of the goddesses. Under Aphrodite's care he then left Oenone and sailed for Sparta, whence he bore away Helen to Troy, thus bringing about the Trojan war. Ida is the name of a mountain range forming the southern boundary of the territory of Troas, or Ilium. It was in these mountains that Paris was brought up by shepherds, having been abandoned there as a baby after his mother dreamed that he would bring ruin on Troy. Gargarus is the name of one of the highest peaks of Ida.

Stands up and takes the morning; but in front
The gorges, opening wide apart, reveal
Troas and Ilion's columned citadel,
The crown of Troas.
             Hither came at noon
Mournful Oenone, wandering forlorn      15
Of Paris, once her playmate on the hills.
Her cheek had lost the rose, and round her
    neck
Floated her hair or seemed to float in rest.
She, leaning on a fragment twined with vine,
Sang to the stillness, till the mountain-shade 20
Sloped downward to her seat from the upper
    cliff.

"O mother Ida, many-fountained Ida,
Dear mother Ida, harken ere I die.
For now the noonday quiet holds the hill;
The grasshopper is silent in the grass;      25
The lizard, with his shadow on the stone,
Rests like a shadow, and the winds are dead.
The purple flower droops, the golden bee
Is lily-cradled; I alone awake.
My eyes are full of tears, my heart of love, 30
My heart is breaking, and my eyes are dim,
And I am all aweary of my life.

"O mother Ida, many-fountained Ida,
Dear mother Ida, harken ere I die.
Hear me, O earth, hear me, O hills, O caves
That house the cold crowned snake! O moun-
    tain brooks,      36
I am the daughter of a River-God,
Hear me, for I will speak, and build up all
My sorrow with my song, as yonder walls
Rose slowly to a music slowly breathed,      40
A cloud that gathered shape; [2] for it may be
That, while I speak of it, a little while
My heart may wander from its deeper woe.

"O mother Ida, many-fountained Ida,
Dear mother Ida, harken ere I die.      45
I waited underneath the dawning hills,
Aloft the mountain lawn was dewy-dark,
And dewy-dark aloft the mountain pine,
Beautiful Paris, evil-hearted Paris,
Leading a jet-black goat white-horned, white-
    hooved,      50
Came up from reedy Simois [3] all alone.

"O mother Ida, harken ere I die.
Far-off the torrent called me from the cleft;
Far up the solitary morning smote
The streaks of virgin snow. With down-dropped
    eyes      55
I sat alone; white-breasted like a star
Fronting the dawn he moved; a leopard skin
Drooped from his shoulder, but his sunny hair
Clustered about his temples like a God's;

---

[2] The walls of Troy were said to have arisen in obedience to Apollo's music.
[3] A stream which rises on Mount Ida.

And his cheek brightened as the foam-bow
   brightens                 60
When the wind blows the foam, and all my
   heart
Went forth to embrace him coming ere he
   came.

  "Dear mother Ida, harken ere I die.
He smiled, and opening out his milk-white
   palm
Disclosed a fruit of pure Hesperian gold,[4]   65
That smelt ambrosially, and while I looked
And listened, the full-flowing river of speech
Came down upon my heart:
    " 'My own Oenone,
Beautiful-browed Oenone, my own soul,
Behold this fruit, whose gleaming rind in-
   graven                  70
"For the most fair," would seem to award it
   thine,
As lovelier than whatever Oread [5] haunt
The knolls of Ida, loveliest in all grace
Of movement, and the charm of married
   brows.'

  "Dear mother Ida, harken ere I die.   75
He pressed the blossom of his lips to mine,
And added, 'This cast was upon the board,
When all the full-faced presence of the Gods
Ranged in the halls of Peleus; whereupon
Rose feud, with question unto whom 'twere
   due;                    80
But light-foot Iris [6] brought it yester-eve,
Delivering, that to me, by common voice
Elected umpire, Herë comes to-day,
Pallas and Aphrodite, claiming each
This meed of fairest. Thou, within the cave [85]
Behind yon whispering tuft of oldest pine,
Mayst well behold them unbeheld, unheard
Hear all, and see thy Paris judge of Gods.'

  "Dear mother Ida, harken ere I die.
It was the deep midnoon; one silvery cloud  90
Had lost his way between the piny sides
Of this long glen. Then to the bower they
   came,
Naked they came to that smooth-swarded
   bower,
And at their feet the crocus brake like fire,
Violets, amaracus, and asphodel,[7]       95
Lotos and lilies; and a wind arose,
And overhead the wandering ivy and vine,
This way and that, in many a wild festoon
Ran riot, garlanding the gnarléd boughs
With bunch and berry and flower through and
   through.             100

  "O mother Ida, harken ere I die.
On the tree-tops a crested peacock lit,

   [4] A golden apple like those which grew in the gardens of the Hesperides.
   [5] Mountain-nymph.      [6] Messenger of the gods.
   [7] Amaracus is the modern marjoram; asphodel is
a lily-shaped plant.

And o'er him flowed a golden cloud, and leaned
Upon him, slowly dropping fragrant dew.
Then first I heard the voice of her to whom 105
Coming through heaven, like a light that grows
Larger and clearer, with one mind the Gods
Rise up for reverence. She to Paris made
Proffer of royal power, ample rule
Unquestioned, overflowing revenue   110
Wherewith to embellish state, 'from many a
   vale
And river-sundered champaign clothed with
   corn,
Or labored mine undrainable of ore.
Honor,' she said, 'and homage, tax and toll,
From many an inland town and haven large, 115
Mast-thronged beneath her shadowing citadel
In glassy bays among her tallest towers.'

  "O mother Ida, harken ere I die.
Still she spake on and still she spake of power,
'Which in all action is the end of all;   120
Power fitted to the season; wisdom-bred
And throned of wisdom—from all neighbor
   crowns
Alliance and allegiance, till thy hand
Fail from the scepter-staff. Such boon from me,
From me, heaven's queen, Paris, to thee king-
   born,                125
A shepherd all thy life but yet king-born,
Should come most welcome, seeing men, in
   power
Only, are likest Gods, who have attained
Rest in a happy place and quiet seats
Above the thunder, with undying bliss   130
In knowledge of their own supremacy.'

  "Dear mother Ida, harken ere I die.
She ceased, and Paris held the costly fruit
Out at arm's-length, so much the thought of
   power
Flattered his spirit; but Pallas where she stood
Somewhat apart, her clear and bared limbs 136
O'erthwarted with the brazen-headed spear
Upon her pearly shoulder leaning cold,
The while, above, her full and earnest eye
Over her snow-cold breast and angry cheek 140
Kept watch, waiting decision, made reply:
'Self-reverence, self-knowledge, self-control,
These three alone lead life to sovereign power.
Yet not for power (power of herself
Would come uncalled for) but to live by law,
Acting the law we live by without fear;  146
And, because right is right, to follow right
Were wisdom in the scorn of consequence.'

  "Dear mother Ida, harken ere I die.
Again she said: 'I woo thee not with gifts. 150
Sequel of guerdon could not alter me
To fairer. Judge thou me by what I am,
So shalt thou find me fairest.
                      Yet, indeed,
If gazing on divinity disrobed
Thy mortal eyes are frail to judge of fair, 155

Unbiased by self-profit, O, rest thee sure
That I shall love thee well and cleave to thee,
So that my vigor, wedded to thy blood,
Shall strike within thy pulses, like a God's,
To push thee forward through a life of shocks,
Danger, and deeds, until endurance grow     161
Sinewed with action, and the full-grown will,
Circled through all experiences, pure law,
Commeasure [8] perfect freedom.'

             "Here she ceased,
And Paris pondered, and I cried, 'O Paris,     165
Give it to Pallas!' but he heard me not,
Or hearing would not hear me, woe is me!

"O mother Ida, many-fountained Ida,
Dear mother Ida, harken ere I die.
Idalian [9] Aphrodite beautiful,     170
Fresh as the foam, new-bathed in Paphian
   wells,
With rosy slender fingers backward drew
From her warm brows and bosom her deep hair
Ambrosial, golden round her lucid throat
And shoulder; from the violets her light foot [175]
Shone rosy-white, and o'er her rounded form
Between the shadows of the vine-bunches
Floated the glowing sunlights, as she moved.

"Dear mother Ida, harken ere I die.
She with a subtle smile in her mild eyes,     180
The herald of her triumph, drawing nigh
Half-whispered in his ear, 'I promise thee
The fairest and most loving wife in Greece.'
She spoke and laughed; I shut my sight for
   fear;
But when I looked, Paris had raised his arm,
And I beheld great Herë's angry eyes,     186
As she withdrew into the golden cloud,
And I was left alone within the bower,
And from that time to this I am alone,
And I shall be alone until I die.     190

"Yet, mother Ida, harken ere I die.
Fairest—why fairest wife? am I not fair?
My love hath told me so a thousand times.
Methinks I must be fair, for yesterday,
When I passed by, a wild and wanton pard,[10]
Eyed like the evening star, with playful tail [196]
Crouched fawning in the weed. Most loving is
   she?
Ah me, my mountain shepherd, that my arms
Were wound about thee, and my hot lips
   pressed
Close, close to thine in that quick-falling dew
Of fruitful kisses, thick as autumn rains     201
Flash in the pools of whirling Simois!

"O mother, hear me yet before I die.
They [11] came, they cut away my tallest pines,

[8] Be equal in measure to.
[9] Idalium and Paphos were towns in Cyprus where
Aphrodite was specially worshipped.
[10] Leopard.
[11] Shipwrights, who cut down the pines to make
ships for Paris's journey to Sparta.

My tall dark pines, that plumed the craggy
   ledge     205
High over the blue gorge, and all between
The snowy peak and snow-white cataract
Fostered the callow eaglet—from beneath
Whose thick mysterious boughs in the dark
   morn
The panther's roar came muffled, while I sat [210]
Low in the valley. Never, never more
Shall lone Oenone see the morning mist
Sweep through them; never see them overlaid
With narrow moonlit slips of silver cloud,
Between the loud stream and the trembling
   stars.     215

"O mother, hear me yet before I die.
I wish that somewhere in the ruined folds,
Among the fragments tumbled from the glens,
Or the dry thickets, I could meet with her
The Abominable,[12] that uninvited came     220
Into the fair Peleïan banquet-hall,
And cast the golden fruit upon the board,
And bred this change; that I might speak my
   mind,
And tell her to her face how much I hate
Her presence, hated both of Gods and men. [225]

"O mother, hear me yet before I die.
Hath he not sworn his love a thousand times,
In this green valley, under this green hill,
Even on this hand, and sitting on this stone?
Sealed it with kisses? watered it with tears? [230]
O happy tears, and how unlike to these!
O happy heaven, how canst thou see my face?
O happy earth, how canst thou bear my weight?
O death, death, death, thou ever-floating cloud,
There are enough unhappy on this earth,     235
Pass by the happy souls, that love to live;
I pray thee, pass before my light of life,
And shadow all my soul, that I may die.
Thou weightest heavy on the heart within,
Weigh heavy on my eyelids; let me die.     240

"O mother, hear me yet before I die.
I will not die alone, for fiery thoughts
Do shape themselves within me, more and
   more,
Whereof I catch the issue, as I hear
Dead sounds at night come from the inmost
   hills,     245
Like footsteps upon wool. I dimly see
My far-off doubtful purpose, as a mother
Conjectures of the features of her child
Ere it is born. Her child!—a shudder comes
Across me: never child be born of me,     250
Unblest, to vex me with his father's eyes!

"O mother, hear me yet before I die.
Hear me, O earth. I will not die alone,
Lest their shrill happy laughter come to me
Walking the cold and starless road of death [255]

[12] Eris, goddess of strife.

Uncomforted, leaving my ancient love
With the Greek woman. I will rise and go
Down into Troy, and ere the stars come forth
Talk with the wild Cassandra,[13] for she says
A fire dances before her, and a sound          260
Rings ever in her ears of arméd men.
What this may be I know not, but I know
That, wheresoe'er I am by night and day,
All earth and air seem only burning fire."

## The Palace of Art [1]

I built my soul a lordly pleasure-house,
   Wherein at ease for aye to dwell.
I said, "O Soul, make merry and carouse,
   Dear soul, for all is well."

A huge crag-platform, smooth as burnished
   brass,                                     5
I chose. The rangéd ramparts bright
From level meadow-bases of deep grass
   Suddenly scaled the light.

Thereon I built it firm. Of ledge or shelf
   The rock rose clear, or winding stair.  10
My soul would live alone unto herself
   In her high palace there.

And "while the world runs round and round,"
   I said,
"Reign thou apart, a quiet king,
Still as, while Saturn whirls, his steadfast shade
   Sleeps on his luminous ring."          16

To which my soul made answer readily:
   "Trust me, in bliss I shall abide
In this great mansion, that is built for me,
   So royal-rich and wide."              20

[13] Daughter of Priam, who predicted the destruction of Troy but was thought to be mad.

[1] Published in 1832, but much altered in later editions. Tennyson prefixed to the poem the following explanation:
I send you here a sort of allegory
(For you will understand it), of a soul,
A sinful soul possessed of many gifts,
A spacious garden full of flowering weeds,
A glorious Devil, large in heart and brain,
That did love Beauty only (Beauty seen
In all varieties of mold and mind)
And Knowledge for its beauty; or if Good,
Good only for its beauty, seeing not
That Beauty, Good, and Knowledge are three sisters
That dote upon each other, friends to man,
Living together under the same roof,
And never can be sundered without tears.
And he that shuts Love out, in turn shall be
Shut out from Love, and on her threshold lie
Howling in outer darkness. Not for this
Was common clay ta'en from the common earth,
Molded by God, and tempered with the tears
Of angels to the perfect shape of man.

Four courts I made, East, West and South and
   North,
In each a squaréd lawn, wherefrom
The golden gorge [2] of dragons spouted forth
   A flood of fountain-foam.

And round the cool green courts there ran a
   row                                      25
   Of cloisters, branched like mighty woods,
Echoing all night to that sonorous flow
   Of spouted fountain-floods;

And round the roofs a gilded gallery
   That lent broad verge to distant lands,   30
Far as the wild swan wings, to where the sky
   Dipped down to sea and sands.

From those four jets four currents in one swell
   Across the mountain streamed below
In misty folds, that floating as they fell      35
   Lit up a torrent-bow.

And high on every peak a statue seemed
   To hang on tiptoe, tossing up
A cloud of incense of all odor steamed
   From out a golden cup.                  40

So that she thought, "And who shall gaze upon
   My palace with unblinded eyes,
While this great bow will waver in the sun,
   And that sweet incense rise?"

For that sweet incense rose and never failed,  45
   And, while day sank or mounted higher,
The light aerial gallery, golden-railed,
   Burned like a fringe of fire.

Likewise the deep-set windows, stained and
   traced,
   Would seem slow-flaming crimson fires   50
From shadowed grots of arches interlaced,
   And tipped with frost-like spires.

Full of long-sounding corridors it was,
   That over-vaulted grateful gloom,
Through which the livelong day my soul did
   pass,                                    55
   Well-pleased, from room to room.

Full of great rooms and small the palace stood,
   All various, each a perfect whole
From living Nature, fit for every mood
   And change of my still soul.            60

For some were hung with arras green and blue,
   Showing a gaudy summer-morn,
Where with puffed cheek the belted hunter
   blew
   His wreathéd bugle-horn.

One seemed all dark and red—a tract of sand,
   And some one pacing there alone,         66

[2] Throat.

Who paced for ever in a glimmering land,
    Lit with a low large moon.

One showed an iron coast and angry waves.
    You seemed to hear them climb and fall  70
And roar rock-thwarted under bellowing caves,
    Beneath the windy wall.

And one, a full-fed river winding slow
    By herds upon an endless plain,
The ragged rims of thunder brooding low  75
    With shadow-streaks of rain.

And one, the reapers at their sultry toil.
    In front they bound the sheaves. Behind
Were realms of upland, prodigal in oil,
    And hoary to the wind.[3]  80

And one a foreground black with stones and
    slags;
Beyond, a line of heights; and higher
All barred with long white cloud the scornful
    crags;
    And highest, snow and fire.

And one, an English home—gray twilight
    poured  85
    On dewy pastures, dewy trees,
Softer than sleep—all things in order stored,
    A haunt of ancient Peace.

Nor these alone, but every landscape fair,
    As fit for every mood of mind,  90
Or gay, or grave, or sweet, or stern, was there,
    Not less than truth designed.

    .    .    .    .

Or the maid-mother by a crucifix,
    In tracts of pasture sunny-warm,
Beneath branch-work of costly sardonyx [4]  95
    Sat smiling, babe in arm.

Or in a clear-walled city on the sea,
    Near gilded organ-pipes, her hair
Wound with white roses, slept Saint Cecily; [5]
    An angel looked at her.  100

Or thronging all one porch of Paradise
    A group of Houris [6] bowed to see
The dying Islamite, with hands and eyes
    That said, We wait for thee.

Or mythic Uther's deeply-wounded son [7]  105
    In some fair space of sloping greens

Lay, dozing in the vale of Avalon,
    And watched by weeping queens.

Or hollowing one hand against his ear,
    To list a foot-fall, ere he saw  110
The wood-nymph, stayed the Ausonian King [8]
    to hear
    Of wisdom and of law.

Or over hills with peaky tops engrailed,
    And many a tract of palm and rice,
The throne of Indian Cama [9] slowly sailed  115
    A summer fanned with spice.

Or sweet Europa's mantle blew unclasped,
    From off her shoulder backward borne;
From one hand drooped a crocus; one hand
    grasped
    The mild bull's golden horn.[10]  120

Or else flushed Ganymede, his rosy thigh
    Half-buried in the eagle's down,
Sole as a flying star shot through the sky
    Above the pillared town.[11]

Nor these alone; but every legend fair  125
    Which the supreme Caucasian mind
Carved out of Nature for itself was there,
    Not less than life designed.

    .    .    .    .

Then in the towers I placed great bells that
    swung,
    Moved of themselves, with silver sound;  130
And with choice paintings of wise men I hung
    The royal dais round.

For there was Milton like a seraph strong,
    Beside him Shakespeare bland and mild;
And there the world-worn Dante grasped his
    song,  135
    And somewhat grimly smiled.

And there the Ionian father of the rest; [12]
    A million wrinkles carved his skin;
A hundred winters snowed upon his breast,
    From cheek and throat and chin.  140

Above, the fair hall-ceiling stately-set
    Many an arch high up did lift,
And angels rising and descending met
    With interchange of gift.

Below was all mosaic choicely planned  145
    With cycles of the human tale

[3] I. e., the whitish underside of the olive leaves turned up by the wind.

[4] Ornamental patterns of a yellow and white polished stone.

[5] St. Cecilia was said to have invented the organ.

[6] The virgins who, according to the Koran, attend upon the faithful Mahometan in Paradise.

[7] King Arthur. Tennyson tells the story of his death in The Passing of Arthur.

[8] Numa, legislator and second king of Rome, was said to have been instructed in the art of government by the wood-nymph Egeria.

[9] The god of love in Hindu mythology.

[10] Europa while gathering flowers was carried off by Zeus under the form of a bull.

[11] Ganymede was carried off by the eagle of Zeus to become Zeus's cup-bearer.

[12] Homer.

Of this wide world, the times of every land
    So wrought they will not fail.

The people here, a beast of burden slow,
    Toiled onward, pricked with goads and
        stings;     150
Here played, a tiger, rolling to and fro
    The heads and crowns of kings;

Here rose, an athlete, strong to break or bind
    All force in bonds that might endure,
And here once more like some sick man de-
        clined,     155
    And trusted any cure.

But over these she trod; and those great bells
    Began to chime. She took her throne;
She sat betwixt the shining oriels,
    To sing her songs alone.     160

And through the topmost oriels' colored flame
    Two godlike faces gazed below;
Plato the wise, and large-browed Verulam,[13]
    The first of those who know.

And all those names that in their motion were
    Full-welling fountain-heads of change,    166
Betwixt the slender shafts were blazoned fair
    In diverse raiment strange;

Through which the lights, rose, amber, emer-
    ald, blue,
    Flushed in her temples and her eyes,    170
And from her lips, as morn from Memnon,[14]
    drew
    Rivers of melodies.

No nightingale delighteth to prolong
    Her low preamble all alone,
More than my soul to hear her echoed song 175
    Throb through the ribbéd stone;

Singing and murmuring in her feastful mirth,
    Joying to feel herself alive,
Lord over Nature, lord of the visible earth,
    Lord of the senses five;    180

Communing with herself: "All these are mine,
    And let the world have peace or wars,
'Tis one to me." She—when young night di-
    vine
    Crowned dying day with stars,

Making sweet close of his delicious toils— 185
    Lit light in wreaths and anadems,[15]
And pure quintessences of precious oils
    In hollowed moons of gems,

To mimic heaven; and clapped her hands and
    cried,
    "I marvel if my still delight    190
In this great house so royal-rich and wide
    Be flattered to the height.

"O all things fair to sate my various eyes!
    O shapes and hues that please me well!
O silent faces of the Great and Wise,    195
    My Gods, with whom I dwell!

"O Godlike isolation which art mine,
    I can but count thee perfect gain,
What time I watch the darkening droves of
    swine
    That range on yonder plain.    200

"In filthy sloughs they roll a prurient skin,
    They graze and wallow, breed and sleep;
And oft some brainless devil enters in,
    And drives them to the deep." [16]

Then of the moral instinct would she prate 205
    And of the rising from the dead,
As hers by right of full-accomplished Fate;
    And at the last she said:

"I take possession of man's mind and deed.
    I care not what the sects may brawl.    210
I sit as God holding no form of creed,
    But contemplating all."

      .     .     .     .

Full oft the riddle of the painful earth
    Flashed through her as she sat alone,
Yet not the less held she her solemn mirth, 215
    And intellectual throne.

And so she throve and prospered; so three years
    She prospered; on the fourth she fell,
Like Herod, when the shout was in his ears,
    Struck through with pangs of hell.[17] 220

Lest she should fall and perish utterly,
    God, before whom ever lie bare
The abysmal deeps of personality,
    Plagued her with sore despair.

When she would think, where'er she turned
    her sight    225
    The airy hand confusion wrought,
Wrote, "Mene, mene," [18] and divided quite
    The kingdom of her thought.

Deep dread and loathing of her solitude
    Fell on her, from which mood was born 230
Scorn of herself; again, from out that mood
    Laughter at her self-scorn.

"What! is not this my place of strength," she
    said,

---

[13] Francis Bacon. The following line translates the epithet Dante applies to Aristotle (*Inferno*, iv, 131).

[14] A colossal Egyptian statue (really of Amenophis) which was said to give forth a musical sound when first struck by the rays of the rising sun.

[15] In lamps arranged like wreaths and garlands.

[16] See St. Mark, 5:13.

[17] See Acts, 12:21–23.

[18] See the account of Belshazzar's feast, Daniel, 5.

"My spacious mansion built for me,
Whereof the strong foundation-stones were
    laid   235
    Since my first memory?"

But in dark corners of her palace stood
  Uncertain shapes; and unawares
On white-eyed phantasms weeping tears of
    blood,
    And horrible nightmares,   240

And hollow shades enclosing hearts of flame,
  And, with dim-fretted [19] foreheads all,
On corpses three-months-old at noon she came,
    That stood against the wall.

A spot of dull stagnation, without light   245
  Or power of movement, seemed my soul,
Mid onward-sloping motions infinite
    Making for one sure goal;

A still salt pool, locked in with bars of sand,
  Left on the shore, that hears all night   250
The plunging seas draw backward from the
    land
    Their moon-led waters white;

A star that with the choral starry dance
  Joined not, but stood, and standing saw
The hollow orb of moving Circumstance   255
    Rolled round by one fixed law.

Back on herself her serpent pride had curled
  "No voice," she shrieked in that lone hall,
"No voice breaks through the stillness of this
    world;
    One deep, deep silence all!"   260

She, moldering with the dull earth's moldering
    sod,
  Inwrapped tenfold in slothful shame,
Lay there exiléd from eternal God,
    Lost to her place and name;

And death and life she hated equally,   265
  And nothing saw, for her despair,
But dreadful time, dreadful eternity,
    No comfort anywhere;

Remaining utterly confused with fears,
  And ever worse with growing time,   270
And ever unrelieved by dismal tears,
    And all alone in crime.

Shut up as in a crumbling tomb, girt round
  With blackness as a solid wall,
Far off she seemed to hear the dully sound [275]
    Of human footsteps fall:

As in strange lands a traveler walking slow,
  In doubt and great perplexity,
A little before moonrise hears the low
    Moan of an unknown sea;   280

[19] Worm-eaten (Tennyson's explanation).

And knows not if it be thunder, or a sound
  Of rocks thrown down, or one deep cry
Of great wild beasts; then thinketh, "I have
    found
    A new land, but I die."

She howled aloud, "I am on fire within.   285
  There comes no murmur of reply.
What is it that will take away my sin,
    And save me lest I die?"

So when four years were wholly finished,
  She threw her royal robes away.   290
"Make me a cottage in the vale," she said,
    "Where I may mourn and pray.

"Yet pull not down my palace towers, that are
  So lightly, beautifully built;
Perchance I may return with others there   295
    When I have purged my guilt."

# The Lotos-Eaters [1]

"Courage!" he [2] said, and pointed toward the
    land,
"This mounting wave will roll us shoreward
    soon."
In the afternoon they came unto a land
In which it seeméd always afternoon.
All round the coast the languid air did swoon, [5]
Breathing like one that hath a weary dream.
Full-faced above the valley stood the moon;
And, like a downward smoke, the slender
    stream
Along the cliff to fall and pause and fall did
    seem.

A land of streams! some, like a downward
    smoke,   10
Slow-dropping veils of thinnest lawn, did go;
And some through wavering lights and shadows
    broke,
Rolling a slumbrous sheet of foam below.
They saw the gleaming river seaward flow
From the inner land; far off, three mountain-
    tops,   15
Three silent pinnacles of agéd snow,
Stood sunset-flushed; and, dewed with showery
    drops,
Up-clomb the shadowy pine above the woven
    copse.

The charméd sunset lingered low adown
In the red West; through mountain clefts the
    dale   20
Was seen far inland, and the yellow down
Bordered with palm, and many a winding vale

[1] Published in 1832. The land of the lotos-eaters
was visited by Ulysses, and Tennyson drew the framework of his poem from the *Odyssey*, IX, 82–97.
The lotos referred to is an African plant, sometimes
called the Cyrenean lotos.

[2] Ulysses.

And meadow, set with slender galingale; [3]
A land where all things always seemed the same!
And round about the keel with faces pale,    25
Dark faces pale against that rosy flame,
The mild-eyed melancholy Lotos-eaters came.

Branches they bore of that enchanted stem,
Laden with flower and fruit, whereof they gave
To each, but whoso did receive of them    30
And taste, to him the gushing of the wave
Far far away did seem to mourn and rave
On alien shores; and if his fellow spake,
His voice was thin, as voices from the grave;
And deep-asleep he seemed, yet all awake,    35
And music in his ears his beating heart did make.

They sat them down upon the yellow sand,
Between the sun and moon upon the shore;
And sweet it was to dream of Fatherland,
Of child, and wife, and slave; but evermore    40
Most weary seemed the sea, weary the oar,
Weary the wandering fields of barren foam.
Then some one said, "We will return no more";
And all at once they sang, "Our island home
Is far beyond the wave; we will no longer roam."    45

### CHORIC SONG

#### I

THERE is sweet music here that softer falls
Than petals from blown roses on the grass,
Or night-dews on still waters between walls
Of shadowy granite, in a gleaming pass;
Music that gentlier on the spirit lies,    5
Than tired eyelids upon tired eyes;
Music that brings sweet sleep down from the blissful skies.
Here are cool mosses deep,
And through the moss the ivies creep,
And in the stream the long-leaved flowers weep,
And from the craggy ledge the poppy hangs in sleep.    11

#### II

Why are we weighed upon with heaviness,
And utterly consumed with sharp distress,
While all things else have rest from weariness?
All things have rest: why should we toil alone,
We only toil, who are the first of things,    16
And make perpetual moan,
Still from one sorrow to another thrown;
Nor ever fold our wings,
And cease from wanderings,    20
Nor steep our brows in slumber's holy balm;
Nor hearken what the inner spirit sings,
"There is no joy but calm!"—
Why should we only toil, the roof and crown of things?

[3] Plant with an aromatic root.

#### III

Lo! in the middle of the wood,    25
The folded leaf is wooed from out the bud
With winds upon the branch, and there
Grows green and broad, and takes no care,
Sun-steeped at noon, and in the moon
Nightly dew-fed; and turning yellow    30
Falls, and floats adown the air.
Lo! sweetened with the summer light,
The full-juiced apple, waxing over-mellow,
Drops in a silent autumn night.
All its allotted length of days    35
The flower ripens in its place,
Ripens and fades, and falls, and hath no toil,
Fast-rooted in the fruitful soil.

#### IV

Hateful is the dark-blue sky,
Vaulted o'er the dark-blue sea.    40
Death is the end of life; ah, why
Should life all labor be?
Let us alone. Time driveth onward fast,
And in a little while our lips are dumb.
Let us alone. What is it that will last?    45
All things are taken from us, and become
Portions and parcels of the dreadful past.
Let us alone. What pleasure can we have
To war with evil? Is there any peace
In ever climbing up the climbing wave?    50
All things have rest, and ripen toward the grave
In silence—ripen, fall, and cease:
Give us long rest or death, dark death, or dreamful ease.

#### V

How sweet it were, hearing the downward stream,
With half-shut eyes ever to seem    55
Falling asleep in a half-dream!
To dream and dream, like yonder amber light,
Which will not leave the myrrh-bush on the height;
To hear each other's whispered speech;
Eating the Lotos day by day,    60
To watch the crisping ripples on the beach,
And tender curving lines of creamy spray;
To lend our hearts and spirits wholly
To the influence of mild-minded melancholy;
To muse and brood and live again in memory,
With those old faces of our infancy    66
Heaped over with a mound of grass,
Two handfuls of white dust, shut in an urn of brass!

#### VI

Dear is the memory of our wedded lives,
And dear the last embraces of our wives    70
And their warm tears; but all hath suffered change;
For surely now our household hearths are cold,
Our sons inherit us, our looks are strange,
And we should come like ghosts to trouble joy.

Or else the island princes over-bold    75
Have eat our substance, and the minstrel sings
Before them of the ten years' war in Troy,
And our great deeds, as half-forgotten things.
Is there confusion in the little isle?
Let what is broken so remain.    80
The Gods are hard to reconcile;
'Tis hard to settle order once again.
There *is* confusion worse than death,
Trouble on trouble, pain on pain,
Long labor unto agèd breath,    85
Sore task to hearts worn out by many wars
And eyes grown dim with gazing on the pilot-
    stars.

### VII

But, propped on beds of amaranth and moly,[4]
How sweet—while warm airs lull us, blowing
    lowly—
With half-dropped eyelid still,    90
Beneath a heaven dark and holy,
To watch the long bright river drawing slowly
His waters from the purple hill—
To hear the dewy echoes calling
From cave to cave through the thick-twined
    vine—    95
To watch the emerald-colored water falling
Through many a woven acanthus-wreath[5] di-
    vine!
Only to hear and see the far-off sparkling brine,
Only to hear were sweet, stretched out beneath
    the pine.

### VIII

The Lotos blooms below the barren peak,    100
The Lotos blows by every winding creek;
All day the wind breathes low with mellower
    tone;
Through every hollow cave and alley lone
Round and round the spicy downs the yellow
    Lotos-dust is blown.
We have had enough of action, and of motion
    we,    105
Rolled to starboard, rolled to larboard, when
    the surge was seething free,
Where the wallowing monster spouted his
    foam-fountains in the sea.
Let us swear an oath, and keep it with an equal
    mind,
In the hollow Lotos-land to live and lie reclined
On the hills like Gods together, careless of man-
    kind.    110
For they lie beside their nectar, and the bolts
    are hurled
Far below them in the valleys, and the clouds
    are lightly curled

---

[4] Amaranth was a fabled unfading flower; moly a
fabled plant with black root and milk-white flower
given by Hermes to Ulysses to protect him from the
draught of Circe (*Odyssey*, X, 305).
[5] Acanthus is a plant with pendant leaves, reproduced on the capitals of Corinthian columns.

Round their golden houses, girdled with the
    gleaming world;
Where they smile in secret, looking over wasted
    lands,
Blight and famine, plague and earthquake,
    roaring deeps and fiery sands,    115
Clanging fights, and flaming towns, and sinking
    ships, and praying hands.
But they smile, they find a music centered in
    a doleful song
Steaming up, a lamentation and an ancient tale
    of wrong,
Like a tale of little meaning though the words
    are strong;
Chanted from an ill-used race of men that
    cleave the soil,    120
Sow the seed, and reap the harvest with endur-
    ing toil,
Storing yearly little dues of wheat, and wine
    and oil;
Till they perish and they suffer—some, 'tis
    whispered—down in hell
Suffer endless anguish, others in Elysian valleys
    dwell,
Resting weary limbs at last on beds of asphodel.
Surely, surely, slumber is more sweet than toil,
    the shore    126
Than labor in the deep mid-ocean, wind and
    wave and oar;
O, rest ye, brother mariners, we will not wander
    more.

# You Ask Me, Why,
# Though Ill at Ease[1]

You ask me, why, though ill at ease,
    Within this region I subsist,
    Whose spirits falter in the mist,
And languish for the purple seas.

It is the land that freemen till,    5
    That sober-suited Freedom chose,
    The land, where girt with friends or foes
A man may speak the thing he will;

A land of settled government,
    A land of just and old renown,    10
    Where Freedom slowly broadens down
From precedent to precedent;

Where faction seldom gathers head,
    But, by degrees to fullness wrought,
    The strength of some diffusive thought    15
Hath time and space to work and spread.

Should banded unions persecute
    Opinion, and induce a time
    When single thought is civil crime,
And individual freedom mute,    20

---

[1] Published in 1842.

Though power should make from land to land
  The name of Britain trebly great—
  Though every channel of the State
Should fill and choke with golden sand—

Yet waft me from the harbor-mouth,      25
  Wild wind! I seek a warmer sky,
  And I will see before I die
The palms and temples of the South.

## Ulysses [1]

It little profits that an idle king,
By this still hearth, among these barren crags,
Matched with an aged wife, I mete [2] and dole
Unequal laws unto a savage race,
That hoard, and sleep, and feed, and know not
    me.                                    5
I cannot rest from travel; I will drink
Life to the lees. All times I have enjoyed
Greatly, have suffered greatly, both with those
That loved me, and alone; on shore, and when
Through scudding drifts the rainy Hyades [3]  10
Vexed the dim sea. I am become a name;
For always roaming with a hungry heart
Much have I seen and known,—cities of men
And manners, climates, councils, governments,
Myself not least, but honored of them all,—  15
And drunk delight of battle with my peers,
Far on the ringing plains of windy Troy.
I am a part of [4] all that I have met;
Yet all experience is an arch wherethrough
Gleams that untraveled world whose margin
    fades                                   20
For ever and for ever when I move.
How dull it is to pause, to make an end,
To rust unburnished, not to shine in use!
As though to breathe were life! Life piled on
    life
Were all too little, and of one to me        25
Little remains; but every hour is saved
From that eternal silence, something more,
A bringer of new things; and vile it were
For some three suns to store and hoard myself,
And this gray spirit yearning in desire      30
To follow knowledge like a sinking star,
Beyond the utmost bound of human thought.
  This is my son, mine own Telemachus,
To whom I leave the scepter and the isle,—
Well-loved of me, discerning to fulfil       35
This labor, by slow prudence to make mild
A rugged people, and through soft degrees
Subdue them to the useful and the good.

---

[1] Published in 1842. This imagined speech of
Ulysses (essentially modern in character) after his
return to Ithaca and Penelope (his "aged wife")
was suggested to Tennyson, not by Homer, but by
Dante's *Inferno*, xxvi, 90–142.

[2] Measure.

[3] A group of seven stars whose rising and setting
were anciently believed to be accompanied by much
rain.

[4] I. e., I am known by.

Most blameless is he, centered in the sphere
Of common duties, decent not to fail       40
In offices of tenderness, and pay
Meet adoration to my household gods,
When I am gone. He works his work, I mine.
  There lies the port; the vessel puffs her sail;
There gloom the dark, broad seas. My mariners,
Souls that have toiled, and wrought, and
    thought with me,—                       46
That ever with a frolic welcome took
The thunder and the sunshine, and opposed
Free hearts, free foreheads,—you and I are old;
Old age hath yet his honor and his toil.    50
Death closes all; but something ere the end,
Some work of noble note, may yet be done,
Not unbecoming men that strove with Gods.
The lights begin to twinkle from the rocks;
The long day wanes; the slow moon climbs; the
    deep                                    55
Moans round with many voices. Come, my
    friends.
'Tis not too late to seek a newer world.
Push off, and sitting well in order smite
The sounding furrows; for my purpose holds
To sail beyond the sunset, and the baths    60
Of all the western stars, until I die.
It may be that the gulfs will wash us down;
It may be we shall touch the Happy Isles,
And see the great Achilles, whom we knew.
Though much is taken, much abides; and
    though                                   65
We are not now that strength which in old days
Moved earth and heaven, that which we are,
    we are,—
One equal temper of heroic hearts,
Made weak by time and fate, but strong in will
To strive, to seek, to find, and not to yield.  70

## Tithonus [1]

The woods decay, the woods decay and fall,
The vapors weep their burthen to the ground,
Man comes and tills the field and lies beneath,
And after many a summer dies the swan.
Me only cruel immortality                    5
Consumes; I wither slowly in thine arms,
Here at the quiet limit of the world,
A white-haired shadow roaming like a dream
The ever-silent spaces of the East,
Far-folded mists, and gleaming halls of morn.
  Alas! for this gray shadow, once a man—   11
So glorious in his beauty and thy choice,
Who madest him thy chosen, that he seemed

---

[1] Published in 1860. The story of this poem is to
be found in the Homeric *Hymn to Aphrodite*, 218–
239. Tithonus was loved by Aurora, goddess of
dawn, who made him immortal at his request. He,
however, had neglected to ask for the perpetuation
of his youth, so that he grew slowly older and more
decrepit until he finally asked the goddess for death.
As she could not give him death, she changed him
into a grasshopper.

To his great heart none other than a God!
I asked thee, "Give me immortality."   15
Then didst thou grant mine asking with a
   smile,
Like wealthy men who care not how they give.
But thy strong Hours [2] indignant worked their
   wills,
And beat me down and marred and wasted me,
And though they could not end me, left me
   maimed   20
To dwell in presence of immortal youth,
Immortal age beside immortal youth,
And all I was in ashes. Can thy love,
Thy beauty, make amends, though even now,
Close over us, the silver star, thy guide,   25
Shines in those tremulous eyes that fill with
   tears
To hear me? Let me go; take back thy gift.
Why should a man desire in any way
To vary from the kindly race of men,
Or pass beyond the goal of ordinance   30
Where all should pause, as is most meet for all?
   A soft air fans the cloud apart; there comes
A glimpse of that dark world where I was
   born.
Once more the old mysterious glimmer steals
From thy pure brows, and from thy shoulders
   pure,   35
And bosom beating with a heart renewed.
Thy cheek begins to redden through the gloom,
Thy sweet eyes brighten slowly close to mine,
Ere yet they blind the stars, and the wild
   team [3]
Which love thee, yearning for thy yoke, arise,
And shake the darkness from their loosened
   manes,   41
And beat the twilight into flakes of fire.
   Lo! ever thus thou growest beautiful
In silence, then before thine answer given
Departest, and thy tears are on my cheek.   45
   Why wilt thou ever scare me with thy
   tears,
And make me tremble lest a saying learnt,
In days far-off, on that dark earth, be true?
"The Gods themselves cannot recall their
   gifts."
   Ay me! ay me! with what another heart   50
In days far-off, and with what other eyes
I used to watch—if I be he that watched—
The lucid outline forming round thee; saw
The dim curls kindle into sunny rings;
Changed with thy mystic change, and felt my
   blood   55
Glow with the glow that slowly crimsoned all
Thy presence and thy portals, while I lay,
Mouth, forehead, eyelids, growing dewy-warm
With kisses balmier than half-opening buds
Of April, and could hear the lips that kissed [60]
Whispering I knew not what of wild and sweet,
Like that strange song I heard Apollo sing,

[2] Goddesses of the seasons.
[3] The horses which drew Dawn's chariot.

While Ilion like a mist rose into towers.[4]
   Yet hold me not for ever in thine East;
How can my nature longer mix with thine?   65
Coldly thy rosy shadows bathe me, cold
Are all thy lights, and cold my wrinkled feet
Upon thy glimmering thresholds, when the
   steam
Floats up from those dim fields about the
   homes
Of happy men that have the power to die,   70
And grassy barrows of the happier dead.
Release me, and restore me to the ground.
Thou seest all things, thou wilt see my grave;
Thou wilt renew thy beauty morn by morn,
I earth in earth forget these empty courts,   75
And thee returning on thy silver wheels.

# Locksley Hall [1]

Comrades, leave me here a little, while as yet
   'tis early morn;
Leave me here and when you want me, sound
   upon the bugle-horn.

'Tis the place, and all around it, as of old, the
   curlews [2] call,
Dreary gleams about the moorland flying over
   Locksley Hall;

Locksley Hall, that in the distance overlooks
   the sandy tracts,   5
And the hollow ocean-ridges roaring into cataracts.

Many a night from yonder ivied casement, ere
   I went to rest,
Did I look on great Orion [3] sloping slowly to
   the west.

Many a night I saw the Pleiads,[4] rising through
   the mellow shade,
Glitter like a swarm of fireflies tangled in a
   silver braid.   10

Here about the beach I wandered, nourishing a
   youth sublime
With the fairy tales of science, and the long result of time;

When the centuries behind me like a fruitful
   land reposed;
When I clung to all the present for the promise that it closed;

When I dipped into the future far as human
   eye could see,   15
Saw the vision of the world and all the wonder
   that would be.—

[4] The walls of Ilion, or Troy, were said to have
arisen in obedience to Apollo's music.
[1] Published in 1842.
[2] Birds of the snipe family.
[3] The constellation.   [4] A group of stars.

In the spring a fuller crimson comes upon the
   robin's breast;
In the spring the wanton lapwing gets himself
   another crest;

In the spring a livelier iris changes on the
   burnished dove;
In the spring a young man's fancy lightly turns
   to thoughts of love.   20

Then her cheek was pale and thinner than
   should be for one so young,
And her eyes on all my motions with a mute
   observance hung.

And I said, "My cousin Amy, speak, and speak
   the truth to me,
Trust me, cousin, all the current of my being
   sets to thee."

On her pallid cheek and forehead came a color
   and a light,   25
As I have seen the rosy red flushing in the
   northern night.

And she turned—her bosom shaken with a sudden storm of sighs—
All the spirit deeply dawning in the dark of
   hazel eyes—

Saying, "I have hid my feelings, fearing they
   should do me wrong";
Saying, "Dost thou love me, cousin?" weeping,
   "I have loved thee long."   30

Love took up the glass of Time, and turned it
   in his glowing hands;
Every moment, lightly shaken, ran itself in
   golden sands.

Love took up the harp of Life, and smote on
   all the chords with might;
Smote the chord of Self, that, trembling, passed
   in music out of sight.

Many a morning on the moorland did we hear
   the copses ring,   35
And her whisper thronged my pulses with the
   fullness of the spring.

Many an evening by the waters did we watch
   the stately ships,
And our spirits rushed together at the touching
   of the lips.

O my cousin, shallow-hearted! O my Amy,
   mine no more!
O the dreary, dreary moorland! O the barren,
   barren shore!   40

Falser than all fancy fathoms, falser than all
   songs have sung,
Puppet to a father's threat, and servile to a
   shrewish tongue!

Is it well to wish thee happy?—having known
   me—to decline
On a range of lower feelings and a narrower
   heart than mine!

Yet it shall be; thou shalt lower to his level
   day by day,   45
What is fine within thee growing coarse to
   sympathize with clay.

As the husband is, the wife is; thou art mated
   with a clown,[5]
And the grossness of his nature will have weight
   to drag thee down.

He will hold thee, when his passion shall have
   spent its novel force,
Something better than his dog, a little dearer
   than his horse.   50

What is this? his eyes are heavy; think not they
   are glazed with wine.
Go to him, it is thy duty; kiss him, take his
   hand in thine.

It may be my lord is weary, that his brain is
   overwrought;
Soothe him with thy finer fancies, touch him
   with thy lighter thought.

He will answer to the purpose, easy things to
   understand—   55
Better thou wert dead before me, though I
   slew thee with my hand!

Better thou and I were lying, hidden from the
   heart's disgrace,
Rolled in one another's arms, and silent in a
   last embrace.

Cursed be the social wants that sin against
   the strength of youth!
Cursed be the social lies that warp us from the
   living truth!   60
Cursed be the sickly forms that err from honest
   Nature's rule!
Cursed be the gold that gilds the straitened
   forehead of the fool!

Well—'tis well that I should bluster!—Hadst
   thou less unworthy proved—
Would to God—for I had loved thee more
   than ever wife was loved.

Am I mad, that I should cherish that which
   bears but bitter fruit?   65
I will pluck it from my bosom, though my
   heart be at the root.

Never, though my mortal summers to such
   length of years should come

---

[5] Countryman.

As the many-wintered crow that leads the
  clanging rookery home.

Where is comfort? in division of the records
  of the mind?
Can I part her from herself, and love her, as
  I knew her, kind?         70

I remember one that perished; sweetly did she
  speak and move;
Such a one do I remember, whom to look at
  was to love.

Can I think of her as dead, and love her for
  the love she bore?
No—she never loved me truly; love is love for
  evermore.

Comfort? comfort scorned of devils! [6] this is
  truth the poet [7] sings,     75
That a sorrow's crown of sorrow is remembering happier things.

Drug thy memories, lest thou learn it, lest thy
  heart be put to proof,
In the dead unhappy night, and when the rain
  is on the roof.

Like a dog, he hunts in dreams, and thou art
  staring at the wall,
Where the dying night-lamp flickers, and the
  shadows rise and fall.    80

Then a hand shall pass before thee, pointing to
  his drunken sleep,
To thy widowed marriage-pillows, to the tears
  that thou wilt weep.

Thou shalt hear the "Never, never," whispered
  by the phantom years,
And a song from out the distance in the ringing of thine ears;

And an eye shall vex thee, looking ancient kindness on thy pain.    85
Turn thee, turn thee on thy pillow; get thee
  to thy rest again.

Nay, but Nature brings thee solace; for a
  tender voice will cry.
'Tis a purer life than thine, a lip to drain thy
  trouble dry.

Baby lips will laugh me down; my latest rival
  brings thee rest.
Baby fingers, waxen touches, press me from
  the mother's breast.    90

O, the child too clothes the father with a dear-
  ness not his due.
Half is thine and half is his; it will be worthy
  of the two.

[6] The allusion is to *Paradise Lost*, Bks. I and II.
[7] Dante, *Inferno*, v, 121–123.

O, I see thee old and formal, fitted to thy petty
  part,
With a little hoard of maxims preaching down
  a daughter's heart.

"They were dangerous guides the feelings—
  she herself was not exempt—   95
Truly, she herself had suffered"—Perish in thy
  self-contempt!

Overlive it—lower yet—be happy! wherefore
  should I care?
I myself must mix with action, lest I wither by
  despair.

What is that which I should turn to, lighting
  upon days like these?
Every door is barred with gold, and opens but
  to golden keys.    100

Every gate is thronged with suitors, all the
  markets overflow,
I have but an angry fancy; what is that which
  I should do?

I had been content to perish, falling on the
  foeman's ground,
When the ranks are rolled in vapor, and the
  winds are laid with sound.

But the jingling of the guinea helps the hurt
  that Honor feels,    105
And the nations do but murmur, snarling at
  each other's heels.

Can I but relive in sadness? I will turn that
  earlier page.
Hide me from my deep emotion, O thou
  wondrous Mother-Age!

Make me feel the wild pulsation that I felt
  before the strife,
When I heard my days before me, and the
  tumult of my life;    110

Yearning for the large excitement that the
  coming years would yield,
Eager-hearted as a boy when first he leaves his
  father's field,

And at night along the dusky highway near and
  nearer drawn,
Sees in heaven the light of London flaring like
  a dreary dawn;

And his spirit leaps within him to be gone
  before him then,    115
Underneath the light he looks at, in among the
  throngs of men;

Men, my brothers, men the workers, ever reaping something new;
That which they have done but earnest of the
  things that they shall do.

For I dipped into the future, far as human eye
    could see,
Saw the Vision of the world, and all the wonder
    that would be;   120

Saw the heavens fill with commerce, argosies of
    magic sails,
Pilots of the purple twilight, dropping down
    with costly bales;

Heard the heavens fill with shouting, and there
    rained a ghastly dew
From the nations' airy navies grappling in the
    central blue;

Far along the world-wide whisper of the south-
    wind rushing warm,   125
With the standards of the peoples plunging
    through the thunder-storm;

Till the war-drum throbbed no longer, and the
    battle-flags were furled
In the Parliament of man, the Federation of the
    world.

There the common sense of most shall hold a
    fretful realm in awe,
And the kindly earth shall slumber, lapped in
    universal law.   130

So I triumphed ere my passion sweeping
    through me left me dry,
Left me with the palsied heart, and left me
    with the jaundiced eye;

Eye, to which all order festers, all things here
    are out of joint.
Science moves, but slowly, slowly, creeping on
    from point to point;

Slowly comes a hungry people, as a lion, creep-
    ing nigher,   135
Glares at one that nods and winks behind a
    slowly-dying fire.

Yet I doubt not through the ages one increasing
    purpose runs,
And the thoughts of men are widened with the
    process of the suns.

What is that to him that reaps not harvest of
    his youthful joys,
Though the deep heart of existence beat for
    ever like a boy's?   140

Knowledge comes, but wisdom lingers, and I
    linger on the shore,
And the individual withers, and the world is
    more and more.

Knowledge comes, but wisdom lingers, and he
    bears a laden breast,
Full of sad experience, moving toward the still-
    ness of his rest.

Hark, my merry comrades call me, sounding on
    the bugle-horn,   145
They to whom my foolish passion were a target
    for their scorn.

Shall it not be scorn to me to harp on such a
    moldered string?
I am shamed through all my nature to have
    loved so slight a thing.

Weakness to be wroth with weakness! woman's
    pleasure, woman's pain—
Nature made them blinder motions bounded in
    a shallower brain.   150

Woman is the lesser man, and all thy passions,
    matched with mine,
Are as moonlight unto sunlight, and as water
    unto wine—

Here at least, where nature sickens, nothing.
    Ah, for some retreat
Deep in yonder shining Orient, where my life
    began to beat,

Where in wild Mahratta-battle [8] fell my father
    evil-starred;—   155
I was left a trampled orphan, and a selfish
    uncle's ward.

Or to burst all links of habit—there to wander
    far away,
On from island unto island at the gateways of
    the day.

Larger constellations burning, mellow moons
    and happy skies,
Breadths of tropic shade and palms in cluster,
    knots of Paradise.   160

Never comes the trader, never floats an Euro-
    pean flag,
Slides the bird o'er lustrous woodland, swings
    the trailer from the crag;

Droops the heavy-blossomed bower, hangs the
    heavy-fruited tree—
Summer isles of Eden lying in dark-purple
    spheres of sea.

There methinks would be enjoyment more than
    in this march of mind,   165
In the steamship, in the railway, in the thoughts
    that shake mankind.

There the passions cramped no longer shall have
    scope and breathing space;
I will take some savage woman, she shall rear
    my dusky race.

Iron-jointed, supple-sinewed, they shall dive,
    and they shall run,

[8] The Mahrattas are a Hindu people.

Catch the wild goat by the hair, and hurl their
lances in the sun;                                       170

Whistle back the parrot's call, and leap the
rainbows of the brooks,
Not with blinded eyesight poring over miserable
books—

Fool, again the dream, the fancy! but I *know*
my words are wild,
But I count the gray barbarian lower than the
Christian child.

I, to herd with narrow foreheads, vacant of our
glorious gains,                                          175
Like a beast with lower pleasures, like a beast
with lower pains!

Mated with a squalid savage—what to me were
sun or clime?
I the heir of all the ages, in the foremost files
of time—

I that rather held it better men should perish
one by one,
Than that earth should stand at gaze like
Joshua's moon in Ajalon! [9]                             180

Not in vain the distance beacons. Forward,
forward, let us range,
Let the great world spin for ever down the
ringing grooves of change. [10]

Through the shadow of the globe we sweep
into the younger day;
Better fifty years of Europe than a cycle of
Cathay. [11]

Mother-Age,—for mine I knew not,—help me
as when life begun;                                      185
Rift the hills, and roll the waters, flash the
lightnings, weigh the sun.

O, I see the crescent promise of my spirit hath
not set.
Ancient founts of inspiration well through all
my fancy yet.

Howsoever these things be, a long farewell to
Locksley Hall!
Now for me the woods may wither, now for me
the roof-tree fall.                                      190

Comes a vapor from the margin, blackening
over heath and holt,
Cramming all the blast before it, in its breast a
thunderbolt.

[9] See Joshua, 10:12–13.
[10] Tennyson explained that when he rode on the
first train from Liverpool to Manchester in 1830 he
supposed that the wheels ran in grooves, and so used
the word in this line.
[11] China.

Let it fall on Locksley Hall, with rain or hail
or fire or snow;
For the mighty wind arises, roaring seaward,
and I go.

# Break, Break, Break [1]

Break, break, break,
  On the cold gray stones, O Sea!
And I would that my tongue could utter
  The thoughts that arise in me.

O well for the fisherman's boy,                          5
  That he shouts with his sister at play!
O well for the sailor lad,
  That he sings in his boat on the bay!

And the stately ships go on
  To their haven under the hill;                         10
But O for the touch of a vanished hand,
  And the sound of a voice that is still!

Break, break, break,
  At the foot of thy crags, O Sea!
But the tender grace of a day that is dead               15
  Will never come back to me.

# Songs from
# The Princess [1]

## I

The splendor falls on castle walls
  And snowy summits old in story;
The long light shakes across the lakes,
  And the wild cataract leaps in glory.
Blow, bugle, blow, set the wild echoes flying, 5
Blow, bugle; answer, echoes, dying, dying,
        dying.

O hark, O hear! how thin and clear,
  And thinner, clearer, farther going!
O sweet and far from cliff and scar [2]
  The horns of Elfland faintly blowing!         10
Blow, let us hear the purple glens replying,
Blow, bugle; answer, echoes, dying, dying,
        dying.

O love, they die in yon rich sky,
  They faint on hill or field or river;
Our echoes roll from soul to soul,             15
  And grow for ever and for ever.
Blow, bugle, blow, set the wild echoes flying,
And answer, echoes, answer, dying, dying,
        dying.

[1] Published in 1842. One of Tennyson's first attempts to express his grief over the death of A. H.
Hallam.
[1] Published in 1847. The first of these songs was,
however, added in 1848, and the third in 1850.
[2] Crag.

II

Tears, idle tears, I know not what they mean,
Tears from the depth of some divine despair
Rise in the heart, and gather to the eyes,
In looking on the happy autumn-fields,
And thinking of the days that are no more. 5

Fresh as the first beam glittering on a sail,
That brings our friends up from the under-
world,
Sad as the last which reddens over one
That sinks with all we love below the verge;
So sad, so fresh, the days that are no more. 10

Ah, sad and strange as in dark summer dawns
The earliest pipe of half-awakened birds
To dying ears, when unto dying eyes
The casement slowly grows a glimmering
square;
So sad, so strange, the days that are no more. 15

Dear as remembered kisses after death,
And sweet as those by hopeless fancy feigned
On lips that are for others; deep as love,
Deep as first love, and wild with all regret,
O Death in Life, the days that are no more! 20

III

Home they brought her warrior dead;
    She nor swooned nor uttered cry.
All her maidens, watching, said,
    "She must weep or she will die."

Then they praised him, soft and low,   5
    Called him worthy to be loved,
Truest friend and noblest foe;
    Yet she neither spoke nor moved.

Stole a maiden from her place,
    Lightly to the warrior stepped,   10
Took the face-cloth from the face;
    Yet she neither moved nor wept.

Rose a nurse of ninety years,
    Set his child upon her knee—
Like summer tempest came her tears—   15
    "Sweet my child, I live for thee."

## In Memoriam A. H. H.[1]

Strong Son of God, immortal Love,
    Whom we, that have not seen thy face,
    By faith, and faith alone, embrace
Believing where we cannot prove;

[1] Published in 1850. The poems were gradually written in the period between the death of Arthur Henry Hallam on 15 September, 1833, and the date of publication. At the time of his death Hallam was engaged to Tennyson's sister Emily. His body was brought to England by sea (he had died in Vienna) and was buried at Clevedon, on the Bristol Channel, on 3 January, 1834. Clevedon Court was

Thine are these orbs of light and shade;   5
    Thou madest Life in man and brute;
    Thou madest Death; and lo, thy foot
Is on the skull which thou hast made.

Thou wilt not leave us in the dust:
    Thou madest man, he knows not why,   10

the residence of Hallam's maternal grandfather. Tennyson says: "It must be remembered that this is a poem, *not* an actual biography. . . . The different moods of sorrow as in a drama are dramatically given, and my conviction that fear, doubts, and suffering will find answer and relief only through Faith in a God of Love. 'I' is not always the author speaking of himself, but the voice of the human race speaking through him." Tennyson also says: "The sections were written at many different places, and as the phases of our intercourse came to my memory and suggested them. I did not write them with any view of weaving them into a whole, or for publication, until I found that I had written so many." This circumstance of the poem's composition has given room for differences of opinion concerning the period of time covered in it. Some, imagining that Tennyson wrote, as it were, an historical record of his grief, and connecting allusions in the sections with actual happenings, hold that the period covered by the poem is 1833–1842. More probably, however, the internal chronology of the poem is independent of the actual order of events, and the period of time covered is not quite three years. The following table indicates the chronology, the Christmas sections marking the major divisions of the poem:

| | |
|---|---|
| Section XI, | Early Autumn, 1833. |
| XV, | Later Autumn. |
| XXVIII–XXX, | Christmas, 1833. |
| XXXVIII–XXXIX, | Spring. |
| LXXII, | First Anniversary, September, 1834. |
| LXXVIII, | Christmas, 1834. |
| LXXXIII, | Delaying Spring. |
| LXXXVI, | |
| LXXXVIII, | Spring. |
| LXXXIX, XCV, | |
| XCVIII, | Summer. |
| XCIX, | Second Anniversary. |
| CIV, CV, | Christmas, 1835. |
| CVI, | New Year's Day. |
| CVII, | Winter. |
| CXV, CXVI, | Spring. |

Tennyson sometimes referred to *In Memoriam* as "The Way of the Soul"; it is "a journey from the first stupor and confusion of grief, through a growing acquiescence often disturbed by the recurrence of pain, to an almost unclouded peace and joy. The anguish of wounded love passes into the triumph of love over sorrow, time, and death. The soul, at first, almost sunk in the feeling of loss, finds itself at last freed from regret and yet strengthened in affection. It pines no longer for the vanished hand and silent voice; it is filled with the consciousness of union with the spirit. The world, which once seemed to it a mere echo of its sorrow, has become the abode of that immortal Love, at once divine and human, which includes the living and the dead" (A. C. Bradley, *Commentary*, p. 27, from which the above table has also been adapted).

He thinks he was not made to die;
And thou hast made him: thou art just.

Thou seemest human and divine,
　The highest, holiest, manhood, thou.
　Our wills are ours, we know not how;　15
Our wills are ours, to make them thine.

Our little systems have their day;
　They have their day and cease to be;
　They are but broken lights of thee,
And thou, O Lord, art more than they.　20

We have but faith: we cannot know,
　For knowledge is of things we see;
　And yet we trust it comes from thee,
A beam in darkness: let it grow.

Let knowledge grow from more to more,　25
　But more of reverence in us dwell;
　That mind and soul, according well,
May make one music as before,

But vaster. We are fools and slight;
　We mock thee when we do not fear:　30
　But help thy foolish ones to bear;
Help thy vain worlds to bear thy light.

Forgive what seemed my sin in me,
　What seemed my worth since I began;
　For merit lives from man to man,　35
And not from man, O Lord, to thee.

Forgive my grief for one removed,
　Thy creature, whom I found so fair.
　I trust he lives in thee, and there
I find him worthier to be loved.　　40

Forgive these wild and wandering cries,
　Confusions of a wasted youth;
　Forgive them where they fail in truth,
And in thy wisdom make me wise.

I

I held it truth, with him[2] who sings
　To one clear harp in divers tones,
　That men may rise on stepping-stones
Of their dead selves to higher things.

But who shall so forecast the years　5
　And find in loss a gain to match?
　Or reach a hand through time to catch
The far-off interest of tears?

Let Love clasp Grief lest both be drowned,
　Let darkness keep her raven gloss.　10
　Ah, sweeter to be drunk with loss,
To dance with Death, to beat the ground,

Than that the victor Hours should scorn
　The long result of love, and boast,

　[2] Tennyson thought, in 1880, that his allusion was to Goethe.

"Behold the man that loved and lost,　15
But all he was is overworn."

II

Old yew, which graspest at the stones
　That name the underlying dead,
　Thy fibers net the dreamless head,
Thy roots are wrapped about the bones.

The seasons bring the flower again,　5
　And bring the firstling to the flock;
　And in the dusk of thee the clock
Beats out the little lives of men.

O, not for thee the glow, the bloom,
　Who changest not in any gale,　10
　Nor branding summer suns avail
To touch thy thousand years of gloom;

And gazing on thee, sullen tree,
　Sick for thy stubborn hardihood,
　I seem to fail from out my blood　15
And grow incorporate into thee.

III

O Sorrow, cruel fellowship,
　O Priestess in the vaults of Death,
　O sweet and bitter in a breath,
What whispers from thy lying lip?

"The stars," she whispers, "blindly run;　5
　A web is woven across the sky;
　From out waste places comes a cry,
And murmurs from the dying sun;

"And all the phantom, Nature, stands—
　With all the music in her tone,　10
　A hollow echo of my own,—
A hollow form with empty hands."

And shall I take a thing so blind,
　Embrace her as my natural good;
　Or crush her, like a vice of blood,　15
Upon the threshold of the mind?

IV

To Sleep I give my powers away;
　My will is bondsman to the dark;
　I sit within a helmless bark,
And with my heart I muse and say:

O heart, how fares it with thee now,　5
　That thou shouldst fail from thy desire,
　Who scarcely darest to inquire,
"What is it makes me beat so low?"

Something it is which thou hast lost,
　Some pleasure from thine early years.　10
　Break, thou deep vase of chilling tears,
That grief hath shaken into frost!

Such clouds of nameless trouble cross
　All night below the darkened eyes;

With morning wakes the will, and cries,   15
  "Thou shalt not be the fool of loss."

### V

I sometimes hold it half a sin
  To put in words the grief I feel;
  For words, like Nature, half reveal
And half conceal the Soul within.

But, for the unquiet heart and brain,   5
  A use in measured language lies;
  The sad mechanic exercise,
Like dull narcotics, numbing pain.

In words, like weeds, I'll wrap me o'er,
  Like coarsest clothes against the cold;   10
  But that large grief which these enfold
Is given in outline and no more.

### VI

One writes, that "other friends remain,"
  That "loss is common to the race"—
  And common is the commonplace,
And vacant chaff well meant for grain.

That loss is common would not make   5
  My own less bitter, rather more.
  Too common! Never morning wore
To evening, but some heart did break.

O father, wheresoe'er thou be,
  Who pledgest now thy gallant son,   10
  A shot, ere half thy draught be done,
Hath stilled the life that beat from thee.

O mother, praying God will save
  Thy sailor,—while thy head is bowed,
  His heavy-shotted hammock-shroud   15
Drops in his vast and wandering grave.

Ye know no more than I who wrought
  At that last hour to please him well;
  Who mused on all I had to tell,
And something written, something thought;   20

Expecting still his advent home;
  And ever met him on his way
  With wishes, thinking, "here to-day,"
Or "here to-morrow will he come."

O, somewhere, meek, unconscious dove,   25
  That sittest ranging golden hair;
  And glad to find thyself so fair,
Poor child, that waitest for thy love!

For now her father's chimney glows
  In expectation of a guest;   30
  And thinking "this will please him best,"
She takes a riband or a rose;

For he will see them on to-night;
  And with the thought her color burns;
  And, having left the glass, she turns   35
Once more to set a ringlet right;

And, even when she turned, the curse
  Had fallen, and her future lord
  Was drowned in passing through the ford,
Or killed in falling from his horse.   40

O, what to her shall be the end?
  And what to me remains of good?
  To her perpetual maidenhood,
And unto me no second friend.

### VII

Dark house,[3] by which once more I stand
  Here in the long unlovely street,
  Doors, where my heart was used to beat
So quickly, waiting for a hand,

A hand that can be clasped no more—   5
  Behold me, for I cannot sleep,
  And like a guilty thing I creep
At earliest morning to the door.

He is not here; but far away
  The noise of life begins again,   10
  And ghastly through the drizzling rain
On the bald street breaks the blank day.

### VIII

A happy lover who has come
  To look on her that loves him well,
  Who 'lights and rings the gateway bell,
And learns her gone and far from home;

He saddens, all the magic light   5
  Dies off at once from bower and hall,
  And all the place is dark, and all
The chambers emptied of delight:

So find I every pleasant spot
  In which we two were wont to meet,   10
  The field, the chamber, and the street,
For all is dark where thou art not.

Yet as that other, wandering there
  In those deserted walks, may find
  A flower beat with rain and wind,   15
Which once she fostered up with care;

So seems it in my deep regret,
  O my forsaken heart, with thee
  And this poor flower of poesy
Which, little cared for, fades not yet.   20

But since it pleased a vanished eye,
  I go to plant it on his tomb,
  That if it can it there may bloom,
Or, dying, there at least may die.

### IX

Fair ship, that from the Italian shore [4]
  Sailest the placid ocean-plains

[3] In which Hallam lived, in London.
[4] Hallam's body was brought to England by sea, from Trieste.

With my lost Arthur's loved remains,
Spread thy full wings, and waft him o'er.

So draw him home to those that mourn    5
In vain; a favorable speed
Ruffle thy mirrored mast, and lead
Through prosperous floods his holy urn.

All night no ruder air perplex
Thy sliding keel, till Phosphor,[5] bright    10
As our pure love, through early light
Shall glimmer on the dewy decks.

Sphere all your lights around, above;
Sleep, gentle heavens, before the prow;
Sleep, gentle winds, as he sleeps now,    15
My friend, the brother of my love;

My Arthur, whom I shall not see
Till all my widowed race be run;
Dear as the mother to the son,
More than my brothers are to me.    20

### X

I hear the noise about thy keel;
I hear the bell struck in the night;
I see the cabin-window bright;
I see the sailor at the wheel.

Thou bring'st the sailor to his wife,    5
And traveled men from foreign lands;
And letters unto trembling hands;
And, thy dark freight, a vanished life.

So bring him; we have idle dreams;
This look of quiet flatters thus    10
Our home-bred fancies. O, to us,
The fools of habit, sweeter seems

To rest beneath the clover sod,
That takes the sunshine and the rains,
Or where the kneeling hamlet drains    15
The chalice of the grapes of God;

Than if with thee the roaring wells
Should gulf him fathom-deep in brine,
And hands so often clasped in mine,
Should toss with tangle and with shells.    20

### XI

Calm is the morn without a sound,
Calm as to suit a calmer grief,
And only through the faded leaf
The chestnut pattering to the ground;

Calm and deep peace on this high wold,[6]    5
And on these dews that drench the furze,
And all the silvery gossamers
That twinkle into green and gold;

Calm and still light on yon great plain
That sweeps with all its autumn bowers,    10

[5] The morning star.    [6] Open country.

And crowded farms and lessening towers,
To mingle with the bounding main;[7]

Calm and deep peace in this wide air,
These leaves that redden to the fall,
And in my heart, if calm at all,    15
If any calm, a calm despair;

Calm on the seas, and silver sleep,
And waves that sway themselves in rest,
And dead calm in that noble breast
Which heaves but with the heaving deep.    20

### XIV

If one should bring me this report,
That thou hadst touched the land to-day,
And I went down unto the quay,
And found thee lying in the port;

And standing, muffled round with woe,    5
Should see thy passengers in rank
Come stepping lightly down the plank,
And beckoning unto those they know;

And if along with these should come
The man I held as half-divine,    10
Should strike a sudden hand in mine,
And ask a thousand things of home;

And I should tell him all my pain,
And how my life had drooped of late,
And he should sorrow o'er my state    15
And marvel what possessed my brain;

And I perceived no touch of change,
No hint of death in all his frame,
But found him all in all the same,
I should not feel it to be strange.    20

### XV

To-night the winds begin to rise
And roar from yonder dropping day;
The last red leaf is whirled away,
The rooks are blown about the skies;

The forest cracked, the waters curled,    5
The cattle huddled on the lea;
And wildly dash'd on tower and tree
The sunbeam strikes along the world:

And but for fancies, which aver
That all thy motions gently pass    10
Athwart a plane of molten glass,[8]
I scarce could brook the strain and stir

That makes the barren branches loud;
And but for fear it is not so,
The wild unrest that lives in woe    15
Would dote and pore on yonder cloud

That rises upward always higher,
And onward drags a laboring breast,

[7] Limiting sea.    [8] Across a calm sea.

And topples round the dreary west,
A looming bastion fringed with fire.   20

. . . . . .

### XIX

The Danube to the Severn gave
    The darkened heart that beat no more;
    They laid him by the pleasant shore,
And in the hearing of the wave.[9]

There twice a day the Severn fills;   5
    The salt sea-water passes by,
    And hushes half the babbling Wye,
And makes a silence in the hills.

The Wye is hushed nor moved along,
    And hushed my deepest grief of all,   10
    When filled with tears that cannot fall,
I brim with sorrow drowning song.

The tide flows down, the wave again
    Is vocal in its wooded walls;
    My deeper anguish also falls,   15
And I can speak a little then.

### XXII

The path by which we twain did go,
    Which led by tracts that pleased us well,
    Through four sweet years arose and fell,
From flower to flower, from snow to snow;

And we with singing cheered the way,   5
    And, crowned with all the season lent,
    From April on to April went,
And glad at heart from May to May.

But where the path we walked began
    To slant the fifth autumnal slope,   10
    As we descended following Hope,
There sat the Shadow feared of man;

Who broke our fair companionship,
    And spread his mantle dark and cold,
    And wrapped thee formless in the fold,   15
And dulled the murmur on thy lip,

And bore thee where I could not see
    Nor follow, though I walk in haste,
    And think that somewhere in the waste
The Shadow sits and waits for me.   20

. . . . . .

### XXVI

Still onward winds the dreary way;
    I with it, for I long to prove
    No lapse of moons can canker Love,
Whatever fickle tongues may say.

And if that eye which watches guilt   5
    And goodness, and hath power to see

[9] Clevedon Churchyard is near the point where the Severn River flows into Bristol Channel.

Within the green the moldered tree,
And towers fallen as soon as built—

O, if indeed that eye foresee
    Or see—in Him is no before—   10
    In more of life true life no more
And Love the indifference to be,

Then might I find, ere yet the morn
    Breaks hither over Indian seas,
    That Shadow waiting with the keys,   15
To shroud me from my proper scorn.

### XXVII

I envy not in any moods
    The captive void of noble rage,
    The linnet born within the cage,
That never knew the summer woods;

I envy not the beast that takes   5
    His license in the field of time,
    Unfettered by the sense of crime,
To whom a conscience never wakes;

Nor, what may count itself as blest,
    The heart that never plighted troth   10
    But stagnates in the weeds of sloth;
Nor any want-begotten rest.

I hold it true, whate'er befall;
    I feel it, when I sorrow most;
    'Tis better to have loved and lost   15
Than never to have loved at all.

### XXVIII

The time draws near the birth of Christ.
    The moon is hid, the night is still;
    The Christmas bells from hill to hill
Answer each other in the mist.

Four voices of four hamlets round,   5
    From far and near, on mead and moor,
    Swell out and fail, as if a door
Were shut between me and the sound;

Each voice four changes on the wind,
    That now dilate, and now decrease,   10
    Peace and goodwill, goodwill and peace,
Peace and goodwill, to all mankind.

This year I slept and woke with pain,
    I almost wished no more to wake,
    And that my hold on life would break   15
Before I heard those bells again;

But they my troubled spirit rule,
    For they controlled me when a boy;
    They bring me sorrow touched with joy,
The merry, merry bells of Yule.   20

### XXIX

With such compelling cause to grieve
    As daily vexes household peace,

And chains regret to his decease,
How dare we keep our Christmas-eve,

Which brings no more a welcome guest      5
   To enrich the threshold of the night
   With showered largess of delight
In dance and song and game and jest?

Yet go, and while the holly boughs
   Entwine the cold baptismal font,      10
   Make one wreath more for Use and Wont,
That guard the portals of the house;

Old sisters of a day gone by,
   Gray nurses, loving nothing new—
   Why should they miss their yearly due      15
Before their time? They too will die.

### XXX

With trembling fingers did we weave
   The holly round the Christmas hearth;
   A rainy cloud possessed the earth,
And sadly fell our Christmas-eve.

At our old pastimes in the hall      5
   We gamboled, making vain pretense
   Of gladness, with an awful sense
Of one mute Shadow watching all.

We paused: the winds were in the beech;
   We heard them sweep the winter land;      10
   And in a circle hand-in-hand
Sat silent, looking each at each.

Then echo-like our voices rang;
   We sung, though every eye was dim,
   A merry song we sang with him      15
Last year; impetuously we sang.

We ceased; a gentler feeling crept
   Upon us: surely rest is meet.
   "They rest," we said, "their sleep is sweet,"
And silence followed, and we wept.      20

Our voices took a higher range;
   Once more we sang: "They do not die
   Nor lose their mortal sympathy,
Nor change to us, although they change;

"Rapt from the fickle and the frail      25
   With gathered power, yet the same,
   Pierces the keen seraphic flame
From orb to orb, from veil to veil."

Rise, happy morn, rise, holy morn,
   Draw forth the cheerful day from night:      30
   O Father, touch the east, and light
The light that shone when Hope was born.

### XXXI

When Lazarus left his charnel-cave,
   And home to Mary's house returned,
   Was this demanded—if he yearned
To hear her weeping by his grave?

"Where wert thou, brother, those four days?"
   There lives no record of reply,      6
   Which telling what it is to die
Had surely added praise to praise.

From every house the neighbors met,
   The streets were filled with joyful sound,      10
   A solemn gladness even crowned
The purple brows of Olivet.

Behold a man raised up by Christ!
   The rest remaineth unrevealed;
   He told it not, or something sealed      15
The lips of that Evangelist.[10]

### XXXII

Her eyes [11] are homes of silent prayer,
   Nor other thought her mind admits
   But, he was dead, and there he sits,
And he that brought him back is there.

Then one deep love doth supersede      5
   All other, when her ardent gaze
   Roves from the living brother's face,
And rests upon the Life indeed.

All subtle thought, all curious fears,
   Borne down by gladness so complete,      10
   She bows, she bathes the Savior's feet
With costly spikenard and with tears.

Thrice blest whose lives are faithful prayers,
   Whose loves in higher love endure;
   What souls possess themselves so pure,      15
Or is there blessedness like theirs?

### XXXIII

O thou that after toil and storm
   Mayst seem to have reached a purer air,
   Whose faith has center everywhere,
Nor cares to fix itself to form,

Leave thou thy sister when she prays      5
   Her early heaven, her happy views;
   Nor thou with shadowed hint confuse
A life that leads melodious days.

Her faith through form is pure as thine,
   Her hands are quicker unto good.      10
   O, sacred be the flesh and blood
To which she links a truth divine!

See thou, that countest reason ripe
   In holding by the law within,
   Thou fail not in a world of sin,      15
And even for want of such a type.

### XXXIV

My own dim life should teach me this,
   That life shall live for evermore,
   Else earth is darkness at the core,
And dust and ashes all that is;

[10] St. John 11:1-44.
[11] The eyes of Mary, the sister of Lazarus.

This round of green, this orb of flame,　5
　Fantastic beauty; such as lurks
　In some wild poet, when he works
Without a conscience or an aim.

What then were God to such as I?
　'Twere hardly worth my while to choose　10
　Of things all mortal, or to use
A little patience ere I die;

'Twere best at once to sink to peace,
　Like birds the charming sepent draws
　To drop head-foremost in the jaws　15
Of vacant darkness and to cease.

### XXXV

Yet if some voice that man could trust
　Should murmur from the narrow house,
　"The cheeks drop in, the body bows;
Man dies, nor is there hope in dust;"

Might I not say? "Yet even here,　5
　But for one hour, O Love, I strive
　To keep so sweet a thing alive."
But I should turn mine ears and hear

The moanings of the homeless sea,
　The sound of streams that swift or slow　10
　Draw down Aeonian [12] hills, and sow
The dust of continents to be;

And Love would answer with a sigh,
　"The sound of that forgetful shore
　Will change my sweetness more and more, 15
Half-dead to know that I shall die."

O me, what profits it to put
　An idle case? If Death were seen
　At first as Death, Love had not been,
Or been in narrowest working shut,　20

Mere fellowship of sluggish moods,
　Or in his coarsest Satyr-shape
　Had bruised the herb and crushed the grape,
And basked and battened [13] in the woods.

### XXXVI

Though truths in manhood darkly join,
　Deep-seated in our mystic frame,
　We yield all blessing to the name
Of Him that made them current coin;

For Wisdom dealt with mortal powers,　5
　Where truth in closest words shall fail,
　When truth embodied in a tale
Shall enter in at lowly doors.

And so the Word had breath, and wrought
　With human hands the creed of creeds　10
　In loveliness of perfect deeds,
More strong than all poetic thought;

Which he may read that binds the sheaf,
　Or builds the house, or digs the grave,
　And those wild eyes that watch the wave　15
In roarings round the coral reef.

### XXXIX

Old warder of these buried bones,
　And answering now my random stroke
　With fruitful cloud and living smoke,
Dark yew, that graspest at the stones

And dippest toward the dreamless head,　5
　To thee too comes the golden hour
　When flower is feeling after flower;
But Sorrow,—fixed upon the dead,

And darkening the dark graves of men,—
　What whispered from her lying lips?　10
　Thy gloom is kindled at the tips,
And passes into gloom again.

### XLVII

That each, who seems a separate whole,
　Should move his rounds, and fusing all
　The skirts of self again, should fall
Remerging in the general Soul,

Is faith as vague as all unsweet.　5
　Eternal form shall still divide
　The eternal soul from all beside;
And I shall know him when we meet;

And we shall sit at endless feast,
　Enjoying each the other's good.　10
　What vaster dream can hit the mood
Of Love on earth? He seeks at least

Upon the last and sharpest height,
　Before the spirits fade away,
　Some landing-place, to clasp and say,　15
"Farewell! We lose ourselves in light."

### XLVIII

If these brief lays, of Sorrow born,
　Were taken to be such as closed
　Grave doubts and answers here proposed,
Then these were such as men might scorn.

Her care is not to part and prove;　5
　She takes, when harsher moods remit,
　What slender shade of doubt may flit,
And makes it vassal unto love;

And hence, indeed, she sports with words,
　But better serves a wholesome law,　10
　And holds it sin and shame to draw
The deepest measure from the chords;

Nor dare she trust a larger lay,
　But rather loosens from the lip

[12] Everlasting.　　　　　　[13] Fed.

Short swallow-flights of song, that dip 15
Their wings in tears, and skim away.

**L**

Be near me when my light is low,
    When the blood creeps, and the nerves prick
And tingle; and the heart is sick,
And all the wheels of being slow.

Be near me when the sensuous frame 5
    Is racked with pangs that conquer trust;
And Time, a maniac scattering dust,
And Life, a Fury slinging flame.

Be near me when my faith is dry,
    And men the flies of latter spring, 10
That lay their eggs, and sting and sing
And weave their petty cells and die.

Be near me when I fade away,
    To point the term of human strife,
And on the low dark verge of life 15
The twilight of eternal day.

**LI**

Do we indeed desire the dead
    Should still be near us at our side?
Is there no baseness we would hide?
No inner vileness that we dread?

Shall he for whose applause I strove, 5
    I had such reverence for his blame,
See with clear eye some hidden shame
And I be lessened in his love?

I wrong the grave with fears untrue.
    Shall love be blamed for want of faith? 10
There must be wisdom with great Death;
The dead shall look me through and through.

Be near us when we climb or fall;
    Ye watch, like God, the rolling hours
With larger other eyes than ours, 15
To make allowance for us all.

**LII**

I cannot love thee as I ought,
    For love reflects the thing beloved;
My words are only words, and moved
Upon the topmost froth of thought.

"Yet blame not thou thy plaintive song," 5
    The Spirit of true love replied;
"Thou canst not move me from thy side,
Nor human frailty do me wrong.

"What keeps a spirit wholly true
    To that ideal which he bears? 10
What record? not the sinless years
That breathed beneath the Syrian blue,[14]

---

[14] Not even the record of the life of Jesus.

"So fret not, like an idle girl,
    That life is dashed with flecks of sin.
Abide; thy wealth is gathered in, 15
When Time hath sundered shell from pearl."

**LIII**

How many a father have I seen,
    A sober man, among his boys,
Whose youth was full of foolish noise,
Who wears his manhood hale and green;

And dare we to this fancy give,[15] 5
    That had the wild oat not been sown,
The soil, left barren, scarce had grown
The grain by which a man may live?

Or, if we held the doctrine sound
    For life outliving heats of youth, 10
Yet who would preach it as a truth
To those that eddy round and round?

Hold thou the good, define it well;
    For fear divine Philosophy
Should push beyond her mark, and be 15
Procuress to the Lords of Hell.

**LIV**

O, yet we trust that somehow good
    Will be the final goal of ill,
To pangs of nature, sins of will,
Defects of doubt, and taints of blood;

That nothing walks with aimless feet; 5
    That not one life shall be destroyed,
Or cast as rubbish to the void,
When God hath made the pile complete;

That not a worm is cloven in vain;
    That not a moth with vain desire 10
Is shriveled in a fruitless fire,
Or but subserves another's gain.

Behold, we know not anything;
    I can but trust that good shall fall
At last—far off—at last, to all, 15
And every winter change to spring.

So runs my dream; but what am I?
    An infant crying in the night;
An infant crying for the light,
And with no language but a cry. 20

**LV**

The wish, that of the living whole
    No life may fail beyond the grave,
Derives it not from what we have
The likest God within the soul?

Are God and Nature then at strife, 5
    That Nature lends such evil dreams?
So careful of the type she seems,
So careless of the single life,

---

[15] Yield.

That I, considering everywhere
  Her secret meaning in her deeds,
  And finding that of fifty seeds     10
She often brings but one to bear,

I falter where I firmly trod,
  And falling with my weight of cares
  Upon the great world's altar-stairs     15
That slope through darkness up to God,

I stretch lame hands of faith, and grope,
  And gather dust and chaff, and call
  To what I feel is Lord of all,
And faintly trust the larger hope.     20

#### LVI

"So careful of the type?" but no.
  From scarpèd cliff and quarried stone
  She cries, "A thousand types are gone;
I care for nothing, all shall go.

"Thou makest thine appeal to me:     5
  I bring to life, I bring to death;
  The spirit does but mean the breath:
I know no more." And he, shall he,

Man, her last work, who seemed so fair,
  Such splendid purpose in his eyes,     10
  Who rolled the psalm to wintry skies,
Who built him fanes of fruitless prayer,

Who trusted God was love indeed
  And love Creation's final law—
  Though Nature, red in tooth and claw     15
With ravine, shrieked against his creed—

Who loved, who suffered countless ills,
  Who battled for the True, the Just,
  Be blown about the desert dust,
Or sealed within the iron hills?     20

No more? A monster then, a dream,
  A discord. Dragons of the prime,[16]
  That tare each other in their slime,
Were mellow music matched with him.

O life as futile, then, as frail!     25
  O for thy voice to soothe and bless!
  What hope of answer, or redress?
Behind the veil, behind the veil.

#### LVII

Peace; come away: the song of woe
  Is after all an earthly song.
  Peace; come away: we do him wrong
To sing so wildly: let us go.

Come; let us go: your cheeks are pale;     5
  But half my life I leave behind.
  Methinks my friend is richly shrined;
But I shall pass, my work will fail.

[16] Prehistoric monsters.

Yet in these ears, till hearing dies,
  One set slow bell will seem to toll     10
  The passing of the sweetest soul
That ever looked with human eyes.

I hear it now, and o'er and o'er,
  Eternal greetings to the dead;
  And "Ave, Ave, Ave," said,     15
"Adieu, adieu," for evermore.

· · · · · ·

#### LIX

O Sorrow, wilt thou live with me
  No casual mistress, but a wife,
  My bosom-friend and half of life;
As I confess it needs must be?

O Sorrow, wilt thou rule my blood,     5
  Be sometimes lovely like a bride,
  And put thy harsher moods aside,
If thou wilt have me wise and good?

My centered passion cannot move,
  Nor will it lessen from to-day;     10
  But I'll have leave at times to play
As with the creature of my love;

And set thee forth, for thou art mine,
  With so much hope for years to come,
  That, howsoe'er I know thee, some     15
Could hardly tell what name were thine.

#### LXVII

When on my bed the moonlight falls,
  I know that in thy place of rest
  By that broad water of the west
There comes a glory on the walls:

Thy marble bright in dark appears,     5
  As slowly steals a silver flame
  Along the letters of thy name,
And o'er the number of thy years.

The mystic glory swims away,
  From off my bed the moonlight dies;     10
  And closing eaves of wearied eyes
I sleep till dusk is dipped in gray;

And then I know the mist is drawn
  A lucid veil from coast to coast,
  And in the dark church like a ghost     15
Thy tablet glimmers in the dawn.

#### LXVIII

When in the down I sink my head,
  Sleep, Death's twin-brother, times my breath;
Sleep, Death's twin-brother, knows not Death,
Nor can I dream of thee as dead.

I walk as ere I walked forlorn,     5
  When all our path was fresh with dew,

And all the bugle breezes blew
Reveillée to the breaking morn.

But what is this? I turn about,
  I find a trouble in thine eye,     10
  Which makes me sad I know not why,
Nor can my dream resolve the doubt;

But ere the lark hath left the lea
  I wake, and I discern the truth;
  It is the trouble of my youth     15
That foolish sleep transfers to thee.

#### LXIX

I dreamed there would be Spring no more,
  That Nature's ancient power was lost;
  The streets were black with smoke and frost,
They chattered trifles at the door;

I wandered from the noisy town,     5
  I found a wood with thorny boughs;
  I took the thorns to bind my brows,
I wore them like a civic crown;

I met with scoffs, I met with scorns
  From youth and babe and hoary hairs:     10
  They called me in the public squares
The fool that wears a crown of thorns.

They called me fool, they called me child:
  I found an angel of the night;
  The voice was low, the look was bright:     15
He looked upon my crown and smiled.

He reached the glory of a hand,
  That seemed to touch it into leaf:
  The voice was not the voice of grief,
The words were hard to understand.     20

#### LXX

I cannot see the features right,
  When on the gloom I strive to paint
  The face I know; the hues are faint
And mix with hollow masks of night;

Cloud-towers by ghostly masons wrought,     5
  A gulf that ever shuts and gapes,
  A hand that points, and palléd shapes
In shadowy thoroughfares of thought;

And crowds that stream from yawning doors,
  And shoals of puckered faces drive;     10
  Dark bulks that tumble half alive,
And lazy lengths on boundless shores:

Till all at once beyond the will
  I hear a wizard music roll,
  And through a lattice on the soul     15
Looks thy fair face and makes it still.

#### LXXIII

So many worlds, so much to do,
  So little done, such things to be,

How know I what had need of thee,
  For thou wert strong as thou wert true?

The fame is quenched that I foresaw,     5
  The head hath missed an earthly wreath:
  I curse not Nature, no, nor Death;
For nothing is that errs from law.

We pass; the path that each man trod
  Is dim, or will be dim, with weeds.     10
  What fame is left for human deeds
In endless age? It rests with God.

O hollow wraith of dying fame,
  Fade wholly, while the soul exults,
  And self-infolds the large results     15
Of force that would have forged a name.

#### LXXVIII

Again at Christmas did we weave
  The holly round the Christmas hearth;
  The silent snow possessed the earth,
And calmly fell our Christmas-eve.

The yule-clog [17] sparkled keen with frost,     5
  No wing of wind the region swept,
  But over all things brooding slept
The quiet sense of something lost.

As in the winters left behind,
  Again our ancient games had place,     10
  The music picture's breathing grace,
And dance and song and hoodman-blind.

Who showed a token of distress?
  No single tear, no mark of pain—
  O sorrow, then can sorrow wane?     15
O grief, can grief be changed to less?

O last regret, regret can die!
  No—mixed with all this mystic frame,
  Her deep relations are the same,
But with long use her tears are dry.     20

#### LXXIX

"More than my brothers are to me,"—
  Let this not vex thee,[18] noble heart!
  I know thee of what force thou art
To hold the costliest love in fee.

But thou and I are one in kind,     5
  As molded like in Nature's mint;
  And hill and wood and field did print
The same sweet forms in either mind.

For us the same cold streamlet curled
  Through all his eddying coves, the same     10
  All winds that roam the twilight came
In whispers of the beauteous world.

---

[17] Log.
[18] Charles, Tennyson's brother. The line within
quotation-marks is the last line of Section IX.

At one dear knee we proffered vows,
  One lesson from one book we learned,
  Ere childhood's flaxen ringlet turned   15
To black and brown on kindred brows.

And so my wealth resembles thine,
  But he was rich where I was poor,
  And he supplied my want the more
As his unlikeness fitted mine.   20

### LXXXII

I wage not any feud with Death
  For changes wrought on form and face;
  No lower life that earth's embrace
May breed with him can fright my faith.

Eternal process moving on,   5
  From state to state the spirit walks;
  And these are but the shattered stalks,
Or ruined chrysalis of one.

Nor blame I Death, because he bare
  The use of virtue out of earth;   10
  I know transplanted human worth
Will bloom to profit, otherwhere.

For this alone on Death I wreak
  The wrath that garners in my heart:
  He put our lives so far apart   15
We cannot hear each other speak.

### LXXXIII

Dip down upon the northern shore,
  O sweet new-year delaying long;
  Thou doest expectant Nature wrong;
Delaying long, delay no more.

What stays thee from the clouded noons,   5
  Thy sweetness from its proper place?
  Can trouble live with April days,
Or sadness in the summer moons?

Bring orchis, bring the foxglove spire,
  The little speedwell's darling blue,   10
  Deep tulips dashed with fiery dew,
Laburnums, dropping-wells of fire.

O thou, new-year, delaying long,
  Delayest the sorrow in my blood,
  That longs to burst a frozen bud   15
And flood a fresher throat with song.

### LXXXV [19]

This truth came borne with bier and pall,
  I felt it, when I sorrowed most,
  'Tis better to have loved and lost,
Than never to have loved at all—

[19] This section is addressed to Edmund Lushington, whose marriage to Tennyson's sister Cecilia is celebrated in the Epilogue which concludes *In Memoriam*.

O true in word, and tried in deed,   5
  Demanding, so to bring relief
  To this which is our common grief,
What kind of life is that I lead;

And whether trust in things above
  Be dimmed of sorrow, or sustained;   10
  And whether love for him have drained
My capabilities of love;

Your words have virtue such as draws
  A faithful answer from the breast,
  Through light reproaches, half expressed,   15
And loyal unto kindly laws.

My blood an even tenor kept,
  Till on mine ear this message falls,
  That in Vienna's fatal walls
God's finger touched him, and he slept.   20

The great Intelligences fair
  That range above our mortal state,
  In circle round the blessèd gate,
Received and gave him welcome there;

And led him through the blissful climes,   25
  And showed him in the fountain fresh
  All knowledge that the sons of flesh
Shall gather in the cycled times.

But I remained, whose hopes were dim,
  Whose life, whose thoughts were little worth,   30
  To wander on a darkened earth,
Where all things round me breathed of him.

O friendship, equal-poised control,
  O heart, with kindliest motion warm,
  O sacred essence, other form,   35
O solemn ghost, O crownèd soul!

Yet none could better know than I,
  How much of act at human hands
  The sense of human will demands
By which we dare to live or die.   40

Whatever way my days decline,
  I felt and feel, though left alone,
  His being working in mine own,
The footsteps of his life in mine;

A life that all the Muses decked   45
  With gifts of grace, that might express
  All-comprehensive tenderness,
All-subtilizing intellect:

And so my passion hath not swerved
  To works of weakness, but I find   50
  An image comforting the mind,
And in my grief a strength reserved.

Likewise the imaginative woe,
  That loved to handle spiritual strife,

Diffused the shock through all my life, 55
But in the present broke the blow.

My pulses therefore beat again
For other friends that once I met;
Nor can it suit me to forget
The mighty hopes that make us men. 60

I woo your love: I count it crime
To mourn for any overmuch;
I, the divided half of such
A friendship as had mastered Time;

Which masters Time indeed, and is 65
Eternal, separate from fears.
The all-assuming months and years
Can take no part away from this;

But Summer on the steaming floods,
And Spring that swells the narrow brooks, 70
And Autumn, with a noise of rooks,
That gather in the waning woods,

And every pulse of wind and wave
Recalls, in change of light or gloom,
My old affection of the tomb, 75
And my prime passion in the grave.

My old affection of the tomb,
A part of stillness, yearns to speak:
"Arise, and get thee forth and seek
A friendship for the years to come. 80

"I watch thee from the quiet shore;
Thy spirit up to mine can reach;
But in dear words of human speech
We two communicate no more."

And I, "Can clouds of nature stain 85
The starry clearness of the free?
How is it? Canst thou feel for me
Some painless sympathy with pain?"

And lightly does the whisper fall:
"'Tis hard for thee to fathom this; 90
I triumph in conclusive bliss,
And that serene result of all."

So hold I commerce with the dead;
Or so methinks the dead would say;
Or so shall grief with symbols play 95
And pining life be fancy-fed.

Now looking to some settled end,
That these things pass, and I shall prove
A meeting somewhere, love with love,
I crave your pardon, O my friend; 100

If not so fresh, with love as true,
I, clasping brother-hands, aver
I could not, if I would, transfer
The whole I felt for him to you.

For which be they that hold apart 105
The promise of the golden hours?
First love, first friendship, equal powers,
That marry with the virgin heart.

Still mine, that cannot but deplore,
That beats within a lonely place, 110
That yet remembers his embrace,
But at his footstep leaps no more,

My heart, though widowed, may not rest
Quite in the love of what is gone,
But seeks to beat in time with one 115
That warms another living breast.

Ah, take the imperfect gift I bring,
Knowing the primrose yet is dear,
The primrose of the later year,
As not unlike to that of Spring. 120

### LXXXVI

Sweet after showers, ambrosial air,
That rollest from the gorgeous gloom
Of evening over brake and bloom
And meadow, slowly breathing bare

The round of space, and rapt below 5
Through all the dewy tasseled wood,
And shadowing down the hornéd [20] flood
In ripples, fan my brows and blow

The fever from my cheek, and sigh
The full new life that feeds thy breath 10
Throughout my frame, till Doubt and Death,
Ill brethren, let the fancy fly

From belt to belt of crimson seas
On leagues of odor streaming far,
To where in yonder orient star 15
A hundred spirits whisper "Peace."

### LXXXVII

I passed beside the reverend walls
In which of old I wore the gown;
I roved at random through the town,
And saw the tumult of the halls;

And heard once more in college fanes 5
The storm their high-built organs make,
And thunder-music, rolling, shake
The prophet blazoned on the panes;

And caught once more the distant shout,
The measured pulse of racing oars 10
Among the willows; paced the shores
And many a bridge, and all about

The same gray flats again, and felt
The same, but not the same; and last
Up that long walk of limes I passed 15
To see the rooms in which he dwelt.

[20] Winding.

Another name was on the door.
  I lingered; all within was noise
  Of songs, and clapping hands, and boys
That crashed the glass and beat the floor;    20

Where once we held debate, a band
  Of youthful friends, on mind and art,
  And labor, and the changing mart,
And all the framework of the land;

When one would aim an arrow fair,    25
  But send it slackly from the string;
  And one would pierce an outer ring,
And one an inner, here and there;

And last the master-bowman, he,
  Would cleave the mark. A willing ear    30
  We lent him. Who but hung to hear
The rapt oration flowing free

From point to point, with power and grace
  And music in the bounds of law,
  To those conclusions when we saw    35
The God within him light his face,

And seem to lift the form, and glow
  In azure orbits heavenly-wise;
  And over those ethereal eyes
The bar of Michael Angelo? [21]    40

### LXXXVIII

Wild bird,[22] whose warble, liquid sweet,
  Rings Eden through the budded quicks,[23]
  O tell me where the senses mix,
O tell me where the passions meet,

Whence radiate: fierce extremes employ    5
  Thy spirits in the darkening leaf,
  And in the midmost heart of grief
Thy passion clasps a secret joy;

And I—my harp would prelude woe—
  I cannot all command the strings;    10
  The glory of the sum of things
Will flash along the chords and go.

### XCIII

I shall not see thee. Dare I say
  No spirit ever brake the band
  That stays him from the native land
Where first he walked when clasped in clay?

No visual shade of some one lost,    5
  But he, the Spirit himself, may come

[21] These lines I wrote from what Arthur Hallam said after reading of the prominent ridge of bone over the eyes of Michael Angelo: "Alfred, look over my eyes; surely I have the bar of Michael Angelo!" (Tennyson.)
[22] Presumably the nightingale.
[23] Hedge-rows formed of living shrubs or small trees.

Where all the nerve of sense is numb,
Spirit to Spirit, Ghost to Ghost.

O, therefore from thy sightless range
  With gods in unconjectured bliss,    10
  O, from the distance of the abyss
Of tenfold-complicated change,

Descend, and touch, and enter; hear
  The wish too strong for words to name,
  That in this blindness of the frame    15
My Ghost may feel that thine is near.

### XCV

By night we lingered on the lawn,
  For underfoot the herb was dry;
  And genial warmth; and o'er the sky
The silvery haze of summer drawn;

And calm that let the tapers burn    5
  Unwavering: not a cricket chirred;
  The brook alone far-off was heard,
And on the board the fluttering urn.

And bats went round in fragrant skies,
  And wheeled or lit the filmy shapes [24]    10
  That haunt the dusk, with ermine capes
And woolly breasts and beaded eyes;

While now we sang old songs that pealed
  From knoll to knoll, where, couched at ease,
  The white kine glimmered, and the trees    15
Laid their dark arms about the field.

But when those others, one by one,
  Withdrew themselves from me and night,
  And in the house light after light
Went out, and I was all alone,    20

A hunger seized my heart; I read
  Of that glad year which once had been,
  In those fallen leaves which kept their green,
The noble letters of the dead.

And strangely on the silence broke    25
  The silent-speaking words, and strange
  Was love's dumb cry defying change
To test his worth; and strangely spoke

The faith, the vigor, bold to dwell
  On doubts that drive the coward back,    30
  And keen through wordy snares to track
Suggestion to her inmost cell.

So word by word, and line by line,
  The dead man touched me from the past,
  And all at once it seemed at last    35
The living soul was flashed on mine,

And mine in this was wound, and whirled
  About empyreal heights of thought,
[24] Night moths (Tennyson).

And came on that which is, and caught
The deep pulsations of the world,          40

Aeonian music measuring out
    The steps of Time—the shocks of Chance—
    The blows of Death. At length my trance
Was canceled, stricken through with doubt.

Vague words! but ah, how hard to frame     45
    In matter-molded forms of speech,
    Or even for intellect to reach
Through memory that which I became;

Till now the doubtful dusk revealed
    The knolls once more where, couched at
        ease,                               50
    The white kine glimmered, and the trees
Laid their dark arms about the field;

And sucked from out the distant gloom
    A breeze began to tremble o'er
    The large leaves of the sycamore,       55
And fluctuate all the still perfume,

And gathering freshlier overhead,
    Rocked the full-foliaged elms, and swung
    The heavy-folded rose, and flung
The lilies to and fro, and said,           60

"The dawn, the dawn," and died away;
    And East and West, without a breath,
    Mixed their dim lights, like life and death,
To broaden into boundless day.

### XCVI

You say, but with no touch of scorn,
    Sweet-hearted, you, whose light-blue eyes
    Are tender over drowning flies,
You tell me, doubt is Devil-born.

I know not: one indeed I knew              5
    In many a subtle question versed,
    Who touched a jarring lyre at first,
But ever strove to make it true;

Perplexed in faith, but pure in deeds,
    At last he beat his music out.          10
    There lives more faith in honest doubt,
Believe me, than in half the creeds.

He fought his doubts and gathered strength,
    He would not make his judgment blind,
    He faced the specters of the mind       15
And laid them; thus he came at length

To find a stronger faith his own,
    And Power was with him in the night,
    Which makes the darkness and the light,
And dwells not in the light alone,         20

But in the darkness and the cloud,
    As over Sinaï's peaks of old,

While Israel made their gods of gold,
Although the trumpet blew so loud.[25]

### XCIX

Risest thou thus, dim dawn, again,
    So loud with voices of the birds,
    So thick with lowings of the herds,
Day, when I lost the flower of men;

Who tremblest through thy darkling red     5
    On yon swollen brook that bubbles fast
    By meadows breathing of the past,
And woodlands holy to the dead;

Who murmurest in the foliaged eaves
    A song that slights the coming care,    10
    And Autumn laying here and there
A fiery finger on the leaves;

Who wakenest with thy balmy breath
    To myriads on the genial earth,
    Memories of bridal, or of birth,        15
And unto myriads more, of death.

O, wheresoever those may be,
    Betwixt the slumber of the poles,
    To-day they count as kindred souls;
They know me not, but mourn with me.       20

### CIII

On that last night before we went
    From out the doors where I was bred,
    I dreamed a vision of the dead,
Which left my after-morn content.

Methought I dwelt within a hall,           5
    And maidens [26] with me; distant hills
    From hidden summits fed with rills
A river sliding by the wall.

The hall with harp and carol rang.
    They sang of what is wise and good      10
    And graceful. In the center stood
A statue veiled, to which they sang;

And which, though veiled, was known to me,
    The shape of him I loved, and love
    For ever. Then flew in a dove           15
And brought a summons from the sea; [27]

And when they learned that I must go,
    They wept and wailed, but led the way
    To where a little shallop lay
At anchor in the flood below;              20

[25] See Exodus, 19 and 22.

[26] They are the muses, poetry, arts—all that made
life beautiful here, which we hope will pass with us
beyond the grave (Tennyson). Tennyson also stated
that the "hidden summits" of the following line
and the "river" of the last line of the stanza mean,
respectively, "the divine" and "life."

[27] Eternity (Tennyson).

And on by many a level mead,
  And shadowing bluff that made the banks,
  We glided winding under ranks
Of iris and the golden reed;

And still as vaster grew the shore [28]          25
  And rolled the floods in grander space,
  The maidens gathered strength and grace
And presence, lordlier than before;

And I myself, who sat apart
  And watched them, waxed in every limb;  30
  I felt the thews of Anakim,[29]
The pulses of a Titan's heart;

As one would sing the death of war,
  And one would chant the history
  Of that great race which is to be,      35
And one the shaping of a star; [30]

Until the forward-creeping tides
  Began to foam, and we to draw
  From deep to deep, to where we saw
A great ship lift her shining sides.      40

The man we loved was there on deck,
  But thrice as large as man he bent
  To greet us. Up the side I went,
And fell in silence on his neck;

Whereat those maidens with one mind      45
  Bewailed their lot; I did them wrong:
  "We served thee here," they said, "so long,
And wilt thou leave us now behind?"

So rapt I was, they could not win
  An answer from my lips, but he          50
  Replying, "Enter likewise ye
And go with us": they entered in.

And while the wind began to sweep
  A music out of sheet and shroud,
  We steered her toward a crimson cloud   55
That landlike slept along the deep.

### CIV

The time draws near the birth of Christ;
  The moon is hid, the night is still;
  A single church below the hill
Is pealing, folded in the mist.

A single peal of bells below,             5
  That wakens at this hour of rest
  A single murmur in the breast,
That these are not the bells I know.

Like strangers' voices here they sound,
  In lands where not a memory strays,    10
  Nor landmark breathes of other days,
But all is new unhallowed ground.

[28] The progress of the Age (Tennyson).
[29] Giants (see Deuteronomy, 9:2).
[30] The great hopes of humanity and science (Tennyson).

### CV

To-night ungathered let us leave
  This laurel, let this holly stand:
  We live within the stranger's land,
And strangely falls our Christmas-eve.

Our father's dust is left alone           5
  And silent under other snows:
  There in due time the woodbine blows,
The violet comes, but we are gone.

No more shall wayward grief abuse
  The genial hour with mask and mime;    10
  For change of place, like growth of time,
Has broke the bond of dying use.

Let cares that petty shadows cast,
  By which our lives are chiefly proved,
  A little spare the night I loved,      15
And hold it solemn to the past.

But let no footstep beat the floor,
  Nor bowl of wassail mantle warm;
  For who would keep an ancient form
Through which the spirit breathes no more?  20

Be neither song, nor game, nor feast;
  Nor harp be touched, nor flute be blown;
  No dance, no motion, save alone
What lightens in the lucid East

Of rising worlds by yonder wood.          25
  Long sleeps the summer in the seed;
  Run out your measured arcs, and lead
The closing cycle rich in good.

### CVI

Ring out, wild bells, to the wild sky,
  The flying cloud, the frosty light:
  The year is dying in the night;
Ring out, wild bells, and let him die.

Ring out the old, ring in the new,        5
  Ring, happy bells, across the snow:
  The year is going, let him go;
Ring out the false, ring in the true.

Ring out the grief that saps the mind,
  For those that here we see no more;    10
  Ring out the feud of rich and poor,
Ring in redress to all mankind.

Ring out a slowly dying cause,
  And ancient forms of party strife;
  Ring in the nobler modes of life,      15
With sweeter manners, purer laws.

Ring out the want, the care, the sin,
  The faithless coldness of the times;
  Ring out, ring out my mournful rimes,
But ring the fuller minstrel in.          20

Ring out false pride in place of blood,
  The civil slander and the spite;
  Ring in the love of truth and right,
Ring in the common love of good.

Ring out old shapes of foul disease;   25
  Ring out the narrowing lust of gold;
  Ring out the thousand wars of old,
Ring in the thousand years of peace.

Ring in the valiant man and free,
  The larger heart, the kindlier hand;   30
  Ring out the darkness of the land,
Ring in the Christ that is to be.

### CVII

It is the day when he was born,[31]
  A bitter day that early sank
  Behind a purple-frosty bank
Of vapor, leaving night forlorn.

The time admits not flowers or leaves   5
  To deck the banquet. Fiercely flies
  The blast of North and East, and ice
Makes daggers at the sharpened eaves,

And bristles all the brakes and thorns
  To yon hard crescent, as she hangs   10
  Above the wood which grides [32] and clangs
Its leafless ribs and iron horns

Together, in the drifts that pass
  To darken on the rolling brine
  That breaks the coast. But fetch the wine,  15
Arrange the board and brim the glass;

Bring in great logs and let them lie,
  To make a solid core of heat;
  Be cheerful-minded, talk and treat
Of all things even as he were by;   20

We keep the day. With festal cheer,
  With books and music, surely we
  Will drink to him, whate'er he be,
And sing the songs he loved to hear.

### CVIII

I will not shut me from my kind,
  And, lest I stiffen into stone,
  I will not eat my heart alone,
Nor feed with sighs a passing wind:

What profit lies in barren faith,   5
  And vacant yearning, though with might
  To scale the heaven's highest height,
Or dive below the wells of death?

What find I in the highest place,
  But mine own phantom chanting hymns?  10
  And on the depths of death there swims
The reflex of a human face.

[31] Hallam's birthday, 1 February.   [32] Scrapes.

I'll rather take what fruit may be
  Of sorrow under human skies:
  'Tis held that sorrow makes us wise,  15
Whatever wisdom sleep with thee.

### CIX

Heart-affluence in discursive talk
  From household fountains never dry;
  The critic clearness of an eye
That saw through all the Muses' walk;

Seraphic intellect and force   5
  To seize and throw the doubts of man;
  Impassioned logic, which outran
The hearer in its fiery course;

High nature amorous of the good,
  But touched with no ascetic gloom;  10
  And passion pure in snowy bloom
Through all the years of April blood;

A love of freedom rarely felt,
  Of freedom in her regal seat
  Of England; not the schoolboy heat,  15
The blind hysterics of the Celt;

And manhood fused with female grace
  In such a sort, the child would twine
  A trustful hand, unasked, in thine,
And find his comfort in thy face;   20

All these have been and thee mine eyes
  Have looked on: if they looked in vain,
  My shame is greater who remain,
Nor let thy wisdom make me wise.

### CX

Thy converse drew us with delight,
  The men of rathe [33] and riper years;
  The feeble soul, a haunt of fears,
Forgot his weakness in thy sight.

On thee the loyal-hearted hung,   5
  The proud was half disarmed of pride,
  Nor cared the serpent at thy side [34]
To flicker with his double tongue.

The stern were mild when thou wert by,
  The flippant put himself to school  10
  And heard thee, and the brazen fool
Was softened, and he knew not why;

While I, thy nearest, sat apart,
  And felt thy triumph was as mine;
  And loved them more, that they were thine,
The graceful tact, the Christian art;  16

Nor mine the sweetness or the skill,
  But mine the love that will not tire,
  And, born of love, the vague desire
That spurs an imitative will.  20

[33] Early.
[34] The envious and venomous slanderer.

### CXIV

Who loves not Knowledge? Who shall rail
  Against her beauty? May she mix
  With men and prosper! Who shall fix
Her pillars? Let her work prevail.

But on her forehead sits a fire;                   5
  She sets her forward countenance
  And leaps into the future chance,
Submitting all things to desire.

Half-grown as yet, a child, and vain—
  She cannot fight the fear of death.          10
  What is she, cut from love and faith,
But some wild Pallas [35] from the brain

Of demons? fiery-hot to burst
  All barriers in her onward race
  For power. Let her know her place;            15
She is the second, not the first.

A higher hand must make her mild,
  If all be not in vain, and guide
  Her footsteps, moving side by side
With Wisdom, like the younger child;          20

For she is earthly of the mind,
  But Wisdom heavenly of the soul.
  O friend, who camest to thy goal
So early, leaving me behind,

I would the great world grew like thee,      25
  Who grewest not alone in power
  And knowledge, but by year and hour
In reverence and in charity.

### CXV

Now fades the last long streak of snow,
  Now burgeons every maze of quick [36]
  About the flowering squares, [37] and thick
By ashen roots the violets blow.

Now rings the woodland loud and long,         5
  The distance takes a lovelier hue,
  And drowned in yonder living blue
The lark becomes a sightless song.

Now dance the lights on lawn and lea,
  The flocks are whiter down the vale,          10
  And milkier every milky sail
On winding stream or distant sea;

Where now the seamew pipes, or dives
  In yonder greening gleam, and fly
  The happy birds, that change their sky         15
To build and brood, that live their lives

From land to land; and in my breast
  Spring wakens too, and my regret

[35] Pallas Athena sprang full-grown and full-armed
from the head of Zeus.
[36] Hedge.    [37] Fields.

Becomes an April violet,
And buds and blossoms like the rest.            20

### CXVI

Is it, then, regret for buried time
  The keenlier in sweet April wakes,
  And meets the year, and gives and takes
The colors of the crescent prime? [38]

Not all: the songs, the stirring air,              5
  The life re-orient out of dust,
  Cry through the sense to hearten trust
In that which made the world so fair.

Not all regret: the face will shine
  Upon me, while I muse alone,                     10
  And that dear voice, I once have known,
Still speak to me of me and mine.

Yet less of sorrow lives in me
  For days of happy commune dead,
  Less yearning for the friendship fled           15
Than some strong bond which is to be.

### CXVII

O days and hours, your work is this,
  To hold me from my proper place,
  A little while from his embrace,
For fuller gain of after bliss;

That out of distance might ensue                  5
  Desire of nearness doubly sweet,
  And unto meeting, when we meet,
Delight a hundredfold accrue,

For every grain of sand that runs, [39]
  And every span of shade that steals,          10
  And every kiss of toothéd wheels, [40]
And all the courses of the suns.

### CXVIII

Contemplate all this work of Time,
  The giant laboring in his youth;
  Nor dream of human love and truth,
As dying Nature's earth and lime;

But trust that those we call the dead             5
  Are breathers of an ampler day
  For ever nobler ends. They say,
The solid earth whereon we tread

In tracts of fluent heat began,
  And grew to seeming-random forms,          10
  The seeming prey of cyclic storms,
Till at the last arose the man;

Who throve and branched from clime to clime,
  The herald of a higher race,
  And of himself in higher place,                    15
If so he type this work of time

[38] Spring.          [39] In allusion to the hour-glass.
[40] The wheels of a clock.

Within himself, from more to more;
  Or, crowned with attributes of woe
  Like glories, move his course, and show
That life is not as idle ore,    20

But iron dug from central gloom,
  And heated hot with burning fears,
  And dipped in baths of hissing tears,
And battered with the shocks of doom

To shape and use. Arise and fly    25
  The reeling Faun, the sensual feast;
  Move upward, working out the beast,
And let the ape and tiger die.

· · · · · · ·

### CXX

I trust I have not wasted breath:
  I think we are not wholly brain,
  Magnetic mockeries; not in vain,
Like Paul with beasts,[41] I fought with Death;

Not only cunning casts in clay:    5
  Let Science prove we are, and then
  What matters Science unto men,
At least to me? I would not stay.

Let him, the wiser man who springs
  Hereafter, up from childhood shape   10
  His action like the greater ape,
But I was *born* to other things.

### CXXI

Sad Hesper [42] o'er the buried sun
  And ready, thou, to die with him,
  Thou watchest all things ever dim
And dimmer, and a glory done.

The team is loosened from the wain,    5
  The boat is drawn upon the shore;
  Thou listenest to the closing door,
And life is darkened in the brain.

Bright Phosphor, fresher for the night,
  By thee the world's great work is heard   10
  Beginning, and the wakeful bird;
Behind thee comes the greater light.

The market boat is on the stream,
  And voices hail it from the brink;
  Thou hear'st the village hammer clink,   15
And see'st the moving of the team.

[41] I Corinthians, 15:32.

[42] Hesper, the evening star, which follows the setting sun and watches the fading light and ending life of day, is also Phosphor, the morning star, which precedes the sun and sees the dawn of light and life. They are the same "planet of Love" (*Maud*), which does but change its place. And so the poet's past and present are in substance one thing (Love), which has merely changed its place in becoming present instead of past (A. C. Bradley).

Sweet Hesper-Phosphor, double name
  For what is one, the first, the last,
  Thou, like my present and my past,
Thy place is changed; thou art the same.   20

### CXXIII

There rolls the deep where grew the tree.
  O earth, what changes hast thou seen!
  There where the long street roars hath been
The stillness of the central sea.

The hills are shadows, and they flow    5
  From form to form, and nothing stands;
  They melt like mist, the solid lands,
Like clouds they shape themselves and go.

But in my spirit will I dwell,
  And dream my dream, and hold it true;   10
  For though my lips may breathe adieu,
I cannot think the thing farewell.

### CXXIV

That which we dare invoke to bless;
  Our dearest faith; our ghastliest doubt;
  He, They, One, All; within, without; [43]
The Power in darkness, whom we guess,—

I found Him not in world or sun,    5
  Or eagle's wing, or insect's eye,
  Nor through the questions men may try,
The petty cobwebs we have spun.

If e'er when faith had fallen asleep,
  I heard a voice, "believe no more,"   10
  And heard an ever-breaking shore
That tumbled in the Godless deep,

A warmth within the breast would melt
  The freezing reason's colder part,
  And like a man in wrath the heart   15
Stood up and answered, "I have felt."

No, like a child in doubt and fear:
  But that blind clamor made me wise;
  Then was I as a child that cries,
But, crying, knows his father near;   20

And what I am beheld again
  What is, and no man understands;
  And out of darkness came the hands
That reach through nature, molding men.

### CXXV

Whatever I have said or sung,
  Some bitter notes my harp would give,
  Yea, though there often seemed to live
A contradiction on the tongue,

Yet Hope had never lost her youth,    5
  She did but look through dimmer eyes;

[43] The Deity, however imagined to exist, whether as conceived by the theist, the polytheist, the monist, or the pantheist, or as inside us or outside us.

Or Love but played with gracious lies,
Because he felt so fixed in truth;

And if the song were full of care,
  He breathed the spirit of the song;   10
And if the words were sweet and strong
He set his royal signet there;

Abiding with me till I sail
  To seek thee on the mystic deeps,
  And this electric force, that keeps   15
A thousand pulses dancing, fail.

### CXXVI

Love is and was my lord and king,
  And in his presence I attend
  To hear the tidings of my friend,
Which every hour his couriers bring.

Love is and was my king and lord,   5
  And will be, though as yet I keep
  Within the court on earth, and sleep
Encompassed by his faithful guard,

And hear at times a sentinel
  Who moves about from place to place,   10
  And whispers to the worlds of space,
In the deep night, that all is well.

### CXXVII

And all is well, though faith and form
  Be sundered in the night of fear;
  Well roars the storm to those that hear
A deeper voice across the storm,

Proclaiming social truth shall spread,   5
  And justice, even though thrice again
  The red fool-fury of the Seine [44]
Should pile her barricades with dead.

But ill for him that wears a crown,
  And him, the lazar, in his rags!   10
  They tremble, the sustaining crags;
The spires of ice are toppled down,

And molten up, and roar in flood;
  The fortress crashes from on high,
  The brute earth lightens to the sky,   15
And the great Aeon [45] sinks in blood,

And compassed by the fires of hell;
  While thou, dear spirit, happy star,
  O'erlook'st the tumult from afar,
And smilest, knowing all is well.   20

### CXXX

Thy voice is on the rolling air;
  I hear thee where the waters run;
  Thou standest in the rising sun,
And in the setting thou art fair.

[44] The violent revolutions in France.
[45] The modern age.

What art thou then? I cannot guess;   5
  But though I seem in star and flower
  To feel thee some diffusive power,
I do not therefore love thee less.

My love involves the love before;
  My love is vaster passion now;   10
  Though mix'd with God and Nature thou,
I seem to love thee more and more.

Far off thou art, but ever nigh;
  I have thee still, and I rejoice;
  I prosper, circled with thy voice;   15
I shall not lose thee though I die.

### CXXXI

O living will that shalt endure
  When all that seems shall suffer shock,
  Rise in the spiritual rock,[46]
Flow through our deeds and make them pure,

That we may lift from out of dust   5
  A voice as unto him that hears,
  A cry above the conquered years
To one that with us works, and trust,

With faith that comes of self-control,
  The truths that never can be proved   10
  Until we close with all we loved,
And all we flow from, soul in soul.

---

O true and tried, so well and long,[47]
  Demand not thou a marriage lay;
  In that it is thy marriage day
Is music more than any song.

Nor have I felt so much of bliss   5
  Since first he told me that he loved
  A daughter of our house, nor proved
Since that dark day a day like this;

Though I since then have numbered o'er
  Some thrice three years; [48] they went and
    came,   10
  Remade the blood and changed the frame,
And yet is love not less, but more;

No longer caring to embalm
  In dying songs a dead regret,
  But like a statue solid-set,   15
And molded in colossal calm.

Regret is dead, but love is more
  Than in the summers that are flown,

[46] I Corinthians, 10:4.
[47] This Epilogue is an epithalamium written to celebrate the marriage of Edmund Lushington to Tennyson's sister Cecilia in 1842. Tennyson said of *In Memoriam*: "It begins with a funeral and ends with a marriage—begins with death and ends in promise of a new life—a sort of *Divine Comedy*, cheerful at the close."
[48] In making this statement Tennyson violates the internal chronology of the poem elsewhere maintained.

For I myself with these have grown
To something greater than before;                    20

Which makes appear the songs I made
As echoes out of weaker times,
As half but idle brawling rimes,
The sport of random sun and shade.

But where is she, the bridal flower,                 25
That must be made a wife ere noon?
She enters, glowing like the moon
Of Eden on its bridal bower.

On me she bends her blissful eyes
And then on thee; they meet thy look     30
And brighten like the star that shook
Betwixt the palms of Paradise.

Oh, when her life was yet in bud,
He [49] too foretold the perfect rose.
For thee she grew, for thee she grows     35
For ever, and as fair as good.

And thou art worthy, full of power;
As gentle; liberal-minded, great,
Consistent; wearing all that weight
Of learning lightly like a flower.[50]          40

But now set out: the noon is near,
And I must give away the bride;
She fears not, or with thee beside
And me behind her, will not fear.

For I that danced her on my knee,            45
That watched her on her nurse's arm,
That shielded all her life from harm,
At last must part with her to thee;

Now waiting to be made a wife,
Her feet, my darling, on the dead;            50
Their pensive tablets round her head,
And the most living words of life

Breathed in her ear. The ring is on,
The "Wilt thou?" answered, and again
The "Wilt thou?" asked, till out of twain  55
Her sweet "I will" has made you one.

Now sign your names, which shall be read,
Mute symbols of a joyful morn,
By village eyes as yet unborn.
The names are signed, and overhead        60

Begins the clash and clang that tells
The joy to every wandering breeze;
The blind wall rocks, and on the trees
The dead leaf trembles to the bells.

O happy hour, and happier hours              65
Await them. Many a merry face

[49] Hallam.
[50] Lushington was a classical scholar, who became
Professor of Greek at Glasgow.

Salutes them—maidens of the place,
That pelt us in the porch with flowers.

O happy hour, behold the bride
With him to whom her hand I gave.           70
They leave the porch, they pass the grave
That has to-day its sunny side.

To-day the grave is bright for me,
For them the light of life increased,
Who stay to share the morning feast,         75
Who rest to-night beside the sea.

Let all my genial spirits advance
To meet and greet a whiter sun;
My drooping memory will not shun
The foaming grape of eastern France.        80

It circles round, and fancy plays,
And hearts are warmed and faces bloom,
As drinking health to bride and groom
We wish them store of happy days.

Nor count me all to blame if I                     85
Conjecture of a stiller guest,
Perchance, perchance, among the rest,
And, though in silence, wishing joy.

But they must go, the time draws on,
And those white-favored horses wait;          90
They rise, but linger; it is late;
Farewell, we kiss, and they are gone.

A shade falls on us like the dark
From little cloudlets on the grass,
But sweeps away as out we pass                    95
To range the woods, to roam the park,

Discussing how their courtship grew,
And talk of others that are wed,
And how she looked, and what he said,
And back we come at fall of dew.               100

Again the feast, the speech, the glee,
The shade of passing thought, the wealth
Of words and wit, the double health,
The crowning cup, the three-times-three,

And last the dance;—till I retire.               105
Dumb is that tower which spake so loud,
And high in heaven the streaming cloud,
And on the downs a rising fire:

And rise, O moon, from yonder down,
Till over down and over dale                      110
All night the shining vapor sail
And pass the silent-lighted town,

The white-faced halls, the glancing rills,
And catch at every mountain head,
And o'er the friths [51] that branch and spread
Their sleeping silver through the hills;      116

[51] Firths, arms of the sea.

And touch with shade the bridal doors,
　With tender gloom the roof, the wall;
　And breaking let the splendor fall
To spangle all the happy shores　120

By which they rest, and ocean sounds,
　And, star and system rolling past,
　A soul shall draw from out the vast
And strike his being into bounds,

And, moved through life of lower phase,　125
　Result in man, be born and think,
　And act and love, a closer link
Betwixt us and the crowning race

Of those that, eye to eye, shall look
　On knowledge; under whose command　130
　Is Earth and Earth's, and in their hand
Is Nature like an open book;

No longer half-akin to brute,
　For all we thought and loved and did,
　And hoped, and suffered, is but seed　135
Of what in them is flower and fruit;

Whereof the man that with me trod
　This planet was a noble type
　Appearing ere the times were ripe,
That friend of mine who lives in God,　140

That God, which ever lives and loves,
　One God, one law, one element,
　And one far-off divine event,
To which the whole creation moves.

# The Charge of the Light Brigade [1]

## I

Half a league, half a league,
Half a league onward,
All in the valley of Death
　Rode the six hundred.
"Forward the Light Brigade!　5
Charge for the guns!" he said.
Into the valley of Death
　Rode the six hundred.

## II

"Forward, the Light Brigade!"
Was there a man dismayed?　10
Not though the soldier knew
　Some one had blundered.
Theirs not to make reply,
Theirs not to reason why,
Theirs but to do and die.　15
Into the valley of Death
　Rode the six hundred.

[1] Published in December, 1854. The charge occurred in the Battle of Balaclava, 1854, an engagement of the Crimean War.

## III

Cannon to right of them,
Cannon to left of them,
Cannon in front of them　20
　Volleyed and thundered;
Stormed at with shot and shell,
Boldly they rode and well,
Into the jaws of Death,
Into the mouth of hell　25
　Rode the six hundred.

## IV

Flashed all their sabers bare,
Flashed as they turned in air
Sab'ring the gunners there,
Charging an army, while　30
　All the world wondered.
Plunged in the battery-smoke
Right through the line they broke;
Cossack and Russian
Reeled from the saber-stroke　35
　Shattered and sundered.
Then they rode back, but not,
　Not the six hundred.

## V

Cannon to right of them,
Cannon to left of them,　40
Cannon behind them
　Volleyed and thundered;
Stormed at with shot and shell,
While horse and hero fell,
They that had fought so well　45
Came through the jaws of Death,
Back from the mouth of hell,
All that was left of them,
　Left of six hundred.

## VI

When can their glory fade?　50
O the wild charge they made!
　All the world wondered.
Honor the charge they made!
Honor the Light Brigade,
　Noble six hundred!　55

# Come into the Garden [1]

## I

Come into the garden, Maud,
　For the black bat, night, has flown,
Come into the garden, Maud,
　I am here at the gate alone;
And the woodbine spices are wafted abroad,　5
　And the musk of the rose is blown.

## II

For a breeze of morning moves,
　And the planet of Love is on high,

[1] From *Maud*, published in 1855.

Beginning to faint in the light that she loves
  On a bed of daffodil sky,      10
To faint in the light of the sun she loves,
  To faint in his light, and to die.

### III

All night have the roses heard
  The flute, violin, bassoon;
All night has the casement jessamine stirred 15
  To the dancers dancing in tune;
Till a silence fell with the waking bird,
  And a hush with the setting moon.

### IV

I said to the lily, "There is but one,
  With whom she has heart to be gay.      20
When will the dancers leave her alone?
  She is weary of dance and play."
Now half to the setting moon are gone,
  And half to the rising day;
Low on the sand and loud on the stone      25
  The last wheel echoes away.

### V

I said to the rose, "The brief night goes
  In babble and revel and wine.
O young lord-lover, what sighs are those,
  For one that will never be thine?      30
But mine, but mine," so I sware to the rose,
  "For ever and ever, mine."

### VI

And the soul of the rose went into my blood
  As the music clashed in the hall;
And long by the garden lake I stood,      35
  For I heard your rivulet fall
From the lake to the meadow and on to the
    wood,
  Our wood, that is dearer than all;

### VII

From the meadow your walks have left so sweet
  That whenever a March-wind sighs      40
He sets the jewel-print of your feet
  In violets blue as your eyes,
To the woody hollows in which we meet
  And the valleys of Paradise.

### VIII

The slender acacia would not shake      45
  One long milk-bloom on the tree;
The white lake-blossom fell into the lake
  As the pimpernel dozed on the lea;
But the rose was awake all night for your sake,
  Knowing your promise to me;      50
The lilies and roses were all awake,
  They sighed for the dawn and thee.

### IX

Queen rose of the rosebud garden of girls,
  Come hither, the dances are done,
In gloss of satin and glimmer of pearls,      55
  Queen lily and rose in one;

Shine out, little head, sunning over with curls,
  To the flowers, and be their sun.

### X

There has fallen a splendid tear
  From the passion-flower at the gate.      60
She is coming, my dove, my dear;
  She is coming, my life, my fate.
The red rose cries, "She is near, she is near";
  And the white rose weeps, "She is late";
The larkspur listens, "I hear, I hear";      65
  And the lily whispers, "I wait."

### XI

She is coming, my own, my sweet;
  Were it ever so airy a tread,
My heart would hear her and beat,
  Were it earth in an earthy bed;      70
My dust would hear her and beat,
  Had I lain for a century dead,
Would start and tremble under her feet,
  And blossom in purple and red.

# Milton [1]

## (*Alcaics*)

O mighty-mouthed inventor of harmonies,
O skilled to sing of Time or Eternity,
  God-gifted organ-voice of England,
    Milton, a name to resound for ages;
Whose Titan angels, Gabriel, Abdiel,      5
Starred from Jehovah's gorgeous armories,
  Tower, as the deep-domed empyrean
    Rings to the roar of an angel onset!
Me rather all that bowery loneliness,
The brooks of Eden mazily murmuring,      10
  And bloom profuse and cedar arches
    Charm, as a wanderer out in ocean,
Where some refulgent sunset of India
Streams o'er a rich ambrosial ocean isle,
  And crimson-hued the stately palm-woods 15
    Whisper in odorous heights of even.

# Flower in the Crannied Wall [1]

Flower in the crannied wall,
I pluck you out of the crannies,
I hold you here, root and all, in my hand,
Little flower—but *if* I could understand
What you are, root and all, and all in all, 5
I should know what God and man is.

# Crossing the Bar [1]

Sunset and evening star,
  And one clear call for me!

[1] Published in December, 1863. One of several attempts made by Tennyson to reproduce in English the effect of classical meters.

[1] Published in 1869.

[1] Published in 1889. Tennyson wished this poem to be placed at the end of all editions of his poems.

And may there be no moaning of the bar,
   When I put out to sea,

But such a tide as moving seems asleep,    5
   Too full for sound and foam,
When that which drew from out the bound-
    less deep
   Turns again home.

Twilight and evening bell,
   And after that the dark!    10

And may there be no sadness of farewell,
   When I embark;

For though from out our bourn [2] of Time and
    Place
   The flood may bear me far,
I hope to see my Pilot face to face    15
   When I have crossed the bar.

[2] Boundary.

# Robert Browning

## 1812-1889

Browning's father was a clerk in the Bank of England who lived in Camberwell, a suburb of London in the early nineteenth century. He was a man in easy circumstances and of unusual culture, interested in art, in music, and in literature. He had a good collection of pictures and a large library containing many curious and out-of-the-way books. In Camberwell Browning was born on 7 May, 1812. His education was almost entirely derived from his parents and the influences of his home. Occasionally he attended near-by schools, and occasionally, when he made it plain that conventional methods of education were not for him, he had a private tutor at home; but his formal training was decidedly irregular. He was enrolled in the University of London, but spent only a short time in university studies and made no attempt to take a degree. All this does not mean that Browning was an idle and ignorant youth; on the contrary, he was very early a man of wide and curious learning, with a cultivated taste in both painting and music. But it means that what he learned came from the influences of his home, from the encouragement of his parents, from reading in his father's library, and from the cultivated friends of his family. He early began the writing of verse and early fell under the influence of Shelley. His first published poem, Pauline, which appeared in 1833 when he was twenty, shows this influence strongly. Pauline made no impression on the public; but Browning's next poem, Paracelsus, published in 1835, while it attracted only a few readers, gained for its author the attention or friendship of a number of men of letters. Among these were Wordsworth, Landor, Leigh Hunt, and Dickens.

Paracelsus also attracted the attention of the actor-manager Macready, and led him to ask the poet for a play. As a result Browning wrote Strafford, which was acted at the Covent Garden Theater in 1837 and published in the same year. He had dramatic genius, as was evident from Paracelsus, and it was natural both for him and for Macready to suppose that he could succeed with plays; yet it is unfortunate that he was led to expend as much time as he did on the effort. Strafford, while it was not a complete failure, had only a very qualified success. Nevertheless, Browning went on to write other plays, hoping for a better result, producing work which shows powerfully some of the elements of dramatic genius, and yet not writing one play which could hold the stage with complete success. This was true even of A Blot in the 'Scutcheon (1843), the best of the half-dozen or more plays he wrote and one which evoked the enthusiastic praise of Dickens. The truth would seem to be that Browning, knowing that he had dramatic genius, did not yet know his limitations, and needed his eight years' trial of play-writing in order to help him to the discovery of the form of poetry which he was soon to make peculiarly his own and in which he did his best work with all his powers in free play. Not all of his time during these years, however, was spent upon "regular" drama. In 1841 he published Pippa Passes, a series of dramatic scenes, which contains poetry that can scarcely be overpraised and at least one scene, the incident of Ottima and Sebald, of tremendous power. And in the late eighteen-thirties he had been working on another long poem into which he put the fruit of much study and for the sake of which he had made his first visit to Italy. This poem, however, Sordello, published in 1840, was a worse failure than were the plays. Largely because of its obscure style it disappointed Browning's friends and alienated from him for many years the general reading public. But two years later, with the publication of Dramatic Lyrics, he showed that he was beginning to find his true work; and this and Dramatic Romances and Lyrics, published in 1845, contained some of his finest poems.

About this time Browning became acquainted with Elizabeth Barrett, herself a gifted writer of poetry, conducted with her a correspondence which has become famous, finally met her and talked with her, and in 1846 married her despite the violent opposition of her father. Partly on account of her delicate health and partly because of difficulties with her father, the Brownings went to Italy and settled in Florence, where they remained until Mrs. Browning's death in 1861. During this period Browning published Christmas Eve and Easter Day (1850) and Men and Women (1855), the latter volume containing some of the best and most widely liked of all his poems. After Mrs. Browning's death he returned to England and for some years spent much time in London. In 1864 he published Dramatis Personae, and in 1868–1869 his longest work and, in the opinion of many, his greatest, The Ring and the Book, a series of poems founded on an account which he had accidentally found of a Roman murder trial of the seventeenth century. In later years Browning published much, including several translations of Greek plays; but as he grew older his style became more difficult and harsh, and a certain waywardness or indifference to the legitimate demands of readers, perhaps always to some extent apparent in his work, increased. The consequence is that much, if not most, of his later work is inferior to the work of his best years and is no longer widely read. Browning died in his son's house at Venice on 12 December, 1889, and was buried in Westminster Abbey.

The form of poetry which Browning, as was said above, made peculiarly his own is commonly known as the dramatic monologue—a kind of poem in which some person speaks to another, or to others, self-revealingly, either narrating an incident or telling the story of his life, but in any case laying bare his soul through what he says. This form of poem gave Browning full scope for his dramatic genius without making apparent his limitations. It enabled him to exercise his dramatic imagination in the creation of a single character and a single scene without calling upon him for a large constructive ability which he did not have. It was the happiest of discoveries; here was a kind of poem apparently designed expressly for him, and he proceeded to put into it all that he had of rich imagination, deep insight, tender or delicate feeling, and curious learning. He even, when he came to write a long poem, cast The Ring and the Book in this form, making it a series of monologues in which the characters of his story and several spectators each tells the story in his own way. This was an extraordinary experiment, bound to result, as it did, in some unevenness of execution and interest, but resulting also in the greatest of his achievements in the dramatic delineation of character.

The best edition of Browning is the "Centenary Edition" ed. F. G. Kenyon (Works, 10 vols., London, 1912). The best one-volume edition is that in the Reynard Library, edited by Simon Nowell-Smith (London, 1950). The Letters of Robert Browning and Elizabeth Barrett Browning, 1845–1846 (London, 1899) has been supplemented by New Letters of Robert Browning, edited by W. C. De Vane and K. L. Knickerbocker (New Haven, 1950). The Life of Robert Browning by H. W. Griffin and H. C. Minchin (London, 1910; later revised) is the standard biography. Other good or useful books are Robert Browning by G. K. Chesterton ("English Men of Letters" series, 1903); Robert Browning by C. H. Herford (London, 1905); Browning's Parleyings; The Autobiography of a Mind by William Clyde De Vane (New Haven, 1927); A Browning Handbook by W. C. De Vane (New York, 1955)—a model of its kind and indispensable; Victorian Temper, by J. H. Buckley (Cambridge, U. S. A., 1951); The Alien Vision of Victorian Poetry, by E. D. H. Johnson (Princeton, 1952); and Robert Browning, a Portrait, by Betty B. Miller (London, 1952).

# Cavalier Tunes [1]

## I. Marching Along

Kentish Sir Byng stood for his King,
Bidding the crop-headed Parliament swing:
And, pressing a troop unable to stoop
And see the rogues flourish and honest folk
    droop,
Marched them along, fifty-score strong,   5
Great-hearted gentlemen, singing this song.

God for King Charles! Pym and such carles [2]
To the Devil that prompts 'em their treasonous
    parles!
Cavaliers, up! Lips from the cup,
Hands from the pasty, nor bite take nor sup  10
Till you're—
    Cho.—Marching along, fifty-score strong,
        Great-hearted gentlemen, singing this
          song.

[1] Published in 1842, the bicentenary of the beginning of the English Civil Wars which supplied Browning's subject.
[2] Churls.

Hampden to hell, and his obsequies' knell.
Serve Hazelrig, Fiennes, and young Harry [3] as
   well!
England, good cheer! Rupert [4] is near!    15
Kentish and loyalists, keep we not here,
  Cho.—Marching along, fifty-score strong,
      Great-hearted gentlemen, singing this
        song?

Then, God for King Charles! Pym and his snarls
To the Devil that pricks on such pestilent
   carles!    20
Hold by the right, you double your might;
So, onward to Nottingham,[5] fresh for the fight,
  Cho.—Marching along, fifty-score strong,
      Great-hearted gentlemen, singing this
        song!

### II. *Give a Rouse*

King Charles, and who'll do him right now?
King Charles, and who's ripe for fight now?
Give a rouse: here's, in hell's despite now,
King Charles!

Who gave me the goods that went since?    5
Who raised me the house that sank once?
Who helped me to gold I spent since?
Who found me in wine you drank once?
  Cho.—King Charles, and who'll do him
      right now?
    King Charles, and who's ripe for
      fight now?    10
    Give a rouse: here's, in hell's despite
      now,
    King Charles!

To whom used my boy George quaff else,
By the old fool's side that begot him?
For whom did he cheer and laugh else,    15
While Noll's [6] damned troopers shot him?
  Cho.—King Charles, and who'll do him
      right now?
    King Charles, and who's ripe for
      fight now?
    Give a rouse: here's, in hell's despite
      now,
    King Charles!    20

### III. *Boot and Saddle*

Boot, saddle, to horse, and away!
Rescue my castle before the hot day
Brightens to blue from its silvery gray.
  Cho.—Boot, saddle, to horse, and away!

Ride past the suburbs, asleep as you'd say;    5
Many's the friend there, will listen and pray
"God's luck to gallants that strike up the lay—
  Cho.—Boot, saddle, to horse, and away!"

[3] Sir Henry Vane the younger.
[4] Prince Rupert, cousin of Charles I, under whom
he served as general.
[5] Here Charles I's standard was raised in 1642.
[6] Cromwell's.

Forty miles off, like a roebuck at bay,
Flouts Castle Brancepeth the Roundheads'
   array:    10
Who laughs, "Good fellows ere this, by my fay,
  Cho.—Boot, saddle, to horse, and away!"

Who? My wife Gertrude; that, honest and gay,
Laughs when you talk of surrendering, "Nay!
I've better counselors; what counsel they?    15
  Cho.—Boot, saddle, to horse, and away!"

# My Last Duchess [1]

### *Ferrara*

That's my last Duchess painted on the wall,
Looking as if she were alive. I call
That piece a wonder, now: Fra Pandolf's [2]
   hands
Worked busily a day, and there she stands.
Will't please you sit and look at her? I said    5
"Fra Pandolf" by design, for never read
Strangers like you that pictured countenance,
The depth and passion of its earnest glance,
But to myself they turned (since none puts by
The curtain I have drawn for you, but I)    10
And seemed as they would ask me, if they
   durst,
How such a glance came there; so, not the first
Are you to turn and ask thus. Sir, 't was not
Her husband's presence only, called that spot
Of joy into the Duchess' cheek: perhaps    15
Fra Pandolf chanced to say, "Her mantle laps
Over my lady's wrist too much," or "Paint
Must never hope to reproduce the faint
Half-flush that dies along her throat": such
   stuff
Was courtesy, she thought, and cause enough
For calling up that spot of joy. She had    21
A heart—how shall I say?—too soon made
   glad,
Too easily impressed: she liked whate'er
She looked on, and her looks went everywhere.
Sir, 't was all one! My favor at her breast,    25
The dropping of the daylight in the West,
The bough of cherries some officious fool
Broke in the orchard for her, the white mule
She rode with round the terrace—all and each
Would draw from her alike the approving
   speech,    30
Or blush, at least. She thanked men,—good!
   but thanked
Somehow—I know not how—as if she ranked
My gift of a nine-hundred-years-old name
With anybody's gift. Who'd stoop to blame
This sort of trifling? Even had you skill    35
In speech—(which I have not)—to make your
   will

[1] Published in 1842. Ferrara is a town in northern
Italy. The character and story of the Duke may be
founded on those of a real, sixteenth century Duke
of Ferrara.
[2] Fra means brother. Pandolf is an imaginary
artist—and monk—of the Renaissance.

Quite clear to such an one, and say, "Just this
Or that in you disgusts me; here you miss,
Or there exceed the mark"—and if she let
Herself be lessoned so, nor plainly set          40
Her wits to yours, forsooth, and made excuse,
—E'en then would be some stooping; and I
    choose
Never to stoop. Oh sir, she smiled, no doubt,
Whene'er I passed her; but who passed without
Much the same smile? This grew; I gave com-
    mands;                                         45
Then all smiles stopped together. There she
    stands
As if alive. Will 't please you rise? We'll meet
The company below, then. I repeat
The Count your master's known munificence
Is ample warrant that no just pretense           50
Of mine for dowry will be disallowed;
Though his fair daughter's self, as I avowed
At starting, is my object. Nay, we'll go
Together down, sir. Notice Neptune, though,
Taming a sea-horse, thought a rarity,            55
Which Claus of Innsbruck [3] cast in bronze for
    me!

# Soliloquy of the
# Spanish Cloister [1]

Gr-r-r—there go, my heart's abhorrence!
    Water your damned flower-pots, do!
If hate killed men, Brother Lawrence,
    God's blood, would not mine kill you!
What? your myrtle-bush wants trimming?        5
    Oh, that rose has prior claims—
Needs its leaden vase filled brimming?
    Hell dry you up with its flames!

At the meal we sit together:
    *Salve tibi!* [2] I must hear            10
Wise talk of the kind of weather,
    Sort of season, time of year:
*Not a plenteous cork-crop: scarcely
    Dare we hope oak-galls,* [3] *I doubt:*
*What's the Latin name for "parsley"?*        15
    What's the Greek name for Swine's Snout?

Whew! We'll have our platter burnished,
    Laid with care on our own shelf!
With a fire-new spoon we're furnished,
    And a goblet for ourself,                 20
Rinsed like something sacrificial
    Ere 'tis fit to touch our chaps—
Marked with L for our initial!
    (He-he! There his lily snaps!)

Saint, forsooth! While brown Dolores          25
    Squats outside the Convent bank
With Sanchicha, telling stories,
    Steeping tresses in the tank,
Blue-black, lustrous, thick like horsehairs,
    —Can't I see his dead eye glow,           30
Bright as 'twere a Barbary corsair's?
    (That is, if he'd let it show!)

When he finishes refection,
    Knife and fork he never lays
Cross-wise, to my recollection,               35
    As do I, in Jesu's praise.
I the Trinity illustrate,
    Drinking watered orange-pulp—
In three sips the Arian [4] frustrate;
    While he drains his at one gulp.          40

Oh, those melons! If he's able
    We're to have a feast! so nice!
One goes to the Abbot's table,
    All of us get each a slice.
How go on your flowers? None double?          45
    Not one fruit-sort can you spy?
Strange!—And I, too, at such trouble
    Keep them close-nipped on the sly!

There's a great text in Galatians, [5]
    Once you trip on it, entails              50
Twenty-nine distinct damnations,
    One sure, if another fails:
If I trip him just a-dying,
    Sure of heaven as sure can be,
Spin him round and send him flying            55
    Off to hell, a Manichee? [6]

Or, my scrofulous French novel
    On gray paper with blunt type!
Simply glance at it, you grovel
    Hand and foot in Belial's gripe:          60
If I double down its pages
    At the woeful sixteenth print,
When he gathers his greengages,
    Ope a sieve and slip it in't?

Or, there's Satan!—one might venture          65
    Pledge one's soul to him, yet leave
Such a flaw in the indenture
    As he'd miss till, past retrieve,
Blasted lay that rose-acacia
    We're so proud of! Hy, Zy, Hine [7] . . . 70
'St, there's Vespers! *Plena gratiâ,*
    *Ave, Virgo!* [8] Gr-r-r—you swine!

[3] Like Pandolf, an imaginary artist.
[1] Published in 1842.
[2] Save you! (a salutation).
[3] Excrescences, made on oak trees by insects, used
in manufacturing ink.

[4] One who holds with Arius (A.D. 256–336) that
Christ is a created being, inferior to God the Father
in nature and dignity.
[5] Probably Galatians, 5:19–21.
[6] Follower of the Persian Manes who maintained
the existence of two supreme principles, light (good)
and darkness (evil).
[7] Sounds perhaps echoing the vesper bell.
[8] Hail, Virgin, full of grace!

# Cristina [1]

She should never have looked at me
    If she meant I should not love her!
There are plenty . . . men, you call such,
    I suppose . . . she may discover
All her soul to, if she pleases,        5
    And yet leave much as she found them:
But I'm not so, and she knew it
    When she fixed me, glancing round them.

What? To fix me thus meant nothing?
    But I can't tell (there's my weakness)    10
What her look said!—no vile cant, sure,
    About "need to strew the bleakness
Of some lone shore with its pearl-seed,
    That the sea feels"—no "strange yearning
That such souls have, most to lavish    15
    Where there's chance of least returning."

Oh, we're sunk enough here, God knows!
    But not quite so sunk that moments,
Sure though seldom, are denied us,
    When the spirit's true endowments    20
Stand out plainly from its false ones,
    And apprise it if pursuing
Or the right way or the wrong way,
    To its triumph or undoing.

There are flashes struck from midnights,    25
    There are fire-flames noondays kindle,
Whereby piled-up honors perish,
    Whereby swollen ambitions dwindle,
While just this or that poor impulse,
    Which for once had play unstifled,    30
Seems the sole work of a lifetime,
    That away the rest have trifled.

Doubt you if, in some such moment,
    As she fixed me, she felt clearly,
Ages past the soul existed,    35
    Here an age 'tis resting merely,
And hence fleets again for ages,
    While the true end, sole and single,
It stops here for is, this love-way,
    With some other soul to mingle?    40

Else it loses what it lived for,
    And eternally must lose it;
Better ends may be in prospect,
    Deeper blisses (if you choose it),
But this life's end and this love-bliss    45
    Have been lost here. Doubt you whether
This she felt as, looking at me,
    Mine and her souls rushed together?

[1] Published in 1842. The title was suggested by
Maria Christina of Naples (1806–1878), who in
1829 became the fourth wife of the aged King
Ferdinand VII of Spain and who, after his death
in 1833, ruled that country for eight years as regent.
She was a coquette of dissolute life.

Oh, observe! Of course, next moment,
    The world's honors, in derision,    50
Trampled out the light for ever:
    Never fear but there's provision
Of the devil's to quench knowledge
    Lest we walk the earth in rapture!
—Making those who catch God's secret    55
    Just so much more prize their capture!

Such am I: the secret's mine now!
    She has lost me, I have gained her;
Her soul's mine: and thus, grown perfect,
    I shall pass my life's remainder.    60
Life will just hold out the proving
    Both our powers, alone and blended:
And then, come the next life quickly!
    This world's use will have been ended.

# The Lost Leader [1]

Just for a handful of silver he left us,
    Just for a riband to stick in his coat—
Found the one gift of which fortune bereft us,
    Lost all the others she lets us devote;
They, with the gold to give, doled him out
        silver,    5
    So much was theirs who so little allowed:
How all our copper had gone for his service!
    Rags—were they purple, his heart had been
        proud!

[1] Published in 1845. Browning was often asked
if Wordsworth was the subject of this poem. The
following letter, written to A. B. Grosart on 24
February, 1875, is one of his replies:

"DEAR MR. GROSART,—I have been asked the
question you now address me with, and as duly
answered it, I can't remember how many times;
there is no sort of objection to one more assurance
or rather confession, on my part, that I *did* in my
hasty youth presume to use the great and venerated
personality of Wordsworth as a sort of painter's
model; one from which this or the other particular
feature may be selected and turned to account; had
I intended more, above all, such a boldness as portraying the entire man, I should not have talked
about 'handfuls of silver and bits of ribbon.' These
never influenced the change of politics in the great
poet, whose defection, nevertheless, accompanied as
it was by a regular face-about of his special party,
was to my juvenile apprehension, and even mature
consideration, an event to deplore. But just as in
the tapestry on my wall I can recognize figures
which have *struck out* a fancy, on occasion, that
though truly enough thus derived, yet would be
preposterous as a copy, so, though I dare not deny
the original of my little poem, I altogether refuse
to have it considered as the 'very effigies' of such a
moral and intellectual superiority.
                    "Faithfully yours,
                    "ROBERT BROWNING."

In 1845, however, Browning's "handful of silver"
and "riband" could only be interpreted as references
to Wordsworth's recent acceptance of a pension and
the laureateship.

We that had loved him so, followed him,
  honored him,
  Lived in his mild and magnificent eye,   10
Learned his great language, caught his clear
  accents,
Made him our pattern to live and to die!
Shakespeare was of us, Milton was for us,
  Burns, Shelley, were with us,—they watch
  from their graves!
He alone breaks from the van and the freemen,
  —He alone sinks to the rear and the slaves!  16
We shall march prospering,—not through his
  presence;
  Songs may inspirit us,—not from his lyre;
Deeds will be done,—while he boasts his
  quiescence,
  Still bidding crouch whom the rest bade
  aspire:   20
Blot out his name, then, record one lost soul
  more,
  One task more declined, one more foot-
  path untrod,
One more devils'-triumph and sorrow for angels,
  One wrong more to man, one more insult to
  God!
Life's night begins: let him never come back to
  us!   25
  There would be doubt, hesitation and pain,
Forced praise on our part—the glimmer of
  twilight,
  Never glad confident morning again!
Best fight on well, for we taught him—strike
  gallantly,
  Menace our heart ere we master his own;  30
Then let him receive the new knowledge and
  wait us,
  Pardoned in heaven, the first by the throne!

## Home Thoughts from Abroad [1]

Oh, to be in England
Now that April's there,
And whoever wakes in England
Sees, some morning, unaware,
That the lowest boughs and the brush-wood
  sheaf   5
Round the elm-tree bole are in tiny leaf,
While the chaffinch sings on the orchard bough
In England—now!

And after April, when May follows,
And the whitethroat builds, and all the swal-
  lows!   10
Hark, where my blossomed pear-tree in the
  hedge
Leans to the field and scatters on the clover
Blossoms and dewdrops—at the bent spray's
  edge—
That's the wise thrush; he sings each song
  twice over,

[1] Published in 1845.

Lest you should think he never could recap-
  ture   15
  The first fine careless rapture!
And though the fields look rough with hoary
  dew,
All will be gay when noontide wakes anew
The buttercups, the little children's dower
—Far brighter than this gaudy melon-flower!  20

## Meeting at Night [1]

The gray sea and the long black land;
And the yellow half-moon large and low;
And the startled little waves that leap
In fiery ringlets from their sleep,
As I gain the cove with pushing prow,   5
And quench its speed i' the slushy sand.

Then a mile of warm sea-scented beach;
Three fields to cross till a farm appears;
A tap at the pane, the quick sharp scratch
And blue spurt of a lighted match,   10
And a voice less loud, through its joys and
  fears,
Than the two hearts beating each to each!

## Parting at Morning [2]

Round the cape of a sudden came the sea,
And the sun looked over the mountain's rim:
And straight was a path of gold for him,[3]
And the need of a world of men for me.

## Love among the Ruins [4]

Where the quiet-colored end of evening smiles
  Miles and miles
On the solitary pastures where our sheep
  Half-asleep
Tinkle homeward through the twilight, stray
  or stop   5
  As they crop—
Was the site once of a city great and gay,
  (So they say)
Of our country's very capital, its prince
  Ages since   10
Held his court in, gathered councils, wielding
  far
  Peace or war.

Now,—the country does not even boast a tree,
  As you see,
To distinguish slopes of verdure, certain rills  15
  From the hills
Intersect and give a name to (else they run
  Into one),
Where the domed and daring palace shot its
  spires
  Up like fires   20
O'er the hundred-gated circuit of a wall
  Bounding all,

[1] Published in 1845.   [2] Published in 1845.
[3] The sun.   [4] Published in 1855.

Made of marble, men might march on nor be
    pressed,
    Twelve abreast.

And such plenty and perfection, see, of grass
    Never was!    26
Such a carpet as, this summer-time, o'er-spreads
    And embeds
Every vestige of the city, guessed alone,
    Stock or stone—    30
Where a multitude of men breathed joy and
    woe
    Long ago;
Lust of glory pricked their hearts up, dread of
    shame
    Struck them tame;
And that glory and that shame alike, the gold 35
    Bought and sold.

Now,—the single little turret that remains
    On the plains,
By the caper overrooted, by the gourd
    Overscored,    40
While the patching houseleek's head of blos-
    som winks
    Through the chinks—
Marks the basement whence a tower in ancient
    time
    Sprang sublime,
And a burning ring, all round, the chariots
    traced    45
    As they raced,
And the monarch and his minions and his
    dames
    Viewed the games.

And I know, while thus the quiet-colored eve
    Smiles to leave    50
To their folding, all our many-tinkling fleece
    In such peace,
And the slopes and rills in undistinguished gray
    Melt away—
That a girl with eager eyes and yellow hair 55
    Waits me there
In the turret whence the charioteers caught
    soul
    For the goal,
When the king looked, where she looks now,
    breathless, dumb
    Till I come.    60

But he looked upon the city, every side,
    Far, and wide,
All the mountains topped with temples, all
    the glades'
    Colonnades,
All the causeys,[5] bridges, aqueducts,—and
    then,    65
    All the men!
When I do come, she will speak not, she will
    stand,
    Either hand

[5] Causeways.

On my shoulder, give her eyes the first em-
    brace
    Of my face,    70
Ere we rush, ere we extinguish sight and speech
    Each on each.

In one year they sent a million fighters forth
    South and North,
And they built their gods a brazen pillar high
    As the sky,    76
Yet reserved a thousand chariots in full force—
    Gold, of course.
Oh heart! oh blood that freezes, blood that
    burns!
    Earth's returns    80
For whole centuries of folly, noise and sin!
    Shut them in
With their triumphs and their glories and the
    rest!
    Love is best.

# Up at a Villa—Down in the City [1]

## (As *Distinguished by an Italian Person of Quality*)

Had I but plenty of money, money enough and
    to spare,
The house for me, no doubt, were a house in
    the city-square;
Ah, such a life, such a life, as one leads at the
    window there!
Something to see, by Bacchus, something to
    hear, at least!
There, the whole day long, one's life is a per-
    fect feast;    5
While up at a villa one lives, I maintain it,
    no more than a beast.

Well now, look at our villa! stuck like the horn
    of a bull
Just on a mountain-edge as bare as the crea-
    ture's skull,
Save a mere shag of a bush with hardly a leaf
    to pull!
—I scratch my own, sometimes, to see if the
    hair's turned wool.    10

But the city, oh the city—the square with the
    houses! Why?
They are stone-faced, white as a curd, there's
    something to take the eye!
Houses in four straight lines, not a single front
    awry;
You watch who crosses and gossips, who
    saunters, who hurries by;
Green blinds, as a matter of course, to draw
    when the sun gets high;    15

[1] Published in 1855. The city is probably Siena, in a villa outside of which the Brownings lived in the autumn of 1850.

And the shops with fanciful signs which are
    painted properly.

What of a villa? Though winter be over in
    March by rights,
'Tis May perhaps ere the snow shall have
    withered well off the heights:
You've the brown plowed land before, where
    the oxen steam and wheeze,
And the hills over-smoked behind by the faint
    gray olive-trees.    20

Is it better in May, I ask you? You've summer
    all at once;
In a day he leaps complete with a few strong
    April suns.
'Mid the sharp short emerald wheat, scarce
    risen three fingers well,
The wild tulip, at end of its tube, blows out its
    great red bell
Like a thin clear bubble of blood, for the
    children to pick and sell.    25

Is it ever hot in the square? There's a fountain
    to spout and splash!
In the shade it sings and springs; in the shine
    such foambows flash
On the horses with curling fish-tails, that prance
    and paddle and pash
Round the lady atop in her conch—fifty gazers
    do not abash,
Though all that she wears is some weeds round
    her waist in a sort of sash.    30

All the year long at the villa, nothing to see
    though you linger,
Except yon cypress that points like death's
    lean lifted forefinger.
Some think fireflies pretty, when they mix i'
    the corn and mingle,
Or thrid [2] the stinking hemp till the stalks of
    it seem a-tingle.
Late August or early September, the stunning
    cicala is shrill,    35
And the bees keep their tiresome whine round
    the resinous firs on the hill.
Enough of the seasons,—I spare you the
    months of the fever and chill.

Ere you open your eyes in the city, the blessed
    church-bells begin:
No sooner the bells leave off than the diligence
    rattles in:
You get the pick of the news, and it costs you
    never a pin.    40
By and by there's the traveling doctor gives
    pills, lets blood, draws teeth;
Or the Pulcinello-trumpet [3] breaks up the
    market beneath.
At the post-office such a scene-picture—the
    new play, piping hot!

[2] Thread.
[3] The trumpet announcing a Punch-and-Judy show.

And a notice how, only this morning, three
    liberal thieves [4] were shot.
Above it, behold the Archbishop's most fatherly
    of rebukes,    45
And beneath, with his crown and his lion, some
    little new law of the Duke's!
Or a sonnet with flowery marge, to the Rev-
    erend Don So-and-so,
Who is [5] Dante, Boccaccio, Petrarca, Saint
    Jerome, and Cicero,
"And moreover," (the sonnet goes riming)
    "the skirts of Saint Paul has reached,
Having preached us those six Lent-lectures
    more unctuous than ever he preached." [50]
Noon strikes,—here sweeps the procession!
    our Lady borne smiling and smart
With a pink gauze gown all spangles, and seven
    swords stuck in her heart! [6]
*Bang-whang-whang* goes the drum, *tootle-te-
tootle* the fife;
No keeping one's haunches still: it's the greatest
    pleasure in life.

But bless you, it's dear—it's dear! fowls, wine,
    at double the rate.    55
They have clapped a new tax upon salt, and
    what oil pays passing the gate [7]
It's a horror to think of. And so, the villa for
    me, not the city!
Beggars can scarcely be choosers: but still—
    ah, the pity, the pity!
Look, two and two go the priests, then the
    monks with cowls and sandals,
And the penitents dressed in white shirts,
    a-holding the yellow candles;    60
One, he carries a flag up straight, and another
    a cross with handles,
And the Duke's guard brings up the rear, for
    the better prevention of scandals:
*Bang-whang-whang* goes the drum, *tootle-te-
tootle* the fife.
Oh, a day in the city-square, there is no such
    pleasure in life!

## Fra Lippo Lippi [1]

I am poor brother Lippo, by your leave!
You need not clap your torches to my face.
Zooks, what's to blame? you think you see a
    monk!
What, 'tis past midnight, and you go the
    rounds,
And here you catch me at an alley's end    5

[4] I. e., those executed were republicans, and
"thieves" indicates the "person of quality's" attitude
towards those whose politics differed from his.
[5] I. e., rivals.
[6] The swords symbolize the Seven Sorrows of our
Lady—the Virgin Mary.
[7] I. e., what tax has to be paid when it is brought
into the city.
[1] Published in 1855. Filippo Lippi's life (1406?–
1469) is to be found in Vasari's *Lives of the Painters.*

Where sportive ladies leave their doors ajar?
The Carmine's [2] my cloister: hunt it up,
Do,—harry out, if you must show your zeal,
Whatever rat, there, haps on his wrong hole,
And nip each softling of a wee white mouse, 10
*Weke, weke,* that's crept to keep him company!
Aha, you know your betters! Then, you'll take
Your hand away that's fiddling on my throat,
And please to know me likewise. Who am I?
Why, one, sir, who is lodging with a friend 15
Three streets off—he's a certain . . . how d'ye call?
Master—a . . . Cosimo of the Medici,[3]
I' the house that caps the corner. Boh! you were best!
Remember and tell me, the day you're hanged,
How you affected such a gullet's-gripe!      20
But you, sir, it concerns you that your knaves
Pick up a manner nor discredit you:
Zooks, are we pilchards, that they sweep the streets
And count fair prize what comes into their net?
He's Judas to a tittle, that man is!      25
Just such a face! Why, sir, you make amends.
Lord, I'm not angry! Bid your hangdogs go
Drink out this quarter-florin to the health
Of the munificent House that harbors me
(And many more beside, lads! more beside!)
And all's come square again. I'd like his face—
His, elbowing on his comrade in the door      32
With the pike and lantern,—for the slave that holds
John Baptist's head a-dangle by the hair
With one hand ("Look you, now," as who should say)      35
And his weapon in the other, yet unwiped!
It's not your chance to have a bit of chalk,
A wood-coal or the like? or you should see!
Yes, I'm the painter, since you style me so.
What, brother Lippo's doings, up and down,
You know them and they take you? Like enough!      41
I saw the proper twinkle in your eye—
'Tell you, I liked your looks at very first.
Let's sit and set things straight now, hip to haunch.
Here's spring come, and the nights one makes up bands      45
To roam the town and sing out carnival,
And I've been three weeks shut within my mew,
A-painting for the great man, saints and saints
And saints again. I could not paint all night—
Ouf! I leaned out of window for fresh air.      50
There came a hurry of feet and little feet,
A sweep of lute-strings, laughs, and whiffs of song,—
*Flower o' the broom,*

*Take away love, and our earth is a tomb!*
*Flower o' the quince,*      55
*I let Lisa go, and what good in life since?*
*Flower o' the thyme* [4]—and so on. Round they went.
Scarce had they turned the corner when a titter
Like the skipping of rabbits by moonlight,—three slim shapes,
And a face that looked up . . . zooks, sir, flesh and blood,      60
That's all I'm made of! Into shreds it went,
Curtain and counterpane and coverlet,
All the bed-furniture—a dozen knots,
There was a ladder! Down I let myself,
Hands and feet, scrambling somehow, and so dropped,      65
And after them. I came up with the fun
Hard by Saint Laurence,[5] hail fellow, well met,—
*Flower o' the rose,*
*If I've been merry, what matter who knows?*
And so as I was stealing back again      70
To get to bed and have a bit of sleep
Ere I rise up to-morrow and go work
On Jerome knocking at his poor old breast
With his great round stone to subdue the flesh,
You snap me of the sudden. Ah, I see!      75
Though your eye twinkles still, you shake your head—
Mine's shaved—a monk, you say—the sting's in that!
If Master Cosimo announced himself,
Mum's the word naturally; but a monk!
Come, what am I a beast for? tell us, now! 80
I was a baby when my mother died
And father died and left me in the street.
I starved there, God knows how, a year or two
On fig-skins, melon-parings, rinds and shucks,
Refuse and rubbish. One fine frosty day,      85
My stomach being empty as your hat,
The wind doubled me up and down I went.
Old Aunt Lapaccia trussed me with one hand
(Its fellow was a stinger as I knew),
And so along the wall, over the bridge,      90
By the straight cut to the convent. Six words there,
While I stood munching my first bread that month:
"So, boy, you're minded," quoth the good fat father,
Wiping his own mouth, 'twas refection-time,—
"To quit this very miserable world?      95
Will you renounce" . . . "the mouthful of bread?" thought I;
By no means! Brief, they made a monk of me;
I did renounce the world, its pride and greed,
Palace, farm, villa, shop, and banking-house,
Trash, such as these poor devils of Medici 100

[2] The monastery of the friars Del Carmine.
[3] Cosimo de' Medici (1389–1464), who built "the house that caps the corner" in 1430. The time of the poem is between that year and 1432, when Fra Lippo left his monastery.

[4] This and the following flower-songs are modeled on the *stornelli* sung by the peasants of Tuscany.
[5] The church of San Lorenzo.

Have given their hearts to—all at eight years
   old.
Well, sir, I found in time, you may be sure,
'Twas not for nothing—the good bellyful,
The warm serge and the rope that goes all
   round,
And day-long blessèd idleness beside!    105
"Let's see what the urchin's fit for"—that came
   next.
Not overmuch their way, I must confess.
Such a to-do! They tried me with their books;
Lord, they'd have taught me Latin in pure
   waste!
*Flower o' the clove,*             110
*All the Latin I construe is "amo," I love!*
But, mind you, when a boy starves in the streets
Eight years together, as my fortune was,
Watching folk's faces to know who will fling
The bit of half-stripped grape-bunch he desires,
And who will curse or kick him for his pains,—
Which gentleman processional and fine,    117
Holding a candle to the Sacrament,
Will wink and let him lift a plate and catch
The droppings of the wax to sell again,    120
Or holla for the Eight[6] and have him
   whipped,—
How say I?—nay, which dog bites, which lets
   drop
His bone from the heap of offal in the street,—
Why, soul and sense of him grow sharp alike,
He learns the look of things, and none the less
For admonition from the hunger-pinch.    126
I had a store of such remarks, be sure,
Which, after I found leisure, turned to use.
I drew men's faces on my copy-books,
Scrawled them within the antiphonary's[7]
   marge,             130
Joined legs and arms to the long music-notes,
Found eyes and nose and chin for A's and B's,
And made a string of pictures of the world
Betwixt the ins and outs of verb and noun,
On the wall, the bench, the door. The monks
   looked black.    135
"Nay," quoth the Prior, "turn him out, d'ye
   say?
In no wise. Lose a crow and catch a lark.
What if at last we get our man of parts,
We Carmelites, like those Camaldolese
And Preaching Friars,[8] to do our church up
   fine    140
And put the front on it that ought to be!"
And hereupon he bade me daub away.
Thank you! my head being crammed, the walls
   a blank,
Never was such prompt disemburdening.
First, every sort of monk, the black and white,
I drew them, fat and lean: then, folk at church,
From good old gossips waiting to confess   147
Their cribs[9] of barrel-dropping, candle-ends,—
To the breathless fellow at the altar-foot,

Fresh from his murder, safe and sitting there[150]
With the little children round him in a row
Of admiration, half for his beard and half
For that white anger of his victim's son
Shaking a fist at him with one fierce arm,
Signing himself with the other because of
   Christ    155
(Whose sad face on the cross sees only this
After the passion of a thousand years)
Till some poor girl, her apron o'er her head,
(Which the intense eyes looked through) came
   at eve
On tiptoe, said a word, dropped in a loaf,   160
Her pair of earrings and a bunch of flowers
(The brute took growling), prayed, and so was
   gone.
I painted all, then cried " 'Tis ask and have;
Choose, for more's ready!"—laid the ladder
   flat,
And showed my covered bit of cloister-wall.   165
The monks closed in a circle and praised loud
Till checked, taught what to see and not to see,
Being simple bodies,—"That's the very man!
Look at the boy who stoops to pat the dog!
That woman's like the Prior's niece who comes
To care about his asthma: it's the life!"    171
But there my triumph's straw-fire flared and
   funked;
Their betters took their turn to see and say:
The Prior and the learnéd pulled a face
And stopped all that in no time. "How? what's
   here?    175
Quite from the mark of painting, bless us all!
Faces, arms, legs, and bodies like the true
As much as pea and pea! it's devil's-game!
Your business is not to catch men with show,
With homage to the perishable clay,    180
But lift them over it, ignore it all,
Make them forget there's such a thing as flesh.
Your business is to paint the souls of men—
Man's soul, and it's a fire, smoke . . . no, it's
   not . . .
It's vapor done up like a new-born babe—   185
(In that shape when you die it leaves your
   mouth)
It's . . . well, what matters talking, it's the
   soul!
Give us no more of body than shows soul!
Here's Giotto,[10] with his Saint a-praising God,
That sets us praising,—why not stop with him?
Why put all thoughts of praise out of our head
With wonder at lines, colors, and what not?[192]
Paint the soul, never mind the legs and arms!
Rub all out, try at it a second time.
Oh, that white smallish female with the breasts,
She's just my niece . . . Herodias,[11] I would
   say,—    196
Who went and danced and got men's heads
   cut off!
Have it all out!" Now, is this sense, I ask?

---

[6] The magistrates who governed Florence.
[7] The Roman service-book.
[8] The Dominicans.         [9] Petty thefts.

[10] Architect and painter (1266–1337).
[11] See St. Matthew, 14:6–11.

A fine way to paint soul, by painting body
So ill, the eye can't stop there, must go further
And can't fare worse! Thus, yellow does for
    white                           201
When what you put for yellow's simply black,
And any sort of meaning looks intense
When all beside itself means and looks naught.
Why can't a painter lift each foot in turn, 205
Left foot and right foot, go a double step,
Make his flesh liker and his soul more like,
Both in their order? Take the prettiest face,
The Prior's niece . . . patron-saint—is it so
    pretty
You can't discover if it means hope, fear, 210
Sorrow or joy? won't beauty go with these?
Suppose I've made her eyes all right and blue,
Can't I take breath and try to add life's flash,
And then add soul and heighten them three-
    fold?
Or say there's beauty with no soul at all—215
(I never saw it—put the case the same—)
If you get simple beauty and naught else,
You get about the best thing God invents:
That's somewhat: and you'll find the soul you
    have missed,
Within yourself, when you return him thanks.
"Rub all out!" Well, well, there's my life, in
    short,                          221
And so the thing has gone on ever since.
I'm grown a man no doubt, I've broken bonds:
You should not take a fellow eight years old
And make him swear to never kiss the girls. 225
I'm my own master, paint now as I please—
Having a friend, you see, in the Corner-
    house! [12]
Lord, it's fast holding by the rings in front—
Those great rings serve more purposes than just
To plant a flag in, or tie up a horse!    230
And yet the old schooling sticks, the old grave
    eyes
Are peeping o'er my shoulder as I work,
The heads shake still—"It's art's decline, my
    son!
You're not of the true painter, great and old;
Brother Angelico's [13] the man, you'll find;   235
Brother Lorenzo stands his single peer:
Fag on at flesh, you'll never make the third!"
*Flower o' the pine,*
*You keep your mistr . . . manners, and I'll*
*stick to mine!*
I'm not the third, then: bless us, they must
    know!                         240
Don't you think they're the likeliest to know,
They with their Latin? So, I swallow my rage,
Clench my teeth, suck my lips in tight, and
    paint

[12] I. e., in the Medici Palace.
[13] Fra Angelico (1387–1455) was a religious
painter, painting the soul and not minding the legs
and arms. He is said to have fasted and prayed
before painting, and to have painted some of his
pictures while kneeling. Lorenzo Monaco (the
monk) was a painter of the Camaldolese.

To please them—sometimes do and sometimes
    don't;
For, doing most, there's pretty sure to come 245
A turn, some warm eve finds me at my saints—
A laugh, a cry, the business of the world—
(*Flower o' the peach,*
*Death for us all, and his own life for each!*)
And my whole soul revolves, the cup runs over,
The world and life's too big to pass for a
    dream,                        251
And I do these wild things in sheer despite,
And play the fooleries you catch me at,
In pure rage! The old mill-horse, out at grass
After hard years, throws up his stiff heels so, 255
Although the miller does not preach to him
The only good of grass is to make chaff.
What would men have? Do they like grass or
    no—
May they or mayn't they? all I want's the thing
Settled for ever one way. As it is,    260
You tell too many lies and hurt yourself:
You don't like what you only like too much,
You do like what, if given you at your word,
You find abundantly detestable.
For me, I think I speak as I was taught;   265
I always see the garden and God there
A-making man's wife: and, my lesson learned,
The value and significance of flesh,
I can't unlearn ten minutes afterwards.

You understand me: I'm a beast, I know. 270
But see, now—why, I see as certainly
As that the morning-star's about to shine,
What will hap some day. We've a youngster
    here
Comes to our convent, studies what I do,
Slouches and stares and lets no atom drop: 275
His name is Guidi [14]—he'll not mind the
    monks—
They call him Hulking Tom, he lets them
    talk—
He picks my practice up—he'll paint apace,
I hope so—though I never live so long,
I know what's sure to follow. You be judge! 280
You speak no Latin more than I, belike;
However, you're my man, you've seen the world
—The beauty and the wonder and the power,
The shapes of things, their colors, lights and
    shades,
Changes, surprises,—and God made it all! 285
—For what? Do you feel thankful, ay or no,
For this fair town's face, yonder river's line,
The mountain round it and the sky above,
Much more the figures of man, woman, child,
These are the frame to? What's it all about?
To be passed over, despised? or dwelt upon, 291
Wondered at? oh, this last of course!—you say.
But why not do as well as say,—paint these
Just as they are, careless what comes of it?

[14] Tommaso Guidi, called Masaccio (1401–1428).
Browning for the sake of his point reverses the historical relationship between him and Fra Lippo.

God's works—paint any one, and count it crime 295
To let a truth slip. Don't object, "His works
Are here already; nature is complete:
Suppose you reproduce her—(which you can't)
There's no advantage! you must beat her, then."
For, don't you mark? we're made so that we love 300
First when we see them painted, things we have passed
Perhaps a hundred times nor cared to see;
And so they are better, painted—better to us,
Which is the same thing. Art was given for that;
God uses us to help each other so, 305
Lending our minds out. Have you noticed, now,
Your cullion's [15] hanging face? A bit of chalk,
And trust me but you should, though! How much more,
If I drew higher things with the same truth!
That were to take the Prior's pulpit-place, 310
Interpret God to all of you! Oh, oh,
It makes me mad to see what men shall do
And we in our graves! This world's no blot for us,
Nor blank; it means intensely, and means good:
To find its meaning is my meat and drink. 315
"Ay, but you don't so instigate to prayer!"
Strikes in the Prior: "when your meaning's plain
It does not say to folk—remember matins,
Or, mind you fast next Friday!" Why, for this
What need of art at all? A skull and bones, 320
Two bits of stick nailed crosswise, or, what's best,
A bell to chime the hour with, does as well.
I painted a Saint Laurence six months since
At Prato, splashed the fresco in fine style:
"How looks my painting, now the scaffold's down?" 325
I ask a brother: "Hugely," he returns—
"Already not one phiz of your three slaves
Who turn the Deacon off his toasted side,[16]
But's scratched and prodded to our heart's content,
The pious people have so eased their own 330
With coming to say prayers there in a rage:
We get on fast to see the bricks beneath.
Expect another job this time next year,
For pity and religion grow i' the crowd—
Your painting serves its purpose!" Hang the fools! 335

—That is—you'll not mistake an idle word
Spoke in a huff by a poor monk, God wot,
Tasting the air this spicy night which turns
The unaccustomed head like Chianti wine!

Oh, the church knows! don't misreport me, now! 340
It's natural a poor monk out of bounds
Should have his apt word to excuse himself:
And hearken how I plot to make amends.
I have bethought me: I shall paint a piece
. . . There's for you! Give me six months, then go, see 345
Something in Sant' Ambrogio's! Bless the nuns!
They want a cast o' my office. I shall paint [17]
God in the midst, Madonna and her babe,
Ringed by a bowery, flowery angel-brood,
Lilies and vestments and white faces, sweet 350
As puff on puff of grated orris-root
When ladies crowd to Church at midsummer.
And then i' the front, of course a saint or two—
Saint John, because he saves the Florentines,
Saint Ambrose, who puts down in black and white 355
The convent's friends and gives them a long day,
And Job, I must have him there past mistake,
The man of Uz (and Us without the z,
Painters who need his patience). Well, all these
Secured at their devotion, up shall come 360
Out of a corner when you least expect,
As one by a dark stair into a great light,
Music and talking, who but Lippo! I!—
Mazed, motionless, and moonstruck—I'm the the man!
Back I shrink—what is this I see and hear? 365
I, caught up with my monk's-things by mistake,
My old serge gown and rope that goes all round,
I, in this presence, this pure company!
Where's a hole, where's a corner for escape?
Then steps a sweet angelic slip of a thing 370
Forward, puts out a soft palm—"Not so fast!"
—Addresses the celestial presence, "nay—
He made you and devised you, after all,
Though he's none of you! Could Saint John there draw—
His camel-hair make up a painting-brush? 375
We come to brother Lippo for all that,
*Iste perfecit opus!*" [18] So, all smile—
I shuffle sideways with my blushing face
Under the cover of a hundred wings
Thrown like a spread of kirtles when you're gay 380
And play hot cockles, all the doors being shut,
Till, wholly unexpected, in there pops
The hothead husband! Thus I scuttle off
To some safe bench behind, not letting go
The palm of her, the little lily thing 385
That spoke the good word for me in the nick,

[17] The picture described is known as "The Coronation of the Virgin." It is now in the Accademia delle Belle Arti at Florence.
[18] This man made the picture (work). The words appear in the picture, on a scroll running from the speaker towards Fra Lippo.

[15] Rascal's.
[16] St. Laurence suffered martyrdom by being burned on a gridiron.

Like the Prior's niece . . . Saint Lucy, I would
  say.
And so all's saved for me, and for the church
A pretty picture gained. Go, six months hence!
Your hand, sir, and good-by: no lights, no
  lights! <sup>390</sup>
The street's hushed, and I know my own way
  back,
Don't fear me! There's the gray beginning.
  Zooks!

## My Star [1]

All that I know
  Of a certain star
Is, it can throw
  (Like the angled spar [2])
Now a dart of red,      5
  Now a dart of blue;
Till my friends have said
  They would fain see, too,
My star that dartles the red and the blue!
Then it stops like a bird; like a flower, hangs
  furled:      10
  They must solace themselves with the Saturn
    above it.
What matter to me if their star is a world?
  Mine has opened its soul to me; therefore
    I love it.

## Respectability [1]

Dear, had the world in its caprice
  Deigned to proclaim "I know you both,
  Have recognized your plighted troth,
Am sponsor for you: live in peace!"—
How many precious months and years      5
  Of youth had passed, that speed so fast,
  Before we found it out at last,
The world, and what it fears!

How much of priceless life were spent
  With men that every virtue decks,      10
  And women models of their sex,
Society's true ornament,—
Ere we dared wander, nights like this,
  Through wind and rain, and watch the Seine,
  And feel the Boulevard break again      15
To warmth and light and bliss!

I know! the world proscribes not love;
  Allows my finger to caress
  Your lips' contour and downiness,
Provided it supply a glove.      20
The world's good word!—the Institute!
  Guizot receives Montalembert! [2]

---

[1] Published in 1855. The star undoubtedly symbolizes Mrs. Browning.
[2] Piece of crystalline mineral with an angular surface.
[1] Published in 1855.
[2] The glove is the body of accepted social conventions. The French Institute symbolizes the rewards

Eli? Down the court three lampions [3] flare:
Put forward your best foot!

## The Statue and the Bust [1]

There's a palace in Florence, the world knows
  well,
And a statue watches it from the square,[2]
And this story of both do our townsmen tell.

Ages ago, a lady there,
  At the farthest window facing the East      5
Asked, "Who rides by with the royal air?"

The bridesmaids' prattle around her ceased;
  She leaned forth, one on either hand;
  They saw how the blush of the bride increased—

They felt by its beats her heart expand—      10
  As one at each ear and both in a breath
Whispered, "The Great-Duke Ferdinand."

That selfsame instant, underneath,
  The Duke rode past in his idle way,
Empty and fine like a swordless sheath.      15

of conventionality. Guizot, although a constitutional royalist who hated the liberalism of Montalembert, welcomed him into the Institute.

[3] Small lamps.
[1] Published in 1855. The following inquiry was once sent to an American newspaper:
"1. When, how, and where did it happen? Browning's divine vagueness lets one gather only that the lady's husband was a Riccardi. 2. Who was the lady? who the duke? 3. The magnificent house wherein Florence lodges her préfet is known to all Florentine ball-goers as the Palazzo Riccardi. It was bought by the Riccardi from the Medici in 1659. From none of its windows did the lady gaze at her more than royal lover. From what window, then, if from any? Are the statue and the bust still in their original positions?"
These questions were found by Mr. Thomas J. Wise, who sent them to Browning. He received from Browning the following reply, written on 8 January, 1887:
"DEAR MR. WISE,—I have seldom met with such a strange inability to understand what seems the plainest matter possible: 'ball-goers' are probably not history-readers, but any guide-book would confirm what is sufficiently stated in the poem. I will append a note or two, however. 1. 'This story the townsmen tell;' 'when, how, and where,' constitutes the subject of the poem. 2. The lady was the wife of Riccardi; and the duke, Ferdinand, just as the poem says. 3. As it was built by, and inhabited by, the Medici till sold, long after, to the Riccardi, it was not from the duke's palace, but a window in that of the Riccardi, that the lady gazed at her lover riding by. The statue is still in its place, looking at the window under which 'now is the empty shrine.' Can anything be clearer? My 'vagueness' leaves what to be 'gathered' when all these things are put down in black and white? Oh, 'ball-goers'!"
[2] The Piazza della Annunziata. The statue is of the Grand Duke Ferdinand I (1549–1608).

Gay he rode, with a friend as gay,
Till he threw his head back—"Who is she?"
—"A bride the Riccardi brings home to-day."

Hair in heaps lay heavily
Over a pale brow spirit-pure—                    20
Carved like the heart of the coal-black tree,

Crisped like a war-steed's encolure—[3]
And vainly sought to dissemble her eyes
Of the blackest black our eyes endure,

And lo, a blade for a knight's emprise      25
Filled the fine empty sheath of a man,—
The Duke grew straightway brave and wise.

He looked at her, as a lover can;
She looked at him, as one who awakes:
The past was a sleep, and her life began.     30

Now, love so ordered for both their sakes,
A feast was held that selfsame night
In the pile which the mighty shadow makes.[4]

(For Via Larga is three-parts light,
But the palace overshadows one,               35
Because of a crime, which may God requite!

To Florence and God the wrong was done,
Through the first republic's murder there
By Cosimo [5] and his curséd son.)

The Duke (with the statue's face in the square)
Turned in the midst of his multitude          41
At the bright approach of the bridal pair.

Face to face the lovers stood
A single minute and no more,
While the bridegroom bent as a man sub-
dued—                                                     45

Bowed till his bonnet brushed the floor—
For the Duke on the lady a kiss conferred,
As the courtly custom was of yore.

In a minute can lovers exchange a word?
If a word did pass, which I do not think,      50
Only one out of a thousand heard.

That was the bridegroom. At day's brink
He and his bride were alone at last
In a bed chamber by a taper's blink.

Calmly he said that her lot was cast,          55
That the door she had passed was shut on her
Till the final catafalk [6] repassed.

[3] Neck and shoulders.
[4] The Palace of Ferdinand.
[5] Cosimo de' Medici (1389–1464). Through him
Florence prospered, while its republican government was undermined. He built the palace later
occupied by Ferdinand.
[6] Funeral canopy.

The world meanwhile, its noise and stir,
Through a certain window facing the East
She could watch like a convent's chronicler.  60

Since passing the door might lead to a feast,
And a feast might lead to so much beside,
He, of many evils, chose the least.

"Freely I choose too," said the bride—
"Your window and its world suffice,"            65
Replied the tongue, while the heart replied—

"If I spend the night with that devil twice,
May his window serve as my loop of hell
Whence a damned soul looks on paradise!

"I fly to the Duke who loves me well,          70
Sit by his side and laugh at sorrow
Ere I count another ave-bell.

"'Tis only the coat of a page to borrow,
And tie my hair in a horse-boy's trim,
And I save my soul—but not to-morrow"—   75

(She checked herself and her eye grew dim)
"My father tarries to bless my state:
I must keep it one day more for him.

"Is one day more so long to wait?
Moreover the Duke rides past, I know;          80
We shall see each other, sure as fate."

She turned on her side and slept. Just so!
So we resolve on a thing and sleep:
So did the lady, ages ago.

That night the Duke said, "Dear or cheap      85
As the cost of this cup of bliss may prove
To body or soul, I will drain it deep."

And on the morrow, bold with love,
He beckoned the bridegroom (close on call,
As his duty bade, by the Duke's alcove)      90

And smiled " 'Twas a very funeral,
Your lady will think, this feast of ours,—
A shame to efface, whate'er befall!

"What if we break from the Arno bowers,
And try if Petraja,[7] cool and green,          95
Cure last night's fault with this morning's
          flowers?"

The bridegroom, not a thought to be seen
On his steady brow and quiet mouth,
Said, "Too much favor for me so mean!

"But, alas! my lady leaves the South; [8]      100
Each wind that comes from the Apennine
Is a menace to her tender youth:

[7] Outside of Florence. The Arno is a river flowing through Florence.
[8] I. e., is from the South. Apennine is the mountain range amidst which Florence is situated.

"Nor a way exists, the wise opine,
If she quits her palace twice this year,
To avert the flower of life's decline."    105

Quoth the Duke, "A sage and a kindly fear.
Moreover Petraja is cold this spring:
Be our feast to-night as usual here!"

And then to himself—"Which night shall
    bring
Thy bride to her lover's embraces, fool—    110
Or I am the fool, and thou art the king!

"Yet my passion must wait a night, nor cool—
For to-night the Envoy arrives from France
Whose heart I unlock with thyself, my tool.

"I need thee still and might miss perchance. 115
To-day is not wholly lost, beside,
With its hope of my lady's countenance:

"For I ride—what should I do but ride?
And passing her palace, if I list,
May glance at its window—well betide!"    120

So said, so done: nor the lady missed
One ray that broke from the ardent brow,
Nor a curl of the lips where the spirit kissed.

Be sure that each renewed the vow,
No morrow's sun should arise and set    125
And leave them then as it left them now.

But next day passed, and next day yet,
With still fresh cause to wait one day more
Ere each leaped over the parapet.

And still, as love's brief morning wore,    130
With a gentle start, half smile, half sigh,
They found love not as it seemed before.

They thought it would work infallibly,
But not in despite of heaven and earth:
The rose would blow when the storm passed
    by.    135

Meantime they could profit in winter's dearth
By store of fruits that supplant the rose:
The world and its ways have a certain worth:

And to press a point while these oppose
Were simple [9] policy; better wait:    140
We lose no friends and we gain no foes.

Meantime, worse fates than a lover's fate,
Who daily may ride and pass and look
Where his lady watches behind the grate!

And she—she watched the square like a book
Holding one picture and only one,    146
Which daily to find she undertook:

[9] Silly.

When the picture was reached the book was
    done,
And she turned from the picture at night to
    scheme
Of tearing it out for herself next sun.    150

So weeks grew months, years; gleam by gleam
The glory dropped from their youth and love,
And both perceived they had dreamed a dream;

Which hovered as dreams do, still above:
But who can take a dream for a truth?    155
Oh, hide our eyes from the next remove!

One day as the lady saw her youth
Depart, and the silver thread that streaked
Her hair, and, worn by the serpent's tooth,

The brow so puckered, the chin so peaked,—
And wondered who the woman was,    161
Hollow-eyed and haggard-cheeked,

Fronting her silent in the glass—
"Summon here," she suddenly said,
"Before the rest of my old self pass,    165

"Him, the Carver, a hand to aid,
Who fashions the clay no love will change,
And fixes a beauty never to fade.

"Let Robbia's craft [10] so apt and strange
Arrest the remains of young and fair,    170
And rivet them while the seasons range,

"Make me a face on the window there,
Waiting as ever, mute the while,
My love to pass below in the square!

"And let me think that it may beguile    175
Dreary days which the dead must spend
Down in their darkness under the aisle,

"To say, 'What matters it at the end?
I did no more while my heart was warm
Than does that image, my pale-faced friend.'

"Where is the use of the lip's red charm,    181
The heaven of hair, the pride of the brow,
And the blood that blues the inside arm—

"Unless we turn, as the soul knows how,
The earthly gift to an end divine?    185
A lady of clay is as good, I trow."

But long ere Robbia's cornice, fine,
With flowers and fruits which leaves enlace,
Was set where now is the empty shrine—

(And, leaning out of a bright blue space,    190
As a ghost might lean from a chink of sky,
The passionate pale lady's face—

[10] Robbia is not here the name of the artist (the
last famous Robbia had died in 1566), but is applied to the kind of work done by the Robbias—
terra-cotta relief work covered with enamel.

Eying ever, with earnest eye
And quick-turned neck at its breathless stretch,
Some one who ever is passing by—)              195

The Duke had sighed like the simplest wretch
In Florence, "Youth—my dream escapes!
Will its record stay?" And he bade them fetch

Some subtle molder of brazen shapes—
"Can the soul, the will, die out of a man      200
Ere his body find the grave that gapes?

"John of Douay shall effect my plan,
Set me on horseback here aloft,
Alive, as the crafty sculptor can,

"In the very square I have crossed so oft:     205
That men may admire, when future suns
Shall touch the eyes to a purpose soft,

"While the mouth and the brow stay brave in
      bronze—
Admire and say, 'When he was alive
How he would take his pleasure once!'          210

"And it shall go hard but I contrive
To listen the while, and laugh in my tomb
At idleness which aspires to strive."

———————

So! While these wait the trump of doom,
How do their spirits pass, I wonder,           215
Nights and days in the narrow room?

Still, I suppose, they sit and ponder
What a gift life was, ages ago,
Six steps out of the chapel yonder.

Only they see not God, I know,                 220
Nor all that chivalry of his,
The soldier-saints who, row on row,

Burn upward each to his point of bliss—
Since, the end of life being manifest,
He had burned his way through the world to
      this.                                     225

I hear you reproach, "But delay was best,
For their end was a crime."—Oh, a crime will
      do
As well, I reply, to serve for a test,

As a virtue golden through and through,
Sufficient to vindicate itself                 230
And prove its worth at a moment's view!

Must a game be played for the sake of pelf?
Where a button goes, 'twere an epigram
To offer the stamp of the very Guelph.[11]

———————

[11] Where a button will pass as readily as real
money ("the stamp of the very Guelph") it would
be absurd ("an epigram," i. e., a matter for satire)
to use the latter.

The true has no value beyond the sham:         235
As well the counter as coin, I submit,
When your table's a hat, and your prize, a
      dram.

Stake your counter as boldly every whit,
Venture as warily, use the same skill,
Do your best, whether winning or losing it, 240
If you chose to play!—is my principle.
Let a man contend to the uttermost
For his life's set prize, be it what it will!

The counter our lovers staked was lost
As surely as if it were lawful coin:           245
And the sin I impute to each frustrate ghost

Is—the unlit lamp and the ungirt loin,
Though the end in sight was a vice, I say.
You of the virtue (we issue join)
How strive you? *De te, fabula!* [12]           250

# The Patriot [1]

### An Old Story

It was roses, roses, all the way,
      With myrtle mixed in my path like mad:
The house-roofs seemed to heave and sway,
      The church-spires flamed, such flags they
      had,
A year ago on this very day.                    5

The air broke into a mist with bells,
      The old walls rocked with the crowd and
      cries.
Had I said, "Good folk, mere noise repels—
      But give me your sun from yonder skies!"
They had answered "And afterward, what else?"

Alack, it was I who leaped at the sun           11
      To give it my loving friends to keep!
Naught man could do, have I left undone:
      And you see my harvest, what I reap
This very day, now a year is run.               15

There's nobody on the house-tops now—
      Just a palsied few at the windows set,
For the best of the sight is, all allow,
      At the Shambles' Gate—or, better yet,
By the very scaffold's foot, I trow.            20

I go in the rain, and, more than needs,
      A rope cuts both my wrists behind;
And I think, by the feel, my forehead bleeds,
      For they fling, whoever has a mind,
Stones at me for my year's misdeeds.            25

Thus I entered, and thus I go!
      In triumphs, people have dropped down
      dead.

[12] The story concerns you.
[1] Published in 1855.

"Paid by the world, what dost thou owe
   Me?"—God might question; now instead,
'Tis God shall repay: I am safer so.    30

## Andrea Del Sarto [1]

### Called "The Faultless Painter"

But do not let us quarrel any more,
No, my Lucrezia; bear with me for once:
Sit down and all shall happen as you wish.
You turn your face, but does it bring your
   heart?
I'll work then for your friend's friend, never
   fear,    5
Treat his own subject after his own way,
Fix his own time, accept too his own price,
And shut the money into this small hand
When next it takes mine. Will it? tenderly?
Oh, I'll content him,—but to-morrow, Love!    10
I often am much wearier than you think,
This evening more than usual, and it seems
As if—forgive now—should you let me sit
Here by the window with your hand in mine
And look a half-hour forth on Fiesole,[2]    15
Both of one mind, as married people use,
Quietly, quietly the evening through,
I might get up to-morrow to my work
Cheerful and fresh as ever. Let us try.
To-morrow, how you shall be glad for this!    20
Your soft hand is a woman of itself,
And mine the man's bared breast she curls in-
   side.
Don't count the time lost, neither; you must
   serve
For each of the five pictures we require:
It saves a model. So! keep looking so—    25
My serpentining beauty, rounds on rounds!
—How could you ever prick those perfect ears,
Even to put the pearl there! oh, so sweet—
My face, my moon, my everybody's moon,
Which everybody looks on and calls his,    30
And, I suppose, is looked on by in turn,
While she looks—no one's: very dear, no less.
You smile? why, there's my picture ready made,
There's what we painters call our harmony!
A common grayness silvers everything,—    35
All in a twilight, you and I alike
—You, at the point of your first pride in me
(That's gone you know),—but I, at every
   point;
My youth, my hope, my art, being all toned
   down
To yonder sober pleasant Fiesole.    40
There's the bell clinking from the chapel-top;
That length of convent-wall across the way
Holds the trees safer, huddled more inside;
The last monk leaves the garden; days decrease,

And autumn grows, autumn in everything.    45
Eh? the whole seems to fall into a shape
As if I saw alike my work and self
And all that I was born to be and do,
A twilight-piece. Love, we are in God's hand.
How strange now looks the life he makes us
   lead;    50
So free we seem, so fettered fast we are!
I feel he laid the fetter: let it lie!
This chamber for example—turn your head—
All that's behind us! You don't understand
Nor care to understand about my art,    55
But you can hear at least when people speak:
And that cartoon, the second from the door
—It is the thing, Love! so such thing should
   be—
Behold Madonna!—I am bold to say.
I can do with my pencil what I know,    60
What I see, what at bottom of my heart
I wish for, if I ever wish so deep—
Do easily, too—when I say, perfectly,
I do not boast, perhaps: yourself are judge,
Who listened to the Legate's talk last week,    65
And just as much they used to say in France.
At any rate 'tis easy, all of it!
No sketches first, no studies, that's long past:
I do what many dream of all their lives,
—Dream? strive to do, and agonize to do,    70
And fail in doing. I could count twenty such
On twice your fingers, and not leave this town,
Who strive—you don't know how the others
   strive
To paint a little thing like that you smeared
Carelessly passing with your robes afloat,—    75
Yet do much less, so much less, Someone says,
(I know his name, no matter)—so much less!
Well, less is more, Lucrezia: I am judged.
There burns a truer light of God in them,
In their vexed beating stuffed and stopped-up
   brain,    80
Heart, or whate'er else, than goes on to prompt
This low-pulsed forthright craftsman's hand of
   mine.
Their works drop groundward, but themselves, I
   know,
Reach many a time a heaven that's shut to me,
Enter and take their place there sure enough,    85
Though they come back and cannot tell the
   world.
My works are nearer heaven, but I sit here.
The sudden blood of these men! at a word—
Praise them, it boils, or blame them, it boils
   too.
I, painting from myself and to myself,    90
Know what I do, am unmoved by men's blame
Or their praise either. Somebody remarks
Morello's outline [3] there is wrongly traced,
His hue mistaken; what of that? or else,
Rightly traced and well ordered; what of that?
Speak as they please, what does the mountain
   care?    96

[1] Published in 1855. Andrea's life (1486–1531)
is to be found in the Lives of the Painters, by
Giorgio Vasari, one of Andrea's pupils.
[2] A small town about three miles west of Florence.

[3] Morello is a mountain of the Apennines, north
of Florence.

Ah, but a man's reach should exceed his grasp,
Or what's a heaven for? All is silver-gray
Placid and perfect with my art: the worse!
I know both what I want and what might gain,
And yet how profitless to know, to sigh    101
"Had I been two, another and myself,
Our head would have o'erlooked the world!"
No doubt.
Yonder's a work now, of that famous youth
The Urbinate [4] who died five years ago.    105
('Tis copied, George Vasari sent it me.)
Well, I can fancy how he did it all,
Pouring his soul, with kings and popes to see,
Reaching, that heaven might so replenish him,
Above and through his art—for it gives way; [110]
That arm is wrongly put—and there again—
A fault to pardon in the drawing's lines,
Its body, so to speak: its soul is right,
He means right—that, a child may understand.
Still, what an arm! and I could alter it:    115
But all the play, the insight and the stretch—
Out of me, out of me! And wherefore out?
Had you enjoined them on me, given me soul,
We might have risen to Rafael, I and you!
Nay, Love, you did give all I asked, I think—
More than I merit, yes, by many times.    121
But had you—oh, with the same perfect brow,
And perfect eyes, and more than perfect mouth,
And the low voice my soul hears, as a bird
The fowler's pipe, and follows to the snare—
Had you, with these the same, but brought a
mind!    126
Some women do so. Had the mouth there
urged,
"God and the glory! never care for gain.
The present by the future, what is that?
Live for fame, side by side with Agnolo! [5]    130
Rafael is waiting: up to God, all three!"
I might have done it for you. So it seems:
Perhaps not. All is as God overrules.
Beside, incentives come from the soul's self;
The rest avail not. Why do I need you?    135
What wife had Rafael, or has Agnolo?
In this world, who can do a thing, will not;
And who would do it, cannot, I perceive:
Yet the will's somewhat—somewhat, too, the
power—
And thus we half-men struggle. At the end,    140
God, I conclude, compensates, punishes.
'Tis safer for me, if the award be strict,
That I am something underrated here,
Poor this long while, despised, to speak the
truth.
I dared not, do you know, leave home all day,
For fear of chancing on the Paris lords.    146
The best is when they pass and look aside;
But they speak sometimes; I must bear it all.
Well may they speak! That Francis, [6] that first
time,

And that long festal year at Fontainebleau! [150]
I surely then could sometimes leave the ground,
Put on the glory, Rafael's daily wear,
In that humane great monarch's golden look,—
One finger in his beard or twisted curl
Over his mouth's good mark that made the
smile,    155
One arm about my shoulder, round my neck,
The jingle of his gold chain in my ear,
I painting proudly with his breath on me,
All his court round him, seeing with his eyes,
Such frank French eyes, and such a fire of
souls    160
Profuse, my hand kept plying by those hearts,—
And, best of all, this, this, this face beyond,
This in the background, waiting on my work,
To crown the issue with a last reward!
A good time, was it not, my kingly days?    165
And had you not grown restless . . . but I
know—
'Tis done and past; 'twas right, my instinct said;
Too live the life grew, golden and not gray,
And I'm the weak-eyed bat no sun should
tempt
Out of the grange whose four walls make his
world.    170
How could it end in any other way?
You called me, and I came home to your heart.
The triumph was—to reach and stay there; since
I reached it ere the triumph, what is lost?
Let my hands frame your face in your hair's
gold,    175
You beautiful Lucrezia that are mine!
"Rafael did this, Andrea painted that;
The Roman's is the better when you pray,
But still the other's Virgin was his wife"—
Men will excuse me. I am glad to judge    180
Both pictures in your presence; clearer grows
My better fortune, I resolve to think.
For, do you know, Lucrezia, as God lives,
Said one day Agnolo, his very self,
To Rafael . . . I have known it all these
years . . .    185
(When the young man was flaming out his
thoughts
Upon a palace-wall for Rome to see,
Too lifted up in heart because of it)
"Friend, there's a certain sorry little scrub
Goes up and down our Florence, none cares
how,    190
Who, were he set to plan and execute
As you are, pricked on by your popes and kings,
Would bring the sweat into that brow of
yours!"
To Rafael's!—And indeed the arm is wrong.
I hardly dare . . . yet, only you to see,    195
Give the chalk here—quick, thus the line
should go!
Ay, but the soul! he's Rafael! rub it out!

---

[4] Raphael (1483–1520), who was born at Urbino.
[5] Michael Angelo (1475–1564).
[6] King Francis I of France, Andrea's patron.

Fontainebleau is a town near Paris, where is situated the royal palace in which Andrea worked.

Still, all I care for, if he spoke the truth,
(What he? why, who but Michel Agnolo?
Do you forget already words like those?)   200
If really there was such a chance, so lost,—
Is, whether you're—not grateful—but more
   pleased.
Well, let me think so. And you smile indeed!
This hour has been an hour! Another smile?
If you would sit thus by me every night   205
I should work better, do you comprehend?
I mean that I should earn more, give you more.
See, it is settled dusk now; there's a star;
Morello's gone, the watch-lights show the wall,
The cue-owls[7] speak the name we call them
   by.   210
Come from the window, love,—come in, at last,
Inside the melancholy little house
We built to be so gay with. God is just.
King Francis may forgive me: oft at nights
When I look up from painting, eyes tired
   out,   215
The walls become illumined, brick from brick
Distinct, instead of mortar, fierce bright gold,
That gold of his I did cement them with!
Let us but love each other. Must you go?
That Cousin here again? he waits outside?   220
Must see you—you, and not with me? Those
   loans?
More gaming debts to pay? you smiled for that?
Well, let smiles buy me! have you more to
   spend?
While hand and eye and something of a heart
Are left me, work's my ware, and what's it
   worth?   225
I'll pay my fancy. Only let me sit
The gray remainder of the evening out,
Idle, you call it, and muse perfectly
How I could paint, were I but back in France,
One picture, just one more—the Virgin's face,
Not yours this time! I want you at my side   231
To hear them—that is, Michel Agnolo—
Judge all I do and tell you of its worth.
Will you? To-morrow, satisfy your friend.
I take the subjects for his corridor,   235
Finish the portrait out of hand—there, there,
And throw him in another thing or two
If he demurs; the whole should prove enough
To pay for this same Cousin's freak. Beside,
What's better and what's all I care about,   240
Get you the thirteen scudi[8] for the ruff!
Love, does that please you? Ah, but what does
   he,
The Cousin! what does he to please you more?

I am grown peaceful as old age to-night.
I regret little, I would change still less.   245
Since there my past life lies, why alter it?
The very wrong to Francis!—it is true
I took his coin, was tempted and complied,
And built this house and sinned, and all is said.
My father and my mother died of want.   250

[7] The scops owl, whose cry sounds like Italian *ciù*.
[8] Coins worth about 97 cents.

Well, had I riches of my own? you see
How one gets rich! Let each one bear his lot.
They were born poor, lived poor, and poor they
   died:
And I have labored somewhat in my time   254
And not been paid profusely. Some good son
Paint my two hundred pictures—let him try!
No doubt, there's something strikes a balance.
   Yes,
You loved me quite enough, it seems to-night.
This must suffice me here. What would one
   have?
In heaven, perhaps, new chances, one more
   chance—   260
Four great walls in the New Jerusalem,
Meted on each side by the angel's reed,
For Leonard,[9] Rafael, Agnolo and me
To cover—the three first without a wife,
While I have mine! So—still they overcome
Because there's still Lucrezia,—as I choose.[266]

Again the Cousin's whistle! Go, my Love.

# A Grammarian's Funeral [1]

### *Shortly After the Revival of Learning in Europe*

Let us begin and carry up this corpse,
   Singing together.
Leave we the common crofts, the vulgar
   thorpes[2]
   Each in its tether
Sleeping safe on the bosom of the plain,   5
   Cared-for till cock-crow:
Look out if yonder be not day again
   Rimming the rock-row!
That's the appropriate country; there, man's
   thought,
   Rarer, intenser,   10
Self-gathered for an outbreak, as it ought,
   Chafes in the censer.
Leave we the unlettered plain its herd and crop;
   Seek we sepulture
On a tall mountain, cited to the top,   15
   Crowded with culture!
All the peaks soar, but one the rest excels;
   Clouds overcome it;
No! yonder sparkle is the citadel's
   Circling its summit.   20
Thither our path lies; wind we up the heights;
   Wait ye the warning?
Our low life was the level's and the night's;
   He's for the morning.
Step to a tune, square chests, erect each head,
   'Ware the beholders!   26
This is our master, famous, calm and dead,
   Borne on our shoulders.

Sleep, crop and herd! sleep, darkling thorpe and
   croft,

[9] Leonardo da Vinci (1452–1519).
[1] Published in 1855.
[2] The common farms, the vulgar villages.

Safe from the weather! 30
He, whom we convoy to his grave aloft,
    Singing together,
He was a man born with thy face and throat,
    Lyric Apollo!
Long he lived nameless: how should Spring
    take note 35
    Winter would follow?
Till lo, the little touch, and youth was gone!
    Cramped and diminished,
Moaned he, "New measures, other feet anon!
    My dance is finished"? 40
No, that's the world's way: (keep the moun-
    tain-side,
    Make for the city!)
He knew the signal, and stepped on with pride
    Over men's pity;
Left play for work, and grappled with the world
    Bent on escaping: 46
"What's in the scroll," quoth he, "thou keep-
    est furled?
    Show me their shaping,
Theirs who most studied man, the bard and
    sage,—
    Give!"—So, he gowned him, 50
Straight got by heart that book to its last page:
    Learned, we found him.
Yea, but we found him bald too, eyes like lead,
    Accents uncertain:
"Time to taste life," another would have said,
    "Up with the curtain!" 56
This man said rather, "Actual life comes next?
    Patience a moment!
Grant I have mastered learning's crabbed text,
    Still there's the comment. 60
Let me know all! Prate not of most or least,
    Painful or easy!
Even to the crumbs I'd fain eat up the feast,
    Ay, nor feel queasy."
Oh, such a life as he resolved to live, 65
    When he had learned it,
When he had gathered all books had to give!
    Sooner, he spurned it.
Imagine the whole, then execute the parts—
    Fancy the fabric 70
Quite, ere you build, ere steel strike fire from
    quartz,
    Ere mortar dab brick!

(Here's the town-gate reached: there's the
    market-place
    Gaping before us.)
Yea, this in him was the peculiar grace 75
    (Hearten our chorus!)
That before living he'd learn how to live—
    No end to learning:
Earn the means first—God surely will contrive
    Use for our earning. 80
Others mistrust and say, "But time escapes:
    Live now or never!"
He said, "What's time? Leave Now for dogs
    and apes!
    Man has Forever."

Back to his book then: deeper drooped his
    head: 85
    *Calculus* [3] racked him:
Leaden before, his eyes grew dross of lead:
    *Tussis* [4] attacked him.
"Now, master, take a little rest!"—not he!
    (Caution redoubled, 90
Step two abreast, the way winds narrowly!)
    Not a whit troubled,
Back to his studies, fresher than at first,
    Fierce as a dragon
He (soul-hydroptic [5] with a sacred thirst) 95
    Sucked at the flagon.
Oh, if we draw a circle premature,
    Heedless of far gain,
Greedy for quick returns of profit, sure
    Bad is our bargain! 100
Was it not great? did not he throw on God,
    (He loves the burthen)—
God's task to make the heavenly period
    Perfect the earthen?
Did not he magnify the mind, show clear 105
    Just what it all meant?
He would not discount life, as fools do here,
    Paid by instalment.
He ventured neck or nothing—heaven's suc-
    cess
    Found, or earth's failure: 110
"Wilt thou trust death or not?" He answered
    "Yes!
    Hence with life's pale lure!"
That low man seeks a little thing to do,
    Sees it and does it:
This high man, with a great thing to pursue,
    Dies ere he knows it. 116
That low man goes on adding one to one,
    His hundred's soon hit:
This high man, aiming at a million,
    Misses an unit. 120
That, has the world here—should he need the
    next,
    Let the world mind him!
This, throws himself on God, and unperplexed
    Seeking shall find him.
So, with the throttling hands of death at strife,
    Ground he at grammar; 126
Still, through the rattle, parts of speech were
    rife;
    While he could stammer
He settled *Hoti's* business—let it be!—
    Properly based *Oun*— 130
Gave us the doctrine of the enclitic *De* [6]

[3] The stone.    [4] A cough.    [5] Soul-thirsty.
[6] These are Greek particles, meaning respectively
*that, therefore,* and *towards.* Concerning the last
Browning wrote to the London *Daily News* on 20
November, 1874: "In a clever article this morning
you speak of 'the doctrine of enclitic De'—'which,
with all deference to Mr. Browning, in point of
fact does not exist.' No, not to Mr. Browning:
but pray defer to Herr Buttmann, whose fifth list
of 'enclitics' ends with 'the inseparable *De*'—or to
Curtius, whose fifth list ends also with '*De* (mean-

Dead from the waist down.
Well, here's the platform, here's the proper
  place:
  Hail to your purlieus,
All ye highfliers of the feathered race,    135
  Swallows and curlews!
Here's the top-peak; the multitude below
  Live, for they can, there:
This man decided not to Live but Know—
  Bury this man there?    140
Here—here's his place, where meteors shoot,
  clouds form,
  Lightnings are loosened,
Stars come and go! Let joy break with the
  storm,
  Peace let the dew send!
Lofty designs must close in like effects:    145
  Loftily lying,
Leave him—still loftier than the world suspects,
  Living and dying.

# Abt Vogler [1]

*(After He Has Been Extemporizing upon
the Musical Instrument of His Invention)*

Would that the structure brave, the manifold
  music I build,
  Bidding my organ obey, calling its keys to
  their work,
Claiming each slave of the sound, at a touch, as
  when Solomon willed
  Armies of angels that soar, legions of demons
  that lurk,
Man, brute, reptile, fly,—alien of end and of
  aim,    5
  Adverse, each from the other heaven-high,
  hell-deep removed,—
Should rush into sight at once as he named the
  ineffable Name,
  And pile him a palace straight, to pleasure
  the princess he loved! [2]

Would it might tarry like his, the beautiful
  building of mine,
  This which my keys in a crowd pressed and
  importuned to raise!    10
Ah, one and all, how they helped, would dispart now and now combine,

ing "*towards*" and as a demonstrative appendage).'
That this is not to be confounded with the accentu-
ated 'De, meaning *but*' was the 'doctrine' which the
Grammarian bequeathed to those capable of receiving it."
  [1] Published in 1864. George Joseph Vogler (1749–
1814), organist and composer, was a native of
Würzburg. He invented an instrument called the
Orchestrion—a compact organ with four keyboards
of five octaves each and a pedal-board of thirty-six
keys. Vogler was a Catholic priest—hence Browning's "Abt."
  [2] Jewish legend gave Solomon such powers as this.
"The ineffable Name" is the unspeakable name of
God.

Zealous to hasten the work, heighten their
  master his praise!
And one would bury his brow with a blind
  plunge down to hell,
  Burrow awhile and build, broad on the roots
  of things,
Then up again swim into sight, having based me
  my palace well,    15
  Founded it, fearless of flame, flat on the
  nether springs.

And another would mount and march, like the
  excellent minion he was,
  Ay, another and yet another, one crowd but
  with many a crest,
Raising my rampired [3] walls of gold as transparent as glass,
  Eager to do and die, yield each his place to
  the rest:    20
For higher still and higher (as a runner tips
  with fire,
  When a great illumination surprises a festal
  night—
Outlining round and round Rome's dome [4]
  from space to spire)
  Up, the pinnacled glory reached, and the
  pride of my soul was in sight.

In sight? Not half! for it seemed, it was certain, to match man's birth,    25
  Nature in turn conceived, obeying an impulse as I;
And the emulous heaven yearned down, made
  effort to reach the earth,
  As the earth had done her best, in my passion, to scale the sky:
Novel splendors burst forth, grew familiar and
  dwelt with mine,
  Not a point nor peak but found and fixed its
  wandering star;    30
Meteor-moons, balls of blaze: and they did not
  pale nor pine,
  For earth had attained to heaven, there was
  no more near nor far.

Nay more; for there wanted not who walked in
  the glare and glow,
  Presences [5] plain in the place; or, fresh from
  the Protoplast, [6]
Furnished for ages to come, when a kindlier
  wind should blow,    35
  Lured now to begin and live, in a house to
  their liking at last;
Or else the wonderful Dead who have passed
  through the body and gone,
  But were back once more to breathe in an
  old world worth their new:
What never had been, was now; what was, as it
  shall be anon;

  [3] Protected with a rampart.    [4] St. Peter's.
  [5] Spirits.
  [6] The thing first formed, as a model to be imitated.

And what is,—shall I say, matched both? for
I was made perfect too.    40

All through my keys that gave their sounds to a
wish of my soul,
All through my soul that praised as its wish
flowed visibly forth,
All through music and me! For think, had I
painted the whole,
Why, there it had stood, to see, nor the
process so wonder-worth:
Had I written the same, made verse—still,
effect proceeds from cause,    45
Ye know why the forms are fair, ye hear how
the tale is told;
It is all triumphant art, but art in obedience to
laws,
Painter and poet are proud in the artist-list
enrolled:—

But here is the finger of God, a flash of the will
that can,
Existent behind all laws, that made them
and, lo, they are!    50
And I know not if, save in this, such gift be allowed to man,
That out of three sounds he frame, not a
fourth sound, but a star.
Consider it well: each tone of our scale in itself
is naught:
It is everywhere in the world—loud, soft,
and all is said:
Give it to me to use! I mix it with two in my
thought:    55
And, there! Ye have heard and seen: consider and bow the head!

Well, it is gone at last, the palace of music I
reared;
Gone! and the good tears start, the praises
that come too slow;
For one is assured at first, one scarce can say
that he feared,
That he even gave it a thought, the gone
thing was to go.    60
Never to be again! But many more of the kind
As good, nay, better perchance: is this your
comfort to me?
To me, who must be saved because I cling with
my mind
To the same, same self, same love, same
God: ay, what was, shall be.

Therefore to whom turn I but to Thee, the in-
effable Name?    65
Builder and maker, Thou, of houses not
made with hands!
What, have fear of change from Thee who art
ever the same?
Doubt that Thy power can fill the heart that
Thy power expands?
There shall never be one lost good! What was,
shall live as before;

The evil is null, is naught, is silence implying sound;    70
What was good shall be good, with, for evil, so
much good more;
On the earth the broken arcs; in the heaven
a perfect round.

All we have willed or hoped or dreamed of good
shall exist;
Not its semblance, but itself; no beauty, nor
good, nor power
Whose voice has gone forth, but each survives
for the melodist    75
When eternity affirms the conception of an
hour.
The high that proved too high, the heroic for
earth too hard,
The passion that left the ground to lose itself
in the sky,
Are music sent up to God by the lover and the
bard;
Enough that he heard it once: we shall hear
it by and by.    80

And what is our failure here but a triumph's
evidence
For the fullness of the days? Have we withered or agonized?
Why else was the pause prolonged but that
singing might issue thence?
Why rushed the discords in, but that harmony should be prized?
Sorrow is hard to bear, and doubt is slow to
clear,    85
Each sufferer says his say, his scheme of the
weal and woe:
But God has a few of us whom he whispers in
the ear;
The rest may reason and welcome: 'tis we
musicians know.

Well, it is earth with me; silence resumes her
reign:
I will be patient and proud, and soberly acquiesce.    90
Give me the keys. I feel for the common
chord [7] again,
Sliding by semitones, till I sink to the
minor,—yes,
And I blunt it into a ninth,[8] and I stand on
alien ground,
Surveying awhile the heights I rolled from
into the deep;
Which, hark, I have dared and done, for my
resting-place is found,    95
The C Major [9] of this life: so, now I will try
to sleep.

[7] A fundamental tone with its major (4 semitones) or minor (3 semitones) third, and a perfect
fifth (7 semitones) above it.
[8] Either an interval containing an octave and two
semitones (major) or one containing an octave and
one semitone (minor).
[9] This scale contains no sharps or flats.

# Rabbi Ben Ezra [1]

Grow old along with me!
The best is yet to be,
The last of life, for which the first was made:
Our times are in His hand
Who saith, "A whole I planned,                                     5
Youth shows but half; trust God: see all, nor
    be afraid!"

Not that, amassing flowers,
Youth sighed, "Which rose make ours,
Which lily leave and then as best recall?"
Not that, admiring stars,                                          10
It yearned, "Nor Jove, nor Mars;
Mine be some figured flame which blends, tran-
    scends them all!"

Not for such hopes and fears
Annulling youth's brief years,
Do I remonstrate: folly wide the mark!                             15
Rather I prize the doubt
Low kinds exist without,
Finished and finite clods, untroubled by a
    spark.

Poor vaunt of life indeed,
Were man but formed to feed                                        20
On joy, to solely seek and find and feast:
Such feasting ended, then
As sure an end to men;
Irks care the crop full bird? Frets doubt the
    maw-crammed beast?

Rejoice we are allied                                              25
To That which doth provide
And not partake, effect and not receive!
A spark disturbs our clod;
Nearer we hold of God
Who gives, than of His tribes that take, I must
    believe.                                                     30

Then, welcome each rebuff
That turns earth's smoothness rough,
Each sting that bids nor sit nor stand but go!
Be our joys three-parts pain!
Strive, and hold cheap the strain;                                 35
Learn, nor account the pang; dare, never grudge
    the throe!

For thence,—a paradox
Which comforts while it mocks,—

Shall life succeed in that it seems to fail:
What I aspired to be,                                              40
And was not, comforts me:
A brute I might have been, but would not sink
    i' the scale.

What is he but a brute
Whose flesh has soul to suit,
Whose spirit works lest arms and legs want
    play?                                                        45
To man, propose this test—
Thy body at its best,
How far can that project thy soul on its lone
    way?

Yet gifts should prove their use:
I own the Past profuse                                             50
Of power each side, perfection every turn:
Eyes, ears took in their dole,
Brain treasured up the whole;
Should not the heart beat once "How good to
    live and learn"?

Not once beat "Praise be thine!                                    55
I see the whole design,
I, who saw power, see now Love perfect too:
Perfect I call Thy plan:
Thanks that I was a man!
Maker, remake, complete,—I trust what Thou
    shalt do!"                                                   60

For pleasant is this flesh;
Our soul, in its rose-mesh
Pulled ever to the earth, still yearns for rest:
Would we some prize might hold
To match those manifold                                            65
Possessions of the brute,—gain most, as we did
    best!

Let us not always say,
"Spite of this flesh to-day
I strove, made head, gained ground upon the
    whole!"
As the bird wings and sings,                                       70
Let us cry, "All good things
Are ours, nor soul helps flesh more, now, than
    flesh helps soul!"

Therefore I summon age
To grant youth's heritage,
Life's struggle having so far reached its term:    75
Thence shall I pass, approved
A man, for aye removed
From the developed brute; a God though in
    the germ.

And I shall thereupon
Take rest, ere I be gone                                           80
Once more on my adventure brave and new:
Fearless and unperplexed,
When I wage battle next,
What weapons to select, what armor to indue. [2]

[1] Published in 1864. Abenezra, or Ibn Ezra (1092–
1167), was one of the most distinguished Jewish
learned men of the Middle Age, and attained eminence as philosopher, astronomer, physician, and
poet, and particularly as grammarian and commen-
tator. Browning derived much in this poem from his
works, though his own views coincided largely with
Ibn Ezra's teaching. It is also probable that *Rabbi
Ben Ezra* was written as a reply to the philosophy
advanced by Edward FitzGerald in *The Rubáiyát
of Omar Khayyám* (1859).

[2] To put on.

Youth ended, I shall try 85
My gain or loss thereby;
Leave the fire ashes, what survives is gold:
And I shall weigh the same,
Give life its praise or blame:
Young, all lay in dispute; I shall know, being old. 90

For note, when evening shuts,
A certain moment cuts
The deed off, calls the glory from the gray:
A whisper from the west
Shoots—"Add this to the rest, 95
Take it and try its worth: here dies another day."

So, still within this life,
Though lifted o'er its strife,
Let me discern, compare, pronounce at last,
"This rage was right i' the main, 100
That acquiescence vain:
The Future I may face now I have proved the Past."

For more is not reserved
To man, with soul just nerved
To act to-morrow what he learns to-day: 105
Here, work enough to watch
The Master work, and catch
Hints of the proper craft, tricks of the tool's true play.

As it was better, youth
Should strive, through acts uncouth, 110
Toward making, than repose on aught found made:
So, better, age, exempt
From strife, should know, than tempt
Further. Thou waitedst age: wait death nor be afraid!

Enough now, if the Right 115
And Good and Infinite
Be named here, as thou callest thy hand thine own,
With knowledge absolute,
Subject to no dispute
From fools that crowded youth, nor let thee feel alone. 120

Be there, for once and all,
Severed great minds from small,
Announced to each his station in the Past!
Was I, the world arraigned,
Were they, my soul disdained, 125
Right? Let age speak the truth and give us peace at last!

Now, who shall arbitrate?
Ten men love what I hate,
Shun what I follow, slight what I receive;
Ten, who in ears and eyes 130
Match me: we all surmise,

They this thing, and I that: whom shall my soul believe?

Not on the vulgar mass
Called "work," must sentence pass,
Things done, that took the eye and had the price; 135
O'er which, from level stand,
The low world laid its hand,
Found straightway to its mind, could value in a trice:

But all, the world's coarse thumb
And finger failed to plumb, 140
So passed in making up the main account;
All instincts immature,
All purposes unsure,
That weighed not as his work, yet swelled the man's amount:

Thoughts hardly to be packed 145
Into a narrow act,
Fancies that broke through language and escaped;
All I could never be,
All, men ignored in me,
This, I was worth to God, whose wheel the pitcher shaped. 150

Ay, note that Potter's wheel,[3]
That metaphor! and feel
Why time spins fast, why passive lies our clay,—
Thou, to whom fools propound,
When the wine makes its round, 155
"Since life fleets, all is change; the Past gone, seize to-day!"

Fool! All that is, at all,
Lasts ever, past recall;
Earth changes, but thy soul and God stand sure:
What entered into thee, 160
*That* was, is, and shall be:
Time's wheel runs back or stops: Potter and clay endure.

He fixed thee 'mid this dance
Of plastic circumstance,
This Present, thou, forsooth, wouldst fain arrest: 165
Machinery just meant
To give thy soul its bent,
Try thee and turn thee forth, sufficiently impressed.

What though the earlier grooves,
Which ran the laughing loves 170
Around thy base, no longer pause and press;
What though, about thy rim,
Skull-things in order grim
Grow out, in graver mood, obey the sterner stress?

[3] See Isaiah, 64:8; also Jeremiah, 18:1–6.

Look not thou down but up!      175
To uses of a cup,
The festal board, lamp's flash and trumpet's
    peal,
The new wine's foaming flow,
The Master's lips aglow!
Thou, heaven's consummate cup, what needst
    thou with earth's wheel?      180

But I need, now as then,
Thee, God, who moldest men;
And since, not even while the whirl was worst,
Did I—to the wheel of life
With shapes and colors rife,      185
Bound dizzily—mistake my end, to slake Thy
    thirst:

So, take and use Thy work:
Amend what flaws may lurk,
What strain o' the stuff, what warpings past the
    aim!
My times be in Thy hand!      190
Perfect the cup as planned!
Let age approve of youth, and death complete
    the same!

## Prospice [1]

Fear death?—to feel the fog in my throat,
    The mist in my face,
When the snows begin, and the blasts denote
    I am nearing the place,
The power of the night, the press of the storm,
    The post of the foe;      6
Where he stands, the Arch Fear in a visible
    form,
    Yet the strong man must go:
For the journey is done and the summit at-
    tained,
    And the barriers fall,      10
Though a battle's to fight ere the guerdon be
    gained,
    The reward of it all.
I was ever a fighter, so—one fight more,
    The best and the last!
I would hate that death bandaged my eyes, and
    forebore,      15
    And bade me creep past.
No! let me taste the whole of it, fare like my
    peers
    The heroes of old,
Bear the brunt, in a minute pay glad life's ar-
    rears
    Of pain, darkness and cold.      20
For sudden the worst turns the best to the
    brave,
    The black minute's at end,
And the elements' rage, the fiend-voices that
    rave,

Shall dwindle, shall blend,
Shall change, shall become first a peace out of
    pain,      25
    Then a light, then thy breast,
O thou soul of my soul! I shall clasp thee again,
    And with God be the rest!

## Never the Time and the Place [2]

Never the time and the place
    And the loved one all together!
This path—how soft to pace!
    This May—what magic weather!
Where is the loved one's face?      5
In a dream that loved one's face meets mine,
    But the house is narrow, the place is bleak
Where, outside, rain and wind combine
    With a furtive ear, if I strive to speak,
    With a hostile eye at my flushing cheek,      10
With a malice that marks each word, each sign!
O enemy sly and serpentine,
    Uncoil thee from the waking man!
    Do I hold the Past
    Thus firm and fast      15
Yet doubt if the Future hold I can?
This path so soft to pace shall lead
Through the magic of May to herself indeed!
Or narrow if needs the house must be,
Outside are the storms and strangers: we—
Oh, close, safe warm sleep I and she,      21
—I and she!

## Epilogue [3]

At the midnight in the silence of the sleep-time,
    When you set your fancies free,
Will they pass to where—by death, fools think,
    imprisoned—
Low he lies who once so loved you, whom you
    loved so,
        —Pity me?      5

Oh to love so, be so loved, yet so mistaken!
    What had I on earth to do
With the slothful, with the mawkish, the un-
    manly?
Like the aimless, helpless, hopeless, did I drivel
        —Being—who?      10

One who never turned his back but marched
    breast forward,
    Never doubted clouds would break,
Never dreamed, though right were worsted,
    wrong would triumph,
Held we fall to rise, are baffled to fight better,
        Sleep to wake.      15

[1] Published in 1864; written in 1861 not long after
Mrs. Browning's death. The title means, Look forward.

[2] Published in 1883, twenty-two years after Mrs.
Browning's death.

[3] Published in 1889. The poem concludes *Aso-
lando*, the last volume Browning published.

No, at noonday in the bustle of man's work-
time
Greet the unseen [4] with a cheer!

[4] Browning when he is dead.

Bid him forward, breast and back as either
should be,
"Strive and thrive!" cry "Speed,—fight on, fare
ever
There as here!"   20

# John Ruskin

## 1819 - 1900

Ruskin's father was a wine-merchant dealing in sherry. He was a Scotchman, a man of unusual practical ability and of considerable fortune, with conventional views, but possessed of fine taste. He married his first cousin, a woman of great power, with a harsh and deeply religious nature. To them John Ruskin, their only child, was born in London on 8 February, 1819. Few youths have been so completely and so long subjected to the influences of their homes as was Ruskin, and something of the general character of his early years may be gathered from the brief autobiographical passages printed below. After a somewhat irregular course of preparation he entered Christ Church, Oxford, at the age of eighteen, as a gentleman-commoner. His work there was interrupted by bad health which forced him to spend a year and a half abroad, chiefly in Italy. He took his B.A. in May, 1842, receiving an honorary fourth class both in classics and in mathematics. His parents had expected him to become a clergyman, and he disappointed them by refusing either to take holy orders or to enter the sherry trade. What he was to do was not yet perhaps entirely clear to himself, yet he had been since boyhood persistently training himself for writing. Nearly every day since his seventh year he had been writing poetry, and his exercises in prose composition had begun almost as early. Likewise he had been from youth an enthusiastic lover of the landscape art of J. M. W. Turner, convinced as he was that Turner alone of contemporary artists saw nature truly and painted what he saw; and at the age of seventeen he had written an eloquent, impassioned essay in defense of Turner against adverse criticism. Now, his academic career concluded and his future at least negatively determined, he settled down in the autumn and winter of 1842 to the writing of "Turner and the Ancients," as he at first intended to entitle his book. The title was later changed to Modern Painters, and the volume

was published anonymously in 1843. It caused a sensation in both the artistic and literary worlds, and it was almost immediately recognized that a new master had appeared. Ruskin was, indeed, by his successive volumes to work a veritable revolution in taste and to rise to a position of authority as an art-critic unexampled in England. What he did, said William Morris, was "to let a flood of daylight into the cloud of sham-twaddle which was once the whole substance of art-criticism." And he did this with an assurance, an eloquence, a wealth of ingenious illustration, and a splendor of language which fairly swept many contemporaries off their feet. The basis of his work, moreover, was exceedingly simple. He preached in his own way essentially the great lesson of Carlyle, by whom he was much influenced;— he preached that better than all things else in the world is truth. He asked of artists only that they should submit themselves, humbly and obediently, to the truth of nature, and told them that in this way, and in this way alone, they could discover the highest inspiration and learn how to use their pencils and their brushes in the noble fashion of the master.

Ruskin was twenty-four when the first volume of Modern Painters was published; despite his manifest genius and his thoughtfulness above his years, he obviously had some things yet to learn. As new chapters in the history of art were opened up to him by travel and study the original plan of Modern Painters was changed and expanded, and in addition Ruskin was more than once drawn aside into other work, with the result that the fifth and final volume did not appear until 1860. In the intervening years occurred his unhappy marriage to Euphemia Chalmers Gray, which took place in April, 1848, and which was a few years later annulled on the petition of Mrs. Ruskin. In those years, too, he wrote The Seven Lamps of Architecture (1849)—Truth, Beauty, Power, Sacrifice, Obedience, Labor, Memory—in which he did for the art of building what he had already done for painting, and The Stones of Venice (1851–1853), which is, so to say, a practical amplification of the Seven Lamps, applying its doctrine to the defense of Gothic architecture.

From the first Ruskin's art-criticism was a consideration of the conditions under which great works of art may come into being, and from the first Ruskin regarded the good, the true, and the beautiful as ultimately one in their nature. In other words, he taught that beauty is at bottom the concomitant or outgrowth of a right and true system of values, and that ugliness consequently must be the expression of a wrong or low or false system of values. And as he went on with his work he saw more and more clearly that this conviction implied that only a good man could be a great artist. Thus it was that the Seven Lamps was written to show, as he later explained, "that certain right states of temper and moral feeling were the magic powers by which all good architecture without exception had been produced. The Stones of Venice had, from beginning to end, no other aim than to show that the Gothic architecture of Venice had arisen out of, and indicated in all its features, a state of pure national faith and of domestic virtue; and that its Renaissance architecture had arisen out of, and in all its features indicated, a state of concealed national infidelity and of domestic corruption." This, then, is the secret of his transition in middle life from the role of art-critic to that of social reformer. The two are ordinarily thought of as very different activities, but in Ruskin the social reformer grew naturally, indeed inevitably, out of the art-critic, and to separate them from each other is in his case to misunderstand both. From the late eighteen-fifties until the close of his active life he gave himself increasingly to social work, and wrote, and spent his money, in the effort to arouse the upper classes to a sense of their responsibilities and to help the poor to rise out of the misery and ugliness which surrounded them. Some of the books which preserve the writings of this period are Unto this Last, Munera Pulveris, Time and Tide, Fors Clavigera, Sesame and Lilies, and The Crown of Wild Olive. In these Ruskin no doubt often wrote rashly, as was indeed his habit in all his work, and he aroused bitter feeling which at the moment seemed to go far towards destroying the reputation he had previously built up for himself. Time has, however, been remarkably on Ruskin's side, and it is today an astonishing and illuminating

thing to count up for one's self the number of his one-time social heresies which have since become accepted commonplaces.

In his later life Ruskin was for some years the Slade Professor of Fine Art at Oxford, where his lectures drew very large audiences. After his retirement from Oxford he wrote those autobiographical sketches which were published under the title Praeterita. He died on 20 January, 1900. He had once said: "Life without industry is guilt, and industry without art is brutality." This sentence sums up better than could any other words the meaning of all his work.

The standard edition, never likely to be superseded, of the complete Works of Ruskin is the "Library Edition," ed. E. T. Cook and Alexander Wedderburn (39 vols., London, 1903–1912). The standard biography is The Life of John Ruskin by E. T. Cook (2 vols., London, 1911). The Diaries of John Ruskin are edited by Joan Evans and John Howard Whitehouse (Oxford, 1956–   ). The most convenient one-volume edition is Selected Writings, edited by Peter Quennell (London, 1952). Biographical and critical studies of Ruskin are numerous, and only a few can be mentioned: John Ruskin, Social Reformer, by J. A. Hobson (London, 1898); John Ruskin by Mrs. Meynell (New York, 1900); John Ruskin by Frederic Harrison ("English Men of Letters" series, 1902); Ruskin, A Study in Personality, by A. C. Benson (New York, 1911); John Ruskin, An Introduction to Further Study of His Life and Work, by R. H. Wilenski (London, 1933); Ruskin, the Great Victorian, by Derrick Leon (London, 1949); John Ruskin, Portrait of a Prophet, by Peter Quennell (London, 1949); and John Ruskin, by Joan Evans (London, 1954).

# Praeterita

## EARLY READING AND SUMMER TRAVEL [1]

I am, and my father was before me, a violent Tory of the old school;—Walter Scott's school, that is to say, and Homer's. I name these two out of the numberless great Tory writers, because they were my own two masters. I had Walter Scott's novels, and the *Iliad* (Pope's translation), for constant reading when I was

[1] *Praeterita* (things gone by) was published in chapters at irregular intervals from 1885 to 1889. This passage is from vol. I, chap. i, which consists of slightly revised passages from *Fors Clavigera*, written 1871–1875.

a child, on week-days: on Sunday, their effect was tempered by *Robinson Crusoe* and the *Pilgrim's Progress*; my mother having it deeply in her heart to make an evangelical clergyman of me. Fortunately, I had an aunt more evangelical than my mother; and my aunt gave me cold mutton for Sunday's dinner, which—as I much preferred it hot—greatly diminished the influence of the *Pilgrim's Progress*; and the end of the matter was, that I got all the noble [10] imaginative teaching of Defoe and Bunyan, and yet—am not an evangelical clergyman.

I had, however, still better teaching than theirs, and that compulsorily, and every day of the week.

Walter Scott and Pope's Homer were reading of my own election, and my mother forced me, by steady daily toil, to learn long chapters of the Bible by heart; as well as to read it every syllable through, aloud, hard names and all, [20] from Genesis to the Apocalypse, about once a year: and to that discipline—patient, accurate, and resolute—I owe, not only a knowledge of the book, which I find occasionally serviceable, but much of my general power of taking pains, and the best part of my taste in literature. From Walter Scott's novels I might easily, as I grew older, have fallen to other people's novels; and Pope might, perhaps, have led me to take Johnson's English, or Gibbon's, as types of lan- [30] guage; but once knowing the 32nd of Deuteronomy, the 119th Psalm, the 15th of 1st Corinthians, the Sermon on the Mount, and most of the Apocalypse, every syllable by heart, and having always a way of thinking with myself what words meant, it was not possible for me, even in the foolishest times of youth, to write entirely superficial or formal English; and the affectation of trying to write like Hooker and George Herbert was the most innocent I could [40] have fallen into.

From my own chosen masters, then, Scott and Homer, I learned the Toryism which my best after-thought has only served to confirm.

That is to say, a most sincere love of kings, and dislike of everybody who attempted to disobey them. Only, both by Homer and Scott, I was taught strange ideas about kings, which I find for the present much obsolete; for, I perceived that both the author of the *Iliad* and [50] the author of *Waverley* made their kings, or king-loving persons, do harder work than anybody else. Tydides or Idomeneus always killed twenty Trojans to other people's one, and Redgauntlet speared more salmon than any of the Solway fishermen; [2] and—which was particu-

larly a subject of admiration to me—I observed that they not only did more, but in proportion to their doings *got* less, than other people—nay, that the best of them were even ready to govern for nothing! and let their followers divide any quantity of spoil or profit. Of late it has seemed to me that the idea of a king has become exactly the contrary of this, and that it has been supposed the duty of superior persons generally to govern less, and get more, than anybody else. So that it was, perhaps, quite as well that in those early days my contemplation of existent kingship was a very distant one.

The aunt who gave me cold mutton on Sundays was my father's sister: she lived at Bridgeend, in the town of Perth, and had a garden full of gooseberry-bushes, sloping down to the Tay, with a door opening to the water, which ran past it, clear-brown over the pebbles three or four feet deep; swift-eddying,—an infinite thing for a child to look down into.

My father began business as a winemerchant, with no capital, and a considerable amount of debts bequeathed him by my grandfather. He accepted the bequest, and paid them all before he began to lay by anything for himself,—for which his best friends called him a fool, and I, without expressing any opinion as to his wisdom, which I knew in such matters to be at least equal to mine, have written on the granite slab over his grave that he was "an entirely honest merchant." As days went on he was able to take a house in Hunter Street, Brunswick Square, No. 54 (the windows of it, fortunately for me, commanded a view of a marvelous iron post, out of which the water-carts were filled through beautiful little trap-doors, by pipes like boa-constrictors; and I was never weary of contemplating that mystery, and the delicious dripping consequent); and as years went on, and I came to be four or five years old, he could command a postchaise and pair for two months in the summer, by help of which, with my mother and me, he went the round of his country customers (who liked to see the principal of the house his own traveler); so that, at a jog-trot pace, and through the panoramic opening of the four windows of a postchaise, made more panoramic still to me because my seat was a little bracket in front (for we used to hire the chaise regularly for the two months out of Long Acre, and so could have it bracketed and pocketed as we

[2] For Diomed (son of Tydeus) see such a pas-

sage in Pope's *Iliad* as x, 560; for Idomeneus, xiii, 457. For Redgauntlet see Letter 4 of Scott's novel of the same name.

liked), I saw all the highroads, and most of the cross ones, of England and Wales; and great part of lowland Scotland, as far as Perth, where every other year we spent the whole summer: and I used to read the *Abbot* at Kinross, and the *Monastery* in Glen Farg, which I confused with "Glendearg," and thought that the White Lady had as certainly lived by the streamlet in that glen of the Ochils, as the Queen of Scots in the island of Loch Leven.

To my farther great benefit, as I grew older, I thus saw nearly all the noblemen's houses in England; in reverent and healthy delight of uncovetous admiration,—perceiving, as soon as I could perceive any political truth at all, that it was probably much happier to live in a small house, and have Warwick Castle to be astonished at, than to live in Warwick Castle and have nothing to be astonished at; but that, at all events, it would not make Brunswick Square in the least more pleasantly habitable, to pull Warwick Castle down. And at this day, though I have kind invitations enough to visit America, I could not, even for a couple of months, live in a country so miserable as to possess no castles.

Nevertheless, having formed my notion of kinghood chiefly from the FitzJames of the *Lady of the Lake,* and of noblesse from the Douglas there, and the Douglas in *Marmion,* a painful wonder soon arose in my child mind, why the castles should now be always empty. Tantallon was there; but no Archibald of Angus:—Stirling, but no Knight of Snowdoun. The galleries and gardens of England were beautiful to see— but his Lordship and her Ladyship were always in town, said the housekeepers and gardeners. Deep yearning took hold of me for a kind of "Restoration," which I began slowly to feel that Charles the Second had not altogether effected, though I always wore a gilded oak-apple very piously in my button-hole on the 29th of May. It seemed to me that Charles the Second's Restoration had been, as compared with the Restoration I wanted, much as that gilded oak-apple to a real apple. And as I grew wiser, the desire for sweet pippins instead of bitter ones, and Living Kings instead of dead ones, appeared to me rational as well as romantic; and gradually it has become the main purpose of my life to grow pippins, and its chief hope, to see Kings.

### DAILY LIFE AT HERNE HILL [1]

When I was about four years old my father found himself able to buy the lease of a house

on Herne Hill, a rustic eminence four miles south of the "Standard in Cornhill"; [2] of which the leafy seclusion remains, in all essential points of character, unchanged to this day: certain Gothic splendors, lately indulged in by our wealthier neighbors, being the only serious innovations; and these are so graciously concealed by the fine trees of their grounds, that the passing viator [3] remains unappalled by them; and I can still walk up and down the piece of road between the Fox tavern and the Herne Hill station, imagining myself four years old.

Our house was the northernmost of a group which stand accurately on the top or dome of the hill, where the ground is for a small space level, as the snows are (I understand), on the dome of Mont Blanc; presently falling, however, in what may be, in the London clay formation, considered a precipitous slope, to our valley of Chamouni (or of Dulwich) on the east; and with a softer descent into Cold Harbor-lane on the west: on the south, no less beautifully declining to the dale of the Effra (doubtless shortened from Effrena, signifying the "Unbridled" river; recently, I regret to say, bricked over for the convenience of Mr. Biffin, chemist, and others); while on the north, prolonged indeed with slight depression some half mile or so, and receiving, in the parish of Lambeth, the chivalric title of "Champion Hill," it plunges down at last to efface itself in the plains of Peckham, and the rural barbarism of Goose Green.

The group, of which our house was the quarter, consisted of two precisely similar partner-couples of houses, gardens and all to match; still the two highest blocks of buildings seen from Norwood on the crest of the ridge; so that the house itself, three-stories, with garrets above, commanded, in those comparatively smokeless days, a very notable view from its garret windows, of the Norwood hills on one side, and the winter sunrise over them; and of the valley of the Thames on the other, with Windsor telescopically clear in the distance, and Harrow, conspicuous always in fine weather to open vision against the summer sunset. It had front and back garden in sufficient proportion to its size; the front, richly set with old evergreens, and well-grown lilac and laburnum;

---

[1] From vol. I, chap. ii, the greater part of which consists of slightly revised passages from *Fors Clavigera,* written 1873–1875.

[2] A standard was a lofty structure containing a vertical conduit pipe with spouts and taps for supplying water to the public. This one, built in 1582, stood near the junction of Cornhill with Leadenhall Street.

[3] Traveler.

the back, seventy yards long by twenty wide, renowned over all the hill for its pears and apples, which had been chosen with extreme care by our predecessor (shame on me to forget the name of a man to whom I owe so much!)— and possessing also a strong old mulberry tree, a tall white-heart cherry tree, a black Kentish one, and an almost unbroken hedge, all round, of alternate gooseberry and currant bush; decked, in due season (for the ground was wholly beneficent), with magical splendor of abundant fruit: fresh green, soft amber, and rough-bristled crimson bending the spinous branches; clustered pearl and pendent ruby joyfully discoverable under the large leaves that looked like vine.

The differences of primal importance which I observed between the nature of this garden, and that of Eden, as I had imagined it, were, that, in this one, *all* the fruit was forbidden; and there were no companionable beasts: in other respects the little domain answered every purpose of Paradise to me; and the climate, in that cycle of our years, allowed me to pass most of my life in it. My mother never gave me more to learn than she knew I could easily get learned, if I set myself honestly to work, by twelve o'clock. She never allowed anything to disturb me when my task was set; if it was not said rightly by twelve o'clock, I was kept in till I knew it, and in general, even when Latin Grammar came to supplement the Psalms, I was my own master for at least an hour before half-past one dinner, and for the rest of the afternoon.

My mother, herself finding her chief personal pleasure in her flowers, was often planting or pruning beside me, at least if I chose to stay beside *her.* I never thought of doing anything behind her back which I would not have done before her face; and her presence was therefore no restraint to me; but, also, no particular pleasure, for, from having always been left so much alone, I had generally my own little affairs to see after; and, on the whole, by the time I was seven years old, was already getting too independent, mentally, even of my father and mother; and, having nobody else to be dependent upon, began to lead a very small, perky, contented, conceited, Cock-Robinson-Crusoe sort of life, in the central point which it appeared to me (as it must naturally appear to geometrical animals) that I occupied in the universe.

This was partly the fault of my father's modesty; and partly of his pride. He had so much more confidence in my mother's judgment as to such matters than in his own, that he never

ventured even to help, much less to cross her, in the conduct of my education; on the other hand, in the fixed purpose of making an ecclesiastical gentleman of me, with the superfinest of manners, and access to the highest circles of fleshly and spiritual society, the visits to Croydon, where I entirely loved my aunt,[4] and young baker-cousins, became rarer and more rare: the society of our neighbors on the hill could not be had without breaking up our regular and sweetly selfish manner of living; and on the whole, I had nothing animate to care for, in a childish way, but myself, some nests of ants, which the gardener would never leave undisturbed for me, and a sociable bird or two; though I never had the sense of perseverance to make one really tame. But that was partly because, if ever I managed to bring one to be the least trustful of me, the cats got it.

Under these circumstances, what powers of imagination I possessed, either fastened themselves on inanimate things—the sky, the leaves, and pebbles, observable within the walls of Eden—or caught at any opportunity of flight into regions of romance, compatible with the objective realities of existence in the nineteenth century, within a mile and a quarter of Camberwell Green.

Herein my father, happily, though with no definite intention other than of pleasing me, when he found he could do so without infringing any of my mother's rules, became my guide. I was particularly fond of watching him shave; and was always allowed to come into his room in the morning (under the one in which I am now writing), to be the motionless witness of that operation. Over his dressing-table hung one of his own water-color drawings, made under the teaching of the elder Nasmyth; I believe, at the High School of Edinburgh. It was done in the early manner of tinting, which, just about the time when my father was at the High School, Dr. Munro[5] was teaching Turner; namely, in gray under-tints of Prussian blue and British ink, washed with warm color afterward on the lights. It represented Conway Castle, with its Frith, and, in the foreground, a cottage, a fisherman, and a boat at the water's edge.

When my father had finished shaving, he always told me a story about this picture. The custom began without any initial purpose of

[4] The sister of Ruskin's mother, who married a baker in Croydon named Richardson.

[5] Thomas Munro (1759–1833), a physician and an early patron of J. M. W. Turner (1775–1851), the landscape artist, who was responsible for Ruskin's beginning *Modern Painters*.

his, in consequence of my troublesome curiosity whether the fisherman lived in the cottage, and where he was going to in the boat. It being settled, for peace' sake, that he *did* live in the cottage, and was going in the boat to fish near the castle, the plot of the drama afterward gradually thickened; and became, I believe, involved with that of the tragedy of *Douglas*, and of the *Castle Specter*,[6] in both of which pieces my father had performed in private theatricals, before my mother, and a select Edinburgh audience, when he was a boy of sixteen, and she, at grave twenty, a model housekeeper, and very scornful and religiously suspicious of theatricals. But she was never weary of telling me, in later years, how beautiful my father looked in his Highland dress, with the high black feathers.

In the afternoons, when my father returned (always punctually) from his business, he dined, at half-past four, in the front parlor, my mother sitting beside him to hear the events of the day, and give counsel and encouragement with respect to the same;—chiefly the last, for my father was apt to be vexed if orders for sherry fell the least short of their due standard, even for a day or two. I was never present at this time, however, and only avouch what I relate by hearsay and probable conjecture; for between four and six it would have been a grave misdemeanor in me if I so much as approached the parlor door. After that, in summer time, we were all in the garden as long as the day lasted; tea under the white-cherry tree; or in winter and rough weather, at six o'clock in the drawing-room,—I having my cup of milk, and slice of bread-and-butter, in a little recess, with a table in front of it, wholly sacred to me; and in which I remained in the evenings as an Idol in a niche, while my mother knitted, and my father read to her,—and to me, so far as I chose to listen.

The series of the Waverley novels, then drawing towards its close, was still the chief source of delight in all households caring for literature; and I can no more recollect the time when I did not know them than when I did not know the Bible; but I have still a vivid remembrance of my father's intense expression of sorrow mixed with scorn, as he threw down *Count Robert of Paris*, after reading three or four pages; and knew that the life of Scott was ended: the scorn being a very complex and bitter feeling in him,—partly, indeed,

⁶ The former by John Home (published in 1757), the latter by M. G. ("Monk") Lewis, played at Drury Lane Theater in 1798.

of the book itself, but chiefly of the wretches who were tormenting and selling the wrecked intellect, and not a little, deep down, of the subtle dishonesty which had essentially caused the ruin. My father never could forgive Scott his concealment of the Ballantyne partnership.

Such being the salutary pleasures of Herne Hill, I have next with deeper gratitude to chronicle what I owe to my mother for the resolutely consistent lessons which so exercised me in the Scriptures as to make every word of them familiar to my ear in habitual music,—yet in that familiarity reverenced, as transcending all thought, and ordaining all conduct.

This she effected, not by her own sayings or personal authority; but simply by compelling me to read the book thoroughly, for myself. As soon as I was able to read with fluency, she began a course of Bible work with me, which never ceased till I went to Oxford. She read alternate verses with me, watching, at first, every intonation of my voice, and correcting the false ones, till she made me understand the verse, if within my reach, rightly, and energetically. It might be beyond me altogether; that she did not care about; but she made sure that as soon as I got hold of it at all, I should get hold of it by the right end.

In this way she began with the first verse of Genesis, and went straight through, to the last verse of the Apocalypse; hard names, numbers, Levitical law, and all; and began again at Genesis the next day. If a name was hard, the better the exercise in pronunciation,—if the chapter was tiresome, the better lesson in patience,—if loathsome, the better lesson in faith that there was some use in its being so outspoken. After our chapters (from two to three a day, according to their length, the first thing after breakfast, and no interruption from servants allowed,—none from visitors, who either joined in the reading or had to stay upstairs,—and none from any visitings or excursions, except real traveling), I had to learn a few verses by heart, or repeat, to make sure I had not lost, something of what was already known; and, with the chapters thus gradually possessed from the first word to the last, I had to learn the whole body of the fine old Scottish paraphrases, which are good, melodious, and forceful verse; and to which, together with the Bible itself, I owe the first cultivation of my ear in sound.

It is strange that of all the pieces of the Bible which my mother thus taught me, that which cost me most to learn, and which was, to my child's mind, chiefly repulsive—the 119th Psalm—has now become of all the most precious to me, in its overflowing and glorious passion of love for the Law of God, in opposition to the abuse of it by modern preachers of what they imagine to be His gospel.

But it is only by deliberate effort that I recall the long morning hours of toil, as regular as sunrise,—toil on both sides equal—by which, year after year, my mother forced me to learn these paraphrases, and chapters (the eighth of 1st Kings being one—try it, good reader, in a leisure hour!), allowing not so much as a syllable to be missed or misplaced; while every sentence was required to be said over and over again till she was satisfied with the accent of it. I recollect a struggle between us of about three weeks, concerning the accent of the "of" in the lines

> Shall any following spring revive
> The ashes of the urn? [7]—

I insisting, partly in childish obstinacy, and partly in true instinct for rhythm (being wholly careless on the subject both of urns and their contents), on reciting it with an accented *of*. It was not, I say, till after three weeks' labor, that my mother got the accent lightened on the "of" and laid on the ashes, to her mind. But had it taken three years she would have done it, having once undertaken to do it. And, assuredly, had she not done it,—well, there's no knowing what would have happened; but I'm very thankful she *did*.

I have just opened my oldest (in use) Bible, —a small, closely, and very neatly printed volume it is, printed in Edinburgh by Sir D. Hunter Blair and J. Bruce, Printers of the King's Most Excellent Majesty, in 1816. Yellow, now, with age; and flexible, but not unclean, with much use; except that the lower corners of the pages at 8th of 1st Kings, and 32nd Deuteronomy, are worn somewhat thin and dark, the learning of these two chapters having cost me much pains. My mother's list of the chapters with which, thus learned, she established my soul in life, has just fallen out of it. I will take what indulgence the incurious reader can give me, for printing the list thus accidentally occurrent:—

Exodus,          chapters 15th and 20th.
2 Samuel,        "    1st, from 17th verse to end.
I Kings,         "    8th.
Psalms,          "    23rd, 32nd, 90th, 91st, 103rd, 112th, 119th, 139th.
Proverbs,        "    2nd, 3rd, 8th, 12th.

[7] By John Logan, in one of the *Scottish Church Paraphrases*.

Isaiah,          "    58th.
Matthew,         "    5th, 6th, 7th.
Acts,            "    26th.
I Corinthians,   "    13th, 15th.
James,           "    4th.
Revelation,      "    5th, 6th.

And, truly, though I have picked up the elements of a little further knowledge—in mathematics, meteorology, and the like, in after life,— and owe not a little to the teaching of many people, this maternal installation of my mind in that property of chapters I count very confidently the most precious, and, on the whole, the one *essential* part of all my education.

# Modern Painters

## DEFINITION OF GREATNESS IN ART [1]

In the 15th Lecture of Sir Joshua Reynolds,[2] incidental notice is taken of the distinction between those excellences in the painter which belong to him *as such*, and those which belong to him in common with all men of intellect, the general and exalted powers of which art is the evidence and expression, not the subject. But the distinction is not there dwelt upon as it should be, for it is owing to the slight attention ordinarily paid to it, that criticism is open to every form of coxcombry, and liable to every phase of error. It is a distinction on which depend all sound judgment of the rank of the artist, and all just appreciation of the dignity of art.

Painting, or art generally, as such, with all its technicalities, difficulties, and particular ends, is nothing but a noble and expressive language, invaluable as the vehicle of thought, but by itself nothing. He who has learned what is commonly considered the whole art of painting, that is, the art of representing any natural object faithfully, has as yet only learned the language by which his thoughts are to be expressed. He has done just as much towards being that which we ought to respect as a great painter, as a man who has learned how to express himself grammatically and melodiously has towards being a great poet. The language is, indeed, more difficult of acquirement in the one case than in the other, and possesses more power of delighting the sense, while it speaks to the intellect; but it is, nevertheless, nothing more than language, and all those excellences

[1] Vol. I (published in 1843), part I, section 1, chapter 2.
[2] During his presidency of the Royal Academy Reynolds delivered a series of lectures, or discourses as they are usually called (1769–1790).

which are peculiar to the painter as such, are merely what rhythm, melody, precision, and force are in the words of the orator and the poet, necessary to their greatness, but not the tests of their greatness. It is not by the mode of representing and saying, but by what is represented and said, that the respective greatness either of the painter or the writer is to be finally determined.

Speaking with strict propriety, therefore, we should call a man a great painter only as he excelled in precision and force in the language of lines, and a great versifier, as he excelled in precision and force in the language of words. A great poet would then be a term strictly, and in precisely the same sense, applicable to both, if warranted by the character of the images or thoughts which each in their respective languages conveyed.

Take, for instance, one of the most perfect poems or pictures (I use the words as synonymous) which modern times have seen:—the "Old Shepherd's Chief-mourner." [3] Here the exquisite execution of the glossy and crisp hair of the dog, the bright sharp touching of the green bough beside it, the clear [4] painting of the wood of the coffin and the folds of the blanket, are language—language clear and expressive in the highest degree. But the close pressure of the dog's breast against the wood, the convulsive clinging of the paws, which has dragged the blanket off the trestle, the total powerlessness of the head laid, close and motionless, upon its folds, the fixed and tearful fall of the eye in its utter hopelessness, the rigidity of repose which marks that there has been no motion nor change in the trance of agony since the last blow was struck on the coffin-lid, the quietness and gloom of the chamber, the spectacles marking the place where the Bible was last closed, indicating how lonely has been the life, how unwatched the departure, of him who is now laid solitary in his sleep;—these are all thoughts—thoughts by which the picture is separated at once from hundreds of equal merit, as far as mere painting goes, by which it ranks as a work of high art, and stamps its author, not as the neat imitator of the texture of a skin, or the fold of a drapery, but as the Man of Mind.

It is not, however, always easy, either in painting or literature, to determine where the influence of language stops, and where that of thought begins. Many thoughts are so dependent upon the language in which they are clothed, that they would lose half their beauty if otherwise expressed. But the highest thoughts are those which are least dependent on language, and the dignity of any composition, and praise to which it is entitled, are in exact proportion to its independency of language or expression. A composition is indeed usually most perfect, when to such intrinsic dignity is added all that expression can do to attract and adorn; but in every case of supreme excellence this all becomes as nothing. We are more gratified by the simplest lines or words which can suggest the idea in its own naked beauty, than by the robe and the gem which conceal while they decorate; we are better pleased to feel by their absence how little they could bestow, than by their presence how much they can destroy.

There is therefore a distinction to be made between what is ornamental in language and what is expressive. That part of it which is necessary to the embodying and conveying of the thought is worthy of respect and attention as necessary to excellence, though not the test of it. But that part of it which is decorative has little more to do with the intrinsic excellence of the picture than the frame or the varnishing of it. And this caution in distinguishing between the ornamental and the expressive is peculiarly necessary in painting: for in the language of words it is nearly impossible for that which is not expressive to be beautiful, except by mere rhythm or melody, any sacrifice to which is immediately stigmatized as error. But the beauty of mere language in painting is not only very attractive and entertaining to the spectator, but requires for its attainment no small exertion of mind and devotion of time by the artist. Hence, in art, men have frequently fancied that they were becoming rhetoricians and poets when they were only learning to speak melodiously, and the judge has over and over again advanced to the honor of authors those who were never more than ornamental writing-masters.

Most pictures of the Dutch school, for instance, excepting always those of Rubens, Vandyke, and Rembrandt, are ostentatious exhibitions of the artist's power of speech, the clear and vigorous elocution of useless and senseless words; while the early efforts of Cimabue [5] and Giotto [6] are the burning messages of prophecy, delivered by the stammering lips of infants. It

---

[3] By Sir Edwin Landseer, now in the Victoria and Albert South Kensington Museum.

[4] "Clear" is printed in all the editions, and so is retained here, but Ruskin originally wrote "clever" and probably never detected the misprint.

[5] Florentine painter (1240?–1302?).

[6] Florentine painter and architect (1276?–1337?).

is not by ranking the former as more than mechanics, or the latter as less than artists, that
the taste of the multitude, always awake to the
lowest pleasures which art can bestow, and
blunt to the highest, is to be formed or elevated. It must be the part of the judicious critic
carefully to distinguish what is language, and
what is thought, and to rank and praise pictures chiefly for the latter, considering the
former as a totally inferior excellence, and one 10
which cannot be compared with nor weighed
against thought in any way or in any degree
whatsoever. The picture which has the nobler
and more numerous ideas, however awkwardly
expressed, is a greater and a better picture than
that which has the less noble and less numerous
ideas, however beautifully expressed. No weight,
nor mass, nor beauty of execution, can outweigh
one grain or fragment of thought. Three pen-
strokes of Raffaelle are a greater and a better 20
picture than the most finished work that ever
Carlo Dolci [7] polished into inanity. A finished
work of a great artist is only better than its
sketch, if the sources of pleasure belonging to
color and realization—valuable in themselves—
are so employed as to increase the impressiveness of the thought. But if one atom of thought
has vanished, all color, all finish, all execution,
all ornament, are too dearly bought. Nothing
but thought can pay for thought, and the in- 30
stant that the increasing refinement or finish of
the picture begins to be paid for by the loss of
the faintest shadow of an idea, that instant all
refinement or finish is an excrescence and a
deformity.

Yet although in all our speculations on art,
language is thus to be distinguished from, and
held subordinate to, that which it conveys, we
must still remember that there are certain ideas
inherent in language itself, and that, strictly 40
speaking, every pleasure connected with art has
in it some reference to the intellect. The mere
sensual pleasure of the eye, received from the
most brilliant piece of coloring, is as nothing
to that which it receives from a crystal prism,
except as it depends on our perception of a
certain meaning and intended arrangement of
color, which has been the subject of intellect.
Nay, the term idea, according to Locke's [8] definition of it, will extend even to the sensual im- 50
pressions themselves as far as they are "things
which the mind occupies itself about in thinking"; that is, not as they are felt by the eye

[7] Tuscan painter (1616–1686).
[8] John Locke (1632–1704). The following quotation comes from Bk. II, chap. i, of the *Essay Concerning Human Understanding.*

only, but as they are received by the mind
through the eye. So that, if I say that the
greatest picture is that which conveys to the
mind of the spectator the greatest number of
the greatest ideas, I have a definition which
will include as subjects of comparison every
pleasure which art is capable of conveying. If
I were to say, on the contrary, that the best
picture was that which most closely imitated
nature, I should assume that art could only
please by imitating nature; and I should cast
out of the pale of criticism those parts of works
of art which are not imitative, that is to say, intrinsic beauties of color and form, and those
works of art wholly, which, like the Arabesques
of Raffaelle in the Loggias,[9] are not imitative
at all. Now, I want a definition of art wide
enough to include all its varieties of aim. I do
not say, therefore, that the art is greatest which
gives most pleasure, because perhaps there is 20
some art whose end is to teach, and not to
please. I do not say that the art is greatest
which teaches us most, because perhaps there
is some art whose end is to please, and not to
teach. I do not say that the art is greatest
which imitates best, because perhaps there is
some art whose end is to create and not to
imitate. But I say that the art is greatest which
conveys to the mind of the spectator, by any
means whatsoever, the greatest number of the 30
greatest ideas; and I call an idea great in proportion as it is received by a higher faculty of
the mind, and as it more fully occupies, and in
occupying, exercises and exalts, the faculty by
which it is received.

If this, then, be the definition of great art,
that of a great artist naturally follows. He is
the greatest artist who has embodied, in the
sum of his works, the greatest number of the
greatest ideas. 40

## LA RICCIA [1]

There is, in the first room of the National
Gallery, a landscape attributed to Gaspar Poussin,[2] called sometimes Aricia, sometimes Le or
La Riccia, according to the fancy of catalogue
printers. Whether it can be supposed to resemble the ancient Aricia, now La Riccia, close to
Albano, I will not take upon me to determine, 50
seeing that most of the towns of these old mas-

[9] Of the Vatican, Rome.
[1] Volume I, part II, section 2, from chapter 2,
"Of Truth of Color."
[2] French landscape painter (1613–1675), brother-
in-law and pupil of the more famous Nicolas Poussin.

ters are quite as like one place as another; but, at any rate, it is a town on a hill, wooded with two-and-thirty bushes, of very uniform size, and possessing about the same number of leaves each. These bushes are all painted in with one dull opaque brown, becoming very slightly greenish toward the lights, and discover in one place a bit of rock, which of course would in nature have been cool and gray beside the lustrous hues of foliage, and which, therefore, being moreover completely in shade, is consistently and scientifically painted of a very clear, pretty, and positive brick red, the only thing like color in the picture. The foreground is a piece of road which, in order to make allowance for its greater nearness, for its being completely in light, and, it may be presumed, for the quantity of vegetation usually present on carriage-roads, is given in a very cool green gray; and the truth of the picture is completed by a number of dots in the sky on the right, with a stalk to them, of a sober and similar brown.[3]

Not long ago, I was slowly descending this very bit of carriage-road, the first turn after you leave Albano, not a little impeded by the worthy successors of the ancient prototypes of Veiento.[4] It had been wild weather when I left Rome, and all across the Campagna the clouds were sweeping in sulphurous blue, with a clap of thunder or two, and breaking gleams of sun along the Claudian aqueduct lighting up the infinity of its arches like the bridge of chaos. But as I climbed the long slope of the Alban Mount, the storm swept finally to the north, and the noble outline of the domes of Albano, and graceful darkness of its ilex grove rose against pure streaks of alternate blue and amber; the upper sky gradually flushing through the last fragments of rain-cloud in deep palpitating azure, half ether and half dew. The noonday sun came slanting down the rocky slopes of La Riccia, and their masses of entangled and tall foliage, whose autumnal tints were mixed with the wet verdure of a thousand evergreens, were penetrated with it as with rain. I cannot call it color, it was conflagration. Purple, and crimson, and scarlet, like the curtains of God's tabernacle, the rejoicing trees sank into the valley in showers of light, every separate leaf quivering with buoyant and burning life; each,

as it turned to reflect or to transmit the sunbeam, first a torch and then an emerald. Far up into the recesses of the valley, the green vistas arched like the hollows of mighty waves of some crystalline sea, with the arbutus flowers dashed along their flanks for foam, and silver flakes of orange spray tossed into the air around them, breaking over the gray walls of rock into a thousand separate stars, fading and kindling alternately as the weak wind lifted and let them fall. Every glade of grass burned like the golden floor of heaven, opening in sudden gleams as the foliage broke and closed above it, as sheet-lightning opens in a cloud at sunset; the motionless masses of dark rock—dark though flushed with scarlet lichen, casting their quiet shadows across its restless radiance, the fountain underneath them filling its marble hollow with blue mist and fitful sound; and over all, the multitudinous bars of amber and rose, the sacred clouds that have no darkness, and only exist to illumine, were seen in fathomless intervals between the solemn and orbed repose of the stone pines, passing to lose themselves in the last, white, blinding luster of the measureless line where the Campagna melted into the blaze of the sea.

## OF MODERN LANDSCAPE [1]

We turn our eyes, therefore, as boldly and as quickly as may be, from these serene fields and skies of medieval art,[2] to the most characteristic examples of modern landscape. And, I believe, the first thing that will strike us, or that ought to strike us, is their *cloudiness*.

Out of perfect light and motionless air, we find ourselves on a sudden brought under somber skies, and into drifting wind; and, with fickle sunbeams flashing in our face, or utterly drenched with sweep of rain, we are reduced to track the changes of the shadows on the grass, or watch the rents of twilight through angry cloud. And we find that whereas all the pleasure of the medieval was in *stability, definiteness*, and *luminousness*, we are expected to rejoice in darkness, and triumph in mutability; to lay the foundation of happiness in things which momentarily change or fade; and to expect the utmost satisfaction and instruction from what it is impossible to arrest, and difficult to comprehend.

We find, however, together with this general delight in breeze and darkness, much atten-

---

[3] It should be said that this picture was very dirty when Ruskin wrote the first volume of *Modern Painters*. In 1880 it was cleaned and varnished.

[4] I. e., by beggars (Ruskin refers to a passage in Juvenal—*Sat.*, IV, 116—where, however, it is one Catullus, and not Veiento, who is described as fit only to beg alms on the Arician road).

[1] Volume III, part IV, from chapter 16.

[2] The preceding chapter is entitled "Of Medieval Landscape."

tion to the real form of clouds, and careful drawing of effects of mist; so that the appearance of objects, as seen through it, becomes a subject of science with us; and the faithful representation of that appearance is made of primal importance, under the name of aërial perspective. The aspects of sunset and sunrise, with all their attendant phenomena of cloud and mist, are watchfully delineated; and in ordinary daylight landscape, the sky is considered of so much importance, that a principal mass of foliage, or a whole foreground, is unhesitatingly thrown into shade merely to bring out the form of a white cloud. So that, if a general and characteristic name were needed for modern landscape art, none better could be invented than "the service of clouds."

And this name would, unfortunately, be characteristic of our art in more ways than one. In the last chapter, I said that all the Greeks spoke kindly about the clouds, except Aristophanes; and he, I am sorry to say (since his report is so unfavorable), is the only Greek who had studied them attentively. He tells us, first, that they are "great goddesses to idle men"; then, that they are "mistresses of disputings, and logic, and monstrosities, and noisy chattering"; declares that whoso believes in their divinity must first disbelieve in Jupiter, and place supreme power in the hands of an unknown god "Whirlwind"; and, finally, he displays their influence over the mind of one of their disciples, in his sudden desire "to speak ingeniously concerning smoke." [3]

There is, I fear, an infinite truth in this Aristophanic judgment applied to our modern cloud-worship. Assuredly, much of the love of mystery in our romances, our poetry, our art, and, above all, in our metaphysics, must come under that definition so long ago given by the great Greek, "speaking ingeniously concerning smoke." And much of the instinct, which, partially developed in painting, may be now seen throughout every mode of exertion of mind,— the easily encouraged doubt, easily excited curiosity, habitual agitation, and delight in the changing and the marvelous, as opposed to the old quiet serenity of social custom and religious faith,—is again deeply defined in those few words, the "dethroning of Jupiter," the "coronation of the whirlwind."

Nor of whirlwind merely, but also of darkness or ignorance respecting all stable facts. That darkening of the foreground to bring out the white cloud, is, in one aspect of it, a type of the subjection of all plain and positive fact, to what is uncertain and unintelligible. And, as we examine farther into the matter, we shall be struck by another great difference between the old and modern landscape, namely, that in the old no one ever thought of drawing anything but as well *as he could*. That might not be *well*, as we have seen in the case of rocks; but it was as well as he *could*, and always distinctly. Leaf, or stone, or animal, or man, it was equally drawn with care and clearness, and its essential characters shown. If it was an oak tree, the acorns were drawn; if a flint pebble, its veins were drawn; if an arm of the sea, its fish were drawn; if a group of figures, their faces and dresses were drawn—to the very last subtlety of expression and end of thread that could be got into the space, far off or near. But now our ingenuity is all "concerning smoke." Nothing is truly drawn but that; all else is vague, slight, imperfect; got with as little pains as possible. You examine your closest foreground, and find no leaves; your largest oak, and find no acorns; your human figure, and find a spot of red paint instead of a face; and in all this, again and again, the Aristophanic words come true, and the clouds seem to be "great goddesses to idle men."

The next thing that will strike us, after this love of clouds, is the love of liberty. Whereas the medieval was always shutting himself into castles, and behind fosses, and drawing brickwork neatly, and beds of flowers primly, our painters delight in getting to the open fields and moors; abhor all hedges and moats; never paint anything but free-growing trees, and rivers gliding "at their own sweet will"; [4] eschew formality down to the smallest detail; break and displace the brickwork which the medieval would have carefully cemented; leave unpruned the thickets he would have delicately trimmed; and, carrying the love of liberty even to license, and the love of wildness even to ruin, take pleasure at last in every aspect of age and desolation which emancipates the objects of nature from the government of men;—on the castle wall displacing its tapestry with ivy, and spreading, through the garden, the bramble for the rose.

Connected with this love of liberty we find a singular manifestation of love of mountains, and see our painters traversing the wildest places of the globe in order to obtain subjects with craggy foregrounds and purple distances. Some few of them remain content with pollards

[3] See the *Clouds* of Aristophanes, ll. 316–318, 320, and 360.

[4] Wordsworth, sonnet *Composed upon Westminster Bridge, 3 September, 1802*, l. 12.

and flat land; but these are always men of third-rate order; and the leading masters, while they do not reject the beauty of the low grounds, reserve their highest powers to paint Alpine peaks or Italian promontories. And it is eminently noticeable, also, that this pleasure in the mountains is never mingled with fear, or tempered by a spirit of meditation, as with the medieval; but is always free and fearless, brightly exhilarating, and wholly unreflective; so that the painter feels that his mountain foreground may be more consistently animated by a sportsman than a hermit; and our modern society in general goes to the mountains, not to fast, but to feast, and leaves their glaciers covered with chicken-bones and egg-shells.

Connected with this want of any sense of solemnity in mountain scenery, is a general profanity of temper in regarding all the rest of nature; that is to say, a total absence of faith in the presence of any deity therein. Whereas the medieval never painted a cloud, but with the purpose of placing an angel in it; and a Greek never entered a wood without expecting to meet a god in it; we should think the appearance of an angel in the cloud wholly unnatural, and should be seriously surprised by meeting a god anywhere. Our chief ideas about the wood are connected with poaching. We have no belief that the clouds contain more than so many inches of rain or hail, and from our ponds and ditches expect nothing more divine than ducks and watercresses.

Finally: connected with this profanity of temper is a strong tendency to deny the sacred element of color, and make our boast in blackness. For though occasionally glaring or violent, modern color is on the whole eminently somber, tending continually to gray or brown, and by many of our best painters consistently falsified, with a confessed pride in what they call chaste or subdued tints; so that, whereas a medieval paints his sky bright blue and his foreground bright green, gilds the towers of his castles, and clothes his figures with purple and white, we paint our sky gray, our foreground black, and our foliage brown, and think that enough is sacrificed to the sun in admitting the dangerous brightness of a scarlet cloak or a blue jacket.

These, I believe, are the principal points which would strike us instantly, if we were to be brought suddenly into an exhibition of modern landscapes out of a room filled with medieval work. It is evident that there are both evil and good in this change; but how much evil, or how much good, we can only estimate by considering, as in the former divisions of our inquiry, what are the real roots of the habits of mind which have caused them.

And first, it is evident that the title "Dark Ages," given to the medieval centuries, is, respecting art, wholly inapplicable. They were, on the contrary, the bright ages; ours are the dark ones. I do not mean metaphysically, but literally. They were the ages of gold; ours are the ages of umber.

This is partly mere mistake in us; we build brown brick walls, and wear brown coats, because we have been blunderingly taught to do so, and go on doing so mechanically. There is, however, also some cause for the change in our own tempers. On the whole, these are much *sadder* ages than the early ones; not sadder in a noble and deep way, but in a dim wearied way,—the way of ennui, and jaded intellect, and uncomfortableness of soul and body. The Middle Ages had their wars and agonies, but also intense delights. Their gold was dashed with blood; but ours is sprinkled with dust. Their life was inwoven with white and purple: ours is one seamless stuff of brown. Not that we are without apparent festivity, but festivity more or less forced, mistaken, embittered, incomplete—not of the heart. How wonderfully, since Shakespeare's time, have we lost the power of laughing at bad jests! The very finish of our wit belies our gayety.

The profoundest reason of this darkness of heart is, I believe, our want of faith. There never yet was a generation of men (savage or civilized) who, taken as a body, so woefully fulfilled the words "having no hope, and without God in the world," [5] as the present civilized European race. A Red Indian or Otaheitan [6] savage has more sense of a divine existence round him, or government over him, than the plurality of refined Londoners and Parisians: and those among us who may in some sense be said to believe, are divided almost without exception into two broad classes, Romanist and Puritan; who, but for the interference of the unbelieving portions of society, would, either of them, reduce the other sect as speedily as possible to ashes; the Romanist having always done so whenever he could, from the beginning of their separation, and the Puritan at this time holding himself in complacent expectation of the destruction of Rome by volcanic fire. Such division as this between persons nominally of one religion, that is to say, believing in the same God, and the same Revelation,

---

[5] Ephesians, 2:12.

[6] Otaheite (Tahiti) is the largest of the Society Islands, in the South Pacific.

cannot but become a stumbling-block of the gravest kind to all thoughtful and far-sighted men,—a stumbling-block which they can only surmount under the most favorable circumstances of early education. Hence, nearly all our powerful men in this age of the world are unbelievers; the best of them in doubt and misery; the worst in reckless defiance; the plurality, in plodding hesitation, doing, as well as they can, what practical work lies ready to their hands. Most of our scientific men are in this last class: our popular authors either set themselves definitely against all religious form, pleading for simple truth and benevolence (Thackeray, Dickens), or give themselves up to bitter and fruitless statements of facts (De Balzac), or surface-painting (Scott), or careless blasphemy, sad or smiling (Byron, Béranger). Our earnest poets and deepest thinkers are doubtful and indignant (Tennyson, Carlyle); one or two, anchored, indeed, but anxious or weeping (Wordsworth, Mrs. Browning); and of these two, the first is not so sure of his anchor, but that now and then it drags with him, even to make him cry out,—

Great God, I had rather be
A Pagan suckled in some creed outworn;
So might I, standing on this pleasant lea,
Have glimpses that would make me less forlorn.[7]

In politics, religion is now a name; in art, a hypocrisy or affectation. Over German religious pictures the inscription, "See how Pious I am," can be read at a glance by any clear-sighted person. Over French and English religious pictures the inscription, "See how Impious I am," is equally legible. All sincere and modest art is, among us, profane.[8]

This faithlessness operates among us according to our tempers, producing either sadness or levity, and being the ultimate root alike of our discontents and of our wantonnesses. It is marvelous how full of contradiction it makes us: we are first dull, and seek for wild and lonely places because we have no heart for the garden; presently we recover our spirits, and build an assembly room among the mountains, because we have no reverence for the desert. I do not know if there be game on Sinai, but I am always expecting to hear of some one's shooting over it.[9]

There is, however, another, and a more innocent root of our delight in wild scenery.

All the Renaissance principles of art tended, as I have before often explained, to the setting Beauty above Truth, and seeking for it always at the expense of truth. And the proper punishment of such pursuit—the punishment which all the laws of the universe rendered inevitable—was, that those who thus pursued beauty should wholly lose sight of beauty. All the thinkers of the age, as we saw previously, declared that it did not exist. The age seconded their efforts, and banished beauty, so far as human effort could succeed in doing so, from the face of the earth, and the form of man. To powder the hair, to patch the cheek, to hoop the body, to buckle the foot, were all part and parcel of the same system which reduced streets to brick walls, and pictures to brown stains. One desert of Ugliness was extended before the eyes of mankind; and their pursuit of the beautiful, so recklessly continued, received unexpected consummation in high-heeled shoes and periwigs,—Gower Street, and Gaspar Poussin.

Reaction from this state was inevitable, if any true life was left in the races of mankind; and, accordingly, though still forced, by rule and fashion, to the producing and wearing all that is ugly, men steal out, half-ashamed of themselves for doing so, to the fields and mountains; and, finding among these the color, and liberty, and variety, and power, which are for ever grateful to them, delight in these to an extent never before known; rejoice in all the wildest shattering of the mountain side, as an opposition to Gower Street, gaze in a rapt manner at sunsets and sunrises, to see there the blue, and gold, and purple, which glow for them no longer on knight's armor or temple porch; and gather with care out of the fields, into their blotted herbaria, the flowers which the five orders of architecture have banished from their doors and casements.

The absence of care for personal beauty, which is another great characteristic of the age, adds to this feeling in a twofold way: first, by turning all reverent thoughts away from human nature; and making us think of men as ridiculous or ugly creatures, getting through the world as well as they can, and spoiling it in doing so; not ruling it in a kingly way and crowning all its loveliness. In the Middle Ages hardly anything but vice could be caricatured, because virtue was always visibly and personally

[7] Sonnet beginning "The world is too much with us; late and soon," ll. 9–12.

[8] Pre-Raphaelitism, of course, excepted, which is a new phase of art, in no wise considered in this chapter. Blake was sincere, but full of wild creeds, and somewhat diseased in brain (Ruskin's note).

[9] Ruskin's expectation was soon fulfilled; see his

description of a drawing by J. F. Lewis, *Academy Notes,* 1856.

noble: now virtue itself is apt to inhabit such poor human bodies, that no aspect of it is invulnerable to jest; and for all fairness we have to seek to the flowers; for all sublimity, to the hills.

The same want of care operates, in another way, by lowering the standard of health, increasing the susceptibility to nervous or sentimental impressions, and thus adding to the other powers of nature over us whatever charm may be felt in her fostering the melancholy fancies of brooding idleness.

It is not, however, only to existing inanimate nature that our want of beauty in person and dress has driven us. The imagination of it, as it was seen in our ancestors, haunts us continually; and while we yield to the present fashions, or act in accordance with the dullest modern principles of economy and utility, we look fondly back to the manners of the ages of chivalry, and delight in painting, to the fancy, the fashions we pretend to despise, and the splendors we think it wise to abandon. The furniture and personages of our romance are sought, when the writer desires to please most easily, in the centuries which we profess to have surpassed in everything; the art which takes us into the present times is considered as both daring and degraded; and while the weakest words please us, and are regarded as poetry, which recall the manners of our forefathers, or of strangers, it is only as familiar and vulgar that we accept the description of our own.

In this we are wholly different from all the races that preceded us. All other nations have regarded their ancestors with reverence as saints or heroes; but have nevertheless thought their own deeds and ways of life the fitting subjects for their arts of painting or of verse. We, on the contrary, regard our ancestors as foolish and wicked, but yet find our chief artistic pleasures in descriptions of their ways of life.

The Greeks and medievals honored, but did not imitate their forefathers; we imitate, but do not honor.

With this romantic love of beauty, forced to seek in history, and in external nature, the satisfaction it cannot find in ordinary life, we mingle a more rational passion, the due and just result of newly awakened powers of attention. Whatever may first lead us to the scrutiny of natural objects, that scrutiny never fails of its reward. Unquestionably they are intended to be regarded by us with both reverence and delight; and every hour we give to them renders their beauty more apparent, and their interest more engrossing. Natural science—which can

hardly be considered to have existed before modern times—rendering our knowledge fruitful in accumulation, and exquisite in accuracy, has acted for good or evil, according to the temper of the mind which received it; and though it has hardened the faithlessness of the dull and proud, has shown new grounds for reverence to hearts which were thoughtful and humble. The neglect of the art of war, while it has somewhat weakened and deformed the body,[10] has given us leisure and opportunity for studies to which, before, time and space were equally wanting; lives which once were early wasted on the battlefield are now passed usefully in the study; nations which exhausted themselves in annual warfare now dispute with each other the discovery of new planets,[11] and the serene philosopher dissects the plants, and analyzes the dust, of lands which were of old only traversed by the knight in hasty march, or by the borderer in heedless rapine.

The elements of progress and decline being thus strangely mingled in the modern mind, we might beforehand anticipate that one of the notable characters of our art would be its inconsistency; that efforts would be made in every direction, and arrested by every conceivable cause and manner of failure; that in all we did, it would become next to impossible to distinguish accurately the grounds for praise or for regret; that all previous canons of practice and methods of thought would be gradually overthrown, and criticism continually defied by successes which no one had expected, and sentiments which no one could define.

Accordingly, while, in our inquiries into Greek and medieval art, I was able to describe, in general terms, what all men did or felt, I find now many characters in many men; some, it seems to me, founded on the inferior and evanescent principles of modernism, on its recklessness, impatience, or faithlessness; others founded on its science, its new affection for nature, its love of openness and liberty. And among all these characters, good or evil, I see that some, remaining to us from old or transitional periods, do not properly belong to us,

[10] Of course this is meant only of the modern citizen or country gentleman, as compared with a citizen of Sparta or old Florence. I leave it to others to say whether the "neglect of the *art* of war" may or may not, in a yet more fatal sense, be predicated of the English nation. War *without* art, we seem, with God's help, able still to wage nobly (Ruskin's note). The "war *without* art" was the Crimean War.

[11] The allusion is to France and England. In each country several minor planets were discovered independently during the years 1854–1856.

and will soon fade away, and others, though not yet distinctly developed, are yet properly our own, and likely to grow forward into greater strength.

For instance: our reprobation of bright color is, I think, for the most part, mere affectation, and must soon be done away with. Vulgarity, dullness, or impiety, will indeed always express themselves through art in brown and gray, as in Rembrandt, Caravaggio,[12] and Salvator;[13] but we are not wholly vulgar, dull, or impious; nor, as moderns, are we necessarily obliged to continue so in any wise. Our greatest men, whether sad or gay, still delight, like the great men of all ages, in brilliant hues. The coloring of Scott and Byron is full and pure; that of Keats and Tennyson rich even to excess. Our practical failures in coloring are merely the necessary consequences of our prolonged want of practice during the periods of Renaissance affectation and ignorance; and the only durable difference between old and modern coloring, is the acceptance of certain hues, by the modern, which please him by expressing that melancholy peculiar to his more reflective or sentimental character, and the greater variety of them necessary to express his greater science.

Again: if we ever become wise enough to dress consistently and gracefully, to make health a principal object in education, and to render our streets beautiful with art, the external charm of past history will in great measure disappear. There is no essential reason, because we live after the fatal seventeenth century, that we should never again be able to confess interest in sculpture, or see brightness in embroidery; nor, because now we choose to make the night deadly with our pleasures, and the day with our labors, prolonging the dance till dawn, and the toil to twilight, that we should never again learn how rightly to employ the sacred trusts of strength, beauty, and time. Whatever external charm attaches itself to the past, would then be seen in proper subordination to the brightness of present life; and the elements of romance would exist, in the earlier ages, only in the attraction which must generally belong to whatever is unfamiliar; in the reverence which a noble nation always pays to its ancestors; and in the enchanted light which races, like individuals, must perceive in looking back to the days of their childhood.

Again: the peculiar levity with which natural scenery is regarded by a large number of modern minds cannot be considered as entirely characteristic of the age, inasmuch as it never can belong to its greatest intellects. Men of any high mental power must be serious, whether in ancient or modern days; a certain degree of reverence for fair scenery is found in all our great writers without exception,—even the one who has made us laugh oftenest, taking us to the valley of Chamouni, and to the sea beach, there to give peace after suffering, and change revenge into pity.[14] It is only the dull, the uneducated, or the worldly, whom it is painful to meet on the hillsides; and levity, as a ruling character, cannot be ascribed to the whole nation, but only to its holiday-making apprentices, and its House of Commons.

We need not, therefore, expect to find any single poet or painter representing the entire group of powers, weaknesses, and inconsistent instincts which govern or confuse our modern life. But we may expect that in the man who seems to be given by Providence as the type of the age (as Homer and Dante were given, as the types of classical and medieval mind), we shall find whatever is fruitful and substantial to be completely present, together with those of our weaknesses, which are indeed nationally characteristic, and compatible with general greatness of mind, just as the weak love of fences, and dislike of mountains, were found compatible with Dante's greatness in other respects.

Farther: as the admiration of mankind is found, in our times, to have in great part passed from men to mountains, and from human emotion to natural phenomena, we may anticipate that the great strength of art will also be warped in this direction; with this notable result for us, that whereas the greatest painters or painter of classical and medieval periods, being wholly devoted to the representation of humanity, furnished us with but little to examine in landscape, the greatest painters or painter of modern times will in all probability be devoted to landscape principally; and farther, because in representing human emotion words surpass painting, but in representing natural scenery painting surpasses words, we may anticipate also that the painter and poet (for convenience' sake I here use the words in opposition) will somewhat change their relations of rank in illustrating the mind of the age; that the painter will be-

[12] Italian painter (1569–1609).
[13] Salvator Rosa (1615?–1673), Neapolitan painter, musician, and satirical poet.

[14] See *David Copperfield*, chaps. lv and lviii (Ruskin's note).

come of more importance, the poet of less; and that the relations between the men who are the types and first-fruits of the age in word and work,—namely, Scott and Turner,—will be, in many curious respects, different from those between Homer and Phidias, or Dante and Giotto.

## The Stones of Venice

### ST. MARK'S [1]

"And so Barnabas took Mark, and sailed unto Cyprus." If as the shores of Asia lessened upon his sight, the spirit of prophecy had entered into the heart of the weak disciple who had turned back when his hand was on the plough, and who had been judged, by the chiefest of Christ's captains, unworthy thenceforward to go forth with him to the work,[2] how wonderful would he have thought it, that by the lion symbol in future ages he was to be represented among men! how woeful, that the war-cry of his name should so often reanimate the rage of the soldier, on those very plains where he himself had failed in the courage of the Christian, and so often dye with fruitless blood that very Cypriot Sea, over whose waves, in repentance and shame, he was following the Son of Consolation!

That the Venetians possessed themselves of his body in the ninth century, there appears no sufficient reason to doubt, nor that it was principally in consequence of their having done so, that they chose him for their patron saint. There exists, however, a tradition that before he went into Egypt he had founded the church at Aquileia, and was thus in some sort the first bishop of the Venetian isles and people. I believe that this tradition stands on nearly as good grounds as that of St. Peter having been the first bishop of Rome; but, as usual, it is enriched by various later additions and embellishments, much resembling the stories told respecting the church of Murano. Thus we find it recorded by the Santo Padre who compiled the *Vite de' Santi spettanti alle Chiese di Venezia*,[3] that "St. Mark having seen the people of Aquileia well grounded in religion,

and being called to Rome by St. Peter, before setting off took with him the holy bishop Hermagoras, and went in a small boat to the marshes of Venice. There were at that period some houses built upon a certain high bank called Rialto, and the boat being driven by the wind was anchored in a marshy place, when St. Mark, snatched into ecstasy, heard the voice of an angel saying to him: 'Peace be to thee, Mark; here shall thy body rest.'" The angel goes on to foretell the building of *una stupenda, ne più veduta Città*;[4] but the fable is hardly ingenious enough to deserve farther relation.

But whether St. Mark was first bishop of Aquileia or not, St. Theodore was the first patron of the city; nor can he yet be considered as having entirely abdicated his early right, as his statue, standing on a crocodile, still companions the winged lion on the opposing pillar of the piazzetta. A church erected to this Saint is said to have occupied, before the ninth century, the site of St. Mark's; and the traveler, dazzled by the brilliancy of the great square, ought not to leave it without endeavoring to imagine its aspect in that early time, when it was a green field, cloister-like and quiet, divided by a small canal, with a line of trees on each side; and extending between the two churches of St. Theodore and St. Geminian, as the little piazza of Torcello lies between its "palazzo" and cathedral.

But in the year 813, when the seat of government was finally removed to the Rialto, a Ducal Palace, built on the spot where the present one stands, with a Ducal Chapel beside it, gave a very different character to the Square of St. Mark; and fifteen years later, the acquisition of the body of the Saint, and its deposition in the Ducal Chapel, perhaps not yet completed, occasioned the investiture of that Chapel with all possible splendor. St. Theodore was deposed from his patronship, and his church destroyed, to make room for the aggrandizement of the one attached to the Ducal Palace, and thenceforward known as "St. Mark's."

This first church was however destroyed by fire, when the Ducal Palace was burned in the revolt against Candiano, in 976. It was partly rebuilt by his successor, Pietro Orseolo, on a larger scale; and, with the assistance of Byzantine architects, the fabric was carried on under successive Doges for nearly a hundred years; the main building

---

[1] Vol. II (published in 1853) entitled "The Sea-Stories," from chapter 4.

[2] Acts, 13:13; 15:38, 39 (Ruskin's note).

[3] By the Holy Father who compiled the *Lives of the Patron Saints of the Venetian Churches* (Ruskin gives the reference: Venice, 1761, I, 126).

[4] A wonderful city, never before seen.

being completed in 1071, but its incrustation with marble not till considerably later. It was consecrated on the 8th of October, 1085, according to Sansovino and the author of the *Chiesa Ducale di S. Marco*,[5] in 1094 according to Lazari, but certainly between 1084 and 1096, those years being the limits of the reign of Vital Falier; I incline to the supposition that it was soon after his accession to the throne in 1085, though Sansovino writes, by mistake, Ordelafo instead of Vital Falier. But, at all events, before the close of the eleventh century the great consecration of the church took place. It was again injured by fire in 1106, but repaired; and from that time to the fall of Venice there was probably no Doge who did not in some slight degree embellish or alter the fabric, so that few parts of it can be pronounced boldly to be of any given date. Two periods of interference are, however, notable above the rest: the first, that in which the Gothic school had superseded the Byzantine towards the close of the fourteenth century, when the pinnacles, upper archivolts, and window traceries were added to the exterior, and the great screen, with various chapels and tabernacle-work, to the interior; the second, when the Renaissance school superseded the Gothic, and the pupils of Titian and Tintoret substituted, over one-half of the church, their own compositions for the Greek mosaics with which it was originally decorated; happily, though with no good-will, having left enough to enable us to imagine and lament what they destroyed. Of this irreparable loss we shall have more to say hereafter; meantime, I wish only to fix in the reader's mind the succession of periods of alterations as firmly and simply as possible.

We have seen that the main body of the church may be broadly stated to be of the eleventh century, the Gothic additions of the fourteenth, and the restored mosaics of the seventeenth. There is no difficulty in distinguishing at a glance the Gothic portions from the Byzantine; but there is considerable difficulty in ascertaining how long, during the course of the twelfth and thirteenth centuries, additions were made to the Byzantine church, which cannot be easily distinguished from the work of the eleventh century, being purposely executed in the same manner. Two of the most important pieces of evidence on this point are, a mosaic in the south transept, and another over the northern door of the

[5] Ducal church of St. Mark.

façade; the first representing the interior, the second the exterior, of the ancient church.

It has just been stated that the existing building was consecrated by the Doge Vital Falier. A peculiar solemnity was given to that act of consecration, in the minds of the Venetian people, by what appears to have been one of the best arranged and most successful impostures ever attempted by the clergy of the Romish Church. The body of St. Mark had, without doubt, perished in the conflagration of 976; but the revenues of the church depended too much upon the devotion excited by these relics to permit the confession of their loss. The following is the account given by Corner, and believed to this day by the Venetians, of the pretended miracle by which it was concealed.

"After the repairs undertaken by the Doge Orseolo, the place in which the body of the holy Evangelist rested had been altogether forgotten; so that the Doge Vital Falier was entirely ignorant of the place of the venerable deposit. This was no light affliction, not only to the pious Doge, but to all the citizens and people; so that at last, moved by confidence in the Divine mercy, they determined to implore, with prayer and fasting, the manifestation of so great a treasure, which did not now depend upon any human effort. A general fast being therefore proclaimed, and a solemn procession appointed for the 25th day of June, while the people assembled in the church interceded with God in fervent prayers for the desired boon, they beheld, with as much amazement as joy, a slight shaking in the marbles of a pillar (near the place where the altar of the Cross is now), which, presently falling to the earth, exposed to the view of the rejoicing people the chest of bronze in which the body of the Evangelist was laid."

Of the main facts of this tale there is no doubt. They were embellished afterward, as usual, by many fanciful traditions; as, for instance, that, when the sacrophagus was discovered, St. Mark extended his hand out of it, with a gold ring on one of the fingers which he permitted a noble of the Dolfin family to remove; and a quaint and delightful story was further invented of this ring, which I shall not repeat here, as it is now as well known as any tale of the Arabian Nights.[6] But the fast and the discovery of

[6] The story tells of the miraculous intervention of St. Mark, with St. George and St. Nicholas, to save Venice from destruction by a great storm in

the coffin, by whatever means effected, are facts; and they are recorded in one of the best-preserved mosaics of the south transept, executed very certainly not long after the event had taken place, closely resembling in its treatment that of the Bayeux tapestry,[7] and showing, in a conventional manner, the interior of the church, as it then was, filled by the people, first in prayer, then in thanksgiving, the pillar standing open before them, and the Doge, in the midst of them, distinguished by his crimson bonnet embroidered with gold, but more unmistakably by the inscription "Dux" over his head, as uniformly is the case in the Bayeux tapestry, and most other pictorial works of the period. The church is, of course, rudely represented, and the two upper stories of it reduced to a small scale in order to form a background to the figures; one of those bold pieces of picture history which we in our pride of perspective, and a thousand things besides, never dare attempt.[8] We should have put in a column or two, of the real or perspective size, and subdued it into a vague background: the old workman crushed the church together that he might get it all in, up to the cupolas; and has, therefore, left us some useful notes of its ancient form, though any one who is familiar with the method of drawing employed at the period will not push the evidence too far. The two pulpits are there, however, as they are at this day, and the fringe of mosaic flowerwork which then encompassed the whole church, but which modern restorers have destroyed, all but one fragment still left in the south aisle. There is no attempt to represent the other mosaics on the roof, the scale being too small to admit of their being represented with any success; but some at least of those mosaics had been executed at that period, and their absence in the representation of the entire church is especially to be observed, in order to show that we must not trust to any negative evidence in such works. M. Lazari has rashly concluded that the central archivolt of St. Mark's *must* be posterior to the year 1205, because it does not appear in the representa-

tion of the exterior of the church over the northern door;[9] but he justly observes that this mosaic (which is the other piece of evidence we possess respecting the ancient form of the building) cannot itself be earlier than 1205, since it represents the bronze horses which were brought from Constantinople in that year. And this one fact renders it very difficult to speak with confidence respecting the date of any part of the exterior of St. Mark's; for we have above seen that it was consecrated in the eleventh century, and yet here is one of its most important exterior decorations assuredly retouched, if not entirely added, in the thirteenth, although its style would have led us to suppose it had been an original part of the fabric. However, for all our purposes, it will be enough for the reader to remember that the earliest parts of the building belong to the eleventh, twelfth, and first part of the thirteenth century; the Gothic portions to the fourteenth; some of the altars and embellishments to the fifteenth and sixteenth; and the modern portion of the mosaics to the seventeenth.

This, however, I only wish him to recollect in order that I may speak generally of the Byzantine architecture of St. Mark's, without leading him to suppose the whole church to have been built and decorated by Greek artists. Its later portions, with the single exception of the seventeenth century mosaics, have been so dexterously accommodated to the original fabric that the general effect is still that of a Byzantine building; and I shall not, except when it is absolutely necessary, direct attention to the discordant points, or weary the reader with anatomical criticism. Whatever in St. Mark's arrests the eye, or affects the feelings, is either Byzantine, or has been modified by Byzantine influence; and our inquiry into its architectural merits need not therefore be disturbed by the anxieties of antiquarianism, or arrested by the obscurities of chronology.

And now I wish that the reader, before I bring him into St. Mark's Place, would imagine himself for a little time in a quiet English cathedral town, and walk with me to the west front of its cathedral.[10] Let us go together up the more retired street, at the end of which we can see the pinnacles of one

---

1340. It is translated in Mrs. Jameson's *Sacred and Legendary Art*.

[7] A representation of episodes in the conquest of England by William of Normandy, dating probably from early in the twelfth century. It is in the Public Library of Bayeux.

[8] I leave this exceedingly ill-written sentence, trusting the reader will think I write better now (Ruskin's note, added in 1879).

[9] In 1879 Ruskin added the note: "He is right, however."

[10] Some have identified this English cathedral with Canterbury, others with Salisbury. Ruskin, however, meant his description to be generic.

of the towers, and then through the low gray gateway, with its battlemented top and small latticed window in the center, into the inner private-looking road or close, where nothing goes in but the carts of the tradesmen who supply the bishop and the chapter, and where there are little shaven grass-plots, fenced in by neat rails, before old-fashioned groups of somewhat diminutive and excessively trim houses, with little oriel and bay windows jut- 10 ting out here and there, and deep wooden cornices and eaves painted cream color and white, and small porches to their doors in the shape of cockle-shells, or little, crooked, thick, indescribable wooden gables warped a little on one side; and so forward till we come to larger houses, also old-fashioned, but of red brick, and with garden behind them, and fruit walls, which show here and there, among the nectarines, the vestiges of 20 an old cloister arch or shaft, and looking in front on the cathedral square itself, laid out in rigid divisions of smooth grass and gravel walk, yet not uncheerful, especially on the sunny side, where the canon's children are walking with their nursery maids. And so, taking care not to tread on the grass, we will go along the straight walk to the west front, and there stand for a time, looking up at its deep-pointed porches and the dark places 30 between their pillars where there were statues once, and where the fragments, here and there, of a stately figure are still left, which has in it the likeness of a king, perhaps indeed a king on earth, perhaps a saintly king long ago in heaven; and so higher and higher up to the great moldering wall of rugged sculpture and confused arcades, shattered, and gray, and grisly with heads of dragons and mocking fiends, worn by the rain and swirl- 40 ing winds into yet unseemlier shape, and colored on their stony scales by the deep russet-orange lichen,[11] melancholy gold; and so, higher still, to the bleak towers, so far above that the eye loses itself among the bosses of their traceries, though they are rude and strong, and only sees like a drift of eddying black points, now closing, now scattering, and now settling suddenly into in-

visible places among the bosses and flowers, the crowd of restless birds that fill the whole square with that strange clangor of theirs, so harsh and yet so soothing, like the cries of birds on a solitary coast between the cliffs and sea.

Think for a little while of that scene, and the meaning of all its small formalisms, mixed with its serene sublimity. Estimate its secluded, continuous, drowsy felicities, and its evidence of the sense and steady performance of such kind of duties as can be regulated by the cathedral clock; and weigh the influence of those dark towers on all who have passed through the lonely square at their feet for centuries, and on all who have seen them rising far away over the wooded plain, or catching on their square masses the last rays of the sunset, when the city at their feet was indicated only by mist at the bend of the river. And then let us quickly recollect that we are in Venice, and land at the extremity of the Calle Lunga San Moisè, which may be considered as there answering to the secluded street that led us to our English cathedral gateway.[12]

We find ourselves in a paved alley, some seven feet wide where it is widest, full of people, and resonant with cries of itinerant salesmen,—a shriek in their beginning, and dying away into a kind of brazen ringing, all the worse for its confinement between the high houses of the passage along which we have to make our way. Over head, an inextricable confusion of rugged shutters, and iron balconies and chimney flues, pushed out on brackets to save room, and arched windows with projecting sills of Istrian stone, and gleams of green leaves here and there where a fig-tree branch escapes over a lower wall from some inner cortile,[13] leading the eye up to the narrow stream of blue sky high over all. On each side, a row of shops, as densely set as may be, occupying, in fact, intervals between the square stone shafts, about eight feet high, which carry the first floors: intervals of which one is narrow and serves as a door; the other is, in the more respectable shops, wainscoted to the height of the counter and glazed above, but in those of the poorer tradesmen left open to the ground, and the wares laid on benches and tables in the open air, the light in all cases entering at the front only, and fading away in a few feet from the threshold into a gloom

---

[11] Alas! all this was described from things now never to be seen more. Read, for "the great moldering wall," and the context of four lines, "the beautiful new parapet by Mr. Scott, with a gross of kings sent down from Kensington" (Ruskin's note, added in 1879). Sir Gilbert Scott restored a number of cathedrals. The restoration of Salisbury was begun in 1862 and 60 new statues were placed on its west front.

[12] The Venetian street has been widened and renamed since this was written.

[13] Courtyard.

which the eye from without cannot penetrate, but which is generally broken by a ray or two from a feeble lamp at the back of the shop, suspended before a print of the Virgin. The less pious shopkeeper sometimes leaves his lamp unlighted, and is contented with a penny print; the more religious one has his print colored and set in a little shrine with a gilded or figured fringe, with perhaps a faded flower or two on each side, and his lamp burning brilliantly. Here, at the fruiterer's, where the dark-green watermelons are heaped upon the counter like cannon balls, the Madonna has a tabernacle of fresh laurel leaves; but the pewterer next door has let his lamp out, and there is nothing to be seen in his shop but the dull gleam of the studded patterns on the copper pans, hanging from his roof in the darkness. Next comes a *Vendita Frittole e Liquori*,[14] where the Virgin, enthroned in a very humble manner beside a tallow candle on a back shelf, presides over certain ambrosial morsels of a nature too ambiguous to be defined or enumerated. But a few steps farther on, at the regular wine-shop of the calle, where we are offered *Vino Nostrani a Soldi* 28.32, the Madonna is in great glory, enthroned above ten or a dozen large red casks of three-year-old vintage, and flanked by goodly ranks of bottles of Maraschino, and two crimson lamps; and for the evening, when the gondoliers will come to drink out, under her auspices, the money they have gained during the day, she will have a whole chandelier.

A yard or two farther, we pass the hostelry of the Black Eagle, and glancing as we pass through the square door of marble, deeply molded, in the outer wall, we see the shadows of its pergola of vines resting on an ancient wall, with a pointed shield carved on its side; and so presently emerge on the bridge and Campo San Moisè, whence to the entrance into St. Mark's Place, called the Bocca di Piazza (mouth of the square), the Venetian character is nearly destroyed, first by the frightful façade of San Moisè, which we will pause at another time to examine,[15] and then by the modernizing of the shops as they near the piazza, and the mingling with the lower Venetian populace of lounging groups of English and Austrians. We will push fast through them into the shadow of the pillars at the end of the Bocca di Piazza, and then we forget them all; for between those pillars there opens a great light, and, in the midst of it, as we advance slowly, the vast tower of St. Mark seems to lift itself visibly forth from the level field of checkered stones; and, on each side, the countless arches prolong themselves into ranged symmetry, as if the rugged and irregular houses that pressed together above us in the dark alley had been struck back into sudden obedience and lovely order, and all their rude casements and broken walls had been transformed into arches charged with goodly sculpture, and fluted shafts of delicate stone.

And well may they fall back, for beyond those troops of ordered arches there rises a vision out of the earth, and all the great square seems to have opened from it in a kind of awe, that we may see it far away;— a multitude of pillars and white domes, clustered into a long low pyramid of colored light; a treasure-heap, it seems, partly of gold, and partly of opal and mother-of-pearl, hollowed beneath into five great vaulted porches, ceiled with fair mosaic, and beset with sculpture of alabaster, clear as amber and delicate as ivory,—sculpture fantastic and involved, of palm leaves and lilies, and grapes and pomegranates, and birds clinging and fluttering among the branches, all twined together into an endless network of buds and plumes; and, in the midst of it, the solemn forms of angels, sceptered, and robed to the feet, and leaning to each other across the gates, their figures indistinct among the gleaming of the golden ground through the leaves beside them, interrupted and dim, like the morning light as it faded back among the branches of Eden, when first its gates were angel-guarded long ago. And round the walls of the porches there are set pillars of variegated stones, jasper and porphyry, and deep-green serpentine spotted with flakes of snow, and marbles, that half refuse and half yield to the sunshine, Cleopatra-like, "their bluest veins to kiss"[16]— the shadow, as it steals back from them, revealing line after line of azure undulation, as a receding tide leaves the waved sand; their capitals rich with interwoven tracery, rotted knots of herbage, and drifting leaves of acanthus and vine, and mystical signs, all beginning and ending in the Cross; and above them, in the broad archivolts, a continuous chain of language and of life—angels, and the signs of heaven, and the labors of men, each in its appointed season upon the earth; and above these, another range of glittering pin-

[14] Fritter and Liquor Shop.

[15] See vol. III, chap. 3.

[16] *Antony and Cleopatra*, II, v, 29.

nacles, mixed with white arches edged with scarlet flowers—a confusion of delight, amidst which the breasts of the Greek horses are seen blazing in their breadth of golden strength, and the St. Mark's lion, lifted on a blue field covered with stars, until at last, as if in ecstasy, the crests of the arches break into a marble foam, and toss themselves far into the blue sky in flashes and wreaths of sculptured spray, as if the breakers on the Lido shore had been frost-bound before they fell, and the sea-nymphs had inlaid them with coral and amethyst.

Between that grim cathedral of England and this, what an interval! There is a type of it in the very birds that haunt them; for, instead of the restless crowd, hoarse-voiced and sable-winged, drifting on the bleak upper air, the St. Mark's porches are full of doves, that nestle among the marble foliage, and mingle the soft iridescense of their living plumes, changing at every motion, with the tints, hardly less lovely, that have stood unchanged for seven hundred years.

And what effect has this splendor on those who pass beneath it? You may walk from sunrise to sunset, to and fro, before the gateway of St. Mark's, and you will not see an eye lifted to it, nor a countenance brightened by it. Priest and layman, soldier and civilian, rich and poor, pass by it alike regardlessly. Up to the very recesses of the porches, the meanest tradesmen of the city push their counters; nay, the foundations of its pillars are themselves the seats—not "of them that sell doves" [17] for sacrifice, but of the vendors of toys and caricatures. Round the whole square in front of the church there is almost a continuous line of cafés, where the idle Venetians of the middle classes lounge, and read empty journals; in its center the Austrian bands play during the time of vespers, their martial music jarring with the organ notes,—the march drowning the miserere, and the sullen crowd thickening round them,—a crowd, which, if it had its will, would stiletto every soldier that pipes to it.[18] And in the recesses of the porches all day long, knots of men of the lowest classes, unemployed and listless, lie basking in the sun like lizards; and unregarded children,—every heavy glance of their young eyes full of desperation and stony depravity, and their throats hoarse with cursing,—gamble, and fight, and snarl, and sleep, hour after

hour, clashing their bruised centesimi [19] upon the marble ledges of the church porch. And the images of Christ and His angels look down upon it continually.

That we may not enter the church out of the midst of the horror of this, let us turn aside under the portico which looks across the sea, and passing round within the two massive pillars brought from St. Jean d'Acre, we shall find the gate of the Baptistery; let us enter there. The heavy door closes behind us instantly, and the light and the turbulence of the Piazzetta are together shut out by it.

We are in a low vaulted room; vaulted, not with arches but with small cupolas starred with gold, and checkered with gloomy figures: in the center is a bronze font charged with rich bas-reliefs, a small figure of the Baptist standing above it in a single ray of light that glances across the narrow room, dying as it falls from a window high in the wall, and the first thing that it strikes, and the only thing that it strikes brightly, is a tomb. We hardly know if it be a tomb indeed; for it is like a narrow couch set beside the window, low-roofed and curtained, so that it might seem, but that it is some height above the pavement, to have been drawn towards the window, that the sleeper might be wakened early;—only there are two angels, who have drawn the curtain back, and are looking down upon him. Let us look also, and thank that gentle light that rests upon his forehead for ever, and dies away upon his breast.

The face is of a man in middle life, but there are two deep furrows right across the forehead, dividing it like the foundations of a tower: the height of it above is bound by the fillet of the ducal cap. The rest of the features are singularly small and delicate, the lips sharp, perhaps the sharpness of death being added to that of the natural lines; but there is a sweet smile upon them, and a deep serenity upon the whole countenance. The roof of the canopy above has been blue, filled with stars; beneath, in the center of the tomb on which the figure rests, is a seated figure of the Virgin, and the border of it all around is of flowers and soft leaves, growing rich and deep, as if in a field in summer.

It is the Doge Andrea Dandolo, a man early great among the great of Venice; and early lost. She chose him for her king in his 36th year; he died ten years later, leaving be-

---

[17] St. Matthew, 21:12; St. John, 2:16.
[18] This was written before 1866, when Venice was surrendered by Austria to the new Kingdom of Italy.

[19] Small coins, normally worth about one-fifth of a cent.

hind him that history to which we owe half of what we know of her former fortunes.[20]

Look round at the room in which he lies. The floor of it is of rich mosaic, encompassed by a low seat of red marble, and its walls are of alabaster, but worn and shattered, and darkly stained with age, almost a ruin,—in places the slabs of marble have fallen away altogether, and the rugged brickwork is seen through the rents, but all beautiful; the ravaging fissures fretting their way among the islands and channeled zones of the alabaster, and the time-stains on its translucent masses darkened into fields of rich golden brown, like the color of seaweed when the sun strikes on it through deep sea. The light fades away into the recess of the chamber towards the altar, and the eye can hardly trace the lines of the bas-relief behind it of the baptism of Christ: but on the vaulting of the roof the figures are distinct, and there are seen upon it two great circles, one surrounded by the "Principalities and powers in heavenly places," [21] of which Milton has expressed the ancient division in the single massy line,

Thrones, Dominations, Princedoms, Virtues, Powers,[22]

and around the other, the Apostles; Christ the center of both: and upon the walls, again and again repeated, the gaunt figure of the Baptist, in every circumstance of his life and death; and the streams of the Jordan running down between their cloven rocks; the ax laid to the root of a fruitless tree that springs up on their shore. "Every tree that bringeth not forth good fruit shall be hewn down, and cast into the fire." [23] Yes, verily: to be baptized with fire, or to be cast therein; it is the choice set before all men. The march-notes still murmur through the grated window, and mingle with the sounding in our ears of the sentence of judgment, which the old Greek has written on the Baptistery wall. Venice has made her choice.

He who lies under that stone canopy would have taught her another choice, in his day, if she would have listened to him; but he and his counsels have long been forgotten by her, and the dust lies upon his lips.

Through the heavy door whose bronze network closes the place of his rest, let us enter the church itself. It is lost in still deeper twilight, to which the eye must be accustomed for some moments before the form of the building can be traced; and then there opens before us a vast cave, hewn out into the form of a Cross, and divided into shadowy aisles by many pillars. Round the domes of its roof the light enters only through narrow apertures like large stars; and here and there a ray or two from some faraway casement wanders into the darkness, and casts a narrow phosphoric stream upon the waves of marble that heave and fall in a thousand colors along the floor. What else there is of light is from torches, or silver lamps, burning ceaselessly in the recesses of the chapels; the roof sheeted with gold, and the polished walls covered with alabaster, give back at every curve and angle some feeble gleaming to the flames; and the glories round the heads of the sculptured saints flash out upon us as we pass them, and sink again into the gloom. Under foot and over head, a continual succession of crowded imagery, one picture passing into another, as in a dream; forms beautiful and terrible mixed together; dragons and serpents, and ravening beasts of prey, and graceful birds that in the midst of them drink from running fountains and feed from vases of crystal; the passions and the pleasures of human life symbolized together, and the mystery of its redemption; for the mazes of interwoven lines and changeful pictures lead always at last to the Cross, lifted and carved in every place and upon every stone; sometimes with the serpent of eternity wrapped round it, sometimes with doves beneath its arms, and sweet herbage growing forth from its feet; but conspicuous most of all on the great rood that crosses the church before the altar, raised in bright blazonry against the shadow of the apse. And although in the recesses of the aisles and chapels, when the mist of the incense hangs heavily, we may see continually a figure traced in faint lines upon their marble, a woman standing with her eyes raised to heaven, and the inscription above her, "Mother of God," she is not here [24] the presiding deity. It is the Cross that is first seen, and always, burning in the center of the temple; and every dome and hollow of its roof has the figure of Christ in the utmost height of it, raised in power, or returning in judgment.

Nor is this interior without effect on the minds of the people. At every hour of the day

---

[20] The *Venetian Chronicle of Andrea Dandolo.* He reigned from 1343 to 1354.
[21] See Ephesians, 3:10.
[22] *Paradise Lost*, v, 601.
[23] St. Matthew, 3:10.

[24] There is an implied reference to the church of San Donato at Murano, described in the preceding chapter, in which the Virgin is "the presiding deity."

there are groups collected before the various shrines, and solitary worshipers scattered through the darker places of the church, evidently in prayer both deep and reverent, and, for the most part, profoundly sorrowful. The devotees at the greater number of the renowned shrines of Romanism may be seen murmuring their appointed prayers with wandering eyes and unengaged gestures; but the step of the stranger does not disturb those who kneel on the pavement of St. Mark's; and hardly a moment passes, from early morning to sunset, in which we may not see some half-veiled figure enter beneath the Arabian porch, cast itself into long abasement on the floor of the temple, and then rising slowly with more confirmed step, and with a passionate kiss and clasp of the arms given to the feet of the crucifix, by which the lamps burn always in the northern aisle, leave the church, as if comforted.

But we must not hastily conclude from this that the nobler characters of the building have at present any influence in fostering a devotional spirit. There is distress enough in Venice to bring many to their knees, without excitement from external imagery; and whatever there may be in the temper of the worship offered in St. Mark's more than can be accounted for by reference to the unhappy circumstances of the city, is assuredly not owing either to the beauty of its architecture or to the impressiveness of the Scripture histories embodied in its mosaics. That it has a peculiar effect, however slight, on the popular mind, may perhaps be safely conjectured from the number of worshipers which it attracts, while the churches of St. Paul and the Frari, larger in size and more central in position, are left comparatively empty.[25] But this effect is altogether to be ascribed to its richer assemblage of those sources of influence which address themselves to the commonest instincts of the human mind, and which, in all ages and countries, have been more or less employed in the support of superstition. Darkness and mystery; confused recesses of building; artificial light employed in small quantity, but maintained with a constancy which seems to give it a kind of sacredness; preciousness of material easily comprehended by the vulgar eye; close air loaded with a sweet and peculiar odor associated only with religious services, solemn music, and tangible idols or images having popular legends attached to them,—these, the stage properties of superstition, which have been from the beginning of the world, and must be to the end of it, employed by all nations, whether openly savage or nominally civilized, to produce a false awe in minds incapable of apprehending the true nature of the Deity, are assembled in St. Mark's to a degree, as far as I know, unexampled in any other European church. The arts of the Magus [26] and the Brahmin are exhausted in the animation of a paralyzed Christianity; and the popular sentiment which these arts excite is to be regarded by us with no more respect than we should have considered ourselves justified in rendering to the devotion of the worshipers at Eleusis, Ellora, or Edfou.[27]

---

[25] The mere warmth of St. Mark's in winter, which is much greater than that of the other two churches above named, must, however, be taken into consideration, as one of the most efficient causes of its being then more frequented (Ruskin's note).

[26] Member of the ancient Persian priestly class.

[27] Ellora is in Hyderabad, India; Edfou in upper Egypt.

# Matthew Arnold

## 1822 - 1888

Arnold was born at Laleham, in Middlesex, on 24 December, 1822. His father, Thomas Arnold, later became famous as the head-master of Rugby School; and the son, widely as his thought came to diverge from his father's, never ceased to feel the influence of the simple and powerful personality who, by his work at Rugby, transformed English public-school life. Arnold was sent first to his father's school, the Wykehamist College of Winchester, but after a year there was brought to Rugby, where he remained four years, until, in 1841, he went up to Balliol College, Oxford, with a classical scholarship. He took his B. A. in 1845. He failed to secure a first class, but nevertheless was soon elected a fellow of Oriel College. This opened up to him the possibility of an academic career; but, deeply as Arnold loved Oxford throughout his life, he seems never seriously to have considered remaining there. In 1847 he became a private secretary to Lord Lansdowne, who was then President of the Privy Council. Four years later Arnold was appointed an inspector of schools. He took this post, as he many years later told an audience of teachers, not because he liked the work or indeed at first knew anything about it, but in order to be able to marry. And shortly thereafter he was married to Miss Frances Lucy Wightman, who made a home for him which during the remainder of his life was his chief resource and stay. Arnold never grew to like the drudgery of his educational post; but he soon came to see the importance of his work and to value his position for the influence it gave him in improving education. His post also gave him various opportunities for travel on the Continent, and enabled him to publish some of the best and wisest writing on education that the nineteenth century saw. He remained an inspector of schools until within a few years of his death on 15 April, 1888.

Arnold began his literary career as a poet, publishing The Strayed Reveler and Other Poems anonymously in 1849, and three years later, also anonymously, Empedocles on Etna and Other Poems. Both volumes were soon withdrawn from sale because of Arnold's dissatisfaction with some of the pieces they contained. In 1853 and 1855, however, the greater number of the earlier poems were re-issued, together with some new ones, among the latter Sohrab and Rustum and The Scholar Gypsy. Merope, a dramatic poem, was published in 1858, and New Poems in 1867. Meanwhile Arnold had been elected Professor of Poetry at Oxford in 1857, a post which he held, as was then possible, for two terms, until 1867. The duties of this position turned his attention definitely to criticism, and from the early eighteen-sixties his work was almost exclusively critical; he wrote little or no poetry after 1867. His lectures On Translating Homer were published in 1861, Essays in Criticism in 1865, and Celtic Literature in 1867. In a famous and often disputed phrase Arnold defined poetry as a "criticism of life." It is a phrase which, at any rate, may stand for the poetry which he valued most highly, and it may stand, too, for his own critical work. Like Ruskin, Arnold was unable to consider artistic excellence as a thing separable from the common life of men, and like Ruskin he was inevitably drawn on from the consideration of art to consideration of the social and moral problems raised by industrial democracies. His major contributions to the discussion of these questions are contained in Culture and Anarchy (1869), St. Paul and Protestantism (1870), Friendship's Garland (1871), Literature and Dogma (1873), God and the Bible (1875), Mixed Essays (1879), and Irish Essays (1882). The Discourses in America (1885) were delivered in a lecture-tour of the United States in the winter of 1883–1884.

In a letter to his mother written in 1869 Arnold says: "My poems represent, on the whole, the main movement of mind of the last

quarter of a century, and thus they will probably have their day as people become conscious
to themselves of what that movement of mind
is, and interested in the literary productions
which reflect it. It might be fairly urged that I
have less poetical sentiment than Tennyson,
and less intellectual vigor and abundance than
Browning; yet, because I have perhaps more of
a fusion of the two than either of them, and
have more regularly applied that fusion to the
main line of modern development, I am likely
enough to have my turn, as they have had
theirs." The passage of years has served to show
that Arnold's verdict on his own poetry was
essentially just. His verse has never been widely
popular, but it securely holds, and will long
hold, the attention of thoughtful people. Likewise his criticism, whether one can agree with
all his conclusions or not, will long be read for
its persuasive charm, its ease and urbanity, its
combined lightness and sureness of touch, and
its honest good faith always showing beneath
the surface of Arnold's playfulness.

Properly speaking, no collected edition of
Arnold's writings has ever been published. A
uniformly and finely printed edition of the volumes by Arnold which Macmillan and Co., of
London, had published appeared in 1903, with
the general title of Works, but this was seriously incomplete. Lists of Arnold's books will
be found in several of the volumes mentioned
below. A convenient one-volume edition of
Arnold's Poems is published by the Oxford
University Press with Introduction by Sir
Arthur Quiller-Couch (revised by C. B. Tinker
and H. F. Lowry, 1950). Another excellent
one-volume selection is Arnold's Poetry and
Prose, edited by John Bryson (Reynard Library,
London, 1954). Poetry and Prose, with Wil-
liam Watson's Poem, and Essays by Lionel
Johnson and H. W. Garrod, is edited by Sir
E. K. Chambers (Oxford, 1939). An excellent,
though unattractively printed, selection from
Arnold's prose, Representative Essays, has been
edited by E. K. Brown (New York, 1936); and
Culture and Anarchy has been notably edited
by J. Dover Wilson (Cambridge, 1932). The
Note Books of Matthew Arnold were edited by
H. F. Lowry, K. Young, and W. H. Dunn
(Oxford, 1952). Arnold's Letters, ed. George
W. E. Russell, were published in two volumes
in 1895. Additional letters have since been
published, the most important being The
Letters of Matthew Arnold to Arthur Hugh
Clough, ed. H. F. Lowry (London, 1932). It
was Arnold's wish that no biography of him
should be written, but his friend G. W. E.

Russell after editing the Letters wrote an account of the effect Arnold produced "on the
thought and action of his age" (Matthew
Arnold, in the series of "Literary Lives," 1904)
which has permanent value. The best appreciative and critical introduction to Arnold, with
many long quotations from his verse and prose,
is Stuart P. Sherman's Matthew Arnold, How
to Know Him (Indianapolis, 1917). Matthew
Arnold by Lionel Trilling (New York, 1949)
is a thorough critical study, scholarly, intelligent, and illuminating. Other recommended
biographical and critical studies are The Poetry
of Matthew Arnold: a Commentary, by C. B.
Tinker and H. F. Lowry (New York, 1940);
Matthew Arnold and the Modern Spirit, by
H. F. Lowry (Princeton, 1941); Matthew
Arnold: a Study, by Sir E. K. Chambers (Oxford, 1947); and Matthew Arnold: a Study in
Conflict, by E. K. Brown (Chicago, 1948). An
interesting critical essay concerning Arnold is
included in The Use of Poetry and the Use of
Criticism, by T. S. Eliot (London, 1933).

# Sweetness and Light [1]

The disparagers of culture make its motive curiosity; sometimes, indeed, they make
its motive mere exclusiveness and vanity. The
culture which is supposed to plume itself
on a smattering of Greek and Latin is a culture
which is begotten by nothing so intellectual as
curiosity; it is valued either out of sheer vanity
and ignorance or else as an engine of social and
class distinction, separating its holder, like a
badge or title, from other people who have not
got it. No serious man would call this culture,
or attach any value to it, as culture, at all. To
find the real ground for the very different estimate which serious people will set upon culture, we must find some motive for culture in
the terms of which may lie a real ambiguity;
and such a motive the word curiosity gives us.

I have before now pointed out that we
English do not, like the foreigners, use this
word in a good sense as well as in a bad
sense. With us the word is always used in
a somewhat disapproving sense. A liberal
and intelligent eagerness about the things of
the mind may be meant by a foreigner when
he speaks of curiosity, but with us the word

[1] The initial essay in Culture and Anarchy, 1869.
In 1867 Arnold had delivered it as his last lecture
as Professor of Poetry at Oxford, and in the same
year it had been published in the Cornhill Magazine;
the original title of the essay was Culture and Its
Enemies.

always conveys a certain notion of frivolous and unedifying activity. In the *Quarterly Review*, some little time ago, was an estimate of the celebrated French critic, M. Sainte-Beuve,[2] and a very inadequate estimate it in my judgment was. And its inadequacy consisted chiefly in this: that in our English way it left out of sight the double sense really involved in the word *curiosity*, thinking enough was said to stamp M. Sainte-Beuve with blame if it was said that he was impelled in his operations as a critic by curiosity, and omitting either to perceive that M. Sainte-Beuve himself, and many other people with him, would consider that this was praiseworthy and not blameworthy, or to point out why it ought really to be accounted worthy of blame and not of praise. For as there is a curiosity about intellectual matters which is futile, and merely a disease, so there is certainly a curiosity,—a desire after the things of the mind simply for their own sakes and for the pleasure of seeing them as they are,—which is, in an intelligent being, natural and laudable. Nay, and the very desire to see things as they are implies a balance and regulation of mind which is not often attained without fruitful effort, and which is the very opposite of the blind and diseased impulse of mind which is what we mean to blame when we blame curiosity. Montesquieu[3] says: "The first motive which ought to impel us to study is the desire to augment the excellence of our nature, and to render an intelligent being yet more intelligent." This is the true ground to assign for the genuine scientific passion, however manifested, and for culture, viewed simply as a fruit of this passion; and it is a worthy ground, even though we let the term *curiosity* stand to describe it.

But there is of culture another view, in which not solely the scientific passion, the sheer desire to see things as they are, natural and proper in an intelligent being, appears as the ground of it. There is a view in which all the love of our neighbor, the impulses towards action, help, and beneficence, the desire for removing human error, clearing human confusion, and diminishing human misery, the noble aspiration to leave the world better and happier than we found it,—motives eminently such as are called social,—come in as part of the grounds of culture, and the main and pre-eminent part. Culture is then

properly described not as having its origin in curiosity, but as having its origin in the love of perfection; it is *a study of perfection*. It moves by the force, not merely or primarily of the scientific passion for pure knowledge, but also of the moral and social passion for doing good. As, in the first view of it, we took for its worthy motto Montesquieu's words: "To render an intelligent being yet more intelligent!" so, in the second view of it, there is no better motto which it can have than these words of Bishop Wilson:[4] "To make reason and the will of God prevail!"

Only, whereas the passion for doing good is apt to be overhasty in determining what reason and the will of God say, because its turn is for acting rather than thinking and it wants to be beginning to act; and whereas it is apt to take its own conceptions, which proceed from its own state of development and share in all the imperfections and immaturities of this, for a basis of action; what distinguishes culture is, that it is possessed by the scientific passion as well as by the passion of doing good; that it demands worthy notions of reason and the will of God, and does not readily suffer its own crude conceptions to substitute themselves for them. And knowing that no action or institution can be salutary and stable which is not based on reason and the will of God, it is not so bent on acting and instituting, even with the great aim of diminishing human error and misery ever before its thoughts, but that it can remember that acting and instituting are of little use, unless we know how and what we ought to act and to institute.

This culture is more interesting and more far-reaching than that other, which is founded solely on the scientific passion for knowing. But it needs times of faith and ardor, times when the intellectual horizon is opening and widening all round us, to flourish in. And is not the close and bounded intellectual horizon within which we have long lived and moved now lifting up, and are not new lights finding free passage to shine in upon us? For a long time there was no passage for them to make their way in upon us, and then it was of no use to think of adapting the world's action to them. Where was the hope of making reason and the will of God prevail among people who had a routine which they had christened reason and

[2] Charles A. Sainte-Beuve (1804–1869), author of the *Causeries du Lundi*.

[3] Charles L. de Secondat de Montesquieu (1689–1755), author of the *De l'Esprit des Lois*.

[4] Thomas Wilson (1663–1755), Bishop of Sodor and Man.

the will of God, in which they were inextricably bound, and beyond which they had no power of looking? But now the iron force of adhesion to the old routine,—social, political, religious—has wonderfully yielded; the iron force of exclusion of all which is new has wonderfully yielded. The danger now is, not that people should obstinately refuse to allow anything but their old routine to pass for reason and the will of God, but either that they should allow some novelty or other to pass for these too easily, or else that they should underrate the importance of them altogether, and think it enough to follow action for its own sake, without troubling themselves to make reason and the will of God prevail therein. Now, then, is the moment for culture to be of service, culture which believes in making reason and the will of God prevail, believes in perfection, is the study and pursuit of perfection, and is no longer debarred, by a rigid invincible exclusion of whatever is new, from getting acceptance for its ideas, simply because they are new.

The moment this view of culture is seized, the moment it is regarded not solely as the endeavor to see things as they are, to draw towards a knowledge of the universal order which seems to be intended and aimed at in the world, and which it is a man's happiness to go along with or his misery to go counter to,—to learn, in short, the will of God,—the moment, I say, culture is considered not merely as the endeavor to *see* and *learn* this, but as the endeavor, also, to make it *prevail*, the moral, social, and beneficent character of culture becomes manifest. The mere endeavor to see and learn the truth for our own personal satisfaction is indeed a commencement for making it prevail, a preparing the way for this, which always serves this, and is wrongly, therefore, stamped with blame absolutely in itself and not only in its caricature and degeneration. But perhaps it has got stamped with blame, and disparaged with the dubious title of curiosity, because in comparison with this wider endeavor of such great and plain utility it looks selfish, petty, and unprofitable.

And religion, the greatest and most important of the efforts by which the human race has manifested its impulse to perfect itself,—religion, that voice of the deepest human experience,—does not only enjoin and sanction the aim which is the great aim of culture, the aim of setting ourselves to ascertain what perfection is and to make it prevail; but also, in determining generally in what human perfection consists, religion comes to a conclusion identical with that which culture,—culture seeking the determination of this question through *all* the voices of human experience which have been heard upon it, of art, science, poetry, philosophy, history, as well as of religion, in order to give a greater fulness and certainty to its solution,—likewise reaches. Religion says: *The kingdom of God is within you;* and culture, in like manner, places human perfection in an *internal* condition, in the growth and predominance of our humanity proper, as distinguished from our animality. It places it in the ever-increasing efficacy and in the general harmonious expansion of those gifts of thought and feeling, which make the peculiar dignity, wealth, and happiness of human nature. As I have said on a former occasion: "It is in making endless additions to itself, in the endless expansion of its powers, in endless growth in wisdom and beauty, that the spirit of the human race finds its ideal. To reach this ideal, culture is an indispensable aid, and that is the true value of culture." Not a having and a resting, but a growing and a becoming, is the character of perfection as culture conceives it; and here, too, it coincides with religion.

And because men are all members of one great whole, and the sympathy which is in human nature will not allow one member to be indifferent to the rest or to have a perfect welfare independent of the rest, the expansion of our humanity, to suit the idea of perfection which culture forms, must be a *general* expansion. Perfection, as culture conceives it, is not possible while the individual remains isolated. The individual is required, under pain of being stunted and enfeebled in his own development if he disobeys, to carry others along with him in his march towards perfection, to be continually doing all he can to enlarge and increase the volume of the human stream sweeping thitherward. And here, once more, culture lays on us the same obligation as religion, which says, as Bishop Wilson has admirably put it, that "to promote the kingdom of God is to increase and hasten one's own happiness."

But, finally, perfection,—as culture from a thorough disinterested study of human nature and human experience learns to conceive it,—is a harmonious expansion of *all* the powers which make the beauty and worth of human nature, and is not consistent with the over-development of any one power at the expense of the rest. Here culture goes beyond religion as religion is generally conceived by us.

If culture, then, is a study of perfection, and of harmonious perfection, general perfection, and perfection which consists in becoming something rather than in having something, in an inward condition of the mind and spirit, not in an outward set of circumstances,—it is clear that culture, instead of being the frivolous and useless thing which Mr. Bright, and Mr. Frederic Harrison,[5] and many other Liberals are apt to call it, has a very important function to fulfil for mankind. And this function is particularly important in our modern world, of which the whole civilization is, to a much greater degree than the civilization of Greece and Rome, mechanical and external, and tends constantly to become more so. But above all in our own country has culture a weighty part to perform, because here that mechanical character, which civilization tends to take everywhere, is shown in the most eminent degree. Indeed nearly all the characters of perfection, as culture teaches us to fix them, meet in this country with some powerful tendency which thwarts them and sets them at defiance. The idea of perfection as an *inward* condition of the mind and spirit is at variance with the mechanical and material civilization in esteem with us, and nowhere, as I have said, so much in esteem as with us. The idea of perfection as a *general* expansion of the human family is at variance with our strong individualism, our hatred of all limits to the unrestrained swing of the individual's personality, our maxim of "every man for himself." Above all, the idea of perfection as a *harmonious* expansion of human nature is at variance with our want of flexibility, with our inaptitude for seeing more than one side of a thing, with our intense energetic absorption in the particular pursuit we happen to be following. So culture has a rough task to achieve in this country. Its preachers have, and are likely long to have, a hard time of it, and they will much oftener be regarded, for a great while

to come, as elegant or spurious Jeremiahs than as friends and benefactors. That, however, will not prevent their doing in the end good service if they persevere. And, meanwhile, the mode of action they have to pursue, and the sort of habits they must fight against, ought to be made quite clear for every one to see, who may be willing to look at the matter attentively and dispassionately.

Faith in machinery is, I said, our besetting danger; often in machinery most absurdly disproportioned to the end which this machinery, if it is to do any good at all, is to serve; but always in machinery, as if it had a value in and for itself. What is freedom but machinery? what is population but machinery? what is coal but machinery? what are railroads but machinery? what is wealth but machinery? what are, even, religious organizations but machinery? Now almost every voice in England is accustomed to speak of these things as if they were precious ends in themselves, and therefore had some of the characters of perfection indisputably joined to them. I have before now noticed Mr. Roebuck's[6] stock argument for proving the greatness and happiness of England as she is, and for quite stopping the mouths of all gainsayers. Mr. Roebuck is never weary of reiterating this argument of his, so I do not know why I should be weary of noticing it. "May not every man in England say what he likes?"—Mr. Roebuck perpetually asks; and that, he thinks, is quite sufficient, and when every man may say what he likes, our aspirations ought to be satisfied. But the aspirations of culture, which is the study of perfection, are not satisfied, unless what men say, when they may say what they like, is worth saying,—has good in it, and more good than bad. In the same way the *Times*,[7] replying to some foreign strictures on the dress, looks, and behavior of the English abroad, urges that the English ideal is that every one should be free to do and look just as he likes. But culture indefatigably tries, not to make what each raw person may like the rule by which he fashions himself; but to draw ever nearer to a sense of what is indeed beautiful, graceful, and becoming, and to get the raw person to like that.

And in the same way with respect to railroads and coal. Every one must have ob-

[5] The Quaker, John Bright (1811–1889), was one of the leading middle-class liberals of his time, a manufacturer, a member of Parliament, and a member of several cabinets. Frederic Harrison (1831–1923) was a writer who devoted much of his energy to the propagation of the positivistic philosophy of Auguste Comte.

[6] The Right Hon. J. A. Roebuck (1801–1879), barrister and politician.

[7] The London *Times*, the most authoritative English newspaper.

served the strange language current during the late discussions as to the possible failure of our supplies of coal. Our coal, thousands of people were saying, is the real basis of our national greatness; if our coal runs short, there is an end of the greatness of England. But what *is* greatness?—culture makes us ask. Greatness is a spiritual condition worthy to excite love, interest, and admiration; and the outward proof of possessing greatness is that we excite love, interest, and admiration. If England were swallowed up by the sea to-morrow, which of the two, a hundred years hence, would most excite the love, interest, and admiration of mankind,—would most, therefore, show the evidences of having possessed greatness,—the England of the last twenty years, or the England of Elizabeth, of a time of splendid spiritual effort, but when our coal, and our industrial operations depending on coal, were very little developed? Well, then, what an unsound habit of mind it must be which makes us talk of things like coal or iron as constituting the greatness of England, and how salutary a friend is culture, bent on seeing things as they are, and thus dissipating delusions of this kind and fixing standards of perfection that are real!

Wealth, again, that end to which our prodigious works for material advantage are directed,—the commonest of commonplaces tells us how men are always apt to regard wealth as a precious end in itself; and certainly they have never been so apt thus to regard it as they are in England at the present time. Never did people believe anything more firmly than nine Englishmen out of ten at the present day believe that our greatness and welfare are proved by our being so very rich. Now, the use of culture is that it helps us, by means of its spiritual standard of perfection, to regard wealth as but machinery, and not only to say as a matter of words that we regard wealth as but machinery, but really to perceive and feel that it is so. If it were not for this purging effect wrought upon our minds by culture, the whole world, the future as well as the present, would inevitably belong to the Philistines. The people who believe most that our greatness and welfare are proved by our being very rich, and who most give their lives and thoughts to becoming rich, are just the very people whom we call Philistines. Culture says: "Consider these people, then, their way of life, their habits, their manners,

the very tones of their voice; look at them attentively; observe the literature they read, the things which give them pleasure, the words which come forth out of their mouths, the thoughts which make the furniture of their minds: would any amount of wealth be worth having with the condition that one was to become just like these people by having it?" And thus culture begets a dissatisfaction which is of the highest possible value in stemming the common tide of men's thoughts in a wealthy and industrial community, and which saves the future, as one may hope, from being vulgarized, even if it cannot save the present.

Population, again, and bodily health and vigor, are things which are nowhere treated in such an unintelligent, misleading, exaggerated way as in England. Both are really machinery; yet how many people all around us do we see rest in them and fail to look beyond them! Why, one has heard people, fresh from reading certain articles of the *Times* on the Registrar-General's returns of marriages and births in this country, who would talk of our large English families in quite a solemn strain, as if they had something in itself beautiful, elevating, and meritorious in them; as if the British Philistine would have only to present himself before the Great Judge with his twelve children, in order to be received among the sheep as a matter of right!

But bodily health and vigor, it may be said, are not to be classed with wealth and population as mere machinery; they have a more real and essential value. True; but only as they are more intimately connected with a perfect spiritual condition than wealth or population are. The moment we disjoin them from the idea of a perfect spiritual condition, and pursue them, as we do pursue them, for their own sake and as ends in themselves, our worship of them becomes as mere worship of machinery, as our worship of wealth or population, and as unintelligent and vulgarizing a worship as that is. Every one with anything like an adequate idea of human perfection has distinctly marked this subordination to higher and spiritual ends of the cultivation of bodily vigor and activity. "Bodily exercise profiteth little; but godliness is profitable unto all things," says the author of the Epistle to Timothy.[8] And the utilitarian Franklin says just as explicitly:— "Eat and drink such an exact quantity as

[8] I Timothy, 4:8.

suits the constitution of thy body, *in reference to the services of the mind."* But the point of view of culture, keeping the mark of human perfection simply and broadly in view, and not assigning to this perfection, as religion or utilitarianism assigns to it, a special and limited character, this point of view, I say, of culture is best given by these words of Epictetus: [9]—"It is a sign of ἀφυία," says he,—that is, of a nature not finely tempered, —"to give yourselves up to things which relate to the body; to make, for instance, a great fuss about exercise, a great fuss about eating, a great fuss about drinking, a great fuss about walking, a great fuss about riding. All these things ought to be done merely by the way: the formation of the spirit and character must be our real concern." This is admirable; and, indeed, the Greek word εὐφυία, a finely tempered nature, gives exactly the notion of perfection as culture brings us to conceive it: a harmonious perfection, a perfection in which the characters of beauty and intelligence are both present, which unites "the two noblest of things,"—as Swift, who of one of the two, at any rate, had himself all too little, most happily calls them in his *Battle of the Books,* —"the two noblest of things, *sweetness and light."* The εὐφυής is the man who tends towards sweetness and light; the ἀφυής, on the other hand, is our Philistine. The immense spiritual significance of the Greeks is due to their having been inspired with this central and happy idea of the essential character of human perfection; and Mr. Bright's misconception of culture, as a smattering of Greek and Latin, comes itself, after all, from this wonderful significance of the Greeks having affected the very machinery of our education, and is in itself a kind of homage to it.

In thus making sweetness and light to be characters of perfection, culture is of like spirit with poetry, follows one law with poetry. Far more than on our freedom, our population, and our industrialism, many amongst us rely upon our religious organizations to save us. I have called religion a yet more important manifestation of human nature than poetry, because it has worked on a broader scale for perfection, and with greater masses of men. But the idea of beauty and of a human nature perfect on all its sides, which is the dominant idea of poetry, is a true and invaluable idea, though it has not yet had the

[9] The Stoic philosopher of the first century A.D.

success that the idea of conquering the obvious faults of our animality, and of a human nature perfect on the moral side,—which is the dominant idea of religion,—has been enabled to have; and it is destined, adding to itself the religious idea of a devout energy, to transform and govern the other.

The best art and poetry of the Greeks, in which religion and poetry are one, in which the idea of beauty and of a human nature perfect on all sides adds to itself a religious and devout energy, and works in the strength of that, is on this account of such surpassing interest and instructiveness for us, though it was,—as, having regard to the human race in general, and, indeed, having regard to the Greeks themselves, we must own,—a premature attempt, an attempt which for success needed the moral and religious fiber in humanity to be more braced and developed than it had yet been. But Greece did not err in having the idea of beauty, harmony, and complete human perfection, so present and paramount. It is impossible to have this idea too present and paramount; only, the moral fiber must be braced too. And we, because we have braced the moral fiber, are not on that account in the right way, if at the same time the idea of beauty, harmony, and complete human perfection, is wanting or misapprehended amongst us; and evidently it *is* wanting or misapprehended at present. And when we rely as we do on our religious organizations, which in themselves do not and cannot give us this idea, and think we have done enough if we make them spread and prevail, then, I say, we fall into our common fault of overvaluing machinery.

Nothing is more common than for people to confound the inward peace and satisfaction which follows the subduing of the obvious faults of our animality with what I may call absolute inward peace and satisfaction,— the peace and satisfaction which are reached as we draw near to complete spiritual perfection, and not merely to moral perfection, or rather to relative moral perfection. No people in the world have done more and struggled more to attain this relative moral perfection than our English race has. For no people in the world has the command to *resist the devil,* to *overcome the wicked one,* in the nearest and most obvious sense of those words, had such a pressing force and reality. And we have had our reward, not only in the great worldly prosperity which our obedience to this command has brought us, but also, and far more, in great inward peace and satisfaction. But to me few things are more pathetic than to see people, on the strength of the inward peace and satisfaction which their rudimentary efforts towards perfection have brought them, employ, concerning their incomplete perfection and the religious organizations within which they have found it, language which properly applies only to complete perfection, and is a far-off echo of the human soul's prophecy of it. Religion itself, I need hardly say, supplies them in abundance 10 with this grand language. And very freely do they use it; yet it is really the severest possible criticism of such an incomplete perfection as alone we have yet reached through our religious organizations.

The impulse of the English race towards moral development and self-conquest has nowhere so powerfully manifested itself as in Puritanism. Nowhere has Puritanism found so adequate an expression as in the religious 20 organization of the Independents.[10] The modern Independents have a newspaper, the *Nonconformist*, written with great sincerity and ability. The motto, the standard, the profession of faith which this organ of theirs carries aloft, is: "The Dissidence of Dissent and the Protestantism of the Protestant religion." There is sweetness and light, and an ideal of complete harmonious human perfection! One need not go to culture and poetry to find language to 30 judge it. Religion, with its instinct for perfection, supplies language to judge it, language, too, which is in our mouths every day. "Finally, be of one mind, united in feeling," says St. Peter.[11] There is an ideal which judges the Puritan ideal: "The Dissidence of Dissent and the Protestantism of the Protestant religion!" And religious organizations like this are what people believe in, rest in, would give their lives for! Such, I say, is the wonderful 40 virtue of even the beginnings of perfection, of having conquered even the plain faults of our animality, that the religious organization which has helped us to do it can seem to us something precious, salutary, and to be propagated, even when it wears such a brand of imperfection on its forehead as this. And men have got such a habit of giving to the language of religion a special application, of making it a mere jargon, that for the condemnation which reli- 50 gion itself passes on the shortcomings of their religious organizations they have no ear; they are sure to cheat themselves and to explain this condemnation away. They can only be reached by the criticism which culture, like poetry, speaking a language not to be sophisticated,

and resolutely testing these organizations by the ideal of a human perfection complete on all sides, applies to them.

But men of culture and poetry, it will be said, are again and again failing, and failing conspicuously, in the necessary first stage to a harmonious perfection, in the subduing of the great obvious faults of our animality, which it is the glory of these religious organizations to have helped us to subdue. True, they do often so fail. They have often been without the virtues as well as the faults of the Puritan; it has been one of their dangers that they so felt the Puritan's faults that they too much neglected the practice of his virtues. I will not, however, exculpate them at the Puritan's expense. They have often failed in morality, and morality is indispensable. And they have been punished for their failure, as the Puritan has been rewarded for his performance. They have been punished wherein they erred; but their ideal of beauty, of sweetness and light, and a human nature complete on all its sides, remains the true ideal of perfection still; just as the Puritan's ideal of perfection remains narrow and inadequate, although for what he did well he has been richly rewarded. Notwithstanding the mighty results of the Pilgrim Fathers' voyage, they and their standard of perfection are rightly judged when we figure to ourselves Shakespeare or Virgil,—souls in whom sweetness and light, and all that in human nature is most humane, were eminent, —accompanying them on their voyage, and think what intolerable company Shakespeare and Virgil would have found them! In the same way let us judge the religious organizations which we see all around us. Do not let us deny the good and the happiness which they have accomplished; but do not let us fail to see clearly that their idea of human perfection is narrow and inadequate, and that the Dissidence of Dissent and the Protestantism of the Protestant religion will never bring humanity to its true goal. As I said with regard to wealth: Let us look at the life of those who live in and for it,—so I say with regard to the religious organizations. Look at the life imaged in such a newspaper as the *Nonconformist*,—a life of jealousy of the Establishment,[12] disputes, tea-meetings, openings of chapels, sermons; and then think of it as an ideal of a human life completing itself on all sides, and aspiring with all its organs after sweetness, light, and perfection!

[10] Congregationalists.    [11] I Peter, 3:8.

[12] The ecclesiastical system of the Church of England, established by law.

Another newspaper, representing, like the *Nonconformist,* one of the religious organizations of this country, was a short time ago giving an account of the crowd at Epsom on the Derby day, and of all the vice and hideousness which was to be seen in that crowd; and then the writer turned suddenly round upon Professor Huxley,[13] and asked him how he proposed to cure all this vice and hideousness without religion. I confess I felt disposed to ask the asker this question: and how do you propose to cure it with such a religion as yours? How is the ideal of a life so unlovely, so unattractive, so incomplete, so narrow, so far removed from a true and satisfying ideal of human perfection, as is the life of your religious organization as you yourself reflect it, to conquer and transform all this vice and hideousness? Indeed, the strongest plea for the study of perfection as pursued by culture, the clearest proof of the actual inadequacy of the idea of perfection held by the religious organizations, —expressing, as I have said, the most widespread effort which the human race has yet made after perfection,—is to be found in the state of our life and society with these in possession of it, and having been in possession of it I know not how many hundred years. We are all of us included in some religious organization or other; we all call ourselves, in the sublime and aspiring language of religion which I have before noticed, *children of God.* Children of God;—it is an immense pretension!—and how are we to justify it? By the works which we do, and the words which we speak. And the work which we collective children of God do, our grand center of life, our *city* which we have builded for us to dwell in, is London! London, with its unutterable external hideousness, and with its internal canker of *publice egestas, privatim opulentia,*[14]—to use the words which Sallust puts into Cato's mouth about Rome,— unequaled in the world! The word, again, which we children of God speak, the voice which most hits our collective thought, the newspaper with the largest circulation in England, nay, with the largest circulation in the whole world, is the *Daily Telegraph!* I say that when our religious organizations,—which I admit to express the most considerable effort

after perfection that our race has yet made,— land us in no better result than this, it is high time to examine carefully their idea of perfection, to see whether it does not leave out of account sides and forces of human nature which we might turn to great use; whether it would not be more operative if it were more complete. And I say that the English reliance on our religious organizations and on their ideas of human perfection just as they stand, is like our reliance on freedom, on muscular Christianity, on population, on coal, on wealth, —mere belief in machinery, and unfruitful; and that it is wholesomely counteracted by culture, bent on seeing things as they are, and on drawing the human race onwards to a more complete, a harmonious perfection.

Culture, however, shows its single-minded love of perfection, its desire simply to make reason and the will of God prevail, its freedom from fanaticism, by its attitude towards all this machinery, even while it insists that it *is* machinery. Fanatics, seeing the mischief men do themselves by their blind belief in some machinery or other,—whether it is wealth and industrialism, or whether it is the cultivation of bodily strength and activity, or whether it is a political organization,—or whether it is a religious organization,—oppose with might and main the tendency to this or that political and religious organization, or to games and athletic exercises, or to wealth and industrialism, and try violently to stop it. But the flexibility which sweetness and light give, and which is one of the rewards of culture pursued in good faith, enables a man to see that a tendency may be necessary, and even, as a preparation for something in the future, salutary, and yet that the generations or individuals who obey this tendency are sacrificed to it, that they fall short of the hope of perfection by following it; and that its mischiefs are to be criticized, lest it should take too firm a hold and last after it has served its purpose.

Mr. Gladstone[15] well pointed out, in a speech at Paris,—and others have pointed out the same thing,—how necessary is the present great movement towards wealth and industrialism, in order to lay broad foundations of material well-being for the society of the future. The worst of these justifications is, that they are generally addressed to the very people engaged, body and soul, in the movement in question; at all events, that they are always seized with the greatest avidity by these people, and taken by

[13] Thomas Henry Huxley (1825–1895), the English writer who did most to popularize the ideas of the new science in Arnold's time.

[14] Public poverty, private wealth. Quoted from the *Bellum Catilinarium* (chap. 56) of Sallust, the Roman historian of the first century B.C.; the words were used by Marcus Porcius Cato (Cato Uticensis) in a speech.

[15] William Ewart Gladstone (1809–1898), several times prime minister.

them as quite justifying their life; and that thus they tend to harden them in their sins. Now, culture admits the necessity of the movement towards fortune-making and exaggerated industrialism, readily allows that the future may derive benefit from it; but insists, at the same time, that the passing generations of industrialists,—forming, for the most part, the stout main body of Philistinism,—are sacrificed to it. In the same way, the result of all the games and sports which occupy the passing generation of boys and young men may be the establishment of a better and sounder physical type for the future to work with. Culture does not set itself against the games and sports; it congratulates the future, and hopes it will make a good use of its improved physical basis; but it points out that our passing generation of boys and young men is, meantime, sacrificed. Puritanism was perhaps necessary to develop the moral fiber of the English race, Nonconformity to break the yoke of ecclesiastical domination over men's minds and to prepare the way for freedom of thought in the distant future; still, culture points out that the harmonious perfection of generations of Puritans and Nonconformists has been, in consequence, sacrificed. Freedom of speech may be necessary for the society of the future, but the young lions of the *Daily Telegraph* in the meanwhile are sacrificed. A voice for every man in his country's government may be necessary for the society of the future, but meanwhile Mr. Beales and Mr. Bradlaugh [16] are sacrificed.

Oxford, the Oxford of the past, has many faults; and she has heavily paid for them in defeat, in isolation, in want of hold upon the modern world. Yet we in Oxford, brought up amidst the beauty and sweetness of that beautiful place, have not failed to seize one truth,— the truth that beauty and sweetness are essential characters of a complete human perfection. When I insist on this, I am all in the faith and tradition of Oxford. I say boldly that this our sentiment for beauty and sweetness, our sentiment against hideousness and rawness, has been at the bottom of our attachment to so many beaten causes, of our opposition to so many triumphant movements. And the sentiment is true, and has never been wholly defeated, and has shown its power even in its defeat. We have not won our political battles,

we have not carried our main points, we have not stopped our adversaries' advance, we have not marched victoriously with the modern world; but we have told silently upon the mind of the country, we have prepared currents of feeling which sap our adversaries' position when it seems gained, we have kept up our own communications with the future. Look at the course of the great movement which shook Oxford to its center some thirty years ago! [17] It was directed, as any one who reads Dr. Newman's *Apology* may see, against what in one word may be called "Liberalism." Liberalism prevailed; it was the appointed force to do the work of the hour; it was necessary, it was inevitable that it should prevail. The Oxford movement was broken, it failed; our wrecks are scattered on every shore:—

Quae regio in terris nostri non plena laboris? [18]

But what was it, this liberalism, as Dr. Newman saw it, and as it really broke the Oxford movement? It was the great middle-class liberalism, which had for the cardinal points of its belief the Reform Bill of 1832, and local self-government, in politics; in the social sphere, free-trade, unrestricted competition, and the making of large industrial fortunes; in the religious sphere, the Dissidence of Dissent and the Protestantism of the Protestant religion. I do not say that other and more intelligent forces than this were not opposed to the Oxford movement: but this was the force which really beat it; this was the force which Dr. Newman felt himself fighting with; this was the force which till only the other day seemed to be the paramount force in this country, and to be in possession of the future; this was the force whose achievements fill Mr. Lowe [19] with such inexpressible admiration, and whose rule he was so horror-struck to see threatened. And where is this great force of Philistinism now? It is thrust into the second rank, it is become a power of yesterday, it has lost the future. A new power has suddenly appeared, a power which it is impossible yet to

[16] Edmond Beales (1803–1881), president of the Reform League, which advocated manhood suffrage; Charles Bradlaugh (1833–1891), who claimed and eventually succeeded in obtaining the right to sit in Parliament without taking an oath on the Bible.

[17] The Oxford Movement (1833–1845), an effort to return to the forms and doctrines of traditional Anglicanism. The most important member of the Movement, Newman, ultimately became a Roman Catholic; his *Apologia pro Vita Sua* (1864) was an explanation and defense of the steps in his conversion.

[18] What region of the earth is not filled with the story of our troubles? (*Aeneid*, I, 460.)

[19] Robert Lowe, later Lord Sherbrooke, leader of the Liberals who broke from their own party in 1866 when it proposed further reforms of a democratic character.

judge fully, but which is certainly a wholly different force from middle-class liberalism; different in its cardinal points of belief, different in its tendencies in every sphere. It loves and admires neither the legislation of middle-class Parliaments, nor the local self-government of middle-class vestries, nor the unrestricted competition of middle-class industrialists, nor the dissidence of middle-class Dissent and the Protestantism of middle-class Protestant religion. I am not now praising this new force, or saying that its own ideals are better; all I say is, that they are wholly different. And who will estimate how much the currents of feeling created by Dr. Newman's movement, the keen desire for beauty and sweetness which it nourished, the deep aversion it manifested to the hardness and vulgarity of middle-class liberalism, the strong light it turned on the hideous and grotesque illusions of middle-class Protestantism,—who will estimate how much all these contributed to swell the tide of secret dissatisfaction which has mined the ground under the self-confident liberalism of the last thirty years, and has prepared the way for its sudden collapse and supersession? It is in this manner that the sentiment of Oxford for beauty and sweetness conquers, and in this manner long may it continue to conquer!

In this manner it works to the same end as culture, and there is plenty of work for it yet to do. I have said that the new and more democratic force which is now superseding our old middle-class liberalism cannot yet be rightly judged. It has its main tendencies still to form. We hear promises of its giving us administrative reform, law reform, reform of education, and I know not what; but those promises come rather from its advocates, wishing to make a good plea for it and to justify it for superseding middle-class liberalism, than from clear tendencies which it has itself yet developed. But meanwhile it has plenty of well-intentioned friends against whom culture may with advantage continue to uphold steadily its ideal of human perfection; that this is *an inward spiritual activity, having for its characters increased sweetness, increased light, increased life, increased sympathy.* Mr. Bright, who has a foot in both worlds, the world of middle-class liberalism and the world of democracy, but who brings most of his ideas from the world of middle-class liberalism in which he was bred, always inclines to inculcate that faith in machinery to which, as we have seen, Englishmen are so prone, and which has been the bane of middle-class liberalism. He complains

with a sorrowful indignation of people who "appear to have no proper estimate of the value of the franchise"; he leads his disciples to believe—what the Englishman is always too ready to believe,—that the having a vote, like the having a large family, or a large business, or large muscles, has in itself some edifying and perfecting effect upon human nature. Or else he cries out to the democracy,—"the men," as he calls them, "upon whose shoulders the greatness of England rests,"—he cries out to them: "See what you have done! I look over this country and see the cities you have built, the railroads you have made, the manufactures you have produced, the cargoes which freight the ships of the greatest mercantile navy the world has ever seen! I see that you have converted by your labors what was once a wilderness, these islands, into a fruitful garden; I know that you have created this wealth, and are a nation whose name is a word of power throughout all the world." Why, this is just the very style of laudation with which Mr. Roebuck or Mr. Lowe debauches the minds of the middle classes, and makes such Philistines of them. It is the same fashion of teaching a man to value himself not on what he *is*, not on his progress in sweetness and light, but on the number of the railroads he has constructed, or the bigness of the tabernacle he has built. Only the middle classes are told they have done it all with their energy, self-reliance, and capital, and the democracy are told they have done it all with their hands and sinews. But teaching the democracy to put its trust in achievements of this kind is merely training them to be Philistines to take the place of the Philistines whom they are superseding; and they, too, like the middle class, will be encouraged to sit down at the banquet of the future without having on a wedding garment, and nothing excellent can then come from them. Those who know their besetting faults, those who have watched them and listened to them, or those who will read the instructive account recently given of them by one of themselves, the *Journeyman Engineer*, will agree that the idea which culture sets before us of perfection, —an increased spiritual activity, having for its characters increased sweetness, increased light, increased life, increased sympathy,—is an idea which the new democracy needs far more than the idea of the blessedness of the franchise, or the wonderfulness of its own industrial performances.

Other well-meaning friends of this new power are for leading it, not in the old ruts of middle-class Philistinism, but in ways which are naturally alluring to the feet of democracy, though in this country they are novel and untried ways. I may call them the ways of Jacobinism.[20] Violent indignation with the past, abstract systems of renovation applied wholesale, a new doctrine drawn up in black and white for elaborating down to the very smallest details a rational society for the future,—these are the ways of Jacobinism. Mr. Frederic Harrison and other disciples of Comte,[21]—one of them, Mr. Congreve, is an old friend of mine, and I am glad to have an opportunity of publicly expressing my respect for his talents and character,—are among the friends of democracy who are for leading it in paths of this kind. Mr. Frederic Harrison is very hostile to culture, and from a natural enough motive; for culture is the eternal opponent of the two things which are the signal marks of Jacobinism,—its fierceness, and its addiction to an abstract system. Culture is always assigning to system-makers and systems a smaller share in the bent of human destiny than their friends like. A current in people's minds sets towards new ideas; people are dissatisfied with their old narrow stock of Philistine ideas, Anglo-Saxon ideas, or any other; and some man, some Bentham[22] or Comte, who has the real merit of having early and strongly felt and helped the new current, but who brings plenty of narrowness and mistakes of his own into his feeling and help of it, is credited with being the author of the whole current, the fit person to be entrusted with its regulation and to guide the human race.

The excellent German historian of the mythology of Rome, Preller,[23] relating the introduction at Rome under the Tarquins of the worship of Apollo, the god of light, healing, and reconciliation, will have us observe that it was not so much the Tarquins who brought to Rome the new worship of Apollo, as a current in the mind of the Roman people which set powerfully at that time towards a new worship of this kind, and away from the old run of Latin and Sabine religious ideas. In a similar way, culture directs our attention to the natural current there is in human affairs, and to its continual working, and will not let us rivet our faith upon any one man and his doings. It makes us see not only his good side, but also how much in him was of necessity limited and transient; nay, it even feels a pleasure, a sense of an increased freedom and of an ampler future, in so doing.

I remember, when I was under the influence of a mind to which I feel the greatest obligations, the mind of a man who was the very incarnation of sanity and clear sense, a man the most considerable, it seems to me, whom America has yet produced,—Benjamin Franklin,—I remember the relief with which, after long feeling the sway of Franklin's imperturbable common-sense, I came upon a project of his for a new version of the Book of Job, to replace the old version, the style of which, says Franklin, has become obsolete, and thence less agreeable. "I give," he continues, "a few verses, which may serve as a sample of the kind of version I would recommend." We all recollect the famous verse in our translation: "Then Satan answered the Lord and said: 'Doth Job fear God for nought?'" Franklin makes this: "Does your Majesty imagine that Job's good conduct is the effect of mere personal attachment and affection?" I well remember how, when first I read that, I drew a deep breath of relief and said to myself: "After all, there is a stretch of humanity beyond Franklin's victorious good sense!"[24] So, after hearing Bentham cried loudly up as the renovator of modern society, and Bentham's mind and ideas proposed as the rulers of our future, I open the *Deontology*. There I read: "While Xenophon was writing his history and Euclid teaching geometry, Socrates and Plato were talking nonsense under pretense of talking wisdom and morality. This morality of theirs consisted in words; this wisdom of theirs was the denial of matters known to every man's experience." From the moment of reading that, I am delivered from the bondage of Bentham! the fanaticism of his adherents can touch me no longer. I feel the inadequacy of his mind and ideas for supplying the rule of human society, for perfection.

Culture tends always thus to deal with the men of a system, of disciples, of a school; with men like Comte, or the late Mr. Buckle, or Mr. Mill.[25] However much it may find to

[20] The ultra-democratic principles of the Jacobins, a political society influential during the French Revolution.

[21] Auguste Comte (1798–1857), the French philosopher, author of the system of positivism, which replaces religion and metaphysics with the ideals of sociological ethics.

[22] Jeremy Bentham (1748–1832), the English utilitarian philosopher.

[23] Ludwig Preller (1809–1861), author of *Römische Mythologie*.

[24] Arnold fails to realize that in the passage to which he refers Franklin is joking.

[25] Henry Thomas Buckle (1821–1862), author of

admire in these personages, or in some of them, it nevertheless remembers the text: "Be not ye called Rabbi!" and it soon passes on from any Rabbi. But Jacobinism loves a Rabbi; it does not want to pass on from its Rabbi in pursuit of a future and still un-reached perfection; it wants its Rabbi and his ideas to stand for perfection, that they may with the more authority recast the world; and for Jacobinism, therefore, culture,—eternally 10 passing onwards and seeking,—is an imperti-nence and an offence. But culture, just because it resists this tendency of Jacobinism to im-pose on us a man with limitations and errors of his own along with the true ideas of which he is the organ, really does the world and Jacobinism itself a service.

So, too, Jacobinism, in its fierce hatred of the past and of those whom it makes liable for the sins of the past, cannot away with 20 the inexhaustible indulgence proper to cul-ture, the consideration of circumstances, the severe judgment of actions joined to the merciful judgment of persons. "The man of culture is in politics," cries Mr. Frederic Harrison, "one of the poorest mortals alive!" Mr. Frederic Harrison wants to be doing business, and he complains that the man of culture stops him with a "turn for small fault-finding, love of selfish ease, and indecision in 30 action." Of what use is culture, he asks, except for "a critic of new books or a professor of *belles lettres?*" Why, it is of use because, in presence of the fierce exasperation which breathes, or rather, I may say, hisses through the whole production in which Mr. Frederic Harrison asks that question, it reminds us that the perfection of human nature is sweetness and light. It is of use, because, like religion,— that other effort after perfection,—it testifies 40 that, where bitter envying and strife are, there is confusion and every evil work.

The pursuit of perfection, then, is the pur-suit of sweetness and light.[26] He who works

for sweetness and light, works to make reason and the will of God prevail. He who works for machinery, he who works for hatred, works only for confusion. Culture looks beyond machinery, culture hates hatred; culture has one great passion, the passion for sweetness and light. It has one even yet greater!—the pas-sion for making them *prevail*. It is not satisfied till we *all* come to a perfect man; it knows that the sweetness and light of the few must be imperfect until the raw and unkindled masses of humanity are touched with sweetness and light. If I have not shrunk from saying that we must work for sweetness and light, so neither have I shrunk from saying that we must have a broad basis, must have sweetness and light for as many as possible. Again and again I have insisted how those are the happy moments of humanity, how those are the marking epochs of a people's life, how those are the flowering times for literature and art and all the creative power of genius, when there is a *national* glow of life and thought, when the whole of society is in the fullest measure permeated by thought, sensible to beauty, intelligent and alive. Only it must be *real* thought and *real* beauty; *real* sweetness and *real* light. Plenty of people will try to give the masses, as they call them, an intellectual food prepared and adapted in the way they think proper for the actual condition of the masses. The ordinary popular literature is an example of this way of working on the masses. Plenty of people will try to indoctrinate the masses with the set of ideas and judgments con-stituting the creed of their own profession or party. Our religious and political organ-izations give an example of this way of work-ing on the masses. I condemn neither way; but culture works differently. It does not try to teach down to the level of inferior classes; it does not try to win them for this or that sect of its own, with ready-made judgments and watchwords. It seeks to do away with classes; to make the best that has been thought and

a *History of Civilization in England*; John Stuart Mill (1806–1873), during the early part of his life a follower of Bentham's utilitarian philosophy.

[26] At this point in earlier versions Arnold had added:

"On this, the last occasion that I am to speak from this place, I have permitted myself, in justify-ing culture and in enforcing the reasons for it, to keep chiefly on ground where I am at one with the central instinct and sympathy of Oxford. The pur-suit of perfection is the pursuit of sweetness and light. Oxford has worked with all the best of her nature for sweetness, for beauty, and I have allowed myself today chiefly to insist on sweetness, on

beauty, as necessary characters of perfection. Light, too, is a necessary character of perfection; Oxford must not suffer herself to forget that! At other times during my passage in this chair I have not failed to remind her, so far as my feeble voice availed, that light is a necessary character of perfection. I never shall cease, so long as anywhere my voice finds any utterance, to insist on the need of light as well as of sweetness. Today I have spoken most of that which Oxford has loved most. But he who works for sweetness, works in the end for light also; he who works for light works in the end for sweetness also."

known in the world current everywhere; to make all men live in an atmosphere of sweetness and light, where they may use ideas, as it uses them itself, freely,—nourished, and not bound by them.

This is the *social idea*; and the men of culture are the true apostles of equality. The great men of culture are those who have had a passion for diffusing, for making prevail, for carrying from one end of society to the other, the best knowledge, the best ideas of their time; who have labored to divest knowledge of all that was harsh, uncouth, difficult, abstract, professional, exclusive; to humanize it, to make it efficient outside the clique of the cultivated and learned, yet still remaining the *best* knowledge and thought of the time, and a true source, therefore, of sweetness and light. Such a man was Abelard [27] in the Middle Ages, in spite of all his imperfections; and thence the boundless emotion and enthusiasm which Abelard excited. Such were Lessing and Herder [28] in Germany, at the end of the last century; and their services to Germany were in this way inestimably precious. Generations will pass, and literary monuments will accumulate, and works far more perfect than the works of Lessing and Herder will be produced in Germany; and yet the names of these two men will fill a German with a reverence and enthusiasm such as the names of the most gifted masters will hardly awaken. And why? Because they *humanized* knowledge; because they broadened the basis of life and intelligence; because they worked powerfully to diffuse sweetness and light, to make reason and the will of God prevail. With Saint Augustine they said: "Let us not leave thee alone to make in the secret of thy knowledge, as thou didst before the creation of the firmament, the division of light from darkness; let the children of thy spirit, placed in their firmament, make their light shine upon the earth, mark the division of night and day, and announce the revolution of the times; for the old order is passed, and the new arises; the night is spent, the day is come forth; and thou shalt crown the year with thy blessing, when thou shalt send forth laborers into thy harvest sown by other hands than theirs; when thou shalt send forth new laborers to new seed-times, whereof the harvest shall be not yet."

[27] The medieval thinker (1079–1142).
[28] Gotthold E. Lessing (1729–1781), critic and dramatist; Johann G. Herder (1744–1803), critic and poet.

# The Study of Poetry

"The future of poetry is immense, because in poetry, where it is worthy of its high destinies, our race, as time goes on, will find an ever surer and surer stay. There is not a creed which is not shaken, not an accredited dogma which is not shown to be questionable, not a received tradition which does not threaten to dissolve. Our religion has materialised itself in the fact, in the supposed fact; it has attached its emotion to the fact, and now the fact is failing it. But for poetry the idea is everything; the rest is a world of illusion, of divine illusion. Poetry attaches its emotion to the idea; the idea *is* the fact. The strongest part of our religion to-day is its unconscious poetry."

Let me be permitted to quote these words of my own, as uttering the thought which should, in my opinion, go with us and govern us in all our study of poetry. In the present work it is the course of one great contributory stream to the world-river of poetry that we are invited to follow. We are here invited to trace the stream of English poetry. But whether we set ourselves, as here, to follow only one of the several streams that make the mighty river of poetry, or whether we seek to know them all, our governing thought should be the same. We should conceive of poetry worthily, and more highly than it has been the custom to conceive of it. We should conceive of it as capable of higher uses, and called to higher destinies, than those which in general men have assigned to it hitherto. More and more mankind will discover that we have to turn to poetry to interpret life for us, to console us, to sustain us. Without poetry, our science will appear incomplete; and most of what now passes with us for religion and philosophy will be replaced by poetry. Science, I say, will appear incomplete without it. For finely and truly does Wordsworth call poetry "the impassioned expression which is in the countenance of all science"; and what is a countenance without its expression? Again, Wordsworth finely and truly calls poetry "the breath and finer spirit of all knowledge": our religion, parading evidences such as those on which the popular mind relies now; our philosophy, pluming itself on its reasonings about causation and finite and infinite being; what are they but the shadows and dreams and false shows of knowledge? The day will come when we shall wonder at ourselves for having trusted to them, for having taken them seriously; and the more we perceive their hollowness, the more we shall prize "the breath and finer spirit of knowledge" offered to us by poetry.

But if we conceive thus highly of the destinies of poetry, we must also set our standard for poetry high, since poetry, to be capable of fulfilling such high destinies, must be poetry of a high order of excellence. We must accustom ourselves to a high standard and to a strict judgment. Sainte-Beuve relates that Napoleon one day said, when somebody was spoken of in his presence as a charlatan: "Charlatan as much as you please; but where is there *not* charlatanism?"—"Yes," answers Sainte-Beuve, "in politics, in the art of governing mankind, that is perhaps true. But in the order of thought, in art, the glory, the eternal honour is that charlatanism shall find no entrance; herein lies the inviolableness of that noble portion of man's being." It is admirably said, and let us hold fast to it. In poetry, which is thought and art in one, it is the glory, the eternal honour, that charlatanism shall find no entrance; that this noble sphere be kept inviolate and inviolable. Charlatanism is for confusing or obliterating the distinctions between excellent and inferior, sound and unsound or only half-sound, true and untrue or only half-true. It is charlatanism, conscious or unconscious, whenever we confuse or obliterate these. And in poetry, more than anywhere else, it is unpermissible to confuse or obliterate them. For in poetry the distinction between excellent and inferior, sound and unsound or only half-sound, true and untrue or only half-true, is of paramount importance. It is of paramount importance because of the high destinies of poetry. In poetry, as a criticism of life under the conditions fixed for such a criticism by the laws of poetic truth and poetic beauty, the spirit of our race will find, we have said, as time goes on and as other helps fail, its consolation and stay. But the consolation and stay will be of power in proportion to the power of the criticism of life. And the criticism of life will be of power in proportion as the poetry conveying it is excellent rather than inferior, sound rather than unsound or half-sound, true rather than untrue or half-true.

The best poetry is what we want; the best poetry will be found to have a power of forming, sustaining, and delighting us, as nothing else can. A clearer, deeper sense of the best in poetry, and of the strength and joy to be drawn from it, is the most precious benefit which we can gather from a poetical collection such as the present. And yet in the very nature and conduct of such a collection there is inevitably something which tends to obscure in us the consciousness of what our benefit should be, and to distract us from the pursuit of it. We should therefore steadily set it before our minds at the outset, and should compel ourselves to revert constantly to the thought of it as we proceed.

Yes; constantly in reading poetry, a sense for the best, the really excellent, and of the strength and joy to be drawn from it, should be present in our minds and should govern our estimate of what we read. But this real estimate, the only true one, is liable to be superseded, if we are not watchful, by two other kinds of estimate, the historic estimate and the personal estimate, both of which are fallacious. A poet or a poem may count to us historically, they may count to us on grounds personal to ourselves, and they may count to us really. They may count to us historically. The course of development of a nation's language, thought, and poetry, is profoundly interesting; and by regarding a poet's work as a stage in this course of development we may easily bring ourselves to make it of more importance as poetry than in itself it really is, we may come to use a language of quite exaggerated praise in criticising it; in short, to over-rate it. So arises in our poetic judgments the fallacy caused by the estimate which we may call historic. Then, again, a poet or a poem may count to us on grounds personal to ourselves. Our personal affinities, likings, and circumstances, have great power to sway our estimate of this or that poet's work, and to make us attach more importance to it as poetry than in itself it really possesses, because to us it is, or has been, of high importance. Here also we over-rate the object of our interest, and apply to it a language of praise which is quite exaggerated. And thus we get the source of a second fallacy in our poetic judgments—the fallacy caused by an estimate which we may call personal.

Both fallacies are natural. It is evident how naturally the study of the history and development of a poetry may incline a man to pause over reputations and works once conspicuous but now obscure, and to quarrel with a careless public for skipping, in obedience to mere tradition and habit, from one famous name or work in its national poetry to another, ignorant of what it misses, and of the reason for keeping what it keeps, and of the whole process of growth in its poetry. The French have become diligent students of their own early poetry, which they long neglected; the study makes many of them dissatisfied with their so-called classical poetry, the court-tragedy of the seventeenth century, a poetry which Pellisson long ago reproached with its want of the true poetic stamp, with its *politesse stérile et rampante*, but which nevertheless has reigned in France as absolutely as if it had been the perfection of classical poetry indeed. The dissatisfaction is natural; yet a lively and accomplished critic, M. Charles d'Héricault, the editor of Clément Marot, goes too far when he says that "the cloud of glory playing round a classic is a mist as dangerous to the future of a literature as it is intolerable for the purposes of history." "It hinders," he goes on, "it hinders us from seeing more than one single point, the culminating and exceptional point; the summary, fictitious and arbitrary, of a thought and of a work. It substitutes a halo for a physiognomy, it puts a statue where there was once a man, and hiding from us all trace of the labour, the attempts, the weaknesses, the failures, it claims not study but veneration; it does not show us how the thing is done, it imposes upon us a model. Above all, for the historian this creation of classic personages is inadmissible; for it withdraws the poet from his time, from his proper life, it breaks historical relationships, it blinds criticism by conventional admiration, and renders the investigation of literary origins unacceptable. It gives us a human personage no longer, but a God seated immovable amidst His perfect work, like Jupiter on Olympus; and hardly will it be possible for the young student, to whom such work is exhibited at such a distance from him, to believe that it did not issue ready made from that divine head."

All this is brilliantly and tellingly said, but we must plead for a distinction. Everything depends on the reality of a poet's classic character. If he is a dubious classic, let us sift him; if he is a false classic, let us explode him. But if he is a real classic, if his work belongs to the class of the very best (for this is the true and right meaning of the word *classic, classical*), then the great thing for us is to feel and enjoy his work as deeply as ever we can, and to appreciate the wide difference between it and all work which has not the same high character. This is what is salutary, this is what is formative; this is the great benefit to be got from the study of poetry. Everything which interferes with it, which hinders it, is injurious.

True, we must read our classic with open eyes, and not with eyes blinded with superstition; we must perceive when his work comes short, when it drops out of the class of the very best, and we must rate it, in such cases, at its proper value. But the use of this negative criticism is not in itself, it is entirely in its enabling us to have a clearer sense and a deeper enjoyment of what is truly excellent. To trace the labour, the attempts, the weaknesses, the failures of a genuine classic, to acquaint oneself with his time and his life and his historical relationships, is mere literary dilettantism unless it has that clear sense and deeper enjoyment for its end. It may be said that the more we know about a classic the better we shall enjoy him; and, if we lived as long as Methuselah and had all of us heads of perfect clearness and wills of perfect steadfastness, this might be true in fact as it is plausible in theory. But the case here is much the same as the case with the Greek and Latin studies of our schoolboys. The elaborate philological groundwork which we require them to lay is in theory an admirable preparation for appreciating the Greek and Latin authors worthily. The more thoroughly we lay the groundwork, the better we shall be able, it may be said, to enjoy the authors. True, if time were not so short, and schoolboys' wits not so soon tired and their power of attention exhausted; only, as it is, the elaborate philological preparation goes on, but the authors are little known and less enjoyed. So with the investigator of "historic origins" in poetry. He ought to enjoy the true classic all the better for his investigations; he often is distracted from the enjoyment of the best, and with the less good he overbusies himself, and is prone to over-rate it in proportion to the trouble which it has cost him.

The idea of tracing historic origins and historical relationships cannot be absent from a compilation like the present. And naturally the poets to be exhibited in it will be assigned to those persons for exhibition who are known to prize them highly, rather than to those who have no special inclination towards them. Moreover the very occupation with an author, and the business of exhibiting him, disposes us to affirm and amplify his importance. In the present work, therefore, we are sure of frequent temptation to adopt the historic estimate, or the personal estimate, and to forget the real estimate; which latter, nevertheless, we must employ if we are to make poetry yield us its full benefit. So high is that benefit, the benefit of clearly feeling and of deeply enjoying the really excellent, the truly classic in poetry, that we do well, I say, to set it fixedly before our minds as our object in studying poets and poetry, and to make the desire of attaining it the one principle to which, as the *Imitation* says, whatever we may read or come to know, we always return. *Cum multa legeris et cognoveris, ad unum semper oportet redire principium.*

The historic estimate is likely in especial to affect our judgment and our language when we are dealing with ancient poets; the personal estimate when we are dealing with poets our contemporaries, or at any rate modern. The exaggerations due to the historic estimate are not in themselves, perhaps, of very much gravity. Their report hardly enters the general ear; probably they do not always impose even on the literary men who adopt them. But they lead to a dangerous abuse of language. So we hear Cædmon, amongst our own poets, compared to Milton. I have already noticed the enthusiasm of one accomplished French critic for "historic origins." Another eminent French critic, M. Vitet, comments upon that famous document of the early poetry of his nation, the *Chanson de Roland.* It is indeed a most interesting document. The *joculator* or *jongleur* Taillefer, who was with William the Conqueror's army at Hastings, marched before the Norman troops, so said the tradition, singing "of Charlemagne and of Roland and of Oliver, and of the vassals who died at Roncevaux"; and it is suggested that in the *Chanson de Roland* by one Turoldus or Théroulde, a poem perserved in a manuscript of the twelfth century in the Bodleian Library at Oxford, we have certainly the matter, perhaps even some of the words, of the chant which Taillefer sang. The poem has vigour and freshness; it is not without pathos. But M. Vitet is not satisfied with seeing in it a document of some poetic value, and of very high historic and linguistic value; he sees in it a grand and beautiful work, a monument of epic genius. In its general design he finds the grandiose conception, in its details he finds the constant union of simplicity with greatness, which are the marks, he truly says, of the genuine epic, and distinguish it from the artificial epic of literary ages. One thinks of Homer; this is the sort of praise which is given to Homer, and justly given. Higher praise there cannot well be, and it is the praise due to epic poetry of the highest order only, and to no other. Let us try, then, the *Chanson de Roland* at its best. Roland, mortally wounded, lays himself down under a pine-tree,

with his face turned towards Spain and the enemy—

> De plusurs choses à remembrer li prist,
> De tantes teres cume li bers cunquist,
> De dulce France, des humes de sun lign,
> De Charlemagne sun seignor ki l'nurrit.[1]

That is primitive work, I repeat, with an undeniable poetic quality of its own. It deserves such praise, and such praise is sufficient for it. But now turn to Homer—

> Ὣς φάτο· τοὺς δ᾽ ἤδη κατέχεν φυσίζοος αἶα
> ἐν Λακεδαίμονι αὖθι, φίλῃ ἐν πατρίδι γαίῃ.[2]

We are here in another world, another order of poetry altogether; here is rightly due such supreme praise as that which M. Vitet gives to the *Chanson de Roland.* If our words are to have any meaning, if our judgments are to have any solidity, we must not heap that supreme praise upon poetry of an order immeasurably inferior.

Indeed there can be no more useful help for discovering what poetry belongs to the class of the truly excellent, and can therefore do us most good, than to have always in one's mind lines and expressions of the great masters, and to apply them as a touchstone to other poetry. Of course we are not to require this other poetry to resemble them; it may be very dissimilar. But if we have any tact we shall find them, when we have lodged them well in our minds, an infallible touchstone for detecting the presence or absence of high poetic quality, and also the degree of this quality, in all other poetry which we may place beside them. Short passages, even single lines, will serve our turn quite sufficiently. Take the two lines which I have just quoted from Homer, the poet's comment on Helen's mention of her brothers;—or take his

> Ἆ δειλώ, τί σφῶϊ δόμεν Πηλῆϊ ἄνακτι
> θνητῷ; ὑμεῖς δ᾽ ἐστὸν ἀγήρω τ᾽ ἀθανάτω τε.
> ἦ ἵνα δυστήνοισι μετ᾽ ἀνδράσιν ἄλγε᾽ ἔχητον;[3]

[1] "Then began he to call many things to remembrance,—all the lands which his valour conquered, and pleasant France, and the men of his lineage, and Charlemagne his liege lord who nourished him."—*Chanson de Roland*, iii, 939–42. (Arnold's note.)

[2] So said she; they long since in Earth's soft arms were reposing,
There, in their own dear land, their fatherland, Lacedæmon.
*Iliad*, iii, 243, 244 (translated by Dr. Hawtrey). (Arnold's note.)

[3] Ah, unhappy pair, why gave we you to King Peleus, to a mortal? but ye are without old age, and immortal. Was it that with men born to misery ye might have sorrow?—*Iliad*, xvii, 443–45. (Arnold's note.)

the address of Zeus to the horses of Peleus;— or take finally his

Καὶ σέ, γέρον, τὸ πρὶν μὲν ἀκούομεν ὄλβιον εἶναι· [4]

the words of Achilles to Priam, a suppliant before him. Take that incomparable line and a half of Dante, Ugolino's tremendous words—

Io no piangeva; sì dentro impietrai.
Piangevan elli . . . [5]

take the lovely words of Beatrice to Virgil—

Io son fatta da Dio, sua mercè, tale,
Che la vostra miseria non mi tange,
Nè fiamma d'esto incendio non m'assale . . . [6]

take the simple, but perfect, single line—

In la sua volontade è nostra pace. [7]

Take of Shakespeare a line or two of Henry the Fourth's expostulation with sleep—

Wilt thou upon the high and giddy mast
Seal up the ship-boy's eyes, and rock his brains
In cradle of the rude imperious surge . . .

and take, as well, Hamlet's dying request to Horatio—

If thou didst ever hold me in thy heart,
Absent thee from felicity awhile,
And in this harsh world draw thy breath in pain
To tell my story . . . .

Take of Milton that Miltonic passage—

Darken'd so, yet shone
Above them all the archangel; but his face
Deep scars of thunder had intrench'd, and care
Sat on his faded cheek . . .

add two such lines as—

And courage never to submit or yield
And what is else not to be overcome . . .

and finish with the exquisite close to the loss of Proserpine, the loss

. . . which cost Ceres all that pain
To seek her through the world.

These few lines, if we have tact and can use them, are enough even of themselves to keep clear and sound our judgments about poetry, to save us from fallacious estimates of it, to conduct us to a real estimate.

[4] "Nay, and thou too, old man, in former days wast, as we hear, happy."—*Iliad*, xxiv, 543. (Arnold's note.)

[5] "I wailed not, so of stone grew I within;—*they* wailed."—*Inferno*, xxxiii, 39, 40. (Arnold's note.)

[6] "Of such sort hath God, thanked be His mercy, made me, that your misery toucheth me not, neither doth the flame of this fire strike me."—*Inferno*, ii, 91–93. (Arnold's note.)

[7] "In His will is our peace."—*Paradiso*, iii, 85. (Arnold's note.)

The specimens I have quoted differ widely from one another, but they have in common this: the possession of the very highest poetical quality. If we are thoroughly penetrated by their power, we shall find that we have acquired a sense enabling us, whatever poetry may be laid before us, to feel the degree in which a high poetical quality is present or wanting there. Critics give themselves great labour to draw out what in the abstract constitutes the characters of a high quality of poetry. It is much better simply to have recourse to concrete examples;—to take specimens of poetry of the high, the very highest quality, and to say: The characters of a high quality of poetry are what is expressed *there*. They are far better recognised by being felt in the verse of the master, than by being perused in the prose of the critic. Nevertheless if we are urgently pressed to give some critical account of them, we may safely, perhaps, venture on laying down, not indeed how and why the characters arise, but where and in what they arise. They are in the matter and substance of the poetry, and they are in its manner and style. Both of these, the substance and matter on the one hand, the style and manner on the other, have a mark, an accent, of high beauty, worth, and power. But if we are asked to define this mark and accent in the abstract, our answer must be: No, for we should thereby be darkening the question, not clearing it. The mark and accent are as given by the substance and matter of that poetry, by the style and manner of that poetry, and of all other poetry which is akin to it in quality.

Only one thing we may add as to the substance and matter of poetry, guiding ourselves by Aristotle's profound observation that the superiority of poetry over history consists in its possessing a higher truth and a higher seriousness (φιλοσοφώτερον χαὶ σπουδαιότερον). Let us add, therefore, to what we have said, this: that the substance and matter of the best poetry acquire their special character from possessing, in an eminent degree, truth and seriousness. We may add yet further, what is in itself evident, that to the style and manner of the best poetry their special character, their accent, is given by their diction, and, even yet more, by their movement. And though we distinguish between the two characters, the two accents, of superiority, yet they are nevertheless vitally connected one with the other. The superior character of truth and seriousness, in the matter and substance of the best poetry, is inseparable from the superiority of diction and movement marking its style and manner. The two superiorities are closely related, and are in steadfast proportion one to the other. So far as high poetic truth and seriousness are wanting to a poet's matter and substance, so far also, we may be sure, will a high poetic stamp of diction and movement be wanting to his style and manner. In proportion as this high stamp of diction and movement, again, is absent from a poet's style and manner, we shall find, also, that high poetic truth and seriousness are absent from his substance and matter.

## To a Friend [1]

Who prop, thou ask'st, in these bad days, my
　　mind?—
He [2] much, the old man, who, clearest-souled
　　of men,
Saw The Wide Prospect,[3] and the Asian Fen,
And Tmolus hill,[4] and Smyrna bay, though
　　blind.
Much he,[5] whose friendship I not long since
　　won,　　　　　　　　　　　　　　　　5
That halting slave, who in Nicopolis
Taught Arrian, when Vespasian's brutal son [6]
Cleared Rome of what most shamed him. But
　　be his [7]
My special thanks, whose even-balanced soul [9]
From first youth tested up to extreme old age,
Business could not make dull, nor passion wild;
Who saw life steadily, and saw it whole;
The mellow glory of the Attic stage,
Singer of sweet Colonus, and its child.

## Shakespeare

Others abide our question. Thou art free.
We ask and ask—Thou smilest and art still,
Out-topping knowledge. For the loftiest hill,
Who to the stars uncrowns his majesty,
Planting his steadfast footsteps in the sea,　　5

[1] Published, as were also the two following sonnets, in 1849.
[2] Homer.
[3] Europe (Εὐρώπη, *the wide prospect*) probably describes the appearance of the European coast to the Greeks on the coast of Asia Minor opposite. The name Asia, again, comes, it has been thought, from the muddy fens of the rivers of Asia Minor such as the Cayster or Maeander, which struck the imagination of the Greeks living near them (Arnold's note).
[4] A mountain range near Smyrna, which is one of the cities that claimed to be Homer's birthplace.
[5] Epictetus, the Stoic.
[6] Domitian, who banished the philosophers from Rome in A.D. 89.
[7] Sophocles's, who was born at Colonus, which he described in his tragedy *Oedipus at Colonus*.

Making the heaven of heavens his dwelling-
　　place,
Spares but the cloudy border of his base
To the foiled searching of mortality;
And thou, who didst the stars and sunbeams
　　know,
Self-schooled, self-scanned, self-honored, self-
　　secure,　　　　　　　　　　　　　　10
Didst walk on earth unguessed at.—Better so!
All pains the immortal spirit must endure,
All weakness which impairs, all griefs which
　　bow,
Find their sole speech in that victorious brow.

## In Harmony with Nature

### To a Preacher

"In harmony with Nature?" Restless fool,
Who with such heat dost preach what were to
　　thee,
When true, the last impossibility—
To be like Nature strong, like Nature cool!
Know, man hath all which Nature hath, but
　　more,　　　　　　　　　　　　　　　5
And in that *more* lie all his hopes of good.
Nature is cruel, man is sick of blood;
Nature is stubborn, man would fain adore;
Nature is fickle, man hath need of rest;
Nature forgives no debt, and fears no grave; 10
Man would be mild, and with safe conscience
　　blest.
Man must begin, know this, where Nature
　　ends;
Nature and man can never be fast friends.
Fool, if thou canst not pass her, rest her slave!

## Requiescat [1]

Strew on her roses, roses,
　　And never a spray of yew!
In quiet she reposes:
　　Ah, would that I did too!

Her mirth the world required;　　　　　5
　　She bathed it in smiles of glee.
But her heart was tired, tired,
　　And now they let her be.

Her life was turning, turning,
　　In mazes of heat and sound.　　　　10
But for peace her soul was yearning,
　　And now peace laps her round.

Her cabined, ample spirit,
　　It fluttered and failed for breath.
To-night it doth inherit　　　　　　15
　　The vasty hall of death.

[1] Published in 1853.

# Resignation [1]

### To Fausta

"To die be given us, or attain!
Fierce work it were, to do again."
So pilgrims, bound for Mecca, prayed
At burning noon; so warriors said,
Scarfed with the cross, who watched the miles 5
Of dust which wreathed their struggling files
Down Lydian mountains; so, when snows
Round Alpine summits, eddying, rose,
The Goth, bound Rome-wards; so the Hun,
Crouched on his saddle, while the sun 10
Went lurid down o'er flooded plains
Through which the groaning Danube strains
To the drear Euxine;—so pray all,
Whom labors, self-ordained, enthrall;
Because they to themselves propose 15
On this side the all-common close
A goal which, gained, may give repose.
So pray they; and to stand again
Where they stood once, to them were pain;
Pain to thread back and to renew 20
Past straits, and currents long steered through.

But milder natures, and more free—
Whom an unblamed serenity
Hath freed from passions, and the state
Of struggle these necessitate; 25
Whom schooling of the stubborn mind
Hath made, or birth hath found, resigned—
These mourn not, that their goings pay
Obedience to the passing day.
These claim not every laughing Hour 30
For handmaid to their striding power;
Each in her turn, with torch upreared,
To await their march; and when appeared,
Through the cold gloom, with measured race,
To usher for a destined space 35
(Her own sweet errands all forgone)
The too imperious traveler on.
These, Fausta, ask not this; nor thou,
Time's chafing prisoner, ask it now!

We left, just ten years since, you say, 40
That wayside inn we left to-day.[2]
Our jovial host, as forth we fare,
Shouts greeting from his easy chair.
High on a bank our leader stands,
Reviews and ranks his motley bands, 45
Makes clear our goal to every eye—
The valley's western boundary.
A gate swings to! our tide hath flowed
Already from the silent road.

[1] Published in 1849.
[2] Those who have been long familiar with the English Lake Country will find no difficulty in recalling, from the description in the text, the roadside inn at Wythburn on the descent from Dunmail Raise towards Keswick; its sedentary landlord of thirty years ago, and the passage over the Wythburn Fells to Watendlath (Arnold's note).

The valley-pastures, one by one, 50
Are threaded, quiet in the sun;
And now beyond the rude stone bridge
Slopes gracious up the western ridge.
Its woody border, and the last
Of its dark upland farms is past— 55
Cool farms, with open-lying stores,
Under their burnished sycamores;
All past! and through the trees we glide,
Emerging on the green hill-side.
There climbing hangs, a far-seen sign, 60
Our wavering, many-colored line;
There winds, upstreaming slowly still
Over the summit of the hill.
And now, in front, behold outspread
Those upper regions we must tread! 65
Mild hollows, and clear heathy swells,
The cheerful silence of the fells.[3]
Some two hours' march with serious air,
Through the deep noontide heats we fare;
The red-grouse, springing at our sound, 70
Skims, now and then, the shining ground;
No life, save his and ours, intrudes
Upon these breathless solitudes.
Oh joy! again the farms appear.
Cool shade is there, and rustic cheer; 75
There springs the brook will guide us down,
Bright comrade, to the noisy town.
Lingering, we follow down; we gain
The town, the highway, and the plain
And many a mile of dusty way, 80
Parched and road-worn, we made that day;
But, Fausta, I remember well,
That as the balmy darkness fell
We bathed our hands with speechless glee,
That night, in the wide-glimmering sea. 85

Once more we tread this self-same road,
Fausta, which ten years since we trod;
Alone we tread it, you and I,
Ghosts of that boisterous company.
Here, where the brook shines, near its head, 90
In its clear, shallow, turf-fringed bed;
Here, whence the eye first sees, far down,
Capped with faint smoke, the noisy town;
Here sit we, and again unroll,
Though slowly, the familiar whole. 95
The solemn wastes of healthy hill
Sleep in the July sunshine still;
The self-same shadows now, as then,
Play through this grassy upland glen;
The loose dark stones on the green way 100
Lie strewn, it seems, where then they lay;
On this mild bank above the stream,
(You crush them!) the blue gentians gleam.
Still this wild brook, the rushes cool,
The sailing foam, the shining pool! 105
These are not changed; and we, you say,
Are scarce more changed, in truth, than they.

The gypsies, whom we met below,
They, too, have long roamed to and fro;

[3] Mountains.

They ramble, leaving, where they pass,        110
Their fragments on the cumbered grass.
And often to some kindly place
Chance guides the migratory race,
Where, though long wanderings intervene,
They recognize a former scene.        115
The dingy tents are pitched; the fires
Give to the wind their wavering spires;
In dark knots crouch round the wild flame
Their children, as when first they came;
They see their shackled beasts again        120
Move, browsing, up the gray-walled lane.
Signs are not wanting, which might raise
The ghost in them of former days—
Signs are not wanting, if they would;
Suggestions to disquietude.        125
For them, for all, time's busy touch,
While it mends little, troubles much.
Their joints grow stiffer—but the year
Runs his old round of dubious cheer;
Chilly they grow—yet winds of March,        130
Still, sharp as ever, freeze and parch;
They must live still—and yet, God knows,
Crowded and keen the country grows;
It seems as if, in their decay,
The law grew stronger every day.        135
So might they reason, so compare,
Fausta, times past with times that are.
But no!—they rubbed through yesterday
In their hereditary way,
And they will rub through, if they can,        140
To-morrow on the self-same plan,
Till death arrive to supersede,
For them, vicissitude and need.

The poet, to whose mighty heart
Heaven doth a quicker pulse impart,        145
Subdues that energy to scan
Not his own course, but that of man.
Though he move mountains, though his day
Be passed on the proud heights of sway,
Though he hath loosed a thousand chains,        150
Though he hath borne immortal pains,
Action and suffering though he know—
He hath not lived, if he lives so.
He sees, in some great-historied land,
A ruler of the people stand,        155
Sees his strong thought in fiery flood
Roll through the heaving multitude,
Exults—yet for no moment's space
Envies the all-regarded place.
Beautiful eyes meet his—and he        160
Bears to admire uncravingly;
They pass—he, mingled with the crowd,
Is in their far-off triumphs proud.
From some high station he looks down,
At sunset, on a populous town;        165
Surveys each happy group, which fleets,
Toil ended, through the shining streets,
Each with some errand of its own—
And does not say, "I am alone."
He sees the gentle stir of birth        170
When morning purifies the earth;

He leans upon a gate and sees
The pastures, and the quiet trees.
Low woody hill, with gracious bound,
Folds the still valley almost round;        175
The cuckoo, loud on some high lawn,
Is answered from the depth of dawn;
In the hedge straggling to the stream,
Pale, dew-drenched, half-shut roses gleam;
But, where the farther side slopes down,        180
He sees the drowsy new-waked clown
In his white quaint-embroidered frock
Make, whistling, towards his mist-wreathed
    flock—
Slowly, behind the heavy tread,
The wet, flowered grass heaves up its head.        185
Leaned on his gate, he gazes—tears
Are in his eyes, and in his ears
The murmur of a thousand years.
Before him he sees life unroll,
A placid and continuous whole—        190
That general life, which does not cease,
Whose secret is not joy, but peace;
That life, whose dumb wish is not missed
If birth proceeds, if things subsist;
The life of plants, and stones, and rain,        195
The life he craves—if not in vain
Fate gave, what chance shall not control,
His sad lucidity of soul.

You listen—but that wandering smile,
Fausta, betrays you cold the while!        200
Your eyes pursue the bells of foam
Washed, eddying, from this bank, their home.
"Those gypsies," so your thoughts I scan,
"Are less, the poet more, than man.
They feel not, though they move and see;        205
Deeply the poet feels; but he
Breathes, when he will, immortal air,
Where Orpheus and where Homer are.
In the day's life, whose iron round
Hems us all in, he is not bound;        210
He leaves his kind, o'erleaps their pen,
And flees the common life of men.
He escapes thence, but we abide—
Not deep the poet sees, but wide."

The world in which we live and move        215
Outlasts aversion, outlasts love,
Outlasts each effort, interest, hope,
Remorse, grief, joy;—and were the scope
Of these affections wider made,
Man still would see, and see dismayed,        220
Beyond his passion's widest range,
Far regions of eternal change.
Nay, and since death, which wipes out man,
Finds him with many an unsolved plan,
With much unknown, and much untried,        225
Wonder not dead, and thirst not dried,
Still gazing on the ever full
Eternal mundane spectacle—
This world in which we draw our breath,
In some sense, Fausta, outlasts death.        230

Blame thou not, therefore, him who dares
Judge vain beforehand human cares;
Whose natural insight can discern
What through experience others learn;
Who needs not love and power, to know     235
Love transient, power an unreal show;
Who treads at ease life's uncheered ways—
Him blame not, Fausta, rather praise!
Rather thyself for some aim pray
Nobler than this, to fill the day;     240
Rather that heart, which burns in thee,
Ask, not to amuse, but to set free;
Be passionate hopes not ill resigned
For quiet, and a fearless mind.
And though fate grudge to thee and me     245
The poet's rapt security,
Yet they, believe me, who await
No gifts from chance, have conquered fate;
They, winning room to see and hear,
And to men's business not too near,     250
Through clouds of individual strife
Draw homeward to the general life.
Like leaves by suns not yet uncurled;
To the wise, foolish; to the world,
Weak,—yet not weak, I might reply,     255
Not foolish, Fausta, in His eye,
To whom each moment in its race,
Crowd as we will its neutral space,
Is but a quiet watershed
Whence, equally, the seas of life and death are
     fed.     260

Enough, we live!—and if a life,
With large results so little rife,
Though bearable, seem hardly worth
This pomp of worlds, this pain of birth;
Yet, Fausta, the mute turf we tread,     265
The solemn hills around us spread,
This stream which falls incessantly,
The strange-scrawled rocks, the lonely sky,
If I might lend their life a voice,
Seem to bear rather than rejoice.     270
And even could the intemperate prayer
Man iterates, while these forbear,
For movement, for an ampler sphere,
Pierce Fate's impenetrable ear;
Not milder is the general lot     275
Because our spirits have forgot,
In action's dizzying eddy whirled,
The something that infects the world.

# The Forsaken Merman [1]

Come, dear children, let us away;
Down and away below!
Now my brothers call from the bay,
Now the great winds shoreward blow,
Now the salt tides seaward flow;     5
Now the wild white horses play,
Champ and chafe and toss in the spray.
Children dear, let us away!
This way, this way!

[1] Published in 1849.

Call her once before you go—     10
Call once yet!
In a voice that she will know:
"Margaret! Margaret!"
Children's voices should be dear
(Call once more) to a mother's ear;     15
Children's voices, wild with pain—
Surely she will come again!
Call her once and come away;
This way, this way!
"Mother dear, we cannot stay!     20
The wild white horses foam and fret."
Margaret! Margaret!

Come, dear children, come away down;
Call no more!
One last look at the white-walled town,     25
And the little gray church on the windy shore;
Then come down!
She will not come though you call all day;
Come away, come away!

Children dear, was it yesterday     30
We heard the sweet bells over the bay?
In the caverns where we lay,
Through the surf and through the swell,
The far-off sound of a silver bell?
Sand-strewn caverns, cool and deep,     35
Where the winds are all asleep;
Where the spent lights quiver and gleam,
Where the salt weed sways in the stream,
Where the sea-beasts, ranged all round,
Feed in the ooze of their pasture-ground;     40
Where the sea-snakes coil and twine,
Dry their mail and bask in the brine;
Where great whales come sailing by,
Sail and sail, with unshut eye,
Round the world for ever and aye?     45
When did music come this way?
Children dear, was it yesterday?

Children dear, was it yesterday
(Call yet once) that she went away?
Once she sat with you and me,     50
On a red gold throne in the heart of the sea,
And the youngest sat on her knee.
She combed its bright hair, and she tended it
     well,
When down swung the sound of a far-off bell.
She sighed, she looked up through the clear
     green sea;     55
She said: "I must go, for my kinsfolk pray
In the little gray church on the shore to-day.
'Twill be Easter-time in the world—ah me!
And I lose my poor soul, Merman! here with
     thee."
I said: "Go up, dear heart, through the waves;
Say thy prayer, and come back to the kind sea-
     caves!"     61
She smiled, she went up through the surf in
     the bay.
Children dear, was it yesterday?

Children dear, were we long alone?
"The sea grows stormy, the little ones moan; 65
Long prayers," I said, "in the world they say;
Come!" I said; and we rose through the surf in
 the bay.
We went up the beach, by the sandy down
Where the sea-stocks bloom, to the white-
 walled town;
Through the narrow paved streets, where all
 was still,    70
To the little gray church on the windy hill.
From the church came a murmur of folk at
 their prayers,
But we stood without in the cold blowing airs.
We climbed on the graves, on the stones worn
 with rains,
And we gazed up the aisle through the small
 leaded panes.    75
She sat by the pillar; we saw her clear:
"Margaret, hist! come quick, we are here!
Dear heart," I said, "we are long alone;
The sea grows stormy, the little ones moan."
But, ah, she gave me never a look,  80
For her eyes were sealed to the holy book!
Loud prays the priest; shut stands the door.
Come away, children, call no more!
Come away, come down, call no more!

Down, down, down!    85
Down to the depths of the sea!
She sits at her wheel in the humming town,
Singing most joyfully.
Hark what she sings: "O joy, O joy,
For the humming street, and the child with its
 toy!    90
For the priest, and the bell, and the holy well;
For the wheel where I spun,
And the blessèd light of the sun!"
And so she sings her fill,
Singing most joyfully,    95
Till the spindle falls from her hand,
And the whizzing wheel stands still.
She steals to the window, and looks at the sand,
And over the sand at the sea;
And her eyes are set in a stare;  100
And anon there breaks a sigh,
And anon there drops a tear,
From a sorrow-clouded eye,
And a heart sorrow-laden,
A long, long sigh;    105
For the cold strange eyes of a little Mer-
 maiden
And the gleam of her golden hair.

Come away, away children;
Come children, come down!
The hoarse wind blows coldly;  110
Lights shine in the town.
She will start from her slumber
When gusts shake the door;
She will hear the winds howling,
Will hear the waves roar.    115
We shall see, while above us

The waves roar and whirl,
A ceiling of amber,
A pavement of pearl.
Singing: "Here came a mortal,  120
But faithless was she!
And alone dwell for ever
The kings of the sea."

But, children, at midnight,
When soft the winds blow,  125
When clear falls the moonlight,
When spring-tides are low;
When sweet airs come seaward
From heaths starred with broom,
And high rocks throw mildly  130
On the blanched sands a gloom;
Up the still, glistening beaches,
Up the creeks we will hie,
Over banks of bright seaweed
The ebb-tide leaves dry.  135
We will gaze, from the sand-hills,
At the white, sleeping town;
At the church on the hill-side—
And then come back down.
Singing: "There dwells a loved one,  140
But cruel is she!
She left lonely for ever
The kings of the sea."

# Switzerland [1]

## 1. Meeting

Again I see my bliss at hand,
The town, the lake are here;
My Marguerite smiles upon the strand,
Unaltered with the year.

I know that graceful figure fair,  5
That cheek of languid hue;
I know that soft, enkerchiefed hair,
And those sweet eyes of blue.

Again I spring to make my choice;
Again in tones of ire  10
I hear a God's tremendous voice:
"Be counseled, and retire."

Ye guiding Powers who join and part,
What would ye have with me?
Ah, warn some more ambitious heart,  15
And let the peaceful be!

## 2. Parting

Ye storm-winds of Autumn!
Who rush by, who shake

[1] The general title was given to this group of
poems in 1853, though some of them were published
in 1852. The third poem was published in 1869, the
fourth in 1857, and the seventh in 1867, though it
was not made a member of this group until 1869.
A final change in arrangement brought the group to
its present form in 1885.

The window, and ruffle
The gleam-lighted lake;
Who cross to the hill-side    5
Thin-sprinkled with farms,
Where the high woods strip sadly
Their yellowing arms—
Ye are bound for the mountains!
Ah! with you let me go    10
Where your cold, distant barrier,
The vast range of snow,
Through the loose clouds lifts dimly
Its white peaks in air—
How deep is their stillness!    15
Ah, would I were there!

But on the stairs what voice is this I hear,
Buoyant as morning, and as morning clear?
Say, has some wet bird-haunted English lawn
Lent it the music of its trees at dawn?    20
Or was it from some sun-flecked mountain-
  brook
That the sweet voice its upland clearness took?
     Ah! it comes nearer—
     Sweet notes, this way!

    Hark! fast by the window    25
    The rushing winds go,
    To the ice-cumbered gorges,
    The vast seas of snow!
    There the torrents drive upward
    Their rock-strangled hum;    30
    There the avalanche thunders
    The hoarse torrent dumb.
    —I come, O ye mountains!
    Ye torrents, I come!

But who is this, by the half-opened door,    35
Whose figure casts a shadow on the floor?
The sweet blue eyes—the soft, ash-colored
  hair—
The cheeks that still their gentle paleness
  wear—
The lovely lips, with their arch smile that tells
The unconquered joy in which her spirit
  dwells—    40
     Ah! they bend nearer—
     Sweet lips, this way!

Hark! The wind rushes past us!
Ah! with that let me go
To the clear, waning hill-side,    45
Unspotted by snow,
There to watch, o'er the sunk vale,
The frore mountain-wall,
Where the niched snow-bed sprays down
Its powdery fall.    50
There its dusky blue clusters
The aconite [2] spreads;
There the pines slope, the cloud-strips
Hung soft in their heads.
No life but, at moments,    55
The mountain-bee's hum.

  [2] The flower, monkshood.

—I come, O ye mountains!
Ye pine-woods, I come!

    Forgive me! forgive me!
    Ah, Marguerite, fain    60
Would these arms reach to clasp thee!
    But see! 'tis in vain.

    In the void air, towards thee,
    My stretched arms are cast;
But a sea rolls between us—    65
    Our different past!

    To the lips, ah! of others
    Those lips have been pressed,
And others, ere I was;
    Were strained to that breast;    70

    Far, far from each other
    Our spirits have grown;
And what heart knows another?
    Ah! who knows his own?

Blow, ye winds! lift me with you!    75
    I come to the wild.
Fold closely, O Nature!
    Thine arms round thy child.

To thee only God granted
    A heart ever new—    80
To all always open,
    To all always true.

Ah! calm me, restore me;
    And dry up my tears
On thy high mountain-platforms,    85
    Where morn first appears;

Where the white mists, for ever,
    Are spread and upfurled—
In the stir of the forces
    Whence issued the world.    90

### 3. *A Farewell*

My horse's feet beside the lake,
Where sweet the unbroken moonbeams lay,
Sent echoes through the night to wake
Each glistening strand, each heath-fringed bay.

The poplar avenue was passed,    5
And the roofed bridge that spans the stream;
Up the steep street I hurried fast,
Led by thy taper's starlike beam.

I came! I saw thee rise!—the blood
Poured flushing to thy languid cheek.    10
Locked in each other's arms we stood,
In tears, with hearts too full to speak.

Days flew;—ah, soon I could discern
A trouble in thine altered air!
Thy hand lay languidly in mine,    15
Thy cheek was grave, thy speech grew rare.

I blame thee not!—this heart, I know,
To be long loved was never framed;
For something in its depths doth glow
Too strange, too restless, too untamed.      20

And women—things that live and move
Mined by the fever of the soul—
They seek to find in those they love
Stern strength, and promise of control.

They ask not kindness, gentle ways—      25
These they themselves have tried and known;
They ask a soul which never sways
With the blind gusts that shake their own.

I too have felt the load I bore
In a too strong emotion's sway;      30
I too have wished, no woman more,
This starting, feverish heart away.

I too have longed for trenchant force,
And will like a dividing spear;
Have praised the keen, unscrupulous course,  35
Which knows no doubt, which feels no fear.

But in the world I learned, what there
Thou too wilt surely one day prove,
That will, that energy, though rare,
Are yet far, far less rare than love.      40

Go, then!—till time and fate impress
This truth on thee, be mine no more!
They will!—for thou, I feel, not less
Than I, wast destined to this lore.

We school our manners, act our parts—     45
But He, who sees us through and through,
Knows that the bent of both our hearts
Was to be gentle, tranquil, true.

And though we wear out life, alas!
Distracted as a homeless wind,      50
In beating where we must not pass,
In seeking what we shall not find;

Yet we shall one day gain, life past,
Clear prospect o'er our being's whole;
Shall see ourselves, and learn at last      55
Our true affinities of soul.

We shall not then deny a course
To every thought the mass ignore;
We shall not then call hardness force,
Nor lightness wisdom any more.      60

Then, in the eternal Father's smile,
Our soothed, encouraged souls will dare
To seem as free from pride and guile,
As good, as generous, as they are.

Then we shall know our friends!—though
     much      65
Will have been lost—the help in strife,

The thousand sweet, still joys of such
As hand in hand face earthly life—

Though these be lost, there will be yet
A sympathy august and pure;      70
Ennobled by a vast regret,
And by contrition sealed thrice sure.

And we, whose ways were unlike here,
May then more neighboring courses ply;
May to each other be brought near,      75
And greet across infinity.

How sweet, unreached by earthly jars,
My sister! to maintain with thee
The hush among the shining stars,
The calm upon the moonlit sea!      80

How sweet to feel, on the boon air,
All our unquiet pulses cease!
To feel that nothing can impair
The gentleness, the thirst for peace—

The gentleness too rudely hurled      85
On this wild earth of hate and fear;
The thirst for peace a raving world
Would never let us satiate here.

### 4. Isolation. To Marguerite

We were apart; yet, day by day,
I bade my heart more constant be.
I bade it keep the world away,
And grow a home for only thee;
Nor feared but thy love likewise grew,      5
Like mine, each day, more tried, more true.

The fault was grave! I might have known
What far too soon, alas! I learned—
The heart can bind itself alone,
And faith may oft be unreturned.      10
Self-swayed our feelings ebb and swell—
Thou lov'st no more;—Farewell! Farewell!

Farewell!—and thou, thou lonely heart,
Which never yet without remorse
Even for a moment didst depart      15
From thy remote and spheréd course
To haunt the place where passions reign—
Back to thy solitude again!

Back! with the conscious thrill of shame
Which Luna [3] felt, that summer night,      20
Flash through her pure immortal frame,
When she forsook the starry height
To hang over Endymion's sleep
Upon the pine-grown Latmian steep.

Yet she, chaste queen, had never proved      25
How vain a thing is mortal love,
Wandering in Heaven, far removed.
But thou hast long had place to prove

[3] Artemis.

This truth—to prove, and make thine own:
"Thou hast been, shalt be, art, alone."    30

Or, if not quite alone, yet they
Which touch thee are unmating things—
Ocean and clouds and night and day;
Lorn autumns and triumphant springs;
And life, and others' joy and pain,    35
And love, if love, of happier men.

Of happier men—for they, at least,
Have *dreamed* two human hearts might blend
In one, and were through faith released
From isolation without end    40
Prolonged; nor knew, although not less
Alone than thou, their loneliness.

### 5. To Marguerite—Continued

Yes! in the sea of life enisled,
With echoing straits between us thrown,
Dotting the shoreless watery wild,
We mortal millions live *alone*.
The islands feel the enclasping flow,    5
And then their endless bounds they know.

But when the moon their hollows lights,
And they are swept by balms of spring,
And in their glens, on starry nights,
The nightingales divinely sing;    10
And lovely notes, from shore to shore,
Across the sounds and channels pour—

Oh! then a longing like despair
Is to their farthest caverns sent;
For surely once, they feel, we were    15
Parts of a single continent!
Now round us spreads the watery plain—
Oh might our marges meet again!

Who ordered, that their longing's fire
Should be, as soon as kindled, cooled?    20
Who renders vain their deep desire?—
A God, a God their severance ruled!
And bade betwixt their shores to be
The unplumbed, salt, estranging sea.

### 6. Absence

In this fair stranger's eyes of gray
Thine eyes, my love! I see.
I shiver; for the passing day
Had borne me far from thee.

This is the curse of life! that not    5
A nobler, calmer train
Of wiser thoughts and feelings blot
Our passions from our brain;

But each day brings its petty dust
Our soon-choked souls to fill,    10
And we forget because we must
And not because we will.

I struggle towards the light; and ye,
Once-longed-for storms of love!
If with the light ye cannot be,    15
I bear that ye remove.

I struggle towards the light—but oh,
While yet the night is chill,
Upon time's barren, stormy flow,
Stay with me, Marguerite, still!    20

### 7. The Terrace at Berne

(COMPOSED TEN YEARS AFTER THE
PRECEDING)

Ten years!—and to my waking eye
Once more the roofs of Berne appear;
The rocky banks, the terrace high,
The stream!—and do I linger here?

The clouds are on the Oberland,    5
The Jungfrau snows look faint and far;
But bright are those green fields at hand,
And through those fields comes down the Aar,

And from the blue twin-lakes it comes,
Flows by the town, the churchyard fair;    10
And 'neath the garden-walk it hums,
The house!—and is my Marguerite there?

Ah, shall I see thee, while a flush
Of startled pleasure floods thy brow,
Quick through the oleanders brush,    15
And clap thy hands, and cry: " 'Tis thou!"

Or hast thou long since wandered back,
Daughter of France! to France, thy home;
And flitted down the flowery track
Where feet like thine too lightly come?    20

Doth riotous laughter now replace
Thy smile; and rouge, with stony glare,
Thy cheeks' soft hue; and fluttering lace
The kerchief that enwound thy hair?

Or is it over?—art thou dead?—    25
Dead!—and no warning shiver ran
Across my heart, to say thy thread
Of life was cut, and closed thy span!

Could from earth's ways that figure slight
Be lost, and I not feel 'twas so?    30
Of that fresh voice the gay delight
Fail from earth's air, and I not know?

Or shall I find thee still, but changed,
But not the Marguerite of thy prime?
With all thy being re-arranged,    35
Passed through the crucible of time;

With spirit vanished, beauty waned,
And hardly yet a glance, a tone,
A gesture—anything—retained
Of all that was my Marguerite's own?    40

I will not know! For wherefore try,
To things by mortal course that live,
A shadowy durability,
For which they were not meant, to give?

Like driftwood spars, which meet and pass 45
Upon the boundless ocean-plain,
So on the sea of life, alas!
Man meets man—meets, and quits again.

I knew it when my life was young;
I feel it still, now youth is o'er.         50
—The mists are on the mountain hung,
And Marguerite I shall see no more.

## Philomela [1]

Hark! ah, the nightingale—
The tawny-throated!
Hark, from that moonlit cedar what a burst!
What triumph! hark!—what pain!

O wanderer from a Grecian shore,         5
Still, after many years, in distant lands,
Still nourishing in thy bewildered brain
That wild, unquenched, deep-sunken, old-world
    pain—
Say, will it never heal?
And can this fragrant lawn         10
With its cool trees, and night,
And the sweet, tranquil Thames,
And moonshine, and the dew,
To thy racked heart and brain
Afford no balm?         15

Dost thou to-night behold
Here, through the moonlight on this English
    grass,
The unfriendly palace in the Thracian wild?
Dost thou again peruse
With hot cheeks and seared eyes         20
The too clear web, and thy dumb sister's
    shame?
Dost thou once more assay
Thy flight, and feel come over thee,
Poor fugitive, the feathery change
Once more, and once more seem to make re-
    sound         25
With love and hate, triumph and agony,
Lone Daulis, and the high Cephissian vale?
Listen, Eugenia—

[1] Philomela was violated by her brother-in-law,
Tereus, King of Daulis, who thereafter cut out her
tongue so that she might not betray the deed. She,
however, made it known to her sister Procne,
Tereus's wife, by weaving words into a robe ("the
too clear web"). Procne killed her son, gave his
body as food to his father, and fled with Philomela.
When Tereus pursued them, and they prayed for
deliverance, the gods changed them into birds—
Philomela into a nightingale. In the poem (published in 1853), Arnold reverses the positions of
Philomela and Procne.

How thick the bursts come crowding through
    the leaves!
Again—thou hearest?         30
Eternal Passion!
Eternal Pain!

## Dover Beach [2]

The sea is calm to-night.
The tide is full, the moon lies fair
Upon the straits;—on the French coast the
    light
Gleams and is gone; the cliffs of England stand,
Glimmering and vast, out in the tranquil bay. 5
Come to the window, sweet is the night-air!
Only, from the long line of spray
Where the sea meets the moon-blanched land,
Listen! you hear the grating roar
Of pebbles which the waves draw back, and
    fling,         10
At their return, up the high strand,
Begin, and cease, and then again begin,
With tremulous cadence slow, and bring
The eternal note of sadness in.

Sophocles long ago         15
Heard it on the Aegean, and it brought
Into his mind the turbid ebb and flow
Of human misery; we
Find also in the sound a thought,
Hearing it by this distant northern sea.         20

The Sea of Faith
Was once, too, at the full, and round earth's
    shore
Lay like the folds of a bright girdle furled.
But now I only hear
Its melancholy, long, withdrawing roar,         25
Retreating, to the breath
Of the night-wind, down the vast edges drear
And naked shingles [3] of the world.

Ah, love, let us be true
To one another! for the world, which seems
To lie before us like a land of dreams,         31
So various, so beautiful, so new,
Hath really neither joy, nor love, nor light,
Nor certitude, nor peace, nor help for pain;
And we are here as on a darkling plain         35
Swept with confused alarms of struggle and
    flight,
Where ignorant armies clash by night.

## Self-Dependence [4]

Weary of myself, and sick of asking
What I am, and what I ought to be,
At this vessel's prow I stand, which bears me
Forwards, forwards, o'er the star-lit sea.

[2] Published in 1867.         [3] Pebbly shores.
[4] Published in 1852.

And a look of passionate desire 5
O'er the sea and to the stars I send:
"Ye who from my childhood up have calmed
   me,
Calm me, ah, compose me to the end!

"Ah, once more," I cried, "ye stars, ye waters,
On my heart your mighty charm renew; 10
Still, still let me, as I gaze upon you,
Feel my soul becoming vast like you!"

From the intense, clear, star-sown vault of
   heaven,
Over the lit sea's unquiet way,
In the rustling night-air came the answer: 15
"Wouldst thou *be* as these are? *Live* as they.

"Unaffrighted by the silence round them,
Undistracted by the sights they see,
These demand not that the things without
   them
Yield them love, amusement, sympathy. 20

"And with joy the stars perform their shining,
And the sea its long moon-silvered roll;
For self-poised they live, nor pine with noting
All the fever of some differing soul.

"Bounded by themselves, and unregardful 25
In what state God's other works may be,
In their own tasks all their powers pouring,
These attain the mighty life you see."

O air-born voice! long since, severely clear,
A cry like thine in my own heart I hear: 30
"Resolve to be thyself; and know that he,
Who finds himself, loses his misery!"

## Morality [5]

We cannot kindle when we will
The fire which in the heart resides;
The spirit bloweth and is still,
In mystery our soul abides.
  But tasks in hours of insight willed 5
  Can be through hours of gloom fulfilled.

With aching hands and bleeding feet
We dig and heap, lay stone on stone;
We bear the burden and the heat
Of the long day, and wish 'twere done. 10
  Not till the hours of light return,
  All we have built do we discern.

Then, when the clouds are off the soul,
When thou dost bask in Nature's eye,
Ask, how *she* viewed thy self-control, 15
Thy struggling, tasked morality—
  Nature, whose free, light, cheerful air,
  Oft made thee, in thy gloom, despair.

And she, whose censure thou dost dread,
Whose eye thou wast afraid to seek,

[5] Published in 1852.

See, on her face a glow is spread,
A strong emotion on her cheek!
  "Ah, child!" she cries, "that strife divine,
  Whence was it, for it is not mine?

"There is no effort on *my* brow—
I do not strive, I do not weep;
I rush with the swift spheres and glow
In joy, and when I will, I sleep.
  Yet that severe, that earnest air,
  I saw, I felt it once—but where? 30

"I knew not yet the gauge of time,
Nor wore the manacles of space;
I felt it in some other clime,
I saw it in some other place.
  'Twas when the heavenly house I trod, 35
  And lay upon the breast of God."

## The Buried Life [1]

Light flows our war of mocking words, and yet,
Behold, with tears mine eyes are wet!
I feel a nameless sadness o'er me roll.
Yes, yes, we know that we can jest,
We know, we know that we can smile! 5
But there's a something in this breast,
To which thy light words bring no rest,
And thy gay smiles no anodyne.
Give me thy hand, and hush awhile,
And turn those limpid eyes on mine, 10
And let me read there, love! thy inmost soul.

Alas! is even love too weak
To unlock the heart, and let it speak?
Are even lovers powerless to reveal
To one another what indeed they feel? 15
I knew the mass of men concealed
Their thoughts, for fear that if revealed
They would by other men be met
With blank indifference, or with blame re-
  proved;
I knew they lived and moved 20
Tricked in disguises, alien to the rest
Of men, and alien to themselves—and yet
The same heart beats in every human breast!

But we, my love!—doth a like spell benumb
Our hearts, our voices?—must we too be dumb?

Ah! well for us, if even we, 26
Even for a moment, can get free
Our heart, and have our lips unchained;
For that which seals them hath been deep-
  ordained!

Fate, which foresaw 30
How frivolous a baby man would be—
By what distractions he would be possessed,
How he would pour himself in every strife,
And well-nigh change his own identity—
That it might keep from his capricious play 35

[1] Published in 1852.

His genuine self, and force him to obey
Even in his own despite his being's law,
Bade through the deep recesses of our breast
The unregarded river of our life
Pursue with indiscernible flow its way;      40
And that we should not see
The buried stream, and seem to be
Eddying at large in blind uncertainty,
Though driving on with it eternally.

But often, in the world's most crowded streets,
But often, in the din of strife,      46
There rises an unspeakable desire
After the knowledge of our buried life;
A thirst to spend our fire and restless force
In tracking out our true, original course;      50
A longing to inquire
Into the mystery of this heart which beats
So wild, so deep in us—to know
Whence our lives come and where they go.
And many a man in his own breast then delves,
But deep enough, alas! none ever mines.      56
And we have been on many thousand lines,[2]
And we have shown, on each, spirit and power;
But hardly have we, for one little hour,
Been on our own line, have we been our-
      selves—      60
Hardly had skill to utter one of all
The nameless feelings that course through our
      breast,
But they course on for ever unexpressed.
And long we try in vain to speak and act
Our hidden self, and what we say and do      65
Is eloquent, is well—but 'tis not true!
And then we will no more be racked
With inward striving, and demand
Of all the thousand nothings of the hour
Their stupefying power;      70
Ah yes, and they benumb us at our call!
Yet still, from time to time, vague and forlorn,
From the soul's subterranean depth upborne
As from an infinitely distant land,
Come airs, and floating echoes, and convey      75
A melancholy into all our day.

Only—but this is rare—
When a belovéd hand is laid in ours,
When, jaded with the rush and glare
Of the interminable hours,      80
Our eyes can in another's eyes read clear,
When our world-deafened ear
Is by the tones of a loved voice caressed—
A bolt is shot back somewhere in our breast,
And a lost pulse of feeling stirs again.      85
The eye sinks inward, and the heart lies plain,
And what we mean, we say, and what we
      would, we know.
A man becomes aware of his life's flow,
And hears its winding murmur; and he sees
The meadows where it glides, the sun, the
      breeze.      90

And there arrives a lull in the hot race
Wherein he doth for ever chase
That flying and elusive shadow, rest.
An air of coolness plays upon his face,
And an unwonted calm pervades his breast.      95
And then he thinks he knows
The hills where his life rose,
And the sea where it goes.

## The Future [1]

A wanderer is man from his birth.
He was born in a ship
On the breast of the river of Time;
Brimming with wonder and joy
He spreads out his arms to the light,      5
Rivets his gaze on the banks of the stream.

As what he sees is, so have his thoughts been.
Whether he wakes,
Where the snowy mountainous pass,
Echoing the screams of the eagles,      10
Hems in its gorges the bed
Of the new-born clear-flowing stream;
Whether he first sees light
Where the river in gleaming rings
Sluggishly winds through the plain;      15
Whether in sound of the swallowing sea—
As is the world on the banks,
So is the mind of the man.

Vainly does each, as he glides,
Fable and dream      20
Of the lands which the river of Time
Had left ere he woke on its breast,
Or shall reach when his eyes have been closed.
Only the tract where he sails
He wots of; only the thoughts,      25
Raised by the objects he passes, are his.

Who can see the green earth any more
As she was by the sources of Time?
Who imagines her fields as they lay
In the sunshine, unworn by the plow?      30
Who thinks as they thought,
The tribes who then roamed on her breast,
Her vigorous, primitive sons?

What girl
Now reads in her bosom as clear      35
As Rebekah read, when she sat
At eve by the palm-shaded well? [2]
Who guards in her breast
As deep, as pellucid a spring
Of feeling, as tranquil, as sure?      40

What bard,
At the height of his vision, can deem
Of God, of the world, of the soul,
With a plainness as near,
As flashing as Moses felt      45

---

[2] Appointed tasks.

[1] Published in 1852.      [2] See Genesis, 24

When he lay in the night by his flock
On the starlit Arabian waste? [3]
Can rise and obey
The beck of the Spirit like him?

This tract which the river of Time          50
Now flows through with us, is the plain.
Gone is the calm of its earlier shore.
Bordered by cities and hoarse
With a thousand cries is its stream.
And we on its breast, our minds          55
Are confused as the cries which we hear,
Changing and shot as the sights which we see.

And we say that repose has fled
For ever the course of the river of Time.
That cities will crowd to its edge          60
In a blacker, incessanter line;
That the din will be more on its banks,
Denser the trade on its stream,
Flatter the plain where it flows,
Fiercer the sun overhead.          65
That never will those on its breast
See an ennobling sight,
Drink of the feeling of quiet again.

But what was before us we know not,
And we know not what shall succeed.          70

Haply, the river of Time—
As it grows, as the towns on its marge
Fling their wavering lights
On a wider, statelier stream—
May acquire, if not the calm          75
Of its early mountainous shore,
Yet a solemn peace of its own.
And the width of the waters, the hush
Of the gray expanse where he floats,
Freshening its current and spotted with foam          80
As it draws to the Ocean, may strike
Peace to the soul of the man on its breast—
As the pale waste widens around him,
As the banks fade dimmer away,
As the stars come out, and the night-wind          85
Brings up the stream
Murmurs and scents of the infinite sea.

# The Scholar-Gypsy [1]

Go, for they call you, shepherd, from the hill;
    Go, shepherd, and untie the wattled cotes! [2]

[3] See Exodus, 3.

[1] "There was very lately a lad in the University of
Oxford, who was by his poverty forced to leave his
studies there; and at last to join himself to a company of vagabond gypsies. Among these extravagant people, by the insinuating subtlety of his
carriage, he quickly got so much of their love and
esteem as that they discovered to him their mystery.
After he had been a pretty while exercised in the
trade, there chanced to ride by a couple of scholars,
who had formerly been of his acquaintance. They
quickly spied out their old friend among the gypsies;
and he gave them an account of the necessity which

No longer leave thy wistful flock unfed,
    Nor let thy bawling fellows rack their
        throats,
    Nor the cropped herbage shoot another
        head.          5
        But when the fields are still,
    And the tired men and dogs all gone to rest,
        And only the white sheep are sometimes
            seen
    Cross and recross the strips of moon-
        blanched green,
    Come, shepherd, and again begin the quest!

Here, where the reaper was at work of late—          11
    In this high field's dark corner, where he
        leaves
        His coat, his basket, and his earthen cruse,
    And in the sun all morning binds the
        sheaves,
        Then here, at noon, comes back his stores
            to use—          15
        Here will I sit and wait,
    While to my ear from uplands far away
        The bleating of the folded flocks is borne,
        With distant cries of reapers in the corn—
    All the live murmur of a summer's day.          20

Screened is this nook o'er the high, half-reaped
        field,
    And here till sun-down, shepherd! will I be.
        Through the thick corn the scarlet poppies
            peep,
    And round green roots and yellowing stalks
        I see
        Pale pink convolvulus in tendrils creep;          25
        And air-swept lindens yield
    Their scent, and rustle down their perfumed
        showers
        Of bloom on the bent grass where I am
            laid,
        And bower me from the August sun with
            shade;
    And the eye travels down to Oxford's towers.

And near me on the grass lies Glanvil's book—
    Come, let me read the oft-read tale again!          32
        The story of the Oxford scholar poor,
    Of pregnant parts and quick inventive brain,
        Who, tired of knocking at preferment's
            door, [3]          35
        One summer morn forsook

drove him to that kind of life, and told them that
the people he went with were not such impostors as
they were taken for, but that they had a traditional
kind of learning among them, and could do wonders
by the power of imagination, their fancy binding
that of others; that himself had learned much of
their art, and when he had compassed the whole
secret, he intended, he said, to leave their company,
and give the world an account of what he had
learned."—Glanvil, *Vanity of Dogmatizing*, 1661
(Arnold's note). The poem was published in 1853.
[2] Sheep-folds.
[3] I. e., of trying to secure a post in the Church.

His friends, and went to learn the gypsy-lore,
  And roamed the world with that wild
      brotherhood,
  And came, as most men deemed, to little
      good,
But came to Oxford and his friends no more.

But once, years after, in the country lanes, 41
  Two scholars, whom at college erst he knew,
  Met him, and of his way of life inquired;
  Whereat he answered, that the gypsy-crew,
    His mates, had arts to rule as they desired
      The workings of men's brains,     46
  And they can bind them to what thoughts
      they will.
  "And I," he said, "the secret of their art,
  When fully learned, will to the world
      impart;
  But it needs heaven-sent moments for this
    skill."       50

This said, he left them, and returned no
    more.—
  But rumors hung about the country-side,
    That the lost Scholar long was seen to
      stray,
  Seen by rare glimpses, pensive and tongue-
      tied,
    In hat of antique shape, and cloak of
      gray,     55
    The same the gypsies wore.
  Shepherds had met him on the Hurst in
      spring;
    At some lone alehouse in the Berkshire
      moors,
    On the warm ingle-bench, the smock-
      frocked boors
  Had found him seated at their entering, 60

But, 'mid their drink and clatter, he would fly.
  And I myself seem half to know thy looks,
    And put the shepherds, wanderer! on thy
      trace;
  And boys who in lone wheatfields scare the
      rooks
  I ask if thou hast passed their quiet place;
    Or in my boat I lie     66
  Moored to the cool bank in the summer
      heats,
    'Mid wide grass meadows which the sun-
      shine fills,
    And watch the warm, green-muffled Cum-
      ner hills,
  And wonder if thou haunt'st their shy re-
    treats.     70

For most, I know, thou lov'st retired ground!
  Thee at the ferry Oxford riders blithe,
    Returning home on summer nights, have
      met
  Crossing the stripling Thames at Bab-lock-
      hithe,

Trailing in the cool stream thy fingers
    wet,     75
  As the punt's rope chops round;
  And leaning backward in a pensive dream,
    And fostering in thy lap a heap of flowers
    Plucked in shy fields and distant Wych-
      wood [4] bowers,
  And thine eyes resting on the moonlit
    stream.     80

And then they land, and thou art seen no
    more!—
  Maidens, who from the distant hamlets come
    To dance around the Fyfield elm in May,
  Oft through the darkening fields have seen
      thee roam,
    Or cross a stile into the public way.   85
    Oft thou hast given them store
  Of flowers—the frail-leafed, white anem-
      one,
    Dark bluebells drenched with dews of
      summer eves,
    And purple orchises with spotted leaves—
  But none hath words she can report of thee.

And, above Godstow Bridge, when hay-time's
    here     91
  In June, and many a scythe in sunshine
      flames,
    Men who through those wide fields of
      breezy grass
  Where black-winged swallows haunt the
      glittering Thames,
    To bathe in the abandoned lasher [5] pass, 95
    Have often passed thee near
  Sitting upon the river bank o'ergrown;
    Marked thine outlandish garb, thy figure
      spare,
    Thy dark vague eyes, and soft abstracted
      air—
  But, when they came from bathing, thou
    wast gone!     100

At some lone homestead in the Cumner hills,
  Where at her open door the housewife darns,
    Thou hast been seen, or hanging on a
      gate
  To watch the threshers in the mossy barns.
    Children, who early range these slopes and
      late     105
    For cresses from the rills,
  Have known thee eying, all an April-day,
    The springing pastures and the feeding
      kine;
    And marked thee, when the stars come
      out and shine,
  Through the long dewy grass move slow
    away.     110

In autumn, on the skirts of Bagley wood—
  Where most the gypsies by the turf-edged
    way

[4] A forest about ten miles from Oxford.
[5] The pool below a dam.

Pitch their smoked tents, and every bush
    you see
With scarlet patches tagged and shreds of
    gray,
    Above the forest ground called Thessaly—
    The blackbird, picking food,    116
Sees thee, nor stops his meal, nor fears at all;
    So often has he known thee past him
    stray,
Rapt, twirling in thy hand a withered
    spray,
And waiting for the spark from heaven to
    fall.    120

And once, in winter, on the causeway chill
    Where home through flooded fields foot-
    travelers go,
    Have I not passed thee on the wooden
    bridge,
Wrapped in thy cloak and battling with the
    snow,
    Thy face tow'rd Hinksey and its wintry
    ridge?    125
    And thou hast climbed the hill
And gained the white brow of the Cumner
    range;
Turned once to watch, while thick the
    snowflakes fall,
The line of festal light in Christ-Church
    hall [6]—
Then sought thy straw in some sequestered
    grange.    130

But what—I dream! Two hundred years are
    flown
Since first thy story ran through Oxford halls,
    And the grave Glanvil did the tale in-
    scribe
That thou wert wandered from the studious
    walls
    To learn strange arts, and join a gypsy-
    tribe;    135
    And thou from earth are gone
Long since, and in some quiet churchyard
    laid—
    Some country-nook, where o'er thy un-
    known grave
Tall grasses and white flowering nettles
    wave,    139
Under a dark, red-fruited yew-tree's shade.

—No, no, thou hast not felt the lapse of hours!
For what wears out the life of mortal men?
    'Tis that from change to change their
    being rolls;
'Tis that repeated shocks, again, again,
    Exhaust the energy of strongest souls 145
    And numb the elastic powers.
Till having used our nerves with bliss and
    teen,[7]

[6] The hall of the college of that name, Oxford.
[7] Suffering.

And tired upon a thousand schemes our
    wit,
    To the just-pausing Genius [8] we remit
    Our worn-out life, and are—what we have
    been.    150

Thou has not lived, why should'st thou perish,
    so?
    Thou hadst *one* aim, *one* business, *one* de-
    sire;
    Else wert thou long since numbered with
    the dead!
Else hadst thou spent, like other men, thy
    fire!
    The generations of thy peers are fled,    155
    And we ourselves shall go;
But thou possessest an immortal lot,
    And we imagine thee exempt from age
    And living as thou liv'st on Glanvil's page,
Because thou hadst—what we, alas! have
    not.    160

For early didst thou leave the world, with
    powers
Fresh, undiverted to the world without,
    Firm to their mark, not spent on other
    things;
Free from the sick fatigue, the languid doubt,
    Which much to have tried, in much been
    baffled, brings.    165
    O life unlike to ours!
Who fluctuate idly without term or scope,
    Of whom each strives, nor knows for what
    he strives,
    And each half lives a hundred different
    lives;
Who wait like thee, but not, like thee, in
    hope.    170

Thou waitest for the spark from heaven! and
    we,
    Light half-believers of our casual creeds,
    Who never deeply felt, nor clearly willed,
Whose insight never has borne fruit in
    deeds,
    Whose vague resolves never have been ful-
    filled;    175
    For whom each year we see
Breeds new beginnings, disappointments
    new;
    Who hesitate and falter life away,
    And lose to-morrow the ground won to-
    day—
Ah! do not we, wanderer! await it too?    180

Yes, we await it!—but it still delays,
    And then we suffer! and amongst us one,[9]
    Who most has suffered, takes dejectedly

[8] Spirit attendant on an individual.
[9] Whether or not Arnold had in mind some contemporary is not known. Carlyle has been suggested and, with much greater plausibility, Tennyson.

His seat upon the intellectual throne;
  And all his store of sad experience he  185
    Lays bare of wretched days;
  Tells us his misery's birth and growth and
    signs,
  And how the dying spark of hope was fed,
  And how the breast was soothed, and how
    the head,
  And all his hourly varied anodynes.   190

This for our wisest! and we others pine,
  And wish the long unhappy dream would
    end,
  And waive all claim to bliss, and try to
    bear;
  With close-lipped patience for our only
    friend,
    Sad patience, too near neighbor to de-
      spair——  195
    But none has hope like thine!
  Thou through the fields and through the
    woods dost stray,
  Roaming the country-side, a truant boy,
  Nursing thy project in unclouded joy,
  And every doubt long blown by time away.

O born in days when wits were fresh and
    clear,   201
  And life ran gayly as the sparkling Thames;
  Before this strange disease of modern life,
  With its sick hurry, its divided aims,
    Its heads o'ertaxed, its palsied hearts, was
      rife——  205
    Fly hence, our contact fear!
  Still fly, plunge deeper in the bowering wood!
  Averse, as Dido did with gesture stern
    From her false friend's approach in Hades
    turn,[10]
  Wave us away, and keep thy solitude!   210

Still nursing the unconquerable hope,
  Still clutching the inviolable shade,
    With a free, onward impulse brushing
    through,
  By night, the silvered branches of the glade—
    Far on the forest skirts, where none pur-
      sue,  215
    On some mild pastoral slope
  Emerge, and resting on the moonlit pales
  Freshen thy flowers as in former years
  With dew, or listen with enchanted ears,
  From the dark dingles, to the nightingales!

But fly our paths, our feverish contact fly!  221
  For strong the infection of our mental strife,
    Which, though it gives no bliss, yet spoils
    for rest;
  And we should win thee from thy own fair
    life,
    Like us distracted, and like us unblest.  225
    Soon, soon thy cheer would die,

[10] The "false friend" was Aeneas; see *Aeneid*, VI,
469.

Thy hopes grow timorous, and unfixed thy
    powers,
  And thy clear aims be cross and shifting
    made;
  And then thy glad perennial youth would
    fade,
  Fade, and grow old at last, and die like ours.

Then fly our greetings, fly our speech and
    smiles!   231
  —As some grave Tyrian trader, from the sea,
    Descried at sunrise an emerging prow
  Lifting the cool-haired creepers stealthily,
    The fringes of a southward-facing brow
      Among the Aegean isles;   236
  And saw the merry Grecian coaster come,
    Freighted with amber grapes, and Chian
    wine,
    Green, bursting figs, and tunnies [11] steeped
      in brine——  239
  And knew the intruders on his ancient home,

The young light-hearted masters of the waves—
  And snatched his rudder, and shook out
    more sail;
  And day and night held on indignantly
  O'er the blue Midland [12] waters with the
    gale,
  Betwixt the Syrtes [13] and soft Sicily,   245
    To where the Atlantic raves
  Outside the western straits; and unbent sails
    There, where down cloudy cliffs, through
    sheets of foam,
    Shy traffickers, the dark Iberians [14] come;
  And on the beach undid his corded bales.  250

## Rugby Chapel [1]

### *November, 1857*

Coldly, sadly descends
The autumn-evening. The field
Strewn with its dank yellow drifts
Of withered leaves, and the elms,
Fade into dimness apace,         5
Silent;—hardly a shout
From a few boys late at their play!
The lights come out in the street,
In the school-room windows;—but cold,
Solemn, unlighted, austere,       10
Through the gathering darkness, arise
The chapel-walls, in whose bound
Thou, my father! art laid.

There thou dost lie, in the gloom
Of the autumn evening. But ah!    14
That word, *gloom*, to my mind

[11] A large oceanic fish.       [12] Mediterranean.
[13] Shoals off the north coast of Africa.
[14] Inhabitants of the Spanish peninsula.
[1] Published in 1867. Arnold's father, Thomas Arnold, died on 12 June, 1842, and was buried in
Rugby Chapel.

Brings thee back, in the light
Of thy radiant vigor, again;
In the gloom of November we passed
Days not dark at thy side;                    20
Seasons impaired not the ray
Of thy buoyant cheerfulness clear.
Such thou wast! and I stand
In the autumn evening, and think
Of bygone autumns with thee.                  25

Fifteen years have gone round
Since thou arosest to tread,
In the summer-morning, the road
Of death, at a call unforeseen,
Sudden. For fifteen years,                    30
We who till then in thy shade
Rested as under the boughs
Of a mighty oak, have endured
Sunshine and rain as we might,
Bare, unshaded, alone,                        35
Lacking the shelter of thee.

O strong soul, by what shore
Tarriest thou now? For that force,
Surely, has not been left vain!
Somewhere, surely, afar,                      40
In the sounding labor-house vast
Of being, is practiced that strength,
Zealous, beneficent, firm!

Yes, in some far-shining sphere,
Conscious or not of the past,                 45
Still thou performest the word
Of the Spirit in whom thou dost live—
Prompt, unwearied, as here!
Still thou upraisest with zeal
The humble good from the ground,              50
Sternly repressest the bad!
Still, like a trumpet, dost rouse
Those who with half-open eyes
Tread the border-land dim
'Twixt vice and virtue; reviv'st,             55
Succorest!—this was thy work,
This was thy life upon earth.

What is the course of the life
Of mortal men on the earth?—
Most men eddy about                           60
Here and there—eat and drink,
Chatter and love and hate,
Gather and squander, are raised
Aloft, are hurled in the dust,
Striving blindly, achieving                   65
Nothing; and then they die—
Perish;—and no one asks
Who or what they have been,
More than he asks what waves,
In the moonlit solitudes mild                 70
Of the midmost Ocean, have swelled,
Foamed for a moment, and gone.

And there are some, whom a thirst
Ardent, unquenchable, fires,

Not with the crowd to be spent,               75
Not without aim to go round
In an eddy of purposeless dust,
Effort unmeaning and vain.
Ah yes! some of us strive
Not without action to die                     80
Fruitless, but something to snatch
From dull oblivion, nor all
Glut the devouring grave!
We, we have chosen our path—
Path to a clear-purposed goal,                85
Path of advance!—but it leads
A long, steep journey, through sunk
Gorges, o'er mountains in snow.
Cheerful, with friends, we set forth—
Then, on the height, comes the storm.         90
Thunder crashes from rock
To rock, the cataracts reply,
Lightnings dazzle our eyes.
Roaring torrents have breached
The track, the stream-bed descends            95
In the place where the wayfarer once
Planted his footstep—the spray
Boils o'er its borders! aloft
The unseen snow-beds dislodge
Their hanging ruin; alas,                      100
Havoc is made in our train!
Friends, who set forth at our side,
Falter, are lost in the storm.
We, we only are left!
With frowning foreheads, with lips            105
Sternly compressed, we strain on,
On—and at nightfall at last
Come to the end of our way,
To the lonely inn 'mid the rocks;
Where the gaunt and taciturn host             110
Stands on the threshold, the wind
Shaking his thin white hairs—
Holds his lantern to scan
Our storm-beat figures, and asks:
Whom in our party we bring?                    115
Whom we have left in the snow?

Sadly we answer: We bring
Only ourselves! we lost
Sight of the rest in the storm.
Hardly ourselves we fought through,           120
Stripped, without friends, as we are.
Friends, companions, and train,
The avalanche swept from our side.

But thou wouldst not *alone*
Be saved, my father! *alone*                  125
Conquer and come to thy goal,
Leaving the rest in the wild.
We were weary, and we
Fearful, and we in our march
Fain to drop down and to die.                  130
Still thou turnedst, and still
Beckonedst the trembler, and still
Gavest the weary thy hand.

If, in the paths of the world,
Stones might have wounded thy feet,           135

Toil or dejection have tried
Thy spirit, of that we saw
Nothing—to us thou wast still
Cheerful, and helpful, and firm!
Therefore to thee it was given                    140
Many to save with thyself;
And, at the end of thy day,
O faithful shepherd! to come,
Bringing thy sheep in thy hand.

And through thee I believe                        145
In the noble and great who are gone;
Pure souls honored and blest
By former ages, who else—
Such, so soulless, so poor,
Is the race of men whom I see—                    150
Seemed but a dream of the heart,
Seemed but a cry of desire.
Yes! I believe that there lived
Others like thee in the past,
Not like the men of the crowd                     155
Who all round me to-day
Bluster or cringe, and make life
Hideous, and arid, and vile;
But souls tempered with fire,
Fervent, heroic, and good,                         160
Helpers and friends of mankind.

Servants of God!—or sons
Shall I not call you? because
Not as servants ye knew
Your Father's innermost mind,                      165
His, who unwillingly sees
One of his little ones lost—
Yours is the praise, if mankind
Hath not as yet in its march
Fainted, and fallen, and died!                     170

See! In the rocks of the world
Marches the host of mankind,
A feeble, wavering line.
Where are they tending?—A God
Marshaled them, gave them their goal.             175
Ah, but the way is so long!
Years they have been in the wild!
Sore thirst plagues them; the rocks,
Rising all round, overawe;
Factions divide them, their host                   180
Threatens to break, to dissolve.
—Ah! keep, keep them combined!
Else, of the myriads who fill
That army, not one shall arrive;
Sole they shall stray; in the rocks                185
Stagger for ever in vain,
Die one by one in the waste.

Then, in such hour of need
Of your fainting, dispirited race,
Ye, like angels, appear,                           190
Radiant with ardor divine!
Beacons of hope, ye appear!
Languor is not in your heart,
Weakness is not in your word,

Weariness not on your brow.                        195
Ye alight in our van! at your voice,
Panic, despair, flee away.
Ye move through the ranks, recall
The stragglers, refresh the outworn,
Praise, re-inspire the brave!                      200
Order, courage, return.
Eyes rekindling, and prayers,
Follow your steps as ye go.
Ye fill up the gaps in our files,
Strengthen the wavering line,                      205
Stablish, continue our march,
On, to the bound of the waste,
On, to the City of God.

# Stanzas from the Grande Chartreuse [1]

Through Alpine meadows soft-suffused
With rain, where thick the crocus blows,
Past the dark forges long disused,
The mule-track from Saint Laurent goes.
The bridge is crossed, and slow we ride,          5
Through forest, up the mountain-side.

The autumnal evening darkens round,
The wind is up, and drives the rain;
While, hark! far down, with strangled sound
Doth the Dead Guier's stream complain             10
Where that wet smoke, among the woods,
Over his boiling caldron broods.

Swift rush the spectral vapors white
Past limestone scars with ragged pines,
Showing—then blotting from our sight!—            15
Halt—through the cloud-drift something shines!
High in the valley, wet and drear,
The huts of Courrerie appear.

*Strike leftward!* cries our guide; and higher
Mounts up the stony forest-way.                    20
At last the encircling trees retire;
Look! through the showery twilight gray
What pointed roofs are these advance?—
A palace of the Kings of France?

Approach, for what we seek is here!                25
Alight, and sparely sup, and wait
For rest in this outbuilding near;
Then cross the sward and reach that gate.
Knock; pass the wicket! Thou art come
To the Carthusians' world-famed home.             30

The silent courts, where night and day
Into their stone-carved basins cold
The splashing icy fountains play—
The humid corridors behold!

[1] Published in 1855. The Grande Chartreuse is the chief monastery of the Carthusian monks, founded in the eleventh century. It is situated in the Alps of southeastern France.

Where, ghostlike in the deepening night,   35
Cowled forms brush by in gleaming white.

The chapel, where no organ's peal
Invests the stern and naked prayer—
With penitential cries they kneel
And wrestle; rising then, with bare   40
And white uplifted faces stand,
Passing the Host from hand to hand;

Each takes, and then his visage wan
Is buried in his cowl once more.
The cells!—the suffering Son of Man   45
Upon the wall—the knee-worn floor—
And where they sleep, that wooden bed,
Which shall their coffin be, when dead!

The library, where tract and tome
Not to feed priestly pride are there,   50
To hymn the conquering march of Rome,
Nor yet to amuse, as ours are!
They paint of souls the inner strife,
Their drops of blood, their death in life.

The garden, overgrown—yet mild,   55
See, fragrant herbs are flowering there!
Strong children of the Alpine wild
Whose culture is the brethren's care;
Of human tasks their only one,
And cheerful works beneath the sun.   60

Those halls too, destined to contain
Each its own pilgrim-host of old,[2]
From England, Germany, or Spain—
All are before me! I behold
The House, the Brotherhood austere!   65
—And what am I, that I am here?

For rigorous teachers seized my youth,
And purged its faith, and trimmed its fire,
Showed me the high, white star of Truth,
There bade me gaze, and there aspire.   70
Even now their whispers pierce the gloom:
*What dost thou in this living tomb?*

Forgive me, masters of the mind!
At whose behest I long ago
So much unlearned, so much resigned—   75
I come not here to be your foe!
I seek these anchorites, not in ruth,
To curse and to deny your truth;

Not as their friend, or child, I speak!
But as, on some far northern strand,   80
Thinking of his own Gods, a Greek
In pity and mournful awe might stand
Before some fallen Runic stone—
For both were faiths, and both are gone.

Wandering between two worlds, one dead,   85
The other powerless to be born,

With nowhere yet to rest my head,
Like these, on earth I wait forlorn.
Their faith, my tears, the world deride—
I come to shed them at their side.   90

Oh, hide me in your gloom profound,
Ye solemn seats of holy pain!
Take me, cowled forms, and fence me round,
Till I possess my soul again;
Till free my thoughts before me roll,   95
Not chafed by hourly false control!

For the world cries your faith is now
But a dead time's exploded dream;
My melancholy, sciolists[3] say,
Is a passed mode, an outworn theme—   100
As if the world had ever had
A faith, or sciolists been sad!

Ah, if it *be* passed, take away,
At least, the restlessness, the pain;
Be man henceforth no more a prey   105
To these out-dated stings again!
The nobleness of grief is gone—
Ah, leave us not the fret alone!

But—if you cannot give us ease—
Last of the race of them who grieve   110
Here leave us to die out with these
Last of the people who believe!
Silent, while years engrave the brow;
Silent—the best are silent now.

Achilles ponders in his tent,[4]   115
The kings of modern thought are dumb;
Silent they are, though not content,
And wait to see the future come.
They have the grief men had of yore,
But they contend and cry no more.   120

Our fathers watered with their tears
This sea of time whereon we sail,
Their voices were in all men's ears
Who passed within their puissant hail.
Still the same ocean round us raves,   125
But we stand mute, and watch the waves.

For what availed it, all the noise
And outcry of the former men?—
Say, have their sons achieved more joys,
Say, is life lighter now than then?   130
The sufferers died, they left their pain—
The pangs which tortured them remain.

What helps it now, that Byron bore,
With haughty scorn which mocked the smart,
Through Europe to the Aetolian shore[5]   135
The pageant of his bleeding heart?
That thousands counted every groan,
And Europe made his woe her own?

[2] Carthusian monks on pilgrimage.

[3] Smatterers.   [4] *Iliad*, Bk. I.
[5] Grecian shore.

What boots it, Shelley! that the breeze
Carried thy lovely wail away,    140
Musical through Italian trees
Which fringe thy soft blue Spezzian bay? [6]
Inheritors of thy distress
Have restless hearts one throb the less?

Or are we easier, to have read,    145
O Obermann! [7] the sad, stern page,
Which tells us how thou hidd'st thy head
From the fierce tempest of thine age
In the lone brakes of Fontainebleau,
Or chalets near the Alpine snow?    150

Ye slumber in your silent grave!—
The world, which for an idle day
Grace to your mood of sadness gave,
Long since hath flung her weeds away.
The eternal trifler breaks your spell;    155
But we—we learned your lore too well!

Years hence, perhaps, may dawn an age,
More fortunate, alas! than we,
Which without hardness will be sage,
And gay without frivolity.    160
Sons of the world, oh, speed those years;
But, while we wait, allow our tears!

Allow them! We admire with awe
The exulting thunder of your race;
You give the universe your law,    165
You triumph over time and space!
Your pride of life, your tireless powers,
We laud them, but they are not ours.

We are like children reared in shade
Beneath some old-world abbey wall,    170
Forgotten in a forest-glade,
And secret from the eyes of all.

[6] Shelley's last days were spent on the shores of the Gulf of Spezzia, in northwestern Italy.
[7] Étienne Pivert de Senancour (1770–1846), whose book is entitled *Obermann*.

Deep, deep the greenwood round them waves,
Their abbey, and its close [8] of graves!

But, where the road runs near the stream,    175
Oft through the trees they catch a glance
Of passing troops in the sun's beam—
Pennon, and plume, and flashing lance!
Forth to the world those soldiers fare,
To life, to cities, and to war!    180

And through the wood, another way,
Faint bugle-notes from far are borne,
Where hunters gather, staghounds bay,
Round some fair forest-lodge at morn.
Gay dames are there, in sylvan green;    185
Laughter and cries—those notes between!

The banners flashing through the trees
Make their blood dance and chain their eyes,
That bugle-music on the breeze
Arrests them with a charmed surprise.    190
Banner by turns and bugle woo:
*Ye shy recluses, follow too!*

O children, what do ye reply?—
"Action and pleasure, will ye roam
Through these secluded dells to cry    195
And call us?—but too late ye come!
Too late for us your call ye blow,
Whose bent was taken long ago.

"Long since we pace this shadowed nave;
We watch those yellow tapers shine,    200
Emblems of hope over the grave,
In the high altar's depth divine;
The organ carries to our ear
Its accents of another sphere.

"Fenced early in this cloistral round    205
Of reverie, of shade, of prayer,
How should we grow in other ground?
How can we flower in foreign air?
—Pass, banners, pass, and bugles, cease;
And leave our desert to its peace!"    210

[8] Enclosed plot.

# Dante Gabriel Rossetti

## 1828-1882

Rossetti was the eldest son of Gabriele Rossetti and Mary Lavinia Polidori, and was born in London on 12 May, 1828. Gabriele was a native of the Kingdom of Naples, where he had been Curator of Antiquities in the Naples Museum, but he had had to flee from that country because of his share in the insurrectionary movements of 1820 and 1821. He had come to England in 1824, where he was for many years Professor of Italian in King's College, London. The environment of his home early stimulated Dante Gabriel Rossetti's powers, and he was writing poetry at the age of five or six. At nine he began attending lectures at King's College, where he remained until he was fourteen. This was the extent of his formal education, though extensive reading done at home was of great importance in his development. When he left King's College in 1842 he determined that painting was to be his profession, and for the next six years he studied drawing at Cary's Drawing Academy and in the antique class of the Royal Academy. In this work he did not make remarkable progress, partly because then, as later, he was impatient for great results and tended to neglect the slow and tiresome drudgery necessary for a thorough foundation in drawing. He also began in this period the writing of poetry, some of his translations from Dante and his contemporaries being made as early as 1845, and several of his most remarkable poems, notably The Blessed Damozel, being written about 1847. In 1848 Rossetti applied to Ford Madox Brown for instruction, and this proved a momentous step. Through Brown he was introduced to a group of young men who were feeling their way to a new movement in art, resolving to abandon the conventionalities inherited from the eighteenth century and to revive the detailed elaboration and mystical interpretation of nature that characterized early medieval art. The best known of these are Woolner, Holman Hunt, and Millais, and they formed themselves,

with Brown, Rossetti, and others, into the so-called Pre-Raphaelite Brotherhood. The literary manifesto of the group was the Germ, four numbers of which appeared in 1850 under the editorship of William Michael Rossetti, a younger brother of Dante Gabriel. In this The Blessed Damozel was printed, as was also Hand and Soul, the only imaginative work in prose which D. G. Rossetti ever completed. About this time he fell in love with Elizabeth Eleanor Siddal, a milliner's assistant who was the daughter of a Sheffield cutler. He became engaged to her probably in 1851, and she served then and later as a model for many of his pictures; but he did not marry her until May, 1860, both because of his scanty means and because of her uncertain, delicate health. For several years his income was increased by Ruskin, who not only defended the aims of the Pre-Raphaelite painters but made an arrangement, which lasted until after 1861, to purchase Rossetti's pictures. Ruskin also stood the expense of the publication of Rossetti's translations from the Early Italian Poets (in later editions entitled Dante and His Circle) in 1861. Another friend who was at this time useful to him was Sir Edward Burne-Jones, who introduced him to Swinburne, William Morris, and others, at Oxford.

When Rossetti married in 1860 it was obvious that his wife could not live long, because of the consumption which had attacked her. She died, however, even sooner than anyone expected, in February, 1862, from an overdose of laudanum taken to relieve neuralgia. Rossetti characteristically expressed his grief by burying with her the manuscripts of his unpublished poems. And there they remained until the fall of 1869, when he consented to their disinterment. His Collected Poems were published in the following year and immediately secured for him a great reputation. The White Ship, the King's Tragedy, and other poems were published under the title Ballads and

Sonnets *in 1881. In the following year he died at Birchington, near Margate, on 10 April.*

*Rossetti was, as Ruskin said, "the chief intellectual force in the establishment of the Modern Romantic School in England." This he was, alike in the fine arts and in poetry. In the latter his chief followers were William Morris and Swinburne. This school voiced a reaction in its own lesser, sensuous way from the materialism and ugliness of the growing industrial civilization of England, just as the earlier romantic writers of the beginning of the century had reacted against the skeptical rationalism of the eighteenth century.*

*The standard edition of Rossetti's* Works *is edited by William Michael Rossetti (London, 1911; this is a revised and enlarged edition in one volume, superseding the* Collected Works *in two volumes, ed. W. M. R., 1886). All of the poems published in Rossetti's life-time, together with selections from his posthumously published verse and his translations, and* Hand and Soul *have been excellently edited by Paull F. Baum (New York, 1937). The standard biography is* Dante Gabriel Rossetti: His Family Letters, with a Memoir, *by W. M. Rossetti (2 vols., London, 1895; Vol. I contains the Memoir, Vol. II the* Letters). *A. C. Benson's* Rossetti ("English Men of Letters" *series, 1904) is a very good short life; also recommended are Max Beerbohm's* Rossetti and His Circle, 1824–54 *(London, 1922);* Evelyn Waugh's Rossetti: His Life and Works *(London, 1928); Oswald Doughty's* D. G. Rossetti, a Victorian Romantic *(New Haven, 1949); and Helen Angeli's* Rossetti, his Friends and his Enemies *(London, 1949). H. C. Marillier's* Dante Gabriel Rossetti: An Illustrated Memorial of His Life and Art *(London, 1899) is indispensable for the study of Rossetti's drawings and paintings. A. C. Swinburne's essay on Rossetti's poems is to be found in his* Essays and Studies *(London, 1875); and there is an essay by Walter Pater in* Appreciations *(London, 1889). Robert Buchanan's provocative attack on Rossetti,* The Fleshly School of Poetry and Other Phenomena of the Day *(London, 1872), has been reprinted in Albert Mordell's* Notorious Literary Attacks *(New York, 1926).*

# Sister Helen [1]

"Why did you melt your waxen man,
　　　Sister Helen?

[1] Published in 1853. The poem is founded on the belief, long and widely held, that if a wax or clay image were roasted the person whose name it bore

To-day is the third since you began."
"The time was long, yet the time ran,
　　　Little brother."　　　　　　　　　5
　　(O Mother, Mary Mother,
*Three days to-day, between Hell and Heaven!*)

"But if you have done your work aright,
　　　Sister Helen,
You'll let me play, for you said I might."　10
"Be very still in your play to-night,
　　　Little brother."
　　(O Mother, Mary Mother,
*Third night, to-night, between Hell and Heaven!*)

"You said it must melt ere vesper-bell,　15
　　　Sister Helen;
If now it be molten, all is well."
"Even so,—nay, peace! you cannot tell,
　　　Little brother."
　　(O Mother, Mary Mother,　　　　20
*O what is this, between Hell and Heaven?*)

"Oh the waxen knave was plump to-day,
　　　Sister Helen;
How like dead folk he has dropped away!"
"Nay now, of the dead what can you say,　25
　　　Little brother?"
　　(O Mother, Mary Mother,
*What of the dead, between Hell and Heaven?*)

"See, see, the sunken pile of wood,
　　　Sister Helen,　　　　　　　　　30
Shines through the thinned wax red as blood!"
"Nay now, when looked you yet on blood,
　　　Little brother?"
　　(O Mother, Mary Mother,
*How pale she is, between Hell and Heaven!*)　35

"Now close your eyes, for they're sick and sore,
　　　Sister Helen,
And I'll play without the gallery door."
"Aye, let me rest,—I'll lie on the floor,
　　　Little brother."　　　　　　　　40
　　(O Mother, Mary Mother,
*What rest to-night, between Hell and Heaven?*)

"Here high up in the balcony,
　　　Sister Helen,
The moon flies face to face with me."　　45
"Aye, look and say whatever you see,
　　　Little brother."
　　(O Mother, Mary Mother,
*What sight to-night, between Hell and Heaven?*)

"Outside it's merry in the wind's wake,　50
　　　Sister Helen;
In the shaken trees the chill stars shake."

would be melted or dried away by continual sickness.

"Hush, heard you a horse-tread, as you spake,
   Little brother?"
  (*O Mother, Mary Mother,*  55
*What sound to-night, between Hell and
 Heaven?*)

"I hear a horse-tread, and I see,
   Sister Helen,
Three horsemen that ride terribly."
"Little brother, whence come the three, 60
   Little brother?"
  (*O Mother, Mary Mother,*
*Whence should they come, between Hell and
 Heaven?*)

"They come by the hill-verge from Boyne Bar,
   Sister Helen, 65
And one draws nigh, but two are afar."
"Look, look, do you know them who they are,
   Little brother?"
  (*O Mother, Mary Mother,*
*Who should they be, between Hell and
 Heaven?*) 70

"Oh, it's Keith of Eastholm rides so fast,
   Sister Helen,
For I know the white mane on the blast."
"The hour has come, has come at last,
   Little brother!" 75
  (*O Mother, Mary Mother,*
*Her hour at last, between Hell and Heaven!*)

"He has made a sign and called Halloo!
   Sister Helen,
And he says that he would speak with you." 80
"Oh tell him I fear the frozen dew,
   Little brother."
  (*O Mother, Mary Mother,*
*Why laughs she thus, between Hell and
 Heaven?*)

"The wind is loud, but I hear him cry, 85
   Sister Helen,
That Keith of Ewern's like to die."
"And he and thou, and thou and I,
   Little brother."
  (*O Mother, Mary Mother,* 90
*And they and we, between Hell and Heaven!*)

"Three days ago, on his marriage-morn,
   Sister Helen,
He sickened, and lies since then forlorn."
"For bridegroom's side is the bride a thorn, 95
   Little brother?"
  (*O Mother, Mary Mother,*
*Cold bridal cheer, between Hell and Heaven!*)

"Three days and nights he has lain abed,
   Sister Helen, 100
And he prays in torment to be dead."
"The thing may chance, if he have prayed,
   Little brother!"
  (*O Mother, Mary Mother,*
*If he have prayed, between Hell and Heaven!*)

"But he has not ceased to cry to-day, 106
   Sister Helen,
That you should take your curse away."
"*My* prayer was heard,—he need but pray,
   Little brother!" 110
  (*O Mother, Mary Mother,*
*Shall God not hear, between Hell and
 Heaven?*)

"But he says, till you take back your ban,[2]
   Sister Helen,
His soul would pass, yet never can." 115
"Nay then, shall I slay a living man,
   Little brother?"
  (*O Mother, Mary Mother,*
*A living soul, between Hell and Heaven!*)

"But he calls for ever on your name, 120
   Sister Helen,
And says that he melts before a flame."
"My heart for his pleasure fared the same,
   Little brother."
  (*O Mother, Mary Mother,* 125
*Fire at the heart, between Hell and Heaven!*)

"Here's Keith of Westholm riding fast,
   Sister Helen,
For I know the white plume on the blast."
"The hour, the sweet hour I forecast, 130
   Little brother!"
  (*O Mother, Mary Mother,*
*Is the hour sweet, between Hell and Heaven?*)

"He stops to speak, and he stills his horse,
   Sister Helen; 135
But his words are drowned in the wind's
 course."
"Nay hear, nay hear, you must hear perforce,
   Little brother!"
  (*O Mother, Mary Mother,*
*What word now heard, between Hell and
 Heaven?*) 140

"Oh he says that Keith of Ewern's cry,
   Sister Helen,
Is ever to see you ere he die."
"In all that his soul sees, there am I,
   Little brother!" 145
  (*O Mother, Mary Mother,*
*The soul's one sight, between Hell and
 Heaven!*)

"He sends a ring and a broken coin,[3]
   Sister Helen,
And bids you mind the banks of Boyne." 150
"What else he broke will he ever join,
   Little brother?"
  (*O Mother, Mary Mother,*
*No, never joined, between Hell and Heaven!*)

[2] Curse.
[3] The two had broken a coin, each keeping half as
a pledge.

"He yields you these and craves full fain,    155
        Sister Helen,
You pardon him in his mortal pain."
"What else he took will he give again,
        Little brother?"
    (*O Mother, Mary Mother,*    160
*Not twice to give, between Hell and Heaven!*)

"He calls your name in an agony,
        Sister Helen,
That even dead Love must weep to see."
"Hate, born of Love, is blind as he,    165
        Little brother!"
    (*O Mother, Mary Mother,*
*Love turned to hate, between Hell and
    Heaven!*)

"Oh it's Keith of Keith now that rides fast,
        Sister Helen,    170
For I know the white hair on the blast."
"The short short hour will soon be past,
        Little brother!"
    (*O Mother, Mary Mother,*
*Will soon be past, between Hell and Heaven!*)

"He looks at me and he tries to speak,    176
        Sister Helen,
But oh! his voice is sad and weak!"
"What here should the mighty Baron seek
        Little brother?"    180
    (*O Mother, Mary Mother,*
*Is this the end, between Hell and Heaven?*)

"Oh his son still cries, if you forgive,
        Sister Helen,
The body dies but the soul shall live."    185
"Fire shall forgive me as I forgive,
        Little brother!"
    (*O Mother, Mary Mother,*
*As she forgives, between Hell and Heaven!*)

"Oh he prays you, as his heart would rive,    190
        Sister Helen,
To save his dear son's soul alive."
"Fire cannot slay it, it shall thrive,
        Little brother!"
    (*O Mother, Mary Mother,*    195
*Alas, alas, between Hell and Heaven!*)

"He cries to you, kneeling in the road,
        Sister Helen,
To go with him for the love of God!"
"The way is long to his son's abode,    200
        Little brother."
    (*O Mother, Mary Mother,*
*The way is long, between Hell and Heaven!*)

"A lady's here, by a dark steed brought,
        Sister Helen,    205
So darkly clad, I saw her not."
"See her now or never see aught,
        Little brother!"
    (*O Mother, Mary Mother,*
*What more to see, between Hell and Heaven?*)

"Her hood falls back, and the moon shines
    fair,    211
        Sister Helen,
On the Lady of Ewern's golden hair."
"Blest hour of my power and her despair,
        Little brother!"    215
    (*O Mother, Mary Mother,*
*Hour blest and banned, between Hell and
    Heaven!*)

"Pale, pale her cheeks, that in pride did glow,
        Sister Helen,
'Neath the bridal-wreath three days ago."    220
"One morn for pride and three days for woe,
        Little brother!"
    (*O Mother, Mary Mother,*
*Three days, three nights, between Hell and
    Heaven!*)

"Her clasped hands stretch from her bending
    head,    225
        Sister Helen;
With the loud wind's wail her sobs are wed."
"What wedding-strains hath her bridal-bed,
        Little brother?"
    (*O Mother, Mary Mother,*    230
*What strain but death's, between Hell and
    Heaven!*)

"She may not speak, she sinks in a swoon,
        Sister Helen,—
She lifts her lips and gasps on the moon."
"Oh! might I but hear her soul's blithe tune,
        Little brother!"    236
    (*O Mother, Mary Mother,*
*Her woe's dumb cry, between Hell and
    Heaven!*)

"They've caught her to Westholm's saddlebow,
        Sister Helen,    240
And her moonlit hair gleams white in its flow."
"Let it turn whiter than winter snow,
        Little brother!"
    (*O Mother, Mary Mother,*
*Woe-withered gold, between Hell and
    Heaven!*)    245

"O Sister Helen, you heard the bell,
        Sister Helen!
More loud than the vesper-chime it fell."
"No vesper-chime, but a dying knell,
        Little brother!"    250
    (*O Mother, Mary Mother,*
*His dying knell, between Hell and Heaven!*)

"Alas! but I fear the heavy sound,
        Sister Helen;
Is it in the sky or in the ground?"    255
"Say, have they turned their horses round,
        Little brother?"
    (*O Mother, Mary Mother,*
*What would she more, between Hell and
    Heaven?*)

"They have raised the old man from his knee,
                    Sister Helen,                261
And they ride in silence hastily."
"More fast the naked soul doth flee,
                    Little brother!"
          (*O Mother, Mary Mother,*          265
*The naked soul, between Hell and Heaven!*)

"Flank to flank are the three steeds gone,
                    Sister Helen,
But the lady's dark steed goes alone."
"And lonely her bridegroom's soul hath flown,
                    Little brother."           271
          (*O Mother, Mary Mother,*
*The lonely ghost, between Hell and Heaven!*)

"Oh the wind is sad in the iron chill,
                    Sister Helen,              275
And weary sad they look by the hill."
"But he and I are sadder still,
                    Little brother!"
          (*O Mother, Mary Mother,*
*Most sad of all, between Hell and Heaven!*)  280

"See, see, the wax has dropped from its place,
                    Sister Helen,
And the flames are winning up apace!"
"Yet here they burn but for a space,
                    Little brother!"           285
          (*O Mother, Mary Mother,*
*Here for a space, between Hell and Heaven!*)

"Ah! what white thing at the door has crossed,
                    Sister Helen?
Ah! what is this that sighs in the frost?"    290
"A soul that's lost as mine is lost,
                    Little brother!"
          (*O Mother, Mary Mother,*
*Lost, lost, all lost, between Hell and Heaven!*)

# The House of Life [1]

## A Sonnet Sequence

A sonnet is a moment's monument,—
    Memorial from the Soul's eternity
    To one dead deathless hour. Look that it be,
Whether for lustral rite or dire portent,
Of its own arduous fullness reverent:         5
    Carve it in ivory or in ebony,
    As Day or Night may rule; and let Time see
Its flowering crest impearled and orient.

A Sonnet is a coin: its face reveals
    The soul,—its converse, to what Power 'tis
        due:—                                 10
Whether for tribute to the august appeals

---
[1] Published in its final form in 1881. Rossetti began writing the sonnets as early as 1848. They were chiefly inspired by Elizabeth Siddal. The title of the sequence was drawn from the astrological division of the heavens into twelve "houses," the first and greatest of which was the "house of life."

Of Life, or dower in Love's high retinue,
It serve; or, 'mid the dark wharf's cavernous
        breath,
In Charon's [2] palm it pay the toll to Death.

## PART I—YOUTH AND CHANGE

### 4. *Lovesight*

When do I see thee most, belovéd one?
    When in the light the spirits of mine eyes
    Before thy face, their altar, solemnize
The worship of that Love through thee made
        known?
Or when in the dusk hours (we two alone),     5
    Close-kissed and eloquent of still replies
    Thy twilight-hidden glimmering visage lies,
And my soul only sees thy soul its own?

O love, my love! if I no more should see
Thyself, nor on the earth the shadow of thee, 10
    Nor image of thine eyes in any spring,—
How then should sound upon Life's darkening
        slope
The ground-whirl of the perished leaves of
        Hope,
    The wind of Death's imperishable wing?

### 19. *Silent Noon*

Your hands lie open in the long fresh grass,—
    The finger-points look through like rosy
        blooms:
    Your eyes smile peace. The pasture gleams
        and glooms
'Neath billowing skies that scatter and amass.
All round our nest, far as the eye can pass,   5
    Are golden kingcup-fields with silver edge
    Where the cow-parsley skirts the hawthorn-
        hedge.
'Tis visible silence, still as the hour-glass.

Deep in the sun-searched growths the dragon-
        fly
Hangs like a blue thread loosened from the
        sky;—                                  10
    So this winged hour is dropped to us from
        above.
Oh! clasp we to our hearts, for deathless dower,
This close-companioned inarticulate hour
    When twofold silence was the song of love.

### 21. *Love-Sweetness*

Sweet dimness of her loosened hair's downfall
    About thy face; her sweet hands round thy
        head
    In gracious fostering union garlanded;
Her tremulous smiles; her glances' sweet recall
Of love; her murmuring sighs memorial;        5
    Her mouth's culled sweetness by thy kisses
        shed
    On cheeks and neck and eyelids, and so led

---
[2] The ferryman of the lower world, who for a coin conveyed the souls of the dead across the rivers Styx and Acheron.

Back to her mouth which answers there for
all:—

What sweeter than these things, except the
thing
  In lacking which all these would lose their
    sweet:—          10
  The confident heart's still fervor: the swift
    beat
And soft subsidence of the spirit's wing,
Then when it feels, in cloud-girt wayfaring,
  The breath of kindred plumes against its
    feet?

### 22. Heart's Haven

Sometimes she is a child within mine arms,
  Cowering beneath dark wings that love must
    chase,—
  With still tears showering and averted face,
Inexplicably filled with faint alarms:
And oft from mine own spirit's hurtling harms
  I crave the refuge of her deep embrace,—  6
  Against all ills the fortified strong place
And sweet reserve of sovereign counter-charms.

And Love, our light at night and shade at noon,
  Lulls us to rest with songs, and turns away 10
  All shafts of shelterless tumultuous day.
Like the moon's growth, his face gleams
    through his tune;
And as soft waters warble to the moon,
  Our answering spirits chime one roundelay.

### 26. Mid-Rapture

Thou lovely and beloved, thou my love;
  Whose kiss seems still the first; whose sum-
    moning eyes,
  Even now, as for our love-world's new sun-
    rise,
Shed very dawn; whose voice, attuned above
All modulation of the deep-bowered dove,    5
  Is like a hand laid softly on the soul;
  Whose hand is like a sweet voice to control
Those worn tired brows it hath the keeping
  of:—

What word can answer to thy word,—what
    gaze
  To thine, which now absorbs within its
    sphere      10
  My worshiping face, till I am mirrored there
Light-circled in a heaven of deep-drawn rays?
What clasp, what kiss mine inmost heart can
    prove,
O lovely and belovéd, O my love?

### 36. Life-in-Love

Not in thy body is thy life at all,
  But in this lady's lips and hands and eyes;
  Through these she yields thee life that vivifies
What else were sorrow's servant and death's
    thrall.

Look on thyself without her, and recall    5
  The waste remembrance and forlorn surmise
  That lived but in a dead-drawn breath of
    sighs
O'er vanished hours and hours eventual.

Even so much life hath the poor tress of hair 9
  Which, stored apart, is all love hath to show
  For heart-beats, and for fire-heats long ago;
Even so much life endures unknown, even
    where,
'Mid change the changeless night environeth,
Lies all that golden hair undimmed in death.

### 55. Stillborn Love

The hour which might have been yet might
    not be,
  Which man's and woman's heart conceived
    and bore
  Yet whereof life was barren,—on what shore
Bides it the breaking of Time's weary sea?
Bondchild of all consummate joys set free,  5
  It somewhere sighs and serves, and mute be-
    fore
  The house of Love, hears through the echo-
    ing door
His hours elect in choral consonancy.

But lo! what wedded souls now hand in hand
Together tread at last the immortal strand    10
  With eyes where burning memory lights love
    home?
Lo! how the little outcast hour has turned
And leaped to them and in their faces
    yearned:—
"I am your child: O Parents, ye have come!"

## PART II—CHANGE AND FATE
### 71, 72, 73. The Choice

#### I

Eat thou and drink; to-morrow thou shalt die.
  Surely the earth, that's wise being very old,
  Needs not our help. Then loose me, love,
    and hold
Thy sultry hair up from my face; that I    4
May pour for thee this golden wine, brim-high,
  Till round the glass thy fingers glow like gold.
  We'll drown all hours: thy song, while hours
    are tolled,
Shall leap, as fountains veil the changing sky.

Now kiss, and think that there are really those,
  My own high-bosomed beauty, who increase
    Vain gold, vain lore, and yet might choose
      our way!    11
    Through many years they toil; then on a
      day
    They die not,—for their life was death,—but
      cease;
And round their narrow lips the mold falls
    close.

## II

Watch thou and fear; to-morrow thou shalt die.
  Or art thou sure thou shalt have time for
    death?
Is not the day which God's word promiseth
To come man knows not when? In yonder sky,
Now while we speak, the sun speeds forth:
    can I      5
  Or thou assure him of his goal? God's breath
  Even at this moment haply quickeneth
The air to a flame; till spirits, always nigh
Though screened and hid, shall walk the day-
    light here.
  And dost thou prate of all that man shall do?
    Canst thou, who hast but plagues, presume
      to be      11
    Glad in his gladness that comes after thee?
Will *his* strength slay *thy* worm in Hell? Go
    to:
Cover thy countenance, and watch, and fear.

## III

Think thou and act; to-morrow thou shalt die.
  Outstretched in the sun's warmth upon the
    shore,
  Thou say'st: "Man's measured path is all
    gone o'er:
Up all his years, steeply, with strain and sigh,
Man clomb until he touched the truth; and I,
  Even I, am he whom it was destined for."   6
  How should this be? Art thou then so much
    more
Than they who sowed, that thou shouldst reap
    thereby?

Nay, come up hither. From this wave-washed
    mound
  Unto the furthest flood-brim look with me;
Then reach on with thy thought till it be
    drowned.      11
  Miles and miles distant though the last line
    be,
  And though thy soul sail leagues and leagues
    beyond,—
    Still, leagues beyond those leagues, there is
      more sea.

### 82. *Hoarded Joy*

I said: "Nay, pluck not,—let the first fruit be:
  Even as thou sayest, it is sweet and red,
  But let it ripen still. The tree's bent head
Sees in the stream its own fecundity
And bides the day of fullness. Shall not we   5
  At the sun's hour that day possess the shade,
  And claim our fruit before its ripeness fade,
And eat it from the branch and praise the
    tree?"

I say: "Alas! our fruit hath wooed the sun
  Too long,—'tis fallen and floats adown the
    stream.      10
Lo, the last clusters! Pluck them every one,

And let us sup with summer; ere the gleam
Of autumn set the year's pent sorrow free,
And the woods wail like echoes from the sea."

### 85. *Vain Virtues*

What is the sorriest thing that enters Hell?
  None of the sins,—but this and that fair
    deed
  Which a soul's sin at length could supersede.
These yet are virgins, whom death's timely
    knell
Might once have sainted; whom the fiends com-
    pel      5
  Together now, in snake-bound shuddering
    sheaves
  Of anguish, while the pit's pollution leaves
Their refuse maidenhood abominable.

Night sucks them down, the tribute of the pit,
  Whose names, half entered in the book of
    Life,      10
    Were God's desire at noon. And as their
      hair
And eyes sink last, the Torturer deigns no whit
  To gaze, but, yearning, waits his destined
    wife,
    The Sin still blithe on earth that sent them
      there.

### 86. *Lost Days*

The lost days of my life until to-day,
  What were they, could I see them on the
    street
  Lie as they fell? Would they be ears of wheat
Sown once for food but trodden into clay?
Or golden coins squandered and still to pay?   5
  Or drops of blood dabbling the guilty feet?
  Or such spilt water as in dreams must cheat
The undying throats of Hell, athirst alway?

I do not see them here; but after death
  God knows I know the faces I shall see,   10
Each one a murdered self, with low last breath.
  "I am thyself,—what hast thou done to me?"
  "And I—and I—thyself" (lo! each one saith)
  "And thou thyself to all eternity!"

### 97. *A Superscription*

Look in my face; my name is Might-have-been;
  I am also called No-more, Too-late, Farewell;
  Unto thine ear I hold the dead-sea shell
Cast up thy Life's foam-fretted feet between;
Unto thine eyes the glass where that is seen   5
  Which had Life's form and Love's, but by
    my spell
  Is now a shaken shadow intolerable,
Of ultimate things unuttered the frail screen.

Mark me, how still I am! But should there dart
  One moment through thy soul the soft sur-
    prise      10
  Of that winged Peace which lulls the breath
    of sighs,—

Then shalt thou see me smile, and turn apart
Thy visage to mine ambush at thy heart
   Sleepless with cold commemorative eyes.

### 101. *The One Hope*

When vain desire at last and vain regret
   Go hand in hand to death, and all is vain,
   What shall assuage the unforgotten pain
And teach the unforgetful to forget?
Shall Peace be still a sunk stream long un-
       met,—               5
   Or may the soul at once in a green plain
   Stoop through the spray of some sweet life-
       fountain
And cull the dew-drenched flowering amulet?

Ah! when the wan soul in that golden air
   Between the scriptured petals softly blown 10
   Peers breathless for the gift of grace un-
       known,—
Ah! let none other alien spell soe'er
But only the one Hope's one name be there,—
   Not less nor more, but even that word alone.

# My Sister's Sleep [1]

She fell asleep on Christmas Eve.
   At length the long-ungranted shade
   Of weary eyelids overweighed
The pain nought else might yet relieve.

Our mother, who had leaned all day     5
   Over the bed from chime to chime,
   Then raised herself for the first time,
And as she sat her down, did pray.

Her little work-table was spread
   With work to finish. For the glare    10
   Made by her candle, she had care
To work some distance from the bed.

Without, there was a cold moon up,
   Of winter radiance sheer and thin;
   The hollow halo it was in    15
Was like an icy crystal cup.

Through the small room, with subtle sound
   Of flame, by vents the fireshine drove
   And reddened. In its dim alcove
The mirror shed a clearness round.    20

I had been sitting up some nights,
   And my tired mind felt weak and blank;
   Like a sharp strengthening wine it drank
The stillness and the broken lights.

Twelve struck. That sound, by dwindling years
   Heard in each hour, crept off; and then   26
   The ruffled silence spread again,
Like water that a pebble stirs.

[1] This and the three following poems were written
not later than 1850.

Our mother rose from where she sat:
   Her needles, as she laid them down,   30
   Met lightly, and her silken gown
Settled: no other noise than that.

"Glory unto the Newly Born!"
   So, as said angels, she did say;
   Because we were in Christmas Day,   35
Though it would still be long till morn.

Just then in the room over us
   There was a pushing back of chairs,
   As some who had sat unawares
So late, now heard the hour, and rose.   40

With anxious softly-stepping haste
   Our mother went where Margaret lay,
   Fearing the sounds o'erhead—should they
Have broken her long watched-for rest!

She stooped an instant, calm, and turned;   45
   But suddenly turned back again;
   And all her features seemed in pain
With woe, and her eyes gazed and yearned.

For my part, I but hid my face,
   And held my breath, and spoke no word:   50
   There was none spoken; but I heard
The silence for a little space.

Our mother bowed herself and wept:
   And both my arms fell, and I said,
   "God knows I knew that she was dead."   55
And there, all white, my sister slept.

Then kneeling, upon Christmas morn
   A little after twelve o'clock,
   We said, ere the first quarter struck,
"Christ's blessing on the newly born!"   60

# The Blessed Damozel

The blesséd damozel leaned out
   From the gold bar of Heaven;
Her eyes were deeper than the depth
   Of waters stilled at even;
She had three lilies in her hand,   5
   And the stars in her hair were seven.

Her robe, ungirt from clasp to hem,
   No wrought flowers did adorn,
But a white rose of Mary's gift,
   For service meetly worn;   10
Her hair that lay along her back
   Was yellow like ripe corn.

Herseemed she scarce had been a day
   One of God's choristers;
The wonder was not yet quite gone   15
   From that still look of hers;
Albeit, to them she left, her day
   Had counted as ten years.

(To one, it is ten years of years.
   . . . Yet now, and in this place,     20
Surely she leaned o'er me—her hair
   Fell all about my face. . . .
Nothing: the autumn-fall of leaves.
   The whole year sets apace.)

It was the rampart of God's house     25
   That she was standing on;
By God built over the sheer depth
   The which is Space begun;
So high, that looking downward thence
   She scarce could see the sun.     30

It lies in Heaven, across the flood,
   Of ether, as a bridge.
Beneath, the tides of day and night
   With flame and darkness ridge
The void, as low as where this earth     35
   Spins like a fretful midge.

Around her, lovers, newly met
   'Mid deathless love's acclaims,
Spoke evermore among themselves
   Their heart-remembered names;     40
And the souls mounting up to God
   Went by her like thin flames.

And still she bowed herself and stooped
   Out of the circling charm;
Until her bosom must have made     45
   The bar she leaned on warm,
And the lilies lay as if asleep
   Along her bended arm.

From the fixed place of Heaven she saw
   Time like a pulse shake fierce     50
Through all the worlds. Her gaze still strove
   Within the gulf to pierce
Its path; and now she spoke as when
   The stars sang in their spheres.

The sun was gone now; the curled moon     55
   Was like a little feather
Fluttering far down the gulf; and now
   She spoke through the still weather.
Her voice was like the voice the stars
   Had when they sang together.     60

(Ah sweet! Even now, in that bird's song,
   Strove not her accents there,
Fain to be hearkened? When those bells
   Possessed the mid-day air,
Strove not her steps to reach my side     65
   Down all the echoing stair?)

"I wish that he were come to me,
   For he will come," she said.
"Have I not prayed in Heaven?—on earth,
   Lord, Lord, has he not prayed?     70
Are not two prayers a perfect strength?
   And shall I feel afraid?

"When round his head the aureole clings,
   And he is clothed in white,
I'll take his hand and go with him     75
   To the deep wells of light;
As unto a stream we will step down,
   And bathe there in God's sight.

"We two will stand beside that shrine,
   Occult, withheld, untrod,     80
Whose lamps are stirred continually
   With prayer sent up to God;
And see our old prayers, granted, melt
   Each like a little cloud.

"We two will lie i' the shadow of     85
   That living mystic tree
Within whose secret growth the Dove
   Is sometimes felt to be,
While every leaf that His plumes touch
   Saith His Name audibly.     90

"And I myself will teach to him,
   I myself, lying so,
The songs I sing here; which his voice
   Shall pause in, hushed and slow,
And find some knowledge at each pause,     95
   Or some new thing to know."

(Alas! we two, we two, thou say'st!
   Yea, one wast thou with me
That once of old. But shall God lift
   To endless unity     100
The soul whose likeness with thy soul
   Was but its love for thee?)

"We two," she said, "will seek the groves
   Where the lady Mary is,
With her five handmaidens, whose names     105
   Are five sweet symphonies,
Cecily, Gertrude, Magdalene,
   Margaret and Rosalys.

"Circlewise sit they, with bound locks
   And foreheads garlanded;     110
Into the fine cloth white like flame
   Weaving the golden thread,
To fashion the birth-robes for them
   Who are just born, being dead.

"He shall fear, haply, and be dumb:     115
   Then will I lay my cheek
To his, and tell about our love,
   Not once abashed or weak:
And the dear Mother will approve
   My pride, and let me speak.     120

"Herself shall bring us, hand in hand,
   To Him round whom all souls
Kneel, the clear-ranged unnumbered heads
   Bowed with their aureoles:
And angels meeting us shall sing     123
   To their citherns and citoles.[1]

[1] Stringed musical instruments.

"There will I ask of Christ the Lord
  Thus much for him and me:—
Only to live as once on earth
  With Love,—only to be,     130
As then awhile, for ever now
  Together, I and he."

She gazed and listened and then said,
  Less sad of speech than mild,—
"All this is when he comes." She ceased.   135
  The light thrilled towards her, filled
With angels in strong level flight.
  Her eyes prayed, and she smiled.

(I saw her smile.) But soon their path
  Was vague in distant spheres:    140
And then she cast her arms along
  The golden barriers,
And laid her face between her hands,
  And wept. (I heard her tears.)

# Sudden Light

I have been here before,
  But when or how I cannot tell:
I know the grass beyond the door,
  The sweet keen smell,
The sighing sound, the lights around the shore.

You have been mine before,—    6
  How long ago I may not know:
But just when at that swallow's soar
  Your neck turned so,
Some veil did fall,—I knew it all of yore.   10
  Has this been thus before?

And shall not thus time's eddying flight
Still with our lives our love restore
  In death's despite,
And day and night yield one delight once
  more?    15

# Walter Pater

## 1839-1894

Walter Horatio Pater was born at Shadwell, in East London, on 4 August, 1839. His father, who was a physician, died so early that in later life Pater could scarcely remember him. At his death the family moved to a house in Chase Side, Enfield, where they remained some fourteen or fifteen years. Pater received his earliest education at a school in Enfield, and at fourteen proceeded to King's School, Canterbury. There he led a happy life—to some extent portrayed in Emerald Uthwart —despite his complete indifference to outdoor games. He did creditable work at school, but was not precocious in his development; as a youth he exhibited a meditative and serious disposition. Just before he left school he came upon Ruskin's Modern Painters, and fell abruptly under the influence of that book. In June, 1858, Pater entered Queen's College, Oxford, with a scholarship from his Canterbury school. In 1862 he took his B. A. with a second class in classics. He had long intended to take holy orders, but had later abandoned the idea, and for a time he now read with private pupils. In 1863 he was elected a member of the "Old Mortality," an essay society through which he became acquainted with Swinburne. In 1864 he was elected a fellow of Brasenose College, and at once went into residence there. He held his fellowship and his rooms at Brasenose through the remainder of his life. He generally spent his long vacations in Germany or northern France, and in 1865 he went to Italy with his friend C. L. Shadwell. In 1882 he also spent the winter in Rome. Save for these journeys and the publication of his essays and books Pater's life was uneventful. He was attacked by rheumatic fever in June, 1894, and died suddenly on the following 30 July.

Pater may be termed the philosopher of the modern or neo-romantic school of Rossetti, Swinburne, and Morris. He sought to think through what they felt and expressed in poetry and art. He saw that their attitude towards life coincided with what, one might contend, was the great lesson of modern philosophy and science in their progress away from ancient and medieval confidence in the ability of human reason to penetrate reality, and in their conclusion that the intellectual life of man is bounded by the impressions of the senses. He concluded that if the sole stuff of life is sense-impressions, Rossetti and his followers were right in their implication that life is fundamentally a problem in aesthetics. Consequently Pater attempted to found an aesthetic criticism in a series of studies and imaginary portraits, the more important of which are contained in Studies in the History of the Renaissance (1873), Imaginary Portraits (1887), and Appreciations (1889). His lectures on Plato and Platonism (1893) are in reality, though less obviously, an effort in the same kind. And his longest and most carefully wrought work, Marius the Epicurean (1885)—to which he gave six years of sustained labor—contains his full exposition, in a form at once literary and meditative, of his aesthetic Epicureanism. Pater's work taken as a whole thus has an important historical interest, and, in addition, his books are full of the rare charm and rightness of a very distinguished and finely cultivated mind. His readers are inevitably struck by his humanity, by the unobtrusiveness of his scholarship, by his never-failing good taste, and by his gift—amounting to genius—for the precise expression of his meaning.

The standard edition of Pater's writings is the "Library Edition" (10 vols., London, 1910). Pieces not included in this edition are to be found in Uncollected Essays (Portland, Maine, 1903) and in Sketches and Reviews, ed. A Mordell (New York, 1919). The best edition of Marius the Epicurean is edited by Joseph Sagmaster (Garden City, N. Y., 1935). A convenient volume is Pater's Selected Works, edited by Richard Aldington (New York,

1948). *The fullest biography is* The Life of Walter Pater *by Thomas Wright (2 vols., London, 1907), but this is an uncritical work and is to be used with caution. The best biographical and critical study is A. C. Benson's* Walter Pater *("English Men of Letters" series, 1906). Ferris Greenslet's shorter and slighter* Walter Pater *(New York, 1903) is also a good introduction. Also recommended are* Walter Pater, *by Arthur Symons (London, 1932), and* The Aesthetic of Pater, *by R. C. Child (New York, 1940). Finally two essays on Pater should be mentioned—those in P. E. More's* The Drift of Romanticism *("Shelburne Essays," Eighth Series, Boston, 1913), and in T. S. Eliot's* Selected Essays, 1917–1932 *(London, 1932).*

## The Child in the House [1]

As Florian Deleal walked, one hot afternoon, he overtook by the wayside a poor aged man, and, as he seemed weary with the road, helped him on with the burden which he carried, a certain distance. And as the man told his story, it chanced that he named the place, a little place in the neighborhood of a great city, where Florian had passed his earliest years, but which he had never since seen, and, the story told, went forward on his journey comforted. And that night, like a reward for his pity, a dream of that place came to Florian, a dream which did for him the office of the finer sort of memory, bringing its object to mind with a great clearness, yet, as sometimes happens in dreams, raised a little above itself, and above ordinary retrospect. The true aspect of the place, especially of the house there in which he had lived as a child, the fashion of its doors, its hearths, its windows, the very scent upon the air of it, was with him in sleep for a season; only, with tints more musically blent on wall and floor, and some finer light and shadow running in and out along its curves and angles, and with all its little carvings daintier. He awoke with a sigh at the thought of almost thirty years which lay between him and that place, yet with a flutter of pleasure still within him at the fair light, as if it were a smile, upon it. And it happened that this accident of his dream was just the thing needed for the beginning of a certain design he then had in view, the noting, namely, of some things

in the story of his spirit—in that process of brain-building by which we are, each one of us, what we are. With the image of the place so clear and favorable upon him, he fell to thinking of himself therein, and how his thoughts had grown up to him. In that half-spiritualized house he could watch the better, over again, the gradual expansion of the soul which had come to be there—of which indeed, through the law which makes the material objects about them so large an element in children's lives, it had actually become a part; inward and outward being woven through and through each other into one inextricable texture—half, tint and trace and accident of homely color and form, from the wood and the bricks; half, mere soul-stuff, floated thither from who knows how far. In the house and garden of his dream he saw a child moving, and could divide the main streams at least of the winds that had played on him, and study so the first stage in that mental journey.

The *old house*, as when Florian talked of it afterwards he always called it (as all children do, who can recollect a change of home, soon enough but not too soon to mark a period in their lives), really was an old house; and an element of French descent in its inmates—descent from Watteau, the old court-painter, one of whose gallant pieces still hung in one of the rooms—might explain, together with some other things, a noticeable trimness and comely whiteness about everything there—the curtains, the couches, the paint on the walls with which the light and shadow played so delicately; might explain also the tolerance of the great poplar in the garden, a tree most often despised by English people, but which French people love, having observed a certain fresh way its leaves have of dealing with the wind, making it sound, in never so slight a stirring of the air, like running water.

The old-fashioned, low wainscoting went round the rooms, and up the staircase with carved balusters and shadowy angles, landing half-way up at a broad window, with a swallow's nest below the sill, and the blossom of an old pear-tree showing across it in late April, against the blue, below which the perfumed juice of the find of fallen fruit in autumn was so fresh. At the next turning came the closet which held on its deep shelves the best china. Little angel faces and reedy flutings stood out round the fireplace of the children's room. And on the top of the

---

[1] Published in *Macmillan's Magazine*, August, 1878, with the title, "Imaginary Portrait. The Child in the House." Reprinted in *Miscellaneous Studies* (1895).

house, above the large attic, where the white mice ran in the twilight—an infinite, unexplored wonderland of childish treasures, glass beads, empty scent-bottles still sweet, thrum [2] of colored silks, among its lumber—a flat space of roof, railed round, gave a view of the neighboring steeples; for the house, as I said, stood near a great city, which sent up heavenwards, over the twisting weathervanes, not seldom, its beds of rolling cloud and smoke, touched with storm or sunshine. But the child of whom I am writing did not hate the fog because of the crimson lights which fell from it sometimes upon the chimneys, and the whites which gleamed through its openings, on summer mornings, on turret or pavement. For it is false to suppose that a child's sense of beauty is dependent on any choiceness or special fineness, in the objects which present themselves to it, though this indeed comes to be the rule with most of us in later life; earlier, in some degree, we see inwardly; and the child finds for itself, and with unstinted delight, a difference for the sense, in those whites and reds through the smoke on very homely buildings, and in the gold of the dandelions at the road-side, just beyond the houses, where not a handful of earth is virgin and untouched, in the lack of better ministries to its desire of beauty.

This house then stood not far beyond the gloom and rumors of the town, among high garden-wall, bright all summer-time with Golden-rod, and brown-and-golden Wallflower—*Flos Parietis*, as the childern's Latin-reading father taught them to call it, while he was with them. Tracing back the threads of his complex spiritual habit, as he was used in after years to do, Florian found that he owed to the place many tones of sentiment afterwards customary with him, certain inward lights under which things most naturally presented themselves to him. The coming and going of travelers to the town along the way, the shadow of the streets, the sudden breath of the neighboring gardens, the singular brightness of bright weather there, its singular darknesses which linked themselves in his mind to certain engraved illustrations in the old big Bible at home, the coolness of the dark, cavernous shops round the great church, with its giddy winding stair up to the pigeons and the bells—a citadel of peace in the heart of the trouble—all this acted on his childish fancy, so that ever afterwards the like aspects and incidents never failed to throw him into a well-recognized imaginative mood, seeming actually to have become a part of the texture of his mind. Also, Florian could trace home to this point a pervading preference in himself for a kind of comeliness and dignity, an *urbanity* literally, in modes of life, which he connected with the pale people of towns, and which made him susceptible to a kind of exquisite satisfaction in the trimness and well-considered grace of certain things and persons he afterwards met with, here and there, in his way through the world.

So the child of whom I am writing lived on there quietly; things without thus ministering to him, as he sat daily at the window with the birdcage hanging below it, and his mother taught him to read, wondering at the ease with which he learned, and at the quickness of his memory. The perfume of the little flowers of the lime-tree fell through the air upon them like rain; while time seemed to move ever more slowly to the murmur of the bees in it, till it almost stood still on June afternoons. How insignificant, at the moment, seem the influences of the sensible things which are tossed and fall and lie about us, so, or so, in the environment of early childhood. How indelibly, as we afterwards discover, they affect us; with what capricious attractions and associations they figure themselves on the white paper, the smooth wax, of our ingenuous souls, as "with lead in the rock for ever," [3] giving form and feature, and as it were assigned house-room in our memory, to early experiences of feeling and thought, which abide with us ever afterwards, thus, and not otherwise. The realities and passions, the rumors of the greater world without, steal in upon us, each by its own special little passage-way, through the wall of custom about us; and never afterwards quite detach themselves from this or that accident, or trick, in the mode of their first entrance to us. Our susceptibilities, the discovery of our powers, manifold experiences—our various experiences of the coming and going of bodily pain, for instance—belong to this or the other well-remembered place in the material habitation —that little white room with the window across which the heavy blossoms could beat so peevishly in the wind, with just that particular catch or throb, such a sense of teasing in it, on gusty mornings; and the early habitation thus gradually becomes a sort of ma-

---

[2] Waste thread.

[3] Job, 19:24.

terial shrine or sanctuary of sentiment; a system of visible symbolism interweaves itself through all our thoughts and passions; and irresistibly, little shapes, voices, accidents—the angle at which the sun in the morning fell on the pillow—become parts of the great chain wherewith we are bound.

Thus far, for Florian, what all this had determined was a peculiarly strong sense of home—so forcible a motive with all of us—prompting to us our customary love of the earth, and the larger part of our fear of death, that revulsion we have from it, as from something strange, untried, unfriendly; though life-long imprisonment, they tell you, and final banishment from home is a thing bitterer still; the looking forward to but a short space, a mere childish *goûter* [4] and dessert of it, before the end, being so great a resource of effort to pilgrims and wayfarers, and the soldier in distant quarters, and lending, in lack of that, some power of solace to the thought of sleep in the home churchyard, at least—dead cheek by dead cheek, and with the rain soaking in upon one from above.

So powerful is this instinct, and yet accidents like those I have been speaking of so mechanically determine it; its essence being indeed the early familiar, as constituting our ideal, or typical conception, of rest and security. Out of so many possible conditions, just this for you and that for me, brings ever the unmistakable realization of the delightful *chez soi*; [5] this for the Englishman, for me and you, with the closely-drawn white curtain and the shaded lamp; that, quite other, for the wandering Arab, who folds his tent every morning, and makes his sleeping-place among haunted ruins, or in old tombs.

With Florian then the sense of home became singularly intense, his good fortune being that the special character of his home was in itself so essentially home-like. As after many wanderings I have come to fancy that some parts of Surrey and Kent are, for Englishmen, the true landscape, true home-counties, by right, partly, of a certain earthy warmth in the yellow of the sand below their gorse-bushes, and of a certain gray-blue mist after rain, in the hollows of the hills there, welcome to fatigued eyes, and never seen farther south; so I think that the sort of house I have described, with precisely those proportions of red-brick and green, and with a just perceptible monotony in the subdued order of it, for its distinguishing note, is for

Englishmen at least typically homelike. And so for Florian that general human instinct was reinforced by this special homelikeness in the place his wandering soul had happened to light on, as, in the second degree, its body and earthly tabernacle; the sense of harmony between his soul and its physical environment became, for a time at least, like perfectly played music, and the life led there singularly tranquil and filled with a curious sense of self-possession. The love of security, of an habitually undisputed standing-ground or sleeping-place, came to count for much in the generation and correcting of his thoughts, and afterwards as a salutary principle of restraint in all his wanderings of spirit. The wistful yearning towards home, in absence from it, as the shadows of evening deepened, and he followed in thought what was doing there from hour to hour, interpreted to him much of a yearning and regret he experienced afterwards, towards he knew not what, out of strange ways of feeling and thought in which, from time to time, his spirit found itself alone; and in the tears shed in such absences there seemed always to be some soul-subduing foretaste of what his last tears might be.

And the sense of security could hardly have been deeper, the quiet of the child's soul being one with the quiet of its home, a place "inclosed" and "sealed." But upon this assured place, upon the child's assured soul which resembled it, there came floating in from the larger world without, as at windows left ajar unknowingly, or over the high garden walls, two streams of impressions, the sentiments of beauty and pain—recognitions of the visible, tangible, audible loveliness of things, as a very real and somewhat tyrannous element in them —and of the sorrow of the world, of grown people and children and animals, as a thing not to be put by in them. From this point he could trace two predominant processes of mental change in him—the growth of an almost diseased sensibility to the spectacle of suffering, and, parallel with this, the rapid growth of a certain capacity of fascination by bright color and choice form—the sweet curvings, for instance, of the lips of those who seemed to him comely persons, modulated in such delicate unison to the things they said or sang,—marking early the activity in him of a more than customary sensuousness, "the lust of the eye," as the Preacher [6] says, which might

---

[4] Luncheon.

[5] Homelikeness (literally, at one's home).

[6] Ecclesiastes. There are several passages which might have suggested the quoted phrase to Pater, but its words are his own.

lead him, one day, how far! Could he have foreseen the weariness of the way! In music sometimes the two sorts of impressions came together, and he would weep, to the surprise of older people. Tears of joy too the child knew, also to older people's surprise; real tears, once, of relief from long-strung, childish expectation, when he found returned at evening, with new roses in her cheeks, the little sister who had been to a place where there was a 10 wood, and brought back for him a treasure of fallen acorns, and black crow's feathers, and his peace at finding her again near him mingled all night with some intimate sense of the distant forest, the rumor of its breezes, with the glossy blackbirds aslant and the branches lifted in them, and of the perfect nicety of the little cups that fell. So those two elementary apprehensions of the tenderness and of the color in things grew apace in him, and were seen by 20 him afterwards to send their roots back into the beginnings of life.

Let me note first some of the occasions of his recognition of the element of pain in things—incidents, now and again, which seemed suddenly to awake in him the whole force of that sentiment which Goethe has called the *Weltschmerz*, and in which the concentrated sorrow of the world seemed suddenly to lie heavy upon him. A book lay in 30 an old book-case, of which he cared to remember one picture—a woman sitting, with hands bound behind her, the dress, the cap, the hair, folded with a simplicity which touched him strangely, as if not by her own hands, but with some ambiguous care of the hands of others—Queen Marie Antoinette, on her way to execution—we all remember David's [7] drawing, meant merely to make her ridiculous. The face that had been so high had learned to be 40 mute and resistless; but out of its very resistlessness, seemed now to call on men to have pity, and forbear; and he took note of that, as he closed the book, as a thing to look at again, if he should at any time find himself tempted to be cruel. Again, he would never quite forget the appeal in the small sister's face, in the garden under the lilacs, terrified at a spider lighted on her sleeve. He could trace back to the look then noted a certain mercy he con- 50 ceived always for people in fear, even of little things, which seemed to make him, though but for a moment, capable of almost any sacrifice of himself. Impressible, susceptible persons,

[7] Jacques Louis David (1748–1825), court-painter to Louis XVI, supporter of the Revolution, and court-painter to Napoleon.

indeed, who had had their sorrows, lived about him; and this sensibility was due in part to the tacit influence of their presence, enforcing upon him habitually the fact that there are those who pass their days, as a matter of course, in a sort of "going quietly." Most poignantly of all he could recall, in unfading minutest circumstance, the cry on the stair, sounding bitterly through the house, and struck into his soul for ever, of an aged woman, his father's sister, come now to announce his death in distant India; how it seemed to make the aged woman like a child again; and, he knew not why, but this fancy was full of pity to him. There were the little sorrows of the dumb animals too— of the white angora, with a dark tail like an ermine's, and a face like a flower, who fell into a lingering sickness, and became quite delicately human in its valetudinarianism, and came to have a hundred different expressions of voice—how it grew worse and worse, till it began to feel the light too much for it, and at last, after one wild morning of pain, the little soul flickered away from the body, quite worn to death already, and now but feebly retaining it.

So he wanted another pet; and as there were starlings about the place, which could be taught to speak, one of them was caught, and he meant to treat it kindly; but in the nights its young ones could be heard crying after it, and the responsive cry of the mother-bird towards them; and at last, with the first light, though not till after some debate with himself, he went down and opened the cage, and saw a sharp bound of the prisoner up to her nestlings; and therewith came the sense of remorse,—that he too was become an accomplice in moving, to the limit of his small power, the springs and handles of that great machine in things, constructed so ingeniously to play pain-fugues on the delicate nerve-work of living creatures.

I have remarked how, in the process of our brain-building, as the house of thought in which we live gets itself together, like some airy bird's-nest of floating thistle-down and chance straws, compact at last, little accidents have their consequence; and thus it happened that, as he walked one evening, a garden gate, usually closed, stood open; and lo! within, a great red hawthorn in full flower, embossing heavily the bleached and twisted trunk and branches, so aged that there were but a few green leaves thereon—a plumage of tender, crimson fire out of the heart of the dry wood. The perfume of the tree had now and again reached him, in the currents of the wind, over the wall, and he had wondered what might be behind it, and was now allowed to fill his arms with the flowers—flowers enough for all the old blue-china pots along the chimney-piece, making *fête* in the children's room. Was it some periodic moment in the expansion of soul within him, or mere trick of heat in the heavily-laden summer air? But the beauty of the thing struck home to him feverishly; and in dreams all night he loitered along a magic roadway of crimson flowers, which seemed to open ruddily in thick, fresh masses about his feet, and fill softly all the little hollows in the banks on either side. Always afterwards summer by summer, as the flowers came on, the blossom of the red hawthorn still seemed to him absolutely the reddest of all things; and the goodly crimson, still alive in the works of old Venetian masters or old Flemish tapestries, called out always from afar the recollection of the flame in those perishing little petals, as it pulsed gradually out of them, kept long in the drawers of an old cabinet. Also then, for the first time, he seemed to experience a passionateness in his relation to fair outward objects, an inexplicable excitement in their presence, which disturbed him, and from which he half longed to be free. A touch of regret or desire mingled all night with the remembered presence of the red flowers, and their perfume in the darkness about him; and the longing for some undivined entire possession of them was the beginning of a revelation to him, growing ever clearer, with the coming of the gracious summer guise of fields and trees and persons in each succeeding year, of a certain, at times seemingly exclusive, predominance in his interests, of beautiful physical things, a kind of tyranny of the senses over him.

In later years he came upon philosophies which occupied him much in the estimate of the proportion of the sensuous and the ideal elements in human knowledge, the relative parts they bear in it; and, in his intellectual scheme, was led to assign very little to the abstract thought, and much to its sensible vehicle or occasion. Such metaphysical speculation did but reinforce what was instinctive in his way of receiving the world, and for him, everywhere, that sensible vehicle or occasion became, perhaps only too surely, the necessary concomitant of any perception of things, real enough to be of any weight or reckoning, in his house of thought. There were times when he could think of the necessity he was under of associating all thoughts to touch and sight,

as a sympathetic link between himself and actual, feeling, living objects; a protest in favor of real men and women against mere gray, unreal abstractions; and he remembered gratefully how the Christian religion, hardly less than the religion of the ancient Greeks, translating so much of its spiritual verity into things that may be seen, condescends in part to sanction this infirmity, if so it be, of our human existence, wherein the world of sense is so much with us, and welcomed this thought as a kind of keeper and sentinel over his soul therein. But certainly, he came more and more to be unable to care for, or think of soul but as in an actual body, or of any world but that wherein are water and trees, and where men and women look, so or so, and press actual hands. It was the trick even his pity learned, fastening those who suffered in anywise to his affections by a kind of sensible attachments. He would think of Julian, fallen into incurable sickness, as spoiled in the sweet blossom of his skin like pale amber, and his honey-like hair; of Cecil, early dead, as cut off from the lilies, from golden summer days, from women's voices; and then what comforted him a little was the thought of the turning of the child's flesh to violets in the turf above him. And thinking of the very poor, it was not the things which most men care most for that he yearned to give them; but fairer roses, perhaps, and power to taste quite as they will, at their ease and not task-burdened, a certain desirable, clear light in the new morning, through which sometimes he had noticed them, quite unconscious of it, on their way to their early toil.

So he yielded himself to these things, to be played upon by them like a musical instrument, and began to note with deepening watchfulness, but always with some puzzled, unutterable longing in his enjoyment, the phases of the seasons and of the growing or waning day, down even to the shadowy changes wrought on bare wall or ceiling—the light cast up from the snow, bringing out their darkest angles; the brown light in the cloud, which meant rain; that almost too austere clearness, in the protracted light of the lengthening day, before warm weather began, as if it lingered but to make a severer workday, with the school-books opened earlier and later; that beam of June sunshine, at last, as he lay awake before the time, a way of gold-dust across the darkness; all the humming, the freshness, the perfume of the garden seemed to lie upon it—and coming in one afternoon in September, along the red gravel walk, to look for a basket of yellow crab-apples left in the cool, old parlor, he remembered it the more, and how the colors struck upon him, because a wasp in one bitten apple stung him, and he felt the passion of sudden, severe pain. For this too brought its curious reflections; and, in relief from it, he would wonder over it—how it had then been with him—puzzled at the depth of the charm or spell over him, which lay, for a little while at least, in the mere absence of pain; once, especially, when an older boy taught him to make flowers of sealing-wax, and he had burned his hand badly at the lighted taper, and been unable to sleep. He remembered that also afterwards, as a sort of typical thing—a white vision of heat about him, clinging closely, through the languid scent of the ointments put upon the place to make it well.

Also, as he felt this pressure upon him of the sensible world, then, as often afterwards, there would come another sort of curious questioning how the last impressions of the eye and ear might happen to him, how they would find him—the scent of the last flower, the soft yellowness of the last morning, the last recognition of some object of affection, hand or voice; it could not be but that the latest look of the eyes, before their final closing, would be strangely vivid; one would go with the hot tears, the cry, the touch of the wistful bystander, impressed how deeply on one! or would it be, perhaps, a mere frail retiring of all things, great or little, away from one, into a level distance?

For with this desire of physical beauty mingled itself early the fear of death—the fear of death intensified by the desire of beauty. Hitherto he had never gazed upon dead faces, as sometimes, afterwards, at the *Morgue* in Paris, or in that fair cemetery at Munich, where all the dead must go and lie in state before burial, behind glass windows, among the flowers and incense and holy candles—the aged clergy with their sacred ornaments, the young men in their dancing-shoes and spotless white linen—after which visits, those waxen resistless faces would always live with him for many days, making the broadest sunshine sickly. The child had heard indeed of the death of his father, and how, in the Indian station, a fever had taken him, so that though not in action he had yet died as a soldier; and hearing of the "resurrection of the just," [8] he could think of him as still abroad in the world, somehow, for his protection—a grand, though perhaps rather terrible figure, in beautiful sol-

dier's things, like the figure in the picture of Joshua's Vision in the Bible [9]—and of that, round which the mourners moved so softly, and afterwards with such solemn singing, as but a worn-out garment left at a deserted lodging. So it was, until on a summer day he walked with his mother through a fair churchyard. In a bright dress he rambled among the graves, in the gay weather, and so came, in one corner, upon an open grave for a child—a dark space on the brilliant grass—the black mold lying heaped up round it, weighing down the little jeweled branches of the dwarf rose-bushes in flower. And therewith came, full-grown, never wholly to leave him, with the certainty that even children do sometimes die, the physical horror of death, with its wholly selfish recoil from the association of lower forms of life, and the suffocating weight above. No benign, grave figure in beautiful soldier's things any longer abroad in the world for his protection! only a few poor, piteous bones; and above them, possibly, a certain sort of figure he hoped not to see. For sitting one day in the garden below an open window, he heard people talking, and could not but listen, how, in a sleepless hour, a sick woman had seen one of the dead sitting beside her, come to call her hence; and from the broken talk evolved with much clearness the notion that not all those dead people had really departed to the churchyard, nor were quite so motionless as they looked, but led a secret, half-fugitive life in their old homes, quite free by night, though sometimes visible in the day, dodging from room to room, with no great good will towards those who shared the place with them. All night the figure sat beside him in the reveries of his broken sleep, and was not quite gone in the morning—an odd, irreconcilable new member of the household, making the sweet familiar chambers unfriendly and suspect by its uncertain presence. He could have hated the dead he had pitied so, for being thus. Afterwards he came to think of those poor, home-returning ghosts, which all men have fancied to themselves—the *revenants*—pathetically, as crying, or beating with vain hands at the doors, as the wind came, their cries distinguishable in it as a wilder inner note. But, always making death more unfamiliar still, that old experience would ever, from time to time, return to him; even in the living he sometimes caught its likeness; at any time or place, in a moment, the faint atmosphere of the chamber of death would be breathed around him, and the image with the

[8] St. Luke, 14:14.

[9] Joshua, 5:13–14.

bound chin, the quaint smile, the straight, stiff feet, shed itself across the air upon the bright carpet, amid the gayest company, or happiest communing with himself.

To most children the somber questionings to which impressions like these attach themselves, if they come at all, are actually suggested by religious books, which therefore they often regard with much secret distaste, and dismiss, as far as possible, from their habitual thoughts as a too depressing element in life. To Florian such impressions, these misgivings as to the ultimate tendency of the years, of the relationship between life and death, had been suggested spontaneously in the natural course of his mental growth by a strong innate sense for the soberer tones in things, further strengthened by actual circumstances; and religious sentiment, that system of biblical ideas in which he had been brought up, presented itself to him as a thing that might soften and dignify, and light up as with a "lively hope," [10] a melancholy already deeply settled in him. So he yielded himself easily to religious impressions, and with a kind of mystical appetite for sacred things; the more as they came to him through a saintly person who loved him tenderly, and believed that this early pre-occupation with them already marked the child out for a saint. He began to love, for their own sakes, church lights, holy days, all that belonged to the comely order of the sanctuary, the secrets of its white linen, and holy vessels, and fonts of pure water; and its hieratic purity and simplicity became the type of something he desired always to have about him in actual life. He pored over the pictures in religious books, and knew by heart the exact mode in which the wrestling angel grasped Jacob, how Jacob looked in his mysterious sleep, how the bells and pomegranates were attached to the hem of Aaron's vestment,[11] sounding sweetly as he glided over the turf of the holy place. His way of conceiving religion came then to be in effect what it ever afterwards remained—a sacred history indeed, but still more a sacred ideal, a transcendent version or representation, under intenser and more expressive light and shade, of human life and its familiar or exceptional incidents, birth, death, marriage, youth, age, tears, joy, rest, sleep, waking—a mirror, towards which men might turn away their eyes from vanity and dullness, and see themselves therein as angels, with their daily meat and drink, even, become a kind of sacred transac-

tion—a complementary strain or burden,[12] applied to our every-day existence, whereby the stray snatches of music in it re-set themselves, and fall into the scheme of some higher and more consistent harmony. A place adumbrated itself in his thoughts, wherein those sacred personalities, which are at once the reflex and the pattern of our nobler phases of life, housed themselves; and this region in his intellectual scheme all subsequent experience did but tend still further to realize and define. Some ideal, hieratic persons he would always need to occupy it and keep a warmth there. And he could hardly understand those who felt no such need at all, finding themselves quite happy without such heavenly companionship, and sacred double of their life, beside them.

Thus a constant substitution of the typical for the actual took place in his thoughts. Angels might be met by the way, under English elm or beech-tree; mere messengers seemed like angels, bound on celestial errands; a deep mysticity brooded over real meetings and partings; marriages were made in heaven; and deaths also, with hands of angels thereupon, to bear soul and body quietly asunder, each to its appointed rest. All the acts and accidents of daily life borrowed a sacred color and significence; the very colors of things became themselves weighty with meanings like the sacred stuffs of Moses' tabernacle,[13] full of penitence or peace. Sentiment, congruous in the first instance only with those divine transactions, the deep effusive unction of the House of Bethany, was assumed as the due attitude for the reception of our every-day existence; and for a time he walked through the world in a sustained, not unpleasurable awe, generated by the habitual recognition, beside every circumstance and event of life, of its celestial correspondent.

Sensibility—the desire of physical beauty —a strange biblical awe, which made any reference to the unseen act on him like solemn music—these qualities the child took away with him, when, at about the age of twelve years, he left the old house, and was taken to live in another place. He had never left home before, and, anticipating much from this change, had long dreamed over it, jealously counting the days till the time fixed for departure should come; had been a little careless about others even, in his strong desire for it— when Lewis fell sick, for instance, and they must wait still two days longer. At last the morning came, very fine; and all things—the

[10] 1 Peter, 1:3.
[11] Genesis, 32:24; 28:11; Exodus, 28:33.
[12] Bass under-part.     [13] Exodus, 26.

very pavement with its dust, at the roadside—seemed to have a white, pearl-like luster in them. They were to travel by a favorite road on which he had often walked a certain distance, and on one of those two prisoner days, when Lewis was sick, had walked farther than ever before, in his great desire to reach the new place. They had started and gone a little way when a pet bird was found to have been left behind, and must even now—so it presented itself to him—have already all the appealing fierceness and wild self-pity at heart of one left by others to perish of hunger in a closed house; and he returned to fetch it, himself in hardly less stormy distress. But as he passed in search of it from room to room, lying so pale, with a look of meekness in their denudation, and at last through that little, stripped white room, the aspect of the place touched him like the face of one dead; and a clinging back towards it came over him, so intense that he knew it would last long, and spoiling all his pleasure in the realization of a thing so eagerly anticipated. And so, with the bird found, but himself in an agony of homesickness, thus capriciously sprung up within him, he was driven quickly away, far into the rural distance, so fondly speculated on, of that favorite country-road.

# Studies in the History of the Renaissance

## Conclusion [1]

Λέγει που Ἡράκλειτος ὅτι πάντα χωρεῖ καὶ οὐδὲν μένει.[2]

To regard all things and principles of things as inconstant modes or fashions has more and more become the tendency of modern thought. Let us begin with that which is without—our physical life. Fix upon it in one of its more exquisite intervals, the moment, for instance, of delicious recoil from the flood of water in summer heat. What is the whole physical life in that moment but a combination of natural

elements to which science gives their names? But those elements, phosphorus and lime and delicate fibers, are present not in the human body alone: we detect them in places most remote from it. Our physical life is a perpetual motion of them—the passage of the blood, the waste and repairing of the lenses of the eye, the modification of the tissues of the brain under every ray of light and sound—processes which science reduces to simpler and more elementary forces. Like the elements of which we are composed, the action of these forces extends beyond us: it rusts iron and ripens corn. Far out on every side of us those elements are broadcast, driven in many currents; and birth and gesture [3] and death and the springing of violets from the grave are but a few out of ten thousand resultant combinations. That clear, perpetual outline of face and limb is but an image of ours, under which we group them—a design in a web, the actual threads of which pass out beyond it. This at least of flamelike our life has, that it is but the concurrence, renewed from moment to moment, of forces parting sooner or later on their ways.

Or if we begin with the inward world of thought and feeling, the whirlpool is still more rapid, the flame more eager and devouring. There is no longer the gradual darkening of the eye, the gradual fading of color from the wall—movements of the shore-side, where the water flows down indeed, though in apparent rest—but the race of the midstream, a drift of momentary acts of sight and passion and thought. At first sight experience seems to bury us under a flood of external objects, pressing upon us with a sharp and importunate reality, calling us out of ourselves in a thousand forms of action. But when reflection begins to play upon those objects they are dissipated under its influence; the cohesive force seems suspended like some trick of magic; each object is loosed into a group of impressions—color, odor, texture—in the mind of the observer. And if we continue to dwell in thought on this world, not of objects in the solidity with which language invests them, but of impressions, unstable, flickering, inconsistent, which burn and are extinguished with our consciousness of them, it contracts still further: the whole scope of observation is dwarfed into the narrow chamber of the individual mind. Experience, already reduced to a group of impressions, is ringed round for each one of us by that thick wall of personality through which no real voice has ever pierced on its way to us, or from

[1] Written in 1868 and printed at the end of *Studies in the History of the Renaissance* in 1873. It was omitted from the second edition of that book (1877), but restored in the third edition (1888) with the following note: "This brief *Conclusion* was omitted in the second edition of this book, as I conceived it might possibly mislead some of those young men into whose hands it might fall. On the whole, I have thought it best to reprint it here, with some slight changes which bring it closer to my original meaning. I have dealt more fully in *Marius the Epicurean* with the thoughts suggested by it."

[2] Heraclitus says that all things give way and nothing remains (Plato, *Cratylus*).

[3] Bearing, behavior.

us to that which we can only conjecture to be without. Every one of those impressions is the impression of the individual in his isolation, each mind keeping as a solitary prisoner its own dream of a world. Analysis goes a step farther still, and assures us that those impressions of the individual mind to which, for each one of us, experience dwindles down, are in perpetual flight; that each of them is limited by time, and that as time is infinitely divisible, each of them is infinitely divisible also, all that is actual in it being a single moment, gone while we try to apprehend it, of which it may ever be more truly said that it has ceased to be than that it is. To such a tremulous wisp constantly reforming itself on the stream, to a single sharp impression, with a sense in it, a relic more or less fleeting, of such moments gone by, what is real in our life fines itself down. It is with this movement, with the passage and dissolution of impressions, images, sensations, that analysis leaves off—that continual vanishing away, that strange, perpetual weaving and unweaving of ourselves.

*Philosophiren*, says Novalis, *ist dephlegmatisiren vivificiren.*[4] The service of philosophy, of speculative culture, towards the human spirit, is to rouse, to startle it to a life of constant and eager observation. Every moment some form grows perfect in hand or face; some tone on the hills or the sea is choicer than the rest; some mood of passion or insight or intellectual excitement is irresistibly real and attractive to us,—for that moment only. Not the fruit of experience, but experience itself, is the end. A counted number of pulses only is given to us of a variegated, dramatic life. How may we see in them all that is to be seen in them by the finest senses? How shall we pass most swiftly from point to point, and be present always at the focus where the greatest number of vital forces unites in their purest energy?

To burn always with this hard, gemlike flame, to maintain this ecstasy, is success in life. In a sense it might even be said that our failure is to form habits: for, after all, habit is relative to a stereotyped world, and meantime it is only the roughness of the eye that makes any two persons, things, situations, seem alike. While all melts under our feet, we may well grasp at any exquisite passion, or any contribution to knowledge that seems by a lifted horizon to set the spirit free for a moment, or any stirring of the senses, strange

dyes, strange colors, and curious odors, or work of the artist's hands, or the face of one's friend. Not to discriminate every moment some passionate attitude in those about us, and in the very brilliancy of their gifts some tragic dividing of forces on their ways, is, on this short day of frost and sun, to sleep before evening. With this sense of the splendor of our experience and of its awful brevity, gathering all we are into one desperate effort to see and touch, we shall hardly have time to make theories about the things we see and touch. What we have to do is to be for ever curiously testing new opinions and courting new impressions, never acquiescing in a facile orthodoxy of Comte, or of Hegel,[5] or of our own. Philosophical theories or ideas, as points of view, instruments of criticism, may help us to gather up what might otherwise pass unregarded by us. "Philosophy is the microscope of thought." The theory or idea or system which requires of us the sacrifice of any part of this experience, in consideration of some interest into which we cannot enter, or some abstract theory we have not identified with ourselves, or of what is only conventional, has no real claim upon us.

One of the most beautiful passages of Rousseau is that in the sixth book of the *Confessions* where he describes the awakening in him of the literary sense. An undefinable taint of death had clung always about him, and now in early manhood he believed himself smitten by mortal disease. He asked himself how he might make as much as possible of the interval that remained; and he was not biased by anything in his previous life when he decided that it must be by intellectual excitement, which he found just then in the clear, fresh writings of Voltaire. Well! we are all *condamnés*, as Victor Hugo says: we are all under sentence of death but with a sort of indefinite reprieve—*les hommes sont tous condamnés à mort avec des sursis indéfinis:* we have an interval, and then our place knows us no more. Some spend this interval in listlessness, some in high passions, the wisest, at least among "the children of this world," in art and song. For our one chance lies in expanding that interval, in getting as many pulsations as possible into the given time. Great passions may give us this quickened sense of life, ecstasy and sorrow and love, the various forms of enthusiastic activity, disinterested or otherwise, which come naturally to many of

---

[4] To be a philosopher is to rid one's self of inertia, to become alive. (Novalis was the pseudonym of Friedrich von Hardenberg, 1772–1801.)

[5] The French thinker, Auguste Comte (1798–1857), and the German, Georg W. F. Hegel (1770–1831). Both were founders of philosophical systems.

us. Only be sure it is passion—that it does yield you this fruit of a quickened, multiplied consciousness. Of such wisdom, the poetic passion, the desire of beauty, the love of art for its own sake, has most. For art comes to you proposing frankly to give nothing but the highest quality to your moments as they pass, and simply for those moments' sake.

# Robert Louis Stevenson

## 1850 - 1894

Stevenson was born in Edinburgh on 13 November, 1850. He was the only child of his parents, and his health was infirm from the beginning of his life. Through his boyhood and youth he suffered from frequent bronchial affections and acute nervous excitability, and was thus prevented from getting much regular or continuous schooling. From 1862 until 1867 he spent a large amount of time in travel on the Continent. In the latter year he entered Edinburgh University and for several years attended classes there with such regularity as his health permitted. He read widely, but did not give much attention to routine college studies. He came of a family of distinguished engineers and was expected to follow this profession. Some of his university studies were directed to this end, but in 1871 it was agreed that his health would not allow of his becoming an engineer. He accordingly turned to the study of the law, and was called to the bar in 1875; but he never attempted to practice. Outwardly his life had been hitherto, and was still to be for several years, that of a semi-invalid and idler; but in reality Stevenson was attempting with the utmost industry to learn the art of writing. And in 1876 the fruits of his industry began to appear, in the shape of a series of essays contributed to the Cornhill Magazine. Two years later his first book was published, An Inland Voyage, an account of a canoe-trip in Belgium and France. A few critical readers, such as Leslie Stephen, promptly recognized Stevenson's promise, perceiving that he "aimed at, and often achieved, those qualities of sustained precision, lucidity, and grace of style which are characteristic of the best French prose, but in English rare in the extreme. He had known how to stamp all he wrote with the impress of a vivid personal charm; had shown himself a master of the apt and animated phrase; and whether in tale or parable, essay or wayside musing, had touched on vital points of experience and feeling with the observation and insight of a true poet and humorist" (S. Colvin, D. N. B.). Nevertheless, he did not win a large audience until 1882, and then only with a story written for boys, Treasure Island.

Meanwhile Stevenson had met in France Mrs. Fanny Osbourne, an American woman then separated from her husband. In 1878 she went to California, and in the following year Stevenson determined to follow her. The journey was exceedingly hard on him and would probably have cost him his life had it not been for the careful nursing of Mrs. Osbourne. By 1880 she had secured a divorce from her husband and was married to Stevenson, who took her back to his home in Scotland in August of that year. She herself had delicate health, but she proved a perfect companion for him and was through the remainder of his life his devoted nurse;—his nurse, for Stevenson never won his battle against consumption, but only delayed the end while he continued despite all ills to write, and write, and write. For several years he continued to seek health, or at least a respite from his disease, at various places in Europe, and then in 1887 sailed for America on the same quest. He spent the winter of 1887–1888 at Saranac Lake in the Adirondacks. In the following June he sailed from San Francisco on a voyage among the island groups of the South Sea; and there he established himself in Samoa, where he remained until his death on 4 December, 1894.

Stevenson's life was one of heroic endeavor in the face of constant illness, with the threat of death ever hovering above him. A few of his many books, in addition to those mentioned above, are: Travels with a Donkey (1879), Virginibus Puerisque (1881), Familiar Studies of Men and Books (1882), The New Arabian Nights (1882), Kidnapped (1886), Memories and Portraits (1887), The Master of Ballantrae (1889), and Across the Plains (1892).

There are several collected editions of Stevenson's writings. The "Pentland Edition" (20 vols., London, 1906–1907) *contains biblio-graphical notes by E. Gosse. The "Swanston Edition" (25 vols., 1911–1912) contains an Introduction by Andrew Lang. Most easily ac-cessible are the volumes of the "Biographical Edition." The* Essays *have been edited by M. Elwin, the* Tales and Essays *by G. B. Stern, and the* Collected Poems *by J. A. Smith, all published in London in 1950, the Stevenson Centenary year. Stevenson's* Letters *have been edited by Sidney Colvin (the last ed., 4 vols., London, 1911, is the fullest). The standard biography is by Stevenson's cousin, Graham Balfour (2 vols., London, 1901; later reprinted in one vol.). New matter is presented and im-portant questions are raised in* Robert Louis Stevenson, A Critical Biography, *by John A. Steuart (2 vols., Boston, 1924), and in the same writer's* The Cap of Youth, Being the Love-Romance of Robert Louis Stevenson *(Philadelphia, 1927). An instructive critical study,* Robert Louis Stevenson *(London, 1923), has been written by Frank Swinnerton. The following books may also be found useful:* An Intimate Portrait of R. L. S. *by Lloyd Os-bourne (New York, 1924);* Robert Louis Ste-venson *by G. K. Chesterton (New York, 1928);* Stevenson *(New York, 1946), and* Stevenson and the Art of Fiction *(New York, 1951), by David Daiches; and* Voyage to Windward: Life of Stevenson, *by J. C. Furnas (New York, 1951).*

## An Apology for Idlers [1]

BOSWELL: We grow weary when idle.

JOHNSON: That is, sir, because others being busy, we want company; but if we were all idle, there would be no growing weary; we should all entertain one another.[2]

Just now, when every one is bound, under pain of a decree in absence convicting them of *lèse*-respectability, to enter on some lucra-tive profession, and labor therein with some-thing not far short of enthusiasm, a cry from the opposite party who are content when they have enough, and like to look on and enjoy in the meanwhile, savors a little of bravado and gasconade. And yet this should not be. Idle-ness so called, which does not consist in doing nothing, but in doing a great deal not recog-

[1] Published in 1877; reprinted in the volume en-titled *Virginibus Puerisque*. This essay, the three following ones, and the selections from *A Child's Garden of Verses* and *Underwoods* by Stevenson are here reprinted with the permission of Charles Scrib-ner's Sons.

[2] Boswell's *Johnson* (Hill's edition, N. Y.), II, 113.

nized in the dogmatic formularies of the ruling class, has as good a right to state its position as industry itself. It is admitted that the presence of people who refuse to enter in the great handicap race for sixpenny pieces, is at once an insult and a disenchantment for those who do. A fine fellow (as we see so many) takes his determination, votes for the sixpences, and in the emphatic Americanism, "goes for" them. And while such an one is plowing dis-tressfully up the road, it is not hard to under-stand his resentment, when he perceives cool persons in the meadows by the wayside, lying with a handkerchief over their ears and a glass at their elbow. Alexander is touched in a very delicate place by the disregard of Diogenes. Where was the glory of having taken Rome for these tumultuous barbarians, who poured into the Senate house, and found the Fathers sitting silent and unmoved by their success? It is a sore thing to have labored along and scaled the arduous hilltops, and when all is done, find humanity indifferent to your achievement. Hence physicists condemn the unphysical; financiers have only a superficial toleration for those who know little of stocks; literary persons despise the unlettered; and people of all pursuits combine to disparage those who have none.

But though this is one difficulty of the sub-ject, it is not the greatest. You could not be put in prison for speaking against industry, but you can be sent to Coventry [3] for speaking like a fool. The greatest difficulty with most sub-jects is to do them well; therefore, please to remember this is an apology. It is certain that much may be judiciously argued in favor of diligence; only there is something to be said against it, and that is what, on the present oc-casion, I have to say. To state one argument is not necessarily to be deaf to all others, and that a man has written a book of travels in Montenegro, is no reason why he should never have been to Richmond.

It is surely beyond a doubt that people should be a good deal idle in youth. For though here and there a Lord Macaulay may escape from school honors with all his wits about him, most boys pay so dear for their medals that they never afterward have a shot in their locker, and begin the world bankrupt. And the same holds true during all the time a lad is educating himself, or suffering others to edu-cate him. It must have been a very foolish old gentleman who addressed Johnson at Oxford

[3] You can be excluded from the society of which you are a member.

in these words: "Young man, ply your book diligently now, and acquire a stock of knowledge; for when years come upon you, you will find that poring upon books will be but an irksome task." The old gentleman seems to have been unaware that many other things besides reading grow irksome, and not a few become impossible, by the time a man has to use spectacles and cannot walk without a stick. Books are good enough in their own way, but 10 they are a mighty bloodless substitute for life. It seems a pity to sit, like the Lady of Shalott, peering into a mirror, with your back turned on all the bustle and glamour of reality. And if a man reads very hard, as the old anecdote reminds us, he will have little time for thoughts.

If you look back on your own education, I am sure it will not be the full, vivid, instructive hours of truantry that you regret; you 20 would rather cancel some lack-luster periods between sleep and waking in the class. For my own part, I have attended a good many lectures in my time. I still remember that the spinning of a top is a case of Kinetic Stability. I still remember that Emphyteusis [4] is not a disease, nor Stillicide [5] a crime. But though I would not willingly part with such scraps of science, I do not set the same store by them as by certain other odds and ends that 30 I came by in the open street while I was playing truant. This is not the moment to dilate on that mighty place of education, which was the favorite school of Dickens and of Balzac, and turns out yearly many inglorious masters in the Science of the Aspects of Life. Suffice it to say this: if a lad does not learn in the streets, it is because he has no faculty of learning. Nor is the truant always in the streets, for if he prefers, he may go out by the gardened 40 suburbs into the country. He may pitch on some tuft of lilacs over a burn, [6] and smoke innumerable pipes to the tune of the water on the stones. A bird will sing in the thicket. And there he may fall into a vein of kindly thought, and see things in a new perspective. Why, if this be not education, what is? We may conceive Mr. Worldly Wiseman accosting such an one, and the conversation that should thereupon ensue: 50

"How now, young fellow, what dost thou here?"

"Truly, sir, I take mine ease."

"Is not this the hour of the class? and should'st thou not be plying thy Book with diligence, to the end thou mayest obtain knowledge?"

"Nay, but thus also I follow after Learning, by your leave."

"Learning, quotha! After what fashion, I pray thee? Is it mathematics?"

"No, to be sure."

"Is it metaphysics?"

"Nor that."

"Is it some language?"

"Nay, it is no language."

"Is it a trade?"

"Nor a trade neither."

"Why, then, what is't?"

"Indeed, sir, as a time may soon come for me to go upon Pilgrimage, I am desirous to note what is commonly done by persons in my case, and where are the ugliest Sloughs and Thickets on the Road; as also, what manner of Staff is of the best service. Moreover, I lie here, by this water, to learn by root-of-heart a lesson which my master teaches me to call Peace, or Contentment."

Hereupon Mr. Worldly Wiseman was much commoved with passion, and shaking his cane with a very threatful countenance, broke forth upon this wise: "Learning, quotha!" said he; "I would have all such rogues scourged by the Hangman!"

And so he would go his way, ruffling out his cravat with a crackle of starch, like a turkey when it spread its feathers.

Now this, of Mr. Wiseman's, is the common opinion. A fact is not called a fact, but 40 a piece of gossip, if it does not fall into one of your scholastic categories. An inquiry must be in some acknowledged direction, with a name to go by; or else you are not inquiring at all, only lounging; and the workhouse is too good for you. It is supposed that all knowledge is at the bottom of a well, or the far end of a telescope. Sainte-Beuve, [7] as he grew older, came to regard all experience as a single great book, in which to study for a few years ere we 50 go hence; and it seemed all one to him whether you should read in Chapter xx, which is the differential calculus, or in Chapter xxxix, which is hearing the band play in the gardens. As a matter of fact, an intelligent person, looking out of his eyes and hearkening in his ears,

---

[4] A kind of conditional grant of a right to the possession and enjoyment of land.

[5] A continual falling or succession of drops. In Roman law, the right to have rain from one's roof drop on another's land or roof, or the right to refuse to allow rain from another's roof to drop on one's own land or roof.

[6] Brook.

[7] Charles A. Sainte-Beuve (1804–1869), French critic and poet.

with a smile on his face all the time, will get more true education than many another in a life of heroic vigils. There is certainly some chill and arid knowledge to be found upon the summits of formal and laborious science; but it is all round about you, and for the trouble of looking, that you will acquire the warm and palpitating facts of life. While others are filling their memory with a lumber of words, one-half of which they will forget before the week be out, your truant may learn some really useful art: to play the fiddle, to know a good cigar, or to speak with ease and opportunity to all varieties of men. Many who have "plied their book diligently," and know all about some one branch or another of accepted lore, come out of the study with an ancient and owl-like demeanor, and prove dry, stockish, and dyspeptic in all the better and brighter parts of life. Many make a large fortune, who remain underbred and pathetically stupid to the last. And meantime there goes the idler, who began life along with them——by your leave, a different picture. He has had time to take care of his health and his spirits; he has been a great deal in the open air, which is the most salutary of all things for both body and mind; and if he has never read the great Book in very recondite places, he has dipped into it and skimmed it over to excellent purpose. Might not the student afford some Hebrew roots, and the business man some of his half-crowns, for a share of the idler's knowledge of life at large, and Art of Living? Nay, and the idler has another and more important quality than these. I mean his wisdom. He who has much looked on at the childish satisfaction of other people in their hobbies, will regard his own with only a very ironical indulgence. He will not be heard among the dogmatists. He will have a great and cool allowance for all sorts of people and opinions. If he finds no out-of-the-way truths, he will identify himself with no very burning falsehood. His way takes him along a by-road, not much frequented, but very even and pleasant, which is called Commonplace Lane, and leads to the Belvedere [8] of Commonsense. Thence he shall command an agreeable, if no very noble prospect; and while others behold the East and West, the Devil and the Sunrise, he will be contentedly aware of a sort of morning hour upon all sublunary things, with an army of shadows running speedily and in many different directions into the great daylight of Eternity. The shadows and the generations, the shrill doctors and the plangent wars, go by into ultimate silence and emptiness; but underneath all this, a man may see, out of the Belvedere windows, much green and peaceful landscape; many firelit parlors; good people laughing, drinking, and making love as they did before the Flood or the French Revolution; and the old shepherd telling his tale under the hawthorn.

Extreme *busyness*, whether at school or college, kirk or market, is a symptom of deficient vitality; and a faculty for idleness implies a catholic appetite and a strong sense of personal identity. There is a sort of dead-alive, hackneyed people about, who are scarcely conscious of living except in the exercise of some conventional occupation. Bring these fellows into the country, or set them aboard ship, and you will see how they pine for their desk or their study. They have no curiosity; they cannot give themselves over to random provocations; they do not take pleasure in the exercise of their faculties for its own sake; and unless Necessity lays about them with a stick, they will even stand still. It is no good speaking to such folk: they *cannot* be idle, their nature is not generous enough; and they pass those hours in a sort of coma, which are not dedicated to furious moiling in the gold-mill. When they do not require to go to the office, when they are not hungry and have no mind to drink, the whole breathing world is a blank to them. If they have to wait an hour or so for a train, they fall into a stupid trance with their eyes open. To see them, you would suppose there was nothing to look at and no one to speak with; you would imagine they were paralyzed or alienated; [9] and yet very possibly they are hard workers in their own way, and have good eyesight for a flaw in a deed or a turn of the market. They have been to school and college, but all the time they had their eye on the medal; they have gone about in the world and mixed with clever people, but all the time they were thinking of their own affairs. As if a man's soul were not too small to begin with, they have dwarfed and narrowed theirs by a life of all work and no play; until here they are at forty, with a listless attention, a mind vacant of all material of amusement, and not one thought to rub against another while they wait for the train. Before he was breeched, he might have clambered on the boxes; when he was twenty, he would have stared at the girls; but now the pipe is smoked

[8] A building commanding a fine prospect.

[9] Mentally deranged.

out, the snuffbox empty, and my gentleman sits bolt upright upon a bench, with lamentable eyes. This does not appeal to me as being Success in Life.

But it is not only the person himself who suffers from his busy habits, but his wife and children, his friends and relations, and down to the very people he sits with in a railway carriage or an omnibus. Perpetual devotion to what a man calls his business is only to be sustained by perpetual neglect of many other things. And it is not by any means certain that a man's business is the most important thing he has to do. To an impartial estimate it will seem clear that many of the wisest, most virtuous, and most beneficent parts that are to be played upon the Theater of Life are filled by gratuitous performers, and pass, among the world at large, as phases of idleness. For in that Theater, not only the walking gentlemen, singing chambermaids, and diligent fiddlers in the orchestra, but those who look on and clap their hands from the benches, do really play a part and fulfill important offices towards the general result. You are no doubt very dependent on the care of your lawyer and stockbroker, of the guards and signalmen who convey you rapidly from place to place, and the policemen who walk the streets for your protection; but is there not a thought of gratitude in your heart for certain other benefactors who set you smiling when they fall in your way, or season your dinner with good company? Colonel Newcome helped to lose his friend's money; Fred Bayham had an ugly trick of borrowing shirts; and yet they were better people to fall among than Mr. Barnes.[10] And though Falstaff was neither sober nor very honest, I think I could name one or two long-faced Barabbases [11] whom the world could better have done without. Hazlitt mentions that he was more sensible of obligation to Northcote,[12] who had never done him anything he could call a service, than to his whole circle of ostentatious friends; for he thought a good companion emphatically the greatest benefactor. I know there are people in the world who cannot feel grateful unless the favor has been done them at the cost of pain and difficulty. But this is a

churlish disposition. A man may send you six sheets of letter-paper covered with the most entertaining gossip, or you may pass half an hour pleasantly, perhaps profitably, over an article of his; do you think the service would be greater, if he had made the manuscript in his heart's blood, like a compact with the devil? Do you really fancy you should be more beholden to your correspondent, if he had been damning you all the while for your importunity? Pleasures are more beneficial than duties because, like the quality of mercy, they are not strained,[13] and they are twice blest. There must always be two to a kiss, and there may be a score in a jest; but wherever there is an element of sacrifice, the favor is conferred with pain, and, among generous people, received with confusion. There is no duty we so much underrate as the duty of being happy. By being happy, we sow anonymous benefits upon the world, which remain unknown even to ourselves, or when they are disclosed, surprise nobody so much as the benefactor. The other day, a ragged, barefoot boy ran down the street after a marble, with so jolly an air that he set everyone he passed into a good-humor; one of these persons, who had been delivered from more than usually black thoughts, stopped the little fellow and gave him some money with this remark: "You see what sometimes comes of looking pleased." If he had looked pleased before, he had now to look both pleased and mystified. For my part, I justify this encouragement of smiling rather than tearful children; I do not wish to pay for tears anywhere but upon the stage; but I am prepared to deal largely in the opposite commodity. A happy man or woman is a better thing to find than a five-pound note. He or she is a radiating focus of good-will; and their entrance into a room is as though another candle had been lighted. We need not care whether they could prove the forty-seventh proposition; [14] they do a better thing than that, they practically demonstrate the great Theorem of the Livableness of Life. Consequently, if a person cannot be happy without remaining idle, idle he should remain. It is a revolutionary precept; but thanks to hunger and the workhouse, one not easily to be abused; and within practical limits, it is one of the most incontestable truths in the

---

[10] Characters in Thackeray's *Newcomes*.

[11] Falstaff appears in *Henry IV, I* and *II*, and in *The Merry Wives of Windsor*. Barabbas was the robber whose freedom, instead of that of Jesus, the Jews demanded of Pilate.

[12] James Northcote (1746–1831), painter and writer.

[13] See *The Merchant of Venice*, IV, i, 184.

[14] Of Bk. I, Euclid's *Elements*—the Pythagorean theorem.

whole Body of Morality. Look at one of your industrious fellows for a moment, I beseech you. He sows hurry and reaps indigestion; he puts a vast deal of activity out to interest, and receives a large measure of nervous derangement in return. Either he absents himself entirely from all fellowship, and lives a recluse in a garret, with carpet slippers and a leaden inkpot; or he comes among people swiftly and bitterly, in a contraction of his whole nervous system, to discharge some temper before he returns to work. I do not care how much or how well he works, this fellow is an evil feature in other people's lives. They would be happier if he were dead. They could easier do without his services in the Circumlocution Office,[15] than they can tolerate his fractious spirits. He poisons life at the well-head. It is better to be beggared out of hand by a scapegrace nephew, than daily hag-ridden by a peevish uncle.

And what, in God's name, is all this pother about? For what cause do they embitter their own and other people's lives? That a man should publish three or thirty articles a year, that he should finish or not finish his great allegorical picture, are questions of little interest to the world. The ranks of life are full; and although a thousand fall, there are always some to go into the breach. When they told Joan of Arc she should be at home minding women's work, she answered there were plenty to spin and wash. And so, even with your own rare gifts! When nature is "so careless of the single life,"[16] why should we coddle ourselves into the fancy that our own is of exceptional importance? Suppose Shakespeare had been knocked on the head some dark night in Sir Thomas Lucy's preserves,[17] the world would have wagged on better or worse, the pitcher gone to the well, the scythe to the corn, and the student to his book; and no one been any the wiser of the loss. There are not many works extant, if you look the alternative all over, which are worth the price of a pound of tobacco to a man of limited means. This is a sobering reflection for the proudest of our earthly vanities. Even a tobacconist may, upon consideration, find no great cause for personal vainglory in the phrase; for

although tobacco is an admirable sedative, the qualities necessary for retailing it are neither rare nor precious in themselves. Alas and alas! you may take it how you will, but the services of no single individual are indispensable. Atlas[18] was just a gentleman with a protracted nightmare! And yet you see merchants who go and labor themselves into a great fortune and thence into the bankruptcy court; scribblers who keep scribbling at little articles until their temper is a cross to all who come about them, as though Pharaoh should set the Israelites to make a pin instead of a pyramid; and fine young men who work themselves into a decline, and are driven off in a hearse with white plumes upon it. Would you not suppose these persons had been whispered, by the Master of the Ceremonies, the promise of some momentous destiny? and that this lukewarm bullet on which they play their farces was the bull's eye and center-point of all the universe? And yet it is not so. The ends for which they gave away their priceless youth, for all they know, may be chimerical or hurtful; the glory and riches they expect may never come, or may find them indifferent; and they and the world they inhabit are so inconsiderable that the mind freezes at the thought.

# Aes Triplex [1]

The changes wrought by death are in themselves so sharp and final, and so terrible and melancholy in their consequences, that the thing stands alone in man's experience, and has no parallel upon earth. It outdoes all other accidents because it is the last of them. Sometimes it leaps suddenly upon its victims like a Thug;[2] sometimes it lays a regular seige and creeps upon their citadel during a score of years. And when the business is done, there is sore havoc made in other people's lives, and a pin knocked out by which many subsidiary friendships hung together. There are empty chairs, solitary walks, and single beds at night. Again, in taking away our friends, death does not take them away utterly, but leaves behind a mocking, tragical, and soon intolerable residue,

[15] See Dickens's *Little Dorrit.*
[16] Tennyson, *In Memoriam*, LV, 8.
[17] The game preserves in the neighborhood of Stratford, where, according to an apocryphal story, young Shakespeare was caught poaching.

[18] Who supported the world on his head.
[1] Published in *Virginibus Puerisque* (1881). *Aes Triplex* may be translatated Triple Bronze and is borrowed from Horace (*Odes*, I, iii, 9), who writes that "Oak and triple bronze must have girt the breast of him who first committed his frail bark to the angry sea" (translation of C. E. Bennett).
[2] One of an association of professional murderers in India.

which must be hurriedly concealed. Hence a whole chapter of sights and customs striking to the mind, from the pyramids of Egypt to the gibbets and dule trees[3] of mediaeval Europe. The poorest persons have a bit of pageant going toward the tomb; memorial stones are set up over the least memorable; and, in order to preserve some show of respect for what remains of our old loves and friendships, we must accompany it with much grimly ludicrous ceremonial, and the hired undertaker parades before the door. All this, and much more of the same sort, accompanied by the eloquence of poets, has gone a great way to put humanity in error; nay, in many philosophies the error has been embodied and laid down with every circumstance of logic; although in real life the bustle and swiftness, in leaving people little time to think, have not left them time enough to go dangerously wrong in practice.

As a matter of fact, although few things are spoken of with more fearful whisperings than this prospect of death, few have less influence on conduct under healthy circumstances. We have all heard of cities in South America built upon the side of fiery mountains, and how, even in this tremendous[4] neighborhood, the inhabitants are not a jot more impressed by the solemnity of mortal conditions than if they were delving gardens in the greenest corner of England. There are serenades and suppers and much gallantry among the myrtles overhead; and meanwhile the foundation shudders underfoot, the bowels of the mountain growl, and at any moment living ruin may leap sky-high into the moonlight, and tumble man and his merry-making in the dust. In the eyes of very young people, and very dull old ones, there is something indescribably reckless and desperate in such a picture. It seems not credible that respectable married people, with umbrellas, should find appetite for a bit of supper within quite a long distance of a fiery mountain; ordinary life begins to smell of high-handed debauch when it is carried on so close to a catastrophe; and even cheese and salad, it seems, could hardly be relished in such circumstances without something like a defiance of the Creator. It should be a place for nobody but hermits dwelling in prayer and maceration, or mere born-devils drowning care in a perpetual carouse.

And yet, when one comes to think upon it calmly, the situation of these South American citizens forms only a very pale figure for the state of ordinary mankind. This world itself, traveling blindly and swiftly in overcrowded space, among a million other worlds traveling blindly and swiftly in contrary directions, may very well come by a knock that would set it into explosion like a penny squib. And what, pathologically looked at, is the human body with all its organs, but a mere bagful of petards?[5] The least of these is as dangerous to the whole economy as the ship's powder-magazine to the ship; and with every breath we breathe, and every meal we eat, we are putting one or more of them in peril. If we clung as devotedly as some philosophers pretend we do to the abstract idea of life, or were half as frightened as they make out we are, for the subversive accident that ends it all, the trumpets might sound by the hour and no one would follow them into battle—the blue peter might fly at the truck;[6] but who would climb into a seagoing ship? Think (if these philosophers were right) with what a preparation of spirit we should affront the daily peril of the dinner-table: a deadlier spot than any battlefield in history, where the far greater proportion of our ancestors have miserably left their bones! What woman would ever be lured into marriage, so much more dangerous than the wildest sea? And what would it be to grow old? For, after a certain distance, every step we take in life we find the ice growing thinner below our feet, and all around us and behind us we see our contemporaries going through. By the time a man gets well into the seventies, his continued existence is a mere miracle; and when he lays his old bones in bed for the night, there is an overwhelming probability that he will never see the day. Do the old men mind it, as a matter of fact? Why, no. They were never merrier; they have their grog at night, and tell the raciest stories; they hear of the death of people about their own age, or even younger, not as if it was a grisly warning, but with a simple childlike pleasure at having outlived someone else; and when a draught might puff them out like a guttering candle, or a bit of a stumble shatter them like so much glass, their old hearts keep sound and unaffrighted, and they go on, bubbling with laughter, through years of man's age compared to which the valley of Balaclava[7] was as safe and peaceful

[3] Trees of sorrow.    [4] Horrible.

[5] Firecrackers.
[6] The flag for departure might fly at the masthead.
[7] The battle, fought in 1854 during the Crimean

as a village cricket-green on Sunday. It may fairly be questioned (if we look to the peril only) whether it was a much more daring feat for Curtius[8] to plunge into the gulf, than for any old gentleman of ninety to doff his clothes and clamber into bed.

Indeed, it is a memorable subject for consideration, with what unconcern and gaiety mankind pricks on along the Valley of the Shadow of Death. The whole way is one wilderness of snares, and the end of it, for those who fear the last pinch, is irrevocable ruin. And yet we go spinning through it all, like a party for the Derby.[9] Perhaps the reader remembers one of the humorous devices of the deified Caligula:[10] how he encouraged a vast concourse of holiday-makers on to his bridge over Baiae bay; and when they were in the height of their enjoyment, turned loose the Praetorian guards among the company, and had them tossed into the sea. This is no bad miniature of the dealings of nature with the transitory race of man. Only, what a checkered picnic we have of it, even while it lasts! and into what great waters, not to be crossed by any swimmer, God's pale Praetorian throws us over in the end!

We live the time that a match flickers; we pop the cork of a ginger-beer bottle, and the earthquake swallows us on the instant. Is it not odd, is it not incongruous, is it not, in the highest sense of human speech, incredible, that we should think so highly of the ginger-beer, and regard so little the devouring earthquake? The love of Life and the fear of Death are two famous phrases that grow harder to understand the more we think about them. It is a well-known fact that an immense proportion of boat accidents would never happen if people held the sheet[11] in their hands instead of making it fast; and yet, unless it be some martinet of a professional mariner or some landsman with shattered nerves, every one of God's creatures makes it fast. A strange instance of man's unconcern and brazen boldness in the face of death!

We confound ourselves with metaphysical phrases, which we import into daily talk with noble inappropriateness. We have no idea of what death is, apart from its circumstances and some of its consequences to others; and although we have some experience of living, there is not a man on earth who has flown so high into abstraction as to have any practical guess at the meaning of the word *life*. All literature, from Job and Omar Khayyám to Thomas Carlyle or Walt Whitman, is but an attempt to look upon the human state with such largeness of view as shall enable us to rise from the consideration of living to the Definition of Life. And our sages give us about the best satisfaction in their power when they say that it is a vapor, or a show, or made of the same stuff with dreams. Philosophy, in its more rigid sense, has been at the same work for ages; and after a myriad bald heads have wagged over the problem, and piles of words have been heaped one upon another into dry and cloudy volumes without end, philosophy has the honor of laying before us, with modest pride, her contribution toward the subject: that life is a Permanent Possibility of Sensation. Truly a fine result! A man may very well love beef, or hunting, or a woman; but surely, surely, not a Permanent Possibility of Sensation! He may be afraid of a precipice, or a dentist, or a large enemy with a club, or even an undertaker's man; but not certainly of abstract death. We may trick with the word *life* in its dozen senses until we are weary of tricking; we may argue in terms of all the philosophies on earth, but one fact remains true throughout—that we do not love life, in the sense that we are greatly preoccupied about its conservation—that we do not, properly speaking, love life at all, but living. Into the views of the least careful there will enter some degree of providence; no man's eyes are fixed entirely on the passing hour; but although we have some anticipation of good health, good weather, wine, active employment, love, and self-approval, the sum of these anticipations does not amount to anything like a general view of life's possibilities and issues; nor are those who cherish them most vividly, at all the most scrupulous of their personal safety. To be deeply interested in the accidents of our existence, to enjoy keenly the mixed texture of human experience, rather leads a man to disregard precautions, and risk his neck against a straw. For surely the love of living is stronger in an Alpine climber roping over a peril, or a hunter

War, in which an English brigade was by mistake thrown against a much larger force of Russians and annihilated.

[8] Mettus Curtius, who according to legend saved Rome in B.C. 362 by jumping into a chasm which had opened in the Forum.

[9] The annual horse-race run at Epsom.

[10] Roman emperor (A.D. 37–41) and madman. Baiae was a resort on the Bay of Naples; the Praetorians, the imperial bodyguard.

[11] Rope controlling the angle of a sail.

riding merrily at a stiff fence, than in a creature who lives upon a diet and walks a measured distance in the interest of his constitution.

There is a great deal of very vile nonsense talked upon both sides of the matter: tearing [12] divines reducing life to the dimensions of a mere funeral procession, so short as to be hardly decent; and melancholy unbelievers yearning for the tomb as if it were a world too far away. Both sides must feel a little ashamed of their performances now and again when they draw in their chairs to dinner. Indeed, a good meal and a bottle of wine is an answer to most standard works upon the question. When a man's heart warms to his viands, he forgets a great deal of sophistry, and soars into a rosy zone of contemplation. Death may be knocking at the door, like the Commander's statue; [13] we have something else in hand, thank God, and let him knock. Passing bells are ringing all the world over. All the world over, and every hour, some one is parting company with all his aches and ecstasies. For us also the trap is laid. But we are so fond of life that we have no leisure to entertain the terror of death. It is a honeymoon with us all through, and none of the longest. Small blame to us if we give our whole hearts to this glowing bride of ours, to the appetites, to honor, to the hungry curiosity of the mind, to the pleasure of the eyes in nature, and the pride of our own nimble bodies.

We all of us appreciate the sensations; but as for caring about the Permanence of the Possibility, a man's head is generally very bald, and his senses very dull, before he comes to that. Whether we regard life as a lane leading to a dead wall—a mere bag's end, as the French say—or whether we think of it as a vestibule or gymnasium, where we wait our turn and prepare our faculties for some more noble destiny; whether we thunder in a pulpit, or pule in little atheistic poetry-books, about its vanity and brevity; whether we look justly for years of health and vigor, or are about to mount into a Bath chair,[14] as a step toward the hearse; in each and all of these views and situations there is but one conclusion possible: that a man should stop his ears against paralyzing terror, and run the race that is set before him with a single mind.

No one surely could have recoiled with more heartache and terror from the thought of death than our respected lexicographer; [15] and yet we know how little it affected his conduct, how wisely and boldly he walked, and in what a fresh and lively vein he spoke of life. Already an old man, he ventured on his Highland tour; and his heart, bound with triple brass, did not recoil before twenty-seven individual cups of tea. As courage and intelligence are the two qualities best worth a good man's cultivation, so it is the first part of intelligence to recognize our precarious estate in life, and the first part of courage to be not at all abashed before the fact. A frank and somewhat headlong carriage, not looking too anxiously before, not dallying in maudlin regret over the past, stamps the man who is well armored for this world.

And not only well armored for himself, but a good friend and a good citizen to boot. We do not go to cowards for tender dealing; there is nothing so cruel as panic; the man who has least fear for his own carcass, has most time to consider others. That eminent chemist who took his walks abroad in tin shoes, and subsisted wholly upon tepid milk, had all his work cut out for him in considerate dealings with his own digestion. So soon as prudence has begun to grow up in the brain, like a dismal fungus, it finds its first expression in a paralysis of generous acts. The victim begins to shrink spiritually; he develops a fancy for parlors with a regulated temperature, and takes his morality on the principle of tin shoes and tepid milk. The care of one important body or soul becomes so engrossing, that all the noises of the outer world begin to come thin and faint into the parlor with the regulated temperature; and the tin shoes go equably forward over blood and rain. To be overwise is to ossify; and the scruple-monger ends by standing stock-still. Now the man who has his heart on his sleeve, and a good whirling weathercock of a brain, who reckons his life as a thing to be dashingly used and cheerfully hazarded, makes a very different acquaintance of the world, keeps all his pulses going true and fast, and gathers impetus as he runs, until, if he be running toward anything better than wildfire, he may shoot up and become a constellation in the end. Lord, look after his health; Lord, have a care of his soul, says he; and he has at the key of the position, and

---

[12] Ranting.

[13] In the Spanish legend: the funeral statue of the Commander, whose daughter Don Juan has ravished, visits the seducer and delivers him over to devils.

[14] Invalid's chair on wheels.

[15] Samuel Johnson.

swashes through incongruity and peril toward his aim. Death is on all sides of him with pointed batteries, as he is on all sides of all of us; unfortunate surprises gird him round; mim-mouthed friends and relations hold up their hands in quite a little elegiacal synod about his path: and what cares he for all this? Being a true lover of living, a fellow with something pushing and spontaneous in his inside, he must, like any other soldier, in any other stirring, deadly warfare, push on at his best pace until he touch the goal. "A peerage or Westminster Abbey!" cried Nelson in his bright, boyish, heroic manner. These are great incentives; not for any of these, but for the plain satisfaction of living, of being about their business in some sort or other, do the brave, serviceable men of every nation tread down the nettle danger, and pass flyingly over all the stumbling-blocks of prudence. Think of the heroism of Johnson, think of that superb indifference to mortal limitation that set him upon his dictionary, and carried him through triumphantly until the end! Who, if he were wisely considerate of things at large, would ever embark upon any work much more considerable than a halfpenny post card? Who would project a serial novel, after Thackeray and Dickens had each fallen in mid-course? [16] Who would find heart enough to begin to live, if he dallied with the consideration of death?

And, after all, what sorry and pitiful quibbling all this is! To forego all the issues of living in a parlor with the regulated temperature—as if that were not to die a hundred times over, and for ten years at a stretch! As if it were not to die in one's own lifetime, and without even the sad immunities of death! As if it were not to die, and yet be the patient spectators of our own

---

[16] Thackeray died without finishing *Denis Duval*; Dickens left *Edwin Drood* incomplete. In the same way, Stevenson himself did not live to complete his masterpiece, *Weir of Hermiston*.

---

pitiable change! The Permanent Possibility is preserved, but the sensations carefully held at arm's length, as if one kept a photographic plate in a dark chamber. It is better to lose health like a spendthrift than to waste it like a miser. It is better to live and be done with it, than to die daily in the sickroom. By all means begin your folio; even if the doctor does not give you a year, even if he hesitates about a month, make one brave push and see what can be accomplished in a week. It is not only in finished undertakings that we ought to honor useful labor. A spirit goes out of the man who means execution, which outlives the most untimely ending. All who have meant good work with their whole hearts, have done good work, although they may die before they have the time to sign it. Every heart that has beat strong and cheerfully has left a hopeful impulse behind it in the world, and bettered the tradition of mankind. And even if death catch people, like an open pitfall, and in mid-career, laying out vast projects, and planning monstrous foundations, flushed with hope, and their mouths full of boastful language, they should be at once tripped up and silenced: is there not something brave and spirited in such a termination? and does not life go down with a better grace, foaming in full body over a precipice, than miserably straggling to an end in sandy deltas? When the Greeks made their fine saying that those whom the gods love die young, I cannot help believing they had this sort of death also in their eye. For surely, at whatever age it overtake the man, this is to die young. Death has not been suffered to take so much as an illusion from his heart. In the hot-fit of life, a-tiptoe on the highest point of being, he passes at a bound on to the other side. The noise of the mallet and chisel is scarcely quenched, the trumpets are hardly done blowing, when, trailing with him coluds of glory, this happy-starred, full-blooded spirit shoots into the spiritual land.

# Algernon Charles Swinburne

## 1837 - 1909

Swinburne was born in London on 5 April, 1837, the eldest child of Admiral Charles Henry Swinburne and the Lady Jane Henrietta, daughter of the third Earl of Ashburnham. It is said that Swinburne's features and something of his mental character were inherited from his mother, who was a woman of unusual accomplishment and widely read in foreign literature. His paternal grandfather, Sir John Edward Swinburne, sixth baronet of Capheaton, Northumberland, who had been born and brought up in France, and who in habits, dress, and modes of thought resembled a French nobleman of the ancien régime, exercised a strong influence over his grandson's youth. The boy was brought up in the Isle of Wight, and from his earliest years was trained by his grandfather and mother in French and Italian. In 1849 he was sent to Eton, where he proceeded to read enormously, devouring everything he could lay his hands on, particularly in the fields of lyric poetry and the Elizabethan drama. By the time he was fourteen many of his life-long partialities and prejudices were fully formed; at that time he was immersed in Shelley, Keats, Landor, the Orlando Furioso, and the tragedies of Corneille, and already he was indifferent to Horace, disliked Racine, and hated Euripides. In 1853 Swinburne left Eton under something of a cloud, because of his rebellious attitude towards one or more of his teachers. There was then some talk in his family of preparing him for the army, but the project was abandoned because of his shortness and slightness, to his own life-long regret. In January, 1856, he entered Balliol College, Oxford. After his first year there his high-church proclivities melted away, and he became, what he remained, a nihilist in religion and a republican. He kept his terms regularly at Oxford until 1858, after which he was there less regularly; and he finally left the University without a degree in the fall of 1859. He was a brilliant though self-willed student, and his attainments in Greek were remarkable; but Benjamin Jowett, who long remained his warm friend, advised his leaving Oxford because of irregular ways of life into which he was drifting.

Late in 1860 Swinburne's first book was published, The Queen Mother and Rosamond, containing two plays. It passed at the time entirely unnoticed both by reviewers and by the public, and it is said that not a single copy was sold until some years afterwards. Early in 1864 he went abroad for the longest journey of his life, traveling through France to Italy, where he saw his idol, Landor, then in his ninetieth year. In April, 1865, Swinburne's second book, Atalanta in Calydon, was published. The magnificent verse of this play did not go unappreciated, and the book became, indeed, the literary sensation of the year. At the end of 1865 a fourth play was published, Chastelard, which also was successful, though it was regarded by a section of the public as an immoral performance. Suspicion concerning his morals was electrified into certainty by the publication in the following year of Poems and Ballads. So violent and universal were the attacks on this book that after a few months it was withdrawn from sale by its publisher. In 1879 Theodore Watts-Dunton brought the poet to his own house, The Pines, Putney, where he lived in retirement until his death from pneumonia on 10 April, 1909. In the years after 1866 Swinburne continued to write voluminously, both plays and lyric poems, and he also published from time to time a number of critical studies written in dithyrambic prose. Among his volumes are: Songs before Sunrise (1871), Bothwell, a Tragedy (1874), Songs of Two Nations (1875), Erechtheus (1876), Poems and Ballads, Second Series (1878), Mary Stuart, a Tragedy (1881), Tristram of Lyonesse, and Other Poems (1882), A Century of Roundels (1883), Poems and Ballads, Third Series (1889), Astrophel and Other Poems (1894), The Tale of Balen (1896), and A Channel Passage, and Other Poems (1904). His critical studies include: William Blake (1868), George

Chapman (1875), Essays and Studies (1875), A Study of Shakespeare (1880), A Study of Victor Hugo (1886), A Study of Ben Jonson (1889), *and* The Age of Shakespeare (1908).

*Swinburne in an essay on Wordsworth and Byron wrote, "It would be an absolute waste of time, for one who assumes it as indisputable, to enter into controversy with one who holds it as disputable, that the two primary and essential qualities of poetry are imagination and harmony; that where these qualities are wanting there can be no poetry, properly so called; and that where these qualities are perceptible in the highest degree, there, even though they should be unaccompanied and unsupported by any other great quality whatever—even though the ethical or critical faculty should be conspicuous by its absence—there, and only there, is the best and highest poetry." This definition of poetry is at least useful to indicate the qualities for which Swinburne's own verse is pre-eminent. Whether or not he had the highest poetical imagination may be a question, but there can be no doubt about his lyrical fervor and his unparalleled mastery of the rhythmical possibilities of the language.*

*The standard edition of Swinburne is the "Bonchurch Edition" of The Complete Works, ed. Sir Edmund Gosse and Thomas James Wise (20 vols, London, 1925–1927). Vol. 18 of this edition contains Letters; Vol. 19, the standard biography by Gosse; and Vol. 20, a bibliography by Wise. There is a volume of Selections from Swinburne, ed. William O. Raymond (New York, 1925); another one-volume selection is The Best of Swinburne, edited by C. K. Hyder and L. Chase (New York, 1937). The Collected Letters are being edited by C. Y. Lang. Harold Nicolson's Swinburne ("English Men of Letters" series, 1926) is a good brief introduction. The following more detailed critical studies are valuable: Swinburne by Samuel C. Chew (Boston, 1929); Swinburne, A Literary Biography by Georges Lafourcade (London, 1932); Swinburne's Literary Career and Fame by Clyde Kenneth Hyder (Durham, N. C., 1933); and Swinburne: a Biographical Approach by H. Hare (London, 1949).*

# Choruses from
## Atalanta in Calydon [1]

### I

When the hounds of spring are on winter's
    traces,

[1] The following poems are reprinted from the

The mother of months [2] in meadow or plain
Fills the shadows and windy places
    With lisp of leaves and ripple of rain;
And the brown bright nightingale amorous    5
Is half assuaged for Itylus, [3]
For the Thracian ships and the foreign faces,
    The tongueless vigil, and all the pain.

Come with bows bent and with emptying of
    quivers,
    Maiden most perfect, lady of light,    10
With a noise of winds and many rivers,
    With a clamor of waters, and with might;
Bind on thy sandals, O thou most fleet,
Over the splendor and speed of thy feet;
For the faint east quickens, the wan west
    shivers,    15
    Round the feet of the day and the feet of
    the night.

Where shall we find her, how shall we sing to
    her,
    Fold our hands round her knees, and cling?
O that man's heart were as fire and could
    spring to her,
    Fire, or the strength of the streams that
    spring!    20
For the stars and the winds are unto her
As raiment, as songs of the harp-player;
For the risen stars and the fallen cling to her,
    And the southwest-wind and the west-wind
    sing.

For winter's rains and ruins are over,    25
    And all the season of snows and sins;
The days dividing lover and lover,
    The light that loses, the night that wins;
And time remembered is grief forgotten,
And frosts are slain and flowers begotten,    30
And in green underwood and cover
    Blossom by blossom the spring begins.

The full streams feed on flower of rushes,
    Ripe grasses trammel a traveling foot,
The faint fresh flame of the young year flushes
    From leaf to flower and flower to fruit;    36
And fruit and leaf are as gold and fire,
And the oat is heard above the lyre,
And the hoofèd heel of a satyr crushes
    The chestnut-husk at the chestnut-root.    40

And Pan by noon and Bacchus by night,
    Fleeter of foot than the fleet-foot kid,
Follows with dancing and fills with delight
    The Maenad and the Bassarid; [4]
And soft as lips that laugh and hide    45

collected edition of Swinburne's poems, in six volumes, by permission of Harper and Brothers.
[2] The moon, Artemis.
[3] See note to Arnold's *Philomela* above. Itylus was the son of Procne, the nephew of Philomela (the nightingale).
[4] Bacchantes, worshipers of Bacchus.

The laughing leaves of the trees divide,
And screen from seeing and leave in sight
    The god pursuing, the maiden hid.

The ivy falls with the Bacchanal's hair
    Over her eyebrows hiding her eyes;    50
The wild vine slipping down leaves bare
    Her bright breast shortening into sighs;
The wild vine slips with the weight of its leaves,
But the berried ivy catches and cleaves
To the limbs that glitter, the feet that scare    55
    The wolf that follows, the fawn that flies.

## II

Before the beginning of years
    There came to the making of man
Time, with a gift of tears;
    Grief, with a glass that ran;
Pleasure, with pain for leaven;    5
    Summer, with flowers that fell;
Remembrance fallen from heaven,
    And madness risen from hell;
Strength without hands to smite;
    Love that endures for a breath:    10
Night, the shadow of light,
    And life, the shadow of death.

And the high gods took in hand
    Fire, and the falling of tears,
And a measure of sliding sand    15
    From under the feet of the years;
And froth and drift of the sea;
    And dust of the laboring earth;
And bodies of things to be
    In the houses of death and of birth;    20
And wrought with weeping and laughter,
    And fashioned with loathing and love,
With life before and after
    And death beneath and above,
For a day and a night and a morrow,    25
    That his strength might endure for a span
With travail and heavy sorrow,
    The holy spirit of man.

From the winds of the north and the south
    They gathered as unto strife;    30
They breathed upon his mouth,
    They filled his body with life;
Eyesight and speech they wrought
    For the veils of the soul therein,
A time for labor and thought,    35
    A time to serve and to sin;
They gave him light in his ways,
    And love, and a space for delight,
And beauty and length of days,
    And night, and sleep in the night.    40
His speech is a burning fire;
    With his lips he travaileth;
In his heart is a blind desire,
    In his eyes foreknowledge of death;
He weaves, and is clothed with derision;    45
    Sows, and he shall not reap;

His life is a watch or a vision
    Between a sleep and a sleep.

## III

We have seen thee, O Love, thou art fair,
    thou art goodly, O Love;
Thy wings make light in the air as the wings
    of a dove.
Thy feet are as winds that divide the stream of
    the sea;
Earth is thy covering to hide thee, the garment
    of thee.
Thou art swift and subtle and blind as a flame
    of fire;    5
Before thee the laughter, behind thee the tears
    of desire;
And twain go forth beside thee, a man with
    a maid;
Her eyes are the eyes of a bride whom delight
    makes afraid;
As the breath in the buds that stir is her bridal
    breath:
But Fate is the name of her; and his name is
    Death.    10

For an evil blossom was born
    Of sea-foam and the frothing of blood,
        Blood-red and bitter of fruit,
            And the seed of it laughter and tears,
And the leaves of it madness and scorn;    15
    A bitter flower from the bud,
        Sprung of the sea without root,
            Sprung without graft from the years.

The weft of the world was untorn
    That is woven of the day on the night,    20
    The hair of the hours was not white
Nor the raiment of time overworn,
    When a wonder, a world's delight,
A perilous goddess was born;
    And the waves of the sea as she came    25
Clove, and the foam at her feet,
    Fawning, rejoiced to bring forth
A fleshly blossom, a flame
Filling the heavens with heat
    To the cold white ends of the north.    30

And in air the clamorous birds,
    And men upon earth that hear
Sweet articulate words
    Sweetly divided apart,
And in shallow and channel and mere    35
The rapid and footless herds,
    Rejoiced, being foolish of heart.

For all they said upon earth,
    She is fair, she is white like a dove,
        And the life of the world in her breath    40
Breathes, and is born at her birth;
    For they knew thee for mother of love,
        And knew thee not mother of death.

What hadst thou to do being born,
    Mother, when winds were at ease,    45

As a flower of the springtime of corn,
    A flower of the foam of the seas?
For bitter thou wast from thy birth,
    Aphrodite, a mother of strife;
For before thee some rest was on earth,    50
    A little respite from tears,
    A little pleasure of life;
For life was not then as thou art,
    But as one that waxeth in years
Sweet-spoken, a fruitful wife;    55
    Earth had no thorn, and desire
No sting, neither death any dart;
    What hadst thou to do among these,
    Thou, clothed with a burning fire,
Thou, girt with sorrow of heart,    60
    Thou, sprung of the seed of the seas
As an ear from a seed of corn,
    As a brand plucked forth of a pyre,
As a ray shed forth of the morn,
    For division of soul and disease,    65
For a dart and a sting and a thorn?
    What ailed thee then to be born?

Was there not evil enough,
    Mother, and anguish on earth
Born with a man at his birth,    70
Wastes underfoot, and above
    Storm out of heaven, and dearth
Shaken down from the shining thereof,
    Wrecks from afar overseas
And peril of shallow and firth,    75
    And tears that spring and increase
In the barren places of mirth,
That thou, having wings as a dove,
    Being girt with desire for a girth,
    That thou must come after these,    80
That thou must lay on him love?

Thou shouldst not so have been born:
    But death should have risen with thee,
    Mother, and visible fear,
    Grief, and the wringing of hands,    85
And noise of many that mourn;
    The smitten bosom, the knee
    Bowed, and in each man's ear
    A cry as of perishing lands,
A moan as of people in prison,    90
    A tumult of infinite griefs;
    And thunder of storm on the sands,
    And wailing of waves on the shore;
And under thee newly arisen
    Loud shoals and shipwrecking reefs,    95
    Fierce air and violent light;
    Sail rent and sundering oar,
    Darkness, and noises of night;
Clashing of streams in the sea,
    Wave against wave as a sword,    100
    Clamor of currents, and foam;
    Rains making ruin on earth,
    Winds that wax ravenous and roam
As wolves in a wolfish horde;
Fruits growing faint in the tree,    105
    And blind things dead in their birth;

Famine, and blighting of corn,
    When thy time was come to be born.

All these we know of; but thee
    Who shall discern or declare?    110
In the uttermost ends of the sea
    The light of thine eyelids and hair,
    The light of thy bosom as fire
    Between the wheel of the sun
And the flying flames of the air?    115
    Wilt thou turn thee not yet nor have pity,
But abide with despair and desire
    And the crying of armies undone,
    Lamentation of one with another
    And breaking of city by city;    120
The dividing of friend against friend,
    The severing of brother and brother;
Wilt thou utterly bring to an end?
    Have mercy, mother!

For against all men from of old    125
    Thou hast set thine hand as a curse,
    And cast out gods from their places.
    These things are spoken of thee.
Strong kings and goodly with gold
    Thou hast found out arrows to pierce,    130
    And made their kingdoms and races
    As dust and surf of the sea.
All these, overburdened with woes
    And with length of their days waxen weak,
    Thou slewest; and sentest moreover    135
    Upon Tyro [5] an evil thing,
Rent hair and a fetter and blows
    Making bloody the flower of the cheek,
    Though she lay by a god as a lover,
    Though fair, and the seed of a king.    140
For of old, being full of thy fire,
    She endured not longer to wear
    On her bosom a saffron vest,
    On her shoulder an ashwood quiver;
Being mixed and made one through desire 145
    With Enipeus, and all her hair
    Made moist with his mouth, and her
        breast
    Filled full of the foam of the river.

## Itylus [1]

Swallow, my sister, O sister swallow,
    How can thine heart be full of the spring?
    A thousand summers are over and dead.
What hast thou found in the spring to follow?
    What hast thou found in thine heart to
        sing?    5

[5] The wife of Cretheus. She was loved by Enipeus, Macedonian river-god.

[1] This and the four following poems are from *Poems and Ballads*, First Series (1866). Concerning Itylus see notes above to the first chorus from *Atalanta in Calydon* and to Arnold's *Philomela*. It is Philomela, the nightingale, not Procne, her "sister swallow" and the mother of Itylus, who here laments the slain boy.

What wilt thou do when the summer is
    shed?

O swallow sister, O fair swift swallow,
  Why wilt thou fly after spring to the south,
    The soft south whither thine heart is set?
Shall not the grief of the old time follow?  10
  Shall not the song thereof cleave to thy
    mouth?
    Hast thou forgotten ere I forget?

Sister, my sister, O fleet sweet swallow,
  Thy way is long to the sun and the south;
    But I, fulfilled of my heart's desire,    15
Shedding my song upon height, upon hollow,
  From tawny body and sweet small mouth
    Feed the heart of the night with fire.

I the nightingale all spring through,
  O swallow, sister, O changing swallow,    20
    All spring through till the spring be done,
Clothed with the light of the night on the dew,
  Sing, while the hours and the wild birds
    follow,
    Take flight and follow and find the sun.

Sister, my sister, O soft light swallow,    25
  Though all things feast in the spring's guest-
    chamber,
    How hast thou heart to be glad thereof
    yet?
For where thou fliest I shall not follow,
  Till life forget and death remember,
    Till thou remember and I forget.    30

Swallow, my sister, O singing swallow,
  I know not how thou hast heart to sing.
    Hast thou the heart? is it all past over?
Thy lord the summer is good to follow,
  And fair the feet of thy lover the spring:  35
    But what wilt thou say to the spring thy
    lover?

O swallow, sister, O fleeting swallow,
  My heart in me is a molten ember
    And over my head the waves have met.
But thou wouldst tarry or I would follow,    40
  Could I forget or thou remember,
    Couldst thou remember and I forget.

O sweet stray sister, O shifting swallow,
  The heart's division divideth us.
    Thy heart is light as a leaf of a tree;  45
But mine goes forth among sea-gulfs hollow
  To the place of the slaying of Itylus,
    The feast of Daulis, the Thracian sea.

O swallow, sister, O rapid swallow,
  I pray thee sing not a little space.    50
    Are not the roofs and the lintels wet?
The woven web that was plain to follow,
  The small slain body, the flowerlike face,
    Can I remember if thou forget?

O sister, sister, thy first-begotten!    55
  The hands that cling and the feet that fol-
    low,
    The voice of the child's blood crying yet:
Who *hath remembered me? who hath for-*
    *gotten?*
  Thou hast forgotten, O summer swallow,
    But the world shall end when I forget.  60

# Satia Te Sanguine [1]

If you loved me ever so little,
  I could bear the bonds that gall,
I could dream the bonds were brittle;
  You do not love me at all.

O beautiful lips, O bosom    5
  More white than the moon's and warm,
A sterile, a ruinous blossom
  Is blown your way in a storm.

As the lost white feverish limbs
  Of the Lesbian Sappho, adrift    10
In foam where the sea-weed swims,
  Swam loose for the streams to lift,

My heart swims blind in a sea
  That stuns me; swims to and fro,
And gathers to windward and lee    15
  Lamentation, and mourning, and woe.

A broken, an emptied boat,
  Sea saps it, winds blow apart,
Sick and adrift and afloat,
  The barren waif of a heart.    20

Where, when the gods would be cruel,
  Do they go for a torture? where
Plant thorns, set pain like a jewel?
  Ah, not in the flesh, not there!

The racks of earth and the rods    25
  Are weak as foam on the sands;
In the heart is the prey for gods,
  Who crucify hearts, not hands.

Mere pangs corrode and consume,
  Dead when life dies in the brain;    30
In the infinite spirit is room
  For the pulse of an infinite pain.

I wish you were dead, my dear;
  I would give you, had I to give,
Some death too bitter to fear;    35
  It is better to die than live.

I wish you were stricken of thunder
  And burnt with a bright flame through,
Consumed and cloven in sunder,
  I dead at your feet like you.    40

[1] Satiate thyself with blood.

If I could but know after all,
  I might cease to hunger and ache,
Though your heart were ever so small,
  If it were not a stone or a snake.

You are crueler, you that we love,  45
  Than hatred, hunger, or death;
You have eyes and breasts like a dove,
  And you kill men's hearts with a breath.

As plague in a poisonous city
  Insults and exults on her dead,  50
So you, when pallid for pity
  Comes love, and fawns to be fed.

As a tame beast writhes and wheedles,
  He fawns to be fed with wiles;
You carve him a cross of needles,  55
  And whet them sharp as your smiles.

He is patient of thorn and whip,
  He is dumb under ax or dart;
You suck with a sleepy red lip
  The wet red wounds in his heart.  60

You thrill as his pulses dwindle,
  You brighten and warm as he bleeds,
With insatiable eyes that kindle
  And insatiable mouth that feeds.

Your hands nailed love to the tree,  65
  You stripped him, scourged him with rods,
And drowned him deep in the sea
  That hides the dead and their gods.

And for all this, die will he not;
  There is no man sees him but I;  70
You came and went and forgot;
  I hope he will some day die.

# A Match

If love were what the rose is,
  And I were like the leaf,
Our lives would grow together
In sad or singing weather,
Blown fields or flowerful closes,  5
  Green pleasure or gray grief;
If love were what the rose is,
  And I were like the leaf.

If I were what the words are,
  And love were like the tune,  10
With double sound and single
Delight our lips would mingle,
With kisses glad as birds are
  That get sweet rain at noon;
If I were what the words are,  15
  And love were like the tune.

If you were life, my darling,
  And I your love were death,
We'd shine and snow together

Ere March made sweet the weather  20
With daffodil and starling
  And hours of fruitful breath;
If you were life, my darling,
  And I your love were death.

If you were thrall to sorrow,  25
  And I were page to joy,
We'd play for lives and seasons
With loving looks and treasons
And tears of night and morrow
  And laughs of maid and boy;  30
If you were thrall to sorrow,
  And I were page to joy.

If you were April's lady,
  And I were lord in May,
We'd throw with leaves for hours  35
And draw for days with flowers,
Till day like night were shady
  And night were bright like day;
If you were April's lady,
  And I were lord in May.  40

If you were queen of pleasure,
  And I were king of pain,
We'd hunt down love together,
Pluck out his flying-feather,
And teach his feet a measure,  45
  And find his mouth a rein;
If you were queen of pleasure,
  And I were king of pain.

# The Garden of Proserpine [1]

Here, where the world is quiet;
  Here, where all trouble seems
Dead winds' and spent waves' riot
  In doubtful dreams of dreams;
I watch the green field growing  5
For reaping folk and sowing,
For harvest-time and mowing,
  A sleepy world of streams.

I am tired of tears and laughter,
  And men that laugh and weep;  10
Of what may come hereafter
  For men that sow to reap:
I am weary of days and hours,
Blown buds of barren flowers,
Desires and dreams and powers  15
  And everything but sleep.

Here life has death for neighbor,
  And far from eye or ear
Wan waves and wet winds labor,
  Weak ships and spirits steer;  20
They drive adrift, and whither
They wot not who make thither;
But no such winds blow hither,
  And no such things grow here.

[1] Proserpine was the wife of Pluto and queen of the lower world.

No growth of moor or coppice, 25
　No heather-flower or vine,
But bloomless buds of poppies,
　Green grapes of Proserpine,
Pale beds of blowing rushes
Where no leaf blooms or blushes 30
Save this whereout she crushes
　For dead men deadly wine.

Pale, without name or number,
　In fruitless fields of corn,
They bow themselves and slumber 35
　All night till light is born;
And like a soul belated,
In hell and heaven unmated,
By cloud and mist abated
　Comes out of darkness morn. 40

Though one were strong as seven,
　He too with death shall dwell,
Nor wake with wings in heaven,
　Nor weep for pains in hell;
Though one were fair as roses, 45
His beauty clouds and closes;
And well though love reposes,
　In the end it is not well.

Pale, beyond porch and portal,
　Crowned with calm leaves, she stands 50
Who gathers all things mortal
　With cold immortal hands;
Her languid lips are sweeter
Than love's who fears to greet her
To men that mix and meet her 55
　From many times and lands.

She waits for each and other,
　She waits for all men born;
Forgets the earth her mother,[2]
　The life of fruits and corn; 60
And spring and seed and swallow
Take wing for her and follow
Where summer song rings hollow
　And flowers are put to scorn.

There go the loves that wither, 65
　The old loves with wearier wings;
And all dead years draw thither,
　And all disastrous things;
Dead dreams of days forsaken,
Blind buds that snows have shaken, 70
Wild leaves that winds have taken,
　Red strays of ruined springs.

We are not sure of sorrow,
　And joy was never sure;
To-day will die to-morrow; 75
　Time stoops to no man's lure;
And love, grown faint and fretful,
With lips but half regretful
Sighs, and with eyes forgetful
　Weeps that no loves endure. 80

　[2] Her mother was Demeter, goddess of the earth.

From too much love of living,
　From hope and fear set free,
We thank with brief thanksgiving
　Whatever gods may be
That no life lives for ever; 85
That dead men rise up never;
That even the weariest river
　Winds somewhere safe to sea.

Then star nor sun shall waken,
　Nor any change of light: 90
Nor sound of waters shaken,
　Nor any sound or sight:
Nor wintry leaves nor vernal,
Nor days nor things diurnal;
Only the sleep eternal 95
　In an eternal night.

# An Interlude

In the greenest growth of the Maytime,
　I rode where the woods were wet,
Between the dawn and the daytime;
　The spring was glad that we met.

There was something the season wanted, 5
　Though the ways and the woods smelt sweet;
The breath at your lips that panted,
　The pulse of the grass at your feet.

You came, and the sun came after,
　And the green grew golden above; 10
And the flag-flowers lightened with laughter,
　And the meadow-sweet shook with love.

Your feet in the full-grown grasses
　Moved soft as a weak wind blows;
You passed me as April passes, 15
　With face made out of a rose.

By the stream where the stems were slender,
　Your bright foot paused at the sedge;
It might be to watch the tender
　Light leaves in the springtime hedge, 20

On boughs that the sweet month blanches
　With flowery frost of May:
It might be a bird in the branches,
　It might be a thorn in the way.

I waited to watch you linger 25
　With foot drawn back from the dew,
Till a sunbeam straight like a finger
　Struck sharp through the leaves at you.

And a bird overhead sang *Follow*,
　And a bird to the right sang *Here*; 30
And the arch of the leaves was hollow,
　And the meaning of May was clear.

I saw where the sun's hand pointed,
　I knew what the bird's note said;

By the dawn and the dewfall anointed,     35
  You were queen by the gold on your head.

As the glimpse of a burnt-out ember
  Recalls a regret of the sun,
I remember, forget, and remember
  What Love saw done and undone.     40

I remember the way we parted,
  The day and the way we met;
You hoped we were both broken-hearted,
  And knew we should both forget.

And May with her world in flower     45
  Seemed still to murmur and smile
As you murmured and smiled for an hour;
  I saw you turn at the stile.

A hand like a white wood-blossom
  You lifted, and waved, and passed,     50
With head hung down to the bosom,
  And pale, as it seemed, at last.

And the best and the worst of this is
  That neither is most to blame
If you've forgotten my kisses     55
  And I've forgotten your name.

# Hertha [1]

I am that which began;
  Out of me the years roll;
Out of me God and man;
  I am equal and whole;
God changes, and man, and the form of them
    bodily; I am the soul.     5

Before ever land was,
  Before ever the sea,
Or soft hair of the grass,
  Or fair limbs of the tree,
Or the flesh-colored fruit of my branches, I
    was, and thy soul was in me.     10

First life on my sources
  First drifted and swam;
Out of me are the forces
  That save it or damn;
Out of me man and woman, and wild-beast
    and bird; before God was, I am.     15

Beside or above me
  Nought is there to go;
Love or unlove me,
  Unknow me or know,

[1] This and the two following poems are from *Songs before Sunrise.* Hertha (of Nerthus) was the Germanic earth-mother, goddess of fertility and growing things. Swinburne himself said, "Of all I have done, I rate *Hertha* highest as a single piece, finding in it the most of lyric force and music combined with the most of condensed and clarified thought."

I am that which unloves me and loves; I am
  stricken, and I am the blow.     20

I the mark that is missed
  And the arrows that miss,
I the mouth that is kissed
  And the breath in the kiss,
The search, and the sought, and the seeker, the
  soul and the body that is.     25

I am that thing which blesses
  My spirit elate;
That which caresses
  With hands uncreate
My limbs unbegotten that measure the length
  of the measure of fate.     30

But what things dost thou now,
  Looking Godward, to cry
"I am I, thou art thou,
  I am low, thou art high"?
I am thou, whom thou seekest to find him; find
  thou but thyself, thou art I.     35

I the grain and the furrow,
  The plow-cloven clod
And the plowshare drawn thorough,
  The germ and the sod,
The deed and the doer, the seed and the sower,
  the dust which is God.     40

Hast thou known how I fashioned thee,
  Child, underground?
Fire that impassioned thee,
  Iron that bound,
Dim changes of water, what thing of all these
  hast thou known of or found?     45

Canst thou say in thine heart
  Thou hast seen with thine eyes
With what cunning of art
  Thou wast wrought in what wise,
By what force of what stuff thou wast shapen,
  and shown on my breast to the skies?     50

Who hath given, who hath sold it thee,
  Knowledge of me?
Hath the wilderness told it thee?
  Hast thou learned of the sea?
Hast thou communed in spirit with night? have
  the winds taken counsel with thee?     55

Have I set such a star
  To show light on thy brow
That thou sawest from afar
  What I show to thee now?
Have ye spoken as brethren together, the sun
  and the mountains and thou?     60

What is here, dost thou know it?
  What was, hast thou known?
Prophet nor poet

Nor tripod nor throne [2]
Nor spirit nor flesh can make answer, but only
    thy mother alone.       65

Mother, not maker,
    Born, and not made;
Though her children forsake her,
    Allured or afraid,
Praying prayers to the God of their fashion, she
    stirs not for all that have prayed.    70

A creed is a rod,
    And a crown is of night;
But this thing is God,
    To be man with thy might,
To grow straight in the strength of thy spirit,
    and live out thy life as the light.   75

I am in thee to save thee,
    As my soul in thee saith;
Give thou as I gave thee,
    Thy life-blood and breath,
Green leaves of thy labor, white flowers of thy
    thought, and red fruit of thy death.  80

Be the ways of thy giving
    As mine were to thee;
The free life of thy living,
    Be the gift of it free;
Not as servant to lord, nor as master to slave,
    shalt thou give thee to me.    85

O children of banishment,
    Souls overcast,
Were the lights ye see vanish meant
    Alway to last,
Ye would know not the sun overshining the
    shadows and stars overpast.    90

I that saw where ye trod
    The dim paths of the night
Set the shadow called God
    In your skies to give light;
But the morning of manhood is risen, and the
    shadowless soul is in sight.    95

The tree many-rooted
    That swells to the sky
With frondage [3] red-fruited,
    The life-tree am I;
In the buds of your lives is the sap of my
    leaves: ye shall live and not die.  100

But the Gods of your fashion
    That take and that give,
In their pity and passion
    That scourge and forgive,
They are worms that are bred in the bark that
    falls off; they shall die and not live. 105

My own blood is what stanches
    The wounds in my bark;

[2] I. e., nor priest nor king.    [3] Foliage.

Stars caught in my branches
    Make day of the dark,
And are worshiped as suns till the sunrise shall
    tread out their fires as a spark.  110

Where dead ages hide under
    The live roots of the tree,
In my darkness the thunder
    Makes utterance of me;
In the clash of my boughs with each other ye
    hear the waves sound of the sea.  115

That noise is of Time,
    As his feathers are spread
And his feet set to climb
    Through the boughs overhead,
And my foliage rings round him and rustles,
    and branches are bent with his tread.

The storm-winds of ages    121
    Blow through me and cease,
The war-wind that rages,
    The spring-wind of peace,
Ere the breath of them roughen my tresses, ere
    one of my blossoms increase.  125

All sounds of all changes,
    All shadows and lights
On the world's mountain-ranges
    And stream-riven heights,
Whose tongue is the wind's tongue and lan-
    guage of storm-clouds on earth-shaking
    nights;    130

All forms of all faces,
    All works of all hands
In unsearchable places
    Of time-stricken lands,
All death and all life, and all reigns and all
    ruins, drop through me as sands.  135

Though sore be my burden
    And more than ye know,
And my growth have no guerdon
    But only to grow,
Yet I fail not of growing for lightnings above
    me or deathworms below.  140

These too have their part in me,
    As I too in these;
Such fire is at heart in me,
    Such sap is this tree's,
Which hath in it all sounds and all secrets of
    infinite lands and of seas.  145

In the spring-colored hours
    When my mind was as May's,
There brake forth of me flowers
    By centuries of days,
Strong blossoms with perfume of manhood,
    shot out from my spirit as rays.  150

And the sound of them springing
    And smell of their shoots

Were as warmth and sweet singing
And strength to my roots;
And the lives of my children made perfect with
freedom of soul were my fruits.    155

I bid you but be;
I have need not of prayer;
I have need of you free
As your mouths of mine air;
That my heart may be greater within me, be-
holding the fruits of me fair.    160

More fair than strange fruit is
Of faiths ye espouse;
In me only the root is
That blooms in your boughs;
Behold now your God that ye made you, to
feed him with faith of your vows.    165

In the darkening and whitening
Abysses adored,
With dayspring and lightning
For lamp and for sword,
God thunders in heaven, and his angels are red
with the wrath of the Lord.    170

O my sons, O too dutiful
Toward Gods not of me,
Was not I enough beautiful?
Was it hard to be free?
For Behold, I am with you, am in you and of
you; look forth now and see.    175

Lo, winged with world's wonders,
With miracles shod,
With the fires of his thunders
For raiment and rod,
God trembles in heaven, and his angels are
white with the terror of God.    180

For his twilight is come on him,
His anguish is here;
And his spirits gaze dumb on him,
Grown gray from his fear;
And his hour taketh hold on him stricken, the
last of his infinite year.    185

Thought made him and breaks him,
Truth slays and forgives;
But to you, as time takes him,
This new thing it gives,
Even love, the beloved Republic, that feeds
upon freedom and lives.    190

For truth only is living,
Truth only is whole,
And the love of his giving
Man's polestar and pole;
Man, pulse of my center, and fruit of my body,
and seed of my soul.    195

One birth of my bosom;
One beam of mine eye;

One topmost blossom
That scales the sky;
Man, equal and one with me, man that is
made of me, man that is I.    200

# To Walt Whitman in America

Send but a song oversea for us,
Heart of their hearts who are free,
Heart of their singer, to be for us
More than our singing can be;
Ours, in the tempest at error,    5
With no light but the twilight of terror;
Send us a song oversea!

Sweet-smelling of pine-leaves and grasses,
And blown as a tree through and through
With the winds of the keen mountain-passes,    10
And tender as sun-smitten dew;
Sharp-tongued as the winter that shakes
The wastes of your limitless lakes,
Wide-eyed as the sea-line's blue.

O strong-winged soul with prophetic    15
Lips hot with the bloodbeats of song,
With tremor of heartstrings magnetic,
With thoughts as thunders in throng,
With consonant ardors of chords
That pierce men's souls as with swords    20
And hale them hearing along,

Make us too music, to be with us
As a word from a world's heart warm,
To sail the dark as a sea with us,
Full-sailed, outsinging the storm,    25
A song to put fire in our ears
Whose burning shall burn up tears,
Whose sign bid battle reform;

A note in the ranks of a clarion,
A word in the wind of cheer,    30
To consume as with lightning the carrion
That makes time foul for us here;
In the air that our dead things infest
A blast of the breath of the west,
Till east way as west way is clear.    35

Out of the sun beyond sunset,
From the evening whence morning shall be,
With the rollers in measureless onset,
With the van of the storming sea,
With the world-wide wind, with the breath    40
That breaks ships driven upon death,
With the passion of all things free,

With the sea-steeds footless and frantic,
White myriads for death to bestride
In the charge of the ruining Atlantic    45
Where deaths by regiments ride,
With clouds and clamors of waters,
With a long note shriller than slaughter's
On the furrowless fields world-wide.

With terror, with ardor and wonder,   50
  With the soul of the season that wakes
When the weight of a whole year's thunder
  In the tidestream of autumn breaks,
Let the flight of the wide-winged word
Come over, come in and be heard,   55
  Take form and fire for our sakes.

For a continent bloodless with travail
  Here toils and brawls as it can,
And the web of it who shall unravel
  Of all that peer on the plan;   60
Would fain grow men, but they grow not,
And fain be free, but they know not
  One name for freedom and man?

One name, not twain for division;
  One thing, not twain, from the birth;   65
Spirit and substance and vision,
  Worth more than worship is worth;
Unbeheld, unadored, undivined,
The cause, the center, the mind,
  The secret and sense of the earth.   70

Here as a weakling in irons,
  Here as a weanling in bands,
As a prey that the stake-net environs,
  Our life that we looked for stands;
And the man-child naked and dear,   75
Democracy, turns on us here
  Eyes trembling with tremulous hands.

It sees not what season shall bring to it
  Sweet fruit of its bitter desire;
Few voices it hears yet sing to it,   80
  Few pulses of hearts reaspire;
Foresees not time, nor forehears
The noises of imminent years,
  Earthquake, and thunder, and fire:

When crowned and weaponed and curbless 85
  It shall walk without helm or shield
The bare burnt furrows and herbless
  Of war's last flame-stricken field,
Till godlike, equal with time,
It stand in the sun sublime,   90
  In the godhead of man revealed.

Round your people and over them
  Light like raiment is drawn,
Close as a garment to cover them
  Wrought not of mail nor of lawn;   95
Here, with hope hardly to wear,
Naked nations and bare
  Swim, sink, strike out for the dawn.

Chains are here, and a prison,
  Kings, and subjects, and shame,   100
If the God upon you be arisen,
  How should our songs be the same?
How, in confusion of change,
How shall we sing, in a strange
  Land, songs praising his name?   105

God is buried and dead to us,
  Even the spirit of earth,
Freedom; so have they said to us,
  Some with mocking and mirth,
Some with heartbreak and tears;   110
And a God without eyes, without ears,
  Who shall sing of him, dead in the birth?

The earth-God Freedom, the lonely
  Face lightening, the footprint unshod,
Not as one man crucified only   115
  Nor scourged with but one life's rod;
The soul that is substance of nations,
Reincarnate with fresh generations;
  The great god Man, which is God.

But in weariest of years and obscurest   120
  Doth it live not at heart of all things,
The one God and one spirit, a purest
  Life, fed from unstanchable springs?
Within love, within hatred it is,
And its seed in the stripe as the kiss,   125
  And in slaves is the germ, and in kings.

Freedom we call it, for holier
  Name of the soul's there is none;
Surlier it labors, if slowlier,
  Than the meters of star or of sun;   130
Slowlier than life into breath,
Surelier than time into death,
  It moves till its labor be done.

Till the motion be done and the measure
  Circling through season and clime,   135
Slumber and sorrow and pleasure,
  Vision of virtue and crime;
Till consummate with conquering eyes,
A soul disembodied, it rise
  From the body transfigured of time.   140

Till it rise and remain and take station
  With the stars of the worlds that rejoice;
Till the voice of its heart's exultation
  Be as theirs an invariable voice;
By no discord of evil estranged,   145
By no pause, by no breach in it changed,
  By no clash in the chord of its choice.

It is one with the world's generations,
  With the spirit, the star, and the sod;   149
With the kingless and king-stricken nations,
  With the cross, and the chain, and the rod;
The most high, the most secret, most lonely,
The earth-soul Freedom, that only
  Lives, and that only is God.

# The Oblation

Ask nothing more of me, sweet;
  All I can give you I give.
    Heart of my heart, were it more,
More would be laid at your feet:

Love that should help you to live, 5
Song that should spur you to soar.

All things were nothing to give
Once to have sense of you more,
Touch you and taste of you, sweet,
Think you and breathe you and live, 10
Swept of your wings as they soar,
Trodden by chance of your feet.

I that have love and no more
Give you but love of you, sweet:
He that hath more, let him give; 15
He that hath wings, let him soar;
Mine is the heart at your feet
Here, that must love you to live.

# Ave Atque Vale [1]

### In Memory of Charles Baudelaire

*Nous devrions pourtant lui porter quelques fleurs;*
*Les morts, les pauvres morts, ont de grandes douleurs,*
*Et quand Octobre souffle, émondeur des vieux arbres,*
*Son vent mélancolique à l'entour de leur marbres,*
*Certe, ils doivent trouver les vivants bien ingrats.* [2]
—Les Fleurs du Mal.

#### I

Shall I strew on thee rose or rue or laurel,
Brother, on this that was the veil of thee?
Or quiet sea-flower molded by the sea,
Or simplest growth of meadow-sweet or sorrel,
Such as the summer-sleepy Dryads [3] weave,
Waked up by snow-soft sudden rains at
eve? 6
Or wilt thou rather, as on earth before,
Half-faded fiery blossoms, pale with heat
And full of bitter summer, but more sweet
To thee than gleanings of a northern shore 10
Trod by no tropic feet?

#### II

For always thee the fervid languid glories
Allured of heavier suns in mightier skies;
Thine ears knew all the wandering watery
sighs
Where the sea sobs round Lesbian promon-
tories, 15
The barren kiss of piteous wave to wave
That knows not where is that Leucadian
grave

Which hides too deep the supreme head of
song. [4]
Ah, salt and sterile as her kisses were,
The wild sea winds her and the green
gulfs bear 20
Hither and thither, and vex and work her
wrong,
Blind gods that cannot spare.

#### III

Thou sawest, in thine old singing season,
brother,
Secrets and sorrows unbeheld of us:
Fierce loves, and lovely leaf-buds poison-
ous 25
Bare to thy subtler eye, but for none other
Blowing by night in some unbreathed-in
clime;
The hidden harvest of luxurious time,
Sin without shape, and pleasure without speech;
And where strange dreams in a tumultuous
sleep 30
Make the shut eyes of stricken spirits
weep;
And with each face thou sawest the shadow on
each,
Seeing as men sow men reap.

#### IV

O sleepless heart and somber soul unsleeping,
That were athirst for sleep and no more
life 35
And no more love, for peace and no more
strife!
Now the dim gods of death have in their keep-
ing
Spirit and body and all the springs of song,
Is it well now where love can do no wrong,
Where stingless pleasure has no foam or fang 40
Behind the unopening closure of her lips?
Is it not well where soul from body slips
And fresh from bone divides without a pang
As dew from flower-bell drips?

#### V

It is enough; the end and the beginning 45
Are one thing to thee, who art past the
end.
O hand unclasped of unbeholden friend,
For thee no fruits to pluck, no palms for win-
ning,
No triumph and no labor and no lust,
Only dead yew-leaves and a little dust. 50
O quiet eyes wherein the light saith nought,
Whereto the day is dumb, nor any night
With obscure finger silences your sight,
Nor in your speech the sudden soul speaks
thought,
Sleep, and have sleep for light. 55

VI

Now all strange hours and all strange loves are
    over,
    Dreams and desires and somber songs and
        sweet,
    Hast thou found place at the great knees
        and feet
Of some pale Titan-woman like a lover,
    Such as thy vision here solicited,[5]    60
    Under the shadow of her fair vast head,
The deep division of prodigious breasts,
    The solemn slope of mighty limbs asleep,
    The weight of awful tresses that still keep
The savor and shade of old-world pine-forests
    Where the wet hill-winds weep?    66

VII

Hast thou found any likeness for thy vision?
    O gardener of strange flowers, what bud,
        what bloom,
    Hast thou found sown, what gathered in
        the gloom?
What of despair, of rapture, of derision,    70
    What of life is there, what of ill or good?
    Are the fruits gray like dust or bright like
        blood?
Does the dim ground grow any seed of ours,
    The faint fields quicken any terrene root,
    In low lands where the sun and moon are
        mute    75
And all the stars keep silence? Are there flow-
    ers
    At all, or any fruit?

VIII

Alas, but though my flying song flies after,
    O sweet strange elder singer, thy more
        fleet
    Singing, and footprints of thy fleeter feet,
Some dim derision of mysterious laughter    81
    From the blind tongueless warders of the
        dead,
    Some gainless glimpse of Proserpine's
        veiled head,
Some little sound of unregarded tears
    Wept by effaced unprofitable eyes,    85
    And from pale mouths some cadence of
        dead sighs—
These only, these the hearkening spirit hears,
    Sees only such things rise.

IX

Thou art far too far for wings of words to fol-
    low,
    Far too far off for thought or any prayer.
    What ails us with thee, who art wind and
        air?    91
What ails us gazing where all seen is hollow?

[5] See Baudelaire's *La Géante.*

Yet with some fancy, yet with some de-
    sire,
Dreams pursue death as winds a flying fire,
Our dreams pursue our dead and do not find.
    Still, and more swift than they, the thin
        flame flies,    96
    The low light fails us in elusive skies,
Still the foiled earnest ear is deaf, and blind
    Are still the eluded eyes.

X

Not thee, O never thee, in all time's changes,
    Not thee, but this the sound of thy sad
        soul,    101
    The shadow of thy swift spirit, this shut
        scroll
I lay my hand on, and not death estranges
    My spirit from communion of thy song—
    These memories and these melodies that
        throng    105
Veiled porches of a Muse funereal—
    These I salute, these touch, these clasp
        and fold
    As though a hand were in my hand to
        hold,
Or through mine ears a mourning musical
    Of many mourners rolled.    110

XI

I among these, I also, in such station
    As when the pyre was charred, and piled
        the sods,
    And offering to the dead made, and their
        gods,
The old mourners had, standing to make liba-
    tion,
    I stand, and to the gods and to the dead
    Do reverence without prayer or praise, and
        shed    116
Offering to these unknown, the gods of gloom,
    And what of honey and spice my seed-
        lands bear,
    And what I may of fruits in this chilled
        air,
And lay, Orestes-like,[6] across the tomb    120
    A curl of severed hair.

XII

But by no hand nor any treason stricken,
    Not like the low-lying head of Him, the
        King,[7]
    The flame that made of Troy a ruinous
        thing,
Thou liest, and on this dust no tears could
    quicken    125
    There fall no tears like theirs that all men
        hear
    Fall tear by sweet imperishable tear

[6] See Aeschylus, *Choëphorae,* 4–8.
[7] Agamemnon.

Down the opening leaves of holy poets' pages.
    Thee not Orestes, not Electra mourns;
    But bending us-ward with memorial urns
The most high Muses that fulfill all ages   131
    Weep, and our God's heart yearns.

### XIII

For, sparing of his sacred strength, not often
    Among us darkling here the lord of light
    Makes manifest his music and his might
In hearts that open and in lips that soften  136
    With the soft flame and heat of songs that
        shine.
    Thy lips indeed he touched with bitter
        wine,
And nourished them indeed with bitter bread;
    Yet surely from his hand thy soul's food
        came,   140
    The fire that scarred thy spirit at his
        flame
Was lighted, and thine hungering heart he fed
    Who feeds our hearts with fame.

### XIV

Therefore he too now at thy soul's sunsetting,
    God of all suns and songs, he too bends
        down   145
    To mix his laurel with thy cypress crown,
And save thy dust from blame and from for-
        getting.
    Therefore he too, seeing all thou wert and
        art,
    Compassionate, with sad and sacred heart,
Mourns thee of many his children the last
        dead,   150
    And hallows with strange tears and alien
        sighs
    Thine unmelodious mouth and sunless
        eyes,
And over thine irrevocable head
    Sheds light from the under skies.

### XV

And one weeps with him in the ways Lethean,
    And stains with tears her changing bosom
        chill:   156
    That obscure Venus of the hollow hill,[8]
That thing transformed which was the Cy-
        therean,
    With lips that lost their Grecian laugh di-
        vine
    Long since, and face no more called
        Erycine;[9]   160
A ghost, a bitter and luxurious god.
    Thee also with fair flesh and singing spell

[8] The Venus of medieval legend, fabled to hold her
court in the recesses of the Venusberg, or Hörsel-
berg, in central Germany.
[9] So called because there was a temple to Aphrodite Urania (the goddess of heavenly love) at Eryx,
in Sicily.

Did she, a sad and second prey, compel
Into the footless places once more trod,
    And shadows hot from hell.   165

### XVI

And now no sacred staff shall break in blos-
    som,[10]
    No choral salutation lure to light
    A spirit sick with perfume and sweet night
And love's tired eyes and hands and barren
        bosom.
    There is no help for these things; none to
        mend   170
    And none to mar; not all our songs, O
        friend,
Will make death clear or make life durable.
    Howbeit with rose and ivy and wild vine
    And with wild notes about this dust of
        thine
At least I fill the place where white dreams
        dwell   175
    And wreathe an unseen shrine.

### XVII

Sleep; and if life was bitter to thee, pardon,
    If sweet, give thanks; thou hast no more to
        live;
    And to give thanks is good, and to forgive.
Out of the mystic and the mournful garden  180
    Where all day through thine hands in bar-
        ren braid
    Wove the sick flowers of secrecy and
        shade,
Green buds of sorrow and sin, and remnants
        gray,
    Sweet-smelling, pale with poison, sanguine-
        hearted,
    Passions that sprang from sleep and
        thoughts that started,   185
Shall death not bring us all as thee one day
    Among the days departed?

### XVIII

For thee, O now a silent soul, my brother,
    Take at my hands this garland, and fare-
        well.
    Thin is the leaf, and chill the wintry smell,
And chill the solemn earth, a fatal mother, 191
    With sadder than the Niobean [11] womb,
    And in the hollow of her breasts a tomb.
Content thee, howsoe'er, whose days are done;
    There lies not any troublous thing before,
    Nor sight nor sound to war against thee
        more,   196
For whom all winds are quiet as the sun,
    All waters as the shore.

[10] Tannhäuser's pilgrimage in search of absolution. See note 11 on p. 1130 below.
[11] Niobe, with fourteen children, boasted of her
superiority to the goddess Latona, with her two,
whereupon all of Niobe's children were slain.

# A Ballad of François Villon [1]

## *Prince of All Ballad-Makers*

Bird of the bitter bright grey golden morn
  Scarce risen upon the dusk of dolorous years,
First of us all and sweetest singer born
    Whose far shrill note the world of new men
      hears
    Cleave the cold shuddering shade as twilight
      clears;        5
When song new-born put off the old world's
    attire
And felt its tune on her changed lips expire,
  Writ foremost on the roll of them that came
Fresh girt for service of the latter lyre,
  Villon, our sad bad glad mad brother's name!

Alas the joy, the sorrow, and the scorn,    11
    That clothed thy life with hopes and sins and
      fears,
And gave thee stones for bread and tares for
    corn
    And plume-plucked gaol-birds for thy starve-
      ling peers
Till death clipt close their flight with shame-
    ful shears;      15
Till shifts came short and loves were hard to
    hire,
  When lilt of song nor twitch of twangling wire
    Could buy thee bread or kisses; when light
      fame
Spurned like a ball and haled through brake
    and briar,
  Villon, our sad bad glad mad brother's
    name!      20

Poor splendid wings so frayed and soiled and
    torn!
    Poor kind wild eyes so dashed with light
      quick tears!
Poor perfect voice, most blithe when most for-
    lorn,
    That rings athwart the sea whence no man
      steers
    Like joy-bells crossed with death-bells in our
      ears!      25
What far delight has cooled the fierce desire
That like some ravenous bird was strong to tire
  On that frail flesh and soul consumed with
    flame,
But left more sweet than roses to respire,
  Villon, our sad bad glad mad brother's
    name?      30

[1] The French lyric poet of the fifteenth century.

### ENVOI

Prince of sweet songs made out of tears and
    fire,
A harlot was thy nurse, a God thy sire;
  Shame soiled thy song, and song assoiled thy
    shame.
But from thy feet now death has washed the
    mire,
Love reads out first at head of all our quire, [35]
  Villon, our sad bad glad mad brother's name.

# First Footsteps [1]

A little way, more soft and sweet
  Than fields aflower with May,
A babe's feet, venturing, scarce complete
  A little way.

  Eyes full of dawning day    5
Look up for mother's eyes to meet,
  Too blithe for song to say.
Glad as the golden spring to greet
  Its first live leaflet's play,
Love, laughing, leads the little feet    10
  A little way.

# The Roundel

A roundel is wrought as a ring or a star-bright
    sphere,
With craft of delight and with cunning of
    sound unsought,
That the heart of the hearer may smile if to
    pleasure his ear
    A roundel is wrought.

Its jewel of music is carven of all or of aught—
Love, laughter, or mourning—remembrance of
    rapture or fear—    6
That fancy may fashion to hang in the ear of
    thought.

As a bird's quick song runs round, and the
    hearts in us hear
Pause answer to pause, and again the same
    strain caught,
So moves the device whence, round as a pearl
    or tear,    10
    A roundel is wrought.

[1] This and the following poem are from *A Century of Roundels.* The roundel, or rondel, is a French lyric form having but two rimes. It commonly has fourteen lines, of which the first two are repeated as the seventh and eighth and as the thirteenth and fourteenth.

# Selected Victorian and Edwardian Poetry

The poets included in the pages immediately following represent nearly as wide a range of style and philosophy as could be imagined. Elizabeth Barrett Browning wrote in the manner of the Romantic poets; her subject-matter is love, treated with an intensity of feeling and a close personal involvement that is comparable to Shelley's in Adonais or Tennyson's in In Memoriam. She was one of the most popular poets of the century; though her husband's appeal and reputation have varied, her poems have consistently found a wide and devoted audience.

Gerard Manley Hopkins, on the other hand, wrote in the manner of the century he was not to live to see: his influence on twentieth-century poetry has been profound. His concern with form and structure, with process in art and in nature, and with the patterns and interactions of patterns in all that he saw points toward much of the best poetry written since the middle of the twentieth century in both England and America. However, he was unknown in his own century; his friend Robert Bridges retained all Hopkins' work until 1918 before publishing, nearly thirty years after the poet's death. By then both the general audience and the critics were more nearly ready to understand and appreciate Hopkins' "sprung rhythm," an echo from Anglo-Saxon verse, in which only the stressed syllables are counted, and there may be any number of unstressed syllables in the line. The term "sprung" Hopkins used to describe what happens or seems to happen when two stressed syllables occur together. In a letter to Bridges, Hopkins wrote:

Why do I employ sprung rhythm at all? Because it is the nearest to the rhythm of prose, that is the native and natural rhythm of speech, the least forced, the most rhetorical and emphatic of all possible rhythms, combining, as it seems to me, opposite and, one wd. have thought, incompatible excellences, markedness of rhythm—that is rhythm's self —and naturalness of expression.

Thus he made his style unique, clearly differentiated—and in style as well as subject-matter expressed his special "admiration for particular things."

Between Mrs. Browning's approach to poetry and Hopkins'—voices of the past and of the future—falls the poetry of George Meredith, Christina Rossetti, Thomas Hardy, William Ernest Henley, Oscar Wilde, Francis Thompson, A. E. Housman, Rudyard Kipling, and John Masefield. Closest to Mrs. Browning is Christina Rossetti, sister of Dante Gabriel Rossetti, whose poems show the intensity of her feeling as she is torn between her own warm humanity and an intense religious dedication.

Meredith and Hardy were both most noted as novelists. A situation is the foundation of many of their most characteristic poems: a man and woman are shown in tragic or ironic relationship, viewing their circumstances from opposed viewpoints. The moment of time described in the poem is a kind of novel in miniature, with both past and future plot implied. Meredith's philosophy is essentially naturalistic; he tried conscientiously to be objective, and his poetry is dominated by the same perfectionism that is apparent in his novels. Hardy is also a naturalist, blending Nature and Fate and a concept of a blighted universe with a deep pity for the suffering which he believes to be inevitable in human life.

Henley and Thompson are opposites in their philosophies. Henley was a rebel; Victorian beliefs, ways, attitudes, and art forms seemed to him superficial, conventional, stultifying. He spoke out for life, here and now; for the independent spirit; for reliance on self, tempered by pity but never by fear. Thompson, on the other hand, was moved by the deeply-felt need to rely on a power greater than self. "To be the poet of the return to Nature," he wrote, "is somewhat; but I would be the poet of the return to God."

*Wilde, the chief spokesman of "the yellow nineties" and their doctrine of "art for art's sake," was celebrated for many reasons: his eccentricity (he had lectured in America while dressed in knee pants and carrying a sunflower), his extremely successful plays (particularly* Lady Windermere's Fan *and* The Importance of Being Earnest*), and his sexual immorality (which made newspaper headlines and sent him to Reading Gaol). "The Ballad of Reading Gaol" is unique; Wilde produced it from the deepest agony of self-evaluation, and wrote nothing else approaching it in intensity or similar to it in subject.*

*Housman's poetry reminds us of Hardy's in tone and outlook. Housman believed that life was essentially a hopeless, humiliating experience, and what he believed to be the essential truth he expressed without compromise. His intense sincerity and the painstaking art with which it is joined give his best lyrics a finality and strength rare in modern writing.*

*When Kipling speaks of Browning's* Fra Lippo Lippi *as "a not too remote . . . ancestor of mine," he is acknowledging the desire to give a bold, unvarnished picture of the natural world which characterizes much of his own work. He combines with this desire the element which lies behind his great popularity in his own time: his ability to express, even to epitomize, the democratic and imperialistic ideals of the generation of Anglo-Saxons for which he wrote.*

*Masefield belongs in two worlds, the Edwardian and the modern. When* Salt-Water Ballads *was published in England in 1902, its realism seemed daring, and its approach original. But as Masefield continued to write, producing a long list of poems and novels of the sea, poems dealing with humble people (including* The Everlasting Mercy *and* Dauber, *his most effective long poems), and poems about fox-hunting and horse-racing, he came to represent the older generation of poets—a still-living voice from the past. Though it is not inevitable, as Yeats proved, it is certainly never surprising to see the modern Edwardian become in time the Edwardian modern.*

The standard edition of the poetry of Elizabeth Barrett Browning is The Complete Poems (London, 1904). There are many volumes of letters. Biographical studies include Elizabeth Barrett Browning: a Life, by Dorothy Hewlett (New York, 1952), and The Life of Elizabeth Barrett Browning, by Gardner B. Taplin (New Haven, 1957).

A *new edition of Meredith's poems would be desirable; an excellent edition of* Modern Love, *with an introduction by C. Day Lewis (London, 1948) is available, but for the other poems there is only* The Poetical Works of George Meredith, *with some notes by G. M. Trevelyan (London, 1912).* The Ordeal of George Meredith, *by Lionel Stevenson (New York, 1953), is a good biographical study; for criticism of his poetry, see "Meredith's Poetry,"* in Essays in Retrospect, *by C. B. Tinker (New Haven, 1948).*

The Poetical Works of Christina Georgina Rossetti, *with a memoir and notes by W. M. Rossetti (London, 1904), is a standard work. Two brief but excellent critical studies appeared in the same year:* Christina Georgina Rossetti, *by Eleanor Walter Thomas (New York, 1931), and* Christina Rossetti, *by Fredegond Shove (Cambridge, 1931). A full biographical study is* Christina Rossetti: a Portrait with Background, *by Marya Zaturenska (New York, 1949).*

Hardy's *Collected Poems (London, 1932) is standard; in addition, several volumes of selections have appeared. The many biographies include* Hardy of Wessex, *by Carl J. Weber (New York, 1940), and* Thomas Hardy, a Critical Biography, *by Evelyn Hardy (London, 1954). A valuable study of Hardy's philosophy is* On a Darkling Plain, *by Harvey Curtis Webster (Chicago, 1947). Studies of the poetry include* The Lyrical Poetry of Hardy, *by Sir M. Bowra (Nottingham, 1947), and* The Poetry of Hardy, *by J. G. Southworth (New York, 1947).*

W. H. Gardner *has edited both* The Poems of Gerard Manley Hopkins, *which reprints the first edition along with its prefaces and notes by Robert Bridges, and adds additional poems and notes (New York, 1956), and the excellent selection of poems and prose in the Penguin Poets series,* Gerard Manley Hopkins (London, 1953). *Three volumes of Hopkins' letters are available, and several biographical studies, including* Gerard Manley Hopkins, Priest and Poet, *by John Pick (London, 1942), and* Gerard Manley Hopkins: a Life, *by Eleanor Ruggles (New York, 1944). An interesting critical study is* Gerard Manley Hopkins: a Study of Poetic Idiosyncrasy in Relation to Poetic Tradition, *by W. H. Gardner (London, 1948–1949). There are two published symposia on Hopkins' work:* Immortal Diamond: Studies in Gerard Manley Hopkins, *edited by Norman Weyand, S. J., and Raymond Schoder, S. J. (New York, 1939), and* Gerard Manley Hopkins, *by the Kenyon Critics* (*Norfolk, Connecticut, 1945*).

The Works of W. E. Henley (*London, 1921*) *is standard. Studies include* W. E. Henley, a Memoir, *by Kennedy Williamson* (*London, 1930*); William Ernest Henley: a Study in the "Counter-Decadence" of the 'Nineties, *by Jerome Hamilton Buckley* (*Princeton, 1945*); *and* William Ernest Henley, *by* "J. Connell" (*London, 1949*).

*The best edition of Oscar Wilde is the* Works, *ed. G. F. Maine* (*London, 1948*). *The most useful of the many biographical studies is* Oscar Wilde, His Life and Wit, *by Hesketh Pearson* (*New York, 1946*). *For a critical interpretation of Wilde's work, see* Oscar Wilde, *by Arthur Ransome* (*London, 1913*).

*The standard edition of Thompson is* The Works of Francis Thompson, *ed. Wilfrid Meynell* (*London, 1913*). *A separate edition of the* Poems *is edited by T. L. Connolly* (*New York, 1941*). *The standard* Life of Francis Thompson *is that by Everard Meynell* (*London, 1926*). *The best study has been written by R. L. Mégroz,* Francis Thompson: the Poet of Earth in Heaven; a Study in Poetic Mysticism and the Evolution of Love-Poetry (*London, 1927*).

*The* Collected Poems of A. E. Housman (*London, 1953*) *is the standard edition. Biographical studies include* A. E. H.: Some Poems, Some Letters and a Personal Memoir by His Brother, *by Laurence Housman* (*London, 1937*); A. E. Housman, a Divided Life, *by George L. Watson* (*London, 1957*); *and* A. E. Housman: Man Behind a Mask, *by Maude M. Hawkins* (*Chicago, 1958*). *A valuable critical study is* Angry Dust: the Poetry of Housman, *by O. Robinson* (*Boston, 1950*).

*Kipling's* Complete Works in Prose and Verse (*London, 1937–39*), *the "Sussex Edition" in 35 volumes, is definitive. The best separate edition of the poems is* Rudyard Kipling's Verse, Inclusive Edition, 1885–1936 (*New York, 1940*). *T. S. Eliot has edited* A Choice of Kipling's Verse (*London, 1941*). *Kipling has supplied an interesting autobiographical fragment,* Something of Myself for My Friends Known and Unknown (*New York, 1937*); *the standard biography is* The Life of Rudyard Kipling, *by C. E. Carrington* (*New York, 1956*). *A brief but valuable interpretation appears in* Prophets and Poets, *by André Maurois* (*New York, 1935*). *A* Handbook to the Poetry of Rudyard Kipling, *by Ralph Durand* (*New York, 1914*), *is still useful.*

*Masefield's* Poems (*New York, 1953*) *is the standard edition. So Long To Learn* (*New York, 1952*) *includes the poet's autobiographical interpretation of his development.* John Masefield, *by Gilbert O. Thomas* (*London, 1932*), *is primarily biographical;* John Masefield, A Popular Study, *by W. H. Hamilton* (*London, 1925*) *is a critical summary.*

# ELIZABETH BARRETT BROWNING

## (1806–1861)

### *From* Sonnets from the Portuguese [1]

#### 1

I thought once how Theocritus had sung
Of the sweet years, the dear and wished-for
    years,
Who each one in a gracious hand appears
To bear a gift for mortals, old or young;
And, as I mused it in his antique tongue,   5
I saw, in gradual vision through my tears,
The sweet, sad years, the melancholy years,
Those of my own life, who by turns had flung
A shadow across me. Straightway I was 'ware,
So weeping, how a mystic Shape did move   10
Behind me, and drew me backward by the
    hair;
And a voice said in mastery, while I strove,—
"Guess now who holds thee?"—"Death," I
    said. But there,
The silver answer rang,—"Not Death, but
    Love."

#### 3

Unlike are we, unlike, O princely Heart!
Unlike our uses and our destinies.
Our ministering two angels look surprise
On one another, as they strike athwart
Their wings in passing. Thou, bethink thee, art
A guest for queens to social pageantries,   6
With gages from a hundred brighter eyes
Than tears even can make mine, to play thy
    part
Of chief musician. What hast *thou* to do
With looking from the lattice-lights at me,  10
A poor, tired, wandering singer, singing through
The dark, and leaning up a cypress tree?
The chrism is on thine head,—on mine, the
    dew,—
And Death must dig the level where these agree.

#### 4

Thou hast thy calling to some palace floor,
Most gracious singer of high poems! where

[1] Published 1850. Mrs. Browning felt that these sonnets were too personal to publish without disguise; so she pretended that they were translated from the Portuguese.

The dancers will break footing, from the care
Of watching up thy pregnant lips for more.
And dost thou lift this house's latch too poor
For hand of thine? and canst thou think and
    bear        6
To let thy music drop here unaware
In folds of golden fulness at my door?
Look up and see the casement broken in,
The bats and owlets builders in the roof!   10
My cricket chirps against thy mandolin.
Hush, call no echo up in further proof
Of desolation! there's a voice within
That weeps . . . as thou must sing . . .
    alone, aloof.

### 6

Go from me. Yet I feel that I shall stand
Henceforward in thy shadow. Nevermore
Alone upon the threshold of my door
Of individual life, I shall command
The uses of my soul, nor lift my hand    5
Serenely in the sunshine as before,
Without the sense of that which I forbore—
Thy touch upon the palm. The widest land
Doom takes to part us, leaves thy heart in mind
With pulses that beat double. What I do   10
And what I dream include thee, as the wine
Must taste of its own grapes. And when I sue
God for myself, He hears that name of thine,
And sees within my eyes the tears of two.

### 7

The face of all the world is changed, I think,
Since first I heard the footsteps of thy soul
Move still, oh, still, beside me, as they stole
Betwixt me and the dreadful outer brink    4
Of obvious death, where I, who thought to sink,
Was caught up into love, and taught the whole
Of life in a new rhythm. The cup of dole
God gave for baptism, I am fain to drink,
And praise its sweetness, Sweet, with thee anear.
The names of country, heaven, are changed
    away    10
For where thou art or shalt be, there or here;
And this . . . this lute and song . . . loved
    yesterday,
(The singing angels know) are only dear
Because thy name moves right in what they say.

### 14

If thou must love me, let it be for nought
Except for love's sake only. Do not say,
"I love her for her smile—her look—her way
Of speaking gently,—for a trick of thought
That falls in well with mine, and certes brought
A sense of pleasant ease on such a day"—   6
For these things in themselves, Belovéd, may
Be changed, or change for thee,—and love, so
    wrought,
May be unwrought so. Neither love me for
Thine own dear pity's wiping my cheeks dry,—
A creature might forget to weep, who bore   11
Thy comfort long, and lose thy love thereby!

But love me for love's sake, that evermore
Thou may'st love on, through love's eternity.

### 20

Belovéd, my Belovéd, when I think
That thou wast in the world a year ago,
What time I sat alone here in the snow
And saw no footprint, heard the silence sink
No moment at thy voice, but, link by link,   5
Went counting all my chains as if that so
They never could fall off at any blow
Struck by thy possible hand,—why, thus I drink
Of life's great cup of wonder! Wonderful,
Never to feel thee thrill the day or night   10
With personal act or speech,—nor ever cull
Some prescience of thee with the blossoms
    white
Thou sawest growing! Atheists are as dull,
Who cannot guess God's presence out of sight.

### 22

When our two souls stand up erect and strong,
Face to face, silent, drawing nigh and nigher,
Until the lengthening wings break into fire
At either curvéd point,—what bitter wrong
Can the earth do to us, that we should not
    long    5
Be here contented? Think. In mounting higher,
The angels would press on us and aspire
To drop some golden orb of perfect song
Into our deep, dear silence. Let us stay
Rather on earth, Belovéd,—where the unfit 10
Contrarious moods of men recoil away
And isolate pure spirits, and permit
A place to stand and love in for a day,
With darkness and the death-hour rounding it.

### 26

I lived with visions for my company,
Instead of men and women, years ago,
And found them gentle mates, nor thought to
    know
A sweeter music than they played to me.
But soon their trailing purple was not free   5
Of this world's dust, their lutes did silent grow,
And I myself grew faint and blind below
Their vanishing eyes. Then THOU didst come
    —to be,
Belovéd, what they seemed. Their shining
    fronts,
Their songs, their splendors (better, yet the
    same,   10
As river-water hallowed into fonts),
Met in thee, and from out thee overcame
My soul with satisfaction of all wants:
Because God's gifts put man's best dreams to
    shame.

### 35

If I leave all for thee, wilt thou exchange
And be all to me? Shall I never miss
Home-talk and blessing and the common kiss

That comes to each in turn, nor count it
    strange,
When I look up, to drop on a new range   5
Of walls and floors, another home than this?
Nay, wilt thou fill that place by me which is
Filled by dead eyes too tender to know change?
That's hardest. If to conquer love, has tried,
To conquer grief, tries more, as all things prove;
For grief indeed is love and grief beside.   11
Alas, I have grieved so I am hard to love.
Yet love me—wilt thou? Open thine heart wide,
And fold within the wet wings of thy dove.

### 43

How do I love thee? Let me count the ways.
I love thee to the depth and breadth and
    height
My soul can reach, when feeling out of sight
For the ends of Being and ideal Grace.
I love thee to the level of everyday's   5
Most quiet need, by sun and candlelight.
I love thee freely, as men strive for Right;
I love thee purely, as they turn from Praise.
I love thee with the passion put to use
In my old griefs, and with my childhood's faith.
I love thee with a love I seemed to lose   11
With my lost saints,—I love thee with the
    breath,
Smiles, tears, of all my life!—and, if God
    choose,
I shall but love thee better after death.

# GEORGE MEREDITH

## (1829–1909)

## *From* Modern Love [1]

### 1

By this he knew she wept with waking eyes:
That, at his hand's light quiver by her head,
The strange low sobs that shook their common
    bed
Were called into her with a sharp surprise,
And strangled mute, like little gaping snakes,
Dreadfully venomous to him. She lay   6
Stone-still, and the long darkness flowed away
With muffled pulses. Then, as midnight makes
Her giant heart of Memory and Tears
Drink the pale drug of silence, and so beat   10
Sleep's heavy measure, they from head to feet
Were moveless, looking through their dead
    black years,
By vain regret scrawled over the blank wall.
Like sculptured effigies they might be seen
Upon their marriage-tomb, the sword between;
Each wishing for the sword that severs all.   16

[1] Published 1862. The poem refers to the poet's
own unhappy marriage.

### 16

In our old shipwrecked days there was an hour,
When in the firelight steadily aglow,
Joined slackly, we beheld the red chasm grow
Among the clicking coals. Our library-bower
That eve was left to us: and hushed we sat   5
As lovers to whom Time is whispering.
From sudden-opened doors we heard them sing;
The nodding elders mixed good wine with chat.
Well knew we that Life's greatest treasure lay
With us, and of it was our talk, "Ah, yes!   10
Love dies!" I said: I never thought it less.
She yearned to me that sentence to unsay.
Then when the fire domed blackening, I found
Her cheek was salt against my kiss, and swift
Up the sharp scale of sobs her breast did
    lift:—   15
Now am I haunted by that taste! that sound!

### 17

At dinner, she is hostess, I am host.
Went the feast ever cheerfuller? She keeps
The Topic over intellectual deeps
In buoyancy afloat. They see no ghost.
With sparkling surface-eyes we ply the ball;   5
It is in truth a most contagious game:
HIDING THE SKELETON shall be its name.
Such play as this the devils might appall!
But here's the greater wonder: in that we,
Enamored of an acting naught can tire,   10
Each other, like true hypocrites, admire;
Warm-lighted looks, Love's ephemerioe,
Shoot gayly o'er the dishes and the wine.
We waken envy of our happy lot.
Fast, sweet, and golden, shows the marriage-
    knot.   15
Dear guests, you now have seen Love's corpse-
    light shine.

### 43

Mark where the pressing wind shoots javelin-
    like
Its skeleton shadow on the broad-backed wave!
Here is a fitting spot to dig Love's grave;
Here where the ponderous breakers plunge and
    strike,
And dart their hissing tongues high up the sand:
In hearing of the ocean, and in sight   6
Of those ribbed wind-streaks running into
    white.
If I the death of Love had deeply planned,
I never could have made it half so sure,
As by the unblest kisses which upbraid   10
The full-waked senses; or failing that, degrade!
'Tis morning: but no morning can restore
What we have forfeited. I see no sin:
The wrong is mixed. In tragic life, God wot,
No villain need be! Passions spin the plot:   15
We are betrayed by what is false within.

### 47

We saw the swallows gathering in the sky,
And in the osier-isle we heard them noise.
We had not to look back on summer joys,
Or forward to a summer of bright dye:
But in the largeness of the evening earth   5
Our spirits grew as we went side by side.
The hour became her husband and my bride.
Love, that had robbed us so, thus blessed our
    dearth!
The pilgrims of the year waxed very loud
In multitudinous chatterings, as the flood   10
Full brown came from the West, and like pale
    blood
Expanded to the upper crimson cloud.
Love, that had robbed us of immortal things,
This little moment mercifully gave,
Where I have seen across the twilight wave 15
The swan sail with her young beneath her wings.

### 50

Thus piteously Love closed what he begat:
The union of this ever-diverse pair!
These two were rapid falcons in a snare,
Condemned to do the flitting of the bat.
Lovers beneath the singing sky of May,   5
They wandered once; clear as the dew on flow-
    ers:
But they fed not on the advancing hours:
Their hearts held cravings for the buried day.
Then each applied to each that fatal knife,
Deep questioning, which probes to endless
    dole.   10
Ah, what a dusty answer gets the soul
When hot for certainties in this our life!—
In tragic hints here see what evermore
Moves dark as yonder midnight ocean's force,
Thundering like ramping hosts of warrior horse,
To throw that faint thin line upon the shore! 16

# CHRISTINA GEORGINA
# ROSSETTI

## (1830–1894)
## Song [1]

When I am dead, my dearest,
  Sing no sad songs for me;
Plant thou no roses at my head,
  Nor shady cypress tree:
Be the green grass above me   5
  With showers and dewdrops wet;
And if thou wilt, remember,
  And if thou wilt, forget.

I shall not see the shadows,
  I shall not feel the rain;   10
I shall not hear the nightingale

[1] Published 1862; written 12 December, 1848.

Sing on as if in pain:
And dreaming through the twilight
  That doth not rise nor set,
Haply I may remember,   15
  And haply may forget.

## A Better Resurrection [2]

I have no wit, no words, no tears;
  My heart within me like a stone
Is numbed too much for hopes or fears.
  Look right, look left, I dwell alone;
I lift mine eyes, but dimmed with grief   5
  No everlasting hills I see;
My life is in the falling leaf;
  O Jesus, quicken me.

My life is like a faded leaf,
  My harvest dwindled to a husk;   10
Truly my life is void and brief
  And tedious in the barren dusk;
My life is like a frozen thing,
  No bud nor greenness can I see;
Yet rise it shall—the sap of Spring;   15
  O Jesus, rise in me.

My life is like a broken bowl,
  A broken bowl that cannot hold
One drop of water for my soul
  Or cordial in the searching cold;   20
Cast in the fire the perished thing;
  Melt and remold it, till it be
A royal cup for Him, my King;
  O Jesus, drink of me.

## A Birthday [3]

My heart is like a singing bird
  Whose nest is in a watered shoot;
My heart is like an apple-tree
  Whose boughs are bent with thickset fruit;
My heart is like a rainbow shell   5
  That paddles in a halcyon sea;
My heart is gladder than all these
  Because my love is come to me.

Raise me a dais of silk and down;
  Hang it with vair and purple dyes;   10
Carve it in doves, and pomegranates,
  And peacocks with a hundred eyes;
Work it in gold and silver grapes,
  In leaves and silver fleurs-de-lys;
Because the birthday of my life   15
  Is come, my love is come to me.

## Life and Death [4]

Life is not sweet. One day it will be sweet
  To shut our eyes and die;
Nor feel the wild flowers blow, nor birds dart by

[2] Published 1862; written 30 June, 1857.
[3] Published 1861; written 18 November, 1857.
[4] Published 1866; written 24 April, 1863.

With flitting butterfly,
Nor grass grow long above our heads and feet,
Nor hear the happy lark that soars sky-high,   6
Nor sigh that spring is fleet and summer fleet,
  Nor mark the waxing wheat,
Nor know who sits in our accustomed seat.

Life is not good. One day it will be good   10
  To die, then live again;
To sleep meanwhile; so, not to feel the wane
Of shrunk leaves dropping in the wood,
Nor hear the foamy lashing of the main,
Nor mark the blackened bean-fields, nor where
    stood                                       15
  Rich ranks of golden grain,
Only dead refuse stubble clothe the plain:
  Asleep from risk, asleep from pain.

## Sleeping at Last [5]

Sleeping at last, the trouble and tumult over,
  Sleeping at last, the struggle and horror past,
Cold and white, out of sight of friend and of
    lover,
    Sleeping at last.

No more a tired heart downcast or overcast,
No more pangs that wring or shifting fears that
    hover,                                       6
Sleeping at last in a dreamless sleep locked
    fast.

Fast asleep. Singing birds in their leafy cover
  Cannot wake her, nor shake her the gusty
    blast.
Under the purple thyme and the purple clover
  Sleeping at last.                              11

# THOMAS HARDY
## (1840–1928)
## Hap [1]

If but some vengeful god would call to me
From up the sky, and laugh: "Thou suffering
    thing,
Know that thy sorrow is my ecstasy,
That thy love's loss is my hate's profiting!"

Then would I bear it, clench myself, and die,
Steeled by the sense of ire unmerited;          6
Half-ease in that a Powerfuller than I
Had willed and meted me the tears I shed.

But not so. How arrives it joy lies slain,
And why unblooms the best hope ever sown?

[5] Published 1896; written about 1893.
[1] The following poems are reprinted with the permission of The Macmillan Company. *Hap* and the two following pieces are from *Wessex Poems and Other Verses* (1898).

—Crass Casualty obstructs the sun and rain,
And dicing Time for gladness casts a
    moan. . . .                                  12
These purblind Doomsters had as readily
    strown
Blisses about my pilgrimage as pain.

## Nature's Questioning

When I look forth at dawning, pool,
  Field, flock, and lonely tree,
  All seem to gaze at me
Like chastened children sitting silent in a
    school;

Their faces dulled, constrained, and worn, [5]
  As though the master's ways
  Through the long teaching days
Had cowed them till their early zest was
    overborne.

Upon them stirs in lippings mere
  (As if once clear in call,                     10
  But now scarce breathed at all)—
"We wonder, ever wonder, why we find us
    here!

"Has some Vast Imbecility,
  Mighty to build and blend,
  But impotent to tend,                          15
Framed us in jest, and left us now to hazardry?

"Or come we of an Automaton
  Unconscious of our pains? . . .
  Or are we live remains
Of Godhead dying downwards, brain and eye
    now gone?                                    20

"Or is it that some high Plan betides,
  As yet not understood,
  Of Evil stormed by Good,
We the Forlorn Hope over which Achievement
    strides?"

Thus things around. No answerer I. . . .
  Meanwhile the winds, and rains,               26
  And Earth's old glooms and pains
Are still the same, and Life and Death are
    neighbors nigh.

## The Slow Nature
### (An Incident of Froom Valley)

"Thy husband—poor, poor Heart!—is dead!
  Dead, out by Moreford Rise;
A bull escaped the barton-shed,[2]
  Gored him, and there he lies!"

—"Ha, ha—go away! 'Tis a tale, methink,   [5]
  Thou joker Kit!" laughed she.
"I've known thee many a year, Kit Twink,
  And ever hast thou fooled me!"

[2] Farmyard-shed.

—"But, Mistress Damon—I can swear
   Thy goodman John is dead!       10
And soon th'lt hear their feet who bear
   His body to his bed."

So unwontedly sad was the merry man's face—
   That face which had long deceived—
That she gazed and gazed; and then could
     trace              15
   The truth there; and she believed.
She laid a hand on the dresser-ledge,
   And scanned far Egdon-side;
And stood; and you heard the wind-swept sedge
   And the rippling Froom; till she cried:  20

"O my chamber's untidied, unmade my bed,
   Though the day has begun to wear!
'What a slovenly hussif!'[3] it will be said,
   When they all go up my stair!"

She disappeared; and the joker stood    25
   Depressed by his neighbor's doom,
And amazed that a wife struck to widowhood
   Thought first of her unkempt room.

But a fortnight thence she could take no food,
   And she pined in a slow decay;    30
While Kit soon lost his mournful mood
   And laughed in his ancient way.

## God-Forgotten [4]

I towered far, and lo! I stood within
   The presence of the Lord Most High,
Sent thither by the sons of Earth, to win
   Some answer to their cry.

—"The Earth, sayest thou? The Human
     race?          5
   By Me created? Sad its lot?
Nay: I have no remembrance of such place:
   Such world I fashioned not."—

—"O Lord, forgive me when I say
   Thou spakest the word that made it all."—
"The Earth of men—let me bethink me . . .
     Yea!         11
   I dimly do recall

"Some tiny sphere I built long back
   (Mid millions of such shapes of mine)
So named . . . It perished, surely—not a
     wrack        15
   Remaining, or a sign?

"It lost my interest from the first,
   My aims therefore succeeding ill;
Haply it died of doing as it durst?"—
     "Lord, it existeth still."    20

[3] Housewife.
[4] This and the following two pieces are from
*Poems of the Past and the Present* (1901).

"Dark, then, its life! For not a cry
   Of aught it bears do I now hear;
Of its own act the threads were snapped whereby
   Its plaints had reached mine ear.

"It used to ask for gifts of good,    25
   Till came its severance, self-entailed,
When sudden silence on that side ensued,
   And has till now prevailed.

"All other orbs have kept in touch;
   Their voicings reach me speedily:   30
Thy people took upon them overmuch
   In sundering them from me!

"And it is strange—though sad enough—
   Earth's race should think that one whose call
Frames, daily, shining spheres of flawless
     stuff       35
   Must heed their tainted ball! . . .

"But sayest it is by pangs distraught,
   And strife, and silent suffering?—
Sore grieved am I that injury should be wrought
   Even on so poor a thing!    40

"Thou shouldst have learned that *Not to
     Mend*
For Me could mean but *Not to Know:*
Hence, Messengers! and straightway put an end
   To what men undergo." . . .

Homing at dawn, I thought to see    45
   One of the Messengers standing by.
—Oh, childish thought! . . . Yet often it
     comes to me
   When trouble hovers nigh.

## On a Fine Morning

Whence comes Solace?—Not from seeing
What is doing, suffering, being,
Not from noting Life's conditions,
Nor from heeding Time's monitions;
   But in cleaving to the Dream,    5
   And in gazing at the gleam
   Whereby gray things golden seem.

Thus do I this heyday, holding
Shadows but as lights unfolding,
As no specious show this moment    10
With its iris-hued embowment;
   But as nothing other than
   Part of a benignant plan;
   Proof that earth was made for man.

## The Well-Beloved

I went by star and planet shine
   Towards the dear one's home
At Kingsbere, there to make her mine
   When the next sun upclomb.

I edged the ancient hill and wood 5
  Beside the Ikling Way,
Nigh where the Pagan temple stood
  In the world's earlier day.

And as I quick and quicker walked
  On gravel and on green, 10
I sang to sky, and tree, or talked
  Of her I called my queen.

—"O faultless is her dainty form,
  And luminous her mind;
She is the God-created norm 15
  Of perfect womankind!"

A shape whereon one star-blink gleamed
  Slid softly by my side,
A woman's; and her motion seemed
  The motion of my bride. 20

And yet methought she'd drawn erstwhile
  Out from the ancient leaze,[5]
Where once were pile and peristyle
  For men's idolatries.

—"O maiden lithe and lone, what may 25
  Thy name and lineage be
Who so resemblest by this ray
  My darling?—Art thou she?"

The Shape: "Thy bride remains within
  Her father's grange and grove." 30
—"Thou speakest rightly," I broke in,
  "Thou art not she I love."

—"Nay: though thy bride remains inside
  Her father's walls," said she,
"The one most dear is with thee here, 35
  For thou dost love but me."

Then I: "But she, my only choice,
  Is now at Kingsbere Grove?"
Again her soft mysterious voice:
  "I am thy only Love." 40

Thus still she vouched, and still I said,
  "O sprite, that cannot be!" . . .
It was as if my bosom bled,
  So much she troubled me.

The sprite resumed: "Thou hast transferred
  To her dull form awhile 46
My beauty, fame, and deed, and word,
  My gestures and my smile.

"O fatuous man, this truth infer,
  Brides are not what they seem; 50
Thou lovest what thou dreamest her;
  I am thy very dream!"

—"O then," I answered miserably,
  Speaking as scarce I knew,
[5] Meadow-land, or common.

"My loved one, I must wed with thee 55
  If what thou sayest be true!"

She, proudly, thinning in the gloom:
  "Though, since troth-plight began,
I have ever stood as bride to groom,
  I wed no mortal man!" 60

Thereat she vanished by the lane
  Adjoining Kingsbere town,
Near where, men say, once stood the Fane
  To Venus, on the Down.

—When I arrived and met my bride 65
  Her look was pinched and thin,
As if her soul had shrunk and died,
  And left a waste within.

# The Curate's Kindness [6]

### A Workhouse Irony

### I

I thought they'd be strangers aroun' me,
  But she's to be there!
Let me jump out o' wagon and go back and
    drown me
  At Pummery or Ten-Hatches Weir.

### II

I thought: "Well, I've come to the Union— 5
  The workhouse at last—
After honest hard work all the week, and Com-
    munion
  O' Zundays, these fifty years past.

### III

" 'Tis hard; but," I thought, "never mind it:
  There's gain in the end: 10
And when I get used to the place I shall find it
  A home, and may find there a friend.

### IV

"Life there will be better than t'other,
  For peace is assured.
*The men in one wing and their wives in an-*
    *other* 15
  Is strictly the rule of the Board."

### V

Just then one young Pa'son arriving
  Steps up out of breath
To the side o' the wagon wherein we were
    driving
  To Union; and calls out and saith: 20

### VI

"Old folks, that harsh order is altered,
  Be not sick of heart!

[6] This and the following five poems are from
*Time's Laughingstocks and Other Verses* (1909).

The Guardians they poohed and they pished
and they paltered
When urged not to keep you apart.

### VII

" 'It is wrong,' I maintained, 'to divide them,
Near forty years wed.'                    26
'Very well, sir. We promised, then, they shall
abide them
In one wing together,' they said."

### VIII

Then I sank—knew 'twas quite a foredone
thing
That misery should be                    30
To the end! . . . . To get freed of her there
was the one thing
Had made the change welcome to me.

### IX

To go there was ending but badly;
'Twas shame and 'twas pain;
"But anyhow," thought I, "thereby I shall
gladly                                    35
Get free of this forty years' chain."

### X

I thought they'd be strangers aroun' me,
But she's to be there!
Let me jump out o' wagon and go back and
drown me
At Pummery or Ten-Hatches Weir.          40

## The Dawn After the Dance

Here is your parents' dwelling with its curtained windows telling
Of no thought of us within it or of our arrival
here;
Their slumbers have been normal after one day
more of formal
Matrimonial commonplace and household life's
mechanic gear.

I would be candid willingly, but dawn draws
on so chillingly                          5
As to render further cheerlessness intolerable
now,
So I will not stand endeavoring to declare a day
for severing,
But will clasp you just as always—just the
olden love avow.

Through serene and surly weather we have
walked the ways together,
And this long night's dance this year's end eve
now finishes the spell;                   10
Yet we dreamed us but beginning a sweet
sempiternal spinning
Of a cord we have spun to breaking—too in-
temperately, too well.

Yes; last night we danced I know, Dear, as we
did that year ago, Dear,
When a new strange bond between our days
was formed, and felt, and heard;
Would that dancing were the worst thing
from the latest to the first thing         15
That the faded year can charge us with; but
what avails a word!

That which makes man's love the lighter and
the woman's burn no brighter
Came to pass with us inevitably while slipped
the shortening year. . . . .
And there stands your father's dwelling with
its blind bleak windows telling
That the vows of man and maid are frail as
filmy gossamere.                          20

## Misconception

I busied myself to find a sure
Snug hermitage
That should preserve my Love secure
From the world's rage;
Where no unseemly saturnals,[7]           5
Or strident traffic-roars,
Or hum of intervolved cabals
Should echo at her doors.

I labored that the diurnal spin
Of vanities                              10
Should not contrive to suck her in
By dark degrees,
And cunningly operate to blur
Sweet teachings I had begun,
And then I went full-heart to her         15
To expound the glad deeds done.

She looked at me, and said thereto
With a pitying smile,
"And *this* is what has busied you
So long a while?                          20
O poor exhausted one, I see
You have worn you old and thin
For naught! Those moils you fear for me
I find most pleasure in!"

## The Homecoming

*Gruffly growled the wind on Toller downland*
*broad and bare,*
*And lonesome was the house, and dark; and*
*few came there.*

"Now don't ye rub your eyes so red; we're
home and have no cares;
Here's a skimmer-cake for supper, peckled
onions, and some pears;
I've got a little keg o' summat strong, too, under stairs:                               5

[7] Periods of unrestrained license and revelry (from
the Roman holiday of Saturn, held in December).

—What, slight your husband's victuals? Other
    brides can tackle theirs!"

*The wind of winter mooed and mouthed their*
    *chimney like a horn,*
*And round the house and past the house 'twas*
    *leafless and lorn,*

"But my dear and tender poppet,[8] then, how
    came ye to agree
In Ivel church this morning? Sure, there-right
    you married me!"                                  10
—"Hoo-hoo!—I don't know—I forgot how
    strange and far 'twould be,
An' I wish I was at home again with dear dad-
    dee!"

*Gruffly growled the wind on Toller downland*
    *broad and bare,*
*And lonesome was the house and dark; and*
    *few came there.*

"I didn't think such furniture as this was all
    you'd own,                                        15
And great black beams for ceiling, and a floor
    o' wretched stone,
And nasty pewter platters, horrid forks of steel
    and bone,
And a monstrous crock in chimney. 'Twas to
    me quite unbeknown!"

*Rattle rattle went the door; down flapped a*
    *cloud of smoke,*
*As shifting north the wicked wind assayed a*
    *smarter stroke.*                                 20

"Now sit ye by the fire, poppet; put yourself
    at ease:
And keep your little thumb out of your mouth,
    dear, please!
And I'll sing to 'ee a pretty song of lovely flow-
    ers and bees,
And happy lovers taking walks within a grove
    o' trees."

*Gruffly growled the wind on Toller Down, so*
    *bleak and bare,*                                 25
*And lonesome was the house, and dark; and*
    *few came there.*

"Now, don't ye gnaw your handkercher; 'twill
    hurt your little tongue,
And if you do feel spitish, 'tis because ye are
    over young;
But you'll be getting older, like us all, ere
    very long,
And you'll see me as I am—a man who never
    did 'ee wrong."                                   30

*Straight from Whit'sheet Hill to Benvill Lane*
    *the blusters pass,*

[8] Doll; dainty person; darling.

*Hitting hedges, milestones, handposts, trees,*
    *and tufts of grass.*

"Well, had I only known, my dear, that this
    was how you'd be,
I'd have married her of riper years that was so
    fond of me.
But since I can't, I've half a mind to run
    away to sea,                                      35
And leave 'ee to go barefoot to your d——d
    daddee!"

*Up one wall and down the other—past each*
    *window-pane—*
*Prance the gusts, and then away down Crim-*
    *mercrock's long lane.*

"I—I—don't know what to say to 't, since
    your wife I've vowed to be;
And as 'tis done, I s'pose here I must bide—
    poor me!                                          40
Aye—as you are ki-ki-kind, I'll try to live along
    with 'ee,
Although I'd fain have stayed at home with
    dear daddee!"

*Gruffly growled the wind on Toller Down, so*
    *bleak and bare,*
*And lonesome was the house and dark; and*
    *few came there.*

"That's right, my Heart! And though on
    haunted Toller Down we be,                        45
And the wind swears things in chimley, we'll to
    supper merrily!
So don't ye tap your shoe so pettish-like; but
    smile at me,
And ye'll soon forget to sock and sigh for dear
    daddee!"

## To Sincerity

O sweet sincerity!—
Where modern methods be
What scope for thine and thee?

Life may be sad past saying,
Its greens for ever graying,                          5
Its faiths to dust decaying;

And youth may have foreknown it,
And riper seasons shown it,
But custom cries: "Disown it:

"Say ye rejoice, though grieving,                     10
Believe, while unbelieving,
Behold, without perceiving!"

—Yet, would men look at true things,
And unilluded view things,
And count to bear undue things,                       15

The real might mend the seeming,
Facts better their foredeeming,
And Life its disesteeming.

## George Meredith

### (1828–1909)

Forty years back, when much had place
That since has perished out of mind,
I heard that voice and saw that face.

He spoke as one afoot will wind
A morning horn ere men awake;                        5
His note was trenchant, turning kind.

He was of those whose wit can shake
And riddle to the very core
The counterfeits that Time will break . . .

Of late, when we two met once more,                  10
The luminous countenance and rare
Shone just as forty years before.

So that, when now all tongues declare
His shape unseen by his green hill,[9]
I scarce believe he sits not there.                  15

No matter. Further and further still
Through the world's vaporous vitiate air
His words wing on—as live words will.

## The Face at the Casement [10]

If ever joy leave
An abiding sting of sorrow,
So befell it on the morrow
Of that May eve. . . .

The traveled sun dropped                             5
To the north-west, low and lower,
The pony's trot grew slower,
Until we stopped.

"This cozy house just by
I must call at for a minute,                          10
A sick man lies within it
Who soon will die.

"He wished to—marry me,
So I am bound, when I drive near him,
To inquire, if but to cheer him,                     15
How he may be."

A message was sent in,
And wordlessly we waited,
Till someone came and stated
The bulletin.                                        20

And that the sufferer said,
For her call no words could thank her;

[9] Box Hill, Surrey, where his home was.
[10] This and the following three poems are from
*Satires of Circumstance. Lyrics and Reveries* (1914).

As his angel he must rank her
Till life's spark fled.

Slowly we drove away,                                25
When I turned my head, although not
Called to: why I turned I know not
Even to this day:

And lo, there in my view
Pressed against an upper lattice                     30
Was a white face, gazing at us
As we withdrew.

And well did I divine
It to be the man's there dying,
Who but lately had been sighing                      35
For her pledged mine.

Then I deigned a deed of hell;
It was done before I knew it;
What devil made me do it
I cannot tell!                                       40

Yes, while he gazed above,
I put my arm about her
That he might see, nor doubt her
My plighted Love.

The pale face vanished quick,                        45
As if blasted, from the casement,
And my shame and self-abasement
Began their prick.

And they prick on, ceaselessly,
For that stab in Love's fierce fashion               50
Which, unfired by lover's passion,
Was foreign to me.

She smiled at my caress,
But why came the soft embowment
Of her shoulder at that moment                       55
She did not guess.

Long long years has he lain
In thy garth,[11] O sad Saint Cleather:
What tears there, bared to weather,
Will cleanse that stain!                             60

Love is long-suffering,
Sweet, prompt, precious as a jewel;
But jealousy is cruel,
Cruel as the grave!

## Lost Love

I play my sweet old airs—
The airs he knew
When our love was true—
But he does not balk
His determined walk,                                 5
And passes up the stairs.

[11] Yard.

I sing my songs once more,
  And presently hear
  His footstep near
  As if it would stay;          10
  But he goes his way,
And shuts a distant door.

So I wait for another morn,
  And another night
  In this soul-sick blight;        15
  And I wonder much
  As I sit, why such
A woman as I was born!

## Ah, Are You Digging on My Grave?

"Ah, are you digging on my grave
  My loved one?—planting rue?"
—"No: yesterday he went to wed
One of the brightest wealth has bred.
It cannot hurt her now, he said,    5
  'That I should not be true.' "

"Then who is digging on my grave?
  My nearest dearest kin?"
—"Ah, no: they sit and think, 'What use!
What good will planting flowers produce?  10
No tendance of her mound can loose
  Her spirit from Death's gin.' "

"But someone digs upon my grave?
  My enemy?—prodding sly?"
—"Nay: when she heard you had passed the
    Gate        15
That shuts on all flesh soon or late,
She thought you no more worth her hate,
  And cares not where you lie."

"Then, who is digging on my grave?
  Say—since I have not guessed!"    20
—"Oh it is I, my mistress dear,
Your little dog, who still lives near,
And much I hope my movements here
  Have not disturbed your rest?"

"Ah, yes! *You* dig upon my grave . . .    25
  Why flashed it not on me
That one true heart was left behind!
What feeling do we ever find
To equal among human kind
  A dog's fidelity!"    30

"Mistress, I dug upon your grave
  To bury a bone, in case
I should be hungry near this spot
When passing on my daily trot.
I am sorry, but I quite forgot    35
  It was your resting-place."

## The Sweet Hussy

In his early days he was quite surprised
When she told him she was compromised

By meetings and lingerings at his whim,
And thinking not of herself but him;
While she lifted orbs aggrieved and round    5
That scandal should so soon abound
(As she had raised them to nine or ten
Of antecedent nice young men):
And in remorse he thought with a sigh,
How good she is, and how bad am I!—    10
It was years before he understood
That she was the wicked one—he the good.

## You Were the Sort That Men Forget [12]

You were the sort that men forget;
  Though I—not yet!—
Perhaps not ever. Your slighted weakness
  Adds to the strength of my regret!

You'd not the art—you never had    5
  For good or bad—
To make men see how sweet your meaning,
  Which, visible, had charmed them glad.

You would, by words inept let fall,
  Offend them all,    10
Even if they saw your warm devotion
  Would hold your life's blood at their call.

You lacked the eye to understand
  Those friends offhand
Whose mode was crude, though whose dim
    purport    15
  Outpriced the courtesies of the bland.

I am now the only being who
  Remembers you
It may be. What a waste that Nature
  Grudged soul so dear the art its due!    20

## To the Moon

"What have you looked at, Moon,
  In your time,
Now long past your prime?"
"O, I have looked at, often looked at
  Sweet, sublime,    5
Sore things, shudderful, night and noon
  In my time."

"What have you mused on, Moon,
  In your day,
So aloof, so far away?"    10
"O, I have mused on, often mused on
  Growth, decay,
Nations alive, dead, mad, aswoon,
  In my day!"

"Have you much wondered, Moon,    15
  On your rounds,

[12] This and the following poems are from *Moments of Vision and Miscellaneous Verses* (1918).

Self-wrapt, beyond Earth's bounds?"
"Yea, I have wondered, often wondered
    At the sounds
Reaching me of the human tune      **20**
    On my rounds."

"What do you think of it, Moon,
    As you go?
Is Life much or no?"
"O I think of it, often think of it
    As a show
God ought surely to shut up soon,
    As I go."

## Life Laughs Onward

Rambling I looked for an old abode
Where, years back, one had lived I knew;
Its site a dwelling duly showed,
    But it was new.

I went where, not so long ago,      **5**
The sod had riven two breasts asunder;
Daisies throve gayly there, as though
    No grave were under.

I walked along a terrace where
Loud children gamboled in the sun;    **10**
The figure that had once sat there
    Was missed by none.

Life laughed and moved on unsubdued,
I saw that Old succumbed to Young:
'Twas well. My too regretful mood   **15**
    Died on my tongue.

# GERARD MANLEY HOPKINS

## (1844–1889)

## God's Grandeur [1]

The world is charged with the grandeur of God.
    It will flame out, like shining from shook
      foil;
    It gathers to a greatness, like the ooze of oil
Crushed. Why do men then now not reck his
    rod?

Generations have trod, have trod, have trod;   **5**
    And all is seared with trade; bleared, smeared
    with toil;

[1] Published in 1918; written in 1877. Hopkins refers to gold foil in the second line, explaining that "shaken goldfoil gives off broad glares like sheet lightning and also . . . a sort of fork lightning too." This and the following seven poems are from *The Poems of Gerard Manley Hopkins*, Third Edition 1948. Reprinted by permission of Oxford University Press.

And wears man's smudge and shares man's
    smell: the soil
Is bare now, nor can foot feel, being shod.

And for all this, nature is never spent;
    There lives the dearest freshness deep down
      things;     **10**
And though the last lights off the black West
    went
    Oh, morning, at the brown brink eastward,
      springs—
Because the Holy Ghost over the bent
    World broods with warm breast and with ah!
      bright wings.

## The Windhover: [2]

### To Christ our Lord

I caught this morning morning's minion, king-
    dom of daylight's dauphin, dapple-dawn-
    drawn Falcon, in his riding
    Of the rolling level underneath him steady
    air, and striding
High there, how he rung upon the rein of a
    wimpling wing
In his ecstasy! then off, off forth on swing,
    As a skate's heel sweeps smooth on a bow-
    bend; the hurl and gliding     **5**
    Rebuffed the big wind. My heart in hiding
Stirred for a bird,—the achieve of, the mastery
    of the thing!

Brute beauty and valor and act, oh, air, pride,
    plume, here
Buckle! AND the fire that breaks from thee
    then, a billion
Times told lovelier, more dangerous, O my
    chevalier!     **10**

No wonder of it: sheer plod makes plough
    down sillion
Shine, and blue-bleak embers, ah my dear,
    Fall, gall themselves, and gash gold-ver-
    milion.

## Pied Beauty [3]

Glory be to God for dappled things—
    For skies of couple-color as a brinded cow;
      For rose-moles all in stipple upon trout
      that swim;
Fresh-firecoal chestnut-falls; finches' wings;
    Landscape plotted and pieced—fold, fallow,
    and plow;     **5**
      And all trades, their gear and tackle and
      trim.

[2] Published in 1918; written 30 May, 1877. Hopkins described "The Windhover" as "the best thing I ever wrote." For citations of explications of the poem see *The Cambridge Bibliography of English Literature.*

[3] Published 1918; written summer, 1877.

All things counter, original, spare, strange;
    Whatever is fickle, freckled (who knows
        how?)
    With swift, slow; sweet, sour; adazzle, dim;
He fathers-forth whose beauty is past change: 10
    Praise him.

## Binsey Poplars [4]

My aspens dear, whose airy cages quelled,
Quelled or quenched in leaves the leaping sun,
Are felled, felled, are all felled;
    Of a fresh and following folded rank
        Not spared, not one    5
        That dandled a sandalled
        Shadow that swam or sank
On meadow and river and wind-wandering
    weed-winding bank.

O if we but knew what we do
        When we delve or hew—    10
Hack and rack the growing green!
        Since country is so tender
    To touch, her being so slender,
    That, like this sleek and seeing ball
    But a prick will make no eye at all,    15
    Where we, even where we mean
        To mend her we end her,
        When we hew or delve:
After-comers cannot guess the beauty been.
    Ten or twelve, only ten or twelve    20
        Stroke of havoc unselve
        The sweet especial scene,
        Rural scene, a rural scene,
        Sweet especial rural scene.

## Spring and Fall: [5]

### *To a Young Child*

Márgarét, are you gríeving
Over Goldengrove unleaving?
Leáves, líke the things of man, you
With your fresh thoughts care for, can you?
Áh! ás the heart grows older    5
It will come to such sights colder
By and by, nor spare a sigh
Though worlds of wanwood leafmeal lie;
And yet you wíll weep and know why.
Now no matter, child, the name:    10
Sórrow's spríngs áre the same.
Nor mouth had, no nor mind, expressed
What heart heard of, ghost guessed:
It ís the blight man was born for,
It is Margaret you mourn for.    15

## As Kingfishers Catch Fire [6]

As kingfishers catch fire, dragonflies draw flame;
As tumbled over rim in roundy wells

[4] Published 1918; written March, 1879.
[5] Published 1918; written 7 September, 1880.
[6] Published 1918. Probably written early in 1882.

Stones ring; like each tucked string tells, each
    hung bell's
Bow swung finds tongue to fling out broad its
    name;
Each mortal thing does one thing and the
    same:    5
Deals out that being indoors each one dwells;
Selves—goes itself; *myself* it speaks and spells,
Crying *What I do is me: for that I came.*

I say more: the just man justices;
Keeps grace: that keeps all his goings graces; 10
Acts in God's eye what in God's eye he is—
Christ—for Christ plays in ten thousand
    places,
Lovely in limbs, and lovely in eyes not his
To the Father through the features of men's
    faces.

## Inversnaid [7]

This darksome burn, horseback brown,
His rollrock highroad roaring down,
In coop and in comb the fleece of his foam
Flutes and low to the lake falls home.

A windpuff-bonnet of fáwn-fróth    5
Turns and twindles over the broth
Of a pool so pitchblack, féll-frówning,
It rounds and rounds Despair to drowning.

Degged with dew, dappled with dew
Are the groins of the braes that the brook
    treads through,    10
Wiry heathpacks, flitches of fern,
And the beadbonny ash that sits over the burn.

What would the world be, once bereft
Of wet and of wildness? Let them be left,
O let them be left, wildness and wet;    15
Long live the weeds and the wilderness yet.

## I Wake and Feel the Fell of Dark [8]

I wake and feel the fell of dark, not day.
What hours, O what black hours we have spent
This night! What sights you, heart, saw; ways
    you went!
And more must, in yet longer light's delay.
    With witness I speak this. But where I say    5
Hours I mean years, mean life. And my lament
Is cries countless, cries like dead letters sent
To dearest him that lives alas! away.

    I am gall, I am heartburn. God's most deep
    decree
Bitter would have me taste: my taste was me; 10
Bones built in me, flesh filled, blood brimmed
    the curse.

[7] Published 1918; written September, 1881.
[8] Published 1918; written 1885.

Selfyeast of spirit a dull dough sours. I see
The lost are like this, and their scourge to be
As I am mine, their sweating selves; but worse.

# WILLIAM ERNEST HENLEY

## (1849–1903)

### *From* In Hospital [1]

#### 1

#### *Enter Patient*

The morning mists still haunt the stony street;
The northern summer air is shrill and cold;
And lo, the Hospital, gray, quiet, old,
Where Life and Death like friendly chafferers meet.
Thro' the loud spaciousness and draughty gloom　　5
A small, strange child—so agéd yet so young!—
Her little arm besplinted and beslung,
Precedes me gravely to the waiting-room.
I limp behind, my confidence all gone.
The gray-haired soldier-porter waves me on, 10
And on I crawl, and still my spirits fail:
A tragic meanness seems so to environ
These corridors and stairs of stone and iron,
Cold, naked, clean—half-workhouse and half-jail.

#### 4

#### *Before*

Behold me waiting—waiting for the knife.
A little while, and at a leap I storm
The thick, sweet mystery of chloroform,
The drunken dark, the little death-in-life.
The gods are good to me: I have no wife,　　5
No innocent child, to think of as I near
The fateful minute; nothing all-too dear
Unmans me for my bout of passive strife.
Yet I am tremulous and a trifle sick,
And, face to face with chance, I shrink a little:
My hopes are strong, my will is something weak.　　11
Here comes the basket? Thank you. I am ready.
But, gentlemen my porters, life is brittle:
You carry Caesar and his fortunes—steady!

#### 28

#### *Discharged*

Carry me out
Into the wind and the sunshine,
Into the beautiful world.

O, the wonder, the spell of the streets!
The stature and strength of the horses,　　5
The rustle and echo of footfalls,

[1] Published 1888; written 1872–75.

The flat roar and rattle of wheels!
A swift tram floats huge on us . . .
It's a dream?
The smell of the mud in my nostrils　　10
Blows brave—like a breath of the sea!

As of old,
Ambulant, undulant drapery,
Vaguely and strangely provocative,
Flutters and beckons. O, yonder—　　15
Is it?—the gleam of a stocking!
Sudden, a spire

Wedged in the mist! O, the houses,
The long lines of lofty, gray houses,
Cross-hatched with shadow and light!　　20
These are the streets. . . .
Each is an avenue leading
Whither I will!

Free . . . !
Dizzy, hysterical, faint,　　25
I sit, and the carriage rolls on with me
Into the wonderful world.

## Invictus [2]

Out of the night that covers me,
　　Black as the Pit from pole to pole,
I thank whatever gods may be
　　For my unconquerable soul.

In the fell clutch of circumstance　　5
　　I have not winced nor cried aloud.
Under the bludgeonings of chance
　　My head is bloody, but unbowed.

Beyond this place of wrath and tears
　　Looms but the Horror of the shade,　　10
And yet the menace of the years
　　Finds, and shall find, me unafraid.

It matters not how strait the gate,
　　How charged with punishments the scroll,
I am the master of my fate;　　15
　　I am the captain of my soul.

## I. M. Margaritae Sorori [3]

A late lark twitters from the quiet skies;
And from the west,
Where the sun, his day's work ended,
Lingers as in content,
There falls on the old, gray city　　5
An influence luminous and serene,
A shining peace.

The smoke ascends
In a rosy-and-golden haze. The spires

[2] Published 1888; written 1875.
[3] Published 1888; written 1886.

Shine, and are changed. In the valley 10
Shadows rise. The lark sings on. The sun,
Closing his benediction,
Sinks, and the darkening air
Thrills with a sense of the triumphing night—
Night with her train of stars 15
And her great gift of sleep.

So be my passing!
My task accomplished and the long day done,
My wages taken, and in my heart
Some late lark singing, 20
Let me be gathered to the quiet west,
The sundown splendid and serene,
Death.

## Space and Dread and the Dark [4]

Space and dread and the dark—
Over a livid stretch of sky
Cloud-monsters crawling, like a funeral train
Of huge, primeval presences
Stooping beneath the weight 5
Of some enormous, rudimentary grief;
While in the haunting loneliness
The far sea waits and wanders with a sound
As of the trailing skirts of Destiny,
Passing unseen 10
To some immitigable end
With her gray henchman, Death.

What larve, what specter is this
Thrilling the wilderness to life
As with the bodily shape of Fear? 15
What but a desperate sense,
A strong foreboding of those dim
Interminable continents, forlorn
And many-silenced, in a dusk
Inviolable utterly, and dead 20
As the poor dead it huddles and swarms and styes
In hugger-mugger through eternity?

Life—life—let there be life!
Better a thousand times the roaring hours
When wave and wind, 25
Like the Arch-Murderer in flight
From the Avenger at his heel,
Storms through the desolate fastnesses
And wild waste places of the world!

Life—give me life until the end, 30
That at the very top of being,
The battle-spirit shouting in my blood,
Out of the reddest hell of the fight
I may be snatched and flung
Into the everlasting lull, 35
The immortal, incommunicable dream.

[4] Published 1892; written about 1890.

# OSCAR WILDE
## (1854–1900)

## Helas! [1]

To drift with every passion till my soul
Is a stringed lute on which all winds can play,
Is it for this that I have given away
Mine ancient wisdom, and austere control?
Methinks my life is a twice-written scroll 5
Scrawled over on some boyish holiday
With idle songs for pipe and virelay,[2]
Which do but mar the secret of the whole.
Surely there was a time I might have trod
The sunlit heights, and from life's dissonance
Struck one clear chord to reach the ears of
God: 11
Is that time dead? lo! with a little rod
I did but touch the honey of romance—
And must I lose a soul's inheritance?

## Symphony in Yellow [3]

An omnibus across the bridge
Crawls like a yellow butterfly,
And, here and there, a passer-by
Shows like a little restless midge.

Big barges full of yellow hay 5
Are moved against the shadowy wharf,
And, like a yellow silken scarf,
The thick fog hangs along the quay.

The yellow leaves begin to fade
And flutter from the Temple [4] elms, 10
And at my feet the pale green Thames
Lies like a rod of rippled jade.

## The Ballad of Reading Gaol [5]

*In Memoriam C. T. W.: Sometime
Trooper of the Royal Horse Guards.
Obiit H. M. Prison, Reading,
Berkshire, July 7th, 1896.*

I

He did not wear his scarlet coat,
For blood and wine are red,
And blood and wine were on his hands
When they found him with the dead,

[1] This sonnet was published in *Poems*, 1881.
[2] A song or short lyric piece, usually written in interlocking stanzas, each limited to two rime sounds.
[3] First published in the *Centennial Magazine* (of Sydney, Australia), February, 1889.
[4] The London legal collegiate societies.
[5] First published in 1898. The "C. T. W." to whose memory the poem is dedicated was Charles T. Wooldridge, who was executed for the murder of his wife.

The poor dead woman whom he loved,    5
  And murdered in her bed.

He walked amongst the Trial Men
  In a suit of shabby gray;
A cricket cap was on his head,
  And his step seemed light and gay;    10
But I never saw a man who looked
  So wistfully at the day.

I never saw a man who looked
  With such a wistful eye
Upon that little tent of blue    15
  Which prisoners call the sky,
And at every drifting cloud that went
  With sails of silver by.

I walked, with other souls in pain,
  Within another ring,    20
And was wondering if the man had done
  A great or little thing,
When a voice behind me whispered low,
  *"That fellow's got to swing."*

Dear Christ! the very prison walls    25
  Suddenly seemed to reel,
And the sky above my head became
  Like a casque of scorching steel;
And, though I was a soul in pain,
  My pain I could not feel.    30

I only knew what hunted thought
  Quickened his step, and why
He looked upon the garish day
  With such a wistful eye;
The man had killed the thing he loved,    35
  And so he had to die.

Yet each man kills the thing he loves,
  By each let this be heard,
Some do it with a bitter look,
  Some with a flattering word,    40
The coward does it with a kiss,
  The brave man with a sword!

Some kill their love when they are young,
  And some when they are old;
Some strangle with the hands of Lust,    45
  Some with the hands of Gold:
The kindest use a knife, because
  The dead so soon grow cold.

Some love too little, some too long,
  Some sell, and others buy;    50
Some do the deed with many tears,
  And some without a sigh:
For each man kills the thing he loves,
  Yet each man does not die.

He does not die a death of shame    55
  On a day of dark disgrace,
Nor have a noose about his neck,
  Nor a cloth upon his face,

Nor drop feet foremost through the floor
  Into an empty space.    60

He does not sit with silent men
  Who watch him night and day;
Who watch him when he tries to weep,
  And when he tries to pray;
Who watch him lest himself should rob    65
  The prison of its prey.

He does not wake at dawn to see
  Dread figures throng his room,
The shivering Chaplain robed in white,
  The Sheriff stern with gloom,    70
And the Governor all in shiny black,
  With the yellow face of Doom.

He does not rise in piteous haste
  To put on convict-clothes,
While some coarse-mouthed Doctor gloats, and notes    75
  Each new and nerve-twitched pose,
Fingering a watch whose little ticks
  Are like horrible hammer-blows.

He does not know that sickening thirst
  That sands one's throat, before    80
The hangman with his gardener's gloves
  Slips through the padded door,
And binds one with three leathern thongs,
  That the throat may thirst no more.

He does not bend his head to hear    85
  The Burial Office read,
Nor while the terror of his soul
  Tells him he is not dead,
Cross his own coffin, as he moves
  Into the hideous shed.    90

He does not stare upon the air
  Through a little roof of glass:
He does not pray with lips of clay
  For his agony to pass;
Nor feel upon his shuddering cheek    95
  The kiss of Caiaphas.

II

Six weeks our guardsman walked the yard,
  In the suit of shabby gray:
His cricket cap was on his head,
  And his step seemed light and gay,
But I never saw a man who looked    5
  So wistfully at the day.

I never saw a man who looked
  With such a wistful eye
Upon that little tent of blue
  Which prisoners call the sky,    10
And at every wandering cloud that trailed
  Its raveled fleeces by.

He did not wring his hands, as do
  Those witless men who dare

To try to rear the changeling Hope    15
  In the cave of black Despair:
He only looked upon the sun,
  And drank the morning air.

He did not wring his hands nor weep,
  Nor did he peek or pine,    20
But he drank the air as though it held
  Some healthful anodyne;
With open mouth he drank the sun
  As though it had been wine!

And I and all the souls in pain,    25
  Who tramped the other ring,
Forgot if we ourselves had done
  A great or little thing,
And watched with gaze of dull amaze
  The man who had to swing.    30

And strange it was to see him pass
  With a step so light and gay,
And strange it was to see him look
  So wistfully at the day,
And strange it was to think that he    35
  Had such a debt to pay.

For oak and elm have pleasant leaves
  That in the spring-time shoot:
But grim to see is the gallows-tree,
  With its adder-bitten root,    40
And, green or dry, a man must die
  Before it bears its fruit!

The loftiest place is that seat of grace
  For which all worldlings try:
But who would stand in hempen band    45
  Upon a scaffold high,
And through a murderer's collar take
  His last look at the sky?

It is sweet to dance to violins
  When Love and Life are fair:    50
To dance to flutes, to dance to lutes
  Is delicate and rare:
But it is not sweet with nimble feet
  To dance upon the air!

So with curious eyes and sick surmise    55
  We watched him day by day,
And wondered if each one of us
  Would end the self-same way,
For none can tell to what red Hell
  His sightless soul may stray.    60

At last the dead man walked no more
  Amongst the Trial Men,
And I knew that he was standing up
  In the black dock's dreadful pen,
And that never would I see his face    65
  In God's sweet world again.

Like two doomed ships that pass in storm
  We had crossed each other's way:

But we made no sign, we said no word,
  We had no word to say;    70
For we did not meet in the holy night,
  But in the shameful day.

A prison wall was round us both,
  Two outcast men we were:
The world had thrust us from its heart,    75
  And God from out His care:
And the iron gin that waits for Sin
  Had caught us in its snare.

III

In Debtor's Yard the stones are hard,
  And the dripping wall is high,
So it was there he took the air
  Beneath the leaden sky,
And by each side a Warder walked,    5
  For fear the man might die.

Or else he sat with those who watched
  His anguish night and day;
Who watched him when he rose to weep,
  And when he crouched to pray;    10
Who watched him lest himself should rob
  Their scaffold of its prey.

The Governor was strong upon
  The Regulations Act:
The Doctor said that Death was but    15
  A scientific fact:
And twice a day the Chaplain called,
  And left a little tract.

And twice a day he smoked his pipe,
  And drank his quart of beer:    20
His soul was resolute, and held
  No hiding-place for fear;
He often said that he was glad
  The hangman's hands were near.

But why he said so strange a thing    25
  No Warder dared to ask:
For he to whom a watcher's doom
  Is given as his task,
Must set a lock upon his lips,
  And make his face a mask.    30

Or else he might be moved, and try
  To comfort or console:
And what should Human Pity do
  Pent up in Murderer's Hole?
What word of grace in such a place    35
  Could help a brother's soul?

With slouch and swing around the ring
  We trod the Fools' Parade!
We did not care: we knew we were
  The Devil's Own Brigade:    40
And shaven head and feet of lead
  Make a merry masquerade.

We tore the tarry rope to shreds
  With blunt and bleeding nails;
We rubbed the doors, and scrubbed the floors,
  And cleaned the shining rails:       46
And, rank by rank, we soaped the plank,
  And clattered with the pails.

We sewed the sacks, we broke the stones,
  We turned the dusty drill:           50
We banged the tins, and bawled the hymns,
  And sweated on the mill:
But in the heart of every man
  Terror was lying still.

So still it lay that every day          55
  Crawled like a weed-clogged wave:
And we forgot the bitter lot
  That waits for fool and knave,
Till once, as we tramped in from work,
  We passed an open grave.             60

With yawning mouth the yellow hole
  Gaped for a living thing;
The very mud cried out for blood
  To the thirsty asphalt ring:
And we knew that ere one dawn grew fair   65
  Some prisoner had to swing.

Right in we went, with soul intent
  On Death and Dread and Doom:
The hangman, with his little bag,
  Went shuffling through the gloom:    70
And each man trembled as he crept
  Into his numbered tomb.

That night the empty corridors
  Were full of forms of Fear,
And up and down the iron town          75
  Stole feet we could not hear,
And through the bars that hide the stars
  White faces seemed to peer.

He lay as one who lies and dreams
  In a pleasant meadow-land,           80
The watchers watched him as he slept,
  And could not understand
How one could sleep so sweet a sleep
  With a hangman close at hand.

But there is no sleep when men must weep  85
  Who never yet have wept:
So we—the fool, the fraud, the knave—
  That endless vigil kept,
And through each brain on hands of pain
  Another's terror crept.              90

Alas! it is a fearful thing
  To feel another's guilt!
For, right within, the sword of Sin
  Pierced to its poisoned hilt,
And as molten lead were the tears we shed  95
  For the blood we had not spilt.

The Warders with their shoes of felt
  Crept by each padlocked door,
And peeped and saw, with eyes of awe,
  Gray figures on the floor,           100
And wondered why men knelt to pray
  Who never prayed before.

All through the night we knelt and prayed,
  Mad mourners of a corse!
The troubled plumes of midnight were   105
  The plumes upon a hearse:
And bitter wine upon a sponge
  Was the savor of Remorse.

The gray cock crew, the red cock crew,
  But never came the day:              110
And crooked shapes of Terror crouched,
  In the corners where we lay:
And each evil sprite that walks by night
  Before us seemed to play.

They glided past, they glided fast,    115
  Like travelers through a mist:
They mocked the moon in a rigadoon [6]
  Of delicate turn and twist,
And with formal pace and loathsome grace
  The phantoms kept their tryst.       120

With mop and mow,[7] we saw them go,
  Slim shadows hand in hand:
About, about, in ghostly rout
  They trod a saraband: [8]
And the damned grotesques made arabesques,
  Like the wind upon the sand!         126

With the pirouettes of marionettes,
  They tripped on pointed tread:
But with flutes of Fear they filled the ear,
  As their grisly masque they led,     130
And loud they sang, and long they sang,
  For they sang to wake the dead.

*"Oho!"* they cried, *"The world is wide,*
  *But fettered limbs go lame!*
*And once, or twice, to throw the dice*   135
  *Is a gentlemanly game,*
*But he does not win who plays with Sin*
  *In the secret House of Shame."*

No things of air these antics were,
  That frolicked with such glee:       140
To men whose lives were held in gyves [9]
  And whose feet might not go free,
Ah! wounds of Christ! they were living things,
  Most terrible to see.

Around, around, they waltzed and wound; [145]
  Some wheeled in smirking pairs;
With the mincing step of a demirep [10]
  Some sidled up the stairs:

----

  [6] A complicated dance.           [7] With grimaces.
  [8] A slow and stately dance.          [9] Shackles.
  [10] An adventuress.

And with subtle sneer, and fawning leer,
  Each helped us at our prayers.   150

The morning wind began to moan,
  But still the night went on:
Through its giant loom the web of gloom
  Crept till each thread was spun:
And, as we prayed, we grew afraid   155
  Of the Justice of the Sun.

The moaning wind went wandering round
  The weeping prison-wall:
Till like a wheel of turning steel
  We felt the minutes crawl:   160
O moaning wind! what had we done
  To have such a seneschal?

At last I saw the shadowed bars,
  Like a lattice wrought in lead,
Move right across the whitewashed wall   165
  That faced my three-plank bed,
And I knew that somewhere in the world
  God's dreadful dawn was red.

At six o'clock we cleaned our cells,
  At seven all was still,   170
But the sough and swing of a mighty wing
  The prison seemed to fill,
For the Lord of Death with icy breath
  Had entered in to kill.

He did not pass in purple pomp,   175
  Nor ride a moon-white steed.
Three yards of cord and a sliding board
  Are all the gallows' need:
So with rope of shame the Herald came
  To do the secret deed.   180

We were as men who through a fen
  Of filthy darkness grope:
We did not dare to breathe a prayer,
  Or to give our anguish scope:
Something was dead in each of us,   185
  And what was dead was Hope.

For Man's grim Justice goes its way,
  And will not swerve aside:
It slays the weak, it slays the strong,
  It has a deadly stride:   190
With iron heel it slays the strong,
  The monstrous parricide!

We waited for the stroke of eight:
  Each tongue was thick with thirst:
For the stroke of eight is the stroke of Fate   195
  That makes a man accursed,
And Fate will use a running noose
  For the best man and the worst.

We had no other thing to do,
  Save to wait for the sign to come:   200
So, like things of stone in a valley lone,
  Quiet we sat and dumb:

But each man's heart beat thick and quick,
  Like a madman on a drum!

With sudden shock the prison-clock   205
  Smote on the shivering air,
And from all the gaol rose up a wail
  Of impotent despair,
Like the sound that frightened marshes hear
  From some leper in his lair.   210

And as one sees most fearful things
  In the crystal of a dream,
We saw the greasy hempen rope
  Hooked to the blackened beam,
And heard the prayer the hangman's snare   215
  Strangled into a scream.

And all the woe that moved him so
  That he gave that bitter cry,
And the wild regrets, and the bloody sweats,
  None knew so well as I:   220
For he who lives more lives than one
  More deaths than one must die.

IV

There is no chapel on the day
  On which they hang a man:
The Chaplain's heart is far too sick,
  Or his face is far too wan,
Or there is that written in his eyes   5
  Which none should look upon.

So they kept us close till nigh on noon,
  And then they rang the bell,
And the Warders with their jingling keys
  Opened each listening cell,   10
And down the iron stair we tramped,
  Each from his separate Hell.

Out into God's sweet air we went,
  But not in wonted way,
For this man's face was white with fear,   15
  And that man's face was gray,
And I never saw sad men who looked
  So wistfully at the day.

I never saw sad men who looked
  With such a wistful eye   20
Upon that little tent of blue
  We prisoners called the sky,
And at every careless cloud that passed
  In happy freedom by.

But there were those amongst us all   25
  Who walked with downcast head,
And knew that, had each got his due,
  They should have died instead:
He had but killed a thing that lived,
  Whilst they had killed the dead.   30

For he who sins a second time
  Wakes a dead soul to pain,
And draws it from its spotted shroud,

And makes it bleed again,
And makes it bleed great gouts of blood,       35
And makes it bleed in vain!

Like ape or clown, in monstrous garb
  With crooked arrows starred,
Silently we went round and round
  The slippery asphalt yard;                   40
Silently we went round and round,
  And no man spoke a word.

Silently we went round and round,
  And through each hollow mind
The Memory of dreadful things                  45
  Rushed like a dreadful wind,
And Horror stalked before each man,
  And Terror crept behind.

The Warders strutted up and down,
  And kept their herd of brutes,               50
Their uniforms were spick and span,
  And they wore their Sunday suits,
But we knew the work they had been at,
  By the quicklime on their boots.

For where a grave had opened wide,             55
  There was no grave at all:
Only a stretch of mud and sand
  By the hideous prison-wall,
And a little heap of burning lime,
  That the man should have his pall.           60

For he has a pall, this wretched man,
  Such as few men can claim:
Deep down below a prison-yard,
  Naked for greater shame,
He lies, with fetters on each foot,            65
  Wrapt in a sheet of flame!

And all the while the burning lime
  Eats flesh and bone away,
It eats the brittle bone by night,
  And the soft flesh by day,                   70
It eats the flesh and bone by turns,
  But it eats the heart alway.

For three long years they will not sow
  Or root or seedling there:
For three long years the unbless'd spot        75
  Will sterile be and bare,
And look upon the wondering sky
  With unreproachful stare.

They think a murderer's heart would taint
  Each simple seed they sow.                   80
It is not true! God's kindly earth
  Is kindlier than men know,
And the red rose would but blow more red,
  The white rose whiter blow.

Out of his mouth a red, red rose!              85
  Out of his heart a white!
For who can say by what strange way,
  Christ brings His will to light,

Since the barren staff the pilgrim bore
  Bloomed in the great Pope's sight? [11]      90

But neither milk-white rose nor red
  May bloom in prison-air;
The shard, the pebble, and the flint,
  Are what they give us there:
For flowers have been known to heal            95
  A common man's despair.

So never will wine-red rose or white,
  Petal by petal, fall
On that stretch of mud and sand that lies
  By the hideous prison-wall,                  100
To tell the men who tramp the yard
  That God's Son died for all.

Yet though the hideous prison-wall
  Still hems him round and round,
And a spirit may not walk by night             105
  That is with fetters bound,
And a spirit may but weep that lies
  In such unholy ground,

He is at peace—this wretched man—
  At peace, or will be soon:                   110
There is no thing to make him mad,
  Nor does Terror walk at noon,
For the lampless Earth in which he lies
  Has neither Sun nor Moon.

They hanged him as a beast is hanged:          115
  They did not even toll
A requiem that might have brought
  Rest to his startled soul,
But hurriedly they took him out.
  And hid him in a hole.                       120

They stripped him of his canvas clothes,
  And gave him to the flies:
They mocked the swollen purple throat,
  And the stark and staring eyes:
And with laughter loud they heaped the shroud
  In which their convict lies.                 126

The Chaplain would not kneel to pray
  By his dishonored grave:
Nor mark it with that blessed Cross
  That Christ for sinners gave,                130
Because the man was one of those
  Whom Christ came down to save.

Yet all is well; he has but passed
  To Life's appointed bourne: [12]

[11] After living with Venus for seven years, Tannhäuser went on a pilgrimage to Rome to seek absolution from the Pope. His Holiness replied that
it was as impossible for Tannhäuser to be forgiven
as for his pilgrim staff to blossom. Three days later,
after the sinner had gone off in despair, his staff
(left in Rome) began to blossom. Then the Pope
sent for him, but he had returned to Venus.

[12] Destination.

And alien tears will fill for him    135
  Pity's long-broken urn,
For his mourners will be outcast men,
  And outcasts always mourn.

V

I know not whether Laws be right,
  Or whether Laws be wrong;
All that we know who lie in gaol
  Is that the wall is strong;
And that each day is like a year,    5
  A year whose days are long.

But this I know, that every Law
  That men have made for Man,
Since first Man took his brother's life,
  And the sad world began,    10
But straws [13] the wheat and saves the chaff
  With a most evil fan.

This too I know—and wise it were
  If each could know the same—
That every prison that men build    15
  Is built with bricks of shame,
And bound with bars lest Christ should see
  How men their brothers maim.

With bars they blur the gracious moon,
  And blind the goodly sun:    20
And they do well to hide their Hell,
  For in it things are done
That Son of God nor son of Man
  Ever should look upon!

The vilest deeds like poison weeds    25
  Bloom well in prison-air:
It is only what is good in Man
  That wastes and withers there:
Pale Anguish keeps the heavy gate,
  And the Warder is Despair.    30

For they starve the little frightened child
  Till it weeps both night and day:
And they scourge the weak, and flog the fool,
  And gibe the old and gray,
And some grow mad, and all grow bad,    35
  And none a word may say.

Each narrow cell in which we dwell
  Is a foul and dark latrine,
And the fetid breath of living Death
  Chokes up each grated screen,    40
And all, but Lust, is turned to dust
  In Humanity's machine.

The brackish water that we drink
  Creeps with a loathsome slime,
And the bitter bread they weigh in scales    45
  Is full of chalk and lime,
And Sleep will not lie down, but walks
  Wild-eyed, and cries to Time.

[13] Throws away like straw.

But though lean Hunger and green Thirst
  Like asp with adder fight,    50
We have little care of prison fare,
  For what chills and kills outright
Is that every stone one lifts by day
  Becomes one's heart by night.

With midnight always in one's heart,    55
  And twilight in one's cell,
We turn the crank, or tear the rope,
  Each in his separate Hell,
And the silence is more awful far
  Than the sound of a brazen bell.    60

And never a human voice comes near
  To speak a gentle word:
And the eye that watches through the door
  Is pitiless and hard:
And by all forgot, we rot and rot,    65
  With soul and body marred.

And thus we rust Life's iron chain
  Degraded and alone:
And some men curse, and some men weep,
  And some men make no moan:    70
But God's eternal Laws are kind
  And break the heart of stone.

And every human heart that breaks,
  In prison-cell or yard,
Is as that broken box that gave    75
  Its treasure to the Lord,
And filled the unclean leper's house
  With the scent of costliest nard. [14]

Ah! happy they whose hearts can break
  And peace of pardon win!    80
How else may man make straight his plan
  And cleanse his soul from Sin?
How else but through a broken heart
  May Lord Christ enter in?

And he of the swollen purple throat,    85
  And the stark and staring eyes,
Waits for the holy hands that took
  The Thief to Paradise;
And a broken and a contrite heart
  The Lord will not despise.    90

The man in red who reads the Law
  Gave him three weeks of life,
Three little weeks in which to heal
  His soul of his soul's strife,
And cleanse from every blot of blood    95
  The hand that held the knife.

And with tears of blood he cleansed the hand,
  The hand that held the steel:
For only blood can wipe out blood,
  And only tears can heal:    100
And the crimson stain that was of Cain
  Became Christ's snow-white seal.

[14] An allusion to the story of Lazarus (St. John,
11).

VI

In Reading gaol by Reading town
　There is a pit of shame,
And in it lies a wretched man
　Eaten by teeth of flame,
In a burning winding-sheet he lies,　　　5
　And his grave has got no name.

And there, till Christ call forth the dead,
　In silence let him lie:
No need to waste the foolish tear,
　Or heave the windy sigh:　　　　　　10
The man had killed the thing he loved,
　And so he had to die.

And all men kill the thing they love,
　By all let this be heard,
Some do it with a bitter look,　　　　　15
　Some with a flattering word,
The coward does it with a kiss,
　The brave man with a sword!

# FRANCIS THOMPSON

## (1859–1907)

## The Hound of Heaven [1]

I fled Him, down the nights and down the
　　days;
　I fled Him, down the arches of the years;
I fled Him, down the labyrinthine ways
　Of my own mind; and in the mist of tears
I hid from Him, and under running laughter.
　　Up vistaed hopes, I sped;　　　　　6
　　And shot, precipitated,
Adown Titanic glooms of chasmèd fears,
From those strong Feet that followed, followed
　　after.
　　But with unhurrying chase,　　　　10
　　And unperturbèd pace,
Deliberate speed, majestic instancy,
　　They beat—and a Voice beat
　　More instant than the Feet:
"All things betray thee, who betrayest Me." 15

　　I pleaded, outlaw-wise,
By many a hearted casement, curtained red,
　Trellised with intertwining charities;
(For, though I knew His love Who followèd,
　　Yet was I sore adread　　　　　　20
Lest, having Him, I must have naught beside).
But, if one little casement parted wide,
　The gust of His approach would clash it to.
　Fear wist not to evade, as Love wist to
　　pursue.
Across the margent of the world I fled,　　25
　And troubled the gold gateways of the stars,
　Smiting for shelter on their clangèd bars;
　　Fretted to dulcet jars

[1] Written in 1889 or 1890; published in *Poems*,
1893.

And silvern chatter the pale ports o' the moon.
I said to Dawn, Be sudden—to Eve, Be soon:
　With thy young skyey blossoms heap me
　　over　　　　　　　　　　　　　31
　From this tremendous Lover—
Float thy vague veil about me, lest He see!
　I tempted all His servitors, but to find
My own betrayal in their constancy,　　35
In faith to Him their fickleness to me,
　Their traitorous trueness, and their loyal
　　deceit.
To all swift things for swiftness did I sue;
　Clung to the whistling mane of every wind.
　　But whether they swept, smoothly
　　　fleet,　　　　　　　　　　　40
　The long savannahs of the blue;
　　Or whether, thunder-driven,
　They clanged His chariot 'thwart a heaven
Plashy with flying lightnings round the spurn
　o' their feet:
　　Fear wist not to evade as Love wist to
　　　pursue.　　　　　　　　　　　45
　　Still with unhurrying chase,
　　And unperturbèd pace,
Deliberate speed, majestic instancy,
　　Came on the following Feet,
　　And a Voice above their beat:　　50
"Naught shelters thee, who wilt not shelter
　　Me."

I sought no more that after which I strayed
　In face of man or maid;
But still within the little children's eyes
　Seems something, something that replies,
*They* at least are for me, surely for me!　56
I turned me to them very wistfully;
But just as their young eyes grew sudden fair
　With dawning answers there,
Their angel plucked them from me by the
　hair.　　　　　　　　　　　　　60
"Come then, ye other children, Nature's,—
　share
With me" (said I) "your delicate fellowship;
　Let me greet you lip to lip,
　Let me twine with you caresses,
　　Wantoning　　　　　　　　　65
　With our Lady-Mother's [2] vagrant tresses;
　　Banqueting
　With her in her wind-walled palace,
　Underneath her azured daïs;
Quaffing, as your taintless way is,　　70
　　From a chalice
Lucent-weeping out of the dayspring."
　So it was done:
*I* in their delicate fellowship was one—
Drew the bolt of Nature's secrecies.　　75
　I knew all the swift importings
　On the willful face of skies;
　I knew how the clouds arise
　Spuméd of the wild sea-snortings—
　　All that's born or dies,　　　　80

[2] I. e., Nature's.

Rose and drooped with; made them shapers
Of mine own moods, or wailful or divine;
   With them joyed and was bereaven.
   I was heavy with the even,
When she lit her glimmering tapers   85
Round the day's dead sanctities;
   I laughed in the morning's eyes.
I triumphed and I saddened with all weather:
   Heaven and I wept together,
And its sweet tears were salt with mortal mine;
Against the red throb of its sunset-heart   91
      I laid my own to beat,
      And share commingling heat.
But not by that, by that, was eased my human smart;
In vain my tears were wet on Heaven's gray cheek.   95
For ah! we know not what each other says,
   These things and I: in sound I speak—
*Their* sound is but their stir, they speak by silences.
Nature, poor stepdame, cannot slake my drouth;
   Let her, if she would owe [3] me,   100
Drop yon blue bosom-veil of sky, and show me
   The breasts o' her tenderness:
Never did any milk of hers once bless
      My thirsting mouth.
   Nigh and nigh draws the chase,   105
   With unperturbéd pace,
Deliberate speed, majestic instancy,
   And past those noiséd Feet
   A Voice comes yet more fleet—
"Lo! naught contents thee, who content'st not Me."   110

Naked I wait Thy love's uplifted stroke!
My harness piece by piece Thou hast hewn from me,
   And smitten me to my knee:
   I am defenseless utterly.
   I slept, methinks, and woke,   115
And, slowly gazing, find me stripped in sleep.
In the rash lustihead of my young powers,
   I shook the pillaring hours
And pulled my life upon me; [4] grimed with smears,
I stand amid the dust o' the mounded years—   119
My mangled youth lies dead beneath the heap.
My days have crackled and gone up in smoke,
Have puffed and burst as sun-starts on a stream.
   Yea, faileth now even dream
The dreamer, and the lute the lutanist;   125
Even the linked fantasies, in whose blossomy twist
I swung the earth a trinket at my wrist,
Are yielding—cords of all too weak account

[3] Own.
[4] In allusion to Samson (Judges, 16:29-30).

For earth, with heavy griefs so overplussed.
   Ah! is Thy love indeed   130
A weed, albeit an amaranthine weed,
Suffering no flowers except its own to mount?
      Ah! must—
      Designer infinite!—
Ah! must Thou char the wood ere Thou canst limn with it?   135
My freshness spent its wavering shower i' the dust;
And now my heart is as a broken fount,
Wherein tear-drippings stagnate, spilt down ever
   From the dank thoughts that shiver
Upon the sighful branches of my mind.   140
   Such is: what is to be?
The pulp so bitter, how shall taste the rind?
I dimly guess what Time in mist confounds;
Yet ever and anon a trumpet sounds
From the hid battlements of Eternity:   145
Those shaken mists a space unsettle, then
Round the half-glimpséd turrets slowly wash again.
   But not ere him who summoneth
   I first have seen, enwound
With glooming robes purpureal, cypress-crowned:   150
His name I know, and what his trumpet saith.
Whether man's heart or life it be which yields
   Thee harvest, must Thy harvest fields
   Be dunged with rotten death?

   Now of that long pursuit   155
   Comes on at hand the bruit;
That Voice is round me like a bursting sea:
   "And is thy earth so marred,
   Shattered in shard on shard?
Lo, all things fly thee, for thou fliest Me!   160
   Strange, piteous, futile thing!
Wherefore should any set thee love apart?
Seeing none but I makes much of naught"
      (He said),
"And human love needs human meriting:
   How hast thou merited—   165
Of all man's clotted clay the dingiest clot?
   Alack, thou knowest not
How little worthy of any love thou art!
Whom wilt thou find to love ignoble thee,
   Save Me, save only Me?   170
All which I took from thee I did but take,
   Not for thy harms,
But just that thou might'st seek it in My arms.
All which thy child's mistake
Fancies as lost, I have stored for thee at home:
   Rise, clasp My hand, and come!"   176

   Halts by me that footfall:
   Is my gloom, after all,
Shade of His hand, outstretched caressingly?—
   "Ah, fondest, blindest, weakest,   180
   I am He Whom thou seekest!
Thou dravest love from thee, who dravest Me."

# ALFRED EDWARD HOUSMAN

(1859–1936)

## A Shropshire Lad [1]

### II

Loveliest of trees, the cherry now
Is hung with bloom along the bough,
And stands about the woodland ride
Wearing white for Eastertide.

Now, of my threescore years and ten,   5
Twenty will not come again,
And take from seventy springs a score,
It only leaves me fifty more.

And since to look at things in bloom
Fifty springs are little room,   10
About the woodlands I will go
To see the cherry hung with snow.

### IV. REVEILLE

Wake: the silver dusk returning
  Up the beach of darkness brims,
And the ship of sunrise burning
  Strands upon the eastern rims.

Wake: the vaulted shadow shatters,   5
  Trampled to the floor it spanned,
And the tent of night in tatters
  Straws [2] the sky-pavilioned land.

Up, lad, up, 'tis late for lying:
  Hear the drums of morning play;   10
Hark, the empty highways crying
  "Who'll beyond the hills away?"

Towns and countries woo together,
  Forelands beacon, belfries call;
Never lad that trod on leather   15
  Lived to feast his heart with all.

Up, lad: thews that lie and cumber
  Sunlit pallets never thrive;
Morns abed and daylight slumber
  Were not meant for man alive.   20

Clay lies still, but blood's a rover;
  Breath's a ware that will not keep.
Up, lad: when the journey's over
  There'll be time enough to sleep.

### VIII

"Farewell to barn and stack and tree,
  Farewell to Severn shore.

[1] Published in 1896.   [2] Strews.

Terence, look your last at me,
  For I come home no more.

"The sun burns on the half-mown hill,   5
  By now the blood is dried;
And Maurice amongst the hay lies still
  And my knife is in his side.

"My mother thinks us long away;
  'Tis time the field were mown.   10
She had two sons at rising day,
  To-night she'll be alone.

"And here's a bloody hand to shake,
  And oh, man, here's good-bye;
We'll sweat no more on scythe and rake,   15
  My bloody hands and I.

"I wish you strength to bring you pride,
  And a love to keep you clean,
And I wish you luck, come Lammastide,
  At racing on the green.   20

"Long for me the rick will wait,
  And long will wait the fold,
And long will stand the empty plate,
  And dinner will be cold."

### XIX. TO AN ATHLETE DYING YOUNG

The time you won your town the race
We chaired you through the market-place;
Man and boy stood cheering by,
And home we brought you shoulder-high.

To-day, the road all runners come,   5
Shoulder-high we bring you home,
And set you at your threshold down,
Townsman of a stiller town.

Smart lad, to slip betimes away
From fields where glory does not stay   10
And early though the laurel grows
It withers quicker than the rose.

Eyes the shady night has shut
Cannot see the record cut,
And silence sounds no worse than cheers   15
After earth has stopped the ears:

Now you will not swell the rout
Of lads that wore their honors out,
Runners whom renown outran
And the name died before the man.   20

So set, before its echoes fade,
The fleet foot on the sill of shade,
And hold to the low lintel up
The still-defended challenge-cup.

And round that early-laureled head   25
Will flock to gaze the strengthless dead,

And find unwithered on its curls
The garland briefer than a girl's.

### XXVII

"Is my team plowing,
That I used to drive
And hear the harness jingle
When I was man alive?"

Ay, the horses trample,           5
The harness jingles now;
No change though you lie under
The land you used to plow.

"Is football playing
Along the river shore,           10
With lads to chase the leather,
Now I stand up no more?"

Ay, the ball is flying,
The lads play heart and soul;
The goal stands up, the keeper   15
Stands up to keep the goal.

"Is my girl happy,
That I thought hard to leave,
And has she tired of weeping
As she lies down at eve?"        20

Ay, she lies down lightly,
She lies not down to weep:
Your girl is well contented.
Be still, my lad, and sleep.

"Is my friend hearty,           25
Now I am thin and pine,
And has he found to sleep in
A better bed than mine?"

Yes, lad, I lie easy,
I lie as lads would choose;      30
I cheer a dead man's sweetheart,
Never ask me whose.

### XXXIV. THE NEW MISTRESS

"Oh, sick I am to see you, will you never let
me be?
You may be good for something but you are
not good for me.
Oh, go where you are wanted, for you are not
wanted here."
And that was all the farewell when I parted
from my dear.

"I will go where I am wanted, to a lady born
and bred                         5
Who will dress me free for nothing in a uniform of red;
She will not be sick to see me if I only keep
it clean:

I will go where I am wanted for a soldier of
the Queen.

"I will go where I am wanted, for the sergeant
does not mind;
He may be sick to see me but he treats me
very kind:                       10
He gives me beer and breakfast and a ribbon
for my cap,
And I never knew a sweetheart spend her
money on a chap.

"I will go where I am wanted, where there's
room for one or two,
And the men are none too many for the work
there is to do;
Where the standing line wears thinner and the
dropping dead lie thick;         15
And the enemies of England they shall see me
and be sick."

### XLVIII

Be still, my soul, be still; the arms you bear are
brittle,
Earth and high heaven are fixed of old and
founded strong.
Think rather,—call to thought, if now you
grieve a little,
The days when we had rest, O soul, for they
were long.

Men loved unkindness then, but lightless in
the quarry                       5
I slept and saw not; tears fell down, I did not
mourn;
Sweat ran and blood sprang out and I was
never sorry:
Then it was well with me, in days ere I was
born.

Now, and I muse for why and never find the
reason,
I pace the earth, and drink the air, and feel
the sun.                         10
Be still, be still, my soul; it is but for a season:
Let us endure an hour and see injustice done.

Aye, look: high heaven and earth ail from the
prime foundation;
All thoughts to rive the heart are here, and
all are vain:
Horror and scorn and hate and fear and indignation—                          15
Oh why did I awake? when shall I sleep
again?

### LIV

With rue my heart is laden
For golden friends I had,
For many a rose-lipt maiden
And many a lightfoot lad.

By brooks too broad for leaping          5
  The lightfoot boys are laid;
The rose-lipt girls are sleeping
  In fields where roses fade.

### LXII

"Terence, this is stupid stuff:
You eat your victuals fast enough;
There can't be much amiss, 'tis clear,
To see the rate you drink your beer.
But oh, good Lord, the verse you make,      5
It gives a chap the belly-ache.
The cow, the old cow, she is dead;
It sleeps well, the horned head:
We poor lads, 'tis our turn now
To hear such tunes as killed the cow.       10
Pretty friendship 'tis to rime
Your friends to death before their time
Moping melancholy mad:
Come, pipe a tune to dance to, lad."

Why, if 'tis dancing you would be,          15
There's brisker pipes than poetry.
Say, for what were hop-yards meant,
Or why was Burton built on Trent? [3]
Oh many a peer of England brews
Livelier liquor than the Muse,              20
And malt does more than Milton can
To justify God's ways to man.
Ale, man, ale's the stuff to drink
For fellows whom it hurts to think:
Look into the pewter pot                     25
To see the world as the world's not.
And faith, 'tis pleasant till 'tis past:
The mischief is that 'twill not last.
Oh I have been to Ludlow fair
And left my necktie God knows where,        30
And carried half way home, or near,
Pints and quarts of Ludlow beer:
Then the world seemed none so bad,
And I myself a sterling lad;
And down in lovely muck I've lain,          35
Happy till I woke again.
Then I saw the morning sky:
Heigho, the tale was all a lie;
The world, it was the old world yet,
I was I, my things were wet,                40
And nothing now remained to do
But begin the game anew.

Therefore, since the world has still
Much good, but much less good than ill,
And while the sun and moon endure          45
Luck's a chance, but trouble's sure,
I'd face it as a wise man would,
And train for ill and not for good.
'Tis true, the stuff I bring for sale
Is not so brisk a brew as ale:              50
Out of a stem that scored the hand
I wrung it in a weary land.

[3] Burton upon Trent is a town famous for the manufacture of beer.

But take it: if the smack is sour,
The better for the embittered hour;
It should do good to heart and head        55
When your soul is in my soul's stead;
And I will friend you, if I may
In the dark and cloudy day.

There was a king reigned in the East:
There, when kings will sit to feast,       60
They get their fill before they think
With poisoned meat and poisoned drink.
He gathered all that springs to birth
From the many-venomed earth;
First a little, thence to more,            65
He sampled all her killing store;
And easy, smiling, seasoned sound,
Sate the king when healths went round.
They put arsenic in his meat
And stared aghast to watch him eat;        70
They poured strychnine in his cup
And shook to see him drink it up:
They shook, they stared as white's their shirt:
Them it was their poison hurt.
—I tell the tale that I heard told.        75
Mithridates, he died old.

## Last Poems [1]

### VII

In valleys green and still
  Where lovers wander maying
They hear from over hill
  A music playing.

Behind the drum and fife,                   5
  Past hawthornwood and hollow,
Through earth and out of life
  The soldiers follow.

The soldier's is the trade:
  In any wind or weather                    10
He steals the heart of maid
  And man together.

The lover and his lass
  Beneath the hawthorn lying
Have heard the soldiers pass,               15
  And both are sighing.

And down the distance they
  With dying note and swelling
Walk the resounding way
  To the still dwelling.                    20

### IX

The chestnut casts his flambeaux, and the
    flowers
  Stream from the hawthorn on the wind away,

[1] Published in 1922. The following selections from *Last Poems* are reprinted by permission of Henry Holt and Company, publishers.

The doors clap to, the pane is blind with
    showers.
    Pass me the can, lad; there's an end of May.

There's one spoilt spring to scant our mortal
    lot,        5
One season ruined of our little store.
May will be fine next year as like as not:
    Oh, aye, but then we shall be twenty-four.

We for a certainty are not the first
    Have sat in taverns while the tempest hurled
Their hopeful plans to emptiness, and cursed  11
    Whatever brute and blackguard made the
    world.

It is in truth iniquity on high
    To cheat our sentenced souls of aught they
    crave,
And mar the merriment as you and I     15
    Fare on our long fool's-errand to the grave.

Iniquity it is; but pass the can.
    My lad, no pair of kings our mothers bore;
Our only portion is the estate of man:
    We want the moon, but we shall get no
    more.    20

If here to-day the cloud of thunder lours
    To-morrow it will hie on far behests;
The flesh will grieve on other bones than ours
    Soon, and the soul will mourn in other
    breasts.

The troubles of our proud and angry dust  25
    Are from eternity, and shall not fail.
Bear them we can, and if we can we must
    Shoulder the sky, my lad, and drink your ale.

## XI

Yonder see the morning blink:
    The sun is up, and up must I,
To wash and dress and eat and drink
And look at things and talk and think
    And work, and God knows why.    5

Oh often have I washed and dressed
    And what's to show for all my pain?
Let me lie abed and rest:
Ten thousand times I've done my best
    And all's to do again.    10

# RUDYARD KIPLING

### (1865–1936)

## Tomlinson [1]

### 1891

Now Tomlinson gave up the ghost in his house
    in Berkeley Square,

[1] This and the following six poems are reprinted

And a Spirit came to his bedside and gripped
    him by the hair—
A Spirit gripped him by the hair and carried
    him far away,
Till he heard as the roar of a rain-fed ford the
    roar of the Milky Way:
Till he heard the roar of the Milky Way die
    down and drone and cease,    5
And they came to the Gate within the Wall
    where Peter holds the keys.
"Stand up, stand up now, Tomlinson, and an-
    swer loud and high
The good that ye did for the sake of men or
    ever ye came to die—
The good that ye did for the sake of men on
    little earth so lone!"
And the naked soul of Tomlinson grew white
    as a rain-washed bone.    10
"Oh I have a friend on earth," he said, "that
    was my priest and guide,
And well would he answer all for me if he
    were at my side."
—"For that ye strove in neighbor-love it shall
    be written fair,
But now ye wait at Heaven's Gate and not in
    Berkeley Square:
Though we called your friend from his bed
    this night, he could not speak for you,    15
For the race is run by one and one and never
    by two and two."
Then Tomlinson looked up and down, and
    little gain was there,
For the naked stars grinned overhead, and he
    saw that his soul was bare.
The Wind that blows between the Worlds, it
    cut him like a knife,
And Tomlinson took up the tale and spoke of
    his good in life.    20
"O this I have read in a book," he said, "and
    that was told to me,
And this I have thought that another man
    thought of a Prince in Muscovy."
The good souls flocked like homing doves and
    bade him clear the path,
And Peter twirled the jangling Keys in weari-
    ness and wrath.
"Ye have read, ye have heard, ye have thought,"
    he said, "and the tale is yet to run:    25
By the worth of the body that once ye had,
    give answer—what ha' ye done?"
Then Tomlinson looked back and forth, and
    little good it bore,
For the darkness stayed at his shoulder-blade
    and Heaven's Gate before:—
"O this I have felt, and this I have guessed,
    and this I have heard men say,
And this they wrote that another man wrote of
    a carl [2] in Norroway."    30
"Ye have read, ye have felt, ye have guessed,

by permission of Mrs. Kipling and of Doubleday,
Doran and Company.

[2] A base fellow.

good lack! Ye have hampered Heaven's
    Gate;
There's little room between the stars in idleness
    to prate!
O none may reach by hired speech of neighbor,
    priest, and kin
Through borrowed deed to God's good meed
    that lies so fair within;
Get hence, get hence to the Lord of Wrong,
    for the doom has yet to run,   35
And . . . . the faith that ye share with Berke-
    ley Square uphold you, Tomlinson!"

The Spirit gripped him by the hair, and sun by
    sun they fell
Till they came to the belt of Naughty Stars that
    rim the mouth of Hell.
The first are red with pride and wrath, the next
    are white with pain,
But the third are black with clinkered sins [3] that
    cannot burn again:   40
They may hold their path, they may leave their
    path, with never a soul to mark,
They may burn or freeze, but they must not
    cease in the Scorn of the Outer Dark.
The Wind that blows between the Worlds, it
    nipped him to the bone,
And he yearned to the flare of Hell-gate there
    as the light of his own hearthstone.
The Devil he sat behind the bars, where the
    desperate legions drew,   45
But he caught the hasting Tomlinson and
    would not let him through.
"Wot ye the price of good pit-coal that I must
    pay?" said he,
"That ye rank yoursel' so fit for Hell and ask
    no leave of me?
I am all o'er-sib [4] to Adam's breed that ye
    should give me scorn,
For I strove with God for your First Father the
    day that he was born.   50
Sit down, sit down upon the slag, and answer
    loud and high
The harm that ye did to the Sons of Men or
    ever you came to die."
And Tomlinson looked up and up, and saw
    against the night
The belly of a tortured star blood-red in Hell-
    Mouth light;
And Tomlinson looked down and down, and
    saw beneath his feet   55
The frontlet of a tortured star milk-white in
    Hell-Mouth heat.
"O I had a love on earth," said he, "that kissed
    me to my fall;
And if ye would call my love to me I know
    she would answer all."
—"All that ye did in love forbid it shall be
    written fair,

But now ye wait at Hell-Mouth Gate and not
    in Berkeley Square:   60
Though we whistled your love from her bed to-
    night, I trow she would not run,
For the sin ye do by two and two ye must pay
    for one by one!"
The Wind that blows between the Worlds, it
    cut him like a knife,
And Tomlinson took up the tale and spake of
    his sins in life:—
"Once I ha' laughed at the power of Love and
    twice at the grip of the Grave,   65
And thrice I ha' patted my God on the head
    that men might call me brave."
The Devil he blew on a brandered soul and set
    it aside to cool:—
"Do ye think I would waste my good pit-coal
    on the hide of a brain-sick fool?
I see no worth in the hobnailed mirth or the
    jolthead jest ye did
That I should waken my gentlemen that are
    sleeping three on a grid."   70
Then Tomlinson looked back and forth, and
    there was little grace.
For Hell-Gate filled the houseless soul with the
    Fear of Naked Space.
"Nay, this I ha' heard," quo' Tomlinson, "and
    this was noised abroad,
And this I ha' got from a Belgian book on the
    word of a dead French lord."
—"Ye ha' heard, ye ha' read, ye ha' got, good
    lack! and the tale begins afresh—   75
Have ye sinned one sin for the pride o' the eye
    or the sinful lust of the flesh?"
Then Tomlinson he gripped the bars and yam-
    mered, "Let me in—
"For I mind that I borrowed my neighbor's
    wife to sin the deadly sin."
The Devil he grinned behind the bars, and
    banked the fires high:
"Did ye read of that sin in a book?" said he;
    and Tomlinson said, "Ay!"   80
The Devil he blew upon his nails, and the little
    devils ran,
And he said: "Go husk this whimpering thief
    that comes in the guise of a man:
Winnow him out 'twixt star and star, and sieve
    his proper worth:
There's sore decline in Adam's line if this be
    spawn of earth."
Empusa's [5] crew, so naked-new they may not
    face the fire,   85
But weep that they bin too small to sin to the
    height of their desire,
Over the coal they chased the Soul, and racked
    it all abroad,
As children rifle a caddis-case or the raven's
    foolish hoard
And back they came with the tattered Thing,
    as children after play,

---

[3] Sins left over like slag from burned coal.
[4] All too closely akin.

[5] In classical mythology a monstrous creature,
reputed to devour human beings.

And they said: "The soul that he got from
   God he has bartered clean away.   90
We have threshed a stook [6] of print and book,
   and winnowed a chattering wind,
And many a soul wherefrom he stole, but his
   we cannot find.
We have handled him, we have dandled him,
   we have seared him to the bone,
And Sire, if tooth and nail show truth he has
   no soul of his own."
The Devil he bowed his head on his breast and
   rumbled deep and low:—   95
"I'm all o'er-sib to Adam's breed that I
   should bid him go.
Yet close we lie, and deep we lie, and if I gave
   him place,
My gentlemen that are so proud would flout
   me to my face;
They'd call my house a common stews and me
   a careless host,
And—I would not anger my gentlemen for the
   sake of a shiftless ghost."   100
The Devil he looked at the mangled Soul that
   prayed to feel the flame,
And he thought of Holy Charity, but he
   thought of his own good name:—
"Now ye could haste my coal to waste, and sit
   ye down to fry.
Did ye think of that theft for yourself?" said
   he; and Tomlinson said, "Ay!"
The Devil he blew an outward breath, for his
   heart was free from care:—   105
"Ye have scarce the soul of a louse," he said,
   "but the roots of sin are there.
And for that sin should ye come in were I the
   lord alone.
But sinful pride has rule inside—ay, mightier
   than my own.
Honor and Wit, fore-damned they sit, to each
   his Priest and Whore;
Nay scarce I dare myself go there, and you
   they'd torture sore.   110
Ye are neither spirit nor spirk," he said; "ye
   are neither book nor brute—
Go, get ye back to the flesh again for the sake
   of Man's repute.
I'm all o'er-sib to Adam's breed that I should
   mock your pain,
But look that ye win to worthier sin ere ye
   come back again.
Get hence, the hearse is at your door—the grim
   black stallions wait—   115
They bear your clay to place to-day. Speed,
   lest ye come too late!
Go back to Earth with a lip unsealed—go back
   with an open eye,
And carry my word to the Sons of Men or ever
   ye come to die:
That the sin they do by two and two they must
   pay for one by one,
And . . . the God that you took from a
   printed book be with you, Tomlinson!"   120

[6] Shock.

# Tommy [7]

I went into a public-'ouse to get a pint o' beer,
The publican 'e up an' sez, "We serve no red-
   coats here."
The girls be'ind the bar they laughed an'
   giggled fit to die,
I outs into the street again an' to myself sez I:
  O it's Tommy this, an' Tommy that, an'
    "Tommy, go away";   5
  But it's "Thank you, Mister Atkins," when
    the band begins to play—
  The band begins to play, my boys, the band
    begins to play,
  O it's "Thank you, Mister Atkins," when the
    band begins to play.

I went into a theater as sober as could be,
They gave a drunk civilian room, but 'adn't
   none for me;   10
They sent me to the gallery or round the
   music-'alls,
But when it comes to fightin', Lord! they'll
   shove me in the stalls!
  For it's Tommy this, an' Tommy that, an'
    "Tommy, wait outside";
  But it's "Special train for Atkins" when the
    trooper's on the tide—
  The troopship's on the tide, my boys, the
    troopship's on the tide,   15
  O it's "Special Train for Atkins" when the
    trooper's on the tide.

Yes, makin' mock o' uniforms that guard you
   while you sleep
Is cheaper than them uniforms, an' they're
   starvation cheap;
An' hustlin' drunken soldiers when they're
   goin' large a bit
Is five times better business the paradin' in
   full kit.   20
  Then it's Tommy this, an' Tommy that, an'
    "Tommy, 'ow's yer soul?"
  But it's "Thin red line of 'eroes" when the
    drums begin to roll—
  The drums begin to roll, my boys, the drums
    begin to roll,
  O it's "Thin red line of 'eroes" when the
    drums begin to roll.

We aren't no thin red 'eroes, nor we aren't no
   blackguards too,   25
But single men in barricks, most remarkable
   like you;
An' if sometimes our conduck isn't all your
   fancy paints;
Why, single men in barricks don't grow into
   plaster saints;
  While it's Tommy this, an' Tommy that,
    an' "Tommy, fall be'ind,"

[7] This and the three following poems were published in *Barrack-Room Ballads* (1892).

But it's "Please to walk in front, sir," when
there's trouble in the wind,           30
There's trouble in the wind, my boys, there's
trouble in the wind,
O it's "Please to walk in front, sir," when
there's trouble in the wind.

You talk o' better food for us, an' schools, an'
fires, an' all:
We'll wait for extry rations if you treat us
rational.
Don't mess about the cook-room slops, but
prove it to our face           35
The Widow's Uniform is not the soldier-man's
disgrace.
For it's Tommy this, an' Tommy that, an'
"Chuck him out, the brute!"
But it's "Savior of 'is country" when the guns
begin to shoot;
An' it's Tommy this, an' Tommy that, an'
anything you please;
An' Tommy ain't a bloomin' fool—you bet
that Tommy sees!           40

## "Fuzzy-Wuzzy"

### (*Sudan Expeditionary Force*)

We've fought with many men acrost the seas,
An' some of 'em was brave an' some was
not:
The Paythan an' the Zulu an' Burmese;
But the Fuzzy was the finest o' the lot.
We never got a ha'porth's [8] change of 'im:     5
'E squatted in the scrub an' 'ocked our
'orses,[9]
'E cut our sentries up at Sua*kim*,
An' 'e played the cat an' banjo with our
forces.
So 'ere's *to* you, Fuzzy-Wuzzy, at your
'ome in the Sudan;
You're a pore benighted 'eathen but a
first-class fightin' man;           10
We gives you your certificate, an' if you
want it signed
We'll come an' 'ave a romp with you
whenever you're inclined.

We took our chanst among the Kyber 'ills,
The Boers knocked us silly at a mile,
The Burman give us Irriwaddy chills,     15
An' a Zulu *impi* [10] dished us up in style:
But all we ever got from such as they
Was pop to what the Fuzzy made us swaller;
We 'eld our bloomin' own, the papers say,
But man for man the Fuzzy knocked us
'oller.           20
Then 'ere's *to* you, Fuzzy-Wuzzy, an' the
missis and the kid;

[8] A halfpenny worth's.
[9] Cut the tendons in the hocks, or joints in the middle of the hind legs, of our horses.
[10] Body of warriors.

Our orders was to break you, an' of course
we went an' did.
We sloshed you with Martinis, an' it
wasn't 'ardly fair;
But for all the odds agin' you, Fuzzy-
Wuz, you broke the square.

'E 'asn't got no papers of 'is own,           25
'E 'asn't got no medals nor rewards,
So *we* must certify the skill 'e's shown,
In usin' of 'is long two-'anded swords:
When 'e's 'oppin' in an' out among the bush
With 'is coffin-'eaded shield an' shovel-spear,
An 'appy day with Fuzzy on the rush     31
Will last an 'ealthy Tommy for a year.
So 'ere's *to* you, Fuzzy-Wuzzy, an' your
friends which are no more,
If we 'adn't lost some messmates we would
'elp you to deplore.
But give an' take's the gospel, an' we'll
call the bargain fair,           35
For if you 'ave lost more than us, you
crumpled up the square!

'E rushes at the smoke when we let drive,
An', before we know, 'e's 'ackin' at our 'ead;
'E's all 'ot sand an' ginger when alive,
An' 'e's generally shammin' when 'e's dead.
'E's a daisy, 'e's a ducky, 'e's a lamb!     41
'E's a injia-rubber idiot on the spree,
'E's the on'y thing that doesn't give a damn
For a Regiment o' British Infantree!
So 'ere's *to* you, Fuzzy-Wuzzy, at your
'ome in the Sudan;           45
You're a pore benighted 'eathen but a
first-class fightin' man;
An' 'ere's *to* you, Fuzzy-Wuzzy, with your
'ayrick 'ead of 'air—
You big black boundin' beggar—for you
broke a British square!

## Gunga Din

You may talk o' gin and beer
When you're quartered safe out 'ere,
An' you're sent to penny-fights an' Aldershot
it;
But when it comes to slaughter
You will do your work on water,           5
An' you'll lick the bloomin' boots of 'im that's
got it.
Now in Injia's sunny clime,
Where I used to spend my time
A-servin' of 'Er Majesty the Queen,
Of all them blackfaced crew           10
The finest man I knew
Was our regimental bhisti,[11] Gunga Din.
He was "Din! Din! Din!
You limpin' lump o' brick-dust, Gunga Din!
Hi! Slippy *hitherao*!           15
Water, get it! *Panee lao* [12]
You squidgy-nosed old idol, Gunga Din."

[11] Water-carrier.           [12] Bring water quickly.

The uniform 'e wore
Was nothin' much before,
An' rather less than 'arf o' that be'ind,                    20
For a piece o' twisty rag
An' a goatskin water-bag
Was all the field-equipment 'e could find.
When the sweatin' troop-train lay
In a sidin' through the day,                                 25
Where the 'eat would make your bloomin'
        eyebrows crawl,
We shouted "Harry By!" [13]
Till our throats were bricky-dry,
Then we wopped 'im 'cause 'e couldn't serve
        us all.
    It was "Din! Din! Din!                                   30
    You 'eathen, where the mischief 'ave you
        been?
    You put some *juldee* [14] in it
    Or I'll *marrow* [15] you this minute
    If you don't fill up my helmet, Gunga Din!"

'E would dot an' carry one                                   35
Till the longest day was done;
An' 'e didn't seem to know the use o' fear.
If we charged or broke or cut,
You could bet your bloomin' nut,
'E'd be waitin' fifty paces right flank rear.               40
With 'is mussick [16] on 'is back,
'E would skip with our attack,
An' watch us till the bugles made "Retire"
An' for all 'is dirty 'ide
'E was white, clear white, inside                           45
When 'e went to tend the wounded under
        fire!
    It was "Din! Din! Din!"
    With the bullets kickin' dust-spots on the
        green
    When the cartridges ran out,
    You could hear the front ranks shout,            50
    "Hi! ammunition-mules an' Gunga Din!"

I sha'n't forgit the night
When I dropped be'ind the fight
With a bullet where my belt-plate should 'a'
        been.
I was chokin' mad with thirst,                              55
An' the man that spied me first
Was our good old grinnin', gruntin' Gunga
        Din.
'E lifted up my 'ead,
An' he plugged me where I bled,
An' 'e guv me 'arf-a-pint o' water green.          60
It was crawlin' and it stunk,
But of all the drinks I've drunk,
I'm gratefullest to one from Gunga Din.
    It was "Din! Din! Din!
    'Ere's a beggar with a bullet through 'is
        spleen;                                              65
    'E's chawin' up the ground,
    An' 'e's kickin' all around:
    For Gawd's sake git the water, Gunga Din!"

[13] O Brother!      [14] Be quick.      [15] Hit you.
[16] Water-skin.

'E carried me away
To where a dooli [17] lay,                                  70
An' a bullet came an' drilled the beggar clean.
'E put me safe inside,
An' just before 'e died,
"I 'ope you liked your drink," sez Gunga Din.
So I'll meet 'im later on                                   75
At the place where 'e is gone—
Where it's always double drill and no canteen.
'E'll be squattin' on the coals
Givin' drink to poor damned souls,
An' I'll get a swig in hell from Gunga Din!        80
    Yes, Din! Din! Din!
    You Lazarushian-leather Gunga Din!
    Though I've belted you and flayed you,
    By the livin' Gawd that made you,
    You're a better man than I am, Gunga
        Din!                                                85

# Mandalay [18]

By the old Moulmein [19] Pagoda, lookin' east-
        ward to the sea,
There's a Burma girl a-settin', and I know she
        thinks o' me;
For the wind is in the palm-trees, and the
        temple-bells they say:
"Come you back, you British soldier; come you
        back to Mandalay!"
        Come you back to Mandalay,            5
        Where the old Flotilla lay:
        Can't you 'ear their paddles chunkin'
                from Rangoon to Mandalay?
        On the road to Mandalay,
        Where the flyin'-fishes play,
        An' the dawn comes up like thunder
                outer China 'crost the Bay!    10

'Er petticoat was yaller an' 'er little cap was
        green,
An' 'er name was Supi-yaw-lat—jes' the same
        as Theebaw's Queen,
An' I seed her first a-smokin' of a whackin'
        white cheroot,
An' a-wastin' Christian kisses on an 'eathen
        idol's foot:
        Bloomin' idol made o' mud—           15
        Wot they called the Great Gawd
                Budd—
        Plucky lot she cared for idols when
                I kissed 'er where she stud!
        On the road to Mandalay . . .

When the mist was on the rice-fields an' the
        sun was droppin' slow,

[17] Litter used in carrying wounded.
[18] Mandalay is the capital of Upper Burma, whose
ruler, Theebaw, provoked hostilities with the British
in 1885. As a result of the expedition sent against
him his country was annexed to India in the following year.
[19] Moulmein and Rangoon are seaports in Lower
Burma.

She'd git 'er little banjo an' she'd sing "*Kulla-
lo-lo!*"                                            20
With 'er arm upon my shoulder an' 'er cheek
  agin my cheek
We useter watch the steamers an' the *hathis*
  pilin' teak.
    Elephants a-pilin' teak
    In the sludgy, squdgy creek,
    Where the silence 'ung that 'eavy
      you was 'arf afraid to speak! 25
    On the road to Mandalay . . .

But that's all shove be'ind me—long ago an'
  fur away,
An' there ain't no 'busses runnin' from the
  Bank to Mandalay;
An' I'm learnin' 'ere in London what the ten-
  year soldier tells:
"If you've 'eard the East a-callin', you won't
  never 'eed naught else."             30
    No! you won't 'eed nothin' else
    But them spicy garlic smells,
    An' the sunshine an' the palm-trees
      an' the tinkly temple-bells;
    On the road to Mandalay . . .

I am sick o' wastin' leather on these gritty
  pavin'-stones,                        35
An' the blasted Henglish drizzle wakes the
  fever in my bones;
'Tho' I walks with fifty 'ousemaids outer
  Chelsea to the Strand,
An' they talks a lot o' lovin', but wot do they
  understand?
    Beefy face an' grubby 'and—
    Law! wot do they understand?    40
    I've a neater, sweeter maiden in a
      cleaner, greener land!
    On the road to Mandalay . . .

Ship me somewheres east of Suez, where the
  best is like the worst,
Where there aren't no Ten Commandments
  an' a man can raise a thirst;
For the temple-bells are callin', an' it's there
  that I would be—                    45
By the old Moulmein Pagoda, looking lazy at
  the sea;
    On the road to Mandalay,
    Where the old Flotilla lay,
    With our sick beneath the awnings
      when we went to Mandalay!
    On the road to Mandalay,      50
    Where the flyin'-fishes play,
    An' the dawn comes up like thunder
      outer China 'crost the Bay!

## Recessional

### 1897

God of our fathers, known of old,
  Lord of our far-flung battle-line,

Beneath whose awful Hand we hold
  Dominion over palm and pine—
Lord God of Hosts, be with us yet,    5
Lest we forget—lest we forget!

The tumult and the shouting dies;
  The Captains and the Kings depart:
Still stands Thine ancient sacrifice,
  An humble and a contrite heart.    10
Lord God of Hosts, be with us yet,
Lest we forget—lest we forget!

Far-called, our navies melt away;
  On dune and headland sinks the fire:
Lo, all our pomp of yesterday        15
  Is one with Nineveh and Tyre!
Judge of the Nations, spare us yet,
Lest we forget—lest we forget!

If, drunk with sight of power, we loose
  Wild tongues that have not Thee in awe, 20
Such boastings as the Gentiles use,
  Or lesser breeds without the Law—
Lord God of Hosts, be with us yet,
Lest we forget—lest we forget!

For heathen heart that puts her trust  25
  In reeking tube and iron shard,[20]
All valiant dust that builds on dust,
  And guarding, calls not Thee to guard,
For frantic boast and foolish word—
Thy mercy on Thy People, Lord!        30

## When 'Omer Smote 'Is Bloomin' Lyre

When 'Omer smote 'is bloomin' lyre,
  He'd 'eard men sing by land an' sea;
An' what he thought 'e might require,
  'E went an' took—the same as me!

The market-girls an' fishermen,        5
  The shepherds an' the sailors, too,
They 'eard old songs turn up again,
  But kep' it quiet—same as you!

They knew 'e stole; 'e knew they knowed.
  They didn't tell, nor make a fuss,    10
But winked at 'Omer down the road,
  An' 'e winked back—the same as us!

## JOHN MASEFIELD

### (1878–)

### Cargoes [1]

Quinquireme of Nineveh from distant Ophir,[2]
Rowing home to haven in sunny Palestine,

[20] In gun and bullet.
[1] This and the following four poems are reprinted
by permission of The Macmillan Company, publishers, and of Mr. Masefield.
[2] The place, probably in southeastern Arabia, from
which the ships of King Solomon brought gold and
precious stones (I Kings, 10:11).

With a cargo of ivory,
And apes and peacocks,
Sandalwood, cedarwood, and sweet white wine.

Stately Spanish galleon coming from the
    Isthmus,                                             6
Dipping through the Tropics by the palm-
    green shores,
With a cargo of diamonds,
Emeralds, amethysts,
Topazes, and cinnamon, and gold moidores.[3] 10

Dirty British coaster with a salt-caked smoke
    stack,
Butting through the Channel in the mad
    March days,
With a cargo of Tyne coal,
Road-rails, pig-lead,
Firewood, iron-ware, and cheap tin trays.    15

## Captain Stratton's Fancy

Oh some are fond of red wine, and some are
    fond of white,
And some are all for dancing by the pale moon-
    light;
But rum alone's the tipple, and the heart's de-
    light
    Of the old bold mate of Henry Morgan.[4]

Oh some are fond of Spanish wine, and some
    are fond of French,                              5
And some'll swallow tay and stuff fit only for
    a wench;
But I'm for right Jamaica till I roll beneath
    the bench,
    Says the old bold mate of Henry Morgan.

Oh some are for the lily, and some are for the
    rose,
But I am for the sugar-cane that in Jamaica
    grows;                                           10
For it's that that makes the bonny drink to
    warm my copper nose,
    Says the old bold mate of Henry Morgan.

Oh some are fond of fiddles, and a song well
    sung,
And some are all for music for to lilt upon the
    tongue;
But mouths were made for tankards, and for
    sucking at the bung,                             15
    Says the old bold mate of Henry Morgan.

Oh some are fond of dancing, and some are
    fond of dice,
And some are all for red lips, and pretty lasses'
    eyes;

[3] Portuguese coins.
[4] Sir Henry Morgan (1635–1688), who was at one
time leader of the West Indian buccaneers, but was
later knighted by Charles II and sent to Jamaica as
lieutenant-governor.

But a right Jamaica puncheon [5] is a finer prize
    To the old bold mate of Henry Morgan.  20

Oh some that's good and godly ones they hold
    that it's a sin
To troll [6] the jolly bowl around, and let the
    dollars spin;
But I'm for toleration and for drinking at the
    inn,
    Says the old bold mate of Henry Morgan.

Oh some are sad and wretched folk that go in
    silken suits,                                    25
And there's a mort [7] of wicked rogues that live
    in good reputes;
So I'm for drinking honestly, and dying in my
    boots,
    Like an old bold mate of Henry Morgan.

## The West Wind

It's a warm wind, the west wind, full of birds'
    cries;
I never hear the west wind but tears are in my
    eyes.
For it comes from the west lands, the old
    brown hills,
And April's in the west wind, and daffodils.

It's a fine land, the west land, for hearts as
    tired as mine,                                   5
Apple orchards blossom there, and the air's like
    wine.
There is cool green grass there, where men
    may lie at rest,
And the thrushes are in song there, fluting
    from the nest.

"Will you not come home, brother? you have
    been long away,
It's April, and blossom time, and white is the
    spray;                                           10
And bright is the sun, brother, and warm is
    the rain,—
Will you not come home, brother, home to us
    again?

"The young corn is green, brother, where the
    rabbits run,
It's blue sky, and white clouds, and warm rain
    and sun.
It's song to a man's soul, brother, fire to a
    man's brain,                                     15
To hear the wild bees and see the merry spring
    again.

"Larks are singing in the west, brother, above
    the green wheat,
So will ye not come home, brother, and rest
    your tired feet?

[5] Cask of Jamaica rum.          [6] Pass.
[7] Great number.

I've a balm for bruised hearts, brother, sleep
    for aching eyes,"
Says the warm wind, the west wind, full of
    birds' cries.    20

It's the white road westwards is the road I
    must tread
To the green grass, the cool grass, and rest for
    heart and head,
To the violets and the brown brooks and the
    thrushes' song,
In the fine land, the west land, the land where
    I belong.

# C. L. M.

In the dark womb where I began
My mother's life made me a man.
Through all the months of human birth
Her beauty fed my common earth.
I cannot see, nor breathe, nor stir,    5
But through the death of some of her.

Down in the darkness of the grave
She cannot see the life she gave.
For all her love, she cannot tell
Whether I use it ill or well,    10
Nor knock at dusty doors to find
Her beauty dusty in the mind.

If the grave's gates could be undone,
She would not know her little son,
I am so grown. If we should meet    15
She would pass by me in the street,
Unless my soul's face let her see
My sense of what she did for me.

What have I done to keep in mind
My debt to her and womankind?    20
What woman's happier life repays
Her for those months of wretched days?
For all my mouthless body leeched
Ere Birth's releasing hell was reached?

What have I done, or tried, or said    25
In thanks to that dear woman dead?
Men triumph over women still,

Men trample women's rights at will,
And man's lust roves the world untamed.

. . . . . .

O grave, keep shut lest I be shamed.    30

# On Growing Old

Be with me Beauty for the fire is dying,
My dog and I are old, too old for roving,
Man, whose young passion sets the spindrift
    flying
Is soon too lame to march, too cold for loving.

I take the book and gather to the fire,    5
Turning old yellow leaves; minute by minute,
The clock ticks to my heart; a withered wire
Moves a thin ghost of music in the spinet.

I cannot sail your seas, I cannot wander,
Your cornland, nor your hill-land nor your
    valleys,    10
Ever again, nor share the battle yonder
Where the young knight the broken squadron
    rallies.

Only stay quiet while my mind remembers
The beauty of fire from the beauty of embers.

Beauty, have pity, for the strong have power,
The rich their wealth, the beautiful their
    grace    16
Summer of man its sunlight and its flower
Spring of man all April in a face.

Only, as in the jostling in the Strand,
Where the mob thrusts or loiters or is loud 20
The beggar with the saucer in his hand
Asks only a penny from the passing crowd.

So, from this glittering world with all its
    fashion
Its fire and play of men, its stir, its march,
Let me have wisdom, Beauty, wisdom and
    passion,    25
Bread to the soul, rain where the summers
    parch.

Give me but these, and though the darkness
    close
Even the night will blossom as the rose.

# VII

# THE PRESENT TIME, 1914-

Now at last, after tracing the stream of English literature and life from their first recorded origins through the ages of Chaucer, Shakespeare, Johnson, Wordsworth, and Tennyson, we are ready to emerge from the vital past into the vital present, and to sample at first hand the literary art of our own time. All history is a curtain-raiser for the present—and now as we read the works of living authors the curtain goes up, and the world of art and the world of our experience share the same time dimension.

There were some comfortable qualities in the great books that we will not find in the literature of contemporary England. For one thing, it is always easier to gain perspective on old books than on new; and our evaluations may be proved over-harsh or over-generous within the generation. For another thing, an author who is no longer living cannot change his mind and become another kind of person entirely (as Aldous Huxley may be said to have done between the early 1920's and the late 1930's), or read our comments and tell us we are wrongheaded. And perhaps most disturbing of all, a contemporary poem or story or play that satirizes society is showing us our own world; Huxley, Auden, and Eliot probe beneath the merciful inattention and aloofness we use to preserve our security of mind, and show us what we often would rather not see.

Yet the chance that we will meet or hear Mr. Auden adds immediacy to his work—and the facts that he is still writing, that his style and approach are still developing, that his most significant contribution to literature may not have been written, may in fact now be in the process of taking form and substance, all

bring us closer to the living artist. Stereotypes and neatly-outlined generalizations do not seem to apply to a man who may yet develop a new style, or enter a different field of literature, or produce a critical work which will reveal new dimensions of his thought.

It is certain, also, that what literature tries to do for its time needs to be done for our time as much as for any time in the past. Literature seeks to interpret life, to show us life from a perspective new or unusual for us, to reach beneath the surface of life to give us understanding of the emotions and feelings, the nature and humanity of man. In contemporary literature these interpretations, perspectives, and understandings have a direct relationship to our own experience and our own actions and decisions; through this relationship we can learn about both life and literature.

Anyone who has read a Shaw play or a Katherine Mansfield story or a Huxley novel knows what it can tell us of life, as it extends and deepens our experience through adding the perspective and sympathy of the author's view of life to our own insight. We learn about literature through observing how the contemporary author treats the world around us—the same world that is the subject-matter of newspaper stories, grade "B" motion pictures, and the articles in *True Confessions* magazine—and how in his treatment he creates something more than life, something of our time and yet not tied to a dateline, something that shares with *Beowulf*, *Everyman*, *Tom Jones*, and "In Memoriam" the qualities of genuineness and universality that make for enduring literature.

### THE SEARCH FOR AN ANSWER

The basic questions "Why is man?" and "What is the good life?" have always engaged the writer, no matter how objective he has tried to be. To the author of *Beowulf*, the highest purpose for the thane was to serve the king with bravery and loyalty; for the king, the highest purposes were to be generous to his thane and to be powerful in war. Some authors in the Middle Ages found their answer to the basic human questions in the Church and in the holy symbols of the Church; others developed the intricate and idealized concept of courtly love. The Renaissance was a return to the Greek ideal of humanism, the worthwhileness of man and of life for their own sake, for what man might achieve and life become. The Reformation drew attention again to the discipline of the Church; John Bunyan perhaps best presents the ideal of steadfastly following the narrow path of the Christian to the rejection of the temptations of the flesh.

The eighteenth century was called The Age of Reason because its answer was moderation, control, restraint, order. The reaction to this kind of answer was the Romantic Movement, which during its long course presented impassioned answers in great variety: deism; romantic love; the nobility of the unspoiled, the savage, the remote; democracy; humanitarianism; transcendentalism, and the forces of the mystic and the supernatural; pure beauty in art; a belief that emotion was a surer guide than intellect, that feeling rather than reason led to right judgments; the revival of religion; even theories of communism and fascism.

The nineteenth century held many hopes for man, and all were expressed in literature. It seemed that the Industrial Revolution would result in greater happiness and a higher level of life for humanity: the machines which made shoes and cloth and tools and books held the promise of a shorter day and relief from drudgery for the worker, and more, better, and cheaper products readily available to all. It seemed that there would be a new level of literateness, a golden age of cultural understanding, as magazines and books became accessible to everyone and as works of art could be mass-produced. The railway and steamboat opened new horizons of travel and cultural accessibility. And certainly some of these benefits were clearly realized—but there were so many offsetting regressions that the progress

could be seen only dimly, if at all. The hopes were smothered in disillusion, and the tone of disillusion remains dominant as we review the literary expression of the Industrial Revolution.

Also, the nineteenth century believed strongly, almost desperately, in political reform. The political structure seemed an adequate tool to achieve the highest hopes for the happiness and felicity of man, if its chinks could just be mended, and a few new laws passed. Universal suffrage was one of the noblest goals of the political reformers; the English Liberals felt that the achievement of a real government by the people would result in a kind of Utopia, and that this achievement was within reach, there and then, in the towns and boroughs of England. But universal suffrage did not result in a real government by the people, nor in a Utopia; and the ambitious Poor Laws and labor laws did not bring perfect felicity to the people, though they did prevent some extreme forms of exploitation.

Science came of age in the nineteenth century, and seemed at last ready to supply the answers not only to the why and whence but also to the whither and how of man. Natural science had the most spectacular answers; the theories developed in one book alone, Darwin's *The Origin of Species*, upset the philosophy, theology, education, and art of the civilized world. Genetics and medical science offered new hope for the improvement of man, and bacteriology promised control of disease. At the same time petroleum geology began to provide the new fuels which were to revolutionize transportation and the economy in the twentieth century. On the tangible and practical level, physical science contributed the telegraph, the telephone, and the electric light, and on the theoretical level, the clearest and purest operational definition of the scientific approach to knowledge. Chemistry also staggered the imagination with syntheses which to the superstitious seemed little less than creation, and biochemistry made its tentative beginnings, hypothesizing a chemistry of life. With all this scientific achievement, however, it became clear that people were not noticeably happier than they had been; if anything, the pushing back of the borders of the unknown made it seem less likely that there was a great benign unknowable force beyond the boundaries of perception. And people still had human problems.

At the end of the nineteenth century, Kipling (and G. A. Henty) celebrated the Briton's pride in the Empire and his sense of responsibility to its increasing millions; the Empire seemed a challenge important enough to engage the best in man. At its height, the Empire covered the staggering total of 16,000,000 square miles, nearly one-third of the land surface of the earth, and included a population of over half a billion. Indeed, the sun never set on the British Empire. Control of this vast quantity of natural and human resources lay in a small island kingdom with a total area almost exactly that of Ohio, and a population of about forty million. It must have seemed to some, for at least a few optimistic years, that the "reason for being" for the Briton was to lead these subject millions to the good life, and through trade with them, to build an even better life for the people of England. Both freedom from want and freedom from fear seemed guaranteed by the power of the Empire. However, as the new century developed, it became increasingly clear that Britannia's rule of the waves had to be shared. After the Boer War there was no unshared British victory in war, and there was no significant extension of the Empire except by the division of the German colonies after the Treaty of Versailles and by the British claims in Antarctica. The process of disintegration of the Empire had begun, actually, before then—with the establishment of the self-governing commonwealths of Canada, Australia, New Zealand, and the Union of South Africa; the power structure of empire, at least, was lost, as the commonwealths were no longer united by need for the paternal strength and support of Britain, but by common interests and tradition. The word "free" in the statute of Westminster indicated the new relationship; the crown had become "the symbol of the free association of the members of the British Commonwealth of Nations."

Thus the Industrial Revolution, politics, science, and the growth of empire glimmered with hope for man, but delivered less than promised. Each at one time seemed the way to Progress, the channel through which England would move "onward and upward toward its glorious destiny." The Idea of Progress itself lost some of its glitter as the successive disappointments came.

## THE CHANGING ROLE OF BRITAIN

We have traced some of the changes which affected Britain in the nineteenth century. It is significant that nearly all these changes grew out of new movements in science, politics, or

technology, themselves largely begun in Britain, and that the movements had a profound effect on the world outside the British Empire. Britain's Industrial Revolution changed world production, and Britain's Darwin profoundly influenced world thought. Britain had been a world leader since the defeat of the Spanish Armada in 1588; throughout the nineteenth century Britain was *the* world leader.

True, Napoleon had achieved great power, but the Duke of Wellington defeated him on land at the Battle of Waterloo, as Lord Nelson had earlier defeated his admirals at sea, at Aboukir and Trafalgar. The United States had won a favorable treaty after the War of 1812, with Britain diverted by greater dangers in Europe and unwilling to carry on a costly long-range war largely as a matter of principle; certainly, however, the United States did not qualify in 1815 or even later in the century as a world power to rank with Britain. Bismarck's Germany did not challenge Britain's strength or her predominant world position.

Britain dominated world markets, as well as the naval fleets of the world, in the nineteenth century. Between 1821 and 1876 the already enormous trade between Great Britain and the rest of the world (including British colonies) increased more than 700%. In the third quarter of the century Britain produced more than half the world's output of pig iron, then the chief basic metal for all machine use, and was by far the largest steel-manufacturing center of the world. British finance also dominated world markets in the nineteenth century; the largest and most influential banks and insurance companies in the world developed in London. The British gold pound was the standard for world monetary exchange.

With the unlimited natural resources and the developing markets of the colonies, the security accompanying domination of the seas, and the advantage of trained and skilled manpower by the millions, it must have seemed to Britons that British leadership had only one way to go—up, to encompass yet more achievement.

Yet in 1872 an event occurred which went practically unnoticed, but which indicated the passing of the peak of British power. British exports began to fall, though imports continued to rise. Britain's population had nearly reached its productive capacity; although production continued to increase, its rate of increase had stabilized, and it could no longer increase as rapidly as the demand of the British market itself, swelled by the steadily rising standard of living. Britain had nearly reached its optimum level of production efficiency, and was helpless to compete with the overwhelming growth of industry in countries which had begun later but which had more room to grow, more people to grow with, and a more efficient location of plants in relation to raw materials and markets. Thus between 1872 and 1913, though British production of pig iron (for example) continued to rise steadily, the British share of world production dropped from half to one-tenth. Germany and the United States were the major gainers.

Of course, if Britain had developed industry in her colonies instead of bringing all raw materials to England for processing and resale, the bottleneck could have been avoided, or at least partly avoided—but it is easy to recognize this fact after the event. Since this book is about literature and not about economics, the important point is not what might have happened, but what did happen, and what effect it had on the creative art of the British people. And what did happen is substantially this: during the years of transition leading into the modern period of English literature, England lost its dominant place in world trade and politics, lost its dynamic movement of expansion of empire and growth of power, lost much of its hope for future greatness. Englishmen accustomed to visualize their country in the leading role had to accept a lesser concept. This changed concept did not destroy English patriotism, but it certainly destroyed "March of Empire" optimism.

### CULTURE AND PERSONALITY

At the same time as the British citizen in the twentieth century learned to accept a lesser role for his country, the new social sciences were developing definitions for "role" and for the concepts that have supplemented Darwinian evolution as ways to look at the world and its people to find new meanings and relationships: "culture" and "personality."

Culture is a major concern of anthropology and sociology; it has little in common with the "culture" of Matthew Arnold's essay or with the meaning "appreciating art and music and poetry," and it is not a value judgment. In the anthropological concept, culture is what people learn from the generations preceding them and pass on to those which follow; the shared knowledge, customs, and beliefs of a group make up their culture. Works of art or poetry are cultural products, but so are eco-

nomic theories, recipes, jokes, superstitions, morality, and language itself. An awareness of culture from this point of view brings new insight into the nature of tradition and of its relationship to change and innovation in human institutions, of its relationships to the form and matter of works of creative art. Just as the idea of evolution created a tension in the Victorian mind, the new concept pulling against the accepted and "known" ideas of creation and divine purpose, so the idea of culture creates a tension in the mind of the person who accepts and believes in a tradition yet can see it as a tradition, a cultural product evolved by a group and maintained by the group, and defensible on only arbitrary grounds.

Personality is a main concern of the comparatively new science of psychology. Just as culture involves a kind of evolution, a shaping process to meet the needs for survival of the group, so the psychology of personality development describes an evolution within the lifetime of a person, a development of patterns of response to meet the needs for survival of the individual, patterns which correspond to traditions in culture, and which, like traditions, resist change, yet remain to some extent open to change. The psychology of human personality development creates a whole series of tensions between the "known" and the new, the static and the dynamic. The tension between the idea of freedom and the idea of responsibility, or between the arbitrary concepts of both freedom and responsibility and the evidence of research in psychology, is one example: the adult who "knew" he was free to think or act and learns that he instead will respond in patterns already strongly determined by his experience knows a tension equivalent to Milton's in his discussion of predestination and free will. Psychology adds dimensions of understanding to sin and guilt, to hate and love and fear. However, to the guardians of tradition these new dimensions of understanding are potentially dangerous and disruptive.

Culture and personality interact, and help shape and explain each other. The sciences which have grown up around them also interact and help explain each other. Philosophy and biology contributed to the development of anthropology and psychology, and have not escaped being influenced in turn. Bergson, Dewey, Russell, and Whitehead in philosophy; William James, Freud, and Jung in psychology; and Tylor, Frazer, Boas, Levy Brühl, Sapir, and Malinowski in anthropology have contributed notably to the modern view of man, and to an understanding of his motives, of the forces which shape him, and of the values, images, and meanings which are both his interpretations of experience and the shapers of his behavior.

## FRAGMENTATION OF CULTURE

As the social sciences developed theories of culture and research methods to study cultural change, the English culture itself was changing more rapidly than ever before in its history.

Tradition is developed to ensure the survival of the culture and the people who hold the culture; it is protected by cultural isolation. When contact between different cultural groups occurs, two alternate traditions may be seen operating, and both are questioned and therefore threatened. The observer may decide he can get along better without either. If there are reasonable and unreasonable parts of a tradition, the observer may discard both, or neither, or either. An observer may develop a well-balanced sense of evaluation of tradition and change, depending partly on the rate of change that is made possible by cross-cultural contact and social control. Forces tending to break down cultural isolation developed with great rapidity following the invention of electricity and the gasoline engine. The telephone, the mass circulation of magazines and newspapers, and the increasing use of the motor car had a strong impact before World War I. The war itself sent millions into training, and other group activities, breaking down regional differences and developing international cultural awareness. After the war tourists descended on all parts of Great Britain, in season and out. The cinema, which had been an interesting novelty before the war, became the dominant art form of the nation even before the addition of sound. In the 1920's and 1930's radio sent standard British pronunciation and a vast array of facts about other ways of life to nearly every British family.

A phenomenon imported first from America, the comic strip, developed a new dimension, the comic book, in the late 1930's. World War II and the years following brought even more international cultural awareness than World War I. After World War II came widespread television, and greatly expanded air travel brought any part of the world within range of a few hours' flight. The printed word was used in diverse ways, far too numerous to list completely—advertising and mail promotion; catalogues; reports and pamphlets distributed to the public; scientific and scholarly journals. At the same time the length of school terms, the total years of school attendance, and the percentage of persons reached by education increased steadily.

The result of all this intercommunication has been notable loss of speech differences and of distinguishing features of regional or rural dress or manner, particularly among the young; much loss of folkways and seasonal customs; and some loss of prejudice toward and distrust of outsiders. Tradition itself has been the main loser; in each decade there has been less respect for tradition, for old places and for history, for the ideals of the nineteenth-century empire, the old morality and the authority-figures who try to enforce it.

The breakdown of tradition is not a new process; it is the theme of Wordsworth's "Michael," and earlier it appeared in works by Defoe and Fielding. Hardy saw that the process was accelerating in the 1870's and 1880's, and dramatized in several novels the conflict of forces for and against tradition. In the twentieth century, however, we have not simply a continuation of a slow process begun long before and likely to be sustained for centuries: we have what seems to be a nearly universal fragmentation of culture, and a readiness to abandon tradition not already abandoned whenever the immediate reward seems to make it worth while. The decline of tradition has moved so far since World War I that Eliot, Aldous Huxley, and other intellectual leaders who helped destroy tradition in the 1920's have turned to an attempt to salvage some of what remains before it is too late.

## THE AGE OF ANXIETY

The new lesser role of Britain, with its loss of security; the new sciences of culture and personality, with their new tensions working against the dogma and authority of the past; the new fragmentation of culture, with its tendency to accept change for its own sake and to throw out the good of tradition with the bad: all these contribute to what Auden called *The Age of Anxiety*. In that play Malon thinks that

We're quite in the dark: we do not
Know the connection between
The clock we are bound to obey
And the miracle we must not despair of. . . .

The key to the age is complexity. The twentieth century is, as Henry Adams indicated, a chaos of multiplicity. Everything is going on at once, and influencing everything else. The tempo of life has been speeded up, so that minutes seem to become of first importance, and saving minutes becomes an end in itself. Quantity of time—or of anything else—is generally more important than quality: hence the dilemma posed in Auden's poem quoted above. In a world of quantity it is hard to keep faith with enduring values, which are always qualitative. There is no meaning in quantity, no unifying thread.

Yet life has always been complex; even in Hrothgar's mead-hall and in the priory of Chaucer's Prioress there were conflicting values and motives, divergent meanings for the same phenomena, combined belief and unbelief, understanding and despair of understanding. Perhaps complexity is the key not of the age but of life itself.

But now in the twentieth century, in the new light of psychology and cultural science, we *know* how complex life is, and we refuse to be misled by oversimplifications. This awareness of complexity can contribute to a kind of multi-dimensional balance based on seeing both sides of situations and events (though sometimes modern man would trade this balanced view for simple faith, and somehow, sometimes he does). Consider a question of morality, for example: if the question is, "Should I or shouldn't I tell a lie to protect a friend?" the answer of the age is not "I should," complicated by feelings of guilt about the lie; or "I shouldn't," complicated by feelings of guilt about disloyalty; but "I should *and* I shouldn't," complicated by the need to decide one way or the other in spite of the multiple awareness. As Eliot indicated in "Gerontion,"

Neither fear nor courage saves us. Unnatural vices
Are fathered by our heroism. Virtues
Are forced upon us by our impudent crimes.
These tears are shaken from the wrath-bearing tree.

To the citizen of the modern world who is imperfectly aware of complexity, and who tries to keep up with the confused chaos of expectations he is certain to meet, there will come anxiety, possibly neurosis, or at best a kind of uneasy adjustment to multiple standards.

A further element of complexity arises in that a situation in life or literature is likely to involve both those who are and those who are not aware of the multiple dimensions of meaning in the situation; Eliot's *Murder in the Cathedral*, for example, shows Thomas Becket,

a man who feels that he should and should not become a martyr, speaking his perceptive line

The last temptation is the greatest treason:
To do the right deed for the wrong reason.

against the counterpoint of a chorus of women who represent preoccupation with surface awareness:

Sometimes the corn has failed us,
Sometimes the harvest is good,
One year is a year of rain,
Another a year of dryness,
One year the apples are abundant,
Another year the plums are lacking.

## INDIVIDUALITY

The twentieth century is above all, in art and literature, the century of the individual. The ready acceptance of Gerard Manley Hopkins by modern poets and critics is a tribute to his individuality, to the particularity and separateness with which he viewed all things. Eliot's individuality is triumphant over all schools and movements, even over the threatened dominance of the arch-individualist of the century, Ezra Pound. Joyce learned to be his own man early; the journal entry for April 26 which ends *Portrait of the Artist as a Young Man* reads

Mother is putting my new secondhand clothes in order. She prays now, she says, that I may learn in my own life and away from home and friends what the heart is and what it feels.

Herbert Read indicated the scope of D. H. Lawrence's individualism when he described him as

the poet-philosopher of a movement which includes, as intellectual counterparts, William James, Bergson and Freud. It is essentially a movement of liberation—liberation from dogma, from static conceptions of life, from unwholesome repressions of instinct.

In "To an Unknown Citizen," Auden satirizes the man who is too bound up in convention and routine to be an individual in his own right:

He was fully sensible to the advantages of the
    Installment Plan
And had everything necessary to the Modern Man,
A phonograph, a radio, a car and a frigidaire.
Our researchers into Public Opinion are content
That he held the proper opinions for the time of
    year;
When there was peace, he was for peace; when there
    was war, he went.

The individualism of Dylan Thomas is akin to that of Whitman; his dominant theme and favorite subject was himself. He held his personality, as it were, in his two hands, and turned it over and over, examining its particularity in something like awe.

Individualism may come from within, as an affirmation of self and the particularity of self, or it may arise in revolt against the forces seemingly allied against individualism in modern society. Industrial labor, office work, commuter trains, Sunday traffic, and countless other patterns of regimentation or routine may cause such a revolt, projecting the creative artist into the development of a style and approach uniquely his own, and of themes of freedom and individualism.

In individuality, also, there is identity, a means of establishing personality through a structure of symbols which once created take on a kind of life of their own. A writer may not know his own mind until he reads his work; he may not know who he really is, what he really stands for, until he hears himself speak through his writing and then makes his considered judgment and evaluation. He may, in other words, feel that he is too close to himself to know himself, and thus he may use his writing to identify his meaning of self. Such a writer is Dylan Thomas, and to a lesser extent Woolf, Lawrence, and Joyce. To such a writer the reader may sometimes be secondary; the writer may seem to say "Here I am; this is myself. Know me or not, understand me or not, I am none the less myself."

Finally, in individuality there are implied the twentieth-century answers to the questions "*who* and *why* is man?" If the answers are not in science or religion, in politics or law, in emotion or reason, in the Greek state or the dynamo, where can man look for answers? To himself, to the potential of his own personality, is the reply of the age. If he will discover that personality, and free it to develop creatively, if he will be open to his experience yet controlled by his past experience and learning, he may establish a beachhead of self on the shore of the future. It is through this beachhead that the great forces of life will shape their human achievement—or fail to find shape at all. Man is a structure, a unique framework of cells in process, holding in his genes and chromosomes and in his cherished seeds of culture the future of all mankind. Yet the filling out of the framework is up to the individual; his choices seem infinite, and through them he may shape the *who* that he thinks man is according to the reason he projects for the *why* of man. He may thus directly express the *why*, in the

process of living—and, if he is a writer, also in the process of writing. Even in an age when nearly all the *why* answers are given by some external authority, each person makes his own synthesis of these answers and his experience; and in an age like the present when external authority is seldom heeded, the synthesis is the more individual.

And now, after exploring several facets of the background of twentieth-century British literature, we are ready to discuss the authors themselves—looking at the forces from within Britain and from outside which shaped them, and considering the nature of their achievement.

## THE IRISH LITERARY RENAISSANCE

The first significant development toward modern British literature came in Ireland, and involved poets, playwrights, and a literary giant who was both, William Butler Yeats (1865–1939).

The stirrings of national feeling in Ireland were strong in Yeats's boyhood, and from 1886 on, the demand for home rule became formidable and at times violent. The political struggle, however, was only one part of the comprehensive national effort. The study of ancient Irish history was undertaken; Irish legends and folklore were collected; and an attempt was made to revive in all Ireland the use of Gaelic, the Celtic language which was still the language of Western Ireland.

Yeats has told how, when he was only a youth, he began to dream of the possibility of uniting the Irish on the level of their best selves through a national literature. When, under the influence of Blake and others, Yeats finally became a mystic, his mystical visions took the forms of shadowy figures out of Irish legend; and the mythological stuff of Irish tradition became a major part of the content of his poetry. His approach was completely subjective, after the style of the French symbolist poets of whom Stéphane Mallarmé (1842–1898) was the leader. These poets were the inheritors of the romantic tendency to subjectivism. They sought to express their own feelings, their own sensations, with perfect fidelity. Their problem was made difficult by the fact that every human being is unique, and, in addition, has different feelings and sensations from moment to moment, even when the objects causing feeling and sensation remain the same. Language, however, as was observed when Blake was under discussion in the preceding chapter, is a generalized medium of communication. The symbolist poets derive their name from the fact that they, like the mystics, can only attain their aim of expression by the use of symbols which do not state, but suggest, their private momentary reactions or moods.

The complexity of Yeats's symbolism, the depth of his awareness, and the beauty of his language have influenced much modern poetry, and seem to have a continuing impact which grows stronger as time passes. Yeats was drawn out into the world of social experience by his desire to participate practically in the creation of a new Irish literature. One of his most fruitful achievements was the founding of the Irish Literary Theater in Dublin, which was established permanently in the Abbey Theater. The most notable of his contemporaries with whom Yeats was associated in the nationalist literary movement were George William Russell, who was a mystic also, and is known by the letters he used as a pseudonym ("A.E."); Lady Gregory, a manager of the theater, playwright, and collector of legends; Douglas Hyde, a collector of tales in Gaelic, later President of Eire; John Millington Synge, the author of *The Playboy of the Western World* and other plays; and George Moore, novelist and storyteller, author of the controversial *Esther Waters*.

### THE NEW DRAMA

Not only did Yeats, Lady Gregory, Synge, and others succeed in creating a new national drama in Ireland; at the same time, upon the groundwork laid by Sir Henry Arthur Jones (1851–1929) and Sir Arthur Wing Pinero (1855–1934), a group of dramatists put new life into the London stage by a succession of effective and significant plays about contemporary life and problems.

The great animating impulse of the new drama came from the Norwegian dramatist Henrik Ibsen (1828–1906), whose work began to be known and praised in England about 1890. Ibsen was realistic, thoughtful, serious, powerful, and emancipated. He tried to look at modern men and women as they are, to expose shams, and to attack moral standards which he thought outworn or vicious. He put on the stage social problems whose representation shocked conventional people, and he reached conclusions which equally shocked them. In this he was a reformer at a time when dissatisfaction with the established order of society was becoming acute. He aroused violent controversy, but won the enthusiastic approval of all those who felt that society had grown rotten through hypocrisy and injustice and must be remolded.

Chief among those in England who were fired by Ibsen's example was an Irishman from Dublin, George Bernard Shaw (1856–1950). After writing some interesting but unsuccessful novels, he turned to journalistic criticism for a living. In 1891 he published a small book entitled *The Quintessence of Ibsenism*, and in the following year he entered on his exciting dramatic career with a play called *Widowers' Houses*, in which he exposed evils connected with the profitable rental of tenements in slum districts.

Shaw delighted in shocking and astonishing the public, and often did so by the simple expedient of following ideas to their extreme logical conclusions. He outraged sentiment, mocked at piety, tore patriotism to shreds, and, generally, shot up the existing state of things —and was greeted with cheers. Many who by no means agreed with him found his wit and his capacity for creating absurd situations irresistibly amusing, and his intellectual liveliness and zest exhilarating. His pose was that of an all-wise, infinitely superior being who looked at men with scorn, seeing nothing but stupidity, hypocrisy, and corruption in their lives, and declared himself able (were he given the opportunity) to set everything right by altering their ideas, practices, and institutions. It may be regarded as one measure of his genius that this pose was not generally resented.

Shaw's witty liquidation of the existing state of things was always subordinated to a constructive purpose, transparently well meant, whether or not it was practicable. The disillusioned generation which preceded him had no convictions and no earnestness. In general, we feel that any positive convictions are better than none; and it is invigorating to encounter a man who faces the facts and the future with cheerful confidence. Shaw's cure-all was the socialist state. He believed, with Darwin and Herbert Spencer, that the race was progressing through evolution. And he had a religion—the worship of the Life-Force, the beneficent creative power which he believed to be at work in the processes of evolution.

A number of studies have been made of Shaw's use of the new science of psychology. Like Ibsen in *A Doll's House*, Shaw recognized the multiple levels of awareness of different participants in a situation, and in *Candida* left the three main characters holding three different interpretations of what has actually happened in the play. The dream sequence "Don Juan in Hell," from *Man and Superman*, and the entire play *Saint Joan* are psychological documents; the Preface to *Saint Joan* is a brilliant study of the psychological basis of mysticism, though as is usual in his prefaces Shaw sounds opinionated and thoroughly unscientific. And of course he was unscientific; he would have considered a scientific psychological study quackery.

Shaw's plays are a series of triumphs over the traditional demands of successful drama. Action is reduced to a minimum, the plots are usually unimportant, and the characterization is often purposely subordinated. Everything else is sacrificed in order to concentrate attention on the brilliant dialogue in which the author's views are set forth. His first play, *Widowers' Houses*, appeared in 1892. His earlier plays were published collectively in 1898 under the title *Plays, Pleasant and Unpleasant* (*Mrs. Warren's Profession, Candida, You Never Can Tell*, and others). Later plays are *Man and Superman* (1903), *Fanny's First Play* (1911), *Pygmalion* (1912), *Heartbreak House* (1917), *Back to Methuselah* (1921), and *Saint Joan* (1923).

## E. M. FORSTER

In 1905 there appeared a novel *Where Angels Fear to Tread*, reminiscent in some ways of Meredith, Butler, and Henry James yet certainly a work to be reckoned with in its own right. E. M. Forster, its author, was 26; in this first book he clearly showed the comic-satiric spirit which was to dominate his five novels and many of his tales. As in all his novels, there are multiple themes, interwoven and interacting. It is an international novel, showing the effect of a foreign culture on English people and their points of view. It is a social novel, criticizing the values and the way of life of the middle class. It is also a psychological novel, showing the causes and effects of complex human relationships and the inner growth and development (in particular) of Caroline Abbott, a woman of high principle who seeks to find real love and real life, and fails, but finds meaning as she accepts despair.

The same multiplicity of effect is found in *The Longest Journey* (1907), a brilliant fictional treatment of the nature of appearance and reality. Rickie Elliot finds unhappiness, disillusion, and finally death through failure to distinguish between real existence, real qualities

of people, and "the subjective product of a diseased imagination, which, to our destruction, we invest with the semblance of reality." He marries a girl whom his imagination has made the personification of his ideal; what he believes her to be is false, a semblance, and these two people, without meaning to, aid each other in their deterioration, failing to know and reach each other or to have real understanding of each other. Rickie "suffered from the Primal Curse, which is not—as the Authorized Version suggests—the knowledge of good and evil, but the knowledge of good-and-evil." Though he recognizes the reality of good and evil existing together in the same thought or event, actually, except in moments of rare greatness, he is unable to act on this awareness. He finds it easier to choose absolute idealism or, to his ruin, an equally absolute practical adjustment to the petty demands of daily life.

*A Room with a View* (1908) is somewhat lighter than *The Longest Journey*, though it is also about the confusion of appearance and reality. Charlotte Bartlett uses all her influence to recruit her young cousin Lucy to

the vast armies of the benighted, who follow neither the heart nor the brain, and march to their destiny by catch-words. The armies are full of pleasant and pious folk. But they have yielded to the only enemy that matters—the enemy within.

Having won Lucy away from her lover, Charlotte, who does and does not want Lucy to be happy, seemingly plots against herself by bringing Lucy and her lover permanently together. *Howards End* (1910) may well be Forster's masterpiece; its theme, "Only connect the prose and the passion, and both will be exalted, and human love will be seen at its height," is a logical outgrowth of the concerns of the earlier novels. The tragic and comic relationships of the Schlegel sisters, the Wilcoxes and the Basts show that it is the inner life—true morality—that is real; the inner life *pays*, Forster insists.

The most popular of Forster's novels is *A Passage to India* (1924). Of the five it is easiest to grasp; it has an almost conventional form, and it is more restrained than the others. Also, the remoteness of its Indian setting permits the reader a perspective of greater objectivity. The theme of the novel is separateness on several levels. First there is the obvious separateness of East and West, of Indian culture and English culture. Then there is the separateness of the people: first of the vaguely-lumped-together mobs of natives and the undifferentiated civil servants, then of the individuals we get to know, Aziz and Fielding, and Adela and Mrs. Moore. The separateness of Aziz and Fielding, who really try to reach each other, is the more tragic in that if their desperate and sensitive effort must fail, there seems no hope for human contact across these cultural barriers. The inevitable separateness of Fielding and Stella, his wife-to-be, is clearly projected, and will grow and widen. Finally, there is the separateness within the self, the walling in of aspects of the self, best shown in the character of Mrs. Moore, who retreats to deep hiding places within herself, and as it were separates herself from the human race and from herself as a member of it.

Forster wrote three volumes of short stories: *The Celestial Omnibus and Other Stories* (1911), *The Story of the Siren* (1920), and *The Eternal Moment and Other Stories* (1928). The major themes from the novels recur; in "The Machine Stops," for example, we find barriers to human contact and understanding, the sacrifice of the inner to the outer life, and the question of appearance and reality. *Aspects of the Novel* (1927) is a major work of literary criticism; the biographies, essays, and literary studies also meet Forster's high standard for his own work. It is interesting to note Forster's statement that if he had lived earlier, he would have chosen the essay instead of the novel as the vehicle of his opinion. In *What I Believe* (1939; reprinted in *Two Cheers for Democracy*, 1947) Forster gives his credo. "I do not believe in Belief. Faith, to my mind, is a stiffening process, a sort of mental starch, which ought to be applied as sparingly as possible." Instead of belief he asks for "tolerance, good temper and sympathy—they are what matter really, and if the human race is not to collapse they must come to the front before long." What he asks for are attitudes, ways of life that provide for openness, awareness of others, restraint; he distrusts systems of order, master plans of progress.

We have dwelt thus at length on Mr. Forster because he is in a real sense the pivotal writer of the modern age. In him speaks the fully matured modern temperament, able to see the multiple interacting lines and planes of contemporary society, and able to cope with them; able to see both sides of the shield at once, and yet able to bear it; above all, able to keep a low, calm voice in the age of anxiety. Other major writers move in sudden shifts from left to right or from despair to faith across the advancing front of modern thought; as we observe the overriding direction the entire front is moving, however, we see that it is the direction Mr. Forster began purposefully to trace while Edward VII was still alive, and has traced with restraint and notable achievement ever since.

## VIRGINIA WOOLF

The so-called stream-of-consciousness technique began in England with the work of Dorothy M. Richardson. She began to use the method in the first book of her interminable *Pilgrimage,* written before the outbreak of the first World War, though not published until 1915, under the title *Pointed Roofs.* She has gone on to write book after book, using the same technique, publishing them as separate volumes with titles of their own, though they all are successive parts of *Pilgrimage.* Dorothy Richardson employs the stream-of-consciousness technique with competence, and her work interests other novelists, who have praised it but have not succeeded in arousing public interest in it.

The case is different with Virginia Woolf (Mrs. Leonard Woolf, 1882–1941), the brilliant and keenly intelligent daughter of Leslie Stephen, the distinguished critic of literature and thought, mentioned in the preceding chapter. Her earliest novels—the first, *The Voyage Out,* appeared in 1915—proved that she was a talented writer with acute perceptions and a sound imagination. She thought Wells, Bennett, and Galsworthy materialistic and superficial; and was impressed, like many others, with the power of Russian writers of fiction—particularly Feodor Dostoevsky (1821–1881) and Anton Chekhov (1860–1904)—to penetrate below the surface of life and lay bare the innermost souls of their characters.

She sought a way to achieve the same depth of penetration and insight, and was moved to experimentation of her own after reading the earliest work of Dorothy Richardson and some portions of Joyce's *Ulysses* which were printed in a periodical before the publication of the complete book.

In two short stories, "Kew Gardens" and "The Mark on the Wall," and in *Jacob's Room* (1922), Mrs. Woolf developed her own poetic and original form of stream-of-consciousness; and in *Mrs. Dalloway* (1925) she achieved a masterpiece. Page after page the sights, sounds, thoughts, impressions, feelings, awarenesses of a selected handful of characters pile in upon the reader, who starts with no plot summary, no helpful description of characters and their relationships, and must slowly build Mrs. Dalloway's self and world through becoming a part of her consciousness:

She had reached the Park gates. She stood for a moment, looking at the omnibuses in Piccadilly.

She would not say of any one in the world now that they were this or were that. She felt very young: at the same time unspeakably aged. She sliced like a knife through everything; at the same time was outside, looking on. She had a perpetual sense, as she watched the taxi cabs, of being out, out, far out to sea and alone; she always had the feeling that it was very, very dangerous to live even one day. Not that she thought herself clever, or much out of the ordinary. How she had got through life on the few twigs of knowledge Fräulein Daniels gave them she could not think. She knew nothing; no language, no history; she scarcely read a book now, except memoirs in bed; and yet to her it was absolutely absorbing; all this; the cabs passing; and she would not say of Peter, she would not say of herself, I am this, I am that.

Thus the reader feels Mrs. Dalloway's openness to her experience, sees with her depth of focus, her sense of being at once inside and outside what she observes. Both *what* she selects to observe and the *way* she observes are passed directly to us as we merge our consciousness with hers.

Virginia Woolf was a friend of E. M. Forster; each wrote sympathetic studies of the other, and subject to many of the same experiences, they had many viewpoints in common. It is thus not surprising to find some of Forster's favorite themes in *Mrs. Dalloway*: the awareness of complexity, of good-and-evil; even the concept of separateness. The appearance-reality concept is shown in a sequence in which Peter Walsh, feeling young and free in spite of his being past fifty, observes and follows an attractive woman with a red carnation. As he watches her "she became the very woman he had always had in mind; young, but stately; merry, but discreet; black, but enchanting." As he followed he became a buccaneer, swift, daring, and then she turned a key, opened a door, and was gone. ". . . It was half made up, as he knew very well; invented, this escapade with the girl; made up, as one makes up the better part of life, he thought—making oneself up; making her up; creating an exquisite amusement, and something more."

*Mrs. Dalloway* is, like Joyce's *Ulysses*, all about one day in one city; also like *Ulysses*, it has no unified plot line, and most of what happens takes place in the characters' minds. It is a masterpiece because of its point of view, its insight, the effectiveness of the cumulative impact of impressions, and the many lines it contains which are themselves masterpieces, memorable in their compressed poetry:

She had a right to his arm, though it was without feeling. He would give her, who was so simple, so impulsive, only twenty-four, without friends in England, who had left Italy for her sake, a piece of bone.

*To the Lighthouse* (1927) and *The Waves* (1931) are equally effective; and the latter contains Mrs. Woolf's magnificent statement of form as abstraction, far in advance of the philosophy of her time:

They come with their violins, said Rhoda; they wait; count; nod; down come their bows. And there is ripples and laughter like the dance of olive trees. . . .

"Like" and "like" and "like"—but what is the thing that lies beneath the semblance of the thing? Now that lightning has gashed the tree and the flowering branch has fallen . . . let me see the thing. There is a square. There is an oblong. The players take the square and place it upon the oblong. They place it very accurately; they make a perfect dwelling-place. Very little is left outside. The structure is now visible; what is inchoate is here stated; we are not so various or so mean; we have made oblongs and stood them upon squares. This is our triumph; this is our consolation.

The symbol that is the structure of Mozart's music is closer to the essence of art than the symbol that is Rhoda's simile of the dance of olive trees. Seeing the symbol of structure is a triumph of the human imagination, akin to Mozart's triumph in shaping the structure originally: it is an ordering of the inchoate, a construction by sheer force of human will of something coherent out of nothingness. And in her image of oblongs and squares Mrs. Woolf touches the thin line where science and art are one.

Mrs. Woolf wrote two more novels, *The Years* (1937) and *Between the Acts* (1941); a fantasy, *Orlando* (1928); and a number of volumes of essays, studies, and sketches, notably *The Common Reader* (1925) and *The Death of a Moth* (1942). Her short stories have been widely reprinted. *Monday or Tuesday* (1921), her first volume of stories and sketches, was printed on a hand press by Leonard and Virginia Woolf, and was illustrated by her sister Vanessa Bell; the Hogarth Press grew to be a highly successful printing venture, with an outstanding list of young authors who were to become significant.

## KATHERINE MANSFIELD

One of the first authors published by the Hogarth Press was Katherine Mansfield, whose *Prelude* appeared in blue paper covers in 1918. One of her books had been published earlier by a publisher who had quickly failed: *In a German Pension* (1911), a volume of short stories. She was still largely unknown in 1920 when another book of short stories appeared: *Bliss and Other Stories. The Garden Party and Other Stories* appeared in 1922; and in January, 1923, Miss Mansfield was dead, at the age of 34. In all, she had finished 73 stories, apart from juvenilia.

The special quality of her stories is derived partly from Chekhov, her most consistent model, and partly from her own intensity of emotion and her ability to select exactly the right detail to underline or accentuate the emotion. She served as co-translator of Chekhov's *Diary* and of his *Letters;* her admiration for Chekhov's writing was second only to her admiration for life itself. She also admired Dostoevsky and Tolstoi; she could never think that any English writer approached them in developing a vision of life consistent with reality.

Though her technique is distinctively different from Virginia Woolf's, Miss Mansfield also often used the stream-of-consciousness method to produce her most characteristic effect, the inner consciousness observing, thinking, feeling, in a setting of objective reality, with concrete details carefully chosen to enhance the impact on the reader. Such a detail is Miss Brill's honey-cake, for example, which she bought on the way from the concert in the park to her solitary room:

It was her Sunday treat. Sometimes there was an almond in her slice, sometimes not. It made a great difference. If there was an almond it was like carrying home a tiny present—a surprise—something that might very well not have been there. She hurried on the almond Sundays and struck the match for the kettle in quite a dashing way.

Miss Mansfield's stories may begin *in media res,* as short stories often do; and many of them, such as "Something Childish but Very Natural," end *in media res* also, and at the moment of climax, so that the reader finds himself projected beyond the story by the story's dynamic. This proves a strongly moving technique, and it may account in part both for her comparatively small audience and for the hauntingly memorable quality of her stories.

## SATIRE: ALDOUS HUXLEY

It might have been expected that the disillusion following the war years 1914–1918 would have produced a wave of satiric writing, but it did not. Several of the later plays of Bernard Shaw have shown the effect of the war and the postwar years on his inveterately satiric spirit; and Wyndham Lewis (1886–    ), in his buoyant and irrepressible way, has announced himself as the leader of a new age of satire, and has written several satirical novels. But, in general, disillusion has thrown poets and novelists back into themselves, and has generated the individualistic self-expression beneath much of the creative work of the age. And the fact is that for effective satire, as for other forms of successful art, there must be points of reference which readers and writers accept, or which writers can take for granted in readers. And in recent years, as we have seen, there are fewer and fewer such points of reference.

Nevertheless, there have appeared since 1918 several writers who have given direct expression to angry or bitter complaint against the times and in whose books there are satirical elements. One of these writers is Richard Aldington (1892–    ), whose *Death of a Hero* (1929) outraged conventional patriotic sentiment in its picture of the state of mind of a returned soldier: he had held himself together through the horrors of war but could not face the horrors of peace, and preferred death.

In *Death of a Hero* and in several subsequent novels, however, Aldington exhibits very little of the spirit of satire. He is merely angry because life is hard and the times are bad. Significantly, in *All Men Are Enemies* (1933), he concludes that this world is no place for sensitive souls, and pictures a battered artist and his battered companion agreeing to retire from it to nurse their dreams and grievances in isolation.

Aldous Leonard Huxley (1894–    ), a grandson of Thomas Henry Huxley and a grand-nephew of Matthew Arnold, has more claim to being considered a satirist than Aldington. In such novels as *Antic Hay* (1923) and *Point Counter Point* (1928) his method is genuinely satirical; and in *Brave New World* (1932) he has sketched a satirical caricature of the collectivist Utopia towards which, he believes, science and industry are leading the way. Yet Huxley is basically not so much a satirist as a moralist. He began by rejecting not only traditional Christianity, but also both the outlook on life and the scale of values enshrined in Christianity; yet at the same time he rejected the worldly alternative—belief in progress through science—towards which modern men have hopefully turned. Huxley treats all institutions equally, rejecting them all: "All modern history is a history of the Idea of Freedom from Institutions. It is also the Fact of Slavery to the Institutions."

None of the popular causes of his age, none of the ready answers to the questions of the *why* and *wherefore* of man satisfied him; the early novels show his unwillingness to accept any of the meanings of life he found others accepting. Yet the facts that he kept on looking, and that although he insisted on meaninglessness he rejected the meaningless cycles of event as well as meanings, indicate that he held standards he had not made explicit. With *Point Counter Point* these standards begin to emerge, and in *Brave New World* it is clear that he considers love a meaning. In *Eyeless in Gaza* (1936), *After Many a Summer Dies the Swan* (1940), *Time Must Have a Stop* (1944), and *Ape and Essence* (1949), he has traveled far from his earlier negation of meaning. As his *The Perennial Philosophy* (1945) shows, he has, in fact, become a believer in mysticism; also, he has further developed his concept of love and friendship as meanings. Moreover, he has himself pointed out that his earlier insistence on the meaninglessness of everything was only a stage in his growth towards maturity, and not a point at which one could stop.

Huxley's development prompts three comments. In the first place, his relatively immature books have seemed more impressive to readers than his later ones. There are more reasons for this than can be mentioned here, but one reason is of particular importance to us. The "philosophy of meaninglessness" gives formal expression to a situation produced by that destruction of old beliefs and standards which seemed to be finally accomplished in the nineteenth century, by the subsequent disintegration of society, and by our contemporary disenchantment with the worldly gospel of progress through science. The gospel of meaninglessness may be considered a confession of collapse and failure of established meanings, and a signal for a fresh start. There are two ways to look at this fresh start: it may

come about through keeping the mind open to individual meanings, without an attempt to systematize meanings for groups or for all of society, or it may come about through the development of new "established meanings" and their superimposition on society. The early Huxley novels speak most strongly to those who wish their fresh start to come through openness; the later Huxley at times speaks to those who seek a new prescription for society in general.

In the second place, Huxley's development is symbolic of the times in that his books are a series of more or less uncertain and provisional experiments. They can be regarded as a set of bulletins from a laboratory, recording stages in the progress of a prolonged piece of research. They enable us to follow an interesting personal growth; they show us a promising artist forced by the times to become a philosopher and finally becoming a prophet.

The third comment is that in his search for a new prescription for society, Huxley is searching for a philosophical or religious-philosophical stability; in so doing he resembles C. E. M. Joad, T. S. Eliot, Graham Greene, Evelyn Waugh, and others whose quests have led them to solutions orthodox or otherwise. Happiness in the material world, says Huxley, is not the goal of life. Through the character of Helmholtz in *Brave New World* he indicates the high value of love, and comes close to saying that the goal of life is a kind of personal salvation through love and the acceptance of pain. More recently, Huxley has explored mysticism and the means of crossing what Santayana called "the bridge of faith."

Although change and the reaction to change are not limited to the twentieth century (witness the change in Wordsworth from his first draft of the *Prelude* to his final draft, or in John Henry Newman through his lifetime), the idea of change as a normal state of affairs is largely a twentieth-century idea. Orthodox critics liked stability, liked things to stay where they were put, and so were highly suspicious even of John Dryden and Daniel Defoe because they had adapted to change in the highly unstable years after the Restoration. Such critics will find no significant writer to meet their standards in the modern age, where Bergson's *flux* is the overriding law. Oddly enough the most consistent British writer of the century is Bernard Shaw, who took an extreme position early and was able to watch the civilization approach him.

## D. H. LAWRENCE

David Herbert Lawrence (1885–1930) and Huxley were intimate friends. Huxley modeled from him a character in one of his novels, and Lawrence was not pleased; but the friendship held fast, and in 1932 Huxley edited *The Letters of D. H. Lawrence* with an Introduction which is one of the best critical explanations of the novelist and poet yet published.

"To be with Lawrence," Huxley has said, "was a kind of adventure, a voyage of discovery into newness and otherness. For, being himself of a different order, he inhabited a different universe from that of common men —a brighter and intenser world, of which, while he spoke, he would make you free."

Lawrence was a man of genius, in the full sense of the word, who, from the beginning of his career, arrested the attention of the discerning and roused their hopes. Almost continuously through the last dozen years of his life he was surrounded by small bands of disciples who looked on him to lead the human race once more out of the wilderness. And he was continually writing; for he was impelled in spite of himself to try to give imaginative form—or, we may say, living reality—to the intense convictions which possessed him and endowed him with energy. Nevertheless, though he was primarily an artist, he remained to the end an imperfect one; and it can be said of his novels, tales, and poems, as it was said of Huxley's books, that they are a series of more or less provisional experiments.

Some have thought of Lawrence as primarily an evangelist or prophet, and only secondarily an artist. And he *was* a prophet, an inspired man, faithful at any cost to his intuitive certainties. He was, in a sense, the creature or servant of "firm persuasions," and was firmly persuaded that his intuitions sprang from a kind of primordial stuff far within, deeper than his conscious self and truer. In fact his intuitions came, he believed, directly from the universal principle of life itself. He believed that matter itself is living, in accordance with a true wisdom dark to us because our temporary lease of individuality and consciousness separates us off, deceptively, from the springs of our being. He therefore valued any experience in which a human being could be lifted out of himself and plunged into direct shuddering contact with that dark "otherness," as he called it, lying below consciousness and individuality, and really real.

A letter he wrote in June, 1914, places his central intuition in a clear light:

Somehow that which is physic—nonhuman in humanity—is more interesting to me than the old-fashioned human element, which causes one to conceive a character in a certain moral scheme and make him consistent. The certain moral scheme is what I object to. In Turgenev, and in Tolstoi, and in Dostoevsky, the moral scheme into which all the characters fit . . . . is dull, old, dead. When Marinetti [author of a manifesto concerning "Futurism"] writes: "It is the solidity of a blade of steel that is interesting by itself, that is, the incomprehending and inhuman alliance of its molecules in resistance to, let us say, a bullet. The heat of a piece of wood or iron is in fact more passionate, for us, than the laughter or tears of a woman"— then I know what he means. He is stupid, as an artist, for contrasting the heat of the iron and the laugh of the woman. Because what is interesting in the laugh of the woman is the same as the binding of the molecules of steel or their action in heat: it is the inhuman will, call it physiology, that fascinates me. I don't so much care for what the woman *feels*, in the ordinary usage of the word. That presumes an *ego* to feel with. I only care about what the woman *is*—what she is—inhumanly, physiologically, materially—according to the use of the word: but for me, what she *is* as a phenomenon (or as representing some greater, inhuman will), instead of what she *feels* according to the human conception. . . . You mustn't look in my novel for the old stable *ego* of the character. There is another *ego*, according to whose action the individual is unrecognizable, and passes through, as it were, allotropic states which it needs a keener sense than any we've been used to exercise, to discover are states of the same single radically unchanged element.

This is an exciting concept, derived in part from biology, anthropology, and psychology, and in part from insight or intuition. It is not necessarily a concept that we can translate into action in our lives; it may not be possible to run a society as Lawrence moves his characters; but it is no less exciting to test the concept in our minds and let it extend the limits of our imaginations. Lawrence indicates here that man —as a complex of living cells, inheriting the past and accepting instinctively the responsibility for the continuation of man in the future, facing the need for survival, functioning as an organism—is expressing a force we barely understand, "another ego" which may be the very nature of the universe but which, whatever it is, is an archetypal and unifying force of vast power, beyond question and classification, a force that shapes being and is the reason for being. Culture, which is also a shaping force, is in comparison weak: it is to Lawrence "the certain moral scheme," dull, old, and dead. The individual, the ego, the self with its differentiating characteristics of which each man is so proud, is largely irrelevant; it is just a form which the vast force assumes, a form changing in small and (to the ultimate purpose) unimportant ways. Neither the self nor the culture should war with the shaping force, which speaks through instinct and might speak more through intuition if conditions were favorable.

Lawrence's burning intensity and the often startling nature of his concepts earn more attention that his technique as a writer. He seemed to mold his books and stories out of fire, working hastily before his ideas cooled; often he seems impatient with the time it takes to write and read words, as if communication through print were too slow to be real. The novels especially are unlike any others in literature, and should perhaps rather be called highly subjective allegories: "autobiographical allegories" is Drieu La Rochelle's term. The most notable—and notorious—are *Sons and Lovers* (1913) and *Lady Chatterley's Lover* (1928). Their theme is love; the first is about a young man whose love for his mother keeps him from giving himself fully in love to any other woman, and the second is about the triumph of an intense physical love over conventionality. Both are masterpieces, as are also *The Plumed Serpent* (1926) and at least four of the short stories.

In novels and stories, letters and poems, Lawrence's answer to the basic question *why?* is not to seek an answer; André Maurois has summarized Lawrence's prescription for living:

> Do not worry about the whole universe; never wonder to what end the world has been created. There is no such end. Life and love are life and love; a bunch of violets is a bunch of violets, and to push an idea of finality with it is utterly destructive. Live and let live. Love and let love. Follow the natural curve of blossoming and fading. . . .

## JAMES JOYCE

Though Lawrence has stirred disagreement in his time, the most controversial writer of the twentieth century is certainly James Joyce (1882–1944). Two of his novels are the widely known and widely misunderstood *Ulysses* (1922) and *Finnegans Wake* (1939). Joyce also, in 1907, published thirty-six short poems under the title *Chamber Music*, and in 1914, after vexatious negotiations and delays, a volume of short stories entitled *Dubliners*. Two years later there appeared an autobiographical narrative thinly disguised as fiction (*A Portrait of the Artist as a Young Man*), and in 1918 a

play called *Exiles*. A further volume of poems, *Pomes Penyeach*, was published in 1927.

All of these books are important for the study of Joyce, and they are all mentioned here because Joyce himself is widely regarded as the only imaginative writer of the very first importance who has developed in the English-speaking world in our time. He was born in Dublin of working-class parents and brought up there, receiving his education in Irish Catholic institutions.

From boyhood he loved words for their own sake, as if they were things having an existence and properties of their own independently of their use to denote meanings. As a young man he sought to work out a purely personal and individual aesthetic as a preparation for using words in a new way, which was to be uniquely his own way. To gain isolation he spent some months in Paris, in the winter of 1902–1903, in dreadful poverty. He was called back to Dublin in the spring of 1903 by the fatal illness of his mother; but in October, 1904, he left Ireland again, this time with a wife to support, and never returned except for one or two brief visits. He taught languages, chiefly at Trieste, until 1914; lived in Zurich, Switzerland, during the war; and later made his home in Paris.

Though he lived an expatriate, the one home of Joyce's imagination was Ireland. There is little evidence that his surroundings following his youth and young manhood made any impression on him. His work suggests that his life in the world ceased with his retreat to the Continent, and that from then on he contemplated and used only his early self. His first experimental poems and stories were objective, but as he withdrew into himself he found that he himself was his own best subject.

In the *Portrait* we see the progress of Stephen Dedalus, who is Joyce, from boyhood to young manhood, his emancipation from beliefs, and the formation of his decision "to discover the mode of life or art whereby his spirit could express itself in unfettered freedom." And in his next major work, the real subject remained Joyce—Joyce the impartial spectator of mankind in all ages and places, encompassing all limited, ephemeral, conflicting beliefs and values, and creating, by a triumph of imaginative insight and of artistic skill, the final picture of Man as he truly is and always has been. But the form had to be altered to fit this conception of the real subject, and autobiographical narrative was abandoned. Stephen remained, but remained only as one of three characters, who were to be presented, inside and out, as they went through a normal day's existence. This is the framework of *Ulysses*. The scene is Dublin. The story begins at 8:00 a.m. on 16 June, 1904, and ends at 2:00 a.m. on the following day. The reader not only sees Stephen, and the principal character, Leopold Bloom, and his wife Molly Bloom, as they go about their business through the day and into the night, but also follows their thoughts and even the inarticulate "stream of consciousness" lying below and around their explicit thoughts. This fullness of presentation requires many words. *Ulysses* runs to nearly eight hundred closely printed pages in the definitive edition published at Hamburg in 1932. Joyce takes nothing for granted, and from the completeness of his transcription of one day's events succeeds in presenting the whole personality of each of the characters.

Every novelist assumes the privilege and and responsibilities of omniscience; he enters into his characters, as we say, and knows more about them than anyone can learn about actual human beings from mere closeness of observation. If he is anxious to preserve verisimilitude, he endeavors to obscure his privileged position, and tends to accept approximately the limitations of the dramatist, who makes his characters reveal themselves through their own action and speech, with some help from the comment of a chorus or of other actors. Joyce, however, goes to the opposite extreme, takes the bull by the horns, and boldly thrusts the novelist's superhuman omniscience in the face of the reader. His most telling instrument of revelation is the so-called interior monologue, in which he puts into words the inarticulate wanderings of the mind when conscious control is relaxed and the "unconscious" rises dimly like some object half-perceived, or less than half-perceived, through a dense fog. The "interior monologue" in Joyce's hands is a marvel of virtuosity. He attempts the impossible, and so nearly succeeds that fellow-artists —themselves engaged in trying to make language do more than it is capable of doing, and hence aware of all the difficulties overcome— hail his achievement as "magical."

This interest for other artists possessed by *Ulysses* is largely aroused, not by the stuff of the "unconscious" used, which is from this point of view a matter of indifference, but by the way it is used, by the technique employed to bring the inarticulate "unconscious" out into the open. And a second feature of the book which gives it interest also arises from the virtuosity of the artist. Joyce wanted to present

Mr. and Mrs. Bloom unsentimentally and nakedly, but this was only the beginning of what he aimed to do. He wanted, in addition, without sacrificing their individualities, to insist constantly throughout his book that in Bloom and his wife, and, generally, in the normal course of Dublin life, we can see all Mankind and all Life in all times and places. He undertook to achieve this further purpose through suggestion, by a complex symbolism. He chose as his chief point of reference the *Odyssey* of Homer. Leopold Bloom, underneath the surface, is Ulysses all over again (and hence the title of Joyce's novel). Further, Joyce's *Ulysses* falls into eighteen parts which correspond to the eighteen principal episodes of the *Odyssey*, the relationship being indicated by covert allusion and the method of treatment. Still further, these parts of *Ulysses* are each governed as to treatment by one of the arts of mankind, and for each a different technique of presentation is adopted, and each has its own symbol. Finally, many of the episodes also are allusively related to parts of the human body, and some of them to colors. Thus the episode in *Ulysses* which corresponds to the Aeolus episode of the *Odyssey* has for its art, rhetoric; for its technique, progress through argument of the kind known in logic as the enthymeme; for its symbol, "Editor"; for its part of the body, lungs; and for its color, red. Even more symbolism of varying kinds pervades the book; for example, in a hospital scene where a woman gives birth to a child, growth is symbolized by passages which reflect the development of English prose style from earliest times to the present.

*Finnegans Wake*, at which Joyce worked for sixteen years, carries still further his pursuit of a wholly individual or "unfettered" medium of expression. In six hundred and twenty-six large pages he puts into words the dreams of a public-house keeper of Dublin during a single night's sleep.

In poems and half-poetry, in language which constantly bubbles over or turns itself inside out, Joyce pursues wild associations of words and meanings, symbols and connotations. He demands of his reader an impossible range of understanding; each page requires either encyclopedic knowledge or fifty footnotes (neither of which are supplied). Nonetheless readers keep accepting the challenge, and many who survive the ordeal call him great.

Joyce's works assume an awareness of complexity, of multiplicity. *Finnegans Wake* projects a universe based on relativity, consistent with the new science: he even speaks (in 1939) of the "Abnihilisation of the etym" and "whorled without aimed." Like Lawrence and Virginia Woolf, he took his art close to the thin edge where science and poetry, where man as force and man as form, meet and merge.

Like Lawrence and Huxley, Joyce wrote significant poetry; however, also like them, he did not find in poetry the range and scope he needed for full expression. *Chamber Music*, especially, and *Pomes Penyeach* seem almost the work of another writer, a key to a lyric quality in Joyce that his experimental prose style sometimes permits the reader to forget. In contrast, Huxley's *Leda and Other Poems* contains the germs of at least the early Huxley novels, imperfectly realized. Of the three only Lawrence would have been considered a major writer had he produced no prose—yet the Lawrence poems do not seem to belong with Yeats's or Eliot's or Auden's, or with the work of any other modern poet. Thus all three of the novelist-poets wrote outside the main streams of poetic style in their age.

## WAR POETS

World War II has been so recently in men's minds, and was so successful in breaking records for size and effectiveness of bombs, speed of planes, and general total effect of frightfulness, that it is sometimes difficult to believe that the emotional impact of any previous war could be significant. As a matter of fact, however, the impact of World War I on the people of England probably caused a more profound change than any other war in modern British history. Earlier victories shifted the concept of empire and the hope for the future from *good to better*; World War II from *bad to worse*; World War I moved the pendulum from white to black, from *good to bad*.

Comparisons of the degree of horror are certainly meaningless, however, as we look at the poetry of Rupert Brooke (1887–1915) and Wilfred Owen (1893–1918), who died in World War I. For each of them the war was too great a thing to know or encompass, too much, far too much to express. Brooke, speaking almost for the hope and the glorious past of England, wrote six short poems about the war in 1914 before he died, facing death without fear. One of the six is "The Soldier," which begins

If I should die, think only this of me:
  That there's some corner of a foreign field
  That is for ever England.

Wilfred Owen, on the other hand, saw and died in the same war, but his feelings remind us of Auden's in the next war, of a voice from the disillusioned present:

If in some smothering dreams, you too could pace
Behind the wagon that we flung him in,
And watch the white eyes writhing in his face,
His hanging face, like a devil's sick of sin;
If you could hear, at every holt, the blood
Come gargling from the froth-corrupted lungs
Bitter as the end
Of vile, incurable sores on innocent tongues,—
My friend, you would not tell with such high zest
To children ardent for some desperate glory,
The old Lie: Dulce et decorum est
Pro patria mori.

Herbert Read was born the same year as Owen, 1893, and served as a captain in the Yorkshire Regiment in World War I. He survived to become a museum curator, a professor of art, and an editor, critic, and writer; his war poems include *The End of a War* (1933) and *A World Within a War* (1944). Reed represents a larger view than Brooke or Owen, an inclusiveness and perspective, almost an objectivity, rare in the highly subjective art of poetry. Read, like Lawrence, Huxley and Joyce, seems outside the main stream of British poetry; he is not an imitator of Pound and Eliot, though some critics have so classified him. His closest resemblances are to the American Wallace Stevens, and to some of the younger poets.

## THE IMAGISTS AND EZRA POUND

Ezra Loomis Pound (1885–    ) and Thomas Stearns Eliot (1888–    ), who between them have inaugurated a distinctive period of English poetry, impress on us forcibly the growing power of America in Europe. The progressive Americanization of England has long been a subject of comment on both sides of the Atlantic. The literary influence of the United States on Europe began early, with Fenimore Cooper (1789–1851), rose to importance with Edgar Allan Poe (1809–1849), Walt Whitman (1819–1892), and Henry James (1843–1916), and remains important today, continuing alongside the influence of American films and popular music.

Not all the Americans who have influenced English literature thought highly of America; Ezra Pound, when he explained his departure from the United States in 1908, wrote contemptuously of our diluted and derivative ideas. Henry James, more urbanely but no less decisively, repudiated the United States when he made his home on the other side of the Atlantic; but the critics of James, of Pound, and of T. S. Eliot have clearly shown that these writers remained fundamentally American. The fact may be considered more curious than important; yet the case of James, Pound, and Eliot usefully reminds us that English literature of every age, including the present, has been no isolated phenomenon, but rather a fusion of native elements with others drawn from abroad.

When Pound left the United States, he abandoned at the same time a design of obtaining the degree of Ph. D. and of entering into a professorial career, and turned instead to poetry. He had at that time some knowledge of French, Italian, and Spanish, and immediately plunged into a study of the twelfth-century poetry of Provence because he regarded an acquaintance with this poetry as an indispensable foundation for the understanding of later European versification. As the years have passed, Pound has worked long and hard to gain skill in languages, in versification and in the use of words. In his earliest poems he could not help echoing the language and rhythms of Swinburne, of Ernest Dowson (1867–1900), of Browning, and of W. B. Yeats. He struggled with considerable success to break through "the crust of dead English" which, he thought, was hindering the poets of his generation, and to achieve a style based on living speech, which should be direct and economical, in the sense that neither his words nor his rhythms should say or imply anything except what he himself wanted to say. His verse, for example, was not to suggest Swinburne by its movement, when its words and statements were not Swinburnian. He wanted a concentrated effect, with all his material freed from adventitious or inappropriate associations and completely under his control for his purposes.

In 1909, while in London, Pound became acquainted with Thomas Ernest Hulme (1883–1917) and with a small group who were gathered round Hulme, and engaged with him in discussion and experimentation looking toward the development of a new technique of poetry. Hulme felt that in the early years of the present century the romantic era was drawing to an inglorious but blessed end, and that the time had come for what he called a new classicism.

As a practical means for bringing in a new classical poetry, Hulme thought there was everything to be said for a definite, even though limited aim. He concentrated his effort, in fact, upon a single point. He thought that the ro-

mantic poets had first blurred and then falsified reality by pretending to see infinity in a grain of sand, eternity in a flower, and so on. They had tried to see things, not as they are, but as they wished to see them. This wishful distortion of reality suggested the first step towards reform. The true poet, Hulme insisted, must engage in disinterested contemplation, and must find in what he sees, a kind of interest sufficient to force him into the attempt to describe accurately the impression made through his senses. Perfect faithfulness in the expression of just that perception which may actually, for a moment, transfix one's whole being, with nothing added, and with not a word, not a syllable, more or less than may be needed for accurate notation—this should be the ideal of the true poet. Both the object perceived and the emotion felt by the poet were to be regarded as matters of indifference:

> It doesn't matter an atom that the emotion produced is not of dignified vagueness, but on the contrary amusing; the point is that exactly the same activity is at work as in the highest verse. That is the avoidance of conventional language in order to get the exact curve of the thing. . . . It isn't the scale or kind of emotion produced that decides, but this one fact: Is there any real zest in it? Did the poet have an actually realized visual object before him in which he delighted? It doesn't matter if it were a lady's shoe or the starry heavens.

Unconventional language is a prime necessity because familiar phrases have acquired general meanings and convey only what is common in all experience. Often enough, long familiarity with certain words and stock comparisons so dulls a reader's attention that a poem conveys no definite or fresh impression. But the one justifying reason for poetry, the one basis for distinguishing true poetry from worthless verse, Hulme thought, is the poet's ability to discover something unique, something not hitherto seen or felt exactly as he sees or feels it, and to express this unique impression so faithfully as to evoke in the reader precisely the poet's own discovery in its every shade of differentiation and with its particular certifying physical sensation. Thus every poet must create his own language and rhythm, absolutely peculiar to himself. When we read any genuine poet, our reward lies in our enlarged and heightened consciousness, secured through their discoveries and through their invention of fresh techniques for the full communication of them.

The practical conclusion which Hulme drew from these considerations was that the true poet in the year 1909, should, by way of discipline and of making a start, attempt the accurate translation of distinct images into words. It appears that Pound, by the time he met Hulme, was well on the way to the same conclusion for much the same reasons. During the next few years he gradually assumed the leadership of a small group consisting principally of F. S. Flint (1885–     ), Richard Aldington (1892–     ), and the American poet H. D. (Hilda Doolittle, 1886–     ). In 1912, when he published five of Hulme's poems, he gave the group a name, "Les Imagistes." In the spring of 1913 they announced three principles on which they were agreed:

(1) Direct treatment of the "thing" whether subjective or objective.

(2) To use absolutely no word that does not contribute to the presentation.

(3) As regards rhythm: to compose in the sequence of the musical phrase, not in the sequence of a metronome.

Early in 1914 *Des Imagistes: An Anthology* appeared under Pound's editorship, containing poems by himself, Flint, H. D., Aldington, and several others, including Amy Lowell (1874–1925). Perhaps the most famous example of imagist poetry is Pound's "In a Station of the Metro":

> The apparition of these faces in the crowd;
> Petals on a wet, black bough.

Obviously, if anything of much significance was to issue from an effort of which this poem is the classic illustration, the effort could not stop with pure imagism. And it did not. Nevertheless, it is essential to dwell on what the imagists were trying to do, and why they were trying to do it, in order to understand the whole poetical development which followed from their experiments. T. S. Eliot's evaluation of Pound is helpful here:

No one living has practiced the art of verse with such austerity and devotion; and no one living has practiced it with more success. . . . A man who devises new rhythms is a man who extends and refines our sensibility; and that is not merely a matter of "technique." . . . He has enabled a few persons, including myself, to improve their verse sense; so that he has improved poetry through other men as well as by himself. I cannot think of anyone writing verse, of our generation and the next, whose verse (if any good) has not been improved by the study of Pound's. His poetry is an inexhaustible reference book of verse form. There is, in fact, no one else to study. . . .

## T. S. ELIOT

By universal consent, T. S. Eliot is the foremost poet of our time. He began to write verse in 1908 or 1909, when he was twenty or twenty-one, in a style which, he says, was "directly drawn" from his study of the French poet Jules Laforgue (1860–1887) "together with the later Elizabethan drama." It was only afterwards that he came under the influence of Ezra Pound. But though he made an independent beginning, he discovered in Pound such kinship of technical purpose that for a period of years in his own poems he often followed Pound's lead.

Eliot's first small volume of poems, *Prufrock and Other Observations*, was published in 1917, though some of the pieces had appeared earlier in magazines. This book was followed in 1920 by another small collection, and in 1922 by *The Waste Land*, a poem in five parts running in all to four hundred and thirty-three lines, with an appendix containing notes.

*The Waste Land* quickly became one of the most controversial poems in the language; it was clearly a major poem, but it was also, clearly, a very hard poem for most readers to take. It was called, and accurately, a poem of overwhelming negation, about a waste land lonely and infertile, a sterile empty land, its people empty, without hope, and that land England. It was also called a poem of intolerable obscurity, insulting its modern readers by parading its learning in the ancient manner: in the five lines of its epigraph and dedication there were four languages, with a total of six used in the poem, and Eliot himself supplied 52 notes to explain passages and identify allusions. Even with the notes, the poem required long and careful reading and a wider background than, say, most college professors have. Much of the obscurity—and in fact the final form in which the poem appeared—may be credited to Pound, who edited the manuscript ruthlessly and cut out half the text. *The Waste Land* is in form and style almost more like one of Pound's *Cantos* than an Eliot poem; in substance, however, it fits into the line of development of Eliot's point of view, and carries significant traces of the Eliot to come.

*Ash Wednesday* (1930) emerges clearly from the shadow of Pound, and reveals also that Eliot is ready to recognize affirmative forces, and has begun seriously looking for them. *Four Quartets* (1943) is his masterpiece of non-dramatic poetry, and is among the finest long poems in the language. In it he seems fully at home in the form and in the language; his sense of structure—the structure of thought, the structure of poetic movement, and the interaction of the two—has seldom been equalled.

In another medium, Eliot projected an "Aristophanic melodrama" in colloquial language and music-hall verse, but never got beyond two fragments which he published, first in a periodical, and then, in 1933, in a small book, under the title *Sweeney Agonistes.* The preoccupation with murder which inspired this abortive experiment stayed with him, and reappeared as the theme of the verse-play entitled *The Family Reunion* (1939). *The Cocktail Party* (1949) is built around a breaking marriage and an omniscient psychiatrist. *The Confidential Clerk,* somewhat less successful, appeared in 1943. In the years between *Sweeney* and *The Family Reunion* Eliot wrote the choruses for a pageant play entitled *The Rock* (1934), and a play concerning the martyrdom of St. Thomas Becket (*Murder in the Cathedral,* 1935), which was performed in Canterbury Cathedral and later had a successful run on the stage.

*Murder in the Cathedral* is a disturbing and significant work, fully in the spirit of the modern age. The Archbishop, Thomas Becket, must decide whether to accept the king's will or hold to principle and be executed. The complexity of the motives of Becket is fully shown, and no arbitrary resolution is imposed. The effect of Becket's fight for principle on the ordinary people of Canterbury is effectively brought in by a chorus of women. The knights who speak for the king present some sound and reasonable arguments, along with some which have a good ring but mean nothing. The knights sound a bit like announcers presenting radio commercials, but that is part of the irony. There is no delusion; the knights, Becket, and even the people see both sides of the issue. There is freedom for Becket to choose, but it is freedom limited and modified as in real life. There is responsibility on several interacting levels, limiting Becket's individualism and shaping his decisions. There are in the play, in other words, about the same mixture of motives and forces, pressures of opinion, self-images and social images that we would find in today's world.

### THE AUDEN GENERATION

T. S. Eliot left America and became a British citizen; for motives of his own, without aiming specifically to complete a trade, W. H. Auden reversed the process, left Britain, and became an American citizen. Auden and the poets of the Auden generation—chiefly Stephen Spender, Louis MacNeice, and C. Day Lewis —were influenced by Yeats and Eliot, by Hopkins and Donne, and by diverse European and American poets. However, it was not long before they began to be thought of as having distinctive styles of their own; and their total output and impact has been significant.

Time and change are recurrent themes in Auden:

> . . . time is inches
> And the heart's changes

The nature of self, the development of the ego, the shaping forces of experience, and the dark unexplored rooms of the mind are important in the Pulitzer-prize-winning eclogue *The Age of Anxiety* (1947) and in the verse plays (in collaboration with Christopher Isherwood) *The Dog Beneath the Skin* (1935), *The Ascent of F.6* (1936), and *On the Frontier* (1938). Complexity and multiplicity, Bergsonian flux, and a multi-dimensional view of human motives and values appear as themes and assumptions. The image concept replaces the appearance-reality theme:

> . . . the world he is true to
> Is his own creation. . . .

Finally, no poet has more fully captured the tone and the idiom, the rhythms and the tensions of the age.

### STEPHEN SPENDER

Stephen Spender has often been compared to Shelley, the poet's poet. He makes the writing of poetry seem easy; the emotion is strong, the words ring true, and the stanzas obviously have the touch of the poet—a touch many of Spender's friends try to conceal in their work. And like Shelley, Spender poured himself into causes, and particularly into causes of revolt. In the thirties many British intellectuals swung far to the left politically; Spender was the most passionate and articulate of the group of poets who tried Marxism and gradually found it wanting. He wrote poems about Russian workers, and published a striking and unusual critical work, *The Destructive Element* (1935), charged throughout with the Marxist point of view yet enough off the party line to displease some of the Marxists, who felt that Spender allowed the artist too much leeway in choice of theme and treatment, too much individuality. And it is true that in all his writing, the early leftist works and the later works as well,

Spender's chief concern is with the individual and his values.

After the great disillusionment following the failure of the left to fulfill its promise, Spender moved back to dead center, keeping as his cause and his main theme the individual consciousness and its relationship to the ideas and ideologies, the tensions and pressures of the outside world. In an important autobiography, *World Within World* (1951), he carefully retraces his own development as a step toward better understanding of the complex relationships that affect the individual. In a second significant critical volume, *The Creative Element* (1953), he completes the synthesis he attempted in *The Destructive Element*, encompassing the viewpoint of the earlier book and moving from it to a fuller perspective and understanding. It contains a valuable analysis of poetry and politics:

The kind of orthodoxy communism requires of writers in fact makes literature impossible, because it selects or dictates inspiration, theme, and attitude, matters in which the directors of the Party Line are more informed than the writer. The propagandist point of view becomes the centre of inspiration. The writers who accepted this dictation soon found themselves unable to write. Those who did not were reaching towards another kind of orthodoxy. Out of the long internecine debate about poetry and politics of the 1930's, various possible attitudes for a poetry of a just society emerged. It is worth listing these, if only because they lead into a better understanding of orthodoxy in literature:

(1) Poetry which crystallized the ideal of a socially just world. Some of my own early poems attempt this.

(2) Poetry (like Auden's *Spain*) which treats socialist interpretation of history as the hypothesis for imagining a contemporary historic conflict. Essentially, *Spain* is dramatic, and one can imagine a poetic drama on the theme of this struggle. My own poetic drama *Trial of a Judge* (1938) is also an experiment of this kind.

(3) Poetry of action about the struggle for human freedom (Cecil Day Lewis's *The Nabara*).

(4) The poetic journal which is a commentary on public and private events, in a situation where the social struggle is felt to be intimately connected with the private life (Louis MacNeice's *Autumn Journal*).

(5) The poetry of those who have consciously uprooted themselves from their own environment and interests, and deliberately joined another class, making its interests their own (John Cornford, Christopher Caudwell, and other poets of the International Brigade; but the example of Orwell shows how this can boomerang on the politicians).

Any one of these attitudes permits the poet to write out of his own thought or experience, while relating it to the idea of the cause which he accepts. Communists, however, object to the first because

it is idealist; and to the second because it may well be ambiguous, like *Spain*, cutting both ways; the third, fourth, and fifth would all be liable to just so much censorship as would prevent the poet from remaining true to his own experience.

C. Day Lewis and Louis MacNeice are the chief among the other poets of the Auden generation; both have, like the others, written poems of revolt and poems focussing on the dilemma of the individual in the modern age. Day Lewis has written significant criticism, also, including *A Hope for Poetry* (1934) and *The Poetic Image* (1947); MacNeice has written poetic dramas for radio.

## DYLAN THOMAS

Although only five years younger than Spender, Dylan Thomas seems a member of another generation entirely. He was only 16 when Auden's *Poems* appeared in 1930, and the full impact of his own work was not to come until the nineteen fifties, enhanced by the legends of his life and death.

The legends have giant dimensions: "Here was no small man," they seem to say. The poems confirm the legends. Thomas decided early that he would write great poetry; that he would, in fact, be a great poet. This approach to his writing no doubt contributed toward the manner of greatness; he wrote with confidence, an intense driving force, a rich and imaginative use of language, a passion for striking metaphor, and a sure mastery of form and structure.

It is hard to compare Thomas's poetry with other poetry, or to determine fully the forces and influences that shaped his style. A list of "influences on Thomas" named by a few of the recent critics seems itself almost too extravagant to credit; they are named here in no particular order: Freud; Henry Vaughan; Thomas Vaughan; surrealist writing; Rimbaud; Dali; Hopkins; Joyce; the Bible; A. E. Housman; Mallarmé and the French symbolists; Hegel; William Empson; Coleridge; Anglo-Saxon verse; Donne; Whitman; Dickens; Thomas Wolfe; Yeats; Wordsworth; Keats; early Welsh poetry. Of these suggested influences, the most relevant are probably Freud, the surrealists, and the symbolists.

Thomas's style is a complex of symbols, images, metaphors, patterns, rhythms, existing at several levels at once. Consider these two lines from *The Map of Love* (January 1939):

In the sniffed and poured snow on the tip of the
tongue of the year

That clouts the spittle like bubbles with broken
  rooms . . . .

There is no rhyme and no regular meter; however, there are free patterns of rhythm, and a characteristic Thomas metrical sequence, "on the tip of the tongue of the year." The most consistent pattern in the two lines (and in the poem) is alliteration; s-s and t-t in the first line, and b-b in the second. Another relatively consistent pattern, of course directly related to the rhythm, is the arrangement of monosyllables and polysyllables. Also, the pair of -ed words in the first line (sniffed and poured) and the pair of doubled-letter words in the second line (spittle like bubbles) are not accidental, and the two pairs complement each other. In addition, Thomas has repeated vowel sounds: sniffed, tip, spittle; snow, broken; tongue, bubbles.

Not all the images are clear, particularly in this fragment out of context. The snow, however, is 1. real snow; 2. the slang name of a drug, generally heroin, which produces a dream-world effect when taken; 3. a symbol of transformation into a dream world. "On the tip of the tongue of the year" is 1. a continuation of the drug image; 2. a time reference, meaning "early in the year" (reworking a time-worn folk-idiom in a strikingly unexpected combination); 3. a compressed image connoting the freshness of the real snow through the added dimension of the sense of touch. It should be said here that Thomas could write un-complicated poetry when he wanted to, though some that seems deceptively simple has a separate existence on another level of meaning.

The ideas in the poems may also be read on more than one level. Some readers seem to see in Thomas only the "I," the particular self at the center of Thomas's self-centered world. "This is how I feel about me and love" or "This is how I feel about me and death" then become Thomas's themes. Julian Symons, criticizing Thomas for not saying enough in his poetry, sees on the other hand the broadest of generalities: "What is said in Mr. Thomas's poetry is that seasons change: that we decrease in vigour as we grow older; that life has no obvious meaning; that love dies. . . . ." Between these readings of the poems is the opportunity of observing Thomas's profound interest in life as a process, in being born and living and growing and loving and changing and dying; and of recognizing that behind the subjective language there is a concept that we have identified as basic in the modern age—the idea of complexity, of life as chaos, multiplicity, impossible to understand in terms of any one image, or to freeze in any static relationship.

## DIVERSE DIRECTIONS

The selection of key figures in any period of literature sooner or later reaches a point of no return. We have talked of Yeats and Shaw, of Forster and Woolf and Joyce, of Eliot and Auden—but what of Orwell and Waugh? What of O'Casey, Rattigan, and Christopher Fry?

The literature of the modern age in Britain has too much richness, too much diversity, too much depth to encompass in brief summary. It would be impossible here to list all the significant writers we might have talked about—but we cannot omit mention among the novelists, of Elizabeth Bowen (1899–    ), Graham Greene (1904–    ), Christopher Isherwood (1904–    ), Somerset Maugham (1874–    ), George Orwell (1903–1950), John Cowper Powys (1872–    ), J. B. Priestley (1894–    ), Evelyn Waugh (1903–    ), and Rebecca West (Cicily Isabel Fairfield, 1892–    ); of three short story writers, A. E. Coppard (1878–    ), Saki (H. H. Munro, 1870–1916), and T. F. Powys (1872–    ); of a writer of fantasies, David Garnett (1892–    ); of five poets, Robert Bridges (1844–1930), Roy Campbell (1901–    ), Alun Lewis (1915–1944), Hugh MacDiarmid (Christopher Murray Grieve, 1892–    ), and Edith Sitwell (1887–    ); and among the dramatists, of Paul Vincent Carroll (1900–    ), Noel Coward (1899–    ), Christopher Fry (1907–    ), Sean O'Casey (1884–    ), Terence Rattigan (1911–    ), John Van Druten (1901–    ), and Emlyn Williams (1905–    ).

That the creative activity of these writers, showing such extremes of difference among themselves as Bridges and Sitwell, O'Casey and Coward, Maugham and Isherwood, could take place at the same time and in the same small country, is further evidence, if any were needed, of the complexity of the age. No general terms of literary classification fit even most of the group, and no great, clear-cut developing trend can be identified.

Finally, it is clear that the great forces at work in England in the modern age are not separable; literary and philosophic influences from France and America, rapid economic and social change, developing science and the resulting technological change, the rise of cultural science and psychology, political shifts and the struggle for power—these and the other dynamics shaping creative expression all work together, interact, cancel and excite each other. At the same time the process of development excites itself; the poetry of Eliot helps create the poetry of Auden, and the early poetry of Auden helps create the late poetry of Auden, just as the first line of "To an Unknown Citizen" helps create the second line, and both help create the third line.

The modern age offers greater freedom for creative development than all past history has known. Openness replaces the rigid traditional frameworks which in the past have shaped the line and the stanza; the plot and the play; concepts of man's nature and purpose; and the values of the good life. The achievement of the age so far is high, but not its least achievement is the development of this open, free creative temper. It will be extremely interesting to see what happens next, as we move from the vital present into the vital future.

# George Bernard Shaw

## 1856-1950

George Bernard Shaw was born in Dublin, 26 July, 1856. His grandfather was sheriff of Kilkenny County, and his father held a civil service post and then became a wholesale merchant. Shaw's schooling included tutoring in classics, a few years at the Wesleyan Connexional school and three other schools in Dublin, and persistent self-education in literature, art, and (with help from his mother) music.

At fifteen Shaw became an office boy, and later a cashier, for a Dublin estate agent. At twenty he went to London, where his mother and sister had preceded him, and tried to become a successful writer. Between 1879 and 1883 he worked on five novels, amazing books that no one seemed to want to publish and that even today seem outspoken and uncontrolled.

In 1882 Shaw was converted to Socialism by Henry George; in 1884 he became a dedicated Fabian Socialist. In 1885 he began his career as a dramatist, though most of his energy was pouring into the demanding work of promoting Fabian Socialism and into newspaper and magazine criticism of music and the drama. He was noted as a critic primarily for his advocacy of Ibsen and of music as an art for all people as well as for specialists and experts. Widowers' Houses, his first play, was performed in 1892; its reception was less than friendly. His next two plays, The Philanderer (1893) and Mrs. Warren's Profession (1893), could not be produced. Then came Arms and the Man (1894), The Devil's Disciple (1897), and Candida (1897), which were successful both in winning popularity and in notably exposing false views and shams of the time.

Caesar and Cleopatra (1898) looks at history from a new perspective. Man and Superman (1901–03), often considered his masterpiece, personifies the Life Force in the woman seeking her mate, and is notable for its dream sequence "Don Juan in Hell," sometimes presented separately. Major Barbara (1905) probes beneath the surface of well-meaning efforts to meet the needs of the poor without understanding the real complexity of those needs. Androcles and the Lion (1911–12) satirizes the martyrs; and the highly successful Pygmalion (also 1912) shows that the culture snobbish people value so highly is a veneer that can be acquired by a Cockney flower girl in a few months. Back to Methuselah (1921) expresses more fully than any of the other plays the Bergsonian-Lamarckian basis of Shaw's philosophy, in which the universe is conceived as being in the process of evolving itself, energized by a God-like Life Force, toward a God-like expression of that Force. Saint Joan (1923) is a multi-dimensional study of the legendary Maid of Orleans, showing the inner forces and the outer forces working toward her destiny.

There were many other plays, some vigorous criticism, and a few book-length political tracts; the most significant work besides the plays, however, was certainly the prefaces he wrote for each play. These were often long, frequently highly controversial, and always interesting. The Prefaces were published separately in 1934.

The best edition is The Collected Works of Bernard Shaw, Ayot St. Lawrence Edition (London, 1930–    ). There are several collections of three or more plays; the most useful one generally available is Nine Plays (New York, 1946). Biographical and critical studies include G. K. Chesterton's George Bernard Shaw (London, 1909); Archibald Henderson's Bernard Shaw, Playboy and Prophet (New York, 1932); Hesketh Pearson's Shaw: his Life and Personality (London, 1942); Eric Bentley's Bernard Shaw (Norfolk, Connecticut, 1947); C. E. M. Joad's Shaw (London, 1949); Sir Desmond McCarthy's Shaw (London, 1951); and A. C. Ward's Shaw (London, 1951).

## Don Juan in Hell [1]

### From Man and Superman

Stillness settles on the Sierra; and the darkness deepens. The fire has again buried itself in

[1] Man and Superman was written between 1901

*white ash and ceased to glow. The peaks shew unfathomably dark against the starry firmament; but now the stars dim and vanish; and the sky seems to steal away out of the universe. Instead of the Sierra there is nothing: omnipresent nothing. No sky, no peaks, no light, no sound, no time nor space, utter void. Then somewhere the beginning of a pallor, and with it a faint throbbing buzz of a ghostly violoncello palpitating on the same note endlessly.* 10 *A couple of ghostly violins presently take advantage of this bass*

*and therewith the pallor reveals a man in the void, an incorporeal but visible man, seated, absurdly enough, on nothing. For a moment he raises his head as the music passes him by.* 20 *Then, with a heavy sigh, he drops in utter dejection; and the violins, discouraged, retrace their melody in despair and at last give it up, extinguished by wailings from uncanny wind instruments, thus:—*

*It is all very odd. One recognizes the Mozartian strain; and on this hint, and by the aid of certain sparkles of violet light in the pallor, the man's costume explains itself as that of a Spanish nobleman of the XV–XVI century. Don Juan, of course; but where? why? how? Besides, in the brief lifting of his face, now hidden by his hat brim, there was a curious suggestion of Tanner. A more critical, fastidious, handsome face, paler and colder, without* 40 *Tanner's impetuous credulity and enthusiasm, and without a touch of his modern plutocratic vulgarity, but still a resemblance, even an identity. The name too: Don Juan Tenorio, John Tanner. Where on earth—or elsewhere—have we got to from the XX century and the Sierra?*

*Another pallor in the void, this time not violet, but a disagreeable smoky yellow. With it, the whisper of a ghostly clarinet turning this tune into infinite sadness:* 50

*and 1903, and published in 1903.* "Don Juan in Hell" *is part of Act III of* Man and Superman; *it has been performed separately, and the play is often acted without it. Reprinted by permission of The Public Trustee and The Society of Authors (London).*

*The yellowish pallor moves: there is an old crone wandering in the void, bent and toothless; draped, as well as one can guess, in the coarse brown frock of some religious order. She wanders and wanders in her slow hopeless way, much as a wasp flies in its rapid busy way, until she blunders against the thing she seeks: companionship. With a sob of relief the poor old creature clutches at the presence of the man and addresses him in her dry unlovely voice, which can still express pride and resolution as well as suffering.*

THE OLD WOMAN. Excuse me; but I am so lonely; and this place is so awful.

DON JUAN. A new comer?

THE OLD WOMAN. Yes: I suppose I died this morning. I confessed; I had extreme unction; I was in bed with my family about me and my eyes fixed on the cross. Then it grew dark; and when the light came back it was this light by which I walk seeing nothing. I have wandered for hours in horrible loneliness.

DON JUAN [*sighing*] Ah! you have not yet lost the sense of time. One soon does, in eternity.

THE OLD WOMAN. Where are we?

DON JUAN. In hell.

THE OLD WOMAN [*proudly*] Hell! I in hell! How dare you?

DON JUAN [*unimpressed*] Why not, Señora?

THE OLD WOMAN. You do not know to whom you are speaking. I am a lady, and a faithful daughter of the Church.

DON JUAN. I do not doubt it.

THE OLD WOMAN. But how then can I be in hell? Purgatory, perhaps: I have not been perfect: who has? But hell! oh, you are lying.

DON JUAN. Hell, Señora, I assure you; hell at its best: that is, its most solitary—though perhaps you would prefer company.

THE OLD WOMAN. But I have sincerely repented; I have confessed—

DON JUAN. How much?

THE OLD WOMAN. More sins than I really committed. I loved confession.

DON JUAN. Ah, that is perhaps as bad as confessing too little. At all events, Señora, whether by oversight or intention, you are certainly damned, like myself; and there is nothing for it now but to make the best of it.

THE OLD WOMAN [*indignantly*] Oh! and I might have been so much wickeder! All my good deeds wasted! It is unjust.

DON JUAN. No: you were fully and clearly warned. For your bad deeds, vicarious atonement, mercy without justice. For your good deeds, justice without mercy. We have many good people here.

THE OLD WOMAN. Were you a good man?

DON JUAN. I was a murderer.

THE OLD WOMAN. A murderer! Oh, how dare they send me to herd with murderers! I was not as bad as that: I was a good woman. There is some mistake: where can I have it set right?

DON JUAN. I do not know whether mistakes can be corrected here. Probably they will not admit a mistake even if they have made one.

THE OLD WOMAN. But whom can I ask?

DON JUAN. I should ask the Devil, Señora: he understands the ways of this place, which is more than I ever could.

THE OLD WOMAN. The Devil! I speak to the Devil!

DON JUAN. In hell, Señora, the Devil is the leader of the best society.

THE OLD WOMAN. I tell you, wretch, I know I am not in hell.

DON JUAN. How do you know?

THE OLD WOMAN. Because I feel no pain.

DON JUAN. Oh, then there is no mistake: you are intentionally damned.

THE OLD WOMAN. Why do you say that?

DON JUAN. Because hell, Señora, is a place for the wicked. The wicked are quite comfortable in it: it was made for them. You tell me you feel no pain. I conclude you are one of those for whom Hell exists.

THE OLD WOMAN. Do you feel no pain?

DON JUAN. I am not one of the wicked, Señora; therefore it bores me, bores me beyond description, beyond belief.

THE OLD WOMAN. Not one of the wicked! You said you were a murderer.

DON JUAN. Only a duel. I ran my sword through an old man who was trying to run his through me.

THE OLD WOMAN. If you were a gentleman, that was not a murder.

DON JUAN. The old man called it murder, because he was, he said, defending his daughter's honor. By this he means that because I foolishly fell in love with her and told her so, she screamed; and he tried to assassinate me after calling me insulting names.

THE OLD WOMAN. You were like all men. Libertines and murderers all, all, all!

DON JUAN. And yet we meet here, dear lady.

THE OLD WOMAN. Listen to me. My father was slain by just such a wretch as you, in just such a duel, for just such a cause. I screamed: it was my duty. My father drew on my assailant: his honor demanded it. He fell: that was the reward of honor. I am here: in hell, you

tell me: that is the reward of duty. Is there justice in heaven?

DON JUAN. No; but there is justice in hell: heaven is far above such idle human personalities. You will be welcome in hell, Señora. Hell is the home of honor, duty, justice, and the rest of the seven deadly virtues. All the wickedness on earth is done in their name: where else but in hell should they have their reward? Have I not told you that the truly damned are those who are happy in hell?

THE OLD WOMAN. And are you happy here?

DON JUAN [*springing to his feet*] No; and that is the enigma on which I ponder in darkness. Why am I here? I, who repudiated all duty, trampled honor underfoot, and laughed at justice!

THE OLD WOMAN. Oh, what do I care why you are here? Why am I here? I, who sacrificed all my inclinations to womanly virtue and propriety!

DON JUAN. Patience, lady: you will be perfectly happy and at home here. As saith the poet, "Hell is a city much like Seville."

THE OLD WOMAN. Happy! here! where I am nothing! where I am nobody!

DON JUAN. Not at all: you are a lady; and wherever ladies are is hell. Do not be surprised or terrified: you will find everything here that a lady can desire, including devils who will serve you from sheer love of servitude, and magnify your importance for the sake of dignifying their service—the best of servants.

THE OLD WOMAN. My servants will be devils!

DON JUAN. Have you ever had servants who were not devils?

THE OLD WOMAN. Never: they were devils, perfect devils, all of them. But that is only a manner of speaking. I thought you meant that my servants here would be real devils.

DON JUAN. No more real devils than you will be a real lady. Nothing is real here. That is the horror of damnation.

THE OLD WOMAN. Oh, this is all madness. This is worse than fire and the worm.

DON JUAN. For you, perhaps, there are consolations. For instance: how old were you when you changed from time to eternity?

THE OLD WOMAN. Do not ask me how old I was—as if I were a thing of the past. I am 77.

DON JUAN. A ripe age, Señora. But in hell old age is not tolerated. It is too real. Here we worship Love and Beauty. Our souls being entirely damned, we cultivate our hearts. As a lady of 77, you would not have a single acquaintance in hell.

THE OLD WOMAN. How can I help my age, man?

DON JUAN. You forget that you have left your age behind you in the realm of time. You are no more 77 than you are 7 or 17 or 27.

THE OLD WOMAN. Nonsense!

DON JUAN. Consider, Señora: was not this true even when you lived on earth? When you were 70, were you really older underneath your wrinkles and your grey hairs than when you were 30?

THE OLD WOMAN. No, younger: at 30 I was a fool. But of what use is it to feel younger and look older?

DON JUAN. You see, Señora, the look was only an illusion. Your wrinkles lied, just as the plump smooth skin of many a stupid girl of 17, with heavy spirits and decrepit ideas, lies about her age! Well, here we have no bodies: we see each other as bodies only because we learnt to think about one another under that aspect when we were alive; and we still think in that way, knowing no other. But we can appear to one another at what age we choose. You have but to will any of your old looks back, and back they will come.

THE OLD WOMAN. It cannot be true.

DON JUAN. Try.

THE OLD WOMAN. *Seventeen!*

DON JUAN. Stop. Before you decide, I had better tell you that these things are a matter of fashion. Occasionally we have a rage for 17; but it does not last long. Just at present the fashionable age is 40—or say 37; but there are signs of a change. If you were at all good-looking at 27, I should suggest your trying that, and setting a new fashion.

THE OLD WOMAN. I do not believe a word you are saying. However, 27 be it. [*Whisk! the old woman becomes a young one, magnificently attired, and so handsome that in the radiance into which her dull yellow halo has suddenly lightened one might almost mistake her for Ann Whitefield*].

DON JUAN. Doña Ana de Ulloa!

ANA. What? You know me!

DON JUAN. And you forget me!

ANA. I cannot see your face. [*He raises his hat*]. Don Juan Tenorio! Monster! You who slew my father! even here you pursue me.

DON JUAN. I protest I do not pursue you. Allow me to withdraw [*going*].

ANA [*seizing his arm*] You shall not leave me alone in this dreadful place.

DON JUAN. Provided my staying be not interpreted as pursuit.

ANA [*releasing him*] You may well wonder how I can endure your presence. My dear, dear father!

DON JUAN. Would you like to see him?

ANA. My father here!!!

DON JUAN. No: he is in heaven.

ANA. I knew it. My noble father! He is looking down on us now. What must he feel to see his daughter in this place, and in conversation with his murderer!

DON JUAN. By the way, if we should meet him—

ANA. How can we meet him? He is in heaven.

DON JUAN. He condescends to look in upon us here from time to time. Heaven bores him. So let me warn you that if you meet him he will be mortally offended if you speak of me as his murderer! He maintains that he was a much better swordsman than I, and that if his foot had not slipped he would have killed me. No doubt he is right: I was not a good fencer. I never dispute the point; so we are excellent friends.

ANA. It is no dishonor to a soldier to be proud of his skill in arms.

DON JUAN. You would rather not meet him, probably.

ANA. How dare you say that?

DON JUAN. Oh, that is the usual feeling here. You may remember that on earth—though of course we never confessed it—the death of anyone we knew, even those we liked best, was always mingled with a certain satisfaction at being finally done with them.

ANA. Monster! Never, never.

DON JUAN [*placidly*] I see you recognize the feeling. Yes: a funeral was always a festivity in black, especially the funeral of a relative. At all events, family ties are rarely kept up here. Your father is quite accustomed to this: he will not expect any devotion from you.

ANA. Wretch: I wore mourning for him all my life.

DON JUAN. Yes: it became you. But a life of mourning is one thing: an eternity of it quite another. Besides, here you are as dead as he. Can anything be more ridiculous than one dead person mourning for another? Do not look shocked, my dear Ana; and do not be alarmed: there is plenty of humbug in hell (indeed there is hardly anything else); but the humbug of death and age and change is dropped because here we are all dead and all eternal. You will pick up our ways soon.

ANA. And will all the men call me their dear Ana?

DON JUAN. No. That was a slip of the tongue. I beg your pardon.

ANA [*almost tenderly*] Juan: did you really love me when you behaved so disgracefully to me?

DON JUAN [*impatiently*] Oh, I beg you not to begin talking about love. Here they talk of nothing else but love: its beauty, its holiness, its 10 spirituality, its devil knows what!—excuse me; but it does so bore me. They dont know what theyre talking about: I do. They think they have achieved the perfection of love because they have no bodies. Sheer imaginative debauchery! Faugh!

ANA. Has even death failed to refine your soul, Juan? Has the terrible judgment of which my father's statue was the minister taught you no reverence? 20

DON JUAN. How is that very flattering statue, by the way? Does it still come to supper with naughty people and cast them into this bottomless pit?

ANA. It has been a great expense to me. The boys in the monastery school would not let it alone: the mischievous ones broke it; and the studious ones wrote their names on it. Three new noses in two years, and fingers without end. I had to leave it to its fate at last; and now 30 I fear it is shockingly mutilated. My poor father!

DON JUAN. Listen! [*Two great chords rolling on syncopated waves of sound break forth. D minor and its dominant: a sound of dreadful joy to all musicians*]. Ha! Mozart's statue music. It is your father. You had better disappear until I prepare him. [*She vanishes*].

*From the void comes a living statue of white marble, designed to represent a majestic old* 40 *man. But he waives his majesty with infinite grace; walks with a feather-like step; and makes every wrinkle in his war worn visage brim over with holiday joyousness. To his sculptor he owes a perfectly trained figure, which he carries erect and trim; and the ends of his moustache curl up, elastic as watchsprings, giving him an air which, but for its Spanish dignity, would be called jaunty. He is on the pleasantest terms with Don Juan. His voice, save for a* 50 *much more distinguished intonation, is so like the voice of Roebuck Ramsden that it calls attention to the fact that they are not unlike one another in spite of their very different fashions of shaving.*

DON JUAN. Ah, here you are, my friend.

Why dont you learn to sing the splendid music Mozart has written for you?

THE STATUE. Unluckily he has written it for a bass voice. Mine is a counter tenor. Well: have you repented yet?

DON JUAN. I have too much consideration for you to repent, Don Gonzalo. If I did, you would have no excuse for coming from heaven to argue with me.

THE STATUE. True. Remain obdurate, my boy. I wish I had killed you, as I should have done but for an accident. Then I should have come here; and you would have had a statue and a reputation for piety to live up to. Any news?

DON JUAN. Yes: your daughter is dead.

THE STATUE [*puzzled*] My daughter? [*Recollecting*] Oh! the one you were taken with. Let me see: what was her name?

DON JUAN. Ana.

THE STATUE. To be sure: Ana. A goodlooking girl, if I recollect aright. Have you warned Whatshisname? her husband.

DON JUAN. My friend Ottavio? No: I have not seen him since Ana arrived.

*Ana comes indignantly to light.*

ANA. What does this mean? Ottavio here and your friend! And you, father, have forgotten my name. You are indeed turned to stone.

THE STATUE. My dear: I am so much more admired in marble than I ever was in my own person that I have retained the shape the sculptor gave me. He was one of the first men of his day: you must acknowledge that.

ANA. Father! Vanity! personal vanity! from you!

THE STATUE. Ah, you outlived that weakness, my daughter: you must be nearly 80 by this time. I was cut off (by an accident) in my 64th year, and am considerably your junior in consequence. Besides, my child, in this place, what our libertine friend here would call the farce of parental wisdom is dropped. Regard me, I beg, as a fellow creature, not as a father.

ANA. You speak as this villain speaks.

THE STATUE. Juan is a sound thinker, Ana. A bad fencer, but a sound thinker.

ANA [*horror creeping upon her*] I begin to understand. These are devils, mocking me. I had better pray.

THE STATUE [*consoling her*] No, no, no, my child: do not pray. If you do, you will throw away the main advantage of this place. Written over the gate here are the words "Leave every hope behind, ye who enter." Only think what a relief that is! For what is hope? A form of moral responsibility. Here there is no hope, and consequently no duty, no work, nothing to be gained by praying, nothing to be lost by doing what you like. Hell, in short, is a place where you have nothing to do but amuse yourself. [*Don Juan sighs deeply*]. You sigh, friend Juan; but if you dwelt in heaven, as I do, you would realize your advantages.

DON JUAN. You are in good spirits today, Commander. You are positively brilliant. What is the matter?

THE STATUE. I have come to a momentous decision, my boy. But first, where is our friend the Devil? I must consult him in the matter. And Ana would like to make his acquaintance, no doubt.

ANA. You are preparing some torment for me.

DON JUAN. All that is superstition, Ana. Reassure yourself. Remember: the devil is not so black as he is painted.

THE STATUE. Let us give him a call.

*At the wave of the statue's hand the great chords roll out again; but this time Mozart's music gets grotesquely adulterated with Gounod's. A scarlet halo begins to glow; and into it the Devil rises, very Mephistophelean, and not at all unlike Mendoza, though not so interesting. He looks older; is getting prematurely bald; and, in spite of an effusion of good-nature and friendliness, is peevish and sensitive when his advances are not reciprocated. He does not inspire much confidence in his powers of hard work or endurance, and is, on the whole, a disagreeably self-indulgent looking person; but he is clever and plausible, though perceptibly less well bred than the two other men, and enormously less vital than the woman.*

THE DEVIL [*heartily*] Have I the pleasure of again receiving a visit from the illustrious Commander of Calatrava? [*Coldly*] Don Juan, your servant. [*Politely*] And a strange lady? My respects, Señora.

ANA. Are you—

THE DEVIL [*bowing*] Lucifer, at your service.

ANA. I shall go mad.

THE DEVIL [*gallantly*] Ah, Señora, do not be anxious. You come to us from earth, full of the prejudices and terrors of that priest-ridden place. You have heard me ill spoken of; and yet, believe me, I have hosts of friends there.

ANA. Yes: you reign in their hearts.

THE DEVIL [*shaking his head*] You flatter me, Señora; but you are mistaken. It is true that the world cannot get on without me; but it never gives me credit for that: in its heart it mistrusts and hates me. Its sympathies are all with misery, with poverty, with starvation of the body, and of the heart. I call on it to sympathize with joy, with love, with happiness, with beauty—

DON JUAN [*nauseated*] Excuse me: I am going. You know I cannot stand this.

THE DEVIL [*angrily*] Yes: I know that you are no friend of mine.

THE STATUE. What harm is he doing you, Juan? It seems to me that he was talking excellent sense when you interrupted him.

THE DEVIL [*warmly patting the statue's hand*] Thank you, my friend: thank you. You have always understood me: he has always disparaged and avoided me.

DON JUAN. I have treated you with perfect courtesy.

THE DEVIL. Courtesy! What is courtesy? I care nothing for mere courtesy. Give me warmth of heart, true sincerity, the bond of sympathy with love and joy—

DON JUAN. You are making me ill.

THE DEVIL. There! [*Appealing to the statue*] You hear, sir! Oh, by what irony of fate was this cold selfish egotist sent to my kingdom, and you taken to the icy mansions of the sky!

THE STATUE. I can't complain. I was a hypocrite; and it served me right to be sent to heaven.

THE DEVIL. Why, sir, do you not join us, and leave a sphere for which your temperament is too sympathetic, your heart too warm, your capacity for enjoyment too generous?

THE STATUE. I have this day resolved to do so. In future, excellent Son of the Morning, I am yours. I have left heaven for ever.

THE DEVIL [*again touching the marble hand*] Ah, what an honor! what a triumph for our cause! Thank you, thank you. And now, my friend—I may call you so at last—could you not persuade him to take the place you have left vacant above?

THE STATUE [*shaking his head*] I cannot conscientiously recommend anybody with whom I am on friendly terms to deliberately make himself dull and uncomfortable.

THE DEVIL. Of course not; but are you sure he would be uncomfortable? Of course you know best: you brought him here originally; and we had the greatest hopes of him. His sentiments were in the best taste of our best people. You remember how he sang? [*He begins to sing in a nasal operatic baritone, tremulous from an eternity of misuse in the French manner*]

Vivan le femmine!
Viva il buon vino!

THE STATUE [*taking up the tune an octave higher in his counter tenor*]
                Sostegno e gloria
                D'umanità.

THE DEVIL. Precisely. Well, he never sings for us now.

DON JUAN. Do you complain of that? Hell is full of musical amateurs: music is the brandy of the damned. May not one lost soul be permitted to abstain?

THE DEVIL. You dare blaspheme against the sublimest of the arts!

DON JUAN [*with cold disgust*] You talk like a hysterical woman fawning on a fiddler.

THE DEVIL. I am not angry. I merely pity you. You have no soul; and you are unconscious of all that you lose. Now you, Señor Commander, are a born musician. How well you sing! Mozart would be delighted if he were still here; but he moped and went to heaven. Curious how these clever men, whom you would have supposed born to be popular here, have turned out social failures, like Don Juan!

DON JUAN. I am really very sorry to be a social failure.

THE DEVIL. Not that we dont admire your intellect, you know. We do. But I look at the matter from your own point of view. You dont get on with us. The place doesnt suit you. The truth is, you have—I wont say no heart; for we know that beneath all your affected cynicism you have a warm one—

DON JUAN [*shrinking*] Dont, please dont.

THE DEVIL [*nettled*] Well, youve no capacity for enjoyment. Will that satisfy you?

DON JUAN. It is a somewhat less insufferable form of cant than the other. But if youll allow me, I'll take refuge, as usual, in solitude.

THE DEVIL. Why not take refuge in heaven? Thats the proper place for you. [*To Ana*] Come, Señora! could you not persuade him for his own good to try change of air?

ANA. But can he go to heaven if he wants to?

THE DEVIL. Whats to prevent him?

ANA. Can anybody—can *I* go to heaven if I want to?

THE DEVIL [*rather contemptuously*] Certainly, if your taste lies that way.

ANA. But why doesnt everybody go to heaven, then?

THE STATUE [*chuckling*] I can tell you that, my dear. It's because heaven is the most angelically dull place in all creation: thats why.

THE DEVIL. His excellency the Commander puts it with military bluntness; but the strain of living in heaven is intolerable. There is a notion that I was turned out of it; but as a matter of fact nothing could have induced me to stay there. I simply left it and organized this place.

THE STATUE. I dont wonder at it. Nobody could stand an eternity of heaven.

THE DEVIL. Oh, it suits some people. Let us be just, Commander: it is a question of temperament. I dont admire the heavenly temperament. I dont understand it: I dont know that I particularly want to understand it; but it takes all sorts to make a universe. There is no accounting for tastes: there are people who like it. I think Don Juan would like it.

DON JUAN. But—pardon my frankness—could you really go back there if you desired to; or are the grapes sour?

THE DEVIL. Back there! I often go back there. Have you never read the book of Job? Have you any canonical authority for assuming that there is any barrier between our circle and the other one?

ANA. But surely there is a great gulf fixed.

THE DEVIL. Dear lady: a parable must not be taken literally. The gulf is the difference between the angelic and the diabolic temperament. What more impassable gulf could you have? Think of what you have seen on earth. There is no physical gulf between the philosopher's class room and the bull ring; but the bull fighters do not come to the class room for all that. Have you ever been in the country where I have the largest following? England. There they have great racecourses, and also concert rooms where they play the classical compositions of his Excellency's friend Mozart. Those who go to the racecourses can stay away from them and go to the classical concerts instead if they like: there is no law against it; for Englishmen never will be slaves: they are free to do whatever the Government and public opinion allow them to do. And the classical concert is admitted to be a higher, more cultivated, poetic, intellectual, ennobling place than the racecourse. But do the lovers of racing desert their sport and flock to the concert room? Not they. They would suffer there all the weariness the Commander has suffered in heaven. There is the great gulf of the parable between the two places. A mere physical gulf they could bridge; or at least I could bridge it for them (the earth is full of Devil's Bridges); but the gulf of dislike is impassable and eternal. And that is the only gulf that separates my friends here from those who are invidiously called the blest.

ANA. I shall go to heaven at once.

THE STATUE. My child: one word of warning first. Let me complete my friend Lucifer's similitude of the classical concert. At every one of these concerts in England you will find rows of weary people who are there, not because they really like classical music, but because they think they ought to like it. Well, there is the same thing in heaven. A number of people sit there in glory, not because they are happy, but because they think they owe it to their position to be in heaven. They are almost all English.

THE DEVIL. Yes: the Southerners give it up and join me just as you have done. But the English really do not seem to know when they are thoroughly miserable. An Englishman thinks he is moral when he is only uncomfortable.

THE STATUE. In short, my daughter, if you go to heaven without being naturally qualified for it, you will not enjoy yourself there.

ANA. And who dares say that I am not naturally qualified for it? The most distinguished princes of the Church have never questioned it. I owe it to myself to leave this place at once.

THE DEVIL [*offended*] As you please, Señora. I should have expected better taste from you.

ANA. Father: I shall expect you to come with me. You cannot stay here. What will people say?

THE STATUE. People! Why, the best people are here—princes of the Church and all. So few go to heaven, and so many come here, that the blest, once called a heavenly host, are a continually dwindling minority. The saints, the fathers, the elect of long ago, are the cranks, the faddists, the outsiders of today.

THE DEVIL. It is true. From the beginning of my career I knew that I should win in the long run by sheer weight of public opinion, in spite of the long campaign of misrepresentation and calumny against me. At the bottom the universe is a constitutional one; and with such a majority as mine I cannot be kept permanently out of office.

DON JUAN. I think, Ana, you had better stay here.

ANA [*jealously*] You do not want me to go with you.

DON JUAN. Surely you do not want to enter heaven in the company of a reprobate like me.

ANA. All souls are equally precious. You repent, do you not?

DON JUAN. My dear Ana, you are silly. Do you suppose heaven is like earth, where people persuade themselves that what is done can be undone by repentance; that what is spoken can be unspoken by withdrawing it; that what is true can be annihilated by a general agreement to give it the lie? No: heaven is the home of the masters of reality: that is why I am going thither.

ANA. Thank you: I am going to heaven for happiness. I have had quite enough of reality on earth.

DON JUAN. Then you must stay here; for hell is the home of the unreal and of the seekers of happiness. It is the only refuge from heaven, which is, as I tell you, the home of the masters of reality, and from earth, which is the home of the slaves of reality. The earth is a nursery in which men and women play at being heroes and heroines, saints and sinners; but they are dragged down from their fool's paradise by their bodies: hunger and cold and thirst, age and decay and disease, death above all, make them slaves of reality: thrice a day meals must be eaten and digested: thrice a century a new generation must be engendered: ages of faith, of romance, and of science are all driven at last to have but one prayer "Make me a healthy animal." But here you escape this tyranny of the flesh; for here you are not an animal at all: you are a ghost, an appearance, an illusion, a convention, deathless, ageless: in a word, bodiless. There are no social questions here, no political questions, no religious questions, best of all, perhaps, no sanitary questions. Here you call your appearance beauty, your emotions love, your sentiments heroism, your aspirations virtue, just as you did on earth; but here there are no hard facts to contradict you, no ironic contrast of your needs with your pretensions, no human comedy, nothing but a perpetual romance, a universal melodrama. As our German friend put it in his poem, "the poetically nonsensical here is good sense; and the Eternal Feminine draws us ever upward and on"— without getting us a step farther. And yet you want to leave this paradise!

ANA. But if hell be so beautiful as this, how glorious must heaven be!

*The Devil, the Statue, and Don Juan all begin to speak at once in violent protest; then stop, abashed.*

DON JUAN. I beg your pardon.

THE DEVIL. Not at all. I interrupted you.

THE STATUE. You were going to say something.

DON JUAN. After you, gentlemen.

THE DEVIL [*to Don Juan*] You have been so eloquent on the advantages of my dominions that I leave you to do equal justice to the drawbacks of the alternative establishment.

DON JUAN. In heaven, as I picture it, dear lady, you live and work instead of playing and pretending. You face things as they are; you escape nothing but glamor; and your steadfastness and your peril are your glory. If the play still goes on here and on earth, and all the world is a stage, heaven is at least behind the scenes. But heaven cannot be described by metaphor. Thither I shall go presently, because there I hope to escape at last from lies and from the tedious, vulgar pursuit of happiness, to spend my eons in contemplation—

THE STATUE. Ugh!

DON JUAN. Señor Commander: I do not blame your disgust: a picture gallery is a dull place for a blind man. But even as you enjoy the contemplation of such romantic mirages as beauty and pleasure; so would I enjoy the contemplation of that which interests me above all things: namely, Life: the force that ever strives to attain greater power of contemplating itself. What made this brain of mine, do you think? Not the need to move my limbs; for a rat with half my brain moves as well as I. Not merely the need to do, but the need to know what I do, lest in my blind efforts to live I should be slaying myself.

THE STATUE. You would have slain yourself in your blind efforts to fence but for my foot slipping, my friend.

DON JUAN. Audacious ribald: your laughter will finish in hideous boredom before morning.

THE STATUE. Ha ha! Do you remember how I frightened you when I said something like that to you from my pedestal in Seville? It sounds rather flat without my trombones.

DON JUAN. They tell me it generally sounds flat with them, Commander.

ANA. Oh, do not interrupt with these frivolities, father. Is there nothing in heaven but contemplation, Juan?

DON JUAN. In the heaven I seek, no other joy. But there is the work of helping Life in its struggle upward. Think of how it wastes and scatters itself, how it raises up obstacles to itself and destroys itself in its ignorance and blindness. It needs a brain, this irresistible force, lest in its ignorance it should resist itself. What a piece of work is man! says the poet. Yes; but what a blunderer! Here is the highest miracle of organization yet attained by life, the most intensely alive thing that exists, the most conscious of all the organisms; and yet, how wretched are his brains! Stupidity made sordid and cruel by the realities learnt from toil and poverty: Imagination resolved to starve sooner than face these realities, piling up illusions to hide them, and calling itself cleverness, genius! And each accusing the other of its own defect: Stupidity accusing Imagination of folly, and Imagination accusing Stupidity of ignorance: whereas, alas! Stupidity has all the knowledge, and Imagination all the intelligence.

THE DEVIL. And a pretty kettle of fish they make of it between them. Did I say, when I was arranging that affair of Faust's, that all Man's reason has done for him is to make him beastlier than any beast. One splendid body is worth the brains of a hundred dyspeptic, flatulent philosophers.

DON JUAN. You forget that brainless magnificence of body has been tried. Things immeasurably greater than man in every respect but brain have existed and perished. The megatherium, the ichthyosaurus have paced the earth with seven-league steps and hidden the day with cloud vast wings. Where are they now? Fossils in museums, and so few and imperfect at that, that a knuckle bone or a tooth of one of them is prized beyond the lives of a thousand soldiers. These things lived and wanted to live; but for lack of brains they did not know how to carry out their purpose, and so destroyed themselves.

THE DEVIL. And is Man any the less destroying himself for all this boasted brain of his? Have you walked up and down upon the earth lately? I have; and I have examined Man's wonderful inventions. And I tell you that in the arts of life man invents nothing; but in the arts of death he outdoes Nature herself, and produces by chemistry and machinery all the slaughter of plague, pestilence, and famine. The peasant I tempt today eats and drinks what was eaten and drunk by the peasants of ten thousand years ago; and the house he lives in has not altered as much in a thousand centuries as the fashion of a lady's bonnet in a score of weeks. But when he goes out to slay, he carries a marvel of mechanism that lets loose at the touch of his finger all the hidden molecular energies, and leaves the javelin, the arrow, the blowpipe of his fathers far behind. In the arts of peace Man is a bungler. I have seen his cotton factories and the like, with machinery that a greedy dog could have invented if it had wanted money instead of food. I know his clumsy typewriters and bungling locomotives and tedious bicycles: they are toys compared to the Maxim gun, the submarine torpedo boat.

There is nothing in Man's industrial machinery but his greed and sloth: his heart is in his weapons. This marvellous force of Life of which you boast is a force of Death: Man measures his strength by his destructiveness. What is his religion? An excuse for hating me. What is his law? An excuse for hanging you. What is his morality? Gentility! an excuse for consuming without producing. What is his art? An excuse for gloating over pictures of slaughter. What are his politics? Either the worship of a despot because a despot can kill, or parliamentary cockfighting. I spent an evening lately in a certain celebrated legislature, and heard the pot lecturing the kettle for its blackness, and ministers answering questions. When I left I chalked upon the door the old nursery saying "Ask no questions and you will be told no lies." I bought a sixpenny family magazine, and found it full of pictures of young men shooting and stabbing one another. I saw a man die: he was a London bricklayer's laborer with seven children. He left seventeen pounds club money; and his wife spent it all on his funeral and went into the workhouse with the children next day. She would not have spent sevenpence on her children's schooling: the law had to force her to let them be taught gratuitously; but on death she spent all she had. Their imagination glows, their energies rise up at the idea of death, these people: they love it; and the more horrible it is the more they enjoy it. Hell is a place far above their comprehension: they derive their notion of it from two of the greatest fools that ever lived, an Italian and an Englishman. The Italian described it as a place of mud, frost, filth, fire, and venomous serpents: all torture. This ass, when he was not lying about me, was maundering about some woman whom he saw once in the street. The Englishman described me as being expelled from heaven by cannons and gunpowder; and to this day every Briton believes that the whole of his silly story is in the Bible. What else he says I do not know; for it is all in a long poem which neither I nor anyone else ever succeeded in wading through. It is the same in everything. The highest form of literature is the tragedy, a play in which everybody is murdered at the end. In the old chronicles you read of earthquakes and pestilences, and are told that these shewed the power and majesty of God and the littleness of Man. Nowadays the chronicles describe battles. In a battle two bodies of men shoot at one another with bullets and explosive shells until one body runs away, when the others chase the fugitives on horseback and cut them to pieces as they fly. And this, the chronicle concludes, shews the greatness and majesty of empires, and the littleness of the vanquished. Over such battles the people run about the streets yelling with delight, and egg their governments on to spend hundreds of millions of money in the slaughter, whilst the strongest Ministers dare not spend an extra penny in the pound against the poverty and pestilence through which they themselves daily walk. I could give you a thousand instances; but they all come to the same thing: the power that governs the earth is not the power of Life but of Death; and the inner need that has nerved Life to the effort of organising itself into the human being is not the need for higher life but for a more efficient engine of destruction. The plague, the famine, the earthquake, the tempest were too spasmodic in their action; the tiger and crocodile were too easily satiated and not cruel enough: something more constantly, more ruthlessly, more ingeniously destructive was needed; and that something was Man, the inventor of the rack, the stake, the gallows, the electric chair; of sword and gun and poison gas: above all, of justice, duty, patriotism, and all the other isms by which even those who are clever enough to be humanely disposed are persuaded to become the most destructive of all the destroyers.

DON JUAN. Pshaw! all this is old. Your weak side, my diabolic friend, is that you have always been a gull: you take Man at his own valuation. Nothing would flatter him more than your opinion of him. He loves to think of himself as bold and bad. He is neither one nor the other: he is only a coward. Call him tyrant, murderer, pirate, bully; and he will adore you, and swagger about with the consciousness of having the blood of the old sea kings in his veins. Call him liar and thief; and he will only take an action against you for libel. But call him coward; and he will go mad with rage: he will face death to outface that stinging truth. Man gives every reason for his conduct save one, every excuse for his crimes save one, every plea for his safety save one; and that one is his cowardice. Yet all his civilization is founded on his cowardice, on his abject tameness, which he calls his respectability. There are limits to what a mule or an ass will stand; but Man will suffer himself to be degraded until his vileness becomes so loathsome to his oppressors that they themselves are forced to reform it.

THE DEVIL. Precisely. And these are the creatures in whom you discover what you call a Life Force!

DON JUAN. Yes; for now comes the most surprising part of the whole business.

THE STATUE. What's that?

DON JUAN. Why, that you can make any of these cowards brave by simply putting an idea into his head.

THE STATUE. Stuff! As an old soldier I admit the cowardice: it's as universal as sea sickness, and matters just as little. But that about putting an idea into a man's head is stuff and nonsense. In a battle all you need to make you fight is a little hot blood and the knowledge that it's more dangerous to lose than to win.

DON JUAN. That is perhaps why battles are so useless. But men never really overcome fear until they imagine they are fighting to further a universal purpose—fighting for an idea, as they call it. Why was the Crusader braver than the pirate? Because he fought, not for himself, but for the Cross. What force was it that met him with a valor as reckless as his own? The force of men who fought, not for themselves, but for Islam. They took Spain from us, though we were fighting for our very hearths and homes; but when we, too, fought for that mighty idea, a Catholic Church, we swept them back to Africa.

THE DEVIL [*ironically*] What! you a Catholic, Señor Don Juan! A devotee! My congratulations.

THE STATUE [*seriously*] Come, come! as a soldier, I can listen to nothing against the Church.

DON JUAN. Have no fear, Commander: this idea of a Catholic Church will survive Islam, will survive the Cross, will survive even that vulgar pageant of incompetent schoolboyish gladiators which you call the Army.

THE STATUE. Juan: you will force me to call you to account for this.

DON JUAN. Useless: I cannot fence. Every idea for which Man will die will be a Catholic idea. When the Spaniard learns at last that he is no better than the Saracen, and his prophet no better than Mahomet, he will arise, more Catholic than ever, and die on a barricade across the filthy slum he starves in, for a universal liberty and equality.

THE STATUE. Bosh!

DON JUAN. What you call bosh is the only thing men dare die for. Later on, Liberty will not be Catholic enough: men will die for human perfection, to which they will sacrifice all their liberty gladly.

THE DEVIL. Ay: they will never be at a loss for an excuse for killing one another.

DON JUAN. What of that? It is not death that matters, but the fear of death. It is not killing and dying that degrades us, but base living, and accepting the wages and profits of degradation. Better ten dead men than one live slave or his master. Men shall yet rise up, father against son and brother against brother, and kill one another for the great Catholic idea of abolishing slavery.

THE DEVIL. Yes, when the Liberty and Equality of which you prate shall have made free white Christians cheaper in the labor market than black heathen slaves sold by auction at the block.

DON JUAN. Never fear! the white laborer shall have his turn too. But I am now defending the illusory forms the great ideas take. I am giving you examples of the fact that this creature Man, who in his own selfish affairs is a coward to the backbone, will fight for an idea like a hero. He may be abject as a citizen; but he is dangerous as a fanatic. He can only be enslaved whilst he is spiritually weak enough to listen to reason. I tell you, gentlemen, if you can shew a man a piece of what he now calls God's work to do, and what he will later on call by many new names, you can make him entirely reckless of the consequences to himself personally.

ANA. Yes: he shirks all his responsibilities, and leaves his wife to grapple with them.

THE STATUE. Well said, daughter. Do not let him talk you out of your common sense.

THE DEVIL. Alas! Señor Commander, now that we have got on to the subject of Women, he will talk more than ever. However, I confess it is for me the one supremely interesting subject.

DON JUAN. To a woman, Señora, man's duties and responsibilities begin and end with the task of getting bread for her children. To her, Man is only a means to the end of getting children and rearing them.

ANA. Is that your idea of a woman's mind? I call it cynical and disgusting animalism.

DON JUAN. Pardon me, Ana: I said nothing about a woman's whole mind. I spoke of her view of Man as a separate sex. It is no more cynical than her view of herself as above all things a Mother. Sexually, Woman is Nature's contrivance for perpetuating its highest achievement. Sexually, Man is Woman's contrivance for fulfilling Nature's behest in the most economical way. She knows by instinct that far back in the evolutional process she invented him, differentiated him, created him in order to produce something better than the single-sexed process can produce. Whilst he fulfils the purpose for which she made him, he is welcome to his dreams, his follies, his ideals, his heroisms, provided that the keystone of them all is the worship of woman, of motherhood, of the family, of the hearth. But how rash and dangerous it was to invent a separate creature whose sole function was her own impregnation! For mark what has happened. First, Man has multiplied on her hands until there are as many men as women; so that she has been unable to employ for her purposes more than a fraction of the immense energy she has left at his disposal by saving him the exhausting labor of gestation. This superfluous energy has gone to his brain and to his muscle. He has become too strong to be controlled by her bodily, and too imaginative and mentally vigorous to be content with mere self-reproduction. He has created civilization without consulting her, taking her domestic labor for granted as the foundation of it.

ANA. That is true, at all events.

THE DEVIL. Yes; and this civilization! what is it, after all?

DON JUAN. After all, an excellent peg to hang your cynical commonplaces on; but before all, it is an attempt on Man's part to make himself something more than the mere instrument of Woman's purpose. So far, the result of Life's continual effort, not only to maintain itself, but to achieve higher and higher organization and completer self-consciousness, is only, at best, a doubtful campaign between its forces and those of Death and Degeneration. The battles in this campaign are mere blunders, mostly won, like actual military battles, in spite of the commanders.

THE STATUE. That is a dig at me. No matter: go on, go on.

DON JUAN. It is a dig at a much higher power than you, Commander. Still, you must have noticed in your profession that even a stupid general can win battles when the enemy's general is a little stupider.

THE STATUE [*very seriously*] Most true, Juan, most true. Some donkeys have amazing luck.

DON JUAN. Well, the Life Force is stupid; but it is not so stupid as the forces of Death and Degeneration. Besides, these are in its pay all the time. And so Life wins, after a fashion. What mere copiousness of fecundity can supply and mere greed preserve, we possess. The survival of whatever form of civilization can produce the best rifle and best fed riflemen is assured.

THE DEVIL. Exactly! the survival, not of the most effective means of Life but of the most effective means of Death. You always come back to my point, in spite of your wrigglings and evasions and sophistries, not to mention the intolerable length of your speeches.

DON JUAN. Oh, come! who began making long speeches? However, if I overtax your intellect, you can leave us and seek the society of love and beauty and the rest of your favorite boredoms.

THE DEVIL [*much offended*] This is not fair, Don Juan, and not civil. I am also on the intellectual plane. Nobody can appreciate it more than I do. I am arguing fairly with you, and, I think, successfully refuting you. Let us go on for another hour if you like.

DON JUAN. Good: let us.

THE STATUE. Not that I see any prospect of your coming to any point in particular, Juan. Still, since in this place, instead of merely killing time we have to kill eternity, go ahead by all means.

DON JUAN [*somewhat impatiently*] My point, you marbleheaded old masterpiece, is only a step ahead of you. Are we agreed that Life is a force which has made innumerable experiments in organizing itself; that the mammoth and the man, the mouse and the megatherium, the flies and the fleas and the Fathers of the Church, are all more or less successful attempts to build up that raw force into higher and higher individuals, the ideal individual being omnipotent, omniscient, infallible, and withal completely, unilludedly self-conscious: in short, a god?

THE DEVIL. I agree, for the sake of argument.

THE STATUE. I agree, for the sake of avoiding argument.

ANA. I most emphatically disagree as regards the Fathers of the Church; and I must beg you not to drag them into the argument.

DON JUAN. I did so purely for the sake of alliteration, Ana; and I shall make no further allusion to them. And now, since we are, with that exception, agreed so far, will you not agree with me further that Life has not measured the success of its attempts at godhead by the beauty or bodily perfection of the result, since in both these respects the birds, as our friend Aristophanes long ago pointed out, are so extraordinarily superior, with their power of flight and their lovely plumage, and, may I add, the touching poetry of their loves and nestings, that it is inconceivable that Life, having once produced them, should, if love and beauty were her object, start off on another line and labor at the clumsy elephant and the hideous ape, whose grandchildren we are?

ANA. Aristophanes was a heathen; and you, Juan, I am afraid, are very little better.

THE DEVIL. You conclude, then, that Life was driving at clumsiness and ugliness?

DON JUAN. No, perverse devil that you are, a thousand times no. Life was driving at brains —at its darling object: an organ by which it can attain not only self-consciousness but self-understanding.

THE STATUE. This is metaphysics, Juan. Why the devil should—[*to The Devil*] I beg your pardon.

THE DEVIL. Pray dont mention it. I have always regarded the use of my name to secure additional emphasis as a high compliment to me. It is quite at your service, Commander.

THE STATUE. Thank you: thats very good of you. Even in heaven, I never quite got out of my old military habits of speech. What I was going to ask Juan was why Life should bother itself about getting a brain. Why should it want to understand itself? Why not be content to enjoy itself?

DON JUAN. Without a brain, Commander, you would enjoy yourself without knowing it, and so lose all the fun.

THE STATUE. True, most true. But I am quite content with brain enough to know that I'm enjoying myself. I dont want to understand why. In fact, I'd rather not. My experience is that one's pleasures dont bear thinking about.

DON JUAN. That is why intellect is so unpopular. But to Life, the force behind the Man, intellect is a necessity, because without it he blunders into death. Just as Life, after ages of struggle, evolved that wonderful bodily organ the eye, so that the living organism could see where it was going and what was coming to help or threaten it, and thus avoid a thousand dangers that formerly slew it, so it is evolving today a mind's eye that shall see, not the physical world, but the purpose of life, and thereby enable the individual to work for that purpose instead of thwarting and baffling it by setting up shortsighted personal aims as at present. Even as it is, only one sort of man has ever been happy, has ever been universally respected among all the conflicts of interests and illusions.

THE STATUE. You mean the military man.

DON JUAN. Commander: I do not mean the military man. When the military man approaches, the world locks up its spoons and packs off its womankind. No: I sing not arms and the hero, but the philosophic man: he who seeks in contemplation to discover the inner will of the world, in invention to discover the means of fulfilling that will, and in action to do that will by the so-discovered means. Of all other sorts of men I declare myself tired. They are tedious failures. When I was on earth, professors of all sorts prowled round me feeling for an unhealthy spot in me on which they could fasten. The doctors of medicine bade me consider what I must do to save my body, and offered me quack cures for imaginary diseases. I replied that I was not a hypochondriac; so they called me Ignoramus and went their way. The doctors of divinity bade me consider what I must do to save my soul; but I was not a spiritual hypochondriac any more than a bodily one, and would not trouble myself about that either; so they called me Atheist and went their way. After them came the politician, who said there was only one purpose in nature, and that was to get him into parliament. I told him I did not care whether he got into parliament or not; so he called me Mugwump and went his way. Then came the romantic man, the Artist, with his love songs and his paintings and his poems; and with him I had great delight for many years, and some profit; for I cultivated my senses for his sake; and his songs taught me to hear better, his paintings to see better, and his poems to feel more deeply. But he led me at last into the worship of Woman.

ANA. Juan!

DON JUAN. Yes: I came to believe that in her voice was all the music of the song, in her face all the beauty of the painting, and in her soul all the emotion of the poem.

ANA. And you were disappointed, I suppose. Well, was it her fault that you attributed all these perfections to her?

DON JUAN. Yes, partly. For with a wonderful instinctive cunning, she kept silent and allowed me to glorify her: to mistake my own visions, thoughts, and feelings for hers. Now my friend the romantic man was often too poor or too timid to approach those women who were beautiful or refined enough to seem to realize his ideal; and so he went to his grave believing in his dream. But I was more favored by nature and circumstance. I was of noble birth and rich; and when my person did not please, my conversation flattered, though I generally found myself fortunate in both.

THE STATUE. Coxcomb!

DON JUAN. Yes; but even my coxcombry pleased. Well, I found that when I had touched a woman's imagination, she would allow me to persuade myself that she loved me; but when my suit was granted she never said "I am happy; my love is satisfied": she always said, first, "At last, the barriers are down," and second, "When will you come again?"

ANA. That is exactly what men say.

DON JUAN. I protest I never said it. But all women say it. Well, these two speeches always alarmed me; for the first meant that the lady's impulse had been solely to throw down my fortifications and gain my citadel; and the second openly announced that henceforth she regarded me as her property, and counted my 10 time as already wholly at her disposal.

THE DEVIL. That is where your want of heart came in.

THE STATUE [*shaking his head*] You shouldnt repeat what a woman says, Juan.

ANA [*severely*] It should be sacred to you.

THE STATUE. Still, they certainly do say it. I never minded the barriers; but there was always a slight shock about the other, unless one was very hard hit indeed. 20

DON JUAN. Then the lady, who had been happy and idle enough before, became anxious, preoccupied with me, always intriguing, conspiring, pursuing, watching, waiting, bent wholly on making sure of her prey: I being the prey, you understand. Now this was not what I had bargained for. It may have been very proper and very natural; but it was not music, painting, poetry, and joy incarnated in a beautiful woman. I ran away from it. I ran away 30 from it very often: in fact I became famous for running away from it.

ANA. Infamous, you mean.

DON JUAN. I did not run away from you. Do you blame me for running away from the others?

ANA. Nonsense, man. You are talking to a woman of 77 now. If you had had the chance, you would have run away from me too—if I had let you. You would not have found it so 40 easy with me as with some of the others. If men will not be faithful to their home and their duties, they must be made to be. I daresay you all want to marry lovely incarnations of music and painting and poetry. Well, you cant have them, because they dont exist. If flesh and blood is not good enough for you, you must go without: thats all. Women have to put up with flesh-and-blood husbands—and little enough of that too, sometimes; and you 50 will have to put up with flesh-and-blood wives. [*The Devil looks dubious. The Statue makes a wry face*]. I see you dont like that, any of you; but it's true, for all that; so if you dont like it you can lump it.

DON JUAN. My dear lady, you have put my whole case against romance into a few sentences. That is just why I turned my back on the romantic man with the artist nature, as he called his infatuation. I thanked him for teaching me to use my eyes and ears; but I told him that his beauty worshipping and happiness hunting and woman idealizing was not worth a dump as a philosophy of life; so he called me Philistine and went his way.

ANA. It seems that Woman taught you something, too, with all her defects.

DON JUAN. She did more: she interpreted all the other teaching for me. Ah, my friends, when the barriers were down for the first time, what an astounding illumination! I had been prepared for infatuation, for intoxication, for all the illusions of love's young dream; and lo! never was my perception clearer, nor my criticism more ruthless. The most jealous rival of my mistress never saw every blemish in her more keenly than I. I was not duped: I took 20 her without chloroform.

ANA. But you did take her.

DON JUAN. That was the revelation. Up to that moment I had never lost the sense of being my own master; never consciously taken a single step until my reason had examined and approved it. I had come to believe that I was a purely rational creature: a thinker! I said, with the foolish philosopher, "I think; therefore I am." It was Woman who taught me to say "I am; therefore I think." And also "I would think more; therefore I must be more."

THE STATUE. This is extremely abstract and metaphysical, Juan. If you would stick to the concrete, and put your discoveries in the form of entertaining anecdotes about your adventures with women, your conversation would be easier to follow.

DON JUAN. Bah! what need I add? Do you not understand that when I stood face to face with Woman, every fibre in my clear critical brain warned me to spare her and save myself. My morals said No. My conscience said No. My chivalry and pity for her said No. My prudent regard for myself said No. My ear, practised on a thousand songs and symphonies; my eye, exercised on a thousand paintings; tore her voice, her features, her color to shreds. I caught all those tell-tale resemblances to her 50 father and mother by which I knew what she would be like in thirty years' time. I noted the gleam of gold from a dead tooth in the laughing mouth: I made curious observations of the strange odors of the chemistry of the nerves. The visions of my romantic reveries, in which I had trod the plains of heaven with a deathless, ageless creature of coral and ivory, deserted me in that supreme hour. I remembered them and desperately strove to recover their illusion; but they now seemed the emptiest of inventions: my judgment was not to be corrupted: my brain still said No on every issue. And whilst I was in the act of framing my excuse to the lady, Life seized me and threw me into her arms as a sailor throws a scrap of fish into the mouth of a seabird.

THE STATUE. You might as well have gone without thinking such a lot about it, Juan. You are like all the clever men: you have more brains than is good for you.

THE DEVIL. And were you not the happier for the experience, Señor Don Juan?

DON JUAN. The happier; not the wiser, yes. That moment introduced me for the first time to myself, and, through myself, to the world. I saw then how useless it is to attempt to impose conditions on the irresistible force of Life; to preach prudence, careful selection, virtue, honor, chastity—

ANA. Don Juan: a word against chastity is an insult to me.

DON JUAN. I say nothing against your chastity, Señora, since it took the form of a husband and twelve children. What more could you have done had you been the most abandoned of women?

ANA. I could have had twelve husbands and no children: thats what I could have done, Juan. And let me tell you that that would have made all the difference to the earth which I replenished.

THE STATUE. Bravo Ana! Juan: you are floored, quelled, annihilated.

DON JUAN. No: for though that difference is the true essential difference—Doña Ana has, I admit, gone straight to the real point—yet it is not a difference of love or chastity, or even constancy; for twelve children by twelve different husbands would have replenished the earth perhaps more effectively. Suppose my friend Ottavio had died when you were thirty, you would never have remained a widow: you were too beautiful. Suppose the successor of Ottavio had died when you were forty, you would still have been irresistible; and a woman who marries twice marries three times if she becomes free to do so. Twelve lawful children borne by one highly respectable lady to three different fathers is not impossible nor condemned by public opinion. That such a lady may be more law abiding than the poor girl whom we used to spurn into the gutter for bearing one unlawful infant is no doubt true; but dare you say she is less self-indulgent?

ANA. She is more virtuous: that is enough for me.

DON JUAN. In that case, what is virtue but the Trade Unionism of the married? Let us face the facts, dear Ana. The Life Force respects marriage only because marriage is a contrivance of its own to secure the greatest number of children and the closest care of them. For honor, chastity, and all the rest of your moral figments it cares not a rap. Marriage is the most licentious of human institutions—

ANA. Juan!

THE STATUE [*protesting*] Really!

DON JUAN [*determinedly*] I say the most licentious of human institutions: that is the secret of its popularity. And a woman seeking a husband is the most unscrupulous of all the beasts of prey. The confusion of marriage with morality has done more to destroy the conscience of the human race than any other single error. Come, Ana! do not look shocked: you know better than any of us that marriage is a mantrap baited with simulated accomplishments and delusive idealizations. When your sainted mother, by dint of scoldings and punishments, forced you to learn how to play half a dozen pieces on the spinet—which she hated as much as you did—had she any other purpose than to delude your suitors into the belief that your husband would have in his home an angel who would fill it with melody, or at least play him to sleep after dinner? You married my friend Ottavio: well, did you ever open the spinet from the hour when the Church united him to you?

ANA. You are a fool, Juan. A young married woman has something else to do than sit at the spinet without any support for her back; so she gets out of the habit of playing.

DON JUAN. Not if she loves music. No: believe me, she only throws away the bait when the bird is in the net.

ANA [*bitterly*] And men, I suppose, never throw off the mask when their bird is in the net. The husband never becomes negligent, selfish, brutal—oh, never!

DON JUAN. What do these recriminations prove, Ana? Only that the hero is as gross an imposture as the heroine.

ANA. It is all nonsense: most marriages are perfectly comfortable.

DON JUAN. "Perfectly" is a strong expression, Ana. What you mean is that sensible people make the best of one another. Send me to the galleys and chain me to the felon whose number happens to be next before mine; and I must accept the inevitable and make the best of the companionship. Many such companionships, they tell me, are touchingly affectionate; and most are at least tolerably friendly. But that does not make a chain a desirable ornament nor the galleys an abode of bliss. Those who talk most about the blessings of marriage and the constancy of its vows are the very people who declare that if the chain were broken and the prisoners left free to choose, the whole social fabric would fly asunder. You cannot have the argument both ways. If the prisoner is happy, why lock him in? If he is not, why pretend that he is?

ANA. At all events, let me take an old woman's privilege again, and tell you flatly that marriage peoples the world and debauchery does not.

DON JUAN. How if a time come when this shall cease to be true? Do you not know that where there is a will there is a way? that whatever Man really wishes to do he will finally discover a means of doing? Well, you have done your best, you virtuous ladies, and others of your way of thinking, to bend Man's mind wholly towards honorable love as the highest good, and to understand by honorable love romance and beauty and happiness in the possession of beautiful, refined, delicate, affectionate women. You have taught women to value their own youth, health, shapeliness, and refinement above all things. Well, what place have squalling babies and household cares in this exquisite paradise of the senses and emotions? Is it not the inevitable end of it all that the human will shall say to the human brain: Invent me a means by which I can have love, beauty, romance, emotion, passion, without their wretched penalties, their expenses, their worries, their trials, their illnesses and agonies and risks of death, their retinue of servants and nurses and doctors and schoolmasters.

THE DEVIL. All this, Señor Don Juan, is realized here in my realm.

DON JUAN. Yes, at the cost of death. Man will not take it at that price: he demands the romantic delights of your hell whilst he is still on earth. Well, the means will be found: the brain will not fail when the will is in earnest. The day is coming when great nations will find their numbers dwindling from census to census; when the six roomed villa will rise in price above the family mansion; when the viciously reckless poor and the stupidly pious rich will delay the extinction of the race only by degrading it; whilst the boldly prudent, the thriftily selfish and ambitious, the imaginative and poetic, the lovers of money and solid comfort, the worshippers of success, of art, and of love, will all oppose to the Force of Life the device of sterility.

THE STATUE. That is all very eloquent, my young friend; but if you had lived to Ana's age, or even to mine, you would have learned that the people who get rid of the fear of poverty and children and all the other family troubles, and devote themselves to having a good time of it, only leave their minds free for the fear of old age and ugliness and impotence and death. The childless laborer is more tormented by his wife's idleness and her constant demands for amusement and distraction than he could be by twenty children; and his wife is more wretched than he. I have had my share of vanity; for as a young man I was admired by women; and as a statue I am praised by art critics. But I confess that had I found nothing to do in the world but wallow in these delights I should have cut my throat. When I married Ana's mother—or perhaps, to be strictly correct, I should rather say when I at last gave in and allowed Ana's mother to marry me—I knew that I was planting thorns in my pillow, and that marriage for me, a swaggering young officer thitherto unvanquished, meant defeat and capture.

ANA [*scandalized*] Father!

THE STATUE. I am sorry to shock you, my love; but since Juan has stripped every rag of decency from the discussion I may as well tell the frozen truth.

ANA. Hmf! I suppose I was one of the thorns.

THE STATUE. By no means: you were often a rose. You see, your mother had most of the trouble you gave.

DON JUAN. Then may I ask, Commander, why you have left heaven to come here and wallow, as you express it, in sentimental beatitudes which you confess would once have driven you to cut your throat?

THE STATUE [*struck by this*] Egad, thats true.

THE DEVIL [*alarmed*] What! You are going back from your word! [*To Don Juan*] And all your philosophizing has been nothing but a mask for proselytizing! [*To the Statue*] Have you forgotten already the hideous dulness from which I am offering you a refuge here? [*To Don Juan*] And does your demonstration of the approaching sterilization and extinction of mankind lead to anything better than making the most of those pleasures of art and love which you yourself admit refined you, elevated you, developed you?

DON JUAN. I never demonstrated the ex-

tinction of mankind. Life cannot will its own
extinction either in its blind amorphous state
or in any of the forms into which it has organized itself. I had not finished when His
Excellency interrupted me.

THE STATUE. I begin to doubt whether you
ever will finish, my friend. You are extremely
fond of hearing yourself talk.

DON JUAN. True; but since you have endured
so much, you may as well endure to the end. 10
Long before this sterilization which I described
becomes more than a clearly foreseen possibility, the reaction will begin. The great central
purpose of breeding the race: ay, breeding it to
heights now deemed superhuman: that purpose
which is now hidden in a mephitic cloud of
love and romance and prudery and fastidiousness, will break through into clear sunlight as
a purpose no longer to be confused with the
gratification of personal fancies, the impossi- 20
ble realization of boys' and girls' dreams of
bliss, or the need of older people for companionship or money. The plain-spoken marriage
services of the vernacular Churches will no
longer be abbreviated and half suppressed as
indelicate. The sober decency, earnestness, and
authority of their declaration of the real purpose of marriage will be honored and accepted,
whilst their romantic vowings and pledgings
and until-death-do-us-partings and the like will 30
be expunged as unbearable frivolities. Do my
sex the justice to admit, Señora, that we have
always recognized that the sex relation is not
a personal or friendly relation at all.

ANA. Not a personal or friendly relation!
What relation is more personal? more sacred?
more holy?

DON JUAN. Sacred and holy, if you like, Ana,
but not personally friendly. Your relation to
God is sacred and holy: dare you call it per- 40
sonally friendly? In the sex relation the universal creative energy, of which the parties are
both the helpless agents, overrides and sweeps
away all personal considerations, and dispenses
with all personal relations. The pair may be utter strangers to one another, speaking different
languages, differing in race and color, in age
and disposition, with no bond between them
but a possibility of that fecundity for the sake
of which the Life Force throws them into one 50
another's arms at the exchange of a glance.
Do we not recognize this by allowing marriages
to be made by parents without consulting the
woman? Have you not often expressed your disgust at the immorality of the English nation, in
which women and men of noble birth become
acquainted and court each other like peasants?

And how much does even the peasant know of
his bride or she of him before he engages himself? Why, you would not make a man your
lawyer or your family doctor on so slight an
acquaintance as you would fall in love with
and marry him!

ANA. Yes, Juan: we know the libertine's
philosophy. Always ignore the consequences to
the woman.

DON JUAN. The consequences, yes: they justify her fierce grip of the man. But surely you
do not call that attachment a sentimental one.
As well call the policeman's attachment to his
prisoner a love relation.

ANA. You see you have to confess that marriage is necessary, though, according to you,
love is the slightest of all human relations.

DON JUAN. How do you know that it is not
the greatest of all human relations? far too
great to be a personal matter. Could your father
have served his country if he had refused to kill
an enemy of Spain unless he personally hated
him? Can a woman serve her country if she
refuses to marry any man she does not personally love? You know it is not so: the woman
of noble birth marries as the man of noble
birth fights, on political and family grounds,
not on personal ones.

THE STATUE [*impressed*] A very clever point
that, Juan: I must think it over. You are really
full of ideas. How did you come to think of
this one?

DON JUAN. I learnt it by experience. When I
was on earth, and made those proposals to
ladies which, though universally condemned,
have made me so interesting a hero of legend,
I was not infrequently met in some such way
as this. The lady would say that she would
countenance my advances, provided they were
honorable. On inquiring what that proviso
meant, I found that it meant that I proposed to
get possession of her property, if she had any,
or to undertake her support for life if she had
not; that I desired her continual companionship, counsel, and conversation to the end of
my days, and would take a most solemn oath
to be always enraptured by them: above all,
that I would turn my back on all other women
for ever for her sake. I did not object to these
conditions because they were exorbitant and
inhuman: it was their extraordinary irrelevance
that prostrated me. I invariably replied with
perfect frankness that I had never dreamt of
any of these things; that unless the lady's character and intellect were equal or superior to
my own, her conversation must degrade and
her counsel mislead me; that her constant com-

panionship might, for all I knew, become intolerably tedious to me; that I could not answer for my feelings for a week in advance, much less to the end of my life; that to cut me off from all natural and unconstrained intercourse with half my fellow-creatures would narrow and warp me if I submitted to it, and, if not, would bring me under the curse of clandestinity; that, finally, my proposals to her 10 were wholly unconnected with any of these matters, and were the outcome of a perfectly simple impulse of my manhood towards her womanhood.

ANA. You mean that it was an immoral impulse.

DON JUAN. Nature, my dear lady, is what you call immoral. I blush for it; but I cannot help it. Nature is a pandar, Time a wrecker, and Death a murderer. I have always preferred to stand up to those facts and build institutions 20 on their recognition. You prefer to propitiate the three devils by proclaiming their chastity, their thrift, and their loving kindness; and to base your institutions on these flatteries. Is it any wonder that the institutions do not work smoothly?

THE STATUE. What used the ladies to say, Juan?

DON JUAN. Oh, come! Confidence for confidence. First tell me what you used to say to 30 the ladies.

THE STATUE. I! Oh, I swore that I would be faithful to the death; that I should die if they refused me; that no woman could ever be to me what she was—

ANA. She! Who?

THE STATUE. Whoever it happened to be at the time, my dear. I had certain things I always said. One of them was that even when I was eighty, one white hair of the woman I loved 40 would make me tremble more than the thickest gold tress from the most beautiful young head. Another was that I could not bear the thought of anyone else being the mother of my children.

DON JUAN [revolted] You old rascal!

THE STATUE [stoutly] Not a bit; for I really believed it with all my soul at the moment. I had a heart: not like you. And it was this sincerity that made me successful.

DON JUAN. Sincerity! To be fool enough to 50 believe a ramping, stamping, thumping lie: that is what you call sincerity! To be so greedy for a woman that you deceive yourself in your eagerness to deceive her: sincerity, you call it!

THE STATUE. Oh, damn your sophistries! I was a man in love, not a lawyer. And the women loved me for it, bless them!

DON JUAN. They made you think so. What will you say when I tell you that though I played the lawyer so callously, they made me think so too? I also had my moments of infatuation in which I gushed nonsense and believed it. Sometimes the desire to give pleasure by saying beautiful things so rose in me on the flood of emotion that I said them recklessly. At other times I argued against myself with a devilish coldness that drew tears. But I found it just as hard to escape when I was cruel as when I was kind. When the lady's instinct was set on me, there was nothing for it but lifelong servitude or flight.

ANA. You dare boast, before me and my father, that every woman found you irresistible.

DON JUAN. Am I boasting? It seems to me that I cut the most pitiable of figures. Besides, I said "when the lady's instinct was set on me." It was not always so; and then, heavens! what transports of virtuous indignation! what overwhelming defiance to the dastardly seducer! what scenes of Imogen and Iachimo!

ANA. I made no scenes. I simply called my father.

DON JUAN. And he came, sword in hand, to vindicate outraged honor and morality by murdering me.

THE STATUE. Murdering! What do you mean? Did I kill you or did you kill me?

DON JUAN. Which of us was the better fencer?

THE STATUE. I was.

DON JUAN. Of course you were. And yet you, the hero of those scandalous adventures you have just been relating to us, you had the effrontery to pose as the avenger of outraged morality and condemn me to death! You would have slain me but for an accident.

THE STATUE. I was expected to, Juan. That is how things were arranged on earth. I was not a social reformer; and I always did what it was customary for a gentleman to do.

DON JUAN. That may account for your attacking me, but not for the revolting hypocrisy of your subsequent proceedings as a statue.

THE STATUE. That all came of my going to heaven.

THE DEVIL. I still fail to see, Señor Don Juan, that these episodes in your earthly career and in that of the Señor Commander in any way discredit my view of life. Here, I repeat, you have all that you sought without anything that you shrank from.

DON JUAN. On the contrary, here I have everything that disappointed me without any that I have not already tried and found wanting. I tell you that as long as I can conceive something better than myself I cannot be easy unless I am striving to bring it into existence or clearing the way for it. That is the law of my life. That is the working within me of Life's incessant aspiration to higher organization, wider, deeper, intenser self-consciousness, and clearer self-understanding. It was the supremacy of this purpose that reduced love 10 for me to the mere pleasure of a moment, art for me to the mere schooling of my faculties, religion for me to a mere excuse for laziness, since it had set up a God who looked at the world and saw that it was good, against the instinct in me that looked through my eyes at the world and saw that it could be improved. I tell you that in the pursuit of my own pleasure, my own health, my own fortune, I have never known happiness. It was not love 20 for Woman that delivered me into her hands: it was fatigue, exhaustion. When I was a child, and bruised my head against a stone, I ran to the nearest woman and cried away my pain against her apron. When I grew up, and bruised my soul against the brutalities and stupidities with which I had to strive, I did again just what I had done as a child. I have enjoyed, too, my rests, my recuperations, my breathing times, my very prostrations after 30 strife; but rather would I be dragged through all the circles of the foolish Italian's Inferno than through the pleasures of Europe. That is what has made this place of eternal pleasures so deadly to me. It is the absence of this instinct in you that makes you that strange monster called a Devil. It is the success with which you have diverted the attention of men from their real purpose, which in one degree or another is the same as mine, to yours, that has 40 earned you the name of The Tempter. It is the fact that they are doing your will, or rather drifting with your want of will, instead of doing their own, that makes them the uncomfortable, false, restless, artificial, petulant, wretched creatures they are.

THE DEVIL [*mortified*] Señor Don Juan: you are uncivil to my friends.

DON JUAN. Pooh! why should I be civil to them or to you? In this Palace of Lies a truth 50 or two will not hurt you. Your friends are all the dullest dogs I know. They are not beautiful: they are only decorated. They are not clean: they are only shaved and starched. They are not dignified: they are only fashionably dressed. They are not educated: they are only

college passmen. They are not religious: they are only pewrenters. They are not moral: they are only conventional. They are not virtuous: they are only cowardly. They are not even vicious: they are only "frail." They are not artistic: they are only lascivious. They are not prosperous: they are only rich. They are not loyal, they are only servile; not dutiful, only sheepish; not public spirited, only patriotic; not 10 courageous, only quarrelsome; not determined, only obstinate; not masterful, only domineering; not self-controlled, only obtuse; not self-respecting, only vain; not kind, only sentimental; not social, only gregarious; not considerate, only polite; not intelligent, only opinionated; not progressive, only factious; not imaginative, only superstitious; not just, only vindictive; not generous, only propitiatory; not disciplined, only cowed; and not truthful 20 at all: liars every one of them, to the very backbone of their souls.

THE STATUE. Your flow of words is simply amazing, Juan. How I wish I could have talked like that to my soldiers.

THE DEVIL. It is mere talk, though. It has all been said before; but what change has it ever made? What notice has the world ever taken of it?

DON JUAN. Yes, it is mere talk. But why is 30 it mere talk? Because, my friend, beauty, purity, respectability, religion, morality, art, patriotism, bravery, and the rest are nothing but words which I or anyone else can turn inside out like a glove. Were they realities, you would have to plead guilty to my indictment; but fortunately for your self-respect, my diabolical friend, they are not realities. As you say, they are mere words, used for duping barbarians into adopting civilization, or the civi- 40 lized poor into submitting to be robbed and enslaved. That is the family secret of the governing caste; and if we who are of that caste aimed at more Life for the world instead of at more power and luxury for our miserable selves, that secret would make us great. Now, since I, being a nobleman, am in the secret too, think how tedious to me must be your unending cant about all these moralistic figments, and how squalidly disastrous your sacrifice of 50 your lives to them! If you even believed in your moral game enough to play it fairly, it would be interesting to watch; but you don't: you cheat at every trick; and if your opponent outcheats you, you upset the table and try to murder him.

THE DEVIL. On earth there may be some

truth in this, because the people are uneducated and cannot appreciate my religion of love and beauty; but here—

DON JUAN. Oh yes: I know. Here there is nothing but love and beauty. Ugh! it is like sitting for all eternity at the first act of a fashionable play, before the complications begin. Never in my worst moments of superstitious terror on earth did I dream that hell was so horrible. I live, like a hairdresser, in the continued contemplation of beauty, toying with silken tresses. I breathe an atmosphere of sweetness, like a confectioner's shopboy. Commander: are there any beautiful women in heaven?

THE STATUE. None. Absolutely none. All dowdies. Not two pennorth of jewellery among a dozen of them. They might be men of fifty.

DON JUAN. I am impatient to get there. Is the word beauty ever mentioned; and are there any artistic people?

THE STATUE. I give you my word they wont admire a fine statue even when it walks past them.

DON JUAN. I go.

THE DEVIL. Don Juan: shall I be frank with you?

DON JUAN. Were you not so before?

THE DEVIL. As far as I went, yes. But I will now go further, and confess to you that men get tired of everything, of heaven no less than of hell; and that all history is nothing but a record of the oscillations of the world between these two extremes. An epoch is but a swing of the pendulum; and each generation thinks the world is progressing because it is always moving. But when you are as old as I am; when you have a thousand times wearied of heaven, like myself and the Commander, and a thousand times wearied of hell, as you are wearied now, you will no longer imagine that every swing from heaven to hell is an emancipation, every swing from hell to heaven an evolution. Where you now see reforms, progress, fulfilment of upward tendency, continual ascent by Man on the stepping stones of his dead selves to higher things, you will see nothing but an infinite comedy of illusion. You will discover the profound truth of the saying of my friend Koheleth, that there is nothing new under the sun. Vanitas vanitatum—

DON JUAN [*out of all patience*] By Heaven, this is worse than your cant about love and beauty. Clever dolt that you are, is a man no better than a worm, or a dog than a wolf, because he gets tired of everything? Shall he give up eating because he destroys his appetite in the act of gratifying it? Is a field idle when it is fallow? Can the Commander expand his hellish energy here without accumulating heavenly energy for his next term of blessedness? Granted that the great Life Force has hit on the device of the clockmaker's pendulum, and uses the earth for its bob; that the history of each oscillation, which seems so novel to us the actors, is but the history of the last oscillation repeated; nay more, that in the unthinkable infinitude of time the sun throws off the earth and catches it again a thousand times as a circus rider throws up a ball, and that our agelong epochs are but the moments between the toss and the catch, has the colossal mechanism no purpose?

THE DEVIL. None, my friend. You think, because you have a purpose, Nature must have one. You might as well expect it to have fingers and toes because you have them.

DON JUAN. But I should not have them if they served no purpose. And I, my friend, am as much a part of Nature as my own finger is a part of me. If my finger is the organ by which I grasp the sword and the mandoline, my brain is the organ by which Nature strives to understand itself. My dog's brain serves only my dog's purposes; but my own brain labors at a knowledge which does nothing for me personally but make my body bitter to me and my decay and death a calamity. Were I not possessed with a purpose beyond my own I had better be a ploughman than a philosopher; for the ploughman lives as long as the philosopher, eats more, sleeps better, and rejoices in the wife of his bosom with less misgiving. This is because the philosopher is in the grip of the Life Force. This Life Force says to him "I have done a thousand wonderful things unconsciously by merely willing to live and following the line of least resistance: now I want to know myself and my destination, and choose my path; so I have made a special brain—a philosopher's brain—to grasp this knowledge for me as the husbandman's hand grasps the plough for me. And this" says the Life Force to the philosopher "must thou strive to do for me until thou diest, when I will make another brain and another philosopher to carry on the work."

THE DEVIL. What is the use of knowing?

DON JUAN. Why, to be able to choose the line of greatest advantage instead of yielding in the direction of the least resistance. Does a ship sail to its destination no better than a log drifts nowhither? The philosopher is Nature's pilot. And there you have our difference: to be in hell is to drift: to be in heaven is to steer.

THE DEVIL. On the rocks, most likely.

DON JUAN. Pooh! which ship goes oftenest on the rocks or to the bottom? the drifting ship or the ship with a pilot on board?

THE DEVIL. Well, well, go your way, Señor Don Juan. I prefer to be my own master and not the tool of any blundering universal force. I know that beauty is good to look at; that music is good to hear; that love is good to feel; and that they are all good to think about and talk about. I know that to be well exercised in these sensations, emotions, and studies is to be a refined and cultivated being. Whatever they may say of me in churches on earth, I know that it is universally admitted in good society that the Prince of Darkness is a gentleman; and that is enough for me. As to your Life Force, which you think irresistible, it is the most resistible thing in the world for a person of any character. But if you are naturally vulgar and credulous, as all reformers are, it will thrust you first into religion, where you will sprinkle water on babies to save their souls from me; then it will drive you from religion into science, where you will snatch the babies from the water sprinkling and innoculate them with disease to save them from catching it accidentally; then you will take to politics, where you will become the catspaw of corrupt functionaries and the henchman of ambitious humbugs; and the end will be despair and decrepitude, broken nerve and shattered hopes, vain regrets for that worst and silliest of wastes and sacrifices, the waste and sacrifice of the power of enjoyment: in a word, the punishment of the fool who pursues the better before he has secured the good.

DON JUAN. But at least I shall not be bored. The service of the Life Force has that advantage, at all events. So fare you well, Señor Satan.

THE DEVIL [*amiably*] Fare you well, Don Juan. I shall often think of our interesting chats about things in general. I wish you every happiness: heaven, as I said before, suits some people. But if you should change your mind, do not forget that the gates are always open here to the repentant prodigal. If you feel at any time that warmth of heart, sincere unforced affection, innocent enjoyment, and warm, breathing, palpitating reality—

DON JUAN. Why not say flesh and blood at once, though we have left those two greasy commonplaces behind us?

THE DEVIL [*angrily*] You throw my friendly farewell back in my teeth, then, Don Juan?

DON JUAN. By no means. But though there is much to be learnt from a cynical devil, I really cannot stand a sentimental one. Señor Commander: you know the way to the frontier of hell and heaven. Be good enough to direct me.

THE STATUE. Oh, the frontier is only the difference between two ways of looking at things. Any road will take you across it if you really want to get there.

DON JUAN. Good. [*Saluting Doña Ana*] Señora: your servant.

ANA. But I am going with you.

DON JUAN. I can find my own way to heaven, Ana; not yours [*he vanishes*].

ANA. How annoying!

THE STATUE [*calling after him*] Bon voyage, Juan! [*He wafts a final blast of his great rolling chords after him as a parting salute. A faint echo of the first ghostly melody comes back in acknowledgment*]. Ah! there he goes. [*Puffing a long breath out through his lips*] Whew! How he does talk! They'll never stand it in heaven.

THE DEVIL [*gloomily*] His going is a political defeat. I cannot keep these Life Worshippers: they all go. This is the greatest loss I have had since that Dutch painter went: a fellow who would paint a hag of 70 with as much enjoyment as a Venus of 20.

THE STATUE. I remember: he came to heaven. Rembrandt.

THE DEVIL. Ay, Rembrandt. There is something unnatural about these fellows. Do not listen to their gospel, Señor Commander: it is dangerous. Beware of the pursuit of the Superhuman: it leads to an indiscriminate contempt for the Human. To a man, horses and dogs and cats are mere species, outside the moral world. Well, to the Superman, men and women are a mere species too, also outside the moral world. This Don Juan was kind to women and courteous to men as your daughter here was kind to her pet cats and dogs; but such kindness is a denial of the exclusively human character of the soul.

THE STATUE. And who the deuce is the Superman?

THE DEVIL. Oh, the latest fashion among the Life Force fanatics. Did you not meet in Heaven, among the new arrivals, that German

Polish madman? what was his name? Nietzsche?

THE STATUE. Never heard of him.

THE DEVIL. Well, he came here first, before he recovered his wits. I had some hopes of him; but he was a confirmed Life Force worshipper. It was he who raked up the Superman, who is as old as Prometheus; and the 20th century will run after this newest of the old crazes when it gets tired of the world, the flesh, and 10 your humble servant.

THE STATUE. Superman is a good cry; and a good cry is half the battle. I should like to see this Nietzsche.

THE DEVIL. Unfortunately he met Wagner here, and had a quarrel with him.

THE STATUE. Quite right, too. Mozart for me!

THE DEVIL. Oh, it was not about music. Wagner once drifted into Life Force worship, 20 and invented a Superman called Siegfried. But he came to his senses afterwards. So when they met here, Nietzsche denounced him as a renegade; and Wagner wrote a pamphlet to prove that Nietzsche was a Jew; and it ended in Nietzsche's going to heaven in a huff. And a good riddance too. And now, my friend, let us hasten to my palace and celebrate your arrival with a grand musical service.

THE STATUE. With pleasure: youre most kind.

THE DEVIL. This way, Commander. We go down the old trap [*he places himself on the grave trap*].

THE STATUE. Good. [*Reflectively*] All the same, the Superman is a fine conception. There is something statuesque about it. [*He places himself on the grave trap beside The Devil. It begins to descend slowly. Red glow from the abyss*]. Ah, this reminds me of old times.

THE DEVIL. And me also.

ANA. Stop! [*The trap stops*].

THE DEVIL. You, Señora, cannot come this way. You will have an apotheosis. But you will be at the palace before us.

ANA. That is not what I stopped you for. Tell me: where can I find the Superman?

THE DEVIL. He is not yet created, Señora.

THE STATUE. And never will be, probably. Let us proceed: the red fire will make me sneeze. [*They descend*].

ANA. Not yet created! Then my work is not yet done. [*Crossing herself devoutly*] I believe in the Life to Come. [*Crying to the universe*] A father! a father for the Superman!

*She vanishes into the void; and again there is nothing: all existence seems suspended infinitely.*

# William Butler Yeats

## 1865-1939

William Butler Yeats was born near Dublin, at Sandymount, 13 June, 1865. J. B. Yeats, his father, was an artist of great ability. The family moved to London shortly after Yeats was born, but the boy spent most of his early years in County Sligo, Ireland, where his mother's family lived. Although he had thought for a time of becoming a painter also, and had studied painting, Yeats was drawn increasingly to poetry, and after publication of The Wanderings of Oisin (1889) he declared himself a literary man by profession.

Yeats kept producing volumes of poetry for the whole of his long life, although he interspersed them with plays and essays. The chief among his collections of poems are The Wind among the Reeds (1899), Responsibilities (1914), The Wild Swans at Coole (1917), Later Poems (1922), and The Tower (1927); the Collected Poems appeared in 1933.

Although the poems vary in form and in depth of symbolism from his early volumes to his later work, the characteristic sound of Yeats's language and the Irish setting are clearly recognizable from first to last. The early poems Yeats describes in his Autobiography (1916) as overcharged with color inherited from the Romantic Movement; dissatisfied with the "yellow and dull green" of The Wanderings of Oisin he consciously reshaped his style, "deliberately sought out an impression as of cold light and tumbling clouds," discarded traditional metaphors and loosened his rhythm, "became as emotional as possible but with an emotion which [he described to himself as] cold." Both the Autobiography and his introduction to The Oxford Book of Modern Verse give valuable insight into Yeats's philosophy of poetry.

The plays to which Yeats gave his name are mainly poetic dramas of great beauty and intensity, such as Cathleen Ni Houlihan (1902) and Deirdre (1907). Oliver St. John Gogarty suggests that Yeats was also largely responsible for many farces and comedies produced by the Abbey Theatre as the work of Lady Gregory. Yeats's critical writings, including The Cutting of an Agate (1903–15) are collected in Essays (1924).

The best text of the poems is The Variorum Edition of the Poems of W. B. Yeats, ed. Peter Allt and Russell K. Alspach (New York, 1957); of the plays, The Collected Plays (New York, 1953). The Letters of W. B. Yeats, ed. Allan Wade (New York, 1955), is a very full selection. Biographical and critical studies include Louis MacNeice, The Poetry of W. B. Yeats (London, 1941); Richard Ellman, Yeats: The Man and the Masks (London, 1948), and The Identity of Yeats (London, 1954); Donald Stauffer, The Golden Nightingale (New York, 1949); The Performance of Yeats, Selected Criticism, ed. James Hall and Martin Steinmann (New York, 1950); T. R. Henn, The Lonely Tower (London, 1950); Virginia Moore, The Unicorn: William Butler Yeats' Search for Reality (New York, 1954); Frank Kermode, Romantic Image (London, 1957); and F. A. C. Wilson, W. B. Yeats and Tradition (London, 1958). John Unterecker, Reader's Guide to William Butler Yeats (New York, 1959), supplies useful background.

## The Meditation of the Old Fisherman [1]

You waves, though you dance by my feet like
    children at play,
Though you glow and you glance, though you
    purr and you dart;
In the Junes that were warmer than these are,
    the waves were more gay,
When I was a boy with never a crack in my
    heart.

The herring are not in the tides as they were
    of old;     5

[1] Published 1886. Yeats's poems appear here in the order preferred by the poet.

My sorrow! for many a creak gave the creel in
    the cart
That carried the take to Sligo town to be sold,
*When I was a boy with never a crack in my*
    *heart.*

And ah, you proud maiden, you are not so fair
    when his oar
Is heard on the water, as they were, the proud
    and apart,           10
Who paced in the eve by the nets on the
    pebbly shore,
*When I was a boy with never a crack in my*
    *heart.*

## To the Rose upon the Rood of Time [2]

Red Rose, proud Rose, sad Rose of all my days!
Come near me, while I sing the ancient ways:
Cuchulain battling with the bitter tide;
The Druid, grey, wood-nurtured, quiet-eyed,
Who cast round Fergus dreams, and ruin un-
    told;              5
And thine own sadness, whereof stars, grown
    old
In dancing silver-sandalled on the sea,
Sing in their high and lonely melody.
Come near, that no more blinded by man's
    fate,
I find under the boughs of love and hate, 10
In all poor foolish things that live a day,
Eternal beauty wandering on her way.

Come near, come near, come near—Ah, leave
    me still
A little space for the rose-breath to fill!
Lest I no more hear common things that crave;
The weak worm hiding down in its small cave,
The field-mouse running by me in the grass, 17
And heavy mortal hopes that toil and pass;
But seek alone to hear the strange things said
By God to the bright hearts of those long dead,
And learn to chaunt a tongue men do not
    know.             21
Come near; I would, before my time to go,
Sing of old Eire and the ancient ways:
Red Rose, proud Rose, sad Rose of all my days.

## The Lake Isle of Innisfree [3]

I will arise and go now, and go to Innisfree,
And a small cabin build there, of clay and
    wattles made:
Nine bean-rows will I have there, a hive for the
    honeybee,
And live alone in the bee-loud glade.

[2] Published 1892. In later editions Yeats dates the
poem 1893.
[3] Published 1890.

And I shall have some peace there, for peace
    comes dropping slow,      5
Dropping from the veils of the morning to
    where the cricket sings;
There midnight's all a glimmer, and noon a
    purple glow,
And evening full of the linnet's wings.
I will arise and go now, for always night and
    day
I hear lake water lapping with low sounds by
    the shore;          10
While I stand on the roadway, or on the pave-
    ments grey,
I hear it in the deep heart's core.

## The Sorrow of Love [4]

The brawling of a sparrow in the eaves,
The brilliant moon and all the milky sky,
And all that famous harmony of leaves,
Had blotted out man's image and his cry.

A girl arose that had red mournful lips   5
And seemed the greatness of the world in tears,
Doomed like Odysseus and the labouring ships
And proud as Priam murdered with his peers;

Arose, and on the instant clamorous eaves,
A climbing moon upon an empty sky,   10
And all that lamentation of the leaves,
Could but compose man's image and his cry.

## When You Are Old [5]

When you are old and grey and full of sleep,
And nodding by the fire, take down this book,
And slowly read, and dream of the soft look
Your eyes had once, and of their shadows deep;

How many loved your moments of glad grace, 5
And loved your beauty with love false or true,
But one man loved the pilgrim soul in you,
And loved the sorrows of your changing face;

And bending down beside the glowing bars,
Murmur, a little sadly, how Love fled   10
And paced upon the mountains overhead
And hid his face amid a crowd of stars.

## The Host of the Air [6]

O'Driscoll drove with a song
The wild duck and the drake
From the tall and the tufted reeds
Of the drear Hart Lake.

And he saw how the reeds grew dark   5
At the coming of night-tide,
And dreamed of the long dim hair
Of Bridget his bride.

[4] Published 1892.     [5] Published 1892.
[6] Written and published 1893.

He heard while he sang and dreamed
A piper piping away,                                      10
And never was piping so sad,
And never was piping so gay.

And he saw young men and young girls
Who danced on a level place,
And Bridget his bride among them,                         15
With a sad and a gay face.

The dancers crowded about him
And many a sweet thing said,
And a young man brought him red wine
And a young girl white bread.                             20

But Bridget drew him by the sleeve
Away from the merry bands,
To old men playing at cards
With a twinkling of ancient hands.

The bread and the wine had a doom,                        25
For these were the host of the air;
He sat and played in a dream
Of her long dim hair.

He played with the merry old men
And thought not of evil chance,                           30
Until one bore Bridget his bride
Away from the merry dance.

He bore her away in his arms,
The handsomest young man there,
And his neck and his breast and his arms                  35
Were drowned in her long dim hair.

O'Driscoll scattered the cards
And out of his dream awoke:
Old men and young men and young girls
Were gone like a drifting smoke;                          40

But he heard high up in the air
A piper piping away,
And never was piping so sad,
And never was piping so gay.

## The Song of Wandering Aengus [7]

I went out to the hazel wood,
Because a fire was in my head,
And cut and peeled a hazel wand,
And hooked a berry to a thread;
And when white moths were on the wing,    5
And moth-like stars were flickering out,
I dropped the berry in a stream
And caught a little silver trout.

When I had laid it on the floor
I went to blow the fire aflame,           10
But something rustled on the floor,
And some one called me by my name:
It had become a glimmering girl
With apple blossom in her hair
Who called me by my name and ran          15
And faded through the brightening air.

[7] Published 1897.

Though I am old with wandering
Through hollow lands and hilly lands,
I will find out where she has gone,
And kiss her lips and take her hands;     20
And walk among long dappled grass,
And pluck till time and times are done
The silver apples of the moon,
The golden apples of the sun.

## The Song of the Old Mother [8]

I rise in the dawn, and I kneel and blow
Till the seed of the fire flicker and glow;
And then I must scrub and bake and sweep
Till stars are beginning to blink and peep;
And the young lie long and dream in their bed
Of the matching of ribbons for bosom and
    head,                                   6
And their day goes over in idleness,
And they sigh if the wind but lift a tress:
While I must work because I am old,
And the seed of the fire gets feeble and cold. 10

## He Mourns for the Change That Has Come upon Him and His Beloved, and Longs for the End of the World [9]

Do you not hear me calling, white deer with
    no horns?
I have been changed to a hound with one red
    ear;
I have been in the Path of Stones and the
    Wood of Thorns,
For somebody hid hatred and hope and desire
    and fear
Under my feet that they follow you night and
    day.                                     5
A man with a hazel wand came without sound;
He changed me suddenly; I was looking an-
    other way;
And now my calling is but the calling of a
    hound;
And Time and Birth and Change are hurrying
    by.
I would that the Boar without bristles had
    come from the West                        10
And had rooted the sun and moon and stars
    out of the sky
And lay in the darkness, grunting, and turning
    to his rest.

## He Remembers Forgotten Beauty [10]

When my arms wrap you round I press
My heart upon the loveliness

[8] Published 1894.
[9] Written and published 1897.
[10] Published 1896.

That has long faded from the world;
The jewelled crowns that kings have hurled
In shadowy pools, when armies fled;      5
The love-tales wrought with silken thread
By dreaming ladies upon cloth
That has made fat the murderous moth;
The roses that of old time were
Woven by ladies in their hair,      10
The dew-cold lilies ladies bore
Through many a sacred corridor
Where such grey clouds of incense rose
That only God's eyes did not close:
For that pale breast and lingering hand      15
Come from a more dream-heavy land,
A more dream-heavy hour than this;
And when you sigh from kiss to kiss
I hear white Beauty sighing, too,
For hours when all must fade like dew,      20
But flame on flame, and deep on deep,
Throne over throne where in half sleep,
Their swords upon their iron knees,
Brood her high lonely mysteries.

## He Wishes for the Cloths of Heaven [11]

Had I the heavens' embroidered cloths,
Enwrought with golden and silver light,
The blue and the dim and the dark cloths
Of night and light and the half-light,
I would spread the cloths under your feet:      5
But I, being poor, have only my dreams;
I have spread my dreams under your feet;
Tread softly because you tread on my dreams.

## He Thinks of His Past Greatness When a Part of the Constellations of Heaven [12]

I have drunk ale from the Country of the
    Young
And weep because I know all things now:
I have been a hazel-tree, and they hung
The Pilot Star and the Crooked Plough
Among my leaves in times out of mind:      5
I became a rush that horses tread:
I became a man, a hater of the wind,
Knowing one, out of all things, alone, that his
    head
May not lie on the breast nor his lips on the
    hair
Of the woman that he loves, until he dies.      10
O beast of the wilderness, bird of the air,
Must I endure your amorous cries?

## The Fiddler of Dooney [13]

When I play on my fiddle in Dooney,
Folk dance like a wave of the sea;

My cousin is priest in Kilvarnet,
My brother in Mocharabuiee.

I passed my brother and cousin:      5
They read in their books of prayer;
I read in my book of songs
I bought at the Sligo fair.

When we come at the end of time
To Peter sitting in state,      10
He will smile on the three old spirits,
But call me first through the gate;

For the good are always the merry,
Save by an evil chance,
And the merry love the fiddle,      15
And the merry love to dance:

And when the folk there spy me,
They will all come up to me,
With 'Here is the fiddler of Dooney!'
And dance like a wave of the sea.      20

## The Wild Swans at Coole [14]

The trees are in their autumn beauty,
The woodland paths are dry,
Under the October twilight the water
Mirrors a still sky;
Upon the brimming water among the stones      5
Are nine-and-fifty swans.

The nineteenth autumn has come upon me
Since I first made my count;
I saw, before I had well finished,
All suddenly mount      10
And scatter wheeling in great broken rings
Upon their clamorous wings.

I have looked upon those brilliant creatures,
And now my heart is sore.
All's changed since I, hearing at twilight,      15
The first time on this shore,
The bell-beat of their wings above my head,
Trod with a lighter tread.

Unwearied still, lover by lover,
They paddle in the cold      20
Companionable streams or climb the air;
Their hearts have not grown old;
Passion or conquest, wander where they will,
Attend upon them still.

But now they drift on the still water,      25
Mysterious, beautiful;
Among what rushes will they build,
By what lake's edge or pool
Delight men's eyes when I awake some day
To find they have flown away?      30

[11] Published 1899.   [12] Published 1898.
[13] Published 1892.

[14] Written 1916, published 1917; in later editions dated 1919. Reprinted by permission of The Macmillan Company.

## Stream and Sun at Glendalough [15]

Through intricate motions ran
Stream and gliding sun
And all my heart seemed gay:
Some stupid thing that I had done
Made my attention stray.                    5

[15] Written and published 1932. Reprinted by permission of The Macmillan Company.

Repentance keeps my heart impure;
But what am I that dare
Fancy that I can
Better conduct myself or have more
Sense than a common man?          10

What motion of the sun or stream
Or eyelid shot the gleam
That pierced my body through?
What made me live like these that seem
Self-born, born anew?          15

# John Millington Synge

## 1871 - 1909

John Millington Synge was born at Rathfarnham, Ireland, 16 April, 1871. He was educated at Trinity College, Dublin. After some years in Paris and elsewhere on the Continent, he took up residence in 1898 on the somewhat remote and primitive Aran Islands of the west coast of Ireland beyond Galway Bay.

He became interested in the life of the Aran Islanders, and in their language; he listened closely to the rhythms and stresses of their speech, until he could reproduce its sound in written dialogue. At first he wrote brief sketches of island life, which were published a number of years later in The Aran Islands (1907). By 1903, however, he had found himself as a writer; in that year he produced a one-act play, The Shadow of the Glen, that captured not only the rhythm of language but the rhythm of life of the island people. Riders to the Sea (1904), another one-act play, is a grimly simple but beautiful tragedy which is about the fatalism and grief of the islanders but is also about the suffering of all mankind.

In 1904 Synge was made a director of a new theatrical enterprise dedicated to the native drama of Ireland, the Abbey Theatre of Dublin. In 1905 he produced his first three-act play, The Well of the Saints, and in 1907 his most famous long play, The Playboy of the Western World. In these and in his unfinished play, Deirdre of the Sorrows (1910), he remained solidly inside the emotional frame of reference of the Irish common people, drawing the universal qualities of his plays up out of the characters themselves rather than imposing externally-derived values. Synge's Poems and Translations was published in 1909, the year of his death.

The best text is the Works of John Millington Synge (London, 1932). There is a one-volume selection (London, 1941) in Everyman's Library. Biographical and critical studies include W. B. Yeats's Synge and the Ireland of His Time (Dundrum, 1911); P. P. Howe's J. M. Synge, a Critical Study (London, 1912); Maurice Bourgeois's John Millington Synge and the Irish Theatre (London, 1913); Daniel Corkery's Synge and Anglo-Irish Literature (Oxford, 1931); and L. A. G. Strong's John Millington Synge (London, 1941).

## In the Shadow of the Glen [1]

Scene. The last cottage at the head of a long glen in County Wicklow. (Cottage kitchen; turf fire on the right; a bed near it against the wall with a body lying on it covered with a sheet. A door is at the other end of the room, with a low table near it, and stools, or wooden chairs. There are a couple of glasses on the table, and a bottle of whisky, as if for a wake, with two cups, a teapot, and a home-made cake. There is another small door near the bed. Nora Burke is moving about the room, settling a few things, and lighting candles on the table, looking now and then at the bed with an uneasy look. Some one knocks softly at the door. She takes up a stocking with money from the table and puts it in her pocket. Then she opens the door.)

TRAMP (outside). Good evening to you, lady of the house.

NORA. Good evening, kindly stranger, it's a wild night. God help you, to be out in the rain falling.

TRAMP. It is, surely, and I walking to Brittas from the Aughrim fair.

NORA. Is it walking on your feet, stranger?

TRAMP. On my two feet, lady of the house, and when I saw the light below I thought maybe if you'd a sup of new milk and a quiet decent corner where a man could sleep. (He looks in past her and sees the dead man.) The Lord have mercy on us all!

NORA. It doesn't matter anyway, stranger, come in out of the rain.

[1] First performed October 8, 1903, in Dublin. Reprinted by permission of Random House.

TRAMP (*coming in slowly and going towards the bed*). Is it departed he is?

NORA. It is, stranger. He's after dying on me, God forgive him, and there I am now with a hundred sheep beyond on the hills, and no turf drawn for the winter.

TRAMP (*looking closely at the dead man*). It's a queer look is on him for a man that's dead.

NORA (*half-humorously*). He was always queer, stranger, and I suppose them that's queer and they living men will be queer bodies after.

TRAMP. Isn't it a great wonder you're letting him lie there, and he is not tidied, or laid out itself?

NORA (*coming to the bed*). I was afeard, stranger, for he put a black curse on me this morning if I'ld touch his body the time he'ld die sudden, or let any one touch it except his sister only, and it's ten miles away she lives in the big glen over the hill.

TRAMP (*looking at her and nodding slowly*). It's a queer story he wouldn't let his own wife touch him, and he dying quiet in his bed.

NORA. He was an old man, and an odd man, stranger, and it's always up on the hills he was thinking thoughts in the dark mist. (*She pulls back a bit of the sheet.*) Lay your hand on him now, and tell me if it's cold he is surely.

TRAMP. Is it getting the curse on me you'ld be, woman of the house? I wouldn't lay my hand on him for the Lough Nahanagan and it filled with gold.

NORA (*looking uneasily at the body*). Maybe cold would be no sign of death with the like of him, for he was always cold, every day since I knew him,—and every night, stranger,—(*she covers up his face and comes away from the bed*); but I'm thinking it's dead he is surely, for he's complaining a while back of a pain in his heart, and this morning, the time he was going off to Brittas for three days or four, he was taken with a sharp turn. Then he went into his bed and he was saying it was destroyed he was, the time the shadow was going up through the glen, and when the sun set on the bog beyond he made a great lep, and let a great cry out of him, and stiffened himself out the like of a dead sheep.

TRAMP (*crosses himself*). God rest his soul.

NORA (*pouring him out a glass of whisky*). Maybe that would do you better than the milk of the sweetest cow in County Wicklow.

TRAMP. The Almighty God reward you, and may it be to your good health.

[*He drinks.*]

NORA (*giving him a pipe and tobacco*). I've no pipes saving his own, stranger, but they're sweet pipes to smoke.

TRAMP. Thank you kindly, lady of the house.

NORA. Sit down now, stranger, and be taking your rest.

TRAMP (*filling a pipe and looking about the room*). I've walked a great way through the world, lady of the house, and seen great wonders, but I never seen a wake till this day with fine spirits, and good tobacco, and the best of pipes, and no one to taste them but a woman only.

NORA. Didn't you hear me say it was only after dying on me he was when the sun went down, and how would I go out into the glen and tell the neighbors, and I a lone woman with no house near me?

TRAMP (*drinking*). There's no offence, lady of the house?

NORA. No offence in life, stranger. How would the like of you, passing in the dark night, know the lonesome way I was with no house near me at all?

TRAMP (*sitting down*). I knew rightly. (*He lights his pipe so that there is a sharp light beneath his haggard face.*) And I was thinking, and I coming in through the door, that it's many a lone woman would be afeard of the like of me in the dark night, in a place wouldn't be as lonesome as this place, where there aren't two living souls would see the little light you have shining from the glass.

NORA (*slowly*). I'm thinking many would be afeard but I never knew what way I'd be afeard of beggar or bishop or any man of you at all. (*She looks towards the window and lowers her voice.*) It's other things than the like of you, stranger, would make a person afeard.

TRAMP (*looking round with a half-shudder*). It is surely, God help us all!

NORA (*looking at him for a moment with curiosity*). You're saying that, stranger, as if you were easy afeard.

TRAMP (*speaking mournfully*). Is it myself, lady of the house, that does be walking round in the long nights, and crossing the hills when the fog is on them, the time a little stick would seem as big as your arm, and a rabbit as big as a bay horse, and a stack of turf as big as a towering church in the city of Dublin? If myself was easily afeard, I'm telling you, it's long ago I'ld have been locked into the Richmond Asylum, or maybe have run up into the back hills with nothing on me but an old shirt, and been eaten with crows the like of Patch Darcy —the Lord have mercy on him—in the year that's gone.

NORA (*with interest*). You knew Darcy?

TRAMP. Wasn't I the last one heard his living voice in the whole world?

NORA. There were great stories of what was heard at that time, but would any one believe the things they do be saying in the glen?

TRAMP. It was no lie, lady of the house. . . . I was passing below on a dark night the like of this night, and the sheep were lying under the ditch and every one of them coughing, and choking, like an old man, with the great rain and the fog. Then I heard a thing talking— queer talk, you wouldn't believe it at all, and you out of your dreams,—and "Merciful God," says I, "if I begin hearing the like of that voice out of the thick mist, I'm destroyed surely." Then I run, and I run, and I run, till I was below in Rathvanna. I got drunk that night, I got drunk in the morning, and drunk the day after,—I was coming from the races beyond— and the third day they found Darcy. . . . Then I knew it was himself I was after hearing, and I wasn't afeard any more.

NORA (*speaking sorrowfully and slowly*). God spare Darcy, he'ld always look in here and he passing up or passing down, and it's very lonesome I was after him a long while (*she looks over at the bed and lowers her voice, speaking very clearly*), and then I got happy again—if it's ever happy we are, stranger,—for I got used to being lonesome.

[*A short pause; then she stands up.*]

NORA. Was there any one on the last bit of the road, stranger, and you coming from Aughrim?

TRAMP. There was a young man with a drift of mountain ewes, and he running after them this way and that.

NORA (*with a half-smile*). Far down, stranger?

TRAMP. A piece only.

[*She fills the kettle and puts it on the fire.*]

NORA. Maybe, if you're not easy afeard, you'ld stay here a short while alone with himself.

TRAMP. I would surely. A man that's dead can do no hurt.

NORA (*speaking with a sort of constraint*). I'm going a little back to the west, stranger, for himself would go there one night and another and whistle at that place, and then the young man you're after seeing—a kind of a farmer has come up from the sea to live in a cottage beyond—would walk round to see if there was a thing we'ld have to be done, and I'm wanting him this night, the way he can go down into the glen when the sun goes up and tell the people that himself is dead.

TRAMP (*looking at the body in the sheet*). It's myself will go for him, lady of the house, and let you not be destroying yourself with the great rain.

NORA. You wouldn't find your way, stranger, for there's a small path only, and it running up between two sluigs where an ass and cart would be drowned. (*She puts a shawl over her head.*) Let you be making yourself easy, and saying a prayer for his soul, and it's not long I'll be coming again.

TRAMP (*moving uneasily*). Maybe if you'd a piece of a grey thread and a sharp needle— there's great safety in a needle, lady of the house—I'ld be putting a little stitch here and there in my old coat, the time I'll be praying for his soul, and it going up naked to the saints of God.

NORA (*takes a needle and thread from the front of her dress and gives it to him*). There's the needle, stranger, and I'm thinking you won't be lonesome, and you used to the black hills, for isn't a dead man itself more company than to be sitting alone, and hearing the winds crying, and you not knowing on what thing your mind would stay?

TRAMP (*slowly*). It's true, surely, and the Lord have mercy on us all!

[*Nora goes out. The Tramp begins stitching one of the tags in his coat, saying the "De Profundis" under his breath. In an instant the sheet is drawn slowly down, and Dan Burke looks out. The Tramp moves uneasily, then looks up, and springs to his feet with a movement of terror.*]

DAN (*with a hoarse voice*). Don't be afeard, stranger; a man that's dead can do no hurt.

TRAMP (*trembling*). I meant no harm, your honour; and won't you leave me easy to be saying a little prayer for your soul?

[*A long whistle is heard outside.*]

DAN (*sitting up in his bed and speaking fiercely*). Ah, the devil mend her. . . . Do you hear that, stranger? Did ever you hear another woman could whistle the like of that with two fingers in her mouth? (*He looks at the table hurriedly.*) I'm destroyed with the drouth, and let you bring me a drop quickly before herself will come back.

TRAMP (*doubtfully*). Is it not dead you are?

DAN. How would I be dead, and I as dry as a baked bone, stranger?

TRAMP (*pouring out the whisky*). What will herself say if she smells the stuff on you, for I'm thinking it's not for nothing you're letting on to be dead?

DAN. It is not, stranger, but she won't be coming near me at all, and it's not long now I'll be letting on, for I've a cramp in my back, and my hip's asleep on me, and there's been the devil's own fly itching my nose. It's near dead I was wanting to sneeze, and you blathering about the rain, and Darcy (*bitterly*)—the devil choke him—and the towering church. (*Crying out impatiently.*) Give me that whisky. Would you have herself come back before I taste a drop at all?

[*Tramp gives him the glass.*]

Dan (*after drinking*). Go over now to that cupboard, and bring me a black stick you'll see in the west corner by the wall.

Tramp (*taking a stick from the cupboard*). Is it that?

Dan. It is, stranger; it's a long time I'm keeping that stick for I've a bad wife in the house.

Tramp (*with a queer look*). Is it herself, master of the house, and she a grand woman to talk?

Dan. It's herself, surely, it's a bad wife she is —a bad wife for an old man, and I'm getting old, God help me, though I've an arm to me still. (*He takes the stick in his hand.*) Let you wait now a short while, and it's a great sight you'll see in this room in two hours or three. (*He stops to listen.*) Is that somebody above?

Tramp (*listening*). There's a voice speaking on the path.

Dan. Put that stick here in the bed and smooth the sheet the way it was lying. (*He covers himself up hastily.*) Be falling to sleep now and don't let on you know anything, or I'll be having your life. I wouldn't have told you at all but it's destroyed with the drouth I was.

Tramp (*covering his head*). Have no fear, master of the house. What is it I know of the like of you that I'd be saying a word or putting out my hand to stay you at all?

[*He goes back to the fire, sits down on a stool with his back to the bed and goes on stitching his coat.*]

Dan (*under the sheet, querulously*). Stranger!

Tramp (*quickly*). Whisht, whisht. Be quiet I'm telling you, they're coming now at the door.

[*Nora comes in with Michael Dara, a tall, innocent young man behind her.*]

Nora. I wasn't long at all, stranger, for I met himself on the path.

Tramp. You were middling long, lady of the house.

Nora. There was no sign from himself?

Tramp. No sign at all, lady of the house.

Nora (*to Michael*). Go over now and pull down the sheet, and look on himself, Michael Dara, and you'll see it's the truth I'm telling you.

Michael. I will not, Nora, I do be afeard of the dead.

[*He sits down on a stool next the table facing the Tramp. Nora puts the kettle on a lower hook of the pothooks, and piles turf under it.*]

Nora (*turning to Tramp*). Will you drink a sup of tea with myself and the young man, stranger, or (*speaking more persuasively*) will you go into the little room and stretch yourself a short while on the bed, I'm thinking it's destroyed you are walking the length of that way in the great rain.

Tramp. Is it to go away and leave you, and you having a wake, lady of the house? I will not surely. (*He takes a drink from his glass which he has beside him.*) And it's none of your tea I'm asking either.

[*He goes on stitching. Nora makes the tea.*]

Michael (*after looking at the Tramp rather scornfully for a moment*). That's a poor coat you have, God help you, and I'm thinking it's a poor tailor you are with it.

Tramp. If it's a poor tailor I am, I'm thinking it's a poor herd does be running back and forward after a little handful of ewes the way I seen yourself running this day, young fellow, and you coming from the fair.

[*Nora comes back to the table.*]

Nora (*to Michael in a low voice*). Let you not mind him at all, Michael Dara, he has a drop taken and it's soon he'll be falling asleep.

Michael. It's no lie he's telling, I was destroyed surely. They were that wilful they were running off into one man's bit of oats, and another man's bit of hay, and tumbling into the red bogs till it's more like a pack of old goats than sheep they were. Mountain ewes is a queer breed, Nora Burke, and I'm not used to them at all.

Nora (*settling the tea things*). There's no one can drive a mountain ewe but the men do be reared in the Glen Malure, I've heard them say, and above by Rathvanna, and the Glen Imaal, men the like of Patch Darcy, God spare his soul, who would walk through five hundred sheep and miss one of them, and he not reckoning them at all.

Michael (*uneasily*). Is it the man went queer in his head the year that's gone?

Nora. It is surely.

Tramp (*plaintively*). That was a great man, young fellow, a great man I'm telling you. There was never a lamb from his own ewes he wouldn't know before it was marked, and he'd run from this to the city of Dublin and never catch for his breath.

NORA (*turning round quickly*). He was a great man surely, stranger, and isn't it a grand thing when you hear a living man saying a good word of a dead man, and he mad dying?

TRAMP. It's the truth I'm saying, God spare his soul.

[*He puts the needle under the collar of his coat, and settles himself to sleep in the chimney-corner. Nora sits down at the table; their backs are turned to the bed.*]

MICHAEL (*looking at her with a queer look*). I heard tell this day, Nora Burke, that it was on the path below Patch Darcy would be passing up and passing down, and I heard them say he'd never pass it night or morning without speaking with yourself.

NORA (*in a low voice*). It was no lie you heard, Michael Dara.

MICHAEL. I'm thinking it's a power of men you're after knowing if it's in a lonesome place you live itself.

NORA (*giving him his tea*). It's in a lonesome place you do have to be talking with some one, and looking for some one, in the evening of the day, and if it's a power of men I'm after knowing they were fine men, for I was a hard child to please, and a hard girl to please (*she looks at him a little sternly*), and it's a hard woman I am to please this day, Michael Dara, and it's no lie I'm telling you.

MICHAEL (*looking over to see that the Tramp is asleep, and then pointing to the dead man*). Was it a hard woman to please you were when you took himself for your man?

NORA. What way would I live and I an old woman if I didn't marry a man with a bit of a farm, and cows on it, and sheep on the back hills?

MICHAEL (*considering*). That's true, Nora, and maybe it's no fool you were, for there's good grazing on it, if it is a lonesome place, and I'm thinking it's a good sum he's left behind.

NORA (*taking the stocking with money from her pocket, and putting it on the table*). I do be thinking in the long nights it was a big fool I was that time, Michael Dara, for what good is a bit of a farm with cows on it, and sheep on the back hills, when you do be sitting looking out from a door the like of that door, and seeing nothing but the mists rolling down the bog, and the mists again, and they rolling up the bog, and hearing nothing but the wind crying out in the bits of broken trees were left from the great storm, and the streams roaring with the rain.

MICHAEL (*looking at her uneasily*). What is it ails you, this night, Nora Burke? I've heard tell it's the like of that talk you do hear from men, and they after being a great while on the back hills.

NORA (*putting out the money on the table*). It's a bad night, and a wild night, Michael Dara, and isn't it a great while I am at the foot of the back hills, sitting up here boiling food for himself, and food for the brood sow, and baking a cake when the night falls? (*She puts up the money, listlessly, in little piles on the table.*) Isn't it a long while I am sitting here in the winter and the summer, and the fine spring, with the young growing behind me and the old passing, saying to myself one time, to look on Mary Brien who wasn't that height (*holding out her hand*), and I a fine girl growing up, and there she is now with two children, and another coming on her in three months or four.

[*She pauses.*]

MICHAEL (*moving over three of the piles*). That's three pounds we have now, Nora Burke.

NORA (*continuing in the same voice*). And saying to myself another time, to look on Peggy Cavanagh, who had the lightest hand at milking a cow that wouldn't be easy, or turning a cake, and there she is now walking round on the roads, or sitting in a dirty old house, with no teeth in her mouth, and no sense and no more hair than you'd see on a bit of a hill and they after burning the furze from it.

MICHAEL. That's five pounds and ten notes, a good sum, surely! . . . It's not that way you'll be talking when you marry a young man, Nora Burke, and they were saying in the fair my lambs were the best lambs, and I got a grand price, for I'm no fool now at making a bargain when my lambs are good.

NORA. What was it you got?

MICHAEL. Twenty pound for the lot, Nora Burke. . . . We'd do right to wait now till himself will be quiet awhile in the Seven Churches, and then you'll marry me in the chapel of Rathvanna, and I'll bring the sheep up on the bit of a hill you have on the back mountain, and we won't have anything we'ld be afeard to let our minds on when the mist is down.

NORA (*pouring him out some whisky*). Why would I marry you, Mike Dara? You'll be getting old and I'll be getting old, and in a little while I'm telling you, you'll be sitting up in your bed—the way himself was sitting—with a shake in your face, and your teeth falling, and the white hair sticking out round you like an old bush where sheep do be leaping a gap.

[*Dan Burke sits up noiselessly from under the sheet, with his hand to his face. His white hair is sticking out round his head.*]

NORA (*goes on slowly without hearing him*). It's a pitiful thing to be getting old, but it's a queer thing surely. It's a queer thing to see an old man sitting up there in his bed with no teeth in him, and a rough word in his mouth, and his chin the way it would take the bark from the edge of an oak board you'ld have building a door. . . . God forgive me, Michael Dara, we'll all be getting old, but it's a queer thing surely.

MICHAEL. It's too lonesome you are from living a long time with an old man, Nora, and you're talking again like a herd that would be coming down from the thick mist (*he puts his arm round her*), but it's a fine life you'll have now with a young man, a fine life surely. . . .

[*Dan sneezes violently. Michael tries to get to the door, but before he can do so, Dan jumps out of the bed in queer white clothes, with his stick in his hand, and goes over and puts his back against it.*]

MICHAEL. Son of God deliver us.

[*Crosses himself, and goes backward across the room.*]

DAN (*holding up his hand at him*). Now you'll not marry her the time I'm rotting below in the Seven Churches, and you'll see the thing I'll give you will follow you on the back mountains when the wind is high.

MICHAEL (*to Nora*). Get me out of it, Nora, for the love of God. He always did what you bid him, and I'm thinking he would do it now.

NORA (*looking at the Tramp*). Is it dead he is or living?

DAN (*turning towards her*). It's little you care if it's dead or living I am, but there'll be an end now of your fine times, and all the talk you have of young men and old men, and of the mist coming up or going down. (*He opens the door.*) You'll walk out now from that door, Nora Burke, and it's not tomorrow, or the next day, or any day of your life, that you'll put in your foot through it again.

TRAMP (*standing up*). It's a hard thing you're saying for an old man, master of the house, and what would the like of her do if you put her out on the roads?

DAN. Let her walk round the like of Peggy Cavanagh below, and be begging money at the cross-road, or selling songs to the men. (*To Nora.*) Walk out now, Nora Burke, and it's soon you'll be getting old with that life, I'm telling you; it's soon your teeth'll be falling and

your head'll be the like of a bush where sheep do be leaping a gap.

[*He pauses: she looks round at Michael.*]

MICHAEL (*timidly*). There's a fine Union below in Rathdrum.

DAN. The like of her would never go there. . . . It's lonesome roads she'll be going and hiding herself away till the end will come, and they find her stretched like a dead sheep with the frost on her, or the big spiders, maybe, and they putting their webs on her, in the butt of a ditch.

NORA (*angrily*). What way will yourself be that day, Daniel Burke? What way will you be that day and you lying down a long while in your grave? For it's bad you are living, and it's bad you'll be when you're dead. (*She looks at him a moment fiercely, then half turns away and speaks plaintively again.*) Yet, if it is itself, Daniel Burke, who can help it at all, and let you be getting up into your bed, and not be taking your death with the wind blowing on you, and the rain with it, and you half in your skin.

DAN. It's proud and happy you'ld be if I was getting my death the day I was shut of yourself. (*Pointing to the door.*) Let you walk out through that door, I'm telling you, and let you not be passing this way if it's hungry you are, or wanting a bed.

TRAMP (*pointing to Michael*). Maybe himself would take her.

NORA. What would he do with me now?

TRAMP. Give you the half of a dry bed, and good food in your mouth.

DAN. Is it a fool you think him, stranger, or is it a fool you were born yourself? Let her walk out of that door, and let you go along with her, stranger—if it's raining itself—for it's too much talk you have surely.

TRAMP (*going over to Nora*). We'll be going now, lady of the house—the rain is falling, but the air is kind and maybe it'll be a grand morning by the grace of God.

NORA. What good is a grand morning when I'm destroyed surely, and I going out to get my death walking the roads?

TRAMP. You'll not be getting your death with myself, lady of the house, and I knowing all the ways a man can put food in his mouth. . . . We'll be going now, I'm telling you, and the time you'll be feeling the cold, and the frost, and the great rain, and the sun again, and the south wind blowing in the glens, you'll not be sitting up on a wet ditch, the way you're after sitting in the place, making yourself old with looking on each day, and it passing you by. You'll be saying one time, "It's a grand evening, by the grace of God," and another time, "It's a wild night, God help us, but it'll pass surely." You'll be saying—

DAN (*goes over to them crying out impatiently*). Go out of that door, I'm telling you, and do your blathering below in the glen.

[*Nora gathers a few things into her shawl.*]

TRAMP (*at the door*). Come along with me now, lady of the house, and it's not my blather you'll be hearing only, but you'll be hearing the herons crying out over the black lakes, and you'll be hearing the grouse and the owls with them, and the larks and the big thrushes when the days are warm, and it's not from the like of them you'll be hearing a talk of getting old like Peggy Cavanagh, and losing the hair off you, and the light of your eyes, but it's fine songs you'll be hearing when the sun goes up, and there'll be no old fellow wheezing, the like of a sick sheep, close to your ear.

NORA. I'm thinking it's myself will be wheezing that time with lying down under the Heavens when the night is cold; but you've a fine bit of talk, stranger, and it's with yourself I'll go. (*She goes towards the door, then turns to Dan.*) You think it's a grand thing you're after doing with your letting on to be dead, but what

is it at all? What way would a woman live in a lonesome place the like of this place, and she not making a talk with the men passing? And what way will yourself live from this day, with none to care for you? What is it you'll have now but a black life, Daniel Burke, and it's not long I'm telling you, till you'll be lying again under that sheet, and you dead surely.

[*She goes out with the Tramp. Michael is slinking after them, but Dan stops him.*]

DAN. Sit down now and take a little taste of the stuff, Michael Dara. There's a great drouth on me, and the night is young.

MICHAEL (*coming back to the table*). And it's very dry I am, surely, with the fear of death you put on me, and I after driving mountain ewes since the turn of the day.

DAN (*throwing away his stick*). I was thinking to strike you, Michael Dara, but you're a quiet man, God help you, and I don't mind you at all.

[*He pours out two glasses of whisky, and gives one to Michael.*]

DAN. Your good health, Michael Dara.

MICHAEL. God reward you, Daniel Burke, and may you have a long life, and a quiet life, and good health with it.

[*They drink.*]

CURTAIN

# E. M. Forster

## 1879-

Edward Morgan Forster was born in London 1 January, 1879, of Welsh parentage. He attended Tonbridge as a day boy, and completed his education at King's College, Cambridge, where the scholar G. Lowes Dickinson was one of his preceptors.

Forster spent many important years of his life abroad, years extremely fruitful in supplying materials for his writing. He has lived in Italy, India, and Egypt, as well as in England.

Where Angels Fear to Tread (1905), The Longest Journey (1907), and A Room With a View (1908) lead up to the more successful novel Howards End (1910), a study of the contemporary propertied class in England. Forster's fifth novel, A Passage to India (1927), is in some ways unlike anything else in modern fiction. Both style and content can best be compared to those of Henry James' novels. The theme is the cultural distance between the ruling class in India and the native Indians; the sincere and sensitive persons who try to reach across this cultural distance find the barriers impossible to penetrate except in brief moments of insight. The complexity of the forces acting on the characters and the even greater complexity of their own attitudes toward these forces and toward each other combine to achieve an unusual sense of reality; Forster seems at all times to avoid oversimplification at any cost. Yet as Forster telescopes the sense of time to achieve his purpose, the reality of the novel sometimes becomes almost a dream-reality, and the impact approaches that of surrealism.

Forster has written at least three short stories which belong in any list of the finest stories in the language: "The Celestial Omnibus," "The Road from Colonus," and "The Machine Stops" all appear in The Collected Tales of E. M. Forster (1947). His historical writings include Alexandria: A History and a Guide (1922), and Pharos and Pharillon (1923). The Hill of Devi (1953) discusses the political background of India. He has written three biographies, Goldsworthy Lowes Dickinson (1934); an excellent brief study of Virginia Woolf (1942); and Marianne Thornton (1956). Abinger Harvest (1936) and Two Cheers for Democracy (1950) contain a wide range of brief studies, reviews, and sketches; the latter reprints "What I Believe," Forster's philosophic credo. It is impossible to speak too highly of the creative theoretical study Aspects of the Novel (1927), probably the best extended statement by a novelist about his approach to the making of literature. Forster's versatility is shown, finally, by his film script Diary for Timothy and his libretto (with Eric Crozier) for Benjamin Britten's opera, Billy Budd (1952). Three critical studies are available, The Writings of E. M. Forster, by Rose Macaulay (London, 1938); E. M. Forster, by Lionel Trilling (Norfolk, Connecticut, 1943); and The Novels of E. M. Forster, by James McConkey (Ithaca, New York, 1957).

## The Machine Stops [1]

### From The Collected Tales of E. M. Forster

#### I. THE AIR-SHIP

Imagine, if you can, a small room, hexagonal in shape, like the cell of a bee. It is lighted neither by window nor by lamp, yet it is filled with a soft radiance. There are no apertures for ventilation, yet the air is fresh. There are no musical instruments, and yet, at the moment that my meditation opens, this room is throbbing with melodious sounds. An armchair is in the centre, by its side a reading-desk—that is all

[1] Published 1928. In a note to the reader of The Eternal Moment and Other Stories, in which "The Machine Stops" first appeared, Forster explains that "these stories were written at various dates previous to 1914." Copyright, 1928, by Harcourt, Brace and Company, Inc.; renewed, 1955, by E. M. Forster. Reprinted by permission of the publishers.

the furniture. And in the arm-chair there sits a swaddled lump of flesh—a woman, about five feet high, with a face as white as a fungus. It is to her that the little room belongs.

An electric bell rang.

The woman touched a switch and the music was silent.

"I suppose I must see who it is," she thought, and set her chair in motion. The chair, like the music, was worked by machinery, and it rolled her to the other side of the room, where the bell still rang importunately.

"Who is it?" she called. Her voice was irritable, for she had been interrupted often since the music began. She knew several thousand people; in certain directions human intercourse had advanced enormously.

But when she listened into the receiver, her white face wrinkled into smiles, and she said:

"Very well. Let us talk, I will isolate myself. I do not expect anything important will happen for the next five minutes—for I can give you fully five minutes, Kuno. Then I must deliver my lecture on 'Music during the Australian Period.'"

She touched the isolation knob, so that no one else could speak to her. Then she touched the lighting apparatus, and the little room was plunged into darkness.

"Be quick!" she called, her irritation returning. "Be quick, Kuno; here I am in the dark wasting my time."

But it was fully fifteen seconds before the round plate that she held in her hands began to glow. A faint blue light shot across it, darkening to purple, and presently she could see the image of her son, who lived on the other side of the earth, and he could see her.

"Kuno, how slow you are."

He smiled gravely.

"I really believe you enjoy dawdling."

"I have called you before, mother, but you were always busy or isolated. I have something particular to say."

"What is it, dearest boy? Be quick. Why could you not send it by pneumatic post?"

"Because I prefer saying such a thing. I want—"

"Well?"

"I want you to come and see me."

Vashti watched his face in the blue plate.

"But I can see you!" she exclaimed. "What more do you want?"

"I want to see you not through the Machine," said Kuno. "I want to speak to you not through the wearisome Machine."

"Oh, hush!" said his mother, vaguely shocked. "You mustn't say anything against the Machine."

"Why not?"

"One mustn't."

"You talk as if a god had made the Machine," cried the other. "I believe that you pray to it when you are unhappy. Men made it, do not forget that. Great men, but men. The Machine is much, but it is not everything. I see something like you in this plate, but I do not see you. I hear something like you through this telephone, but I do not hear you. That is why I want you to come. Come and stop with me. Pay me a visit, so that we can meet face to face, and talk about the hopes that are in my mind."

She replied that she could scarcely spare the time for a visit.

"The air-ship barely takes two days to fly between me and you."

"I dislike air-ships."

"Why?"

"I dislike seeing the horrible brown earth, and the sea, and the stars when it is dark. I get no ideas in an air-ship."

"I do not get them anywhere else."

"What kind of ideas can the air give you?"

He paused for an instant.

"Do you know four big stars that form an oblong, and three stars close together in the middle of the oblong, and hanging from these stars, three other stars?"

"No, I do not. I dislike the stars. But did they give you an idea? How interesting; tell me."

"I had an idea that they were like a man."

"I do not understand."

"The four big stars are the man's shoulders and his knees. The three stars in the middle are like the belts that men wore once, and the three stars hanging are like a sword."

"A sword?"

"Men carried swords about with them, to kill animals and other men."

"It does not strike me as a very good idea, but it is certainly original. When did it come to you first?"

"In the air-ship—" He broke off and she fancied that he looked sad. She could not be sure, for the Machine did not transmit *nuances* of expression. It only gave a general idea of people—an idea that was good enough for all practical purposes, Vashti thought. The imponderable bloom, declared by a discredited philosophy to be the actual essence of intercourse, was rightly ignored by the Machine, just as the imponderable bloom of the grape was ignored by the manufacturers of artificial fruit. Something "good enough" had long since been accepted by our race.

"The truth is," he continued, "that I want to see these stars again. They are curious stars. I want to see them not from the air-ship, but from the surface of the earth, as our ancestors did, thousands of years ago. I want to visit the surface of the earth."

She was shocked again.

"Mother, you must come, if only to explain to me what is the harm of visiting the surface of the earth."

"No harm," she replied, controlling herself. "But no advantage. The surface of the earth is only dust and mud, no life remains on it, and you would need a respirator, or the cold of the outer air would kill you. One dies immediately in the outer air."

"I know; of course I shall take all precautions."

"And besides—"

"Well?"

She considered, and chose her words with care. Her son had a queer temper, and she wished to dissuade him from the expedition.

"It is contrary to the spirit of the age," she asserted.

"Do you mean by that, contrary to the Machine?"

"In a sense, but—"

His image in the blue plate faded.

"Kuno!"

He had isolated himself.

For a moment Vashti felt lonely.

The she generated the light, and the sight of her room, flooded with radiance and studded with electric buttons, revived her. There were buttons and switches everywhere—buttons to call for food, for music, for clothing. There was the hot-bath button, by pressure of which a basin of (imitation) marble rose out of the floor, filled to the brim with a warm deodorized liquid. There was the cold-bath button. There was the button that produced literature. And there were of course the buttons by which she communicated with her friends. The room, though it contained nothing, was in touch with all that she cared for in the world.

Vashti's next move was to turn off the isolation-switch, and all the accumulations of the last three minutes burst upon her. The room was filled with the noise of bells, and speaking-tubes. What was the new food like? Could she recommend it? Had she had any ideas lately? Might one tell her one's own ideas? Would she make an engagement to visit the public

nurseries at an early date?—say this day month.

To most of these questions she replied with irritation—a growing quality in that accelerated age. She said that the new food was horrible. That she could not visit the public nurseries through press of engagements. That she had no ideas of her own but had just been told one —that four stars and three in the middle were like a man: she doubted there was much in it. Then she switched off her correspondents, for it was time to deliver her lecture on Australian music.

The clumsy system of public gatherings had been long since abandoned; neither Vashti nor her audience stirred from their rooms. Seated in her arm-chair she spoke, while they in their arm-chairs heard her, fairly well, and saw her, fairly well. She opened with a humorous account of music in the pre-Mongolian epoch, and went on to describe the great outburst of song that followed the Chinese conquest. Remote and primeval as were the methods of I-San-So and the Brisbane school, she yet felt (she said) that study of them might repay the musician of today: they had freshness; they had, above all, ideas.

Her lecture, which lasted ten minutes, was well received, and at its conclusion she and many of her audience listened to a lecture on the sea; there were ideas to be got from the sea; the speaker had donned a respirator and visited it lately. Then she fed, talked to many friends, had a bath, talked again, and summoned her bed.

The bed was not to her liking. It was too large, and she had a feeling for a small bed. Complaint was useless, for beds were of the same dimension all over the world, and to have had an alternative size would have involved vast alterations in the Machine. Vashti isolated herself—it was necessary, for neither day nor night existed under the ground—and reviewed all that had happened since she had summoned the bed last. Ideas? Scarcely any. Events—was Kuno's invitation an event?

By her side, on the little reading-desk, was a survival from the ages of litter—one book. This was the Book of the Machine. In it were instructions against every possible contingency. If she was hot or cold or dyspeptic or at loss for a word, she went to the book, and it told her which button to press. The Central Committee published it. In accordance with a growing habit, it was richly bound.

Sitting up in the bed, she took it reverently in her hands. She glanced round the glowing room as if some one might be watching her.

Then, half ashamed, half joyful, she murmured "O Machine! O Machine!" and raised the volume to her lips. Thrice she kissed it, thrice inclined her head, thrice she felt the delirium of acquiescence. Her ritual performed, she turned to page 1367, which gave the times of the departure of the air-ships from the island in the southern hemisphere, under whose soil she lived, to the island in the northern hemisphere, whereunder lived her son.

She thought, "I have not the time."

She made the room dark and slept; she awoke and made the room light; she ate and exchanged ideas with her friends, and listened to music and attended lectures; she made the room dark and slept. Above her, beneath her, and around her, the Machine hummed eternally; she did not notice the noise, for she had been born with it in her ears. The earth, carrying her, hummed as it sped through silence, turning her now to the invisible sun, now to the invisible stars. She awoke and made the room light.

"Kuno!"

"I will not talk to you," he answered, "until you come."

"Have you been on the surface of the earth since we spoke last?"

His image faded.

Again she consulted the book. She became very nervous and lay back in her chair palpitating. Think of her as without teeth or hair. Presently she directed the chair to the wall, and pressed an unfamiliar button. The wall swung apart slowly. Through the opening she saw a tunnel that curved slightly, so that its goal was not visible. Should she go to see her son, here was the beginning of the journey.

Of course she knew all about the communication-system. There was nothing mysterious in it. She would summon a car and it would fly with her down the tunnel until it reached the lift that communicated with the air-ship station: the system had been in use for many, many years, long before the universal establishment of the Machine. And of course she had studied the civilization that had immediately preceded her own—the civilization that had mistaken the functions of the system, and had used it for bringing people to things, instead of for bringing things to people. Those funny old days, when men went for change of air instead of changing the air in their rooms! And yet—she was frightened of the tunnel: she had not seen it since her last child was born. It curved—but not quite as she remembered; it was brilliant—but not quite as brilliant as a lecturer had suggested. Vashti was seized with the terrors of direct experience. She shrank back into the room, and the wall closed up again.

"Kuno," she said, "I cannot come to see you. I am not well."

Immediately an enormous apparatus fell on to her out of the ceiling, a thermometer was automatically inserted between her lips, a stethoscope was automatically laid upon her heart. She lay powerless. Cool pads soothed her forehead. Kuno had telegraphed to her doctor.

So the human passions still blundered up and down in the Machine. Vashti drank the medicine that the doctor projected into her mouth, and the machinery retired into the ceiling. The voice of Kuno was heard asking how she felt.

"Better." Then with irritation: "But why do you not come to me instead?"

"Because I cannot leave this place."

"Why?"

"Because, any moment, something tremendous may happen."

"Have you been on the surface of the earth yet?"

"Not yet."

"Then what is it?"

"I will not tell you through the Machine."

She resumed her life.

But she thought of Kuno as a baby, his birth, his removal to the public nurseries, her one visit to him there, his visits to her—visits which stopped when the Machine had assigned him a room on the other side of the earth. "Parents, duties of," said the book of the Machine, "cease at the moment of birth. P. 422327483." True, but there was something special about Kuno—indeed there had been something special about all her children—and, after all, she must brave the journey if he desired it. And "something tremendous might happen." What did that mean? The nonsense of a youthful man, no doubt, but she must go. Again she pressed the unfamiliar button, again the wall swung back, and she saw the tunnel that curved out of sight. Clasping the Book, she rose, tottered on to the platform, and summoned the car. Her room closed behind her: the journey to the northern hemisphere had begun.

Of course it was perfectly easy. The car approached and in it she found arm-chairs exactly like her own. When she signalled, it stopped, and she tottered into the lift. One other passenger was in the lift, the first fellow creature she had seen face to face for months. Few travelled in these days, for, thanks to the advance of science, the earth was exactly alike all over. Rapid intercourse, from which the previous civilization had hoped so much, had ended by defeating itself. What was the good of going to Pekin when it was just like Shrewsbury? Why return to Shrewsbury when it would be just like Pekin? Men seldom moved their bodies; all unrest was concentrated in the soul.

The air-ship service was a relic from the former age. It was kept up, because it was 10 easier to keep it up than to stop it or to diminish it, but it now far exceeded the wants of the population. Vessel after vessel would rise from the vomitories of Rye or of Christchurch (I use the antique names), would sail into the crowded sky, and would draw up at the wharves of the south—empty. So nicely adjusted was the system, so independent of meteorology, that the sky, whether calm or cloudy, resembled a vast kaleidoscope whereon 20 the same patterns periodically recurred. The ship on which Vashti sailed started now at sunset, now at dawn. But always, as it passed above Rheims, it would neighbour the ship that served between Helsingfors and the Brazils, and, every third time it surmounted the Alps, the fleet of Palermo would cross its track behind. Night and day, wind and storm, tide and earthquake, impeded man no longer. He had harnessed Leviathan. All the old literature, with 30 its praise of Nature, and its fear of Nature, rang false as the prattle of a child.

Yet as Vashti saw the vast flank of the ship, stained with exposure to the outer air, her horror of direct experience returned. It was not quite like the air-ship in the cinematophote. For one thing it smelt—not strongly or unpleasantly, but it did smell, and with her eyes shut she should have known that a new thing was close to her. Then she had to walk 40 to it from the lift, had to submit to glances from the other passengers. The man in front dropped his Book—no great matter, but it disquieted them all. In the rooms, if the Book was dropped, the floor raised it mechanically, but the gangway to the air-ship was not so prepared, and the sacred volume lay motionless. They stopped—the thing was unforeseen—and the man, instead of picking up his property, felt the muscles of his arm to see how they had 50 failed him. Then some one actually said with direct utterance: "We shall be late"—and they trooped on board, Vashti treading on the pages as she did so.

Inside, her anxiety increased. The arrangements were old-fashioned and rough. There was even a female attendant, to whom she would have to announce her wants during the voyage. Of course a revolving platform ran the length of the boat, but she was expected to walk from it to her cabin. Some cabins were better than others, and she did not get the best. She thought the attendant had been unfair, and spasms of rage shook her. The glass valves had closed, she could not go back. She saw, at the end of the vestibule, the lift in which she had ascended going quietly up and down, empty. Beneath those corridors of shining tiles were rooms, tier below tier, reaching far into the earth, and in each room there sat a human being, eating, or sleeping, or producing ideas. And buried deep in the hive was her own room. Vashti was afraid.

"O Machine! O Machine!" she murmured, and caressed her Book, and was comforted.

Then the sides of the vestibule seemed to melt together, as do the passages that we see in dreams, the lift vanished, the Book that had been dropped slid to the left and vanished, polished tiles rushed by like a stream of water, there was a slight jar, and the air-ship, issuing from its tunnel, soared above the waters of a tropical ocean.

It was night. For a moment she saw the coast of Sumatra edged by the phosphorescence of waves, and crowned by lighthouses, still sending forth their disregarded beams. These also vanished, and only the stars distracted her. They were not motionless, but swayed to and fro above her head, thronging out of one skylight into another, as if the universe and not the airship was careening. And, as often happens, on clear nights, they seemed now to be in perspective, now on a plane; now piled tier beyond tier into the infinite heavens, now concealing infinity, a roof limiting for ever the visions of men. In either case they seemed intolerable. "Are we to travel in the dark?" called the passengers angrily, and the attendant, who had been careless, generated the light, and pulled down the blinds of pliable metal. When the airships had been built, the desire to look direct at things still lingered in the world. Hence the extraordinary number of skylights and windows, and the proportionate discomfort to those who were civilized and refined. Even in Vashti's cabin one star peeped through a flaw in the blind, and after a few hours' uneasy slumber, she was disturbed by an unfamiliar glow, which was the dawn.

Quick as the ship had sped westwards, the earth had rolled eastwards quicker still, and had dragged back Vashti and her companions towards the sun. Science could prolong the night, but only for a little, and those high hopes of neutralizing the earth's diurnal revolution had passed, together with hopes that were possibly higher. "To keep pace with the sun," or even to outstrip it, had been the aim of the civilization preceding this. Racing aeroplanes had been built for the purpose, capable of enormous speed, and steered by the greatest intellects of the epoch. Round the globe they went, round and round, westward, westward, round and round, amidst humanity's applause. In vain. The globe went eastward quicker still, horrible accidents occurred, and the Committee of the Machine, at the time rising into prominence, declared the pursuit illegal, unmechanical, and punishable by Homelessness.

Of Homelessness more will be said later.

Doubtless the Committee was right. Yet the attempt to "defeat the sun" aroused the last common interest that our race experienced about the heavenly bodies, or indeed about anything. It was the last time that men were compacted by thinking of a power outside the world. The sun had conquered, yet it was the end of his spiritual dominion. Dawn, midday, twilight, the zodiacal path, touched neither men's lives nor their hearts, and science retreated into the ground, to concentrate herself upon problems that she was certain of solving.

So when Vashti found her cabin invaded by a rosy finger of light, she was annoyed, and tried to adjust the blind. But the blind flew up altogether, and she saw through the skylight small pink clouds, swaying against a background of blue, and as the sun crept higher, its radiance entered direct, brimming down the wall, like a golden sea. It rose and fell with the air-ship's motion, just as waves rise and fall, but it advanced steadily, as a tide advances. Unless she was careful, it would strike her face. A spasm of horror shook her and she rang for the attendant. The attendant too was horrified, but she could do nothing; it was not her place to mend the blind. She could only suggest that the lady should change her cabin, which she accordingly prepared to do.

People were almost exactly alike all over the world, but the attendant of the air-ship, perhaps owing to her exceptional duties, had grown a little out of the common. She had often to address passengers with direct speech, and this had given her a certain roughness and originality of manner. When Vashti swerved away from the sunbeams with a cry, she behaved barbarically—she put out her hand to steady her.

"How dare you!" exclaimed the passenger. "You forget yourself!"

The woman was confused, and apologized for not having let her fall. People never touched one another. The custom had become obsolete, owing to the Machine.

"Where are we now?" asked Vashti haughtily.

"We are over Asia," said the attendant, anxious to be polite.

"Asia?"

"You must excuse my common way of speaking. I have got into the habit of calling places over which I pass by their unmechanical names."

"Oh, I remember Asia. The Mongols came from it."

"Beneath us, in the open air, stood a city that was once called Simla."

"Have you ever heard of the Mongols and of the Brisbane school?"

"No."

"Brisbane also stood in the open air."

"Those mountains to the right—let me show you them." She pushed back a metal blind. The main chain of the Himalayas was revealed. "They were once called the Roof of the World, those mountains."

"What a foolish name!"

"You must remember that, before the dawn of civilization, they seemed to be an impenetrable wall that touched the stars. It was supposed that no one but the gods could exist above their summits. How we have advanced, thanks to the Machine!"

"How we have advanced, thanks to the Machine!" said Vashti.

"How we have advanced, thanks to the Machine!" echoed the passenger who had dropped his Book the night before, and who was standing in the passage.

"And that white stuff in the cracks?—what is it?"

"I have forgotten its name."

"Cover the window, please. These mountains give me no ideas."

The northern aspect of the Himalayas was in deep shadow: on the Indian slope the sun had just prevailed. The forests had been destroyed during the literature epoch for the purpose of making newspaper-pulp, but the snows were awakening to their morning glory, and clouds still hung on the breasts of Kinchinjunga. In the plain were seen the ruins of cities, with diminished rivers creeping by their walls, and by the sides of these were sometimes the signs of vomitories, marking the cities of today. Over the whole prospect air-ships rushed, crossing and intercrossing with incredible *aplomb,* and rising nonchalantly when they desired to escape the perturbations of the lower atmosphere and to traverse the Roof of the World.

"We have indeed advanced, thanks to the Machine," repeated the attendant, and hid the Himalayas behind a metal blind.

The day dragged wearily forward. The passengers sat each in his cabin, avoiding one another with an almost physical repulsion and longing to be once more under the surface of the earth. There were eight or ten of them, mostly young males, sent out from the public nurseries to inhabit the rooms of those who had died in various parts of the earth. The man who had dropped his Book was on the homeward journey. He had been sent to Sumatra for the purpose of propagating the race. Vashti alone was travelling by her private will.

At midday she took a second glance at the earth. The air-ship was crossing another range of mountains, but she could see little, owing to clouds. Masses of black rock hovered below her, and merged indistinctly into gray. Their shapes were fantastic; one of them resembled a prostrate man.

"No ideas here," murmured Vashti, and hid the Caucasus behind a metal blind.

In the evening she looked again. They were crossing a golden sea, in which lay many small islands and one peninsula.

She repeated, "No ideas here," and hid Greece behind a metal blind.

## II. THE MENDING APPARATUS

By a vestibule, by a lift, by a tubular railway, by a platform, by a sliding door—by reversing all the steps of her departure did Vashti arrive at her son's room, which exactly resembled her own. She might well declare that the visit was superfluous. The buttons, the knobs, the reading-desk with the Book, the temperature, the atmosphere, the illumination —all were exactly the same. And if Kuno himself, flesh of her flesh, stood close beside her at last, what profit was there in that? She was too well-bred to shake him by the hand.

Averting her eyes, she spoke as follows:

"Here I am. I have had the most terrible journey and greatly retarded the development of my soul. It is not worth it, Kuno, it is not worth it. My time is too precious. The sunlight almost touched me, and I have met with the

rudest people. I can only stop a few minutes. Say what you want to say, and then I must return."

"I have been threatened with Homelessness," said Kuno.

She looked at him now.

"I have been threatened with Homelessness, and I could not tell you such a thing through the Machine."

Homelessness means death. The victim is exposed to the air, which kills him.

"I have been outside since I spoke to you last. The tremendous thing has happened, and they have discovered me."

"But why shouldn't you go outside!" she exclaimed. "It is perfectly legal, perfectly mechanical, to visit the surface of the earth. I have lately been to a lecture on the sea; there is no objection to that; one simply summons a respirator and gets an Egression-permit. It is not the kind of thing that spiritually-minded people do, and I begged you not to do it, but there is no legal objection to it."

"I did not get an Egression-permit."

"Then how did you get out?"

"I found out a way of my own."

The phrase conveyed no meaning to her, and he had to repeat it.

"A way of your own?" she whispered. "But that would be wrong."

"Why?"

The question shocked her beyond measure.

"You are beginning to worship the Machine," he said coldly. "You think it irreligious of me to have found out a way of my own. It was just what the Committee thought, when they threatened me with Homelessness."

At this she grew angry. "I worship nothing!" she cried. "I am most advanced. I don't think you irreligious, for there is no such thing as religion left. All the fear and the superstition that existed once have been destroyed by the Machine. I only meant that to find out a way of your own was— Besides, there is no new way out."

"So it is always supposed."

"Except through the vomitories, for which one must have an Egression-permit, it is impossible to get out. The Book says so."

"Well, the Book's wrong, for I have been out on my feet."

For Kuno was possessed of a certain physical strength.

By these days it was a demerit to be muscular. Each infant was examined at birth, and all who promised undue strength were destroyed. Humanitarians may protest, but it would have been no true kindness to let an athlete live; he would never have been happy in that state of life to which the Machine had called him; he would have yearned for trees to climb, rivers to bathe in, meadows and hills against which he might measure his body. Man must be adapted to his surroundings, must he not? In the dawn of the world our weakly must be exposed on Mount Taygetus, in its twilight our strong will suffer euthanasia, that the Machine may 10 progress, that the Machine may progress, that the Machine may progress eternally.

"You know that we have lost the sense of space. We say 'space is annihilated,' but we have annihilated not space, but the sense thereof. We have lost a part of ourselves. I determined to recover it, and I began by walking up and down the platform of the railway outside my room. Up and down, until I was tired, and so did recapture the meaning of 20 'Near' and 'Far.' 'Near' is a place to which I can get quickly *on my feet,* not a place to which the train or the air-ship will take me quickly. 'Far' is a place to which I cannot get quickly on my feet; the vomitory is 'far,' though I could be there in thirty-eight seconds by summoning the train. Man is the measure. That was my first lesson, Man's feet are the measure for distance, his hands are the measure for ownership, his body is the measure for all that is lovable and 30 desirable and strong. Then I went further: it was then that I called to you for the first time, and you would not come.

"This city, as you know, is built deep beneath the surface of the earth, with only the vomitories protruding. Having paced the platform outside my own room, I took the lift to the next platform and paced that also, and so with each in turn, until I came to the topmost, above which begins the earth. All the platforms 40 were exactly alike, and all that I gained by visiting them was to develop my sense of space and my muscles. I think I should have been content with this—it is not a little thing —but as I walked and brooded, it occurred to me that our cities had been built in the days when men still breathed the outer air, and that there had been ventilation shafts for the workmen. I could think of nothing but these ventilation shafts. Had they been destroyed 50 by all the food-tubes and medicine tubes and music tubes that the Machine has evolved lately? Or did traces of them remain? One thing was certain. If I came upon them anywhere, it would be in the railway-tunnels of the topmost story. Everywhere else, all space was accounted for.

"I am telling my story quickly, but don't think that I was not a coward or that your answers never depressed me. It is not the proper thing, it is not mechanical, it is not decent to walk along a railway-tunnel. I did not fear that I might tread upon a live rail and be killed. I feared something far more intangible—doing what was not contemplated by the Machine. Then I said to myself, 'Man is the measure,' and I went, and after many visits I found an opening.

"The tunnels, of course, were lighted. Everything is light, artificial light; darkness is the exception. So when I saw a black gap in the tiles, I knew that it was an exception, and rejoiced. I put in my arm—I could put in no more at first—and waved it round and round in ecstasy. I loosened another tile, and put in my head, and shouted into the darkness: 'I am coming, I shall do it yet,' and my voice reverberated down endless passages. I seemed to hear the spirits of those dead workmen who had returned each evening to the starlight and to their wives, and all the generations who had lived in the open air called back to me, 'You will do it yet, you are coming.'"

He paused, and, absurd as he was, his last words moved her. For Kuno had lately asked to be a father, and his request had been refused by the Committee. His was not a type that the Machine desired to hand on.

"Then a train passed. It brushed by me, but I thrust my head and arms into the hole. I had done enough for one day, so I crawled back to the platform, went down in the lift, and summoned my bed. Ah, what dreams! And again I called you, and again you refused."

She shook her head and said:

"Don't. Don't talk of these terrible things. You make me miserable. You are throwing civilization away."

"But I had got back the sense of space and a man cannot rest then. I determined to get in at the hole and climb the shaft. And so I exercised my arms. Day after day I went through ridiculous movements, until my flesh ached, and I could hang by my hands and hold the pillow of my bed outstretched for many minutes. Then I summoned a respirator, and started.

"It was easy at first. The mortar had somehow rotted, and I soon pushed some more tiles in, and clambered after them into the darkness, and the spirit of the dead comforted me. I don't know what I mean by that. I just say what I felt. I felt, for the first time, that a protest had been lodged against corruption, and that even as the dead were comforting me, so I was comforting the unborn. I felt that humanity existed, and that it existed without clothes. How can I possibly explain this? It was naked, humanity seemed naked, and all these tubes and buttons and machineries neither came into the world with us, nor will they follow us out, nor do they matter supremely while we are here. Had I been strong, I would have torn off every garment I had, and gone out into the outer air unswaddled. But this is not for me, nor perhaps for my generation. I climbed with my respirator and my hygienic clothes and my dietetic tabloids! Better thus than not at all.

"There was a ladder, made of some primeval metal. The light from the railway fell upon its lowest rungs, and I saw that it led straight upwards out of the rubble at the bottom of the shaft. Perhaps our ancestors ran up and down it a dozen times daily, in their building. As I climbed, the rough edges cut through my gloves so that my hands bled. The light helped me for a little, and then came darkness and, worse still, silence which pierced my ears like a sword. The Machine hums! Did you know that? Its hum penetrates our blood, and may even guide our thoughts. Who knows! I was getting beyond its power. Then I thought: 'This silence means that I am doing wrong.' But I heard voices in the silence, and again they strengthened me." He laughed. "I had need of them. The next moment I cracked my head against something."

She sighed.

"I had reached one of those pneumatic stoppers that defend us from the outer air. You may have noticed them on the air-ship. Pitch dark, my feet on the rungs of an invisible ladder, my hands cut; I cannot explain how I lived through this part, but the voices still comforted me, and I felt for fastenings. The stopper, I suppose, was about eight feet across. I passed my hand over it as far as I could reach. It was perfectly smooth. I felt it almost to the centre. Not quite to the centre, for my arm was too short. Then the voice said: 'Jump. It is worth it. There may be a handle in the centre, and you may catch hold of it and so come to us your own way. And if there is no handle, so that you may fall and are dashed to pieces—it is still worth it: you will still come to us your own way.' So I jumped. There was a handle, and—"

He paused. Tears gathered in his mother's eyes. She knew that he was fated. If he did not die today he would die to-morrow. There was

not room for such a person in the world. And with her pity disgust mingled. She was ashamed at having borne such a son, she who had always been so respectable and so full of ideas. Was he really the little boy to whom she had taught the use of his stops and buttons, and to whom she had given his first lessons in the Book? The very hair that disfigured his lips showed that he was reverting to some savage type. On atavism the Machine can have no mercy.

"There was a handle, and I did catch it. I hung tranced over the darkness and heard the hum of these workings as the last whisper in a dying dream. All the things I had cared about and all the people I had spoken to through tubes appeared infinitely little. Meanwhile the handle revolved. My weight had set something in motion and I span slowly, and then—

"I cannot describe it. I was lying with my face to the sunshine. Blood poured from my nose and ears and I heard a tremendous roaring. The stopper, with me clinging to it, had simply been blown out of the earth, and the air that we make down here was escaping through the vent into the air above. It burst up like a fountain. I crawled back to it—for the upper air hurts—and, as it were, I took great sips from the edge. My respirator had flown goodness knows where, my clothes were torn. I just lay with my lips close to the hole, and I sipped until the bleeding stopped. You can imagine nothing so curious. This hollow in the grass—I will speak of it in a minute,—the sun shining into it, not brilliantly but through marbled clouds,—the peace, the nonchalance, the sense of space, and, brushing my cheek, the roaring fountain of our artificial air! Soon I spied my respirator, bobbing up and down in the current high above my head, and higher still were many air-ships. But no one ever looks out of air-ships, and in my case they could not have picked me up. There I was stranded. The sun shone a little way down the shaft, and revealed the topmost rung of the ladder, but it was hopeless trying to reach it. I should either have been tossed up again by the escape, or else have fallen in, and died. I could only lie on the grass, sipping and sipping, and from time to time glancing around me.

"I knew that I was in Wessex, for I had taken care to go to a lecture on the subject before starting. Wessex lies above the room in which we are talking now. It was once an important state. Its kings held all the southern coast from the Andredswald to Cornwall, while the Wansdyke protected them on the north, running over the high ground. The lecturer was only concerned with the rise of Wessex, so I do not know how long it remained an international power, nor would the knowledge have assisted me. To tell the truth I could do nothing but laugh, during this part. There was I, with a pneumatic stopper by my side and a respirator bobbling over my head, imprisoned, all three of us, in a grass-grown hollow that was edged with fern."

Then he grew grave again.

"Lucky for me that it was a hollow. For the air began to fall back into it and to fill it as water fills a bowl. I could crawl about. Presently I stood. I breathed a mixture, in which the air that hurts predominated whenever I tried to climb the sides. This was not so bad. I had not lost my tabloids and remained ridiculously cheerful, and as for the Machine, I forgot about it altogether. My one aim now was to get to the top, where the ferns were, and to view whatever objects lay beyond.

"I rushed the slope. The new air was still too bitter for me and I came rolling back, after a momentary vision of something gray. The sun grew very feeble, and I remembered that he was in Scorpio—I had been to a lecture on that too. If the sun is in Scorpio and you are in Wessex, it means that you must be as quick as you can, or it will get too dark. (This is the first bit of useful information I have ever got from a lecture, and I expect it will be the last.) It made me try frantically to breathe the new air, and to advance as far as I dared out of my pond. The hollow filled so slowly. At times I thought that the fountain played with less vigour. My respirator seemed to dance nearer the earth; the roar was decreasing."

He broke off.

"I don't think this is interesting you. The rest will interest you even less. There are no ideas in it, and I wish that I had not troubled you to come. We are too different, mother."

She told him to continue.

"It was evening before I climbed the bank. The sun had very nearly slipped out of the sky by this time, and I could not get a good view. You, who have just crossed the Roof of the World, will not want to hear an account of the little hills that I saw—low colourless hills. But to me they were living and the turf that covered them was a skin, under which their muscles rippled, and I felt that those hills had called with incalculable force to men in the past, and that men had loved them. Now they sleep—perhaps for ever. They commune with

humanity in dreams. Happy the man, happy the woman, who awakes the hills of Wessex. For though they sleep, they will never die."

His voice rose passionately.

"Cannot you see, cannot all your lecturers see, that it is we who are dying, and that down here the only thing that really lives is the Machine? We created the Machine, to do our will, but we cannot make it do our will now. It has robbed us of the sense of space and of the sense of touch, it has blurred every human relation and narrowed down love to a carnal act, it has paralyzed our bodies and our wills, and now it compels us to worship it. The Machine develops—but not on our lines. The Machine proceeds—but not to our goal. We only exist as the blood corpuscles that course through its arteries, and if it could work without us, it would let us die. Oh, I have no remedy—or, at least, only one—to tell men again and again that I have seen the hills of Wessex as Ælfrid saw them when he overthrew the Danes.

"So the sun set. I forgot to mention that a belt of mist lay between my hill and other hills, and that it was the colour of pearl."

He broke off for the second time.

"Go on," said his mother wearily.

He shook his head.

"Go on. Nothing that you say can distress me now. I am hardened."

"I had meant to tell you the rest, but I cannot: I know that I cannot: good-bye."

Vashti stood irresolute. All her nerves were tingling with his blasphemies. But she was also inquisitive.

"This is unfair," she complained. "You have called me across the world to hear your story, and hear it I will. Tell me—as briefly as possible, for this is a disastrous waste of time—tell me how you returned to civilization."

"Oh—that!" he said, starting. "You would like to hear about civilization. Certainly. Had I got to where my respirator fell down?"

"No—but I understand everything now. You put on your respirator, and managed to walk along the surface of the earth to a vomitory, and there your conduct was reported to the Central Committee."

"By no means."

He passed his hand over his forehead, as if dispelling some strong impression. Then, resuming his narrative, he warmed to it again.

"My respirator fell about sunset. I had mentioned that the fountain seemed feebler, had I not?"

"Yes."

"About sunset, it let the respirator fall. As I said, I had entirely forgotten about the Machine, and I paid no great attention at the time, being occupied with other things. I had my pool of air, into which I could dip when the outer keenness became intolerable, and which would possibly remain for days, provided that no wind sprang up to disperse it. Not until it was too late, did I realize what the stoppage of the escape implied. You see—the gap in the tunnel had been mended; the Mending Apparatus; the Mending Apparatus, was after me.

"One other warning I had, but I neglected it. The sky at night was clearer than it had been in the day, and the moon, which was about half the sky behind the sun, shone into the dell at moments quite brightly. I was in my usual place—on the boundary between the two atmospheres—when I thought I saw something dark move across the bottom of the dell, and vanish into the shaft. In my folly, I ran down. I bent over and listened, and I thought I heard a faint scraping noise in the depths.

"At this—but it was too late—I took alarm. I determined to put on my respirator and to walk right out of the dell. But my respirator had gone. I knew exactly where it had fallen—between the stopper and the aperture—and I could even feel the mark that it had made in the turf. It had gone, and I realized that something evil was at work, and I had better escape to the outer air, and, if I must die, die running towards the cloud that had been the colour of a pearl. I never started. Out of the shaft—it is too horrible. A worm, a long white worm, had crawled out of the shaft and was gliding over the moonlit grass.

"I screamed. I did everything that I should not have done, I stamped upon the creature instead of flying from it, and it at once curled round the ankle. Then we fought. The worm let me run all over the dell, but edged up my leg as I ran. 'Help!' I cried. (That part is too awful. It belongs to the part that you will never know.) 'Help!' I cried. (Why cannot we suffer in silence?) 'Help!' I cried. Then my feet were wound together, I fell, I was dragged away from the dear ferns and the living hills, and past the great metal stopper (I can tell you this part), and I thought it might save me again if I caught hold of the handle. It also was enwrapped, it also. Oh, the whole dell was full of the things. They were searching it in all directions, they were denuding it, and the white snouts of others peeped out of the hole, ready if needed. Everything that could

be moved they brought—brushwood, bundles of fern, everything, and down we all went intertwined into hell. The last things that I saw, ere the stopper closed after us, were certain stars, and I felt that a man of my sort lived in the sky. For I did fight, I fought till the very end, and it was only my head hitting against the ladder that quieted me. I woke up in this room. The worms had vanished. I was surrounded by artificial air, artificial light, artificial peace, and my friends were calling to me down speaking-tubes to know whether I had come across any new ideas lately."

Here his story ended. Discussion of it was impossible, and Vashti turned to go.

"It will end in Homelessness," she said quietly.

"I wish it would," retorted Kuno.

"The Machine has been most merciful."

"I prefer the mercy of God."

"By that superstitious phrase, do you mean that you could live in the outer air?"

"Yes."

"Have you ever seen, round the vomitories, the bones of those who were extruded after the Great Rebellion?"

"Yes."

"They were left where they perished for our edification. A few crawled away, but they perished, too—who can doubt it? And so with the Homeless of our own day. The surface of the earth supports life no longer."

"Indeed."

"Ferns and a little grass may survive, but all higher forms have perished. Has any air-ship detected them?"

"No."

"Has any lecturer dealt with them?"

"No."

"Then why this obstinacy?"

"Because I have seen them," he exploded.

"Seen *what?*"

"Because I have seen her in the twilight—because she came to my help when I called—because she, too, was entangled by the worms, and, luckier than I, was killed by one of them piercing her throat."

He was mad. Vashti departed, nor, in the troubles that followed, did she ever see his face again.

## III. THE HOMELESS

During the years that followed Kuno's escapade, two important developments took place in the Machine. On the surface they were revolutionary, but in either case men's minds had been prepared beforehand, and they did but express tendencies that were latent already.

The first of these was the abolition of respirators.

Advanced thinkers, like Vashti, had always held it foolish to visit the surface of the earth. Air-ships might be necessary, but what was the good of going out for mere curiosity and crawling along for a mile or two in a terrestrial motor? The habit was vulgar and perhaps faintly improper: it was unproductive of ideas, and had no connection with the habits that really mattered. So respirators were abolished, and with them, of course, the terrestrial motors, and except for a few lecturers, who complained that they were debarred access to their subject-matter, the development was accepted quietly. Those who still wanted to know what the earth was like had after all only to listen to some gramophone, or to look into some cinematophote. And even the lecturers acquiesced when they found that a lecture on the sea was none the less stimulating when compiled out of other lectures that had already been delivered on the same subject. "Beware of first-hand ideas!" exclaimed one of the most advanced of them. "First-hand ideas do not really exist. They are but the physical impressions produced by love and fear, and on this gross foundation who could erect a philosophy? Let your ideas be second-hand, and if possible tenth-hand, for then they will be far removed from the disturbing element—direct observation. Do not learn anything about this subject of mine—the French Revolution. Learn instead what I think that Enicharmon thought Urizen thought Gutch thought Ho-Yung thought Chi-Bo-Sing thought Lafcadio Hearn thought Carlyle thought Mirabeau said about the French Revolution. Through the medium of these eight great minds, the blood that was shed at Paris and the windows that were broken at Versailles will be clarified to an idea which you may employ most profitably in your daily lives. But be sure that the intermediates are many and varied, for in history one authority exists to counteract another. Urizen must counteract the scepticism of Ho-Yung and Enicharmon, I must myself counteract the impetuosity of Gutch. You who listen to me are in a better position to judge about the French Revolution than I am. Your descendants will be even in a better position than you, for they will learn what you think I think, and yet another intermediate will be added to the chain. And in time"—his voice rose— "there will come a generation that has got beyond facts, beyond impressions, a generation absolutely colourless, a generation

'scraphically free
From taint of personality.'

which will see the French Revolution not as it happened, nor as they would like it to have happened, but as it would have happened, had it taken place in the days of the Machine."

Tremendous applause greeted this lecture, which did but voice a feeling already latent in the minds of men—a feeling that terrestrial facts must be ignored, and that the abolition of respirators was a positive gain. It was even suggested that air-ships should be abolished too. This was not done, because air-ships had somehow worked themselves into the Machine's system. But year by year they were used less, and mentioned less by thoughtful men.

The second great development was the re-establishment of religion.

This, too, had been voiced in the celebrated lecture. No one could mistake the reverent tone in which the peroration had concluded, and it awakened a responsive echo in the heart of each. Those who had long worshipped silently, now began to talk. They described the strange feeling of peace that came over them when they handled the Book of the Machine, the pleasure that it was to repeat certain numerals out of it, however little meaning those numerals conveyed to the outward ear, the ecstasy of touching a button, however unimportant, or of ringing an electric bell, however superfluously.

"The Machine," they exclaimed, "feeds us and clothes us and houses us; through it we speak to one another, through it we see one another, in it we have our being. The Machine is the friend of ideas and the enemy of superstition: the Machine is omnipotent, eternal; blessed is the Machine." And before long this allocution was printed on the first page of the Book, and in subsequent editions the ritual swelled into a complicated system of praise and prayer. The word "religion" was sedulously avoided, and in theory the Machine was still the creation and the implement of man. But in practice all, save a few retrogrades, worshipped it as divine. Nor was it worshipped in unity. One believer would be chiefly impressed by the blue optic plates, through which he saw other believers; another by the mending apparatus, which sinful Kuno had compared to worms; another by the lifts, another by the Book. And each would pray to this or to that, and ask it to intercede for him with the Machine as a whole. Persecution—that also was present. It did not break out, for reasons that will be set forward shortly. But it was latent, and all who did not accept the minimum known as "undenominational Mechanism" lived in danger of Homelessness, which means death, as we know.

To attribute these two great developments to the Central Committee, is to take a very narrow view of civilization. The Central Committee announced the developments, it is true, but they were no more the cause of them than were the kings of the imperialistic period the cause of war. Rather did they yield to some invincible pressure, which came no one knew whither, and which, when gratified, was succeeded by some new pressure equally invincible. To such a state of affairs it is convenient to give the name of progress. No one confessed the Machine was out of hand. Year by year it was served with increased efficiency and decreased intelligence. The better a man knew his own duties upon it, the less he understood the duties of his neighbour, and in all the world there was no one who understood the monster as a whole. Those master brains had perished. They had left full directions, it is true, and their successors had each of them mastered a portion of those directions. But Humanity, in its desire for comfort, had overreached itself. It had exploited the riches of nature too far. Quietly and complacently, it was sinking into decadence, and progress had come to mean the progress of the Machine.

As for Vashti, her life went peacefully forward until the final disaster. She made her room dark and slept; she awoke and made the room light. She lectured and attended lectures. She exchanged ideas with her innumerable friends and believed she was growing more spiritual. At times a friend was granted Euthanasia, and left his or her room for the homelessness that is beyond all human conception. Vashti did not much mind. After an unsuccessful lecture, she would sometimes ask for Euthanasia herself. But the death-rate was not permitted to exceed the birth-rate and the Machine had hitherto refused it to her.

The troubles began quietly, long before she was conscious of them.

One day she was astonished at receiving a message from her son. They never communicated, having nothing in common, and she had only heard indirectly that he was still alive, and had been transferred from the northern hemisphere, where he had behaved so mischievously, to the southern—indeed, to a room not far from her own.

"Does he want me to visit him?" she thought. "Never again, never. And I have not the time."

No, it was madness of another kind.

He refused to visualize his face upon the blue plate, and speaking out of the darkness with solemnity said:

"The Machine stops."

"What do you say?"

"The Machine is stopping, I know it, I know the signs."

She burst into a peal of laughter. He heard her and was angry, and they spoke no more.

"Can you imagine anything more absurd?" she cried to a friend. "A man who was my son believes that the Machine is stopping. It would be impious if it was not mad."

"The Machine is stopping?" her friend replied. "What does that mean? The phrase conveys nothing to me."

"Nor to me."

"He does not refer, I suppose, to the trouble there has been lately with the music?"

"Oh no, of course not. Let us talk about music."

"Have you complained to the authorities?"

"Yes, and they say it wants mending, and referred me to the Committee of the Mending Apparatus. I complained of those curious gasping sighs that disfigure the symphonies of the Brisbane school. They sound like some one in pain. The Committee of the Mending Aparatus say that it shall be remedied shortly."

Obscurely worried, she resumed her life. For one thing, the defect in the music irritated her. For another thing, she could not forget Kuno's speech. If he had known that the music was out of repair—he could not know it, for he detested music—if he had known that it was wrong, "the Machine stops" was exactly the venomous sort of remark he would have made. Of course he had made it at a venture, but the coincidence annoyed her, and she spoke with some petulance to the Committee of the Mending Apparatus.

They replied, as before, that the defect would be set right shortly.

"Shortly! At once!" she retorted. "Why should I be worried by imperfect music? Things are always put right at once. If you do not mend it at once, I shall complain to the Central Committee."

"No personal complaints are received by the Central Committee," the Committee of the Mending Apparatus replied.

"Through whom am I to make my complaint, then?"

"Through us."

"I complain then."

"Your complaint shall be forwarded in its turn."

"Have others complained?"

This question was unmechanical, and the Committee of the Mending Apparatus refused to answer it.

"It is too bad!" she exclaimed to another of her friends. "There never was such an unfortunate woman as myself. I can never be sure of my music now. It gets worse and worse each time I summon it."

"I too have my troubles," the friend replied. "Sometimes my ideas are interrupted by a slight jarring noise."

"What is it?"

"I do not know whether it is inside my head, or inside the wall."

"Complain, in either case."

"I have complained, and my complaint will be forwarded in its turn to the Central Committee."

Time passed, and they resented the defects no longer. The defects had not been remedied, but the human tissues in that latter day had become so subservient, that they readily adapted themselves to every caprice of the Machine. The sigh at the crisis of the Brisbane symphony no longer irritated Vashti; she accepted it as part of the melody. The jarring noise, whether in the head or in the wall, was no longer resented by her friend. And so with the mouldy artificial fruit, so with the bath water that began to stink, so with the defective rhymes that the poetry machine had taken to emit. All were bitterly complained of at first, and then acquiesced in and forgotten. Things went from bad to worse unchallenged.

It was otherwise with the failure of the sleeping apparatus. That was a more serious stoppage. There came a day when over the whole world—in Sumatra, in Wessex, in the innumerable cities of Courland and Brazil—the beds, when summoned by their tired owners, failed to appear. It may seem a ludicrous matter, but from it we may date the collapse of humanity. The Committee responsible for the failure was assailed by complaints, whom it referred, as usual, to the Committee of the Mending Apparatus, who in its turn assured them that their complaints would be forwarded to the Central Committee. But the discontent grew, for mankind was not yet sufficiently adaptable to do without sleeping.

"Some one is meddling with the Machine—" they began.

"Some one is trying to make himself king, to reintroduce the personal element."

"Punish that man with Homelessness."

"To the rescue! Avenge the Machine! Avenge the Machine!"

"War! Kill the man!"

But the Committee of the Mending Apparatus now came forward, and allayed the panic with well-chosen words. It confessed that the Mending Apparatus was itself in need of repair.

The effect of this frank confession was admirable.

"Of course," said a famous lecturer—he of the French Revolution, who gilded each new decay with splendour—"of course we shall not press our complaints now. The Mending Apparatus has treated us so well in the past that we all sympathize with it, and will wait patiently for its recovery. In its own good time it will resume its duties. Meanwhile let us do without our beds, our tabloids, our other little wants. Such, I feel sure, would be the wish of the Machine."

Thousands of miles away his audience applauded. The Machine still linked them. Under the seas, beneath the roots of the mountains, ran the wires through which they saw and heard, the enormous eyes and ears that were their heritage, and the hum of many workings clothed their thoughts in one garment of subserviency. Only the old and the sick remained ungrateful, for it was rumoured that Euthanasia, too, was out of order, and that pain had reappeared among men.

It became difficult to read. A blight entered the atmosphere and dulled its luminosity. At times Vashti could scarcely see across her room. The air, too, was foul. Loud were the complaints, impotent the remedies, heroic the tone of the lecturer as he cried: "Courage, courage! What matter so long as the Machine goes on? To it the darkness and the light are one." And though things improved again after a time, the old brilliancy was never recaptured, and humanity never recovered from its entrance into twilight. There was an hysterical talk of "measures," of "provisional dictatorship," and the inhabitants of Sumatra were asked to familiarize themselves with the workings of the central power station, the said power station being situated in France. But for the most part panic reigned, and men spent their strength praying to their Books, tangible proofs of the Machine's omnipotence. There were gradations of terror—at times came rumours of hope—the Mending Apparatus was almost mended—the enemies of the Machine had been got under—new "nerve-centres" were evolving which would do the work even more magnificently than before. But there came a day when, without the slightest warning, without any previous hint of feebleness, the entire communication-system broke down, all over the world, and the world, as they understood it, ended.

Vashti was lecturing at the time and her earlier remarks had been punctuated with applause. As she proceeded the audience became silent, and at the conclusion there was no sound. Somewhat displeased, she called to a friend who was a specialist in sympathy. No sound: doubtless the friend was sleeping. And so with the next friend whom she tried to summon, and so with the next, until she remembered Kuno's cryptic remark, "The Machine stops."

The phrase still conveyed nothing. If Eternity was stopping it would of course be set going shortly.

For example, there was still a little light and air—the atmosphere had improved a few hours previously. There was still the Book, and while there was the Book there was security.

Then she broke down, for with the cessation of activity came an unexpected terror—silence.

She had never known silence, and the coming of it nearly killed her—it did kill many thousands of people outright. Ever since her birth she had been surrounded by the steady hum. It was to the ear what artificial air was to the lungs, and agonizing pains shot across her head. And scarcely knowing what she did, she stumbled forward and pressed the unfamiliar button, the one that opened the door of her cell.

Now the door of the cell worked on a simple hinge of its own. It was not connected with the central power station, dying far away in France. It opened, rousing immoderate hopes in Vashti, for she thought that the Machine had been mended. It opened, and she saw the dim tunnel that curved far away towards freedom. One look, and then she shrank back. For the tunnel was full of people—she was almost the last in that city to have taken alarm.

People at any time repelled her, and these were nightmares from her worst dreams. People were crawling about, people were screaming, whimpering, gasping for breath, touching each other, vanishing in the dark, and ever and anon being pushed off the platform on to the live rail. Some were fighting around the electric bells, trying to summon trains which could not be summoned. Others were yelling for Euthanasia or for respirators, or blaspheming the Machine. Others stood at the doors of their cells fearing, like herself, either to stop in them or to leave them. And behind all the uproar was silence—the silence which is the voice of the earth and of the generations who have gone.

No—it was worse than solitude. She closed the door again and sat down to wait for the end. The disintegration went on, accompanied by horrible cracks and rumbling. The valves that restrained the Medical Apparatus must have been weakened, for it ruptured and hung hideously from the ceiling. The floor heaved and fell and flung her from her chair. A tube oozed towards her serpent fashion. And at last the final horror approached—light began to ebb, and she knew that civilization's long day was closing.

She whirled round, praying to be saved from this, at any rate, kissing the Book, pressing button after button. The uproar outside was increasing, and even penetrated the wall. Slowly the brilliancy of her cell was dimmed, the reflections faded from her metal switches. Now she could not see the reading-stand, now not the Book, though she held it in her hand. Light followed the flight of sound, air was following light, and the original void returned to the cavern from which it had been so long excluded. Vashti continued to whirl, like the devotees of an earlier religion, screaming, praying, striking at the buttons with bleeding hands.

It was thus that she opened her prison and escaped—escaped in the spirit: at least so it seems to me, ere my meditation closes. That she escapes in the body—I cannot perceive that. She struck, by chance, the switch that released the door, and the rush of foul air on her skin, the loud throbbing whispers in her ears, told her that she was facing the tunnel again, and that tremendous platform on which she had seen men fighting. They were not fighting now. Only the whispers remained, and the little whimpering groans. They were dying by hundreds out in the dark.

She burst into tears.

Tears answered her.

They wept for humanity, those two, not for themselves. They could not bear that this should be the end. Ere silence was completed their hearts were opened, and they knew what had been important on the earth. Man, the flower of all flesh, the noblest of all creatures visible, man who had once made god in his image, and had mirrored his strength on the constellations, beautiful naked man was dying, strangled in the garments that he had woven. Century after century had he toiled, and here was his reward. Truly the garment had seemed heavenly at first, shot with the colours of culture, sewn with the threads of self-denial. And heavenly it had been so long as it was a garment and no more, so long as man could shed it at will and live by the essence that is his soul, and the essence, equally divine, that is his body. The sin against the body—it was for that they wept in chief; the centuries of wrong against the muscles and the nerves, and those five portals by which we can alone apprehend —glozing it over with talk of evolution, until the body was white pap, the home of ideas as colourless, last sloshy stirrings of a spirit that had grasped the stars.

"Where are you?" she sobbed.

His voice in the darkness said, "Here."

"Is there any hope, Kuno?"

"None for us."

"Where are you?"

She crawled towards him over the bodies of the dead. His blood spurted over her hands.

"Quicker," he gasped, "I am dying—but we touch, we talk, not through the Machine."

He kissed her.

"We have come back to our own. We die, but we have recaptured life, as it was in Wessex, when Aelfrid overthrew the Danes. We know what they know outside, they who dwelt in the cloud that is the colour of a pearl."

"But, Kuno, is it true? Are there still men on the surface of the earth? Is this—this tunnel, this poisoned darkness—really not the end?"

He replied:

"I have seen them, spoken to them, loved them. They are hiding in the mist and the ferns until our civilization stops. To-day they are the Homeless—to-morrow—"

"Oh, to-morrow—some fool will start the Machine again, to-morrow."

"Never," said Kuno, "never. Humanity has learnt its lesson."

As he spoke, the whole city was broken like a honeycomb. An airship had sailed in through the vomitory into a ruined wharf. It crashed downwards, exploding as it went, rending gallery after gallery with its wings of steel. For a moment they saw the nations of the dead, and, before they joined them, scraps of the untainted sky.

# Virginia Woolf

## 1882 - 1941

Virginia Stephen was born in 1882 at 13 Hyde Park South in London. Her father was Sir Leslie Stephen, scholar and editor of the Dictionary of National Biography. Hardy, Stevenson, Ruskin, John Morley, George Meredith, and many other giants of literature and scholarship were friends and visitors during her childhood. She was educated at home, where she explored the riches of her father's great library and followed her interests freely whether in Greek, music, art, or poetry. In 1912 she married Leonard Woolf, an historian and political essayist.

In 1917 the couple set by hand the first Hogarth Press book, Two Stories by "L. and V. Woolf." The Press was a hobby and labor of love; it was dedicated to quality of content and to attractive and distinctive book production. In 1918 the Press published Katherine Mansfield's Prelude; also in 1918, T. S. Eliot's Poems and Virginia Woolf's Kew Gardens. In 1920 came E. M. Forster's The Story of the Siren.

As Virginia Woolf's development as a writer continued, she relied more heavily and confidently on a method she had experimented with in sketches and stories, the stream-of-consciousness technique. Jacob's Room (1922) was a modified artistic success; Mrs. Dalloway (1925) was a triumph, moving smoothly on a free-flowing flux of emotions, feelings, sensations, and thoughts to permit the reader a viewpoint within the consciousness of the characters. To the Lighthouse (1927) and The Waves (1931) continued the triumph; after The Waves, Mrs. Woolf evidently felt that she had made her point, and discontinued her experimental exploration of the nature and potential of fiction. The Years (1937) was a popular success, but was much less in the style and spirit of her best work. Her short stories appeared in two collections after her first book in 1917: Monday or Tuesday (1921) and A Haunted House (1947).

Mrs. Woolf's essays are among the finest of the century. The Common Reader (1925) and The Second Common Reader (1932) are collections of personal essays on literary subjects. The Death of the Moth (1942) and other posthumous collections of essays show the wide range of their author's interests and the light, easy mastery of language that she possessed.

A Writer's Diary (London, 1953) is a valuable source of insight into the mind and art of the novelist. The best introduction to the novels is E. M. Forster's brief analysis, Virginia Woolf (London, 1942). Other critical and biographical studies include David Daiches's Virginia Woolf (Norfolk, Connecticut, 1942); Joan Bennett's Virginia Woolf, Her Art as a Novelist (New York, 1945); R. L. Chambers's The Novels of Virginia Woolf (London, 1947); Bernard Blackstone's Virginia Woolf, a Commentary (New York, 1949); Winifred Holtby's Virginia Woolf (London, 1952); and James Hafley's The Glass Roof: Virginia Woolf as Novelist (Berkeley and Los Angeles, 1954).

## The Death of the Moth [1]

Moths that fly by day are not properly to be called moths; they do not excite that pleasant sense of dark autumn nights and ivy-blossom which the commonest yellow-underwing asleep in the shadow of the curtain never fails to rouse in us. They are hybrid creatures, neither gay like butterflies nor sombre like their own species. Nevertheless the present specimen, with his narrow hay-coloured wings, fringed with a tassel of the same colour, seemed to be content with life. It was a pleasant morning, mid-September, mild, benignant, yet with a keener breath than that of the summer months. The plough was already scoring the field opposite the window, and where the share had been, the earth was pressed flat and gleamed with moisture. Such vigour came rolling in from the fields and the down beyond that it was difficult to keep the eyes strictly turned upon the book. The rooks too were keeping one of their annual festivities; soaring round the tree tops until it looked as if a vast net with thousands of black knots in it had been cast up into the air; which, after a few moments sank slowly down upon the trees until every twig seemed to have a knot at the end of it. Then, suddenly, the net would be thrown into the air again in a wider circle this time, with the utmost clamour and vociferation, as though to be thrown into the air and settle slowly down upon the tree tops were a tremendously exciting experience.

The same energy which inspired the rooks, the ploughmen, the horses, and even, it seemed, the lean bare-backed downs, sent the moth fluttering from side to side of his square of the window-pane. One could not help watching him. One was, indeed, conscious of a queer feeling of pity for him. The possibilities of pleasure seemed that morning so enormous and so various that to have only a moth's part in life, and a day moth's at that, appeared a hard fate, and his zest in enjoying his meagre opportunities to the full, pathetic. He flew vigorously to one corner of his compartment, and, after waiting there a second, flew across to the other. What remained for him but to fly to a third corner and then to a fourth? That was all he could do, in spite of the size of the downs, the width of the sky, the far-off smoke of houses, and the romantic voice, now and then, of a steamer out at sea. What he could do he did. Watching him, it seemed as if a fibre, very thin but pure, of the enormous energy of the world had been thrust into his frail and diminutive body. As often as he crossed the pane, I could fancy that a thread of vital light became visible. He was little or nothing but life.

Yet, because he was so small, and so simple a form of the energy that was rolling in at the open window and driving its way through so many narrow and intricate corridors in my own brain and in those of other human beings, there was something marvellous as well as pathetic about him. It was as if someone had taken a tiny bead of pure life and decking it as lightly as possible with down and feathers, had set it dancing and zigzagging to show us the true nature of life. Thus displayed one could not get over the strangeness of it. One is apt to forget all about life, seeing it humped

and bossed and garnished and cumbered so that it has to move with the greatest circumspection and dignity. Again, the thought of all that life might have been had he been born in any other shape caused one to view his simple activities with a kind of pity.

After a time, tired by his dancing apparently, he settled on the window ledge in the sun, and, the queer spectacle being at an end, I forgot about him. Then, looking up, my eye was caught by him. He was trying to resume his dancing, but seemed either so stiff or so awkward that he could only flutter to the bottom of the window-pane; and when he tried to fly across it he failed. Being intent on other matters I watched these futile attempts for a time without thinking, unconsciously waiting for him to resume his flight, as one waits for a machine, that has stopped momentarily, to start again without considering the reason of its failure. After perhaps a seventh attempt he slipped from the wooden ledge and fell, fluttering his wings, on to his back on the window sill. The helplessness of his attitude roused me. It flashed upon me that he was in difficulties; he could no longer raise himself; his legs struggled vainly. But, as I stretched out a pencil, meaning to help him to right himself, it came over me that the failure and awkwardness were the approach of death. I laid the pencil down again.

The legs agitated themselves once more. I looked as if for the enemy against which he struggled. I looked out of doors. What had happened there? Presumably it was midday, and work in the fields had stopped. Stillness and quiet had replaced the previous animation. The birds had taken themselves off to feed in the brooks. The horses stood still. Yet the power was there all the same, massed outside indifferent, impersonal, not attending to anything in particular. Somehow it was opposed to the little hay-coloured moth. It was useless to try to do anything. One could only watch the extraordinary efforts made by those tiny legs against an oncoming doom which could, had it chosen, have submerged an entire city, not merely a city, but masses of human beings; nothing, I knew had any chance against death. Nevertheless after a pause of exhaustion the legs fluttered again. It was superb this last protest, and so frantic that he succeeded at last in righting himself. One's sympathies, of course, were all on the side of life. Also, when there was nobody to care or to know, this gigantic effort on the part of an insignificant little moth, against a power of such magnitude, to retain what no one else valued or desired to keep, moved one strangely. Again, somehow, one saw life, a pure bead. I lifted the pencil again, useless though I knew it to be. But even as I did so, the unmistakable tokens of death showed themselves. The body relaxed, and instantly grew stiff. The struggle was over. The insignificant little creature now knew death. As I looked at the dead moth, this minute wayside triumph of so great a force over so mean an antagonist filled me with wonder. Just as life had been strange a few minutes before, so death was now as strange. The moth having righted himself now lay most decently and uncomplainingly composed. O yes, he seemed to say, death is stronger than I am.

## The New Dress [1]

Mabel had her first serious suspicion that something was wrong as she took her cloak off and Mrs. Barnet, while handing her the mirror and touching the brushes and thus drawing her attention, perhaps rather markedly, to all the appliances for tidying and improving hair, complexion, clothes, which existed on the dressing table, confirmed the suspicion—that it was not right, not quite right, which growing stronger as she went upstairs and springing at her, with conviction as she greeted Clarissa Dalloway, she went straight to the far end of the room, to a shaded corner where a looking-glass hung and looked. No! It was not *right*. And at once the misery which she always tried to hide, the profound dissatisfaction—the sense she had had, ever since she was a child, of being inferior to other people—set upon her, relentlessly, remorselessly, with an intensity which she could not beat off, as she would when she woke at night at home, by reading Borrow or Scott; for oh these men, oh these women, all were thinking—"What's Mabel wearing? What a fright she looks! What a hideous new dress!" —their eyelids flickering as they came up and then their lids shutting rather tight. It was her own appalling inadequacy; her cowardice; her mean, water-sprinkled blood that depressed her. And at once the whole of the room where, for ever so many hours, she had planned with the little dressmaker how it was to go, seemed sordid, repulsive; and her own drawing-room so shabby, and herself, going out, puffed up with vanity as she touched the letters on the

[1] Published 1927. From *A Haunted House and Other Stories* by Virginia Woolf, copyright, 1944, by Harcourt, Brace and Company, Inc., and used with their permission.

hall table and said: "How dull!" to show off— all this now seemed unutterably silly, paltry, and provincial. All this had been absolutely destroyed, shown up, exploded, the moment she came into Mrs. Dalloway's drawing-room.

What she had thought that evening when, sitting over the teacups, Mrs. Dalloway's invitation came, was that, of course, she could not be fashionable. It was absurd to pretend it even—fashion meant cut, meant style, meant thirty guineas at least—but why not be original? Why not be herself, anyhow? And, getting up, she had taken that old fashion book of her mother's, a Paris fashion book of the time of the Empire, and had thought how much prettier, more dignified, and more womanly they were then, and so set herself— oh, it was foolish—trying to be like them, pluming herself in fact, upon being modest and old-fashioned and very charming, giving herself up, no doubt about it, to an orgy of self-love, which deserved to be chastised, and so rigged herself out like this.

But she dared not look in the glass. She could not face the whole horror—the pale yellow, idiotically old-fashioned silk dress with its long skirt and its high sleeves and its waist and all the things that looked so charming in the fashion book, but not on her, not among all these ordinary people. She felt like a dressmaker's dummy standing there, for young people to stick pins into.

"But, my dear, it's perfectly charming!" Rose Shaw said, looking her up and down with that little satirical pucker of the lips which she expected—Rose herself being dressed in the height of the fashion, precisely like everybody else, always.

"We are all like flies trying to crawl over the edge of the saucer," Mabel thought, and repeated the phrase as if she were crossing herself, as if she were trying to find some spell to annul this pain, to make this agony endurable. Tags of Shakespeare, lines from books she had read ages ago, suddenly came to her when she was in agony, and she repeated them over and over again. "Flies trying to crawl," she repeated. If she could say that over often enough and make herself see the flies, she would become numb, chill, frozen, dumb. Now she could see flies crawling slowly out of a saucer of milk with their wings stuck together; and she strained and strained (standing in front of the looking-glass, listening to Rose Shaw) to make herself see Rose Shaw and all the other people there as flies, trying to hoist themselves out of something, or into something, meagre, insignificant, toiling flies. But she could not see them like that, nor other people. She saw herself like that —she was a fly, but the others were dragonflies, skimming, while she alone dragged herself up out of the saucer. (Envy and spite, the most detestable of the vices, were her chief faults.)

"I feel like some dowdy, decrepit, horribly dingy old fly," she said, making Robert Haydon stop just to hear her say that, just to reassure herself by furbishing up a poor weak-kneed 10 phrase and so showing how detached she was, how witty, that she did not feel in the least out of anything. And, of course, Robert Haydon answered something quite polite, quite insincere, which she saw through instantly, and said to herself, directly he went (again from some book), "Lies, lies, lies!" For a party makes things either much more real, or much less real, she thought; she saw in a flash to the bottom of Robert Haydon's heart; she saw 20 through everything. She saw the truth. *This* was true, this drawing-room, this self, and the other false. Miss Milan's little work-room was really terribly hot, stuffy, sordid. It smelt of clothes and cabbage cooking; and yet, when Miss Milan put the glass in her hand, and she looked at herself with the dress on, finished, an extraordinary bliss shot through her heart. Suffused with light, she sprang into existence. Rid of cares and wrinkles, what she had 30 dreamed of herself was there—a beautiful woman. Just for a second (she had not dared look longer, Miss Milan wanted to know about the length of the skirt), there looked at her, framed in the scrolloping mahogany, a grey-white, mysteriously smiling, charming girl, the core of herself, the soul of herself; and it was not vanity only, not only self-love that made her think it good, tender, and true. Miss Milan said that the skirt could not well be longer; if 40 anything the skirt, said Miss Milan, puckering her forehead, considering with all her wits about her, must be shorter; and she felt, suddenly, honestly, full of love for Miss Milan, much, much fonder of Miss Milan than of anyone in the whole world, and could have cried for pity that she should be crawling on the floor with her mouth full of pins, and her face red and her eyes bulging—that one human being should be doing this for another, and 50 she saw them all as human beings merely, and herself going off to her party, and Miss Milan pulling the cover over the canary's cage, or letting him pick a hemp-seed from between her lips, and the thought of it, of this side of human nature and its patience and its endurance and its being content with such miser-

able, scanty, sordid, little pleasures filled her eyes with tears.

And now the whole thing had vanished. The dress, the room, the love, the pity, the scrolloping looking-glass, and the canary's cage—all had vanished, and here she was in a corner of Mrs. Dalloway's drawing-room, suffering tortures, woken wide awake to reality.

But it was all so paltry, weak-blooded, and petty-minded to care so much at her age with two children, to be still so utterly dependent on people's opinions and not have principles or convictions, not to be able to say as other people did, "There's Shakespeare! There's death! We're all weevils in a captain's biscuit" —or whatever it was that people did say.

She faced herself straight in the glass; she pecked at her left shoulder; she issued out into the room, as if spears were thrown at her yellow dress from all sides. But instead of looking fierce or tragic, as Rose Shaw would have done —Rose would have looked like Boadicea—she looked foolish and self-conscious, and simpered like a schoolgirl and slouched across the room, positively slinking, as if she were a beaten mongrel, and looked at a picture, an engraving. As if one went to a party to look at a picture! Everybody knew why she did it—it was from shame, from humiliation.

"Now the fly's in the saucer," she said to herself, "right in the middle, and can't get out, and the milk," she thought, rigidly staring at the picture, "is sticking its wings together."

"It's so old-fashioned," she said to Charles Burt, making him stop (which by itself he hated) on his way to talk to someone else.

She meant, or she tried to make herself think that she meant, that it was the picture and not her dress, that was old-fashioned. And one word of praise, one word of affection from Charles would have made all the difference to her at the moment. If he had only said, "Mabel, you're looking charming tonight!" it would have changed her life. But then she ought to have been truthful and direct. Charles said nothing of the kind, of course. He was malice itself. He always saw through one, especially if one were feeling particularly mean, paltry, or feeble-minded.

"Mabel's got a new dress!" he said, and the poor fly was absolutely shoved into the middle of the saucer. Really, he would like her to drown, she believed. He had no heart, no fundamental kindness, only a veneer of friendliness. Miss Milan was much more real, much kinder. If only one could feel that and stick to it, always. "Why," she asked herself—

replying to Charles much too pertly, letting him see that she was out of temper, or "ruffled" as he called it ("Rather ruffled?" he said and went on to laugh at her with some woman over there)—"Why," she asked herself, "can't I feel one thing always, feel quite sure that Miss Milan is right, and Charles wrong and stick to it, feel sure about the canary and pity and love and not be whipped all round in a second by coming into a room full of people?" It was her odious, weak, vacillating character again, always giving at the critical moment and not being seriously interested in conchology, etymology, botany, archeology, cutting up potatoes and watching them fructify like Mary Dennis, like Violet Searle.

Then Mrs. Holman, seeing her standing there, bore down upon her. Of course a thing like a dress was beneath Mrs. Holman's notice, with her family always tumbling downstairs or having the scarlet fever. Could Mabel tell her if Elmthorpe was ever let for August and September? Oh, it was a conversation that bored her unutterably!—it made her furious to be treated like a house agent or a messenger boy, to be made use of. Not to have value, that was it, she thought, trying to grasp something hard, something real, while she tried to answer sensibly about the bathroom and the south aspect and the hot water to the top of the house; and all the time she could see little bits of her yellow dress in the round looking-glass which made them all the size of boot-buttons or tadpoles; and it was amazing to think how much humiliation and agony and self-loathing and effort and passionate ups and downs of feeling were contained in a thing the size of a threepenny bit. And what was still odder, this thing, this Mabel Waring, was separate, quite disconnected; and though Mrs. Holman (the black button) was leaning forward and telling her how her eldest boy had strained his heart running, she could see her, too, quite detached in the looking-glass, and it was impossible that the black dot, leaning forward, gesticulating, should make the yellow dot, sitting solitary, self-centred, feel what the black dot was feeling, yet they pretended.

"So impossible to keep boys quiet"—that was the kind of thing one said.

And Mrs. Holman, who could never get enough sympathy and snatched what little there was greedily, as if it were her right (but she deserved much more for there was her little girl who had come down this morning with a swollen knee-joint), took this miserable offering and looked at it suspiciously, grudgingly, as if it were a half-penny when it ought to have been a pound and put it away in her purse, must put up with it, mean and miserly though it was, times being hard, so very hard; and on she went, creaking, injured Mrs. Holman, about the girl with the swollen joints. Ah, it was tragic, this greed, this clamour of human beings, like a row of cormorants, barking and flapping their wings for sympathy—it was tragic, could one have felt it and not merely pretended to feel it!

But in her yellow dress tonight she could not wring out one drop more; she wanted it all, all for herself. She knew (she kept on looking into the glass, dipping into that dreadfully showing-up blue pool) that she was condemned, despised, left like this in a backwater, because of her being like this a feeble, vacillating creature; and it seemed to her that the yellow dress was a penance which she had deserved, and if she had been dressed like Rose Shaw, in lovely, clinging green with a ruffle of swansdown, she would have deserved that; and she thought that there was no escape for her—none whatever. But it was not her fault altogether, after all. It was being one of a family of ten; never having money enough, always skimping and paring; and her mother carrying great cans, and the linoleum worn on the stair edges, and one sordid little domestic tragedy after another—nothing catastrophic, the sheep farm failing, but not utterly; her eldest brother marrying beneath him but not very much—there was no romance, nothing extreme about them all. They petered out respectably in sea-side resorts; every watering-place had one of her aunts even now asleep in some lodging with the front windows not quite facing the sea. That was so like them—they had to squint at things always. And she had done the same—she was just like her aunts. For all her dreams of living in India, married to some hero like Sir Henry Lawrence, some empire builder (still the sight of a native in a turban filled her with romance), she had failed utterly. She had married Hubert, with his safe, permanent underling's job in the Law Courts, and they managed tolerably in a smallish house, without proper maids, and hash when she was alone or just bread and butter, but now and then—Mrs. Holman was off, thinking her the most dried-up, unsympathetic twig she had ever met, absurdly dressed, too, and would tell everyone about Mabel's fantastic appearance—now and then, thought Mabel Waring, left alone on the blue sofa, punching the cushion in order to look occupied, for she would not join Charles

Burt and Rose Shaw, chattering like magpies and perhaps laughing at her by the fireplace— now and then, there did come to her delicious moments, reading the other night in bed, for instance, or down by the sea on the sand in the sun, at Easter—let her recall it—a great tuft of pale sand-grass standing all twisted like a shock of spears against the sky, which was blue like a smooth china egg, so firm, so hard, and then the melody of the waves—"Hush, hush," they said, and the children's shouts paddling— yes, it was a divine moment, and there she lay, she felt, in the hand of the Goddess who was the world; rather a hard-hearted, but very beautiful Goddess, a little lamb laid on the altar (one did think these silly things, and it didn't matter so long as one never said them). And also with Hubert sometimes she had quite unexpectedly—carving the mutton for Sunday lunch, for no reason, opening a letter, coming into a room—divine moments, when she said to herself (for she would never say this to anybody else), "This is it. This has happened. This is it!" And the other way about it was equally surprising—that is, when everything was arranged—music, weather, holidays, every reason for happiness was there—then nothing happened at all. One wasn't happy. It was flat, just flat, that was all.

Her wretched self again, no doubt! She had always been a fretful, weak, unsatisfactory mother, a wobbly wife, lolling about in a kind of twilight existence with nothing very clear or very bold, or more one thing than another, like all her brothers and sisters, except perhaps Herbert—they were all the same poor water-veined creatures who did nothing. Then in the midst of this creeping, crawling life, suddenly she was on the crest of a wave. That wretched fly—where had she read the story that kept coming into her mind about the fly and the saucer?—struggled out. Yes, she had those moments. But now that she was forty, they might come more and more seldom. By degrees

she would cease to struggle any more. But that was deplorable! That was not to be endured! That made her feel ashamed of herself!

She would go to the London Library tomorrow. She would find some wonderful, helpful, astonishing book, quite by chance, a book by a clergyman, by an American no one had ever heard of; or she would walk down the Strand and drop, accidentally, into a hall where a miner was telling about the life in the pit, and suddenly she would become a new person. She would be absolutely transformed. She would wear a uniform; she would be called Sister Somebody; she would never give a thought to clothes again. And forever after she would be perfectly clear about Charles Burt and Miss Milan and this room and that room; and it would be always, day after day, as if she were lying in the sun or carving the mutton. It would be it!

So she got up from the blue sofa, and the yellow button in the looking-glass got up too, and she waved her hand to Charles and Rose to show them she did not depend on them one scrap, and the yellow button moved out of the looking-glass, and all the spears were gathered into her breast as she walked towards Mrs. Dalloway and said, "Good night."

"But it's too early to go," said Mrs. Dalloway, who was always so charming.

"I'm afraid I must," said Mabel Waring. "But," she added in her weak, wobbly voice which only sounded ridiculous when she tried to strengthen it, "I have enjoyed myself enormously."

"I have enjoyed myself," she said to Mr. Dalloway, whom she met on the stairs.

"Lies, lies, lies!" she said to herself, going downstairs, and "Right in the saucer!" she said to herself as she thanked Mrs. Barnet for helping her and wrapped herself, round and round and round, in the Chinese cloak she had worn these twenty years.

# James Joyce

## 1882 - 1941

James Augustine Aloysius Joyce was born 2 February, 1882 in Rathgar, a suburb of Dublin. His father, John Stanislaus Joyce, after investing in an unsuccessful distillery became Collector of Rates of the City of Dublin. James was the eldest of 16 or 17 children. He attended three Jesuit schools: Congowes Wood College, Clane, from 1888–1893; Bewedere College, Dublin, 1893–1898; and University College, Dublin, 1898–1902. At University College his interest in language developed, and he read Latin, Italian, French, and Norwegian. In 1901 his pamphlet The Day of the Rabblement appeared.

Joyce left Ireland for Paris in October, 1902, and began attending lectures at the Collège de Mèdecine, but soon had to drop out for lack of funds. In 1903 he returned to Dublin, and his mother died; in 1904 he again left Dublin, with Nora Barnacle, and took a job teaching English at the Berlitz School in Trieste. His Chamber Music, a slender volume of lyric poems, was rejected by four publishers before it was accepted in 1907. Dubliners, a collection of sketches and stories of Irish life considered by some his finest work, was completed by 1905, but publishers were afraid to print it; it finally appeared in 1914. In 1915 the Joyces settled in Zurich. The autobiographical A Portrait of The Artist as a Young Man appeared in 1916, and Joyce's only play, Exiles, in 1918. In 1920 the Joyces moved to Paris. The 1920's and 1930's were spent in controversy about Ulysses (1922) and in completion of Finnegans Wake (1939). The first publication of Ulysses in Paris let loose a storm of protest and praise. Joyce's symbolic prose epic of a day in a city (Dublin, 16 June, 1904) is unlike anything that had been written before; many writers and readers found it exciting, many found it obscure, and many found it revolting. Its publication, its sale, and even its importation into English-speaking countries was prohibited, and it became a game among intellectuals to smuggle a copy from France. Not until 1933,

after stormy trial scenes, was American publication permitted. Finnegans Wake required 16 years to complete; as Ulysses had recorded "the day and the conscious mind," Finnegans Wake recorded "the night and the subconscious." Where Ulysses had been considered difficult, Finnegans Wake was considered nearly impossible to read, for its language was highly individual and included denotations, connotations, and symbolic meanings on several levels.

After fleeing from the German invasion of France in 1940, Joyce was ill and beset by trouble until his death in Zurich (13 January, 1941). His posthumous Stephen Hero (1944) is largely autobiographical.

The only critical edition of any of Joyce's works is the fully collated Chamber Music edited by William York Tindall (New York, 1954). The Collected Poems (New York, 1937) is available, and there is a useful selection, The Portable James Joyce (New York, 1947). The Letters have been edited by Stuart Gilbert (New York, 1957). James Joyce's Critical Writings, ed. Richard Ellmann and Ellsworth Mason (New York, 1959), includes much hitherto unpublished material. The authorized biography is Herbert Gorman's James Joyce (New York, 1939). David Daiches, The Novel in the Modern World (Chicago, 1939), contains an excellent analysis of Dubliners. Other biographical and critical studies include James Joyce: Two Decades of Criticism, ed. Seon Givens (New York, 1948); Hugh Kenner, Dublin's Joyce (London, 1955); and Marvin Magalaner and Richard M. Kain, Joyce: The Man, the Work, the Reputation (New York, 1956), containing a useful bibliography.

## The Sisters [1]

### (From Dubliners)

There was no hope for him this time: it was the third stroke. Night after night I had passed

[1] Completed 1905; published 1914. From Dubliners in The Portable James Joyce. Copyright 1946,

the house (it was vacation time) and studied the lighted square of window: and night after night I had found it lighted in the same way, faintly and evenly. If he was dead, I thought, I would see the reflection of candles on the darkened blind, for I knew that two candles must be set at the head of a corpse. He had often said to me: 'I am not long for this world,' and I had thought his words idle. Now I knew they were true. Every night as I gazed up at the window I said softly to myself the word *paralysis*. It had always sounded strangely in my ears, like the word *gnomon* in the Euclid and the word *simony* in the Catechism. But now it sounded to me like the name of some maleficent and sinful being. It filled me with fear, and yet I longed to be nearer to it and to look upon its deadly work.

Old Cotter was sitting at the fire, smoking, when I came downstairs to supper. While my aunt was ladling out my stirabout he said, as if returning to some former remark of his:

'No, I wouldn't say he was exactly . . . but there was something queer . . . there was something uncanny about him. I'll tell you my opinion. . . .'

He began to puff at his pipe, no doubt arranging his opinion in his mind. Tiresome old fool! When we knew him first he used to be rather interesting, talking of faints and worms; but I soon grew tired of him and his endless stories about the distillery.

'I have my own theory about it,' he said. 'I think it was one of those . . . peculiar cases. . . . But it's hard to say. . . .'

He began to puff again at his pipe without giving us his theory. My uncle saw me staring and said to me:

'Well, so your old friend is gone, you'll be sorry to hear.'

'Who?' said I.

'Father Flynn.'

'Is he dead?'

'Mr. Cotter here has just told us. He was passing by the house.'

I knew that I was under observation, so I continued eating as if the news had not interested me. My uncle explained to old Cotter.

'The youngster and he were great friends. The old chap taught him a great deal, mind you; and they say he had a great wish for him.'

'God have mercy on his soul,' said my aunt piously.

Old Cotter looked at me for a while. I felt that his little beady black eyes were examining

me, but I would not satisfy him by looking up from my plate. He returned to his pipe and finally spat rudely into the grate.

'I wouldn't like children of mine,' he said, 'to have too much to say to a man like that.'

'How do you mean, Mr. Cotter?' asked my aunt.

'What I mean is,' said old Cotter, 'it's bad for children. My idea is: let a young lad run about and play with young lads of his own age and not be . . . Am I right, Jack?'

'That's my principle, too,' said my uncle. 'Let him learn to box his corner. That's what I'm always saying to that Rosicrucian there: take exercise. Why, when I was a nipper every morning of my life I had a cold bath, winter and summer. And that's what stands to me now. Education is all very fine and large. . . . Mr. Cotter might take a pick of that leg of mutton,' he added to my aunt.

'No, no, not for me,' said old Cotter.

My aunt brought the dish from the safe and put it on the table.

'But why do you think it's not good for children, Mr. Cotter?' she asked.

'It's bad for children,' said old Cotter, 'because their minds are so impressionable. When children see things like that, you know, it has an effect. . . .'

I crammed my mouth with stirabout for fear I might give utterance to my anger. Tiresome old red-nosed imbecile!

It was late when I fell asleep. Though I was angry with old Cotter for alluding to me as a child, I puzzled my head to extract meaning from his unfinished sentences. In the dark of my room I imagined that I saw again the heavy grey face of the paralytic. I drew the blankets over my head and tried to think of Christmas. But the grey face still followed me. It murmured; and I understood that it desired to confess something. I felt my soul receding into some pleasant and vicious region; and there again I found it waiting for me. It began to confess to me in a murmuring voice and I wondered why it smiled continually and why the lips were so moist with spittle. But then I remembered that it had died of paralysis and I felt that I too was smiling feebly, as if to absolve the simoniac of his sin.

The next morning after breakfast I went down to look at the little house in Great Britain Street. It was an unassuming shop, registered under the vague name of *Drapery*. The drapery consisted mainly of children's bootees and umbrellas; and on ordinary days a notice used to hang in the window, saying: *Umbrellas Re-*

*covered.* No notice was visible now, for the shutters were up. A crape bouquet was tied to the door-knocker with ribbon. Two poor women and a telegram boy were reading the card pinned on the crape. I also approached and read:

July 1st, 1895
The Rev. James Flynn (formerly of
S. Catherine's Church,
Meath Street), aged sixty-five years.
R.I.P.

The reading of the card persuaded me that he was dead and I was disturbed to find myself at check. Had he not been dead I would have gone into the little dark room behind the shop to find him sitting in his arm-chair by the fire, nearly smothered in his great-coat. Perhaps my aunt would have given me a packet of High Toast for him, and this present would have roused him from his stupefied doze. It was always I who emptied the packet into his black snuff-box, for his hands trembled too much to allow him to do this without spilling half the snuff about the floor. Even as he raised his large trembling hand to his nose little clouds of smoke dribbled through his fingers over the front of his coat. It may have been these constant showers of snuff which gave his ancient priestly garments their green faded look, for the red handkerchief, blackened, as it always was, with the snuff-stains of a week, with which he tried to brush away the fallen grains, was quite inefficacious.

I wished to go in and look at him, but I had not the courage to knock. I walked away slowly along the sunny side of the street, reading all the theatrical advertisements in the shop-windows as I went. I found it strange that neither I nor the day seemed in a mourning mood and I felt even annoyed at discovering in myself a sensation of freedom as if I had been freed from something by his death. I wondered at this for, as my uncle had said the night before, he had taught me a great deal. He had studied in the Irish college in Rome and he had taught me to pronounce Latin properly. He had told me stories about the catacombs and about Napoleon Bonaparte, and he had explained to me the meaning of the different ceremonies of the Mass and of the different vestments worn by the priest. Sometimes he had amused himself by putting difficult questions to me, asking me what one should do in certain circumstances or whether such and such sins were mortal or venial or only imperfections. His questions showed me how complex and mysterious were certain insti-

tutions of the Church which I had always regarded as the simplest acts. The duties of the priest towards the Eucharist and towards the secrecy of the confessional seemed so grave to me that I wondered how anybody had ever found in himself the courage to undertake them; and I was not surprised when he told me that the fathers of the Church had written books as thick as the *Post Office Directory* and as closely printed as the law notices in the newspaper, elucidating all these intricate questions. Often when I thought of this I could make no answer or only a very foolish and halting one, upon which he used to smile and nod his head twice or thrice. Sometimes he used to put me through the responses of the Mass, which he had made me learn by heart; and, as I pattered, he used to smile pensively and nod his head, now and then pushing huge pinches of snuff up each nostril alternately. When he smiled he used to uncover his big discoloured teeth and let his tongue lie upon his lower lip—a habit which had made me feel uneasy in the beginning of our acquaintance before I knew him well.

As I walked along in the sun I remembered old Cotter's words and tried to remember what had happened afterwards in the dream. I remembered that I had noticed long velvet curtains and a swinging lamp of antique fashion. I felt that I had been very far away, in some land where the customs were strange—in Persia, I thought. . . . But I could not remember the end of the dream.

In the evening my aunt took me with her to visit the house of mourning. It was after sunset; but the window-panes of the houses that looked to the west reflected the tawny gold of a great bank of clouds. Nannie received us in the hall; and, as it would have been unseemly to have shouted at her, my aunt shook hands with her for all. The old woman pointed upwards interrogatively and, on my aunt's nodding, proceeded to toil up the narrow staircase before us, her bowed head being scarcely above the level of the banister-rail. At the first landing she stopped and beckoned us forward encouragingly towards the open door of the dead-room. My aunt went in and the old woman, seeing that I hesitated to enter, began to beckon to me again repeatedly with her hand.

I went in on tiptoe. The room through the lace end of the blind was suffused with dusky golden light amid which the candles looked like pale thin flames. He had been coffined. Nannie gave the lead and we three knelt down at the foot of the bed. I pretended to pray but

I could not gather my thoughts because the old woman's mutterings distracted me. I noticed how clumsily her skirt was hooked at the back and how the heels of her cloth boots were trodden down all to one side. The fancy came to me that the old priest was smiling as he lay there in his coffin.

But no. When we rose and went up to the head of the bed I saw that he was not smiling. There he lay, solemn and copious, vested as for the altar, his large hands loosely retaining a chalice. His face was very truculent, grey and massive, with black cavernous nostrils and circled by a scanty white fur. There was a heavy odour in the room—the flowers.

We crossed ourselves and came away. In the little room downstairs we found Eliza seated in his arm-chair in state. I groped my way towards my usual chair in the corner while Nannie went to the sideboard and brought out a decanter of sherry and some wine-glasses. She set these on the table and invited us to take a little glass of wine. Then, at her sister's bidding, she filled out the sherry into the glasses and passed them to us. She pressed me to take some cream crackers also, but I declined because I thought I would make too much noise eating them. She seemed to be somewhat disappointed at my refusal and went over quietly to the sofa, where she sat down behind her sister. No one spoke: we all gazed at the empty fireplace.

My aunt waited until Eliza sighed and then said:

'Ah, well, he's gone to a better world.'

Eliza sighed again and bowed her head in assent. My aunt fingered the stem of her wine-glass before sipping a little.

'Did he . . . peacefully?' she asked.

'Oh, quite peacefully, ma'am,' said Eliza. 'You couldn't tell when the breath went out of him. He had a beautiful death, God be praised.'

'And everything . . . ?'

'Father O'Rourke was in with him a Tuesday and anointed him and prepared him and all.'

'He knew then?'

'He was quite resigned.'

'He looks quite resigned,' said my aunt.

'That's what the woman we had in to wash him said. She said he just looked as if he was asleep, he looked that peaceful and resigned. No one would think he'd make such a beautiful corpse.'

'Yes, indeed,' said my aunt.

She sipped a little more from her glass and said:

'Well, Miss Flynn, at any rate it must be a great comfort for you to know that you did all you could for him. You were both very kind to him, I must say.'

Eliza smoothed her dress over her knees.

'Ah, poor James!' she said. 'God knows we done all we could, as poor as we are—we wouldn't see him want anything while he was in it.'

Nannie had leaned her head against the sofa-pillow and seemed about to fall asleep.

'There's poor Nannie,' said Eliza, looking at her, 'she's wore out. All the work we had, she and me, getting in the woman to wash him and then laying him out and then the coffin and then arranging about the Mass in the chapel. Only for Father O'Rourke I don't know what we'd done at all. It was him brought us all them flowers and them two candlesticks out of the chapel, and wrote out the notice for the *Freeman's General* and took charge of all the papers for the cemetery and poor James's insurance.'

'Wasn't that good of him?' said my aunt.

Eliza closed her eyes and shook her head slowly.

'Ah, there's no friends like the old friends,' she said, 'when all is said and done, no friends that a body can trust.'

'Indeed, that's true,' said my aunt. 'And I'm sure now that he's gone to his eternal reward he won't forget you and all your kindness to him.'

'Ah, poor James!' said Eliza. 'He was no great trouble to us. You wouldn't hear him in the house any more than now. Still, I know he's gone and all to that. . . .'

'It's when it's all over that you'll miss him,' said my aunt.

'I know that,' said Eliza. 'I won't be bringing him in his cup of beef tea any more, nor you, ma'am, send him his snuff. Ah, poor James!'

She stopped, as if she were communing with the past, and then said shrewdly:

'Mind you, I noticed there was something queer coming over him latterly. Whenever I'd bring in his soup to him there, I'd find him with his breviary fallen to the floor, lying back in the chair and his mouth open.'

She laid a finger against her nose and frowned: then she continued:

'But still and all he kept on saying that before the summer was over he'd go out for a drive one fine day just to see the old house again where we were all born down in Irishtown, and take me and Nannie with him. If we could only get one of them new-fangled carriages that makes no noise that Father O'Rourke told him about, them with the rheumatic wheels, for the day cheap—he said, at Johnny Rush's over the way there and drive out the three of us together of a Sunday evening. He had his mind set on that. . . . Poor James!'

'The Lord have mercy on his soul!' said my aunt.

Eliza took out her handkerchief and wiped 10 her eyes with it. Then she put it back again in her pocket and gazed into the empty grate for some time without speaking.

'He was too scrupulous always,' she said. 'The duties of the priesthood was too much for him. And then his life was, you might say, crossed.'

'Yes,' said my aunt. 'He was a disappointed man. You could see that.'

A silence took possession of the little room 20 and, under cover of it, I approached the table and tasted my sherry and then returned quietly to my chair in the corner. Eliza seemed to have fallen into a deep reverie. We waited respectfully for her to break the silence: and after a long pause she said slowly:

'It was that chalice he broke. . . . That was the beginning of it. Of course, they say it was all right, that it contained nothing, I mean. But still. . . . They say it was the boy's fault. 30 But poor James was so nervous, God be merciful to him!'

'And was that it?' said my aunt. 'I heard something. . . .'

Eliza nodded.

'That affected his mind,' she said. 'After that he began to mope by himself, talking to no one and wandering about by himself. So one night he was wanted for to go on a call and they couldn't find him anywhere. They looked high 40 up and low down; and still they couldn't see a sight of him anywhere. So then the clerk suggested to try the chapel. So then they got the keys and opened the chapel, and the clerk and Father O'Rourke and another priest that was there brought in a light for to look for him. . . . And what do you think but there he was, sitting up by himself in the dark in his confession-box, wide-awake and laughing-like softly to himself?'

She stopped suddenly as if to listen. I too 50 listened; but there was no sound in the house: and I knew that the old priest was lying still in his coffin as we had seen him, solemn and truculent in death, an idle chalice on his breast. Eliza resumed:

'Wide-awake and laughing-like to himself.

. . . So then, of course, when they saw that, that made them think that there was something gone wrong with him. . . .'

# *From* Chamber Music [1]

## II

The twilight turns from amethyst
    To deep and deeper blue,
The lamp fills with a pale green glow
    The trees of the avenue.

The old piano plays an air,    5
    Sedate and slow and gay;
She bends upon the yellow keys,
    Her head inclines this way.

Shy thoughts and grave wide eyes and hands
    That wander as they list—    10
The twilight turns to darker blue
    With lights of amethyst.

## IV

When the shy star goes forth in heaven
    All maidenly, disconsolate,
Hear you amid the drowsy even
    One who is singing by your gate.
His song is softer than the dew    5
And he is come to visit you.

O bend no more in revery
    When he at eventide is calling,
Nor muse: Who may this singer be
    Whose song about my heart is falling?    10
Know you by this, the lover's chant,
'Tis I that am your visitant.

## VII

My love is in a light attire
    Among the apple-trees,
Where the gay winds do most desire
    To run in companies.

There, where the gay winds stay to woo    5
    The young leaves as they pass,
My love goes slowly, bending to
    Her shadow on the grass;

And where the sky's a pale blue cup
    Over the laughing land,    10
My love goes lightly, holding up
    Her dress with dainty hand.

## VIII

Who goes amid the green wood
    With springtide all adorning her?
Who goes amid the merry green wood
    To make it merrier?

Who passes in the sunlight     5
  By ways that know the light footfall?
Who passes in the sweet sunlight
  With mien so virginal?

The ways of all the woodland
  Gleam with a soft and golden fire—    10
For whom does all the sunny woodland
  Carry so brave attire?

O, it is for my own true love,
  The woods their rich apparel wear—   15
O, it is for my true love
  That is so young and fair.

### XXXV

All day I hear the noise of waters
  Making moan,
Sad as the sea-bird is, when going
  Forth alone,
He hears the winds cry to the waters'    5
  Monotone.

The grey winds, the cold winds are blowing
  Where I go.
I hear the noise of many waters    10
  Far below.

All day, all night, I hear them flowing
  To and fro.

### XXXVI

I hear an army charging upon the land,
  And the thunder of horses plunging, foam
    about their knees:
Arrogant, in black armour, behind them stand,
  Disdaining the reins, with fluttering whips,
    the charioteers.

They cry unto the night their battle-name:   5
  I moan in sleep when I hear afar their
    whirling laughter.
They cleave the gloom of dreams, a blinding
    flame,
  Clanging, clanging upon the heart as upon
    an anvil.

They come shaking in triumph their long,
    green hair:
  They come out of the sea and run shouting
    by the shore.   10
My heart, have you no wisdom thus to despair?
  My love, my love, my love, why have you
    left me alone?

# D. H. Lawrence

## 1885 - 1930

David Herbert Lawrence was born 11 September, 1885 at Eastwood in the coal-mining district of Nottinghamshire. His father was John Arthur Lawrence, a miner, and his mother was a teacher; Lawrence was one of five children. Throughout his life he was subject to ill health, a burning intellect in a frail body subject to pneumonia and finally to tuberculosis. His early life was unpleasant; he was devoted to his mother, and his father was often brutal to mother and children alike. The poverty he knew in his early life continued almost until his death.

At 13 he entered Nottingham High School on a scholarship; at 16 he became a clerk, and then a pupil and teacher at the British School at Eastwood. At 18 he entered University College, Nottingham, continued his work for two years until he had earned a teaching certificate, and at 20 began to teach at an elementary school in Croydon. Soon he was publishing poetry in the English Review. His first novel, The White Peacock, appeared in 1911.

During the next 19 years Lawrence wrote a series of significant novels, notably Sons and Lovers (1913), The Rainbow (1915), Women in Love (1920), The Plumed Serpent (1926), and Lady Chatterley's Lover (1928). He produced volume after volume of poetry also, and a number of significant short stories. He lived, with his wife Frieda, in Sicily; in Taos, New Mexico; in Mexico; and in Italy; he died March 2, 1930, of tuberculosis.

Lawrence's early life was dominated by his love for his mother, an emotional involvement which made any other close permanent attachment impossible for him. His middle and later life was dominated by his driving mission to achieve freedom and harmony, both for himself and for others, and to find a way of life in which freedom and harmony are possible without the conflicts of forces commonly found in modern society. The harmony Lawrence sought was a harmony of nature and culture, of instinct and intellect—and toward the end of his life he found himself the prophet of a group who made a kind of religion out of their own search for this harmony.

The best text of the poems is The Complete Poems (London, 1957). The Letters of D. H. Lawrence have been edited by Aldous Huxley (New York, 1932); however, a fuller edition of the letters, bearing the same title, is being completed by Harry Moore. Excellent essays on Lawrence appear in André Maurois, Prophets and Poets (New York, 1935), and in Stephen Spender, The Destructive Element (London, 1953). Other critical and biographical studies include Stephen Potter, D. H. Lawrence: A First Study (London, 1930); Horace Gregory, Pilgrim of the Apocalypse: A Critical Study of D. H. Lawrence (New York, 1934); Richard Aldington, D. H. Lawrence: Portrait of a Genius But . . . (New York, 1950); Harry T. Moore, The Life and Works of D. H. Lawrence (New York, 1951), and The Intelligent Heart (New York, 1954); Frederick J. Hoffman and Harry T. Moore, editors, The Achievement of D. H. Lawrence (Norman, Oklahoma, 1953); F. R. Leavis, D. H. Lawrence: Novelist (London, 1955); Graham Hough, The Dark Sun (New York, 1957); Edward Nehls, editor and compiler, D. H. Lawrence: A Composite Biography (Madison, Wisconsin, 1957–1958); and Harry Moore, editor, A D. H. Lawrence Miscellany (Carbondale, Illinois, 1959).

## The Rocking-Horse Winner [1]

There was a woman who was beautiful, who started with all the advantages, yet she had no luck. She married for love, and the love turned to dust. She had bonny children, yet she felt

[1] Published 1926. From The Lovely Lady by D. H. Lawrence. Copyright 1933 by the Estate of D. H. Lawrence. Reprinted by permission of The Viking Press, Inc., New York.

they had been thrust upon her, and she could not love them. They looked at her coldly, as if they were finding fault with her. And hurriedly she felt she must cover up some fault in herself. Yet what it was that she must cover up she never knew. Nevertheless, when her children were present, she always felt the centre of her heart go hard. This troubled her, and in her manner she was all the more gentle and anxious for her children, as if she loved them very much. Only she herself knew that at the centre of her heart was a hard little place that could not feel love, no, not for anybody. Everybody else said of her: "She is such a good mother. She adores her children." Only she herself, and her children themselves, knew it was not so. They read it in each other's eyes.

There were a boy and two girls. They lived in a pleasant house, with a garden, and they had discreet servants, and felt themselves superior to anyone in the neighbourhood.

Although they lived in style, they felt always an anxiety in the house. There was never enough money. The mother had a small income, and the father had a small income, but not nearly enough for the social position which they had to keep up. The father went into town to some office. But though he had good prospects, these prospects never materialized. There was always the grinding sense of the shortage of money, though the style was always kept up.

At last the mother said: "I will see if I can't make something." But she did not know where to begin. She racked her brains, and tried this thing and the other, but could not find anything successful. The failure made deep lines come into her face. Her children were growing up, they would have to go to school. There must be more money, there must be more money. The father, who was always very handsome and expensive in his tastes, seemed as if he never would be able to do anything worth doing. And the mother, who had a great belief in herself, did not succeed any better, and her tastes were just as expensive.

And so the house came to be haunted by the unspoken phrase: There must be more money! There must be more money! The children could hear it all the time, though nobody said it aloud. They heard it at Christmas, when the expensive and splendid toys filled the nursery. Behind the shining modern rocking-horse, behind the smart doll's-house, a voice would start whispering: "There must be more money! There must be more money!" And the children

would stop playing, to listen for a moment. They would look into each other's eyes, to see if they had all heard. And each one saw in the eyes of the other two that they too had heard. "There must be more money! There must be more money!"

It came whispering from the springs of the still-swaying rocking-horse, and even the horse, bending his wooden, champing head, heard it. The big doll, sitting so pink and smirking in her new pram, could hear it quite plainly, and seemed to be smirking all the more self-consciously because of it. The foolish puppy, too, that took the place of the teddy-bear, he was looking so extraordinarily foolish for no other reason but that he heard the secret whisper all over the house: "There must be more money!"

Yet nobody ever said it aloud. The whisper was everywhere, and therefore no one spoke it. Just as no one ever says: "We are breathing!" in spite of the fact that breath is coming and going all the time.

"Mother," said the boy Paul one day, "why don't we keep a car of our own? Why do we always use uncle's, or else a taxi?"

"Because we're the poor members of the family," said the mother.

"But why are we, mother?"

"Well—I suppose," she said slowly and bitterly, "it's because your father has no luck."

The boy was silent for some time.

"Is luck money, mother?" he asked, rather timidly.

"No, Paul. Not quite. It's what causes you to have money."

"Oh!" said Paul vaguely. "I thought when Uncle Oscar said filthy lucker, it meant money."

"Filthy lucre does mean money," said the mother. "But it's lucre, not luck."

"Oh!" said the boy. "Then what is luck, mother?"

"It's what causes you to have money. If you're lucky you have money. That's why it's better to be born lucky than rich. If you're rich, you may lose your money. But if you're lucky, you will always get more money."

"Oh! Will you? And is father not lucky?"

"Very unlucky, I should say," she said bitterly.

The boy watched her with unsure eyes.

"Why?" he asked.

"I don't know. Nobody ever knows why one person is lucky and another unlucky."

"Don't they? Nobody at all? Does nobody know?"

"Perhaps God. But He never tells."

"He ought to, then. And aren't you lucky either, mother?"

"I can't be, if I married an unlucky husband."

"But by yourself, aren't you?"

"I used to think I was, before I married. Now I think I am very unlucky indeed."

"Why?"

"Well—never mind! Perhaps I'm not really," she said.

The child looked at her, to see if she meant it. But he saw, by the lines of her mouth, that she was only trying to hide something from him.

"Well, anyhow," he said stoutly, "I'm a lucky person."

"Why?" said his mother, with a sudden laugh.

He stared at her. He didn't even know why he had said it.

"God told me," he asserted, brazening it out.

"I hope He did, dear!" she said, again with a laugh, but rather bitter.

"He did, mother!"

"Excellent!" said the mother, using one of her husband's exclamations.

The boy saw she did not believe him; or, rather, that she paid no attention to his assertion. This angered him somewhat, and made him want to compel her attention.

He went off by himself, vaguely, in a childish way, seeking for the clue to "luck." Absorbed, taking no heed of other people, he went about with a sort of stealth, seeking inwardly for luck. He wanted luck, he wanted it, he wanted it. When the two girls were playing dolls in the nursery, he would sit on his big rocking-horse, charging madly into space, with a frenzy that made the little girls peer at him uneasily. Wildly the horse careered, the waving dark hair of the boy tossed, his eyes had a strange glare in them. The little girls dared not speak to him.

When he had ridden to the end of his mad little journey, he climbed down and stood in front of his rocking-horse, staring fixedly into its lowered face. Its red mouth was slightly open, its big eye was wide and glassy-bright.

"Now!" he would silently command the snorting steed. "Now, take me to where there is luck! Now take me!"

And he would slash the horse on the neck with the little whip he had asked Uncle Oscar for. He knew the horse could take him to where there was luck, if only he forced it. So he would mount again, and start on his furious ride, hop-

ing at last to get there. He knew he could get there.

"You'll break your horse, Paul!" said the nurse.

"He's always riding like that! I wish he'd leave off!" said his elder sister Joan.

But he only glared down on them in silence. Nurse gave him up. She could make nothing of him. Anyhow he was growing beyond her.

One day his mother and his Uncle Oscar came in when he was on one of his furious rides. He did not speak to them.

"Halloo, you young jockey! Riding a winner?" said his uncle.

"Aren't you growing too big for a rocking-horse? You're not a very little boy any longer, you know," said his mother.

But Paul only gave a blue glare from his big, rather close-set eyes. He would speak to nobody when he was in full tilt. His mother watched him with an anxious expression on her face.

At last he suddenly stopped forcing his horse into the mechanical gallop, and slid down.

"Well, I got there!" he announced fiercely, his blue eyes still flaring, and his sturdy long legs straddling apart.

"Where did you get to?" asked his mother.

"Where I wanted to go," he flared back at her.

"That's right, son!" said Uncle Oscar. "Don't you stop till you get there. What's the horse's name?"

"He doesn't have a name," said the boy.

"Gets on without all right?" asked the uncle.

"Well, he has different names. He was called Sansovino last week."

"Sansovino, eh? Won the Ascot. How did you know his name?"

"He always talks about horse-races with Bassett," said Joan.

The uncle was delighted to find that his small nephew was posted with all the racing news. Bassett, the young gardener, who had been wounded in the left foot in the war and had got his present job through Oscar Cresswell, whose batman he had been, was a perfect blade of the "turf." He lived in the racing events, and the small boy lived with him.

Oscar Cresswell got it all from Bassett.

"Master Paul comes and asks me, so I can't do more than tell him, sir," said Bassett, his face terribly serious, as if he were speaking of religious matters.

"And does he ever put anything on a horse he fancies?"

"Well—I don't want to give him away—he's a young sport, a fine sport, sir. Would you mind asking him yourself? He sort of takes a pleasure in it, and perhaps he'd feel I was giving him away, sir, if you don't mind."

Bassett was serious as a church.

The uncle went back to his nephew, and took him off for a ride in the car.

"Say, Paul, old man, do you ever put anything on a horse?" the uncle asked.

The boy watched the handsome man closely.

"Why, do you think I oughtn't to?" he parried.

"Not a bit of it! I thought perhaps you might give me a tip for the Lincoln."

The car sped on into the country, going down to Uncle Oscar's place in Hampshire.

"Honour bright?" said the nephew.

"Honour bright, son!" said the uncle.

"Well, then, Daffodil."

"Daffodil! I doubt it, sonny. What about Mirza?"

"I only know the winner," said the boy. "That's Daffodil."

"Daffodil, eh?"

There was a pause. Daffodil was an obscure horse comparatively.

"Uncle!"

"Yes, son?"

"You won't let it go any further, will you? I promised Bassett."

"Bassett be damned, old man! What's he got to do with it?"

"We're partners. We've been partners from the first. Uncle, he lent me my first five shillings, which I lost. I promised him, honour bright, it was only between me and him; only you gave me that ten-shilling note I started winning with, so I thought you were lucky. You won't let it go any further, will you?"

The boy gazed at his uncle from those big, hot, blue eyes, set rather close together. The uncle stirred and laughed uneasily.

"Right you are, son! I'll keep your tip private. Daffodil, eh? How much are you putting on him?"

"All except twenty pounds," said the boy. "I keep that in reserve."

The uncle thought it a good joke.

"You keep twenty pounds in reserve, do you, you young romancer? What are you betting, then?"

"I'm betting three hundred," said the boy gravely. "But it's between you and me, Uncle Oscar! Honour bright?"

The uncle burst into a roar of laughter.

"It's between you and me all right, you young Nat Gould," he said, laughing. "But where's your three hundred?"

"Bassett keeps it for me. We're partners."

"You are, are you! And what is Bassett putting on Daffodil?"

"He won't go quite as high as I do, I expect. Perhaps he'll go a hundred and fifty."

"What, pennies?" laughed the uncle.

"Pounds," said the child, with a surprised look at his uncle. "Bassett keeps a bigger reserve than I do."

Between wonder and amusement Uncle Oscar was silent. He pursued the matter no further, but he determined to take his nephew with him to the Lincoln races.

"Now, son," he said, "I'm putting twenty on Mirza, and I'll put five for you on any horse you fancy. What's your pick?"

"Daffodil, uncle."

"No, not the fiver on Daffodil!"

"I should if it was my own fiver," said the child.

"Good! Good! Right you are! A fiver for me and a fiver for you on Daffodil."

The child had never been to a race-meeting before, and his eyes were blue fire. He pursed his mouth tight, and watched. A Frenchman just in front had put his money on Lancelot. Wild with excitement, he flayed his arms up and down, yelling "Lancelot! Lancelot!" in his French accent.

Daffodil came in first, Lancelot second, Mirza third. The child, flushed and with eyes blazing, was curiously serene. His uncle brought him four five-pound notes, four to one.

"What am I to do with these?" he cried, waving them before the boy's eyes.

"I suppose we'll talk to Bassett," said the boy. "I expect I have fifteen hundred now; and twenty in reserve; and this twenty."

His uncle studied him for some moments.

"Look here, son!" he said. "You're not serious about Bassett and that fifteen hundred, are you?"

"Yes, I am. But it's between you and me, uncle. Honour bright!"

"Honour bright all right, son! But I must talk to Bassett."

"If you'd like to be a partner, uncle, with Bassett and me, we could all be partners. Only, you'd have to promise, honour bright, uncle, not to let it go beyond us three. Bassett and I are lucky, and you must be lucky, because it was your ten shillings I started winning with. . . ."

Uncle Oscar took both Bassett and Paul into Richmond Park for an afternoon, and there they talked.

"It's like this, you see, sir," Bassett said.

"Master Paul would get me talking about racing events, spinning yarns, you know, sir. And he was always keen on knowing if I'd made or if I'd lost. It's about a year since, now, that I put five shillings on Blush of Dawn for him—and we lost. Then the luck turned, with that ten shillings he had from you, that we put on Singhalese. And since that time, it's been pretty steady, all things considering. What do you say, Master Paul?"

"We're all right when we're sure," said Paul. "It's when we're not quite sure that we go down."

"Oh, but we're careful then," said Bassett.

"But when are you sure?" smiled Uncle Oscar.

"It's Master Paul, sir," said Bassett, in a secret, religious voice. "It's as if he had it from heaven. Like Daffodil, now, for the Lincoln. That was as sure as eggs."

"Did you put anything on Daffodil?" asked Oscar Cresswell.

"Yes, sir. I made my bit."

"And my nephew?"

Bassett was obstinately silent, looking at Paul.

"I made twelve hundred, didn't I, Bassett? I told uncle I was putting three hundred on Daffodil."

"That's right," said Bassett, nodding.

"But where's the money?" asked the uncle.

"I keep it safe locked up, sir. Master Paul he can have it any minute he likes to ask for it."

"What, fifteen hundred pounds?"

"And twenty! And forty, that is, with the twenty he made on the course."

"It's amazing!" said the uncle.

"If Master Paul offers you to be partners, sir, I would, if I were you; if you'll excuse me," said Bassett.

Oscar Cresswell thought about it.

"I'll see the money," he said.

They drove home again, and sure enough, Bassett came round to the garden-house with fifteen hundred pounds in notes. The twenty pounds reserve was left with Joe Glee, in the Turf Commission deposit.

"You see, it's all right, uncle, when I'm sure! Then we go strong, for all we're worth. Don't we, Bassett?"

"We do that, Master Paul."

"And when are you sure?" said the uncle, laughing.

"Oh, well, sometimes I'm absolutely sure, like about Daffodil," said the boy; "and sometimes I have an idea; and sometimes I haven't even an idea, have I, Bassett? Then we're careful, because we mostly go down."

"You do, do you! And when you're sure, like about Daffodil, what makes you sure, sonny?"

"Oh, well, I don't know," said the boy uneasily. "I'm sure, you know, uncle; that's all."

"It's as if he had it from heaven, sir," Bassett reiterated.

"I should say so!" said the uncle.

But he became a partner. And when the Leger was coming on, Paul was "sure" about Lively Spark, which was a quite inconsiderable horse. The boy insisted on putting a thousand on the horse, Bassett went for five hundred, and Oscar Cresswell two hundred. Lively Spark came in first, and the betting had been ten to one against him. Paul had made ten thousand.

"You see," he said, "I was absolutely sure of him."

Even Oscar Cresswell had cleared two thousand.

"Look here, son," he said, "this sort of thing makes me nervous."

"It needn't, uncle! Perhaps I shan't be sure again for a long time."

"But what are you going to do with your money?" asked the uncle.

"Of course," said the boy, "I started it for mother. She said she had no luck, because father is unlucky, so I thought if I was lucky, it might stop whispering."

"What might stop whispering?"

"Our house. I hate our house for whispering."

"What does it whisper?"

"Why—why"—the boy fidgeted—"why, I don't know. But it's always short of money, you know, uncle."

"I know it, son, I know it."

"You know people send mother writs, don't you, uncle?"

"I'm afraid I do," said the uncle.

"And then the house whispers, like people laughing at you behind your back. It's awful, that is! I thought if I was lucky . . ."

"You might stop it," added the uncle.

The boy watched him with big blue eyes that had an uncanny cold fire in them, and he said never a word.

"Well, then!" said the uncle. "What are we doing?"

"I shouldn't like mother to know I was lucky," said the boy.

"Why not, son?"

"She'd stop me."

"I don't think she would."

"Oh!"—and the boy writhed in an odd way—"I don't want her to know, uncle."

"All right, son! We'll manage it without her knowing."

They managed it very easily. Paul, at the other's suggestion, handed over five thousand pounds to his uncle, who deposited it with the family lawyer, who was then to inform Paul's mother that a relative had put five thousand pounds into his hands, which sum was to be paid out a thousand pounds at a time, on the mother's birthday, for the next five years.

"So she'll have a birthday present of a thousand pounds for five successive years," said Uncle Oscar. "I hope it won't make it all the harder for her later."

Paul's mother had her birthday in November. The house had been "whispering" worse than ever lately, and, even in spite of his luck, Paul could not bear up against it. He was very anxious to see the effect of the birthday letter, telling his mother about the thousand pounds.

When there were no visitors, Paul now took his meals with his parents, as he was beyond the nursery control. His mother went into town nearly every day. She had discovered that she had an odd knack of sketching furs and dress materials, so she worked secretly in the studio of a friend who was the chief "artist" for the leading drapers. She drew the figures of ladies in furs and ladies in silk and sequins for the newspaper advertisements. This young woman artist earned several thousand pounds a year, but Paul's mother only made several hundreds, and she was again dissatisfied. She so wanted to be first in something, and she did not succeed, even in making sketches for drapery advertisements.

She was down to breakfast on the morning of her birthday. Paul watched her face as she read her letters. He knew the lawyer's letter. As his mother read it, her face hardened and became more expressionless. Then a cold, determined look came on her mouth. She hid the letter under the pile of others, and said not a word about it.

"Didn't you have anything nice in the post for your birthday, mother?" said Paul.

"Quite moderately nice," she said, her voice cold and absent.

She went away to town without saying more.

But in the afternoon Uncle Oscar appeared. He said Paul's mother had had a long interview with the lawyer, asking if the whole five thousand could be advanced at once, as she was in debt.

"What do you think, uncle?" said the boy.

"I leave it to you, son."

"Oh, let her have it, then! We can get some more with the other," said the boy.

"A bird in the hand is worth two in the bush, laddie!" said Uncle Oscar.

"But I'm sure to know for the Grand National; or the Lincolnshire; or else the Derby. I'm sure to know for one of them," said Paul.

So Uncle Oscar signed the agreement, and Paul's mother touched the whole five thousand. Then something very curious happened. The voices in the house suddenly went mad, like a chorus of frogs on a spring evening. There were certain new furnishings, and Paul had a tutor. He was really going to Eton, his father's school, in the following autumn. There were flowers in the winter, and a blossoming of the luxury Paul's mother had been used to. And yet the voices in the house, behind the sprays of mimosa and almond blossom, and from under the piles of iridescent cushions, simply trilled and screamed in a sort of ecstasy: "There must be more money! Oh-h-h, there must be more money. Oh, now, now-w! Now-w-w—there must be more money!—more than ever! More than ever!"

It frightened Paul terribly. He studied away at his Latin and Greek with his tutors. But his intense hours were spent with Bassett. The Grand National had gone by: he had not "known," and had lost a hundred pounds. Summer was at hand. He was in agony for the Lincoln. But even for the Lincoln he didn't "know" and he lost fifty pounds. He became wild-eyed and strange, as if something were going to explode in him.

"Let it alone, son! Don't you bother about it!" urged Uncle Oscar. But it was as if the boy couldn't really hear what his uncle was saying.

"I've got to know for the Derby! I've got to know for the Derby!" the child reiterated, his big blue eyes blazing with a sort of madness.

His mother noticed how overwrought he was.

"You'd better go to the seaside. Wouldn't you like to go now to the seaside, instead of waiting? I think you'd better," she said, looking down at him anxiously, her heart curiously heavy because of him.

But the child lifted his uncanny blue eyes.

"I couldn't possibly go before the Derby, mother!" he said. "I couldn't possibly!"

"Why not?" she said, her voice becoming heavy when she was opposed. "Why not? You can still go from the seaside to see the Derby with your Uncle Oscar, if that's what you wish. No need for you to wait here. Besides, I think you care too much about these races. It's a bad sign. My family has been a gambling family, and you won't know till you grow up how much damage it has done. But it has done damage. I shall have to send Bassett away, and ask Uncle Oscar not to talk racing to you, unless you promise to be reasonable about it; go away to the seaside and forget it. You're all nerves!"

"I'll do what you like, mother, so long as you don't send me away till after the Derby," the boy said.

"Send you away from where? Just from this house?"

"Yes," he said, gazing at her.

"Why, you curious child, what makes you care about this house so much, suddenly? I never knew you loved it."

He gazed at her without speaking. He had a secret within a secret, something he had not divulged, even to Bassett or to his Uncle Oscar.

But his mother, after standing undecided and a little bit sullen for some moments, said:

"Very well, then! Don't go to the seaside till after the Derby, if you don't wish it. But promise me you won't let your nerves go to pieces. Promise you won't think so much about horse-racing and events, as you call them!"

"Oh, no," said the boy casually. "I won't think much about them, mother. You needn't worry. I wouldn't worry, mother, if I were you."

"If you were me and I were you," said his mother, "I wonder what we should do!"

"But you know you needn't worry, mother, don't you?" the boy repeated.

"I should be awfully glad to know it," she said wearily.

"Oh, well, you can, you know. I mean, you ought to know you needn't worry," he insisted.

"Ought I? Then I'll see about it," she said.

Paul's secret of secrets was his wooden horse, that which had no name. Since he was emancipated from a nurse and a nursery-governess, he had had his rocking-horse removed to his own bedroom at the top of the house.

"Surely, you're too big for a rocking-horse!" his mother had remonstrated.

"Well, you see, mother, till I can have a real horse, I like to have some sort of animal about," had been his quaint answer.

"Do you feel he keeps you company?" she laughed.

"Oh, yes! He's very good, he always keeps me company, when I'm there," said Paul.

So the horse, rather shabby, stood in an arrested prance in the boy's bedroom.

The Derby was drawing near, and the boy grew more and more tense. He hardly heard what was spoken to him, he was very frail, and

his eyes were really uncanny. His mother had sudden seizures of uneasiness about him. Sometimes, for half-an-hour, she would feel a sudden anxiety about him that was almost anguish. She wanted to rush to him at once, and know he was safe.

Two nights before the Derby, she was at a big party in town, when one of her rushes of anxiety about her boy, her first-born, gripped her heart till she could hardly speak. She fought with the feeling, might and main, for she believed in common sense. But it was too strong. She had to leave the dance and go downstairs to telephone to the country. The children's nursery-governess was terribly surprised and startled at being rung up in the night.

"Are the children all right, Miss Wilmot?"

"Oh, yes, they are quite all right."

"Master Paul? Is he all right?"

"He went to bed as right as a trivet. Shall I run up and look at him?"

"No," said Paul's mother reluctantly. "No! don't trouble. It's all right. Don't sit up. We shall be home fairly soon." She did not want her son's privacy intruded upon.

"Very good," said the governess.

It was about one o'clock when Paul's mother and father drove up to their house. All was still. Paul's mother went to her room and slipped off her white fur cloak. She had told her maid not to wait up for her. She heard her husband downstairs, mixing a whisky-and-soda.

And then, because of the strange anxiety at her heart, she stole upstairs to her son's room. Noiselessly she went along the upper corridor. Was there a faint noise? What was it?

She stood, with arrested muscles, outside his door, listening. There was a strange, heavy, and yet not loud noise. Her heart stood still. It was a soundless noise, yet rushing and powerful. Something huge, in violent, hushed motion. What was it? What in God's name was it? She ought to know. She felt that she knew the noise. She knew what it was.

Yet she could not place it. She couldn't say what it was. And on and on it went, like a madness.

Softly, frozen with anxiety and fear, she turned the doorhandle.

The room was dark. Yet in the space near the window, she heard and saw something plunging to and fro. She gazed in fear and amazement.

Then suddenly she switched on the light, and saw her son, in his green pyjamas, madly surging on the rocking-horse. The blaze of light suddenly lit him up, as he urged the wooden horse, and lit her up, as she stood, blonde, in her dress of pale green and crystal, in the doorway.

"Paul!" she cried. "Whatever are you doing?"

"It's Malabar!" he screamed, in a powerful, strange voice. "It's Malabar."

His eyes blazed at her for one strange and senseless second, as he ceased urging his wooden horse. Then he fell with a crash to 10 the ground, and she, all her tormented motherhood flooding upon her, rushed to gather him up.

But he was unconscious, and unconscious he remained, with some brain-fever. He talked and tossed, and his mother sat stonily by his side.

"Malabar! It's Malabar! Bassett, Bassett, I know! It's Malabar!"

So the child cried, trying to get up and urge 20 the rocking-horse that gave him his inspiration.

"What does he mean by Malabar?" asked the heart-frozen mother.

"I don't know," said the father stonily.

"What does he mean by Malabar?" she asked her brother Oscar.

"It's one of the horses running for the Derby," was the answer.

And in spite of himself, Oscar Cresswell spoke to Bassett, and himself put a thousand 30 on Malabar: at fourteen to one.

The third day of the illness was critical: they were waiting for a change. The boy, with his rather long, curly hair, was tossing ceaselessly on the pillow. He neither slept nor regained consciousness, and his eyes were like blue stones. His mother sat, feeling her heart had gone, turned actually into a stone.

In the evening, Oscar Cresswell did not come, but Bassett sent a message, saying could 40 he come up for one moment, just one moment? Paul's mother was very angry at the intrusion, but on second thought she agreed. The boy was the same. Perhaps Bassett might bring him to consciousness.

The gardener, a shortish fellow with a little brown moustache, and sharp little brown eyes, tiptoed into the room, touched his imaginary cap to Paul's mother, and stole to the bedside, staring with glittering, smallish eyes, at the 50 tossing, dying child.

"Master Paul!" he whispered. "Master Paul! Malabar come in first all right, a clean win. I did as you told me. You've made over seventy thousand pounds, you have; you've got over eighty thousand. Malabar came in all right, Master Paul."

"Malabar! Malabar! Did I say Malabar, mother? Did I say Malabar? Do you think I'm lucky, mother? I knew Malabar, didn't I? Over eighty thousand pounds! I call that lucky, don't you, mother? Over eighty thousand pounds! I knew, didn't I know I knew? Malabar came in all right. If I ride my horse till I'm sure, then I tell you, Bassett, you can go as high as you like. Did you go for all you were worth, Bassett?"

"I went a thousand on it, Master Paul."

"I never told you, mother, that if I can ride my horse, and get there, then I'm absolutely sure—oh, absolutely! Mother, did I ever tell you? I am lucky."

"No, you never did," said the mother.

But the boy died in the night.

And even as he lay dead, his mother heard her brother's voice saying to her: "My God, Hester, you're eighty-odd thousand to the good and a poor devil of a son to the bad. But, poor devil, poor devil, he's best gone out of a life where he rides his rocking-horse to find a winner."

# A Winter's Tale [1]

Yesterday the fields were only grey with scattered snow,
And now the longest grass-leaves hardly emerge;
Yet her deep footsteps mark the snow, and go
On towards the pines at the hill's white verge.

I cannot see her, since the mist's pale scarf   5
Obscures the dark wood and the dull orange sky;
But she's waiting, I know, impatient and cold, half
Sobs struggling into her frosty sigh.

Why does she come so promptly, when she must know
She's only the nearer to the inevitable farewell?
The hill is steep, on the snow my steps are slow—   11
Why does she come, when she knows what I have to tell?

# Troth with the Dead

The moon is broken in twain, and half a moon
Beyond me lies on the low, still floor of the sky;

[1] This and the three following poems are printed in the order of writing, as Lawrence arranged them in *Collected Poems* (1929). All four were written between 1908 and 1917. These and "The English Are So Nice" are from *Collected Poems* by D. H. Lawrence, copyright 1929 by Jonathan Cape and Harrison Smith, Inc., 1957 by Frieda Lawrence Ravagli. Reprinted by permission of The Viking Press, Inc., New York.

The other half of the broken coin of troth
Is buried away in the dark, where the dead all
   lie.

They buried her half in the grave when they
   laid her away;     5
Pushed gently away and hidden in the thick of
   her hair
Where it gathered towards the plait, on that
   very last day;
And like a moon unshowing it must still shine
   there.

So half lies on the sky, for a general sign
Of the troth with the dead that we are pledged
   to keep;     10
Turning its broken edge to the dark, its shine
Ends like a broken love, that turns to the dark
   of sleep.

And half lies there in the dark where the dead
   all lie
Lost and yet still connected; and between the
   two
Strange beams must travel still, for I feel that I
Am lit beneath my heart with a half-moon,
   weird and blue.     16

## Reading a Letter

She sits on the recreation ground
   Under an oak whose yellow buds dot the
   pale blue sky.
The young grass twinkles in the wind, and the
   sound
   Of the wind in the knotted buds makes a
   canopy.

So sitting under the knotted canopy     5
   Of the wind, she is lifted and carried away
   as in a balloon
Across the insensible void, till she stoops to see
   The sandy desert beneath her, the dreary
   platoon.

She knows the waste all dry beneath her, in one
   place
   Stirring with earth-coloured life, ever turning
   and stirring.     10
But never the motion has a human face
   Nor sound, only intermittent machinery
   whirring.

And so again, on the recreation ground
   She alights a stranger, wondering, unused to
   the scene;
Suffering at sight of the children playing
   around,     15
   Hurt at the chalk-coloured tulips, and the
   evening-green.

## Song of a Man Who Has Come Through

Not I, not I, but the wind that blows through
   me!

A fine wind is blowing the new direction of
   Time.
If only I let it bear me, carry me, if only it
   carry me!
If only I am sensitive, subtle, oh, delicate, a
   winged gift!
If only, most lovely of all, I yield myself and
   am borrowed     5
By the fine, fine wind that takes its course
   through the chaos of the world
Like a fine, an exquisite chisel, a wedge-blade
   inserted;
If only I am keen and hard like the sheer tip
   of a wedge
Driven by invisible blows,
The rock will split, we shall come at the won-
   der, we shall find the Hesperides.     10

Oh, for the wonder that bubbles into my soul,
I would be a good fountain, a good well-head,
Would blur no whisper, spoil no expression.

What is the knocking?
What is the knocking at the door in the night?
It is somebody wants to do us harm.     16
No, no, it is the three strange angels.
Admit them, admit them.

## The English Are So Nice! [1]

The English are so nice
so awfully nice
they are the nicest people in the world.

And what's more, they're very nice about being
   nice
about your being nice as well!     5
If you're not nice they soon make you feel it.

American and French and Germans and so on
they're all very well
but they're not *really* nice, you know.
They're not nice in *our* sense of the word, are
   they now?     10

That's why one doesn't have to take them seriously.
We must be nice to them, of course,
of course, naturally.
But it doesn't really matter what you say to
   them,
they don't really understand     15
you can just say anything to them:
be nice, you know, just nice
but you must never take them seriously, they
   wouldn't understand,
just be nice, you know! oh, fairly nice,
not too nice of course, they take advantage     20
but nice enough, just nice enough
to let them feel they're not quite as nice as
   they might be.

[1] Discovered in a notebook dated 1928, and included in the posthumous *Last Poems* (1933).

# Katherine Mansfield

## 1888 - 1923

Kathleen Mansfield Beauchamp ("Katherine Mansfield") was born 14 October, 1888 at Wellington, New Zealand. Her father was Harold Beauchamp, a banker and industrialist. She received her early schooling at Karori, near Wellington, and was sent to London in 1903 to attend Queen's College. She became an excellent cellist, edited the college magazine, and formed a strong attachment for London.

At seventeen she returned to New Zealand, and at twenty secured permission from her family to return to England to develop her interests and talent in music and the arts. She lived a Bohemian life after a brief and unsatisfactory marriage; she poured her energy into writing, and after 1911 into her attachment for John Middleton Murry, whom she was unable to marry until 1918, when her divorce from her first husband was final.

In 1907 she began writing the sketches of German life and human experience which were to become In a German Pension (1911). In 1912 and 1913 she wrote stories and poems for John Middleton Murry's Rhythm and its successor The Blue Review, and wrote but did not at the time publish "Something Childish But Very Natural"; in 1915 she worked on a novel which apparently she did not finish, and published several stories in Signature, a new magazine—publishing venture of the D. H. Lawrences and the Murrys. In 1917 she wrote several pieces for The New Age, including "Pictures," and completed The Prelude—published by Virginia and Leonard Woolfs' Hogarth Press.

When Murry became editor of The Athenaeum in 1919, Katherine Mansfield contributed verse, a collaborative translation of The Diary of Anton Tchehov, and The Letters of Anton Tchehov, and many critical reviews. Meanwhile she continued to write stories, and her first collection for a major publisher, Bliss, appeared in December 1920. The Garden Party appeared in 1922. January 9, 1933, she died at age 34, near Fountainbleau, of tuberculosis.

Katherine Mansfield combined gamin, pixy, child-woman, with faithful and careful observer, sensitive and perceptive friend of humanity, sure and spontaneous literary artist in the spirit and manner of Chekhov, with an individual flavor and intensity added that is peculiarly her own.

The Short Stories of Katherine Mansfield (New York, 1937) includes all the complete stories and some fragments. J. Middleton Murry has edited the Journal of Katherine Mansfield (New York, 1954), The Letters of Katherine Mansfield (New York, 1929), Novels and Novelists (New York, 1930), The Scrapbook of Katherine Mansfield (New York, 1940), and Letters to John Middleton Murry, 1913–1922 (New York, 1951). The biographical and critical works are R. E. Mantz and J. Middleton Murry, The Life of Katherine Mansfield (London, 1933); Sylvia Berkman, Katherine Mansfield, a Critical Study (New Haven, 1951); and Antony Alpers, Katherine Mansfield (New York, 1953).

## Something Childish but Very Natural [1]

Whether he had forgotten what it felt like, or his head had really grown bigger since the summer before, Henry could not decide. But his straw hat hurt him: it pinched his forehead and started a dull ache in the two bones just over the temples. So he chose a corner seat in a third-class "smoker," took off his hat and put it in the rack with his large black cardboard portfolio and his Aunt B's Christmas-present gloves. The carriage smelt horribly of wet indiarubber and soot. There were ten minutes to spare before the train went, so Henry decided to go and have a look at the bookstall. Sunlight darted through the glass roof of the station in long beams of blue and gold; a little boy ran up and down carrying a tray of primroses; there was something about the people—about the women especially—something idle and yet eager. The most thrilling day of the year, the first real day of Spring had unclosed its warm delicious beauty even to London eyes. It had put a spangle in every colour and a new tone in every voice, and city folks walked as though they carried real live bodies under their clothes with real live hearts pumping the stiff blood through.

Henry was a great fellow for books. He did not read many nor did he possess above half-a-dozen. He looked at all in the Charing Cross Road during lunch-time and at any odd time in London; the quantity with which he was on nodding terms was amazing. By his clean neat handling of them and by his nice choice of phrase when discussing them with one or another bookseller you would have thought that he had taken his pap with a tome propped before his nurse's bosom. But you would have been quite wrong. That was only Henry's way with everything he touched or said. That afternoon it was an anthology of English poetry, and he turned over the pages until a title struck his eye—*Something Childish but very Natural!*

> Had I but two little wings,
> And were a little feathery bird,
> To you I'd fly, my dear,
> But thoughts like these are idle things,
> And I stay here.
>
> But in my sleep to you I fly,
> I'm always with you in my sleep,
> The world is all one's own,
> But then one wakes and where am I?
> All, all alone.
>
> Sleep stays not though a monarch bids,
> So I love to wake at break of day,
> For though my sleep be gone,
> Yet while 'tis dark one shuts one's lids,
> And so, dreams on.

He could not have done with the little poem. It was not the words so much as the whole air of it that charmed him! He might have written it lying in bed, very early in the morning, and watching the sun dance on the ceiling. "It is *still*, like that," thought Henry, "I am sure he wrote it when he was half-awake some time, for it's got a smile of a dream on it." He stared at the poem and then looked away and repeated it by heart, missed a word in the third

verse and looked again, and again until he became conscious of shouting and shuffling, and he looked up to see the train moving slowly.

"God's thunder!" Henry dashed forward. A man with a flag and a whistle had his hand on a door. He clutched Henry somehow . . . Henry was inside with the door slammed, in a carriage that wasn't a "smoker," that had not a trace of his straw hat or the black portfolio or his Aunt B's Christmas-present gloves. Instead, in the opposite corner, close against the wall, there sat a girl. Henry did not dare to look at her, but he felt certain she was staring at him. "She must think I'm mad," he thought, "dashing into a train without even a hat, and in the evening, too." He felt so funny. He didn't know how to sit or sprawl. He put his hands in his pockets and tried to appear quite indifferent and frown at a large photograph of Bolton Abbey. But feeling her eyes on him he gave her just the tiniest glance. Quick she looked away out of the window, and then Henry, careful of her slightest movement, went on looking. She sat pressed against the window, her cheek and shoulder half hidden by a long wave of marigold-coloured hair. One little hand in a grey cotton glove held a leather case on her lap with the initials E. M. on it. The other hand she had slipped through the window-strap, and Henry noticed a silver bangle on the wrist with a Swiss cow-bell and a silver shoe and a fish. She wore a green coat and a hat with a wreath round it. All this Henry saw while the title of the new poem persisted in his brain—*Something Childish but very Natural.* "I suppose she goes to some school in London," thought Henry. "She might be in an office. Oh, no, she is too young. Besides she'd have her hair up if she was. It isn't even down her back." He could not keep his eyes off that beautiful waving hair. " 'My eyes are like two drunken bees. . . .' Now, I wonder if I read that or made it up?"

That moment the girl turned round and, catching his glance, she blushed. She bent her head to hide the red colour that flew in her cheeks, and Henry, terribly embarrassed, blushed too. "I shall have to speak—have to—have to!" He started putting up his hand to raise the hat that wasn't there. He thought that funny; it gave him confidence.

"I'm—I'm most awfully sorry," he said, smiling at the girl's hat. "But I can't go on sitting in the same carriage with you and not explaining why I dashed in like that, without my hat even. I'm sure I gave you a fright, and just now I was staring at you—but that's only an awful fault of mine; I'm a terrible starer! If you'd like me to explain—how I got in here—not about the staring, of course,"—he gave a little laugh—"I will."

For a minute she said nothing, then in a low, shy voice—"It doesn't matter."

The train had flung behind the roofs and chimneys. They were swinging into the country, past little black woods and fading fields and pools of water shining under an apricot 10 evening sky. Henry's heart began to thump and beat to the beat of the train. He couldn't leave it like that. She sat so quiet, hidden in her fallen hair. He felt that it was absolutely necessary that she should look up and understand him—understand him at least. He leant forward and clasped his hands round his knees.

"You see I'd just put all my things—a portfolio—into a third-class 'smoker' and was having a look at the book-stall," he explained. 20

As he told the story she raised her head. He saw her grey eyes under the shadow of her hat and her eyebrows like two gold feathers. Her lips were faintly parted. Almost unconsciously he seemed to absorb the fact that she was wearing a bunch of primroses and that her throat was white—the shape of her face wonderfully delicate against all that burning hair. "How beautiful she is! How simply beautiful she is!" sang Henry's heart, and swelled with 30 the words, bigger and bigger and trembling like a marvellous bubble—so that he was afraid to breathe for fear of breaking it.

"I hope there was nothing valuable in the portfolio," said she, very grave.

"Oh, only some silly drawings that I was taking back from the office," answered Henry, airily. "And—I was rather glad to lose my hat. It had been hurting me all day."

"Yes," she said, "it's left a mark," and she 40 nearly smiled.

Why on earth should those words have made Henry feel so free suddenly and so happy and so madly excited? What was happening between them? They said nothing, but to Henry their silence was alive and warm. It covered him from his head to his feet in a trembling wave. Her marvellous words, "It's made a mark," had in some mysterious fashion established a bond between them. They could not 50 be utter strangers to each other if she spoke so simply and so naturally. And now she was really smiling. The smile danced in her eyes, crept over cheeks to her lips and stayed there. He leant back. The words flew from him.—"Isn't life wonderful!"

At that moment the train dashed into a tun-nel. He heard her voice raised against the noise. She leant forward.

"I don't think so. But then I've been a fatalist for a long time now"—a pause—"months."

They were shattering through the dark. "Why?" called Henry.

"Oh. . . ."

Then she shrugged, and smiled and shook her head, meaning she could not speak against the noise. He nodded and leant back. They came out of the tunnel into a sprinkle of lights and houses. He waited for her to explain. But she got up and buttoned her coat and put her hands to her hat, swaying a little. "I get out here," she said. That seemed quite impossible to Henry.

The train slowed down and the lights outside grew brighter. She moved towards his end of the carriage.

"Look here!" he stammered. "Shan't I see you again?" He got up, too, and leant against the rack with one hand. "I *must* see you again." The train was stopping.

She said breathlessly, "I come down from London every evening."

"You—you—you do—really?" His eagerness frightened her. He was quick to curb it. "Shall we or shall we not shake hands?" raced through his brain. One hand was on the doorhandle, the other held the little bag. The train stopped. Without another word or glance she was gone.

§

Then came Saturday—a half day at the office —and Sunday between. By Monday evening Henry was quite exhausted. He was at the station far too early, with a pack of silly thoughts at his heels as it were driving him up and down. "She didn't say she came by this train!" "And supposing I go up and she cuts me." "There may be somebody with her." "Why do you suppose she's ever thought of you again?" "What are you going to say if you do see her?" He even prayed "Lord if it be Thy will, let us meet."

But nothing helped. White smoke floated against the roof of the station—dissolved and came again in swaying wreaths. Of a sudden, as he watched it, so delicate and so silent, moving with such mysterious grace above the crowd and the scuffle, he grew calm. He felt very tired—he only wanted to sit down and shut his eyes—she was not coming—a forlorn relief breathed in the words. And then he saw her quite near to him walking towards the train with the same little leather case in her hand.

Henry waited. He knew, somehow, that she had seen him, but he did not move until she came close to him and said in her low, shy voice—"Did you get them again?"

"Oh, yes, thank you, I got them again," and with a funny half gesture he showed her the portfolio and the gloves. They walked side by side to the train and into an empty carriage. They sat down opposite to each other, smiling timidly but not speaking, while the train moved slowly, and slowly gathered speed and smoothness. Henry spoke first.

"It's so silly," he said, "not knowing your name." She put back a big piece of hair that had fallen on her shoulder, and he saw how her hand in the grey glove was shaking. Then he noticed that she was sitting very stiffly with her knees pressed together—and he was, too—both of them trying not to tremble so. She said, "My name is Edna."

"And mine is Henry."

In the pause they took possession of each other's names and turned them over and put them away, a shade less frightened after that.

"I want to ask you something else now," said Henry. He looked at Edna, his head a little on one side. "How old are you?"

"Over sixteen," she said, "and you?"

"I'm nearly eighteen. . . ."

"Isn't it hot?" she said suddenly, and pulled off her grey gloves and put her hands to her cheeks and kept them there. Their eyes were not frightened—they looked at each other with a sort of desperate calmness. If only their bodies would not tremble so stupidly! Still half hidden by her hair, Edna said:

"Have you ever been in love before?"

"No, never! Have you?"

"Oh, never in all my life." She shook her head. "I never even thought it possible."

His next words came in a rush. "Whatever have you been doing since last Friday evening? Whatever did you do all Saturday and all Sunday and to-day?"

But she did not answer—only shook her head and smiled and said, "No, you tell *me.*"

"I?" cried Henry—and then he found he couldn't tell her either. He couldn't climb back to those mountains of days, and he had to shake his head, too.

"But it's been agony," he said, smiling brilliantly—"agony." At that she took away her hands and started laughing, and Henry joined her. They laughed until they were tired.

"It's so—so extraordinary," she said. "So suddenly, you know, and I feel as if I'd known you for years."

"So do I . . . ." said Henry. "I believe it must be the Spring. I believe I've swallowed a butterfly—and it's fanning its wings just here." He put his hand on his heart.

"And the really extraordinary thing is," said Edna, "that I had made up my mind that I didn't care for—men at all. I mean all the girls at College—"

"Were you at College?"

She nodded. "A training college, learning to be a secretary." She sounded scornful.

"I'm in an office," said Henry. "An architect's office—such a funny little place up one hundred and thirty stairs. We ought to be building nests instead of houses, I always think."

"Do you like it?"

"No, of course I don't. I don't want to do anything, do you?"

"No, I hate it. . . . And," she said, "my mother is a Hungarian—I believe that makes me hate it even more."

That seemed to Henry quite natural. "It would," he said.

"Mother and I are exactly alike. I haven't a thing in common with my father; he's just . . . . a little man in the City—but mother has got wild blood in her and she's given it to me. She hates our life just as much as I do." She paused and frowned. "All the same, we don't get on a bit together—that's funny—isn't it? But I'm absolutely alone at home."

Henry was listening—in a way he was listening, but there was something else he wanted to ask her. He said, very shyly, "Would you—would you take off your hat?"

She looked startled. "Take off my hat?"

"Yes—it's your hair. I'd give anything to see your hair properly."

She protested. "It isn't really . . . ."

"Oh, it *is,*" cried Henry, and then, as she took off the hat and gave her head a little toss, "Oh, Edna! it's the loveliest thing in the world."

"Do you like it?" she said, smiling and very pleased. She pulled it round her shoulders like a cape of gold. "People generally laugh at it. It's such an absurd colour." But Henry would not believe that. She leaned her elbows on her knees and cupped her chin in her hands. "That's how I often sit when I'm angry and then I feel it burning me up. . . . Silly?"

"No, no, not a bit," said Henry. "I knew you did. It's your sort of weapon against all the dull horrid things."

"However did you know that? Yes, that's just it. But however did you know?"

"Just knew," smiled Henry. "My God!" he cried, "what fools people are! All the little pollies that you know and that I know. Just look at you and me. Here we are—that's all there is to be said. I know about you and you know about me—we've just found each other—quite simply—just by being natural. That's all life is—something childish and very natural. Isn't it?"

"Yes—yes," she said eagerly. "That's what I've always thought."

"It's people that make things so—silly. As long as you can keep away from them you're safe and you're happy."

"Oh, I've thought that for a long time."

"Then you're just like me," said Henry. The wonder of that was so great that he almost wanted to cry. Instead he said very solemnly: "I believe we're the only two people alive who think as we do. In fact, I'm sure of it. Nobody understands me. I feel as though I were living in a world of strange beings—do you?"

"Always."

"We'll be in that loathsome tunnel again in a minute," said Henry. "Edna! can I—just touch your hair?"

She drew back quickly. "Oh, no, please don't," and as they were going into the dark she moved a little away from him.

§

"Edna! I've bought the tickets. The man at the concert hall didn't seem at all surprised that I had the money. Meet me outside the gallery doors at three, and wear that cream blouse and the corals—will you? I love you. I don't like sending these letters to the shop. I always feel those people with 'Letters received' in their window keep a kettle in their back parlour that would steam open an elephant's ear of an envelope. But it really doesn't matter, does it, darling? Can you get away on Sunday? Pretend you are going to spend the day with one of the girls from the office, and let's meet at some little place and walk or find a field where we can watch the daisies uncurling. I do love you, Edna. But Sundays without you are simply impossible. Don't get run over before Saturday, and don't eat anything out of a tin or drink anything from a public fountain. That's all, darling."

"My dearest, yes, I'll be there on Saturday—and I've arranged about Sunday, too. That is one great blessing. I'm quite free at home. I have just come in from the garden. It's such a lovely evening. Oh, Henry, I could sit and cry, I love you so to-night. Silly—isn't it? I either feel so happy I can hardly stop laughing or else so sad I can hardly stop crying and both for the same reason. But we are so young to have found each other, aren't we? I am sending you a violet. It is quite warm. I wish you were here now, just for a minute even. Good-night, darling. I am Edna."

§

"Safe," said Edna, "safe! And excellent places, aren't they, Henry?"

She stood up to take off her coat and Henry made a movement to help her. "No—no—it's off." She tucked it under the seat. She sat down beside him. "Oh, Henry, what have you got there? Flowers?"

"Only two tiny little roses." He laid them in her lap.

"Did you get my letter all right?" asked Edna, unpinning the paper.

"Yes," he said, "and the violet is growing beautifully. You should see my room. I planted a little piece of it in every corner and one on my pillow and one in the pocket of my pyjama jacket."

She shook her hair at him. "Henry, give me the program."

"Here it is—you can read it with me. I'll hold it for you."

"No, let me have it."

"Well, then, I'll read it for you."

"No, you can have it after."

"Edna," he whispered.

"Oh, please don't," she pleaded. "Not here—the people."

Why did he want to touch her so much and why did she mind? Whenever he was with her he wanted to hold her hand or take her arm when they walked together, or lean against her—not hard—just lean lightly so that his shoulder should touch her shoulder—and she wouldn't even have that. All the time that he was away from her he was hungry, he craved the nearness of her. There seemed to be comfort and warmth breathing from Edna that he needed to keep him calm. Yes, that was it. He couldn't get calm with her because she wouldn't let him touch her. But she loved him. He knew that. Why did she feel so curiously about it? Every time he tried to or even asked for her hand she shrank back and looked at him with pleading frightened eyes as though he wanted to hurt her. They could say anything to each other. And there wasn't any question of their belonging to each other. And yet he couldn't touch her. Why, he couldn't even help her off with her coat. Her voice dropped into his thoughts.

"Henry!" He leaned to listen, setting his lips. "I want to explain something to you. I will—I will—I promise—after the concert."

"All right." He was still hurt.

"You're not sad, are you?" she said.

He shook his head.

"Yes, you are, Henry."

"No, really not." He looked at the roses lying in her hands.

"Well, are you happy?"

"Yes. Here comes the orchestra."

It was twilight when they came out of the hall. A blue net of light hung over the streets and houses, and pink clouds floated in a pale sky. As they walked away from the hall Henry felt they were very little and alone. For the first time since he had known Edna his heart was heavy.

"Henry!" She stopped suddenly and stared at him. "Henry, I'm not coming to the station with you. Don't—don't wait for me. Please, please leave me."

"My God!" cried Henry, and started, "what's the matter—Edna—darling—Edna, what have I done?"

"Oh, nothing—go away," and she turned and ran across the street into a square and leaned up against the square railings—and hid her face in her hands.

"Edna—Edna—my little love—you're crying. Edna, my baby girl!"

She leaned her arms along the railings and sobbed distractedly.

"Edna—stop—it's all my fault. I'm a fool— I'm a thundering idiot. I've spoiled your afternoon. I've tortured you with my idiotic mad bloody clumsiness. That's it. Isn't it, Edna? For God's sake."

"Oh," she sobbed, "I do hate hurting you so. Every time you ask me to let—let you hold my hand or—or kiss me I could kill myself for not doing it—for not letting you. I don't know why I don't even." She said wildly, "It's not that I'm frightened of you—it's not that—it's only a feeling, Henry, that I can't understand myself even. Give me your handkerchief, darling." He pulled it from his pocket. "All through the concert I've been haunted by this, and every time we meet I know it's bound to come up. Somehow I feel if once we did that—you know—held each other's hands and kissed it would be all changed—and I feel we wouldn't be free like we are—we'd be doing something secret. We wouldn't be children any

more . . . silly, isn't it? I'd feel awkward with you, Henry, and I'd feel shy, and I do so feel that just because you and I are you and I, we don't need that sort of thing." She turned and looked at him, pressing her hands to her cheeks in the way he knew so well, and behind her as in a dream he saw the sky and half a white moon and the trees of the square with their unbroken buds. He kept twisting, twisting up in his hands the concert program. "Henry! You do understand me—don't you?"

"Yes, I think I do. But you're not going to be frightened any more, are you?" He tried to smile. "We'll forget, Edna. I'll never mention it again. We'll bury the bogy in this square— now—you and I—won't we?"

"But," she said, searching his face—"will it make you love me less?"

"Oh, no," he said. "Nothing could—nothing on earth could do that."

§

London became their play-ground. On Saturday afternoons they explored. They found their own shops where they bought cigarettes and sweets for Edna—and their own tea-shop with their own table—their own streets—and one night when Edna was supposed to be at a lecture at the Polytechnic they found their own village. It was the name that made them go there. "There's white geese in that name," said Henry, telling it to Edna. "And a river and little low houses with old men sitting outside them—old sea captains with wooden legs winding up their watches, and there are little shops with lamps in the windows."

It was too late for them to see the geese or the old men, but the river was there and the houses and even the shops with lamps. In one a woman sat working a sewing-machine on the counter. They heard the whirring hum and they saw her big shadow filling the shop. "Too full for a single customer," said Henry. "It is a perfect place."

The houses were small and covered with creepers and ivy. Some of them had worn wooden steps leading up to the doors. You had to go down a little flight of steps to enter some of the others; and just across the road— to be seen from every window—was the river, with a walk beside it and some high poplar trees.

"This is the place for us to live in," said Henry. "There's a house to let, too. I wonder if it would wait if we asked it. I'm sure it would."

"Yes, I would like to live there," said Edna. They crossed the road and she leaned against the trunk of a tree and looked up at the empty house, with a dreamy smile.

"There is a little garden at the back, dear," said Henry, "a lawn with one tree on it and some daisy bushes round the wall. At night the stars shine in the tree like tiny candles. And inside there are two rooms downstairs and a big room with folding doors upstairs and above that an attic. And there are eight stairs to the kitchen—very dark, Edna. You are rather frightened of them, you know. 'Henry, dear, would you mind bringing the lamp? I just want to make sure that Euphemia has raked out the fire before we go to bed.' "

"Yes," said Edna. "Our bedroom is at the very top—that room with the two square windows. When it is quiet we can hear the river flowing and the sound of the poplar trees far, far away, rustling and flowing in our dreams, darling."

"You're not cold—are you?" he said suddenly.

"No—no, only happy."

"The room with the folding doors is yours." Henry laughed. "It's a mixture—it isn't a room at all. It's full of your toys and there's a big blue chair in it where you sit curled up in front of the fire with the flames in your curls— because though we're married you refuse to put your hair up and only tuck it inside your coat for the church service. And there's a rug on the floor for me to lie on, because I'm so lazy. Euphemia—that's our servant—only comes in the day. After she's gone we go down to the kitchen and sit on the table and eat an apple, or perhaps we make some tea, just for the sake of hearing the kettle sing. That's not joking. If you listen to a kettle right through it's like an early morning in Spring."

"Yes, I know," she said. "All the different kinds of birds."

A little cat came through the railings of the empty house and into the road. Edna called it and bent down and held out her hands— "Kitty! Kitty!" The little cat ran to her and rubbed against her knees.

"If we're going for a walk just take the cat and put it inside the front door," said Henry, still pretending. "I've got the key."

They walked across the road and Edna stood stroking the cat in her arms while Henry went up the steps and pretended to open the door.

He came down again quickly. "Let's go away at once. It's going to turn into a dream."

The night was dark and warm. They did not want to go home. "What I feel so certain of is," said Henry, "that we ought to be living there, now. We oughtn't to wait for things. What's age? You're as old as you'll ever be and so am I. You know," he said, "I have a feeling often and often that it's dangerous to wait for things—that if you wait for things they only go further and further away."

"But, Henry,—money! You see we haven't any money."

"Oh, well,—perhaps if I disguised myself as an old man we could get a job as caretakers in some large house—that would be rather fun. I'd make up a terrific history of the house if anyone came to look over it and you could dress up and be the ghost moaning and wringing your hands in the deserted picture gallery, to frighten them off. Don't you ever feel that money is more or less accidental—that if one really wants things it's either there or it doesn't matter?"

She did not answer that—she looked up at the sky and said, "Oh dear, I don't want to go home."

"Exactly—that's the whole trouble—and we oughtn't to go home. We ought to be going back to the house and find an odd saucer to give the cat the dregs of the milk-jug in. I'm not really laughing—I'm not even happy. I'm lonely for you, Edna—I would give anything to lie down and cry" . . . and he added limply, "with my head in your lap and your darling cheek in my hair."

"But, Henry," she said, coming closer, "you have faith, haven't you? I mean you are absolutely certain that we shall have a house like that and everything we want—aren't you?"

"Not enough—that's not enough. I want to be sitting on those very stairs and taking off these very boots this very minute. Don't you? Is faith enough for you?"

"If only we weren't so young . . ." she said miserably. "And yet," she sighed, "I'm sure I don't feel very young—I feel twenty at least."

§

Henry lay on his back in the little wood. When he moved the dead leaves rustled beneath him, and above his head the new leaves quivered like fountains of green water steeped in sunlight. Somewhere out of sight Edna was gathering primroses. He had been so full of dreams that morning that he could not keep pace with her delight in the flowers. "Yes, love, you go and come back for me. I'm too lazy." She had thrown off her hat and knelt beside him, and by and by her voice and her footsteps had grown fainter. Now the wood was silent except for the leaves, but he knew that she was not far away and he moved so that the tips of his fingers touched her pink jacket. Ever since waking he had felt so strangely that he was not really awake at all, but just dreaming. The time before, Edna was a dream and now he and she were dreaming together and somewhere in some dark place another dream waited for him. "No, that can't be true because I can't ever imagine the world without us. I feel that we two together mean something that's got to be there just as naturally as trees or birds or clouds." He tried to remember what it had felt like without Edna, but he could not get back to those days. They were hidden by her; Edna, with the marigold hair and strange, dreamy smile filled him up to the brim. He breathed her; he ate and drank her. He walked about with a shining ring of Edna keeping the world away or touching whatever it lighted on with its own beauty. "Long after you have stopped laughing," he told her, "I can hear your laugh running up and down my veins—and yet—are we a dream?" And suddenly he saw himself and Edna as two very small children walking through the streets, looking through windows, buying things and playing with them, talking to each other, smiling—he saw even their gestures and the way they stood, so often, quite still, face to face— and then he rolled over and pressed his face in the leaves—faint with longing. He wanted to kiss Edna, and to put his arms round her and press her to him and feel her cheek hot against his kiss and kiss her until he'd no breath left and so stifle the dream.

"No, I can't go on being hungry like this," said Henry, and jumped up and began to run in the direction she had gone. She had wandered a long way. Down in a green hollow he saw her kneeling, and when she saw him she waved and said—"Oh, Henry—such beauties! I've never seen such beauties. Come and look." By the time he had reached her he would have cut off his hand rather than spoil her happiness. How strange Edna was that day! All the time she talked to Henry her eyes laughed; they were sweet and mocking. Two little spots of colour like strawberries glowed on her cheeks and "I wish I could feel tired," she kept saying. "I want to walk over the whole world until I die. Henry—come along. Walk faster— Henry! If I start flying suddenly, you'll promise to catch hold of my feet, won't you? Otherwise I'll never come down." And "Oh," she

cried, "I am so happy. I'm so frightfully happy!" They came to a weird place, covered with heather. It was early afternoon and the sun streamed down upon the purple.

"Let's rest here a little," said Edna, and she waded into the heather and lay down. "Oh, Henry, it's so lovely. I can't see anything except the little bells and the sky."

Henry knelt down by her and took some primroses out of her basket and made a long chain to go round her throat. "I could almost fall asleep," said Edna. She crept over to his knees and lay hidden in her hair just beside him. "It's like being under the sea, isn't it, dearest, so sweet and so still?"

"Yes," said Henry, in a strange husky voice. "Now I'll make you one of violets." But Edna sat up. "Let's go in," she said.

They came back to the road and walked a long way. Edna said, "No, I couldn't walk over the world—I'm tired now." She trailed on the grass edge of the road. "You and I are tired, Henry! How much further is it?"

"I don't know—not very far," said Henry, peering into the distance. Then they walked in silence.

"Oh," she said at last, "it really is too far, Henry, I'm tired and I'm hungry. Carry my silly basket of primroses." He took them without looking at her.

At last they came to a village and a cottage with a notice "Teas Provided."

"This is the place," said Henry. "I've often been here. You sit on the little bench and I'll go and order the tea." She sat down on the bench, in the pretty garden all white and yellow with spring flowers. A woman came to the door and leaned against it watching them eat. Henry was very nice to her, but Edna did not say a word. "You haven't been here for a long spell," said the woman.

"No—the garden's looking wonderful."

"Fair," said she. "Is the young lady your sister?" Henry nodded Yes, and took some jam.

"There's a likeness," said the woman. She came down into the garden and picked a head of white jonquils and handed it to Edna. "I suppose you don't happen to know anyone who wants a cottage," said she. "My sister's taken ill and she left me hers. I want to let it."

"For a long time?" asked Henry, politely.

"Oh," said the woman vaguely, "that depends."

Said Henry, "Well—I might know of somebody—could we go and look at it?"

"Yes, it's just a step down the road, the little

one with the apple trees in front—I'll fetch you the key."

While she was away Henry turned to Edna and said, "Will you come?" She nodded.

They walked down the road and in through the gate and up the grassy path between the pink and white trees. It was a tiny place—two rooms downstairs and two rooms upstairs. Edna leaned out of the top window, and Henry stood at the doorway. "Do you like it?" he asked.

"Yes," she called, and then made a place for him at the window. "Come and look. It's so sweet."

He came and leant out of the window. Below them were the apple trees tossing in a faint wind that blew a long piece of Edna's hair across his eyes. They did not move. It was evening—the pale green sky was sprinkled with stars. "Look!" she said—"stars, Henry."

"There will be a moon in two T"s," said Henry.

She did not seem to move and yet she was leaning against Henry's shoulders; he put his arm round her—"Are all those trees down there—apple?" she asked in a shaky voice.

"No, darling," said Henry. "Some of them are full of angels and some of them are full of sugar almonds—but evening light is awfully deceptive." She sighed. "Henry—we mustn't stay here any longer."

He let her go and she stood up in the dusky room and touched her hair. "What has been the matter with you all day?" she said—and then did not wait for an answer but ran to him and put her arms round his neck, and pressed his head into the hollow of her shoulder. "Oh," she breathed, "I do love you. Hold me, Henry." He put his arms round her, and she leaned against him and looked into his eyes. "Hasn't it been terrible, all to-day?" said Edna. "I knew what was the matter and I've tried every way I could to tell you that I wanted you to kiss me—that I'd quite got over the feeling."

"You're perfect, perfect, perfect," said Henry.

§

"The thing is," said Henry, "how am I going to wait until evening?" He took his watch out of his pocket, went into the cottage and popped it into a china jar on the mantelpiece. He'd looked at it seven times in one hour, and now he couldn't remember what time it was. Well, he'd look once again. Half-past four. Her train arrived at seven. He'd have to start for

the station at half-past six. Two hours more to wait. He went through the cottage again—downstairs and upstairs. "It looks lovely," he said. He went into the garden and picked a round bunch of white pinks and put them in a vase on the little table by Edna's bed. "I don't believe this," thought Henry. "I don't believe this for a minute. It's too much. She'll be here in two hours and we'll walk home, and then I'll take that white jug off the kitchen table and go across to Mrs. Biddie's and get the milk, and then come back, and when I come back she'll have lighted the lamp in the kitchen and I'll look through the window and see her moving about in the pool of lamplight. And then we shall have supper, and after supper (Bags I washing up!) I shall put some wood on the fire and we'll sit on the hearthrug and watch it burning. There won't be a sound except the wood and perhaps the wind will creep round the house once. . . . And then we shall change our candles and she will go up first with her shadow on the wall beside her, and she will call out, Good-night, Henry—and I shall answer—Good-night, Edna. And then I shall dash upstairs and jump into bed and watch the tiny bar of light from her room brush my door, and the moment it disappears will shut my eyes and sleep until morning. Then we'll have all to-morrow and to-morrow and to-morrow night. Is she thinking all this, too? Edna, come quickly!

> *Had I two little wings,*
> *And were a little feathery bird,*
> *To you I'd fly, my dear—*

"No, no, dearest. . . . Because the waiting is a sort of Heaven, too, darling. If you can understand that. Did you ever know a cottage could stand on tip-toe. This one is doing it now."

He was downstairs and sat on the doorstep with his hands clasped round his knees. That night when they found the village—and Edna said, "Haven't you faith, Henry?" "I hadn't then. Now I have," he said, "I feel just like God."

He leaned his head against the lintel. He could hardly keep his eyes open, not that he was sleepy, but . . . for some reason . . . and a long time passed.

Henry thought he saw a big white moth flying down the road. It perched on the gate. No, it wasn't a moth. It was a little girl in a pinafore. What a nice little girl, and he smiled in his sleep, and she smiled, too, and turned in her toes as she walked. "But she can't be living here," thought Henry. "Because this is ours. Here she comes."

When she was quite close to him she took her hand from under her pinafore and gave him a telegram and smiled and went away. There's a funny present! thought Henry, staring at it. "Perhaps it's only a make-believe one, and it's got one of those snakes inside it that fly

up at you." He laughed gently in the dream and opened it very carefully. "It's just a folded paper." He took it out and spread it open.

The garden became full of shadows—they span a web of darkness over the cottage and the trees and Henry and the telegram. But Henry did not move.

# T. S. Eliot

## 1888-

Thomas Stearns Eliot was born at St. Louis, Missouri, 26 September, 1888. His grandfather, William Greenleaf Eliot, had come West from New England, founded a Unitarian church in St. Louis and served as its pastor; in 1893 he founded Washington University and became its chancellor. T. S. Eliot's father was a prominent businessman and for a time was vice-chancellor of Washington University.

In 1906 T. S. Eliot entered Harvard, where he came to know and admire professors Irving Babbitt and George Santayana. He edited The Harvard Advocate, and contributed nine poems to it besides the Harvard class ode for 1910. He graduated from Harvard in 1909 while yet twenty, took his M. A. in philosophy, spent a year at the Sorbonne and returned to Harvard for three more years of advanced study in philosophy, philology, and Sanskrit. In 1914 he studied in Germany on a summer fellowship, and in the fall moved on to Merton College, Oxford, for his last months of formal academic study. During the years 1909–1914 he had come to know as teachers Alain-Fournier, Bergson, Josiah Royce, and Bertrand Russell. He completed his doctoral dissertation (on the philosopher Bradley) after his marriage.

By the summer of 1915 he had determined that he would live in England permanently. He tried teaching, briefly at the High Wycombe Grammar School and for four terms at the Highgate School. From 1916 to 1925 he held a position in Lloyd's Bank; in 1925 he joined the publishing firm of Faber and Gwyer (now Faber and Faber), of which he is currently a director. He served as assistant editor of The Egoist before establishing The Criterion, which he edited from 1922 to 1939. In addition he had held important lectureships in England and America, including the post of Charles Eliot Norton Professor of Poetry at Harvard in 1932–33. In 1927 he was confirmed as a member of the Church of England and was made a British subject.

In 1909–10 Eliot wrote the first of his more important poems, "Portrait of a Lady." Two of the four "Preludes" were completed in the same period, and the other two in 1911. Eliot began writing "The Love Song of J. Alfred Prufrock" at Harvard in 1910, and finished it in Europe in 1911. These early poems show a complex blending of poetic influences with the intellectual individuality of Eliot; the French symbolists, particularly Jules Laforgue, suggested some aspects of form and approach, and there are in the content traces of Byron and Shakespeare, Andrew Marvell and Dostoevsky, in fact of Eliot's whole broad background in literature and philosophy.

Eliot first met Ezra Pound in 1914; Pound "discovered" him and persuaded Harriet Monroe to publish "Prufrock" in Poetry (1915). The widely-discussed influence of Pound on Eliot is shown in a number of lesser-known poems written during the war years, in the Sweeney poems ("Sweeney Among the Nightingales" was written in 1918), in "Gerontion" (1919) and in The Waste Land (1921). Pound's influence on The Waste Land was direct as well as indirect: he slashed Eliot's original version with such a vigorous editorial pencil that only about half of the poem is left. Again, however, it is a mistake to oversimplify the tracing of influences. Eliot's notes to The Waste Land cite scores of sources for form, style, and content. There are few poems in the language which make such omnivorous use of the author's learning.

The Waste Land caused much excitement on both sides of the Atlantic because of both its power and its obscurity, and it remains Eliot's best-known poem. It is probably safe to say that most persons who read it fail to see what Eliot meant to do, though to any reader many phrases make sense and have power, and there is a general effect of hopelessness and despair. Beneath the erudite imagery of The Waste Land and "The Hollow

*Men"* (1925), *there is elaborate complexity
of structure, irony of approach, and depth of
philosophic content.* The Waste Land *challenges complete interpretation; the critics do
not always agree.*

To the reader who stops with the poems before 1927, the Eliot negatives seem dominant.
With Ash Wednesday (1930), however, another Eliot begins to emerge, and we see that
he has been there all along. The mature Eliot
has learned from Dante and Dryden, and has
read with deep sympathy the mystic St. John
of the Cross. In Landscapes (1933–34) the
affirmative voice is stronger; the aridity of The
Waste Land seems part of another world from
that shown in these landscapes. From this
time on affirmatives are always mixed with
Eliot's negatives; sometimes, as in "Five-Finger
Exercises" (1933) and Old Possum's Book of
Practical Cats (1939), the light touch is the
dominant tone.

Four Quartets (1943) show Eliot in calm
mastery of poetic structure and philosophic
structure. The year before in his essay The
Music of Poetry he had said "There are possibilities for verse which bear some analogy to
the development of a theme by different groups
of instruments; there are possibilities of transitions in a poem comparable to the different
movements of a symphony or a quartet; there
are possibilities of contrapuntal arrangements
of subject-matter." Both sound and theme in
Four Quartets show that Eliot could successfully put his theory into practice.

Had Eliot written no non-dramatic poetry his
reputation could stand comfortably on his verse
plays. Murder in the Cathedral (1935) about
the martyrdom of St. Thomas à Becket, is the
best known and the least complex: it has perhaps the greatest unity of effect of any of Eliot's
works.

The Family Reunion (1939), The Cocktail
Party (1949), The Confidential Clerk (1953),
and The Elder Statesman (1959) are all verse
dramas of the contemporary scene. In each the
conversation is brilliant, and the interaction of
characters seems to occur on several levels.

As a scholar and essayist Eliot has explored
literature, religion, and culture; the range of his
thinking is shown in the list of his prose
works:* Ezra Pound: His Metric and Poetry
(1917), Andrew Marvell (1922), Homage to
Dryden (1924), Shakespeare and the Stoicism
of Seneca (1927), Dante (1929), Tradition
and Experiment in Present-Day Literature
(1929), Thoughts after Lambeth (1931), Selected Essays, 1917–1932 (1932), John Dry-

den (1932), Elizabethan Essays (1934), The
Idea of a Christian Society (1940), Notes
Towards the Definition of Culture (1949), On
Poetry and Poets (1957).

*Nearly all of Eliot's verse, including all the
dramas except* The Confidential Clerk *and* The
Elder Statesman, *appears in* The Complete
Poems and Plays (1952).

*Critical studies include T. McGreevy,
Thomas Stearns Eliot (London, 1931); A.
Oras, The Critical Ideas of T. S. Eliot (Lon-
don, 1932); H. R. Williamson, The Poetry of
T. S. Eliot (London, 1932); F. O. Matthies-
sen, The Achievement of T. S. Eliot (New
York, 1947); E. Drew, T. S. Eliot: The Design
of His Poetry (New York, 1949); George Wil-
liamson, A Reader's Guide to T. S. Eliot (New
York, 1953); and Grover Smith, T. S. Eliot's
Poetry and Plays (Chicago, 1956).*

# The Love Song of
# J. Alfred Prufrock [1]

*S'io credesse che mia risposta fosse
A persona che mai tornasse al mondo,
Questa fiamma staria senza piu scosse.
Ma perciocche giammai di questo fondo
Non torno vivo alcun, s'i'odo il vero,
Senza tema d'infamia ti rispondo.*

Let us go then, you and I,
When the evening is spread out against the sky
Like a patient etherised upon a table;
Let us go, through certain half-deserted streets,
The muttering retreats    5
Of restless nights in one-night cheap hotels
And sawdust restaurants with oyster-shells:
Streets that follow like a tedious argument
Of insidious intent
To lead you to an overwhelming question . . .
Oh, do not ask, "What is it?"    11
Let us go and make our visit

In the room the women come and go
Talking of Michelangelo.

The yellow fog that rubs its back upon the
    window-panes,    15
The yellow smoke that rubs its muzzle on the
    window-panes
Licked its tongue into the corners of the eve-
    ning,
Lingered upon the pools that stand in drains,
Let fall upon its back the soot that falls from
    chimneys,
Slipped by the terrace, made a sudden leap,    20

[1] This and the four following poems from *Collected Poems 1909–1935* by T. S. Eliot, copyright,
1936, by Harcourt, Brace and Company, Inc., and
used with their permission.

And seeing that it was a soft October night,
Curled once about the house, and fell asleep.

And indeed there will be time
For the yellow smoke that slides along the
     street,
Rubbing its back upon the window-panes; 25
There will be time, there will be time
To prepare a face to meet the faces that you
     meet;
There will be time to murder and create,
And time for all the works and days of hands
That lift and drop a question on your plate; 30
Time for you and time for me,
And time yet for a hundred indecisions,
And for a hundred visions and revisions,
Before the taking of a toast and tea.

In the room the women come and go 35
Talking of Michelangelo.

And indeed there will be time
To wonder, "Do I dare?" and, "Do I dare?"
Time to turn back and descend the stair,
With a bald spot in the middle of my hair— 40
(They will say: "How his hair is growing
     thin!")
My morning coat, my collar mounting firmly to
     the chin,
My necktie rich and modest, but asserted by a
     simple pin—
(They will say: "But how his arms and legs are
     thin!")
Do I dare 45
Disturb the universe?
In a minute there is time
For decisions and revisions which a minute will
     reverse.

For I have known them all already, known
     them all:—
Have known the evenings, mornings, after-
     noons, 50
I have measured out my life with coffee spoons;
I know the voices dying with a dying fall
Beneath the music from a farther room.
     So how should I presume?

And I have known the eyes already, known
     them all— 55
The eyes that fix you in a formulated phrase,
And when I am formulated, sprawling on a pin,
When I am pinned and wriggling on the wall,
Then how should I begin
To spit out all the butt-ends of my days and
     ways? 60
     And how should I presume?

And I have known the arms already, known
     them all—
Arms that are braceleted and white and bare
(But in the lamplight, downed with light
     brown hair!)

Is it perfume from a dress 65
That makes me so digress?
Arms that lie along a table, or wrap about a
     shawl.
     And should I then presume?
     And how should I begin?

          .     .     .     .     .     .

Shall I say, I have gone at dusk through nar-
     row streets 70
And watched the smoke that rises from the
     pipes
Of lonely men in shirt-sleeves, leaning out of
     windows?

I should have been a pair of ragged claws
Scuttling across the floors of silent seas.

          .     .     .     .     .     .

And the afternoon, the evening, sleeps so peace-
     fully! 75
Smoothed by long fingers,
Asleep . . . tired . . . or it malingers,
Stretched on the floor, here beside you and me.
Should I, after tea and cakes and ices,
Have the strength to force the moment to its
     crisis? 80
But though I have wept and fasted, wept and
     prayed,
Though I have seen my head (grown slightly
     bald) brought in upon a platter,
I am no prophet—and here's no great matter;
I have seen the moment of my greatness flicker,
And I have seen the eternal Footman hold my
     coat, and snicker, 85
And in short, I was afraid.

And would it have been worth it, after all,
After the cups, the marmalade, the tea,
Among the porcelain, among some talk of you
     and me,
Would it have been worth while, 90
To have bitten off the matter with a smile,
To have squeezed the universe into a ball
To roll it toward some overwhelming question,
To say: "I am Lazarus, come from the dead,
Come back to tell you all, I shall tell you all"—
If one, settling a pillow by her head, 96
     Should say: "That is not what I meant at all.
     That is not it, at all."

And would it have been worth it, after all,
Would it have been worth while, 100
After the sunsets and the dooryards and the
     sprinkled streets,
After the novels, after the teacups, after the
     skirts that trail along the floor—
And this, and so much more?—
It is impossible to say just what I mean!
But as if a magic lantern threw the nerves in
     patterns on a screen: 105
Would it have been worth while

If one, settling a pillow or throwing off a
    shawl,
And turning toward the window, should say:
    "That is not it at all,
    That is not what I meant, at all."   110

No! I am not Prince Hamlet, nor was meant to
    be;
Am an attendant lord, one that will do
To swell a progress, start a scene or two,
Advise the prince; no doubt, an easy tool,
Deferential, glad to be of use,   115
Politic, cautious, and meticulous;
Full of high sentence, but a bit obtuse;
At times, indeed, almost ridiculous—
Almost, at times, the Fool.

I grow old . . . I grow old . . .   120
I shall wear the bottoms of my trousers rolled.

Shall I part my hair behind? Do I dare to eat
    a peach?
I shall wear white flannel trousers, and walk
    upon the beach.
I have heard the mermaids singing, each to
    each.

I do not think that they will sing to me.   125

I have seen them riding seaward on the waves
Combing the white hair of the waves blown
    back
When the wind blows the water white and
    black.

We have lingered in the chambers of the sea
By sea-girls wreathed with seaweed red and
    brown   130
Till human voices wake us, and we drown.

## Animula

'Issues from the hand of God, the simple soul'
To a flat world of changing lights and noise,
To light, dark, dry or damp, chilly or warm;
Moving between the legs of tables and of
    chairs,
Rising or falling, grasping at kisses and toys, 5
Advancing boldly, sudden to take alarm,
Retreating to the corner of arm and knee,
Eager to be reassured, taking pleasure
In the fragrant brilliance of the Christmas
    tree,
Pleasure in the wind, the sunlight and the sea;
Studies the sunlit pattern on the floor   11
And running stags around a silver tray;
Confounds the actual and the fanciful,
Content with playing-cards and kings and
    queens,
What the fairies do and what the servants say.
The heavy burden of the growing soul   16
Perplexes and offends more, day by day;
Week by week, offends and perplexes more

With the imperatives of 'is and seems'
And may and may not, desire and control.   20
The pain of living and the drug of dreams
Curl up the small soul in the window seat
Behind the *Encyclopaedia Britannica.*
Issues from the hand of time the simple soul
Irresolute and selfish, misshapen, lame,   25
Unable to fare forward or retreat,
Fearing the warm reality, the offered good,
Denying the importunity of the blood,
Shadow of its own shadows, spectre in its own
    gloom,
Leaving disordered papers in a dusty room;   30
Living first in the silence after the viaticum.

Pray for Guiterriez, avid of speed and power,
For Boudin, blown to pieces,
For this one who made a great fortune,
And that one who went his own way.   35
Pray for Floret, by the boarhound slain be-
    tween the yew trees,
Pray for us now and at the hour of our birth.

## From *Ash Wednesday*

### III

At the first turning of the second stair
I turned and saw below
The same shape twisted on the banister
Under the vapour in the fetid air
Struggling with the devil of the stairs who
    wears   5
The deceitful face of hope and of despair.

At the second turning of the second stair
I left them twisting, turning below;
There were no more faces and the stair was
    dark,
Damp, jaggèd, like an old man's mouth drivel-
    ling, beyond repair,   10
Or the toothed gullet of an agèd shark.

At the first turning of the third stair
Was a slotted window bellied like the fig's fruit
And beyond the hawthorn blossom and a pas-
    ture scene   14
The broadbacked figure drest in blue and green
Enchanted the maytime with an antique flute.
Blown hair is sweet, brown hair over the mouth
    blown,
Lilac and brown hair;
Distraction, music of the flute, stops and steps
    of the mind over the third stair,
Fading, fading; strength beyond hope and
    despair   20
Climbing the third stair.

Lord, I am not worthy
Lord, I am not worthy

      but speak the word only.

## V

If the lost word is lost, if the spent word is
    spent     25
If the unheard, unspoken
Word is unspoken, unheard;
Still is the unspoken word, the Word unheard,
The Word without a word, the Word within
The world and for the world;     30
And the light shone in darkness and
Against the Word the unstilled world still
    whirled
About the centre of the silent Word.

O my people, what have I done unto thee.

Where shall the word be found, where will the
    word     35
Resound? Not here, there is not enough silence
Not on the sea or on the islands, not
On the mainland, in the desert or the rain land,
For those who walk in darkness
Both in the day time and in the night time  40
The right time and the right place are not here
No place of grace for those who avoid the face
No time to rejoice for those who walk among
    noise and deny the voice

Will the veiled sister pray for
Those who walk in darkness, who chose thee
    and oppose thee,     45
Those who are torn on the horn between sea-
    son and season, time and time, between
Hour and hour, word and word, power and
    power, those who wait
In darkness? Will the veiled sister pray
For children at the gate
Who will not go away and cannot pray:   50
Pray for those who chose and oppose

O my people, what have I done unto thee.

Will the veiled sister between the slender
Yew trees pray for those who offend her
And are terrified and cannot surrender   55
And affirm before the world and deny between
    the rocks
In the last desert between the last blue rocks
The desert in the garden the garden in the
    desert
Of drouth, spitting from the mouth the with-
    ered apple-seed.

O my people.     60

## VI

Although I do not hope to turn again
Although I do not hope
Although I do not hope to turn

Wavering between the profit and the loss
In this brief transit where the dreams cross  65

The dreamcrossed twilight between birth and
    dying
(Bless me father) though I do not wish to
    wish these things
From the wide window towards the granite
    shore
The white sails still fly seaward, seaward flying
Unbroken wings     70

And the lost heart stiffens and rejoices
In the lost lilac and the lost sea voices
And the weak spirit quickens to rebel
For the bent golden-rod and the lost sea smell
Quickens to recover     75
The cry of quail and the whirling plover
And the blind eye creates
The empty forms between the ivory gates
And smell renews the salt savour of the sandy
    earth

This is the time of tension between dying and
    birth     80
The place of solitude where three dreams cross
Between blue rocks
But when the voices shaken from the yew-tree
    drift away
Let the other yew be shaken and reply.

Blessèd sister, holy mother, spirit of the foun-
    tain, spirit of the garden,     85
Suffer us not to mock ourselves with falsehood
Teach us to care and not to care
Teach us to sit still
Even among these rocks,
Our peace in His will     90
And even among these rocks
Sister, mother
And spirit of the river, spirit of the sea,
Suffer me not to be separated

And let my cry come unto Thee.     95

# Burnt Norton [1]

τοῦ λόγου δ'ἐόντος ξυνοῦ ζώουσιν οἱ πολλοὶ ὡς ἰδίαν
ἔχοντες φρόνησιν [Although reason is a common possession, most men live thinking that they have intelligence peculiarly their own].

                        I. p. 77. Fr. 2.

ὁδὸς ἄνω κάτω μία καὶ ὡυτή [The journey up and down
is one and the same].

                     I. p. 89. Fr. 60.

Diels: *Die Fragmente der Vorsokratiker* (Hera-
kleitos).

### I

Time present and time past
Are both perhaps present in time future,
And time future contained in time past.
If all time is eternally present

[1] From *Four Quartets*, copyright 1943 by T. S.
Eliot. Reprinted by permission of Harcourt, Brace
and Company, Inc.

All time is unredeemable.                                    5
What might have been is an abstraction
Remaining a perpetual possibility
Only in a world of speculation.
What might have been and what has been
Point to one end, which is always present.   10
Footfalls echo in the memory
Down the passage which we did not take
Towards the door we never opened
Into the rose-garden. My words echo
Thus, in your mind.                          15
                        But to what purpose
Disturbing the dust on a bowl of rose-leaves
I do not know.
                        Other echoes
Inhabit the garden. Shall we follow?         20
Quick, said the bird, find them, find them,
Round the corner. Through the first gate,
Into our first world, shall we follow
The deception of the thrush? Into our first
world.
There they were, dignified, invisible,       25
Moving without pressure, over the dead leaves,
In the autumn heat, through the vibrant air,
And the bird called, in response to
The unheard music hidden in the shrubbery,
And the unseen eyebeam crossed, for the roses
Had the look of flowers that are looked at.   31
There they were as our guests, accepted and ac-
    cepting.
So we moved, and they, in a formal pattern,
Along the empty alley, into the box circle,
To look down into the drained pool.           35
Dry the pool, dry concrete, brown edged,
And the pool was filled with water out of sun-
    light,
And the lotos rose, quietly, quietly,
The surface glittered out of heart of light,  39
And they were behind us, reflected in the pool.
Then a cloud passed, and the pool was empty.
Go, said the bird, for the leaves were full of
    children,
Hidden excitedly, containing laughter.
Go, go, go, said the bird: human kind
Cannot bear very much reality.                45
Time past and time future
What might have been and what has been
Point to one end, which is always present.

                        II

Garlic and sapphires in the mud
Clot the bedded axle-tree.                     50
The trilling wire in the blood
Sings below inveterate scars
And reconciles forgotten wars.
The dance along the artery
The circulation of the lymph                   55
Are figured in the drift of stars
Ascend to summer in the tree
We move above the moving tree
In light upon the figured leaf
And hear upon the sodden floor                 60

Below, the boarhound and the boar
Pursue their pattern as before
But reconciled among the stars.

At the still point of the turning world. Neither
    flesh nor fleshless;
Neither from nor towards; at the still point,
    there the dance is,                        65
But neither arrest nor movement. And do not
    call it fixity,
Where past and future are gathered. Neither
    movement from nor towards,
Neither ascent nor decline. Except for the
    point, the still point,
There would be no dance, and there is only the
    dance.
I can only say, *there* we have been: but I can-
    not say where.                             70
And I cannot say, how long, for that is to place
    it in time.

The inner freedom from the practical desire,
The release from action and suffering, release
    from the inner
And the outer compulsion, yet surrounded
By a grace of sense, a white light still and mov-
    ing,                                       75
*Erhebung* without motion, concentration
Without elimination, both a new world
And the old made explicit, understood
In the completion of its partial ecstasy,
The resolution of its partial horror.          80
Yet the enchainment of past and future
Woven in the weakness of the changing body,
Protects mankind from heaven and damnation
Which flesh cannot endure.
                        Time past and time future
Allow but a little consciousness.              86
To be conscious is not to be in time
But only in time can the moment in the rose-
    garden,
The moment in the arbour where the rain beat,
The moment in the draughty church at smoke-
    fall                                       90
Be remembered; involved with past and future.
Only through time time is conquered.

                        III

Here is a place of disaffection
Time before and time after
In a dim light: neither daylight               95
Investing form with lucid stillness
Turning shadow into transient beauty
With slow rotation suggesting permanence
Nor darkness to purify the soul
Emptying the sensual with deprivation          100
Cleansing affection from the temporal.
Neither plenitude nor vacancy. Only a flicker
Over the strained time-ridden faces
Distracted from distraction by distraction
Filled with fancies and empty of meaning       105
Tumid apathy with no concentration

Men and bits of paper, whirled by the cold
  wind
That blows before and after time,
Wind in and out of unwholesome lungs
Time before and time after.          110
Eructation of unhealthy souls
Into the faded air, the torpid
Driven on the wind that sweeps the gloomy
  hills of London,
Hampstead and Clerkenwell, Campden and
  Putney,
Highgate, Primrose and Ludgate. Not here 115
Not here the darkness, in this twittering world.

Descend lower, descend only
Into the world of perpetual solitude,
World not world, but that which is not world,
Internal darkness, deprivation          120
And destitution of all property,
Desiccation of the world of sense,
Evacuation of the world of fancy,
Inoperancy of the world of spirit;
This is the one way, and the other          125
Is the same, not in movement
But abstention from movement; while the
  world moves
In appetency, on its metalled ways
Of time past and time future.

### IV

Time and the bell have buried the day,          130
The black cloud carries the sun away.
Will the sunflower turn to us, will the clema-
  tis
Stray down, bend to us; tendril and spray
Clutch and cling?
Chill          135
Fingers of yew be curled
Down on us? After the kingfisher's wing
Has answered light to light, and is silent, the
  light is still
At the still point of the turning world.

### V

Words move, music moves          140
Only in time; but that which is only living
Can only die. Words, after speech, reach
Into the silence. Only by the form, the pattern,
Can words or music reach
The stillness, as a Chinese jar still          145
Moves perpetually in its stillness.
Not the stillness of the violin, while the note
  lasts,
Not that only, but the co-existence,
Or say that the end precedes the beginning,
And the end and the beginning were always
  there          150
Before the beginning and after the end.
And all is always now. Words strain,
Crack and sometimes break, under the burden,
Under the tension, slip, slide, perish,

Decay with imprecision, will not stay in place,
Will not stay still. Shrieking voices          156
Scolding, mocking, or merely chattering,
Always assail them. The Word in the desert
Is most attacked by voices of temptation,
The crying shadow in the funeral dance,          160
The loud lament of the disconsolate chimera.

The detail of the pattern is movement,
As in the figure of the ten stairs.
Desire itself is movement
Not in itself desirable;          165
Love is itself unmoving,
Only the cause and end of movement,
Timeless, and undesiring
Except in the aspect of time
Caught in the form of limitation          170
Between un-being and being.
Sudden in a shaft of sunlight
Even while the dust moves
There rises the hidden laughter
Of children in the foliage          175
Quick now, here, now, always—
Ridiculous the waste sad time
Stretching before and after.

# Murder in the Cathedral [1]

This play was written for production (in an
abbreviated form) at the Canterbury Festival,
June 1935. For help in its construction I am
much indebted to Mr. E. Martin Browne, the
producer, and to Mr. Rupert Doone; and for
incidental criticisms, to Mr. F. V. Morley, and
Mr. John Hayward.
*April 1935*

In the second edition a chorus was substituted for the introits which, in the first edition,
constituted the opening of Part II. To this third
edition the introits have been added as an appendix, and may be used instead of that chorus
in productions of the play.
At the suggestion of Mr. E. Martin Browne,
I have in Part II reassigned most of the lines
formerly attributed to the Fourth Knight.
When, as was originally intended, the parts of
the Tempters are doubled with those of the
Knights, the advantage of these alterations
should be obvious.
*June 1937*

In this fourth edition certain further rear-
rangements and deletions have been made,
which have been found advisable by experiment in the course of production.
*March 1938*          **T. S. E.**

[1] Copyright, 1935, by Harcourt, Brace and Company, Inc., and used with their permission.

## PART I

### Characters

A Chorus of Women of Canterbury
Three Priests of the Cathedral
A Messenger
Archbishop Thomas Becket
Four Tempters
Attendants

*The Scene is the Archbishop's Hall,
on December 2nd, 1170*

#### Chorus

Here let us stand, close by the cathedral. Here
    let us wait.
Are we drawn by danger? Is it the knowledge
    of safety, that draws our feet
Towards the cathedral? What danger can be
For us, the poor, the poor women of Canter-
    bury? What tribulation
With which we are not already familiar? There
    is no danger     5
For us, and there is no safety in the cathedral.
    Some presage of an act
Which our eyes are compelled to witness, has
    forced our feet
Towards the cathedral. We are forced to bear
    witness.

Since golden October declined into sombre
    November
And the apples were gathered and stored, and
    the land became brown sharp points of
    death in a waste of water and mud,   10
The New Year waits, breathes, waits, whispers
    in darkness.
While the labourer kicks off a muddy boot and
    stretches his hand to the fire,
The New Year waits, destiny waits for the
    coming.
Who has stretched out his hand to the fire and
    remembered the Saints at All Hallows,
Remembered the martyrs and saints who wait?
    And who shall     15
Stretch out his hand to the fire, and deny his
    master? Who shall be warm
By the fire, and deny his master?

Seven years and the summer is over,
Seven years since the Archbishop left us,
He who was always kind to his people.     20
But it would not be well if he should return.
King rules or barons rule;
We have suffered various oppression,
But mostly we are left to our own devices,
And we are content if we are left alone.     25
We try to keep our households in order;
The merchant, shy and cautious, tries to
    compile a little fortune,
And the labourer bends to his piece of earth,
    earth-colour, his own colour,
Preferring to pass unobserved.

Now I fear disturbance of the quiet seasons:   30
Winter shall come bringing death from the
    sea,
Ruinous spring shall beat at our doors,
Root and shoot shall eat our eyes and our ears,
Disastrous summer burn up the beds of our
    streams
And the poor shall wait for another decaying
    October.     35
Why should the summer bring consolation
For autumn fires and winter fogs?
What shall we do in the heat of summer
But wait in barren orchards for another
    October?
Some malady is coming upon us. We wait, we
    wait,     40
And the saints and martyrs wait, for those who
    shall be martyrs and saints.
Destiny waits in the hand of God, shaping the
    still unshapen:
I have seen these things in a shaft of sunlight.
Destiny waits in the hand of God, not in the
    hands of statesmen
Who do, some well, some ill, planning and
    guessing,     45
Having their aims which turn in their hands
    in the pattern of time.
Come, happy December, who shall observe
    you, who shall preserve you?
Shall the Son of Man be born again in the
    litter of scorn?
For us, the poor, there is no action,
But only to wait and to witness.     50
[*Enter* Priests.]

#### First Priest

Seven years and the summer is over.
Seven years since the Archbishop left us.

#### Second Priest

What does the Archbishop do, and our Sover-
    eign Lord the Pope
With the stubborn King and the French King
In ceaseless intrigue, combinations,     55
In conference, meetings accepted, meetings
    refused,
Meetings unended or endless
At one place or another in France?

#### Third Priest

I see nothing quite conclusive in the art of
    temporal government,
But violence, duplicity and frequent malversa-
    tion.     60
King rules or barons rule:
The strong man strongly and the weak man by
    caprice.
They have but one law, to seize the power and
    keep it,
And the steadfast can manipulate the greed
    and lust of others,
The feeble is devoured by his own.     65

FIRST PRIEST

Shall these things not end
Until the poor at the gate
Have forgotten their friend, their Father in
    God, have forgotten
That they had a friend?
[*Enter* MESSENGER.]

MESSENGER

Servants of God, and watchers of the temple, 70
I am here to inform you, without circumlocu-
    tion:
The Archbishop is in England, and is close
    outside the city.
I was sent before in haste
To give you notice of his coming, as much as
    was possible,
That you may prepare to meet him.      75

FIRST PRIEST

What, is the exile ended, is our Lord Arch-
    bishop
Reunited with the King? What reconciliation
Of two proud men?

THIRD PRIEST
                What peace can be found
To grow between the hammer and the anvil?

SECOND PRIEST
                            Tell us,
Are the old disputes at an end, is the wall of
    pride cast down      80
That divided them? Is it peace or war?

FIRST PRIEST
                            Does he come
In full assurance, or only secure
In the power of Rome, the spiritual rule,
The assurance of right, and the love of the
    people?

MESSENGER

You are right to express a certain incredulity.
He comes in pride and sorrow, affirming all his
    claims,      86
Assured, beyond doubt, of the devotion of the
    people,
Who receive him with scenes of frenzied
    enthusiasm,
Lining the road and throwing down their capes,
Strewing the way with leaves and late flowers
    of the season.      90
The streets of the city will be packed to suf-
    focation,
And I think that his horse will be deprived of
    its tail,
A single hair of which becomes a precious relic.
He is at one with the Pope, and with the King
    of France,
Who indeed would have liked to detain him in
    his kingdom:      95
But as for our King, that is another matter.

FIRST PRIEST

But again, is it war or peace?

MESSENGER
            Peace, but not the kiss of peace.
A patched up affair, if you ask my opinion.
And if you ask me, I think the Lord Archbishop
Is not the man to cherish any illusions,      100
Or yet to diminish the least of his pretensions.
If you ask my opinion, I think that this peace
Is nothing like an end, or like a beginning.
It is common knowledge that when the Arch-
    bishop
Parted from the King, he said to the King, 105
My Lord, he said, I leave you as a man
Whom in this life I shall not see again.
I have this, I assure you, on the highest
    authority;
There are several opinions as to what he meant,
But no one considers it a happy prognostic. 110
                            [*Exit.*]

FIRST PRIEST

I fear for the Archbishop, I fear for the Church,
I know that the pride bred of sudden prosperity
Was but confirmed by bitter adversity.
I saw him as Chancellor, flattered by the King,
Liked or feared by courtiers, in their overbear-
    ing fashion,      115
Despised and despising, always isolated,
Never one among them, always insecure;
His pride always feeding upon his own virtues,
Pride drawing sustenance from impartiality,
Pride drawing sustenance from generosity, 120
Loathing power given by temporal devolution,
Wishing subjection to God alone.
Had the King been greater, or had he been
    weaker
Things had perhaps been different for Thomas.

SECOND PRIEST

Yet our lord is returned. Our lord has come
    back to his own again.      125
We have had enough of waiting, from Decem-
    ber to dismal December.
The Archbishop shall be at our head, dispelling
    dismay and doubt.
He will tell us what we are to do, he will give
    us our orders, instruct us.
Our Lord is at one with the Pope, and also the
    King of France.
We can lean on a rock, we can feel a firm foot-
    hold      130
Against the perpetual wash of tides of balance
    of forces of barons and landholders.
The rock of God is beneath our feet. Let us
    meet the Archbishop with cordial thanks-
    giving:
Our lord, our Archbishop returns. And when
    the Archbishop returns
Our doubts are dispelled. Let us therefore
    rejoice,

I say rejoice, and show a glad face for his wel-
  come.                                            135
I am the Archbishop's man. Let us give the
  Archbishop welcome!

#### Third Priest

For good or ill, let the wheel turn.
The wheel has been still, these seven years, and
  no good.
For ill or good, let the wheel turn.
For who knows the end of good or evil?          140
Until the grinders cease
And the door shall be shut in the street,
And all the daughters of music shall be brought
  low.

#### Chorus

Here is no continuing city, here is no abiding
  stay.
Ill the wind, ill the time, uncertain the profit,
  certain the danger.                            145
O late late late, late is the time, late too late,
  and rotten the year;
Evil the wind, and bitter the sea, and grey the
  sky, grey grey grey.
O Thomas, return, Archbishop; return, return
  to France.
Return. Quickly. Quietly. Leave us to perish
  in quiet.
You come with applause, you come with rejoicing, but you come bringing death into
  Canterbury:                                     150
A doom on the house, a doom on yourself, a
  doom on the world.

We do not wish anything to happen.
Seven years we have lived quietly,
Succeeded in avoiding notice,
Living and partly living.                        155
There have been oppression and luxury,
There have been poverty and licence,
There has been minor injustice.
Yet we have gone on living,
Living and partly living.                        160
Sometimes the corn has failed us,
Sometimes the harvest is good,
One year is a year of rain,
Another a year of dryness,
One year the apples are abundant,                165
Another year the plums are lacking.
Yet we have gone on living,
Living and partly living.
We have kept the feasts, heard the masses,
We have brewed beer and cyder,                   170
Gathered wood against the winter,
Talked at the corner of the fire,
Talked at the corners of streets,
Talked not always in whispers,
Living and partly living.                        175
We have seen births, deaths and marriages,
We have had various scandals,
We have been afflicted with taxes,
We have had laughter and gossip,

Several girls have disappeared                   180
Unaccountably, and some not able to.
We have all had our private terrors,
Our particular shadows, our secret fears.
But now a great fear is upon us, a fear not of
  one but of many,
A fear like birth and death, when we see birth
  and death alone                                185
In a void apart. We
Are afraid in a fear which we cannot know,
  which we cannot face, which none under-
  stands,
And our hearts are torn from us, our brains
  unskinned like the layers of an onion, our
  selves are lost lost
In a final fear which none understands. O
  Thomas Archbishop,
O Thomas our Lord, leave us and leave us be,
  in our humble and tarnished frame of
  existence, leave us; do not ask us           190
To stand to the doom on the house, the doom
  on the Archbishop, the doom on the
  world.
Archbishop, secure and assured of your fate,
  unaffrayed among the shades, do you
  realise what you ask, do you realise what
  it means
To the small folk drawn into the pattern of
  fate, the small folk who live among small
  things,
The strain on the brain of the small folk who
  stand to the doom of the house, the doom
  of their lord, the doom of the world?
O Thomas Archbishop, leave us, leave us, leave
  sullen Dover, and set sail for France.
  Thomas our Archbishop still our Archbishop even in France. Thomas Archbishop, set the white sail between the grey
  sky and the bitter sea, leave us, leave us for
  France.                                         195

#### Second Priest

What a way to talk at such a juncture!
You are foolish, immodest and babbling
  women.
Do you not know that the good Archbishop
Is likely to arrive at any moment?
The crowds in the streets will be cheering and
  cheering,                                       200
You go on croaking like frogs in the treetops:
But frogs at least can be cooked and eaten.
Whatever you are afraid of, in your craven ap-
  prehension,
Let me ask you at the least to put on pleasant
  faces,
And give a hearty welcome to our good Arch-
  bishop.                                         205
[Enter Thomas.]

#### Thomas

Peace. And let them be, in their exaltation.
They speak better than they know, and beyond
  your understanding.

They know and do not know, what it is to act
or suffer.
They know and do not know, that action is
suffering
And suffering is action. Neither does the agent
suffer                                               210
Nor the patient act. But both are fixed
In an eternal action, an eternal patience
To which all must consent that it may be willed
And which all must suffer that they may will it,
That the pattern may subsist, for the pattern
is the action                                        215
And the suffering, that the wheel may turn and
still
Be forever still.

### SECOND PRIEST

O my Lord, forgive me, I did not see you
coming,
Engrossed by the chatter of these foolish
women.
Forgive us, my Lord, you would have had a
better welcome                                       220
If we had been sooner prepared for the event.
But your Lordship knows that seven years of
waiting,
Seven years of prayer, seven years of emptiness,
Have better prepared our hearts for your
coming,
Than seven days could make ready Canterbury.
However, I will have fires laid in all your rooms
To take the chill off our English December, 227
Your Lordship now being used to a better
climate.
Your Lordship will find your rooms in order as
you left them.

### THOMAS

And will try to leave them in order as I find
them.                                                230
I am more than grateful for all your kind at-
tentions.
These are small matters. Little rest in Canter-
bury
With eager enemies restless about us.
Rebellious bishops, York, London, Salisbury,
Would have intercepted our letters,                  235
Filled the coast with spies and sent to meet me
Some who hold me in bitterest hate.
By God's grace aware of their prevision
I sent my letters on another day,
Had fair crossing, found at Sandwich              240
Broc, Warenne, and the Sheriff of Kent,
Those who had sworn to have my head from
me
Only John, the Dean of Salisbury,
Fearing for the King's name, warning against
treason,                                             244
Made them hold their hands. So for the time
We are unmolested.

### FIRST PRIEST
But do they follow after?

### THOMAS

For a little time the hungry hawk
Will only soar and hover, circling lower,
Waiting excuse, pretence, opportunity.
End will be simple, sudden, God-given.            250
Meanwhile the substance of our first act
Will be shadows, and the strife with shadows.
Heavier the interval than the consummation.
All things prepare the event. Watch.
[*Enter* FIRST TEMPTER.]

### FIRST TEMPTER

You see, my Lord, I do not wait upon cere-
mony:                                                255
Here I have come, forgetting all acrimony,
Hoping that your present gravity
Will find excuse for my humble levity
Remembering all the good time past.
Your Lordship won't despise an old friend out
of favour?                                           260
Old Tom, gay Tom, Becket of London,
Your Lordship won't forget that evening on the
river
When the King, and you and I were all friends
together?
Friendship should be more than biting Time
can sever.
What, my Lord, now that you recover            265
Favour with the King, shall we say that sum-
mer's over
Or that the good time cannot last?
Fluting in the meadows, viols in the hall,
Laughter and apple-blossom floating on the
water,
Singing at nightfall, whispering in chambers, 270
Fires devouring the winter season,
Eating up the darkness, with wit and wine and
wisdom!
Now that the King and you are in amity,
Clergy and laity may return to gaiety,           274
Mirth and sportfulness need not walk warily.

### THOMAS

You talk of seasons that are past. I remember
Not worth forgetting.

### TEMPTER
And of the new season.
Spring has come in winter. Snow in the
branches
Shall float as sweet as blossoms. Ice along the
ditches
Mirror the sunlight. Love in the orchard        280
Send the sap shooting. Mirth matches mel-
ancholy.

### THOMAS

We do not know very much of the future
Except that from generation to generation
The same things happen again and again.
Men learn little from others' experience.      285
But in the life of one man, never

The same time returns. Sever
The cord, shed the scale. Only
The fool, fixed in his folly, may think
He can turn the wheel on which he turns.    290

TEMPTER

My Lord, a nod is as good as a wink.
A man will often love what he spurns.
For the good times past, that are come again
I am your man.

THOMAS

Not in this train
Look to your behaviour. You were safer    295
Think of penitence and follow your master.

TEMPTER

Not at this gait!
If you go so fast, others may go faster.
Your Lordship is too proud!
The safest beast is not the one that roars most
loud,    300
This was not the way of the King our master!
You were not used to be so hard upon sinners
When they were your friends. Be easy, man!
The easy man lives to eat the best dinners.
Take a friend's advice. Leave well alone,    305
Or your goose may be cooked and eaten to the
bone.

THOMAS

You come twenty years too late.

TEMPTER

Then I leave you to your fate.
I leave you to the pleasures of your higher vices,
Which will have to be paid for at higher prices.
Farewell, my Lord, I do not wait upon cere-
mony,    311
I leave as I came, forgetting all acrimony,
Hoping that your present gravity
Will find excuse for my humble levity.
If you will remember me, my Lord, at your
prayers,    315
I'll remember you at kissing-time below the
stairs.

THOMAS

Leave-well-alone, the springtime fancy,
So one thought goes whistling down the wind.
The impossible is still temptation.
The impossible, the undesirable,    320
Voices under sleep, waking a dead world,
So that the mind may not be whole in the
present.
[*Enter* SECOND TEMPTER.]

SECOND TEMPTER

Your Lordship has forgotten me, perhaps. I
will remind you.
We met at Clarendon, at Northampton,
And last at Montmirail, in Maine. Now that I
have recalled them,    325

Let us but set these not too pleasant memories
In balance against other, earlier
And weightier ones: those of the Chancellor-
ship.
See how the late ones rise! You, master of
policy
Whom all acknowledged, should guide the
state again.    330

THOMAS

Your meaning?

TEMPTER

The Chancellorship that you resigned
When you were made Archbishop—that was a
mistake
On your part—still may be regained. Think,
my Lord,
Power obtained grows to glory,
Life lasting, a permanent possession.    335
A templed tomb, monument of marble.
Rule over men reckon no madness.

THOMAS

To the man of God what gladness?

TEMPTER

Sadness
Only to those giving love to God alone.
Shall he who held the solid substance    340
Wander waking with deceitful shadows?
Power is present. Holiness hereafter.

THOMAS

Who then?

TEMPTER

The Chancellor. King and Chancellor.
King commands. Chancellor richly rules.    345
This is a sentence not taught in the schools.
To set down the great, protect the poor,
Beneath the throne of God can man do more?
Disarm the ruffian, strengthen the laws,
Rule for the good of the better cause,    350
Dispensing justice make all even,
Is thrive on earth, and perhaps in heaven.

THOMAS

What means?

TEMPTER

Real power
Is purchased at price of a certain submission.
Your spiritual power is earthly perdition.    355
Power is present, for him who will wield.

THOMAS

Who shall have it?

TEMPTER

He who will come.

THOMAS

What shall be the month?

TEMPTER
>    The last from the first. 360

THOMAS
What shall we give for it?

TEMPTER
>    Pretence of priestly power.

THOMAS
Why should we give it?

TEMPTER
>    For the power and the glory.

THOMAS
No! 365

TEMPTER
>    Yes! or bravery will be broken,
Cabined in Canterbury, realmless ruler,
Self-bound servant of a powerless Pope,
The old stag, circled with hounds.

THOMAS
No! 370

TEMPTER
>    Yes! men must manœuvre. Monarchs also,
Waging war abroad, need fast friends at home.
Private policy is public profit;
Dignity still shall be dressed with decorum.

THOMAS
You forget the bishops 375
Whom I have laid under excommunication.

TEMPTER
Hungry hatred
Will not strive against intelligent self-interest.

THOMAS
You forget the barons. Who will not forget
Constant curbing of petty privilege. 380

TEMPTER
Against the barons
Is King's cause, churl's cause, Chancellor's
>    cause.

THOMAS
No! shall I, who keep the keys 384
Of heaven and hell, supreme alone in England,
Who bind and loose, with power from the
>    Pope,
Descend to desire a punier power?
Delegate to deal the doom of damnation, 389
To condemn kings, not serve among their
>    servants,
Is my open office. No! Go.

TEMPTER
Then I leave you to your fate. 394
Your sin soars sunward, covering kings' falcons.

THOMAS
Temporal power, to build a good world,
To keep order, as the world knows order.
Those who put their faith in worldly order
Not controlled by the order of God,
In confident ignorance, but arrest disorder, 400
Make it fast, breed fatal disease,
Degrade what they exalt. Power with the
>    King—
I *was* the King, his arm, his better reason.
But what was once exaltation 405
Would now be only mean descent.
[*Enter* THIRD TEMPTER.]

THIRD TEMPTER
I am an unexpected visitor.

THOMAS
>    I expected you.

TEMPTER
But not in this guise, or for my present purpose.

THOMAS
No purpose brings surprise. 410

TEMPTER
>    Well, my Lord,
I am no trifler, and no politician.
To idle or intrigue at court
I have no skill. I am no courtier.
I know a horse, a dog, a wench; 415
I know how to hold my estates in order,
A country-keeping lord who minds his own
>    business.
It is we country lords who know the country
And we who know what the country needs.
It is our country. We care for the country. 420
We are the backbone of the nation.
We, not the plotting parasites
About the King. Excuse my bluntness:
I am a rough straightforward Englishman.

THOMAS
Proceed straight forward. 425

TEMPTER
>    Purpose is plain.
Endurance of friendship does not depend
Upon ourselves, but upon circumstance.
But circumstance is not undetermined.
Unreal friendship may turn to real 430
But real friendship, once ended, cannot be
>    mended.
Sooner shall enmity turn to alliance.
The enmity that never knew friendship
Can sooner know accord.

THOMAS
>    For a countryman
You wrap your meaning in as dark generality
As any courtier. 436

TEMPTER

This is the simple fact!
You have no hope of reconciliation
With Henry the King. You look only
To blind assertion in isolation.
That is a mistake.                          440

THOMAS

O Henry, O my King!

TEMPTER

Other friends
May be found in the present situation.
King in England is not all-powerful;
King is in France, squabbling in Anjou;
Round him waiting hungry sons.              445
We are for England. We are in England.
You and I, my Lord, are Normans.
England is a land for Norman
Sovereignty. Let the Angevin
Destroy himself, fighting in Anjou.         450
He does not understand us, the English barons.
We are the people.

THOMAS

To what does this lead?

TEMPTER

To a happy coalition
Of intelligent interests.

THOMAS

But what have you—
If you do speak for barons—                 455

TEMPTER

For a powerful party
Which has turned its eyes in your direction—
To gain from you, your Lordship asks.
For us, Church favour would be an advantage,
Blessing of Pope powerful protection
In the fight for liberty. You, my Lord,     460
In being with us, would fight a good stroke
At once, for England and for Rome,
Ending the tyrannous jurisdiction
Of king's court over bishop's court,
Of king's court over baron's court.         465

THOMAS

Which I helped to found.

TEMPTER

Which you helped to found.
But time past is time forgotten.
We expect the rise of a new constellation.

THOMAS

And if the Archbishop cannot trust the
King,                                       470
How can he trust those who work for King's
undoing?

TEMPTER

Kings will allow no power but their own;
Church and people have good cause against
the throne.

THOMAS

If the Archbishop cannot trust the Throne,
He has good cause to trust none but God
alone.                                      475
I ruled once as Chancellor
And men like you were glad to wait at my door.
Not only in the court, but in the field
And in the tilt-yard I made many yield.
Shall I who ruled like an eagle over doves  480
Now take the shape of a wolf among wolves?
Pursue your treacheries as you have done be-
fore:
No one shall say that I betrayed a king.

TEMPTER

Then, my Lord, I shall not wait at your door.
And I well hope, before another spring      485
The King will show his regard for your loyalty.

THOMAS

To make, then break, this thought has come
before,
The desperate exercise of failing power.
Samson in Gaza did no more.
But if I break, I must break myself alone.  490
[*Enter* FOURTH TEMPTER.]

FOURTH TEMPTER

Well done, Thomas, your will is hard to bend.
And with me beside you, you shall not lack a
friend.

THOMAS

Who are you? I expected
Three visitors, not four.

TEMPTER

Do not be surprised to receive one more.    495
Had I been expected, I had been here before.
I always precede expectation.

THOMAS

Who are you?

TEMPTER

As you do not know me, I do not need a name,
And, as you know me, that is why I come.    500
You know me, but have never seen my face.
To meet before was never time or place.

THOMAS

Say what you come to say.

TEMPTER

It shall be said at last.
Hooks have been baited with morsels of the
past.                                       505

Wantonness is weakness. As for the King,
His hardened hatred shall have no end.
You know truly, the King will never trust
Twice, the man who has been his friend.
Borrow use cautiously, employ          510
Your services as long as you have to lend.
You would wait for trap to snap
Having served your turn, broken and crushed.
As for barons, envy of lesser men
Is still more stubborn than king's anger.     515
Kings have public policy, barons private profit,
Jealousy raging possession of the fiend.
Barons are employable against each other;
Greater enemies must kings destroy.

THOMAS

What is your counsel?          520

TEMPTER
          Fare forward to the end.
All other ways are closed to you
Except the way already chosen.
But what is pleasure, kingly rule,
Or rule of men beneath a king,          525
With craft in corners, stealthy stratagem,
To general grasp of spiritual power?
Man oppressed by sin, since Adam fell—
You hold the keys of heaven and hell.
Power to bind and loose: bind, Thomas, bind,
King and bishop under your heel.          531
King, emperor, bishop, baron, king:
Uncertain mastery of melting armies,
War, plague, and revolution,
New conspiracies, broken pacts;          535
To be master or servant within an hour,
This is the course of temporal power.
The Old King shall know it, when at last
          breath,
No sons, no empire, he bites broken teeth.
You hold the skein: wind, Thomas, wind     540
The thread of eternal life and death.
You hold this power, hold it.

THOMAS
          Supreme, in this land?

TEMPTER

Supreme, but for one.          544

THOMAS
          That I do not understand.

TEMPTER
It is not for me to tell you how this may be so;
I am only here, Thomas, to tell you what you
          know.

THOMAS

How long shall this be?

TEMPTER

Save what you know already, ask nothing of me.
But think, Thomas, think of glory after death.

When king is dead, there's another king, 551
And one more king is another reign.
King is forgotten, when another shall come:
Saint and Martyr rule from the tomb.
Think, Thomas, think of enemies dismayed, 555
Creeping in penance, frightened of a shade;
Think of pilgrims, standing in line
Before the glittering jewelled shrine,
From generation to generation
Bending the knee in supplication,          560
Think of the miracles, by God's grace,
And think of your enemies, in another place.

THOMAS

I have thought of these things.

TEMPTER
          That is why I tell you,
Your thoughts have more power than kings to
          compel you.          565
You have also thought, sometimes at your
          prayers,
Sometimes hesitating at the angles of stairs,
And between sleep and waking, early in the
          morning,
When the bird cries, have thought of further
          scorning.
That nothing lasts, but the wheel turns,     570
The nest is rifled, and the bird mourns;
That the shrine shall be pillaged, and the gold
          spent,
The jewels gone for light ladies' ornament,
The sanctuary broken, and its stores
Swept into the laps of parasites and whores. 575
When miracles cease, and the faithful desert
          you,
And men shall only do their best to forget you.
And later is worse, when men will not hate you
Enough to defame or to execrate you,
But pondering the qualities that you lacked 580
Will only try to find the historical fact.
When men shall declare that there was no
          mystery
About this man who played a certain part in
          history.

THOMAS

But what is there to do? What is left to be
          done?
Is there no enduring crown to be won?     585

TEMPTER

Yes, Thomas, yes; you have thought of that
          too.
What can compare with glory of Saints
Dwelling forever in presence of God?
What earthly glory, of king or emperor,
What earthly pride, that is not poverty     590
Compared with richness of heavenly grandeur?
Seek the way of martyrdom, make yourself the
          lowest
On earth, to be high in heaven.

And see far off below you, where the gulf is
   fixed,
Your persecutors, in timeless torment,     595
Parched passion, beyond expiation.

#### THOMAS

                    No!
Who are you, tempting with my own desires?
Others have come, temporal tempters,
With pleasure and power at palpable price.   600
What do you offer? What do you ask?

#### TEMPTER

I offer what you desire. I ask
What you have to give. Is it too much
For such a vision of eternal grandeur?

#### THOMAS

Others offered real goods, worthless     605
But real. You only offer
Dreams to damnation.

#### TEMPTER

             You have often dreamt them.

#### THOMAS

Is there no way, in my soul's sickness,
Does not lead to damnation in pride?     610
I well know that these temptations
Mean present vanity and future torment.
Can sinful pride be driven out
Only by more sinful? Can I neither act nor
   suffer
Without perdition?     615

#### TEMPTER

You know and do not know, what it is to act
   or suffer.
You know and do not know, that action is
   suffering,
And suffering action. Neither does the agent
   suffer
Nor the patient act. But both are fixed
In an eternal action, an eternal patience   620
To which all must consent that it may be
   willed
And which all must suffer that they may will it,
That the pattern may subsist, that the wheel
   may turn and still
Be forever still.

#### CHORUS

There is no rest in the house. There is no rest
   in the street.     625
I hear restless movement of feet. And the air
   is heavy and thick.
Thick and heavy the sky. And the earth presses
   up against our feet.
What is the sickly smell, the vapour? The dark
   green light from a cloud on a withered
   tree? The earth is heaving to parturition of
   issue of hell. What is the sticky dew that
   forms on the back of my hand?

#### THE FOUR TEMPTERS

Man's life is a cheat and a disappointment;
All things are unreal,     630
Unreal or disappointing:
The Catherine wheel, the pantomime cat,
The prizes given at the children's party,
The prize awarded for the English Essay,
The scholar's degree, the statesman's decora-
   tion.     635
All things become less real, man passes
From unreality to unreality.
This man is obstinate, blind, intent
On self-destruction,
Passing from deception to deception,     640
From grandeur to grandeur to final illusion,
Lost in the wonder of his own greatness,
The enemy of society, enemy of himself.

#### THE THREE PRIESTS

O Thomas my Lord do not fight the intractable
   tide,
Do not sail the irresistible wind; in the storm,
Should we not wait for the sea to subside, in
   the night     646
Abide the coming of day, when the traveller
   may find his way,
The sailor lay course by the sun?

CHORUS, PRIESTS *and* TEMPTERS *alternately*

C. Is it the owl that calls, or a signal between
   the trees?
P. Is the window-bar made fast, is the door
   under lock and bolt?     650
T. Is it rain that taps at the window, is it wind
   that pokes at the door?
C. Does the torch flame in the hall, the candle
   in the room?
P. Does the watchman walk by the wall?
T. Does the mastiff prowl by the gate?
C. Death has a hundred hands and walks by a
   thousand ways.     655
P. He may come in the sight of all, he may
   pass unseen unheard.
T. Come whispering through the ear, or a sud-
   den shock on the skull.
C. A man may walk with a lamp at night, and
   yet be drowned in a ditch.
P. A man may climb the stair in the day, and
   slip on a broken step.
T. A man may sit at meat, and feel the cold
   in his groin.     660

#### CHORUS

We have not been happy, my Lord, we have
   not been too happy.
We are not ignorant women, we know what
   we must expect and not expect.
We know of oppression and torture,
We know of extortion and violence,
Destitution, disease,     665
The old without fire in winter,
The child without milk in summer,
Our labour taken away from us,

Our sins made heavier upon us.
We have seen the young man mutilated, 670
The torn girl trembling by the mill-stream.
And meanwhile we have gone on living,
Living and partly living,
Picking together the pieces,
Gathering faggots at nightfall, 675
Building a partial shelter,
For sleeping, and eating and drinking and
    laughter.

God gave us always some reason, some hope;
    but now a new terror has soiled us, which
    none can avert, none can avoid, flowing
    under our feet and over the sky;
Under doors and down chimneys, flowing in at
    the ear and the mouth and the eye.
God is leaving us, God is leaving us, more
    pang, more pain than birth or death. 680
Sweet and cloying through the dark air
Falls the stifling scent of despair;
The forms take shape in the dark air:
Puss-purr of leopard, footfall of padding bear,
Palm-pat of nodding ape, square hyaena wait-
    ing 685
For laughter, laughter, laughter. The Lords of
    Hell are here.
They curl round you, lie at your feet, swing and
    wing through the dark air.
O Thomas Archbishop, save us, save us, save
    yourself that we may be saved;
Destroy yourself and we are destroyed. 689

#### THOMAS

Now is my way clear, now is the meaning plain:
Temptation shall not come in this kind again.
The last temptation is the greatest treason:
To do the right deed for the wrong reason.
The natural vigour in the venial sin
Is the way in which our lives begin. 695
Thirty years ago, I searched all the ways
That lead to pleasure, advancement and praise.
Delight in sense, in learning and in thought,
Music and philosophy, curiosity,
The purple bullfinch in the lilac tree, 700
The tilt-yard skill, the strategy of chess,    10
Love in the garden, singing to the instrument,
Were all things equally desirable.
Ambition comes when early force is spent
And when we find no longer all things possible.
Ambition comes behind and unobservable. 706
Sin grows with doing good. When I imposed
    the King's law
In England, and waged war with him against
    Toulouse,
I beat the barons at their own game. I
Could then despise the men who thought me   20
    most contemptible, 710
The raw nobility, whose manners matched their
    fingernails.
While I ate out of the King's dish
To become servant of God was never my wish.
Servant of God has chance of greater sin

And sorrow, than the man who serves a king.
For those who serve the greater cause may
    make the cause serve them, 716
Still doing right: and striving with political
    men
May make that cause political, not by what
    they do
But by what they are. I know
What yet remains to show you of my history
Will seem to most of you at best futility, 721
Senseless self-slaughter of a lunatic,
Arrogant passion of a fanatic.
I know that history at all times draws
The strangest consequence from remotest
    cause. 725
But for every evil, every sacrilege,
Crime, wrong, oppression and the axe's edge,
Indifference, exploitation, you, and you,
And you, must all be punished. So must you.
I shall no longer act or suffer, to the sword's
    end. 730
Now my good Angel, whom God appoints
To be my guardian, hover over the swords'
    points.

### INTERLUDE

#### THE ARCHBISHOP
*preaches in the Cathedral on Christmas*
*Morning, 1170*

'Glory to God in the highest, and on earth peace
to men of good will.' *The fourteenth verse of the
second chapter of the Gospel according to Saint
Luke.* In the Name of the Father, and of the Son,
and of the Holy Ghost. Amen.

Dear children of God, my sermon this
Christmas morning will be a very short one.
I wish only that you should meditate in your
hearts the deep meaning and mystery of our
masses of Christmas Day. For whenever Mass
is said, we re-enact the Passion and Death of
Our Lord; and on this Christmas Day we do
this in celebration of His Birth. So that at
the same moment we rejoice in His coming
for the salvation of men, and offer again to
God His Body and Blood in sacrifice, oblation
and satisfaction for the sins of the whole world.
It was in this same night that has just passed,
that a multitude of the heavenly host appeared
before the shepherds at Bethlehem, saying
'Glory to God in the highest, and on earth
peace to men of good will'; at this same time
of all the year that we celebrate at once the
Birth of Our Lord and His Passion and Death
upon the Cross. Beloved, as the World sees,
this is to behave in a strange fashion. For who
in the World will both mourn and rejoice at
once and for the same reason? For either joy
will be overborne by mourning, or mourning
will be cast out by joy; so it is only in these
our Christian mysteries that we can rejoice and
mourn at once for the same reason. Now think
for a moment about the meaning of this word

'peace.' Does it seem strange to you that the angels should have announced Peace, when ceaselessly the world has been stricken with War and the fear of War? Does it seem to you that the angelic voices were mistaken, and that the promise was a disappointment and a cheat?

Reflect now, how Our Lord Himself spoke of Peace. He said to His disciples, 'My peace I leave with you, my peace I give unto you.' Did He mean peace as we think of it: the kingdom of England at peace with its neighbours, the barons at peace with the King, the householder counting over his peaceful gains, the swept hearth, his best wine for a friend at the table, his wife singing to the children? Those men His disciples knew no such things: they went forth to journey afar, to suffer by land and sea, to know torture, imprisonment, disappointment, to suffer death by martyrdom. What then did He mean? If you ask that, remember then that He said also, 'Not as the world gives, give I unto you.' So then, He gave to His disciples peace, but not peace as the world gives.

Consider also one thing of which you have probably never thought. Not only do we at the feast of Christmas celebrate at once Our Lord's Birth and His Death: but on the next day we celebrate the martyrdom of His first martyr, the blessed Stephen. Is it an accident, do you think, that the day of the first martyr follows immediately the day of the Birth of Christ? By no means. Just as we rejoice and mourn at once, in the Birth and in the Passion of Our Lord; so also, in a smaller figure, we both rejoice and mourn in the death of martyrs. We mourn, for the sins of the world that has martyred them; we rejoice, that another soul is numbered among the Saints in Heaven, for the glory of God and for the salvation of men.

Beloved, we do not think of a martyr simply as a good Christian who has been killed because he is a Christian: for that would be solely to mourn. We do not think of him simply as a good Christian who has been elevated to the company of the Saints: for that would be simply to rejoice: and neither our mourning nor our rejoicing is as the world's is. A Christian martyrdom is never an accident, for Saints are not made by accident. Still less is a Christian martyrdom the effect of a man's will to become a Saint, as a man by willing and contriving may become a ruler of men. A martyrdom is always the design of God, for His love of men, to warn them and to lead them, to bring them back to His ways. It is never the design of man; for the true martyr is he who has become the instrument of God, who has lost his will in the will of God, and who no longer desires anything for himself, not even the glory of being a martyr. So thus as on earth the Church mourns and rejoices at once, in a fashion that the world cannot understand; so in Heaven the Saints are most high, having made themselves most low, and are seen, not as we see them, but in the light of the Godhead from which they draw their being.

I have spoken to you to-day, dear children of God, of the martyrs of the past, asking you to remember especially our martyr of Canterbury, the blessed Archbishop Elphege; because it is fitting, on Christ's birth day, to remember what is that Peace which He brought; and because, dear children, I do not think I shall ever preach to you again; and because it is possible that in a short time you may have yet another martyr, and that one perhaps not the last. I would have you keep in your hearts these words that I say, and think of them at another time. In the Name of the Father, and of the Son, and of the Holy Ghost. Amen.

### PART II

*Characters*

THREE PRIESTS
FOUR KNIGHTS
ARCHBISHOP THOMAS BECKET
CHORUS OF WOMEN OF CANTERBURY
ATTENDANTS

*The first scene is in the Archbishop's Hall,
the second scene is in the Cathedral,
on December 29th, 1170*

CHORUS

Does the bird sing in the South?
Only the sea-bird cries, driven inland by the
 storm.
What sign of the spring of the year?
Only the death of the old: not a stir, not a
 shoot, not a breath.
Do the days begin to lengthen?                   5
Longer and darker the day, shorter and colder
 the night.
Still and stifling the air: but a wind is stored
 up in the East.
The starved crow sits in the field, attentive; and
 in the wood
The owl rehearses the hollow note of death.
What signs of a bitter spring?                  10
The wind stored up in the East.
What, at the time of the birth of Our Lord, at
 Christmastide,
Is there not peace upon earth, goodwill among
 men?
The peace of this world is always uncertain,
 unless men keep the peace of God.
And war among men defiles this world, but
 death in the Lord renews it,                    15
And the world must be cleaned in the winter,
 or we shall have only
A sour spring, a parched summer, an empty
 harvest.
Between Christmas and Easter what work shall
 be done?
The ploughman shall go out in March and
 turn the same earth

He has turned before, the bird shall sing the
    same song.                                                    20
When the leaf is out on the tree, when the
    elder and may
Burst over the stream, and the air is clear and
    high,
And voices trill at windows, and children tum-
    ble in front of the door,
What work shall have been done, what wrong
Shall the bird's song cover, the green tree
    cover, what wrong                                    25
Shall the fresh earth cover? We wait, and the
    time is short
But waiting is long.
[*Enter the* FIRST PRIEST *with a banner of St.*
   *Stephen borne before him. The lines sung*
          *are in italics.*]

### FIRST PRIEST
Since Christmas a day: and the day of St.
    Stephen, First Martyr.
*Princes moreover did sit, and did witness falsely*
    *against me.*
A day that was always most dear to the Arch-
    bishop Thomas.                                        30
And he kneeled down and cried with a loud
    voice:
Lord, lay not this sin to their charge.
*Princes moreover did sit.*
          [*Introit of St. Stephen is heard.*]
[*Enter the* SECOND PRIEST, *with a banner of*
   *St. John the Apostle borne before him.*]

### SECOND PRIEST
Since St. Stephen a day: and the day of St.
    John the Apostle.
*In the midst of the congregation he opened his*
    *mouth.*                                                      35
That which was from the beginning, which we
    have heard,
Which we have seen with our eyes, and our
    hands have handled
Of the word of life; that which we have seen
    and heard
Declare we unto you.
*In the midst of the congregation.*
          [*Introit of St. John is heard.*]
[*Enter the* THIRD PRIEST, *with a banner of the*
   *Holy Innocents borne before him.*]

### THIRD PRIEST
Since St. John the Apostle a day: and the day
    of the Holy Innocents.                              40
*Out of the mouth of very babes, O God.*
As the voice of many waters, of thunder, of
    harps,
They sung as it were a new song.
The blood of thy saints have they shed like
    water,
And there was no man to bury them. Avenge,
    O Lord,                                                         45
The blood of thy saints. In Rama, a voice
    heard, weeping.

*Out of the mouth of very babes, O God!*
[THE PRIESTS *stand together with the banners*
        *behind them.*]

### FIRST PRIEST
Since the Holy Innocents a day: the fourth
    day from Christmas.

### THE THREE PRIESTS
*Rejoice we all, keeping holy day.*

### FIRST PRIEST
As for the people, so also for himself, he offer-
    eth for sins.                                                 50
He lays down his life for the sheep.

### THE THREE PRIESTS
*Rejoice we all, keeping holy day.*

### FIRST PRIEST
                To-day?

### SECOND PRIEST
To-day, what is to-day? For the day is half
    gone.

### FIRST PRIEST
To-day, what is to-day? But another day, the
    dusk of the year.                                         55

### SECOND PRIEST
To-day, what is to-day? Another night, and an-
    other dawn.

### THIRD PRIEST
What day is the day that we know that we
    hope for or fear for?
Every day is the day we should fear from or
    hope from. One moment
Weighs like another. Only in retrospection,
    selection,
We say, that was the day. The critical mo-
    ment                                                             60
That is always now, and here. Even now, in
    sordid particulars
The eternal design may appear.
[*Enter the* FOUR KNIGHTS. *The banners disap-*
        *pear.*]

### FIRST KNIGHT
Servants of the King.

### FIRST PRIEST
            And known to us.
You are welcome. Have you ridden far?      65

### FIRST KNIGHT
Not far to-day, but matters urgent
Have brought us from France. We rode hard,
Took ship yesterday, landed last night,
Having business with the Archbishop.

### SECOND KNIGHT
Urgent business.                                            70

THIRD KNIGHT
From the king.

SECOND KNIGHT
By the King's order.

FIRST KNIGHT
Our men are outside.

FIRST PRIEST
You know the Archbishop's hospitality.
We are about to go to dinner.                          75
The good Archbishop would be vexed
If we did not offer you entertainment
Before your business. Please dine with us.
Your men shall be looked after also.
Dinner before business. Do you like roast
        pork?                                           80

FIRST KNIGHT
Business before dinner. We will roast your pork
First, and dine upon it after.

SECOND KNIGHT
We must see the Archbishop.

THIRD KNIGHT
                    Go, tell the Archbishop
We have no need of his hospitality.                    85
We will find our own dinner.

FIRST PRIEST [*to attendant*]
Go, tell His Lordship.

FOURTH KNIGHT
  How much longer will you keep us waiting?
[*Enter* THOMAS.]

THOMAS [*to* PRIESTS]
However certain our expectation
The moment foreseen may be unexpected     90
When it arrives. It comes when we are
Engrossed with matters of other urgency.
On my table you will find
The papers in order, and the documents signed.
[*To* KNIGHTS.]
You are welcome, whatever your business may
        be.                                             95
You say, from the King?

FIRST KNIGHT
                    Most surely from the King.
We must speak with you alone.

THOMAS [*to* PRIESTS]
                    Leave us then alone.
Now what is the matter?                               100

FIRST KNIGHT
                    This is the matter.

THE THREE KNIGHTS
You are the Archbishop in revolt against the
        King; in rebellion to the King and the
        law of the land;

You are the Archbishop who was made by the
        King; whom he set in your place to carry
        out his command.
You are his servant, his tool, and his jack,
You wore his favours on your back,                     105
You had your honours all from his hand; from
        him you had the power, the seal and the
        ring.
This is the man who was the tradesman's son:
        the backstairs brat who was born in
        Cheapside;
This is the creature that crawled upon the
        King; swollen with blood and swollen
        with pride.
Creeping out of the London dirt,
Crawling up like a louse on your shirt,                110
The man who cheated, swindled, lied; broke his
        oath and betrayed his King.

THOMAS
This is not true.
Both before and after I received the ring
I have been a loyal subject to the king.
Saving my order, I am at his command,                  115
As his most faithful vassal in the land.

FIRST KNIGHT
Saving your order! let your order save you—
As I do not think it is like to do.
Saving your ambition is what you mean,
Saving your pride, envy and spleen.                    120

SECOND KNIGHT
Saving your insolence and greed.
Won't you ask us to pray to God for you, in
        your need?

THIRD KNIGHT
Yes, we'll pray for you!

FIRST KNIGHT
                    Yes, we'll pray for you!

THE THREE KNIGHTS
Yes, we'll pray that God may help you!     125

THOMAS
But, gentlemen, your business
Which you said so urgent, is it only
Scolding and blaspheming?

FIRST KNIGHT
                    That was only
Our indignation, as loyal subjects.               130

THOMAS
Loyal? To whom?

FIRST KNIGHT
                    To the King!

SECOND KNIGHT
                            The King!

THIRD KNIGHT

The King!

THE THREE KNIGHTS

God bless him!                                                    135

THOMAS

Then let your new coat of loyalty be worn
Carefully, so it get not soiled or torn.
Have you something to say?

FIRST KNIGHT

By the King's command.
Shall we say it now?                                           140

SECOND KNIGHT

Without delay,
Before the old fox is off and away.

THOMAS

What you have to say
By the King's command—if it be the King's
command—
Should be said in public. If you make charges,
Then in public I will refute them.          146

FIRST KNIGHT

No! here and now!
[*They make to attack him, but the priests and
attendants return and quietly interpose
themselves.*]

THOMAS

Now and here!

FIRST KNIGHT

Of your earlier misdeeds I shall make no men-
tion.
They are too well known. But after dissension
Had ended, in France, and you were endued 151
With your former privilege, how did you show
your gratitude?
You had fled from England, not exiled
Or threatened, mind you; but in the hope
Of stirring up trouble in the French dominions.
You sowed strife abroad, you reviled       156
The King to the King of France, to the Pope,
Raising up against him false opinions.

SECOND KNIGHT

Yet the King, out of his charity,
And urged by your friends, offered clemency,
Made a pact of peace, and all dispute ended 160
Sent you back to your See as you demanded.

THIRD KNIGHT

And burying the memory of your transgressions
Restored your honours and your possessions.
All was granted for which you sued:          165
Yet how, I repeat, did you show your gratitude?

FIRST KNIGHT

Suspending those who had crowned the young
prince,
Denying the legality of his coronation.

SECOND KNIGHT

Binding with the chains of anathema.

THIRD KNIGHT

Using every means in your power to evince 170
The King's faithful servants, every one who
transacts
His business in his absence, the business of the
nation.

FIRST KNIGHT

These are the facts.
Say therefore if you will be content
To answer in the King's presence. Therefore    175
were we sent.

THOMAS

Never was it my wish
To uncrown the King's son, or to diminish
His honour and power. Why should he wish
To deprive my people of me and keep me from
my own
And bid me sit in Canterbury, alone?            180
I would wish him three crowns rather than one,
And as for the bishops, it is not my yoke
That is laid upon them, or mine to revoke.
Let them go to the Pope. It was he who
condemned them.

FIRST KNIGHT

Through you they were suspended.         185

SECOND KNIGHT

By you be this amended.

THIRD KNIGHT

Absolve them.

FIRST KNIGHT

Absolve them.

THOMAS

I do not deny
That this was done through me. But it is not I
Who can loose whom the Pope has bound. 191
Let them go to him, upon whom redounds
Their contempt towards me, their contempt
towards the Church shown.

FIRST KNIGHT

Be that as it may, here is the King's command:
That you and your servants depart from this
land.                                                          195

THOMAS

If that *is* the King's command, I will be bold
To say: seven years were my people without
My presence; seven years of misery and pain.
Seven years a mendicant on foreign charity
I lingered abroad: seven years is no brevity. 200
I shall not get those seven years back again.
Never again, you must make no doubt,
Shall the sea run between the shepherd and his
fold.

FIRST KNIGHT

The King's justice, the King's majesty,
You insult with gross indignity;                            205
Insolent madman, whom nothing deters
From attainting his servants and ministers.

THOMAS

It is not I who insult the King,
And there is higher than I or the King.
It is not I, Becket from Cheapside,                        210
It is not against me, Becket, that you strive.
It is not Becket who pronounces doom,
But the Law of Christ's Church, the judgement
    of Rome.

FIRST KNIGHT

Priest, you have spoken in peril of your life.

SECOND KNIGHT

Priest, you have spoken in danger of the knife.

THIRD KNIGHT

Priest, you have spoken treachery and treason.

THE THREE KNIGHTS

Priest! traitor, confirmed in malfeasance.      217

THOMAS

I submit my cause to the judgement of Rome.
But if you kill me, I shall rise from my tomb
To submit my cause before God's throne. 220
                                              [*Exit.*]

FOURTH KNIGHT

Priest! monk! and servant! take, hold, detain,
Restrain this man, in the King's name.

FIRST KNIGHT

Or answer with your bodies.

SECOND KNIGHT

                              Enough of words.

THE FOUR KNIGHTS

We come for the King's justice, we come with
    swords.                                            225
                                            [*Exeunt.*]

CHORUS

I have smelt them, the death-bringers, senses
    are quickened
By subtile forebodings; I have heard
Fluting in the night-time, fluting and owls,
    have seen at noon
Scaly wings slanting over, huge and ridiculous.
    I have tasted
The savour of putrid flesh in the spoon. I have
    felt                                                  230
The heaving of earth at nightfall, restless,
    absurd. I have heard
Laughter in the noises of beasts that make
    strange noises; jackal, jackass, jackdaw; the

scurrying noise of mouse and jerboa; the
    laugh of the loon, the lunatic bird. I have
    seen
Grey necks twisting, rat tails twining, in the
    thick light of dawn. I have eaten
Smooth creatures still living, with the strong
    salt taste of living things under sea; I have
    tasted
The living lobster, the crab, the oyster, the
    whelk and the prawn; and they live and
    spawn in my bowels, and my bowels dis-
    solve in the light of dawn. I have smelt 235
Death in the rose, death in the hollyhock,
    sweet pea, hyacinth, primrose and cowslip.
    I have seen
Trunk and horn, tusk and hoof, in odd places;
I have lain on the floor of the sea and breathed
    with the breathing of the sea-anemone,
    swallowed with ingurgitation of the
    sponge. I have lain in the soil and criti-
    cised the worm. In the air
Flirted with the passage of the kite, I have
    plunged with the kite and cowered with
    the wren. I have felt
The horn of the beetle, the scale of the viper,
    the mobile hard insensitive skin of the
    elephant, the evasive flank of the fish. I
    have smelt                                       240
Corruption in the dish, incense in the latrine,
    the sewer in the incense, the smell of
    sweet soap in the woodpath, a hellish
    sweet scent in the woodpath, while the
    ground heaved. I have seen
Rings of light coiling downwards, descending
To the horror of the ape. Have I not known,
    not known
What was coming to be? It was here, in the
    kitchen, in the passage,
In the mews in the barn in the byre in the
    market place                                     245
In our veins our bowels our skulls as well
As well as in the plottings of potentates
As well as in the consultations of powers.
What is woven on the loom of fate
What is woven in the councils of princes     250
Is woven also in our veins, our brains,
Is woven like a pattern of living worms
In the guts of the women of Canterbury.

I have smelt them, the death-bringers; now is
    too late
For action, too soon for contrition.            255
Nothing is possible but the shamed swoon
Of those consenting to the last humiliation.
I have consented, Lord Archbishop, have con-
    sented.
Am torn away, subdued, violated,
United to the spiritual flesh of nature,        260
Mastered by the animal powers of spirit,
Dominated by the lust of self-demolition,
By the final utter uttermost death of spirit,
By the final ecstasy of waste and shame,
O Lord Archbishop, O Thomas Archbishop,

forgive us, forgive us, pray for us that we
    may pray for you, out of our shame. 265
[*Enter* THOMAS.]

THOMAS

Peace, and be at peace with your thoughts and
    visions.
These things had to come to you and you to
    accept them.
This is your share of the eternal burden,
The perpetual glory. This is one moment,
But know that another          270
Shall pierce you with a sudden painful joy
When the figure of God's purpose is made
    complete.
You shall forget these things, toiling in the
    household,
You shall remember them, droning by the fire,
When age and forgetfulness sweeten memory
Only like a dream that has often been told 276
And often been changed in the telling. They
    will seem unreal.
Human kind cannot bear very much reality.
[*Enter* PRIESTS.]

PRIESTS [*severally*]

My Lord, you must not stop here. To the
    minster.
Through the cloister. No time to waste. They
    are coming back, armed. To the altar, to
    the altar.          280

THOMAS

All my life they have been coming, these feet.
    All my life
I have waited. Death will come only when I
    am worthy,
And if I am worthy, there is no danger.
I have therefore only to make perfect my will.

PRIESTS

My Lord, they are coming. They will break
    through presently.          285
You will be killed. Come to the altar.
Make haste, my Lord. Don't stop here talking.
    It is not right.
What shall become of us, my Lord, if you are
    killed; what shall become of us?

THOMAS

Peace! be quiet! remember where you are, and
    what is happening;
No life here is sought for but mine,          290
And I am not in danger: only near to death.

PRIESTS

My Lord, to vespers! You must not be absent
    from vespers. You must not be absent from
    the divine office. To vespers. Into the
    cathedral!

THOMAS

Go to vespers, remember me at your prayers.
They shall find the shepherd here; the flock
    shall be spared.

I have had a tremour of bliss, a wink of heaven,
    a whisper,          295
And I would no longer be denied; all things
Proceed to a joyful consummation.

[*In the cathedral. THOMAS and PRIESTS.*]

PRIESTS

Seize him! force him! drag him!

THOMAS

Keep your hands off!

PRIESTS

To vespers! Hurry.          300
[*They drag him off. While the* CHORUS *speak,
    the scene is changed to the cathedral.*]

CHORUS [*While a* Dies Iræ *is sung in Latin by
    a choir in the distance.*]
Numb the hand and dry the eyelid,
Still the horror, but more horror
Than when tearing in the belly.

Still the horror, but more horror
Than when twisting in the fingers,          305
Than when splitting in the skull.

More than footfall in the passage,
More than shadow in the doorway,
More than fury in the hall.

The agents of hell disappear, the human, they
    shrink and dissolve          310
Into dust on the wind, forgotten, unmemor-
    able; only is here
The white flat face of Death, God's silent
    servant,
And behind the face of Death the Judgement
And behind the Judgement the Void, more
    horrid than active shapes of hell;
Emptiness, absence, separation from God; 315
The horror of the effortless journey, to the
    empty land
Which is no land, only emptiness, absence, the
    Void,
Where those who were men can no longer turn
    the mind
To distraction, delusion, escape into dream,
    pretence,
Where the soul is no longer deceived, for there
    are no objects, no tones,          320
No colours, no forms to distract, to divert the
    soul
From seeing itself, foully united forever,
    nothing with nothing,
Not what we call death, but what beyond
    death is not death,
We fear, we fear. Who shall then plead for
    me,
Who intercede for me, in my most need? 325

Dead upon the tree, my Saviour,
Let not be in vain Thy labour;
Help me, Lord, in my last fear.

Dust I am, to dust am bending,
From the final doom impending    330
Help me, Lord, for death is near.

[*In the cathedral.* THOMAS *and* PRIESTS.]

PRIESTS

Bar the door. Bar the door.
The door is barred.
We are safe. We are safe.
They dare not break in.    335
They cannot break in. They have not the force.
We are safe. We are safe.

THOMAS

Unbar the doors! throw open the doors!
I will not have the house of prayer, the church
of Christ,
The sanctuary, turned into a fortress.    340
The Church shall protect her own, in her own
way, not
As oak and stone; stone and oak decay,
Give no stay, but the Church shall endure.
The church shall be open, even to our enemies.
Open the door!

PRIESTS

My Lord! these are not men, these come not
as men come, but    345
Like maddened beasts. They come not like
men, who
Respect the sanctuary, who kneel to the Body
of Christ,
But like beasts. You would bar the door
Against the lion, the leopard, the wolf or the
boar,
Why not more    350
Against beasts with the souls of damned men,
against men
Who would damn themselves to beasts. My
Lord! My Lord!

THOMAS

You think me reckless, desperate and mad.
You argue by results, as this world does,
To settle if an act be good or bad.    355
You defer to the fact. For every life and every
act
Consequence of good and evil can be shown.
And as in time results of many deeds are
blended
So good and evil in the end become con-
founded.
It is not in time that my death shall be known;
It is out of time that my decision is taken    361
If you call that decision
To which my whole being gives entire consent.
I give my life
To the Law of God above the Law of Man.    365
Unbar the door! unbar the door!
We are not here to triumph by fighting, by
stratagem, or by resistance,

Not to fight with beasts as men. We have
fought the beast
And have conquered. We have only to conquer
Now, by suffering. This is the easier victory.    370
Now is the triumph of the Cross, now
Open the door! I command it. OPEN THE DOOR!
[*The door is opened. The* KNIGHTS *enter,
slightly tipsy.*]

PRIESTS

This way, my Lord! Quick. Up the stair. To
the roof.
To the crypt. Quick. Come. Force him.

KNIGHTS

Where is Becket, the traitor to the King?    375
Where is Becket, the meddling priest?
Come down Daniel to the lions' den,
Come down Daniel for the mark of the
beast.

Are you washed in the blood of the Lamb?
Are you marked with the mark of the beast?
Come down Daniel to the lions' den,    381
Come down Daniel and join in the feast.

Where is Becket the Cheapside brat?
Where is Becket the faithless priest?
Come down Daniel to the lions' den,    385
Come down Daniel and join in the feast.

THOMAS

It is the just man who
Like a bold lion, should be without fear.
I am here.
No traitor to the King. I am a priest,    390
A Christian, saved by the blood of Christ,
Ready to suffer with my blood.
This is the sign of the Church always,
The sign of blood. Blood for blood.
His blood given to buy my life,    395
My blood given to pay for His death,
My death for His death.

FIRST KNIGHT

Absolve all those you have excommunicated.

SECOND KNIGHT

Resign the powers you have arrogated.

THIRD KNIGHT

Restore to the King the money you appropriated.    400

FIRST KNIGHT

Renew the obedience you have violated.

THOMAS

For my Lord I am now ready to die,
That His Church may have peace and liberty.
Do with me as you will, to your hurt and
shame;
But none of my people, in God's name,    405

Whether layman or clerk, shall you touch.
This I forbid.

KNIGHTS

Traitor! traitor! traitor!

THOMAS

You, Reginald, three times traitor you:
Traitor to me as my temporal vassal,    410
Traitor to me as your spiritual lord,
Traitor to God in desecrating His Church.

FIRST KNIGHT

No faith do I owe to a renegade,
And what I owe shall now be paid.

THOMAS

   Now to Almighty God, to the Blessed Mary
ever Virgin, to the blessed John the Baptist,
the holy apostles Peter and Paul, to the blessed
martyr Denys, and to all the Saints, I commend my cause and that of the Church.    415
   *While the* KNIGHTS *kill him, we hear the*    10

CHORUS

Clear the air! clean the sky! wash the wind!
   take stone from stone and wash them.
The land is foul, the water is foul, our beasts
   and ourselves defiled with blood.
A rain of blood has blinded my eyes. Where is
   England? Where is Kent? Where is
   Canterbury?
O far far far far in the past; and I wander in
   a land of barren boughs: if I break them,    20
   they bleed; I wander in a land of dry
   stones: if I touch them they bleed.
How how can I ever return, to the soft quiet
   seasons?    420
Night stay with us, stop sun, hold season, let
   the day not come, let the spring not come.
Can I look again at the day and its common
   things, and see them all smeared with
   blood, through a curtain of falling blood?
We did not wish anything to happen.
We understood the private catastrophe,    30
The personal loss, the general misery,    425
Living and partly living;
The terror by night that ends in daily action,
The terror by day that ends in sleep;
But the talk in the market-place, the hand on
   the broom,
The night-time heaping of the ashes,    430
The fuel laid on the fire at daybreak,
These acts marked a limit to our suffering.
Every horror had its definition,
Every sorrow had a kind of end:    435
In life there is not time to grieve long.    435
But this, this is out of life, this is out of time,
An instant eternity of evil and wrong.
We are soiled by a filth that we cannot clean,
   united to supernatural vermin,
It is not we alone, it is not the house, it is
   not the city that is defiled,

But the world that is wholly foul.    440
Clear the air! clean the sky! wash the wind!
   take the stone from the stone, take the
   skin from the arm, take the muscle from
   the bone, and wash them. Wash the stone,
   wash the bone, wash the brain, wash the
   soul, wash them wash them!
[*The* KNIGHTS, *having completed the murder,
advance to the front of the stage and address
   the audience.*]

FIRST KNIGHT

   We beg you to give us your attention for a
few moments. We know that you may be
disposed to judge unfavourably of our action.
You are Englishmen, and therefore you believe
in fair play: and when you see one man being
set upon by four, then your sympathies are all
with the under dog. I respect such feelings, I
share them. Nevertheless, I appeal to your
sense of honour. You are Englishmen, and
therefore will not judge anybody without hearing both sides of the case. That is in accordance
with our long-established principle of Trial by
Jury. I am not myself qualified to put our case
to you. I am a man of action and not of words.
For that reason I shall do no more than introduce the other speakers, who, with their various
abilities, and different points of view, will be
able to lay before you the merits of this extremely complex problem. I shall call upon our
eldest member to speak first, my neighbour
in the country: Baron William de Traci.

THIRD KNIGHT

   I am afraid I am not anything like such an
experienced speaker as my old friend Reginald
Fitz Urse would lead you to believe. But there
is one thing I should like to say, and I might
as well say it at once. It is this: in what we
have done, and whatever you may think of it,
we have been perfectly disinterested. [*The
other* KNIGHTS: 'Hear! hear!'.] *We* are not getting anything out of this. We have much more
to lose than to gain. We are four plain Englishmen who put our country first. I dare say that
we didn't make a very good impression when
we came in just now. The fact is that we knew
we had taken on a pretty stiff job; I'll only
speak for myself, but I had drunk a good deal—
I am not a drinking man ordinarily—to brace
myself up for it. When you come to the point,
it does go against the grain to kill an Archbishop, especially when you have been brought
up in good Church traditions. So if we seemed
a bit rowdy, you will understand why it was;
and for my part I am awfully sorry about it.
We realised this was our duty, but all the same
we had to work ourselves up to it. And, as I
said, *we* are not getting a penny out of this.
We know perfectly well how things will turn
out. King Henry—God bless him—will have
to say, for reasons of state, that he never meant

this to happen; and there is going to be an awful row; and at the best we shall have to spend the rest of our lives abroad. And even when reasonable people come to see that the Archbishop *had* to be put out of the way—and personally I had a tremendous admiration for him—you must have noticed what a good show he put up at the end—they won't give *us* any glory. No, we have done for ourselves, there's no mistake about that. So, as I said at the be-10 ginning, please give us at least the credit for being completely disinterested in this business. I think that is about all I have to say.

### FIRST KNIGHT

I think we will all agree that William de Traci has spoken well and has made a very important point. The gist of his argument is this: that we have been completely dis-interested. But our act itself needs more justifi-cation than that; and you must hear our other speakers. I shall next call upon Hugh de 20 Morville, who has made a special study of statecraft and constitutional law. Sir Hugh de Morville.

### SECOND KNIGHT

I should like first to recur to a point that was very well put by our leader, Reginald Fitz Urse: that you are Englishmen, and therefore your sympathies are always with the under dog. It is the English spirit of fair play. Now the worthy Archbishop, whose good qualities I very 30 much admired, has throughout been presented as the under dog. But is this really the case? I am going to appeal not to your emotions but to your reason. You are hard-headed sensible people, as I can see, and not to be taken in by emotional clap-trap. I therefore ask you to consider soberly: what were the Archbishop's aims? And what are King Henry's aims? In the answer to these questions lies the key to the problem.

The King's aim has been perfectly consistent. 40 During the reign of the late Queen Matilda and the irruption of the unhappy usurper Stephen, the kingdom was very much divided. Our King saw that the one thing needful was to restore order: to curb the excessive powers of local government, which were usually exercised for selfish and often for seditious ends, and to reform the legal system. He therefore intended that Becket, who had proved himself an ex-tremely able administrator—no one denies that —should unite the offices of Chancellor and 50 Archbishop. Had Becket concurred with the King's wishes, we should have had an almost ideal State: a union of spiritual and temporal administration, under the central government. I knew Becket well, in various official relations; and I may say that I have never known a man so well qualified for the highest rank of the Civil Service. And what happened? The mo-

ment that Becket, at the King's instance, had been made Archbishop, he resigned the office of Chancellor, he became more priestly than the priests, he ostentatiously and offensively adopted an ascetic manner of life, he affirmed immediately that there was a higher order than that which our King, and he as the King's servant, had for so many years striven to estab-lish; and that—God knows why—the two orders were incompatible.

You will agree with me that such interference by an Archbishop offends the instincts of a people like ours. So far, I know that I have your approval: I read it in your faces. It is only with the measures we have had to adopt, in order to set matters to rights, that you take issue. No one regrets the necessity for violence more than we do. Unhappily, there are times when violence is the only way in which social justice can be secured. At another time, you would condemn an Archbishop by vote of Parliament and execute him formally as a traitor, and no one would have to bear the burden of being called murderer. And at a later time still, even such temperate measures as these would become unnecessary. But, if you have now arrived at a just subordination of the pretensions of the Church to the welfare of the State, remember that it is we who took the first step. We have been instrumental in bringing about the state of affairs that you approve. We have served your interests; we merit your applause; and if there is any guilt whatever in the matter, you must share it with us.

### FIRST KNIGHT

Morville has given us a great deal to think about. It seems to me that he has said almost the last word, for those who have been able to follow his very subtle reasoning. We have, however, one more speaker, who has I think another point of view to express. If there are any who are still unconvinced, I think that Richard Brito, coming as he does of a family distinguished for its loyalty to the Church, will be able to convince them. Richard Brito.

### FOURTH KNIGHT

The speakers who have preceded me, to say nothing of our leader, Reginald Fitz Urse, have all spoken very much to the point. I have nothing to add along their particular lines of argument. What I have to say may be put in the form of a question: *Who killed the Arch-bishop?* As you have been eye-witnesses of this lamentable scene, you may feel some surprise at my putting it in this way. But consider the course of events. I am obliged, very briefly, to go over the ground traversed by the last speaker. While the late Archbishop was Chancellor, no one, under the King, did more to weld the country together, to give it the unity, the stability, order, tranquillity, and justice that it so badly needed. From the moment he became Archbishop, he completely reversed his policy; he showed himself to be utterly indifferent to the fate of the country, to be, in fact, a monster of egotism. This egotism grew upon him, until it became at last an undoubted mania. I have unimpeachable evidence to the effect that before he left France he clearly prophesied, in the presence of numerous witnesses, that he had not long to live, and that he would be killed in England. He used every means of provocation; from his conduct, step by step, there can be no inference except that he had determined upon a death by martyrdom. Even at the last, he could have given us reason: you have seen how he evaded our questions. And when he had deliberately exasperated us beyond human endurance, he could still have easily escaped; he could have kept himself from us long enough to allow our righteous anger to cool. That was just what he did not wish to happen; he insisted, while we were still inflamed with wrath, that the doors should be opened. Need I say more? I think, with these facts before you, you will unhesitatingly render a verdict of Suicide while of Unsound Mind. It is the only charitable verdict you can give, upon one who was, after all, a great man.

#### FIRST KNIGHT

Thank you, Brito, I think that there is no more to be said; and I suggest that you now disperse quietly to your homes. Please be careful not to loiter in groups at street corners, and do nothing that might provoke any public outbreak.

[*Exeunt* KNIGHTS.]

#### FIRST PRIEST

O father, father, gone from us, lost to us,
How shall we find you, from what far place
Do you look down on us? You now in Heaven,
Who shall now guide us, protect us, direct us?
After what journey through what further dread
Shall we recover your presence? When inherit
Your strength? The Church lies bereft,   452
Alone, descrated, desolated, and the heathen
    shall build on the ruins,
Their world without God. I see it. I see it.

#### THIRD PRIEST

No. For the Church is stronger for this action,
Triumphant in adversity. It is fortified   456
By persecution: supreme, so long as men will
    die for it.
Go, weak sad men, lost erring souls, homeless
    in earth or heaven.
Go where the sunset reddens the last grey rock
Of Brittany, or the Gates of Hercules.   460
Go venture shipwreck on the sullen coasts
Where blackamoors make captive Christian
    men;

Go to the northern seas confined with ice
Where the dead breath makes numb the hand,
    makes dull the brain;
Find an oasis in the desert sun,   465
Go seek alliance with the heathen Saracen,
To share his filthy rites, and try to snatch
Forgetfulness in his libidinous courts,
Oblivion in the fountain by the date-tree;
Or sit and bite your nails in Aquitaine.   470
In the small circle of pain within the skull
You still shall tramp and tread one endless
    round
Of thought, to justify your action to yourselves,
Weaving a fiction which unravels as you weave,
Pacing forever in the hell of make-believe   475
Which never is belief: this is your fate on earth
And we must think no further of you.

#### FIRST PRIEST

                              O my lord
The glory of whose new state is hidden from us,
Pray for us of your charity.   480

#### SECOND PRIEST

                    Now in the sight of God
Conjoined with all the saints and martyrs gone
    before you,
Remember us.

#### THIRD PRIEST

                    Let our thanks ascend
To God, who has given us another Saint in
    Canterbury.   485

CHORUS [*While a* Te Deum *is sung in Latin
    by a choir in the distance.*]
We praise Thee, O God, for Thy glory dis-
    played in all the creatures of the earth,
In the snow, in the rain, in the wind, in the
    storm; in all of Thy creatures, both the
    hunters and the hunted.
For all things exist only as seen by Thee, only
    as known by Thee, all things exist
Only in Thy light, and Thy glory is declared
    even in that which denies Thee; the dark-
    ness declares the glory of light.
Those who deny Thee could not deny, if Thou
    didst not exist; and their denial is never
    complete, for if it were so, they would not
    exist.   490
They affirm Thee in living; all things affirm
    Thee in living; the bird in the air, both
    the hawk and the finch; the beast on the
    earth, both the wolf and the lamb; the
    worm in the soil and the worm in the
    belly.
Therefore man, whom Thou hast made to be
    conscious of Thee, must consciously praise
    Thee, in thought and in word and in deed.
Even with the hand to the broom, the back
    bent in laying the fire, the knee bent in
    cleaning the hearth, we, the scrubbers
    and sweepers of Canterbury,

The back bent under toil, the knee bent under
   sin, the hands to the face under fear, the
   head bent under grief,
Even in us the voices of seasons, the snuffle of
   winter, the song of spring, the drone of
   summer, the voices of beasts and of birds,
   praise Thee.            495
We thank Thee for Thy mercies of blood, for
   Thy redemption by blood. For the blood
   of Thy martyrs and saints
Shall enrich the earth, shall create the holy  10
   places.
For wherever a saint has dwelt, wherever a
   martyr has given his blood for the blood of
   Christ,
There is holy ground, and the sanctity shall
   not depart from it
Though armies trample over it, though sight-
   seers come with guide-books looking over
   it;            500
From where the western seas gnaw at the coast
   of Iona,        20
To the death in the desert, the prayer in forgotten places by the broken imperial
   column,
From such ground springs that which forever
   renews the earth
Though it is forever denied. Therefore, O God,
   we thank Thee
Who hast given such blessing to Canterbury.

Forgive us, O Lord, we acknowledge ourselves
   as type of the common man,   506  30
Of the men and women who shut the door and
   sit by the fire;
Who fear the blessing of God, the loneliness
   of the night of God, the surrender required, the deprivation inflicted;
Who fear the injustice of men less than the
   justice of God;
Who fear the hand at the window, the fire in
   the thatch, the fist in the tavern, the push
   into the canal,      510
Less than we fear the love of God.   40
We acknowledge our trespass, our weakness,
   our fault; we acknowledge
That the sin of the world is upon our heads;
   that the blood of the martyrs and the
   agony of the saints
Is upon our heads.
Lord, have mercy upon us.
Christ, have mercy upon us.     515
Lord, have mercy upon us.
Blessed Thomas, pray for us.

# Tradition and the Individual Talent [1]

In English writing we seldom speak of tradition, though we occasionally apply its name

---

[1] From *Selected Essays* by T. S. Eliot, copyright,

in deploring its absence. We cannot refer to
"the tradition" or to "a tradition"; at most, we
employ the adjective in saying that the poetry
of So-and-so is "traditional" or even "too traditional." Seldom, perhaps, does the word
appear except in a phrase of censure. If otherwise, it is vaguely approbative, with the implication, as to the work approved, of some
pleasing archaeological reconstruction. You can
hardly make the word agreeable to English ears
without this comfortable reference to the re-
assuring science of archaeology.

    Certainly the word is not likely to appear in
our appreciations of living or dead writers.
Every nation, every race, has not only its own
creative, but its own critical turn of mind; and
is even more oblivious of the shortcomings and
limitations of its critical habits than of those
of its creative genius. We know, or think we
know, from the enormous mass of critical writing that has appeared in the French language
the critical method or habit of the French; we
only conclude (we are such unconscious people) that the French are "more critical" than
we, and sometimes even plume ourselves a
little with the fact, as if the French were the
less spontaneous. Perhaps they are; but we
might remind ourselves that criticism is as inevitable as breathing, and that we should be
none the worse for articulating what passes in
our minds when we read a book and feel an
emotion about it, for criticizing our own minds
in their work of criticism. One of the facts
that might come to light in this process is our
tendency to insist, when we praise a poet,
upon those aspects of his work in which he
least resembles any one else. In these aspects
or parts of his work we pretend to find what is
individual, what is the peculiar essence of the
man. We dwell with satisfaction upon the
poet's difference from his predecessors, especially his immediate predecessors; we endeavour
to find something that can be isolated in order
to be enjoyed. Whereas if we approach a poet
without this prejudice we shall often find that
not only the best, but the most individual parts
of his work may be those in which the dead
poets, his ancestors, assert their immortality
most vigorously. And I do not mean the impressionable period of adolescence, but the
period of full maturity.

    Yet if the only form of tradition, of handing
down, consisted in following the ways of the
immediate generation before us in a blind or
timid adherence to its successes, "tradition"

should positively be discouraged. We have seen many such simple currents soon lost in the sand; and novelty is better than repetition. Tradition is a matter of much wider significance. It cannot be inherited, and if you want it you must obtain it by great labour. It involves, in the first place, the historical sense, which we may call nearly indispensable to any one who would continue to be a poet beyond his twenty-fifth year; and the historical sense 10 involves a perception, not only of the pastness of the past, but of its presence; the historical sense compels a man to write not merely with his own generation in his bones, but with a feeling that the whole of the literature of Europe from Homer and within it the whole of the literature of his own country has a simultaneous existence and composes a simultaneous order. This historical sense, which is a sense of the timeless as well as of the tem- 20 poral and of the timeless and of the temporal together, is what makes a writer traditional. And it is at the same time what makes a writer most acutely conscious of his place in time, of his own contemporaneity.

No poet, no artist of any art, has his complete meaning alone. His significance, his appreciation is the appreciation of his relation to the dead poets and artists. You cannot value him alone; you must set him, for contrast and 30 comparison, among the dead. I mean this as a principle of aesthetic, not merely historical, criticism. The necessity that he shall conform, that he shall cohere, is not one-sided; what happens when a new work of art is created is something that happens simultaneously to all the works of art which preceded it. The existing monuments form an ideal order among themselves, which is modified by the introduction of the new (the really new) work of art 40 among them. The existing order is complete before the new work arrives; for order to persist after the supervention of novelty, the *whole* existing order must be, if ever so slightly, altered; and so the relations, proportions, values of each work of art toward the whole are readjusted; and this is conformity between the old and the new. Whoever has approved this idea of order, of the form of European, of English literature will not find it preposterous that the 50 past should be altered by the present as much as the present is directed by the past. And the poet who is aware of this will be aware of great difficulties and responsibilities.

In a peculiar sense he will be aware also that he must inevitably be judged by the standards of the past. I say judged, not amputated, by

them; not judged to be as good as, or worse or better than, the dead; and certainly not judged by the canons of dead critics. It is a judgment, a comparison, in which two things are measured by each other. To conform merely would be for the new work not really to conform at all; it would not be new, and would therefore not be a work of art. And we do not quite say that the new is more valuable because it fits in; but its fitting in is a test of its value— a test, it is true, which can only be slowly and cautiously applied, for we are none of us infallible judges of conformity. We say: it appears to conform, and is perhaps individual, or it appears individual, and may conform; but we are hardly likely to find that it is one and not the other.

To proceed to a more intelligible exposition of the relation of the poet to the past: he can neither take the past as a lump, an indiscriminate bolus, nor can he form himself wholly on one or two private admirations, nor can he form himself wholly upon one preferred period. The first course is inadmissible, the second is an important experience of youth, and the third is a pleasant and highly desirable supplement. The poet must be very conscious of the main current, which does not at all flow invariably through the most distinguished reputations. He must be quite aware of the obvious fact that art never improves, but that the material of art is never quite the same. He must be aware that the mind of Europe—the mind of his own country—a mind which he learns in time to be much more important than his own private mind—is a mind which changes, and that this change is a development which abandons nothing *en route,* which does not superannuate either Shakespeare, or Homer, or the rock drawing of the Magdalenian draughtsmen. That this development, refinement perhaps, complication certainly, is not, from the point of view of the artist, any improvement. Perhaps not even an improvement from the point of view of the psychologist or not to the extent which we imagine; perhaps only in the end based upon a complication in economics and machinery. But the difference between the present and the past is that the conscious present is an awareness of the past in a way and to an extent which the past's awareness of itself cannot show.

Some one said: "The dead writers are remote from us because we *know* so much more than they did." Precisely, and they are that which we know.

I am alive to a usual objection to what is

clearly part of my programme for the *métier* of poetry. The objection is that the doctrine requires a ridiculous amount of erudition (pedantry), a claim which can be rejected by appeal to the lives of poets in any pantheon. It will even be affirmed that much learning deadens or perverts poetic sensibility. While, however, we persist in believing that a poet ought to know as much as will not encroach upon his necessary receptivity and necessary laziness, it is not desirable to confine knowledge to whatever can be put into a useful shape for examinations, drawing-rooms, or the still more pretentious modes of publicity. Some can absorb knowledge, the more tardy must sweat for it. Shakespeare acquired more essential history from Plutarch than most men could from the whole British Museum. What is to be insisted upon is that the poet must develop or procure the consciousness of the past and that he should continue to develop this consciousness throughout his career.

What happens is a continual surrender of himself as he is at the moment to something which is more valuable. The progress of an artist is a continual self-sacrifice, a continual extinction of personality.

There remains to define this process of depersonalization and its relation to the sense of tradition. It is in this depersonalization that art may be said to approach the condition of science. I, therefore, invite you to consider, as a suggestive analogy, the action which takes place when a bit of finely filiated platinum is introduced into a chamber containing oxygen and sulphur dioxide.

## II

Honest criticism and sensitive appreciation are directed not upon the poet but upon the poetry. If we attend to the confused cries of the newspaper critics and the *susurrus* of popular repetition that follows, we shall hear the names of poets in great numbers; if we seek not Blue-book knowledge but the enjoyment of poetry, and ask for a poem, we shall seldom find it. I have tried to point out the importance of the relation of the poem to other poems by other authors, and suggested the conception of poetry as a living whole of all the poetry that has ever been written. The other aspect of this Impersonal theory of poetry is the relation of the poem to its author. And I hinted, by an analogy, that the mind of the mature poet differs from that of the immature one not precisely in any valuation of "personality," not being necessarily more interesting, or having "more to say," but rather by being a more

finely perfected medium in which special, or very varied, feelings are at liberty to enter into new combinations.

The analogy was that of the catalyst. When the two gases previously mentioned are mixed in the presence of a filament of platinum, they form sulphurous acid. This combination takes place only if the platinum is present; nevertheless the newly formed acid contains no trace of platinum, and the platinum itself is apparently unaffected; has remained inert, neutral, and unchanged. The mind of the poet is the shred of platinum. It may partly or exclusively operate upon the experience of the man himself; but, the more perfect the artist, the more completely separate in him will be the man who suffers and the mind which creates; the more perfectly will the mind digest and transmute the passions which are its material.

The experience, you will notice, the elements which enter the presence of the transforming catalyst, are of two kinds: emotions and feelings. The effect of a work of art upon the person who enjoys it is an experience different in kind from any experience not of art. It may be formed out of one emotion, or may be a combination of several; and various feelings, inhering for the writer in particular words or phrases or images, may be added to compose the final result. Or great poetry may be made without the direct use of any emotion whatever: composed out of feelings solely. Canto xv of the *Inferno* (Brunetto Latini) is a working up of the emotion evident in the situation; but the effect, though single as that of any work of art, is obtained by considerable complexity of detail. The last quatrain gives an image, a feeling attaching to an image, which "came," which did not develop simply out of what precedes, but which was probably in suspension in the poet's mind until the proper combination arrived for it to add itself to. The poet's mind is in fact a receptacle for seizing and storing up numberless feelings, phrases, images, which remain there until all the particles which can unite to form a new compound are present together.

If you compare several representative passages of the greatest poetry you see how great is the variety of types of combination, and also how completely any semi-ethical criterion of "sublimity" misses the mark. For it is not the "greatness," the intensity, of the emotions, the components, but the intensity of the artistic process, the pressure, so to speak, under which the fusion takes place, that counts. The episode of Paolo and Francesca employs a definite emotion, but the intensity of the poetry is something quite different from whatever intensity in the supposed experience it may give the impression of. It is no more intense, furthermore, than Canto XXVI, the voyage of Ulysses, which has not the direct dependence upon an emotion. Great variety is possible in the process of transmutation of emotion: the murder of Agamemnon, or the agony of Othello, gives an artistic effect apparently closer to a possible original than the scenes from Dante. In the *Agamemnon*, the artistic emotion approximates to the emotion of an actual spectator; in *Othello* to the emotion of the protagonist himself. But the difference between art and the event is always absolute; the combination which is the murder of Agamemnon is probably as complex as that which is the voyage of Ulysses. In either case there has been a fusion of elements. The ode of Keats contains a number of feelings which have nothing particular to do with the nightingale, but which the nightingale, partly, perhaps, because of its attractive name, and partly because of its reputation, served to bring together.

The point of view which I am struggling to attack is perhaps related to the metaphysical theory of the substantial unity of the soul: for my meaning is, that the poet has, not a "personality" to express, but a particular medium, which is only a medium and not a personality, in which impressions and experiences combine in peculiar and unexpected ways. Impressions and experiences which are important for the man may take no place in the poetry, and those which become important in the poetry may play quite a negligible part in the man, the personality.

I will quote a passage which is unfamiliar enough to be regarded with fresh attention in the light—or darkness—of these observations:

> And now methinks I could e'en chide myself
> For doating on her beauty, though her death
> Shall be revenged after no common action.
> Does the silkworm expend her yellow labours
> For thee? For thee does she undo herself?
> Are lordships sold to maintain ladyships
> For the poor benefit of a bewildering minute?
> Why does yon fellow falsify highways,
> And put his life between the judge's lips,
> To refine such a thing—keeps horse and men
> To beat their valours for her? . . .

In this passage (as is evident if it is taken in its context) there is a combination of positive and negative emotions: an intensely strong attraction toward beauty and an equally intense fascination by the ugliness which is contrasted with it and which destroys it. This balance of contrasted emotion is in the dramatic situation to which the speech is pertinent, but that situation alone is inadequate to it. This is, so to speak, the structural emotion, provided by the drama. But the whole effect, the dominant one, is due to the fact that a number of floating feelings, having an affinity to this emotion by no means superficially evident, have combined with it to give us a new art emotion.

It is not in his personal emotions, the emotions provoked by particular events in his life, that the poet is in any way remarkable or interesting. His particular emotions may be simple, or crude, or flat. The emotion in his poetry will be a very complex thing, but not with the complexity of the emotions of people who have very complex or unusual emotions in life. One error, in fact, of eccentricity in poetry is to seek for new human emotions to express; and in this search for novelty in the wrong place it discovers the perverse. The business of the poet is not to find new emotions, but to use the ordinary ones and, in working them up into poetry, to express feelings which are not in actual emotions at all. And emotions which he has never experienced will serve his turn as well as those familiar to him. Consequently, we must believe that "emotion recollected in tranquillity" is an inexact formula. For it is neither emotion, nor recollection, nor, without distortion of meaning, tranquillity. It is a concentration, and a new thing resulting from the concentration, of a very great number of experiences which to the practical and active person would not seem to be experiences at all; it is a concentration which does not happen consciously or of deliberation. These experiences are not "recollected," and they finally unite in an atmosphere which is "tranquil" only in that it is a passive attending upon the event. Of course this is not quite the whole story. There is a great deal, in the writing of poetry, which must be conscious and deliberate. In fact, the bad poet is usually unconscious where he ought to be conscious, and conscious where he ought to be unconscious. Both errors tend to make him "personal." Poetry is not a turning loose of emotion, but an escape from emotion; it is not the expression of personality but an escape from personality. But, of course, only those who have personality and emotions know what it means to want to escape from these things.

III ὁ δὲ νοῦς ἴσως Θειότερόν τι χαὶ ἀπαθές ἐστιν.

This essay proposes to halt at the frontier of metaphysics or mysticism, and confine itself to such practical conclusions as can be applied by the responsible person interested in poetry. To divert interest from the poet to the poetry is a laudable aim: for it would conduce to a juster estimation of actual poetry, good and bad. There are many people who appreciate the expression of sincere emotion in verse, and there is a smaller number of people who can appreciate technical excellence. But very few know when there is an expression of *significant* emotion, emotion which has its life in the poem and not in the history of the poet. The

emotion of art is impersonal. And the poet cannot reach this impersonality without surrendering himself wholly to the work to be done. And he is not likely to know what is to be done unless he lives in what is not merely the present, but the present moment of the past, unless he is conscious, not of what is dead, but of what is already living.

# Rupert Brooke
## 1887 - 1915

# Wilfred Owen
## 1893 - 1918

# Herbert Read
## 1893 -

Rupert Brooke was born 3 August, 1887 at Rugby. His father was William Parker Brooke, a Housemaster at Rugby School; Rupert was entered at School Field, Rugby, his father's House, and in 1906 entered King's College, Cambridge. He was deputized as head of the House on his father's death in 1911. In the same year he published Poems. He continued to write, and began also to travel; in September 1914, on the outbreak of World War I, he was commissioned in the Royal Naval Division. He died in Greece, on the island of Scyros, April 23, 1915. The Collected Poems of Rupert Brooke were published in 1918. Arthur Stringer's Red Wine of Youth (Indianapolis, 1948) is the only biography.

Wilfred Owen was born 18 March, 1893 at Oswestry, Shropshire. He was educated at Birkenhead Institute, Liverpool; he read widely in poetry and was especially attached to Keats. From 1913 to 1915 he lived in France because of delicate health, but he entered the service in spite of his infirmity and was killed in France at the Sambre Canal November 4, 1918—just a week before the Armistice. His Poems were published posthumously in 1920, edited by Siegfried Sassoon; his complete Poems were published in 1931 with an introduction and memoir by Edmund Blunden.

Herbert Read was born at Muscoates, Kirbymoorshire, Yorkshire, 4 December, 1893. He attended Crossley's School, Halifax, and the University of Leeds. He was a captain in the Yorkshire Regiment in World War I. Since that time he has been a writer, editor, museum keeper, professor of art, and publisher. His first volume of poems was Songs of Chaos (1915); the latest of his dozen volumes of poetry is Moon's Farm (1956). Collected Poems (1951) includes the best of his poems up to that date. He has written a novel, The Green Child (1935), and many significant critical works, including The Meaning of Art (1931), The Innocent Eye (1947), Form in Modern Poetry (1948), and The Tenth Muse (1958). Henry Treece's Herbert Read (London, 1944) is the best critical study.

## The Great Lover [1]

### By RUPERT BROOKE

I have been so great a lover: filled my days
So proudly with the splendour of Love's praise,
The pain, the calm, and the astonishment,
Desire illimitable, and still content,
And all dear names men use, to cheat despair,
For the perplexed and viewless streams that
    bear    6
Our hearts at random down the dark of life.
Now, ere the unthinking silence on that strife
Steals down, I would cheat drowsy Death so
    far,
My night shall be remembered for a star   10
That outshone all the suns of all men's days.
Shall I not crown them with immortal praise
Whom I have loved, who have given me, dared
    with me
High secrets, and in darkness knelt to see
The inenarrable godhead of delight?   15
Love is a flame;—we have beaconed the
    world's night.
A city:—and we have built it, these and I.
An emperor:—we have taught the world to
    die.

[1] Written in Tahiti, 1914; published, 1918. Reprinted by permission of Dodd, Mead & Company from The Collected Poems of Rupert Brooke. Copyright 1915 by Dodd, Mead & Company, Inc. Copyright 1943 by Edward Marsh.

So, for their sakes I lived, ere I go hence,
And the high cause of Love's magnificence,    20
And to keep loyalties young, I'll write those
    names
Golden for ever, eagles, crying flames,
And set them as a banner, that men may know,
To dare the generations, burn, and blow
Out on the wind of Time, shining and stream-
    ing. . . .    25


These I have loved:
            White plates and cups, clean-gleaming,
Ringed with blue lines; and feathery, faery
    dust;
Wet roofs, beneath the lamplight; the strong
    crust
Of friendly bread and many-tasting food;
Rainbows; and the blue bitter smoke of wood;
And radiant raindrops couching in cool flowers;
And flowers themselves, that sway through
    sunny hours,    32
Dreaming of moths that drink them under the
    moon;
Then, the cool kindliness of sheets, that soon
Smooth away trouble; and the rough male kiss
Of blankets; grainy wood; live hair that is    36
Shining and free; blue-massing clouds; the keen
Unpassioned beauty of a great machine;
The benison of hot water; furs to touch;
The good smell of old clothes; and other
    such—    40
The comfortable smell of friendly fingers,
Hair's fragrance, and the musty reek that lingers
About dead leaves and last year's ferns. . . .

                        Dear names,
And thousand other throng to me! Royal
    flames;
Sweet water's dimpling laugh from tap or
    spring;    45
Holes in the ground; and voices that do sing;
Voices in laughter, too; and body's pain,
Soon turned to peace; and the deep-panting
    train;
Firm sands; the little dulling edge of foam
That browns and dwindles as the wave goes
    home;    50
And washen stones, gay for an hour; the cold
Graveness of iron; moist black earthen mould;
Sleep; and high places; footprints in the dew;
And oaks; and brown horse-chestnuts, glossy-
    new;
And new-peeled stocks; and shining pools on
    grass;—    55
All these have been my loves. And these shall
    pass,
Whatever passes not, in the great hour,
Nor all my passion, all my prayers, have power
To hold them with me through the gate of
    Death.
They'll play deserter, turn with the traitor
    breath,    60

Break the high bond we made, and sell Love's
    trust
And sacramented covenant to the dust.
—Oh, never a doubt but, somewhere, I shall
    wake,
And give what's left of love again, and make
New friends, now strangers. . . .
                        But the best I've known,
Stays here, and changes, breaks, grows old, is
    blown    66
Above the winds of the world, and fades from
    brains
Of living men, and dies.
                        Nothing remains.

O dear my loves, O faithless, once again
This one last gift I give: that after men    70
Shall know, and later lovers, far-removed,
Praise you, "All these were lovely"; say, "He
    loved."

## Strange Meeting [1]

### By WILFRED OWEN

It seemed that out of battle I escaped
Down some profound dull tunnel, long since
    scooped
Through granites which titanic wars had
    groined.
Yet also there encumbered sleepers groaned,
Too fast in thought or death to be bestirred.    [5]
Then, as I probed them, one sprang up, and
    stared
With piteous recognition in fixed eyes,
Lifting distressful hands as if to bless.
And by his smile, I knew that sullen hall,
By his dead smile I knew we stood in Hell.    [10]
With a thousand pains that vision's face was
    grained;
Yet no blood reached there from the upper
    ground,
And no guns thumped, or down the flues made
    moan.
"Strange friend," I said, "here is no cause to
    mourn."
"None," said the other, "save the undone
    years,    [15]
The hopelessness. Whatever hope is yours,
Was my life also; I went hunting wild
After the wildest beauty in the world,
Which lies not calm in eyes, or braided hair,
But mocks the steady running of the hour,    [20]
And if it grieves, grieves richlier than here.
For by my glee might many men have laughed,
And of my weeping something had been left,
Which must die now. I mean the truth untold,
The pity of war, the pity war distilled.    [25]
Now men will go content with what we spoiled.
Or, discontent, boil bloody, and be spilled.
They will be swift with swiftness of the tigress,

None will break ranks, though nations trek
    from progress.
Courage was mine, and I had mystery,    30
Wisdom was mine, and I had mastery;
To miss the march of this retreating world
Into vain citadels that are not walled.
Then, when much blood had clogged their
    chariot-wheels
I would go up and wash them from sweet wells,
Even with truths that lie too deep for taint. 36
I would have poured my spirit without stint
But not through wounds; not on the cess of
    war.
Foreheads of men have bled where no wounds
    were.
I am the enemy you killed, my friend.    40
I knew you in this dark; for so you frowned
Yesterday through me as you jabbed and killed.
I parried; but my hands were loath and cold.
Let me sleep now. . . ."

# A World within a War [1]

### By HERBERT READ

L'espérance est le seul bien que le dégoût
respecte.       VAUVENARGUES

### I

Sixteen years ago I built this house
By an oak tree on an acre of wild land
Its walls white against the beechwood
Its roof of Norfolk reed and sedge.

The mossy turf I levelled for a lawn    5
But for the most part left the acre wild
Knowing I could never live
From its stony soil. My work is within
Between three stacks of books. My window
Looks out on a long line of elms.    10

A secular and insecure retreat—
The alien world is never far away.
Over the ridge, beyond the elms
The railway runs: a passing train
Sends a faint tremor through the ground    15
Enough to sever a rotted picture-cord
Or rattle the teaspoon against my cup.
A dozen times a day a red bus
Trundles down the lane: there is the screech
    and scuttle
Of minor traffic: voices rise    20
Suddenly from silent wheels.
But such dusty veins drain the land
And leave an interstitial stillness.

The hedgehog and the grass-snake
Still haunt my wood. Winter    25
Brings the starved wildings nearer: once

[1] Published 1944. From *A World within a War*
by Herbert Read, copyright, 1945, by Harcourt,
Brace and Company, Inc. and used with their permission.

We woke to find a fox's tracks
Printed on the crisp film of snow.
It was the first year of my second war
When every night a maddened yaffle    30
Thrummed on the icicled thatch.
Another day a reckless kestrel
Dashed against a gable and fell
Dead at my feet: the children
Watched its dying flutter and the fiery eye    35
Slowly eclipsed under a dim grey lid.

For years the city like a stream of lava
Crept towards us: now its flow
Is frozen in fear. To the sere earth
The ancient ritual returns: the months    40
Have their heraldic labours once again.
A tractor chugs through the frozen clods
And gold buds bead the gorse.
In coppices where besom-heads are cut.
Hedges are trimmed again and primroses    45
Bunch in splendour on the open banks.
The sparring rooks pick twigs
From shockhead nests built high
In the dark tracery of the elms.
April and the nightingales will come    50
From an alien world. The squirrels
Chatter in the green hazel-trees.
The nuthatch inspects the oak's ribbed bark
While the robin jumps round his own domain.
The hay is mown in June. With summer    55
Comes all ripeness, rusty, red and gold
To die in September. The reaper
Spirals round the blanched fields
The corn diminishing until at last
The expected moment comes and rabbits    60
Zigzag across the glistening stubble
Pursued by yelping dogs and sudden guns.
In December the corn is thrashed:
In the frosty evening the engine's smoke
Trails slowly above the berried twigs    65
And meets the rising mist.

### II

Sedate within this palisade
Which unforethinking I have made

Of brittle leaves and velvet flowers,
I re-indite a Book of Hours—    70

Would emulate the Lombard School
(Crisp as medals, bright but cool)

Talk mainly of the Human Passion
That made us in a conscious fashion

Strive to control our human fate:    75
But in the margins interpolate

Apes and angels playing tunes
On harpsichords or saxophones

Throughout the story thus maintain
Under a sacred melody the bass profane.    80

My saints were often silly men
Fond of wine and loose with women.

When they rose to holy stature
They kept the whims of human nature

Were mystics in their London gardens      85
Or wore instead of hairshirts burdens

Of a mild domestic sort: but so devout
That suddenly they would go out

And die for freedom in the street
Or fall like partridges before a butt      90

Of ambushed tyranny and hate.

Other legends will relate

The tale of men whose only love
Was simple work: whose usual lives

Were formed in mirth and music, or in words
Whose golden echoes are wild rewards      96

For all our suffering, unto death . . .

On the last page a colophon
Would conclude the liberal plan

Showing Man within a frame      100
Of trophies stolen from a dream.

### III

The busy routine kills the flowers
That blossom only on the casual path.
The gift is sacrificed to gain: the gain
Is ploughed into the hungry ground.      105
The best of life is sparely spent
In contemplation of those laws
Illustrious in leaves, in tiny webs
Spun by the ground-spider: in snailshells
And mushroom gills: in acorns and gourds—
The design everywhere evident      111
The purpose still obscure.

In a free hour
I walk through the woods with God
When the air is calm and the midges      115
Hover in the netted sun and stillness.
Deep then I sink in reverie. There is rest
Above the beating heart: the body
Settles round its axis: mind simulates
The crystal in the cooling rock      120
The theorem in the beetle's eye—
After the day's mutations
Finds the silver node of sleep. . . .

In that peace
Mind looks into a mirror poised      125
Above body: sees in perspective
Guts, bones and glands: the make of a man.

Out of that labyrinth
The man emerges: becomes
What he is: by no grace      130
Can become other: can only seize
The pattern in the bone, in branching veins
In clever vesicles and valves
And imitate in acts that beauty.

His nature is God's nature: but torn      135
How torn and fretted by vain energies
The darting images of eye and ear
Veiled in the web of memory
Drifts of words that deaden
The subtle manuals of sense.      140

But the pattern once perceived and held
Is then viable: in good gait and going
In fine song and singular sign: in all
God's festival of perfect form.

### IV

Here is my cell: here my houselings      145
Gentle in love, excelling hate, extending
Tokens of friendship to free hearts.

But well we know there is a world without
Of alarm and horror and extreme distress
Where pity is a bond of fear      150
And only the still heart has grace.

An ancient road winds through the wood
The wood is dark: a chancel where the mind
Sways in terror of the formal foe.

Their feet upon the peat and sand      155
Make no sound. But sounds were everywhere
     around
Life rustled under fallen leaves, rotted twigs
Snapped like rafters above the heads
Of those friars preachers, constant and firm,
Who in charity advanced against the Arian
     hate      160
Ambushed against them. See now
The falchion falls: the martyred limbs
Lie like trimmed branches on the ground.

The ancient road winds through the wood
A path obscure and frail.      165

The martyr takes it and the man
Who makes the martyr by his deed.

Death waits on evil and on holiness
Death waits in the leafy labyrinth.

There is a grace to still the blood      170
Of those who take the daring path:

There is a grace that fills the dying eye
With pity for the wielder of the axe.

There is a grace that nulls the pain
Of martyrs in their hour of death.    175

Death is no pain to desperate men.

Vision itself is desperate: the act
Is born of the ideal: the hand
Must seize the hovering grail.
The sense of glory stirs the heart    180
Out of its stillness: a white light
Is in the hills and the thin cry
Of a hunter's horn. We shall act: we shall
    build
A crystal city in the age of peace
Setting out from an island of calm    185
A limpid source of love.

## V

The branches break. The beaters
Are moving in: lie still my loves
Like deer: let the lynx
Glide through the dappled underwoods.    190
Lie still: he cannot hear: he may not see.

Should the ravening death descend
We will be calm: die like the mouse
Terrified but tender. The claw
Will meet no satisfaction in our sweet flesh 195
And we shall have known peace.

In a house beneath a beechwood
In an acre of wild land.

# Aldous Huxley

## 1894-

Aldous Huxley was born in Godalming, Surrey, 26 July, 1894. His father was Leonard Huxley, eldest son of the scientist Thomas Henry Huxley; his mother was Julia Arnold, daughter of Thomas Arnold, Matthew Arnold's brother.

While at Eton the boy Huxley developed eye trouble, and became for a time almost completely blind; he has indicated that the resulting isolation from ordinary boys' activities required him to live mainly on his inner resources. He attended Balliol College, Oxford, and then became a literary journalist in London, working with John Middleton Murry on The Athenaeum and reviewing plays for the Westminster Gazette before moving to Italy in 1923. Since 1930 he has lived in France, England, and America.

His first books were volumes of poetry: The Burning Wheel (1916) and The Defeat of Youth (1918). The strange, elaborate, and often grotesque poems of Leda (1920) apparently carried him as far as he felt poetry could take him. Also in 1920 came Limbo, six stories and one play; and in 1922 came Mortal Coils, which includes two of the most famous short stories, "Green Tunnels" and "The Giaconda Smile." Underlying the elaborate shadow play of personality and the brilliant dialogue of the stories are the questions of the purpose and meaning of life and the nature and meaning of love, the questions for which Huxley in 1922 felt there were no positive answers.

The first of the novels, Crome Yellow, appeared in 1921; its line "We all know that there's no ultimate point" states its theme. Antic Hay followed in 1923, a kaleidoscopic shifting of scenes and people, men and women whose desperate but futile causes draw them hopelessly in circles without end. Those Barren Leaves (1925) and Point Counter Point (1928) begin the intrusion of meaning into Huxley's universe, and Brave New World (1932), the most widely read of his novels, combines science fiction with Swift-like satire to imply to discerning readers a basic change in Huxley's viewpoint, an awareness of the positive values of love.

Eyeless in Gaza (1936), After Many a Summer (1939), Time Must Have a Stop (1944), and Ape and Essence (1949) retain some of the bizarre trappings of the earlier novels, though their satire is more intensive and the light touch sometimes found earlier has practically disappeared. Yet in what they say, they might almost have been written by a different author from the Huxley of Antic Hay. Philo Buck has stated the prescription for humanity Huxley offers in his new role as prophet, as shown in Eyeless in Gaza and After Many a Summer: "Eradicate greed and make the fruits of benevolence prevail by founding societies of friends." Ape and Essence, written in the form of a scenario, is a savage document with human characters reminiscent of the Yahoos in Gulliver's Travels, yet it too implies much the same prescription.

Besides the short stories already mentioned, Huxley has published three collections, Little Mexican (1924), Two or Three Graces (1926), and Brief Candles (1930). Collected Short Stories appeared in 1957. There are several volumes of travel, of which the best known is Jesting Pilate (1926); Grey Eminence, A Biography of Father Joseph (1941); and a long list of volumes on philosophy, society, and the arts, including Proper Studies (1927), The Olive Tree (1936), and Ends and Means (1937). The best exposition of his mysticism is The Perennial Philosophy (New York, 1945).

Studies by André Maurois appear in Private Universe (London, 1932) and in Prophets and Poets (New York, 1935). Alexander Henderson's critical study Aldous Huxley (New York, 1935) was written before many of Huxley's most revealing statements of philosophy and intent were made. Aldous Huxley: a Literary

Study, *by John Atkins (London, 1956) is recommended.*

## Green Tunnels [1]

"In the Italian gardens of the thirteenth century . . . " Mr. Buzzacott interrupted himself to take another helping of the risotto which was being offered him. "Excellent risotto this," he observed. "Nobody who was not born in Milan can make it properly. So they say."

"So they say," Mr. Topes repeated in his sad, apologetic voice, and helped himself in his turn.

"Personally," said Mrs. Topes, with decision, "I find all Italian cooking abominable. I don't like the oil—especially hot. No, thank you." She recoiled from the proffered dish.

After the first mouthful Mr. Buzzacott put down his fork. "In the Italian gardens of the thirteenth century," he began again, making with his long, pale hand a curved and flowery gesture that ended with a clutch at his beard, "a frequent and most felicitous use was made of green tunnels."

"Green tunnels?" Barbara woke up suddenly from her tranced silence. "Green tunnels?"

"Yes, my dear," said her father. "Green tunnels. Arched alleys covered with vines or other creeping plants. Their length was often very considerable."

But Barbara had once more ceased to pay attention to what he was saying. Green tunnels —the word had floated down to her, through profound depths of reverie, across great spaces of abstraction, startling her like the sound of a strange-voiced bell. Green tunnels—what a wonderful idea. She would not listen to her father explaining the phrase into dullness. He made everything dull; an inverted alchemist, turning gold into lead. She pictured caverns in a great aquarium, long vistas between rocks and scarcely swaying weeds and pale, discoloured corals; endless dim green corridors with huge lazy fishes loitering aimlessly along them. Green-faced monsters with goggling eyes and mouths that slowly opened and shut. Green tunnels . . .

"I have seen them illustrated in illuminated manuscripts of the period," Mr. Buzzacott went on; once more he clutched his pointed brown beard—clutched and combed it with his long fingers.

Mr. Topes looked up. The glasses of his round owlish spectacles flashed as he moved his head. "I know what you mean," he said.

"I have a very good mind to have one planted in my garden here."

"It will take a long time to grow," said Mr. Topes. "In this sand, so close to the sea, you will only be able to plant vines. And they come up very slowly—very slowly indeed." He shook his head and the points of light danced wildly in his spectacles. His voice drooped hopelessly, his grey moustache drooped, his whole person drooped. Then, suddenly, he pulled himself up. A shy, apologetic smile appeared on his face. He wriggled uncomfortably. Then, with a final rapid shake of the head, he gave vent to a quotation:

"But at my back I always hear
Time's winged chariot hurrying near."

He spoke deliberately, and his voice trembled a little. He always found it painfully difficult to say something choice and out of the ordinary; and yet what a wealth of remembered phrase, what apt new coinages were always surging through his mind!

"They don't grow so slowly as all that," said Mr. Buzzacott confidently. He was only just over fifty, and looked a handsome thirty-five. He gave himself at least another forty years; indeed, he had not yet begun to contemplate the possibility of ever concluding.

"Miss Barbara will enjoy it, perhaps—your green tunnel." Mr. Topes sighed and looked across the table at his host's daughter.

Barbara was sitting with her elbows on the table, her chin in her hands, staring in front of her. The sound of her own name reached her faintly. She turned her head in Mr. Topes's direction and found herself confronted by the glitter of his round, convex spectacles. At the end of the green tunnel—she stared at the shining circles—hung the eyes of a goggling fish. They approached, floating, closer and closer, along the dim submarine corridor.

Confronted by this fixed regard, Mr. Topes looked away. What thoughtful eyes! He couldn't remember ever to have seen eyes so full of thought. There were certain Madonnas of Montagna, he reflected, very like her: mild little blonde Madonnas with slightly snub noses and very, very young. But he was old; it would be many years, in spite of Buzzacott, before the vines grew up into a green tunnel. He took a sip of wine; then, mechanically, sucked his drooping grey moustache.

"Arthur!"

At the sound of his wife's voice Mr. Topes

[1] Published 1922. From *Mortal Coils* by Aldous Huxley, copyright 1922, 1950 by Aldous Huxley. Reprinted by permission of Harper & Brothers.

started, raised his napkin to his mouth. Mrs. Topes did not permit the sucking of moustaches. It was only in moments of absent-mindedness that he ever offended, now.

"The Marchese Prampolini is coming here to take coffee," said Mr. Buzzacott suddenly. "I almost forgot to tell you."

"One of these Italian marquises, I suppose," said Mrs. Topes, who was no snob, except in England. She raised her chin with a little jerk.

Mr. Buzzacott executed an upward curve of the hand in her direction. "I assure you, Mrs. Topes, he belongs to a very old and distinguished family. They are Genoese in origin. You remember their palace, Barbara? Built by Alessi."

Barbara looked up. "Oh yes," she said vaguely. "Alessi. I know." Alessi: Aleppo— where a malignant and a turbaned Turk. *And* a turbaned; that had always seemed to her very funny.

"Several of his ancestors," Mr. Buzzacott went on, "distinguished themselves as viceroys of Corsica. They did good work in the suppression of rebellion. Strange, isn't it"—he turned parenthetically to Mr. Topes—"the way in which sympathy is always on the side of rebels? What a fuss people made of Corsica! That ridiculous book of Gregorovius, for example. And the Irish, and the Poles, and all the rest of them. It always seems to me very superfluous and absurd."

"Isn't it, perhaps, a little natural?" Mr. Topes began timorously and tentatively; but his host went on without listening.

"The present marquis," he said, "is the head of the local Fascisti. They have done no end of good work in this district in the way of preserving law and order and keeping the lower classes in their place."

"Ah, the Fascisti," Mrs. Topes repeated approvingly. "One would like to see something of the kind in England. What with all these strikes . . ."

"He has asked me for a subscription to the funds of the organisation. I shall give him one, of course."

"Of course." Mrs. Topes nodded. "My nephew, the one who was a major during the war, volunteered in the last coal strike. He was sorry, I know, that it didn't come to a fight. 'Aunt Annie,' he said to me, when I saw him last, 'if there had been a fight we should have knocked them out completely—completely.'"

In Aleppo, the Fascisti, malignant *and* turbaned, were fighting, under the palm trees.

Weren't they palm trees, those tufted green plumes?

"What, no ice to-day? *Niente gelato?*" inquired Mr. Buzzacott as the maid put down the compote of peaches on the table.

Concetta apologised. The ice-making machine in the village had broken down. There would be no ice till to-morrow.

"Too bad," said Mr. Buzzacott. "*Troppo male*, Concetta."

Under the palm trees, Barbara saw them: they pranced about, fighting. They were mounted on big dogs, and in the trees were enormous many-coloured birds.

"Goodness me, the child's asleep." Mrs. Topes was proffering the dish of peaches. "How much longer am I to hold this in front of your nose, Barbara?"

Barbara felt herself blushing. "I'm so sorry," she mumbled, and took the dish clumsily.

"Day-dreaming. It's a bad habit."

"It's one we all succumb to sometimes," put in Mr. Topes deprecatingly, with a little nervous tremble of the head.

"You may, my dear," said his wife. "I do not."

Mr. Topes lowered his eyes to his plate and went on eating.

"The *marchese* should be here at any moment now," said Mr. Buzzacott, looking at his watch. "I hope he won't be late. I find I suffer so much from any postponement of my siesta. This Italian heat," he added, with growing plaintiveness, "one can't be too careful."

"Ah, but when I was with my father in India," began Mrs. Topes in a tone of superiority: "he was an Indian civilian, you know . . ."

Aleppo, India—always the palm trees. Cavalcades of big dogs, and tigers too.

Concetta ushered in the marquis. Delighted. Pleased to meet. Speak English? Yés, yéss. *Pocchino.* Mrs. Topes: and Mr. Topes, the distinguished antiquarian. Ah, of course; know his name very well. My daughter. Charmed. Often seen the signorina bathing. Admired the way she dives. Beautiful—the hand made a long, caressing gesture. These athletic English signorine. The teeth flashed astonishingly white in the brown face, the dark eyes glittered. She felt herself blushing again, looked away, smiled foolishly. The marquis had already turned back to Mr. Buzzacott.

"So you have decided to settle in our Carrarese."

Well, not settled exactly; Mr. Buzzacot

wouldn't go so far as to say settled. A villino for the summer months. The winter in Rome. One was forced to live abroad. Taxation in England . . . Soon they were all talking. Barbara looked at them. Beside the marquis they all seemed half dead. His face flashed as he talked; he seemed to be boiling with life. Her father was limp and pale, like something long buried from the light; and Mr. Topes was all dry and shrivelled; and Mrs. Topes looked more than ever like something worked by clockwork. They were talking about Socialism and Fascisti, and all that. Barbara did not listen to what they were saying; but she looked at them, absorbed.

Good-bye, good-bye. The animated face with its flash of a smile was turned like a lamp from one to another. Now it was turned on her. Perhaps one evening she would come, with her father, and the Signora Topes. He and his sister gave little dances sometimes. Only the gramophone, of course. But that was better than nothing, and the signorina must dance divinely—another flash—he could see that. He pressed her hand again. Good-bye.

It was time for the siesta.

"Don't forget to pull down the mosquito netting, my dear," Mr. Buzzacott exhorted. "There is always a danger of anophylines."

"All right, father." She moved towards the door without turning round to answer him. He was always terribly tiresome about mosquito nets. Once they had driven through the Campagna in a hired cab, completely enclosed in an improvised tent of netting. The monuments along the Appian Way had loomed up mistily as through bridal veils. And how everyone had laughed. But her father, of course, hadn't so much as noticed it. He never noticed anything.

"Is it at Berlin, that charming little Madonna of Montagna's?" Mr. Topes abruptly asked. "The one with the Donor kneeling in the left-hand corner as if about to kiss the foot of the Child." His spectacles flashed in Mr. Buzzacott's direction.

"Why do you ask?"

"I don't know. I was just thinking of it."

"I think you must mean the one in the Mond Collection."

"Ah, yes; very probably. In the Mond . . . "

Barbara opened the door and walked into the twilight of her shuttered room. It was hot even here; for another three hours it would hardly be possible to stir. And that old idiot, Mrs. Topes, always made a fuss if one came in to lunch with bare legs and one's after-bathing tunic. "In India we always made a point of being properly and adequately dressed. An Englishwoman must keep up her position with natives, and to all intents and purposes Italians *are* natives." And so she always had to put on shoes and stockings and a regular frock just at the hottest hour of the day. What an old ass that woman was! She slipped off her clothes as fast as she could. That was a little better.

Standing in front of the long mirror in the wardrobe door she came to the humiliating conclusion that she looked like of piece of badly toasted bread. Brown face, brown neck and shoulders, brown arms, brown legs from the knee downwards; but all the rest of her was white, silly, effeminate, townish white. If only one could run about with no clothes on till one was like those little coppery children who rolled and tumbled in the burning sand! Now she was just underdone, half-baked, and wholly ridiculous. For a long time she looked at her pale image. She saw herself running, bronzed all over, along the sand; or through a field of flowers, narcissus and wild tulips; or in soft grass under grey olive trees. She turned round with a sudden start. There, in the shadows behind her . . . No, of course there was nothing. It was that awful picture in a magazine she had looked at, so many years ago, when she was a child. There was a lady sitting at her dressing-table, doing her hair in front of the glass; and a huge, hairy black monkey creeping up behind her. She always got the creeps when she looked at herself in a mirror. It was very silly. But still. She turned away from the mirror, crossed the room, and, without lowering the mosquito curtains, lay down on her bed. The flies buzzed about her, settled incessantly on her face. She shook her head, flapped at them angrily with her hands. There would be peace if she let down the netting. But she thought of the Appian Way seen mistily through the bridal veil and preferred to suffer the flies. In the end she had to surrender; the brutes were too much for her. But, at any rate, it wasn't the fear of anophylines that made her lower the netting.

Undisturbed now and motionless, she lay stretched stiffly out under the transparent bell of gauze. A specimen under a glass case. The fancy possessed her mind. She saw a huge museum with thousands of glass cases, full of fossils and butterflies and stuffed birds and mediaeval spoons and armour and Florentine jewellery and mummies and carved ivory and illuminated manuscripts. But in one of the cases was a human being, shut up there alive.

All of a sudden she became horribly miserable. "Boring, boring, boring," she whispered, formulating the words aloud. Would it never stop being boring? The tears came into her eyes. How awful everything was! And perhaps it would go on being as bad as this all her life. Seventeen from seventy was fifty-three. Fifty-three years of it. And if she lived to a hundred 10 there would be more than eighty.

The thought depressed her all the evening. Even her bath after tea did her no good. Swimming far out, far out, she lay there, floating on the warm water. Sometimes she looked at the sky, sometimes she turned her head towards the shore. Framed in their pinewoods, the villas looked as small and smug as the advertisement of a seaside resort. But behind them, across the level plain, were the mountains. Sharp, bare 20 peaks of limestone, green woodland slopes and grey-green expanses of terraced olive trees— they seemed marvellously close and clear in this evening light. And beautiful, beautiful beyond words. But that, somehow, only made things worse. And Shelley had lived a few miles farther up the coast, there, behind the headland guarding the Gulf of Spezia. Shelley had been drowned in this milk-warm sea. That made it worse too. 30

The sun was getting very low and red over the sea. She swam slowly in. On the beach Mrs. Topes waited, disapprovingly. She had known somebody, a strong man, who had caught cramp from staying in too long. He sank like a stone. Like a stone. The queer people Mrs. Topes had known! And the funny things they did, the odd things that happened to them!

Dinner that evening was duller than ever. 40 Barbara went early to bed. All night long the same old irritating cicada scraped and scraped among the pine trees, monotonous and regular as clockwork. Zip zip, zip zip zip. Boring, boring. Was the animal never bored by its own noise? It seemed odd that it shouldn't be. But, when she came to think of it, nobody ever did get bored with their own noise. Mrs. Topes, for example; she never seemed to get bored. Zip zip, zip zip zip. The cicada went on with- 50 out pause.

Concetta knocked at the door at half-past seven. The morning was as bright and cloudless as all the mornings were. Barbara jumped up, looked from one window at the mountains, from the other at the sea; all seemed to be well with them. All was well with her, too, this

morning. Seated at the mirror, she did not so much as think of the big monkey in the far obscure corner of the room. A bathing dress and a bath-gown, sandals, a handkerchief round her head, and she was ready. Sleep had left no recollection of last night's mortal boredom. She ran downstairs.

"Good morning, Mr. Topes."

Mr. Topes was walking in the garden among the vines. He turned round, took off his hat, 10 smiled a greeting.

"Good morning, Miss Barbara." He paused. Then, with an embarrassed wriggle of introduction he went on; a queer little falter came into his voice. "A real Chaucerian morning, Miss Barbara. A May-day morning—only it happens to be September. Nature is fresh and bright, and there is at least one specimen in this dream garden"—he wriggled more uncomfortably 20 than ever, and there was a tremulous glitter in his round spectacle lenses—"of the poet's 'yonge fresshe folkes.'" He bowed in her direction, smiled deprecatingly, and was silent. The remark, it seemed to him, now that he had finished speaking, was somehow not as good as he had thought it would be.

Barbara laughed. "Chaucer! They used to make us read the *Canterbury Tales* at school. But they always bored me. Are you going to 30 bathe?"

"Not before breakfast." Mr. Topes shook his head. "One is getting a little old for that."

"Is one?" Why did the silly old man always say 'one' when he meant 'I'? She couldn't help laughing at him. "Well, I must hurry, or else I shall be late for breakfast again, and you know how I catch it."

She ran out, through the gate in the garden wall, across the beach, to the striped red-and- 40 white bathing cabin that stood before the house. Fifty yards away she saw the Marchese Prampolini, still dripping from the sea, running up towards his bathing hut. Catching sight of her, he flashed a smile in her direction, gave a military salute. Barbara waved her hand, then thought that the gesture had been too familiar —but at this hour of the morning it was difficult not to have bad jolly manners—and added the corrective of a stiff bow. After all, 50 she had only met him yesterday. Soon she was swimming out to sea, and, ugh! what a lot of horrible huge jelly-fish there were.

Mr. Topes had followed her slowly through the gate and across the sand. He watched her running down from the cabin, slender as a boy, with long, bounding strides. He watched her go jumping with great splashes through the deepening water, then throw herself forward and begin to swim. He watched her till she was no more than a small dark dot far out.

Emerging from his cabin, the marquis met him walking slowly along the beach, his head bent down and his lips slightly moving as though he were repeating something, a prayer or a poem, to himself.

"Good morning, signore." The marquis shook him by the hand with a more than English cordiality.

"Good morning," replied Mr. Topes, allowing his hand to be shaken. He resented this interruption of his thoughts.

"She swims very well, Miss Buzzacott."

"Very," assented Mr. Topes, and smiled to himself to think what beautiful, poetical things he might have said, if he had chosen.

"Well, so, so," said the marquis, too colloquial by half. He shook hands again, and the two men went their respective ways.

Barbara was still a hundred yards from the shore when she heard the crescendo and dying boom of the gong floating out from the villa. Damn! she'd be late again. She quickened her stroke and came splashing out through the shallows, flushed and breathless. She'd be ten minutes late, she calculated; it would take her at least that to do her hair and dress. Mrs. Topes would be on the warpath again; though what business that old woman had to lecture her as she did, goodness only knew. She always succeeded in making herself horribly offensive and unpleasant.

The beach was quite deserted as she trotted, panting, across it, empty to right and left as far as she could see. If only she had a horse to go galloping at the water's edge, miles and miles. Right away down to Bocca d'Arno she'd go, swim the river—she saw herself crouching on the horse's back, as he swam, with legs tucked up on the saddle, trying not to get her feet wet—and gallop on again, goodness only knew where.

In front of the cabin she suddenly halted. There in the ruffled sand she had seen a writing. Big letters, faintly legible, sprawled across her path.

## O CLARA D'ELLÉBEUSE.

She pieced the dim letters together. They hadn't been there when she started out to bathe. Who? . . . She looked round. The beach was quite empty. And what was the meaning? "O Clara d'Ellébeuse." She took her bath-gown from the cabin, slipped on her sandals, and ran back towards the house as fast as she could. She felt most horribly frightened.

It was a sultry, headachey sort of morning, with a hot sirocco that stirred the bunting on the flagstaffs. By midday the thunderclouds had covered half the sky. The sun still blazed on the sea, but over the mountains all was black and indigo. The storm broke noisily overhead just as they were drinking their after-luncheon coffee.

"Arthur," said Mrs. Topes, painfully calm, "shut the shutters, please."

She was not frightened, no. But she preferred not to see the lightning. When the room was darkened, she began to talk suavely and incessantly.

Lying back in her deep arm-chair, Barbara was thinking of Clara d'Ellébeuse. What did it mean and who was Clara d'Ellébeuse? And why had he written it there for her to see? He—for there could be no doubt who had written it. The flash of teeth and eyes, the military salute; she knew she oughtn't to have waved to him. He had written it there while she was swimming out. Written it and then run away. She rather liked that—just an extraordinary word on the sand, like the footprint in *Robinson Crusoe.*

"Personally," Mrs. Topes was saying, "I prefer Harrod's."

The thunder crashed and rattled. It was rather exhilarating, Barbara thought; one felt, at any rate, that something was happening for a change. She remembered the little room halfway up the stairs at Lady Thingumy's house, with the bookshelves and the green curtains and the orange shade on the light; and that awful young man like a white slug who had tried to kiss her there, at the dance last year. But that was different—not at all serious; and the young man had been so horribly ugly. She saw the marquis running up the beach, quick and alert. Copper coloured all over, with black hair. He was certainly very handsome. But as for being in love, well . . . what did that exactly mean? Perhaps when she knew him better. Even now she fancied she detected something. O Clara d'Ellébeuse. What an extraordinary thing it was!

With his long fingers Mr. Buzzacott combed his beard. This winter, he was thinking, he would put another thousand into Italian money when the exchange was favourable. In the spring it always seemed to drop back again. One could clear three hundred pounds on one's capital if the exchange went down to seventy.

The income on three hundred was fifteen pounds a year, and fifteen pounds was now fifteen hundred lire. And fifteen hundred lire, when you came to think of it, was really sixty pounds. That was to say that one would make an addition of more than one pound a week to one's income by this simple little speculation. He became aware that Mrs. Topes had asked him a question.

"Yes, yes, perfectly," he said.

Mrs. Topes talked on; she was keeping up her morale. Was she right in believing that the thunder sounded a little less alarmingly loud and near?

Mr. Topes sat, polishing his spectacles with a white silk handkerchief. Vague and myopic between their puckered lids, his eyes seemed lost, homeless, unhappy. He was thinking about beauty. There were certain relations between the eyelids and the temples, between the breast and the shoulder; there were certain successions of sounds. But what about them? Ah, that was the problem—that was the problem. And there was youth, there was innocence. But it was all very obscure, and there were so many phrases, so many remembered pictures and melodies; he seemed to get himself entangled among them. And he was after all so old and so ineffective.

He put on his spectacles again, and definition came into the foggy world beyond his eyes. The shuttered room was very dark. He could distinguish the Renaissance profile of Mr. Buzzacott, bearded and delicately featured. In her deep arm-chair Barbara appeared, faintly white, in an attitude relaxed and brooding. And Mrs. Topes was nothing more than a voice in the darkness. She had got on to the marriage of the Prince of Wales. Who would they eventually find for him?

Clara d'Ellébeuse, Clara d'Ellébeuse. She saw herself so clearly as the *marchesa*. They would have a house in Rome, a palace. She saw herself in the Palazzo Spada—it had such a lovely vaulted passage leading from the courtyard to the gardens at the back. "MARCHESA PRAMPOLINI, PALAZZO SPADA, ROMA" —a great big visiting-card beautifully engraved. And she would go riding every day in the Pincio. "*Mi porta il mio cavallo,*" she would say to the footman, who answered the bell. *Porta?* Would that be quite correct? Hardly. She'd have to take some proper Italian lessons to talk to the servants. One must never be ridiculous before servants. "*Voglio il mio cavallo.*" Haughtily one would say it sitting at one's writing-table in a riding-habit, without

turning round. It would be a green riding-habit, with a black tricorne hat, braided with silver.

"*Prendero la mia collazione al letto.*" Was that right for breakfast? Because she would have breakfast in bed, always. And when she got up there would be lovely looking-glasses with three panels where one could see oneself sideface. She saw herself leaning forward, powdering her nose, carefully, scientifically. With the monkey creeping up behind? Ooh! Horrible! *Ho paura di questa scimmia, questo scimmione.*

She would come back to lunch after her ride. Perhaps Prampolini would be there; she had rather left him out of the picture so far. "*Dov'è il Marchese?*" "*Nella sala di pranza, signora.*" I began without you, I was so hungry. *Pasta asciutta.* Where have you been, my love? Riding, my dove. She supposed they'd get into the habit of saying that sort of thing. Everyone seemed to. And you? I have been out with the Fascisti.

Oh, these Fascisti! Would life be worth living when he was always going out with pistols and bombs and things? They would bring him back one day on a stretcher. She saw it. Pale, pale, with blood on him. *Il signore è ferito. Nel petto. Gravamente. E morto.*

How could she bear it? It was too awful; too, too terrible. Her breath came in a kind of sob; she shuddered as though she had been hurt. *E morto. E morto.* The tears came into her eyes.

She was roused suddenly by a dazzling light. The storm had receded far enough into the distance to permit of Mrs. Topes's opening the shutters.

"It's quite stopped raining."

To be disturbed in one's intimate sorrow and self-abandonment at a death-bed by a stranger's intrusion, an alien voice . . . Barbara turned her face away from the light and surreptitiously wiped her eyes. They might see and ask her why she had been crying. She hated Mrs. Topes for opening the shutters; at the inrush of the light something beautiful had flown, an emotion had vanished, irrecoverably. It was a sacrilege.

Mr. Buzzacott looked at his watch. "Too late, I fear, for a siesta now," he said. "Suppose we ring for an early tea."

"An endless succession of meals," said Mr. Topes, with a tremolo and a sigh. "That's what life seems to be—real life."

"I have been calculating"—Mr. Buzzacott turned his pale green eyes towards his guest—

"that I may be able to afford that pretty little *cinque* cassone, after all. It would be a bit of a squeeze." He played with his beard. "But still . . ."

After tea, Barbara and Mr. Topes went for a walk along the beach. She didn't much want to go, but Mrs. Topes thought it would be good for her; so she had to. The storm had passed and the sky over the sea was clear. But the waves were still breaking with an incessant clamour on the outer shallows, driving wide sheets of water high up the beach, twenty or thirty yards above the line where, on a day of calm, the ripples ordinarily expired. Smooth, shining expanses of water advanced and receded like steel surfaces moved out and back by a huge machine. Through the rain-washed air the mountains appeared with an incredible clarity. Above them hung huge masses of cloud.

"Clouds over Carrara," said Mr. Topes, deprecating his remark with a little shake of the head and a movement of the shoulders. "I like to fancy sometimes that the spirits of the great sculptors lodge among these marble hills, and that it is their unseen hands that carve the clouds into these enormous splendid shapes. I imagine their ghosts"—his voice trembled—"feeling about among superhuman conceptions, planning huge groups and friezes and monumental figures with blowing draperies; planning, conceiving, but never quite achieving. Look, there's something of Michelangelo in that white cloud with the dark shadows underneath it." Mr. Topes pointed, and Barbara nodded and said, "Yes, yes," though she wasn't quite sure which cloud he meant. "It's like Night on the Medici tomb; all the power and passion are brooding inside it, pent up. And there, in that sweeping, gesticulating piece of vapour—you see the one I mean—there's a Bernini. All the passion's on the surface, expressed; the gesture's caught at its most violent. And that sleek, smug white fellow over there, that's a delicious absurd Canova." Mr. Topes chuckled.

"Why do you always talk about art?" said Barbara. "You bring these dead people into everything. What do I know about Canova or whoever it is?" They were none of them alive. She thought of that dark face, bright as a lamp with life. He at least wasn't dead. She wondered whether the letters were still there in the sand before the cabin. No, of course not; the rain and the wind would have blotted them out.

Mr. Topes was silent; he walked with slightly bent knees and his eyes were fixed on the ground; he wore a speckled black-and-white straw hat. He always thought of art; that was what was wrong with him. Like an old tree he was; built up of dead wood, with only a few fibres of life to keep him from rotting away. They walked on for a long time in silence.

"Here's the river," said Mr. Topes at last.

A few steps more and they were on the bank of a wide stream that came down slowly through the plain to the sea. Just inland from the beach it was fringed with pine trees; beyond the trees one could see the plain, and beyond the plain were the mountains. In this calm light after the storm everything looked strange. The colours seemed deeper and more intense than at ordinary times. And though all was so clear, there was a mysterious air of remoteness about the whole scene. There was no sound except the continuous breathing of the sea. They stood for a little while, looking; then turned back.

Far away along the beach two figures were slowly approaching. White flannel trousers, a pink skirt.

"Nature," Mr. Topes enunciated, with a shake of the head. "One always comes back to nature. At a moment such as this, in surroundings like these, one realises it. One lives now—more quietly, perhaps, but more profoundly. Deep waters. Deep waters . . ."

The figures drew closer. Wasn't it the marquis? And who was with him? Barbara strained her eyes to see.

"Most of one's life," Mr. Topes went on, "is one prolonged effort to prevent oneself thinking. Your father and I, we collect pictures and read about the dead. Other people achieve the same results by drinking, or breeding rabbits, or doing amateur carpentry. Anything rather than think calmly about the important things."

Mr. Topes was silent. He looked about him, at the sea, at the great clouds, at his companion. A frail Montagna madonna, with the sea and the westering sun, the mountains and the storm, all eternity as a background. And he was sixty, with all a life, immensely long and yet timelessly short, behind him, an empty life. He thought of death and the miracles of beauty; behind his round, glittering spectacles he felt inclined to weep.

The approaching couple were quite near now.

"What a funny old walrus," said the lady.

"Walrus? Your natural history is quite wrong." The marquis laughed. "He's much too dry to be a walrus. I should suggest some sort of an old cat."

"Well, whatever he is, I'm sorry for that

poor little girl. Think of having nobody better to go about with!"

"Pretty, isn't she?"

"Yes, but too young, of course."

"I like innocence."

"Innocence? Cher ami! These English girls. Oh, la la! They may look innocent. But, believe me . . . ."

"Sh, sh. They'll hear you."

"Pooh, they don't understand Italian."

The marquis raised his hand. "The old walrus . . . ." he whispered; then addressed himself loudly and jovially to the newcomers.

"Good evening, signorina. Good evening, Mr. Topes. After a storm the air is always the purest, don't you find, eh?"

Barbara nodded, leaving Mr. Topes to answer. It wasn't his sister. It was the Russian woman, the one of whom Mrs. Topes used to say that it was a disgrace she should be allowed to stay at the hotel. She had turned away, dissociating herself from the conversation; Barbara looked at the line of her averted face. Mr. Topes was saying something about the Pastoral Symphony. Purple face powder in the daylight; it looked hideous.

"Well, au revoir."

The flash of the marquis's smile was directed at them. The Russian woman turned back from the sea, slightly bowed, smiled languidly. Her heavy white eyelids were almost closed; she seemed the prey of an enormous ennui.

"They jar a little," said Mr. Topes when they were out of earshot—"they jar on the time, on the place, on the emotion. They haven't the innocence for this . . . this . . . ." —he wriggled and tremoloed out the just, the all too precious word—"this prelapsarian landscape."

He looked sideways at Barbara and wondered what she was so thoughtfully frowning over. Oh, lovely and delicate young creature? What could he adequately say of death and beauty and tenderness? Tenderness . . . .

"All this," he went on desperately, and waved his hand to indicate the sky, the sea, the mountains, "this scene is like something remembered, clear and utterly calm; remembered across great gulfs of intervening time."

But that was not really what he wanted to say.

"You see what I mean?" he asked dubiously. She made no reply. How could she see? "This scene is so clear and pure and remote; you need the corresponding emotion. Those people were out of harmony. They weren't clear and pure enough." He seemed to be getting more muddled than ever. "It's an emotion of the young and of the old. You could feel it. I could feel it. Those people couldn't." He was feeling his way through obscurities. Where would he finally arrive? "Certain poems express it. You know Francis Jammes? I have thought so much of his work lately. Art instead of life, as usual; but then I'm made that way. I can't help thinking of Jammes. Those delicate, exquisite things he wrote about Clara d'Ellébeuse."

"Clara d'Ellébeuse?" She stopped and stared at him.

"You know the lines?" Mr. Topes smiled delightedly. "This makes me think, you make me think of them. *'J'aime dans les temps Clara d'Ellébeuse . . .'* But, my dear Barbara, what is the matter?"

She had started crying, for no reason whatever.

# W. H. Auden

## 1907 -

Wystan Hugh Auden was born in York 21 February, 1907, the third son of George A. Auden M.D., a retired medical officer. Auden was educated at Gresham's School, Holt, and at Christ Church College, Oxford. For a time he was employed as a schoolmaster.

Part of 1928–9 he spent in Berlin, as did Isherwood and Spender. In 1935 he married Erika Mann, daughter of Thomas Mann. In 1936 he visited Spain, where his sympathies were strongly with the republicans in the civil war. He received the King's Gold Medal for Poetry in 1937, visited China in 1938, and took up permanent residence in America in 1939; he is now an American citizen. In 1956 he was appointed Professor of Poetry at the University of Oxford.

Auden had edited Oxford Poetry in 1926 and 1927; in 1928 he produced the verse charade Paid on Both Sides. Poems appeared in 1930, with a second edition in 1932. Among the collections of poetry since published are Look Stranger (1936), Another Time (1940), New Year Letter (1941), For the Time Being (1944), Nones (1951), Mountains (1954), The Shield of Achilles (1955), and The Old Man's Road (1956). With Christopher Isherwood, Auden wrote three unusual verse plays, The Dog Beneath the Skin (1935), The Ascent of F. 6 (1936), and On the Frontier (1938), as well as Journey to a War (1939), a non-dramatic collaboration in verse and prose.

With Louis MacNeice, Auden wrote Letters from Iceland, in verse and prose. Auden's Spain (1937) is an essentially-dramatic longer poem, as is the Pulitzer-Prize-winning The Age of Anxiety (1948), which Auden calls "a baroque eclogue." The total effect of the dramatic and non-dramatic poetry of Auden is that of a significant and substantial body of work, representative of the complexity and variety, the intensity of feeling, and the expanding knowledge of the twentieth century.

Auden has selected the Collected Shorter Poems 1930–1944 (London, 1950). The Mak-ing of the Auden Canon, by Joseph Warren Beach (Minneapolis, 1957), is one of the best textual studies of a modern author extant. Auden and After, by Francis Scarfe (London, 1942), deals with the "Auden generation." Auden: An Introductory Essay, by Richard Hoggart (New Haven, 1951) is a useful study.

## Pur [1]

This lunar beauty
Has no history,
Is complete and early;
If beauty later
Bear any feature,                                    5
It had a lover
And is another.

This like a dream
Keeps other time,
And daytime is                                       10
The loss of this;
For time is inches
And the heart's changes,
Where ghost has haunted,
Lost and wanted.                                     15

But this was never
A ghost's endeavour
Nor, finished this,
Was ghost at ease;
And till it pass                                     20
Love shall not near
The sweetness here,
Nor sorrow take
His endless look.

## A Summer Night 1933 [2]

### (To Geoffrey Hoyland)

Out on the lawn I lie in bed,
Vega conspicuous overhead

[1] Published 1930. From The Collected Poetry of W. H. Auden. Copyright 1934 by The Modern Library, Inc. Reprinted by permission of Random House, Inc.

[2] Published 1934. From The Collected Poetry of W. H. Auden. Copyright 1937 by Random House, Inc. Reprinted by permission.

In the windless nights of June,
As congregated leaves complete
Their day's activity; my feet
    Point to the rising moon.

Lucky, this point in time and space
Is chosen as my working-place,
    Where the sexy airs of summer,
The bathing hours and the bare arms,
The leisured drives through a land of farms
    Are good to the newcomer.

Equal with colleagues in a ring
I sit on each calm evening
    Enchanted as the flowers
The opening lights draws out of hiding
With all its gradual dove-like pleading,
    Its logic and its powers

That later we, though parted then,
May still recall these evenings when
    Fear gave his watch no look;
The lion griefs loped from the shade
And on our knees their muzzles laid,
    And Death put down his book

Now north and south and east and west
Those I love lie down to rest;
    The moon looks on them all,
The healers and the brilliant talkers
The eccentrics and the silent walkers,
    The dumpy and the tall.

She climbs the European sky,
Churches and power-station lie
    Alike among earth's fixtures:
Into the galleries she peers
And blankly as a butcher stares
    Upon the marvellous pictures

To gravity attentive, she
Can notice nothing here, though we
    Whom hunger does not move,
From gardens where we feel secure
Look up and with a sigh endure
    The tyrannies of love:

And, gentle, do not care to know,
Where Poland draws her eastern bow,
    What violence is done,
Nor ask what doubtful act allows
Our freedom in this English house,
    Our picnics in the sun.

Soon, soon, through dykes of our content
The crumpling flood will force a rent
    And, taller than a tree,
Hold sudden death before our eyes
Whose river dreams long hid the size
    And vigours of the sea.

But when the waters make retreat
And through the black mud first the wheat

In shy green stalks appears,
When stranded monsters gasping lie,
And sounds of riveting terrify
    Their whorled unsubtle ears,

May these delights we dread to lose,
This privacy, need no excuse
    But to that strength belong,
As through a child's rash happy cries
The drowned parental voices rise
    In unlamenting song.

After discharges of alarm
All unpredicted let them calm
    The pulse of nervous nations,
Forgive the murderer in his glass,
Tough in their patience to surpass
    The tigress her swift motions.

## Casino [3]

Only the hands are living; to the wheel attracted,
Are moved as deer trek desperately towards a creek
    Through the dust and scrub of the desert, or gently
    As sunflowers turn to the light.

And, as the night takes up the cries of feverish children,
The cravings of lions in dens, the loves of dons,
    Gathers them all and remains the night, the
    Great room is full of their prayers

To the last feast of isolation self-invited
They flock, and in the rite of disbelief are joined;
    From numbers all their stars are recreated,
    The enchanted, the world, the sad.

Without, the rivers flow among the wholly living,
Quite near their trysts; and the mountains part them; and the bird
    Deep in the greens and moistures of summer
    Sings towards their work.

But here no nymph comes naked to the youngest shepherd;
The fountain is deserted; the laurel will not grow;
    The labyrinth is safe but endless, and broken
    Is Ariadne's thread.

As deeper in these hands is grooved their fortune: 'Lucky
Were few, and it is possible that none was loved;
    And what was godlike in this generation
    Was never to be born.'

# As I Walked Out One Evening [4]

As I walked out one evening,
    Walking down Bristol Street,
The crowds upon the pavement
    Were fields of harvest wheat.

And down by the brimming river    5
    I heard a lover sing
Under an arch of the railway:
    'Love has no ending.

'I'll love you, dear, I'll love you
    Till China and Africa meet,    10
And the river jumps over the mountain
    And the salmon sing in the street.

'I'll love you till the ocean
    Is folded and hung up to dry
And the seven stars go squawking    15
    Like geese about the sky.

'The years shall run like rabbits,
    For in my arms I hold
The Flower of the Ages,
    And the first love of the world.'    20

But all the clocks in the city
    Began to whirr and chime:
'O let not Time deceive you,
    You cannot conquer Time.

'In the burrows of the Nightmare    25
    Where Justice naked is,
Time watches from the shadow
    And coughs when you would kiss.

'In the headaches and in worry
    Vaguely life leaks away,    30
And Time will have his fancy
    To-morrow or to-day.

'Into many a green valley
    Drifts the appalling snow;
Time breaks the threaded dances    35
    And the diver's brilliant bow.

'O plunge your hands in water,
    Plunge them in up to the wrist;
Stare, stare in the basin
    And wonder what you've missed.    40

'The glacier knocks in the cupboard,
    The desert sighs in the bed,
And the crack in the tea-cup opens
    A lane to the land of the dead.

'Where the beggars raffle the banknotes    45
    And the Giant is enchanting to Jack,

And the Lily-white Boy is a Roarer,
    And Jill goes down on her back.

'O look, look in the mirror,
    O look in your distress;    50
Life remains a blessing
    Although you cannot bless.

'O stand, stand at the window
    As the tears scald and start;
You shall love your crooked neighbour    55
    With your crooked heart.'

It was late, late in the evening,
    The lovers they were gone;
The clocks had ceased their chiming,
    And the deep river ran on.    60

# The Unknown Citizen [5]

*(To JS/07/M/378*
*This Marble Monument*
*Is Erected by the State)*

He was found by the Bureau of Statistics to be
One against whom there was no official com-
    plaint,
And all the reports on his conduct agree
That, in the modern sense of an old-fashioned
    word, he was a saint,
For in everything he did he served the Greater
    Community.    5
Except for the War till the day he retired
He worked in a factory and never got fired,
But satisfied his employers, Fudge Motors Inc.
Yet he wasn't a scab or odd in his views,
For his Union reports that he paid his dues, 10
(Our report on his Union shows it was sound)
And our Social Psychology workers found
That he was popular with his mates and liked
    a drink.
The Press are convinced that he bought a
    paper every day
And that his reactions to advertisements were
    normal in every way.    15
Policies taken out in his name prove that he
    was fully insured,
And his Health-card shows he was once in hos-
    pital but left it cured.
Both Producers Research and High-Grade Liv-
    ing declare
He was fully sensible to the advantages of the
    Instalment Plan
And had everything necessary to the Modern
    Man,    20
A phonograph, a radio, a car and a frigidaire.
Our researchers into Public Opinion are con-
    tent
That he held the proper opinions for the time
    of year;

When there was peace, he was for peace; when
    there was war, he went.
He was married and added five children to the
    population,     25
Which our Eugenist says was the right number
    for a parent of his generation,
And our teachers report that he never inter-
    fered with their education.
Was he free? Was he happy? The question is
    absurd:
Had anything been wrong, we should certainly
    have heard.

## *From* In Time of War [6]

### XVII

They are and suffer; that is all they do;
A bandage hides the place where each is living,
His knowledge of the world restricted to
The treatment that the instruments are giving.

And lie apart like epochs from each other    5
—Truth in their sense is how much they can
    bear;
It is not talk like ours, but groans they
    smother—
And are remote as plants; we stand elsewhere.

For who when healthy can become a foot?
Even a scratch we can't recall when cured,    10
But are boist'rous in a moment and believe

In the common world of the uninjured, and
    cannot
Imagine isolation. Only happiness is shared,
And anger, and the idea of love.

### XXI

The life of man is never quite completed;    15
The daring and the chatter will go on:
But, as an artist feels his power gone,
These walk the earth and know themselves de-
    feated.

Some could not bear nor break the young and
    mourn for
The wounded myths that once made nations
    good,    20
Some lost a world they never understood,
Some saw too clearly all that man was born for.

Loss is their shadow-wife, Anxiety
Receives them like a grand hotel; but where
They may regret they must; their life, to hear

The call of the forbidden cities, see    26
The stranger watch them with a happy stare,
And Freedom hostile in each home and tree.

## Our Bias [7]

The hour-glass whispers to the lion's paw,
The clock-towers tell the gardens day and night,
How many errors Time has patience for,
How wrong they are in being always right.

Yet Time, however loud its chimes or deep,    5
However fast its falling torrent flows,
Has never put the lion off his leap
Nor shaken the assurance of the rose.

For they, it seems, care only for success:
While we choose words according to their
    sound    10
And judge a problem by its awkwardness;

And Time with us was always popular.
When have we not preferred some going round
To going straight to where we are?

## *From* The Sea and the Mirror [8]

### PREFACE

### (*The Stage Manager to the Critics*)

The aged catch their breath,
For the nonchalant couple go
Waltzing across the tightrope
As if there were no death
Or hope of falling down;    5
The wounded cry as the clown
Doubles his meaning, and O
How the dear little children laugh
When the drums roll and the lovely
Lady is sawn in half.    10

O what authority gives
Existence its surprise?
Science is happy to answer
That the ghosts who haunt our lives
Are handy with mirrors and wire,    15
That song and sugar and fire,
Courage and come-hither eyes
Have a genius for taking pains.
But how does one think up a habit?
Our wonder, our terror remains.    20

Art open the fishiest eye
To the Flesh and the Devil who heat
The Chamber of Temptation
Where heroes roar and die.
We are wet with sympathy now;    25
Thanks for the evening; but how

Shall we satisfy when we meet,
Between Shall-I and I-Will,
The lion's mouth whose hunger
No metaphors can fill?                                         30

Well, who in his own backyard
Has not opened his heart to the smiling
Secret he cannot quote?

Which goes to show that the Bard
Was sober when he wrote                                       35
That this world of fact we love
Is insubstantial stuff:
All the rest is silence
On the other side of the wall;
And the silence ripeness,                                     40
And the ripeness all.

# Stephen Spender

## 1909-

Stephen Spender was born in London 28 February, 1909. His father was Edwin H. Spender, journalist and lecturer. Spender was educated at University College School and at University College, Oxford. He spent several months a year in Germany between 1929 and 1932; in those years in Germany and in London, with Auden, Isherwood, Day Lewis, and MacNeice, he helped shape the "Auden generation." Spender and Day Lewis were the poet-critics of the group; in books and articles they outlined the group's purposes and fit those purposes into the larger pattern of development of modern poetry. From time to time, too, they paused to look back at the accomplishment so far, to analyze and to evaluate. Spender's The Destructive Element (1935) has been referred to often in our discussion of other writers; the fact that it is one of the most significant critical studies of the century remains unaffected by Spender's major change of political viewpoint, from left to center, since its publication. As co-editor of (1939–41) and as contributor to Horizon, and as author of critical articles and reviews in other magazines, Spender continued his documentation of the intellectual temper and poetic temperament of the age. In The Creative Element (1953), the Elliston Chair of Poetry lectures at the University of Cincinnati, he brought The Destructive Element into the perspective of his mature thinking, and in addition expressed more fully than he had done before his individual poetic belief. Life and the Poet (1942) and the perceptive autobiography World within World (1951) both give additional insight into the philosophy of poetry of both the poet himself and his generation.

20 Poems appeared in 1930, Poems in 1930, Poems in 1933, Vienna in 1934. Spender is a selective poet; his standards for his own work are high. As he considered these, and the later slender volumes The Still Centre (1939), Ruins and Visions (1942), Poems of Dedication (1946) and The Edge of Being (1949), for inclusion in Collected Poems 1928–1953 (1955), he showed these standards and his deep awareness of the relationship of poet to reader and of the responsibility of poet to his own earlier self.

Spender's short stories were published in The Burning Cactus (1936); he has written one novel, The Backward Son (1940) and a verse play, Trial of a Judge (1938).

## Acts Passed beyond the Boundary of Mere Wishing [1]

Acts passed beyond the boundary of mere wishing
Not privy looks, hedged words, at times you saw.
These, blundering, heart-surrendered troopers were
Small presents made, and waiting for the tram.
Then once you said: 'Waiting was very kind',   5
And looked surprised. Surprising for me, too,
Whose every movement has been missionary,
A pleading tongue unheard. I had not thought
That you, who nothing else saw, would see this.

So 'very kind' was merest overflow     10
Something I had not reckoned in myself,
A chance deserter from my force. When we touched hands,
I felt the whole rebel, feared mutiny
And turned away,
Thinking, if these were tricklings through a dam,   15
I must have love enough to run a factory on,
Or give a city power, or drive a train.

## I Hear the Cries of Evening, While the Paw

I hear the cries of evening, while the paw
Of dark creeps up the turf;

[1] This and the nine poems which follow published in 1934. They are from Collected Poems 1928–1953, by Stephen Spender, and were copyrighted 1934 by

Sheep's bleating, swaying gulls' cry, the rook's
   caw,
The hammering surf.

I am inconstant yet this constancy     5
Of natural rest twangs at my heart;
Town-bred, I feel the roots of each earth-cry
Tear me apart.

These are the creakings of the dusty day
When the dog night bites sharp,     10
These fingers grip my soul and tear away
And pluck me like a harp.

I feel this huge sphere turn, the great wheel
   sing
While beasts move to their ease:
Sheep's love, gulls' peace—I feel my chattering
Uncared by these.     16

## Different Living Is Not Living in Different Places

Different living is not living in different places
But creating in the mind a map
And willing on that map a desert
Pinnacled mountain, or saving resort.

When I frowned, making desert, Time only  5
Shook once his notchless column, as when Ape
Centuries before, with furrowed hand
Fumbled at stone, discerning new use:
Setting his mark against mind's progress;
Shaking Time, but with no change of Place.  10

## An 'I' Can Never Be Great Man

An 'I' can never be great man.
This known great one has weakness
To friends is most remarkable for weakness:
His ill-temper at meals, dislike of being contra-
   dicted,
His only real pleasure fishing in ponds,     5
His only real wish—forgetting.

To advance from friends to the composite self,
Central 'I' is surrounded by 'I eating',
'I loving', 'I angry', 'I excreting',
And the great 'I' planted in him     10
Has nothing to do with all these,

Can never claim its true place
Resting in the forehead, and calm in his gaze.
The great 'I' is an unfortunate intruder
Quarrelling with 'I tiring' and 'I sleeping'   15
And all those other 'I's who long for 'We
   dying'.

## My Parents Kept Me from Children Who Were Rough

My parents kept me from children who were
   rough
Who threw words like stones and who wore torn
   clothes.
Their thighs showed through rags. They ran in
   the street
And climbed cliffs and stripped by the country
   streams.

I feared more than tigers their muscles like iron
Their jerking hands and their knees tight on my
   arms.     6
I feared the salt coarse pointing of those boys
Who copied my lisp behind me on the road.

They were lithe, they sprang out behind hedges
Like dogs to bark at my world. They threw
   mud     10
While I looked the other way, pretending to
   smile.
I longed to forgive them, but they never smiled.

## What I Expected, Was Thunder, Fighting

What I expected, was
Thunder, fighting,
Long struggles with men
And climbing.
After continual straining     5
I should grow strong;
Then the rocks would shake,
And I rest long.

What I had not foreseen
Was the gradual day     10
Weakening the will
Leaking the brightness away,
The lack of good to touch,
The fading of body and soul
—Smoke before wind,     15
Corrupt, unsubstantial.

The wearing of Time,
And the watching of cripples pass
With limbs shaped like questions
In their odd twist,     20
The pulverous grief
Melting the bones with pity,
The sick falling from earth—
These, I could not foresee.

Expecting always     25
Some brightness to hold in trust,
Some final innocence
Exempt from dust,
That, hanging solid,

Would dangle through all,                                    30
Like the created poem,
Or faceted crystal.

## I Think Continually of Those Who Were Truly Great

I think continually of those who were truly
    great.
Who, from the womb, remembered the soul's
    history
Through corridors of light where the hours are
    suns,
Endless and singing. Whose lovely ambition
Was that their lips, still touched with fire,  5
Should tell of the Spirit, clothed from head
    to foot in song.
And who hoarded from the Spring branches
The desire falling across their bodies like blos-
    soms.

What is precious, is never to forget
The essential delight of the blood drawn from
    ageless springs                                        10
Breaking through rocks in worlds before our
    earth.
Never to deny its pleasure in the morning
    simple light
Nor its grave evening demand for love.
Never to allow gradually the traffic to smother
With noise and fog, the flowering of the Spirit.

Near the snow, near the sun, in the highest
    fields,                                                16
See how these names are fêted by the waving
    grass
And by the streamers of white cloud
And whispers of wind in the listening sky.
The names of those who in their lives fought
    for life.                                              20
Who wore at their hearts the fire's centre.
Born of the sun, they travelled a short while
    toward the sun,
And left the vivid air signed with their honour.

## The Express

After the first powerful, plain manifesto
The black statement of pistons, without more
    fuss
But gliding like a queen, she leaves the station.
Without bowing and with restrained unconcern
She passes the houses which humbly crowd
    outside,                                               5
The gasworks, and at last the heavy page
Of death, printed by gravestones in the ceme-
    tery.
Beyond the town, there lies the open country
Where, gathering speed, she acquires mystery,
The luminous self-possession of ships on ocean.
It is now she begins to sing—at first quite
    low                                                    11

Then loud, and at last with a jazzy madness—
The song of her whistle screaming at curves,
Of deafening tunnels, brakes, innumerable
    bolts.
And always light, aerial, underneath,          15
Retreats the elate metre of her wheels.
Steaming through metal landscape on her lines,
She plunges new eras of white happiness,
Where speed throws up strange shapes, broad
    curves
And parallels clean like trajectories from guns.
At last, further than Edinburgh or Rome,     21
Beyond the crest of the world, she reaches night
Where only a low stream-line brightness
Of phosphorus on the tossing hills is light.
Ah, like a comet through flame, she moves en-
    tranced,                                               25
Wrapt in her music no bird song, no, nor
    bough
Breaking with honey buds, shall ever equal.

## The Landscape near an Aerodrome

More beautiful and soft than any moth
With burring furred antennae feeling its huge
    path
Through dusk, the air liner with shut-off en-
    gines
Glides over suburbs and the sleeves set trailing
    tall
To point the wind. Gently, broadly, she falls, 5
Scarcely disturbing charted currents of air.

Lulled by descent, the travellers across sea
And across feminine land indulging its easy
    limbs
In miles of softness, now let their eyes trained
    by watching
Penetrate through dusk the outskirts of this
    town                                                   10
Here where industry shows a fraying edge.
Here they may see what is being done.

Beyond the winking masthead light
And the landing ground, they observe the out-
    posts
Of work: chimneys like lank black fingers     15
Or figures, frightening and mad: and squat
    buildings
With their strange air behind trees, like wom-
    en's faces
Shattered by grief. Here where few houses
Moan with faint light behind their blinds,
They remark the unhomely sense of complaint,
    like a dog                                             20
Shut out, and shivering at the foreign moon.

In the last sweep of love, they pass over fields
Behind the aerodrome, where boys play all day
Hacking dead grass: whose cries, like wild birds,
Settle upon the nearest roofs                    25
But soon are hid under the loud city.

Then, as they land, they hear the tolling bell
Reaching across the landscape of hysteria,
To where, louder than all those batteries
And charcoaled towers against that dying sky, 30
Religion stands, the Church blocking the sun.

## The Pylons

The secret of these hills was stone, and cottages
Of that stone made,
And crumbling roads
That turned on sudden hidden villages.

Now over these small hills, they have built the
    concrete 5
That trails black wire;
Pylons, those pillars
Bare like nude giant girls that have no secret.

The valley with its gilt and evening look
And the green chestnut 10
Of customary root,
Are mocked dry like the parched bed of a
    brook.

But far above and far as sight endures
Like whips of anger
With lightning's danger 15
There runs the quick perspective of the future.

This dwarfs our emerald country by its trek
So tall with prophecy:
Dreaming of cities
Where often clouds shall lean their swan-white
    neck. 20

## The Double Shame [1]

You must live through the time when every-
    thing hurts
When the space of the ripe, loaded afternoon
Expands to a landscape of white heat frozen
And trees are weighed down with hearts of
    stone
And green stares back where you stare alone, 5
And the walking eyes throw flinty comments,
And the words which carry most knives are the
    blind
Phrases searching to be kind.

Solid and usual objects are ghosts
The furniture carries cargoes of memory, 10
The staircase has corners which remember
As fire blows reddest in gusty embers,
And each empty dress cuts out an image
In fur and evening and summer and spring
Of her who was different in each. 15

Pull down the blind and lie on the bed
And clasp the hour in the glass of one room

Against your mouth like a crystal doom.
Take up the book and stare at the letters
Hieroglyphs on sand and as meaningless— 20
Here birds crossed once and a foot once trod
In a mist where sight and sound are blurred.

The story of others who made their mistakes
And of one whose happiness pierced like a star
Eludes and evades between sentences 25
And the letters break into eyes which read
The story life writes now in your head
As though the characters sought for some clue
To their being transcendently living and dead
In your history, worse than theirs, but true. 30

Set in the mind of their poet, they compare
Their tragic sublime with your tawdry despair
And they have fingers which accuse
You of the double way of shame.
At first you did not love enough 35
And afterwards you loved too much
And you lacked the confidence to choose
And you have only yourself to blame.

## Seascape [1]

### *In Memoriam, M.A.S.*

There are some days the happy ocean lies
Like an unfingered harp, below the land.
Afternoon gilds all the silent wires
Into a burning music for the eyes.
On mirrors flashing between fine-strung fires 5
The shore, heaped up with roses, horses, spires,
Wanders on water, walking above ribbed sand.

The motionlessness of the hot sky tires
And a sigh, like a woman's, from inland
Brushes the instrument with shadowing hand 10
Drawing across its wires some gull's sharp cries
Or bell, or shout, from distant, hedged-in shires;
These, deep as anchors, the hushing wave
    buries.

Then from the shore, two zig-zag butterflies,
Like errant dog-roses, cross the bright strand 15
Spiralling over sea in foolish gyres
Until they fall into reflected skies.
They drown. Fishermen understand
Such wings sunk in such ritual sacrifice,

Recalling legends of undersea, drowned cities.
What voyagers, oh what heroes, flamed like
    pyres 21
With helmets plumed, have set forth from
    some island
And them the sea engulfed. Their eyes,
Contorted by the cruel waves' desires
Glitter with coins through the tide scarcely
    scanned, 25
While, above them, that harp assumes their
    sighs.

# Dylan Thomas

## 1914-1953

Dylan Thomas was born in Carmarthenshire, Wales, 27 October, 1914. He was educated at Swansea Grammar School, where his father was the English master. He gave early promise of an unsettled and irresponsible career, and told anyone who urged him to work or study that he was going to be a poet. He sought his real education in experience, sensation, action, emotion; the sketches in Portrait of the Artist as a Young Dog (1940) record this education that poured in through the poet's senses:

There was nowhere like the farm-yard in all the slapdash county, nowhere so poor and grand and dirty as that square of mud and rubbish and bad wood and falling stone, where a bucketful of old and bedraggled hens scratched and laid small eggs.

And again,

I liked the taste of the beer, its live, white lather, its brass-bright depths, the sudden world through the wet brown walls of the glass, the tilted rush to the lips and the slow swallowing down to the lapping belly, the salt on the tongue, the foam at the corners.

Dylan Thomas's career was living, as fully as he could live, and writing poetry. His first published volume was 18 Poems (1935), in which the primary preoccupation is sex, the forces of generation and life, the relationship of the individual to the energy represented by these forces within him. In "If I were tickled by the rub of love" the poet asks "Man be my metaphor": he can imagine no better image of change, of mutability, of the flux of life, than man.

25 Poems, published in 1936, is more diverse in theme; Thomas in this volume evidently felt the responsibility of the poet to treat varied serious themes, and tried hard to meet this responsibility, with mixed success. Only a few of the pieces, notably "And death shall have no dominion," "Why east wind chills," and "The hand that signed the paper," show the success and evoke the response of the poet's best work.

The Map of Love, containing sixteen poems

and seven prose tales, was published in 1939. In 1946 came the finest of the poetry volumes, Deaths and Entrances, including "Poem in October," "Fern Hill," and "In my Craft or Sullen Art." The Collected Poems 1934–1952, published in 1953, added six poems to the Thomas canon.

For a living, and because the possibilities of the art forms pleased him, Thomas wrote for radio and the films. His broadcast on the stories of Walter de la Mare was published as part of a symposium in 1947. He prepared a propaganda film Our Country during World War II, and a script for a film about oil, as well as a number of scripts for popular movies. His two more creative and ambitious dramatic projects were The Doctor and the Devils (1953), a screen play, and Under Milk Wood, a radio script. Under Milk Wood is the more exciting of the two; it uses the language of poetry effectively and is driven on by an overriding exuberance and enthusiasm.

The Collected Poems 1934–1952 (London, 1953) is the best text for the poems. There are several volumes of letters and three careful book-length studies, Dylan Thomas, by Henry Treece (London, 1956); Dylan Thomas: A Literary Study, by Derek Stanford (New York, 1954); and The Poetry of Dylan Thomas, by Elder Olson (Chicago, 1954). There are excellent brief studies by Edith Sitwell (Atlantic Monthly, February, 1954); David Aivaz (Hudson Review, Autumn, 1950); and many others.

## And Death Shall Have No Dominion [1]

And death shall have no dominion.
Dead men naked they shall be one
With the man in the wind and the west moon;

[1] Published 1936. All these poems by Thomas copyright 1952, 1953 by Dylan Thomas. Reprinted by permission of New Directions.

1304

When their bones are picked clean and the
    clean bones gone,
They shall have stars at elbow and foot;     5
Though they go mad they shall be sane,
Though they sink through the sea they shall
    rise again;
Though lovers be lost love shall not;
And death shall have no dominion.

And death shall have no dominion.    10
Under the windings of the sea
They lying long shall not die windily;
Twisting on racks when sinews give way,
Strapped to a wheel, yet they shall not break;
Faith in their hands shall snap in two,    15
And the unicorn evils run them through;
Split all ends up they shan't crack;
And death shall have no dominion.

And death shall have no dominion.
No more may gulls cry at their ears    20
Or waves break loud on the seashores;
Where blew a flower may a flower no more
Lift its head to the blows of the rain;
Though they be made and dead as nails,
Heads of the characters hammer through
    daisies;    25
Break in the sun till the sun breaks down,
And death shall have no dominion.

## Fern Hill [2]

Now as I was young and easy under the apple
    boughs
About the lilting house and happy as the grass
    was green,
    The night above the dingle starry,
      Time let me hail and climb
    Golden in the heydays of his eyes,    5
And honoured among wagons I was prince of
    the apple towns
And once below a time I lordly had the trees
    and leaves
      Trail with daisies and barley
    Down the rivers of the windfall light.

And as I was green and carefree, famous among
    the barns    10
About the happy yard and singing as the farm
    was home,
    In the sun that is young once only,
      Time let me play and be
    Golden in the mercy of his means,
And green and golden I was huntsman and
    herdsman, the calves    15
Sang to my horn, the foxes on the hills barked
    clear and cold,
      And the sabbath rang slowly
    In the pebbles of the holy streams.

[2] This and the two poems which follow published
1946.

All the sun long it was running, it was lovely,
    the hay
Fields high as the house, the tunes from the
    chimneys, it was air    20
    And playing, lovely and watery
      And fire green as grass.
And nightly under the simple stars
As I rode to sleep the owls were bearing the
    farm away,
All the moon long I heard, blessed among
    stables, the night-jars    25
    Flying with the ricks, and the horses
      Flashing into the dark.

And then to awake, and the farm, like a wan-
    derer white
With the dew, come back, the cock on his
    shoulder: it was all
    Shining, it was Adam and maiden,    30
      The sky gathered again
And the sun grew round that very day.
So it must have been after the birth of the
    simple light
In the first, spinning place, the spellbound
    horses walking warm
    Out of the whinnying green stable    35
      On to the fields of praise.

And honoured among foxes and pheasants by
    the gay house
Under the new made clouds and happy as the
    heart was long,
    In the sun born over and over,
      I ran my heedless ways,    40
    My wishes raced through the house high hay
And nothing I cared, at my sky blue trades,
    that time allows
In all his tuneful turning so few and such
    morning songs
    Before the children green and golden
      Follow him out of grace,    45

Nothing I cared, in the lamb white days, that
    time would take me
Up to the swallow thronged loft by the shadow
    of my hand,
    In the moon that is always rising,
      Nor that riding to sleep
    I should hear him fly with the high fields    50
And wake to the farm forever fled from the
    childless land.
Oh as I was young and easy in the mercy of his
    means,
    Time held me green and dying
    Though I sang in my chains like the sea.

## In My Craft or Sullen Art

In my craft or sullen art
Exercised in the still night
When only the moon rages
And the lovers lie abed
With all their griefs in their arms,    5

I labour by singing light
Not for ambition or bread
Or the strut and trade of charms
On the ivory stages
But for the common wages          10
Of their most secret heart.

Not for the proud man apart
From the raging moon I write
On these spindrift pages
Nor for the towering dead          15
With their nightingales and psalms
But for the lovers, their arms
Round the griefs of the ages,
Who pay no praise or wages
Nor heed my craft or art.          20

## Poem in October

It was my thirtieth year to heaven
Woke to my hearing from harbour and neigh-
    bour wood
And the mussel pooled and the heron
    Priested shore
    The morning beckon          5
With water praying and call of seagull and
    rook
And the knock of sailing boats on the net
    webbed wall
    Myself to set foot
    That second
In the still sleeping town and set forth.          10

My birthday began with the water-
Birds and the birds of the winged trees flying
    my name
Above the farms and the white horses
    And I rose
    In rainy autumn          15
And walked abroad in a shower of all my days.
High tide and the heron dived when I took the
    road
    Over the border
    And the gates
Of the town closed as the town awoke.          20

A springful of larks in a rolling
Cloud and the roadside bushes brimming with
    whistling
Blackbirds and the sun of October
    Summery
    On the hill's shoulder,          25
Here were fond climates and sweet singers sud-
    denly
Come in the morning where I wandered and
    listened
    To the rain wringing
    Wind blow cold
In the wood faraway under me.          30

Pale rain over the dwindling harbour
And over the sea wet church the size of a snail

With its horns through mist and the castle
    Brown as owls
    But all the gardens          35
Of spring and summer were blooming in the
    tall tales
Beyond the border and under the lark full
    cloud.
    There could I marvel
    My birthday
Away but the weather turned around.          40

It turned away from the blithe country
And down the other air and the blue altered
    sky
Streamed again a wonder of summer
    With apples
    Pears and red currants          45
And I saw in the turning so clearly a child's
Forgotten mornings when he walked with his
    mother
    Through the parables
    Of sun light
And the legends of the green chapels          50

And the twice told fields of infancy
That his tears burned my cheeks and his heart
    moved in mine.
These were the woods the river and sea
    Where a boy
    In the listening          55
Summertime of the dead whispered the truth of
    his joy
To the trees and the stones and the fish in the
    tide.
    And the mystery
    Sang alive
Still in the water and singingbirds.          60

And there could I marvel my birthday
Away but the weather turned around. And the
    true
Joy of the long dead child sang burning
    In the sun.
    It was my thirtieth          65
Year to heaven stood there then in the summer
    noon
Though the town below lay leaved with
    October blood.
    O may my heart's truth
    Still be sung
On this high hill in a year's turning.          70

## Do Not Go Gentle into That Good Night [3]

Do not go gentle into that good night,
Old age should burn and rave at close of day;
Rage, rage against the dying of the light.

[3] Published 1951.

Though wise men at their end know dark is
right,
Because their words had forked no lightning
they                                                    5
Do not go gentle into that good night.

Good men, the last wave by, crying how bright
Their frail deeds might have danced in a green
bay,
Rage, rage against the dying of the light.

Wild men who caught and sang the sun in
flight,                                                  10

And learn, too late, they grieved it on its way,
Do not go gentle into that good night.

Grave men, near death, who see with blinding
sight
Blind eyes could blaze like meteors and be gay,
Rage, rage against the dying of the light.      15

And you, my father, there on the sad height,
Curse, bless, me now with your fierce tears, I
pray.
Do not go gentle into that good night.
Rage, rage against the dying of the light.

# CHRONOLOGICAL OUTLINE

*Abbreviations: c.* (for *circa*) prefixed to a date means "about"; *fl.* (for *floruit*) following a person's name means that he was in middle age at about the year given.

| POLITICAL, SOCIAL, RELIGIOUS | | LITERARY, PHILOSOPHICAL |
|---|---|---|
| St. Patrick. | 373–463 | |
| St. Patrick consecrated Bishop of Ireland. | 405 | |
| Traditional date for the departure of the Roman legions from Britain. | 410 | |
| Traditional date for the Anglo-Saxon invasion of Britain. | 449 | |
| | c.510 | Date at which the action of the first part of *Beowulf* is conjectured to have been laid. |
| | 516?–570? | Gildas, author of *De Excidio Britanniae.* |
| Battle of Mount Badon, victory of the Britons over invading Saxons. | 516? | |
| Battle of Camlan, in which Arthur was later said to have fallen. | 537? | |
| St. Columba at Iona. | 563 | |
| Papacy of St. Gregory the Great. | 590–604 | |
| Reign of Ethelbert of Kent. | c.560–616 | |
| St. Augustine's mission to Kent. | 597 | |
| Reign of Edwin of Northumbria. | 617–633 | |
| St. Aidan sets forth for Lindisfarne. | 635 | |
| | 639–709 | Aldhelm. |
| Synod of Whitby. | 664 | |
| | 670 | Caedmon, author of *Hymns, fl.* |
| | 672?–735 | Bede. |
| | 679–800 | *Historia Britonum,* first account of Arthur. |
| Death of Abbess Hilda of Whitby. | 680 | |
| | c.690 | Adamnan's *Life of St. Columba.* |
| | c.700 | *Genesis, Daniel,* and *Exodus,* the so-called Caedmon group. |
| | c.725 | *Deor's Lament.* |
| | | *The Seafarer.* |
| | | *Widsith.* |
| | | *The Wanderer.* |
| | 731 | Bede's *Ecclesiastical History.* |
| | 735–804 | Alcuin. |
| | c.740 | *Beowulf.* |
| Charlemagne. | 742–814 | |
| Beginning of the Danish raids. | c.790 | |
| | 796 | Nennius, reviser of the *Historia Britonum, fl.* |
| | c.800 | Cynewulf's *Juliana, Elene,* and *Fates of the Apostles.* |

| POLITICAL, SOCIAL, RELIGIOUS | | LITERARY, PHILOSOPHICAL |
|---|---|---|
| | | Cynewulfian *Crist, Phoenix, Andreas, Dream of the Rood.* |
| | c.825 | *Heliand*, translation of the four Gospels. |
| | 856 or 915? | *Judith.* |
| Reign of Alfred. | 871–899 | Alfred's translations of Bede's *Ecclesiastical History*, Gregory's *Pastoral Care*, and Boethius's *Consolation of Philosophy.* |
| | c.875 | First *Quem Quaeritis?* trope (beginning of medieval drama). |
| Beginning of the Norman raids on northern France. | 886 | |
| | c.887 | Asser's *Life of Alfred the Great.* |
| | c.890–1154 | *Anglo-Saxon Chronicle.* |
| Rollo becomes Duke of Normandy. | 911 | |
| Reign of Aethelstan. | 924–939 | |
| | c.937 | *Battle of Brunanburh.* |
| | 971 | *Blickling Homilies.* |
| | c.991 | *Battle of Maldon.* |
| | c.1000 | British Museum Manuscript *Vitellius A.xv*, containing *Beowulf, Judith.* |
| | | *The Exeter Book*, manuscript containing *Deor's Lament, The Seafarer, The Wanderer, Widsith.* |
| | | *The Vercelli Book*, manuscript containing *Andreas, Elene, Dream of the Rood.* |
| | 1000–1100 | *Chanson de Roland.* |
| | 1006 | Aelfric, translator of *Genesis*, author of *Homilies* and *Lives of the Saints, fl.* |
| Reign of Canute. | 1017–1035 | |
| Reign of Edward the Confessor. | 1042–1066 | |
| Battle of Hastings. | 1066 | |
| Reign of William I (the Conqueror, first of the Norman kings). | 1066–1087 | |
| | 1079–1142 | Abelard. |
| | 1084?–1155 | Henry of Huntingdon, chronicler. |
| *Doomesday Book.* | 1086 | |
| Reign of William II (Rufus). | 1087–1100 | |
| Anselm appointed Archbishop of Canterbury. | 1093 | |
| | c.1095–1143 | William of Malmesbury, chronicler. |
| First Crusade. | 1096–1099 | |
| | c.1100 | Earliest Norse sagas. |
| | | Earliest tales in the Welsh *Mabinogion.* |
| Reign of Henry I. | 1100–1135 | |
| | 1100?–1154 | Geoffrey of Monmouth, author of the *Historia Regum Britanniae* (first appearance of King Arthur as a romantic hero). |
| Reign of Stephen. | 1135–1154 | |
| | 1136–1198? | William of Newburgh, author of the *Historia Rerum Anglicarum.* |
| Civil wars of Stephen and Matilda. | 1139–1153 | |
| | c.1140 | Eadmer's *Life of Anselm.* |
| | 1146?–1220? | Giraldus Cambrensis, author of the *Expugnatio Hibernica* and the *Itinerarium Cambriae.* |
| Second Crusade. | 1147 | |
| Reign of Henry II (first of the Plantagenet kings). | 1154–1189 | |
| | c.1154 | Wace of Jersey's *Geste des Bretons* (based on Geoffrey of Monmouth). |

| POLITICAL, SOCIAL, RELIGIOUS | | LITERARY, PHILOSOPHICAL |
|---|---|---|
| | c.1160 | Benoît de Sainte Maure's *Roman de Troie* (based on Dares Phrygius and Dictys Cretensis; first romantic treatment of Troilus and Cressida). |
| First English invasion of Ireland. | 1170 | |
| Murder of St. Thomas à Becket. | | |
| | 1175–1253 | Robert Grosseteste. |
| | 1180 | Death of John of Salisbury, author of the *Policraticus*. |
| Third Crusade. | 1189–1192 | |
| Reign of Richard I (the Lion-Hearted). | 1189–1199 | |
| Reign of John. | 1199–1216 | |
| | 1200 | Walter Map or Mapes, *fl.* |
| | c.1200 | Orm's *Ormulum* (paraphrases of the Gospels in English). |
| | | Layamon's *Brut* (first important poem in Middle English; fairy element added to Arthurian legends). |
| | 1201? | Death of Roger of Hoveden, chronicler. |
| King John acknowledges the overlordship of the Pope. | 1213 | |
| Battle of Bouvines (defeat of the English pretensions in France). | 1214 | |
| | c.1214–1292 | Roger Bacon |
| *Magna Charta.* | 1215 | |
| Reign of Henry III. | 1216–1272 | |
| | c.1225 | "Sumer is Icumen In" (earliest secular lyric extant in English). |
| | c.1225–1274 | St. Thomas Aquinas. |
| Death of Stephen Langton, Archbishop of Canterbury. | 1228 | |
| | c.1230 | First part of the *Roman de la Rose*, by Guillaume de Lorris. |
| Foundation of University College (first college at Oxford). | 1249 | |
| | c.1250 | *The Owl and the Nightingale.* |
| | | *Gesta Romanorum.* |
| | | *King Horn* (earliest verse romance extant in English). |
| Murder of Hugh of Lincoln. | 1255 | |
| Henry III begins to use English as well as French in proclamations. | 1258 | |
| | 1259 | Death of Matthew Paris, chronicler. |
| Simon de Montfort's Parliament (first representation of towns). | 1265 | |
| | 1265–1308 | John Duns Scotus. |
| | 1265–1321 | Dante. |
| | c.1270 | Second part of the *Roman de la Rose*, by Jean de Meung. |
| Reign of Edward I. | 1272–1307 | |
| | 1280–c.1347 | William of Ockham. |
| | 1281–1345 | Richard de Bury, author of the *Philobiblion*. |
| Conquest of Wales completed. | 1284 | |
| | 1287 | Guido della Colonna's *Historia Troiana* (based on Benoît de Sainte Maure). |
| Model Parliament. | 1295 | |
| Confirmation of the Charters (restriction of the royal power of taxation by Parliament). | 1297 | |

| POLITICAL, SOCIAL, RELIGIOUS | | LITERARY, PHILOSOPHICAL |
|---|---|---|
| | c.1300 | Manuscript of "Judas" (earliest ballad extant in English). |
| | | *Amis and Amiloun, Bevis of Hampton, Guy of Warwick, Havelok the Dane* (verse romances). |
| | | *Cursor Mundi* (religious history in didactic verse). |
| | c.1300–1320 | Dante's *Divina Commedia*. |
| | c.1300–1349 | Richard Rolle of Hampole. |
| | 1304–1374 | Petrarch. |
| Babylonian Captivity of the Papacy. | 1305–1376 | |
| Edward le Bruce crowned in Scotland. | 1306 | |
| Reign of Edward II. | 1307–1327 | |
| Feast of Corpus Christi established. | 1311 | Beginning of the guild cycle plays, of which the earliest extant are probably those performed at York. |
| | 1313–1375 | Boccaccio. |
| Battle of Bannockburn. | 1314 | |
| John Wiclif. | c.1320–1384 | |
| | c.1325–1408 | John Gower. |
| Reign of Edward III. | 1327–1377 | |
| | c.1328 | Chester cycle of guild plays composed. |
| Hundred Years' War. | 1338–1453 | |
| | c.1338 | Boccaccio's *Filostrato* (founded on Benoît de Sainte Maure and Guido della Colonna). |
| Battle of Sluys (first important English victory in the Hundred Years' War). | 1340 | |
| | c.1340–1400 | Geoffrey Chaucer. |
| Battle of Crécy. | 1346 | |
| Capture of Calais. | 1347 | |
| First epidemic of the Black Death. | 1348–1350 | |
| | 1348–1358 | Boccaccio's *Decamerone*. |
| Statute of Laborers. | 1349 | |
| Order of the Garter established. | | |
| English replaces French in the schools. | c.1350 | |
| Battle of Poitiers. | 1356 | |
| English used in opening Parliament. | 1362 | |
| | c.1362 | *Piers Plowman*, A-text. |
| | 1364 | Death of Ranulf Higden, author of the *Polychronicon*. |
| | 1367 | John de Trevisa's English translation of Higden's *Polychronicon*. |
| | c.1370 | Chaucer's *Book of the Duchess*. |
| | | *Sir Gawain and the Green Knight*. |
| | | *The Pearl*. |
| | 1372–1373 | Chaucer's first trip to Italy. |
| | c.1375 | John Barbour's *Bruce*. |
| Reign of Richard II. | 1377–1399 | |
| | c.1377 | *Piers Plowman*, B-text (first allusion to Robin Hood). |
| Great Schism. | 1378–1417 | |
| | 1378 | Chaucer's second trip to Italy. |
| | c.1378 | Gower's *Speculum Meditantis* (in French). |
| | c.1380 | Chaucer's *Hous of Fame*. |
| | | Wiclif's translation of the Bible. |
| Peasants' Revolt. | 1381 | |
| | c.1382 | Chaucer's *Parlement of Foules*. |
| | | Gower's *Vox Clamantis*. |

| POLITICAL, SOCIAL, RELIGIOUS | | LITERARY, PHILOSOPHICAL |
|---|---|---|
| | *c.*1385 | Chaucer's *Troilus and Criseyde* (founded on Boccaccio's *Filostrato*), *Legend of Good Women* (early version), and the "Knightes Tale" in the *Canterbury Tales*. |
| | 1387 | Departure of Canterbury pilgrims from the Tabard Inn, Southwark, on 17 April. |
| | *c.*1387 | In Chaucer's *Canterbury Tales* the "Prologue" and the "Prioresses Tale." |
| | | Thomas Usk's *Testament of Love.* |
| Battle of Otterburn, described in the ballad *The Hunting of the Cheviot*. | 1388 | |
| | 1390 | Gower's *Confessio Amantis* (in English). |
| | *c.*1390 | *Piers Plowman*, C-text. |
| | 1390–1447 | Humphrey, Duke of Gloucester, patron of letters. |
| | *c.*1393 | The "Pardoners Tale" in Chaucer's *Canterbury Tales*. |
| | 1393–1464 | John Capgrave, chronicler. |
| | *c.*1395 | The "Nonne Preestes Tale" in Chaucer's *Canterbury Tales*. |
| | | Chaucer's *Legend of Good Women* (revised version). |
| | 1396 | Death of Walter Hilton, author of the *Scala Perfectionis*. |
| Reign of Henry IV (first of the Lancastrian kings). | 1399–1413 | |
| | *c.*1400 | Froissart's *Chroniques*. |
| | 1400–1425 | Two English translations of *The Voiage and Travaile of Sir John Maundeville* (another, quite imperfect, may be earlier). |
| | 1400–1500 | Composition of the best of the English and Scottish popular ballads. |
| | *c.*1412 | Thomas Occleve's *De Regimine Principum* (in English). |
| Reign of Henry V. | 1413–1422 | |
| Battle of Agincourt. | 1415 | |
| Reign of Henry VI. | 1422–1461 | |
| | 1422–1509 | *Paston Letters.* |
| | *c.*1423 | *The Kingis Quair* of James I of Scotland. |
| | *c.*1425 | *Castle of Perseverance* (first complete morality play extant). |
| | | *The Pride of Life* (early fragment of a morality play). |
| | | Wakefield (Towneley) cycle of guild plays. |
| Capture and execution of Joan of Arc. | 1430–1431 | |
| | 1430?–1506 | Robert Henryson, Scottish Chaucerian. |
| | 1438 | John Lydgate's *Falls of Princes* (founded on Boccaccio's *De Casibus Virorum Illustrium*). |
| | 1446?–1519 | William Grocyn. |
| Jack Cade's rebellion. | 1450 | |
| | 1455 | Reginald Pecock's *Repressor of Over-Much Blaming of the Clergy.* |
| Wars of the Roses. | 1455–1485 | |
| | 1456 | The Gutenberg Bible. |
| | 1460?–1524 | Thomas Linacre. |
| | *c.*1460–1529 | John Skelton. |

| POLITICAL, SOCIAL, RELIGIOUS | | LITERARY, PHILOSOPHICAL |
|---|---|---|
| | c.1460–c.1530 | William Dunbar, Scottish Chaucerian. |
| Reign of Edward IV (first of the Yorkist kings). | 1461–1483 | |
| | 1466–1536 | Erasmus. |
| | c.1467–1519 | John Colet. |
| | 1469 or 1470 | Sir Thomas Malory's *Morte d'Arthur* completed. |
| | 1469–1527 | Machiavelli. |
| | 1471 | Death of Sir Thomas Malory. |
| Thomas Wolsey. | 1471–1530 | |
| | c.1474 | Caxton prints at Bruges the *Recuyell of the Histories of Troy* (first book printed in English). |
| | 1474–1533 | Ariosto. |
| | 1477 | *Dictes and Seyings of the Philosophers* printed by Caxton at Westminster (the first dated book printed in England). |
| | 1478–1535 | St. Thomas More. |
| Reign of Edward V. | 1483 | |
| Reign of Richard III. | 1483–1485 | |
| | 1483–1540 | Guicciardini. |
| | 1483–1546 | Luther. |
| Battle of Bosworth Field. | 1485 | Caxton publishes Malory's *Morte d'Arthur*. |
| Reign of Henry VII (first of the Tudor kings). | 1485–1509 | |
| Thomas Cranmer. | 1489–1556 | |
| | c.1490 | Henry Medwall's *Fulgens and Lucrece* (first extant interlude). |
| | c.1490–1536 | William Tyndale. |
| | 1491 | Greek taught at Oxford. |
| First voyage of Columbus. | 1492 | |
| | 1493–1537 | Earliest editions of *Everyman*. |
| | 1495?–1553 | Rabelais. |
| Vasco da Gama reaches India by the Cape of Good Hope. | 1497–1498 | |
| John Cabot in America. | | |
| | 1497–1499 | |
| | 1499–1500 | First visit of Erasmus to England. |
| | 1503?–1542 | Sir Thomas Wyatt. |
| | c.1505 | Skelton's *Bowge of Court* written. |
| | 1505–1506 | Second visit of Erasmus to England. |
| | 1509 | Alexander Barclay's *Ship of Fools*. Erasmus's *Praise of Folly*. Stephen Hawes's *Pastime of Pleasure*. |
| | 1509–1514 | Third visit of Erasmus to England. |
| Reign of Henry VIII. | 1509–1547 | |
| Calvin. | 1509–1564 | |
| Battle of Flodden Field. | 1513 | |
| Wolsey chief minister of State. | 1515–1529 | |
| | 1515–1568 | Roger Ascham. |
| | 1516 | More's *Utopia* (in Latin). |
| | 1516–1532 | Ariosto's *Orlando Furioso*. |
| Luther posts his theses in Wittenberg. | 1517 | |
| | 1517?–1547 | Henry Howard, Earl of Surrey. |
| Circumnavigation of the earth by Magellan's fleet. | 1519–1522 | |
| William Cecil, Lord Burghley. | 1520–1598 | |
| Diet of Worms. | 1521 | |
| | 1523 | Skelton's *Garland of Laurel* published. |
| | 1523–1525 | Lord Berners's English translation of Froissart's *Chronicles*. |

| POLITICAL, SOCIAL, RELIGIOUS | | LITERARY, PHILOSOPHICAL |
|---|---|---|
| | 1524–1585 | Ronsard. |
| | 1525–1526 | Tyndale's New Testament (published in Germany). |
| | 1525?–1577 | George Gascoigne. |
| | 1528 | Castiglione's *Book of the Courtier*. |
| | 1529 | Simon Fish's *Supplication of Beggars*. |
| | 1530 | Tyndale's Pentateuch. |
| | 1531 | Sir Thomas Elyot's *Governour*. |
| | 1532 | Chaucer's *Works*, ed. William Thynne. |
| | | Machiavelli's *Prince* published. |
| | 1532–1548 | Rabelais's *Pantagruel* and *Gargantua*. |
| Henry VIII marries Anne Boleyn. | 1533 | |
| Separation of the English Church from Rome. | | |
| Thomas Cromwell in power. | 1533–1540 | |
| | 1533–1592 | Montaigne. |
| Act of Supremacy (Henry VIII head of the Church of England). | 1534 | |
| | 1535 | Miles Coverdale's first complete English Bible. |
| | 1536 | Calvin's *Institutes of the Christian Religion*. |
| | 1536–1608 | Thomas Sackville, Lord Buckhurst. |
| | 1539 | The Great Bible (prepared under Cranmer). |
| | 1540 | Sir David Lindsay's *Satyr of Three Estates*. |
| | c.1540 | Nicholas Udall's *Ralph Roister Doister* written. |
| | 1542–1550 | Edward Hall's *Chronicle*. |
| | 1543–1607 | Sir Edward Dyer. |
| | 1545 | Ascham's *Toxophilus*. |
| | c.1545 | John Heywood's *Four P. P.* published. |
| Council of Trent. | 1546–1563 | |
| Reign of Edward VI. | 1547–1553 | |
| | 1547–1562 | English version of the Psalms by Thomas Sternhold and John Hopkins. |
| | 1547–1616 | Cervantes. |
| First Book of Common Prayer and Act of Uniformity. | 1549 | Joachim Du Bellay's *Défense et Illustration de la Langue Française*. |
| | 1551 | Translation of More's *Utopia* into English by Ralph Robinson. |
| Second Book of Common Prayer and Second Act of Uniformity. | 1552 | |
| | 1552?–1599 | Edmund Spenser. |
| | 1552?–1618 | Sir Walter Ralegh. |
| | 1553 | Thomas Wilson's *Arte of Rhetorique*. |
| Reign of Mary I (Mary Tudor). | 1553–1558 | |
| Marriage of Mary and Philip of Spain. | 1554 | |
| Execution of Lady Jane Grey. | | |
| | 1554–1586 | Sir Philip Sidney. |
| | 1554?–1606 | John Lyly. |
| | c.1555 | George Cavendish's *Life of Cardinal Wolsey* written. |
| | | William Roper's *Life of Sir Thomas More* written. |
| Mary's religious executions. | 1555–1558 | |
| | 1557 | St. Thomas More's English *Works* (ed. William Rastell). |
| | | *Songs and Sonnets* (*Tottel's Miscellany*). |

POLITICAL, SOCIAL, RELIGIOUS

LITERARY, PHILOSOPHICAL

|  |  |  |
|---|---|---|
|  |  | Surrey's blank verse translation of the *Aeneid*, Books II and IV, published. |
| Loss of Calais. | 1558 | John Knox's *First Blast of the Trumpet against the Monstrous Regiment of Women.* |
|  | 1558–1562 | Thomas Phaer's English translation of the *Aeneid.* |
| Reign of Elizabeth. | 1558–1603 |  |
|  | 1558?–1597? | George Peele. |
| Elizabethan Prayer Book. | 1559 |  |
| Elizabethan Acts of Supremacy and Uniformity. |  |  |
|  | 1559–1610 | *Mirror for Magistrates.* |
|  | 1559?–1634 | George Chapman. |
|  | c.1560 | *Gammer Gurton's Needle.* |
|  |  | Geneva Bible. |
|  | 1560?–1592 | Robert Greene. |
|  | 1561 | Sir Thomas Hoby's English translation of Castiglione's *Cortegiano* (*The Courtier*). |
|  |  | Thomas Norton's English translation of Calvin's *Institutes.* |
|  |  | Sackville and Norton's *Gorboduc* acted. |
|  |  | Joseph Scaliger's *Poetics.* |
|  | 1561–1626 | Francis Bacon. |
|  | 1562 | Richard Grafton's *Abridgement of the Chronicles of England.* |
| Wars of Religion in France. | 1562–1598 |  |
|  | 1562–1619 | Samuel Daniel. |
|  | 1563 | John Foxe's *Actes and Monuments* (*The Book of Martyrs*). |
|  |  | Sackville's *Induction* to the *Mirror for Magistrates.* |
|  | 1563–1631 | Michael Drayton. |
|  | 1564–1593 | Christopher Marlowe. |
|  | 1564–1616 | William Shakespeare. |
|  | 1565 | John Stow's *Summarie of English Chronicles.* |
|  | 1565–1567 | Arthur Golding's English translation of Ovid's *Metamorphoses.* |
|  | 1566 | Gascoigne's *Supposes* and *Jocasta.* |
|  | 1566–1567 | William Painter's *Palace of Pleasure.* |
|  | 1567–1619 | Thomas Campion. |
| Battle of Langside (Mary of Scotland surrenders to Elizabeth). | 1568 |  |
| Northern Rising. | 1569 |  |
| Pius V excommunicates Elizabeth. | 1570 | Ascham's *Scholemaster.* |
|  | 1570?–1632? | Thomas Dekker. |
| Thirty-nine Articles issued. | 1571 |  |
| Massacre of St. Bartholomew. | 1572 | Gascoigne's *Hundred Sundry Flowers.* |
|  | 1572–1637 | Ben Jonson. |
|  | 1572?–1631 | John Donne. |
| William Laud. | 1573–1645 |  |
| First executions of Catholic missionaries. | 1575 |  |
|  | 1576 | Gascoigne's *Steel Glass.* |
|  |  | A *Paradise of Dainty Devices* (ed. Richard Edwards). |
|  |  | George Pettie's *Petite Palace of Pettie his Pleasure.* |
|  |  | The Theater built (first London playhouse). |

POLITICAL, SOCIAL, RELIGIOUS                    LITERARY, PHILOSOPHICAL

Sir Francis Drake circumnavigates the  1577–1580
earth in the *Golden Hind*.

1578    A *Gorgeous Gallery of Gallant Inven-*
        *tions*.
        Raphael Holinshed's *Chronicles* (revised
        edition 1586–1587).
        Lyly's *Euphues, the Anatomy of Wit*.

1579    Stephen Gosson's *School of Abuse*.
        Sir Thomas North's English translation
        of Plutarch's *Lives*.
        Spenser's *Shepherd's Calendar*.

1579–1625    John Fletcher.
1580         Lyly's *Euphues and his England*.
1580         John Stowe's *Chronicles of England*.
c.1580       Sidney's *Arcadia* and *Astrophel and*
             *Stella* written; his *Defense of Poesy*
             begun.

1580–1597    Montaigne's *Essays*.
1581         Tasso's *Jerusalem Delivered*.
             English translation of Seneca's *Trage-*
             *dies*, by Thomas Newton and others.

c.1581       Peele's *Arraignment of Paris* written.
1582         Richard Stanyhurst's translation of Vir-
             gil's *Aeneid*, Books I–IV.

1583         Philip Stubbes's *Anatomie of Abuses*.
1584         Lyly's *Alexander and Campaspe*.
             A *Handful of Pleasant Delights* (ed.
             Clement Robinson).
             Reginald Scot's *Discovery of Witch-*
             *craft*.

1584–1616    Francis Beaumont.
1586         William Webbe's *Discourse of English*
             *Poetrie*.
             William Warner's *Albion's England*.
             William Camden's *Britannia*.

Execution of Mary Queen of Scots.  1587
                                   c.1587    Marlowe's *Tamburlaine*, Part I, written.
                                             Thomas Kyd's *Spanish Tragedy* written.

Defeat of the Spanish Armada.  1588
                               c.1588      Marlowe's *Doctor Faustus* written.
                               1588–1589   Martin Marprelate tracts.
                               1588–1679   Thomas Hobbes.
                               1589        Greene's *Menaphon*.
                                           George Puttenham's *Art of English*
                                           *Poesie*.
                                           Richard Hakluyt's *Principall Naviga-*
                                           *tions, Voyages, and Discoveries of the*
                                           *English Nation* (enlarged 1598–1600).

1590         Thomas Lodge's *Rosalynde*.
             Spenser's *Faerie Queene*, Books I–III.
c.1590       Greene's *James IV* performed.
             Peele's *Old Wives' Tale* written.

1590–1593    Sidney's *Arcadia* published (earlier,
             shorter version first printed, from
             manuscript, 1926).

1591         John Harington's English translation of
             Ariosto's *Orlando Furioso*.
             Sidney's *Astrophel and Stella* published.
             Spenser's *Complaints*.

1591–1592    Greene's Conny-Catching pamphlets.
1591–1674    Robert Herrick.
1592         Daniel's *Delia*.

| POLITICAL, SOCIAL, RELIGIOUS | | LITERARY, PHILOSOPHICAL |
|---|---|---|
| | 1593 | *The Phoenix' Nest.* |
| | | Shakespeare's *Venus and Adonis.* |
| | 1593–1633 | George Herbert. |
| | 1593–1683 | Izaak Walton. |
| | 1594 | Drayton's *Idea.* |
| | | Thomas Nashe's *Unfortunate Traveler.* |
| | | Shakespeare's *Rape of Lucrece.* |
| | 1594–1595 | Shakespeare's *Romeo and Juliet* probably written. |
| | 1594–1597 | Richard Hooker's *Of Ecclesiastical Polity*, Books I–V. |
| | 1595 | Daniel's *Civil Wars.* |
| | | Sidney's *Defense of Poesy* published. |
| | | Spenser's *Amoretti* and *Epithalamion.* |
| Cadiz Expedition (under Essex and Ralegh). | 1596 | Ralegh's *Discovery of Guiana.* |
| | | Spenser's *Faerie Queene*, Books IV–VI. |
| | *c.*1596 | Thomas Deloney's *Thomas of Reading.* |
| | 1597 | Bacon's *Essays* (first edition, ten essays). |
| | | Drayton's *Heroical Epistles.* |
| | 1597–1598 | Shakespeare's *Henry IV* probably written. |
| Edict of Nantes. | 1598 | Jonson's *Every Man in His Humor.* |
| | | Francis Meres's *Palladis Tamia.* |
| | | John Stow's *Survey of London.* |
| | 1598–1600 | Shakespeare's *As You Like It, Twelfth Night, Julius Caesar,* and *Hamlet* probably written. |
| The rebellion of Hugh O'Neill, Earl of Tyrone. | 1598–1603 | |
| | 1598–1611 | Chapman's English translation of the *Iliad.* |
| | 1599 | Sir John Davies's *Nosce Teipsum.* |
| | | The Globe Theater built. |
| Oliver Cromwell. | 1599–1658 | |
| | 1600 | *England's Helicon* (ed. John Bodenham). |
| | | *England's Parnassus* (ed. Robert Allot). |
| | | Dekker's *Shoemakers' Holiday* and *Old Fortunatus* published. |
| Elizabethan Poor Law. | 1601 | |
| Execution of the Earl of Essex. | | |
| | 1602 | Founding of the Bodleian Library. |
| | | Campion's *Observations in the Art of English Poesie.* |
| | | *Poetical Rhapsody* (ed. Francis and Walter Davison). |
| | *c.*1602 | Daniel's *Defense of Ryme.* |
| | 1603 | John Florio's English translation of Montaigne's *Essays.* |
| | | Thomas Heywood's *Woman Killed with Kindness* acted. |
| Reign of James I (first of the Stuart kings). | 1603–1625 | |
| Hampton Court Conference. | 1604 | |
| | 1604–1605 | Shakespeare's *Othello* probably written. |
| | 1604 | Dekker's *Honest Whore*, Part I. |
| Gunpowder Plot. | 1605 | Bacon's *Advancement of Learning.* |
| | 1605–1615 | Cervantes's *Don Quixote.* |
| | 1605–1682 | Sir Thomas Browne. |
| | 1606 | Jonson's *Volpone* written. |
| | 1606–1607 | Shakespeare's *Macbeth, King Lear,* and *Antony and Cleopatra* probably written. |

| POLITICAL, SOCIAL, RELIGIOUS | | LITERARY, PHILOSOPHICAL |
|---|---|---|
| | 1606–1668 | Sir William Davenant. |
| | 1606–1684 | Corneille. |
| | 1606–1687 | Edmund Waller. |
| First settlement in Virginia. | 1607 | Chapman's *Bussy D'Ambois.* |
| | c.1608 | John Webster's *White Devil* acted. |
| | 1608–1661 | Thomas Fuller. |
| | 1608–1674 | John Milton. |
| | 1609 | Shakespeare's *Sonnets* published. |
| | | Dekker's *Gull's Hornbook* and *Four Birds of Noah's Ark.* |
| | c.1609 | Beaumont and Fletcher's *Knight of the Burning Pestle* and *Philaster* acted. |
| | 1609–1642 | Sir John Suckling. |
| | 1609–1674 | Edward Hyde, Earl of Clarendon (*History of the Rebellion* published 1702–1704). |
| | 1610 | Giles Fletcher's *Christ's Victory and Triumph.* |
| | | Jonson's *Alchemist* written. |
| | 1611 | King James Bible, often referred to as the Authorized Version. |
| | 1611–1612 | Shakespeare's *Tempest* probably written. |
| | 1612 | Bacon's *Essays* (second edition, thirty-eight essays). |
| | | Donne's *Second Anniversary.* |
| | | Thomas Shelton's English translation of Cervantes's *Don Quixote.* |
| | 1612–1622 | Drayton's *Polyolbion.* |
| | 1612–1680 | Samuel Butler. |
| | 1612?–1649 | Richard Crashaw. |
| | 1613–1616 | William Browne of Tavistock's *Britannia's Pastorals.* |
| | 1614 | Sir Thomas Overbury's *Characters.* |
| | | Ralegh's *History of the World.* |
| | c.1614 | John Webster's *Duchess of Malfi* acted. |
| | 1614–1615 | Chapman's English translation of the *Odyssey.* |
| Bacon made Lord Chancellor. | 1618 | |
| Synod of Dort. | | |
| Thirty Years' War. | 1618–1648 | |
| | 1618–1658 | Richard Lovelace. |
| | 1618–1667 | Abraham Cowley. |
| Pilgrim Fathers establish Plymouth. | 1620 | Bacon's *Novum Organum.* |
| | 1620–1706 | John Evelyn (*Diary* first published 1818). |
| | 1621 | Robert Burton's *Anatomy of Melancholy.* |
| | 1621–1678 | Andrew Marvell. |
| | 1622–1673 | Molière. |
| | 1622–1695 | Henry Vaughan. |
| | 1623 | First folio of Shakespeare's *Plays.* |
| | | Thomas Middleton's *Changeling* acted. |
| | 1625 | Bacon's *Essays* (third edition, fifty-eight essays). |
| Reign of Charles I. | 1625–1649 | |
| | 1626 | Bacon's *New Atlantis.* |
| Duke of Buckingham murdered. | 1628 | Sir Edward Coke's *Institutes of the Laws of England.* |
| | 1628–1688 | John Bunyan. |
| | 1629 | Milton's *On the Morning of Christ's Nativity* written. |
| Personal government of Charles I. | 1629–1640 | |

| POLITICAL, SOCIAL, RELIGIOUS | | LITERARY, PHILOSOPHICAL |
|---|---|---|
| | 1650–1651 | Jeremy Taylor's *Holy Living* and *Holy Dying*. |
| | 1650–1655 | Vaughan's *Silex Scintillans*. |
| John Churchill, Duke of Marlborough. | 1650–1722 | |
| Battle of Worcester. | 1651 | Davenant's *Gondibert*. |
| Navigation Act. | | Hobbes's *Leviathan*. |
| | | Milton's *Pro Populo Anglicano Defensio*. |
| First Dutch Naval War. | 1652–1654 | Dorothy Osborne's *Letters* written (first published 1888). |
| Rump Parliament ejected. | 1653 | Walton's *Compleat Angler*, Part I. |
| Barebone's Parliament. | | |
| Cromwell Lord Protector. | | |
| | 1656 | Cowley's *Davideis* and *Pindaric Odes*. |
| | | Davenant's *Siege of Rhodes*. |
| | 1658 | Browne's *Hydriotaphia*. |
| | | Dryden's *Stanzas on the Death of Cromwell*. |
| Restoration. | 1660 | |
| | 1660–1669 | Pepys's *Diary* written (first published 1825). |
| Reign of Charles II. | 1660–1685 | |
| | 1660–1672 | Bunyan's first imprisonment. |
| | 1660?–1731 | Daniel Defoe. |
| | 1661 | Joseph Glanvill's *Vanity of Dogmatizing*. |
| Final version of the Prayer Book. | 1662 | Fuller's *Worthies of England*. |
| | | Royal Society chartered. |
| | 1662–1678 | Samuel Butler's *Hudibras*. |
| | 1663 | Third Folio of Shakespeare's *Plays*. |
| | | Drury Lane Theater built. |
| Great Plague. | 1665 | Dryden and Sir Robert Howard's *Indian Queen*. |
| Second Dutch War. | 1665–1667 | |
| Great Fire of London. | 1666 | Bunyan's *Grace Abounding*. |
| | | Molière's *Misanthrope*. |
| | 1667 | Dryden's *Annus Mirabilis*. |
| | | Milton's *Paradise Lost* (first edition, in ten books). |
| | | Molière's *Tartuffe*. |
| | | Thomas Sprat's *History of the Royal Society*. |
| | 1667–1745 | Jonathan Swift. |
| | 1668 | Dryden's *Essay of Dramatic Poesy*. |
| | | Sir Charles Sedley's *Mulberry Garden*. |
| | 1668–1688 | Dryden poet laureate. |
| | 1668–1694 | La Fontaine's *Fables*. |
| Secret Treaty of Dover. | 1670 | Pascal's *Pensées*. |
| | 1670–1672 | Dryden's *Conquest of Granada*. |
| | 1670–1729 | William Congreve. |
| | 1671 | Milton's *Paradise Regained* and *Samson Agonistes*. |
| | | *The Rehearsal* acted (the work of George Villiers, Duke of Buckingham, and others). |
| | 1672–1719 | Joseph Addison. |
| | 1672–1729 | Sir Richard Steele. |
| | 1674 | Boileau's *Art Poétique*. |
| | | Milton's *Paradise Lost* (second edition, in twelve books). |
| | c.1674 | Wycherley's *Plain-Dealer* acted. |
| | 1676 | Charles Cotton's *Compleat Angler*, Part II. |

| POLITICAL, SOCIAL, RELIGIOUS | | LITERARY, PHILOSOPHICAL |
|---|---|---|
| | | Etherege's *Man of Mode*. |
| | 1677 | Mme. de Lafayette's *Princesse de Clèves*. |
| | | Nathaniel Lee's *Rival Queens*. |
| | | Racine's *Phèdre*. |
| | | Wycherley's *Plain-Dealer* published. |
| Popish Plot. | 1678 | Dryden's *All for Love*. |
| | | Thomas Rymer's *Tragedies of the Last Age Considered*. |
| | | Bunyan's *Pilgrim's Progress*, Part I. |
| | c.1678 | Mrs. Aphra Behn's *Oroonoko*. |
| | 1679–1714 | Gilbert Burnet's *History of the Reformation*. |
| | 1680 | Bunyan's *Life and Death of Mr. Badman*. |
| | 1681–1682 | Dryden's *Absalom and Achitophel*. |
| | 1682 | Dryden's *Mac Flecknoe* and *Religio Laici*. |
| | | Thomas Otway's *Venice Preserved*. |
| | 1684 | Bunyan's *Pilgrim's Progress*, Part II. |
| Monmouth's Rebellion. | 1685 | |
| Revocation of the Edict of Nantes. | | |
| Reign of James II. | 1685–1688 | |
| | 1685–1753 | George Berkeley. |
| | 1687 | Newton's *Principia*. |
| | | Dryden's *Hind and the Panther*. |
| Glorious or Bloodless Revolution. | 1688 | George Savile, Marquis of Halifax's *Character of a Trimmer*. |
| | 1688–1692 | Thomas Shadwell poet laureate. |
| Reign of William III and Mary II. | 1688–1694 | |
| | 1688–1744 | Alexander Pope. |
| Bill of Rights. | 1689 | |
| Toleration Act. | | |
| | 1689–1761 | Samuel Richardson. |
| | 1690 | Locke's *Essay Concerning the Human Understanding*. |
| | 1691–1692 | Anthony à Wood's *Athenae Oxonienses*. |
| A society for the reformation of manners founded. | 1692 | Thomas Rymer's *Short View of Tragedy*. |
| | | Sir William Temple's *Essays*. |
| | 1692–1699 | English Quarrel of the Ancients and the Moderns. |
| | 1692–1715 | Nahum Tate poet laureate. |
| | 1693 | Locke's *Thoughts concerning Education*. |
| | 1694 | William Wotton's *Reflections on Ancient and Modern Learning*. |
| Reign of William III. | 1694–1702 | |
| | 1694–1773 | Philip Stanhope, Earl of Chesterfield. |
| | 1694–1778 | Voltaire. |
| | 1695 | Congreve's *Love for Love*. |
| | 1696 | John Toland's *Christianity not Mysterious*. |
| Treaty of Ryswick. | 1697 | Dryden's *Alexander's Feast*. |
| | | Sir John Vanbrugh's *Relapse*. |
| | 1697–1698 | Swift's *Tale of a Tub* and *Battle of the Books* written. |
| | 1698 | Jeremy Collier's *Short View of the Immorality and Profaneness of the English Stage*. |
| | 1698–1703 | Edward Ward's *London Spy*. |
| | 1699 | Samuel Garth's *Dispensary*. |
| | 1700 | Congreve's *Way of the World*. |
| | | Dryden's *Fables*. |
| | | John Pomfret's *Choice*. |

| POLITICAL, SOCIAL, RELIGIOUS | | LITERARY, PHILOSOPHICAL |
|---|---|---|
| | | Tom Brown's *Amusements Serious and Comical.* |
| Act of Settlement. | 1701 | Defoe's *True-Born Englishman.* |
| | | Steele's *Christian Hero.* |
| War of the Spanish Succession. | 1701–1714 | |
| | 1702 | Defoe's *Shortest Way with the Dissenters.* |
| | 1702–1704 | Clarendon's *History of the Rebellion and Civil Wars in England* first published. |
| Reign of Queen Anne. | 1702–1714 | |
| | 1703 | Nicholas Rowe's *Fair Penitent.* |
| | | Steele's *Lying Lover.* |
| John Wesley. | 1703–1791 | |
| Capture of Gibraltar. | 1704 | Swift's *Tale of a Tub* and *Battle of the Books* published. |
| Battles of Blenheim and Malaga. | | |
| | 1705 | Addison's *Campaign.* |
| | | Steele's *Tender Husband.* |
| Parliamentary Union of England and Scotland. | 1707 | George Farquhar's *Beaux' Stratagem.* |
| | 1707–1754 | Henry Fielding. |
| William Pitt, Earl of Chatham. | 1708–1778 | |
| | 1709 | Pope's *Pastorals.* |
| | 1709–1711 | The *Tatler.* |
| | 1709–1784 | Samuel Johnson. |
| | 1710–1713 | Swift's *Journal to Stella* written. |
| | 1711 | Pope's *Essay on Criticism.* |
| | | Anthony Ashley Cooper, Earl of Shaftesbury's *Characteristics of Men and Manners.* |
| | 1711–1712 | The *Spectator.* |
| | 1711–1776 | David Hume. |
| | 1712–1714 | Pope's *Rape of the Lock.* |
| | 1712–1778 | Rousseau. |
| Treaty of Utrecht. | 1713 | Pope's *Windsor Forest.* |
| | | Scriblerus Club formed. |
| | | Addison's *Cato.* |
| | | Berkeley's *Dialogues between Hylas and Philonous.* |
| | | Steele's *Guardian.* |
| | | Anne Finch, Countess of Winchilsea's *Miscellany Poems.* |
| | 1713–1768 | Laurence Sterne. |
| | 1714–1723 | Bernard Mandeville's *Fable of the Bees.* |
| Reign of George I (first of the Hanoverian kings). | 1714–1727 | |
| George Whitefield. | 1714–1770 | |
| First Jacobite Rebellion. | 1715 | Isaac Watts's *Divine Songs for Children.* |
| | 1715–1718 | Nicholas Rowe poet laureate. |
| | 1715–1720 | Pope's translation of the *Iliad.* |
| | 1716 | John Gay's *Trivia.* |
| | 1716–1771 | Thomas Gray. |
| | 1717–1779 | David Garrick. |
| | 1717–1797 | Horace Walpole. |
| | 1718–1730 | Laurence Eusden poet laureate. |
| | 1719 | Defoe's *Robinson Crusoe.* |
| | | Isaac Watts's *Psalms of David.* |
| South Sea Bubble. | 1720 | |
| Sir Robert Walpole head of the cabinet. | 1721–1742 | |
| | 1721–1771 | Tobias Smollett. |

| POLITICAL, SOCIAL, RELIGIOUS | | LITERARY, PHILOSOPHICAL |
|---|---|---|
| | 1722 | Defoe's *Journal of the Plague Year* and *Moll Flanders*. |
| | | Steele's *Conscious Lovers* acted. |
| | 1723–1734 | Gilbert Burnet's *History of My Own Time*. |
| | 1723–1792 | Sir Joshua Reynolds. |
| | 1724 | *The Evergreen* (collection of old Scotch poetry, ed. Allan Ramsay). |
| | | Swift's *Drapier's Letters*. |
| | 1724–1804 | Kant. |
| | 1725 | Allan Ramsay's *Gentle Shepherd*. |
| | | Pope's edition of Shakespeare. |
| | 1725–1726 | Pope's translation of the *Odyssey*. |
| Robert Clive, Lord Clive. | 1725–1774 | |
| | 1726 | Swift's *Gulliver's Travels*. |
| | 1726–1727 | John Dyer's *Grongar Hill*. |
| | 1726–1729 | Voltaire's visit to England. |
| | 1726–1730 | James Thomson's *Seasons*. |
| | 1727–1737 | The period covered in the *Memoirs of the Reign of George II* by Lord Hervey (first published 1848). |
| | 1727–1750 | John Gay's *Fables*. |
| Reign of George II. | 1727–1760 | |
| | 1728 | John Gay's *Beggar's Opera*. |
| | | William Law's *Serious Call to a Devout and Holy Life*. |
| | 1728–1743 | Pope's *Dunciad*. |
| | 1728–1774 | Oliver Goldsmith. |
| | 1729 | Swift's *Modest Proposal*. |
| | 1729–1797 | Edmund Burke. |
| | 1730–1731 | Fielding's *Tom Thumb*. |
| | 1730–1757 | Colley Cibber poet laureate. |
| | 1731 | George Lillo's *London Merchant, or George Barnwell*. |
| | 1731–1800 | William Cowper. |
| | 1731–1914 | The *Gentleman's Magazine*. |
| | 1732 | Covent Garden Theater built. |
| Warren Hastings. | 1732–1818 | |
| | 1733 | Pope's *Essay on Man*. |
| | 1734 | Lewis Theobald's edition of Shakespeare. |
| | 1735 | Pope's *Epistle to Dr. Arbuthnot*. |
| | 1736 | Joseph Butler's *Analogy of Religion*. |
| | 1737 | William Shenstone's *Schoolmistress*. |
| | | Act for licensing the theaters. |
| | | Wesley's *Psalms and Hymns*. |
| | 1737–1741 | William Warburton's *Divine Legation of Moses*. |
| | 1737–1768 | Chesterfield's *Letters to His Natural Son* written. |
| | 1737–1794 | Edward Gibbon. |
| | 1738 | Johnson's *London*. |
| | 1739–1740 | Hume's *Treatise of Human Nature*. |
| | 1739–1741 | Gray's trip to the Continent with Horace Walpole. |
| | 1740 | Colley Cibber's *Apology for the Life of Colley Cibber*. |
| | | Richardson's *Pamela, or Virtue Rewarded*. |
| War of the Austrian Succession. | 1740–1748 | |
| | 1740–1795 | James Boswell. |
| | 1742 | Fielding's *Joseph Andrews*. |

| POLITICAL, SOCIAL, RELIGIOUS | | LITERARY, PHILOSOPHICAL |
|---|---|---|
| | | Edward Young's *Complaint, or Night Thoughts.* |
| | 1743 | Robert Blair's *Grave.* |
| | | Fielding's *Jonathan Wild the Great.* |
| | 1744 | Mark Akenside's *Pleasures of Imagination.* |
| Second Jacobite Rebellion. | 1745–1746 | |
| Battle of Culloden. | 1746 | William Collins's *Odes.* |
| | | Joseph Warton's *Odes.* |
| | 1747 | Thomas Warton's *Pleasures of Melancholy.* |
| | 1748 | James Thomson's *Castle of Indolence.* |
| | | Richardson's *Clarissa Harlowe.* |
| | | Smollett's *Roderick Random.* |
| | | Hume's *Inquiry concerning Human Understanding.* |
| | | Montesquieu's *Esprit des Lois.* |
| | 1748–1832 | Jeremy Bentham. |
| | 1749 | Fielding's *Tom Jones.* |
| | | Henry St. John, Lord Bolingbroke's *Idea of a Patriot King.* |
| | | Johnson's *Vanity of Human Wishes.* |
| Charles James Fox. | 1749–1806 | |
| | 1749–1832 | Goethe. |
| | 1750–1752 | Johnson's *Rambler.* |
| | 1751 | Gray's *Elegy Written in a Country Churchyard.* |
| | | Fielding's *Amelia.* |
| | | Smollett's *Peregrine Pickle.* |
| | 1751–1816 | Richard Brinsley Sheridan. |
| Gregorian Calendar adopted by act of Parliament. | 1752 | |
| | 1752–1770 | Thomas Chatterton. |
| | 1753 | British Museum chartered. |
| | 1753–1754 | Richardson's *Sir Charles Grandison.* |
| | 1754 | Thomas Warton's *Observations on the Fairie Queene of Spenser.* |
| | 1754–1762 | Hume's *History of England.* |
| | 1754–1832 | George Crabbe. |
| | 1755 | Johnson's *English Dictionary.* |
| Black Hole of Calcutta. | 1756 | John Home's *Douglas* acted. |
| William Pitt the elder, head of the cabinet. | 1756–1761 | |
| Seven Years' War. | 1756–1763 | |
| | 1756–1782 | Joseph Warton's *Genius and Writings of Pope.* |
| Clive's victory at Plassey. | 1757 | Gray's *Odes* (*The Bard* and *The Progress of Poesy*). |
| | 1757–1785 | William Whitehead poet laureate. |
| | 1757–1827 | William Blake. |
| Capture of Louisburg. | 1758 | |
| | 1758–1760 | Johnson's *Idler.* |
| Wolfe takes Quebec. | 1759 | Goldsmith's *Bee.* |
| | | Johnson's *Rasselas.* |
| | | Voltaire's *Candide.* |
| | | British Museum opened. |
| | 1759–1796 | Robert Burns. |
| | 1759–1805 | Schiller. |
| | 1760 | James Macpherson's *Fragments of Ancient Poetry* (*Ossian*). |
| | | Rousseau's *Nouvelle Héloïse.* |

| POLITICAL, SOCIAL, RELIGIOUS | | LITERARY, PHILOSOPHICAL |
|---|---|---|
| | 1760–1761 | Goldsmith's *Citizen of the World* (*Chinese Letters*). |
| | 1760–1767 | Sterne's *Tristram Shandy*. |
| Reign of George III. | 1760–1820 | |
| | 1761 | Charles Churchill's *Rosciad*. |
| | 1762 | Richard Hurd's *Letters on Chivalry and Romance*. |
| | | Rousseau's *Contrat Social*. |
| | 1762–1763 | Smollett's *Briton*. |
| | | John Wilkes's *North Briton*. |
| | 1763 | Boswell meets Johnson, 16 May. |
| | 1763–1766 | Boswell's visit to the Continent. |
| Spinning jenny invented by James Hargreaves. | 1764 | Goldsmith's *Traveler*. |
| | | The Literary Club established. |
| | | Walpole's *Castle of Otranto*. |
| Invention of the steam engine by James Watt. | 1765 | Johnson's edition of Shakespeare. |
| | | Thomas Percy's *Reliques of Ancient English Poetry*. |
| | 1765–1769 | Sir William Blackstone's *Commentaries on the Laws of England*. |
| | 1766 | Goldsmith's *Vicar of Wakefield*. |
| | | Lessing's *Laokoön*. |
| | 1766–1767 | Rousseau's visit to England. |
| | 1768 | Boswell's *Account of Corsica*. |
| | | Goldsmith's *Good-Natured Man*. |
| | | Hugh Kelly's *False Delicacy*. |
| | | Sterne's *Sentimental Journey*. |
| | 1768–1772 | *Letters of Junius* (perhaps by Sir Philip Francis). |
| | 1768–1840 | Francis Burney's *Letters and Diaries* written (first published 1842–1889). |
| | 1768–1848 | Chateaubriand. |
| | 1769 | William Robertson's *History of Charles V.* |
| Controversy over the election of John Wilkes for Middlesex. | 1769–1774 | |
| | 1769–1790 | Reynold's *Discourses to the Royal Academy*. |
| | 1770 | Burke's *Thoughts on the Present Discontent*. |
| | | Goldsmith's *Deserted Village*. |
| Lord North head of the cabinet. | 1770–1782 | |
| | 1770–1850 | William Wordsworth. |
| | 1771 | Henry Mackenzie's *Man of Feeling*. |
| | | Smollett's *Humphry Clinker*. |
| | 1771–1774 | James Beattie's *Minstrel*. |
| | 1771–1832 | Sir Walter Scott. |
| | 1772 | Richard Graves's *Spiritual Quixote*. |
| | 1772–1834 | Samuel Taylor Coleridge. |
| | 1773 | Goldsmith's *She Stoops to Conquer*. |
| | 1773–1779 | Robert Fergusson's *Poems*. |
| | 1774 | Chesterfield's *Letters to His Natural Son* published. |
| | | Goethe's *Sorrows of Werther*. |
| | 1774–1781 | Thomas Warton's *History of English Poetry*. |
| | 1774–1843 | Robert Southey. |
| | 1775 | Burke's *Speech on Conciliation*. |
| | | Sheridan's *Rivals* performed. |
| War with the American Colonies. | 1775–1783 | |
| | 1775–1817 | Jane Austen. |

| POLITICAL, SOCIAL, RELIGIOUS | | LITERARY, PHILOSOPHICAL |
|---|---|---|
| | 1775–1834 | Charles Lamb. |
| | 1775–1864 | Walter Savage Landor. |
| Declaration of American Independence. | 1776 | Thomas Paine's *Common Sense*. |
| | | Adam Smith's *Wealth of Nations*. |
| | 1776–1788 | Gibbon's *Decline and Fall of the Roman Empire*. |
| | 1777 | Chatterton's *Rowley Poems* published. |
| | | Maurice Morgann's *Essay on the Character of Falstaff*. |
| | | Clara Reeve's *Champion of Virtue* (*The Old English Baron*). |
| | | Sheridan's *School for Scandal* performed. |
| | 1778 | Frances Burney's *Evelina*. |
| | 1778–1830 | William Hazlitt. |
| | 1779 | Hume's *Natural History of Religion*. |
| | | Cowper and John Newton's *Olney Hymns*. |
| | 1779–1781 | Johnson's *Lives of the Poets*. |
| Gordon Riots. | 1780 | |
| | 1781 | Charles Macklin's *Man of the World* acted. |
| | | Sheridan's *Critic*. |
| | | Kant's *Critique of Pure Reason*. |
| | 1781–1788 | Rousseau's *Confessions*. |
| | 1782 | Cowper's *Poems* and *Diverting History of John Gilpin*. |
| | 1783 | William Blake's *Poetical Sketches*. |
| | | George Crabbe's *Village*. |
| | | Joseph Ritson's *Collection of English Songs*. |
| William Pitt the younger, head of the cabinet. | 1783–1801 | |
| | 1784–1859 | Leigh Hunt. |
| | 1785 | Boswell's *Journal of a Tour to the Hebrides*. |
| | | Cowper's *Poems* (including *The Task*). |
| | 1785–1790 | Thomas Warton poet laureate. |
| | 1785–1859 | Thomas De Quincey. |
| | 1785–1873 | Manzoni. |
| | 1786 | William Beckford's *Vathek* (English translation from original French). |
| | | Burns's *Poems* (published at Kilmarnock). |
| American Constitution signed. | 1787 | Goethe's *Iphigenie auf Tauris*. |
| Society for the Abolition of the Slave-trade founded (under William Wilberforce). | | |
| Trial of Warren Hastings. | 1788–1795 | |
| | 1788–1824 | George Noel Gordon, Lord Byron. |
| Fall of the Bastille (beginning of the French Revolution). | 1789 | Blake's *Songs of Innocence*. |
| | | William Lisle Bowles's *Fourteen Sonnets*. |
| | | Gilbert White's *Natural History of Selborne*. |
| | 1789–1792 | Erasmus Darwin's *Botanic Garden*. |
| | 1790 | Blake's *Marriage of Heaven and Hell*. |
| | | Burke's *Reflections on the French Revolution*. |
| | | Ann Radcliffe's *Sicilian Romance*. |
| | | Wordsworth's first visit to the Continent. |
| | | Goethe's *Faust* (first published version). |
| | 1790–1813 | Henry James Pye poet laureate. |

| POLITICAL, SOCIAL, RELIGIOUS | | LITERARY, PHILOSOPHICAL |
|---|---|---|
| | 1791 | Boswell's *Life of Johnson*. |
| | | Cowper's translation of the *Iliad* and the *Odyssey*. |
| | 1791–1792 | Thomas Paine's *Rights of Man*. |
| | 1791–1793 | Wordsworth's second visit to the Continent. |
| | 1792 | Thomas Holcroft's *Anna St. Ives*. |
| | | Mary Wollstonecraft's *Rights of Woman*. |
| | | Arthur Young's *Travels in France*. |
| | 1792–1822 | Percy Bysshe Shelley. |
| Louis XVI executed. | 1793 | William Godwin's *Political Justice*. |
| England enters the first coalition against France. | | Wordsworth's *Evening Walk* and *Descriptive Sketches*. |
| Reign of Terror in France. | 1793–1794 | |
| Fall of Robespierre. | 1794 | William Godwin's *Caleb Williams*. |
| | | Ann Radcliffe's *Mysteries of Udolpho*. |
| | | Blake's *Songs of Experience*. |
| | | Thomas Paine's *Age of Reason* (Part II, 1795; Part III, 1811). |
| | 1795 | Matthew Lewis's *Monk*. |
| | | First meeting of Wordsworth and Coleridge. |
| | 1795–1796 | Goethe's *Wilhelm Meister*. |
| | 1795–1821 | John Keats. |
| | 1795–1881 | Thomas Carlyle. |
| Napoleon's Italian campaign. | 1796 | Gibbon's *Memoirs* (ed. Earl of Sheffield) published. |
| | | William Roscoe's *Life of Lorenzo de' Medici*. |
| | | Scott's *William and Helen* (translation of Bürger's *Leonore*). |
| | 1797 | Coleridge's *Kubla Khan* written. |
| | 1797–1801 | Coleridge's *Christabel* written. |
| | 1797–1856 | Heine. |
| Battle of the Nile. | 1798 | Landor's *Gebir*. |
| | | Malthus's *Essay on Population*. |
| | 1798 | Wordsworth and Coleridge's *Lyrical Ballads*. |
| | | Wordsworth and Coleridge go to Germany. |
| | 1798–1805 | Wordsworth's *Prelude* written. |
| | 1798–1828 | Dorothy Wordsworth's *Journals* written. |
| | 1798–1837 | Leopardi. |
| Napoleon First Consul. | 1799–1804 | |
| Parliamentary Union of England and Ireland. | 1800 | Maria Edgeworth's *Castle Rackrent*. |
| | | Wordsworth and Coleridge's *Lyrical Ballads* (second edition, with Preface). |
| | 1800–1859 | Thomas Babington, Lord Macaulay. |
| | 1801 | Chateaubriand's *Atala*. |
| | | Southey's *Thalaba*. |
| | 1801–1890 | John Henry, Cardinal Newman. |
| Peace of Amiens. | 1802 | Chateaubriand's *Génie du Christianisme*. |
| | | *Edinburgh Review* founded. |
| | | *Minstrelsy of the Scottish Border* (ed. Scott). |
| | 1802–1885 | Victor Hugo. |
| War with France renewed. | 1803 | Jane Porter's *Thaddeus of Warsaw*. |
| | 1803–1873 | Edward Bulwer, Lord Lytton. |
| | 1803–1882 | Emerson. |
| | 1804–1869 | Sainte-Beuve. |
| Benjamin Disraeli, Earl of Beaconsfield. | 1804–1881 | |

| POLITICAL, SOCIAL, RELIGIOUS | | LITERARY, PHILOSOPHICAL |
|---|---|---|
| Battles of Austerlitz and Trafalgar. | 1805 | Scott's *Lay of the Last Minstrel*. |
| | 1805–1812 | Henry Cary's translation of the *Divina Commedia*. |
| Ministry of All the Talents. | 1806–1807 | |
| | 1806–1861 | Elizabeth Barrett Browning. |
| | 1806–1873 | John Stuart Mill. |
| Abolition of the slave trade. | 1807 | Byron's *Hours of Idleness*. |
| | | Charles and Mary Lamb's *Tales from Shakespeare*. |
| | | Wordsworth's *Poems in Two Volumes*. |
| | 1808 | Scott's *Marmion*. |
| | | Lamb's *Specimens of the English Dramatic Poets*. |
| | | August Wilhelm von Schlegel's lectures on Shakespeare. |
| Peninsular Campaign. | 1808–1814 | |
| | 1808–1832 | Goethe's *Faust*. |
| | 1809 | Thomas Campbell's *Gertrude of Wyoming and Other Poems*. |
| | | Byron's *English Bards and Scotch Reviewers*. |
| | | Hannah More's *Coelebs in Search of a Wife*. |
| | | *Quarterly Review* founded. |
| | 1809–1810 | Coleridge's *Friend*. |
| | 1809–1882 | Charles Darwin. |
| | 1809–1883 | Edward FitzGerald. |
| | 1809–1892 | Alfred, Lord Tennyson. |
| William Ewart Gladstone. | 1809–1898 | |
| | 1810 | Coleridge's lectures on Shakespeare (first published 1849). |
| | | Crabbe's *Borough*. |
| | | Jane Porter's *Scottish Chiefs*. |
| | | Scott's *Lady of the Lake*. |
| | 1811 | Jane Austen's *Sense and Sensibility*. |
| Regency of Prince of Wales (later George IV). | 1811–1820 | |
| | 1811–1833 | Goethe's *Dichtung und Wahrheit*. |
| | 1811–1863 | William Makepeace Thackeray. |
| Napoleon's Russian campaign. | 1812 | |
| War with the United States. | 1812–1815 | |
| | 1812–1816 | Hegel's *Logic*. |
| | 1812–1818 | Byron's *Childe Harold*. |
| | 1812–1870 | Charles Dickens. |
| | 1812–1889 | Robert Browning. |
| Battle of Leipsic. | 1813 | Robert Owen's *New View of Society*. |
| | | Shelley's *Queen Mab*. |
| | | Southey's *Life of Nelson*. |
| | | Jane Austen's *Pride and Prejudice*. |
| | 1813–1843 | Southey poet laureate. |
| Napoleon's abdication. | 1814 | Jane Austen's *Mansfield Park*. |
| | | Scott's *Waverley*. |
| | | Wordsworth's *Excursion*. |
| | | Shelley's departure from England to the Continent. |
| Congress of Vienna. | 1814–1815 | |
| Return of Napoleon from Elba. | 1815 | Scott's *Guy Mannering*. |
| Battle of Waterloo. | | Wordsworth's *White Doe of Rylstone*. |
| | 1815–1882 | Anthony Trollope. |
| | 1816 | Jane Austen's *Emma*. |
| | | Byron's departure from England to the Continent. |

| POLITICAL, SOCIAL, RELIGIOUS | | LITERARY, PHILOSOPHICAL |
|---|---|---|
| | | Coleridge's *Christabel* and *Kubla Khan* published. |
| | | Leigh Hunt's *Story of Rimini.* |
| | | Shelley's *Alastor.* |
| | 1816–1855 | Charlotte Brontë. |
| | 1817 | Byron's *Manfred.* |
| | | Thomas Moore's *Lalla Rookh.* |
| | | Coleridge's *Biographia Literaria* and *Sibylline Leaves.* |
| | | Shelley's *Laon and Cythna (Revolt of Islam).* |
| | | Keats's *Poems.* |
| | | Hazlitt's *Characters of Shakespeare's Plays.* |
| | | *Blackwood's Magazine* founded. |
| | | David Ricardo's *Principles of Political Economy and Taxation.* |
| | 1818 | Byron's *Beppo.* |
| | | Keats's *Endymion.* |
| | | Mary Shelley's *Frankenstein.* |
| | | Attack on Keats in the *Quarterly Review.* |
| | 1818 | Jane Austen's *Northanger Abbey* and *Persuasion.* |
| | | Thomas Love Peacock's *Nightmare Abbey.* |
| | | Scott's *Heart of Midlothian.* |
| | | Hazlitt's *Lectures on the English Poets.* |
| | 1818–1848 | Emily Brontë. |
| Peterloo Massacre. | 1819 | Scott's *Ivanhoe.* |
| | | Crabbe's *Tales of the Hall.* |
| | | Shelley's *Cenci.* |
| | | Schopenhauer's *World as Will and Idea.* |
| | 1819–1824 | Byron's *Don Juan.* |
| | 1819–1861 | Arthur Hugh Clough. |
| | 1819–1875 | Charles Kingsley. |
| | 1819–1880 | Mary Ann Evans (George Eliot). |
| | 1819–1900 | John Ruskin. |
| | 1820 | Keats's *Lamia, Isabella, The Eve of St. Agnes, Hyperion, and Other Poems.* |
| | | Shelley's *Prometheus Unbound.* |
| | | John Clare's *Poems Descriptive of Rural Life.* |
| | | Lamartine's *Méditations Poétiques.* |
| Reign of George IV. | 1820–1830 | |
| | 1820–1903 | Herbert Spencer. |
| | 1821 | Scott's *Kenilworth.* |
| | | Shelley's *Adonais* and *Epipsychidion.* |
| | | Southey's *Vision of Judgment.* |
| | 1821–1880 | Flaubert. |
| | 1821–1881 | Dostoevsky. |
| | 1822 | Byron's *Vision of Judgment.* |
| | | De Quincey's *Confessions of an English Opium-Eater* (first version). |
| | 1822–1888 | Matthew Arnold. |
| | 1823 | Lamb's *Essays of Elia.* |
| | | Scott's *Quentin Durward.* |
| | 1824 | Carlyle's translation of Goethe's *Wilhelm Meister.* |
| | 1824–1829 | Landor's *Imaginary Conversations.* |
| | 1824–1832 | Mary Mitford's *Our Village.* |
| Completion of the first railroad line in England. | 1825 | Coleridge's *Aids to Reflection.* |
| | | Macaulay's *Milton.* |

| POLITICAL, SOCIAL, RELIGIOUS | | LITERARY, PHILOSOPHICAL |
|---|---|---|
| | 1825–1895 | Thomas Henry Huxley. |
| | 1827 | De Quincey's *Murder as One of the Fine Arts*. |
| | | Heine's *Buch der Lieder*. |
| | | John Keble's *Christian Year*. |
| Catholic Emancipation Act. | 1828 | Bulwer Lytton's *Pelham*. |
| | | Carlyle's *Burns*. |
| | 1828–1882 | Dante Gabriel Rossetti. |
| | 1828–1909 | George Meredith. |
| | 1828–1910 | Tolstoy. |
| | 1829 | William Cobbett's *Advice to Young Men*. |
| July Revolution in France. | 1830 | William Cobbett's *Rural Rides* published. |
| | | Hugo's *Hernani*. |
| | | Tennyson's *Poems, Chiefly Lyrical*. |
| | 1830 | Attack on Tennyson in the *Quarterly Review*. |
| | 1830–1833 | Sir Charles Lyell's *Principles of Geology*. |
| Reign of William IV. | 1830–1837 | |
| | 1830–1894 | Christina Rossetti. |
| | 1831 | Macaulay's *Samuel Johnson* and *Boswell*. |
| Reform Bill passed. | 1832 | Bulwer Lytton's *Eugene Aram*. |
| | | Tennyson's *Poems*. |
| Factory Acts. | 1833 | Death of Arthur Hallam. |
| | | Lamb's *Last Essays of Elia*. |
| | | Browning's *Pauline*. |
| | | Newman's *Arians of the Fourth Century*. |
| | 1833–1834 | Carlyle's *Sartor Resartus* published in *Fraser's Magazine*. |
| | 1833–1841 | *Tracts for the Times* (by Newman and others). |
| Oxford Movement. | 1833–1845 | |
| | 1833–1850 | Tennyson's *In Memoriam* written. |
| Poor Law. | 1834 | Sir Henry Taylor's *Philip van Artevelde*. |
| | | Frederick Marryat's *Peter Simple* and *Jacob Faithful*. |
| | | Bulwer Lytton's *Last Days of Pompeii*. |
| | 1834–1896 | William Morris. |
| | 1835 | Browning's *Paracelsus*. |
| | | Bulwer Lytton's *Rienzi*. |
| | | Vigny's *Chatterton*. |
| | 1835–1902 | Samuel Butler. |
| | 1835–1907 | Carducci. |
| | 1836 | Carlyle's *Sartor Resartus* published as a book (in Boston, U. S. A.). |
| | | Emerson's *Nature*. |
| | | Dickens's *Pickwick Papers* and *Sketches by Boz*. |
| | 1836–1838 | John Lockhart's *Life of Scott*. |
| | 1837 | Carlyle's *French Revolution*. |
| | 1837–1838 | Dickens's *Oliver Twist*. |
| Reign of Victoria. | 1837–1901 | |
| | 1837–1909 | Algernon Charles Swinburne. |
| Chartist Movement. | 1838–1848 | |
| | 1839 | William Harrison Ainsworth's *Jack Sheppard*. |
| | | De Quincey's *Klosterheim*. |
| Opium War. | 1839–1842 | |
| | 1839–1894 | Walter Pater. |
| | 1840 | Browning's *Sordello*. |

POLITICAL, SOCIAL, RELIGIOUS

LITERARY, PHILOSOPHICAL

Poe's *Tales of the Grotesque and Arabesque*.

Shelley's *Letters and Miscellaneous Prose* (including the *Defense of Poetry*) published.

|  |  |
|---|---|
| 1840–1847 | Richard Barham's *Ingolsby Legends*. |
| 1840–1928 | Thomas Hardy. |
| 1841 | Browning's *Pippa Passes*. |
|  | Carlyle's *Heroes and Hero-Worship*. |
|  | Charles J. Lever's *Charles O'Malley*. |
|  | Macaulay's *Warren Hastings*. |
|  | Newman's *Tract XC*. |
| 1841–1922 | William Henry Hudson. |
| 1842 | Browning's *Dramatic Lyrics*. |
|  | Macaulay's *Lays of Ancient Rome*. |
|  | Tennyson's *Poems*. |
| 1843 | Carlyle's *Past and Present*. |
|  | Thomas Hood's *Song of the Shirt* (in *Punch*). |
|  | Macaulay's *Essays* (first authorized collection). |
| 1843–1850 | Wordsworth poet laureate. |
| 1843–1860 | Ruskin's *Modern Painters*. |
| 1843–1916 | Henry James. |

Opening of the first co-operative shop in Rochdale.

| 1844 | William Barnes's *Poems of Rural Life*. |
|---|---|
|  | Disraeli's *Coningsby*. |
|  | Dumas's *Three Musketeers*. |
|  | Alexander Kinglake's *Eothen*. |
| 1844–1889 | Gerard Manley Hopkins (*Poems* first published 1918). |
| 1844–1930 | Robert Bridges. |
| 1845 | Carlyle's *Oliver Cromwell's Letters and Speeches*. |
|  | Dickens's *Cricket on the Hearth*. |
|  | Newman's entry into the Roman Catholic Church. |

Corn Laws repealed.

| 1846 | Marriage of Elizabeth Barrett and Robert Browning. |
|---|---|
|  | *Poems* of the Brontë sisters. |
|  | Bulwer Lytton's *New Timon*. |
| 1846–1856 | George Grote's *History of Greece*. |
| 1847 | C. Brontë's *Jane Eyre*. |
|  | E. Brontë's *Wuthering Heights*. |
|  | Tennyson's *Princess*. |
| 1847–1848 | Thackeray's *Vanity Fair*. |
| 1848 | Clough's *Bothie of Toper-na-Fuosich*. |
|  | Elizabeth Gaskell's *Mary Barton*. |
| 1848–1850 | Thackeray's *Pendennis*. |
| 1848–1861 | Macaulay's *History of England, from the Accession of James the Second*. |
| 1849 | Arnold's *Strayed Reveler and Other Poems*. |
|  | Ruskin's *Seven Lamps of Architecture*. |
| 1849–1850 | Dickens's *David Copperfield*. |
| 1850 | E. B. Browning's *Sonnets from the Portuguese*. |
|  | Browning's *Christmas Eve and Easter Day*. |
|  | Carlyle's *Latter Day Pamphlets*. |
|  | Emerson's *Representative Men*. |
|  | *The Germ* (Rossetti and others). |

POLITICAL, SOCIAL, RELIGIOUS | LITERARY, PHILOSOPHICAL

Hawthorne's *Scarlet Letter.*
Kingsley's *Alton Locke.*

1850    Tennyson's *In Memoriam* published.
Wordsworth's *Prelude* published.

1850–1892    Tennyson poet laureate.
1850–1894    Robert Louis Stevenson.

Great Exhibition at the Crystal Palace. 1851    Thomas Lovell Beddoes's *Death's Jest Book.*

*Coup d'État* of Louis Napoleon (Napoleon III).    George Borrow's *Lavengro.*
Carlyle's *Life of John Sterling.*
FitzGerald's *Euphranor.*
Melville's *Moby Dick.*

1851–1853    Ruskin's *Stones of Venice.*
1852    Arnold's *Empedocles on Etna and Other Poems.*
Newman's lectures *On the Scope and Nature of University Education.*
Thackeray's *Henry Esmond.*

1852–1853    Dickens's *Bleak House.*
1852–1933    George Moore.
1853    Arnold's *Poems* (including *The Scholar Gypsy*).
C. Brontë's *Villette.*
Elizabeth Gaskell's *Cranford.*
Kingsley's *Hypatia.*
Landor's *Last Fruit off an Old Tree.*
Thackeray's *English Humorists* published.

1853–1855    Thackeray's *Newcomes.*
Crimean War.    1853–1856
Cecil John Rhodes.    1853–1902
1854    Dickens's *Hard Times.*
Thoreau's *Walden.*

1854–1862    Coventry Patmore's *Angel in the House.*
1854–1900    Oscar Wilde.
1855    Browning's *Men and Women.*
Kingsley's *Westward Ho.*
Spencer's *Principles of Psychology.*
Tennyson's *Maud.*
Trollope's *Warden.*
Whitman's *Leaves of Grass.*

Second Chinese War.    1855–1860
1856    Dinah Mulock's *John Halifax, Gentleman.*
De Quincey's *Confessions of an English Opium-Eater* (enlarged edition).
*The Oxford and Cambridge Magazine* (Morris and others).

1856–1870    James Anthony Froude's *History of England.*
1856–1950    George Bernard Shaw.
1857    Henry Thomas Buckle's *History of Civilization in England.*
E. B. Browning's *Aurora Leigh.*
Flaubert's *Madame Bovary.*
Thomas Hughes's *Tom Brown's School Days.*
Trollope's *Barchester Towers.*

Sepoy Mutiny.    1857–1858
1857–1903    George Gissing.
1857–1924    Joseph Conrad.
1858    Eliot's *Scenes of Clerical Life.*

| POLITICAL, SOCIAL, RELIGIOUS | | LITERARY, PHILOSOPHICAL |
|---|---|---|
| | | Morris's *Defense of Guinevere*. |
| | 1858–1865 | Carlyle's *Frederick the Great*. |
| | 1859 | Darwin's *Origin of Species*. |
| | | Dickens's *Tale of Two Cities*. |
| | | FitzGerald's *Rubáiyát of Omar Khayyám* (first edition). |
| | | Meredith's *Ordeal of Richard Feverel*. |
| | | Mill's *On Liberty*. |
| | | Eliot's *Adam Bede*. |
| | | Newman's *Idea of a University*. |
| Unification of Italy. | 1859–1871 | |
| | 1859–1880 | David Masson's *Life of Milton*. |
| | 1859–1885 | Tennyson's *Idyls of the King*. |
| | 1859–1907 | Francis Thompson. |
| | 1859–1936 | Alfred E. Housman. |
| | 1860 | Wilkie Collins's *Woman in White*. |
| | | Eliot's *Mill on the Floss*. |
| | 1860–1937 | James M. Barrie. |
| Death of Prince Albert. | 1861 | Arnold's *On Translating Homer*. |
| | | Eliot's *Silas Marner*. |
| | | Reade's *Cloister and the Hearth*. |
| American Civil War. | 1861–1865 | |
| | 1861–1874 | James Spedding's *Life and Letters of Francis Bacon*. |
| | 1862 | Meredith's *Modern Love and Other Poems*. |
| | | C. Rossetti's *Goblin Market and Other Poems*. |
| | | Ruskin's *Unto This Last*. |
| | | Spencer's *First Principles*. |
| | | Turgenev's *Fathers and Sons*. |
| | 1863 | Eliot's *Romola*. |
| | | Huxley's *Man's Place in Nature*. |
| | | Kingsley's *Water Babies*. |
| | | Renan's *Vie de Jésus*. |
| | 1863–1864 | Taine's *Histoire de la Littérature Anglaise*. |
| | 1864 | Browning's *Dramatis Personae*. |
| | | Newman's *Apologia pro Vita Sua*. |
| | | Tennyson's *Enoch Arden*. |
| | 1865 | Arnold's *Essays in Criticism* (First Series). |
| | | Lewis Carroll's (Charles L. Dodgson's) *Alice's Adventures in Wonderland*. |
| | | Swinburne's *Atalanta in Calydon*. |
| | 1865–1868 | Ruskin's *Sesame and Lilies*. |
| | 1865–1872 | Tolstoy's *War and Peace*. |
| | 1865–1936 | Rudyard Kipling. |
| | 1865–1939 | William Butler Yeats. |
| | 1866 | Dostoevsky's *Crime and Punishment*. |
| | | Ruskin's *Crown of Wild Olive*. |
| | 1866 | Swinburne's *Poems and Ballads* (First Series). |
| | 1866–1946 | Herbert George Wells. |
| Factory Acts. | 1867 | Arnold's *New Poems* (including *Thyrsis*). |
| Reform Act. | | Bagehot's *English Constitution*. |
| | | Morris's *Life and Death of Jason*. |
| | | Thomas William Robertson's *Caste* acted. |
| | 1867–1905 | Marx and Engels's *Kapital*. |
| | 1867–1933 | John Galsworthy. |

| POLITICAL, SOCIAL, RELIGIOUS | | LITERARY, PHILOSOPHICAL |
|---|---|---|
| | 1868 | Wilkie Collins's *Moonstone*. |
| | | FitzGerald's *Rubáiyát of Omar Khayyám* (second and much altered edition). |
| | 1868–1869 | Browning's *Ring and the Book*. |
| | 1868–1870 | Morris's *Earthly Paradise*. |
| | 1868–1952 | Norman Douglas. |
| Gladstone head of the cabinet. | 1868–1874 | |
| Suez Canal opened. | 1869 | Arnold's *Culture and Anarchy*. |
| | | William Edward Lecky's *History of European Morals*. |
| | | Richard D. Blackmore's *Lorna Doone*. |
| | | Clough's *Dipsychus*. |
| Elementary Education Act. | 1870 | Rossetti's *Collected Poems*. |
| | | Huxley's *Lay Sermons*. |
| Franco-Prussian War. | 1870–1871 | |
| Abolition of the religious tests at Oxford and Cambridge. | 1871 | Robert Buchanan's *Fleshly School of Poetry* (magazine article attacking Rossetti). |
| | | Darwin's *Descent of Man*. |
| | | Swinburne's *Songs before Sunrise*. |
| | | Benjamin Jowett's translation of Plato's *Dialogues*. |
| | 1871–1872 | Eliot's *Middlemarch*. |
| | 1871–1884 | Ruskin's *Fors Clavigera*. |
| | 1871–1909 | John Millington Synge. |
| | 1871–1922 | Marcel Proust. |
| Act providing for the use of the Australian ballot. | 1872 | Butler's *Erewhon*. |
| | | Hardy's *Under the Greenwood Tree*. |
| | 1873 | Arnold's *Literature and Dogma*. |
| | | John Stuart Mill's *Autobiography*. |
| | | Pater's *Studies in the History of the Renaissance*. |
| | 1874 | Hardy's *Far from the Madding Crowd*. |
| | | James Thomson's *City of Dreadful Night*. |
| | 1874– | W. Somerset Maugham. |
| Disraeli head of the cabinet. | 1874–1880 | |
| Employers' and Workmen's Act. | 1875 | |
| | 1875–1876 | Tolstoy's *Anna Karenina*. |
| | 1875– | Thomas Mann. |
| | 1875– | Theodore F. Powys. |
| | 1876 | Bridges's *Growth of Love*. |
| | | Sir Leslie Stephen's *English Thought in the Eighteenth Century*. |
| | 1877 | James's *American*. |
| Congress of Berlin. | 1878 | Hardy's *Return of the Native*. |
| | | Lecky's *History of England in the Eighteenth Century*. |
| | 1878 | Swinburne's *Poems and Ballads* (Second Series). |
| | 1878– | John Masefield. |
| | 1879 | Edwin Arnold's *Light of Asia*. |
| | | Walter Bagehot's *Literary Studies*. |
| | | Ibsen's *Doll's House*. |
| | | Meredith's *Egoist*. |
| | 1879– | E. M. Forster. |
| | 1880 | Dostoevsky's *Brothers Karamazov*. |
| | | Wilfred Scawen Blunt's *Love Sonnets of Proteus*. |
| | | Gissing's *Workers in the Dawn*. |
| | | Lewis Wallace's *Ben Hur*. |
| | 1881 | Ibsen's *Ghosts*. |

| POLITICAL, SOCIAL, RELIGIOUS | | LITERARY, PHILOSOPHICAL |
|---|---|---|
| | | James's *Portrait of a Lady*. |
| | | Rossetti's *Ballads and Sonnets*. |
| | | Stevenson's *Virginibus Puerisque*. |
| | | Wilde's *Poems*. |
| Triple Alliance. | 1882 | Stevenson's *New Arabian Nights* and *Treasure Island*. |
| | 1882–1941 | James Joyce. |
| | 1882–1941 | Virginia Woolf. |
| | 1882– | Alan A. Milne. |
| | 1883 | Richard Jefferies's *Story of My Heart*. |
| | 1883–1917 | Thomas E. Hulme. |
| Fall of Khartoum. | 1885 | Sir William Gilbert and Sir Arthur Sullivan's *Mikado*. |
| | | Meredith's *Diana of the Crossways*. |
| | | Pater's *Marius the Epicurean*. |
| | | Stevenson's *Child's Garden of Verses*. |
| | 1885–1889 | Ruskin's *Praeterita*. |
| | 1885–1930 | David Herbert Lawrence. |
| | 1886 | Kipling's *Departmental Ditties*. |
| | | Hardy's *Mayor of Casterbridge*. |
| | | Stevenson's *Doctor Jekyll and Mr. Hyde* and *Kidnapped*. |
| | | Tennyson's *Locksley Hall Sixty Years After*. |
| | 1887–1915 | Rupert Brooke. |
| | 1887– | Edith Sitwell. |
| | 1888 | Arnold's *Essays in Criticism* (Second Series). |
| | | Charles Montagu Doughty's *Travels in Arabia Deserta*. |
| | | Hardy's *Wessex Tales*. |
| | | Kipling's *Soldiers Three*. |
| | | Mrs. Humphry Ward's *Robert Elsmere*. |
| | 1888–1935 | Thomas Edward Lawrence. |
| | 1888– | Thomas Stearns Eliot. |
| | 1888–1923 | Katherine Mansfield. |
| | 1889 | Browning's *Asolando*. |
| | | FitzGerald's *Letters and Literary Remains*. |
| | | Pater's *Appreciations*. |
| | | Stevenson's *Master of Ballantrae*. |
| | | Yeats's *Wanderings of Oisin and Other Poems*. |
| Fall of Bismarck. | 1890 | Sir James George Frazer's *Golden Bough* (first edition; later much enlarged). |
| | | Sir William Watson's *Wordsworth's Grave*. |
| | 1890– | Aldous Huxley. |
| | 1890– | Sean O'Casey. |
| | 1891 | Barrie's *Little Minister*. |
| | | Gissing's *New Grub Street*. |
| | | Hardy's *Tess of the D'Urbervilles*. |
| | | Morris's *News from Nowhere*. |
| | | Wilde's *House of Pomegranates, Picture of Dorian Gray*, and *Intentions*. |
| | 1892 | Kipling's *Barrack-Room Ballads*. |
| | | Wilde's *Lady Windermere's Fan* acted. |
| | 1892–1896 | Austen Dobson's *Eighteenth-Century Vignettes*. |
| | 1892– | Richard Aldington. |
| | 1893 | Anatole France's *La Rôtisserie de la Reine Pedauque*. |

| POLITICAL, SOCIAL, RELIGIOUS | | LITERARY, PHILOSOPHICAL |
|---|---|---|
| | | William Ernest Henley's *London Voluntaries*. |
| | | Sir Arthur Pinero's *Second Mrs. Tanqueray* acted. |
| | | Pater's *Plato and Platonism*. |
| | | Thompson's *Poems* (including *The Hound of Heaven*). |
| | | Yeats's *The Rose*. |
| | 1893– | Herbert Read. |
| | 1893– | Wilfred Owen. |
| | 1893– | I. A. Richards. |
| Dreyfus Trial. | 1894 | John Davidson's *Ballads and Songs*. |
| | | Kipling's *Jungle Book*. |
| | | George Moore's *Esther Waters*. |
| | 1894–1897 | *The Yellow Book* (Aubrey Beardsley and others). |
| | 1894– | John B. Priestley. |
| | 1895 | Stephen Crane's *Red Badge of Courage*. |
| | 1895 | Hardy's *Jude the Obscure*. |
| | | Lionel Johnson's *Poems*. |
| | | Wilde's *Importance of Being Earnest* acted. |
| | 1896 | Housman's *Shropshire Lad*. |
| | | Stevenson's *Weir of Hermiston*. |
| | 1896–1913 | Alfred Austin poet laureate. |
| | 1896– | Liam O'Flaherty. |
| Diamond Jubilee of Queen Victoria. | 1897 | Conrad's *Nigger of the Narcissus*. |
| | | Henry Arthur Jones's *Liars*. |
| | | Meredith's *Essay on Comedy*. |
| | 1898 | Hardy's *Wessex Poems*. |
| | | Maurice Hewlett's *Forest Lovers*. |
| | | James's *Two Magics* (including *The Turn of the Screw*). |
| | | Shaw's *Plays: Pleasant and Unpleasant*. |
| | | Wilde's *Ballad of Reading Gaol*. |
| | 1899– | Noel Coward. |
| Boxer Uprising. | 1899–1900 | |
| Boer War. | 1899–1902 | |
| | 1900 | Conrad's *Lord Jim*. |
| | 1901 | Kipling's *Kim*. |
| | | Shaw's *Three Plays for Puritans*. |
| Reign of Edward VII. | 1901–1910 | |
| | 1902 | Conrad's *Youth*. |
| | | James's *Wings of the Dove*. |
| | | Thomas Mann's *Buddenbrooks*. |
| | | Masefield's *Saltwater Ballads*. |
| | | Yeats's *Cathleen ni Hoolihan*. |
| | 1903 | Chekhov's *Cherry Orchard*. |
| | | Conrad's *Typhoon and Other Stories*. |
| | | John, Viscount Morley's *Life of William Ewart Gladstone*. |
| | | Butler's *Way of All Flesh*. |
| | | Gissing's *Private Papers of Henry Ryecroft*. |
| | | James's *Ambassadors*. |
| | | Shaw's *Man and Superman*. |
| | 1903–1908 | Hardy's *Dynasts*. |
| | 1903– | Evelyn Waugh. |
| *Entente Cordiale* between France and Britain. | 1904 | Barrie's *Peter Pan*. |
| | | Conrad's *Nostromo*. |
| | | Hudson's *Green Mansions*. |
| | | James's *Golden Bowl*. |

POLITICAL, SOCIAL, RELIGIOUS | | LITERARY, PHILOSOPHICAL
---|---|---
| 1904–1912 | Romain Rolland's *Jean-Christophe*.
| 1905 | Ernest Dowson's *Poems*.
| 1905 | Forster's *Where Angels Fear to Tread*.
| | H. A. Jones's *Mrs. Dane's Defence*.
| | Synge's *Riders to the Sea*.
Algeciras Crisis. | 1905–1906 | George Santayana's *Life of Reason*.
| 1906 | Kipling's *Puck of Pook's Hill*.
| 1906–1922 | Galsworthy's *Forsyte Saga*.
Triple Entente. | 1907 | Max Beerbohm's *A Book of Caricatures*.
| | Sir John E. E. Dalberg, Lord Acton's *History of Freedom*.
| | Joyce's *Chamber Music*.
| | George Russell's *Deirdre*.
| | Synge's *Playboy of the Western World*.
| | Yeats's *Deirdre*.
| 1907– | W. H. Auden.
| 1907– | Louis MacNeice.
| 1908 | Arnold Bennett's *Old Wives' Tale*.
| | G. K. Chesterton's *The Man Who Was Thursday*.
| | Forster's *A Room with a View*.
| | Anatole France's *Penguin Island*.
| | Sir Arthur W. Pinero's *Thunderbolt*.
Lloyd George's budget. | 1909 | Galsworthy's *Justice*.
| | Lady Augusta Gregory's *Seven Short Plays*.
| | H. G. Wells's *Tono Bungay*.
| 1909– | Stephen Spender.
| 1910 | Aldington's *Images*.
| | Arnold Bennett's *Clayhanger*.
| | Lord Dunsany's *A Dreamer's Tales*.
| | Forster's *Howard's End*.
| | Alfred Noyes's *Collected Poems*.
Reign of George V. | 1910–1936 |
Agadir Crisis. | 1911 | Beerbohm's *Zuleika Dobson*.
| | Rupert Brooke's *Poems*.
| | Chesterton's *The Innocence of Father Brown*.
| | Jeffrey Farnol's *The Broad Highway*.
| | Forster's *The Celestial Omnibus and Other Stories*.
| | D. H. Lawrence's *The White Peacock*.
| | Masefield's *Everlasting Mercy*.
| | Pinero's *Mid-Channel*.
| | Wells's *New Machiavelli*.
| | Yeats's *Celtic Twilight*.
| 1911–1913 | Moore's *Hail and Farewell*.
| 1912 | Beerbohm's *Christmas Garland*.
| 1912 | Robert Bridges's *Poetical Works*.
| | Walter De la Mare's *Listeners*.
| | Galsworthy's *The Pigeon*.
| | Masefield's *Widow in the Bye Street*.
| | Bertrand Russell's *The Problems of Philosophy*.
| | James Stephens's *Crock of Gold*.
| 1913 | Lawrence's *Sons and Lovers*.
| | Masefield's *Dauber*.
| 1913–1925 | Proust's *À la Recherche du Temps Perdu*.
| 1913–1930 | Bridges poet laureate.
Assassination of Archduke Ferdinand at Sarajevo. | 1914 | James Barrie's *Admirable Crichton*.
| | Hardy's *Satires of Circumstance*.

| POLITICAL, SOCIAL, RELIGIOUS | | LITERARY, PHILOSOPHICAL |
|---|---|---|
| First Trans-Atlantic Flight. | 1927 | George Russell's *Collected Poems*.<br>T. E. Lawrence's *Revolt in the Desert*.<br>Woolf's *To the Lighthouse*. |
|  | 1928 | Eliot's *For Lancelot Andrewes*.<br>Forster's *The Eternal Moment*.<br>Aldous Huxley's *Point Counter Point*.<br>D. H. Lawrence's *The Collected Poems of D. H. Lawrence* and *Lady Chatterly's Lover*.<br>Powys's *Mr. Weston's Good Wine*.<br>Waugh's *Decline and Fall*. |
| Crash of American stock market, with world-wide effects. | 1929 | Bridges's *The Testament of Beauty*.<br>Galsworthy's *A Modern Comedy*.<br>MacNeice's *Blind Fireworks*.<br>Powys's *Wolf Solent*.<br>Priestley's *The Good Companions*.<br>I. A. Richards's *Practical Criticism* |
|  | 1930 | Coward's *Private Lives*.<br>Eliot's *Ash Wednesday*.<br>Masefield's *Collected Poems*.<br>Edith Sitwell's *Collected Poems*. |
|  | 1930–1931 | John Masefield poet laureate.<br>D. H. Lawrence's *The Man Who Died*.<br>Read's *The Meaning of Art*.<br>Osbert Sitwell's *Collected Satires and Poems*.<br>Woolf's *The Waves*. |
|  | 1932 | Auden's *The Orators*.<br>Coward's *Cavalcade*.<br>Aldous Huxley's *Brave New World*.<br>Maugham's *Rain*. |
|  | 1933 | Auden's *Dance of Death*.<br>Federico Garcia Lorca's *Blood Wedding*.<br>Spender's *Poems*.<br>Yeats's *Collected Poems*.<br>Eliot's *After Strange Gods* and *The Rock*.<br>Galsworthy's *End of the Chapter*.<br>Dylan Thomas's *Eighteen Poems*.<br>Waugh's *A Handful of Dust*. |
| Invasion of Ethiopia by Mussolini. | 1935 | Auden and Isherwood's *The Dog Beneath the Skin*.<br>Eliot's *Murder in the Cathedral*.<br>C. Day Lewis's *A Time to Dance*.<br>MacNeice's *Poems*.<br>Read's *The Green Child*. |
| First television broadcast. | 1936 | Eliot's *Four Quartets*.<br>Forster's *Abinger Harvest*.<br>Aldous Huxley's *Eyeless in Gaza*.<br>Spender's *The Destructive Element*.<br>Thomas's *Twenty-Five Poems*. |
| Reign of Edward VIII. | 1–20–36 to<br>12–11–36 |  |
| Reign of George VI. | 1936–1952 |  |
|  | 1937 | Auden's *On This Island*.<br>Woolf's *The Years*. |
| Munich Conference. | 1838 | Yeats's *Autobiography of Wm. Butler Yeats*. |
| German Invasion of Poland. | 1939 | Eliot's *Old Possum's Book of Practical Cats* and *The Family Reunion*.<br>Aldous Huxley's *After Many a Summer*.<br>Joyce's *Finnegans Wake*.<br>MacNeice's *Autumn Journal*. |

| POLITICAL, SOCIAL, RELIGIOUS | | LITERARY, PHILOSOPHICAL |
|---|---|---|
| World War II. | 1939–1945 | |
| | 1940 | Dylan Thomas's *A Portrait of the Artist as a Young Dog.* |
| | | Woolf's *Between the Acts.* |
| | 1941 | |
| Adoption of Beveridge Plan. | 1942 | |
| | 1944 | Auden's *For the Time Being.* |
| | | Waugh's *Brideshead Revisited.* |
| Clement Atlee's Labor Government. | 1945 | Auden's *The Collected Poetry of W. H. Auden.* |
| First use of atomic bomb. | | Christopher Isherwood's *Prater Violet.* |
| Establishment of United Nations. | | Read's *A World Within a War.* |
| | 1946 | MacNeice's *The Dark Tower.* |
| | | Thomas's *Deaths and Entrances.* |
| Establishment of independent India. | 1947 | Auden's *The Age of Anxiety.* |
| | | Read's *The Innocent Eye.* |
| | 1948 | Eliot's *Notes towards the Definition of Culture.* |
| | | Christopher Fry's *The Lady's Not for Burning.* |
| | | Graham Greene's *The Heart of the Matter.* |
| | 1949 | Edith Sitwell's *The Canticle of the Sun.* |
| | | MacNeice's *Collected Poems: 1925–1948.* |
| | | Spender's *The Edge of Being.* |
| | 1950 | Eliot's *The Cocktail Party.* |
| | | Fry's *Venus Observed.* |
| Korean War. | 1950–1953 | |
| | 1951 | Spender's *World within World.* |
| | 1952 | Auden's *Nones.* |
| | | Thomas's *Collected Poems.* |
| Reign of Elizabeth II. | 1952– | |
| | 1953 | Eliot's *The Confidential Clerk.* |
| | 1954 | Auden's *Mountains.* |
| | | Fry's *The Dark is Light Enough.* |
| | | Spender's *The Creative Element.* |
| | | Thomas's *Under Milk Wood.* |
| | 1955 | Auden's *The Shield of Achilles.* |
| Suez Crisis. | 1956 | Auden's *The Old Man's Road.* |
| Establishment of independent Ghana. | 1957 | Eliot's *On Poetry and Poets.* |
| | 1958 | Huxley's *Brave New World Revisited.* |
| | 1959 | Eliot's *The Elder Statesman.* |

# GLOSSARY

(Words are included which occur in the poems by Chaucer, in the *Popular Ballads*, and in Book I of Spencer's *Faerie Queene*. Words unfamiliar only by reason of their spelling, whose meaning can be determined by pronunciation, are not included. Unfamiliar words not contained in any good modern dictionary which occur in texts other than those mentioned above are explained in footnotes.)

**a**, one; of.
**a'**, all.
**abon**, above.
**about**, out of.
**abrayde**, awoke.
**abused**, deceived.
**abye**, pay for.
**accident**, outward appearance.
**accordaunt**, according.
**achat**, buying.
**achatours**, buyers.
**acord**, agree; agreement.
**acquite**, release.
**addrest**, prepared; ready; directed.
**admired**, wondered at.
**adrad**, afraid.
**advauncing**, praising.
**afferm**, establish as true.
**afflicted**, downcast.
**affray**, alarm; panic; terror.
**affyle his tonge**, polish his speech.
**after**, along; according to.
**agayn**, toward; in.
**agayns**, when you meet.
**ageyn**, against.
**aghast**, frightened.
**ago**, gone.
**agraste**, favored.
**agrief**, amiss.
**al**, although; awl.
**albe**, although.
**alday**, at any time.
**alderbest**, best of all.
**ale-stake**, a stake projecting horizontally from a house to indicate that ale could be bought there.
**algate**, in every case; nevertheless.
**Algezir**, Algeciras in north Africa.
**Alisaundre**, Alexandria.
**alkin**, of every kind.
**alle and somme**, one and all.
**aller**, of all.
**almner**, giver of alms.
**als**, also.
**al-so**, as.
**amate**, dismay; dishearten.
**amazed**, bewildered.
**amazement**, perplexity.
**amblere**, pacer.
**amende**, improve.
**amis**, hood; cape; wrongly.
**a-morwe**, on the morrow.
**amoved**, stirred.
**an(d)**, if.

**and**, an.
**ane**, one.
**anlas**, dagger.
**annoy**, distress.
**anon**, instantly.
**antiphoner**, anthem-book.
**ape**, fool; dupe.
**applyde**, accommodated.
**approving**, proving.
**apyked**, sharpened; trimmed.
**archery**, archers.
**aread**, point out; tell; make known.
**areeds**, counsels.
**areste**, stop.
**arette**, impute; consider.
**aright**, wholly; well.
**arise**, depart.
**armory**, armor.
**arras**, tapestry.
**array**, dress.
**arrayed**, ordered; dressed.
**aryve**, disembarcation of troops.
**ascendent**, part of the zodiac rising above the horizon.
**aslake**, appease.
**aspire**, grow up.
**aspye**, spy.
**assay**, try; touch; assail; attack; value.
**assent**, conspiracy.
**assoile**, pardon.
**assoilling**, absolution.
**assured**, secure.
**assynd**, pointed out.
**asterte**, escape.
**as that**, as one who.
**aston(ie)d**, stunned.
**attaint**, dim.
**attained**, broached.
**atte beste**, in the best fashion.
**attempree**, temperate.
**Austin**, St. Augustine.
**avale**, fall.
**avaunce**, profit.
**avaunt**, boast.
**avauntour**, boaster.
**Ave-Mary**, prayer to the Virgin.
**avenge**, take vengeance on.
**aventure**, chance.
**avision**, vision.
**avize**, perceive; consider.
**avouchen**, prove.
**avys**, opinion.
**avysed**, well advised.
**awkwarde**, backhanded.
**axe**, ask.

**ay**, always.

**ba**, ball.
**bachelere**, young aspirant to knighthood.
**bains**, banns.
**bairn**, child.
**baite**, feed.
**baith**, both.
**bake mete**, meat pie.
**bale**, injury; evil influence; sorrow; fire.
**ballade**, poem consisting of one or more triplets of seven or eight-line stanzas, each ending with the same refrain, and an envoy.
**bands**, bonds.
**banes**, banns.
**bar**, bore.
**barne**, man.
**barres**, stripes; ornaments.
**baser**, too humble.
**basnites**, light helmets.
**bastard**, ignoble.
**batailed**, battlemented.
**battailous**, warlike.
**bawdrik**, belt worn over one shoulder.
**be**, by.
**beadmen**, men of prayer.
**beare up**, put the helm up.
**become**, gone.
**bed**, command.
**beggestere**, beggar-woman.
**beguiled of**, disappointed in.
**beguyld**, foiled.
**behight**, call; name; entrusted.
**behot**, held out hope for; promised.
**bekke**, nod.
**bel amy**, fair friend.
**belive**, quickly.
**Belmarye**, Benmarin, a district in north Africa.
**bemes**, trumpets.
**ben**, are.
**bene**, bean; jot.
**Beneit**, St. Benedict.
**bent**, coarse grass; field; purpose; levelled.
**bequeathed**, entrusted.
**beseene, well**, good looking.
**bestedd**, sorely pressed; situated.
**bet**, beaten; better.
**bet, go**, go as quickly as possible.
**betake**, deliver.

bete, relieve.
beth, be.
bethinkes, determines.
bethrall, enslave.
betide, happen.
bever, visor.
bewray, disclose.
beye, buy.
bicched bones, cursed dice.
bidding bedes, saying prayers.
biknowe, acknowledge.
bile, bill; beak.
bilive, quickly; immediately.
birk, birch.
bisette, set to work.
bismotered, stained.
bisy, anxious.
bisyde, of, from near.
bisydes, him, near him.
bit, commands.
bits, food.
biwraye, reveal.
blakeberied, a-, blackberrying.
blame, injury.
blane, stopped.
blankmanger, creamed fowl.
blaze, proclaim.
blent, blinds; blinded; deceived; stained.
bless, preserve; brandish.
blubbred, tear-stained.
Boece, Boethius.
boght, redeemed.
boist, box.
bokeler, small shield.
boles, bulls.
boot, help; remedy; avail.
bootelesse, unavailing.
bord bigonne, sat at the head of the table.
borne, brook.
borrow, ransom.
bosses, knobs.
bote, boot; remedy; salvation.
boughtes, coils.
bounty, virtue.
bour, bedroom.
bourde, jest.
bouzing can, drinking cup.
bowne, make ready; ready.
bowr, bedroom; house; muscle.
boys, bows.
bracer, guard for the arm in archery.
brae, hillside.
braid, broad; long; written on a long sheet.
brand, sword.
bras, money.
brast, broke; burst.
braun, muscle.
braw, fine.
bray, cry out.
breach, breaking.
bred, were born.
breem, fresh-water fish.
brend, burned.
brenninge, burning.
bret-ful, brimful.
brimstoon, sulphur.
brode, plainly.
brook, enjoy.

brotch, brooch.
brouke, enjoy the use of.
bryttlynge, cutting up.
buckle, make ready.
buffe, blow.
bugle, wild ox.
bulte it to the bren, sift it to the bran.
burdoun, bass.
burn, brook.
buske, bush; make ready.
buskin, high boot.
but, unless.
but-if, unless.
buxom, yielding.
buxumnesse, submission.
by, along; pay for.
by and by, immediately.
byckarte, attacked.
byddys, abides.
byde, endure.
byears, biers.
bylive, quickly; immediately.
bylle, sword.
byre, cow-house.
bystode, hard pressed.

caas, legal cases.
caityf, captive; wretch.
cake, round loaf of bread.
call, netted head-dress.
can, did; know; began.
cancred, venomous; corrupt.
canon bitt, smooth, round bit.
capull-hyde, horse-hide.
car'd, cared for.
car'd for, shrank from.
cardiacle, pain in the heart.
carefull, full of care.
carelesse, uncared for.
carke, anxiety.
carl(e), fellow.
carline, old; low-born.
carpe, talk; joke.
carpyng, discussion.
carver, used for carving.
cas, accident.
cast, intend; devise; plan.
casuelly, by chance.
catapuce, spurge.
catel, property.
caytive, captive; wretch.
ceint, girdle.
celle, subordinate convent.
centaure, centaury.
centonell, sentinel.
certes, certainly.
ceruce, lead ointment.
chaffare, merchandise.
channerin, fretting.
chapman, merchant.
charge, memory; care.
chauffed, heated; rubbed.
chaunce, term in the game of hazard.
chaunterie, endowment to pay for masses.
chaw, jaw; chew.
cheare, countenance; behavior.
chearen, cheer himself.
cheffe, chief.

chere, countenance; behavior; appearance.
cherl, fellow.
chevisaunce, dealing for profit.
chide, champ.
chiknes, chickens.
chivachye, military expedition.
chivalrye, knighthood.
cink, five.
clappeth, chatters.
clause, in a, briefly.
clepen, call.
clere, bright; pure.
clergeon, choir-boy.
clerk, scholar.
clinke, tinkle.
clos(s), enclosure.
cloutes, rags; clothes.
clowe, claw; clutch.
coast, region.
cod, bag; stomach.
coillons, testicles.
cokewold, cuckold.
cold, baneful; could.
colera, bile.
colerik, of a bilious temperament.
col-fox, fox with black in its fur.
colpons, shreds.
combred, impeded.
combrous, harassing.
comfortlesse, helpless.
commonly, sociably.
commune, as in, alike.
compeer, comrade.
compeld, summoned.
complecciouns, collections of humors; temperaments.
composicioun, arrangement.
comyn-bell, town-bell.
condicioun, rank.
confiture, mixture.
conne, learn; know how.
conning, skill; knowledge.
conscience, tenderness.
conseil, secret.
consort, accord.
constraint, distress.
construe, translate.
contek, strife.
contenaunce, outward show.
contrairie, foe.
cop, top; tip.
cope, priest's cloak.
coppe, cup.
corages, hearts.
cordial, heart stimulant.
corn, grain.
corny, strong in corn or malt.
corpus bones, bones of the Lord's body.
corrosives, remedies.
cors(e), body.
cote, small house.
couch, set; place.
coude, knew how to.
counterfesaunce, imposture.
counterfete, imitate.
countour, king's legal representative in a county.
courtepy, short upper coat.
courting, courtier-like.

couthe, known; knew; best knew how.
coveityse, covetousness.
covenaunt, contract.
coverchiefs, coverings for the head.
covyne, trickery.
coy, quiet.
craftes, handicrafts.
crew, company.
crime, reproach.
cristofre, figure of St. Christopher.
crokke, earthenware pot.
crop, reward.
crope, crept.
croppes, shoots.
croslet, small cross.
crounyng, tonsure.
crowned, capital.
crownes with cups, salutes with full cups.
croys, cross.
cruddy, curdled.
crudled, curdled.
crulle, curled.
cryke, creek.
curat, parish-priest.
cure, cure of souls; care.
curious, careful.
cursednesse, malice.
curst turne, spiteful feat.
cut, lot.

daint, choice.
dainty dear, exceedingly precious.
dalliance, amorous talk; trifling; social entertainment.
dam(e), mother.
darrayne, prepare for battle; prove by battle.
date, term of life.
daun, master.
daunce, dance; game.
daunger, control; risk.
daungerous, overbearing.
daunte, tame; subdue.
dayesye, daisy.
deadly, deathlike.
deadly made, mortal.
deare, injury.
debate, quarrel; fight.
debonaire, gracious.
deceivable, deceitful.
deceived, cheated.
dee, do.
deel, bit.
dees, dice.
deeth, the, the pestilence.
deface, disgrace.
defame, dishonor.
defaute, fault.
defeasaunce, defeat.
defenden, forbid.
defye, renounce.
degree, rank; order.
delices, pleasures.
deliver, active; set free.
deliverly, quickly.
delyces, pleasures.
demen, judge.
departed, divided.

depeint, painted.
dere, injury.
derive, divert.
descryde, declared.
despight, anger; ill treatment.
despit(e) ous, cruel; malicious; scornful.
desport, amusement.
devys, decision.
devyse, relate; describe.
dewties, dues.
deye, dairy-woman.
deyntee, good.
deys, dais.
diamond, adamant.
dight, adorn; put on.
dighted, wiped.
digne, worthy; haughty.
dint, stroke.
disaventrous, unfortunate.
dischevele, disheveled.
discolourd, many-colored.
disdaine, that which would excite disdain.
disdainfull, indignant.
disese, grief.
dishonesty, unchastity.
dismaid, overcame.
dispart, divide.
dispence, make amends; expenditure.
dispence, esy of, spending little.
dispiteous, cruel.
disple, subject to penance.
disport, amusement; pleasantry.
dispredden, spread out.
disputisoun, disputation.
disseized, deprived.
dissolute, enfeebled.
distayned, stained.
distraine, afflict.
dites, lifts.
ditty, theme.
diverse, distracting; perverse.
divide, play an elaborate passage in music.
doctryne, teaching.
documents, lessons.
doen to, betake.
doghtren, daughters.
dois, does.
dokked, cut short.
dolour, grief; pain.
dome, judgment.
doune, ended.
doome, decree.
doon us honge, have us hanged.
dormant, table, a side-table kept permanently filled with food.
dorste, dared.
doted, imbecile.
doubtfull, fearful.
dre, endured.
dreadfull, full of dread.
drecched, troubled.
drede, doubt; fear.
dree, can do.
dreed, object of reverence.
drenched, drowned.
drere, sadness.
dreriment, gloom; sorrow.

drery, bloody; ghastly.
dresse, set in order.
dreynt, drowned.
drie, feel; endure.
drift, impetus; plot.
dronkelewe, addicted to drink.
drouped, were draggled.
drumlie, gloomy.
dryve, pass.
dugs, breasts.
dule, grief.
dye, hazard.
dynte, stroke.

each where, everywhere.
earne, yearn.
earst, formerly.
edifyde, built.
ee, eye.
eek, also.
eeke, increase.
eft, then.
eftsoones, forthwith.
eke, also.
eld, old age.
ellebor, hellabore.
elles, otherwise.
else, already.
elyng, miserable.
embalme, anoint.
embard, imprisoned.
embay, enclose; bathe.
embosse, plunge.
embost, driven to extremity; encased.
embowd, arched over.
emboyled, agitated; heated.
embrouded, embroidered.
emmove, move.
empeach, hinder.
emperst, penetrated.
emprize, enterprise.
emys, uncle's.
enchace, serve as setting for.
encombred, involved.
encounter, go to meet.
endyte, write.
enfouldred, thunderous.
engorged, devoured.
engrave, bury.
engyned, put on the rack for torture.
enhaunst, raised; exalted.
enraged, frantic.
ensample, example.
ensewen, follow; befall.
entente, mind.
entire, with full vigor.
entraile, twisted coil.
entune, intone.
envious, envied.
envoy, postscript of a poem.
envyned, well provided of wine.
equall, impartial.
erbe yve, ground ivy.
erme, grief.
erst, first.
ese, doon, provide entertainment.
esloyne, withdraw.
espye, perceive.
essoyne, excuse; exemption.
estatlich, stately.

eugh, yew.
even(e), smooth; medium.
ever-dying dread, constant fear of death.
everich, every.
everichon, everyone.
everilkon, everyone.
ever-mo, continually.
every-deel, in every respect.
ewghen, of yew.
excheat, gain.
expire, come to a term; breathe out.
extirpe, extirpate.
ey, egg.
eyas, young hawk, newly fledged.
eyne, eyes.

fa', fall.
fact, deed.
facultee, as by his, considering his authority or disposition.
fade, decay.
fader, father's.
faine, glad.
fairlies, wonders.
fairnesse, honesty of life.
faitor, villain; impostor.
falding, coarse cloth.
fanglenesse, showy modernity.
faren, gone.
farsed, stuffed.
fashes, troubles.
faste, close; soundly; intently.
fatal, prophetic.
faynd, disguised.
faytor, impostor.
feare, object of fear; make afraid.
fearefull, full of fear.
fee, wealth.
fell, befell; fierce.
felly, fiercely; cruelly.
fen, chapter of a book by Avicenna.
ferd, fear.
fere, mate; comrade.
fere, on, together.
fered, frightened.
ferly, wonder.
ferme, rent.
ferne, distant.
ferre, further.
ferreste, furthest.
ferthing, small portion.
fest, fist.
fet, feeds; fetched.
fetis, neat; graceful.
fetisly, gracefully.
fey, faith.
feyne, invent.
ffaine, glad.
ffare, go.
ffarley, strange.
ffetteled, made ready.
fil, befell.
file, smoothe.
fille, fell.
finch, pulle a, pluck a dupe (?).
find, provide for; choose.
fit, division of a song; strain of music; emotion; condition.
fithele, fiddle.

flaggy, drooping.
flake, flash.
flatour, flatterer.
flee, fly.
fleigh, flew.
fleshly, carnally.
flit, give way; move.
florin, English coin, first coined at Florence.
flowen, flew.
floytinge, fluting.
foile, thin sheet of metal.
fond, foolish; provided for.
fone, foes.
food, feud.
foole-happie, blindly lucky.
foot-mantel, outer skirt.
for, against; why.
for that, because.
for-by, past.
fordonne, ruined; overcome.
for-dronke, very drunk.
foreby, near.
forecast, pause to reflect.
forelifting, lifting up in front.
forespent, utterly wasted.
forlete, give up; abandon.
forlorne, utterly lost; abandoned.
forn-cast, premeditated.
forneys, furnace.
for-pyned, wasted away by torment.
fors, matter.
fors, do no, take no account.
forsake, avoid.
for-sleuthen, waste in idleness.
forster, forester.
forth right, straight.
for-thi, therefore.
fortunen, forecast; give a good or bad fortune to.
forwandred, tired out with wandering.
forward, agreement.
for-wearied, utterly wearied.
for-why, because.
forwiting, foreknowledge.
forworne, worn out.
forwoot, knows beforehand.
forwrapped, wrapped up; concealed.
fother, load.
fou, dry measure varying from two to six Winchester, or slightly less than standard, bushels.
foulys, birds.
frame, steady.
francklin, freeman; freeholder; substantial farmer.
fraternitee, guild.
fray, frighten.
frayneth, beseeches.
freck, bold man.
fredom, liberality.
free, generous; noble.
frend, friend; help.
frend, to, as friend.
fret, gnaw.
freyke, bold man.
frie, good.
frounce, gather in folds.

fruytesteres, female fruit-sellers.
fry, swarm.
ful, very.
fume, harmful vapor rising from stomach to brain.
fumetere, fumitory.
fumositee, fumes caused by drunkenness.
funerall, death.
furlong, eighth of a mile.
fustian, coarse cloth.
fynde, end; finish (?).

gabbe, jest; prate.
gae, go.
gage, pledge.
gain, serve.
galingale, spice made from the root of sweet cyperus.
gall, gall-bladder.
game, in, jokingly.
gamed, it pleased.
gamen, play.
gan, began; did.
gang, go.
gar, make.
gare, ready.
garget, throat.
garlande, wreath hung on a wand for a target in archery.
gate, way; path.
gat-tothed, with teeth widely spaced; goat-toothed and so lascivious (?).
gaude, trick.
gauded, fitted with gauds or beads that in a rosary marked the five joys of the Virgin.
gaytres beryies, berries of the buckthorn.
gede, went.
gent, gentle.
gentils, gentlefolk.
gere, utensils; apparel.
german, brother.
Gernade, Granada.
gerner, garner.
gest, exploit.
ghost, soul; spirit.
gied, gave.
gin, instrument of torture; begin; if.
gipoun, short coat worn under the armor.
gipser, wallet.
girles, young people of both sexes.
giternes, guitars.
glade, rejoice.
glede, glowing coal; fire.
glee, cheer; entertainment.
glent, glanced; darted.
glister, shine.
glosed, commented on; explained.
gnarre, growl; snarl.
go, walk.
gobbet, piece; fragment.
golett, throat; part covering the throat.
goliardeys, buffoon.
good, income; property.
good, knew his, knew how to act

gorge, throat; what has been swallowed.

gory blood, clotted blood.

gossib, friend; relative.

gost, soul; spirit.

governaunce, control; manner.

government, control; self-control.

gowe, go we.

graile, gravel.

graine, died in, dyed thoroughly.

grate, chafe.

gree, favor.

green, grass plot.

greetin, weeping.

Grete See, Mediterranean.

grette, greeted.

greved, grew angry.

grevis, groves.

greyn, grain; corn.

griesie, gray; grizzled.

griple, grasp; tenacious.

grisly, horrible.

grith, peace; charter of peace.

grope, test.

grosse, heavy.

grotes, four-penny pieces.

ground, land; earth; texture.

grucche, murmur.

gruf, on his face.

gryfon, fabulous animal; vulture (?).

gryping, grasp.

grys, gray fur.

gryte, great.

guerdon, reward.

guise, behavior.

gypon, short coat.

gyse, way.

ha', hall.

habergeoun, coat of mail.

hable, powerful; able.

hagard hauke, untamed hawk.

hals, neck.

halse, beseech.

halwes, saints; shrines of saints.

halyde, hauled.

han, have.

handeling, usage.

harbour, shelter.

hardily, certainly.

hardiment, courage.

hardly, with difficulty.

harlot, rogue.

harlotryes, ribald actions or tales.

harneised, equipped.

harre, hinge.

harrow, help.

hasard, game of hazard.

hasardrye, gambling.

haughtie, lofty; high-pitched.

haunt, limit; usual resort; skill.

haunteden, practiced.

hauteyn, loud.

hawe, yard.

he(e), high.

heben, ebony.

heep, crowd.

heft, raised.

heig, high.

heigh ymaginacioun, Heaven's foreknowledge.

heled, hidden.

helpless, unavoidable.

hem, them.

hende, noble; gracious.

hente, obtain; seize.

her(e), their.

herbergage, lodging.

herberwe, harbor; inn.

herde, shepherd.

herien, praise.

heryinge, praising.

heste, command.

hethenesse, heathen lands.

hevinesse, sorrow.

hew, shape; condition; pretense; expression.

hight, commanded; called; promise.

hight, on, aloud.

hind, deer.

hinde, courteous.

hindreste, hindmost.

hir, their; her.

hit, it.

hold, possession.

holde, wager.

holland, a kind of linen.

holme, evergreen oak; holly (?).

holpen, helped.

holt, wood.

hond, out of, at once.

honest, honorable.

hoomly, simply.

hoor, gray.

hord, treasure.

hore, frosty; hoary.

horned, horny.

horrid, bristling; rough.

horro, roughness.

hors, horses.

hot, was called.

houped, whooped.

houres, astrological hours.

housbondrye, economy.

housling, sacramental.

hove, rise.

humour, one of the four chief fluids of the body (blood, phlegm, bile, and black bile) in Gelenical medicine.

hurtlen, rush jostling.

hussyfskap, housewifery.

hyne, farm servant.

hyre, reward.

ilk(e), each; every; same.

ilkone, each one.

imbrew, shed blood.

impe, scion; offspring.

implyes, enfolds.

improvided, unforeseen.

in, dwelling.

incontinent, at once.

infect, invalidated.

infected, ingrained.

infest, attack; make hostile.

inspire, breathe in.

intended, stretched forth.

intendiment, careful consideration; knowledge.

intent, purpose; gaze; pleasure.

intreat, persuade.

invent, find.

inwith, within.

irkesome, troubled; weary.

Ise, I shall.

ith, in the.

Jacob's staff, pilgrim's staff.

janglere, babbler.

jangleth, chatters.

jape, trick; deception.

japers, jesters.

jaw, wave.

jet, fashion.

jolif, merry.

jolitee, comfort; smartness.

jolly, brave; gallant; handsome.

jordanes, pots.

jott, least bit.

journall, daily.

juste, joust.

justyse, judge; administration of justice.

keep(e), heed; watch.

keeping, be at your, be on your guard.

ken, know.

kepe, protect; care.

kest, cast.

kind(e), nature.

kind, beastly, in the nature of a beast.

kindly, natural.

kirk, church.

kirtle, tunic; cloak.

kithe, of the same country or people.

kitte, cut.

knarre, stump of a fellow.

knave, servant-boy.

knees, jagged projections of the rock.

knobbes, swellings.

knowes, knees.

kyn, cows.

laas, cord.

Lacidomie, Lacedaemonia.

lady, lady's.

lafte, leave; leave off.

laike, play.

laith, loath.

lake, pit; cavity.

lap, leaped.

large, coarsely.

last, loads.

lat be, do away with.

later, late.

latoun, alloy similar in appearance to brass.

laude, praise.

laugte, caught.

launcht, pierced.

lauriol, spurge-laurel.

lay, lodged.

layn, lying.

lay-stall, refuse-heap.

lazar, leper.

lea, grassy field.

leach, physician.

leaned, lay.

learne, teach.

leasing, lie.
leche, physician.
leed, stationary cauldron above a furnace.
leet, caused; left; let.
leman, lover.
lemes, flames.
lene, lend.
lere, teach; learn.
lesinges, lies.
lessoun, reading from Scripture.
lest, delight.
leste, pleased.
let, prevent; hinder; hindrance; obstacle.
leten, allowed; considered.
lette, stop; wait; hindered.
letterure, learning.
Lettow, Lithuania.
letuaries, prescriptions.
leute, loyalty.
leve, cease; grant; permission; dear.
leved, believed.
leven, lawn.
lever, rather.
lewed, ignorant; rude; common.
lewte, loyalty.
leye, wager.
libbard, leopard.
libbying, living.
licentiat, provided with a papal license to hear confession.
licour, sap.
lief(e), loved one; dear.
liggen, lie.
light, quickly; easily; befall.
likerous, dainty; gluttonous.
lilled, lolled; put out.
lillie, lovely.
limitour, one licensed to beg within certain limits.
lin, cease.
line, in a, by a cord.
lipsed, lisped.
list, pleased.
litarge, ointment made from protoxide of lead.
lith, limb.
lively, living.
loathed, disgusted.
lodemenage, pilotage.
loe, love.
loft, roof.
logge, resting-place.
loken, locked.
lond, in, away.
lond, up-on, in the country.
long a, many a.
long of, owing to.
longs, belongs.
lordinges, gentlemen.
lore, doctrine; learning.
lorn(e), lost; deserted.
losengeour, flatterer.
loset, loosed.
lough, laughed; lake.
lout, bow.
love-dayes, days appointed for the settlement of disputes.
lovely, affectionate; amorously.
lowe, hill.

lowed, stooped.
lowly, modest; humble.
Loy, St. Eligius.
luce, carp.
lucre of vilanye, vile gain.
lumpish, dull.
lust, delight; desire.
lustlesse, feeble.
lusty, gay.
Lyde, Lydia.
Lyes, Ayas in Asiatic Turkey.
lyking, pleasure; desire.
lynde, linden-tree.
lyne, linden; lineage.
lyng, furze; bent grass.
lyte, small.
lyvinge, manner of life.

magger of, in spite of.
maile, link armor.
maine, force.
maistrye, for the, to take the prize; as regards authority.
make, mate.
making, composition; poetry.
male, wallet.
mall, club.
maner, kind of.
manly, human.
many, multitude.
March-parti, borders.
mark, money worth two thirds of a pound.
marshal, master of ceremonies.
Mart, Mars.
mart, trade.
Martinmass, 11 November.
mary, marrow.
mase, state of confusion; confused fancy.
masteryes, feats of skill.
mated, stupefied; overcome.
maugree your heed, in spite of all you can do.
maun, must.
maunciple, officer who purchased victuals for an inn or college.
Maure, St. Maur, a disciple of St. Benedict.
may, maid.
mayne, strength; force.
maynly, violently.
mealt'h, melteth.
meany, troop.
mede, field; reward.
mell, mingle.
menage, control.
ment, mingled; joined.
mercenarie, hireling.
Mercenrike, Mercia.
merciable, merciful.
mery, pleasant.
meschief, mishap.
mesurable, moderate.
mete, measure.
meten, dream.
mew(e), coop; den.
meynee, followers.
minisht, diminished.
ministres, officers of justice.
mirk, murky.
mirkesome, dark.

mirthe, amusement.
mischieves, misfortunes.
misdeeming, misleading.
misdeem'd, misjudged.
misfeigning, feigning with evil purpose.
misseeming, unseemly; false show.
mistake, mislead.
misweening, misjudgment.
mister, kind of; trade.
miteyn, glove.
mo, more.
mochel, much; many.
moder, mother's.
molde, earth.
momme, mumbling.
moniments, relics; traces.
moot, men, one should.
mormal, running sore.
morne milk, morning milk.
mort, note on a horn to announce the death of a deer.
mortall, deadly.
mortreux, stew.
morwe, morning.
moss, bog.
moste, might.
mote, may; must.
mottelee, parti-colored costume.
mould, form; shape.
mountance, amount.
mowe(n), way.
moyste, new.
muche, great.
muchell, much.
muckle, much.
myd, with.
mykel, much.
myllan, Milan steel.
mylner, miller.
myneyeple, gauntlet (?).

name, by; especially.
name, great, great value.
namely, especially.
namo, no more.
narette, do not impute.
nas, was not.
natheles, nevertheless.
neare, close.
nedely, of necessity.
needments, things needed.
neet, cattle.
nere, were not.
never-a-del, not a bit.
newe, afresh.
nextin, next.
nicer, too nice.
nicetie, reserve.
nightertale, night-time.
ni'll, will not.
nis, is not.
niste, did not know.
nobles, coins worth a third of a pound.
noblesse, nobleness.
noder, none other.
nolde, would not.
nominate, call.
nones, for the, for the occasion.
nonne pre(e)st, nun's priest.

noot, know not.
nose-thirles, nostrils.
nosethrill, nostril.
notabilitee, notable fact.
note, know not.
not-heed, cropped head.
nould, would not.
noursled, trained; reared.
nouthe, as, just now.
nouther, neither.
noyd, vexed; grieved.
noyous, harmful.
ny, close.
nyce, scrupulous; foolish.

o, one.
observe, favor.
of, by.
offring, the offering by the congregation of the bread and wine to be consecrated in the mass; voluntary gifts to a parish-priest from his congregation.
ofspring, family.
oght, at all.
on, one.
onely, mere; especial.
ones, united in design.
onis, once.
oon, alwey after, uniform in quality.
oon, ever in, ever alike.
oppyned, opened.
or, ere.
origane, wild marjoram (?).
original, source; cause.
orlogge, clock.
ought, owned; aught.
ounces, bunches.
oures, hours of the breviary.
out of, without.
outrage, clamor; violence.
outragious, violent.
outrely, utterly.
out-rydere, inspector of the farms of a monastery.
over, besides.
over-al, everywhere.
overcraw, exult over.
overest, uppermost.
overlepe, outrun; catch.
oversight, escape.
owches, gems.
oweth, owns.
o-wher, somewhere.

paas, a, at a footpace.
pace, proceed; surpass; steps.
paire, impair.
Palatye, Palathia in Anatolia.
paled, fenced with pales.
palfrey, saddle-horse, especially for ladies.
pall, cloak.
palmer, pilgrim.
par, by.
paramours, lovers.
parbreake, vomit.
pardale, panther.
pardee, par dieux, a common oath.
pardoner, one who sold indulgences.
parfourned, performed.

parisshens, parishioners.
parti, upon a, aside.
parvys, church porch, especially that of St. Paul's in London.
pas, foot-pace; pace.
passion, suffering.
passionate, express with feeling.
pastes, pasties.
patente, letter of privilege.
Pater-Noster, Our Father (the Lord's Prayer).
patrone, preserver.
paynim, pagan.
peece, structure; fabric; fortified place.
peire, series; set.
pennes, feathers.
perceable, penetrable.
peren, appear.
pers, dark shade of blue or crimson.
persant, piercing.
persoun, parson.
peyne, take trouble.
pight, placed; struck.
piled, thin.
pilwe-beer, pillowcase.
pin, whit.
pinche at, find fault with.
pinched, pleated.
pine, suffering; sorrow.
pined, exhausted by suffering.
pitaunce, charitable gift.
pitous, compassionate.
pitty, fill with pity.
place, rank.
place, in, present; to the spot.
plat, flat; plainly; interfolded; entwined.
platane, oriental plane-tree.
plate, plate armor.
pledges, children.
plenteous, plenteous.
pleyen, play; joke.
pleyn, full; unlimited.
plight, plait; fold; pledge.
point, whit.
point, in good, in good condition.
point, to, completely; exactly.
pokkes, pustules.
pollicie, Machiavellian tactics.
pomely, dappled.
poraille, poor people.
portesse, portable breviary.
post, pillar.
potage, broth.
poudre-marchant, flavoring powder.
pouldred, powdered; pulverized.
pounces, talons.
pouped, puffed.
pourtraiture, image.
povert, poverty.
povre, poor.
poyse, force.
practicke, artful.
prancke, adjust.
praunce, stalk.
pray, preying; ravage.
prease, strive; press; crowd.
predicacioun, preaching.
prees, crowd.

presage, point out beforehand.
presence, chamber in which a sovereign receives guests.
presently, immediately.
presse, device for pressing; mould.
pretence, importance.
prevaile, avail.
pricasour, hard rider.
price, pay the price of.
pricke-wande, rod used as a mark in archery.
prickes, rods used as marks in archery.
pricking, riding; spurring.
priefe, experience; power.
priketh, incites.
prime, nine o'clock in the morning; spring-time.
privily, secretly.
properly, exactly.
propre, own; well-made.
propretee, peculiar quality.
prouder, too proud.
prove, test; try.
provost, chief magistrate.
prow, brave; profit.
Pruce, Prussia.
prys, renown.
puddings, sausages.
puiccccion, peculiar.
puissance, might.
pulled, plucked.
purchas(e), proceeds from begging; acquisition.
purchasing, conveyancing.
purchasour, conveyancer.
purf(i)led, fringed; decorated with an ornamental border.
purposes, discourses.
purtreye, draw.
purveyaunce, provision.
pyned, tortured.

quad, bad.
quaile, become dismayed.
quayd, subdued.
quell, frighten; kill.
quick, alive.
quight, release.
quit, release.
quited, requited.
quyrry, slaughtered game.
quyte, requite.

rablement, mob.
radly, quickly.
raft, struck off.
rage, romp.
raile, flow.
ramp, tear; attack.
rank, bold.
rape, haste.
rapt, carried off.
rare, thin; faint.
raskall, base; worthless.
rather, earlier; sooner.
ratones, small rats.
raug(h)te, reached; obtained
ravin, plunder; booty.
ravisedest, didst draw.
raw, unstrung.
rawbone, excessively lean.

rawstye by the roote, rusted at the end with blood (?).
reacheles on, heedless about.
read, counsel; advice; advise.
reas, rouse.
reave, take away.
rebownded, reverberated.
rebutte, recoil; drive back.
recche, direct.
recchelees, heedless.
recorde, call to mind.
recoyle, retreat; retire.
recure, restore.
red, named; known.
rede, read; advise.
redily, quickly.
redound, overflow.
redresse, heal.
reed, counsel; adviser.
reele, roll.
refrain, restrain.
rekeninges, bills.
rekke, care.
remes, realms.
renne, run.
rente, income; burst.
renverst, upside down.
repast, refreshment.
repining, indignant.
repleccioun, over-eating.
reprevable, reprehensible.
repreve, shame.
repriefe, reproach.
requere, request.
resons, opinions.
respire, take breath.
restore, reward.
rethor, rhetorician.
retyrd, withdrawn.
reve, steward.
revenging will, desire for revenge.
reverence, respectful manner.
revers(e), contrary; bring back.
rew, pity; be sorry.
reysed, gone on a military expedition.
ribaudye, ribaldry.
richesse, wealth.
riddes, dispatches.
rife, strong; strongly.
rift, split; fissure; rent asunder.
right, straight ahead.
rightwisnesse, righteousness.
rigorous, violent.
rigour, violence.
ring, hammer of a door-knocker.
riotise, riotous living.
ritt, runs about; rides.
rive, split; tear.
rode, harbor; rood.
roghte, cared.
roome, station.
roste, roast meat.
rote, root; stringed instrument.
rouncy, farm horse.
round lists, enclosed ground for set combats as distinguished from open fields.
route, band.
rouze, shake up.
rove, shoot an arrow from an elevation.

rowels, polling parts of a bit.
rowd, rolled.
Ruce, Russia.
rue, pity.
ruefulnesse, pathos.
rueth, cause to pity.
ruffin, disorderly; ruffian.
ruine, fall.
rule, taking on.
ruth, pity; grief.
ryden out, go on expeditions.
ryotour, roisterer.
ryve, pierce.

sacred, accursed.
sad, serious; sober; firm.
saffron with, color.
sair, sore.
sallow, variety of willow.
salue, salute.
salvage, savage.
sam, together.
sanguin, red.
sangwyn, of a complexion, according to Galenical medicine, which implied jollity and generosity.
sapience, wisdom.
Satalye, Adalia in Asiatic Turkey.
sautrye, psaltery.
savour, have a relish for.
sawcefleem, covered with pimples caused by an excess of the salty humor.
sawten, assault.
say, fine woolen cloth; saw.
sayling, used for masts.
scad, scald.
scald, scab.
scalle, scab.
scalled, scabby.
scalpe, skull.
Scariot, Judas Iscariot.
scarlot, rich cloth.
scarsly, economically.
scath(e), harm; injury; pity.
schrewe, sinner.
science, knowledge; learned writing.
scole, manner.
scoleye, attend the university.
scored, inscribed.
scowre, run; pursue.
scrip, bag.
scriveyn, scribe.
scryne, chest for keeping books and papers.
se, protect; saw.
seare, burning.
seasd, penetrated.
second tenor, melody of lower pitch.
secree, able to keep secrets.
securly, surely.
see, save.
seeled, closed.
seely, innocent.
seeming meet, seemly.
seeming wise, appearance.
seigh, saw.
seintuarie, consecrated object.

seised, reached.
seke, sick.
selde, seldom.
selle, barter.
sely, innocent; good; simple.
sembled, met.
semi-cope, short cloak worn by priests.
seminge, to my, as it seems to me.
sen, since.
sendal, thin silk.
sene, visible.
sent, sense.
sentence, meaning; subject; judgment.
sermone, preach.
servisable, willing to serve.
sete, inflicted.
sethe, boil.
sette, care.
sette hir aller cappe, made fools of them all.
settyng, planting.
sew, follow; pursue.
seye, was to, meant.
seynd, broiled.
shapen, plan.
shaply, fit.
share, slice.
shaume, musical instrument similar to an oboe.
shawes, woods.
shear, several.
sheeldes, French crowns.
sheene, bright; beautiful.
shend, reproach.
shent(e), scolded; injured.
shepe, shepherd.
shete a peny, shoot for a penny.
sheugh, trench; furrow.
shewes, appearances; marks.
shiten, defiled.
shone, shoes.
shoop, planned.
shopen, arrayed.
shorte with, shorten.
shradds, coppices.
shrewe, curse; rascal.
shrighte, shrieked.
shroggs, wands serving for marks.
shroudes, garments.
shrowd, take shelter.
sic, such.
sight, of in appearance.
signe, watch-word.
sike, sick.
siker, sure.
sikerer, surer.
sikerly, surely.
silly, simple; harmless; innocent.
sin, since.
sinfull hire, service to sin.
sinke, deposit.
sits, fits.
sith, afterward; since.
sithens, since.
slade, valley.
slake, moderate; abate.
slawe, slain.
sleighte, craft; trick.
sleuthe, sloth.

slight, trick; device.
slon, slay.
smale fowles, little birds; nightingales (?).
smart, agony.
smerte, sharply; hurt.
snibben, rebuke.
snubbes, snags; knobs.
softly, gently.
solas, amusement; pleasure.
solempne, important; cheerful.
solempnely, importantly.
som-del, somewhat.
somnour, officer who cited culprits before an ecclesiastical
court.
somtyme, once.
soothly, truly.
sop in wyn, bread or cake broken
in wine.
sort, chance; manner.
sorwe, with, bad luck to him; to
his harm.
sote, sweet.
soth, truth.
sothfastnesse, truth.
souce, strike; swoop upon.
souded, confirmed.
soukinge, sucking.
soun, sound.
souninge in, tending to.
soust, dipped; steeped.
sovereygne, excellent.
sovereynly, chiefly.
sownd, clash; wield.
sowne, sound.
space, length of time; course.
spanne, about nine inches.
sparred, shut.
spendyd, got ready.
spent, worn out.
spersed, dispersed.
spies, glances; thrusts.
spill, destroy.
sporne, kick.
spousd, betrothed.
sprente, sprang; spurted.
spreyned, sprinkled.
spright, spirit.
spring, flood.
spurn, kick (?); encounter (?).
spyced, over-fastidious.
spyrred, asked.
stadle, prop.
stage, at a, from a floor.
stal, stole away.
stape in age, advanced in years.
starke, stiff.
stayd, caused to stay.
sted, place.
stelths, thefts.
stemed, shone.
stepe, prominent; bulging.
stere, steersman; rudder.
sterlinges, silver coins.
sterne, stern; men.
sterte, move quickly; leap.
sterve, die.
steven, voice.
steven, unsett, unexpected time.
stew(e), hot place; fish-pond;
brothel.

stiked, stuck.
still, ever.
stinte, stop.
stockes, posts; stumps.
stole, mantle.
stoor, farm-stock.
stop, obstacle.
storie, series of readings from
Scripture.
storven, died.
stot, hack; cob.
stound, stunned; moment; time;
peril; trouble.
stour, brawl: fight.
stowre, conflict; danger; distress.
straunge, foreign.
streightes, closes.
streit, strict; stinted; cramped.
streite, tightly; drawn.
stremes, currents.
streyneth, constrains.
strete and stalle, on the road
and housed (?).
streyte, strictly.
strike, hank.
stroke, moved rapidly forward.
strowd, scattered.
stryving, strife.
stub, stock of a tree.
studieth, meditate; delay.
sturre, disturbance; tumult.
stye, alley; mount.
subject, underlying.
subtilly, secretly.
suffisaunce, contentment.
suffised, satisfied.
suffyce unto, be content with.
suppress, overcome.
surcote, upper coat.
sure, genuine.
suspect, fear.
sustened, maintained.
swaid, swung.
swaine, youth.
swal, swelled.
swapte, smote with swords.
swat, were sweating.
sway, swing.
swelt, swelled; raged; fainted.
swevene, dream.
sweyved, sounded.
swich, such.
swinged, singed.
swink, toil.
swinken, work.
swonken, worked.
swote, sweet.
swouwn(d) e, swoon.
swythe, quickly.
syen, see.
syke, ditch; trench.
syne, afterwards.
sythes, times.

tabard, rough coat worn by
laborers.
table, picture.
tackles, equipment of a ship;
rigging.
taffetie, fine silk.
taille, by, on account.

take in hand, maintain.
takel, archery-gear; arrows.
talants, claws.
tale, tell, give heed.
talen, tell stories.
talent, desire.
tapicer, upholsterer.
tappestere, barmaid.
targe, small shield.
Tartary, Tartarus; hell.
taught, told.
teade, torch.
tear, there (?).
teene, affliction; grief.
telle no store, set no store.
tellen, count over.
tempest thee, distress thyself
severely.
temple, college of law.
tempred, accommodated.
termes, in, in set phrases; ver-
batim.
tett, lock of hair.
than, then.
that, so that; when; what.
the, they.
the(e), so mot I, so may I thrive.
thee'ch, so, so may I thrive.
thegither, together.
then, than.
ther-as, where.
there, where.
ther-to, in addition.
thewes, manners; habits.
thilke, that.
thing, make a, draw up a writ.
tho, the; those; then.
thombe of gold, thumb of a good
miller.
thral, slave.
thraldome, slavery.
thrast, pressed.
three square, with three equal
sides.
thriftily, carefully.
thrill, pierce; penetrate.
thrillant, piercing.
throly, strenuously.
tide, time.
tikelnesse, instability.
timely, measured.
tipet, hood.
tire, dress; head-dress; train;
crew.
toft, exposed elevation.
told, counted.
tollen, take toll.
tombesteres, female tumblers.
ton, one.
tool, weapon.
toon, toes.
to-rente, tore asunder; torn
asunder.
tort, wrong.
to-swinke, work much.
to-tere, tear asunder.
touch, touchstone.
toun, farm.
toy, sport.
trace, walk.
tract, trace; track.
traine, tail; trickery.

**Tramissene, Tremeyen,** a district in north Africa.
**transmew,** transmute.
**trayne,** artifice; snare.
**treachour,** traitor.
**treatie,** diplomacy.
**treen mould,** form of a tree.
**trenchand,** sharp; piercing.
**trespas,** sin; wrong.
**tretys,** well-proportioned.
**treye,** three.
**triacle,** sovereign remedy.
**trielich,** choicely.
**trinall,** threefold.
**tristil-tre,** tree used as a meeting-place.
**trowe,** believe.
**truncked,** beheaded.
**trusse,** seize and carry away.
**twinn, in,** in twain; in two's; apart.
**twinne,** depart from; separate; deprive.
**twyne,** band.
**tyde,** time.
**tyne,** pain; sorrow.
**type of thine,** symbol of thee.
**tyre,** head-dress.

**unacquainted,** unaccustomed.
**unbid,** unprayed for.
**unbrent,** unburned.
**uncoupled,** loose.
**uncouth,** strange.
**undern,** noon; from nine to twelve.
**undertake,** conduct an enterprise.
**undight,** unfastened; removed.
**uneasie,** uncomfortable; disturbed.
**uneath,** difficult; with difficulty; almost.
**unhardy,** timid.
**unkinde,** unnatural.
**unkindly,** against nature; unnatural.
**unlese,** unloose.
**unnethe(s),** scarcely.
**unprovided,** unforeseen.
**unthrifty,** wicked; destructive.
**untill,** towards; unto.
**unty,** loosen.
**unused,** from disuse.
**unwary,** unexpected.
**unweeting,** unconscious; unknowing.
**upright,** flat on the back.
**up so doun,** upside down.
**upstaring,** bristling; upstarting.

**vavasour,** sub-vassal; landholder.
**veiwe,** yew.
**venerye,** hunting.
**verament,** truly.
**vere,** turn.
**vernicle,** copy of the Veronica picture of Christ.
**verraily,** truly.
**verray,** true; very.
**vers,** verses.

**vertu,** quickening power; valor.
**vertuous,** virtuous; efficacious; manly.
**vew,** appearance.
**viage,** journey.
**viewe,** yew.
**vigilyës,** ceremonies held the evening before a festival.
**vilde,** vile.
**vile,** lowly.
**vileinye,** rudeness; unfit speech.
**visour,** mask; disguise.
**vitaille,** victuals.
**voyage,** journey.

**wade,** go.
**wafereres,** confectioners.
**wage,** pledge.
**wake,** watch; wake.
**wallowd,** rolled.
**wan,** pale; gloomy.
**wane,** number (?); vehicle for a missile (?).
**wanto(w)n,** wild; playful.
**war,** aware; cautious.
**war him,** let him beware.
**ward,** guard.
**wardles make,** earthly mate.
**wardrobe,** privy.
**ware,** guard; wary; sharp.
**warely,** carefully.
**warente,** protect.
**warison,** reward.
**warrayd,** made war upon.
**warsle,** wrestle.
**waryce,** cure.
**wast,** useless.
**wastel-breed,** fine white bread.
**wastfull,** barren.
**watering,** brook or watering-place for horses.
**Watte,** Walter.
**wayne,** chariot.
**wayted,** observed.
**wayted after,** demanded; expected.
**wayting,** watching.
**weaker,** too weak.
**weal,** clench hard.
**weare,** spend.
**webbe,** weaver.
**weeds,** clothes.
**weene,** think.
**weet,** know; wet.
**wel,** fully; very.
**welawey,** alas.
**weld,** wield.
**wele,** happiness.
**welke,** fade; wane.
**welked,** withered.
**welkin,** sky.
**well to donne,** well-doing.
**wende,** would have supposed.
**wenden,** go.
**wenen,** think.
**wered,** wore.
**werken,** act.
**werre,** war.
**wex,** grow; wax.
**whally,** streaked.
**what,** why.
**whelkes,** pustules.

**whelp,** puppy.
**wher,** whether.
**whereas,** where.
**whether,** which.
**whiche,** what sort.
**whilom,** formerly; ever.
**whot,** hot.
**whyleare,** erewhile; lately.
**whylom,** formerly; ever.
**wi,** with.
**wide,** away.
**wif,** woman.
**wight,** man; person; strong.
**wighty,** strong.
**wike,** week.
**wikke,** wicked.
**wilfull,** ignorant.
**wilfully,** by choice.
**will or nill,** willy-nilly.
**wimpel,** covering for the head.
**wimpled,** pleated.
**win,** go.
**winne,** gain.
**winning,** profit.
**wis,** surely.
**wise,** manner.
**wisly,** surely.
**wist,** knew.
**wit,** bit of wisdom; genius; intelligence; judgment.
**with,** by.
**with-alle,** withal; however.
**withouten,** besides.
**withseye,** oppose.
**witing,** knowledge.
**wize,** manner.
**wlatsom,** loathsome.
**wolden,** wished.
**wombe,** belly.
**won,** overcome.
**wone,** custom; number; plenty; one.
**won(n)e,** dwell; live; abide.
**woning,** dwelling.
**wood,** mad.
**woodnesse,** madness.
**woodweele,** woodlark (?).
**woot,** know.
**worm,** snake; dragon.
**worship,** honor.
**wortes,** herbs.
**worth,** be.
**worthy,** noble; distinguished.
**wot,** know.
**wouche,** evil.
**woxen,** grown; become.
**wrattheth,** becomes angry.
**wreke,** avenge.
**wrighte,** workman.
**wring,** distress.
**wrizled,** wrinkled; shriveled.
**wrocken,** avenged.
**wroghte,** contrived.
**wyde,** aside; away.
**wyde, a little,** a short distance away.
**wyf,** woman.
**wyld,** deer.
**wynning,** profit.
**wys, to make it,** to make it a subject for deliberation.
**wysly,** surely.

y-, a prefix used especially with the past participles of verbs.

ȝaf, gave.

yblent, blinded.

y-chaped, with the metal point of a scabbard; mounted.

y-corven, cut.

ydel, in vain.

ydrad, dreaded.

yĕ, eyes.

yeddinges, songs.

yede, go.

yeldéd, yelled.

yeldhalle, guildhall.

yemen, yeomen.

yerde, switch.

yerle, earl.

yerly, early.

yerne, briskly.

yersel, yourself.

yes, you shall.

yeve, give.

yfere, together.

yiftes, gifts.

yive, give.

y-lad, carried.

ymages, wax images of the patient (?); signs of the zodiac (?).

ympe, scion; offspring.

yod, went.

ypight, placed.

yplaste, placed.

Ypocras, Hippocrates.

y-preved, proved.

y-sene, visible.

y-wimpled, covered with a wimple.

y-wis, certainly.

# INDEX OF AUTHORS, TITLES, AND FIRST LINES OF POEMS

Names of authors are printed in CAPITALS, and titles are printed in *italics*.
Titles beginning with "A," "An," or "The" are indexed under their second words.
In cases where the title of a poem is identical with its first line, or with the initial
portion of it, the title only is indexed.